20 BICYCLE TOURS
in and around
NEW YORK CITY

**Dan Carlinsky
and David Heim**

Revised Edition

Backcountry Publications
Woodstock, Vermont

An Invitation to the Reader—Although it is unlikely that the roads you cycle on these tours will change much with time, some road signs, landmarks, and other items may. If you find that changes have occurred on these routes, please let us know so we may correct them in future editions. The authors and publisher also welcome other comments and suggestions. Address all correspondence to:

Editor, *Bicycle Tours*
Backcountry Publications, Inc.
P.O. Box 175
Woodstock, Vermont 05091

Text and cover design by Richard Widhu
Maps by Richard Widhu, © 1984, 1988 Backcountry Publications

Library of Congress Cataloging in Publication Data

Carlinsky, Dan.
   20 bicycle tours in and around New York City.

   1. Bicycle touring — New York Metropolitan Area — Guide book . 2. New York Metropolitan Area — Description and travel — Guide-books. I. Heim, David, 1946- II. Title. III. Title: Twenty bicycle tours in and around New York City.
GV1045.5.N72N493   1988   917.47'1   88-19391
ISBN 0-88150-123-9 (pbk.)

Dedication

Thanks to Nancy Carlinsky and Katherine Foran; Chris Lloyd, Carl Taylor, Jr., Amy Ullrich, and Dick Widhu; Ken Andresen, Alinda Barth, Richard Bograd, Steve Casey, Carol Cirignano, Maggie Clarke, George Heitman, Bill Hoffman, Bonnie Jockel, Bob Keene, Gene Tani, Irv Weisman, and any other helpers whose names may have been inadvertently left out.

Contents

Introduction   6
1. **The Mayor's Special:** Gracie Mansion to City Hall and Wall Street   14
2. **Upper Manhattan:** Morningside Heights to Inwood   21
3. **The Plaza Hotel to Coney Island:** From the Sublime to the Ridiculous   27
4. **Staten Island:** The Rural Borough   34
5. **Picnic Across the Hudson:** to Tallman Mountain Park   41
6. **The Long Island Quickie:** Eisenhower Memorial Park and Old Westbury Gardens   46
7. **Southern Nassau:** Five Towns Area   50

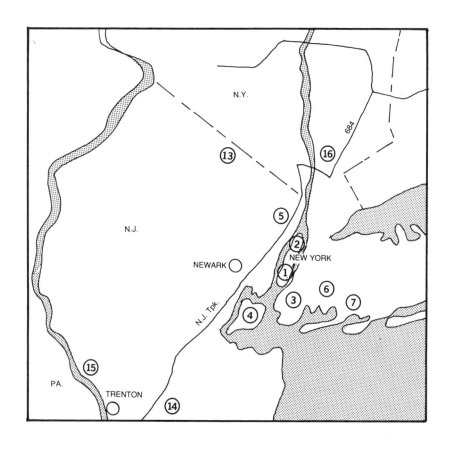

8. **The North Shore:** to the Beach at Bayville   55
9. **A Bully Tour:** to Teddy Roosevelt's Home and Oyster Bay   60
10. **Western Suffolk:** Smith-Haven Mall to Heckscher State Park   65
11. **Southampton Area:** An Easy Tour   70
12. **Eastern Long Island:** Far from New York   75
13. **To Greenwood Lake:** An Interstate Overnight   84
14. **Jersey Farm Country:** Cranbury to New Egypt   91
15. **Crossing the Delaware:** Princeton to New Hope   96
16. **Westchester County:** Three Bodies of Water   102
17. **Back Roads of Westchester:** Armonk to Bedford   106
18. **Westchester and Fairfield:** A Challenging Ride   111
19. **To Ridgefield:** A Hard Day Trip (or an Overnight)   118
20. **The Pro's Overnight:** 111 Miles in Westchester and Connecticut
    Lake Country   125
Appendix: Bike Clubs   132

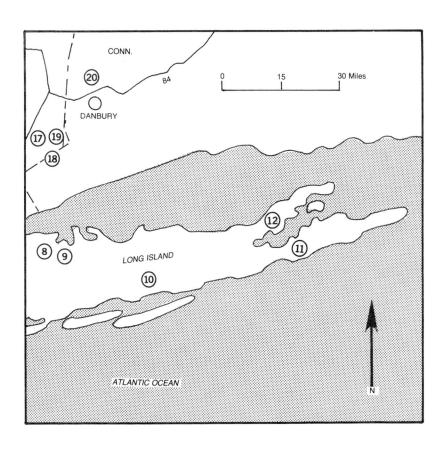

Introduction

A Few Words

Cyclists everywhere ask the same question: Where to ride? New Yorkers soon find that on nice weekends Central Park is nearly as mobbed as Grand Central Terminal; besides, it can be boring after the forty-fifth time around. Suburbanites, too, are often at a loss to find safe, interesting routes. And so we wrote this book, which does the planning for you.

What's in This Book

We've suggested twenty basic tours within 100 miles of New York City. Although a few are in the city itself, most are in the surrounding area, with emphasis on back roads. Some routes can be covered in only two or three hours; some take two full days. Most are good for all-day trips; all are planned to take you in a circle, with minimum path retracing. Included are turn-by-turn instructions, minutely detailed maps, running mileage, area bike shops, and descriptions of points of interest along the route. Picnic spots, restaurants, and—on the longer tours—overnight accommodations are suggested. Restaurants, don't forget, have rest room facilities as well as food.

Several of the tours make figure eights, so it's easy to ride just one part if you want to make a shorter tour. Other routes are also easily abridged; just check the map before you go. Try reversing direction for variety, or invent your own variations.

Planning Your Times

At the start of each entry is the tour's total mileage, a capsule description of the terrain you'll encounter ("flat," "mostly flat," "moderately hilly," or "very hilly"), and "minimum cycling time." Consider this last as a rough guideline only. Generally, the "minimum cycling time" is for an average cyclist stopping perhaps ten minutes each hour for rest or a visit to a point of interest. If you choose to linger at several stopping points or if you like three-hour lunches, you'd be wise to add on some time. If you're the masochistic type who won't be happy until you see the finish line, you can certainly complete the tour in less than the "minimum." On day trips lasting several hours, you'll have to start shortly after sunrise. On very hot days even the short trips will have to begin early, since you won't want to ride much during the noon-to-3 p.m. heat. Autumn is a wonderful time for bike touring in this region, but days do grow short; think ahead.

Five Smart Moves

1. Cyclist, know thyself. If you're new to bicycle touring, don't pick out one of the longer trips for a first try. Take a baby tour and work up to the overnights. If you've never done much cycling, get out and practice. Start by going around the block, then around two.

2. Adjust your seat so that your leg is nearly straight when the pedal is in its lowest position; keep the handlebars lower than the seat.

3. Pedal on the balls of the feet, not the arches.

4. Shift to a lower gear *before* you start uphill.

5. Eat *before* you're really hungry.

About the Points of Interest

On these tours the diversions are many and varied. Your cycling will bring you to unusual museums, old homes, a great old country store, a superb candy shop, gardens, ponds, lakes, beaches, a covered bridge, and a horse's grave—plus a hundred more. Hours and admission charges (if any) are usually listed, but both are liable to change; never set your heart on one special sight. Obviously, these spots can't all be everyone's cup of tea. Stop at those that interest you, nod at the others as you go by. But do remember that you won't find things like this if you're driving a car on a superhighway. Even if you *could* safely bike on the Long Island Expressway, the New Jersey Turnpike, or I-684, you'd hardly find interesting touring there. More than half the pleasure of cycle touring is seeing a world you just don't see from the highway.

Maps

The maps in this book are good maps. The directions are good directions. But let's face it—you still might get lost. If you don't panic, losing your way can become one of the most memorably pleasant parts of a tour because it forces you to talk to people (or, in the most desperate of circumstances, animals).

If you're at all worried that you might never find your way home again, since you can't leave a trail of breadcrumbs, buy a county map of the area you'll be visiting. (Gas station maps, you'll discover, are only rarely useful; they simply don't include the back roads that are best for cycling.)

Trains and Buses

The PATH trains from lower Manhattan to New Jersey allow bikes during nonpeak hours (*not* 6-9:30 a.m. or 3-6:30 p.m.), but you have to call first for information and to arrange a free permit. Information: 212-466-7649. Long Island Rail Road allows bikes off-peak, but says no on holidays like Mother's Day and Christmas Eve. First you need to buy a $5 permit from any LIRR ticket office. Information: 718-990-8228. You also need a $5 permit (available at Grand Central Terminal, stationmaster's office) for Metro North trains. There's a four-bikes-per-train limit. Information: 212-340-2144. Officially, bicycles aren't allowed on New York City buses and subways, but depending on the time of day and which conductor you run into, you *may* be able to bring your bike aboard. Your best bet is to collapse the bike first and pick quiet times. But it's a gamble, so it's wise to have an alternate escape plan.

Safety

   1. Ride on the right, with the auto traffic.

   2. Observe stop signs, traffic lights, and other warnings.

   3. Ride single file only, close to the curb, three or four lengths behind other cyclists.

   4. Yield to cars (they're bigger) and walkers (they're helpless).

   5. Be alert; constantly change your gaze from near to far, from down at the road to straight ahead.

   6. Use hand signals on turns.

   7. Don't let downhills get out of hand; use your brakes to keep your speed reasonable.

   8. At rest stops, get your bike all the way off the road.

   9. Wear light- or bright-colored clothing.

   10. Have reflectors and lights with you in case you're caught at night.

   Rule number 1 is the single most important law of safe cycling. Failure to obey it is the cause of countless accidents and deaths. The logic is undeniable: On the right, you can see cars coming around left-hand bends and, most crucial, you reduce the chance of a head-on collision. (On one-way city streets, it's okay to keep left to avoid buses.)

Hazards to Watch For

   In the city: double-parked cars, doors swinging open on parked cars, wandering buses, careening taxis, pieces of glass, potholes, pedestrians crossing against the light, other cyclists riding the wrong way, grates with wide openings going the same way as your tires.

   In the country: soft shoulders, no shoulders, sand or gravel on the pavement, wet leaves, railroad tracks, blind driveways, spirited dogs. (When a dog menaces, remember that he's probably just being territorial. Outrun him if you can; otherwise stop, dismount, and slowly walk past with the bike between you and the mutt. Don't be afraid to try a firm "No!")

What to Take Along

   Your bicycle. There are too many opinions about what constitutes a good touring bike. It's safe to say that folks on lesser, cheaper bikes can have just as much fun as folks on $1,500 jobs. Tours rated "flat" or "mostly flat" can be negotiated on a three-speed (or even one-speed) model; the hillier routes require a ten-speed.

Toe clips. They look dangerous and uncomfortable; they are neither. They force you to pedal with the balls of your feet (which is the proper way), and if you learn to point your toes up at the twelve o'clock position and down at six o'clock (it's called "ankling") to make use of upward motion as well as downward, you'll make your pedaling nearly one-third easier. It's surprisingly simple to get accustomed to clips.

Bike carrier for your car. Any number of models are available. The roof type saves the bike in case of rear-end collision, keeps the driver's rear view clear, and makes parking easier; the rear-bumper type cuts wind drag, prevents clearance problems, and simplifies loading. Take your choice. Handy types can fashion their own in an afternoon. Look at some store models, then go home and copy.

Lock. Unless you stop only in places where you can take your bike in with you, you must have a lock of some sort. Many cyclists find the chainless Kryptonite or Citadel locks convenient and comfortingly strong, if expensive. Any time you can take your bike inside (to restaurants, say), do so; just ask first. Otherwise, lock up in a visible, well-traveled spot.

Bags. Unless you thrill to the sound of the word "backpacker," you'll find packs awkward for cycling. Their one advantage—the fact that you don't have to unpack your cycle every time you lock and leave—is matched by using quickly removable lightweight bags that attach to front or rear. Do try to find bags that are truly easy-on and easy-off. Camping out, of course, requires all sorts of extra gear.

Reflectors. You need a good reflector in back, and it doesn't hurt to have more on the sides as well. Night touring doesn't appeal to most, but you may want a light in case you get caught with the sun down; get a battery model.

Horn. Although they're the law, purists don't believe in them. Yell, they say, and save weight. But sometimes it's tough to shout above the traffic in a pinch. Better to have some mechanical sounding device, the uglier and louder the better. Rubber-ball squawk horns are pretty effective.

Rearview mirror. It's not a bad safety device. Handlebar models aren't as good as a tiny dental mirror (or a cycle-shop version) attached to the visor of a cap or to eyeglass frames.

Speedometers, odometers. These add a little extra weight and drag, but they're nice if you like statistics and helpful for following the directions for the tours.

Baby seat. Use the papoose style for ages 1 to 3, rear-seat carrier (safer than handlebar-mounted) for three and up. Any way is scary.

Clothing. Take a nylon windbreaker or rain parka if conditions dictate. Gloves can help. In warm weather, shorts and a jersey are best. If you're not wearing shorts, don't forget clips to keep your pant legs out of the chain. Don't wear jeans; their thick seams rub too much. Cycling shoes really aren't a must. No matter how hot the weather, keep your shirt on. Don't forget a handkerchief.

Liquids. Carry a clip-on plastic bottle with water, sugared if you like for an energy jolt. Keep away from anything carbonated. Beer or wine for lunch? At your own risk; it'll probably go straight to your legs and make the return trip seem three times as long.

Food. Keep it simple, keep it light. Eat frequently in small doses— nibble and sip. You can always buy food on the road, but it's nice to have a little something for emergencies. Bananas, oranges, and tangerines are convenient, since they come in their own wrappers and need no washing. Some riders favor raisins for a pick-me-up; others, honey.

First aid kit. You'll need antiseptic, a few bandages, perhaps a couple of aspirins, and sunscreen lotion or ointment in season.

Small change. Having coins can be important for an emergency phone call.

Helmet. You like your head? Treat it well.

Tools. Carry a pump and air-pressure gauge, small screwdriver, ap- propriate-sized wrenches, pliers, tire irons, patch kit, spare tube, small rag or paper towels.

Spare paper or plastic bags. These are useful for garbage, dirty socks, or whatever.

Penknife. You never know when you may need to cut something.

Soap or small packaged moistened towelettes. You never know when you may need to wash something.

Dog repellent. Just in case, a clip-on can of harmless spray is nice to have.

String, rubber bands. You'll know why you took them along the first time you use them.

Use your head. If there are two or more of you going, double up when- ever you can: one pump, one tool set, one first aid kit, and so on. When you're through loading up, if you can't lift your bike and carry it up a flight of stairs, either you're in terrible shape or you've packed too much.

Repairs on the Road

Buy a bicycle repair book and use it. For starters, learn how to check over your bike before you take off so you can spot potential trouble.

Preventive maintenance is crucial, but breakdowns will happen. Here's how to deal with two of the simplest and most common snafus.

Flats. Never ride on a flat tire; get off your bike and fix it right away. If you have a sudden blowout, chances are good you can find the leak easily by pumping some air into the tire and listening for the hiss; squeeze

A touch of the sublime—hansom cabs at The Plaza.   Dan Carlinsky

to make the escaping air more audible. Then deflate the tire completely by pressing in the valve stem. Use your tire irons to pry one side of the tire loose from its rim for several inches on each side of the leak. Pull out that part of the tube, locate the hole, and patch it according to instructions on your patch kit. Make sure to remove the cause of the blowout—glass shard, nail, sharp stone, or whatever. Replace the tube, force the tire back onto the rim, and inflate it to normal pressure. (Never pump up a tube while it's outside the tire.) If the patch doesn't hold, if you can't readily locate the source of the leak, or if the leak is in or around the valve itself, replace the tube. (You're out for a ride, not for a day of repair work.) To remove the defective tube, you'll have to take off the wheel and loosen the tire all the way around. Stuff the spare inside the tire, valve first, keeping kinks out of the tube and making sure the valve stays straight. Force the tire back into place and inflate it.

Thrown chains. If your chain falls off the sprockets, put it back on the rear sprocket first (on a ten-speed, put it on the smallest rear sprocket), then press the chain down onto the teeth at the top of the front sprocket. (If your bike has a chain guard, you'll probably have to remove it.) Hold the chain in place and crank the pedals by hand as if you were riding the bike. The chain should slip back into place. Unless you hit something that knocks the chain off, a thrown chain is usually a sign that the gears need adjusting or that the chain is so old it needs to be replaced.

If you meet with a mishap you can't handle alone, know when you're licked and look for help. For example, don't ride if you severely bend a wheel, the frame, or the front fork. Flag down another cyclist or a passing motorist and get to the nearest bike shop; several in the area are listed at the end of each tour. If there's no shop nearby, lock your bicycle securely, get yourself home, and come back for the bike later.

If you do fall, make sure *you're* okay before you check your bike.

Learning More About Cycling in the Area

The League of American Wheelmen, one of the oldest cycling organizations, offers a handy cycling almanac as a premium to new members. Among many other things, it lists hospitality houses (good for individual wayfaring cyclists), maps and bicycling books for each state, plus clubs. A year's individual membership costs $22. For ordering information, write the League of American Wheelmen, 6707 Whitestone Road, Suite 209, Baltimore, MD 21207.

The New York Bicycle Touring Guide is a series of strip maps designating routes that crisscross the Empire State. They cover popular touring areas and major cities. For a free descriptive brochure, write William N. Hoffman, 53 Claire Avenue, #5B, New Rochelle, NY 10804.

The Connecticut Bicycle Book is an encyclopedia about cycling in the Nutmeg State. The book includes 17 tours plus a listing of bike shops and cycling organizations. It's available for $2.60 from Coalition of Connecticut Bicyclists, P.O. Box 121, Middletown, CT 06457.

New Jersey Bicycling Information is a free handout that also has some good listings and other help. Get your copy from William Feldman, Pedestrian/Bicycle Advocate, New Jersey Department of Transportation, 1035 Parkway Avenue—CN600, Trenton, NJ 08625.

Bicycling in New York State isn't as useful as the first two listed here, but it is free, from Kathleen B. Cramer, Trails Coordinator, Office of Parks, Recreation, and Historic Preservation, Empire State Plaza, Agency Building 1, Albany, NY 12238.

Happy cycling.

Dan Carlinsky
David Heim

1

The Mayor's Special:
Gracie Mansion to City Hall and Wall Street

Round-trip distance pedaled: 15 miles
Terrain: flat
Minimum cycling time: 2 hours

Here's a short, easy circuit with plenty to stop and look at along the way. You can complete the tour in a couple of hours, or you can easily stretch it out to an all-day affair. If the mayor biked to work each morning, he'd pass through Yorkville, Sutton Place, Turtle Bay, Kips Bay, the Lower East Side, and Chinatown, and then pedal down Broadway to his office to read the mail and maybe give an impromptu news conference or two. Later, he could bike down to Wall Street, where the real power is, pass by the World Trade Center, get a whiff of Greenwich Village, take in the United Nations Headquarters buildings, and head home. That's quite a lot of Manhattan Island. This tour is best on Sunday mornings, when in-town traffic is at its lightest. Start at Gracie Mansion, where the mayor hangs his coat, at 89th Street and East End Avenue.

0.0 *From Gracie Mansion in Carl Schurz Park, head south on East End Avenue.*

Hizzoner lives here in a frequently remodeled big white house that was a country residence when it was built, in 1799. The mayor's backyard is Carl Schurz Park. Named after the most prominent German immigrant of the nineteenth century (he was, at various times, a general, minister, senator, secretary of the interior, and newspaper editor), this is a small, well-mannered parcel. The most popular spot is John Finley Walk, a promenade that affords a panoramic view of the East River, the Triborough and Hell Gate bridges, and Queens. You can sit on a bench and watch barges chug down toward New York Harbor, you can scout around and try to find a rare black squirrel, you can socialize with neighborhood kibitzers . . . but you can't ride your bike here.

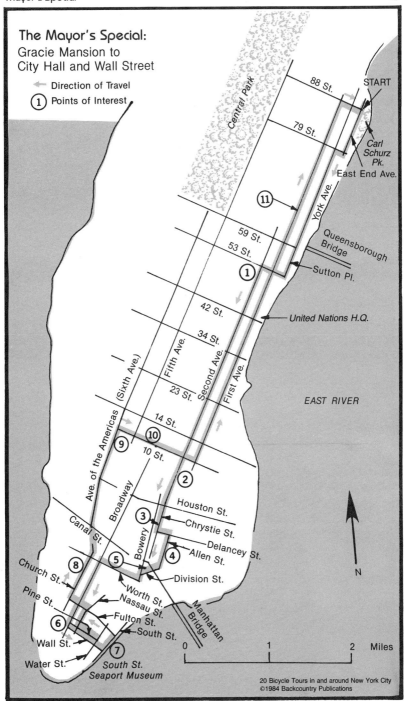

The Mayor's Special:
Gracie Mansion to
City Hall and Wall Street

← Direction of Travel
① Points of Interest

Central Park

88 St.   START

79 St.

Carl
Schurz
Pk.
East End Ave.

⑪   York Ave.

59 St.   Queensborough
53 St.   Bridge
①   Sutton Pl.

42 St.

United Nations H.Q.

34 St.

(Sixth Ave.)   Fifth Ave.   Second Ave.   First Ave.

23 St.

EAST RIVER

14 St.

⑨ ⑩

Ave. of the Americas   Broadway   10 St.

②

Houston St.

③   Chrystie St.

Canal St.   Bowery   Delancey St.
                                   Allen St.
⑧   ⑤   ④

Division St.

Church St.

Worth St.
Nassau St.
Pine St.   Manhattan
                                         Bridge
⑥   Fulton St.

Wall St.   South St.

⑦

Water St.   South St.
                Seaport Museum

N

0   1   2   Miles

20 Bicycle Tours in and around New York City
©1984 Backcountry Publications

0.5 *RIGHT onto 79th Street for just a block.*

0.6 *LEFT onto York Avenue.*

On the left at 72nd Street, you'll pass a branch of Sotheby's, the world-famous antiques and art auction house. Inside, experts evaluate everything from armor to snuff bottles.

In the 60s is the New York Hospital–Cornell Medical Center, a stolid cluster of buildings housing one of New York's largest hospitals as well as a variety of specialized medical facilities and a major teaching and research center. Next door: Rockefeller University, a high-powered graduate school known for its enviable number of Nobel laureates.

As you pass 59th Street, look up and see if a tram is crossing to or from Roosevelt Island. Thousands of islanders take the four-minute ride on the aerial cablecar daily, leaving their apartments on a bit of land that was once a farm, later was a complex of hospitals and jails, and now is just another middle-class New York neighborhood that happens to be in the middle of a river.

Below 59th Street, York Avenue becomes Sutton Place, one of Manhattan's truly high-class streets. The prettiest view is from Riverview Terrace—detour left a few dozen yards at 58th Street.

1.9 *RIGHT onto 53rd Street.*

2.2 *LEFT onto Second Avenue for the ride downtown.*

At 51st Street, you can make an optional detour right for part of a block to visit Greenacre Park (1), one of several vest-pocket oases in Manhattan, meant purely for relaxed urban lounging. This one has a twenty-five-foot-high waterfall and honey locust trees.

On your left just off the avenue, stretching between 43rd and 42nd streets, is the Ford Foundation building, headquarters of the Fort Knox of foundations. This strikingly modern building has a big enclosed garden that includes New York's tallest indoor tree, a three-story-high Southern magnolia.

On the left at 35th Street is St. Vartan's Armenian Cathedral, easy to spot because of its gilt-trimmed steeple. Pause to examine the stained glass and relief work outside.

At 10th Street you'll find another of Manhattan's unusual churches—St. Mark's-in-the-Bowery, which began in 1799 as a plain Georgian building and has been greatly altered and restored. "Peg Leg Pete" Stuyvesant, the early Dutch governor, is buried in the yard, and there are those who insist that his ghost—among others—still shows up for services now and then.

At 7th Street is Kiev (2), a twenty-four-hour restaurant of the simple ethnic school, where you can devour blini and pirogi at any hour.

4.9 *Below Houston Street stay STRAIGHT as Second Avenue be-*

comes Chrystie Street.

At Rivington Street, on your right, is Sammy's Famous Roumanian Restaurant (3). "Pure Chicken Schmaltz Served with Above Orders," boasts the menu of this below-the-sidewalk eatery on the fringes of the Lower East Side. Besides chicken fat you can stuff yourself with kasha varnishkes, chopped liver, kishka, stuffed cabbage, and other tasty, leaden fare, washed down with a Dr. Brown's soda. It's not for lunch, however; the restaurant is open only from 4:30 p.m. to 10:30 p.m. daily, later on weekends, often with entertainment. The chief problem with this kind of meal, as the comedians say, is that three days later you're hungry again.

5.1 *LEFT onto Delancey Street.*

5.3 *RIGHT onto Allen Street.*

You're in the bargain center of the Lower East Side (4). You want shirts? We got. Some nice linens? Of course, linens. If you want to pay full price for a dress at Lord & Taylor or towels at Bloomingdale's, that's your business—but don't say we didn't tell you where to get it cheaper. You might lunch here on bagels and lox, or just grab a knish and wheel away. The narrow, old-world, shop-lined streets are fun for a cyclist except on supercrowded Sundays; peddlers and pedalers don't mix.

5.6 *RIGHT onto Division Street.*

5.8 *LEFT onto Bowery, quickly bearing RIGHT as you pass the flank of Chinatown.*

You'll find a mind-boggling collection of potential lunch spots in Chinatown (5), which may have the world's highest density of restaurants. Representing all regions, all styles, they're jammed into an intriguing maze of street life with an Oriental flavor. As on the Lower East Side, Sunday is the big day here—although Saturday isn't exactly serene either. Chinatown is always worth a detour.

5.9 *RIGHT onto Worth Street.*

6.3 *LEFT onto Broadway.*

A few blocks down on your left is where the mayor works—City Hall, a smart Federal building with French Renaissance detail, completed in 1811. The surrounding park was a pasture in the days of the Dutch and later a public execution site. Now it's nice for ceremonies or just schmoozing.

Across the street stands the Woolworth Building, which, at 729 feet, was the tallest in the world through this century's teens and twenties. (In 1930 the Chrysler Building took the title for a while.) A business tower modeled after the grand churches of Europe, it was nicknamed the Cathedral of Commerce. Look up to find the decorative faces and the oaks and acorns (which remind us that mighty fortunes from nickels and dimes grow).

A few blocks farther on Broadway, to your right at Vesey Street, is St. Paul's Chapel, New York's oldest public building. Built in 1766 (the steeple went up thirty years later), this was the church attended by Washington during the first year of his presidency, when New York was the nation's capital. No records exist of the sermons of the day, but given the proclivity of colonial ministers to speak at length, it's possible that George Washington slept here.

Pedaling down Broadway a few more blocks brings you to the graceful old, black-spired Trinity Church (6), on the right at the head of Wall Street. Three bronze doors depict scenes of the Bible and of Manhattan history. Alexander Hamilton and Robert "Steamboat" Fulton are buried out back in the grassy graveyard. Walk through the winding stone paths there and gaze up at the surrounding skyscrapers.

7.0 *LEFT onto Wall Street.*

The symbol of American big business known the world over, Wall Street was named for an actual wall of wood built by the Dutch in 1653 to protect their settlement against Indian attack. On the left-hand sidewalk in front of 70 Wall a plaque reads: "On this site the New York Stock Exchange was founded May 17, 1792, by 24 merchants and brokers who agreed to meet daily to buy and sell stocks and bonds under an old buttonwood tree which stood here."

An optional two-block detour will take you to the South Street Seaport (7) on the East River waterfront. To see this ambitious, ongoing reclamation of New York's old downtown waterfront properly will require a return trip of several hours. The complex is part re-creation and restoration, part introduction of the chic and trendy. Thus the visitor finds shops and restaurants with the feel of Madison—or Columbus—Avenue in nineteenth-century row houses across the street from tall ships.

7.3 *LEFT onto Water Street, then fast LEFT onto Pine Street.*

On Pine Street, you'll pass the distinctive Chase Manhattan Plaza, a huge, silvery skyscraper with a courtyard designed by Isamu Noguchi. In the corner is a fanciful sculpture by Jean Dubuffet, *Four Trees* (1972).

7.6 *RIGHT onto Nassau Street.*

Part of narrow Nassau Street is closed to cars on weekdays, making it a shopping mecca for thousands of financial district workers. Weekends, it's blissfully deserted.

7.8 *LEFT onto Fulton Street.*

8.0 *RIGHT onto Church Street.*

The World Trade Center is straight ahead as you turn. Up Church

Street, on the left, is the Job Lot Trading Co. and The Pushcart (8), the ultimate general store, with nearly everything at discount. It's hopelessly mobbed on Saturdays.

8.5 *Bear LEFT to Avenue of the Americas.*
On the right at 9th Street is Balducci's (9), the downtown Zabar's,

Exploring Wall Street under the gaze of George Washington.			Dan Carlinsky

where you can inhale the smells of foods from all corners of the world.

9.8 *RIGHT onto 10th Street.*

Tenth Street epitomizes the extremes of Greenwich Village: chic at the start, the street's townhouses become shabbier the farther east you go.

At Broadway, on your left, is Grace Church (10), a handsome Gothic Episcopal church with a welcome bonus for all (when it works)—a rare sidewalk drinking fountain.

10.7 *LEFT onto First Avenue.*

Take the overpass at 42nd Street as you go by the United Nations complex on your right; stop to count the flags on the plaza.

At 66th Street, on the left, Peppermint Park (11) serves lunches of the yogurt-quiche-crêpe-salad variety every day, plus a great selection of desserts and ice creams for a ride's-end treat.

14.7 *RIGHT onto 88th Street and head back to Gracie Mansion.*

Bicycle Shops

Bicycle Discount House, 332 East 14th Street (between First and Second avenues) (212-228-4344)

Bicycles Plus, 204 East 85th Street (between Second and Third avenues) (212-794-2201)

Bikes by George, 413 East 12th Street (between First Avenue and Avenue A) (212-533-0203)

Conrad's Bike Shop, 25 Tudor City Place (41st Street east of Second Avenue) (212-697-6966)

Emmey's 25th Street Bike Shop, 162 East 25th Street (between Lexington and Third avenues) (212-689-5186)

Gene's Bikes, 242 East 79th Street (between Second and Third avenues) (212-249-9218)

John's Mini-Bike and Bicycle Shop, 151 East Houston (between First and Second avenues) (212-982-5310)

Metro Bicycles, 1311 Lexington Avenue (88th Street) (212-427-4450)

Pedal Pusher Bicycles, 1306 Second Avenue (68th Street) (212-879-0740)

2

Upper Manhattan: Morningside Heights to Inwood

Round-trip distance pedaled: 15 miles
Terrain: moderately hilly
Minimum cycling time: 2 hours

Here's a fairly short city trip with a few good hills to put you in condition for the longer voyages to come. This route starts at the academic community of Morningside Heights, where, if you come by car, Sunday street parking is fairly easy. The tour leads through some of the lesser-known upper reaches of Manhattan, including two lush parks: peaceful Fort Tryon, with the extraordinary Cloisters museum and a great view of the Palisades, and Inwood Hill, where the Hudson and Harlem rivers meet, a big patch of surprisingly rough woodland in the midst of Manhattan's northernmost neighborhood.

0.0 *From Columbia University, cross Broadway and go downhill on 116th Street.*

Before you leave (or on your return), give at least a fast peek at the Columbia campus (1). Once a Revolutionary War battleground, later an area of sheep farms and goat pastures, still later the location of the Bloomingdale Asylum for the Insane, the site is now the home of a major world university. Columbia (founded in 1754) was one of the first colleges in the colonies; it was moved here in 1897. Most of the earliest campus buildings are of red brick, in Italian Renaissance style, with copper roofs that the years have turned green. Low Memorial Library, at campus center, is a great domed limestone building with Ionic columns that owes a lot to the Pantheon of Rome; a panel of noted architecture critics once named it one of America's ten most beautiful buildings. In front of Low is the much-photographed Alma Mater, created by Daniel Chester French, who designed the Lincoln Memorial statue in Washington; find the owl in the folds of Alma's skirts, as students have been doing for luck for more than eighty-five years. To the right as you face Low is a little brick house dating to 1820, the oldest building on campus. Just behind it is Columbia's chapel, with entry columns topped by cherub heads carved by Gutzon Borglum, who also

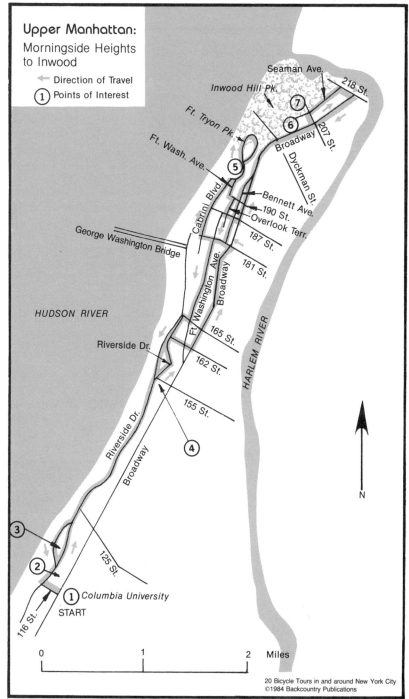

Upper Manhattan:
Morningside Heights
to Inwood

← Direction of Travel
① Points of Interest

Seaman Ave.
Inwood Hill Pk.
Ft. Tryon Pk.
Ft. Wash. Ave.
218 St.
⑦
⑥
207 St.
Broadway
Dyckman St.
⑤
Bennett Ave.
190 St.
Overlook Terr.
Cabrini Blvd.
187 St.
George Washington Bridge
181 St.
Ft. Washington Ave.
Broadway
165 St.
HUDSON RIVER
162 St.
Riverside Dr.
HARLEM RIVER
155 St.
④
Riverside Dr.
Broadway
N
③
125 St.
②
① Columbia University
START
116 St.

0   1   2   Miles

20 Bicycle Tours in and around New York City
©1984 Backcountry Publications

carved the heads at Mount Rushmore. Behind you as you face Low are lawns once used as athletic fields. Oldtimers like to tell how a student named Lou Gehrig used to hit long drives from home plate, near the lone tennis court, to the steps of Low, about 550 feet away. Unlikely, but it's a nice story just the same. The campus is tough to bike through because it's built on several levels, with connecting steps, but if you want to see more you can lock your bike to a rack and stroll through the ivy. Check the outdoor sculptures by Henry Moore and Jacques Lipchitz on the terrace that spans Amsterdam Avenue at 117th Street.

0.1 *RIGHT at the end of 116th Street onto Riverside Drive.*

On your right at 120th Street, you'll pass Riverside Church (2), built mostly with Rockefeller money. The largest building on Riverside Drive, the church is a gothic mass of Indiana limestone with a stately 392-foot tower housing the world's largest carillon: seventy-four bells ranging in weight from ten pounds to twenty tons. Sundays at 10:45 a.m. you can hear the call to worship sounded; Saturdays and Sundays, the bells chime every twenty minutes; on the hour weekdays.

Just beyond the church is International House, a melting-pot student residence, and, across the drive, one of the city's big tourist draws: Grant's Tomb (3). The tomb is a Greek-style temple, rather pompous but impressive nonetheless. Groucho used to ask who's buried here; you can go inside and find out. Grant's Tomb is open from 9 a.m. to 5 p.m. except Mondays and Tuesdays, and admission is free. Outside you can appreciate a great view of the Hudson River, nice lawns for kite-flying when the winds are right, and a colorful if jarring set of mosaic-tile benches done in 1973 by local residents.

2.1 *RIGHT onto 155th Street.*

On your right is Trinity Cemetery. Buried here are Clement Clarke Moore, author of "A Visit from St. Nicholas" (you know it as "The Night Before Christmas"), and John James Audubon, of bird fame.

An optional one-block detour will take you to the Audubon Terrace museum group (4) on 155th Street, a cluster of good specialty museums well worth a stop if you're interested in the subjects.

The Museum of the American Indian has a great three-story collection of masks, baskets, tools, dolls, silver, and gold fashioned by Indians of North, Central, and South America and the West Indies, plus art of the Arctic. You'll see tomahawks and wampum belts, carvings and weavings, Geronimo's carbine, Sitting Bull's medicine drum, and Crazy Horse's war bonnet. The Indian Information Center will answer all your questions. Open 10 a.m. to 5 p.m. Tuesdays through Saturdays, 1 p.m. to 5 p.m. Sundays; closed Mondays and holidays. Admission is $3 for adults, $2 for students and seniors with ID. Kids under 7 and native Americans get in free.

The Hispanic Society of America museum displays items ranging from centuries-old ivory boxes and ornate velvet-covered chests to giant door knockers from old Spanish castles and oils by El Greco, Goya, and Velásquez. The major artwork here is a room whose four walls are covered with 196 feet of murals, depicting life in different parts of Spain. Open 10 a.m. to 4:30 p.m. Tuesdays through Saturdays, 1 p.m. to 4 p.m. Sundays; closed Mondays and holidays. Admission is free.

The American Numismatic Society museum has more coins than $crooge McDuck: medals, decorations, and metal currency from modern times back to the sixth century. And for collectors searching for some arcane bit of numismatic minutia, there's a huge library of coin books. Open 9 a.m. to 4:30 p.m. Tuesdays through Saturdays, 1 p.m. to 3 p.m. Sundays; closed Mondays and holidays. Admission is free.

2.2 *Quickly bear LEFT, then RIGHT, following Riverside Drive signs.*

2.4 *LEFT onto the upper level of Riverside Drive.*

2.9 *RIGHT onto 162nd Street.*
The way here is cobblestoned and fairly steep, but bear with it—it doesn't last long.

3.1 *LEFT onto Broadway.*
Columbia Presbyterian Medical Center is on your left, starting at 165th Street. Columbia's medical school and the affiliated hospital form one of the preeminent medical teaching, treatment, and research centers in the country.

At 175th Street, look right to see the sprawling, garish United Palace, once a Loews Theater and now the home church of the noted healer and blesser known as Reverend Ike.

4.0 *LEFT onto 181st Street.*

4.2 *RIGHT onto Cabrini Boulevard.*
A block to your right is Bennett Park, with a rock outcropping that is the highest point in Manhattan, 267.75 feet above sea level. No wonder your legs hurt.

Cabrini Boulevard winds right and brings you to Fort Tryon Park, another Rockefeller gift to New York. The park consists of sixty-two peaceful acres of lawns for picnicking and paths lined with trees, flowering bushes, and gorgeous gardens in season. It's a favorite of neighboring German-speaking immigrants.

The pride of Fort Tryon is the Cloisters (5), also a Rockefeller present, which houses an extensive medieval art collection—part of the Metropolitan Museum—in an impressive hodgepodge of period monasteries and parts of a twelfth-century Romanesque church, transported from Europe to New York piecemeal. The highlight is a group of six tapestries of the fifteenth century, portraying the Hunt of the Unicorn. This is a wonderful spot for restful contemplation, as you walk down the cool stone-walled corridors admiring the art. Glorious medieval music is piped throughout at 12:30 p.m. and 2:30 p.m. Open 9:30 a.m. to 4:45 p.m. Tuesdays through Sundays from November through February; March through October closing time is 5:15 p.m. Always closed Mondays. Pay what you wish, but the official suggestion is $5 for adults, $2.50 for students and seniors. Kids under 12 go free, if they're with an adult.

Stay right leaving the Cloisters to avoid Henry Hudson Parkway.

6.1 *Leaving the park, go south on Fort Washington Avenue.*

6.4 *LEFT onto 190th Street.*

6.5 *RIGHT onto Overlook Terrace, a very steep downhill.*

6.7 *LEFT onto 187th Street.*

Low Plaza, the classical center of Columbia University's campus. Columbia University

6.9 *LEFT onto Broadway.*

On your left at 204th Street is Dyckman House (6), the last remaining eighteenth-century farmhouse in New York. This wood-and-stone gambrel-roofed 1783 dwelling looks thoroughly out of place amid upper Manhattan's standard fare of apartment blocks and stores. Behind is a fieldstone wall nearly two feet thick. Inside, you can see the original Dyckman family furniture and bric-a-brac—British, American, and Dutch furnishings—and a farmwife's dream kitchen. Nearby is a replica of a British army hut done up with trappings of the Revolutionary era. Open from 11 a.m. to 4 p.m. Tuesdays through Sundays; closed Mondays and holidays. Admission is free.

8.3 *LEFT onto 207th Street.*

At the end of 207th Street is Inwood Hill Park (7), where Indians once lived in caves. Today you'll find serious birdwatchers and other nature lovers who have come to appreciate the most natural spot in Manhattan: 196 hilly, rocky, heavily wooded acres with huge yellow poplars and oaks and all manner of wildflowers. Lock your bike and walk around. Look by the water for the boulder with a plaque marking the spot where Peter Minuit is supposed to have purchased Manhattan from an Indian tribe in 1626, paying with baubles and beads estimated at $24.

8.4 *Exit the park and turn LEFT up Seaman Avenue.*

8.7 *RIGHT at the end onto 218th Street.*

You're passing Baker Field, where Columbia competes in baseball, crew, soccer, tennis, track, and, in its 17,500-seat stadium, Ivy League football. The previous football stadium, demolished in 1983 at age 55, was the oldest major all-wood stadium in the country. The new one is nicer.

8.9 *RIGHT onto Broadway.*

10.3 *RIGHT onto Bennett Avenue.*

11.0 *RIGHT onto 181st Street.*

11.4 *LEFT onto Fort Washington Avenue.*

11.9 *RIGHT onto 165th Street and down a short, steep hill.*

12.0 *LEFT at the end onto Riverside Drive and back to the start.*

Bicycle Shops

Sid's Bike Shop, 215 West 230th Street (west of Broadway), Bronx (212-549-8247)
Simms Bicycle Store, 1619 Amsterdam Avenue (140th Street) (212-368-8860)
West Side Bicycle Discount House, 231 West 96th Street (Broadway)
   (212-663-7531)

3

The Plaza Hotel to Coney Island: From the Sublime to the Ridiculous

Round-trip distance pedaled: 35 miles
Terrain: flat
Minimum cycling time: 4 hours

Bike thirty-five miles just for a hot dog? Why not? This tour takes you from luxurious Fifth Avenue to rickety Coney Island. Two more opposite urban areas are hard to imagine. In between, you'll see plenty of lower Manhattan and the heart of Brooklyn, including a long, easily pedaled straightaway on the carless Ocean Parkway pedestrian mall. You might pack fishing gear and see what you can catch at Sheepshead bay, or check out the great aquarium at Coney Island, or stop in for an exhibit at the Brooklyn Museum. You'll probably be tempted to buy a hot dog or two, for that's what Coney Island is all about.

Start at the Plaza Hotel, corner of Fifth Avenue and 59th Street. The Plaza (1) is a New York version of a French Renaissance château. It's super-impressive, like a European grand hotel, with all those horses and drivers out front and all those snazzy customers trotting up and down the steps. Go inside, if you like, and stroll around the lobby for a taste of the sublime. Be sure to get a look at the chic Palm Court, but don't try to brunch there if you're dressed like a cyclist.

When you've had your fill, wave goodbye to General Sherman's statue on the square. Try to figure out if he's riding *out of* Central Park on his way downtown or backing *into* the park. Why doesn't he get off the horse and let the lady ride?

0.0 *South on Fifth Avenue to 8th Street.*

This portion of Fifth Avenue (2) is the most famous shopping strip in the United States. First comes the jewelers' half-mile, with the shops of Van Cleef & Arpels, Tiffany, Harry Winston, Buccellati, Cartier, and more, displaying zillions of dollars' worth of stones behind glass. At 57th Street, glance up to your left and see Atlas holding Tiffany's clock; if you like diamonds, walk inside to check out the wall display case holding the world's largest yellow diamond, a 128-carat boulder that's so valuable it's not for sale. Next door is the glassy Trump Tower, the city's highest concrete building, with its six-story marble atrium and costumed guards who appear to be auditioning for some high-budget Hollywood epic.

At 53rd Street, try to find the dollar sign over the Bridal Door of St. Thomas' Church; it was carved there by an impish stonemason who was making fun of wealthy parishioners. You're in shouting distance here of three notable museums. Across Fifth Avenue is the Museum of Broadcasting, where you can dig into the archives and listen to Fred Allen or watch Edward R. Murrow. Behind the church, toward Sixth Avenue, are the landmark Museum of Modern Art and the Museum of American Folk Art. This is Manhattan at its best.

Pass the Gothic St. Patrick's Cathedral, dwarfed by the surrounding skyscrapers, then Rockefeller Center. Look right at 47th Street to the colorful diamond block, where old-world merchants and traders put together hundreds of millions of dollars' worth of deals every day.

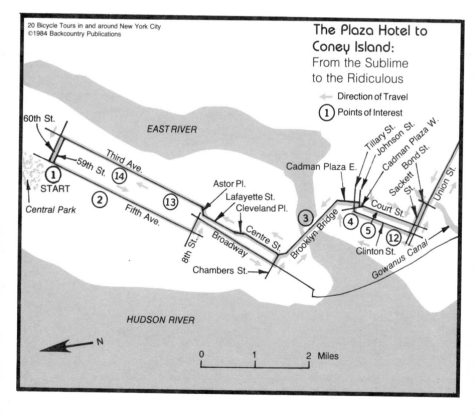

The Plaza Hotel to Coney Island: From the Sublime to the Ridiculous

In front of Wallach's clothiers at 46th Street is a little marble water trough for the refreshment of strolling dogs. Think about taking a lap or two, but don't.

At 42nd Street is the temple of the printed word, the New York Public Library. At 34th Street is King Kong's old stomping ground, the Empire State Building. And the slender wedge of a structure at 23rd Street is the Flatiron Building; bear right past it to stay on Fifth Avenue.

2.6 *LEFT onto 8th Street.*

2.8 *RIGHT onto Broadway.*

Below Houston Street, Broadway takes you through the heart of the Cast-Iron District, an area of commercial buildings with cast-iron facades, much loved by architecture students.

The Broadway building on your left on the near side of Broome Street houses the world's first practical passenger elevator; there's even a special door for it on the Broadway side, marked "Elevator."

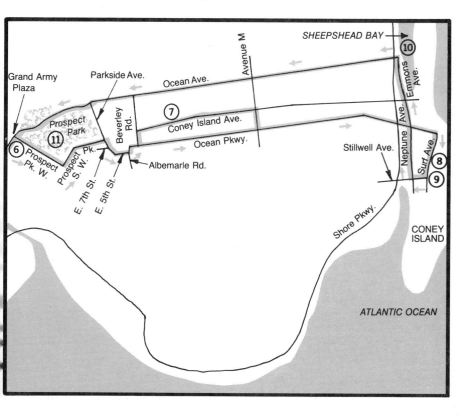

4.3 *LEFT onto Chambers Street.*

The city's police headquarters, a modern, red-brick building, is visible through the massive arches of the Municipal Building, straight ahead.

4.4 *RIGHT onto Centre Street.*

4.5 *LEFT, across Centre Street, onto the central pedestrian path of the Brooklyn Bridge (3).*

On July 23, 1886, so the story goes, a 23-year-old newsboy with a wife, three children, a girlfriend, and a stack of debts jumped off the bridge and won a $20 bet and a flock of sideshow offers. He was Steve Brodie, and his name is now in the dictionary, a "brodie" being defined as a suicidal leap.

Carry your bike down the steps as you leave the bridge in Brooklyn.

5.6 *RIGHT onto Cadman Plaza East.*

6.0 *RIGHT at the end onto Johnson Street, then first LEFT onto Cadman Plaza West.*

To your right, should you care to make a detour, is Brooklyn Heights (4). This was New York's first suburb, a Dutch settlement called Breukelen. It's still a lovely neighborhood, with residents who are very chauvinistic about its European blend of homey architecture and interesting shops, and its topnotch views of the lower Manhattan skyline.

Cadman Plaza West becomes Court Street.

There's another optional detour to the right on Atlantic Avenue (5) for a two-block stretch of Middle Eastern food shops and restaurants—everything from felafel to nuts.

7.0 *LEFT onto Union Street and over the Gowanus Canal.*

The canal, named for the Indian chief Gouwane, was once an important shipping byway, as well as a way of retreat for George Washington, who didn't always have the upper hand on the British. Don't inhale too deeply going across the water. The neighborhood here is run-down, but the route improves in a mile or so.

8.6 *RIGHT at Grand Army Plaza to Prospect Park West.*

This was plain old Ninth Avenue until it became fashionably lined with chic townhouses fronting on Prospect Park, when an upgrading name change seemed appropriate. (You can visit the park on the return trip.) For a gorgeous look at Brooklyn brownstone living at its best, peek into Montgomery Place (6), a few blocks down on your right, where there's a variety of well-kept old rowhouses.

9.5 *LEFT onto Prospect Park Southwest via the traffic circle (Bartel-Pritchard Square).*

10.3 *RIGHT at the first street off the next traffic circle, following a large overhead sign to "Bkln. Battery Tun.," which leads you onto the Ocean Parkway service road.*

10.5 *Walk your bike up the curved ramp on your left at East 7th Street.*

10.6 *LEFT onto East 5th Street, the first street off the ramp.*

10.9 *LEFT onto Albemarle Road.*

11.0 *First RIGHT onto the Ocean Parkway service road again.*
    Pick up the wide, shady pedestrian/bike mall on Ocean Parkway and pedal for five miles through the midsection of Brooklyn. The path, incidentally, was America's first for bikers, built in the 1890s from donations.
    An optional detour leads you to the antiques district (7) on Coney Island Avenue, which parallels Ocean Parkway a few blocks to the left. You'll find good browsing at the shops here, stretching south of Beverley Road.

16.1 *Follow Ocean Parkway as it swings right and becomes Surf Avenue at Coney Island.*
    Early in the century the subway brought all of New York here for the rides, the fun, and the nickel franks. Today the old-time amusement area is faded and a bit seedy, but even honky-tonk is worth a visit now and then. Tightly packed Surf Avenue is the main street. (The area, according to some, got its name from the rabbits—or conies—that once lived here.)
    On your left at West 8th Street is the New York Aquarium (8), where you can see penguins, seals, sharks, dolphins,and other sea life. Open 10 a.m. to 4:45 p.m. every day; $3.75 for adults, $1.50 for kids (anyone under 16 has to be with a grown-up), free after 2 p.m. on weekdays only for those over 65.
    Also on your left, at Stillwell Avenue, is the original Nathan's Famous (9). It was in 1916 that Nathan Handwerker quit his job as a pushcart hot-dog vendor to open his own stand, shrewdly charging a nickel instead of a dime for a frank. The rest is socio-culinary history. You can buy chicken, ribs, corn on the cob, and other assorted mouth-stuffers at Nathan's. Actually, just watching the action can be a treat. Patrons don't merely eat; they shovel it all in.

16.8 *Leaving Nathan's, go up Stillwell Avenue toward the elevated tracks.*

17.1 *RIGHT onto Neptune Avenue, which becomes Emmons Avenue at Sheepshead Bay (10).*
    Fishing, fishing, fishing. Emmons Avenue, the main drag, is a mar-

velous mix of sea sounds and smells. On the piers side, take a whiff of true ocean air; across the road, where restaurants and open-air snack stands line the way, the odor of seafood and garlic rules. On pleasant days, gulls scream, baby carriages squeak, boats chug and honk, the voices of men in rubber boots sound from pier to pier over the slapping of miniwaves: "We got fresh blackfish here! Here! Plenty of fish here! Hey, we got fish!" And so they do. At the storefront seafood counters you can snack on little-necks and cherrystones, on the halfshell or baked, garlicky and loaded with breadcrumbs: noshing by the sea.

19.0 *LEFT onto Ocean Avenue (not Ocean Parkway) back to Prospect Park.*

24.2 *LEFT when you reach the corner of the park (at unmarked Parkside Avenue) to enter.*

If you don't know Prospect Park (11), take some time to look around and be impressed. Its 526 acres were laid out by the designer of Central Park, and many think this landscape is even better. There's a lake to your left, the fine Brooklyn Museum and the lush Botanic Garden to your right, and lawns and trees everywhere.

Follow the park drive to the exit at Grand Army Plaza, where you'll come out upon the grand Soldiers and Sailors Memorial Arch, with its sculpture of a flag-draped Victory in a horse-drawn chariot flanked by trumpet-playing winged heralds. It's quite a sight.

25.6 *First LEFT, across Prospect Park West onto the street to the left of a dark brown, narrow apartment building, putting you onto Union Street.*

26.8 *RIGHT onto Bond Street.*

26.9 *LEFT onto Sackett Street.*

27.4 *RIGHT onto Clinton Street through the heart of the Cobble Hill Historic District (12).*

A tree-shaded section with fine old rowhouses of varying styles with some beautiful iron grillwork, Cobble Hill has a charming nineteenth-century atmosphere. Many of the houses date from the 1840s and 1850s and have been lavishly restored or renovated within.

28.3 *Clinton Street curves right to become Tillary Street.*

28.4 *LEFT onto Cadman Plaza East and back to the mall of the Brooklyn Bridge.*

29.9 *First RIGHT off the bridge in Manhattan, onto Centre Street, which runs into Cleveland Place and then Lafayette Street in less than a mile.*

31.3 *RIGHT onto Astor Place.*

31.4 *LEFT onto Third Avenue.*

Detour left, if you like, at 20th Street to visit Gramercy Park (13), a genteel, London-like residential square.

If you want to make one final stop before tour's end, try Seashells Unlimited (14), on the left side of Third Avenue between 38th and 39th Streets. Here you'll find more than 2,000 varieties of shells, coral, and other natural treasures of the deep. Open 11 a.m. to 6 p.m. every day but Sunday. Only in New York.

34.0 *LEFT onto 60th Street, back to Central Park and the Plaza Hotel.*

Bicycle Shops

Manhattan

Bicycle Habitat, 244 Lafayette Street (between Spring and Prince streets (212-431-3315)

Conrad's Bike Shop, 25 Tudor City Place (41st Street east of Second Avenue) (212-697-6966)

Emmey's 25th Street Bike Shop, 162 East 25th Street (between Lexington and Third avenues) (212-689-5186)

Manhattan Express Bicycle Shop, 40 Great Jones Street (3rd Street, between Bowery and Second Avenue) (212-420-1515)

Sixth Avenue Bicycles, 546 Avenue of the Americas (at 15th Street) (212-255-5100)

Brooklyn

Ace Cycles, 1120 Cortelyou Road (two blocks east of Coney Island Avenue) (718-462-7713)

Boerum Hill Cycles, 1278 Atlantic Avenue (at Smith Street) (718-625-9633)

Brooklyn Bicycle Center, 717 Coney Island Avenue (near Cortelyou Road) (718-941-9095)

Dixon's Bicycle Shop, 792 Union Street (near Sixth Avenue) (718-636-0067)

Kings Highway Cycle, 728 Kings Highway (at East 8th Street) (718-339-9830)

Roy's Sheepshead Cycle, 2679, Coney Island Avenue (at Avenue X) (718-646-9430)

Sizzling Cycles, 3100 Ocean Parkway (at Brighton Beach Avenue) (718-372-8985)

4
Staten Island: The Rural Borough

Round-trip distance pedaled: 23 miles
Terrain: moderately hilly
Minimum cycling time: 3 hours, plus 1 hour for ferry rides and waits

Back in the old days, so an ancient story maintains, New York won Staten Island from New Jersey in a boat race. The Staten Island Historical Society says it ain't so (ruining a nice tale), but if it *were* true, it was a pretty nice prize from cyclists' point of view. If you come over from Manhattan on one of the huge ferry boats, you'll feel as though you've come into a small seaside town. Then, just a few blocks later, you'll be into hill country. You can rush through this tour in a few hours, but how much better to allot a full day and take in all the sights—a Tibetan temple and gardens (on Staten Island!), ocean views, harbor views, houses and crafts shops more than 200 years old. For good measure, there's a little zoo and a spunky arts center. Begin at South Ferry in Manhattan. The boat ride costs a quarter each way.

0.0 *Leave the ferry (1) by the ramp and take the first LEFT onto Bay Street (2).*

For the 25 cents you pay on the return ferry trip, you get to ride close to the water, usually with a crowd of other island-bound bikers. During the twenty-minute trip, you'll pass the Statue of Liberty and marvel at the impressive view of the lower Manhattan skyline. You'll also catch a glimpse of the sweeping, 4,260-foot Verrazano-Narrows Bridge, linking Staten Island and Brooklyn. (Until 1980 it was the longest suspension bridge in the world, but the 4,626-foot Humber Estuary Bridge in England now holds the title.) Once you're cycling on wide, flat Bay Street, you'll be able to spot the dramatic bridge from several points. There's also an antiques row here that can be worth a pause.

Just past the intersection of Bay Street and Victory Boulevard, you can detour along the side streets to see the Stapleton neighborhood (3). Now a quiet, polyglot neighborhood of new apartment buildings and nineteenth-century Victorian houses, Stapleton in the old days was home to

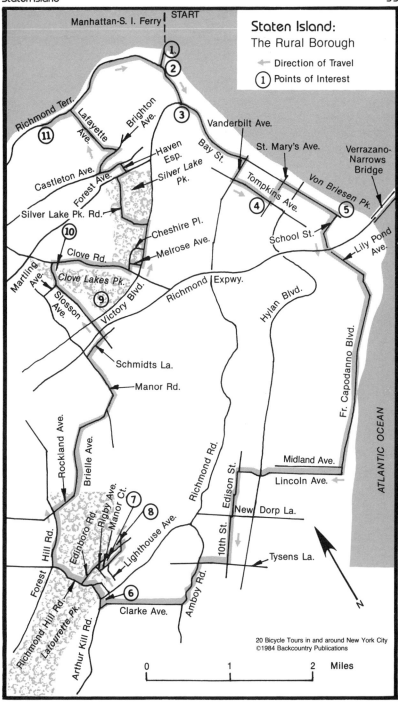

Staten Island   START
Manhattan-S. I. Ferry

Staten Island:
The Rural Borough

← Direction of Travel
① Points of Interest

Richmond Terr.
Lafayette Ave.
Brighton Ave.
Castleton Ave.
Forest Ave.
Haven Esp.
Silver Lake Pk.
Bay St.
Vanderbilt Ave.
St. Mary's Ave.
Verrazano-Narrows Bridge
Tompkins Ave.
Von Briesen Pk.
Silver Lake Pk. Rd.
Cheshire Pl.
Melrose Ave.
School St.
Lily Pond Ave.
Clove Rd.
Clove Lakes Pk.
Martling Ave.
Slosson Ave.
Victory Blvd.
Richmond Expwy.
Hylan Blvd.
Fr. Capodanno Blvd.
ATLANTIC OCEAN
Schmidts La.
Manor Rd.
Rockland Ave.
Brielle Ave.
Richmond Rd.
Edison St.
Midland Ave.
Lincoln Ave. ←
Edinboro Rd.
Rigby Ave.
Manor Ct.
Lighthouse Ave.
New Dorp La.
10th St.
Tysens La.
Forest Hill Rd.
Richmond Hill Rd.
Latourette Pk.
Arthur Kill Rd.
Clarke Ave.
Amboy Rd.

N

20 Bicycle Tours in and around New York City
©1984 Backcountry Publications

0   1   2   Miles

several breweries (many with *Biergarten* attached), a vaudeville theater, and at least one famous New Yorker — Cornelius Vanderbilt, the shipping tycoon.

1.5 *RIGHT onto Vanderbilt Avenue.*

1.8 *LEFT at a traffic light onto Tompkins Avenue.*
At number 420, stop at the Garibaldi-Meucci Memorial Museum (4), in a two-story white frame house surrounded by an iron fence and a large lawn. Giuseppe Garibaldi, the nineteenth-century Italian patriot, soldier, and expatriate, lived here for two years; Antonio Meucci, who claimed to have invented the telephone, was his roommate. Documents inside give Meucci's version of phone history. The house is open 10 a.m. to 5 p.m. Tuesdays through Fridays, 1 p.m. to 5 p.m. Saturdays and Sundays; closed Mondays; no charge.

2.2 *RIGHT onto Tompkins Avenue leaving the museum, then immediate LEFT onto St. Mary's Avenue.*

2.6 *RIGHT back onto Bay Street.*
On your left at the end of Bay Street is Von Briesen Park (5), where you can take a close-up look at the Narrows and the Verrazano bridge.

3.3 *Leaving the park, cross Bay Street to pick up unmarked School Street, which curves left and goes under a highway overpass; follow the bike lane markings on the pavement toward Route 278 East. School Street becomes Lily Pond Avenue.*
As you go along School Street under the approach to the bridge, look up to your left. The bridge toll plaza is built on the site of the former grounds of the Staten Island Cricket and Baseball Club. There, in 1874, on a court modeled after one seen in Bermuda, America's first game of lawn tennis was played.

4.8 *Lily Pond Avenue curves left and becomes Fr. Capodanno Boulevard.*
You can stay on the road, or follow the bike path on the landward side of the boulevard, or cross to the pedestrian walkway. The view of the Atlantic Ocean is hard to beat.

6.7 *RIGHT onto Lincoln Avenue, one block past Midland Avenue.*

7.7 *LEFT onto Edison Street.*

8.3 *RIGHT onto New Dorp Lane, then immediate LEFT onto 10th Street.*

8.8 *RIGHT at the first light onto Tysens Lane.*

9.2 *LEFT onto Amboy Road.*

9.6 *RIGHT at the second traffic light onto Clarke Avenue.*

Coming up on your right is the Richmondtown Restoration (6), a perfect place to lunch and learn. Richmondtown, in the eighteenth century, was the largest community on the island. With an eye to the past, the superb and still-developing restored village of two dozen buildings gives a good picture of life here during the eighteenth and nineteenth centuries.

You can park at the bike racks in front of the first stop—the Staten Island Historical Society Museum, a building that dates from 1848. Nearby you'll see a carriage house, a military goods store, a print shop (with the oldest operating press in the United States), a carpentry shop, a tinsmith's shop, and a general store stocked with patent medicines, candles, snowshoes, household items, and other necessities of the Dutch colonial village. Craft demonstrations— harness making, spinning, tinsmithing, weaving, and the like—are always part of the show, with the demonstrators dressed in period clothes. The most noteworthy building is the Voorlezer's House, a National Historic Landmark. This clapboard house on Richmond Hill Road is the oldest surviving elementary school in the States, circa 1695. (The *Voorlezer,* in Dutch settlements, was a teacher and lay prayer leader.) It's been restored to the period.

You can easily spend an hour or two at Richmondtown, especially if you make the picnic area near the museum your lunch stop. Buildings are open from 10 a.m. to 5 p.m. Mondays through Fridays, 1 p.m. to 5 p.m. weekends. Free entry to the grounds, $4 to go inside.

10.6 *Leaving the restoration on Clarke Avenue, go RIGHT at a traffic light onto Arthur Kill Road, which quickly runs into Richmond Hill Road.*

You'll puff and pedal uphill, through a public golf course. Islanders call this winding stretch Snake Hill. It's the steepest hill of the tour.

11.0 *RIGHT, at the crest, following the sign to the Clubhouse Cafe.*

11.1 *Bear RIGHT, following the road past the cafe and out of the golf course; pick up unmarked Edinboro Road, noting the lighthouse straight ahead.*

11.3 *First RIGHT onto Rigby Avenue, following the road as it curves.*

11.5 *At the end of Rigby Avenue, pick up cobblestoned Manor Court for just a few yards, then LEFT onto Lighthouse Avenue.*

Note the strikingly modern house on your right, at number 48 Manor Court. It's the only residence in New York City designed by Frank Lloyd Wright.

Take a short uphill climb on Lighthouse Avenue to one of Staten Island's most unexpected attractions: the Jacques Marchais Center of Tibetan Art (7). Here, in New York, is a close copy of a Tibetan temple with gardens. The museum is the creation of an American actress who, as a child, was given some small bronze Tibetan deities as dolls, sparking a life-long love affair with Tibetan art and culture. Although she never visited the country, she managed to amass perhaps the largest privately owned collection of

Hilltop lighthouse on Staten Island.   Carol Cirignano

Tibetan art outside Tibet. She chose the hilltop location so its views would remind visitors of the Himalayas. The center is open Fridays through Sundays from 1 p.m. to 5 p.m. in April, October, and November; same hours Wednesdays through Sundays from May through September. Admission is $2.50 for adults, $2 for seniors, $1 for children under 12. Past the Tibetan museum, continue uphill on Lighthouse Avenue.

11.8 *LEFT onto Edinboro Road.*
About half a mile down the road on your left you'll see a lighthouse (8) planted in the middle of a lawn. Why? Simple. You're on a hill, high above New York Harbor; the light is used to guide ships. It's been doing its job since 1912, and the Coast Guard recently refurbished its brick and limestone facade. You can't go into the house itself, but you can stop and take a breather on the lawn. Continue on Edinboro Road past the lighthouse and back into the golf course.

12.6 *RIGHT onto Richmond Hill Road.*

13.0 *RIGHT at the first traffic light onto Forest Hill Road.*

13.7 *RIGHT at the next light onto Rockland Avenue.*

14.1 *First LEFT onto unmarked Brielle Avenue.*

15.3 *LEFT at the end onto Manor Road.*

16.0 *RIGHT, at the third traffic light, onto Schmidts Lane, just before Manor Road goes under an expressway overpass.*

16.3 *LEFT at the next traffic light onto Slosson Avenue.*

17.1 *RIGHT at the end of Slosson Avenue onto Martling Avenue.*
You're cutting through a corner of Clove Lakes Park (9), a pleasantly bucolic spot little known off the island. To your right are playing fields, a couple of lakes, and some quiet little grassy areas good for informal picnics; to your left, a brook-fed lake and even a small waterfall.

17.4 *RIGHT onto Clove Road.*
The Staten Island Zoo (10) comes up immediately. Here's some of what's there: mammoth turtles, slithering iguanas, snarling alligators, and the world's largest rattlesnake collection. Feeding times: mammals daily at 3 p.m.; reptiles, Sundays at 3 p.m. The zoo is open daily from 10 a.m. to 4:45 p.m.; entry is free on Wednesdays (and free every day for those under 3 or over 65); other days, the price is $1. There's a special little kids' zoo.

18.2 *LEFT onto Cheshire Place.*

18.3 *First RIGHT onto Melrose Avenue.*

18.5 *LEFT onto Victory Boulevard.*

18.9 *LEFT onto unmarked Silver Lake Park Road (closed to cars on weekends) and through the park.*

19.6 *RIGHT leaving the park onto Forest Avenue, uphill.*

19.7 *LEFT onto Haven Esplanade; bear RIGHT.*

19.9 *LEFT at the end onto Castleton Avenue, downhill.*

20.2 *RIGHT at the first traffic light onto Brighton Avenue.*

20.5 *LEFT at a caution light onto Lafayette Avenue.*

21.2 *RIGHT at the end of Lafayette Avenue onto Richmond Terrace (also known as Bay Street).*

Three blocks to the left is an optional detour: the Snug Harbor Cultural Center (11). Snug Harbor was opened in the 1830s as a retirement spot for "aged, decrepit, and worn-out sailors." Old tars lived at the eighty-acre retreat until 1976, when they were moved to new quarters in North Carolina and the city took over the grounds and the Greek Revival buildings. Seven of the structures—including the beautiful nineteenth-century wrought-iron fence that surrounds the center—are National Historic Landmarks. There are art galleries open Wednesdays through Sundays, noon to 5 p.m., plus a snack bar, a museum for children, gift shops, a botanical garden, and eighty acres of lawn and meadow open daily for strolling or relaxing. Frequent concerts and other performances are often free. Turn right leaving the center.

23.1 *LEFT to return to the ferry terminal for the sail back to Manhattan.*

Bicycle Shops
Bennett's Bicycles Inc., 517 Jewett Avenue (near Forest Avenue) (718-447-8652)
Roald Bike Shop, 1434 Richmond Road (near Raritan Avenue) (718-351-7575)

5

Picnic Across The Hudson: To Tallman Mountain Park

Round-trip distance pedaled: 49 miles
Terrain: mostly flat
Minimum cycling time: 6 hours

This is a long but fairly easy interstate ride with a delightful picnic stop at the halfway point. There are some good things to see as you head up Riverside Drive, and you'll find crossing the George Washington Bridge on two wheels a thrill if the view is clear. The New Jersey part of the ride is mostly quiet, uninterrupted pedaling through a string of suburban towns. Leave early to allow enough time for proper alfresco dining and a bit of frolic in the park before you head for home.

0.0 *Start at the corner of Broadway and 80th Street.*

There's a smart reason for beginning here: This corner is home to Zabar's (1), a fine place to stock up on picnic fixings of various persuasions. (For fresh fruits and vegetables you'll do best at one of the outdoor stands in the neighborhood.) If you're a bagel lover, pop into H & H bagels across 80th Street, if only for the smells.

0.1 *Up Broadway and LEFT onto 81st Street.*

0.2 *RIGHT at the end onto Riverside Drive.*

Riverside Drive, in the view of many, is New York's best-looking street. On one side you'll see a string of huge, expensive apartment houses of differing architectural styles; on the other side, wonderful river vistas.

On your left at 89th Street is the Soldiers' and Sailors' Monument, a Riverside Drive landmark. It's a Grecian-style memorial, honoring the memory of Union soldiers in the Civil War. Surrounding the columned tower is a terrace with a great view of Riverside Park and the Hudson River. In front, for whatever reason, there are ornamental cannon aimed at New Jersey. Several more monuments pop up over the next mile or so. That's Joan of Arc at 93rd Street.

Many of the apartment buildings on the Drive have eye-catching facades. One that looks ordinary but isn't if you look more closely is at the

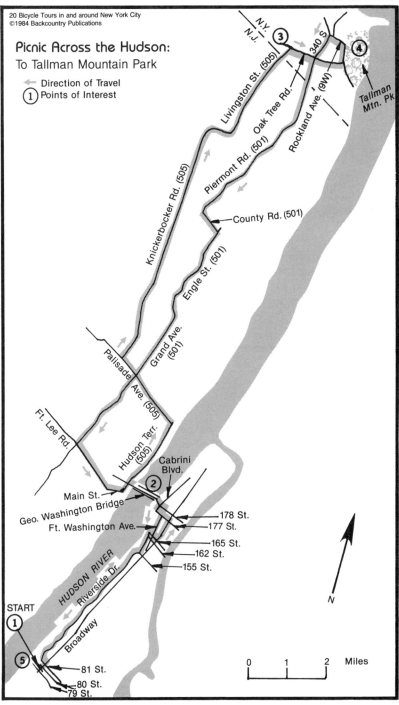

20 Bicycle Tours in and around New York City
©1984 Backcountry Publications

Picnic Across the Hudson:
To Tallman Mountain Park

← Direction of Travel
① Points of Interest

N.Y.
N.J.

③ 340 S. ④

Livingston St. (505)
Oak Tree Rd.
Piermont Rd. (501)
Rockland Ave. (9W)

Tallman
Mtn. Pk

Knickerbocker Rd. (505)

County Rd. (501)

Engle St. (501)

Grand Ave.
(501)

Palisade Ave. (505)

Ft. Lee Rd.

Hudson Terr.
(505)

Cabrini
Blvd.

②

Main St.

Geo. Washington Bridge

Ft. Washington Ave.

178 St.
177 St.

165 St.
162 St.

155 St.

HUDSON RIVER

Riverside Dr.

START
①

Broadway

⑤

81 St.

80 St.
79 St.

N

0   1   2   Miles

northeast corner of 96th Street. It's the Cliff Dweller's Apartments, a thin, orange-brick tower with some Art Deco touches. Look above the second story and you'll see a frieze with carvings of buffalo heads, mountain lions, and other Western creatures—charmingly out of place on the West Side of Manhattan.

At 107th Street you're greeted by a triple-life-size statue in front of a townhouse that houses the New York Buddhist Church. He's a Buddhist saint, Shinran Shonin (1173–1262), given by the people of Hiroshima. If you come by at the right times, you can drop in for chanting or meditation.

Just up the hill at 116th Street is Columbia University's main campus. At 120th Street is the stately Riverside Church, and two blocks later, Grant's Tomb.

4.2 *RIGHT onto 155th Street for a few seconds, then bear left and then right to follow Riverside Drive signs. Next, turn LEFT onto the upper level of Riverside Drive.*

On your right on 155th Street is Trinity Cemetery, resting place of Clement Clarke Moore, who wrote "A Visit from St. Nicholas," and of John James Audubon, the bird man.

4.9 *RIGHT onto 162nd Street, a short but steep cobbled hill.*

5.1 *LEFT onto Broadway.*

5.7 *LEFT onto 177th Street.*

5.9 *RIGHT onto Cabrini Boulevard, then a quick LEFT onto the sidewalk at 178th Street.*

6.0 *LEFT through the gate on the pedestrian ramp leading to the George Washington Bridge (2).*

Le Corbusier once called this "the most beautiful bridge in the world . . . blessed . . . the only seat of grace in the disordered city"—but that was before the lower level was added. It's still a nice bridge. The ride over is a full mile; savor the views.

7.3 *RIGHT onto the first road off the bridge on the New Jersey side — unmarked Hudson Terrace (Route 505).*

9.3 *LEFT onto Palisade Avenue, keeping to Route 505.*

11.6 *RIGHT onto Knickerbocker Road, still Route 505.*

17.7 *RIGHT onto Livingston Street, still Route 505.*

In a couple of miles you'll be out of New Jersey and into Rockland County, New York.

21.1 *RIGHT onto Oak Tree Road.*

Here you can make a detour two blocks to your left on Oak Tree to the De Wint House (3), a national landmark. Once the home of a West Indian planter, the house served several times as George Washington's headquarters. Open 10 a.m. to 4 p.m. every day but Sundays; free admission.

22.8 *LEFT onto Route 9W (Rockland Avenue).*

24.0 *RIGHT into Tallman Mountain Park.*
Part of the Palisades Interstate Park chain of greenery, Tallman (4) offers a choice of picnic grounds. The north area, three-quarters of a mile from the entrance, gives a spectacular view of the widening Hudson River and of Washington Irving territory on the other side. Except on summer Sundays, which can be crowded here, this is a good, relaxing spot for a cycling break.

25.5 *Leaving the park, turn RIGHT to continue up Route 9W.*

25.7 *LEFT, downhill, onto Route 340 South; at the bottom, bear LEFT to stay on 340.*
As you recross the state line into New Jersey, Route 340 switches to Route 501 (Piermont Road). Stay on 501 through a series of pleasant residential areas into the town of Leonia; street names change often, but the 501 signs keep you on course.

39.5 *LEFT onto Fort Lee Road at Parkway Motors Toyota; signs point to the town of Fort Lee.*
The road is a monstrous uphill climb; many before you have walked their bikes up it. As you enter downtown Fort Lee, the name of the road changes to Main Street.

41.4 *LEFT at the end of Main Street onto Hudson Terrace, a very steep downhill.*

41.5 *RIGHT, about a block later, at the "Pedestrians to New York" sign, and back across the George Washington Bridge. Leave the bridge by the same ramp you took on the way over.*

42.9 *RIGHT at the foot of the ramp onto 178th Street.*

43.1 *RIGHT onto Fort Washington Avenue, downhill past the Columbia Presbyterian Medical Center.*

43.7 *RIGHT, downhill, onto 165th Street.*

43.8 *LEFT at the foot of the hill and back down Riverside Drive.*
For an optional end-of-tour detour, go down to 79th Street, turn right, and bike under the Henry Hudson Parkway to the Boat Basin (5). All kinds of vessels, from sailing yachts to little putt-putts, are anchored here.

There's even a small community of fulltime houseboat-dwellers, who refer to the West Side as "over in New York." The nautical atmosphere is pleasant, and on clear days there's a good view up the river to George's bridge.

Bicycle Shops
Bicycle Renaissance, 491 Amsterdam Avenue (84th Street) (212-724-2350)
Eddie's Bicycle Shop, 490 Amsterdam Avenue (84th Street) (212-580-2011)
Simms Bicycle Store, 1619 Amsterdam Avenue (140th Street) (212-368-8860)
West Side Bicycle Discount House, 231 West 96th Street (Broadway)
    (212-663-7531)

Sampling the world of boating at the 79th Street Boat Basin.   Dan Carlinsky

6

The Long Island Quickie:
Eisenhower Memorial Park
and Old Westbury Gardens

Round-trip distance pedaled: 13 miles
Terrain: flat
Minimum cycling time: 2 hours

This is a perfect starter tour for those with questionable leg power. The route is 95 percent hill-free, not long at all, and mostly pleasant country riding to boot. You can spend some time in Eisenhower Memorial Park, bike a ways, spend some more time at pretty Old Westbury Gardens, bike some more, and relax at an out-of-the-way duck pond before you head back. Nassau County residents may leave their cars in the park; others will have to try the shopping center lots on the other side of the Bethpage-Hempstead Turnpike. The park is at exit M5 of the Meadowbrook Parkway, in East Meadow.

0.0 *Follow Park Boulevard for a mile and a half through the park to the Merrick Avenue exit, or take time to mosey about the park before you set out on the tour.*

Eisenhower Memorial Park (1) has four miles of very flat bike paths, just right for warming up the legs. The paths are unmarked, so you'd be wise to pick up a park map at the Field House at Parking Field number 2. In the park itself, visit the Nassau County Historical Museum, which details Long Island's development from glacial times through Nassau's first settlement in 1643 to modern times. There are convenient bike racks at the door. The museum is open 9 a.m. to 4:45 p.m. Wednesdays through Sundays; admission is 25 cents. Look around and you'll find other diversions, including a driving range, where you might stop and hit a bucket of golf balls as far as you can.

1.5 *Leave the park by turning RIGHT onto busy Merrick Avenue.*

That's Roosevelt Raceway, the trotters track, on your left as you go up the avenue.

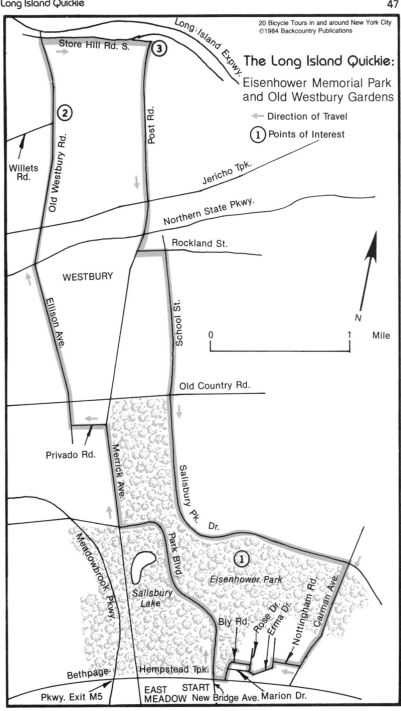

20 Bicycle Tours in and around New York City
©1984 Backcountry Publications

The Long Island Quickie:

Eisenhower Memorial Park and Old Westbury Gardens

← Direction of Travel

① Points of Interest

Long Island Expwy.

Store Hill Rd. S. ③

②

Willets Rd.

Old Westbury Rd.

Post Rd.

Jericho Tpk.

Northern State Pkwy.

Rockland St.

WESTBURY

Ellison Ave.

School St.

0 _____ 1 Mile

N

Old Country Rd.

Privado Rd.

Merrick Ave.

Salisbury Pk. Dr.

Meadowbrook Pkwy.

Park Blvd.

Salisbury Lake

① Eisenhower Park

Rose Dr.
Erma Dr.

Bly Rd.

Nottingham Rd.

Carman Ave.

Bethpage-

Pkwy. Exit M5

EAST MEADOW

Hempstead Tpk.

START New Bridge Ave. Marion Dr.

2.2 *LEFT at the first traffic light onto Privado Road.*

2.5 *RIGHT onto Ellison Avenue, which becomes Old Westbury Road as you cross Jericho Turnpike.*

In 2.2 miles, stop at the huge iron gates of Old Westbury Gardens (2), on your right. No cycling is allowed on the grounds, but you can leave your bike locked to one of the big oak trees near the ticket booth, under the watchful eyes of a guard, and stroll through the 100 acres of trees, gardens, pools, and statues. You'll pass through eight distinctively de-signed gardens, patterned after the great eighteenth-century English parks. Depending on the season, look for exotic water lilies, veronica, Japanese iris, phlox,and a rainbow of other flowers. Admission is $4.50 ($1 for children 6 to 12). An extra $3 (another $1.50 for kids) entitles you to inspect the impressive Georgian manor, built in 1906. Senior citizens pay $3.50 for both. The gates are open Wednesdays through Sundays and Monday holidays, May through October, 10 a.m. to 5 p.m. Picnicking is allowed. Leaving the gardens, turn right and continue on Old Westbury Road.

5.1 *RIGHT onto Store Hill Road South (the Long Island Expressway service road).*

This is the trip's only serious hill; if you're on a single-speed bike you'll probably want to dismount and walk for a short while.

6.0 *RIGHT along a tiny duck pond onto Post Road.*

Stop at the pond (3) to catch your breath and talk to the ducks. This is a nice spot for a picnic if you've brought food along.

7.6 *LEFT onto Rockland Street, just after crossing Jericho Turnpike and the Northern State Parkway.*

7.8 *RIGHT onto School Street, which becomes Salisbury Park Drive as you cross Old Country Road; follow along the edge of a lush county golf course.*

10.7 *RIGHT onto Carman Avenue, at the park's edge.*

11.5 *RIGHT onto Nottingham Road.*

11.7 *LEFT onto Erma Drive.*

11.8 *RIGHT onto Marion Drive; immediate RIGHT onto Rose Drive.*

11.9 *LEFT onto Bly Road.*

12.2 *RIGHT onto Hempstead-Bethpage Turnpike and back to the Eisenhower Memorial Park entrance.*

Bicycle Shops
East Meadow Bike & Mower, 353 Merrick Avenue, East Meadow (516-481-1880)

7
Southern Nassau: Five Towns Area

Round-trip distance pedaled: 38 miles
Terrain: flat
Minimum cycling time: 4 hours

This quiet, simple tour goes from eastern Queens through some fairly fancy South Shore real estate down to the beaches on the Atlantic. Early on a weekend morning is probably the best time for the trip, particularly if you follow this route in summer. That way you'll have more elbow room, more delightful sea breezes, and smooth rolling in general. The starting point is in Hollis, at the shopping center at the corner of Hillside Avenue and Francis Lewis Boulevard. Drivers take the Long Island Expressway exit to Francis Lewis Boulevard and follow it to Hillside Avenue.

0.0 *From the shopping center lot, cross Hillside Avenue and pick up Francis Lewis Boulevard.*
This first stretch of the tour consists of row houses and more row houses—pure Queens. But have patience; the scenery improves. Francis Lewis, in case the name doesn't ring a bell, was a Welsh-born colonial bigshot, member of the Continental Congress, signer of the Declaration of Independence, and all that.

2.0 *Crossing Springfield Boulevard, stay STRAIGHT between 217th Street and 119th Avenue to keep on Francis Lewis Boulevard.*

2.4 *LEFT at a wide intersection with several stop signs to stay on Francis Lewis Boulevard.*

3.0 *Skirt Montefiore Cemetery, on your right, then turn RIGHT at the edge of the cemetery and keep following the signs to stay on Francis Lewis Boulevard.*

5.4 *Francis Lewis Boulevard runs into unmarked Hook Creek Boulevard.*

5.5 *Bear RIGHT for a very short block, then a quick LEFT onto Hungry Harbor Road, which becomes Rosedale Road.*

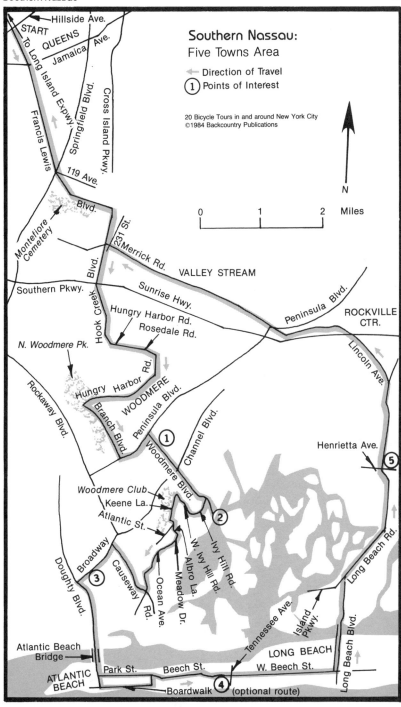

Southern Nassau:
Five Towns Area

⬅ Direction of Travel
① Points of Interest

20 Bicycle Tours in and around New York City
©1984 Backcountry Publications

0   1   2   Miles

N

You're in Nassau County now, and, as promised, the scenery has improved.

6.2 *RIGHT onto Hungry Harbor Road again.*

7.7 *Follow the road to the LEFT past a park, where Hungry Harbor Road becomes Branch Boulevard.*

8.5 *LEFT at the end of Branch Boulevard onto Peninsula Boulevard.*

9.4 *RIGHT onto Woodmere Boulevard, past Woodmere Academy on your left.*

This is Woodmere (1). If you're a fan of lovely homes, take some time to go off the path and see how people here live. If you feel like taking a rest at the quarter-way-through mark, the place to stop is beneath the huge weeping willow on the academy's front lawn.

10.7 *Bear LEFT at the intersection with Channel Boulevard to stay on Woodmere Boulevard.*

11.1 *At the end of Woodmere Boulevard is a small town dock and the Keystone Yacht Club.*

The dock is open and paved, with a few benches. The Keystone Yacht Club (2) is a bit more impressive, and private—but not so private you can't sneak a look. In boating season, it's worth a few minutes. When you're done, retrace your path one-tenth of a mile to the right up Woodmere Boulevard.

12.0 *LEFT at a stop sign onto Ivy Hill Road, which winds and becomes West Ivy Hill Road.*

12.4 *Just past the entrance to The Woodmere Club, turn LEFT onto Keene Lane.*

12.8 *Swing RIGHT as Keene Lane becomes Atlantic Street, then immediate LEFT onto Albro Lane.*

13.0 *RIGHT, two blocks later, onto Meadow Drive, which becomes Ocean Avenue.*

Along this part of the trip you'll see more lovely homes. Here, in fact, they're veritable mansions, with sumptuous grounds and, often, servants' houses out back.

14.1 *RIGHT onto Causeway Road.*

15.0 *LEFT at the end of Causeway Road onto Broadway; on your left, next to Lawrence Junior High School, is Rock Hall Museum.*

Rock Hall (3) is an architectural gem, say the experts. This beautifully maintained Georgian mansion was a summer home from 1767 to 1948, kept by just two families in all that time. Today it is a museum displaying period household utensils, Chippendale furniture, early toys, a venerable harpsichord, and more—some of it original to the house. Open April through November, noon to 4 p.m. on Sundays, 10 a.m. to 4 p.m. weekdays and Saturdays; closed Tuesdays. Admission is free.

16.1 *LEFT around a traffic circle, following signs to the Atlantic Beach Bridge by way of Doughty Boulevard.*

16.7 *Bear LEFT, toward Atlantic Beach and Long Beach.*

17.0 *Over the Atlantic Beach Bridge.*

Pay 5 cents a bike for crossing. (And you thought a nickel didn't buy anything these days.)

17.4 *Bear LEFT off the bridge and onto Park Street, or keep on straight and pick up the boardwalk.*

You can ride at least partway along the boardwalk; if you love salt air and surf, you'll be that much closer to them.

Park Street becomes Beech Street, then West Beech Street as you ride past the varied houses of Atlantic Beach and Long Beach. Atlantic Beach, where Enrico Caruso and Rudy Vallee used to summer, guards its waterfront on both the ocean and the bay sides; residents, who pay a quarter-million dollars or so for oceanfront condos, and more for stucco cottages with a California look, want the beach to themselves. Long Beach, just east, is open to the masses. Look to your right at Tennessee Avenue (4) and you'll see a public beach entrance; the charge is $5, but you won't always find an attendant on duty to collect it.

In flat territory, the recumbent bicycle shines.   Dan Carlinsky

22.4 *Off West Beech Street, turn LEFT onto Long Beach Boulevard, through a commercial strip of gas stations and stores, then over a free bridge back to the mainland.*

23.2 *Across the bridge, bear LEFT on Long Beach Road, following the sign toward Island Park.*

23.8 *Bear RIGHT at the intersection with Island Parkway to stay on Long Beach Road.*
   On your right at Henrietta Avenue is the South Shore Farmers Market (5), open seven days a week to peddle edibles such as fruit, vegetables, and hot bagels. Buy a snack for now or stock up for the trip home.

27.4 *LEFT, just beyond a funeral home on your right, onto Lincoln Avenue.*

28.2 *At the end of Lincoln Avenue, ignore the green highway signs to Merrick Road; instead, take the lower road, to the right of Roma Furniture. Then make an immediate LEFT onto the Sunrise Highway and follow signs there to pick up Merrick Road for almost five miles.*
   Merrick Road, a broad, commercial thoroughfare, leads back into Queens.

33.0 *RIGHT, just beyond 231st Street, onto Francis Lewis Boulevard. Follow the boulevard, retracing the route five miles back to Hillside Avenue and the shopping center.*

Bicycle Shops
Central Bicycle & Mower Shop, 126 North Central Avenue, Valley Stream (516-825-6091)
Kreitzman's Bicycle & Toy Shop, 755 East Park Avenue, Long Beach (516-432-9632)
Laurelton Bicycle & Carriage Shop, 232–20 Merrick Boulevard, Laurelton, Queens (718-528-6886)
Park Avenue Cycle Shop, 148 North Park Avenue, Rockville Centre (516-536-5353)
Rockville Centre Bicycle, 17 North Park Avenue, Rockville Centre (516-678-6918)
Valley Stream Bicycle, 95 East Merrick Road, Valley Stream (516-825-8181)
Woodmere Bicycle, 1067 Broadway, Woodmere (516-374-0606)

8
The North Shore: To the Beach at Bayville

Round-trip distance pedaled: 29 miles
Terrain: moderately hilly
Minimum cycling time: 4 hours

This route is a favorite of members of the the New York Cycle Club. The tour begins at the I.U. Willets Road School in Roslyn. Take Long Island Expressway exit 39S, go eight-tenths of a mile down Guinea Woods Road, and turn right just a tenth of a mile to the school, where you can park in the lot. You're likely to find other cyclists readying for the trip — or their cars, recognizable by the telltale roof racks. The route goes north over some pretty roads to Bayville on Long Island Sound, where you can swim, lunch on fresh seafood, or just look around. There are possible stops at two of Long Island's fine arboretums, along with few other points of interest. Except for weekday rush hours and heavy summer beach times, almost the whole route is lightly traveled by autos, which makes for enjoyable cycling.

0.0 *RIGHT, leaving the school, onto I.U. Willets Road.*

1.4 *LEFT onto Old Westbury Road.*
On your right just after you turn is Old Westbury Gardens (1). A splendid variety of plant life lives on the 100 acres behind the huge gates, and you can pay a visit Wednesdays through Sundays and Monday holidays from May through October, from 10 a.m. to 5 p.m.; entry costs $4.50 ($1.50 for children 6 to 12). For an extra $3 ($1.50 more for children) you can visit the 1906 manor house, furnished with English antiques, in the center of the gardens. Senior citizens can see house and gardens both for just $3.50. Picnics are allowed, but no bikes beyond the ticket booth.

1.8 *Cross the Long Island Expressway, then go LEFT onto Store Hill Road North (the expressway service road).*

2.0 *First RIGHT onto Wheatley Road.*

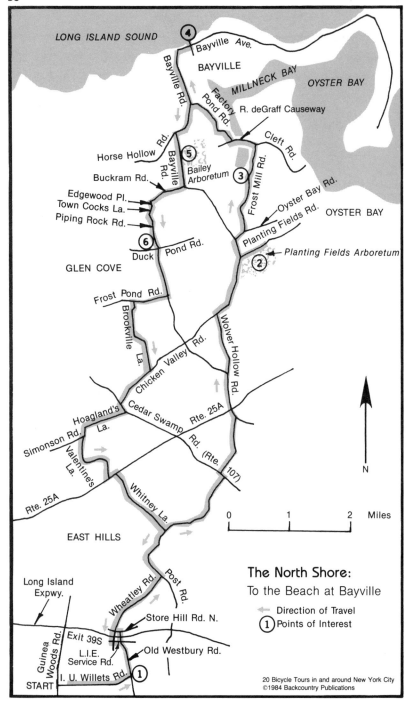

LONG ISLAND SOUND

Bayville Ave.

BAYVILLE

MILLNECK BAY

OYSTER BAY

Bayville Rd.

Factory Pond Rd.

R. deGraff Causeway

Cleft Rd.

Horse Hollow Rd.

Bayville Rd.

Bailey Arboretum

Frost Mill Rd.

Buckram Rd.

Edgewood Pl.
Town Cocks La.
Piping Rock Rd.

Oyster Bay Rd.

Planting Fields Rd.

OYSTER BAY

Duck Pond Rd.

Planting Fields Arboretum

GLEN COVE

Frost Pond Rd.

Brookville La.

Wolver Hollow Rd.

Chicken Valley Rd.

Hoagland's La.

Cedar Swamp

Rte. 25A

Simonson Rd.

Valentine's La.

Rd. (Rte. 107)

Rte. 25A

Whitney La.

EAST HILLS

N

0   1   2   Miles

Long Island Expwy.

Wheatley Rd.

Post Rd.

The North Shore:

To the Beach at Bayville

Store Hill Rd. N.

Exit 39S

← Direction of Travel
① Points of Interest

L.I.E. Service Rd.

Old Westbury Rd.

Guinea Woods Rd.

I. U. Willets Rd.

START

20 Bicycle Tours in and around New York City
©1984 Backcountry Publications

3.4 *LEFT at Post Road to stay on Wheatley Road, then bear RIGHT at the intersection with Whitney Lane to stay on Wheatley Road.*

5.8 *STRAIGHT across Cedar Swamp Road (Route 107) to remain on Wheatley Road.*

6.8 *Bear LEFT at Brookville Reformed Church to remain on Wheatley Road.*

7.0 *STRAIGHT across Route 25A onto Wolver Hollow Road.*

8.5 *RIGHT onto Chicken Valley Road; follow signs toward Bailey Arboretum.*
You'll visit Bailey later on the tour, but you can take an optional detour to another arboretum just a mile up Chicken Valley Road. Turn right at Planting Fields Road and travel less than a mile to Planting Fields Arboretum (2). Open every day but Christmas, it changes offerings with the season, of course. Two hundred of the 400 acres — once a working farm — are preserved as natural woodlands and fields; the rest are sprawling lawns and beautiful plantings, including an acre and a half of spectacularly colorful tropical plants in greenhouses. The Arboretum has great orchids, hibiscus, rhododendrons, azaleas, Japanese cherries, monumental linden and copper beech trees, and cacti you won't believe. Admission is $1.50 for adults; free for children under 12 with an adult. (During daylight-saving months, a fee is charged only on weekends and holidays.) Leaving the arboretum, retrace your path along Planting Fields Road and turn right onto Chicken Valley Road to pick up the route.

9.7 *First RIGHT onto unmarked Oyster Bay Road; you'll see a small pond on your left.*

9.8 *First LEFT onto Frost Mill Road.*
A little more than a mile after you pick up Frost Mill Road, you'll pass the Charles B. Church Wildlife Refuge (3). It's open every day but Fridays throughout the year. You can lock your bike at the entrance and explore the two walking trails. No charge.

11.6 *LEFT at the end of Frost Mill Road onto Cleft Road and over the Robert F. deGraff Causeway.*
Slow down to gaze at the huge estates along the way. And stop along the causeway; chances are better than even that you'll spy a few ducks or swans just off the road. If you've packed some bird feed, now's your chance to be kind to your web-footed friends.

12.1 *First RIGHT past the causeway onto Factory Pond Road.*

13.1 *RIGHT at the end onto Bayville Road, which curves right and becomes Bayville Avenue at the water.*

On Bayville Avenue, Charles E. Ransom Beach (4) is to your left, a strip of restaurants to your right. The beach is still known to residents by its former name: Oak Neck Beach. You can lock your bike, strip down to your swimsuit, and take a dip in Long Island Sound, opposite the Connecticut towns of Greenwich and Stamford. Nonresidents are supposed to pay $1 in season, but the rule is cyclists go for free. There are bike racks down Bayville Avenue a bit, at Stehli Beach. Across the road are several restaurants and sidewalk stands, featuring mostly local seafood, of course. The Tides, the first one you'll see as you make the turn at the Sound, caters to a lot of cyclists. It's a motel restaurant offering steaks, seafood, and sandwiches. As you leave the beach, retrace your path along Bayville Avenue and uphill on Bayville Road.

15.6 *Bear LEFT at a traffic light to avoid Horse Hollow Road. Follow signs to Bailey Arboretum, on your left in two-tenths of a mile.*

The arboretum (5) is a lush forty-two-acre estate with serene ponds and an astonishing variety of plantings, some of them very rare. If old and exotic trees are your passion, a stop here will be particularly rewarding. Open 9 a.m. to 4 p.m. from mid-April to mid-November, but closed Mondays; admission is $1 for adults.

16.5 *RIGHT onto Buckram Road.*

17.1 *LEFT at Edgewood Place and under a stone arch, onto Town Cocks Lane.*

17.9 *Bear LEFT to pick up Piping Rock Road.*

On your right, just before Duck Pond Road, is the Matinecock Meeting House (6). It's still used regularly for Quaker meetings. The original 1725 house, said to be one of the oldest Friends houses of worship in the United States, was destroyed by fire in the mid-1980s; the house you see is a faithful reproduction.

18.7 *RIGHT onto Frost Pond Road.*

19.2 *LEFT onto Brookville Lane, uphill.*

As you travel on Brookville Lane, you're going deep into country club territory. There are golf courses all over the area.

20.4 *RIGHT at the end onto Chicken Valley Road.*

21.0 *LEFT onto Cedar Swamp Road (Route 107 South).*

21.2 *RIGHT onto Hoagland's Lane.*

21.9 *LEFT onto Valentine's Lane.*

22.1 *Bear LEFT at Simonson Road to stay on Valentine's Lane.*

23.1 *LEFT onto Route 25A, then immediate RIGHT to pick up Whitney Lane.*

24.4 *RIGHT at the end onto Wheatley Road.*

25.5 *RIGHT at Post Road to stay on Wheatley Road.*

26.8 *Cross the Long Island Expressway and turn LEFT onto the expressway service road.*

27.0 *First RIGHT onto Old Westbury Road.*

27.4 *RIGHT onto I.U. Willets Road.*

28.8 *LEFT into the school parking lot.*

Bicycle Shops
Bikeworks, 118 Glen Cove Road, East Hills (516-484-4422)

Warmly dressed for a cool fall ride to Bayville.   George Heitman

9

A Bully Tour: To Teddy Roosevelt's Home and Oyster Bay

Round-trip distance pedaled: 21 miles
Terrain: moderately hilly
Minimum cycling time: 4 hours

Theodore Roosevelt may or may not have bicycled around Oyster Bay and Cove Neck on Long Island's North Shore. If he never did, he missed something. T.R. had exquisite taste in countryside, for Sagamore Hill is one of the loveliest spots on Long Island. The tour starts at a good place to park your car—the railroad station in the center of Syosset, on Jackson Avenue just south of Muttontown Road. There are several serious hills—notably on the way from Oyster Bay to the Roosevelt estate and in the few miles after you leave Oyster Bay on your way back to the start—but the ride isn't all that strenuous and it *is* all that pleasant.

0.0 *Leave the railroad station parking lot by the north exit, turning LEFT onto Syosset–Cold Spring Harbor Road.*

0.1 *Bear RIGHT, toward the Friendly Ice Cream shop, to stay on route.*

0.2 *RIGHT, at a five-way intersection, onto Berry Hill Road and continue for three and a half miles.*
This part of the tour is an immediate contrast to downtown Syosset. You travel through a pleasant stretch of pastures and horse farms. Some nice overhanging trees line the road. The rolling is easy.

3.8 *RIGHT onto South Street.*

4.4 *RIGHT onto East Main Street, which becomes Cove Road.*
In 1.3 miles, at the corner of Cove Road and Cove Neck Road, stop at Theodore Roosevelt's grave and the Theodore Roosevelt Sanctuary (1) on your right. The gravesite has a bike rack in the parking area; lock your bike and walk through the iron gates and up a shady, steep hill, then up

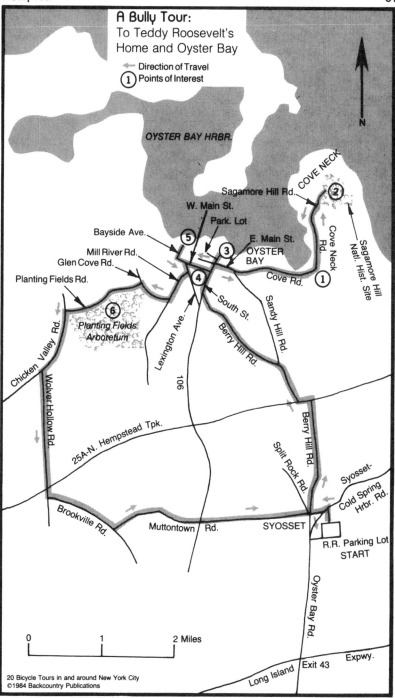

A Bully Tour:
To Teddy Roosevelt's
Home and Oyster Bay

⟵ Direction of Travel
① Points of Interest

N

OYSTER BAY HRBR.

COVE NECK

Sagamore Hill Rd.   ②

W. Main St.

Park. Lot

Cove Neck Rd.

Sagamore Hill Natl. Hist. Site

Bayside Ave.   ⑤

E. Main St.
OYSTER
BAY

Mill River Rd.   ③

Glen Cove Rd.   ④

Planting Fields Rd.   ①
                                            Cove Rd.

⑥

Planting Fields
Arboretum

Lexington Ave.

South St.

Sandy Hill Rd.

Chicken Valley Rd.

Wolver Hollow Rd.

106

Berry Hill Rd.

25A-N. Hempstead Tpk.

Berry Hill Rd.

Split Rock Rd.

Syosset-
Cold Spring
Hrbr. Rd.

Brookville Rd.

Muttontown   Rd.

SYOSSET

R.R. Parking Lot
START

Oyster Bay Rd.

0   1   2 Miles

Long Island   Exit 43   Expwy.

20 Bicycle Tours in and around New York City
©1984 Backcountry Publications

a flight of brick and cement steps to the sheltered graves of T.R. and his wife, Edith. The steps number twenty-six, signifying that T.R. was the twenty-sixth U.S. president. The surrounding burial ground—started by English colonists—dates from 1658. Opposite the iron fence enclosing the Roosevelt graves is a small stone with a quotation from T.R.: "Keep your eyes on the stars and keep your feet on the ground." Unless, of course, they're on the pedals.

The land surrounding the cemetery is a wildlife sanctuary, the oldest in the National Audubon Society chain, appropriately donated by a Roosevelt cousin in T.R.'s name. (The president was a great outdoorsman and conservationist.) Leave your bike at the cemetery and follow the signs to the sanctuary on foot. You can explore the main trail of wood chips through the twelve-acre site in about half an hour. Along the way, you'll come upon a lot of benches for sitting and contemplating, plus a bird blind where you can hide to peek at feathered occupants drinking and bathing in a nearby pool. Most of the foliage you'll see—both native and imported species—was planted specifically to attract wildlife. The visitors center at the beginning of the trail is open weekdays 9 a.m. to 5 p.m. and most weekend afternoons. The walk is free, but there's a box for donations.

5.7 *LEFT onto Cove Neck Road.*
Eyes left for splendid glimpses of Oyster Bay Harbor.

6.7 *RIGHT onto Sagamore Hill Road and uphill.*
Sagamore Hill National Historic Site (2) was T.R.'s home and, during his terms as president, the summer White House. Park your bike at the racks next to the kiosk in the parking lot and head for the house itself. Admission is $1 (free for those under 16 or over 62); the house is open 9:30 a.m. to 5 p.m. every day. Roosevelt built Sagamore Hill in 1884 and 1885, while he was in his twenties, at a cost of $16,975. It remained his permanent home until he died in 1919. The Victorian house is of wood and brick, with twenty-three rooms and a gorgeous wraparound piazza; there are original furnishings throughout, including a batch of T.R.'s hunting trophies.

There is also a Roosevelt museum on the grounds, in Old Orchard, the Georgian house that T.R., Jr., built in 1937–1938 on the site of his father's apple orchard.

7.3 *Leaving the Roosevelt homestead, go downhill on Sagamore Hill Road, then LEFT at the foot of the hill onto Cove Neck Road again.*

10.1 *RIGHT onto Cove Road, which becomes East Main Street.*
Note the historical marker on your right as you turn. It's a simple note saying that George Washington "rested" here April 23–24, 1790. Apparently, he didn't sleep.

11.4 *LEFT onto South Street, then fast RIGHT onto West Main Street.*

The hamlet of Oyster Bay is worth a look-see for its shops and for its peace and quiet. There are plenty of eating places around South and Main streets.

For a fast optional detour, turn right onto South Street from East Main Street, then take the first left, following the sign to the municipal parking lot. You'll come to a local attraction that's a boon to bicyclists: fresh well water (3). It's on your right, and you'll likely find it cold, clear, and tasty. Retrace your path back to South Street to pick up the route.

On West Main Street, just past South Street, is Raynham Hall (4), which was occupied by a small group of Redcoats during the Revolution. The much-altered saltbox is now a museum, open Tuesdays through Sundays from 1 p.m. to 5 p.m.; admission is $1 for adults, 50 cents for seniors and students, nothing for accompanied children.

11.9 *RIGHT onto Bayside Avenue.*

At the end of this short street, overlooking Oyster Bay Harbor, is Roosevelt Memorial Park (5). From mid-June through Labor Day, only residents are allowed in the swimming area — officially. Off-season, outsiders may come in. There's a picnic area, too.

12.1 *Leaving the park, retrace your path on Bayside Avenue.*

12.3 *LEFT at the end onto West Main Street.*

Teddy Roosevelt's bully summer White House.   Dan Carlinsky

12.4 *Second RIGHT onto Lexington Avenue.*

12.5 *First RIGHT onto Mill River Road.*

12.9 *RIGHT, uphill, onto Glen Cove Road.*

13.5 *LEFT onto unmarked Planting Fields Road, following the signs to Planting Fields Arboretum.*
   The 400-acre arboretum (6) boasts an amazing assortment of rhododendrons, azaleas, orchids, begonias, cacti, banana plants, dogwoods, Japanese cherries, magnolias—more trees, shrubs, and flowers than you can name. There are garden paths, rolling lawns, and wooded slopes, colorful foliage in fall, blooming colors in spring and summer. It's open 9 a.m. to 4:30 p.m. every day year-round; admission is $1.50 (accompanied children under 12 free). During daylight-saving months a fee is charged only on weekends and holidays. Park at the bike racks to your right near the entrance.

14.5 *LEFT at the end of Planting Fields Road onto unmarked Chicken Valley Road.*

15.6 *LEFT onto Wolver Hollow Road. Bear LEFT crossing Route 25A, as Wolver Hollow Road becomes Brookville Road.*

18.2 *LEFT onto Muttontown Road.*
   It's easy pedaling for the last three miles. Large, forested estates are on both sides of the road—some with a few horses and other paraphernalia of the rich. Watch for pheasants and other game scooting across the road.

21.1 *Back in Syosset, stay STRAIGHT through the five-way intersection you encountered at the start. Then turn RIGHT into the railroad station parking lot.*

Bicycle Shops
Syosset Bicycle Shop, 328 Jackson Avenue, Syosset (516-921-3225)

10

Western Suffolk: Smith-Haven Mall to Heckscher State Park

Round-trip distance pedaled: 33 miles
Terrain: flat
Minimum cycling time: 4 hours

This is an easy thirty-three miles through some pleasant parts of western Suffolk County, with a beach visit on Great South Bay and an optional spin through a fascinating old artists' colony. There's plenty of time to dally on a short tour like this, so pick a time when the weather is conducive to noodling around. On warm autumn days the swimming area is uncrowded and appealing. The tour starts at the Smith-Haven Mall, a large shopping center at the Smithtown-Brookhaven line that's easily reached via Nichols Road and Moriches Road north from exit 58 of the Long Island Expressway.

0.0 *Start in front of the RKO Century Mall Theater.*

0.4 *Cross Middle Country Road and head down Moriches Road.*

0.7 *RIGHT, just past the tan dormitories of the Lake Grove School on your left, onto Nichols Road.*
Nichols is variously spelled as Nichols, Nicolls, and Nicholls. However it's written, the road provides very flat pedaling through several housing developments.

4.5 *Cross over the Long Island Expressway and continue STRAIGHT.*

5.6 *LEFT onto Veterans Highway.*

6.1 *First RIGHT onto Connetquot Avenue, which becomes Great River Road.*
About four miles along on Connetquot Avenue you'll pass, on your right, a war memorial (1) set in a small plaza with benches; it's a good place to stop for a rest. Along the avenue are various delis and other food stores for a midmorning snack or a later picnic lunch.

A couple of miles later, at 11.8 on your odometer, you'll see a small town park (2) on your left at the edge of the Connetquot River. Even if you

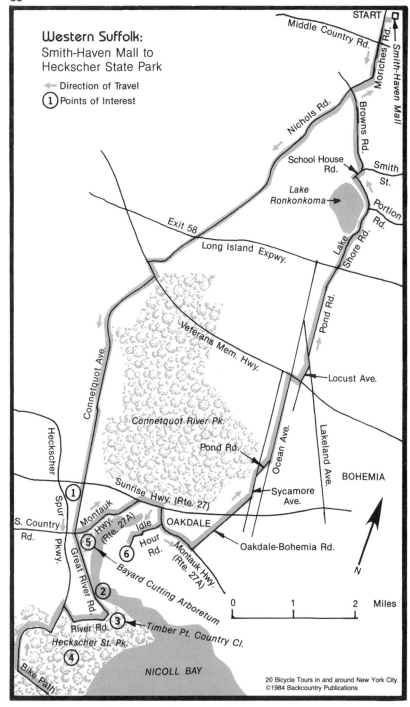

Western Suffolk:
Smith-Haven Mall to
Heckscher State Park

← Direction of Travel
① Points of Interest

START

Middle Country Rd.

Moriches Rd.

Smith-Haven Mall

Nichols Rd.

Browns Rd.

School House Rd.

Smith St.

Lake Ronkonkoma

Portion Rd.

Exit 58

Long Island Expwy.

Lake Shore Rd.

Veterans Mem. Hwy.

Pond Rd.

Connetquot Ave.

Locust Ave.

Connetquot River Pk.

Pond Rd.

Ocean Ave.

Lakeland Ave.

BOHEMIA

Heckscher

Sunrise Hwy. (Rte. 27)

Sycamore Ave.

①

Spur

Montauk Hwy. (Rte. 27A)

Idle

OAKDALE

Oakdale-Bohemia Rd.

S. Country Rd.

Pkwy.

⑤

⑥

Hour Rd.

Montauk Hwy. (Rte. 27A)

N

Great River Rd.

Bayard Cutting Arboretum

②

River Rd.

③   Timber Pt. Country Cl.

Heckscher St. Pk.

④

Bike Path

NICOLL BAY

0   1   2   Miles

20 Bicycle Tours in and around New York City
©1984 Backcountry Publications

don't need to catch your breath, you should stop for the view.

The Timber Point Country Club (3) is a mile beyond, at the mouth of the river. Golfing is officially for Suffolk County residents and their guests only, but cyclists can take a two-mile detour around the tees and fairways to watch the golfers duff amid flocks of waterfowl. Timber Point does have a restaurant that's open to all, serving breakfast and lunch at reasonable prices. It's closed from mid-December to mid-March.

12.7 *Leaving the country club, turn LEFT onto River Road. The road will take you uphill over a parkway.*

14.1 *LEFT onto a pedestrian/bicycle path into Heckscher State Park.*

The path at Heckscher State Park (4) is nearly two miles long overall and closed to cars. It leads through the woods and past large picnic grounds to a couple of bathing areas and a big pool. Swimming is free in the bay, 50 cents in the pool. There are bike racks by the West Bath House and at Overlook Bathing Area. You can rent lockers, umbrellas, and beach chairs, but not swimsuits. To leave, retrace your route on the bike path back to River Road. Then go right on River Road, back over the parkway, past the country club, and then left onto Great River Road.

20.7 *RIGHT onto the very busy Montauk Highway (Route 27A).*

In less than half a mile, on your right, enter the Bayard Cutting Arboretum (5), a 690-acre oasis of trees and colorful wildflowers. The arboretum was begun in 1887 according to plans drawn by Frederick Law ("Central Park") Olmsted. Many varieties of aquatic birds can be found along the adjacent Connetquot River. Biking isn't allowed (racks are provided near the ticket booth), but walking is encouraged. Five distinct nature walks, ranging from twenty-five to sixty minutes long, are marked in different areas of the grounds. Refreshments are available in the main building (former home of the founder, William Bayard Cutting), along with a small nature museum that features a large collection of stuffed birds. It's all open Wednesdays through Sundays from 10 a.m. to 5 p.m. (until 4 p.m. during standard time). From April through Labor Day, admission is $1.50 for adults; from Labor Day through November, admission is charged only on weekends; kids under 12 always go for free.

21.1 *RIGHT leaving the arboretum and back onto the Montauk High-way, which merges briefly with Route 27 East; follow the green sign for Route 27A to stay on the Montauk Highway.*

In one and a half miles you can make an optional detour to the Oak-dale artists' colony (6), definitely worth seeing if you have the time. Turn right onto Idle Hour Road, a winding little street less than a mile long that takes you past the imposing buildings of Dowling College and on to an un-usual ivy-covered red-brick cylindrical tower—residence of some lucky people. Behind the tower are two-story buildings that used to be chicken coops on the huge Vanderbilt estate. In the 1930s they were used by artists, but now they're populated mostly by ordinary folks (although a few artists' studios do remain). The whole riverside area has the flavor of a small English village. Check out several of the side streets before you go back up Idle Hour Road to continue on Route 27A.

23.3 *LEFT, just past the railroad station, onto Oakdale-Bohemia Road.*

24.7 *Bear LEFT past the modern Sycamore Elementary School onto Sycamore Avenue.*

25.0 *First RIGHT onto Pond Road, which soon runs into Ocean Avenue.*

25.7 *RIGHT onto busy Veterans Memorial Highway.*

26.8 *First LEFT onto Locust Avenue.*

27.2 *Cross Lakeland Avenue and go STRAIGHT onto Pond Road.*

28.8 *Go under the Long Island Expressway, staying STRAIGHT on Pond Road.*

29.2 *Pond Road becomes Lake Shore Road as the route passes Lake Ronkonkoma.*
   Once (more than half a century ago) this was a fashionable, elegant, almost ritzy resort favored by Manhattanites. Now, it's not so fashionable, not so elegant, definitely not ritzy. The swank have long since switched to the Hamptons.

30.1 *LEFT at Portion Road to stay on Lake Shore Road.*

Flocking together on a quiet day.   George Heitman

30.6 *RIGHT at a traffic light onto School House Road.*

30.7 *LEFT at the fork with Smith Street to stay on School House Road.*

30.8 *LEFT again two blocks later onto Browns Road.*

31.9 *RIGHT onto Nichols Road at a five-way intersection. Follow signs to the Smith-Haven Mall.*

32.4 *LEFT at the end of Nichols onto Moriches Road.*

32.9 *Follow Moriches Road back to the shopping center.*

Bicycle Shops
Byron Lake Schwinn Cyclery, 4551 Sunrise Highway, Bohemia (516-589-3912)
Smithtown Bicycle and Fitness, 11 West Main Street, Smithtown (516-265-5900)

11

Southampton Area: An Easy Tour

Round-trip distance pedaled: 25 miles
Terrain: mostly flat
Minimum cycling time: 3 hours

This is a simple route through part of Long Island's South Fork, the area around Southampton and Bridgehampton. You'll have plenty of easy cycling through flat farmland and peaceful winding roads. Suggested stops include a nineteenth-century windmill, a bayside beach, and a wildlife refuge with its own little-known swimming area, plus three fine, small museums on a short optional detour. Despite the directions and the map, count on getting off-track at least once or twice. With some street signs missing, others that can be read only from the opposite direction, and confusing street names (Seven Ponds Road, Lower Seven Ponds Road, Head of Pond Road), you can't help coming up bewildered. Just stay cool and you'll find your way back on course. The route begins at the Long Island Rail Road station in Southampton. To drive to the starting point, take Route 27 (Sunrise Highway Extension) to town. Go right on North Sea Road, left on Prospect Street, then left on North Main Street; finally, a quick right on Railroad Plaza will bring you to the station and its parking lot.

0.0 *From the station, head east along Powell Avenue, framed by trees that line the road and meet overhead.*

0.4 *LEFT at the end onto David White's Lane; cross the railroad tracks, then cross County Road 39.*

0.9 *Bear RIGHT at the first intersection onto Seven Ponds Road.*
You're in farm country now. This region, in fact, has a long agricultural history; America's first cattle ranch was in Suffolk County. Today, farming in these parts leans to fruit, potatoes, cauliflower, and cabbage.

1.6 *LEFT onto Lower Seven Ponds Road.*
This intersection is confusing—Seven Ponds Road, Upper Seven Ponds Road, and Lower Seven Ponds Road meet here—check the street signs to be sure you're on *Lower* Seven Ponds Road.

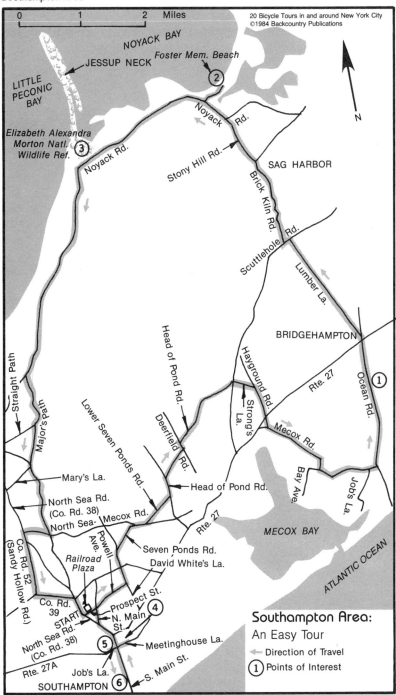

NOYACK BAY

JESSUP NECK

Foster Mem. Beach

②

20 Bicycle Tours in and around New York City
©1984 Backcountry Publications

0   1   2   Miles

LITTLE
PECONIC
BAY

N

*Elizabeth Alexandra
Morton Natl.
Wildlife Ref.*
③

Noyack Rd.

Noyack Rd.

Stony Hill Rd.

SAG HARBOR

Brick Kiln Rd.

Scuttlehole Rd.

Lumber La.

BRIDGEHAMPTON

Head of Pond Rd.

Hayground Rd.

Strong's La.

Rte. 27

Ocean Rd.

①

Straight Path

Major's Path

Lower Seven Ponds Rd.

Deerfield Rd.

Mecox Rd.

Bay Ave.

Job's La.

Mary's La.

North Sea Rd.
(Co. Rd. 38)

Head of Pond Rd.

North Sea-

Mecox Rd.

Rte. 27

MECOX BAY

Co. Rd. 52
(Sandy Hollow Rd.)

Powell
Ave.

*Railroad
Plaza*

Seven Ponds Rd.

David White's La.

ATLANTIC OCEAN

Co. Rd.
39

Prospect St.

④

START

N. Main
St.

North Sea Rd.
(Co. Rd. 38)

⑤

Meetinghouse La.

Rte. 27A

Job's La.

S. Main St.

SOUTHAMPTON

⑥

Southampton Area:

An Easy Tour

← Direction of Travel

① Points of Interest

2.1 *LEFT at the end of Lower Seven Ponds Road to pick up unmarked Head of Pond Road.*

2.4 *Bear RIGHT to stay on Head of Pond Road.*
Along the route you'll begin to see bits of old windmills (or reproductions) near houses. It's a local fashion.

3.0 *At the end, go LEFT onto Deerfield Road, then a quick RIGHT to pick up Head of Pond Road again.*
The road here is narrow with no shoulders; be careful.

4.5 *RIGHT onto Strong's Lane.*
You'll begin to notice that the Hamptons area has a mix of very old and very new houses.

4.9 *RIGHT at the end onto unmarked Hayground Road.*
In a little bit you'll pass the tracks of the Long Island Rail Road.

5.6 *LEFT at the end of Hayground Road onto unmarked Mecox Road.*

6.7 *Bear LEFT at Bay Avenue to stay on Mecox Road.*

7.4 *Bear LEFT at Job's Lane to stay on Mecox Road.*

7.6 *LEFT onto Ocean Road.*
In about three quarters of a mile, on the right at the corner of Bridge Lane, is Bridgehampton's oldest house, a handsome, weathered, shingled saltbox built in 1680.

In another three quarters of a mile, you'll pass on your right the Bridgehampton Golf Club, and shortly after that you'll come to a big wooden windmill on a small lawn (1). This is one of several real, complete old windmills in the area; they're all from the early nineteenth century (this one is from 1820), when the power they harnessed was used to grind corn and flour or to saw wood. Beyond, you can see a huge showplace of an estate house from the 1920s.

9.5 *Cross Route 27 and immediately turn LEFT onto Lumber Lane.*

11.4 *LEFT at the end of Lumber Lane onto Scuttlehole Road, then immediate RIGHT onto unmarked Brick Kiln Road.*

13.0 *Bear LEFT for Stony Hill Road as Brick Kiln Road turns right; Stony Hill Road runs into Noyack Road.*
In a mile you can take an optional half-mile detour to Foster Memorial Beach (2), turning onto the road on your right at the Salty Dog restaurant. Foster is a good stretch of gravel beach, with lifeguards during the summer. You might snack at the Oasis, a typical beachy honky-tonk luncheonette, or, if it's Sunday (when the Oasis is closed) have some seafood back at

the Salty Dog. Leaving the beach, turn right at the Salty Dog to get back on route.

After two more hilly miles on Noyack Road, stop at the Elizabeth Alexandra Morton National Wildlife Refuge (3) on your right. The refuge, on a long narrow finger of land that juts into Noyack Bay, includes nature trails and such, with frequent sightings of waterfowl, deer, cottontail, fox, weasel, raccoon, and opossum. There's also a secluded beach (you have to walk through half a mile of wooded trail to reach it) that seems to be crowd-free even on summer holiday weekends. Open daylight hours every day; free. Leaving the refuge, turn right back onto Noyack Road.

20.0 *LEFT onto Major's Path.*

An early look at one of Bridgehampton's windmills.   Southampton Town Historian

20.7 *Bear LEFT at the first fork to stay on Major's Path.*

21.4 *Bear LEFT again at the next fork, just past Straight Path, to stay on Major's Path. (Don't go onto Mary's Lane.)*

22.5 *RIGHT onto North Sea–Mecox Road.*

22.9 *LEFT at the end onto County Road 38 (North Sea Road); you'll see a sign to New York and Riverhead.*

23.1 *Immediately bear RIGHT, following the signs to Riverhead, onto Country Road 52 (Sandy Hollow Road).*

23.9 *LEFT onto County Road 39.*

24.6 *First RIGHT at a traffic light onto unmarked North Sea Road (County Road 38), following the green sign to Southampton.*

24.9 *Cycle under the railroad trestle, then first LEFT onto Prospect Street.*

25.2 *LEFT at the end onto unmarked North Main Street.*

If you have time, you might first go *right* down North Main Street onto South Main Street. Pause at the intersection where Meeting House Lane goes left and Job's Lane goes right.

On Meeting House Lane is the Southampton Historical Museum (4), with exhibits on old whalers and on Long Island in the time of the Revolution; open mid-June to mid-September, 11 a.m. to 5 p.m. except Mondays; admission $2 (50 cents for young children).

On Job's Lane is the Parrish Art Museum (5), which has changing exhibits of American artists of the nineteenth and twentieth centuries; open year-round, 10 a.m. to 5 p.m. Mondays and Thursdays through Saturdays, 1 p.m. to 5 p.m. Sundays; $2 donation suggested.

A bit farther down South Main Street toward the ocean, on your right, is the 1648 Old Halsey Homestead (6), the oldest frame house in New York State. It's a shingled house with leaded windows and a huge brick chimney. Inside it's authentically furnished and set up as though a seventeenth-century family were inhabiting it. Open mid-June to mid-September, 11 a.m. to 5 p.m. except Mondays; admission $2 (50 cents for kids).

25.3 *RIGHT onto Railroad Plaza and back to the station.*

Bicycle Shops

Kid Stuff of Southampton, 45 Main Street, Southampton (516-727-4164)
Rotations, 32 Windmill Lane, Southampton (516-283-2890)
The Bikeman, Lumber Lane, Bridgehampton (516-537-0226, 537-3688)

12

€astern Long Island:
Far from New York

Round-trip distance pedaled: 78 miles (31 the first day, 47 the second)
Terrain: mostly flat
Minimum cycling time: 2 days

Here's a plan for two days of easy cycling, with plenty of time to slow down and savor Suffolk County's scenic beauty or go for a swim. See the green potato farms of the North Fork (with its New England flavor), the busy docks of Greenport, away-from-it-all Shelter Island, newly trendy Sag Harbor, and a stretch of the famous Hamptons beach area. Along the way, you can stop at a winery, perhaps, or a beautiful lighthouse high above Long Island Sound. There are seafood restaurants, of course, and much more. From the end of the Long Island Expressway, take Route 25 to the center of Riverhead. The tour starts at the free municipal parking lot at East Main Street and Peconic Avenue.

First Day
Find yourself some breakfast before you leave town (1). The Riverhead Grill on East Main Street near the parking lot is open six mornings a week. Sundays you can fortify yourself at the Riverboat, at the traffic circle just over the bridge.

0.0 *RIGHT, leaving the parking lot, onto East Main Street.*

1.0 *RIGHT onto Hubbard Avenue, riding parallel to the railroad tracks.*

2.8 *RIGHT at the end, across the tracks, and pick up unmarked Meetinghouse Creek Road.*

3.2 *LEFT onto Peconic Bay Boulevard.*
Flat roads lead through modest neighborhoods and small farms with front-yard produce stands along the way. About six miles along on Peconic Bay Boulevard, there's a pond on the left; you should see, atop a pole in the water, a house for osprey, practically the official bird of the area. The

roost is used every summer, and local bird fanciers love to watch the activity around it.

9.5 *Follow the road LEFT onto Bay Avenue, just past Veterans Memorial Park on the right.*

10.2 *RIGHT onto Main Road (Route 25).*

10.7 *LEFT onto Wickham Avenue.*

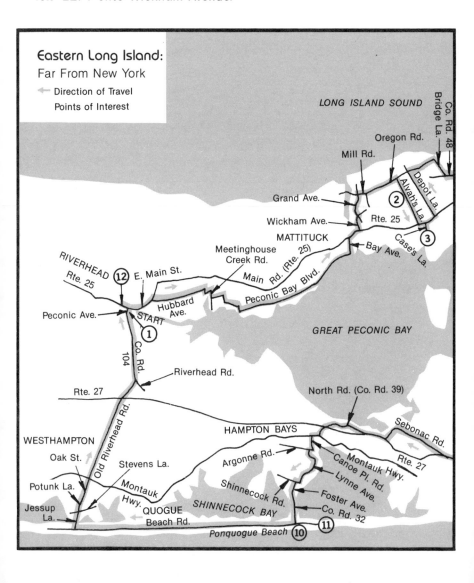

11.3 *Stay LEFT just past Bayer Road to pick up Grand Avenue.*

12.1 *RIGHT, at the first major intersection, onto Mill Road.*

12.4 *Bear LEFT at the first fork to pick up unmarked Oregon Road.*
    Now you're riding through large, flat farms with only an isolated farm-house to give variation.

13.8 *RIGHT onto Alvah's Lane.*

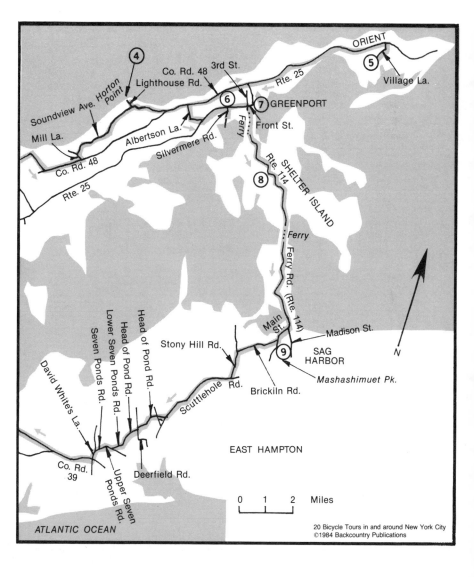

At the first intersection is Hargrave Vineyard (2), the first Long Island winemaker. On eighty-four acres once planted with potatoes, Hargrave grows high-quality grapes and turns out several highly respectable varieties of reds and whites. If you happen to hit at the right time, you might pick up on a tour of the growing area and the cellars, or a tasting. Cyclists shouldn't take more than a few sips—there are many more miles to pedal today.

15.7 *LEFT onto Route 25.*

16.1 *RIGHT onto Case's Lane.*
Just off Main Road, in a small cluster of old buildings on the village green, is Old House (3), a weathered clapboard house of English design. In this instance, "old" really means old: 1649. It's furnished with household items of the day. You can visit in summer, Saturdays, Sundays, and Mondays only. Admission is $1 (half price for children under 12). Even if you arrive too early to go in, peek through the windows to see beamed walls and ceilings, bare wood floors, a huge fireplace and a kitchen table set for dinner. Across the road is an old schoolhouse, with rows of uncomfortable desks and a great old potbelly stove. Leaving the historic buildings, turn right to continue on Route 25.

16.6 *LEFT onto Depot Lane.*

18.6 *RIGHT onto Oregon Road again.*

19.7 *RIGHT at the end of Oregon Road onto Bridge Lane.*

20.4 *First LEFT onto County Road 48.*
It's busy, but the right-hand lane is wide.

22.0 *LEFT onto Mill Lane, the road just past the* second *sign to Peconic.*

22.3 *RIGHT at the first fork onto Soundview Avenue.*
You're cycling parallel to the shore of Long Island Sound now. You'll hit a few easy hills in this wooded section of the North Fork.

25.3 *LEFT, just past a white bridge, onto Lighthouse Road.*
At the end of the road is the Horton Point Lighthouse (4), commissioned by George Washington in 1790 but not built until 1857. Take the wooden stairway down the ragged bluff to the waters of Long Island Sound, or stay up top and just admire the Sound and the spread of grass by the lighthouse. Picturesque is the word. Retrace your path up Lighthouse Road.

25.8 *LEFT, uphill, onto Soundview Avenue.*

27.2 *Soundview Avenue runs into County Road 48; follow it along the water.*

If you're running very early, consider going to the end of the North Fork. It's an eight-mile detour to Orient (5), via County Road 48 and Route 25. Scout around and find Village Lane, on your right behind a tan Civil War marker. It's an almost-hidden street of houses of the seventeenth and eighteenth centuries. Some are still private residences, others are open to the public on summer afternoons. You can pick up the tour again by heading back along Route 25 and following it to the Greenport dock.

28.0 *RIGHT onto Albertson Lane. (Left, if you are returning from the side trip to Orient.)*

28.9 *LEFT at the end onto Route 25.*

In season, if you want help with hotel rooms or area happenings, you can stop at the Chamber of Commerce information booth (6) on your left opposite Silvermere Road. But it's much smarter to have a room booked in advance. Shelter Island, just ahead on the tour, is a soothing and convenient place to spend the night.

30.8 *RIGHT onto 3rd Street to the ferry landing. (Ignore the ferry signs that try to send you down another street.)*

30.9 *Park and lock your bike by the ferry terminal and explore Greenport (7), the North Fork's chief town.*

A century ago, Greenport's business was whaling. This century's world wars made shipbuilding the big game in town. (Between the wars, Prohibition made Greenport a center for rum-runners from Connecticut.) Lately, it's been discovered—somewhat—by New Yorkers trying to escape from the trendier and more crowded South Fork summer spots.

Walk up 3rd Street to Front Street, where you'll find arts and crafts shops. Turn right onto Main Street and you'll pass a variety of boating supply shops and all the other little businesses you'd expect in a harbor town. Claudio's Restaurant, at the docks, calls itself the oldest continuously family-owned restaurant in the United States.

Return to the ferry terminal, retrieve your bike, and go for an eight-minute, $1 ride to Shelter Island.

The island (8), which first saw white settlers in the seventeenth century, is today favored by vacationers who have something of the escapist in them. Because the only access from either of Long Island's forks is by ferry, summer mobs are blissfully absent. Route 114 is the main street of the island, running north to south, from ferry landing to ferry landing. Many of the businesses distribute the Chamber of Commerce's free map of the island, which can be very helpful in exploring.

The boat from Greenport lands at Shelter Island Heights, an area with a bustling town dock and side streets of Victorian houses. Crescent Beach, to the west, is a good spot for a picnic at sunset.

The large, white Chequit Inn, less than half a mile down Route 114 from the ferry stop, is an old-style inn, complete with an ample veranda. It's open May through October and charges about $42 to $50 for a single room, $50 to $80 for a double. (Phone: 516-749-0018). Out of season, the only choice is the elaborate Shelter Island Resort Motel, at Crescent Beach, where a room—single or double— runs $60 or more. In season the price doubles. (Phone: 516-749-2001.)

Down Route 114 a piece and just off the road to your left is an old Quaker cemetery with headstones that can be used to make rubbings.

Farther on Route 114, on the way to South Ferry, is the Haven House, a lovely, old, white-shingled house built as a saltbox in 1743 but enlarged and remodeled nearly a century later in the Federal style.

Don't miss the joys of meandering through the quiet lanes and peaceful beaches of the southern part of the island.

Second Day

0.0 *To continue on route, follow Route 114 down the island to the landing at South Ferry and take a seven-minute ride across to the South Fork. The trip costs $1.25. If you've stayed at the Chequit, you'll ride nearly six miles to the ferry.*

5.8 *Off the ferry, pick up Route 114 again, here called Ferry Road.*

7.3 *Ferry Road will take you to a short but busy bridge; walk your bike across and into the town of Sag Harbor (9).*

In its day, which was around 1840, Sag Harbor was a leading whaling port, and there's a whaling museum on Main Street to prove it. The white-columned museum building was the mansion of a whaling tycoon, and huge whalebones form an arch at the doorway. Inside are five rooms filled with harpoons and other ship's tools, log books, scrimshaw (artistic carvings done by whalemen at sea to pass the time), and a real whaleboat. Entry costs $1.50 ($1 for children, 75 cents for seniors). Hours are 11 a.m. to 5 p.m. every day but Mondays. The museum is closed during the winter.

A block from the museum is Madison Street, with an interesting row of antiques and crafts shops. If you scout around you'll also see lovely old sea captains' houses and some good eating places.

8.3 *Leaving Sag Harbor via Main Street, go RIGHT opposite the entrance to Mashashimuet Park onto Brickiln Road (here and there misspelled as "Bricklin").*

9.7 *LEFT at the end onto winding Stony Hill Road.*

Expect to lose your way in this farm country—the street markings are not the finest.

11.0 *RIGHT at the end onto unmarked Scuttlehole Road.*

13.3 *RIGHT just past a small white garage onto unmarked Head of Pond Road.*

14.7 *LEFT at the end onto Deerfield Road.*

14.8 *Immediate RIGHT to pick up Head of Pond Road again.*

15.6 *Second RIGHT onto Lower Seven Ponds Road.*

16.1 *STRAIGHT onto Upper Seven Ponds Road, which becomes Seven Ponds Road.*

16.9 *At a four-way intersection, STRAIGHT to pick up unmarked David White's Lane.*

17.1 *RIGHT at a stop sign onto unmarked County Road 39, which becomes Route 27.*

18.6 *Bear RIGHT onto Sebonac Road, which runs back into Route 27.*

22.3 *RIGHT, following a green sign, onto North Road.*

23.5 *Bear LEFT, following signs back to Route 27 West; the road goes under a railroad trestle.*

A house on Long Island, 1649 style.   Ken Andresen

24.3 *RIGHT onto Montauk Highway West.*
You'll go over the Shinnecock Canal. Stop on the bridge to take in a splendid view in both directions.

24.6 *First LEFT over the bridge onto Canoe Place Road.*

25.1 *RIGHT at the end onto Argonne Road.*
Again, check out the view, just after you turn.

25.2 *Immediate LEFT onto Lynne Avenue, uphill.*

26.9 *RIGHT at the end onto Shinnecock Road.*

27.0 *Immediate LEFT onto Foster Avenue, which curves left and then right, and becomes County Road 32.*

28.7 *LEFT at the end onto Ponquogue Beach (10).*
You can go for a fast swim or a wade here. Bike racks are at the parking lot entrance, and there's a snack bar at the beach house. For restaurant lunching, make an optional one-mile detour to your left to the eating spots (11) at the end of the road. At the Deck Restaurant you can eat outdoors overlooking the water.

Retrace your path to the entrance to Ponquogue Beach and continue west on Beach Road (unmarked) for several miles.

The first half of the beach ride is desolate, but there's plenty to look at when you hit the town of Quogue. You'll get a quick free survey course in Modern Beach Architecture, Hamptons style, as you note the large, often bizarre beach houses built atop the dunes. Don't spend too much time gawking, though, for the road is narrow and can be dangerous if there's traffic.

37.3 *RIGHT, opposite the Swordfish Beach Club, onto Jessup Lane; go over a drawbridge.*

38.0 *RIGHT at the end of Jessup Lane onto Stevens Lane. Immediate LEFT onto Potunk Lane.*

38.7 *At a six-way intersection, cross to the left of the Hampton Arts Theater to continue STRAIGHT onto Oak Street.*

39.2 *Across the Montauk Highway, Oak Street becomes Old Riverhead Road.*
That's Westhampton Airport coming up on your right.

43.3 *Bear LEFT, picking up County Road 104 North into Riverhead.*

45.0 *Bear LEFT to stay on 104.*

46.3 *Go around a traffic circle and pick up Peconic Avenue.*

46.4 *RIGHT onto East Main Street (Route 25) and back to the municipal lot.*

Optional final detour: If you return early enough and with strength left in your legs, go left on Main Street half a mile to the Suffolk County Historical Society museum (12), on your right. There's lots to see here—old medical recipes, Indian artifacts, antique toys, and some very old bicycles you may have to ask to view. There's also a packed gift shop downstairs. The museum is open 12:30 p.m. to 4:30 p.m. year-round, except Sundays. Donate what you wish.

Bicycle Shops
Bermuda Bikes Plus, 36 Gingerbread Lane, East Hampton (516-324-6688)
Bike 'n' Kite, 112 Potunk Lane, Westhampton Beach (516-288-1210)
Bike Stop, 200 Front Street, Greenport (516-477-2432)
Country Time Bike Shop, Main Road, Mattituck (516-298-8700)
Kid Stuff of Riverhead, 209 East Main Street, Riverhead (516-727-4164)
P & M Bicycles & Equipment, 38 East Montauk Highway, Hampton Bays (516-728-6686)
Piccozzi Bros. Garage, Bridge Street, Shelter Island (516-749-0520)
Rotations, 32 Windmill Lane, Southampton (516-283-2890)

13

To Greenwood Lake:
An Interstate Overnight

Round-trip distance pedaled: 91 miles (45 the first day, 46 the second)
Terrain: very hilly
Minimum cycling time: two 8-hour days

The beauty of this trip—aside from some lovely country—is that you can abridge it in two or three different ways to make an easier two-day affair or even a one-day jaunt. Just look at the map and your own shortened versions will pop readily to mind. If you do choose to take the full trip as outlined here, leave early; each day requires a full eight hours' pedaling, since some of the hills are tough going. You'll go through some affluent New Jersey suburbs, some country areas, and some little lake towns. This route is particularly recommended for autumn touring. Start at Bloomingdale's parking lot on Route 4 in Hackensack, about five miles northwest of the George Washington Bridge. It's not too hard to reach the starting point by bike from Manhattan: Go south a block or so on Hudson Terrace, the first road off the bridge, and then use a county map to work your way west and north a bit. Avoid Route 4 itself until you reach Bloomingdale's.

First Day

0.0 *From Bloomingdale's parking lot, head out to the RIGHT toward the Bradlee's store onto Hackensack Avenue (Route 503 North).*

0.3 *Swing RIGHT to make a LEFT turn onto Main Street.*

0.4 *RIGHT at the first traffic light onto Kinderkamack Road (still Route 503). Follow the Route 503 signs as you head north.*
As you cross Oradell Avenue, three miles up the road, note the blue-and-white sign on your right, a space-age historical marker proclaiming: "Oradell—Home of Commander Walter M. Schirra Jr., USN, the first Jerseyman to orbit the earth, October 3, 1962."
In another mile and a half, just after you cross some railroad tracks,

look left and you'll spy the Cookie Cupboard (1). It's a great snack shop, selling delicious handmade Pennsylvania Dutch mints and all sorts of fancy and unusual cookies and candles. Closed Mondays; open other days at 10 a.m.

5.8 *LEFT at a traffic light onto Old Hook Road (Route 502); follow the Route 502 signs west.*
Here come your first hills; the worst is after the Garden State Parkway.

Along the way, Route 502 is known variously as Washington Avenue, Werimus Road, East Saddle River Road, Hollywood Avenue, and Franklin Avenue.

On North Franklin Turnpike, in Ho-ho-kus, note the Hermitage (2) on your left. George Washington spent some time here. Aaron Burr was married here. A prominent Dutch-style homestead in the eighteenth century, it was altered in the 1840s to a Gothic Revival form, unusual for the area. The brown sandstone exterior is in this mid-nineteenth-century style, while the inside is part colonial farmhouse and part nineteenth-century, with a turn-of-the-century kitchen just like Grandma's. Open only Wednesdays and the first and third Sundays of each month, from 1 p.m. to 4 p.m. Suggested donation: $1.50.

Three miles or so along on your right is Zabriskie's Pond (3), a peaceful spot with weeping willows and, usually, some ducks. Two blocks later comes Quackenbush Avenue; make all the jokes you want.

16.2 *LEFT onto unmarked Ewing Avenue at the junction with Routes 3 and 4 to stay on Route 502.*

17.4 *RIGHT at Franklin Lake Road to stay on Route 502.*

18.2 *As you head through a traffic circle, pick up Long Hill Road to stay on Route 502.*

20.2 *Continue STRAIGHT on Long Hill Road as Route 502 turns left.*

21.2 *At a traffic light, pick up Route 202 South for a couple of blocks.*

21.5 *RIGHT onto Doty Road.*

21.9 *Cross over a narrow metal bridge, then make a sharp left onto unmarked West Oakland Avenue at the end of Doty Road. West Oakland Avenue becomes Colfax Avenue and goes into Pompton Lakes.*

23.7 *RIGHT at the end onto Wanaque ("Wanna-cue") Avenue, across a bridge.*

24.1 *RIGHT, just past a shopping center, onto Ringwood Avenue.*

29.1 *LEFT onto Westbrook Road.*

Westbrook Road leads across the large Wanaque Reservoir, offering especially nice looks at the wooded hills around the water.

30.5 *Bear RIGHT at the first fork onto Stontown Road (here marked "Stontown"); it's hilly.*

34.5 *LEFT at a stop sign, uphill onto Greenwood Lake Turnpike (Route 511).*

37.8 *Bear RIGHT to stay on Route 511; avoid Marshall Hill Road.*

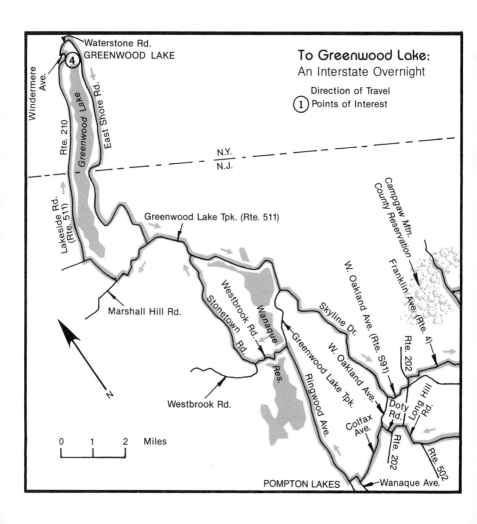

39.2 *After you glimpse the southern end of Greenwood Lake, turn RIGHT to stay on Route 511 (here unmarked Lakeside Road). The road soon becomes Route 210 over the border in Rockland County, New York.*

At the northern end of the lake, in the town of Greenwood Lake, you'll find a place to stay the night — Dieber's Breezy Point Inn (4), on the right side of Route 210 as you head north. This medium-sized motel offers rooms with double beds for $40 a night. For reservations call 914-477-8513. The inn also has a large dining room overlooking the lake, where hearty German-style food is served every day but Wednesdays.

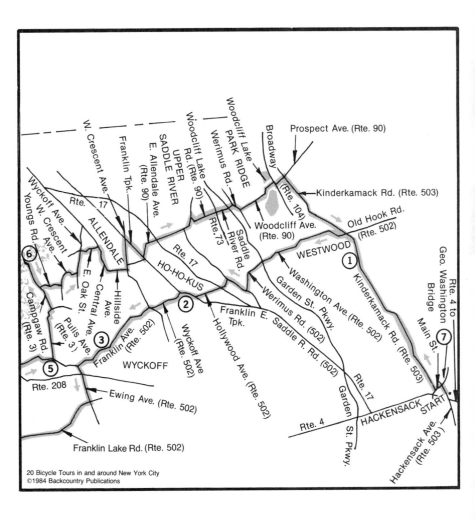

20 Bicycle Tours in and around New York City
©1984 Backcountry Publications

Second Day

0.0 *Continue on Route 210, turning LEFT onto Windermere Avenue.*

0.1 *Fast RIGHT onto Waterstone Road.*

0.8 *Cross a small bridge and bear RIGHT onto unmarked East Shore Road.*
You're coming back into Passaic County, New Jersey, now.

8.1 *LEFT at the end onto Greenwood Lake Turnpike.*

13.5 *LEFT onto Skyline Drive, which is very hilly.*

18.6 *LEFT as you reach the bottom of the mountain, at the end of Skyline Drive, onto West Oakland Avenue to pick up Route S91.*

19.2 *RIGHT at the entrance ramp to Route 208, avoiding Route 208 and keeping on West Oakland Avenue.*

19.4 *LEFT at a stop sign onto Route 202.*

19.7 *RIGHT at a traffic light onto Franklin Avenue (Route 4).*
About a mile and a half down Franklin Avenue you'll find a small food store or two (5). This is your best bet for edible supplies on this portion of the tour.

21.8 *LEFT onto Pulis Avenue (Route 3 North).*

23.4 *LEFT onto Campgaw Road to stay on Route 3.*
In a couple of miles the road will take you into the Campgaw Mountain County Reservation (6), where you'll find convenient picnic tables and marked hiking trails that lead up and down slopes that are used for skiing in winter.

26.0 *Retrace your path back down Campgaw Road, then turn LEFT onto Youngs Road.*

27.1 *Bear RIGHT at a fork onto West Crescent Avenue.*

27.3 *LEFT at a T intersection to stay on West Crescent Avenue (here unmarked).*

27.5 *LEFT at the end onto Wyckoff Avenue.*

28.2 *RIGHT onto East Oak Street.*

28.8 *RIGHT onto Central Avenue, which becomes Hillside Avenue as you pedal into the borough of Allendale.*

30.1 *LEFT at a traffic light onto West Crescent Avenue.*

31.0 *RIGHT at a traffic light onto Franklin Turnpike. (There's a "No Right Turn" sign; walk your bike through the turn.)*

31.8 *LEFT at a traffic light onto East Allendale Avenue (Route 90). (The only street sign you'll see is on your right, for West Allendale Avenue.)*

34.0 *RIGHT onto Woodcliff Lake Road, keeping to Route 90, going uphill.*

34.4 *Pass the intersection with Route 73 and stay on Route 90.*

35.0 *RIGHT onto Saddle River Road to stay on route.*

35.4 *RIGHT at the end of Saddle River Road onto Werimus Road.*

35.6 *LEFT onto Woodcliff Avenue, opposite Old Mill Road on the right, to pick up Route 90 again.*
The road leads straight through the midsection of Woodcliff Lake and Reservoir.

Some of northern New Jersey's finest scenery.   Bill Hoffman

37.0 *RIGHT at the end of Woodcliff Avenue, just after some railroad tracks, onto Broadway (Route 104).*

37.1 *Fast LEFT onto Prospect Avenue (Route 90).*

37.4 *RIGHT at a traffic light onto Kinderkamack Road (Route 503).*

45.3 *LEFT at a traffic light onto Main Street in North Hackensack to stay on Route 503.*

Here you can take an optional detour to the von Steuben house (7) on Main Street beyond Hackensack Avenue. The two-story stone house, built in the 1750s, was owned by a Tory but seized during the Revolutionary War and given to Baron von Steuben, Washington's drillmaster. Inside, you can look at pottery, furniture, toys, and other objects made or used in Bergen County from the 1680s to the 1850s. Also take a look at the rare Indian dugout canoe, thought to be three hundred years old; it was found buried in mud in Hackensack back in 1868. Open 10 a.m. to 5 p.m., with the noon hour off for lunch, Wednesdays through Saturdays, 2 p.m. to 5 p.m. only on Sundays; admission is free. From the house, retrace your path along Main Street and turn left onto Hackensack Avenue.

45.4 *Fast RIGHT at a traffic light onto Hackensack Avenue.*

45.7 *RIGHT onto Route 4 West, then bear LEFT for the ramp crossing Hackensack Avenue into Bloomingdale's parking lot.*

Bicycle Shops

A & R Cyclery, 141 Newark-Pompton Turnpike, Pequannock, NJ (201-696-3413)
Albert's Westwood Cycle Store, 182 Third Avenue, Westwood, NJ (201-664-1688)
Cyclesport, 1 Hawthorne Avenue, Park Ridge, NJ (201-391-5269)
Schwinn Bicycle Agency Sales & Service, 231 Everett Avenue, Wyckoff, NJ (201-891-8339)

14

Jersey Farm Country: Cranbury to New Egypt

Round-trip distance pedaled: 53 miles
Terrain: mostly flat
Minimum cycling time: 6 hours

Fairly flat and mostly bucolic, this route winds through farmland in west-central New Jersey. Take it slowly, stopping where you will, and count on a full day. If you're at all interested in collectibles, you'll want to make the trip on a Wednesday or a weekend, so you can catch the New Egypt Farmers Market in action—not that you'll have all that much room on your bike for purchases, but just to see the incredible maze of stuff for sale. Find the starting point by leaving the New Jersey Turnpike (always a pleasure) at exit 8A and following signs to Cranbury. The route begins at the Midlantic National Bank parking lot, on your left on Main Street, just past Park Place.

In Cranbury, you can breakfast at Teddy's Luncheonette (1), to the right across from the bank parking lot on Main Street. This place is good for early birds—it opens every morning at 5. You may run into other bikers here.

0.0 *LEFT, leaving the bank parking lot, onto Main Street.*

0.6 *Bear RIGHT onto unmarked Old Hightstown Road, following the sign to East Windsor and Trenton.*

0.7 *STRAIGHT at the next fork; this time, ignore the sign to East Windsor and Trenton.*

1.9 *STRAIGHT at a traffic light to pick up unmarked Old Cranbury Road into Hightstown.*

2.2 *RIGHT onto North Main Street.*

3.2 *Bear LEFT to pick up Route 539 South into Allentown, where it's called North Main Street and then South Main Street. Go straight through Allentown and take Old York Road to the village of North Crosswicks.*

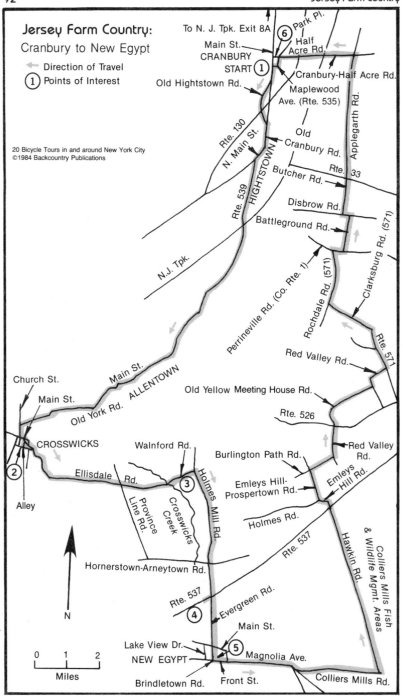

Jersey Farm Country:
Cranbury to New Egypt

← Direction of Travel
① Points of Interest

20 Bicycle Tours in and around New York City
©1984 Backcountry Publications

To N. J. Tpk. Exit 8A
Park Pl.
⑥
Half
Acre Rd.
Main St.
CRANBURY
START ①
Cranbury-Half Acre Rd.
Old Hightstown Rd.
Maplewood
Ave. (Rte. 535)
Old
Cranbury Rd.
Rte. 130
N. Main St.
HIGHTSTOWN
Butcher Rd.
Rte. 33
Applegarth Rd.
Rte. 539
Disbrow Rd.
Battleground Rd.
Clarksburg Rd. (571)
N.J. Tpk.
Perrineville Rd. (Co. Rte. 1)
Rochdale Rd. (571)
Red Valley Rd.
Rte. 571
Main St.
ALLENTOWN
Old Yellow Meeting House Rd.
Church St.
Old York Rd.
Rte. 526
Main St.
Red Valley
Rd.
CROSSWICKS
Walnford Rd.
Burlington Path Rd.
Emleys
Hill Rd.
② Ellisdale Rd.
③
Holmes Mill Rd.
Emleys Hill-
Prospertown Rd.
Alley
Province Line Rd.
Crosswicks Creek
Holmes Rd.
Colliers Mills Fish & Wildlife Mgmt. Areas
Rte. 537
Hawkin Rd.
Hornerstown-Arneytown Rd.
N
Rte. 537
④
Evergreen Rd.
Main St.
Lake View Dr.
⑤
Magnolia Ave.
NEW EGYPT
0 1 2
Miles
Brindletown Rd.
Front St.
Colliers Mills Rd.

14.4 *LEFT at the end of Old York Road onto Church Street in North Crosswicks.*

14.6 *LEFT onto Main Street in Crosswicks.*

14.8 *RIGHT downhill in an alley, where you'll see a deli called the Thistle Stop.*

You might stop here to pick up picnic fixings if the weather and mood are right.

14.9 *First RIGHT after the Thistle Stop to a large compound on a green.*

The red brick building farthest from the road is a Friends Meeting House (2) built in 1773. Embedded in its north side is a cannonball—a reminder of a 1778 skirmish between colonial and British troops.

15.0 *Retrace your path to the Thistle Stop, then turn RIGHT to continue on Main Street, heading out of town. Main Street becomes Ellisdale Road.*

18.9 *STRAIGHT as you cross Province Line Road, to pick up Walnford Road.*

After a nice downhill run you'll come to Crosswicks Creek (3), a beautiful, serene spot. If you could use a rest, this is the place for it.

20.2 *Bear LEFT on the bridge over the creek.*

20.3 *First RIGHT across the bridge, uphill onto an unmarked, unpaved road.*

21.1 *RIGHT onto unmarked, hilly Holmes Mill Road.*

24.8 *RIGHT, just past Hornerstown-Arneytown Road, onto unmarked Route 537.*

On your left in a tenth of a mile is the New Egypt Auction & Farmers Market (4), an amazing ten-acre shantytown of antiques stalls, market stands, junk dealers, and who knows what. The market operates Wednesdays, Saturdays, and Sundays. The lion's share of the action is over by one o'clock. Auctions are held Wednesdays and Sundays at noon. Rest rooms, a snack bar, and a pay phone are handy. Retrace your path on Route 537.

25.0 *First RIGHT onto Evergreen Road.*

26.3 *You've reached New Egypt, the halfway mark. It's time for lunch and relaxation.*

In New Egypt (5), local cyclists like to lunch at the very informal Tootie's Diner. Once you hit town, turn right onto Main Street; Tootie's, open every day, is a tenth of a mile down on your left. The best in-town picnic site is the grassy bank of Oakford Lake on Lake View Drive.

From Evergreen Road, cross Main Street and continue down Brindle-town Road, then take a quick LEFT onto Front Street, which be-comes Magnolia Avenue. Follow Magnolia Avenue out of town.

28.0 *LEFT at a three-way fork onto Colliers Mills Road.*

30.6 *LEFT onto unmarked Hawkin Road, to follow one edge of the Colliers Mills Fish and Wildlife Management Areas. (Watch for hunters crossing the road; hope they watch for bikers.) Hawkin Road becomes Emleys Hill Road as you cross Route 537.*

35.3 *RIGHT at the first fork onto unmarked Emleys Hill–Prospertown Road, avoiding Holmes Road.*

36.2 *RIGHT, at a white church and graveyard, onto Burlington Path Road.*

37.0 *LEFT at a fork onto Red Valley Road.*

37.8 *STRAIGHT across Route 526 to pick up Old Yellow Meeting House Road.*

39.8 *LEFT at the end onto Red Valley Road again.*

40.7 *LEFT at the first stop sign onto Route 571.*

41.2 *RIGHT to stay on Route 571, here called Clarksburg Road.*

43.4 *RIGHT again to stay on Route 571, now called Rochdale Road.*

44.9 *RIGHT onto Perrineville Road (County Route 1).*

45.2 *First LEFT onto Battleground Road.*

46.3 *LEFT at the end onto unmarked Disbrow Road.*

46.5 *RIGHT onto Butcher Road, which soon becomes Applegarth Road.*

50.8 *LEFT, at a four-way stop, onto Cranbury–Half Acre Road, which becomes Half Acre Road.*

52.8 *LEFT at the end onto Maplewood Avenue (Route 535 South).*

53.1 *Bear LEFT to stay on Maplewood Avenue.*

53.2 *RIGHT, into the bank parking lot.*

   If you finish early enough on a Saturday or Sunday, stop at the little Cranbury Historical Museum (6) around the corner from Main Street on Park Place. It's in a typical village house of the 1800s; the rear was built about 1820, the front added after the Civil War. Inside are some interesting furnishings, mostly donated by old Cranbury families from among their heirlooms. Of special interest are a 1720 rocker and a great old spinning wheel. The museum is open weekends only, from 1 p.m. to 4 p.m.; there is no charge.

Bicycle Shops
Bicycle Trails, Route 206, Bordentown (609-298-2747)
Speedway Bicycle Shop, Route 33 (Mercer Street), Hightstown (609-443-3320)

A late summer pleasure—counting out the ears.   Dan Carlinsky

15

Crossing the Delaware: Princeton to New Hope

Round-trip distance pedaled: 58 miles
Terrain: moderately hilly
Minimum cycling time: 8 hours

This full day of cycling takes you through spectacular areas of New Jersey and eastern Pennsylvania, offering something for everyone. For ecofreaks, there's mile after mile of woodland, farms, and waterways; for history buffs, lots of Washington-stopped-here spots, including the site where he crossed the Delaware; for shoppers, a town full of slick gifts and fancy foods; for serious cyclists, some good, stiff hills. Start this tour in Princeton Junction. Take exit 8 off the New Jersey Turnpike, then Route 33 westbound to County Road 571. Turn left on Wallace Road just before the railroad tracks and park at the Princeton Junction station (50 cents for a day).

For an optional breakfast or picnic-supplies detour, a left turn onto Wallace Road as you leave the parking lot will bring you to the Gourmet Delicatessen and Bakery Shop (1), at the intersection with County Road 571. You'll find coffee and sandwiches to go and an assortment of snacks for the country roads ahead. Closed Sundays. You can breakfast outdoors in a park about ten minutes into the tour.

0.0 *RIGHT, leaving the parking lot, onto Wallace Road.*

0.3 *Bear RIGHT at a yield sign onto Alexander Road, which quickly becomes North Post Road.*

2.5 *RIGHT at a stop sign onto Village Road West.*
You're skirting the large Mercer County Central Park; time for that open-air breakfast, if you like.

4.2 *LEFT at the end of Village Road West onto Quakerbridge Road.*

5.2 *RIGHT at a traffic light onto Youngs Road.*
Immediately around the bend on Youngs Road, note on your left a

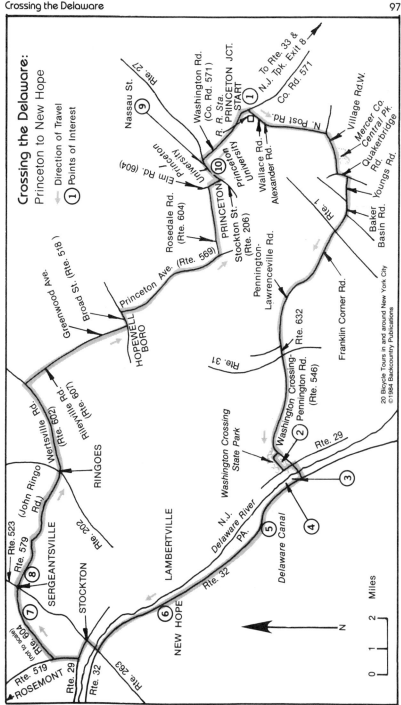

Crossing the Delaware:
Princeton to New Hope

→ Direction of Travel
① Points of Interest

20 Bicycle Tours in and around New York City
©1984 Backcountry Publications

rough stone column marking the route of "Washington's march by night from Trenton to Princeton and victory" on January 3, 1777.

6.2 *Bear LEFT at a stop sign onto Baker Basin Road.*

In about a mile, Baker Basin Road becomes Franklin Corner Road as you cross Route 1. A couple of miles later, you pass through Lawrenceville Prep School territory and the road changes name again—to Pennington-Lawrenceville Road. The ride here is very flat and goes through small clusters of homes. In season, you'll notice an abundance of roadside farm stands.

11.8 *LEFT onto unmarked Route 632. (A sign for Route 31 is the only clue to where to make this turn.)*

12.4 *RIGHT around a traffic circle to pick up Route 546 West, Washington Crossing–Pennington Road.*

16.2 *RIGHT on the first road into Washington Crossing State Park.*

Cars pay to get in on summer weekends and holidays; bikes don't. You'll wind left and right through the trees for about half a mile. Take half an hour to check out the free historical displays in three park buildings. During the famous Delaware crossing, Washington's men were in and out of the two-story Ferry House all evening (the operation took nine hours, what with 2,400 troops and their gear); now the house, furnished with eighteenth-century antiques, is open for inspection from 9 a.m. to 4 p.m. Wednesdays through Saturdays and 1 p.m. to 4 p.m. Sundays. In the Nelson House, a sturdy stone structure on the river bank near the Washington Crossing bridge, there's a flag display to see from 10 a.m. to 5 p.m. during the summer months only. And at the park's visitors' center you can look at Revolution-era weapons, uniforms, documents, and other memorabilia from 9 a.m. to 4:30 p.m. Wednesdays through Sundays. All are free entry.

16.8 *LEFT, from the Ferry House, onto the park road.*

17.2 *Bear LEFT to the walk bridge leading over Route 29.*

17.3 *RIGHT onto the iron bridge across the Delaware River.*

On your right, just as you get off the bridge in Pennsylvania, is the Old Ferry Inn (3), one of many buildings and sights that make up Pennsylvania's Washington Crossing State Park. Washington and his staff came by in 1776, but they camped out instead of renting rooms. Much of the paneling and woodwork inside is original. One story says that George had dinner here just before he crossed the Delaware. The inn is open every day (afternoons only on Sundays); entry costs $1.50, but seniors pay $1 and kids 6 to 17 pay just 50 cents. The ticket also lets you inspect an

1816 house on the grounds and an early farmhouse, the Thompson-Neely House, about five miles ahead.

17.6 *RIGHT onto Route 32 North.*

A tenth of a mile after you make the turn, you'll come to the Memorial Building (4) on your right. Inside, for free, you can see a copy of Emanuel Leutze's famous painting, *Washington Crossing the Delaware.* (The original hangs in the American Wing of New York's Metropolitan Museum.) Outside, there's a pool surrounded by flags of the thirteen colonies, a "Betsy Ross flag," and a statue of you-know-who.

In another couple of miles, the road turns left, away from the river; you'll cross the Delaware Canal (5). Stop here to enjoy the natural beauty at part of a sixty-mile-long scenic waterway that roughly parallels the river.

In a couple of miles more, you'll see a miniature stone tower on your left, marking the road to Bowman Hill. A mile-long side road leads to the lookout post where rebel sentries climbed to keep an eye on the Jersey side of the river.

Route 32 takes you into the compact center of 300-year-old New Hope (6), Pennsylvania's answer to Quincy Market in Boston and Georgetown in Washington, D.C. Main Street is lined with boutiques, galleries, craft shops (particularly leather and jewelry), restaurants, and snackeries. Bridge Street is the place to shop for antiques. An artists' colony at the turn of the century, New Hope is still pleasant enough, but it's now a tourist town from start to finish, catering to Philadelphians and New Yorkers out for a country drive; even the ice cream is expensive. If you need help sorting it all out, call the town's information center at 215-862-5880. Take time off from the rampant consumption, if you like, by hiking along the old towpath, which parallels the river. Follow Route 32 out of town.

28.0 *RIGHT at the junction with Route 263, crossing the river to Stockton, New Jersey.*

28.3 *LEFT at a stop sign onto Route 29 North.*

Here you pass Colligan's Stockton Inn, where "Small Hotel," a song from the Broadway musical *On Your Toes*, was written. Just as the song says, there's a wishing well—in a garden on the left side of the inn.

28.9 *RIGHT onto Route 519 North, uphill.*

30.9 *RIGHT at the end, following the sign for Baptistown, to stay on Route 519.*

31.1 *RIGHT onto Route 604.*

At the intersection is the Rosemont General Store (closed Sundays), which dates from about 1845.

About a mile and a half along Route 604—at the end of a great downhill stretch—you'll come to Green Sergeant's Bridge (7), the last public covered bridge in New Jersey. It was rebuilt in 1872 on foundations that date from 1750. Bridge traffic is restricted to one-way now—opposite to the direction of this tour—so you'll have to cross via the adjacent ugly modern bridge and circle back to see the inside. Nearby is a small white house (c. 1792) that was probably the toll collector's home. Go uphill after leaving the bridge, through the sleepy town of Sergeantsville.

A mile beyond the bridge you'll pass the Sergeantsville Inn and, across the street, another nineteenth-century general store.

38.0 *RIGHT, at a stop sign, onto Route 579 South (John Ringo Road), toward the town of Ringoes.*

In less than half a mile, you'll pass the Black River and Western Railroad (8), New Jersey's only profit-making passenger line. There's a one-room train museum to see for free, and if you have time you can see the landscape from the tracks by taking a train ride, available Saturdays, Sundays, and holidays from mid-April through November (every day but Monday during July and August). Starting times are 10:45 a.m. and 12:15, 1:45, 3:15, and 4:45 p.m. Price of the hour-and-ten-minute ride—north to Flemington and back — is $5 ($2.50 for kids 5 to 12). There's no problem in taking bikes along.

39.0 *LEFT, just past Mom's Restaurant in Ringoes, onto Wertsville Road (Route 602).*

There are more nice rolling hills on this stretch.

42.6 *RIGHT onto Route 607 South (unmarked Rileyville Road).*

The street name changes to Greenwood Avenue in Hopewell.

47.1 *LEFT at a traffic light in Hopewell Boro onto Broad Street (Route 518 East).*

47.3 *RIGHT at a traffic light two blocks later onto Route 569 (unmarked Princeton Avenue).*

In roughly three and a half miles you'll go by the headquarters of the Educational Testing Service. They're the folks who drive high school kids crazy with the College Board exams every year.

51.0 *LEFT onto Rosedale Road (Route 604), following the sign toward Princeton.*

53.4 *RIGHT at a traffic light onto Elm Road (still Route 604).*

53.9 *LEFT at a traffic light onto busy Stockton Street (Route 206 North).*

On your right in a couple of short blocks, at 32 Edgehill Street, is the Barracks, thought to be the oldest building in Princeton. Built in 1695, it got its name because it was reportedly used as a military outpost during the Revolution. The Stockton family, which lived in the place before soldiers took over, includes a signer of the Declaration of Independence.

54.4 *Stay STRAIGHT at a traffic light to pick up Nassau Street (Route 27 North).*

Before exploring Nassau Street, you can make a short optional detour to the right down Mercer Street, to number 112—the house where Einstein lived.

Nassau Street (9) is the main drag of Princeton University. Several informal eateries here are popular with Tigers, among them the Annex, at 128½ Nassau. It's a friendly downstairs spot serving good sandwiches and hearty Italian food at reasonable prices. For more imposing surroundings and fancier eats, there's the Nassau Inn. Generations of Princetonians have carved their initials in the massive oak tables of its Yankee Doodle Tap Room (named for the large Normal Rockwell painting that hangs there). For desserts or end-of-tour snacks, the popular spot is Thomas Sweet, where specialties like Grand Marnier ice cream and chocolate-dipped fruit draw raves.

Unless you began early and pedaled very fast, you probably won't have much time for a full tour of the Princeton University campus (10). But try to take at least a fast stroll through the ivy. As you meander, note some of the twenty modern sculptures (a Calder, a Picasso, and a Moore among them) spotted around the grounds. If you can, stop at:

Nassau Hall. When it was built, in 1756, it was the largest building in the colonies. The British took it over for a barracks and hospital during the Revolution and the rebels won it back, ending the Battle of Princeton. Later, it briefly housed the Continental Congress.

The University Art Museum. Its collection includes pre-Columbian artifacts, classical and Oriental pieces, and African and American folk art.

Prospect Garden. A quiet flower garden behind the faculty club. A spot for unwinding.

University Chapel. A neo-Gothic building with striking stained-glass windows.

54.8 *From Nassau Street, RIGHT onto County Road 571 East (Washington Road).*

57.6 *Bear LEFT over a bridge, following signs toward Hightstown and Freehold, to stay on route.*

57.9 *RIGHT at a traffic light onto Wallace Road.*

58.1 *RIGHT into the station parking lot.*

Bicycle Shops
Jay's Cycles, 249 Nassau Street, Princeton (609-924-7233)
Kopp's Cycle, 38 Spring Street, Princeton (609-924-1052)
The Nickel, Princeton Shopping Center, North Harrison Street, Princeton (609-921-6078)

16

Westchester County: Three Bodies of Water

Round-trip distance pedaled: 30 miles
Terrain: moderately hilly
Minimum cycling time: 4 hours

Start this tour in Mount Kisco, where you can park at the train station, which is just off Main Street and offers long-term parking meters ($1.25 for ten hours) six days and free parking on Sundays. This is mostly easy country cycling, although part of the road — around Byram Lake Reservoir — is dirt. The toughest hill leads up to the lake, but you'll probably decide that climbing it was worth the effort when you take the long coast down through the trees to the water.

0.0 *Leaving the train station, turn RIGHT onto Main Street (Route 117).*

0.2 *Bear RIGHT to stay on Route 117 south, uphill through Mount Kisco center.*
    Just after Gregory Avenue, on your right, you'll pass the United Methodist Church, a distinctive white wood building, dating from 1868, with curious stained-glass windows and a pair of fancy shingled steeples.
    Beyond, an old cemetery (1) contains faded and broken headstones from the late 1700s on. History buffs may want to search for a small marker in the southeast corner; it indicates that soldiers from the Revolutionary War are buried here.

1.3 *One block past the cemetery, turn LEFT onto Byram Lake Road, opposite Lloyd Lumber Company, and skirt Byram Lake Reservoir (2).*
    The road leading to the lake is mostly uphill and lined with old low stone fences, horse farms, refreshing rills, and trickling brooks. If it gets to be too much for you, do what the experts do to avoid strain: Get off your bike and walk. As you reach the hill's crest, you'll glimpse Byram Lake through the trees. Take the steep downhill run to the water slowly, for the road twists and turns suddenly; again, walk the bike if the going gets too rough. Just past the boathouse at the bottom of the hill, the pavement

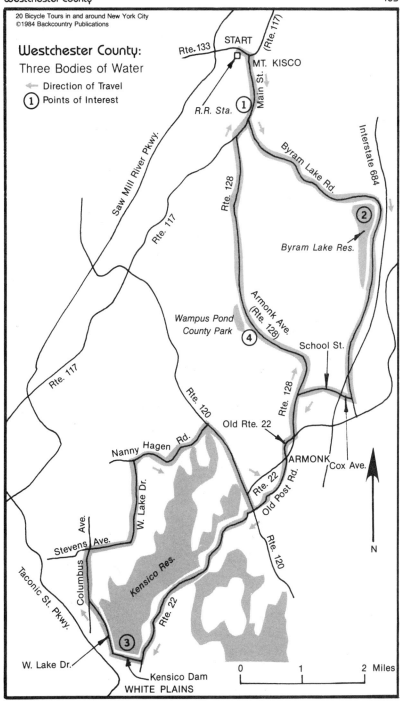

20 Bicycle Tours in and around New York City
©1984 Backcountry Publications

Westchester County:
Three Bodies of Water

← Direction of Travel
① Points of Interest

ends. The dirt is easy to bike on, though, and about a mile past the boathouse you'll pick up paved road again.

7.6 *Take a hairpin RIGHT onto Cox Avenue.*

8.1 *Cross over busy I-684, then bear LEFT two-tenths of a mile later onto unmarked School Street.*

8.5 *LEFT at the end of School Street onto Route 128 and into Armonk, IBM territory.*

9.3 *RIGHT, just past town, at the sign for Old Route 22.*

9.9 *Carefully cross busy Route 22 onto Old Post Road.*

10.7 *Cross Route 120, then turn LEFT at a traffic light onto Route 22, along the edge of the Kensico Reservoir.*
On your right you'll notice a large stone marker commemorating Reuben Wright's Mills, where George Washington made his headquarters for a time in 1778. The mills are now under water.

14.0 *RIGHT at a traffic light and a green sign for West Lake Drive, crossing over the Kensico Dam.*
The dam (3) was completed about the time of World War I. As you pedal across, gaze to your right at the Kensico Reservoir, which, via a long pipeline, supplies denizens of New York City. Midway over, park on the sidewalk and check out the better view from across the road.

15.4 *Bear RIGHT onto Columbus Avenue.*

16.0 *RIGHT at the second traffic light onto Stevens Avenue, which swings left and becomes unmarked West Lake Drive again.*

18.1 *RIGHT at the end onto Nanny Hagen Road.*

19.7 *RIGHT at the end onto Route 120.*

21.0 *Route 120 merges with Route 22. Bear RIGHT to stay on track.*

21.3 *LEFT at the first traffic light, then immediately LEFT again, making a wide U-turn to wind up on Old Post Road, a narrow street diagonally opposite the light.*

22.2 *Cross Route 22 again, picking up Old Route 22.*

22.8 *LEFT onto Route 128 (Armonk Avenue).*
On your left in about two and one-half miles is Wampus Pond County Park (4), a tiny, shaded green nook that's perfect for a rest and a snack before the final leg of the tour. Smallest of the three bodies of water on this tour, Wampus Pond is most conducive to lying on the bank and snooz-

ing. Picnic tables, a good drinking fountain, and rest rooms are provided by the county. There's a lone phone booth, too, in case you miss somebody. If you care to exercise different muscles, you can rent a small boat. The park is open in season (April through October) from 9 a.m. to 5 p.m. on weekdays, 7 a.m. to 6 p.m. on weekends and holidays; the rest of the year, 10 a.m. to dusk.

28.1 *Pick up Route 117 North back into Mount Kisco.*

29.6 *Bear LEFT at the Routes 117/133 fork. The train station will be on the left, just past a traffic light.*

Bicycle Shops
Bicycle World, 141 Main Street (Route 117), Mount Kisco (914-666-4044)
County Bike Center, 144 Bedford Road, Armonk (914-273-3454)
Paulding's Cycle Store, 98 West Post Road, White Plains (914-949-5527)
Yeager's Cycle Store, 14 East Post Road, White Plains (914-949-3305)

The view from the shore.   Steve Casey

17

Back Roads of Westchester: Armonk to Bedford

Round-trip distance pedaled: 27 miles
Terrain: moderately hilly
Minimum cycling time: 4 hours

Here's a tour that happily manages to stick to roads that don't see too many autos. Some sections are unpaved—dirt and gravel roads, one with some pretty deep ruts—but don't let that deter you. There are just a handful of formal attractions along the way, but the scenery is superb and the unbusy atmosphere relaxing. It's a pleasure to ride in an area so well protected from suburban sprawl. History buffs will enjoy the preserved buildings around the Bedford Village green. A good starting point is the spacious parking lot of the A&P on Route 128 in Armonk, opposite Annadale Street.

0.0 *Leaving the A&P, go LEFT; bear RIGHT to pick up Old Route 22.*
Four-tenths of a mile from the start, on your right, is the Cider Mill (1), an open-air produce stand with a snack bar next door. Both open at 8:30 every morning except fall and winter Tuesdays, when the whole thing is closed. Sip fresh, sweet cider in season, and if you show up on a Saturday or Sunday, watch doughnuts being made.

Retrace your path past the A&P and proceed along Route 128. You'll pass Orchard Drive, Old Mount Kisco Road, School Street, and Old Mount Kisco Road again.

1.7 *RIGHT, just after you pass Old Mount Kisco Road for the second time, then a fast LEFT onto High Street.*

3.1 *RIGHT at a fork (half a mile after Sarles Street) onto Sheather Road, which is unpaved and unmarked. It's the only bad stretch on the tour.*

4.3 *Hairpin RIGHT at the first intersection onto Westwood Drive.*
This road is also unpaved part of the way. Stop to search for a huge, vine-covered rock (2) behind a wire fence to your left, where Tripp Street,

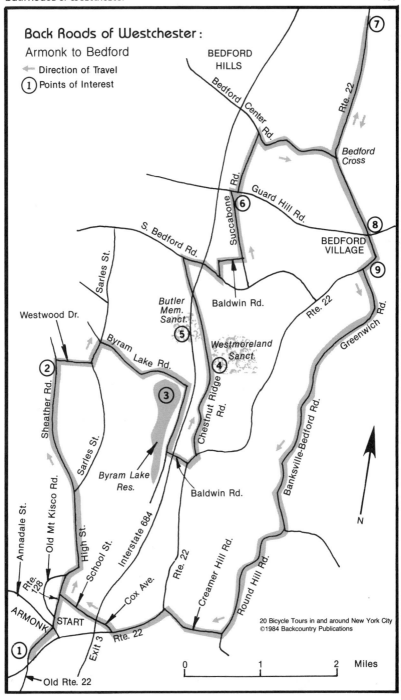

Back Roads of Westchester:
Armonk to Bedford

← Direction of Travel
(1) Points of Interest

BEDFORD HILLS

Bedford Center Rd.

Rte. 22

Bedford Cross

Guard Hill Rd.

Succabone Rd.

(6)

(7)

(8)

BEDFORD VILLAGE

(9)

S. Bedford Rd.

Sarles St.

Westwood Dr.

Byram Lake Rd.

Butler Mem. Sanct.

Baldwin Rd.

(5)

Westmoreland Sanct.

(4)

Rte. 22

Greenwich Rd.

(2)

Sheather Rd.

(3)

Chestnut Ridge Rd.

Byram Lake Res.

Baldwin Rd.

Banksville-Bedford Rd.

N

Sarles St.

Annadale St.

Old Mt Kisco Rd.

Rte. 128

High St.

School St.

Interstate 684

Cox Ave.

Rte. 22

Creamer Hill Rd.

Round Hill Rd.

20 Bicycle Tours in and around New York City
©1984 Backcountry Publications

ARMONK

(1)

START

Exit 3

Rte. 22

Old Rte. 22

0   1   2   Miles

Sheather Road, and Westwood Drive meet. The boulder has a tablet embedded in it that says, "Hungry Jim Hunter Died May 6 1902." Hungry Jim, according to folks who claim to know, was a horse.

4.8 *LEFT at the end onto Sarles Street.*

5.3 *RIGHT at a stop sign onto Byram Lake Road.*
The road leads downhill around Byram Lake Reservoir (3). Take it easy coasting on the long approach to the water, both for safety's sake and to savor the glorious view. You'll be on a paved road for about a mile; once you pass the boathouse, the road becomes unpaved for an uphill stretch.

7.6 *LEFT at the first intersection after the reservoir onto unmarked Baldwin Road.*

8.0 *LEFT at the end onto Route 22.*

8.1 *Immediate LEFT onto Chestnut Ridge Road.*
About one and one-half miles down the road, pay a visit to Westmoreland Sanctuary (4) on the right or continue on to Butler Memorial Sanctuary (5) just down the road on the left.

At Westmoreland, fifteen miles of marked trails wind through more than 625 acres and take in habitats ranging from open field to mature forest. Dabblers can stroll a quarter-mile easy loop and see the little lake and old graveyard, all near the entrance. A small nature museum on the grounds is in a 1783 church that was moved piece by piece from nearby Bedford Village and rebuilt here. The trails are open daily, dawn to dusk; the museum is open 9 a.m. to 5 p.m. Wednesdays through Saturdays, 10:30 a.m. to 5 p.m. on Sundays. It's all free.

The 350-acre Butler Sanctuary is another refuge for plants and wildlife. Posted on the wall of an information booth near the parking area are page after page listing the flowers that bloom on the grounds, from such exotica as tearthumb and loosestrife to eleven types of violets and thirteen varieties of goldenrod. Maps of the sanctuary's seven miles of hiking trails are available at the booth. The only sour note is that the roar of traffic from I-684 can be intrusive in some spots. The sanctuary is open daily, dawn to dusk, and entry is free.

Leaving either sanctuary, continue up Chestnut Ridge Road.

10.5 *RIGHT at the stop sign onto South Bedford Road, which passes under I-684.*

11.9 *Hairpin LEFT onto Baldwin Road.*

12.5 *First LEFT onto Succabone Road.*

13.2 *Dogleg RIGHT on Guard Hill Road, past the Sutton Memorial Tower on your right, to stay on Succabone Road.*

The tower (6) is a handsome, tall, brick affair with metal clock faces on top, surmounted by a weathervane. The clock is a windup, operated by weights. It's not as accurate as your electronic digital, but close enough.

14.5 *RIGHT onto Bedford Center Road.*

16.1 *Bedford Center Road brings you to Bedford Cross, a large stone cross in the middle of a lawn, at the intersection with Route 22.*
At this point you can take an optional detour two miles to the left along Route 22, to the John Jay Homestead State Historic Site (7). In 1801, having been a Founding Father, president of the Continental Congress, first chief justice of the United States, governor and chief justice of New York, and minister to Spain, Jay retired to this farm. The land, once owned by the Indian sachem Katonah, had already been in the Jay family for a century. Five generations of Jays maintained the spread as a working farm, periodically remodeling the house to keep up with fashion and adding outbuildings here and there. The current count includes four barns—one of stone, with elaborate wood supports for the roof—stables, a carriage shed and coachman's house, and a stone schoolhouse that John built for his grandchildren. The farmhouse has been restored to an early-nineteenth-century look, with family antiques in ten rooms. Other buildings on the sixty-acre site are being restored as well. Guided tours are available, and the grounds are open for walks, picnics, and weekend concerts and such. Admission is free, but hours change with the season. If you're interested, best call ahead for more information: 914-232-5651.

From Bedford Center Road, bear RIGHT at the cross onto Route 22.
About one and one-quarter miles after the cross, look to your left for the Bedford Oak (8), a massive white oak thought to be 500 years old. The much-loved old tree, in a clearing, serves as a symbol of Bedford Village's preservation-mindedness.

17.6 *Follow Route 22 through Bedford Village past the village green and out of town.*
The center of Bedford Village (9), a district listed in the National Register of Historic Places, has an impressive collection of eighteenth- and nineteenth- century buildings clustered around the well-manicured village green. If it looks typically New England, perhaps that's because when the village was founded, in 1680, it belonged to Connecticut. Twenty years later, Britain's King William decided to rearrange the colonial boundaries, and Bedford ended up as part of New York.
During the 1700s it became the most important and prosperous community in the region, until the British army burned most of the village in 1779. The buildings you see, including a restored 1787 courthouse, the oldest surviving government building in Westchester County, are later re-

placements. On the second floor of the white clapboard courthouse are two old jail cells and the Bedford Museum. Admission of $1 (50 cents for children) brings a guided tour of the museum and of an 1829 one-room schoolhouse. The buildings are open from 2 p.m. to 5 p.m. Wednesdays through Sundays, mid-April to mid-November. Other sites around the green include a 1681 burial ground, the resting place of townspeople from slaves to prominent citizens, and Historical Hall, which, according to a sign, was moved to its present site in 1837 "by 20 yoke of oxen." On Route 22 near the green is the Center Store Deli, a convenient twentieth-century refreshment spot. Just beyond is The Butcher and The Baker Restaurant (open from 11:30 a.m. Mondays through Saturdays, from 11 a.m. on Sundays), for classier victuals.

17.9 *LEFT, just outside of town, onto Greenwich Road, which becomes Banksville-Bedford Road.*

21.9 *RIGHT onto Round Hill Road.*

24.0 *RIGHT onto Creamer Hill Road (also known as Creemer Road).* Careful on the downhill.

25.2 *LEFT at the end onto busy Route 22.*

25.7 *RIGHT onto Cox Avenue at the flashing yellow light; the Modern Furniture Barn is on your right.*

25.9 *Bear LEFT to stay on Cox Avenue.*

26.4 *Cross over I-684, then bear LEFT two-tenths of a mile later at the Old Methodist Burial Ground onto unmarked School Street.*

26.9 *LEFT onto Route 128, back to the A&P, or on to the Cider Mill again for a well-deserved snack.*

Bicycle Shops
Big Cycle, 9 Norm Avenue, Bedford Hills (914-666-3549)
Country Bike Center, 144 Bedford Road, Armonk (914-273-3454)

18

Westchester and Fairfield: A Challenging Ride

Round-trip distance pedaled: 47 miles
Terrain: very hilly
Minimum cycling time: 8 hours

This tour starts at the Westchester County Airport in White Plains (exit 2 of I-684), scoots across the corner of the Nutmeg State, loops through Bedford Village in upper Westchester, and swings back through New Canaan, Connecticut, to the starting point. The region offers history, nature, culture, and, best of all, an always varied terrain—surely among the best cycling areas in the country. Note, however, that some of the roads are poorly marked and many are narrow and twisty, so ride with special care. And the many hills make this a tough ride for those not in condition. But if you do things right, this trip is worth the effort.

0.0 *Leaving the airport terminal, follow the green sign toward Green-wich uphill into Connecticut on unmarked Rye Lake Avenue.*

0.2 *LEFT at a traffic light onto King Street (Route 120A). The street is marked but the sign may be hard to find.*

0.3 *First RIGHT onto Cliffdale Road.*
Cliffdale Road passes through a municipal golf course. (Note signs that warn of golf carts crossing.) Take a short but very steep and winding downhill run, carefully cross a small brook on a wooden bridge, then climb up a ways.

1.4 *RIGHT at the end of Cliffdale Road onto unmarked Riversville Road, following a stone fence.*

1.9 *First LEFT onto Porchuck Road.*

2.6 *LEFT onto hilly North Porchuck Road.*

3.3 *Just past Old Mill Road, stop at the Audubon Fairchild Garden.*
The garden (1) features a wide selection of native and introduced species, with many pharmaceutical plants. Admission — $2 for adults, $1

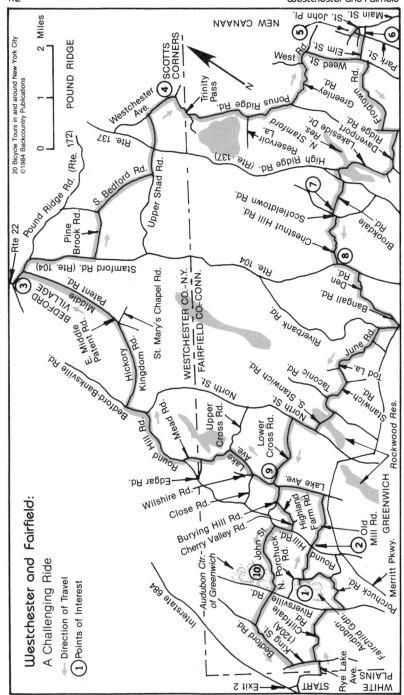

Westchester and Fairfield:
A Challenging Ride

→ Direction of Travel
① Points of Interest

20 Bicycle Tours in and around New York City
©1984 Backcountry Publications

0   1   2 Miles

POUND RIDGE

NEW CANAAN

for kids and seniors, free for Audubon Society members — is also good for the Audubon Center of Greenwich, which you'll reach later on the tour. The garden is open from dawn to dusk every day. As you leave the garden, turn right onto North Porchuck Road.

3.4 *LEFT onto Old Mill Road.*
Along Old Mill Road you'll pass a gorgeous private pond with a quiet waterfall. Then you'll go uphill. As you cross Round Hill Road you'll see, on your right, the Round Hill Store (2), an old-style general store dating from 1801. This little place has a fine old rolltop desk and wood display cases, and a counter for sandwiches and coffee. It's closed Sundays.

5.2 *LEFT at the end of Old Mill Road onto Lake Avenue.*

6.1 *Bear RIGHT at Burying Hill Road, then take a fast LEFT at Lower Cross Road to stay on Lake Avenue.*

6.6 *Bear RIGHT at Close and Wilshire roads to stay on Lake Avenue.*

7.3 *LEFT at a fork with Upper Cross Road to stay on Lake Avenue.*
As you cross back into New York at Edgar Road, Lake Avenue is unpaved for a short stretch and then becomes unmarked Mead Road.

8.7 *RIGHT at the end onto unmarked Round Hill Road.*

9.6 *LEFT at the end onto Bedford-Banksville Road, following the green sign for Bedford.*

10.3 *Second RIGHT up a steep hill onto winding Hickory Kingdom Road.*

12.2 *Continue STRAIGHT onto East Middle Patent Road, then Middle Patent Road.*

14.4 *LEFT at the end onto Pound Ridge Road (Route 172).*

14.9 *RIGHT, following the sign for Route 22 north.*
Bedford Village (3) is a favorite lunch stop for Westchester cyclists, for good reason. The village is a gem from one side of its tidy green to the other. A National Historic Landmark, the main district includes buildings of the eighteenth and nineteenth centuries. The old courthouse (1787), including two jail cells upstairs, has been restored. Poke around the 1681 graveyard and see how many of the older tombstones you can find and decipher.

15.1 *Leaving the green, follow the sign to Pound Ridge along Route 172 eastbound (Pound Ridge Road).*

15.7 *RIGHT, following the green sign toward Stamford, onto Route 104 (Stamford Road).*

16.9 *LEFT onto Pine Brook Road (a white wooden street sign is on your right).*

17.9 *RIGHT at the end onto South Bedford Road (another white sign).*

19.6 *LEFT at the end onto Upper Shad Road; cross Route 137.*

20.6 *RIGHT at the end onto Westchester Avenue, which takes you past a small shopping center, Scotts Corners.*

Described as "the shopping center of historic Pound Ridge," Scotts Corners (4) has several small shops selling everything from antiques to natural foods. Most stores stay closed on Sundays.

21.1 *RIGHT, next to a Shell gas station, onto Trinity Pass (street sign hidden).*

21.8 *LEFT, downhill, onto Ponus Ridge Road.*

23.0 *LEFT at Reservoir Lane to stay on route.*

24.0 *LEFT at a triangular traffic island onto Greenley (sometimes spelled without the third "e") Road.*

25.1 *Bear RIGHT onto West Road (you'll see a yield sign on your right and a street sign on your left).*

25.2 *First RIGHT at a triangular traffic island onto Weed Street.*

26.3 *LEFT onto Elm Street, past high stone walls on both sides.*

26.8 *LEFT onto Park Street in New Canaan, just past the train station on your right.*

26.9 *RIGHT, downhill, onto St. John Place.*

27.0 *LEFT onto unmarked Main Street, which loops right and enters the New Canaan historic district.*

The historic district (5) includes several buildings worth a visit. A white wood house dating from 1825 contains a costume display and an 1845 apothecary with all its contents. Next door is an 1833 Lutheran church (the town's oldest), and nearby is the Hanford-Silliman House, a restored 1764 home with period furnishings. To the rear is a tool museum and a print shop with a hand press more than 150 years old. Also in the historic district are a 1799 schoolhouse and a sculptor's studio from Victorian times. Two dollars will get you into everything (free if you're under 16). The buildings are open Wednesdays, Thursdays, and Sundays from 2 p.m. to 4 p.m., plus other hours at certain periods; phone ahead: 203-966-1776.

27.1 *LEFT onto Park Street.*

27.3 *RIGHT onto Elm Street, past the train station.*

There are restaurants and food shops on Elm Street (6), including an ice cream store that's open on Sundays.

27.8 *LEFT at the end onto Weed Street.*

28.0 *First RIGHT onto Frogtown Road.*

29.6 *LEFT at the end onto unmarked Ponus Ridge Road.*

29.9 *RIGHT at a traffic island with a stone marker onto Davenport Ridge Road.*

The rough-hewn stone marker in the island at the turn commemorates the homesite and traditional tomb of Ponus, sachem of the Rippowams, c. 1640.

30.6 *RIGHT at a kidney-shaped traffic island onto Lakeside Drive.*

31.9 *Bear LEFT at a stop sign after a land bridge over North Stamford Reservoir to stay on Lakeside Drive.*

32.1 *LEFT at the end onto unmarked High Ridge Road (Route 137).*

32.2 *Fast RIGHT onto Brookdale Road.*

A quarter-mile ahead on your right is Bartlett Arboretum (7), sixty-two acres featuring a collection of dwarf conifers and, in spring, azaleas and rhododendrons. The arboretum also has natural trails through untouched land, good for half an hour or so of exploring nature. Open every day from

On Route 22 in elegant Bedford Village. Bedford Historical Society

8:30 a.m. to sunset; no admission charge. Free maps are available in a box near the entrance.

32.8 *LEFT at the end of Brookdale Road onto unmarked Scofield-town Road.*

32.9 *Next RIGHT onto Chestnut Hill Road.*

Here, you can rest or picnic at the leafy park (8) behind the stone fence to your left.

34.0 *LEFT at the end of Chestnut Hill Road onto unmarked Route 104.*

34.5 *RIGHT onto curvy Den Road.*

35.8 *Bear RIGHT at unmarked Bangall Road, just past Hardesty Lane.*

36.0 *RIGHT at a fork onto unmarked Riverbank Road. (The road to the left has a sign for Merritt Parkway eastbound.)*

36.3 *LEFT at the first major road onto June Road, crossing over a small bridge.*

36.5 *RIGHT at the first fork to stay on June Road.*

37.5 *LEFT onto Tod Lane.*

37.8 *RIGHT at the end onto unmarked Stanwich Road.*

38.4 *STRAIGHT ahead as the street name changes to Taconic Road.*

38.7 *RIGHT onto South Stanwich Road, crossing Rockwood Reservoir.*

39.3 *RIGHT at the end onto unmarked North Street, uphill.*

39.7 *LEFT at a wide intersection onto Lower Cross Road.*

About a mile and a half down Lower Cross Road, you'll pass the Art Barn (9) on your right. It's an arts-and-crafts center with a gallery of for-sale works by local professionals. No regular hours; phone for information about special shows: 203-661-9048.

41.2 *LEFT at a small traffic island onto Lake Avenue.*

41.3 *First RIGHT onto Burying Hill Road.*

41.7 *LEFT onto Highland Farm Road, just before Burying Hill Road turns uphill.*

42.2 *RIGHT at the end onto unmarked Cherry Valley Road.*

42.4 *RIGHT at the end onto Round Hill Road.*

42.7 *LEFT at the First Church of Round Hill onto unmarked John Street, a very steep cimb.*

At the intersection with Riversville Road is the Audubon Center of Greenwich (10), a 477-acre sanctuary with seven miles of self-guiding hiking trails, a viewing area where you can peer at feeding birds through scopes provided, and a fascinating "environmental bookshop." Adults pay $2, children and seniors pay $1, Audubon Society members pay nothing; admission covers the center and the Audubon Fairchild Garden (1). Open 9 a.m. to 5 p.m. Tuesdays through Sundays.

44.9 *LEFT at the end of John Street onto Bedford Road.*

46.0 *LEFT at the end onto King Street.*

There are a couple of good roadside fruit and vegetable stands on King Street.

46.5 *RIGHT at a traffic light onto Rye Lake Avenue.*

46.7 *LEFT to return to the airport.*

Bicycle Shops

Big Cycle, 9 Norm Avenue, Bedford Hills, NY (914-666-3549)
Stamford Cycle Centre, 1492 High Ridge Road, Stamford, CT (203-968-1100)

19

To Ridgefield: A Hard Day Trip (or an Overnight)

Round-trip distance pedaled: 65 miles
Terrain: very hilly
Minimum cycling time: 10 hours

Like the tour "Westchester and Fairfield: A Challenging Ride," this route begins at the Westchester County Airport in White Plains (exit 2 on I-684) and goes into Connecticut. But while this tour goes through the same type of pretty countryside, only more so, there's no more than an occasional brief overlap between the two. Following a trail that meanders back and forth over state lines several times, you explore an unusually scenic part of the greater New York region. The hardy may want to stop overnight at the Ward Pound Ridge Reservation, which has lean-tos for rent; those looking for more comfort could stay in Ridgefield, one of Connecticut's loveliest towns, at the pleasant old Elms Inn. A seasoned cyclist might make the trip in one day of very hard pedaling and just a few stops, but it's much more pleasant as an overnight. There are plenty of places that cry for a pause and a gaze, and there are some hills that are rough on the tendons.

0.0 *Leaving the airport terminal, follow the green sign toward Greenwich uphill into Connecticut on unmarked Rye Lake Avenue.*

0.2 *RIGHT at a traffic light onto King Street.*
The road is marked, but the sign may be hard to find, not an uncommon problem in these parts.

1.9 *LEFT onto Sherwood Avenue, noting the modern, round St. Paul's Catholic Church on your right.*

2.9 *RIGHT at the end of Sherwood Avenue, under a concrete overpass, onto unmarked Riversville Road.*
The highway above is the Merritt Parkway, built in the 1930s—a pretty road as highways go, but not as scenic as the roads on this route.

4.3 *LEFT onto hilly Pecksland Road at a broad intersection.*

To Ridgefield:
A Hard Day Trip
(Or an Overnight)

Rte. 116 (N. Salem Rd.)

North St.

Gilbert St.

Ramapo Rd.

High Ridge Ave.

Peaceable Hill Rd.

Peaceable St.

S. Salem Rd.

Rte. 35 (Old Post Rd.)

← Direction of Travel
(1) Points of Interest

NORTH
SALEM

Main St.

Rte. 102

④

Rte. 35

⑤

RIDGEFIELD

Rte. 35

West La.

BEDFORD HILLS

Rte. 35

③

Reservation
Rd.

Ward Pound
Ridge Res.

Conant Valley Rd.

Rte. 123

Elmwood Dr.

Rte. 22

Old Church La.

East Woods
Rd.

⑥

Old Post Rd. (Rte. 121)

Trinity Pass

SCOTTS
CORNERS

BEDFORD
VILLAGE

②

Poundridge Rd.

⑦

West chester
Ave.

Rte. 29

Old Post Rd. (Rte. 22)

Greenwich Rd.

Rte. 104

Rte. 137 (High Ridge Rd.)

Bedford-Banksville Rd.

WESTCHESTER CO.–N.Y.
FAIRFIELD CO.–CONN.

Mayapple Rd.

Rockrimmon Rd.

Old Long Ridge Rd.

Creamer
Hill Rd.

S. Stanwich
Rd. North St.

Tod La.

June Rd.

Riverbank
Rd.

Rte. 104

STAMFORD

Close Rd.

Taconic Rd.

Rockwood
Lake Res.

Merritt Pkwy.

Interstate 684

Old Mill Rd.

①

Stanwich Rd.

N

Exit 2

Clapboard
Ridge Rd.

Sherwood Ave.

Round Hill Rd.

Peckland Rd.

Riversville Rd.

King St.

START

Lake Ave.

Grahampton La.

Rye Lake Ave.

WHITE
PLAINS

GREENWICH

0   1   2   Miles

20 Bicycle Tours in and around New York City
©1984 Backcountry Publications

5.8 *LEFT at the end onto Round Hill Road.*

The Round Hill Store (1) is two and a half miles along, at the corner of Old Mill Road. It's a great old place that's been a general store since 1801; only two families have been in charge in all that time. Some of the nineteenth-century furnishings (wood cabinets, a safe, a rolltop desk) are still in place. The furniture isn't for sale, but other things are, including coffee, soft drinks, and wedges (a local label for hero, or submarine, sandwiches). Closed Sundays.

9.9 *Bear LEFT at Close Road to stay on Round Hill Road.*

10.8 *Bear RIGHT at Creamer Hill Road to stay on Round Hill.*

You're passing back into New York State again.

12.9 *LEFT at a stop sign onto Bedford-Banksville Road, which becomes Greenwich Road. A sign at the corner points you on the way to Bedford.*

16.8 *RIGHT onto Old Post Road (Route 22), through Bedford Village. As you approach the village green, you'll come to a fork in the road; bear LEFT to stay on Route 22.*

It's worth stopping and tethering your bike so you can walk around the Bedford Village green (2), a historic grouping of clapboard houses with very much of a New England flavor. Read the informative signs on some of the old buildings, poke around the even older burial ground, visit the museum upstairs in the restored colonial courthouse, mosey into an antiques shop. Go grocery shopping, if you like, to prepare for a picnic ahead.

17.4 *RIGHT onto Route 121 (also called Old Post Road).*

In four and a half miles you can make an optional detour to the Ward Pound Ridge Reservation (3) on your right. It's less than a mile from Route 121 to the entrance, along Reservation Road. The reservation is a gorgeous 4,500 acres, with plenty of picnic space, tables, grills, and such, plus a refreshment stand, hiking trails, a nature museum, and gardens. Overnighters can put up in rustic lean-tos with fireplaces and dirt floors; renting is from 9 a.m. to 5 p.m. — first-come, first-served — with a charge of $15 for up to eight in a shelter. Reservations are possible if two weeks' notice is given, to allow for the mailing of paperwork; phone 914-763-3493 for information. If you need food, continue on Route 121 past the reservation entrance, turn right onto Route 35 East, and you'll find the Fifth Division Market, open Mondays through Fridays 8 a.m. to 8 p.m., Saturdays 8 a.m. to 6 p.m., Sundays 9 a.m. to 5 p.m.

22.1 *RIGHT at the end of Route 121 onto Route 35 East (again called Old Post Road); stay straight on Route 35.*

27.4 *LEFT onto Peaceable Street, opposite the junction with Route 123.*

You'll cross the border into Connecticut again in two-tenths of a mile; look for a boundary stone on the left side of the road.

27.7 *First LEFT to stay on Peaceable Street (here unmarked). Avoid South Salem Road, which goes straight.*

28.3 *First RIGHT to stay on Peaceable Street. Avoid Peaceable Hill Road, which goes straight.*

29.3 *LEFT at a stop sign onto High Ridge Avenue.*

29.9 *RIGHT to avoid Ramapoo (also called Ramapo) Road, picking up Gilbert Street.*

Bedford Village's historic general store. Bedford Historical Society

30.2 *LEFT at the end onto Main Street, stopping for the night, if you wish, at the Elms Inn.*

The well-known Elms (4) is Ridgefield's oldest continuously functioning hostelry. The sprawling white clapboard house, built in 1760, has been open to lodgers since 1799. You'll spend about $90 for a double room with continental breakfast; there's a $10 break for solo guests. The Elms has a fine reputation in these parts for its continental-style cuisine; the restaurant is closed Wednesdays. Most of the year room reservations are a must; phone 203-438-2541. Leaving the inn, continue up Main Street.

30.5 *Bear LEFT for Route 116 (North Salem Road).*

30.6 *First RIGHT onto North Street past an old cemetery on your left.*

30.9 *RIGHT onto Copps Hill Road past another cemetery as you turn.*

31.3 *RIGHT at a traffic light onto Main Street (Route 35). The road isn't well marked, so note the large Copps Hill Plaza shopping center on your right.*

31.9 *Bear LEFT to stay on Route 35.*

On your left in about a mile, just past Market Street, is the Aldrich Museum of Contemporary Art (5). Paintings by nationally known artists are the feature here, with exhibitions changing four times a year. The museum is open Friday, Saturday, and Sunday afternoons, with occasional extra days in summer; the admission charge is $2 for adults, $1 for seniors and students. At any time, for no charge, you can walk out back and look at an extensive collection of modern sculpture arrayed on an expanse of lawn. Leaving the museum, continue on Route 35 (Main Street).

33.2 *RIGHT at the junction with Route 33 to stay on Route 35 (here called West Lane).*

33.9 *LEFT, at a fork in the road (there's a small red schoolhouse straight ahead) to stay on West Lane.*

In just a mile you'll cross the state line into New York again.

35.2 *LEFT at a triangular traffic island onto Elmwood Drive.*

37.6 *LEFT at a stop sign onto Route 123.*

On your left is the striking gray-shingled Rockwell Memorial Chapel of St. Paul (Episcopal) (6), with very attractive blue English stained-glass windows. The windows over the altar, though unsigned, are thought to be Tiffany creations. The bells in the tower were given by old-time New York City politico Boss Tweed, who used to summer hereabouts.

37.8 *First RIGHT onto unmarked Conant Valley Road, a winding lane.*

38.6 *LEFT at the end onto unmarked Old Church Lane.*

39.2 *RIGHT at the end onto East Woods Road.*

40.6 *LEFT at the end onto Trinity Pass.*

40.7 *Bear LEFT at a fork in the road to stay on Trinity Pass.*

A mile or so after the fork, there's a shopping center (7) on your left. This is Scotts Corners, where you'll find a couple of food stores, in case you're ready for sustenance, and an antiques shop, if you feel like browsing through the past. A bit later you're back into Connecticut again.

43.7 *LEFT at the end onto unmarked High Ridge Road (Route 137).*

43.8 *First RIGHT, at a blinking traffic light, onto Mayapple Road.*

Half a mile down the road, start looking right. Behind a wire fence you may see a llama or another of an assortment of nonsuburban animals kept in a private preserve.

44.7 *RIGHT, at a three-way intersection, onto Rockrimmon Road.*

46.0 *LEFT at the end onto unmarked Old Long Ridge Road.*

47.3 *At the end of Old Long Ridge Road, cross Route 104 diagonally to the RIGHT onto Riverbank Road.*

50.5 *RIGHT, at a sharp leftward curve, onto unmarked June Road and across a short bridge over the Mianus River.*

50.7 *Bear RIGHT at the first fork to stay on June Road.*

51.7 *LEFT onto Tod Lane.*

52.0 *RIGHT at the end onto unmarked Stanwich Road.*

52.6 *At a triangular traffic island, pick up Taconic Road, which joins the route from the right.*

52.9 *First RIGHT onto South Stanwich Road, which crosses Rockwood Lake Reservoir on a land bridge.*

53.5 *LEFT at the end onto unmarked North Street.*

56.1 *RIGHT onto Clapboard Ridge Road.*

As you make the turn, you'll see a stone marker on your left. It commemorates the first transatlantic shortwave radio message, sent from here to Scotland by an amateur radio station in 1921.

56.4 *Stay STRAIGHT to pick up Grahampton Lane as Clapboard*

Ridge Road turns right.

57.0 *LEFT at the end (opposite the entrance to private Khakum Wood Road) onto unmarked Lake Avenue.*

58.4 *Sharp RIGHT at a small traffic circle onto Round Hill Road.*

59.4 *Sharp LEFT onto Pecksland Road (street sign on your left).*

60.9 *RIGHT at the end onto Riversville Road.*

62.3 *LEFT just beyond a concrete overpass onto Sherwood Avenue.*

63.3 *RIGHT at the end onto King Street.*
Note the striking old stone gates across King Street as you turn.

65.2 *LEFT at a traffic light onto Rye Lake Avenue.*

65.4 *LEFT at the bottom of the hill and into the airport parking lot.*

Bicycle Shops
Big Cycle, 9 Norm Avenue, Bedford Hills, NY (914-666-3549)
Ridgefield Cycle Centre, 56 Danbury Road, Ridgefield, CT (203-431-6365)

20

The Pro's Overnight: 111 Miles in Westchester and Connecticut Lake Country

Round-trip distance pedaled: 111 miles
Terrain: very hilly
Minimum cycling time: two long days (about 10 hours' cycling each day)

This tour is a big one—a century plus. There are some tremendous hills, some stretches of dirt road, and an awful lot of pedaling. It's at least a two-day affair, and you *must* be in top condition before you attempt it. Start at the shopping center parking lot at the northern split between Routes 35 and 121 in Cross River (find Route 35 at exit 6 of I-684). The trip begins with a nice ride north and east across the Connecticut border and through Danbury into lake territory. In season you'll find fruit and vegetable stands for on-the-road snacks. The route goes up the western edge of Candlewood Lake, a huge summer play area, and on to more serene Bantam Lake; spend the night in the vicinity. The second day, like the first, should begin by 7 a.m. if you expect to complete your appointed rounds before sundown. Repeat: This trip takes two very long days of cycling and is only for experienced cyclists in top condition.

0.0 *LEFT leaving the shopping center onto Route 121 North; later, Route 116 will merge with Route 121.*

6.4 *LEFT, at center of North Salem, to stay on Route 121.*

7.6 *RIGHT, at a group of stores, onto Dingle Ridge Road.*

7.8 *First RIGHT onto Finch Lane.*

8.3 *Keep on STRAIGHT onto an unmarked dirt road, Chestnut Hill Road.*

You're crossing into Fairfield County, Connecticut in seven-tenths of a mile; the road becomes paved again.

10.1 *LEFT onto the first major paved street, unmarked Old Ridgebury Road.*

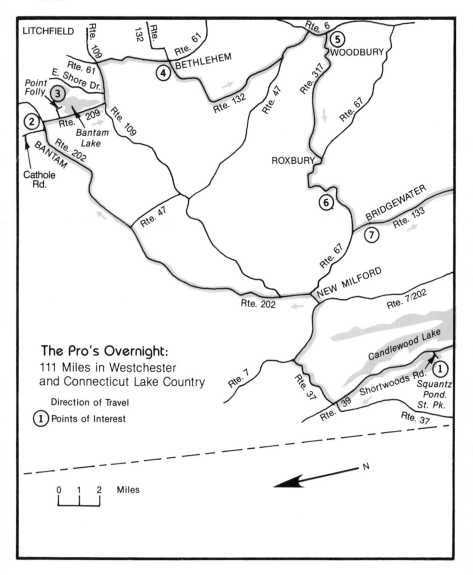

The Pro's Overnight:
111 Miles in Westchester
and Connecticut Lake Country

Direction of Travel

① Points of Interest

0 1 2 Miles

10.9 *RIGHT onto George Washington Highway; turn when you see the white Ridgebury Congregational Church on your left.*

12.0 *Bear RIGHT at the intersection with Briar Ridge Road to stay on George Washington Highway.*

12.6 *Bear LEFT at Miry Brook Road onto Backus Avenue.*

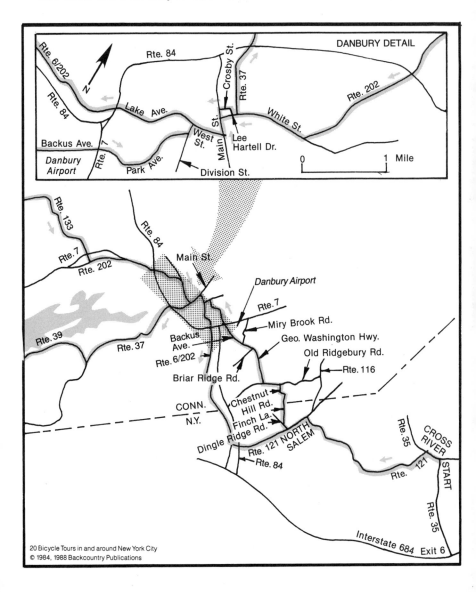

20 Bicycle Tours in and around New York City
© 1984, 1988 Backcountry Publications

In less than a mile you'll pass Danbury Airport on the right and, several hundred yards later across the street, the site of the old Danbury Fair, for decades one of the nation's largest country expositions. The show is no more; progress means a gigantic shopping mall.

14.0 *After you pass under Route 7, Backus Avenue becomes residential Park Avenue.*

15.2 *LEFT at the end onto unmarked Division Street.*

15.3 *RIGHT, at a traffic island with a monument, onto West Street.*

15.7 *LEFT at a traffic light, just beyond another small island with a monument, onto unmarked Main Street.*

16.5 *RIGHT onto Route 37 North.*

21.5 *RIGHT onto Route 39 North.*
You're going up the west side of Candlewood Lake, a dam-made body of water whose shores swell in population each summer.

25.5 *LEFT onto Shortwoods Road.*
You're now in Squantz Pond State Park (1). Rest and picnic here if you wish. But do go in and look around; this is one of the most scenic state parks, with good beaches and trails. Turn left leaving the park, back onto Route 39.

30.4 *RIGHT where Routes 39 and 37 merge; stay on Route 37.*
In a couple of miles you'll cross into Litchfield County, Connecticut's most rural corner, and start a fantastic mile-and-a-half-long downhill run into the town of New Milford.

33.9 *RIGHT at the end to pick up Route 7 South.*

36.5 *LEFT at a traffic circle to pick up Route 202 East; stay on 202 for nearly sixteen lovely miles of rolling hills to Bantam.*
Bantam (2) is a mostly rural borough of the town of Litchfield, the county seat. It's roughly the halfway point of this tour. Where to stay the night? Three very different choices—a gracious country inn, a simple lakeside campground, and a very secluded B&B:
• For the inn, detour off-route a couple of miles east along Route 202 to the full-comfort Litchfield Inn, where a good-sized room with private bath costs $95 for a double, $85 for a single, including Continental breakfast; $15 less from December through April. Full restaurant. (For reservations: 203-567-4503.)
• The White Memorial Family Campground, just beyond Bantam center, is run by a nonprofit foundation that maintains a surrounding nature preserve. Bare-bones campsites cost $9.25 seven days a week. Open mid-April through Columbus Day. Book (by mail) well in advance. First,

phone: 203-567-0089. If this is your overnight stop, you can choose from among several informal dinner possibilities in Bantam center. There's a pub with Italian-American food, a pizza house, and the Bantam Inn, with a full New England menu (closed Mondays in the summer, Mondays through Wednesdays in winter). And there's the well-stocked Big Value supermarket if you prefer to pick up fixin's.

• You'll find the Dutch Moccasin bed-and-breakfast on a country lane about ten miles ahead in Bethlehem. (It's a couple of miles off the route, but otherwise in the direction you're headed.) The 18th-century house offers three rooms (one with a waterbed) at prices ranging from $45 to $65, full breakfast included. If you're not too tired from your long day, there are several diversions on the premises: reading rooms, TV, VCR, piano, boccie. The owner, who's "into cooking," will prepare dinner for guests with advance planning. Rooms, too, should be reserved; phone 203-266-7364. If you choose the B&B but don't choose to dine there, you can stop at the German-flavored Deer Island Gate (closed Mondays and Tuesdays) on the way, just ahead on Route 209. (If you do opt for dinner at the Gate and bed at the Dutch Moccasin, be sure to eat early; you'll have several miles to go after dinner, and you'll want to finish the ride before dark.)

Unless you're super-flexible and not at all given to frustration, don't leave home without an overnight reservation.

52.3 *RIGHT, in the center of Bantam, onto Route 209 South along Bantam Lake (3).*

Bantam is the state's largest natural lake. Its rare feature: more than half the lakeside property is untouchable, being part of a 4,000-acre preserve set up by a local brother and sister in 1913, a time when few were thinking of preserving the environment. The donors' vision then makes Bantam Lake pleasantly uncommercial today. The Point Folly campground is on North Shore Road, a left turn nearly a mile down Route 209. The Deer Island Gate restaurant is another mile down the road.

55.2 *At the end of Route 209 turn LEFT onto Route 109.*

There are a few bad hills on this stretch; you are, after all, in the foothills of the Berkshires, close to 1,000 feet above sea level. These hills, at least, are short and bikeable, if tough.

56.7 *RIGHT, just before a traffic blinker, onto Route 61 South.*

59.9 *RIGHT, at the next blinker, onto Route 132.*

Before you make this turn, stop and look around. You're at the center of the town of Bethlehem (4). Directly ahead is a typical New England village green. To your left, the little house with the bell on the lawn is the town historical society's tiny museum—again typical, in that it's open just a few hours a week. Over your right shoulder, behind white picket fences and thick trees, is the splendid Joseph Bellamy estate, built about 1760 by a prominent minister of the time. Young Aaron Burr attended Bellamy's theological school here just before the Revolution, but apparently lost the calling; after a year under Bellamy's tutelage he quit and went to law school. Now turn right. The Dutch Moccasin B&B is a detour off 132; if you're staying there, be sure to ask directions when you book.

66.6 *LEFT at a stop sign onto Route 47 South.*

68.0 *RIGHT at a traffic light onto Route 6.*
You're in Woodbury (5) now, the antiques capital of the state. This town's shops are packed with super-high-priced American and British golden oldies.

68.7 *RIGHT at a traffic light onto Route 317, which runs into Route 67 North at the town of Roxbury.*
There's a long steep uphill on this stretch, the toughest of the return journey. But there's an equally long—and very steep and curvy—downhill to compensate.

74.8 *RIGHT to stay on Route 67.*
In about a mile and three-quarters, you'll go downhill past Hodge Park (6) on your right. You can stop here for a snack on the banks of the Shepaug River, or you can wait a while to eat.

79.8 *LEFT onto Route 133 South and into the town of Bridgewater.*
Stop, if you like, to pick up eats at the Village Store (7), on the right in the center of town; a mile or two later on your right is a perfect spot to stop to picnic and take in a great view of the surrounding valley and farm-land. If you prefer restaurants, keep going; there are some about eight miles ahead.

86.8 *LEFT, then an immediate RIGHT to stay on Route 133.*

87.5 *RIGHT, under some railroad tracks, to stay on Route 133.*

88.1 *LEFT at the end onto Route 202.*
You'll find several eateries on this stretch of Route 202, most being of the franchised fast-food variety.

92.4 *Bear RIGHT at a traffic light onto unmarked White Street.*

93.3 *RIGHT, following the one-way traffic pattern, onto Lee Hartell Drive.*

93.4 *Next LEFT onto unmarked Crosby Street.*

93.5 *LEFT two blocks later onto Main Street.*

93.8 *RIGHT, at a triangular island with a white column marking the memory of the Defenders of the Union, onto unmarked West Street. West Street becomes Lake Avenue, which goes under an I-84 highway bridge and runs into Route 6/202. (The road here is busy, but you can use the shoulders.)*

101.2 *LEFT, after you cross the state line back into New York, onto Route 121.*

104.9 *RIGHT, in the town of North Salem, where Route 116 starts to overlap with Route 121; keep to 121.*

111.2 *RIGHT into the shopping center in Cross River, where the tour began.*

Bicycle Shops
The Bike Express, 73A Bridge Street, New Milford, CT (203-354-1466)
The Bike Express, 76 West Street, Danbury, CT (203-792-5460)

Typical small farm in Litchfield County.   Dan Carlinsky

Bike Clubs

The following are among the cycle touring clubs in the Greater New York area. There are others; ask at your friendly neighborhood bike shop.

Connecticut

Clinton
Nova Cycle Club
88 East Main Street
Clinton 06413
203-453-4749; 663-2420

Gales Ferry
Pequot Cyclists
1538 Route 12, Apt. 11
Gales Ferry 06335-0505

Greenwich
Brno Velo
P.O. Box 4378
Greenwich 06830
914-939-6683

Hartford
Yankee Council, AYH
118 Oak Street
Hartford 06106
203-247-6356

Kensington
Metacomet Cycling Club
22 Chamberlain Highway
Kensington 06037
203-828-5808; 800-637-2453

Manchester
Exposition Wheelmen
c/o Manchester Cycle Shop
178 West Middle Turnpike
Manchester 06040
203-649-BIKE

Middletown
Middlesex Bicycle Club
c/o Andy Raymond
126 Highland Avenue
Middletown 06457
203-347-0798

Norwalk
Sound Cyclists Bicycle Club
D/3 Camelot Drive
Norwalk 06850
203-847-5541

Vernon
Cycling Touring Club
c/o Cycle Center of Vernon
352 Hartford Turnpike
Rte. 30 Post Road Plaza
Vernon 06066
203-872-7740

Wallingford
Appalachian Mountain Club
c/o Trish Niece
810 N. Farms Road
Wallingford 06492

New Jersey

Budd Lake
Morris Area Freewheelers
c/o Jack Kelly
31 Elizabeth Lane
Budd Lake 07828
201-691-9275

Cherry Hill
South Jersey Spoke Folks
c/o Danzeisen & Quigley
1720 East Route 70
Cherry Hill 08003
609-424-5969

Delran
Outdoor Club of South Jersey
Box 1508
Delran 08075
609-346-2242

Emerson
Bicycle Touring Club of North Jersey
73 Ross Avenue
Emerson 07630
201-599-9880

Fords
Central Jersey Bicycle Club
c/o Jerry Glick
3 Tracy Drive
Fords 08863
908-225-1463

Manasquan
Atlantic Bicycle Club
c/o Doug Mitchell
2606 Woodchuck Lane
Manasquan 08736
908-528-7198

Montclair
Appalachian Mountain Club Bicycle
    Committee (NY-North Jersey
    chapter)
c/o Roger McFarland
56 Gates Avenue
Montclair 07042
201-746-2105

Princeton
Princeton Freewheelers
P.O. Box 1204
Princeton 08542
609-393-1206

Red Bank
Jersey Shore Touring Society
c/o Brian Schmult
P.O. Box 8581
Red Bank 07701
908-747-8206

South Vineland
South Jersey Wheelmen
P.O. Box 2705
South Vineland 08360
609-327-1336

New York

Brooklyn and New York City
New York Cycle Club
P.O. Box 020877
Brooklyn 11202
212-242-3900

Hauppauge
Suffolk Bicycle Riders Association
P.O. Box 983
Hauppauge 11788

Hicksville
Paumonok Bicycle Club
P.O. Box 7159
Hicksville 11802
516-842-4699

Huntington Station
Huntington Bicycle Club
P.O. Box 322
Huntington Station 11746
516-754-1066

Massapequa Park
Massapequa Park Bicycle Club
P.O. Box 231
Massapequa Park 11758

New City
Rockland Bicycle Club
Box 307
New City 10956
914-634-7595

New York City
Metropolitan New York Council AYH
75 Spring Street
New York 10012
212-431-7100

Staten Island
Staten Island Bicycling Association
P.O. Box 14106
Staten Island 10314
718-448-9197

White Plains
Country Cycle Club
1 Willowbrook Road
White Plains 10605
717-560-3636; 337-5623

National

American Youth Hostels
P.O. Box 37613
Washington, DC 20013
202-783-4943

International Bicycle Touring Society
P.O. Box 6979
La Jolla, CA 92106
619-226-TOUR

League of American Wheelmen
6707 Whitestone Road, Suite 209
Baltimore, MD 21207
301-944-3399

Also from Backcountry Publications and Countryman Press

Backcountry Publications and Countryman Press, long known for fine books on travel and outdoor recreation, offer a range of practical and readable guides. These carefully prepared books feature detailed trail and tour directions, notes on points of interest and natural highlights, maps, and photographs.

Biking Series

25 Bicycle Tours on Delmarva, $9.95
25 Bicycle Tours in the Finger Lakes, Second Edition $9.95
20 Bicycle Tours in the Five Boroughs (New York City), $8.95
25 Bicycle Tours in the Hudson Valley, $9.95
25 Bicycle Tours in Southern Indiana, $10.95
25 Bicycle Tours in Maine, Second Edition $9.95
30 Bicycle Tours in New Hampshire, Third Edition $10.95
25 Bicycle Tours in New Jersey, $9.95
20 Bicycle Tours in and around New York City, $7.95
25 Bicycle Tours in Ohio's Western Reserve, $11.95
25 Bicycle Tours in Eastern Pennsylvania, Second Edition $8.95
25 Bicycle Tours in Vermont, Second Edition $9.95
25 Bicycle Tours in and around Washington, D.C., $9.95
25 Mountain Bike Tours in Massachusetts, $9.95
25 Mountain Bike Tours in Vermont, $9.95

A sampling of other guides

Best Festivals Mid-Atlantic: Over 250 Festivals from New York State to Virginia, $12.95
Canoeing Central New York, $10.95
Discover the Adirondack High Peaks, $14.95
Family Resorts of the Northeast, $12.95
Keep on Pedaling: The Complete Guide to Adult Bicycling, $12.95
Fifty Hikes in the Adirondacks, Second Edition $12.95
Fifty Hikes in Central New York, $11.95
Fifty Hikes in the Hudson Valley, $12.95
Fifty Hikes in Western New York, $12.95
New England's Special Places, Revised Edition $12.95
Walks & Rambles in Dutchess and Putnam Counties (NY), $10.95

Our travel and outdoor recreation guides are available through bookstores and specialty shops. For a free catalog write: The Countryman Press, Inc., Dept. APB, PO Box 175, Woodstock, VT 05091.

Andrew Marvell
David Mason
Suiko Matsushita
Matthew
Claude McKay
Rod McKuen
Samuel Menashe
Thomas Merton
W. S. Merwin
Robert Mezey
Edna St. Vincent Millay
Tedi López Mills
John Milton
N. Scott Momaday
Marianne Moore
Arakida Moritake
Howard Moss
Marilyn Nelson
Pablo Neruda
Lorine Niedecker
Sharon Olds
Mary Oliver

Michael Ortiz
Wilfred Owen
Neiji Ozawa
José Emilio Pacheco
Dorothy Parker
Octavio Paz
Robert Pinsky
Sylvia Plath
Edgar Allan Poe
Alexander Pope
Ezra Pound
Craig Raine
Dudley Randall
Henry Reed
Alastair Reid
Adrienne Rich
Edwin Arlington Robinson
Theodore Roethke
Christina Rossetti
Kay Ryan
Benjamin Alire Sáenz

Carl Sandburg
Carole Satyamurti
Pedro Serrano
Anne Sexton
William Shakespeare
Julie Sheehan
Percy Bysshe Shelley
Charles Simic
Paul Simon
Bessie Smith
Stevie Smith
Gary Snyder
Sor Juana
William Stafford
A. E. Stallings
James Stephens
Wallace Stevens
Michael Stillman
Alfred, Lord Tennyson
Diane Thiel
Dylan Thomas

Jean Toomer
Natasha Trethewey
Brian Turner
John Updike
Gina Valdés
César Vallejo
Hakuro Wada
Derek Walcott
Arthur Waley
Edmund Waller
Eliot Weinberger
Walt Whitman
Richard Wilbur
Clarence Williams
William Carlos Williams
William Wordsworth
James Wright
Mary Sidney Wroth
William Butler Yeats
Kevin Young

PLAYWRIGHTS

Susan Glaspell
David Henry Hwang
Henrik Ibsen
David Ives

Edward Bok Lee
Christopher Marlowe
Jane Martin
Milcha Sanchez-Scott

William Shakespeare
Anna Deavere Smith
Sophocles

Tennessee Williams
August Wilson

CRITICS

Elizabeth Ammons
Claire Asquith
W. H. Auden
Houston Baker
Maud Bodkin
Anthony Burgess
Barbara Christian
Louise S. Cowan
E. R. Dodds
Denis Donoghue
Rita Dove
Maud Ellmann

Judith Farr
Stanley Fish
Juliann Fleenor
Dean Flower
Sigmund Freud
Sandra Gilbert
Susan Gubar
A. E. Haigh
Geoffrey Hartman
Philip R. Headings
Onwuchekwa Jemie
Thomas H. Johnson

Ben Jonson
Alfred Kazin
Robert Langbaum
Brett Millier
Marilyn Nelson
Camille Paglia
Charlotte Pierce-Baker
Darryl Pinckney
Ezra Pound
Arnold Rampersad
R. J. R. Rockwood
Mary Jane Schenck

Gretchen Schulz
Kathryn Lee Seidel
Elaine Showalter
Nina Pelikan Straus
J. O. Tate
Virginia Mason Vaughan
Edmond Volpe
Mary Helen Washington
Richard Wilbur
David Wiles
Cynthia Griffin Wolff

Why Do You Need This New Edition?

Here are six great reasons!

1. **New stories.** Ten new stories that tell tales from revenge to mistaken identity, including Anne Tyler's "Teenage Wasteland," Ray Bradbury's "A Sound of Thunder," and ZZ Packer's "Brownies."

2. **A new chapter "Reading Long Stories and Novels"** features Franz Kafka's chilling story *The Metamorphosis*.

3. **New poems.** Nearly sixty new poems appear in this edition, ranging from classic selections by John Keats and Gwendolyn Brooks to fresh contemporary works by Kay Ryan, Rafael Campo, and Julie Sheehan.

4. **New plays.** Four new plays give you a chance to experience the pleasure of reading drama in a one-act format, including two short comedies, David Ives's *Sure Thing* and Jane Martin's *Beauty*.

5. **New audio version of *Trifles*.** Experience live theater by tuning in to a new audio production of Susan Glaspell's *Trifles* available for you to download in *MyLiteratureLab.com*.

6. **New writing assignments.** New writing suggestions have been introduced in many chapters to help you discover ideas and topics to write about.

Tell Us What You Think!

Make a difference by sharing your opinions with the authors of this book—X. J. Kennedy and Dana Gioia. Have you read a story that you loved? Disliked? Found boring? What content did you find most helpful? Is there anything you would change? The authors want to hear what you liked and what you didn't. Log on to **https://www.surveymonkey.com/s/KennedyLiterature** to provide your feedback.

PEARSON

LITERATURE

SEVENTH COMPACT EDITION

LITERATURE

An Introduction to Fiction,
Poetry, Drama, and Writing

INTERACTIVE EDITION

SEVENTH COMPACT EDITION

X. J. Kennedy

Dana Gioia
University of Southern California

PEARSON

Boston Columbus Indianapolis New York San Francisco Upper Saddle River
Amsterdam Cape Town Dubai London Madrid Milan Munich Paris Montreal Toronto
Delhi Mexico City São Paulo Sydney Hong Kong Seoul Singapore Taipei Tokyo

Vice President and Editor in Chief: Joe Terry
Director of Development: Mary Ellen Curley
Senior Development Editor: Katharine Glynn
Executive Marketing Manager: Joyce Nilsen
Senior Supplements Editor: Donna Campion
Production Manager: Savoula Amanatidis
Project Coordination, Text Design, and Electronic Page Makeup: Cenveo Publisher Services
Cover Designer/Manager: John Callahan
Cover Image: *Cliffs and Sailboats at Pourville* (oil on canvas), Monet, Claude (1840–1926)/Private
    Collection/Photo © Christie's Images/The Bridgeman Art Library International
Photo Research: PreMedia Global USA
Senior Manufacturing Buyer: Roy L. Pickering, Jr.
Printer and Binder: RR Donnelley Crawfordsville, In
Cover Printer: Lehigh-Phoenix Color Corporation–Hagerstown

Cataloging-in-Publication Data is on file at the Library of Congress.

10 9 8 7 6 5 4 3 —DOC—15 14 13

www.pearsonhighered.com

PEARSON

(Compact)
ISBN 13: 978-0-205-22941-3; ISBN 10: 0-205-22941-7
(Compact Interactive)
ISBN-13: 978-0-205-22984-0; ISBN-10: 0-205-22984-0

CONTENTS

Preface   xxxvi
To the Instructor   xxxix
About the Authors   xlix

FICTION

TALKING WITH *Amy Tan*   2

1   READING A STORY   5

THE ART OF FICTION   5

TYPES OF SHORT FICTION   6

W. Somerset Maugham, The Appointment in Samarra   6
*A servant tries to gallop away from Death in this brief sardonic fable retold in
memorable form by a popular storyteller.*

Aesop, The Fox and the Grapes   7
*Ever wonder where the phrase "sour grapes" comes from? Find out in this
classic fable.*

Bidpai, The Camel and His Friends   8
With friends like these, you can guess what the camel doesn't need.

Chuang Tzu, Independence   11
*The Prince of Ch'u asks the philosopher Chuang Tzu to become his advisor and gets
a surprising reply in this classic Chinese fable.*

Jakob and Wilhelm Grimm, Godfather Death   12
*Neither God nor the Devil came to the christening. In this stark folktale,
a young man receives magical powers with a string attached.*

PLOT   14

THE SHORT STORY   16

John Updike, A & P   17
*In walk three girls in nothing but bathing suits, and Sammy finds himself no longer an
aproned checkout clerk but an armored knight.*

WRITING EFFECTIVELY
John Updike on Writing, Why Write?   22
THINKING ABOUT PLOT   23
CHECKLIST: Writing About Plot   24

WRITING ASSIGNMENT ON PLOT 24
MORE TOPICS FOR WRITING 24
TERMS FOR REVIEW 25

2 POINT OF VIEW 27

IDENTIFYING POINT OF VIEW 28

TYPES OF NARRATORS 28

STREAM OF CONSCIOUSNESS 30

William Faulkner, A Rose for Emily 31
Proud, imperious Emily Grierson defied the town from the fortress of her mansion. Who could have guessed the secret that lay within?

ZZ Packer, Brownies 38
A Brownie troop of African American girls at camp declare war on a rival troop only to discover their humiliating mistake.

Edgar Allan Poe, The Tell-Tale Heart 52
The smoldering eye at last extinguished, a murderer finds that, despite all his attempts at a cover-up, his victim will be heard.

James Baldwin, Sonny's Blues 56
Two brothers in Harlem see life differently. The older brother is the sensible family man, but Sonny wants to be a jazz musician.

WRITING EFFECTIVELY
James Baldwin on Writing, Race and the African American Writer 77
THINKING ABOUT POINT OF VIEW 78
CHECKLIST: Writing About Point of View 78
WRITING ASSIGNMENT ON POINT OF VIEW 78
MORE TOPICS FOR WRITING 79
TERMS FOR REVIEW 79

3 CHARACTER 81

TYPES OF CHARACTERS 82

Katherine Anne Porter, The Jilting of Granny Weatherall 83
For sixty years Ellen Weatherall has fought back the memory of that terrible day, but now once more the priest waits in the house.

Nathaniel Hawthorne, Young Goodman Brown 90
Urged on through deepening woods, a young Puritan sees—or dreams he sees—good villagers hasten toward a diabolic rite.

Katherine Mansfield, Miss Brill   100
Sundays had long brought joy to solitary Miss Brill, until one fateful day when she happened to share a bench with two lovers in the park.

Raymond Carver, Cathedral   103
He had never expected to find himself trying to describe a cathedral to a blind man. He hadn't even wanted to meet this odd, old friend of his wife.

WRITING EFFECTIVELY
Raymond Carver on Writing, Commonplace but Precise Language   114
   THINKING ABOUT CHARACTER   115
   CHECKLIST: Writing About Character   115
   WRITING ASSIGNMENT ON CHARACTER   116
   MORE TOPICS FOR WRITING   116
   TERMS FOR REVIEW   117

4 SETTING   118

ELEMENTS OF SETTING   118

HISTORICAL FICTION   119

REGIONALISM   120

NATURALISM   120

   Kate Chopin, The Storm   121
   Even with her husband away, Calixta feels happily, securely married. Why then should she not shelter an old admirer from the rain?

   Jack London, To Build a Fire   125
   Seventy-five degrees below zero. Alone except for one mistrustful wolf dog, a man finds himself battling a relentless force.

   Ray Bradbury, A Sound of Thunder   135
   In 2055, you can go on a Time Safari to hunt dinosaurs 60 million years ago. But put one foot wrong, and suddenly the future's not what it used to be.

   Amy Tan, A Pair of Tickets   144
   A young woman flies with her father to China to meet two half sisters she never knew existed.

WRITING EFFECTIVELY
Amy Tan on Writing, Setting the Voice   158
   THINKING ABOUT SETTING   159
   CHECKLIST: Writing About Setting   159
   WRITING ASSIGNMENT ON SETTING   159
   MORE TOPICS FOR WRITING   160
   TERMS FOR REVIEW   160

5 TONE AND STYLE 161

TONE 162

STYLE 162

DICTION 163

Ernest Hemingway, A Clean, Well-Lighted Place 165
All by himself each night, the old man lingers in the bright café. What does he need more than brandy?

William Faulkner, Barn Burning 168
This time when Ab Snopes wields his blazing torch, his son Sarty faces a dilemma: whether to obey or defy the vengeful old man.

IRONY 180

O. Henry, The Gift of the Magi 182
A young husband and wife find ingenious ways to buy each other Christmas presents, in the classic story that defines the word "irony."

Anne Tyler, Teenage Wasteland 186
With her troubled son, his teachers, and a peculiar tutor all giving her their own versions of what's going on with him, what's a mother to do?

WRITING EFFECTIVELY
Ernest Hemingway on Writing, The Direct Style 193
THINKING ABOUT TONE AND STYLE 194
CHECKLIST: Writing About Tone and Style 195
WRITING ASSIGNMENT ON TONE AND STYLE 195
MORE TOPICS FOR WRITING 195
TERMS FOR REVIEW 196

6 THEME 197

PLOT VERSUS THEME 197

THEME AS A UNIFYING DEVICE 198

FINDING THE THEME 199

Chinua Achebe, Dead Men's Path 199
The new headmaster of the village school was determined to fight superstition, but the villagers did not agree.

Alice Munro, How I Met My Husband 202
When Edie meets the carnival pilot, her life gets more complicated than she expects.

Luke 15:11–32, The Parable of the Prodigal Son 214
A father has two sons. One demands his inheritance now and leaves to spend it with ruinous results.

Kurt Vonnegut Jr., Harrison Bergeron 216
*Are you handsome? Off with your eyebrows! Are you brainy? Let a transmitter
sound thought-shattering beeps inside your ear.*

WRITING EFFECTIVELY
Kurt Vonnegut Jr. on Writing, The Themes of Science Fiction 221

THINKING ABOUT THEME 222

CHECKLIST: Writing About Theme 222

WRITING ASSIGNMENT ON THEME 222

MORE TOPICS FOR WRITING 223

TERMS FOR REVIEW 223

7   SYMBOL 224

ALLEGORY 224

SYMBOLS 225

RECOGNIZING SYMBOLS 226

John Steinbeck, The Chrysanthemums 227
*Fenced-in Elisa feels emotionally starved—then her life promises to blossom with the
arrival of the scissors-grinding man.*

D. H. Lawrence, The Rocking-Horse Winner 234
*Wild-eyed "as if something were going to explode in him," the boy predicts each
winning horse, and gamblers rush to bet a thousand pounds.*

Ursula K. Le Guin, The Ones Who Walk Away from Omelas 245
*Omelas is the perfect city. All of its inhabitants are happy. But everyone's prosperity
depends on a hidden evil.*

Shirley Jackson, The Lottery 250
*Splintered and faded, the sinister black box had worked its annual terror for longer
than anyone in town could remember.*

WRITING EFFECTIVELY
Shirley Jackson on Writing, Biography of a Story 257

THINKING ABOUT SYMBOLS 259

CHECKLIST: Writing About Symbols 259

WRITING ASSIGNMENT ON SYMBOLS 259

Sample Student Paper, An Analysis of the Symbolism in Steinbeck's
"The Chrysanthemums" 260

MORE TOPICS FOR WRITING 262

TERMS FOR REVIEW 262

8   READING LONG STORIES AND NOVELS 263

ORIGINS OF THE NOVEL 263

NOVELISTIC METHODS 265

READING NOVELS 267

Franz Kafka, The Metamorphosis 268
"When Gregor Samsa awoke one morning from troubled dreams, he found himself transformed in his bed into a monstrous insect." Kafka's famous opening sentence introduces one of the most chilling stories in world literature.

WRITING EFFECTIVELY
  Franz Kafka on Writing, Discussing *The Metamorphosis* 298
    THINKING ABOUT LONG STORIES AND NOVELS 299
    CHECKLIST: Writing About Long Stories and Novels 300
    WRITING ASSIGNMENT FOR A RESEARCH PAPER 300
  Sample Student Research Paper, Kafka's Greatness 300
    MORE TOPICS FOR WRITING 305
    TERMS FOR REVIEW 306

9   CRITICAL CASEBOOK
Flannery O'Connor 307

FLANNERY O'CONNOR 308
  A Good Man Is Hard to Find 308
  Wanted: The Misfit, a cold-blooded killer. An ordinary family vacation leads to horror—and one moment of redeeming grace.
  Revelation 319
  Mrs. Turpin thinks herself Jesus's favorite child, until she meets a troubled college girl. Soon violence flares in a doctor's waiting room.

FLANNERY O'CONNOR ON WRITING 333
  From "On Her Own Work" 333
  On Her Catholic Faith 335
  From "The Grotesque in Southern Fiction" 336

CRITICS ON FLANNERY O'CONNOR
  J. O. Tate, A Good Source Is Not So Hard to Find: The Real Life
    Misfit 337
  Mary Jane Schenck, Deconstructing "A Good Man Is Hard to Find" 340
  Louise S. Cowan, The Character of Mrs. Turpin in "Revelation" 341
  Dean Flower, Listening to Flannery O'Connor 342

WRITING EFFECTIVELY
  TOPICS FOR WRITING 343

10   CRITICAL CASEBOOK
Two Stories in Depth 344

CHARLOTTE PERKINS GILMAN 344

The Yellow Wallpaper 345
A doctor prescribes a "rest cure" for his wife after the birth of their child. The new mother tries to settle in to life in the isolated and mysterious country house they have rented for the summer. The cure proves worse than the disease in this Gothic classic.

CHARLOTTE PERKINS GILMAN ON WRITING 356

Why I Wrote "The Yellow Wallpaper" 356
Whatever Is 357
The Nervous Breakdown of Women 357

CRITICS ON "THE YELLOW WALLPAPER" 358

Juliann Fleenor, Gender and Pathology in "The Yellow Wallpaper" 358
Sandra M. Gilbert and Susan Gubar, Imprisonment and Escape:
The Psychology of Confinement 360
Elizabeth Ammons, Biographical Echoes in "The Yellow Wallpaper" 361

ALICE WALKER 363

Everyday Use 363
When successful Dee visits from the city, she has changed her name to reflect her African roots. Her mother and sister notice other things have changed, too.

ALICE WALKER ON WRITING 369

The Black Woman Writer in America 369
Reflections on Writing and Women's Lives 371

CRITICS ON "EVERYDAY USE" 371

Barbara T. Christian, "Everyday Use" and the Black Power
Movement 371
Mary Helen Washington, "Everyday Use" as a Portrait of the
Artist 374
Houston A. Baker and Charlotte Pierce-Baker, Stylish vs. Sacred in
"Everyday Use" 375
Elaine Showalter, Quilt as Metaphor in "Everyday Use" 377

WRITING EFFECTIVELY

TOPICS FOR WRITING 379

11 STORIES FOR FURTHER READING 380

Sherman Alexie, This Is What It Means to Say Phoenix, Arizona 380
The only one who can help Victor when his father dies is a childhood friend he's been avoiding for years.

Isabel Allende, The Judge's Wife 388
Revenge can take many different forms, but few are as strange as the revenge taken in this passionate tale.

Margaret Atwood, Happy Endings 394
John and Mary meet. What happens next? This witty experimental story offers five different outcomes.

Ambrose Bierce, An Occurrence at Owl Creek Bridge 397
At last, Peyton Farquhar's neck is in the noose. Reality mingles with dream in this classic story of the American Civil War.

Jorge Luis Borges, The Gospel According to Mark 404
A young man from Buenos Aires is trapped by a flood on an isolated ranch. To pass the time, he reads the Gospel to a family with unforeseen results.

T. Coraghessan Boyle, Greasy Lake 408
Murky and strewn with beer cans, the lake appears a wasteland. On its shore three "dangerous characters" learn a lesson one grim night.

Kate Chopin, The Story of an Hour 415
"There was something coming to her and she was waiting for it, fearfully. What was it? She did not know; it was too subtle and elusive to name."

Gabriel García Márquez, A Very Old Man with Enormous
       Wings 417
What do you do when a worn-out angel crashes in your yard? Sell tickets or call the priest?

Zora Neale Hurston, Sweat 421
Delia's hard work paid for her small house. Now her drunken husband Sykes has promised it to another woman.

James Joyce, Araby 430
If only he can find her a token, she might love him in return. As night falls, a Dublin boy hurries to make his dream come true.

Jamaica Kincaid, Girl 435
"Try to walk like a lady, and not like the slut you are so bent on becoming." An old-fashioned mother tells her daughter how to live.

Jhumpa Lahiri, Interpreter of Maladies 436
Mr. Kapasi's life had settled into a quiet pattern—and then Mrs. Das and her family came into it.

Joyce Carol Oates, Where Are You Going, Where Have
       You Been? 451
Alone in the house, Connie finds herself helpless before the advances of Arnold Friend, a spellbinding imitation teenager.

Tim O'Brien, The Things They Carried 462
What each soldier carried into the combat zone was largely determined by necessity, but each man's necessities differed.

Eudora Welty, A Worn Path 474
When the man said to old Phoenix, "you must be a hundred years old, and scared of nothing," he might have been exaggerating, but not by much.

POETRY

TALKING WITH *Kay Ryan* 482

12 READING A POEM 487

POETRY OR VERSE 487

READING A POEM 488

PARAPHRASE 488

    William Butler Yeats, The Lake Isle of Innisfree 489

LYRIC POETRY 491

    Robert Hayden, Those Winter Sundays 491
    Adrienne Rich, Aunt Jennifer's Tigers 492

NARRATIVE POETRY 492

    Anonymous, Sir Patrick Spence 493
    Robert Frost, "Out, Out—" 494

DRAMATIC POETRY 495

    Robert Browning, My Last Duchess 496

DIDACTIC POETRY 497

WRITING EFFECTIVELY
    Adrienne Rich on Writing, Recalling "Aunt Jennifer's Tigers" 498
      THINKING ABOUT PARAPHRASING 498
    William Stafford, Ask Me 499
    William Stafford, A Paraphrase of "Ask Me" 499
      CHECKLIST: Writing a Paraphrase 500
      WRITING ASSIGNMENT ON PARAPHRASING 500
      MORE TOPICS FOR WRITING 500
      TERMS FOR REVIEW 500

13 LISTENING TO A VOICE 501

TONE 501

    Theodore Roethke, My Papa's Waltz 501
    Countee Cullen, For a Lady I Know 502
    Anne Bradstreet, The Author to Her Book 503
    Walt Whitman, To a Locomotive in Winter 504
    Emily Dickinson, I like to see it lap the Miles 504
    Benjamin Alire Sáenz, To the Desert 505

Gwendolyn Brooks, Speech to the Young. Speech to the Progress-
Toward   506

Weldon Kees, For My Daughter   506

THE PERSON IN THE POEM   507

Natasha Trethewey, White Lies   507

Edwin Arlington Robinson, Luke Havergal   509

Ted Hughes, Hawk Roosting   510

Anonymous, Dog Haiku   510

William Wordsworth, I Wandered Lonely as a Cloud   511

Dorothy Wordsworth, Journal Entry   512

Anne Sexton, Her Kind   513

William Carlos Williams, The Red Wheelbarrow   513

IRONY   514

Robert Creeley, Oh No   514

W. H. Auden, The Unknown Citizen   515

Sharon Olds, Rite of Passage   516

Julie Sheehan, Hate Poem   517

Edna St. Vincent Millay, Second Fig   518

Thomas Hardy, The Workbox   519

FOR REVIEW AND FURTHER STUDY   520

William Blake, The Chimney Sweeper   520

William Stafford, At the Un-National Monument Along the Canadian
Border   520

Richard Lovelace, To Lucasta   521

Wilfred Owen, Dulce et Decorum Est   521

WRITING EFFECTIVELY

Wilfred Owen on Writing, War Poetry   522

THINKING ABOUT TONE   523

CHECKLIST: Writing About Tone   523

WRITING ASSIGNMENT ON TONE   524

Sample Student Paper, Word Choice, Tone, and Point of View in
Roethke's "My Papa's Waltz"   524

MORE TOPICS FOR WRITING   527

TERMS FOR REVIEW   527

14 WORDS   528

LITERAL MEANING: WHAT A POEM SAYS FIRST   528

William Carlos Williams, This Is Just to Say   528

DICTION   529

Marianne Moore, Silence   530

Robert Graves, Down, Wanton, Down! 530
John Donne, Batter my heart, three-personed God, for You 531

THE VALUE OF A DICTIONARY 532

Henry Wadsworth Longfellow, Aftermath 533
Kay Ryan, Mockingbird 533
J. V. Cunningham, Friend, on this scaffold Thomas More
lies dead 535
Samuel Menashe, Bread 535
Carl Sandburg, Grass 535

WORD CHOICE AND WORD ORDER 536

Robert Herrick, Upon Julia's Clothes 537
Thomas Hardy, The Ruined Maid 538
Wendy Cope, Lonely Hearts 539

FOR REVIEW AND FURTHER STUDY 540

E. E. Cummings, anyone lived in a pretty how town 540
Billy Collins, The Names 541
Anonymous, Carnation Milk 543
Gina Valdés, English con Salsa 543
Lewis Carroll, Jabberwocky 544

WRITING EFFECTIVELY
Lewis Carroll, Humpty Dumpty Explicates "Jabberwocky" 545

THINKING ABOUT DICTION 546
CHECKLIST: Writing About Diction 547
WRITING ASSIGNMENT ON WORD CHOICE 547
MORE TOPICS FOR WRITING 547
TERMS FOR REVIEW 548

15 SAYING AND SUGGESTING 549

DENOTATION AND CONNOTATION 549

William Blake, London 550
Wallace Stevens, Disillusionment of Ten O'Clock 552
Gwendolyn Brooks, The Bean Eaters 552
E. E. Cummings, next to of course god america i 553
Robert Frost, Fire and Ice 553
Diane Thiel, The Minefield 553
H. D., Storm 554
Alfred, Lord Tennyson, Tears, Idle Tears 555
Richard Wilbur, Love Calls Us to the Things of This World 555

WRITING EFFECTIVELY
Richard Wilbur on Writing, Concerning "Love Calls Us to the
Things of This World" 557

THINKING ABOUT DENOTATION AND CONNOTATION 557

CHECKLIST: Writing About What a Poem Says and Suggests 558

WRITING ASSIGNMENT ON DENOTATION AND CONNOTATION 559

MORE TOPICS FOR WRITING 559

TERMS FOR REVIEW 559

16 IMAGERY 560

Ezra Pound, In a Station of the Metro 560
Taniguchi Buson, The piercing chill I feel 560

IMAGERY 561

T. S. Eliot, The winter evening settles down 562
Theodore Roethke, Root Cellar 562
Elizabeth Bishop, The Fish 563
Emily Dickinson, A Route of Evanescence 565
Jean Toomer, Reapers 565
Gerard Manley Hopkins, Pied Beauty 565

ABOUT HAIKU 566

Arakida Moritake, The falling flower 566
Matsuo Basho, Heat-lightning streak 567
Matsuo Basho, In the old stone pool 567
Taniguchi Buson, On the one-ton temple bell 567
Taniguchi Buson, Moonrise on mudflats 567
Kobayashi Issa, only one guy 567
Kobayashi Issa, Cricket 567

HAIKU FROM JAPANESE INTERNMENT CAMPS 567

Suiko Matsushita, Rain shower from mountain 568
Suiko Matsushita, Cosmos in bloom 568
Hakuro Wada, Even the croaking of frogs 568
Neiji Ozawa, The war—this year 568

CONTEMPORARY HAIKU 568

Etheridge Knight, Making jazz swing in 568
Gary Snyder, After weeks of watching the roof leak 568
Adelle Foley, Learning to Shave 568
Garry Gay, Hole in the ozone 568

FOR REVIEW AND FURTHER STUDY 569

John Keats, Bright star! would I were steadfast as thou art 569
Walt Whitman, The Runner 569
H. D., Oread 570
William Carlos Williams, El Hombre 570
Robert Bly, Driving to Town Late to Mail a Letter 570
Stevie Smith, Not Waving but Drowning 570

WRITING EFFECTIVELY
  Ezra Pound on Writing, The Image 571
    THINKING ABOUT IMAGERY 571
    CHECKLIST: Writing About Imagery 572
    WRITING ASSIGNMENT ON IMAGERY 573
  Sample Student Paper, Faded Beauty: Elizabeth Bishop's Use
    of Imagery in "The Fish" 573
    MORE TOPICS FOR WRITING 576
    TERMS FOR REVIEW 576

17 FIGURES OF SPEECH 577

WHY SPEAK FIGURATIVELY? 577
  Alfred, Lord Tennyson, The Eagle 578
  William Shakespeare, Shall I compare thee to a
    summer's day? 578
  Howard Moss, Shall I Compare Thee to a Summer's Day? 579

METAPHOR AND SIMILE 579
  Emily Dickinson, My Life had stood – a Loaded Gun 581
  Alfred, Lord Tennyson, Flower in the Crannied Wall 581
  William Blake, To see a world in a grain of sand 582
  Sylvia Plath, Metaphors 582
  N. Scott Momaday, Simile 582
  Jill Alexander Essbaum, The Heart 583
  Craig Raine, A Martian Sends a Postcard Home 583

OTHER FIGURES OF SPEECH 585
  James Stephens, The Wind 585
  Robinson Jeffers, Hands 586
  Margaret Atwood, You fit into me 588
  Dana Gioia, Money 588
  Carl Sandburg, Fog 589

FOR REVIEW AND FURTHER STUDY 589
  Robert Frost, The Silken Tent 589
  Jane Kenyon, The Suitor 590
  Robert Frost, The Secret Sits 590
  A. R. Ammons, Coward 590
  Kay Ryan, Turtle 591
  Emily Brontë, Love and Friendship 591
  Robert Burns, Oh, my love is like a red, red rose 591

WRITING EFFECTIVELY
  Robert Frost on Writing, The Importance of Poetic
    Metaphor 592

THINKING ABOUT METAPHORS   593

CHECKLIST: Writing About Metaphors   593

WRITING ASSIGNMENT ON FIGURES OF SPEECH   593

MORE TOPICS FOR WRITING   593

TERMS FOR REVIEW   594

18   SONG   595

SINGING AND SAYING   595

Ben Jonson, To Celia   596
James Weldon Johnson, Sence You Went Away   597
William Shakespeare, Fear no more the heat o' the sun   598
Edwin Arlington Robinson, Richard Cory   599
Paul Simon, Richard Cory   600

BALLADS   601

Anonymous, Bonny Barbara Allan   601
Dudley Randall, Ballad of Birmingham   604

BLUES   605

Bessie Smith with Clarence Williams, Jailhouse Blues   606
W. H. Auden, Funeral Blues   606

RAP   607

FOR REVIEW AND FURTHER STUDY   608

Bob Dylan, The Times They Are a-Changin'   608
Aimee Mann, Deathly   609

WRITING EFFECTIVELY

Bob Dylan on Writing, The Term "Protest Singer" Didn't Exist   610

THINKING ABOUT POETRY AND SONG   611

CHECKLIST: Writing About Song Lyrics   612

WRITING ASSIGNMENT ON SONG LYRICS   612

MORE TOPICS FOR WRITING   612

TERMS FOR REVIEW   613

19   SOUND   614

SOUND AS MEANING   614

William Butler Yeats, Who Goes with Fergus?   616
William Wordsworth, A Slumber Did My Spirit Seal   616
Aphra Behn, When maidens are young   617

ALLITERATION AND ASSONANCE   617

A. E. Housman, Eight O'Clock   618

James Joyce, All day I hear 618
Alfred, Lord Tennyson, The splendor falls on castle walls 619

RIME 619

William Cole, On my boat on Lake Cayuga 620
Hilaire Belloc, The Hippopotamus 622
Bob Kaufman, No More Jazz at Alcatraz 622
William Butler Yeats, Leda and the Swan 623
Gerard Manley Hopkins, God's Grandeur 624
Robert Frost, Desert Places 624

READING AND HEARING POEMS ALOUD 625

Michael Stillman, In Memoriam John Coltrane 626
Kevin Young, Doo Wop 626
T. S. Eliot, Virginia 627

WRITING EFFECTIVELY
T. S. Eliot on Writing, The Music of Poetry 627
THINKING ABOUT A POEM'S SOUND 628
CHECKLIST: Writing About a Poem's Sound 629
WRITING ASSIGNMENT ON SOUND 629
MORE TOPICS FOR WRITING 629
TERMS FOR REVIEW 629

20 RHYTHM 631

STRESSES AND PAUSES 631

Gwendolyn Brooks, We Real Cool 635
Alfred, Lord Tennyson, Break, Break, Break 635
Dorothy Parker, Résumé 636

METER 636

Edna St. Vincent Millay, Counting-out Rhyme 641
A. E. Housman, When I was one-and-twenty 641
William Carlos Williams, Smell! 642
Walt Whitman, Beat! Beat! Drums! 642
David Mason, Song of the Powers 643
Langston Hughes, Dream Boogie 643

WRITING EFFECTIVELY
Gwendolyn Brooks on Writing, Hearing "We Real Cool" 644
THINKING ABOUT RHYTHM 645
CHECKLIST: Scanning a Poem 646
WRITING ASSIGNMENT ON RHYTHM 646
MORE TOPICS FOR WRITING 646
TERMS FOR REVIEW 647

21 CLOSED FORM 648

FORMAL PATTERNS 649

John Keats, This living hand, now warm and capable 649
Robert Graves, Counting the Beats 651
John Donne, Song ("Go and catch a falling star") 652

THE SONNET 653

William Shakespeare, Let me not to the marriage of true minds 654
Edna St. Vincent Millay, What lips my lips have kissed, and where, and why 654
Robert Frost, Acquainted with the Night 655
A. E. Stallings, Sine Qua Non 656
Amit Majmudar, Rites to Allay the Dead 656
R. S. Gwynn, Shakespearean Sonnet 657

THE EPIGRAM 657

Sir John Harrington, Of Treason 657
Langston Hughes, Two Somewhat Different Epigrams 658
Dorothy Parker, The Actress 658

POETWEETS 658

Lawrence Bridges, Two Poetweets 659
Robert Pinsky, Low Pay Piecework 659

OTHER FORMS 659

Dylan Thomas, Do not go gentle into that good night 659
Robert Bridges, Triolet 660
Elizabeth Bishop, Sestina 661

WRITING EFFECTIVELY
A. E. Stallings on Writing, On Form and Artifice 662
   THINKING ABOUT A SONNET 663
   CHECKLIST: Writing About a Sonnet 664
   WRITING ASSIGNMENT ON A SONNET 664
   MORE TOPICS FOR WRITING 664
   TERMS FOR REVIEW 665

22 OPEN FORM 666

Denise Levertov, Ancient Stairway 666

FREE VERSE 667

W. S. Merwin, For the Anniversary of My Death 669

E. E. Cummings, Buffalo Bill 's 670
William Carlos Williams, The Dance 670
Stephen Crane, The Wayfarer 672
Walt Whitman, Cavalry Crossing a Ford 672
Wallace Stevens, Thirteen Ways of Looking at a Blackbird 673

PROSE POETRY 675

Charles Simic, The Magic Study of Happiness 675

VISUAL POETRY 676

George Herbert, Easter Wings 676
John Hollander, Swan and Shadow 677

FOR REVIEW AND FURTHER STUDY 678

E. E. Cummings, in Just- 678
Francisco X. Alarcón, Frontera / Border 679
Carole Satyamurti, I Shall Paint My Nails Red 679
Alice Fulton, What I Like 680

WRITING EFFECTIVELY
Walt Whitman on Writing, The Poetry of the Future 680

THINKING ABOUT FREE VERSE 681

CHECKLIST: Writing About Line Breaks 681

WRITING ASSIGNMENT ON OPEN FORM 682

MORE TOPICS FOR WRITING 682

TERMS FOR REVIEW 682

23 SYMBOL 683

THE MEANINGS OF A SYMBOL 683

T. S. Eliot, The *Boston Evening Transcript* 684
Emily Dickinson, The Lightning is a yellow Fork 685

IDENTIFYING SYMBOLS 685

Thomas Hardy, Neutral Tones 686

ALLEGORY 687

Matthew 13:24–30, The Parable of the Good Seed 687
George Herbert, Redemption 688
Robert Frost, The Road Not Taken 689
Antonio Machado, Proverbios y Cantares (XXIX) 689
   Translated by Dana Gioia, Traveler 689
Christina Rossetti, Uphill 690

FOR REVIEW AND FURTHER STUDY 690

William Carlos Williams, The Young Housewife 691
Ted Kooser, Carrie 691
Mary Oliver, Wild Geese 691

Tami Haaland, Lipstick 692
Lorine Niedecker, Popcorn-can cover 693
Wallace Stevens, The Snow Man 693
Wallace Stevens, Anecdote of the Jar 693

WRITING EFFECTIVELY
William Butler Yeats on Writing, Poetic Symbols 694
    THINKING ABOUT SYMBOLS 694
    CHECKLIST: Writing About Symbols 695
    WRITING ASSIGNMENT ON SYMBOLISM 695
    MORE TOPICS FOR WRITING 695
    TERMS FOR REVIEW 696

24 MYTH AND NARRATIVE 697

ORIGINS OF MYTH 698
    Robert Frost, Nothing Gold Can Stay 699
    William Wordsworth, The world is too much with us 699
    H. D., Helen 700
    Edgar Allan Poe, To Helen 700

ARCHETYPE 701
    Louise Bogan, Medusa 702
    John Keats, La Belle Dame sans Merci 702

PERSONAL MYTH 704
    William Butler Yeats, The Second Coming 705

MYTH AND POPULAR CULTURE 706
    A. E. Stallings, First Love: A Quiz 706
    Anne Sexton, Cinderella 707

WRITING EFFECTIVELY
Anne Sexton on Writing, Transforming Fairy Tales 710
    THINKING ABOUT MYTH 711
    CHECKLIST: Writing About Myth 712
    WRITING ASSIGNMENT ON MYTH 712
Sample Student Paper, The Bonds Between Love and Hatred in H.D.'s "Helen" 712
    MORE TOPICS FOR WRITING 716
    TERMS FOR REVIEW 716

25 POETRY AND PERSONAL IDENTITY 717

CONFESSIONAL POETRY 718
    Sylvia Plath, Lady Lazarus 718

IDENTITY POETICS 721

   Rhina Espaillat, Bilingual/*Bilingüe* 721

CULTURE, RACE, AND ETHNICITY 722

   Claude McKay, America 722
   Shirley Geok-lin Lim, Riding into California 723
   Judith Ortiz Cofer, Quinceañera 724
   Yusef Komunyakaa, Facing It 725

GENDER 726

   Carolyn Kizer, Bitch 726
   Rafael Campo, For J. W. 727
   Donald Justice, Men at Forty 728
   Adrienne Rich, Women 729

FOR REVIEW AND FURTHER STUDY 729

   Brian Turner, The Hurt Locker 729
   Andrew Hudgins, Elegy for My Father, Who Is Not Dead 730
   Philip Larkin, Aubade 731

WRITING EFFECTIVELY
   Rhina Espaillat on Writing, Being a Bilingual Writer 732
      THINKING ABOUT POETIC VOICE AND IDENTITY 733
      CHECKLIST: Writing About Voice and Personal Identity 734
      WRITING ASSIGNMENT ON PERSONAL IDENTITY 734
      MORE TOPICS FOR WRITING 734

26 POETRY IN SPANISH: LITERATURE OF LATIN AMERICA 736

   Sor Juana, Presente en que el Cariño Hace Regalo la Llaneza 737
      Translated by Diane Thiel, A Simple Gift Made Rich by
         Affection 738
   Pablo Neruda, Muchos Somos 738
      Translated by Alastair Reid, We Are Many 739
   Jorge Luis Borges, On his blindness 740
      Translated by Robert Mezey, On His Blindness 741
   Octavio Paz, Con los ojos cerrados 741
      Translated by Eliot Weinberger, With eyes closed 742

SURREALISM IN LATIN AMERICAN POETRY 742

   Frida Kahlo, The Two Fridas 743
   César Vallejo, La cólera que quiebra al hombre en niños 744
      Translated by Thomas Merton, Anger 744

CONTEMPORARY MEXICAN POETRY 745

   José Emilio Pacheco, Alta Traición 745
      Translated by Alastair Reid, High Treason 745

Pedro Serrano, Golondrinas 745
   Translated by Anna Crowe, Swallows 746
Tedi López Mills, Convalecencia 746
   Translated by Cheryl Clark, Convalescence 746

WRITING EFFECTIVELY
Alastair Reid on Writing, Translating Neruda 747
   WRITING ASSIGNMENT ON SPANISH POETRY 747
   MORE TOPICS FOR WRITING 747

27 RECOGNIZING EXCELLENCE 748

Anonymous, O Moon, when I gaze on thy
   beautiful face 749
Emily Dickinson, A Dying Tiger – moaned
   for Drink 750

SENTIMENTALITY 751

Rod McKuen, Thoughts on Capital Punishment 752
William Stafford, Traveling Through the Dark 753

RECOGNIZING EXCELLENCE 753

William Butler Yeats, Sailing to Byzantium 754
Arthur Guiterman, On the Vanity of Earthly
   Greatness 756
Percy Bysshe Shelley, Ozymandias 756
Robert Hayden, Frederick Douglass 757
Elizabeth Bishop, One Art 758
John Keats, Ode to a Nightingale 759
Walt Whitman, O Captain! My Captain! 762
Dylan Thomas, In My Craft or Sullen Art 763
Paul Laurence Dunbar, We Wear the Mask 764
Emma Lazarus, The New Colossus 765
Edgar Allan Poe, Annabel Lee 765

WRITING EFFECTIVELY
Edgar Allan Poe on Writing, A Long Poem Does
   Not Exist 767
   THINKING ABOUT EVALUATING A POEM 767
   CHECKLIST: Writing an Evaluation 768
   WRITING ASSIGNMENT ON EVALUATING A POEM 768
   MORE TOPICS FOR WRITING 768
   TERMS FOR REVIEW 768

28 WHAT IS POETRY? 769

Archibald MacLeish, Ars Poetica 769
**Dante, Samuel Johnson, Samuel Taylor Coleridge, William
 Wordsworth, Thomas Hardy, Emily Dickinson, Gerard Manley
 Hopkins, Robert Frost, Wallace Stevens, Mina Loy, T. S. Eliot,
 W. H. Auden, José García Villa, Christopher Fry,
 Elizabeth Bishop, Joy Harjo, Lucille Clifton, Charles Simic,**
 Some Definitions of Poetry 770–771

29 TWO CRITICAL CASEBOOKS
Emily Dickinson and Langston Hughes 772

EMILY DICKINSON 773

Success is counted sweetest 773
I taste a liquor never brewed 774
Wild Nights – Wild Nights! 774
I felt a Funeral, in my Brain 774
I'm Nobody! Who are you? 775
The Soul selects her own Society 775
After great pain, a formal feeling comes 775
Much Madness is divinest Sense 776
This is my letter to the World 776
I heard a Fly buzz – when I died 776
Because I could not stop for Death 777
Tell all the Truth but tell it slant 777

EMILY DICKINSON ON EMILY DICKINSON 778

Recognizing Poetry 778
Self-Description 778

CRITICS ON EMILY DICKINSON 780

Thomas H. Johnson, The Discovery of Emily Dickinson's Manuscripts
 780
Richard Wilbur, The Three Privations of Emily Dickinson 781
Cynthia Griffin Wolff, Dickinson and Death (A Reading of "Because
 I could not stop for Death") 782
Judith Farr, A Reading of "My Life had stood – a Loaded Gun" 784
Sandra M. Gilbert and Susan Gubar, The Freedom of Emily
 Dickinson 785

LANGSTON HUGHES 787

The Negro Speaks of Rivers 787
My People 788
Mother to Son 788
Dream Variations 789
I, Too 789

The Weary Blues 790
Song for a Dark Girl 791
Ballad of the Landlord 791
Theme for English B 792
Nightmare Boogie 793
Harlem [Dream Deferred] 793
Homecoming 794

LANGSTON HUGHES ON WRITING 795

The Negro Artist and the Racial Mountain 795
The Harlem Renaissance 796

CRITICS ON LANGSTON HUGHES 798

Arnold Rampersad, Hughes as an Experimentalist 798
Rita Dove and Marilyn Nelson, The Voices in Langston Hughes 799
Darryl Pinckney, Black Identity in Langston Hughes 801
Onwuchekwa Jemie, A Reading of "Dream Deferred" 802

WRITING EFFECTIVELY
    TOPICS FOR WRITING 803

30 CRITICAL CASEBOOK
T. S. Eliot's "The Love Song of J. Alfred Prufrock" 804

T. S. ELIOT 805

The Love Song of J. Alfred Prufrock 806

T. S. ELIOT ON WRITING 810

Poetry and Emotion 810
The Objective Correlative 811

CRITICS ON "PRUFROCK" 812

Denis Donoghue, One of the Irrefutable Poets 812
Philip R. Headings, The Pronouns in the Poem: "One," "You,"
    and "I" 813
Maud Ellmann, Will There Be Time? 814

WRITING EFFECTIVELY
    TOPICS FOR WRITING 815

31 POEMS FOR FURTHER READING 816

Aaron Abeyta, thirteen ways of looking at a tortilla 816
Anonymous, Lord Randall 817
Matthew Arnold, Dover Beach 818
John Ashbery, At North Farm 819
Margaret Atwood, Siren Song 820

W. H. Auden, As I Walked Out One Evening 821

W. H. Auden, Musée des Beaux Arts 823

Elizabeth Bishop, Filling Station 823

William Blake, The Tyger 824

William Blake, The Sick Rose 826

Gwendolyn Brooks, the mother 826

Gwendolyn Brooks, the rites for Cousin Vit 827

Elizabeth Barrett Browning, How Do I Love Thee? Let Me Count
    the Ways 827

Robert Browning, Soliloquy of the Spanish Cloister 828

Charles Bukowski, Dostoevsky 830

Lorna Dee Cervantes, Cannery Town in August 831

Samuel Taylor Coleridge, Kubla Khan 831

Billy Collins, Care and Feeding 833

Hart Crane, My Grandmother's Love Letters 833

E. E. Cummings, somewhere i have never
    travelled,gladly beyond 834

Marisa de los Santos, Perfect Dress 835

John Donne, Death be not proud 836

John Donne, The Flea 836

John Donne, A Valediction: Forbidding Mourning 837

Rita Dove, Daystar 838

T. S. Eliot, Journey of the Magi 839

Robert Frost, Birches 840

Robert Frost, Mending Wall 841

Robert Frost, Stopping by Woods on a Snowy Evening 842

Allen Ginsberg, A Supermarket in California 843

Thomas Hardy, The Convergence of the Twain 844

Thomas Hardy, The Darkling Thrush 845

Seamus Heaney, Digging 846

George Herbert, Love 847

Robert Herrick, To the Virgins, to Make Much of Time 847

Gerard Manley Hopkins, Spring and Fall 848

Gerard Manley Hopkins, The Windhover 848

A. E. Housman, Loveliest of trees, the cherry now 849

A. E. Housman, To an Athlete Dying Young 849

Randall Jarrell, The Death of the Ball Turret Gunner 850

Robinson Jeffers, Rock and Hawk 851

Ha Jin, Missed Time 851

Ben Jonson, On My First Son 852

Donald Justice, On the Death of Friends in Childhood 852

John Keats, Ode on a Grecian Urn 852

John Keats, When I have fears that I may cease to be 854

John Keats, To Autumn 855

Ted Kooser, Abandoned Farmhouse 856

Philip Larkin, Home is so Sad 856

Philip Larkin, Poetry of Departures 857

D. H. Lawrence, Piano 857

Denise Levertov, O Taste and See 858

Li Po, Translated by Arthur Waley, Drinking Alone by
  Moonlight 858
Shirley Geok-lin Lim, Learning to love America 859
Robert Lowell, Skunk Hour 860
Andrew Marvell, To His Coy Mistress 861
Edna St. Vincent Millay, Recuerdo 862
John Milton, When I consider how my light is spent 863
Marianne Moore, Poetry 863
Marilyn Nelson, A Strange Beautiful Woman 864
Sharon Olds, The One Girl at the Boys' Party 865
Wilfred Owen, Anthem for Doomed Youth 865
Sylvia Plath, Daddy 866
Alexander Pope, A little Learning is a dang'rous Thing 868
Ezra Pound, The River-Merchant's Wife: A Letter 869
Henry Reed, Naming of Parts 869
Adrienne Rich, Living in Sin 870
Edwin Arlington Robinson, Miniver Cheevy 871
Theodore Roethke, Elegy for Jane 872
William Shakespeare, When to the sessions of sweet
  silent thought 873
William Shakespeare, That time of year thou mayst
  in me behold 873
William Shakespeare, My mistress' eyes are nothing like
  the sun 874
Charles Simic, Butcher Shop 874
William Stafford, The Farm on the Great Plains 875
Wallace Stevens, The Emperor of Ice-Cream 876
Alfred, Lord Tennyson, Ulysses 876
Dylan Thomas, Fern Hill 878
John Updike, Ex-Basketball Player 879
Derek Walcott, Sea Grapes 880
Edmund Waller, Go, Lovely Rose 881
Walt Whitman, from Song of the Open Road 881
Walt Whitman, I Hear America Singing 882
Richard Wilbur, The Writer 883
William Carlos Williams, Spring and All 884
William Carlos Williams, Queen-Anne's-Lace 884
William Wordsworth, Composed upon Westminster
  Bridge 885
James Wright, Autumn Begins in Martins Ferry, Ohio 886
Mary Sidney Wroth, In this strange labyrinth 886
William Butler Yeats, Crazy Jane Talks with the Bishop 887
William Butler Yeats, The Magi 887
William Butler Yeats, When You Are Old 888

DRAMA

TALKING WITH *David Ives* 890

32 READING A PLAY 893

THEATRICAL CONVENTIONS 894

ELEMENTS OF A PLAY 894

Susan Glaspell, Trifles 895
Was Minnie Wright to blame for the death of her husband? While the menfolk try to unravel a mystery, two women in the kitchen turn up revealing clues.

ANALYZING *TRIFLES* 906

WRITING EFFECTIVELY
Susan Glaspell on Writing, Creating *Trifles* 910
    THINKING ABOUT A PLAY 911
    CHECKLIST: Writing About a Play 912
    WRITING ASSIGNMENT ON CONFLICT 912
Sample Student Paper, Outside *Trifles* 912
    MORE TOPICS FOR WRITING 916
    TERMS FOR REVIEW 916

33 MODES OF DRAMA
Tragedy and Comedy 918

TRAGEDY 918

Christopher Marlowe, Scene from Doctor Faustus
    (Act 2, Scene 1) 920
In this scene from the classic drama, a brilliant scholar sells his soul to the devil. How smart is that?

COMEDY 926

David Ives, Sure Thing 928
Bill wants to pick up Betty in a cafe, but he makes every mistake in the book. Luckily, he not only gets a second chance, but a third and a fourth as well.

WRITING EFFECTIVELY
David Ives on Writing, On the One-Act Play 938
    THINKING ABOUT COMEDY 939
    CHECKLIST: Writing About Comedy 939
    WRITING ASSIGNMENT ON COMEDY 939
    TOPICS FOR WRITING ABOUT TRAGEDY 940

TOPICS FOR WRITING ABOUT COMEDY 940

TERMS FOR REVIEW 940

34 CRITICAL CASEBOOK
Sophocles 941

THE THEATER OF SOPHOCLES 942

THE CIVIC ROLE OF GREEK DRAMA 944

ARISTOTLE'S CONCEPT OF TRAGEDY 945

SOPHOCLES 947

THE ORIGINS OF *OEDIPUS THE KING* 947

Sophocles, Oedipus the King
   (***Translated by Dudley Fitts and Robert Fitzgerald***) 949
"Who is the man proclaimed / by Delphi's prophetic rock / as the bloody handed murderer / the doer of deeds that none dare name? / . . . Terribly close on his heels are the Fates that never miss."

CRITICS ON SOPHOCLES 987
   Aristotle, Defining Tragedy 987
   Sigmund Freud, The Destiny of Oedipus 988
   E. R. Dodds, On Misunderstanding Oedipus 989
   A. E. Haigh, The Irony of Sophocles 990
   David Wiles, The Chorus as Democrat 991

WRITING EFFECTIVELY
   Robert Fitzgerald on Writing, Translating Sophocles into English 992
      THINKING ABOUT GREEK TRAGEDY 992
      CHECKLIST: Writing About Greek Drama 993
      WRITING ASSIGNMENT ON SOPHOCLES 993
      MORE TOPICS FOR WRITING 993
      TERMS FOR REVIEW 994

35 CRITICAL CASEBOOK
Shakespeare 996

THE THEATER OF SHAKESPEARE 997

WILLIAM SHAKESPEARE 998

A NOTE ON *OTHELLO* 999

PICTURING *OTHELLO* 1000

William Shakespeare, Othello, the Moor of Venice 1002
Here is a story of jealousy, that "green-eyed monster which doth mock / The meat it feeds on"—of a passionate, suspicious man and his blameless wife, of a serpent masked as a friend.

CRITICS ON SHAKESPEARE 1105
  Anthony Burgess, An Asian Culture Looks at Shakespeare 1105
  W. H. Auden, Iago as a Triumphant Villain 1106
  Maud Bodkin, Lucifer in Shakespeare's *Othello* 1107
  Virginia Mason Vaughan, Black and White in *Othello* 1107
  Clare Asquith, Shakespeare's Language as a Hidden
      Political Code 1108

WRITING EFFECTIVELY
  Ben Jonson on Writing, On His Friend and Rival
      William Shakespeare 1110
  UNDERSTANDING SHAKESPEARE 1110
  CHECKLIST: Writing About Shakespeare 1111
  WRITING ASSIGNMENT ON TRAGEDY 1111
  Sample Student Paper, Othello: Tragedy or Soap Opera? 1112
  MORE TOPICS FOR WRITING 1115

36 THE MODERN THEATER 1116

REALISM 1116

NATURALISM 1117

SYMBOLISM AND EXPRESSIONISM 1118

AMERICAN MODERNISM 1118

Henrik Ibsen, A Doll's House (*Translated by R. Farquharson Sharp,
    revised by Viktoria Michelsen*) 1119
*The founder of modern drama portrays a troubled marriage. Helmer, the bank
manager, regards his wife Nora as a "little featherbrain"—not knowing the truth may
shatter his smug world.*

Henrik Ibsen on Writing, Correspondence on the Final Scene of
    A Doll's House 1172

Tennessee Williams, The Glass Menagerie 1174
*Painfully shy and retiring, shunning love, Laura dwells in a world as fragile as her
collection of tiny figurines—until one memorable night a gentleman comes to call.*

Tennessee Williams on Writing, How to Stage *The Glass Menagerie*
    1221

TRAGICOMEDY AND THE ABSURD 1222

RETURN TO REALISM 1223

EXPERIMENTAL DRAMA 1224

Milcha Sanchez-Scott, The Cuban Swimmer 1224
*Nineteen-year-old Margarita Suárez wants to win a Southern California distance
swimming race. Is her family behind her? Quite literally!*

Milcha Sanchez-Scott on Writing, Writing *The Cuban Swimmer* 1237

DOCUMENTARY DRAMA 1238

Anna Deavere Smith, Scenes from Twilight: Los Angeles, 1992 1238
The violence that tore apart a city, in the words of those who were there.

Anna Deavere Smith on Writing, A Call to the Community 1248

WRITING EFFECTIVELY
    THINKING ABOUT DRAMATIC REALISM 1250
    CHECKLIST: Writing About a Realist Play 1250
    WRITING ASSIGNMENT ON REALISM 1251
Sample Student Paper, Helmer vs. Helmer 1251
    MORE TOPICS FOR WRITING 1254
    TERMS FOR REVIEW 1254

37 PLAYS FOR FURTHER READING 1256

David Henry Hwang, The Sound of a Voice 1256
A strange man arrives at a solitary woman's home in the remote countryside. As they fall in love, they discover disturbing secrets about one another's past.

David Henry Hwang on Writing, Multicultural Theater 1270

Edward Bok Lee, El Santo Americano 1272
A wrestler and his unhappy wife drive through the desert to a surprising conclusion.

Edward Bok Lee on Writing, On Being a Korean American Writer 1276

Jane Martin, Beauty 1277
We've all wanted to be someone else at one time or another. But what would happen if we got our wish?

August Wilson, Fences 1282
A proud man's love for his family is choked by his rigidity and self-righteousness, in this powerful drama by one of the great American playwrights of our time.

August Wilson on Writing, A Look into Black America 1331

WRITING

38 WRITING ABOUT LITERATURE 1335

READ ACTIVELY 1335
Robert Frost, Nothing Gold Can Stay 1336

PLAN YOUR ESSAY 1337

PREWRITING: DISCOVER YOUR IDEAS 1337

Sample Student Prewriting Exercises 1338–1341

DEVELOP A LITERARY ARGUMENT 1341

CHECKLIST: Developing an Argument 1343

WRITE A ROUGH DRAFT 1343

Sample Student Paper, Rough Draft 1344

REVISE YOUR DRAFT 1346

CHECKLIST: Revising Your Draft 1349

FINAL ADVICE ON REWRITING 1350

Sample Student Paper, Revised Draft 1351

DOCUMENT SOURCES TO AVOID PLAGIARISM 1353

THE FORM OF YOUR FINISHED PAPER 1354

SPELL-CHECK AND GRAMMAR-CHECK PROGRAMS 1354

Anonymous (after a poem by Jerrold H. Zar), A Little Poem
Regarding Computer Spell Checkers 1355

39 WRITING ABOUT A STORY 1356

READ ACTIVELY 1356

THINK ABOUT THE STORY 1358

PREWRITING: DISCOVER YOUR IDEAS 1358

Sample Student Prewriting Exercises 1358–1360

WRITE A ROUGH DRAFT 1361

CHECKLIST: Writing a Rough Draft 1362

REVISE YOUR DRAFT 1362

CHECKLIST: Revising Your Draft 1363

WHAT'S YOUR PURPOSE? COMMON APPROACHES
TO WRITING ABOUT FICTION 1363

Explication 1364
Sample Student Paper, Explication 1365

Analysis 1367
Sample Student Paper, Analysis 1368

The Card Report 1370
Sample Student Card Report 1371

Comparison and Contrast 1372
Sample Student Paper, Comparison and Contrast 1374

        Response Paper 1376
        Sample Student Response Paper 1377

    TOPICS FOR WRITING 1379

40 WRITING ABOUT A POEM 1381

    READ ACTIVELY 1381
       Robert Frost, Design 1382

    THINK ABOUT THE POEM 1383

    PREWRITING: DISCOVER YOUR IDEAS 1383
       Sample Student Prewriting Exercises 1383–1386

    WRITE A ROUGH DRAFT 1386
          CHECKLIST: Writing a Rough Draft 1387

    REVISE YOUR DRAFT 1387
          CHECKLIST: Revising Your Draft 1389

    COMMON APPROACHES TO WRITING ABOUT POETRY 1389

       Explication 1389
       Sample Student Paper, Explication 1390

       A Critic's Explication of Frost's "Design" 1392

       Analysis 1393
       Sample Student Paper, Analysis 1394

       Comparison and Contrast 1395
       Abbie Huston Evans, Wing-Spread 1396
       Sample Student Paper, Comparison and Contrast 1396

    HOW TO QUOTE A POEM 1398

    TOPICS FOR WRITING 1400

       Robert Frost, In White 1401

41 WRITING ABOUT A PLAY 1403

    READ CRITICALLY 1403

    COMMON APPROACHES TO WRITING ABOUT DRAMA 1404

       Explication 1405

       Analysis 1405

       Comparison and Contrast 1405

       Card Report 1405
       Sample Student Card Report 1407

A Drama Review 1408
Sample Student Drama Review 1410

HOW TO QUOTE A PLAY 1411

TOPICS FOR WRITING 1412

42 WRITING A RESEARCH PAPER 1414

BROWSE THE RESEARCH 1414

CHOOSE A TOPIC 1415

BEGIN YOUR RESEARCH 1415
Print Resources 1415
Online Databases 1416
Reliable Web Sources 1416
CHECKLIST: Finding Reliable Sources 1417
Visual Images 1417
CHECKLIST: Using Visual Images 1418

EVALUATE YOUR SOURCES 1419
Print Resources 1419
Web Resources 1419
CHECKLIST: Evaluating Your Sources 1420

ORGANIZE YOUR RESEARCH 1420

REFINE YOUR THESIS 1423

ORGANIZE YOUR PAPER 1423

WRITE AND REVISE 1423

MAINTAIN ACADEMIC INTEGRITY 1424

ACKNOWLEDGE ALL SOURCES 1424
Using Quotations 1425
Citing Ideas 1425

DOCUMENT SOURCES USING MLA STYLE 1426
List of Sources 1426
Parenthetical References 1426
Works-Cited List 1427
Citing Print Sources in MLA Style 1428
Citing Web Sources in MLA Style 1429
Sample List of Works Cited 1430

ENDNOTES AND FOOTNOTES 1431

SAMPLE STUDENT RESEARCH PAPER 1423

Sample Student Research Paper, (*See Chapter 8, page 300*)

CONCLUDING THOUGHTS 1432

REFERENCE GUIDE FOR MLA CITATIONS 1433

43 WRITING AN ESSAY EXAM 1439

CHECKLIST: Taking an Essay Exam 1443

44 CRITICAL APPROACHES TO LITERATURE 1444

FORMALIST CRITICISM 1445

Robert Langbaum, On Robert Browning's "My Last Duchess" 1445

BIOGRAPHICAL CRITICISM 1447

Brett C. Millier, On Elizabeth Bishop's "One Art" 1448

HISTORICAL CRITICISM 1449

Kathryn Lee Seidel, The Economics of Zora Neale Hurston's "Sweat" 1450

PSYCHOLOGICAL CRITICISM 1452

Gretchen Schulz and R. J. R. Rockwood, Fairy Tale Motifs in "Where Are You Going, Where Have You Been?" 1452

MYTHOLOGICAL CRITICISM 1454

Edmond Volpe, Myth in Faulkner's "Barn Burning" 1455

SOCIOLOGICAL CRITICISM 1457

Alfred Kazin, Walt Whitman and Abraham Lincoln 1457

GENDER CRITICISM 1458

Nina Pelikan Straus, Transformations in *The Metamorphosis* 1459

READER-RESPONSE CRITICISM 1460

Stanley Fish, An Eskimo "A Rose for Emily" 1461

DECONSTRUCTIONIST CRITICISM 1462

Geoffrey Hartman, On Wordsworth's "A Slumber Did My Spirit Seal" 1463

CULTURAL STUDIES 1464

Camille Paglia, A Reading of William Blake's "The Chimney
Sweeper" 1466

TERMS FOR REVIEW 1468

Glossary of Literary Terms 1469

Literary Credits 1499

Photo Credits 1513

Index of Major Themes 1515

Index of First Lines of Poetry 1521

Index of Authors and Titles 1525

Index of Literary Terms 1540

PREFACE

*L*iterature, Seventh Compact Edition—the book in your hands—is really four interlocking volumes sharing one cover. Each of the first three sections is devoted to one of the major literary forms—fiction, poetry, and drama. The fourth section is a comprehensive introduction to critical writing. All together, the book is an attempt to provide the college student with a reasonably compact introduction to the study and appreciation of stories, poems, and plays—as well as practical advice on the sort of writing expected in a college English course.

We assume that appreciation begins in delighted attention to words on a page. Speed reading has its uses; but at times, as Robert Frost said, the person who reads for speed "misses the best part of what a good writer puts into it." Close reading, then, is essential. Still, we do not believe that close reading tells us everything, that it is wrong to read a literary work by any light except that of the work itself. At times we suggest different approaches such as referring to the facts of an author's life, looking for myth, or seeing the conventions that typify a kind of writing—noticing, for instance, that an old mansion, cobwebbed and creaking, is the setting for a Gothic horror story.

Although we cannot help having a few convictions about the meanings of stories, poems, and plays, we have tried to step back and give you room to make up your own mind. Here and there, in the wording of a question, our opinions may occasionally stick out. If you should notice any, please feel free to ignore them. Be assured that no one interpretation, laid down by authority, is the only right one for any work of literature. Trust your own interpretation—provided that in making it you have looked clearly and carefully at the evidence.

Reading literature often will provide you with a reason to write. Following the fiction, poetry, and drama sections, there are several chapters that give the student writer some practical advice. It will guide you, step by step, in finding a topic, planning an essay, writing, revising, and putting your paper into finished form. Further, you will find there specific help in writing about fiction, poetry, and drama. There are also short features at the end of most chapters that provide help and perspective on writing about literature. In a few places we have even offered some suggestions about writing your own stories or poems—in case reading the selections in this book inspires you to try your hand at imaginative writing.

A WORD ABOUT CAREERS

Most students agree that to read celebrated writers such as William Faulkner, Emily Dickinson, and William Shakespeare is probably good for the spirit. Most students even take some pleasure in the experience. But many, not planning to teach English and impatient to begin some other career, wonder if the study of literature, however enjoyable, isn't a waste of time—or at least, an annoying obstacle.

This objection may seem reasonable at first glance, but it rests on a shaky assumption. Success in a career does not depend merely on learning the specialized information and skills required to join a profession. In most careers, according to one senior business executive, people often fail not because they don't understand their jobs, but because they don't understand their co-workers, their clients, or their customers. They don't ever see the world from another person's point of view. Their problem is a failure of imagination.

To leap over the wall of self and to look through another's eyes is valuable experience that literature offers. If you are lucky, you may never meet (or have to do business with) anyone exactly like Mrs. Turpin in the story "Revelation," and yet you will learn much about the kind of person she is from Flannery O'Connor's fictional portrait of her. What is it like to be black, a white may wonder? James Baldwin, Gwendolyn Brooks, Rita Dove, Langston Hughes, Zora Neale Hurston, Alice Walker, August Wilson, and others have knowledge to impart. What is it like to be a woman? If a man would like to learn, let him read (for a start) Kate Chopin, Susan Glaspell, Alice Munro, Sylvia Plath, Katherine Anne Porter, Flannery O'Connor, Adrienne Rich, and Amy Tan, and perhaps, too, Henrik Ibsen's *A Doll's House* and John Steinbeck's "The Chrysanthemums."

Plodding single-mindedly toward careers, some people are like horses wearing blinders. For many, the goals look fixed and predictable. Competent nurses, accountants, and dental technicians seem always in demand. Others may find that in our society some careers, like waves in the sea, will rise or fall unexpectedly. Think how many professions we now take for granted, which a few years ago didn't even exist: genetic engineering, energy conservation, digital editing, and website design. Others that once looked like lifetime meal tickets have been cut back and nearly ruined: shoe repairing, commercial fishing, railroading.

In a perpetually changing society, it may be risky to lock yourself on one track to a career, refusing to consider any other. "We are moving," writes John Naisbitt in *Megatrends*, a study of our changing society, "from the specialist, soon obsolete, to the generalist who can adapt." Perhaps the greatest opportunity in your whole life lies in a career that has yet to be invented. If you do change your career as you go along, you will be like most people. According to a U.S. Bureau of Labor Statistics survey conducted in September 2010, the average American holds over eleven jobs between the ages of 18 and 44—often completely changing his or her basic occupation. When for some unforeseen reason you have to make such a change, basic skills—and a knowledge of humanity—may be your most valuable credentials.

Literature has much practical knowledge to offer you. An art of words, it can help you become more sensitive to language—both your own and other people's. It can make you aware of the difference between the word that is exactly right and the word that is merely good enough—Mark Twain calls it "the difference between the lightning and the lightning-bug." Read a fine work of literature alertly, and some of its writer's sensitivity to words may grow on you. A Supreme Court Justice, John Paul Stevens, once remarked that the best preparation for law school is to study poetry. Why? George D. Gopen, an English professor with a law degree, says it may be because "no other discipline so closely replicates the central question asked in the study of legal thinking: Here is a text; in how many ways can it have meaning?"

Many careers today, besides law, call for close reading and clear writing—as well as careful listening and thoughtful speech. Lately, college placement directors have reported more demand for graduates who are good readers and writers. The reason is evident: Employers need people who can handle words. In a survey conducted by Cornell University, business executives were asked to rank in importance the traits they look for when hiring. Leadership was first, but skill in writing and speaking came in fourth, ahead of both managerial and analytical skills. Times change, but to think cogently and to express yourself well will always be the abilities the world needs.

KEY LITERARY TERMS

Every discipline has its own terminology. This book introduces a large range of critical terms that may help you in both your reading and writing. When these important words and phrases are first defined, they are printed in **boldface.** If you find a critical term anywhere in this book you don't know or don't recall (for example, what is a *carpe diem* poem or a *dramatic question?*), just check the Index of Literary Terms in the back of the book, and you'll see the page where the term is discussed; or look it up in the Glossary of Literary Terms, also at the back of the book.

TEXTS AND DATES

Every effort has been made to supply each selection in its most accurate text and (where necessary) in a lively, faithful translation. For the reader who wishes to know when a work was written, at the right of each title appears the date of its first publication in book form. Parentheses around a date indicate the work's date of composition or first magazine publication, given when it was composed much earlier than when it was first published in book form.

But enough housekeeping—let's enjoy ourselves and read some unforgettable stories, poems, and plays.

X. J. K. AND D. G.

TO THE
INSTRUCTOR

*L*iterature is a book with two major goals. First, it introduces college students to the appreciation and experience of literature in its major forms. Second, the book tries to develop the student's ability to think critically and communicate effectively through writing.

Both editors of this volume are writers. We believe that textbooks should be not only informative and accurate but also lively, accessible, and engaging. In education, it never hurts to have a little fun. Our intent has always been to write a book that students will read eagerly and enjoy.

WHAT'S NEW TO THIS EDITION?

- **Ten new stories**—including Isabel Allende's "The Judge's Wife," Jack London's "To Build a Fire," Eudora Welty's "A Worn Path," Alice Munro's "How I Met My Husband," Anne Tyler's "Teenage Wasteland," Ray Bradbury's now-classic "A Sound of Thunder," and ZZ Packer's "Brownies," as well as new fables by Aesop and Bidpai.
- **New chapter on "Reading Long Stories and Novels"**—featuring Franz Kafka's powerful and popular novella *The Metamorphosis*.
- **Nearly sixty new poems**—ranging from classic selections by John Keats, Emily Dickinson, Gwendolyn Brooks, Jorge Luis Borges, Robert Hayden, Antonio Machado, H.D., Robinson Jeffers, and William Shakespeare to fresh contemporary works by Kay Ryan, Rafael Campo, Derek Walcott, Lorna Dee Cervantes, Carolyn Kizer, Amit Majmudar, and Julie Sheehan.
- **Four new one-act plays**—providing greater flexibility in studying diverse contemporary trends in a crowded curriculum. The new works include two short comedies, David Ives's *Sure Thing* and Jane Martin's *Beauty*, as well as Milcha Sanchez-Scott's *The Cuban Swimmer* and Edward Bok Lee's experimental *El Santo Americano*.
- **New audio version of *Trifles***—specially created for this edition by the celebrated L.A. Theatre Works. To help students less familiar with the experience of live theater, we offer this new audio production of Susan Glaspell's *Trifles* (featured in our introductory "Reading a Play" chapter). This play is introduced with commentary by Dana Gioia and is available for students to download in *MyLiteratureLab*.
- **New writing assignments**—new writing ideas have been introduced in many chapters.
- **Updated MLA coverage**—our concise Reference Guide for MLA Citations has been updated and expanded to reflect the latest MLA guidelines and illustrate a greater variety of online sources.

Overall, we have tried to create a book to help readers develop sensitivity to language, culture, and identity, to lead them beyond the boundaries of their own selves, and to see the world through the eyes of others. This book is built on the assumption that great literature can enrich and enlarge the lives it touches.

KEY FEATURES

We have revised this edition of *Literature* with the simple aim of introducing useful new features and selections without losing the best-liked material. We have been guided in this effort by scores of instructors and students who use the book in their classrooms. Teaching is a kind of conversation between instructor and student and between reader and text. By revising *Literature*, we try to help keep this conversation fresh by mixing the classic with the new and the familiar with the unexpected.

- **Wide variety of popular and provocative stories, poems, plays, and critical prose**—offers traditional favorites with exciting and sometimes surprising contemporary selections.
  - **50 stories, 10 new selections**—diverse and exciting stories from authors new and old from around the globe.
  - **366 poems, nearly 60 new selections**—great poems, familiar and less well known, mixing classic favorites with engaging contemporary work from a wonderful range of poets.
  - **13 plays, 4 new selections**—a rich array of drama from classical Greek tragedy to Shakespeare to contemporary work by August Wilson and Anna Deavere Smith.
  - **92 critical prose pieces, 9 new selections**—extensive selections help students think about different approaches to reading, interpreting, and writing about literature.
- **"Talking with Writers"**—Exclusive conversations between Dana Gioia and celebrated fiction writer Amy Tan, former U.S. Poet Laureate Kay Ryan, and contemporary playwright David Ives offer students an insider's look into the importance of literature and reading in the lives of three modern masters.
- **Eight casebooks on major authors and literary masterpieces**—provide students with a variety of material, including biographies, photographs, critical commentaries, and author statements, to begin an in-depth study of writers and works frequently used for critical analyses or research papers.
  - Flannery O'Connor
  - Emily Dickinson
  - Langston Hughes
  - Sophocles
  - William Shakespeare
  - Charlotte Perkins Gilman's "The Yellow Wallpaper"
  - Alice Walker's "Everyday Use"
  - T. S. Eliot's "The Love Song of J. Alfred Prufrock"
- **Chapter on Latin American Poetry in Spanish**—presents some of the finest authors of the region, including Sor Juana, Jorge Luis Borges, and Octavio Paz. This important and unique chapter will not only broaden most students' knowledge of world literature but will also recognize the richness of Spanish language poetry in the literature of the Americas—a very relevant subject in today's multicultural classrooms. The bilingual selections will also allow your Spanish-speaking students a chance to bring their native language into their coursework.

■ *Othello,* **richly illustrated**—production photos of every major scene and character make Shakespeare more accessible to students who have never seen a live production, helping them to visualize the play's action (as well as break up the long blocks of print to make the play's text less intimidating).

- "Picturing *Othello*" photo montage—offers students a pictorial introduction to the play with a visual preview of the key scenes and the characters.

■ **Audio version of Susan Glaspell's** *Trifles*—specially created for this book.

■ **Terms for Review at the end of every major chapter**—provides students a simple study guide to go over key concepts and terms in each chapter.

■ **Writing Effectively feature in every major chapter** of Fiction, Poetry, and Drama has four elements designed to make the writing process easier, clearer, and less intimidating:

- **Writers on Writing** personalizes the composition process
- **Thinking About** _____ discusses the specific topic of the chapter
- **Checklist** provides a step-by-step approach to composition and critical thinking
- **Writing Assignment** plus **More Topics for Writing** provide a rich source of ideas for writing a paper.

■ **Writing About Literature**—seven full writing chapters provide comprehensive coverage of the composition and research process, in general and by genre. All chapters have been edited for increased clarity and accessibility. Our chief aim has been to make the information and structure of the writing chapters more visual for today's Internet-oriented students. (We strive to simplify the text but not to dumb it down. Clarity and concision are never out of place in a textbook, but condescension is fatal.)

■ **Student writing**—sixteen sample papers by students with annotations, prewriting exercises and rough drafts, plus a journal entry, provide credible examples of how to write about literature. Includes many samples of student work-in-progress that illustrate the writing process, including a step-by-step presentation of the development of a topic, idea generation, and the formulation of a strong thesis and argument. Samples include several types of papers:

- Argument papers
- Explication papers
- Analysis papers
- Comparison and contrast papers
- Response paper
- Research paper

■ **Updated MLA guidelines**—provide students source citation requirements from the seventh edition of the *MLA Handbook* and incorporates them in all sample student papers.

■ **Accessible, easy-to-use format**—section titles and subtitles help web-oriented students navigate easily from topic to topic in every chapter. Additionally, all chapters have been reviewed and updated to include relevant cultural references.

■ **Critical Approaches to Literature, a chapter with 10 prose selections**—provides depth and flexibility for instructors who prefer to incorporate literary theory and criticism into their introductory courses. Includes an example for every major critical school, carefully chosen both to illustrate the major theoretical approaches and to be accessible to beginning students, focusing on literary works found in the present edition.

■ **Glossary of Literary Terms**—Over 350 terms defined, including those high-lighted in boldface throughout the text as well as other important terms. Provides clear and accurate definitions, usually with cross references to related terms.

OTHER EDITIONS AVAILABLE

Literature *Still Available*

The full, hardbound edition of *Literature: An Introduction to Fiction, Poetry, Drama, and Writing,* Twelfth Edition, continues to delight professors and students.

Portable Edition

This edition provides all the content of the hardcover *Literature* text in four lightweight paperback volumes—*Fiction, Poetry, Drama,* and *Writing*—packed in a slipcase.

Interactive Editions

Both *Compact,* Seventh Edition, and *Literature,* Twelfth Edition, are published as interactive editions and come with access to *MyLiteratureLab.com* (as described in the following section) for instructors who want to incorporate media into their class.

Backpack Edition

There is an even more compact edition of this book, which we have titled *Backpack Literature,* Fourth Edition. This much briefer anthology contains only the most essential selections and writing apparatus, and it is published in a smaller format to create a more travel-friendly book.

Fiction and Poetry Available Separately

Instructors who wish to use only the fiction section or only the poetry section of this book are directed to *An Introduction to Fiction,* Eleventh Edition, and *An Introduction to Poetry,* Thirteenth Edition. Each book has writing chapters applicable to its subject, as well as the chapters "Writing a Research Paper" and "Critical Approaches to Literature."

RESOURCES FOR STUDENTS AND INSTRUCTORS

For Students

MyLiteratureLab.com

MyLiteratureLab is a state-of-the-art, web-based, interactive learning resource for use in literature courses, either as a media supplement, or as a management system to completely administer a course online. It provides a wealth of resources geared to meet the diverse teaching and learning needs of today's instructors and students. *MyLiteratureLab* adds a new dimension to the study of literature with Longman Lectures—evocative, richly illustrated audio readings along with suggestions on how to read, interpret, and write about literary works from our roster of Longman authors (including X. J. Kennedy). This powerful program also features an eAnthology with 200 additional selections, feature-length films from Films for the Humanities and Sciences, a composing space with a "Writer's Toolkit," Interactive Readings with clickable prompts, "Writers on Writing" (video interviews with distinguished authors that inspire students to explore their creativity), grammar diagnostics, which produce personalized study plans, sample student papers, Literature Timelines, Avoiding Plagiarism, and more.

Audio Production of Trifles

So many students today have limited experience attending live theater that we thought it would be useful to offer a complete audio version of our opening play, Susan Glaspell's *Trifles*, which we use to teach the elements of drama. The audio version was produced especially for this edition by the celebrated L.A. Theatre Works for students to download in *MyLiteratureLab*. It includes an introduction and commentary by Dana Gioia.

Handbook of Literary Terms

Handbook of Literary Terms by X. J. Kennedy, Dana Gioia, and Mark Bauerlein is a user-friendly primer of over 350 critical terms brought to life with literary examples, pronunciation guides, and scholarly yet accessible explanations. Aimed at undergraduates getting their first taste of serious literary study, the volume will help students engage with the humanities canon and become critical readers and writers ready to experience the insights and joys of great fiction, poetry, and drama.

Responding to Literature: A Writer's Journal (ISBN 0321095421)

This journal provides students with their own personal space for writing and is available at no additional cost when packaged with this anthology. Helpful writing prompts for responding to fiction, poetry, and drama are also included.

Evaluating Plays on Film and Video (ISBN 0321187946)

This guide walks students through the process of analyzing and writing about plays on film, whether in a short review or a longer essay. It covers each stage of the process, from preparing and analyzing material through writing the piece. The four appendixes include writing and editing tips and a glossary of film terms. The final section of the guide offers worksheets to help students organize their notes and thoughts before they begin writing.

Evaluating a Performance (ISBN 0321095413)

Perfect for the student assigned to review a local production, this supplement offers students a convenient place to record their evaluations and is available at no additional cost when packaged with this anthology. Useful tips and suggestions of things to consider when evaluating a production are included.

For Instructors

Instructor's Manual

A separate *Instructor's Manual* is available to instructors. If you have never seen our *Instructor's Manual* before, don't prejudge it. We actually write much of the manual ourselves, and we work hard to make it as interesting, lively, and informed as the parent text. It offers commentary and teaching ideas for every selection in the book. It also contains additional commentary, debate, qualifications and information—

including scores of classroom ideas—from over 100 teachers and authors. As you will see, our *Instructor's Manual* is no ordinary supplement.

Penguin Discount Paperback Program

In cooperation with Penguin Group USA, Pearson is proud to offer a variety of Penguin paperbacks, such as Tennessee Williams's *A Streetcar Named Desire*, George Orwell's *Animal Farm*, and Charlotte Brontë's *Jane Eyre*, at a significant discount—almost sixty percent off the retail price—when packaged with any Pearson title. To review the list of titles available, visit the Pearson Penguin Group USA website at *www.pearsonhighered.com/penguin*.

Video Program

For qualified adopters, an impressive selection of videos is available to enrich students' experience of literature. The videos include selections from William Shakespeare, Sylvia Plath, Ezra Pound, Alice Walker, and many more. Contact your Pearson sales representative to see if you qualify.

The Longman Electronic Testbank for Literature

This electronic testbank features various objective questions on major works of fiction, short fiction, poetry, and drama. It's available as a download from the Instructor Resource Center located at *www.pearsonhighered.com*.

CONTACT US

For examination copies of any of these books, videos, and programs, contact your Pearson sales representative, or write to Literature Marketing Manager, Pearson Higher Education, 51 Madison Avenue, New York, NY 10010. For examination copies only, call (800) 922-0579.

To order an examination copy online, go to *http://www.pearsonhighered.com* or send an e-mail to *exam.copies@pearsonhighered.com*.

THANKS

The collaboration necessary to create this new edition goes far beyond the partnership of its two editors. The new compact edition of *Literature: An Introduction to Fiction, Poetry, Drama, and Writing* has once again been revised, corrected, and shaped by wisdom and advice from instructors who actually put it to the test—and also from a number who, in teaching literature, preferred other textbooks to it, but who generously criticized this book anyway and made suggestions for it. (Some responded to the book in part, focusing their comments on the previous editions of *An Introduction to Poetry* and *An Introduction to Fiction*.) Deep thanks to the following individuals:

Alvaro Aleman, University of Florida

Jonathan Alexander, University of Southern Colorado

Ann P. Allen, Salisbury State University

Karla Alwes, SUNY Cortland

Brian Anderson, Central Piedmont Community College

Kimberly Green Angel, Georgia State University

Carmela A. Arnoldt, Glendale Community College

Herman Asarnow, University of Portland

Beverly Bailey, Seminole Community College

Carolyn Baker, San Antonio College

Rosemary Baker, SUNY Morrisville

Lee Barnes, Community College of Southern Nevada, Las Vegas

Sandra Barnhill, South Plains College

Bob Baron, Mesa Community College

Melinda Barth, El Camino Community College

Robin Barrow, University of Iowa

Joseph Bathanti, Mitchell Community College

Judith Baumel, Adelphi University

Anis Bawarski, University of Kansas

Bruce Beckum, Colorado Mountain College

Elaine Bender, El Camino Community College

Pamela Benson, Tarrant County Junior College

Jennifer Black, McLennan Community College

Brian Blackley, North Carolina State University

Debbie Borchers, Pueblo Community College

Alan Braden, Tacoma Community College

Glenda Bryant, South Plains College

Paul Buchanan, Biola University

Andrew Burke, University of Georgia

Jolayne Call, Utah Valley State College

Stasia Callan, Monroe Community College

Uzzie T. Cannon, University of North Carolina at Greensboro

Al Capovilla, Folsom Lake Community College

Eleanor Carducci, Sussex County Community College

Thomas Carper, University of Southern Maine

Jean W. Cash, James Madison University

Michael Cass, Mercer University

Patricia Cearley, South Plains College

Fred Chancey, Chemeketa Community College

Kitty Chen, Nassau Community College

Edward M. Cifelli, County College of Morris

Marc Cirigliano, Empire State College

Bruce Clary, McPherson College

Maria Clayton, Middle Tennessee State University

Cheryl Clements, Blinn College

Jerry Coats, Tarrant County Community College

Peggy Cole, Arapahoe Community College

Doris Colter, Henry Ford Community College

Dean Cooledge, University of Maryland Eastern Shore

Patricia Connors, University of Memphis

Steve Cooper, California State University, Long Beach

Cynthia Cornell, DePauw University

Ruth Corson, Norwalk Community Technical College, Norwalk

James Finn Cotter, Mount St. Mary College

Dessa Crawford, Delaware Community College

Janis Adams Crowe, Furman University

Allison M. Cummings, University of Wisconsin, Madison

Elizabeth Curtin, Salisbury State University

Robert Darling, Keuka College

Denise David, Niagara County Community College

Alan Davis, Moorhead State University

Michael Degen, Jesuit College Preparatory School, Dallas

Kathleen De Grave, Pittsburgh State University

Apryl Denny, Viterbo University

Fred Dings, University of South Carolina

Leo Doobad, Stetson University

Stephanie Dowdle, Salt Lake Community College

Dennis Driewald, Laredo Community College

David Driscoll, Benedictine College

John Drury, University of Cincinnati

Tony D'Souza, Shasta College

Victoria Duckworth, Santa Rosa Junior College

Ellen Dugan-Barrette, Brescia University

Dixie Durman, Chapman University

Bill Dynes, University of Indianapolis

Janet Eber, County College of Morris

Terry Ehret, Santa Rosa Junior College

George Ellenbogen, Bentley College

Peggy Ellsberg, Barnard College

Toni Empringham, El Camino Community College

Lin Enger, Moorhead State University

Alexina Fagan, Virginia Commonwealth University

Lynn Fauth, Oxnard College

Annie Finch, University of Southern Maine

Katie Fischer, Clarke College

Susan Fitzgerald, University of Memphis

Juliann Fleenor, Harper College

Richard Flynn, Georgia Southern University

Billy Fontenot, Louisiana State University at Eunice

Deborah Ford, University of Southern Mississippi

Doug Ford, Manatee Community College

James E. Ford, University of Nebraska, Lincoln

Peter Fortunato, Ithaca College

Ray Foster, Scottsdale Community College

Maryanne Garbowsky, County College of Morris

John Gery, University of New Orleans

Mary Frances Gibbons, Richland College

Maggie Gordon, University of Mississippi

Joseph Green, Lower Columbia College

William E. Gruber, Emory University

Huey Guagliardo, Louisiana State University
R. S. Gwynn, Lamar University
Steven K. Hale, DeKalb College
Renée Harlow, Southern Connecticut State
   University
David Harper, Chesapeake College
John Harper, Seminole Community College
Iris Rose Hart, Santa Fe Community College
Karen Hatch, California State University, Chico
Jim Hauser, William Patterson College
Kevin Hayes, Essex County College
Jennifer Heller, Johnson County Community
   College
Hal Hellwig, Idaho State University
Gillian Hettinger, William Paterson University
Mary Piering Hiltbrand, University of Southern
   Colorado
Martha Hixon, Middle Tennessee State
   University
Jan Hodge, Morningside College
David E. Hoffman, Averett University
Mary Huffer, Lake-Sumter Community College
Patricia Hymson, Delaware County Community
   College
Carol Ireland, Joliet Junior College
Alan Jacobs, Wheaton College
Ann Jagoe, North Central Texas College
Kimberlie Johnson, Seminole Community College
Peter Johnson, Providence College
Ted E. Johnston, El Paso Community College
Cris Karmas, Graceland University
Howard Kerner, Polk Community College
Lynn Kerr, Baltimore City Community College
D. S. Koelling, Northwest College
Dennis Kriewald, Laredo Community College
Paul Lake, Arkansas Technical University
Susan Lang, Southern Illinois University
Greg LaPointe, Elmira College
Tracy Lassiter, Eastern Arizona College
Sherry Little, San Diego State University
Alfred Guy Litton, Texas Woman's University
Heather Lobban-Viravong, Grinnell College
Karen Locke, Lane Community College
Eric Loring, Scottsdale Community College
Deborah Louvar, Seminole State College
Gerald Luboff, County College of Morris
Susan Popkin Mach, UCLA
Samuel Maio, California State University,
   San Jose
Jim Martin, Mount Ida College
Paul Marx, University of New Haven
David Mason, Colorado College
Mike Matthews, Tarrant County Junior College

Beth Maxfield, Henderson State University
Janet McCann, Texas A&M University
Susan McClure, Indiana University of
   Pennsylvania
Kim McCollum-Clark, Millersville University
David McCracken, Texas A&M University
Nellie McCrory, Gaston College
William McGee, Jr., Joliet Junior College
Kerri McKeand, Joliet Junior College
Robert McPhillips, Iona College
Jim McWilliams, Dickinson State University
Elizabeth Meador, Wayne Community College
Bruce Meyer, Laurentian University
Tom Miller, University of Arizona
Joseph Mills, University of California at Davis
Cindy Milwe, Santa Monica High School
Dorothy Minor, Tulsa Community College
Mary Alice Morgan, Mercer University
Samantha Morgan, University of Tennessee
Bernard Morris, Modesto Junior College
Brian T. Murphy, Burlington Community College
William Myers, University of Colorado at
   Colorado Springs
Madeleine Mysko, Johns Hopkins University
Kevin Nebergall, Kirkwood Community College
Eric Nelson, Georgia Southern University
Jeff Newberry, University of West Florida
Marsha Nourse, Dean College
Hillary Nunn, University of Akron
James Obertino, Central Missouri State University
Julia O'Brien, Meredith College
Sally O'Friel, John Carroll University
Elizabeth Oness, Viterbo College
Regina B. Oost, Wesleyan College
Mike Osborne, Central Piedmont Community
   College
Jim Owen, Columbus State University
Jeannette Palmer, Motlow State Community
   College
Mark Palmer, Tacoma Community College
Dianne Peich, Delaware County Community
   College
Betty Jo Peters, Morehead State University
Timothy Peters, Boston University
Norm Peterson, County College of Morris
Susan Petit, College of San Mateo
Louis Phillips, School of Visual Arts
Robert Phillips, University of Houston
Jason Pickavance, Salt Lake Community College
Teresa Point, Emory University
Deborah Prickett, Jacksonville State University
William Provost, University of Georgia
Wyatt Prunty, University of the South, Sewanee

Allen Ramsey, Central Missouri State University
Ron Rash, Tri-County Technical College
Michael W. Raymond, Stetson University
Mary Anne Reiss, Elizabethtown Community
  College
Barbara Rhodes, Central Missouri State University
Diane Richard-Alludya, Lynn University
Gary Richardson, Mercer University
Fred Robbins, Southern Illinois University
Douglas Robillard Jr., University of Arkansas at
  Pine Bluff
Daniel Robinson, Colorado State University
Dawn Rodrigues, University of Texas, Brownsville
Linda C. Rollins, Motlow State Community
  College
Mark Rollins, Ohio University
Laura Ross, Seminole Community College
Jude Roy, Madisonville Community College
M. Runyon, Saddleback College
Mark Sanders, College of the Mainland
Kay Satre, Carroll College
Ben Sattersfield, Mercer University
SueAnn Schatz, University of New Mexico
Roy Scheele, Doane College
Bill Schmidt, Seminole Community College
Beverly Schneller, Millersville University
Meg Schoerke, San Francisco State University
Janet Schwarzkopf, Western Kentucky University
William Scurrah, Pima Community College
Susan Semrow, Northeastern State University
Tom Sexton, University of Alaska, Anchorage
Chenliang Sheng, Northern Kentucky University
Roger Silver, University of Maryland–Asian
  Division

Phillip Skaar, Texas A&M University
Michael Slaughter, Illinois Central College
Martha K. Smith, University of Southern Indiana
Richard Spiese, California State, Long Beach
Lisa S. Starks, Texas A&M University
John R. Stephenson, Lake Superior State
  University
Jack Stewart, East Georgia College
Dabney Stuart, Washington and Lee University
David Sudol, Arizona State University
Stan Sulkes, Raymond Walters College
Gerald Sullivan, Savio Preparatory School
Henry Taylor, American University
Jean Tobin, University of Wisconsin Center,
  Sheboygan County
Linda Travers, University of Massachusetts, Amherst
Tom Treffinger, Greenville Technical College
Peter Ulisse, Housatonia Community College
Lee Upton, Lafayette College
Rex Veeder, St. Cloud University
Deborah Viles, University of Colorado, Boulder
Joyce Walker, Southern Illinois
  University–Carbondale
Sue Walker, University of South Alabama
Irene Ward, Kansas State University
Penelope Warren, Laredo Community College
Barbara Wenner, University of Cincinnati
Terry Witek, Stetson University
Sallie Wolf, Arapahoe Community College
Beth Rapp Young, University of Alabama
William Zander, Fairleigh Dickinson University
Tom Zaniello, Northern Kentucky University
Guanping Zeng, Pensacola Junior College
John Zheng, Mississippi Valley State University

Ongoing thanks go to our friends and colleagues who helped with earlier editions: Michael Palma, who scrupulously examined and updated every chapter of the previous edition; Diane Thiel of the University of New Mexico, who originally helped develop the Latin American poetry chapter; Susan Balée of Temple University, who contributed to the chapter on writing a research paper; April Lindner of Saint Joseph's University in Philadelphia, Pennsylvania, who served as associate editor for the writing sections; Mark Bernier of Blinn College in Brenham, Texas, who helped improve the writing material; Joseph Aimone of Santa Clara University, who helped integrate web-based materials and research techniques; and John Swensson of De Anza College, who provided excellent practical suggestions from the classroom.

On the publisher's staff, Joseph Terry, Katharine Glynn, and Joyce Nilsen made many contributions to the development and revision of the new edition. Savoula Amanatidis and Lois Lombardo directed the complex job of managing the production of the book in all of its many versions from the manuscript to the final printed form. Beth Keister handled the difficult job of permissions. Rona Tuccillo and Jennifer Nonenmacher supervised the expansion of photographs in the new edition.

Mary Gioia was involved in every stage of planning, editing, and execution. Not only could the book not have been done without her capable hand and careful eye, but her expert guidance made every chapter better.

Past debts that will never be repaid are outstanding to hundreds of instructors named in prefaces past and to Dorothy M. Kennedy.

X. J. K. AND D. G.

ABOUT THE
AUTHORS

X. J. KENNEDY, after graduation from Seton Hall and Columbia, became a journalist second class in the Navy ("Actually, I was pretty eighth class"). His poems, some published in the *New Yorker*, were first collected in *Nude Descending a Staircase* (1961). Since then he has published seven more collections, including a volume of new and selected poems in 2007, several widely adopted literature and writing textbooks, and seventeen books for children, including two novels. He has taught at Michigan, North Carolina (Greensboro), California (Irvine), Wellesley, Tufts, and Leeds. Cited in *Bartlett's Familiar Quotations* and reprinted in some 200 anthologies, his verse has brought him a Guggenheim fellowship, a Lamont Award, a Los Angeles Times Book Prize, an award from the American Academy and Institute of Arts and Letters, an Aiken-Taylor prize, and the Award for Poetry for Children from the National Council of Teachers of English. He now lives in Lexington, Massachusetts, where he and his wife Dorothy have collaborated on five books and five children.

DANA GIOIA is a poet, critic, and teacher. Born in Los Angeles of Italian and Mexican ancestry, he attended Stanford and Harvard before taking a detour into business. ("Not many poets have a Stanford M.B.A., thank goodness!") After years of writing and reading late in the evenings after work, he quit a vice presidency to write and teach. He has published four collections of poetry, *Daily Horoscope* (1986), *The Gods of Winter* (1991), *Interrogations at Noon* (2001), which won the American Book Award, and *Pity the Beautiful* (2012); and three critical volumes, including *Can Poetry Matter?* (1992), an influential study of poetry's place in contemporary America. Gioia has taught at Johns Hopkins, Sarah Lawrence, Wesleyan (Connecticut), Mercer, and Colorado College. From 2003 to 2009 he served as the Chairman of the National Endowment for the Arts. At the NEA he created the largest literary programs in federal history, including Shakespeare in American Communities and Poetry Out Loud, the national high school poetry recitation contest. He also led the campaign to restore active literary reading by creating The Big Read, which helped reverse a quarter century of decline in U.S. reading. He is currently the Judge Widney Professor of Poetry and Public Culture at the University of Southern California.

(The surname Gioia is pronounced JOY-A. As some of you may have already guessed, Gioia is the Italian word for joy.)

LITERATURE

SEVENTH COMPACT EDITION

Amy Tan in Chinatown, San Francisco, 1989.

FICTION

TALKING WITH *Amy Tan*

"Life Is Larger Than We Think"
Dana Gioia Interviews Amy Tan

Q: You were born in Oakland in a family where both parents had come from China. Were you raised bilingually?

AMY TAN: Until the age of five, my parents spoke to me in Chinese or a combination of Chinese and English, but they didn't force me to speak Mandarin. In retrospect, this was sad, because they believed that my chance of doing well in America hinged on my fluency in English. Later, as an adult, I wanted to learn Chinese. Now I make an effort when I am with my sisters, who don't speak English well.

Amy Tan with her mother.

Q: What books do you remember reading early in your childhood?

AMY TAN: I read every fairy tale I could lay my hands on at the public library. It was a wonderful world to escape to. I say "escape" deliberately, because I look back and I feel that my childhood was filled with a lot of tensions in the house, and I was able to go to another place. These stories were also filled with their own kinds of dangers and tensions, but they weren't mine. And they were usually solved in the end. This was something satisfying. You could go through these things and then suddenly, you would have some kind of ending. I think that every lonely kid loves to escape through stories. And what kids never thought that they were lonely at some point in their life?

Q: Your mother—to put it mildly—did not approve of your ambition to be a writer.

AMY TAN: My mother and father were immigrants and they were practical people. They wanted us to do well in the new country. They didn't want us to be starving artists. Going into the arts was considered a luxury—that was something you did if you were born to wealth. When my mother found out that I had switched from pre-med to English literature, she imagined that I would lead this life of poverty, that this was a dream that couldn't possibly lead to anything. I didn't know what it would lead to. It just occurred to me I could finally make a choice when I was in college. I didn't have to follow what my parents had set out for me from the age of six—to become a doctor.

Q: What did your mother think of *The Joy Luck Club?*

AMY TAN: Well, by the time I wrote *The Joy Luck Club*, she had changed her opinion. I was making a very good living as a business writer, enough to buy a house for her to live in. When you can do that for your parents they think you're doing fairly well. That was the goal, to become a doctor and be able to make enough money to take care of my mother in her old age. Because I was able to do that as a business writer, she thought it was great. When I decided to write fiction and I said I needed to interview her for stories from her past, she thought that was even better. Then when I got published, and it became a success, she said, "I always knew she was going to be a writer, because she had a wild imagination."

Q: *The Joy Luck Club* is a book of enormous importance, because it brought the complex history of Chinese immigration into the mainstream of American literature. Writing this book, did you have any sense that you were opening up a whole new territory?

AMY TAN: No, I had no idea this was going to be anything but weird stories about a weird family that was unique to us. To think that they would apply to other people who would find similarities to their own families or conflicts was beyond my imagination, and I have a very good imagination.

I wanted to write this book for very personal reasons. One of them, of course, was to learn the craft of writing. The other reason was to understand myself, to figure out who I was. A lot of writers use writing as a way of finding their own personal meaning. I wrote out of total chaos and personal history, which did not seem like something that would ever be used by other people as a way of understanding their lives.

Q: Did you have any literary models in writing your short stories or putting them together as a book? Or did you just do it on intuition?

AMY TAN: I look back, and there were unconscious models—fairy tales, the Bible, especially the cadence of the Bible. There was a book called *Little House in the Big Woods,* by Laura Ingalls Wilder. Wilder wrote this fictional story based on her life as a lonely little girl, moving from place to place. She lived 100 years ago, but that was my life.

The other major influence was my parents. My father wrote sermons and he read them aloud to me, as his test audience. They were not the kind of hell and brimstone sermons. They were stories about himself and his doubts, what he wanted and how he tried to do it.

Then, of course, there was my mother, who told stories as though they were happening right in front of her. She would remember what happened to her in life and act them out in front of me. That's oral storytelling at its best.

Q: Is there anything else that you'd like to say?

AMY TAN: I think reading is really important. It provided for me a refuge, especially during difficult times. It provided me with the notion that I could find an ending that was different from what was happening to me at the time. When you read about the lives of other people, people of different circumstances or similar circumstances, you are part of their lives for that moment. You inhabit their lives and you feel what they're feeling and that is compassion.

Life is larger than we think it is. Certain events can happen that we don't understand. We can take it as faith or as superstition, or as a fairy tale. The possibilities are wide open as to how we look at them.

It's a wonderful part of life to come to a situation and think that it can offer all kinds of possibilities and you get to choose them. I look at what's happened to me as a published writer, and sometimes I think it's a fairy tale.

Here is a story, one of the shortest ever written and one of the most difficult to forget:

> A woman is sitting in her old, shuttered house. She knows that she is alone in the whole world; every other thing is dead.
> The doorbell rings.

In a brief space this small tale of terror, credited to Thomas Bailey Aldrich, makes itself memorable. It sets a promising scene—is this a haunted house?—introduces a character, and places her in a strange and intriguing situation. Although in reading a story that is over so quickly we don't come to know the character well, for a moment we enter her thoughts and begin to share her feelings. Then something amazing happens. The story leaves us to wonder: who or what rang that bell?

Like many richer, longer, more complicated stories, this one, in its few words, engages the imagination. Evidently, how much a story contains and suggests doesn't depend on its size. In the opening chapter of this book, we will look first at other brief stories—examples of three ancient kinds of fiction, a fable, a parable, and a tale—then at a contemporary short story. We will consider the elements of fiction one after another. By seeing a few short stories broken into their parts, you will come to a keener sense of how a story is put together. Not all stories are short, of course; later in the book, you will find a chapter on reading long stories and novels.

All in all, here are fifty stories. Among them, may you find at least a few you'll enjoy and care to remember.

1

READING A STORY

When I read a good book ... I wish that life were
three thousand years long.

—RALPH WALDO EMERSON

After the shipwreck that marooned him on his desert island, Robinson Crusoe, in the novel by Daniel Defoe, stood gazing over the water where pieces of cargo from his ship were floating by. Along came "two shoes, not mates." It is the qualification *not mates* that makes the detail memorable. We could well believe that a thing so striking and odd must have been seen, and not invented. But in truth Defoe, like other masters of the art of fiction, had the power to make us believe his imaginings. Borne along by the art of the storyteller, we trust what we are told, even though the story may be sheer fantasy.

THE ART OF FICTION

Fiction (from the Latin *fictio*, "a shaping, a counterfeiting") is a name for stories not entirely factual, but at least partially shaped, made up, imagined. It is true that in some fiction, such as a historical novel, a writer draws on factual information in presenting scenes, events, and characters. But the factual information in a historical novel, unlike that in a history book, is of secondary importance.

Many firsthand accounts of the American Civil War were written by men who had fought in it, but few eyewitnesses give us so keen a sense of actual life on the battlefront as the author of *The Red Badge of Courage*, Stephen Crane, who was born after the war was over. In fiction, the "facts" may or may not be true, and a story is none the worse for their being entirely imaginary. We expect from fiction a sense of how people act, not an authentic chronicle of how, at some past time, a few people acted.

Human beings love stories. We put them everywhere—not only in books, films, and plays, but also in songs, news articles, cartoons, and video games. There seems to be a general human curiosity about how other lives, both real and imaginary, take shape and unfold. Some stories provide simple and predictable pleasures according to a conventional plan. Each episode of *Law & Order* or *The Simpsons*, for instance, follows a roughly similar structure, so that regular viewers feel comfortably engaged and entertained. But other stories may seek to challenge rather than comfort us, by finding new and exciting ways to tell a tale, or delving deeper into the mysteries of human nature, or both.

Literary Fiction

Literary fiction calls for close attention. Reading a short story by Ernest Hemingway instead of watching an episode of *Grey's Anatomy* is a little like playing chess rather than checkers. It isn't that Hemingway isn't entertaining. Great literature provides deep and genuine pleasures. But it also requires great attention and skilled engagement from the reader. We are not necessarily led on by the promise of thrills; we do not keep reading mainly to find out what happens next. Indeed, a literary story might even disclose in its opening lines everything that happened, then spend the rest of its length revealing what that happening meant.

Reading literary fiction is not merely a passive activity, but is one that demands both attention and insight-lending participation. In return, it offers rewards. In some works of literary fiction, such as Flannery O'Connor's "Revelation," we see more deeply into the minds and hearts of the characters than we ever see into those of our families, our close friends, our lovers—or even ourselves.

TYPES OF SHORT FICTION

Modern literary fiction in English has been dominated by two forms: the novel and the short story. The two have many elements in common. Perhaps we will be able to define the short story more meaningfully—for it has traits more essential than just a particular length—if first, for comparison, we consider some related varieties of fiction: the fable, the parable, and the tale. Ancient forms whose origins date back to the time of word-of-mouth storytelling, the fable and the tale are relatively simple in structure; in them we can plainly see elements also found in the short story (and in the novel).

Fable

The **fable** is a brief, often humorous narrative told to illustrate a moral. The characters in a fable are often animals who represent specific human qualities. An ant, for example, may represent a hard-working type of person, or a lion nobility. But fables can also present human characters. To begin, here is a fable by W. Somerset Maugham (1874–1965), an English novelist and playwright, that retells an Arabian folk story. The narrator of the story is Death. (Samarra, by the way, is a city sixty miles from Baghdad.)

W. Somerset Maugham

The Appointment in Samarra   1933

Death speaks: There was a merchant in Baghdad who sent his servant to market to buy provisions and in a little while the servant came back, white and trembling, and said, Master, just now when I was in the marketplace I was jostled by a woman in the crowd and when I turned I saw it was Death that jostled me. She looked at me and made a threatening gesture; now, lend me your horse, and I will ride away from this city and avoid my fate. I will go to Samarra and there Death will not find me. The merchant lent him his horse, and the servant mounted it, and he dug his spurs in its flanks and as fast as the horse could gallop he went. Then the merchant went down to the marketplace and he saw me standing in the crowd and he came to me and said, Why did you make a threatening gesture to my servant when you saw him this morning? That was not a threatening gesture, I said, it was only a start of surprise. I was astonished to see him in Baghdad, for I had an appointment with him tonight in Samarra.

Elements of Fable

This brief story seems practically all skin and bones; that is, it contains little decoration. For in a fable everything leads directly to the **moral,** or message, sometimes stated at the end (moral: "Haste makes waste"). In "The Appointment in Samarra" the moral isn't stated outright, it is merely implied. How would you state it in your own words?

You are probably acquainted with some of the fables credited to the Greek slave Aesop (about 620–560 B.C.), whose stories seem designed to teach lessons about human life. Such is the fable of "The Goose That Laid the Golden Eggs," in which the owner of this marvelous creature slaughters her to get at the great treasure that he thinks is inside her, but finds nothing (implied moral: "Be content with what you have"). Another is the fable of "The Tortoise and the Hare" (implied moral: "Slow, steady plodding wins the race"). The characters in a fable may be talking animals (as in many of Aesop's fables), inanimate objects, or people and supernatural beings (as in "The Appointment in Samarra"). Whoever they may be, these characters are merely sketched, not greatly developed. Evidently, it would not have helped Maugham's fable to make its point if he had portrayed the merchant, the servant, and Death in fuller detail. A more elaborate description of the marketplace would not have improved the story. Probably, such a description would strike us as unnecessary and distracting. By its very bareness and simplicity, a fable fixes itself—and its message—in memory.

Aesop

The Fox and the Grapes

6th century B.C.

Translated by V. S. Vernon Jones

Very little is known with certainty about the man called Aesop, but several accounts and many traditions survive from antiquity. According to the Greek historian Herodotus, Aesop was a slave on the island of Samos. He gained great fame from his fables, but he somehow met his death at the hands of the people of Delphi. According to one tradition, Aesop was an ugly and misshapen man who charmed and amused people with his stories. No one knows if Aesop himself wrote down any of his fables, but they circulated widely in ancient Greece and were praised by Plato, Aristotle, and many other authors. His short and witty tales with their incisive morals have remained constantly popular and influenced innumerable later writers.

A hungry fox saw some fine bunches of grapes hanging from a vine that was trained along a high trellis, and did his best to reach them by jumping as high as he could into the air. But it was all in vain, for they were just out of reach: so he gave up trying, and walked away with an air of dignity and unconcern, remarking, "I thought those grapes were ripe, but I see now they are quite sour."

Moral: It is easy to despise what you cannot get.

Questions

1. In fables, the fox is usually clever and frequently successful. Is that the case here?
2. The original Greek word for the fox's description of the grapes is *omphakes*, which more precisely means "unripe." Does the translator's use of the word "sour" add any further level of meaning to the fable?
3. How well does the closing moral fit the fable?

Aesop's fox and the grapes.

We are so accustomed to the phrase *Aesop's fables* that we might almost start to think the two words inseparable, but in fact there have been fabulists (creators or writers of fables) in virtually every culture throughout recorded history. Here is another fable from many centuries ago, this time from India.

Bidpai

The Camel and His Friends   c. 4th century

Retold in English by Arundhati Khanwalkar

The Panchatantra *(Pañca-tantra), a collection of beast fables from India, is attributed to its narrator, a sage named Bidpai, who is a legendary figure about whom almost nothing is known for certain. The* Panchatantra, *which means the "Five Chapters" in Sanskrit, is based on earlier*

The Lion, the King of the Animals from "The Fables of Bidpai," c.1480 (vellum). Musée Condé, Chantilly, France/The Bridgeman Art Library.

oral folklore. The collection was composed some time between 100 B.C. and 500 A.D. in a Sanskrit original now lost, and is primarily known through an Arabic version of the eighth century and a twelfth-century Hebrew translation, which is the source of most Western versions of the tales. Other translations spread the fables as far as central Europe, Asia, and Indonesia.

Like many collections of fables, the Panchatantra is a frame tale, with an introduction containing verse and aphorisms spoken by an eighty-year-old Brahmin teacher named Vishnusharman, who tells the stories over a period of six months for the edification of three foolish princes named Rich-Power, Fierce-Power, and Endless-Power. The stories are didactic, teaching niti, the wise conduct of life, and artha, practical wisdom that stresses cleverness and self-reliance above more altruistic virtues.

Once a merchant was leading a caravan of heavily-laden camels through a jungle when one of them, overcome by fatigue, collapsed. The merchant decided to leave the camel in the jungle and go on his way. Later, when the camel recovered his strength, he realized that he was alone in a strange jungle. Fortunately there was plenty of grass, and he survived.

One day the king of the jungle, a lion, arrived along with his three friends—a leopard, a fox, and a crow. The king lion wondered what the camel was doing in the jungle! He came near the camel and asked how he, a creature of the desert, had ended up in the hostile jungle. The camel tearfully explained what happened. The lion took pity on him and said, "You have nothing to fear now. Henceforth, you are under my protection and can stay with us." The camel began to live happily in the jungle.

Then one day the lion was wounded in a fight with an elephant. He retired to his cave and stayed there for several days. His friends came to offer their sympathy. They tried to catch prey for the hungry lion but failed. The camel had no problem as he lived on grass while the others were starving.

The fox came up with a plan. He secretly went to the lion and suggested that the camel be sacrificed for the good of the others. The lion got furious, "I can never kill an animal who is under my protection."

The fox humbly said, "But Lord, you have provided us food all the time. If any   5
one of us voluntarily offered himself to save your life, I hope you won't mind!" The hungry lion did not object to that and agreed to take the offer.

The fox went back to his companions and said, "Friends, our king is dying of starvation. Let us go and beg him to eat one of us. It is the least we can do for such a noble soul."

So they went to the king and the crow offered his life. The fox interrupted, and said, "You are a small creature, the master's hunger will hardly be appeased by eating you. May I humbly offer my life to satisfy my master's hunger."

The leopard stepped forward and said, "You are no bigger than the crow, it is me whom our master should eat."

The foolish camel thought, "Everyone has offered to lay down their lives for the king, but he has not hurt any one. It is now my turn to offer myself." So he stepped forward and said, "Stand aside friend leopard, the king and you have close family ties. It is me whom the master must eat."

An ominous silence greeted the camel's offer. Then the king gladly said, "I ac-   10
cept your offer, O noble camel." And in no time he was killed by the three rogues, the false friends.

Moral: Be careful in choosing your friends.

Parable

Another traditional form of storytelling is the **parable.** Like the fable, a parable is a brief narrative that teaches a moral, but unlike the fable, its plot is plausibly realistic, and the main characters are human rather than anthropomorphized animals or natural forces. The other key difference is that parables usually possess a more mysterious and suggestive tone. A fable customarily ends by explicitly stating its moral, but parables often present their morals implicitly, and their meanings can be open to several interpretations.

In the Western tradition, the literary conventions of the parable are largely based on the brief stories told by Jesus in his preaching. The forty-three parables recounted in the four Gospels reveal how frequently he used the form to teach. Jesus designed his parables to have two levels of meaning—a literal story that could immediately be understood by the crowds he addressed and a deeper meaning fully comprehended only by his disciples, an inner circle who understood the nature of his ministry. (You can see the richness of interpretations suggested by Jesus's parables by reading and analyzing "The Parable of the Prodigal Son" from St. Luke's Gospel, which appears in Chapter 6.) The parable was also widely used by Eastern philosophers.

The Taoist sage Chuang Tzu often portrayed the principles of Tao—which he called the "Way of Nature"—in witty parables such as the following one, traditionally titled "Independence."

Chuang Tzu

Independence   Chou Dynasty (4th century B.C.)

Translated by Herbert Giles

Chuang Chou, usually known as Chuang Tzu (approximately 390–365 B.C.), was one of the great philosophers of the Chou period in China. He was born in the Sung feudal state and received an excellent education. Unlike most educated men, however, Chuang Tzu did not seek public office or political power. Influenced by Taoist philosophy, he believed that individuals should transcend their desire for success and wealth, as well as their fear of failure and poverty. True freedom, he maintained, came from escaping the distractions of worldly affairs. Chuang Tzu's writings have been particularly praised for their combination of humor and wisdom. His parables and stories are classics of Chinese literature.

Chuang Tzu was one day fishing, when the Prince of Ch'u sent two high officials to interview him, saying that his Highness would be glad of Chuang Tzu's assistance in the administration of his government. The latter quietly fished on, and without looking round, replied, "I have heard that in the State of Ch'u there is a sacred tortoise, which has been dead three thousand years, and which the prince keeps packed up in a box on the altar in his ancestral shrine. Now do you think that tortoise would rather be dead and have its remains thus honoured, or be alive and wagging its tail in the mud?" The two officials answered that no doubt it would rather be alive and wagging its tail in the mud; whereupon Chuang Tzu cried out "Begone! I too elect to remain wagging my tail in the mud."

Questions

1. What part of this story is the exposition? How many sentences does Chuang Tzu use to set up the dramatic situation?
2. Why does the protagonist change the subject and mention the sacred tortoise? Why doesn't he answer the request directly and immediately? Does it serve any purpose that Chuang Tzu makes the officials answer a question to which he knows the answer?
3. What does this story tell us about the protagonist Chuang Tzu's personality?

Tale

The name *tale* (from the Old English *talu,* "speech") is sometimes applied to any story, whether short or long, true or fictitious. *Tale* being a more evocative name than *story,* writers sometimes call their stories "tales" as if to imply something handed down from the past. But defined in a more limited sense, a **tale** is a story, usually short, that sets forth strange and wonderful events in more or less bare summary, without detailed character-drawing. "Tale" is pretty much synonymous with "yarn," for it implies a story in which the goal is revelation of the marvelous rather than revelation of character. In the English folktale "Jack and the Beanstalk," we take away a more vivid impression of the miraculous beanstalk and the giant who dwells at its top than of Jack's mind or personality. Because such venerable stories were told aloud before someone set them down in writing, the storytellers had to limit themselves to brief descriptions. Probably spoken around a fire or hearth, such a tale tends to be less complicated and less closely detailed than a story written for the printed page, whose reader can linger over it. Still, such tales *can* be complicated. It is not merely greater length that makes a short story different from a tale or a fable: one mark of a short story is a fully delineated character.

Types of Tales

Even modern tales favor supernatural or fantastic events: for instance, the **tall tale,** a variety of folk story that recounts the deeds of a superhero (Paul Bunyan, John Henry, Sally Ann Thunder) or of the storyteller. If the storyteller is describing his or her own imaginary experience, the bragging yarn is usually told with a straight face to listeners who take pleasure in scoffing at it. Although the **fairy tale,** set in a world of magic and enchantment, is sometimes the work of a modern author (notably Hans Christian Andersen), well-known examples are those German folktales that probably originated in the Middle Ages, collected by the Brothers Grimm. The label *fairy tale* is something of an English misnomer, for in the Grimm stories, though witches and goblins abound, fairies are a minority.

Jakob and Wilhelm Grimm

Godfather Death
1812 (from oral tradition)

Translated by Dana Gioia

Jakob Grimm (1785–1863) and Wilhelm Grimm (1786–1859), brothers and scholars, were born near Frankfurt am Main, Germany. For most of their lives they worked together—lived together, too, even when in 1825 Wilhelm married. In 1838, as librarians, they began toiling on their Deutsch Wörterbuch, or German dictionary, a vast project that was to outlive them by a century. (It was completed only in 1960.) In 1840 King Friedrich Wilhelm IV appointed both brothers to the Royal Academy of Sciences, and both taught at the University of Berlin for the rest of their days.

Jakob and Wilhelm Grimm

The name Grimm is best known to us for that splendid collection of ancient German folk stories we call Grimm's Fairy Tales—*in German,* Kinder- und Hausmärchen *("Childhood and Household Tales," 1812–15). This classic work spread German children's stories around the world. Many tales we hear early in life were collected by the Grimms: "Hansel and Gretel," "Snow White and the Seven Dwarfs," "Rapunzel," "Tom Thumb," "Little Red Riding Hood," "Rumpelstiltskin." Versions of some of these tales had been written down as early as the sixteenth century, but mainly the brothers relied on the memories of Hessian peasants who recited the stories aloud for them.*

A poor man had twelve children and had to work day and night just to give them bread. Now when the thirteenth came into the world, he did not know what to do, so he ran out onto the main highway intending to ask the first one he met to be the child's godfather.

The first person he met was the good Lord God, who knew very well what was weighing on the man's heart. And He said to him, "Poor man, I am sorry for you. I will hold your child at the baptismal font. I will take care of him and fill his days with happiness."

The man asked, "Who are you?"

"I am the good Lord."

"Then I don't want you as godfather. You give to the rich and let the poor 5 starve."

The man spoke thus because he did not know how wisely God portions out wealth and poverty. So he turned away from the Lord and went on.

Then the Devil came up to him and said, "What are you looking for? If you take me as your child's sponsor, I will give him gold heaped high and wide and all the joys of this world."

The man asked, "Who are you?"

"I am the Devil."

"Then I don't want you as godfather," said the man. "You trick men and lead 10 them astray."

He went on, and bone-thin Death strode up to him and said, "Choose me as godfather."

The man asked, "Who are you?"

"I am Death, who makes all men equal."

Then the man said, "You are the right one. You take the rich and the poor without distinction. You will be the godfather."

Death answered, "I will make your child rich and famous. Whoever has me as a 15 friend shall lack for nothing."

The man said, "The baptism is next Sunday. Be there on time."

Death appeared just as he had promised and stood there as a proper godfather.

When the boy had grown up, his godfather walked in one day and said to come along with him. Death led him out into the woods, showed him an herb, and said, "Now you are going to get your christening present. I am making you a famous doctor. When you are called to a patient, I will always appear to you. If I stand next to the sick person's head, you may speak boldly that you will make him healthy again. Give him some of this herb, and he will recover. But if you see me standing by the sick person's feet, then he is mine. You must say that nothing can be done and that no doctor in the world can save him. But beware of using the herb against my will, or it will turn out badly for you."

It was not long before the young man was the most famous doctor in the whole world. "He needs only to look at the sick person," everyone said, "and then he knows how things stand—whether the patient will get well again or whether he must die." People came from far and wide to bring their sick and gave him so much gold that he quickly became quite rich.

Now it soon happened that the king grew ill, and the doctor was summoned to 20 say whether a recovery was possible. But when he came to the bed, Death was standing at the sick man's feet, and now no herb grown could save him.

"If I cheat Death this one time," thought the doctor, "he will be angry, but since I am his godson, he will turn a blind eye, so I will risk it." He took up the sick man and turned him around so that his head was now where Death stood. Then he gave the king some of the herb. The king recovered and grew healthy again.

But Death then came to the doctor with a dark and angry face and threatened him with his finger. "You have hoodwinked me this time," he said. "And I will forgive you once because you are my godson. But if you try such a thing again, it will be your neck, and I will take you away with me."

Not long after, the king's daughter fell into a serious illness. She was his only child, and he wept day and night until his eyes went blind. He let it be known that whoever saved her from death would become her husband and inherit the crown.

When the doctor came to the sick girl's bed, he saw Death standing at her feet. He should have remembered his godfather's warning, but the princess's great beauty and the happy prospect of becoming her husband so infatuated him that he flung all caution to the wind. He didn't notice that Death stared at him angrily or that he raised his hand and shook his bony fist. The doctor picked up the sick girl and turned her around to place her head where her feet had been. He gave her the herb, and right away her cheeks grew rosy and she stirred again with life.

When Death saw that he had been cheated out of his property a second time, he   25
strode with long steps up to the doctor and said, "It is all over for you. Now it's your turn." Death seized him so firmly with his ice-cold hand that the doctor could not resist. He led him into an underground cavern. There the doctor saw thousands and thousands of candles burning in endless rows. Some were tall, others medium-sized, and others quite small. Every moment some went out and others lit up, so that the tiny flames seemed to jump to and fro in perpetual motion.

"Look," said Death, "these are the life lights of mankind. The tall ones belong to children, the middle-size ones to married people in the prime of life, and the short ones to the very old. But sometimes even children and young people have only a short candle."

"Show me my life light," said the doctor, assuming it would be very tall.

Death pointed to a small stub that seemed about to flicker out.

"Oh, dear godfather!" cried the terrified doctor. "Light a new candle for me. If you love me, do it, so that I may enjoy my life, become king, and marry the beautiful princess."

"That I cannot do," Death replied. "One candle must first go out before a new   30
one is lighted."

"Then put my old one on top of a new candle that will keep burning when the old one goes out," begged the doctor.

Death acted as if he were going to grant the wish and picked up a tall new candle. But because he wanted revenge, he deliberately fumbled in placing the new candle, and the stub toppled over and went out. The doctor immediately dropped to the ground and fell into the hands of Death.

PLOT

Like a fable, the Grimm brothers' tale seems stark in its lack of detail and in the swiftness of its telling. Compared with the fully portrayed characters of many modern stories, the characters of father, son, king, princess, and even Death himself seem hardly more than stick figures. It may have been that to draw ample characters would not have contributed to the storytellers' design; that, indeed, to have done so would have been inartistic. Yet "Godfather Death" is a compelling story. By what methods does it arouse and sustain our interest?

Elements of Plot

Plot sometimes refers simply to the events in a story. In this book, though, **plot** will mean the artistic arrangement of those events. From the opening sentence of "Godfather Death," we watch the unfolding of a **dramatic situation:** a person is involved in some **conflict.** First, this character is a poor man with children to feed, in conflict with the world; very soon, we find him in conflict with God and with the Devil besides. Drama in fiction occurs in any clash of wills, desires, or powers—whether it be a conflict of character against character, character against society, character against some natural force, or, as in "Godfather Death," character against some supernatural entity.

Like any shapely tale, "Godfather Death" has a beginning, a middle, and an end. In fact, it is unusual to find a story so clearly displaying the elements of structure that critics have found in many classic works of fiction and drama. The tale begins with an **exposition:** the opening portion that sets the scene (if any), introduces the main characters, tells us what happened before the story opened, and provides any other background information that we need in order to understand and care about the events to follow. In "Godfather Death," the exposition is brief—all in the opening paragraph. The middle section of the story begins with Death's giving the herb to the boy and his warning not to defy him. This moment introduces a new conflict (a **complication**), and by this time it is clear that the son and not the father is to be the central human character of the story.

Protagonist Versus Antagonist

Death's godson is the principal person who strives: the **protagonist** (a better term than **hero**, for it may apply equally well to a central character who is not especially brave or virtuous). The **suspense,** the pleasurable anxiety we feel that heightens our attention to the story, resides in our wondering how it will all turn out. Will the doctor triumph over Death? Even though we suspect, early in the story, that the doctor stands no chance against such a superhuman **antagonist,** we want to see for ourselves the outcome of his defiance.

Crisis and Climax

When the doctor defies his godfather for the first time—when he saves the king—we have a **crisis,** a moment of high tension. The tension is momentarily resolved when Death lets him off. Then an even greater crisis—the turning point in the action—occurs with the doctor's second defiance in restoring the princess to life. In the last section of the story, with the doctor in the underworld, events come to a **climax,** the moment of greatest tension at which the outcome is to be decided, when the terrified doctor begs for a new candle. Will Death grant him one? Will he live, become king, and marry the princess? The outcome or **conclusion**—also called the **resolution** or **dénouement** (French for "the untying of the knot")—quickly follows as Death allows the little candle to go out.

Narrative Techniques

The treatment of plot is one aspect of an author's artistry. Different arrangements of the same material are possible. A writer might decide to tell of the events in chronological order, beginning with the earliest; or he or she might open the story with the last event, then tell what led up to it. Sometimes a writer chooses to skip rapidly over the exposition and begin *in medias res* (Latin for "in the midst of things"), first presenting some exciting or significant moment, then filling in what happened earlier. This method is by no means a modern invention: Homer begins the *Odyssey* with his hero mysteriously late in returning from war and his son searching for him; John Milton's *Paradise Lost* opens with Satan already defeated in his revolt against the Lord. A device useful to writers for filling in what happened earlier is the **flashback** (or **retrospect**), a scene relived in a character's memory. Alternatively, a storyteller can try to incite our anticipation by giving us some **foreshadowing** or indication of events to come. In "Godfather Death" the foreshadowings are apparent in Death's warnings ("But if you try such a thing again, it will be your neck").

THE SHORT STORY

The teller of tales relies heavily on the method of **summary:** terse, general narration. In a **short story**, a form more realistic than the tale and of modern origin, the writer usually presents the main events in greater fullness. Fine writers of short stories, although they may use summary at times (often to give some portion of a story less emphasis), are skilled in rendering a **scene:** a vivid or dramatic moment described in enough detail to create the illusion that the reader is practically there. Avoiding long summary, they try to *show* rather than simply to *tell,* as if following Mark Twain's advice to authors: "Don't say, 'The old lady screamed.' Bring her on and let her scream."

A short story is more than just a sequence of happenings. A finely wrought short story has the richness and conciseness of an excellent lyric poem. Spontaneous and natural as the finished story may seem, the writer has crafted it so artfully that there is meaning in even seemingly casual speeches and apparently trivial details. If we skim it hastily, skipping the descriptive passages, we miss significant parts.

Some literary short stories, unlike commercial fiction in which the main interest is in physical action or conflict, tell of an **epiphany:** some moment of insight, discovery, or revelation by which a character's life, or view of life, is greatly altered. The term, which means "showing forth" in Greek, was first used in Christian theology to signify the manifestation of God's presence in the world. This theological idea was adapted by James Joyce to refer to a heightened moment of secular revelation. (For such moments in fiction, see the stories in this book by Joyce, John Steinbeck, and Joyce Carol Oates.) Other short stories tell of a character initiated into experience or maturity: one such **story of initiation** is William Faulkner's "Barn Burning" (Chapter 5), in which a boy finds it necessary to defy his father and suddenly to grow into manhood. Less obviously dramatic, perhaps, than "Godfather Death," such a story may be no less powerful.

The fable and the tale are ancient forms; the short story is of more recent origin. In the nineteenth century, writers of fiction were encouraged by a large, literate audience of middle-class readers who wanted to see their lives reflected in faithful mirrors. Skillfully representing ordinary life, many writers perfected the art of the short story: in Russia, Anton Chekhov; in France, Honoré de Balzac and Guy de Maupassant; and in America, Nathaniel Hawthorne and Edgar Allan Poe (although the Americans seem less fond of everyday life than of dream and fantasy). It would be false to claim that, in passing from the fable and the tale to the short story, fiction has made a triumphant progress; or to claim that, because short stories are modern, they are superior to fables and tales. Fable, tale, and short story are distinct forms, each achieving its own effects. Far from being extinct, fable and tale have enjoyed a resurgence in recent years. Jorge Luis Borges, Italo Calvino, and Gabriel García Márquez have all used fable and folktale to create memorable and very modern fiction. All forms of fiction are powerful in the right authorial hands.

Let's begin with a contemporary short story whose protagonist undergoes an initiation into maturity. To notice the difference between a short story and a tale, you may find it helpful to compare John Updike's "A & P" with "Godfather Death." Although Updike's short story is centuries distant from the Grimm tale in its method of telling and in its setting, you may be reminded of "Godfather Death" in the main character's dramatic situation. To defend a young woman, a young man has to defy his mentor—here, the boss of a supermarket! In so doing, he places himself in jeopardy. Updike has the protagonist tell his own story, amply and with humor. How does it differ from a tale?

John Updike

A & P   1961

John Updike (1932–2009) was born in Pennsylvania, received his B.A. from Harvard, then went to Oxford to study drawing and fine art. In the mid-1950s he worked on the staff of the New Yorker, *at times doing errands for the aged James Thurber. Although he left the magazine to become a full-time writer, Updike continued to supply it with memorable stories, witty light verse, and searching reviews. A famously prolific writer, he published more than fifty books. Updike is best known as a hardworking, versatile, highly productive writer of fiction. For his novel* The Centaur *(1963) he received a National Book Award, and for* Rabbit Is Rich *(1982) a Pulitzer Prize and an American Book Award. The fourth and last Rabbit Angstrom novel,* Rabbit at Rest *(1990), won him a second Pulitzer. Updike is one of the few Americans ever to be awarded both the National Medal of Arts (1989) and the National Humanities Medal (2003)—the nation's highest honors in each respective field. His many other books include* The Witches of Eastwick *(1984), made into a successful film starring Jack Nicholson,* Terrorist *(2006), and his final novel,* The Widows of Eastwick *(2008).*

Almost uniquely among contemporary American writers, Updike moved back and forth successfully among a variety of literary genres: light verse, serious poetry, drama, criticism, children's books, novels, and short stories. But it is perhaps in short fiction that he did his finest work. Some critics, such as Washington Post writer Jonathan Yardley, believe that "It is in his short stories that we find Updike's most assured work, and no doubt it is upon the best of them that his reputation ultimately will rest."

In walks three girls in nothing but bathing suits. I'm in the third check-out slot, with my back to the door, so I don't see them until they're over by the bread. The one that caught my eye first was the one in the plaid green two-piece. She was a chunky kid, with a good tan and a sweet broad soft-looking can with those two crescents of white just under it, where the sun never seems to hit, at the top of the backs of her legs. I stood there with my hand on a box of HiHo crackers trying to remember if I rang it up or not. I ring it up again and the customer starts giving me hell. She's one of these cash-register-watchers, a witch about fifty with rouge on her cheekbones and no eyebrows, and I know it made her day to trip me up. She'd been watching cash registers for fifty years and probably never seen a mistake before.

By the time I got her feathers smoothed and her goodies into a bag—she gives me a little snort in passing, if she'd been born at the right time they would have burned her over in Salem—by the time I get her on her way the girls had circled around the bread and were coming back, without a pushcart, back my way along the counters, in the aisle between the check-outs and the Special bins. They didn't even have shoes on. There was this chunky one, with the two-piece—it was bright green and the seams on the bra were still sharp and her belly was still pretty pale so I guessed she just got it (the suit)—there was this one, with one of those chubby berry-faces, the lips all bunched together under her nose, this one, and a tall one, with black hair that hadn't quite frizzed right, and one of these sunburns right across under the eyes, and a chin that was too long—you know, the kind of girl other girls think is very "striking" and "attractive" but never quite makes it, as they very well know, which is why they like her so much—and then the third one, that wasn't quite so tall. She was the queen. She kind of led them, the other two peeking around and making their shoulders round. She didn't look around, not this queen, she just walked straight on slowly, on these long white prima-donna legs. She came down a little hard on her heels, as if she didn't walk in her bare feet that much, putting down her heels and then letting the weight move along to her toes as if she was testing the floor with every step, putting a little deliberate extra action into it. You never know for sure how girls' minds work (do you really think it's a mind in there or just a little buzz like a bee in a glass jar?) but you got the idea she had talked the other two into coming in here with her, and now she was showing them how to do it, walk slow and hold yourself straight.

She had on a kind of dirty-pink—beige maybe, I don't know—bathing suit with a little nubble all over it and, what got me, the straps were down. They were off her shoulders looped loose around the cool tops of her arms, and I guess as a result the suit had slipped a little on her, so all around the top of the cloth there was this shining rim. If it hadn't been there you wouldn't have known there could have been anything whiter than those shoulders. With the straps pushed off, there was nothing between the top of the suit and the top of her head except just *her*, this clean bare plane of the top of her chest down from the shoulder bones like a dented sheet of metal tilted in the light. I mean, it was more than pretty.

She had sort of oaky hair that the sun and salt had bleached, done up in a bun that was unraveling, and a kind of prim face. Walking into the A & P with your straps down, I suppose it's the only kind of face you *can* have. She held her head so high her neck, coming up out of those white shoulders, looked kind of stretched, but I didn't mind. The longer her neck was, the more of her there was.

She must have felt in the corner of her eye me and over my shoulder Stokesie in the second slot watching, but she didn't tip. Not this queen. She kept her eyes moving across the racks, and stopped, and turned so slow it made my stomach rub the inside of my apron, and buzzed to the other two, who kind of huddled against her for relief, and they all three of them went up the cat-and-dog-food-breakfast-cereal-macaroni-rice-raisins-seasonings-spreads-spaghetti-soft-drinks-crackers-and-cookies aisle. From the third slot I look straight up this aisle to the meat counter, and I watched them all the

5

way. The fat one with the tan sort of fumbled with the cookies, but on second thought she put the packages back. The sheep pushing their carts down the aisle—the girls were walking against the usual traffic (not that we have one-way signs or anything)— were pretty hilarious. You could see them, when Queenie's white shoulders dawned on them, kind of jerk, or hop, or hiccup, but their eyes snapped back to their own baskets and on they pushed. I bet you could set off dynamite in an A & P and the people would by and large keep reaching and checking oatmeal off their lists and muttering "Let me see, there was a third thing, began with A, asparagus, no, ah, yes, applesauce!" or whatever it is they do mutter. But there was no doubt, this jiggled them. A few houseslaves in pin curlers even looked around after pushing their carts past to make sure what they had seen was correct.

You know, it's one thing to have a girl in a bathing suit down on the beach, where what with the glare nobody can look at each other much anyway, and another thing in the cool of the A & P, under the fluorescent lights, against all those stacked packages, with her feet padding along naked over our checkerboard green-and-cream rubber-tile floor.

"Oh Daddy," Stokesie said beside me. "I feel so faint."

"Darling," I said. "Hold me tight." Stokesie's married, with two babies chalked up on his fuselage already, but as far as I can tell that's the only difference. He's twenty-two, and I was nineteen this April.

"Is it done?" he asks, the responsible married man finding his voice. I forgot to say he thinks he's going to be manager some sunny day, maybe in 1990 when it's called the Great Alexandrov and Petrooshki Tea Company or something.

What he meant was, our town is five miles from a beach, with a big summer colony out on the Point, but we're right in the middle of town, and the women generally put on a shirt or shorts or something before they get out of the car into the street. And anyway these are usually women with six children and varicose veins mapping their legs and nobody, including them, could care less. As I say, we're right in the middle of town, and if you stand at our front doors you can see two banks and the Congregational church and the newspaper store and three real-estate offices and about twenty-seven old freeloaders tearing up Central Street because the sewer broke again. It's not as if we're on the Cape; we're north of Boston and there's people in this town haven't seen the ocean for twenty years. The girls had reached the meat counter and were asking McMahon something. He pointed, they pointed, and they shuffled out of sight behind a pyramid of Diet Delight peaches. All that was left for us to see was old McMahon patting his mouth and looking after them sizing up their joints. Poor kids, I began to feel sorry for them, they couldn't help it.

Now here comes the sad part of the story, at least my family says it's sad but I don't think it's sad myself. The store's pretty empty, it being Thursday afternoon, so there was nothing much to do except lean on the register and wait for the girls to show up again. The whole store was like a pinball machine and I didn't know which tunnel they'd come out of. After a while they come around out of the far aisle, around the light bulbs, records at discount of the Caribbean Six or Tony Martin Sings or some such gunk you wonder they waste the wax on, six-packs of candy bars, and plastic toys done up in cellophane that fall apart when a kid looks at them anyway. Around they come, Queenie still leading the way, and holding a little gray jar in her hand. Slots Three through Seven are unmanned and I could see her wondering between Stokes and me, but Stokesie with his usual luck draws an old party in baggy gray pants who stumbles up with four giant cans of pineapple juice (what do these bums *do* with all that pineapple juice? I've often asked myself) so the girls come to me. Queenie puts down the jar and I take it into my fingers icy cold. Kingfish Fancy Herring Snacks in Pure Sour Cream: 49¢. Now her hands are empty, not a ring or a bracelet, bare as God made them, and I wonder where the money's coming from. Still with that prim look she lifts a folded dollar bill out of the hollow at the center of her nubbled pink top. The jar went heavy in my hand. Really, I thought that was so cute.

Then everybody's luck begins to run out. Lengel comes in from haggling with a truck full of cabbages on the lot and is about to scuttle into that door marked MANAGER behind which he hides all day when the girls touch his eye. Lengel's pretty dreary, teaches Sunday school and the rest, but he doesn't miss that much. He comes over and says, "Girls, this isn't the beach."

Queenie blushes, though maybe it's just a brush of sunburn I was noticing for the first time, now that she was so close. "My mother asked me to pick up a jar of herring snacks." Her voice kind of startled me, the way voices do when you see the people first, coming out so flat and dumb yet kind of tony, too, the way it ticked over "pick up" and "snacks." All of a sudden I slid right down her voice into her living room. Her father and the other men were standing around in ice-cream coats and bow ties and the women were in sandals picking up herring snacks on toothpicks off a big plate and they were all holding drinks the color of water with olives and sprigs of mint in them. When my parents have somebody over they get lemonade and if it's a real racy affair Schlitz in tall glasses with "They'll Do It Every Time" cartoons stencilled on.

"That's all right," Lengel said. "But this isn't the beach." His repeating this struck me as funny, as if it had just occurred to him, and he had been thinking all these years the A & P was a great big dune and he was the head lifeguard. He didn't like my smiling—as I say he doesn't miss much—but he concentrates on giving the girls that sad Sunday-school-superintendent stare.

Queenie's blush is no sunburn now, and the plump one in plaid, that I liked bet-   15
ter from the back—a really sweet can—pipes up, "We weren't doing any shopping. We just came in for the one thing."

"That makes no difference," Lengel tells her, and I could see from the way his eyes went that he hadn't noticed she was wearing a two-piece before. "We want you decently dressed when you come in here."

"We *are* decent," Queenie says suddenly, her lower lip pushing, getting sore now that she remembers her place, a place from which the crowd that runs the A & P must look pretty crummy. Fancy Herring Snacks flashed in her very blue eyes.

"Girls, I don't want to argue with you. After this come in here with your shoulders covered. It's our policy." He turns his back. That's policy for you. Policy is what the kingpins want. What the others want is juvenile delinquency.

All this while, the customers had been showing up with their carts but, you know, sheep, seeing a scene, they had all bunched up on Stokesie, who shook open a paper bag as gently as peeling a peach, not wanting to miss a word. I could feel in the silence everybody getting nervous, most of all Lengel, who asks me, "Sammy, have you rung up this purchase?"

I thought and said "No" but it wasn't about that I was thinking. I go through the punches, 4, 9, GROC, TOT—it's more complicated than you think, and after you do it often enough, it begins to make a little song, that you hear words to, in my case "Hello (*bing*) there, you (*gung*) hap-py *pee-*pul (*splat*)!"—the *splat* being the drawer flying out. I uncrease the bill, tenderly as you may imagine, it just having come from between the two smoothest scoops of vanilla I had ever known were there, and pass a half and a penny into her narrow pink palm, and nestle the herrings in a bag and twist its neck and hand it over, all the time thinking.

The girls, and who'd blame them, are in a hurry to get out, so I say "I quit" to Lengel quick enough for them to hear, hoping they'll stop and watch me, their unsuspected hero. They keep right on going, into the electric eye; the door flies open and they flicker across the lot to their car, Queenie and Plaid and Big Tall Goony-Goony (not that as raw material she was so bad), leaving me with Lengel and a kink in his eyebrow.

"Did you say something, Sammy?"

"I said I quit."

"I thought you did."

"You didn't have to embarrass them."

"It was they who were embarrassing us."

I started to say something that came out "Fiddle-de-doo." It's a saying of my grandmother's, and I know she would have been pleased.

"I don't think you know what you're saying," Lengel said.

"I know you don't," I said. "But I do." I pull the bow at the back of my apron and start shrugging it off my shoulders. A couple customers that had been heading for my slot begin to knock against each other, like scared pigs in a chute.

Lengel sighs and begins to look very patient and old and gray. He's been a friend of my parents for years. "Sammy, you don't want to do this to your Mom and Dad," he tells me. It's true, I don't. But it seems to me that once you begin a gesture it's fatal not to go through with it. I fold the apron, "Sammy" stitched in red on the pocket, and put it on the counter, and drop the bow tie on top of it. The bow tie is theirs, if you've ever wondered. "You'll feel this for the rest of your life," Lengel says, and I know that's true, too, but remembering how he made that pretty girl blush makes me so scrunchy inside I punch the No Sale tab and the machine whirs "pee-pul" and the drawer splats out. One advantage to this scene taking place in summer, I can follow this up with a clean exit, there's no fumbling around getting your coat and galoshes, I just saunter into the electric eye in my white shirt that my mother ironed the night before, and the door heaves itself open, and outside the sunshine is skating around on the asphalt.

I look around for my girls, but they're gone, of course. There wasn't anybody but some young married screaming with her children about some candy they didn't get by the door of a powder-blue Falcon station wagon. Looking back in the big windows, over the bags of peat moss and aluminum lawn furniture stacked on the pavement, I could see Lengel in my place in the slot, checking the sheep through. His face was dark gray and his back stiff, as if he'd just had an injection of iron, and my stomach kind of fell as I felt how hard the world was going to be to me hereafter.

Questions

1. Notice how artfully Updike arranges details to set the story in a perfectly ordinary supermarket. What details stand out for you as particularly true to life? What does this close attention to detail contribute to the story?

2. How fully does Updike draw the character of Sammy? What traits (admirable or otherwise) does Sammy show? Is he any less a hero for wanting the girls to notice his heroism? To what extent is he more thoroughly and fully portrayed than the doctor in "Godfather Death"?

3. What part of the story seems to be the exposition? (See the definition of *exposition* in the discussion of plot earlier in the chapter.) Of what value to the story is the carefully detailed portrait of Queenie, the leader of the three girls?

4. As the story develops, do you detect any change in Sammy's feelings toward the girls?

5. Where in "A & P" does the dramatic conflict become apparent? What moment in the story brings the crisis? What is the climax of the story?

6. Why, exactly, does Sammy quit his job?

7. Does anything lead you to *expect* Sammy to make some gesture of sympathy for the three girls? What incident earlier in the story (before Sammy quits) seems a foreshadowing?

8. What do you understand from the conclusion of the story? What does Sammy mean when he acknowledges "how hard the world was going to be . . . hereafter"?

9. What comment does Updike—through Sammy—make on supermarket society?

■ WRITING *effectively*

John Updike on Writing

Why Write? 1975

Most people sensibly assume that writing is propaganda. Of course, they admit, there is bad propaganda, like the boy-meets-tractor novels of socialist realism, and old-fashioned propaganda, like Christian melodrama and the capitalist success stories of Horatio Alger or Samuel Smiles. But that some message is intended, wrapped in the story like a piece of crystal carefully mailed in cardboard and excelsior, is not doubted. Scarcely a day passes in my native land that I don't receive some letter from a student or teacher asking me *what I meant to say* in such a book, asking me to elaborate more fully on some sentence I deliberately

John Updike

whittled into minimal shape, or inviting me to speak on some topic, usually theological or sexual, on which it is pleasantly assumed I am an expert. The writer as hero, as Hemingway or Saint-Exupéry or D'Annunzio, a tradition of which Camus was perhaps the last example, has been replaced in America by the writer as educationist. Most writers teach, a great many teach writing; writing is furiously taught in the colleges even as the death knell of the book and the written word is monotonously tolled; any writer, it is assumed, can give a lecture, and the purer products of his academic mind, the "writings" themselves, are sifted and, if found of sufficient quality, installed in their places on the assembly belt of study, as objects of educational contemplation.

How dare one confess, to the politely but firmly inquiring letter-writer who takes for granted that as a remote but functioning element of his education you are duty-bound to provide the information and elucidating essay that will enable him to complete his term paper, or his Ph.D. thesis, or his critical *opus*—how dare one confess that the absence of a swiftly expressible message is, often, *the* message; that reticence is as important a tool to the writer as expression; that the hasty filling out of a questionnaire is not merely irrelevant but *inimical* to the writer's proper activity; that this activity is rather curiously private and finicking, a matter of exorcism and manufacture rather than of toplofty proclamation; that what he makes is ideally as ambiguous and opaque as life itself.

From "Why Write?"

THINKING ABOUT PLOT

A day without conflict is pleasant, but a story without conflict is boring. The plot of every short story, novel, or movie derives its energy from conflict. A character desperately wants something he or she can't have, or is frantic to avoid an unpleasant (or deadly) event. In most stories, conflict is established and tension builds, leading to a crisis and, finally, a resolution of some sort. When analyzing a story, be sure to remember these points:

- **Plotting isn't superficial.** Although plot might seem like the most obvious and superficial part of a story, it is an important expressive device. Plot combines with the other elements of fiction—imagery, style, and symbolism, for example—to create an emotional response in the reader: suspense, humor, sadness, excitement, terror.

- **Small events can have large consequences.** In most short stories, plot depends less on large external events than on small occurrences that set off large internal changes in the main character.

- **Action reveals character.** Good stories are a lot like life: the protagonist's true nature is usually revealed not just by what he or she says but also by what he or she does. Stories often show how the protagonist comes to a personal turning point, or how his or her character is tested or revealed by events.

- **Plot is about cause and effect.** Plot is more than just a sequence of events ("First A happens, and then B, and then C . . . "). The actions, events, and situations described in most stories are related to each other by more than just accident ("First A happens, which causes B to happen, which makes C all the more surprising, or inevitable, or ironic . . . ").

CHECKLIST: Writing About Plot

☐ What is the story's central conflict?

☐ Who is the protagonist? What does he or she want?

☐ What is at stake for the protagonist in the conflict?

☐ What stands in the way of the protagonist's easily achieving his or her goal?

☐ What are the main events that take place in the story? How does each event relate to the protagonist's struggle?

☐ Where do you find the story's climax, or crisis?

☐ How is the conflict resolved?

☐ Does the protagonist succeed in achieving his or her goals?

☐ What is the impact of success, failure, or a surprising outcome on the protagonist?

WRITING ASSIGNMENT ON PLOT

Choose and read a story from this collection, and write a brief description of its plot and main characters. Then write at length about how the protagonist is changed or tested by the story's events. What do the main character's actions reveal about his or her personality? Some possible story choices are Updike's "A & P," Alice Walker's "Everyday Use," Alice Munro's "How I Met My Husband," and T. C. Boyle's "Greasy Lake."

MORE TOPICS FOR WRITING

1. Briefly list the events described in "A & P." Now write several paragraphs about the ways in which the story adds up to more than the sum of its events. Why should the reader care about Sammy's thoughts and decisions?

2. How do Sammy's actions in "A & P" reveal his character? In what ways are his thoughts and actions at odds with each other?

3. Write a brief fable modeled on either "The Appointment in Samarra," "The Fox and the Grapes," or "The Camel and His Friends." Begin with a familiar proverb—"A penny saved is a penny earned" or "Too many cooks spoil the broth"—and invent a story to make the moral convincing.

4. With "Godfather Death" in mind, write a fairy tale set in the present, in a town or city much like your own. After you've completed your fairy tale, write a paragraph explaining what aspects of the fairy tale by the Brothers Grimm you hoped to capture in your story.

5. The Brothers Grimm collected and wrote down many of our best-known fairy tales—"Cinderella," "Snow White and the Seven Dwarfs," and "Little Red Riding Hood," for example. If you have strong childhood recollections of one of these stories—perhaps based on picture books or on the animated Disney versions—find and read the Brothers Grimm version. Are you surprised by the differences? Write a brief essay contrasting the original with your remembered version. What does the original offer that the adaptation does not?

▶ TERMS FOR *review*

Types of Short Fiction

Fable ▶ A brief, often humorous narrative told to illustrate a moral. The characters in fables are traditionally animals whose personality traits symbolize human traits.

Parable ▶ A brief, usually allegorical narrative that teaches a moral. In parables, unlike fables (where the moral is explicitly stated within the narrative), the moral themes are implicit and can often be interpreted in several ways.

Tale ▶ A short narrative without a complex plot. Tales are an ancient form of narrative found in folklore, and traditional tales often contain supernatural elements. A tale differs from a short story by its tendency toward lesser-developed characters and linear plotting.

Tall tale ▶ A humorous short narrative that provides a wildly exaggerated version of events. Originally an oral form, the tall tale usually assumes that its audience knows the narrator is distorting the events. The form is often associated with the American frontier.

Fairy tale, folktale ▶ A traditional form of short narrative folklore, originally transmitted orally, which features supernatural characters such as witches, giants, fairies, or animals with human personality traits. Fairy tales often feature a hero or heroine who strives to achieve some desirable fate—such as marrying royalty or finding great wealth.

Short story ▶ A prose narrative too brief to be published in a separate volume—as novellas and novels frequently are. The short story is usually a focused narrative that presents one or two characters involved in a single compelling action.

Initiation story ▶ (also called **coming-of-age story**) A narrative in which the main character, usually a child or adolescent, undergoes an important experience (or "rite of passage") that prepares him or her for adulthood.

Elements of Plot

Protagonist ▶ The main or central character in a narrative. The protagonist usually initiates the main action of the story, often in conflict with the antagonist.

Antagonist ▶ The most significant character or force that opposes the protagonist in a narrative. The antagonist may be another character, society itself, a force of nature, or even—in modern literature—conflicting impulses within the protagonist.

Exposition ▶ The opening portion of a narrative. In the exposition, the scene is set, the protagonist is introduced, and the author discloses any other background information necessary for the reader to understand the events that follow.

Conflict ▶ The central struggle between two or more forces in a story. Conflict generally occurs when some person or thing prevents the protagonist from achieving his or her goal. Conflict is the basic material out of which most plots are made.

Complication ▶ The introduction of a significant development in the central conflict between characters (or between a character and his or her situation). Complications may be external (an outside problem that the characters cannot avoid) or internal (a complication that originates in some important aspect of a character's values or personality).

Crisis ▶ The point in a narrative when the crucial action, decision, or realization must take place. From the Greek word *krisis*, meaning "decision."

Climax ▶ The moment of greatest intensity in a story, which almost inevitably occurs toward the end of the work. The climax often takes the form of a decisive confrontation between the protagonist and antagonist.

Conclusion ► In plotting, the logical end or outcome of a unified plot, shortly following the climax. Also called **resolution** or **dénouement** ("the untying of the knot"), as in resolving—or untying the knots created by—plot complications earlier in the narrative.

Narrative Techniques

Foreshadowing ► An indication of events to come in a narrative. The author may introduce specific words, images, or actions in order to suggest significant later events.

Flashback ► A scene relived in a character's memory. Flashbacks may be related by the narrator in a summary, or they may be experienced by the characters themselves. Flashbacks allow the author to include significant events that occurred before the opening of the story.

Epiphany ► A moment of profound insight or revelation by which a character's life is greatly altered.

In medias res ► A Latin phrase meaning "in the midst of things"; refers to the narrative device of beginning a story midway in the events it depicts (usually at an exciting or significant moment) before explaining the context or preceding actions.

2

POINT OF VIEW

*An author in his book must be like God in his universe,
present everywhere and visible nowhere.*
—GUSTAVE FLAUBERT

In the opening lines of *The Adventures of Huckleberry Finn*, Mark Twain takes care to separate himself from the leading character, who is to tell his own story:

> You don't know about me, without you have read a book by the name of *The Adventures of Tom Sawyer*, but that ain't no matter. That book was made by Mr. Mark Twain, and he told the truth, mainly.

Twain wrote the novel, but the **narrator** or speaker is Huck Finn, a fictional character who supposedly tells the story. Obviously, in *Huckleberry Finn*, the narrator of the story is not the same person as the "real-life" author. In employing Huck as his narrator, Twain selects a special angle of vision: not his own, exactly, but that of a resourceful boy moving through the thick of events, with a mind at times shrewd, at other times innocent. Through Huck's eyes, Twain takes in certain scenes, actions, and characters and—as only Huck's angle of vision could have enabled Twain to do so well—records them memorably.

Not every narrator in fiction is, like Huck Finn, a main character, one in the thick of events. Some narrators play only minor parts in the stories they tell; others take no active part at all. In the tale of "Godfather Death," we have a narrator who does not participate in the events he recounts. He is not a character in the story but is someone not even named, who stands at some distance from the action recording what the main characters say and do; recording also, at times, what they think, feel, or desire. He seems to have unlimited knowledge: he even knows the mind of Death, who "because he wanted revenge" let the doctor's candle go out.

More humanly restricted in their knowledge, other narrators can see into the mind of only one character. They may be less willing to express opinions than the narrator of "Godfather Death" ("He ought to have remembered his godfather's warning"). A story may even be told by a narrator who seems so impartial and aloof that he limits himself to reporting only overheard conversation and to describing, without comment or opinion, the appearances of things.

IDENTIFYING POINT OF VIEW

Narrators come in many forms; however, because stories usually are told by someone, almost every story has some kind of narrator. Some theorists reserve the term *narrator* for a character who tells a story in the first person. We use it in a wider sense, to mean a recording consciousness that an author creates, who may or may not be a participant in the events of the story. It is rare in modern fiction for the "real-life" author to try to step away from the keyboard and tell the story. Real persons can tell stories, but when such a story is *written*, the result is usually *nonfiction*: a memoir, an account of travels, an autobiography.

To identify a story's **point of view,** describe the role the narrator plays in the events and any limits placed on his or her knowledge of the events. In a short story, it is usual for the writer to maintain one point of view from beginning to end, but there is nothing to stop him or her from introducing other points of view as well. In his long, panoramic novel *War and Peace*, encompassing the vast drama of Napoleon's invasion of Russia, Leo Tolstoy freely shifts the point of view in and out of the minds of many characters, among them Napoleon himself.

TYPES OF NARRATORS

Theoretically, a great many points of view are possible. A narrator's knowledge might vary in gradations from total omniscience to almost total ignorance. But in reading fiction, again and again we encounter familiar and recognizable points of view. Here is a list of them—admittedly just a rough abstraction—that may provide a few terms with which to discuss the stories that you read and to describe their points of view:

Participant Narrator

■ Writes in the first person ("I")
■ Can be either a major or minor character

Nonparticipant Narrator

■ Writes in the third person ("he," "she")
■ Can possess different levels of knowledge about characters
  • **All-knowing** or **omniscient** (sees into any or all of the characters)
  • **Limited omniscience** (sees into one character)
  • **Objective** (does not see into any characters, reports events from outside)

When the narrator is cast as a **participant** in the events of the story, he or she is a dramatized character who says "I." Such a narrator may be the protagonist (Huck Finn) or may be an **observer,** a minor character standing a little to one side, watching a story unfold that mainly involves someone else. A famous example of a participant narrator occurs in F. Scott Fitzgerald's *The Great Gatsby*. The novel's narrator is not Jay Gatsby, but his friend Nick Carraway, who knows only portions of Gatsby's mysterious life.

A narrator who remains a **nonparticipant** does not appear in the story as a character. Viewing the characters, perhaps seeing into the minds of one or more of them, such a narrator refers to them as "he," "she," or "they."

How Much Does a Narrator Know?

The **all-knowing** (or **omniscient**) narrator sees into the minds of all (or some) char-acters, moving when necessary from one to another. This is the point of view in "Godfather Death," in which the narrator knows the feelings and motives of the fa-ther, of the doctor, and even of Death himself. Since he adds an occasional comment or opinion, this narrator may be said also to show **editorial omniscience** (as we can tell from his disapproving remark that the doctor "should have remembered" and his observation that the father did not understand "how wisely God shares out wealth and poverty"). A narrator who shows **impartial omniscience** presents the thoughts and actions of the characters, but does not judge them or comment on them.

When a nonparticipating narrator sees events through the eyes of a single character, whether a major character or a minor one, the resulting point of view is sometimes called **limited omniscience** or **selective omniscience.** The author, of course, selects which character to see through; the omniscience is his and not the narrator's. In William Faulkner's "Barn Burning" (Chapter 5), the narrator is almost entirely confined to knowing the thoughts and perceptions of a boy, the central character.

In the **objective point of view,** the narrator does not enter the mind of any char-acter but describes events from the outside. Telling us what people say and how their faces look, he or she leaves us to infer their thoughts and feelings. So inconspicuous is the narrator that this point of view has been called "the fly on the wall." This metaphor assumes the existence of a fly with a highly discriminating gaze, who knows which details to look for to communicate the deepest meaning. Some critics would say that in the objective point of view, the narrator disappears altogether. Consider this passage by a writer famous for remaining objective, Dashiell Hammett, in his mystery novel *The Maltese Falcon,* describing his private detective Sam Spade:

> Spade's thick fingers made a cigarette with deliberate care, sifting a measured quantity of tan flakes down into curved paper, spreading the flakes so that they lay equal at the ends with a slight depression in the middle, thumbs rolling the paper's inner edge down and up under the outer edge as forefingers pressed it over, thumb and fingers sliding to the paper cylinder's ends to hold it even while tongue licked the flap, left forefinger and thumb pinching their ends while right forefinger and thumb smoothed the damp seam, right fore-finger and thumb twisting their end and lifting the other to Spade's mouth.

In Hammett's novel, this sentence comes at a moment of crisis: just after Spade has been roused from bed in the middle of the night by a phone call telling him that his partner has been murdered. Even in times of stress (we infer) Spade is deliberate, cool, efficient, and painstaking. Hammett refrains from applying all those adjectives to Spade; to do so would be to exercise editorial omniscience and to destroy the objective point of view.

Other Narrative Points of View

Besides the common points of view just listed, uncommon points of view are possible. In *Flush,* a fictional biography of Elizabeth Barrett Browning, Virginia Woolf em-ploys an unusual observer as narrator: the poet's pet cocker spaniel. In "The Circular Valley," a short story by Paul Bowles, a man and a woman are watched by a sinister spirit trying to take possession of them, and we see the human characters through the spirit's vague consciousness.

Also possible, but unusual, is a story written in the second person, *you*. This point of view results in an attention-getting directness, as in Jay McInerney's novel *Bright Lights, Big City* (1985), which begins:

> You are not the kind of guy who would be at a place like this at this time of the morning. But here you are, and you cannot say that the terrain is entirely unfamiliar, although the details are fuzzy. You are at a nightclub talking to a girl with a shaved head.

The attitudes and opinions of a narrator aren't necessarily those of the author; in fact, we may notice a lively conflict between what we are told and what, apparently, we are meant to believe. A story may be told by an **innocent narrator** or a **naive narrator,** a character who fails to understand all the implications of the story. One such innocent narrator (despite his sometimes shrewd perceptions) is Huckleberry Finn. Because Huck accepts without question the morality and lawfulness of slavery, he feels guilty about helping Jim, a runaway slave. But, far from condemning Huck for his defiance of the law—"All right, then, I'll *go* to hell," Huck tells himself, deciding against returning Jim to captivity—the author, and the reader along with him, silently applaud.

Naive in the extreme is the narrator of one part of William Faulkner's novel *The Sound and the Fury*, the idiot Benjy, a grown man with the intellect of a child. In a story told by an **unreliable narrator,** the point of view is that of a person who, we perceive, is deceptive, self-deceptive, deluded, or deranged. As though seeking ways to be faithful to uncertainty, contemporary writers have been particularly fond of unreliable narrators.

STREAM OF CONSCIOUSNESS

Virginia Woolf compared life to "a luminous halo, a semi-transparent envelope surrounding us from the beginning of consciousness to the end." To capture such a reality, modern writers of fiction have employed many strategies. One is the method of writing called **stream of consciousness,** from a phrase coined by psychologist William James to describe the procession of thoughts passing through the mind. In fiction, the stream of consciousness is a kind of selective omniscience: the presentation of thoughts and sense impressions in a lifelike fashion—not in a sequence arranged by logic, but mingled randomly. When in his novel *Ulysses* James Joyce takes us into the mind of Leopold Bloom, an ordinary Dublin mind well-stocked with trivia and fragments of odd learning, the reader may have an impression not of a smoothly flowing stream but of an ocean of miscellaneous things, all crowded and jostling.

> As he set foot on O'Connell bridge a puffball of smoke plumed up from the parapet. Brewery barge with export stout. England. Sea air sours it, I heard. Be interesting some day to get a pass through Hancock to see the brewery. Regular world in itself. Vats of porter, wonderful. Rats get in too. Drink themselves bloated as big as a collie floating.

Perceptions—such as the smoke from the brewery barge—trigger Bloom's reflections. A moment later, as he casts a crumpled paper ball off the bridge, he recalls a bit of science he learned in school, the rate of speed of a falling body: "thirty-two feet per sec."

Stream-of-consciousness writing usually occurs in relatively short passages, but in *Ulysses* Joyce employs it extensively. Similar in method, an **interior monologue** is an extended presentation of a character's thoughts, not in the seemingly helter-skelter order of a stream of consciousness, but in an arrangement as if the character were speaking out loud to himself, for us to overhear.

Every point of view has limitations. Even **total omniscience**, a knowledge of the minds of all the characters, has its disadvantages. Such a point of view requires high skill to manage, without the storyteller's losing his or her way in a multitude of perspectives. In fact, there are evident advantages in having a narrator not know everything. We are accustomed to seeing the world through one pair of eyes, to having truths gradually occur to us. Henry James, whose theory and practice of fiction have been influential, held that an excellent way to tell a story was through the fine but bewildered mind of an observer. "It seems probable," James wrote, "that if we were never bewildered there would never be a story to tell about us; we should partake of the superior nature of the all-knowing immortals whose annals are dreadfully dull so long as flurried humans are not, for the positive relief of bored Olympians, mixed up with them."

By using a particular point of view, an author may artfully withhold information, if need be, rather than immediately present it to us. If, for instance, the suspense in a story depends on our not knowing until the end that the protagonist is a spy, the author would be ill advised to tell the story from the protagonist's point of view. Clearly, the author makes a fundamental decision in selecting, from many possibilities, a story's point of view.

Here is a short story memorable for many reasons, among them its point of view.

William Faulkner

A Rose for Emily   1931

William Faulkner (1897–1962) spent most of his days in Oxford, Mississippi, where he attended the University of Mississippi and where he served as postmaster until angry townspeople ejected him because they had failed to receive mail. During World War I he served with the Royal Canadian Air Force and afterward worked as a feature writer for the New Orleans Times-Picayune. Faulkner's private life was a long struggle to stay solvent: even after fame came to him, he had to write Hollywood scripts and teach at the University of Virginia to support himself. His violent comic novel Sanctuary *(1931) caused a stir and turned a profit, but critics tend most to admire* The Sound and the Fury *(1929), a tale partially told through the eyes of an idiot;* As I Lay Dying *(1930);* Light in August *(1932);* Absalom, Absalom *(1936); and* The Hamlet *(1940). Beginning with* Sartoris *(1929), Faulkner in his fiction imagines a Mississippi county named Yoknapatawpha and traces the fortunes of several of its families, including the aristocratic Compsons*

William Faulkner

and Sartorises and the white-trash, dollar-grabbing Snopeses, from the Civil War to modern times. His influence on his fellow Southern writers (and others) has been profound. In 1950 he received the Nobel Prize in Literature. Although we think of Faulkner primarily as a novelist, he wrote nearly a hundred short stories. Forty-two of the best are available in his Collected Stories *(1950; 1995).*

I

When Miss Emily Grierson died, our whole town went to her funeral: the men through a sort of respectful affection for a fallen monument, the women mostly out of curiosity to see the inside of her house, which no one save an old manservant—a combined gardener and cook—had seen in at least ten years.

It was a big, squarish frame house that had once been white, decorated with cupolas and spires and scrolled balconies in the heavily lightsome style of the seventies, set on what had once been our most select street. But garages and cotton gins had encroached and obliterated even the august names of that neighborhood; only Miss Emily's house was left, lifting its stubborn and coquettish decay above the cotton wagons and the gasoline pumps—an eyesore among eyesores. And now Miss Emily had gone to join the representatives of those august names where they lay in the cedar-bemused cemetery among the ranked and anonymous graves of Union and Confederate soldiers who fell at the battle of Jefferson.

Alive, Miss Emily had been a tradition, a duty, and a care; a sort of hereditary obligation upon the town, dating from that day in 1894 when Colonel Sartoris, the mayor—he who fathered the edict that no Negro woman should appear on the streets without an apron—remitted her taxes, the dispensation dating from the death of her father on into perpetuity. Not that Miss Emily would have accepted charity. Colonel Sartoris invented an involved tale to the effect that Miss Emily's father had loaned money to the town, which the town, as a matter of business, preferred this way of repaying. Only a man of Colonel Sartoris' generation and thought could have invented it, and only a woman could have believed it.

When the next generation, with its more modern ideas, became mayors and aldermen, this arrangement created some little dissatisfaction. On the first of the year they mailed her a tax notice. February came, and there was no reply. They wrote her a formal letter, asking her to call at the sheriff's office at her convenience. A week later the mayor wrote her himself, offering to call or to send his car for her, and received in reply a note on paper of an archaic shape, in a thin, flowing calligraphy in faded ink, to the effect that she no longer went out at all. The tax notice was also enclosed, without comment.

They called a special meeting of the Board of Aldermen. A deputation waited upon   5
her, knocked at the door through which no visitor had passed since she ceased giving china-painting lessons eight or ten years earlier. They were admitted by the old Negro into a dim hall from which a stairway mounted into still more shadow. It smelled of dust and disuse—a close, dank smell. The Negro led them into the parlor. It was furnished in heavy, leather-covered furniture. When the Negro opened the blinds of one window, they could see that the leather was cracked; and when they sat down, a faint dust rose sluggishly about their thighs, spinning with slow motes in the single sun-ray. On a tarnished gilt easel before the fireplace stood a crayon portrait of Miss Emily's father.

They rose when she entered—a small, fat woman in black, with a thin gold chain descending to her waist and vanishing into her belt, leaning on an ebony cane with a tarnished gold head. Her skeleton was small and spare; perhaps that was why what would have been merely plumpness in another was obesity in her. She looked bloated, like a body long submerged in motionless water, and of that pallid hue. Her eyes, lost in the fatty ridges of her face, looked like two small pieces of coal pressed into a lump of dough as they moved from one face to another while the visitors stated their errand.

She did not ask them to sit. She just stood in the door and listened quietly until the spokesman came to a stumbling halt. Then they could hear the invisible watch ticking at the end of the gold chain.

Her voice was dry and cold. "I have no taxes in Jefferson. Colonel Sartoris explained it to me. Perhaps one of you can gain access to the city records and satisfy yourselves."

"But we have. We are the city authorities, Miss Emily. Didn't you get a notice from the sheriff, signed by him?"

"I received a paper, yes," Miss Emily said. "Perhaps he considers himself the sheriff . . . I have no taxes in Jefferson." 10

"But there is nothing on the books to show that, you see. We must go by the—"

"See Colonel Sartoris. I have no taxes in Jefferson."

"But, Miss Emily—"

"See Colonel Sartoris." (Colonel Sartoris had been dead almost ten years.) "I have no taxes in Jefferson. Tobe!" The Negro appeared. "Show these gentlemen out."

II

So she vanquished them, horse and foot, just as she had vanquished their fathers thirty years before about the smell. That was two years after her father's death and a short time after her sweetheart—the one we believed would marry her—had deserted her. After her father's death she went out very little; after her sweetheart went away, people hardly saw her at all. A few of the ladies had the temerity to call, but were not received, and the only sign of life about the place was the Negro man—a young man then—going in and out with a market basket. 15

"Just as if a man—any man—could keep a kitchen properly," the ladies said; so they were not surprised when the smell developed. It was another link between the gross, teeming world and the high and mighty Griersons.

A neighbor, a woman, complained to the mayor, Judge Stevens, eighty years old.

"But what will you have me do about it, madam?" he said.

"Why, send her word to stop it," the woman said. "Isn't there a law?"

"I'm sure that won't be necessary," Judge Stevens said. "It's probably just a snake or a rat that nigger of hers killed in the yard. I'll speak to him about it." 20

The next day he received two more complaints, one from a man who came in diffident deprecation. "We really must do something about it, Judge. I'd be the last one in the world to bother Miss Emily, but we've got to do something." That night the Board of Aldermen met—three graybeards and one younger man, a member of the rising generation.

"It's simple enough," he said. "Send her word to have her place cleaned up. Give her a certain time to do it in, and if she don't . . ."

"Dammit, sir," Judge Stevens said, "will you accuse a lady to her face of smelling bad?"

So the next night, after midnight, four men crossed Miss Emily's lawn and slunk about the house like burglars, sniffing along the base of the brickwork and at the cellar openings while one of them performed a regular sowing motion with his hand out of a sack slung from his shoulder. They broke open the cellar door and sprinkled lime there, and in all the outbuildings. As they recrossed the lawn, a window that had been dark was lighted and Miss Emily sat in it, the light behind her, and her upright torso motionless as that of an idol. They crept quietly across the lawn and into the shadow of the locusts that lined the street. After a week or two the smell went away.

That was when people had begun to feel really sorry for her. People in our town, remembering how old lady Wyatt, her great-aunt, had gone completely crazy at last, believed that the Griersons held themselves a little too high for what they really were. None of the young men were quite good enough for Miss Emily and such. We had long thought of them as a tableau, Miss Emily a slender figure in white in the background, her father a spraddled silhouette in the foreground, his back to her and clutching a horsewhip, the two of them framed by the back-flung front door. So when she got to be thirty and was still single, we were not pleased exactly, but vindicated; even with insanity in the family she wouldn't have turned down all of her chances if they had really materialized.

When her father died, it got about that the house was all that was left to her; and in a way, people were glad. At last they could pity Miss Emily. Being left alone, and a pauper, she had become humanized. Now she too would know the old thrill and the old despair of a penny more or less.

The day after his death all the ladies prepared to call at the house and offer condolence and aid, as is our custom. Miss Emily met them at the door, dressed as usual and with no trace of grief on her face. She told them that her father was not dead. She did that for three days, with the ministers calling on her, and the doctors, trying to persuade her to let them dispose of the body. Just as they were about to resort to law and force, she broke down, and they buried her father quickly.

We did not say she was crazy then. We believed she had to do that. We remembered all the young men her father had driven away, and we knew that with nothing left, she would have to cling to that which had robbed her, as people will.

III

She was sick for a long time. When we saw her again, her hair was cut short, making her look like a girl, with a vague resemblance to those angels in colored church windows—sort of tragic and serene.

The town had just let the contracts for paving the sidewalks, and in the summer after her father's death they began the work. The construction company came with niggers and mules and machinery, and a foreman named Homer Barron, a Yankee—a big, dark, ready man, with a big voice and eyes lighter than his face. The little boys would follow in groups to hear him cuss the niggers, and the niggers singing in time to the rise and fall of picks. Pretty soon he knew everybody in town. Whenever you heard a lot of laughing anywhere about the square, Homer Barron would be in the center of the group. Presently we began to see him and Miss Emily on Sunday afternoons driving in the yellow-wheeled buggy and the matched team of bays from the livery stable.

At first we were glad that Miss Emily would have an interest, because the ladies all said, "Of course a Grierson would not think seriously of a Northerner, a day laborer." But there were still others, older people, who said that even grief could not cause a real lady to forget *noblesse oblige*°—without calling it *noblesse oblige*. They just said, "Poor Emily. Her kinsfolk should come to her." She had some kin in Alabama; but years ago her father had fallen out with them over the estate of old lady Wyatt,

---

noblesse oblige: the obligation of a member of the nobility to behave with honor and dignity.

the crazy woman, and there was no communication between the two families. They had not even been represented at the funeral.

And as soon as the old people said, "Poor Emily," the whispering began. "Do you suppose it's really so?" they said to one another. "Of course it is. What else could . . ." This behind their hands; rustling of craned silk and satin behind jalousies closed upon the sun of Sunday afternoon as the thin, swift clop-clop-clop of the matched team passed: "Poor Emily."

She carried her head high enough—even when we believed that she was fallen. It was as if she demanded more than ever the recognition of her dignity as the last Grierson; as if it had wanted that touch of earthiness to reaffirm her imperviousness. Like when she bought the rat poison, the arsenic. That was over a year after they had begun to say "Poor Emily," and while the two female cousins were visiting her.

"I want some poison," she said to the druggist. She was over thirty then, still a slight woman, though thinner than usual, with cold, haughty black eyes in a face the flesh of which was strained across the temples and about the eye-sockets as you imagine a lighthouse-keeper's face ought to look. "I want some poison," she said.

"Yes, Miss Emily. What kind? For rats and such? I'd recom—"   35

"I want the best you have. I don't care what kind."

The druggist named several. "They'll kill anything up to an elephant. But what you want is—"

"Arsenic," Miss Emily said. "Is that a good one?"

"Is . . . arsenic? Yes, ma'am. But what you want—"

"I want arsenic."   40

The druggist looked down at her. She looked back at him, erect, her face like a strained flag. "Why, of course," the druggist said. "If that's what you want. But the law requires you to tell what you are going to use it for."

Miss Emily just stared at him, her head tilted back in order to look him eye for eye, until he looked away and went and got the arsenic and wrapped it up. The Negro delivery boy brought her the package; the druggist didn't come back. When she opened the package at home there was written on the box, under the skull and bones: "For rats."

IV

So the next day we all said, "She will kill herself"; and we said it would be the best thing. When she had first begun to be seen with Homer Barron, we had said, "She will marry him." Then we said, "She will persuade him yet," because Homer himself had remarked—he liked men, and it was known that he drank with the younger men in the Elks' Club—that he was not a marrying man. Later we said, "Poor Emily," behind the jalousies as they passed on Sunday afternoon in the glittering buggy, Miss Emily with her head high and Homer Barron with his hat cocked and a cigar in his teeth, reins and whip in a yellow glove.

Then some of the ladies began to say that it was a disgrace to the town and a bad example to the young people. The men did not want to interfere, but at last the ladies forced the Baptist minister—Miss Emily's people were Episcopal—to call upon her. He would never divulge what happened during that interview, but he refused to go back again. The next Sunday they again drove about the streets, and the following day the minister's wife wrote to Miss Emily's relations in Alabama.

So she had blood-kin under her roof again and we sat back to watch develop-   45
ments. At first nothing happened. Then we were sure that they were to be married.

We learned that Miss Emily had been to the jeweler's and ordered a man's toilet set in silver, with the letters H.B. on each piece. Two days later we learned that she had bought a complete outfit of men's clothing, including a nightshirt, and we said, "They are married." We were really glad. We were glad because the two female cousins were even more Grierson than Miss Emily had ever been.

So we were not surprised when Homer Barron—the streets had been finished some time since—was gone. We were a little disappointed that there was not a public blowing-off, but we believed that he had gone on to prepare for Miss Emily's coming, or to give her a chance to get rid of the cousins. (By that time it was a cabal, and we were all Miss Emily's allies to help circumvent the cousins.) Sure enough, after another week they departed. And, as we had expected all along, within three days Homer Barron was back in town. A neighbor saw the Negro man admit him at the kitchen door at dusk one evening.

And that was the last we saw of Homer Barron. And of Miss Emily for some time. The Negro man went in and out with the market basket, but the front door remained closed. Now and then we would see her at a window for a moment, as the men did that night when they sprinkled the lime, but for almost six months she did not appear on the streets. Then we knew that this was to be expected too; as if that quality of her father which had thwarted her woman's life so many times had been too virulent and too furious to die.

When we next saw Miss Emily, she had grown fat and her hair was turning gray. During the next few years it grew grayer and grayer until it attained an even pepper-and-salt iron-gray, when it ceased turning. Up to the day of her death at seventy-four it was still that vigorous iron-gray, like the hair of an active man.

From that time on her front door remained closed, save for a period of six or seven years, when she was about forty, during which she gave lessons in china-painting. She fitted up a studio in one of the downstairs rooms, where the daughters and granddaughters of Colonel Sartoris' contemporaries were sent to her with the same regularity and in the same spirit that they were sent to church on Sundays with a twenty-five-cent piece for the collection plate. Meanwhile her taxes had been remitted.

Then the newer generation became the backbone and the spirit of the town, and the painting pupils grew up and fell away and did not send their children to her with boxes of color and tedious brushes and pictures cut from the ladies' magazines. The front door closed upon the last one and remained closed for good. When the town got free postal delivery, Miss Emily alone refused to let them fasten the metal numbers above her door and attach a mailbox to it. She would not listen to them. 50

Daily, monthly, yearly we watched the Negro grow grayer and more stooped, going in and out with the market basket. Each December we sent her a tax notice, which would be returned by the post office a week later, unclaimed. Now and then we would see her in one of the downstairs windows—she had evidently shut up the top floor of the house—like the carven torso of an idol in a niche, looking or not looking at us, we could never tell which. Thus she passed from generation to generation—dear, inescapable, impervious, tranquil, and perverse.

And so she died. Fell ill in the house filled with dust and shadows, with only a doddering Negro man to wait on her. We did not even know she was sick; we had long since given up trying to get any information from the Negro. He talked to no one, probably not even to her, for his voice had grown harsh and rusty, as if from disuse.

She died in one of the downstairs rooms, in a heavy walnut bed with a curtain, her gray head propped on a pillow yellow and moldy with age and lack of sunlight.

V

The Negro met the first of the ladies at the front door and let them in, with their hushed, sibilant voices and their quick, curious glances, and then he disappeared. He walked right through the house and out the back and was not seen again.

The two female cousins came at once. They held the funeral on the second day, with the town coming to look at Miss Emily beneath a mass of bought flowers, with the crayon face of her father musing profoundly above the bier and the ladies sibilant and macabre; and the very old men—some in their brushed Confederate uniforms— on the porch and the lawn, talking of Miss Emily as if she had been a contemporary of theirs, believing that they had danced with her and courted her perhaps, confusing time with its mathematical progression, as the old do, to whom all the past is not a diminishing road but, instead, a huge meadow which no winter ever quite touches, divided from them now by the narrow bottleneck of the most recent decade of years.

Already we knew that there was one room in that region above stairs which no one had seen in forty years, and which would have to be forced. They waited until Miss Emily was decently in the ground before they opened it.

The violence of breaking down the door seemed to fill this room with pervading dust. A thin, acrid pall as of the tomb seemed to lie everywhere upon this room decked and furnished as for a bridal: upon the valance curtains of faded rose color, upon the rose-shaded lights, upon the dressing table, upon the delicate array of crystal and the man's toilet things backed with tarnished silver, silver so tarnished that the monogram was obscured. Among them lay collar and tie, as if they had just been removed, which, lifted, left upon the surface a pale crescent in the dust. Upon a chair hung the suit, carefully folded; beneath it the two mute shoes and the discarded socks.

The man himself lay in the bed.

For a long while we just stood there, looking down at the profound and fleshless grin. The body had apparently once lain in the attitude of an embrace, but now the long sleep that outlasts love, that conquers even the grimace of love, had cuckolded him. What was left of him, rotted beneath what was left of the nightshirt, had become inextricable from the bed in which he lay; and upon him and upon the pillow beside him lay that even coating of the patient and biding dust.

Then we noticed that in the second pillow was the indentation of a head. One of us lifted something from it, and leaning forward, that faint and invisible dust dry and acrid in the nostrils, we saw a long strand of iron-gray hair.

Questions

1. What is meaningful in the final detail that the strand of hair on the second pillow is "iron-gray"?
2. Who is the unnamed narrator? For whom does he (or she?) profess to be speaking?
3. Why does "A Rose for Emily" seem better told from his or her point of view than if it were told (like John Updike's "A & P") from the point of view of the main character?
4. What foreshadowings of the discovery of the body of Homer Barron are we given earlier in the story? Share your experience in reading "A Rose for Emily": did the foreshadowings give away the ending for you? Did they heighten your interest?
5. What contrasts does the narrator draw between changing reality and Emily's refusal or inability to recognize change?
6. How do the character and background of Emily Grierson differ from those of Homer Barron? What general observations about the society that Faulkner depicts can be made from his portraits of these two characters and from his account of life in this one Mississippi town?
7. Does the story seem to you totally grim, or do you find any humor in it?

8. What do you infer to be the author's attitude toward Emily Grierson? Is she simply a murderous madwoman? Why do you suppose Faulkner calls his story "A Rose . . ."?

ZZ Packer

Brownies°   2003

ZZ Packer (b. 1973) was born in Chicago, Illinois, but grew up in Atlanta, Georgia, and Louisville, Kentucky. Her given name was Zuwena, the Swahili term for "good," but it was so often mispronounced that she began calling herself "ZZ." Packer became interested in writing in high school, and published her first story in Seventeen magazine while still a senior at Yale University. She did graduate work at Johns Hopkins and the University of Iowa, and eventually became a Stegner fellow at Stanford University. "Brownies" is the opening story of her first collection of short stories, Drinking Coffee Elsewhere (2003), which has been translated into five languages. Packer currently lives in the San Francisco Bay area.

ZZ Packer

By our second day at Camp Crescendo, the girls in my Brownie troop had decided to kick the asses of each and every girl in Brownie Troop 909. Troop 909 was doomed from the first day of camp; they were white girls, their complexions a blend of ice cream: strawberry, vanilla. They turtled out from their bus in pairs, their rolled-up sleeping bags chromatized with Disney characters: Sleeping Beauty, Snow White, Mickey Mouse; or the generic ones cheap parents bought: washed-out rainbows, unicorns, curly-eyelashed frogs. Some clutched Igloo coolers and still others held on to stuffed toys like pacifiers, looking all around them like tourists determined to be dazzled.

Our troop was wending its way past their bus, past the ranger station, past the colorful trail guide drawn like a treasure map, locked behind glass.

"Man, did you smell them?" Arnetta said, giving the girls a slow once-over, "They smell like Chihuahuas. *Wet* Chihuahuas." Their troop was still at the entrance, and though we had passed them by yards, Arnetta raised her nose in the air and grimaced.

Arnetta said this from the very rear of the line, far away from Mrs. Margolin, who always strung our troop behind her like a brood of obedient ducklings. Mrs. Margolin even looked like a mother duck—she had hair cropped close to a small ball of a head, almost no neck, and huge, miraculous breasts. She wore enormous belts that looked like the kind that weightlifters wear, except hers would be cheap metallic gold or rabbit fur or covered with gigantic fake sunflowers, and often these belts would become nature lessons in and of themselves. "See," Mrs. Margolin once said to us, pointing to her belt, "this one's made entirely from the feathers of baby pigeons."

The belt layered with feathers was uncanny enough, but I was more disturbed by the realization that I had never actually *seen* a baby pigeon. I searched weeks for one, in vain—scampering after pigeons whenever I was downtown with my father.

5

Brownies: Girl Scout program for 2nd and 3rd graders. (In this story, however, the author puts the Brownies in the fourth grade.)

But nature lessons were not Mrs. Margolin's top priority. She saw the position of troop leader as an evangelical post. Back at the A.M.E. church° where our Brownie meetings were held, Mrs. Margolin was especially fond of imparting religious aphorisms by means of acrostics—"Satan" was the "Serpent Always Tempting and Noisome"; she'd refer to the "Bible" as "Basic Instructions Before Leaving Earth." Whenever she quizzed us on these, expecting to hear the acrostics parroted back to her, only Arnetta's correct replies soared over our vague mumblings. "Jesus?" Mrs. Margolin might ask expectantly, and Arnetta alone would dutifully answer, "Jehovah's Example, Saving Us Sinners."

Arnetta always made a point of listening to Mrs. Margolin's religious talk and giving her what she wanted to hear. Because of this, Arnetta could have blared through a megaphone that the white girls of Troop 909 were "wet Chihuahuas" without so much as a blink from Mrs. Margolin. Once, Arnetta killed the troop goldfish by feeding it a french fry covered in ketchup, and when Mrs. Margolin demanded that she explain what had happened, claimed the goldfish had been eyeing her meal for *hours*, then the fish—giving in to temptation—had leapt up and snatched a whole golden fry from her fingertips.

"*Serious* Chihuahua," Octavia added, and though neither Arnetta nor Octavia could *spell* "Chihuahua," had ever *seen* a Chihuahua, trisyllabic words had gained a sort of exoticism within our fourth-grade set at Woodrow Wilson Elementary. Arnetta and Octavia would flip through the dictionary, determined to work the vulgar-sounding ones like "Djibouti" and "asinine" into conversation.

"*Caucasian* Chihuahuas," Arnetta said.

That did it. The girls in my troop turned elastic: Drema and Elise doubled up on one another like inextricably entwined kites; Octavia slapped her belly; Janice jumped straight up in the air, then did it again, as if to slam-dunk her own head. They could not stop laughing. No one had laughed so hard since a boy named Martez had stuck a pencil in the electric socket and spent the whole day with a strange grin on his face. | 10

"Girls, girls," said our parent helper, Mrs. Hedy. Mrs. Hedy was Octavia's mother, and she wagged her index finger perfunctorily, like a windshield wiper. "Stop it, now. Be good." She said this loud enough to be heard, but lazily, bereft of any feeling or indication that she meant to be obeyed, as though she could say these words again at the exact same pitch if a button somewhere on her were pressed.

But the rest of the girls didn't stop; they only laughed louder. It was the word "Caucasian" that got them all going. One day at school, about a month before the Brownie camping trip, Arnetta turned to a boy wearing impossibly high-ankled floodwater jeans and said, "What are you? *Caucasian?*" The word took off from there, and soon everything was Caucasian. If you ate too fast you ate like a Caucasian, if you ate too slow you ate like a Caucasian. The biggest feat anyone at Woodrow Wilson could do was to jump off the swing in midair, at the highest point in its arc, and if you fell (as I had, more than once) instead of landing on your feet, knees bent Olympic gymnast-style, Arnetta and Octavia were prepared to comment. They'd look at each other with the silence of passengers who'd narrowly escaped an accident, then nod their heads, whispering with solemn horror, "*Caucasian.*"

Even the only white kid in our school, Dennis, got in on the Caucasian act. That time when Martez stuck a pencil in the socket, Dennis had pointed and yelled, "That was *so* Caucasian!"

A.M.E. church: African Methodist Episcopal Church, a Protestant denomination founded by people of African descent.

*

When you lived in the south suburbs of Atlanta, it was easy to forget about whites. Whites were like those baby pigeons: real and existing, but rarely seen or thought about. Everyone had been to Rich's to go clothes shopping, everyone had seen white girls and their mothers coo-cooing over dresses; everyone had gone to the downtown library and seen white businessmen swish by importantly, wrists flexed in front of them to check the time as though they would change from Clark Kent into Superman at any second. But those images were as fleeting as cards shuffled in a deck, whereas the ten white girls behind us—*invaders*, Arnetta would later call them—were instantly real and memorable, with their long, shampoo-commercial hair, straight as spaghetti from the box. This alone was reason for envy and hatred. The only black girl most of us had ever seen with hair that long was Octavia, whose hair hung past her butt like a Hawaiian hula dancer's. The sight of Octavia's mane prompted other girls to listen to her reverentially, as though whatever she had to say would somehow activate their own follicles. For example, when, on the first day of camp, Octavia made as if to speak, and everyone fell silent. "Nobody," Octavia said, "calls us niggers."

At the end of that first day, when half of our troop made their way back to the cabin after tag-team restroom visits, Arnetta said she'd heard one of the Troop 909 girls call Daphne a nigger. The other half of the girls and I were helping Mrs. Margolin clean up the pots and pans from the campfire ravioli dinner. When we made our way to the restrooms to wash up and brush our teeth, we met up with Arnetta midway. 15

"Man, I completely heard the girl," Arnetta reported. "Right, Daphne?"

Daphne hardly ever spoke, but when she did, her voice was petite and tinkly, the voice one might expect from a shiny new earring. She'd written a poem once, for Langston Hughes Day, a poem brimming with all the teacher-winning ingredients— trees and oceans, sunsets and moons—but what cinched the poem for the grown-ups, snatching the win from Octavia's musical ode to Grandmaster Flash and the Furious Five, were Daphne's last lines:

> You are my father, the veteran
> When you cry in the dark
> It rains and rains and rains in my heart

She'd always worn clean, though faded, jumpers and dresses when Chic jeans were the fashion, but when she went up to the dais to receive her prize journal, pages trimmed in gold, she wore a new dress with a velveteen bodice and a taffeta skirt as wide as an umbrella. All the kids clapped, though none of them understood the poem. I'd read encyclopedias the way others read comics, and I didn't get it. But those last lines pricked me, they were so eerie, and as my father and I ate cereal, I'd whisper over my Froot Loops, like a mantra, "*You are my father, the veteran. You are my father, the veteran, the veteran, the veteran,*" until my father, who acted in plays as Caliban and Othello and was not a veteran, marched me up to my teacher one morning and said, "Can you tell me what's wrong with this kid?"

I thought Daphne and I might become friends, but I think she grew spooked by me whispering those lines to her, begging her to tell me what they meant, and I soon understood that two quiet people like us were better off quiet alone.

"Daphne? Didn't you hear them call you a nigger?" Arnetta asked, giving Daphne a nudge. 20

The sun was setting behind the trees, and their leafy tops formed a canopy of black lace for the flame of the sun to pass through. Daphne shrugged her shoulders at first, then slowly nodded her head when Arnetta gave her a hard look.

Twenty minutes later, when my restroom group returned to the cabin, Arnetta was still talking about Troop 909. My restroom group had passed by some of the 909 girls. For the most part, they deferred to us, waving us into the restrooms, letting us go even though they'd gotten there first.

We'd seen them, but from afar, never within their orbit enough to see whether their faces were the way all white girls appeared on TV—ponytailed and full of energy, bubbling over with love and money. All I could see was that some of them rapidly fanned their faces with their hands, though the heat of the day had long passed. A few seemed to be lolling their heads in slow circles, half purposefully, as if exercising the muscles of their necks, half ecstatically, like Stevie Wonder.

"We can't let them get away with that," Arnetta said, dropping her voice to a laryngitic whisper. "We can't let them get away with calling us niggers. I say we teach them a lesson." She sat down crosslegged on a sleeping bag, an embittered Buddha, eyes glimmering acrylic-black. "We can't go telling Mrs. Margolin, either. Mrs. Margolin'll say something about doing unto others and the path of righteousness and all. Forget that shit." She let her eyes flutter irreverently till they half closed, as though ignoring an insult not worth returning. We could all hear Mrs. Margolin outside, gathering the last of the metal campware.

Nobody said anything for a while. Usually people were quiet after Arnetta spoke. 25 Her tone had an upholstered confidence that was somehow both regal and vulgar at once. It demanded a few moments of silence in its wake, like the ringing of a church bell or the playing of taps. Sometimes Octavia would ditto or dissent to whatever Arnetta had said, and this was the signal that others could speak. But this time Octavia just swirled a long cord of hair into pretzel shapes.

"*Well?*" Arnetta said. She looked as if she had discerned the hidden severity of the situation and was waiting for the rest of us to catch up. Everyone looked from Arnetta to Daphne. It was, after all, Daphne who had supposedly been called the name, but Daphne sat on the bare cabin floor, flipping through the pages of the Girl Scout handbook, eyebrows arched in mock wonder, as if the handbook were a catalogue full of bright and startling foreign costumes. Janice broke the silence. She clapped her hands to broach her idea of a plan.

"They gone be sleeping," she whispered conspiratorially, "then we gone sneak into they cabin, then we'll put daddy longlegs in they sleeping bags. Then they'll wake up. Then we gone beat 'em up till they're as flat as frying pans!" She jammed her fist into the palm of her hand, then made a sizzling sound.

Janice's country accent was laughable, her looks homely, her jumpy acrobatics embarrassing to behold. Arnetta and Octavia volleyed amused, arrogant smiles whenever Janice opened her mouth, but Janice never caught the hint, spoke whenever she wanted, fluttered around Arnetta and Octavia futilely offering her opinions to their departing backs. Whenever Arnetta and Octavia shooed her away, Janice loitered until the two would finally sigh and ask, "What *is* it, Miss Caucausoid? What do you *want?*"

"Shut up, Janice," Octavia said, letting a fingered loop of hair fall to her waist as though just the sound of Janice's voice had ruined the fun of her hair twisting.

Janice obeyed, her mouth hung open in a loose grin, unflappable, unhurt. 30

"All right," Arnetta said, standing up. "We're going to have a secret meeting and talk about what we're going to do."

Everyone gravely nodded her head. The word "secret" had a built-in importance, the modifier form of the word carried more clout than the noun. A secret meant nothing; it was like gossip: just a bit of unpleasant knowledge about someone who happened to be someone other than yourself. A secret *meeting*, or a secret *club* was entirely different.

That was when Arnetta turned to me as though she knew that doing so was both a compliment and a charity.

"Snot, you're not going to be a bitch and tell Mrs. Margolin, are you?"

I had been called "Snot" ever since first grade, when I'd sneezed in class and two 35
long ropes of mucus had splattered a nearby girl.

"Hey," I said. "Maybe you didn't hear them right—I mean—"

"Are you gonna tell on us or not?" was all Arnetta wanted to know, and by the time the question was asked, the rest of our Brownie troop looked at me as though they'd already decided their course of action, me being the only impediment.

Camp Crescendo used to double as a high-school-band and field hockey camp until an arcing field hockey ball landed on the clasp of a girl's metal barrette, knifing a skull nerve and paralyzing the right side of her body. The camp closed down for a few years and the girl's teammates built a memorial, filling the spot on which the girl fell with hockey balls, on which they had painted—all in nail polish—get-well tidings, flowers, and hearts. The balls were still stacked there, like a shrine of ostrich eggs embedded in the ground.

On the second day of camp, Troop 909 was dancing around the mound of hockey balls, their limbs jangling awkwardly, their cries like the constant summer squeal of an amusement park. There was a stream that bordered the field hockey lawn, and the girls from my troop settled next to it, scarfing down the last of lunch: sandwiches made from salami and slices of tomato that had gotten waterlogged from the melting ice in the cooler. From the stream bank, Arnetta eyed the Troop 909 girls, scrutinizing their movements to glean inspiration for battle.

"Man," Arnetta said, "we could bumrush them right now if that damn lady 40
would *leave*."

The 909 troop leader was a white woman with the severe pageboy hairdo of an ancient Egyptian. She lay on a picnic blanket, sphinx-like, eating a banana, sometimes holding it out in front of her like a microphone. Beside her sat a girl slowly flapping one hand like a bird with a broken wing. Occasionally, the leader would call out the names of girls who'd attempted leapfrogs and flips, or of girls who yelled too loudly or strayed far from the circle.

"I'm just glad Big Fat Mama's not following us here," Octavia said. "At least we don't have to worry about her." Mrs. Margolin, Octavia assured us, was having her Afternoon Devotional, shrouded in mosquito netting, in a clearing she'd found. Mrs. Hedy was cleaning mud from her espadrilles in the cabin.

"I handled them." Arnetta sucked on her teeth and proudly grinned. "I told her we was going to gather leaves."

"Gather leaves," Octavia said, nodding respectfully. "That's a good one. Especially since they're so mad-crazy about this camping thing." She looked from ground to sky, sky to ground. Her hair hung down her back in two braids like a squaw's. "I mean, I really don't know why it's even called *camping*—all we ever do with Nature is find some twigs and say something like, 'Wow, this fell from a tree.'" She then studied her sandwich. With two disdainful fingers, she picked out a slice of dripping tomato, the sections congealed with red slime. She pitched it into the stream embrowned with dead leaves and the murky effigies of other dead things, but in the opaque water, a group of small silver-brown fish appeared. They surrounded the tomato and nibbled.

"Look!" Janice cried. "Fishes! Fishes!" As she scrambled to the edge of the stream to watch, a covey of insects threw up tantrums from the wheatgrass and nettle, a throng of tiny electric machines, all going at once. Octavia sneaked up behind Janice as if to push her in. Daphne and I exchanged terrified looks. It seemed as though only we knew that Octavia was close enough—and bold enough—to actually push Janice into the stream. Janice turned around quickly, but Octavia was already staring serenely into the still water as though she was gathering some sort of courage from it. "What's so funny?" Janice said, eyeing them all suspiciously.

Elise began humming the tune to "Karma Chameleon," all the girls joining in, their hums light and facile. Janice also began to hum, against everyone else, the high-octane opening chords of "Beat It."

"I love me some Michael Jackson," Janice said when she'd finished humming, smacking her lips as though Michael Jackson were a favorite meal. "I *will* marry Michael Jackson."

Before anyone had a chance to impress upon Janice the impossibility of this, Arnetta suddenly rose, made a sun visor of her hand, and watched Troop 909 leave the field hockey lawn.

"Dammit!" she said. "We've got to get them *alone*."

"They won't ever be alone," I said. All the rest of the girls looked at me, for I usually kept quiet. If I spoke even a word, I could count on someone calling me Snot. Everyone seemed to think that we could beat up these girls; no one entertained the thought that they might fight *back*. "The only time they'll be unsupervised is in the bathroom."

"Oh shut up, Snot," Octavia said.

But Arnetta slowly nodded her head. "The bathroom," she said. "The bathroom," she said, again and again. "The bathroom! The bathroom!"

According to Octavia's watch, it took us five minutes to hike to the restrooms, which were midway between our cabin and Troop 909's. Inside, the mirrors above the sinks returned only the vaguest of reflections, as though someone had taken a scouring pad to their surfaces to obscure the shine. Pine needles, leaves, and dirty, flattened wads of chewing gum covered the floor like a mosaic. Webs of hair matted the drain in the middle of the floor. Above the sinks and below the mirrors, stacks of folded white paper towels lay on a long metal counter. Shaggy white balls of paper towels sat on the sinktops in a line like corsages on display. A thread of floss snaked from a wad of tissues dotted with the faint red-pink of blood. One of those white girls, I thought, had just lost a tooth.

Though the restroom looked almost the same as it had the night before, it somehow seemed stranger now. We hadn't noticed the wooden rafters coming together in great V's. We were, it seemed, inside a whale, viewing the ribs of the roof of its mouth.

"Wow. It's a mess," Elise said.

"You can say that again."

Arnetta leaned against the doorjamb of a restroom stall. "This is where they'll be again," she said. Just seeing the place, just having a plan seemed to satisfy her. "We'll go in and talk to them. You know, 'How you doing? How long'll you be here?' That sort of thing. Then Octavia and I are gonna tell them what happens when they call any one of us a nigger."

"I'm going to say something, too," Janice said.

Arnetta considered this. "Sure," she said. "Of course. Whatever you want."

Janice pointed her finger like a gun at Octavia and rehearsed the line she'd   60
thought up, "'We're gonna teach you a *lesson*!' That's what I'm going to say." She
narrowed her eyes like a TV mobster. "'We're gonna teach you little girls a lesson!'"

With the back of her hand, Octavia brushed Janice's finger away. "You couldn't teach me to shit in a toilet."

"But," I said, "what if they say, 'We didn't say that? We didn't call anyone an N-I-G-G-E-R.'"

"Snot," Arnetta said, and then sighed. "Don't think. Just fight. If you even know how."

Everyone laughed except Daphne. Arnetta gently laid her hand on Daphne's shoulder. "Daphne. You don't have to fight. We're doing this for you."

Daphne walked to the counter, took a clean paper towel, and carefully unfolded   65
it like a map. With it, she began to pick up the trash all around. Everyone watched.

"C'mon," Arnetta said to everyone. "Let's beat it." We all ambled toward the doorway, where the sunshine made one large white rectangle of light. We were immediately blinded, and we shielded our eyes with our hands and our forearms.

"Daphne?" Arnetta asked. "Are you coming?"

We all looked back at the bending girl, the thin of her back hunched like the back of a custodian sweeping a stage, caught in limelight. Stray strands of her hair were lit near-transparent, thin fiber-optic threads. She did not nod yes to the question, nor did she shake her head no. She abided, bent. Then she began again, picking up leaves, wads of paper, the cotton fluff innards from a torn stuffed toy. She did it so methodically, so exquisitely, so humbly, she must have been trained. I thought of those dresses she wore, faded and old, yet so pressed and clean. I then saw the poverty in them; I then could imagine her mother, cleaning the houses of others, returning home, weary.

"I guess she's not coming."

We left her and headed back to our cabin, over pine needles and leaves, taking   70
the path full of shade.

"What about our secret meeting?" Elise asked.

Arnetta enunciated her words in a way that defied contradiction: "We just had it."

It was nearing our bedtime but the sun had not yet set.

"Hey, your mama's coming," Arnetta said to Octavia when she saw Mrs. Hedy walk toward the cabin, sniffling. When Octavia's mother wasn't giving bored, parochial orders, she sniffled continuously, mourning an imminent divorce from her husband. She might begin a sentence, "I don't know what Robert will do when Octavia and I are gone. Who'll buy him cigarettes?" and Octavia would hotly whisper, "*Mama*," in a way that meant: Please don't talk about our problems in front of everyone. Please shut up.

But when Mrs. Hedy began talking about her husband, thinking about her hus-   75
band, seeing clouds shaped like the head of her husband, she couldn't be quiet, and no one could dislodge her from the comfort of her own woe. Only one thing could perk her up—Brownie songs. If the girls were quiet, and Mrs. Hedy was in her dopey, sorrowful mood, she would say, "Y'all know I like those songs, girls. Why don't you

sing one?" Everyone would groan, except me and Daphne. I, for one, liked some of the songs.

"C'mon, everybody," Octavia said drearily. "She likes the Brownie song best."

We sang, loud enough to reach Mrs. Hedy:

"I've got something in my pocket;
It belongs across my face.
And I keep it very close at hand
    in a most convenient place.
I'm sure you couldn't guess it
If you guessed a long, long while.
So I'll take it out and put it on—
It's a great big Brownie smile!"

The Brownie song was supposed to be sung cheerfully, as though we were elves in a workshop, singing as we merrily cobbled shoes, but everyone except me hated the song so much that they sang it like a maudlin record, played on the most sluggish of rpms.

"That was good," Mrs. Hedy said, closing the cabin door behind her. "Wasn't that nice, Linda?"

"Praise God," Mrs. Margolin answered without raising her head from the chore   80
of counting out Popsicle sticks for the next day's craft session.

"Sing another one," Mrs. Hedy said. She said it with a sort of joyful aggression, like a drunk I'd once seen who'd refused to leave a Korean grocery.

"God, Mama, get over it," Octavia whispered in a voice meant only for Arnetta, but Mrs. Hedy heard it and started to leave the cabin.

"Don't go," Arnetta said. She ran after Mrs. Hedy and held her by the arm. "We haven't finished singing." She nudged us with a single look. "Let's sing the 'Friends Song.' For Mrs. Hedy."

Although I liked some of the songs, I hated this one:

Make new friends
But keep the o-old.
One is silver
And the other gold.

If most of the girls in the troop could be any type of metal, they'd be bunched-up   85
wads of tinfoil, maybe, or rusty iron nails you had to get tetanus shots for.

"No, no, no," Mrs. Margolin said before anybody could start in on the "Friends Song." "An uplifting song. Something to lift her up and take her mind off all these earthly burdens."

Arnetta and Octavia rolled their eyes. Everyone knew what song Mrs. Margolin was talking about, and no one, no one, wanted to sing it.

"Please, no," a voice called out. "Not 'The Doughnut Song.'"

"Please not 'The Doughnut Song,'" Octavia pleaded.

"I'll brush my teeth two times if I don't have to sing 'The Doughnut—'"   90

"Sing!" Mrs. Margolin demanded.

We sang:

"Life without Jesus is like a do-ough-nut!
Like a do-ooough-nut!
Like a do-ooough-nut!
Life without Jesus is like a do-ough-nut!
There's a hole in the middle of my soul!"

There were other verses, involving other pastries, but we stopped after the first one and cast glances toward Mrs. Margolin to see if we could gain a reprieve. Mrs. Margolin's eyes fluttered blissfully. She was half asleep.

"Awww," Mrs. Hedy said, as though giant Mrs. Margolin were a cute baby, "Mrs. Margolin's had a long day."

"Yes indeed," Mrs. Margolin answered. "If you don't mind, I might just go to the 95 lodge where the beds are. I haven't been the same since the operation."

I had not heard of this operation, or when it had occurred, since Mrs. Margolin had never missed the once-a-week Brownie meeting, but I could see from Daphne's face that she was concerned, and I could see that the other girls had decided that Mrs. Margolin's operation must have happened long ago in some remote time unconnected to our own. Nevertheless, they put on sad faces. We had all been taught that adulthood was full of sorrow and pain, taxes and bills, dreaded work and dealings with whites, sickness and death. I tried to do what the others did. I tried to look silent.

"Go right ahead, Linda," Mrs. Hedy said. "I'll watch the girls." Mrs. Hedy, seemed to forget about divorce for a moment; she looked at us with dewy eyes, as if we were mysterious, furry creatures. Meanwhile, Mrs. Margolin walked through the maze of sleeping bags until she found her own. She gathered a neat stack of clothes and pajamas slowly, as though doing so was almost painful. She took her toothbrush, her toothpaste, her pillow. "All right!" Mrs. Margolin said, addressing us all from the threshold of the cabin. "Be in bed by nine." She said it with a twinkle in her voice, letting us know she was allowing us to be naughty and stay up till nine-fifteen.

"C'mon, everybody," Arnetta said after Mrs. Margolin left. "Time for us to wash up."

Everyone watched Mrs. Hedy closely, wondering whether she would insist on coming with us since it was night, making a fight with Troop 909 nearly impossible. Troop 909 would soon be in the bathroom, washing their faces, brushing their teeth—completely unsuspecting of our ambush.

"We won't be long," Arnetta said. "We're old enough to go to the restrooms by 100 ourselves."

Mrs. Hedy pursed her lips at this dilemma. "Well, I guess you Brownies are almost Girl Scouts, right?"

"Right!"

"Just one more badge," Drema said.

"And about," Octavia droned, "a million more cookies to sell."

Octavia looked at all of us. *Now's our chance*, her face seemed to say, but our 105 chance to do *what*, I didn't exactly know.

Finally, Mrs. Hedy walked to the doorway where Octavia stood dutifully waiting to say goodbye but looking bored doing it. Mrs. Hedy held Octavia's chin. "You'll be good?"

"Yes, Mama."

"And remember to pray for me and your father? If I'm asleep when you get back?"

"Yes, Mama."

When the other girls had finished getting their toothbrushes and washcloths and   110
flashlights for the group restroom trip, I was drawing pictures of tiny birds with too
many feathers. Daphne was sitting on her sleeping bag, reading.

"You're not going to come?" Octavia asked.

Daphne shook her head.

"I'm gonna stay, too," I said. "I'll go to the restroom when Daphne and Mrs. Hedy go."

Arnetta leaned down toward me and whispered so that Mrs. Hedy, who had
taken over Mrs. Margolin's task of counting Popsicle sticks, couldn't hear. "No, Snot.
If we get in trouble, you're going to get in trouble with the rest of us."

We made our way through the darkness by flashlight. The tree branches that had   115
shaded us just hours earlier, along the same path, now looked like arms sprouting menacing hands. The stars sprinkled the sky like spilled salt. They seemed fastened to the
darkness, high up and holy, their places fixed and definite as we stirred beneath them.

Some, like me, were quiet because we were afraid of the dark; others were talking
like crazy for the same reason.

"Wow!" Drema said, looking up. "Why are all the stars out here? I never see stars
back on Oneida Street."

"It's a camping trip, that's why," Octavia said. "You're supposed to see stars on
camping trips."

Janice said, "This place smells like my mother's air freshener."

"These woods are *pine*," Elise said. "Your mother probably uses *pine* air freshener."   120

Janice mouthed an exaggerated "Oh," nodding her head as though she just then
understood one of the world's great secrets.

No one talked about fighting. Everyone was afraid enough just walking through
the infinite deep of the woods. Even though I didn't fight to fight, was afraid of fighting, I felt I was part of the rest of the troop; like I was defending something. We
trudged against the slight incline of the path, Arnetta leading the way.

"You know," I said, "their leader will be there. Or they won't even be there. It's
dark already. Last night the sun was still in the sky. I'm sure they're already finished."

Arnetta acted as if she hadn't heard me. I followed her gaze with my flashlight, and
that's when I saw the squares of light in the darkness. The bathroom was just ahead.

But the girls were there. We could hear them before we could see them.   125

"Octavia and I will go in first so they'll think that there's just two of us, then wait
till I say, 'We're gonna teach you a lesson,'" Arnetta said. "Then, bust in. That'll
surprise them."

"That's what I was supposed to say," Janice said.

Arnetta went inside, Octavia next to her. Janice followed, and the rest of us
waited outside.

They were in there for what seemed like whole minutes, but something was
wrong. Arnetta hadn't given the signal yet. I was with the girls outside when I heard
one of the Troop 909 girls say, "NO. That did NOT happen!"

That was to be expected, that they'd deny the whole thing. What I hadn't ex-   130
pected was *the voice* in which the denial was said. The girl sounded as though her
tongue were caught in her mouth. "That's a BAD word!" the girl continued. "We
don't say BAD words!"

"Let's go in," Elise said.

"No," Drema said, "I don't want to. What if we get beat up?"

"Snot?" Elise turned to me, her flashlight blinding. It was the first time anyone had asked my opinion, though I knew they were just asking because they were afraid.

"I say we go inside, just to see what's going on."

"But Arnetta didn't give us the signal," Drema said. "She's supposed to say, 135 'We're gonna teach you a lesson,' and I didn't hear her say it."

"C'mon," I said. "Let's just go in."

We went inside. There we found the white girls—about five girls huddled up next to one big girl. I instantly knew she was the owner of the voice we'd heard. Arnetta and Octavia inched toward us as soon as we entered.

"Where's Janice?" Elise asked, then we heard a flush. "Oh."

"I think," Octavia said, whispering to Elise, "they're retarded."

"We ARE NOT retarded!" the big girl said, though it was obvious that she was. 140 That they all were. The girls around her began to whimper.

"They're just pretending," Arnetta said, trying to convince herself. "I know they are."

Octavia turned to Arnetta. "Arnetta. Let's just leave."

Janice came out of a stall, happy and relieved, then she suddenly remembered her line, pointed to the big girl, and said, "We're gonna teach you a lesson."

"Shut up, Janice," Octavia said, but her heart was not in it. Arnetta's face was set in a lost, deep scowl. Octavia turned to the big girl and said loudly, slowly, as if they were all deaf, "We're going to leave. It was nice meeting you, O.K.? You don't have to tell anyone that we were here. O.K.?"

"Why not?" said the big girl, like a taunt. When she spoke, her lips did not meet, 145 her mouth did not close. Her tongue grazed the roof of her mouth, like a little pink fish. "You'll get in trouble. I know. *I* know."

Arnetta got back her old cunning. "If you said anything, then you'd be a tattletale."

The girl looked sad for a moment, and then perked up quickly. A flash of genius crossed her face. "I *like* tattletale."

"It's all right, girls. It's gonna be all right!" the 909 troop leader said. All of Troop 909 burst into tears. It was as though someone had instructed them all to cry at once. The troop leader had girls under her arm, and all the rest of the girls crowded around her. It reminded me of a hog I'd seen on a field trip, where all the little hogs gathered about the mother at feeding time, latching onto her teats. The 909 troop leader had come into the bathroom, shortly after the big girl had threatened to tell. Then the ranger came, then, once the ranger had radioed the station, Mrs. Margolin arrived with Daphne in tow.

The ranger had left the restroom area, but everybody else was huddled just outside, swatting mosquitoes.

"Oh. They *will* apologize," Mrs. Margolin said to the 909 troop leader, but she 150 said this so angrily, I knew she was speaking more to us than to the other troop leader. "When their parents find out, every one a them will be on punishment."

"It's all right, it's all right," the 909 troop leader reassured Mrs. Margolin. Her voice lilted in the same way it had when addressing the girls. She smiled the whole time she talked. She was like one of those TV-cooking-show women who talk and dice onions and smile all at the same time.

"See. It could have happened. I'm not calling your girls fibbers or anything." She shook her head ferociously from side to side, her Egyptian-style pageboy flapping against her cheeks like heavy drapes. "It *could* have happened. See. Our girls are *not* retarded. They are *delayed* learners." She said this in a syrupy instructional voice, as though our troop might be delayed learners as well. "We're from the Decatur Children's Academy. Many of them just have special needs."

"Now we won't be able to walk to the bathroom by ourselves!" the big girl said.

"Yes you will," the troop leader said, "but maybe we'll wait till we get back to Decatur—"

"I don't want to wait!" the girl said. "I want my Independence badge!"   155

The girls in my troop were entirely speechless. Arnetta looked stoic, as though she were soon to be tortured but was determined not to appear weak. Mrs. Margolin pursed her lips solemnly and said, "Bless them, Lord. Bless them."

In contrast, the Troop 909 leader was full of words and energy. "Some of our girls are echolalic—" She smiled and happily presented one of the girls hanging onto her, but the girl widened her eyes in horror, and violently withdrew herself from the center of attention, sensing she was being sacrificed for the village sins. "Echolalic," the troop leader continued. "That means they will say whatever they hear, like an echo—that's where the word comes from. It comes from 'echo.'" She ducked her head apologetically. "I mean, not all of them have the most *progressive* of parents, so if they heard a bad word, they might have repeated it. But I guarantee it would not have been *intentional*."

Arnetta spoke. "I saw her say the word. I heard her." She pointed to a small girl, smaller than any of us, wearing an oversized T-shirt that read, "Eat Bertha's Mussels."

The troop leader shook her head and smiled, "That's impossible. She doesn't speak. She can, but she doesn't."

Arnetta furrowed her brow. "No. It wasn't her. That's right. It was *her*."   160

The girl Arnetta pointed to grinned as though she'd been paid a compliment. She was the only one from either troop actually wearing a full uniform: The mocha-colored A-line shift, the orange ascot, the sash covered with badges, though all the same one— the Try-It patch. She took a few steps toward Arnetta and made a grand sweeping gesture toward the sash. "See," she said, full of self-importance, "I'm a Brownie." I had a hard time imagining this girl calling anyone a "nigger"; the girl looked perpetually delighted, as though she would have cuddled up with a grizzly if someone had let her.

On the fourth morning, we boarded the bus to go home.

The previous day had been spent building miniature churches from Popsicle sticks. We hardly left the cabin. Mrs. Margolin and Mrs. Hedy guarded us so closely, almost no one talked for the entire day.

Even on the day of departure from Camp Crescendo, all was serious and silent. The bus ride began quietly enough. Arnetta had to sit beside Mrs. Margolin; Octavia had to sit beside her mother. I sat beside Daphne, who gave me her prize journal without a word of explanation.

"You don't want it?"   165

She shook her head no. It was empty.

Then Mrs. Hedy began to weep. "Octavia," Mrs. Hedy said to her daughter without looking at her, "I'm going to sit with Mrs. Margolin. All right?"

Arnetta exchanged seats with Mrs. Hedy. With the two women up front, Elise felt it safe to speak. "Hey," she said, then she set her face into a placid, vacant stare, trying to imitate that of a Troop 909 girl. Emboldened, Arnetta made a gesture of mock pride toward an imaginary sash, the way the girl in full uniform had done. Then they all made a game of it, trying to do the most exaggerated imitations of the Troop 909 girls, all without speaking, all without laughing loud enough to catch the women's attention.

Daphne looked down at her shoes, white with sneaker polish. I opened the journal she'd given me. I looked out the window, trying to decide what to write, searching for lines, but nothing could compare with what Daphne had written, "My *father, the veteran,*" my favorite line of all time. It replayed itself in my head, and I gave up trying to write.

By then, it seemed that the rest of the troop had given up making fun of the girls   170 in Troop 909. They were now quietly gossiping about who had passed notes to whom in school. For a moment the gossiping fell off, and all I heard was the hum of the bus as we sped down the road and the muffled sounds of Mrs. Hedy and Mrs. Margolin talking about serious things.

"You know," Octavia whispered, "why did *we* have to be stuck at a camp with retarded girls? You know?"

"*You* know why," Arnetta answered. She narrowed her eyes like a cat. "My mama and I were in the mall in Buckhead, and this white lady just kept looking at us. I mean, like we were foreign or something. Like we were from China."

"What did the woman say?" Elise asked.

"Nothing," Arnetta said. "She didn't say nothing."

A few girls quietly nodded their heads.   175

"There was this time," I said, "when my father and I were in the mall and—"

"Oh shut up, Snot," Octavia said.

I stared at Octavia, then rolled my eyes from her to the window. As I watched the trees blur, I wanted nothing more than to be through with it all: the bus ride, the troop, school—all of it. But we were going home. I'd see the same girls in school the next day. We were on a bus, and there was nowhere else to go.

"Go on, Laurel," Daphne said to me. It seemed like the first time she'd spoken the whole trip, and she'd said my name. I turned to her and smiled weakly so as not to cry, hoping she'd remember when I'd tried to be her friend, thinking maybe that her gift of the journal was an invitation of friendship. But she didn't smile back. All she said was, "What happened?"

I studied the girls, waiting for Octavia to tell me to shut up again before I even   180 had a chance to utter another word, but everyone was amazed that Daphne had spoken. The bus was silent. I gathered my voice. "Well," I said. "My father and I were in this mall, but *I* was the one doing the staring." I stopped and glanced from face to face. I continued. "There were these white people dressed like Puritans or something, but they weren't Puritans. They were Mennonites.° They're these people who, if you ask them to do a favor, like paint your porch or something, they have to do it. It's in their rules."

"That sucks," someone said.

"C'mon," Arnetta said. "You're lying."

"I am not."

"How do you know that's not just some story someone made up?" Elise asked, her head cocked full of daring. "I mean, who's gonna do whatever you ask?"

Mennonites: Highly traditional Christian denomination whose core beliefs include nonviolence and peace. Some sects incorporate very simple living and separation from the modern world—including old-fashioned dress.

"It is not made up. I know because when I was looking at them, my father said, 185
'See those people? If you ask them to do something, they'll do it. Anything you want.'"

No one would call anyone's father a liar—then they'd have to fight the person.
But Drema parsed her words carefully. "How does your *father* know that's not just
some story? Huh?"

"Because," I said, "he went up to the man and asked him would he paint our
porch, and the man said yes. It's their religion."

"Man, I'm glad I'm a Baptist," Elise said, shaking her head in sympathy for the
Mennonites.

"So did the guy do it?" Drema asked, scooting closer to hear if the story got juicy.

"Yeah," I said. "His whole family was with him. My dad drove them to our house. 190
They all painted our porch. The woman and girl were in bonnets and long, long
skirts with buttons up to their necks. The guy wore this weird hat and these huge
suspenders."

"Why," Arnetta asked archly, as though she didn't believe a word, "would someone pick a *porch*? If they'll do anything, why not make them paint the whole *house*?
Why not ask for a hundred bucks?"

I thought about it, and then remembered the words my father had said about
them painting our porch, though I had never seemed to think about his words after
he'd said them.

"He said," I began, only then understanding the words as they uncoiled from my
mouth, "it was the only time he'd have a white man on his knees doing something for
a black man for free."

I now understand what he meant, and why he did it, though I didn't like it.
When you've been made to feel bad for so long, you jump at the chance to do it to
others. I remembered the Mennonites bending the way Daphne had bent when she
was cleaning the restroom. I remembered the dark blue of their bonnets, the black of
their shoes. They painted the porch as though scrubbing a floor. I was already trembling before Daphne asked quietly, "Did he thank them?"

I looked out the window. I could not tell which were the thoughts and which 195
were the trees. "No," I said, and suddenly knew there was something mean in the
world that I could not stop.

Arnetta laughed. "If I asked them to take off their long skirts and bonnets and
put on some jeans, would they do it?"

And Daphne's voice, quiet, steady: "Maybe they would. Just to be nice."

Questions

1. What is the effect of having Laurel (nicknamed "Snot") narrate the story?
2. How does the setting of the story affect the action? How is the Brownie camp different
   from the girls' everyday world?
3. What is Laurel's opinion of Arnetta? Does it change in the course of the story?
4. How does the narrator initially view the white Brownie troop? Does her background
   influence her initial perspective? Consult the text for examples.
5. Much of "Brownies" is very funny. What role does humor have in the story?
6. What realization does the narrator have at the end of the story? How does this change her
   understanding of her father and of racial dynamics more generally?
7. What does this story suggest about racial stereotyping?

Edgar Allan Poe

The Tell-Tale Heart

(1843) 1850

Edgar Allan Poe

Edgar Poe was born in Boston in January 1809, the second son of actors Eliza and David Poe. Edgar inherited his family's legacy of artistic talent, financial instability, and social inferiority (actors were not considered respectable in the nineteenth century), as well as his father's problems with alcohol. David Poe abandoned his family after the birth of Edgar's little sister, Rosalie, and Eliza died of tuberculosis in a Richmond, Virginia, boarding-house before Edgar turned three. He was taken in by the wealthy John and Frances Allan of Richmond, whose name he added to his own. Allan educated Poe at first-rate schools, where he excelled in all subjects. But he grew into a moody adolescent, and his relationship with his foster father deteriorated.

Poe's first year at the University of Virginia was marked by scholastic success, alcoholic binges, and gambling debts. Disgraced, he fled to Boston and joined the army under the name Edgar Perry. He performed well as an enlisted man and published his first collection of poetry, Tamerlane and Other Poems, *at the age of eighteen. After an abortive stint at West Point led to a final break with Allan, Poe embarked on a full-time literary career. A respected critic and editor, he sharply improved both the content and circulation of every magazine with which he was associated. But, morbidly sensitive to criticism, paranoid and belligerent when drunk, he left or was fired from every post he held. Poorly paid as both an editor and a writer, he earned almost nothing from the works that made him famous, such as "The Fall of the House of Usher" and "The Raven."*

After the break with his foster family, Poe rediscovered his own. From 1831, he lived with his father's widowed sister, Maria Clemm, and her daughter, Virginia. In 1836 Poe married this thirteen-year-old first cousin. These women provided him with much-needed emotional stability. However, like his mother, Poe's wife died of tuberculosis at age twenty-four, her demise doubtless hastened by poverty. Afterward, Poe's life came apart; his drinking intensified, as did his self-destructive tendencies. In October 1849 he died in mysterious circumstances, a few days after being found sick and incoherent on a Baltimore street.

True!—nervous—very, very dreadfully nervous I had been and am; but why *will* you say that I am mad? The disease had sharpened my senses—not destroyed—not dulled them. Above all was the sense of hearing acute. I heard all things in the heaven and in the earth. I heard many things in hell. How, then, am I mad? Hearken! and observe how healthily—how calmly, I can tell you the whole story.

It is impossible to say how first the idea entered my brain; but once conceived, it haunted me day and night. Object there was none. Passion there was none. I loved the old man. He had never wronged me. He had never given me insult. For his gold I had no desire. I think it was his eye! yes, it was this! One of his eyes resembled that of a vulture—a pale blue eye, with a film over it. Whenever it fell upon me, my blood ran cold; and so by degrees—very gradually—I made up my mind to take the life of the old man, and thus rid myself of the eye forever.

Now this is the point. You fancy me mad. Madmen know nothing. But you should have seen *me*. You should have seen how wisely I proceeded—with what caution—with what foresight—with what dissimulation I went to work! I was never kinder to the old man than during the whole week before I killed him. And every night, about midnight, I turned the latch of his door and opened it—oh, so gently! And then, when I had made an opening sufficient for my head, I put in a dark lantern, all closed, closed, so that no light shone out, and then I thrust in my head. Oh, you would have laughed to see how cunningly I thrust it in! I moved it slowly— very, very slowly, so that I might not disturb the old man's sleep. It took me an hour to place my whole head within the opening so far that I could see him as he lay upon his bed. Ha!—would a madman have been so wise as this? And then, when my head was well in the room, I undid the lantern cautiously—oh, so cautiously—cautiously (for the hinges creaked)—I undid it just so much that a single thin ray fell upon the vulture eye. And this I did for seven long nights—every night just at midnight—but I found the eye always closed; and so it was impossible to do the work; for it was not the old man who vexed me, but his Evil Eye. And every morning, when the day broke, I went boldly into the chamber, and spoke courageously to him, calling him by name in a hearty tone, and inquiring how he had passed the night. So you see he would have been a very profound old man, indeed, to suspect that every night, just at twelve, I looked in upon him while he slept.

Upon the eighth night I was more than usually cautious in opening the door. A watch's minute hand moves more quickly than did mine. Never before that night had I *felt* the extent of my own powers—of my sagacity. I could scarcely contain my feelings of triumph. To think that there I was, opening the door, little by little, and he not even to dream of my secret deeds or thoughts. I fairly chuckled at the idea; and perhaps he heard me; for he moved on the bed suddenly, as if startled. Now you may think that I drew back—but no. His room was as black as pitch with the thick darkness (for the shutters were close fastened, through fear of robbers), and so I knew that he could not see the opening of the door, and I kept pushing it on steadily, steadily.

I had my head in, and was about to open the lantern, when my thumb slipped upon the tin fastening, and the old man sprang up in the bed, crying out—"Who's there?"

I kept quite still and said nothing. For a whole hour I did not move a muscle, and in the meantime I did not hear him lie down. He was still sitting up in the bed, listening;—just as I have done, night after night, hearkening to the death watches° in the wall.

Presently I heard a slight groan, and I knew it was the groan of mortal terror. It was not a groan of pain or of grief—oh, no!—it was the low stifled sound that arises from the bottom of the soul when overcharged with awe. I knew the sound very well. Many a night, just at midnight, when all the world slept, it has welled up from my own bosom, deepening, with its dreadful echo, the terrors that distracted me. I say I knew it well. I knew what the old man felt, and pitied him, although I chuckled at heart. I knew that he had been lying awake ever since the first slight noise, when he had turned in the bed. His fears had been ever since growing upon him. He had been trying to fancy them causeless, but could not. He had been saying to himself—"It is nothing but the wind in the chimney—it is only a mouse crossing the floor," or "it is merely a cricket which has made a single chirp." Yes, he had been trying to comfort himself with these suppositions;

death watches: beetles that infest timbers. Their clicking sound was thought to be an omen of death.

but he had found all in vain. *All in vain*; because Death, in approaching him, had stalked with his black shadow before him, and enveloped the victim. And it was the mournful influence of the unperceived shadow that caused him to feel—although he neither saw nor heard—to *feel* the presence of my head within the room.

When I had waited a long time, very patiently, without hearing him lie down, I resolved to open a little—a very, very little crevice in the lantern. So I opened it—you cannot imagine how stealthily, stealthily—until, at length, a single dim ray, like the thread of the spider, shot from out of the crevice and fell upon the vulture eye.

It was open—wide, wide open—and I grew furious as I gazed upon it. I saw it with perfect distinctness—all a dull blue, with a hideous veil over it that chilled the very marrow in my bones; but I could see nothing else of the old man's face or person: for I had directed the ray as if by instinct, precisely upon the damned spot.

And now have I not told you that what you mistake for madness is but over-acuteness of the senses?—now, I say, there came to my ears a low, dull, quick sound, such as a watch makes when enveloped in cotton. I knew *that* sound well, too. It was the beating of the old man's heart. It increased my fury, as the beating of a drum stimulates the soldier into courage.

But even yet I refrained and kept still. I scarcely breathed. I held the lantern motionless. I tried how steadily I could maintain the ray upon the eye. Meantime the hellish tattoo of the heart increased. It grew quicker and quicker, and louder and louder every instant. The old man's terror *must* have been extreme! It grew louder, I say, louder every moment!—do you mark me well? I have told you that I am nervous: so I am. And now at the dead hour of the night, amid the dreadful silence of that old house, so strange a noise as this excited me to uncontrollable terror. Yet, for some minutes longer I refrained and stood still. But the beating grew louder, louder! I thought the heart must burst. And now a new anxiety seized me—the sound would be heard by a neighbor! The old man's hour had come! With a loud yell, I threw open the lantern and leaped into the room. He shrieked once—once only. In an instant I dragged him to the floor, and pulled the heavy bed over him. I then smiled gaily, to find the deed so far done. But, for many minutes, the heart beat on with a muffled sound. This, however, did not vex me; it would not be heard through the wall. At length it ceased. The old man was dead. I removed the bed and examined the corpse. Yes, he was stone, stone dead. I placed my hand upon the heart and held it there many minutes.

If still you think me mad, you will think so no longer when I describe the wise precautions I took for the concealment of the body. The night waned, and I worked hastily, but in silence. First of all I dismembered the corpse. I cut off the head and the arms and the legs.

I then took up three planks from the flooring of the chamber, and deposited all between the scantlings. I then replaced the boards so cleverly, so cunningly, that no human eye—not even *his*—could have detected anything wrong. There was nothing to wash out—no stain of any kind—no blood-spot whatever. I had been too wary for that. A tub had caught all—ha! ha!

When I had made an end of these labors, it was four o'clock—still dark as midnight. As the bell sounded the hour, there came a knocking at the street door. I went down to open it with a light heart,—for what had I *now* to fear? There entered three men, who introduced themselves, with perfect suavity, as officers of the police. A shriek had been heard by a neighbor during the night; suspicion of foul play had been

10

aroused, information had been lodged at the police office, and they (the officers) had been deputed to search the premises.

I smiled,—for *what* had I to fear? I bade the gentlemen welcome. The shriek, I said, was my own in a dream. The old man, I mentioned, was absent in the country. I took my visitors all over the house. I bade them search—search *well*. I led them, at length, to *his* chamber. I showed them his treasures, secure, undisturbed. In the enthusiasm of my confidence, I brought chairs into the room, and desired them *here* to rest from their fatigues, while I myself, in the wild audacity of my perfect triumph, placed my own seat upon the very spot beneath which reposed the corpse of the victim.

The officers were satisfied. My *manner* had convinced them. I was singularly at ease. They sat, and while I answered cheerily, they chatted of familiar things. But, ere long, I felt myself getting pale and wished them gone. My head ached, and I fancied a ringing in my ears: but still they sat and still they chatted. The ringing became more distinct:—it continued and became more distinct: I talked more freely to get rid of the feeling: but it continued and gained definitiveness—until, at length, I found that the noise was *not* within my ears.

No doubt I now grew *very* pale:—but I talked more fluently, and with a heightened voice. Yet the sound increased—and what could I do? It was a *low, dull, quick sound—much such a sound as a watch makes when enveloped in cotton.* I gasped for breath—and yet the officers heard it not. I talked more quickly—more vehemently; but the noise steadily increased. I arose and argued about trifles, in a high key and with violent gesticulations; but the noise steadily increased. Why *would* they not be gone? I paced the floor to and fro with heavy strides, as if excited to fury by the observations of the men—but the noise steadily increased. Oh God! what *could* I do? I foamed—I raved—I swore! I swung the chair upon which I had been sitting, and grated it upon the boards, but the noise arose over all and continually increased. It grew louder—louder—*louder!* And still the men chatted pleasantly, and smiled. Was it possible they heard not? Almighty God!—no, no! They heard!—they suspected!—they *knew!*—they were making a mockery of my horror!—this I thought, and this I think. But anything was better than this agony! Anything was more tolerable than this derision! I could bear those hypocritical smiles no longer! I felt that I must scream or die!—and now—again!—hark! louder! louder! louder! *louder!*—

"Villains!" I shrieked, "dissemble no more! I admit the deed!—tear up the planks!—here, here!—it is the beating of his hideous heart!"

Questions

1. From what point of view is Poe's story told? Why is this point of view particularly effective for "The Tell-Tale Heart"?
2. Point to details in the story that identify its speaker as an unreliable narrator.
3. What do we know about the old man in the story? What motivates the narrator to kill him?
4. In spite of all his precautions, the narrator does not commit the perfect crime. What trips him up?
5. How do you account for the police officers' chatting calmly with the murderer instead of reacting to the sound that stirs the murderer into a frenzy?
6. See the student essays on this story in the chapter "Writing About a Story" later in the book. What do they point out that enlarges your own appreciation of Poe's art?

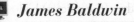

James Baldwin

Sonny's Blues   1957

James Baldwin (1924–1987) was born in Harlem, in New York City. His father was a
Pentecostal minister, and the young Baldwin initially planned to become a clergyman. While
still in high school, he preached sermons in a storefront church. At seventeen, however, he
left home to live in Greenwich Village, where he worked at menial jobs and began publishing
articles in Commentary *and the* Nation. *Later he embarked on a series of travels that even-*
tually brought him to France. Baldwin soon regarded France as a second home, a country in
which he could avoid the racial discrimination he felt in America. His first novel, Go Tell It
on the Mountain *(1953), which described a single day in the lives of the members of a*
Harlem church, immediately earned him a position as a leading African American writer.
His next two novels, Giovanni's Room *(1956) and* Another Country *(1962), dealt with*
homosexual themes and drew criticism from some of his early champions. His collection of
essays Notes of a Native Son *(1955) remains one of the key books of the civil rights move-*
ment. His short stories were not collected until Going to Meet the Man *was published in*
1965. Although he spent nearly forty years in France, Baldwin still considered himself an
American. He was not an expatriate, he claimed, but a "commuter." He died in St. Paul de
Vence, France, but was buried in Ardsley, New York.

I read about it in the paper, in the subway, on my way to work. I read it, and I
couldn't believe it, and I read it again. Then perhaps I just stared at it, at the
newsprint spelling out his name, spelling out the story. I stared at it in the swinging
lights of the subway car, and in the faces and bodies of the people, and in my own
face, trapped in the darkness which roared outside.

It was not to be believed and I kept telling myself that, as I walked from the subway
station to the high school. And at the same time I couldn't doubt it. I was scared, scared
for Sonny. He became real to me again. A great block of ice got settled in my belly and
kept melting there slowly all day long, while I taught my classes algebra. It was a special
kind of ice. It kept melting, sending trickles of ice water all up and down my veins, but it
never got less. Sometimes it hardened and seemed to expand until I felt my guts were going to come spilling out or that I was going to choke or scream. This would always be at
a moment when I was remembering some specific thing Sonny had once said or done.

When he was about as old as the boys in my classes his face had been bright and
open, there was a lot of copper in it; and he'd had wonderfully direct brown eyes, and
great gentleness and privacy. I wondered what he looked like now. He had been
picked up, the evening before, in a raid on an apartment downtown, for peddling and
using heroin.

I couldn't believe it: but what I mean by that is that I couldn't find any room for
it anywhere inside me. I had kept it outside me for a long time. I hadn't wanted to
know. I had had suspicions, but I didn't name them, I kept putting them away. I told
myself that Sonny was wild, but he wasn't crazy. And he'd always been a good boy, he
hadn't ever turned hard or evil or disrespectful, the way kids can, so quick, so quick,
especially in Harlem. I didn't want to believe that I'd ever see my brother going
down, coming to nothing, all that light in his face gone out, in the condition I'd already seen so many others. Yet it had happened and here I was, talking about algebra
to a lot of boys who might, every one of them for all I knew, be popping off needles
every time they went to the head. Maybe it did more for them than algebra could.

I was sure that the first time Sonny had ever had horse,° he couldn't have been   5
much older than these boys were now. These boys, now, were living as we'd been living then, they were growing up with a rush and their heads bumped abruptly against
the low ceiling of their actual possibilities. They were filled with rage. All they really
knew were two darknesses, the darkness of their lives, which was now closing in on
them, and the darkness of the movies, which had blinded them to that other darkness, and in which they now, vindictively, dreamed, at once more together than they
were at any other time, and more alone.

When the last bell rang, the last class ended, I let out my breath. It seemed I'd
been holding it for all that time. My clothes were wet—I may have looked as though
I'd been sitting in a steam bath, all dressed up, all afternoon. I sat alone in the classroom a long time. I listened to the boys outside, downstairs, shouting and cursing and
laughing. Their laughter struck me for perhaps the first time. It was not the joyous
laughter which—God knows why—one associates with children. It was mocking and
insular, its intent to denigrate. It was disenchanted, and in this, also, lay the authority of their curses. Perhaps I was listening to them because I was thinking about my
brother and in them I heard my brother. And myself.

One boy was whistling a tune, at once very complicated and very simple, it
seemed to be pouring out of him as though he were a bird, and it sounded very cool
and moving through all that harsh, bright air, only just holding its own through all
those other sounds.

I stood up and walked over to the window and looked down into the courtyard.
It was the beginning of the spring and the sap was rising in the boys. A teacher passed
through them every now and again, quickly, as though he or she couldn't wait to get
out of that courtyard, to get those boys out of their sight and off their minds. I started
collecting my stuff. I thought I'd better get home and talk to Isabel.

The courtyard was almost deserted by the time I got downstairs. I saw this boy
standing in the shadow of a doorway, looking just like Sonny. I almost called his
name. Then I saw that it wasn't Sonny, but somebody we used to know, a boy from
around our block. He'd been Sonny's friend. He'd never been mine, having been too
young for me, and, anyway, I'd never liked him. And now, even though he was a
grown-up man, he still hung around that block, still spent hours on the street corners, was always high and raggy. I used to run into him from time to time and he'd often work around to asking me for a quarter or fifty cents. He always had some real
good excuse, too, and I always gave it to him, I don't know why.

But now, abruptly, I hated him. I couldn't stand the way he looked at me,   10
partly like a dog, partly like a cunning child. I wanted to ask him what the hell he
was doing in the school courtyard.

He sort of shuffled over to me, and he said, "I see you got the papers. So you
already know about it."

"You mean about Sonny? Yes, I already know about it. How come they didn't get
you?"

He grinned. It made him repulsive and it also brought to mind what he'd looked
like as a kid. "I wasn't there. I stay away from them people."

"Good for you." I offered him a cigarette and I watched him through the smoke.
"You come all the way down here just to tell me about Sonny?"

horse: heroin.

"That's right." He was sort of shaking his head and his eyes looked strange, as   15
though they were about to cross. The bright sun deadened his damp dark brown skin
and it made his eyes look yellow and showed up the dirt in his kinked hair. He
smelled funky. I moved a little away from him and I said, "Well, thanks. But I already
know about it and I got to get home."

"I'll walk you a little ways," he said. We started walking. There were a couple of
kids still loitering in the courtyard and one of them said goodnight to me and looked
strangely at the boy beside me.

"What're you going to do?" he asked me. "I mean, about Sonny?"

"Look. I haven't seen Sonny for over a year. I'm not sure I'm going to do anything. Anyway, what the hell *can* I do?"

"That's right," he said quickly, "ain't nothing you can do. Can't much help old
Sonny no more, I guess."

It was what I was thinking and so it seemed to me he had no right to say it.   20

"I'm surprised at Sonny, though," he went on—he had a funny way of talking, he
looked straight ahead as though he were talking to himself—"I thought Sonny was a
smart boy, I thought he was too smart to get hung."

"I guess he thought so too," I said sharply, "and that's how he got hung. And how
about you? You're pretty goddamn smart, I bet."

Then he looked directly at me, just for a minute. "I ain't smart," he said. "If I was
smart, I'd have reached for a pistol a long time ago."

"Look. Don't tell *me* your sad story, if it was up to me, I'd give you one." Then I felt
guilty—guilty, probably, for never having supposed that the poor bastard *had* a story of his
own, much less a sad one, and I asked, quickly, "What's going to happen to him now?"

He didn't answer this. He was off by himself some place. "Funny thing," he said,   25
and from his tone we might have been discussing the quickest way to get to Brooklyn,
"when I saw the papers this morning, the first thing I asked myself was if I had anything to do with it. I felt sort of responsible."

I began to listen more carefully. The subway station was on the corner, just before us, and I stopped. He stopped, too. We were in front of a bar and he ducked
slightly, peering in, but whoever he was looking for didn't seem to be there. The juke
box was blasting away with something black and bouncy and I half watched the barmaid as she danced her way from the juke box to her place behind the bar. And I
watched her face as she laughingly responded to something someone said to her, still
keeping time to the music. When she smiled one saw the little girl, one sensed the
doomed, still-struggling woman beneath the battered face of the semiwhore.

"I never *give* Sonny nothing," the boy said finally, "but a long time ago I come to
school high and Sonny asked me how it felt." He paused, I couldn't bear to watch
him, I watched the barmaid, and I listened to the music which seemed to be causing
the pavement to shake. "I told him it felt great." The music stopped, the barmaid
paused and watched the juke box until the music began again. "It did."

All this was carrying me some place I didn't want to go. I certainly didn't want to
know how it felt. It filled everything, the people, the houses, the music, the dark,
quicksilver barmaid, with menace; and this menace was their reality.

"What's going to happen to him now?" I asked again.

"They'll send him away some place and they'll try to cure him." He shook his   30
head. "Maybe he'll even think he's kicked the habit. Then they'll let him loose"—he
gestured, throwing his cigarette into the gutter. "That's all."

"What do you mean, that's *all?*"

But I knew what he meant.

"I *mean,* that's *all.*" He turned his head and looked at me, pulling down the corners of his mouth. "Don't you know what I mean?" he asked, softly.

"How the hell *would* I know what you mean?" I almost whispered it, I don't know why.

"That's right," he said to the air, "how would *he* know what I mean?" He turned toward me again, patient and calm, and yet I somehow felt him shaking, shaking as though he were going to fall apart. I felt that ice in my guts again, the dread I'd felt all afternoon; and again I watched the barmaid, moving about the bar, washing glasses, and singing. "Listen. They'll let him out and then it'll just start all over again. That's what I mean."

"You mean—they'll let him out. And then he'll just start working his way back in again. You mean he'll never kick the habit. Is that what you mean?"

"That's right," he said, cheerfully. "*You* see what I mean."

"Tell me," I said at last, "why does he want to die? He must want to die, he's killing himself, why does he want to die?"

He looked at me in surprise. He licked his lips. "He don't want to die. He wants to live. Don't nobody want to die, ever."

Then I wanted to ask him—too many things. He could not have answered, or if he had, I could not have borne the answers. I started walking. "Well, I guess it's none of my business."

"It's going to be rough on old Sonny," he said. We reached the subway station. "This is your station?" he asked. I nodded. I took one step down. "Damn!" he said, suddenly. I looked up at him. He grinned again. "Damn it if I didn't leave all my money home. You ain't got a dollar on you, have you? Just for a couple of days, is all."

All at once something inside gave and threatened to come pouring out of me. I didn't hate him any more. I felt that in another moment I'd start crying like a child.

"Sure," I said. "Don't sweat." I looked in my wallet and didn't have a dollar, I only had a five. "Here," I said. "That hold you?"

He didn't look at it—he didn't want to look at it. A terrible closed look came over his face, as though he were keeping the number on the bill a secret from him and me. "Thanks," he said, and now he was dying to see me go. "Don't worry about Sonny. Maybe I'll write him or something."

"Sure," I said. "You do that. So long."

"Be seeing you," he said. I went on down the steps.

And I didn't write Sonny or send him anything for a long time. When I finally did, it was just after my little girl died, he wrote me back a letter which made me feel like a bastard.

Here's what he said:

Dear brother,

You don't know how much I needed to hear from you. I wanted to write you many a time but I dug how much I must have hurt you and so I didn't write. But now I feel like a man who's been trying to climb up out of some deep, real deep and funky hole and just saw the sun up there, outside. I got to get outside.

I can't tell you much about how I got here. I mean I don't know how to tell you. I guess I was afraid of something or I was trying to escape from something and you know I have never been very strong in the head (smile). I'm glad Mama and Daddy are dead and can't see what's happened to their son and I swear if I'd known what I was doing I would never have hurt you so, you and a lot of other fine people who were nice to me and who believed in me.

I don't want you to think it had anything to do with me being a musician. It's more than that. Or maybe less than that. I can't get anything straight in my head down here and I try not to think about what's going to happen to me when I get outside again. Sometime I think I'm going to flip and *never* get outside and sometime I think I'll come straight back. I tell you one thing, though, I'd rather blow my brains out than go through this again. But that's what they all say, so they tell me. If I tell you when I'm coming to New York and if you could meet me, I sure would appreciate it. Give my love to Isabel and the kids and I was sure sorry to hear about little Gracie. I wish I could be like Mama and say the Lord's will be done, but I don't know it seems to me that trouble is the one thing that never does get stopped and I don't know what good it does to blame it on the Lord. But maybe it does some good if you believe it.

> Your brother,
> Sonny

Then I kept in constant touch with him and I sent him whatever I could and I went to meet him when he came back to New York. When I saw him many things I thought I had forgotten came flooding back to me. This was because I had begun, finally, to wonder about Sonny, about the life that Sonny lived inside. This life, whatever it was, had made him older and thinner and it had deepened the distant stillness in which he had always moved. He looked very unlike my baby brother. Yet, when he smiled, when we shook hands, the baby brother I'd never known looked out from the depths of his private life, like an animal waiting to be coaxed into the light.

"How you been keeping?" he asked me.   50

"All right. And you?"

"Just fine." He was smiling all over his face. "It's good to see you again."

"It's good to see you."

The seven years' difference in our ages lay between us like a chasm: I wondered if these years would ever operate between us as a bridge. I was remembering, and it made it hard to catch my breath, that I had been there when he was born; and I had heard the first words he had ever spoken. When he started to walk, he walked from our mother straight to me. I caught him just before he fell when he took the first steps he ever took in this world.

"How's Isabel?"   55

"Just fine. She's dying to see you."

"And the boys?"

"They're fine, too. They're anxious to see their uncle."

"Oh, come on. You know they don't remember me."

"Are you kidding? Of course they remember you."   60

He grinned again. We got into a taxi. We had a lot to say to each other, far too much to know how to begin.

As the taxi began to move, I asked, "You still want to go to India?"

He laughed. "You still remember that. Hell, no. This place is Indian enough for me."

"It used to belong to them," I said.

And he laughed again. "They damn sure knew what they were doing when they 65 got rid of it."

Years ago, when he was around fourteen, he'd been all hipped on the idea of going to India. He read books about people sitting on rocks, naked, in all kinds of weather, but mostly bad, naturally, and walking barefoot through hot coals and arriving at wisdom. I used to say that it sounded to me as though they were getting away from wisdom as fast as they could. I think he sort of looked down on me for that.

"Do you mind," he asked, "if we have the driver drive alongside the park? On the west side—I haven't seen the city in so long."

"Of course not," I said. I was afraid that I might sound as though I were humoring him, but I hoped he wouldn't take it that way.

So we drove along, between the green of the park and the stony, lifeless elegance of hotels and apartment buildings, toward the vivid, killing streets of our childhood. These streets hadn't changed, though housing projects jutted up out of them now like rocks in the middle of a boiling sea. Most of the houses in which we had grown up had vanished, as had the stores from which we had stolen, the basements in which we had first tried sex, the rooftops from which we had hurled tin cans and bricks. But houses exactly like the houses of our past yet dominated the landscape, boys exactly like the boys we once had been found themselves smothering in these houses, came down into the streets for light and air and found themselves encircled by disaster. Some escaped the trap, most didn't. Those who got out always left something of themselves behind, as some animals amputate a leg and leave it in the trap. It might be said, perhaps, that I had escaped, after all, I was a school teacher; or that Sonny had, he hadn't lived in Harlem for years. Yet, as the cab moved uptown through streets which seemed, with a rush, to darken with dark people, and as I covertly studied Sonny's face, it came to me that what we both were seeking through our separate cab windows was that part of ourselves which had been left behind. It's always at the hour of trouble and confrontation that the missing member aches.

We hit 110th Street and started rolling up Lenox Avenue. And I'd known this 70 avenue all my life, but it seemed to me again, as it had seemed on the day I'd first heard about Sonny's trouble, filled with a hidden menace which was its very breath of life.

"We almost there," said Sonny.

"Almost." We were both too nervous to say anything more.

We live in a housing project. It hasn't been up long. A few days after it was up it seemed uninhabitably new, now, of course, it's already rundown. It looks like a parody of the good, clean, faceless life—God knows the people who live in it do their best to make it a parody. The beat-looking grass lying around isn't enough to make their lives green, the hedges will never hold out the streets, and they know it. The big windows fool no one, they aren't big enough to make space out of no space. They don't bother with the windows, they watch the TV screen instead. The playground is most popular with the children who don't play at jacks, or skip rope, or roller skate, or swing, and they can be found in it after dark. We moved in partly because it's not too far from where I teach, and partly for the kids; but it's really just like the houses in which Sonny and I grew up. The same things happen, they'll have the same things to remember. The moment Sonny and I started into the house I had the feeling that I was simply bringing him back into the danger he had almost died trying to escape.

Sonny has never been talkative. So I don't know why I was sure he'd be dying to talk to me when supper was over the first night. Everything went fine, the oldest boy remembered him, and the youngest boy liked him, and Sonny had remembered to bring something for each of them; and Isabel, who is really much nicer than I am, more open and giving, had gone to a lot of trouble about dinner and was genuinely glad to see him. And she's always been able to tease Sonny in a way that I haven't. It was nice to see her face so vivid again and to hear her laugh and watch her make Sonny laugh. She wasn't, or, anyway, she didn't seem to be, at all uneasy or embarrassed. She chatted as though there were no subject which had to be avoided and she got Sonny past his first, faint stiffness. And thank God she was there, for I was filled with that icy dread again. Everything I did seemed awkward to me, and everything I said sounded freighted with hidden meaning. I was trying to remember everything I'd heard about dope addiction and I couldn't help watching Sonny for signs. I wasn't doing it out of malice. I was trying to find out something about my brother. I was dying to hear him tell me he was safe.

"Safe!" my father grunted, whenever Mama suggested trying to move to a neighborhood which might be safer for children. "Safe, hell! Ain't no place safe for kids, nor nobody."

He always went on like this, but he wasn't, ever, really as bad as he sounded, not even on weekends, when he got drunk. As a matter of fact, he was always on the lookout for "something a little better," but he died before he found it. He died suddenly, during a drunken weekend in the middle of the war, when Sonny was fifteen. He and Sonny hadn't ever got on too well. And this was partly because Sonny was the apple of his father's eye. It was because he loved Sonny so much and was frightened for him, that he was always fighting with him. It doesn't do any good to fight with Sonny. Sonny just moves back, inside himself, where he can't be reached. But the principal reason that they never hit it off is that they were so much alike. Daddy was big and rough and loud-talking, just the opposite of Sonny, but they both had—that same privacy.

Mama tried to tell me something about this, just after Daddy died. I was home on leave from the army.

This was the last time I ever saw my mother alive. Just the same, this picture gets all mixed up in my mind with pictures I had of her when she was younger. The way I always see her is the way she used to be on a Sunday afternoon, say, when the old folks were talking after the big Sunday dinner. I always see her wearing pale blue. She'd be sitting on the sofa. And my father would be sitting in the easy chair, not far from her. And the living room would be full of church folks and relatives. There they sit, in chairs all around the living room, and the night is creeping up outside, but nobody knows it yet. You can see the darkness growing against the windowpanes and you hear the street noises every now and again, or maybe the jangling beat of a tambourine from one of the churches close by, but it's real quiet in the room. For a moment nobody's talking, but every face looks darkening, like the sky outside. And my mother rocks a little from the waist, and my father's eyes are closed. Everyone is looking at something a child can't see. For a minute they've forgotten the children. Maybe a kid is lying on the rug, half asleep. Maybe somebody's got a kid in his lap and is absent-mindedly stroking the kid's head. Maybe there's a kid, quiet and big-eyed, curled up in a big chair in the corner. The silence, the darkness coming, and the darkness in the faces frightens the child obscurely. He hopes that the hand which strokes his forehead will never stop—will never die. He hopes that there will never come a time when the old folks won't be sitting around the living room, talking about where they've come from, and what they've seen, and what's happened to them and their kinfolk.

But something deep and watchful in the child knows that this is bound to end, is already ending. In a moment someone will get up and turn on the light. Then the old folks will remember the children and they won't talk any more that day. And when light fills the room, the child is filled with darkness. He knows that every time this happens he's moved just a little closer to that darkness outside. The darkness outside is what the old folks have been talking about. It's what they've come from. It's what they endure. The child knows that they won't talk any more because if he knows too much about what's happened to *them*, he'll know too much too soon, about what's going to happen to *him*.

The last time I talked to my mother, I remember I was restless. I wanted to get out and see Isabel. We weren't married then and we had a lot to straighten out between us.

There Mama sat, in black, by the window. She was humming an old church song, *Lord, you brought me from a long ways off.* Sonny was out somewhere. Mama kept watching the streets.

"I don't know," she said, "if I'll ever see you again, after you go off from here. But I hope you'll remember the things I tried to teach you."

"Don't talk like that," I said, and smiled. "You'll be here a long time yet."

She smiled, too, but she said nothing. She was quiet for a long time. And I said, "Mama, don't you worry about nothing. I'll be writing all the time, and you be getting the checks . . ."

"I want to talk to you about your brother," she said, suddenly. "If anything happens to me he ain't going to have nobody to look out for him."

"Mama," I said, "ain't nothing going to happen to you *or* Sonny. Sonny's all right. He's a good boy and he's got good sense."

"It ain't a question of his being a good boy," Mama said, "nor of his having good sense. It ain't only the bad ones, nor yet the dumb ones that gets sucked under." She stopped, looking at me. "Your Daddy once had a brother," she said, and she smiled in a way that made me feel she was in pain. "You didn't never know that, did you?"

"No," I said, "I never knew that," and I watched her face.

"Oh, yes," she said, "your Daddy had a brother." She looked out of the window again. "I know you never saw your Daddy cry. But *I* did—many a time, through all these years."

I asked her, "What happened to his brother? How come nobody's ever talked about him?"

This was the first time I ever saw my mother look old.

"His brother got killed," she said, "when he was just a little younger than you are now. I knew him. He was a fine boy. He was maybe a little full of the devil, but he didn't mean nobody no harm."

Then she stopped and the room was silent, exactly as it had sometimes been on those Sunday afternoons. Mama kept looking out into the streets.

"He used to have a job in the mill," she said, "and, like all young folks, he just liked to perform on Saturday nights. Saturday nights, him and your father would drift around to different places, go to dances and things like that, or just sit around with people they knew, and your father's brother would sing, he had a fine voice, and play along with himself on his guitar. Well, this particular Saturday night, him and your father was coming home from some place, and they were both a little drunk and there was a moon that night, it was bright like day. Your father's brother was feeling kind of good, and he was whistling to himself, and he had his guitar slung over his shoulder. They was coming down a hill and beneath them was a road that turned off from the highway. Well, your father's brother, being always kind of frisky, decided to run down this hill, and he did, with that guitar banging and clanging behind him, and he ran across the road, and he was making water behind a tree. And your father was sort of amused at him and he was still coming down the hill, kind of slow. Then he heard a car motor and that same minute his brother stepped from behind the tree, into the road, in the moonlight. And he started to cross the road. And your father started to run down the hill, he says he don't know why. This car was full of white men. They was all drunk, and when they seen your father's brother they let out a great whoop and holler and they aimed the car straight at him. They was having fun, they just wanted to scare him, the way they do sometimes, you know. But they was drunk. And I guess the boy, being drunk, too, and scared, kind of lost his head. By the time he jumped it was too late. Your father says he heard his brother scream when the car rolled over him, and he heard the wood of that guitar when it give, and he heard them strings go flying, and he heard them white men shouting, and the car kept on a-going and it ain't stopped till this day. And, time your father got down the hill, his brother weren't nothing but blood and pulp."

Tears were gleaming on my mother's face. There wasn't anything I could say.   95

"He never mentioned it," she said, "because I never let him mention it before you children. Your Daddy was like a crazy man that night and for many a night thereafter. He says he never in his life seen anything as dark as that road after the lights of that car had gone away. Weren't nothing, weren't nobody on that road, just your Daddy and his brother and that busted guitar. Oh, yes. Your Daddy never did really get right again. Till the day he died he weren't sure but that every white man he saw was the man that killed his brother."

She stopped and took out her handkerchief and dried her eyes and looked at me.

"I ain't telling you all this," she said, "to make you scared or bitter or to make you hate nobody. I'm telling you this because you got a brother. And the world ain't changed."

I guess I didn't want to believe this. I guess she saw this in my face. She turned away from me, toward the window again, searching those streets.

"But I praise my Redeemer," she said at last, "that He called your Daddy home   100 before me. I ain't saying it to throw no flowers at myself, but, I declare, it keeps me from feeling too cast down to know I helped your father get safely through this world. Your father always acted like he was the roughest, strongest man on earth. And everybody took him to be like that. But if he hadn't had *me* there—to see his tears!"

She was crying again. Still, I couldn't move. I said, "Lord, Lord, Mama, I didn't know it was like that."

"Oh, honey," she said, "there's a lot that you don't know. But you are going to find it out." She stood up from the window and came over to me. "You got to hold on to your brother," she said, "and don't let him fall, no matter what it looks like is happening to him and no matter how evil you gets with him. You going to be evil with him many a time. But don't you forget what I told you, you hear?"

"I won't forget," I said. "Don't you worry, I won't forget. I won't let nothing happen to Sonny."

My mother smiled as though she were amused at something she saw in my face. Then, "You may not be able to stop nothing from happening. But you got to let him know you's *there*."

Two days later I was married, and then I was gone. And I had a lot of things on   105
my mind and I pretty well forgot my promise to Mama until I got shipped home on a
special furlough for her funeral.

And, after the funeral, with just Sonny and me alone in the empty kitchen, I
tried to find out something about him.

"What do you want to do?" I asked him.

"I'm going to be a musician," he said.

For he had graduated, in the time I had been away, from dancing to the juke box
to finding out who was playing what, and what they were doing with it, and he had
bought himself a set of drums.

"You mean, you want to be a drummer?" I somehow had the feeling that being a   110
drummer might be all right for other people but not for my brother Sonny.

"I don't think," he said, looking at me very gravely, "that I'll ever be a good
drummer. But I think I can play a piano."

I frowned. I'd never played the role of the older brother quite so seriously before,
had scarcely ever, in fact, *asked* Sonny a damn thing. I sensed myself in the presence
of something I didn't really know how to handle, didn't understand. So I made my
frown a little deeper as I asked: "What kind of musician do you want to be?"

He grinned. "How many kinds do you think there are?"

"Be *serious*," I said.

He laughed, throwing his head back, and then looked at me. "I *am* serious."   115

"Well, then, for Christ's sake, stop kidding around and answer a serious question. I
mean, do you want to be a concert pianist, you want to play classical music and all that,
or—or what?" Long before I finished he was laughing again. "For Christ's *sake*, Sonny!"

He sobered, but with difficulty. "I'm sorry. But you sound so—*scared!*" and he
was off again.

"Well, you may think it's funny now, baby, but it's not going to be so funny
when you have to make your living at it, let me tell you *that*." I was furious because I
knew he was laughing at me and I didn't know why.

"No," he said, very sober now, and afraid, perhaps, that he'd hurt me, "I don't
want to be a classical pianist. That isn't what interests me. I mean"—he paused,
looking hard at me, as though his eyes would help me to understand, and then gestured helplessly, as though perhaps his hand would help—"I mean, I'll have a lot of
studying to do, and I'll have to study *everything*, but, I mean, I want to play *with*—jazz
musicians." He stopped. "I want to play jazz," he said.

Well, the word had never before sounded as heavy, as real, as it sounded that   120
afternoon in Sonny's mouth. I just looked at him and I was probably frowning a real
frown by this time. I simply couldn't see why on earth he'd want to spend his time
hanging around nightclubs, clowning around on bandstands, while people pushed
each other around a dance floor. It seemed—beneath him, somehow. I had never
thought about it before, had never been forced to, but I suppose I had always put jazz
musicians in a class with what Daddy called "goodtime people."

"Are you *serious*?"

"Hell, *yes*, I'm serious."

He looked more helpless than ever, and annoyed, and deeply hurt.

I suggested, helpfully: "You mean—like Louis Armstrong?"°

Louis Armstrong: jazz trumpeter and vocalist (1900–1971) born in New Orleans. In the 1950s his music
would have been considered conservative by progressive jazz fans.

His face closed as though I'd struck him. "No. I'm not talking about none of that 125
old-time, down home crap."

"Well, look, Sonny, I'm sorry, don't get mad. I just don't altogether get it, that's
all. Name somebody—you know, a jazz musician you admire."

"Bird."

"Who?"

"Bird! Charlie Parker!° Don't they teach you nothing in the goddamn army?"

I lit a cigarette. I was surprised and then a little amused to discover that I was 130
trembling. "I've been out of touch," I said. "You'll have to be patient with me. Now.
Who's this Parker character?"

"He's just one of the greatest jazz musicians alive," said Sonny, sullenly, his
hands in his pockets, his back to me. "Maybe *the* greatest," he added, bitterly, "that's
probably why *you* never heard of him."

"All right," I said, "I'm ignorant. I'm sorry. I'll go out and buy all the cat's records
right away, all right?"

"It don't," said Sonny, with dignity, "make any difference to me. I don't care
what you listen to. Don't do me no favors."

I was beginning to realize that I'd never seen him so upset before. With another
part of my mind I was thinking that this would probably turn out to be one of those
things kids go through and that I shouldn't make it seem important by pushing it too
hard. Still, I didn't think it would do any harm to ask: "Doesn't all this take a lot of
time? Can you make a living at it?"

He turned back to me and half leaned, half sat, on the kitchen table. "Every- 135
thing takes time," he said, "and—well, yes, sure, I can make a living at it. But what I
don't seem to be able to make you understand is that it's the only thing I want to do."

"Well, Sonny," I said, gently, "you know people can't always do exactly what
they *want* to do—"

"*No*, I don't know that," said Sonny, surprising me. "I think people *ought* to do
what they want to do, what else are they alive for?"

"You getting to be a big boy," I said desperately, "it's time you started thinking
about your future."

"I'm thinking about my future," said Sonny, grimly. "I think about it all the time."

I gave up. I decided, if he didn't change his mind, that we could always talk 140
about it later. "In the meantime," I said, "you got to finish school." We had already
decided that he'd have to move in with Isabel and her folks. I knew this wasn't the
ideal arrangement because Isabel's folks are inclined to be dicty° and they hadn't especially wanted Isabel to marry me. But I didn't know what else to do. "And we have
to get you fixed up at Isabel's."

There was a long silence. He moved from the kitchen table to the window.
"That's a terrible idea. You know it yourself."

"Do you have a *better* idea?"

He just walked up and down the kitchen for a minute. He was as tall as I was. He
had started to shave. I suddenly had the feeling that I didn't know him at all.

He stopped at the kitchen table and picked up my cigarettes. Looking at me with
a kind of mocking, amused defiance, he put one between his lips. "You mind?"

Charlie Parker: a jazz saxophonist (1920–1955) who helped create the progressive jazz style called bebop.
Parker was a heroin addict who died at an early age. *dicty:* slang word for stylish, high-class; snobbish.

"You smoking already?" 145

He lit the cigarette and nodded, watching me through the smoke. "I just wanted to see if I'd have the courage to smoke in front of you." He grinned and blew a great cloud of smoke to the ceiling. "It was easy." He looked at my face. "Come on, now. I bet you was smoking at my age, tell the truth."

I didn't say anything but the truth was on my face, and he laughed. But now there was something very strained in his laugh. "Sure. And I bet that ain't all you was doing."

He was frightening me a little. "Cut the crap," I said. "We already decided that you was going to go and live at Isabel's. Now what's got into you all of a sudden?"

"*You* decided it," he pointed out. "I didn't decide nothing." He stopped in front of me, leaning against the stove, arms loosely folded. "Look, brother. I don't want to stay in Harlem no more, I really don't." He was very earnest. He looked at me, then over toward the kitchen window. There was something in his eyes I'd never seen before, some thoughtfulness, some worry all his own. He rubbed the muscle of one arm. "It's time I was getting out of here."

"Where do you want to *go*, Sonny?" 150

"I want to join the army. Or the navy, I don't care. If I say I'm old enough, they'll believe me."

Then I got mad. It was because I was so scared. "You must be crazy. You goddamn fool, what the hell do you want to go and join the *army* for?"

"I just told you. To get out of Harlem."

"Sonny, you haven't even finished *school*. And if you really want to be a musician, how do you expect to study if you're in the *army*?"

He looked at me, trapped, and in anguish. "There's ways. I might be able to work 155 out some kind of deal. Anyway, I'll have the G.I. Bill when I come out."

"*If* you come out." We stared at each other. "Sonny, please. Be reasonable. I know the setup is far from perfect. But we got to do the best we can."

"I ain't learning nothing in school," he said. "Even when I go." He turned away from me and opened the window and threw his cigarette out into the narrow alley. I watched his back. "At least, I ain't learning nothing you'd want me to learn." He slammed the window so hard I thought the glass would fly out, and turned back to me. "And I'm sick of the stink of these garbage cans!"

"Sonny," I said, "I know how you feel. But if you don't finish school now, you're going to be sorry later that you didn't." I grabbed him by the shoulders. "And you only got another year. It ain't so bad. And I'll come back and I swear I'll help you do *whatever* you want to do. Just try to put up with it till I come back. Will you please do that? For me?"

He didn't answer and he wouldn't look at me.

"Sonny. You hear me?" 160

He pulled away. "I hear you. But you never hear anything *I* say."

I didn't know what to say to that. He looked out of the window and then back at me. "OK," he said, and sighed. "I'll try."

Then I said, trying to cheer him up a little, "They got a piano at Isabel's. You can practice on it."

And as a matter of fact, it did cheer him up for a minute. "That's right," he said to himself. "I forgot that." His face relaxed a little. But the worry, the thoughtfulness, played on it still, the way shadows play on a face which is staring into the fire.

*

But I thought I'd never hear the end of that piano. At first, Isabel would write   165
me, saying how nice it was that Sonny was so serious about his music and how, as
soon as he came in from school, or wherever he had been when he was supposed to
be at school, he went straight to that piano and stayed there until suppertime. And,
after supper, he went back to that piano and stayed there until everybody went to
bed. He was at the piano all day Saturday and all day Sunday. Then he bought a
record player and started playing records. He'd play one record over and over again,
all day long sometimes, and he'd improvise along with it on the piano. Or he'd play
one section of the record, one chord, one change, one progression, then he'd do it on
the piano. Then back to the record. Then back to the piano.

Well, I really don't know how they stood it. Isabel finally confessed that it wasn't
like living with a person at all, it was like living with sound. And the sound didn't
make any sense to her, didn't make any sense to any of them—naturally. They began,
in a way, to be afflicted by this presence that was living in their home. It was as
though Sonny were some sort of god, or monster. He moved in an atmosphere which
wasn't like theirs at all. They fed him and he ate, he washed himself, he walked in
and out of their door; he certainly wasn't nasty or unpleasant or rude, Sonny isn't any
of those things; but it was as though he were all wrapped up in some cloud, some fire,
some vision all his own; and there wasn't any way to reach him.

At the same time, he wasn't really a man yet, he was still a child, and they had to watch
out for him in all kinds of ways. They certainly couldn't throw him out. Neither did they
dare to make a great scene about that piano because even they dimly sensed, as I sensed,
from so many thousands of miles away, that Sonny was at that piano playing for his life.

But he hadn't been going to school. One day a letter came from the school board
and Isabel's mother got it—there had, apparently, been other letters but Sonny had
torn them up. This day, when Sonny came in, Isabel's mother showed him the letter
and asked where he'd been spending his time. And she finally got it out of him that
he'd been down in Greenwich Village, with musicians and other characters, in a
white girl's apartment. And this scared her and she started to scream at him and what
came up, once she began—though she denies it to this day—was what sacrifices they
were making to give Sonny a decent home and how little he appreciated it.

Sonny didn't play the piano that day. By evening, Isabel's mother had calmed down
but then there was the old man to deal with, and Isabel herself. Isabel says she did her
best to be calm but she broke down and started crying. She says she just watched
Sonny's face. She could tell, by watching him, what was happening with him. And what
was happening was that they penetrated his cloud, they had reached him. Even if their
fingers had been a thousand times more gentle than human fingers ever are, he could
hardly help feeling that they had stripped him naked and were spitting on that naked-
ness. For he also had to see that his presence, that music, which was life or death to him,
had been torture for them and that they had endured it, not at all for his sake, but only
for mine. And Sonny couldn't take that. He can take it a little better today than he
could then but he's still not very good at it and, frankly, I don't know anybody who is.

The silence of the next few days must have been louder than the sound of all the   170
music ever played since time began. One morning, before she went to work, Isabel
was in his room for something and she suddenly realized that all of his records were
gone. And she knew for certain that he was gone. And he was. He went as far as the
navy would carry him. He finally sent me a postcard from some place in Greece and

that was the first I knew that Sonny was still alive. I didn't see him any more until we were both back in New York and the war had long been over.

He was a man by then, of course, but I wasn't willing to see it. He came by the house from time to time, but we fought almost every time we met. I didn't like the way he carried himself, loose and dreamlike all the time, and I didn't like his friends, and his music seemed to be merely an excuse for the life he led. It sounded just that weird and disordered.

Then we had a fight, a pretty awful fight, and I didn't see him for months. By and by I looked him up, where he was living, in a furnished room in the Village, and I tried to make it up. But there were lots of people in the room and Sonny just lay on his bed, and he wouldn't come downstairs with me, and he treated these other people as though they were his family and I weren't. So I got mad and then he got mad, and then I told him that he might just as well be dead as live the way he was living. Then he stood up and he told me not to worry about him any more in life, that he *was* dead as far as I was concerned. Then he pushed me to the door and the other people looked on as though nothing were happening, and he slammed the door behind me. I stood in the hallway, staring at the door. I heard somebody laugh in the room and then the tears came to my eyes. I started down the steps, whistling to keep from crying, I kept whistling to myself, *You going to need me, baby, one of these cold, rainy days.*

I read about Sonny's trouble in the spring. Little Grace died in the fall. She was a beautiful little girl. But she only lived a little over two years. She died of polio and she suffered. She had a slight fever for a couple of days, but it didn't seem like anything and we just kept her in bed. And we would certainly have called the doctor, but the fever dropped, she seemed to be all right. So we thought it had just been a cold. Then, one day, she was up, playing, Isabel was in the kitchen fixing lunch for the two boys when they'd come in from school, and she heard Grace fall down in the living room. When you have a lot of children you don't always start running when one of them falls, unless they start screaming or something. And, this time, Grace was quiet. Yet, Isabel says that when she heard that *thump* and then that silence, something happened in her to make her afraid. And she ran to the living room and there was little Grace on the floor, all twisted up, and the reason she hadn't screamed was that she couldn't get her breath. And when she did scream, it was the worst sound, Isabel says, that she'd ever heard in all her life, and she still hears it sometimes in her dreams. Isabel will sometimes wake me up with a low, moaning, strangled sound and I have to be quick to awaken her and hold her to me and where Isabel is weeping against me seems a mortal wound.

I think I may have written Sonny the very day that little Grace was buried. I was sitting in the living room in the dark, by myself, and I suddenly thought of Sonny. My trouble made his real.

One Saturday afternoon, when Sonny had been living with us, or, anyway, been in our house, for nearly two weeks, I found myself wandering aimlessly about the living room, drinking from a can of beer, and trying to work up the courage to search Sonny's room. He was out, he was usually out whenever I was home, and Isabel had taken the children to see their grandparents. Suddenly I was standing still in front of the living room window, watching Seventh Avenue. The idea of searching Sonny's room made me still. I scarcely dared to admit to myself what I'd be searching for. I didn't know what I'd do if I found it. Or if I didn't.

On the sidewalk across from me, near the entrance to a barbecue joint, some people were holding an old-fashioned revival meeting. The barbecue cook, wearing a dirty white apron, his conked hair reddish and metallic in the pale sun, and a cigarette between his lips, stood in the doorway, watching them. Kids and older people paused in their errands and stood there, along with some older men and a couple of very tough-looking women who watched everything that happened on the avenue, as though they owned it, or were maybe owned by it. Well, they were watching this, too. The revival was being carried on by three sisters in black, and a brother. All they had were their voices and their Bibles and a tambourine. The brother was testifying and while he testified two of the sisters stood together, seeming to say, amen, and the third sister walked around with the tambourine outstretched and a couple of people dropped coins into it. Then the brother's testimony ended and the sister who had been taking up the collection dumped the coins into her palm and transferred them to the pocket of her long black robe. Then she raised both hands, striking the tambourine against the air, and then against one hand, and she started to sing. And the two other sisters and the brother joined in.

It was strange, suddenly, to watch, though I had been seeing these street meetings all my life. So, of course, had everybody else down there. Yet, they paused and watched and listened and I stood still at the window. "*Tis the old ship of Zion,*" they sang, and the sister with the tambourine kept a steady, jangling beat, "*it has rescued many a thousand!*" Not a soul under the sound of their voices was hearing this song for the first time, not one of them had been rescued. Nor had they seen much in the way of rescue work being done around them. Neither did they especially believe in the holiness of the three sisters and the brother, they knew too much about them, knew where they lived, and how. The woman with the tambourine, whose voice dominated the air, whose face was bright with joy, was divided by very little from the woman who stood watching her, a cigarette between her heavy, chapped lips, her hair a cuckoo's nest, her face scarred and swollen from many beatings, and her black eyes glittering like coal. Perhaps they both knew this, which was why, when, as rarely, they addressed each other, they addressed each other as Sister. As the singing filled the air the watching, listening faces underwent a change, the eyes focusing on something within; the music seemed to soothe a poison out of them; and time seemed, nearly, to fall away from the sullen, belligerent, battered faces, as though they were fleeing back to their first condition, while dreaming of their last. The barbecue cook half shook his head and smiled, and dropped his cigarette and disappeared into his joint. A man fumbled in his pockets for change and stood holding it in his hand impatiently, as though he had just remembered a pressing appointment further up the avenue. He looked furious. Then I saw Sonny, standing on the edge of the crowd. He was carrying a wide, flat notebook with a green cover, and it made him look, from where I was standing, almost like a schoolboy. The coppery sun brought out the copper in his skin, he was very faintly smiling, standing very still. Then the singing stopped, the tambourine turned into a collection plate again. The furious man dropped in his coins and vanished, so did a couple of the women, and Sonny dropped some change in the plate, looking directly at the woman with a little smile. He started across the avenue, toward the house. He has a slow, loping walk, something like the way Harlem hipsters walk, only he's imposed on this his own half-beat. I had never really noticed it before.

I stayed at the window, both relieved and apprehensive. As Sonny disappeared from my sight, they began singing again. And they were still singing when his key turned in the lock.

"Hey," he said.

"Hey, yourself. You want some beer?" 180

"No. Well, maybe." But he came up to the window and stood beside me, looking out. "What a warm voice," he said.

They were singing *If I could only hear my mother pray again!*

"Yes," I said, "and she can sure beat that tambourine."

"But what a terrible song," he said, and laughed. He dropped his notebook on the sofa and disappeared into the kitchen. "Where's Isabel and the kids?"

"I think they went to see their grandparents. You hungry?" 185

"No." He came back into the living room with his can of beer. "You want to come some place with me tonight?"

I sensed, I don't know how, that I couldn't possibly say no. "Sure. Where?"

He sat down on the sofa and picked up his notebook and started leafing through it. "I'm going to sit in with some fellows in a joint in the Village."

"You mean, you're going to play, tonight?"

"That's right." He took a swallow of his beer and moved back to the window. He 190 gave me a sidelong look. "If you can stand it."

"I'll try," I said.

He smiled to himself and we both watched as the meeting across the way broke up. The three sisters and the brother, heads bowed, were singing *God be with you till we meet again*. The faces around them were very quiet. Then the song ended. The small crowd dispersed. We watched the three women and the lone man walk slowly up the avenue.

"When she was singing before," said Sonny, abruptly, "her voice reminded me for a minute of what heroin feels like sometimes—when it's in your veins. It makes you feel sort of warm and cool at the same time. And distant. And—and sure." He sipped his beer, very deliberately not looking at me. I watched his face. "It makes you feel—in control. Sometimes you've got to have that feeling."

"Do you?" I sat down slowly in the easy chair.

"Sometimes." He went to the sofa and picked up his notebook again. "Some people 195 do."

"In order," I asked, "to play?" And my voice was very ugly, full of contempt and anger.

"Well"—he looked at me with great, troubled eyes, as though, in fact, he hoped his eyes would tell me things he could never otherwise say—"they *think* so. And if they think so—!"

"And what do *you* think?" I asked.

He sat on the sofa and put his can of beer on the floor. "I don't know," he said, and I couldn't be sure if he were answering my question or pursuing his thoughts. His face didn't tell me. "It's not so much to *play*. It's to *stand* it, to be able to make it at all. On any level." He frowned and smiled: "In order to keep from shaking to pieces."

"But these friends of yours," I said, "they seem to shake themselves to pieces 200 pretty goddamn fast."

"Maybe." He played with the notebook. And something told me that I should curb my tongue, that Sonny was doing his best to talk, that I should listen. "But of course you only know the ones that've gone to pieces. Some don't—or at least they haven't *yet* and that's just about all *any* of us can say." He paused. "And then there are some who just live, really, in hell, and they know it and they see what's happening and they go right on. I don't know." He sighed, dropped the notebook, folded his arms. "Some guys, you can tell from the way they play, they on something *all* the time. And you can see that, well, it makes something real for them. But of course," he picked up his beer from the floor and sipped it and put the can down again, "they *want* to, too, you've got to see that. Even some of them that say they don't—*some*, not all."

"And what about you?" I asked—I couldn't help it. "What about you? Do *you* want to?"

He stood up and walked to the window and remained silent for a long time. Then he sighed. "Me," he said. Then: "While I was downstairs before, on my way here, listening to that woman sing, it struck me all of a sudden how much suffering she must have had to go through—to sing like that. It's *repulsive* to think you have to suffer that much."

I said: "But there's no way not to suffer—is there, Sonny?"

"I believe not," he said and smiled, "but that's never stopped anyone from try-   205 ing." He looked at me. "Has it?" I realized, with this mocking look, that there stood between us, forever, beyond the power of time or forgiveness, the fact that I had held silence—so long!—when he had needed human speech to help him. He turned back to the window. "No, there's no way not to suffer. But you try all kinds of ways to keep from drowning in it, to keep on top of it, and to make it seem—well, like *you*. Like you did something, all right, and now you're suffering for it. You know?" I said noth- ing. "Well you know," he said, impatiently, "why *do* people suffer? Maybe it's better to do something to give it a reason, *any* reason."

"But we just agreed," I said, "that there's no way not to suffer. Isn't it better, then, just to—take it?"

"But nobody just takes it," Sonny cried, "that's what I'm telling you! *Everybody* tries not to. You're just hung up on the *way* some people try—it's not *your* way!"

The hair on my face began to itch, my face felt wet. "That's not true," I said, "that's not true. I don't give a damn what other people do, I don't even care how they suffer. I just care how *you* suffer." And he looked at me. "Please believe me," I said, "I don't want to see you—die—trying not to suffer."

"I won't," he said, flatly, "die trying not to suffer. At least, not any faster than anybody else."

"But there's no need," I said, trying to laugh, "is there? in killing yourself."   210

I wanted to say more, but I couldn't. I wanted to talk about will power and how life could be—well, beautiful. I wanted to say that it was all within; but was it? or, rather, wasn't that exactly the trouble? And I wanted to promise that I would never fail him again. But it would all have sounded—empty words and lies.

So I made the promise to myself and prayed that I would keep it.

"It's terrible sometimes, inside," he said, "that's what's the trouble. You walk these streets, black and funky and cold, and there's not really a living ass to talk to, and there's nothing shaking, and there's no way of getting it out—that storm inside. You can't talk it and you can't make love with it, and when you finally try to get with it and play it, you realize *nobody's* listening. So *you've* got to listen. You got to find a way to listen."

And then he walked away from the window and sat on the sofa again, as though all the wind had suddenly been knocked out of him. "Sometimes you'll do *anything* to play, even cut your mother's throat." He laughed and looked at me. "Or your brother's." Then he sobered. "Or your own." Then: "Don't worry. I'm all right now and I think I'll *be* all right. But I can't forget—where I've been. I don't mean just the physical place I've been, I mean where I've *been*. And *what* I've been."

"What have you been, Sonny?" I asked.

He smiled—but sat sideways on the sofa, his elbow resting on the back, his fingers playing with his mouth and chin, not looking at me. "I've been something I didn't recognize, didn't know I could be. Didn't know anybody could be." He stopped, looking inward, looking helplessly young, looking old. "I'm not talking about it now because I feel *guilty* or anything like that—maybe it would be better if I did, I don't know. Anyway, I can't really talk about it. Not to you, not to anybody," and now he turned and faced me. "Sometimes, you know, and it was actually when I was most *out* of the world, I felt that I was in it, that I was *with* it, really, and I could play or I didn't really have to *play*, it just came out of me, it was there. And I don't know how I played, thinking about it now, but I know I did awful things, those times, sometimes, to people. Or it wasn't that I *did* anything to them—it was that they weren't real." He picked up the beer can; it was empty; he rolled it between his palms: "And other times—well, I needed a fix, I needed to find a place to lean, I needed to clear a space to *listen*—and I couldn't find it, and I—went crazy, I did terrible things to *me*, I was terrible *for* me." He began pressing the beer can between his hands, I watched the metal begin to give. It glittered, as he played with it, like a knife, and I was afraid he would cut himself, but I said nothing. "Oh well. I can never tell you. I was all by myself at the bottom of something, stinking and sweating and crying and shaking, and I smelled it, you know? *my* stink, and I thought I'd die if I couldn't get away from it and yet, all the same, I knew that everything I was doing was just locking me in with it. And I didn't know," he paused, still flattening the beer can, "I didn't know, I still *don't* know, something kept telling me that maybe it was good to smell your own stink, but I didn't think that *that* was what I'd been trying to do—and—who can stand it?" and he abruptly dropped the ruined beer can, looking at me with a small, still smile, and then rose, walking to the window as though it were the lodestone rock. I watched his face, he watched the avenue. "I couldn't tell you when Mama died—but the reason I wanted to leave Harlem so bad was to get away from drugs. And then, when I ran away, that's what I was running from—really. When I came back, nothing had changed, *I* hadn't changed, I was just—older." And he stopped, drumming with his fingers on the windowpane. The sun had vanished, soon darkness would fall. I watched his face. "It can come again," he said, almost as though speaking to himself. Then he turned to me. "It can come again," he repeated. "I just want you to know that."

"All right," I said, at last. "So it can come again. All right."

He smiled, but the smile was sorrowful. "I had to try to tell you," he said.

"Yes," I said. "I understand that."

"You're my brother," he said, looking straight at me, and not smiling at all.

"Yes," I repeated, "yes. I understand that."

He turned back to the window, looking out. "All that hatred down there," he said, "all that hatred and misery and love. It's a wonder it doesn't blow the avenue apart."

We went to the only nightclub on a short, dark street, downtown. We squeezed through the narrow, chattering, jam-packed bar to the entrance of the big room, where the bandstand was. And we stood there for a moment, for the lights were very dim in this room and we couldn't see. Then, "Hello, boy," said a voice and an enormous black man, much older than Sonny or myself, erupted out of all that atmospheric lighting and put an arm around Sonny's shoulder. "I been sitting right here," he said, "waiting for you."

He had a big voice, too, and heads in the darkness turned toward us.

Sonny grinned and pulled a little away, and said, "Creole, this is my brother. I   225
told you about him."

Creole shook my hand. "I'm glad to meet you, son," he said, and it was clear that he was glad to meet me *there*, for Sonny's sake. And he smiled, "You got a real musician in *your* family," and he took his arm from Sonny's shoulder and slapped him, lightly, affectionately, with the back of his hand.

"Well. Now I've heard it all," said a voice behind us. This was another musician, and a friend of Sonny's, a coal-black, cheerful-looking man, built close to the ground. He immediately began confiding to me, at the top of his lungs, the most terrible things about Sonny, his teeth gleaming like a lighthouse and his laugh coming up out of him like the beginning of an earthquake. And it turned out that everyone at the bar knew Sonny, or almost everyone; some were musicians, working there, or nearby, or not working, some were simply hangers-on, and some were there to hear Sonny play. I was introduced to all of them and they were all very polite to me. Yet, it was clear that, for them, I was only Sonny's brother. Here, I was in Sonny's world. Or, rather: his kingdom. Here, it was not even a question that his veins bore royal blood.

They were going to play soon and Creole installed me, by myself, at a table in a dark corner. Then I watched them, Creole, and the little black man, and Sonny, and the others, while they horsed around, standing just below the bandstand. The light from the bandstand spilled just a little short of them and, watching them laughing and gesturing and moving about, I had the feeling that they, nevertheless, were being most careful not to step into that circle of light too suddenly: that if they moved into the light too suddenly, without thinking, they would perish in flame. Then, while I watched, one of them, the small, black man, moved into the light and crossed the bandstand and started fooling around with his drums. Then—being funny and being, also, extremely ceremonious—Creole took Sonny by the arm and led him to the piano. A woman's voice called Sonny's name and a few hands started clapping. And Sonny, also being funny and being ceremonious, and so touched, I think, that he could have cried, but neither hiding it nor showing it, riding it like a man, grinned, and put both hands to his heart and bowed from the waist.

Creole then went to the bass fiddle and a lean, very bright-skinned brown man jumped up on the bandstand and picked up his horn. So there they were, and the atmosphere on the bandstand and in the room began to change and tighten. Someone stepped up to the microphone and announced them. Then there were all kinds of murmurs. Some people at the bar shushed others. The waitress ran around, frantically getting in the last orders, guys and chicks got closer to each other, and the lights on the bandstand, on the quartet, turned to a kind of indigo. Then they all looked different there. Creole looked about him for the last time, as though he were making certain that all his chickens were in the coop, and then he—jumped and struck the fiddle. And there they were.

All I know about music is that not many people ever really hear it. And even then,   230
on the rare occasions when something opens within, and the music enters, what we mainly hear, or hear corroborated, are personal, private, vanishing evocations. But the man who creates the music is hearing something else, is dealing with the roar rising from the void and imposing order on it as it hits the air. What is evoked in him, then, is of another order, more terrible because it has no words, and triumphant, too, for that

same reason. And his triumph, when he triumphs, is ours. I just watched Sonny's face. His face was troubled, he was working hard, but he wasn't with it. And I had the feeling that, in a way, everyone on the bandstand was waiting for him, both waiting for him and pushing him along. But as I began to watch Creole, I realized that it was Creole who held them all back. He had them on a short rein. Up there, keeping the beat with his whole body, wailing on the fiddle, with his eyes half closed, he was listening to everything, but he was listening to Sonny. He was having a dialogue with Sonny. He wanted Sonny to leave the shoreline and strike out for the deep water. He was Sonny's witness that deep water and drowning were not the same thing—he had been there, and he knew. And he wanted Sonny to know. He was waiting for Sonny to do the things on the keys which would let Creole know that Sonny was in the water.

And, while Creole listened, Sonny moved, deep within, exactly like someone in torment. I had never before thought of how awful the relationship must be between the musician and his instrument. He has to fill it, this instrument, with the breath of life, his own. He has to make it do what he wants it to do. And a piano is just a piano. It's made out of so much wood and wires and little hammers and big ones, and ivory. While there's only so much you can do with it, the only way to find this out is to try; to try and make it do everything.

And Sonny hadn't been near a piano for over a year. And he wasn't on much better terms with his life, not the life that stretched before him now. He and the piano stammered, started one way, got scared, stopped; started another way, panicked, marked time, started again; then seemed to have found a direction, panicked again, got stuck. And the face I saw on Sonny I'd never seen before. Everything had been burned out of it, and, at the same time, things usually hidden were being burned in, by the fire and fury of the battle which was occurring in him up there.

Yet, watching Creole's face as they neared the end of the first set, I had the feeling that something had happened, something I hadn't heard. Then they finished, there was scattered applause, and then, without an instant's warning, Creole started into something else, it was almost sardonic, it was *Am I Blue*. And, as though he commanded, Sonny began to play. Something began to happen. And Creole let out the reins. The dry, low, black man said something awful on the drums, Creole answered, and the drums talked back. Then the horn insisted, sweet and high, slightly detached perhaps, and Creole listened, commenting now and then, dry, and driving, beautiful and calm and old. Then they all came together again, and Sonny was part of the family again. I could tell this from his face. He seemed to have found, right there beneath his fingers, a damn brand-new piano. It seemed that he couldn't get over it. Then, for awhile, just being happy with Sonny, they seemed to be agreeing with him that brand-new pianos certainly were a gas.

Then Creole stepped forward to remind them that what they were playing was the blues. He hit something in all of them, he hit something in me, myself, and the music tightened and deepened, apprehension began to beat the air. Creole began to tell us what the blues were all about. They were not about anything very new. He and his boys up there were keeping it new, at the risk of ruin, destruction, madness, and death, in order to find new ways to make us listen. For, while the tale of how we suffer, and how we are delighted, and how we may triumph is never new, it always must be heard. There isn't any other tale to tell, it's the only light we've got in all this darkness.

And this tale, according to that face, that body, those strong hands on those 235 strings, has another aspect in every country, and a new depth in every generation.

Listen, Creole seemed to be saying, listen. Now these are Sonny's blues. He made the little black man on the drums know it, and the bright, brown man on the horn. Creole wasn't trying any longer to get Sonny in the water. He was wishing him Godspeed.° Then he stepped back, very slowly, filling the air with the immense suggestion that Sonny speak for himself.

Then they all gathered around Sonny and Sonny played. Every now and again one of them seemed to say, amen. Sonny's fingers filled the air with life, his life. But that life contained so many others. And Sonny went all the way back, he really began with the spare, flat statement of the opening phrase of the song. Then he began to make it his. It was very beautiful because it wasn't hurried and it was no longer a lament. I seemed to hear with what burning he had made it his, with what burning we had yet to make it ours, how we could cease lamenting. Freedom lurked around us and I understood, at last, that he could help us to be free if we would listen, that he would never be free until we did. Yet, there was no battle in his face now. I heard what he had gone through, and would continue to go through until he came to rest in earth. He had made it his: that long line, of which we knew only Mama and Daddy. And he was giving it back, as everything must be given back, so that, passing through death, it can live forever. I saw my mother's face again, and felt, for the first time, how the stones of the road she had walked on must have bruised her feet. I saw the moon-lit road where my father's brother died. And it brought something else back to me, and carried me past it. I saw my little girl again and felt Isabel's tears again, and I felt my own tears begin to rise. And I was yet aware that this was only a moment, that the world waited outside, as hungry as a tiger, and that trouble stretched above us, longer than the sky.

Then it was over. Creole and Sonny let out their breath, both soaking wet, and grinning. There was a lot of applause and some of it was real. In the dark, the girl came by and I asked her to take drinks to the bandstand. There was a long pause, while they talked up there in the indigo light and after awhile I saw the girl put a Scotch and milk on top of the piano for Sonny. He didn't seem to notice it, but just before they started playing again, he sipped from it and looked toward me, and nodded. Then he put it back on top of the piano. For me, then, as they began to play again, it glowed and shook above my brother's head like the very cup of trembling.°

Questions

1. From whose point of view is "Sonny's Blues" told? How do the narrator's values and experiences affect his view of the story?
2. What is the older brother's profession? Does it suggest anything about his personality?
3. How would this story change if it were told by Sonny?
4. What event prompts the narrator to write to his brother?
5. What does the narrator's mother ask him to do for Sonny? Does the older brother keep his promise?
6. The major characters in this story are called Mama, Daddy, and Sonny (the older brother is never named or even nicknamed). How do these names affect our sense of the story?
7. Reread the last four paragraphs and explain the significance of the statement "Now these are Sonny's blues." How has Sonny made this music his own?

---

wishing him Godspeed: wishing success.   *cup of trembling:* image of redemptive suffering from Isaiah 51:15-22—"See, I have taken out of your hand the cup of trembling, the dregs of the cup of My fury; you shall no longer drink it."

■ WRITING *effectively*

James Baldwin on Writing

Race and the African American Writer   1955

I know, in any case, that the most crucial time in my own development came when I was forced to recognize that I was a kind of bastard of the West; when I followed the line of my past I did not find myself in Europe but in Africa. And this meant that in some subtle way, in a really profound way, I brought to Shakespeare, Bach, Rembrandt, to the stones of Paris, to the cathedral at Chartres, and to the Empire State Building, a special attitude. These were not really my creations, they did not contain my history; I might search in them in vain forever for any reflection of myself. I was an interloper; this was not my heritage. At the same time I had no other heritage which I could possibly hope to use—I had certainly been unfitted for the jungle or the tribe. I would have to appropri-

James Baldwin

ate these white centuries, I would have to make them mine—I would have to accept my special attitude, my special place in this scheme—otherwise I would have no place in *any* scheme. What was the most difficult was the fact that I was forced to admit something I had always hidden from myself, which the American Negro has had to hide from himself as the price of his public progress; that I hated and feared the world. And this meant, not only that I thus gave the world an altogether murderous power over me, but also that in such a self-destroying limbo I could never hope to write.

One writes out of one thing only—one's own experience. Everything depends on how relentlessly one forces from this experience the last drop, sweet or bitter, it can possibly give. This is the only real concern of the artist, to recreate out of the disorder of life that order which is art. The difficulty then, for me, of being a Negro writer was the fact that I was, in effect, prohibited from examining my own experience too closely by the tremendous demands and the very real dangers of my social situation.

I don't think the dilemma outlined above is uncommon. I do think, since writers work in the disastrously explicit medium of language, that it goes a little way towards explaining why, out of the enormous resources of Negro speech and life, and despite the example of Negro music, prose written by Negroes has been generally speaking so pallid and so harsh. I have not written about being a Negro at such length because I expect that to be my only subject, but only because it was the gate I had to unlock before I could hope to write about anything else.

From "Autobiographical Notes"

THINKING ABOUT POINT OF VIEW

When we hear an outlandish piece of news, something that doesn't quite add up, we're well advised, as the saying goes, to consider the source. The same is true when we read a short story.

- **Consider who is telling the story.** A story's point of view determines how much confidence a reader should have in the events related. A story told from a third-person omniscient point of view generally provides a sense of authority and stability that makes the narrative seem reliable.
- **Ask why the narrator is telling the story.** The use of a first-person narrator, on the other hand, often suggests a certain bias, especially when the narrator relates events in which he or she has played a part. In such cases the narrator sometimes has an obvious interest in the audience's accepting his or her version of the story as truth.
- **Think about whether anything important is being left out of the story.** Is something of obvious importance to the situation not being reported? Understanding the limits of a narrator's point of view is key to interpreting what a story says.

CHECKLIST: Writing About Point of View

- ☐ How is the story narrated? Is it told in the third or the first person?
- ☐ If the story is told in the third person, is the point of view omniscient or does it confine itself to what is perceived by a particular character?
- ☐ What is gained by this choice?
- ☐ If the story is told by a first-person narrator, what is the speaker's main reason for telling the story? What does the narrator have to gain by making us believe his or her account?
- ☐ Does the first-person narrator fully understand his or her own motivations? Is there some important aspect of the narrator's character or situation that is being overlooked?
- ☐ Is there anything peculiar about the first-person narrator? Does this peculiarity create any suspicions about the narrator's accuracy or reliability?
- ☐ What does the narrator's perspective add? Would the story seem as memorable if related from another narrative angle?

WRITING ASSIGNMENT ON POINT OF VIEW

Choose a story from this book and analyze how point of view contributes to the story's overall meaning. Come up with a thesis sentence, and back up your argument with specific observations about the text. Incorporate at least three quotations, and document them, as explained in the writing chapters at the end of the book. Some stories that might lend themselves well to this assignment are "Sonny's Blues," "Cathedral," "The Tell-Tale Heart," and "Greasy Lake."

MORE TOPICS FOR WRITING

1. Retell the events in "A & P" from the point of view of one of the story's minor characters: Lengel, or Stokesie, or one of the girls. How does the story's emphasis change?

2. Here is another writing exercise to help you sense what a difference point of view makes. Write a short statement from the point of view of one of these characters: William Faulkner's Homer Barron (on "My Affair with Miss Emily") or ZZ Packer's Brownie Arnetta (on "I Was Framed: Why Does No One Believe Me?").

3. Imagine a story such as "A & P" or "A Rose for Emily" told by an omniscient third-person narrator. Write several paragraphs about what would be lost (or gained) by such a change.

4. Choose any tale from "Stories for Further Reading," and, in a paragraph or two, describe how point of view colors the general meaning. If you like, you may argue that the story might be told more effectively from an alternate point of view.

5. Think back to a confrontation in your own life, and describe that event from a point of view contrary to your own. Try to imagine yourself inside your speaker's personality, and present the facts as that person would, as convincingly as you can.

6. With "Sonny's Blues" in mind, write about a family member or friend from your own point of view, allowing, as Baldwin does, an understanding of that person's perspective to slowly develop.

7. Tell the story of a confrontation—biographical or fictional—from the point of view of a minor character peripheral to the central action. You could, for instance, tell the story of a disastrous first date from the point of view of the unlucky waitress who serves the couple dinner.

▶ TERMS FOR *review*

Points of View

Total omniscience ▶ Point of view in which the narrator knows everything about all of the characters and events in a story. A narrator with total omniscience can move freely from one character to another. Generally, a totally omniscient narrative is written in the third person.

Limited or selective omniscience ▶ Point of view in which the narrator sees into the minds of some but not all of the characters. Most typically, limited omniscience sees through the eyes of one major or minor character.

Impartial omniscience ▶ Point of view employed when an omniscient narrator, who presents the thoughts and actions of the characters, does not judge them or comment on them.

Editorial omniscience ▶ Point of view employed when an omniscient narrator goes beyond reporting the thoughts of his characters to make a critical judgment or commentary, making explicit the narrator's own thoughts or attitudes.

Objective point of view ▶ Point of view in which the third-person narrator merely reports dialogue and action with little or no interpretation or access to the characters' minds.

Types of Narrators

Omniscient or all-knowing narrator ▶ A narrator who has the ability to move freely through the consciousness of any character. The omniscient narrator also has complete knowledge of all of the external events in a story.

Participant or first-person narrator ▶ A narrator who is a participant in the action. Such a narrator refers to himself or herself as "I" and may be a major or minor character in the story.

Observer ▶ A first-person narrator who is relatively detached from or plays only a minor role in the events described.

Nonparticipant or third-person narrator ▶ A narrator who does not appear in the story as a character but is usually capable of revealing the thoughts and motives of one or more characters.

Innocent or naive narrator ▶ A character who fails to understand all the implications of the story he or she tells. The innocent narrator—often a child or childlike adult—is frequently used by an author to generate irony, sympathy, or pity by creating a gap between what the narrator perceives and what the reader knows.

Unreliable narrator ▶ A narrator who—intentionally or unintentionally—relates events in a subjective or distorted manner. The author usually provides some indication early on in such stories that the narrator is not to be completely trusted.

Narrative Techniques

Interior monologue ▶ An extended presentation of a character's thoughts in a narrative. Usually written in the present tense and printed without quotation marks, an interior monologue reads as if the character were speaking aloud to himself or herself, for the reader to overhear.

Stream of consciousness ▶ A type of modern narration that uses various literary devices, especially interior monologue, in an attempt to duplicate the subjective and associative nature of human consciousness.

3

CHARACTER

*Show me a character without anxieties
and I will show you a boring book.*

—MARGARET ATWOOD

From popular fiction and drama, both classic and contemporary, we are acquainted with many stereotyped characters. Called **stock characters**, they are often known by some outstanding trait or traits: the *bragging* soldier of Greek and Roman comedy, the Prince *Charming* of fairy tales, the *mad* scientist of horror movies, the *fearlessly reckless* police detective of urban action films, the *brilliant but alcoholic* brain surgeon of medical thrillers on television. Stock characters are especially convenient for writers of commercial fiction: they require little detailed portraiture, for we already know them well. Most writers of the literary story, however, attempt to create characters who strike us not as stereotypes but as unique individuals. Although stock characters tend to have single dominant virtues and vices, characters in the finest contemporary short stories tend to have many facets, like people we meet.

A **character**, then, is presumably an imagined person who inhabits a story—although that simple definition may admit to a few exceptions. In George Stewart's novel *Storm*, the protagonist is the wind; in Richard Adams's *Watership Down*, the main characters are rabbits. But usually we recognize, in the main characters of a story, human personalities that become familiar to us. If the story seems "true to life," we generally find that its characters act in a reasonably consistent manner and that the author has provided them with **motivation**: sufficient reason to behave as they do. Should a character behave in a sudden and unexpected way, seeming to deny what we have been told about his or her nature or personality, we trust that there was a reason for this behavior and that sooner or later we will discover it.

In good fiction, characters sometimes change or develop. In *A Christmas Carol*, Charles Dickens tells how Ebenezer Scrooge, a tightfisted miser, reforms overnight, suddenly gives to the poor, and endeavors to assist his clerk's struggling family. But Dickens amply demonstrates why Scrooge had such a change of heart: four ghostly visitors, stirring kind memories the old miser had forgotten and also warning him of the probable consequences of his habits, provide the character (and hence the story) with adequate motivation.

TYPES OF CHARACTERS

To borrow the useful terms of the English novelist E. M. Forster, characters may seem **flat** or **round**, depending on whether a writer sketches or sculpts them. A flat character has only one outstanding trait or feature, or at most a few distinguishing marks: for example, the familiar stock character of the mad scientist, with his lust for absolute power and his crazily gleaming eyes. Flat characters, however, need not be stock characters: in all of literature there is probably only one Tiny Tim, though his functions in *A Christmas Carol* are mainly to invoke blessings and to remind others of their Christian duties.

Some writers, notably Balzac, who peopled his many novels with hosts of characters, try to distinguish the flat ones by giving each a single odd physical feature or mannerism— a nervous twitch, a piercing gaze, an obsessive fondness for oysters. Round characters, however, present us with more facets—that is, their authors portray them in greater depth and in more generous detail. Such a round character may appear to us only as he appears to the other characters in the story. If their views of him differ, we will see him from more than one side. In other stories, we enter a character's mind and come to know him through his own thoughts, feelings, and perceptions.

Flat characters tend to stay the same throughout a story, but round characters often change—learn or become enlightened, grow or deteriorate. In William Faulkner's "Barn Burning" (Chapter 5), the boy Sarty Snopes, driven to defy his proud and violent father, becomes at the story's end more knowing and more mature. (Some critics call a fixed character **static**; a changing one, **dynamic**.) This is not to damn a flat character as an inferior creation. In most fiction—even the greatest—minor characters tend to be flat instead of round. Why? Rounding them would cost time and space; and so enlarged, they might only distract us from the main characters.

"A character, first of all, is the noise of his name," according to novelist William Gass. Names, chosen artfully, can indicate natures. A simple illustration is the completely virtuous Squire Allworthy, the foster father in *Tom Jones* by Henry Fielding. Subtler, perhaps, is the custom of giving a character a name that makes an **allusion**: a reference to some famous person, place, or thing. For his central characters in *Moby-Dick*, Herman Melville chose names from the Old Testament, calling his tragic and domineering Ahab after a biblical tyrant who came to a bad end, and his wandering narrator Ishmael after a biblical outcast. Whether or not it includes such a reference, a good name often reveals the character of the character. Charles Dickens, a vigorous and richly suggestive christener, named a couple of shyster lawyers Dodgson and Fogg (suggesting dodging evasiveness and foglike obfuscation), and named two heartless educators, who grimly drill their schoolchildren in "hard facts," Gradgind and M'Choakumchild.

Hero Versus Antihero

Instead of a hero, many a recent novel has featured an **antihero**: a protagonist conspicuously lacking in one or more of the usual attributes of a traditional **hero**, bravery, skill, idealism, sense of purpose. The antihero is an ordinary, unglorious citizen of the modern world, usually drawn (according to the Irish short story writer Sean O'Faolain) as someone "groping, puzzled, cross, mocking, frustrated, and isolated."

If epic poets once drew their heroes as decisive leaders of their people, embodying their people's highest ideals, antiheroes tend to be loners, without admirable qualities, just barely able to survive. A gulf separates Leopold Bloom, antihero of James Joyce's novel *Ulysses*, from the hero of the Greek *Odyssey*. In Homer's epic,

Ulysses wanders the Mediterranean, battling monsters and overcoming enchantments. In Joyce's novel, Bloom wanders the littered streets of Dublin, peddling advertising space. Meursault, the title character of Albert Camus's novel *The Stranger*, is so alienated from his own life that he is unmoved at the news of his mother's death.

Many contemporary writers of fiction would deny even that people have definite selves to alter. Following Sigmund Freud and other modern psychologists, they assume that a large part of human behavior is shaped in the unconscious—that, for instance, a person might fear horses, not because of a basically timid nature, but because of unconscious memories of having been nearly trampled by a horse when a child. To some writers it now appears that personality is more vulnerable to change from such causes as age, disease, neurosis, psychic shock, or brainwashing than was once believed.

Characterization, as practiced by nineteenth-century novelists, almost entirely disappears in Franz Kafka's *The Castle*, whose protagonist has no home, no family, no definite appearance—not even a name, just the initial K. Characters are things of the past, insisted the modern French novelist Alain Robbe-Grillet. Still, nearly all writers of fiction go on portraying them.

Katherine Anne Porter

The Jilting of Granny Weatherall

1930

Katherine Anne Porter (1890–1980) was born in Indian Creek, Texas. Her mother died when she was two, and Porter was raised by a grandmother who surrounded the growing girl with books. At sixteen she ran away from school and soon married a railway clerk in Louisiana. Three years later, she divorced her husband and began supporting herself as a reporter in Chicago, Denver, and Fort Worth, and sometimes as an actress and ballad singer while traveling through the South. Sojourns in Europe and in Mexico supplied her with material for some of her finest stories. Her brilliant, sensitive short fiction, first collected in Flowering Judas *(1930), won her a high reputation. Her one novel,* Ship of Fools *(1962), with which she*

Katherine Anne Porter

had struggled for twenty years, received harsh critical notices, but proved a commercial success. In 1965 her Collected Stories *received a Pulitzer Prize and a National Book Award.*

She flicked her wrist neatly out of Doctor Harry's pudgy careful fingers and pulled the sheet up to her chin. The brat ought to be in knee breeches. Doctoring around the country with spectacles on his nose! "Get along now, take your schoolbooks and go. There's nothing wrong with me."

Doctor Harry spread a warm paw like a cushion on her forehead where the forked green vein danced and made her eyelids twitch. "Now, now, be a good girl, and we'll have you up in no time."

"That's no way to speak to a woman nearly eighty years old just because she's down. I'd have you respect your elders, young man."

"Well, Missy, excuse me." Doctor Harry patted her cheek. "But I've got to warn you, haven't I? You're a marvel, but you must be careful or you're going to be good and sorry."

"Don't tell me what I'm going to be. I'm on my feet now, morally speaking. It's Cornelia. I had to go to bed to get rid of her."   5

Her bones felt loose, and floated around in her skin, and Doctor Harry floated like a balloon around the foot of the bed. He floated and pulled down his waistcoat and swung his glasses on a cord. "Well, stay where you are, it certainly can't hurt you."

"Get along and doctor your sick," said Granny Weatherall. "Leave a well woman alone. I'll call for you when I want you. . . . Where were you forty years ago when I pulled through milk-leg and double pneumonia? You weren't even born. Don't let Cornelia lead you on," she shouted, because Doctor Harry appeared to float up to the ceiling and out. "I pay my own bills, and I don't throw my money away on nonsense!"

She meant to wave good-by, but it was too much trouble. Her eyes closed of themselves, it was like a dark curtain drawn around the bed. The pillow rose and floated under her, pleasant as a hammock in a light wind. She listened to the leaves rustling outside the window. No, somebody was swishing newspapers: no, Cornelia and Doctor Harry were whispering together. She leaped broad awake, thinking they whispered in her ear.

"She was never like this, *never* like this!" "Well, what can we expect?" "Yes, eighty years old. . . ."

Well, and what if she was? She still had ears. It was like Cornelia to whisper   10
around doors. She always kept things secret in such a public way. She was always being tactful and kind. Cornelia was dutiful; that was the trouble with her. Dutiful and good: "So good and dutiful," said Granny, "that I'd like to spank her." She saw herself spanking Cornelia and making a fine job of it.

"What'd you say, Mother?"

Granny felt her face tying up in hard knots.

"Can't a body think, I'd like to know?"

"I thought you might want something."

"I do. I want a lot of things. First off, go away and don't whisper."   15

She lay and drowsed, hoping in her sleep that the children would keep out and let her rest a minute. It had been a long day. Not that she was tired. It was always pleasant to snatch a minute now and then. There was always so much to be done, let me see: tomorrow.

Tomorrow was far away and there was nothing to trouble about. Things were finished somehow when the time came; thank God there was always a little margin over for peace: then a person could spread out the plan of life and tuck in the edges orderly. It was good to have everything clean and folded away, with the hair brushes and tonic bottles sitting straight on the white embroidered linen: the day started without fuss and the pantry shelves laid out with rows of jelly glasses and brown jugs and white stone-china jars with blue whirligigs and words painted on them: coffee, tea, sugar, ginger, cinnamon, allspice: and the bronze clock with the lion on top nicely dusted off. The dust that lion could collect in twenty-four hours! The box in the attic with all those letters tied up, well, she'd have to go through that tomorrow. All those letters—George's letters and John's letters and her letters to them both— lying around for the children to find afterwards made her uneasy. Yes, that would be tomorrow's business. No use to let them know how silly she had been once.

While she was rummaging around she found death in her mind and it felt clammy and unfamiliar. She had spent so much time preparing for death there was no need for bringing it up again. Let it take care of itself now. When she was sixty she had felt very old, finished, and went around making farewell trips to see her children and grandchildren, with a secret in her mind: This is the very last of your mother, children! Then she made her will and came down with a long fever. That was all just a notion like a lot of other things, but it was lucky too, for she had once for all got over the idea of dying for a long time. Now she couldn't be worried. She hoped she had better sense now. Her father had lived to be one hundred and two years old and had drunk a noggin of strong hot toddy on his last birthday. He told the reporters it was his daily habit, and he owed his long life to it. He had made quite a scandal and was very pleased about it. She believed she'd just plague Cornelia a little.

"Cornelia! Cornelia!" No footsteps, but a sudden hand on her cheek. "Bless you, where have you been?"

"Here, Mother."

"Well, Cornelia, I want a noggin of hot toddy."

"Are you cold, darling?"

"I'm chilly, Cornelia. Lying in bed stops the circulation. I must have told you that a thousand times."

Well, she could just hear Cornelia telling her husband that Mother was getting a little childish and they'd have to humor her. The thing that most annoyed her was that Cornelia thought she was deaf, dumb, and blind. Little hasty glances and tiny gestures tossed around her and over her head saying, "Don't cross her, let her have her way, she's eighty years old," and she sitting there as if she lived in a thin glass cage. Sometimes Granny almost made up her mind to pack up and move back to her own house where nobody could remind her every minute that she was old. Wait, wait, Cornelia, till your own children whisper behind your back!

In her day she had kept a better house and had got more work done. She wasn't too old yet for Lydia to be driving eighty miles for advice when one of the children jumped the track, and Jimmy still dropped in and talked things over: "Now, Mammy, you've a good business head, I want to know what you think of this? . . ." Old. Cornelia couldn't change the furniture around without asking. Little things, little things! They had been so sweet when they were little. Granny wished the old days were back again with the children young and everything to be done over. It had been a hard pull, but not too much for her. When she thought of all the food she had cooked, and all the clothes she had cut and sewed, and all the gardens she had made—well, the children showed it. There they were, made out of her, and they couldn't get away from that. Sometimes she wanted to see John again and point to them and say, Well, I didn't do so badly, did I? But that would have to wait. That was for tomorrow. She used to think of him as a man, but now all the children were older than their father, and he would be a child beside her if she saw him now. It seemed strange and there was something wrong in the idea. Why, he couldn't possibly recognize her. She had fenced in a hundred acres once, digging the post holes herself and clamping the wires with just a negro boy to help. That changed a woman. John would be looking for a young woman with the peaked Spanish comb in her hair and the painted fan. Digging post holes changed a woman. Riding country roads in the winter when women had their babies was another thing: sitting up nights with sick horses and sick negroes and sick children and hardly ever losing one. John, I hardly ever lost one of them! John would see that in a minute, that would be something he could understand, she wouldn't have to explain anything!

It made her feel like rolling up her sleeves and putting the whole place to rights again. No matter if Cornelia was determined to be everywhere at once, there were a great many things left undone on this place. She would start tomorrow and do them. It was good to be strong enough for everything, even if all you made melted and changed and slipped under your hands, so that by the time you finished you almost forgot what you were working for. What was it I set out to do? she asked herself intently, but she could not remember. A fog rose over the valley, she saw it marching across the creek swallowing the trees and moving up the hill like an army of ghosts. Soon it would be at the near edge of the orchard, and then it was time to go in and light the lamps. Come in, children, don't stay out in the night air.

Lighting the lamps had been beautiful. The children huddled up to her and breathed like little calves waiting at the bars in the twilight. Their eyes followed the match and watched the flame rise and settle in a blue curve, then they moved away from her. The lamp was lit, they didn't have to be scared and hang on to mother any more. Never, never, never more. God, for all my life I thank Thee. Without Thee, my God, I could never have done it. Hail, Mary, full of grace.

I want you to pick all the fruit this year and see that nothing is wasted. There's always someone who can use it. Don't let good things rot for want of using. You waste life when you waste good food. Don't let things get lost. It's bitter to lose things. Now, don't let me get to thinking, not when I am tired and taking a little nap before supper. . . .

The pillow rose about her shoulders and pressed against her heart and the memory was being squeezed out of it: oh, push down the pillow, somebody: it would smother her if she tried to hold it. Such a fresh breeze blowing and such a green day with no threats in it. But he had not come, just the same. What does a woman do when she has put on the white veil and set out the white cake for a man and he doesn't come? She tried to remember. No, I swear he never harmed me but in that. He never harmed me but in that . . . and what if he did? There was the day, the day, but a whirl of dark smoke rose and covered it, crept up and over into the bright field where everything was planted so carefully in orderly rows. That was hell, she knew hell when she saw it. For sixty years she had prayed against remembering him and against losing her soul in the deep pit of hell, and now the two things were mingled in one and the thought of him was a smoky cloud from hell that moved and crept in her head when she had just got rid of Doctor Harry and was trying to rest a minute. Wounded vanity, Ellen, said a sharp voice in the top of her mind. Don't let your wounded vanity get the upper hand of you. Plenty of girls get jilted. You were jilted, weren't you? Then stand up to it. Her eyelids wavered and let in streamers of blue-gray light like tissue paper over her eyes. She must get up and pull the shades down or she'd never sleep. She was in bed again and the shades were not down. How could that happen? Better turn over, hide from the light, sleeping in the light gave you nightmares. "Mother, how do you feel now?" and a stinging wetness on her forehead. But I don't like having my face washed in cold water!

Hapsy? George? Lydia? Jimmy? No, Cornelia, and her features were swollen and full of little puddles. "They're coming, darling, they'll all be here soon." Go wash your face, child, you look funny.   30

Instead of obeying, Cornelia knelt down and put her head on the pillow. She seemed to be talking but there was no sound. "Well, are you tongue-tied? Whose birthday is it? Are you going to give a party?"

Cornelia's mouth moved urgently in strange shapes. "Don't do that, you bother me, daughter."

"Oh, no, Mother. Oh, no. . . ."

Nonsense. It was strange about children. They disputed your every word. "No what, Cornelia?"

"Here's Doctor Harry." 35

"I won't see that boy again. He just left three minutes ago."

"That was this morning, Mother. It's night now. Here's the nurse."

"This is Doctor Harry, Mrs. Weatherall. I never saw you look so young and happy!"

"Ah, I'll never be young again—but I'd be happy if they'd let me lie in peace and get rested."

She thought she spoke up loudly, but no one answered. A warm weight on her 40 forehead, a warm bracelet on her wrist, and a breeze went on whispering, trying to tell her something. A shuffle of leaves in the everlasting hand of God. He blew on them and they danced and rattled. "Mother, don't mind, we're going to give you a little hypodermic." "Look here, daughter, how do ants get in this bed? I saw sugar ants yesterday." Did you send for Hapsy too?

It was Hapsy she really wanted. She had to go a long way back through a great many rooms to find Hapsy standing with a baby on her arm. She seemed to herself to be Hapsy also, and the baby on Hapsy's arm was Hapsy and himself and herself, all at once, and there was no surprise in the meeting. Then Hapsy melted from within and turned flimsy as gray gauze and the baby was a gauzy shadow, and Hapsy came up close and said, "I thought you'd never come," and looked at her very searchingly and said, "You haven't changed a bit!" They leaned forward to kiss, when Cornelia began whispering from a long way off, "Oh, is there anything you want to tell me? Is there anything I can do for you?"

Yes, she had changed her mind after sixty years and she would like to see George. I want you to find George. Find him and be sure to tell him I forgot him. I want him to know I had my husband just the same and my children and my house like any other woman. A good house too and a good husband that I loved and fine children out of him. Better than I hoped for even. Tell him I was given back everything he took away and more. Oh, no, oh, God, no, there was something else besides the house and the man and the children. Oh, surely they were not all? What was it? Something not given back. . . . Her breath crowded down under her ribs and grew into a monstrous frightening shape with cutting edges; it bored up into her head, and the agony was unbelievable: Yes, John, get the Doctor now, no more talk, my time has come.

When this one was born it should be the last. The last. It should have been born first, for it was the one she had truly wanted. Everything came in good time. Nothing left out, left over. She was strong, in three days she would be as well as ever. Better. A woman needed milk in her to have her full health.

"Mother, do you hear me?"

"I've been telling you—" 45

"Mother, Father Connolly's here."

"I went to Holy Communion only last week. Tell him I'm not so sinful as all that."

"Father just wants to speak to you."

He could speak as much as he pleased. It was like him to drop in and inquire about her soul as if it were a teething baby, and then stay on for a cup of tea and a round of cards and gossip. He always had a funny story of some sort, usually about an Irishman who made his little mistakes and confessed them, and the point lay in some absurd thing he would blurt out in the confessional showing his struggles between native piety and original sin. Granny felt easy about her soul. Cornelia, where are your manners? Give Father Connolly a chair. She had her secret comfortable understanding with a few favorite saints who cleared a straight road to God for her. All as surely signed and sealed as the papers for the new Forty Acres. Forever . . . heirs and assigns forever. Since the day the wedding cake was not cut, but thrown out and wasted. The whole bottom dropped out of the world, and there she was blind and sweating with nothing under her feet and the walls falling away. His hand had caught her under the breast, she had not fallen, there was the freshly polished floor with the green rug on it, just as before. He had cursed like a sailor's parrot and said, "I'll kill him for you." Don't lay a hand on him, for my sake leave something to God. "Now, Ellen, you must believe what I tell you. . . ."

So there was nothing, nothing to worry about any more, except sometimes in the   50
night one of the children screamed in a nightmare, and they both hustled out shaking and hunting for the matches and calling, "There, wait a minute, here we are!" John, get the doctor now, Hapsy's time has come. But there was Hapsy standing by the bed in a white cap. "Cornelia, tell Hapsy to take off her cap. I can't see her plain."

Her eyes opened very wide and the room stood out like a picture she had seen somewhere. Dark colors with the shadows rising towards the ceiling in long angles. The tall black dresser gleamed with nothing on it but John's picture, enlarged from a little one, with John's eyes very black when they should have been blue. You never saw him, so how do you know how he looked? But the man insisted the copy was perfect, it was very rich and handsome. For a picture, yes, but it's not my husband. The table by the bed had a linen cover and a candle and a crucifix. The light was blue from Cornelia's silk lampshades. No sort of light at all, just frippery. You had to live forty years with kerosene lamps to appreciate honest electricity. She felt very strong and she saw Doctor Harry with a rosy nimbus around him.

"You look like a saint, Doctor Harry, and I vow that's as near as you'll ever come to it."

"She's saying something."

"I heard you, Cornelia. What's all this carrying-on?"

"Father Connolly's saying—"   55

Cornelia's voice staggered and bumped like a cart in a bad road. It rounded corners and turned back again and arrived nowhere. Granny stepped up in the cart very lightly and reached for the reins, but a man sat beside her and she knew him by his hands, driving the cart. She did not look in his face, for she knew without seeing, but looked instead down the road where the trees leaned over and bowed to each other and a thousand birds were singing a Mass. She felt like singing too, but she put her hand in the bosom of her dress and pulled out a rosary, and Father Connolly murmured Latin in a very solemn voice and tickled her feet. My God, will you stop that nonsense? I'm a married woman. What if he did run away and leave me to face the priest by myself? I found another a whole world better. I wouldn't have exchanged my husband for anybody except St. Michael himself, and you may tell him that for me with a thank you in the bargain.

Light flashed on her closed eyelids, and a deep roaring shook her. Cornelia, is that lightning? I hear thunder. There's going to be a storm. Close all the windows. Call the children in. . . . "Mother, here we are, all of us." "Is that you, Hapsy?" "Oh, no, I'm Lydia. We drove as fast as we could." Their faces drifted above her, drifted away.

The rosary fell out of her hands and Lydia put it back. Jimmy tried to help, their hands fumbled together, and Granny closed two fingers around Jimmy's thumb. Beads wouldn't do, it must be something alive. She was so amazed her thoughts ran round and round. So, my dear Lord, this is my death and I wasn't even thinking about it. My children have come to see me die. But I can't, it's not time. Oh, I always hated surprises. I wanted to give Cornelia the amethyst set—Cornelia, you're to have the amethyst set, but Hapsy's to wear it when she wants, and, Doctor Harry, do shut up. Nobody sent for you. Oh, my dear Lord, do wait a minute. I meant to do something about the Forty Acres, Jimmy doesn't need it and Lydia will later on, with that worthless husband of hers. I meant to finish the altar cloth and send six bottles of wine to Sister Borgia for her dyspepsia. I want to send six bottles of wine to Sister Borgia, Father Connolly, now don't let me forget.

Cornelia's voice made short turns and tilted over and crashed, "Oh, Mother, oh, Mother, oh, Mother. . . ."

"I'm not going, Cornelia. I'm taken by surprise. I can't go."

You'll see Hapsy again. What about her? "I thought you'd never come." Granny 60 made a long journey outward, looking for Hapsy. What if I don't find her? What then? Her heart sank down and down, there was no bottom to death, she couldn't come to the end of it. The blue light from Cornelia's lampshade drew into a tiny point in the center of her brain, it flickered and winked like an eye, quietly it fluttered and dwindled. Granny lay curled down within herself, amazed and watchful, staring at the point of light that was herself; her body was now only a deeper mass of shadow in an endless darkness and this darkness would curl around the light and swallow it up. God, give a sign!

For the second time there was no sign. Again no bridegroom and the priest in the house. She could not remember any other sorrow because this grief wiped them all away. Oh, no, there's nothing more cruel than this—I'll never forgive it. She stretched herself with a deep breath and blew out the light.

Questions

1. In the very first paragraph, what does the writer tell us about Ellen (Granny) Weatherall?

2. What does the name of Weatherall have to do with Granny's nature (or her life story)? What other traits or qualities do you find in her?

3. "Her bones felt loose, and floated around in her skin, and Doctor Harry floated like a balloon" (paragraph 6). What do you understand from this statement? By what other remarks does the writer indicate Granny's condition? In paragraph 56, why does Father Connolly tickle Granny's feet? At what other moments in the story does she fail to understand what is happening, or confuse the present with the past?

4. Exactly what happened to Ellen Weatherall sixty years earlier? What effects did this event have on her?

5. In paragraph 49, whom do you guess to be the man who "cursed like a sailor's parrot"? In paragraph 56, whom do you assume to be the man driving the cart? Is the fact that these persons are not clearly labeled and identified a failure on the author's part?

6. What is stream of consciousness? Would you call "The Jilting of Granny Weatherall" a stream-of-consciousness story? Refer to the story in your reply.

7. Sum up the character of the daughter Cornelia.

8. Why doesn't Granny's last child, Hapsy, come to her mother's deathbed?

9. Would you call the character of Doctor Harry "flat" or "round"? Why is his flatness (or roundness) appropriate to the story?

10. How is this the story of another "jilting"? What similarities are there between that fateful day of sixty years ago (described in paragraphs 29, 49, and 61) and the moment when Granny is dying? This time, who is the "bridegroom" not in the house?

11. "This is the story of an eighty-year-old woman lying in bed, getting groggy, and dying. I can't see why it should interest anybody." How would you answer this critic?

Nathaniel Hawthorne

Young Goodman Brown   (1835) 1846

Nathaniel Hawthorne (1804–1864) was born in the clipper-ship seaport of Salem, Massachusetts, son of a merchant captain (who died when the future novelist was only four years old) and great-great-grandson of a magistrate involved in the notorious Salem witchcraft trials. Hawthorne takes a keen interest in New England's sin-and-brimstone Puritan past in many of his stories, especially "Young Goodman Brown," and in the classic novel The Scarlet Letter *(1850), his deepest exploration of his major themes of conscience, sin, and guilt. In 1825 Hawthorne graduated from Bowdoin College; one of his classmates—and his lifelong best friend—was Franklin Pierce, who in 1852 would be elected president of the United States.*

Nathaniel Hawthorne

After college, Hawthorne lived at home and trained to be a writer. His first novel, Fanshawe *(1828), begun while he was still an undergraduate, was published anonymously and at his own expense. During this period, Hawthorne also experienced great difficulty in trying to publish his short fiction, both in magazines and in book form, until the appearance of* Twice-Told Tales *(1837). In 1841, he was appointed to a position in the Boston Custom House; in the following year he married Sophia Peabody. The newlyweds settled in the Old Manse in Concord, Massachusetts. Three more novels followed:* The House of the Seven Gables *(1851, the story of a family curse, tinged with nightmarish humor),* The Blithedale Romance *(1852, drawn from his short, irritating stay at a Utopian commune, Brook Farm), and* The Marble Faun *(1860, inspired by a stay in Italy). When Franklin Pierce ran for president, Hawthorne wrote his campaign biography. After taking office, Pierce appointed his old friend American consul at Liverpool, England. Depressed by ill health and the terrible toll of the Civil War, Hawthorne died suddenly while on a tour with Pierce of New Hampshire's White Mountains. With his contemporary Edgar Allan Poe, Hawthorne transformed the American short story from popular magazine filler into a major literary form.*

Young Goodman° Brown came forth, at sunset, into the street of Salem village,° but put his head back, after crossing the threshold, to exchange a parting kiss with his young wife. And Faith, as the wife was aptly named, thrust her own pretty head into

Goodman: title given by Puritans to a male head of a household; a farmer or other ordinary citizen.
Salem village: in England's Massachusetts Bay Colony.

the street, letting the wind play with the pink ribbons of her cap, while she called to Goodman Brown.

"Dearest heart," whispered she, softly and rather sadly, when her lips were close to his ear, "pray thee, put off your journey until sunrise, and sleep in your own bed to-night. A lone woman is troubled with such dreams and such thoughts, that she's afraid of herself, sometimes. Pray, tarry with me this night, dear husband, of all nights in the year!"

"My love and my Faith," replied young Goodman Brown, "of all nights in the year, this one night must I tarry away from thee. My journey, as thou callest it, forth and back again, must needs be done 'twixt now and sunrise. What, my sweet, pretty wife, dost thou doubt me already, and we but three months married!"

"Then, God bless you!" said Faith, with the pink ribbons, "and may you find all well, when you come back."

"Amen!" cried Goodman Brown. "Say thy prayers, dear Faith, and go to bed at dusk, and no harm will come to thee." 5

So they parted; and the young man pursued his way, until, being about to turn the corner by the meeting-house, he looked back, and saw the head of Faith still peeping after him, with a melancholy air, in spite of her pink ribbons.

"Poor little Faith!" thought he, for his heart smote him. "What a wretch am I, to leave her on such an errand! She talks of dreams, too. Methought, as she spoke, there was trouble in her face, as if a dream had warned her what work is to be done to-night. But, no, no! 'twould kill her to think it. Well; she's a blessed angel on earth; and after this one night, I'll cling to her skirts and follow her to Heaven."

With this excellent resolve for the future, Goodman Brown felt himself justified in making more haste on his present evil purpose. He had taken a dreary road, darkened by all the gloomiest trees of the forest, which barely stood aside to let the narrow path creep through, and closed immediately behind. It was all as lonely as could be; and there is this peculiarity in such a solitude, that the traveller knows not who may be concealed by the innumerable trunks and the thick boughs overhead; so that, with lonely footsteps, he may yet be passing through an unseen multitude.

"There may be a devilish Indian behind every tree," said Goodman Brown, to himself; and he glanced fearfully behind him, as he added, "What if the devil himself should be at my very elbow!"

His head being turned back, he passed a crook of the road, and looking forward again, beheld the figure of a man, in grave and decent attire, seated at the foot of an old tree. He arose, at Goodman Brown's approach, and walked onward, side by side with him. 10

"You are late, Goodman Brown," said he. "The clock of the Old South was striking as I came through Boston; and that is full fifteen minutes agone."°

"Faith kept me back awhile," replied the young man, with a tremor in his voice, caused by the sudden appearance of his companion, though not wholly unexpected.

It was now deep dusk in the forest, and deepest in that part of it where these two were journeying. As nearly as could be discerned, the second traveller was about fifty years old, apparently in the same rank of life as Goodman Brown, and bearing a considerable resemblance to him, though perhaps more in expression than features. Still, they might have been taken for father and son. And yet, though the elder person was as simply clad as the younger, and as simple in manner too, he had an indescribable air

---

full fifteen minutes agone: Apparently this mystery man has traveled in a flash from Boston's Old South Church all the way to the woods beyond Salem—as the crow flies, a good sixteen miles.

of one who knew the world, and would not have felt abashed at the governor's dinner-table, or in King William's court,° were it possible that his affairs should call him thither. But the only thing about him, that could be fixed upon as remarkable, was his staff, which bore the likeness of a great black snake, so curiously wrought, that it might almost be seen to twist and wriggle itself, like a living serpent. This, of course, must have been an ocular deception, assisted by the uncertain light.

"Come, Goodman Brown!" cried his fellow-traveller, "this is a dull pace for the beginning of a journey. Take my staff, if you are so soon weary."

"Friend," said the other, exchanging his slow pace for a full stop, "having kept covenant by meeting thee here, it is my purpose now to return whence I came. I have scruples, touching the matter thou wot'st° of."   15

"Sayest thou so?" replied he of the serpent, smiling apart. "Let us walk on, never-theless, reasoning as we go, and if I convince thee not, thou shalt turn back. We are but a little way in the forest, yet."

"Too far, too far!" exclaimed the goodman, unconsciously resuming his walk. "My father never went into the woods on such an errand, nor his father before him. We have been a race of honest men and good Christians, since the days of the martyrs.° And shall I be the first of the name of Brown, that ever took this path, and kept—"

"Such company, thou wouldst say," observed the elder person, interpreting his pause. "Well said, Goodman Brown! I have been as well acquainted with your fam-ily as with ever a one among the Puritans; and that's no trifle to say. I helped your grandfather, the constable, when he lashed the Quaker woman so smartly through the streets of Salem. And it was I that brought your father a pitch-pine knot, kin-dled at my own hearth, to set fire to an Indian village, in King Philip's war.° They were my good friends, both; and many a pleasant walk have we had along this path, and returned merrily after midnight. I would fain be friends with you, for their sake."

"If it be as thou sayest," replied Goodman Brown, "I marvel they never spoke of these matters. Or, verily, I marvel not, seeing that the least rumor of the sort would have driven them from New England. We are a people of prayer, and good works, to boot, and abide no such wickedness."

"Wickedness or not," said the traveller with the twisted staff, "I have a very general acquaintance here in New England. The deacons of many a church have drunk the communion wine with me; the selectmen, of divers towns, make me their chairman; and a majority of the Great and General Court are firm supporters of my interest. The governor and I, too—but these are state-secrets."   20

"Can this be so!" cried Goodman Brown, with a stare of amazement at his undis-turbed companion. "Howbeit, I have nothing to do with the governor and council; they have their own ways, and are no rule for a simple husbandman, like me. But, were I to go on with thee, how should I meet the eye of that good old man, our minister, at Salem village? Oh, his voice would make me tremble, both Sabbath-day and lecture-day!"°

King William's court: back in England, where William III reigned from 1689 to 1702. *wot'st*: know. *days of the martyrs*: a time when many forebears of the New England Puritans had given their lives for religious convictions—when Mary I (Mary Tudor, nicknamed "Bloody Mary"), queen of England from 1553 to 1558, briefly reestablished the Roman Catholic Church in England and launched a campaign of persecu-tion against Protestants. *King Philip's war*: Metacomet, or King Philip (as the English called him), chief of the Wampanoag Indians, had led a bitter, widespread uprising of several New England tribes (1675–78). Metacomet died in the war, as did one out of every ten white male colonists. *lecture-day*: a weekday when everyone had to go to church to hear a sermon or Bible-reading.

Thus far, the elder traveller had listened with due gravity, but now burst into a fit of irrepressible mirth, shaking himself so violently, that his snake-like staff actually seemed to wriggle in sympathy.

"Ha! ha! ha!" shouted he, again and again; then composing himself, "Well, go on, Goodman Brown, go on; but pray thee, don't kill me with laughing!"

"Well, then, to end the matter at once," said Goodman Brown, considerably nettled, "there is my wife, Faith. It would break her dear little heart; and I'd rather break my own!"

"Nay, if that be the case," answered the other, "e'en go thy ways, Goodman Brown. I would not, for twenty old women like the one hobbling before us, that Faith should come to any harm." 25

As he spoke, he pointed his staff at a female figure on the path, in whom Goodman Brown recognized a very pious and exemplary dame, who had taught him his catechism, in youth, and was still his moral and spiritual adviser, jointly with the minister and Deacon Gookin.

"A marvel, truly, that Goody° Cloyse should be so far in the wilderness, at nightfall!" said he. "But, with your leave, friend, I shall take a cut through the woods, until we have left this Christian woman behind. Being a stranger to you, she might ask whom I was consorting with, and whither I was going."

"Be it so," said his fellow-traveller. "Betake you to the woods, and let me keep the path."

Accordingly, the young man turned aside, but took care to watch his companion, who advanced softly along the road, until he had come within a staff's length of the old dame. She, meanwhile, was making the best of her way, with singular speed for so aged a woman, and mumbling some indistinct words, a prayer, doubtless, as she went. The traveller put forth his staff, and touched her withered neck with what seemed the serpent's tail.

"The devil!" screamed the pious old lady. 30

"Then Goody Cloyse knows her old friend?" observed the traveller, confronting her, and leaning on his writhing stick.

"Ah, forsooth, and is it your worship, indeed?" cried the good dame. "Yea, truly is it, and in the very image of my old gossip,° Goodman Brown, the grandfather of the silly fellow that now is. But—would your worship believe it?—my broomstick hath strangely disappeared, stolen, as I suspect, by that unhanged witch, Goody Cory, and that, too, when I was all anointed with the juice of smallage and cinquefoil and wolf's bane°—"

"Mingled with fine wheat and the fat of a new-born babe," said the shape of old Goodman Brown.

"Ah, your worship knows the receipt,"° cried the old lady, cackling aloud. "So, as I was saying, being all ready for the meeting, and no horse to ride on, I made up my mind to foot it; for they tell me, there is a nice young man to be taken into communion

---

Goody: short for Goodwife, title for a married woman of ordinary station. In his story, Hawthorne borrows from history the names of two "Goodys"—Goody Cloyse and Goody Cory—and one unmarried woman, Martha Carrier. In 1692 Hawthorne's great-great-grandfather John Hathorne, a judge in the Salem witchcraft trials, had condemned all three to be hanged. *gossip*: friend or kinsman. *smallage and cinquefoil and wolf's bane*: wild plants—here, ingredients for a witch's brew. *receipt*: recipe.

to-night. But now your good worship will lend me your arm, and we shall be there in a twinkling."

"That can hardly be," answered her friend. "I may not spare you my arm, Goody Cloyse, but here is my staff, if you will."   35

So saying, he threw it down at her feet, where, perhaps, it assumed life, being one of the rods which its owner had formerly lent to the Egyptian Magi.° Of this fact, however, Goodman Brown could not take cognizance. He had cast up his eyes in astonishment, and looking down again, beheld neither Goody Cloyse nor the serpentine staff, but his fellow-traveller alone, who waited for him as calmly as if nothing had happened.

"That old woman taught me my catechism!" said the young man; and there was a world of meaning in this simple comment.

They continued to walk onward, while the elder traveller exhorted his companion to make good speed and persevere in the path, discoursing so aptly, that his arguments seemed rather to spring up in the bosom of his auditor, than to be suggested by himself. As they went, he plucked a branch of maple, to serve for a walking-stick, and began to strip it of the twigs and little boughs, which were wet with evening dew. The moment his fingers touched them, they became strangely withered and dried up, as with a week's sunshine. Thus the pair proceeded, at a good free pace, until suddenly, in a gloomy hollow of the road, Goodman Brown sat himself down on the stump of a tree, and refused to go any farther.

"Friend," said he, stubbornly, "my mind is made up. Not another step will I budge on this errand. What if a wretched old woman do choose to go to the devil, when I thought she was going to Heaven! Is that any reason why I should quit my dear Faith, and go after her?"

"You will think better of this, by-and-by," said his acquaintance, composedly.   40
"Sit here and rest yourself awhile; and when you feel like moving again, there is my staff to help you along."

Without more words, he threw his companion the maple stick, and was as speed-ily out of sight, as if he had vanished into the deepening gloom. The young man sat a few moments, by the road-side, applauding himself greatly, and thinking with how clear a conscience he should meet the minister, in his morning-walk, nor shrink from the eye of good old Deacon Gookin. And what calm sleep would be his, that very night, which was to have been spent so wickedly, but purely and sweetly now, in the arms of Faith! Amidst these pleasant and praiseworthy meditations, Goodman Brown heard the tramp of horses along the road, and deemed it advisable to conceal himself within the verge of the forest, conscious of the guilty purpose that had brought him thither, though now so happily turned from it.

On came the hoof-tramps and the voices of the riders, two grave old voices, con-versing soberly as they drew near. These mingled sounds appeared to pass along the road, within a few yards of the young man's hiding-place; but owing, doubtless, to the depth of the gloom, at that particular spot, neither the travellers nor their steeds were visible. Though their figures brushed the small boughs by the way-side, it could not be seen that they intercepted, even for a moment, the faint gleam from the strip of

---

Egyptian Magi: In the Bible, Pharaoh's wise men and sorcerers who by their magical powers changed their rods into live serpents. (This incident, part of the story of Moses and Aaron, is related in Exodus 7:8–12.)

bright sky, athwart which they must have passed. Goodman Brown alternately crouched and stood on tip-toe, pulling aside the branches, and thrusting forth his head as far as he durst, without discerning so much as a shadow. It vexed him the more, because he could have sworn, were such a thing possible, that he recognized the voices of the minister and Deacon Gookin, jogging along quietly, as they were wont to do, when bound to some ordination or ecclesiastical council. While yet within hearing, one of the riders stopped to pluck a switch.

"Of the two, reverend Sir," said the voice like the deacon's, "I had rather miss an ordination-dinner than to-night's meeting. They tell me that some of our community are to be here from Falmouth and beyond, and others from Connecticut and Rhode Island; besides several of the Indian powows,° who, after their fashion, know almost as much deviltry as the best of us. Moreover, there is a goodly young woman to be taken into communion."

"Mighty well, Deacon Gookin!" replied the solemn old tones of the minister. "Spur up, or we shall be late. Nothing can be done, you know, until I get on the ground."

The hoofs clattered again, and the voices, talking so strangely in the empty air, passed on through the forest, where no church had ever been gathered, nor solitary Christian prayed. Whither, then, could these holy men be journeying, so deep into the heathen wilderness? Young Goodman Brown caught hold of a tree, for support, being ready to sink down on the ground, faint and overburdened with the heavy sickness of his heart. He looked up to the sky, doubting whether there really was a Heaven above him. Yet, there was the blue arch, and the stars brightening in it.

"With Heaven above, and Faith below, I will yet stand firm against the devil!" cried Goodman Brown.

While he still gazed upward, into the deep arch of the firmament, and had lifted his hands to pray, a cloud, though no wind was stirring, hurried across the zenith, and hid the brightening stars. The blue sky was still visible, except directly overhead, where this black mass of cloud was sweeping swiftly northward. Aloft in the air, as if from the depths of the cloud, came a confused and doubtful sound of voices. Once, the listener fancied that he could distinguish the accents of town's-people of his own, men and women, both pious and ungodly, many of whom he had met at the communion-table, and had seen others rioting at the tavern. The next moment, so indistinct were the sounds, he doubted whether he had heard aught but the murmur of the old forest, whispering without a wind. Then came a stronger swell of those familiar tones, heard daily in the sunshine, at Salem village, but never, until now, from a cloud of night. There was one voice, of a young woman, uttering lamentations, yet with an uncertain sorrow, and entreating for some favor, which, perhaps, it would grieve her to obtain. And all the unseen multitude, both saints and sinners, seemed to encourage her onward.

"Faith!" shouted Goodman Brown, in a voice of agony and desperation; and the echoes of the forest mocked him, crying—"Faith! Faith!" as if bewildered wretches were seeking her, all through the wilderness.

The cry of grief, rage, and terror, was yet piercing the night, when the unhappy husband held his breath for a response. There was a scream, drowned immediately in

powows: Indian priests or medicine men.

a louder murmur of voices, fading into far-off laughter, as the dark cloud swept away, leaving the clear and silent sky above Goodman Brown. But something fluttered lightly down through the air, and caught on the branch of a tree. The young man seized it, and beheld a pink ribbon.

"My Faith is gone!" cried he, after one stupefied moment. "There is no good on earth; and sin is but a name. Come, devil! for to thee is this world given." 50

And maddened with despair, so that he laughed loud and long, did Goodman Brown grasp his staff and set forth again, at such a rate, that he seemed to fly along the forest-path, rather than to walk or run. The road grew wilder and drearier, and more faintly traced, and vanished at length, leaving him in the heart of the dark wilderness, still rushing onward, with the instinct that guides mortal man to evil. The whole forest was peopled with frightful sounds; the creaking of the trees, the howling of wild beasts, and the yell of Indians; while, sometimes, the wind tolled like a distant church-bell, and sometimes gave a broad roar around the traveller, as if all Nature were laughing him to scorn. But he was himself the chief horror of the scene, and shrank not from its other horrors.

"Ha! ha! ha!" roared Goodman Brown, when the wind laughed at him. "Let us hear which will laugh loudest! Think not to frighten me with your deviltry! Come witch, come wizard, come Indian powow, come devil himself! and here comes Goodman Brown. You may as well fear him as he fear you!"

In truth, all through the haunted forest, there could be nothing more frightful than the figure of Goodman Brown. On he flew, among the black pines, brandishing his staff with frenzied gestures, now giving vent to an inspiration of horrid blasphemy, and now shouting forth such laughter, as set all the echoes of the forest laughing like demons around him. The fiend in his own shape is less hideous, than when he rages in the breast of man. Thus sped the demoniac on his course, until, quivering among the trees, he saw a red light before him, as when the felled trunks and branches of a clearing have been set on fire, and throw up their lurid blaze against the sky, at the hour of midnight. He paused, in a lull of the tempest that had driven him onward, and heard the swell of what seemed a hymn, rolling solemnly from a distance, with the weight of many voices. He knew the tune; it was a familiar one in the choir of the village meeting-house. The verse died heavily away, and was lengthened by a chorus, not of human voices, but of all the sounds of the benighted wilderness, pealing in awful harmony together. Goodman Brown cried out; and his cry was lost to his own ear, by its unison with the cry of the desert.

In the interval of silence, he stole forward, until the light glared full upon his eyes. At one extremity of an open space, hemmed in by the dark wall of the forest, arose a rock, bearing some rude, natural resemblance either to an altar or a pulpit, and surrounded by four blazing pines, their tops aflame, their stems untouched, like candles at an evening meeting. The mass of foliage, that had overgrown the summit of the rock, was all on fire, blazing high into the night, and fitfully illuminating the whole field. Each pendent twig and leafy festoon was in a blaze. As the red light arose and fell, a numerous congregation alternately shone forth, then disappeared in shadow, and again grew, as it were, out of the darkness, peopling the heart of the solitary woods at once.

"A grave and dark-clad company!" quoth Goodman Brown. 55

In truth, they were such. Among them, quivering to-and-fro, between gloom and splendor, appeared faces that would be seen, next day, at the council-board of the province, and others which, Sabbath after Sabbath, looked devoutly heaven-ward, and benignantly over the crowded pews, from the holiest pulpits in the land. Some affirm that the lady of the governor was there. At least, there were high dames well known to her, and wives of honored husbands, and widows, a great multitude, and ancient maidens, all of excellent repute, and fair young girls, who trembled, lest their mothers should espy them. Either the sudden gleams of light, flashing over the obscure field, bedazzled Goodman Brown, or he recognized a score of the church-members of Salem village, famous for their especial sanctity. Good old Deacon Gookin had arrived, and waited at the skirts of that venerable saint, his revered pas-tor. But, irreverently consorting with these grave, reputable, and pious people, these elders of the church, these chaste dames and dewy virgins, there were men of dis-solute lives and women of spotted fame, wretches given over to all mean and filthy vice, and suspected even of horrid crimes. It was strange to see, that the good shrank not from the wicked, nor were the sinners abashed by the saints. Scattered, also, among their pale-faced enemies, were the Indian priests, or powows, who had often scared their native forest with more hideous incantations than any known to English witchcraft.

"But, where is Faith?" thought Goodman Brown; and, as hope came into his heart, he trembled.

Another verse of the hymn arose, a slow and mournful strain, such as the pious love, but joined to words which expressed all that our nature can conceive of sin, and darkly hinted at far more. Unfathomable to mere mortals is the lore of fiends. Verse after verse was sung, and still the chorus of the desert swelled between, like the deepest tone of a mighty organ. And, with the final peal of that dreadful anthem, there came a sound, as if the roaring wind, the rushing streams, the howling beasts, and every other voice of the unconverted wilderness, were mingling and according with the voice of guilty man, in homage to the prince of all. The four blazing pines threw up a loftier flame, and obscurely discovered shapes and visages of horror on the smoke-wreaths, above the impious assembly. At the same moment, the fire on the rock shot redly forth, and formed a glowing arch above its base, where now appeared a figure. With reverence be it spoken, the figure bore no slight similitude, both in garb and manner, to some grave divine of the New England churches.

"Bring forth the converts!" cried a voice, that echoed through the field and rolled into the forest.

At the word, Goodman Brown stepped forth from the shadow of the trees, and approached the congregation, with whom he felt a loathful brotherhood, by the sym-pathy of all that was wicked in his heart. He could have well nigh sworn, that the shape of his own dead father beckoned him to advance, looking downward from a smoke-wreath, while a woman, with dim features of despair, threw out her hand to warn him back. Was it his mother? But he had no power to retreat one step, nor to resist, even in thought, when the minister and good old Deacon Gookin seized his arms, and led him to the blazing rock. Thither came also the slender form of a veiled female, led between Goody Cloyse, that pious teacher of the catechism, and Martha Carrier, who had received the devil's promise to be queen of hell. A rampant hag was she! And there stood the proselytes,° beneath the canopy of fire.

60

proselytes: new converts.

"Welcome, my children," said the dark figure, "to the communion of your race! Ye have found, thus young, your nature and your destiny. My children, look behind you!"

They turned; and flashing forth, as it were, in a sheet of flame, the fiend-worshippers were seen; the smile of welcome gleamed darkly on every visage.

"There," resumed the sable form, "are all whom ye have reverenced from youth. Ye deemed them holier than yourselves, and shrank from your own sin, contrasting it with their lives of righteousness, and prayerful aspirations heavenward. Yet, here are they all, in my worshipping assembly! This night it shall be granted you to know their secret deeds; how hoary-bearded elders of the church have whispered wanton words to the young maids of their households; how many a woman, eager for widow's weeds, has given her husband a drink at bedtime, and let him sleep his last sleep in her bosom; how beardless youths have made haste to inherit their fathers' wealth; and how fair damsels—blush not, sweet ones!—have dug little graves in the garden, and bidden me, the sole guest, to an infant's funeral. By the sympathy of your human hearts for sin, ye shall scent out all the places—whether in church, bed-chamber, street, field, or forest—where crime has been committed, and shall exult to behold the whole earth one stain of guilt, one mighty bloodspot. Far more than this! It shall be yours to penetrate, in every bosom, the deep mystery of sin, the fountain of all wicked arts, and which inexhaustibly supplies more evil impulses than human power—than my power, at its utmost!—can make manifest in deeds. And now, my children, look upon each other."

They did so; and, by the blaze of the hell-kindled torches, the wretched man beheld his Faith, and the wife her husband, trembling before that unhallowed altar.

"Lo! there ye stand, my children," said the figure, in a deep and solemn tone, almost sad, with its despairing awfulness, as if his once angelic nature could yet mourn for our miserable race. "Depending upon one another's hearts, ye had still hoped, that virtue were not all a dream. Now are ye undeceived! Evil is the nature of mankind. Evil must be your only happiness. Welcome, again, my children, to the communion of your race!"

"Welcome!" repeated the fiend-worshippers, in one cry of despair and triumph.

And there they stood, the only pair, as it seemed, who were yet hesitating on the verge of wickedness, in this dark world. A basin was hollowed, naturally, in the rock. Did it contain water, reddened by the lurid light? or was it blood? or, perchance, a liquid flame? Herein did the Shape of Evil dip his hand, and prepare to lay the mark of baptism upon their foreheads, that they might be partakers of the mystery of sin, more conscious of the secret guilt of others, both in deed and thought, than they could now be of their own. The husband cast one look at his pale wife, and Faith at him. What polluted wretches would the next glance show them to each other, shuddering alike at what they disclosed and what they saw!

"Faith! Faith!" cried the husband. "Look up to Heaven, and resist the Wicked one!"

Whether Faith obeyed, he knew not. Hardly had he spoken, when he found himself amid calm night and solitude, listening to a roar of the wind, which died heavily away through the forest. He staggered against the rock and felt it chill and damp, while a hanging twig, that had been all on fire, besprinkled his cheek with the coldest dew.

65

The next morning, young Goodman Brown came slowly into the street of 70
Salem village, staring around him like a bewildered man. The good old minister
was taking a walk along the grave-yard, to get an appetite for breakfast and meditate his sermon, and bestowed a blessing, as he passed, on Goodman Brown. He
shrank from the venerable saint, as if to avoid an anathema.° Old Deacon Good-
kin was at domestic worship, and the holy words of his prayer were heard through
the open window. "What God doth the wizard pray to?" quoth Goodman Brown.
Goody Cloyse, that excellent old Christian, stood in the early sunshine, at her
own lattice, catechizing a little girl, who had brought her a pint of morning's
milk. Goodman Brown snatched away the child, as from the grasp of the fiend
himself. Turning the corner by the meeting-house, he spied the head of Faith,
with the pink ribbons, gazing anxiously forth, and bursting into such joy at sight
of him, that she skipt along the street, and almost kissed her husband before the
whole village. But, Goodman Brown looked sternly and sadly into her face, and
passed on without a greeting.

Had Goodman Brown fallen asleep in the forest, and only dreamed a wild dream
of a witch-meeting?

Be it so, if you will. But, alas! it was a dream of evil omen for young Goodman
Brown. A stern, a sad, a darkly meditative, a distrustful, if not a desperate man, did
he become, from the night of that fearful dream. On the Sabbath-day, when the
congregation were singing a holy psalm, he could not listen, because an anthem of
sin rushed loudly upon his ear, and drowned all the blessed strain. When the minister spoke from the pulpit, with power and fervid eloquence, and, with his hand on
the open Bible, of the sacred truths of our religion, and of saint-like lives and triumphant deaths, and of future bliss or misery unutterable, then did Goodman
Brown turn pale, dreading, lest the roof should thunder down upon the gray blas-
phemer and his hearers. Often, awakening suddenly at midnight, he shrank from
the bosom of Faith, and at morning or even-tide, when the family knelt down at
prayer, he scowled, and muttered to himself, and gazed sternly at his wife, and
turned away. And when he had lived long, and was borne to his grave, a hoary
corpse, followed by Faith, an aged woman, and children and grandchildren, a
goodly procession, besides neighbors, not a few, they carved no hopeful verse upon
his tombstone; for his dying hour was gloom.

Questions

1. Hawthorne's story is set in Salem, Massachusetts. What historical associations does this
   setting suggest to the reader?
2. Why is Brown's new bride Faith "aptly named" according to the narrator? What does the
   name "Goodman Brown" suggest about the character of the protagonist?
3. Is there any significance to the fact that the old man in the woods seems to resemble
   Brown?
4. As Brown and the stranger proceed deeper into the woods, what does Brown find out that
   troubles him? When the pink ribbon flutters to the ground, as though fallen from something airborne (paragraph 49), what does Brown assume? What effect does this event
   have upon his determination to resist the devil?

anathema: an official curse, a decree that casts one out of a church and bans him or her from receiving the
sacraments.

5. Is it significant that most of the story's action takes place at night and in the woods?
6. What is the nature of the ceremony going on in the woods? What is being transacted between the old man and the townspeople?
7. What power does the devil promise to give his communicants (paragraph 63)?
8. Is Brown's experience in the woods real? If not, what other explanation can you provide?
9. What would be lost if the last three paragraphs of the tale were omitted?

Katherine Mansfield

Miss Brill   1922

Katherine Mansfield

Katherine Mansfield Beauchamp (1888–1923), who shortened her byline, was born into a sedate Victorian family in New Zealand, the daughter of a successful businessman. At fifteen, she emigrated to England to attend school and did not ever permanently return Down Under. In 1918, after a time of wild-oat sowing in bohemian London, she married the journalist and critic John Middleton Murry. All at once, Mansfield found herself struggling to define her sexual identity, to earn a living by her pen, to endure World War I (in which her brother was killed in action), and to survive the ravages of tuberculosis. She died at thirty-four, in France, at a spiritualist commune where she had sought to regain her health. Mansfield wrote no novels, but during her brief career concentrated on the short story, in which form of art she has few peers. Bliss (1920) and The Garden-Party and Other Stories (1922) were greeted with an acclaim that has continued; her collected short stories were published in 1937. Some of her stories celebrate life, others wryly poke fun at it. Many reveal, in ordinary lives, small incidents that open like doorways into significances.

Although it was so brilliantly fine—the blue sky powdered with gold and great spots of light like white wine splashed over the Jardins Publiques—Miss Brill was glad that she had decided on her fur. The air was motionless, but when you opened your mouth there was just a faint chill, like a chill from a glass of iced water before you sip, and now and again a leaf came drifting—from nowhere, from the sky. Miss Brill put up her hand and touched her fur. Dear little thing! It was nice to feel it again. She had taken it out of its box that afternoon, shaken out the moth-powder, given it a good brush, and rubbed the life back into the dim little eyes. "What has been happening to me?" said the sad little eyes. Oh, how sweet it was to see them snap at her again from the red eiderdown! . . . But the nose, which was of some black composition, wasn't at all firm. It must have had a knock, somehow. Never mind—a little dab of black sealing-wax when the time came—when it was absolutely necessary. . . . Little rogue! Yes, she really felt like that about it. Little rogue biting its tail just by her left ear. She could have taken it off and laid it on her lap and stroked it. She felt a tingling in her hands and arms, but that came from walking, she supposed. And when she breathed, something light and sad—no, not sad, exactly—something gentle seemed to move in her bosom.

There were a number of people out this afternoon, far more than last Sunday. And the band sounded louder and gayer. That was because the Season had begun. For although the band played all year round on Sundays, out of season it was never the same. It was like some one playing with only the family to listen; it didn't care how it played if there weren't any strangers present. Wasn't the conductor wearing a new coat, too? She was sure it was new. He scraped with his foot and flapped his arms like a rooster about to crow, and the bandsmen sitting in the green rotunda blew out their cheeks and glared at the music. Now there came a little "flutey" bit—very pretty!—a little chain of bright drops. She was sure it would be repeated. It was; she lifted her head and smiled.

Only two people shared her "special" seat: a fine old man in a velvet coat, his hands clasped over a huge carved walking-stick, and a big old woman, sitting upright, with a roll of knitting on her embroidered apron. They did not speak. This was disappointing, for Miss Brill always looked forward to the conversation. She had become really quite expert, she thought, at listening as though she didn't listen, at sitting in other people's lives just for a minute while they talked round her.

She glanced, sideways, at the old couple. Perhaps they would go soon. Last Sunday, too, hadn't been as interesting as usual. An Englishman and his wife, he wearing a dreadful Panama hat and she button boots. And she'd gone on the whole time about how she ought to wear spectacles; she knew she needed them; but that it was no good getting any; they'd be sure to break and they'd never keep on. And he'd been so patient. He'd suggested everything—gold rims, the kind that curved round your ears, little pads inside the bridge. No, nothing would please her. "They'll always be sliding down my nose!" Miss Brill wanted to shake her.

The old people sat on the bench, still as statues. Never mind, there was always the crowd to watch. To and fro, in front of the flower-beds and the band rotunda, the couples and groups paraded, stopped to talk, to greet, to buy a handful of flowers from the old beggar who had his tray fixed to the railings. Little children ran among them, swooping and laughing; little boys with big white silk bows under their chins, little girls, little French dolls, dressed up in velvet and lace. And sometimes a tiny staggerer came suddenly rocking into the open from under the trees, stopped, stared, as suddenly sat down "flop," until its small high-stepping mother, like a young hen, rushed scolding to its rescue. Other people sat on the benches and green chairs, but they were nearly always the same, Sunday after Sunday, and—Miss Brill had often noticed—there was something funny about nearly all of them. They were odd, silent, nearly all old, and from the way they stared they looked as though they'd just come from dark little rooms or even—even cupboards!

Behind the rotunda the slender trees with yellow leaves down drooping, and through them just a line of sea, and beyond the blue sky with gold-veined clouds.

Tum-tum-tum tiddle-um! tiddle-um! tum tiddley-um tum ta! blew the band.

Two young girls in red came by and two young soldiers in blue met them, and they laughed and paired and went off arm-in-arm. Two peasant women with funny straw hats passed, gravely, leading beautiful smoke-colored donkeys. A cold, pale nun hurried by. A beautiful woman came along and dropped her bunch of violets, and a little boy ran after to hand them to her, and she took them and threw them away as if they'd been poisoned. Dear me! Miss Brill didn't know whether to admire that or not! And now an ermine toque and a gentleman in grey met just in front of her. He

5

was tall, stiff, dignified, and she was wearing the ermine toque she'd bought when her hair was yellow. Now everything, her hair, her face, even her eyes, was the same color as the shabby ermine, and her hand, in its cleaned glove, lifted to dab her lips, was a tiny yellowish paw. Oh, she was so pleased to see him—delighted! She rather thought they were going to meet that afternoon. She described where she'd been— everywhere, here, there, along by the sea. The day was so charming—didn't he agree? And wouldn't he, perhaps? . . . But he shook his head, lighted a cigarette, slowly breathed a great deep puff into her face, and, even while she was still talking and laughing, flicked the match away and walked on. The ermine toque was alone; she smiled more brightly than ever. But even the band seemed to know what she was feeling and played more softly, played tenderly, and the drum beat, "The Brute! The Brute!" over and over. What would she do? What was going to happen now? But as Miss Brill wondered, the ermine toque turned, raised her hand as though she'd seen some one else, much nicer, just over there, and pattered away. And the band changed again and played more quickly, more gaily than ever, and the old couple on Miss Brill's seat got up and marched away, and such a funny old man with long whiskers hobbled along in time to the music and was nearly knocked over by four girls walking abreast.

Oh, how fascinating it was! How she enjoyed it! How she loved sitting here, watching it all! It was like a play. It was exactly like a play. Who could believe the sky at the back wasn't painted? But it wasn't till a little brown dog trotted on solemn and then slowly trotted off, like a little "theatre" dog, a little dog that had been drugged, that Miss Brill discovered what it was that made it so exciting. They were all on the stage. They weren't only the audience, not only looking on; they were acting. Even she had a part and came every Sunday. No doubt somebody would have noticed if she hadn't been there; she was part of the performance after all. How strange she'd never thought of it like that before! And yet it explained why she made such a point of starting from home at just the same time each week—so as not to be late for the performance—and it also explained why she had quite a queer, shy feeling at telling her English pupils how she spent her Sunday afternoons. No wonder! Miss Brill nearly laughed out loud. She was on the stage. She thought of the old invalid gentleman to whom she read the newspaper four afternoons a week while he slept in the garden. She had got quite used to the frail head on the cotton pillow, the hollowed eyes, the open mouth and the high pinched nose. If he'd been dead she mightn't have noticed for weeks; she wouldn't have minded. But suddenly he knew he was having the paper read to him by an actress! "An actress!" The old head lifted; two points of light quivered in the old eyes. "An actress—are ye?" And Miss Brill smoothed the newspaper as though it were the manuscript of her part and said gently: "Yes, I have been an actress for a long time."

The band had been having a rest. Now they started again. And what they played   10 was warm, sunny, yet there was just a faint chill—a something, what was it?—not sadness—no, not sadness—a something that made you want to sing. The tune lifted, lifted, the light shone; and it seemed to Miss Brill that in another moment all of them, all the whole company, would begin singing. The young ones, the laughing ones who were moving together, they would begin, and the men's voices, very resolute and brave, would join them. And then she too, she too, and the others on the benches—they would come in with a kind of accompaniment—something low, that scarcely rose or fell, something so beautiful—moving . . . And Miss Brill's eyes filled with tears and she looked smiling at all the other members of the company. Yes, we understand, we understand, she thought—though what they understood she didn't know.

Just at that moment a boy and a girl came and sat down where the old couple had been. They were beautifully dressed; they were in love. The hero and heroine, of course, just arrived from his father's yacht. And still soundlessly singing, still with that trembling smile, Miss Brill prepared to listen.

"No, not now," said the girl. "Not here, I can't."

"But why? Because of that stupid old thing at the end there?" asked the boy. "Why does she come here at all—who wants her? Why doesn't she keep her silly old mug at home?"

"It's her fu-fur which is so funny," giggled the girl. "It's exactly like a fried whiting."

"Ah, be off with you!" said the boy in an angry whisper. Then: "Tell me, my petite   15
chérie—"

"No, not here," said the girl. "Not yet."

On her way home she usually bought a slice of honeycake at the baker's. It was her Sunday treat. Sometimes there was an almond in her slice, sometimes not. It made a great difference. If there was an almond it was like carrying home a tiny present—a surprise—something that might very well not have been there. She hurried on the almond Sundays and struck the match for the kettle in quite a dashing way.

But today she passed the baker's boy, climbed the stairs, went into the little dark room—her room like a cupboard—and sat down on the red eiderdown. She sat there for a long time. The box that the fur came out of was on the bed. She unclasped the necklet quickly; quickly, without looking, laid it inside. But when she put the lid on she thought she heard something crying.

Questions

1. What details provide insight into Miss Brill's character and lifestyle?
2. What point of view is used in "Miss Brill"? How does this method improve the story?
3. Where and in what season does the story take place? Would the effect be the same if the story were set, say, in a remote Alaskan village in the winter?
4. What draws Miss Brill to the park every Sunday? What is the nature of the startling revelation that delights her on the day the story takes place?
5. Miss Brill's sense of herself is at least partly based on her attitudes toward others. Give instances of this tendency, showing also how it is connected with her drastic change of mood.
6. What explanations might there be for Miss Brill's thinking, in the last line of the story, that she "heard something crying"?

Raymond Carver

Cathedral   1983

Raymond Carver (1938–1988) was born in Clatskanie, Oregon. When he was three, his family moved to Yakima, Washington, where his father worked in a sawmill. In his early years Carver worked briefly at a lumber mill and at other unskilled jobs, including a stint as a tulip-picker. Married with two children before he was twenty, he experienced blue-collar desperation more intimately than most American writers, though he once quipped that, until he read critics' reactions to his works, he never realized that the characters in his stories

"were so bad off." In 1963 Carver earned a degree from Humboldt State College (now California State University, Humboldt). He briefly attended the Writers' Workshop of the University of Iowa, but, needing to support his family, he returned to California, working for three years as a hospital custodian before finding a job editing textbooks. In 1967 he met Gordon Lish, the influential editor who would publish several of his stories in Esquire. Under Lish's demanding tutelage, Carver learned to pare his fiction to the essentials. In the early 1970s, though plagued with bankruptcies, increasing dependency on alcohol, and marital problems, he taught at several universities.

Carver's publishing career began with a volume of poems, Near Klamath (1968). His books of short stories include Will You Please Be Quiet, Please? (1977), What We Talk About When We Talk About Love (1981), Cathedral (1983), and Where I'm Calling From (1988), which contained new and selected work. The compression of language he learned as a poet may in part account for the lean quality of his prose, often called "minimalist," a term Carver did not like. In his last decade Carver taught creative writing at Syracuse University, and lived with the poet Tess Gallagher, whom he married in 1988. He divided his final years between Syracuse and Port Angeles, Washington. Carver's personal victory in 1977 over decades of alcoholism underscored the many professional triumphs of his final decade. He once said, "I'm prouder of that, that I quit drinking, than I am of anything in my life." His reputation as a master craftsman of the contemporary short story was still growing when he died, after a struggle with lung cancer.

This blind man, an old friend of my wife's, he was on his way to spend the night. His wife had died. So he was visiting the dead wife's relatives in Connecticut. He called my wife from his in-laws'. Arrangements were made. He would come by train, a five-hour trip, and my wife would meet him at the station. She hadn't seen him since she worked for him one summer in Seattle ten years ago. But she and the blind man had kept in touch. They made tapes and mailed them back and forth. I wasn't enthusiastic about his visit. He was no one I knew. And his being blind bothered me. My idea of blindness came from the movies. In the movies, the blind moved slowly and never laughed. Sometimes they were led by seeing-eye dogs. A blind man in my house was not something I looked forward to.

That summer in Seattle she had needed a job. She didn't have any money. The man she was going to marry at the end of the summer was in officers' training school. He didn't have any money, either. But she was in love with the guy, and he was in love with her, etc. She'd seen something in the paper: HELP WANTED—*Reading to Blind Man*, and a telephone number. She phoned and went over, was hired on the spot. She'd worked with this blind man all summer. She read stuff to him, case studies, reports, that sort of thing. She helped him organize his little office in the county social-service department. They'd become good friends, my wife and the blind man. How do I know these things? She told me. And she told me something else. On her last day in the office, the blind man asked if he could touch her face. She agreed to this. She told me he touched his fingers to every part of her face, her nose—even her neck! She never forgot it. She even tried to write a poem about it. She was always trying to write a poem. She wrote a poem or two every year, usually after something really important had happened to her.

When we first started going out together, she showed me the poem. In the poem, she recalled his fingers and the way they had moved around over her face. In the poem, she talked about what she had felt at the time, about what went through her mind when the blind man touched her nose and lips. I can remember I didn't think much of the poem. Of course, I didn't tell her that. Maybe I just don't understand poetry. I admit it's not the first thing I reach for when I pick up something to read.

Anyway, this man who'd first enjoyed her favors, the officer-to-be, he'd been her childhood sweetheart. So okay. I'm saying that at the end of the summer she let the blind man run his hands over her face, said good-bye to him, married her childhood etc., who was now a commissioned officer, and she moved away from Seattle. But they'd kept in touch, she and the blind man. She made the first contact after a year or so. She called him up one night from an Air Force base in Alabama. She wanted to talk. They talked. He asked her to send a tape and tell him about her life. She did this. She sent the tape. On the tape, she told the blind man about her husband and about their life together in the military. She told the blind man she loved her husband but she didn't like it where they lived and she didn't like it that he was part of the military-industrial thing. She told the blind man she'd written a poem and he was in it. She told him that she was writing a poem about what it was like to be an Air Force officer's wife. The poem wasn't finished yet. She was still writing it. The blind man made a tape. He sent her the tape. She made a tape. This went on for years. My wife's officer was posted to one base and then another. She sent tapes from Moody AFB, McGuire, McConnell, and finally Travis, near Sacramento, where one night she got to feeling lonely and cut off from people she kept losing in that moving-around life. She got to feeling she couldn't go it another step. She went in and swallowed all the pills and capsules in the medicine chest and washed them down with a bottle of gin. Then she got into a hot bath and passed out.

But instead of dying, she got sick. She threw up. Her officer—why should he   5 have a name? he was the childhood sweetheart, and what more does he want?—came home from somewhere, found her, and called the ambulance. In time, she put it all on a tape and sent the tape to the blind man. Over the years, she put all kinds of stuff on tapes and sent the tapes off lickety-split. Next to writing a poem every year, I think it was her chief means of recreation. On one tape, she told the blind man she'd decided to live away from her officer for a time. On another tape, she told him about her divorce. She and I began going out, and of course she told her blind man about it. She told him everything, or so it seemed to me. Once she asked me if I'd like to hear the latest tape from the blind man. This was a year ago. I was on the tape, she said. So I said okay, I'd listen to it. I got us drinks and we settled down in the living room. We made ready to listen. First she inserted the tape into the player and adjusted a couple of dials. Then she pushed a lever. The tape squeaked and someone began to talk in this loud voice. She lowered the volume. After a few minutes of harmless chitchat, I heard my own name in the mouth of this stranger, this blind man I didn't even know! And then this: "From all you've said about him, I can only conclude—" But we were interrupted, a knock at the door, something, and we didn't ever get back to the tape. Maybe it was just as well. I'd heard all I wanted to.

Now this same blind man was coming to sleep in my house.

"Maybe I could take him bowling," I said to my wife. She was at the draining board doing scalloped potatoes. She put down the knife she was using and turned around.

"If you love me," she said, "you can do this for me. If you don't love me, okay. But if you had a friend, any friend, and the friend came to visit, I'd make him feel comfortable." She wiped her hands with the dish towel.

"I don't have any blind friends," I said.

"You don't have *any* friends," she said. "Period. Besides," she said, "goddamn it,   10
his wife's just died! Don't you understand that? The man's lost his wife!"

I didn't answer. She'd told me a little about the blind man's wife. Her name was
Beulah. Beulah! That's a name for a colored woman.

"Was his wife a Negro?" I asked.

"Are you crazy?" my wife said. "Have you just flipped or something?" She picked
up a potato. I saw it hit the floor, then roll under the stove. "What's wrong with you?"
she said. "Are you drunk?"

"I'm just asking," I said.

Right then my wife filled me in with more detail than I cared to know. I made a   15
drink and sat at the kitchen table to listen. Pieces of the story began to fall into place.

Beulah had gone to work for the blind man the summer after my wife had
stopped working for him. Pretty soon Beulah and the blind man had themselves a
church wedding. It was a little wedding—who'd want to go to such a wedding in
the first place?—just the two of them, plus the minister and the minister's wife.
But it was a church wedding just the same. It was what Beulah had wanted, he'd
said. But even then Beulah must have been carrying the cancer in her glands. After they had been inseparable for eight years—my wife's word, *inseparable*—
Beulah's health went into a rapid decline. She died in a Seattle hospital room, the
blind man sitting beside the bed and holding on to her hand. They'd married,
lived and worked together, slept together—had sex, sure—and then the blind
man had to bury her. All this without his having ever seen what the goddamned
woman looked like. It was beyond my understanding. Hearing this, I felt sorry for
the blind man for a little bit. And then I found myself thinking what a pitiful life
this woman must have led. Imagine a woman who could never see herself as she
was seen in the eyes of her loved one. A woman who could go on day after day and
never receive the smallest compliment from her beloved. A woman whose husband could never read the expression on her face, be it misery or something better. Someone who could wear makeup or not—what difference to him? She could,
if she wanted, wear green eye-shadow around one eye, a straight pin in her nostril,
yellow slacks, and purple shoes, no matter. And then to slip off into death, the
blind man's hand on her hand, his blind eyes streaming tears—I'm imagining
now—her last thought maybe this: that he never even knew what she looked like,
and she on an express to the grave. Robert was left with a small insurance policy
and a half of a twenty-peso Mexican coin. The other half of the coin went into
the box with her. Pathetic.

So when the time rolled around, my wife went to the depot to pick him up. With
nothing to do but wait—sure, I blamed him for that—I was having a drink and
watching the TV when I heard the car pull into the drive. I got up from the sofa with
my drink and went to the window to have a look.

I saw my wife laughing as she parked the car. I saw her get out of the car and shut
the door. She was still wearing a smile. Just amazing. She went around to the other
side of the car to where the blind man was already starting to get out. This blind man,
feature this, he was wearing a full beard! A beard on a blind man! Too much, I say.
The blind man reached into the backseat and dragged out a suitcase. My wife took
his arm, shut the car door, and, talking all the way, moved him down the drive and
then up the steps to the front porch. I turned off the TV. I finished my drink, rinsed
the glass, dried my hands. Then I went to the door.

My wife said, "I want you to meet Robert. Robert, this is my husband. I've told you all about him." She was beaming. She had this blind man by his coat sleeve.

The blind man let go of his suitcase and up came his hand. 20

I took it. He squeezed hard, held my hand, and then he let it go.

"I feel like we've already met," he boomed.

"Likewise," I said. I didn't know what else to say. Then I said, "Welcome. I've heard a lot about you." We began to move then, a little group, from the porch into the living room, my wife guiding him by the arm. The blind man was carrying his suitcase in his other hand. My wife said things like, "To your left here, Robert. That's right. Now watch it, there's a chair. That's it. Sit down right here. This is the sofa. We just bought this sofa two weeks ago."

I started to say something about the old sofa. I'd liked that old sofa. But I didn't say anything. Then I wanted to say something else, small-talk, about the scenic ride along the Hudson. How going *to* New York, you should sit on the right-hand side of the train, and coming *from* New York, the left-hand side.

"Did you have a good train ride?" I said. "Which side of the train did you sit on, 25 by the way?"

"What a question, which side!" my wife said. "What's it matter which side?" she said.

"I just asked," I said.

"Right side," the blind man said. "I hadn't been on a train in nearly forty years. Not since I was a kid. With my folks. That's been a long time. I'd nearly forgotten the sensation. I have winter in my beard now," he said. "So I've been told, anyway. Do I look distinguished, my dear?" the blind man said to my wife.

"You look distinguished, Robert," she said. "Robert," she said. "Robert, it's just so good to see you."

My wife finally took her eyes off the blind man and looked at me. I had the feel- 30 ing she didn't like what she saw. I shrugged.

I've never met, or personally known, anyone who was blind. This blind man was late forties, a heavy-set, balding man with stooped shoulders, as if he carried a great weight there. He wore brown slacks, brown shoes, a light-brown shirt, a tie, a sports coat. Spiffy. He also had this full beard. But he didn't use a cane and he didn't wear dark glasses. I'd always thought dark glasses were a must for the blind. Fact was, I wished he had a pair. At first glance, his eyes looked like anyone else's eyes. But if you looked close, there was something different about them. Too much white in the iris, for one thing, and the pupils seemed to move around in the sockets without his know-ing it or being able to stop it. Creepy. As I stared at his face, I saw the left pupil turn in toward his nose while the other made an effort to keep in one place. But it was only an effort, for that eye was on the roam without his knowing it or wanting it to be.

I said, "Let me get you a drink. What's your pleasure? We have a little of every-thing. It's one of our pastimes."

"Bub, I'm a Scotch man myself," he said fast enough in this big voice.

"Right," I said. Bub! "Sure you are. I knew it."

He let his fingers touch his suitcase, which was sitting alongside the sofa. He was 35 taking his bearings. I didn't blame him for that.

"I'll move that up to your room," my wife said.

"No, that's fine," the blind man said loudly. "It can go up when I go up."

"A little water with the Scotch?" I said.

"Very little," he said.

"I knew it," I said.

He said, "Just a tad. The Irish actor, Barry Fitzgerald? I'm like that fellow. When I drink water, Fitzgerald said, I drink water. When I drink whiskey, I drink whiskey." My wife laughed. The blind man brought his hand up under his beard. He lifted his beard slowly and let it drop.

I did the drinks, three big glasses of Scotch with a splash of water in each. Then we made ourselves comfortable and talked about Robert's travels. First the long flight from the West Coast to Connecticut, we covered that. Then from Connecticut up here by train. We had another drink concerning that leg of the trip.

I remembered having read somewhere that the blind didn't smoke because, as speculation had it, they couldn't see the smoke they exhaled. I thought I knew that much and that much only about blind people. But this blind man smoked his cigarette down to the nubbin and then lit another one. This blind man filled his ashtray and my wife emptied it.

When we sat down at the table for dinner, we had another drink. My wife heaped Robert's plate with cube steak, scalloped potatoes, green beans. I buttered him up two slices of bread. I said, "Here's bread and butter for you." I swallowed some of my drink. "Now let us pray," I said, and the blind man lowered his head. My wife looked at me, her mouth agape. "Pray the phone won't ring and the food doesn't get cold," I said.

We dug in. We ate everything there was to eat on the table. We ate like there was no tomorrow. We didn't talk. We ate. We scarfed. We grazed that table. We were into serious eating. The blind man had right away located his foods, he knew just where everything was on his plate. I watched with admiration as he used his knife and fork on the meat. He'd cut two pieces of meat, fork the meat into his mouth, and then go all out for the scalloped potatoes, the beans next, and then he'd tear off a hunk of buttered bread and eat that. He'd follow this up with a big drink of milk. It didn't seem to bother him to use his fingers once in a while, either.

We finished everything, including half a strawberry pie. For a few moments, we sat as if stunned. Sweat beaded on our faces. Finally, we got up from the table and left the dirty plates. We didn't look back. We took ourselves into the living room and sank into our places again. Robert and my wife sat on the sofa. I took the big chair. We had us two or three more drinks while they talked about the major things that had come to pass for them in the past ten years. For the most part, I just listened. Now and then I joined in. I didn't want him to think I'd left the room, and I didn't want her to think I was feeling left out. They talked of things that had happened to them—to them!—these past ten years. I waited in vain to hear my name on my wife's sweet lips: "And then my dear husband came into my life"—something like that. But I heard nothing of the sort. More talk of Robert. Robert had done a little of everything, it seemed, a regular blind jack-of-all-trades. But most recently he and his wife had had an Amway distributorship, from which, I gathered, they'd earned their living, such as it was. The blind man was also a ham radio operator. He talked in his loud voice about conversations he'd had with fellow operators in Guam, in the Philippines, in Alaska, and even in Tahiti. He said he'd have a lot of friends there if he ever wanted to go visit those places. From time to time, he'd turn his blind face toward me, put his hand under his beard, ask me something. How long had I been in my present position? (Three

40

45

years.) Did I like my work? (I didn't.) Was I going to stay with it? (What were the options?) Finally, when I thought he was beginning to run down, I got up and turned on the TV.

My wife looked at me with irritation. She was heading toward a boil. Then she looked at the blind man and said, "Robert, do you have a TV?"

The blind man said, "My dear, I have two TVs. I have a color set and a black-and-white thing, an old relic. It's funny, but if I turn the TV on, and I'm always turning it on, I turn on the color set. It's funny, don't you think?"

I didn't know what to say to that. I had absolutely nothing to say to that. No opinion. So I watched the news program and tried to listen to what the announcer was saying.

"This is a color TV," the blind man said. "Don't ask me how, but I can tell." 50

"We traded up a while ago," I said.

The blind man had another taste of his drink. He lifted his beard, sniffed it, and let it fall. He leaned forward on the sofa. He positioned his ashtray on the coffee table, then put the lighter to his cigarette. He leaned back on the sofa and crossed his legs at the ankles.

My wife covered her mouth, and then she yawned. She stretched. She said, "I think I'll go upstairs and put on my robe. I think I'll change into something else. Robert, you make yourself comfortable," she said.

"I'm comfortable," the blind man said.

"I want you to feel comfortable in this house," she said. 55

"I am comfortable," the blind man said.

After she'd left the room, he and I listened to the weather report and then to the sports roundup. By that time, she'd been gone so long I didn't know if she was going to come back. I thought she might have gone to bed. I wished she'd come back downstairs. I didn't want to be left alone with a blind man. I asked him if he wanted another drink, and he said sure. Then I asked if he wanted to smoke some dope with me. I said I'd just rolled a number. I hadn't, but I planned to do so in about two shakes.

"I'll try some with you," he said.

"Damm right," I said. "That's the stuff."

I got our drinks and sat down on the sofa with him. Then I rolled us two fat 60 numbers. I lit one and passed it. I brought it to his fingers. He took it and inhaled.

"Hold it as long as you can," I said. I could tell he didn't know the first thing.

My wife came back downstairs wearing her pink robe and her pink slippers.

"What do I smell?" she said.

"We thought we'd have us some cannabis," I said.

My wife gave me a savage look. Then she looked at the blind man and said, 65 "Robert, I didn't know you smoked."

He said, "I do now, my dear. There's a first time for everything. But I don't feel anything yet."

"This stuff is pretty mellow," I said. "This stuff is mild. It's dope you can reason with," I said. "It doesn't mess you up."

"Not much it doesn't, bub," he said, and laughed.

My wife sat on the sofa between the blind man and me. I passed her the number. She took it and toked and then passed it back to me. "Which way is this going?" she said. Then she said, "I shouldn't be smoking this. I can hardly keep my eyes open as it is. That dinner did me in. I shouldn't have eaten so much."

"It was the strawberry pie," the blind man said. "That's what did it," he said, and he laughed his big laugh. Then he shook his head. 70

"There's more strawberry pie," I said.

"Do you want some more, Robert?" my wife said.

"Maybe in a little while," he said.

We gave our attention to the TV. My wife yawned again. She said, "Your bed is made up when you feel like going to bed, Robert. I know you must have had a long day. When you're ready to go to bed, say so." She pulled his arm. "Robert?"

He came to and said, "I've had a real nice time. This beats tapes, doesn't it?" 75

I said, "Coming at you," and I put the number between his fingers. He inhaled, held the smoke, and then let it go. It was like he'd been doing it since he was nine years old.

"Thanks, bub," he said. "But I think this is all for me. I think I'm beginning to feel it," he said. He held the burning roach out for my wife.

"Same here," she said. "Ditto. Me, too." She took the roach and passed it to me. "I may just sit here for a while between you two guys with my eyes closed. But don't let me bother you, okay? Either one of you. If it bothers you, say so. Otherwise, I may just sit here with my eyes closed until you're ready to go to bed," she said. "Your bed's made up, Robert, when you're ready. It's right next to our room at the top of the stairs. We'll show you up when you're ready. You wake me up now, you guys, if I fall asleep." She said that and then she closed her eyes and went to sleep.

The news program ended. I got up and changed the channel. I sat back down on the sofa. I wished my wife hadn't pooped out. Her head lay across the back of the sofa, her mouth open. She'd turned so that her robe slipped away from her legs, exposing a juicy thigh. I reached to draw her robe back over her, and it was then that I glanced at the blind man. What the hell! I flipped the robe open again.

"You say when you want some strawberry pie," I said. 80

"I will," he said.

I said, "Are you tired? Do you want me to take you up to your bed? Are you ready to hit the hay?"

"Not yet," he said. "No, I'll stay up with you, bub. If that's all right. I'll stay up until you're ready to turn in. We haven't had a chance to talk. Know what I mean? I feel like me and her monopolized the evening." He lifted his beard and he let it fall. He picked up his cigarettes and his lighter.

"That's all right," I said. Then I said, "I'm glad for the company."

And I guess I was. Every night I smoked dope and stayed up as long as I could before I fell asleep. My wife and I hardly ever went to bed at the same time. When I did go to sleep, I had these dreams. Sometimes I'd wake up from one of them, my heart going crazy. 85

Something about the church and the Middle Ages was on the TV. Not your run-of-the-mill TV fare. I wanted to watch something else. I turned to the other channels. But there was nothing on them, either. So I turned back to the first channel and apologized.

"Bub, it's all right," the blind man said. "It's fine with me. Whatever you want to watch is okay. I'm always learning something. Learning never ends. It won't hurt me to learn something tonight. I got ears," he said.

*

We didn't say anything for a time. He was leaning forward with his head turned at me, his right ear aimed in the direction of the set. Very disconcerting. Now and then his eyelids drooped and then they snapped open again. Now and then he put his fingers into his beard and tugged, like he was thinking about something he was hearing on the television.

On the screen, a group of men wearing cowls was being set upon and tormented by men dressed in skeleton costumes and men dressed as devils. The men dressed as devils wore devil masks, horns, and long tails. This pageant was part of a procession. The Englishman who was narrating the thing said it took place in Spain once a year. I tried to explain to the blind man what was happening.

"Skeletons," he said. "I know about skeletons," he said, and he nodded.   90

The TV showed this one cathedral. Then there was a long, slow look at another one. Finally, the picture switched to the famous one in Paris, with its flying buttresses and its spires reaching up to the clouds. The camera pulled away to show the whole of the cathedral rising above the skyline.

There were times when the Englishman who was telling the thing would shut up, would simply let the camera move around the cathedrals. Or else the camera would tour the countryside, men in fields walking behind oxen. I waited as long as I could. Then I felt I had to say something. I said, "They're showing the outside of this cathedral now. Gargoyles. Little statues carved to look like monsters. Now I guess they're in Italy. Yeah, they're in Italy. There's paintings on the walls of this one church."

"Are those fresco paintings, bub?" he asked, and he sipped from his drink.

I reached for my glass. But it was empty. I tried to remember what I could remember. "You're asking me are those frescoes?" I said. "That's a good question. I don't know."

The camera moved to a cathedral outside Lisbon. The differences in the Por-   95
tuguese cathedral compared with the French and Italian were not that great. But they were there. Mostly the interior stuff. Then something occurred to me, and I said, "Something has occurred to me. Do you have any idea what a cathedral is? What they look like, that is? Do you follow me? If somebody says cathedral to you, do you have any notion what they're talking about? Do you know the difference between that and a Baptist church, say?"

He let the smoke dribble from his mouth. "I know they took hundreds of workers fifty or a hundred years to build," he said. "I just heard the man say that, of course. I know generations of the same families worked on a cathedral. I heard him say that, too. The men who began their life's work on them, they never lived to see the completion of their work. In that wise, bub, they're no different from the rest of us, right?" He laughed. Then his eyelids drooped again. His head nodded. He seemed to be snoozing. Maybe he was imagining himself in Portugal. The TV was showing another cathedral now. This one was in Germany. The Englishman's voice droned on. "Cathedrals," the blind man said. He sat up and rolled his head back and forth. "If you want the truth, bub, that's about all I know. What I just said. What I heard him say. But maybe you could describe one to me? I wish you'd do it. I'd like that. If you want to know, I really don't have a good idea."

I stared hard at the shot of the cathedral on the TV. How could I even begin to describe it? But say my life depended on it. Say my life was being threatened by an insane guy who said I had to do it or else.

I stared some more at the cathedral before the picture flipped off into the countryside. There was no use. I turned to the blind man and said, "To begin with, they're very tall." I was looking around the room for clues. "They reach way up. Up and up. Toward the sky. They're so big, some of them, they have to have these supports. To help hold them up, so to speak. These supports are called buttresses. They remind me of viaducts, for some reason. But maybe you don't know viaducts, either? Sometimes the cathedrals have devils and such carved into the front. Sometimes lords and ladies. Don't ask me why this is," I said.

He was nodding. The whole upper part of his body seemed to be moving back and forth.

"I'm not doing so good, am I?" I said.

He stopped nodding and leaned forward on the edge of the sofa. As he listened to me, he was running his fingers through his beard. I wasn't getting through to him, I could see that. But he waited for me to go on just the same. He nodded, like he was trying to encourage me. I tried to think what else to say. "They're really big," I said. "They're massive. They're built of stone. Marble, too, sometimes. In those olden days, when they built cathedrals, men wanted to be close to God. In those olden days, God was an important part of everyone's life. You could tell this from their cathedral-building. I'm sorry," I said, "but it looks like that's the best I can do for you. I'm just no good at it."

"That's all right, bub," the blind man said. "Hey, listen. I hope you don't mind my asking you. Can I ask you something? Let me ask you a simple question, yes or no. I'm just curious and there's no offense. You're my host. But let me ask if you are in any way religious? You don't mind my asking?"

I shook my head. He couldn't see that, though. A wink is the same as a nod to a blind man. "I guess I don't believe in it. In anything. Sometimes it's hard. You know what I'm saying?"

"Sure, I do," he said.

"Right," I said.

The Englishman was still holding forth. My wife sighed in her sleep. She drew a long breath and went on with her sleeping.

"You'll have to forgive me," I said. "But I can't tell you what a cathedral looks like. It just isn't in me to do it. I can't do any more than I've done."

The blind man sat very still, his head down, as he listened to me.

I said, "The truth is, cathedrals don't mean anything special to me. Nothing. Cathedrals. They're something to look at on late-night TV. That's all they are."

It was then that the blind man cleared his throat. He brought something up. He took a handkerchief from his back pocket. Then he said, "I get it, bub. It's okay. It happens. Don't worry about it," he said. "Hey, listen to me. Will you do me a favor? I got an idea. Why don't you find us some heavy paper? And a pen. We'll do something. We'll draw one together. Get us a pen and some heavy paper. Go on, bub, get the stuff," he said.

So I went upstairs. My legs felt like they didn't have any strength in them. They felt like they did after I'd done some running. In my wife's room I looked around. I found some ballpoints in a little basket on her table. And then I tried to think where to look for the kind of paper he was talking about.

Downstairs, in the kitchen, I found a shopping bag with onion skins in the bottom of the bag. I emptied the bag and shook it. I brought it into the living room and sat down with it near his legs. I moved some things, smoothed the wrinkles from the bag, spread it out on the coffee table.

The blind man got down from the sofa and sat next to me on the carpet.

He ran his fingers over the paper. He went up and down the sides of the paper. The edges, even the edges. He fingered the corners.

"All right," he said. "All right, let's do her."

He found my hand, the hand with the pen. He closed his hand over my hand. "Go ahead, bub, draw," he said. "Draw. You'll see. I'll follow along with you. It'll be okay. Just begin now like I'm telling you. You'll see. Draw," the blind man said.

So I began. First I drew a box that looked like a house. It could have been the house I lived in. Then I put a roof on it. At either end of the roof, I drew spires. Crazy.

"Swell," he said. "Terrific. You're doing fine," he said. "Never thought anything like this could happen in your lifetime, did you, bub? Well, it's a strange life, we all know that. Go on now. Keep it up."

I put in windows with arches. I drew flying buttresses. I hung great doors. I couldn't stop. The TV station went off the air. I put down the pen and closed and opened my fingers. The blind man felt around over the paper. He moved the tips of his fingers over the paper, all over what I had drawn, and he nodded.

"Doing fine," the blind man said.

I took up the pen again, and he found my hand. I kept at it. I'm no artist. But I kept drawing just the same.

My wife opened up her eyes and gazed at us. She sat up on the sofa, her robe hanging open. She said, "What are you doing? Tell me, I want to know."

I didn't answer her.

The blind man said, "We're drawing a cathedral. Me and him are working on it. Press hard," he said to me. "That's right. That's good," he said. "Sure. You got it, bub, I can tell. You didn't think you could. But you can, can't you? You're cooking with gas now. You know what I'm saying? We're going to really have us something here in a minute. How's the old arm?" he said. "Put some people in there now. What's a cathedral without people?"

My wife said, "What's going on? Robert, what are you doing? What's going on?"

"It's all right," he said to her. "Close your eyes now," the blind man said to me. I did it. I closed them just like he said.

"Are they closed?" he said. "Don't fudge."

"They're closed," I said.

"Keep them that way," he said. He said, "Don't stop now. Draw."

So we kept on with it. His fingers rode my fingers as my hand went over the paper. It was like nothing else in my life up to now.

Then he said, "I think that's it. I think you got it," he said. "Take a look. What do you think?"

But I had my eyes closed. I thought I'd keep them that way for a little longer. I thought it was something I ought to do.

"Well?" he said. "Are you looking?"

My eyes were still closed. I was in my house. I knew that. But I didn't feel like I was inside anything.

"It's really something," I said.

Questions

1. What details in "Cathedral" make clear the narrator's initial attitude toward blind people? What hints does the author give about the reasons for this attitude? At what point in the story do the narrator's preconceptions about blind people start to change?
2. For what reason does the wife keep asking Robert if he'd like to go to bed (paragraphs 74–78)? What motivates the narrator to make the same suggestion in paragraph 82? What effect does Robert's reply have on the narrator?
3. What makes the narrator start explaining what he's seeing on television?
4. How does the point of view contribute to the effectiveness of the story?
5. At the end, the narrator has an epiphany. How would you describe it?
6. Would you describe the narrator as an antihero? Use specific details from the story to back up your response.
7. Is the wife a flat or a round character? What about Robert? Support your conclusion about each of them.
8. In a good story, a character doesn't suddenly become a completely different sort of person. Find details early in the story that show the narrator's more sensitive side and thus help to make his development credible and persuasive.

■ WRITING *effectively*

Raymond Carver on Writing

Commonplace but Precise Language   1983

It's possible, in a poem or short story, to write about commonplace things and objects using commonplace but precise language, and to endow those things—a chair, a window curtain, a fork, a stone, a woman's earring— with immense, even startling power. It is possible to write a line of seemingly innocuous dialogue and have it send a chill along the reader's spine—the source of artistic delight, as Nabokov would have it. That's the kind of writing that most interests me. I hate sloppy or haphazard writing whether it flies under the banner of experimentation or else is just clumsily rendered realism. In Isaac Babel's wonderful short story, "Guy de Maupassant," the narrator has this to say about the writing of fiction: "No iron can

Raymond Carver

pierce the heart with such force as a period put just at the right place." This too ought to go on a three-by-five.

Evan Connell said once that he knew he was finished with a short story when he found himself going through it and taking out commas and then going through the story again and putting commas back in the same places. I like that way of working on something. I respect that kind of care for what is being done. That's all we have, finally, the words, and they had better be the right ones, with the punctuation in the right places so that they can best say what they are meant to say. If the words are heavy with the writer's own unbridled emotions, or if they are imprecise and inaccurate for some reason—if the words are in any way blurred—the reader's eyes will slide right over them and nothing will be achieved.

From "On Writing"

THINKING ABOUT CHARACTER

Although readers usually consider plot the central element of fiction, writers usually remark that stories begin with characters.

- **Identify the most important character.** The central character is the one who must deal with the plot complications and the central crisis of the story. The choices made by this character communicate his or her attitudes as well as the story's themes.
- **Consider the ways the characters' personalities and values are communicated.** Note that the way characters speak can immediately reveal important things about their personalities, beliefs, and behavior. A single line of dialogue can tell the audience a great deal, as in an old film in which the comedian W. C. Fields confides, "A woman drove me to drink and I never even had the courtesy to thank her."
- **Consider how the story's action grows out of its central character.** A story's action usually grows out of the personality of its protagonist and the situation he or she faces. As novelist Phyllis Bottome observed, "If a writer is true to his characters, they will give him his plot."

CHECKLIST: Writing About Character

- ☐ Who is the main character or protagonist of the story?
- ☐ Make a quick list of the character's physical, mental, moral, or behavioral traits. Which seem especially significant to the action of the story?
- ☐ Does the main character have an antagonist in the story? How do they differ?
- ☐ Does the way the protagonist speaks reveal anything about his or her personality?
- ☐ If the story is told in the first person, what is revealed about how the protagonist views his or her surroundings?
- ☐ What is the character's primary motivation? Does this motivation seem reasonable to you?
- ☐ Does the protagonist fully understand his or her motivations?
- ☐ In what ways is the protagonist changed or tested by the events of the story?

WRITING ASSIGNMENT ON CHARACTER

Choose a story with a dynamic protagonist. (See the beginning of this chapter for a discussion of dynamic characters.) Write an essay exploring how that character evolves over the course of the story, providing evidence from the story to back up your argument. Some good story choices might be Faulkner's "Barn Burning," Carver's "Cathedral," Baldwin's "Sonny's Blues," and Packer's "Brownies."

MORE TOPICS FOR WRITING

1. Using a story from this book, write a short essay that explains why a protagonist takes a crucial life-changing action. What motivates this character to do something that seems bold or surprising? You might consider:

   ▪ What motivates the narrator to overcome his instinctive antipathy to the blind man in "Cathedral"?

   ▪ What motivates the older brother to write to Sonny during his incarceration in "Sonny's Blues"?

   ▪ Why doesn't Miss Brill buy her usual slice of honeycake on her way home at the end of "Miss Brill"?

2. It is sometimes suggested that "Young Goodman Brown" is a story about an innocent young man who becomes disillusioned about human nature. How innocent is Goodman Brown at the beginning of the tale? Use details from the text to back up your conclusion.

3. Choose a minor character from any of the stories in this book, and write briefly on what the story reveals about that person, reading closely for even the smallest of details. Is he or she a stock character? Why or why not?

4. Choose a story in which the main character has an obvious antagonist, such as "Cathedral" or "A & P." (You can even choose a story with a nonhuman antagonist, such as "To Build a Fire.") What role does this second character play in bringing the protagonist to a new awareness of life?

5. Choose a dynamic character from one of the stories you've read so far. Write a brief essay on how the events in the story relate to your chosen character's strengths or shortcomings.

6. Choose a favorite character from a television show you watch regularly. What details are provided (either in the show's dialogue or in its visuals) to communicate the personality of this character? Would you say this person is a stock character or a rounded one? Write a brief essay making a case for your position.

7. Browse through magazines and newspapers to find a picture of a person you can't identify. Cut out the picture. Create a character based on the picture. As many writers do, make a list of characteristics, from the large (her life's ambition) to the small (his favorite breakfast cereal). As you build your list, make sure your details add up to a rounded character.

► TERMS FOR *review*

Characterization ► The techniques a writer uses to create, reveal, or develop the characters in a narrative.

Character description ► An aspect of characterization through which the author overtly relates either physical or mental traits of a character. This description is almost invariably a sign of what lurks beneath the surface of the character.

Character development ► The process by which a character is introduced, advanced, and possibly transformed in a story.

Character motivation ► What a character in a narrative wants, the reasons an author provides for a character's actions. Motivation can be either *explicit* (these reasons are specifically stated in a story) or *implicit* (the reasons are only hinted at or partially revealed).

Flat character ► A term coined by English novelist E. M. Forster to describe a character with only one outstanding trait. Flat characters are rarely the central characters in a narrative and stay the same throughout a story.

Round character ► A term also coined by E. M. Forster to describe a complex character who is presented in depth in a narrative. Round characters are those who change significantly during the course of a narrative or whose full personalities are revealed gradually throughout the story.

Stock character ► A common or stereotypical character. Examples of stock characters are the mad scientist, the battle-scarred veteran, and the strong but silent cowboy.

4

SETTING

ELEMENTS OF SETTING

By the **setting** of a story, we mean its time and place. The word might remind you of the metal that holds a diamond in a ring, or of a set used in a play—perhaps a bare chair in front of a slab of painted canvas. But often, in an effective short story, setting may figure as more than mere background or underpinning. It can make things happen. It can prompt characters to act, bring them to realizations, or cause them to reveal their inmost natures.

Place

To be sure, the idea of setting includes the physical environment of a story: a house, a street, a city, a landscape, a region. (*Where* a story takes place is sometimes called its **locale**.) Physical places mattered so greatly to French novelist Honoré de Balzac that sometimes, before writing a story set in a particular town, he would visit that town, select a few houses, and describe them in detail, down to their very smells.

Time

In addition to place, setting may crucially involve the time of the story—the hour, year, or century. It might matter greatly that a story takes place at dawn, or on the day of the first moon landing. When we begin to read a historical novel, we are soon made aware that we aren't reading about life in the twenty-first century. In *The Scarlet Letter*, nineteenth-century author Nathaniel Hawthorne, by a long introduction and a vivid opening scene at a prison door, prepares us to witness events in the Puritan community of Boston in the earlier seventeenth century. This setting, together with scenes of Puritan times we recall from high school history, helps us understand what happens in the novel. We can appreciate the shocked agitation in town when a woman is accused of adultery: she has given illegitimate birth. Such an event might seem common to-day, but in the stern, God-fearing New England Puritan community, it was a flagrant defiance of church and state, which were all-powerful (and were all one). That reader will make no sense of *The Scarlet Letter* who ignores its setting—if it is even possible to ignore the setting, given how much attention Hawthorne pays to it.

The fact that Hawthorne's novel takes place in a time remote from our own leads us to expect different customs and different attitudes. Some critics and teachers regard the setting of a story as its whole society, including the beliefs and assumptions of its characters. Still, we suggest that for now you keep your working definition of *setting* simple. Call it time and place. If later you should feel that your definition needs widening and deepening, you can always expand it.

Weather

Besides time and place, setting may also include the weather, which in some stories may be crucial. Climate seems as substantial as any character in William Faulkner's "Dry September." After sixty-two rainless days, a long unbroken spell of late-summer heat has frayed every nerve in a small town and caused the main character, a hotheaded white supremacist, to feel more and more irritated. The weather, someone remarks, is "enough to make a man do anything." When a false report circulates that a white woman has been raped by a black man, the rumor, like a match flung into a dry field, ignites rage and provokes a lynching. Evidently, to understand the story we have to recognize its locale, a small town in Mississippi in the 1930s during an infernal heat wave. Fully to take in the meaning of Faulkner's story, we have to take in the setting in its entirety.

Atmosphere

Atmosphere is the dominant mood or feeling that pervades all parts of a literary work. Atmosphere refers to the total effect conveyed by the author's use of language, images, and physical setting. But as the term *atmosphere* suggests, aspects of the physical setting (place, time, and weather) are usually crucial elements in achieving the author's intention. In some stories, a writer will seem to draw a setting mainly to evoke atmosphere. In such a story, setting starts us feeling whatever the storyteller would have us feel. In "The Tell-Tale Heart," Poe's setting the action in an old, dark, lantern-lit house greatly contributes to our sense of unease—and so helps the story's effectiveness.

HISTORICAL FICTION

One obvious example of how time can become a major element of setting is in **historical fiction**, where the story is set in another time and place. In historical fiction the author usually tries to recreate a faithful picture of daily life during the period. The historical period might be long ago, such as ancient Rome in Robert Graves's novel *I, Claudius* (1934), or it may be more recent, as in the setting of early twentieth-century Britain in Ian McEwan's *Atonement* (2001). Historical fiction sometimes introduces well-known figures from the past. Thornton Wilder's *Ides of March* (1948) includes Julius Caesar and Cleopatra among its many characters. Ron Hansen's *Exiles* (2008) depicts the life of English poet Gerard Manley Hopkins. More often, historical fiction presents imaginary characters in a carefully reconstructed version of a particular period of the past. Part of the pleasure of reading this sort of fiction comes from experiencing the many details of another time, just as films carefully set in a particular historical moment, such as Ridley Scott's *Gladiator* (2000) and James Cameron's *Titanic* (1997), let us see meticulously recreated settings of another time and place.

REGIONALISM

Physical place, by the way, is especially vital to a **regional writer**, who usually sets stories (or other work) in one geographic area. Such a writer, often a native of the place, tries to bring it alive to readers who live elsewhere. William Faulkner, a distinguished regional writer, almost always sets his novels and stories in his native Mississippi. Though born in St. Louis, Kate Chopin became known as a regional writer because she wrote about Louisiana in many of her short stories and in her novel *The Awakening*. Willa Cather, for her novels of frontier Nebraska, sometimes is regarded as another outstanding regionalist (though she also set fiction in Quebec, the Southwest, and, in "Paul's Case," in Pittsburgh and New York).

There is often something arbitrary, however, about calling an author a regional writer. The label sometimes has a political tinge; it means that the author describes an area outside the political and economic centers of a society. In a sense, we might think of James Joyce as a regional writer, in that all his fiction takes place in the city of Dublin, but instead we usually call him an Irish author.

As such writers show, a place can profoundly affect the character of someone who grew up in it. Willa Cather is fond of portraying strong-minded, independent women, such as the heroine of her novel *My Antonia*, strengthened in part by years of coping with the hardships of life on the wind-lashed prairie.

NATURALISM

Some writers consider the social and economic setting the most important element in the story. They present social environment as the determining factor in human behavior. Their approach is called **naturalism**—fiction of grim realism, in which the writer observes human characters like a scientist observing ants, seeing them as the products and victims of environment and heredity. Naturalism was first consciously developed in fiction in the late nineteenth century by French novelist Émile Zola. Important American Naturalists include Jack London, Theodore Dreiser, and Stephen Crane. Dreiser's novel *The Financier* (1912) begins in a city setting. A young boy (who will grow up to be a ruthless industrialist) is watching a battle to the death between a lobster and a squid in a fish-market tank. Dented for the rest of his life by this grim scene, he decides that's exactly the way human society functions.

Setting usually operates more subtly than that fish tank. Often, setting and character will reveal each other. Recall how Faulkner, at the start of "A Rose for Emily," depicts Emily Grierson's house, once handsome but now "an eyesore among eyesores" surrounded by gas stations. Still standing, refusing to yield its old-time horse-and-buggy splendor to the age of the automobile, the house in "its stubborn and coquettish decay" embodies the character of its owner. In John Steinbeck's "The Chrysanthemums" (Chapter 7), the story begins with a fog that has sealed off a valley from the rest of the world—a fog like the lid on a pot. That physical setting helps convey the isolation and loneliness of the protagonist's situation.

But be warned: you'll meet stories in which setting appears hardly to matter. In W. Somerset Maugham's fable "The Appointment in Samarra," all we need to be told about the setting is that it is a marketplace in Baghdad. In that brief fable, the inevitability of death is the point, not an exotic setting. In this chapter, though, you will meet four fine stories in which setting, for one reason or another, counts greatly. Without it, none of these stories could take place.

Kate Chopin

The Storm   (1898)

Kate Chopin (1851–1904) was born Katherine O'Flaherty in St. Louis, daughter of an Irish immigrant grown wealthy in retailing. On his death, young Kate was raised by her mother's family: aristocratic Creoles, descendants of the French and Spaniards who had colonized Louisiana. She received a convent schooling, and at nineteen married Oscar Chopin, a Creole cotton broker from New Orleans. Later, the Chopins lived on a plantation near Cloutierville, Louisiana, a region whose varied people— Creoles, Cajuns, blacks—Kate Chopin was later to write about with loving care in Bayou Folk (1894) and A Night in Arcadie (1897). The shock of her husband's sudden death in 1883, which left her with the raising of six children, seems to have plunged Kate Chopin

Kate Chopin

into writing. She read and admired fine woman writers of her day, such as the Maine realist Sarah Orne Jewett. She also read Maupassant, Zola, and other new (and scandalous) French naturalist writers. She began to bring into American fiction some of their hard-eyed observation and their passion for telling unpleasant truths. Determined, in defiance of her times, frankly to show the sexual feelings of her characters, Chopin suffered from neglect and censorship. When her major novel, The Awakening, appeared in 1899, critics were outraged by her candid portrait of a woman who seeks sexual and professional indepen- dence. After causing such a literary scandal, Chopin was unable to get her later work published, and wrote little more before she died. The Awakening and many of her stories had to wait seven decades for a sympathetic audience.

I

The leaves were so still that even Bibi thought it was going to rain. Bobinôt, who was accustomed to converse on terms of perfect equality with his little son, called the child's attention to certain somber clouds that were rolling with sinister intention from the west, accompanied by a sullen, threatening roar. They were at Friedheimer's store and decided to remain there till the storm had passed. They sat within the door on two empty kegs. Bibi was four years old and looked very wise.

"Mama'll be 'fraid, yes," he suggested with blinking eyes.

"She'll shut the house. Maybe she got Sylvie helpin' her this evenin'," Bobinôt responded reassuringly.

"No; she ent got Sylvie. Sylvie was helpin' her yistiday," piped Bibi.

Bobinôt arose and going across to the counter purchased a can of shrimps, of   5 which Calixta was very fond. Then he returned to his perch on the keg and sat stolidly holding the can of shrimps while the storm burst. It shook the wooden store and seemed to be ripping great furrows in the distant field. Bibi laid his little hand on his father's knee and was not afraid.

II

Calixta, at home, felt no uneasiness for their safety. She sat at a side window sewing furiously on a sewing machine. She was greatly occupied and did not notice the approaching storm. But she felt very warm and often stopped to mop her face on which the perspiration gathered in beads. She unfastened her white sacque at the throat. It began to grow dark, and suddenly realizing the situation she got up hurriedly and went about closing windows and doors.

Out on the small front gallery she had hung Bobinôt's Sunday clothes to air and she hastened out to gather them before the rain fell. As she stepped outside, Alcée Laballière rode in at the gate. She had not seen him very often since her marriage, and never alone. She stood there with Bobinôt's coat in her hands, and the big rain drops began to fall. Alcée rode his horse under the shelter of a side projection where the chickens had huddled and there were plows and a harrow piled up in the corner.

"May I come and wait on your gallery till the storm is over, Calixta?" he asked.

"Come 'long in, M'sieur Alcée."

His voice and her own startled her as if from a trance, and she seized Bobinôt's vest. Alcée, mounting to the porch, grabbed the trousers and snatched Bibi's braided jacket that was about to be carried away by a sudden gust of wind. He expressed an intention to remain outside, but it was soon apparent that he might as well have been out in the open: the water beat in upon the boards in driving sheets, and he went inside, closing the door after him. It was even necessary to put something beneath the door to keep the water out.

"My! what a rain! It's good two years since it rain' like that," exclaimed Calixta as she rolled up a piece of bagging and Alcée helped her to thrust it beneath the crack.

She was a little fuller of figure than five years before when she married; but she had lost nothing of her vivacity. Her blue eyes still retained their melting quality; and her yellow hair, dishevelled by the wind and rain, kinked more stubbornly than ever about her ears and temples.

The rain beat upon the low, shingled roof with a force and clatter that threatened to break an entrance and deluge them there. They were in the dining room—the sitting room—the general utility room. Adjoining was her bed room, with Bibi's couch along side her own. The door stood open, and the room with its white, monumental bed, its closed shutters, looked dim and mysterious.

Alcée flung himself into a rocker and Calixta nervously began to gather up from the floor the lengths of a cotton sheet which she had been sewing.

"If this keeps up, *Dieu sait*° if the levees goin' to stan' it!" she exclaimed.

"What have you got to do with the levees?"

"I got enough to do! An' there's Bobinôt with Bibi out in that storm—if he only didn' left Friedheimer's!"

"Let us hope, Calixta, that Bobinôt's got sense enough to come in out of a cyclone."

She went and stood at the window with a greatly disturbed look on her face. She wiped the frame that was clouded with moisture. It was stiflingly hot. Alcée got up and joined her at the window, looking over her shoulder. The rain was coming down in sheets obscuring the view of far-off cabins and enveloping the distant wood in a gray mist. The playing of the lightning was incessant. A bolt struck a tall chinaberry

10

15

Dieu sait: God only knows.

tree at the edge of the field. It filled all visible space with a blinding glare and the crash seemed to invade the very boards they stood upon.

Calixta put her hands to her eyes, and with a cry, staggered backward. Alcée's   20 arm encircled her, and for an instant he drew her close and spasmodically to him.

"*Bonté!*"° she cried, releasing herself from his encircling arm and retreating from the window, "the house'll go next! If I only knew w'ere Bibi was!" She would not compose herself; she would not be seated. Alcée clasped her shoulders and looked into her face. The contact of her warm, palpitating body when he had unthinkingly drawn her into his arms, had aroused all the old-time infatuation and desire for her flesh.

"Calixta," he said, "don't be frightened. Nothing can happen. The house is too low to be struck, with so many tall trees standing about. There! aren't you going to be quiet? say, aren't you?" He pushed her hair back from her face that was warm and steaming. Her lips were as red and moist as pomegranate seed. Her white neck and a glimpse of her full, firm bosom disturbed him powerfully. As she glanced up at him the fear in her liquid blue eyes had given place to a drowsy gleam that unconsciously betrayed a sensuous desire. He looked down into her eyes and there was nothing for him to do but gather her lips in a kiss. It reminded him of Assumption.°

"Do you remember—in Assumption, Calixta?" he asked in a low voice broken by passion. Oh! she remembered; for in Assumption he had kissed her and kissed and kissed her; until his senses would well nigh fail, and to save her he would resort to a desperate flight. If she was not an immaculate dove in those days, she was still inviolate; a passionate creature whose very defenselessness had made her defense, against which his honor forbade him to prevail. Now—well, now—her lips seemed in a manner free to be tasted, as well as her round, white throat and her whiter breasts.

They did not heed the crashing torrents, and the roar of the elements made her laugh as she lay in his arms. She was a revelation in that dim, mysterious chamber; as white as the couch she lay upon. Her firm, elastic flesh that was knowing for the first time its birthright, was like a creamy lily that the sun invites to contribute its breath and perfume to the undying life of the world.

The generous abundance of her passion, without guile or trickery, was like a   25 white flame which penetrated and found response in depths of his own sensuous nature that had never yet been reached.

When he touched her breasts they gave themselves up in quivering ecstasy, inviting his lips. Her mouth was a fountain of delight. And when he possessed her, they seemed to swoon together at the very borderland of life's mystery.

He stayed cushioned upon her, breathless, dazed, enervated, with his heart beating like a hammer upon her. With one hand she clasped his head, her lips lightly touching his forehead. The other hand stroked with a soothing rhythm his muscular shoulders.

The growl of the thunder was distant and passing away. The rain beat softly upon the shingles, inviting them to drowsiness and sleep. But they dared not yield.

The rain was over; and the sun was turning the glistening green world into a palace of gems. Calixta, on the gallery, watched Alcée ride away. He turned and smiled at her with a beaming face; and she lifted her pretty chin in the air and laughed aloud.

III

Bobinôt and Bibi, trudging home, stopped without at the cistern to make themselves presentable.   30

Bonté!: Heavens!   *Assumption:* a parish west of New Orleans.

"My! Bibi, w'at will yo' mama say! You ought to be ashame'. You oughtn' put on those good pants. Look at 'em! An' that mud on yo' collar! How you got that mud on yo' collar, Bibi? I never saw such a boy!" Bibi was the picture of pathetic resignation. Bobinôt was the embodiment of serious solicitude as he strove to remove from his own person and his son's the signs of their tramp over heavy roads and through wet fields. He scraped the mud off Bibi's bare legs and feet with a stick and carefully removed all traces from his heavy brogans. Then, prepared for the worst—the meeting with an overscrupulous housewife, they entered cautiously at the back door.

Calixta was preparing supper. She had set the table and was dripping coffee at the hearth. She sprang up as they came in.

"Oh, Bobinôt! You back! My! but I was uneasy. W'ere you been during the rain? An' Bibi? he ain't wet? he ain't hurt?" She had clasped Bibi and was kissing him effusively. Bobinôt's explanations and apologies which he had been composing all along the way, died on his lips as Calixta felt him to see if he were dry, and seemed to express nothing but satisfaction at their safe return.

"I brought you some shrimps, Calixta," offered Bobinôt, hauling the can from his ample side pocket and laying it on the table.

"Shrimps! Oh, Bobinôt! you too good fo' anything!" and she gave him a smacking kiss on the cheek that resounded. *"J'vous réponds,°* we'll have a feas' to night! umph-umph!"

Bobinôt and Bibi began to relax and enjoy themselves, and when the three seated themselves at table they laughed much and so loud that anyone might have heard them as far away as Laballière's.

IV

Alcée Laballière wrote to his wife, Clarisse, that night. It was a loving letter, full of tender solicitude. He told her not to hurry back, but if she and the babies liked it at Biloxi, to stay a month longer. He was getting on nicely; and though he missed them, he was willing to bear the separation a while longer—realizing that their health and pleasure were the first things to be considered.

V

As for Clarisse, she was charmed upon receiving her husband's letter. She and the babies were doing well. The society was agreeable; many of her old friends and acquaintances were at the bay. And the first free breath since her marriage seemed to restore the pleasant liberty of her maiden days. Devoted as she was to her husband, their intimate conjugal life was something which she was more than willing to forego for a while.

So the storm passed and everyone was happy.

Questions

1. Exactly where does Chopin's story take place? How can you tell?
2. What circumstances introduced in Part I turn out to have a profound effect on events in the story?
3. What details in "The Storm" emphasize the fact that Bobinôt loves his wife? What details reveal how imperfectly he comprehends her nature?

J'vous réponds: Let me tell you.

4. What general attitudes toward sex, love, and marriage does Chopin imply? Cite evidence to support your answer.
5. What meanings do you find in the title "The Storm"?
6. In the story as a whole, how do setting and plot reinforce each other?

Jack London

To Build a Fire

1910

Jack London

Jack London (1876–1916), born in San Francisco, won a large popular audience for his novels of the sea and the Yukon: The Call of the Wild (1903), The Sea-Wolf (1904), and White Fang (1906). Like Ernest Hemingway, he was a writer who lived a strenuous life. In 1893, he marched cross-country in Coxey's Army, an organized protest of the unemployed; in 1897, he took part in the Klondike gold rush; and later, as a reporter, he covered the Russo-Japanese War and the Mexican Revolution. Son of an unmarried mother and a father who denied his paternity, London grew up in poverty. At fourteen, he began holding hard jobs: working in a canning factory and a jute-mill, serving as a deck hand, pirating oysters in San Francisco Bay. These experiences persuaded him to join the Socialist Labor Party and crusade for workers' rights. In his political novel The Iron Heel (1908), London envisions a grim totalitarian America. Like himself, the hero of his novel Martin Eden (1909) is a man of brief schooling who gains fame as a writer, works for a cause, loses faith in it, and finds life without meaning. Though endowed with immense physical energy—he wrote fifty volumes—London drank hard, spent fast, and played out early. While his reputation as a novelist may have declined since his own day, some of his short stories have lasted triumphantly.

Day had broken cold and gray, exceedingly cold and gray, when the man turned aside from the main Yukon trail and climbed the high earth-bank, where a dim and little-travelled trail led eastward through the fat spruce timberland. It was a steep bank, and he paused for breath at the top, excusing the act to himself by looking at his watch. It was nine o'clock. There was no sun nor hint of sun, though there was not a cloud in the sky. It was a clear day, and yet there seemed an intangible pall over the face of things, a subtle gloom that made the day dark, and that was due to the absence of sun. This fact did not worry the man. He was used to the lack of sun. It had been days since he had seen the sun, and he knew that a few more days must pass before that cheerful orb, due south, would just peep above the sky line and dip immediately from view.

The man flung a look back along the way he had come. The Yukon lay a mile wide and hidden under three feet of ice. On top of this ice were as many feet of snow. It was all pure white, rolling in gentle undulations where the ice jams of the freeze-up had formed. North and south, as far as the eye could see, it was unbroken white, save for a dark hairline that curved and twisted from around the spruce-covered island to the south, and that curved and twisted away into the north, where it disappeared behind another spruce-covered island. This dark hairline was the trail—the main trail—that led south five hundred miles to the Chilcoot Pass, Dyea, and salt water; and that led north seventy miles to Dawson, and still on to the north a thousand miles to Nulato, and finally to St. Michael, on Bering Sea, a thousand miles and half a thousand more.

But all this—the mysterious, far-reaching hairline trail, the absence of sun from the sky, the tremendous cold, and the strangeness and weirdness of it all—made no impression on the man. It was not because he was long used to it. He was a newcomer in the land, a *chechaquo*, and this was his first winter. The trouble with him was that he was without imagination. He was quick and alert in the things of life, but only in the things, and not in the significances. Fifty degrees below zero meant eighty-odd degrees of frost. Such fact impressed him as being cold and uncomfortable, and that was all. It did not lead him to meditate upon his frailty as a creature of temperature, and upon man's frailty in general, able only to live within certain narrow limits of heat and cold; and from there on it did not lead him to the conjectural field of immortality and man's place in the universe. Fifty degrees below zero stood for a bite of frost that hurt and that must be guarded against by the use of mittens, ear flaps, warm moccasins, and thick socks. Fifty degrees below zero was to him just precisely fifty degrees below zero. That there should be anything more to it than that was a thought that never entered his head.

As he turned to go on, he spat speculatively. There was a sharp, explosive crackle that startled him. He spat again. And again, in the air, before it could fall to the snow, the spittle crackled. He knew that at fifty below spittle crackled on the snow, but this spittle had crackled in the air. Undoubtedly it was colder than fifty below—how much colder he did not know. But the temperature did not matter. He was bound for the old claim on the left fork of Henderson Creek, where the boys were already. They had come over across the divide from the Indian Creek country, while he had come the roundabout way to take a look at the possibilities of getting out logs in the spring from the islands in the Yukon. He would be in to camp by six o'clock; a bit after dark, it was true, but the boys would be there, a fire would be going, and a hot supper would be ready. As for lunch, he pressed his hand against the protruding bundle under his jacket. It was also under his shirt, wrapped up in a handkerchief and lying against the naked skin. It was the only way to keep the biscuits from freezing. He smiled agreeably to himself as he thought of those biscuits, each cut open and sopped in bacon grease, and each enclosing a generous slice of fried bacon.

He plunged in among the big spruce trees. The trail was faint. A foot of snow had fallen since the last sled had passed over, and he was glad he was without a sled, travelling light. In fact, he carried nothing but the lunch wrapped in the handkerchief. He was surprised, however, at the cold. It certainly was cold, he concluded, as he rubbed his numb nose and cheekbones with his mittened hand. He was a warm-whiskered man, but the hair on his face did not protect the high cheekbones and the eager nose that thrust itself aggressively into the frosty air.

At the man's heels trotted a dog, a big native husky, the proper wolf dog, gray-coated and without any visible or temperamental difference from its brother, the wild wolf. The animal was depressed by the tremendous cold. It knew that it was no time for travelling. Its instinct told it a truer tale than was told to the man by the man's

5

judgment. In reality, it was not merely colder than fifty below zero; it was colder than sixty below, than seventy below. It was seventy-five below zero. Since the freezing point is thirty-two above zero, it meant that one hundred and seven degrees of frost obtained. The dog did not know anything about thermometers. Possibly in its brain there was no sharp consciousness of a condition of very cold such as was in the man's brain. But the brute had its instinct. It experienced a vague but menacing apprehension that subdued it and made it slink along at the man's heels, and that made it question eagerly every unwonted movement of the man as if expecting him to go into camp or to seek shelter somewhere and build a fire. The dog had learned fire, and it wanted fire, or else to burrow under the snow and cuddle its warmth away from the air.

The frozen moisture of its breathing had settled on its fur in a fine powder of frost, and especially were its jowls, muzzle, and eyelashes whitened by its crystalled breath. The man's red beard and mustache were likewise frosted, but more solidly, the deposit taking the form of ice and increasing with every warm, moist breath he exhaled. Also, the man was chewing tobacco, and the muzzle of ice held his lips so rigidly that he was unable to clear his chin when he expelled the juice. The result was that a crystal beard of the color and solidity of amber was increasing its length on his chin. If he fell down it would shatter itself, like glass, into brittle fragments. But he did not mind the appendage. It was the penalty all tobacco chewers paid in that country, and he had been out before in two cold snaps. They had not been so cold as this, he knew, but by the spirit thermometer at Sixty Mile he knew they had been registered at fifty below and at fifty-five.

He held on through the level stretch of woods for several miles, crossed a wide flat, and dropped down a bank to the frozen bed of a small stream. This was Henderson Creek, and he knew he was ten miles from the forks. He looked at his watch. It was ten o'clock. He was making four miles an hour, and he calculated that he would arrive at the forks at half-past twelve. He decided to celebrate that event by eating his lunch there.

The dog dropped in again at his heels, with a tail drooping discouragement, as the man swung along the creek bed. The furrow of the old sled trail was plainly visible, but a dozen inches of snow covered the marks of the last runners. In a month no man had come up or down that silent creek. The man held steadily on. He was not much given to thinking, and just then particularly he had nothing to think about save that he would eat lunch at the forks and that at six o'clock he would be in camp with the boys. There was nobody to talk to; and, had there been, speech would have been impossible because of the ice muzzle on his mouth. So he continued monotonously to chew tobacco and to increase the length of his amber beard.

Once in a while the thought reiterated itself that it was very cold and that he   10
had never experienced such cold. As he walked along he rubbed his cheekbones and nose with the back of his mittened hand. He did this automatically, now and again changing hands. But, rub as he would, the instant he stopped his cheekbones were numb, and the following instant the end of his nose went numb. He was sure to frost his cheeks; he knew that, and experienced a pang of regret that he had not devised a nose strap of the sort Bud wore in cold snaps. Such a strap passed across the cheeks, as well, and saved them. But it didn't matter much, after all. What were frosted cheeks? A bit painful, that was all; they were never serious.

Empty as the man's mind was of thoughts, he was keenly observant, and he noticed the changes in the creek, the curves and bends and timber jams, and always he sharply noted where he placed his feet. Once, coming around a bend, he shied abruptly, like a startled horse, curved away from the place where he had been walking, and retreated several paces back along the trail. The creek he knew was frozen clear to the bottom—no creek could contain water in that arctic winter—but he knew also that there were springs that bubbled out from the hillsides and ran along under the snow and on top the ice of the creek. He knew that the coldest snaps never froze these springs, and he knew likewise their danger. They were traps. They hid pools of water under the snow that might be three inches deep, or three feet. Sometimes a skin of ice half an inch thick covered them, and in turn was covered by the snow. Sometimes there were alternate layers of water and ice skin, so that when one broke through he kept on breaking through for a while, sometimes wetting himself to the waist.

That was why he had shied in such panic. He had felt the give under his feet and heard the crackle of a snow-hidden ice skin. And to get his feet wet in such a temperature meant trouble and danger. At the very least it meant delay, for he would be forced to stop and build a fire, and under its protection to bare his feet while he dried his socks and moccasins. He stood and studied the creek bed and its banks, and decided that the flow of water came from the right. He reflected awhile, rubbing his nose and cheeks, then skirted to the left, stepping gingerly and testing the footing for each step. Once clear of the danger, he took a fresh chew of tobacco and swung along at his four-mile gait.

In the course of the next two hours he came upon several similar traps. Usually the snow above the hidden pools had a sunken, candied appearance that advertised the danger. Once again, however, he had a close call; and once, suspecting danger, he compelled the dog to go on in front. The dog did not want to go. It hung back until the man shoved it forward, and then it went quickly across the white, unbroken surface. Suddenly it broke through, floundered to one side, and got away to firmer footing. It had wet its forefeet and legs, and almost immediately the water that clung to it turned to ice. It made quick efforts to lick the ice off its legs, then dropped down in the snow and began to bite out the ice that had formed between the toes. This was a matter of instinct. To permit the ice to remain would mean sore feet. It did not know this. It merely obeyed the mysterious prompting that arose from the deep crypts of its being. But the man knew, having achieved a judgment on the subject, and he removed the mitten from his right hand and helped tear out the ice particles. He did not expose his fingers more than a minute, and was astonished at the swift numbness that smote them. It certainly was cold. He pulled on the mitten hastily, and beat the hand savagely across his chest.

At twelve o'clock the day was at its brightest. Yet the sun was too far south on its winter journey to clear the horizon. The bulge of the earth intervened between it and Henderson Creek, where the man walked under a clear sky at noon and cast no shadow. At half-past twelve, to the minute, he arrived at the forks of the creek. He was pleased at the speed he had made. If he kept it up, he would certainly be with the boys by six. He unbuttoned his jacket and shirt and drew forth his lunch. The action consumed no more than a quarter of a minute, yet in that brief moment the numbness laid hold of the exposed fingers. He did not put the mitten on, but, instead, struck the fingers a dozen sharp smashes against his leg. Then he sat down on a snow-covered log to eat. The sting that followed upon the striking of his fingers against his leg ceased so quickly that he was startled. He had had no chance to take a bite of biscuit. He struck the fingers repeatedly and returned them to the mitten, baring the other hand for the purpose of eating. He tried to take a mouthful, but the ice muzzle prevented. He had forgotten to build a fire and thaw out. He chuckled at his foolishness, and as he chuckled he noted the numbness creeping into the exposed fingers. Also, he noted that the stinging which had first come to his toes when he sat down was already passing away. He wondered whether the toes were warm or numb. He moved them inside the moccasins and decided that they were numb.

He pulled the mitten on hurriedly and stood up. He was a bit frightened. He stamped up and down until the stinging returned into the feet. It certainly was cold, was his thought. That man from Sulphur Creek had spoken the truth when telling how cold it sometimes got in the country. And he had laughed at him at the time! That showed one must not be too sure of things. There was no mistake about it, it *was* cold. He strode up and down, stamping his feet and threshing his arms, until reassured by the returning warmth. Then he got out matches and proceeded to make a fire. From the undergrowth, where high water of the previous spring had lodged a supply of seasoned twigs, he got his firewood. Working carefully from a small beginning, he soon had a roaring fire, over which he thawed the ice from his face and in the protection of which he ate his biscuits. For the moment the cold of space was outwitted. The dog took satisfaction in the fire, stretching out close enough for warmth and far enough away to escape being singed.

When the man had finished, he filled his pipe and took his comfortable time over a smoke. Then he pulled on his mittens, settled the ear flaps of his cap firmly about his ears, and took the creek trail up the left fork. The dog was disappointed and yearned back toward the fire. This man did not know cold. Possibly all the generations of his ancestry had been ignorant of cold, of real cold, of cold one hundred and seven degrees below freezing point. But the dog knew; all its ancestry knew, and it had inherited the knowledge. And it knew that it was not good to walk abroad in such fearful cold. It was the time to lie snug in a hole in the snow and wait for a curtain of cloud to be drawn across the face of outer space whence this cold came. On the other hand, there was no keen intimacy between the dog and the man. The one was the toil slave of the other, and the only caresses it had ever received were the caresses of the whip lash and of harsh and menacing throat sounds that threatened the whip lash. So the dog made no effort to communicate its apprehension to the man. It was not concerned in the welfare of the man; it was for its own sake that it yearned back toward the fire. But the man whistled, and spoke to it with the sound of whip lashes, and the dog swung in at the man's heels and followed after.

The man took a chew of tobacco and proceeded to start a new amber beard. Also, his moist breath quickly powdered with white his mustache, eyebrows, and lashes. There did not seem to be so many springs on the left fork of the Henderson, and for half an hour the man saw no signs of any. And then it happened. At a place where there were no signs, where the soft, unbroken snow seemed to advertise solidity beneath, the man broke through. It was not deep. He wet himself halfway to the knees before he floundered out to the firm crust.

He was angry, and cursed his luck aloud. He had hoped to get into camp with the boys at six o'clock, and this would delay him an hour, for he would have to build a fire and dry out his footgear. This was imperative at that low temperature—he knew that much; and he turned aside to the bank, which he climbed. On top, tangled in the underbrush about the trunks of several small spruce trees, was a high-water deposit of dry firewood—sticks and twigs, principally, but also larger portions of seasoned branches and fine, dry, last year's grasses. He threw down several large pieces on top of the snow. This served for a foundation and prevented the young flame from drowning itself in the snow it otherwise would melt. The flame he got by touching a match to a small shred of birch bark that he took from his pocket. This burned even more readily than paper. Placing it on the foundation, he fed the young flame with wisps of dry grass and with the tiniest dry twigs.

He worked slowly and carefully, keenly aware of his danger. Gradually, as the flame grew stronger, he increased the size of the twigs with which he fed it. He squatted in the snow, pulling the twigs out from their entanglement in the brush and feeding directly to the flame. He knew there must be no failure. When it is seventy-five below zero, a man must not fail in his first attempt to build a fire—that is, if his feet are wet. If his feet are dry, and he fails, he can run along the trail for half a mile and restore his circulation. But the circulation of wet and freezing feet cannot be restored by running when it is seventy-five below. No matter how fast he runs, the wet feet will freeze the harder.

All this the man knew. The old-timer on Sulphur Creek had told him about it 20 the previous fall, and now he was appreciating the advice. Already all sensation had gone out of his feet. To build the fire he had been forced to remove his mittens, and the fingers had quickly gone numb. His pace of four miles an hour had kept his heart pumping blood to the surface of his body and to all the extremities. But the instant he stopped, the action of the pump eased down. The cold of space smote the unprotected tip of the planet, and he, being on that unprotected tip, received the full force of the blow. The blood of his body recoiled before it. The blood was alive, like the dog, and like the dog it wanted to hide away and cover itself up from the fearful cold. So long as he walked four miles an hour, he pumped that blood, willy-nilly, to the surface; but now it ebbed away and sank down into the recesses of his body. The extremities were the first to feel its absence. His wet feet froze the faster, and his exposed fingers numbed the faster, though they had not yet begun to freeze. Nose and cheeks were already freezing, while the skin of all his body chilled as it lost its blood.

But he was safe. Toes and nose and cheeks would be only touched by the frost, for the fire was beginning to burn with strength. He was feeding it with twigs the size of his finger. In another minute he would be able to feed it with branches the size of his wrist, and then he could remove his wet footgear, and, while it dried, he could keep his naked feet warm by the fire, rubbing them at first, of course, with snow. The fire was a success. He was safe. He remembered the advice of the old-timer on Sulphur Creek, and smiled. The old-timer had been very serious in laying down the law that no man must travel alone in the Klondike after fifty below. Well, here he was; he had had the accident; he was alone; and he had saved himself. Those old-timers were rather womanish, some of them, he thought. All a man had to do was to keep his head, and he was all right. Any man who was a man could travel alone. But it was surprising, the rapidity with which his cheeks and nose were freezing. And he had not thought his fingers could go lifeless in so short a time. Lifeless they were, for he could scarcely make them move together to grip a twig, and they seemed remote from his body and from him. When he touched a twig, he had to look and see whether or not he had hold of it. The wires were pretty well down between him and his finger ends.

All of which counted for little. There was the fire, snapping and crackling and promising life with every dancing flame. He started to untie his moccasins. They were coated with ice; the thick German socks were like sheaths of iron halfway to the knees; and the moccasin strings were like rods of steel all twisted and knotted as by some conflagration. For a moment he tugged with his numb fingers, then, realizing the folly of it, he drew his sheath knife.

But before he could cut the strings, it happened. It was his own fault or, rather, his mistake. He should not have built the fire under the spruce tree. He should have built it in the open. But it had been easier to pull the twigs from the brush and drop them directly on the fire. Now the tree under which he had done this carried a weight of snow on its boughs. No wind had blown for weeks, and each bough was fully freighted. Each time he had pulled a twig he had communicated a slight agitation to the tree—an imperceptible agitation, so far as he was concerned, but an agitation sufficient to bring about the disaster. High up in the tree one bough capsized its load of snow. This fell on the boughs beneath, capsizing them. This process continued, spreading out and involving the whole tree. It grew like an avalanche, and it descended without warning upon the man and the fire, and the fire was blotted out! Where it had burned was a mantle of fresh and disordered snow.

The man was shocked. It was as though he had just heard his own sentence of death. For a moment he sat and stared at the spot where the fire had been. Then he grew very calm. Perhaps the old-timer on Sulphur Creek was right. If he had only had a trail mate he would have been in no danger now. The trail mate could have built the fire. Well, it was up to him to build the fire over again, and this second time there must be no failure. Even if he succeeded, he would most likely lose some toes. His feet must be badly frozen by now, and there would be some time before the second fire was ready.

Such were his thoughts, but he did not sit and think them. He was busy all the time they were passing through his mind. He made a new foundation for a fire, this time in the open, where no treacherous tree could blot it out. Next he gathered dry grasses and tiny twigs from the high-water flotsam. He could not bring his fingers together to pull them out, but he was able to gather them by the handful. In this way he got many rotten twigs and bits of green moss that were undesirable, but it was the best he could do. He worked methodically, even collecting an armful of the larger branches to be used later when the fire gathered strength. And all the while the dog sat and watched him, a certain yearning wistfulness in its eye, for it looked upon him as the fire provider, and the fire was slow in coming.

When all was ready, the man reached in his pocket for a second piece of birch bark. He knew the bark was there, and, though he could not feel it with his fingers, he could hear its crisp rustling as he fumbled for it. Try as he would, he could not clutch hold of it. And all the time, in his consciousness, was the knowledge that each instant his feet were freezing. This thought tended to put him in a panic, but he fought against it and kept calm. He pulled on his mittens with his teeth, and threshed his arms back and forth, beating his hands with all his might against his sides. He did this sitting down, and he stood up to do it; and all the while the dog sat in the snow, its wolf brush of a tail curled around warmly over its forefeet, its sharp wolf ears pricked forward intently as it watched the man. And the man, as he beat and threshed with his arms and hands, felt a great surge of envy as he regarded the creature that was warm and secure in its natural covering.

After a time he was aware of the first faraway signals of sensation in his beaten fingers. The faint tingling grew stronger till it evolved into a stinging ache that was excruciating, but which the man hailed with satisfaction. He stripped the mitten from his right hand and fetched forth the birch bark. The exposed fingers were quickly going numb again. Next he brought out his bunch of sulphur matches. But the tremendous cold had already driven the life out of his fingers. In his effort to separate one match from the others, the whole bunch fell in the snow. He tried to pick it out of the snow, but failed. The dead fingers could neither touch nor clutch. He

25

was very careful. He drove the thought of his freezing feet, and nose, and cheeks, out of his mind, devoting his whole soul to the matches. He watched, using the sense of vision in place of that of touch, and when he saw his fingers on each side the bunch, he closed them—that is, he willed to close them, for the wires were down, and the fingers did not obey. He pulled the mitten on the right hand, and beat it fiercely against his knee. Then, with both mittened hands, he scooped the bunch of matches, along with much snow, into his lap. Yet he was no better off.

After some manipulation he managed to get the bunch between the heels of his mittened hands. In this fashion he carried it to his mouth. The ice crackled and snapped when by a violent effort he opened his mouth. He drew the lower jaw in, curled the upper lip out of the way, and scraped the bunch with his upper teeth in order to separate a match. He succeeded in getting one, which he dropped on his lap. He was no better off. He could not pick it up. Then he devised a way. He picked it up in his teeth and scratched it on his leg. Twenty times he scratched before he succeeded in lighting it. As it flamed he held it with his teeth to the birch bark. But the burning brimstone went up his nostrils and into his lungs, causing him to cough spasmodically. The match fell into the snow and went out.

The old-timer on Sulphur Creek was right, he thought in the moment of controlled despair that ensued: after fifty below, a man should travel with a partner. He beat his hands, but failed in exciting any sensation. Suddenly he bared both hands, removing the mittens with his teeth. He caught the whole bunch between the heels of his hands. His arm muscles not being frozen enabled him to press the hand heels tightly against the matches. Then he scratched the bunch along his leg. It flared into flame, seventy sulphur matches at once! There was no wind to blow them out. He kept his head to one side to escape the strangling fumes, and held the blazing bunch to the birch bark. As he so held it, he became aware of sensation in his hand. His flesh was burning. He could smell it. Deep down below the surface he could feel it. The sensation developed into pain that grew acute. And still he endured it, holding the flame of the matches clumsily to the bark that would not light readily because his own burning hands were in the way, absorbing most of the flame.

At last, when he could endure no more, he jerked his hands apart. The blazing 30
matches fell sizzling into the snow, but the birch bark was alight. He began laying dry grasses and the tiniest twigs on the flame. He could not pick and choose, for he had to lift the fuel between the heels of his hands. Small pieces of rotten wood and green moss clung to the twigs, and he bit them off as well as he could with his teeth. He cherished the flame carefully and awkwardly. It meant life, and it must not perish. The withdrawal of blood from the surface of his body now made him begin to shiver, and he grew more awkward. A large piece of green moss fell squarely on the little fire. He tried to poke it out with his fingers, but his shivering frame made him poke too far, and he disrupted the nucleus of the little fire, the burning grasses and tiny twigs separating and scattering. He tried to poke them together again, but in spite of the tenseness of the effort, his shivering got away from him, and the twigs were hopelessly scattered. Each twig gushed a puff of smoke and went out. The fire provider had failed. As he looked apathetically about him, his eyes chanced on the dog, sitting across the ruins of the fire from him, in the snow, making restless, hunching movements, slightly lifting one forefoot and then the other, shifting its weight back and forth on them with wistful eagerness.

The sight of the dog put a wild idea into his head. He remembered the tale of the man, caught in the blizzard, who killed a steer and crawled inside the carcass, and so was saved. He would kill the dog and bury his hands in the warm body until the numbness went out of them. Then he could build another fire. He spoke to the dog, calling it to him; but in his voice was a strange note of fear that frightened the animal, who had never known the man to speak in such a way before. Something was the matter, and its suspicious nature sensed danger—it knew not what danger, but somewhere, somehow, in its brain arose an apprehension of the man. It flattened its ears down at the sound of the man's voice, and its restless, hunching movements and the liftings and shiftings of its forefeet became more pronounced; but it would not come to the man. He got on his hands and knees and crawled toward the dog. This unusual posture again excited suspicion, and the animal sidled mincingly away.

The man sat up in the snow for a moment and struggled for calmness. Then he pulled on his mittens, by means of his teeth, and got upon his feet. He glanced down at first in order to assure himself that he was really standing up, for the absence of sensation in his feet left him unrelated to the earth. His erect position in itself started to drive the webs of suspicion from the dog's mind; and when he spoke peremptorily, with the sound of whip lashes in his voice, the dog rendered its customary allegiance and came to him. As it came within reaching distance, the man lost his control. His arms flashed out to the dog, and he experienced genuine surprise when he discovered that his hands could not clutch, that there was neither bend nor feeling in the fingers. He had forgotten for the moment that they were frozen and that they were freezing more and more. All this happened quickly, and before the animal could get away, he encircled its body with his arms. He sat down in the snow, and in this fashion held the dog, while it snarled and whined and struggled.

But it was all he could do, hold its body encircled in his arms and sit there. He realized that he could not kill the dog. There was no way to do it. With his helpless hands he could neither draw nor hold his sheath knife nor throttle the animal. He released it, and it plunged wildly away, with tail between its legs, and still snarling. It halted forty feet away and surveyed him curiously, with ears sharply pricked forward.

The man looked down at his hands in order to locate them, and found them hanging on the ends of his arms. It struck him as curious that one should have to use his eyes in order to find out where his hands were. He began threshing his arms back and forth, beating the mittened hands against his sides. He did this for five minutes, violently, and his heart pumped enough blood up to the surface to put a stop to his shivering. But no sensation was aroused in the hands. He had an impression that they hung like weights on the ends of his arms, but when he tried to run the impression down, he could not find it.

A certain fear of death, dull and oppressive, came to him. This fear quickly became poignant as he realized that it was no longer a mere matter of freezing his fingers and toes, or of losing his hands and feet, but that it was a matter of life and death with the chances against him. This threw him into a panic, and he turned and ran up the creek bed along the old, dim trail. The dog joined in behind and kept up with him. He ran blindly, without intention, in fear such as he had never known in his life. Slowly, as he plowed and floundered through the snow, he began to see things again—the banks of the creek, the old timber jams, the leafless aspens, and the sky. The running made him feel better. He did not shiver. Maybe, if he ran on, his feet would thaw out; and anyway, if he ran far enough, he would reach camp and the boys. Without doubt he would lose some fingers and toes and some of his face; but the boys would take care of him, and save the rest of him when he got there. And at the same time there was another thought in his mind that said he would never get to the camp and the boys; that it was too many miles away, that the freezing had too great a start on him, and that he would soon be stiff and dead. This thought he kept in the background and refused to consider. Sometimes it pushed itself forward and demanded to be heard, but he thrust it back and strove to think of other things.

It struck him as curious that he could run at all on feet so frozen that he could not feel them when they struck the earth and took the weight of his body. He seemed to himself to skim along above the surface, and to have no connection with the earth. Somewhere he had once seen a winged Mercury, and he wondered if Mercury felt as he felt when skimming over the earth.

His theory of running until he reached the camp and the boys had one flaw in it: he lacked the endurance. Several times he stumbled, and finally he tottered, crumpled up, and fell. When he tried to rise, he failed. He must sit and rest, he decided, and next time he would merely walk and keep on going. As he sat and regained his breath, he noted that he was feeling quite warm and comfortable. He was not shivering, and it even seemed that a warm glow had come to his chest and trunk. And yet, when he touched his nose and cheeks, there was no sensation. Running would not thaw them out. Nor would it thaw out his hands and feet. Then the thought came to him that the frozen portions of his body must be extending. He tried to keep this thought down, to forget it, to think of something else; he was aware of the panicky feeling that it caused, and he was afraid of the panic. But the thought asserted itself, and persisted, until it produced a vision of his body totally frozen. This was too much, and he made another wild run along the trail. Once he slowed down to a walk, but the thought of the freezing extending itself made him run again.

And all the time the dog ran with him, at his heels. When he fell down a second time, it curled its tail over its forefeet and sat in front of him, facing him, curiously eager and intent. The warmth and security of the animal angered him, and he cursed it till it flattened down its ears appeasingly. This time the shivering came more quickly upon the man. He was losing in his battle with the frost. It was creeping into his body from all sides. The thought of it drove him on, but he ran no more than a hundred feet, when he staggered and pitched headlong. It was his last panic. When he had recovered his breath and control, he sat up and entertained in his mind the conception of meeting death with dignity. However, the conception did not come to him in such terms. His idea of it was that he had been making a fool of himself, running around like a chicken with its head cut off—such was the simile that occurred to him. Well, he was bound to freeze anyway, and he might as well take it decently. With this new-found peace of mind came the first glimmerings of drowsiness. A good idea, he thought, to sleep off to death. It was like taking an anesthetic. Freezing was not so bad as people thought. There were lots worse ways to die.

He pictured the boys finding his body next day. Suddenly he found himself with them, coming along the trail and looking for himself. And, still with them, he came around a turn in the trail and found himself lying in the snow. He did not belong with himself any more, for even then he was out of himself, standing with the boys and looking at himself in the snow. It certainly was cold, was his thought. When he got back to the States he could tell the folks what real cold was. He drifted on from this to a vision of the old-timer on Sulphur Creek. He could see him quite clearly, warm and comfortable, and smoking a pipe.

"You were right, old hoss; you were right," the man mumbled to the old-timer of   40
Sulphur Creek.

Then the man drowsed off into what seemed to him the most comfortable and satisfying sleep he had ever known. The dog sat facing him and waiting. The brief day drew to a close in a long, slow twilight. There were no signs of a fire to be made, and, besides, never in the dog's experience had it known a man to sit like that in the snow and make no fire. As the twilight drew on, its eager yearning for the fire mastered it, and with a great lifting and shifting of forefeet, it whined softly, then flattened its ears down in anticipation of being chidden by the man. But the man remained silent. Later the dog whined loudly. And still later it crept close to the man and caught the scent of death. This made the animal bristle and back away. A little longer it delayed, howling under the stars that leaped and danced and shone brightly in the cold sky. Then it turned and trotted up the trail in the direction of the camp it knew, where were the other food providers and fire providers.

Questions

1. Roughly how much of London's story is devoted to describing the setting? What particular details make it memorable?
2. To what extent does setting determine what happens in this story?
3. From what point of view is London's story told?
4. In "To Build a Fire" the man is never given a name. What is the effect of his being called simply "the man" throughout the story?
5. From the evidence London gives us, what stages are involved in the process of freezing to death? What does the story gain from London's detailed account of the man's experience with each successive stage?
6. What are the most serious mistakes the man makes? To what factors do you attribute these errors?

Ray Bradbury

A Sound of Thunder   1953

Raymond Douglas Bradbury was born in 1920 in Waukegan, Illinois, a small Midwestern town he has frequently evoked in his fiction. His mother was a Swedish immigrant, his father an electrical lineman. In 1934 his unemployed father could find no work in Depression-ravaged Illinois and moved the family to Los Angeles, where his son entered high school. The young Bradbury soon discovered science fiction and began publishing stories in his high school magazine. In 1939 he even started his own fanzine, Futuria Fantasia, *which lasted four issues. Unable to afford college, Bradbury took odd jobs while he tried to make his way as a writer. By 1941 he was publishing fiction in commercial magazines and very quickly developed a personal style that was strikingly unlike the conventional science fiction of the era. His stories*

Ray Bradbury

were quietly poetic, evocatively detailed, overtly symbolic, and often suffused with nostalgia. His first collection, Dark Carnival *(1947), made a modest impression, but his 1950 cycle of stories about mankind's doomed colonization of Mars,* The Martian Chronicles, *was immediately recognized as a classic of science fiction. The success of* The Martian Chronicles *made Bradbury the first American science-fiction writer to cross over into the mainstream literary market.*

His novels became both critical and popular successes, especially Fahrenheit 451 *(1953),* Dandelion Wine *(1957), and* Something Wicked This Way Comes *(1962), but he is best known for his short stories, which were collected in volumes like* The Illustrated Man *(1951),* The Golden Apples of the Sun *(1953),* A Medicine for Melancholy *(1959),* The Machineries of Joy *(1964), and* I Sing the Body Electric! *(1969). Bradbury's literary vision has also been disseminated though film, television, and theater. A huge number of his novels and stories have been filmed. His ongoing connection with Hollywood was a natural extension of his literary career since Bradbury has lived his entire adult life in Los Angeles. In one sense, however, he has remained a very odd Angelino—Bradbury has never learned to drive a car. Although at his best an elegant stylist, Bradbury is perhaps primarily a myth-maker. His science fiction and fantasy narratives have given contemporary readers (and viewers) the stories, situations, images, and symbols necessary to a complex, and rapidly changing, technology-driven society. Bradbury has received many honors, including the National Medal of Arts in 2004 and a lifetime Pulitzer Prize in 2007.*

The sign on the wall seemed to quaver under a film of sliding warm water. Eckels felt his eyelids blink over his stare, and the sign burned in this momentary darkness:

TIME SAFARI, INC.
SAFARIS TO ANY YEAR IN THE
PAST.
YOU NAME THE ANIMAL.
WE TAKE YOU THERE.
YOU SHOOT IT.

A warm phlegm gathered in Eckels' throat; he swallowed and pushed it down. The muscles around his mouth formed a smile as he put his hand slowly out upon the air, and in that hand waved a check for ten thousand dollars to the man behind the desk.

"Does this safari guarantee I come back alive?"

"We guarantee nothing," said the official, "except the dinosaurs." He turned. "This is Mr. Travis, your Safari Guide in the Past. He'll tell you what and where to shoot. If he says no shooting, no shooting. If you disobey instructions, there's a stiff penalty of another ten thousand dollars, plus possible government action, on your return."

Eckels glanced across the vast office at a mass and tangle, a snaking and humming of wires and steel boxes, at an aurora that flickered now orange, now silver, now blue. There was a sound like a gigantic bonfire burning all of Time, all the years and all the parchment calendars, all the hours piled high and set aflame.

A touch of the hand and this burning would, on the instant, beautifully reverse itself. Eckels remembered the wording in the advertisements to the letter. Out of chars and ashes, out of dust and coals, like golden salamanders, the old years, the green years, might leap; roses sweeten the air, white hair turn Irish-black, wrinkles vanish; all, everything fly back to seed, flee death, rush down to their beginnings, suns rise in

5

western skies and set in glorious easts, moons eat themselves opposite to the custom, all and everything cupping one in another like Chinese boxes, rabbits into hats, all and everything returning to the fresh death, the seed death, the green death, to the time before the beginning. A touch of a hand might do it, the merest touch of a hand.

"Unbelievable." Eckels breathed, the light of the Machine on his thin face. "A real Time Machine." He shook his head. "Makes you think, If the election had gone badly yesterday, I might be here now running away from the results. Thank God Keith won. He'll make a fine President of the United States."

"Yes," said the man behind the desk. "We're lucky. If Deutscher had gotten in, we'd have the worst kind of dictatorship. There's an anti everything man for you, a militarist, anti-Christ, anti-human, anti-intellectual. People called us up, you know, joking but not joking. Said if Deutscher became President they wanted to go live in 1492. Of course it's not our business to conduct Escapes, but to form Safaris. Anyway, Keith's President now. All you got to worry about is—"

"Shooting my dinosaur," Eckels finished it for him.

"A *Tyrannosaurus rex*. The Tyrant Lizard, the most incredible monster in his- 10
tory. Sign this release. Anything happens to you, we're not responsible. Those dinosaurs are hungry."

Eckels flushed angrily. "Trying to scare me!"

"Frankly, yes. We don't want anyone going who'll panic at the first shot. Six Safari leaders were killed last year, and a dozen hunters. We're here to give you the severest thrill a *real* hunter ever asked for. Traveling you back sixty million years to bag the biggest game in all of Time. Your personal check's still there. Tear it up."

Mr. Eckels looked at the check. His fingers twitched.

"Good luck," said the man behind the desk. "Mr. Travis, he's all yours."

They moved silently across the room, taking their guns with them, toward the 15
Machine, toward the silver metal and the roaring light.

First a day and then a night and then a day and then a night, then it was day-night-day-night-day. A week, a month, a year, a decade! A.D. 2055. A.D. 2019. 1999! 1957! Gone! The Machine roared.

They put on their oxygen helmets and tested the intercoms.

Eckels swayed on the padded seat, his face pale, his jaw stiff. He felt the trembling in his arms and he looked down and found his hands tight on the new rifle. There were four other men in the Machine. Travis, the Safari Leader, his assistant, Lesperance, and two other hunters, Billings and Kramer. They sat looking at each other, and the years blazed around them.

"Can these guns get a dinosaur cold?" Eckels felt his mouth saying.

"If you hit them right," said Travis on the helmet radio. "Some dinosaurs have 20
two brains, one in the head, another far down the spinal column. We stay away from those. That's stretching luck. Put your first two shots into the eyes, if you can, blind them, and go back into the brain."

The Machine howled. Time was a film run backward. Suns fled and ten million moons fled after them. "Think," said Eckels. "Every hunter that ever lived would envy us today. This makes Africa seem like Illinois."

The Machine slowed; its scream fell to a murmur. The Machine stopped.

The sun stopped in the sky.

The fog that had enveloped the Machine blew away and they were in an old time, a very old time indeed, three hunters and two Safari Heads with their blue metal guns across their knees.

"Christ isn't born yet," said Travis. "Moses has not gone to the mountain to talk 25 with God. The Pyramids are still in the earth, waiting to be cut out and put up. *Remember* that. Alexander, Caesar, Napoleon, Hitler—none of them exists."

The man nodded.

"That"—Mr. Travis pointed—"is the jungle of sixty million two thousand and fifty-five years before President Keith."

He indicated a metal path that struck off into green wilderness, over streaming swamp, among giant ferns and palms.

"And that," he said, "is the Path, laid by Time Safari for your use. It floats six inches above the earth. Doesn't touch so much as one grass blade, flower, or tree. It's an anti-gravity metal. Its purpose is to keep you from touching this world of the past in any way. Stay on the Path. Don't go off it. I repeat. *Don't go off.* For *any* reason! If you fall off, there's a penalty. And don't shoot any animal we don't okay."

"Why?" asked Eckels. 30

They sat in the ancient wilderness. Far birds' cries blew on a wind, and the smell of tar and an old salt sea, moist grasses, and flowers the color of blood.

"We don't want to change the Future. We don't belong here in the Past. The government doesn't *like* us here. We have to pay big graft to keep our franchise. A Time Machine is finicky business. Not knowing it, we might kill an important animal, a small bird, a roach, a flower even, thus destroying an important link in a growing species."

"That's not clear," said Eckels.

"All right," Travis continued, "say we accidentally kill one mouse here. That means all the future families of this one particular mouse are destroyed, right?"

"Right." 35

"And all the families of the families of the families of that one mouse! With a stamp of your foot, you annihilate first one, then a dozen, then a thousand, a million, a billion possible mice!"

"So they're dead," said Eckels. "So what?"

"So what?" Travis snorted quietly. "Well, what about the foxes that'll need those mice to survive? For want of ten mice, a fox dies. For want of ten foxes a lion starves. For want of a lion, all manner of insects, vultures, infinite billions of life forms are thrown into chaos and destruction. Eventually it all boils down to this: fifty-nine million years later, a caveman, one of a dozen on the *entire world*, goes hunting wild boar or saber-toothed tiger for food. But you, friend, have stepped on all the tigers in that region. By stepping on *one* single mouse. So the caveman starves. And the caveman, please note, is not just *any* expendable man, no! He is an *entire future nation.* From his loins would have sprung ten sons. From their loins one hundred sons, and thus onward to a civilization. Destroy this one man, and you destroy a race, a people, an entire history of life. It is comparable to slaying some of Adam's grandchildren. The stomp of your foot, on one mouse, could start an earthquake, the effects of which could shake our earth and destinies down through Time, to their very foundations. With the death of that one caveman, a billion others yet unborn are throttled in the womb. Perhaps Rome never rises on its seven hills. Perhaps Europe is forever a dark forest, and only Asia waxes healthy and teeming. Step on a mouse and you crush the Pyramids. Step on a mouse and you leave your print, like a Grand Canyon, across Eternity. Queen Elizabeth might never be born, Washington might not cross the Delaware, there might never be a United States at all. So be careful. Stay on the Path. *Never* step off!"

"I see," said Eckels. "Then it wouldn't pay for us even to touch the *grass?*"

"Correct. Crushing certain plants could add up infinitesimally. A little error here would multiply in sixty million years, all out of proportion. Of course maybe our theory is wrong. Maybe Time *can't* be changed by us. Or maybe it can be changed only in little subtle ways. A dead mouse here makes an insect imbalance there, a population disproportion later, a bad harvest further on, a depression, mass starvation, and finally, a change in *social* temperament in far-flung countries. Something much more subtle, like that. Perhaps only a soft breath, a whisper, a hair, pollen on the air, such a slight, slight change that unless you looked close you wouldn't see it. Who knows? Who really can say he knows? We don't know. We're guessing. But until we do know for certain whether our messing around in Time *can* make a big roar or a little rustle in history, we're being careful. This Machine, this Path, your clothing and bodies, were sterilized, as you know, before the journey. We wear these oxygen helmets so we can't introduce our bacteria into an ancient atmosphere."

"How do we know which animals to shoot?"

"They're marked with red paint," said Travis. "Today, before our journey, we sent Lesperance here back with the Machine. He came to this particular era and followed certain animals."

"Studying them?"

"Right," said Lesperance. "I track them through their entire existence, noting which of them lives longest. Very few. How many times they mate. Not often. Life's short, When I find one that's going to die when a tree falls on him, or one that drowns in a tar pit, I note the exact hour, minute, and second. I shoot a paint bomb. It leaves a red patch on his side. We can't miss it. Then I correlate our arrival in the Past so that we meet the Monster not more than two minutes before he would have died anyway. This way, we kill only animals with no future, that are never going to mate again. You see how *careful* we are?"

"But if you came back this morning in Time," said Eckels eagerly, you must've bumped into *us*, our Safari! How did it turn out? Was it successful? Did all of us get through—alive?"

Travis and Lesperance gave each other a look.

"That'd be a paradox," said the latter. "Time doesn't permit that sort of mess—a man meeting himself. When such occasions threaten, Time steps aside. Like an airplane hitting an air pocket. You felt the Machine jump just before we stopped? That was us passing ourselves on the way back to the Future. We saw nothing. There's no way of telling if this expedition was a success, if we got our monster, or whether all of us—meaning *you*, Mr. Eckels—got out alive."

Eckels smiled palely.

"Cut that," said Travis sharply. "Everyone on his feet!"

They were ready to leave the Machine.

The jungle was high and the jungle was broad and the jungle was the entire world forever and forever. Sounds like music and sounds like flying tents filled the sky, and those were pterodactyls soaring with cavernous gray wings, gigantic bats of delirium and night fever.

Eckels, balanced on the narrow Path, aimed his rifle playfully.

"Stop that!" said Travis. "Don't even aim for fun, blast you! If your guns should go off—"

Eckels flushed. "Where's our *Tyrannosaurus?*"

Lesperance checked his wristwatch. "Up ahead, We'll bisect his trail in sixty sec- 55
onds. Look for the red paint! Don't shoot till we give the word. Stay on the Path.
Stay on the Path!"

They moved forward in the wind of morning.

"Strange," murmured Eckels. "Up ahead, sixty million years, Election Day over.
Keith made President. Everyone celebrating. And here we are, a million years lost,
and they don't exist. The things we worried about for months, a lifetime, not even
born or thought of yet."

"Safety catches off, everyone!" ordered Travis. "You, first shot, Eckels. Second,
Billings, Third, Kramer."

"I've hunted tiger, wild boar, buffalo, elephant, but now, this is *it*," said Eckels.
"I'm shaking like a kid."

"Ah," said Travis. 60

Everyone stopped.

Travis raised his hand. "Ahead," he whispered. "In the mist. There he is. There's
His Royal Majesty now."

The jungle was wide and full of twitterings, rustlings, murmurs, and sighs.

Suddenly it all ceased, as if someone had shut a door.

Silence. 65

A sound of thunder.

Out of the mist, one hundred yards away, came *Tyrannosaurus rex*.

"It," whispered Eckels. "It . . ."

"Sh!"

It came on great oiled, resilient, striding legs. It towered thirty feet above half of 70
the trees, a great evil god, folding its delicate watchmaker's claws close to its oily reptilian chest. Each lower leg was a piston, a thousand pounds of white bone, sunk in
thick ropes of muscle, sheathed over in a gleam of pebbled skin like the mail of a terrible warrior. Each thigh was a ton of meat, ivory, and steel mesh. And from the great
breathing cage of the upper body those two delicate arms dangled out front, arms
with hands which might pick up and examine men like toys, while the snake neck
coiled. And the head itself, a ton of sculptured stone, lifted easily upon the sky. Its
mouth gaped, exposing a fence of teeth like daggers. Its eyes rolled, ostrich eggs,
empty of all expression save hunger. It closed its mouth in a death grin. It ran, its
pelvic bones crushing aside trees and bushes, its taloned feet clawing damp earth,
leaving prints six inches deep wherever it settled its weight.

It ran with a gliding ballet step, far too poised and balanced for its ten tons. It
moved into a sunlit area warily, its beautifully reptilian hands feeling the air.

"Why, why," Eckels twitched his mouth. "It could reach up and grab the
moon."

"Sh!" Travis jerked angrily. "He hasn't seen us yet."

"It can't be killed," Eckels pronounced this verdict quietly, as if there could be
no argument. He had weighed the evidence and this was his considered opinion. The
rifle in his hands seemed a cap gun. "We were fools to come. This is impossible."

"Shut up!" hissed Travis. 75

"Nightmare."

"Turn around," commanded Travis. "Walk quietly to the Machine. We'll remit
half your fee."

"I didn't realize it would be this *big*," said Eckels. "I miscalculated, that's all. And now I want out."

"It *sees* us!"

"There's the red paint on its chest!"

The Tyrant Lizard raised itself. Its armored flesh glittered like a thousand green coins. The coins, crusted with slime, steamed. In the slime, tiny insects wriggled, so that the entire body seemed to twitch and undulate, even while the monster itself did not move. It exhaled. The stink of raw flesh blew down the wilderness.

"Get me out of here," said Eckels. "It was never like this before. I was always sure I'd come through alive. I had good guides, good safaris, and safety. This time, I figured wrong. I've met my match and admit it. This is too much for me to get hold of."

"Don't run," said Lesperance. "Turn around. Hide in the Machine."

"Yes." Eckels seemed to be numb. He looked at his feet as if trying to make them move. He gave a grunt of helplessness.

"Eckels!"

He took a few steps, blinking, shuffling.

"Not *that* way!"

The Monster, at the first motion, lunged forward with a terrible scream. It covered one hundred yards in six seconds. The rifles jerked up and blazed fire. A windstorm from the beast's mouth engulfed them in the stench of slime and old blood. The Monster roared, teeth glittering with sun.

Eckels, not looking back, walked blindly to the edge of the Path, his gun limp in his arms, stepped off the Path, and walked, not knowing it, in the jungle. His feet sank into green moss. His legs moved him, and he felt alone and remote from the events behind.

The rifles cracked again, Their sound was lost in shriek and lizard thunder. The great level of the reptile's tail swung up, lashed sideways. Trees exploded in clouds of leaf and branch. The Monster twitched its jeweler's hands down to fondle at the men, to twist them in half, to crush them like berries, to cram them into its teeth and its screaming throat. Its boulderstone eyes leveled with the men. They saw themselves mirrored. They fired at the metallic eyelids and the blazing black iris.

Like a stone idol, like a mountain avalanche, *Tyrannosaurus* fell. Thundering, it clutched trees, pulled them with it. It wrenched and tore the metal Path. The men flung themselves back and away. The body hit, ten tons of cold flesh and stone. The guns fired. The Monster lashed its armored tail, twitched its snake jaws, and lay still. A fount of blood spurted from its throat. Somewhere inside, a sac of fluids burst. Sickening gushes drenched the hunters. They stood, red and glistening.

The thunder faded.

The jungle was silent. After the avalanche, a green peace. After the nightmare, morning.

Billings and Kramer sat on the pathway and threw up. Travis and Lesperance stood with smoking rifles, cursing steadily.

In the Time Machine, on his face, Eckels lay shivering. He had found his way back to the Path, climbed into the Machine.

Travis came walking, glanced at Eckels, took cotton gauze from a metal box, and returned to the others, who were sitting on the Path.

"Clean up."

They wiped the blood from their helmets. They began to curse too. The Monster lay, a hill of solid flesh. Within, you could hear the sighs and murmurs as the furthest chambers of it died, the organs malfunctioning, liquids running a final instant from pocket to sac to spleen, everything shutting off, closing up forever. It was like standing by a wrecked locomotive or a steam shovel at quitting time, all valves being released or levered tight. Bones cracked; the tonnage of its own flesh, off balance, dead weight, snapped the delicate forearms, caught underneath. The meat settled, quivering.

Another cracking sound. Overhead, a gigantic tree branch broke from its heavy mooring, fell. It crashed upon the dead beast with finality.

"There." Lesperance checked his watch. "Right on time. That's the giant tree   100
that was scheduled to fall and kill this animal originally." He glanced at the two hunters. "You want the trophy picture?"

"What?"

"We can't take a trophy back to the Future. The body has to stay right here where it would have died originally, so the insects, birds, and bacteria can get at it, as they were intended to. Everything in balance. The body stays. But we *can* take a picture of you standing near it."

The two men tried to think, but gave up, shaking their heads.

They let themselves be led along the metal Path. They sank wearily into the Machine cushions. They gazed back at the ruined Monster, the stagnating mound, where already strange reptilian birds and golden insects were busy at the steaming armor. A sound on the floor of the Time Machine stiffened them. Eckels sat there, shivering.

"I'm sorry," he said at last.   105

"Get up!" cried Travis.

Eckels got up.

"Go out on that Path alone," said Travis. He had his rifle pointed, "You're not coming back in the Machine. We're leaving you here!"

Lesperance seized Travis's arm. "Wait—"

"Stay out of this!" Travis shook his hand away. "This fool nearly killed us. But it   110
isn't *that* so much, no. It's his *shoes!* Look at them! He ran off the Path. That *ruins* us! We'll forfeit! Thousands of dollars of insurance! We guarantee no one leaves the Path. He left it. Oh, the fool! I'll have to report to the government. They might revoke our license to travel. Who knows *what* he's done to Time, to History!"

"Take it easy, all he did was kick up some dirt."

"How do we *know?*" cried Travis. "We don't know anything! It's all a mystery! Get out of here, Eckels!"

Eckels fumbled his shirt. "I'll pay anything. A hundred thousand dollars!"

Travis glared at Eckels' checkbook and spat. "Go out there. The Monster's next to the Path. Stick your arms up to your elbows in his mouth. Then you can come back with us."

"That's unreasonable!"   115

"The Monster's dead, you idiot. The bullets! The bullets can't be left behind. They don't belong in the Past; they might change anything. Here's my knife. Dig them out!"

The jungle was alive again, full of the old tremorings and bird cries. Eckels turned slowly to regard the primeval garbage dump, that hill of nightmares and terror. After a long time, like a sleepwalker he shuffled out along the Path.

He returned, shuddering, five minutes later, his arms soaked and red to the elbows. He held out his hands. Each held a number of steel bullets. Then he fell. He lay where he fell, not moving.

"You didn't have to make him do that," said Lesperance.

"Didn't I? It's too early to tell." Travis nudged the still body. "He'll live. Next 120
time he won't go hunting game like this. Okay." He jerked his thumb wearily at Lesperance. "Switch on. Let's go home."

1492. 1776. 1812.

They cleaned their hands and faces. They changed their caking shirts and pants.
Eckels was up and around again, not speaking. Travis glared at him for a full ten minutes.

"Don't look at me," cried Eckels. "I haven't done anything."

"Who can tell?"

"Just ran off the Path, that's all, a little mud on my shoes—what do you want me 125
to do—get down and pray?"

"We might need it. I'm warning you, Eckels, I might kill you yet. I've got my gun
ready."

"I'm innocent. I've done nothing!"

1999. 2000. 2055.

The Machine stopped.

"Get out," said Travis. 130

The room was there as they had left it. But not the same as they had left it. The
same man sat behind the same desk. But the same man did not quite sit behind the
same desk. Travis looked around swiftly. "Everything okay here?" he snapped.

"Fine. Welcome home!"

Travis did not relax. He seemed to be looking through the one high window.

"Okay, Eckels, get out. Don't ever come back." Eckels could not move.

"You heard me," said Travis. "What're you *staring* at?" 135

Eckels stood smelling of the air, and there was a thing to the air, a chemical taint
so subtle, so slight, that only a faint cry of his subliminal senses warned him it was
there. The colors, white, gray, blue, orange, in the wall, in the furniture, in the sky
beyond the window, were . . . were. . . . And there was a *feel*. His flesh twitched. His
hands twitched. He stood drinking the oddness with the pores of his body. Somewhere, someone must have been screaming one of those whistles that only a dog can
hear. His body screamed silence in return. Beyond this room, beyond this wall, beyond this man who was not quite the same man seated at this desk that was not quite
the same desk . . . lay an entire world of streets and people. What sort of world it was
now, there was no telling. He could feel them moving there, beyond the walls, almost, like so many chess pieces blown in a dry wind. . . .

But the immediate thing was the sign painted on the office wall, the same sign
he had read earlier today on first entering. Somehow, the sign had changed:

TYME SEFARI INC.
SEFARIS TU ANY YEER EN THE
PAST.
YU NAIM THE ANIMALL.
WEE TAEKYUTHAIR.
YU SHOOT ITT.

Eckels felt himself fall into a chair. He fumbled crazily at the thick slime on his boots.
He held up a clod of dirt, trembling, "No, it *can't* be. Not a *little* thing like that. No!"

Embedded in the mud, glistening green and gold and black, was a butterfly, very
beautiful and very dead.

"Not a little thing like *that!* Not a butterfly!" cried Eckels.   140

It fell to the floor, an exquisite thing, a small thing that could upset balances and knock down a line of small dominoes and then big dominoes and then gigantic dominoes, all down the years across Time. Eckels' mind whirled. It *couldn't* change things. Killing one butterfly couldn't be *that* important! Could it?

His face was cold. His mouth trembled, asking: "Who—who won the presidential election yesterday?"

The man behind the desk laughed. "You joking? You know very well. Deutscher, of course! Who else? Not that fool weakling Keith. We got an iron man now, a man with guts!" The official stopped. "What's wrong?"

Eckels moaned. He dropped to his knees. He scrabbled at the golden butterfly with shaking fingers. "Can't we," he pleaded to the world, to himself, to the officials, to the Machine, "can't we take it *back*, can't we *make* it alive again? Can't we start over? Can't we—"

He did not move. Eyes shut, he waited, shivering. He heard Travis breathe loud in   145 the room; he heard Travis shift his rifle, click the safety catch, and raise the weapon.

There was a sound of thunder.

Questions

1. What are the two main settings of Bradbury's story? What is unusual about both settings?
2. How does the plot of the story depend on the setting? Would it be possible to tell this story in different settings?
3. Why does the government not approve of time travel? How does Time Safari Inc. deal with governmental obstacles?
4. When Eckels returns to the altered present, when does he first sense that something has changed?
5. In what specific ways has the present been changed by the trip?
6. What happens in the last three paragraphs of the story?
7. "A Sound of Thunder" is not a realistic story, but it seems to convey a pertinent message about humanity's relation to the natural world. How would you summarize that message?

Amy Tan

A Pair of Tickets   1989

Amy Tan was born in Oakland, California, in 1952. Both of her parents were recent Chinese immigrants. Her father was an electrical engineer (as well as a Baptist minister); her mother was a vocational nurse. When her father and older brother both died of brain tumors, the fifteen-year-old Tan moved with her mother and younger brother to Switzerland, where she attended high school. On their return to the United States Tan attended Linfield College, a Baptist school in Oregon, but she eventually transferred to San Jose State University. At this time Tan and her mother argued about her future. The mother insisted her daughter pursue premedical studies in preparation for becoming a neurosurgeon, but Tan wanted to do something else. For six months the two did not speak to one another. Tan worked for IBM writing computer manuals and also wrote freelance business articles under a pseudonym. In 1987 she and her mother visited China together. This experience, which is reflected in "A Pair of Tickets," deepened Tan's sense of her Chinese American identity. "As soon as my feet touched China," she wrote, "I became Chinese." Soon after, she began writing her first novel, The Joy Luck Club *(1989), which consists of sixteen interrelated stories about a group of Chinese American mothers and their daughters. (The club of the title is a woman's social group.)* The Joy Luck Club *became both a critical success and a best seller, and was made into a movie in 1993. In 1991 Tan published her second novel,* The Kitchen God's Wife. *Her later novels include* The Bonesetter's Daughter *(2001) and* Saving Fish from Drowning *(2005). Tan performs with a "vintage garage" band called the Rock Bottom Remainders, which also includes, among others, Stephen King, Dave Barry, and Scott Turow. She lives outside San Francisco with her husband.*

The minute our train leaves the Hong Kong border and enters Shenzhen, China, I feel different. I can feel the skin on my forehead tingling, my blood rushing through a new course, my bones aching with a familiar old pain. And I think, My mother was right. I am becoming Chinese.

"Cannot be helped," my mother said when I was fifteen and had vigorously denied that I had any Chinese whatsoever below my skin. I was a sophomore at Galileo High in San Francisco, and all my Caucasian friends agreed: I was about as Chinese as they were. But my mother had studied at a famous nursing school in Shanghai, and she said she knew all about genetics. So there was no doubt in her mind, whether I agreed or not: Once you are born Chinese, you cannot help but feel and think Chinese.

"Someday you will see," said my mother. "It is in your blood, waiting to be let go."

And when she said this, I saw myself transforming like a werewolf, a mutant tag of DNA suddenly triggered, replicating itself insidiously into a *syndrome,*° a cluster of telltale Chinese behaviors, all those things my mother did to embarrass me—haggling with store owners, pecking her mouth with a toothpick in public, being color-blind to the fact that lemon yellow and pale pink are not good combinations for winter clothes.

But today I realize I've never really known what it means to be Chinese. I am thirty-six years old. My mother is dead and I am on a train, carrying with me her dreams of coming home. I am going to China.

We are first going to Guangzhou, my seventy-two-year-old father, Canning Woo, and I, where we will visit his aunt, whom he has not seen since he was ten years old. And I don't know whether it's the prospect of seeing his aunt or if it's because he's back in China, but now he looks like he's a young boy, so innocent and happy I want to button his sweater and pat his head. We are sitting across from each other, separated by a little table with two cold cups of tea. For the first time I can ever remember, my father has tears in his eyes, and all he is seeing out the train window is a sectioned field of yellow, green, and brown, a narrow canal flanking the tracks, low rising hills, and three people in blue jackets riding an ox-driven cart on this early October morning. And I can't help myself. I also have misty eyes, as if I had seen this a long, long time ago, and had almost forgotten.

In less than three hours, we will be in Guangzhou, which my guidebook tells me is how one properly refers to Canton these days. It seems all the cities I have heard of, except Shanghai, have changed their spellings. I think they are saying China has changed in other ways as well. Chungking is Chongqing. And Kweilin is Guilin. I

syndrome: a group of symptoms that occur together as the sign of a particular disease or abnormality.

have looked these names up, because after we see my father's aunt in Guangzhou, we will catch a plane to Shanghai, where I will meet my two half-sisters for the first time.

They are my mother's twin daughters from her first marriage, little babies she was forced to abandon on a road as she was fleeing Kweilin for Chungking in 1944. That was all my mother had told me about these daughters, so they had remained babies in my mind, all these years, sitting on the side of a road, listening to bombs whistling in the distance while sucking their patient red thumbs.

And it was only this year that someone found them and wrote with this joyful news. A letter came from Shanghai, addressed to my mother. When I first heard about this, that they were alive, I imagined my identical sisters transforming from little babies into six-year-old girls. In my mind, they were seated next to each other at a table, taking turns with the fountain pen. One would write a neat row of characters: *Dearest Mama. We are alive.* She would brush back her wispy bangs and hand the other sister the pen, and she would write: *Come get us. Please hurry.*

Of course they could not know that my mother had died three months before,   10 suddenly, when a blood vessel in her brain burst. One minute she was talking to my father, complaining about the tenants upstairs, scheming how to evict them under the pretense that relatives from China were moving in. The next minute she was holding her head, her eyes squeezed shut, groping for the sofa, and then crumpling softly to the floor with fluttering hands.

So my father had been the first one to open the letter, a long letter it turned out. And they did call her Mama. They said they always revered her as their true mother. They kept a framed picture of her. They told her about their life, from the time my mother last saw them on the road leaving Kweilin to when they were finally found.

And the letter had broken my father's heart so much—these daughters calling my mother from another life he never knew—that he gave the letter to my mother's old friend Auntie Lindo and asked her to write back and tell my sisters, in the gentlest way possible, that my mother was dead.

But instead Auntie Lindo took the letter to the Joy Luck Club and discussed with Auntie Ying and Auntie An-mei what should be done, because they had known for many years about my mother's search for her twin daughters, her endless hope. Auntie Lindo and the others cried over this double tragedy, of losing my mother three months before, and now again. And so they couldn't help but think of some miracle, some possible way of reviving her from the dead, so my mother could fulfill her dream.

So this is what they wrote to my sisters in Shanghai: "Dearest Daughters, I too have never forgotten you in my memory or in my heart. I never gave up hope that we would see each other again in a joyous reunion. I am only sorry it has been too long. I want to tell you everything about my life since I last saw you. I want to tell you this when our family comes to see you in China. . . ." They signed it with my mother's name.

It wasn't until all this had been done that they first told me about my sisters, the   15 letter they received, the one they wrote back.

"They'll think she's coming, then," I murmured. And I had imagined my sisters now being ten or eleven, jumping up and down, holding hands, their pigtails bouncing, excited that their mother—*their* mother—was coming, whereas my mother was dead.

"How can you say she is not coming in a letter?" said Auntie Lindo. "She is their mother. She is your mother. You must be the one to tell them. All these years, they have been dreaming of her." And I thought she was right.

But then I started dreaming, too, of my mother and my sisters and how it would be if I arrived in Shanghai. All these years, while they waited to be found, I had lived with my mother and then had lost her. I imagined seeing my sisters at the airport. They would be standing on their tip-toes, looking anxiously, scanning from one dark head to another as we got off the plane. And I would recognize them instantly, their faces with the identical worried look.

"Jyejye, Jyejye. Sister, Sister. We are here," I saw myself saying in my poor version of Chinese.

"Where is Mama?" they would say, and look around, still smiling, two flushed   20
and eager faces. "Is she hiding?" And this would have been like my mother, to stand behind just a bit, to tease a little and make people's patience pull a little on their hearts. I would shake my head and tell my sisters she was not hiding.

"Oh, that must be Mama, no?" one of my sisters would whisper excitedly, pointing to another small woman completely engulfed in a tower of presents. And that, too, would have been like my mother, to bring mountains of gifts, food, and toys for children—all bought on sale—shunning thanks, saying the gifts were nothing, and later turning the labels over to show my sisters, "Calvin Klein, 100% wool."

I imagined myself starting to say, "Sisters, I am sorry, I have come alone . . ." and before I could tell them—they could see it in my face—they were wailing, pulling their hair, their lips twisted in pain, as they ran away from me. And then I saw myself getting back on the plane and coming home.

After I had dreamed this scene many times—watching their despair turn from horror into anger—I begged Auntie Lindo to write another letter. And at first she refused.

"How can I say she is dead? I cannot write this," said Auntie Lindo with a stubborn look.

"But it's cruel to have them believe she's coming on the plane," I said. "When   25
they see it's just me, they'll hate me."

"Hate you? Cannot be." She was scowling. "You are their own sister, their only family."

"You don't understand," I protested.

"What I don't understand?" she said.

And I whispered, "They'll think I'm responsible, that she died because I didn't appreciate her."

And Auntie Lindo looked satisfied and sad at the same time, as if this were true   30
and I had finally realized it. She sat down for an hour, and when she stood up she handed me a two-page letter. She had tears in her eyes. I realized that the very thing I had feared, she had done. So even if she had written the news of my mother's death in English, I wouldn't have had the heart to read it.

"Thank you," I whispered.

The landscape has become gray, filled with low flat cement buildings, old factories, and then tracks and more tracks filled with trains like ours passing by in the opposite direction. I see platforms crowded with people wearing drab Western clothes, with spots of bright colors: little children wearing pink and yellow, red and peach. And there are soldiers in olive green and red, and old ladies in gray tops and pants that stop mid-calf. We are in Guangzhou.

Before the train even comes to a stop, people are bringing down their belongings from above their seats. For a moment there is a dangerous shower of heavy suitcases laden with gifts to relatives, half-broken boxes wrapped in miles of string to keep the contents from spilling out, plastic bags filled with yarn and vegetables and packages of dried mushrooms, and camera cases. And then we are caught in a stream of people rushing, shoving, pushing us along, until we find ourselves in one of a dozen lines waiting to go through customs. I feel as if I were getting on the number 30 Stockton bus in San Francisco. I am in China, I remind myself. And somehow the crowds don't bother me. It feels right. I start pushing too.

I take out the declaration forms and my passport. "Woo," it says at the top, and below that, "June May," who was born in "California, U.S.A.," in 1951. I wonder if the customs people will question whether I'm the same person in the passport photo. In this picture, my chin-length hair is swept back and artfully styled. I am wearing false eyelashes, eye shadow, and lip liner. My cheeks are hollowed out by bronze blusher. But I had not expected the heat in October. And now my hair hangs limp with the humidity. I wear no makeup; in Hong Kong my mascara had melted into dark circles and everything else had felt like layers of grease. So today my face is plain, unadorned except for a thin mist of shiny sweat on my forehead and nose.

Even without makeup, I could never pass for true Chinese. I stand five-foot-six, 35 and my head pokes above the crowd so that I am eye level only with other tourists. My mother once told me my height came from my grandfather, who was a northerner, and may have even had some Mongol blood. "This is what your grandmother once told me," explained my mother. "But now it is too late to ask her. They are all dead, your grandparents, your uncles, and their wives and children, all killed in the war, when a bomb fell on our house. So many generations in one instant."

She had said this so matter-of-factly that I thought she had long since gotten over any grief she had. And then I wondered how she knew they were all dead.

"Maybe they left the house before the bomb fell," I suggested.

"No," said my mother. "Our whole family is gone. It is just you and I."

"But how do you know? Some of them could have escaped."

"Cannot be," said my mother, this time almost angrily. And then her frown was 40 washed over by a puzzled blank look, and she began to talk as if she were trying to remember where she had misplaced something. "I went back to that house. I kept looking up to where the house used to be. And it wasn't a house, just the sky. And below, underneath my feet, were four stories of burnt bricks and wood, all the life of our house. Then off to the side I saw things blown into the yard, nothing valuable. There was a bed someone used to sleep in, really just a metal frame twisted up at one corner. And a book, I don't know what kind, because every page had turned black. And I saw a teacup which was unbroken but filled with ashes. And then I found my doll, with her hands and legs broken, her hair burned off. . . . When I was a little girl, I had cried for that doll, seeing it all alone in the store window, and my mother had bought it for me. It was an American doll with yellow hair. It could turn its legs and arms. The eyes moved up and down. And when I married and left my family home, I gave the doll to my youngest niece, because she was like me. She cried if that doll was not with her always. Do you see? If she was in the house with that doll, her parents were there, and so everybody was there, waiting together, because that's how our family was."

The woman in the customs booth stares at my documents, then glances at me briefly, and with two quick movements stamps everything and sternly nods me along. And soon my father and I find ourselves in a large area filled with thousands of people and suitcases. I feel lost and my father looks helpless.

"Excuse me," I say to a man who looks like an American. "Can you tell me where I can get a taxi?" He mumbles something that sounds Swedish or Dutch.

"Syau Yen! Syau Yen!" I hear a piercing voice shout from behind me. An old woman in a yellow knit beret is holding up a pink plastic bag filled with wrapped trinkets. I guess she is trying to sell us something. But my father is staring down at this tiny sparrow of a woman, squinting into her eyes. And then his eyes widen, his face opens up and he smiles like a pleased little boy.

"Aiyi! Aiyi!"—Auntie Auntie!—he says softly.

"Syau Yen!" coos my great-aunt. I think it's funny she has just called my father 45
"Little Wild Goose." It must be his baby milk name, the name used to discourage ghosts from stealing children.

They clasp each other's hands—they do not hug—and hold on like this, taking turns saying, "Look at you! You are so old. Look how old you've become!" They are both crying openly, laughing at the same time, and I bite my lip, trying not to cry. I'm afraid to feel their joy. Because I am thinking how different our arrival in Shanghai will be tomorrow, how awkward it will feel.

Now Aiyi beams and points to a Polaroid picture of my father. My father had wisely sent pictures when he wrote and said we were coming. See how smart she was, she seems to intone as she compares the picture to my father. In the letter, my father had said we would call her from the hotel once we arrived, so this is a surprise, that they've come to meet us. I wonder if my sisters will be at the airport.

It is only then that I remember the camera. I had meant to take a picture of my father and his aunt the moment they met. It's not too late.

"Here, stand together over here," I say, holding up the Polaroid. The camera flashes and I hand them the snapshot. Aiyi and my father still stand close together, each of them holding a corner of the picture, watching as their images begin to form. They are almost reverentially quiet. Aiyi is only five years older than my father, which makes her around seventy-seven. But she looks ancient, shrunken, a mummified relic. Her thin hair is pure white, her teeth are brown with decay. So much for stories of Chinese women looking young forever, I think to myself.

Now Aiyi is crooning to me: "Jandale." So big already. She looks up at me, at my 50
full height, and then peers into her pink plastic bag—her gifts to us, I have figured out—as if she is wondering what she will give to me, now that I am so old and big. And then she grabs my elbow with her sharp pincerlike grasp and turns me around. A man and woman in their fifties are shaking hands with my father, everybody smiling and saying, "Ah! Ah!" They are Aiyi's oldest son and his wife, and standing next to them are four other people, around my age, and a little girl who's around ten. The introductions go by so fast, all I know is that one of them is Aiyi's grandson, with his wife, and the other is her granddaughter, with her husband. And the little girl is Lili, Aiyi's great-granddaughter.

Aiyi and my father speak the Mandarin dialect from their childhood, but the rest of the family speaks only the Cantonese of their village. I understand only Mandarin but can't speak it that well. So Aiyi and my father gossip unrestrained in Mandarin, exchanging news about people from their old village. And they stop only occasionally to talk to the rest of us, sometimes in Cantonese, sometimes in English.

"Oh, it is as I suspected," says my father, turning to me. "He died last summer." And I already understood this. I just don't know who this person, Li Gong, is. I feel as if I were in the United Nations and the translators had run amok.

"Hello," I say to the little girl. "My name is Jing-mei." But the little girl squirms to look away, causing her parents to laugh with embarrassment. I try to think of Cantonese words I can say to her, stuff I learned from friends in Chinatown, but all I can think of are swear words, terms for bodily functions, and short phrases like "tastes good," "tastes like garbage," and "she's really ugly." And then I have another plan: I hold up the Polaroid camera, beckoning Lili with my finger. She immediately jumps forward, places one hand on her hip in the manner of a fashion model, juts out her chest, and flashes me a toothy smile. As soon as I take the picture she is standing next to me, jumping and giggling every few seconds as she watches herself appear on the greenish film.

By the time we hail taxis for the ride to the hotel, Lili is holding tight onto my hand, pulling me along.

In the taxi, Aiyi talks nonstop, so I have no chance to ask her about the different sights we are passing by.

"You wrote and said you would come only for one day," says Aiyi to my father in an agitated tone. "One day! How can you see your family in one day! Toishan is many hours' drive from Guangzhou. And this idea to call us when you arrive. This is nonsense. We have no telephone."

My heart races a little. I wonder if Auntie Lindo told my sisters we would call from the hotel in Shanghai?

Aiyi continues to scold my father. "I was so beside myself, ask my son, almost turned heaven and earth upside down trying to think of a way! So we decided the best was for us to take the bus from Toishan and come into Guangzhou—meet you right from the start."

And now I am holding my breath as the taxi driver dodges between trucks and buses, honking his horn constantly. We seem to be on some sort of long freeway overpass, like a bridge above the city. I can see row after row of apartments, each floor cluttered with laundry hanging out to dry on the balcony. We pass a public bus, with people jammed in so tight their faces are nearly wedged against the window. Then I see the skyline of what must be downtown Guangzhou. From a distance, it looks like a major American city, with high rises and construction going on everywhere. As we slow down in the more congested part of the city, I see scores of little shops, dark inside, lined with counters and shelves. And then there is a building, its front laced with scaffolding made of bamboo poles held together with plastic strips. Men and women are standing on narrow platforms, scraping the sides, working without safety straps or helmets. Oh, would OSHA° have a field day here, I think.

Aiyi's shrill voice rises up again: "So it is a shame you can't see our village, our house. My sons have been quite successful, selling our vegetables in the free market. We had enough these last few years to build a big house, three stories, all of new brick, big enough for our whole family and then some. And every year, the money is even better. You Americans aren't the only ones who know how to get rich!"

The taxi stops and I assume we've arrived, but then I peer out at what looks like a grander version of the Hyatt Regency. "This is communist China?" I wonder out loud. And then I shake my head toward my father. "This must be the wrong hotel." I quickly

OSHA: Occupational Safety and Health Administration, a U.S. federal agency that regulates and monitors workplace safety conditions.

pull out our itinerary, travel tickets, and reservations. I had explicitly instructed my travel agent to choose something inexpensive, in the thirty-to-forty-dollar range. I'm sure of this. And there it says on our itinerary: Garden Hotel, Huanshi Dong Lu. Well, our travel agent had better be prepared to eat the extra, that's all I have to say.

The hotel is magnificent. A bellboy complete with uniform and sharp-creased cap jumps forward and begins to carry our bags into the lobby. Inside, the hotel looks like an orgy of shopping arcades and restaurants all encased in granite and glass. And rather than be impressed, I am worried about the expense, as well as the appearance it must give Aiyi, that we rich Americans cannot be without our luxuries even for one night.

But when I step up to the reservation desk, ready to haggle over this booking mistake, it is confirmed. Our rooms are prepaid, thirty-four dollars each. I feel sheepish, and Aiyi and the others seem delighted by our temporary surroundings. Lili is looking wide-eyed at an arcade filled with video games.

Our whole family crowds into one elevator, and the bellboy waves, saying he will meet us on the eighteenth floor. As soon as the elevator door shuts, everybody becomes very quiet, and when the door finally opens again, everybody talks at once in what sounds like relieved voices. I have the feeling Aiyi and the others have never been on such a long elevator ride.

Our rooms are next to each other and are identical. The rugs, drapes, bedspreads are all in shades of taupe. There's a color television with remote-control panels built into the lamp table between the two twin beds. The bathroom has marble walls and floors. I find a built-in wet bar with a small refrigerator stocked with Heineken beer, Coke Classic, and Seven-Up, mini-bottles of Johnnie Walker Red, Bacardi rum, and Smirnoff vodka, and packets of M & M's, honey-roasted cashews, and Cadbury chocolate bars. And again I say out loud, "This is communist China?" 65

My father comes into my room. "They decided we should just stay here and visit," he says, shrugging his shoulders. "They say, Less trouble that way. More time to talk."

"What about dinner?" I ask. I have been envisioning my first real Chinese feast for many days already, a big banquet with one of those soups steaming out of a carved winter melon, chicken wrapped in clay, Peking duck, the works.

My father walks over and picks up a room service book next to a *Travel & Leisure* magazine. He flips through the pages quickly and then points to the menu. "This is what they want," says my father.

So it's decided. We are going to dine tonight in our rooms, with our family, sharing hamburgers, french fries, and apple pie à la mode.

Aiyi and her family are browsing the shops while we clean up. After a hot ride on the train, I'm eager for a shower and cooler clothes. 70

The hotel has provided little packets of shampoo which, upon opening, I discover is the consistency and color of hoisin sauce. This is more like it, I think. This is China. And I rub some in my damp hair.

Standing in the shower, I realize this is the first time I've been by myself in what seems like days. But instead of feeling relieved, I feel forlorn. I think about what my mother said, about activating my genes and becoming Chinese. And I wonder what she meant.

Right after my mother died, I asked myself a lot of things, things that couldn't be answered, to force myself to grieve more. It seemed as if I wanted to sustain my grief, to assure myself that I had cared deeply enough.

But now I ask the questions mostly because I want to know the answers. What was that pork stuff she used to make that had the texture of sawdust? What were the names of the uncles who died in Shanghai? What had she dreamt all these years about her other daughters? All the times when she got mad at me, was she really thinking about them? Did she wish I were they? Did she regret that I wasn't?

At one o'clock in the morning, I awake to tapping sounds on the window. I must   75
have dozed off and now I feel my body uncramping itself. I'm sitting on the floor, leaning against one of the twin beds. Lili is lying next to me. The others are asleep, too, sprawled out on the beds and floor. Aiyi is seated at a little table, looking very sleepy. And my father is staring out the window, tapping his fingers on the glass. The last time I listened my father was telling Aiyi about his life since he last saw her. How he had gone to Yenching University, later got a post with a newspaper in Chungking, met my mother there, a young widow. How they later fled together to Shanghai to try to find my mother's family house, but there was nothing there. And then they traveled eventually to Canton and then to Hong Kong, then Haiphong and finally to San Francisco. . . .

"Suyuan didn't tell me she was trying all these years to find her daughters," he is now saying in a quiet voice. "Naturally, I did not discuss her daughters with her. I thought she was ashamed she had left them behind."

"Where did she leave them?" asks Aiyi. "How were they found?"

I am wide awake now. Although I have heard parts of this story from my mother's friends.

"It happened when the Japanese took over Kweilin," says my father.

"Japanese in Kweilin?" says Aiyi. "That was never the case. Couldn't be. The   80
Japanese never came to Kweilin."

"Yes, that is what the newspapers reported. I know this because I was working for the news bureau at the time. The Kuomintang often told us what we could say and could not say. But we knew the Japanese had come into Kwangsi Province. We had sources who told us how they had captured the Wuchang-Canton railway. How they were coming overland, making very fast progress, marching toward the provincial capital."

Aiyi looks astonished. "If people did not know this, how could Suyuan know the Japanese were coming?"

"An officer of the Kuomintang secretly warned her," explains my father. "Suyuan's husband also was an officer and everybody knew that officers and their families would be the first to be killed. So she gathered a few possessions and, in the middle of the night, she picked up her daughters and fled on foot. The babies were not even one year old."

"How could she give up those babies!" sighs Aiyi. "Twin girls. We have never had such luck in our family." And then she yawns again.

"What were they named?" she asks. I listen carefully. I had been planning on us-   85
ing just the familiar "Sister" to address them both. But now I want to know how to pronounce their names.

"They have their father's surname, Wang," says my father. "And their given names are Chwun Yu and Chwun Hwa."

"What do the names mean?" I ask.

"Ah." My father draws imaginary characters on the window. "One means 'Spring Rain,' the other 'Spring Flower,'" he explains in English, "because they born in the spring, and of course rain come before flower, same order these girls are born. Your mother like a poet, don't you think?"

I nod my head. I see Aiyi nod her head forward, too. But it falls forward and stays there. She is breathing deeply, noisily. She is asleep.

"And what does Ma's name mean?" I whisper.

"'Suyuan,'" he says, writing more invisible characters on the glass. "The way she write it in Chinese, it mean 'Long-Cherished Wish.' Quite a fancy name, not so ordinary like flower name. See this first character, it mean something like 'Forever Never Forgotten.' But there is another way to write 'Suyuan.' Sound exactly the same, but the meaning is opposite." His finger creates the brushstrokes of another character. "The first part look the same: 'Never Forgotten.' But the last part add to first part make the whole word mean 'Long-Held Grudge.' Your mother get angry with me, I tell her her name should be Grudge."

My father is looking at me, moist-eyed. "See, I pretty clever, too, hah?"

I nod, wishing I could find some way to comfort him. "And what about my name," I ask, "what does 'Jing-mei' mean?"

"Your name also special," he says. I wonder if any name in Chinese is not something special. "'Jing' like excellent *jing*. Not just good, it's something pure, essential, the best quality. *Jing* is good leftover stuff when you take impurities out of something like gold, or rice, or salt. So what is left—just pure essence. And 'Mei,' this is common *mei*, as in *meimei*, 'younger sister.'"

I think about this. My mother's long-cherished wish. Me, the younger sister who was supposed to be the essence of the others. I feed myself with the old grief, wondering how disappointed my mother must have been. Tiny Aiyi stirs suddenly, her head rolls and then falls back, her mouth opens as if to answer my question. She grunts in her sleep, tucking her body more closely into the chair.

"So why did she abandon those babies on the road?" I need to know, because now I feel abandoned too.

"Long time I wondered this myself," says my father. "But then I read that letter from her daughters in Shanghai now, and I talk to Auntie Lindo, all the others. And then I knew. No shame in what she done. None."

"What happened?"

"Your mother running away—" begins my father.

"No, tell me in Chinese," I interrupt. "Really, I can understand."

He begins to talk, still standing at the window, looking into the night.

After fleeing Kweilin, your mother walked for several days trying to find a main road. Her thought was to catch a ride on a truck or wagon, to catch enough rides until she reached Chungking, where her husband was stationed.

She had sewn money and jewelry into the lining of her dress, enough, she thought, to barter rides all the way. If I am lucky, she thought, I will not have to trade the heavy gold bracelet and jade ring. These were things from her mother, your grandmother.

By the third day, she had traded nothing. The roads were filled with people, everybody running and begging for rides from passing trucks. The trucks rushed by, afraid to stop. So your mother found no rides, only the start of dysentery pains in her stomach.

Her shoulders ached from the two babies swinging from scarf slings. Blisters grew   105
on her palms from holding two leather suitcases. And then the blisters burst and began to bleed. After a while, she left the suitcases behind, keeping only the food and a few clothes. And later she also dropped the bags of wheat flour and rice and kept walking like this for many miles, singing songs to her little girls, until she was delirious with pain and fever.

Finally, there was not one more step left in her body. She didn't have the strength to carry those babies any farther. She slumped to the ground. She knew she would die of her sickness, or perhaps from thirst, from starvation, or from the Japanese, who she was sure were marching right behind her.

She took the babies out of the slings and sat them on the side of the road, then lay down next to them. You babies are so good, she said, so quiet. They smiled back, reaching their chubby hands for her, wanting to be picked up again. And then she knew she could not bear to watch her babies die with her.

She saw a family with three young children in a cart going by. "Take my babies, I beg you," she cried to them. But they stared back with empty eyes and never stopped.

She saw another person pass and called out again. This time a man turned around, and he had such a terrible expression—your mother said it looked like death itself—she shivered and looked away.

When the road grew quiet, she tore open the lining of her dress, and stuffed   110
jewelry under the shirt of one baby and money under the other. She reached into her pocket and drew out the photos of her family, the picture of her father and mother, the picture of herself and her husband on their wedding day. And she wrote on the back of each the names of the babies and this same message: "Please care for these babies with the money and valuables provided. When it is safe to come, if you bring them to Shanghai, 9 Weichang Lu, the Li family will be glad to give you a generous reward. Li Suyuan and Wang Fuchi."

And then she touched each baby's cheek and told her not to cry. She would go down the road to find them some food and would be back. And without looking back, she walked down the road, stumbling and crying, thinking only of this one last hope, that her daughters would be found by a kindhearted person who would care for them. She would not allow herself to imagine anything else.

She did not remember how far she walked, which direction she went, when she fainted, or how she was found. When she awoke, she was in the back of a bouncing truck with several other sick people, all moaning. And she began to scream, thinking she was now on a journey to Buddhist hell. But the face of an American missionary lady bent over her and smiled, talking to her in a soothing language she did not understand. And yet she could somehow understand. She had been saved for no good reason, and it was now too late to go back and save her babies.

When she arrived in Chungking, she learned her husband had died two weeks before. She told me later she laughed when the officers told her this news, she was so delirious with madness and disease. To come so far, to lose so much and to find nothing.

I met her in a hospital. She was lying on a cot, hardly able to move, her dysentery had drained her so thin. I had come in for my foot, my missing toe, which was cut off by a piece of falling rubble. She was talking to herself, mumbling.

"Look at these clothes," she said, and I saw she had on a rather unusual dress for 115
wartime. It was silk satin, quite dirty, but there was no doubt it was a beautiful dress.

"Look at this face," she said, and I saw her dusty face and hollow cheeks, her eyes
shining back. "Do you see my foolish hope?"

"I thought I had lost everything, except these two things," she murmured.
"And I wondered which I would lose next. Clothes or hope? Hope or clothes?"

"But now, see here, look what is happening," she said, laughing, as if all her
prayers had been answered. And she was pulling hair out of her head as easily as one
lifts new wheat from wet soil.

It was an old peasant woman who found them. "How could I resist?" the peasant
woman later told your sisters when they were older. They were still sitting obediently
near where your mother had left them, looking like little fairy queens waiting for
their sedan to arrive.

The woman, Mei Ching, and her husband, Mei Han, lived in a stone cave. 120
There were thousands of hidden caves like that in and around Kweilin so secret that
the people remained hidden even after the war ended. The Meis would come out of
their cave every few days and forage for food supplies left on the road, and sometimes
they would see something that they both agreed was a tragedy to leave behind. So
one day they took back to their cave a delicately painted set of rice bowls, another
day a little footstool with a velvet cushion and two new wedding blankets. And once,
it was your sisters.

They were pious people, Muslims, who believed the twin babies were a sign of
double luck, and they were sure of this when, later in the evening, they discovered
how valuable the babies were. She and her husband had never seen rings and
bracelets like those. And while they admired the pictures, knowing the babies
came from a good family, neither of them could read or write. It was not until
many months later that Mei Ching found someone who could read the writing on
the back. By then, she loved these baby girls like her own.

In 1952 Mei Han, the husband, died. The twins were already eight years old, and
Mei Ching now decided it was time to find your sisters' true family.

She showed the girls the picture of their mother and told them they had been born
into a great family and she would take them back to see their true mother and grandparents. Mei Ching told them about the reward, but she swore she would refuse it. She
loved these girls so much, she only wanted them to have what they were entitled to—a
better life, a fine house, educated ways. Maybe the family would let her stay on as the
girls' amah. Yes, she was certain they would insist.

Of course, when she found the place at 9 Weichang Lu, in the old French Concession, it was something completely different. It was the site of a factory building,
recently constructed, and none of the workers knew what had become of the family
whose house had burned down on that spot.

Mei Ching could not have known, of course, that your mother and I, her new 125
husband, had already returned to that same place in 1945 in hopes of finding both
her family and her daughters.

Your mother and I stayed in China until 1947. We went to many different
cities—back to Kweilin, to Changsha, as far south as Kunming. She was always looking out of one corner of her eye for twin babies, then little girls. Later we went to
Hong Kong, and when we finally left in 1949 for the United States, I think she was

even looking for them on the boat. But when we arrived, she no longer talked about them. I thought, At last, they have died in her heart.

When letters could be openly exchanged between China and the United States, she wrote immediately to old friends in Shanghai and Kweilin. I did not know she did this. Auntie Lindo told me. But of course, by then, all the street names had changed. Some people had died, others had moved away. So it took many years to find a contact. And when she did find an old schoolmate's address and wrote asking her to look for her daughters, her friend wrote back and said this was impossible, like looking for a needle on the bottom of the ocean. How did she know her daughters were in Shanghai and not somewhere else in China? The friend, of course, did not ask, How do you know your daughters are still alive?

So her schoolmate did not look. Finding babies lost during the war was a matter of foolish imagination, and she had no time for that.

But every year, your mother wrote to different people. And this last year, I think she got a big idea in her head, to go to China and find them herself. I remember she told me, "Canning, we should go, before it is too late, before we are too old." And I told her we were already too old, it was already too late.

I just thought she wanted to be a tourist! I didn't know she wanted to go and look for her daughters. So when I said it was too late, that must have put a terrible thought in her head that her daughters might be dead. And I think this possibility grew bigger and bigger in her head, until it killed her.

Maybe it was your mother's dead spirit who guided her Shanghai schoolmate to find her daughters. Because after your mother died, the schoolmate saw your sisters, by chance, while shopping for shoes at the Number One Department Store on Nanjing Dong Road. She said it was like a dream, seeing these two women who looked so much alike, moving down the stairs together. There was something about their facial expressions that reminded the schoolmate of your mother.

She quickly walked over to them and called their names, which of course, they did not recognize at first, because Mei Ching had changed their names. But your mother's friend was so sure, she persisted. "Are you not Wang Chwun Yu and Wang Chwun Hwa?" she asked them. And then these double-image women became very excited, because they remembered the names written on the back of an old photo, a photo of a young man and woman they still honored, as their much-loved first parents, who had died and become spirit ghosts still roaming the earth looking for them.

At the airport, I am exhausted. I could not sleep last night. Aiyi had followed me into my room at three in the morning, and she instantly fell asleep on one of the twin beds, snoring with the might of a lumberjack. I lay awake thinking about my mother's story, realizing how much I have never known about her, grieving that my sisters and I had both lost her.

And now at the airport, after shaking hands with everybody, waving good-bye, I think about all the different ways we leave people in this world. Cheerily waving good-bye to some at airports, knowing we'll never see each other again. Leaving others on the side of the road, hoping that we will. Finding my mother in my father's story and saying good-bye before I have a chance to know her better.

Aiyi smiles at me as we wait for our gate to be called. She is so old. I put one arm around her and one around Lili. They are the same size, it seems. And then it's time.

130

135

As we wave good-bye one more time and enter the waiting area, I get the sense I am going from one funeral to another. In my hand I'm clutching a pair of tickets to Shanghai. In two hours we'll be there.

The plane takes off. I close my eyes. How can I describe to them in my broken Chinese about our mother's life? Where should I begin?

"Wake up, we're here," says my father. And I awake with my heart pounding in my throat. I look out the window and we're already on the runway. It's gray outside.

And now I'm walking down the steps of the plane, onto the tarmac and toward the building. If only, I think, if only my mother had lived long enough to be the one walking toward them. I am so nervous I cannot even feel my feet. I am just moving somehow.

Somebody shouts, "She's arrived!" And then I see her. Her short hair. Her small body. And that same look on her face. She has the back of her hand pressed hard against her mouth. She is crying as though she had gone through a terrible ordeal and were happy it is over.

And I know it's not my mother, yet it is the same look she had when I was five 140 and had disappeared all afternoon, for such a long time, that she was convinced I was dead. And when I miraculously appeared, sleepy-eyed, crawling from underneath my bed, she wept and laughed, biting the back of her hand to make sure it was true.

And now I see her again, two of her, waving, and in one hand there is a photo, the Polaroid I sent them. As soon as I get beyond the gate, we run toward each other, all three of us embracing, all hesitations and expectations forgotten.

"Mama, Mama," we all murmur, as if she is among us.

My sisters look at me, proudly. *"Meimei jandale,"* says one sister proudly to the other. "Little Sister has grown up." I look at their faces again and I see no trace of my mother in them. Yet they still look familiar. And now I also see what part of me is Chinese. It is so obvious. It is my family. It is in our blood. After all these years, it can finally be let go.

My sisters and I stand, arms around each other, laughing and wiping the tears from each other's eyes. The flash of the Polaroid goes off and my father hands me the snapshot. My sisters and I watch quietly together, eager to see what develops.

The gray-green surface changes to the bright colors of our three images, sharpen- 145 ing and deepening all at once. And although we don't speak, I know we all see it: Together we look like our mother. Her same eyes, her same mouth, open in surprise to see, at last, her long-cherished wish.

Questions

1. How is the external setting of "A Pair of Tickets" essential to what happens internally to the narrator in the course of this story?
2. How does the narrator's view of her father change by seeing him in a different setting?
3. In what ways does the narrator feel at home in China? In what ways does she feel foreign?
4. What do the narrator and her half-sisters have in common? How does this element relate to the theme of the story?
5. In what ways does the story explore specifically Chinese American experiences? In what other ways is the story grounded in universal family issues?

▪ WRITING *effectively*

Amy Tan on Writing

Setting the Voice   1989

Lately, I've been giving more thought to the kind of English my mother speaks. Like others, I have described it to people as "broken" or "fractured" English. But I wince when I say that. It has always bothered me that I can think of no way to describe it other than "broken," as if it were damaged and needed to be fixed, as if it lacked a certain wholeness and soundness. I've heard other terms used, "limited English," for example. But they seem just as bad, as if everything is limited, including people's perceptions of the limited English speaker.

I know this for a fact, because when I was growing up, my mother's "limited" English limited *my* perception of her. I was

Amy Tan

ashamed of her English. I believed that her English reflected the quality of what she had to say. That is, because she expressed them imperfectly, her thoughts were imperfect. And I had plenty of empirical evidence to support me: the fact that people in department stores, at banks, and at restaurants did not take her seriously, did not give her good service, pretended not to understand her, or even acted as if they did not hear her.

• • •

But it wasn't until 1985 that I finally began to write fiction. And at first I wrote using what I thought to be wittily crafted sentences, sentences that would finally prove I had mastery over the English language. Here's an example from the first draft of a story that later made its way into *The Joy Luck Club*, but without this line: "That was my mental quandary in its nascent state." A terrible line, which I can barely pronounce.

Fortunately, for reasons I won't get into today, I later decided I should envision a reader for the stories I would write. And the reader I decided upon was my mother, because these were stories about mothers. So with this reader in mind—and in fact she did read my early drafts—I began to write stories using all the Englishes I grew up with: the English I spoke to my mother, which for lack of a better term might be described as "simple"; the English she used with me, which for lack of a better term might be described as "broken"; my translation of her Chinese, which could certainly be described as "watered down"; and what I imagined to be her translation of her Chinese if she could speak in perfect English, her internal language, and for that I sought to preserve the essence, but neither an English nor a Chinese structure. I wanted to capture what language ability tests can never reveal: her intent, her passion, her imagery, the rhythms of her speech and the nature of her thoughts.

Apart from what any critic had to say about my writing, I knew I had succeeded where it counted when my mother finished reading my book and gave me her verdict: "So easy to read."

From "Mother Tongue"

THINKING ABOUT SETTING

The time and place in which a story is set serve as more than mere backdrop. When preparing to write about a story, be sure to consider where and when it is set, and what role the setting plays.

- **Ask whether setting helps motivate the plot.** The external pressure of the setting is often the key factor that compels or invites the protagonist into action. Setting can play as large a role as plot and characters do by prompting a protagonist into an action he or she might not otherwise take.
- **Consider whether the external setting suggests the character's inner reality.** A particular setting can create a mood or provide clues to a protagonist's nature. To write about a story's setting, therefore, invites you to study not only the time and place but also their relation to the protagonist. Does the external reality provide a clue to the protagonist's inner reality?
- **Notice whether the setting changes as the plot progresses.** The settings in a story are not static. Characters can move from place to place, and their actions may bring them into significantly different external and internal places.

CHECKLIST: Writing About Setting

- ☐ Where does the story take place?
- ☐ What does the setting suggest about the characters' lives?
- ☐ Are there significant differences in the settings for different characters? What does this suggest about each person?
- ☐ When does the story take place? Is the time of year or time of day significant?
- ☐ Does the weather play a meaningful role in the story's action?
- ☐ What is the protagonist's relationship to the setting?
- ☐ Does the setting of the story in some way compel the protagonist into action?
- ☐ Does the story's time or place suggest something about the character of the protagonist?
- ☐ Does a change in setting during the story suggest some internal change in the protagonist?

WRITING ASSIGNMENT ON SETTING

Choose a story from this chapter, and explore how character and setting are interrelated. A possible topic would be to describe the significance of setting to the protagonist in "A Pair of Tickets" or "A Sound of Thunder." How does the setting of the climax of the story contribute to a change in the character's personal perspective?

MORE TOPICS FOR WRITING

1. Write about how setting functions as a kind of character in "To Build a Fire." Do the landscape and weather act as the antagonist in the story's plot?

2. Write about how the two imaginary settings (near future and distant past) in "A Sound of Thunder" contribute to the larger meaning of the story. (You might possibly discuss how two settings create possibilities to dramatize ideas more powerfully than a single setting might.)

3. Take any story in this chapter and analyze how the author presents the key setting. Don't pay special attention to the protagonist or other human characters, but focus on the setting that surrounds him or her and how it emerges as a force in the story.

4. Think of a place—on campus or beyond—to which you often return. If possible, go there. Make a list of every physical detail you can think of to describe that place. Then look the list over and write a paragraph on what sort of mood is suggested by it. If you were to describe your emotional connection to the place, which three details would you choose? Why?

5. Choose any story in this book, and pay careful attention to setting as you read it. Write several paragraphs reflecting on the following questions: What details in the story suggest the time and place in which it is set? Is setting central to the story? If the action were transplanted to some other place and time, how would the story change?

▶ TERMS FOR *review*

Setting ▶ The time and place of a story. The setting may also include the climate and even the social, psychological, or spiritual state of the characters.

Locale ▶ The location where a story takes place.

Atmosphere ▶ The dominant mood or feeling that pervades all or part of a literary work. Atmosphere is the total effect conveyed by the author's use of language, images, and physical setting.

Regionalism ▶ The literary representation of a specific locale that consciously uses the particulars of geography, custom, history, folklore, or speech. In regional narratives, the locale plays a crucial role in the presentation and progression of the story.

Naturalism ▶ A type of fiction in which the characters are presented as products or victims of environment and heredity. Naturalism is considered an extreme form of **realism** (the attempt to reproduce faithfully the surface appearance of life, especially that of ordinary people in everyday situations).

5

TONE AND STYLE

In many Victorian novels it was customary for some commentator, presumably the author, to interrupt the story from time to time, remarking on the action, offering philosophical asides, or explaining the procedures to be followed in telling the story.

> Two hours later, Dorothea was seated in an inner room or boudoir of a handsome apartment in the Via Sistina. I am sorry to add that she was sobbing bitterly. . . .
> —George Eliot in *Middlemarch* (1873)

> But let the gentle-hearted reader be under no apprehension whatsoever. It is not destined that Eleanor shall marry Mr. Slope or Bertie Stanhope.
> —Anthony Trollope in *Barchester Towers* (1857)

Of course, the voice of this commentator was not identical with that of the "real-life" author—the one toiling over an inkpot, worrying about publication deadlines and whether the rent would be paid. At times the living author might have been far different in personality from that usually wise and cheerful intruder who kept addressing the reader of the book. Much of the time, to be sure, the author probably agreed with whatever attitudes this alter ego expressed. But, in effect, the author created the character of a commentator to speak for him or her and artfully sustained that character's voice throughout the novel.

Such intrusions, although sometimes useful to the "real" author and enjoyable to the reader, are today rare. Modern storytellers, carefully keeping out of sight, seldom comment on their plots and characters. Apparently they agree with Anton Chekhov that a writer should not judge the characters but should serve as their "impartial witness." And yet, no less definitely than Victorian novelists who introduced commentators, modern writers of effective stories no doubt have feelings toward their characters and events. The authors make us see these people in such a way that we, too, will care about them.

Although many modern writers have adopted Chekhov's "impartial" methods, they are rarely impartial witnesses. They merely embed their own feelings more deeply into the story so that those reactions emerge indirectly for the reader. For example, when at the beginning of the short story "In Exile" Chekhov introduces us to a character, he does so with a description that arouses sympathy:

> The Tartar was worn out and ill, and wrapping himself in his rags, he talked about how good it was in the province of Simbirsk, and what a beautiful and clever wife he had left at home. He was not more than twenty-five, and in the firelight his pale, sickly face and woebegone expression made him seem like a boy.

Other than the comparison of the Tartar to a child, the details in this passage seem mostly factual: the young man's illness, ragged clothes, facial expression, and topics of conversation. But these details form a portrait that stirs pity. By his selection of these imaginary details out of countless others that he might have included, Chekhov firmly directs our feelings about the Tartar, so miserable and pathetic in his sickness and his homesickness. We cannot know, of course, exactly what the living Chekhov felt; but at least we can be sure that we are supposed to share the compassion and tenderness of the narrator—Chekhov's impartial (but human) witness.

TONE

Not only the author's choice of details may lead us to infer his or her attitude, but also choice of characters, events, and situations, and choice of words. When the narrator of Joseph Conrad's *Heart of Darkness* comes upon an African outpost littered with abandoned machines and notices "a boiler wallowing in the grass," the exact word *wallowing* conveys an attitude: that there is something swinish about this scene of careless waste.

Whatever leads us to infer the author's attitude is commonly called **tone.** Like a tone of voice, the tone of a story may communicate amusement, anger, affection, sorrow, contempt. It implies the feelings of the author, so far as we can sense them. Those feelings may be similar to feelings expressed by the narrator of the story (or by any character), but sometimes they may be dissimilar, even sharply opposed. The characters in a story may regard an event as sad, but we sense that the author regards it as funny. To understand the tone of a story, then, is to understand some attitude more fundamental to the story than whatever attitudes the characters explicitly declare.

The tone of a story, like a tone of voice, may convey not simply one attitude, but a medley. Reading "A & P" (Chapter 1), we have mingled feelings about Sammy: delight in his wicked comments about other people and his skewering of hypocrisy; irritation at his smugness and condescension; admiration for his readiness to take a stand; sympathy for the pain of his disillusionment. Often the tone of a literary story will be too rich and complicated to sum up in one or two words. But to try to describe the tone of such a story may be a useful way to penetrate to its center and to grasp the whole of it.

STYLE

One of the clearest indications of the tone of a story is the **style** in which it is written. In general, style refers to the individual traits or characteristics of a piece of writing: to a writer's particular ways of managing words that we come to recognize as habitual or customary. A distinctive style marks the work of a fine writer: we can tell his or her work from that of anyone else. From one story to another, however, the writer may fittingly change style; and in some stories, style may be altered meaningfully as the story goes along. In his novel *As I Lay Dying*, William Faulkner changes narrators with every chapter, and he distinguishes the narrators one from another by giving each an individual style or manner of speaking. Though each narrator has his or her own style, the book as a whole demonstrates Faulkner's style as well. For instance, one chapter is written from the point of view of a small boy, Vardaman Bundren, member of a family of poor Mississippi tenant farmers, whose view of a horse in a barn reads like this:

> It is as though the dark were resolving him out of his integrity, into an unrelated scattering of components—snuffings and stampings; smells of cooling flesh and ammoniac hair; an illusion of a co-ordinated whole of splotched hide and strong bones within which, detached and secret and familiar, an *is* different from my *is*.

How can a small boy unaccustomed to libraries use words like *integrity, components, illusion,* and *co-ordinated*? Elsewhere in the story, Vardaman says aloud, with no trace of literacy, "Hit was a-laying right there on the ground." Apparently, in the passage it is not the voice of the boy that we are hearing, but something resembling the voice of William Faulkner, elevated and passionate, expressing the boy's thoughts in a style that admits Faulknerian words.

DICTION

Usually, *style* indicates a mode of expression: the language a writer uses. In this sense, the notion of style includes such traits as the length and complexity of sentences, and **diction,** or choice of words: abstract or concrete, bookish ("unrelated scattering of components") or close to speech ("Hit was a-laying right there on the ground"). Involved in the idea of style, too, is any habitual use of imagery, patterns of sound, figures of speech, or other devices.

Several writers of realistic fiction, called **minimalists**—Ann Beattie, Raymond Carver, Bobbie Ann Mason—have written with a flat, laid-back, unemotional tone, in an appropriately bare, unadorned style. Minimalists seem to give nothing but facts drawn from ordinary life, sometimes in picayune detail. Here is a sample passage from Raymond Carver's story "A Small, Good Thing":

> She pulled into the driveway and cut the engine. She closed her eyes and leaned her head against the wheel for a minute. She listened to the ticking sounds the engine made as it began to cool. Then she got out of the car. She could hear the dog barking inside the house. She went to the front door, which was unlocked. She went inside and turned on lights and put on a kettle of water for tea. She opened some dog food and fed Slug on the back porch. The dog ate in hungry little smacks. It kept running into the kitchen to see that she was going to stay.

Explicit feeling and showy language are kept at a minimum here. Notice how Carver's diction relies on everyday words—most words of only one and two syllables. Taken out of context, this description may strike you as banal, as if the writer himself were bored; but it works effectively as a part of Carver's entire story. As in all good writing, the style here seems a faithful mirror of what is said in it. At its best, such writing achieves "a hard-won reduction, a painful stripping away of richness, a baring of bone."[1]

Two Examples of Style: Hemingway Versus Faulkner

To see what style means, compare the stories in this chapter by William Faulkner ("Barn Burning") and by Ernest Hemingway ("A Clean, Well-Lighted Place"). Faulkner frequently falls into a style in which a statement, as soon as it is uttered, is followed by another statement expressing the idea in a more emphatic way. Sentences are interrupted with parenthetical elements (asides, like this) thrust into them unexpectedly. At times, Faulkner writes of seemingly ordinary matters as if giving a speech in a towering passion. Here, from "Barn Burning," is a description of how a boy's father delivers a rug:

> "Don't you want me to help?" he whispered. His father did not answer and now he heard again that stiff foot striking the hollow portico with that wooden and clocklike deliberation, that outrageous overstatement of the weight it carried. The rug, hunched, not flung (the boy could tell that even in the darkness) from his father's shoulder struck the angle of wall and floor with a sound unbelievably loud, thunderous, then the foot again, unhurried and enormous; a light came on in the house and the boy sat, tense, breathing steadily and quietly and just a little fast, though the foot itself did not increase its beat at all, descending the steps now; now the boy could see him.

Faulkner is not merely indulging in language for its own sake. As you will find when you read the whole story, this rug delivery is vital to the story, and so too is the father's profound defiance—indicated by his walk. By devices of style—by *metaphor* and *simile* ("wooden and clocklike"), by exact qualification ("not flung"), by emphatic adjectives ("loud, thunderous")—Faulkner is carefully placing his emphases.

By the words he selects to describe the father's stride, Faulkner directs how we feel toward the man and perhaps also indicates his own wondering but skeptical attitude toward a character whose very footfall is "outrageous" and "enormous." (Fond of long sentences like the last one in the quoted passage, Faulkner remarked that there are sentences that need to be written in the way a circus acrobat pedals a bicycle on a high wire: rapidly, so as not to fall off.)

Hemingway's famous style includes both short sentences and long, but when the sentences are long, they tend to be relatively simple in construction. Hemingway likes long compound sentences (clause plus clause plus clause), sometimes joined with "and"s. He interrupts such a sentence with a dependent clause or a parenthetical element much less frequently than Faulkner does. The effect is like listening to speech:

> In the day time the street was dusty, but at night the dew settled the dust and the old man liked to sit late because he was deaf and now at night it was quiet and he felt the difference.

Hemingway is a master of swift, terse dialogue, and often casts whole scenes in the form of conversation. As if he were a closemouthed speaker unwilling to let his feelings loose, the narrator of a Hemingway story often addresses us in understatement, implying greater depths of feeling than he puts into words. Read the following story and you will see that its style and tone cannot be separated.

[1]Letter in the *New York Times Book Review*, 5 June 1988.

Ernest Hemingway

A Clean, Well-Lighted Place

1933

Ernest Hemingway (1899–1961), born in Oak Park, Illinois, bypassed college to be a cub reporter. In World War I, as an eighteen-year-old volunteer ambulance driver in Italy, he was wounded in action. In 1922 he settled in Paris, then aswarm with writers; he later recalled that time in A Moveable Feast *(1964). Hemingway won swift acclaim for his early stories,* In Our Time *(1925), and for his first, perhaps finest, novel,* The Sun Also Rises *(1926), portraying a "lost generation" of postwar American drifters in France and Spain. For Whom the Bell Tolls *(1940) depicts life during the Spanish Civil War. Hemingway became a celebrity, often photographed as a marlin fisherman or a lion hunter. A fan of bullfighting, he wrote two nonfiction books on the subject:* Death in the Afternoon *(1932) and* The Dangerous Summer *(posthumously published in 1985). After World War II, with his fourth wife, journalist Mary Welsh, he made his home in Cuba, where he wrote* The Old Man and the Sea *(1952). The Nobel Prize in Literature came his way in 1954. In 1961, mentally distressed and physically ailing, he shot himself. Hemingway brought a hard-bitten realism to American fiction. His heroes live dangerously, by personal codes of honor, courage, and endurance. Hemingway's distinctively crisp, unadorned style left American literature permanently changed.*

It was late and every one had left the café except an old man who sat in the shadow the leaves of the tree made against the electric light. In the day time the street was dusty, but at night the dew settled the dust and the old man liked to sit late because he was deaf and now at night it was quiet and he felt the difference. The two waiters inside the café knew that the old man was a little drunk, and while he was a good client they knew that if he became too drunk he would leave without paying, so they kept watch on him.

"Last week he tried to commit suicide," one waiter said.

"Why?"

"He was in despair."

"What about?"

"Nothing."   5

"How do you know it was nothing?"

"He has plenty of money."

They sat together at a table that was close against the wall near the door of the café and looked at the terrace where the tables were all empty except where the old man sat in the shadow of the leaves of the tree that moved slightly in the wind. A girl and a soldier went by in the street. The street light shone on the brass number on his collar. The girl wore no head covering and hurried beside him.

"The guard will pick him up," one waiter said.   10

"What does it matter if he gets what he's after?"

"He had better get off the street now. The guard will get him. They went by five minutes ago."

The old man sitting in the shadow rapped on his saucer with his glass. The younger waiter went over to him.

"What do you want?"

The old man looked at him. "Another brandy," he said.   15

"You'll be drunk," the waiter said. The old man looked at him. The waiter went away.

"He'll stay all night," he said to his colleague. "I'm sleepy now. I never get into bed before three o'clock. He should have killed himself last week."

The waiter took the brandy bottle and another saucer from the counter inside the café and marched out to the old man's table. He put down the saucer and poured the glass full of brandy.

"You should have killed yourself last week," he said to the deaf man. The old man motioned with his finger. "A little more," he said. The waiter poured on into the glass so that the brandy slopped over and ran down the stem into the top saucer of the pile. "Thank you," the old man said. The waiter took the bottle back inside the café. He sat down at the table with his colleague again.

"He's drunk now," he said.   20

"He's drunk every night."°

"What did he want to kill himself for?"

"How should I know?"

"How did he do it?"

"He hung himself with a rope."   25

"Who cut him down?"

"His niece."

"Why did they do it?"

"Fear for his soul."

"How much money has he got?"   30

"He's got plenty."

"He must be eighty years old."

"Anyway I should say he was eighty."°

"I wish he would go home. I never get to bed before three o'clock. What kind of hour is that to go to bed?"

"He stays up because he likes it."   35

"He's lonely. I'm not lonely. I have a wife waiting in bed for me."

"He had a wife once too."

"A wife would be no good to him now."

"You can't tell. He might be better with a wife."

"His niece looks after him."   40

"I know. You said she cut him down."

"I wouldn't want to be that old. An old man is a nasty thing."

"Not always. This old man is clean. He drinks without spilling. Even now, drunk. Look at him."

"I don't want to look at him. I wish he would go home. He has no regard for those who must work."

The old man looked from his glass across the square, then over at the waiters.   45

"Another brandy," he said, pointing to his glass. The waiter who was in a hurry came over.

"Finished," he said, speaking with that omission of syntax stupid people employ when talking to drunken people or foreigners. "No more tonight. Close now."

"Another," said the old man.

"He's drunk now," he said. "He's drunk every night": The younger waiter perhaps says both these lines. A device of Hemingway's style is sometimes to have a character pause, then speak again—as often happens in actual speech. *"He must be eighty years old." "Anyway I should say he was eighty"*: Is this another instance of the same character's speaking twice? Clearly, it is the younger waiter who says the next line, "I wish he would go home."

"No. Finished." The waiter wiped the edge of the table with a towel and shook his head.

The old man stood up, slowly counted the saucers, took a leather coin purse from his pocket and paid for the drinks, leaving half a peseta tip.

The waiter watched him go down the street, a very old man walking unsteadily but with dignity.

"Why didn't you let him stay and drink?" the unhurried waiter asked. They were putting up the shutters. "It is not half-past two."

"I want to go home to bed."

"What is an hour?"

"More to me than to him."

"An hour is the same."

"You talk like an old man yourself. He can buy a bottle and drink at home."

"It's not the same."

"No, it is not," agreed the waiter with a wife. He did not wish to be unjust. He was only in a hurry.

"And you? You have no fear of going home before the usual hour?"

"Are you trying to insult me?"

"No, hombre, only to make a joke."

"No," the waiter who was in a hurry said, rising from pulling down the metal shutters. "I have confidence. I am all confidence."

"You have youth, confidence, and a job," the older waiter said. "You have everything."

"And what do you lack?"

"Everything but work."

"You have everything I have."

"No. I have never had confidence and I am not young."

"Come on. Stop talking nonsense and lock up."

"I am of those who like to stay late at the café," the older waiter said. "With all those who do not want to go to bed. With all those who need a light for the night."

"I want to go home and into bed."

"We are of two different kinds," the older waiter said. He was not dressed to go home. "It is not only a question of youth and confidence although those things are very beautiful. Each night I am reluctant to close up because there may be some one who needs the café."

"Hombre, there are bodegas° open all night long."

"You do not understand. This is a clean and pleasant café. It is well lighted. The light is very good and also, now, there are shadows of the leaves."

"Good night," said the younger waiter.

"Good night," the other said. Turning off the electric light he continued the conversation with himself. It is the light of course but it is necessary that the place be clean and pleasant. You do not want music. Certainly you do not want music. Nor can you stand before a bar with dignity although that is all that is provided for these hours. What did he fear? It was not fear or dread. It was a nothing that he knew too well. It was all a nothing and a man was nothing too. It was only that and light was all it needed and a certain cleanness and order. Some lived in it and never felt it but he

bodegas: wineshops.

knew it all was nada y pues nada y nada y pues nada.° Our nada who art in nada, nada be thy name thy kingdom nada thy will be nada in nada as it is in nada. Give us this nada our daily nada and nada us our nada as we nada our nadas and nada us not into nada but deliver us from nada; pues nada. Hail nothing full of nothing, nothing is with thee. He smiled and stood before a bar with a shining steam pressure coffee machine.

"What's yours?" asked the barman.

"Nada."

"Otro loco más,"° said the barman and turned away.

"A little cup," said the waiter.   80

The barman poured it for him.

"The light is very bright and pleasant but the bar is unpolished," the waiter said.

The barman looked at him but did not answer. It was too late at night for conversation.

"You want another copita?"° the barman asked.

"No, thank you," said the waiter and went out. He disliked bars and bodegas. A   85
clean, well-lighted café was a very different thing. Now, without thinking further, he would go home to his room. He would lie in the bed and finally, with daylight, he would go to sleep. After all, he said to himself, it is probably only insomnia. Many must have it.

Questions

1. What besides insomnia makes the older waiter reluctant to go to bed? Comment especially on his meditation with its *nada* refrain. Why does he understand so well the old man's need for a café? What does the café represent for the two of them?

2. Compare the younger waiter and the older waiter in their attitudes toward the old man. Whose attitude do you take to be closer to that of the author? Even though Hemingway does not editorially state his own feelings, how does he make them clear to us?

3. Point to sentences that establish the style of the story. What is distinctive in them? What repetitions of words or phrases seem particularly effective? Does Hemingway seem to favor a simple or an erudite vocabulary?

4. What is the story's point of view? Discuss its appropriateness.

William Faulkner

Barn Burning   1939

William Faulkner (1897–1962) receives a capsule biography in Chapter 2, page 31, along with his story "A Rose for Emily." "Barn Burning" is among his many contributions to the history of Yoknapatawpha, an imaginary Mississippi county in which the Sartorises and the de Spains are landed aristocrats living by a code of honor and the Snopeses—most of them— are shiftless ne'er-do-wells.

The store in which the Justice of the Peace's court was sitting smelled of cheese. The boy, crouched on his nail keg at the back of the crowded room, knew he smelled cheese, and more: from where he sat he could see the ranked shelves close-packed

---

nada y pues ... nada: nothing and then nothing and nothing and then nothing.   *Otro loco más:* another lunatic.   *copita:* little cup.

with the solid, squat, dynamic shapes of tin cans whose labels his stomach read, not from the lettering which meant nothing to his mind but from the scarlet devils and the silver curve of fish—this, the cheese which he knew he smelled and the hermetic meat which his intestines believed he smelled coming in intermittent gusts momentary and brief between the other constant one, the smell and sense just a little of fear because mostly of despair and grief, the old fierce pull of blood. He could not see the table where the Justice sat and before which his father and his father's enemy (*our enemy* he thought in that despair: *ourn! mine and hisn both! He's my father!*) stood, but he could hear them, the two of them that is, because his father had said no word yet:

"But what proof have you, Mr. Harris?"

"I told you. The hog got into my corn. I caught it up and sent it back to him. He had no fence that would hold it. I told him so, warned him. The next time I put the hog in my pen. When he came to get it I gave him enough wire to patch up his pen. The next time I put the hog up and kept it. I rode down to his house and saw the wire I gave him still rolled on to the spool in his yard. I told him he could have the hog when he paid me a dollar pound fee. That evening a nigger came with the dollar and got the hog. He was a strange nigger. He said, 'He say to tell you wood and hay kin burn.' I said, 'What?' 'That whut he say to tell you,' the nigger said. 'Wood and hay kin burn.' That night my barn burned. I got the stock out but I lost the barn."

"Where's the nigger? Have you got him?"

"He was a strange nigger, I tell you. I don't know what became of him."   5

"But that's not proof. Don't you see that's not proof?"

"Get that boy up here. He knows." For a moment the boy thought too that the man meant his older brother until Harris said, "Not him. The little one. The boy," and, crouching, small for his age, small and wiry like his father, in patched and faded jeans even too small for him, with straight, uncombed, brown hair and eyes gray and wild as storm scud, he saw the men between himself and the table part and become a lane of grim faces, at the end of which he saw the Justice, a shabby, collarless, graying man in spectacles, beckoning him. He felt no floor under his bare feet; he seemed to walk beneath the palpable weight of the grim turning faces. His father, still in his black Sunday coat donned not for the trial but for the moving, did not even look at him. *He aims for me to lie,* he thought, again with that frantic grief and despair. *And I will have to do hit.*

"What's your name, boy?" the Justice said.

"Colonel Sartoris Snopes," the boy whispered.

"Hey?" the Justice said. "Talk louder. Colonel Sartoris? I reckon anybody named   10
for Colonel Sartoris in this country can't help but tell the truth, can they?" The boy said nothing. *Enemy! Enemy!* he thought; for a moment he could not even see, could not see that the Justice's face was kindly nor discern that his voice was troubled when he spoke to the man named Harris: "Do you want me to question this boy?" But he could hear, and during those subsequent long seconds while there was absolutely no sound in the crowded little room save that of quiet and intent breathing it was as if he had swung outward at the end of a grape vine, over a ravine, and at the top of the swing had been caught in a prolonged instant of mesmerized gravity, weightless in time.

"No!" Harris said violently, explosively. "Damnation! Send him out of here!" Now time, the fluid world, rushed beneath him again, the voices coming to him again through the smell of cheese and sealed meat, the fear and despair and the old grief of blood:

"This case is closed. I can't find against you, Snopes, but I can give you advice. Leave this country and don't come back to it."

His father spoke for the first time, his voice cold and harsh, level, without emphasis: "I aim to. I don't figure to stay in a country among people who . . ." he said something unprintable and vile, addressed to no one.

"That'll do," the Justice said. "Take your wagon and get out of this country before dark. Case dismissed."

His father turned, and he followed the stiff black coat, the wiry figure walking a little stiffly from where a Confederate provost's man's musket ball had taken him in the heel on a stolen horse thirty years ago, followed the two backs now, since his older brother had appeared from somewhere in the crowd, no taller than the father but thicker, chewing tobacco steadily, between the two lines of grim-faced men and out of the store and across the worn gallery and down the sagging steps and among the dogs and half-grown boys in the mild May dust, where as he passed a voice hissed: "Barn burner!"

Again he could not see, whirling; there was a face in a red haze, moonlike, bigger than the full moon, the owner of it half again his size, he leaping in the red haze toward the face, feeling no blow, feeling no shock when his head struck the earth, scrabbling up and leaping again, feeling no blow this time either and tasting no blood, scrabbling up to see the other boy in full flight and himself already leaping into pursuit as his father's hand jerked him back, the harsh, cold voice speaking above him: "Go get in the wagon."

It stood in a grove of locusts and mulberries across the road. His two hulking sisters in their Sunday dresses and his mother and her sister in calico and sunbonnets were already in it, sitting on and among the sorry residue of the dozen and more movings which even the boy could remember—the battered stove, the broken beds and chairs, the clock inlaid with mother-of-pearl, which would not run, stopped at some fourteen minutes past two o'clock of a dead and forgotten day and time, which had been his mother's dowry. She was crying, though when she saw him she drew her sleeve across her face and began to descend from the wagon. "Get back," the father said.

"He's hurt. I got to get some water and wash his . . ."

"Get back in the wagon," his father said. He got in too, over the tail-gate. His father mounted to the seat where the older brother already sat and struck the gaunt mules two savage blows with the peeled willow, but without heat. It was not even sadistic; it was exactly that same quality which in later years would cause his descendants to over-run the engine before putting a motor car into motion, striking and reining back in the same movement. The wagon went on, the store with its quiet crowd of grimly watching men dropped behind; a curve in the road hid it. *Forever* he thought. *Maybe he's done satisfied now, now that he has . . .* stopping himself, not to say it aloud even to himself. His mother's hand touched his shoulder.

"Does hit hurt?" she said.

"Naw," he said. "Hit don't hurt. Lemme be."

"Can't you wipe some of the blood off before hit dries?"

"I'll wash to-night," he said. "Lemme be, I tell you."

The wagon went on. He did not know where they were going. None of them ever did or ever asked, because it was always somewhere, always a house of sorts waiting for them a day or two days or even three days away. Likely his father had already arranged to make a crop on another farm before he . . . Again he had to stop himself. He (the father) always did. There was something about his wolflike independence and even courage when the advantage was at least neutral which impressed strangers, as if they got from his latent ravening ferocity not so much a sense of dependability as a feeling that his ferocious conviction in the rightness of his own actions would be of advantage to all whose interest lay with his.

That night they camped, in a grove of oaks and beeches where a spring ran. The nights were still cool and they had a fire against it, of a rail lifted from a nearby fence and cut into lengths—a small fire, neat, niggard almost, a shrewd fire; such fires were his father's habit and custom always, even in freezing weather. Older, the boy might have remarked this and wondered why not a big one; why should not a man who had not only seen the waste and extravagance of war, but who had in his blood an inherent voracious prodigality with material not his own, have burned everything in sight? Then he might have gone a step farther and thought that that was the reason: that niggard blaze was the living fruit of nights passed during those four years in the woods hiding from all men, blue and gray, with his strings of horses (captured horses, he called them). And older still, he might have divined the true reason: that the element of fire spoke to some deep mainspring of his father's being, as the element of steel or of powder spoke to other men, as the one weapon for the preservation of integrity, else breath were not worth the breathing, and hence to be regarded with respect and used with discretion.

But he did not think this now and he had seen those same niggard blazes all his life. He merely ate his supper beside it and was already half asleep over his iron plate when his father called him, and once more he followed the stiff back, the stiff and ruthless limp, up the slope and on to the starlit road where, turning, he could see his father against the stars but without face or depth—a shape black, flat, and bloodless as though cut from tin in the iron folds of the frockcoat which had not been made for him, the voice harsh like tin and without heat like tin:

"You were fixing to tell them. You would have told him." He didn't answer. His father struck him with the flat of his hand on the side of the head, hard but without heat, exactly as he had struck the two mules at the store, exactly as he would strike either of them with any stick in order to kill a horse fly, his voice without heat or anger: "You're getting to be a man. You got to learn. You got to learn to stick to your own blood or you ain't going to have any blood to stick to you. Do you think either of them, any man there this morning, would? Don't you know all they wanted was a chance to get at me because they knew I had them beat? Eh?" Later, twenty years later, he was to tell himself, "If I had said they wanted only truth, justice, he would have hit me again." But now he said nothing. He was not crying. He just stood there. "Answer me," his father said.

"Yes," he whispered. His father turned.

"Get on to bed. We'll be there tomorrow."

Tomorrow they were there. In the early afternoon the wagon stopped before a paintless two-room house identical almost with the dozen others it had stopped before even in the boy's ten years, and again, as on the other dozen occasions, his mother and aunt got down and began to unload the wagon, although his two sisters and his father and brother had not moved.

"Likely hit ain't fitten for hawgs," one of the sisters said.

"Nevertheless, fit it will and you'll hog it and like it," his father said. "Get out of them chairs and help your Ma unload."

The two sisters got down, big, bovine, in a flutter of cheap ribbons; one of them drew from the jumbled wagon bed a battered lantern, the other a worn broom. His

30

father handed the reins to the older son and began to climb stiffly over the wheel. "When they get unloaded, take the team to the barn and feed them." Then he said, and at first the boy thought he was still speaking to his brother: "Come with me."

"Me?" he said.   35

"Yes," his father said. "You."

"Abner," his mother said. His father paused and looked back—the harsh level stare beneath the shaggy, graying, irascible brows.

"I reckon I'll have a word with the man that aims to begin to-morrow owning me body and soul for the next eight months."

They went back up the road. A week ago—or before last night, that is—he would have asked where they were going, but not now. His father had struck him before last night but never before had he paused afterward to explain why; it was as if the blow and the following calm, outrageous voice still rang, repercussed, divulging nothing to him save the terrible handicap of being young, the light weight of his few years, just heavy enough to prevent his soaring free of the world as it seemed to be ordered but not heavy enough to keep him footed solid in it, to resist it and try to change the course of its events.

Presently he could see the grove of oaks and cedars and the other flowering trees   40 and shrubs where the house would be, though not the house yet. They walked beside a fence massed with honeysuckle and Cherokee roses and came to a gate swinging open between two brick pillars, and now, beyond a sweep of drive, he saw the house for the first time and at that instant he forgot his father and the terror and despair both, and even when he remembered his father again (who had not stopped) the terror and despair did not return. Because, for all the twelve movings, they had sojourned until now in a poor country, a land of small farms and fields and houses, and he had never seen a house like this before. *Hit's big as a courthouse* he thought quietly, with a surge of peace and joy whose reason he could not have thought into words, being too young for that: *They are safe from him. People whose lives are a part of this peace and dignity are beyond his touch, he no more to them than a buzzing wasp: capable of stinging for a little moment but that's all; the spell of this peace and dignity rendering even the barns and stable and cribs which belong to it impervious to the puny flames he might contrive . . .* this, the peace and joy, ebbing for an instant as he looked again at the stiff black back, the stiff and implacable limp of the figure which was not dwarfed by the house, for the reason that it had never looked big anywhere and which now, against the serene columned backdrop, had more than ever that impervious quality of something cut ruthlessly from tin, depthless, as though, sidewise to the sun, it would cast no shadow. Watching him, the boy remarked the absolutely undeviating course which his father held and saw the stiff foot come squarely down in a pile of fresh droppings where a horse had stood in the drive and which his father could have avoided by a simple change of stride. But it ebbed only a moment, though he could not have thought this into words either, walking on in the spell of the house, which he could even want but without envy, without sorrow, certainly never with that ravening and jealous rage which unknown to him walked in the ironlike black coat before him: *Maybe he will feel it too. Maybe it will even change him now from what maybe he couldn't help but be.*

They crossed the portico. Now he could hear his father's stiff foot as it came down on the boards with clocklike finality, a sound out of all proportion to the displacement of the body it bore and which was not dwarfed either by the white door before it, as though it had attained to a sort of vicious and ravening minimum not to be dwarfed by anything—the flat, wide, black hat, the formal coat of broadcloth which had once been black but which had now that friction-glazed greenish cast of the bodies of old house flies, the lifted sleeve which was too large, the lifted hand like a curled claw. The door opened so promptly that the boy knew the Negro must have been watching them all the time, an old man with neat grizzled hair, in a linen jacket, who stood barring the door with his body, saying, "Wipe yo foots, white man, fo you come in here. Major ain't home nohow."

"Get out of my way, nigger," his father said, without heat too, flinging the door back and the Negro also and entering, his hat still on his head. And now the boy saw the prints of the stiff foot on the doorjamb and saw them appear on the pale rug behind the machinelike deliberation of the foot which seemed to bear (or transmit) twice the weight which the body compassed. The Negro was shouting "Miss Lula! Miss Lula!" somewhere behind them, then the boy, deluged as though by a warm wave by a suave turn of the carpeted stair and a pendant glitter of chandeliers and a mute gleam of gold frames, heard the swift feet and saw her too, a lady—perhaps he had never seen her like before either—in a gray, smooth gown with lace at the throat and an apron tied at the waist and the sleeves turned back, wiping cake or biscuit dough from her hands with a towel as she came up the hall, looking not at his father at all but at the tracks on the blond rug with an expression of incredulous amazement.

"I tried," the Negro cried. "I tole him to . . ."

"Will you please go away?" she said in a shaking voice. "Major de Spain is not at home. Will you please go away?"

His father had not spoken again. He did not speak again. He did not even look   45 at her. He just stood stiff in the center of the rug, in his hat, the shaggy iron-gray brows twitching slightly above the pebble-colored eyes as he appeared to examine the house with brief deliberation. Then with the same deliberation he turned; the boy watched him pivot on the good leg and saw the stiff foot drag around the arc of the turning, leaving a final long and fading smear. His father never looked at it, he never once looked down at the rug. The Negro held the door. It closed behind them, upon the hysteric and indistinguishable woman-wail. His father stopped at the top of the steps and scraped his boot clean on the edge of it. At the gate he stopped again. He stood for a moment, planted stiffly on the stiff foot, looking back at the house. "Pretty and white, ain't it?" he said. "That's sweat. Nigger sweat. Maybe it ain't white enough yet to suit him. Maybe he wants to mix some white sweat with it."

Two hours later the boy was chopping wood behind the house within which his mother and aunt and the two sisters (the mother and aunt, not the two girls, he knew that; even at this distance and muffled by walls the flat loud voices of the two girls emanated an incorrigible idle inertia) were setting up the stove to prepare a meal, when he heard the hooves and saw the linen-clad man on a fine sorrel mare, whom he recognized even before he saw the rolled rug in front of the Negro youth following on a fat bay carriage horse—a suffused, angry face vanishing, still at full gallop, beyond the corner of the house where his father and brother were sitting in the two tilted chairs; and a moment later, almost before he could have put the axe down, he heard the hooves again and watched the sorrel mare go back out of the yard, already galloping again. Then his father began to shout one of the sisters' names, who presently emerged backward from the kitchen door dragging the rolled rug along the ground by one end while the other sister walked behind it.

"If you ain't going to tote, go on and set up the wash pot," the first said.

"You, Sarty!" the second shouted. "Set up the wash pot!" His father appeared at the door, framed against that shabbiness, as he had been against that other bland perfection, impervious to either, the mother's anxious face at his shoulder.

"Go on," the father said. "Pick it up." The two sisters stooped, broad, lethargic; stooping, they presented an incredible expanse of pale cloth and a flutter of tawdry ribbons.

"If I thought enough of a rug to have to git hit all the way from France I wouldn't   50
keep hit where folks coming in would have to tromp on hit," the first said. They raised the rug.

"Abner," the mother said. "Let me do it."

"You go back and git dinner," his father said. "I'll tend to this."

From the woodpile through the rest of the afternoon the boy watched them, the rug spread flat in the dust beside the bubbling wash pot, the two sisters stooping over it with that profound and lethargic reluctance, while the father stood over them in turn, implacable and grim, driving them though never raising his voice again. He could smell the harsh homemade lye they were using; he saw his mother come to the door once and look toward them with an expression not anxious now but very like despair; he saw his father turn, and he fell to with the axe and saw from the corner of his eye his father raise from the ground a flattish fragment of field stone and examine it and return to the pot, and this time his mother actually spoke: "Abner. Abner. Please don't. Please, Abner."

Then he was done too. It was dusk; the whippoorwills had already begun. He could smell coffee from the room where they would presently eat the cold food remaining from the mid-afternoon meal, though when he entered the house he realized they were having coffee again probably because there was a fire on the hearth, before which the rug now lay spread over the backs of the two chairs. The tracks of his father's foot were gone. Where they had been were now long, water-cloudy scoriations resembling the sporadic course of a lilliputian mowing machine.

It still hung there while they ate the cold food and then went to bed, scattered   55
without order or claim up and down the two rooms, his mother in one bed, where his father would later lie, the older brother in the other, himself, the aunt, and the two sisters on pallets on the floor. But his father was not in bed yet. The last thing the boy remembered was the depthless, harsh silhouette of the hat and coat bending over the rug and it seemed to him that he had not even closed his eyes when the silhouette was standing over him, the fire almost dead behind it, the stiff foot prodding him awake. "Catch up the mule," his father said.

When he returned with the mule his father was standing in the back door, the rolled rug over his shoulder. "Ain't you going to ride?" he said.

"No. Give me your foot."

He bent his knee into his father's hand, the wiry, surprising power flowed smoothly, rising, he rising with it, on to the mule's bare back (they had owned a saddle once; the boy could remember it though not when or where) and with the same effortlessness his father swung the rug up in front of him. Now in the starlight they retraced the afternoon's path, up the dusty road rife with honeysuckle, through the gate and up the black tunnel of the drive to the lightless house, where he sat on the mule and felt the rough warp of the rug drag across his thighs and vanish.

"Don't you want me to help?" he whispered. His father did not answer and now he heard again that stiff foot striking the hollow portico with that wooden and clocklike deliberation, that outrageous overstatement of the weight it carried. The rug, hunched, not flung (the boy could tell that even in the darkness) from his father's shoulder struck the angle of wall and floor with a sound unbelievably loud, thunderous, then the foot again, unhurried and enormous; a light came on in the house and the boy sat, tense, breathing steadily and quietly and just a little fast, though the foot itself did not increase its beat at all, descending the steps now; now the boy could see him.

"Don't you want to ride now?" he whispered. "We kin both ride now," the light 60 within the house altering now, flaring up and sinking. *He's coming down the stairs now,* he thought. He had already ridden the mule up beside the horse block; presently his father was up behind him and he doubled the reins over and slashed the mule across the neck, but before the animal could begin to trot the hard, thin arm came around him, the hard, knotted hand jerking the mule back to a walk.

In the first red rays of the sun they were in the lot, putting plow gear on the mules. This time the sorrel mare was in the lot before he heard it at all, the rider collarless and even bareheaded, trembling, speaking in a shaking voice as the woman in the house had done, his father merely looking up once before stooping again to the hame he was buckling, so that the man on the mare spoke to his stooping back:

"You must realize you have ruined that rug. Wasn't there anybody here, any of your women . . ." he ceased, shaking, the boy watching him, the older brother leaning now in the stable door, chewing, blinking slowly and steadily at nothing apparently. "It cost a hundred dollars. But you never had a hundred dollars. You never will. So I'm going to charge you twenty bushels of corn against your crop. I'll add it in your contract and when you come to the commissary you can sign it. That won't keep Mrs. de Spain quiet but maybe it will teach you to wipe your feet off before you enter her house again."

Then he was gone. The boy looked at his father, who still had not spoken or even looked up again, who was now adjusting the logger-head in the hame.

"Pap," he said. His father looked at him—the inscrutable face, the shaggy brows beneath where the gray eyes glinted coldly. Suddenly the boy went toward him, fast, stopping as suddenly. "You done the best you could!" he cried. "If he wanted hit done different why didn't he wait and tell you how? He won't git no twenty bushels! He won't git none! We'll gather hit and hide hit! I kin watch . . ."

"Did you put the cutter back in that straight stock like I told you?"   65

"No, sir," he said.

"Then go do it."

That was Wednesday. During the rest of that week he worked steadily, at what was within his scope and some which was beyond it, with an industry that did not need to be driven nor even commanded twice; he had this from his mother, with the difference that some at least of what he did he liked to do, such as splitting wood with the half-size axe which his mother and aunt had earned, or saved money somehow, to present him with at Christmas. In company with the two older women (and on one afternoon, even one of the sisters), he built pens for the shoat and the cow which were a part of his father's contract with the landlord, and one afternoon, his father being absent, gone somewhere on one of the mules, he went to the field.

They were running a middle buster now, his brother holding the plow straight while he handled the reins, and walking beside the straining mule, the rich black soil shearing cool and damp against his bare ankles, he thought *Maybe this is the end of it. Maybe even that twenty bushels that seems hard to have to pay for just a rug will be a cheap price for him to stop forever and always from being what he used to be;* thinking, dreaming now, so that his brother had to speak sharply to him to mind the mule: *Maybe he even won't collect the twenty bushels. Maybe it will all add up and balance and vanish—corn, rug, fire; the terror and grief; the being pulled two ways like between two teams of horses—gone, done with for ever and ever.*

Then it was Saturday; he looked up from beneath the mule he was harnessing 70 and saw his father in the black coat and hat. "Not that," his father said. "The wagon gear." And then, two hours later, sitting in the wagon bed behind his father and brother on the seat, the wagon accomplished a final curve, and he saw the weathered paintless store with its tattered tobacco- and patent-medicine posters and the teth-ered wagons and saddle animals below the gallery. He mounted the gnawed steps be-hind his father and brother, and there again was the lane of quiet, watching faces for the three of them to walk through. He saw the man in spectacles sitting at the plank table and he did not need to be told this was a Justice of the Peace; he sent one glare of fierce, exultant, partisan defiance at the man in collar and cravat now, whom he had seen but twice before in his life, and that on a galloping horse, who now wore on his face an expression not of rage but of amazed unbelief which the boy could not have known was at the incredible circumstance of being sued by one of his own ten-ants, and came and stood against his father and cried at the Justice: "He ain't done it! He ain't burnt . . ."

"Go back to the wagon," his father said.

"Burnt?" the Justice said. "Do I understand this rug was burned too?"

"Does anybody here claim it was?" his father said. "Go back to the wagon." But he did not, he merely retreated to the rear of the room, crowded as that other had been, but not to sit down this time, instead, to stand pressing among the motionless bodies, listening to the voices:

"And you claim twenty bushels of corn is too high for the damage you did to the rug?"

"He brought the rug to me and said he wanted the tracks washed out of it. I 75 washed the tracks out and took the rug back to him."

"But you didn't carry the rug back to him in the same condition it was in before you made the tracks on it."

His father did not answer, and now for perhaps half a minute there was no sound at all save that of breathing, the faint, steady suspiration of complete and intent listening.

"You decline to answer that, Mr. Snopes?" Again his father did not answer. "I'm going to find against you, Mr. Snopes. I'm going to find that you were responsible for the injury to Major de Spain's rug and hold you liable for it. But twenty bushels of corn seems a little high for a man in your circumstances to have to pay. Major de Spain claims it cost a hundred dollars. October corn will be worth about fifty cents. I figure that if Major de Spain can stand a ninety-five dollar loss on something he paid cash for, you can stand a five-dollar loss you haven't earned yet. I hold you in damages to Major de Spain to the amount of ten bushels of corn over and above your contract with him, to be paid to him out of your crop at gathering time. Court adjourned."

It had taken no time hardly, the morning was but half begun. He thought they would return home and perhaps back to the field, since they were late, far behind all other farmers. But instead his father passed on behind the wagon, merely indicating with his hand for the older brother to follow with it, and crossed the road toward the blacksmith shop opposite, pressing on after his father, overtaking him, speaking, whispering up at the harsh, calm face beneath the weathered hat: "He won't git no

ten bushels either. He won't git one. We'll . . ." until his father glanced for an instant down at him, the face absolutely calm, the grizzled eyebrows tangled above the
cold eyes, the voice almost pleasant, almost gentle:

"You think so? Well, we'll wait till October anyway."

80

The matter of the wagon—the setting of a spoke or two and the tightening of
the tires—did not take long either, the business of the tires accomplished by driving
the wagon into the spring branch behind the shop and letting it stand there, the
mules nuzzling into the water from time to time, and the boy on the seat with the idle
reins, looking up the slope and through the sooty tunnel of the shed where the slow
hammer rang and where his father sat on an upended cypress bolt, easily, either talking or listening, still sitting there when the boy brought the dripping wagon up out of
the branch and halted it before the door.

"Take them on to the shade and hitch," his father said. He did so and returned.
His father and the smith and a third man squatting on his heels inside the door were
talking, about crops and animals; the boy, squatting too in the ammoniac dust and
hoof-parings and scales of rust, heard his father tell a long and unhurried story out of
the time before the birth of the older brother even when he had been a professional
horsetrader. And then his father came up beside him where he stood before a tattered
last year's circus poster on the other side of the store, gazing rapt and quiet at the
scarlet horses, the incredible poisings and convulsions of tulle and tights and the
painted leers of comedians, and said, "It's time to eat."

But not at home. Squatting beside his brother against the front wall, he watched
his father emerge from the store and produce from a paper sack a segment of cheese
and divide it carefully and deliberately into three with his pocket knife and produce
crackers from the same sack. They all three squatted on the gallery and ate, slowly,
without talking; then in the store again, they drank from a tin dipper tepid water
smelling of the cedar bucket and of living beech trees. And still they did not go home.
It was a horse lot this time, a tall rail fence upon and along which men stood and sat
and out of which one by one horses were led, to be walked and trotted and then can-
tered back and forth along the road while the slow swapping and buying went on and
the sun began to slant westward, they—the three of them—watching and listening,
the older brother with his muddy eyes and his steady, inevitable tobacco, the father
commenting now and then on certain of the animals, to no one in particular.

It was after sundown when they reached home. They ate supper by lamplight,
then, sitting on the doorstep, the boy watched the night fully accomplish, listening
to the whippoorwills and the frogs, when he heard his mother's voice: "Abner! No!
No! Oh, God. Oh, God. Abner!" and he rose, whirled, and saw the altered light
through the door where a candle stub now burned in a bottle neck on the table and
his father, still in the hat and coat, at once formal and burlesque as though dressed
carefully for some shabby and ceremonial violence, emptying the reservoir of the
lamp back into the five-gallon kerosene can from which it had been filled, while the
mother tugged at his arm until he shifted the lamp to the other hand and flung her
back, not savagely or viciously, just hard, into the wall, her hands flung out against
the wall for balance, her mouth open and in her face the same quality of hopeless
despair as had been in her voice. Then his father saw him standing in the door.

"Go to the barn and get that can of oil we were oiling the wagon with," he said.
The boy did not move. Then he could speak.

85

"What . . ." he cried. "What are you . . ."

"Go get that oil," his father said. "Go."

Then he was moving, running, outside the house, toward the stable: this the old habit, the old blood which he had not been permitted to choose for himself, which had been bequeathed him willy nilly and which had run for so long (and who knew where, battening on what of outrage and savagery and lust) before it came to him. *I could keep on*, he thought. *I could run on and on and never look back, never need to see his face again. Only I can't. I can't*, the rusted can in his hand now, the liquid sploshing in it as he ran back to the house and into it, into the sound of his mother's weeping in the next room, and handed the can to his father.

"Ain't you going to even send a nigger?" he cried. "At least you sent a nigger before!"

This time his father didn't strike him. The hand came even faster than the blow   90
had, the same hand which had set the can on the table with almost excruciating care flashing from the can toward him too quick for him to follow it, gripping him by the back of his shirt and on to tiptoe before he had seen it quit the can, the face stooping at him in breathless and frozen ferocity, the cold, dead voice speaking over him to the older brother who leaned against the table, chewing with that steady, curious, sidewise motion of cows:

"Empty the can into the big one and go on. I'll catch up with you."

"Better tie him up to the bedpost," the brother said.

"Do like I told you," the father said. Then the boy was moving, his bunched shirt and the hard, bony hand between his shoulder-blades, his toes just touching the floor, across the room and into the other one, past the sisters sitting with spread heavy thighs in the two chairs over the cold hearth, and to where his mother and aunt sat side by side on the bed, the aunt's arm about his mother's shoulders.

"Hold him," the father said. The aunt made a startled movement. "Not you," the father said. "Lennie. Take hold of him. I want to see you do it." His mother took him by the wrist. "You'll hold him better than that. If he gets loose don't you know what he is going to do? He will go up yonder." He jerked his head toward the road. "Maybe I'd better tie him."

"I'll hold him," his mother whispered.   95

"See you do then." Then his father was gone, the stiff foot heavy and measured upon the boards, ceasing at last.

Then he began to struggle. His mother caught him in both arms, he jerking and wrenching at them. He would be stronger in the end, he knew that. But he had no time to wait for it. "Lemme go!" he cried. "I don't want to have to hit you!"

"Let him go!" the aunt said. "If he don't go, before God, I am going up there myself!"

"Don't you see I can't?" his mother cried. "Sarty! Sarty! No! No! Help me, Lizzie!"

Then he was free. His aunt grasped at him but it was too late. He whirled, run-   100
ning, his mother stumbled forward on to her knees behind him, crying to the nearer sister: "Catch him, Net! Catch him!" But that was too late too, the sister (the sisters were twins, born at the same time, yet either of them now gave the impression of be-ing, encompassing as much living meat and volume and weight as any other two of the family) not yet having begun to rise from the chair, her head, face, alone merely turned, presenting to him in the flying instant an astonishing expanse of young fe-male features untroubled by any surprise even, wearing only an expression of bovine interest. Then he was out of the room, out of the house, in the mild dust of the starlit

road and the heavy rifeness of honeysuckle, the pale ribbon unspooling with terrific slowness under his running feet, reaching the gate at last and turning in, running, his heart and lungs drumming, on up the drive toward the lighted house, the lighted door. He did not knock, he burst in, sobbing for breath, incapable for the moment of speech; he saw the astonished face of the Negro in the linen jacket without knowing when the Negro had appeared.

"De Spain!" he cried, panted. "Where's . . ." then he saw the white man too emerging from a white door down the hall. "Barn!" he cried. "Barn!"

"What?" the white man said. "Barn?"

"Yes!" the boy cried. "Barn!"

"Catch him!" the white man shouted.

But it was too late this time too. The Negro grasped his shirt, but the entire sleeve, rotten with washing, carried away, and he was out that door too and in the drive again, and had actually never ceased to run even while he was screaming into the white man's face.

Behind him the white man was shouting, "My horse! Fetch my horse!" and he thought for an instant of cutting across the park and climbing the fence into the road, but he did not know the park nor how high the vine-massed fence might be and he dared not risk it. So he ran on down the drive, blood and breath roaring; presently he was in the road again though he could not see it. He could not hear either: the galloping mare was almost upon him before he heard her, and even then he held his course, as if the very urgency of his wild grief and need must in a moment more find him wings, waiting until the ultimate instant to hurl himself aside and into the weed-choked roadside ditch as the horse thundered past and on, for an instant in furious silhouette against the stars, the tranquil early summer night sky which, even before the shape of the horse and rider vanished, stained abruptly and violently upward: a long, swirling roar incredible and soundless, blotting the stars, and he springing up and into the road again, running again, knowing it was too late yet still running even after he heard the shot and, an instant later, two shots, pausing now without knowing he had ceased to run, crying, "Pap! Pap!", running again before he knew he had begun to run, stumbling, tripping over something and scrabbling up again without ceasing to run, looking backward over his shoulder at the glare as he got up, running on among the invisible trees, panting, sobbing, "Father! Father!"

At midnight he was sitting on the crest of a hill. He did not know it was midnight and he did not know how far he had come. But there was no glare behind him now and he sat now, his back toward what he had called home for four days anyhow, his face toward the dark woods which he would enter when breath was strong again, small, shaking steadily in the chill darkness, hugging himself into the remainder of his thin, rotten shirt, the grief and despair now no longer terror and fear but just grief and despair. *Father. My father*, he thought. "He was brave!" he cried suddenly, aloud but not loud, no more than a whisper. "He was! He was in the war! He was in Colonel Sartoris' cav'ry!" not knowing that his father had gone to that war a private in the fine old European sense, wearing no uniform, admitting the authority of and giving fidelity to no man or army or flag, going to war as Malbrouck° himself did: for booty—it meant nothing and less than nothing to him if it were enemy booty or his own.

Malbrouck: John Churchill, Duke of Marlborough (1650–1722), English general victorious in the Battle of Blenheim (1704), a triumph that drove the French army out of Germany. The French called him Malbrouck, a name they found easier to pronounce.

The slow constellations wheeled on. It would be dawn and then sun-up after a while and he would be hungry. But that would be to-morrow and now he was only cold, and walking would cure that. His breathing was easier now and he decided to get up and go on, and then he found that he had been asleep because he knew it was almost dawn, the night almost over. He could tell that from the whippoorwills. They were everywhere now among the dark trees below him, constant and inflectioned and ceaseless, so that, as the instant for giving over to the day birds drew nearer and nearer, there was no interval at all between them. He got up. He was a little stiff, but walking would cure that too as it would the cold, and soon there would be the sun. He went on down the hill, toward the dark woods within which the liquid silver voices of the birds called unceasing—the rapid and urgent beating of the urgent and quiring heart of the late spring night. He did not look back.

Questions

1. After delivering his warning to Major de Spain, the boy Snopes does not actually witness what happens to his father and brother, or what happens to the Major's barn. But what do you assume happens? What evidence is given in the story?

2. What do you understand to be Faulkner's opinion of Abner Snopes? Make a guess, indicating details in the story that convey attitudes.

3. Which adjectives best describe the general tone of the story: *calm, amused, disinterested, scornful, marveling, excited, impassioned*? Point out passages that may be so described. What do you notice about the style in which these passages are written?

4. In tone and style, how does "Barn Burning" compare with Faulkner's story "A Rose for Emily" (Chapter 2)? To what do you attribute any differences?

5. Suppose that, instead of "Barn Burning," Faulkner had written a story told by Abner Snopes in the first person. Why would such a story need a style different from that of "Barn Burning"? (Suggestion: Notice Faulkner's descriptions of Abner Snopes's voice.)

6. Although "Barn Burning" takes place some thirty years after the Civil War, how does the war figure in it?

IRONY

If a friend declares, "Oh, sure, I just *love* to have four papers due on the same day," you detect that the statement contains **irony.** This is **verbal irony,** the most familiar kind, in which we understand the speaker's meaning to be far from the usual meaning of the words—in this case, quite the opposite. (When the irony is found, as here, in a somewhat sour statement tinged with mockery, it is called **sarcasm.)**

Irony, of course, occurs in writing as well as in conversation. When in a comic moment in Isaac Bashevis Singer's "Gimpel the Fool" the sexton announces, "The wealthy Reb Gimpel invites the congregation to a feast in honor of the birth of a son," the people at the synagogue burst into laughter. They know that Gimpel, in contrast to the sexton's words, is not a wealthy man but a humble baker; that the son is not his own but his wife's lover's; and that the birth brings no honor to anybody. Verbal irony, then, implies a contrast or discrepancy between what is *said* and what is *meant*.

Dramatic Irony

There are also times when the speaker, unlike the reader, does not realize the ironic dimension of his or her words; such instances are known as **dramatic irony.** The most famous example occurs in Sophocles's tragic drama *Oedipus the King*, when Oedipus vows to find and punish the murderer of King Laius, unaware that he himself is the man he seeks, and adds: "if by any chance / he proves to be an intimate of our house, / here at my hearth, with my full knowledge, / may the curse I just called down on him strike me!" Dramatic irony may also be used, of course, for lighter purposes: for example, Daisy Coble, the mother in Anne Tyler's "Teenage Wasteland," whose attitudes and moods shift constantly according to what others tell her, responds to the idea that *she* should be less strict with her son by saying, "But see, he's still so suggestible." Stories often contain other kinds of irony besides such verbal irony. A situation, for example, can be ironic if it contains some wry contrast or incongruity. In Jack London's "To Build a Fire" (Chapter 4), it is ironic that a freezing man, desperately trying to strike a match to light a fire and save himself, accidentally ignites all his remaining matches.

Irony as Point of View

An entire story may be told from an **ironic point of view.** Whenever we sense a sharp distinction between the narrator of a story and the author, irony is likely to occur—especially when the narrator is telling us something that we are clearly expected to doubt or to interpret very differently. In "A & P," Sammy (who tells his own story) makes many smug and cruel observations about the people around him; but the author makes clear to us that much of his superiority is based on immaturity and lack of self-knowledge. (This irony, by the way, does not negate the fact that Sammy makes some very telling comments about society's superficial values and rigid and judgmental attitudes, comments that Updike seems to endorse and wants us to endorse as well.) And when we read Hemingway's "A Clean, Well-Lighted Place," surely we feel that most of the time the older waiter speaks for the author. Though the waiter gives us a respectful, compassionate view of a lonely old man, and we don't doubt that the view is Hemingway's, still, in the closing lines of the story we are reminded that author and waiter are not identical. Musing on the sleepless night ahead of him, the waiter tries to shrug off his problem—"After all, it is probably only insomnia" —but the reader, who recalls the waiter's bleak view of *nada*, nothingness, knows that it certainly isn't mere insomnia that keeps him awake but a dread of solitude and death. At that crucial moment, Hemingway and the older waiter part company, and we perceive an ironic point of view, and also a verbal irony, "After all, it is probably only insomnia."

Cosmic Irony

Storytellers are sometimes fond of ironic twists of fate—developments that reveal a terrible distance between what people deserve and what they get, between what is and what ought to be. In the novels of Thomas Hardy, some hostile fate keeps playing tricks to thwart the main characters. In *Tess of the D'Urbervilles*, an all-important letter, thrust under a door, by chance slides beneath a carpet and is not received. Such an irony is sometimes called an **irony of fate** or a **cosmic irony,** for it suggests that some malicious fate (or other spirit in the universe) is deliberately frustrating human efforts. Evidently, there is an irony of fate in the servant's futile attempt to escape Death in the fable "The Appointment in Samarra," and perhaps in the flaring up of the all-precious matches in "To Build a Fire" as well. To notice an irony gives pleasure. It may move us to laughter, make us feel wonder, or arouse our sympathy. By so involving us, irony—whether in a statement, a situation, an unexpected event, or a point of view—can render a story more likely to strike us, to affect us, and to be remembered.

A famous example of O. Henry's irony is the following story, perhaps the best-known and most-loved of his many tales.

O. Henry (William Sydney Porter)

The Gift of the Magi   1906

O. Henry

William Sydney Porter (1862–1910), known to the world as O. Henry, was born in Greensboro, North Carolina. He began writing in his mid-twenties, contributing humorous sketches to various periodicals. In 1896 he was indicted for embezzlement from the First National Bank of Austin, Texas; he fled to Honduras before his trial, but returned when he found that his wife was terminally ill. He was convicted, and served three years of a five-year sentence; his guilt or innocence has never been definitively established. Released in 1901, he moved to New York the following year. Already a well-known writer, for the next three years he produced a story every week for the New York World while also contributing tales and sketches to magazines. Beginning with Cabbages and Kings in 1904, his stories were published in nine highly successful collections in the few remaining years of his life, as well as in three posthumously issued volumes. Financial extravagance and alcoholism darkened his last days, culminating in his death from tuberculosis at the age of forty-seven. Ranked during his lifetime with Hawthorne and Poe, O. Henry is more likely now to be invoked in negative terms, for his sentimentality and especially for his reliance on frequently forced trick endings, but the most prestigious annual volume of the best American short fiction is still called The O. Henry Prize Stories, and the best of his own work is loved by millions of readers.

One dollar and eighty-seven cents. That was all. And sixty cents of it was in pennies. Pennies saved one and two at a time by bulldozing the grocer and the vegetable man and the butcher until one's cheeks burned with the silent imputation of parsimony that such close dealing implied. Three times Della counted it. One dollar and eighty-seven cents. And the next day would be Christmas.

There was clearly nothing to do but flop down on the shabby little couch and howl. So Della did it. Which instigates the moral reflection that life is made up of sobs, sniffles, and smiles, with sniffles predominating.

While the mistress of the home is gradually subsiding from the first stage to the second, take a look at the home. A furnished flat at $8 per week. It did not exactly beggar description, but it certainly had that word on the lookout for the mendicancy squad.

In the vestibule below was a letter-box into which no letter would go, and an electric button from which no mortal finger could coax a ring. Also appertaining thereunto was a card bearing the name "Mr. James Dillingham Young."

The "Dillingham" had been flung to the breeze during a former period of prosperity when its possessor was being paid $30 per week. Now, when the income was shrunk to $20, the letters of "Dillingham" looked blurred, as though they were thinking seriously of contracting to a modest and unassuming D. But whenever Mr. James Dillingham Young came home and reached his flat above he was called "Jim" and greatly hugged by Mrs. James Dillingham Young, already introduced to you as Della. Which is all very good.

5

Della finished her cry and attended to her cheeks with the powder rag. She stood by the window and looked out dully at a grey cat walking a grey fence in a grey backyard. Tomorrow would be Christmas Day, and she had only $1.87 with which to buy Jim a present. She had been saving every penny she could for months, with this result. Twenty dollars a week doesn't go far. Expenses had been greater than she had calculated. They always are. Only $1.87 to buy a present for Jim. Her Jim. Many a happy hour she had spent planning for something nice for him. Something fine and rare and sterling— something just a little bit near to being worthy of the honor of being owned by Jim.

There was a pier-glass between the windows of the room. Perhaps you have seen a pier-glass in an $8 flat. A very thin and very agile person may, by observing his re- flection in a rapid sequence of longitudinal strips, obtain a fairly accurate conception of his looks. Della, being slender, had mastered the art.

Suddenly she whirled from the window and stood before the glass. Her eyes were shining brilliantly, but her face had lost its color within twenty seconds. Rapidly she pulled down her hair and let it fall to its full length.

Now, there were two possessions of the James Dillingham Youngs in which they both took a mighty pride. One was Jim's gold watch that had been his father's and his grandfather's. The other was Della's hair. Had the Queen of Sheba lived in the flat across the airshaft, Della would have let her hair hang out the window some day to dry just to depreciate Her Majesty's jewels and gifts. Had King Solomon been the janitor, with all his treasures piled up in the basement, Jim would have pulled out his watch every time he passed, just to see him pluck at his beard from envy.

So now Della's beautiful hair fell about her, rippling and shining like a cascade of brown waters. It reached below her knee and made itself almost a garment for her. And then she did it up again nervously and quickly. Once she faltered for a minute and stood still while a tear or two splashed on the worn red carpet.

On went her old brown jacket; on went her old brown hat. With a whirl of skirts and with the brilliant sparkle still in her eyes, she fluttered out the door and down the stairs to the street.

Where she stopped the sign read: "Mme. Sofronie. Hair Goods of All Kinds." One flight up Della ran, and collected herself, panting. Madame, large, too white, chilly, hardly looked the "Sofronie."

"Will you buy my hair?" asked Della.

"I buy hair," said Madame. "Take yer hat off and let's have a sight at the looks of it."

Down rippled the brown cascade.

"Twenty dollars," said Madame, lifting the mass with a practiced hand.

"Give it to me quick," said Della.

Oh, and the next two hours tripped by on rosy wings. Forget the hashed metaphor. She was ransacking the stores for Jim's present.

She found it at last. It surely had been made for Jim and no one else. There was no other like it in any of the stores, and she had turned all of them inside out. It was a platinum fob chain simple and chaste in design, properly proclaiming its value by substance alone and not by meretricious ornamentation—as all good things should do. It was even worthy of The Watch. As soon as she saw it she knew that it must be Jim's. It was like him. Quietness and value—the description applied to both. Twenty- one dollars they took from her for it, and she hurried home with the 87 cents. With that chain on his watch Jim might be properly anxious about the time in any company.

Grand as the watch was, he sometimes looked at it on the sly on account of the old leather strap that he used in place of a chain.

When Della reached home her intoxication gave way a little to prudence and 20 reason. She got out her curling irons and lighted the gas and went to work repairing the ravages made by generosity added to love. Which is always a tremendous task, dear friends—a mammoth task.

Within forty minutes her head was covered with tiny, close-lying curls that made her look wonderfully like a truant schoolboy. She looked at her reflection in the mirror long, carefully, and critically.

"If Jim doesn't kill me," she said to herself, "before he takes a second look at me, he'll say I look like a Coney Island chorus girl. But what could I do—oh! What could I do with a dollar and eighty-seven cents?"

At 7 o'clock the coffee was made and the frying-pan was on the back of the stove hot and ready to cook the chops.

Jim was never late. Della doubled the fob chain in her hand and sat on the corner of the table near the door that he always entered. Then she heard his step on the stair away down on the first flight, and she turned white for just a moment. She had a habit of saying little silent prayers about the simplest everyday things, and now she whispered: "Please God, make him think I am still pretty."

The door opened and Jim stepped in and closed it. He looked thin and very seri- 25 ous. Poor fellow, he was only twenty-two—and to be burdened with a family! He needed a new overcoat and he was without gloves.

Jim stopped inside the door, as immovable as a setter at the scent of quail. His eyes were fixed upon Della, and there was an expression in them that she could not read, and it terrified her. It was not anger, nor surprise, nor disapproval, nor horror, nor any of the sentiments that she had been prepared for. He simply stared at her fixedly with that peculiar expression on his face.

Della wriggled off the table and went for him.

"Jim, darling," she cried, "don't look at me that way. I had my hair cut off and sold because I couldn't have lived through Christmas without giving you a present. It'll grow out again—you won't mind, will you? I just had to do it. My hair grows awfully fast. Say 'Merry Christmas!' Jim, and let's be happy. You don't know what a nice—what a beautiful, nice gift I've got for you."

"You've cut off your hair?" asked Jim, laboriously, as if he had not arrived at that patent fact yet even after the hardest mental labor.

"Cut it off and sold it," said Della. "Don't you like me just as well, anyhow? I'm 30 me without my hair, ain't I?"

Jim looked about the room curiously.

"You say your hair is gone?" he said, with an air almost of idiocy.

"You needn't look for it," said Della. "It's sold, I tell you—sold and gone, too. It's Christmas Eve, boy. Be good to me, for it went for you. Maybe the hairs of my head were numbered," she went on with a sudden serious sweetness, "but nobody could ever count my love for you. Shall I put the chops on, Jim?"

Out of his trance Jim seemed quickly to wake. He enfolded his Della. For ten seconds let us regard with discreet scrutiny some inconsequential object in the other direction. Eight dollars a week or a million a year—what is the difference? A mathe-matician or a wit would give you the wrong answer. The magi brought valuable gifts, but that was not among them. This dark assertion will be illuminated later on.

Jim drew a package from his overcoat pocket and threw it upon the table. 35

"Don't make any mistake, Dell," he said, "about me. I don't think there's anything in the way of a haircut or a shave or a shampoo that could make me like my girl any less. But if you'll unwrap that package you may see why you had me going a while at first."

White fingers and nimble tore at the string and paper. And then an ecstatic scream of joy; and then, alas! a quick feminine change to hysterical tears and wails, necessitating the immediate employment of all the comforting powers of the lord of the flat.

For there lay The Combs—the set of combs, side and back, that Della had worshipped for long in a Broadway window. Beautiful combs, pure tortoise shell, with jewelled rims—just the shade to wear in the beautiful vanished hair. They were expensive combs, she knew, and her heart had simply craved and yearned over them without the least hope of possession. And now, they were hers, but the tresses that should have adorned the coveted adornments were gone.

But she hugged them to her bosom, and at length she was able to look up with dim eyes and a smile and say: "My hair grows so fast, Jim!"

And then Della leaped up like a little singed cat and cried, "Oh, oh!" 40

Jim had not yet seen his beautiful present. She held it out to him eagerly upon her open palm. The dull precious metal seemed to flash with a reflection of her bright and ardent spirit.

"Isn't it a dandy, Jim? I hunted all over town to find it. You'll have to look at the time a hundred times a day now. Give me your watch. I want to see how it looks on it."

Instead of obeying, Jim tumbled down on the couch and put his hands under the back of his head and smiled.

"Dell," said he, "let's put our Christmas presents away and keep 'em a while. They're too nice to use just at present. I sold the watch to get the money to buy your combs. And now suppose you put the chops on."

The magi, as you know, were wise men—wonderfully wise men—who brought 45
gifts to the Babe in the manger. They invented the art of giving Christmas presents. Being wise, their gifts were no doubt wise ones, possibly bearing the privilege of exchange in case of duplication. And here I have lamely related to you the uneventful chronicle of two foolish children in a flat who most unwisely sacrificed for each other the greatest treasures of their house. But in a last word to the wise of these days let it be said that of all who give gifts these two were the wisest. Of all who give and receive gifts, such as they are wisest. Everywhere they are wisest. They are the magi.

Questions

1. How would you describe the style of this story? Does the author's tone tell you anything about his attitude toward the characters and events of the narrative?

2. What do the details in paragraph 7 tell you about Della and Jim's financial situation?

3. O. Henry tells us that Jim "needed a new overcoat and he was without gloves" (paragraph 25). Why do you think Della didn't buy him these things for Christmas instead of a watch chain?

4. "Eight dollars a week or a million a year—what is the difference? A mathematician or a wit would give you the wrong answer" (paragraph 34). What, in your view, is "the wrong answer," and why is it wrong? What might the right answer be?

5. What is ironic about the story's ending? Is this plot twist the most important element of the conclusion? If not, what is?

Anne Tyler

Teenage Wasteland

1983

Anne Tyler was born in 1941 in Minneapolis, Minnesota, and was raised in North Carolina. Her parents, a chemist and a social worker, were Quakers who home-schooled Tyler and her three younger brothers until she was eleven, at which time they entered the public school system. She earned a bachelor's degree in Russian from Duke University when she was nineteen. In 1963, she married Taghi Modarressi, an Iranian physician. The couple had two daughters, one of whom has provided the illustrations for Tyler's two children's books. Her husband died in 1997. Beginning with If Morning Ever Comes in 1964, Tyler has published eighteen well-written, solidly crafted novels that explore themes of loneliness, alienation, the desperate search for love and acceptance, and the difficult adjustments of marriage and other family

Anne Tyler

relationships. Although she deals unflinchingly with the pain and loss that can dominate and often overwhelm our lives, her work presents a gallery of vivid, strong-willed personalities whose affirmative approach suggests possibilities of hope and renewal. Dinner at the Homesick Restaurant (1982) is perhaps her most highly regarded work, and her personal favorite among her books. Its successor, The Accidental Tourist (1985), won the National Book Critics Circle Award and was made into a film starring William Hurt and Geena Davis, who won an Academy Award for her performance. Her next novel, Breathing Lessons (1988), won the Pulitzer Prize. Her most recent novels are Digging to America (2006) and Noah's Compass (2010). She has published several stories in magazines ("Teenage Wasteland" appeared in Seventeen in 1983) but has not yet collected her short fiction into a book. Tyler avoids the lecture circuit and the other trappings of literary celebrity, preferring to concentrate on her writing. She lives in Baltimore.

He used to have very blond hair—almost white—cut shorter than other children's so that on his crown a little cowlick always stood up to catch the light. But this was when he was small. As he grew older, his hair grew darker, and he wore it longer—past his collar even. It hung in lank, taffy-colored ropes around his face, which was still an endearing face, fine-featured, the eyes an unusual aqua blue. But his cheeks, of course, were no longer round, and a sharp new Adam's apple jogged in his throat when he talked.

In October, they called from the private school he attended to request a conference with his parents. Daisy went alone; her husband was at work. Clutching her purse, she sat on the principal's couch and learned that Donny was noisy, lazy, and disruptive; always fooling around with his friends, and he wouldn't respond in class.

In the past, before her children were born, Daisy had been a fourth-grade teacher. It shamed her now to sit before this principal as a parent, a delinquent parent, a parent who struck Mr. Lanham, no doubt, as unseeing or uncaring. "It isn't that we're not concerned," she said. "Both of us are. And we've done what we could, whatever we could think of. We don't let him watch TV on school nights. We don't let him talk on the phone till he's finished his homework. But he tells us he doesn't *have* any homework or he did it all in study hall. How are we to know what to believe?"

From early October through November, at Mr. Lanham's suggestion, Daisy checked Donny's assignments every day. She sat next to him as he worked, trying to be encouraging, sagging inwardly as she saw the poor quality of everything he did—the sloppy mistakes in math, the illogical leaps in his English themes, the history questions left blank if they required any research.

Daisy was often late starting supper, and she couldn't give as much attention to Donny's younger sister. "You'll never guess what happened at . . ." Amanda would begin, and Daisy would have to tell her, "Not now, honey."   5

By the time her husband, Matt, came home, she'd be snappish. She would recite the day's hardships—the fuzzy instructions in English, the botched history map, the morass of unsolvable algebra equations. Matt would look surprised and confused, and Daisy would gradually wind down. There was no way, really, to convey how exhausting all this was.

In December, the school called again. This time, they wanted Matt to come as well. She and Matt had to sit on Mr. Lanham's couch like two bad children and listen to the news: Donny had improved only slightly, raising a D in history to a C, and a C in algebra to a B-minus. What was worse, he had developed new problems. He had cut classes on at least three occasions. Smoked in the furnace room. Helped Sonny Barnett break into a freshman's locker. And last week, during athletics, he and three friends had been seen off the school grounds; when they returned, the coach had smelled beer on their breath.

Daisy and Matt sat silent, shocked. Matt rubbed his forehead with his fingertips. Imagine, Daisy thought, how they must look to Mr. Lanham: an overweight housewife in a cotton dress and a too-tall, too-thin insurance agent in a baggy, frayed suit. Failures, both of them—the kind of people who are always hurrying to catch up, missing the point of things that everyone else grasps at once. She wished she'd worn nylons instead of knee socks.

It was arranged that Donny would visit a psychologist for testing. Mr. Lanham knew just the person. He would set this boy straight, he said.

When they stood to leave, Daisy held her stomach in and gave Mr. Lanham a firm, responsible handshake.   10

Donny said the psychologist was a jackass and the tests were really dumb; but he kept all three of his appointments, and when it was time for the follow-up conference with the psychologist and both parents, Donny combed his hair and seemed unusually sober and subdued. The psychologist said Donny had no serious emotional problems. He was merely going through a difficult period in his life. He required some academic help and a better sense of self-worth. For this reason, he was suggesting a man named Calvin Beadle, a tutor with considerable psychological training.

In the car going home, Donny said he'd be damned if he'd let them drag him to some stupid fairy tutor. His father told him to watch his language in front of his mother.

That night, Daisy lay awake pondering the term "self-worth." She had always been free with her praise. She had always told Donny he had talent, was smart, was good with his hands. She had made a big to-do over every little gift he gave her. In fact, maybe she had gone too far, although, Lord knows, she had meant every word. Was that his trouble?

She remembered when Amanda was born. Donny had acted lost and bewildered. Daisy had been alert to that, of course, but still, a new baby keeps you so busy. Had she really done all she could have? She longed—she ached—for a time machine. Given one more chance, she'd do it perfectly—hug him more, praise him more, or perhaps praise him less. Oh, who can say . . .

The tutor told Donny to call him Cal. All his kids did, he said. Daisy thought for a 15
second that he meant his own children, then realized her mistake. He seemed too young, anyhow, to be a family man. He wore a heavy brown handlebar mustache. His hair was as long and stringy as Donny's, and his jeans as faded. Wire-rimmed spectacles slid down his nose. He lounged in a canvas director's chair with his fingers laced across his chest, and he casually, amiably questioned Donny, who sat upright and glaring in an armchair.

"So they're getting on your back at school," said Cal. "Making a big deal about anything you do wrong."

"Right," said Donny.

"Any idea why that would be?"

"Oh, well, you know, stuff like homework and all," Donny said.

"You don't do your homework?" 20

"Oh, well, I might do it sometimes but not just exactly like they want it." Donny sat forward and said, "It's like a prison there, you know? You've got to go to every class, you can never step off the school grounds."

"You cut classes sometimes?"

"Sometimes," Donny said, with a glance at his parents.

Cal didn't seem perturbed. "Well," he said, "I'll tell you what. Let's you and me try working together three nights a week. Think you can handle that? We'll see if we can show that school of yours a thing or two. Give it a month; then if you don't like it, we'll stop. If I don't like it, we'll stop. I mean, sometimes people just don't get along, right? What do you say to that?"

"Okay," Donny said. He seemed pleased. 25

"Make it seven o'clock till eight, Monday, Wednesday, and Friday," Cal told Matt and Daisy. They nodded. Cal shambled to his feet, gave them a little salute, and showed them to the door.

This was where he lived as well as worked, evidently. The interview had taken place in the dining room, which had been transformed into a kind of office. Passing the living room, Daisy winced at the rock music she had been hearing, without registering it, ever since she had entered the house. She looked in and saw a boy about Donny's age lying on a sofa with a book. Another boy and a girl were playing Ping-Pong in front of the fireplace. "You have several here together?" Daisy asked Cal.

"Oh, sometimes they stay on after their sessions, just to rap. They're a pretty sociable group, all in all. Plenty of goof-offs like young Donny here."

He cuffed Donny's shoulder playfully. Donny flushed and grinned.

Climbing into the car, Daisy asked Donny, "Well? What do you think?" 30

But Donny had returned to his old evasive self. He jerked his chin toward the garage. "Look," he said. "He's got a basketball net."

Now on Mondays, Wednesdays, and Fridays, they had supper early—the instant Matt came home. Sometimes, they had to leave before they were really finished. Amanda would still be eating her dessert. "Bye, honey. Sorry," Daisy would tell her.

Cal's first bill sent a flutter of panic through Daisy's chest, but it was worth it, of course. Just look at Donny's face when they picked him up: alight and full of interest.

The principal telephoned Daisy to tell her how Donny had improved. "Of course, it hasn't shown up in his grades yet, but several of the teachers have noticed how his attitude's changed. Yes, sir, I think we're onto something here."

At home, Donny didn't act much different. He still seemed to have a low opinion of his parents. But Daisy supposed that was unavoidable—part of being fifteen. He said his parents were too "controlling"—a word that made Daisy give him a sudden look. He said they acted like wardens. On weekends, they enforced a curfew. And any time he went to a party, they always telephoned first to see if adults would be supervising. "For God's sake!" he said. "Don't you trust me?"

"It isn't a matter of trust, honey . . ." But there was no explaining to him. 35

His tutor called one afternoon. "I get the sense," he said, "that this kid's feeling . . . underestimated, you know? Like you folks expect the worst of him. I'm thinking we ought to give him more rope."

"But see, he's still so suggestible," Daisy said. "When his friends suggest some mischief—smoking or drinking or such—why, he just finds it hard not to go along with them."

"Mrs. Coble," the tutor said, "I think this kid is hurting. You know? Here's a serious, sensitive kid, telling you he'd like to take on some grown-up challenges, and you're giving him the message that he can't be trusted. Don't you understand how that hurts?"

"Oh," said Daisy.

"It undermines his self-esteem—don't you realize that?" 40

"Well, I guess you're right," said Daisy. She saw Donny suddenly from a whole new angle: his pathetically poor posture, that slouch so forlorn that his shoulders seemed about to meet his chin . . . oh, wasn't it awful being young? She'd had a miserable adolescence herself and had always sworn no child of hers would ever be that unhappy.

They let Donny stay out later, they didn't call ahead to see if the parties were supervised, and they were careful not to grill him about his evening. The tutor had set down so many rules! They were not allowed any questions at all about any aspect of school, nor were they to speak with his teachers. If a teacher had some complaint, she should phone Cal. Only one teacher disobeyed—the history teacher, Miss Evans. She called one morning in February. "I'm a little concerned about Donny, Mrs. Coble."

"Oh, I'm sorry, Miss Evans, but Donny's tutor handles these things now . . ."

"I always deal directly with the parents. You are the parent," Miss Evans said, speaking very slowly and distinctly. "Now, here is the problem. Back when you were helping Donny with his homework, his grades rose from to D to a C, but now they've slipped back, and they're closer to an F."

"They are?" 45

"I think you should start overseeing his homework again."

"But Donny's tutor says . . ."

"It's nice that Donny has a tutor, but you should still be in charge of his homework. With you, he learned it. Then he passed his tests. With the tutor, well, it seems the tutor is more of a crutch. 'Donny,' I say, 'a quiz is coming up on Friday. Hadn't you better be listening instead of talking?' 'That's okay, Miss Evans,' he says. 'I have a tutor now.' Like a talisman! I really think you ought to take over, Mrs. Coble."

"I see," said Daisy. "Well, I'll think about that. Thank you for calling."

Hanging up, she felt a rush of anger at Donny. A talisman! For a talisman, she'd 50 given up all luxuries, all that time with her daughter, her evenings at home!

She dialed Cal's number. He sounded muzzy. "I'm sorry if I woke you," she told him, "but Donny's history teacher just called. She says he isn't doing well."

"She should have dealt with me."

"She wants me to start supervising his homework again. His grades are slipping."

"Yes," said the tutor, "but you and I both know there's more to it than mere grades, don't we? I care about the *whole* child—his happiness, his self-esteem. The grades will come. Just give them time."

When she hung up, it was Miss Evans she was angry at. What a narrow woman!   55

It was Cal this, Cal that, Cal says this, Cal and I did that. Cal lent Donny an album by The Who. He took Donny and two other pupils to a rock concert. In March, when Donny began to talk endlessly on the phone with a girl named Miriam, Cal even let Miriam come to one of the tutoring sessions. Daisy was touched that Cal would grow so involved in Donny's life, but she was also a little hurt, because she had offered to have Miriam to dinner and Donny had refused. Now he asked them to drive her to Cal's house without a qualm.

This Miriam was an unappealing girl with blurry lipstick and masses of rough red hair. She wore a short, bulky jacket that would not have been out of place on a motorcycle. During the trip to Cal's she was silent, but coming back, she was more talkative. "What a neat guy, and what a house! All those kids hanging out, like a club. And the stereo playing rock . . . gosh, he's not like a grown-up at all! Married and divorced and everything, but you'd think he was our own age."

"Mr. Beadle was married?" Daisy asked.

"Yeah, to this really controlling lady. She didn't understand him a bit."

"No, I guess not," Daisy said.   60

Spring came, and the students who hung around at Cal's drifted out to the basketball net above the garage. Sometimes, when Daisy and Matt arrived to pick up Donny, they'd find him there with the others—spiky and excited, jittering on his toes beneath the backboard. It was staying light much longer now, and the neighboring fence cast narrow bars across the bright grass. Loud music would be spilling from Cal's windows. Once it was The Who, which Daisy recognized from the time that Donny had borrowed the album. "*Teenage Wasteland*,"° she said aloud, identifying the song, and Matt gave a short, dry laugh. "It certainly is," he said. He'd misunderstood; he thought she was commenting on the scene spread before them. In fact, she might have been. The players looked like hoodlums, even her son. Why, one of Cal's students had recently been knifed in a tavern. One had been shipped off to boarding school in midterm; two had been withdrawn by their parents. On the other hand, Donny had mentioned someone who'd been studying with Cal for five years. "Five years!" said Daisy. "Doesn't anyone ever stop needing him?"

Donny looked at her. Lately, whatever she said about Cal was read as criticism. "You're just feeling competitive," he said. "And controlling."

She bit her lip and said no more.

In April, the principal called to tell her that Donny had been expelled. There had been a locker check, and in Donny's locker they found five cans of beer and half a pack of cigarettes. With Donny's previous record, his offense meant expulsion.

"*Teenage Wasteland*": the song is actually titled "Baba O'Riley," by Pete Townshend, from The Who's album *Who's Next* (1971); it is also the theme song of the television series *CSI: NY*.

Daisy gripped the receiver tightly and said, "Well, where is he now?"   65

"We've sent him home," said Mr. Lanham. "He's packed up all his belongings, and he's coming home on foot."

Daisy wondered what she would say to him. She felt him looming closer and closer, bringing this brand-new situation that no one had prepared her to handle. What other place would take him? Could they enter him in public school? What were the rules? She stood at the living room window, waiting for him to show up. Gradually, she realized that he was taking too long. She checked the clock. She stared up the street again.

When an hour had passed, she phoned the school. Mr. Lanham's secretary answered and told her in a grave, sympathetic voice that yes, Donny Coble had most definitely gone home. Daisy called her husband. He was out of the office. She went back to the window and thought awhile, and then she called Donny's tutor.

"Donny's been expelled from school," she said, "and now I don't know where he's gone. I wonder if you've heard from him?"

There was a long silence. "Donny's with me, Mrs. Coble," he finally said.   70

"With you? How'd he get there?"

"He hailed a cab, and I paid the driver."

"Could I speak to him, please?"

There was another silence. "Maybe it'd be better if we had a conference," Cal said.

"I don't *want* a conference. I've been standing at the window picturing him dead   75
or kidnapped or something, and now you tell me you want a—"

"Donny is very, very upset. Understandably so," said Cal. "Believe me, Mrs. Coble, this is not what it seems. Have you asked Donny's side of the story?"

"Well, of course not, how could I? He went running off to you instead."

"Because he didn't feel he'd be listened to."

"But I haven't even—"

"Why don't you come out and talk? The three of us," said Cal, "will try to get   80
this thing in perspective."

"Well, all right," Daisy said. But she wasn't as reluctant as she sounded. Already, she felt soothed by the calm way Cal was taking this.

Cal answered the doorbell at once. He said, "Hi, there," and led her into the dining room. Donny sat slumped in a chair, chewing the knuckle of one thumb. "Hello, Donny," Daisy said. He flicked his eyes in her direction.

"Sit here, Mrs. Coble," said Cal, placing her opposite Donny. He himself remained standing, restlessly pacing. "So," he said.

Daisy stole a look at Donny. His lips were swollen, as if he'd been crying.

"You know," Cal told Daisy, "I kind of expected something like this. That's a   85
very punitive school you've got him in—you realize that. And any half-decent lawyer will tell you they've violated his civil rights. Locker checks! Where's their search warrant?"

"But if the rule is—" Daisy said.

"Well, anyhow, let him tell you his side."

She looked at Donny. He said, "It wasn't my fault. I promise."

"They said your locker was full of beer."

"It was a put-up job! See, there's this guy that doesn't like me. He put all these   90
beers in my locker and started a rumor going, so Mr. Lanham ordered a locker check."

"What was the boy's name?" Daisy asked.

"Huh?"

"Mrs. Coble, take my word, the situation is not so unusual," Cal said. "You can't imagine how vindictive kids can be sometimes."

"What was the boy's *name*," said Daisy, "so that I can ask Mr. Lanham if that's who suggested he run a locker check."

"You don't believe me," Donny said.   95

"And how'd this boy get your combination in the first place?"

"Frankly," said Cal, "I wouldn't be surprised to learn the school was in on it. Any kid that marches to a different drummer, why, they'd just love an excuse to get rid of him. The school is where I lay the blame."

"Doesn't *Donny* ever get blamed?"

"Now, Mrs. Coble, you heard what he—"

"Forget it," Donny told Cal. "You can see she doesn't trust me."   100

Daisy drew in a breath to say that of course she trusted him—a reflex. But she knew that bold-faced, wide-eyed look of Donny's. He had worn that look when he was small, denying some petty misdeed with the evidence plain as day all around him. Still, it was hard for her to accuse him outright. She temporized and said, "The only thing I'm sure of is that they've kicked you out of school, and now I don't know what we're going to do."

"We'll fight it," said Cal.

"We can't. Even you must see we can't."

"I could apply to Brantly," Donny said.

Cal stopped his pacing to beam down at him. "Brantly! Yes. They're really onto   105
where a kid is coming from, at Brantly. Why, *I* could get you into Brantly. I work with a lot of their students."

Daisy had never heard of Brantly, but already she didn't like it. And she didn't like Cal's smile, which struck her now as feverish and avid—a smile of hunger.

On the fifteenth of April, they entered Donny in a public school, and they stopped his tutoring sessions. Donny fought both decisions bitterly. Cal, surprisingly enough, did not object. He admitted he'd made no headway with Donny and said it was because Donny was emotionally disturbed.

Donny went to his new school every morning, plodding off alone with his head down. He did his assignments, and he earned average grades, but he gathered no friends, joined no clubs. There was something exhausted and defeated about him.

The first week in June, during final exams, Donny vanished. He simply didn't come home one afternoon, and no one at school remembered seeing him. The police were reassuring, and for the first few days, they worked hard. They combed Donny's sad, messy room for clues; they visited Miriam and Cal. But then they started talking about the number of kids who ran away every year. Hundreds, just in this city. "He'll show up if he wants to," they said. "If he doesn't, he won't."

Evidently, Donny didn't want to.   110

It's been three months now and still no word. Matt and Daisy still look for him in every crowd of awkward, heartbreaking teenage boys. Every time the phone rings, they imagine it might be Donny. Both parents have aged. Donny's sister seems to be staying away from home as much as possible.

At night, Daisy lies awake and goes over Donny's life. She is trying to figure out what went wrong, where they made their first mistake. Often, she finds herself blaming Cal, although she knows he didn't begin it. Then at other times she excuses him, for without him, Donny might have left earlier. Who really knows? In the end, she can only sigh and search for a cooler spot on the pillow. As she falls asleep, she occasionally glimpses something in the corner of her vision. It's something fleet and round, a ball—a basketball. It flies up, it sinks through the hoop, descends, lands in a yard littered with last year's leaves and striped with bars of sunlight as white as bones, bleached and parched and cleanly picked.

Questions

1. From whose point of view is the story told? How would you characterize the method employed—omniscient, limited omniscient, or objective?
2. What is the significance of the opening paragraph of the story?
3. Daisy is extremely self-conscious and concerned about how others view her. Find instances of this trait in the text. How does it affect her approach to raising her children?
4. Why is it ironic that Daisy was once a teacher?
5. What is ironic about the tutor Cal's appearance and behavior? What about Cal's attitude toward grades?
6. Daisy's attitude toward Cal undergoes frequent and at times rapid changes. Find examples in the text. What does she seem to think of him by the end of the story?
7. How does the portrayal of Donny's sister, Amanda, help to clarify the larger concerns of the story?
8. How do the other students tutored by Cal turn out? What is ironic about their outcomes?
9. Would you describe Tyler's presentation of Daisy as satirical or sympathetic? Can it be both at once? Explain.

■ WRITING *effectively*

Ernest Hemingway on Writing

The Direct Style   1964

"When you write," he [Hemingway] said, "your object is to convey every sensation, sight, feeling, emotion, to the reader. So you have to work over what you write. If you use a pencil, you get three different views of it to see if you are getting it across the way you want to. First, when you read it over, then when it is typed, and again in proof. And it keeps it fluid longer so that you can improve it easier."

"How do you ever learn to convey every sensation, sight and feeling to the reader? Just keep working at it for forty-odd years the way you have? Are there any tricks?"

Ernest Hemingway

"No. The hardest trade in the world to do is the writing of straight, honest prose about human beings. But there are ways you can train yourself."

"How?"

"When you walk into a room and you get a certain feeling or emotion, remember back until you see exactly what it was that gave you the emotion. Remember what the noises and smells were and what was said. Then write it down, making it clear so the reader will see it too and have the same feeling you had. And watch people, observe, try to put yourself in somebody else's head. If two men argue, don't just think who is right and who is wrong. Think what both their sides are. As a man, you know who is right and who is wrong; you have to judge. As a writer, you should not judge, you should understand."

From "An Afternoon with Hemingway" by Edward Stafford

THINKING ABOUT TONE AND STYLE

If you look around a crowded classroom, you will notice—consciously or not—the styles of your fellow students. The way they dress, talk, and even sit conveys information about their attitudes. A haircut, T-shirt, tattoo, or piece of jewelry all silently say something. Similarly, a writer's style—his or her own distinct voice—can give the reader crucial extra information. To analyze a writer's style, think about:

- **Diction: Consider the flavor of words chosen by the author for a particular story.** In "A Clean, Well-Lighted Place," for example, Hemingway favors simple, unemotional, and descriptive language, whereas in "The Storm," Chopin uses extravagant and emotionally charged diction. Each choice reveals something important about the story.

- **Sentence structure: Look for patterns in a story's sentence structure.** Hemingway is famous for his short, clipped sentences, which often repeat certain key words. Faulkner, however, favors complex, elaborate syntax that immerses the reader in the emotion of the narrative.

- **Tone: Try to determine the writer's attitude toward the story he or she is telling.** In "The Gospel According to Mark," Borges uses dispassionate restraint to present a central irony, a tragic misunderstanding that will doom his protagonist. Tan's "A Pair of Tickets," by contrast, creates a tone of hushed excitement and direct emotional involvement.

- **Organization: Examine the order in which information is presented.** Borges tells his story in a straightforward, chronological manner, which eventually makes it possible for us to appreciate the tale's complex undercurrents. Other stories (for example, Atwood's "Happy Endings") present the narrative's events in more complicated and surprising ways.

CHECKLIST: Writing About Tone and Style

☐ Does the writer use word choice in a distinctive way?

☐ Is the diction unusual in any way?

☐ Does the author tend toward long or short—even fragmented— sentences?

☐ How would you characterize the writer's voice? Is it formal or casual? Distant or intimate? Impassioned or restrained?

☐ Can the narrator's words be taken at face value? Is there anything ironic about the narrator's voice?

☐ How does the writer arrange the material? Is information delivered chronologically, or is the organization more complex?

☐ What is the writer's attitude toward the material?

WRITING ASSIGNMENT ON TONE AND STYLE

Examine a short story with a style you admire. Write an essay in which you analyze the author's approach toward diction, sentence structure, tone, and organization. How do these elements work together to create a certain mood? How does that mood contribute to the story's meaning? If your chosen story has a first-person narrator, how do stylistic choices help to create a sense of that particular character?

MORE TOPICS FOR WRITING

1. Write a brief analysis of irony in "Teenage Wasteland," "The Gift of the Magi," or "The Jilting of Granny Weatherall." What sorts of irony does your story employ?

2. Consider a short story in which the narrator is the central character, perhaps "A & P," "Greasy Lake," "Araby," or "Cathedral." In a brief essay, show how the character of the narrator determines the style of the story. Examine language in particular—words or phrases, slang expressions, figures of speech, local or regional usage.

3. Write a page in which you describe eating a meal in the company of others. Using sensory details, convey a sense of the setting, the quality of the food, and the presence of your dining companions. Now rewrite your paragraph as Ernest Hemingway. Finally, rewrite it as William Faulkner.

4. In a paragraph, describe a city street as seen through the eyes of a college graduate who has just moved to the city to start a new career. Now describe that same street in the voice of an old woman walking home from the hospital where her husband has just died. Finally, describe the street in the voice of a teenage runaway. In each paragraph, refrain from identifying your character or saying anything about his or her circumstances. Simply present the street as each character would perceive it.

▶ TERMS FOR *review*

Tone ▶ The attitude toward a subject conveyed in a literary work. No single stylistic device creates tone; it is the net result of the various elements an author brings to creating the work's feeling and manner.

Style ▶ All the distinctive ways in which an author uses language to create a literary work. An author's style depends on his or her characteristic use of diction, imagery, tone, syntax, and figurative language.

Diction ▶ Word choice or vocabulary. Diction refers to the class of words that an author decides is appropriate to use in a particular work.

Irony ▶ A literary device in which a discrepancy of meaning is masked beneath the surface of the language. Irony is present when a writer says one thing but means something quite the opposite.

Dramatic irony ▶ Where the reader understands the implication and meaning of a situation and may foresee the oncoming disaster or triumph while the character does not.

Cosmic irony or irony of fate ▶ A type of situational irony that emphasizes the discrepancy between what characters deserve and what they get, between a character's aspirations and the treatment he or she receives at the hands of fate.

Verbal irony ▶ A statement in which the speaker or writer says the opposite of what is really meant. For example, a friend might say, "How graceful!" after you trip clumsily on a stair.

Sarcasm ▶ A conspicuously bitter form of irony in which the ironic statement is designed to hurt or mock its target.

6

THEME

To produce a mighty book,
you must choose a mighty theme.

—HERMAN MELVILLE

The **theme** of a story is whatever general idea or insight the entire story reveals. In some stories the theme is unmistakable. At the end of Aesop's fable about the council of the mice that can't decide who will bell the cat, the theme is stated in the moral: *It is easier to propose a thing than to carry it out.* In a work of commercial fiction, too, the theme (if any) is usually obvious. Consider a typical detective thriller in which, say, a rookie police officer trained in scientific methods of crime detection sets out to solve a mystery sooner than his or her rival, a veteran sleuth whose only laboratory is carried under his hat. Perhaps the veteran solves the case, leading to the conclusion (and the theme), "The old ways are the best ways after all." Another story by the same writer might dramatize the same rivalry but reverse the outcome, having the rookie win, thereby reversing the theme: "The times are changing! Let's shake loose from old-fashioned ways." In such commercial entertainments, a theme is like a length of rope with which the writer, patently and mechanically, trusses the story neatly (usually too neatly) into meaningful shape.

PLOT VERSUS THEME

In literary fiction, a theme is seldom so obvious. That is, a theme need not be a moral or a message; it may be what the events add up to, what the story is about. When we come to the end of a finely wrought short story such as Ernest Hemingway's "A Clean, Well-Lighted Place" (Chapter 5), it may be easy to sum up the plot—to say what happens—but it is more difficult to sum up the story's main idea. Evidently, Hemingway relates events—how a younger waiter gets rid of an old man and how an older waiter then goes to a coffee bar—but in themselves these events seem relatively slight, though the story as a whole seems large (for its size) and full of meaning. A **summary,** a brief condensation of the main idea or plot of a literary work, may be helpful, but it tends to focus on the surface events of a story. A theme aims for a deeper and more comprehensive statement of its larger meaning.

For the meaning, we must look to other elements in the story besides what happens in it. It is clear that Hemingway is most deeply interested in the thoughts and feelings of the older waiter, the character who has more and more to say as the story progresses, until at the end the story is entirely confined to his thoughts and perceptions. What is meaningful in these thoughts and perceptions? The older waiter understands the old man and sympathizes with his need for a clean, well-lighted place. If we say that, we are still talking about what happens in the story, though we have gone beyond merely recording its external events. But a theme is usually stated in *general* words. Another try: "Solitary people who cannot sleep need a cheerful, orderly place where they can drink with dignity." That's a little better. We have indicated, at least, that Hemingway's story is about more than just an old man and a couple of waiters. But what about the older waiter's meditation on *nada*, nothingness? Coming near the end of the story, it is given great emphasis, and probably no good statement of Hemingway's theme can leave it out. Still another try at a statement: "Solitary people need a place of refuge from their terrible awareness that their lives (or, perhaps, human lives) are essentially meaningless." Neither this nor any other statement of the story's theme is unarguably right, but at least the sentence helps the reader to bring into focus one primary idea that Hemingway seems to be driving at.

When we finish reading "A Clean, Well-Lighted Place," we feel that there is such a theme, a unifying vision, even though we cannot reduce it absolutely to a tag. Like some freshwater lake alive with creatures, Hemingway's story is a broad expanse, reflecting in many directions. No wonder that many readers will view it in different ways.

Moral inferences may be drawn from the story, no doubt, for Hemingway is indirectly giving us advice about properly regarding and sympathizing with the lonely, the uncertain, and the old. But the story doesn't set forth a lesson that we are supposed to put into practice. One could argue that "A Clean, Well-Lighted Place" contains *several* themes, and other statements could be made to include Hemingway's views of love, of communication between people, of dignity. Great short stories, like great symphonies, frequently have more than one theme.

THEME AS A UNIFYING DEVICE

In many a fine short story, theme is the center, the moving force, the principle of unity. Clearly, such a theme is something other than the characters and events of its story. To say of James Joyce's "Araby" (Chapter 11) that it is about a boy who goes to a bazaar to buy a gift for a young woman, only to arrive too late, is to summarize plot, not theme. (The theme *might* be put, "The illusions of a romantic youth are vulnerable," or it might be put in any of a few hundred other ways.) Although the title of Shirley Jackson's "The Lottery" (Chapter 7), with its hint of the lure of easy riches, may arouse pleasant expectations, which the neutral tone of the narrative does nothing to dispel, the theme—the larger realization that the story leaves us with—has to do with the ways in which cruel and insensitive attitudes can come to seem like normal and natural ones.

Sometimes you will hear it said that the theme of a story (say, Faulkner's "Barn Burning") is "loss of innocence" or "initiation into maturity," or that the theme of some other story (Hurston's "Sweat," for instance) is "the revolt of the downtrodden." This is to use theme in a larger and more abstract sense than we use it here. Although such general descriptions of theme can be useful—as in sorting a large number of stories into rough categories—we suggest that, in the beginning, you look for whatever truth or insight you think the writer of a story reveals. Try to sum it up *in a sentence.* By doing so, you will find yourself looking closely at the story, trying to define its principal meaning.

FINDING THE THEME

You may find it helpful, in making a sentence-statement of theme, to consider these questions:

1. Look back once more at the title of the story. From what you have read, what does it indicate?
2. Does the main character change in any way over the course of the story? Does this character arrive at any eventual realization or understanding? Are you left with any realization or understanding you did not have before?
3. Does the author make any general observations about life or human nature? Do the characters make any? (Caution: Characters now and again will utter opinions with which the reader is not necessarily supposed to agree.)
4. Does the story contain any especially curious objects, mysterious flat characters, significant animals, repeated names, song titles, or whatever, that hint at meanings larger than such things ordinarily have? In literary stories, such symbols may point to central themes.
5. When you have worded your statement of theme, have you cast it into general language, not just given a plot summary?
6. Does your statement hold true for the story as a whole, not for just part of it?

In distilling a statement of theme from a rich and complicated story, we have, of course, no more encompassed the whole story than a paleontologist taking a plaster mold of a petrified footprint has captured a living stegosaurus. A writer (other than a fabulist) does not usually set out with theme in hand, determined to make every detail in the story work to demonstrate it. Well then, the skeptical reader may ask, if only *some* stories have themes, if those themes may be hard to sum up, and if readers will probably disagree in their summations, why bother to state themes? Isn't it too much trouble? Surely it is, unless the effort to state a theme ends in pleasure and profit. Trying to sum up the point of a story in our own words is merely one way to make ourselves better aware of whatever we may have understood vaguely and tentatively. Attempted with loving care, such statements may bring into focus our scattered impressions of a rewarding story, may help to clarify and hold fast whatever wisdom the storyteller has offered us.

Chinua Achebe

Dead Men's Path

(1953) 1972

Chinua Achebe was born in Ogidi, a village in eastern Nigeria, in 1930. His father was a missionary schoolteacher, and Achebe had a devout Christian upbringing. A member of the Ibo tribe, the future writer grew up speaking Igbo, but at the age of eight, he began learning English. He went abroad to study at London University but returned to Africa to complete his B.A. at the University College of Ibadan in 1953. Achebe worked for years in Nigerian radio. Shortly after Nigeria's independence from Great Britain in 1963, civil war broke out, and the new nation split in two. Achebe left his job to join the Ministry of Information for Biafra, the new country

Chinua Achebe

created from eastern Nigeria. It was not until 1970 that the bloody civil war ended. Approximately one million Ibos lay dead from war, disease, and starvation as the defeated Biafrans reunited with Nigeria. Achebe is often considered Africa's premier novelist. His novels include Things Fall Apart *(1958),* No Longer at Ease *(1962),* A Man of the People *(1966), and* Anthills of the Savannah *(1987). His short stories have been collected in* Girls at War *(1972). He has also published poetry, children's stories, and several volumes of essays, the most recent of which is* Home and Exile *(2000). In 1990 Achebe suffered massive injuries in a car accident outside Lagos that left him paralyzed from the waist down. Following the accident, he taught at Bard College in upstate New York for almost nineteen years. In 1999 he visited Nigeria again after a deliberate nine-year absence to protest government dictatorship, and his homecoming became a national event. In 2007 he was awarded the second Man Booker International Prize for his lifetime contribution to world literature. He is currently at Brown University.*

Michael Obi's hopes were fulfilled much earlier than he had expected. He was appointed headmaster of Ndume Central School in January 1949. It had always been an unprogressive school, so the Mission authorities decided to send a young and energetic man to run it. Obi accepted this responsibility with enthusiasm. He had many wonderful ideas and this was an opportunity to put them into practice. He had had sound secondary school education which designated him a "pivotal teacher" in the official records and set him apart from the other headmasters in the mission field. He was outspoken in his condemnation of the narrow views of these older and often less-educated ones.

"We shall make a good job of it, shan't we?" he asked his young wife when they first heard the joyful news of his promotion.

"We shall do our best," she replied. "We shall have such beautiful gardens and everything will be just *modern* and delightful . . ." In their two years of married life she had become completely infected by his passion for "modern methods" and his denigration of "these old and superannuated people in the teaching field who would be better employed as traders in the Onitsha market." She began to see herself already as the admired wife of the young headmaster, the queen of the school.

The wives of the other teachers would envy her position. She would set the fashion in everything . . . Then, suddenly, it occurred to her that there might not be other wives. Wavering between hope and fear, she asked her husband, looking anxiously at him.

"All our colleagues are young and unmarried," he said with enthusiasm which for once she did not share. "Which is a good thing," he continued. 5

"Why?"

"Why? They will give all their time and energy to the school."

Nancy was downcast. For a few minutes she became skeptical about the new school; but it was only for a few minutes. Her little personal misfortune could not blind her to her husband's happy prospects. She looked at him as he sat folded up in a chair. He was stoop-shouldered and looked frail. But he sometimes surprised people with sudden bursts of physical energy. In his present posture, however, all his bodily strength seemed to have retired behind his deep-set eyes, giving them an extraordinary power of penetration. He was only twenty-six, but looked thirty or more. On the whole, he was not unhandsome.

"A penny for your thoughts, Mike," said Nancy after a while, imitating the woman's magazine she read.

"I was thinking what a grand opportunity we've got at last to show these people 10 how a school should be run."

*

Ndume School was backward in every sense of the word. Mr. Obi put his whole life into the work, and his wife hers too. He had two aims. A high standard of teaching was insisted upon, and the school compound was to be turned into a place of beauty. Nancy's dream-gardens came to life with the coming of the rains, and blossomed. Beautiful hibiscus and allamanda hedges in brilliant red and yellow marked out the carefully tended school compound from the rank neighborhood bushes.

One evening as Obi was admiring his work he was scandalized to see an old woman from the village hobble right across the compound, through a marigold flower-bed and the hedges. On going up there he found faint signs of an almost disused path from the village across the school compound to the bush on the other side.

"It amazes me," said Obi to one of his teachers who had been three years in the school, "that you people allowed the villagers to make use of this footpath. It is simply incredible." He shook his head.

"The path," said the teacher apologetically, "appears to be very important to them. Although it is hardly used, it connects the village shrine with their place of burial."

"And what has that got to do with the school?" asked the headmaster.   15

"Well, I don't know," replied the other with a shrug of the shoulders. "But I remember there was a big row some time ago when we attempted to close it."

"That was some time ago. But it will not be used now," said Obi as he walked away. "What will the Government Education Officer think of this when he comes to inspect the school next week? The villagers might, for all I know, decide to use the schoolroom for a pagan ritual during the inspection."

Heavy sticks were planted closely across the path at the two places where it entered and left the school premises. These were further strengthened with barbed wire.

Three days later the village priest of *Ani* called on the headmaster. He was an old man and walked with a slight stoop. He carried a stout walking-stick which he usually tapped on the floor, by way of emphasis, each time he made a new point in his argument.

"I have heard," he said after the usual exchange of cordialities, "that our ances-   20
tral footpath has recently been closed . . ."

"Yes," replied Mr. Obi. "We cannot allow people to make a highway of our school compound."

"Look here, my son," said the priest bringing down his walking-stick, "this path was here before you were born and before your father was born. The whole life of this village depends on it. Our dead relatives depart by it and our ancestors visit us by it. But most important, it is the path of children coming in to be born . . ."

Mr. Obi listened with a satisfied smile on his face.

"The whole purpose of our school," he said finally, "is to eradicate just such beliefs as that. Dead men do not require footpaths. The whole idea is just fantastic. Our duty is to teach your children to laugh at such ideas."

"What you say may be true," replied the priest, "but we follow the practices of   25
our fathers. If you reopen the path we shall have nothing to quarrel about. What I always say is: let the hawk perch and let the eagle perch." He rose to go.

"I am sorry," said the young headmaster. "But the school compound cannot be a thoroughfare. It is against our regulations. I would suggest your constructing another path, skirting our premises. We can even get our boys to help in building it. I don't suppose the ancestors will find the little detour too burdensome."

"I have no more words to say," said the old priest, already outside.

Two days later a young woman in the village died in childbed. A diviner was immediately consulted and he prescribed heavy sacrifices to propitiate ancestors insulted by the fence.

Obi woke up next morning among the ruins of his work. The beautiful hedges were torn up not just near the path but right round the school, the flowers trampled to death and one of the school buildings pulled down . . . That day, the white Supervisor came to inspect the school and wrote a nasty report on the state of the premises but more seriously about the "tribal-war situation developing between the school and the village, arising in part from the misguided zeal of the new headmaster."

Questions

1. How would you describe the personalities of the main characters Michael Obi and the village priest?
2. What are the headmaster's motivations for wanting to improve the school?
3. Why does the village priest visit the school? What choices does he offer the headmaster?
4. What significance do you see in the story's title, "Dead Men's Path"?
5. What ironies do you see in the story?
6. What theme in the story seems most important to you? Is it stated anywhere in the story?

Alice Munro

How I Met My Husband   1974

Alice Munro, one of the most widely admired contemporary Canadian writers, was born of farm parents in 1931 in Wingham, in southwestern Ontario, an area in which she has spent most of her life. Its small-town people figure in many of her stories. For two years, she attended the University of Western Ontario, but dropped out at twenty, after her first marriage. The mother of three daughters, Munro is a particularly sensitive explorer of the relations between parents and children, yet she ranges widely in choosing her themes. She has published over a dozen remarkable collections of short fiction, including Dance of the Happy Shades *(1968),* The Beggar Maid *(1982),* The Love of a Good Woman *(1998), and* Too Much Happiness *(2009). Munro's* Selected Stories

Alice Munro

appeared in 1996, confirming her position as one of the greatest living masters of short fiction. Three of her books have won Canada's prestigious Governor General's Literary Award; in the United States she has won the National Book Critics Circle Award. The short story is her true medium, and she has declared her preference for "the story that will zero in and give you intense, but not connected, moments of experience."

We heard the plane come over at noon, roaring through the radio news, and we were sure it was going to hit the house, so we all ran out into the yard. We saw it come in over the treetops, all red and silver, the first close-up plane I ever saw. Mrs. Peebles screamed.

"Crash landing," their little boy said. Joey was his name.

"It's okay," said Dr. Peebles. "He knows what he's doing." Dr. Peebles was only an animal doctor, but had a calming way of talking, like any doctor.

This was my first job—working for Dr. and Mrs. Peebles, who had bought an old house out on the Fifth Line, about five miles out of town. It was just when the trend was starting of town people buying up old farms, not to work them but to live on them.

We watched the plane land across the road, where the fairgrounds used to be. It did make a good landing field, nice and level for the old race track, and the barns and display sheds torn down now for scrap lumber so there was nothing in the way. Even the old grandstand bays had burned.

"All right," said Mrs. Peebles, snappy as she always was when she got over her nerves. "Let's go back in the house. Let's not stand here gawking like a set of farmers."

She didn't say that to hurt my feelings. It never occurred to her.

I was just setting the dessert down when Loretta Bird arrived, out of breath, at the screen door.

"I thought it was going to crash into the house and kill youse all!"

She lived on the next place and the Peebleses thought she was a country-woman, they didn't know the difference. She and her husband didn't farm, he worked on the roads and had a bad name for drinking. They had seven children and couldn't get credit at the HiWay Grocery. The Peebleses made her welcome, not knowing any better, as I say, and offered her dessert.

Dessert was never anything to write home about, at their place. A dish of Jell-O or sliced bananas or fruit out of a tin. "Have a house without a pie, be ashamed until you die," my mother used to say, but Mrs. Peebles operated differently.

Loretta Bird saw me getting the can of peaches.

"Oh, never mind," she said. "I haven't got the right kind of a stomach to trust what comes out of those tins, I can only eat home canning."

I could have slapped her. I bet she never put down fruit in her life.

"I know what he's landed here for," she said. "He's got permission to use the fair-grounds and take people up for rides. It costs a dollar. It's the same fellow who was over at Palmerston° last week and was up the lakeshore before that. I wouldn't go up, if you paid me."

"I'd jump at the chance," Dr. Peebles said. "I'd like to see this neighborhood from the air."

Mrs. Peebles said she would just as soon see it from the ground. Joey said he wanted to go and Heather did, too. Joey was nine and Heather was seven.

"Would you, Edie?" Heather said.

I said I didn't know. I was scared, but I never admitted that, especially in front of children I was taking care of.

"People are going to be coming out here in their cars raising dust and trampling your property, if I was you I would complain," Loretta said. She hooked her legs around the chair rung and I knew we were in for a lengthy visit. After Dr. Peebles went back to his office or out on his next call and Mrs. Peebles went for her nap, she

Palmerston: a town in southern Ontario, Canada.

would hang around me while I was trying to do the dishes. She would pass remarks about the Peebleses in their own house.

"She wouldn't find time to lay down in the middle of the day, if she had seven kids like I got."

She asked me did they fight and did they keep things in the dresser drawer not to have babies with. She said it was a sin if they did. I pretended I didn't know what she was talking about.

I was fifteen and away from home for the first time. My parents had made the effort and sent me to high school for a year, but I didn't like it. I was shy of strangers and the work was hard, they didn't make it nice for you or explain the way they do now. At the end of the year the averages were published in the paper, and mine came out at the very bottom, 37 percent. My father said that's enough and I didn't blame him. The last thing I wanted, anyway, was to go on and end up teaching school. It happened the very day the paper came out with my disgrace in it, Dr. Peebles was staying at our place for dinner, having just helped one of the cows have twins, and he said I looked smart to him and his wife was looking for a girl to help. He said she felt tied down, with the two children, out in the country. I guess she would, my mother said, being polite, though I could tell from her face she was wondering what on earth it would be like to have only two children and no barn work, and then to be complaining.

When I went home I would describe to them the work I had to do, and it made everybody laugh. Mrs. Peebles had an automatic washer and dryer, the first I ever saw. I have had those in my own home for such a long time now it's hard to remember how much of a miracle it was to me, not having to struggle with the wringer and hang up and haul down. Let alone not having to heat water. Then there was practically no baking. Mrs. Peebles said she couldn't make pie crust, the most amazing thing I ever heard a woman admit. I could, of course, and I could make light biscuits and a white cake and dark cake, but they didn't want it, she said they watched their figures. The only thing I didn't like about working there, in fact, was feeling half hungry a lot of the time. I used to bring back a box of doughnuts made out at home, and hide them under my bed. The children found out, and I didn't mind sharing, but I thought I better bind them to secrecy.

The day after the plane landed Mrs. Peebles put both children in the car and drove over to Chesley, to get their hair cut. There was a good woman then at Chesley for doing hair. She got hers done at the same place, Mrs. Peebles did, and that meant they would be gone a good while. She had to pick a day Dr. Peebles wasn't going out into the country, she didn't have her own car. Cars were still in short supply then, after the war.

I loved being left in the house alone, to do my work at leisure. The kitchen was all white and bright yellow, with fluorescent lights. That was before they ever thought of making the appliances all different colors and doing the cupboards like dark old wood and hiding the lighting. I loved light. I loved the double sink. So would anybody new-come from washing dishes in a dishpan with a rag-plugged hole on an oilcloth-covered table by light of a coal-oil lamp. I kept everything shining.

The bathroom too. I had a bath in there once a week. They wouldn't have minded if I took one oftener, but to me it seemed like asking too much, or maybe risking making it less wonderful. The basin and the tub and the toilet were all pink, and there were glass doors with flamingoes painted on them, to shut off the tub. The light had a rosy cast and the mat sank under your feet like snow, except that it was warm. The mirror was three-way. With the mirror all steamed up and the air like a perfume cloud, from things I was allowed to use, I stood up on the side of the tub and admired myself naked, from three directions. Sometimes I thought about the way we lived out at home and the way we lived

25

here and how one way was so hard to imagine when you were living the other way. But I thought it was still a lot easier, living the way we lived at home, to picture something like this, the painted flamingoes and the warmth and the soft mat, than it was anybody knowing only things like this to picture how it was the other way. And why was that?

I was through my jobs in no time, and had the vegetables peeled for supper and sitting in cold water besides. Then I went into Mrs. Peebles' bedroom. I had been in there plenty of times, cleaning, and I always took a good look in her closet, at the clothes she had hanging there. I wouldn't have looked in her drawers, but a closet is open to anybody. That's a lie. I would have looked in drawers, but I would have felt worse doing it and been more scared she could tell.

Some clothes in her closet she wore all the time, I was quite familiar with them. Others she never put on, they were pushed to the back. I was disappointed to see no wedding dress. But there was one long dress I could just see the skirt of, and I was hungering to see the rest. Now I took note of where it hung and lifted it out. It was satin, a lovely weight on my arm, light bluish-green in color, almost silvery. It had a fitted, pointed waist and a full skirt and an off-the-shoulder fold hiding the little sleeves.

Next thing was easy. I got out of my own things and slipped it on. I was slimmer at fifteen than anybody would believe who knows me now and the fit was beautiful. I didn't, of course, have a strapless bra on, which was what it needed, I just had to slide my straps down my arms under the material. Then I tried pinning up my hair, to get the effect. One thing led to another. I put on rouge and lipstick and eyebrow pencil from her dresser. The heat of the day and the weight of the satin and all the excitement made me thirsty, and I went out to the kitchen, got-up as I was, to get a glass of ginger ale with ice cubes from the refrigerator. The Peebleses drank ginger ale, or fruit drinks, all day, like water, and I was getting so I did too. Also there was no limit on ice cubes, which I was so fond of I would even put them in a glass of milk.

I turned from putting the ice tray back and saw a man watching me through the screen. It was the luckiest thing in the world I didn't spill the ginger ale down the front of me then and there.

"I never meant to scare you. I knocked but you were getting the ice out, you didn't hear me."

I couldn't see what he looked like, he was dark the way somebody is pressed up against a screen door with the bright daylight behind them. I only knew he wasn't from around here.

"I'm from the plane over there. My name is Chris Watters and what I was wondering was if I could use that pump."

There was a pump in the yard. That was the way the people used to get their water. Now I noticed he was carrying a pail.

"You're welcome," I said. "I can get it from the tap and save you pumping." I guess I wanted him to know we had piped water, didn't pump ourselves.

"I don't mind the exercise." He didn't move, though, and finally he said, "Were you going to a dance?"

Seeing a stranger there had made me entirely forget how I was dressed.

"Or is that the way ladies around here generally get dressed up in the afternoon?" I didn't know how to joke back then. I was too embarrassed.

"You live here? Are you the lady of the house?"

"I'm the hired girl."

Some people change when they find that out, their whole way of looking at you and speaking to you changes, but his didn't.

"Well, I just wanted to tell you you look very nice. I was so surprised when I looked in the door and saw you. Just because you looked so nice and beautiful."

I wasn't even old enough then to realize how out of the common it is, for a man to say something like that to a woman, or somebody he is treating like a woman. For a man to say a word like *beautiful*. I wasn't old enough to realize or to say anything back, or in fact to do anything but wish he would go away. Not that I didn't like him, but just that it upset me so, having him look at me, and me trying to think of something to say.

He must have understood. He said good-bye, and thanked me, and went and started filling his pail from the pump. I stood behind the Venetian blinds in the dining room, watching him. When he had gone, I went into the bedroom and took the dress off and put it back in the same place. I dressed in my own clothes and took my hair down and washed my face, wiping it on Kleenex, which I threw in the wastebasket.

The Peebleses asked me what kind of man he was. Young, middle-aged, short, tall? I couldn't say.

"Good-looking?" Dr. Peebles teased me.

I couldn't think a thing but that he would be coming to get his water again, he would be talking to Dr. or Mrs. Peebles, making friends with them, and he would mention seeing me that first afternoon, dressed up. Why not mention it? He would think it was funny. And no idea of the trouble it would get me into.

After supper the Peebleses drove into town to go to a movie. She wanted to go somewhere with her hair fresh done. I sat in my bright kitchen wondering what to do, knowing I would never sleep. Mrs. Peebles might not fire me, when she found out, but it would give her a different feeling about me altogether. This was the first place I ever worked but I already had picked up things about the way people feel when you are working for them. They like to think you aren't curious. Not just that you aren't dishonest, that isn't enough. They like to feel you don't notice things, that you don't think or wonder about anything but what they liked to eat and how they liked things ironed, and so on. I don't mean they weren't kind to me, because they were. They had me eat my meals with them (to tell the truth I expected to, I didn't know there were families who don't) and sometimes they took me along in the car. But all the same.

I went up and checked on the children being asleep and then I went out. I had to do it. I crossed the road and went in the old fairgrounds gate. The plane looked unnatural sitting there, and shining with the moon. Off at the far side of the fairgrounds where the bush was taking over, I saw his tent.

He was sitting outside it smoking a cigarette. He saw me coming.

"Hello, were you looking for a plane ride? I don't start taking people up till tomorrow." Then he looked again and said, "Oh, it's you. I didn't know you without your long dress on."

My heart was knocking away, my tongue was dried up. I had to say something. But I couldn't. My throat was closed and I was like a deaf-and-dumb.

"Did you want a ride? Sit down. Have a cigarette."

I couldn't even shake my head to say no, so he gave me one.

"Put it in your mouth or I can't light it. It's a good thing I'm used to shy ladies."

I did. It wasn't the first time I had smoked a cigarette, actually. My girlfriend out home, Muriel Lowe, used to steal them from her brother.

"Look at your hand shaking. Did you just want to have a chat, or what?"

In one burst I said, "I wisht you wouldn't say anything about that dress."

"What dress? Oh, the long dress."

"It's Mrs. Peebles'."

"Whose? Oh, the lady you work for? She wasn't home so you got dressed up in her dress, eh? You got dressed up and played queen. I don't blame you. You're not smoking the cigarette right. Don't just puff. Draw it in. Did anybody ever show you how to inhale? Are you scared I'll tell on you? Is that it?"

I was so ashamed at having to ask him to connive this way I couldn't nod. I just looked at him and he saw yes.

"Well I won't. I won't in the slightest way mention it or embarrass you. I give you my word of honor."

Then he changed the subject, to help me out, seeing I couldn't even thank him. "What do you think of this sign?"

It was a board sign lying practically at my feet.

SEE THE WORLD FROM THE SKY. ADULTS $1.00, CHILDREN 50¢. QUALIFIED PILOT.

"My old sign was getting pretty beat up, I thought I'd make a new one. That's what I've been doing with my time today."

The lettering wasn't all that handsome, I thought. I could have done a better one in half an hour.

"I'm not an expert at sign making."

"It's very good," I said.

"I don't need it for publicity, word of mouth is usually enough. I turned away two carloads tonight. I felt like taking it easy. I didn't tell them ladies were dropping in to visit me."

Now I remembered the children and I was scared again, in case one of them had waked up and called me and I wasn't there.

"Do you have to go so soon?"

I remembered some manners. "Thank you for the cigarette."

"Don't forget. You have my word of honor."

I tore off across the fairgrounds, scared I'd see the car heading home from town. My sense of time was mixed up, I didn't know how long I'd been out of the house. But it was all right, it wasn't late, the children were asleep. I got in my bed myself and lay thinking what a lucky end to the day, after all, and among things to be grateful for I could be grateful Loretta Bird hadn't been the one who caught me.

The yard and borders didn't get trampled, it wasn't as bad as that. All the same it seemed very public, around the house. The sign was on the fairgrounds gate. People came mostly after supper but a good many in the afternoon, too. The Bird children all came without fifty cents between them and hung on the gate. We got used to the excitement of the plane coming in and taking off, it wasn't excitement anymore. I never went over, after that one time, but would see him when he came to get his water. I would be out on the steps doing sitting-down work, like preparing vegetables, if I could.

"Why don't you come over? I'll take you up in my plane."

"I'm saving my money," I said, because I couldn't think of anything else.

"For what? For getting married?"

I shook my head.

"I'll take you up for free if you come sometime when it's slack. I thought you would come, and have another cigarette." 85

I made a face to hush him, because you never could tell when the children would be sneaking around the porch, or Mrs. Peebles herself listening in the house. Sometimes she came out and had a conversation with him. He told her things he hadn't bothered to tell me. But then I hadn't thought to ask. He told her he had been in the war, that was where he learned to fly a plane, and how he couldn't settle down to ordinary life, this was what he liked. She said she couldn't imagine anybody liking such a thing. Though sometimes, she said, she was almost bored enough to try anything herself, she wasn't brought up to living in the country. It's all my husband's idea, she said. This was news to me.

"Maybe you ought to give flying lessons," she said.

"Would you take them?"

She just laughed.

Sunday was a busy flying day in spite of it being preached against from two pulpits. We were all sitting out watching. Joey and Heather were over on the fence with the Bird kids. Their father had said they could go, after their mother saying all week they couldn't. 90

A car came down the road past the parked cars and pulled up right in the drive. It was Loretta Bird who got out, all importance, and on the driver's side another woman got out, more sedately. She was wearing sunglasses.

"This is a lady looking for the man that flies the plane," Loretta Bird said. "I heard her inquire in the hotel coffee shop where I was having a Coke and I brought her out."

"I'm sorry to bother you," the lady said. "I'm Alice Kelling, Mr. Watters' fiancée."

This Alice Kelling had on a pair of brown and white checked slacks and a yellow top. Her bust looked to me rather low and bumpy. She had a worried face. Her hair had had a permanent, but had grown out, and she wore a yellow band to keep it off her face. Nothing in the least pretty or even young-looking about her. But you could tell from how she talked she was from the city, or educated, or both.

Dr. Peebles stood up and introduced himself and his wife and me and asked her to be seated. 95

"He's up in the air right now, but you're welcome to sit and wait. He gets his water here and he hasn't been yet. He'll probably take his break about five."

"That is him, then?" said Alice Kelling, wrinkling and straining at the sky.

"He's not in the habit of running out on you, taking a different name?" Dr. Peebles laughed. He was the one, not his wife, to offer iced tea. Then she sent me into the kitchen to fix it. She smiled. She was wearing sunglasses too.

"He never mentioned his fiancée," she said.

I loved fixing iced tea with lots of ice and slices of lemon in tall glasses. I ought to have mentioned before, Dr. Peebles was an abstainer, at least around the house, or I wouldn't have been allowed to take the place. I had to fix a glass for Loretta Bird too, though it galled me, and when I went out she had settled in my lawn chair, leaving me the steps. 100

"I knew you was a nurse when I first heard you in that coffee shop."

"How would you know a thing like that?"

"I get my hunches about people. Was that how you met him, nursing?"

"Chris? Well yes. Yes, it was."

"Oh, were you overseas?" said Mrs. Peebles. 105

"No, it was before he went overseas. I nursed him when he was stationed at Centralia and had a ruptured appendix. We got engaged and then he went overseas. My, this is refreshing, after a long drive."

"He'll be glad to see you," Dr. Peebles said. "It's a rackety kind of life, isn't it, not staying one place long enough to really make friends."

"Youse've had a long engagement," Loretta Bird said.

Alice Kelling passed that over. "I was going to get a room at the hotel, but when I was offered directions I came on out. Do you think I could phone them?"

"No need," Dr. Peebles said. "You're five miles away from him if you stay at the 110 hotel. Here, you're right across the road. Stay with us. We've got rooms on rooms, look at this big house."

Asking people to stay, just like that, is certainly a country thing, and maybe seemed natural to him now, but not to Mrs. Peebles, from the way she said, oh yes, we have plenty of room. Or to Alice Kelling, who kept protesting, but let herself be worn down. I got the feeling it was a temptation to her, to be that close. I was trying for a look at her ring. Her nails were painted red, her fingers were freckled and wrinkled. It was a tiny stone. Muriel Lowe's cousin had one twice as big.

Chris came to get his water, late in the afternoon just as Dr. Peebles had predicted. He must have recognized the car from a way off. He came smiling.

"Here I am chasing after you to see what you're up to," called Alice Kelling. She got up and went to meet him and they kissed, just touched, in front of us.

"You're going to spend a lot on gas that way," Chris said.

Dr. Peebles invited Chris to stay for supper, since he had already put up the sign 115 that said: NO MORE RIDES TILL 7 P.M. Mrs. Peebles wanted it served in the yard, in spite of the bugs. One thing strange to anybody from the country is this eating outside. I had made a potato salad earlier and she had made a jellied salad, that was one thing she could do, so it was just a matter of getting those out, and some sliced meat and cucumbers and fresh leaf lettuce. Loretta Bird hung around for some time saying, "Oh, well, I guess I better get home to those yappers," and, "It's so nice just sitting here, I sure hate to get up," but nobody invited her, I was relieved to see, and finally she had to go.

That night after rides were finished Alice Kelling and Chris went off somewhere in her car. I lay awake till they got back. When I saw the car lights sweep my ceiling I got up to look down on them through the slats of my blind. I don't know what I thought I was going to see. Muriel Lowe and I used to sleep on her front veranda and watch her sister and her sister's boy friend saying good night. Afterward we couldn't get to sleep, for longing for somebody to kiss us and rub against us and we would talk about suppose you were out in a boat with a boy and he wouldn't bring you in to shore unless you did it, or what if somebody got you trapped in a barn, you would have to, wouldn't you, it wouldn't be your fault. Muriel said her two girl cousins used to try with a toilet paper roll that one of them was a boy. We wouldn't do anything like that; just lay and wondered.

All that happened was that Chris got out of the car on one side and she got out on the other and they walked off separately—him toward the fairgrounds and her toward the house. I got back in bed and imagined about me coming home with him, not like that.

Next morning Alice Kelling got up late and I fixed a grapefruit for her the way I had learned and Mrs. Peebles sat down with her to visit and have another cup of coffee. Mrs. Peebles seemed pleased enough now, having company. Alice Kelling said she guessed she better get used to putting in a day just watching Chris take off and come down, and Mrs. Peebles said she didn't know if she should suggest it because

Alice Kelling was the one with the car, but the lake was only twenty-five miles away and what a good day for a picnic.

Alice Kelling took her up on the idea and by eleven o'clock they were in the car, with Joey and Heather and a sandwich lunch I had made. The only thing was that Chris hadn't come down, and she wanted to tell him where they were going.

"Edie'll go over and tell him," Mrs. Peebles said. "There's no problem."   120

Alice Kelling wrinkled her face and agreed.

"Be sure and tell him we'll be back by five!"

I didn't see that he would be concerned about knowing this right away, and I thought of him eating whatever he ate over there, alone, cooking on his camp stove, so I got to work and mixed up a crumb cake and baked it, in between the other work I had to do; then, when it was a bit cooled, wrapped it in a tea towel. I didn't do anything to myself but take off my apron and comb my hair. I would like to have put some makeup on, but I was too afraid it would remind him of the way he first saw me, and that would humiliate me all over again.

He had come and put another sign on the gate: NO RIDES THIS P.M. APOLOGIES. I worried that he wasn't feeling well. No sign of him outside and the tent flap was down. I knocked on the pole.

"Come in," he said, in a voice that would just as soon have said *Stay out*.   125

I lifted the flap.

"Oh, it's you. I'm sorry. I didn't know it was you."

He had been just sitting on the side of the bed, smoking. Why not at least sit and smoke in the fresh air?

"I brought a cake and hope you're not sick," I said.

"Why would I be sick? Oh—that sign. That's all right. I'm just tired of talking to   130
people. I don't mean you. Have a seat." He pinned back the tent flap. "Get some fresh air in here."

I sat on the edge of the bed, there was no place else. It was one of those foldup cots, really; I remembered and gave him his fiancée's message.

He ate some of the cake. "Good."

"Put the rest away for when you're hungry later."

"I'll tell you a secret. I won't be around here much longer."

"Are you getting married?"   135

"Ha ha. What time did you say they'd be back?"

"Five o'clock."

"Well, by that time this place will have seen the last of me. A plane can get further than a car." He unwrapped the cake and ate another piece of it, absentmindedly.

"Now you'll be thirsty."

"There's some water in the pail."   140

"It won't be very cold. I could bring some fresh. I could bring some ice from the refrigerator."

"No," he said. "I don't want you to go. I want a nice long time of saying good-bye to you."

He put the cake away carefully and sat beside me and started those little kisses, so soft, I can't ever let myself think about them, such kindness in his face and lovely kisses, all over my eyelids and neck and ears, all over, then me kissing back as well as I could (I had only kissed a boy on a dare before, and kissed my own arms for practice) and we lay back on the cot and pressed together, just gently, and he did some other things, not bad things or not in a bad way. It was lovely in the tent, that smell of grass and hot tent cloth with the sun beating down on it, and he said, "I wouldn't do you any harm for the world." Once, when he had rolled on top of me and we were sort of rocking together on the cot, he said softly, "Oh, no," and freed himself and jumped up and got the water pail. He splashed some of it on his neck and face, and the little bit left, on me lying there.

"That's to cool us off, miss."

When we said good-bye I wasn't at all sad, because he held my face and said, 145
"I'm going to write you a letter. I'll tell you where I am and maybe you can come and see me. Would you like that? Okay then. You wait." I was really glad I think to get away from him, it was like he was piling presents on me I couldn't get the pleasure of till I considered them alone.

No consternation at first about the plane being gone. They thought he had taken somebody up, and I didn't enlighten them. Dr. Peebles had phoned he had to go to the country, so there was just us having supper, and then Loretta Bird thrusting her head in the door and saying, "I see he's took off."

"What?" said Alice Kelling, and pushed back her chair.

"The kids come and told me this afternoon he was taking down his tent. Did he think he'd run through all the business there was around here? He didn't take off without letting you know, did he?"

"He'll send me word," Alice Kelling said. "He'll probably phone tonight. He's terribly restless, since the war."

"Edie, he didn't mention to you, did he?" Mrs. Peebles said. "When you took 150
over the message?"

"Yes," I said. So far so true.

"Well why didn't you say?" All of them were looking at me. "Did he say where he was going?"

"He said he might try Bayfield," I said. What made me tell such a lie? I didn't intend it.

"Bayfield, how far is that?" said Alice Kelling.

Mrs. Peebles said, "Thirty, thirty-five miles." 155

"That's not far. Oh, well, that's really not far at all. It's on the lake, isn't it?"

You'd think I'd be ashamed of myself, setting her on the wrong track. I did it to give him more time, whatever time he needed. I lied for him, and also, I have to admit, for me. Women should stick together and not do things like that. I see that now, but didn't then. I never thought of myself as being in any way like her, or coming to the same troubles, ever.

She hadn't taken her eyes off me. I thought she suspected my lie.

"When did he mention this to you?"

"Earlier." 160

"When you were over at the plane?"

"Yes."

"You must've stayed and had a chat." She smiled at me, not a nice smile. "You must've stayed and had a little visit with him."

"I took a cake," I said, thinking that telling some truth would spare me telling the rest.

"We didn't have a cake," said Mrs. Peebles rather sharply. 165

"I baked one."

Alice Kelling said, "That was very friendly of you."

"Did you get permission," said Loretta Bird. "You never know what these girls'll do next," she said. "It's not they mean harm so much, as they're ignorant."

"The cake is neither here nor there," Mrs. Peebles broke in. "Edie, I wasn't aware you knew Chris that well."

I didn't know what to say.

"I'm not surprised," Alice Kelling said in a high voice. "I knew by the look of her as soon as I saw her. We get them at the hospital all the time." She looked hard at me with her stretched smile. "Having their babies. We have to put them in a special ward because of their diseases. Little country tramps. Fourteen and fifteen years old. You should see the babies they have, too."

"There was a bad woman here in town had a baby that pus was running out of its eyes," Loretta Bird put in.

"Wait a minute," said Mrs. Peebles. "What is this talk? Edie. What about you and Mr. Watters? Were you intimate with him?"

"Yes," I said. I was thinking of us lying on the cot and kissing, wasn't that intimate? And I would never deny it.

They were all one minute quiet, even Loretta Bird.

"Well," said Mrs. Peebles. "I am surprised. I think I need a cigarette. This is the first of any such tendencies I've seen in her," she said, speaking to Alice Kelling, but Alice Kelling was looking at me.

"Loose little bitch." Tears ran down her face. "Loose little bitch, aren't you? I knew as soon as I saw you. Men despise girls like you. He just made use of you and went off, you know that, don't you? Girls like you are just nothing, they're just public conveniences, just filthy little rags!"

"Oh, now," said Mrs. Peebles.

"Filthy," Alice Kelling sobbed. "Filthy little rags!"

"Don't get yourself upset," Loretta Bird said. She was swollen up with pleasure at being in on this scene. "Men are all the same."

"Edie, I'm very surprised," Mrs. Pebbles said. "I thought your parents were so strict. You don't want to have a baby, do you?"

I'm still ashamed of what happened next. I lost control, just like a six-year-old, I started howling. "You don't get a baby from just doing that!"

"You see. Some of them are that ignorant," Loretta Bird said.

But Mrs. Peebles jumped up and caught my arms and shook me.

"Calm down. Don't get hysterical. Calm down. Stop crying. Listen to me. Listen. I'm wondering, if you know what being intimate means. Now tell me. What did you think it meant?"

"Kissing," I howled.

She let go. "Oh, Edie. Stop it. Don't be silly. It's all right. It's all a misunderstanding. Being intimate means a lot more than that. Oh, I *wondered*."

"She's trying to cover up, now," said Alice Kelling. "Yes. She's not so stupid. She sees she got herself in trouble."

"I believe her," Mrs. Peebles said. "This is an awful scene."

"Well there is one way to find out," said Alice Kelling, getting up. "After all, I am a nurse."

Mrs. Peebles drew a breath and said, "No. No. Go to your room, Edie. And stop that noise. This is too disgusting."

I heard the car start in a little while. I tried to stop crying, pulling back each wave as it started over me. Finally I succeeded, and lay heaving on the bed.

Mrs. Peebles came and stood in the doorway.

"She's gone," she said. "That Bird woman too. Of course, you know you should never have gone near that man and that is the cause of all this trouble. I have a headache. As soon as you can, go and wash your face in cold water and get at the dishes and we will not say any more about this."

Nor we didn't. I didn't figure out till years later the extent of what I had been saved from. Mrs. Peebles was not very friendly to me afterward, but she was fair. Not very friendly is the wrong way of describing what she was. She had never been very friendly. It was just that now she had to see me all the time and it got on her nerves, a little.

As for me, I put it all out of my mind like a bad dream and concentrated on waiting for my letter. The mail came every day except Sunday, between one-thirty and two in the afternoon, a good time for me because Mrs. Peebles was always having her nap. I would get the kitchen all cleaned and then go up to the mailbox and sit in the grass, waiting. I was perfectly happy, waiting. I forgot all about Alice Kelling and her misery and awful talk and Mrs. Peebles and her chilliness and the embarrassment of whether she told Dr. Peebles and the face of Loretta Bird, getting her fill of other people's troubles. I was always smiling when the mailman got there, and continued smiling even after he gave me the mail and I saw today wasn't the day. The mailman was a Carmichael. I knew by his face because there are a lot of Carmichaels living out by us and so many of them have a sort of sticking-out top lip. So I asked his name (he was a young man, shy, but good-humored, anybody could ask him anything) and then I said, "I knew by your face!" He was pleased by that and always glad to see me and got a little less shy. "You've got the smile I've been waiting for all day!" he used to holler out the car window.

It never crossed my mind for a long time a letter might not come. I believed in it coming just like I believed the sun would rise in the morning. I just put off my hope from day to day, and there was the goldenrod out around the mailbox and the children gone back to school, and the leaves turning, and I was wearing a sweater when I went to wait. One day walking back with the hydro bill stuck in my hand, that was all, looking across at the fairgrounds with the full-blown milkweed and dark teasels, so much like fall, it just struck me: *No letter was ever going to come.* It was an impossible idea to get used to. No, not impossible. If I thought about Chris's face when he said he was going to write me, it was impossible, but if I forgot that and thought about the actual tin mailbox, empty, it was plain and true. I kept on going to meet the mail, but my heart was heavy now like a lump of lead. I only smiled because I thought of the mailman counting on it, and he didn't have an easy life, with the winter driving ahead.

Till it came to me one day there were women doing this with their lives, all over. There were women just waiting and waiting by mailboxes for one letter or another. I imagined me making this journey day after day and year after year, and my hair starting to get gray, and I thought, I was never made to go on like that. So I stopped meeting the mail. If there were women all through life waiting, and women busy and not waiting, I knew which I had to be. Even though there might be things the second kind of women have to pass up and never know about, it still is better.

I was surprised when the mailman phoned the Peebleses' place in the evening and asked for me. He said he missed me. He asked if I would like to go to Goderich, where some well-known movie was on, I forget now what. So I said yes, and I went out with him for two years and he asked me to marry him, and we were engaged a year more while I got my things together, and then we did marry. He always tells the children the story of how I went after him by sitting by the mailbox every day, and naturally I laugh and let him, because I like for people to think what pleases them and makes them happy.

Questions

1. What is your attitude toward Edie, the narrator—sympathy, condescension, disapproval, or something more complicated? Explain.
2. What aspects of Mrs. Peebles and her life does Edie admire or envy? What things about Mrs. Peebles does she find off-putting?
3. Why does Edie dislike Loretta Bird so much?
4. Reread the description of Alice Kelling in paragraph 94. What details does Edie notice about her, and why are these qualities important to Edie?
5. It is interesting that the story contains no description of Chris Watters's personal appearance. Why not, do you think? What are the things about him that really matter to Edie?
6. The twist at the end of the story may remind you of "The Gift of the Magi." Is there here, as there is in O. Henry's tale, more to the conclusion than just a clever surprise?
7. How would you state the theme of this story? Explain.

Luke

The Parable of the Prodigal Son   (King James Version, 1611)

Luke (first century) is traditionally considered the author of the Gospel bearing his name and the Acts of the Apostles in the New Testament. A physician who lived in the Greek city of Antioch (now in Syria), Luke accompanied the Apostle Paul on some of his missionary journeys. Luke's elegantly written Gospel includes some of the Bible's most beloved parables, including that of the Good Samaritan and the Prodigal Son.

And he said, A certain man had two sons: And the younger of them said to his father, Father, give me the portion of goods that falleth to me. And he divided unto them his living. And not many days after the younger son gathered all together, and took his journey into a far country, and there wasted his substance with riotous living. And when he had spent all, there arose a mighty famine in that land; and he began to be in want. And he went and joined himself to a citizen of that country; and he sent him into his fields to feed swine. And he would fain have filled his belly with the husks that the swine did eat: and no man gave unto him. And when he came to himself, he said, How many hired servants of my father's have bread enough and to spare, and I perish with hunger! I will arise and go to my father, and will say unto him, Father I have sinned against heaven, and before thee, and am no more worthy to be called thy son; make me as one of thy hired servants. And he arose, and came to his father. But when he was yet a great way off, his father saw him, and had compassion, and ran, and fell on his neck, and kissed him. And the son said unto him, Father I have sinned against heaven, and in thy sight, and am no more worthy to be called thy son. But the father said to his servants, Bring forth the best robe, and put it on him; and put a ring on his hand, and shoes on his feet: And bring hither the fatted calf, and kill it; and let us eat, and be merry: For this my son was dead, and is alive again; he was lost, and is found. And they began to be merry. Now his elder son was in the field: and he came and drew nigh to the house, he heard music and dancing. And he called

The Prodigal Son, woodcut by Gustave Doré, 1865.

one of the servants, and asked what these things meant. And he said unto him, Thy brother is come; and thy father hath killed the fatted calf, because he hath received him safe and sound. And he was angry, and would not go in: therefore came his father out, and entreated him. And he answering said to his father, Lo, these many years do I serve thee, neither transgressed I at any time thy commandment; and yet thou never gavest me a kid, that I might make merry with my friends: But as soon as this thy son was come, which hath devoured thy living with harlots, thou hast killed for him the fatted calf. And he said unto him, Son thou art ever with me, and all that I have is thine. It was meet that we should make merry, and be glad: for this thy brother was dead, and is alive again; and was lost, and is found.

—Luke 15:11-32

Questions

1. This story has traditionally been called "The Parable of the Prodigal Son." What does *prodigal* mean? Which of the two brothers is prodigal?

2. What position does the younger son expect when he returns to his father's house? What does the father give him?

3. When the older brother sees the celebration for his younger brother's return, he grows angry. He makes a very reasonable set of complaints to his father. He has indeed been a loyal and moral son, but what virtue does the older brother lack?

4. Is the father fair to the elder son? Explain your answer.
5. Theologians have discussed this parable's religious significance for two thousand years. What, in your own words, is the human theme of the story?

Kurt Vonnegut Jr.

Harrison Bergeron   1961

Kurt Vonnegut Jr. (1922–2007) was born in Indianapolis. During the Depression his father, a well-to-do architect, had virtually no work, and the family lived in reduced circumstances. Vonnegut attended Cornell University, where he majored in chemistry and was also managing editor of the daily student newspaper. In 1943 he enlisted in the U.S. Army. During the Battle of the Bulge he was captured by German troops and interned as a prisoner of war in Dresden, where he survived the massive Allied firebombing, which killed tens of thousands of people, mostly civilians. (The firebombing of Dresden became the central incident in Vonnegut's best-selling 1969 novel, Slaughterhouse-Five.*) After the war, Vonnegut worked as a reporter and later as a public relations man for General Electric in Schenectady, New York. He quit his job in 1951 to write full-time after publishing several science fiction stories in national magazines. His first novel,* Player Piano, *appeared in 1952, followed by* Sirens of Titan *(1959) and his first best seller,* Cat's Cradle *(1963)—all now considered classics of literary science fiction. Among his many other books are* Mother Night *(1961),* Jailbird *(1979), and a book of biographical essays,* A Man Without a Country *(2005). His short fiction is collected in* Welcome to the Monkey House *(1968) and* Bagombo Snuff Box *(1999). Vonnegut is a singular figure in modern American fiction. An ingenious comic writer, he combined the popular genre of science fiction with the literary tradition of dark satire—a combination splendidly realized in "Harrison Bergeron."*

The year was 2081, and everybody was finally equal. They weren't only equal before God and the law. They were equal every which way. Nobody was smarter than anybody else. Nobody was better looking than anybody else. Nobody was stronger or quicker than anybody else. All this equality was due to the 211th, 212th, and 213th Amendments to the Constitution, and to the unceasing vigilance of agents of the United States Handicapper General.

Some things about living still weren't quite right, though. April, for instance, still drove people crazy by not being springtime. And it was in that clammy month that the H-G men took George and Hazel Bergeron's fourteen-year-old son, Harrison, away.

It was tragic, all right, but George and Hazel couldn't think about it very hard. Hazel had a perfectly average intelligence, which meant she couldn't think about anything except in short bursts. And George, while his intelligence was way above normal, had a little mental handicap radio in his ear. He was required by law to wear it at all times. It was tuned to a government transmitter. Every twenty seconds or so, the transmitter would send out some sharp noise to keep people like George from taking unfair advantage of their brains.

George and Hazel were watching television. There were tears on Hazel's cheeks, but she'd forgotten for the moment what they were about.

On the television screen were ballerinas.   5

A buzzer sounded in George's head. His thoughts fled in panic, like bandits from a burglar alarm.

"That was a real pretty dance, that dance they just did," said Hazel.

"Huh?" said George.

"That dance—it was nice," said Hazel.

"Yup," said George. He tried to think a little about the ballerinas. They weren't really very good—no better than anybody else would have been, anyway. They were burdened with sashweights and bags of birdshot, and their faces were masked, so that no one, seeing a free and graceful gesture or a pretty face, would feel like something the cat drug in. George was toying with the vague notion that maybe dancers shouldn't be handicapped. But he didn't get very far with it before another noise in his ear radio scattered his thoughts.

George winced. So did two out of the eight ballerinas.

Hazel saw him wince. Having no mental handicap herself, she had to ask George what the latest sound had been.

"Sounded like somebody hitting a milk bottle with a ball peen hammer," said George.

"I'd think it would be real interesting, hearing all the different sounds," said Hazel, a little envious. "All the things they think up."

"Um," said George.

"Only, if I was Handicapper General, you know what I would do?" said Hazel. Hazel, as a matter of fact, bore a strong resemblance to the Handicapper General, a woman named Diana Moon Glampers. "If I was Diana Moon Glampers," said Hazel, "I'd have chimes on Sunday—just chimes. Kind of in honor of religion."

"I could think, if it was just chimes," said George.

"Well—maybe make 'em real loud," said Hazel. "I think I'd make a good Handicapper General."

"Good as anybody else," said George.

"Who knows better'n I do what normal is?" said Hazel.

"Right," said George. He began to think glimmeringly about his abnormal son who was now in jail, about Harrison, but a twenty-one-gun salute in his head stopped that.

"Boy!" said Hazel, "that was a doozy, wasn't it?"

It was such a doozy that George was white and trembling, and tears stood on the rims of his red eyes. Two of the eight ballerinas had collapsed to the studio floor, were holding their temples.

"All of a sudden you look so tired," said Hazel. "Why don't you stretch out on the sofa, so's you can rest your handicap bag on the pillows, honeybunch." She was referring to the forty-seven pounds of birdshot in a canvas bag, which was padlocked around George's neck. "Go on and rest the bag for a little while," she said. "I don't care if you're not equal to me for a while."

George weighed the bag with his hands. "I don't mind it," he said. "I don't notice it any more. It's just a part of me."

"You been so tired lately—kind of wore out," said Hazel. "If there was just some way we could make a little hole in the bottom of the bag, and just take out a few of them lead balls. Just a few."

"Two years in prison and two thousand dollars fine for every ball I took out," said George. "I don't call that a bargain."

"If you could just take a few out when you came home from work," said Hazel. "I mean—you don't compete with anybody around here. You just set around."

"If I tried to get away with it," said George, "then other people'd get away with it—and pretty soon we'd be right back to the dark ages again, with everybody competing against everybody else. You wouldn't like that, would you?"

"I'd hate it," said Hazel. 30

"There you are," said George. "The minute people start cheating on laws, what do you think happens to society?"

If Hazel hadn't been able to come up with an answer to this question, George couldn't have supplied one. A siren was going off in his head.

"Reckon it'd fall all apart," said Hazel.

"What would?" said George blankly.

"Society," said Hazel uncertainly. "Wasn't that what you just said?" 35

"Who knows?" said George.

The television program was suddenly interrupted for a news bulletin. It wasn't clear at first as to what the bulletin was about, since the announcer, like all announcers, had a serious speech impediment. For about half a minute, and in a state of high excitement, the announcer tried to say, "Ladies and gentlemen—"

He finally gave up, handed the bulletin to a ballerina to read.

"That's all right—" Hazel said of the announcer, "he tried. That's the big thing. He tried to do the best he could with what God gave him. He should get a nice raise for trying so hard."

"Ladies and gentlemen—" said the ballerina, reading the bulletin. She must 40 have been extraordinarily beautiful, because the mask she wore was hideous. And it was easy to see that she was the strongest and most graceful of all the dancers, for her handicap bags were as big as those worn by two-hundred-pound men.

And she had to apologize at once for her voice, which was a very unfair voice for a woman to use. Her voice was a warm, luminous, timeless melody. "Excuse me—" she said, and she began again, making her voice absolutely uncompetitive.

"Harrison Bergeron, age fourteen," she said in a grackle squawk, "has just escaped from jail, where he was held on suspicion of plotting to overthrow the government. He is a genius and an athlete, is under-handicapped, and should be regarded as extremely dangerous."

A police photograph of Harrison Bergeron was flashed on the screen upside down, then sideways, upside down again, then right side up. The picture showed the full length of Harrison against a background calibrated in feet and inches. He was exactly seven feet tall.

The rest of Harrison's appearance was Halloween and hardware. Nobody had ever borne heavier handicaps. He had outgrown hindrances faster than the H-G men could think them up. Instead of a little ear radio for a mental handicap, he wore a tremendous pair of earphones, and spectacles with thick wavy lenses. The spectacles were intended to make him not only half blind, but to give him whanging headaches besides.

Scrap metal was hung all over him. Ordinarily, there was a certain symmetry, 45 a military neatness to the handicaps issued to strong people, but Harrison looked like a walking junkyard. In the race of life, Harrison carried three hundred pounds.

And to offset his good looks, the H-G men required that he wear at all times a red rubber ball for a nose, keep his eyebrows shaved off, and cover his even white teeth with black caps at snaggle-tooth random.

"If you see this boy," said the ballerina, "do not—I repeat, do not—try to reason with him."

There was the shriek of a door being torn from its hinges.

Screams and barking cries of consternation came from the television set. The photograph of Harrison Bergeron on the screen jumped again and again, as though dancing to the tune of an earthquake.

George Bergeron correctly identified the earthquake, and well he might have—   50
for many was the time his own home had danced to the same crashing tune. "My
God—" said George, "that must be Harrison!"

The realization was blasted from his mind instantly by the sound of an automobile collision in his head.

When George could open his eyes again, the photograph of Harrison was gone.
A living, breathing Harrison filled the screen.

Clanking, clownish, and huge, Harrison stood in the center of the studio. The
knob of the uprooted studio door was still in his hand. Ballerinas, technicians, musicians, and announcers cowered on their knees before him, expecting to die.

"I am the Emperor!" cried Harrison. "Do you hear? I am the Emperor! Everybody
must do what I say at once!" He stamped his foot and the studio shook.

"Even as I stand here—" he bellowed, "crippled, hobbled, sickened—I am a greater   55
ruler than any man who ever lived! Now watch me become what I *can* become!"

Harrison tore the straps of his handicap harness like wet tissue paper, tore straps
guaranteed to support five thousand pounds.

Harrison's scrap-iron handicaps crashed to the floor.

Harrison thrust his thumbs under the bar of the padlock that secured his head
harness. The bar snapped like celery. Harrison smashed his headphones and spectacles against the wall.

He flung away his rubber-ball nose, revealed a man that would have awed Thor,
the god of thunder.

"I shall now select my Empress!" he said, looking down on the cowering people.   60
"Let the first woman who dares rise to her feet claim her mate and her throne!"

A moment passed, and then a ballerina arose, swaying like a willow.

Harrison plucked the mental handicap from her ear, snapped off her physical
handicaps with marvelous delicacy. Last of all, he removed her mask.

She was blindingly beautiful.

"Now—" said Harrison, taking her hand, "shall we show the people the meaning
of the word dance? Music!" he commanded.

The musicians scrambled back into their chairs, and Harrison stripped them of   65
their handicaps, too. "Play your best," he told them, "and I'll make you barons and
dukes and earls."

The music began. It was normal at first—cheap, silly, false. But Harrison snatched
two musicians from their chairs, waved them like batons as he sang the music as he
wanted it played. He slammed them back into their chairs.

The music began again and was much improved.

Harrison and his Empress merely listened to the music for a while—listened
gravely, as though synchronizing their heartbeats with it.

They shifted their weights to their toes.

Harrison placed his big hands on the girl's tiny waist, letting her sense the   70
weightlessness that would soon be hers.

And then, in an explosion of joy and grace, into the air they sprang!

Not only were the laws of the land abandoned, but the law of gravity and the
laws of motion as well.

They reeled, whirled, swiveled, flounced, capered, gamboled, and spun.

They leaped like deer on the moon.

The studio ceiling was thirty feet high, but each leap brought the dancers nearer to it.   75

It became their obvious intention to kiss the ceiling.

They kissed it.

And then, neutralizing gravity with love and pure will, they remained suspended in air inches below the ceiling, and they kissed each other for a long, long time.

It was then that Diana Moon Glampers, the Handicapper General, came into the studio with a double-barreled ten-gauge shotgun. She fired twice, and the Emperor and the Empress were dead before they hit the floor.

Diana Moon Glampers loaded the gun again. She aimed it at the musicians and   80
told them they had ten seconds to get their handicaps back on.

It was then that the Bergerons' television tube burned out.

Hazel turned to comment about the blackout to George. But George had gone out into the kitchen for a can of beer.

George came back in with the beer, paused while a handicap signal shook him up. And then he sat down again. "You been crying?" he said to Hazel.

"Yup," she said.

"What about?" he said.   85

"I forget," she said. "Something real sad on television."

"What was it?" he said.

"It's all kind of mixed up in my mind," said Hazel.

"Forget sad things," said George.

"I always do," said Hazel.   90

"That's my girl," said George. He winced. There was the sound of a rivetting gun in his head.

"Gee—I could tell that one was a doozy," said Hazel.

"You can say that again," said George.

"Gee—" said Hazel, "I could tell that one was a doozy."

Questions

1. What tendencies in present-day American society is Vonnegut satirizing? Does the story argue *for* anything? How would you sum up its theme?

2. Is Diana Moon Glampers a "flat" or a "round" character? (If you need to review these terms, see the discussion of character in Chapter 3.) Would you call Vonnegut's characterization of her "realistic"? If not, why doesn't it need to be?

3. From what point of view is the story told? Why is it more effective than if Harrison Bergeron had told his own story in the first person?

4. Two sympathetic critics of Vonnegut's work, Karen and Charles Wood, have said of his stories: "Vonnegut proves repeatedly . . . that men and women remain fundamentally the same, no matter what technology surrounds them." Try applying this comment to "Harrison Bergeron." Do you agree?

5. Stanislaw Lem, Polish author of *Solaris* and other novels, once made this thoughtful criticism of many of his contemporaries among science fiction writers:

   The revolt against the machine and against civilization, the praise of the "aesthetic" nature of catastrophe, the dead-end course of human civilization—these are their foremost problems, the intellectual content of their works. Such SF is as it were *a priori* vitiated by pessimism, in the sense that anything that may happen will be for the worse. ("The Time-Travel Story and Related Matters of SF Structuring," *Science Fiction Studies* 1 [1974], 143–54.)

   How might Lem's objection be raised against "Harrison Bergeron"? In your opinion, does it negate the value of Vonnegut's story?

■ WRITING *effectively*

Kurt Vonnegut Jr. on Writing

The Themes of Science Fiction

1971, 1973

Interviewer: You talked a lot about the difficulties you had when you first began. For instance, I think you gave one of the reasons for using the science fiction form as the fact that you were a professional writer and had to do something which was popular.

Vonnegut: In the beginning I was writing about what concerned me, and what was all around me was machinery. I myself had had some training in engineering and chemistry rather than in the arts and I was working for General Electric in a big factory city, Schenectady. So the first book I wrote was about Schenectady, which is full of machinery and engineers. And I was classified as a sci-

Kurt Vonnegut Jr.

ence fiction writer. Well, in the past, science fiction writers have been beneath the attention of any serious critic. That is, far above you are the people dealing with the really important, beautiful issues and using great skills and so forth. It used to be that if you were a science fiction writer you really didn't belong in the arts at all, and other artists wouldn't talk to you. You just had this scruffy little gang of your own.

• • •

Interviewer: What attracted you to using the form [of science fiction] yourself?

Vonnegut: . . . I saw a milling machine for cutting the rotors on jet engines, gas turbines. This was a very expensive thing for a machinist to do, to cut what is essentially one of those Brancusi forms. So they had a computer-operated milling machine built to cut the blades, and I was fascinated by that. This was in 1949 and the guys who were working on it were foreseeing all sorts of machines being run by little boxes and punched cards. *Player Piano* was my response to the implications of having everything run by little boxes. The idea of doing that, you know, made sense, perfect sense. To have a little clicking box make all the decisions wasn't a vicious thing to do. But it was too bad for the human beings who got their dignity from their jobs.

Interviewer: So science fiction seemed like the best way to write about your thoughts on the subject.

Vonnegut: There was no avoiding it, since General Electric Company *was* science fiction.

From interviews with Laurie Clancy and David Standish

THINKING ABOUT THEME

A clear, precise statement about a story's theme can serve as a promising thesis for a writing assignment. After you read a short story, you will probably have some vague sense of its theme—the central unifying idea, or the point of the story. How do you hone that vague sense of theme into a sharp and intriguing thesis?

■ **Start by making a list of all the story's possible themes.** If you are discussing Chinua Achebe's "Dead Men's Path," your list might say:

> Old ways vs. new
> Tradition vs. progress
> Resistance to change
> Intellectual arrogance
> Warning: pride goes before a fall
> Insensitivity to others' feelings
> Live and let live

■ **Determine which points seem most important; then formulate a single sentence in which you combine them.** For Achebe, you might have circled: "tradition vs. progress," "pride goes before a fall," and "insensitivity to others' feelings," and your summary might be: "The central theme of 'Dead Men's Path' is that progress is best made in a spirit of compromise, not by insensitivity to the feelings of those who follow the old ways."

■ **Try to capture the story's essence in a single sentence.** Remember, your goal is to transcend a mere one-sentence plot summary. How can you clearly express the central theme in a few words?

CHECKLIST: Writing About Theme

☐ List as many possible themes as you can.

☐ Circle the two or three most important points and try to combine them into a sentence.

☐ Relate particular details of the story to the theme you have spelled out. Consider plot details, dialogue, setting, point of view, title—any elements that seem especially pertinent.

☐ Check whether all the elements of the story fit your thesis.

☐ Have you missed an important aspect of the story? Or, have you chosen to focus on a secondary idea, overlooking the central one?

☐ If necessary, rework your thesis until it applies to every element in the story.

WRITING ASSIGNMENT ON THEME

Choose a story that catches your attention, and go through the steps outlined above to develop a strong thesis sentence about the story's theme. Then flesh out your argument into an essay, supporting your thesis with evidence from the text, including quotations. Some good story choices might be "A Clean, Well-Lighted Place," "The Chrysanthemums," "A Good Man Is Hard to Find," and "The Lottery."

MORE TOPICS FOR WRITING

1. Define the central theme of "Harrison Bergeron." Is Vonnegut's early 1960s vision of the future still relevant today? Why or why not?

2. Think of a social trend that worries you. With "Harrison Bergeron" in mind, write a brief science fiction parable to warn against this danger to society. Try to pick a less familiar or surprising trend instead of one of the hot-button social issues that immediately pop into your mind.

3. In 500 words or more, discuss Achebe's views on the modernization of tribal Africa and its effects as demonstrated in "Dead Men's Path."

4. What does "How I Met My Husband" have to say about first love? Back up your response with specific evidence from the story.

5. Write a brief personal narrative about your first crush. Use dialogue and sensory detail to capture a sense of time, place, and the personalities involved. Your narrative should have a thematic focus—for example, the sting of first love, or its many delights.

6. A recent *Time* magazine article describes a young California woman who distanced herself from her Chinese heritage until reading *The Joy Luck Club* "turned her into a 'born-again Asian.' It gave her new insights into why her mom was so hard on her and why the ways she showed love—say, through food—were different from those of the families [she] saw on TV, who seemed to say 'I love you' all day long." Have you ever had a similar experience, in which something you read gave you a better understanding of a loved one, or even yourself?

▶ TERMS FOR *review*

Summary ▶ A brief condensation of the main idea or plot of a literary work. A summary is similar to a paraphrase, but less detailed.

Theme ▶ The main idea or larger meaning of a work of literature. A theme may be a message or a moral, but it is more likely to be a central, unifying insight or viewpoint.

7 SYMBOL

*All you have to do is close your eyes
and wait for the symbols.*

—TENNESSEE WILLIAMS

In F. Scott Fitzgerald's novel *The Great Gatsby*, a huge pair of bespectacled eyes stares across a wilderness of ash heaps, from a billboard advertising the services of an oculist. Repeatedly entering into the story, the advertisement comes to mean more than simply the availability of eye examinations. Fitzgerald has a character liken it to the eyes of God; he hints that some sad, compassionate spirit is brooding as it watches the passing procession of humanity. Such an object is a **symbol**: in literature, a person, place, or thing that suggests more than its literal meaning. Symbols generally do not "stand for" any one meaning, nor for anything absolutely definite; they point, they hint, or, as Henry James put it, they cast long shadows. To take a large example: in Herman Melville's *Moby-Dick*, the great white whale of the book's title apparently means more than the literal dictionary-definition meaning of an aquatic mammal. He also suggests more than the devil, to whom some of the characters liken him. The great whale, as the story unfolds, comes to imply an amplitude of meanings, among them the forces of nature and the whole created universe.

ALLEGORY

This indefinite multiplicity of meanings is characteristic of a symbolic story and distinguishes it from an **allegory,** a story in which persons, places, and things form a system of clearly labeled equivalents. In a simple allegory, characters and other elements often stand for other definite meanings, which are often abstractions. You have met such a character in another story in this book, Nathaniel Hawthorne's "Young Goodman Brown." This tale's main female character, Faith, represents the religious virtue suggested by her name. Supreme allegories are found in some biblical parables ("The Kingdom of Heaven is like a man who sowed good seed in his field . . . ," Matthew 13:24–30).

A classic allegory is the medieval play *Everyman*, whose hero represents us all, and who, deserted by false friends called Kindred and Goods, faces the judgment of

God accompanied only by a faithful friend called Good Deeds. In John Bunyan's seventeenth-century allegory *Pilgrim's Progress*, the protagonist, Christian, struggles along the difficult road toward salvation, meeting along the way persons such as Mr. Worldly Wiseman, who directs him into a more comfortable path (a wrong turn), and the residents of a town called Fair Speech, among them a hypocrite named Mr. Facing-both-ways. Not all allegories are simple: Dante's *Divine Comedy*, written during the Middle Ages, continues to reveal new meanings to careful readers. Allegory was much beloved in the Middle Ages, but in contemporary fiction it is rare. One modern instance is George Orwell's long fable *Animal Farm*, in which (among its double meanings) barnyard animals stand for human victims and totalitarian oppressors.

SYMBOLS

Symbols in fiction are not generally abstract terms such as *love* or *truth*, but are likely to be perceptible objects (or worded descriptions that cause us to imagine them). In William Faulkner's "A Rose for Emily" (Chapter 2), Miss Emily's invisible watch ticking at the end of a golden chain not only indicates the passage of time, but also suggests that time passes without even being noticed by the watch's owner, and the golden chain carries suggestions of wealth and authority. Objects (and creatures) that seem insignificant in themselves can take on a symbolic importance in the larger context: in Jhumpa Lahiri's "Interpreter of Maladies" (Chapter 11) the piece of gum that Mrs. Das gives Mr. Kapasi—"As soon as Mr. Kapasi put the gum in his mouth a thick sweet liquid burst onto his tongue"—underscores her effect on his slumbering senses.

Often the symbols we meet in fiction are inanimate objects, but other things also may function symbolically. In James Joyce's "Araby" (Chapter 11), the very name of the bazaar, Araby—the poetic name for Arabia—suggests magic, romance, and *The Arabian Nights*; its syllables (the narrator tells us) "cast an Eastern enchantment over me." Even a locale, or a feature of physical topography, can provide rich suggestions. Recall Ernest Hemingway's "A Clean, Well-Lighted Place" (Chapter 5), in which the café is not merely a café, but an island of refuge from night, chaos, loneliness, old age, and impending death.

Symbolic Characters

In some novels and stories, symbolic characters make brief cameo appearances. Such characters often are not well-rounded and fully known, but are seen fleetingly and remain slightly mysterious. In *Heart of Darkness*, a short novel by Joseph Conrad, a steamship company that hires men to work in the Congo maintains in its waiting room two women who knit black wool—like the classical Fates. Usually such a symbolic character is more a portrait than a person—or somewhat portraitlike, as Faulkner's Miss Emily, who twice appears at a window of her house "like the carven torso of an idol in a niche." Though Faulkner invests Miss Emily with life and vigor, he also clothes her in symbolic hints: she seems almost to personify the vanishing aristocracy of the antebellum South, still maintaining a black servant and being ruthlessly betrayed by a moneymaking Yankee. Sometimes a part of a character's body or an attribute may convey symbolic meaning: a baleful eye, as in Edgar Allan Poe's "The Tell-Tale Heart" (Chapter 2).

Symbolic Acts

Much as a symbolic whale holds more meaning than an ordinary whale, a **symbolic act** is a gesture with larger significance than usual. For the boy's father in Faulkner's "Barn Burning" (Chapter 5), the act of destroying a barn is no mere act of spite, but an expression of his profound hatred for anything not belonging to him. Faulkner adds that burning a barn reflects the father's memories of the "waste and extravagance of war," and further adds that "the element of fire spoke to some deep mainspring" in his being. A symbolic act, however, doesn't have to be a gesture as large as starting a conflagration. Before setting out in pursuit of the great white whale, Melville's Captain Ahab in *Moby-Dick* deliberately snaps his tobacco pipe and throws it away, as if to suggest (among other things) that he will let no pleasure or pastime distract him from his vengeance.

Why do writers have to symbolize—why don't they tell us outright? One advantage of a symbol is that it is so compact, and yet so fully laden. Both starkly concrete and slightly mysterious, like Miss Emily's invisible ticking watch, it may impress us with all the force of something beheld in a dream or in a nightmare. The watch suggests, among other things, the slow and invisible passage of time. What this symbol says, it says more fully and more memorably than could be said, perhaps, in a long essay on the subject.

To some extent (it may be claimed), all stories are symbolic. Merely by holding up for our inspection these characters and their actions, the writer lends them *some* special significance. But this is to think of *symbol* in an extremely broad and inclusive way. For the usual purposes of reading a story and understanding it, there is probably little point in looking for symbolism in every word, in every stick or stone, in every striking of a match, in every minor character. Still, to be on the alert for symbols when reading fiction is perhaps wiser than to ignore them. Not to admit that symbolic meanings may be present, or to refuse to think about them, would be another way to misread a story—or to read no further than its outer edges.

RECOGNIZING SYMBOLS

How, then, do you recognize a symbol in fiction when you meet it? Fortunately, the storyteller often gives the symbol particular emphasis. It may be mentioned repeatedly throughout the story; it may even supply the story with a title ("Barn Burning," "A Clean, Well-Lighted Place," "Araby"). At times, a crucial symbol will open a story or end it. Unless an object, act, or character is given some such special emphasis and importance, we may generally feel safe in taking it at face value. Probably it isn't a symbol if it points clearly and unmistakably toward some one meaning, like a whistle in a factory, whose blast at noon means lunch. But an object, an act, or a character is surely symbolic (and almost as surely displays high literary art) if, when we finish the story, we realize that it was that item—that gigantic eye; that clean, well-lighted café; that burning of a barn—which led us to the author's theme, the essential meaning.

John Steinbeck

The Chrysanthemums

1938

John Steinbeck (1902–1968) was born in Salinas, California, in the fertile valley he remembers in "The Chrysanthemums." Off and on, he attended Stanford University, then sojourned in New York as a reporter and a bricklayer. After years of struggle to earn his living by fiction, Steinbeck reached a large audience with Tortilla Flat *(1935), a loosely woven novel portraying Mexican Americans in Monterey with fondness and sympathy. Great acclaim greeted* The Grapes of Wrath *(1939), the story of a family of Oklahoma farmers who, ruined by dust storms in the 1930s, join a mass migration to California. In 1962 he became the seventh American to win the Nobel Prize in Literature, but critics have never placed Steinbeck on the same high shelf as Faulkner and Hemingway. He wrote much, not all good, and yet his best work adds up to an*

John Steinbeck

impressive total. Besides The Grapes of Wrath, *it includes* In Dubious Battle *(1936), a novel of an apple-pickers' strike;* Of Mice and Men *(1937), a powerful short novel of comradeship between a hobo and a retarded man; and the short stories in* The Long Valley *(1938). Throughout the fiction he wrote in his prime, Steinbeck maintains an appealing sympathy for the poor and downtrodden, the lonely and dispossessed.*

The high grey-flannel fog of winter closed off the Salinas Valley° from the sky and from all the rest of the world. On every side it sat like a lid on the mountains and made of the great valley a closed pot. On the broad, level land floor the gang plows bit deep and left the black earth shining like metal where the shares had cut. On the foothill ranches across the Salinas River, the yellow stubble fields seemed to be bathed in pale cold sunshine, but there was no sunshine in the valley now in December. The thick willow scrub along the river flamed with sharp and positive yellow leaves.

It was a time of quiet and of waiting. The air was cold and tender. A light wind blew up from the southwest so that the farmers were mildly hopeful of a good rain before long; but fog and rain do not go together.

Across the river, on Henry Allen's foothill ranch there was little work to be done, for the hay was cut and stored and the orchards were plowed up to receive the rain deeply when it should come. The cattle on the higher slopes were becoming shaggy and rough-coated.

Elisa Allen, working in her flower garden, looked down across the yard and saw Henry, her husband, talking to two men in business suits. The three of them stood by the tractor shed, each man with one foot on the side of the little Fordson. They smoked cigarettes and studied the machine as they talked.

Elisa watched them for a moment and then went back to her work. She was thirty-five. Her face was lean and strong and her eyes were as clear as water. Her figure looked blocked and heavy in her gardening costume, a man's black hat pulled low

5

Salinas Valley: south of San Francisco in the Coast Ranges region of California.

down over her eyes, clodhopper shoes, a figured print dress almost completely covered by a big corduroy apron with four big pockets to hold the snips, the trowel and scratcher, the seeds and the knife she worked with. She wore heavy leather gloves to protect her hands while she worked.

She was cutting down the old year's chrysanthemum stalks with a pair of short and powerful scissors. She looked down toward the men by the tractor shed now and then. Her face was eager and mature and handsome; even her work with the scissors was over-eager, over-powerful. The chrysanthemum stems seemed too small and easy for her energy.

She brushed a cloud of hair out of her eyes with the back of her glove, and left a smudge of earth on her cheek in doing it. Behind her stood the neat white farm house with red geraniums close-banked around it as high as the windows. It was a hard-swept looking little house with hard-polished windows, and a clean mud-mat on the front steps.

Elisa cast another glance toward the tractor shed. The strangers were getting into their Ford coupe. She took off a glove and put her strong fingers down into the forest of new green chrysanthemum sprouts that were growing around the old roots. She spread the leaves and looked down among the close-growing stems. No aphids were there, no sowbugs or snails or cutworms. Her terrier fingers destroyed such pests before they could get started.

Elisa started at the sound of her husband's voice. He had come near quietly, and he leaned over the wire fence that protected her flower garden from cattle and dogs and chickens.

"At it again," he said. "You've got a strong new crop coming."   10

Elisa straightened her back and pulled on the gardening glove again. "Yes. They'll be strong this coming year." In her tone and on her face there was a little smugness.

"You've got a gift with things," Henry observed. "Some of those yellow chrysanthemums you had this year were ten inches across. I wish you'd work out in the orchard and raise some apples that big."

Her eyes sharpened. "Maybe I could do it, too. I've a gift with things, all right. My mother had it. She could stick anything in the ground and make it grow. She said it was having planters' hands that knew how to do it."

"Well, it sure works with flowers," he said.

"Henry, who were those men you were talking to?"   15

"Why, sure, that's what I came to tell you. They were from the Western Meat Company. I sold those thirty head of three-year-old steers. Got nearly my own price, too."

"Good," she said. "Good for you."

"And I thought," he continued, "I thought how it's Saturday afternoon, and we might go into Salinas for dinner at a restaurant, and then to a picture show—to celebrate, you see."

"Good," she repeated. "Oh, yes. That will be good."

Henry put on his joking tone. "There's fights tonight. How'd you like to go to   20
the fights?"

"Oh, no," she said breathlessly. "No, I wouldn't like fights."

"Just fooling, Elisa. We'll go to a movie. Let's see. It's two now. I'm going to take Scotty and bring down those steers from the hill. It'll take us maybe two hours. We'll go in town about five and have dinner at the Cominos Hotel. Like that?"

"Of course I'll like it. It's good to eat away from home."

"All right, then. I'll go get up a couple of horses."

She said, "I'll have plenty of time to transplant some of these sets, I guess."   25

She heard her husband calling Scotty down by the barn. And a little later she saw the two men ride up the pale yellow hillside in search of the steers.

There was a little square sandy bed kept for rooting the chrysanthemums. With her trowel she turned the soil over and over, and smoothed it and patted it firm. Then she dug ten parallel trenches to receive the sets. Back at the chrysanthemum bed she pulled out the little crisp shoots, trimmed off the leaves of each one with her scissors and laid it on a small orderly pile.

A squeak of wheels and plod of hoofs came from the road. Elisa looked up. The country road ran along the dense bank of willows and cottonwoods that bordered the river, and up this road came a curious vehicle, curiously drawn. It was an old spring-wagon, with a round canvas top on it like the cover of a prairie schooner. It was drawn by an old bay horse and a little grey-and-white burro. A big stubble-bearded man sat between the cover flaps and drove the crawling team. Underneath the wagon, between the hind wheels, a lean and rangy mongrel dog walked sedately. Words were painted on the canvas, in clumsy, crooked letters. "Pots, pans, knives, sisors, lawn mores, Fixed." Two rows of articles, and the triumphantly definitive "Fixed" below. The black paint had run down in little sharp points beneath each letter.

Elisa, squatting on the ground, watched to see the crazy, loose-jointed wagon pass by. But it didn't pass. It turned into the farm road in front of her house, crooked old wheels skirling and squeaking. The rangy dog darted from between the wheels and ran ahead. Instantly the two ranch shepherds flew out at him. Then all three stopped, and with stiff and quivering tails, with taut straight legs, with ambassadorial dignity, they slowly circled, sniffing daintily. The caravan pulled up to Elisa's wire fence and stopped. Now the newcomer dog, feeling out-numbered, lowered his tail and retired under the wagon with raised hackles and bared teeth.

The man on the wagon seat called out, "That's a bad dog in a fight when he gets started." 30

Elisa laughed. "I see he is. How soon does he generally get started?"

The man caught up her laughter and echoed it heartily. "Sometimes not for weeks and weeks," he said. He climbed stiffly down, over the wheel. The horse and the donkey drooped like unwatered flowers.

Elisa saw that he was a very big man. Although his hair and beard were greying, he did not look old. His worn black suit was wrinkled and spotted with grease. The laughter had disappeared from his face and eyes the moment his laughing voice ceased. His eyes were dark, and they were full of the brooding that gets in the eyes of teamsters and of sailors. The calloused hands he rested on the wire fence were cracked, and every crack was a black line. He took off his battered hat.

"I'm off my general road, ma'am," he said. "Does this dirt road cut over across the river to the Los Angeles highway?"

Elisa stood up and shoved the thick scissors in her apron pocket. "Well, yes, it 35 does, but it winds around and then fords the river. I don't think your team could pull through the sand."

He replied with some asperity, "It might surprise you what them beasts can pull through."

"When they get started?" she asked.

He smiled for a second. "Yes. When they get started."

"Well," said Elisa, "I think you'll save time if you go back to the Salinas road and pick up the highway there."

He drew a big finger down the chicken wire and made it sing. "I ain't in any 40
hurry, ma'am. I go from Seattle to San Diego and back every year. Takes all my time.
About six months each way. I aim to follow nice weather."

Elisa took off her gloves and stuffed them in the apron pocket with the scissors.
She touched the under edge of her man's hat, searching for fugitive hairs. "That
sounds like a nice kind of a way to live," she said.

He leaned confidentially over the fence. "Maybe you noticed the writing on my
wagon. I mend pots and sharpen knives and scissors. You got any of them things to do?"

"Oh, no," she said quickly. "Nothing like that." Her eyes hardened with resistance.

"Scissors is the worst thing," he explained. "Most people just ruin scissors trying
to sharpen 'em, but I know how. I got a special tool. It's a little bobbit kind of thing,
and patented. But it sure does the trick."

"No. My scissors are all sharp." 45

"All right, then. Take a pot," he continued earnestly, "a bent pot, or a pot with a
hole. I can make it like new so you don't have to buy no new ones. That's a saving for
you."

"No," she said shortly. "I tell you I have nothing like that for you to do."

His face fell to an exaggerated sadness. His voice took on a whining undertone.
"I ain't had a thing to do today. Maybe I won't have no supper tonight. You see I'm
off my regular road. I know folks on the highway clear from Seattle to San Diego.
They save their things for me to sharpen up because they know I do it so good and
save them money."

"I'm sorry," Elisa said irritably. "I haven't anything for you to do."

His eyes left her face and fell to searching the ground. They roamed about until 50
they came to the chrysanthemum bed where she had been working. "What's them
plants, ma'am?"

The irritation and resistance melted from Elisa's face. "Oh, those are chrysanthemums, giant whites and yellows. I raise them every year, bigger than anybody around
here."

"Kind of a long-stemmed flower? Looks like a quick puff of colored smoke?" he asked.

"That's it. What a nice way to describe them."

"They smell kind of nasty till you get used to them," he said.

"It's a good bitter smell," she retorted, "not nasty at all." 55

He changed his tone quickly. "I like the smell myself."

"I had ten-inch blooms this year," she said.

The man leaned farther over the fence. "Look. I know a lady down the road a
piece, has got the nicest garden you ever seen. Got nearly every kind of flower but no
chrysanthemums. Last time I was mending a copper-bottom washtub for her (that's a
hard job but I do it good), she said to me, 'If you ever run acrost some nice chrysanthemums I wish you'd try to get me a few seeds.' That's what she told me."

Elisa's eyes grew alert and eager. "She couldn't have known much about chrysanthemums. You *can* raise them from seed, but it's much easier to root the little sprouts
you see there."

"Oh," he said. "I s'pose I can't take none to her, then." 60

"Why yes you can," Elisa cried. "I can put some in damp sand, and you can carry
them right along with you. They'll take root in the pot if you keep them damp. And
then she can transplant them."

"She'd sure like to have some, ma'am. You say they're nice ones?"

"Beautiful," she said. "Oh, beautiful." Her eyes shone. She tore off the battered hat and shook out her dark pretty hair. "I'll put them in a flower pot, and you can take them right with you. Come into the yard."

While the man came through the picket gate Elisa ran excitedly along the geranium-bordered path to the back of the house. And she returned carrying a big red flower pot. The gloves were forgotten now. She kneeled on the ground by the starting bed and dug up the sandy soil with her fingers and scooped it into the bright new flower pot. Then she picked up the little pile of shoots she had prepared. With her strong fingers she pressed them in the sand and tamped around them with her knuckles. The man stood over her. "I'll tell you what to do," she said. "You remember so you can tell the lady."

"Yes, I'll try to remember."

"Well, look. These will take root in about a month. Then she must set them out, about a foot apart in good rich earth like this, see?" She lifted a handful of dark soil for him to look at. "They'll grow fast and tall. Now remember this: In July tell her to cut them down, about eight inches from the ground."

"Before they bloom?" he asked.

"Yes, before they bloom." Her face was tight with eagerness. "They'll grow right up again. About the last of September the buds will start."

She stopped and seemed perplexed. "It's the budding that takes the most care," she said hesitantly. "I don't know how to tell you." She looked deep into his eyes, searchingly. Her mouth opened a little, and she seemed to be listening. "I'll try to tell you," she said. "Did you ever hear of planting hands?"

"Can't say I have, ma'am."

"Well, I can only tell you what it feels like. It's when you're picking off the buds you don't want. Everything goes right down into your fingertips. You watch your fingers work. They do it themselves. You can feel how it is. They pick and pick the buds. They never make a mistake. They're with the plant. Do you see? Your fingers and the plant. You can feel that, right up your arm. They know. They never make a mistake. You can feel it. When you're like that you can't do anything wrong. Do you see that? Can you understand that?"

She was kneeling on the ground looking up at him. Her breast swelled passionately.

The man's eyes narrowed. He looked away self-consciously. "Maybe I know," he said. "Sometimes in the night in the wagon there—"

Elisa's voice grew husky. She broke in on him, "I've never lived as you do, but I know what you mean. When the night is dark—why, the stars are sharp-pointed, and there's quiet. Why, you rise up and up! Every pointed star gets driven into your body. It's like that. Hot and sharp and—lovely."

Kneeling there, her hand went out toward his legs in the greasy black trousers. Her hesitant fingers almost touched the cloth. Then her hand dropped to the ground. She crouched low like a fawning dog.

He said, "It's nice, just like you say. Only when you don't have no dinner, it ain't."

She stood up then, very straight, and her face was ashamed. She held the flower pot out to him and placed it gently in his arms. "Here. Put it in your wagon, on the seat, where you can watch it. Maybe I can find something for you to do."

At the back of the house she dug in the can pile and found two old and battered aluminum saucepans. She carried them back and gave them to him. "Here, maybe you can fix these."

His manner changed. He became professional. "Good as new I can fix them." At the back of his wagon he set a little anvil, and out of an oily tool box dug a small machine hammer. Elisa came through the gate to watch him while he pounded out the dents in the kettles. His mouth grew sure and knowing. At a difficult part of the work he sucked his under-lip.

"You sleep right in the wagon?" Elisa asked.   80

"Right in the wagon, ma'am. Rain or shine I'm dry as a cow in there."

"It must be nice," she said. "It must be very nice. I wish women could do such things."

"It ain't the right kind of a life for a woman."

Her upper lip raised a little, showing her teeth. "How do you know? How can you tell?" she said.

"I don't know, ma'am," he protested. "Of course I don't know. Now here's your 85 kettles, done. You don't have to buy no new ones."

"How much?"

"Oh, fifty cents'll do. I keep my prices down and my work good. That's why I have all them satisfied customers up and down the highway."

Elisa brought him a fifty-cent piece from the house and dropped it in his hand. "You might be surprised to have a rival some time. I can sharpen scissors, too. And I can beat the dents out of little pots. I could show you what a woman might do."

He put his hammer back in the oily box and shoved the little anvil out of sight. "It would be a lonely life for a woman, ma'am, and a scarey life, too, with animals creeping under the wagon all night." He climbed over the singletree, steadying himself with a hand on the burro's white rump. He settled himself in the seat, picked up the lines. "Thank you kindly, ma'am," he said. "I'll do like you told me; I'll go back and catch the Salinas road."

"Mind," she called, "if you're long in getting there, keep the sand damp."   90

"Sand, ma'am? . . . Sand? Oh, sure. You mean around the chrysanthemums. Sure I will." He clucked his tongue. The beasts leaned luxuriously into their collars. The mongrel dog took his place between the back wheels. The wagon turned and crawled out the entrance road and back the way it had come, along the river.

Elisa stood in front of her wire fence watching the slow progress of the caravan. Her shoulders were straight, her head thrown back, her eyes half-closed, so that the scene came vaguely into them. Her lips moved silently, forming the words "Good-bye—good-bye." Then she whispered, "That's a bright direction. There's a glowing there." The sound of her whisper startled her. She shook herself free and looked about to see whether anyone had been listening. Only the dogs had heard. They lifted their heads toward her from their sleeping in the dust, and then stretched out their chins and settled asleep again. Elisa turned and ran hurriedly into the house.

In the kitchen she reached behind the stove and felt the water tank. It was full of hot water from the noonday cooking. In the bathroom she tore off her soiled clothes and flung them into the corner. And then she scrubbed herself with a little block of pumice, legs and thighs, loins and chest and arms, until her skin was scratched and red. When she had dried herself she stood in front of a mirror in her bedroom and looked at her body. She tightened her stomach and threw out her chest. She turned and looked over her shoulder at her back.

After a while she began to dress, slowly. She put on her newest underclothing and her nicest stockings and the dress which was the symbol of her prettiness. She worked carefully on her hair, penciled her eyebrows and rouged her lips.

Before she was finished she heard the little thunder of hoofs and the shouts of 95
Henry and his helper as they drove the red steers into the corral. She heard the gate
bang shut and set herself for Henry's arrival.

His step sounded on the porch. He entered the house calling, "Elisa, where are you?"

"In my room, dressing. I'm not ready. There's hot water for your bath. Hurry up.
It's getting late."

When she heard him splashing in the tub, Elisa laid his dark suit on the bed, and
shirt and socks and tie beside it. She stood his polished shoes on the floor beside the
bed. Then she went to the porch and sat primly and stiffly down. She looked toward
the river road where the willow-line was still yellow with frosted leaves so that under
the high grey fog they seemed a thin band of sunshine. This was the only color in the
grey afternoon. She sat unmoving for a long time. Her eyes blinked rarely.

Henry came banging out of the door, shoving his tie inside his vest as he came.
Elisa stiffened and her face grew tight. Henry stopped short and looked at her.
"Why—why, Elisa. You look so nice!"

"Nice? You think I look nice? What do you mean by 'nice'?" 100

Henry blundered on. "I don't know. I mean you look different, strong and happy."

"I am strong? Yes, strong. What do you mean 'strong'?"

He looked bewildered. "You're playing some kind of a game," he said helplessly.
"It's a kind of a play. You look strong enough to break a calf over your knee, happy
enough to eat it like a watermelon."

For a second she lost her rigidity. "Henry! Don't talk like that. You didn't know
what you said." She grew complete again. "I'm strong," she boasted. "I never knew
before how strong."

Henry looked down toward the tractor shed, and when he brought his eyes back 105
to her, they were his own again. "I'll get out the car. You can put on your coat while
I'm starting."

Elisa went into the house. She heard him drive to the gate and idle down his motor, and then she took a long time to put on her hat. She pulled it here and pressed it
there. When Henry turned the motor off she slipped into her coat and went out.

The little roadster bounced along on the dirt road by the river, raising the birds
and driving the rabbits into the brush. Two cranes flapped heavily over the willow-
line and dropped into the river-bed.

Far ahead on the road Elisa saw a dark speck. She knew.

She tried not to look as they passed it, but her eyes would not obey. She whispered to herself sadly, "He might have thrown them off the road. That wouldn't have
been much trouble, not very much. But he kept the pot," she explained. "He had to
keep the pot. That's why he couldn't get them off the road."

The roadster turned a bend and she saw the caravan ahead. She swung full 110
around toward her husband so she could not see the little covered wagon and the
mismatched team as the car passed them.

In a moment it was over. The thing was done. She did not look back.

She said loudly, to be heard above the motor, "It will be good, tonight, a good dinner."

"Now you're changed again," Henry complained. He took one hand from the
wheel and patted her knee. "I ought to take you in to dinner oftener. It would be
good for both of us. We get so heavy out on the ranch."

"Henry," she asked, "could we have wine at dinner?"

"Sure we could. Say! That will be fine." 115

She was silent for a while; then she said, "Henry, at those prize fights, do the men hurt each other very much?"

"Sometimes a little, not often. Why?"

"Well, I've read how they break noses, and blood runs down their chests. I've read how the fighting gloves get heavy and soggy with blood."

He looked around at her. "What's the matter, Elisa? I didn't know you read things like that." He brought the car to a stop, then turned to the right over the Salinas River bridge.

"Do any women ever go to the fights?" she asked.

"Oh, sure, some. What's the matter, Elisa? Do you want to go? I don't think you'd like it, but I'll take you if you really want to go."

She relaxed limply in the seat. "Oh, no. No. I don't want to go. I'm sure I don't." Her face was turned away from him. "It will be enough if we can have wine. It will be plenty." She turned up her coat collar so he could not see that she was crying weakly— like an old woman.

Questions

1. When we first meet Elisa Allen in her garden, with what details does Steinbeck delineate her character for us?

2. Elisa works inside a "wire fence that protected her flower garden from cattle and dogs and chickens" (paragraph 9). What does this wire fence suggest?

3. How would you describe Henry and Elisa's marriage? Cite details from the story.

4. With what motive does the traveling salesman take an interest in Elisa's chrysanthemums? What immediate effect does his interest have on Elisa?

5. For what possible purpose does Steinbeck give us such a detailed account of Elisa's preparations for her evening out? Notice her tearing off her soiled clothes and her scrubbing her body with pumice (paragraphs 93–94).

6. Of what significance to Elisa is the sight of the contents of the flower pot discarded in the road? Notice that, as her husband's car overtakes the covered wagon, Elisa averts her eyes; and then Steinbeck adds, "In a moment it was over. The thing was done. She did not look back" (paragraph 111). Explain this passage.

7. How do you interpret Elisa's asking for wine with dinner? How do you account for her new interest in prizefights?

8. In a sentence, try to state this short story's theme.

9. Why are Elisa Allen's chrysanthemums so important to this story? Sum up what you understand them to mean.

D. H. Lawrence

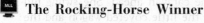

The Rocking-Horse Winner   1933

David Herbert Lawrence (1885–1930) was born in Nottinghamshire, England, child of a coal miner and a schoolteacher who hated her husband's toil and vowed that her son should escape it. He took up fiction writing, attaining early success. During World War I, Lawrence and his wife were unjustly suspected of treason (he because of his pacifism, she because of her aristocratic German birth). After the armistice they left England and, seeking a climate healthier for Lawrence, who suffered from tuberculosis, wandered in Italy, France, Australia, Mexico, and the American Southwest.

Lawrence is an impassioned spokesman for our unconscious instinctive natures, which we moderns (he argues) have neglected in favor of our overweening intellects. In Lady

Chatterley's Lover (1928), *he strove to restore explicit sexuality to English fiction. The book, which today seems tame and repetitious, was long banned in Britain and the United States. Deeper Lawrence novels include* Sons and Lovers *(1913), a veiled account of his breaking away from his fiercely possessive mother;* The Rainbow *(1915);* Women in Love *(1921); and* The Plumed Serpent *(1926), about a revival of pagan religion in Mexico. Besides fiction, Lawrence left a rich legacy of poetry, essays, criticism (*Studies in Classic American Literature, *1923, is especially shrewd and funny), and travel writing. Lawrence exerted deep influence on others, both by the message in his work and by his personal magnetism.*

D. H. Lawrence

There was a woman who was beautiful, who started with all the advantages, yet she had no luck. She married for love, and the love turned to dust. She had bonny children, yet she felt they had been thrust upon her, and she could not love them. They looked at her coldly, as if they were finding fault with her. And hurriedly she felt she must cover up some fault in herself. Yet what it was that she must cover up she never knew. Nevertheless, when her children were present, she always felt the center of her heart go hard. This troubled her, and in her manner she was all the more gentle and anxious for her children, as if she loved them very much. Only she herself knew that at the center of her heart was a hard little place that could not feel love, no, not for anybody. Everybody else said of her: "She is such a good mother. She adores her children." Only she herself, and her children themselves, knew it was not so. They read it in each other's eyes.

There were a boy and two little girls. They lived in a pleasant house, with a garden, and they had discreet servants, and felt themselves superior to anyone in the neighborhood.

Although they lived in style, they felt always an anxiety in the house. There was never enough money. The mother had a small income, and the father had a small income, but not nearly enough for the social position which they had to keep up. The father went into town to some office. But though he had good prospects, these prospects never materialized. There was always the grinding sense of the shortage of money, though the style was always kept up.

At last the mother said: "I will see if *I* can't make something." But she did not know where to begin. She racked her brains, and tried this thing and the other, but could not find anything successful. The failure made deep lines come into her face. Her children were growing up, they would have to go to school. There must be more money, there must be more money. The father, who was always very handsome and expensive in his tastes, seemed as if he never *would* be able to do anything worth doing. And the mother, who had a great belief in herself, did not succeed any better, and her tastes were just as expensive.

And so the house came to be haunted by the unspoken phrase: *There must be more money! There must be more money!* The children could hear it all the time, though nobody said it aloud. They heard it at Christmas, when the expensive and splendid toys filled the nursery. Behind the shining modern rocking-horse, behind

5

the smart doll's house, a voice would start whispering: "There *must* be more money! There *must* be more money!" And the children would stop playing, to listen for a moment. They would look into each other's eyes, to see if they had all heard. And each one saw in the eyes of the other two that they too had heard. "There *must* be more money! There *must* be more money!"

It came whispering from the springs of the still-swaying rocking-horse, and even the horse, bending his wooden, champing head, heard it. The big doll, sitting so pink and smirking in her new pram, could hear it quite plainly, and seemed to be smirking all the more self-consciously because of it. The foolish puppy, too, that took the place of the teddy-bear, he was looking so extraordinarily foolish for no other reason but that he heard the secret whisper all over the house: "There *must* be more money!"

Yet nobody ever said it aloud. The whisper was everywhere, and therefore no one spoke it. Just as no one ever says: "We are breathing!" in spite of the fact that breath is coming and going all the time.

"Mother," said the boy Paul one day, "why don't we keep a car of our own? Why do we always use uncle's, or else a taxi?"

"Because we're the poor members of the family," said the mother.

"But why *are* we, mother?"   10

"Well—I suppose," she said slowly and bitterly, "it's because your father has no luck."

The boy was silent for some time.

"Is luck money, mother?" he asked rather timidly.

"No, Paul. Not quite. It's what causes you to have money."

"Oh!" said Paul vaguely. "I thought when Uncle Oscar said *filthy lucker*, it meant   15
money."

"*Filthy lucre* does mean money," said the mother. "But it's lucre, not luck."

"Oh!" said the boy. "Then what *is* luck, mother?"

"It's what causes you to have money. If you're lucky you have money. That's why it's better to be born lucky than rich. If you're rich, you may lose your money. But if you're lucky, you will always get more money."

"Oh! Will you? And is father not lucky?"

"Very unlucky, I should say," she said bitterly.   20

The boy watched her with unsure eyes.

"Why?" he asked.

"I don't know. Nobody ever knows why one person is lucky and another unlucky."

"Don't they? Nobody at all? Does *nobody* know?"

"Perhaps God. But He never tells."   25

"He ought to, then. And aren't you lucky either, mother?"

"I can't be, if I married an unlucky husband."

"But by yourself, aren't you?"

"I used to think I was, before I married. Now I think I am very unlucky indeed."

"Why?"   30

"Well—never mind! Perhaps I'm not really," she said.

The child looked at her to see if she meant it. But he saw, by the lines of her mouth, that she was only trying to hide something from him.

"Well, anyhow," he said stoutly, "I'm a lucky person."

"Why?" said his mother, with a sudden laugh.

He stared at her. He didn't even know why he had said it.   35

"God told me," he asserted, brazening it out.

"I hope He did, dear!" she said, again with a laugh, but rather bitter.

"He did, mother!"

"Excellent!" said the mother, using one of her husband's exclamations.

The boy saw she did not believe him; or, rather, that she paid no attention to his assertion. This angered him somewhat, and made him want to compel her attention.

He went off by himself, vaguely, in a childish way, seeking for the clue to "luck." Absorbed, taking no heed of other people, he went about with a sort of stealth, seeking inwardly for luck. He wanted luck, he wanted it, he wanted it. When the two girls were playing dolls in the nursery, he would sit on his big rocking-horse, charging madly into space, with a frenzy that made the little girls peer at him uneasily. Wildly the horse careered, the waving dark hair of the boy tossed, his eyes had a strange glare in them. The little girls dared not speak to him.

When he had ridden to the end of his mad little journey, he climbed down and stood in front of his rocking-horse, staring fixedly into its lowered face. Its red mouth was slightly open, its big eye was wide and glassy-bright.

"Now!" he would silently command the snorting steed. "Now, take me to where there is luck! Now take me!"

And he would slash the horse on the neck with the little whip he had asked Uncle Oscar for. He *knew* the horse could take him to where there was luck, if only he forced it. So he would mount again, and start on his furious ride, hoping at last to get there. He knew he could get there.

"You'll break your horse, Paul!" said the nurse.

"He's always riding like that! I wish he'd leave off!" said his elder sister Joan.

But he only glared down on them in silence. Nurse gave him up. She could make nothing of him. Anyhow he was growing beyond her.

One day his mother and his Uncle Oscar came in when he was on one of his furious rides. He did not speak to them.

"Hallo, you young jockey! Riding a winner?" said his uncle.

"Aren't you growing too big for a rocking-horse? You're not a very little boy any longer, you know," said his mother.

But Paul only gave a blue glare from his big, rather close-set eyes. He would speak to nobody when he was in full tilt. His mother watched him with an anxious expression on her face.

At last he suddenly stopped forcing his horse into the mechanical gallop and slid down.

"Well, I got there!" he announced fiercely, his blue eyes still flaring, and his sturdy long legs straddling apart.

"Where did you get to?" asked his mother.

"Where I wanted to go," he flared back at her.

"That's right, son!" said Uncle Oscar. "Don't you stop till you get there. What's the horse's name?"

"He doesn't have a name," said the boy.

"Gets on without all right?" asked the uncle.

"Well, he has different names. He was called Sansovino last week."

"Sansovino, eh? Won the Ascot. How did you know his name?"

"He always talks about horse-races with Bassett," said Joan.

The uncle was delighted to find that his small nephew was posted with all the racing news. Bassett, the young gardener, who had been wounded in the left foot in the war and had got his present job through Oscar Cresswell, whose batman° he had been, was a perfect blade of the "turf." He lived in the racing events, and the small boy lived with him.

Oscar Cresswell got it all from Bassett.

"Master Paul comes and asks me, so I can't do more than tell him, sir," said Bassett, his face terribly serious, as if he were speaking of religious matters.

"And does he ever put anything on a horse he fancies?"   65

"Well—I don't want to give him away—he's a young sport, a fine sport, sir. Would you mind asking him himself? He sort of takes a pleasure in it, and perhaps he'd feel I was giving him away, sir, if you don't mind."

Bassett was serious as a church.

The uncle went back to his nephew and took him off for a ride in the car.

"Say, Paul, old man, do you ever put anything on a horse?" the uncle asked.

The boy watched the handsome man closely.   70

"Why, do you think I oughtn't to?" he parried.

"Not a bit of it. I thought perhaps you might give me a tip for the Lincoln."

The car sped on into the country, going down to Uncle Oscar's place in Hampshire.

"Honor bright?" said the nephew.

"Honor bright, son!" said the uncle.   75

"Well, then, Daffodil."

"Daffodil! I doubt it, sonny. What about Mirza?"

"I only know the winner," said the boy. "That's Daffodil."

"Daffodil, eh?"

There was a pause. Daffodil was an obscure horse comparatively.   80

"Uncle!"

"Yes, son?"

"You won't let it go any further, will you? I promised Bassett."

"Bassett be damned, old man! What's he got to do with it?"

"We're partners. We've been partners from the first. Uncle, he lent me my first   85
five shillings, which I lost. I promised him, honor bright, it was only between me and him; only you gave me that ten-shilling note I started winning with, so I thought you were lucky. You won't let it go any further, will you?"

The boy gazed at his uncle from those big, hot, blue eyes, set rather to-gether. The uncle stirred and laughed uneasily.

"Right you are, son! I'll keep your tip private. Daffodil, eh? How much are you putting on him?"

"All except twenty pounds," said the boy. "I keep that in reserve."

The uncle thought it a good joke.

"You keep twenty pounds in reserve, do you, you young romancer? What are you   90
betting, then?"

"I'm betting three hundred," said the boy gravely. "But it's between you and me, Uncle Oscar! Honor bright?"

The uncle burst into a roar of laughter.

---

batman: an enlisted man who serves as valet to a cavalry officer.

"It's between you and me all right, you young Nat Gould,"° he said, laughing. "But where's your three hundred?"

"Bassett keeps it for me. We're partners."

"You are, are you! And what is Bassett putting on Daffodil?"   95

"He won't go quite as high as I do, I expect. Perhaps he'll go a hundred and fifty."

"What, pennies?" laughed the uncle.

"Pounds," said the child, with a surprised look at his uncle. "Bassett keeps a bigger reserve than I do."

Between wonder and amusement Uncle Oscar was silent. He pursued the matter no further, but he determined to take his nephew with him to the Lincoln races.

"Now, son," he said, "I'm putting twenty on Mirza, and I'll put five for you on   100 any horse you fancy. What's your pick?"

"Daffodil, uncle."

"No, not the fiver on Daffodil!"

"I should if it was my own fiver," said the child.

"Good! Good! Right you are! A fiver for me and a fiver for you on Daffodil."

The child had never been to a race-meeting before, and his eyes were blue fire.   105 He pursed his mouth tight, and watched. A Frenchman just in front had put his money on Lancelot. Wild with excitement, he flayed his arms up and down, yelling "*Lancelot! Lancelot!*" in his French accent.

Daffodil came in first, Lancelot second, Mirza third. The child, flushed and with eyes blazing, was curiously serene. His uncle brought him four five-pound notes, four to one.

"What am I to do with these?" he cried, waving them before the boy's eyes.

"I suppose we'll talk to Bassett," said the boy. "I expect I have fifteen hundred now; and twenty in reserve; and this twenty."

His uncle studied him for some moments.

"Look here, son!" he said. "You're not serious about Bassett and that fifteen hun-   110 dred, are you?"

"Yes, I am. But it's between you and me, uncle. Honor bright!"

"Honor bright all right, son! But I must talk to Bassett."

"If you'd like to be a partner, uncle, with Bassett and me, we could all be partners. Only, you'd have to promise, honor bright, uncle, not to let it go beyond us three. Bassett and I are lucky, and you must be lucky, because it was your ten shillings I started winning with . . ."

Uncle Oscar took both Bassett and Paul into Richmond Park for an afternoon, and there they talked.

"It's like this, you see, sir," Bassett said. "Master Paul would get me talking about   115 racing events, spinning yarns, you know, sir. And he was always keen on knowing if I'd made or if I'd lost. It's about a year since, now, that I put five shillings on Blush of Dawn for him: and we lost. Then the luck turned, and with that ten shillings he had from you: that we put on Singhalese. And since that time, it's been pretty steady, all things considering. What do you say, Master Paul?"

"We're all right when we're sure," said Paul. "It's when we're not quite sure that we go down."

"Oh, but we're careful then," said Bassett.

Nat Gould: celebrated English gambler of the 1920s.

"But when are you *sure?*" smiled Uncle Oscar.

"It's Master Paul, sir," said Bassett, in a secret, religious voice. "It's as if he had it from heaven. Like Daffodil, now, for the Lincoln. That was as sure as eggs."

"Did you put anything on Daffodil?" asked Oscar Cresswell.   120

"Yes, sir. I made my bit."

"And my nephew?"

Bassett was obstinately silent, looking at Paul.

"I made twelve hundred, didn't I, Bassett? I told uncle I was putting three hundred on Daffodil."

"That's right," said Bassett, nodding.   125

"But where's the money?" asked the uncle.

"I keep it safe locked up, sir. Master Paul he can have it any minute he likes to ask for it."

"What, fifteen hundred pounds?"

"And twenty! And *forty*, that is, with the twenty he made on the course."

"It's amazing!" said the uncle.   130

"If Master Paul offers you to be partners, sir, I would, if I were you: if you'll excuse me," said Bassett.

Oscar Cresswell thought about it.

"I'll see the money," he said.

They drove home again, and, sure enough, Bassett came round to the garden-house with fifteen hundred pounds in notes. The twenty pounds reserve was left with Joe Glee, in the Turf Commission deposit.

"You see, it's all right, uncle, when I'm *sure!* Then we go strong, for all we're 135
worth. Don't we, Bassett!"

"We do that, Master Paul."

"And when are you sure?" said the uncle, laughing.

"Oh, well, sometimes I'm *absolutely* sure, like about Daffodil," said the boy; "and sometimes I have an idea; and sometimes I haven't even an idea, have I, Bassett? Then we're careful, because we mostly go down."

"You do, do you! And when you're sure, like about Daffodil, what makes you sure, sonny?"

"Oh, well, I don't know," said the boy uneasily. "I'm sure, you know, uncle; that's all." 140

"It's as if he had it from heaven, sir," Bassett reiterated.

"I should say so!" said the uncle.

But he became a partner. And when the Leger was coming on, Paul was "sure" about Lively Spark, which was a quite inconsiderable horse. The boy insisted on putting a thousand on the horse, Bassett went for five hundred, and Oscar Cresswell two hundred. Lively Spark came in first, and the betting had been ten to one against him. Paul had made ten thousand.

"You see," he said, "I was absolutely sure of him."

Even Oscar Cresswell had cleared two thousand.   145

"Look here, son," he said, "this sort of thing makes me nervous."

"It needn't, uncle! Perhaps I shan't be sure again for a long time."

"But what are you going to do with your money?" asked the uncle.

"Of course," said the boy, "I started it for mother. She said she had no luck, because father is unlucky, so I thought if *I* was lucky, it might stop whispering."

"What might stop whispering?"   150

"Our house. I *hate* our house for whispering."

"What does it whisper?"

"Why—why"—the boy fidgeted—"why, I don't know. But it's always short of money, you know, uncle."

"I know it, son, I know it."

"You know people send mother writs, don't you, uncle?"   155

"I'm afraid I do," said the uncle.

"And then the house whispers, like people laughing at you behind your back. It's awful, that is! I thought if I was lucky—"

"You might stop it," added the uncle.

The boy watched him with big blue eyes, that had an uncanny cold fire in them, and he said never a word.

"Well, then!" said the uncle. "What are we doing?"   160

"I shouldn't like mother to know I was lucky," said the boy.

"Why not, son?"

"She'd stop me."

"I don't think she would."

"Oh!"—and the boy writhed in an odd way—"I *don't* want her to know, uncle."   165

"All right, son! We'll manage it without her knowing."

They managed it very easily. Paul, at the other's suggestion, handed over five thousand pounds to his uncle, who deposited it with the family lawyer, who was then to inform Paul's mother that a relative had put five thousand pounds into his hands, which sum was to be paid out a thousand pounds at a time, on the mother's birthday, for the next five years.

"So she'll have a birthday present of a thousand pounds for five successive years," said Uncle Oscar. "I hope it won't make it all the harder for her later."

Paul's mother had her birthday in November. The house had been "whispering" worse than ever lately, and, even in spite of his luck, Paul could not bear up against it. He was very anxious to see the effect of the birthday letter, telling his mother about the thousand pounds.

When there were no visitors, Paul now took his meals with his parents, as he was   170
beyond the nursery control. His mother went into town nearly every day. She had discovered that she had an odd knack of sketching furs and dress materials, so she worked secretly in the studio of a friend who was the chief "artist" for the leading drapers. She drew the figures of ladies in furs and ladies in silk and sequins for the newspaper advertisements. This young woman artist earned several thousand pounds a year, but Paul's mother only made several hundreds, and she was again dissatisfied. She so wanted to be first in something, and she did not succeed, even in making sketches for drapery advertisements.

She was down to breakfast on the morning of her birthday. Paul watched her face as she read her letters. He knew the lawyer's letter. As his mother read it, her face hardened and became more expressionless. Then a cold, determined look came on her mouth. She hid the letter under the pile of others, and said not a word about it.

"Didn't you have anything nice in the post for your birthday, mother?" said Paul.

"Quite moderately nice," she said, her voice cold and absent.

She went away to town without saying more.

But in the afternoon Uncle Oscar appeared. He said Paul's mother had had a   175
long interview with the lawyer, asking if the whole five thousand could not be advanced at once, as she was in debt.

"What do you think, uncle?" said the boy.

"I leave it to you, son."

"Oh, let her have it, then! We can get some more with the other," said the boy.

"A bird in the hand is worth two in the bush, laddie!" said Uncle Oscar.

"But I'm sure to *know* for the Grand National; or the Lincolnshire; or else the Derby. I'm sure to know for *one* of them," said Paul. 180

So Uncle Oscar signed the agreement, and Paul's mother touched the whole five thousand. Then something very curious happened. The voices in the house suddenly went mad, like a chorus of frogs on a spring evening. There were certain new furnishings, and Paul had a tutor. He was *really* going to Eton, his father's school, in the following autumn. There were flowers in the winter, and a blossoming of the luxury Paul's mother had been used to. And yet the voices in the house, behind the sprays of mimosa and almond blossom, and from under the piles of iridescent cushions, simply trilled and screamed in a sort of ecstasy: "There *must* be more money! Oh-h-h; there *must* be more money. Oh, now, now-w! Now-w-w—there *must* be more money!—more than ever! More than ever!"

It frightened Paul terribly. He studied away at his Latin and Greek with his tutor. But his intense hours were spent with Bassett. The Grand National had gone by: he had not "known," and had lost a hundred pounds. Summer was at hand. He was in agony for the Lincoln. But even for the Lincoln he didn't "know," and he lost fifty pounds. He became wild-eyed and strange, as if something were going to explode in him.

"Let it alone, son! Don't you bother about it!" urged Uncle Oscar. But it was as if the boy couldn't really hear what his uncle was saying.

"I've got to know for the Derby! I've got to know for the Derby!" the child reiterated, his big blue eyes blazing with a sort of madness.

His mother noticed how overwrought he was. 185

"You'd better go to the seaside. Wouldn't you like to go now to the seaside, instead of waiting? I think you'd better," she said, looking down at him anxiously, her heart curiously heavy because of him.

But the child lifted his uncanny blue eyes.

"I couldn't possibly go before the Derby, mother!" he said. "I couldn't possibly!"

"Why not?" she said, her voice becoming heavy when she was opposed. "Why not? You can still go from the seaside to see the Derby with your Uncle Oscar, if that's what you wish. No need for you to wait here. Besides, I think you care too much about these races. It's a bad sign. My family has been a gambling family, and you won't know till you grow up how much damage it has done. But it has done damage. I shall have to send Bassett away, and ask Uncle Oscar not to talk racing to you, unless you promise to be reasonable about it: go away to the seaside and forget it. You're all nerves!"

"I'll do what you like, mother, so long as you don't send me away till after the Derby," the boy said. 190

"Send you away from where? Just from this house?"

"Yes," he said, gazing at her.

"Why, you curious child, what makes you care about this house so much, suddenly? I never knew you loved it."

He gazed at her without speaking. He had a secret within a secret, something he had not divulged, even to Bassett or to his Uncle Oscar.

But his mother, after standing undecided and a little bit sullen for some moments, said:

"Very well, then! Don't go to the seaside till after the Derby, if you don't wish it. But promise me you won't let your nerves go to pieces. Promise you won't think so much about horse-racing and *events*, as you call them!"

"Oh, no," said the boy casually. "I won't think much about them, mother. You needn't worry. I wouldn't worry, mother, if I were you."

"If you were me and I were you," said his mother, "I wonder what we *should* do!"

"But you know you needn't worry, mother, don't you?" the boy repeated.

"I should be awfully glad to know it," she said wearily.

"Oh, well, you *can*, you know. I mean, you *ought* to know you needn't worry," he insisted.

"Ought I? Then I'll see about it," she said.

Paul's secret of secrets was his wooden horse, that which had no name. Since he was emancipated from a nurse and a nursery-governess, he had had his rocking-horse removed to his own bedroom at the top of the house.

"Surely, you're too big for a rocking-horse!" his mother had remonstrated.

"Well, you see, mother, till I can have a *real* horse, I like to have *some* sort of animal about," had been his quaint answer.

"Do you feel he keeps you company?" she laughed.

"Oh, yes! He's very good, he always keeps me company, when I'm there," said Paul.

So the horse, rather shabby, stood in an arrested prance in the boy's bedroom.

The Derby was drawing near, and the boy grew more and more tense. He hardly heard what was spoken to him, he was very frail, and his eyes were really uncanny. His mother had sudden strange seizures of uneasiness about him. Sometimes, for half an hour, she would feel a sudden anxiety about him that was almost anguish. She wanted to rush to him at once, and know he was safe.

Two nights before the Derby, she was at a big party in town, when one of her rushes of anxiety about her boy, her first-born, gripped her heart till she could hardly speak. She fought with the feeling, might and main, for she believed in common sense. But it was too strong. She had to leave the dance and go downstairs to telephone to the country. The children's nursery-governess was terribly surprised and startled at being rung up in the night.

"Are the children all right, Miss Wilmot?"

"Oh, yes, they are quite all right."

"Master Paul? Is he all right?"

"He went to bed as right as a trivet. Shall I run up and look at him?"

"No," said Paul's mother reluctantly. "No! Don't trouble. It's all right. Don't sit up. We shall be home fairly soon." She did not want her son's privacy intruded upon.

"Very good," said the governess.

It was about one-o'clock when Paul's mother and father drove up to their house. All was still. Paul's mother went to her room and slipped off her white fur cloak. She had told her maid not to wait up for her. She heard her husband downstairs, mixing a whisky and soda.

And then, because of the strange anxiety at her heart, she stole upstairs to her son's room. Noiselessly she went along the upper corridor. Was there a faint noise? What was it?

She stood, with arrested muscles, outside his door, listening. There was a strange, heavy, and yet not loud noise. Her heart stood still. It was a soundless noise, yet rushing and powerful. Something huge, in violent, hushed motion. What was it? What in God's name was it? She ought to know. She felt that she knew the noise. She knew what it was.

Yet she could not place it. She couldn't say what it was. And on and on it went, like a madness.   220

Softly, frozen with anxiety and fear, she turned the door-handle.

The room was dark. Yet in the space near the window, she heard and saw something plunging to and fro. She gazed in fear and amazement.

Then suddenly she switched on the light, and saw her son, in his green pajamas, madly surging on the rocking-horse. The blaze of light suddenly lit him up, as he urged the wooden horse, and lit her up, as she stood, blonde, in her dress of pale green and crystal, in the doorway.

"Paul!" she cried. "Whatever are you doing?"

"It's Malabar!" he screamed, in a powerful, strange voice. "It's Malabar!"   225

His eyes blazed at her for one strange and senseless second, as he ceased urging his wooden horse. Then he fell with a crash to the ground, and she, all her tormented motherhood flooding upon her, rushed to gather him up.

But he was unconscious, and unconscious he remained, with some brain-fever. He talked and tossed, and his mother sat stonily by his side.

"Malabar! It's Malabar! Bassett, Bassett, I *know*! It's Malabar!"

So the child cried, trying to get up and urge the rocking-horse that gave him his inspiration.

"What does he mean by Malabar?" asked the heart-frozen mother.   230

"I don't know," said the father stonily.

"What does he mean by Malabar?" she asked her brother Oscar.

"It's one of the horses running for the Derby," was the answer.

And, in spite of himself, Oscar Cresswell spoke to Bassett, and himself put a thousand on Malabar: at fourteen to one.

The third day of the illness was critical: they were waiting for a change. The boy,   235
with his rather long, curly hair, was tossing ceaselessly on the pillow. He neither slept nor regained consciousness, and his eyes were like blue stones. His mother sat, feeling her heart had gone, turned actually into a stone.

In the evening, Oscar Cresswell did not come, but Bassett sent a message, saying could he come up for one moment, just one moment? Paul's mother was very angry at the intrusion, but on second thoughts she agreed. The boy was the same. Perhaps Bassett might bring him to consciousness.

The gardener, a shortish fellow with a little brown moustache and sharp little brown eyes, tiptoed into the room, touched his imaginary cap to Paul's mother, and stole to the bedside, staring with glittering, smallish eyes, at the tossing, dying child.

"Master Paul!" he whispered. "Master Paul! Malabar came in first all right, a clean win. I did as you told me. You've made over seventy thousand pounds, you have; you've got over eighty thousand. Malabar came in all right, Master Paul."

"Malabar! Malabar! Did I say Malabar, mother? Did I say Malabar? Do you think I'm lucky, mother? I knew Malabar, didn't I? Over eighty thousand pounds! I call that lucky, don't you, mother? Over eighty thousand pounds! I knew, didn't I know I knew? Malabar came in all right. If I ride my horse till I'm sure, then I tell you, Bassett, you can go as high as you like. Did you go for all you were worth, Bassett?"

"I went a thousand on it, Master Paul."

"I never told you, mother, that if I can ride my horse, and *get there*, then I'm absolutely sure—oh, absolutely! Mother, did I ever tell you? I *am* lucky!"

"No, you never did," said his mother.

But the boy died in the night.

And even as he lay dead, his mother heard her brother's voice saying to her: "My God, Hester, you're eighty-odd thousand to the good, and a poor devil of a son to the bad. But, poor devil, poor devil, he's best gone out of a life where he rides his rocking-horse to find a winner."

Questions

1. Which details in the story are rooted in fantasy and which in realism?
2. What are the secrets hidden by each character and by the family house?
3. What do we know of Paul's father? Why does he barely figure in the story while Oscar Cresswell, Paul's uncle, plays a more dominant role?
4. What does each character desire? What is Paul's obsession truly for?
5. Why do the voices in the house become louder once Paul has given his mother the five thousand pounds?
6. How are the last words of the story, spoken by Oscar Cresswell, a sad but fitting epitaph for Paul?
7. Why is the rocking-horse the perfect symbolic vehicle for Paul's mad quest?

Ursula K. Le Guin

The Ones Who Walk Away from Omelas   1975

Ursula Kroeber Le Guin was born in 1929 on St. Ursula's Day (October 21) in Berkeley, California, the only daughter and youngest child of Theodora Kroeber, a folklorist, and Alfred Kroeber, a renowned anthropologist. Le Guin attended Radcliffe College, where she graduated Phi Beta Kappa, and then entered Columbia University to do graduate work in French and Italian literature. While completing her M.A., she wrote her first stories. On a Fulbright fellowship to France, she met Charles Le Guin, a professor of French history, whom she married in Paris in 1953. Over the next decade Le Guin reared three children and worked on her writing in private.

Ursula K. Le Guin

In the early sixties Le Guin began publishing in both science fiction pulp magazines and academic journals. In 1966 her first novel, Rocannon's World, was published as an Ace science fiction paperback original—hardly a respectable format for the debut of one of America's premier writers. In 1968 Le Guin published A Wizard of Earthsea, the first novel in her Earthsea Trilogy, now considered a classic of children's literature. The next two volumes, The Tombs of Atuan (1971), which won a Newbery citation, and The Farthest Shore (1972), which won a National Book Award, brought Le Guin mainstream acclaim.

Le Guin's novels The Left Hand of Darkness *(1969) and* The Dispossessed *(1974) won both the Hugo and the Nebula awards, science fiction's two most prized honors. She also twice won the Hugo for best short story, including the 1974 award for "The Ones Who Walk Away from Omelas." Le Guin has published more than thirty novels and many volumes of short stories, poetry, and essays. Her most recent novel is the Locus Award-winning* Lavinia *(2008). Le Guin lives in Portland, Oregon.*

One of the few science fiction writers whose work has earned general critical acclaim, Le Guin belongs most naturally in the company of major novelists of ideas such as Aldous Huxley, George Orwell, and Anthony Burgess, who have used the genre of science fiction to explore the possible consequences of ideological rather than technological change. Le Guin has been especially concerned with issues of social justice and equality. In her short stories— such as "The Ones Who Walk Away from Omelas"—she creates complex imaginary civilizations, envisioned with anthropological authority, and her aim is less to imagine alien cultures than to explore humanity.

With a clamor of bells that set the swallows soaring, the Festival of Summer came to the city Omelas, bright-towered by the sea. The rigging of the boats in harbor sparkled with flags. In the streets between houses with red roofs and painted walls, between old moss-grown gardens and under avenues of trees, past great parks and public buildings, processions moved. Some were decorous: old people in long stiff robes of mauve and grey, grave master workmen, quiet, merry women carrying their babies and chatting as they walked. In other streets the music beat faster, a shimmering of gong and tambourine, and the people went dancing, the procession was a dance. Children dodged in and out, their high calls rising like the swallows' crossing flights over the music and the singing. All the processions wound towards the north side of the city, where on the great water-meadow called the Green Fields boys and girls, naked in the bright air, with mud-stained feet and ankles and long, lithe arms, exercised their restive horses before the race. The horses wore no gear at all but a halter without bit. Their manes were braided with streamers of silver, gold, and green. They flared their nostrils and pranced and boasted to one another; they were vastly excited, the horse being the only animal who has adopted our ceremonies as his own. Far off to the north and west the mountains stood up half encircling Omelas on her bay. The air of morning was so clear that the snow still crowning the Eighteen Peaks burned with white-gold fire across the miles of sunlit air, under the dark blue of the sky. There was just enough wind to make the banners that marked the racecourse snap and flutter now and then. In the silence of the broad green meadows one could hear the music winding through the city streets, farther and nearer and ever approaching, a cheerful faint sweetness of the air that from time to time trembled and gathered together and broke out into the great joyous clanging of the bells.

Joyous! How is one to tell about joy? How describe the citizens of Omelas?

They were not simple folk, you see, though they were happy. But we do not say the words of cheer much any more. All smiles have become archaic. Given a description such as this one tends to make certain assumptions. Given a description such as this one tends to look next for the King, mounted on a splendid stallion and surrounded by his noble knights, or perhaps in a golden litter borne by great-muscled slaves. But there was no king. They did not use swords, or keep slaves. They were not barbarians. I do not know the rules and laws of their society, but I suspect that they were singularly few. As they did without monarchy and slavery, so they also got on without the stock exchange, the advertisement, the secret police, and the bomb. Yet I repeat that these were not simple folk, not dulcet shepherds, noble savages, bland utopians. They were not less complex than us. The trouble is that we have a bad habit, encouraged by pedants and sophisticates, of considering happiness as something rather stupid. Only pain is intellectual, only evil interesting. This is the treason of the artist: a refusal to admit the banality of evil and the terrible boredom of pain. If you can't lick 'em, join 'em. If it hurts, repeat it. But to praise despair is to condemn delight, to embrace violence is to lose hold of everything else. We have almost lost hold; we can no longer describe a happy man, nor make any celebration of joy. How can I tell you about the people of Omelas? They were not naïve and happy children— though their children were, in fact, happy. They were mature, intelligent, passionate adults whose lives were not wretched. O miracle! but I wish I could describe it better. I wish I could convince you. Omelas sounds in my words like a city in a fairy tale, long ago and far away, once upon a time. Perhaps it would be best if you imagined it as your own fancy bids, assuming it will rise to the occasion, for certainly I cannot suit you all. For instance, how about technology? I think that there would be no cars or helicopters in and above the streets; this follows from the fact that the people of Omelas are happy people. Happiness is based on a just discrimination of what is necessary, what is neither necessary nor destructive, and what is destructive. In the middle category, however—that of the unnecessary but undestructive, that of comfort, luxury, exuberance, etc.—they could perfectly well have central heating, subway trains, washing machines, and all kinds of marvelous devices not yet invented here, floating light-sources, fuelless power, a cure for the common cold. Or they could have none of that: it doesn't matter. As you like it. I incline to think that people from towns up and down the coast have been coming in to Omelas during the last days before the Festival on very fast little trains and double-decked trams, and that the train station of Omelas is actually the handsomest building in town, though plainer than the magnificent Farmers' Market. But even granted trains, I fear that Omelas so far strikes some of you as goody-goody. Smiles, bells, parades, horses, bleh. If so, please add an orgy. If an orgy would help, don't hesitate. Let us not, however, have temples from which issue beautiful nude priests and priestesses already half in ecstasy and ready to copulate with any man or woman, lover or stranger, who desires union with the deep godhead of the blood, although that was my first idea. But really it would be better not to have any temples in Omelas—at least, not manned temples. Religion yes, clergy no. Surely the beautiful nudes can just wander about, offering themselves like divine soufflés to the hunger of the needy and the rapture of the flesh. Let them join the processions. Let tambourines be struck above the copulations, and the glory of desire be proclaimed upon the gongs, and (a not unimportant point) let the offspring of these delightful rituals be beloved and looked after by all. One thing I know there is none of in Omelas is guilt. But what else should there be? I thought at first there were no drugs, but that is puritanical. For those who like it, the faint insistent sweetness of *drooz* may perfume the ways of the city, *drooz* which first brings a great lightness and brilliance to the mind and limbs, and then after some hours a dreamy languor, and wonderful visions at last of the very arcana and inmost secrets of the Universe, as well as exciting the pleasure of sex beyond all belief; and it is not habit-forming. For more modest tastes I think there ought to be beer. What else, what else belongs in the joyous city? The sense of victory, surely, the celebration of courage. But as we did without clergy, let us do without soldiers. The joy built upon successful slaughter is not the right kind of joy; it will not do; it is fearful and it is trivial. A boundless and generous contentment, a magnanimous triumph felt not against some outer enemy but in communion with the finest and fairest in the souls of all men everywhere and the splendor of the world's summer: this is what swells the hearts of the people of Omelas, and the victory they celebrate is that of life. I really don't think many of them need to take *drooz*.

Most of the processions have reached the Green Fields by now. A marvelous smell of cooking goes forth from the red and blue tents of the provisioners. The faces of small children are amiably sticky; in the benign grey beard of a man a couple of crumbs of rich pastry are entangled. The youths and girls have mounted their horses and are beginning to group around the starting line of the course. An old woman, small, fat, and laughing, is passing out flowers from a basket, and tall young men wear her flowers in their shining hair. A child of nine or ten sits at the edge of the crowd, alone, playing on a wooden flute. People pause to listen, and they smile, but they do not speak to him, for he never ceases playing and never sees them, his dark eyes wholly rapt in the sweet, thin magic of the tune.

He finishes, and slowly lowers his hands holding the wooden flute.   5

As if that little private silence were the signal, all at once a trumpet sounds from the pavilion near the starting line: imperious, melancholy, piercing. The horses rear on their slender legs, and some of them neigh in answer. Sober-faced, the young riders stroke the horses' necks and soothe them, whispering, "Quiet, quiet, there my beauty, my hope. . . ." They begin to form in rank along the starting line. The crowds along the racecourse are like a field of grass and flowers in the wind. The Festival of Summer has begun.

Do you believe? Do you accept the festival, the city, the joy? No? Then let me describe one more thing.

In a basement under one of the beautiful public buildings of Omelas, or perhaps in the cellar of one of its spacious private homes, there is a room. It has one locked door, and no window. A little light seeps in dustily between cracks in the boards, secondhand from a cobwebbed window somewhere across the cellar. In one corner of the little room a couple of mops, with stiff, clotted, foul-smelling heads, stand near a rusty bucket. The floor is dirt, a little damp to the touch, as cellar dirt usually is. The room is about three paces long and two wide: a mere broom closet or disused tool room. In the room a child is sitting. It could be a boy or a girl. It looks about six, but actually is nearly ten. It is feeble-minded. Perhaps it was born defective, or perhaps it has become imbecile through fear, malnutrition, and neglect. It picks its nose and occasionally fumbles vaguely with its toes or genitals, as it sits hunched in the corner farthest from the bucket and the two mops. It is afraid of the mops. It finds them horrible. It shuts its eyes, but it knows the mops are still standing there; and the door is locked; and nobody will come. The door is always locked; and nobody ever comes, except that sometimes—the child has no understanding of time or interval—sometimes the door rattles terribly and opens, and a person, or several people, are there. One of them may come in and kick the child to make it stand up. The others never come close, but peer in at it with frightened, disgusted eyes. The food bowl and the water jug are hastily filled, the door is locked, the eyes disappear. The people at the door never say anything, but the child, who has not always lived in the tool room, and can remember sunlight and its mother's voice, sometimes speaks. "I will be good," it says. "Please let me out. I will be good!" They never answer. The child used to scream for help at night, and cry a good deal, but now it only makes a kind of whining, "eh-haa, eh-haa," and it speaks less and less often. It is so thin there are no calves to its legs; its belly protrudes; it lives on a half-bowl of corn meal and grease a day. It is naked. Its buttocks and thighs are a mass of festered sores, as it sits in its own excrement continually.

They all know it is there, all the people of Omelas. Some of them have come to see it, others are content merely to know it is there. They all know that it has to be there. Some of them understand why, and some do not, but they all understand that their happiness, the beauty of their city, the tenderness of their friendships, the health of their children, the wisdom of their scholars, the skill of their makers, even the abundance of their harvest and the kindly weathers of their skies, depend wholly on this child's abominable misery.

This is usually explained to children when they are between eight and twelve, 10 whenever they seem capable of understanding; and most of those who come to see the child are young people, though often enough an adult comes, or comes back, to see the child. No matter how well the matter has been explained to them, these young spectators are always shocked and sickened at the sight. They feel disgust, which they had thought themselves superior to. They feel anger, outrage, impotence, despite all the explanations. They would like to do something for the child. But there is nothing they can do. If the child were brought up into the sunlight out of that vile place, if it were cleaned and fed and comforted, that would be a good thing, indeed; but if it were done, in that day and hour all the prosperity and beauty and delight of Omelas would wither and be destroyed. Those are the terms. To exchange all the goodness and grace of every life in Omelas for that single, small improvement: to throw away the happiness of thousands for the chance of the happiness of one: that would be to let guilt within the walls indeed.

The terms are strict and absolute; there may not even be a kind word spoken to the child.

Often the young people go home in tears, or in a tearless rage, when they have seen the child and faced this terrible paradox. They may brood over it for weeks or years. But as time goes on they begin to realize that even if the child could be released, it would not get much good of its freedom: a little vague pleasure of warmth and food, no doubt, but little more. It is too degraded and imbecile to know any real joy. It has been afraid too long ever to be free of fear. Its habits are too uncouth for it to respond to humane treatment. Indeed, after so long it would probably be wretched without walls about it to protect it, and darkness for its eyes, and its own excrement to sit in. Their tears at the bitter injustice dry when they begin to perceive the terrible justice of reality, and to accept it. Yet it is their tears and anger, the trying of their generosity and the acceptance of their helplessness, which are perhaps the true source of the splendor of their lives. Theirs is no vapid, irresponsible happiness. They know that they, like the child, are not free. They know compassion. It is the existence of the child, and their knowledge of its existence, that makes possible the nobility of their architecture, the poignancy of their music, the profundity of their science. It is because of the child that they are so gentle with children. They know that if the wretched one were not there snivelling in the dark, the other one, the flute-player, could make no joyful music as the young riders line up in their beauty for the race in the sunlight of the first morning of summer.

Now do you believe in them? Are they not more credible? But there is one more thing to tell, and this is quite incredible.

At times one of the adolescent girls or boys who go to see the child does not go home to weep or rage, does not, in fact, go home at all. Sometimes also a man or woman much older falls silent for a day or two, and then leaves home. These people go out into the street, and walk down the street alone. They keep walking, and walk straight out of the city of Omelas, through the beautiful gates. They keep walking across the farmlands of Omelas. Each one goes alone, youth or girl, man or woman. Night falls; the traveler must pass down village streets, between the houses with yellow-lit windows, and on out into the darkness of the fields. Each alone, they go west or north, toward the mountains. They go on. They leave Omelas, they walk ahead into the darkness, and they do not come back. The place they go towards is a place even less imaginable to most of us than the city of happiness. I cannot describe it at all. It is possible that it does not exist. But they seem to know where they are going, the ones who walk away from Omelas.

Questions

1. Does the narrator live in Omelas? What do we know about the narrator's society?
2. What is the narrator's opinion of Omelas? Does the author seem to share that opinion?
3. What is the narrator's attitude toward "the ones who walk away from Omelas"? Would the narrator have been one of those who walked away?
4. How do you account for the narrator's willingness to let readers add anything they like to the story?—"If an orgy would help, don't hesitate" (paragraph 3). Doesn't Ursula Le Guin care what her story includes?
5. What is suggested by the locked, dark cellar in which the child sits? What other details in the story are suggestive enough to be called symbolic?
6. Do you find in the story any implied criticism of our own society?

Shirley Jackson

The Lottery   1948

*Shirley Jackson (1919–1965), a native of San Francisco, moved in her teens to Rochester, New York. She started college at the University of Rochester, but had to drop out, stricken by severe depression, a problem that was to recur at intervals throughout her life. Later she graduated from Syracuse University. With her husband, Stanley Edgar Hyman, a literary critic, she settled in Bennington, Vermont, in a sprawling house built in the nineteenth century. There Jackson conscientiously set herself to produce a fixed number of words each day. She wrote novels—*The Road Through the Wall *(1948)— and three psychological thrillers—*Hangsaman *(1951),* The Haunting of Hill House *(1959), and* We Have Always Lived in the Castle *(1962).* She wrote light, witty arti- cles for* Good Housekeeping *and other popular magazines about the horrors of house- keeping and rearing four children, collected in* Life Among the Savages *(1953) and* Raising Demons *(1957); but she claimed to have written these only for money. When "The Lottery" appeared in the* New Yorker *in 1948, that issue of the magazine quickly sold out. Her purpose in writing the story, Jackson declared, had been "to shock the story's readers with a graphic demonstration of the pointless violence and general inhu- manity in their own lives."*

The morning of June 27th was clear and sunny, with the fresh warmth of a full-summer day; the flowers were blossoming profusely and the grass was richly green. The people of the village began to gather in the square, between the post office and the bank, around ten o'clock; in some towns there were so many people that the lottery took two days and had to be started on June 26th, but in this village, where there were only about three hundred people, the whole lottery took less than two hours, so it could begin at ten o'clock in the morning and still be through in time to allow the villagers to get home for noon dinner.

The children assembled first, of course. School was recently over for the summer, and the feeling of liberty sat uneasily on most of them; they tended to gather together quietly for a while before they broke into boisterous play, and their talk was still of the classroom and the teacher, of books and reprimands. Bobby Martin had already stuffed his pockets full of stones, and the other boys soon followed his example, selecting the smoothest and roundest stones; Bobby and Harry Jones and Dickie Delacroix—the villagers pronounced this name "Dellacroy"—eventually made a great pile of stones in one corner of the square and guarded it against the raids of the other boys. The girls stood aside, talking among themselves, looking over their shoulders at the boys, and the very small children rolled in the dust or clung to the hands of their older brothers or sisters.

Soon the men began to gather, surveying their own children, speaking of planting and rain, tractors and taxes. They stood together, away from the pile of stones in the corner, and their jokes were quiet and they smiled rather than laughed. The women, wearing faded house dresses and sweaters, came shortly after their menfolk. They greeted one another and exchanged bits of gossip as they went to join their husbands. Soon the women, standing by their husbands, began to call to their children, and the children came reluctantly, having to be called four or five times. Bobby Martin ducked under his mother's grasping hand and ran, laughing, back to the pile of stones. His father spoke up sharply, and Bobby came quickly and took his place between his father and his oldest brother.

The lottery was conducted—as were the square dances, the teenage club, the Halloween program—by Mr. Summers, who had time and energy to devote to civic activities. He was a roundfaced, jovial man and he ran the coal business, and people were sorry for him, because he had no children and his wife was a scold. When he arrived in the square, carrying the black wooden box, there was a murmur of conversation among the villagers and he waved and called, "Little late today, folks." The postmaster, Mr. Graves, followed him, carrying a three-legged stool, and the stool was put in the center of the square and Mr. Summers set the black box down on it. The villagers kept their distance, leaving a space between themselves and the stool, and when Mr. Summers said, "Some of you fellows want to give me a hand?" there was a hesitation before two men, Mr. Martin and his oldest son, Baxter, came forward to hold the box steady on the stool while Mr. Summers stirred up the papers inside it.

The original paraphernalia for the lottery had been lost long ago, and the black box now resting on the stool had been put into use even before Old Man Warner, the oldest man in town, was born. Mr. Summers spoke frequently to the villagers about making a new box, but no one liked to upset even as much tradition as was represented by the black box. There was a story that the present box had been made with some pieces of the box that had preceded it, the one that had been constructed when the first people settled down to make a village here. Every year, after the lottery, Mr. Summers began talking again about a new box, but every year the subject was allowed to fade off without anything's being done. The black box grew shabbier each year; by now it was no longer completely black but splintered badly along one side to show the original wood color, and in some places faded or stained.

5

Mr. Martin and his oldest son, Baxter, held the black box securely on the stool until Mr. Summers had stirred the papers thoroughly with his hand. Because so much of the ritual had been forgotten or discarded, Mr. Summers had been successful in having slips of paper substituted for the chips of wood that had been used for generations. Chips of wood, Mr. Summers had argued, had been all very well when the village was tiny, but now that the population was more than three hundred and likely to keep on growing, it was necessary to use something that would fit more easily into the black box. The night before the lottery, Mr. Summers and Mr. Graves made up the slips of paper and put them in the box, and it was then taken to the safe of Mr. Summers's coal company and locked up until Mr. Summers was ready to take it to the square next morning. The rest of the year, the box was put away, sometimes one place, sometimes another; it had spent one year in Mr. Graves's barn and another year underfoot in the post office, and sometimes it was set on a shelf in the Martin grocery and left there.

There was a great deal of fussing to be done before Mr. Summers declared the lottery open. There were lists to make up—of heads of families, heads of households in each family, members of each household in each family. There was the proper swearing-in of Mr. Summers by the postmaster, as the official of the lottery; at one time, some people remembered, there had been a recital of some sort, performed by the official of the lottery, a perfunctory, tuneless chant that had been rattled off duly each year; some people believed that the official of the lottery used to stand just so when he said or sang it, others believed that he was supposed to walk among the people, but years and years ago this part of the ritual had been allowed to lapse. There had been, also, a ritual salute, which the official of the lottery had had to use in addressing each person who came up to draw from the box, but this also had changed with time, until now it was felt necessary only for the official to speak to each person approaching. Mr. Summers was very good at all this; in his clean white shirt and blue jeans, with one hand resting carelessly on the black box, he seemed very proper and important as he talked interminably to Mr. Graves and the Martins.

Just as Mr. Summers finally left off talking and turned to the assembled villagers, Mrs. Hutchinson came hurriedly along the path to the square, her sweater thrown over her shoulders, and slid into place in the back of the crowd. "Clean forgot what day it was," she said to Mrs. Delacroix, who stood next to her, and they both laughed softly. "Thought my old man was out back stacking wood," Mrs. Hutchinson went on, "and then I looked out the window and the kids were gone, and then I remembered it was the twenty-seventh and came a-running." She dried her hands on her apron, and Mrs. Delacroix said, "You're in time, though. They're still talking away up there."

Mrs. Hutchinson craned her neck to see through the crowd and found her husband and children standing near the front. She tapped Mrs. Delacroix on the arm as a farewell and began to make her way through the crowd. The people separated good-humoredly to let her through; two or three people said, in voices just loud enough to be heard across the crowd, "Here comes your Missus, Hutchinson," and "Bill, she made it after all." Mrs. Hutchinson reached her husband, and Mr. Summers, who had been waiting, said cheerfully, "Thought we were going to have to get on without you, Tessie." Mrs. Hutchinson said, grinning, "Wouldn't have me leave m'dishes in the sink, now would you, Joe?" and soft laughter ran through the crowd as the people stirred back into position after Mrs. Hutchinson's arrival.

"Well, now," Mr. Summers said soberly, "guess we better get started, get this over   10
with, so's we can go back to work. Anybody ain't here?"

"Dunbar," several people said. "Dunbar, Dunbar."

Mr. Summers consulted his list. "Clyde Dunbar," he said. "That's right. He's
broke his leg, hasn't he? Who's drawing for him?"

"Me, I guess," a woman said, and Mr. Summers turned to look at her. "Wife
draws for her husband," Mr. Summers said. "Don't you have a grown boy to do it for
you, Janey?" Although Mr. Summers and everyone else in the village knew the
answer perfectly well, it was the business of the official of the lottery to ask such
questions formally. Mr. Summers waited with an expression of polite interest while
Mrs. Dunbar answered.

"Horace's not but sixteen yet," Mrs. Dunbar said regretfully. "Guess I gotta fill in
for the old man this year."

"Right," Mr. Summers said. He made a note on the list he was holding. Then he   15
asked, "Watson boy drawing this year?"

A tall boy in the crowd raised his hand. "Here," he said. "I'm drawing for m'mother
and me." He blinked his eyes nervously and ducked his head as several voices in the
crowd said things like "Good fellow, Jack," and "Glad to see your mother's got a man to
do it."

"Well," Mr. Summers said, "guess that's everyone. Old Man Warner make it?"

"Here," a voice said, and Mr. Summers nodded.

A sudden hush fell on the crowd as Mr. Summers cleared his throat and looked
at the list. "All ready?" he called. "Now, I'll read the names—heads of families
first—and the men come up and take a paper out of the box. Keep the paper folded
in your hand without looking at it until everyone has had a turn. Everything clear?"

The people had done it so many times that they only half listened to the direc-   20
tions; most of them were quiet, wetting their lips, not looking around. Then
Mr. Summers raised one hand high and said, "Adams." A man disengaged himself from
the crowd and came forward. "Hi, Steve," Mr. Summers said, and Mr. Adams said,
"Hi, Joe." They grinned at one another humorlessly and nervously. Then Mr. Adams
reached into the black box and took out a folded paper. He held it firmly by one
corner as he turned and went hastily back to his place in the crowd, where he stood a
little apart from his family, not looking down at his hand.

"Allen," Mr. Summers said. "Anderson. . . . Bentham."

"Seems like there's no time at all between lotteries any more," Mrs. Delacroix
said to Mrs. Graves in the back row. "Seems like we got through with the last one
only last week."

"Time sure goes fast," Mrs. Graves said.

"Clark. . . . Delacroix."

"There goes my old man," Mrs. Delacroix said. She held her breath while her   25
husband went forward.

"Dunbar," Mr. Summers said, and Mrs. Dunbar went steadily to the box while
one of the women said, "Go on, Janey," and another said, "There she goes."

"We're next," Mrs. Graves said. She watched while Mr. Graves came around
from the side of the box, greeted Mr. Summers gravely, and selected a slip of paper
from the box. By now, all through the crowd there were men holding the small folded

papers in their large hands, turning them over and over nervously. Mrs. Dunbar and her two sons stood together, Mrs. Dunbar holding the slip of paper.

"Harburt. . . . Hutchinson."

"Get up there, Bill," Mrs. Hutchinson said, and the people near her laughed.

"Jones." 30

"They do say," Mr. Adams said to Old Man Warner, who stood next to him, "that over in the north village they're talking of giving up the lottery."

Old Man Warner snorted. "Pack of crazy fools," he said. "Listening to the young folks, nothing's good enough for *them*. Next thing you know, they'll be wanting to go back to living in caves, nobody work any more, live *that* way for a while. Used to be a saying about 'Lottery in June, corn be heavy soon.' First thing you know, we'd all be eating stewed chickweed and acorns. There's *always* been a lottery," he added petulantly. "Bad enough to see young Joe Summers up there joking with everybody."

"Some places have already quit lotteries," Mrs. Adams said.

"Nothing but trouble in *that*," Old Man Warner said stoutly. "Pack of young fools."

"Martin." And Bobby Martin watched his father go forward. "Overdyke. . . . Percy." 35

"I wish they'd hurry," Mrs. Dunbar said to her older son. "I wish they'd hurry."

"They're almost through," her son said.

"You get ready to run tell Dad," Mrs. Dunbar said.

Mr. Summers called his own name and then stepped forward precisely and selected a slip from the box. Then he called, "Warner."

"Seventy-seventh year I been in the lottery," Old Man Warner said as he went 40 through the crowd. "Seventy-seventh time."

"Watson." The tall boy came awkwardly through the crowd. Someone said, "Don't be nervous, Jack," and Mr. Summers said, "Take your time, son."

"Zanini."

After that, there was a long pause, a breathless pause, until Mr. Summers, holding his slip of paper in the air, said, "All right, fellows." For a minute, no one moved, and then all the slips of paper were opened. Suddenly, all the women began to speak at once, saying, "Who is it?" "Who's got it?" "Is it the Dunbars?" "Is it the Watsons?" Then the voices began to say, "It's Hutchinson. It's Bill." "Bill Hutchinson's got it."

"Go tell your father," Mrs. Dunbar said to her older son.

People began to look around to see the Hutchinsons. Bill Hutchinson was stand- 45 ing quiet, staring down at the paper in his hand. Suddenly, Tessie Hutchinson shouted to Mr. Summers, "You didn't give him time enough to take any paper he wanted. I saw you. It wasn't fair!"

"Be a good sport, Tessie," Mrs. Delacroix called, and Mrs. Graves said, "All of us took the same chance."

"Shut up, Tessie," Bill Hutchinson said.

"Well, everyone," Mr. Summers said, "that was done pretty fast, and now we've got to be hurrying a little more to get done in time." He consulted his next list. "Bill," he said, "you draw for the Hutchinson family. You got any other households in the Hutchinsons?"

"There's Don and Eva," Mrs. Hutchinson yelled. "Make them take their chance!"

"Daughters draw with their husbands' families, Tessie," Mr. Summers said 50 gently. "You know that as well as anyone else."

"It wasn't fair," Tessie said.

"I guess not, Joe," Bill Hutchinson said regretfully. "My daughter draws with her husband's family, that's only fair. And I've got no other family except the kids."

"Then, as far as drawing for families is concerned, it's you," Mr. Summers said in explanation, "and as far as drawing for households is concerned, that's you, too. Right?"

"Right," Bill Hutchinson said.

"How many kids, Bill?" Mr. Summers asked formally.

"Three," Bill Hutchinson said. "There's Bill, Jr., and Nancy, and little Dave. And Tessie and me."

"All right, then," Mr. Summers said. "Harry, you got their tickets back?"

Mr. Graves nodded and held up the slips of paper. "Put them in the box, then," Mr. Summers directed. "Take Bill's and put it in."

"I think we ought to start over," Mrs. Hutchinson said, as quietly as she could. "I tell you it wasn't *fair*. You didn't give him time enough to choose. *Everybody* saw that."

Mr. Graves had selected the five slips and put them in the box, and he dropped all the papers but those onto the ground, where the breeze caught them and lifted them off.

"Listen, everybody," Mrs. Hutchinson was saying to the people around her.

"Ready, Bill?" Mr. Summers asked, and Bill Hutchinson, with one quick glance around at his wife and children, nodded.

"Remember," Mr. Summers said, "take the slips and keep them folded until each person has taken one. Harry, you help little Dave." Mr. Graves took the hand of the little boy, who came willingly with him up to the box. "Take a paper out of the box, Davy," Mr. Summers said. Davy put his hand into the box and laughed. "Take just *one* paper," Mr. Summers said. "Harry, you hold it for him." Mr. Graves took the child's hand and removed the folded paper from the tight fist and held it while little Dave stood next to him and looked up at him wonderingly.

"Nancy next," Mr. Summers said. Nancy was twelve, and her school friends breathed heavily as she went forward, switching her skirt, and took a slip daintily from the box. "Bill, Jr.," Mr. Summers said, and Billy, his face red and his feet over-large, nearly knocked the box over as he got a paper out. "Tessie," Mr. Summers said. She hesitated for a minute, looking around defiantly, and then set her lips and went up to the box. She snatched a paper out and held it behind her.

"Bill," Mr. Summers said, and Bill Hutchinson reached into the box and felt around, bringing his hand out at last with the slip of paper in it.

The crowd was quiet. A girl whispered, "I hope it's not Nancy," and the sound of the whisper reached the edges of the crowd.

"It's not the way it used to be," Old Man Warner said clearly. "People ain't the way they used to be."

"All right," Mr. Summers said. "Open the papers. Harry, you open little Dave's."

Mr. Graves opened the slip of paper and there was a general sigh through the crowd as he held it up and everyone could see that it was blank. Nancy and Bill, Jr., opened theirs at the same time, and both beamed and laughed, turning around to the crowd and holding their slips of paper above their heads.

"Tessie," Mr. Summers said. There was a pause, and then Mr. Summers looked at Bill Hutchinson, and Bill unfolded his paper and showed it. It was blank.

"It's Tessie," Mr. Summers said, and his voice was hushed. "Show us her paper, Bill."

Bill Hutchinson went over to his wife and forced the slip of paper out of her hand. It had a black spot on it, the black spot Mr. Summers had made the night before with the heavy pencil in the coal-company office. Bill Hutchinson held it up, and there was a stir in the crowd.

"All right, folks," Mr. Summers said, "Let's finish quickly."

Although the villagers had forgotten the ritual and lost the original black box, they still remembered to use stones. The pile of stones the boys had made earlier was ready; there were stones on the ground with the blowing scraps of paper that had come out of the box. Mrs. Delacroix selected a stone so large she had to pick it up with both hands and turned to Mrs. Dunbar. "Come on," she said. "Hurry up."

Mrs. Dunbar had small stones in both hands, and she said, gasping for breath, 75 "I can't run at all. You'll have to go ahead and I'll catch up with you."

The children had stones already, and someone gave little Davy Hutchinson a few pebbles.

Tessie Hutchinson was in the center of a cleared space by now, and she held her hands out desperately as the villagers moved in on her. "It isn't fair," she said. A stone hit her on the side of the head.

Old Man Warner was saying, "Come on, come on, everyone." Steve Adams was in the front of the crowd of villagers, with Mrs. Graves beside him.

"It isn't fair, it isn't right," Mrs. Hutchinson screamed, and then they were upon her.

Questions

1. Where do you think "The Lottery" takes place? What purpose do you suppose the writer has in making this setting appear so familiar and ordinary?

2. What details in paragraphs 2 and 3 foreshadow the ending of the story?

3. Take a close look at Jackson's description of the black wooden box (paragraph 5) and of the black spot on the fatal slip of paper (paragraph 72). What do these objects suggest to you? Are there any other symbols in the story?

4. What do you understand to be the writer's own attitude toward the lottery and the stoning? Exactly what in the story makes her attitude clear to us?

5. What do you make of Old Man Warner's saying, "Lottery in June, corn be heavy soon" (paragraph 32)?

6. What do you think Shirley Jackson is driving at? Consider each of the following interpretations and, looking at the story, see if you can find any evidence for it:

   Jackson takes a primitive fertility rite and playfully transfers it to a small town in North America.

   Jackson, writing her story soon after World War II, indirectly expresses her horror at the Holocaust. She assumes that the massacre of the Jews was carried out by unwitting, obedient people, like these villagers.

   Jackson is satirizing our own society, in which men are selected for the army by lottery.

   Jackson is just writing a memorable story that signifies nothing at all.

■ WRITING *effectively*

Shirley Jackson on Writing

Biography of a Story (1960) 1968

Shirley Jackson

My agent did not care for the story, but—as she said in her note at the time—her job was to sell it, not to like it. She sent it at once to the *New Yorker*, and about a week after the story had been written I received a telephone call from the fiction editor of the *New Yorker*; it was quite clear that he did not really care for the story, either, but the *New Yorker* was going to buy it. He asked for one change— that the date mentioned in the story be changed to coincide with the date of the issue of the magazine in which the story would ap- pear, and I said of course. He then asked, hes- itantly, if I had any particular interpretation of my own for the story; Mr. Harold Ross, then the editor of the *New Yorker*, was not al- together sure that he understood the story, and wondered if I cared to enlarge upon its meaning. I said no. Mr. Ross, he said, thought that the story might be puzzling to some people, and in case anyone telephoned the magazine, as sometimes happened, or wrote in asking about the story, was there anything in particular I wanted them to say? No, I said, nothing in particular; it was just a story I wrote.

I had no more preparation than that. I went on picking up the mail every morning, pushing my daughter up and down the hill in her stroller, anticipating pleasurably the check from the *New Yorker*, and shopping for groceries. The weather stayed nice and it looked as though it was going to be a good summer. Then, on June 28, the *New Yorker* came out with my story.

Things began mildly enough with a note from a friend at the *New Yorker*: "Your story has kicked up quite a fuss around the office," he wrote. I was flattered; it's nice to think that your friends notice what you write. Later that day there was a call from one of the magazine's editors; they had had a couple of people phone in about my story, he said, and was there anything I particularly wanted him to say if there were any more calls? No, I said, nothing particular; anything he chose to say was perfectly all right with me; it was just a story.

I was further puzzled by a cryptic note from another friend: "Heard a man talking about a story of yours on the bus this morning," she wrote. "Very exciting. I wanted to tell him I knew the author, but after I heard what he was saying I decided I'd better not."

One of the most terrifying aspects of publishing stories and books is the real- ization that they are going to be read, and read by strangers. I had never fully realized this before, although I had of course in my imagination dwelt lovingly upon the thought of millions and millions of people who were going to be uplifted and enriched and delighted by the stories I wrote. It had simply never occurred to me that these millions and millions of people might be so far from being uplifted that they would sit down and write me letters I was downright scared to open; of the three-hundred-odd letters that I received that summer I can count only thirteen that spoke kindly to me, and they were mostly from friends. Even my mother scolded me: "Dad and I did not care at all for your story in the *New Yorker*," she wrote sternly; "it does seem, dear, that this gloomy kind of story is what all you young people think about these days. Why don't you write something to cheer people up?"

By mid-July I had begun to perceive that I was very lucky indeed to be safely in Vermont, where no one in our small town had ever heard of the *New Yorker*, much less read my story. Millions of people, and my mother, had taken a pronounced dislike to me.

The magazine kept no track of telephone calls, but all letters addressed to me care of the magazine were forwarded directly to me for answering, and all letters addressed to the magazine—some of them addressed to Harold Ross personally; these were the most vehement—were answered at the magazine and then the letters were sent me in great batches, along with carbons of the answers written at the magazine. I have all the letters still, and if they could be considered to give any accurate cross section of the reading public, or the reading public of the *New Yorker*, or even the reading public of one issue of the *New Yorker*, I would stop writing now.

Judging from these letters, people who read stories are gullible, rude, frequently illiterate, and horribly afraid of being laughed at. Many of the writers were positive that the *New Yorker* was going to ridicule them in print; and the most cautious letters were headed, in capital letters: NOT FOR PUBLICATION or PLEASE DO NOT PRINT THIS LETTER, or, at best, THIS LETTER MAY BE PUBLISHED AT YOUR USUAL RATES OF PAYMENT. Anonymous letters, of which there were a few, were destroyed. The *New Yorker* never published any comment of any kind about the story in the magazine, but did issue one publicity release saying that the story had received more mail than any piece of fiction they had ever published; this was after the newspapers had gotten into the act, in midsummer, with a front-page story in the San Francisco *Chronicle* begging to know what the story meant, and a series of columns in New York and Chicago papers pointing out that *New Yorker* subscriptions were being canceled right and left.

Curiously, there are three main themes which dominate the letters of that first summer—three themes which might be identified as bewilderment, speculation, and plain old-fashioned abuse. In the years since then, during which the story has been anthologized, dramatized, televised, and even—in one completely mystifying transformation—made into a ballet, the tenor of letters I receive has changed. I am addressed more politely, as a rule, and the letters largely confine themselves to questions like what does this story mean? The general tone of the early letters, however, was a kind of wide-eyed, shocked innocence. People at first were not so much concerned with what the story meant; what they wanted to know was where these lotteries were held, and whether they could go there and watch.

From *Come Along with Me*

THINKING ABOUT SYMBOLS

One danger in analyzing a story's symbolism is the temptation to read symbolic meaning into *everything*. An image acquires symbolic resonance because it is organically important to the actions and emotions of the story.

- **Consider a symbolic object's relevance to the plot.** What events, characters, and ideas are associated with it? It also helps to remember that some symbols arrive with cultural baggage. Any great white whale that swims into a work of contemporary fiction will inevitably summon up the symbolic associations of Melville's Moby Dick.

- **Ask yourself what the symbol means to the protagonist of your story.** Writers don't simply assign arbitrary meanings to items in their stories; generally, a horse is a horse, and a hammer is just a hammer. Sometimes, though, an object means something more to a character. Think of the flowers in "The Chrysanthemums."

- **Remember: in literature, few symbols are hidden.** Don't go on a symbol hunt. As you read or reread a story, any real symbol will usually find you. If an object appears time and again, or is tied inextricably to the story's events, it is likely to suggest something beyond itself. When an object, an action, or a place has emotional or intellectual power beyond its literal importance, then it is a genuine symbol.

CHECKLIST: Writing About Symbols

- ☐ Which objects, actions, or places seem unusually significant?
- ☐ List the specific objects, people, and ideas with which a particular symbol is associated.
- ☐ Locate the exact place in the story where the symbol links itself to the other thing.
- ☐ Ask whether each symbol comes with ready-made cultural associations.
- ☐ Avoid far-fetched interpretations. Focus first on the literal things, places, and actions in the story.
- ☐ Don't make a symbol mean too much or too little. Don't limit it to one narrow association or claim it summons up many different things.
- ☐ Be specific. Identify the exact place in the story where a symbol takes on a deeper meaning.

WRITING ASSIGNMENT ON SYMBOLS

From the stories in this book, choose one with a strong central symbol. Explain how the symbol helps to communicate the story's meaning, citing specific moments in the text. Here is an example of a paper written on that topic by Samantha L. Brown, a student of Melinda Barth's at El Camino College.

SAMPLE STUDENT PAPER

Samantha L. Brown

Professor Barth

English 210

26 Nov. 2011

An Analysis of the Symbolism in Steinbeck's

"The Chrysanthemums"

Thesis sentence

In a work of literature a symbol is something that suggests more than its surface meaning. In his short story "The Chrysanthemums," John Steinbeck uses the flowers of the title for both realistic and symbolic purposes. On the realistic level, the chrysanthemums advance the plot because they are the basis for the

Clarification and elaboration of thesis

story's central action. They also help define the character of Elisa, provide a greater understanding of the setting, and play a vital part in revealing the story's theme.

Topic sentence

The chrysanthemums provide the reader with insight into Elisa. When we first see her, she is in her flower garden working with her chrysanthemums. She

Development of thesis

is putting a great deal of energy into the relatively simple job of tending to the flowers. Elisa and her husband, Henry, have no children. They do not appear to

Textual evidence

have a very intense or passionate relationship. He praises her skill at growing flowers, but says that he wishes she would work in the orchard and grow larger apples for him. His interests are practical and financial. The beauty of the flowers, which also symbolizes her beauty as a woman, is not important to him.

Further development of thesis

"The Chrysanthemums" is set in rural Monterey, California, in the 1930s. The ranch where Elisa and Henry live is in an isolated area. The flower garden is isolated from the rest of the ranch. The reader sees that Elisa is unhappy and frustrated, emotionally isolated from her husband and the life of their ranch. The flower garden is also surrounded by a wire fence, which symbolizes Elisa's

Textual evidence

feelings of being fenced in. She shows such feelings later in the story when she envies the free and easy life of the tinker and wishes that women could live that way.

Further development of thesis

The symbolic significance of the chrysanthemums is especially brought out in Elisa's conversation with the tinker. At first she resists his attempts to repair something for her, but then she responds to him because he admires her flowers. When he describes them in a poetic-sounding way, she feels she has met someone like herself that she can share an emotional bond with. The feelings he arouses in her are passionate—even sexual, as we see when she stops herself from reaching out and touching his pants. This is also shown after he leaves, when she takes off her mannish gardening clothes, bathes, and looks at her body in the mirror.

Textual evidence

The last and most painful symbolic use of the flowers comes toward the end of the story, when Elisa and her husband are driving into town for their evening out. Even before she can see it clearly, she knows that the speck by the side of the road is the chrysanthemum sprouts she gave the tinker to give to the (probably fictitious) woman he told her about. This is so upsetting to her that she turns around toward her husband so as not to see the tinker again as the car passes his wagon.

Topic sentence announces culmination of thesis

If we read the story only on the surface level, we won't be able to understand why Elisa is so upset. So a cunning traveler has manipulated her love of flowers to soften her up into giving him some work. Maybe he made a fool of her, but it's in the middle of the Depression, and he has to eat, too. What's the big deal? Only when we understand the symbolic importance of the chrysanthemums do we understand why this is so painful for her. She had felt that someone understood her, maybe even felt that life was richer in possibilities than it had seemed. This illusion is shattered, however, when she sees the plant sprouts. The discarded, dying plants symbolize her diminished life, her failure to find anyone who can understand her needs and feelings.

Topic sentence on significance of symbolism

Elaboration of significance of symbolism

The chrysanthemums are vital to Steinbeck's presentation of the theme. At the beginning, Elisa is presented as a strong woman, strong enough to break the back of a calf. At the end, she is seen huddled like an old woman, crying weakly. The newly revealed Elisa is not the strong woman that she or her husband thought she was. It wasn't until she saw the discarded plant sprouts that she felt the sting of her rejection and isolation. Until that moment, her gardening had protected—or at least distracted—her from her loneliness, isolation, and feelings of inadequacy. Finally, the theme emerges from our understanding of this woman and the importance of her chrysanthemums. Understanding Steinbeck's symbolism, therefore, is essential to understanding how the story works.

Elaboration of how symbol reveals theme

Conclusion sums up main idea without simply restating it

MORE TOPICS FOR WRITING

1. Choose a story from this chapter. Describe your experience of reading that story, and of encountering its symbols. At what point did the main symbol's meaning become clear? What in the story indicated the larger importance of that symbol?

2. From any story in this book, select an object, or place, or action that seems clearly symbolic. How do you know? Now select an object, place, or action from the same story that clearly seems to signify no more than itself. How can you tell?

3. Analyze the symbolism in a story from another chapter in this book. Some good choices might be "Dead Men's Path," "The Story of an Hour," and "Where Are You Going, Where Have You Been?" Choose a symbol that recurs over the course of the story, and look closely at each appearance it makes. How does the story's use of the symbol evolve?

4. In an essay of 600 to 800 words, compare and contrast the symbolic use of the scapegoat in "The Lottery" and "The Ones Who Walk Away from Omelas."

▶ TERMS FOR *review*

Symbol ▶ A person, place, or thing in a narrative that suggests meanings beyond its literal sense. Symbol is related to allegory, but it works more complexly. A symbol often contains multiple meanings and associations.

Conventional symbol ▶ A literary symbol that has a conventional or customary meaning for most readers—for example, a black cat crossing a path or a young bride in a white dress.

Symbolic act ▶ An action whose significance goes well beyond its literal meaning. In literature, symbolic acts often involve some conscious or unconscious ritual element such as rebirth, purification, forgiveness, vengeance, or initiation.

Allegory ▶ A narrative in which the literal events (persons, places, and things) consistently point to a parallel sequence of symbolic equivalents. This narrative strategy is often used to dramatize abstract ideas, historical events, religious systems, or political issues. An allegory has two levels of meaning: a literal level that tells a surface story and a symbolic level in which the abstract ideas unfold.

8 READING LONG STORIES AND NOVELS

The novel is the one bright book of life.

—D. H. LAWRENCE

A mong the forms of imaginative literature in our language, the novel has been the favorite of both writers and readers for more than two hundred years. Broadly defined, a **novel** is a book-length fictional story in prose, whose author tries to create the sense that while we read, we experience actual life.

This sense of actuality, also found in artful short stories, may be the quality that sets the novel apart from other long prose narratives. Why do we not apply the name *novel* to, for instance, *Gulliver's Travels*? In his marvel-filled account of Lemuel Gulliver's voyages among pygmies, giants, civilized horses, and noxious humanoid swine, Jonathan Swift does not seem primarily to care if we find his story credible. Though he arrays the adventures of Gulliver in painstaking detail (and, ironically, has Gulliver swear to the truth of them), Swift neither attempts nor achieves a convincing illusion of life. For his book is a fantastic satire that finds resemblances between noble horses and man's reasoning faculties, between debased apes and man's kinship with the beasts.

ORIGINS OF THE NOVEL

Unlike other major literary forms—drama, lyric, ballad, and epic—the novel is a relative newcomer. Originally, the drama in ancient Greece came alive only when actors performed it; the epic or heroic poem (from the classic *Iliad* through the Old English *Beowulf*), only when a bard sang or chanted it. But the English novel came to maturity in literate times, in the eighteenth century, and by its nature was something different: a story to be communicated silently in printed books, at whatever moment and at whatever pace (whether quickly or slowly and meditatively) the reader desired.

Some definitions of the novel would more strictly define the form. "The Novel is a picture of real life and manners, and of the time in which it was written," declared Clara Reeve in 1785. By so specifying that the novel depicts life in the present day, the critic was probably observing the derivation of the word *novel*. Akin to the French word for "news" (*nouvelles*), it comes from the Italian *novella* ("something new and small"), a term applied to a newly made story taking place in recent times, and not a traditional story taking place long ago.

Romances

The novel, which is principally a realistic form, is often contrasted with the other major prose tradition of narrative, the **romance.** In general terms, romance is a narrative mode that employs exotic adventure and idealized emotion rather than realistic depiction of character and action. In the romantic mode—out of which most popular genre fictions develop—people, actions, and events are depicted more as we wish them to be (heroes are very brave, villains are very bad) than as the complex entities they usually are. Medieval romances (in both prose and verse) presented chivalric tales of kings, knights, and aristocratic ladies. Modern romances, emerging in the nineteenth century, were represented by adventure novels such as Sir Walter Scott's *Ivanhoe* which embodied the symbolic quests and idealized characters of earlier, chivalric tales in slightly more realistic terms, a tradition carried on in contemporary popular works such as the *Stars Wars* and James Bond films.

Novels Versus Romances

Also drawing a line between novel and romance, Nathaniel Hawthorne, in his preface to *The House of the Seven Gables* (1851), restricted the novel "not merely to the possible, but to the probable and ordinary course of man's experience." A romance had no such limitations. Such a definition would deny the name of *novel* to any fantastic or speculative story—to, say, the Gothic novel and the science fiction novel. Carefully bestowed, the labels *novel* and *romance* may be useful to distinguish between the true-to-life story of usual people in ordinary places (such as George Eliot's *Silas Marner* or Amy Tan's *The Joy Luck Club*) and the larger-than-life story of daring deeds and high adventure, set in the past or future or in some timeless land (such as Walter Scott's *Ivanhoe* or J. R. R. Tolkien's *The Lord of the Rings*). This sense of the actual is, perhaps, the hallmark of a novel, whether or not the events it relates are literally possible.

A student shouldn't worry too much about the differences between the novel and romance. In everyday conversation people usually refer to any book-length fictional narratives as "novels." The important thing to remember is that there are two fundamentally different ways of telling a story. The novelistic method stresses the everyday, realistic aspects. The romantic method stresses the aspects of adventure, surprise, and wish fulfillment. It is particularly interesting to see the rare occasions when authors deliberately stray across the boundary between the two modes. In Franz Kafka's *The Metamorphosis*, for example, the story begins with a fantastic premise—Gregor Samsa wakes to discover himself turned into a giant insect. This bizarre transformation would seem the very stuff of romance, but after the first sentence Kafka tells the story in the most matter-of-fact and realistic way. The stunning quality of Kafka's masterpiece comes from his novelistic manner of telling his seemingly unrealistic tale.

Novels and Journalism

Since both the novel and journalism try to capture the fabric of everyday life, there has long been a close relationship between the two literary forms. Many novelists, among them Ernest Hemingway, Stephen Crane, and Jack London, began their writing careers as cub reporters. Ambrose Bierce was the most influential newspaper satirist of his day.

The two modes of writing, however, remain different. "Literature is the art of writing something that will be read twice," commented critic and novelist Cyril Connolly, "journalism what will be grasped at once." Journalism greatly influences how novelists depict the world around them. Stephen Crane's "The Open Boat" began as a newspaper account of his actual experiences in a small rowboat after the sinking of the *Commodore* in 1897. A journalist might have been content with such a gripping first-person story of surviving a shipwreck, but a great fiction writer has the gift of turning personal bad luck into art, and Crane eventually created a masterpiece of fiction based on fact.

NOVELISTIC METHODS

Many early novels were told in the form of letters. Sometimes these **epistolary novels** contained letters by only one character; often they contained letters exchanged by several of the characters in the book. By casting his novel *Pamela* (1740) into the form of personal letters, Samuel Richardson helped give the story the appearance of being not invented but discovered from real documents. Alice Walker's *The Color Purple* (1982) is a more recent epistolary novel, though some of the letters that tell the story are addressed to God.

Another method favored by novelists is to write as though setting down a memoir or an autobiography. Daniel Defoe, whose skill in feigning such memoirs was phenomenal, succeeded in writing the supposedly true confessions of a woman retired from a life of crime, *Moll Flanders* (1722), and in maintaining a vivid truthfulness:

> Going through Aldersgate Street, there was a pretty little child who had been at a dancing-school, and was going home all alone: and my prompter, like a true devil, set me upon this innocent creature. I talked to it, and it prattled to me again, and I took it by the hand and led it along till I came to a paved alley that goes into Bartholomew Close, and I led it in there. The child said that was not its way home. I said, "Yes, my dear, it is; I'll show you the way home." The child had a little necklace on of gold beads, and I had my eye upon that, and in the dark of the alley I stooped, pretending to mend the child's clog that was loose, and took off her necklace, and the child never felt it, and so led the child on again. Here, I say, the devil put me upon killing the child in the dark alley, that it might not cry, but the very thought frighted me so that I was ready to drop down; but I turned the child about and bade it go back again. . . . The last affair left no great concern upon me, for as I did the poor child no harm, I only said to myself, I had given the parents a just reproof for their negligence in leaving the poor little lamb to come home by itself, and it would teach them to take more care of it another time.

What could sound more like the voice of an experienced child-robber than this manner of excusing her crime, and even justifying it?

Some novelists place great emphasis on research and notetaking. James A. Michener, the internationally best-selling author of novels such as *Centennial* (which tracks life in Colorado from prehistory through modern times) and *Chesapeake* (which describes 400 years of events on Maryland's Eastern Shore), started work on a book by studying everything available about his chosen subject. He also traveled to locations that might appear in the book, interviewed local people, and compiled immense amounts of scientific, historical, and cultural data. Research alone, however, is not enough to produce a novel. A novel grows to completion only through the slow mental process of creation, selection, and arrangement. But raw facts can sometimes provide a beginning. Many novels started when the author read some arresting episode in a newspaper or magazine. Theodore Dreiser's impressive study of a murder, *An American Tragedy* (1925), for example, was inspired by a journalist's account of a real-life case.

Nonfiction Novels

In the 1960s there was a great deal of talk about the **nonfiction novel,** in which the author presents actual people and events in story form. The vogue of the nonfiction novel was created by Truman Capote's *In Cold Blood* (1966), which depicts an actual multiple murder and the resulting trial in Kansas. Capote traveled to the scene of the crime and interviewed all of the principal parties, including the murderers. Norman Mailer wrote a similar novel, *The Executioner's Song* (1979), chronicling the life and death of Gary Gilmore, the Utah murderer who demanded his own execution. More recently, John Berendt's darkly comic 1994 account of the upper class and under class of Savannah, Georgia, *Midnight in the Garden of Good and Evil* (which also centers on a murder and the subsequent trial), revived interest in the form.

Perhaps the name "nonfiction novel" (Capote's term for it) is newer than the form. In the past, writers of autobiography have cast their memoirs into what looks like novel form: Richard Wright in *Black Boy* (1945), William Burroughs in *Junkie* (1953). Derived from his reporting, John Hersey's *Hiroshima* (1946) reconstructs the lives of six survivors of the atom bomb as if they were fictional. In reading such works we may nearly forget we are reading literal truth, so well do the techniques of the novel lend an air of immediacy to remembered facts.

Historical Novels

A familiar kind of fiction that claims a basis in fact is the **historical novel,** a detailed reconstruction of life in another time, perhaps in another place. In some historical novels the author attempts a faithful picture of daily life in another era, as does Robert Graves in *I, Claudius* (1934), a novel of patrician Rome. More often, history is a backdrop for an exciting story of love and heroic adventure. Nathaniel Hawthorne's *The Scarlet Letter* (set in Puritan Boston) and Stephen Crane's *The Red Badge of Courage* (set on the battlefields of the Civil War) are historical novels in that their authors lived considerably later than the scenes and events that they depicted, and strove for truthfulness, by imaginative means.

Other Types of Novels

Other varieties of novel will be familiar to anyone who browses in bookstores: the mystery or detective novel, the Western novel, the science fiction novel, and other enduring types. Novels are sometimes said to belong to a category if they contain some recognizable kind of structure or theme. Such a category is the **Bildungsroman** (German for a "novel of growth and development"), sometimes called the **apprenticeship novel** after its classic example, *Wilhelm Meister's Apprenticeship* (1796) by Johann Wolfgang von Goethe. This is the kind of novel in which a youth struggles toward maturity, seeking, perhaps, some consistent worldview or philosophy of life. Sometimes the apprenticeship novel is evidently derived from the author's recollection of his own early life: James Joyce's *A Portrait of the Artist as a Young Man* (1916) and Tobias Wolff's *Old School* (2003).

Picaresques

In a **picaresque** (another famous category), a likable scoundrel wanders through adventures, living by his wits, duping the straight citizenry. The name comes from

Spanish: *pícaro*, "rascal" or "rogue." The classic picaresque novel is the anonymous Spanish *Life of Lazarillo de Tormes* (1554), imitated by many English writers, among them Henry Fielding in his story of a London thief and racketeer, *Jonathan Wild* (1743). Mark Twain's *Huckleberry Finn* (1885) owes something to the tradition; like early picaresque novels, it is told in episodes rather than in one all-unifying plot and is narrated in the first person by a hero at odds with respectable society ("dismal regular and decent," Huck Finn calls it). In Twain's novel, however, the traveling swindlers who claim to be a duke and a dauphin are much more typical rogues of picaresque fiction than Huck himself, an honest innocent. Modern novels worthy of the name include Saul Bellow's *The Adventures of Augie March* (1953), J. P. Donleavy's *The Ginger Man* (1965), Erica Jong's *Fanny* (1981), and Seth Morgan's *Homeboy* (1990).

Short Novels and Novellas

The term **short novel** (or **novella**) mainly describes the size of a narrative; it refers to a narrative midway in length between a short story and a novel. (E. M. Forster once said that a novel should be at least 50,000 words in length, and most editors and publishers would agree with that definition.) Generally a short novel, like a short story, focuses on just one or two characters; but, unlike a short story, it has room to examine them in great depth and detail. A short novel also often explores its characters over a greater period of time.

Many writers, such as Thomas Mann, Henry James, Joseph Conrad, and Willa Cather, favored the novella as a perfect medium between the necessary compression of the short story and the potential sprawl of the novel. Franz Kafka's famous novella *The Metamorphosis* is included in this chapter. When the term **novelette** is used, it usually refers (often disapprovingly) to a short novel written for a popular magazine, especially in such fields as science fiction, romance, the Western, and horror.

READING NOVELS

Trying to perceive a novel as a whole, we may find it helpful to look for the same elements that we have noticed in reading short stories. By asking ourselves leading questions, we may be drawn more deeply into the novel's world, and may come to recognize and appreciate the techniques of the novelist. Does the novel have themes, or an overall theme? Who is its main character? What is the author's kind of narrative voice? How would we describe the tone, style, and use of irony? Why is this novel written from one point of view rather than from another? If the novel in question is large and thickly populated, it may help to read it with a pencil and take brief notes. Forced to put the novel aside and later return to it, we may find that the notes refresh the memory. Once our reading of a novel is finished and we prepare to discuss it or write about it, it may be a good idea to browse through it again, rereading brief portions. This method of overall browsing may also help when first approaching a bulky and difficult novel. Just as an explorer mapping unfamiliar territory may find it best to begin by taking an aerial view of it, so too the reader approaching an exceptionally thick and demanding novel may wish, at the start, to look for its general shape. There is, of course, no shortcut to novel reading, and probably the best method is to settle in comfort and read the book through: with your own eyes, not with the borrowed glasses of literary criticism.

The Future of the Novel

The death of the novel has been frequently announced. Competition from television, DVDs, video games, and the Internet, some critics claim, will overwhelm the habit of reading; the public is lazy and will follow the easiest route available for entertainment. But in England and America television and films have been sending people back in vast numbers to the books they dramatize. Jane Austen has never lacked readers, but films such as *Pride and Prejudice, Emma, Persuasion,* and *Sense and Sensibility* (not to mention *Clueless,* a teenage version of *Emma* set in Beverly Hills, or *Bride and Prejudice,* a singing and dancing Bollywood treatment set in modern-day India) made her one of the world's best-selling novelists. Stylish adaptations of Philip K. Dick's offbeat science fiction, including *Blade Runner, Total Recall,* and *Minority Report,* have created a cult for his once neglected work. Sometimes Hollywood even helps bring a good book into print. No one would publish Thomas M. Disch's sophisticated children's novella *The Brave Little Toaster,* until Walt Disney turned it into a cartoon movie. A major publisher then not only rushed it into print, but commissioned a sequel.

Meanwhile, each year new novels by the hundreds continue to appear, their authors wistfully looking for a public. Some of these books reach a mass audience. To forecast the end of the novel seems risky, for the novel exercises the imagination of the beholder. At any hour, at a touch of the hand, it opens and (with no warmup) begins to speak. Once printed, it consumes no further energy. Often so small that it may be carried in a pocket, it may yet survive by its ability to contain multitudes (a "capacious vessel," Henry James called it): a thing that is both a work of art and an amazingly compact system for the storage and retrieval of imagined life.

Franz Kafka

The Metamorphosis   1915

Translated by John Siscoe

Franz Kafka (1883–1924) was born into a German-speaking Jewish family in Prague, Czechoslovakia (then part of the Austro-Hungarian empire). He was the only surviving son of a domineering, successful father. After earning a law degree, Kafka worked as a claims investigator for the state accident insurance company. He worked on his stories at night, especially during his frequent bouts of insomnia. He never married, and lived mostly with his parents. Kafka was such a careful and self-conscious writer that he found it difficult to finish his work and send it out for publication. During his lifetime he published only a few thin volumes of short fiction, most notably The Metamorphosis *(1915) and* In the Penal Colony *(1919). He never finished to his own satisfaction any of his three novels (all published posthumously):* The Trial *(1925),* The Castle *(1926), and* Amerika *(1927). As Kafka was dying of tuberculosis, he begged his friend and literary executor Max Brod to burn his uncompleted manuscripts. Brod*

Franz Kafka

pondered this request but luckily didn't obey. Kafka's two major novels, The Trial *and* The Castle, *both depict huge, remote, bumbling, irresponsible bureaucracies in whose power the individual feels helpless and blind. Kafka's works appear startlingly prophetic to readers looking back on them in the later light of Stalinism, World War II, and the Holocaust. His haunting vision of an alienated modern world led the poet W. H. Auden to remark at midcentury, "Had one to name the author who comes nearest to bearing the same kind of relation to our age as Dante, Shakespeare, and Goethe bore to theirs, Kafka is the first one would think of."* The Metamorphosis, *which arguably has the most famous opening sentence in twentieth-century literature, shows Kafka's dreamlike fiction at its most brilliant and most disturbing.*

I

When Gregor Samsa awoke one morning from troubled dreams, he found himself transformed in his bed into a monstrous insect. He was lying on his back, which was hard, as if plated in armor, and when he lifted his head slightly he could see his belly: rounded, brown, and divided into stiff arched segments; on top of it the blanket, about to slip off altogether, still barely clinging. His many legs, which seemed pathetically thin when compared to the rest of his body, flickered helplessly before his eyes.

"What's happened to me?" he thought. It was no dream. His room, a normal though somewhat small human bedroom, lay quietly within its four familiar walls. Above the table on which his unpacked fabric samples were spread—Samsa was a traveling salesman—hung the picture he had recently cut out of an illustrated magazine and had set in a lovely gilt frame. It showed a lady wearing a fur hat and a fur stole, sitting upright, and thrusting out to the viewer a thick fur muff, into which her whole forearm had disappeared.

Gregor's glance then fell on the window, and the overcast sky—one could hear raindrops drumming on the tin sheeting of the windowsill—made him feel profoundly sad. "What if I went back to sleep for a while and forgot all this nonsense," he thought. But that wasn't to be, for he was used to sleeping on his right side and in his present state was unable to get into that position. No matter how hard he threw himself to his right, he would immediately roll onto his back again. He must have tried a hundred times, shutting his eyes so as not to see his wriggling legs, not stopping until he began to feel in his side a slight dull pain that he had never felt before.

"My God," he thought, "what an exhausting job I've chosen! Always on the go, day in and day out. There are far more worries on the road than at the office, what with the constant travel, the nuisance of making your train connections, the wretched meals eaten at odd hours, and the casual acquaintances you meet only in passing, never to see again, never to become intimate friends. To hell with it all!" He felt a slight itch on the surface of his belly. Slowly he shoved himself on his back closer to the bedpost so that he could lift his head more easily. He found the place where it itched. It was covered with small white spots he did not understand. He started to touch it with one of his legs, but pulled back immediately, for the contact sent a cold shiver through him.

He slid back down to his former position. "Getting up this early," he thought, "would turn anyone into an idiot. A man needs his sleep. Other salesmen live like harem women. For example, when I get back to the hotel in the morning to write up the sales I've made, these gentlemen are sitting down to breakfast. If I tried that with my director, I'd be fired on the spot. Actually, that might not be such a bad idea. If I didn't have to curb my tongue because of my parents, I'd have given notice long ago.

5

I'd have gone up to the director and told him from the bottom of my heart exactly what I thought. That would have knocked him from his desk! It's an odd way to run things, this sitting high at a desk and talking down to employees, especially when, since the director is hard of hearing, they have to approach so near. Well, there's hope yet; as soon as I've saved enough money to pay back what my parents owe him—that should take another five or six years—I'll go do it for sure. Then, I'll cut myself completely free. Right now, though, I'd better get up, as my train leaves at five."

He looked at the alarm clock ticking on top of the chest of drawers. "God Almighty!" he thought. It was half past six and the hands were quietly moving forward, it was later than half past, it was nearly a quarter to seven. Hadn't the alarm clock gone off? You could see from the bed that it had been correctly set for four o'clock; of course it must have gone off. Yes, but could he really have slept peacefully through that ear-splitting racket? Well, if he hadn't slept peacefully, he'd slept deeply all the same. But what was he to do now? The next train left at seven, to make it he would have to rush like mad, and his samples weren't even packed, and he himself wasn't feeling particularly spry or alert. And even if he were to make the train, there would be no avoiding a scene with the director. The office messenger would've been waiting for the five o'clock train and would've long since reported his not showing up. The messenger, dim-witted and lacking a will of his own, was a tool of the director. Well, what if he were to call in sick? But that would look embarrassing and suspicious since in his five years with the firm Gregor had not been sick once. The director himself was sure to come over with the health insurance doctor, would upbraid his parents for their son's laziness, and would cut short all excuses by deferring to the doctor, who believed that everyone in the world was a perfectly healthy layabout. And really, would he be so wrong in this case? Apart from a drowsiness that was hard to account for after such a long sleep, Gregor really felt quite well, and in fact was exceptionally hungry.

As he was thinking all this at top speed, without being able to make up his mind to get out of bed—the alarm clock had just struck a quarter to seven—a cautious tap sounded on the door behind his head. "Gregor," said a voice—it was his mother—"it's a quarter to seven. Don't you have a train to catch?" That gentle voice! Gregor was shocked when he heard his own voice answering hers; unmistakably his own voice, true, but mixed in with it, like an undertone, a miserable squeaking that allowed the words to be clearly heard only for a moment before rising up, reverberating, to drown out their meaning, so that no one could be sure if he had heard them correctly. Gregor wanted to answer fully and give a complete explanation, but under the circumstances he merely said, "Yes, yes, thank you, Mother, I'm just getting up." Through the wooden door between them the change in Gregor's voice was probably not obvious, for his mother, quietly accepting his words, shuffled away. However, this brief exchange had made the rest of the family aware that Gregor, surprisingly, was still in the house, and already at one of the side doors his father was knocking, softly, yet with his fist. "Gregor, Gregor," he called, "what's the matter?" Before long he called once more in a deeper voice, "Gregor? Gregor?" From the other side door came the sound of his sister's voice, gentle and plaintive. "Gregor, aren't you feeling well? Is there anything I can get you?" Gregor answered the two of them at the same time: "I'm almost ready." He tried hard to keep his voice from sounding strange by enunciating the words with great care, and by inserting long pauses between the words. His father went back to his breakfast but his sister whispered, "Gregor, please, open the door." But Gregor had no intention of opening the door, and was thankful for having formed, while traveling, the prudent habit of keeping all his doors locked at night, even at home.

What he wanted to do now was to get up quietly and calmly, to get dressed, and above all to eat his breakfast. Only then would he think about what to do next, for he understood that mulling things over in bed would lead him nowhere. He remembered how often in the past he had felt some small pain in bed, perhaps caused by lying in an uncomfortable position, which as soon as he had gotten up had proven to be purely imaginary, and he looked forward to seeing how this morning's fancies would gradually fade and disappear. As for the change in his voice, he hadn't the slightest doubt that it was nothing more than the first sign of a severe cold, an occupational hazard of traveling salesmen.

Throwing off the blanket was easy enough; he had only to puff himself up a little and it slipped right off. But the next part was difficult, especially as he was so unusually wide. He would have needed arms and legs to lift himself up; instead he had only these numerous little legs that never stopped moving and over which he had no control at all. As soon as he tried to bend one of them it would straighten itself out, and if he finally succeeded in making it do as he wished, all the others, as if set free, would waggle about in a high degree of painful agitation. "But what's the point of lying uselessly in bed?" Gregor said to himself.

He thought that he might start by easing the lower part of his body out of bed first, but this lower part, which incidentally he hadn't yet seen and of which he couldn't form a clear picture, turned out to be very difficult to budge—it went so slowly. When finally, almost in a frenzy, he gathered his strength and pushed forward desperately, he miscalculated his direction and bumped sharply against the post at the foot of the bed, and the searing pain he felt told him that, for right now at least, it was exactly this lower part of his body that was perhaps the most tender.

So he tried getting the top part of his body out first, and cautiously turned his head towards the side of the bed. This proved easy enough, and eventually, despite its breadth and weight the bulk of his body slowly followed the turning of his head. But when he finally got his head out over the edge of the bed he felt too afraid to go any farther, for if he were to let himself fall from this position only a miracle would prevent him from hurting his head. And it was precisely now, at all costs, that he must not lose consciousness; he would be better off staying in bed.

But when after repeating his efforts he lay, sighing, in his former position, and once more watched his little legs struggling with one another more furiously than ever, if that were possible, and saw no way of bringing calm and order into this mindless confusion, he again told himself that it was impossible to stay in bed and that the wisest course would be to stake everything on the hope, however slight, of getting away from the bed. At the same time he didn't forget to remind himself that the calmest of calm reflection was much better than frantic resolutions. During this time he kept his eyes fixed as firmly as possible on the window, but unfortunately the morning fog, which shrouded even the other side of the narrow street, gave him little comfort and cheer. "Already seven o'clock," he said to himself when the alarm clock chimed again, "already seven and still such a thick fog." And for some time he lay still, breathing quietly, as if in the hope that utter stillness would bring all things back to how they really and normally were.

But then he said to himself: "I must make sure that I'm out of bed before it strikes a quarter past seven. Anyway, by then someone from work will have come to check on me, since the office opens before seven." And he immediately set the whole length of his body rocking with a rhythmic motion in order to swing out of bed. If he tumbled out this way he could prevent his head from being injured by keeping it tilted upward as he fell. His back seemed to be hard; the fall onto the carpet would probably not hurt it. His greatest worry was the thought of the loud crash he was bound to make; it would probably cause anxiety, if not outright fear, on the other side of the doors. Yet he had to take the chance.

When Gregor was already half out of bed—his new technique made it more of a game than a struggle, since all he had to do was to edge himself across by rocking back and forth—it struck him how simple it would be if he could get someone to help him. Two strong people—he thought of his father and the maid—would be more than enough. All they would have to do would be to slip their arms under his curved back, lift him out of bed, bend down with their burden, and then wait patiently while he flipped himself right side up onto the floor, where, one might hope, his little legs would acquire some purpose. Well then, aside from the fact that the doors were locked, wouldn't it be a good idea to call for help? In spite of his misery, he could not help smiling at the thought.

He had reached the point where, if he rocked any harder, he was in danger of losing his balance, and very soon he would have to commit himself, because in five minutes it would be a quarter past seven—when the doorbell rang. "It's someone from the office," he said to himself, and almost froze, while his little legs danced even faster. For a moment everything remained quiet. "They won't open the door," Gregor said to himself, clutching at an absurd sort of hope. But then, of course, the maid, as usual, went with her firm tread to the door and opened it. Gregor had only to hear the visitor's first word of greeting to know at once who it was—the office manager himself. Why was Gregor condemned to work for a firm where the most insignificant failure to appear instantly provoked the deepest suspicion? Were the employees, one and all, nothing but scoundrels? Wasn't there among them one man who was true and loyal, who if, one morning, he were to waste an hour or so of the firm's time, would become so conscience-stricken as to be driven out of his mind and actually rendered incapable of leaving his bed? Wouldn't it have been enough to send an office boy to ask—that is, if such prying were necessary at all? Did the office manager have to come in person, and thus demonstrate to an entire family of innocent people that he was the only one wise enough to properly investigate this suspicious affair? And it was more from the anxiety caused by these thoughts than by any act of will that Gregor swung himself out of bed with all his might. There was a loud thump, but not really a crash. The carpet broke his fall somewhat, and his back too was more elastic than he had thought, so there was only a muffled thud that was relatively unobtrusive. However, he had not lifted his head carefully enough and had banged it; he twisted it and rubbed it against the carpet in frustration and pain.

"Something fell down in there," said the office manager in the room on the left. Gregor tried to imagine whether something like what had happened to him today might one day happen to the office manager; really, one had to admit that it was possible. But as if in a blunt reply to this question the office manager took several determined steps in the next room and his patent leather boots creaked. From the room on the right his sister was whispering to let him know what was going on: "Gregor, the office manager is here." "I know," said Gregor to himself, but he didn't dare speak loudly enough for his sister to hear him.

"Gregor," his father now said from the room on the left, "the office manager is here and he wants to know why you weren't on the early train. We don't know what

15

to tell him. Besides, he wants to speak to you in person. So please open the door. I'm sure he'll be kind enough to excuse any untidiness in your room." "Good morning, Mr. Samsa," the manager was calling out amiably. "He isn't feeling well," said his mother to the manager, while his father was still speaking at the door. "He's not well, sir, believe me. Why else would Gregor miss his train? The boy thinks of nothing but his work. It nearly drives me to distraction the way he never goes out in the evening; he's been here the last eight days, and every single evening he's stayed at home. He just sits here at the table with us quietly reading the newspapers or looking over train schedules. The only enjoyment he gets is when he's working away with his fretsaw.° For example, he spent two or three evenings cutting out a little picture frame, you'd be surprised at how pretty it is, it's hanging in his room, you'll see it in a minute as soon as Gregor opens the door. By the way, I'm glad you've come, sir, we would've never have gotten him to unlock the door by ourselves, he's so stubborn; and I'm sure he's sick, even though he wouldn't admit it this morning." "I'm coming right now," said Gregor, slowly and carefully and not moving an inch for fear of missing a single word of the conversation. "I can't imagine any other explanation, madam," said the office manager, "I hope it's nothing serious. But on the other hand businessmen such as ourselves—fortunately or unfortunately—very often have to ignore any minor indisposition, since the demands of business come first." "So, can the office manager come in now?" asked Gregor's father impatiently, once more knocking on the door. "No," said Gregor. In the room on the left there was an embarrassed silence; in the room on the right his sister began to sob.

But why didn't his sister go and join the others? Probably because she had just gotten out of bed and hadn't even begun to dress yet. Then why was she crying? Because he was in danger of losing his job, and because the director would start once again dunning his parents for the money they owed him? Yet surely these were matters one didn't need to worry about just now. Gregor was still here, and hadn't the slightest intention of deserting the family. True, at the moment he was lying on the carpet, and no one aware of his condition could seriously expect him to let the office manager in. But this minor discourtesy, for which in good time an appropriate excuse could easily be found, was unlikely to result in Gregor's being fired on the spot. And it seemed to Gregor far more sensible for them now to leave him in peace than to bother him with their tears and entreaties. But the uncertainty that preyed upon them excused their behavior.

"Mr. Samsa," the office manager now called in a louder voice, "what's the matter with you? You've barricaded yourself in your room, giving only yes or no answers, causing your parents a great deal of needless grief and neglecting—I mention this only in passing—neglecting your business responsibilities to an unbelievable degree. I am speaking now in the name of your parents and of your director, and I beg you in all seriousness to give me a complete explanation at once. I'm amazed at you, simply amazed. I took you for a calm and reliable person, and now all at once you seem determined to make a ridiculous spectacle of yourself. Earlier this morning the director did suggest to me a possible explanation for your disappearance—I'm referring to the sums of cash that were recently entrusted to you—but I practically swore on my solemn word of honor that this could not be. However, now when I see how incredibly stubborn you are, I no longer have the slightest desire to defend you. And your

---

fretsaw: saw with a long, narrow, fine-toothed blade, for cutting thin wooden boards or metal plates into patterns.

position with the firm is by no means secure. I came intending to tell you all this in private, but since you're so pointlessly wasting my time I don't see why your parents shouldn't hear it as well. For some time now your work has left much to be desired. We are aware, of course, that this is not the prime season for doing business; but a season for doing no business at all—that, Mr. Samsa, does not and must not exist."

"But sir," Gregor called out distractedly, forgetting everything else in his excite-   20
ment, "I'm on the verge of opening the door right now. A slight indisposition, a dizzy spell, has prevented me from getting up. I'm still in bed. But I'm feeling better already. I'm getting up now. Please be patient for just a moment. It seems I'm not quite as well as I thought. But really I'm all right. Something like this can come on so suddenly! Only last night I was feeling fine, as my parents can tell you, or actually I did have a slight premonition. I must have shown some sign of it. Oh, why didn't I report it to the office! But one always thinks one can get better without having to stay at home. Please, sir, have mercy on my parents! None of what you've just accused me of has any basis in fact; no one has even spoken a word to me about it. Perhaps you haven't seen the latest orders I've sent in. Anyway, I can still make the eight o'clock train. Don't let me keep you, sir, I'll be showing up at the office very soon. Please be kind enough to inform them, and convey my best wishes to the director."

And while hurriedly blurting all this out, hardly knowing what he was saying, Gregor had reached the chest of drawers easily enough, perhaps because of the practice he had already gotten in bed, and was now trying to use it to lift himself upright. For he actually wanted to open the door, actually intended to show himself, and to talk with the manager; he was eager to find out what the others, who now wanted to see him so much, would say at the sight of him. If they recoiled in horror then he would take no further responsibility and could remain peaceably where he was. But if they took it all in stride then he too had no reason to be upset, and, if he hurried, could even get to the station by eight. The first few times, he slipped down the polished surface of the chest, but finally with one last heave he stood upright. He no longer paid attention to the burning pains in his abdomen, no matter how they hurt. Then, allowing himself to fall against the backrest of a nearby chair, he clung to its edges with his little legs. Now he was once more in control of himself; he fell silent, and was able to hear what the manager was saying.

"Did you understand a single word?" the office manager was asking his parents. "He's not trying to make fools of us, is he?" "My God," cried his mother, already in tears, "maybe he's seriously ill and we're tormenting him. Grete! Grete!" she shouted then. "Mother?" called his sister from the other side. They were calling to each other across Gregor's room. "You must go to the doctor at once. Gregor is sick. Go get the doctor now. Did you hear how Gregor was speaking?" "That was the voice of an animal," said the manager in a tone that was noticeably restrained compared to his mother's shrillness. "Anna! Anna!" his father shouted through the hall to the kitchen, clapping his hands, "get a locksmith and hurry!" And the two girls, their skirts rustling, were already running down the hall—how could his sister have gotten dressed so quickly?—and were pulling the front door open. There was no sound of its being shut; evidently they had left it standing open, as is the custom in houses stricken by some great sorrow.

But Gregor now felt much calmer. Though the words he spoke were apparently no longer understandable, they seemed clear enough to him, even clearer than before, perhaps because his hearing had grown accustomed to their sound. In any case, people were now convinced that something was wrong with him, and were ready to help him. The confidence and assurance with which these first measures had been taken comforted him. He felt himself being drawn back into the human circle and hoped for marvelous and astonishing results from both doctor and locksmith, without really drawing a distinction between them. To ready his voice for the crucial discussion that was now almost upon him, to make it sound as clear as possible, he coughed slightly, as quietly as he could, since for all he knew it might sound different from human coughing. Meanwhile in the next room there was utter silence. Perhaps his parents and the manager were sitting at the table, whispering; perhaps they were, all of them, leaning against the door, listening.

Gregor slowly advanced on the door, pushing the chair in front of him. Then he let go of it, grabbed onto the door for support—the pads at the end of his little legs were somewhat sticky—and, leaning against it, rested for a moment after his efforts. Then he started to turn the key in the lock with his mouth. Unfortunately, he didn't really have any teeth—how was he going to grip the key?—but to make up for that he clearly had very powerful jaws; with their help he was in fact able to start turning the key, paying no attention to the fact that he was surely hurting them somehow, for a brown liquid poured out of his mouth, flowed over the key, and dripped onto the floor. "Listen," said the manager on the other side of the door, "he's turning the key." This was a great encouragement to Gregor, but they should all have been cheering him on, his mother and his father too. "Come on, Gregor," they should have been shouting, "keep at it, hold on to that key!" And, imagining that they were all intently following his efforts, he grimly clamped his jaws on the key with all his might. As the key continued to turn he danced around the lock, holding himself by his mouth alone, either hanging onto the key or pressing down on it with the full weight of his body, as the situation required. The sharper sound of the lock as it finally snapped free woke Gregor up completely. With a sigh of relief he said to himself, "So I didn't need the locksmith after all," and he pressed his head down on the handle to open one wing of the double door.

Because he had to pull the wing in towards him, even when it stood wide open he remained hidden from view. He had to edge slowly around this wing and to do it very carefully or he would fall flat on his back as he made his entrance. He was still busy carrying out this maneuver, with no time to notice anything else, when he heard the manager give a loud "Oh!"—it sounded like a gust of wind—and now he could see him, standing closest to the door, his hand over his open mouth, slowly backing away as if propelled by the relentless pressure of some invisible force. His mother—in spite of the manager's presence, she was standing there with her hair still unpinned and sticking out in all directions—first folded her hands and looked at Gregor's father, then took two steps forward and sank to the floor, her skirts billowing out all around her and her face completely buried in her breast. His father, glowering, clenched his fist, as if he intended to drive Gregor back into his room; then he looked around the living room with uncertainty, covered his eyes with his hands, and wept so hard his great chest shook.

Now Gregor made no attempt to enter the living room, but leaned against the locked wing of the double door, so that only half of his body was visible, with his head above it cocked to one side, peering at the others. Meanwhile the daylight had grown much brighter; across the street one could clearly see a section of the endless, dark gray building opposite—it was a hospital—with a row of uniform windows starkly punctuating its facade. The rain was still falling, but only in large, visibly separate drops that looked as though they were being flung, one by one, onto the earth.

On the table the breakfast dishes were set out in lavish profusion, for breakfast was the most important meal of the day for Gregor's father, who lingered over it for hours while reading various newspapers. Hanging on the opposite wall was a photograph of Gregor from his army days, showing him as a lieutenant, with his hand on his sword and his carefree smile demanding respect for his bearing and his rank. The door to the hall stood open, and as the front door was open too, one could see the landing beyond and the top of the stairs going down.

"Well," said Gregor, who was perfectly aware that he was the only one who had kept his composure, "I'll go now and get dressed, pack up my samples, and be on my way. You will, you will let me go, won't you? You can see, sir, that I'm not stubborn and I'm willing to work; the life of a traveling salesman is hard, but I couldn't live without it. Where are you going, sir? To the office? You are? Will you give an honest report about all this? A man may be temporarily unable to work, but that's just the time to remember the service he has rendered in the past, and to bear in mind that later on, when the present problem has been resolved, he is sure to work with even more energy and diligence than before. As you know very well, I am deeply obligated to the director. At the same time, I'm responsible for my parents and my sister. I'm in a tight spot right now, but I'll get out of it. Don't make things more difficult for me than they already are. Stand up for me at the office! People don't like traveling salesmen, I know. They think they make scads of money and lead lives of luxury. And there's no compelling reason for them to revise this prejudice. But you, sir, have a better understanding of things than the rest of the staff, a better understanding, if I may say so, than even the director himself, who, since he is the owner, can be easily swayed against an employee. You also know very well that a traveling salesman, who is away from the office for most of the year, can so easily fall victim to gossip and bad luck and groundless accusations, against which he is powerless to defend himself since he knows nothing about them until, returning home exhausted from his journeys, he suffers personally from evil consequences that can no longer be traced back to their origins. Sir, please don't go away without giving me some word to show that you think that I'm at least partly right!"

But the office manager had turned away at Gregor's first words, and was looking at him now over one twitching shoulder, his mouth agape. And during Gregor's speech he didn't stand still for even a moment, but without once taking his eyes off him kept edging towards the door, yet very slowly, as if there were some secret injunction against his leaving the room. He was already in the hall, and from the suddenness with which he took his last step out of the living room, one might have thought he had burned the sole of his foot. But once in the hall, he stretched out his right hand as far as possible in the direction of the staircase, as if some supernatural rescuer awaited him there.

Gregor realized that he could not let the manager leave in this frame of mind, or his position with the firm would be in extreme jeopardy. His parents were incapable of clearly grasping this; over the years they had come to believe that Gregor was set for life with this firm, and besides they were now so preoccupied with their immediate problems that they had lost the ability to foresee events. But Gregor had this ability. The manager must be overtaken, calmed, swayed, and finally convinced; the future of Gregor and of his family depended on it! If only his sister were here—she was perceptive; she had already begun to cry while Gregor was still lying calmly on his back. And surely the manager, that ladies' man, would've listened to her; she would've shut the door behind them and in the hall talked him out of his fright. But his sister wasn't there, and he would have to handle this himself. And forgetting that he had no idea what his powers of movement were, and forgetting as well that once again his words would possibly, even probably, be misunderstood, he let go of the door, pushed his way through the opening, and started towards the manager, who by now was on the landing, clinging in a ridiculous manner to the banister with both hands. But as Gregor reached out for support, he immediately fell down with a little cry onto his numerous legs. The moment this happened he felt, for the first time that morning, a sense of physical well-being. His little legs had solid ground under them, and, he noticed with joy, they were at his command, and were even eager to carry him in whatever direction he might desire; and he already felt sure that the final recovery from all his misery was at hand. But at that very moment, as he lay on the floor rocking with suppressed motion, not far from his mother and just opposite her, she, who had seemed so completely overwhelmed, leapt to her feet, stretched her arms out wide, spread her fingers, and cried, "Help! For God's sake, help!" She then craned her neck forward as if to see Gregor better, but at the same time, inconsistently, backed away from him. Forgetting that the table with all its dishes was behind her, she sat down on it, and, as if in a daze when she bumped into it, seemed utterly unaware that the large coffee pot next to her had tipped over and was pouring out a flood of coffee onto the carpet.

"Mother, Mother," said Gregor gently, looking up at her. For the moment he had completely forgotten the office manager; on the other hand, he couldn't resist snapping his jaws a few times at the sight of the streaming coffee. This made his mother scream again; she ran from the table and into the outstretched arms of his father, who came rushing to her. But Gregor had no time now for his parents. The manager had already reached the staircase; with his chin on the banister railing, he was looking back for the last time. Gregor darted forward, to be as sure as possible of catching up with him, but the manager must have guessed his intention, for he sprinted down several steps and disappeared. He was still yelling "Oohh!" and the sound echoed throughout the stairwell.

Unfortunately the manager's escape seemed to make his father, who until now had seemed reasonably calm, lose all sense of proportion. Instead of running after the man himself, or at least not interfering with Gregor's pursuit, he grabbed with his right hand the manager's cane, which he had left behind, together with his hat and overcoat, on the chair; with his left hand he snatched up a large newspaper from the table. He began stamping his feet and waving the cane and newspaper in order to drive Gregor back into his room. Nothing Gregor said made any difference, indeed, nothing he said was even understood. No matter how humbly he lowered his head his father only stamped the louder. Behind his father his mother, despite the cold, had flung open a window and was leaning far outside it, her face in her hands. A strong breeze from the street blew across the room to the stairwell, the window curtains billowed inwards, the newspapers fluttered on the table, stray pages skittered across the floor. His father, hissing like a savage, mercilessly drove him back. But as Gregor had had no practice in walking backwards, it was a very slow process. If he had been given a chance to turn around then he would've gotten back into his room at once, but he was afraid that the length of time it would take him to turn around would exasperate his father and that at any moment the cane in his father's hand might deal him a fatal blow on his back or his head. In the end, though, he had no choice, for he noticed to his horror that while moving backwards he couldn't even keep a straight course. And so, looking back anxiously, he began turning around as quickly as possible, which in reality was very slowly. Perhaps his father divined his good intentions, for he did not interfere,

30

and even helped to direct the maneuver from afar with the tip of his cane. If only he would stop that unbearable hissing! It made Gregor completely lose his concentration. He had turned himself almost all the way around when, confused by this hissing, he made a mistake and started turning back the wrong way. But when at last he'd succeeded in getting his head in front of the doorway, he found that his body was too wide to make it through. Of course his father, in the state he was in, couldn't even begin to consider opening the other wing of the door to let Gregor in. His mind was on one thing only: to drive Gregor back into his room as quickly as possible. He would never have permitted the complicated preparations necessary for Gregor to haul himself upright and in that way perhaps slip through. Instead, making even more noise, he urged Gregor forward as if the way were clear. To Gregor the noise behind him no longer sounded like the voice of merely one father; this really wasn't a joke, and Gregor squeezed himself into the doorway, heedless of the consequences. One side of his body lifted up, he was pitched at an angle in the doorway; the other side was scraped raw, ugly blotches stained the white door. Soon he was stuck fast and couldn't have moved any further by himself. On one side his little legs hung trembling in the air, while those on the other were painfully crushed against the floor—when, from behind, his father gave him a hard blow that was truly a deliverance, and bleeding profusely, he flew far into his room. Behind him the door was slammed shut with the cane, and then at last everything was still.

II

It was already dusk when Gregor awoke from a deep, almost comatose sleep. Surely, even if he hadn't been disturbed he would've soon awakened by himself, since he'd rested and slept long enough; yet it seemed to him that he'd been awakened by the sound of hurried steps and the furtive closing of the hallway door. The light from the electric streetlamps cast pale streaks here and there on the ceiling and the upper part of the furniture, but down below, where Gregor was, it was dark. Groping awkwardly with the feelers which he was only now beginning to appreciate, he slowly pushed himself over to the door to see what had been going on there. His left side felt as if it were one long, painfully tightening scar, and he was actually limping on his two rows of legs. One little leg, moreover, had been badly hurt during the morning's events—it was nearly miraculous that only one had been hurt—and it trailed along lifelessly.

Only when he reached the door did he realize what had impelled him forward—the smell of something to eat. For there stood a bowl full of fresh milk, in which floated small slices of white bread. He could almost have laughed for joy, since he was even hungrier now than he'd been during the morning, and he immediately dipped his head into the milk, almost up to his eyes. But he soon drew it back in disappointment; not only did he find it difficult to eat because of the soreness in his left side—and he was capable of eating only if his whole gasping body cooperated—but also because he didn't like the milk at all, although it had once been his favorite drink, which, no doubt, was why his sister had brought it in. In fact, he turned away from the bowl almost in disgust, and crawled back to the middle of the room.

In the living room, as Gregor could see through the crack in the door, the gaslight had been lit. But while this was the hour when his father would usually be reading the afternoon paper in a loud voice to his mother and sometimes to his sister as well, now there wasn't a sound to be heard. Well, perhaps this custom of reading aloud, which his sister was always telling him about or mentioning in her letters, had recently been discontinued. Still, though the apartment was completely silent, it was scarcely deserted. "What a quiet life the family's been leading," said Gregor to himself, and, staring fixedly into the darkness, he felt a genuine pride at having been able to provide his parents and his sister with such a life in such a nice apartment. But what if all this calm, prosperity, and contentment were to end in horror? So as not to give in to such thoughts, Gregor set himself in motion, and he crawled up and down the room.

Once during the long evening first one of the side doors and then the other was opened a crack and then quickly shut. Someone, it seemed, had wanted to come in but then had thought better of it. Gregor now stationed himself so as to somehow get the hesitant visitor to come in or at least to find out who it might be. But the door did not open again and he waited in vain. That morning when the doors had been locked, everyone had wanted to come in, but now after he'd unlocked one of the doors himself—and the others had evidently been unlocked during the day—nobody came in, and the keys, too, were now on the outside.

It was late at night before the light was put out in the living room, and it was easy for Gregor to tell that his parents and sister had stayed up all the while, since he could plainly hear the three of them as they tiptoed away. As it was obvious that no one would be visiting Gregor before morning, he had plenty of time in which to contemplate, undisturbed, how best to rearrange his life. But the open, high-ceilinged room in which he was forced to lie flat on the floor filled him with a dread which he couldn't account for—since it was, after all, the room he had lived in for the past five years. Almost unthinkingly, and not without a faint sense of shame, he scurried under the couch. There, although his back was slightly cramped and he could no longer raise his head, he immediately felt very much at home, and his only regret was that his body was too wide to fit completely under the couch.

There he spent the rest of the night, now in a doze from which hunger pangs kept awakening him with a start, now preoccupied with worries and vague hopes, all of which, however, led to the same conclusion: that for the time being he must remain calm and, by being patient and showing every consideration, try to help his family bear the burdens that his present condition had placed upon them.

Early the next morning—the night was barely over—Gregor got an opportunity to test the strength of his newly-made resolutions, because his sister, who was almost fully dressed, opened the hallway door and looked in expectantly. She didn't see him at first, but when she spotted him underneath the couch—well, my God, he had to be somewhere, he couldn't just fly away—she was so surprised that she lost her self-control and slammed the door shut again. But, as if she felt sorry for her behavior, she opened it again right away and tiptoed in, as if she were in the presence of someone who was very ill, or who was a stranger. Gregor had moved his head forward almost to the edge of the couch and was watching her. Would she notice that he'd let the milk sit there, and not from lack of hunger, and would she bring him some other food that was more to his taste? If she wasn't going to do it on her own, he'd sooner starve than call her attention to it, although in fact he was feeling a tremendous urge to dash out from under the couch, fling himself at his sister's feet, and beg her for something good to eat. But his sister immediately noticed to her astonishment that the bowl was still full, with only a little milk spilt around it. She picked up the bowl at once—not, it's true, with her bare hands but using a rag—and carried it out. Gregor was extremely curious to find out what she would bring in its place, and he speculated at length as to what it might be. But he never would have guessed what his sister, in the goodness of her heart, actually did. She brought him a wide range of choices, all spread out on an old newspaper. There were old, half-rotten vegetables; bones left over from dinner, covered with a congealed white sauce; some raisins and almonds; a piece of cheese which Gregor two days ago had declared inedible; a slice of plain bread, a slice of bread and butter, and a slice with butter and salt. In addition to all this she replaced the bowl, now evidently reserved for Gregor, filled this time with water. And out of a sense of delicacy, since she knew that Gregor wouldn't eat in front of her, she left in a hurry, even turning the key in the lock in order that Gregor might know that he was free to make himself as comfortable as possible. Gregor's legs whirred as they propelled him toward the food. Besides, his wounds must have healed completely, for he no longer felt handicapped, which amazed him. He thought of how, a month ago, he'd cut his finger slightly with his knife and how only the day before yesterday that little wound had still hurt. "Am I less sensitive now?" he wondered, greedily sucking on the cheese, to which, above all the other dishes, he was immediately and strongly attracted. Tears of joy welled up in his eyes as he devoured the cheese, the vegetables, and the sauce. The fresh foods, on the other hand, were not to his liking; in fact, he couldn't stand to smell them and he actually dragged the food he wanted to eat a little way off. He'd long since finished eating, and was merely lying lazily in the same spot, when his sister began to slowly turn the key in the lock as a signal for him to withdraw. He got up at once, although he'd almost fallen asleep, and scurried back under the couch. But it took a great deal of self-control for him to remain under the couch even for the brief time his sister was in the room, for his heavy meal had swollen his body to some extent and he could scarcely breathe in that confined space. Between little fits of suffocation he stared with slightly bulging eyes as his unsuspecting sister took a broom and swept away not only the scraps of what he'd eaten, but also the food that he'd left untouched—as if these too were no longer any good—and hurriedly dumped everything into a bucket, which she covered with a wooden lid and carried away. She'd hardly turned her back before Gregor came out from under the couch to stretch and puff himself out.

So this was how Gregor was fed each day, once in the morning when his parents and the maid were still asleep, and again after the family's midday meal, while his parents took another brief nap and his sister could send the maid away on some errand or other. His parents didn't want Gregor to starve any more than his sister did, but perhaps for them to be directly involved in his feeding was more than they could bear, or perhaps his sister wanted to shield them even from what might prove to be no more than a minor discomfort, for they were surely suffering enough as it was.

Gregor was unable to discover what excuses had served to get rid of the doctor and the locksmith that first morning. Since the others couldn't understand what he said it never occurred to them, not even to his sister, that he could understand them, so when his sister was in the room, he had to be satisfied with occasionally hearing her sighs and her appeals to the saints. Only later, after she began to get used to the situation—of course she could never become completely used to it—would Gregor sometimes hear a remark that was intended to be friendly or could be so interpreted. "He really liked it today," she'd say when Gregor had polished off a good portion, and when the opposite was the case, which began to happen more and more often, she'd say almost sadly, "Once again, he didn't touch a thing."

But while Gregor wasn't able to get any news directly, he could overhear a considerable amount from the adjoining rooms, and as soon as he would hear the sound of voices he would immediately run to the appropriate door and press his whole body

40

against it. In the early days especially, there wasn't a conversation that didn't in some way, if only indirectly, refer to him. For two whole days, at every meal, the family discussed what they should do, and they kept on doing so between meals as well, for at least two members of the family were now always at home, probably because nobody wanted to be in the apartment alone, and it would be unthinkable to leave it empty. Furthermore, on the very first day the cook—it wasn't completely clear how much she knew of what had happened—had on her knees begged Gregor's mother to dismiss her immediately, and when she said her goodbyes a quarter of an hour later, she thanked them for her dismissal with tears in her eyes, as if this had been the greatest favor ever bestowed on her in the house, and without having to be asked she made a solemn vow never to breathe a word of this to anyone.

So now his sister, together with his mother, had to do all the cooking as well, though in fact this wasn't too much of a chore, since the family ate practically nothing. Gregor kept hearing them vainly urging one another to eat, without receiving any reply except "No thanks, I've had enough," or some similar remark. They didn't seem to drink anything, either. His sister would often ask his father if he'd like some beer, and would gladly offer to go out and get it herself. When he wouldn't respond she'd say, in order to remove any hesitation on his part, that she could always send the janitor's wife, but at that point the father would finally utter an emphatic "No" and that would be the end of the matter.

It was on the very first day that his father gave a full account, to both mother and sister, of the family's financial situation and prospects. Every now and then he would get up from the table and take a receipt or notebook from out of the small safe he'd salvaged from the collapse of his business five years before. He could be heard opening the complicated lock and then securing it again after taking out whatever he'd been looking for. The account that his father gave, or at least part of it, was the first encouraging news that Gregor had heard since being imprisoned. He'd always had the impression that his father had failed to save a penny from the ruin of his business; at least his father had never told him otherwise, and Gregor, for that matter, had never asked him about it. At that time Gregor's only concern had been to do his utmost to make the family forget as quickly as possible the business failure that had plunged them all into a state of total despair. And so he had set to work with tremendous zeal, and had risen almost overnight from junior clerk to become a traveling salesman, which naturally opened up completely new financial opportunities so that in no time at all his success was instantly translated, by way of commissions, into hard cash, which could be laid out on the table under the eyes of his astonished and delighted family. Those had been wonderful times, and they had never returned, at least not with the same glory, even though later on Gregor had been earning enough to pay the entire family's expenses, and in fact had been doing so. They'd simply gotten used to it, both family and Gregor; they had gratefully accepted the money, and he had given it gladly, but no special warmth went with it. Gregor had remained close only to his sister, and it was his secret plan that she, who unlike Gregor loved music and could play the violin with deep feeling, should next year attend the Conservatory, despite the expense which, great as it was, would have to be met in some way. During Gregor's brief stays in the city the subject of the Conservatory would often come up in his conversations with his sister, but always only as a beautiful dream that wasn't meant to come true. His parents weren't happy to hear even these innocent remarks, but Gregor's ideas on the subject were firm and he had intended to make a solemn announcement on Christmas Eve.

Such were the thoughts, so futile in his present condition, that ran through his mind as he stood there, pressed against the door, listening. Sometimes he would grow so thoroughly weary that he couldn't listen any more and would carelessly let his head bump against the door, and though he'd pull it back immediately, even the slight noise he'd made would be heard in the next room, causing everyone to fall silent. "What's he up to now?" his father would say after a pause, obviously looking at the door, and only then would the interrupted conversation gradually be resumed.

Gregor now learned with considerable thoroughness—for his father tended to re- 45
peat his explanations several times, partly because he hadn't dealt with these matters in a long time, and partly because his mother didn't understand everything the first time through—that despite their catastrophic ruin a certain amount of capital, a very small amount, it's true, had survived intact from the old days, and thanks to the interest being untouched had even increased slightly. And what was more, the money which Gregor had been bringing home every month—he'd kept only a small sum for himself—hadn't been completely spent and had grown into a tidy sum. Gregor nodded eagerly behind his door, delighted to hear of this unexpected foresight and thrift. Of course he might have been able to use this extra money to pay off more of his father's debt to the director, and thus have brought nearer the day when he could quit his current job, but, given the present circumstances, things were better the way his father had arranged them.

Now the sum of this money wasn't nearly large enough for the family to live off the interest; the principal might support them for a year, or two at the most, but that was all. So this was really only a sum that was not to be touched, but saved instead for emergencies. As for money to live on—that would have to be earned. Though Gregor's father was indeed still healthy, nevertheless he was an old man who hadn't worked for five years and one from whom not too much should be expected in any case. During those five years, the first ones of leisure in his hard-working but unsuccessful life, he had put on a lot of weight and consequently had grown somewhat sluggish. And as for Gregor's elderly mother, was she supposed to start bringing in money, burdened as she was by her asthma which made it a strain for her to even walk across the apartment and which kept her gasping for breath every other day on the couch by the open window? Or should his sister go to work instead—she who though seventeen was still a child and one moreover whom it would be cruel to deprive of the life she'd led up until now, a life of wearing pretty clothes, sleeping late, helping around the house, enjoying a few modest pleasures, and above all playing the violin? At first, whenever their conversation turned to the need to earn money, Gregor would let go of the door and fling himself down on the cool leather couch which stood beside it, for he felt hot with grief and shame.

Often he would lie there all night long, not sleeping a wink, scratching at the leather couch for hours. Or, undaunted by the great effort it required, he would push the chair over to the window. Then he would crawl up to the sill and, propped up by the chair, would lean against the pane, apparently inspired by some memory of the sense of freedom that gazing out a window used to give him. For in truth objects only a short distance away were now, each day, becoming more indistinct; the hospital across the street, which he used to curse because he could see it all too clearly, was now completely outside his field of vision, and if he hadn't known for a fact that he lived on Charlotte Street—a quiet but nevertheless urban street—he could have imagined that he was looking out his window at a wasteland where gray sky and gray earth had indistinguishably merged as one. His observant sister needed only to notice twice that the armchair had been moved to the window. From then on, whenever she cleaned the room, she carefully placed the chair back by the window, and even began leaving the inner casement open.

If only Gregor had been able to speak to his sister and thank her for everything she'd had to do for him, he could have borne her kindnesses more easily, but as it was they were painful to him. Of course his sister tried her best to ease the general embarrassment, and naturally as time passed she grew better and better at it. But Gregor too, over time, gained a clearer sense of what was involved. Even the way in which she entered the room was a torture to him. No sooner had she stepped in when—not even pausing to shut the door, despite the care she normally would take in sparing others the sight of Gregor's room—she would run straight over to the window and tear it open with impatient fingers, almost as if she were suffocating, and she would remain for some time by the window, even in the coldest weather, breathing deeply. Twice a day she would terrify Gregor with all this noise and rushing around. He would cower under the couch the entire time, knowing full well that she surely would have spared him this if only she could have stood being in the room with him with the windows closed.

Once, about a month after Gregor's metamorphosis—so there was really no particular reason for his sister to be upset by his appearance—she came in earlier than usual and caught Gregor as he gazed out the window, terrifying in his stillness. It wouldn't have surprised Gregor if she'd decided not to come in, since his position prevented her from opening the window right away, but not only did she not come in, she actually jumped back and shut the door—a stranger might have thought that Gregor had been planning to ambush her and bite her. Of course he immediately hid under the couch, but he had to wait until noon before she came back, and this time she seemed much more nervous than usual. In this way he came to realize that the sight of him disgusted her, and likely would always disgust her, and that she probably had to steel herself not to run away at the sight of even the tiny portion of his body that stuck out from under the couch. So, one day, to spare her even this, he carried the bedsheet on his back over to the couch— it took him four hours—and spread it so that he was completely covered and his sister wouldn't be able to see him even if she bent down. If she felt this sheet wasn't necessary then of course she could remove it, since obviously Gregor wasn't shutting himself away so completely in order to amuse himself. But she left the sheet alone, and Gregor even thought that he caught a look of gratitude when he cautiously lifted the sheet a little with his head in order to see how his sister was taking to this new arrangement.

During the first two weeks, his parents couldn't bring themselves to come in to see him, and he frequently heard them remarking how much they appreciated his sister's efforts, whereas previously they'd often been annoyed with her for being, in their eyes, somewhat useless. But now both father and mother had fallen into the habit of waiting outside Gregor's door while his sister cleaned up the room, and as soon as she emerged she would have to tell them every detail of the room's condition, what Gregor had eaten, how he'd behaved this time, and whether he'd perhaps shown a little improvement. It wasn't long before his mother began to want to visit Gregor, but his father and sister were at first able to dissuade her by rational arguments to which Gregor listened with great care, and with which he thoroughly agreed. But as time went by she had to be restrained by force, and when she cried out "Let me go to Gregor, he's my unhappy boy! Don't you understand that I have to go to him?" Gregor began to think that it might be a good idea if his mother did come in after all, not every day, naturally, but, say, once a week. She was really a much more capable person

50

than his sister, who, for all her courage, was still only a child and had perhaps taken on such a difficult task only out of a childish impulsiveness.

Gregor's wish to see his mother was soon fulfilled. During the day Gregor didn't want to show himself at the window, if only out of consideration for his parents. But his few square meters of floor gave him little room to crawl around in, he found it hard to lie still even at night, and eating soon ceased to give him any pleasure. So in order to distract himself he fell into the habit of crawling all over the walls and the ceiling. He especially enjoyed hanging from the ceiling; it was completely different from lying on the floor. He could breathe more freely, a faint pulsing coursed through his body, and in his state of almost giddy absentmindedness up there, Gregor would sometimes, to his surprise, lose his grip and tumble onto the floor. But now, of course, since he had much better control over his body, even such a great fall didn't hurt him. His sister noticed right away the new pastime Gregor had discovered for himself—he'd left sticky traces where he'd been crawling—and so she got it into her head to provide Gregor with as much room as possible to crawl around in by removing all the furniture that was in the way—especially the chest of drawers and the desk. But she couldn't manage this by herself; she didn't dare ask her father for help; the maid wouldn't be of any use, for while this girl, who was around sixteen, was brave enough to stay on after the cook had left, she'd asked to be allowed to always keep the kitchen door locked, opening it only when specifically asked to do so. This left his sister with no choice but, one day when her father was out, to ask her mother for help. And indeed, her mother followed her with joyful, excited cries, although she fell silent when they reached the door to Gregor's room. Naturally his sister first made sure that everything in the room was as it should be; only then did she let her mother come in. Gregor had hurriedly pulled his sheet even lower and had folded it more tightly and it really did look as if it had been casually tossed over the couch. This time Gregor also refrained from peeking out from under the sheet; he denied himself the pleasure of seeing his mother for now and was simply glad that she'd come after all. "Come on in, he's nowhere in sight," said his sister, apparently leading his mother in by the hand. Now Gregor could hear the two delicate women moving the heavy chest of drawers away from its place, his sister stubbornly insisting on doing the hardest work, ignoring the warnings of her mother, who was afraid her daughter would overstrain herself. The work took a very long time. After struggling for over a quarter of an hour, his mother suggested that they might leave the chest where it was; in the first place, it was just too heavy, they'd never be done before his father came home and they'd have to leave it in the middle of the room, blocking Gregor's movements in every direction; in the second place, it wasn't at all certain that they were doing Gregor a favor in removing the furniture. It seemed to her that the opposite was true, the sight of the bare walls broke her heart; and why shouldn't Gregor feel the same since he'd been used to this furniture for so long and would feel abandoned in the empty room? "And wouldn't it look as if," his mother concluded very softly—in fact, she'd been almost whispering the entire time, as if she wanted to prevent Gregor, whose exact whereabouts she didn't know, from hearing the sound of her voice (she was convinced that he couldn't understand her words)—"as if by removing his furniture we were telling him that we'd given up all hope of his getting better, and were callously leaving him to his own devices? I think the best course would be to try to keep the room exactly the way it was, so that when Gregor does come back to us he'll find everything the same, making it easier for him to forget what has happened in the meantime."

When he heard his mother's words, Gregor realized that, over the past two months, the lack of having anyone to converse with, together with the monotonous life within the family, must have befuddled his mind; there wasn't any other way he could explain to himself how he could have ever seriously wanted his room cleared out. Did he really want this warm room of his, so comfortably furnished with family heirlooms, transformed into a lair where he'd be perfectly free to crawl around in every direction, but only at the cost of simultaneously forgetting his human past, swiftly and utterly? Just now he'd been on the brink of forgetting, and only his mother's voice, which he hadn't heard for so long, had brought him back. Nothing should be removed; everything must stay. He couldn't do without the furniture's soothing influence on his state of mind, and if the furniture were to impede his senselessly crawling around, that wouldn't be a loss but rather a great advantage.

But unfortunately his sister thought otherwise. She'd become accustomed, and not without some justification, to assuming the role of the acknowledged expert whenever she and her parents discussed Gregor's affairs; so her mother's advice was enough for her to insist now not merely on her original plan of moving the chest and the desk, but on the removal of every bit of furniture except for the indispensable couch. Her resolve, to be sure, didn't stem merely from childish stubbornness or from the self-confidence she had recently and unexpectedly gained at such great cost. For in fact she'd noticed that while Gregor needed plenty of room to crawl around in, on the other hand, as far as she could tell, he never used the furniture at all. Perhaps too, the sentimental enthusiasm of girls her age, which they indulge themselves in at every opportunity, now tempted Grete to make Gregor's situation all the more terrifying so that she might be able to do more for him. No one but Grete would ever be likely to enter a room where Gregor ruled the bare walls all alone.

And so she refused to give in to her mother, who in any case, from the sheer anxiety caused by being in Gregor's room, seemed unsure of herself. She soon fell silent and began as best she could to help her daughter remove the chest of drawers. Well, if he must, then Gregor could do without the chest, but the desk had to stay. And no sooner had the two women, groaning and squeezing, gotten the chest out of the room than Gregor poked his head out from under the couch to see how he might intervene as tactfully as possible. But unfortunately it was his mother who came back first, leaving Grete in the next room, gripping the chest with her arms and rocking it back and forth without, of course, being able to budge it from the spot. His mother wasn't used to the sight of him—it might make her sick; so Gregor, frightened, scuttled backwards to the far end of the couch, but he couldn't prevent the front of the sheet from stirring slightly. That was enough to catch his mother's attention. She stopped, stood still for a moment, and then went back to Grete.

Gregor kept telling himself that nothing unusual was happening, that only a few 55 pieces of furniture were being moved around. But he soon had to admit that all this coming and going of the two women, their little calls to one another, the scraping of the furniture across the floor, affected him as if it were some gigantic commotion rushing in on him from every side, and though he tucked in his head and legs and pressed his body against the floor, he had to accept the fact that he wouldn't be able to stand it much longer. They were cleaning out his room, taking away from him everything that he loved; already they'd carried off his chest, where he kept his fretsaw and his other tools; now they were trying to pry his writing desk loose—it was practically embedded in the floor—the same desk where he'd always done his homework when he'd been a student at business school, in high school, and even in elementary school. He really no longer had any time left in which to weigh the good intentions of these two women whose existence, for that matter, he'd almost forgotten, since they were so exhausted by now that they worked in silence, the only sound being that of their weary, plodding steps.

And so, while the women were in the next room, leaning against the desk and trying to catch their breath, he broke out, changing his direction four times—since he really didn't know what to rescue first—when he saw, hanging conspicuously on the otherwise bare wall, the picture of the lady all dressed in furs. He quickly crawled up to it and pressed himself against the glass, which held him fast, soothing his hot belly. Now that Gregor completely covered it, this picture at least wasn't about to be carried away by anyone. He turned his head towards the living room door, so that he could watch the women when they returned.

They hadn't taken much of a rest and were already coming back. Grete had put her arm around her mother and was almost carrying her. "Well, what should we take next?" said Grete, looking around. And then her eyes met Gregor's, looking down at her from the wall. Probably only because her mother was there, she kept her composure, bent her head down to her mother to prevent her from glancing around, and said, though in a hollow, quavering voice: "Come on, let's go back to the living room for a minute." To Gregor, her intentions were obvious: she wanted to get his mother to safety and then chase him down from the wall. Well, just let her try! He clung to his picture and he wasn't going to give it up. He'd rather fly at Grete's face.

But Grete's words had made her mother even more anxious; she stepped aside, glimpsed the huge brown blotch on the flowered wallpaper, and before she fully understood that what she was looking at was Gregor, she cried out, "Oh God, oh God!" in a hoarse scream of a voice, and, as if giving up completely, fell with outstretched arms across the couch, and lay there without moving. "You! Gregor!" cried his sister, raising her fist and glaring at him. These were the first words she had addressed directly to him since his metamorphosis. She ran into the next room to get some spirits to revive her mother from her faint. Gregor also wanted to help—he could rescue the picture another time—but he was stuck to the glass and had to tear himself free. He then scuttled into the next room as if to give some advice, as he used to, to his sister. Instead, he had to stand behind her uselessly while she rummaged among various little bottles. When she turned around she was startled, a bottle fell to the floor, a splinter of glass struck Gregor in the face, some sort of corrosive medicine splashed on him, and Grete, without further delay, grabbing as many of the little bottles as she could carry, ran inside with them to her mother, and slammed the door shut behind her with her foot. Now Gregor was cut off from his mother, who was perhaps near death because of him. He didn't dare open the door for fear of scaring his sister, who had to remain with his mother. There wasn't anything for him to do but wait; and so, tormented by guilt and anxiety, he began crawling. He crawled over everything, walls, furniture, and ceiling, until finally, in despair, the room beginning to spin around him, he collapsed onto the middle of the large table.

A short time passed; Gregor lay there stupefied. Everything was quiet around him; perhaps that was a good sign. Then the doorbell rang. The maid, of course, stayed locked up in her kitchen, so Grete had to answer the door. His father was back. "What's happened?" were his first words. Grete's expression must've told him everything. Her answers came in muffled tones—she was obviously burying her face in her father's chest. "Mother fainted, but she's better now. Gregor's broken loose." "I knew it," her father said. "I told you this would happen, but you women refuse to listen." It was clear to

Gregor that his father had put the worst construction on Grete's all too brief account and had assumed that Gregor was guilty of some violent act. That meant that he must calm his father down, since he had neither the time nor the ability to explain things to him. So he fled to the door of his room and pressed himself against it in order that his father might see, as soon as he entered the living room, that Gregor had every intention of returning immediately to his own room and there was no need to force him back. All they had to do was to open the door and he would disappear at once.

But his father wasn't in the mood to notice such subtleties; "Ah!" he roared as he entered, in a voice that sounded at once furious and gleeful. Gregor turned his head from the door and lifted it towards his father. He really hadn't imagined that his father would look the way he did standing before him now; true, Gregor had become too absorbed lately by his new habit of crawling to bother about whatever else might be going on in the apartment, and he should have anticipated that there would be some changes. And yet, and yet, could this really be his father? Was this the same man who used to lie sunk in bed, exhausted, whenever Gregor would set out on one of his business trips; who would greet him upon his return in the evening while sitting in his bathrobe in the armchair; who was hardly capable of getting to his feet, and to show his joy could only lift up his arms; and who, on those rare times when the whole family went out for a walk—on the occasional Sunday or on a legal holiday—used to painfully shuffle along between Gregor and his mother, who were slow walkers themselves, and yet he was always slightly slower than they, wrapped up in his old overcoat, carefully planting his crook-handled cane before him with every step, and almost invariably stopping and gathering his escort around him whenever he wanted to say something? Now, however, he held himself very erect, dressed up in a closely-fitting blue uniform with gold buttons, of the kind worn by bank messengers. His heavy chin thrust out over the stiff collar of his jacket; his black eyes stared, sharp and bright, from under his bushy eyebrows; his white hair, once so rumpled, was combed flat, it gleamed, and the part was meticulously exact. He tossed his cap—which bore a gold monogram, probably that of some bank—in an arc across the room so that it landed on the couch, and with his hands in his pockets, the tails of his uniform's long jacket flung back, his face grim, he went after Gregor. He probably didn't know himself what he was going to do, but he lifted his feet unusually high, and Gregor was amazed at the immense size of the soles of his boots. However, Gregor didn't dwell on these reflections, for he had known from the very first day of his new life that his father considered only the strictest measures to be appropriate in dealing with him. So he ran ahead of his father, stopped when he stood still, and scurried on again when he made the slightest move. In this way they circled the room several times without anything decisive happening; in fact, their movements, because of their slow tempo, did not suggest those of a chase. So Gregor kept to the floor for the time being, especially since he was afraid that his father might consider any flight to the walls or ceiling to be particularly offensive. All the same, Gregor had to admit that he wouldn't be able to keep up even this pace for long, since whenever his father took a single step, Gregor had to perform an entire series of movements. He was beginning to get winded, since even in his former life his lungs had never been strong. As he kept staggering on like this, so weary he could barely keep his eyes open, since he was saving all his strength for running; not even thinking, dazed as he was, that there might be any other way to escape than by running; having almost forgotten that he was free to use the walls, though against these walls, admittedly, were placed bits of intricately carved furniture, bristling with spikes and sharp corners—suddenly something sailed overhead, hit the floor nearby, and rolled right in front of him. It was an apple; at once a second one came flying after it. Gregor stopped, petrified with fear; it was useless to keep on running, for his father had decided to bombard him. He had filled his pockets with the fruit from the bowl on the sideboard and now he was throwing one apple after another, for now at least without bothering to take good aim. These little red apples, colliding with one another, rolled around on the floor as if electrified. One weakly-thrown apple grazed Gregor's back, rolling off without causing harm. But another one that came flying immediately afterwards actually imbedded itself in Gregor's back. Gregor wanted to drag himself onward, as if this shocking and unbelievable pain might disappear if he could only keep moving, but he felt as if he were nailed to the spot, and he splayed himself out in the utter confusion of his senses. With his last glance he saw the door of his room burst open, and his mother, wearing only her chemise—his sister had removed her dress to help her breathe after she'd fainted—rush out, followed by his screaming sister. He saw his mother run toward his father, her loosened underskirts slipping one by one onto the floor. Stumbling over her skirts she flung herself upon his father, embraced him, was as one with him—but now Gregor's sight grew dim—and with her arms clasped around his father's neck, begged for Gregor's life.

III

Gregor's serious wound, which made him suffer for over a month—the apple remained imbedded in his flesh as a visible reminder, no one having the courage to remove it—seemed to have persuaded even his father that Gregor, despite his present pathetic and disgusting shape, was a member of the family who shouldn't be treated as an enemy. On the contrary, familial duty required them to swallow their disgust and to endure him, to endure him and nothing more.

And though his wound probably had caused Gregor to suffer a permanent loss of mobility, and though it now took him, as if he were some disabled war veteran, many a long minute to creep across his room—crawling above ground level was out of the question—yet in return for this deterioration of his condition he was granted a compensation which satisfied him completely: each day around dusk the living room door—which he was in the habit of watching closely for an hour or two ahead of time—was opened, and lying in the darkness of his room, invisible from the living room, he could see the whole family sitting at the table lit by the lamp and could listen to their conversation as if by general consent, instead of the way he'd done before.

True, these were no longer the lively conversations of old, those upon which Gregor had mused somewhat wistfully as he'd settled wearily into his damp bed in some tiny hotel room. Things were now very quiet for the most part. Soon after dinner his father would fall asleep in his armchair, while his mother and sister would admonish each other to be quiet; his mother, bending forward under the light, would sew fine lingerie for a fashion store; his sister, who had found work as a salesgirl, would study shorthand and French in the evenings, hoping to obtain a better job in the future. Sometimes his father would wake up, as if he hadn't the slightest idea that he'd been asleep, and would say to his mother, "Look how long you've been sewing again today!" and then would fall back to sleep, while his mother and sister would exchange weary smiles.

With a kind of perverse obstinacy his father refused to take off his messenger's uniform even in the apartment; while his robe hung unused on the clothes hook, he would sleep fully dressed in his chair, as if he were always ready for duty and were waiting even here for the voice of his superior. As a result his uniform, which hadn't been new in the first place, began to get dirty in spite of all his mother and sister could do to care for it, and Gregor would often spend entire evenings gazing at this garment covered with stains and with its constantly polished buttons gleaming, in which the old man would sit, upright and uncomfortable, yet peacefully asleep.

As soon as the clock would strike ten, his mother would try to awaken his father with soft words of encouragement and then persuade him to go to bed, for this wasn't any place in which to get a decent night's sleep, and his father badly needed his rest, since he had to be at work at six in the morning. But with the stubbornness that had possessed him ever since he'd become a bank messenger he would insist on staying at the table a little while longer, though he invariably would fall asleep again, and then it was only with the greatest difficulty that he could be persuaded to trade his chair for bed. No matter how much mother and sister would urge him on with little ad-monishments, he'd keep shaking his head for a good fifteen minutes, his eyes closed, and wouldn't get up. Gregor's mother would tug at his sleeve, whisper sweet words into his ear; and his sister would leave her homework to help her mother, but it was all useless. He only sank deeper into his armchair. Not until the two women would lift him up by the arms would he open his eyes, look now at one, now at the other, and usually say, "What a life. So this is the peace of my old age." And leaning on the two women he would get up laboriously, as if he were his own greatest burden, and would allow the women to lead him to the door, where, waving them aside, he con-tinued on his own, while Gregor's mother abandoned her sewing and his sister her pen so that they might run after his father and continue to look after him.

Who in this overworked and exhausted family had time to worry about Gregor any more than was absolutely necessary? Their resources grew more limited; the maid was now dismissed after all; a gigantic bony cleaning woman with white hair fluttering about her head came in the mornings and evenings to do the roughest work; Gregor's mother took care of everything else, in addition to her sewing. It even happened that certain pieces of family jewelry which his mother and sister had worn with such plea-sure at parties and celebrations in days gone by, were sold, as Gregor found out one evening by listening to a general discussion of the prices they'd gone for. But their greatest complaint was that they couldn't give up the apartment, which was too big for their current needs, since no one could figure out how they would move Gregor. But Gregor understood clearly enough that it wasn't simply consideration for him which prevented them moving, since he could have easily been transported in a suitable crate equipped with a few air holes. The main reason preventing them from moving was their utter despair and the feeling that they had been struck by a misfortune far greater than any that had ever visited their friends and relatives. What the world de-mands of the poor they did to the utmost: his father fetched breakfast for the bank's minor officials, his mother sacrificed herself for the underwear of strangers, his sister ran back and forth behind the counters at the beck and call of customers; but they lacked the strength for anything beyond this. And the wound in Gregor's back began to ache once more when his mother and sister, after putting his father to bed, returned to the room, ignored their work, and sat huddled together cheek to cheek, and his mother said, "Close that door, Grete," so that Gregor was back in the dark, while in the next room the women wept together or simply stared at the table with dry eyes.

Gregor spent the days and nights almost entirely without sleep. Sometimes he imagined that the next time the door opened he would once again assume control of the family's affairs, as he'd done in the old days. Now, after a long absence, there

65

reappeared in his thoughts the director and the manager, the salesmen and the apprentices, the remarkably stupid errand runner, two or three friends from other firms, a chambermaid at one of the provincial hotels—a sweet, fleeting memory—a cashier at a hat store whom he'd courted earnestly but too slowly—they all came to him mixed up with strangers and with people whom he'd already forgotten. But instead of helping him and his family they were all unapproachable, and he was glad when they faded away. At other times he was in no mood to worry about his family; he was utterly filled with rage at how badly he was being treated, and although he couldn't imagine anything that might tempt his appetite, he nevertheless tried to think up ways of getting into the pantry to take what was rightfully his, even if he wasn't hungry. No longer bothering to consider what Gregor might like as a treat, his sister, before she hurried off to work in the morning and after lunch, would shove any sort of food into Gregor's room with her foot. In the evening, regardless of whether the food had been picked at, or—as was more often the case—left completely untouched, she would sweep it out with a swish of the broom. Nowadays she would clean the room in the evening, and she couldn't have done it any faster. Streaks of grime ran along the walls, balls of dust and dirt lay here and there on the floor. At first, whenever his sister would come in, Gregor would station himself in some corner that was particularly objectionable, as if his presence there might serve as a reproach to her. But he probably could have remained there for weeks without her mending her ways; she obviously could see the dirt as clearly as he could, but she'd made up her mind to leave it. At the same time she made certain—with a touchiness that was completely new to her and which indeed was infecting the entire family—that the cleaning of Gregor's room was to remain her prerogative. On one occasion Gregor's mother had subjected his room to a thorough cleaning, which she managed to accomplish only with the aid of several buckets of water—all this dampness being a further annoyance to Gregor, who lay flat, unhappy, and motionless on the couch. But his mother's punishment was not long in coming. For that evening, as soon as Gregor's sister noticed the difference in his room, she ran, deeply insulted, into the living room, and without regard for his mother's uplifted, beseeching hands, burst into a fit of tears. Both parents—the father, naturally, had been startled out of his armchair—at first looked on with helpless amazement, and then they joined in, the father on his right side blaming the mother: she shouldn't have interfered with the sister's cleaning of the room, while on his left side yelling at the sister that she'd never be allowed to clean Gregor's room again. The mother was trying to drag the father, who was half out of his mind, into their bedroom while the sister, shaking with sobs, pounded the table with her little fists, and Gregor hissed loudly with rage because not one of them had thought to close the door and spare him this scene and this commotion.

But even if his sister, worn out by her job at the store, had gotten tired of taking care of Gregor as she once had, it wasn't really necessary for his mother to take her place so that Gregor wouldn't be neglected. For now the cleaning woman was there. This ancient widow, whose powerful bony frame had no doubt helped her through the hard times in her long life, wasn't at all repelled by Gregor. Without being the least bit inquisitive, she had once, by chance, opened the door to Gregor's room and at the sight of Gregor—who, taken completely by surprise, began running back and forth although no one was chasing him—stood there in amazement, her hands folded over her belly. From then on, morning and evening, she never failed to open his door a crack and peek in on him. At first she also would call him to her, using phrases she probably meant to be friendly, such as "Come on over here, you old dung beetle!" or

"Just look at that old dung beetle!" Gregor wouldn't respond to such forms of address, but would remain motionless where he was as if the door had never been opened. If only this cleaning woman, instead of pointlessly disturbing him whenever she felt like it, had been given orders to clean his room every day! Once, early in the morning, when a heavy rain, perhaps a sign of the already approaching spring, was beating against the window panes, Gregor became so exasperated when the cleaning woman started in with her phrases that he made as if to attack her, though, of course, in a slow and feeble manner. But instead of being frightened, the cleaning woman simply picked up a chair by the door and, lifting it high in the air, stood there with her mouth wide open. Obviously she didn't plan on shutting it until the chair in her hands had first come crashing down on Gregor's back. "So you're not going through with it?" she asked as Gregor turned back while she calmly set the chair down again in the corner.

By now Gregor was eating next to nothing. Only when he happened to pass by the food set out for him would he take a bite, hold it in his mouth for hours, and then spit most of it out again. At first he imagined that it was his anguish at the state of his room that kept him from eating, but it was those very changes to which he had quickly become accustomed. The family had fallen into the habit of using the room to store things for which there wasn't any place anywhere else, and there were many of these things now, since one room in the apartment had been rented to three boarders. These serious gentlemen—all three of them had full beards, as Gregor once noted, peering through a crack in the door—had a passion for neatness, not only in their room but since they were now settled in as boarders, throughout the entire apartment, and especially in the kitchen. They couldn't abide useless, let alone dirty, junk. Besides, they'd brought most of their own household goods along with them. This meant that many objects were now superfluous, which, while clearly without any resale value, couldn't just be thrown out either. All these things ended up in Gregor's room, and so did the ash bucket and the garbage can from the kitchen. Anything that wasn't being used at the moment was simply tossed into Gregor's room by the cleaning woman, who was always in a tremendous hurry. Fortunately, Gregor generally saw only the object in question and the hand that held it. Perhaps the cleaning woman intended to come back for these things when she had the time, or perhaps she planned on throwing them all out, but in fact there they remained, wherever they'd happened to land, except for Gregor's disturbing them as he squeezed his way through the junk pile. At first he did so simply because he was forced to, since there wasn't any other space to crawl in, but later he took a growing pleasure in these rambles even though they left him dead tired and so sad that he would lie motionless for hours. Since the boarders would sometimes have their dinner at home in the shared living room, on those evenings the door between that room and Gregor's would remain shut. But Gregor didn't experience the door's not being open as a hardship; in fact there had been evenings when he'd ignored the open door and had lain, unnoticed by the family, in the darkest corners of his room. But one time the cleaning woman left the door slightly ajar, and it remained ajar when the boarders came in that evening and the lamp was lit. They sat down at the head of the table, where Gregor, his mother and his father had sat in the old days; they unfolded their napkins, and picked up their knives and forks. At once his mother appeared at the kitchen door carrying a platter of meat and right behind her came his sister carrying a platter piled high with potatoes. The steaming food gave off a thick vapor. The platters were set down in front of the boarders, who bent over them as if to examine them before eating, and in fact the one sitting in the middle, who was apparently looked up to as an authority by the other two, cut into a piece of meat while it was still on the platter, evidently to determine if it was tender enough or whether perhaps it should be sent back to the kitchen. He was satisfied, and both mother and daughter, who'd been watching anxiously, breathed a sigh of relief and began to smile.

The family itself ate in the kitchen. Even so, before going to the kitchen his fa- ther came into the living room, bowed once and, cap in hand, walked around the table. The boarders all rose together and mumbled something into their beards. When they were once more alone, they ate in almost complete silence. It seemed strange to Gregor that, out of all the noises produced by eating, he distinctly heard the sound of their teeth chewing; it was as if he were being told you needed teeth in order to eat and that even with the most wonderful toothless jaws, you wouldn't be able to accomplish a thing. "Yes, I'm hungry enough," Gregor told himself sadly, "but not for those things. How well these boarders feed themselves, while I waste away."

That very evening—during this whole time Gregor couldn't once remember hearing the violin—the sound of violin playing came from the kitchen. The boarders had already finished their dinner, the one in the middle had pulled out a newspaper, handed one sheet each to the other two, and now they were leaning back, reading and smoking. When the violin began to play, they noticed it, stood up, and tiptoed to the hall doorway where they stood together in a tight group. They must have been heard in the kitchen for his father called, "Does the playing bother you, gentlemen? We can stop it at once." "On the contrary," said the gentleman in the middle, "wouldn't the young lady like to come and play in here where it's much more roomy and comfortable?" "Why, certainly," called Gregor's father, as if he were the violinist. Soon his father came in carrying the music stand, his mother the sheet music, and his sister the violin. His sister calmly got everything ready for playing; his parents—who had never rented out rooms before and so were overly polite to the boarders—didn't even dare to sit down in their own chairs. His father leaned against the door, slipping his right hand between the buttons of his uniform's jacket, which he'd kept buttoned up; but his mother was offered a chair by one of the gentlemen, and, leaving it where he happened to have placed it, she sat off to one side, in the corner.

His sister began to play; his father and mother, on either side, closely followed the movements of her hands. Gregor, attracted by the playing, had moved a little far- ther forward and already had his head in the living room. He was hardly surprised that recently he'd shown so little concern for others, although in the past he'd taken pride in being considerate. Now more than ever he had good reason to remain hid- den, since he was completely covered with the dust that lay everywhere in his room and was stirred up by the slightest movement. Moreover, threads, hairs, and scraps of food clung to his back and sides, his indifference to everything was much too great for him to have gotten onto his back and rubbed himself clean against the carpet, as he had once done several times a day. And despite his condition he wasn't ashamed to edge his way a little further across the spotless living room floor.

To be sure, no one took any notice of him. The family was completely absorbed by the violin-playing. The boarders, however, who had at first placed themselves, their hands in their pockets, much too close to the music stand—close enough for every one of them to have followed the score, which surely must have flustered his sister—soon retreated to the window, muttering to one another, with their heads lowered. And there they remained while his father watched them anxiously. It seemed all too obvious that they had been disappointed in their hopes of hearing good or entertaining violin-playing; they had had enough of the entire performance, and it was only out of politeness that they continued to let their peace be disturbed. It was especially obvious, by the way they blew their smoke out of their mouths and noses—it floated upwards to the ceiling—just how ill at ease they were. And yet his sister was playing so beautifully. Her face was inclined to one side, and her sad eyes carefully followed the notes of the music. Gregor crawled forward a little farther, keeping his head close to the floor so that their eyes might possibly meet. Was he an animal, that music could move him so? He felt that he was being shown the way to an unknown nourishment he yearned for. He was determined to press on until he reached his sister, to tug at her skirt, and to let her know in this way that she should bring her violin into his room, for no one here would honor her playing as he would. He would never let her out of his room again, at least not for as long as he lived; at last his horrifying appearance would be useful; he would be at every door of his room at once, hissing and spitting at the attackers. His sister, however, wouldn't be forced to remain with him, she would do so of her own free will. She would sit beside him on the couch, leaning towards him and listening as he confided that he had firmly intended to send her to the Conservatory, and if the misfortune hadn't intervened, he would've announced this to everyone last Christmas—for hadn't Christmas come and gone by now?—without paying the slightest attention to any objection. After this declaration his sister would be so moved that she would burst into tears, and Gregor would lift himself up to her shoulder and kiss her on her neck, which, since she had started her job, she had kept bare, without ribbon or collar.

"Mr. Samsa!" cried the middle gentleman to Gregor's father, and without wasting another word pointed with his index finger at Gregor, who was slowly advancing. The violin stopped, the middle gentleman, shaking his head, smiled first at his friends and then looked at Gregor again. Instead of driving Gregor away, his father seemed to think it more important to soothe the boarders, although they weren't upset at all and appeared to consider Gregor more entertaining than the violin-playing. His father rushed over to them and with outstretched arms tried to herd them back into their room and at the same time block their view of Gregor with his body. Now they actually got a little angry—it wasn't clear whether this was due to his father's behavior or to their dawning realization that they had had all along, without knowing it, a next-door neighbor like Gregor. They demanded explanations from his father, raised their own arms now as well, tugged nervously at their beards, and only slowly backed away toward their room. Meanwhile his sister had managed to overcome the bewildered state into which she'd fallen when her playing had been so abruptly interrupted, and after some moments spent holding the violin and bow in her slackly dangling hands and staring at the score as if she were still playing, she suddenly pulled herself together, placed her instrument on her mother's lap—she was still sitting in her chair with her lungs heaving, gasping for breath—and ran into the next room, which the boarders, under pressure from her father, were ever more swiftly approaching. One could see pillows and blankets flying high in the air and then neatly arranging themselves under his sister's practical hands. Before the gentlemen had even reached their room, she had finished making the beds and had slipped out.

Once again a perverse stubbornness seemed to grip Gregor's father, to the extent that he forgot to pay his tenants the respect still due them. He kept on pushing and shoving until the middle gentleman, who was already standing in the room's doorway, brought him up short with a thunderous stamp of his foot. "I hereby declare," he said, raising his hand and looking around for Gregor's mother and sister as well, "that considering the disgusting conditions prevailing in this apartment and in this family"—here he suddenly spat on the floor— "I'm giving immediate notice. Naturally I'm not going to pay a penny for the time I've spent here; on the contrary, I shall be seriously considering bringing some sort of action against you with claims that—I assure you—will be very easy to substantiate." He stopped speaking and stared ahead of him, as if expecting something. And indeed his two friends chimed right in, saying "We're giving immediate notice too." Whereupon he grabbed the doorknob and slammed the door shut with a crash.

Gregor's father, groping his way and staggering forward, collapsed into his armchair; it looked as if he were stretching himself out for his usual evening nap, but his heavily drooping head, looking as if it had lost all means of support, showed that he was anything but asleep. All this time Gregor had lain quietly right where the boarders had first seen him. His disappointment over the failure of his plan, and perhaps also the weakness caused by eating so little for so long, made movement an impossibility. He feared with some degree of certainty that at the very next moment the whole catastrophe would fall on his head, and he waited. He wasn't even startled when the violin slipped from his mother's trembling fingers and fell off her lap with a reverberating clatter.

"Dear parents," said his sister, pounding the table with her hand by way of preamble, "we can't go on like this. Maybe you don't realize it, but I do. I refuse to utter my brother's name in the presence of this monster, and so all I have to say is: we've got to try to get rid of it. We've done everything humanly possible to take care of it and put up with it; I don't think anyone can blame us in the least."

"She's absolutely right," said his father to himself. His mother, still trying to catch her breath, with a wild look in her eyes, began to cough, her cupped hand muffling the sound.

His sister rushed over to his mother and held her forehead. His father seemed to have been led to more definite thoughts by Grete's words; he was sitting up straight and toying with his messenger's cap, which lay on the table among the dishes left over from the boarders' dinner. From time to time he would glance over at Gregor's motionless form.

"We must try to get rid of it," said his sister, speaking only to her father since her mother's coughing was such that she was incapable of hearing a word. "It will be the death of you both. I can see it coming. People who have to work as hard as we do can't stand this constant torture at home. I can't stand it anymore either." And she burst out sobbing so violently that her tears ran down onto her mother's face, where she wiped them away mechanically with her hand. 80

"But, my child," said her father with compassion and remarkable understanding, "what should we do?"

Gregor's sister could only shrug her shoulders as a sign of the helplessness that had overcome her while she wept, in contrast to her earlier self-confidence.

"If he could understand us," said her father tentatively; Gregor's sister, through her tears, shook her hand violently to indicate how impossible that was.

"If he could understand us," repeated her father, closing his eyes so as to take in his daughter's belief that this was impossible, "then perhaps we might be able to reach some agreement with him, but the way things are—"

"He's got to go," cried Gregor's sister, "it's the only way, Father. You just have to 85 get rid of the idea that this is Gregor. Our real misfortune is having believed it for so long. But how can it be Gregor? If it were, he would've realized a long time ago that it's impossible for human beings to live with a creature like that, and he would've left of his own accord. Then we would've lost a brother, but we'd have been able to go on living and honor his memory. But the way things are, this animal persecutes us, drives away our boarders, obviously it wants to take over the whole apartment and make us sleep in the gutter. Look, Father," she suddenly screamed, "he's at it again!" And in a panic which Gregor found incomprehensible his sister abandoned his mother, and actually pushing herself from the chair as if she would rather sacrifice her mother than remain near Gregor, she rushed behind her father, who, startled by this behavior, got up as well, half raising his arms in front of Grete as if to protect her.

Gregor hadn't the slightest desire to frighten anyone, least of all his sister. He had merely started to turn around in order to go back to his room, a procedure which admittedly looked strange, since in his weakened condition he had to use his head to help him in this difficult maneuver, several times raising it and then knocking it against the floor. He stopped and looked around. His good intentions seemed to have been understood; the panic had only been temporary. Now, silent and sad, they all looked at him. His mother lay in her armchair with her legs outstretched and pressed together, her eyes almost closed from exhaustion. His father and sister sat side by side, and his sister had put her arm around her father's neck.

"Now maybe they'll let me turn around," thought Gregor, resuming his efforts. He couldn't stop panting from the strain, and he also had to rest from time to time. At least no one harassed him and he was left alone. When he had finished turning around, he immediately began to crawl back in a straight line. He was amazed at the distance between him and his room and couldn't understand how, weak as he was, he'd covered the same stretch of ground only a little while ago almost without being aware of it. Completely intent on crawling rapidly, he scarcely noticed that neither a word nor an exclamation came from his family to interrupt his progress. Only when he reached the doorway did he turn his head; not all the way, for he felt his neck growing stiff, but enough to see that behind him all was as before except that his sister had gotten to her feet. His last glimpse was of his mother, who by now was fast asleep.

He was barely inside the room before the door was slammed shut, bolted, and locked. Gregor was so frightened by the sudden noise behind him that his little legs collapsed underneath him. It was his sister who had been in such a hurry. She'd been standing there, ready and waiting, and then had sprung swiftly forward, before Gregor had even heard her coming. "At last!" she cried to her parents as she turned the key in the lock.

"And now?" Gregor asked himself, looking around in the darkness. He soon discovered that he was no longer able to move. This didn't surprise him; rather it seemed to him strange that until now he'd actually been able to propel himself with these thin little legs. In other respects he felt relatively comfortable. It was true that his entire body ached, but the pain seemed to him to be growing fainter and fainter and soon would go away altogether. The rotten apple in his back and the inflamed area around it, completely covered with fine dust, hardly bothered him anymore. He recalled his family with deep emotion and love. His own belief that he must disappear was, if anything, even firmer than his sister's. He remained in this state of empty and peaceful reflection until the tower clock struck three in the morning. He could still just sense the general brightening outside his window. Then, involuntarily, his head sank all the way down, and from his nostrils came his last feeble breath.

Early that morning, when the cleaning woman appeared—out of sheer energy and impatience she always slammed all the doors, no matter how often she'd been asked not to, so hard that sleep was no longer possible anywhere in the apartment once she'd arrived—she didn't notice anything peculiar when she paid Gregor her usual brief visit.

90

She thought that he was lying there so still on purpose, pretending that his feelings were hurt; she considered him to be very clever. As she happened to be holding a long broom, she tried to tickle Gregor with it from the doorway. When this too had no effect, she became annoyed and jabbed it into Gregor a little, and it was only when she shoved him from his place without meeting resistance that she began to take notice. Quickly realizing how things stood, she opened her eyes wide, gave a soft whistle, and without wasting any time she tore open the bedroom door and yelled at the top of her lungs into the darkness: "Come and look, it's had it, it's lying there, dead and done for."

Mr. and Mrs. Samsa sat up in their marriage bed, trying to absorb the shock the cleaning woman had given them and yet at first unable to comprehend the meaning of her words. Then they quickly climbed out of bed, Mr. Samsa on one side, Mrs. Samsa on the other. Mr. Samsa threw a blanket over his shoulders, Mrs. Samsa wore only her nightgown; dressed in this fashion they entered Gregor's room. Meanwhile the door to the living room, where Grete had been sleeping since the boarders' arrival, opened as well. Grete was fully dressed, as if she'd never gone to bed, and the pallor of her face seemed to confirm this. "Dead?" asked Mrs. Samsa and looked inquiring at the cleaning woman, although she could have checked for herself, or guessed at the truth without having to investigate. "That's for sure," said the cleaning woman, and to prove it she pushed Gregor's corpse a good way to one side with her broom. Mrs. Samsa made a move as if to stop her, then let it go. "Well," said Mr. Samsa, "now thanks be to God." He crossed himself, and the three women followed his example. Grete, who never took her eyes off the corpse, said, "Just look how thin he was. It's been a long time since he's eaten anything. The food came out just as it was when it came in." Indeed, Gregor's body was completely flat and dry; this was only now obvious because the body was no longer raised on its little legs and nothing else distracted the eye.

"Come to our room with us for a little while, Grete," said Mrs. Samsa with a sad smile, and Grete, not without a look back at the corpse, followed her parents into the bedroom. The cleaning woman shut the door and opened the windows wide. Although it was early in the morning, there was a certain mildness in the fresh air. After all, these were the last days of March.

The three boarders came out of their rooms and looked around in amazement for their breakfast; they had been forgotten. "Where's our breakfast?" the middle gentleman asked the cleaning woman in a sour tone. But she put her finger to her lips, and then quickly and quietly beckoned to the gentlemen to enter Gregor's room. So they did, and, with their hands in the pockets of their somewhat threadbare jackets, they stood in a circle around Gregor's corpse in the now sunlit room.

At that point the bedroom door opened and Mr. Samsa, wearing his uniform, appeared with his wife on one arm and his daughter on the other. They all looked a little tearful; from time to time Grete would press her face against her father's sleeve.

"Leave my home at once," Mr. Samsa told the three gentlemen, pointing to the door without letting go of the women. "What do you mean?" said the middle gentleman, who, somewhat taken aback, smiled a sugary smile. The other two held their hands behind their backs, and kept rubbing them together as if cheerfully anticipating a major argument which they were bound to win. "I mean just what I say," replied Mr. Samsa, and advanced in a line with his two companions directly on the middle boarder. At first this gentleman stood still, looking at the floor as if the thoughts inside his head were arranging themselves in a new pattern. "Well, so we'll be off," he then said, looking up at Mr. Samsa as if, suddenly overcome with humility, he was asking permission for even this decision. Mr. Samsa, his eyes glowering, merely gave him a few brief nods. With that the gentleman, taking long strides, actually set off in the direction of the hall; his two friends, who had been listening for some time with their hands quite still, now went hopping right along after him, as if they were afraid that Mr. Samsa might reach the hall before them and cut them off from their leader. Once in the hall the three of them took their hats from the coat rack, pulled their canes from the umbrella stand, bowed silently, and left the apartment. Impelled by a suspicion that would turn out to be utterly groundless, Mr. Samsa led the two women out onto the landing; leaning against the banister railing they watched the three gentlemen as they marched slowly but steadily down the long staircase, disappearing at every floor when the staircase made a turn and then after a few moments reappearing once again. The lower they descended the more the Samsas' interest in them waned; and when a butcher's boy with a basket on his head came proudly up the stairs towards the gentlemen and then swept on past them, Mr. Samsa and the women quickly left the banister and, as if relieved, returned to the apartment.

They decided to spend this day resting and going for a walk; not only did they deserve this break from work, they absolutely needed it. And so they sat down at the table to write their three letters excusing themselves, Mr. Samsa to the bank manager, Mrs. Samsa to her employer, and Grete to the store's owner. While they were writing, the cleaning woman came by to say that she was leaving now, since her morning's work was done. At first the three letter writers merely nodded without looking up, but when the cleaning woman made no move to go, they looked up at her, annoyed. "Well?" asked Mr. Samsa. The cleaning woman stood in the doorway, smiling as if she had some wonderful news for the family, news she wasn't about to share until they came right out and asked her to. The little ostrich feathers in her hat, which stood up nearly straight in the air and which had irritated Mr. Samsa the entire time she had worked for them, swayed gently in every direction. "What can we do for you?" asked Mrs. Samsa, whom the cleaning woman respected the most. "Well," the cleaning woman replied, with such good-humored laughter that she had to pause before continuing, "you don't have to worry about getting rid of that thing in the next room. It's already been taken care of." Mrs. Samsa and Grete bent over their letters as if they intended to keep on writing; Mr. Samsa, who realized that the cleaning woman was about to go into the details, stopped her firmly with an outstretched hand. Seeing that she wasn't going to be allowed to tell her story, she suddenly remembered that she was in a great hurry; clearly insulted, she called out, "Bye, everybody," whirled around wildly, and left the apartment with a terrible slamming of doors.

"She'll be dismissed tonight," said Mr. Samsa, but without getting a reply from his wife or his daughter, for the cleaning woman seemed to have ruined their tenuous peace of mind. They got up, went to the window, and remained there holding each other tightly. Mr. Samsa turned around in his chair toward them and watched them quietly for some time. Then he called out, "Come on now, come over here. Let those old troubles alone. And have a little consideration for me, too." The two women promptly obeyed him, hurried over to him, caressed him, and quickly finished their letters.

Then all three of them left the apartment together, something they hadn't done in months, and took a streetcar out to the open country on the outskirts of the city. Their car, which they had all to themselves, was completely bathed in warm sunlight. Leaning comfortably back in their seats they discussed their prospects for the future, which on closer inspection seemed to be not so bad, since all three of them had jobs which—though they'd never asked one another about them in any detail—

were in each case very advantageous and promising. Of course the greatest immediate improvement in their situation would quickly come about when they found a new apartment, one that was smaller, cheaper, and in every way easier to maintain than their current one, which Gregor had chosen for them. As they were talking on in this way, it occurred to both Mr. and Mrs. Samsa, almost simultaneously, as they watched their daughter become more and more vivacious, that in spite of all the recent troubles that had turned her cheeks pale, she had blossomed into a pretty and shapely girl. Growing quieter now, communicating almost unconsciously through glances, they reflected that soon it would be time to find her a good husband. And it was as if in confirmation of their new dreams and good intentions that at the end of their ride their daughter got up first and stretched her young body.

Questions

1. What was Gregor's occupation before his transformation? How did he come to his particular job? What kept him working for his firm?
2. When Gregor wakes to discover he has become a gigantic insect, he is mostly intent on the practical implications of his metamorphosis—how to get out of bed, how to get to his job, and so on. He never wonders why or how he has been changed. What does this odd reaction suggest about Gregor?
3. When Gregor's parents first see the gigantic insect (paragraph 25), do they recognize it as their son? What do their initial reactions suggest about their attitude toward their son?
4. How does each family member react to Gregor after his transformation? How do their reactions differ from one another? What do they have in common?
5. What things about Gregor have been changed? What seems to have remained the same? List specific qualities.
6. *The Metamorphosis* takes place almost entirely in the Samsa family apartment. How does the story's setting shape its themes?
7. Which family member first decides that the family must "get rid of" the insect? What rationale is given? In what specific ways does the family's decision affect Gregor?
8. How does the family react to Gregor's death?
9. Does Grete change in the course of the story? If so, how does she change?
10. In what ways is Gregor's metamorphosis symbolic?

▪ WRITING *effectively*

Franz Kafka on Writing

Discussing *The Metamorphosis*   c. 1920

My friend Alfred Kämpf . . . admired Kafka's story *The Metamorphosis*. He described the author as "a new, more profound and therefore more significant Edgar Allan Poe."

During a walk with Franz Kafka on the Altstädter Ring° I told him about this new admirer of his, but aroused neither interest nor understanding. On the contrary, Kafka's expression showed that any discussion of his book was distasteful to him. I, however, was filled with a zeal for discoveries, and so I was tactless.

Altstädter Ring: a major street in Prague.

"The hero of the story is called Samsa," I said. "It sounds like a cryptogram for Kafka. Five letters in each word. The S in the word Samsa has the same position as the K in the word Kafka. The A . . ."

Kafka interrupted me.

"It is not a cryptogram. Samsa is not merely Kafka, and nothing else. *The Metamorphosis* is not a confession, although it is—in a certain sense—an indiscretion."

"I know nothing about that."

"Is it perhaps delicate and discreet to talk about the bugs in one's own family?"

"It isn't usual in good society."

"You see what bad manners I have."

Kafka smiled. He wished to dismiss the subject. But I did not wish to.

"It seems to me that the distinction between good and bad manners hardly applies here," I said. "*The Metamorphosis* is a terrible dream, a terrible conception."

Kafka stood still.

"The dream reveals the reality, which conception lags behind. That is the horror of life—the terror of art. But now I must go home."

From Conversations with Kafka by Gustav Janouch

THINKING ABOUT LONG STORIES AND NOVELS

Writing about a long story or novella may seem overwhelming. There can seem to be so much to analyze and consider. You may despair of being able to master the material and discuss it coherently, but if you focus your attention on some central concerns, you will be surprised at how easily you can develop and express your responses to the work.

- **Be aware that characters in a longer narrative often have more complex personalities.** In a short story, characters are often presented in terms of two or three basic personality traits. But in a long story or novella, characters are usually drawn with more depth and shading—and sometimes even contradictory elements—to their personalities. In reading a long story, you should be alert to all the different aspects of a character's nature.

- **Consider that a longer narrative allows for more development.** Often the intention of a short story is to reveal a personality or a situation as it is, much in the manner of showing a snapshot or drawing back a curtain. But a longer story requires movement and development to sustain the reader's interest. As you read, notice the—often subtle—changes that may take place in the protagonist as he or she initiates or otherwise experiences the events of the narrative.

- **Review the work.** As a long story or novella unfolds, your recollections of the earlier parts of the text may be pushed aside as new events and situations occur. A first-rate work of fiction will yield a wealth of interconnections of language, images, actions, and ideas. After you finish reading the work, by going through the text again you may often see much more in the story than you did the first time around.

CHECKLIST: Writing About Long Stories and Novels

- ☐ What is the protagonist's situation at the beginning of the work?
- ☐ What is the protagonist's main objective at the beginning?
- ☐ What changes take place in the protagonist's situation as the narrative proceeds?
- ☐ How does the protagonist react to these changes? How does his or her response to stress reveal the protagonist's basic nature?
- ☐ Who are the story's other important characters, and what are their relationships to the protagonist?
- ☐ Can anyone be described as an antagonist?
- ☐ Compare and contrast the beginning of the story with its conclusion.
- ☐ Don't try to put everything in your essay. Focus on the main points and be selective in the choice of textual details.
- ☐ Try to put your ideas in some logical order.
- ☐ Outline the main points of your argument to see clearly what is relevant to that argument and what is not.

WRITING ASSIGNMENT FOR A RESEARCH PAPER

This challenging assignment for a research paper comes from Professor Michael Cass of Mercer University. Select a writer from your reading list whose work impresses you, and write a research paper defending that author's claim to literary greatness. Present clear reasons why the author is a major writer, using at least five critical sources and supporting your argument with both examples from the writer's work and statements from critics. Here is a short research paper by a student of Professor Cass, Stephanie Crowe, who discussed why she believed that Franz Kalka was a great writer.

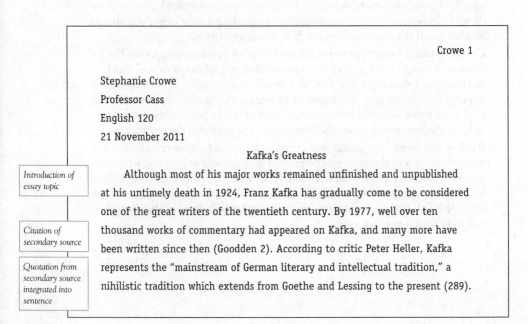

Crowe 1

Stephanie Crowe

Professor Cass

English 120

21 November 2011

Kafka's Greatness

Introduction of essay topic

Although most of his major works remained unfinished and unpublished at his untimely death in 1924, Franz Kafka has gradually come to be considered one of the great writers of the twentieth century. By 1977, well over ten

Citation of secondary source

thousand works of commentary had appeared on Kafka, and many more have been written since then (Goodden 2). According to critic Peter Heller, Kafka

Quotation from secondary source integrated into sentence

represents the "mainstream of German literary and intellectual tradition," a nihilistic tradition which extends from Goethe and Lessing to the present (289).

Crowe 2

Not only is Kafka generally considered one of the greatest fiction writers of the modern era, he is also indisputably one of the most influential. In his 1989 study, *After Kafka*, Shimon Sandbank discusses Kafka's influence on a dozen modern writers, including Sartre, Camus, Beckett, Borges, and Ionesco. His effects on these writers differ. Some borrow his understated, almost passive prose style while others adopt his recurrent images and themes. Whatever the specific elements they use, however, Kafka's ability to influence these writers is another measure of his stature.

Topic sentence on Kafka as influence

Great literature often gives us the stories and images to understand our own age, a process that necessarily includes understanding our deepest problems. The twentieth century, to borrow a phrase from W. H. Auden, was mostly an "Age of Anxiety." Most modern people are no longer bound to follow the occupations, behaviors, and beliefs of their parents, but they gain this newfound freedom at the expense of a constant, difficult search for identity. The personal quest for meaningful identity often leads to despair. This "existential crisis" is the basis for many contemporary problems including the decline of religion, the rise of totalitarianism, the breakdown of social identity, and the decay of traditional family structure.

Assumptions explained

Kafka's works dramatize these problems memorably because they provide us with myths, images, stories, and situations that describe the particular crises of the early twentieth century. When faced with the modern challenge of not having a predetermined social or religious identity, Kafka's characters desperately attempt to find certainty. The problem, however, is that they are usually afraid to do anything decisive because everything is uncertain. Auden observed:

Topic sentence on Kafka's relationship to his time

> Far from being confident of success, the Kafka hero is convinced from the start that he is doomed to fail, as he is also doomed, being who he is, to make prodigious and unending efforts to reach it [the goal]. Indeed, the mere desire to reach the goal is itself a proof, not that he is one of the elect, but that he is under a special curse. (162)

Quotation from secondary source, set off from text

One way that Kafka memorably dramatizes the modern struggle for identity is by reversing the traditional quest story. In a quest story, the hero knows the goal that he wants to achieve and has some confidence that he will be able to achieve it. As he tries to reach the goal, he must overcome various enemies and obstacles. "In a typical Kafka story, on the other hand, the goal is peculiar to the hero himself: he has no competitors" (Auden 162). His question then becomes

Topic sentence elaborates on how Kafka's work reflects his time

Verbatim quotation from secondary source

Crowe 3

not a practical "Can I succeed?" but instead a vague and problematic "What should I do?" Unable to answer this question satisfactorily, the hero becomes increasingly alienated from his own surroundings. This alienation is yet another symptom of "the inhumanity of modern society" that Kafka so memorably portrayed (Kuna 62).

Topic sentence on relationship between Kafka's era and his style

Kafka also distinguishes himself as a great writer because he created a distinctive style that effectively dramatizes modern problems. Although Kafka's fiction often describes extreme situations, his prose usually seems strangely calm and detached. He uses "clear and simple language" that paints "concrete pictures of human beings, pictures that, in a sense, have to speak for themselves" (Cooper 19). These haunting images (the unreachable castle, the unknown laws, the unspecified trial) dramatize the mysterious struggles of the characters.

Topic sentence on Kafka's style incorporates critical view

Kafka also uses his style to separate himself from his characters, a technique that develops a contrast between the calmness of his style and the nervous desperation of his characters (Heller 237). For example, the opening of Kafka's novella *The Metamorphosis*, which is perhaps the most famous first sentence in modern fiction, describes an outrageous event—a young man who wakes up transformed into a giant bug—in a strangely matter-of-fact tone. This contrast is important because it reminds us of the desperation of modern man imprisoned in a world he can neither understand nor control.

Topic sentence on Kafka's style of ambiguity

Perhaps the most interesting feature of Kafka's style is his ability to create works that cannot be explained by a single interpretation. Because he allows his pictures to "speak for themselves," "Kafka's texts have been subject to a variety of widely divergent approaches" (Heller 236). Another critic, speaking directly of *The Metamorphosis*, agrees: "Gregor's transformation has a double meaning: it is both an escape from his oppressive life and a representation or even an intensification of it" (Goldfarb). Therefore, no single interpretation can adequately explain an entire work of Kafka's. Most interpretations may illuminate particular moments in a work, but inevitably they lead to a dead end when pressed to explain the whole narrative. Whether one is reading on a social, moral, psychological, metaphysical, theological, or existential level, Kafka "tends to suspend all distinction and thus to revert to total ambiguity" (Heller 285). According to Heller, this characteristic mysteriousness becomes "the epitome of his art" (230).

Auden believed that the impossibility of interpreting Kafka's work is essential in defining him as an important and influential writer. He says that "Kafka is a great, perhaps the greatest, master of the pure parable, a literary genre about which a critic can say very little worth saying" (159). Since the meaning of a parable is different for each individual, critics cannot explain them without revealing their own visions and values. Kafka develops stories with important symbols that are easily identified; attempting to interpret these symbols, however, only leads to frustration.

Topic sentence on Kafka's complexity

The frustration that comes from trying to interpret Kafka's works exemplifies his recurrent, and particularly twentieth-century, theme, which Peter Heller has described as man's "ever frustrated, ever defeated striving for self-realization in an inhuman human universe in which he is alienated from himself and from the world he lives in" (305). Kafka uses his characteristic difficult symbolism and ambiguity, along with his theme of hopelessness and despair, as a common thread that binds all of his works together.

Topic sentence on Kafka's central theme incorporates quotation from secondary source

Kafka's book *The Great Wall of China* contains several short pieces which have a slightly less desperate tone than that of *The Metamorphosis*. Many of the stories in *The Great Wall of China*, however, still present the theme of hopelessness. In the reflection entitled "The Problem of Our Laws," Kafka examines the origins and legitimacy of law. This parable begins with the narrator stating, "Our laws are not generally known; they are kept secret by the small group of nobles who rule us" (147). Next, the narrator goes through a laborious process of rationally questioning why only the nobility knows the laws, whether the laws really exist, and whether it will ever be possible for common men to know the laws. He finally concludes that the only way to know the law would be a quiet revolution that ends nobility. But even this solution, he realizes, is futile. The nobility cannot be eliminated because they provide the only order that exists. While this parable makes several interesting points, its structure is essentially static. The narrator ends where he began—trapped in an unknowable world.

Topic sentence on tone

Quotation from primary source

One of Kafka's unfinished novels, *The Trial*, also concentrates on the unknown symbol of the Law. In the novel, Joseph K. is arrested for a crime that no one ever knows. Joseph, like most of Kafka's characters, is a common man with an uneventful life who admits that he knows little of the Law. The drama of the novel is the protagonist's hopeless attempts to master an unknown and impossible situation. Joseph K.'s life itself becomes a trial, although he is never

Topic sentence on theme

sentenced. Finally, one year after his arrest, two men come and murder him. Instead of trying to understand the Law, "In the end he appears to accept the verdict as a release from the condition of despair," and "dies like an animal, without comprehending the rationale of the Law which condemns him" (Heller 280-81). Like many men, before his death K. is struggling to discover his identity in relation to the Law that governs him; however, K.'s hopeless life ends with a pointless murder.

Topic sentence on theme

Kafka's other great, unfinished novel, *The Castle*, also concentrates on the theme of unknowability and despair. Instead of trying to understand the Law, K. in *The Castle* has another impossible quest, his attempt to enter the castle of the local ruler to report for duty as a land surveyor. His constant efforts, however, prove futile. As in *The Trial*, the protagonist is at the mercy of an arbitrary and unknowable Law:

> In many ways the castle functions like a secret court system: the officials decide and carry out policies that are conceived as stipulations of law; they lean on their law books, try to serve the law, and know the clandestine ways of law. Many decisions are arrived at arbitrarily and remain secret; even legal actions such as an official indictment can be kept hidden for some time. (Heidsieck 3)

Only when K. lies on his deathbed does a call from the castle come, giving him permission to live in the town. Once again, the protagonist suffers hopelessly and dies in despair.

While *The Trial* emphasizes political and psychological themes characteristic of the twentieth century, *The Castle* focuses on the religious identity crisis. *The Metamorphosis* examines similar themes of identity on a personal and family level. All of these works focus on modern humanity's difficult struggle to define its place in existence.

Conclusion sums up argument

Kafka, through his works, accurately describes the modern condition of many by using memorable images and a distinctive style. This characteristic style influenced many twentieth-century writers and readers. While difficult and somewhat bleak, Kafka's often ambiguous, yet understated dramatizations of man's condition, along with his lasting influence, form the foundation of his greatness.

Thesis sentence makes debatable claim

Crowe 6

Works Cited

Auden, W. H. "The I Without a Self." *The Dyer's Hand*. New York: Random, 1989. 159–70. Print.

Cooper, Gabriele Bon Natzmer. *Kafka and Language: In the Stream of Thoughts and Life*. Riverside: Ariadne, 1991. Print.

Goldfarb, Sheldon. "Critical Essay on *The Metamorphosis*." *Short Stories for Students*. Ed. Jennifer Smith. Vol. 12. Detroit: Gale, 2001. N. pag. *Literature Resource Center*. Gale. Web. 19 September 2011.

Goodden, Christina. "Points of Departure." *The Kafka Debate: New Perspectives for Our Time*. Ed. Angel Flores. New York: Gordian, 1988. 2–9. Print.

Heidsieck, Arnold. "Community, Delusion and Anti-Semitism in Kafka's *The Castle*." *German Studies Program*. German Dept., U of Southern California, n.d. Web. 19 September 2011. <http://www.usc.edu/dept/LAS/german/track/heidsiec/KafkaAntisemitism/KafkaAntisemitism.pdf>.

Heller, Peter. "Kafka: The Futility of Striving." *Dialectics and Nihilism*. Amherst: U of Massachusetts P, 1966. 227–306. Print.

Kafka, Franz. "The Problem of Our Laws." *The Great Wall of China*. New York: Schocken, 1946. 147–49. Print.

Kuna, Franz. *Franz Kafka: Literature as Corrective Punishment*. Bloomington: Indiana UP, 1974. Print.

Sandbank, Shimon. *After Kafka: The Influence of Kafka's Fiction*. Athens: U of Georgia P, 1989. Print.

MORE TOPICS FOR WRITING

1. Choose a thematic concern of *The Metamorphosis*; some possibilities are work, romantic love, and the family. Develop a thesis about what it has to say on your chosen theme. Now choose three key moments from the story to back up your argument. Make your case in a medium-length paper (600 to 1,000 words); be sure to quote as needed from the text.

2. Is *The Metamorphosis* a horror story? What elements does Kafka's story share with horror fiction or films you have known? How does *The Metamorphosis* differ?

3. Compare and contrast Gregor Samsa's relationships with the people in his life to Miss Emily's relationships with those around her in "A Rose for Emily."

4. Explore how Gregor Samsa's metamorphosis into a giant insect is symbolic of his earlier life and relations with his family. (For a discussion of literary symbols, see Chapter 7, "Symbol.")

5. Write a metamorphosis story of your own. Imagine a character who turns overnight into something quite other than himself or herself. As you describe that character's struggles, try for a mix of tragedy and grotesque comedy, as found in *The Metamorphosis*.

► TERMS FOR *review*

Novel ► An extended work of fictional prose narrative. The term *novel* usually implies a book-length narrative.

Novella ► In modern terms, a prose narrative longer than a short story but shorter than a novel. Unlike a short story, a novella is long enough to be published independently as a brief book.

Romance ► In general terms, romance is a narrative mode that employs exotic adventure and idealized emotion rather than realistic depiction of character and action. In the romantic mode, people, actions, and events are depicted more as we wish them to be (heroes are very brave, villains are very bad) than in the complex forms in which they usually exist. Most popular fiction genres—such as mystery, horror, adventure, science fiction—develop from this mode.

Historical fiction ► A type of fiction in which the narrative is set in another time or place. In historical fiction, the author often attempts to recreate a faithful picture of daily life during the period. While it may depict real historical figures, more often it places imaginary characters in a carefully reconstructed version of a particular era.

Nonfiction novel ► A genre in which actual events are presented as a novel-length story, using the techniques of fiction.

Picaresque ► A type of narrative, usually a novel, that presents the life of a likable scoundrel at odds with respectable society. The narrator of a picaresque was originally a *pícaro* (Spanish for "rascal" or "rogue") who recounts his or her adventures tricking the rich and gullible. This type of narrative rarely has a tightly constructed plot, and the episodes or adventures follow in a loose chronological order.

Epistolary novel ► Novel in which the story is told by way of letters written by one or more of the characters. This form often lends an authenticity to the story, an illusion that the author may have discovered these letters, even though they are a product of the author's imagination.

***Bildungsroman* ►** German for "novel of growth and development." Sometimes called an **apprenticeship novel**, this genre depicts a youth who struggles toward maturity and the forming of a worldview or philosophy of life.

CRITICAL CASEBOOK
Flannery O'Connor

**Flannery O'Connor and her *Self-Portrait with
Pheasant Cock*, 1962**

> *The main concern of the fiction writer is with mystery
> as it is incarnated in real life.*
>
> —FLANNERY O'CONNOR

FLANNERY O'CONNOR

Mary Flannery O'Connor (1925–1964) was born in Savannah, Georgia, but spent most of her life in the small town of Milledgeville. While attending Georgia State College for Women, she won a local reputation for her fledgling stories and satiric cartoons. After graduating in 1945, she went on to study at the University of Iowa, where she earned an M.F.A. in 1947. Diagnosed in 1950 with disseminated lupus, the same incurable illness that had killed her father, O'Connor returned home and spent the last decade of her life living with her mother in Milledgeville. Back on the family dairy farm, she wrote, maintained an extensive literary correspondence, raised peacocks, and underwent medical treatment. When her illness occasionally went into a period of remission, she made trips to lecture and read her stories to college audiences. Her health declined rapidly after surgery early in 1964 for an unrelated complaint. She died at thirty-nine.

Flannery O'Connor

O'Connor is unusual among modern American writers in the depth of her Christian vision. A devout Roman Catholic, she attended mass daily while growing up and living in the largely Protestant South. As a latter-day satirist in the manner of Jonathan Swift, O'Connor levels the eye of an uncompromising moralist on the violence and spiritual disorder of the modern world, focusing on what she calls "the action of grace in territory held largely by the devil." She is sometimes called a "Southern Gothic" writer because of her fascination with grotesque incidents and characters. Throughout her career she depicted the South as a troubled region in which the social, racial, and religious status quo that had existed since before the Civil War was coming to a violent end. Despite the inherent seriousness of her religious and social themes, O'Connor's mordant and frequently outrageous humor is everywhere apparent. Her combination of profound vision and dark comedy is the distinguishing characteristic of her literary sensibilities.

O'Connor's published work includes two short novels, Wise Blood *(1952) and* The Violent Bear It Away *(1960), and two collections of short stories,* A Good Man Is Hard to Find *(1955) and* Everything That Rises Must Converge, *published posthumously in 1965. A collection of essays and miscellaneous prose,* Mystery and Manners *(1969), and her selected letters,* The Habit of Being *(1979), reveal an innate cheerfulness and engaging personal warmth that are not always apparent in her fiction.* The Complete Stories *of Flannery O'Connor was posthumously awarded the National Book Award in 1971.*

STORIES

A Good Man Is Hard to Find

1955

The grandmother didn't want to go to Florida. She wanted to visit some of her connections in east Tennessee and she was seizing at every chance to change Bailey's mind. Bailey was the son she lived with, her only boy. He was sitting on the edge of his chair at the table, bent over the orange sports section of the *Journal*. "Now look here, Bailey," she said, "see here, read this," and she stood with one hand on her thin hip and the other rattling the newspaper at his bald head. "Here this fellow that calls himself The Misfit is aloose from the Federal Pen and headed toward Florida and you read here what it says he did to these people. Just you read it. I wouldn't take my children in any direction with a criminal like that aloose in it. I couldn't answer to my conscience if I did."

Bailey didn't look up from his reading so she wheeled around then and faced the children's mother, a young woman in slacks, whose face was as broad and innocent as a cabbage and was tied around with a green head-kerchief that had two points on the top like rabbit's ears. She was sitting on the sofa, feeding the baby his apricots out of a jar. "The children have been to Florida before," the old lady said. "You all ought to take them somewhere else for a change so they would see different parts of the world and be broad. They never have been to east Tennessee."

The children's mother didn't seem to hear her but the eight-year-old boy, John Wesley, a stocky child with glasses, said, "If you don't want to go to Florida, why dontcha stay at home?" He and the little girl, June Star, were reading the funny papers on the floor.

"She wouldn't stay at home to be queen for a day," June Star said without raising her yellow head.

"Yes and what would you do if this fellow, The Misfit, caught you?" the grand- 5 mother said.

"I'd smack his face," John Wesley said.

"She wouldn't stay at home for a million bucks," June Star said. "Afraid she'd miss something. She has to go everywhere we go."

"All right, Miss," the grandmother said. "Just remember that the next time you want me to curl your hair."

June Star said her hair was naturally curly.

The next morning the grandmother was the first one in the car, ready to go. She 10 had her big black valise that looked like the head of a hippopotamus in one corner, and underneath it she was hiding a basket with Pitty Sing, the cat, in it. She didn't intend for the cat to be left alone in the house for three days because he would miss her too much and she was afraid he might brush against one of the gas burners and accidentally asphyxiate himself. Her son, Bailey, didn't like to arrive at a motel with a cat.

She sat in the middle of the back seat with John Wesley and June Star on either side of her. Bailey and the children's mother and the baby sat in front and they left Atlanta at eight forty-five with the mileage on the car at 55890. The grandmother wrote this down because she thought it would be interesting to say how many miles they had been when they got back. It took them twenty minutes to reach the outskirts of the city.

The old lady settled herself comfortably, removing her white cotton gloves and putting them up with her purse on the shelf in front of the back window. The children's mother still had on slacks and still had her hair tied up in a green kerchief, but the grandmother had on a navy blue straw sailor hat with a bunch of white violets on the brim and a navy blue dress with a small white dot in the print. Her collars and cuffs were white organdy trimmed with lace and at her neckline she had pinned a purple spray of cloth violets containing a sachet. In case of an accident, anyone seeing her dead on the highway would know at once that she was a lady.

She said she thought it was going to be a good day for driving, neither too hot nor too cold, and she cautioned Bailey that the speed limit was fifty-five miles an hour and that the patrolmen hid themselves behind billboards and small clumps of trees and sped out after you before you had a chance to slow down. She pointed out interesting details of the scenery: Stone Mountain; the blue granite that in some places came up to both sides of the highway; the brilliant red clay banks slightly streaked with purple; and the various crops that made rows of green lace-work on the ground. The trees were full of silver-white sunlight and the meanest of them sparkled. The children were reading comic magazines and their mother had gone back to sleep.

"Let's go through Georgia fast so we won't have to look at it much," John Wesley said.

"If I were a little boy," said the grandmother, "I wouldn't talk about my native 15 state that way. Tennessee has the mountains and Georgia has the hills."

"Tennessee is just a hillbilly dumping ground," John Wesley said, "and Georgia is a lousy state too."

"You said it," June Star said.

"In my time," said the grandmother, folding her thin veined fingers, "children were more respectful of their native states and their parents and everything else. People did right then. Oh look at the cute little pickaninny!" she said and pointed to a Negro child standing in the door of a shack. "Wouldn't that make a picture, now?" she asked and they all turned and looked at the little Negro out of the back window. He waved.

"He didn't have any britches on," June Star said.

"He probably didn't have any," the grandmother explained. "Little niggers in the 20 country don't have things like we do. If I could paint, I'd paint that picture," she said.

The children exchanged comic books.

The grandmother offered to hold the baby and the children's mother passed him over the front seat to her. She set him on her knee and bounced him and told him about the things they were passing. She rolled her eyes and screwed up her mouth and stuck her leathery thin face into his smooth bland one. Occasionally he gave her a far-away smile. They passed a large cotton field with five or six graves fenced in the middle of it, like a small island. "Look at the graveyard!" the grandmother said, pointing it out. "That was the old family burying ground. That belonged to the plantation."

"Where's the plantation?" John Wesley asked.

"Gone With the Wind," said the grandmother. "Ha. Ha."

When the children finished all the comic books they had brought, they opened 25 the lunch and ate it. The grandmother ate a peanut butter sandwich and an olive and would not let the children throw the box and the paper napkins out the window. When there was nothing else to do they played a game by choosing a cloud and making the other two guess what shape it suggested. John Wesley took one the shape of a cow and June Star guessed a cow and John Wesley said, no, an automobile, and June Star said he didn't play fair, and they began to slap each other over the grandmother.

The grandmother said she would tell them a story if they would keep quiet. When she told a story, she rolled her eyes and waved her head and was very dramatic. She said once when she was a maiden lady she had been courted by a Mr. Edgar Atkins Teagarden from Jasper, Georgia. She said he was a very good-looking man and a gentleman and that he brought her a watermelon every Saturday afternoon with his initials cut in it, E. A. T. Well, one Saturday, she said, Mr. Teagarden brought the watermelon and there was nobody at home and he left it on the front porch and returned in his buggy to Jasper, but she never got the watermelon, she said, because a nigger boy ate it when he saw the initials, E. A. T.! This story tickled John Wesley's funny bone and he giggled and giggled but June Star didn't think it was any good. She said she wouldn't marry a man that just brought her a watermelon on Saturday. The grandmother said she would have done well to marry Mr. Teagarden because he was a gentleman and had bought Coca-Cola stock when it first came out and that he had died only a few years ago, a very wealthy man.

They stopped at The Tower for barbecued sandwiches. The Tower was a part stucco and part wood filling station and dance hall set in a clearing outside of Timothy. A fat man named Red Sammy Butts ran it and there were signs stuck here and there on the building and for miles up and down the highway saying, TRY RED SAMMY'S FAMOUS BARBECUE. NONE LIKE FAMOUS RED SAMMY'S! RED SAM! THE FAT BOY WITH THE HAPPY LAUGH. A VETERAN! RED SAMMY'S YOUR MAN!

Red Sammy was lying on the bare ground outside The Tower with his head under a truck while a gray monkey about a foot high, chained to a small chinaberry tree, chattered nearby. The monkey sprang back into the tree and got on the highest limb as soon as he saw the children jump out of the car and run toward him.

Inside, The Tower was a long dark room with a counter at one end and tables at the other and dancing space in the middle. They all sat down at a board table next to the nickelodeon and Red Sam's wife, a tall burnt-brown woman with hair and eyes lighter than her skin, came and took their order. The children's mother put a dime in the machine and played "The Tennessee Waltz," and the grandmother said that tune always made her want to dance. She asked Bailey if he would like to dance but he only glared at her. He didn't have a naturally sunny disposition like she did and trips made him nervous. The grandmother's brown eyes were very bright. She swayed her head from side to side and pretended she was dancing in her chair. June Star said play something she could tap to so the children's mother put in another dime and played a fast number and June Star stepped out onto the dance floor and did her tap routine.

"Ain't she cute?" Red Sam's wife said, leaning over the counter. "Would you like   30
to come be my little girl?"

"No I certainly wouldn't," June Star said. "I wouldn't live in a broken-down place like this for a million bucks!" and she ran back to the table.

"Ain't she cute?" the woman repeated, stretching her mouth politely.

"Aren't you ashamed?" hissed the grandmother.

Red Sam came in and told his wife to quit lounging on the counter and hurry up with these people's order. His khaki trousers reached just to his hip bones and his stomach hung over them like a sack of meal swaying under his shirt. He came over and sat down at a table nearby and let out a combination sigh and yodel. "You can't win," he said. "You can't win," and he wiped his sweating red face off with a gray handkerchief. "These days you don't know who to trust," he said. "Ain't that the truth?"

"People are certainly not nice like they used to be," said the grandmother.   35

"Two fellers come in here last week," Red Sammy said, "driving a Chrysler. It was a old beat-up car but it was a good one and these boys looked all right to me. Said they worked at the mill and you know I let them fellers charge the gas they bought? Now why did I do that?"

"Because you're a good man!" the grandmother said at once.

"Yes'm, I suppose so," Red Sam said as if he were struck with this answer.

His wife brought the orders, carrying the five plates all at once without a tray, two in each hand and one balanced on her arm. "It isn't a soul in this green world of God's that you can trust," she said. "And I don't count nobody out of that, not nobody," she repeated, looking at Red Sammy.

"Did you read about that criminal, The Misfit, that's escaped?" asked the grand-   40
mother.

"I wouldn't be a bit surprised if he didn't attact this place right here," said the woman. "If he hears about it being here, I wouldn't be none surprised to see him. If he hears it's two cent in the cash register, I wouldn't be a-tall surprised if he . . ."

"That'll do," Red Sam said. "Go bring these people their Co'-Colas," and the woman went off to get the rest of the order.

"A good man is hard to find," Red Sammy said. "Everything is getting terrible. I remember the day you could go off and leave your screen door unlatched. Not no more."

He and the grandmother discussed better times. The old lady said that in her opinion Europe was entirely to blame for the way things were now. She said the way Europe acted you would think we were made of money and Red Sam said it was no use talking about it, she was exactly right. The children ran outside into the white sunlight and looked at the monkey in the lacy chinaberry tree. He was busy catching fleas on himself and biting each one carefully between his teeth as if it were a delicacy.

They drove off again into the hot afternoon. The grandmother took cat naps and   45
woke up every five minutes with her own snoring. Outside of Toombsboro she woke up and recalled an old plantation that she had visited in this neighborhood once when she was a young lady. She said the house had six white columns across the front and that there was an avenue of oaks leading up to it and two little wooden trellis arbors on either side in front where you sat down with your suitor after a stroll in the garden. She recalled exactly which road to turn off to get to it. She knew that Bailey would not be willing to lose any time looking at an old house, but the more she talked about it, the more she wanted to see it once again and find out if the little twin arbors were still standing. "There was a secret panel in this house," she said craftily, not telling the truth but wishing that she were, "and the story went that all the family silver was hidden in it when Sherman° came through but it was never found . . ."

"Hey!" John Wesley said. "Let's go see it! We'll find it! We'll poke all the woodwork and find it! Who lives there? Where do you turn off at? Hey, Pop, can't we turn off there?"

"We never have seen a house with a secret panel!" June Star shrieked. "Let's go to the house with the secret panel! Hey Pop, can't we go see the house with the secret panel!"

"It's not far from here, I know," the grandmother said. "It wouldn't take over twenty minutes."

Bailey was looking straight ahead. His jaw was as rigid as a horseshoe. "No," he said.

The children began to yell and scream that they wanted to see the house with   50
the secret panel. John Wesley kicked the back of the front seat and June Star hung over her mother's shoulder and whined desperately into her ear that they never had any fun even on their vacation, that they could never do what THEY wanted to do. The baby began to scream and John Wesley kicked the back of the seat so hard that his father could feel the blows in his kidney.

"All right!" he shouted and drew the car to a stop at the side of the road. "Will you all shut up? Will you all just shut up for one second? If you don't shut up, we won't go anywhere."

Sherman: General William Tecumseh Sherman, Union commander, whose troops burned Atlanta in 1864, then made a devastating march to the sea.

"It would be very educational for them," the grandmother murmured.

"All right," Bailey said, "but get this: this is the only time we're going to stop for anything like this. This is the one and only time."

"The dirt road that you have to turn down is about a mile back," the grand-mother directed. "I marked it when we passed."

"A dirt road," Bailey groaned.   55

After they had turned around and were headed toward the dirt road, the grand-mother recalled other points about the house, the beautiful glass over the front door-way and the candle-lamp in the hall. John Wesley said that the secret panel was probably in the fireplace.

"You can't go inside this house," Bailey said. "You don't know who lives there."

"While you all talk to the people in front, I'll run around behind and get in a window," John Wesley suggested.

"We'll all stay in the car," his mother said.

They turned onto the dirt road and the car raced roughly along in a swirl of pink   60
dust. The grandmother recalled the times when there were no paved roads and thirty miles was a day's journey. The dirt road was hilly and there were sudden washes in it and sharp curves on dangerous embankments. All at once they would be on a hill, looking down over the blue tops of trees for miles around, then the next minute, they would be in a red depression with the dust-coated trees looking down on them.

"This place had better turn up in a minute," Bailey said, "or I'm going to turn around."

The road looked as if no one had traveled on it for months.

"It's not much farther," the grandmother said and just as she said it, a horrible thought came to her. The thought was so embarrassing that she turned red in the face and her eyes dilated and her feet jumped up, upsetting her valise in the corner. The instant the valise moved, the newspaper top she had over the basket under it rose with a snarl and Pitty Sing, the cat, sprang onto Bailey's shoulder.

The children were thrown to the floor and their mother, clutching the baby, was thrown out the door onto the ground; the old lady was thrown into the front seat. The car turned over once and landed right-side-up in a gulch off the side of the road. Bailey remained in the driver's seat with the cat—gray-striped with a broad white face and an orange nose—clinging to his neck like a caterpillar.

As soon as the children saw they could move their arms and legs, they scram-   65
bled out of the car, shouting, "We've had an ACCIDENT!" The grandmother was curled up under the dashboard, hoping she was injured so that Bailey's wrath would not come down on her all at once. The horrible thought she had had before the ac-cident was that the house she had remembered so vividly was not in Georgia but in Tennessee.

Bailey removed the cat from his neck with both hands and flung it out the win-dow against the side of a pine tree. Then he got out of the car and started looking for the children's mother. She was sitting against the side of the red gutted ditch, hold-ing the screaming baby, but she only had a cut down her face and a broken shoulder. "We've had an ACCIDENT!" the children screamed in a frenzy of delight.

"But nobody's killed," June Star said with disappointment as the grandmother limped out of the car, her hat still pinned to her head but the broken front brim stand-ing up at a jaunty angle and the violet spray hanging off the side. They all sat down in the ditch, except the children, to recover from the shock. They were all shaking.

"Maybe a car will come along," said the children's mother hoarsely.

"I believe I have injured an organ," said the grandmother, pressing her side, but no one answered her. Bailey's teeth were clattering. He had on a yellow sport shirt with bright blue parrots designed in it and his face was as yellow as the shirt. The grandmother decided that she would not mention that the house was in Tennessee.

The road was about ten feet above and they could see only the tops of the trees on the other side of it. Behind the ditch they were sitting in there were more woods, tall and dark and deep. In a few minutes they saw a car some distance away on top of a hill, coming slowly as if the occupants were watching them. The grandmother stood up and waved both her arms dramatically to attract their attention. The car continued to come on slowly, disappeared around a bend and appeared again, moving even slower, on top of the hill they had gone over. It was a big black battered hearse-like automobile. There were three men in it. 70

It came to a stop just over them and for some minutes, the driver looked down with a steady expressionless gaze to where they were sitting, and didn't speak. Then he turned his head and muttered something to the other two and they got out. One was a fat boy in black trousers and a red sweat shirt with a silver stallion embossed on the front of it. He moved around on the right side of them and stood staring, his mouth partly open in a kind of loose grin. The other had on khaki pants and a blue striped coat and a gray hat pulled down very low, hiding most of his face. He came around slowly on the left side. Neither spoke.

The driver got out of the car and stood by the side of it, looking down at them. He was an older man than the other two. His hair was just beginning to gray and he wore silver-rimmed spectacles that gave him a scholarly look. He had a long creased face and didn't have on any shirt or undershirt. He had on blue jeans that were too tight for him and was holding a black hat and a gun. The two boys also had guns.

"We've had an ACCIDENT!" the children screamed.

The grandmother had the peculiar feeling that the bespectacled man was some-one she knew. His face was as familiar to her as if she had known him all her life but she could not recall who he was. He moved away from the car and began to come down the embankment, placing his feet carefully so that he wouldn't slip. He had on tan and white shoes and no socks, and his ankles were red and thin. "Good after-noon," he said. "I see you all had you a little spill."

"We turned over twice!" said the grandmother. 75

"Oncet," he corrected. "We seen it happen. Try their car and see will it run, Hiram," he said quietly to the boy with the gray hat.

"What you got that gun for?" John Wesley asked. "Whatcha gonna do with that gun?"

"Lady," the man said to the children's mother, "would you mind calling them children to sit down by you? Children make me nervous. I want all you all to sit down right together there where you're at."

"What are you telling US what to do for?" June Star asked.

Behind them the line of woods gaped like a dark open mouth. "Come here," said their mother. 80

"Look here now," Bailey began suddenly, "we're in a predicament! We're in . . ."

The grandmother shrieked. She scrambled to her feet and stood staring. "You're The Misfit!" she said. "I recognized you at once!"

"Yes'm," the man said, smiling slightly as if he were pleased in spite of himself to be known, "but it would have been better for all of you, lady, if you hadn't of reckernized me."

Bailey turned his head sharply and said something to his mother that shocked even the children. The old lady began to cry and The Misfit reddened.

"Lady," he said, "don't you get upset. Sometimes a man says things he don't 85 mean. I don't reckon he meant to talk to you thataway."

"You wouldn't shoot a lady, would you?" the grandmother said and removed a clean handkerchief from her cuff and began to slap at her eyes with it.

The Misfit pointed the toe of his shoe into the ground and made a little hole and then covered it up again. "I would hate to have to," he said.

"Listen," the grandmother almost screamed, "I know you're a good man. You don't look a bit like you have common blood. I know you must come from nice people!"

"Yes mam," he said, "finest people in the world." When he smiled he showed a row of strong white teeth. "God never made a finer woman than my mother and my daddy's heart was pure gold," he said. The boy with the red sweat shirt had come around behind them and was standing with his gun at his hip. The Misfit squatted down on the ground. "Watch them children, Bobby Lee," he said. "You know they make me nervous." He looked at the six of them huddled together in front of him and he seemed to be embarrassed as if he couldn't think of anything to say. "Ain't a cloud in the sky," he remarked, looking up at it. "Don't see no sun but don't see no cloud neither."

"Yes, it's a beautiful day," said the grandmother. "Listen," she said, "you shouldn't 90 call yourself The Misfit because I know you're a good man at heart. I can just look at you and tell."

"Hush!" Bailey yelled. "Hush! Everybody shut up and let me handle this!" He was squatting in the position of a runner about to sprint forward but he didn't move.

"I pre-chate that, lady," The Misfit said and drew a little circle in the ground with the butt of his gun.

"It'll take a half a hour to fix this here car," Hiram called, looking over the raised hood of it.

"Well, first you and Bobby Lee get him and that little boy to step over yonder with you," The Misfit said, pointing to Bailey and John Wesley. "The boys want to ast you something," he said to Bailey. "Would you mind stepping back in them woods there with them?"

"Listen," Bailey began, "we're in a terrible predicament! Nobody realizes what 95 this is," and his voice cracked. His eyes were as blue and intense as the parrots in his shirt and he remained perfectly still.

The grandmother reached up to adjust her hat brim as if she were going to the woods with him but it came off in her hand. She stood staring at it and after a second she let it fall on the ground. Hiram pulled Bailey up by the arm as if he were assisting an old man. John Wesley caught hold of his father's hand and Bobby Lee followed. They went off toward the woods and just as they reached the dark edge, Bailey turned and supporting himself against a gray naked pine trunk, he shouted, "I'll be back in a minute, Mamma, wait on me!"

"Come back this instant!" his mother shrilled but they all disappeared into the woods.

"Bailey Boy!" the grandmother called in a tragic voice but she found she was looking at The Misfit squatting on the ground in front of her. "I just know you're a good man," she said desperately. "You're not a bit common!"

"Nome, I ain't a good man," The Misfit said after a second as if he had considered her statement carefully, "but I ain't the worst in the world neither. My daddy said I was a different breed of dog from my brothers and sisters. 'You know,' Daddy said, 'it's some that can live their whole life out without asking about it and it's others has to know why it is, and this boy is one of the latters. He's going to be into everything!'" He put on his black hat and looked up suddenly and then away deep into the woods as if he were embarrassed again. "I'm sorry I don't have on a shirt before you ladies," he said, hunching his shoulders slightly. "We buried our clothes that we had on when we escaped and we're just making do until we can get better. We borrowed these from some folks we met," he explained.

"That's perfectly all right," the grandmother said. "Maybe Bailey has an extra 100
shirt in his suitcase."

"I'll look and see terrectly," The Misfit said.

"Where are they taking him?" the children's mother screamed.

"Daddy was a card himself," The Misfit said. "You couldn't put anything over on him. He never got in trouble with the Authorities though. Just had the knack of handling them."

"You could be honest too if you'd only try," said the grandmother. "Think how wonderful it would be to settle down and live a comfortable life and not have to think about somebody chasing you all the time."

The Misfit kept scratching in the ground with the butt of his gun as if he were 105
thinking about it. "Yes'm, somebody is always after you," he murmured.

The grandmother noticed how thin his shoulder blades were just behind his hat because she was standing up looking down on him. "Do you ever pray?" she asked.

He shook his head. All she saw was the black hat wiggle between his shoulder blades. "Nome," he said.

There was a pistol shot from the woods, followed closely by another. Then silence. The old lady's head jerked around. She could hear the wind move through the tree tops like a long satisfied insuck of breath. "Bailey Boy!" she called.

"I was a gospel singer for a while," The Misfit said. "I been most everything. Been in the arm service, both land and sea, at home and abroad, been twict married, been an undertaker, been with the railroads, plowed Mother Earth, been in a tornado, seen a man burnt alive oncet," and he looked up at the children's mother and the little girl who were sitting close together, their faces white and their eyes glassy; "I even seen a woman flogged," he said.

"Pray, pray," the grandmother began, "pray, pray . . ." 110

"I never was a bad boy that I remember of," The Misfit said in an almost dreamy voice, "but somewheres along the line I done something wrong and got sent to the penitentiary. I was buried alive," and he looked up and held her attention to him by a steady stare.

"That's when you should have started to pray," she said. "What did you do to get sent to the penitentiary that first time?"

"Turn to the right, it was a wall," The Misfit said, looking up again at the cloudless sky. "Turn to the left, it was a wall. Look up it was a ceiling, look down it was a floor. I forget what I done, lady. I set there and set there, trying to remember what it was I done and I ain't recalled it to this day. Oncet in a while, I would think it was coming to me, but it never come."

"Maybe they put you in by mistake," the old lady said vaguely.

"Nome," he said. "It wasn't no mistake. They had the papers on me." 115

"You must have stolen something," she said.

The Misfit sneered slightly. "Nobody had nothing I wanted," he said. "It was a head-doctor at the penitentiary said what I had done was kill my daddy but I known that for a lie. My daddy died in nineteen ought nineteen of the epidemic flu and I never had a thing to do with it. He was buried in the Mount Hopewell Baptist churchyard and you can go there and see for yourself."

"If you would pray," the old lady said, "Jesus would help you."

"That's right," The Misfit said.

"Well then, why don't you pray?" she asked trembling with delight suddenly.   120

"I don't want no hep," he said. "I'm doing all right by myself."

Bobby Lee and Hiram came ambling back from the woods. Bobby Lee was dragging a yellow shirt with bright blue parrots in it.

"Thow me that shirt, Bobby Lee," The Misfit said. The shirt came flying at him and landed on his shoulder and he put it on. The grandmother couldn't name what the shirt reminded her of. "No, lady," The Misfit said while he was buttoning it up, "I found out the crime don't matter. You can do one thing or you can do another, kill a man or take a tire off his car, because sooner or later you're going to forget what it was you done and just be punished for it."

The children's mother had begun to make heaving noises as if she couldn't get her breath. "Lady," he asked, "would you and that little girl like to step off yonder with Bobby Lee and Hiram and join your husband?"

"Yes, thank you," the mother said faintly. Her left arm dangled helplessly and she   125
was holding the baby, who had gone to sleep, in the other. "Hep that lady up, Hiram," The Misfit said as she struggled to climb out of the ditch, "and Bobby Lee, you hold onto that little girl's hand."

"I don't want to hold hands with him," June Star said. "He reminds me of a pig."

The fat boy blushed and laughed and caught her by the arm and pulled her off into the woods after Hiram and her mother.

Alone with The Misfit, the grandmother found that she had lost her voice. There was not a cloud in the sky nor any sun. There was nothing around her but woods. She wanted to tell him that he must pray. She opened and closed her mouth several times before anything came out. Finally she found herself saying, "Jesus. Jesus," meaning, Jesus will help you, but the way she was saying it, it sounded as if she might be cursing.

"Yes'm," The Misfit said as if he agreed. "Jesus thown everything off balance. It was the same case with Him as with me except He hadn't committed any crime and they could prove I had committed one because they had the papers on me. Of course," he said, "they never shown me my papers. That's why I sign myself now. I said long ago, you get you a signature and sign everything you do and keep a copy of it. Then you'll know what you done and you can hold up the crime to the punishment and see do they match and in the end you'll have something to prove you ain't been treated right. I call myself The Misfit," he said, "because I can't make what all I done wrong fit what all I gone through in punishment."

There was a piercing scream from the woods, followed closely by a pistol report.   130
"Does it seem right to you, lady, that one is punished a heap and another ain't punished at all?"

"Jesus!" the old lady cried. "You've got good blood! I know you wouldn't shoot a lady! I know you come from nice people! Pray! Jesus, you ought not to shoot a lady. I'll give you all the money I've got!"

"Lady," The Misfit said, looking beyond her far into the woods, "there never was a body that give the undertaker a tip."

There were two more pistol reports and the grandmother raised her head like a parched old turkey hen crying for water and called, "Bailey Boy, Bailey Boy!" as if her heart would break.

"Jesus was the only One that ever raised the dead," The Misfit continued, "and He shouldn't have done it. He thown everything off balance. If He did what He said, then it's nothing for you to do but thow away everything and follow Him, and if He didn't, then it's nothing for you to do but enjoy the few minutes you got left the best way you can—by killing somebody or burning down his house or doing some other meanness to him. No pleasure but meanness," he said and his voice had become almost a snarl.

"Maybe He didn't raise the dead," the old lady mumbled, not knowing what she   135 was saying and feeling so dizzy that she sank down in the ditch with her legs twisted under her.

"I wasn't there so I can't say He didn't," The Misfit said. "I wisht I had of been there," he said, hitting the ground with his fist. "It ain't right I wasn't there because if I had of been there I would of known. Listen lady," he said in a high voice, "if I had of been there I would of known and I wouldn't be like I am now." His voice seemed about to crack and the grandmother's head cleared for an instant. She saw the man's face twisted close to her own as if he were going to cry and she murmured, "Why you're one of my babies. You're one of my own children!" She reached out and touched him on the shoulder. The Misfit sprang back as if a snake had bitten him and shot her three times through the chest. Then he put his gun down on the ground and took off his glasses and began to clean them.

Hiram and Bobby Lee returned from the woods and stood over the ditch, looking down at the grandmother who half sat and half lay in a puddle of blood with her legs crossed under her like a child's and her face smiling up at the cloudless sky.

Without his glasses, The Misfit's eyes were red-rimmed and pale and defenseless-looking. "Take her off and thow her where you thown the others," he said, picking up the cat that was rubbing itself against his leg.

"She was a talker, wasn't she?" Bobby Lee said, sliding down the ditch with a yodel.

"She would of been a good woman," The Misfit said, "if it had been somebody   140 there to shoot her every minute of her life."

"Some fun!" Bobby Lee said.

"Shut up, Bobby Lee," The Misfit said. "It's no real pleasure in life."

Questions

1. How early in the story does O'Connor foreshadow what will happen in the end? What further hints does she give us along the way? How does the scene at Red Sammy's Barbecue advance the story toward its conclusion?

2. When we first meet the grandmother, what kind of person is she? What do her various remarks reveal about her? Does she remain a static character, or does she change in any way as the story goes on?

3. When the grandmother's head clears for an instant (paragraph 136), what does she suddenly understand? Reread this passage carefully and prepare to discuss what it means.

4. What do we learn from the conversation between The Misfit and the grandmother while the others go out to the woods? How would you describe The Misfit's outlook on the world? Compare it with the author's, from whatever you know about Flannery O'Connor and from the story itself.

5. How would you respond to a reader who complained, "The title of this story is just an obvious platitude"?

Revelation   1965

The doctor's waiting room, which was very small, was almost full when the Turpins entered and Mrs. Turpin, who was very large, made it look even smaller by her presence. She stood looming at the head of the magazine table set in the center of it, a living demonstration that the room was inadequate and ridiculous. Her little bright black eyes took in all the patients as she sized up the seating situation. There was one vacant chair and a place on a sofa occupied by a blond child in a dirty blue romper who should have been told to move over and make room for the lady. He was five or six, but Mrs. Turpin saw at once that no one was going to tell him to move over. He was slumped down in the seat, his arms idle at his sides and his eyes idle in his head; his nose ran unchecked.

Mrs. Turpin put a firm hand on Claud's shoulder and said in a voice that included anyone who wanted to listen, "Claud, you sit in that chair there," and gave him a push down into the vacant one. Claud was florid and bald and sturdy, somewhat shorter than Mrs. Turpin, but he sat down as if he were accustomed to doing what she told him to.

Mrs. Turpin remained standing. The only man in the room besides Claud was a lean stringy old fellow with a rusty hand spread out on each knee, whose eyes were closed as if he were asleep or dead or pretending to be so as not to get up and offer her his seat. Her gaze settled agreeably on a well-dressed grey-haired lady whose eyes met hers and whose expression said: if that child belonged to me, he would have some manners and move over—there's plenty of room there for you and him too.

Claud looked up with a sigh and made as if to rise.

"Sit down," Mrs. Turpin said. "You know you're not supposed to stand on that   5
leg. He has an ulcer on his leg," she explained.

Claud lifted his foot onto the magazine table and rolled his trouser leg up to reveal a purple swelling on a plump marble-white calf.

"My!" the pleasant lady said. "How did you do that?"

"A cow kicked him," Mrs. Turpin said.

"Goodness!" said the lady.

Claud rolled his trouser leg down.   10

"Maybe the little boy would move over," the lady suggested, but the child did not stir.

"Somebody will be leaving in a minute," Mrs. Turpin said. She could not understand why a doctor—with as much money as they made charging five dollars a day to just stick their head in the hospital door and look at you—couldn't afford a decent-sized waiting room. This one was hardly bigger than a garage. The table was cluttered with limp-looking magazines and at one end of it there was a big green glass ash tray full of cigaret butts and cotton wads with little blood spots on them. If she had had anything to do with the running of the place, that would have been emptied every so often. There were no chairs against the wall at the head of the room. It had a rectangular-shaped panel in it that permitted a view of the office where the nurse came and went and the secretary listened to the radio. A plastic fern in a gold pot sat in the opening and trailed its fronds down almost to the floor. The radio was softly playing gospel music.

Just then the inner door opened and a nurse with the highest stack of yellow hair Mrs. Turpin had ever seen put her face in the crack and called for the next patient. The woman sitting beside Claud grasped the two arms of her chair and hoisted herself up; she pulled her dress free from her legs and lumbered through the door where the nurse had disappeared.

Mrs. Turpin eased into the vacant chair, which held her tight as a corset. "I wish I could reduce," she said, and rolled her eyes and gave a comic sigh.

"Oh, *you* aren't fat," the stylish lady said.   15

"Ooooo I am too," Mrs. Turpin said. "Claud he eats all he wants to and never weighs over one hundred and seventy-five pounds, but me I just look at something good to eat and I gain some weight," and her stomach and shoulders shook with laughter. "You can eat all you want to, can't you, Claud?" she asked, turning to him.

Claud only grinned.

"Well, as long as you have such a good disposition," the stylish lady said, "I don't think it makes a bit of difference what size you are. You just can't beat a good disposition."

Next to her was a fat girl of eighteen or nineteen, scowling into a thick blue book which Mrs. Turpin saw was entitled *Human Development*. The girl raised her head and directed her scowl at Mrs. Turpin as if she did not like her looks. She appeared annoyed that anyone should speak while she tried to read. The poor girl's face was blue with acne and Mrs. Turpin thought how pitiful it was to have a face like that at that age. She gave the girl a friendly smile but the girl only scowled the harder. Mrs. Turpin herself was fat but she had always had good skin, and, though she was forty-seven years old, there was not a wrinkle in her face except around her eyes from laughing too much.

Next to the ugly girl was the child, still in exactly the same position, and next to   20
him was a thin leathery old woman in a cotton print dress. She and Claud had three sacks of chicken feed in their pump house that was in the same print. She had seen from the first that the child belonged with the old woman. She could tell by the way they sat—kind of vacant and white-trashy, as if they would sit there until Doomsday if nobody called and told them to get up. And at right angles but next to the well-dressed pleasant lady was a lank-faced woman who was certainly the child's mother. She had on a yellow sweat shirt and wine-colored slacks, both gritty-looking, and the rims of her lips were stained with snuff. Her dirty yellow hair was tied behind with a little piece of red paper ribbon. Worse than niggers any day, Mrs. Turpin thought.

The gospel hymn playing was, "When I looked up and He looked down," and Mrs. Turpin, who knew it, supplied the last line mentally, "And wona these days I know I'll we-eara crown."

Without appearing to, Mrs. Turpin always noticed people's feet. The well-dressed lady had on red and grey suede shoes to match her dress. Mrs. Turpin had on her good black patent leather pumps. The ugly girl had on Girl Scout shoes and heavy socks. The old woman had on tennis shoes and the white-trashy mother had on what appeared to be bedroom slippers, black straw with gold braid threaded through them—exactly what you would have expected her to have on.

Sometimes at night when she couldn't go to sleep, Mrs. Turpin would occupy herself with the question of who she would have chosen to be if she couldn't have been herself. If Jesus had said to her before he made her, "There's only two places available for you. You can either be a nigger or white-trash," what would she have said? "Please, Jesus, please," she would have said, "just let me wait until there's another place available," and he would have said, "No, you have to go right now and I have only those two places so make up your mind." She would have wiggled and squirmed and begged and pleaded but it would have been no use and finally she would have said, "All right, make me a nigger then—but that don't mean a trashy one." And he would have made her a neat clean respectable Negro woman, herself but black.

Next to the child's mother was a red-headed youngish woman, reading one of the magazines and working a piece of chewing gum, hell for leather, as Claud would say. Mrs. Turpin could not see the woman's feet. She was not white-trash, just common. Sometimes Mrs. Turpin occupied herself at night naming the classes of people. On the bottom of the heap were most colored people, not the kind she would have been if she had been one, but most of them; then next to them—not above, just away from—were the white-trash; then above them were the home-owners, and above them the home-and-land owners, to which she and Claud belonged. Above she and Claud were people with a lot of money and much bigger houses and much more land. But here the complexity of it would begin to bear in on her, for some of the people with a lot of money were common and ought to be below she and Claud and some of the people who had good blood had lost their money and had to rent and then there were colored people who owned their homes and land as well. There was a colored dentist in town who had two red Lincolns and a swimming pool and a farm with registered white-face cattle on it. Usually by the time she had fallen asleep all the classes of people were moiling and roiling around in her head, and she would dream they were all crammed in together in a box car, being ridden off to be put in a gas oven.

"That's a beautiful clock," she said and nodded to her right. It was a big wall clock, the face encased in a brass sunburst. 25

"Yes, it's very pretty," the stylish lady said agreeably. "And right on the dot too," she added, glancing at her watch.

The ugly girl beside her cast an eye upward at the clock, smirked, then looked directly at Mrs. Turpin and smirked again. Then she returned her eyes to her book. She was obviously the lady's daughter because, although they didn't look anything alike as to disposition, they both had the same shape of face and the same blue eyes. On the lady they sparkled pleasantly but in the girl's seared face they appeared alternately to smolder and to blaze.

What if Jesus had said, "All right, you can be white-trash or a nigger or ugly"!

Mrs. Turpin felt an awful pity for the girl, though she thought it was one thing to be ugly and another to act ugly.

The woman with the snuff-stained lips turned around in her chair and looked up 30 at the clock. Then she turned back and appeared to look a little to the side of Mrs. Turpin. There was a cast in one of her eyes. "You want to know wher you can get you one of themther clocks?" she asked in a loud voice.

"No, I already have a nice clock," Mrs. Turpin said. Once somebody like her got a leg in the conversation, she would be all over it.

"You can get you one with green stamps," the woman said. "That's most likely wher he got hisn. Save you up enough, you can get you most anythang. I got me some joo'ry."

Ought to have got you a wash rag and some soap, Mrs. Turpin thought.

"I get contour sheets with mine," the pleasant lady said.

The daughter slammed her book shut. She looked straight in front of her, directly through Mrs. Turpin and on through the yellow curtain and the plate glass window which made the wall behind her. The girl's eyes seemed lit all of a sudden with a peculiar light, an unnatural light like night road signs give. Mrs. Turpin turned her head to see if there was anything going on outside that she should see, but 35 she could not see anything. Figures passing cast only a pale shadow through the curtain. There was no reason the girl should single her out for her ugly looks.

"Miss Finley," the nurse said, cracking the door. The gum-chewing woman got up and passed in front of her and Claud and went into the office. She had on red high-heeled shoes.

Directly across the table, the ugly girl's eyes were fixed on Mrs. Turpin as if she had some very special reason for disliking her.

"This is wonderful weather, isn't it?" the girl's mother said.

"It's good weather for cotton if you can get the niggers to pick it," Mrs. Turpin said, "but niggers don't want to pick cotton any more. You can't get the white folks to pick it and now you can't get the niggers—because they got to be right up there with the white folks."

"They gonna *try* anyways," the white-trash woman said, leaning forward. 40

"Do you have one of those cotton-picking machines?" the pleasant lady asked.

"No," Mrs. Turpin said, "they leave half the cotton in the field. We don't have much cotton anyway. If you want to make it farming now, you have to have a little of everything. We got a couple of acres of cotton and a few hogs and chickens and just enough white-face that Claud can look after them himself."

"One thang I don't want," the white-trash woman said, wiping her mouth with the back of her hands. "Hogs. Nasty stinking things, a-gruntin and a-rootin all over the place."

Mrs. Turpin gave her the merest edge of her attention. "Our hogs are not dirty and they don't stink," she said. "They're cleaner than some children I've seen. Their feet never touch the ground. We have a pig-parlor—that's where you raise them on concrete," she explained to the pleasant lady, "and Claud scoots them down with the hose every afternoon and washes off the floor." Cleaner by far than that child right there, she thought. Poor nasty little thing. He had not moved except to put the thumb of his dirty hand into his mouth.

The woman turned her face away from Mrs. Turpin. "I know I wouldn't scoot 45
down no hog with no hose," she said to the wall.

You wouldn't have no hog to scoot down, Mrs. Turpin said to herself.

"A-gruntin and a-rootin and a-groanin," the woman muttered.

"We got a little of everything," Mrs. Turpin said to the pleasant lady. "It's no use in having more than you can handle yourself with help like it is. We found enough niggers to pick our cotton this year but Claud he has to go after them and take them home again in the evening. They can't walk that half a mile. No they can't. I tell you," she said and laughed merrily, "I sure am tired of buttering up niggers, but you got to love em if you want em to work for you. When they come in the morning, I run out and I say, 'Hi yawl this morning?' and when Claud drives them off to the field I just wave to beat the band and they just wave back." And she waved her hand rapidly to illustrate.

"Like you read out of the same book," the lady said, showing she understood perfectly.

"Child, yes," Mrs. Turpin said. "And when they come in from the field, I run out 50
with a bucket of icewater. That's the way it's going to be from now on," she said. "You may as well face it."

"One thang I know," the white-trash woman said. "Two thangs I ain't going to do: love no niggers or scoot down no hog with no hose." And she let out a bark of contempt.

The look that Mrs. Turpin and the pleasant lady exchanged indicated they both understood that you had to *have* certain things before you could *know* certain things.

But every time Mrs. Turpin exchanged a look with the lady, she was aware that the ugly girl's peculiar eyes were still on her, and she had trouble bringing her attention back to the conversation.

"When you got something," she said, "you got to look after it." And when you ain't got a thing but breath and britches, she added to herself, you can afford to come to town every morning and just sit on the Court House coping and spit.

A grotesque revolving shadow passed across the curtain behind her and was thrown palely on the opposite wall. Then a bicycle clattered down against the outside of the building. The door opened and a colored boy glided in with a tray from the drug store. It had two large red and white paper cups on it with tops on them. He was a tall, very black boy in discolored white pants and a green nylon shirt. He was chewing gum slowly, as if to music. He set the tray down in the office opening next to the fern and stuck his head through to look for the secretary. She was not in there. He rested his arms on the ledge and waited, his narrow bottom stuck out, swaying slowly to the left and right. He raised a hand over his head and scratched the base of his skull.

"You see that button there, boy?" Mrs. Turpin said. "You can punch that and she'll come. She's probably in the back somewhere." 55

"Is thas right?" the boy said agreeably, as if he had never seen the button before. He leaned to the right and put his finger on it. "She sometime out," he said and twisted around to face his audience, his elbows behind him on the counter. The nurse appeared and he twisted back again. She handed him a dollar and he rooted in his pocket and made the change and counted it out to her. She gave him fifteen cents for a tip and he went out with the empty tray. The heavy door swung to slowly and closed at length with the sound of suction. For a moment no one spoke.

"They ought to send all them niggers back to Africa," the white-trash woman said. "That's wher they come from in the first place."

"Oh, I couldn't do without my good colored friends," the pleasant lady said.

"There's a heap of things worse than a nigger," Mrs. Turpin agreed. "It's all kinds of them just like it's all kinds of us."

"Yes, and it takes all kinds to make the world go round," the lady said in her musical voice. 60

As she said it, the raw-complexioned girl snapped her teeth together. Her lower lip turned downwards and inside out, revealing the pale pink inside of her mouth. After a second it rolled back up. It was the ugliest face Mrs. Turpin had ever seen anyone make and for a moment she was certain that the girl had made it at her. She was looking at her as if she had known and disliked her all her life—all of Mrs. Turpin's life, it seemed too, not just all the girl's life. Why, girl, I don't even know you, Mrs. Turpin said silently.

She forced her attention back to the discussion. "It wouldn't be practical to send them back to Africa," she said. "They wouldn't want to go. They got it too good here."

"Wouldn't be what they wanted—if I had anythang to do with it," the woman said.

"It wouldn't be a way in the world you could get all the niggers back over there," Mrs. Turpin said. "They'd be hiding out and lying down and turning sick on you and wailing and hollering and raring and pitching. It wouldn't be a way in the world to get them over there."

"They got over here," the trashy woman said. "Get back like they got over." 65
"It wasn't so many of them then," Mrs. Turpin explained.

The woman looked at Mrs. Turpin as if here was an idiot indeed but Mrs. Turpin was not bothered by the look, considering where it came from.

"Nooo," she said, "they're going to stay here where they can go to New York and marry white folks and improve their color. That's what they all want to do, every one of them, improve their color."

"You know what comes of that, don't you?" Claud asked.

"No, Claud, what?" Mrs. Turpin said. 70

Claud's eyes twinkled. "White-faced niggers," he said with never a smile.

Everybody in the office laughed except the white-trash and the ugly girl. The girl gripped the book in her lap with white fingers. The trashy woman looked around her from face to face as if she thought they were all idiots. The old woman in the feed sack dress continued to gaze expressionless across the floor at the hightop shoes of the man opposite her, the one who had been pretending to be asleep when the Turpins came in. He was laughing heartily, his hands still spread out on his knees. The child had fallen to the side and was lying now almost face down in the old woman's lap.

While they recovered from their laughter, the nasal chorus on the radio kept the room from silence.

"You go to blank blank
And I'll go to mine
But we'll all blank along
To-geth-ther,
And all along the blank
We'll hep eachother out
Smile-ling in any kind of
Weath-ther!"

Mrs. Turpin didn't catch every word but she caught enough to agree with the 75 spirit of the song and it turned her thoughts sober. To help anybody out that needed it was her philosophy of life. She never spared herself when she found somebody in need, whether they were white or black, trash or decent. And of all she had to be thankful for, she was most thankful that this was so. If Jesus had said, "You can be high society and have all the money you want and be thin and svelte-like, but you can't be a good woman with it," she would have had to say, "Well don't make me that then. Make me a good woman and it don't matter what else, how fat or how ugly or how poor!" Her heart rose. He had not made her a nigger or white-trash or ugly! He had made her herself and given her a little of everything. Jesus, thank you! she said. Thank you thank you thank you! Whenever she counted her blessings she felt as buoyant as if she weighed one hundred and twenty-five pounds instead of one hundred and eighty.

"What's wrong with your little boy?" the pleasant lady asked the white-trashy woman.

"He has a ulcer," the woman said proudly. "He ain't give me a minute's peace since he was born. Him and her are just alike," she said, nodding at the old woman, who was running her leathery fingers through the child's pale hair. "Look like I can't get nothing down them two but Co' Cola and candy."

That's all you try to get down em, Mrs. Turpin said to herself. Too lazy to light the fire. There was nothing you could tell her about people like them that she didn't know already. And it was not just that they didn't have anything. Because if you gave them everything, in two weeks it would all be broken or filthy or they would have chopped it up for lightwood. She knew all this from her own experience. Help them you must, but help them you couldn't.

All at once the ugly girl turned her lips inside out again. Her eyes were fixed like two drills on Mrs. Turpin. This time there was no mistaking that there was something urgent behind them.

Girl, Mrs. Turpin exclaimed silently, I haven't done a thing to you! The girl might be confusing her with somebody else. There was no need to sit by and let herself be intimidated. "You must be in college," she said boldly, looking directly at the girl. "I see you reading a book there."

The girl continued to stare and pointedly did not answer.

Her mother blushed at this rudeness. "The lady asked you a question, Mary Grace," she said under her breath.

"I have ears," Mary Grace said.

The poor mother blushed again. "Mary Grace goes to Wellesley College," she explained. She twisted one of the buttons on her dress. "In Massachusetts," she added with a grimace. "And in the summer she just keeps right on studying. Just reads all the time, a real book worm. She's done real well at Wellesley; she's taking English and Math and History and Psychology and Social Studies," she rattled on, "and I think it's too much. I think she ought to get out and have fun."

The girl looked as if she would like to hurl them all through the plate glass window.

"Way up north," Mrs. Turpin murmured and thought, well, it hasn't done much for her manners.

"I'd almost rather to have him sick," the white-trash woman said, wrenching the attention back to herself. "He's so mean when he ain't. Look like some children just take natural to meanness. It's some gets bad when they get sick but he was the opposite. Took sick and turned good. He don't give me no trouble now. It's me waitin to see the doctor," she said.

If I was going to send anybody back to Africa, Mrs. Turpin thought, it would be your kind, woman. "Yes, indeed," she said aloud, but looking up at the ceiling, "it's a heap of things worse than a nigger." And dirtier than a hog, she added to herself.

"I think people with bad dispositions are more to be pitied than anyone on earth," the pleasant lady said in a voice that was decidedly thin.

"I thank the Lord he has blessed me with a good one," Mrs. Turpin said. "The day has never dawned that I couldn't find something to laugh at."

"Not since she married me anyways," Claud said with a comical straight face.

Everybody laughed except the girl and the white-trash.

Mrs. Turpin's stomach shook. "He's such a caution," she said, "that I can't help but laugh at him."

The girl made a loud ugly noise through her teeth.

Her mother's mouth grew thin and straight. "I think the worst thing in the world," she said, "is an ungrateful person. To have everything and not appreciate it. I know a girl," she said, "who has parents who would give her anything, a little brother who loves her dearly, who is getting a good education, who wears the best clothes, but who can never say a kind word to anyone, who never smiles, who just criticizes and complains all day long."

"Is she too old to paddle?" Claud asked.

(marginal line numbers: 80, 85, 90, 95)

The girl's face was almost purple.

"Yes," the lady said, "I'm afraid there's nothing to do but leave her to her folly. Some day she'll wake up and it'll be too late."

"It never hurt anyone to smile," Mrs. Turpin said. "It just makes you feel better all over."

"Of course," the lady said sadly, "but there are just some people you can't tell 100 anything to. They can't take criticism."

"If it's one thing I am," Mrs. Turpin said with feeling, "it's grateful. When I think who all I could have been besides myself and what all I got, a little of everything, and a good disposition besides, I just feel like shouting, 'Thank you, Jesus, for making everything the way it is!' It could have been different!" For one thing, somebody else could have got Claud. At the thought of this, she was flooded with gratitude and a terrible pang of joy ran through her. "Oh thank you, Jesus, Jesus, thank you!" she cried aloud.

The book struck her directly over her left eye. It struck almost at the same instant that she realized the girl was about to hurl it. Before she could utter a sound, the raw face came crashing across the table toward her, howling. The girl's fingers sank like clamps into the soft flesh of her neck. She heard the mother cry out and Claud shout, "Whoa!" There was an instant when she was certain that she was about to be in an earthquake.

All at once her vision narrowed and she saw everything as if it were happening in a small room far away, or as if she were looking at it through the wrong end of a telescope. Claud's face crumpled and fell out of sight. The nurse ran in, then out, then in again. Then the gangling figure of the doctor rushed out of the inner door. Magazines flew this way and that as the table turned over. The girl fell with a thud and Mrs. Turpin's vision suddenly reversed itself and she saw everything large instead of small. The eyes of the white-trashy woman were staring hugely at the floor. There the girl, held down on one side by the nurse and on the other by her mother, was wrenching and turning in their grasp. The doctor was kneeling astride her, trying to hold her arm down. He managed after a second to sink a long needle into it.

Mrs. Turpin felt entirely hollow except for her heart which swung from side to side as if it were agitated in a great empty drum of flesh.

"Somebody that's not busy call for the ambulance," the doctor said in the off- 105 hand voice young doctors adopt for terrible occasions.

Mrs. Turpin could not have moved a finger. The old man who had been sitting next to her skipped nimbly into the office and made the call, for the secretary still seemed to be gone.

"Claud!" Mrs. Turpin called.

He was not in his chair. She knew she must jump up and find him but she felt like some one trying to catch a train in a dream, when everything moves in slow motion and the faster you try to run the slower you go.

"Here I am," a suffocated voice, very unlike Claud's, said.

He was doubled up in the corner on the floor, pale as paper, holding his leg. She 110 wanted to get up and go to him but she could not move. Instead, her gaze was drawn slowly downward to the churning face on the floor, which she could see over the doctor's shoulder.

The girl's eyes stopped rolling and focused on her. They seemed a much lighter blue than before, as if a door that had been tightly closed behind them was now open to admit light and air.

Mrs. Turpin's head cleared and her power of motion returned. She leaned forward until she was looking directly into the fierce brilliant eyes. There was no doubt in her mind that the girl did know her, knew her in some intense and personal way, beyond time and place and condition. "What you got to say to me?" she asked hoarsely and held her breath, waiting, as for a revelation.

The girl raised her head. Her gaze locked with Mrs. Turpin's. "Go back to hell where you came from, you old wart hog," she whispered. Her voice was low but clear. Her eyes burned for a moment as if she saw with pleasure that her message had struck its target.

Mrs. Turpin sank back in her chair.

After a moment the girl's eyes closed and she turned her head wearily to the side. 115

The doctor rose and handed the nurse the empty syringe. He leaned over and put both hands for a moment on the mother's shoulders, which were shaking. She was sitting on the floor, her lips pressed together, holding Mary Grace's hand in her lap. The girl's fingers were gripped like a baby's around her thumb. "Go on to the hospital," he said. "I'll call and make the arrangements."

"Now let's see that neck," he said in a jovial voice to Mrs. Turpin. He began to inspect her neck with his first two fingers. Two little moon-shaped lines like pink fish bones were indented over her windpipe. There was the beginning of an angry red swelling above her eye. His fingers passed over this also.

"Lea' me be," she said thickly and shook him off. "See about Claud. She kicked him."

"I'll see about him in a minute," he said and felt her pulse. He was a thin grey-haired man, given to pleasantries. "Go home and have yourself a vacation the rest of the day," he said and patted her on the shoulder.

Quit your pattin me, Mrs. Turpin growled to herself. 120

"And put an ice pack over that eye," he said. Then he went and squatted down beside Claud and looked at his leg. After a moment he pulled him up and Claud limped after him into the office.

Until the ambulance came, the only sounds in the room were the tremulous moans of the girl's mother, who continued to sit on the floor. The white-trash woman did not take her eyes off the girl. Mrs. Turpin looked straight ahead at nothing. Presently the ambulance drew up, a long dark shadow, behind the curtain. The attendants came in and set the stretcher down beside the girl and lifted her expertly onto it and carried her out. The nurse helped the mother gather up her things. The shadow of the ambulance moved silently away and the nurse came back in the office.

"That ther girl is going to be a lunatic, ain't she?" the white-trash woman asked the nurse, but the nurse kept on to the back and never answered her.

"Yes, she's going to be a lunatic," the white-trash woman said to the rest of them.

"Po' critter," the old woman murmured. The child's face was still in her lap. His 125 eyes looked idly out over her knees. He had not moved during the disturbance except to draw one leg up under him.

"I thank Gawd," the white-trash woman said fervently, "I ain't a lunatic."

Claud came limping out and the Turpins went home.

As their pick-up truck turned into their own dirt road and made the crest of the hill, Mrs. Turpin gripped the window ledge and looked out suspiciously. The land sloped gracefully down through a field dotted with lavender weeds and at the start of the rise their small yellow frame house, with its little flower beds spread out around it like a fancy apron, sat primly in its accustomed place between two giant hickory trees. She would not have been startled to see a burnt wound between two blackened chimneys.

Neither of them felt like eating so they put on their house clothes and lowered the shade in the bedroom and lay down, Claud with his leg on a pillow and herself with a damp washcloth over her eye. The instant she was flat on her back, the image of a razor-backed hog with warts on its face and horns coming out behind its ears snorted into her head. She moaned, a low quiet moan.

"I am not," she said tearfully, "a wart hog. From hell." But the denial had no 130
force. The girl's eyes and her words, even the tone of her voice, low but clear, directed only to her, brooked no repudiation. She had been singled out for the message, though there was trash in the room to whom it might justly have been applied. The full force of this fact struck her only now. There was a woman there who was neglecting her own child but she had been overlooked. The message had been given to Ruby Turpin, a respectable, hard-working, church-going woman. The tears dried. Her eyes began to burn instead with wrath.

She rose on her elbow and the washcloth fell into her hand. Claud was lying on his back, snoring. She wanted to tell him what the girl had said. At the same time, she did not wish to put the image of herself as a wart hog from hell into his mind.

"Hey, Claud," she muttered and pushed his shoulder.

Claud opened one pale baby blue eye.

She looked into it warily. He did not think about anything. He just went his way.

"Wha, whasit?" he said and closed the eye again. 135

"Nothing," she said. "Does your leg pain you?"

"Hurts like hell," Claud said.

"It'll quit terreckly," she said and lay back down. In a moment Claud was snoring again. For the rest of the afternoon they lay there. Claud slept. She scowled at the ceiling. Occasionally she raised her fist and made a small stabbing motion over her chest as if she was defending her innocence to invisible guests who were like the comforters of Job, reasonable-seeming but wrong.

About five-thirty Claud stirred. "Got to go after those niggers," he sighed, not moving.

She was looking straight up as if there were unintelligible handwriting on the 140
ceiling. The protuberance over her eye had turned a greenish-blue. "Listen here," she said.

"What?"

"Kiss me."

Claud leaned over and kissed her loudly on the mouth. He pinched her side and their hands interlocked. Her expression of ferocious concentration did not change. Claud got up, groaning and growling, and limped off. She continued to study the ceiling.

She did not get up until she heard the pick-up truck coming back with the Negroes. Then she rose and thrust her feet in her brown oxfords, which she did not bother to lace, and stumped out onto the back porch and got her red plastic bucket. She emptied a tray of ice cubes into it and filled it half full of water and went out into the back yard. Every afternoon after Claud brought the hands in, one of the boys helped him put out hay and the rest waited in the back of the truck until he was ready to take them home. The truck was parked in the shade under one of the hickory trees.

"Hi yawl this evening?" Mrs. Turpin asked grimly, appearing with the bucket 145
and the dipper. There were three women and a boy in the truck.

"Us doin nicely," the oldest woman said. "Hi you doin?" and her gaze stuck immediately on the dark lump on Mrs. Turpin's forehead. "You done fell down, ain't you?" she asked in a solicitous voice. The old woman was dark and almost toothless. She had on an old felt hat of Claud's set back on her head. The other two women were younger and lighter and they both had new bright green sun hats. One of them had hers on her head; the other had taken hers off and the boy was grinning beneath it.

Mrs. Turpin set the bucket down on the floor of the truck. "Yawl hep yourselves," she said. She looked around to make sure Claud had gone. "No. I didn't fall down," she said, folding her arms. "It was something worse than that."

"Ain't nothing bad happen to you!" the old woman said. She said it as if they all knew Mrs. Turpin was protected in some special way by Divine Providence. "You just had you a little fall."

"We were in town at the doctor's office for where the cow kicked Mr. Turpin," Mrs. Turpin said in a flat tone that indicated they could leave off their foolishness. "And there was this girl there. A big fat girl with her face all broke out. I could look at that girl and tell she was peculiar but I couldn't tell how. And me and her mama were just talking and going along and all of a sudden WHAM! She throws this big book she was reading at me and . . ."

"Naw!" the old woman cried out. 150

"And then she jumps over the table and commences to choke me."

"Naw!" they all exclaimed, "naw!"

"Hi come she do that?" the old woman asked. "What ail her?"

Mrs. Turpin only glared in front of her.

"Somethin ail her," the old woman said. 155

"They carried her off in an ambulance," Mrs. Turpin continued, "but before she went she was rolling on the floor and they were trying to hold her down to give her a shot and she said something to me." She paused. "You know what she said to me?"

"What she say?" they asked.

"She said," Mrs. Turpin began, and stopped, her face very dark and heavy. The sun was getting whiter and whiter, blanching the sky overhead so that the leaves of the hickory tree were black in the face of it. She could not bring forth the words. "Something real ugly," she muttered.

"She sho shouldn't said nothin ugly to you," the old woman said. "You so sweet. You the sweetest lady I know."

"She pretty too," the one with the hat on said. 160

"And stout," the other one said. "I never knowed no sweeter white lady."

"That's the truth befo' Jesus," the old woman said. "Amen! You des as sweet and pretty as you can be."

Mrs. Turpin knew just exactly how much Negro flattery was worth and it added to her rage. "She said," she began again and finished this time with a fierce rush of breath, "that I was an old wart hog from hell."

There was an astounded silence.

"Where she at?" the youngest woman cried in a piercing voice. 165

"Lemme see her. I'll kill her!"

"I'll kill her with you!" the other one cried.

"She b'long in the sylum," the old woman said emphatically. "You the sweetest white lady I know."

"She pretty too," the other two said. "Stout as she can be and sweet. Jesus satisfied with her!"

"Deed he is," the old woman declared. 170

Idiots! Mrs. Turpin growled to herself. You could never say anything intelligent to a nigger. You could talk at them but not with them. "Yawl ain't drunk your water," she said shortly. "Leave the bucket in the truck when you're finished with it. I got more to do than just stand around and pass the time of day," and she moved off and into the house.

She stood for a moment in the middle of the kitchen. The dark protuberance over her eye looked like a miniature tornado cloud which might any moment sweep across the horizon of her brow. Her lower lip protruded dangerously. She squared her massive shoulders. Then she marched into the front of the house and out the side door and started down the road to the pig parlor. She had the look of a woman going single-handed, weaponless, into battle.

The sun was a deep yellow now like a harvest moon and was riding westward very fast over the far tree line as if it meant to reach the hogs before she did. The road was rutted and she kicked several good-sized stones out of her path as she strode along. The pig parlor was on a little knoll at the end of a lane that ran off from the side of the barn. It was a square of concrete as large as a small room, with a board fence about four feet high around it. The concrete floor sloped slightly so that the hog wash could drain off into a trench where it was carried to the field for fertilizer. Claud was standing on the outside, on the edge of the concrete, hanging onto the top board, hosing down the floor inside. The hose was connected to the faucet of a water trough nearby.

Mrs. Turpin climbed up beside him and glowered down at the hogs inside. There were seven long-snouted bristly shoats in it—tan with liver-colored spots—and an old sow a few weeks off from farrowing. She was lying on her side grunting. The shoats were running about shaking themselves like idiot children, their little slit pig eyes searching the floor for anything left. She had read that pigs were the most intelligent animal. She doubted it. They were supposed to be smarter than dogs. There had even been a pig astronaut. He had performed his assignment perfectly but died of a heart attack afterwards because they left him in his electric suit, sitting upright throughout his examination when naturally a hog should be on all fours.

A-gruntin and a-rootin and a-groanin. 175

"Gimme that hose," she said, yanking it away from Claud. "Go on and carry them niggers home and then get off that leg."

"You look like you might have swallowed a mad dog," Claud observed, but he got down and limped off. He paid no attention to her humors.

Until he was out of earshot, Mrs. Turpin stood on the side of the pen, holding the hose and pointing the stream of water at the hind quarters of any shoat that looked as if it might try to lie down. When he had had time to get over the hill, she turned her head slightly and her wrathful eyes scanned the path. He was nowhere in sight. She turned back again and seemed to gather herself up. Her shoulders rose and she drew in her breath.

"What do you send me a message like that for?" she said in a low fierce voice, barely above a whisper but with the force of a shout in its concentrated fury. "How am I a hog and me both? How am I saved and from hell too?" Her free fist was knotted and with the other she gripped the hose, blindly pointing the stream of water in and out of the eye of the old sow whose outraged squeal she did not hear.

The pig parlor commanded a view of the back pasture where their twenty beef   180
cows were gathered around the hay-bales Claud and the boy had put out. The freshly cut pasture sloped down to the highway. Across it was their cotton field and beyond that a dark green dusty wood which they owned as well. The sun was behind the wood, very red, looking over the paling of trees like a farmer inspecting his own hogs.

"Why me?" she rumbled. "It's no trash around here, black or white, that I haven't given to. And break my back to the bone every day working. And do for the church."

She appeared to be the right size woman to command the arena before her. "How am I a hog?" she demanded. "Exactly how am I like them?" and she jabbed the stream of water at the shoats. "There was plenty of trash there. It didn't have to be me."

"If you like trash better, go get yourself some trash then," she railed. "You could have made me trash. Or a nigger. If trash is what you wanted why didn't you make me trash?" She shook her fist with the hose in it and a watery snake appeared momentarily in the air. "I could quit working and take it easy and be filthy," she growled. "Lounge about the sidewalks all day drinking root beer. Dip snuff and spit in every puddle and have it all over my face. I could be nasty."

"Or you could have made me a nigger. It's too late for me to be a nigger," she said with deep sarcasm, "but I could act like one. Lay down in the middle of the road and stop traffic. Roll on the ground."

In the deepening light everything was taking on a mysterious hue. The pasture   185
was growing a peculiar glassy green and the streak of highway had turned lavender. She braced herself for a final assault and this time her voice rolled out over the pasture. "Go on," she yelled, "call me a hog! Call me a hog again. From hell. Call me a wart hog from hell. Put that bottom rail on top. There'll still be a top and bottom!"

A garbled echo returned to her.

A final surge of fury shook her and she roared, "Who do you think you are?"

The color of everything, field and crimson sky, burned for a moment with a transparent intensity. The question carried over the pasture and across the highway and the cotton field and returned to her clearly like an answer from beyond the wood.

She opened her mouth but no sound came out of it.

A tiny truck, Claud's, appeared on the highway, heading rapidly out of sight. Its   190
gears scraped thinly. It looked like a child's toy. At any moment a bigger truck might smash into it and scatter Claud's and the niggers' brains all over the road.

Mrs. Turpin stood there, her gaze fixed on the highway, all her muscles rigid, until in five or six minutes the truck reappeared, returning. She waited until it had had time to turn into their own road. Then like a monumental statue coming to life, she bent her head slowly and gazed, as if through the very heart of mystery, down into the pig parlor at the hogs. They had settled all in one corner around the old sow who was grunting softly. A red glow suffused them. They appeared to pant with a secret life.

Until the sun slipped finally behind the tree line, Mrs. Turpin remained there with her gaze bent to them as if she were absorbing some abysmal life-giving knowledge. At last she lifted her head. There was only a purple streak in the sky, cutting through a field of crimson and leading, like an extension of the highway, into the descending dusk. She raised her hands from the side of the pen in a gesture hieratic and profound. A visionary light settled in her eyes. She saw the streak as a vast swinging bridge extending upward from the earth through a field of living fire. Upon it a vast horde of souls were rumbling toward heaven. There were whole companies of white-trash, clean for the first time in their lives, and bands of black niggers in white robes, and battalions of freaks and lunatics shouting and clapping and leaping like frogs. And bringing up the end of the procession was a tribe of people whom she recognized at once as those who, like herself and Claud, had always had a little of everything and the God-given wit to use it right. She leaned forward to observe them closer. They were marching behind the others with great dignity, accountable as they had always been for good order and common sense and respectable behavior. They alone were on key. Yet she could see by their shocked and altered faces that even their virtues were being burned away. She lowered her hands and gripped the rail of the hog pen, her eyes small but fixed unblinkingly on what lay ahead. In a moment the vision faded but she remained where she was, immobile.

At length she got down and turned off the faucet and made her slow way on the darkening path to the house. In the woods around her the invisible cricket choruses had struck up, but what she heard were the voices of the souls climbing upward into the starry field and shouting hallelujah.

Questions

1. How does Mrs. Turpin see herself before Mary Grace calls her a wart hog?
2. What is the narrator's attitude toward Mrs. Turpin in the beginning of the story? How can you tell? Does this attitude change, or stay the same, at the end?
3. Describe the relationship between Mary Grace and her mother. What annoying platitudes does the mother mouth? Which of Mrs. Turpin's opinions seem especially to anger Mary Grace?
4. Sketch the plot of the story. What moment or event do you take to be the crisis, or turning point? What is the climax? What is the conclusion?
5. What do you infer from Mrs. Turpin's conversation with the black farm workers? Is she their friend? Why does she now find their flattery unacceptable ("Jesus satisfied with her")?
6. When, near the end of the story, Mrs. Turpin roars "Who do you think you are?" an echo "returned to her clearly like an answer from beyond the wood" (paragraph 188). Explain.
7. What is the final revelation given to Mrs. Turpin? (To state it is to state the theme of the story.) What new attitude does the revelation impart? (How is Mrs. Turpin left with a new vision of humanity?)
8. Other stories in this book contain revelations: "Young Goodman Brown," "The Gospel According to Mark." If you have read them, try to sum up the supernatural revelation made to the central character in each story. In each, is the revelation the same as a statement of the story's main theme?

FLANNERY O'CONNOR ON WRITING

Flannery O'Connor at her mother's Georgia farm where she raised peacocks; c. 1962.

Excerpt from "On Her Own Work":   1963
Insights into "A Good Man Is Hard to Find"

A story really isn't any good unless it successfully resists paraphrase, unless it hangs on and expands in the mind. Properly, you analyze to enjoy, but it's equally true that to analyze with any discrimination, you have to have enjoyed already, and I think that the best reason to hear a story read is that it should stimulate that primary enjoyment.

I don't have any pretensions to being an Aeschylus or Sophocles and providing you in this story with a cathartic experience out of your mythic background, though this story I'm going to read certainly calls up a good deal of the South's mythic background, and it should elicit from you a degree of pity and terror, even though its way of being serious is a comic one. I do think, though, that like the Greeks you should know what is going to happen in this story so that any element of suspense in it will be transferred from its surface to its interior.

I would be most happy if you had already read it, happier still if you knew it well, but since experience has taught me to keep my expectations along these lines modest, I'll tell you that this is the story of a family of six which, on its way driving to Florida, gets wiped out by an escaped convict who calls himself the Misfit. The family is made up of the Grandmother and her son, Bailey, and his children, John Wesley and June Star and the baby, and there is also the cat and the children's mother. The cat is named Pitty Sing, and the Grandmother is taking him with them, hidden in a basket.

Now I think it behooves me to try to establish with you the basis on which reason operates in this story. Much of my fiction takes its character from a reasonable use of the unreasonable, though the reasonableness of my use of it may not always be apparent. The assumptions that underlie this use of it, however, are those of the central Christian mysteries. These are assumptions to which a large part of the modern audience takes exception. About this I can only say that there are perhaps other ways than my own in which this story could be read, but none other by which it could have been written. Belief, in my own case anyway, is the engine that makes perception operate.

The heroine of this story, the Grandmother, is in the most significant position life offers the Christian. She is facing death. And to all appearances she, like the rest of us, is not too well prepared for it. She would like to see the event postponed. Indefinitely.

I've talked to a number of teachers who use this story in class and who tell their students that the Grandmother is evil, that in fact, she's a witch, even down to the cat. One of these teachers told me that his students, and particularly his Southern students, resisted this interpretation with a certain bemused vigor, and he didn't understand why. I had to tell him that they resisted it because they all had grandmothers or great-aunts just like her at home, and they knew, from personal experience, that the old lady lacked comprehension, but that she had a good heart. The Southerner is usually tolerant of those weaknesses that proceed from innocence, and he knows that a taste for self-preservation can be readily combined with the missionary spirit.

This same teacher was telling his students that morally the Misfit was several cuts above the Grandmother. He had a really sentimental attachment to the Misfit. But then a prophet gone wrong is almost always more interesting than your grandmother, and you have to let people take their pleasures where they find them.

It is true that the old lady is a hypocritical old soul; her wits are no match for the Misfit's, nor is her capacity for grace equal to his; yet I think the unprejudiced reader will feel that the Grandmother has a special kind of triumph in this story which instinctively we do not allow to someone altogether bad.

I often ask myself what makes a story work, and what makes it hold up as a story, and I have decided that it is probably some action, some gesture of a character that is unlike any other in the story, one which indicates where the real heart of the story lies. This would have to be an action or a gesture which was both totally right and totally unexpected; it would have to be one that was both in character and beyond character; it would have to suggest both the world and eternity. The action or gesture I'm talking about would have to be on the anagogical level, that is, the level which has to do with the Divine life and our participation in it. It would be a gesture that transcended any neat allegory that might have been intended or any pat moral categories a reader could make. It would be a gesture which somehow made contact with mystery.

There is a point in this story where such a gesture occurs. The Grandmother is at last alone, facing the Misfit. Her head clears for an instant and she realizes, even in her limited way, that she is responsible for the man before her and joined to him by ties of kinship which have their roots deep in the mystery she has been merely prattling about so far. And at this point, she does the right thing, she makes the right gesture.

I find that students are often puzzled by what she says and does here, but I think myself that if I took out this gesture and what she says with it, I would have no story. What was left would not be worth your attention. Our age not only does not have a very sharp eye for the almost imperceptible intrusions of grace, it no longer has much feeling for the nature of the violences which precede and follow them. The devil's greatest wile, Baudelaire has said, is to convince us that he does not exist.

I suppose the reasons for the use of so much violence in modern fiction will differ with each writer who uses it, but in my own stories I have found that violence is strangely capable of returning my characters to reality and preparing them to accept their moment of grace. Their heads are so hard that almost nothing else will do the work. This idea, that reality is something to which we must be returned at considerable cost, is one which is seldom understood by the casual reader, but it is one which is implicit in the Christian view of the world.

I don't want to equate the Misfit with the devil. I prefer to think that, however unlikely this may seem, the old lady's gesture, like the mustard-seed, will grow to be a great crow-filled tree in the Misfit's heart, and will be enough of a pain to him there to turn him into the prophet he was meant to become. But that's another story.

This story has been called grotesque, but I prefer to call it literal. A good story is literal in the same sense that a child's drawing is literal. When a child draws, he doesn't intend to distort but to set down exactly what he sees, and as his gaze is direct, he sees the lines that create motion. Now the lines of motion that interest the writer are usually invisible. They are lines of spiritual motion. And in this story you should be on the lookout for such things as the action of grace in the Grandmother's soul, and not for the dead bodies.

We hear many complaints about the prevalence of violence in modern fiction, and it is always assumed that this violence is a bad thing and meant to be an end in itself. With the serious writer, violence is never an end in itself. It is the extreme situation that best reveals what we are essentially, and I believe these are times when writers are more interested in what we are essentially than in the tenor of our daily lives. Violence is a force which can be used for good or evil, and among other things taken by it is the kingdom of heaven. But regardless of what can be taken by it, the man in the violent situation reveals those qualities least dispensable in his personality, those qualities which are all he will have to take into eternity with him; and since the characters in this story are all on the verge of eternity, it is appropriate to think of what they take with them. In any case, I hope that if you consider these points in connection with the story, you will come to see it as something more than an account of a family murdered on the way to Florida.

From "On Her Own Work"

On Her Catholic Faith   1955

I write the way I do because (not though) I am a Catholic. This is a fact and nothing covers it like the bald statement. However, I am a Catholic peculiarly possessed of the modern consciousness, the thing Jung describes as unhistorical, solitary, and guilty. To possess this within the Church is to bear a burden, the necessary burden for the conscious Catholic. It's to feel the contemporary situation at the ultimate level. I think that the Church is the only thing that is going to make the terrible world we are coming to endurable; the only thing that makes the Church endurable is that it is somehow the body of Christ and that on this we are fed. It seems to be a fact that you suffer as much from the Church as for it but if you believe in the divinity of Christ, you have to cherish the world at the same time that you struggle to endure it. This may explain the lack of bitterness in the stories.

From a letter (July 20, 1955) in *The Habit of Being*

Excerpt from "The Grotesque in Southern Fiction": 1960
The Serious Writer and the Tired Reader

Those writers who speak for and with their age are able to do so with a great deal more ease and grace than those who speak counter to prevailing attitudes. I once received a letter from an old lady in California who informed me that when the tired reader comes home at night, he wishes to read something that will lift up his heart. And it seems her heart had not been lifted up by anything of mine she had read. I think that if her heart had been in the right place, it would have been lifted up.

You may say that the serious writer doesn't have to bother about the tired reader, but he does, because they are all tired. One old lady who wants her heart lifted up wouldn't be so bad, but you multiply her two hundred and fifty thousand times and what you get is a book club. I used to think it should be possible to write for some supposed elite, for the people who attend the universities and sometimes know how to read, but I have since found that though you may publish your stories in *Botteghe Oscure,*° if they are any good at all, you are eventually going to get a letter from some old lady in California, or some inmate of the Federal Penitentiary or the state insane asylum or the local poorhouse, telling you where you have failed to meet his needs.

And his need, of course, is to be lifted up. There is something in us, as storytellers and as listeners to stories, that demands the redemptive act, that demands that what falls at least be offered the chance to be restored. The reader of today looks for this motion, and rightly so, but what he has forgotten is the cost of it. His sense of evil is diluted or lacking altogether and so he has forgotten the price of restoration. When he reads a novel, he wants either his senses tormented or his spirits raised. He wants to be transported, instantly, either to a mock damnation or a mock innocence.

I am often told that the model of balance for the novelist should be Dante, who divided his territory up pretty evenly between hell, purgatory, and paradise. There can be no objection to this, but also there can be no reason to assume that the result of doing it in these times will give us the balanced picture that it gave in Dante's. Dante lived in the 13th century when that balance was achieved in the faith of his age. We live now in an age which doubts both fact and value, which is swept this way and that by momentary convictions. Instead of reflecting a balance from the world around him, the novelist now has to achieve one from a felt balance inside himself. There are ages when it is possible to woo the reader; there are others when something more drastic is necessary.

Botteghe Oscure: a distinguished and expensive literary magazine published in Rome from 1949 to 1960 by the Princess Marguerite Caetani for a small, sophisticated audience.

There is no literary orthodoxy that can be prescribed as settled for the fiction writer, not even that of Henry James who balanced the elements of traditional realism and romance so admirably within each of his novels. But this much can be said. The great novels we get in the future are not going to be those that the public thinks it wants, or those that critics demand. They are going to be the kind of novels that interest the novelist. And the novels that interest the novelist are those that have not already been written. They are those that put the greatest demands on him, that require him to operate at the maximum of his intelligence and his talents, and to be true to the particularities of his own vocation. The direction of many of us will be toward concentration and the distortion that is necessary to get our vision across; it will be more toward poetry than toward the traditional novel.

The problem for such a novelist will be to know how far he can distort without destroying, and in order not to destroy, he will have to descend far enough into himself to reach those underground springs that give life to his work. This descent into himself will, at the same time, be a descent into his region. It will be a descent through the darkness of the familiar into a world where, like the blind man cured in the gospels, he sees men as if they were trees, but walking. This is the beginning of vision, and I feel it is a vision which we in the South must at least try to understand if we want to participate in the continuance of a vital Southern literature. I hate to think that in twenty years Southern writers too may be writing about men in grey flannel suits and may have lost their ability to see that these gentlemen are even greater freaks than what we are writing about now. I hate to think of the day when the Southern writer will satisfy the tired reader.

From "The Grotesque in Southern Fiction"

CRITICS ON FLANNERY O'CONNOR

J. O. Tate

A Good Source Is Not So Hard to Find: The Real Life Misfit   1980

The mounting evidence of O'Connor's use of items from the Milledgeville and Atlanta newspapers will interest those who realize that these sources, in and of themselves, have nothing to do with the Gothic, the grotesque, the American Romance tradition, Southwestern humor, Southern literature, adolescent aggression, the New Hermeneutics, the anxiety of influence, structuralism, pentecostal Gnosticism, medieval theology, Christian humanism, existentialism, or the Roman Catholic Church.

I. On "The Misfit" as Name and Word

The text of an Atlanta *Constitution* article of November 6, 1952, p. 29, identifies for us the source of a celebrated sobriquet. This newspaper reference was reprinted in *The Flannery O'Connor Bulletin*, Volume III, Autumn 1974. The headline says enough: "'The Misfit' Robs Office, Escapes With $150." Flannery O'Connor took a forgotten criminal's alias and used it for larger purposes: *her* Misfit was out of place in a grander way than the original. But we should not forget O'Connor's credentials as "a literalist of the imagination." There is always "a little lower layer." She meant to mock pop psychology by exploiting the original Misfit's exploitation of a

'The Misfit' Robs Office, Escapes With $150

A bandit who told his victims he was "The Misfit," held up the Atlanta Federal Savings and Loan Association office at 22 Marietta St., N. W., and escaped with $150 cash in a daring daylight raid Wednesday afternoon.

The man was described as being 30 years old, six feet tall and 175 pounds in weight. He carried a nickel-steel .32-caliber revolver, according to J. F. Clemmer, assistant vice-president of the company.

Clemmer told Det. Y. H. Allen the man shoved an envelope through the w i n d o w where a cashier, Mrs. Beverly Bradshaw of 1919 Sylvan Ridge Dr., S. W., was at work. A crudely lettered message on the envelope read: "Put $150 in here and don't say anything. I have a gun, and I am 'The Misfit.' "

Mrs. Bradshaw ducked behind the counter. Clemmer said. Clemmer told another cashier to "do whatever the man wanted." Then he told the robber he'd "better go—we're protected by the FBI." The bandit then fled on Marietta St.

Detectives said the description of the man tallied with that of one who Tuesday night held up a hotel clerk at 87 Harris St., N. W., and fled with $50. FBI agents joined Atlanta police in a search.

The article in the Atlanta *Constitution*, November 6, 1952, that provided Flannery O'Connor with the criminal nickname "The Misfit."

socio-psychological "excuse" for aberrant behavior. But even a little lower: the original meaning of the word "misfit" has to do with clothing. We should not fail, therefore, to note that The Misfit's "borrowed" blue jeans are too tight. He leaves the story, of course, wearing Bailey's shirt.

II. On the Identity and Destiny of the Original Misfit

By November 15, 1952, The Misfit had been apprehended; he had also advanced himself to page three of the Atlanta *Journal*. The Misfit was a twenty-five-year old named James C. Yancey. He "was found to be of unsound mind" and committed to the state mental hospital at—Milledgeville. Where else?

III. On The Misfit's Notoriety, Peregrinations, Good Manners, Eye-glasses, Companions, and Mental Hygiene

The original Misfit was, as criminals go, small potatoes. He was an unambitious thief, no more. O'Connor took nothing from him but his imposing signature. But it just so happens that there was another well-publicized criminal aloose in Tennessee and Georgia just before the time that O'Connor appropriated the Misfit's name. This other hold-up artist had four important qualities in common with *her* Misfit. First, he inspired a certain amount of terror through several states. Second, he had, or claimed to have, a certain *politesse*. Third, he wore spectacles. Fourth, he had two accomplices, in more than one account.

James Francis ("Three-Gun") Hill, the sinister celebrity of the front pages, much more closely resembles the object of the grandmother's warnings than the original Misfit. Various articles tell of "a fantastic record of 26 kidnappings in four states, as many robberies, 10 car thefts, and a climactic freeing of four Florida convicts from a prison gang—all in two kaleidoscopic weeks." He had advanced "from an obscure hoodlum to top billing as a public enemy" (The Atlanta *Constitution*, November 1, p. 1). Such headlines as the grandmother had in mind screamed of Hill (though not in the sports section that Bailey was reading): "Maniac's Gang Terrorizes Hills" (*Constitution*, October 24, p. 2, from Sparta, Tenn.); "Search for Kidnap-Robbery Trio Centers in Atlanta and Vicinity" (October 25, p. 1, from Atlanta); "Chattanooga Is Focal Point for Manhunt" (October 27, p. 26); "2nd of Terror Gang Seized In Florida/Pal Said Still In Atlanta Area" (October 29, p. 32); "Self-Styled 3-Gun Maniac Frees 4 Road Gang Convicts at Gunpoint" (October 31, p. 1, from Bartow, Florida). It is quite clear that O'Connor, imagining through the grandmother's point of view, was, like the newspapers, assuming an Atlanta locale and orientation. The southward trip was in the same direction as Hill's last run.

The article of October 24 gives us a bit of color: "A fantastic band of highwaymen, led by a self-styled 'maniac' who laughed weirdly while he looted his victims, spread terror through the Cumberland hills today. . . . [The leader] boasted that he had escaped from the Utah State Prison and 'killed two people' . . . 'They call me a three-gun maniac, and brother, they got the picture straight,' the head bandit was quoted by victims." The October 31 article hints at the rustic setting of O'Connor's story: "The escapees and Hill . . . drove up a dead-end road and abandoned the car. They fled into thick woods on foot. . . ."

The *Constitution* of November 1 speaks of Hill on the front page as "the bespectacled, shrunken-cheeked highwayman." A later article gives us, as it gave O'Connor, a clue to her Misfit's respectful modes of address ("Good afternoon . . . I pre-chate that, lady . . . Nome . . . I'm sorry I don't have on a shirt before you ladies . . . Yes'm . . ."): We read of the trial of "Accused kidnapper, James Francis (Three-Gun) Hill, who says he's a 'gentleman-bandit' because 'I didn't cuss in front of ladies. . . .'" This Associated Press wire story from Chattanooga was on page 26 of the November 13 Atlanta *Journal*.

The *Constitution* of the same date says "Hearing Delayed for 'Maniac' Hill and 2 Cronies," and goes on to mention "James Francis Hill, self-styled 'three-gun maniac.'" We may observe that both Yancey and Hill were referred to in the newspapers as "self-styled," an arresting phrase perhaps to an author attuned to extravagances of self. I think we may also recognize here the genesis of Hiram and Bobby Lee.

The result of Hill's plea of guilty was perhaps not as forthright as his intention: "'Maniac' Hill Is Adjudged Incompetent" (*Constitution*, November 18). Like Yancey, The Misfit, Hill was sent to a mental institution—in Tennessee, this time. (His cronies were sentenced to jail.) The diagnosis of both Yancey and Hill as mentally ill may have suggested O'Connor's Misfit's experiences with the "head-doctor."

IV. On the Misfit, Memory, and Guilt

The fictional Misfit was not easily freudened: he knew perfectly well that he had not killed his daddy. Yet he insisted there was no balance between guilt and punishment—if memory served.

The issues of accuracy of memory, consciousness of guilt, and conscience were also raised in an odd "human-interest" story that was published in those same days when O'Connor was gathering so much material from the newspapers. The Misfit's claim that he was punished for crimes he did not remember may have been inspired by this account of a man who was *not* punished for a crime he *did* remember—but remembered wrongly.

The *Journal* of November 5, 1952 carried the article, written from Brookhaven, New York, on page 12: "'Murder' Didn't Happen, House Painter Free." Louis Roberts had shot a policeman in 1928; he assumed he had killed him. Over twenty years later, his conscience finally forced him to confess. When his tale was investigated, it was discovered that the policeman had survived after all. There was no prosecution for, as an authority was quoted as saying, "His conscience has punished him enough."

From "A Good Source Is Not So Hard to Find"

Mary Jane Schenck (b. 1944)

Deconstructing "A Good Man Is Hard to Find" 1988

"A Good Man Is Hard to Find" presents a masterful portrait of a woman who creates a self and a world through language. From the outset, the grandmother relies on "texts" to structure her reality. The newspaper article about The Misfit mentioned in the opening paragraph of the story is a written text which has a particular status in the narrative. It refers to events outside and prior to the primary *récit*, but it stands as an unrecognized prophecy of the events which occur at the end. For Bailey, the newspaper story is not important or meaningful, and for the grandmother it does not represent a real threat but is part of a ploy to get her own way. It is thus the first one of her "fictions," one which ironically comes true. The grandmother's whole personality is built upon the fictions she tells herself and her family. Although she knows Bailey would object if she brought her cat on the trip, the grandmother sneaks the cat into the car, justifying her behavior by imagining "he would miss her too much and she was afraid he might brush himself against one of the gas burners and accidentally asphyxiate himself." She also carefully cultivates a fiction about the past when people were good and when "children were more respectful of their native states and their parents and everything else." As she tells Red Sam at the Tower when they stop to eat, "People are certainly not nice like they used to be."

The grandmother reads fictional stories to the children, tells them ostensibly true stories, and provides a continual gloss on the physical world they are passing. "Little niggers in the country don't have things like we do. If I could paint, I'd paint that picture." Lacking that skill, the grandmother nevertheless verbally "creates" a whole universe as they ride along. "'Look at the graveyard!' the grandmother said, pointing it out. 'That was the old family burying ground. That belonged to the plantation.'" She creates the stories behind the visual phenomena she sees and explains relationships between events or her own actions which have no logic other than that which she lends them.

Her most important fiction is, of course, the story of the old plantation house which becomes more of an imperative as she tells it. The more she talks about it, the more she wants to see it again, so she does not hesitate to self-consciously lie about it. "'There was a secret panel in this house,' she said craftily, not telling the truth but wishing she were." At this point we see clearly the performative quality of the grandmother's language. At first it motivates her own desire, then spills over onto the children, finally culminating in their violent outburst of screaming and kicking to get their father to stop the car. The performative quality of her language becomes even more crucial when she realizes that she has fantasized the location of the house. She does not admit it, but her thoughts manifest themselves physically: "The thought was so embarrassing that she turned red in the face and her eyes dilated and her feet jumped up, upsetting her valise in the corner." Of course, it is her physical action which frees the cat and causes the accident. After the accident, she again fictionalizes about her condition, hoping she is injured so she can deflect Bailey's anger, and she cannot even manage to tell the truth about the details of the accident.

The scene with The Misfit is the apogee of the grandmother's use of "fictions" to explain and control reality, attempts that are thwarted by her encounter with a character who understands there is no reality behind her words. When the grandmother recognizes The Misfit, he tells her it would have been better if she hadn't, but she has *named* him, thus forcing him to become what is behind his self-selected name. In a desperate attempt to cope with the threat posed by the murderer, the grandmother runs through her litany of convenient fictions. She believes that there are class distinctions ("I know you're a good man. You don't look a bit like you have common blood"), that appearance reflects reality ("You shouldn't call yourself The Misfit because I know you're a good man at heart. I can just look at you and tell"), that redemption can be achieved through work ("You could be honest too if you'd only try. . . . Think how wonderful it would be to settle down . . ."), and finally, that prayer will change him ("'Pray, pray,' she commanded him").

From "Deconstructing Meaning in Two Short Stories by Flannery O'Connor"

Louise S. Cowan (b. 1916)

The Character of Mrs. Turpin in "Revelation"   2005

O'Connor held that serious writers cannot produce their works simply from their own ideas and conscious convictions; rather, if they are to produce anything of value, they must submit to a larger body of customs and manners of which they are a part. "As far as the creation of a body of fiction is concerned," she writes, "the social is superior to the purely personal." The writer whose themes are religious particularly needs a region where the themes find a response in the life of the people. "What the Southern Catholic writer is apt to find when he descends within his imagination is not Catholic life but the life of his region in which he is both native and alien." For O'Connor, then, the South presented the region to which she could devote her genius. It was out of step with the rest of the nation, since it was still largely agrarian, retaining in the early twentieth century traces in it of an older worldview. Further, as she saw, it still had a "folk," both white and black, who maintained an outlook fundamentally religious. It was likely to be from these groups that the prophetic figures in her fiction could emerge. In the South the general conception of man is still, O'Connor maintained, theological:

> The Bible is known by the ignorant as well as the educated and it is always the *mythos* which the poor hold in common that is most valuable to the fiction writer. When the poor hold sacred history in common, they have ties to the universal and the holy which allows the meaning of their every action to be heightened and seen under the aspect of eternity.

· · ·

"Revelation"

The short story "Revelation," which won first prize in the 1964 O. Henry Awards, is one of O'Connor's last-written pieces and one of her most accomplished. It is about her familiar theme of Pharisaism;° and the epiphany with which it ends is no less devastating for occurring while the protagonist, Mrs. Turpin, is hosing down one of her prize hogs.

O'Connor's favorite target is the respectable, moral person who has lived a good and sensible life. The main character in "Revelation," Ruby Turpin, is such a figure, innocently falling into the pattern of self-satisfaction that finally assumes God himself must be impressed with her virtue. It is a mistake, however, to construe O'Connor's

---

Pharisaism: hypocritical self-righteousness.

keen portrayals as pitiless. Her pharisaical characters are unaware of their self-love; they conduct themselves with kindness and courtesy, as good decent people should do. Mrs. Turpin in "Revelation" is such a naively self-righteous person, convinced that her righteousness makes her a special friend of Jesus. One of O'Connor's worries about the story "Revelation," as a matter of fact, was that people would think she was disapproving of Mrs. Turpin. "You got to be a very big woman to shout at the Lord across a hog pen," she wrote in a letter to a friend.

Ruby Turpin is one of O'Connor's masterpieces. Essentially good-hearted, she is blind to her own pride and self-satisfaction. She passes judgment on everyone she meets, sometimes occupying herself with naming over the classes of people. "On the bottom of the heap were most colored people . . . then next to them, not above, just away from—were the white trash, then above them the home-owners, and above them the home-and-land owners to which she and Claud belonged." She naively congratulates herself on having been born as who she is, a good respectable white woman who, with her husband, makes do with what they have and takes care of their property. But there are people who own more property—and people over them, and some of them are not morally good; so Mrs. Turpin's neat little scale of measurement becomes blurry and leaves her puzzled.

The crucial event in Ruby Turpin's life begins in a doctor's office. . . . She has been singled out, she knows, for a message. And, afterwards, the more she thinks about it in her isolation (for she can't bring herself to ask her husband about it; and the black servants who work for her merely flatter her), the more the incident seems to have some sort of divine import. "The message had been given to Ruby Turpin, a respectable, hard-working, church-going woman." Angry, she makes her way to the hogpen; and as she is watering down a white sow she begins her questioning of God that turns into a challenge: "Go on, call me a hog! Call me a hog again. From hell. Call me a wart hog from hell." And finally the blasphemous, "Who do you think you are?"

It is this direct challenge to the Almighty that produces the real revelation for Ruby Turpin. And in the vision that she receives, the question she had always stumbled over—the complexity of categorizing the classes of people—is answered, with a revelation at once grotesque and sublime.

From "Passing by the Dragon: Flannery O'Connor's Art of Revelation"

Dean Flower

Listening to Flannery O'Connor   2011

Readers of course do not have to be distracted by a writer's actual speaking voice. Sometimes, as in Faulkner's deliberately toneless reading of the Reverend Shegog's sermon in *The Sound and the Fury*, or Eudora Welty's much-too-fast rendition of "Why I Live at the P.O.," hearing the author can be a disappointment. But I am happy to say that this is not the case with Flannery O'Connor. Her voice was recorded, so far as anyone knows, only once—at Vanderbilt University on April 22, 1959, when she gave a reading of her most famous shocker, "A Good Man Is Hard to Find," prefacing it with a few remarks about her work.[3] . . . Although the recording quality is low, O'Connor's voice in 1959 was mellow and rounded, not whiny or nasal or flat. By then she had

---

[3]Available in a DVD reissue of John Huston's 1979 film *Wise Blood* (Criterion Collection #470).

considerable experience in lecturing and giving readings, so no doubt her poise is way greater than it could have been at Iowa or Yaddo. But I was surprised by its warmth. You hear her quiet irony, of course, especially in her introductory remarks, but also— very unexpectedly to me—a youthful spiritedness. Despite its apparent gravity, her voice conveys something close to exuberance in its relish and delight in words. She gets loud laughter in observing that the labels "degenerate" and "gothic" and "grotesque" have been inflicted on her so often she feels "like Bre'er Rabbit stuck on the Tar Baby." Everybody knows that story. But nobody laughs when she offers the following:

> It was suggested to me that I would want to preface this reading tonight with a short statement about my philosophy of writing. Of course I don't want to do anything of the kind. My approach to literary problems is very much like the one Dr. Johnson's° blind housekeeper used when she poured tea for him. She put her finger inside the cup.

What could be clearer, wittier, and more self-deprecating about her craft? Leave it to O'Connor to identify herself—unobtrusively—with the blind Annie Williams, on whom Johnson took such compassion.

From "Listening to Flannery O'Connor"

■ WRITING *effectively*

TOPICS FOR WRITING

1. Compare and contrast a pair of characters from two different stories who feel conceptually related. A good choice might be Mrs. Turpin from "Revelation" and the grandmother in "A Good Man Is Hard to Find." Do these characters play similar roles in their respective stories?

2. Both O'Connor stories are about revelations of one kind or another. How do these revelations relate to each other? Back up your argument with evidence from the stories.

3. In the excerpt from "On Her Own Work," O'Connor writes:

> I often ask myself what makes a story work, and what makes it hold up as a story, and I have decided that it is probably some action, some gesture of a character that is unlike any other in the story, one which indicates where the real heart of the story lies. This would have to be an action or a gesture which was both totally right and totally unexpected; it would have to be one that was both in character and beyond character; it would have to suggest both the world and eternity. . . . It would be a gesture which somehow made contact with mystery.

   While O'Connor is speaking specifically about "A Good Man Is Hard to Find," her words can be applied to her other stories. Choose a gesture from "Revelation" or any other O'Connor story that fits this description, and explain your choice.

4. "In most good stories it is the character's personality that creates the action of the story," O'Connor declares in her essay "Writing Short Stories." "If you start with a real personality, a real character, then something is bound to happen." Discuss this statement as it applies to one or more of the O'Connor stories you have read. Do O'Connor's characters seem to you to be real people, or do you see them as mere vessels for the author's religious views?

5. In 750 to 1,000 words, comment on O'Connor's use of humor. How does comedy help her say what she has to say?

Dr. Johnson: Samuel Johnson (1709-1784), the celebrated English essayist, poet, and lexicographer.

10 CRITICAL CASEBOOK
Two Stories in Depth

Charlotte Perkins Gilman ▪ *The Yellow Wallpaper*
Alice Walker ▪ *Everyday Use*

CHARLOTTE PERKINS GILMAN

Charlotte Perkins Gilman (1860–1935) was born in Hartford, Connecticut. Her father was the writer Frederick Beecher Perkins (a nephew of reformer-novelist Harriet Beecher Stowe, author of Uncle Tom's Cabin, *and abolitionist minister Henry Ward Beecher), but he abandoned the family shortly after his daughter's birth. Raised in meager surroundings, the young Gilman adopted her intellectual Beecher aunts as role models. Because she and her mother moved from one relation to another, Gilman's early education was neglected—at fifteen, she had had only four years of schooling. In 1878 she studied commercial art at the Rhode Island School of Design. In 1884 she married Walter Stetson, an artist. After the birth of her one daughter, she experienced a severe depression. The rest cure her doctor prescribed became the basis of her most famous story, "The Yellow Wallpaper." This tale combines standard elements of*

Charlotte Perkins Gilman

Gothic fiction (the isolated country mansion, the brooding atmosphere of the room, the aloof but dominating husband) with the fresh clarity of Gilman's feminist perspective. Gilman's first marriage ended in an amicable divorce. A celebrated essayist and public speaker, she became an important early figure in American feminism. Her study Women and Economics *(1898) stressed the importance of both sexes having a place in the working world. Her feminist-Utopian novel* Herland *(1915) describes a thriving nation of women without men. In 1900 Gilman married a second time—this time, more happily—to her cousin George Houghton Gilman. Following his sudden death in 1934, Gilman discovered she had inoperable breast cancer. After finishing her autobiography, she killed herself with chloroform in Pasadena, California.*

The Yellow Wallpaper   1892

It is very seldom that mere ordinary people like John and myself secure ancestral halls for the summer.

A colonial mansion, a hereditary estate, I would say a haunted house and reach the height of romantic felicity—but that would be asking too much of fate!

Still I will proudly declare that there is something queer about it.

Else, why should it be let so cheaply? And why have stood so long untenanted?

John laughs at me, of course, but one expects that.   5

John is practical in the extreme. He has no patience with faith, an intense horror of superstition, and he scoffs openly at any talk of things not to be felt and seen and put down in figures.

John is a physician, and *perhaps*—(I would not say it to a living soul, of course, but this is dead paper and a great relief to my mind)—*perhaps* that is one reason I do not get well faster.

You see, he does not believe I am sick! And what can one do?

If a physician of high standing, and one's own husband, assures friends and relatives that there is really nothing the matter with one but temporary nervous depression—a slight hysterical tendency—what is one to do?

My brother is also a physician, and also of high standing, and he says the same thing.   10

So I take phosphates or phosphites—whichever it is—and tonics, and air and exercise, and journeys, and am absolutely forbidden to "work" until I am well again.

Personally, I disagree with their ideas.

Personally, I believe that congenial work, with excitement and change, would do me good.

But what is one to do?

I did write for a while in spite of them; but it *does* exhaust me a good deal—having   15 to be so sly about it, or else meet with heavy opposition.

I sometimes fancy that in my condition, if I had less opposition and more society and stimulus—but John says the very worst thing I can do is to think about my condition, and I confess it always makes me feel bad.

So I will let it alone and talk about the house.

The most beautiful place! It is quite alone, standing well back from the road, quite three miles from the village. It makes me think of English places that you read about, for there are hedges and walls and gates that lock, and lots of separate little houses for the gardeners and people.

There is a *delicious* garden! I never saw such a garden—large and shady, full of box-bordered paths, and lined with long grape-covered arbors with seats under them.

There were greenhouses, but they are all broken now.   20

There was some legal trouble, I believe, something about the heirs and co-heirs; anyhow, the place has been empty for years.

That spoils my ghostliness, I am afraid, but I don't care—there is something strange about the house—I can feel it.

I even said so to John one moonlight evening, but he said what I felt was a *draught,* and shut the window.

I get unreasonably angry with John sometimes. I'm sure I never used to be so sensitive. I think it is due to this nervous condition.

But John says if I feel so I shall neglect proper self-control; so I take pains to control myself—before him, at least, and that makes me very tired. [25]

I don't like our room a bit. I wanted one downstairs that opened onto the piazza and had roses all over the window, and such pretty old-fashioned chintz hangings! But John would not hear of it.

He said there was only one window and not room for two beds, and no near room for him if he took another.

He is very careful and loving, and hardly lets me stir without special direction.

I have a schedule prescription for each hour in the day; he takes all care from me, and so I feel basely ungrateful not to value it more.

He said he came here solely on my account, that I was to have perfect rest and all the air I could get. "Your exercise depends on your strength, my dear," said he, "and your food somewhat on your appetite; but air you can absorb all the time." So we took the nursery at the top of the house. [30]

It is a big, airy room, the whole floor nearly, with windows that look all ways, and air and sunshine galore. It was a nursery first, and then playroom and gymnasium, I should judge, for the windows are barred for little children, and there are rings and things in the walls.

The paint and paper look as if a boys' school had used it. It is stripped off—the paper—in great patches all around the head of my bed, about as far as I can reach, and in a great place on the other side of the room low down. I never saw a worse paper in my life. One of those sprawling, flamboyant patterns committing every artistic sin.

It is dull enough to confuse the eye in following, pronounced enough constantly to irritate and provoke study, and when you follow the lame uncertain curves for a little distance they suddenly commit suicide—plunge off at outrageous angles, destroy themselves in unheard-of contradictions.

The color is repellent, almost revolting: a smouldering unclean yellow, strangely faded by the slow-turning sunlight. It is a dull yet lurid orange in some places, a sickly sulphur tint in others.

No wonder the children hated it! I should hate it myself if I had to live in this room long. [35]

There comes John, and I must put this away—he hates to have me write a word.

We have been here two weeks, and I haven't felt like writing before, since that first day.

I am sitting by the window now, up in this atrocious nursery, and there is nothing to hinder my writing as much as I please, save lack of strength.

John is away all day, and even some nights when his cases are serious.

I am glad my case is not serious! [40]

But these nervous troubles are dreadfully depressing.

John does not know how much I really suffer. He knows there is no *reason* to suffer, and that satisfies him.

Of course it is only nervousness. It does weigh on me so not to do my duty in any way!

I meant to be such a help to John, such a real rest and comfort, and here I am a comparative burden already!

Nobody would believe what an effort it is to do what little I am able—to dress and entertain, and order things. [45]

It is fortunate Mary is so good with the baby. Such a dear baby!

And yet I *cannot* be with him, it makes me so nervous.

I suppose John never was nervous in his life. He laughs at me so about this wallpaper!

At first he meant to repaper the room, but afterward he said that I was letting it get the better of me, and that nothing was worse for a nervous patient than to give way to such fancies.

He said that after the wallpaper was changed it would be the heavy bedstead, 50 and then the barred windows, and then that gate at the head of the stairs, and so on.

"You know the place is doing you good," he said, "and really, dear, I don't care to renovate the house just for a three months' rental."

"Then do let us go downstairs," I said. "There are such pretty rooms there."

Then he took me in his arms and called me a blessed little goose, and said he would go down to the cellar, if I wished, and have it whitewashed into the bargain.

But he is right enough about the beds and windows and things.

It is as airy and comfortable a room as anyone need wish, and, of course, I would 55 not be so silly as to make him uncomfortable just for a whim.

I'm really getting quite fond of the big room, all but that horrid paper.

Out of one window I can see the garden—those mysterious deep-shaded arbors, the riotous old-fashioned flowers, and bushes and gnarly trees.

Out of another I get a lovely view of the bay and a little private wharf belonging to the estate. There is a beautiful shaded lane that runs down there from the house. I always fancy I see people walking in these numerous paths and arbors, but John has cautioned me not to give way to fancy in the least. He says that with my imaginative power and habit of story-making, a nervous weakness like mine is sure to lead to all manner of excited fancies, and that I ought to use my will and good sense to check the tendency. So I try.

I think sometimes that if I were only well enough to write a little it would relieve the press of ideas and rest me.

But I find I get pretty tired when I try. 60

It is so discouraging not to have any advice and companionship about my work. When I get really well, John says we will ask Cousin Henry and Julia down for a long visit; but he says he would as soon put fireworks in my pillow-case as to let me have those stimulating people about now.

I wish I could get well faster.

But I must not think about that. This paper looks to me as if it *knew* what a vicious influence it had!

There is a recurrent spot where the pattern lolls like a broken neck and two bulbous eyes stare at you upside down.

I get positively angry with the impertinence of it and the everlastingness. Up 65 and down and sideways they crawl, and those absurd unblinking eyes are everywhere. There is one place where two breadths didn't match, and the eyes go all up and down the line, one a little higher than the other.

I never saw so much expression in an inanimate thing before, and we all know how much expression they have! I used to lie awake as a child and get more entertainment and terror out of blank walls and plain furniture than most children could find in a toy-store.

I remember what a kindly wink the knobs of our big old bureau used to have, and there was one chair that always seemed like a strong friend.

I used to feel that if any of the other things looked too fierce I could always hop into that chair and be safe.

The furniture in this room is no worse than inharmonious, however, for we had to bring it all from downstairs. I suppose when this was used as a playroom they had to take the nursery things out, and no wonder! I never saw such ravages as the children have made here.

The wallpaper, as I said before, is torn off in spots, and it sticketh closer than a brother—they must have had perseverance as well as hatred. 70

Then the floor is scratched and gouged and splintered, the plaster itself is dug out here and there, and this great heavy bed, which is all we found in the room, looks as if it had been through the wars.

But I don't mind it a bit—only the paper.

There comes John's sister. Such a dear girl as she is, and so careful of me! I must not let her find me writing.

She is a perfect and enthusiastic housekeeper, and hopes for no better profession. I verily believe she thinks it is the writing which made me sick!

But I can write when she is out, and see her a long way off from these windows. 75

There is one that commands the road, a lovely shaded winding road, and one that just looks off over the country. A lovely country, too, full of great elms and velvet meadows.

This wallpaper has a kind of sub-pattern in a different shade, a particularly irritating one, for you can only see it in certain lights, and not clearly then.

But in the places where it isn't faded and where the sun is just so—I can see a strange, provoking, formless sort of figure that seems to skulk about behind that silly and conspicuous front design.

There's sister on the stairs!

Well, the Fourth of July is over! The people are all gone, and I am tired out. John 80 thought it might do me good to see a little company, so we just had Mother and Nellie and the children down for a week.

Of course I didn't do a thing. Jennie sees to everything now.

But it tired me all the same.

John says if I don't pick up faster he shall send me to Weir Mitchell° in the fall.

But I don't want to go there at all. I had a friend who was in his hands once, and she says he is just like John and my brother, only more so!

Besides, it is such an undertaking to go so far. 85

I don't feel as if it was worthwhile to turn my hand over for anything, and I'm getting dreadfully fretful and querulous.

I cry at nothing, and cry most of the time.

Of course I don't when John is here, or anybody else, but when I am alone.

And I am alone a good deal just now. John is kept in town very often by serious cases, and Jennie is good and lets me alone when I want her to.

So I walk a little in the garden or down that lovely lane, sit on the porch under 90 the roses, and lie down up here a good deal.

I'm getting really fond of the room in spite of the wallpaper. Perhaps *because* of the wallpaper.

It dwells in my mind so!

Weir Mitchell (1829–1914): famed nerve specialist who actually treated the author, Charlotte Perkins Gilman, for nervous prostration with his well-known "rest cure." (The cure was not successful.) Also the author of *Diseases of the Nervous System, Especially of Women* (1881).

I lie here on this great immovable bed—it is nailed down, I believe—and follow that pattern about by the hour. It is as good as gymnastics, I assure you. I start, we'll say, at the bottom, down in the corner over there where it has not been touched, and I determine for the thousandth time that I *will* follow that pointless pattern to some sort of a conclusion.

I know a little of the principle of design, and I know this thing was not arranged on any laws of radiation,° or alternation, or repetition, or symmetry, or anything else that I ever heard of.

It is repeated, of course, by the breadths, but not otherwise.   95

Looked at in one way, each breadth stands alone; the bloated curves and flour-ishes—a kind of "debased Romanesque" with *delirium tremens*—go waddling up and down in isolated columns of fatuity.

But, on the other hand, they connect diagonally, and the sprawling outlines run off in great slanting waves of optic horror, like a lot of wallowing sea-weeds in full chase.

The whole thing goes horizontally, too, at least it seems so, and I exhaust myself trying to distinguish the order of its going in that direction.

They have used a horizontal breadth for a frieze, and that adds wonderfully to the confusion.

There is one end of the room where it is almost intact, and there, when the   100
crosslights fade and the low sun shines directly upon it, I can almost fancy radiation after all—the interminable grotesque seems to form around a common center and rush off in headlong plunges of equal distraction.

It makes me tired to follow it. I will take a nap, I guess.

I don't know why I should write this.

I don't want to.

I don't feel able.

And I know John would think it absurd. But I *must* say what I feel and think in   105
some way—it is such a relief!

But the effort is getting to be greater than the relief.

Half the time now I am awfully lazy, and lie down ever so much. John says I mustn't lose my strength, and has me take cod liver oil and lots of tonics and things, to say nothing of ale and wines and rare meat.

Dear John! He loves me very dearly, and hates to have me sick. I tried to have a real earnest reasonable talk with him the other day, and tell him how I wish he would let me go and make a visit to Cousin Henry and Julia.

But he said I wasn't able to go, nor able to stand it after I got there; and I did not make out a very good case for myself, for I was crying before I had finished.

It is getting to be a great effort for me to think straight. Just this nervous weak-   110
ness, I suppose.

And dear John gathered me up in his arms, and just carried me upstairs and laid me on the bed, and sat by me and read to me till it tired my head.

He said I was his darling and his comfort and all he had, and that I must take care of myself for his sake, and keep well.

---

laws of radiation: a principle of design in which all elements are arranged in some circular pattern around a center.

He says no one but myself can help me out of it, that I must use my will and self-control and not let any silly fancies run away with me.

There's one comfort—the baby is well and happy, and does not have to occupy this nursery with the horrid wallpaper.

If we had not used it, that blessed child would have! What a fortunate escape! 115 Why, I wouldn't have a child of mine, an impressionable little thing, live in such a room for worlds.

I never thought of it before, but it is lucky that John kept me here after all; I can stand it so much easier than a baby, you see.

Of course I never mention it to them any more—I am too wise—but I keep watch for it all the same.

There are things in the wallpaper that nobody knows about but me, or ever will.

Behind that outside pattern the dim shapes get clearer every day.

It is always the same shape, only very numerous. 120

And it is like a woman stooping down and creeping about behind that pattern. I don't like it a bit. I wonder—I begin to think—I wish John would take me away from here!

It is so hard to talk with John about my case, because he is so wise, and because he loves me so.

But I tried it last night.

It was moonlight. The moon shines in all around just as the sun does.

I hate to see it sometimes, it creeps so slowly, and always comes in by one win- 125 dow or another.

John was asleep and I hated to waken him, so I kept still and watched the moonlight on that undulating wallpaper till I felt creepy.

The faint figure behind seemed to shake the pattern, just as if she wanted to get out.

I got up softly and went to feel and see if the paper *did* move, and when I came back John was awake.

"What is it, little girl?" he said. "Don't go walking about like that—you'll get cold."

I thought it was a good time to talk, so I told him that I really was not gaining 130 here, and that I wished he would take me away.

"Why, darling!" said he. "Our lease will be up in three weeks, and I can't see how to leave before.

"The repairs are not done at home, and I cannot possibly leave town just now. Of course, if you were in any danger, I could and would, but you really are better, dear, whether you can see it or not. I am a doctor, dear, and I know. You are gaining flesh and color, your appetite is better, I feel really much easier about you."

"I don't weigh a bit more," said I, "nor as much; and my appetite may be better in the evening when you are here but it is worse in the morning when you are away!"

"Bless her little heart!" said he with a big hug. "She shall be as sick as she pleases! But now let's improve the shining hours by going to sleep, and talk about it in the morning!"

"And you won't go away?" I asked gloomily. 135

"Why, how can I, dear? It is only three weeks more and then we will take a nice little trip for a few days while Jennie is getting the house ready. Really, dear, you are better!"

"Better in body perhaps—" I began, and stopped short, for he sat up straight and looked at me with such a stern, reproachful look that I could not say another word.

"My darling," said he, "I beg you, for my sake and for our child's sake, as well as for your own, that you will never for one instant let that idea enter your mind! There is nothing so dangerous, so fascinating, to a temperament like yours. It is a false and foolish fancy. Can you trust me as a physician when I tell you so?"

So of course I said no more on that score, and we went to sleep before long. He thought I was asleep first, but I wasn't, and lay there for hours trying to decide whether that front pattern and the back pattern really did move together or separately.

On a pattern like this, by daylight, there is a lack of sequence, a defiance of law,   140 that is a constant irritant to a normal mind.

The color is hideous enough, and unreliable enough, and infuriating enough, but the pattern is torturing.

You think you have mastered it, but just as you get well under way in following, it turns a back-somersault and there you are. It slaps you in the face, knocks you down, and tramples upon you. It is like a bad dream.

The outside pattern is a florid arabesque,° reminding one of a fungus. If you can imagine a toadstool in joints, an interminable string of toadstools, budding and sprouting in endless convolutions—why, that is something like it.

That is, sometimes!

There is one marked peculiarity about this paper, a thing nobody seems to notice   145 but myself, and that is that it changes as the light changes.

When the sun shoots in through the east window—I always watch for that first long, straight ray—it changes so quickly that I never can quite believe it.

That is why I watch it always.

By moonlight—the moon shines in all night when there is a moon—I wouldn't know it was the same paper.

At night in any kind of light, in twilight, candlelight, lamplight, and worst of all by moonlight, it becomes bars! The outside pattern, I mean, and the woman behind it is as plain as can be.

I didn't realize for a long time what the thing was that showed behind, that dim   150 sub-pattern, but now I am quite sure it is a woman.

By daylight she is subdued, quiet. I fancy it is the pattern that keeps her so still. It is so puzzling. It keeps me quiet by the hour.

I lie down ever so much now. John says it is good for me, and to sleep all I can.

Indeed he started the habit by making me lie down for an hour after each meal.

It is a very bad habit, I am convinced, for you see, I don't sleep.

And that cultivates deceit, for I don't tell them I'm awake—oh, no!   155

The fact is I am getting a little afraid of John.

He seems very queer sometimes, and even Jennie has an inexplicable look.

It strikes me occasionally, just as a scientific hypothesis, that perhaps it is the paper!

I have watched John when he did not know I was looking, and come into the room suddenly on the most innocent excuses, and I've caught him several times *looking at the paper!* And Jennie too. I caught Jennie with her hand on it once.

She didn't know I was in the room, and when I asked her in a quiet, a very quiet   160 voice, with the most restrained manner possible, what she was doing with the paper,

---

arabesque: a type of ornamental style (Arabic in origin) that uses flowers, foliage, fruit, or other figures to create an intricate pattern of interlocking shapes and lines.

she turned around as if she had been caught stealing, and looked quite angry—asked me why I should frighten her so!

Then she said that the paper stained everything it touched, that she had found yellow smooches° on all my clothes and John's and she wished we would be more careful!

Did not that sound innocent? But I know she was studying that pattern, and I am determined that nobody shall find it out but myself!

Life is very much more exciting now than it used to be. You see, I have something more to expect, to look forward to, to watch. I really do eat better, and am more quiet than I was.

John is so pleased to see me improve! He laughed a little the other day, and said I seemed to be flourishing in spite of my wallpaper.

I turned it off with a laugh. I had no intention of telling him it was *because* of the   165
wallpaper—he would make fun of me. He might even want to take me away.

I don't want to leave now until I have found it out. There is a week more, and I think that will be enough.

I'm feeling so much better!

I don't sleep much at night, for it is so interesting to watch developments; but I sleep a good deal during the daytime.

In the daytime it is tiresome and perplexing.

There are always new shoots on the fungus, and new shades of yellow all over it.   170
I cannot keep count of them, though I have tried conscientiously.

It is the strangest yellow, that wallpaper! It makes me think of all the yellow things I ever saw—not beautiful ones like buttercups, but old, foul, bad yellow things.

But there is something else about that paper—the smell! I noticed it the moment we came into the room, but with so much air and sun it was not bad. Now we have had a week of fog and rain, and whether the windows are open or not, the smell is here.

It creeps all over the house.

I find it hovering in the dining-room, skulking in the parlor, hiding in the hall, lying in wait for me on the stairs.

It gets into my hair.   175

Even when I go to ride, if I turn my head suddenly and surprise it—there is that smell!

Such a peculiar odor, too! I have spent hours in trying to analyze it, to find what it smelled like.

It is not bad—at first—and very gentle, but quite the subtlest, most enduring odor I ever met.

In this damp weather it is awful. I wake up in the night and find it hanging over me.

It used to disturb me at first. I thought seriously of burning the house—to reach   180
the smell.

But now I am used to it. The only thing I can think of that it is like is the *color* of the paper! A yellow smell.

There is a very funny mark on this wall, low down, near the mopboard. A streak that runs round the room. It goes behind every piece of furniture, except the bed, a long, straight, even *smooch,* as if it had been rubbed over and over.

---

smooches: smudges or smears.

I wonder how it was done and who did it, and what they did it for. Round and round and round—round and round and round—it makes me dizzy!

I really have discovered something at last.

Through watching so much at night, when it changes so, I have finally found out. 185
The front pattern *does* move—and no wonder! The woman behind shakes it!

Sometimes I think there are a great many women behind, and sometimes only one, and she crawls around fast, and her crawling shakes it all over.

Then in the very bright spots she keeps still, and in the very shady spots she just takes hold of the bars and shakes them hard.

And she is all the time trying to climb through. But nobody could climb through that pattern—it strangles so; I think that is why it has so many heads.

They get through and then the pattern strangles them off and turns them upside 190
down, and makes their eyes white!

If those heads were covered or taken off it would not be half so bad.

I think that woman gets out in the daytime!

And I'll tell you why—privately—I've seen her!

I can see her out of every one of my windows!

It is the same woman, I know, for she is always creeping, and most women do not 195
creep by daylight.

I see her in that long shaded lane, creeping up and down. I see her in those dark grape arbors, creeping all round the garden.

I see her on that long road under the trees, creeping along, and when a carriage comes she hides under the blackberry vines.

I don't blame her a bit. It must be very humiliating to be caught creeping by daylight!

I always lock the door when I creep by daylight. I can't do it at night, for I know John would suspect something at once.

And John is so queer now that I don't want to irritate him. I wish he would take 200
another room! Besides, I don't want anybody to get that woman out at night but myself.

I often wonder if I could see her out of all the windows at once.

But, turn as fast as I can, I can only see out of one at one time.

And though I always see her, she *may* be able to creep faster than I can turn! I have watched her sometimes away off in the open country, creeping as fast as a cloud shadow in a wind.

If only that top pattern could be gotten off from the under one! I mean to try it, little by little.

I have found out another funny thing, but I shan't tell it this time! It does not do 205
to trust people too much.

There are only two more days to get this paper off, and I believe John is beginning to notice. I don't like the look in his eyes.

And I heard him ask Jennie a lot of professional questions about me. She had a very good report to give.

She said I slept a good deal in the daytime.

John knows I don't sleep very well at night, for all I'm so quiet!

He asked me all sorts of questions too, and pretended to be very loving and kind. 210

As if I couldn't see through him!

Still, I don't wonder he acts so, sleeping under this paper for three months.

It only interests me, but I feel sure John and Jennie are affected by it.

Hurrah! This is the last day, but it is enough. John is to stay in town over night, and won't be out until this evening.

Jennie wanted to sleep with me—the sly thing; but I told her I should undoubt-   215
edly rest better for a night all alone.

That was clever, for really I wasn't alone a bit! As soon as it was moonlight and that poor thing began to crawl and shake the pattern, I got up and ran to help her.

I pulled and she shook. I shook and she pulled, and before morning we had peeled off yards of that paper.

A strip about as high as my head and half around the room.

And then when the sun came and that awful pattern began to laugh at me, I declared I would finish it today!

We go away tomorrow, and they are moving all my furniture down again to leave   220
things as they were before.

Jennie looked at the wall in amazement, but I told her merrily that I did it out of pure spite at the vicious thing.

She laughed and said she wouldn't mind doing it herself, but I must not get tired.

How she betrayed herself that time!

But I am here, and no person touches this paper but me—not *alive!*

She tried to get me out of the room—it was too patent! But I said it was so quiet   225
and empty and clean now that I believed I would lie down again and sleep all I could, and not to wake me even for dinner—I would call when I woke.

So now she is gone, and the servants are gone, and the things are gone, and there is nothing left but that great bedstead nailed down, with the canvas mattress we found on it.

We shall sleep downstairs tonight, and take the boat home tomorrow.

I quite enjoy the room, now it is bare again.

How those children did tear about here!

This bedstead is fairly gnawed!   230

But I must get to work.

I have locked the door and thrown the key down into the front path.

I don't want to go out, and I don't want to have anybody come in, till John comes.

I want to astonish him.

I've got a rope up here that even Jennie did not find. If that woman does get out,   235
and tries to get away, I can tie her!

But I forgot I could not reach far without anything to stand on!

This bed will *not* move!

I tried to lift and push it until I was lame, and then I got so angry I bit off a little piece at one corner—but it hurt my teeth.

Then I peeled off all the paper I could reach standing on the floor. It sticks horribly and the pattern just enjoys it! All those strangled heads and bulbous eyes and waddling fungus growths just shriek with derision!

I am getting angry enough to do something desperate. To jump out of the win-   240
dow would be admirable exercise, but the bars are too strong even to try.

Besides I wouldn't do it. Of course not. I know well enough that a step like that is improper and might be misconstrued.

I don't like to *look* out of the windows even—there are so many of those creeping women, and they creep so fast.

I wonder if they all come out of that wallpaper as I did!

But I am securely fastened now by my well-hidden rope—you don't get *me* out in the road there!

I suppose I shall have to get back behind the pattern when it comes night, and that is hard! 245

It is so pleasant to be out in this great room and creep around as I please!

I don't want to go outside. I won't, even if Jennie asks me to.

For outside you have to creep on the ground, and everything is green instead of yellow.

But here I can creep smoothly on the floor, and my shoulder just fits in that long smooch around the wall, so I cannot lose my way.

Why, there's John at the door! 250

It is no use, young man, you can't open it!

How he does call and pound!

Now he's crying to Jennie for an axe.

It would be a shame to break down that beautiful door!

"John, dear!" said I in the gentlest voice. "The key is down by the front steps, un- der a plantain leaf!" 255

That silenced him for a few moments.

Then he said, very quietly indeed, "Open the door, my darling!"

"I can't," said I. "The key is down by the front door under a plantain leaf!" And then I said it again, several times, very gently and slowly, and said it so often that he had to go and see, and he got it of course, and came in. He stopped short by the door.

"What is the matter?" he cried. "For God's sake, what are you doing!"

I kept on creeping just the same, but I looked at him over my shoulder. 260

"I've got out at last," said I, "in spite of you and Jane. And I've pulled off most of the paper, so you can't put me back!"

Now why should that man have fainted? But he did, and right across my path by the wall, so that I had to creep over him every time!

Questions

1. Several times at the beginning of the story, the narrator says such things as "What is one to do?" and "What can one do?" What do these comments refer to? What, if anything, do they suggest about women's roles at the time the story was written?

2. The narrator says, "I get unreasonably angry with John sometimes" (paragraph 24). How unreasonable is her anger at him? What does the fact that she feels it is unreasonable say about her?

3. What do her changing feelings about the wallpaper tell us about the changes in her condition?

4. "It is so hard to talk with John about my case, because he is so wise, and because he loves me so" (paragraph 122). His wisdom is, to say the least, open to question, but what about his love? Do you think he suffers merely from a failure of perception, or is there a failure of affection as well? Explain your response.

5. Where precisely in the story do you think it becomes clear that she has begun to hallucinate?

6. What does the woman behind the wallpaper represent? Why does the narrator come to identify with her?

7. How ill does the narrator seem at the beginning of the story? How ill does she seem at the end? How do you account for the change in her condition?

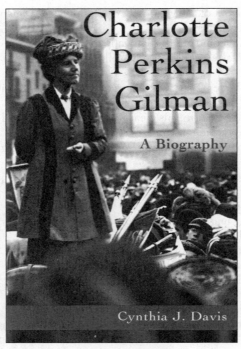

Charlotte Perkins Gilman: A Biography by Cynthia Davis.

CHARLOTTE PERKINS GILMAN ON WRITING

Why I Wrote "The Yellow Wallpaper" 1913

Many and many a reader has asked that. When the story first came out, in the *New England Magazine* about 1891, a Boston physician made protest in *The Transcript*. Such a story ought not to be written, he said; it was enough to drive anyone mad to read it.

Another physician, in Kansas I think, wrote to say that it was the best description of incipient insanity he had ever seen, and—begging my pardon—had I been there?

Now the story of the story is this: For many years I suffered from a severe and continuous nervous breakdown tending to melancholia—and beyond. During about the third year of this trouble I went, in devout faith and some faint stir of hope, to a noted specialist in nervous diseases, the best known in the country. This wise man put me to bed and applied the rest cure, to which a still-good physique responded so promptly that he concluded there was nothing much the matter with me, and sent me home with solemn advice to "live as domestic a life as far as possible," to "have but two hours' intellectual life a day," and "never to touch pen, brush, or pencil again" as long as I lived. This was in 1887.

I went home and obeyed those directions for some three months, and came so near the borderline of utter mental ruin that I could see over.

Then, using the remnants of intelligence that remained, and helped by a wise friend, I cast the noted specialist's advice to the winds and went to work again—work, the normal life of every human being; work, in which is joy and growth and service, without which one is a pauper and a parasite—ultimately recovering some measure of power.

Being naturally moved to rejoicing by this narrow escape, I wrote "The Yellow Wallpaper," with its embellishments and additions, to carry out the ideal (I never had hallucinations or objections to my mural decorations) and sent a copy to the physician who so nearly drove me mad. He never acknowledged it.

The little book is valued by alienists and as a good specimen of one kind of literature. It has, to my knowledge, saved one woman from a similar fate—so terrifying her family that they let her out into normal activity and she recovered.

But the best result is this. Many years later I was told that the great specialist had admitted to friends of his that he had altered his treatment of neurasthenia since reading "The Yellow Wallpaper."

It was not intended to drive people crazy, but to save people from being driven crazy, and it worked.

From *The Forerunner*, October 1913

Whatever Is   1903

Whatever is we only know
As in our minds we find it so;
   No staring fact is half so clear
   As one dim, preconceived idea—
No matter how the fact may glow.   5

Vainly may Truth her trumpet blow
To stir our minds; like heavy dough
   They stick to what they think—won't hear
      Whatever is.

Our ancient myths in solid row   10
Stand up—we simply have to go
   And choke each fiction old and dear
   Before the modest facts appear;
Then we may grasp, reluctant, slow,
      Whatever is.   15

The Nervous Breakdown of Women   1916

[A]s a hindrance they [women] have to meet something which men have never met—the cold and cruel opposition of the other sex. In every step of their long upward path men have had women with them, never against them. In hardship, in privation, in danger, in the last test of religious martyrdom, in the pains and terrors of warfare, in rebellions and revolutions, men have had women with them. Individual women have no doubt been a hindrance to individual men, and the economic dependence of women is a drag upon men's freedom of action; but at no step of man's difficult advance has he had to meet the scorn, the neglect, the open vilification of massed womanhood.

No one has seemed to notice the cost of this great artificial barrier to the advance of woman, the effect upon her nervous system of opposition and abuse from the quarter where nature and tradition had taught her to expect aid and comfort. She has had to keep pace with him in meeting the demands of our swiftly changing times. She has had to meet the additional demands of her own even more swiftly changing conditions. And she has had to do this in the face not only of the organized opposition of the other sex, entrenched in secure possession of all the advantageous positions of church and state, buttressed by law and custom, fully trained and experienced, and holding all the ammunition—the "sinews of war"—the whole money power of the world; but besides this her slow, difficult, conscientious efforts to make the changes she knew were right, or which were forced upon her by conditions, have too often cost her man's love, respect and good will.

This is a heavy price to pay for progress.

We should be more than gentle with the many women who cannot yet meet it.

We should be more than grateful for those strong men who are more human than male, who can feel, think and act above the limitations of their sex, and who have helped women in their difficult advance.

Also we should deeply honor those great women of the last century, who met all demands, paid every exaction, faced all opposition and made the way easier for us now.

But we should not be surprised at the "nervous breakdown" of some women, nor attribute it to weakness.

Only the measureless strength of the mother sex could have enabled women to survive the sufferings of yesterday and to meet the exactions of today.

From *The Forerunner*, July–August 1916

CRITICS ON "THE YELLOW WALLPAPER"

Juliann Fleenor (b. 1942)

Gender and Pathology in "The Yellow Wallpaper" 1983

Although it is not generally known, Gilman wrote at least two other Gothic stories around the same time as "The Yellow Wallpaper." All three were published in the *New England Magazine*. At the time that "The Rocking Chair" and "The Giant Wistaria" were written, Gilman and her young daughter, Katherine, were living in the warmth of Pasadena, separated from her husband, Charles Walter Stetson. Gilman later noted in her papers: "'The Yellow Wallpaper' was written in two days, with the thermometer at one hundred and three in Pasadena, Ca." Her husband was living on the east coast, and, perhaps coincidentally, all three stories appear to be set in a nameless eastern setting, one urban and two rural. All three display similar themes, and all three are evidence that the conflict, central to Gilman's Gothic fiction and later to her autobiography, was a conflict with the mother, with motherhood, and with creation.

In all three stories women are confined within the home; it is their prison, their insane asylum, even their tomb. A sense of the female isolation which Gilman felt, of exclusion from the public world of work and of men, is contained in the anecdote related by Zona Gale in her introduction to Gilman's autobiography. After watching the approach of several locomotives to a train platform in a small town in Wisconsin, Gilman said, "'All that, . . . and women have no part in it. Everything done by men, working together, while women worked on alone within their four walls!'" Female exclusion, women denied the opportunity to work, or their imprisonment behind four walls, led to madness. Her image, interestingly, does not suggest a female subculture of women working together; Gilman was working against her own culture's definition of women, and her primary antagonists were women like her own mother.

A Massachusetts hospital for the insane in the era of Charlotte Perkins Gilman's "The Yellow Wallpaper."

Diseased maternity is explicit in Gilman's third Gothic story. The yellow wallpaper symbolizes more than confinement, victimization, and the inability to write. It suggests a disease within the female self. When the narrator peels the wallpaper off, "It sticks horribly and the pattern just enjoys it! All those strangled heads and bulbous eyes and waddling fungus growths just shriek with derision." This passage describes more than the peeling of wallpaper: the "strangled heads and bulbous eyes and waddling fungus" imply something strange and terrible about birth and death conjoined, about female procreation, and about female physiology. Nature is perverted here, too. The narrator thinks of "old, foul, bad yellow things." The smell "creeps all over the house." She finds it "hovering in the dining-room, skulking in the parlor, hiding in the hall, lying in wait for me on the stairs." Finally, "it gets into my hair."

The paper stains the house in a way that suggests the effect of afterbirth. The house, specifically this room, becomes more than a symbol of a repressive society; it represents the physical self of the narrator as well. She is disgusted, perhaps awed, perhaps frightened of her own bodily processes. The story establishes a sense of fear and disgust, the skin crawls and grows clammy with the sense of physiological fear that Ellen Moers refers to as the Female Gothic.

My contention is that one of the major themes in the story, punishment for becoming a mother (as well as punishment for being female), is supported by the absence of the child. The child is taken away from the mother, almost in punishment, as was the child in "The Giant Wistaria." This differs from Gilman's experience; she had been told to keep her child with her at all times. In both the story and in Gilman's life, a breakdown occurs directly after the birth of a child. The narrator is confined as if she had committed a crime. Maternity—the creation of a child—is combined with writing—the creation of writing—in a way that suggests they are interrelated and perhaps symbiotic, as are the strange toadstools behind the wallpaper.

The pathological nature of both experiences is not surprising, given the treatment Gilman received, and given the fact that maternity reduced women to mothers and not writers. Childbirth has long been a rite of passage for women. But the question is, where does that passage lead? Becoming a mother leads to a child-like state. The narrator becomes the absent child.

From "The Gothic Prism"

Sandra M. Gilbert (b. 1936) and Susan Gubar (b. 1944)

Imprisonment and Escape: The Psychology of Confinement   1979

["The Yellow Wallpaper" is a] striking story of female confinement and escape, a paradigmatic tale which (like *Jane Eyre*) seems to tell *the* story that all literary women would tell if they could speak their "speechless woe." "The Yellow Wallpaper," which Gilman herself called "a description of a case of nervous breakdown," recounts in the first person the experiences of a woman who is evidently suffering from a severe postpartum psychosis. Her husband, a censorious and paternalistic physician, is treating her according to methods by which S. Weir Mitchell, a famous "nerve specialist," treated Gilman herself for a similar problem. He has confined her to a large garret room in an "ancestral hall" he has rented, and he has forbidden her to touch pen to paper until she is well again, for he feels, says the narrator, "that with my imaginative power and habit of story-making, a nervous weakness like mine is sure to lead to all manner of excited fancies, and that I ought to use my will and good sense to check the tendency."

The cure, of course, is worse than the disease, for the sick woman's mental condition deteriorates rapidly. "I think sometimes that if I were only well enough to write a little it would relieve the press of ideas and rest me," she remarks, but literally confined in a room she thinks is a one-time nursery because it has "rings and things" in the walls, she is literally locked away from creativity. The "rings and things," although reminiscent of children's gymnastic equipment, are really the paraphernalia of confinement, like the gate at the head of the stairs, instruments that definitively indicate her imprisonment. Even more tormenting, however, is the room's wallpaper: a sulfurous yellow paper, torn off in spots, and patterned with "lame uncertain curves" that "plunge off at outrageous angles" and "destroy themselves in unheard-of contradictions." Ancient, smoldering, "unclean" as the oppressive structures of the society in which she finds herself, this paper surrounds the narrator like an inexplicable text, censorious and overwhelming as her physician husband, haunting as the "hereditary estate" in which she is trying to survive. Inevitably she studies its suicidal implications—and inevitably, because of her "imaginative power and habit of story-making," she revises it, projecting her own passion for escape into its otherwise incomprehensible hieroglyphics. "This wallpaper," she decides, at a key point in her story,

has a kind of sub-pattern in a different shade, a particularly irritating one, for you can only see it in certain lights, and not clearly then.
But in the places where it isn't faded and where the sun is just so—I can see a strange, provoking, formless sort of figure that seems to skulk about behind that silly and conspicuous front design.

As time passes, this figure concealed behind what corresponds (in terms of what we have been discussing) to the facade of the patriarchal text becomes clearer and clearer. By moonlight the pattern of the wallpaper "becomes bars! The outside pattern I mean, and the woman behind it is as plain as can be." And eventually, as the narrator sinks more deeply into what the world calls madness, the terrifying implications of both the paper and the figure imprisoned behind the paper begin to permeate—that is, to *haunt*—the rented ancestral mansion in which she and her husband are immured. The "yellow smell" of the paper "creeps all over the house," drenching every room in its subtle aroma of decay. And the woman creeps too—through the house, in the house, and out of the house, in the garden and "on that long road under the trees." Sometimes, indeed, the narrator confesses, "I think there are a great many women" both behind the paper and creeping in the garden,

> and sometimes only one, and she crawls around fast, and her crawling shakes [the paper] all over. . . . And she is all the time trying to climb through. But nobody could climb through that pattern—it strangles so; I think that is why it has so many heads.

Eventually it becomes obvious to both reader and narrator that the figure creeping through and behind the wallpaper is both the narrator and the narrator's double. By the end of the story, moreover, the narrator has enabled this double to escape from her textual/architectural confinement: "I pulled and she shook, I shook and she pulled, and before morning we had peeled off yards of that paper." Is the message of the tale's conclusion mere madness? Certainly the righteous Doctor John—whose name links him to the anti-hero of Charlotte Bronte's *Villette*—has been temporarily defeated, or at least momentarily stunned. "Now why should that man have fainted?" the narrator ironically asks as she creeps around her attic. But John's unmasculine swoon of surprise is the least of the triumphs Gilman imagines for her madwoman. More significant are the madwoman's own imaginings and creations, mirages of health and freedom with which her author endows her like a fairy godmother showering gold on a sleeping heroine. The woman from behind the wallpaper creeps away, for instance, creeps fast and far on the long road, in broad daylight. "I have watched her sometimes away off in the open country," says the narrator, "creeping as fast as a cloud shadow in a high wind."

Indistinct and yet rapid, barely perceptible but inexorable, the progress of that cloud shadow is not unlike the progress of nineteenth-century literary women out of the texts defined by patriarchal poetics into the open spaces of their own authority. That such an escape from the numb world behind the patterned walls of the text was a flight from disease into health was quite clear to Gilman herself. When "The Yellow Wallpaper" was published she sent it to Weir Mitchell, whose strictures had kept her from attempting the pen during her own breakdown, thereby aggravating her illness, and she was delighted to learn, years later, that "he had changed his treatment of nervous prostration since reading" her story. "If that is a fact," she declared, "I have not lived in vain."

From *The Madwoman in the Attic*

Elizabeth Ammons

Biographical Echoes in "The Yellow Wallpaper"   1991

"The Yellow Wallpaper" probably had deep roots in Gilman's childhood. In her autobiography, the account she gives of her growing up focuses on the misery of her mother, a woman who adored her husband and loved having babies, only to have her husband leave and her babies grow up. Deserted, Gilman's mother—in the daughter's telling—grew bitter and fiercely repressed, deciding not to show any affection for her daughter in order to toughen the child. Life, as Gilman's mother had come to know it, brought women terrible disappointment and denial. Only in the dead of night would she allow herself to hug her daughter.

As a story about her mother, the early portions of Gilman's autobiography construct a family drama in which sexual desire in a woman leads to babies and death. (According to Gilman, her mother was warned that one more pregnancy would kill her, at which point the father left the family.) On the other hand, denial of sexual desire, the celibate life that Mary Fitch Perkins knew when her husband left, resulted in furious repression and frustration. Either way, female sexual desire, motherhood, and masculine power were bitterly entangled for Gilman's mother, who even after years of separation and rejection remained her husband's prisoner, calling for him on her deathbed. Looked at from the child's point of view, Charlotte Perkins Gilman clearly both admired and hated her father. Frederick Beecher Perkins's power over his wife was so strong that she had to stamp out all that was free and physical and warm in herself, and try to do the same to her daughter. In a sense the woman on her knees at the end of "The Yellow Wallpaper," the prisoner of a charming man and an ugly empty domestic life that she cannot escape, is Gilman's mother as the child experienced her while growing up—humiliated, angry, crushed.

The drama of patriarchal control in "The Yellow Wallpaper" is the same one that Charlotte Perkins Gilman felt as a child, saw in her mother's life, and then experienced again herself as a young wife and mother. The story is not limited to just one stage of her life as a woman, but applies potentially to all stages, from childhood to old age. It is not, moreover, simply a story about the desire for escape from male control. It is also a story about the desire to escape to a female world, a desire to unite with the mother, indeed with all women creeping and struggling in growing numbers, through the paper, behind the wall.

From Conflicting Stories: American Women Writers
at the Turn into the Twentieth Century

ALICE WALKER

Alice Walker, a leading black writer and social activist, was born in 1944 in Eatonton, Georgia, the youngest of eight children. Her father, a sharecropper and dairy farmer, usually earned about $300 a year; her mother helped by working as a maid. Both entertained their children by telling stories. When Alice Walker was eight, she was accidentally struck by a pellet from a brother's BB gun. She lost the sight of her right eye because the Walkers had no car to rush her to the hospital. Later she attended Spelman College in Atlanta and finished college at Sarah Lawrence College on a scholarship. While working for the civil rights movement in Mississippi, she met a young lawyer, Melvyn Leventhal. In 1967 they settled in Jackson, Mississippi, the first legally married interracial couple in town. They returned to New York in 1974 and

Alice Walker

were later divorced. First known as a poet, Walker has published eight books of her verse. She also has edited a collection of the work of the then-neglected black writer Zora Neale Hurston, and has written a study of Langston Hughes. In a collection of essays, In Search of Our Mothers' Gardens: Womanist Prose *(1983), she recalls her mother and addresses her own daughter. (By* womanist *she means "black feminist.") But the largest part of Walker's reading audience knows her fiction: four story collections, including* In Love and Trouble *(1973), from which "Everyday Use" is taken, and her many novels. Her best-known novel,* The Color Purple *(1982), won a Pulitzer Prize and was made into a film by Steven Spielberg in 1985. Her recent novels include* By the Light of My Father's Smile *(1998) and* Now Is the Time to Open Your Heart *(2004). Walker lives in Northern California.*

Everyday Use

1973

for your grandmama

I will wait for her in the yard that Maggie and I made so clean and wavy yesterday afternoon. A yard like this is more comfortable than most people know. It is not just a yard. It is like an extended living room. When the hard clay is swept clean as a floor and the fine sand around the edges lined with tiny, irregular grooves, anyone can come and sit and look up into the elm tree and wait for the breezes that never come inside the house.

Maggie will be nervous until after her sister goes: she will stand hopelessly in corners, homely and ashamed of the burn scars down her arms and legs, eyeing her sister with a mixture of envy and awe. She thinks her sister has held life always in the palm of one hand, that "no" is a word the world never learned to say to her.

You've no doubt seen those TV shows where the child who has "made it" is confronted, as a surprise, by her own mother and father, tottering in weakly from backstage. (A pleasant surprise, of course: What would they do if parent and child came on the show only to curse out and insult each other?) On TV mother and child embrace and smile into each other's faces. Sometimes the mother and father weep, the child wraps them in her arms and leans across the table to tell how she would not have made it without their help. I have seen these programs.°

Sometimes I dream a dream in which Dee and I are suddenly brought together on a TV program of this sort. Out of a dark and soft-seated limousine I am ushered into a bright room filled with many people. There I meet a smiling, gray, sporty man like Johnny Carson who shakes my hand and tells me what a fine girl I have. Then we are on the stage and Dee is embracing me with tears in her eyes. She pins on my dress a large orchid, even though she has told me once that she thinks orchids are tacky flowers.

In real life I am a large, big-boned woman with rough, man-working hands. In   5
the winter I wear flannel nightgowns to bed and overalls during the day. I can kill and clean a hog as mercilessly as a man. My fat keeps me hot in zero weather. I can work outside all day, breaking ice to get water for washing. I can eat pork liver cooked over the open fire minutes after it comes steaming from the hog. One winter I knocked a bull calf straight in the brain between the eyes with a sledge hammer and had the meat hung up to chill before nightfall. But of course all this does not show on television. I am the way my daughter would want me to be: a hundred pounds lighter, my skin like an uncooked barley pancake. My hair glistens in the hot bright lights. Johnny Carson has much to do to keep up with my quick and witty tongue.

But that is a mistake. I know even before I wake up. Who ever knew a Johnson with a quick tongue? Who can even imagine me looking a strange white man in the eye? It seems to me I have talked to them always with one foot raised in flight, with my head turned in whichever way is farthest from them. Dee, though. She would always look anyone in the eye. Hesitation was no part of her nature.

"How do I look, Mama?" Maggie says, showing just enough of her thin body enveloped in pink skirt and red blouse for me to know she's there, almost hidden by the door.

"Come out into the yard," I say.

Have you ever seen a lame animal, perhaps a dog run over by some careless person rich enough to own a car, sidle up to someone who is ignorant enough to be kind to him? That is the way my Maggie walks. She has been like this, chin on chest, eyes on ground, feet in shuffle, ever since the fire that burned the other house to the ground.

Dee is lighter than Maggie, with nicer hair and a fuller figure. She's a woman   10
now, though sometimes I forget. How long ago was it that the other house burned? Ten, twelve years? Sometimes I can still hear the flames and feel Maggie's arms sticking to me, her hair smoking and her dress falling off her in little black papery flakes. Her eyes seemed stretched open, blazed open by the flames reflected in them. And Dee. I see her standing off under the sweet gum tree she used to dig gum out of; a look of concentration on her face as she watched the last dingy gray board of the house fall in toward the red-hot brick chimney. Why don't you do a dance around the ashes? I'd wanted to ask her. She had hated the house that much.

I used to think she hated Maggie, too. But that was before we raised the money, the church and me, to send her to Augusta to school. She used to read to us without pity; forcing words, lies, other folks' habits, whole lives upon us two, sitting trapped

---

these programs: On the NBC television show *This Is Your Life,* people were publicly and often tearfully reunited with friends, relatives, and teachers they had not seen in years.

and ignorant underneath her voice. She washed us in a river of make-believe, burned us with a lot of knowledge we didn't necessarily need to know. Pressed us to her with the serious way she read, to shove us away at just the moment, like dimwits, we seemed about to understand.

Dee wanted nice things. A yellow organdy dress to wear to her graduation from high school; black pumps to match a green suit she'd made from an old suit somebody gave me. She was determined to stare down any disaster in her efforts. Her eyelids would not flicker for minutes at a time. Often I fought off the temptation to shake her. At sixteen she had a style of her own: and knew what style was.

I never had an education myself. After second grade the school was closed down. Don't ask me why: in 1927 colored asked fewer questions than they do now. Sometimes Maggie reads to me. She stumbles along good-naturedly but can't see well. She knows she is not bright. Like good looks and money, quickness passed her by. She will marry John Thomas (who has mossy teeth in an earnest face) and then I'll be free to sit here and I guess just sing church songs to myself. Although I never was a good singer. Never could carry a tune. I was always better at a man's job. I used to love to milk till I was hoofed in the side in '49. Cows are soothing and slow and don't bother you, unless you try to milk them the wrong way.

I have deliberately turned my back on the house. It is three rooms, just like the one that burned, except the roof is tin; they don't make shingle roofs any more. There are no real windows, just some holes cut in the sides, like the portholes in a ship, but not round and not square, with rawhide holding the shutters up on the outside. This house is in a pasture, too, like the other one. No doubt when Dee sees it she will want to tear it down. She wrote me once that no matter where we "choose" to live, she will manage to come see us. But she will never bring her friends. Maggie and I thought about this and Maggie asked me, "Mama, when did Dee ever *have* any friends?"

She had a few. Furtive boys in pink shirts hanging about on washday after   15
school. Nervous girls who never laughed. Impressed with her they worshiped the well-turned phrase, the cute shape, the scalding humor that erupted like bubbles in lye. She read to them.

When she was courting Jimmy T she didn't have much time to pay to us, but turned all her faultfinding power on him. He *flew* to marry a cheap city girl from a family of ignorant flashy people. She hardly had time to recompose herself.

When she comes I will meet—but there they are!

Maggie attempts to make a dash for the house, in her shuffling way, but I stay her with my hand. "Come back here," I say. And she stops and tries to dig a well in the sand with her toe.

It is hard to see them clearly through the strong sun. But even the first glimpse of leg out of the car tells me it is Dee. Her feet were always neat-looking, as if God himself had shaped them with a certain style. From the other side of the car comes a short, stocky man. Hair is all over his head a foot long and hanging from his chin like a kinky mule tail. I hear Maggie suck in her breath. "Uhnnnh," is what it sounds like. Like when you see the wriggling end of a snake just in front of your foot on the road. "Uhnnnh."

Dee next. A dress down to the ground, in this hot weather. A dress so loud it   20
hurts my eyes. There are yellows and oranges enough to throw back the light of the sun. I feel my whole face warming from the heat waves it throws out. Earrings, too,

gold and hanging down to her shoulders. Bracelets dangling and making noises when she moves her arm up to shake the folds of the dress out of her armpits. The dress is loose and flows, and as she walks closer, I like it. I hear Maggie go "Uhnnnh" again. It is her sister's hair. It stands straight up like the wool on a sheep. It is black as night and around the edges are two long pigtails that rope about like small lizards disappearing behind her ears.

"Wa-su-zo-Tean-o!"° she says, coming on in that gliding way the dress makes her move. The short stocky fellow with the hair to his navel is all grinning and he follows up with "Asalamalakim,° my mother and sister!" He moves to hug Maggie but she falls back, right up against the back of my chair. I feel her trembling there and when I look up I see the perspiration falling off her chin.

"Don't get up," says Dee. Since I am stout it takes something of a push. You can see me trying to move a second or two before I make it. She turns, showing white heels through her sandals, and goes back to the car. Out she peeks next with a Polaroid. She stoops down quickly and lines up picture after picture of me sitting there in front of the house with Maggie cowering behind me. She never takes a shot without making sure the house is included. When a cow comes nibbling around the edge of the yard she snaps it and me and Maggie *and* the house. Then she puts the Polaroid in the back seat of the car, and comes up and kisses me on the forehead.

Meanwhile Asalamalakim is going through the motions with Maggie's hand. Maggie's hand is as limp as a fish, and probably as cold, despite the sweat, and she keeps trying to pull it back. It looks like Asalamalakim wants to shake hands but wants to do it fancy. Or maybe he don't know how people shake hands. Anyhow, he soon gives up on Maggie.

"Well," I say. "Dee."

"No, Mama," she says. "Not 'Dee,' Wangero Leewanika Kemanjo!"   25

"What happened to 'Dee'?" I wanted to know.

"She's dead," Wangero said. "I couldn't bear it any longer, being named after the people who oppress me."

"You know as well as me you was named after your aunt Dicie," I said. Dicie is my sister. She named Dee. We called her "Big Dee" after Dee was born.

"But who was *she* named after?" asked Wangero.

"I guess after Grandma Dee," I said.   30

"And who was she named after?" asked Wangero.

"Her mother," I said, and saw Wangero was getting tired. "That's about as far back as I can trace it," I said. Though, in fact, I probably could have carried it back beyond the Civil War through the branches.

"Well," said Asalamalakim, "there you are."

"Uhnnnh," I heard Maggie say.

"There I was not," I said, "before 'Dicie' cropped up in our family, so why should   35
I try to trace it that far back?"

He just stood there grinning, looking down on me like somebody inspecting a Model A car.° Every once in a while he and Wangero sent eye signals over my head.

"How do you pronounce this name?" I asked.

"You don't have to call me by it if you don't want to," said Wangero.

"Why shouldn't I?" I asked. "If that's what you want us to call you, we'll call you."

Wa-su-zo-Tean-o!: salutation in Swahili, an African language. Notice that Dee has to sound it out, syllable by syllable. *Asalamalakim*: salutation in Arabic: "Peace be upon you." *Model A car*: popular low-priced automobile introduced by the Ford Motor Company in 1927.

"I know it might sound awkward at first," said Wangero.   40

"I'll get used to it," I said. "Ream it out again."

Well, soon we got the name out of the way. Asalamalakim had a name twice as long and three times as hard. After I tripped over it two or three times he told me to just call him Hakim-a-barber. I wanted to ask him was he a barber, but I didn't really think he was, so I didn't ask.

"You must belong to those beef-cattle peoples down the road," I said. They said "Asalamalakim" when they met you, too, but they didn't shake hands. Always too busy: feeding the cattle, fixing the fences, putting up salt-lick shelters, throwing down hay. When the white folks poisoned some of the herd the men stayed up all night with rifles in their hands. I walked a mile and a half just to see the sight.

Hakim-a-barber said, "I accept some of their doctrines, but farming and raising cattle is not my style." (They didn't tell me, and I didn't ask, whether Wangero (Dee) had really gone and married him.)

We sat down to eat and right away he said he didn't eat collards and pork was   45
unclean. Wangero, though, went on through the chitlins and corn bread, the greens and everything else. She talked a blue streak over the sweet potatoes. Everything delighted her. Even the fact that we still used the benches her daddy made for the table when we couldn't afford to buy chairs.

"Oh, Mama!" she cried. Then turned to Hakim-a-barber. "I never knew how lovely these benches are. You can feel the rump prints," she said, running her hands underneath her and along the bench. Then she gave a sigh and her hand closed over Grandma Dee's butter dish. "That's it!" she said. "I knew there was something I wanted to ask you if I could have." She jumped up from the table and went over in the corner where the churn stood, the milk in it clabber° by now. She looked at the churn and looked at it.

"This churn top is what I need," she said. "Didn't Uncle Buddy whittle it out of a tree you all used to have?"

"Yes," I said.

"Uh huh," she said happily. "And I want the dasher, too."

"Uncle Buddy whittle that, too?" asked the barber.   50

Dee (Wangero) looked up at me.

"Aunt Dee's first husband whittled the dash," said Maggie so low you almost couldn't hear her. "His name was Henry, but they called him Stash."

"Maggie's brain is like an elephant's," Wangero said, laughing. "I can use the churn top as a centerpiece for the alcove table," she said, sliding a plate over the churn, "and I'll think of something artistic to do with the dasher."

When she finished wrapping the dasher the handle stuck out. I took it for a moment in my hands. You didn't even have to look close to see where hands pushing the dasher up and down to make butter had left a kind of sink in the wood. In fact, there were a lot of small sinks; you could see where thumbs and fingers had sunk into the wood. It was beautiful light yellow wood, from a tree that grew in the yard where Big Dee and Stash had lived.

After dinner Dee (Wangero) went to the trunk at the foot of my bed and started   55
rifling through it. Maggie hung back in the kitchen over the dishpan. Out came Wangero with two quilts. They had been pieced by Grandma Dee and then Big Dee and me had hung them on the quilt frames on the front porch and quilted them. One was in the Lone Star pattern. The other was Walk Around the Mountain. In both of them were scraps

clabber: sour milk or buttermilk.

of dresses Grandma Dee had worn fifty and more years ago. Bits and pieces of Grandpa Jarrell's paisley shirts. And one teeny faded blue piece, about the size of a penny matchbox, that was from Great Grandpa Ezra's uniform that he wore in the Civil War.

"Mama," Wangero said sweet as a bird. "Can I have these old quilts?"

I heard something fall in the kitchen, and a minute later the kitchen door slammed.

"Why don't you take one or two of the others?" I asked. "These old things was just done by me and Big Dee from some tops your grandma pieced before she died."

"No," said Wangero. "I don't want those. They are stitched around the borders by machine."

"That'll make them last better," I said.

"That's not the point," said Wangero. "These are all pieces of dresses Grandma used to wear. She did all this stitching by hand. Imagine!" She held the quilts securely in her arms, stroking them.

"Some of the pieces, like those lavender ones, come from old clothes her mother handed down to her," I said, moving up to touch the quilts. Dee (Wangero) moved back just enough so that I couldn't reach the quilts. They already belonged to her.

"Imagine!" she breathed again, clutching them closely to her bosom.

"The truth is," I said, "I promised to give them quilts to Maggie, for when she marries John Thomas."

She gasped like a bee had stung her.

"Maggie can't appreciate these quilts!" she said. "She'd probably be backward enough to put them to everyday use."

"I reckon she would," I said. "God knows I been saving 'em for long enough with nobody using 'em. I hope she will!" I didn't want to bring up how I had offered Dee (Wangero) a quilt when she went away to college. Then she had told me they were old-fashioned, out of style.

"But they're *priceless!*" she was saying now, furiously; for she has a temper. "Maggie would put them on the bed and in five years they'd be in rags. Less than that!"

"She can always make some more," I said. "Maggie knows how to quilt."

Dee (Wangero) looked at me with hatred. "You just will not understand. The point is these quilts, *these* quilts!"

"Well," I said, stumped. "What would *you* do with them?"

"Hang them," she said. As if that was the only thing you *could* do with quilts.

Maggie by now was standing in the door. I could almost hear the sound her feet made as they scraped over each other.

"She can have them, Mama," she said, like somebody used to never winning anything, or having anything reserved for her. "I can 'member Grandma Dee without the quilts."

I looked at her hard. She had filled her bottom lip with checkerberry snuff and it gave her face a kind of dopey, hangdog look. It was Grandma Dee and Big Dee who taught her how to quilt herself. She stood there with her scarred hands hidden in the folds of her skirt. She looked at her sister with something like fear but she wasn't mad at her. This was Maggie's portion. This was the way she knew God to work.

When I looked at her like that something hit me in the top of my head and ran down to the soles of my feet. Just like when I'm in church and the spirit of God touches me and I get happy and shout. I did something I never had done before: hugged Maggie to me, then dragged her on into the room, snatched the quilts out of Miss Wangero's hands and dumped them into Maggie's lap. Maggie just sat there on my bed with her mouth open.

"Take one or two of the others," I said to Dee.

But she turned without a word and went out to Hakim-a-barber.

"You just don't understand," she said, as Maggie and I came out to the car.

"What don't I understand?" I wanted to know.   80

"Your heritage," she said. And then she turned to Maggie, kissed her, and said, "You ought to try to make something of yourself, too, Maggie. It's really a new day for us. But from the way you and Mama still live you'd never know it."

She put on some sunglasses that hid everything above the tip of her nose and her chin.

Maggie smiled; maybe at the sunglasses. But a real smile, not scared. After we watched the car dust settle I asked Maggie to bring me a dip of snuff. And then the two of us sat there just enjoying, until it was time to go in the house and go to bed.

Questions

1. What is the basic conflict in "Everyday Use"?
2. What is the tone of Walker's story? By what means does the author communicate it?
3. From whose point of view is "Everyday Use" told? What does the story gain from being told from this point of view—instead of, say, from the point of view of Dee (Wangero)?
4. What does the narrator of the story feel toward Dee? What seems to be Dee's present attitude toward her mother and sister?
5. What do you take to be the author's attitude toward each of her characters? How does she convey it?
6. What levels of meaning do you find in the story's title?
7. Contrast Dee's attitude toward her heritage with the attitudes of her mother and sister. How much truth is there in Dee's accusation that her mother and sister don't understand their heritage?
8. Does the knowledge that "Everyday Use" was written by a black writer in any way influence your reactions to it? Explain.

ALICE WALKER ON WRITING

The Black Woman Writer in America   1973

Interview by John O'Brien

Interviewer: Why do you think that the black woman writer has been so ignored in America? Does she have even more difficulty than the black male writer, who perhaps has just begun to gain recognition?

Walker: There are two reasons why the black woman writer is not taken as seriously as the black male writer. One is that she's a woman. Critics seem unusually ill-equipped to intelligently discuss and analyze the works of black women. Generally, they do not even make the attempt; they prefer, rather, to talk about the lives of black women writers, not about what they write. And, since black women writers are not—it would

Alice Walker

seem—very likable—until recently they were the least willing worshipers of male supremacy—comments about them tend to be cruel.

In Nathan Huggins's very readable book, *Harlem Renaissance*, he hardly refers to Zora Neale Hurston's work, except negatively. He quotes from Wallace Thurman's novel, *Infants of the Spring*, at length, giving us the words of a character, "Sweetie Mae Carr," who is allegedly based on Zora Neale Hurston. "Sweetie Mae" is a writer noted more "for her ribald wit and personal effervescence than for any actual literary work. She was a great favorite among those whites who went in for Negro prodigies." Mr. Huggins goes on for several pages, never quoting Zora Neale Hurston herself, but rather the opinions of others about her character. He does say that she was "a master of dialect," but adds that "Her greatest weakness was carelessness or indifference to her art."

Having taught Zora Neale Hurston, and of course, having read her work myself, I am stunned. Personally, I do not care if Zora Hurston was fond of her white women friends. When she was a child in Florida, working for nickels and dimes, two white women helped her escape. Perhaps this explains it. But even if it doesn't, so what? Her work, far from being done carelessly, is done (especially in *Their Eyes Were Watching God*) almost too perfectly. She took the trouble to capture the beauty of rural black expression. She saw poetry where other writers merely saw failure to cope with English. She was so at ease with her blackness it never occurred to her that she should act one way among blacks and another among whites (as her more sophisticated black critics apparently did).

It seems to me that black writing has suffered, because even black critics have assumed that a book that deals with the relationships between members of a black family—or between a man and a woman—is less important than one that has white people as a primary antagonist. The consequences of this is that many of our books by "major" writers (always male) tell us little about the culture, history, or future, imagination, fantasies, etc., of black people, and a lot about isolated (often improbable) or limited encounters with a nonspecific white world. Where is the book, by an American black person (aside from *Cane*), that equals Elechi Amadi's *The Concubine*, for example? A book that exposes the *subconscious* of a people, because the people's dreams, imaginings, rituals, legends, etc., are known to be important, are known to contain the accumulated collective reality of the people themselves. Or, in *The Radiance of the King*, the white person is shown to be the outsider he is, because the culture he enters into in Africa *itself* [expels] him. Without malice, but as nature expels what does not suit. The white man is mysterious, a force to be reckoned with, but he is not glorified to such an extent that the Africans turn their attention away from themselves and their own imagination and culture. Which is what often happens with "protest literature." The superficial becomes—for a time—the deepest reality, and replaces the still waters of the collective subconscious.

When my own novel was published, a leading black monthly admitted (the editor did) that the book itself was never read; but the magazine ran an item stating that a *white* reviewer had praised the book (which was, in itself, an indication that the book was no good—such went the logic) and then hinted that the reviewer had liked my book because of my life-style. When I wrote to the editor to complain, he wrote me a small sermon on the importance of my "image," of what is "good" for others to see. Needless to say, what others "see" of me is the least of my worries, and I assumed that "others" are intelligent enough to recover from whatever shocks my presence might cause.

Women writers are supposed to be intimidated by male disapprobation. What they write is not important enough to be read. How they live, however, their "image," they owe to the race. Read the reason Zora Neale Hurston gave for giving up her writing. See what "image" the Negro press gave her, innocent as she was. I no longer read articles or reviews unless they are totally about the work. I trust that someday a generation of men and women will arise who will forgive me for such wrong as I do not agree I do, and will read my work because it is a true account of my feelings, my perceptions, and my imagination, and because it will reveal something to them of their own selves. They will also be free to toss it—and me—out of a high window. They can do what they like.

From *Interviews with Black Writers*

Reflections on Writing and Women's Lives   (mid-1990s) 2004

Interview by William R. Ferris

If you think of the early stories, it's true that the women end badly, but it's because they belong to the generation of my mother and grandmother, when they were suspended because they had nowhere to go. All of them couldn't be Bessie Smith or Billie Holiday, so they ended up doing all kinds of destructive things. Most of that generation didn't have any fame or glory. But notice that all of those women are much older than I am. They exist in an historical place that is removed from my generation of women. . . . I wrote about these women in *In Search of Our Mothers' Gardens*. The women who have not had anything, have been, almost of necessity, self-destructive. They've just been driven insane. And the ones who have managed have been the ones who could focus their enormous energies on art forms that were not necessarily recognized as art forms—on quilting, on flowers, on making things. It's a very human need, to make things, to create. To think that women didn't need that—that by having a baby you fulfill your whole function—is absurd and demeaning.

From *Southern Cultures*

CRITICS ON "EVERYDAY USE"

Barbara T. Christian   (1943–2000)

"Everyday Use" and the Black Power Movement   1994

"Everyday Use" is, in part, Alice Walker's response to the concept of heritage as articulated by the black movements of the 1960s. In that period, many African Americans, disappointed by the failure of integration, gravitated to the philosophy of cultural nationalism as the means to achieve liberation. In contrast to the veneration of Western ideas and ideals by many integrationists of the 1950s, Black Power ideologues emphasized the African cultural past as the true heritage of African Americans. The acknowledgment and appreciation of that heritage, which had too often been denigrated by African Americans themselves as well as by Euro-Americans, was a major tenet of the revolutionary movements of the period. Many blacks affirmed their African roots by changing their "slave names" to African names, and by wearing Afro styles and African clothing. Yet, ideologues of the period also lambasted older African Americans, opposing them to the lofty mythical models of the ancient past. These older men and women, they claimed, had become Uncle Toms and Aunt Jemimas who displayed little awareness of their culture and who, as a result of their slave past, had internalized the white man's view of blacks. So while these 1960s ideologues extolled an unknown ancient history, they denigrated the known and recent past. The tendency to idealize an ancient African past while ignoring the recent African American past still persists in the Afrocentric movements of the 1990s.

In contrast to that tendency, Walker's "Everyday Use" is dedicated to "your grandmama." And the story is told by a woman many African Americans would recognize as their grandmama, that supposedly backward Southern ancestor the cultural nationalists of the North probably visited during the summers of their youth and probably considered behind the times. Walker stresses those physical qualities which suggest such a person, qualities often demeaned by cultural nationalists. For this grandmama, like the stereotypical mammy of slavery, is "a large big-boned woman with rough, man-working hands," who wears "flannel nightgowns to bed and overalls during the day," and whose "fat keeps [her] hot in zero weather." Nor is this grandmama politically conscious according to the fashion of the day; she never had an education after the second grade, she knows nothing about African names, and she eats pork. In having the grandmama tell this story, Walker gives voice to an entire maternal ancestry often silenced by the political rhetoric of the period. Indeed, Walker tells us in "In Search of Our Mothers' Gardens" that her writing is part of her mother's legacy to her, that many of her stories are based on stories *her* mother told her. Thus, Walker's writing is her way of breaking silences and stereotypes about her grandmothers', mothers', sisters' lives. In effect, her work is a literary continuation of a distinctly oral tradition in which African American women have been and still are pivotal participants.

Alice Walker is well aware of the restrictions of the African American Southern past, for she is the eighth child of Georgia sharecroppers. Born in 1944, she grew up during the period when, as she put it, apartheid existed in America. For in the 1940s and 1950s, when segregation was the law of the South, opportunities for economic and social advancement were legally denied to Southern blacks. Walker was fortunate to come to adulthood during the social and political movements of the late fifties and sixties. Of her siblings, only she, and a slightly older sister, Molly, were able even to imagine the possibility of moving beyond the poverty of their parents. It is unlikely that Alice Walker would have been able to go to college—first at Spelman, the African American women's college in Atlanta, and then at Sarah Lawrence, the white women's college near New York City—if it had not been for the changes that came about as a result of the Civil Rights Movement. Nor is it likely that she, a Southern black woman from a poor family, would have been able to become the writer that she did without the changes resulting from the ferment of the Black and Women's Movements of the 1960s and early 1970s.

While Walker was a participant in these movements, she was also one of their most astute critics. As a Southerner, she was aware of the ways in which black Southern culture was often thought of as backward by predominantly Northern Black Power ideologues, even as they proclaimed their love for black people. She was also acutely aware of the ways in which women were oppressed within the Black Power Movement itself, even as the very culture its participants revered was so often passed on by women. Walker had also visited Africa during her junior year of college and had personally experienced the gap between the Black Power advocates' idealization of Africa and the reality of the African societies she visited.

• • •

Names are extremely important in African and African American culture as a means of indicating a person's spirit. During the 1960s Walker criticized the tendency among some African Americans to give up the names their parents gave them—names which embodied the history of their recent past—for African names that did not relate to a single person they knew. Hence the mother in "Everyday Use" is amazed that Dee would give up her name for the name Wangero. For Dee was the name of her great-grandmother, a woman who had kept her family together against great odds. Wangero might have sounded authentically African but it had no relationship to a person she knew, nor to the personal history that had sustained her.

• • •

In "Everyday Use," by contrasting a sister who has the opportunity to go to college with a sister who stays at home, Walker reminds us of the challenges that contemporary African American women face as they discover what it means to be truly educated. The same concern appears in many of her works. For example, in "For My Sister Molly Who in the Fifties," she explores the conflicts that can result from an education that takes a woman away from her cultural source. Like Molly, Dee/Wangero in "Everyday Use" is embarrassed by her folk. She has been to the North, wears an Afro, and knows the correct political rhetoric of the 1960s, but she has little regard for her relatives who have helped to create that heritage. Thus, she does not know how to quilt and can only conceive of her family's quilts as priceless artifacts, as things, which she intends to hang on her wall as a means of demonstrating to others that she has "heritage." On the other hand, Maggie, the supposedly uneducated sister, who has been nowhere beyond the supposedly uneducated black South, loves and understands her family and can appreciate its history. She knows how to quilt and would put the precious quilts to "everyday use," which is precisely what, Walker suggests, one needs to do with one's heritage. For Maggie, the quilts are an embodiment of the spirit her folks have passed on to her.

From introduction to *Everyday Use*

Lyne Odums as Mama and Rachel Luttrell as Dee in 2003 film of *Everyday Use*.

Mary Helen Washington

"Everyday Use" as a Portrait of the Artist   1994

In 1994 Rutgers University Press brought out a collection of critical essays on Walker's "Everyday Use" in its Women Writers: Texts and Contexts *series. The book reprinted an earlier essay by Mary Helen Washington on Walker's work, along with an addendum she entitled "A Postscript to My 1979 Essay on Alice Walker." This excerpt comes from that 1994 postscript.*

One of the most interesting and glaring omissions of my earlier Walker essay is Walker's statement in the 1973 interview (which took place in her home in Jackson, Mississippi) of the way she sees the story "Everyday Use" as a reflection of her own struggles as an artist, an admission that suggests that female conflicts over art are not so easily resolved as they are in "A Sudden Trip Home . . ."° In "Everyday Use" (published in 1973) all three women characters are artists: Mama, as the narrator, tells her own story; Maggie is the quiltmaker, the creator of art for "everyday use"; Dee, the photographer and collector of art, has designed her jewelry, dress, and hair so deliberately and self-consciously that she appears in the story as a self-creation. Walker says in the interview that she thinks of these three characters as herself split into three parts:

> I really see that story as almost about one person, the old woman and two daughters being one person. The one who stays and sustains—this is the older woman—who has on the one hand a daughter who is the same way, who stays and abides and loves, plus the part of them—*the autonomous person*, the part of them that also wants to go out into the world to see change and be changed. . . . I do in fact have an African name that was given to me, and I love it and use it when I want to, and I love my Kenyan gowns and my Ugandan gowns—the whole bit—it's a part of me. But, on the other hand, my parents and grandparents were part of it, and they take precedence.[1]

Walker is most closely aligned in the story with the "bad daughter," Dee, "this autonomous person," the one who goes out in the world and returns with African clothes and an African name. Like Dee, Walker leaves the community, appropriating the oral tradition in order to turn it into a written artifact, which will no longer be available for "everyday use" by its originators. Everywhere in the story the fears and self-doubts of the woman artist are revealed. The narrator-mother remains hostile to Dee and partial to the homely daughter, Maggie, setting up the opposition between the two daughters that Walker says mirrors her own internal struggles.

• • •

The oppositions in "Everyday Use," between mother and daughters and sisters, between art for everyday use and art for art's sake, between insider and outsider, certainly capture [a] sense of contradiction and conflict. The story ends with Mama choosing Maggie and rejecting Dee, but Dee, who represents Walker herself as the artist who returns home, at least imaginatively, in order to collect the material for her art, certainly cannot be repressed. In this story, as in her essays, Walker shows that the quiltmaker, who has female precursors and female guidance, has an easier relationship

---

°*A Sudden Trip Home . . .":* "A Sudden Trip Home in the Spring," a later Walker story about a black college student returning home from the north to Georgia for her father's funeral.

[1]Mary Helen Washington, "Interview with Alice Walker," June 1973, *Black-Eyed Susans: Classic Stories By and About Black Women* (Garden City: Doubleday, 1975).

with her art than the "deviant" female who finds herself outside of acceptable boundaries. Unlike quiltmaking and garden making and even blues singing, which are part of women's traditions, the writing of fiction is still done under the shadow of men, without female authority. The self-assurance of "A Sudden Trip Home in the Spring" is acquired through an alliance with that male authority. "Everyday Use" tells a different, more threatening tale of the woman writer's fears, of the difficulty of reconciling home and art, particularly when the distance from home has been enlarged by education, by life among the "gentlefolk," and by literary recognition.

From "A Postscript to My 1979 Essay on Alice Walker"

Houston A. Baker (b. 1943)
and Charlotte Pierce-Baker (b. 1943)

Stylish vs. Sacred in "Everyday Use" 1985

The Johnson women, who populate the generations represented in Walker's short story "Everyday Use," are inhabitants of southern cabins who have always worked with "scraps" and seen what they could make of them. The result of their labor has been a succession of mothers and daughters surviving the ignominies of Jim Crow life and passing on ancestral blessings to descendants. The guardians of the Johnson homestead when the story commences are the mother—"a large, big-boned woman with rough, man-working hands"—and her daughter Maggie, who has remained with her "chin on chest, eyes on ground, feet in shuffle, ever since the fire that burned the other house to the ground" ten or twelve years ago. The mood at the story's beginning is one of ritualistic "waiting": "I will wait for her in the yard that Maggie and I made so clean and wavy yesterday afternoon." The subject awaited is the other daughter, Dee. Not only has the yard (as ritual ground) been prepared for the arrival of a goddess, but the sensibilities and costumes of Maggie and her mother have been appropriately attuned for the occasion. The mother daydreams of television shows where parents and children are suddenly— and pleasantly—reunited, banal shows where chatty hosts oversee tearful reunions. In her fantasy, she weighs a hundred pounds less, is several shades brighter in complexion, and possesses a devastatingly quick tongue. She returns abruptly to real life meditation, reflecting on her own heroic, agrarian accomplishments in slaughtering hogs and cattle and preparing their meat for winter nourishment. She is a robust provider who has gone to the people of her church and raised money to send her light-complexioned, lithe-figured, and ever-dissatisfied daughter Dee to college. Today, as she waits in the purified yard, she notes the stark differences between Maggie and Dee and recalls how the "last dingy gray board of the house [fell] in toward the red-hot brick chimney" when her former domicile burned. Maggie was scarred horribly by the fire, but Dee, who had hated the house with an intense fury, stood "off under the sweet gum tree . . . a look of concentration on her face." A scarred and dull Maggie, who has been kept at home and confined to everyday offices, has but one reaction to the fiery and vivacious arrival of her sister: "I hear Maggie suck in her breath. 'Uhnnnh,' is what it sounds like. Like when you see the wriggling end of a snake just in front of your foot on the road. 'Uhnnnh.'"

Indeed, the question raised by Dee's energetic arrival is whether there are words adequate to her flair, her brightness, her intense colorfulness of style which veritably blocks the sun. She wears "a dress so loud it hurts my eyes. There are yellows and oranges enough to throw back the light of the sun. I feel my whole face warming from the heat waves it throws out." Dee is both serpent and fire introduced with bursting esprit into the calm pasture that contains the Johnsons' tin-roofed, three-room, windowless shack and grazing cows. She has joined the radical, black nationalists of the 1960s and 1970s, changing her name from Dee to Wangero and cultivating a suddenly fashionable, or stylish, interest in what she passionately describes as her "heritage." If there is one quality that Dee (Wangero) possesses in abundance, it is "style": "At sixteen she had a style of her own: and knew what style was."

But in her stylishness, Dee is not an example of the indigenous rapping and styling out of Afro-America. Rather, she is manipulated by the style-makers, the fashion designers whose semiotics the French writer Roland Barthes has so aptly characterized. "Style" for Dee is the latest vogue—the most recent fantasy perpetuated by American media. When she left for college, her mother had tried to give her a quilt whose making began with her grandmother Dee, but the bright daughter felt such patched coverings were "old-fashioned and out of style." She has returned at the commencement of "Everyday Use," however, as one who now purports to know the value of the work of black women as holy patchers.

The dramatic conflict of the story surrounds the definition of holiness. The ritual purification of earth and expectant atmosphere akin to that of Beckett's famous drama ("I will wait for her in the yard that Maggie and I made so clean and wavy yesterday afternoon.") prepare us for the narrator's epiphanic experience at the story's conclusion.

Near the end of "Everyday Use," the mother (who is the tale's narrator) realizes that Dee (a.k.a. Wangero) is a *fantasy* child, a perpetrator and victim of: "words, lies, other folks's habits." The energetic daughter is as frivolously careless of other people's lives as the fiery conflagration that she had watched ten years previously. Assured by the makers of American fashion that "black" is currently "beautiful," she has conformed her own "style" to that notion. Hers is a trendy "blackness" cultivated as "art" and costume. She wears "a dress down to the ground . . . bracelets dangling and making noises when she moves her arm up to shake the folds of the dress out of her armpits." And she says of quilts she has removed from a trunk at the foot of her mother's bed: "Maggie can't appreciate these quilts! She'd probably be backward enough to put them to everyday use." "Art" is, thus, juxtaposed with "everyday use" in Walker's short story, and the fire goddess Dee, who has achieved literacy only to burn "us with a lot of knowledge we didn't necessarily need to know," is revealed as a perpetuator of institutional theories of aesthetics.

• • •

Quilts designed for everyday use, pieced wholes defying symmetry and pattern, are signs of the scarred generations of women who have always been alien to a world of literate words and stylish fantasies. The crafted fabric of Walker's story is the very weave of blues and jazz traditions in the Afro-American community, daringly improvisational modes that confront breaks in the continuity of melody (or theme) by riffing. The asymmetrical quilts of southern black women are like the off-centered stomping of the jazz solo or the innovative musical showmanship of the blues interlude. They speak a world in which the deceptively shuffling Maggie is capable of a quick change into goddess, an unlikely holy figure whose dues are paid in full. Dee's anger at her mother is occasioned principally by the mother's insistence that paid dues make Maggie a more likely bearer of sacredness, tradition, and true value than the "brighter" sister. "You just don't understand," she says to her mother. Her assessment is surely correct where institutional theories and systems of "art" are concerned. The mother's cognition contains no categories for framed art. The mother works according to an entirely different scale of use and value, finally assigning proper weight to the virtues of Maggie and to the ancestral importance of the pieced quilts that she has kept out of use for so many years. Smarting, perhaps, from Dee's designation of the quilts as "old-fashioned," the mother has buried the covers away in a trunk. At the end of Walker's story, however, she has become aware of her own mistaken value judgments, and she pays homage that is due to Maggie. The unlikely daughter is a *griot*° of the vernacular who remembers actors and events in a distinctively black "historical" drama.

Before Dee departs, she "put on some sunglasses that hid everything above the tip of her nose and her chin." Maggie smiles at the crude symbolism implicit in this act, for she has always known that her sister saw "through a glass darkly." But it is the mother's conferral of an ancestral blessing (signaled by her deposit of the quilts in Maggie's lap) that constitutes the occasion for the daughter's first "real smile." Maggie knows that it is only communal recognition by elders of the tribe that confers ancestral privileges on succeeding generations. The mother's holy recognition of the scarred daughter's sacred status as quilter is the best gift of a hard-pressed womankind to the fragmented goddess of the present.

At the conclusion of "Everyday Use," which is surely a fitting precursor to *The Color Purple,* with its sewing protagonist and its scenes of sisterly quilting, Maggie and her mother relax in the ritual yard after the dust of Dee's departing car has settled. They dip snuff in the manner of African confreres sharing cola nuts. The moment is past when a putatively "new" generation has confronted scenes of black, everyday life. A change has taken place, but it is a change best described by Amiri Baraka's designation for Afro-American music's various styles and discontinuities. The change in Walker's story is the "changing same." What has been reaffirmed at the story's conclusion is the value of the quiltmaker's motion and strategy in the precincts of a continuously undemocratic South.

From "Patches: Quilts and Community in
Alice Walker's 'Everyday Use'"

Elaine Showalter (b. 1941)

Quilt as Metaphor in "Everyday Use"   1991

For Alice Walker, piecing and quilting have come to represent both the aesthetic heritage of Afro-American women and the model for what she calls a "Womanist," or black feminist, writing of reconciliation and connection; in her essay "In Search of Our Mothers' Gardens," Walker identified the quilt as a major form of creative expression for black women in the South. "In the Smithsonian Institution in Washington, D.C.," Walker writes,

> there hangs a quilt unlike another in the world. In fanciful, inspired, and yet simple and identifiable figures, it portrays the story of the Crucifixion . . . Though it follows no known pattern of quiltmaking, and though it is made of bits and pieces of worthless rags, it is obviously the work of a person of powerful imagination and deep spiritual feeling. Below this quilt I saw a note that says it was made by "an anonymous Black woman in Alabama a hundred years ago."

---

griot: African storyteller, guardian of the people's history [authors' note].

Lone Star quilt pattern: "Out came Wangero with two quilts. . . . One was in the Lone Star pattern" (paragraph 55).

The quilt Walker is describing from memory is in fact one of two extant narrative quilts by Harriet Powers (1836–1911), born a slave in Georgia. The Powers quilt at the Smithsonian illustrates Bible stories, while the one in the Boston Museum of Fine Arts mingles Bible tales with folklore and astronomical events such as shooting stars and meteor showers.[2] For Walker, genuine imagination and feeling can be recognized without the legitimacy conferred by the labels of "art" or the approval of museums. Paradoxically this heritage survives because it has been preserved in museums; but it can be a living art only if it is practiced.

The theme of Walker's quilt aesthetic is most explicitly presented in her early story "Everyday Use." Like much of her work, it uses a contrast between two sisters to get at the meaning of the concept of "heritage": a privileged one who escapes from Southern black culture, and a suffering one who stays or is left behind. The younger daughter, Maggie, has stayed at home since she was horribly scarred in a house fire ten years before. Dee is the bright and confident sister, the one with "faultfinding power." Dee has learned fast how to produce herself: "At sixteen she had a style of her own: and knew what style was." Now having chosen the style of radical black nationalism, her name changed to "Wangero," and spouting Swahili, Dee returns to claim her heritage from her mother in the form of "folk art": the worn benches made by her father, the butter churn whittled by an uncle, and especially the quilts pieced by her grandmother. "Maggie can't appreciate these quilts," Dee exclaims. "She'd probably be backward enough to put them to everyday use." Walker thus establishes

[2]See Marie Jean Adams, "The Harriet Powers Pictorial Quilts," *Black Art 3* (1982) 12–28.

a contrast between "everyday use" and "institutional theories of aesthetics."[3] In a moment of epiphanic insight, the mother, who has always been intimidated by Dee's intelligence and sophistication, decides to give the quilts to Maggie. "She can always make some more," the mother responds. "Maggie knows how to quilt." Maggie cannot speak glibly about her "heritage" or about "priceless" artifacts, but, unlike Dee, she understands the quilt as a process rather than as a commodity; she can read its meaning in a way Dee never will, because she knows the contexts of its pieces, and loves the women who have made it. The meaning of an aesthetic heritage, according to Walker's story, lies in continual renewal rather than in the rhetoric of nostalgia or appreciation. In writing *The Color Purple*, Walker herself took up quilt-making as well as using it as a central metaphor in the novel.

From *Sister's Choice: Tradition and Change in American Women's Writing*

■ WRITING *effectively*

TOPICS FOR WRITING ABOUT "THE YELLOW WALLPAPER"

1. "The Yellow Wallpaper" is cast in the form of the journal written by its central character. Consider how the use of this narrative device enriches—or impoverishes—the story.
2. Thomas L. Erskine and Connie L. Richards have written of "the aesthetic problem with much of Gilman's literary work; often her sociopolitical agenda overwhelms the characters, who become one-dimensional mouthpieces for different ideas. Propaganda all too often threatens art." Discuss whether or not you think these concerns apply to "The Yellow Wallpaper."
3. Think of a contemporary issue that involves women's feelings of being confined or thwarted by the male power structure. Then write a brief treatment of that issue in the style of "The Yellow Wallpaper."
4. Discuss the larger implications of the conclusion of "The Yellow Wallpaper." In the end, has the narrator triumphed by escaping her oppression, or has she been crushed by it?

TOPICS FOR WRITING ABOUT "EVERYDAY USE"

1. Write a brief version of the encounter in "Everyday Use" from Dee's point of view. Is it possible to present a nonironic affirmation of her values over those of her mother and sister? Why or why not?
2. Have you grown apart from a friend or relative with whom you once had a close relationship? Imagine an encounter with that person, and write a first-person description of it from the other person's point of view.
3. Alice Walker has suggested that one of her principal intentions in her writing is "nurturing and healing the reader." Is "nurturing and healing" one of the primary aims of "Everyday Use"?
4. How does the use of a first-person narrator function in "Everyday Use"? Are there places in which the reader is expected to understand more than the narrator does, or is everything that she says and sees to be accepted at face value?

---

[3]Houston A. Baker and Charlotte Pierce-Baker, "Patches: Quilts and Community in Alice Walker's 'Everyday Use.'" *Southern Review* 21:3 (Summer 1985) 716.

STORIES FOR
FURTHER READING

*The novel tends to tell us everything, whereas the short
story tells us only one thing and that intensely.*

—V. S. PRITCHETT

Sherman Alexie

This Is What It Means to Say Phoenix, Arizona   1993

*Sherman Alexie was born in 1966 on the
Spokane Indian Reservation in Wellpinit,
Washington. Hydrocephalic at birth, he underwent surgery at the age of six months. At
first he was expected not to survive; when that
prognosis proved wrong, it was predicted,
again wrongly, that he would be severely retarded. Alexie attended Gonzaga University
in Spokane and graduated from Washington
State University with a degree in American
studies. His first book, a collection of poems
called The Business of Fancydancing,
appeared in 1991, and he has published prolif-
ically since then, averaging a book a year. He
is the author of eleven volumes of poetry as
well as four collections of stories—The Lone
Ranger and Tonto Fistfight in Heaven*

Sherman Alexie

*(1993), The Toughest Indian in the World (2000), Ten Little Indians (2003),
and War Dances (2009)—and three novels—Reservation Blues (1995), Indian
Killer (1996), and Flight (2007). In addition to his writing, Alexie won the World
Heavyweight Poetry Bout competition an unprecedented four consecutive times
(1998–2001); he has appeared on television discussion programs hosted by Bill Maher,
Bill Moyers, and Jim Lehrer (a 1998 "Dialogue on Race" whose participants also in-
cluded President Bill Clinton); he has performed frequently as a stand-up comedian;
and he co-produced and wrote the 1998 feature film Smoke Signals, based on "This Is
What It Means to Say Phoenix, Arizona." Alexie lives with his wife and two sons in
Seattle, Washington.*

Just after Victor lost his job at the BIA,° he also found out that his father had died of a heart attack in Phoenix, Arizona. Victor hadn't seen his father in a few years, only talked to him on the telephone once or twice, but there still was a genetic pain, which was soon to be pain as real and immediate as a broken bone.

Victor didn't have any money. Who does have money on a reservation, except the cigarette and fireworks salespeople? His father had a savings account waiting to be claimed, but Victor needed to find a way to get to Phoenix. Victor's mother was just as poor as he was, and the rest of his family didn't have any use at all for him. So Victor called the Tribal Council.

"Listen," Victor said. "My father just died. I need some money to get to Phoenix to make arrangements."

"Now, Victor," the council said. "You know we're having a difficult time financially."

"But I thought the council had special funds set aside for stuff like this."   5

"Now, Victor, we do have some money available for the proper return of tribal members' bodies. But I don't think we have enough to bring your father all the way back from Phoenix."

"Well," Victor said. "It ain't going to cost all that much. He had to be cremated. Things were kind of ugly. He died of a heart attack in his trailer and nobody found him for a week. It was really hot, too. You get the picture."

"Now, Victor, we're sorry for your loss and the circumstances. But we can really only afford to give you one hundred dollars."

"That's not even enough for a plane ticket."

"Well, you might consider driving down to Phoenix."   10

"I don't have a car. Besides, I was going to drive my father's pickup back up here."

"Now, Victor," the council said. "We're sure there is somebody who could drive you to Phoenix. Or is there somebody who could lend you the rest of the money?"

"You know there ain't nobody around with that kind of money."

"Well, we're sorry, Victor, but that's the best we can do."

Victor accepted the Tribal Council's offer. What else could he do? So he   15
signed the proper papers, picked up his check, and walked over to the Trading Post to cash it.

While Victor stood in line, he watched Thomas Builds-the-Fire standing near the magazine rack, talking to himself. Like he always did. Thomas was a storyteller that nobody wanted to listen to. That's like being a dentist in a town where everybody has false teeth.

Victor and Thomas Builds-the-Fire were the same age, had grown up and played in the dirt together. Ever since Victor could remember, it was Thomas who always had something to say.

Once, when they were seven years old, when Victor's father still lived with the family, Thomas closed his eyes and told Victor this story: "Your father's heart is weak. He is afraid of his own family. He is afraid of you. Late at night he sits in the dark. Watches the television until there's nothing but that white noise. Sometimes he feels like he wants to buy a motorcycle and ride away. He wants to run and hide. He doesn't want to be found."

Thomas Builds-the-Fire had known that Victor's father was going to leave, knew it before anyone. Now Victor stood in the Trading Post with a one-hundred-dollar

---

BIA: Bureau of Indian Affairs, a federal agency responsible for management of Indian lands and concerns.

check in his hand, wondering if Thomas knew that Victor's father was dead, if he
knew what was going to happen next.

Just then Thomas looked at Victor, smiled, and walked over to him. 20

"Victor, I'm sorry about your father," Thomas said.

"How did you know about it?" Victor asked.

"I heard it on the wind. I heard it from the birds. I felt it in the sunlight. Also,
your mother was just in here crying."

"Oh," Victor said and looked around the Trading Post. All the other Indians
stared, surprised that Victor was even talking to Thomas. Nobody talked to Thomas
anymore because he told the same damn stories over and over again. Victor was embarrassed, but he thought that Thomas might be able to help him. Victor felt a sudden
need for tradition.

"I can lend you the money you need," Thomas said suddenly. "But you have to 25
take me with you."

"I can't take your money," Victor said. "I mean, I haven't hardly talked to you in
years. We're not really friends anymore."

"I didn't say we were friends. I said you had to take me with you."

"Let me think about it."

Victor went home with his one hundred dollars and sat at the kitchen table. He
held his head in his hands and thought about Thomas Builds-the-Fire, remembered
little details, tears and scars, the bicycle they shared for a summer, so many stories.

Thomas Builds-the-Fire sat on the bicycle, waited in Victor's yard. He was ten 30
years old and skinny. His hair was dirty because it was the Fourth of July.

"Victor," Thomas yelled. "Hurry up. We're going to miss the fireworks."

After a few minutes, Victor ran out of his house, jumped the porch railing, and
landed gracefully on the sidewalk.

"And the judges award him a 9.95, the highest score of the summer," Thomas
said, clapped, laughed.

"That was perfect, cousin," Victor said. "And it's my turn to ride the bike."

Thomas gave up the bike and they headed for the fairgrounds. It was nearly dark 35
and the fireworks were about to start.

"You know," Thomas said. "It's strange how us Indians celebrate the Fourth of
July. It ain't like it was *our* independence everybody was fighting for."

"You think about things too much," Victor said. "It's just supposed to be fun.
Maybe Junior will be there."

"Which Junior? Everybody on this reservation is named Junior."

And they both laughed.

The fireworks were small, hardly more than a few bottle rockets and a fountain. 40
But it was enough for two Indian boys. Years later, they would need much more.

Afterwards, sitting in the dark, fighting off mosquitoes, Victor turned to Thomas
Builds-the-Fire.

"Hey," Victor said. "Tell me a story."

Thomas closed his eyes and told this story: "There were these two Indian boys who
wanted to be warriors. But it was too late to be warriors in the old way. All the horses
were gone. So the two Indian boys stole a car and drove to the city. They parked the
stolen car in front of the police station and then hitchhiked back home to the reservation. When they got back, all their friends cheered and their parents' eyes shone with
pride. *You were very brave*, everybody said to the two Indian boys. *Very brave*."

"Ya-hey," Victor said. "That's a good one. I wish I could be a warrior." 45

"Me, too," Thomas said.

They went home together in the dark, Thomas on the bike now, Victor on foot. They walked through shadows and light from streetlamps.

"We've come a long ways," Thomas said. "We have outdoor lighting."

"All I need is the stars," Victor said. "And besides, you still think about things too much."

They separated then, each headed for home, both laughing all the way.

Victor sat at his kitchen table. He counted his one hundred dollars again and 50 again. He knew he needed more to make it to Phoenix and back. He knew he needed Thomas Builds-the-Fire. So he put his money in his wallet and opened the front door to find Thomas on the porch.

"Ya-hey, Victor," Thomas said. "I knew you'd call me."

Thomas walked into the living room and sat down on Victor's favorite chair.

"I've got some money saved up," Thomas said. "It's enough to get us down there, but you have to get us back."

"I've got this hundred dollars," Victor said. "And my dad had a savings account I'm going to claim."

"How much in your dad's account?" 55

"Enough. A few hundred."

"Sounds good. When we leaving?"

When they were fifteen and had long since stopped being friends, Victor and Thomas got into a fistfight. That is, Victor was really drunk and beat Thomas up for no reason at all. All the other Indian boys stood around and watched it happen. Junior was there and so were Lester, Seymour, and a lot of others. The beating might have gone on until Thomas was dead if Norma Many Horses hadn't come along and stopped it.

"Hey, you boys," Norma yelled and jumped out of her car. "Leave him alone."

If it had been someone else, even another man, the Indian boys would've just 60 ignored the warnings. But Norma was a warrior. She was powerful. She could have picked up any two of the boys and smashed their skulls together. But worse than that, she would have dragged them all over to some tipi and made them listen to some elder tell a dusty old story.

The Indian boys scattered, and Norma walked over to Thomas and picked him up.

"Hey, little man, are you okay?" she asked.

Thomas gave her a thumbs up.

"Why they always picking on you?"

Thomas shook his head, closed his eyes, but no stories came to him, no words or 65 music. He just wanted to go home, to lie in his bed and let his dreams tell his stories for him.

Thomas Builds-the-Fire and Victor sat next to each other in the airplane, coach section. A tiny white woman had the window seat. She was busy twisting her body into pretzels. She was flexible.

"I have to ask," Thomas said, and Victor closed his eyes in embarrassment.

"Don't," Victor said.

"Excuse me, miss," Thomas asked. "Are you a gymnast or something?"

"There's no something about it," she said. "I was first alternate on the 1980   70
Olympic team."

"Really?" Thomas asked.

"Really."

"I mean, you used to be a world-class athlete?" Thomas asked.

"My husband still thinks I am."

Thomas Builds-the-Fire smiled. She was a mental gymnast, too. She pulled her   75
leg straight up against her body so that she could've kissed her kneecap.

"I wish I could do that," Thomas said.

Victor was ready to jump out of the plane. Thomas, that crazy Indian storyteller
with ratty old braids and broken teeth, was flirting with a beautiful Olympic gymnast.
Nobody back home on the reservation would ever believe it.

"Well," the gymnast said. "It's easy. Try it."

Thomas grabbed at his leg and tried to pull it up into the same position as the
gymnast. He couldn't even come close, which made Victor and the gymnast laugh.

"Hey," she asked. "You two are Indian, right?"   80

"Full-blood," Victor said.

"Not me," Thomas said. "I'm half magician on my mother's side and half clown
on my father's."

They all laughed.

"What are your names?" she asked.

"Victor and Thomas."   85

"Mine is Cathy. Pleased to meet you all."

The three of them talked for the duration of the flight. Cathy the gymnast
complained about the government, how they screwed the 1980 Olympic team by
boycotting.°

"Sounds like you all got a lot in common with Indians," Thomas said.

Nobody laughed.

After the plane landed in Phoenix and they had all found their way to the termi-   90
nal, Cathy the gymnast smiled and waved good-bye.

"She was really nice," Thomas said.

"Yeah, but everybody talks to everybody on airplanes," Victor said. "It's too bad
we can't always be that way."

"You always used to tell me I think too much," Thomas said. "Now it sounds like
you do."

"Maybe I caught it from you."

"Yeah."   95

Thomas and Victor rode in a taxi to the trailer where Victor's father died.

"Listen," Victor said as they stopped in front of the trailer. "I never told you I
was sorry for beating you up that time."

"Oh, it was nothing. We were just kids and you were drunk."

"Yeah, but I'm still sorry."

"That's all right."   100

Victor paid for the taxi and the two of them stood in the hot Phoenix summer.
They could smell the trailer.

---

they screwed the 1980 Olympic team by boycotting: in an international movement led by the United States
at the direction of President Jimmy Carter, some sixty nations boycotted the 1980 Summer Olympic
Games in Moscow as a protest against the Soviet invasion of Afghanistan in December 1979.

"This ain't going to be nice," Victor said. "You don't have to go in."

"You're going to need help."

Victor walked to the front door and opened it. The stink rolled out and made them both gag. Victor's father had lain in that trailer for a week in hundred-degree temperatures before anyone found him. And the only reason anyone found him was because of the smell. They needed dental records to identify him. That's exactly what the coroner said. They needed dental records.

"Oh, man," Victor said. "I don't know if I can do this."   105

"Well, then don't."

"But there might be something valuable in there."

"I thought his money was in the bank."

"It is. I was talking about pictures and letters and stuff like that."

"Oh," Thomas said as he held his breath and followed Victor into the trailer.   110

When Victor was twelve, he stepped into an underground wasp nest. His foot was caught in the hole, and no matter how hard he struggled, Victor couldn't pull free. He might have died there, stung a thousand times, if Thomas Builds-the-Fire had not come by.

"Run," Thomas yelled and pulled Victor's foot from the hole. They ran then, hard as they ever had, faster than Billy Mills, faster than Jim Thorpe,° faster than the wasps could fly.

Victor and Thomas ran until they couldn't breathe, ran until it was cold and dark outside, ran until they were lost and it took hours to find their way home. All the way back, Victor counted his stings.

"Seven," Victor said. "My lucky number."

Victor didn't find much to keep in the trailer. Only a photo album and a stereo.   115
Everything else had that smell stuck in it or was useless anyway.

"I guess this is all," Victor said. "It ain't much."

"Better than nothing," Thomas said.

"Yeah, and I do have the pickup."

"Yeah," Thomas said. "It's in good shape."

"Dad was good about that stuff."   120

"Yeah, I remember your dad."

"Really?" Victor asked. "What do you remember?"

Thomas Builds-the-Fire closed his eyes and told this story: "I remember when I had this dream that told me to go to Spokane, to stand by the Falls in the middle of the city and wait for a sign. I knew I had to go there but I didn't have a car. Didn't have a license. I was only thirteen. So I walked all the way, took me all day, and I finally made it to the Falls. I stood there for an hour waiting. Then your dad came walking up. *What the hell are you doing here?* he asked me. I said, *Waiting for a vision.* Then your father said, *All you're going to get here is mugged.* So he drove me over to Denny's, bought me dinner, and then drove me home to the reservation. For a long time I was

---

Billy Mills . . . Jim Thorpe: William Mervin "Billy" Mills (born 1938), a member of the Sioux tribe, won a gold medal in the 10,000-meter run at the 1964 Summer Olympic Games in Tokyo, Japan. Jacobus Franciscus "Jim" Thorpe (1888–1953), of the Sac and Fox tribe, is widely regarded as one of the greatest American athletes of the twentieth century; he won gold medals in the pentathlon and decathlon at the 1912 Summer Olympic Games in Stockholm, Sweden. He also played professional football, baseball, and basketball.

mad because I thought my dreams had lied to me. But they didn't. Your dad was my vision. *Take care of each other* is what my dreams were saying. *Take care of each other*."

Victor was quiet for a long time. He searched his mind for memories of his father, found the good ones, found a few bad ones, added it all up, and smiled.

"My father never told me about finding you in Spokane," Victor said.   125

"He said he wouldn't tell anybody. Didn't want me to get in trouble. But he said I had to watch out for you as part of the deal."

"Really?"

"Really. Your father said you would need the help. He was right."

"That's why you came down here with me, isn't it?" Victor asked.

"I came because of your father."   130

Victor and Thomas climbed into the pickup, drove over to the bank, and claimed the three hundred dollars in the savings account.

Thomas Builds-the-Fire could fly.

Once, he jumped off the roof of the tribal school and flapped his arms like a crazy eagle. And he flew. For a second, he hovered, suspended above all the other Indian boys who were too smart or too scared to jump.

"He's flying," Junior yelled, and Seymour was busy looking for the trick wires or mirrors. But it was real. As real as the dirt when Thomas lost altitude and crashed to the ground.

He broke his arm in two places.   135

"He broke his wing," Victor chanted, and the other Indian boys joined in, made it a tribal song.

"He broke his wing, he broke his wing, he broke his wing," all the Indian boys chanted as they ran off, flapping their wings, wishing they could fly, too. They hated Thomas for his courage, his brief moment as a bird. Everybody has dreams about flying. Thomas flew.

One of his dreams came true for just a second, just enough to make it real.

Victor's father, his ashes, fit in one wooden box with enough left over to fill a cardboard box.

"He always was a big man," Thomas said.   140

Victor carried part of his father and Thomas carried the rest out to the pickup. They set him down carefully behind the seats, put a cowboy hat on the wooden box and a Dodgers cap on the cardboard box. That's the way it was supposed to be.

"Ready to head back home," Victor asked.

"It's going to be a long drive."

"Yeah, take a couple days, maybe."

"We can take turns," Thomas said.   145

"Okay," Victor said, but they didn't take turns. Victor drove for sixteen hours straight north, made it halfway up Nevada toward home before he finally pulled over.

"Hey, Thomas," Victor said. "You got to drive for a while."

"Okay."

Thomas Builds-the-Fire slid behind the wheel and started off down the road. All through Nevada, Thomas and Victor had been amazed at the lack of animal life, at the absence of water, of movement.

"Where is everything?" Victor had asked more than once.   150

Now when Thomas was finally driving they saw the first animal, maybe the only animal in Nevada. It was a long-eared jackrabbit.

"Look," Victor yelled. "It's alive."

Thomas and Victor were busy congratulating themselves on their discovery when the jackrabbit darted out into the road and under the wheels of the pickup.

"Stop the goddamn car," Victor yelled, and Thomas did stop, backed the pickup to the dead jackrabbit.

"Oh, man, he's dead," Victor said as he looked at the squashed animal.   155

"Really dead."

"The only thing alive in this whole state and we just killed it."

"I don't know," Thomas said. "I think it was suicide."

Victor looked around the desert, sniffed the air, felt the emptiness and loneliness, and nodded his head.

"Yeah," Victor said. "It had to be suicide."   160

"I can't believe this," Thomas said. "You drive for a thousand miles and there ain't even any bugs smashed on the windshield. I drive for ten seconds and kill the only living thing in Nevada."

"Yeah," Victor said. "Maybe I should drive."

"Maybe you should."

Thomas Builds-the-Fire walked through the corridors of the tribal school by himself. Nobody wanted to be anywhere near him because of all those stories. Story after story.

Thomas closed his eyes and this story came to him: "We are all given one thing   165
by which our lives are measured, one determination. Mine are the stories which can change or not change the world. It doesn't matter which as long as I continue to tell the stories. My father, he died on Okinawa in World War II, died fighting for this country, which had tried to kill him for years. My mother, she died giving birth to me, died while I was still inside her. She pushed me out into the world with her last breath. I have no brothers or sisters. I have only my stories which came to me before I even had the words to speak. I learned a thousand stories before I took my first thousand steps. They are all I have. It's all I can do."

Thomas Builds-the-Fire told his stories to all those who would stop and listen. He kept telling them long after people had stopped listening.

Victor and Thomas made it back to the reservation just as the sun was rising. It was the beginning of a new day on earth, but the same old shit on the reservation.

"Good morning," Thomas said.

"Good morning."

The tribe was waking up, ready for work, eating breakfast, reading the newspa-   170
per, just like everybody else does. Willene LeBret was out in her garden wearing a bathrobe. She waved when Thomas and Victor drove by.

"Crazy Indians made it," she said to herself and went back to her roses.

Victor stopped the pickup in front of Thomas Builds-the-Fire's HUD house.° They both yawned, stretched a little, shook dust from their bodies.

"I'm tired," Victor said.

"Of everything," Thomas added.

HUD house: housing subsidized by the U.S. Department of Housing and Urban Development.

They both searched for words to end the journey. Victor needed to thank 175
Thomas for his help, for the money, and make the promise to pay it all back.

"Don't worry about the money," Thomas said. "It don't make any difference anyhow."

"Probably not, enit?"

"Nope."

Victor knew that Thomas would remain the crazy storyteller who talked to dogs
and cars, who listened to the wind and pine trees. Victor knew that he couldn't really
be friends with Thomas, even after all that had happened. It was cruel but it was real.
As real as the ashes, as Victor's father, sitting behind the seats.

"I know how it is," Thomas said. "I know you ain't going to treat me any better 180
than you did before. I know your friends would give you too much shit about it."

Victor was ashamed of himself. Whatever happened to the tribal ties, the sense
of community? The only real thing he shared with anybody was a bottle and broken
dreams. He owed Thomas something, anything.

"Listen," Victor said and handed Thomas the cardboard box which contained
half of his father. "I want you to have this."

Thomas took the ashes and smiled, closed his eyes, and told this story: "I'm going to
travel to Spokane Falls one last time and toss these ashes into the water. And your father
will rise like a salmon, leap over the bridge, over me, and find his way home. It will be
beautiful. His teeth will shine like silver, like a rainbow. He will rise, Victor, he will rise."

Victor smiled.

"I was planning on doing the same thing with my half," Victor said. "But I didn't 185
imagine my father looking anything like a salmon. I thought it'd be like cleaning the
attic or something. Like letting things go after they've stopped having any use."

"Nothing stops, cousin," Thomas said. "Nothing stops."

Thomas Builds-the-Fire got out of the pickup and walked up his driveway. Victor
started the pickup and began the drive home.

"Wait," Thomas yelled suddenly from his porch. "I just got to ask one favor."

Victor stopped the pickup, leaned out the window, and shouted back. "What do
you want?"

"Just one time when I'm telling a story somewhere, why don't you stop and listen?" 190
Thomas asked.

"Just once?"

"Just once."

Victor waved his arms to let Thomas know that the deal was good. It was a fair
trade, and that was all Victor had ever wanted from his whole life. So Victor drove
his father's pickup toward home while Thomas went into his house, closed the door
behind him, and heard a new story come to him in the silence afterwards.

Isabel Allende

The Judge's Wife   1988

Translated by Margaret Sayers Peden

*Isabel Allende was born in 1942 in Lima, Peru; her father, Tomás, was a Chilean diplomat
and a cousin of Salvador Allende, who would be elected president of Chile in 1970. When
Isabel was only three years old, her parents' marriage ended, and she and her two siblings returned to Chile with their mother to live with their grandfather. In 1953 her mother married*

another Chilean diplomat, and the family spent the next five years in Bolivia and in Beirut, Lebanon. After completing her high school education in Chile, she worked for a United Nations organization in Santiago, and later as a magazine and television journalist. She and her family left Chile in 1975 because of the political situation following the coup that overthrew the Allende government in 1973. They spent the next thirteen years in Venezuela, where she continued to work as a journalist and writer. In 1981, upon learning that her ninety-nine-year-old grandfather was dying, she began to write him a letter, which evolved into her first novel, The House of the Spirits. *Published in Spain in 1982 and in English translation three years later, it became an international best seller. Her later novels are* Of Love and Shadows *(1987),*

Isabel Allende

Eva Luna *(1988),* Daughter of Fortune *(1999), and* Portrait in Sepia *(2000). She has also published* The Stories of Eva Luna *(1991), a collection of short fiction that includes "The Judge's Wife";* Paula *(1995), an autobiography and family history begun during her daughter's ultimately fatal illness;* Aphrodite: A Memoir of the Senses *(1997), a paean to pleasure in all its manifestations; and most recently,* Island Beneath the Sea *(2010), a historical novel about a mulatto girl who is sold as a slave in eighteenth-century Santo Domingo. Her novels, written in a lyrical style and blending fantasy and legend with family and social history, have made her one of the most prominent practitioners of magical realism. Her books have been translated into over twenty languages and have sold millions of copies worldwide. In 2010 Allende was awarded Chile's National Literature Prize. She currently lives with her husband in San Rafael, California.*

Nicolas Vidal always knew he would lose his head over a woman. So it was foretold on the day of his birth, and later confirmed by the Turkish woman in the corner shop the one time he allowed her to read his fortune in the coffee grounds. Little did he imagine though that it would be on account of Casilda, Judge Hidalgo's wife. It was on her wedding day that he first glimpsed her. He was not impressed, preferring his women dark-haired and brazen. This ethereal slip of a girl in her wedding gown, eyes filled with wonder, and fingers obviously unskilled in the art of rousing a man to pleasure, seemed to him almost ugly. Mindful of his destiny, he had always been wary of any emotional contact with women, hardening his heart and restricting himself to the briefest of encounters whenever the demands of manhood needed satisfying. Casilda, however, appeared so insubstantial, so distant, that he cast aside all precaution and, when the fateful moment arrived, forgot the prediction that usually weighed in all his decisions. From the roof of the bank, where he was crouching with two of his men, Nicolas Vidal peered down at this young lady from the capital. She had a dozen equally pale and dainty relatives with her, who spent the whole of the ceremony fanning themselves with an air of utter bewilderment, then departed straight away, never to return. Along with everyone else in the town, Vidal was convinced the young bride would not withstand the climate, and that within a few months the old women would be dressing her up again, this time for her funeral. Even if she did survive the heat and the dust that filtered in through every pore to lodge itself in the soul, she would be bound to succumb to the fussy habits of her confirmed bachelor of a husband. Judge Hidalgo was twice her age, and had slept alone for so many years he didn't have the slightest notion of how to go about pleasing a woman. The severity and stubbornness with which he executed the law even at the expense of justice had made him feared throughout the province. He refused to apply any common sense in the exercise of his profession, and was equally harsh in his condemnation of the theft of a chicken as of a premeditated murder. He dressed formally in black, and, despite the all-pervading dust in this godforsaken town, his boots always shone with beeswax. A man such as he was never meant to be a husband, and yet not only did the gloomy wedding-day prophecies remain unfulfilled, but Casilda emerged happy and smiling from three pregnancies in rapid succession. Every Sunday at noon she would go to mass with her husband, cool and collected beneath her Spanish mantilla, seemingly untouched by our pitiless summer, as wan and frail-looking as on the day of her arrival: a perfect example of delicacy and refinement. Her loudest words were a soft-spoken greeting; her most expressive gesture was a graceful nod of the head. She was such an airy, diaphanous creature that a moment's carelessness might mean she disappeared altogether. So slight an impression did she make that the changes noticeable in the Judge were all the more remarkable. Though outwardly he remained the same—he still dressed as black as a crow and was as stiff-necked and brusque as ever—his judgments in court altered dramatically. To general amazement, he found the youngster who robbed the Turkish shopkeeper innocent, on the grounds that she had been selling him short for years, and the money he had taken could therefore be seen as compensation. He also refused to punish an adulterous wife, arguing that since her husband himself kept a mistress he did not have the moral authority to demand fidelity. Word in the town had it that the Judge was transformed the minute he crossed the threshold at home: that he flung off his gloomy apparel, rollicked with his children, chuckled as he sat Casilda on his lap. Though no one ever succeeded in confirming these rumors, his wife got the credit for his newfound kindness, and her reputation grew accordingly. None of this was of the slightest interest to Nicolas Vidal, who as a wanted man was sure there would be no mercy shown him the day he was brought in chains before the Judge. He paid no heed to the talk about Doña Casilda, and the rare occasions he glimpsed her from afar only confirmed his first impression of her as a lifeless ghost.

Born thirty years earlier in a windowless room in the town's only brothel, Vidal was the son of Juana the Forlorn and an unknown father. The world had no place for him. His mother knew it, and so tried to wrench him from her womb with sprigs of parsley, candle butts, douches of ashes, and other violent purgatives, but the child clung to life. Once, years later, Juana was looking at her mysterious son and realized that, while all her infallible methods of aborting might have failed to dislodge him, they had none the less tempered his soul to the hardness of iron. As soon as he came into the world, he was lifted in the air by the midwife who examined him by the light of an oil lamp. She saw he had four nipples.

"Poor creature: he'll lose his head over a woman," she predicted, drawing on her wealth of experience.

Her words rested on the boy like a deformity. Perhaps a woman's love would have made his existence less wretched. To atone for all her attempts to kill him before birth, his mother chose him a beautiful first name, and an imposing family name picked at random. But the lofty name of Nicolas Vidal was no protection against the fateful cast of his destiny. His face was scarred from knife fights before he reached his teens, so it came as no surprise to decent folk that he ended up a bandit. By the age of twenty, he had become the leader of a band of desperadoes. The habit of violence toughened his sinews. The solitude he was condemned to for fear of falling prey to a woman lent his face a doleful expression. As soon as they saw him, everyone in the town knew from his eyes, clouded by tears he would never allow to fall, that he was the son of Juana the Forlorn. Whenever there was an outcry after a crime had been committed in the region, the police set out with dogs to track him down, but after scouring the hills invariably returned empty-handed. In all honesty they preferred it that way, because they could never have fought him. His gang gained such a fearsome reputation that the surrounding villages and estates paid to keep them away. This money would have been plenty for his men, but Nicolas Vidal kept them constantly on horseback in a whirlwind of death and destruction so they would not lose their taste for battle. Nobody dared take them on. More than once, Judge Hidalgo had asked the government to send troops to reinforce the police, but after several useless forays the soldiers returned to their barracks and Nicolas Vidal's gang to their exploits. On one occasion only did Vidal come close to falling into the hands of justice, and then he was saved by his hardened heart.

Weary of seeing the laws flouted, Judge Hidalgo resolved to forget his scruples and set a trap for the outlaw. He realized that to defend justice he was committing an injustice, but chose the lesser of two evils. The only bait he could find was Juana the Forlorn, as she was Vidal's sole known relative. He had her dragged from the brothel where by now, since no clients were willing to pay for her exhausted charms, she scrubbed floors and cleaned out the lavatories. He put her in a specially made cage which was set up in the middle of the Plaza de Armas, with only a jug of water to meet her needs. 5

"As soon as the water's finished, she'll start to squawk. Then her son will come running, and I'll be waiting for him with the soldiers," Judge Hidalgo said.

News of this torture, unheard of since the days of slavery, reached Nicolas Vidal's ears shortly before his mother drank the last of the water. His men watched as he received the report in silence, without so much as a flicker of emotion on his blank lone wolf's face, or a pause in the sharpening of his dagger blade on a leather strap. Though for many years he had had no contact with Juana, and retained few happy childhood memories, this was a question of honor. No man can accept such an insult, his gang reasoned as they got guns and horses ready to rush into the ambush and, if need be, lay down their lives. Their chief showed no sign of being in a hurry. As the hours went by tension mounted in the camp. The perspiring, impatient men stared at each other, not daring to speak. Fretful, they caressed the butts of their revolvers and their horses' manes, or busied themselves coiling their lassos. Night fell. Nicolas Vidal was the only one in the camp who slept. At dawn, opinions were divided. Some of the men reckoned he was even more heartless than they had ever imagined, while others maintained their leader was planning a spectacular ruse to free his mother. The one thing that never crossed any of their minds was that his courage might have failed him, for he had always proved he had more than enough to spare. By noon, they could bear the suspense no longer, and went to ask him what he planned to do.

"I'm not going to fall into his trap like an idiot," he said.

"What about your mother?"

"We'll see who's got more balls, the Judge or me," Nicolas Vidal coolly replied. 10

*

By the third day, Juana the Forlorn's cries for water had ceased. She lay curled on the cage floor, with wildly staring eyes and swollen lips, moaning softly whenever she regained consciousness, and the rest of the time dreaming she was in hell. Four armed guards stood watch to make sure nobody brought her water. Her groans penetrated the entire town, filtering through closed shutters or being carried by the wind through the cracks in doors. They got stuck in corners, where dogs worried at them, and passed them on in their howls to the newly born, so that whoever heard them was driven to distraction. The Judge couldn't prevent a steady stream of people filing through the square to show their sympathy for the old woman, and was powerless to stop the prostitutes going on a sympathy strike just as the miners' fortnight holiday was beginning. That Saturday, the streets were thronged with lusty workmen desperate to unload their savings, who now found nothing in town apart from the spectacle of the cage and this universal wailing carried mouth to mouth down from the river to the coast road. The priest headed a group of Catholic ladies to plead with Judge Hidalgo for Christian mercy and to beg him to spare the poor old innocent woman such a frightful death, but the man of the law bolted his door and refused to listen to them. It was then they decided to turn to Doña Casilda.

The Judge's wife received them in her shady living room. She listened to their pleas looking, as always, bashfully down at the floor. Her husband had not been home for three days, having locked himself in his office to wait for Nicolas Vidal to fall into his trap. Without so much as glancing out of the window, she was aware of what was going on, for Juana's long-drawn-out agony had forced its way even into the vast rooms of her residence. Doña Casilda waited until her visitors had left, dressed her children in their Sunday best, tied a black ribbon round their arms as a token of mourning, then strode out with them in the direction of the square. She carried a food hamper and a bottle of fresh water for Juana the Forlorn. When the guards spotted her turning the corner, they realized what she was up to, but they had strict orders, and barred her way with their rifles. When, watched now by a small crowd, she persisted, they grabbed her by the arms. Her children began to cry.

Judge Hidalgo sat in his office overlooking the square. He was the only person in the town who had not stuffed wax in his ears, because his mind was intent on the ambush and he was straining to catch the sound of horses' hoofs, the signal for action. For three long days and nights he put up with Juana's groans and the insults of the townspeople gathered outside the courtroom, but when he heard his own children start to wail he knew he had reached the bounds of his endurance. Vanquished, he walked out of the office with his three days' beard, his eyes bloodshot from keeping watch, and the weight of a thousand years on his back. He crossed the street, turned into the square and came face to face with his wife. They gazed at each other sadly. In seven years, this was the first time she had gone against him, and she had chosen to do so in front of the whole town. Easing the hamper and the bottle from Casilda's grasp, Judge Hidalgo himself opened the cage to release the prisoner.

"Didn't I tell you he wouldn't have the balls?" laughed Nicolas Vidal when the news reached him.

His laughter turned sour the next day, when he heard that Juana the Forlorn had hanged herself from the chandelier in the brothel where she had spent her life, overwhelmed by the shame of her only son leaving her to fester in a cage in the middle of the Plaza de Armas.

"That Judge's hour has come," said Vidal.

He planned to take the Judge by surprise, put him to a horrible death, then dump him in the accursed cage for all to see. The Turkish shopkeeper sent him word that the Hidalgo family had left that same night for a seaside resort to rid themselves of the bitter taste of defeat.

The Judge learned he was being pursued when he stopped to rest at a wayside inn. There was little protection for him there until an army patrol could arrive, but he had a few hours' start, and his motor car could outrun the gang's horses. He calculated he could make it to the next town and summon help there. He ordered his wife and children into the car, put his foot down on the accelerator, and sped off along the road. He ought to have arrived with time to spare, but it had been ordained that Nicolas Vidal was that day to meet the woman who would lead him to his doom.

Overburdened by the sleepless nights, the townspeople's hostility, the blow to his pride, and the stress of this race to save his family, Judge Hidalgo's heart gave a massive jolt, then split like a pomegranate. The car ran out of control, turned several somersaults and finally came to a halt in the ditch. It took Doña Casilda some minutes to work out what had happened. Her husband's advancing years had often led her to think what it would be like to be left a widow, yet she had never imagined he would leave her at the mercy of his enemies. She wasted little time dwelling on her situation, knowing she must act at once to get her children to safety. When she gazed around her, she almost burst into tears. There was no sign of life in the vast plain baked by a scorching sun, only barren cliffs beneath an unbounded sky bleached colorless by the fierce light. A second look revealed the dark shadow of a passage or cave on a distant slope, so she ran towards it with two children in her arms and the third clutching her skirts.

One by one she carried her children up the cliff. The cave was a natural one, typical of many in the region. She peered inside to be certain it wasn't the den of some wild animal, sat her children against its back wall, then, dry-eyed, kissed them good-bye.

"The troops will come to find you a few hours from now. Until then, don't for any reason whatsoever come out of here, even if you hear me screaming—do you understand?"

Their mother gave one final glance at the terrified children clinging to each other, then clambered back down to the road. She reached the car, closed her husband's eyes, smoothed back her hair and settled down to wait. She had no idea how many men were in Nicolas Vidal's gang, but prayed there were a lot of them so it would take them all the more time to have their way with her. She gathered strength pondering on how long it would take her to die if she determined to do it as slowly as possible. She willed herself to be desirable, luscious, to create more work for them and thus gain time for her children.

Casilda did not have long to wait. She soon saw a cloud of dust on the horizon and heard the gallop of horses' hoofs. She clenched her teeth. Then, to her astonishment, she saw there was only one rider, who stopped a few yards from her, gun at the ready. By the scar on his face she recognized Nicolas Vidal, who had set out all alone in pursuit of Judge Hidalgo, as this was a private matter between the two men. The Judge's wife understood she was going to have to endure something far worse than a lingering death.

A quick glance at her husband was enough to convince Vidal that the Judge was safely out of his reach in the peaceful sleep of death. But there was his wife, a shimmering presence in the plain's glare. He leapt from his horse and strode over to her. She did not flinch or lower her gaze, and to his amazement he realized that for the first time in his life another person was facing him without fear. For several seconds that stretched to eternity, they sized each other up, trying to gauge the other's strength, and their own powers of resistance. It gradually dawned on both of them that they were up against a formidable opponent. He lowered his gun. She smiled.

Casilda won each moment of the ensuing hours. To all the wiles of seduction   25
known since the beginning of time she added new ones born of necessity to bring this man to the heights of rapture. Not only did she work on his body like an artist, stimulating his every fiber to pleasure, but she brought all the delicacy of her spirit into play on her side. Both knew their lives were at stake, and this added a new and terrifying dimension to their meeting. Nicolas Vidal had fled from love since birth, and knew nothing of intimacy, tenderness, secret laughter, the riot of the senses, the joy of shared passion. Each minute brought the detachment of troops and the noose that much nearer, but he gladly accepted this in return for her prodigious gifts. Casilda was a passive, demure, timid woman who had been married to an austere old man in front of whom she had never even dared appear naked. Not once during that unforgettable afternoon did she forget that her aim was to win time for her children, and yet at some point, marveling at her own possibilities, she gave herself completely, and felt something akin to gratitude towards him. That was why, when she heard the soldiers in the distance, she begged him to flee to the hills. Instead, Nicolas Vidal chose to fold her in a last embrace, thus fulfilling the prophecy that had sealed his fate from the start.

Margaret Atwood

Happy Endings   1983

Born in Ottawa, Ontario, in 1939, Margaret Eleanor Atwood was the daughter of an entomologist and spent her childhood summers in the forests of northern Quebec, where her father carried out research. Atwood began writing at the age of five and had already seriously entertained thoughts of becoming a professional writer before she finished high school. She graduated from the University of Toronto in 1961, and got a master's degree from Radcliffe. Atwood initially gained prominence as a poet. Her first full-length collection of poems, The Circle Game (1966), was awarded a Governor General's Award, Canada's most prestigious literary honor, and she has since published nearly twenty volumes of verse. Atwood also began to write fiction seriously in graduate school, and her short

Margaret Atwood

stories were first collected in Dancing Girls *(1977), followed by numerous additional collections, most recently* Moral Disorder *(2006).*

A dedicated feminist, Atwood's works of fiction explore the complex relations between the sexes, most incisively in The Handmaid's Tale *(1985), a futuristic novel about a world in which gender roles are ruthlessly enforced by a society based on religious fundamentalism. In 1986 Atwood was named Woman of the Year by* Ms. *magazine. Subsequent novels include* Cat's Eye *(1988),* The Robber Bride *(1993),* The Blind Assassin *(2000), and* The Year of the Flood *(2009). Atwood has served as writer-in-residence at many universities, and she is widely in demand for appearances at symposia devoted to literature and women's issues.*

John and Mary meet.
What happens next?
If you want a happy ending, try A.

A

John and Mary fall in love and get married. They both have worthwhile and remunerative jobs which they find stimulating and challenging. They buy a charming house. Real estate values go up. Eventually, when they can afford live-in help, they have two children, to whom they are devoted. The children turn out well. John and Mary have a stimulating and challenging sex life and worthwhile friends. They go on fun vacations together. They retire. They both have hobbies which they find stimulating and challenging. Eventually they die. This is the end of the story.

B

Mary falls in love with John but John doesn't fall in love with Mary. He merely   5
uses her body for selfish pleasure and ego gratification of a tepid kind. He comes to her apartment twice a week and she cooks him dinner, you'll notice that he doesn't even consider her worth the price of a dinner out, and after he's eaten the dinner he fucks her and after that he falls asleep, while she does the dishes so he won't think she's untidy, having all those dirty dishes lying around, and puts on fresh lipstick so she'll look good when he wakes up, but when he wakes up he doesn't even notice, he puts on his socks and his shorts and his pants and his shirt and his tie and his shoes, the reverse order from the one in which he took them off. He doesn't take off Mary's clothes, she takes them off herself, she acts as if she's dying for it every time, not because she likes sex exactly, she doesn't, but she wants John to think she does because if they do it often enough surely he'll get used to her, he'll come to depend on her and they will get married, but John goes out the door with hardly so much as a goodnight and three days later he turns up at six o'clock and they do the whole thing over again.

Mary gets run down. Crying is bad for your face, everyone knows that and so does Mary but she can't stop. People at work notice. Her friends tell her John is a rat, a pig, a dog, he isn't good enough for her, but she can't believe it. Inside John, she thinks, is another John, who is much nicer. This other John will emerge like a butterfly from a cocoon, a Jack from a box, a pit from a prune, if the first John is only squeezed enough.

One evening John complains about the food. He has never complained about the food before. Mary is hurt.

Her friends tell her they've seen him in a restaurant with another woman, whose name is Madge. It's not even Madge that finally gets to Mary; it's the restaurant. John has never taken Mary to a restaurant. Mary collects all the sleeping pills and aspirins she can find, and takes them and a half a bottle of sherry. You can see what kind of a woman she is by the fact that it's not even whiskey. She leaves a note for John. She hopes he'll discover her and get her to the hospital in time and repent and then they can get married, but this fails to happen and she dies.

John marries Madge and everything continues as in A.

C

John, who is an older man, falls in love with Mary, and Mary, who is only twenty-two, feels sorry for him because he's worried about his hair falling out. She sleeps with him even though she's not in love with him. She met him at work. She's in love with someone called James, who is twenty-two also and not yet ready to settle down.

John on the contrary settled down long ago: this is what is bothering him. John has a steady, respectable job and is getting ahead in his field, but Mary isn't impressed by him, she's impressed by James, who has a motorcycle and a fabulous record collection. But James is often away on his motorcycle, being free. Freedom isn't the same for girls, so in the meantime Mary spends Thursday evenings with John. Thursdays are the only days John can get away.

John is married to a woman called Madge and they have two children, a charming house which they bought just before the real estate values went up, and hobbies which they find stimulating and challenging, when they have the time. John tells Mary how important she is to him, but of course, he can't leave his wife because a commitment is a commitment. He goes on about this more than is necessary and Mary finds it boring, but older men can keep it up longer so on the whole she has a fairly good time.

One day James breezes in on his motorcycle with some top-grade California hybrid and James and Mary get higher than you'd believe possible and they climb into bed. Everything becomes very underwater, but along comes John, who has a key to Mary's apartment. He finds them stoned and entwined. He's hardly in any position to be jealous, considering Madge, but nevertheless he's overcome with despair. Finally he's middle-aged, in two years he'll be bald as an egg and he can't stand it. He purchases a handgun, saying he needs it for target practice—this is the thin part of the plot, but it can be dealt with later—and shoots the two of them and himself.

Madge, after a suitable period of mourning, marries an understanding man called Fred and everything continues as in A, but under different names.

D

Fred and Madge have no problems. They get along exceptionally well and are good at working out any little difficulties that may arise. But their charming house is by the seashore and one day a giant tidal wave approaches. Real estate values go down. The rest of the story is about what caused the tidal wave and how they escape from it. They do, though thousands drown, but Fred and Madge are virtuous and lucky. Finally on high ground they clasp each other, wet and dripping and grateful, and continue as in A.

E

Yes, but Fred has a bad heart. The rest of the story is about how kind and understanding they both are until Fred dies. Then Madge devotes herself to charity work until the end of A. If you like, it can be "Madge," "cancer," "guilty and confused," and "bird watching."

F

If you think this is all too bourgeois, make John a revolutionary and Mary a counterespionage agent and see how far that gets you. Remember, this is Canada. You'll still end up with A, though in between you may get a lustful brawling saga of passionate involvement, a chronicle of our times, sort of.

You'll have to face it, the endings are the same however you slice it. Don't be deluded by any other endings, they're all fake, either deliberately fake, with malicious intent to deceive, or just motivated by excessive optimism if not by downright sentimentality.

The only authentic ending is the one provided here:

John and Mary die. John and Mary die. John and Mary die.   20

So much for endings. Beginnings are always more fun. True connoisseurs, however, are known to favor the stretch in between, since it's the hardest to do anything with.

That's about all that can be said for plots, which anyway are just one thing after another, a what and a what and a what.

Now try How and Why.

Ambrose Bierce

An Occurrence at Owl Creek Bridge   1891

Ambrose Bierce (1842–1914?) was born in Horse Cave Creek, Ohio, the youngest child of nine in an impoverished farm family. A year at Kentucky Military Academy was his only formal schooling. Enlisting as a drummer boy in the Union Army, Bierce saw action at Shiloh and Chickamauga, took part in Sherman's March to the Sea, and came out of the army a brevet major. Then he became a writer, later an editor, for San Francisco newspapers. For a while Bierce thrived. He and his wife, on her ample dowry, lived five years in London, where Bierce wrote for London papers, honed his style, and cultivated his wit. But his wife left him, his two sons died (one of gunfire and the other of alcoholism), and late in life Bierce came to deserve his nickname "Bitter Bierce." In 1913, at seventy-one, he trekked off to Mexico and vanished without a trace, although one report

Ambrose Bierce

had him riding with the forces of revolutionist Pancho Villa. Bierce, who regarded the novel as "a short story padded," favored shorter lengths: short story, fable, newspaper column, aphorism. Sardonically, in The Devil's Dictionary (1911), he defines diplomacy as "the patriotic art of lying for one's country" and saint as "a dead sinner revised and edited." Master of both realism and the ghost story, he collected his best Civil War fiction, including "An Occurrence at Owl Creek Bridge," in Tales of Soldiers and Civilians (1891), later retitled In the Midst of Life.

I

A man stood upon a railroad bridge in northern Alabama, looking down into the swift water twenty feet below. The man's hands were behind his back, the wrists bound with a cord. A rope closely encircled his neck. It was attached to a stout cross-timber above his head and the slack fell to the level of his knees. Some loose boards laid upon the sleepers supporting the metals of the railway supplied a footing for him and his executioners—two private soldiers of the Federal army, directed by a sergeant who in civil life may have been a deputy sheriff. At a short remove upon the same temporary platform was an officer in the uniform of his rank, armed. He was a captain. A sentinel at each end of the bridge stood with his rifle in the position known as "support," that is to say, vertical in front of the left shoulder, the hammer resting on the forearm thrown straight across the chest—a formal and unnatural position, enforcing an erect carriage of the body. It did not appear to be the duty of these two men to know what was occurring at the center of the bridge; they merely blockaded the two ends of the foot planking that traversed it.

Beyond one of the sentinels nobody was in sight; the railroad ran straight away into a forest for a hundred yards, then, curving, was lost to view. Doubtless there was an outpost farther along. The other bank of the stream was open ground—a gentle acclivity topped with a stockade of vertical tree trunks, loop-holed for rifles, with a single embrasure through which protruded the muzzle of a brass cannon commanding the bridge. Midway of the slope between bridge and fort were the spectators—a single company of infantry in line, at "parade rest," the butts of the rifles on the ground, the barrels inclining slightly backward against the right shoulder, the hands crossed upon the stock. A lieutenant stood at the right of the line, the point of his sword upon the ground, his left hand resting upon his right. Excepting the group of four at the center of the bridge, not a man moved. The company faced the bridge, staring stonily, motionless. The sentinels, facing the banks of the stream, might have been statues to adorn the bridge. The captain stood with folded arms, silent, observing the work of his subordinates, but making no sign. Death is a dignitary who when he comes announced is to be received with formal manifestations of respect, even by those most familiar with him. In the code of military etiquette silence and fixity are forms of deference.

The man who was engaged in being hanged was apparently about thirty-five years of age. He was a civilian, if one might judge from his habit, which was that of a planter. His features were good—a straight nose, firm mouth, broad forehead, from which his long, dark hair was combed straight back, falling behind his ears to the collar of his well-fitting frock-coat. He wore a mustache and pointed beard, but no whiskers; his eyes were large and dark gray, and had a kindly expression which one would hardly have expected in one whose neck was in the hemp. Evidently this was no vulgar assassin. The liberal military code makes provision for hanging many kinds of persons, and gentlemen are not excluded.

The preparations being complete, the two private soldiers stepped aside and each drew away the plank upon which he had been standing. The sergeant turned to the captain, saluted and placed himself immediately behind that officer, who in turn moved apart one pace. These movements left the condemned man and the sergeant standing on the two ends of the same plank, which spanned three of the cross-ties of the bridge. The end upon which the civilian stood almost, but not quite, reached a fourth. This plank had been held in place by the weight of the captain; it was now held by that of the sergeant. At a signal from the former the latter would step aside, the plank would tilt and the condemned man go down between two ties. The arrangement commended itself to his judgment as simple and effective. His face had not been covered nor his eyes bandaged. He looked a moment at his "unsteadfast footing," then let his gaze wander to the swirling water of the stream racing madly beneath his feet. A piece of dancing driftwood caught his attention and his eyes followed it down the current. How slowly it appeared to move! What a sluggish stream!

He closed his eyes in order to fix his last thoughts upon his wife and children. 5 The water, touched to gold by the early sun, the brooding mists under the banks at some distance down the stream, the fort, the soldiers, the piece of drift—all had distracted him. And now he became conscious of a new disturbance. Striking through the thought of his dear ones was a sound which he could neither ignore nor understand, a sharp, distinct, metallic percussion like the stroke of a blacksmith's hammer upon the anvil; it had the same ringing quality. He wondered what it was, and whether immeasurably distant or near by—it seemed both. Its recurrence was regular, but as slow as the tolling of a death knell. He awaited each stroke with impatience and—he knew not why—apprehension. The intervals of silence grew progressively longer; the delays became maddening. With their greater infrequency the sounds increased in strength and sharpness. They hurt his ear like the thrust of a knife; he feared he would shriek. What he heard was the ticking of his watch.

He unclosed his eyes and saw again the water below him. "If I could free my hands," he thought, "I might throw off the noose and spring into the stream. By diving I could evade the bullets and, swimming vigorously, reach the bank, take to the woods and get away home. My home, thank God, is as yet outside their lines; my wife and little ones are still beyond the invader's farthest advance."

As these thoughts, which have here to be set down in words, were flashed into the doomed man's brain rather than evolved from it the captain nodded to the sergeant. The sergeant stepped aside.

II

Peyton Farquhar was a well-to-do planter, of an old and highly respected Alabama family. Being a slave owner and like other slave owners a politician he was naturally an original secessionist and ardently devoted to the Southern cause. Circumstances of an imperious nature, which it is unnecessary to relate here, had prevented him from taking service with the gallant army that had fought the disastrous campaigns ending with the fall of Corinth, and he chafed under the inglorious restraint, longing for the release of his energies, the larger life of the soldier, the opportunity for distinction. That opportunity, he felt, would come, as it comes to all in war time. Meanwhile he did what he could. No service was too humble to him to perform in aid of the South, no adventure too perilous for him to undertake if consistent with the character of a civilian who was at heart a soldier, and who in good faith and without too much qualification assented to at least a part of the frankly villainous dictum that all is fair in love and war.

One evening while Farquhar and his wife were sitting on a rustic bench near the entrance to his grounds, a gray-clad soldier rode up to the gate and asked for a drink of water. Mrs. Farquhar was only too happy to serve him with her own white hands. While she was fetching the water her husband approached the dusty horseman and inquired eagerly for news from the front.

"The Yanks are repairing the railroads," said the man, "and are getting ready for another advance. They have reached the Owl Creek bridge, put it in order and built a stockade on the north bank. The commandant has issued an order, which is posted everywhere, declaring that any civilian caught interfering with the railroad, its bridges, tunnels or trains will be summarily hanged. I saw the order."   10

"How far is it to the Owl Creek bridge?" Farquhar asked.

"About thirty miles."

"Is there no force on this side the creek?"

"Only a picket post half a mile out, on the railroad, and a single sentinel at this end of the bridge."

"Suppose a man—a civilian and student of hanging—should elude the picket post and perhaps get the better of the sentinel," said Farquhar, smiling, "what could he accomplish?"   15

The soldier reflected. "I was there a month ago," he replied. "I observed that the flood of last winter had lodged a great quantity of driftwood against the wooden pier at this end of the bridge. It is now dry and would burn like tow."

The lady had now brought the water, which the soldier drank. He thanked her ceremoniously, bowed to her husband and rode away. An hour later, after nightfall, he repassed the plantation, going northward in the direction from which he had come. He was a Federal scout.

III

As Peyton Farquhar fell straight downward through the bridge he lost consciousness and was as one already dead. From this state he was awakened—ages later, it seemed to him—by the pain of a sharp pressure upon his throat, followed by a sense of suffocation. Keen, poignant agonies seemed to shoot from his neck downward through every fiber of his body and limbs. These pains appeared to flash along well-defined lines of ramification and to beat with an inconceivably rapid periodicity. They seemed like streams of pulsating fire heating him to an intolerable temperature. As to his head, he was conscious of nothing but a feeling of fulness—of congestion. These sensations were unaccompanied by thought. The intellectual part of his nature was already effaced; he had power only to feel, and feeling was torment. He was conscious of motion. Encompassed in a luminous cloud, of which he was now merely the fiery heart, without material substance, he swung through unthinkable arcs of oscillation, like a vast pendulum. Then all at once, with terrible suddenness, the light about him shot upward with the noise of a loud plash; a frightful roaring was in his ears, and all was cold and dark. The power of thought was restored; he knew that the rope had broken and he had fallen into the stream. There was no additional strangulation; the noose about his neck was already suffocating him and kept the water from his lungs. To die of hanging at the bottom of a river!—the idea seemed to him ludicrous. He opened his eyes in the darkness and saw above him a gleam of light, but how distant, how inaccessible! He was still sinking, for the light became fainter and fainter until it was a mere glimmer. Then it began to grow and brighten, and he knew that he was rising toward the surface—knew it with reluctance, for he was now very comfortable. "To be hanged and drowned," he thought, "that is not so bad; but I do not wish to be shot. No; I will not be shot; that is not fair."

He was not conscious of an effort, but a sharp pain in his wrist apprised him that he was trying to free his hands. He gave the struggle his attention, as an idler might observe the feat of a juggler, without interest in the outcome. What splendid effort!—what magnificent, what superhuman strength! Ah, that was a fine endeavor! Bravo! The cord fell away; his arms parted and floated upward, the hands dimly seen on each side in the growing light. He watched them with a new interest as first one and then the other pounced upon the noose at his neck. They tore it away and thrust it fiercely aside, its undulations resembling those of a water-snake. "Put it back, put it back!" He thought he shouted these words to his hands, for the undoing of the noose had been succeeded by the direst pang that he had yet experienced. His neck ached horribly; his brain was on fire; his heart, which had been fluttering faintly, gave a great leap, trying to force itself out at his mouth. His whole body was racked and wrenched with an insupportable anguish! But his disobedient hands gave no heed to the command. They beat the water vigorously with quick, downward strokes, forcing him to the surface. He felt his head emerge; his eyes were blinded by the sunlight; his chest expanded convulsively, and with a supreme and crowning agony his lungs engulfed a great draught of air, which instantly he expelled in a shriek!

He was now in full possession of his physical senses. They were, indeed, preternat- 20
urally keen and alert. Something in the awful disturbance of his organic system had so exalted and refined them that they made record of things never before perceived. He felt the ripples upon his face and heard their separate sounds as they struck. He looked at the forest on the bank of the stream, saw the individual trees, the leaves and the veining of each leaf—saw the very insects upon them: the locusts, the brilliant-bodied flies, the gray spiders stretching their webs from twig to twig. He noted the prismatic colors in all the dewdrops upon a million blades of grass. The humming of the gnats that danced above the eddies of the stream, the beating of the dragon-flies' wings, the strokes of the water-spiders' legs, like oars which had lifted their boat—all these made audible music. A fish slid along beneath his eyes and he heard the rush of its body parting the water.

He had come to the surface facing down the stream; in a moment the visible world seemed to wheel slowly round, himself the pivotal point, and he saw the bridge, the fort, the soldiers upon the bridge, the captain, the sergeant, the two privates, his executioners. They were in silhouette against the blue sky. They shouted and gesticulated, pointing at him. The captain had drawn his pistol, but did not fire; the others were unarmed. Their movements were grotesque and horrible, their forms gigantic.

Suddenly he heard a sharp report and something struck the water smartly within a few inches of his head, spattering his face with spray. He heard a second report, and saw one of the sentinels with his rifle at his shoulder, a light cloud of blue smoke rising from the muzzle. The man in the water saw the eye of the man on the bridge gazing into his own through the sights of the rifle. He observed that it was a gray eye and remembered having read that gray eyes were keenest, and that all famous marksmen had them. Nevertheless, this one had missed.

A counter-swirl had caught Farquhar and turned him half round; he was again looking into the forest on the bank opposite the fort. The sound of a clear, high voice in a monotonous singsong now rang out behind him and came across the water with a distinctness that pierced and subdued all other sounds, even the beating of the ripples in his ears. Although no soldier, he had frequented camps enough to know the dread significance of that deliberate, drawling, aspirated chant; the lieutenant on shore was taking a part in the morning's work. How coldly and pitilessly—with what an even, calm intonation, presaging, and enforcing tranquility in the men—with what accurately measured intervals fell those cruel words:

"Attention, company! . . . Shoulder arms! . . . Ready! . . . Aim! . . . Fire!"

Farquhar dived—dived as deeply as he could. The water roared in his ears like 25
the voice of Niagara, yet he heard the dulled thunder of the volley and, rising again toward the surface, met shining bits of metal, singularly flattened, oscillating slowly downward. Some of them touched him on the face and hands, then fell away, continuing their descent. One lodged between his collar and neck; it was uncomfortably warm and he snatched it out.

As he rose to the surface, gasping for breath, he saw that he had been a long time under water; he was perceptibly farther down stream—nearer to safety. The soldiers had almost finished reloading; the metal ramrods flashed all at once in the sunshine as they were drawn from the barrels, turned in the air, and thrust into their sockets. The two sentinels fired again, independently and ineffectually.

The hunted man saw all this over his shoulder; he was now swimming vigorously with the current. His brain was as energetic as his arms and legs; he thought with the rapidity of lightning.

"The officer," he reasoned, "will not make that martinet's error a second time. It is as easy to dodge a volley as a single shot. He has probably already given the command to fire at will. God help me, I cannot dodge them all!"

An appalling plash within two yards of him was followed by a loud, rushing sound, *diminuendo,*° which seemed to travel back through the air to the fort and died in an explosion which stirred the very river to its deeps! A rising sheet of water curved over him, fell down upon him, blinded him, strangled him! The cannon had taken a hand in the game. As he shook his head free from the commotion of the smitten water he heard the deflected shot humming through the air ahead, and in an instant it was cracking and smashing the branches in the forest beyond.

"They will not do that again," he thought; "the next time they will use a charge 30
of grape. I must keep my eye upon the gun; the smoke will apprise me—the report arrives too late; it lags behind the missile. That is a good gun."

Suddenly he felt himself whirled round and round—spinning like a top. The water, the banks, the forests, the now distant bridge, fort and men—all were commingled and blurred. Objects were represented by their colors only; circular horizontal streaks of color—that was all he saw. He had been caught in a vortex and was being whirled on with a velocity of advance and gyration that made him giddy and sick. In

---

diminuendo: diminishing (Italian); a term from music indicating a gradual decrease in loudness or force.

a few moments he was flung upon the gravel at the foot of the left bank of the stream—the southern bank—and behind a projecting point which concealed him from his enemies. The sudden arrest of his motion, the abrasion of one of his hands on the gravel, restored him, and he wept with delight. He dug his fingers into the sand, threw it over himself in handfuls and audibly blessed it. It looked like diamonds, rubies, emeralds; he could think of nothing beautiful which it did not resemble. The trees upon the bank were giant garden plants; he noted a definite order in their arrangement, inhaled the fragrance of their blooms. A strange, roseate light shone through the spaces among their trunks and the wind made in their branches the music of aeolian harps. He had no wish to perfect his escape—was content to remain in that enchanting spot until retaken.

A whiz and rattle of grapeshot among the branches high above his head roused him from his dream. The baffled cannoneer had fired him a random farewell. He sprang to his feet, rushed up the sloping bank, and plunged into the forest.

All that day he traveled, laying his course by the rounding sun. The forest seemed interminable; nowhere did he discover a break in it, not even a woodman's road. He had not known that he lived in so wild a region. There was something uncanny in the revelation.

By nightfall he was fatigued, footsore, famishing. The thought of his wife and children urged him on. At last he found a road which led him in what he knew to be the right direction. It was as wide and straight as a city street, yet it seemed untraveled. No fields bordered it, no dwelling anywhere. Not so much as the barking of a dog suggested human habitation. The black bodies of the trees formed a straight wall on both sides, terminating on the horizon in a point, like a diagram in a lesson in perspective. Overhead, as he looked up through this rift in the wood, shone great golden stars looking unfamiliar and grouped in strange constellations. He was sure they were arranged in some order which had a secret and malign significance. The wood on either side was full of singular noises, among which—once, twice, and again—he distinctly heard whispers in an unknown tongue.

His neck was in pain and lifting his hand to it he found it horribly swollen. He knew that it had a circle of black where the rope had bruised it. His eyes felt congested; he could no longer close them. His tongue was swollen with thirst; he relieved its fever by thrusting it forward from between his teeth into the cold air. How softly the turf had carpeted the untraveled avenue—he could no longer feel the roadway beneath his feet! 35

Doubtless, despite his suffering, he had fallen asleep while walking, for now he sees another scene—perhaps he has merely recovered from a delirium. He stands at the gate of his own home. All is as he left it, and all bright and beautiful in the morning sunshine. He must have traveled the entire night. As he pushes open the gate and passes up the wide white walk, he sees a flutter of female garments; his wife, looking fresh and cool and sweet, steps down from the veranda to meet him. At the bottom of the steps she stands waiting, with a smile of ineffable joy, an attitude of matchless grace and dignity. Ah, how beautiful she is! He springs forward with extended arms. As he is about to clasp her he feels a stunning blow upon the back of the neck; a blinding white light blazes all about him with a sound like the shock of a cannon—then all is darkness and silence!

Peyton Farquhar was dead; his body, with a broken neck, swung gently from side to side beneath the timbers of the Owl Creek bridge.

Jorge Luis Borges

The Gospel According to Mark
1970

Translated by Andrew Hurley

Jorge Luis Borges

Jorge Luis Borges (1899–1986), an outstanding modern writer of Latin America, was born in Buenos Aires into a family prominent in Argentine history. His father, with whom he had a very close relationship, was a lawyer and teacher. Borges grew up bilingual, learning English from his English grandmother and receiving his early education from an English tutor. In later years, he would translate work by Poe, Melville, Whitman, Faulkner, and others into Spanish. Caught in Europe by the outbreak of World War I, Borges lived in Switzerland—where he learned French and taught himself German—and later Spain, where he joined the Ultraists, a group of experimental poets who renounced realism. On returning to Argentina, he edited a poetry magazine printed in the form of a poster and affixed to city walls. In his early writings, Borges favored the style of Criollismo (regionalism), but by the mid-1930s he had begun to take a more cosmopolitan and internationalist approach; in this same period, his principal literary emphasis began to shift from poetry to fiction. In 1946, for his opposition to the regime of Colonel Juan Perón, Borges was forced to resign his post as a librarian and was mockingly offered a job as a chicken inspector. In 1955, after Perón was deposed, Borges became director of the National Library and professor of English literature at the University of Buenos Aires. A sufferer since childhood from poor eyesight, Borges eventually went blind. His eye problems may have encouraged him to work mainly in short, highly crafted forms: stories, essays, fables, and lyric poems full of elaborate music. His short stories, in Ficciones (1944), El hacedor (1960; translated as Dreamtigers, 1964), and Labyrinths (1962), have been admired worldwide.

The incident took place on the Los Alamos ranch, south of the small town of Junín, in late March of 1928. Its protagonist was a medical student named Baltasar Espinosa. We might define him for the moment as a Buenos Aires youth much like many others, with no traits worthier of note than the gift for public speaking that had won him more than one prize at the English school° in Ramos Mejía and an almost unlimited goodness. He didn't like to argue; he preferred that his interlocutor rather than he himself be right. And though he found the chance twists and turns of gambling interesting, he was a poor gambler, because he didn't like to win. He was intelligent and open to learning, but he was lazy; at thirty-three he had not yet completed the last requirements for his degree. (The work he still owed, incidentally, was for his favorite class.) His father, like all the gentlemen of his day a freethinker,°

English school: a prep school that emphasized English (well-to-do Argentineans of this era wanted their children to learn English).   *freethinker:* person who rejects traditional beliefs, especially religious dogma, in favor of rational inquiry.

had instructed Espinosa in the doctrines of Herbert Spencer,° but once, before he set off on a trip to Montevideo, his mother had asked him to say the Lord's Prayer every night and make the sign of the cross, and never in all the years that followed did he break that promise. He did not lack courage; one morning, with more indifference than wrath, he had traded two or three blows with some of his classmates that were trying to force him to join a strike at the university. He abounded in debatable habits and opinions, out of a spirit of acquiescence: his country mattered less to him than the danger that people in other countries might think the Argentines still wore feathers; he venerated France but had contempt for the French; he had little respect for Americans but took pride in the fact that there were skyscrapers in Buenos Aires; he thought that the gauchos° of the plains were better horsemen than the gauchos of the mountains. When his cousin Daniel invited him to spend the summer at Los Alamos, he immediately accepted—not because he liked the country but out of a natural desire to please, and because he could find no good reason for saying no.

The main house at the ranch was large and a bit run-down; the quarters for the foreman, a man named Gutre, stood nearby. There were three members of the Gutre family: the father, the son (who was singularly rough and unpolished), and a girl of uncertain paternity. They were tall, strong, and bony, with reddish hair and Indian features. They rarely spoke. The foreman's wife had died years before.

In the country, Espinosa came to learn things he hadn't known, had never even suspected; for example, that when you're approaching a house there's no reason to gallop and that nobody goes out on a horse unless there's a job to be done. As the summer wore on, he learned to distinguish birds by their call.

Within a few days, Daniel had to go to Buenos Aires to close a deal on some livestock. At the most, he said, the trip would take a week. Espinosa, who was already a little tired of his cousin's *bonnes fortunes* and his indefatigable interest in the vagaries of men's tailoring, stayed behind on the ranch with his textbooks. The heat was oppressive, and not even nightfall brought relief. Then one morning toward dawn, he was awakened by thunder. Wind lashed the casuarina trees. Espinosa heard the first drops of rain and gave thanks to God. Suddenly the wind blew cold. That afternoon, the Salado overflowed.

The next morning, as he stood on the porch looking out over the flooded plains, Baltasar Espinosa realized that the metaphor equating the pampas with the sea was not, at least that morning, an altogether false one, though Hudson° had noted that the sea seems the grander of the two because we view it not from horseback or our own height, but from the deck of a ship. The rain did not let up; the Gutres, helped (or hindered) by the city dweller, saved a good part of the livestock, though many animals were drowned. There were four roads leading to the ranch; all were under water. On the third day, when a leaking roof threatened the foreman's house, Espinosa gave the Gutres a room at the back of the main house, alongside the toolshed. The move brought Espinosa and the Gutres closer, and they began to eat together in the large dining room. Conversation was not easy; the Gutres, who knew so much about things in the country, did not know how to explain them. One night Espinosa asked them if people still remembered anything about the Indian raids, back when the military

5

Herbert Spencer: a British philosopher (1820–1903) who championed the theory of evolution.   *gauchos*: South American cowboys.   *W. H. Hudson*: an English naturalist and author (1841–1922) who wrote extensively about South America.

command for the frontier had been in Junín. They told him they did, but they would have given the same answer if he had asked them about the day Charles I° had been beheaded. Espinosa recalled that his father used to say that all the cases of longevity that occur in the country are the result of either poor memory or a vague notion of dates—gauchos quite often know neither the year they were born in nor the name of the man that fathered them.

In the entire house, the only reading material to be found were several copies of a farming magazine, a manual of veterinary medicine, a deluxe edition of the romantic verse drama *Tabaré*, a copy of *The History of the Shorthorn in Argentina*, several erotic and detective stories, and a recent novel that Espinosa had not read—*Don Segundo Sombra*, by Ricardo Güiraldes. In order to put some life into the inevitable after-dinner attempt at conversation, Espinosa read a couple of chapters of the novel to the Gutres, who did not know how to read or write. Unfortunately, the foreman had been a cattle drover himself, and he could not be interested in the adventures of another such a one. It was easy work, he said; they always carried along a pack mule with everything they might need. If he had not been a cattle drover, he announced, he'd never have seen Lake Gómez, or the Bragado River, or even the Núñez ranch, in Chacabuco. . . .

In the kitchen there was a guitar; before the incident I am narrating, the laborers would sit in a circle and someone would pick up the guitar and strum it, though never managing actually to play it. That was called "giving it a strum."

Espinosa, who was letting his beard grow out, would stop before the mirror to look at his changed face; he smiled to think that he'd soon be boring the fellows in Buenos Aires with his stories about the Salado overrunning its banks. Curiously, he missed places in the city he never went, and would never go: a street corner on Cabrera where a mailbox stood; two cement lions on a porch on Calle Jujuy a few blocks from the Plaza del Once; a tile-floored corner grocery-store-and-bar (whose location he couldn't quite remember). As for his father and his brothers, by now Daniel would have told them that he had been isolated—the word was etymologically precise—by the floodwaters.

Exploring the house still cut off by the high water, he came upon a Bible printed in English. On its last pages the Guthries (for that was their real name) had kept their family history. They had come originally from Inverness° and had arrived in the New World—doubtlessly as peasant laborers—in the early nineteenth century; they had intermarried with Indians. The chronicle came to an end in the eighteen-seventies; they no longer knew how to write. Within a few generations they had forgotten their English; by the time Espinosa met them, even Spanish gave them some difficulty. They had no faith, though in their veins, alongside the superstitions of the pampas, there still ran a dim current of the Calvinist's harsh fanaticism. Espinosa mentioned his find to them, but they hardly seemed to hear him.

He leafed through the book, and his fingers opened it to the first verses of the   10
Gospel According to St. Mark. To try his hand at translating, and perhaps to see if they might understand a little of it, he decided that that would be the text he read the Gutres after dinner. He was surprised that they listened first attentively and then with mute fascination. The presence of gold letters on the binding may have given it increased authority. "It's in their blood," he thought. It also occurred to him that

Charles I: King of England, beheaded in 1649.   *Inverness*: a county in Scotland.

throughout history, humankind has told two stories: the story of a lost ship sailing the Mediterranean seas in quest of a beloved isle, and the story of a god who allows himself to be crucified on Golgotha. He recalled his elocution classes in Ramos Mejía, and he rose to his feet to preach the parables.

In the following days, the Gutres would wolf down the spitted beef and canned sardines in order to arrive sooner at the Gospel.

The girl had a little lamb; it was her pet, and she prettied it with a sky blue ribbon. One day it cut itself on a piece of barbed wire; to stanch the blood, the Gutres were about to put spiderwebs on the wound, but Espinosa treated it with pills. The gratitude awakened by that cure amazed him. At first, he had not trusted the Gutres and had hidden away in one of his books the two hundred forty pesos he'd brought; now, with Daniel gone, he had taken the master's place and begun to give timid orders, which were immediately followed. The Gutres would trail him through the rooms and along the hallway, as though they were lost. As he read, he noticed that they would sweep away the crumbs he had left on the table. One afternoon, he surprised them as they were discussing him in brief, respectful words. When he came to the end of the Gospel According to St. Mark, he started to read another of the three remaining gospels, but the father asked him to reread the one he'd just finished, so they could understand it better. Espinosa felt they were like children, who prefer repetition to variety or novelty. One night he dreamed of the Flood (which is not surprising) and was awakened by the hammering of the building of the Ark, but he told himself it was thunder. And in fact the rain, which had let up for a while, had begun again; it was very cold. The Gutres told him the rain had broken through the roof of the toolshed; when they got the beams repaired, they said, they'd show him where. He was no longer a stranger, a foreigner, and they all treated him with respect; he was almost spoiled. None of them liked coffee, but there was always a little cup for him, with spoonfuls of sugar stirred in.

That second storm took place on a Tuesday. Thursday night there was a soft knock on his door; because of his doubts about the Gutres he always locked it. He got up and opened the door; it was the girl. In the darkness he couldn't see her, but he could tell by her footsteps that she was barefoot, and afterward, in the bed, that she was naked—that in fact she had come from the back of the house that way. She did not embrace him, or speak a word; she lay down beside him and she was shivering. It was the first time she had lain with a man. When she left, she did not kiss him; Espinosa realized that he didn't even know her name. Impelled by some sentiment he did not attempt to understand, he swore that when he returned to Buenos Aires, he'd tell no one of the incident.

The next day began like all the others, except that the father spoke to Espinosa to ask whether Christ had allowed himself to be killed in order to save all mankind. Espinosa, who was a freethinker like his father but felt obliged to defend what he had read them, paused.

"Yes," he finally replied. "To save all mankind from hell."

"What *is* hell?" Gutre then asked him.

"A place underground where souls will burn in fire forever."

"And those that drove the nails will also be saved?"

"Yes," replied Espinosa, whose theology was a bit shaky. (He had worried that the foreman wanted to have a word with him about what had happened last night with his daughter.)

After lunch they asked him to read the last chapters again.

Espinosa had a long siesta that afternoon, although it was a light sleep, interrupted by persistent hammering and vague premonitions. Toward evening he got up and went out into the hall.

"The water's going down," he said, as though thinking out loud. "It won't be long now."

"Not long now," repeated Gutre, like an echo.

The three of them had followed him. Kneeling on the floor, they asked his blessing. Then they cursed him, spat on him, and drove him to the back of the house. The girl was weeping. Espinosa realized what awaited him on the other side of the door. When they opened it, he saw the sky. A bird screamed; *it's a goldfinch*, Espinosa thought. There was no roof on the shed; they had torn down the roof beams to build the Cross.

T. Coraghessan Boyle

Greasy Lake   1985

T. Coraghessan Boyle (the T. stands for Tom) was born in 1948 in Peekskill, New York, the son of Irish immigrants. He grew up, he recalls, "as a sort of pampered punk" who did not read a book until he was eighteen. After a brief period as a high school teacher, he studied in the University of Iowa Writers' Workshop, submitting a collection of stories for his Ph.D. His stories in Esquire, Paris Review, *the* Atlantic, *and other magazines quickly won him notice for their outrageous macabre humor and bizarre inventiveness. Boyle has published nine volumes of short stories, including* Greasy Lake *(1985), T. C. Boyle Stories (1998), and Tooth and Claw (2005). He has also published over a dozen novels that are quite unlike anything else in*

T. Coraghessan Boyle

contemporary American fiction. The subjects of some Boyle novels reveal his wide-ranging and idiosyncratic interests. Budding Prospects *(1984) is a picaresque romp among adventurous marijuana growers.* East Is East *(1990) is a half-serious, half-comic story of a Japanese fugitive in an American writers' colony.* The Road to Wellville *(1993) takes place in 1907 in a sanitarium run by Dr. John Harvey Kellogg of corn flakes fame, with cameo appearances by Henry Ford, Thomas Edison, and Harvey Firestone. His most recent novel is* When the Killing's Done *(2011). Boyle is Distinguished Professor of English at University of Southern California.*

> *It's about a mile down on the dark side of Route 88.*
> —BRUCE SPRINGSTEEN

There was a time when courtesy and winning ways went out of style, when it was good to be bad, when you cultivated decadence like a taste. We were all dangerous characters then. We wore torn-up leather jackets, slouched around with toothpicks in our mouths, sniffed glue and ether and what somebody claimed was cocaine. When we wheeled our parents' whining station wagons out onto the street we left a patch of rubber half a block long. We drank gin and grape juice, Tango, Thunderbird, and Bali Hai. We were nineteen. We were bad. We read André Gide° and struck elaborate poses to show that we didn't give a shit about anything. At night, we went up to Greasy Lake.

Through the center of town, up the strip, past the housing developments and shopping malls, street lights giving way to the thin streaming illumination of the headlights, trees crowding the asphalt in a black unbroken wall: that was the way out to Greasy Lake. The Indians had called it Wakan, a reference to the clarity of its waters. Now it was fetid and murky, the mud banks glittering with broken glass and strewn with beer cans and the charred remains of bonfires. There was a single ravaged island a hundred yards from shore, so stripped of vegetation it looked as if the air force had strafed it. We went up to the lake because everyone went there, because we wanted to snuff the rich scent of possibility on the breeze, watch a girl take off her clothes and plunge into the festering murk, drink beer, smoke pot, howl at the stars, savor the incongruous full-throated roar of rock and roll against the primeval susurrus of frogs and crickets. This was nature.

I was there one night, late, in the company of two dangerous characters. Digby wore a gold star in his right ear and allowed his father to pay his tuition at Cornell; Jeff was thinking of quitting school to become a painter/musician/head-shop proprietor. They were both expert in the social graces, quick with a sneer, able to manage a Ford with lousy shocks over a rutted and gutted blacktop road at eighty-five while rolling a joint as compact as a Tootsie Roll Pop stick. They could lounge against a bank of booming speakers and trade "man"s with the best of them or roll out across the dance floor as if their joints worked on bearings. They were slick and quick and they wore their mirror shades at breakfast and dinner, in the shower, in closets and caves. In short, they were bad.

I drove. Digby pounded the dashboard and shouted along with Toots & the Maytals while Jeff hung his head out the window and streaked the side of my mother's Bel Air with vomit. It was early June, the air soft as a hand on your cheek, the third night of summer vacation. The first two nights we'd been out till dawn, looking for something we never found. On this, the third night, we'd cruised the strip sixty-seven times, been in and out of every bar and club we could think of in a twenty-mile radius, stopped twice for bucket chicken and forty-cent hamburgers, debated going to a party at the house of a girl Jeff's sister knew, and chucked two dozen raw eggs at mailboxes and hitchhikers. It was 2:00 A.M.; the bars were closing. There was nothing to do but take a bottle of lemon-flavored gin up to Greasy Lake.

The taillights of a single car winked at us as we swung into the dirt lot with its tufts of weed and washboard corrugations; '57 Chevy, mint, metallic blue. On the far side of the lot, like the exoskeleton of some gaunt chrome insect, a chopper leaned against its kickstand. And that was it for excitement: some junkie halfwit biker and a car freak pumping his girlfriend. Whatever it was we were looking for, we weren't about to find it at Greasy Lake. Not that night.   5

André Gide: controversial French writer (1869–1951) whose novels, including *The Counterfeiters* and *Lafcadio's Adventures*, often show individuals in conflict with accepted morality.

But then all of a sudden Digby was fighting for the wheel. "Hey, that's Tony Lovett's car! Hey!" he shouted, while I stabbed at the brake pedal and the Bel Air nosed up to the gleaming bumper of the parked Chevy. Digby leaned on the horn, laughing, and instructed me to put my brights on. I flicked on the brights. This was hilarious. A joke. Tony would experience premature withdrawal and expect to be confronted by grim-looking state troopers with flashlights. We hit the horn, strobed the lights, and then jumped out of the car to press our witty faces to Tony's windows; for all we knew we might even catch a glimpse of some little fox's tit, and then we could slap backs with red-faced Tony, roughhouse a little, and go on to new heights of adventure and daring.

The first mistake, the one that opened the whole floodgate, was losing my grip on the keys. In the excitement, leaping from the car with the gin in one hand and a roach clip in the other, I spilled them in the grass—in the dark, rank, mysterious nighttime grass of Greasy Lake. This was a tactical error, as damaging and irreversible in its way as Westmoreland's decision to dig in at Khe Sanh.° I felt it like a jab of intuition, and I stopped there by the open door, peering vaguely into the night that puddled up round my feet.

The second mistake—and this was inextricably bound up with the first—was identifying the car as Tony Lovett's. Even before the very bad character in greasy jeans and engineer boots ripped out of the driver's door, I began to realize that this chrome blue was much lighter than the robin's-egg of Tony's car, and that Tony's car didn't have rear-mounted speakers. Judging from their expressions, Digby and Jeff were privately groping toward the same inevitable and unsettling conclusion as I was.

In any case, there was no reasoning with this bad greasy character—clearly he was a man of action. The first lusty Rockette° kick of his steel-toed boot caught me under the chin, chipped my favorite tooth, and left me sprawled in the dirt. Like a fool, I'd gone down on one knee to comb the stiff hacked grass for the keys, my mind making connections in the most dragged-out, testudineous way, knowing that things had gone wrong, that I was in a lot of trouble, and that the lost ignition key was my grail and my salvation. The three or four succeeding blows were mainly absorbed by my right buttock and the tough piece of bone at the base of my spine.

Meanwhile, Digby vaulted the kissing bumpers and delivered a savage kung-fu blow   10
to the greasy character's collarbone. Digby had just finished a course in martial arts for phys-ed credit and had spent the better part of the past two nights telling us apocryphal tales of Bruce Lee types and of the raw power invested in lightning blows shot from coiled wrists, ankles, and elbows. The greasy character was unimpressed. He merely backed off a step, his face like a Toltec mask, and laid Digby out with a single whistling roundhouse blow . . . but by now Jeff had got into the act, and I was beginning to extricate myself from the dirt, a tinny compound of shock, rage, and impotence wadded in my throat.

Jeff was on the guy's back, biting at his ear. Digby was on the ground, cursing. I went for the tire iron I kept under the driver's seat. I kept it there because bad characters always keep tire irons under the driver's seat, for just such an occasion as this. Never mind that I hadn't been involved in a fight since sixth grade, when a kid with a sleepy eye and two streams of mucus depending from his nostrils hit me in the

---

Westmoreland's decision . . . Khe Sanh: General William C. Westmoreland commanded U.S. troops in Vietnam (1964–68). In late 1967 the North Vietnamese and Viet Cong forces attacked Khe Sanh (or Khesanh) with a show of strength, causing Westmoreland to expend great effort to defend a plateau of relatively little tactical importance.   *Rockette:* member of a dance troupe in the stage show at Radio City Music Hall, New York, famous for its ability to kick fast and high with wonderful coordination.

knee with a Louisville slugger,° never mind that I'd touched the tire iron exactly twice before, to change tires: it was there. And I went for it.

I was terrified. Blood was beating in my ears, my hands were shaking, my heart turning over like a dirtbike in the wrong gear. My antagonist was shirtless, and a single cord of muscle flashed across his chest as he bent forward to peel Jeff from his back like a wet overcoat. "Motherfucker," he spat, over and over, and I was aware in that instant that all four of us—Digby, Jeff, and myself included—were chanting "motherfucker, motherfucker," as if it were a battle cry. (What happened next? the detective asks the murderer from beneath the turned-down brim of his porkpie hat. I don't know, the murderer says, something came over me. Exactly.)

Digby poked the flat of his hand in the bad character's face and I came at him like a kamikaze, mindless, raging, stung with humiliation—the whole thing, from the initial boot in the chin to this murderous primal instant involving no more than sixty hyperventilating, gland-flooding seconds—I came at him and brought the tire iron down across his ear. The effect was instantaneous, astonishing. He was a stunt man and this was Hollywood, he was a big grimacing toothy balloon and I was a man with a straight pin. He collapsed. Wet his pants. Went loose in his boots.

A single second, big as a zeppelin, floated by. We were standing over him in a circle, gritting our teeth, jerking our necks, our limbs and hands and feet twitching with glandular discharges. No one said anything. We just stared down at the guy, the car freak, the lover, the bad greasy character laid low. Digby looked at me; so did Jeff. I was still holding the tire iron, a tuft of hair clinging to the crook like dandelion fluff, like down. Rattled, I dropped it in the dirt, already envisioning the headlines, the pitted faces of the police inquisitors, the gleam of handcuffs, clank of bars, the big black shadows rising from the back of the cell . . . when suddenly a raw torn shriek cut through me like all the juice in all the electric chairs in the country.

It was the fox. She was short, barefoot, dressed in panties and a man's shirt. "Animals!" she screamed, running at us with her fists clenched and wisps of blow-dried hair in her face. There was a silver chain round her ankle, and her toenails flashed in the glare of the headlights. I think it was the toenails that did it. Sure, the gin and the cannabis and even the Kentucky Fried may have had a hand in it, but it was the sight of those flaming toes that set us off—the toad emerging from the loaf in *Virgin Spring*,° lipstick smeared on a child; she was already tainted. We were on her like Bergman's deranged brothers—see no evil, hear none, speak none—panting, wheezing, tearing at her clothes, grabbing for flesh. We were bad characters, and we were scared and hot and three steps over the line—anything could have happened. 15

It didn't.

Before we could pin her to the hood of the car, our eyes masked with lust and greed and the purest primal badness, a pair of headlights swung into the lot. There we were, dirty, bloody, guilty, dissociated from humanity and civilization, the first of the Ur-crimes behind us, the second in progress, shreds of nylon panty and spandex brassiere dangling from our fingers, our flies open, lips licked—there we were, caught in the spotlight. Nailed.

We bolted. First for the car, and then, realizing we had no way of starting it, for the woods. I thought nothing. I thought escape. The headlights came at me like accusing fingers. I was gone.

Louisville slugger: a brand of baseball bat. *Virgin Spring:* film about a rape by Swedish director Ingmar Bergman (1960).

Ram-bam-bam, across the parking lot, past the chopper and into the feculent undergrowth at the lake's edge, insects flying up in my face, weeds whipping, frogs and snakes and red-eyed turtles splashing off into the night: I was already ankle-deep in muck and tepid water and still going strong. Behind me, the girl's screams rose in intensity, disconsolate, incriminating, the screams of the Sabine women,° the Christian martyrs, Anne Frank° dragged from the garret. I kept going, pursued by those cries, imagining cops and bloodhounds. The water was up to my knees when I realized what I was doing: I was going to swim for it. Swim the breadth of Greasy Lake and hide myself in the thick clot of woods on the far side. They'd never find me there.

I was breathing in sobs, in gasps. The water lapped at my waist as I looked out   20
over the moon-burnished ripples, the mats of algae that clung to the surface like scabs. Digby and Jeff had vanished. I paused. Listened. The girl was quieter now, screams tapering to sobs, but there were male voices, angry, excited, and the high-pitched ticking of the second car's engine. I waded deeper, stealthy, hunted, the ooze sucking at my sneakers. As I was about to take the plunge—at the very instant I dropped my shoulder for the first slashing stroke—I blundered into something. Something unspeakable, obscene, something soft, wet, moss-grown. A patch of weed? A log? When I reached out to touch it, it gave like a rubber duck, it gave like flesh.

In one of those nasty little epiphanies for which we are prepared by films and TV and childhood visits to the funeral home to ponder the shrunken painted forms of dead grandparents, I understood what it was that bobbed there so inadmissibly in the dark. Understood, and stumbled back in horror and revulsion, my mind yanked in six different directions (I was nineteen, a mere child, an infant, and here in the space of five minutes I'd struck down one greasy character and blundered into the waterlogged carcass of a second), thinking, The keys, the keys, why did I have to go and lose the keys? I stumbled back, but the muck took hold of my feet—a sneaker snagged, balance lost—and suddenly I was pitching face forward into the buoyant black mass, throwing out my hands in desperation while simultaneously conjuring the image of reeking frogs and muskrats revolving in slicks of their own deliquescing juices. AAAAArrrgh! I shot from the water like a torpedo, the dead man rotating to expose a mossy beard and eyes cold as the moon. I must have shouted out, thrashing around in the weeds, because the voices behind me suddenly became animated.

"What was that?"

"It's them, it's them: they tried to, tried to . . . *rape* me!" Sobs.

A man's voice, flat Midwestern accent. "You sons a bitches, we'll kill you!"

Frogs, crickets.   25

Then another voice, harsh, r-less, Lower East Side: "Motherfucker!" I recognized the verbal virtuosity of the bad greasy character in the engineer boots. Tooth chipped, sneakers gone, coated in mud and slime and worse, crouching breathless in the weeds waiting to have my ass thoroughly and definitively kicked and fresh from the hideous stinking embrace of a three-days-dead-corpse, I suddenly felt a rush of joy and vindication: the son of a bitch was alive! Just as quickly, my bowels turned to ice.

Sabine women: members of an ancient tribe in Italy, according to legend, forcibly carried off by the early Romans under Romulus to be their wives. The incident is depicted in a famous painting, "The Rape of the Sabine Women," by seventeenth-century French artist Nicolas Poussin.   *Anne Frank:* German Jewish girl (1929–1945) whose diary written during the Nazi occupation of the Netherlands later became world-famous. She hid with her family in a secret attic in Amsterdam, but was caught by the Gestapo and sent to the concentration camp at Belsen, where she died.

"Come on out of there, you pansy mothers!" the bad greasy character was screaming. He shouted curses till he was out of breath.

The crickets started up again, then the frogs. I held my breath. All at once there was a sound in the reeds, a swishing, a splash: thunk-a-thunk. They were throwing rocks. The frogs fell silent. I cradled my head. Swish, swish, thunk-a-thunk. A wedge of feldspar the size of a cue ball glanced off my knee. I bit my finger.

It was then that they turned to the car. I heard a door slam, a curse, and then the sound of the headlights shattering—almost a good-natured sound, celebratory, like corks popping from the necks of bottles. This was succeeded by the dull booming of the fenders, metal on metal, and then the icy crash of the windshield. I inched forward, elbows and knees, my belly pressed to the muck, thinking of guerrillas and commandos and *The Naked and the Dead*.° I parted the weeds and squinted the length of the parking lot.

The second car—it was a Trans-Am—was still running, its high beams washing the scene in a lurid stagy light. Tire iron flailing, the greasy bad character was laying into the side of my mother's Bel Air like an avenging demon, his shadow riding up the trunks of the trees. Whomp. Whomp. Whomp-whomp. The other two guys— blond types, in fraternity jackets—were helping out with tree branches and skull-sized boulders. One of them was gathering up bottles, rocks, muck, candy wrappers, used condoms, poptops, and other refuse and pitching it through the window on the driver's side. I could see the fox, a white bulb behind the windshield of the '57 Chevy. "Bobbie," she whined over the thumping, "come on." The greasy character paused a moment, took one good swipe at the left taillight, and then heaved the tire iron halfway across the lake. Then he fired up the '57 and was gone.

Blond head nodded at blond head. One said something to the other, too low for me to catch. They were no doubt thinking that in helping to annihilate my mother's car they'd committed a fairly rash act, and thinking too that there were three bad characters connected with that very car watching them from the woods. Perhaps other possibilities occurred to them as well—police, jail cells, justices of the peace, reparations, lawyers, irate parents, fraternal censure. Whatever they were thinking, they suddenly dropped branches, bottles, and rocks and sprang for their car in unison, as if they'd choreographed it. Five seconds. That's all it took. The engine shrieked, the tires squealed, a cloud of dust rose from the rutted lot and then settled back on darkness.

I don't know how long I lay there, the bad breath of decay all around me, my jacket heavy as a bear, the primordial ooze subtly reconstituting itself to accommodate my upper thighs and testicles. My jaws ached, my knee throbbed, my coccyx was on fire. I contemplated suicide, wondered if I'd need bridgework, scraped the recesses of my brain for some sort of excuse to give my parents—a tree had fallen on the car, I was blinded by a bread truck, hit and run, vandals had got to it while we were playing chess at Digby's. Then I thought of the dead man. He was probably the only person on the planet worse off than I was. I thought about him, fog on the lake, insects chirring eerily, and felt the tug of fear, felt the darkness opening up inside me like a set of jaws. Who was he, I wondered, this victim of time and circumstance bobbing sorrowfully in the lake at my back. The owner of the chopper, no doubt, a bad older character come to this. Shot during a murky drug deal, drowned while drunkenly frolicking in the lake. Another headline. My car was wrecked; he was dead.

The Naked and the Dead: novel (1948) by Norman Mailer, about U.S. Army life in World War II.

When the eastern half of the sky went from black to cobalt and the trees began to separate themselves from the shadows, I pushed myself up from the mud and stepped out into the open. By now the birds had begun to take over for the crickets, and dew lay slick on the leaves. There was a smell in the air, raw and sweet at the same time, the smell of the sun firing buds and opening blossoms. I contemplated the car. It lay there like a wreck along the highway, like a steel sculpture left over from a vanished civilization. Everything was still. This was nature.

I was circling the car, as dazed and bedraggled as the sole survivor of an air blitz, when Digby and Jeff emerged from the trees behind me. Digby's face was cross-hatched with smears of dirt; Jeff's jacket was gone and his shirt was torn across the shoulder. They slouched across the lot, looking sheepish, and silently came up beside me to gape at the ravaged automobile. No one said a word. After a while Jeff swung open the driver's door and began to scoop the broken glass and garbage off the seat. I looked at Digby. He shrugged. "At least they didn't slash the tires," he said.

It was true: the tires were intact. There was no windshield, the headlights were staved in, and the body looked as if it had been sledge-hammered for a quarter a shot at the county fair, but the tires were inflated to regulation pressure. The car was drivable. In silence, all three of us bent to scrape the mud and shattered glass from the interior. I said nothing about the biker. When we were finished, I reached in my pocket for the keys, experienced a nasty stab of recollection, cursed myself, and turned to search the grass. I spotted them almost immediately, no more than five feet from the open door, glinting like jewels in the first tapering shaft of sunlight. There was no reason to get philosophical about it: I eased into the seat and turned the engine over.

It was at that precise moment that the silver Mustang with the flame decals rumbled into the lot. All three of us froze; then Digby and Jeff slid into the car and slammed the door. We watched as the Mustang rocked and bobbed across the ruts and finally jerked to a halt beside the forlorn chopper at the far end of the lot. "Let's go," Digby said. I hesitated, the Bel Air wheezing beneath me.

Two girls emerged from the Mustang. Tight jeans, stiletto heels, hair like frozen fur. They bent over the motorcycle, paced back and forth aimlessly, glanced once or twice at us, and then ambled over to where the reeds sprang up in a green fence round the perimeter of the lake. One of them cupped her hands to her mouth. "Al," she called. "Hey, Al!"

"Come on," Digby hissed. "Let's get out of here."

But it was too late. The second girl was picking her way across the lot, unsteady on her heels, looking up at us and then away. She was older—twenty-five or -six— and as she came closer we could see there was something wrong with her: she was stoned or drunk, lurching now and waving her arms for balance. I gripped the steering wheel as if it were the ejection lever of a flaming jet, and Digby spat out my name, twice, terse and impatient.

"Hi," the girl said.

We looked at her like zombies, like war veterans, like deaf-and-dumb pencil peddlers.

She smiled, her lips cracked and dry. "Listen," she said, bending from the waist to look in the window, "you guys seen Al?" Her pupils were pinpoints, her eyes glass. She jerked her neck. "That's his bike over there—Al's. You seen him?"

Al. I didn't know what to say. I wanted to get out of the car and retch, I wanted to go home to my parents' house and crawl into bed. Digby poked me in the ribs. "We haven't seen anybody," I said.

35

40

The girl seemed to consider this, reaching out a slim veiny arm to brace herself against the car. "No matter," she said, slurring the *t*'s, "he'll turn up." And then, as if she'd just taken stock of the whole scene—the ravaged car and our battered faces, the desolation of the place—she said: "Hey, you guys look like some pretty bad characters—been fightin', huh?" We stared straight ahead, rigid as catatonics. She was fumbling in her pocket and muttering something. Finally she held out a handful of tablets in glassine wrappers: "Hey, you want to party, you want to do some of these with me and Sarah?"

I just looked at her. I thought I was going to cry. Digby broke the silence. "No, thanks," he said, leaning over me. "Some other time."

I put the car in gear and it inched forward with a groan, shaking off pellets of   45
glass like an old dog shedding water after a bath, heaving over the ruts on its worn springs, creeping toward the highway. There was a sheen of sun on the lake. I looked back. The girl was still standing there, watching us, her shoulders slumped, hand outstretched.

Kate Chopin

The Story of an Hour   1894

Kate Chopin (1851–1904) demonstrates again, as in "The Storm" in Chapter 4, her ability to write short stories of compressed intensity. For a brief biography and a portrait see page 121.

Knowing that Mrs. Mallard was afflicted with a heart trouble, great care was taken to break to her as gently as possible the news of her husband's death.

It was her sister Josephine who told her, in broken sentences; veiled hints that revealed in half concealing. Her husband's friend Richards was there, too, near her. It was he who had been in the newspaper office when intelligence of the railroad disaster was received, with Brently Mallard's name leading the list of "killed." He had only taken the time to assure himself of its truth by a second telegram, and had hastened to forestall any less careful, less tender friend in bearing the sad message.

She did not hear the story as many women have heard the same, with a paralyzed inability to accept its significance. She wept at once, with sudden, wild abandonment, in her sister's arms. When the storm of grief had spent itself she went away to her room alone. She would have no one follow her.

There stood, facing the open window, a comfortable, roomy armchair. Into this she sank, pressed down by a physical exhaustion that haunted her body and seemed to reach into her soul.

She could see in the open square before her house the tops of trees that were all   5
aquiver with the new spring life. The delicious breath of rain was in the air. In the street below a peddler was crying his wares. The notes of a distant song which some one was singing reached her faintly, and countless sparrows were twittering in the eaves.

There were patches of blue sky showing here and there through the clouds that had met and piled one above the other in the west facing her window.

She sat with her head thrown back upon the cushion of the chair, quite motionless, except when a sob came up into her throat and shook her, as a child who has cried itself to sleep continues to sob in its dreams.

She was young, with a fair, calm face, whose lines bespoke repression and even a certain strength. But now there was a dull stare in her eyes, whose gaze was fixed away off yonder on one of those patches of blue sky. It was not a glance of reflection, but rather indicated a suspension of intelligent thought.

There was something coming to her and she was waiting for it, fearfully. What was it? She did not know; it was too subtle and elusive to name. But she felt it, creeping out of the sky, reaching toward her through the sounds, the scents, the color that filled the air.

Now her bosom rose and fell tumultuously. She was beginning to recognize this   10
thing that was approaching to possess her, and she was striving to beat it back with her will—as powerless as her two white slender hands would have been.

When she abandoned herself a little whispered word escaped her slightly parted lips. She said it over and over under her breath: "free, free, free!" The vacant stare and the look of terror that had followed it went from her eyes. They stayed keen and bright. Her pulses beat fast, and the coursing blood warmed and relaxed every inch of her body.

She did not stop to ask if it were or were not a monstrous joy that held her. A clear and exalted perception enabled her to dismiss the suggestion as trivial.

She knew that she would weep again when she saw the kind, tender hands folded in death; the face that had never looked save with love upon her, fixed and gray and dead. But she saw beyond that bitter moment a long procession of years to come that would belong to her absolutely. And she opened and spread her arms out to them in welcome.

There would be no one to live for her during those coming years; she would live for herself. There would be no powerful will bending hers in that blind persistence with which men and women believe they have a right to impose a private will upon a fellow-creature. A kind intention or a cruel intention made the act seem no less a crime as she looked upon it in that brief moment of illumination.

And yet she had loved him—sometimes. Often she had not. What did it matter!   15
What could love, the unsolved mystery, count for in face of this possession of self-assertion which she suddenly recognized as the strongest impulse of her being!

"Free! Body and soul free!" she kept whispering.

Josephine was kneeling before the closed door with her lips to the keyhole, imploring for admission. "Louise, open the door! I beg; open the door—you will make yourself ill. What are you doing, Louise? For heaven's sake open the door."

"Go away. I am not making myself ill." No; she was drinking in a very elixir of life through that open window.

Her fancy was running riot along those days ahead of her. Spring days, and summer days, and all sorts of days that would be her own. She breathed a quick prayer that life might be long. It was only yesterday she had thought with a shudder that life might be long.

She arose at length and opened the door to her sister's importunities. There was   20
a feverish triumph in her eyes, and she carried herself unwittingly like a goddess of Victory. She clasped her sister's waist, and together they descended the stairs. Richards stood waiting for them at the bottom.

Some one was opening the front door with a latchkey. It was Brently Mallard who entered, a little travel-stained, composedly carrying his grip-sack and umbrella. He had been far from the scene of the accident, and did not even know there had been one. He stood amazed at Josephine's piercing cry; at Richards' quick motion to screen him from the view of his wife.

But Richards was too late.

When the doctors came they said she had died of heart disease—of joy that kills.

Gabriel García Márquez

A Very Old Man with Enormous Wings

1968

Translated by Gregory Rabassa

Gabriel García Márquez, among the most emi-
nent of living Latin American writers, was born in
1928 in Aracataca, a Caribbean port in Colom-
bia, one of sixteen children of an impoverished
telegraph operator. For a time he studied law in
Bogotá, then became a newspaper reporter. Al-
though he never joined the Communist Party,
García Márquez outspokenly advocated many
left-wing proposals for reform. In 1954, despair-
ing of any prospect for political change, he left
Colombia to live in Mexico City. Though at nine-
teen he had already completed a book of short sto-
ries, La hojarasca (Leaf Storm), *he waited until*
1955 to publish it. Soon he began to build a tower-
ing reputation among readers of Spanish. His
celebrated novel Cien años de soledad (1967),
published in English as One Hundred Years of
Solitude (1969), *traces the history of a Colom-*
bian family through six generations. Called by

Gabriel García Márquez

Chilean poet Pablo Neruda "the greatest revelation in the Spanish language since Don
Quixote," the book has sold more than thirty million copies in thirty-five languages. In 1982
García Márquez was awarded the Nobel Prize in Literature. His fiction, rich in myth and
invention, has reminded American readers of the work of William Faulkner, another ex-
plorer of his native ground; indeed, García Márquez has called Faulkner "my master." His
later novels include Love in the Time of Cholera (1988), The General in His
Labyrinth (1990), Of Love and Other Demons (1995), *and* Memories of My Melancholy Whores (2005). *His* Collected Stories *was published in 1994.* Living to Tell the
Tale (2003), *the first volume of an autobiographical trilogy, traces the author's life up to*
the beginning of his journalistic career, and offers many insights into the sources and tech-
niques of his works of fiction. García Márquez still lives in Mexico City.

A Tale for Children

On the third day of rain they had killed so many crabs inside the house that Pelayo
had to cross his drenched courtyard and throw them into the sea, because the newborn
child had a temperature all night and they thought it was due to the stench. The world
had been sad since Tuesday. Sea and sky were a single ash-gray thing and the sands of
the beach, which on March nights glimmered like powdered light, had become a stew
of mud and rotten shellfish. The light was so weak at noon that when Pelayo was coming back to the house after throwing away the crabs, it was hard for him to see what it
was that was moving and groaning in the rear of the courtyard. He had to go very close
to see that it was an old man, a very old man, lying face down in the mud, who, in spite
of his tremendous efforts, couldn't get up, impeded by his enormous wings.

Frightened by that nightmare, Pelayo ran to get Elisenda, his wife, who was putting compresses on the sick child, and he took her to the rear of the courtyard. They both looked at the fallen body with mute stupor. He was dressed like a rag-picker. There were only a few faded hairs left on his bald skull and very few teeth in his mouth, and his pitiful condition of a drenched great-grandfather had taken away any sense of grandeur he might have had. His huge buzzard wings, dirty and half-plucked, were forever entangled in the mud. They looked at him so long and so closely that Pelayo and Elisenda very soon overcame their surprise and in the end found him familiar. Then they dared speak to him, and he answered in an incomprehensible dialect with a strong sailor's voice. That was how they skipped over the inconvenience of the wings and quite intelligently concluded that he was a lonely castaway from some foreign ship wrecked by the storm. And yet, they called in a neighbor woman who knew everything about life and death to see him, and all she needed was one look to show them their mistake.

"He's an angel," she told them. "He must have been coming for the child, but the poor fellow is so old that the rain knocked him down."

On the following day everyone knew that a flesh-and-blood angel was held captive in Pelayo's house. Against the judgment of the wise neighbor woman, for whom angels in those times were the fugitive survivors of a celestial conspiracy, they did not have the heart to club him to death. Pelayo watched over him all afternoon from the kitchen, armed with his bailiff's club, and before going to bed he dragged him out of the mud and locked him up with the hens in the wire chicken coop. In the middle of the night, when the rain stopped, Pelayo and Elisenda were still killing crabs. A short time afterward the child woke up without a fever and with a desire to eat. Then they felt magnanimous and decided to put the angel on a raft with fresh water and provisions for three days and leave him to his fate on the high seas. But when they went out into the courtyard with the first light of dawn, they found the whole neighborhood in front of the chicken coop having fun with the angel, without the slightest reverence, tossing him things to eat through the openings in the wire as if he weren't a supernatural creature but a circus animal.

Father Gonzaga arrived before seven o'clock, alarmed at the strange news. By that time onlookers less frivolous than those at dawn had already arrived and they were making all kinds of conjectures concerning the captive's future. The simplest among them thought that he should be named mayor of the world. Others of sterner mind felt that he should be promoted to the rank of five-star general in order to win all wars. Some visionaries hoped that he could be put to stud in order to implant on earth a race of winged wise men who could take charge of the universe. But Father Gonzaga, before becoming a priest, had been a robust woodcutter. Standing by the wire, he reviewed his catechism in an instant and asked them to open the door so that he could take a close look at that pitiful man who looked more like a huge decrepit hen among the fascinated chickens. He was lying in a corner drying his open wings in the sunlight among the fruit peels and breakfast leftovers that the early risers had thrown him. Alien to the impertinences of the world, he only lifted his antiquarian eyes and murmured something in his dialect when Father Gonzaga went into the chicken coop and said good morning to him in Latin. The parish priest had his first suspicion of an impostor when he saw that he did not understand the language of God or know how to greet His ministers. Then he noticed that seen close up he was much too human: he had an unbearable smell of the outdoors, the back side of his wings was strewn with parasites and his main feathers had been mistreated by terrestrial winds, and nothing

5

about him measured up to the proud dignity of angels. Then he came out of the chicken coop and in a brief sermon warned the curious against the risks of being ingenuous. He reminded them that the devil had the bad habit of making use of carnival tricks in order to confuse the unwary. He argued that if wings were not the essential element in determining the difference between a hawk and an airplane, they were even less so in the recognition of angels. Nevertheless, he promised to write a letter to his bishop so that the latter would write to his primate so that the latter would write to the Supreme Pontiff in order to get the final verdict from the highest courts.

His prudence fell on sterile hearts. The news of the captive angel spread with such rapidity that after a few hours the courtyard had the bustle of a marketplace and they had to call in troops with fixed bayonets to disperse the mob that was about to knock the house down. Elisenda, her spine all twisted from sweeping up so much marketplace trash, then got the idea of fencing in the yard and charging five cents admission to see the angel.

The curious came from far away. A traveling carnival arrived with a flying acrobat who buzzed over the crowd several times, but no one paid any attention to him because his wings were not those of an angel but, rather, those of a sidereal bat. The most unfortunate invalids on earth came in search of health: a poor woman who since childhood had been counting her heartbeats and had run out of numbers; a Portuguese man who couldn't sleep because the noise of the stars disturbed him; a sleepwalker who got up at night to undo the things he had done while awake; and many others with less serious ailments. In the midst of that shipwreck disorder that made the earth tremble, Pelayo and Elisenda were happy with fatigue, for in less than a week they had crammed their rooms with money and the line of pilgrims waiting their turn to enter still reached beyond the horizon.

The angel was the only one who took no part in his own act. He spent his time trying to get comfortable in his borrowed nest, befuddled by the hellish heat of the oil lamps and sacramental candles that had been placed along the wire. At first they tried to make him eat some mothballs, which, according to the wisdom of the wise neighbor woman, were the food prescribed for angels. But he turned them down, just as he turned down the papal lunches that the penitents brought him, and they never found out whether it was because he was an angel or because he was an old man that in the end ate nothing but eggplant mush. His only supernatural virtue seemed to be patience. Especially during the first days, when the hens pecked at him, searching for the stellar parasites that proliferated in his wings, and the cripples pulled out feathers to touch their defective parts with, and even the most merciful threw stones at him, trying to get him to rise so they could see him standing. The only time they succeeded in arousing him was when they burned his side with an iron for branding steers, for he had been motionless for so many hours that they thought he was dead. He awoke with a start, ranting in his hermetic language and with tears in his eyes, and he flapped his wings a couple of times, which brought on a whirlwind of chicken dung and lunar dust and a gale of panic that did not seem to be of this world. Although many thought that his reaction had been one not of rage but of pain, from then on they were careful not to annoy him, because the majority understood that his passivity was not that of a hero taking his ease but that of a cataclysm in repose.

Father Gonzaga held back the crowd's frivolity with formulas of maidservant inspiration while awaiting the arrival of a final judgment on the nature of the captive. But the mail from Rome showed no sense of urgency. They spent their time finding out if the prisoner had a navel, if his dialect had any connection with Aramaic, how many times he could fit on the head of a pin,° or whether he wasn't just a Norwegian with wings. Those meager letters might have come and gone until the end of time if a providential event had not put an end to the priest's tribulations.

It so happened that during those days, among so many other carnival attractions,   10
there arrived in town the traveling show of the woman who had been changed into a spider for having disobeyed her parents. The admission to see her was not only less than the admission to see the angel, but people were permitted to ask her all manner of questions about her absurd state and to examine her up and down so that no one would ever doubt the truth of her horror. She was a frightful tarantula the size of a ram and with the head of a sad maiden. What was most heart-rending, however, was not her outlandish shape but the sincere affliction with which she recounted the details of her misfortune. While still practically a child she had sneaked out of her parents' house to go to a dance, and while she was coming back through the woods after having danced all night without permission, a fearful thunderclap rent the sky in two and through the crack came the lightning bolt of brimstone that changed her into a spider. Her only nourishment came from the meatballs that charitable souls chose to toss into her mouth. A spectacle like that, full of so much human truth and with such a fearful lesson, was bound to defeat without even trying that of a haughty angel who scarcely deigned to look at mortals. Besides, the few miracles attributed to the angel showed a certain mental disorder, like the blind man who didn't recover his sight but grew three new teeth, or the paralytic who didn't get to walk but almost won the lottery, and the leper whose sores sprouted sunflowers. Those consolation miracles, which were more like mocking fun, had already ruined the angel's reputation when the woman who had been changed into a spider finally crushed him completely. That was how Father Gonzaga was cured forever of his insomnia and Pelayo's courtyard went back to being as empty as during the time it had rained for three days and crabs walked through the bedrooms.

The owners of the house had no reason to lament. With the money they saved they built a two-story mansion with balconies and gardens and high netting so that crabs wouldn't get in during the winter, and with iron bars on the windows so that angels wouldn't get in. Pelayo also set up a rabbit warren close to town and gave up his job as bailiff for good, and Elisenda bought some satin pumps with high heels and many dresses of iridescent silk, the kind worn on Sunday by the most desirable women in those times. The chicken coop was the only thing that didn't receive any attention. If they washed it down with creolin° and burned tears of myrrh inside it every so often, it was not in homage to the angel but to drive away the dungheap stench that still hung everywhere like a ghost and was turning the new house into an old one. At first, when the child learned to walk, they were careful that he not get too close to the chicken coop. But then they began to lose their fears and got used to the smell, and before the child got his second teeth he'd gone inside the chicken coop to play, where the wires were falling apart. The angel was no less standoffish with him than with other mortals, but he tolerated the most ingenious infamies with the patience of a dog who had no illusions. They both came down with chicken pox at the same time. The doctor who took care of the child couldn't resist the temptation to listen to the angel's heart, and he found so much whistling in the heart and so many sounds in his kidneys that it seemed impossible for him to be alive. What surprised him most, however, was the logic of his wings. They seemed so natural on that completely human organism that he couldn't understand why other men didn't have them too.

fit on the head of a pin: this allusion refers to the famous medieval arguments about how many angels (who had no physical bodies) could dance on the head of a pin.   *creolin:* a type of cleaning product.

When the child began school it had been some time since the sun and rain had caused the collapse of the chicken coop. The angel went dragging himself about here and there like a stray dying man. They would drive him out of the bedroom with a broom and a moment later find him in the kitchen. He seemed to be in so many places at the same time that they grew to think that he'd been duplicated, that he was reproducing himself all through the house, and the exasperated and unhinged Elisenda shouted that it was awful living in that hell full of angels. He could scarcely eat and his antiquarian eyes had also become so foggy that he went about bumping into posts. All he had left were the bare cannulae° of his last feathers. Pelayo threw a blanket over him and extended him the charity of letting him sleep in the shed, and only then did they notice that he had a temperature at night, and was delirious with the tongue twisters of an old Norwegian. That was one of the few times they became alarmed, for they thought he was going to die and not even the wise neighbor woman had been able to tell them what to do with dead angels.

And yet he not only survived his worst winter, but seemed improved with the first sunny days. He remained motionless for several days in the farthest corner of the courtyard, where no one would see him, and at the beginning of December some large, stiff feathers began to grow on his wings, the feathers of a scarecrow, which looked more like another misfortune of decrepitude. But he must have known the reason for those changes, for he was quite careful that no one should notice them, that no one should hear the sea chanteys that he sometimes sang under the stars. One morning Elisenda was cutting some bunches of onions for lunch when a wind that seemed to come from the high seas blew into the kitchen. Then she went to the window and caught the angel in his first attempts at flight. They were so clumsy that his fingernails opened a furrow in the vegetable patch and he was on the point of knocking the shed down with the ungainly flapping that slipped on the light and couldn't get a grip on the air. But he did manage to gain altitude. Elisenda let out a sigh of relief, for herself and for him, when she saw him pass over the last houses, holding himself up in some way with the risky flapping of a senile vulture. She kept watching him even when she was through cutting the onions and she kept on watching until it was no longer possible for her to see him, because then he was no longer an annoyance in her life but an imaginary dot on the horizon of the sea.

Zora Neale Hurston

Sweat — 1926

Zora Neale Hurston (1901?–1960) was born in Eatonville, Florida, but no record of her actual date of birth exists (best guesses range from 1891 to 1901). Hurston was one of eight children. Her father, a carpenter and Baptist preacher, was also the three-term mayor of Eatonville, the first all-black town incorporated in the United States. When Hurston's mother died in 1912, the father moved the children from one relative to another. Consequently, Hurston never finished grammar school, although in 1918 she began taking classes at Howard University, paying her way through school by working as a manicurist and maid. While at Howard, she published her first story. In early 1925 she moved to New York, arriving with "$1.50, no job, no friends, and a lot of hope." She soon became an important

---

cannulae: the Latin word for tubes; it refers to the tubelike quills that attach feathers to a body.

member of the Harlem Renaissance, a group of young black artists (including Langston Hughes, Countee Cullen, Jean Toomer, and Claude McKay) who sought "spiritual emancipation" for African Americans by exploring black heritage and identity in the arts. Hurston eventually became, according to critic Laura Zaidman, "the most prolific black American woman writer of her time." In 1925 she became the first African American student at Barnard College, where she completed a B.A. in anthropology. Hurston's most famous story, "Sweat," appeared in the only issue of Fire!!, a 1926 avant-garde Harlem Renaissance magazine edited by Hurston, Hughes, and Wallace Thur-man. This powerful story of an unhappy marriage

Zora Neale Hurston

turned murderous was particularly noteworthy for having the characters speak in the black country dialect of Hurston's native Florida. Hurston achieved only modest success during her lifetime, despite the publication of her memorable novel Their Eyes Were Watching God *(1937) and her many contributions to the study of African American folklore. She died, poor and neglected, in a Florida welfare home and was buried in an unmarked grave. In 1973 novelist Alice Walker erected a gravestone for her carved with the words:*

> Zora Neale Hurston
> *"A Genius of the South"*
> *1901–1960*
> *Novelist, Folklorist*
> *Anthropologist*

I

It was eleven o'clock of a Spring night in Florida. It was Sunday. Any other night, Delia Jones would have been in bed for two hours by this time. But she was a washwoman, and Monday morning meant a great deal to her. So she collected the soiled clothes on Saturday when she returned the clean things. Sunday night after church, she sorted and put the white things to soak. It saved her almost a half-day's start. A great hamper in the bedroom held the clothes that she brought home. It was so much neater than a number of bundles lying around.

She squatted on the kitchen floor beside the great pile of clothes, sorting them into small heaps according to color, and humming a song in a mournful key, but wondering through it all where Sykes, her husband, had gone with her horse and buckboard.°

Just then something long, round, limp, and black fell upon her shoulders and slithered to the floor beside her. A great terror took hold of her. It softened her knees and dried her mouth so that it was a full minute before she could cry out or move. Then she saw that it was the big bull whip her husband liked to carry when he drove.

---

buckboard: a four-wheeled open carriage with the seat resting on a spring platform.

She lifted her eyes to the door and saw him standing there bent over with laughter at her fright. She screamed at him.

"Sykes, what you throw dat whip on me like dat? You know it would skeer me—   5
looks just like a snake, an' you knows how skeered Ah is of snakes."

"Course Ah knowed it! That's how come Ah done it." He slapped his leg with his hand and almost rolled on the ground in his mirth. "If you such a big fool dat you got to have a fit over a earth worm or a string, Ah don't keer how bad Ah skeer you."

"You ain't got no business doing it. Gawd knows it's a sin. Some day Ah'm goin-tuh drop dead from some of yo' foolishness. 'Nother thing, where you been wid mah rig? Ah feeds dat pony. He ain't fuh you to be drivin' wid no bull whip."

"You sho' is one aggravatin' nigger woman!" he declared and stepped into the room. She resumed her work and did not answer him at once. "Ah done tole you time and again to keep them white folks' clothes outa dis house."

He picked up the whip and glared at her. Delia went on with her work. She went out into the yard and returned with a galvanized tub and set it on the wash-bench. She saw that Sykes had kicked all of the clothes together again, and now stood in her way truculently, his whole manner hoping, *praying*, for an argument. But she walked calmly around him and commenced to re-sort the things.

"Next time, Ah'm gointer kick 'em outdoors," he threatened as he struck a   10
match along the leg of his corduroy breeches.

Delia never looked up from her work, and her thin, stooped shoulders sagged further.

"Ah ain't for no fuss t'night Sykes. Ah just come from taking sacrament at the church house."

He snorted scornfully. "Yeah, you just come from de church house on a Sunday night, but heah you is gone to work on them clothes. You ain't nothing but a hypocrite. One of them amen-corner Christians—sing, whoop, and shout, then come home and wash white folks' clothes on the Sabbath."

He stepped roughly upon the whitest pile of things, kicking them helter-skelter as he crossed the room. His wife gave a little scream of dismay, and quickly gathered them together again.

"Sykes, you quit grindin' dirt into these clothes! How can Ah git through by   15
Sat'day if Ah don't start on Sunday?"

"Ah don't keer if you never git through. Anyhow, Ah done promised Gawd and a couple of other men, Ah ain't gointer have it in mah house. Don't gimme no lip neither, else Ah'll throw 'em out and put mah fist up side yo' head to boot."

Delia's habitual meekness seemed to slip from her shoulders like a blown scarf. She was on her feet; her poor little body, her bare knuckly hands bravely defying the strapping hulk before her.

"Looka heah, Sykes, you done gone too fur. Ah been married to you fur fifteen years, and Ah been takin' in washin' fur fifteen years. Sweat, sweat, sweat! Work and sweat, cry and sweat, pray and sweat!"

"What's that got to do with me?" he asked brutally.

"What's it got to do with you, Sykes? Mah tub of suds is filled yo' belly with vit-   20
tles more times than yo' hands is filled it. Mah sweat is done paid for this house and Ah reckon Ah kin keep on sweatin' in it."

She seized the iron skillet from the stove and struck a defensive pose, which act surprised him greatly, coming from her. It cowed him and he did not strike her as he usually did.

"Naw you won't," she panted, "that ole snaggle-toothed black woman you runnin' with ain't comin' heah to pile up on *mah* sweat and blood. You ain't paid for nothin' on this place, and Ah'm gointer stay right heah till Ah'm toted out foot foremost."

"Well, you better quit gittin' me riled up, else they'll be totin' you out sooner than you expect. Ah'm so tired of you Ah don't know whut to do. Gawd! How Ah hates skinny wimmen!"

A little awed by this new Delia, he sidled out of the door and slammed the back gate after him. He did not say where he had gone, but she knew too well. She knew very well that he would not return until nearly daybreak also. Her work over, she went on to bed but not to sleep at once. Things had come to a pretty pass!

She lay awake, gazing upon the debris that cluttered their matrimonial trail. Not   25 an image left standing along the way. Anything like flowers had long ago been drowned in the salty stream that had been pressed from her heart. Her tears, her sweat, her blood. She had brought love to the union and he had brought a longing after the flesh. Two months after the wedding, he had given her the first brutal beating. She had the memory of his numerous trips to Orlando with all of his wages when he had returned to her penniless, even before the first year had passed. She was young and soft then, but now she thought of her knotty, muscled limbs, her harsh knuckly hands, and drew herself up into an unhappy little ball in the middle of the big feather bed. Too late now to hope for love, even if it were not Bertha it would be someone else. This case differed from the others only in that she was bolder than the others. Too late for everything except her little home. She had built it for her old days, and planted one by one the trees and flowers there. It was lovely to her, lovely.

Somehow, before sleep came, she found herself saying aloud: "Oh well, whatever goes over the Devil's back, is got to come under his belly. Sometime or ruther, Sykes, like everybody else, is gointer reap his sowing." After that she was able to build a spiritual earthworks° against her husband. His shells could no longer reach her. AMEN. She went to sleep and slept until he announced his presence in bed by kicking her feet and rudely snatching the covers away.

"Gimme some kivah heah, an' git yo' damn foots over on yo' own side! Ah oughter mash you in yo' mouf fuh drawing dat skillet on me."

Delia went clear to the rail without answering him. A triumphant indifference to all that he was or did.

II

The week was full of work for Delia as all other weeks, and Saturday found her behind her little pony, collecting and delivering clothes.

It was a hot, hot day near the end of July. The village men on Joe Clarke's   30 porch even chewed cane listlessly. They did not hurl the cane-knots as usual. They let them dribble over the edge of the porch. Even conversation had collapsed under the heat.

"Heah come Delia Jones," Jim Merchant said, as the shaggy pony came 'round the bend of the road toward them. The rusty buckboard was heaped with baskets of crisp, clean laundry.

spiritual earthworks: earthworks are military fortifications made of earth; here Hurston uses it metaphorically to mean Delia's emotional defenses.

"Yep," Joe Lindsay agreed. "Hot or col', rain or shine, jes'ez reg'lar ez de weeks roll roun' Delia carries 'em an' fetches 'em on Sat'day."

"She better if she wanter eat," said Moss. "Syke Jones ain't wuth de shot an' powder hit would tek tuh kill 'im. Not to *huh* he ain't."

"He sho' ain't," Walter Thomas chimed in. "It's too bad, too, cause she wuz a right pretty li'l trick when he got huh. Ah'd uh mah'ied huh mahself if he hadnter beat me to it."

Delia nodded briefly at the men as she drove past.   35

"Too much knockin' will ruin *any* 'oman. He done beat huh 'nough tuh kill three women, let 'lone change they looks," said Elijah Moseley. "How Syke kin stommuck dat big black greasy Mogul he's layin' roun' wid, gits me. Ah swear dat eight-rock couldn't kiss a sardine can Ah done thowed out de back do' 'way las' yeah."

"Aw, she's fat, thass how come. He's allus been crazy 'bout fat women," put in Merchant. "He'd a' been tied up wid one long time ago if he could a' found one tuh have him. Did Ah tell yuh 'bout him come sidlin' roun' *mah* wife—bringin' her a basket uh peecans outa his yard fuh a present? Yessir, mah wife! She tol' him tuh take 'em right straight back home, 'cause Delia works so hard ovah dat washtub she reckon everything on de place taste lak sweat an' soapsuds. Ah jus' wisht Ah'd a' caught 'im 'roun' dere! Ah'd a' made his hips ketch on fiah down dat shell road."

"Ah know he done it, too. Ah sees 'im grinnin' at every 'oman dat passes," Walter Thomas said. "But even so, he useter eat some mighty big hunks uh humble pie tuh git dat li'l 'oman he got. She wuz ez pritty ez a speckled pup! Dat wuz fifteen years ago. He useter be so skeered uh losin' huh, she could make him do some parts of a husband's duty. Dey never wuz de same in de mind."

"There oughter be a law about him," said Lindsay. "He ain't fit tuh carry guts tuh a bear."

Clarke spoke for the first time. "Tain't no law on earth dat kin make a man be   40
decent if it ain't in 'im. There's plenty men dat takes a wife lak dey do a joint uh sugar-cane. It's round, juicy, an' sweet when dey gits it. But dey squeeze an' grind, squeeze an' grind an' wring tell dey wring every drop uh pleasure dat's in 'em out. When dey's satisfied dat dey is wrung dry, dey treats 'em jes' lak dey do a cane-chew. Dey thows 'em away. Dey knows whut dey is doin' while dey is at it, an' hates theirselves fuh it but they keeps on hangin' after huh tell she's empty. Den dey hates huh fuh bein' a cane-chew an' in de way."

"We oughter take Syke an' dat stray 'oman uh his'n down in Lake Howell swamp an' lay on de rawhide till they cain't say Lawd a' mussy. He allus wuz uh ovahbearin niggah, but since dat white 'oman from up north done teached 'im how to run a automobile, he done got too biggety to live—an' we oughter kill 'im," Old Man Anderson advised.

A grunt of approval went around the porch. But the heat was melting their civic virtue and Elijah Moseley began to bait Joe Clarke.

"Come on, Joe, git a melon outa dere an' slice it up for yo' customers. We'se all sufferin' wid de heat. De bear's done got *me!*"

"Thass right, Joe, a watermelon is jes' whut Ah needs tuh cure de eppizudicks," Walter Thomas joined forces with Moseley. "Come on dere, Joe. We all is steady customers an' you ain't set us up in a long time. Ah chooses dat long, bowlegged Floridy favorite."

"A god, an' be dough. You all gimme twenty cents and slice away," Clarke re-   45
torted. "Ah needs a col' slice m'self. Heah, everybody chip in. Ah'll lend y'all mah
meat knife."

The money was all quickly subscribed and the huge melon brought forth. At that
moment, Sykes and Bertha arrived. A determined silence fell on the porch and the
melon was put away again.

Merchant snapped down the blade of his jackknife and moved toward the store
door.

"Come on in, Joe, an' gimme a slab uh sow belly an' uh pound uh coffee—almost
fuhgot 'twas Sat'day. Got to git on home." Most of the men left also.

Just then Delia drove past on her way home, as Sykes was ordering magnificently
for Bertha. It pleased him for Delia to see.

"Git whutsoever yo' heart desires, Honey. Wait a minute, Joe. Give huh two bottles   50
uh strawberry soda-water, uh quart parched ground-peas, an' a block uh chewin' gum."

With all this they left the store, with Sykes reminding Bertha that this was his
town and she could have it if she wanted it.

The men returned soon after they left, and held their watermelon feast.

"Where did Syke Jones git da 'oman from nohow?" Lindsay asked.

"Ovah Apopka. Guess dey musta been cleanin' out de town when she lef'. She
don't look lak a thing but a hunk uh liver wid hair on it."

"Well, she sho' kin squall," Dave Carter contributed. "When she gits ready tuh laff,   55
she jes' opens huh mouf an' latches it back tuh de las' notch. No ole granpa alligator
down in Lake Bell ain't got nothin' on huh."

III

Bertha had been in town three months now. Sykes was still paying her room-
rent at Della Lewis'—the only house in town that would have taken her in. Sykes
took her frequently to Winter Park to "stomps." He still assured her that he was the
swellest man in the state.

"Sho' you kin have dat li'l ole house soon's Ah git dat 'oman outadere. Everything b'longs tuh me an' you sho' kin have it. Ah sho' 'bominates uh skinny 'oman.
Lawdy, you sho' is got one portly shape on you! You kin git *anything* you wants. Dis is
mah town an' you sho' kin have it."

Delia's work-worn knees crawled over the earth in Gethsemane° and up the
rocks of Calvary° many, many times during these months. She avoided the villagers
and meeting places in her efforts to be blind and deaf. But Bertha nullified this to a
degree, by coming to Delia's house to call Sykes out to her at the gate.

Delia and Sykes fought all the time now with no peaceful interludes. They slept
and ate in silence. Two or three times Delia had attempted a timid friendliness, but
she was repulsed each time. It was plain that the breaches must remain agape.

The sun had burned July to August. The heat streamed down like a million hot   60
arrows, smiting all things living upon the earth. Grass withered, leaves browned,
snakes went blind in shedding, and men and dogs went mad. Dog days!

Delia came home one day and found Sykes there before her. She wondered, but
started to go on into the house without speaking, even though he was standing in the

---

Gethsemane: the garden outside Jerusalem that was the scene of Jesus's agony and arrest (see Matthew
26:36–57); hence, a scene of great suffering. *Calvary:* the hill outside Jerusalem where Jesus was crucified.

kitchen door and she must either stoop under his arm or ask him to move. He made no room for her. She noticed a soap box beside the steps, but paid no particular attention to it, knowing that he must have brought it there. As she was stooping to pass under his outstretched arm, he suddenly pushed her backward, laughingly.

"Look in de box dere, Delia, Ah done brung yuh somethin'!"

She nearly fell upon the box in her stumbling, and when she saw what it held, she all but fainted outright.

"Syke! Syke, mah Gawd! You take dat rattlesnake 'way from heah! You *gottuh*. Oh, Jesus, have mussy!"

"Ah ain't got tuh do nuthin' uh de kin'—fact is Ah ain't got tuh do nothin' but 65 die. Tain't no use uh you puttin' on airs makin' out lak you skeered uh dat snake—he's gointer stay right heah tell he die. He wouldn't bite me cause Ah knows how tuh handle 'im. Nohow he wouldn't risk breakin' out his fangs 'gin yo skinny laigs."

"Naw, now Syke, don't keep dat thing 'round tryin' tuh skeer me tuh death. You knows Ah'm even feared uh earth worms. Thass de biggest snake Ah evah did see. Kill 'im, Syke, please."

"Doan ast me tuh do nothin' fuh yuh. Goin' 'round tryin' tuh be so damn asterperious.° Naw, Ah ain't gonna kill it. Ah think uh damn sight mo' uh him dan you! Dat's a nice snake an' anybody doan lak 'im kin jes' hit de grit."

The village soon heard that Sykes had the snake, and came to see and ask questions.

"How de hen-fire did you ketch dat six-foot rattler, Syke?" Thomas asked.

"He's full uh frogs so he cain't hardly move, thass how Ah eased up on 'im. But 70 Ah'm a snake charmer an' knows how tuh handle 'em. Shux, dat ain't nothin'. Ah could ketch one eve'y day if Ah so wanted tuh."

"Whut he needs is a heavy hick'ry club leaned real heavy on his head. Dat's de bes' way tuh charm a rattlesnake."

"Naw, Walt, y'all jes' don't understand dese diamon' backs lak Ah do," said Sykes in a superior tone of voice.

The village agreed with Walter, but the snake stayed on. His box remained by the kitchen door with its screen wire covering. Two or three days later it had digested its meal of frogs and literally came to life. It rattled at every movement in the kitchen or the yard. One day as Delia came down the kitchen steps she saw his chalky-white fangs curved like scimitars hung in the wire meshes. This time she did not run away with averted eyes as usual. She stood for a long time in the doorway in a red fury that grew bloodier for every second that she regarded the creature that was her torment.

That night she broached the subject as soon as Sykes sat down to the table.

"Syke, Ah wants you tuh take dat snake 'way fum heah. You done starved me an' 75 Ah put up widcher, you done beat me an Ah took dat, but you done kilt all mah insides bringin' dat varmint heah."

Sykes poured out a saucer full of coffee and drank it deliberately before he answered her.

"A whole lot Ah keer 'bout how you feels inside uh out. Dat snake ain't goin' no damn wheah till Ah gits ready fuh 'im tuh go. So fur as beatin' is concerned, yuh ain't took near all dat you gointer take ef yuh stay 'round *me*."

Delia pushed back her plate and got up from the table. "Ah hates you, Sykes," she said calmly. "Ah hates you tuh de same degree dat Ah useter love yuh. Ah done took

asterperious: haughty

an' took till mah belly is full up tuh mah neck. Dat's de reason Ah got mah letter fum
de church an' moved mah membership tuh Woodbridge—so Ah don't haftuh take no
sacrament wid yuh. Ah don't wantuh see yuh 'round me atall. Lay 'round wid dat
'oman all yuh wants tuh, but gwan 'way fum me an' mah house. Ah hates yuh lak uh
suck-egg dog."

Sykes almost let the huge wad of corn bread and collard greens he was chewing
fall out of his mouth in amazement. He had a hard time whipping himself up to the
proper fury to try to answer Delia.

"Well, Ah'm glad you does hate me. Ah'm sho' tiahed uh you hangin' ontuh me.   80
Ah don't want yuh. Look at yuh stringey ole neck! Yo' rawbony laigs an' arms is
enough tuh cut uh man tuh death. You looks jes' lak de devvul's doll-baby tuh *me*.
You cain't hate me no worse dan Ah hates you. Ah been hatin' *you* fuh years."

"Yo' ole black hide don't look lak nothin' tuh me, but uh passle uh wrinkled up
rubber, wid yo' big ole yeahs flappin' on each side lak uh paih uh buzzard wings.
Don't think Ah'm gointuh be run 'way fum mah house neither. Ah'm goin' tuh de
white folks 'bout *you*, mah young man, de very nex' time you lay yo' han's on me.
Mah cup is done run ovah." Delia said this with no signs of fear and Sykes departed
from the house, threatening her, but made not the slightest move to carry out any of
them.

That night he did not return at all, and the next day being Sunday, Delia was
glad she did not have to quarrel before she hitched up her pony and drove the four
miles to Woodbridge.

She stayed to the night service—"love feast"—which was very warm and full of
spirit. In the emotional winds her domestic trials were borne far and wide so that she
sang as she drove homeward,

> *Jurden water,°* *black an' col*
> *Chills de body, not de soul*
> *An' Ah wantah cross Jurden in uh calm time.*

She came from the barn to the kitchen door and stopped.

"Whut's de mattah, ol' Satan, you ain't kickin' up yo' racket?" She addressed the   85
snake's box. Complete silence. She went on into the house with a new hope in its
birth struggles. Perhaps her threat to go to the white folks had frightened Sykes! Perhaps he was sorry! Fifteen years of misery and suppression had brought Delia to the
place where she would hope *anything* that looked towards a way over or through her
wall of inhibitions.

She felt in the match-safe behind the stove at once for a match. There was only
one there.

"Dat niggah wouldn't fetch nothin' heah tuh save his rotten neck, but he kin run
thew whut Ah brings quick enough. Now he done toted off nigh on tuh haff uh box
uh matches. He done had dat 'oman heah in mah house, too."

Nobody but a woman could tell how she knew this even before she struck the
match. But she did and it put her into a new fury.

Jurden water: black Southern dialect for the River Jordan, which represents the last boundary before entering heaven. It comes from the Old Testament, when the Jews had to cross the River Jordan to reach the
Promised Land.

Presently she brought in the tubs to put the white things to soak. This time she decided she need not bring the hamper out of the bedroom; she would go in there and do the sorting. She picked up the pot-bellied lamp and went in. The room was small and the hamper stood hard by the foot of the white iron bed. She could sit and reach through the bedposts—resting as she worked.

"*Ah wantah cross Jurden in uh calm time.*" She was singing again. The mood of the 90 "love feast" had returned. She threw back the lid of the basket almost gaily. Then, moved by both horror and terror, she sprang back toward the door. *There lay the snake in the basket!* He moved sluggishly at first, but even as she turned round and round, jumped up and down in an insanity of fear, he began to stir vigorously. She saw him pouring his awful beauty from the basket upon the bed, then she seized the lamp and ran as fast as she could to the kitchen. The wind from the open door blew out the light and the darkness added to her terror. She sped to the darkness of the yard, slamming the door after her before she thought to set down the lamp. She did not feel safe even on the ground, so she climbed up in the hay barn.

There for an hour or more she lay sprawled upon the hay a gibbering wreck.

Finally she grew quiet, and after that came coherent thought. With this stalked through her a cold, bloody rage. Hours of this. A period of introspection, a space of retrospection, then a mixture of both. Out of this an awful calm.

"Well, Ah done de bes' Ah could. If things ain't right, Gawd knows tain't mah fault."

She went to sleep—a twitch sleep—and woke up to a faint gray sky. There was a loud hollow sound below. She peered out. Sykes was at the wood-pile, demolishing a wire-covered box.

He hurried to the kitchen door, but hung outside there some minutes before he 95 entered, and stood some minutes more inside before he closed it after him.

The gray in the sky was spreading. Delia descended without fear now, and crouched beneath the low bedroom window. The drawn shade shut out the dawn, shut in the night. But the thin walls held back no sound.

"Dat ol' scratch° is woke up now!" She mused at the tremendous whirr inside, which every woodsman knows, is one of the sound illusions. The rattler is a ventriloquist. His whirr sounds to the right, to the left, straight ahead, behind, close under foot—everywhere but where it is. Woe to him who guesses wrong unless he is prepared to hold up his end of the argument! Sometimes he strikes without rattling at all.

Inside, Sykes heard nothing until he knocked a pot lid off the stove while trying to reach the match-safe in the dark. He had emptied his pockets at Bertha's.

The snake seemed to wake up under the stove and Sykes made a quick leap into the bedroom. In spite of the gin he had had, his head was clearing now.

"Mah Gawd!" he chattered, "ef Ah could on'y strack uh light!" 100

The rattling ceased for a moment as he stood paralyzed. He waited. It seemed that the snake waited also.

"Oh, fuh de light! Ah thought he'd be too sick"—Sykes was muttering to himself when the whirr began again, closer, right underfoot this time. Long before this, Sykes' ability to think had been flattened down to primitive instinct and he leaped—onto the bed.

---

scratch: a folk expression for the devil.

Outside Delia heard a cry that might have come from a maddened chimpanzee, a stricken gorilla. All the terror, all the horror, all the rage that man possibly could express, without a recognizable human sound.

A tremendous stir inside there, another series of animal screams, the intermittent whirr of the reptile. The shade torn violently down from the window, letting in the red dawn, a huge brown hand seizing the window stick, great dull blows upon the wooden floor punctuating the gibberish of sound long after the rattle of the snake had abruptly subsided. All this Delia could see and hear from her place beneath the window, and it made her ill. She crept over to the four-o'clocks and stretched herself on the cool earth to recover.

She lay there. "Delia, Delia!" She could hear Sykes calling in a most despairing tone 105 as one who expected no answer. The sun crept on up, and he called. Delia could not move—her legs had gone flabby. She never moved, he called, and the sun kept rising.

"Mah Gawd!" She heard him moan, "Mah Gawd fum Heben!" She heard him stumbling about and got up from her flower-bed. The sun was growing warm. As she approached the door she heard him call out hopefully, "Delia, is dat you Ah heah?"

She saw him on his hands and knees as soon as she reached the door. He crept an inch or two toward her—all that he was able, and she saw his horribly swollen neck and his one open eye shining with hope. A surge of pity too strong to support bore her away from that eye that must, could not, fail to see the tubs. He would see the lamp. Orlando with its doctors was too far. She could scarcely reach the chinaberry tree, where she waited in the growing heat while inside she knew the cold river was creeping up and up to extinguish that eye which must know by now that she knew.

James Joyce

Araby 1914

James Joyce (1882–1941) quit Ireland at twenty to spend his mature life in voluntary exile on the continent, writing of nothing but Dublin, where he was born. In Trieste, Zurich, and Paris, he supported his family with difficulty, sometimes teaching in Berlitz language schools, until his writing won him fame and wealthy patrons. At first Joyce met difficulty in getting his work printed and circulated. Publication of Dubliners *(1914), the collection of stories that includes "Araby," was delayed seven years because its prospective Irish publisher feared libel suits. (The book depicts local citizens, some of them recognizable, and views Dubliners mostly as a thwarted, self-deceived lot.) A Portrait of the*

James Joyce

Artist as a Young Man (1916), a novel of thinly veiled autobiography, recounts a young intellectual's breaking away from country, church, and home. Joyce's immense comic novel Ulysses *(1922), a parody of the* Odyssey, *spans eighteen hours in the life of a wandering Jew, a Dublin seller of advertising. Frank about sex but untitillating, the book was banned at one time by the U.S. Post Office. Joyce's later work stepped up its demands on readers. The challenging* Finnegans Wake *(1939), if read aloud, sounds as though a*

learned comic poet were sleep-talking, jumbling several languages. Joyce was an innova-
tor whose bold experiments showed many other writers possibilities in fiction that had not
earlier been imagined.

North Richmond Street, being blind,° was a quiet street except at the hour
when the Christian Brothers' School set the boys free. An uninhabited house of two
stories stood at the blind end, detached from its neighbors in a square ground. The
other houses of the street, conscious of decent lives within them, gazed at one
another with brown imperturbable faces.

The former tenant of our house, a priest, had died in the back drawing-room.
Air, musty from having been long enclosed, hung in all the rooms, and the waste
room behind the kitchen was littered with old useless papers. Among these I
found a few paper-covered books, the pages of which were curled and damp: *The
Abbot*, by Walter Scott, *The Devout Communicant* and *The Memoirs of Vidocq*.° I
liked the last best because its leaves were yellow. The wild garden behind the
house contained a central apple-tree and a few straggling bushes under one of
which I found the late tenant's rusty bicycle-pump. He had been a very charitable
priest: in his will he had left all his money to institutions and the furniture of his
house to his sister.

When the short days of winter came dusk fell before we had well eaten our din-
ners. When we met in the street the houses had grown somber. The space of sky
above us was the color of ever-changing violet and towards it the lamps of the street
lifted their feeble lanterns. The cold air stung us and we played till our bodies glowed.
Our shouts echoed in the silent street. The career of our play brought us through the
dark muddy lanes behind the houses where we ran the gauntlet of the rough tribes
from the cottages, to the back doors of the dark dripping gardens where odors arose
from the ashpits, to the dark odorous stables where a coachman smoothed and
combed the horse or shook music from the buckled harness. When we returned to
the street light from the kitchen windows had filled the areas. If my uncle was seen
turning the corner we hid in the shadow until we had seen him safely housed. Or if
Mangan's sister° came out on the doorstep to call her brother in to his tea we
watched her from our shadow peer up and down the street. We waited to see whether
she would remain or go in and, if she remained, we left our shadow and walked up to
Mangan's steps resignedly. She was waiting for us, her figure defined by the light from
the half-opened door. Her brother always teased her before he obeyed and I stood by
the railings looking at her. Her dress swung as she moved her body and the soft rope
of her hair tossed from side to side.

Every morning I lay on the floor in the front parlor watching her door. The
blind was pulled down within an inch of the sash so that I could not be seen. When
she came out on the doorstep my heart leaped. I ran to the hall, seized my books
and followed her. I kept her brown figure always in my eye and, when we came near
the point at which our ways diverged, I quickened my pace and passed her. This

---

being blind: being a dead-end street. *The Abbot . . . Vidocq:* a popular historical romance (1820); a book of
pious meditations by an eighteenth-century English Franciscan, Pacificus Baker; and the autobiography of
François-Jules Vidocq (1775–1857), a criminal who later turned detective. *Mangan's sister:* an actual young
woman in this story, but the phrase recalls Irish poet James Clarence Mangan (1803–1849) and his best-
known poem, "Dark Rosaleen," which personifies Ireland as a beautiful woman for whom the poet yearns.

happened morning after morning. I had never spoken to her, except for a few casual words, and yet her name was like a summons to all my foolish blood.

Her image accompanied me even in places the most hostile to romance. On Saturday evenings when my aunt went marketing I had to go to carry some of the parcels. We walked through the flaring streets, jostled by drunken men and bargaining women, amid the curses of laborers, the shrill litanies of shopboys who stood on guard by the barrels of pigs' cheeks, the nasal chanting of street-singers, who sang a *come-all-you* about O'Donovan Rossa,° or a ballad about the troubles in our native land. These noises converged in a single sensation of life for me: I imagined that I bore my chalice safely through a throng of foes. Her name sprang to my lips at moments in strange prayers and praises which I myself did not understand. My eyes were often full of tears (I could not tell why) and at times a flood from my heart seemed to pour itself out into my bosom. I thought little of the future. I did not know whether I would ever speak to her or not or, if I spoke to her, how I could tell her of my confused adoration. But my body was like a harp and her words and gestures were like fingers running upon the wires.

One evening I went into the back drawing-room in which the priest had died. It was a dark rainy evening and there was no sound in the house. Through one of the broken panes I heard the rain impinge upon the earth, the fine incessant needles of water playing in the sodden beds. Some distant lamp or lighted window gleamed below me. I was thankful that I could see so little. All my senses seemed to desire to veil themselves and, feeling that I was about to slip from them, I pressed the palms of my hands together until they trembled, murmuring: *O love! O love!* many times.

At last she spoke to me. When she addressed the first words to me I was so confused that I did not know what to answer. She asked me was I going to *Araby*. I forget whether I answered yes or no. It would be a splendid bazaar, she said; she would love to go.

—And why can't you? I asked.

While she spoke she turned a silver bracelet round and round her wrist. She could not go, she said, because there would be a retreat that week in her convent.° Her brother and two other boys were fighting for their caps and I was alone at the railings. She held one of the spikes, bowing her head towards me. The light from the lamp opposite our door caught the white curve of her neck, lit up her hair that rested there and, falling, lit up the hand upon the railing. It fell over one side of her dress and caught the white border of a petticoat, just visible as she stood at ease.

—It's well for you, she said.

—If I go, I said, I will bring you something.

What innumerable follies laid waste my waking and sleeping thoughts after that evening! I wished to annihilate the tedious intervening days. I chafed against the work of school. At night in my bedroom and by day in the classroom her image came between me and the page I strove to read. The syllables of the word *Araby* were called to me through the silence in which my soul luxuriated and cast an Eastern enchantment over me. I asked for leave to go to the bazaar on Saturday night. My aunt was surprised and hoped it was not some Freemason° affair. I answered few

---

come-all-you about O'Donovan Rossa: the street singers earned their living by singing timely songs that usually began, "Come all you gallant Irishmen / And listen to my song." Their subject, also called Dynamite Rossa, was a popular hero jailed by the British for advocating violent rebellion. *a retreat . . . in her convent:* a week devoted to religious observances more intense than usual, at the convent school Miss Mangan attends; probably she will have to listen to a number of hellfire sermons. *Freemason:* Catholics in Ireland viewed the Masonic order as a Protestant conspiracy against them.

questions in class. I watched my master's face pass from amiability to sternness; he hoped I was not beginning to idle. I could not call my wandering thoughts together. I had hardly any patience with the serious work of life which, now that it stood between me and my desire, seemed to me child's play, ugly monotonous child's play.

On Saturday morning I reminded my uncle that I wished to go to the bazaar in the evening. He was fussing at the hallstand, looking for the hatbrush, and answered me curtly:

—Yes, boy, I know.

As he was in the hall I could not go into the front parlor and lie at the window. I left the house in bad humor and walked slowly towards the school. The air was pitilessly raw and already my heart misgave me.

When I came home to dinner my uncle had not yet been home. Still it was early. I sat staring at the clock for some time and, when its ticking began to irritate me, I left the room. I mounted the staircase and gained the upper part of the house. The high cold empty gloomy rooms liberated me and I went from room to room singing. From the front window I saw my companions playing below in the street. Their cries reached me weakened and indistinct and, leaning my forehead against the cool glass, I looked over at the dark house where she lived. I may have stood there for an hour, seeing nothing but the brown-clad figure cast by my imagination, touched discreetly by the lamplight at the curved neck, at the hand upon the railings and at the border below the dress.

When I came downstairs again I found Mrs. Mercer sitting at the fire. She was an old garrulous woman, a pawnbroker's widow, who collected used stamps for some pious purpose. I had to endure the gossip of the tea-table. The meal was prolonged beyond an hour and still my uncle did not come. Mrs. Mercer stood up to go: she was sorry she couldn't wait any longer, but it was after eight o'clock and she did not like to be out late, as the night air was bad for her. When she had gone I began to walk up and down the room, clenching my fists. My aunt said:

—I'm afraid you may put off your bazaar for this night of Our Lord.

At nine o'clock I heard my uncle's latchkey in the halldoor. I heard him talking to himself and heard the hallstand rocking when it had received the weight of his overcoat. I could interpret these signs. When he was midway through his dinner I asked him to give me the money to go to the bazaar. He had forgotten.

—The people are in bed and after their first sleep now, he said.

I did not smile. My aunt said to him energetically:

—Can't you give him the money and let him go? You've kept him late enough as it is.

My uncle said he was very sorry he had forgotten. He said he believed in the old saying: *All work and no play makes Jack a dull boy.* He asked me where I was going and, when I had told him a second time he asked me did I know *The Arab's Farewell to His Steed.°* When I left the kitchen he was about to recite the opening lines of the piece to my aunt.

15

20

The Arab's Farewell to His Steed: This sentimental ballad by a popular poet, Caroline Norton (1808–1877), tells the story of a nomad of the desert who, in a fit of greed, sells his beloved horse, then regrets the loss, flings away the gold he had received, and takes back his horse. Notice the echo of "Araby" in the song title.

I held a florin tightly in my hands as I strode down Buckingham Street towards the station. The sight of the streets thronged with buyers and glaring with gas recalled to me the purpose of my journey. I took my seat in a third-class carriage of a deserted train. After an intolerable delay the train moved out of the station slowly. It crept onward among ruinous houses and over the twinkling river. At Westland Row Station a crowd of people pressed to the carriage doors; but the porters moved them back, saying that it was a special train for the bazaar. I remained alone in the bare carriage. In a few minutes the train drew up beside an improvised wooden platform. I passed out on to the road and saw by the lighted dial of a clock that it was ten minutes to ten. In front of me was a large building which displayed the magical name.

I could not find any sixpenny entrance and, fearing that the bazaar would be   25
closed, I passed in quickly through a turnstile, handing a shilling to a weary-looking man. I found myself in a big hall girdled at half its height by a gallery. Nearly all the stalls were closed and the greater part of the hall was in darkness. I recognized a silence like that which pervades a church after a service. I walked into the center of the bazaar timidly. A few people were gathered about the stalls which were still open. Before a curtain, over which the words *Café Chantant*° were written in colored lamps, two men were counting money on a salver.° I listened to the fall of the coins.

Remembering with difficulty why I had come I went over to one of the stalls and examined porcelain vases and flowered tea-sets. At the door of the stall a young lady was talking and laughing with two young gentlemen. I remarked their English accents and listened vaguely to their conversation.

—O, I never said such a thing!

—O, but you did!

—O, but I didn't!

—Didn't she say that?   30

—Yes. I heard her.

—O, there's a . . . fib!

Observing me the young lady came over and asked me did I wish to buy anything. The tone of her voice was not encouraging; she seemed to have spoken to me out of a sense of duty. I looked humbly at the great jars that stood like eastern guards at either side of the dark entrance to the stall and murmured:

—No, thank you.

The young lady changed the position of one of the vases and went back to the   35
two young men. They began to talk of the same subject. Once or twice the young lady glanced at me over her shoulder.

I lingered before her stall, though I knew my stay was useless, to make my interest in her wares seem the more real. Then I turned away slowly and walked down the middle of the bazaar. I allowed the two pennies to fall against the sixpence in my pocket. I heard a voice call from one end of the gallery that the light was out. The upper part of the hall was now completely dark.

Gazing up into the darkness I saw myself as a creature driven and derided by vanity; and my eyes burned with anguish and anger.

Café Chantant: name for a Paris nightspot featuring topical songs.   *salver:* a tray like that used in serving Holy Communion.

Jamaica Kincaid

Girl   1983

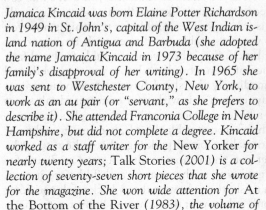

Jamaica Kincaid was born Elaine Potter Richardson in 1949 in St. John's, capital of the West Indian island nation of Antigua and Barbuda (she adopted the name Jamaica Kincaid in 1973 because of her family's disapproval of her writing). In 1965 she was sent to Westchester County, New York, to work as an au pair (or "servant," as she prefers to describe it). She attended Franconia College in New Hampshire, but did not complete a degree. Kincaid worked as a staff writer for the New Yorker for nearly twenty years; Talk Stories (2001) is a collection of seventy-seven short pieces that she wrote for the magazine. She won wide attention for At the Bottom of the River *(1983), the volume of her stories that includes "Girl." In 1985 she published* Annie John, *an interlocking cycle of short stories about growing up in Antigua.* Lucy *(1990) was her first novel; it was followed by* The Autobiography of My Mother *(1996) and* Mr. Potter *(2002), novels inspired by the lives of her parents. Kincaid is also the author of* A Small Place *(1988), a memoir of her homeland and meditation on the destructiveness of colonialism, and* My Brother *(1997), a reminiscence of her brother Devon, who died of AIDS at thirty-three. Her most recent work is* Among Flowers: A Walk in the Himalaya *(2005), a travel book. A naturalized U.S. citizen, Kincaid has said of her adopted country: "It's given me a place to be myself—but myself as I was formed somewhere else." She currently teaches at Claremont McKenna College in Southern California.*

Jamaica Kincaid

Wash the white clothes on Monday and put them on the stone heap; wash the color clothes on Tuesday and put them on the clothesline to dry; don't walk barehead in the hot sun; cook pumpkin fritters in very hot sweet oil; soak your little cloths right after you take them off; when buying cotton to make yourself a nice blouse, be sure that it doesn't have gum on it, because that way it won't hold up well after a wash; soak salt fish overnight before you cook it; is it true that you sing benna° in Sunday school?; always eat your food in such a way that it won't turn someone else's stomach; on Sundays try to walk like a lady and not like the slut you are so bent on becoming; don't sing benna in Sunday school; you mustn't speak to wharf-rat boys, not even to give directions; don't eat fruits on the street—flies will follow you; *but I don't sing benna on Sundays at all and never in Sunday school;* this is how to sew on a button; this is how to make a buttonhole for the button you have just sewed on; this is how to hem a dress when you see the hem coming down and so to prevent yourself from looking like the slut I know you are so bent on becoming; this is how you iron your father's khaki shirt so that it doesn't have a crease; this is how you iron your father's khaki pants so that they don't have a crease; this is how you grow okra—far from the house, because okra tree harbors red ants; when you are growing

benna: Kincaid defined this word, for two editors who inquired, as meaning "songs of the sort your parents didn't want you to sing, at first calypso and later rock and roll" (quoted by Sylvan Barnet and Marcia Stubbs, *The Little Brown Reader,* 2nd ed. [Boston: Little, 1980] 74).

dasheen, make sure it gets plenty of water or else it makes your throat itch when you are eating it; this is how you sweep a corner; this is how you sweep a whole house; this is how you sweep a yard; this is how you smile to someone you don't like too much; this is how you smile to someone you don't like at all; this is how you smile to someone you like completely; this is how you set a table for tea; this is how you set a table for dinner; this is how you set a table for dinner with an important guest; this is how you set a table for lunch; this is how you set a table for breakfast; this is how to behave in the presence of men who don't know you very well, and this way they won't recognize immediately the slut I have warned you against becoming; be sure to wash every day, even if it is with your own spit; don't squat down to play marbles—you are not a boy, you know; don't pick people's flowers— you might catch something; don't throw stones at blackbirds, because it might not be a blackbird at all; this is how to make a bread pudding; this is how to make doukona; this is how to make pepper pot; this is how to make a good medicine for a cold; this is how to make a good medicine to throw away a child before it even becomes a child; this is how to catch a fish; this is how to throw back a fish you don't like, and that way something bad won't fall on you; this is how to bully a man; this is how a man bullies you; this is how to love a man, and if this doesn't work there are other ways, and if they don't work don't feel too bad about giving up; this is how to spit up in the air if you feel like it, and this is how to move quick so that it doesn't fall on you; this is how to make ends meet; always squeeze bread to make sure it's fresh; *but what if the baker won't let me feel the bread?*; you mean to say that after all you are really going to be the kind of woman who the baker won't let near the bread?

Jhumpa Lahiri

Interpreter of Maladies

1999

Jhumpa Lahiri was born in London in 1967 and grew up in Rhode Island. Her father, a librarian, and her mother, a teacher, had emigrated from their native India, to which Lahiri has made a number of extended visits. After writing a great deal of fiction as a child and teenager, she wrote none at all during her college years. She graduated from Barnard College with a B.A. in English literature, and after all her graduate school applications had been rejected, she went to work as a research assistant for a nonprofit or-ganization. She began staying late after work to use her office computer to write short stories, on the strength of which she was accepted into the creative writing program at Boston University. Earning an M.A. in creative writ-ing, Lahiri stayed on to complete an M.A. in English, an M.A. in comparative literature and the arts, and a Ph.D. in Renaissance studies. "In the process," she has said, "it became clear to me that I was not meant to be a scholar. It was something I did out of a sense of duty and practicality, but it was never something I loved." Lahiri's first book of stories, Interpreter of

Jhumpa Lahiri

Maladies, was published in 1999 to excellent reviews and won the Pulitzer Prize for fiction. Its title story was also selected for both an O. Henry Award and publication in The Best American Short Stories. *Her first novel,* The Namesake *(2003), was made into a film (2006) directed by Mira Nair. Her second collection of stories,* Unaccustomed Earth *(2008), also received glowing reviews, and debuted at Number 1 on the* New York Times *best-seller list. Lahiri has taught creative writing at Boston University and the Rhode Island School of Design. She lives in New York.*

At the tea stall Mr. and Mrs. Das bickered about who should take Tina to the toilet. Eventually Mrs. Das relented when Mr. Das pointed out that he had given the girl her bath the night before. In the rearview mirror Mr. Kapasi watched as Mrs. Das emerged slowly from his bulky white Ambassador, dragging her shaved, largely bare legs across the back seat. She did not hold the little girl's hand as they walked to the rest room.

They were on their way to see the Sun Temple at Konarak. It was a dry, bright Saturday, the mid-July heat tempered by a steady ocean breeze, ideal weather for sightseeing. Ordinarily Mr. Kapasi would not have stopped so soon along the way, but less than five minutes after he'd picked up the family that morning in front of Hotel Sandy Villa, the little girl had complained. The first thing Mr. Kapasi had noticed when he saw Mr. and Mrs. Das, standing with their children under the portico of the hotel, was that they were very young, perhaps not even thirty. In addition to Tina they had two boys, Ronny and Bobby, who appeared very close in age and had teeth covered in a network of flashing silver wires. The family looked Indian but dressed as foreigners did, the children in stiff, brightly colored clothing and caps with translucent visors. Mr. Kapasi was accustomed to foreign tourists; he was assigned to them regularly because he could speak English. Yesterday he had driven an elderly couple from Scotland, both with spotted faces and fluffy white hair so thin it exposed their sunburnt scalps. In comparison, the tanned, youthful faces of Mr. and Mrs. Das were all the more striking. When he'd introduced himself, Mr. Kapasi had pressed his palms together in greeting, but Mr. Das squeezed hands like an American so that Mr. Kapasi felt it in his elbow. Mrs. Das, for her part, had flexed one side of her mouth, smiling dutifully at Mr. Kapasi, without displaying any interest in him.

As they waited at the tea stall, Ronny, who looked like the older of the two boys, clambered suddenly out of the back seat, intrigued by a goat tied to a stake in the ground.

"Don't touch it," Mr. Das said. He glanced up from his paperback tour book, which said "INDIA" in yellow letters and looked as if it had been published abroad. His voice, somehow tentative and a little shrill, sounded as though it had not yet settled into maturity.

"I want to give it a piece of gum," the boy called back as he trotted ahead.   5

Mr. Das stepped out of the car and stretched his legs by squatting briefly to the ground. A clean-shaven man, he looked exactly like a magnified version of Ronny. He had a sapphire blue visor, and was dressed in shorts, sneakers, and a T-shirt. The camera slung around his neck, with an impressive telephoto lens and numerous buttons and markings, was the only complicated thing he wore. He frowned, watching as Ronny rushed toward the goat, but appeared to have no intention of intervening. "Bobby, make sure that your brother doesn't do anything stupid."

"I don't feel like it," Bobby said, not moving. He was sitting in the front seat beside Mr. Kapasi, studying a picture of the elephant god taped to the glove compartment.

"No need to worry," Mr. Kapasi said. "They are quite tame." Mr. Kapasi was forty-six years old, with receding hair that had gone completely silver, but his butter-scotch complexion and his unlined brow, which he treated in spare moments to dabs of lotus-oil balm, made it easy to imagine what he must have looked like at an earlier age. He wore gray trousers and a matching jacket-style shirt, tapered at the waist, with short sleeves and a large pointed collar, made of a thin but durable synthetic material. He had specified both the cut and the fabric to his tailor—it was his pre-ferred uniform for giving tours because it did not get crushed during his long hours behind the wheel. Through the windshield he watched as Ronny circled around the goat, touched it quickly on its side, then trotted back to the car.

"You left India as a child?" Mr. Kapasi asked when Mr. Das had settled once again into the passenger seat.

"Oh, Mina and I were both born in America," Mr. Das announced with an air of sudden confidence. "Born and raised. Our parents live here now, in Assansol.° They retired. We visit them every couple years." He turned to watch as the little girl ran toward the car, the wide purple bows of her sundress flopping on her narrow brown shoulders. She was holding to her chest a doll with yellow hair that looked as if it had been chopped, as a punitive measure, with a pair of dull scissors. "This is Tina's first trip to India, isn't it, Tina?"

"I don't have to go to the bathroom anymore," Tina announced.

"Where's Mina?" Mr. Das asked.

Mr. Kapasi found it strange that Mr. Das should refer to his wife by her first name when speaking to the little girl. Tina pointed to where Mrs. Das was purchasing something from one of the shirtless men who worked at the tea stall. Mr. Kapasi heard one of the shirtless men sing a phrase from a popular Hindi love song as Mrs. Das walked back to the car, but she did not appear to understand the words of the song, for she did not express irritation, or embarrassment, or react in any other way to the man's declarations.

He observed her. She wore a red-and-white-checkered skirt that stopped above her knees, slip-on shoes with a square wooden heel, and a close-fitting blouse styled like a man's undershirt. The blouse was decorated at chest-level with a calico appliqué in the shape of a strawberry. She was a short woman, with small hands like paws, her frosty pink fingernails painted to match her lips, and was slightly plump in her figure. Her hair, shorn only a little longer than her husband's, was parted far to one side. She was wearing large dark brown sunglasses with a pinkish tint to them, and carried a big straw bag, almost as big as her torso, shaped like a bowl, with a water bottle poking out of it. She walked slowly, carrying some puffed rice tossed with peanuts and chili peppers in a large packet made from newspapers. Mr. Kapasi turned to Mr. Das.

"Where in America do you live?"

"New Brunswick, New Jersey."

"Next to New York?"

"Exactly. I teach middle school there."

10

15

Assansol: a city in the state of West Bengal in northeastern India.

"What subject?"

"Science. In fact, every year I take my students on a trip to the Museum of Natural History in New York City. In a way we have a lot in common, you could say, you and I. How long have you been a tour guide, Mr. Kapasi?"

"Five years."

Mrs. Das reached the car. "How long's the trip?" she asked, shutting the door.

"About two and a half hours," Mr. Kapasi replied.

At this Mrs. Das gave an impatient sigh, as if she had been traveling her whole life without pause. She fanned herself with a folded Bombay film magazine written in English.

"I thought that the Sun Temple is only eighteen miles north of Puri," Mr. Das said, tapping on the tour book.

"The roads to Konarak are poor. Actually it is a distance of fifty-two miles," Mr. Kapasi explained.

Mr. Das nodded, readjusting the camera strap where it had begun to chafe the back of his neck.

Before starting the ignition, Mr. Kapasi reached back to make sure the cranklike locks on the inside of each of the back doors were secured. As soon as the car began to move the little girl began to play with the lock on her side, clicking it with some effort forward and backward, but Mrs. Das said nothing to stop her. She sat a bit slouched at one end of the back seat, not offering her puffed rice to anyone. Ronny and Tina sat on either side of her, both snapping bright green gum.

"Look," Bobby said as the car began to gather speed. He pointed with his finger to the tall trees that lined the road. "Look."

"Monkeys!" Ronny shrieked. "Wow!"

They were seated in groups along the branches, with shining black faces, silver bodies, horizontal eyebrows, and crested heads. Their long gray tails dangled like a series of ropes among the leaves. A few scratched themselves with black leathery hands, or swung their feet, staring as the car passed.

"We call them the hanuman," Mr. Kapasi said. "They are quite common in the area."

As soon as he spoke, one of the monkeys leaped into the middle of the road, causing Mr. Kapasi to brake suddenly. Another bounced onto the hood of the car, then sprang away. Mr. Kapasi beeped his horn. The children began to get excited, sucking in their breath and covering their faces partly with their hands. They had never seen monkeys outside of a zoo, Mr. Das explained. He asked Mr. Kapasi to stop the car so that he could take a picture.

While Mr. Das adjusted his telephoto lens, Mrs. Das reached into her straw bag and pulled out a bottle of colorless nail polish, which she proceeded to stroke on the tip of her index finger.

The little girl stuck out a hand. "Mine too. Mommy, do mine too."

"Leave me alone," Mrs. Das said, blowing on her nail and turning her body slightly. "You're making me mess up."

The little girl occupied herself by buttoning and unbuttoning a pinafore on the doll's plastic body.

"All set," Mr. Das said, replacing the lens cap.

The car rattled considerably as it raced along the dusty road, causing them all to pop up from their seats every now and then, but Mrs. Das continued to polish her nails. Mr. Kapasi eased up on the accelerator, hoping to produce a smoother ride. When he reached for the gearshift the boy in front accommodated him by swinging his hairless knees out of the way. Mr. Kapasi noted that this boy was slightly paler than the other children. "Daddy, why is the driver sitting on the wrong side in this car, too?" the boy asked.

"They all do that here, dummy," Ronny said.   40

"Don't call your brother a dummy," Mr. Das said. He turned to Mr. Kapasi. "In America, you know . . . . it confuses them."

"Oh yes, I am well aware," Mr. Kapasi said. As delicately as he could, he shifted gears again, accelerating as they approached a hill in the road. "I see it on *Dallas,*° the steering wheels are on the left-hand side."

"What's *Dallas?*" Tina asked, banging her now naked doll on the seat behind Mr. Kapasi.

"It went off the air," Mr. Das explained. "It's a television show."

They were all like siblings, Mr. Kapasi thought as they passed a row of date   45
trees. Mr. and Mrs. Das behaved like an older brother and sister, not parents. It seemed that they were in charge of the children only for the day; it was hard to believe they were regularly responsible for anything other than themselves. Mr. Das tapped on his lens cap, and his tour book, dragging his thumbnail occasionally across the pages so that they made a scraping sound. Mrs. Das continued to polish her nails. She had still not removed her sunglasses. Every now and then Tina renewed her plea that she wanted her nails done, too, and so at one point Mrs. Das flicked a drop of polish on the little girl's finger before depositing the bottle back inside her straw bag.

"Isn't this an air-conditioned car?" she asked, still blowing on her hand. The window on Tina's side was broken and could not be rolled down.

"Quit complaining," Mr. Das said. "It isn't so hot."

"I told you to get a car with air-conditioning," Mrs. Das continued. "Why do you do this, Raj, just to save a few stupid rupees. What are you saving us, fifty cents?"

Their accents sounded just like the ones Mr. Kapasi heard on American television programs, though not like the ones on *Dallas.*

"Doesn't it get tiresome, Mr. Kapasi, showing people the same thing every day?"   50
Mr. Das asked, rolling down his own window all the way. "Hey, do you mind stopping the car. I just want to get a shot of this guy."

Mr. Kapasi pulled over to the side of the road as Mr. Das took a picture of a barefoot man, his head wrapped in a dirty turban, seated on top of a cart of grain sacks pulled by a pair of bullocks.° Both the man and the bullocks were emaciated. In the back seat Mrs. Das gazed out another window, at the sky, where nearly transparent clouds passed quickly in front of one another.

"I look forward to it, actually," Mr. Kapasi said as they continued on their way. "The Sun Temple is one of my favorite places. In that way it is a reward for me. I give tours on Fridays and Saturdays only. I have another job during the week."

"Oh? Where?" Mr. Das asked.

Dallas: extremely popular 1980s television drama centered on the professional and romantic affairs of unscrupulous oil baron J. R. Ewing and his family.   *bullocks:* young or castrated bulls; steers.

"I work in a doctor's office."

"You're a doctor?"

"I am not a doctor. I work with one. As an interpreter."

"What does a doctor need an interpreter for?"

"He has a number of Gujarati patients. My father was Gujarati, but many people do not speak Gujarati in this area, including the doctor. And so the doctor asked me to work in his office, interpreting what the patients say."

"Interesting. I've never heard of anything like that," Mr. Das said.

Mr. Kapasi shrugged. "It is a job like any other."

"But so romantic," Mrs. Das said dreamily, breaking her extended silence. She lifted her pinkish brown sunglasses and arranged them on top of her head like a tiara. For the first time, her eyes met Mr. Kapasi's in the rearview mirror: pale, a bit small, their gaze fixed but drowsy.

Mr. Das craned to look at her. "What's so romantic about it?"

"I don't know. Something." She shrugged, knitting her brows together for an instant. "Would you like a piece of gum, Mr. Kapasi?" she asked brightly. She reached into her straw bag and handed him a small square wrapped in green-and-white-striped paper. As soon as Mr. Kapasi put the gum in his mouth a thick sweet liquid burst onto his tongue.

"Tell us more about your job, Mr. Kapasi," Mrs. Das said.

"What would you like to know, madame?"

"I don't know," she shrugged, munching on some puffed rice and licking the mustard oil from the corners of her mouth. "Tell us a typical situation." She settled back in her seat, her head tilted in a patch of sun, and closed her eyes. "I want to picture what happens."

"Very well. The other day a man came in with a pain in his throat."

"Did he smoke cigarettes?"

"No. It was very curious. He complained that he felt as if there were long pieces of straw stuck in his throat. When I told the doctor he was able to prescribe the proper medication."

"That's so neat."

"Yes," Mr. Kapasi agreed after some hesitation.

"So these patients are totally dependent on you," Mrs. Das said. She spoke slowly, as if she were thinking aloud. "In a way, more dependent on you than the doctor."

"How do you mean? How could it be?"

"Well, for example, you could tell the doctor that the pain felt like a burning, not straw. The patient would never know what you had told the doctor, and the doctor wouldn't know that you had told the wrong thing. It's a big responsibility."

"Yes, a big responsibility you have there, Mr. Kapasi," Mr. Das agreed.

Mr. Kapasi had never thought of his job in such complimentary terms. To him it was a thankless occupation. He found nothing noble in interpreting people's maladies, assiduously translating the symptoms of so many swollen bones, countless cramps of bellies and bowels, spots on people's palms that changed color, shape, or size. The doctor, nearly half his age, had an affinity for bell-bottom trousers and made humorless jokes about the Congress party.° Together they worked in a stale little infirmary where

the Congress party: India's governing party for five decades after independence in 1947, widely perceived as corrupt.

Mr. Kapasi's smartly tailored clothes clung to him in the heat, in spite of the blackened blades of a ceiling fan churning over their heads.

The job was a sign of his failings. In his youth he'd been a devoted scholar of foreign languages, the owner of an impressive collection of dictionaries. He had dreamed of being an interpreter for diplomats and dignitaries, resolving conflicts between people and nations, settling disputes of which he alone could understand both sides. He was a self-educated man. In a series of notebooks, in the evenings before his parents settled his marriage, he had listed the common etymologies of words, and at one point in his life he was confident that he could converse, if given the opportunity, in English, French, Russian, Portuguese, and Italian, not to mention Hindi, Bengali, Orissi, and Gujarati. Now only a handful of European phrases remained in his memory, scattered words for things like saucers and chairs. English was the only non-Indian language he spoke fluently anymore. Mr. Kapasi knew it was not a remarkable talent. Sometimes he feared that his children knew better English than he did, just from watching television. Still, it came in handy for the tours.

He had taken the job as an interpreter after his first son, at the age of seven, contracted typhoid—that was how he had first made the acquaintance of the doctor. At the time Mr. Kapasi had been teaching English in a grammar school, and he bartered his skills as an interpreter to pay the increasingly exorbitant medical bills. In the end the boy had died one evening in his mother's arms, his limbs burning with fever, but then there was the funeral to pay for, and the other children who were born soon enough, and the newer, bigger house, and the good schools and tutors, and the fine shoes and the television, and the countless other ways he tried to console his wife and to keep her from crying in her sleep, and so when the doctor offered to pay him twice as much as he earned at the grammar school, he accepted. Mr. Kapasi knew that his wife had little regard for his career as an interpreter. He knew it reminded her of the son she'd lost, and that she resented the other lives he helped, in his own small way, to save. If ever she referred to his position, she used the phrase "doctor's assistant," as if the process of interpretation were equal to taking someone's temperature, or changing a bedpan. She never asked him about the patients who came to the doctor's office, or said that his job was a big responsibility.

For this reason it flattered Mr. Kapasi that Mrs. Das was so intrigued by his job. Unlike his wife, she had reminded him of its intellectual challenges. She had also used the word "romantic." She did not behave in a romantic way toward her husband, and yet she had used the word to describe him. He wondered if Mr. and Mrs. Das were a bad match, just as he and his wife were. Perhaps they, too, had little in common apart from three children and a decade of their lives. The signs he recognized from his own marriage were there—the bickering, the indifference, the protracted silences. Her sudden interest in him, an interest she did not express in either her husband or her children, was mildly intoxicating. When Mr. Kapasi thought once again about how she had said "romantic," the feeling of intoxication grew.

He began to check his reflection in the rearview mirror as he drove, feeling grateful that he had chosen the gray suit that morning and not the brown one, which tended to sag a little in the knees. From time to time he glanced through the mirror at Mrs. Das. In addition to glancing at her face he glanced at the strawberry between her breasts, and the golden brown hollow in her throat. He decided to tell Mrs. Das

80

about another patient, and another: the young woman who had complained of a sensation of raindrops in her spine, the gentleman whose birthmark had begun to sprout hairs. Mrs. Das listened attentively, stroking her hair with a small plastic brush that resembled an oval bed of nails, asking more questions, for yet another example. The children were quiet, intent on spotting more monkeys in the trees, and Mr. Das was absorbed by his tour book, so it seemed like a private conversation between Mr. Kapasi and Mrs. Das. In this manner the next half hour passed, and when they stopped for lunch at a roadside restaurant that sold fritters and omelette sandwiches, usually something Mr. Kapasi looked forward to on his tours so that he could sit in peace and enjoy some hot tea, he was disappointed. As the Das family settled together under a magenta umbrella fringed with white and orange tassels, and placed their orders with one of the waiters who marched about in tricornered caps, Mr. Kapasi reluctantly headed toward a neighboring table.

"Mr. Kapasi, wait. There's room here," Mrs. Das called out. She gathered Tina onto her lap, insisting that he accompany them. And so, together, they had bottled mango juice and sandwiches and plates of onions and potatoes deep-fried in graham-flour batter. After finishing two omelette sandwiches Mr. Das took more pictures of the group as they ate.

"How much longer?" he asked Mr. Kapasi as he paused to load a new roll of film in the camera.

"About half an hour more."

By now the children had gotten up from the table to look at more monkeys perched in a nearby tree, so there was a considerable space between Mrs. Das and Mr. Kapasi. Mr. Das placed the camera to his face and squeezed one eye shut, his tongue exposed at one corner of his mouth. "This looks funny. Mina, you need to lean in closer to Mr. Kapasi."

She did. He could smell a scent on her skin, like a mixture of whiskey and rosewater. He worried suddenly that she could smell his perspiration, which he knew had collected beneath the synthetic material of his shirt. He polished off his mango juice in one gulp and smoothed his silver hair with his hands. A bit of the juice dripped onto his chin. He wondered if Mrs. Das had noticed.

She had not. "What's your address, Mr. Kapasi?" she inquired, fishing for something inside her straw bag.

"You would like my address?"

"So we can send you copies," she said. "Of the pictures." She handed him a scrap of paper which she had hastily ripped from a page of her film magazine. The blank portion was limited, for the narrow strip was crowded by lines of text and a tiny picture of a hero and heroine embracing under a eucalyptus tree.

The paper curled as Mr. Kapasi wrote his address in clear, careful letters. She would write to him, asking about his days interpreting at the doctor's office, and he would respond eloquently, choosing only the most entertaining anecdotes, ones that would make her laugh out loud as she read them in her house in New Jersey. In time she would reveal the disappointment of her marriage, and he his. In this way their friendship would grow, and flourish. He would possess a picture of the two of them, eating fried onions under a magenta umbrella, which he would keep, he decided, safely tucked between the pages of his Russian grammar. As his mind raced, Mr. Kapasi experienced a mild and pleasant shock. It was similar to a feeling he used to experience long ago when, after months of translating with the aid of a dictionary, he would finally read a passage from a French novel, or an Italian sonnet, and understand the words, one after another, unencumbered by his own efforts. In those moments Mr. Kapasi used to believe that all was right with the world, that all struggles were rewarded, that all of life's mistakes made sense in the end. The promise that he would hear from Mrs. Das now filled him with the same belief.

When he finished writing his address Mr. Kapasi handed her the paper, but as soon as he did so he worried that he had either misspelled his name, or accidentally reversed the numbers of his postal code. He dreaded the possibility of a lost letter, the photograph never reaching him, hovering somewhere in Orissa,° close but ultimately unattainable. He thought of asking for the slip of paper again, just to make sure he had written his address accurately, but Mrs. Das had already dropped it into the jumble of her bag.

They reached Konarak at two-thirty. The temple, made of sandstone, was a massive pyramid-like structure in the shape of a chariot. It was dedicated to the great master of life, the sun, which struck three sides of the edifice as it made its journey each day across the sky. Twenty-four giant wheels were carved on the north and south sides of the plinth. The whole thing was drawn by a team of seven horses, speeding as if through the heavens. As they approached, Mr. Kapasi explained that the temple had been built between A.D. 1243 and 1255, with the efforts of twelve hundred artisans, by the great ruler of the Ganga dynasty, King Narasimhadeva the First, to commemorate his victory against the Muslim army.

"It says the temple occupies about a hundred and seventy acres of land," Mr. Das said, reading from his book.

"It's like a desert," Ronny said, his eyes wandering across the sand that stretched on all sides beyond the temple.

"The Chandrabhaga River once flowed one mile north of here. It is dry now," Mr. Kapasi said, turning off the engine.

They got out and walked toward the temple, posing first for pictures by the pair of lions that flanked the steps. Mr. Kapasi led them next to one of the wheels of the chariot, higher than any human being, nine feet in diameter.

"'The wheels are supposed to symbolize the wheel of life,'" Mr. Das read. "'They depict the cycle of creation, preservation, and achievement of realization.' Cool." He turned the page of his book. "'Each wheel is divided into eight thick and thin spokes, dividing the day into eight equal parts. The rims are carved with designs of birds and animals, whereas the medallions in the spokes are carved with women in luxurious poses, largely erotic in nature.'"

What he referred to were the countless friezes of entwined naked bodies, making love in various positions, women clinging to the necks of men, their knees wrapped eternally around their lovers' thighs. In addition to these were assorted scenes from daily life, of hunting and trading, of deer being killed with bows and arrows and marching warriors holding swords in their hands.

It was no longer possible to enter the temple, for it had filled with rubble years ago, but they admired the exterior, as did all the tourists Mr. Kapasi brought there, slowly strolling along each of its sides. Mr. Das trailed behind, taking pictures. The children ran ahead, pointing to figures of naked people, intrigued in particular by

Orissa: a state on the southwest border of West Bengal.

the Nagamithunas, the half-human, half-serpentine couples who were said, Mr. Kapasi told them, to live in the deepest waters of the sea. Mr. Kapasi was pleased that they liked the temple, pleased especially that it appealed to Mrs. Das. She stopped every three or four paces, staring silently at the carved lovers, and the processions of elephants, and the topless female musicians beating on two-sided drums.

Though Mr. Kapasi had been to the temple countless times, it occurred to him, as he, too, gazed at the topless women, that he had never seen his own wife fully naked. Even when they had made love she kept the panels of her blouse hooked together, the string of her petticoat knotted around her waist. He had never admired the backs of his wife's legs the way he now admired those of Mrs. Das, walking as if for his benefit alone. He had, of course, seen plenty of bare limbs before, belonging to the American and European ladies who took his tours. But Mrs. Das was different. Unlike the other women, who had an interest only in the temple, and kept their noses buried in a guidebook, or their eyes behind the lens of a camera, Mrs. Das had taken an interest in him.

Mr. Kapasi was anxious to be alone with her, to continue their private conversa-   100
tion, yet he felt nervous to walk at her side. She was lost behind her sunglasses, ignoring her husband's requests that she pose for another picture, walking past her children as if they were strangers. Worried that he might disturb her, Mr. Kapasi walked ahead, to admire, as he always did, the three life-sized bronze avatars of Surya, the sun god, each emerging from its own niche on the temple facade to greet the sun at dawn, noon, and evening. They wore elaborate headdresses, their languid, elongated eyes closed, their bare chests draped with carved chains and amulets. Hibiscus petals, offerings from previous visitors, were strewn at their gray-green feet. The last statue, on the northern wall of the temple, was Mr. Kapasi's favorite. This Surya had a tired expression, weary after a hard day of work, sitting astride a horse with folded legs. Even his horse's eyes were drowsy. Around his body were smaller sculptures of women in pairs, their hips thrust to one side.

"Who's that?" Mrs. Das asked. He was startled to see that she was standing beside him.

"He is the Astachala-Surya," Mr. Kapasi said. "The setting sun."

"So in a couple of hours the sun will set right here?" She slipped a foot out of one of her square-heeled shoes, rubbed her toes on the back of her other leg.

"That is correct."

She raised her sunglasses for a moment, then put them back on again. "Neat."   105

Mr. Kapasi was not certain exactly what the word suggested, but he had a feeling it was a favorable response. He hoped that Mrs. Das had understood Surya's beauty, his power. Perhaps they would discuss it further in their letters. He would explain things to her, things about India, and she would explain things to him about America. In its own way this correspondence would fulfill his dream, of serving as an interpreter between nations. He looked at her straw bag, delighted that his address lay nestled among its contents. When he pictured her so many thousands of miles away he plummeted, so much so that he had an overwhelming urge to wrap his arms around her, to freeze with her, even for an instant, in an embrace witnessed by his favorite Surya. But Mrs. Das had already started walking.

"When do you return to America?" he asked, trying to sound placid.

"In ten days."

He calculated: A week to settle in, a week to develop the pictures, a few days to compose her letter, two weeks to get to India by air. According to his schedule, allowing room for delays, he would hear from Mrs. Das in approximately six weeks' time.

The family was silent as Mr. Kapasi drove them back, a little past four-thirty, to   110
Hotel Sandy Villa. The children had bought miniature granite versions of the chariot's wheels at a souvenir stand, and they turned them round in their hands. Mr. Das continued to read his book. Mrs. Das untangled Tina's hair with her brush and divided it into two little ponytails.

Mr. Kapasi was beginning to dread the thought of dropping them off. He was not prepared to begin his six-week wait to hear from Mrs. Das. As he stole glances at her in the rearview mirror, wrapping elastic bands around Tina's hair, he wondered how he might make the tour last a little longer. Ordinarily he sped back to Puri using a shortcut, eager to return home, scrub his feet and hands with sandalwood soap, and enjoy the evening newspaper and a cup of tea that his wife would serve him in silence. The thought of that silence, something to which he'd long been resigned, now oppressed him. It was then that he suggested visiting the hills at Udayagiri and Khandagiri, where a number of monastic dwellings were hewn out of the ground, facing one another across a defile. It was some miles away, but well worth seeing, Mr. Kapasi told them.

"Oh yeah, there's something mentioned about it in this book," Mr. Das said. "Built by a Jain° king or something."

"Shall we go then?" Mr. Kapasi asked. He paused at a turn in the road. "It's to the left."

Mr. Das turned to look at Mrs. Das. Both of them shrugged.

"Left, left," the children chanted.   115

Mr. Kapasi turned the wheel, almost delirious with relief. He did not know what he would do or say to Mrs. Das once they arrived at the hills. Perhaps he would tell her what a pleasing smile she had. Perhaps he would compliment her strawberry shirt, which he found irresistibly becoming. Perhaps, when Mr. Das was busy taking a picture, he would take her hand.

He did not have to worry. When they got to the hills, divided by a steep path thick with trees, Mrs. Das refused to get out of the car. All along the path, dozens of monkeys were seated on stones, as well as on the branches of the trees. Their hind legs were stretched out in front and raised to shoulder level, their arms resting on their knees.

"My legs are tired," she said, sinking low in her seat. "I'll stay here."

"Why did you have to wear those stupid shoes?" Mr. Das said. "You won't be in the pictures."

"Pretend I'm there."   120

"But we could use one of these pictures for our Christmas card this year. We didn't get one of all five of us at the Sun Temple. Mr. Kapasi could take it."

"I'm not coming. Anyway, those monkeys give me the creeps."

"But they're harmless," Mr. Das said. He turned to Mr. Kapasi. "Aren't they?"

"They are more hungry than dangerous," Mr. Kapasi said. "Do not provoke them with food, and they will not bother you."

Jain: an adherent of Jainism, a dualistic, ascetic religion founded in the sixth century B.C. in revolt against the Hindu caste system.

Mr. Das headed up the defile with the children, the boys at his side, the little girl   125
on his shoulders. Mr. Kapasi watched as they crossed paths with a Japanese man and
woman, the only other tourists there, who paused for a final photograph, then
stepped into a nearby car and drove away. As the car disappeared out of view some of
the monkeys called out, emitting soft whooping sounds, and then walked on their flat
black hands and feet up the path. At one point a group of them formed a little ring
around Mr. Das and the children. Tina screamed in delight. Ronny ran in circles
around his father. Bobby bent down and picked up a fat stick on the ground. When
he extended it, one of the monkeys approached him and snatched it, then briefly
beat the ground.

"I'll join them," Mr. Kapasi said, unlocking the door on his side. "There is much
to explain about the caves."

"No. Stay a minute," Mrs. Das said. She got out of the back seat and slipped in
beside Mr. Kapasi. "Raj has his dumb book anyway." Together, through the windshield, Mrs. Das and Mr. Kapasi watched as Bobby and the monkey passed the stick
back and forth between them.

"A brave little boy," Mr. Kapasi commented.

"It's not so surprising," Mrs. Das said.

"No?"   130

"He's not his."

"I beg your pardon?"

"Raj's. He's not Raj's son."

Mr. Kapasi felt a prickle on his skin. He reached into his shirt pocket for the
small tin of lotus-oil balm he carried with him at all times, and applied it to three
spots on his forehead. He knew that Mrs. Das was watching him, but he did not turn
to face her. Instead he watched as the figures of Mr. Das and the children grew
smaller, climbing up the steep path, pausing every now and then for a picture, surrounded by a growing number of monkeys.

"Are you surprised?" The way she put it made him choose his words with care.   135

"It's not the type of thing one assumes," Mr. Kapasi replied slowly. He put the tin
of lotus-oil balm back in his pocket.

"No, of course not. And no one knows, of course. No one at all. I've kept it a secret for eight whole years." She looked at Mr. Kapasi, tilting her chin as if to gain a
fresh perspective. "But now I've told you."

Mr. Kapasi nodded. He felt suddenly parched, and his forehead was warm and
slightly numb from the balm. He considered asking Mrs. Das for a sip of water, then
decided against it.

"We met when we were very young," she said. She reached into her straw bag in
search of something, then pulled out a packet of puffed rice. "Want some?"

"No, thank you."   140

She put a fistful in her mouth, sank into the seat a little, and looked away from
Mr. Kapasi, out the window on her side of the car. "We married when we were still in
college. We were in high school when he proposed. We went to the same college, of
course. Back then we couldn't stand the thought of being separated, not for a day,
not for a minute. Our parents were best friends who lived in the same town. My entire life I saw him every weekend, either at our house or theirs. We were sent upstairs
to play together while our parents joked about our marriage. Imagine! They never
caught us at anything, though in a way I think it was all more or less a setup. The

things we did those Friday and Saturday nights, while our parents sat downstairs drinking tea . . . I could tell you stories, Mr. Kapasi."

As a result of spending all her time in college with Raj, she continued, she did not make many close friends. There was no one to confide in about him at the end of a difficult day, or to share a passing thought or a worry. Her parents now lived on the other side of the world, but she had never been very close to them, anyway. After marrying so young she was overwhelmed by it all, having a child so quickly, and nursing, and warming up bottles of milk and testing their temperature against her wrist while Raj was at work, dressed in sweaters and corduroy pants, teaching his students about rocks and dinosaurs. Raj never looked cross or harried, or plump as she had become after the first baby.

Always tired, she declined invitations from her one or two college girlfriends, to have lunch or shop in Manhattan. Eventually the friends stopped calling her, so that she was left at home all day with the baby, surrounded by toys that made her trip when she walked or wince when she sat, always cross and tired. Only occasionally did they go out after Ronny was born, and even more rarely did they entertain. Raj didn't mind; he looked forward to coming home from teaching and watching television and bouncing Ronny on his knee. She had been outraged when Raj told her that a Punjabi° friend, someone whom she had once met but did not remember, would be staying with them for a week for some job interviews in the New Brunswick area.

Bobby was conceived in the afternoon, on a sofa littered with rubber teething toys, after the friend learned that a London pharmaceutical company had hired him, while Ronny cried to be freed from his playpen. She made no protest when the friend touched the small of her back as she was about to make a pot of coffee, then pulled her against his crisp navy suit. He made love to her swiftly, in silence, with an expertise she had never known, without the meaningful expressions and smiles Raj always insisted on afterward. The next day Raj drove the friend to JFK. He was married now, to a Punjabi girl, and they lived in London still, and every year they exchanged Christmas cards with Raj and Mina, each couple tucking photos of their families into the envelopes. He did not know that he was Bobby's father. He never would.

"I beg your pardon, Mrs. Das, but why have you told me this information?" Mr. Kapasi asked when she had finally finished speaking, and had turned to face him once again. 145

"For God's sake, stop calling me Mrs. Das. I'm twenty-eight. You probably have children my age."

"Not quite." It disturbed Mr. Kapasi to learn that she thought of him as a parent. The feeling he had had toward her, that had made him check his reflection in the rearview mirror as they drove, evaporated a little.

"I told you because of your talents." She put the packet of puffed rice back into her bag without folding over the top.

"I don't understand," Mr. Kapasi said.

"Don't you see? For eight years I haven't been able to express this to anybody, not to friends, certainly not to Raj. He doesn't even suspect it. He thinks I'm still in love with him. Well, don't you have anything to say?" 150

"About what?"

Punjabi: a native of Punjab, a state in northwest India.

"About what I've just told you. About my secret, and about how terrible it makes me feel. I feel terrible looking at my children, and at Raj, always terrible. I have terrible urges, Mr. Kapasi, to throw things away. One day I had the urge to throw everything I own out the window, the television, the children, everything. Don't you think it's unhealthy?"

He was silent.

"Mr. Kapasi, don't you have anything to say? I thought that was your job."

"My job is to give tours, Mrs. Das." 155

"Not that. Your other job. As an interpreter."

"But we do not face a language barrier. What need is there for an interpreter?"

"That's not what I mean. I would never have told you otherwise. Don't you realize what it means for me to tell you?"

"What does it mean?"

"It means that I'm tired of feeling so terrible all the time. Eight years, Mr. Kapasi, 160 I've been in pain eight years. I was hoping you could help me feel better, say the right thing. Suggest some kind of remedy."

He looked at her, in her red plaid skirt and strawberry T-shirt, a woman not yet thirty, who loved neither her husband nor her children, who had already fallen out of love with life. Her confession depressed him, depressed him all the more when he thought of Mr. Das at the top of the path, Tina clinging to his shoulders, taking pictures of ancient monastic cells cut into the hills to show his students in America, unsuspecting and unaware that one of his sons was not his own. Mr. Kapasi felt insulted that Mrs. Das should ask him to interpret her common, trivial little secret. She did not resemble the patients in the doctor's office, those who came glassy-eyed and desperate, unable to sleep or breathe or urinate with ease, unable, above all, to give words to their pains. Still, Mr. Kapasi believed it was his duty to assist Mrs. Das. Perhaps he ought to tell her to confess the truth to Mr. Das. He would explain that honesty was the best policy. Honesty, surely, would help her feel better, as she'd put it. Perhaps he would offer to preside over the discussion, as a mediator. He decided to begin with the most obvious question, to get to the heart of the matter, and so he asked, "Is it really pain you feel, Mrs. Das, or is it guilt?"

She turned to him and glared, mustard oil thick on her frosty pink lips. She opened her mouth to say something, but as she glared at Mr. Kapasi some certain knowledge seemed to pass before her eyes, and she stopped. It crushed him; he knew at that moment that he was not even important enough to be properly insulted. She opened the car door and began walking up the path, wobbling a little on her square wooden heels, reaching into her straw bag to eat handfuls of puffed rice. It fell through her fingers, leaving a zigzagging trail, causing a monkey to leap down from a tree and devour the little white grains. In search of more, the monkey began to follow Mrs. Das. Others joined him, so that she was soon being followed by about half a dozen of them, their velvety tails dragging behind.

Mr. Kapasi stepped out of the car. He wanted to holler, to alert her in some way, but he worried that if she knew they were behind her, she would grow nervous. Perhaps she would lose her balance. Perhaps they would pull at her bag or her hair. He began to jog up the path, taking a fallen branch in his hand to scare away the monkeys. Mrs. Das continued walking, oblivious, trailing grains of puffed rice. Near the top of the incline, before a group of cells fronted by a row of squat stone pillars, Mr. Das was kneeling on the ground focusing the lens of his camera. The children stood under the arcade, now hiding, now emerging from view.

"Wait for me," Mrs. Das called out. "I'm coming."

Tina jumped up and down. "Here comes Mommy!"   165

"Great," Mr. Das said without looking up. "Just in time. We'll get Mr. Kapasi to take a picture of the five of us."

Mr. Kapasi quickened his pace, waving his branch so that the monkeys scampered away, distracted, in another direction.

"Where's Bobby?" Mrs. Das asked when she stopped.

Mr. Das looked up from the camera. "I don't know. Ronny, where's Bobby?"

Ronny shrugged, "I thought he was right here."   170

"Where is he?" Mrs. Das repeated sharply. "What's wrong with all of you?"

They began calling his name, wandering up and down the path a bit. Because they were calling, they did not initially hear the boy's screams. When they found him, a little farther down the path under a tree, he was surrounded by a group of monkeys, over a dozen of them, pulling at his T-shirt with their long black fingers. The puffed rice Mrs. Das had spilled was scattered at his feet, raked over by the monkeys' hands. The boy was silent, his body frozen, swift tears running down his startled face. His bare legs were dusty and red with welts from where one of the monkeys struck him repeatedly with the stick he had given to it earlier.

"Daddy, the monkey's hurting Bobby," Tina said.

Mr. Das wiped his palms on the front of his shorts. In his nervousness he accidentally pressed the shutter on his camera; the whirring noise of the advancing film excited the monkeys, and the one with the stick began to beat Bobby more intently. "What are we supposed to do? What if they start attacking?"

"Mr. Kapasi," Mrs. Das shrieked, noticing him standing to one side. "Do some-   175
thing, for God's sake, do something!"

Mr. Kapasi took his branch and shooed them away, hissing at the ones that remained, stomping his feet to scare them. The animals retreated slowly, with a measured gait, obedient but unintimidated. Mr. Kapasi gathered Bobby in his arms and brought him back to where his parents and siblings were standing. As he carried him he was tempted to whisper a secret into the boy's ear. But Bobby was stunned, and shivering with fright, his legs bleeding slightly where the stick had broken the skin. When Mr. Kapasi delivered him to his parents, Mr. Das brushed some dirt off the boy's T-shirt and put the visor on him the right way. Mrs. Das reached into her straw bag to find a bandage which she taped over the cut on his knee. Ronny offered his brother a fresh piece of gum. "He's fine. Just a little scared, right, Bobby?" Mr. Das said, patting the top of his head.

"God, let's get out of here," Mrs. Das said. She folded her arms across the strawberry on her chest. "This place gives me the creeps."

"Yeah. Back to the hotel, definitely," Mr. Das agreed.

"Poor Bobby," Mrs. Das said. "Come here a second. Let Mommy fix your hair." Again she reached into her straw bag, this time for her hairbrush, and began to run it around the edges of the translucent visor. When she whipped out the hairbrush, the slip of paper with Mr. Kapasi's address on it fluttered away in the wind. No one but Mr. Kapasi noticed. He watched as it rose, carried higher and higher by the breeze, into the trees where the monkeys now sat, solemnly observing the scene below. Mr. Kapasi observed it too, knowing that this was the picture of the Das family he would preserve forever in his mind.

Joyce Carol Oates

Where Are You Going, Where Have You Been?   1970

*Joyce Carol Oates was born in 1938 into a blue
collar, Catholic family in Lockport, New York.
As an undergraduate at Syracuse University,
she won a* Mademoiselle *magazine award for
fiction. After graduating with top honors, she
took a master's degree in English at the University of Wisconsin and went on to teach at several
universities: Detroit, Windsor, and Princeton.
A remarkably prolific writer, Oates has produced
more than twenty-five collections of stories,
including* High Lonesome: Stories 1966–2006,
and forty novels, including them, *winner of a
National Book Award in 1970,* Because It Is
Bitter, *and* Because It Is My Heart *(1990),
and more recently,* Black Girl/White Girl
(2006), The Gravedigger's Daughter
(2007), and A Fair Maiden *(2010). She also
writes poetry, plays, and literary criticism. On*

Joyce Carol Oates

Boxing *(1987) is her nonfiction memoir and
study of fighters and fighting.* Foxfire *(1993), her twenty-second novel, is the story of a girl
gang in upstate New York. Her 1996 Gothic novella,* First Love, *is a bizarre tale of terror
and torture. Violence and the macabre may inhabit her best stories, but Oates has insisted
that these elements in her work are never gratuitous. The 1985 film* Smooth Talk, *directed
by Joyce Chopra, was based on "Where Are You Going, Where Have You Been?"*

For Bob Dylan

Her name was Connie. She was fifteen and she had a quick nervous giggling
habit of craning her neck to glance into mirrors, or checking other people's faces to
make sure her own was all right. Her mother, who noticed everything and knew
everything and who hadn't much reason any longer to look at her own face, always
scolded Connie about it. "Stop gawking at yourself, who are you? You think you're so
pretty?" she would say. Connie would raise her eyebrows at these familiar complaints
and look right through her mother, into a shadowy vision of herself as she was right
at that moment: she knew she was pretty and that was everything. Her mother had
been pretty once too, if you could believe those old snapshots in the album, but now
her looks were gone and that was why she was always after Connie.

"Why don't you keep your room clean like your sister? How've you got your hair
fixed—what the hell stinks? Hair spray? You don't see your sister using that junk."

Her sister June was twenty-four and still lived at home. She was a secretary in
the high school Connie attended, and if that wasn't bad enough—with her in the
same building—she was so plain and chunky and steady that Connie had to hear her
praised all the time by her mother and her mother's sisters. June did this, June did
that, she saved money and helped clean the house and cooked and Connie couldn't
do a thing, her mind was all filled with trashy daydreams. Their father was away at
work most of the time and when he came home he wanted supper and he read the

newspaper at supper and after supper he went to bed. He didn't bother talking much to them, but around his bent head Connie's mother kept picking at her until Connie wished her mother was dead and she herself was dead and it was all over. "She makes me want to throw up sometimes," she complained to her friends. She had a high, breathless, amused voice which made everything she said sound a little forced, whether it was sincere or not.

There was one good thing: June went places with girl friends of hers, girls who were just as plain and steady as she, and so when Connie wanted to do that her mother had no objections. The father of Connie's best girl friend drove the girls the three miles to town and left them off at a shopping plaza, so that they could walk through the stores or go to a movie, and when he came to pick them up again at eleven he never bothered to ask what they had done.

They must have been familiar sights, walking around that shopping plaza in their shorts and flat ballerina slippers that always scuffed the sidewalk, with charm bracelets jingling on their thin wrists; they would lean together to whisper and laugh secretly if someone passed by who amused or interested them. Connie had long dark blond hair that drew anyone's eye to it, and she wore part of it pulled up on her head and puffed out and the rest of it she let fall down her back. She wore a pull-over jersey blouse that looked one way when she was at home and another way when she was away from home. Everything about her had two sides to it, one for home and one for anywhere that was not home: her walk that could be childlike and bobbing, or languid enough to make anyone think she was hearing music in her head, her mouth which was pale and smirking most of the time, but bright and pink on these evenings out, her laugh which was cynical and drawling at home—"Ha, ha, very funny"—but high-pitched and nervous anywhere else, like the jingling of the charms on her bracelet.

Sometimes they did go shopping or to a movie, but sometimes they went across the highway, ducking fast across the busy road, to a drive-in restaurant where older kids hung out. The restaurant was shaped like a big bottle, though squatter than a real bottle, and on its cap was a revolving figure of a grinning boy who held a hamburger aloft. One night in mid-summer they ran across, breathless with daring, and right away someone leaned out a car window and invited them over, but it was just a boy from high school they didn't like. It made them feel good to be able to ignore him. They went up through the maze of parked and cruising cars to the bright-lit, fly-infested restaurant, their faces pleased and expectant as if they were entering a sacred building that loomed out of the night to give them what haven and what blessing they yearned for. They sat at the counter and crossed their legs at the ankles, their thin shoulders rigid with excitement, and listened to the music that made everything so good: the music was always in the background like music at a church service, it was something to depend upon.

A boy named Eddie came in to talk with them. He sat backwards on his stool, turning himself jerkily around in semi-circles and then stopping and turning again, and after a while he asked Connie if she would like something to eat. She said she did and so she tapped her friend's arm on her way out—her friend pulled her face up into a brave droll look—and Connie said she would meet her at eleven, across the way. "I just hate to leave her like that," Connie said earnestly, but the boy said that she wouldn't be alone for long. So they went out to his car and on the way Connie couldn't help but let her eyes wander over the windshields and faces all around her, her face gleaming with a joy that had nothing to do with Eddie or even this place; it might have been the music. She drew her shoulders up and sucked in her breath with the pure pleasure of being alive, and just at that moment she happened to glance at a face just a few feet from hers. It was a boy with shaggy black hair, in a convertible jalopy painted gold. He stared at her and then his lips widened into a grin. Connie slit her eyes at him and turned away, but she couldn't help glancing back and there he was still watching her. He wagged a finger and laughed and said, "Gonna get you, baby," and Connie turned away again without Eddie noticing anything.

She spent three hours with him, at the restaurant where they ate hamburgers and drank Cokes in wax cups that were always sweating, and then down an alley a mile or so away, and when he left her off at five to eleven only the movie house was still open at the plaza. Her girl friend was there, talking with a boy. When Connie came up the two girls smiled at each other and Connie said, "How was the movie?" and the girl said, "*You* should know." They rode off with the girl's father, sleepy and pleased, and Connie couldn't help but look at the darkened shopping plaza with its big empty parking lot and its signs that were faded and ghostly now, and over at the drive-in restaurant where cars were still circling tirelessly. She couldn't hear the music at this distance.

Next morning June asked her how the movie was and Connie said, "So-so."

She and that girl and occasionally another girl went out several times a week that way, and the rest of the time Connie spent around the house—it was summer vacation—getting in her mother's way and thinking, dreaming, about the boys she met. But all the boys fell back and dissolved into a single face that was not even a face, but an idea, a feeling, mixed up with the urgent insistent pounding of the music and the humid night air of July. Connie's mother kept dragging her back to the daylight by finding things for her to do or saying, suddenly, "What's this about the Pettinger girl?"

And Connie would say nervously, "Oh, her. That dope." She always drew thick clear lines between herself and such girls, and her mother was simple and kindly enough to believe her. Her mother was so simple, Connie thought, that it was maybe cruel to fool her so much. Her mother went scuffling around the house in old bedroom slippers and complained over the telephone to one sister about the other, then the other called up and the two of them complained about the third one. If June's name was mentioned her mother's tone was approving, and if Connie's name was mentioned it was disapproving. This did not really mean she disliked Connie and actually Connie thought that her mother preferred her to June because she was prettier, but the two of them kept up a pretense of exasperation, a sense that they were tugging and struggling over something of little value to either of them. Sometimes, over coffee, they were almost friends, but something would come up—some vexation that was like a fly buzzing suddenly around their heads—and their faces went hard with contempt.

One Sunday Connie got up at eleven—none of them bothered with church—and washed her hair so that it could dry all day long, in the sun. Her parents and sister were going to a barbecue at an aunt's house and Connie said no, she wasn't interested, rolling her eyes to let her mother know just what she thought of it. "Stay home alone then," her mother said sharply. Connie sat out back in a lawn chair and watched them drive away, her father quiet and bald, hunched around so that he could back the car out, her mother with a look that was still angry and not at all softened through the windshield, and in the back seat poor old June all dressed up as if she didn't know what a barbecue was, with all the running yelling kids and the flies. Connie sat with her eyes closed in the sun, dreaming and dazed with the warmth about her as if this

10

were a kind of love, the caresses of love, and her mind slipped over onto thoughts of the boy she had been with the night before and how nice he had been, how sweet it always was, not the way someone like June would suppose but sweet, gentle, the way it was in movies and promised in songs; and when she opened her eyes she hardly knew where she was, the back yard ran off into weeds and a fence-line of trees and behind it the sky was perfectly blue and still. The asbestos "ranch house" that was now three years old startled her—it looked small. She shook her head as if to get awake.

It was too hot. She went inside the house and turned on the radio to drown out the quiet. She sat on the edge of her bed, barefoot, and listened for an hour and a half to a program called XYZ Sunday Jamboree, record after record of hard, fast, shrieking songs she sang along with, interspersed by exclamations from "Bobby King": "An' look here you girls at Napoleon's—Son and Charley want you to pay real close attention to this song coming up!"

And Connie paid close attention herself, bathed in a glow of slow-pulsed joy that seemed to rise mysteriously out of the music itself and lay languidly about the airless little room, breathed in and breathed out with each gentle rise and fall of her chest.

After a while she heard a car coming up the drive. She sat up at once, startled, be-   15
cause it couldn't be her father so soon. The gravel kept crunching all the way in from the road—the driveway was long—and Connie ran to the window. It was a car she didn't know. It was an open jalopy, painted a bright gold that caught the sunlight opaquely. Her heart began to pound and her fingers snatched at her hair, checking it, and she whispered "Christ, Christ," wondering how bad she looked. The car came to a stop at the side door and the horn sounded four short taps as if this were a signal Connie knew.

She went into the kitchen and approached the door slowly, then hung out the screen door, her bare toes curling down off the step. There were two boys in the car and now she recognized the driver: he had shaggy, shabby black hair that looked crazy as a wig and he was grinning at her.

"I ain't late, am I?" he said.

"Who the hell do you think you are?" Connie said.

"Toldja I'd be out, didn't I?"

"I don't even know who you are."   20

She spoke sullenly, careful to show no interest or pleasure, and he spoke in a fast bright monotone. Connie looked past him to the other boy, taking her time. He had fair brown hair, with a lock that fell onto his forehead. His sideburns gave him a fierce, embarrassed look, but so far he hadn't even bothered to glance at her. Both boys wore sunglasses. The driver's glasses were metallic and mirrored everything in miniature.

"You wanta come for a ride?" he said.

Connie smirked and let her hair fall loose over one shoulder.

"Don'tcha like my car? New paint job," he said. "Hey."

"What?"   25

"You're cute."

She pretended to fidget, chasing flies away from the door.

"Don'tcha believe me, or what?" he said.

"Look, I don't even know who you are," Connie said in disgust.

"Hey, Ellie's got a radio, see. Mine's broke down." He lifted his friend's arm and   30
showed her the little transistor the boy was holding, and now Connie began to hear the music. It was the same program that was playing inside the house.

"Bobby King?" she said.

"I listen to him all the time. I think he's great."

"He's kind of great," Connie said reluctantly.

"Listen, that guy's *great*. He knows where the action is."

Connie blushed a little, because the glasses made it impossible for her to see just 35
what this boy was looking at. She couldn't decide if she liked him or if he was just a
jerk, and so she dawdled in the doorway and wouldn't come down or go back inside.
She said, "What's all that stuff painted on your car?"

"Can'tcha read it?" He opened the door very carefully, as if he was afraid it
might fall off. He slid out just as carefully, planting his feet firmly on the ground,
the tiny metallic world in his glasses slowing down like gelatine hardening and in
the midst of it Connie's bright green blouse. "This here is my name, to begin
with," he said. ARNOLD FRIEND was written in tarlike black letters on the side, with
a drawing of a round grinning face that reminded Connie of a pumpkin, except it
wore sunglasses. "I wanta introduce myself, I'm Arnold Friend and that's my real
name and I'm gonna be your friend, honey, and inside the car's Ellie Oscar, he's
kinda shy." Ellie brought his transistor radio up to his shoulder and balanced it
there. "Now these numbers are a secret code, honey," Arnold Friend explained.
He read off the numbers 33, 19, 17 and raised his eyebrows at her to see what she
thought of that, but she didn't think much of it. The left rear fender had been
smashed and around it was written, on the gleaming gold background: DONE BY
CRAZY WOMAN DRIVER. Connie had to laugh at that. Arnold Friend was pleased at
her laughter and looked up at her. "Around the other side's a lot more—you
wanta come and see them?"

"No."

"Why not?"

"Why should I?"

"Don'tcha wanta see what's on the car? Don'tcha wanta go for a ride?"   40

"I don't know."

"Why not?"

"I got things to do."

"Like what?"

"Things."   45

He laughed as if she had said something funny. He slapped his thighs. He was
standing in a strange way, leaning back against the car as if he were balancing himself. He wasn't tall, only an inch or so taller than she would be if she came down to
him. Connie liked the way he was dressed, which was the way all of them dressed:
tight faded jeans stuffed into black, scuffed boots, a belt that pulled his waist in and
showed how lean he was, and a white pull-over shirt that was a little soiled and
showed the hard small muscles of his arms and shoulders. He looked as if he probably did hard work, lifting and carrying things. Even his neck looked muscular. And
his face was a familiar face, somehow: the jaw and chin and cheeks slightly darkened, because he hadn't shaved for a day or two, and the nose long and hawk-like,
sniffing as if she were a treat he was going to gobble up and it was all a joke.

"Connie, you ain't telling the truth. This is your day set aside for a ride with me
and you know it," he said, still laughing. The way he straightened and recovered from
his fit of laughing showed that it had been all fake.

"How do you know what my name is?" she said suspiciously.

"It's Connie."

"Maybe and maybe not."

"I know my Connie," he said, wagging his finger. Now she remembered him even   50
better, back at the restaurant, and her cheeks warmed at the thought of how she
sucked in her breath just at the moment she passed him—how she must have looked
to him. And he had remembered her. "Ellie and I come out here especially for you,"
he said. "Ellie can sit in back. How about it?"

"Where?"

"Where what?"

"Where're we going?"

He looked at her. He took off the sunglasses and she saw how pale the skin   55
around his eyes was, like holes that were not in shadow but instead in light. His eyes
were chips of broken glass that catch the light in an amiable way. He smiled. It was as
if the idea of going for a ride somewhere, to some place, was a new idea to him.

"Just for a ride, Connie sweetheart."

"I never said my name was Connie," she said.

"But I know what it is. I know your name and all about you, lots of things,"
Arnold Friend said. He had not moved yet but stood still leaning back against the
side of his jalopy. "I took a special interest in you, such a pretty girl, and found out all
about you like I know your parents and sister are gone somewheres and I know where
and how long they're going to be gone, and I know who you were with last night, and
your best girl friend's name is Betty. Right?"

He spoke in a simple lilting voice, exactly as if he were reciting the words to a
song. His smile assured her that everything was fine. In the car Ellie turned up the
volume on his radio and did not bother to look around at them.

"Ellie can sit in the back seat," Arnold Friend said. He indicated his friend with   60
a casual jerk of his chin, as if Ellie did not count and she should not bother with him.

"How'd you find out all that stuff?" Connie said.

"Listen: Betty Schultz and Tony Fitch and Jimmy Pettinger and Nancy Pettinger," he said, in a chant. "Raymond Stanley and Bob Hutter—"

"Do you know all those kids?"

"I know everybody."

"Look, you're kidding. You're not from around here."   65

"Sure."

"But—how come we never saw you before?"

"Sure you saw me before," he said. He looked down at his boots, as if he were a
little offended. "You just don't remember."

"I guess I'd remember you," Connie said.

"Yeah?" He looked up at this, beaming. He was pleased. He began to mark time   70
with the music from Ellie's radio, tapping his fists lightly together. Connie looked
away from his smile to the car, which was painted so bright it almost hurt her eyes to
look at it. She looked at that name, ARNOLD FRIEND. And up at the front fender was
an expression that was familiar—MAN THE FLYING SAUCERS. It was an expression kids
had used the year before, but didn't use this year. She looked at it for a while as if the
words meant something to her that she did not yet know.

"What're you thinking about? Huh?" Arnold Friend demanded. "Not worried
about your hair blowing around in the car, are you?"

"No."

"Think I maybe can't drive good?"

"How do I know?"

"You're a hard girl to handle. How come?" he said. "Don't you know I'm your   75
friend? Didn't you see me put my sign in the air when you walked by?"

"What sign?"

"My sign." And he drew an X in the air, leaning out toward her. They were maybe
ten feet apart. After his hand fell back to his side the X was still in the air, almost visible. Connie let the screen door close and stood perfectly still inside it, listening to the
music from her radio and the boy's blend together. She stared at Arnold Friend. He
stood there so stiffly relaxed, pretending to be relaxed, with one hand idly on the door
handle as if he were keeping himself up that way and had no intention of ever moving
again. She recognized most things about him, the tight jeans that showed his thighs
and buttocks and the greasy leather boots and the tight shirt, and even that slippery
friendly smile of his, that sleepy dreamy smile that all the boys used to get across ideas
they didn't want to put into words. She recognized all this and also the singsong way
he talked, slightly mocking, kidding, but serious and a little melancholy, and she recognized the way he tapped one fist against the other in homage to the perpetual music
behind him. But all these things did not come together.

She said suddenly, "Hey, how old are you?"

His smile faded. She could see then that he wasn't a kid, he was much older—
thirty, maybe more. At this knowledge her heart began to pound faster.

"That's a crazy thing to ask. Can'tcha see I'm your own age?"   80

"Like hell you are."

"Or maybe a coupla years older, I'm eighteen."

"Eighteen?" she said doubtfully.

He grinned to reassure her and lines appeared at the corners of his mouth. His teeth
were big and white. He grinned so broadly his eyes became slits and she saw how thick
the lashes were, thick and black as if painted with a black tarlike material. Then he
seemed to become embarrassed, abruptly, and looked over his shoulder at Ellie. "*Him*,
he's crazy," he said. "Ain't he a riot, he's a nut, a real character." Ellie was still listening
to the music. His sunglasses told nothing about what he was thinking. He wore a bright
orange shirt unbuttoned halfway to show his chest, which was a pale, bluish chest and
not muscular like Arnold Friend's. His shirt collar was turned up all around and the very
tips of the collar pointed out past his chin as if they were protecting him. He was pressing the transistor radio up against his ear and sat there in a kind of daze, right in the sun.

"He's kinda strange," Connie said.   85

"Hey, she says you're kinda strange! Kinda strange!" Arnold Friend cried. He
pounded on the car to get Ellie's attention. Ellie turned for the first time and Connie saw
with shock that he wasn't a kid either—he had a fair, hairless face, cheeks reddened
slightly as if the veins grew too close to the surface of his skin, the face of a forty-year-old
baby. Connie felt a wave of dizziness rise in her at this sight and she stared at him as if
waiting for something to change the shock of the moment, make it all right again. Ellie's
lips kept shaping words, mumbling along with the words blasting in his ear.

"Maybe you two better go away," Connie said faintly.

"What? How come?" Arnold Friend cried. "We come out here to take you for a
ride. It's Sunday." He had the voice of the man on the radio now. It was the same
voice, Connie thought. "Don'tcha know it's Sunday all day and honey, no matter
who you were with last night today you're with Arnold Friend and don't you forget

it!—Maybe you better step out here," he said, and this last was in a different voice. It was a little flatter, as if the heat was finally getting to him.

"No. I got things to do."

"Hey."

"You two better leave."

"We ain't leaving until you come with us."

"Like hell I am—"

"Connie, don't fool around with me. I mean, I mean, don't fool *around*," he said, shaking his head. He laughed incredulously. He placed his sunglasses on top of his head, carefully, as if he were indeed wearing a wig, and brought the stems down behind his ears. Connie stared at him, another wave of dizziness and fear rising in her so that for a moment he wasn't even in focus but was just a blur, standing there against his gold car, and she had the idea that he had driven up the driveway all right but had come from nowhere before that and belonged nowhere and that everything about him and even about the music that was so familiar to her was only half real.

"If my father comes and sees you—"

"He ain't coming. He's at a barbecue."

"How do you know that?"

"Aunt Tillie's. Right now they're—uh—they're drinking. Sitting around," he said vaguely, squinting as if he were staring all the way to town and over to Aunt Tillie's backyard. Then the vision seemed to get clear and he nodded energetically. "Yeah. Sitting around. There's your sister in a blue dress, huh? And high heels, the poor sad bitch—nothing like you, sweetheart! And your mother's helping some fat woman with the corn, they're cleaning the corn—husking the corn—"

"What fat woman?" Connie cried.

"How do I know what fat woman. I don't know every goddam fat woman in the world!" Arnold Friend laughed.

"Oh, that's Mrs. Hornby. . . . Who invited her?" Connie said. She felt a little light-headed. Her breath was coming quickly.

"She's too fat. I don't like them fat. I like them the way you are, honey," he said, smiling sleepily at her. They stared at each other for a while, through the screen door. He said softly, "Now what you're going to do is this: you're going to come out that door. You're going to sit up front with me and Ellie's going to sit in the back, the hell with Ellie, right? This isn't Ellie's date. You're my date. I'm your lover, honey."

"What? You're crazy—"

"Yes, I'm your lover. You don't know what that is but you will," he said. "I know that too. I know all about you. But look: it's real nice and you couldn't ask for nobody better than me, or more polite. I always keep my word. I'll tell you how it is, I'm always nice at first, the first time. I'll hold you so tight you won't think you have to try to get away or pretend anything because you'll know you can't. And I'll come inside you where it's all secret and you'll give in to me and you'll love me—"

"Shut up! You're crazy!" Connie said. She backed away from the door. She put her hands against her ears as if she'd heard something terrible, something not meant for her. "People don't talk like that, you're crazy," she muttered. Her heart was almost too big now for her chest and its pumping made sweat break out all over her. She looked out to see Arnold Friend pause and then take a step toward the porch lurching. He almost fell. But, like a clever drunken man, he managed to catch his balance. He wobbled in his high boots and grabbed hold of one of the porch posts.

90

95

100

105

"Honey?" he said. "You still listening?"

"Get the hell out of here!"

"Be nice, honey. Listen."

"I'm going to call the police——"

He wobbled again and out of the side of his mouth came a fast spat curse, an   110
aside not meant for her to hear. But even this "Christ!" sounded forced. Then he began to smile again. She watched this smile come, awkward as if he were smiling from
inside a mask. His whole face was a mask, she thought wildly, tanned down onto his
throat but then running out as if he had plastered makeup on his face but had forgotten about his throat.

"Honey——? Listen, here's how it is. I always tell the truth and I promise you this:
I ain't coming in that house after you."

"You better not! I'm going to call the police if you—if you don't——"

"Honey," he said, talking right through her voice, "honey, I'm not coming in
there but you are coming out here. You know why?"

She was panting. The kitchen looked like a place she had never seen before,
some room she had run inside but which wasn't good enough, wasn't going to help
her. The kitchen window had never had a curtain, after three years, and there were
dishes in the sink for her to do—probably—and if you ran your hand across the table
you'd probably feel something sticky there.

"You listening, honey? Hey?"   115

"——going to call the police——"

"Soon as you touch the phone I don't need to keep my promise and can come inside. You won't want that."

She rushed forward and tried to lock the door. Her fingers were shaking. "But
why lock it," Arnold Friend said gently, talking right into her face. "It's just a screen
door. It's just nothing." One of his boots was at a strange angle, as if his foot wasn't in
it. It pointed out to the left, bent at the ankle. "I mean, anybody can break through a
screen door and glass and wood and iron or anything else if he needs to, anybody at
all and specially Arnold Friend. If the place got lit up with a fire honey you'd come
running out into my arms, right into my arms and safe at home—like you knew I was
your lover and'd stopped fooling around. I don't mind a nice shy girl but I don't like
no fooling around." Part of those words were spoken with a slight rhythmic lilt, and
Connie somehow recognized them—the echo of a song from last year, about a girl
rushing into her boyfriend's arms and coming home again——

Connie stood barefoot on the linoleum floor, staring at him. "What do you
want?" she whispered.

"I want you," he said.   120

"What?"

"Seen you that night and thought, that's the one, yes sir. I never needed to look
any more."

"But my father's coming back. He's coming to get me. I had to wash my hair
first——" She spoke in a dry, rapid voice, hardly raising it for him to hear.

"No, your daddy is not coming and yes, you had to wash your hair and you
washed it for me. It's nice and shining and all for me, I thank you, sweetheart," he
said, with a mock bow, but again he almost lost his balance. He had to bend and adjust his boots. Evidently his feet did not go all the way down; the boots must have
been stuffed with something so that he would seem taller. Connie stared out at him

and behind him Ellie in the car, who seemed to be looking off toward Connie's right, into nothing. This Ellie said, pulling the words out of the air one after another as if he were just discovering them, "You want me to pull out the phone?"

"Shut your mouth and keep it shut," Arnold Friend said, his face red from bend- 125
ing over or maybe from embarrassment because Connie had seen his boots. "This ain't none of your business."

"What—what are you doing? What do you want?" Connie said. "If I call the po-lice they'll get you, they'll arrest you—"

"Promise was not to come in unless you touch that phone, and I'll keep that promise," he said. He resumed his erect position and tried to force his shoulders back. He sounded like a hero in a movie, declaring something important. He spoke too loudly and it was as if he were speaking to someone behind Connie. "I ain't made plans for coming in that house where I don't belong but just for you to come out to me, the way you should. Don't you know who I am?"

"You're crazy," she whispered. She backed away from the door but did not want to go into another part of the house, as if this would give him permission to come through the door. "What do you . . . You're crazy, you . . ."

"Huh? What're you saying, honey?"

Her eyes darted everywhere in the kitchen. She could not remember what it was, 130
this room.

"This is how it is, honey: you come out and we'll drive away, have a nice ride. But if you don't come out we're gonna wait till your people come home and then they're all going to get it."

"You want that telephone pulled out?" Ellie said. He held the radio away from his ear and grimaced, as if without the radio the air was too much for him.

"I toldja shut up, Ellie," Arnold Friend said, "you're deaf, get a hearing aid, right? Fix yourself up. This little girl's no trouble and's gonna be nice to me, so Ellie keep to yourself, this ain't your date—right? Don't hem in on me. Don't hog. Don't crush. Don't bird dog. Don't trail me," he said in a rapid meaningless voice, as if he were running through all the expressions he'd learned but was no longer sure which one of them was in style, then rushing on to new ones, making them up with his eyes closed, "Don't crawl under my fence, don't squeeze in my chipmunk hole, don't sniff my glue, suck my popsicle, keep your own greasy fingers on yourself!" He shaded his eyes and peered in at Connie, who was backed against the kitchen table. "Don't mind him honey he's just a creep. He's a dope. Right? I'm the boy for you and like I said you come out here nice like a lady and give me your hand, and nobody else gets hurt, I mean, your nice old bald-headed daddy and your mummy and your sister in her high heels. Because listen: why bring them in this?"

"Leave me alone," Connie whispered.

"Hey, you know that old woman down the road, the one with the chickens and 135
stuff—you know her?"

"She's dead!"

"Dead? What? You know her?" Arnold Friend said.

"She's dead—"

"Don't you like her?"

"She's dead—she's—she isn't here any more—" 140

"But don't you like her, I mean, you got something against her? Some grudge or something?" Then his voice dipped as if he were conscious of a rudeness. He touched the sunglasses perched on top of his head as if to make sure they were still there. "Now you be a good girl."

"What are you going to do?"

"Just two things, or maybe three," Arnold Friend said. "But I promise it won't last long and you'll like me that way you get to like people you're close to. You will. It's all over for you here, so come on out. You don't want your people in any trouble, do you?"

She turned and bumped against a chair or something, hurting her leg, but she ran into the back room and picked up the telephone. Something roared in her ear, a tiny roaring, and she was so sick with fear that she could do nothing but listen to it—the telephone was clammy and very heavy and her fingers groped down to the dial but were too weak to touch it. She began to scream into the phone, into the roaring. She cried out, she cried for her mother, she felt her breath start jerking back and forth in her lungs as if it were something Arnold Friend were stabbing her with again and again with no tenderness. A noisy sorrowful wailing rose all about her and she was locked inside it the way she was locked inside the house.

After a while she could hear again. She was sitting on the floor with her wet 145 back against the wall.

Arnold Friend was saying from the door, "That's a good girl. Put the phone back."

She kicked the phone away from her.

"No, honey. Pick it up. Put it back right."

She picked it up and put it back. The dial tone stopped.

"That's a good girl. Now come outside." 150

She was hollow with what had been fear, but what was now just an emptiness. All that screaming had blasted it out of her. She sat, one leg cramped under her, and deep inside her brain was something like a pinpoint of light that kept going and would not let her relax. She thought, I'm not going to see my mother again. She thought, I'm not going to sleep in my bed again. Her bright green blouse was all wet.

Arnold Friend said, in a gentle-loud voice that was like a stage voice, "The place where you came from ain't there any more, and where you had in mind to go is cancelled out. This place you are now—inside your daddy's house—is nothing but a cardboard box I can knock down any time. You know that and always did know it. You hear me?"

She thought, I have got to think. I have to know what to do.

"We'll go out to a nice field, out in the country here where it smells so nice and it's sunny," Arnold Friend said. "I'll have my arms around you so you won't need to try to get away and I'll show you what love is like, what it does. The hell with this house! It looks solid all right," he said. He ran a fingernail down the screen and the noise did not make Connie shiver, as it would have the day before. "Now put your hand on your heart, honey. Feel that? That feels solid too but we know better, be nice to me, be sweet like you can because what else is there for a girl like you but to be sweet and pretty and give in?—and get away before her people come back?"

She felt her pounding heart. Her hand seemed to enclose it. She thought for the 155 first time in her life that it was nothing that was hers, that belonged to her, but just a pounding, living thing inside this body that wasn't really hers either.

"You don't want them to get hurt," Arnold Friend went on. "Now get up, honey. Get up all by yourself."

She stood up.

"Now turn this way. That's right. Come over here to me—Ellie, put that away, didn't I tell you? You dope. You miserable creepy dope," Arnold Friend said. His words were not angry but only part of an incantation. The incantation was kindly. "Now come out through the kitchen to me honey and let's see a smile, try it, you're a brave sweet little girl and now they're eating corn and hotdogs cooked to bursting over an outdoor fire, and they don't know one thing about you and never did and honey you're better than them because not a one of them would have done this for you."

Connie felt the linoleum under her feet; it was cool. She brushed her hair back out of her eyes. Arnold Friend let go of the post tentatively and opened his arms for her, his elbows pointing in toward each other and his wrists limp, to show that this was an embarrassed embrace and a little mocking, he didn't want to make her self-conscious.

She put out her hand against the screen. She watched herself push the door   160
slowly open as if she were safe back somewhere in the other doorway, watching this body and this head of long hair moving out into the sunlight where Arnold Friend waited.

"My sweet little blue-eyed girl," he said, in a half-sung sigh that had nothing to do with her brown eyes but was taken up just the same by the vast sunlit reaches of the land behind him and on all sides of him, so much land that Connie had never seen before and did not recognize except to know that she was going to it.

Tim O'Brien

The Things They Carried   1990

Tim O'Brien was born in 1946 in Austin, Min-nesota. Immediately after graduating summa cum laude from Macalester College in 1968, he was drafted into the U.S. Army. Serving as an in-fantryman in Vietnam, O'Brien attained the rank of sergeant and was awarded a Purple Heart after being wounded by shrapnel. Upon his discharge in 1970, he began graduate work at Harvard. In 1973 he published If I Die in a Combat Zone, Box Me Up and Ship Me Home, *a mixture of memoir and fiction about his wartime experiences. His 1978 novel* Going After Cacciato *won the National Book Award, and is considered by some critics to be the best book of American fiction*

Tim O'Brien

about the Vietnam War. "The Things They Carried" *was first published in* Esquire *in 1986, and later became the title piece in a book of interlocking short stories published in 1990. His other novels include* The Nuclear Age (1985), In the Lake of the Woods (1994), Tomcat in Love (1998) *and* July, July (2002). *O'Brien currently teaches at Texas State University–San Marcos.*

First Lieutenant Jimmy Cross carried letters from a girl named Martha, a junior at Mount Sebastian College in New Jersey. They were not love letters, but Lieu-tenant Cross was hoping, so he kept them folded in plastic at the bottom of his ruck-sack. In the late afternoon, after a day's march, he would dig his foxhole, wash his hands under a canteen, unwrap the letters, hold them with the tips of his fingers, and spend the last hour of light pretending. He would imagine romantic camping trips into the White Mountains in New Hampshire. He would sometimes taste the envelope flaps, knowing her tongue had been there. More than anything, he wanted Martha to love him as he loved her, but the letters were mostly chatty, elusive on the matter of love. She was a virgin, he was almost sure. She was an English major at Mount Sebastian, and she wrote beautifully about her professors and roommates and midterm exams, about her respect for Chaucer and her great affection for Virginia Woolf. She often quoted lines of poetry; she never mentioned the war, except to say, Jimmy, take care of yourself. The letters weighed 10 ounces. They were signed Love, Martha, but Lieutenant Cross understood that Love was only a way of signing and did not mean what he sometimes pretended it meant. At dusk, he would carefully return the letters to his rucksack. Slowly, a bit distracted, he would get up and move among his men, checking the perimeter; then at full dark he would return to his hole and watch the night and wonder if Martha was a virgin.

The things they carried were largely determined by necessity. Among the necessities or near-necessities were P-38 can openers, pocket knives, heat tabs, wristwatches, dog tags, mosquito repellent, chewing gum, candy, cigarettes, salt tablets, packets of Kool-Aid, lighters, matches, sewing kits, Military Payment Certificates, C rations, and two or three canteens of water. Together, these items weighed between 15 and 20 pounds, depending upon a man's habits or rate of metabolism. Henry Dobbins, who was a big man, carried extra rations; he was especially fond of canned peaches in heavy syrup over pound cake. Dave Jensen, who practiced field hygiene, carried a toothbrush, dental floss, and several hotel-sized bars of soap he'd stolen on R&R° in Sydney, Australia. Ted Lavender, who was scared, carried tranquilizers until he was shot in the head outside the village of Than Khe in mid-April. By necessity, and because it was SOP,° they all carried steel helmets that weighed 5 pounds including the liner and camouflage cover. They carried the standard fatigue jackets and trousers. Very few carried underwear. On their feet they carried jungle boots— 2.1 pounds—and Dave Jensen carried three pairs of socks and a can of Dr. Scholl's foot powder as a precaution against trench foot. Until he was shot, Ted Lavender carried six or seven ounces of premium dope, which for him was a necessity. Mitchell Sanders, the RTO,° carried condoms. Norman Bowker carried a diary. Rat Kiley carried comic books. Kiowa, a devout Baptist, carried an illustrated New Testament that had been presented to him by his father, who taught Sunday school in Oklahoma City, Oklahoma. As a hedge against bad times, however, Kiowa also carried his grandmother's distrust of the white man, his grandfather's old hunting hatchet. Necessity dictated. Because the land was mined and booby-trapped, it was SOP for each man to carry a steel-centered, nylon-covered flak jacket, which weighed 6.7 pounds, but which on hot days seemed much heavier. Because you could die so quickly, each man carried at least one large compress bandage, usually in the helmet band for easy access. Because the nights were cold, and because the monsoons were wet, each carried a green plastic poncho that could be used as a raincoat or groundsheet or makeshift tent. With its quilted liner, the poncho weighed almost two pounds, but it

---

R&R: the military abbreviation for "rest and relaxation," a brief vacation from active service.   SOP: standard operating procedure.   RTO: radio and telephone operator.

was worth every ounce. In April, for instance, when Ted Lavender was shot, they used his poncho to wrap him up, then to carry him across the paddy, then to lift him into the chopper that took him away.

They were called legs or grunts.

To carry something was to hump it, as when Lieutenant Jimmy Cross humped his love for Martha up the hills and through the swamps. In its intransitive form, to hump meant to walk, or to march, but it implied burdens far beyond the intransitive.

Almost everyone humped photographs. In his wallet, Lieutenant Cross carried   5
two photographs of Martha. The first was a Kodacolor snapshot signed Love, though he knew better. She stood against a brick wall. Her eyes were gray and neutral, her lips slightly open as she stared straight-on at the camera. At night, sometimes, Lieutenant Cross wondered who had taken the picture, because he knew she had boyfriends, because he loved her so much, and because he could see the shadow of the picture-taker spreading out against the brick wall. The second photograph had been clipped from the 1968 Mount Sebastian yearbook. It was an action shot— women's volleyball—and Martha was bent horizontal to the floor, reaching, the palms of her hands in sharp focus, the tongue taut, the expression frank and competitive. There was no visible sweat. She wore white gym shorts. Her legs, he thought, were almost certainly the legs of a virgin, dry and without hair, the left knee cocked and carrying her entire weight, which was just over one hundred pounds. Lieutenant Cross remembered touching that left knee. A dark theater, he remembered, and the movie was *Bonnie and Clyde*, and Martha wore a tweed skirt, and during the final scene, when he touched her knee, she turned and looked at him in a sad, sober way that made him pull his hand back, but he would always remember the feel of the tweed skirt and the knee beneath it and the sound of the gunfire that killed Bonnie and Clyde, how embarrassing it was, how slow and oppressive. He remembered kissing her good night at the dorm door. Right then, he thought, he should've done something brave. He should've carried her up the stairs to her room and tied her to the bed and touched that left knee all night long. He should've risked it. Whenever he looked at the photographs, he thought of new things he should've done.

What they carried was partly a function of rank, partly of field specialty.

As a first lieutenant and platoon leader, Jimmy Cross carried a compass, maps, code books, binoculars, and a .45-caliber pistol that weighed 2.9 pounds fully loaded. He carried a strobe light and the responsibility for the lives of his men.

As an RTO, Mitchell Sanders carried the PRC-25 radio, a killer, 26 pounds with its battery.

As a medic, Rat Kiley carried a canvas satchel filled with morphine and plasma and malaria tablets and surgical tape and comic books and all the things a medic must carry, including M&M's for especially bad wounds, for a total weight of nearly 20 pounds.

As a big man, therefore a machine gunner, Henry Dobbins carried the M-60,   10
which weighed 23 pounds unloaded, but which was almost always loaded. In addition, Dobbins carried between 10 and 15 pounds of ammunition draped in belts across his chest and shoulders.

As PFCs or Spec 4s, most of them were common grunts and carried the standard M-16 gas-operated assault rifle. The weapon weighed 7.5 pounds unloaded, 8.2 pounds with its full 20-round magazine. Depending on numerous factors, such as topography and psychology, the riflemen carried anywhere from 12 to 20 magazines, usually in cloth bandoliers, adding on another 8.4 pounds at minimum, 14 pounds at maximum. When it was available, they also carried M-16 maintenance gear—rods and steel brushes and swabs and tubes of LSA oil—all of which weighed about a pound. Among the grunts, some carried the M-79 grenade launcher, 5.9 pounds unloaded, a reasonably light weapon except for the ammunition, which was heavy. A single round weighed 10 ounces. The typical load was 25 rounds. But Ted Lavender, who was scared, carried 34 rounds when he was shot and killed outside Than Khe, and he went down under an exceptional burden, more than 20 pounds of ammunition, plus the flak jacket and helmet and rations and water and toilet paper and tranquilizers and all the rest, plus the unweighed fear. He was dead weight. There was no twitching or flopping. Kiowa, who saw it happen, said it was like watching a rock fall, or a big sandbag or something—just boom, then down—not like the movies where the dead guy rolls around and does fancy spins and goes ass over teakettle—not like that, Kiowa said, the poor bastard just flat-fuck fell. Boom. Down. Nothing else. It was a bright morning in mid-April. Lieutenant Cross felt the pain. He blamed himself. They stripped off Lavender's canteens and ammo, all the heavy things, and Rat Kiley said the obvious, the guy's dead, and Mitchell Sanders used his radio to report one U.S. KIA° and to request a chopper. Then they wrapped Lavender in his poncho. They carried him out to a dry paddy, established security, and sat smoking the dead man's dope until the chopper came. Lieutenant Cross kept to himself. He pictured Martha's smooth young face, thinking he loved her more than anything, more than his men, and now Ted Lavender was dead because he loved her so much and could not stop thinking about her. When the dustoff arrived, they carried Lavender aboard. Afterward they burned Than Khe. They marched until dusk, then dug their holes, and that night Kiowa kept explaining how you had to be there, how fast it was, how the poor guy just dropped like so much concrete. Boom-down, he said. Like cement.

In addition to the three standard weapons—the M-60, M-16, and M-79—they carried whatever presented itself, or whatever seemed appropriate as a means of killing or staying alive. They carried catch-as-catch-can. At various times, in various situations, they carried M-14s and CAR-15s and Swedish Ks and grease guns and captured AK-47s and Chi-Coms and RPGs and Simonov carbines and black market Uzis and .38-caliber Smith & Wesson handguns and 66 mm LAWs and shotguns and silencers and blackjacks and bayonets and C-4 plastic explosives. Lee Strunk carried a slingshot; a weapon of last resort, he called it. Mitchell Sanders carried brass knuckles. Kiowa carried his grandfather's feathered hatchet. Every third or fourth man carried a Claymore antipersonnel mine—3.5 pounds with its firing device. They all carried fragmentation grenades—14 ounces each. They all carried at least one M-18 colored smoke grenade—24 ounces. Some carried CS or tear gas grenades. Some carried white phosphorus grenades. They carried all they could bear, and then some, including a silent awe for the terrible power of the things they carried.

KIA: killed in action.

*

In the first week of April, before Lavender died, Lieutenant Jimmy Cross received a good-luck charm from Martha. It was a simple pebble, an ounce at most. Smooth to the touch, it was a milky white color with flecks of orange and violet, oval-shaped, like a miniature egg. In the accompanying letter, Martha wrote that she had found the pebble on the Jersey shoreline, precisely where the land touched water at high tide, where things came together but also separated. It was this separate-but-together quality, she wrote, that had inspired her to pick up the pebble and to carry it in her breast pocket for several days, where it seemed weightless, and then to send it through the mail, by air, as a token of her truest feelings for him. Lieutenant Cross found this romantic. But he wondered what her truest feelings were, exactly, and what she meant by separate-but-together. He wondered how the tides and waves had come into play on that afternoon along the Jersey shoreline when Martha saw the pebble and bent down to rescue it from geology. He imagined bare feet. Martha was a poet, with the poet's sensibilities, and her feet would be brown and bare, the toenails unpainted, the eyes chilly and somber like the ocean in March, and though it was painful, he wondered who had been with her that afternoon. He imagined a pair of shadows moving along the strip of sand where things came together but also separated. It was phantom jealousy, he knew, but he couldn't help himself. He loved her so much. On the march, through the hot days of early April, he carried the pebble in his mouth, turning it with his tongue, tasting sea salt and moisture. His mind wandered. He had difficulty keeping his attention on the war. On occasion he would yell at his men to spread out the column, to keep their eyes open, but then he would slip away into daydreams, just pretending, walking barefoot along the Jersey shore, with Martha, carrying nothing. He would feel himself rising. Sun and waves and gentle winds, all love and lightness.

What they carried varied by mission.

When a mission took them to the mountains, they carried mosquito netting, machetes, canvas tarps, and extra bug juice.

15

If a mission seemed especially hazardous, or if it involved a place they knew to be bad, they carried everything they could. In certain heavily mined AOs,° where the land was dense with Toe Poppers and Bouncing Betties, they took turns humping a 28-pound mine detector. With its headphones and big sensing plate, the equipment was a stress on the lower back and shoulders, awkward to handle, often useless because of the shrapnel in the earth, but they carried it anyway, partly for safety, partly for the illusion of safety.

On ambush, or other night missions, they carried peculiar little odds and ends. Kiowa always took along his New Testament and a pair of moccasins for silence. Dave Jensen carried night-sight vitamins high in carotene. Lee Strunk carried his slingshot; ammo, he claimed, would never be a problem. Rat Kiley carried brandy and M&M's candy. Until he was shot, Ted Lavender carried the starlight scope, which weighed 6.3 pounds with its aluminum carrying case. Henry Dobbins carried his girlfriend's pantyhose wrapped around his neck as a comforter. They all carried ghosts. When dark came, they would move out single file across the meadows and paddies to their ambush coordinates, where they would quietly set up the Claymores and lie down and spend the night waiting.

AOs: areas of operation.

Other missions were more complicated and required special equipment. In mid-April, it was their mission to search out and destroy the elaborate tunnel complexes in the Than Khe area south of Chu Lai. To blow the tunnels, they carried one-pound blocks of pentrite high explosives, four blocks to a man, 68 pounds in all. They carried wiring, detonators, and battery-powered clackers. Dave Jensen carried earplugs. Most often, before blowing the tunnels, they were ordered by higher command to search them, which was considered bad news, but by and large they just shrugged and carried out orders. Because he was a big man, Henry Dobbins was excused from tunnel duty. The others would draw numbers. Before Lavender died there were 17 men in the platoon, and whoever drew the number 17 would strip off his gear and crawl in head-first with a flashlight and Lieutenant Cross's .45-caliber pistol. The rest of them would fan out as security. They would sit down or kneel, not facing the hole, listening to the ground beneath them, imagining cobwebs and ghosts, whatever was down there—the tunnel walls squeezing in—how the flashlight seemed impossibly heavy in the hand and how it was tunnel vision in the very strictest sense, compression in all ways, even time, and how you had to wiggle in—ass and elbows—a swallowed-up feeling—and how you found yourself worrying about odd things: Will your flashlight go dead? Do rats carry rabies? If you screamed, how far would the sound carry? Would your buddies hear it? Would they have the courage to drag you out? In some respects, though not many, the waiting was worse than the tunnel itself. Imagination was a killer.

On April 16, when Lee Strunk drew the number 17, he laughed and muttered something and went down quickly. The morning was hot and very still. Not good, Kiowa said. He looked at the tunnel opening, then out across a dry paddy toward the village of Than Khe. Nothing moved. No clouds or birds or people. As they waited, the men smoked and drank Kool-Aid, not talking much, feeling sympathy for Lee Strunk but also feeling the luck of the draw. You win some, you lose some, said Mitchell Sanders, and sometimes you settle for a rain check. It was a tired line and no one laughed.

Henry Dobbins ate a tropical chocolate bar. Ted Lavender popped a tranquilizer   20 and went off to pee.

After five minutes, Lieutenant Jimmy Cross moved to the tunnel, leaned down, and examined the darkness. Trouble, he thought—a cave-in maybe. And then suddenly, without willing it, he was thinking about Martha. The stresses and fractures, the quick collapse, the two of them buried alive under all that weight. Dense, crushing love. Kneeling, watching the hole, he tried to concentrate on Lee Strunk and the war, all the dangers, but his love was too much for him, he felt paralyzed, he wanted to sleep inside her lungs and breathe her blood and be smothered. He wanted her to be a virgin and not a virgin, all at once. He wanted to know her. Intimate secrets: Why poetry? Why so sad? Why that grayness in her eyes? Why so alone? Not lonely, just alone—riding her bike across campus or sitting off by herself in the cafeteria—even dancing, she danced alone—and it was the aloneness that filled him with love. He remembered telling her that one evening. How she nodded and looked away. And how, later, when he kissed her, she received the kiss without returning it, her eyes wide open, not afraid, not a virgin's eyes, just flat and uninvolved.

Lieutenant Cross gazed at the tunnel. But he was not there. He was buried with Martha under the white sand at the Jersey shore. They were pressed together, and the pebble in his mouth was her tongue. He was smiling. Vaguely, he was aware of how quiet the day was, the sullen paddies, yet he could not bring himself to worry about matters of security. He was beyond that. He was just a kid at war, in love. He was twenty-four years old. He couldn't help it.

A few moments later Lee Strunk crawled out of the tunnel. He came up grinning, filthy but alive. Lieutenant Cross nodded and closed his eyes while the others clapped Strunk on the back and made jokes about rising from the dead.

Worms, Rat Kiley said. Right out of the grave. Fuckin' zombie.

The men laughed. They all felt great relief.   25

Spook city, said Mitchell Sanders.

Lee Strunk made a funny ghost sound, a kind of moaning, yet very happy, and right then, when Strunk made that high happy moaning sound, when he went *Ahhooooo*, right then Ted Lavender was shot in the head on his way back from peeing. He lay with his mouth open. The teeth were broken. There was a swollen black bruise under his left eye. The cheekbone was gone. Oh shit, Rat Kiley said, the guy's dead. The guy's dead, he kept saying, which seemed profound—the guy's dead. I mean really.

The things they carried were determined to some extent by superstition. Lieutenant Cross carried his good-luck pebble. Dave Jensen carried a rabbit's foot. Norman Bowker, otherwise a very gentle person, carried a thumb that had been presented to him as a gift by Mitchell Sanders. The thumb was dark brown, rubbery to the touch, and weighed four ounces at most. It had been cut from a VC corpse, a boy of fifteen or sixteen. They'd found him at the bottom of an irrigation ditch, badly burned, flies in his mouth and eyes. The boy wore black shorts and sandals. At the time of his death he had been carrying a pouch of rice, a rifle, and three magazines of ammunition.

You want my opinion, Mitchell Sanders said, there's a definite moral here.

He put his hand on the dead boy's wrist. He was quiet for a time, as if counting a   30
pulse, then he patted the stomach, almost affectionately, and used Kiowa's hunting hatchet to remove the thumb.

Henry Dobbins asked what the moral was.

Moral?

You know. *Moral.*

Sanders wrapped the thumb in toilet paper and handed it across to Norman Bowker. There was no blood. Smiling, he kicked the boy's head, watched the flies scatter, and said, It's like with that old TV show—Paladin. Have gun, will travel.

Henry Dobbins thought about it.   35

Yeah, well, he finally said. I don't see no moral.

There it *is*, man.

Fuck off.

They carried USO stationery and pencils and pens. They carried Sterno, safety pins, trip flares, signal flares, spools of wire, razor blades, chewing tobacco, liberated joss sticks and statuettes of the smiling Buddha, candles, grease pencils, *The Stars and Stripes*, fingernail clippers, Psy Ops leaflets, bush hats, bolos, and much more. Twice a week, when the resupply choppers came in, they carried hot chow in green mermite cans and large canvas bags filled with iced beer and soda pop. They carried plastic water containers, each with a two-gallon capacity. Mitchell Sanders carried a set of starched tiger fatigues for special occasions. Henry Dobbins carried Black Flag insecticide. Dave Jensen carried empty sandbags that could be filled at night for added protection. Lee Strunk carried tanning lotion. Some things they carried in common. Taking turns, they carried the big PRC-77 scrambler radio, which weighed 30 pounds with its battery. They shared the weight of memory. They took up what others could no longer bear. Often, they carried each other, the wounded or weak. They carried infections. They carried chess sets, basketballs, Vietnamese-English dictionaries, insignia of rank, Bronze Stars and Purple Hearts, plastic cards imprinted with the Code of Conduct. They carried diseases, among them malaria and dysentery. They carried lice and ring-worm and leeches and paddy algae and various rots and molds. They carried the land it-self—Vietnam, the place, the soil—a powdery orange-red dust that covered their boots and fatigues and faces. They carried the sky. The whole atmosphere, they carried it, the humidity, the monsoons, the stink of fungus and decay, all of it, they carried gravity. They moved like mules. By daylight they took sniper fire, at night they were mortared, but it was not battle, it was just the endless march, village to village, without purpose, nothing won or lost. They marched for the sake of the march. They plodded along slowly, dumbly, leaning forward against the heat, unthinking, all blood and bone, simple grunts, soldiering with their legs, toiling up the hills and down into the paddies and across the rivers and up again and down, just humping, one step and then the next and then another, but no volition, no will, because it was automatic, it was anatomy, and the war was entirely a matter of posture and carriage, the hump was everything, a kind of inertia, a kind of emptiness, a dullness of desire and intellect and conscience and hope and human sensibility. Their principles were in their feet. Their calculations were biological. They had no sense of strategy or mission. They searched the villages without knowing what to look for, not caring, kicking over jars of rice, frisking children and old men, blowing tunnels, sometimes setting fires and sometimes not, then forming up and moving on to the next village, then other villages, where it would always be the same. They carried their own lives. The pressures were enormous. In the heat of early afternoon, they would remove their helmets and flak jackets, walking bare, which was dangerous but which helped ease the strain. They would often discard things along the route of march. Purely for comfort, they would throw away rations, blow their Clay-mores and grenades, no matter, because by nightfall the resupply choppers would arrive with more of the same, then a day or two later still more, fresh watermelons and crates of ammunition and sunglasses and woolen sweaters—the resources were stunning—sparklers for the Fourth of July, colored eggs for Easter—it was the great American war chest—the fruits of science, the smokestacks, the canneries, the arsenals at Hartford, the Minnesota forests, the machine shops, the vast fields of corn and wheat—they carried like freight trains; they carried it on their backs and shoulders—and for all the ambiguities of Vietnam, all the mysteries and unknowns, there was at least the single abiding certainty that they would never be at a loss for things to carry.

After the chopper took Lavender away, Lieutenant Jimmy Cross led his men into the village of Than Khe. They burned everything. They shot chickens and dogs, they trashed the village well, they called in artillery and watched the wreckage, then they marched for several hours through the hot afternoon, and then at dusk, while Kiowa explained how Lavender died, Lieutenant Cross found himself trembling. 40

He tried not to cry. With his entrenching tool, which weighed five pounds, he began digging a hole in the earth.

He felt shame. He hated himself. He had loved Martha more than his men, and as a consequence Lavender was now dead, and this was something he would have to carry like a stone in his stomach for the rest of the war.

All he could do was dig. He used his entrenching tool like an ax, slashing, feeling both love and hate, and then later, when it was full dark, he sat at the bottom of his foxhole and wept. It went on for a long while. In part, he was grieving for Ted Lavender, but mostly it was for Martha, and for himself, because she belonged to another world, which was not quite real, and because she was a junior at Mount Sebastian College in New Jersey, a poet and a virgin and uninvolved, and because he realized she did not love him and never would.

Like cement, Kiowa whispered in the dark. I swear to God—boom, down. Not a word.

I've heard this, said Norman Bowker.

A pisser, you know? Still zipping himself up. Zapped while zipping.

All right, fine. That's enough.

Yeah, but you had to see it, the guy just—

I *heard*, man. Cement. So why not shut the fuck *up?*

Kiowa shook his head sadly and glanced over at the hole where Lieutenant Jimmy Cross sat watching the night. The air was thick and wet. A warm dense fog had settled over the paddies and there was the stillness that precedes rain.

After a time Kiowa sighed.

One thing for sure, he said. The lieutenant's in some deep hurt. I mean that crying jag—the way he was carrying on—it wasn't fake or anything, it was real heavy-duty hurt. The man cares.

Sure, Norman Bowker said.

Say what you want, the man does care.

We all got problems.

Not Lavender.

No, I guess not, Bowker said. Do me a favor, though.

Shut up?

That's a smart Indian. Shut up.

Shrugging, Kiowa pulled off his boots. He wanted to say more, just to lighten up his sleep, but instead he opened his New Testament and arranged it beneath his head as a pillow. The fog made things seem hollow and unattached. He tried not to think about Ted Lavender, but then he was thinking how fast it was, no drama, down and dead, and how it was hard to feel anything except surprise. It seemed unchristian. He wished he could find some great sadness, or even anger, but the emotion wasn't there and he couldn't make it happen. Mostly he felt pleased to be alive. He liked the smell of the New Testament under his cheek, the leather and ink and paper and glue, whatever the chemicals were. He liked hearing the sounds of night. Even his fatigue, it felt fine, the stiff muscles and the prickly awareness of his own body, a floating feeling. He enjoyed not being dead. Lying there, Kiowa admired Lieutenant Jimmy Cross's capacity for grief. He wanted to share the man's pain, he wanted to care as Jimmy Cross cared. And yet when he closed his eyes, all he could think was Boom-down, and all he could feel was the pleasure of having his boots off and the fog curling in around him and the damp soil and the Bible smells and the plush comfort of night.

After a moment Norman Bowker sat up in the dark.

What the hell, he said. You want to talk, *talk*. Tell it to me.

Forget it.

No, man, go on. One thing I hate, it's a silent Indian.

*

For the most part they carried themselves with poise, a kind of dignity. Now and then, however, there were times of panic, when they squealed or wanted to squeal but couldn't, when they twitched and made moaning sounds and covered their heads and said Dear Jesus and flopped around on the earth and fired their weapons blindly and cringed and sobbed and begged for the noise to stop and went wild and made stupid promises to themselves and to God and to their mothers and fathers, hoping not to die. In different ways, it happened to all of them. Afterward, when the firing ended, they would blink and peek up. They would touch their bodies, feeling shame, then quickly hiding it. They would force themselves to stand. As if in slow motion, frame by frame, the world would take on the old logic—absolute silence, then the wind, then sunlight, then voices. It was the burden of being alive. Awkwardly, the men would reassemble themselves, first in private, then in groups, becoming soldiers again. They would repair the leaks in their eyes. They would check for casualties, call in dustoffs, light cigarettes, try to smile, clear their throats and spit and begin cleaning their weapons. After a time someone would shake his head and say, No lie, I almost shit my pants, and someone else would laugh, which meant it was bad, yes, but the guy had obviously not shit his pants, it wasn't that bad, and in any case nobody would ever do such a thing and then go ahead and talk about it. They would squint into the dense, oppressive sunlight. For a few moments, perhaps, they would fall silent, lighting a joint and tracking its passage from man to man, inhaling, holding in the humiliation. Scary stuff, one of them might say. But then someone else would grin or flick his eyebrows and say, Roger-dodger, almost cut me a new asshole, *almost*.

There were numerous such poses. Some carried themselves with a sort of wistful resignation, others with pride or stiff soldierly discipline or good humor or macho zeal. They were afraid of dying but they were even more afraid to show it.

They found jokes to tell.

They used a hard vocabulary to contain the terrible softness. *Greased,* they'd say. *Offed, lit up, zapped while zipping.* It wasn't cruelty, just stage presence. They were actors. When someone died, it wasn't quite dying, because in a curious way it seemed scripted, and because they had their lines mostly memorized, irony mixed with tragedy, and because they called it by other names, as if to encyst and destroy the reality of death itself. They kicked corpses. They cut off thumbs. They talked grunt lingo. They told stories about Ted Lavender's supply of tranquilizers, how the poor guy didn't feel a thing, how incredibly tranquil he was.

There's a moral here, said Mitchell Sanders.

They were waiting for Lavender's chopper, smoking the dead man's dope.   70

The moral's pretty obvious, Sanders said, and winked. Stay away from drugs. No joke, they'll ruin your day every time.

Cute, said Henry Dobbins.

Mind blower, get it? Talk about wiggy. Nothing left, just blood and brains.

They made themselves laugh.

There it is, they'd say. Over and over—there it is, my friend, there it is—as if the   75
repetition itself were an act of poise, a balance between crazy and almost crazy, knowing without going, there it is, which meant be cool, let it ride, because Oh yeah, man, you can't change what can't be changed, there it is, there it absolutely and positively and fucking well *is*.

They were tough.

They carried all the emotional baggage of men who might die. Grief, terror, love, longing—these were intangibles, but the intangibles had their own mass and specific gravity, they had tangible weight. They carried shameful memories. They carried the common secret of cowardice barely restrained, the instinct to run or freeze or hide, and in many respects this was the heaviest burden of all, for it could never be put down, it required perfect balance and perfect posture. They carried their reputations. They carried the soldier's greatest fear, which was the fear of blushing. Men killed, and died, because they were embarrassed not to. It was what had brought them to the war in the first place, nothing positive, no dreams of glory or honor, just to avoid the blush of dishonor. They died so as not to die of embarrassment. They crawled into tunnels and walked point and advanced under fire. Each morning, despite the unknowns, they made their legs move. They endured. They kept humping. They did not submit to the obvious alternative, which was simply to close the eyes and fall. So easy, really. Go limp and tumble to the ground and let the muscles unwind and not speak and not budge until your buddies picked you up and lifted you into the chopper that would roar and dip its nose and carry you off to the world. A mere matter of falling, yet no one fell. It was not courage, exactly; the object was not valor. Rather, they were too frightened to be cowards.

By and large they carried these things inside, maintaining the masks of composure. They sneered at sick call. They spoke bitterly about guys who had found release by shooting off their own toes or fingers. Pussies, they'd say. Candy-asses. It was fierce, mocking talk, with only a trace of envy or awe, but even so the image played itself out behind their eyes.

They imagined the muzzle against flesh. So easy: squeeze the trigger and blow away a toe. They imagined it. They imagined the quick, sweet pain, then the evacuation to Japan, then a hospital with warm beds and cute geisha nurses.

And they dreamed of freedom birds.   80

At night, on guard, staring into the dark, they were carried away by jumbo jets. They felt the rush of takeoff. *Gone!* they yelled. And then velocity—wings and engines—a smiling stewardess—but it was more than a plane, it was a real bird, a big sleek silver bird with feathers and talons and high screeching. They were flying. The weights fell off; there was nothing to bear. They laughed and held on tight, feeling the cold slap of wind and altitude, soaring, thinking *It's over, I'm gone!*—they were naked, they were light and free—it was all lightness, bright and fast and buoyant, light as light, a helium buzz in the brain, a giddy bubbling in the lungs as they were taken up over the clouds and the war, beyond duty, beyond gravity and mortification and global entanglements—*Sin loi!*° they yelled. *I'm sorry, mother-fuckers, but I'm out of it, I'm goofed, I'm on a space cruise, I'm gone!*—and it was a restful, unencumbered sensation, just riding the light waves, sailing that big silver freedom bird over the mountains and oceans, over America, over the farms and great sleeping cities and cemeteries and highways and the golden arches of McDonald's, it was flight, a kind of fleeing, a kind of falling, falling higher and higher, spinning off the edge of the earth and beyond the sun and through the vast, silent vacuum where there were no burdens and where everything weighed exactly nothing—*Gone!* they screamed. *I'm sorry but I'm gone!*—and so at night, not quite dreaming, they gave themselves over to lightness, they were carried, they were purely borne.

Sin loi: Vietnamese for sorry.

*

On the morning after Ted Lavender died, First Lieutenant Jimmy Cross crouched at the bottom of his foxhole and burned Martha's letters. Then he burned the two photographs. There was a steady rain falling, which made it difficult, but he used heat tabs and Sterno to build a small fire, screening it with his body, holding the photographs over the tight blue flame with the tips of his fingers.

He realized it was only a gesture. Stupid, he thought. Sentimental, too, but mostly just stupid.

Lavender was dead. You couldn't burn the blame.

Besides, the letters were in his head. And even now, without photographs, Lieutenant Cross could see Martha playing volleyball in her white gym shorts and yellow T-shirt. He could see her moving in the rain.

When the fire died out, Lieutenant Cross pulled his poncho over his shoulders and ate breakfast from a can.

There was no great mystery, he decided.

In those burned letters Martha had never mentioned the war, except to say, Jimmy, take care of yourself. She wasn't involved. She signed the letters Love, but it wasn't love, and all the fine lines and technicalities did not matter. Virginity was no longer an issue. He hated her. Yes, he did. He hated her. Love, too, but it was a hard, hating kind of love.

The morning came up wet and blurry. Everything seemed part of everything else, the fog and Martha and the deepening rain.

He was a soldier, after all.

Half smiling, Lieutenant Jimmy Cross took out his maps. He shook his head hard, as if to clear it, then bent forward and began planning the day's march. In ten minutes, or maybe twenty, he would rouse the men and they would pack up and head west, where the maps showed the country to be green and inviting. They would do what they had always done. The rain might add some weight, but otherwise it would be one more day layered upon all the other days.

He was realistic about it. There was that new hardness in his stomach. He loved her but he hated her.

No more fantasies, he told himself.

Henceforth, when he thought about Martha, it would be only to think that she belonged elsewhere. He would shut down the daydreams. This was not Mount Sebastian, it was another world, where there were no pretty poems or midterm exams, a place where men died because of carelessness and gross stupidity. Kiowa was right. Boom-down, and you were dead, never partly dead.

Briefly, in the rain, Lieutenant Cross saw Martha's gray eyes gazing back at him.

He understood.

It was very sad, he thought. The things men carried inside. The things men did or felt they had to do.

He almost nodded at her, but didn't.

Instead he went back to his maps. He was now determined to perform his duties firmly and without negligence. It wouldn't help Lavender, he knew that, but from this point on he would comport himself as an officer. He would dispose of his good-luck pebble. Swallow it, maybe, or use Lee Strunk's slingshot, or just drop it along the trail. On the march he would impose strict field discipline. He would be careful to send out flank security, to prevent straggling or bunching up, to keep his troops moving at the proper pace and at the proper interval. He would insist on clean weapons.

He would confiscate the remainder of Lavender's dope. Later in the day, perhaps, he would call the men together and speak to them plainly. He would accept the blame for what had happened to Ted Lavender. He would be a man about it. He would look them in the eyes, keeping his chin level, and he would issue the new SOPs in a calm, impersonal tone of voice, a lieutenant's voice, leaving no room for argument or discussion. Commencing immediately, he'd tell them, they would no longer abandon equipment along the route of march. They would police up their acts. They would get their shit together, and keep it together, and maintain it neatly and in good working order.

He would not tolerate laxity. He would show strength, distancing himself.   100

Among the men there would be grumbling, of course, and maybe worse, because their days would seem longer and their loads heavier, but Lieutenant Jimmy Cross reminded himself that his obligation was not to be loved but to lead. He would dispense with love; it was not now a factor. And if anyone quarreled or complained, he would simply tighten his lips and arrange his shoulders in the correct command posture. He might give a curt little nod. Or he might not. He might just shrug and say, Carry on, then they would saddle up and form into a column and move out toward the villages west of Than Khe.

Eudora Welty

A Worn Path   1941

Eudora Welty (1909–2001) was born in Jackson, Mississippi, daughter of an insurance company president. Like William Faulkner, another Mississippi writer, she stayed close to her roots for practically all her life, except for short sojourns at the University of Wisconsin, where she took her B.A., and in New York City, where she studied advertising. She lived most of her life in her childhood home in Jackson, within a stone's throw of the state capitol. Although Welty was a novelist distinguished for The Robber Bridegroom *(1942),* Delta Wedding *(1946),* The Ponder Heart *(1954),* Losing Battles *(1970), and* The Optimist's Daughter *(1972), many critics think her finest work was in the short-story form. The Collected Stories*

Eudora Welty

of Eudora Welty (1980) gathers the work of more than forty years. Welty's other books include a memoir, One Writer's Beginnings *(1984), and* The Eye of the Story *(1977), a book of sympathetic criticism on the fiction of other writers, including Willa Cather, Virginia Woolf, Katherine Anne Porter, and Isak Dinesen.* One Time, One Place, *a book of photographs of everyday life that Welty took in Mississippi during the Depression, was republished in a revised edition in 1996.*

It was December—a bright frozen day in the early morning. Far out in the country there was an old Negro woman with her head tied in a red rag, coming along a path through the pinewoods. Her name was Phoenix Jackson. She was very old and small and she walked slowly in the dark pine shadows, moving a little from side to side in her steps, with the balanced heaviness and lightness of a pendulum in a grandfather clock. She carried a thin, small cane made from an umbrella, and with this she kept tapping the frozen earth in front of her. This made a grave and persistent noise in the still air, that seemed meditative like the chirping of a solitary little bird.

She wore a dark striped dress reaching down to her shoe tops, and an equally long apron of bleached sugar sacks, with a full pocket: all neat and tidy, but every time she took a step she might have fallen over her shoelaces, which dragged from her unlaced shoes. She looked straight ahead. Her eyes were blue with age. Her skin had a pattern all its own of numberless branching wrinkles and as though a whole little tree stood in the middle of her forehead, but a golden color ran underneath, and the two knobs of her cheeks were illumined by a yellow burning under the dark. Under the red rag her hair came down on her neck in the frailest of ringlets, still black, and with an odor like copper.

Now and then there was a quivering in the thicket. Old Phoenix said, "Out of my way, all you foxes, owls, beetles, jack rabbits, coons and wild animals! . . . Keep out from under these feet, little bob-whites. . . . Keep the big wild hogs out of my path. Don't let none of those come running my direction. I got a long way." Under her small black-freckled hand her cane, limber as a buggy whip, would switch at the brush as if to rouse up any hiding things.

On she went. The woods were deep and still. The sun made the pine needles almost too bright to look at, up where the wind rocked. The cones dropped as light as feathers. Down in the hollow was the mourning dove—it was not too late for him.

The path ran up a hill. "Seem like there is chains about my feet, time I get this far," she said, in the voice of argument old people keep to use with themselves. "Something always take a hold of me on this hill—pleads I should stay." 5

After she got to the top she turned and gave a full, severe look behind her where she had come. "Up through pines," she said at length. "Now down through oaks."

Her eyes opened their widest, and she started down gently. But before she got to the bottom of the hill a bush caught her dress.

Her fingers were busy and intent, but her skirts were full and long, so that before she could pull them free in one place they were caught in another. It was not possible to allow the dress to tear. "I in the thorny bush," she said. "Thorns, you doing your appointed work. Never want to let folks pass, no sir. Old eyes thought you was a pretty little green bush."

Finally, trembling all over, she stood free, and after a moment dared to stoop for her cane.

"Sun so high!" she cried, leaning back and looking, while the thick tears went over her eyes. "The time getting all gone here." 10

At the foot of this hill was a place where a log was laid across the creek.

"Now comes the trial," said Phoenix.

Putting her right foot out, she mounted the log and shut her eyes. Lifting her skirt, leveling her cane fiercely before her, like a festival figure in some parade, she began to march across. Then she opened her eyes and she was safe on the other side.

"I wasn't as old as I thought," she said.

But she sat down to rest. She spread her skirts on the bank around her and folded her hands over her knees. Up above her was a tree in a pearly cloud of mistletoe. She did not dare to close her eyes, and when a little boy brought her a plate with a slice of 15 marble-cake on it she spoke to him. "That would be acceptable," she said. But when she went to take it there was just her own hand in the air.

So she left that tree, and had to go through a barbed-wire fence. There she had to creep and crawl, spreading her knees and stretching her fingers like a baby trying to climb the steps. But she talked loudly to herself: she could not let her dress be torn now, so late in the day, and she could not pay for having her arm or her leg sawed off if she got caught fast where she was.

At last she was safe through the fence and risen up out in the clearing. Big dead trees, like black men with one arm, were standing in the purple stalks of the withered cotton field. There sat a buzzard.

"Who you watching?"

In the furrow she made her way along.

"Glad this not the season for bulls," she said, looking sideways, "and the good   20
Lord made his snakes to curl up and sleep in the winter. A pleasure I don't see no two-headed snake coming around that tree, where it come once. It took a while to get by him, back in the summer."

She passed through the old cotton and went into a field of dead corn. It whispered and shook and was taller than her head. "Through the maze now," she said, for there was no path.

Then there was something tall, black, and skinny there, moving before her.

At first she took it for a man. It could have been a man dancing in the field. But she stood still and listened, and it did not make a sound. It was as silent as a ghost.

"Ghost," she said sharply, "who be you the ghost of? For I have heard of nary death close by."

But there was no answer—only the ragged dancing in the wind.   25

She shut her eyes, reached out her hand, and touched a sleeve. She found a coat and inside that an emptiness, cold as ice.

"You scarecrow," she said. Her face lighted. "I ought to be shut up for good," she said with laughter. "My senses is gone. I too old. I the oldest people I ever know. Dance, old scarecrow," she said, "while I dancing with you."

She kicked her foot over the furrow, and with mouth drawn down, shook her head once or twice in a little strutting way. Some husks blew down and whirled in streamers about her skirts.

Then she went on, parting her way from side to side with the cane, through the whispering field. At last she came to the end, to a wagon track where the silver grass blew between the red ruts. The quail were walking around like pullets, seeming all dainty and unseen.

"Walk pretty," she said. "This the easy place. This the easy going."   30

She followed the track, swaying through the quiet bare fields, through the little strings of trees silver in their dead leaves, past cabins silver from weather, with the doors and windows boarded shut, all like old women under a spell sitting there. "I walking in their sleep," she said, nodding her head vigorously.

In a ravine she went where a spring was silently flowing through a hollow log. Old Phoenix bent and drank. "Sweet-gum makes the water sweet," she said, and drank more. "Nobody know who made this well, for it was here when I was born."

The track crossed a swampy part where the moss hung as white as lace from every limb. "Sleep on, alligators, and blow your bubbles." Then the track went into the road.

Deep, deep the road went down between the high green-colored banks. Overhead the live-oaks met, and it was as dark as a cave.

A black dog with a lolling tongue came up out of the weeds by the ditch. She   35
was meditating, and not ready, and when he came at her she only hit him a little
with her cane. Over she went in the ditch, like a little puff of milkweed.

Down there, her senses drifted away. A dream visited her, and she reached her
hand up, but nothing reached down and gave her a pull. So she lay there and presently
went to talking. "Old woman," she said to herself, "that black dog come up out of the
weeds to stall you off, and now there he sitting on his fine tail, smiling at you."

A white man finally came along and found her—a hunter, a young man, with his
dog on a chain.

"Well, Granny!" he laughed. "What are you doing there?"

"Lying on my back like a June-bug waiting to be turned over, mister," she said,
reaching up her hand.

He lifted her up, gave her a swing in the air, and set her down. "Anything bro-   40
ken, Granny?"

"No sir, them old dead weeds is springy enough," said Phoenix, when she had got
her breath. "I thank you for your trouble."

"Where do you live, Granny?" he asked, while the two dogs were growling at
each other.

"Away back yonder, sir, behind the ridge. You can't even see it from here."

"On your way home?"

"No sir, I going to town."   45

"Why, that's too far! That's as far as I walk when I come out myself, and I get
something for my trouble." He patted the stuffed bag he carried, and there hung
down a little closed claw. It was one of the bob-whites, with its beak hooked bitterly
to show it was dead. "Now you go on home, Granny!"

"I bound to go to town, mister," said Phoenix. "The time come around."

He gave another laugh, filling the whole landscape. "I know you old colored
people! Wouldn't miss going to town to see Santa Claus!"

But something held old Phoenix very still. The deep lines in her face went into a
fierce and different radiation. Without warning, she had seen with her own eyes a
flashing nickel fall out of the man's pocket onto the ground.

"How old are you, Granny?" he was saying.   50

"There is no telling, mister," she said, "no telling."

Then she gave a little cry and clapped her hands and said, "Git on away from
here, dog! Look! Look at that dog!" She laughed as if in admiration. "He ain't scared
of nobody. He a big black dog." She whispered, "Sic him!"

"Watch me get rid of that cur," said the man. "Sic him, Pete! Sic him!"

Phoenix heard the dogs fighting, and heard the man running and throwing sticks.
She even heard a gunshot. But she was slowly bending forward by that time, further
and further forward, the lids stretched down over her eyes, as if she were doing this in
her sleep. Her chin was lowered almost to her knees. The yellow palm of her hand
came out from the fold of her apron. Her fingers slid down and along the ground under
the piece of money with the grace and care they would have in lifting an egg from under a setting hen. Then she slowly straightened up, she stood erect, and the nickel was
in her apron pocket. A bird flew by. Her lips moved. "God watching me the whole
time. I come to stealing."

The man came back, and his own dog panted about them. "Well, I scared him   55
off that time," he said, and then he laughed and lifted his gun and pointed it at
Phoenix.

She stood straight and faced him.

"Doesn't the gun scare you?" he said, still pointing it.

"No, sir, I seen plenty go off closer by, in my day, and for less than what I done," she said, holding utterly still.

He smiled, and shouldered the gun. "Well, Granny," he said, "you must be a hundred years old, and scared of nothing. I'd give you a dime if I had any money with me. But you take my advice and stay home, and nothing will happen to you."

"I bound to go on my way, mister," said Phoenix. She inclined her head in the red rag. Then they went in different directions, but she could hear the gun shooting again and again over the hill.

She walked on. The shadows hung from the oak trees to the road like curtains. Then she smelled wood-smoke, and smelled the river, and she saw a steeple and the cabins on their steep steps. Dozens of little black children whirled around her. There ahead was Natchez shining. Bells were ringing. She walked on.

In the paved city it was Christmas time. There were red and green electric lights strung and crisscrossed everywhere, and all turned on in the daytime. Old Phoenix would have been lost if she had not distrusted her eyesight and depended on her feet to know where to take her.

She paused quietly on the sidewalk where people were passing by. A lady came along in the crowd, carrying an armful of red-, green- and silver-wrapped presents; she gave off perfume like the red roses in hot summer, and Phoenix stopped her.

"Please, missy, will you lace up my shoe?" She held up her foot.

"What do you want, Grandma?"

"See my shoe," said Phoenix. "Do all right for out in the country, but wouldn't look right to go in a big building."

"Stand still then, Grandma," said the lady. She put her packages down on the sidewalk beside her and laced and tied both shoes tightly.

"Can't lace 'em with a cane," said Phoenix, "Thank you, missy. I doesn't mind asking a nice lady to tie up my shoe, when I gets out on the street."

Moving slowly and from side to side, she went into the big building, and into a tower of steps, where she walked up and around and around until her feet knew to stop.

She entered a door, and there she saw nailed up on the wall the document that had been stamped with the gold seal and framed in the gold frame, which matched the dream that was hung up in her head.

"Here I be," she said. There was a fixed and ceremonial stiffness over her body.

"A charity case, I suppose," said an attendant who sat at the desk before her.

But Phoenix only looked above her head. There was sweat on her face, the wrinkles in her skin shone like a bright net.

"Speak up, Grandma," the woman said. "What's your name? We must have your history, you know. Have you been here before? What seems to be the trouble with you?"

Old Phoenix only gave a twitch to her face as if a fly were bothering her.

"Are you deaf?" cried the attendant.

But then the nurse came in.

"Oh, that's just old Aunt Phoenix," she said. "She doesn't come for herself—she has a little grandson. She makes these trips just as regular as clockwork. She lives away back off the Old Natchez Trace." She bent down. "Well, Aunt Phoenix, why don't you just take a seat? We won't keep you standing after your long trip." She pointed.

The old woman sat down, bolt upright in the chair.

"Now, how is the boy?" asked the nurse.

Old Phoenix did not speak.

"I said, how is the boy?"

But Phoenix only waited and stared straight ahead, her face very solemn and withdrawn into rigidity.

"Is his throat any better?" asked the nurse. "Aunt Phoenix, don't you hear me? Is your grandson's throat any better since the last time you came for the medicine?"

With her hands on her knees, the old woman waited, silent, erect and motionless, just as if she were in armor.

"You mustn't take up our time this way, Aunt Phoenix," the nurse said. "Tell us quickly about your grandson, and get it over. He isn't dead, is he?"

At last there came a flicker and then a flame of comprehension across her face, and she spoke.

"My grandson. It was my memory had left me. There I sat and forgot why I made my long trip."

"Forgot?" The nurse frowned. "After you came so far?"

Then Phoenix was like an old woman begging a dignified forgiveness for waking up frightened in the night. "I never did go to school, I was too old at the Surrender," she said in a soft voice. "I'm an old woman without an education. It was my memory fail me. My little grandson, he is just the same, and I forgot it in the coming."

"Throat never heals, does it?" said the nurse, speaking in a loud, sure voice to old Phoenix. By now she had a card with something written on it, a little list. "Yes. Swallowed lye. When was it?—January—two-three years ago—"

Phoenix spoke unasked now. "No, missy, he not dead, he just the same. Every little while his throat begin to close up again, and he not able to swallow. He not get his breath. He not able to help himself. So the time come around, and I go on another trip for the soothing medicine."

"All right. The doctor said as long as you came to get it, you could have it," said the nurse. "But it's an obstinate case."

"My little grandson, he sit up there in the house all wrapped up, waiting by himself," Phoenix went on. "We is the only two left in the world. He suffer and it don't seem to put him back at all. He got a sweet look. He going to last. He wear a little patch quilt and peep out holding his mouth open like a little bird. I remembers so plain now. I not going to forget him again, no, the whole enduring time. I could tell him from all the others in creation."

"All right." The nurse was trying to hush her now. She brought her a bottle of medicine. "Charity," she said, making a check mark in a book.

Old Phoenix held the bottle close to her eyes, and then carefully put it into her pocket.

"I thank you," she said.

"It's Christmas time, Grandma," said the attendant. "Could I give you a few pennies out of my purse?"

"Five pennies is a nickel," said Phoenix stiffly.

"Here's a nickel," said the attendant.

Phoenix rose carefully and held out her hand. She received the nickel and then fished the other nickel out of her pocket and laid it beside the new one. She stared at her palm closely, with her head on one side.

Then she gave a tap with her cane on the floor.

"This is what come to me to do," she said. "I going to the store and buy my child a little windmill they sells, made out of paper. He going to find it hard to believe there such a thing in the world. I'll march myself back where he waiting, holding it straight up in this hand."

She lifted her free hand, gave a little nod, turned around, and walked out of the doctor's office. Then her slow step began on the stairs, going down

Kay Ryan, U.S. Poet Laureate, 2008–2010.

POETRY

TALKING WITH *Kay Ryan*

"Language That Lasts"
Dana Gioia Interviews Former U.S. Poet Laureate Kay Ryan

Q: When did you start writing poetry?

KAY RYAN: In a way I'd say I started writing poetry when I started collecting language, which was as soon as I could. I loved hearing a new word or phrase, and I had a private game of trying to say things differently than I'd said them before. I remember when I was quite advanced in this language study, in ninth grade, I went on a summer trip with my friend and her parents down to Texas. I was sitting there quietly in the small hot living room of my friend's aunt, listening to the adult conversation. Someone said something irritated along the lines of, "Tracy totaled Teddy's Toronado, and Tyler tattled it to Tina!" and I just burst out laughing: that accidental string of T's nobody else seemed to notice. Language brought me constant, secret pleasure, and it was free; I could have as much as I wanted, which is nice if you're poor.

As to writing-writing, I fooled around with writing poetry during high school and college and even after I'd become a community college teacher, trying to keep it at arm's length because I didn't want to be exposed the way poetry makes you exposed. I wanted to stay superficial. But by the time I was thirty I could see that poetry was eating away at my mind anyhow. Why not accept it and try to get really good at it? So, either I started writing poetry at three or thirty.

Q: Did poetry play much of a part in your childhood?

KAY RYAN: I guess the short answer would be no. But my mother had one lovely poem about a dead kitten that she liked to say. I always enjoyed feeling tender and sad when she did; it was a kind of intimacy with a mother who wasn't very intimate. And my mother's mother liked to recite poems when she came to visit. They made me feel very serious, and that is a lovely feeling for a child: "Life is real! Life is earnest! / And the grave is not its goal; / Dust thou art, to dust returnest / Was not spoken of the soul!" My grandmother grew up in a time when people really memorized poetry for pleasure, and I loved hearing it.

My only other contact with poetry—but it was an important one—was in sixth grade. My enlightened teacher, Mrs. Kimball, at Roosevelt Elementary School in Bakersfield, California, had us do "choral reading," meaning the whole class memorized poems and stood up on the stage like a chorus at assemblies and recited them with great gusto. So I got a chance, like my grandmother, to memorize poetry for pleasure and have the pleasure of saying it aloud.

Q: Whom do you write for?

KAY RYAN: This is a devilish question. I'll have to answer it in parts.

First, when I write a poem I'm completely occupied with trying to net some elusive fish; I'm desperate to get the net (made of words) knotted in such a way that it will catch this desired fish (a half-formed idea, a wisp of a feeling). I'm not thinking of anything but that; I'm not thinking of me, I'm not thinking of you.

But then later, after I've finished writing the poem and have let it sit for days or months and look back to see if there's a fish in the net after all (many times, I'm sorry to say, there is no fish), I begin thinking of you. Have I put the necessary connections in the poem, or are some of them still in my head? Have I shaped the lines so they will present the reader with the most pleasure in discovering the secret rhymes? Have I removed self-indulgences? Because a poem, by its nature, must please others. If it doesn't, it can't last; and if it doesn't last it wasn't a poem, because poems are language that lasts.

Q: What gives you pleasure in writing?

KAY RYAN: People have dreams where they begin noticing that their house is lots bigger than they knew; they realize there is a maze of rooms behind the ones they've been occupying. The dreamer (I've had this dream) doesn't know why she hasn't noticed this before, because it's fascinating.

Writing a poem is like this; I go back behind my usual mind and find places I didn't know about, places that only the activity of writing a poem can let me into.

Q: Who are your favorite poets?

Kay Ryan with Dana Gioia

KAY RYAN: My favorite American poets are Emily Dickinson and Robert Frost. British favorites include John Donne, Gerard Manley Hopkins, Philip Larkin, and Stevie Smith. Favorites in other languages are Fernando Pessoa and Constantine Cavafy.

Q: Did a poem ever change your life?

KAY RYAN: A dream poem might have. When I was around ten, I dreamed that a piece of white paper was blowing around and I was chasing it. I knew it had the most beautiful poem in the world written on it. I couldn't catch it.

I never forgot that dream, although at the time I wasn't even thinking of trying to write poetry. Still, maybe some deep part of me was busy at it even then. I'm still trying to catch that piece of paper.

Q: What is the purpose of poetry? Why do people need poetry?

KAY RYAN: The secret, long-term purpose of poetry is to create more space between everything. Poetry is the main engine of the expanding universe. You yourself will have noticed how reading a poem that really strikes you (that will be one in 25, if you're lucky; a poem can be great and still not strike YOU) makes you feel freer and less burdened, even if it's about death. You feel fresher, more awake. This proves my point; your atoms have been subtly distanced from each other, like a breeze is blowing through your DNA. That's poetry loosening you.

W hat is poetry? Pressed for an answer, Robert Frost made a classic reply: "Poetry is the kind of thing poets write." In all likelihood, Frost was trying not merely to evade the question but to chide his questioner into thinking for himself. A trouble with definitions is that they may stop thought. If Frost had said, "Poetry is a rhythmical composition of words expressing an attitude, designed to surprise and delight, and to arouse an emotional response," the questioner might have settled back in his chair, content to have learned the truth about poetry. He would have learned nothing, or not so much as he might learn by continuing to wonder.

The nature of poetry eludes simple definitions. (In this respect it is rather like jazz. Asked after one of his concerts "What is jazz?", Louis Armstrong replied, "Man, if you gotta ask, you'll never know.") Definitions will be of little help at first, if we are to know poetry and respond to it. We have to go to it willing to see and hear. For this reason, you are asked in reading this book not to be in any hurry to decide what poetry is, but instead to study poems and to let them grow in your mind. At the end of our discussions of poetry, the problem of definition will be taken up again (for those who may wish to pursue it).

Confronted with a formal introduction to poetry, you may be wondering "Who needs it?" and you may well be right. It's unlikely that you have avoided meeting poetry before; and perhaps you already have a friendship, or at least a fair acquaintance, with some of the greatest English-speaking poets of all time. What this book provides is an introduction to the *study* of poetry. It tries to help you look at a poem closely, to offer you a wider and more accurate vocabulary with which to express what poems say to you. It will suggest ways to judge for yourself the poems you read. It may set forth some poems new to you.

A frequent objection is that poetry ought not to be studied at all. In this view, a poem is either a series of gorgeous noises to be funneled into one ear and out the other without being allowed to trouble the mind, or an experience so holy that to analyze it in a classroom is as cruel and mechanical as dissecting a hummingbird. To the first view, it might be countered that a good poem has something to say that is well worth listening to. To the second view, it might be argued that poems are much less perishable than hummingbirds, and luckily, we can study them in flight. The risk of a poem's dying from observation is not nearly so great as the risk of not really seeing it at all. It is doubtful that any excellent poem has ever vanished from human memory because people have read it too closely.

That poetry matters to the people who write it has been shown unmistakably by the ordeal of Soviet poet Irina Ratushinskaya. Sentenced to prison for three and a half years, she was given paper and pencil only twice a month to write letters to her husband and her parents and was not allowed to write anything else. Nevertheless, Ratushinskaya composed more than two hundred poems in her cell, engraving them with a burnt match in a bar of soap, then memorizing the lines. "I would read the poem and read it," she said, "until it was committed to memory—then with one washing of my hands, it would be gone."

Good poetry is something that readers can care about. In fact, an ancient persuasion of humankind is that the hearing of a poem, as well as the making of a poem, can be a religious act. Poetry, in speech and song, was part of classic Greek drama, which for playwright, actor, and spectator alike was a holy-day ceremony. The Greeks' belief that a poet writes a poem only by supernatural assistance is clear from the invocations to the Muse that begin the *Iliad* and the *Odyssey* and from the opinion of Socrates (in Plato's *Ion*) that a poet has no powers of invention until divinely inspired. Among the ancient Celts, poets were regarded as magicians and priests, and whoever insulted one of them might expect to receive a curse in rime potent enough to afflict him with boils and to curdle the milk of his cows. Such identifications between the poet and the magician are less common these days, although we know that poetry is involved in the primitive white magic of children, who bring themselves good luck in a game with the charm "Roll, roll, Tootsie-roll! / Roll the marble in the hole!" and who warn against a hex while jumping along a sidewalk: "Step on a crack, / Break your mother's back." To read a poem, we have to be willing to offer it responses *besides* a logical understanding. Whether we attribute the effect of a poem to a divine spirit or to the reactions of our glands and cortexes, we have to take the reading of poetry seriously (not solemnly), if only because—as some of the poems in this book may demonstrate—few other efforts can repay us so generously, both in wisdom and in joy.

If, as we hope you will do, you sometimes browse in the book for fun, you may be annoyed to see so many questions following the poems. Should you feel this way, try reading with a slip of paper to cover up the questions. You will then—if the Muse should inspire you—have paper in hand to write a poem.

To the Muse

Give me leave, Muse, in plain view to array
Your shift and bodice by the light of day.
I would have brought an epic. Be not vexed
Instead to grace a niggling schoolroom text;
Let down your sanction, help me to oblige
Those who would lead fresh devots to your liege,
And at your altar, grant that in a flash
Readers and I know incense from dead ash.

—X. J. K.

12 READING A POEM

*Every good poem begins as the poet's
but ends as the reader's.*

—MILLER WILLIAMS

ow do you read a poem? The literal-minded might say, "Just let your eye light on it"; but there is more to poetry than meets the eye. What Shakespeare called "the mind's eye" also plays a part. Many a reader who has no trouble understanding and enjoying prose finds poetry difficult. This is to be expected. At first glance, a poem usually will make some sense and give some pleasure, but it may not yield everything at once. Poetry is not to be galloped over like the daily news: a poem differs from most prose in that it is to be read slowly, carefully, and attentively. Not all poems are difficult, of course, and some can be understood and enjoyed on first encounter. But good poems yield more if read twice; and the best poems—after ten, twenty, or a hundred readings—still go on yielding.

POETRY OR VERSE

Approaching a thing written in lines and surrounded with white space, we need not expect it to be a poem just because it is verse. (Any composition in lines of more or less regular rhythm, often ending in rimes, is **verse**.) Here, for instance, is a specimen of verse that few will call poetry:

> Thirty days hath September,
> April, June, and November;
> All the rest have thirty-one
> Excepting February alone,
> To which we twenty-eight assign
> Till leap year makes it twenty-nine.

To a higher degree than that classic memory-tickler, poetry appeals to the mind and arouses feelings. Poetry may state facts, but, more important, it makes imaginative statements that we may value even if its facts are incorrect. Coleridge's error in placing a star within the horns of the crescent moon in "The Rime of the Ancient Mariner" does not stop the passage from being good poetry, though it is faulty astronomy. According to poet Gerard Manley Hopkins, poetry is "to be heard for its own sake and interest even over and above its interest of meaning." There are other elements in a poem besides plain prose sense: sounds, images, rhythms, figures of speech. These may strike us and please us even before we ask, "But what does it all mean?"

This is a truth not readily grasped by anyone who regards a poem as a kind of puzzle written in secret code with a message slyly concealed. The effect of a poem (our whole mental and emotional response to it) consists of much more than simply a message. By its musical qualities, by its suggestions, it can work on the reader's unconscious. T. S. Eliot put it well when he said in *The Use of Poetry and the Use of Criticism* that the prose sense of a poem is chiefly useful in keeping the reader's mind "diverted and quiet, while the poem does its work upon him." Eliot went on to liken the meaning of a poem to the bit of meat a burglar brings along to throw to the family dog. What is the work of a poem? To touch us, to stir us, to make us glad, and possibly even to tell us something.

READING A POEM

How to set about reading a poem? Here are a few suggestions. To begin with, read the poem once straight through, with no particular expectations; read open-mindedly. Let yourself experience whatever you find, without worrying just yet about the large general and important ideas the poem contains (if indeed it contains any). Don't dwell on a troublesome word or difficult passage—just push on. Some of the difficulties may seem smaller when you read the poem for a second time; at least, they will have become parts of a whole for you.

On the second reading, read for the exact sense of all the words; if there are words you don't understand, look them up in a dictionary. Dwell on any difficult parts as long as you need to.

If you read the poem silently, sound its words in your mind. Better still, read the poem aloud, or listen to someone else reading it. You may discover meanings you didn't perceive in it before. To decide how to speak a poem can be an excellent method of getting to understand it.

PARAPHRASE

Try to **paraphrase** the poem as a whole, or perhaps just the more difficult lines. In paraphrasing, we put into our own words what we understand the poem to say, restating ideas that seem essential, coming out and stating what the poem may only suggest. This may sound like a heartless thing to do to a poem, but good poems can stand it. In fact, to compare a poem to its paraphrase is a good way to see the distance between poetry and prose. In making a paraphrase, we generally work through a poem or a passage line by line. The statement that results may take as many words as the original, if not more. A paraphrase, then, is ampler than a **summary,** a brief condensation of gist, main idea, or story. (Click the "Info" button on your TV remote control, and you'll get a movie summary like: "Scientist seeks revenge by creating giant man-eating cockroaches.") Here is a poem worth considering line by line. The poet writes of an island in a lake in the west of Ireland, in a region where he spent many summers as a boy.

William Butler Yeats (1865–1939)

The Lake Isle of Innisfree

1892

I will arise and go now, and go to Innisfree,
And a small cabin build there, of clay and wattles made:
Nine bean-rows will I have there, a hive for the honey-bee,
And live alone in the bee-loud glade.

And I shall have some peace there, for peace comes dropping slow,   5
Dropping from the veils of the morning to where the cricket sings;
There midnight's all a glimmer, and noon a purple glow,
And evening full of the linnet's wings.

I will arise and go now, for always night and day
I hear lake water lapping with low sounds by the shore;   10
While I stand on the roadway, or on the pavements gray,
I hear it in the deep heart's core.

Though relatively simple, this poem is far from simple-minded. We need to absorb it slowly and thoughtfully. At the start, for most of us, it raises problems: what
are *wattles,* from which the speaker's dream-cabin is to be made? We might guess, but
in this case it will help to consult a dictionary: they are "poles interwoven with sticks
or branches, formerly used in building as frameworks to support walls or roofs."
Evidently, this getaway house will be built in an old-fashioned way: it won't be a pre-
fabricated log cabin or A-frame house, nothing modern or citified. The phrase *bee-loud
glade* certainly isn't commonplace language, but right away, we can understand it, at
least partially: it's a place loud with bees. What is a *glade?* Experience might tell us
that it is an open space in woods, but if that word stops us, we can look it up. Although the *linnet* doesn't live in North America, it is a creature with wings—a songbird of the finch family, adds the dictionary. But even if we don't make a special trip
to the dictionary to find *linnet,* we probably recognize that the word means "bird,"
and the line makes sense to us.

A paraphrase of the whole poem might go something like this (in language easier to forget than that of the original): "I'm going to get up now, go to Innisfree, build
a cabin, plant beans, keep bees, and live peacefully by myself amid nature and beautiful light. I want to because I can't forget the sound of that lake water. When I'm in
the city, a gray and dingy place, I seem to hear it deep inside me."

These dull remarks, roughly faithful to what Yeats is saying, seem a long way
from poetry. Nevertheless, they make certain things clear. For one, they spell out
what the poet merely hints at in his choice of the word *gray:* that he finds the city
dull and depressing. He stresses the word; instead of saying *gray pavements,* in the
usual word order, he turns the phrase around and makes *gray* stand at the end of the
line, where it rimes with *day* and so takes extra emphasis. The grayness of the city
therefore seems important to the poem, and the paraphrase tries to make its meaning
obvious.

Theme and Subject

Whenever you paraphrase, you stick your neck out. You affirm what the poem gives
you to understand. And making a paraphrase can help you see the central thought of

the poem, its **theme.** The theme isn't the same as the **subject,** which is the main topic, whatever the poem is "about." In Yeats's poem, the subject is the lake isle of Innisfree, or a wish to retreat to it. But the theme is, "I yearn for an ideal place where I will find perfect peace and happiness."

Themes can be stated variously, depending on what you believe matters most in the poem. Taking a different view of the poem, placing more weight on the speaker's wish to escape the city, you might instead state the theme: "This city is getting me down—I want to get back to nature." But after taking a second look at that statement, you might want to sharpen it. After all, this Innisfree seems a special, particular place, where the natural world means more to the poet than just any old trees and birds he might see in a park. Perhaps a stronger statement of theme, one closer to what matters most in the poem, might be: "I want to quit the city for my heaven on earth." That, of course, is saying in an obvious way what Yeats says more subtly, more memorably.

Limits of Paraphrase

A paraphrase never tells *all* that a poem contains, nor will every reader agree that a particular paraphrase is accurate. We all make our own interpretations, and sometimes the total meaning of a poem evades even the poet who wrote it. Asked to explain a passage in one of his poems, Robert Browning replied that when he had written the poem, only God and he knew what it meant; but "Now, only God knows." Still, to analyze a poem *as if* we could be certain of its meaning is, in general, more fruitful than to proceed as if no certainty could ever be had. A useful question might be, "What can we understand from the poem's very words?"

All of us bring personal associations to the poems we read. "The Lake Isle of Innisfree" might give you special pleasure if you have ever vacationed on a small island or on the shore of a lake. Such associations are inevitable, even to be welcomed, as long as they don't interfere with our reading the words on the page. We need to distinguish irrelevant responses from those the poem calls for. The reader who can't stand "The Lake Isle of Innisfree" because she is afraid of bees isn't reading a poem by Yeats, but one of her own invention.

Now and again we meet a poem—perhaps startling and memorable—into which the method of paraphrase won't take us far. Some portion of any deep poem resists explanation, but certain poems resist it almost entirely. Many poems by religious mystics seem closer to dream than waking. So do poems that purport to record drug experiences, such as Coleridge's "Kubla Khan" (page 831). So do nonsense poems, translations of primitive folk songs, and surreal poems. Such poetry may move us and give pleasure (although not, perhaps, the pleasure of intellectual understanding). We do it no harm by trying to paraphrase it, though we may fail. Whether logically clear or strangely opaque, good poems appeal to the intelligence and do not shrink from it.

So far, we have taken for granted that poetry differs from prose; yet all our strategies for reading poetry—plowing straight on through and then going back, isolating difficulties, trying to paraphrase, reading aloud, using a dictionary—are no different from those we might employ in unraveling a complicated piece of prose. Poetry, after all, is similar to prose in most respects. At the very least, it is written in the same language. Like prose, poetry shares knowledge with us. It tells us, for instance, of a beautiful island in Lake Gill, County Sligo, Ireland, and of how one man feels toward it.

LYRIC POETRY

Originally, as its Greek name suggests, a *lyric* was a poem sung to the music of a lyre. This earlier meaning—a poem made for singing—is still current today, when we use *lyrics* to mean the words of a popular song. But the kind of printed poem we now call a *lyric* is usually something else, for over the past five hundred years the nature of lyric poetry has changed greatly. Ever since the invention of the printing press in the fifteenth century, poets have written less often for singers, more often for readers. In general, this tendency has made lyric poems contain less word-music and (since they can be pondered on a page) more thought—and perhaps more complicated feelings.

What Is a Lyric Poem?

Here is a rough definition of a **lyric** as it is written today: a short poem expressing the thoughts and feelings of a single speaker. Often a poet will write a lyric in the first person ("I will arise and go now, and go to Innisfree"), but not always. A lyric can also be in the first person plural, as in Paul Laurence Dunbar's "We Wear the Mask" (page 764). Or, a lyric might describe an object or recall an experience without the speaker's ever bringing himself or herself into it. (For an example of such a lyric, one in which the poet refrains from saying "I," see Theodore Roethke's "Root Cellar" on page 562 or Gerard Manley Hopkins's "Pied Beauty" on page 565.)

Perhaps because, rightly or wrongly, some people still think of lyrics as lyre-strummings, they expect a lyric to be an outburst of feeling, somewhat resembling a song, at least containing musical elements such as rime, rhythm, or sound effects. Such expectations are fulfilled in "The Lake Isle of Innisfree," that impassioned lyric full of language rich in sound. Many contemporary poets, however, write short poems in which they voice opinions or complicated feelings—poems that no reader would dream of trying to sing.

But in the sense in which we use it, *lyric* will usually apply to a kind of poem you can easily recognize. Here, for instance, are two lyrics. They differ sharply in subject and theme, but they have traits in common: both are short, and (as you will find) both set forth one speaker's definite, unmistakable feelings.

Robert Hayden (1913–1980)

Those Winter Sundays   1962

Sundays too my father got up early
and put his clothes on in the blueblack cold,
then with cracked hands that ached
from labor in the weekday weather made
banked fires blaze. No one ever thanked him.   5

I'd wake and hear the cold splintering, breaking.
When the rooms were warm, he'd call,
and slowly I would rise and dress,
fearing the chronic angers of that house,

Speaking indifferently to him,   10
who had driven out the cold
and polished my good shoes as well.
What did I know, what did I know
of love's austere and lonely offices?

Questions

1. Jot down a brief paraphrase of this poem. In your paraphrase, clearly show what the speaker finds himself remembering.
2. What are the speaker's various feelings? What do you understand from the words "chronic angers" and "austere"?
3. With what specific details does the poem make the past seem real?
4. What is the subject of Hayden's poem? How would you state its theme?

Adrienne Rich (1929-2012)

Aunt Jennifer's Tigers 1951

Aunt Jennifer's tigers prance across a screen,
Bright topaz denizens of a world of green.
They do not fear the men beneath the tree;
They pace in sleek chivalric certainty.

Aunt Jennifer's fingers fluttering through her wool 5
Find even the ivory needle hard to pull.
The massive weight of Uncle's wedding band
Sits heavily upon Aunt Jennifer's hand.

When Aunt is dead, her terrified hands will lie
Still ringed with ordeals she was mastered by. 10
The tigers in the panel that she made
Will go on prancing, proud and unafraid.

Compare

"Aunt Jennifer's Tigers" with Adrienne Rich's critical comments on the poem reprinted in the "Writing Effectively" section at the end of this chapter.

NARRATIVE POETRY

Although a lyric sometimes relates an incident, or like "Those Winter Sundays" draws a scene, it does not usually relate a series of events. That happens in a **narrative poem,** one whose main purpose is to tell a story.

Narrative poetry dates back to the Babylonian *Epic of Gilgamesh* (composed before 2000 B.C.) and Homer's epics the *Iliad* and the *Odyssey* (composed before 700 B.C.). It may well have originated much earlier. In England and Scotland, storytelling poems have long been popular; in the late Middle Ages, ballads—or storytelling songs—circulated widely. Some, such as "Sir Patrick Spence" and "Bonny Barbara Allan," survive in our day, and folksingers sometimes perform them.

Evidently the art of narrative poetry invites the skills of a writer of fiction: the ability to draw characters and settings, to engage attention, to shape a plot. Needless to say, it calls for all the skills of a poet as well. In the English language today, lyrics seem more plentiful than other kinds of poetry. Although there has recently been a revival of interest in writing narrative poems, they have a far smaller audience than the readership enjoyed by long verse narratives, such as Henry Wadsworth Longfellow's *Evangeline* and Alfred, Lord Tennyson's *Idylls of the King,* in the nineteenth century.

Here are two narrative poems: one medieval, one modern. How would you paraphrase the stories they tell? How do they hold your attention on their stories?

Anonymous (traditional Scottish ballad)

Sir Patrick Spence

The king sits in Dumferling toune,
   Drinking the blude-reid wine:
"O whar will I get guid sailor
   To sail this schip of mine?"

Up and spak an eldern knicht,°   *knight* 5
   Sat at the kings richt kne:
"Sir Patrick Spence is the best sailor
   That sails upon the se."

The king has written a braid letter,
   And signed it wi' his hand,
And sent it to Sir Patrick Spence,   10
   Was walking on the sand.

The first line that Sir Patrick red,
   A loud lauch lauchèd he;
The next line that Sir Patrick red,   15
   The teir blinded his ee.

"O wha° is this has don this deid,   *who*
   This ill deid don to me,
To send me out this time o' the yeir,
   To sail upon the se!   20

"Mak haste, mak haste, my mirry men all,
   Our guid schip sails the morne."
"O say na sae,° my master deir,   *so*
   For I feir a deadlie storme.

"Late late yestreen I saw the new moone,   25
   Wi' the auld moone in hir arme,
And I feir, I feir, my deir master,
   That we will cum to harme."

O our Scots nobles wer richt laith°   *loath*
   To weet° their cork-heild schoone,°   *wet; shoes* 30
Bot lang owre° a' the play wer playd,   *long before*
   Their hats they swam aboone.°   *above (their heads)*

O lang, lang may their ladies sit,
   Wi' their fans into their hand,
Or ere° they se Sir Patrick Spence   *before* 35
   Cum sailing to the land.

O lang, lang may the ladies stand,
   Wi' their gold kems° in their hair,   *combs*
Waiting for their ain° deir lords,   *own*
   For they'll se thame na mair.   40

Haf owre,° haf owre to Aberdour,   *halfway over*
   It's fiftie fadom deip,
And thair lies guid Sir Patrick Spence,
   Wi' the Scots lords at his feit.

SIR PATRICK SPENCE. *9 braid:* Broad, but broad in what sense? Among guesses are *plain-spoken*, *official*, and *on wide paper*.

Questions

1. That the king drinks "blude-reid wine" (line 2)—what meaning do you find in that detail? What does it hint, or foreshadow?

2. What do you make of this king and his motives for sending Spence and the Scots lords into an impending storm? Is he a fool, is he cruel and inconsiderate, is he deliberately trying to drown Sir Patrick and his crew, or is it impossible for us to know? Let your answer depend on the poem alone, not on anything you read into it.

3. Comment on this ballad's methods of storytelling. Is the story told too briefly for us to care what happens to Spence and his men, or are there any means by which the poet makes us feel compassion for them? Do you resent the lack of a detailed account of the shipwreck?

4. Lines 25–28—the new moon with the old moon in her arm—have been much admired as poetry. What does this stanza contribute to the story as well?

Robert Frost (1874–1963)

"Out, Out—"   1916

The buzz-saw snarled and rattled in the yard
And made dust and dropped stove-length sticks of wood,
Sweet-scented stuff when the breeze drew across it.
And from there those that lifted eyes could count
Five mountain ranges one behind the other   5
Under the sunset far into Vermont.
And the saw snarled and rattled, snarled and rattled,
As it ran light, or had to bear a load.
And nothing happened: day was all but done.
Call it a day, I wish they might have said   10
To please the boy by giving him the half hour
That a boy counts so much when saved from work.
His sister stood beside them in her apron
To tell them "Supper." At the word, the saw,
As if to prove saws knew what supper meant,   15
Leaped out at the boy's hand, or seemed to leap—
He must have given the hand. However it was,
Neither refused the meeting. But the hand!
The boy's first outcry was a rueful laugh,
As he swung toward them holding up the hand   20
Half in appeal, but half as if to keep
The life from spilling. Then the boy saw all—
Since he was old enough to know, big boy
Doing a man's work, though a child at heart—
He saw all spoiled. "Don't let him cut my hand off—   25
The doctor, when he comes. Don't let him, sister!"

So. But the hand was gone already.
The doctor put him in the dark of ether.
He lay and puffed his lips out with his breath.
And then—the watcher at his pulse took fright.   30
No one believed. They listened at his heart.
Little—less—nothing!—and that ended it.
No more to build on there. And they, since they
Were not the one dead, turned to their affairs.

"OUT, OUT—." The title of this poem echoes the words of Shakespeare's Macbeth on receiving news that
his queen is dead: "Out, out, brief candle! / Life's but a walking shadow, a poor player / That struts and frets
his hour upon the stage / And then is heard no more. It is a tale / Told by an idiot, full of sound and fury, /
Signifying nothing" (*Macbeth* 5.5.23–28).

Questions

1. How does Frost make the buzz-saw appear sinister? How does he make it seem, in another
   way, like a friend?
2. What do you make of the people who surround the boy—the "they" of the poem? Who
   might they be? Do they seem to you concerned and compassionate, cruel, indifferent, or
   what?
3. What does Frost's reference to *Macbeth* contribute to your understanding of "'Out, Out—'"?
   How would you state the theme of Frost's poem?
4. Set this poem side by side with "Sir Patrick Spence." How does "'Out, Out—'" resemble
   that medieval folk ballad in subject, or differ from it? How is Frost's poem similar or
   different in its way of telling a story?

DRAMATIC POETRY

A third kind of poetry is **dramatic poetry,** which presents the voice of an imaginary
character (or characters) speaking directly, without any additional narration by the
author.

A dramatic poem, according to T. S. Eliot, does not consist of "what the poet
would say in his own person, but only what he can say within the limits of one imaginary character addressing another imaginary character." Strictly speaking, the term
dramatic poetry describes any verse written for the stage (and until a few centuries ago
most playwrights, like Shakespeare and Molière, wrote their plays mainly in verse).

Dramatic Monologue

The term *dramatic poetry* most often refers to the **dramatic monologue,** a poem written as a speech made by a character (other than the author) at some decisive moment.
A dramatic monologue is usually addressed by the speaker to some other character
who remains silent. If the listener replies, the poem becomes a dialogue (such as
Thomas Hardy's "The Ruined Maid" on page 538) in which the story unfolds in the
conversation between two speakers.

The Victorian poet Robert Browning, who developed the form of the dramatic
monologue, liked to put words in the mouths of characters who were conspicuously
nasty, weak, reckless, or crazy: see, for instance, Browning's "Soliloquy of the Spanish
Cloister" (page 828), in which the speaker is an obsessively proud and jealous
monk. The dramatic monologue has been a popular form among American poets, including Edwin Arlington Robinson, Robert Frost, Ezra Pound, Randall Jarrell, Sylvia
Plath, and David Mason. The most famous dramatic monologue ever written is

probably Browning's "My Last Duchess," in which the poet creates a Renaissance Italian duke whose words reveal much more about himself than the aristocratic speaker intends.

Robert Browning (1812–1889)

My Last Duchess   1842

Ferrara

That's my last Duchess painted on the wall,
Looking as if she were alive. I call
That piece a wonder, now: Frà Pandolf's hands
Worked busily a day, and there she stands.
Will't please you sit and look at her? I said   5
"Frà Pandolf" by design, for never read
Strangers like you that pictured countenance,
The depth and passion of its earnest glance,
But to myself they turned (since none puts by
The curtain I have drawn for you, but I)   10
And seemed as they would ask me, if they durst,
How such a glance came there; so, not the first
Are you to turn and ask thus. Sir, 'twas not
Her husband's presence only, called that spot
Of joy into the Duchess' cheek: perhaps   15
Frà Pandolf chanced to say, "Her mantle laps
Over my lady's wrist too much," or "Paint
Must never hope to reproduce the faint
Half-flush that dies along her throat": such stuff
Was courtesy, she thought, and cause enough   20
For calling up that spot of joy. She had
A heart—how shall I say?—too soon made glad,
Too easily impressed; she liked whate'er
She looked on, and her looks went everywhere.
Sir, 'twas all one! My favor at her breast,   25
The dropping of the daylight in the West,
The bough of cherries some officious fool
Broke in the orchard for her, the white mule
She rode with round the terrace—all and each
Would draw from her alike the approving speech,   30
Or blush, at least. She thanked men,—good! but thanked
Somehow—I know not how—as if she ranked
My gift of a nine-hundred-years-old name
With anybody's gift. Who'd stoop to blame
This sort of trifling? Even had you skill   35
In speech—(which I have not)—to make your will
Quite clear to such an one, and say, "Just this
Or that in you disgusts me; here you miss,
Or there exceed the mark"—and if she let
Herself be lessoned so, nor plainly set   40

Her wits to yours, forsooth, and made excuse,
—E'en then would be some stooping; and I choose
Never to stoop. Oh sir, she smiled, no doubt,
Whene'er I passed her; but who passed without
Much the same smile? This grew; I gave commands;   45
Then all smiles stopped together. There she stands
As if alive. Will't please you rise? We'll meet
The company below, then. I repeat,
The Count your master's known munificence
Is ample warrant that no just pretense   50
Of mine for dowry will be disallowed;
Though his fair daughter's self, as I avowed
At starting, is my object. Nay, we'll go
Together down, sir. Notice Neptune, though,
Taming a sea-horse, thought a rarity,   55
Which Claus of Innsbruck cast in bronze for me!   •

MY LAST DUCHESS. Ferrara, a city in northern Italy, is the scene. Browning may have modeled his speaker after Alonzo, Duke of Ferrara (1533–1598). 3 *Frà Pandolf* and 56 *Claus of Innsbruck:* names of fictitious artists.

Questions

1. Whom is the Duke addressing? What is this person's business in Ferrara?
2. What is the Duke's opinion of his last Duchess's personality? Do we see her character differently?
3. If the Duke was unhappy with the Duchess's behavior, why didn't he make his displeasure known? Cite a specific passage to explain his reticence.
4. How much do we know about the fate of the last Duchess? Would it help our understanding of the poem to know more?
5. Does Browning imply any connection between the Duke's art collection and his attitude toward his wife?

DIDACTIC POETRY

More fashionable in former times was a fourth variety of poetry, **didactic poetry:** a poem written to state a message or teach a body of knowledge. In a lyric, a speaker may express sadness; in a didactic poem, he or she may explain that sadness is inherent in life. Poems that impart a body of knowledge, such as Ovid's *Art of Love* and Lucretius's *On the Nature of Things,* are didactic. Such instructive poetry was favored especially by classical Latin poets and by English poets of the eighteenth century. In *The Fleece* (1757), John Dyer celebrated the British woolen industry and included practical advice on raising sheep:

> In cold stiff soils the bleaters oft complain
> Of gouty ails, by shepherds termed the halt:
> Those let the neighboring fold or ready crook
> Detain, and pour into their cloven feet
> Corrosive drugs, deep-searching arsenic,
> Dry alum, verdigris, or vitriol keen.

One might agree with Dr. Johnson's comment on Dyer's effort: "The subject, Sir, cannot be made poetical." But it may be argued that the subject of didactic poetry does not make it any less poetical. Good poems, it seems, can be written about anything under the sun. Like Dyer, John Milton described sick sheep in "Lycidas," a poem few readers have thought unpoetic:

> The hungry sheep look up, and are not fed,
> But, swoll'n with wind and the rank mist they draw,
> Rot inwardly, and foul contagion spread . . .

What makes Milton's lines better poetry than Dyer's is, among other things, a difference in attitude. Sick sheep to Dyer mean the loss of a few shillings and pence; to Milton, whose sheep stand for English Christendom, they mean a moral catastrophe.

■ WRITING *effectively*

Adrienne Rich on Writing

Recalling "Aunt Jennifer's Tigers"   1971

I know that my style was formed first by male poets: by the men I was reading as an undergraduate—Frost, Dylan Thomas, Donne, Auden, MacNeice, Stevens, Yeats. What I chiefly learned from them was craft. But poems are like dreams: in them you put what you don't know you know. Looking back at poems I wrote before I was 21, I'm startled because beneath the conscious craft are glimpses of the split I even then experienced between the girl who wrote poems, who defined herself in writing poems, and the girl who was to define herself by her relationships with men. "Aunt Jennifer's Tigers," written while I was a student, looks with deliberate detachment at this split. In writing this poem, composed and apparently cool as it is, I

Adrienne Rich

thought I was creating a portrait of an imaginary woman. But this woman suffers from the opposition of her imagination, worked out in tapestry, and her life-style, "ringed with ordeals she was mastered by." It was important to me that Aunt Jennifer was a person as distinct from myself as possible—distanced by the formalism of the poem, by its objective, observant tone—even by putting the woman in a different generation.

In those years formalism was part of the strategy—like asbestos gloves, it allowed me to handle materials I couldn't pick up bare-handed.

From "When We Dead Awaken: Writing as Re-Vision"

THINKING ABOUT PARAPHRASING

A poet takes pains to choose each word of a poem for both its sound and its exact shade of meaning. Since a poem's full effect is so completely wedded to its exact wording, some would say that no poem can be truly paraphrased. But even though it represents an imperfect approximation of the real thing, a paraphrase can be useful to write and read. It can clearly map out a poem's key images, actions, and ideas. A map is no substitute for a landscape, but a good map often helps us find our way through the landscape without getting lost.

William Stafford (1914–1993)

Ask Me 1975

Some time when the river is ice ask me
mistakes I have made. Ask me whether
what I have done is my life. Others
have come in their slow way into
my thought, and some have tried to help 5
or to hurt—ask me what difference
their strongest love or hate has made.

I will listen to what you say.
You and I can turn and look
at the silent river and wait. We know 10
the current is there, hidden; and there
are comings and goings from miles away
that hold the stillness exactly before us.
What the river says, that is what I say.

William Stafford (1914–1993)

A Paraphrase of "Ask Me" 1977

I think my poem can be paraphrased—and that any poem can be paraphrased. But every pass through the material, using other words, would have to be achieved at certain costs, either in momentum, or nuance, or dangerously explicit (and therefore misleading in tone) adjustments. I'll try one such pass through the poem:

> When it's quiet and cold and we have some chance to interchange without hurry, confront me if you like with a challenge about whether I think I have made mistakes in my life—and ask me, if you want to, whether to me my life is actually the sequence of events or exploits others would see. Well, those others tag along in my living, and some of them in fact have played significant roles in the narrative run of my world; they have intended either helping or hurting (but by implication in the way I am saying this you will know that neither effort is conclusive). So—ask me how important their good or bad intentions have been (both intentions get a drastic *leveling* judgment from this cool stating of it all). You, too, will be entering that realm of maybe-help-maybe-hurt, by entering that far into my life by asking this serious question—so: I will stay still and consider. Out there will be the world confronting us both; we will both know we are surrounded by mystery, tremendous things that do not reveal themselves to us. That river, that world—and our lives—all share the depth and stillness of much more significance than our talk, or intentions. There is a steadiness and somehow a solace in knowing that what is around us so greatly surpasses our human concerns.

From "Ask Me"

CHECKLIST: Writing a Paraphrase

☐ **Read the poem closely.** It is important to read it more than once to understand it well.

☐ **Go through it line by line.** Don't skip lines or stanzas or any key details. In your own words, what does each line say?

☐ **Write your paraphrase as prose.**

☐ **State the poem's literal meaning.** Don't worry about deeper meanings.

☐ **Reread your statement to see if you have missed anything important.** Check to see if you have captured the overall significance of the poem along with the details.

WRITING ASSIGNMENT ON PARAPHRASING

Paraphrase any short poem from the chapter "Poems for Further Reading." Be sure to do a careful line-by-line reading. Include the most vital points and details, and state the poem's main thought or theme without quoting any original passage.

MORE TOPICS FOR WRITING

1. In a paragraph, contrast William Stafford's poem with his paraphrase. What does the poem offer that the paraphrase does not? What, then, is the value of the paraphrase?

2. Write a two-page paraphrase of the events described in "'Out, Out—.'" Then take your paraphrase further: summarize the poem's message in a single sentence.

▶ TERMS FOR *review*

Analytic Terms

Verse ▶ This term has two major meanings. It refers to any single line of poetry or any composition written in separate lines of more or less regular rhythm, in contrast to prose.

Paraphrase ▶ The restatement in one's own words of what one understands a poem to say or suggest. A paraphrase is similar to a summary, although not as brief or simple.

Summary ▶ A brief condensation of the main idea or plot of a work. A summary is similar to a paraphrase, but less detailed.

Subject ▶ The main topic of a work, whatever the work is "about."

Theme ▶ A generally recurring subject or idea noticeably evident in a literary work. Not all subjects in a work can be considered themes, only the central one(s).

Types of Poetry

Lyric poem ▶ A short poem expressing the thoughts and feelings of a single speaker. Often written in the first person, it traditionally has a songlike immediacy and emotional force.

Narrative poem ▶ A poem that tells a story. **Ballads** and **epics** are two common forms of narrative poetry.

Dramatic monologue ▶ A poem written as a speech made by a character at some decisive moment. The speaker is usually addressing a silent listener.

Didactic poem ▶ A poem intended to teach a moral lesson or impart a body of knowledge.

13

LISTENING TO A VOICE

*Irony is that little pinch of salt
which alone makes the dish palatable.*
—JOHANN WOLFGANG VON GOETHE

TONE

In old Western movies, when one hombre taunts another, it is customary for the second to drawl, "Smile when you say that, pardner" or "Mister, I don't like your tone of voice." Sometimes in reading a poem, although we can neither see a face nor hear a voice, we can infer the poet's attitude from other evidence.

Like tone of voice, **tone** in literature often conveys an attitude toward the person addressed. Like the manner of a person, the manner of a poem may be friendly or belligerent toward its reader, condescending or respectful. Again like tone of voice, the tone of a poem may tell us how the speaker feels about himself or herself: cocksure or humble, sad or glad. But usually when we ask "What is the tone of a poem?" we mean "What attitude does the poet take toward a theme or a subject?" Is the poet being affectionate, hostile, earnest, playful, sarcastic, or what? We may never be able to know, of course, the poet's personal feelings. All we need know is how to feel when we read the poem.

Strictly speaking, tone isn't an attitude; it is whatever in the poem makes an attitude clear to us: the choice of certain words instead of others, the picking out of certain details. In A. E. Housman's "Loveliest of trees," for example, the poet communicates his admiration for a cherry tree's beauty by singling out its white blossoms for attention; had he wanted to show his dislike for the tree, he might have concentrated on its broken branches, birdlime, or snails. To perceive the tone of a poem rightly, we need to read the poem carefully, paying attention to whatever suggestions we find in it.

Theodore Roethke (1908–1963)

My Papa's Waltz

1948

The whiskey on your breath
Could make a small boy dizzy;
But I hung on like death:
Such waltzing was not easy.

We romped until the pans   5
Slid from the kitchen shelf;
My mother's countenance
Could not unfrown itself.

The hand that held my wrist
Was battered on one knuckle;   10
At every step you missed
My right ear scraped a buckle.

You beat time on my head
With a palm caked hard by dirt,
Then waltzed me off to bed   15
Still clinging to your shirt.

What is the tone of this poem? Most readers find the speaker's attitude toward his father critical, but nonetheless affectionate. They take this recollection of childhood to be an odd but happy one. Other readers, however, concentrate on other details, such as the father's rough manners and drunkenness. One reader has written that "Roethke expresses his resentment for his father, a drunken brute with dirty hands and whiskey breath who carelessly hurt the child's ear and manhandled him." Although this reader accurately noticed some of the events in the poem and perceived that there was something desperate in the son's hanging onto the father "like death," he simplifies the tone of the poem and so misses its humorous side.

While "My Papa's Waltz" contains the dark elements of manhandling and drunkenness, the tone remains grotesquely comic. The rollicking rhythms of the poem underscore Roethke's complex humor—half loving and half censuring of the unwashed, intoxicated father. The humor is further reinforced by playful rimes such as *dizzy* and *easy*, *knuckle* and *buckle*, as well as the joyful suggestions of the words *waltz*, *waltzing*, and *romped*. The scene itself is comic, with kitchen pans falling because of the father's roughhousing while the mother looks on unamused. However much the speaker satirizes the overly rambunctious father, he does not have the boy identify with the soberly disapproving mother. Not all comedy is comfortable and reassuring. Certainly, this small boy's family life has its frightening side, but the last line suggests the boy is *still clinging* to his father with persistent if also complicated love.

Satiric Poetry

"My Papa's Waltz," though it includes lifelike details that aren't pretty, has a tone relatively easy to recognize. So does **satiric poetry,** a kind of comic poetry that generally conveys a message. Usually its tone is one of detached amusement, withering contempt, and implied superiority. In a satiric poem, the poet ridicules some person or persons (or perhaps some kind of human behavior), examining the victim by the light of certain principles and implying that the reader, too, ought to feel contempt for the victim.

Countee Cullen (1903–1946)

For a Lady I Know   1925

She even thinks that up in heaven
    Her class lies late and snores,
While poor black cherubs rise at seven
    To do celestial chores.

Questions

1. What is Cullen's message?
2. How would you characterize the tone of this poem? Wrathful? Amused?

A Spectrum of Tones

In some poems the poet's attitude may be plain enough, while in other poems attitudes may be so mingled that it is hard to describe them tersely without doing injustice to the poem. Does Andrew Marvell in "To His Coy Mistress" (page 861) take a serious or playful attitude toward the fact that he and his lady are destined to be food for worms? No one-word answer will suffice. And what of T. S. Eliot's "The Love Song of J. Alfred Prufrock" (page 806)? In his attitude toward his redemption-seeking hero who wades with trousers rolled, Eliot is seriously funny. Such a mingled tone may be seen in the following poem by the wife of a governor of the Massachusetts Bay Colony and the earliest American poet of note. Anne Bradstreet's first book, *The Tenth Muse Lately Sprung Up in America* (1650), had been published in England without her consent. She wrote these lines to preface a second edition:

Anne Bradstreet (1612?–1672)

The Author to Her Book   1678

Thou ill-formed offspring of my feeble brain,
Who after birth did'st by my side remain,
Till snatched from thence by friends, less wise than true,
Who thee abroad exposed to public view;
Made thee in rags, halting, to the press to trudge,   5
Where errors were not lessened, all may judge.
At thy return my blushing was not small,
My rambling brat (in print) should mother call;
I cast thee by as one unfit for light,
Thy visage was so irksome in my sight;   10
Yet being mine own, at length affection would
Thy blemishes amend, if so I could:
I washed thy face, but more defects I saw,
And rubbing off a spot, still made a flaw.
I stretched thy joints to make thee even feet,   15
Yet still thou run'st more hobbling than is meet;
In better dress to trim thee was my mind,
But nought save homespun cloth in the house I find.
In this array, 'mongst vulgars may'st thou roam;
In critics' hands beware thou dost not come;   20
And take thy way where yet thou are not known.
If for thy Father asked, say thou had'st none;
And for thy Mother, she alas is poor,
Which caused her thus to send thee out of door.

In the author's comparison of her book to an illegitimate ragamuffin, we may be struck by the details of scrubbing and dressing a child: details that might well occur to a mother who had scrubbed and dressed many. As she might feel toward such a child, so she feels toward her book. She starts by deploring it but, as the poem goes on, cannot deny it her affection. Humor enters (as in the pun in line 15). She must dress the creature in *homespun cloth,* something both crude and serviceable. By the end of her poem, Bradstreet seems to regard her book-child with tenderness, amusement, and a certain indulgent awareness of its faults. To read this poem is to sense its mingling of several attitudes. A poet can be merry and in earnest at the same time.

Walt Whitman   (1819–1892)

To a Locomotive in Winter   1881

Thee for my recitative,
Thee in the driving storm even as now, the snow, the winter-day
    declining,
Thee in thy panoply,° thy measur'd dual throbbing and thy beat   *suit of armor*
    convulsive,
Thy black cylindric body, golden brass and silvery steel,
Thy ponderous side-bars, parallel and connecting rods, gyrating,   5
    shuttling at thy sides,
Thy metrical, now swelling pant and roar, now tapering in the distance,
Thy great protruding head-light fix'd in front,
Thy long, pale, floating vapor-pennants, tinged with delicate purple,
The dense and murky clouds out-belching from thy smoke-stack,
Thy knitted frame, thy springs and valves, the tremulous twinkle of thy   10
    wheels,
Thy train of cars behind, obedient, merrily following,
Through gale or calm, now swift, now slack, yet steadily careering;
Type of the modern—emblem of motion and power—pulse of the continent,
For once come serve the Muse and merge in verse, even as here I see thee,
With storm and buffeting gusts of wind and falling snow,   15
By day thy warning ringing bell to sound its notes,
By night thy silent signal lamps to swing.

Fierce-throated beauty!
Roll through my chant with all thy lawless music, thy swinging lamps at night,
Thy madly-whistled laughter, echoing, rumbling like an earth-quake,   20
    rousing all,
Law of thyself complete, thine own track firmly holding,
(No sweetness debonair of tearful harp or glib piano thine,)
Thy trills of shrieks by rocks and hills return'd,
Launch'd o'er the prairies wide, across the lakes,
To the free skies unpent and glad and strong.   25

Emily Dickinson   (1830–1886)

I like to see it lap the Miles   (about 1862)

I like to see it lap the Miles –
And lick the Valleys up –
And stop to feed itself at Tanks –
And then – prodigious step

Around a Pile of Mountains –
And supercilious peer
In Shanties – by the sides of Roads –
And then a Quarry pare   5

To fit its Ribs
And crawl between
Complaining all the while   10
In horrid – hooting stanza –
Then chase itself down Hill –

And neigh like Boanerges –
Then – punctual as a Star   15
Stop – docile and omnipotent
At its own stable door–

Questions

1. What differences in tone do you find between Whitman's and Dickinson's poems? Point out whatever in each poem contributes to these differences.

2. *Boanerges* in Dickinson's last stanza means "sons of thunder," a name given by Jesus to the disciples John and James (see Mark 3:17). How far should the reader work out the particulars of this comparison? Does it make the tone of the poem serious?

3. In Whitman's opening line, what is a *recitative*? What other specialized terms from the vocabulary of music and poetry does each poem contain? How do they help underscore Whitman's theme?

4. Poets and songwriters probably have regarded the locomotive with more affection than they have shown most other machines. Why do you suppose this is so? Can you think of any other poems or songs as examples?

5. What do these two poems tell you about locomotives that you would not be likely to find in a technical book on railroading?

6. Are the subjects of the two poems identical? Discuss.

Benjamin Alire Sáenz (b. 1954)

To the Desert   1995

I came to you one rainless August night.
You taught me how to live without the rain.
You are thirst and thirst is all I know.
You are sand, wind, sun, and burning sky,
The hottest blue. You blow a breeze and brand   5
Your breath into my mouth. You reach—then *bend*
Your force, to break, blow, burn, and make me new.
You wrap your name tight around my ribs
And keep me warm. I was born for you.
Above, below, by you, by you surrounded.   10
I wake to you at dawn. Never break your
Knot. Reach, rise, blow, *Sálvame, mi dios,*
Trágame, mi tierra. Salva, traga, Break me,
I am bread. I will be the water for your thirst.

To the Desert. 6–7 *bend . . . make me new:* quoted from John Donne's "Batter my heart" (page 531). 12–13 *Sálvame, mi dios . . . traga:* Spanish for "Save me, my god, / Take me, my land. Save me, take me." (*Trágame* literally means "swallow me.")

Questions

1. How does the speaker feel about the land being described? What words in the poem suggest or convey those feelings?
2. What effect does the speaker's sudden switch into Spanish create? What is the tone of the Spanish?
3. Of what kind of language do the last few lines of the poem remind you?

Gwendolyn Brooks   (1917–2000)

Speech to the Young. Speech to the Progress-Toward   1970/1987

(Among them Nora and Henry III)

Say to them,
say to the down-keepers,
the sun-slappers,
the self-soilers,
the harmony-hushers,   5
"Even if you are not ready for day
it cannot always be night."
You will be right.
For that is the hard home-run.

Live not for battles won.   10
Live not for the-end-of-the-song.
Live in the along.

SPEECH TO THE YOUNG. SPEECH TO THE PROGRESS-TOWARD. *Nora and Henry III*: Brooks's two children, Nora (b. 1951) and Henry III (b. 1940).

Questions

1. This poem was the concluding text in Brooks's 1970 chapbook *Family Pictures*. In what sense, then, is this a poem about family relationships?
2. Explain, in the context of the poem, the epithets in lines 2–5.
3. Why is the attitude affirmed in the poem described as "hard" (line 9)?
4. How would you paraphrase the theme of this poem?

Weldon Kees   (1914–1955)

For My Daughter   1940

Looking into my daughter's eyes I read
Beneath the innocence of morning flesh
Concealed, hintings of death she does not heed.
Coldest of winds have blown this hair, and mesh
Of seaweed snarled these miniatures of hands;   5
The night's slow poison, tolerant and bland,
Has moved her blood. Parched years that I have seen
That may be hers appear: foul, lingering

Death in certain war, the slim legs green.
Or, fed on hate, she relishes the sting   10
Of others' agony; perhaps the cruel
Bride of a syphilitic or a fool.
These speculations sour in the sun.
I have no daughter. I desire none.

Questions

1. How does the last line of this sonnet affect the meaning of the poem?
2. "For My Daughter" was first published in 1940. What considerations might a potential American parent have felt at that time? Are these historical concerns mirrored in the poem?
3. Donald Justice has said that "Kees is one of the bitterest poets in history." Is bitterness the only attitude the speaker reveals in this poem?

THE PERSON IN THE POEM

The tone of a poem, we said, is like tone of voice in that both communicate feelings. Still, this comparison raises a question: when we read a poem, whose "voice" speaks to us?

"The poet's" is one possible answer; and in the case of many a poem that answer may be right. Reading Anne Bradstreet's "The Author to Her Book," we can be reasonably sure that the poet speaks of her very own book, and of her own experiences. In order to read a poem, we seldom need to read a poet's biography; but in truth there are certain poems whose full effect depends upon our knowing at least a fact or two of the poet's life. Here is one such poem.

Natasha Trethewey (b. 1966)

White Lies   2000

The lies I could tell,
when I was growing up
light-bright, near-white,
high-yellow, red-boned
in a black place,   5
were just white lies.

I could easily tell the white folks
that we lived uptown,
not in that pink and green
shanty-fied shotgun section   10
along the tracks. I could act
like my homemade dresses
came straight out the window
of Maison Blanche. I could even
keep quiet, quiet as kept,   15
like the time a white girl said
(squeezing my hand), *Now
we have three of us in this class.*

But I paid for it every time
Mama found out.
She laid her hands on me,   20
then washed out my mouth
with Ivory soap. *This
is to purify,* she said,
and cleanse your lying tongue.   25
Believing her, I swallowed suds
thinking they'd work
from the inside out.

Through its pattern of vivid color imagery, Trethewey's poem tells of a black child light enough to "pass for white" in a society that was still extremely race-sensitive. But knowing the author's family background gives us a deeper insight into the levels of meaning in the poem. Trethewey was born in Mississippi in 1966, at a time when her parents' interracial marriage was a criminal act in that state. On her birth certificate, her mother's race was given as "colored"; in the box intended to record the race of her father—who was white and had been born in Nova Scotia—appeared the word "Canadian" (although her parents divorced before she began grade school, she remained extremely close to both of them). Trethewey has said of her birth certificate: "Something is left out of the official record that way. The irony isn't lost on me. Even in documenting myself as a person there is a little fiction." "White Lies" succeeds admirably on its own, but these biographical details allow us to read it as an even more complex meditation on issues of racial definition and personal identity in America.

Persona

Most of us can tell the difference between a person we meet in life and a person we meet in a work of art. And yet, in reading poems, we are liable to temptation. When the poet says "I," we may want to assume that he or she is making a personal statement. But reflect: do all poems have to be personal? Here is a brief poem inscribed on the tombstone of an infant in Burial Hill Cemetery, Plymouth, Massachusetts:

Since I have been so quickly done for,
I wonder what I was begun for.

We do not know who wrote those lines, but it is clear that the poet was not a short-lived infant writing from personal experience. In other poems, the speaker is obviously a **persona,** or fictitious character: not the poet, but the poet's creation. As a grown man, William Blake, a skilled professional engraver, wrote a poem in the voice of a boy, an illiterate chimney sweeper. (The poem appears later in this chapter.)

Let's consider a poem spoken not by a poet, but by a persona—in this case a mysterious one. Edwin Arlington Robinson's "Luke Havergal" is a dramatic monologue, but the identity of the speaker is never clearly stated. In 1905, upon first reading the poem in Robinson's *The Children of the Night* (1897), President Theodore Roosevelt was so moved that he wrote an essay about the book that made the author famous. Roosevelt, however, admitted that he found the musically seductive poem difficult. "I am not sure I understand 'Luke Havergal,'" he wrote, "but I am entirely sure I like it." Possibly what most puzzled our twenty-sixth president was who was speaking in the poem. How much does Robinson let us know about the voice and the person it addresses?

Edwin Arlington Robinson (1869–1935)

Luke Havergal

1897

Go to the western gate, Luke Havergal,
There where the vines cling crimson on the wall,
And in the twilight wait for what will come.
The leaves will whisper there of her, and some,
Like flying words, will strike you as they fall;   5
But go, and if you listen she will call.
Go to the western gate, Luke Havergal—
Luke Havergal.

No, there is not a dawn in eastern skies
To rift the fiery night that's in your eyes;   10
But there, where western glooms are gathering,
The dark will end the dark, if anything:
God slays Himself with every leaf that flies,
And hell is more than half of paradise.
No, there is not a dawn in eastern skies—   15
In eastern skies.

Out of a grave I come to tell you this,
Out of a grave I come to quench the kiss
That flames upon your forehead with a glow
That blinds you to the way that you must go.   20
Yes, there is yet one way to where she is,
Bitter, but one that faith may never miss.
Out of a grave I come to tell you this—
To tell you this.

There is the western gate, Luke Havergal,   25
There are the crimson leaves upon the wall.
Go, for the winds are tearing them away,—
Nor think to riddle the dead words they say,
Nor any more to feel them as they fall;
But go, and if you trust her she will call.   30
There is the western gate, Luke Havergal—
Luke Havergal.

Questions

1. Who is the speaker of the poem? What specific details does the author reveal about the speaker?
2. What does the speaker ask Luke Havergal to do?
3. What do you understand "the western gate" to be?
4. Would you advise Luke Havergal to follow the speaker's advice? Why or why not?

No literary law decrees that the speaker in a poem even has to be human. Good poems have been uttered by clouds, pebbles, clocks, and cats. Here is a poem spoken by a hawk, a dramatic monologue that expresses the animal's thoughts and attitudes in a way consciously designed to emphasize how different its worldview is from a human perspective.

Ted Hughes (1930–1998)

Hawk Roosting

1960

I sit in the top of the wood, my eyes closed.
Inaction, no falsifying dream
Between my hooked head and hooked feet:
Or in sleep rehearse perfect kills and eat.

The convenience of the high trees! 5
The air's buoyancy and the sun's ray
Are of advantage to me;
And the earth's face upward for my inspection.

My feet are locked upon the rough bark.
It took the whole of Creation 10
To produce my foot, my each feather:
Now I hold Creation in my foot

Or fly up, and revolve it all slowly—
I kill where I please because it is all mine.
There is no sophistry in my body: 15
My manners are tearing off heads—

The allotment of death.
For the one path of my flight is direct
Through the bones of the living.
No arguments assert my right: 20

The sun is behind me.
Nothing has changed since I began.
My eye has permitted no change.
I am going to keep things like this.

Questions

1. Find three observations the hawk makes about its world that a human would probably not make. What do these remarks tell us about the bird's character?
2. In what ways does Ted Hughes create an unrealistic portrayal of the hawk's true mental powers? What statements in the poem would an actual hawk be unlikely to make? Do these passages add anything to the poem's impact? What would be lost if they were omitted?

Anonymous

Dog Haiku

2001

Today I sniffed
Many dog behinds—I celebrate
By kissing your face.

*

I sound the alarm!
Garbage man—come to kill us all—
Look! Look! Look! Look! Look! 5

*

How do I love thee?
The ways are numberless as
My hairs on the rug.

*

I sound the alarm!   10
Paper boy—come to kill us all—
Look! Look! Look! Look! Look!

*

I am your best friend,
Now, always, and especially
When you are eating.   15

Questions

1. Who is the "I" in the poem? Who is the "you"?
2. Do you recognize the allusion in lines 7–9?
3. What elements create the humorous effect of the poem?

A Classic Poem and Its Source

In a famous definition, William Wordsworth calls poetry "the spontaneous overflow
of powerful feelings . . . recollected in tranquillity." But in the case of the following
poem, Wordsworth's feelings weren't all his; they didn't just overflow spontaneously;
and the process of tranquil recollection had to go on for years.

William Wordsworth (1770–1850)

I Wandered Lonely as a Cloud   1807

I wandered lonely as a cloud
That floats on high o'er vales and hills,
When all at once I saw a crowd,
A host, of golden daffodils,
Beside the lake, beneath the trees,   5
Fluttering and dancing in the breeze.

Continuous as the stars that shine
And twinkle on the milky way,
They stretched in never-ending line
Along the margin of a bay: 10
Ten thousand saw I at a glance,
Tossing their heads in sprightly dance.

The waves beside them danced; but they
Out-did the sparkling waves in glee;
A poet could not but be gay,   15
In such a jocund company;
I gazed—and gazed—but little thought
What wealth the show to me had brought:

For oft, when on my couch I lie
In vacant or in pensive mood,   20

They flash upon that inward eye
Which is the bliss of solitude;
And then my heart with pleasure fills,
And dances with the daffodils.

Between the first printing of the poem in 1807 and the version of 1815 given here, Wordsworth made several deliberate improvements. He changed *dancing* to *golden* in line 4, *Along* to *Beside* in line 5, *Ten thousand* to *Fluttering and* in line 6, *laughing* to *jocund* in line 16, and he added a whole stanza (the second). In fact, the writing of the poem was unspontaneous enough for Wordsworth, at a loss for lines 21–22, to take them from his wife, Mary. It is likely that the experience of daffodil-watching was not entirely his to begin with but was derived in part from the recollections his sister, Dorothy Wordsworth, had set down in her journal on April 15, 1802, two years before he first drafted his poem.

Dorothy Wordsworth (1771–1855)

Journal Entry   1802

When we were in the woods beyond Gowbarrow Park we saw a few daffodils close to the water-side. We fancied that the lake had floated the seeds ashore, and that the little colony had so sprung up. But as we went along there were more and yet more; and at last, under the boughs of the trees, we saw that there was a long belt of them along the shore, about the breadth of a country turnpike road. I never saw daffodils so beautiful. They grew among the mossy stones about and about them; some rested their heads upon these stones as on a pillow for weariness; and the rest tossed and reeled and danced, and seemed as if they verily laughed with the wind, that blew upon them over the Lake; they looked so gay, ever glancing, ever changing. This wind blew directly over the Lake to them. There was here and there a little knot, and a few stragglers a few yards higher up; but they were so few as not to disturb the simplicity, unity, and life of that one busy highway.

Notice that Wordsworth's poem echoes a few of his sister's observations. Weaving poetry out of their mutual memories, Wordsworth has offered the experience as if it were altogether his own, made himself lonely, and left Dorothy out. The point is not that Wordsworth is a liar or a plagiarist but that, like any other good poet, he has transformed ordinary life into art. A process of interpreting, shaping, and ordering had to intervene between the experience of looking at daffodils and the finished poem.

The Art of Imagination

We need not deny that a poet's experience can contribute to a poem or that the emotion in the poem can indeed be the poet's. Still, to write a good poem one has to do more than live and feel. Writing poetry takes skill and imagination—qualities that extensive travel and wide experience do not necessarily give. Emily Dickinson seldom strayed from her family's house and grounds in Amherst, Massachusetts; yet her rimed life studies of a snake, a bee, and a hummingbird contain more poetry than we find in any firsthand description (so far) of the surface of the moon.

Anne Sexton (1928–1974)

Her Kind   1960

I have gone out, a possessed witch,
haunting the black air, braver at night;
dreaming evil, I have done my hitch
over the plain houses, light by light:
lonely thing, twelve-fingered, out of mind.   5
A woman like that is not a woman, quite.
I have been her kind.

I have found the warm caves in the woods,
filled them with skillets, carvings, shelves,
closets, silks, innumerable goods;   10
fixed the suppers for the worms and the elves:
whining, rearranging the disaligned.
A woman like that is misunderstood.
I have been her kind.

I have ridden in your cart, driver,   15
waved my nude arms at villages going by,
learning the last bright routes, survivor
where your flames still bite my thigh
and my ribs crack where your wheels wind.
A woman like that is not ashamed to die.   20
I have been her kind.

Questions

1. Who is the speaker of this poem? What do we know about her?
2. What does the speaker mean by ending each stanza with the statement, "I have been her kind"?
3. Who are the figures with whom the speaker identifies? What do these figures tell us about the speaker's state of mind?

William Carlos Williams (1883–1963)

The Red Wheelbarrow   1923

so much depends
upon

a red wheel
barrow

glazed with rain   5
water

beside the white
chickens

Experiment: Reading With and Without Biography

1. Write a paragraph summing up your initial reactions to "The Red Wheelbarrow."
2. Now write a second paragraph with the benefit of this snippet of biographical information: Inspiration for this poem apparently came to Dr. Williams as he was gazing from the window of a house where one of his patients, a small girl, lay suspended between life and death.[1] How does this information affect your reading of the poem?

IRONY

To see a distinction between the poet and the words of a fictitious character—between Robert Browning and "My Last Duchess"—is to be aware of **irony:** a manner of speaking that implies a discrepancy. If the mask says one thing and we sense that the writer is in fact saying something else, the writer has adopted an **ironic point of view.** No finer illustration exists in English than Jonathan Swift's "A Modest Proposal," an essay in which Swift speaks as an earnest, humorless citizen who sets forth his reasonable plan to aid the Irish poor. The plan is so monstrous no sane reader can assent to it: the poor are to sell their children as meat for the tables of their landlords. From behind his false face, Swift is actually recommending not cannibalism but love and Christian charity.

A poem is often made complicated and more interesting by another kind of irony. **Verbal irony** occurs whenever words say one thing but mean something else, usually the opposite. The word *love* means *hate* here: "I just *love* to stay home and do my hair on a Saturday night!"

Sarcasm

If verbal irony is conspicuously bitter, heavy-handed, and mocking, it is **sarcasm:** "Oh, he's the biggest spender in the world, all right!" (The sarcasm, if that statement were spoken, would be underscored by the speaker's tone of voice.) A famous instance of sarcasm occurs in Shakespeare's *Julius Caesar* in Mark Antony's oration over the body of the slain Caesar: "Brutus is an honorable man." Antony repeats this line until the enraged populace begins shouting exactly what he means to call Brutus and the other conspirators: traitors, villains, murderers. We had best be alert for irony on the printed page, for if we miss it, our interpretations of a poem may go wild.

Robert Creeley (1926–2005)

Oh No   1959

If you wander far enough
you will come to it
and when you get there
they will give you a place to sit
for yourself only, in a nice chair,   5
and all your friends will be there
with smiles on their faces
and they will likewise all have places.

---

[1]This account, from the director of the public library in Williams's native Rutherford, New Jersey, is given by Geri M. Rhodes in "The Paterson Metaphor in William Carlos Williams's *Paterson*," master's thesis, Tufts University, 1965.

This poem is rich in verbal irony. The title helps point out that between the speaker's words and attitude lie deep differences. In line 2, what is *it*? Old age? The wandering suggests a conventional metaphor: the journey of life. Is *it* literally a rest home for "senior citizens," or perhaps some naïve popular concept of heaven (such as we meet in comic strips: harps, angels with hoops for halos) in which the saved all sit around in a ring, smugly congratulating one another? We can't be sure, but the speaker's attitude toward this final sitting-place is definite. It is a place for the selfish, as we infer from the phrase *for yourself only*. And *smiles on their faces* may hint that the smiles are unchanging and forced. There is a difference between saying "They had smiles on their faces" and "They smiled": the latter suggests that the smiles came from within. The word *nice* is to be regarded with distrust. If we see through this speaker, as Creeley implies we can do, we realize that, while pretending to be sweet-talking us into a seat, actually he is revealing the horror of a little hell. And the title is the poet's reaction to it (or the speaker's unironic, straightforward one): "Oh no! Not *that*!"

Dramatic Irony

Dramatic irony, like verbal irony, contains an element of contrast, but it usually refers to a situation in a play wherein a character whose knowledge is limited says, does, or encounters something of greater significance than he or she knows. We, the spectators, realize the meaning of this speech or action, for the playwright has afforded us superior knowledge. In Sophocles's *King Oedipus*, when Oedipus vows to punish whoever has brought down a plague upon the city of Thebes, we know—as he does not—that the man he would punish is himself. The situation of Oedipus also contains **cosmic irony,** or **irony of fate:** some Fate with a grim sense of humor seems cruelly to trick a human being. Cosmic irony clearly exists in poems in which fate or the Fates are personified and seen as hostile, as in Thomas Hardy's "The Convergence of the Twain" (page 844); and it may be said to occur also in Robinson's "Richard Cory" (page 599). Obviously it is a twist of fate for the most envied man in town to kill himself.

To sum up: the effect of irony depends on the reader's noticing some incongruity or discrepancy between two things. In *verbal irony*, there is a contrast between the speaker's words and meaning; in an *ironic point of view*, between the writer's attitude and what is spoken by a fictitious character; in *dramatic irony*, between the limited knowledge of a character and the fuller knowledge of the reader or spectator; in *cosmic irony*, between a character's position or aspiration and the treatment he or she receives at the hands of Fate. Although, in the work of an inept poet, irony can be crude and obvious sarcasm, it is invaluable to a poet of more complicated mind, who imagines more than one perspective.

W. H. Auden (1907–1973)

The Unknown Citizen   1940

(To JS/07/M/378
This Marble Monument Is Erected by the State)

He was found by the Bureau of Statistics to be
One against whom there was no official complaint,
And all the reports on his conduct agree
That, in the modern sense of an old-fashioned word, he was a saint,

For in everything he did he served the Greater Community.   5
Except for the War till the day he retired
He worked in a factory and never got fired,
But satisfied his employers, Fudge Motors Inc.
Yet he wasn't a scab or odd in his views,
For his Union reports that he paid his dues,   10
(Our report on his Union shows it was sound)
And our Social Psychology workers found
That he was popular with his mates and liked a drink.
The Press are convinced that he bought a paper every day
And that his reactions to advertisements were normal in every way.   15
Policies taken out in his name prove that he was fully insured,
And his Health-card shows he was once in hospital but left it cured.
Both Producers Research and High-Grade Living declare
He was fully sensible to the advantages of the Installment Plan
And had everything necessary to the Modern Man,   20
A phonograph, a radio, a car and a frigidaire.
Our researchers into Public Opinion are content
That he held the proper opinions for the time of year;
When there was peace, he was for peace; when there was war, he went.
He was married and added five children to the population,   25
Which our Eugenist says was the right number for a parent of his
      generation,
And our teachers report that he never interfered with their education.
Was he free? Was he happy? The question is absurd:
Had anything been wrong, we should certainly have heard.

Questions

1. Read the two-line epitaph at the beginning of the poem as carefully as you read what follows. How does the epitaph help establish the voice by which the rest of the poem is spoken?
2. Who is speaking?
3. What ironic discrepancies do you find between the speaker's attitude toward the subject and that of the poet himself? By what is the poet's attitude made clear?
4. In the phrase "The Unknown Soldier" (of which "The Unknown Citizen" reminds us), what does the word "unknown" mean? What does it mean in the title of Auden's poem?
5. What tendencies in our civilization does Auden satirize?
6. How would you expect the speaker to define a Modern Man, if an iPod, a radio, a car, and a refrigerator are "everything" a Modern Man needs?

Sharon Olds (b. 1942)

Rite of Passage   1983

As the guests arrive at my son's party
they gather in the living room—
short men, men in first grade
with smooth jaws and chins.

Hands in pockets, they stand around 5
jostling, jockeying for place, small fights
breaking out and calming. One says to another
How old are you? Six. I'm seven. So?
They eye each other, seeing themselves
tiny in the other's pupils. They clear their 10
throats a lot, a room of small bankers,
they fold their arms and frown. *I could beat you
up,* a seven says to a six,
the dark cake, round and heavy as a
turret, behind them on the table. My son, 15
freckles like specks of nutmeg on his cheeks,
chest narrow as the balsa keel of a
model boat, long hands
cool and thin as the day they guided him
out of me, speaks up as a host 20
for the sake of the group.
We could easily kill a two-year-old,
he says in his clear voice. The other
men agree, they clear their throats
like Generals, they relax and get down to 25
playing war, celebrating my son's life.

Questions

1. What is ironic about the way the speaker describes the first-grade boys at her son's birth-day party?
2. What other irony does the author underscore in the last two lines?
3. Does this mother sentimentalize her own son by seeing him as better than the other boys?

Julie Sheehan (b. 1964)

Hate Poem   2005

I hate you truly. Truly I do.
Everything about me hates everything about you.
The flick of my wrist hates you.
The way I hold my pencil hates you.
The sound made by my tiniest bones were they trapped in the jaws of a moray 5
    eel hates you.
Each corpuscle singing in its capillary hates you.

Look out! Fore! I hate you.

The blue-green jewel of sock lint I'm digging from under my third toenail,
    left foot, hates you.
The history of this keychain hates you.
My sigh in the background as you explain relational databases hates you. 10

The goldfish of my genius hates you.
My aorta hates you. Also my ancestors.

A closed window is both a closed window and an obvious symbol of how I
    hate you.

My voice curt as a hairshirt: hate.
My hesitation when you invite me for a drive: hate.   15
My pleasant "good morning": hate.
You know how when I'm sleepy I nuzzle my head under your arm? Hate.

The whites of my target-eyes articulate hate. My wit practices it.
My breasts relaxing in their holster from morning to night hate you.
Layers of hate, a parfait.   20
Hours after our latest row, brandishing the sharp glee of hate,
I dissect you cell by cell, so that I might hate each one individually and at
    leisure.
My lungs, duplicitous twins, expand with the utter validity of my hate,
    which can never have enough of you,
Breathlessly, like two idealists in a broken submarine.

Questions

1. What is the relationship between the speaker of this poem and the object of her hatred? What details in the text support this assumption?
2. Does this poem exemplify the old saying that "There is a thin line between love and hate"?
3. Is the poem more effective, or less so, for never providing any reasons for the hatred it expresses?
4. What do you understand the poem's last two lines to mean?
5. In what ways is the poem ironic?
6. Does the speaker really hate the person she addresses? Support your assertions.

Edna St. Vincent Millay (1892–1950)

Second Fig   1920

Safe upon the solid rock the ugly houses stand:
Come and see my shining palace built upon the sand!

Question

Do you think the author is making fun of the speaker's attitude or agreeing with it?

Exercise: Detecting Irony

Point out the kinds of irony that occur in "The Workbox."

Thomas Hardy (1840–1928)

The Workbox   1914

"See, here's the workbox, little wife,
    That I made of polished oak."
He was a joiner,° of village life;   *carpenter*
    She came of borough folk.

He holds the present up to her   5
    As with a smile she nears
And answers to the profferer,
    "'Twill last all my sewing years!"

"I warrant it will. And longer too.
    'Tis a scantling that I got   10
Off poor John Wayward's coffin, who
    Died of they knew not what.

"The shingled pattern that seems to cease
    Against your box's rim
Continues right on in the piece   15
    That's underground with him.

"And while I worked it made me think
    Of timber's varied doom:
One inch where people eat and drink,
    The next inch in a tomb.   20

"But why do you look so white, my dear,
    And turn aside your face?
You knew not that good lad, I fear,
    Though he came from your native place?"

"How could I know that good young man,   25
    Though he came from my native town,
When he must have left far earlier than
    I was a woman grown?"

"Ah, no. I should have understood!
    It shocked you that I gave   30
To you one end of a piece of wood
    Whose other is in a grave?"

"Don't, dear, despise my intellect,
    Mere accidental things
Of that sort never have effect   35
    On my imaginings."

Yet still her lips were limp and wan,
    Her face still held aside,
As if she had known not only John,
    But known of what he died.   40

FOR REVIEW AND FURTHER STUDY

William Blake (1757–1827)

The Chimney Sweeper   1789

When my mother died I was very young,
And my father sold me while yet my tongue
Could scarcely cry "'weep! 'weep! 'weep! 'weep!"
So your chimneys I sweep, and in soot I sleep.

There's little Tom Dacre, who cried when his head,   5
That curled like a lamb's back, was shaved: so I said
"Hush, Tom! never mind it, for when your head's bare
You know that the soot cannot spoil your white hair."

And so he was quiet, and that very night,
As Tom was a-sleeping, he had such a sight!   10
That thousands of sweepers, Dick, Joe, Ned, and Jack,
Were all of them locked up in coffins of black.

And by came an Angel who had a bright key,
And he opened the coffins and set them all free;
Then down a green plain leaping, laughing, they run,   15
And wash in a river, and shine in the sun.

Then naked and white, all their bags left behind,
They rise upon clouds and sport in the wind;
And the Angel told Tom, if he'd be a good boy,
He'd have God for his father, and never want° joy.   lack   20

And so Tom awoke; and we rose in the dark,
And got with our bags and our brushes to work.
Though the morning was cold, Tom was happy and warm;
So if all do their duty they need not fear harm.

Questions

1. What does Blake's poem reveal about conditions of life in the London of his day?
2. Sum up your impressions of the speaker's character. What does he say and do that displays it to us?
3. What pun do you find in line 3? Is its effect comic or serious?
4. In Tom Dacre's dream (lines 11–20), what wishes come true? Do you understand them to be the wishes of the chimney sweepers, of the poet, or of both?
5. In the last line, what is ironic in the speaker's assurance that the dutiful "need not fear harm"? What irony is there in his urging all to "do their duty"? (Who have failed in their duty to him?)
6. What is the tone of Blake's poem? Angry? Hopeful? Sorrowful? Compassionate? (Don't feel obliged to sum it up in a single word.)

William Stafford (1914–1993)

At the Un-National Monument Along the Canadian Border   1977

This is the field where the battle did not happen,
where the unknown soldier did not die.

This is the field where grass joined hands,
where no monument stands,
and the only heroic thing is the sky. 5

Birds fly here without any sound,
unfolding their wings across the open.
No people killed—or were killed—on this ground
hallowed by neglect and an air so tame
that people celebrate it by forgetting its name. 10

Questions

1. What non-event does this poem celebrate? What is the speaker's attitude toward it?
2. The speaker describes an empty field. What is odd about the way in which he describes it?
3. What words does the speaker appear to use ironically?

Exercise: Telling Tone

Here are two radically different poems on a similar subject. Try stating the theme of each poem in your own words. How is the tone (the speaker's attitude) different in the two poems?

Richard Lovelace (1618–1658)

To Lucasta 1649

> *On Going to the Wars*

Tell me not, Sweet, I am unkind
   That from the nunnery
Of thy chaste breast and quiet mind,
   To war and arms I fly.

True, a new mistress now I chase, 5
   The first foe in the field;
And with a stronger faith embrace
   A sword, a horse, a shield.

Yet this inconstancy is such
   As you too shall adore; 10
I could not love thee, Dear, so much,
   Loved I not Honor more.

Wilfred Owen (1893–1918)

Dulce et Decorum Est 1920

Bent double, like old beggars under sacks,
Knock-kneed, coughing like hags, we cursed through sludge,
Till on the haunting flares we turned our backs
And towards our distant rest began to trudge.
Men marched asleep. Many had lost their boots 5
But limped on, blood-shod. All went lame; all blind;
Drunk with fatigue; deaf even to the hoots
Of tired, outstripped Five-Nines that dropped behind.

Gas! GAS! Quick, boys!—An ecstasy of fumbling,
Fitting the clumsy helmets just in time;   10
But someone still was yelling out and stumbling,
And flound'ring like a man in fire or lime . . .
Dim, through the misty panes and thick green light,
As under a green sea, I saw him drowning.

In all my dreams, before my helpless sight,   15
He plunges at me, guttering, choking, drowning.

If in some smothering dreams you too could pace
Behind the wagon that we flung him in,
And watch the white eyes writhing in his face,
His hanging face, like a devil's sick of sin;   20
If you could hear, at every jolt, the blood
Come gargling from the froth-corrupted lungs,
Obscene as cancer, bitter as the cud
Of vile, incurable sores on innocent tongues,—
My friend, you would not tell with such high zest   25
To children ardent for some desperate glory,
The old Lie: Dulce et decorum est
Pro patria mori.

DULCE ET DECORUM EST. Owen's title is the beginning of the famous Latin quotation from the Roman
poet Horace with which he ends this poem: "*Dulce et decorum est pro patria mori.*" It is translated as "It is
sweet and proper to die for your country." 8 *Five-Nines:* German howitzers often used to shoot poison gas
shells. 17 *you too:* Some manuscript versions of this poem carry the dedication "To Jessie Pope" (a writer of
patriotic verse) or "To a certain Poetess."

■ WRITING *effectively*

Wilfred Owen on Writing

*Wilfred Owen was only twenty-one years old
when World War I broke out in 1914. Twice
wounded in battle, he was rapidly promoted and
eventually became a company commander. The
shocking violence of modern war summoned up
his poetic genius, and in a two-year period he
grew from a negligible minor poet into the most
important English-language poet of World War
I. Owen, however, did not live to see his talent
recognized. He was killed one week before the
end of the war; he was twenty-five years old.
Owen published only four poems during his lifetime. Shortly before his death he drafted a few
lines of prose for the preface of a book of poems.*

Wilfred Owen

War Poetry   (1917?)

    This book is not about heroes. English poetry is not yet fit to speak of them.

    Nor is it about deeds, or lands, nor anything about glory, honour, might, majesty, dominion, or power, except War.

    Above all I am not concerned with Poetry.

    My subject is War, and the pity of War.

    The Poetry is in the pity.

    Yet these elegies are to this generation in no sense consolatory. They may be to the next. All a poet can do today is warn. That is why the true Poets must be truthful.

From *Collected Poems*

THINKING ABOUT TONE

To understand the tone of a poem, we need to listen to the words, as we might listen to an actual conversation. The key is to hear not only *what* is being said but also *how* it is being said. Does the speaker sound noticeably surprised, angry, nostalgic, or tender? Begin with an obvious but often overlooked question: who is speaking? Don't assume that every poem is spoken by its author.

- **Look for the ways—large and small—in which the speaker reveals aspects of his or her character.** Attitudes may be revealed directly or indirectly. Often, emotions must be intuited. The details a poet chooses to convey can reveal much about a speaker's stance toward his or her subject matter.
- **Consider also how the speaker addresses the listener.** Again, listen to the sound of the poem as you would listen to the sound of someone's voice—is it shrill, or soothing, or sarcastic?
- **Look for an obvious difference between the speaker's attitude and your own honest reaction toward what is happening in the poem.** If the gap between the two responses is wide, the poem may be taken as ironic.
- **Remember that many poets strive toward understatement, writing matter-of-factly about matters of intense sorrow, horror, or joy.** In poems, as in conversation, understatement can be a powerful tool, more convincing—and often more moving—than hyperbole.

CHECKLIST: Writing About Tone

- ☐ Who is speaking the poem?
- ☐ Is the narrator's voice close to the poet's or is it the voice of a fictional or historical person?
- ☐ How does the speaker address the listener?
- ☐ Does the poem directly reveal an emotion or attitude?
- ☐ Does it indirectly reveal any attitudes or emotions?
- ☐ Does your reaction to what is happening in the poem differ widely from that of the speaker? If so, what does that difference suggest? Is the poem in some way ironic?
- ☐ What adjectives would best describe the poem's tone?

WRITING ASSIGNMENT ON TONE

Choose a poem from this chapter, and analyze its speaker's attitude toward the poem's main subject. Examine the author's choice of specific words and images to create the particular tone used to convey the speaker's attitudes. (Possible subjects include Wilfred Owen's attitude toward war in "Dulce et Decorum Est," the tone and imagery of Weldon Kees's "For My Daughter," Ted Hughes's view of the workings of nature in "Hawk Roosting," and Anne Bradstreet's attitude toward her own poetry in "The Author to Her Book.")

Here is an example of an essay written for this assignment by Kim Larsen, a student of Karen Locke's at Lane Community College in Eugene, Oregon.

SAMPLE STUDENT PAPER

Larsen 1

Kim Larsen

Professor Locke

English 110

16 January 2012

Word Choice, Tone, and Point of View in Roethke's

"My Papa's Waltz"

Title gives sense of the paper's focus

Name of author and work

Some readers may find Theodore Roethke's "My Papa's Waltz" a reminiscence of a happy childhood scene. I believe, however, that the poem depicts a more painful and complicated series of emotions. By examining the choice of words that Roethke uses to convey the tone of his scene, I will demonstrate that beneath the seemingly comic situation of the poem is a darker story. The true point of view of "My Papa's Waltz" is that of a resentful adult reliving his fear of a domineering parent.

Thesis sentence

The first clue that the dance may not have been a mutually enjoyable experience is in the title itself. The author did not title the poem "Our Waltz" or "Waltzing with My Papa," either of which would set an initial tone for readers to expect a shared, loving sentiment. It does not even have a neutral title, such as "The Waltz." The title specifically implies that the waltz was exclusively the father's. Since a waltz normally involves two people, it can be reasoned that the father dances his waltz without regard for his young partner.

Topic sentence on title's significance

Larsen 2

Examining each stanza of the poem offers numerous examples where the choice of words sustains the tone implied in the title. The first line, "The whiskey on your breath," conjures up an olfactory image that most would find unpleasant. The small boy finds it so overpowering he is made "dizzy." This stanza contains the only simile in the poem, "I hung on like death" (3), which creates a ghastly and stark visual image. There are many choices of similes to portray hanging on: a vine, an infant, an animal cub, all of which would have illustrated a lighthearted romp. The choice of "death" was purposefully used to convey an intended image. The first stanza ends by stating the "waltzing was not easy." The definitions of *easy*, as found in *Merriam-Webster's Collegiate Dictionary*, include "free from pain, annoyance or anxiety," and "not difficult to endure or undergo" ("Easy"). Obviously the speaker did not find those qualities in the waltz.

Further evidence of this harsh and oppressive scene is brought to mind by reckless disregard for "the pans / Slid from the kitchen shelf" (5–6), which the reader can almost hear crashing on the floor in loud cacophony, and the "mother's countenance," which "[c]ould not unfrown itself" (7, 8). If this were only a silly, playful romp between father and son, even a stern, fastidious mother might be expected to at least make an unsuccessful attempt to suppress a grin. Instead, the reader gets a visual image of a silent, unhappy woman, afraid, probably because of past experience, to interfere in the domestic destruction around her. Once more, this detail suggests a domineering father who controls the family.

The third stanza relates the father's "battered" hand holding the boy's wrist. The tactile image of holding a wrist suggests dragging or forcing an unwilling person, not holding hands as would be expected with a mutual dance partner. Further disregard for the son's feelings is displayed by the lines "At every step you missed / My right ear scraped a buckle" (11–12). In each missed step, probably due to his drunkenness, the father causes the boy physical pain.

The tone continues in the final stanza as the speaker recalls "You beat time on my head / With a palm caked hard by dirt" (13–14). The visual and tactile image of a dirt-hardened hand beating on a child's head as if it were a drum is distinctly unpleasant. The last lines, "Then waltzed me off to bed / Still clinging to your shirt" (15–16), are the most ambiguous in the poem. It can be reasoned, as

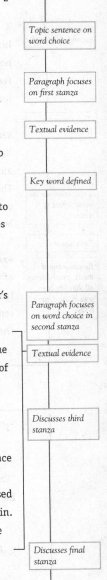

Topic sentence on word choice

Paragraph focuses on first stanza

Textual evidence

Key word defined

Paragraph focuses on word choice in second stanza

Textual evidence

Discusses third stanza

Discusses final stanza

Quotation from secondary source

X. J. Kennedy and Dana Gioia do, that the lines suggest "the boy is *still clinging* to his father with persistent if also complicated love" (502). On the other hand, if one notices the earlier dark images, the conclusion could describe a boy clinging out of fear, the physical fear of being dropped by one who is drunk and the emotional fear of not being loved and nurtured as a child needs to be by his father.

Transitional phrase

It can also be argued that the poem's rollicking rhythm contributes to a sense of fun, and in truth, the poem can be read in that fashion. On the other hand, it can be read in such a way as to de-emphasize the rhythm, as the author himself does in his recording of "My Papa's Waltz" (Roethke, *Reads*).

Topic sentence on ironic effect of meter

The joyful, rollicking rhythm can be seen as ironic. By reminding readers of a waltzing tempo, it is highlighting the discrepancy between what a waltz should be and the bleak, frightening picture painted in the words.

Conclusion

While "My Papa's Waltz" can be read as a roughhouse comedy, by examining Roethke's title and choice of words closely to interpret the meaning of their images and sounds, it is also plausible to hear an entirely different

Restatement of thesis, synthesizing all that has been said in the essay's body.

tone. I believe "My Papa's Waltz" employs the voice of an embittered adult remembering a harsh scene in which both he and his mother were powerless in the presence of a drunk and domineering father.

Works Cited

"Easy." *Merriam-Webster's Collegiate Dictionary.* 11th ed. 2003. Print.

Kennedy, X. J., and Dana Gioia, eds. *Literature: An Introduction to Fiction, Poetry, Drama, and Writing.* 7th Compact ed. New York: Pearson, 2013. 502. Print.

Roethke, Theodore. "My Papa's Waltz." *Literature: An Introduction to Fiction, Poetry, Drama, and Writing.* Ed. X. J. Kennedy and Dana Gioia. 7th Compact ed. New York: Pearson, 2013. 501–02. Print.

---. *Theodore Roethke Reads His Poetry.* Audio forum, 2006. CD.

MORE TOPICS FOR WRITING

1. Describe the tone of W. H. Auden's "The Unknown Citizen," quoting as necessary to back up your argument. How does the poem's tone contribute to its meaning?

2. Write an analysis of Thomas Hardy's "The Workbox," focusing on what the poem leaves unsaid.

3. In an essay of 250 to 500 words, compare and contrast the tone of two poems on a similar subject. You might examine how Walt Whitman and Emily Dickinson treat the subject of locomotives, or how Richard Lovelace and Wilfred Owen write about war. (For advice on writing about poetry by the method of comparison and contrast, see the chapter "Writing About a Poem.")

4. Write a poem of your own in which the speaker's attitude toward the subject is revealed not by what the poem says but by the tone in which it is said. William Blake's "The Chimney Sweeper," W. H. Auden's "The Unknown Citizen," and Sharon Olds's "Rite of Passage" provide some good models.

5. Look closely at any poem in this chapter. Going through it line by line, make a list of the sensory details the poem provides. Now write briefly about how those details combine to create a particular tone. Two choices are William Stafford's "At the Un-National Monument Along the Canadian Border" and Sharon Olds's "Rite of Passage."

▶ TERMS FOR *review*

Tone ▶ The mood or manner of expression in a literary work, which conveys an attitude toward the work's subject, which may be playful, sarcastic, ironic, sad, solemn, or any other possible attitude. Tone helps to establish the reader's relationship to the characters or ideas presented in the work.

Satiric poetry ▶ Poetry that blends criticism with humor to convey a message, usually through the use of irony and a tone of detached amusement, withering contempt, and implied superiority.

Persona ▶ Latin for "mask." A fictitious character created by an author to be the speaker of a literary work.

Types of Irony

Irony ▶ In language, a discrepancy between what is said and what is meant. In life, a discrepancy between what is expected and what occurs.

Verbal irony ▶ A mode of expression in which the speaker or writer says the opposite of what is really meant, such as saying "Great story!" in response to a boring, pointless anecdote.

Sarcasm ▶ A style of bitter irony intended to hurt or mock its target.

Dramatic irony ▶ A situation in which the larger implications of character's words, actions, or situation are unrealized by that character but seen by the author and the reader or audience.

Cosmic irony ▶ The contrast between a character's position or aspiration and the treatment he or she receives at the hands of a seemingly hostile fate; also called **irony of fate**.

14 WORDS

*We all write poems; it is simply that poets are
the ones who write in words.*

—JOHN FOWLES

LITERAL MEANING: WHAT A POEM SAYS FIRST

Although successful as a painter, Edgar Degas found poetry discouragingly hard to
write. To his friend, the poet Stéphane Mallarmé, he complained, "What a business!
My whole day gone on a blasted sonnet, without getting an inch further . . . and it
isn't ideas I'm short of . . . I'm full of them, I've got too many . . ."

"But Degas," said Mallarmé, "you can't make a poem with ideas—you make it
with *words!*"

Like the celebrated painter, some people assume that all it takes to make a poem
is a bright idea. Poems state ideas, to be sure, and sometimes the ideas are invaluable;
and yet the most impressive idea in the world will not make a poem, unless its words
are selected and arranged with loving art. Some poets take great pains to find the
right word. Unable to fill a two-syllable gap in an unfinished line that went, "The
seal's wide——gaze toward Paradise," Hart Crane paged through an unabridged dictionary. When he reached *S*, he found the object of his quest in *spindrift:* "spray
skimmed from the sea by a strong wind." The word is exact and memorable.

In reading a poem, some people assume that its words can be skipped over rapidly,
and they try to leap at once to the poem's general theme. It is as if they fear being
thought clods unless they can find huge ideas in the poem (whether or not there are
any). Such readers often ignore the literal meanings of words: the ordinary, matter-of-
fact sense to be found in a dictionary. (As you will see in the next chapter, "Saying
and Suggesting," words possess not only dictionary meanings—denotations—but also
many associations and suggestions—connotations.) Consider the following poem and
see what you make of it.

 William Carlos Williams (1883–1963)

This Is Just to Say

1934

I have eaten
the plums
that were in
the icebox

528

and which
you were probably
saving
for breakfast

Forgive me
they were delicious
so sweet
and so cold

Some readers distrust a poem so simple and candid. They think, "What's wrong with me? There has to be more to it than this!" But poems seldom are puzzles in need of solutions. We can begin by accepting the poet's statements, without suspecting the poet of trying to hoodwink us. On later reflection, of course, we might possibly decide that the poet is playfully teasing or being ironic; but Williams gives us no reason to think that. There seems no need to look beyond the literal sense of his words, no profit in speculating that the plums symbolize worldly joys and that the icebox stands for the universe. Clearly, a reader who held such a grand theory would have over-looked (in eagerness to find a significant idea) the plain truth that the poet makes clear to us: that ice-cold plums are a joy to taste.

To be sure, Williams's small poem is simpler than most poems are; and yet in reading any poem, no matter how complicated, you will do well to reach slowly and reluctantly for a theory to explain it by. To find the general theme of a poem, you first need to pay attention to its words. Recall Yeats's "The Lake Isle of Innisfree" (page 489), a poem that makes a statement—crudely summed up, "I yearn to leave the city and retreat to a place of ideal peace and happiness." And yet before we can realize this theme, we have to notice details: nine bean rows, a glade loud with bees, "lake water lapping with low sounds by the shore," the gray of a pavement. These details and not some abstract remark make clear what the poem is saying: that the city is drab, while the island hideaway is sublimely beautiful.

Poets often strive for words that point to physical details and solid objects. They may do so even when speaking of an abstract idea:

Beauty is but a flower
Which wrinkles will devour;
Brightness falls from the air,
Queens have died young and fair,
Dust hath closed Helen's eye.
I am sick, I must die:
    Lord, have mercy on us!

In these lines by Thomas Nashe, the abstraction *beauty* has grown petals that shrivel. Brightness may be a general name for light, but Nashe succeeds in giving it the weight of a falling body.

DICTION

If a poem says *daffodils* instead of *plant life*, *diaper years* instead of *infancy*, we call its **diction,** or choice of words, **concrete** rather than **abstract.** Concrete words refer to what we can immediately perceive with our senses: *dog, actor, chemical,* or particular individuals who belong to those general classes: *Bonzo the fox terrier, Clint Eastwood,* *hydrogen sulfate*. Abstract words express ideas or concepts: *love, time, truth*. In abstracting, we leave out some characteristics found in each individual, and instead observe a quality common to many. The word *beauty*, for instance, denotes what may be observed in numerous persons, places, and things.

Ezra Pound gave a famous piece of advice to his fellow poets: "Go in fear of abstractions." This is not to say that a poet cannot employ abstract words, nor that all poems have to be about physical things. Much of T. S. Eliot's *Four Quartets* is concerned with time, eternity, history, language, reality, and other things that cannot be physically handled. But Eliot, however high he may soar for a larger view, keeps returning to earth. He makes us aware of *things*.

Marianne Moore (1887–1972)

Silence   1924

My father used to say,
"Superior people never make long visits,
have to be shown Longfellow's grave
or the glass flowers at Harvard.
Self-reliant like the cat—   5
that takes its prey to privacy,
the mouse's limp tail hanging like a shoelace from its mouth—
they sometimes enjoy solitude,
and can be robbed of speech
by speech which has delighted them.   10
The deepest feeling always shows itself in silence;
not in silence, but restraint."
Nor was he insincere in saying, "Make my house your inn."
Inns are not residences.

Questions

1. Almost all of "Silence" consists of quotation. What are some possible reasons why the speaker prefers using another person's words?
2. What are the words the father uses to describe people he admires?
3. The poem makes an important distinction between two similar words (lines 13–14). Explain the distinction Moore implies.
4. Why is "Silence" an appropriate title for this poem?

Robert Graves (1895–1985)

Down, Wanton, Down!   1933

Down, wanton, down! Have you no shame
That at the whisper of Love's name,
Or Beauty's, presto! up you raise
Your angry head and stand at gaze?

Poor bombard-captain, sworn to reach   5
The ravelin and effect a breach—
Indifferent what you storm or why,
So be that in the breach you die!

Love may be blind, but Love at least
Knows what is man and what mere beast;   10
Or Beauty wayward, but requires
More delicacy from her squires.

Tell me, my witless, whose one boast
Could be your staunchness at the post,
When were you made a man of parts   15
To think fine and profess the arts?

Will many-gifted Beauty come
Bowing to your bald rule of thumb,
Or Love swear loyalty to your crown?
Be gone, have done! Down, wanton, down!   20

DOWN, WANTON, DOWN! 5 *bombard-captain*: officer in charge of a bombard, an early type of cannon that hurled stones. 6 *ravelin*: fortification with two faces that meet in a protruding angle. *effect a breach*: break an opening through (a fortification). 15 *man of parts*: man of talent or ability.

Questions

1. How do you define a "wanton"?
2. What wanton does the poet address?
3. Explain the comparison drawn in the second stanza.
4. In line 14, how many meanings do you find in "staunchness at the post"?
5. Explain any other puns you find in lines 15–19.
6. Do you take this to be a cynical poem making fun of Love and Beauty, or is Graves making fun of stupid, animal lust?

John Donne (1572–1631)

Batter my heart, three-personed God, for You   (about 1610)

Batter my heart, three-personed God, for You
As yet but knock, breathe, shine, and seek to mend.
That I may rise and stand, o'erthrow me, and bend
Your force to break, blow, burn, and make me new.
I, like an usurped town to another due,   5
Labor to admit You, but Oh! to no end.
Reason, Your viceroy in me, me should defend,
But is captived, and proves weak or untrue.
Yet dearly I love You, and would be lovèd fain,
But am betrothed unto Your enemy;   10
Divorce me, untie or break that knot again;
Take me to You, imprison me, for I,
Except You enthrall me, never shall be free,
Nor ever chaste, except You ravish me.

Questions

1. In the last line of this sonnet, to what does Donne compare the onslaught of God's love? Do you think the poem is weakened by the poet's comparing a spiritual experience to something so grossly carnal? Discuss.

2. Explain the seeming contradiction in the last line: in what sense can a ravished person be "chaste"? Explain the seeming contradictions in lines 3–4 and 12–13: how can a person thrown down and destroyed be enabled to "rise and stand"; an imprisoned person be "free"?

3. In lines 5–6 the speaker compares himself to a "usurped town" trying to throw off its conqueror by admitting an army of liberation. Who is the "usurper" in this comparison?

4. Explain the comparison of "Reason" to a "viceroy" (lines 7–8).

5. Sum up in your own words the message of Donne's poem. In stating its theme, did you have to read the poem for literal meanings, figurative comparisons, or both?

THE VALUE OF A DICTIONARY

Use the dictionary. It's better than the critics.

—ELIZABETH BISHOP TO HER STUDENTS

If a poet troubles to seek out the best words available, the least we can do is to find out what the words mean. The dictionary is a firm ally in reading poems; if the poems are more than a century old, it is indispensable. Meanings change. When the Elizabethan poet George Gascoigne wrote, "O Abraham's brats, O brood of blessed seed," the word *brats* implied neither irritation nor contempt. When in the seventeenth century Andrew Marvell imagined two lovers' "vegetable love," he referred to a vegetative or growing love, not one resembling a lettuce. And when Queen Anne, in a famous anecdote, called the just-completed Saint Paul's Cathedral "awful, artificial, and amusing," its architect, Sir Christopher Wren, was overwhelmed with joy and gratitude, for what she had told him was that it was awe-inspiring, artful, and stimulating to contemplate (or *muse* upon).

In reading poetry, there is nothing to be done about the inevitable tendency of language to change except to watch out for it. If you suspect that a word has shifted in meaning over the years, most standard desk dictionaries will be helpful, an unabridged dictionary more helpful still, and most helpful of all the *Oxford English Dictionary (OED)*, which gives, for each definition, successive examples of the word's written use through the past thousand years. You need not feel a grim obligation to keep interrupting a poem in order to rummage in the dictionary; but if the poem is worth reading very closely, you may wish any aid you can find.

"Every word which is used to express a moral or intellectual fact," said Emerson in his study *Nature*, "if traced to its root, is found to be borrowed from some material appearance. *Right* means straight; *wrong* means twisted. *Spirit* primarily means wind; *transgression*, the crossing of a line; *supercilious*, the raising of an eyebrow." Browse in a dictionary and you will discover such original concretenesses. These are revealed in your dictionary's etymologies, or brief notes on the derivation of words, given in most dictionaries near the beginning of an entry on a word; in some dictionaries, at the end of the entry. Look up *squirrel*, for instance, and you will find it comes from two Greek words meaning "shadow-tail." For another example of a common word that originally contained a poetic metaphor, look up the origin of *daisy*.

Experiment: **Use the Dictionary to Read Longfellow's "Aftermath"**

The following short poem seems very simple and straightforward, but much of its total effect depends on the reader knowing the literal meanings of several words. The most crucial word is in the title—"aftermath." Most readers today will assume that they know what that word means, but in this poem Longfellow uses it in both its current sense and its original, more literal meaning. Read the poem twice—first without a dictionary, then a second time after looking up the meanings of "aftermath," "fledged," "rowen," and "mead." How does knowing the exact meanings of these words add to both your literal and critical reading of the poem?

Henry Wadsworth Longfellow (1807–1882)

Aftermath   1873

When the summer fields are mown,
When the birds are fledged and flown,
   And the dry leaves strew the path;
With the falling of the snow,
With the cawing of the crow,   5
Once again the fields we mow
   And gather in the aftermath.

Not the sweet, new grass with flowers
In this harvesting of ours;
   Not the upland clover bloom;   10
But the rowen mixed with weeds,
Tangled tufts from marsh and meads,
Where the poppy drops its seeds
   In the silence and the gloom.

Questions

1. How do the etymology and meaning of "aftermath" help explain this poem? (Look the word up in your dictionary.)
2. What is the meaning of "fledged" (line 2) and "rowen" (line 11)?
3. Once you understand the literal meaning of the poem, do you think that Longfellow intended any further significance to it?

Kay Ryan (b. 1945)

Mockingbird   2000

Nothing whole
is so bold,
we sense. Nothing
not cracked is
so exact and   5
of apiece. He's
the distempered
emperor of parts,
the king of patch,
the master of   10

pastiche, who so
hashes other birds'
laments, so minces
their capriccios, that
the dazzle of dispatch   15
displaces the originals.
As though brio
really does beat feeling,
the way two aces
beat three hearts   20
when it's cards
you're dealing.

Questions

1. What is the origin of the mockingbird's name? What does it tell us about the bird's song?
2. Look up "pastiche," "capriccio," and "brio" in the dictionary. What do those musical terms add to the poem?
3. What aspects of the mockingbird's song does the verb "hashes" (line 12) describe?
4. What does Ryan imply when she wonders if "brio / really does beat feeling"? What is the distinction the author draws between "brio" and "feeling"?
5. In poker, two aces obviously beat three hearts. Why do you think that Ryan reminds the reader that hearts can't win a game?
6. What seems to be Ryan's attitude toward the mockingbird?

Allusion

An **allusion** is an indirect reference to any person, place, or thing—fictitious, historical, or actual. Sometimes, to understand an allusion in a poem, we have to find out something we didn't know before. But usually the poet asks of us only common knowledge. When, in his poem "To Helen," Edgar Allan Poe refers to "the glory that was Greece / And the grandeur that was Rome," he assumes that we have heard of those places. He also expects that we will understand his allusion to the cultural achievements of those ancient nations and perhaps even catch the subtle contrast between those two similar words *glory* and *grandeur*, with its suggestion that, for all its merits, Roman civilization was also more pompous than Greek.

Allusions not only enrich the meaning of a poem, they also save space. In "The Love Song of J. Alfred Prufrock," T. S. Eliot, by giving a brief introductory quotation from the speech of a damned soul in Dante's *Inferno*, is able to suggest that his poem will be the confession of a soul in torment, who sees no chance of escape and who feels the need to confide in someone but trusts that his secrets will be kept safe.

Often in reading a poem, you will meet a name you don't recognize, on which the meaning of a line (or perhaps a whole poem) seems to depend. In this book, most such unfamiliar references and allusions are glossed or footnoted, but when you venture out on your own in reading poems, you may find yourself needlessly perplexed unless you look up such names, the way you look up any other words. Unless the name is one that the poet made up, you will probably find it in one of the larger desk dictionaries, such as *Merriam-Webster's Collegiate Dictionary* or the *American Heritage Dictionary*. If you don't solve your problem there, try an online search of the word or phrase as some allusions are quotations from other poems.

Exercise: **Catching Allusions**

From your knowledge, supplemented by a dictionary or other reference work if need be, explain the allusions in the following poems.

J. V. Cunningham (1911–1985)

Friend, on this scaffold Thomas More lies dead 1960

Friend, on this scaffold Thomas More lies dead
Who would not cut the Body from the Head.

Samuel Menashe (1925–2011)

Bread 1985

Thy will be done
By crust and crumb
And loaves left over
The sea is swollen
With the bread I throw   5
Upon the water

Questions

1. Can you identify the two allusions Menashe uses in this poem? (Hint: The first allusion occurs in line 1; the second in lines 5–6).
2. Paraphrase the content of the poem in a few sentences.
3. How do you think these references add meaning to this very short poem?

Carl Sandburg (1878–1967)

Grass 1918

Pile the bodies high at Austerlitz and Waterloo.
Shovel them under and let me work—
    I am the grass; I cover all.

And pile them high at Gettsyburg
And pile them high at Ypres and Verdun.   5
Shovel them under and let me work.

Two years, ten years, and passengers ask the conductor:
    What place is this?
    Where are we now?

I am the grass.   10
Let me work.

Questions

1. What do the five proper nouns in Sandburg's poem have in common?
2. How much does the reader need to understand about the allusions in "Grass" to appreciate their importance to the literal meaning of the poem?

WORD CHOICE AND WORD ORDER

Even if Samuel Johnson's famous *Dictionary* of 1755 had been as thick as Webster's unabridged, an eighteenth-century poet searching through it for words to use would have had a narrower choice. For in English literature of the neoclassical period, many poets subscribed to a belief in **poetic diction**: "A system of words," said Dr. Johnson, "refined from the grossness of domestic use." The system admitted into a serious poem only certain words and subjects, excluding others as violations of **decorum** (propriety). Accordingly, such common words as *rat, cheese, big, sneeze,* and *elbow,* although admissible to satire, were thought inconsistent with the loftiness of tragedy, epic, ode, and elegy. Dr. Johnson's biographer, James Boswell, tells how a poet writing an epic reconsidered the word "rats" and instead wrote "the whiskered vermin race." Johnson himself objected to Lady Macbeth's allusion to her "keen knife," saying that "we do not immediately conceive that any crime of importance is to be committed with a knife; or who does not, at last, from the long habit of connecting a knife with sordid offices, feel aversion rather than terror?"

Anglo-Saxon Versus Latinate Diction

When Wordsworth, in his Preface to *Lyrical Ballads,* asserted that "the language really spoken by men," especially by humble rustics, is plainer and more emphatic, and conveys "elementary feelings . . . in a state of greater simplicity," he was, in effect, advocating a new poetic diction. Wordsworth's ideas invited freshness into English poetry and, by admitting words that neoclassical poets would have called "low" ("His poor old *ankles* swell"), helped rid poets of the fear of being thought foolish for mentioning a commonplace.

This theory of the superiority of rural diction was, as Coleridge pointed out, hard to adhere to, and, in practice, Wordsworth was occasionally to write a language as Latinate and citified as these lines on yew trees:

> Huge trunks!—and each particular trunk a growth
> Of intertwisted fibers serpentine
> Up-coiling, and inveterately convolved . . .

Language so Latinate sounds pedantic to us, especially the phrase *inveterately convolved.* In fact, some poets, notably Gerard Manley Hopkins, have subscribed to the view that English words derived from Anglo-Saxon (Old English) have more force and flavor than their Latin equivalents. *Kingly,* one may feel, has more power than *regal.* One argument for this view is that so many words of Old English origin—*man, wife, child, house, eat, drink, sleep*—are basic to our living speech. Yet Latinate diction is not necessarily elevated. We use Latinate words every day, such as *station, office, order,* and *human.* None of these terms seem "inveterately convolved." Word choice is a subtle and flexible art.

Levels of Diction

When E. E. Cummings begins a poem, "mr youse needn't be so spry/concernin questions arty," we recognize another kind of diction available to poetry: **vulgate** (speech not much affected by schooling). Handbooks of grammar sometimes distinguish various **levels of diction.** A sort of ladder is imagined, on whose rungs words, phrases, and sentences may be ranked in an ascending order of formality, from the curses of an illiterate thug to the commencement-day address of a doctor of divinity. These levels range from vulgate through **colloquial** (the casual conversation or informal writing of literate people) and **general English** (most literate speech and writing, more studied than colloquial but not pretentious), up to **formal English** (the impersonal language of educated persons, usually only written, possibly spoken on dignified occasions). Recently, however, lexicographers have been shunning such labels. The designation *colloquial* was expelled from *Webster's Third New International Dictionary* on the grounds that "it is impossible to know whether a word out of context is colloquial or not" and that the diction of Americans nowadays is more fluid than the labels suggest. Aware that we are being unscientific, we may find the labels useful. They may help roughly to describe what happens when, as in the following poem, a poet shifts from one level of usage to another.

Robert Herrick (1591–1674)

Upon Julia's Clothes   1648

Whenas in silks my Julia goes,
Then, then, methinks, how sweetly flows
That liquefaction of her clothes.

Next, when I cast mine eyes and see
That brave vibration each way free,   5
O how that glittering taketh me!

Even in so short a poem as "Upon Julia's Clothes," we see how a sudden shift in the level of diction can produce a surprising and memorable effect. One word in each stanza—*liquefaction* in the first, *vibration* in the second—stands out from the standard, but not extravagant, language that surrounds it. Try to imagine the entire poem being written in such formal English, in mostly unfamiliar words of several syllables each: the result, in all likelihood, would be merely an oddity, and a turgid one at that. But by using such terms sparingly, Herrick allows them to take on a greater strength and significance through their contrast with the words that surround them. It is *liquefaction* in particular that strikes the reader: like a great catch by an outfielder, it impresses both for its appropriateness in the situation and for its sheer beauty as a demonstration of superior skill. Once we have read the poem, we realize that the effect would be severely compromised, if not ruined, by the substitution of any other word in its place.

Dialect

At present, most poetry in English avoids elaborate literary expressions such as "fleecy care" in favor of more colloquial language. In many English-speaking areas, such as Scotland, there has even been a movement to write poems in regional dialects. (A **dialect** is a particular variety of language spoken by an identifiable regional group or social class of persons.) Dialect poets frequently try to capture the freshness and authenticity of the language spoken in their immediate locale.

Sentence Structure

Not only the poet's choice of words makes a poem seem more formal, or less, but also the way the words are arranged into sentences. Compare these lines

Jack and Jill went up the hill
To fetch a pail of water.
Jack fell down and broke his crown
And Jill came tumbling after.

with Milton's account of a more significant downfall:

> Earth trembled from her entrails, as again
> In pangs, and Nature gave a second groan;
> Sky loured and, muttering thunder, some sad drops
> Wept at completing of the mortal sin
> Original; while Adam took no thought,
> Eating his fill, nor Eve to iterate
> Her former trespass feared, the more to soothe
> Him with her loved society, that now
> As with new wine intoxicated both
> They swim in mirth, and fancy that they feel
> Divinity within them breeding wings
> Wherewith to scorn the Earth.

Not all the words in Milton's lines are bookish: indeed, many of them can be found in nursery rimes. What helps, besides diction, to distinguish this account of the biblical fall from "Jack and Jill" is that Milton's nonstop sentence seems further removed from usual speech in its length (83 words), in its complexity (subordinate clauses), and in its word order ("with new wine intoxicated both" rather than "both intoxicated with new wine"). Should we think less (or more) highly of Milton for choosing a style so elaborate and formal? No judgment need be passed: both Mother Goose and the author of *Paradise Lost* use language appropriate to their purposes.

Coleridge offered two "homely definitions of prose and poetry; that is, *prose:* words in their best order; *poetry:* the best words in the best order." If all goes well, a poet may fasten the right word into the right place, and the result may be—as T. S. Eliot said in "Little Gidding"—a "complete consort dancing together."

Thomas Hardy (1840–1928)

The Ruined Maid

1901

"O 'Melia, my dear, this does everything crown!
Who could have supposed I should meet you in Town?
And whence such fair garments, such prosperi-ty?"—
"O didn't you know I'd been ruined?" said she.

—"You left us in tatters, without shoes or socks,
Tired of digging potatoes, and spudding up docks;°   *spading up dockweed*   5
And now you've gay bracelets and bright feathers three!"—
"Yes: that's how we dress when we're ruined," said she.

—"At home in the barton° you said 'thee' and 'thou,'   *farmyard*
And 'thik oon,' and 'theäs oon,' and 't'other'; but now   10
Your talking quite fits 'ee for high compa-ny!"—
"Some polish is gained with one's ruin," said she.

—"Your hands were like paws then, your face blue and bleak
But now I'm bewitched by your delicate cheek,
And your little gloves fit as on any la-dy!"—   15
"We never do work when we're ruined," said she.

—"You used to call home-life a hag-ridden dream,
And you'd sigh, and you'd sock;° but at present you seem   *groan*
To know not of megrims° or melancho-ly!"—   *blues*
"True. One's pretty lively when ruined," said she.   20

—"I wish I had feathers, a fine sweeping gown,
And a delicate face, and could strut about Town!"—
"My dear—a raw country girl, such as you be,
Cannot quite expect that. You ain't ruined," said she.

Questions

1. Where does this dialogue take place? Who are the two speakers?
2. Comment on Hardy's use of the word *ruined*. What is the conventional meaning of the word when applied to a woman? As 'Melia applies it to herself, what is its meaning?
3. Sum up the attitude of each speaker toward the other. What details of the new 'Melia does the first speaker most dwell on? Would you expect Hardy to be so impressed by all these details, or is there, between his view of the characters and their view of themselves, any hint of an ironic discrepancy?
4. In losing her country dialect ("thik oon" and "theäs oon" for "this one" and "that one"), 'Melia is presumed to have gained in sophistication. What does Hardy suggest by her "ain't" in the last line?

Wendy Cope (b. 1945)

Lonely Hearts   1986

Can someone make my simple wish come true?
Male biker seeks female for touring fun.
Do you live in North London? Is it you?

Gay vegetarian whose friends are few,
I'm into music, Shakespeare and the sun.   5
Can someone make my simple wish come true?

Executive in search of something new—
Perhaps bisexual woman, arty, young.
Do you live in North London? Is it you?

Successful, straight and solvent? I am too—   10
Attractive Jewish lady with a son.
Can someone make my simple wish come true?

I'm Libran, inexperienced and blue—
Need slim non-smoker, under twenty-one.
Do you live in North London? Is it you?   15

Please write (with photo) to Box 152.
Who knows where it may lead once we've begun?
Can someone make my simple wish come true?
Do you live in North London? Is it you?

LONELY HEARTS. This poem has a double form: the rhetorical, a series of "lonely heart" personal ads from a newspaper, and metrical, a **villanelle,** a fixed form developed by French courtly poets in imitation of Italian folk song. For other villanelles, see Elizabeth Bishop's "One Art" (page 758) and Dylan Thomas's "Do not go gentle into that good night" (page 659). In the villanelle, the first and the third lines are repeated in a set pattern throughout the poem.

Questions

1. What sort of language does Wendy Cope borrow for this poem?
2. The form of the villanelle requires that the poet end each stanza with one of two repeating lines. What special use does the author make of these mandatory repetitions?
3. How many speakers are there in the poem? Does the author's voice ever enter or is the entire poem spoken by individuals in personal ads?
4. The poem seems to begin satirically. Does the poem ever move beyond the critical, mocking tone typical of satire?

FOR REVIEW AND FURTHER STUDY

E. E. Cummings (1894–1962)

anyone lived in a pretty how town   1940

anyone lived in a pretty how town
(with up so floating many bells down)
spring summer autumn winter
he sang his didn't he danced his did.

Women and men(both little and small)   5
cared for anyone not at all
they sowed their isn't they reaped their same
sun moon stars rain

children guessed(but only a few
and down they forgot as up they grew   10
autumn winter spring summer)
that noone loved him more by more

when by now and tree by leaf
she laughed his joy she cried his grief
bird by snow and stir by still   15
anyone's any was all to her

someones married their everyones
laughed their cryings and did their dance
(sleep wake hope and then)they
said their nevers they slept their dream   20

stars rain sun moon
(and only the snow can begin to explain
how children are apt to forget to remember
with up so floating many bells down)

one day anyone died i guess   25
(and noone stooped to kiss his face)

busy folk buried them side by side
little by little and was by was

all by all and deep by deep
and more by more they dream their sleep   30
noone and anyone earth by april
wish by spirit and if by yes.

Women and men(both dong and ding)
summer autumn winter spring
reaped their sowing and went their came   35
sun moon stars rain

Questions

1. Summarize the story told in this poem. Who are the characters?
2. Rearrange the words in the two opening lines into the order you would expect them usually to follow. What effect does Cummings obtain by his unconventional word order?
3. Another of Cummings's strategies is to use one part of speech as if it were another; for instance, in line 4, *didn't* and *did* ordinarily are verbs, but here they are used as nouns. What other words in the poem perform functions other than their expected ones?

Billy Collins (b. 1941)

The Names   2002

Yesterday, I lay awake in the palm of the night.
A soft rain stole in, unhelped by any breeze,
And when I saw the silver glaze on the windows,
I started with A, with Ackerman, as it happened,
Then Baxter and Calabro,   5
Davis and Eberling, names falling into place
As droplets fell through the dark.

Names printed on the ceiling of the night.
Names slipping around a watery bend.
Twenty-six willows on the banks of a stream.   10

In the morning, I walked out barefoot
Among thousands of flowers
Heavy with dew like the eyes of tears,
And each had a name—
Fiori inscribed on a yellow petal   15
Then Gonzalez and Han, Ishikawa and Jenkins.

Names written in the air
And stitched into the cloth of the day.
A name under a photograph taped to a mailbox.
Monogram on a torn shirt,   20
I see you spelled out on storefront windows
And on the bright unfurled awnings of this city.
I say the syllables as I turn a corner—
Kelly and Lee,
Medina, Nardella, and O'Connor.   25

When I peer into the woods,
I see a thick tangle where letters are hidden
As in a puzzle concocted for children.
Parker and Quigley in the twigs of an ash,
Rizzo, Schubert, Torres, and Upton,   30
Secrets in the boughs of an ancient maple.

Names written in the pale sky.
Names rising in the updraft amid buildings.
Names silent in stone
Or cried out behind a door.   35
Names blown over the earth and out to sea.

In the evening—weakening light, the last swallows.
A boy on a lake lifts his oars.
A woman by a window puts a match to a candle,
And the names are outlined on the rose clouds—   40
Vanacore and Wallace,
(let X stand, if it can, for the ones unfound)
Then Young and Ziminsky, the final jolt of Z.

Names etched on the head of a pin.
One name spanning a bridge, another undergoing a tunnel.   45
A blue name needled into the skin.
Names of citizens, workers, mothers and fathers,
The bright-eyed daughter, the quick son.
Alphabet of names in a green field.
Names in the small tracks of birds.   50
Names lifted from a hat
Or balanced on the tip of the tongue.
Names wheeled into the dim warehouse of memory.
So many names, there is barely room on the walls of the heart.

THE NAMES. This poem originally appeared in the *New York Times* on September 11, 2002. On that same day its author, the Poet Laureate of the United States, read the poem before a joint session of Congress specially convened in New York City to mark the one-year anniversary of the attack on the World Trade Center.

Questions

1. Occasional poetry—verse written to commemorate a public or historical occasion—is generally held in low esteem because such poems tend to be self-important and over-written. Does Collins avoid these pitfalls?
2. Discuss the level of diction in "The Names." Is it appropriate to the subject? Explain.

Exercise: Different Kinds of English

Read the following poems and see what kinds of diction and word order you find in them. Which poems are least formal in their language and which most formal? Is there any use of vulgate English? Any dialect? What does each poem achieve that its own kind of English makes possible?

Anonymous (American oral verse)

Carnation Milk (about 1900?)

Carnation Milk is the best in the land;
Here I sit with a can in my hand—
No tits to pull, no hay to pitch,
You just punch a hole in the son of a bitch.

CARNATION MILK. "This quatrain is imagined as the caption under a picture of a rugged-looking cowboy seated upon a bale of hay," notes William Harmon in his *Oxford Book of American Light Verse* (New York: Oxford UP, 1979). Possibly the first to print this work was David Ogilvy (1911–1999), who quotes it in his *Confessions of an Advertising Man* (New York: Atheneum, 1963).

Gina Valdés (b. 1943)

English con Salsa 1993

Welcome to ESL 100, English Surely Latinized,
inglés con chile y cilantro, English as American
as Benito Juárez. Welcome, muchachos from Xochicalco,
learn the language of dólares and Dolores, of kings
and queens, of Donald Duck and Batman. Holy Toluca!   5
In four months you'll be speaking like George Washington,
in four weeks you can ask, More coffee? In two months
you can say, May I take your order? In one year you
can ask for a raise, cool as the Tuxpan River.

Welcome, muchachas from Teocaltiche, in this class   10
we speak English refrito, English con sal y limón,
English thick as mango juice, English poured from
a clay jug, English tuned like a requinto from Uruapan,
English lighted by Oaxacan dawns, English spiked
with mezcal from Mitla, English with a red cactus   15
flower blooming in its heart.

Welcome, welcome, amigos del sur, bring your Zapotec
tongues, your Nahuatl tones, your patience of pyramids,
your red suns and golden moons, your guardian angels,
your duendes, your patron saints, Santa Tristeza,   20
Santa Alegría, Santo Todolopuede. We will sprinkle
holy water on pronouns, make the sign of the cross
on past participles, jump like fish from Lake Pátzcuaro
on gerunds, pour tequila from Jalisco on future perfects,
say shoes and shit, grab a cool verb and a pollo loco   25
and dance on the walls like chapulines.

When a teacher from La Jolla or a cowboy from Santee
asks you, Do you speak English? You'll answer, Sí,
yes, simón, of course, I love English!
                              And you'll hum
A Mixtec chant that touches la tierra and the heavens.   30

ENGLISH CON SALSA. 3 *Benito Juárez:* Mexican statesman (1806–1872), president of Mexico in the 1860s and 1870s.

Lewis Carroll
[Charles Lutwidge Dodgson] (1832–1898)

Jabberwocky   1871

'Twas brillig, and the slithy toves
    Did gyre and gimble in the wabe:
All mimsy were the borogoves,
    And the mome raths outgrabe.

"Beware the Jabberwock, my son!   5
    The jaws that bite, the claws that catch!
Beware the Jubjub bird, and shun
    The frumious Bandersnatch!"

He took his vorpal sword in hand:
    Long time the manxome foe he sought—   10
So rested he by the Tumtum tree
    And stood awhile in thought.

And, as in uffish thought he stood,
    The Jabberwock, with eyes of flame,
Came whiffling through the tulgey wood,   15
    And burbled as it came!

One, two! One, two! And through and through
    The vorpal blade went snicker-snack!
He left it dead, and with its head
    He went galumphing back.   20

"And hast thou slain the Jabberwock?
    Come to my arms, my beamish boy!
O frabjous day! Callooh, Callay!"
    He chortled in his joy.

'Twas brillig, and the slithy toves   25
    Did gyre and gimble in the wabe:
All mimsy were the borogoves,
    And the mome raths outgrabe.

JABBERWOCKY. Fussy about pronunciation, Carroll in his preface to *The Hunting of the Snark* declares: "The first 'o' in 'borogoves' is pronounced like the 'o' in 'borrow.' I have heard people try to give it the sound of the 'o' in 'worry.' Such is Human Perversity." *Toves*, he adds, rimes with *groves*.

Questions

1. Look up *chortled* (line 24) in your dictionary and find out its definition and origin.
2. In *Through the Looking Glass*, Alice seeks the aid of Humpty Dumpty to decipher the meaning of this nonsense poem. "*Brillig*," he explains, "means four o'clock in the afternoon—the time when you begin *broiling* things for dinner." Does "brillig" sound like any other familiar word?
3. "*Slithy*," the explanation goes on, "means 'lithe and slimy.' 'Lithe' is the same as 'active.' You see it's like a portmanteau—there are two meanings packed up into one word." "Mimsy" is supposed to pack together both "flimsy" and "miserable." In the rest of the poem, what other portmanteau—or packed suitcase—words can you find?

■ WRITING *effectively*

Lewis Carroll on Writing

Humpty Dumpty Explicates "Jabberwocky" 1871

"You seem very clever at explaining words, Sir," said Alice. "Would you kindly tell me the meaning of the poem called 'Jabberwocky'?"

"Let's hear it," said Humpty Dumpty. "I can explain all the poems that ever were invented—and a good many that haven't been invented just yet."

This sounded very hopeful, so Alice repeated the first verse:—

Lewis Carroll

"'Twas brillig, and the slithy toves
  Did gyre and gimble in the wabe:
All mimsy were the borogoves,
  And the mome raths outgrabe."

"That's enough to begin with," Humpty Dumpty interrupted: "there are plenty of hard words there. '*Brillig*' means four o'clock in the afternoon—the time when you begin *broiling* things for dinner."

"That'll do very well," said Alice. "And '*slithy*'?"

"Well, '*slithy*' means 'lithe and slimy.' 'Lithe' is the same as 'active.' You see it's like a portmanteau—there are two meanings packed up into one word."

"I see it now," Alice remarked thoughtfully. "And what are '*toves*'?"

"Well, '*toves*' are something like badgers—they're something like lizards—and they're something like corkscrews."

"They must be very curious-looking creatures."

"They are that," said Humpty Dumpty, "also they make their nests under sundials—also they live on cheese."

"And what's to '*gyre*' and to '*gimble*'?"

"To '*gyre*' is to go round and round like a gyroscope. To '*gimble*' is to make holes like a gimlet."

"And '*the wabe*' is the grass-plot round a sun-dial, I suppose?" said Alice, surprised at her own ingenuity.

"Of course it is. It's called '*wabe*,' you know, because it goes a long way before it, and a long way behind it."

"And a long way beyond it on each side," Alice added.

"Exactly so. Well, then, '*mimsy*' is 'flimsy and miserable' (there's another portmanteau for you). And a '*borogove*' is a thin shabby-looking bird with its feathers sticking out all round—something like a live mop."

"And then '*mome raths*'?" said Alice. "I'm afraid I'm giving you a great deal of trouble."

"Well, a '*rath*' is a sort of green pig: but '*mome*' I'm not certain about. I think it's short for 'from home'—meaning that they'd lost their way, you know."

"And what does '*outgrabe*' mean?"

"Well, 'outgribing' is something between bellowing and whistling, with a kind of sneeze in the middle: however, you'll hear it done, maybe—down in the wood yonder—and, when you've once heard it, you'll be *quite* content. Who's been repeating all that hard stuff to you?"

"I read it in a book," said Alice.

From *Through the Looking Glass*

Humpty Dumpty Explicates "Jabberwocky." This celebrated passage is the origin of the term **portmanteau word,** an artificial word that combines parts of other words to express some combination of their qualities. (*Brunch,* for example, is a meal that combines aspects of both breakfast and lunch.) A portmanteau is a large suitcase that opens up into two separate compartments.

THINKING ABOUT DICTION

Although a poem may contain images and ideas, it is made up of words. Language is the medium of poetry, and a poem's diction—its exact wording—is the chief source of its power. Writers labor to shape each word and phrase to create particular effects. Poets choose words for their meanings, their associations, and even their sounds. Changing a single word may ruin a poem's effect, just as changing one number in an online password makes all the other numbers useless.

▪ **As you prepare to write about a poem, ask yourself if some particular word or combination of words gives you particular pleasure or especially intrigues you.** Don't worry yet about why the word or words impress you. Don't even worry about the meaning. Just underline the words in your book.

▪ **Try to determine what about the word or phrase commanded your attention.** Maybe a word strikes you as being unexpected but just right. A phrase might seem especially musical or it might call forth a vivid picture in your imagination.

▪ **Consider your underlined words and phrases in the context of the poem.** How does each relate to the words around it? What does it add to the poem?

▪ **Think about the poem as a whole.** What sort of language does it rely on? Many poems favor the plain, straightforward language people use in everyday conversation, but others reach for more elegant diction. Choices such as these contribute to the poem's distinctive flavor, as well as to its ultimate meaning.

CHECKLIST: Writing About Diction

- ☐ As you read, underline words or phrases that appeal to you or seem especially significant.
- ☐ What is it about each underlined word or phrase that appeals to you?
- ☐ How does the word or phrase relate to the other lines? What does it contribute to the poem's effect?
- ☐ How does the sound of a word you've chosen add to the poem's mood?
- ☐ What would be lost if synonyms were substituted for your favorite words?
- ☐ What sort of diction does the poem use? Conversational? Lofty? Monosyllabic? Polysyllabic? Concrete? Abstract?
- ☐ How does diction contribute to the poem's flavor and meaning?

WRITING ASSIGNMENT ON WORD CHOICE

Find two poems in this book that use very different sorts of diction to address similar subjects. You might choose one with formal and elegant language and another with very down-to-earth or slangy word choices. Some good choices include John Milton's "When I consider how my light is spent" and Seamus Heaney's "Digging"; Dylan Thomas's "Do not go gentle into that good night" and Ted Kooser's "Carrie"; and Robert Hayden's "Frederick Douglass" and Langston Hughes's "I, Too." In a short essay (750 to 1000 words), discuss how the difference in diction affects the tones of the two poems.

MORE TOPICS FOR WRITING

1. Browse through the chapter "Poems for Further Reading," for a poem that catches your interest. Within that poem, find a word or phrase that particularly intrigues you. Write a paragraph on what the word or phrase adds to the poem, how it shades the meaning and contributes to the overall effect.

2. Choose a brief poem from this chapter. Type the poem out, substituting synonyms for each of its nouns and verbs, using a thesaurus if necessary. Next, write a one-page analysis of the difference in feel and meaning between the original and your creation.

3. Choose a poem that strikes you as particularly inventive or unusual in its language, such as E. E. Cummings's "anyone lived in a pretty how town," Gerard Manley Hopkins's "The Windhover," or Wendy Cope's "Lonely Hearts," and write a brief analysis of it. Concentrate on the diction of the poem and word order. For what possible purposes does the poet depart from standard English or incorporate unusual vocabulary?

4. Writers are notorious word junkies who often jot down interesting words they stumble across in daily life. Over the course of a day, keep a list of any intriguing words you run across in your reading, music listening, or television viewing. Even street signs and advertisements can supply surprising words. After twenty-four hours of list-keeping, choose your five favorites. Write a five line poem, incorporating your five words, letting them take you where they will. Then write a page-long description of the process. What appealed to you in the words you chose? What did you learn about the process of composing a poem?

► TERMS FOR *review*

Diction and Allusion

Diction ► Word choice or vocabulary. *Diction* refers to the class of words that an author chooses as appropriate for a particular work.

Concrete diction ► Words that specifically name or describe things or persons. Concrete words refer to what we can immediately perceive with our senses.

Abstract diction ► Words that express general ideas or concepts.

Poetic diction ► Strictly speaking, *poetic diction* means any language deemed suitable for verse, but the term generally refers to elevated language intended for poetry rather than common use.

Allusion ► A brief, sometimes indirect, reference in a text to a person, place, or thing. Allusions imply a common body of knowledge between reader and writer and act as a literary shorthand to enrich the meaning of a text.

Levels of Diction

Vulgate ► The lowest level of diction, vulgate is the language of the common people. Not necessarily containing foul or inappropriate language, it refers simply to unschooled, everyday speech. The term comes from the Latin word *vulgus*, "mob" or "common people."

Colloquial English ► The casual or informal but correct language of ordinary native speakers. Conversational in tone, it may include contractions, slang, and shifts in grammar, vocabulary, and diction.

General English ► The ordinary speech of educated native speakers. Most literate speech and writing is general English. Its diction is more educated than **colloquial English,** yet not as elevated as **formal English.**

Formal English ► The heightened, impersonal language of educated persons, usually only written, although possibly spoken on dignified occasions.

Dialect ► A particular variety of language spoken by an identifiable regional group or social class.

15 SAYING AND SUGGESTING

*To name an object is to take away three-fourths
of the pleasure given by a poem. . . .
to suggest it, that is the ideal.*

—STÉPHANE MALLARMÉ

To write so clearly that they might bring "all things as near the mathematical plainness" as possible—that was the goal of scientists, according to Bishop Thomas Sprat, who lived in the seventeenth century. Such an effort would seem bound to fail, because words, unlike numbers, are ambiguous indicators. Although it may have troubled Bishop Sprat, the tendency of a word to have multiplicity of meaning rather than mathematical plainness opens broad avenues to poetry.

DENOTATION AND CONNOTATION

Every word has at least one **denotation:** a meaning as defined in a dictionary. But the English language has many a common word with so many denotations that a reader may need to think twice to see what it means in a specific context. The noun *field,* for instance, can denote a piece of ground, a sports arena, the scene of a battle, part of a flag, a profession, and a number system in mathematics. Further, the word can be used as a verb ("he fielded a grounder") or an adjective ("field trip," "field glasses").

A word also has **connotations:** overtones or suggestions of additional meaning that it gains from all the contexts in which we have met it in the past. The word *skeleton,* according to a dictionary, denotes "the bony framework of a human being or other vertebrate animal, which supports the flesh and protects the organs." But by its associations, the word can rouse thoughts of war, of disease and death, or (possibly) of one's plans to go to medical school. Think, too, of the difference between "Old Doc Jones" and "Theodore E. Jones, M.D." In the mind's eye, the former appears in his shirtsleeves; the latter has a gold nameplate on his door.

That some words denote the same thing but have sharply different connotations is pointed out in this anonymous Victorian jingle:

Here's a little ditty that you really ought to know:
Horses "sweat" and men "perspire," but ladies only "glow."

The terms *druggist*, *pharmacist*, and *apothecary* all denote the same occupation, but apothecaries lay claim to special distinction.

Poets aren't the only people who care about the connotations of language. Advertisers know that connotations make money. Nowadays many automobile dealers advertise their secondhand cars not as "used" but as "pre-owned," as if fearing that "used car" would connote an old heap with soiled upholstery and mysterious engine troubles. "Pre-owned," however, suggests that the previous owner has kindly taken the trouble of breaking in the car for you. Not long ago prune-packers, alarmed by a slump in sales, sponsored a survey to determine the connotations of prunes in the public consciousness. Asked, "What do you think of when you hear the word *prunes?*" most people replied, "dried up," "wrinkled," or "constipated." Dismayed, the packers hired an advertising agency to create a new image for prunes, in hopes of inducing new connotations. Soon, advertisements began to show prunes in brightly colored settings, in the company of bikinied bathing beauties.

In imaginative writing, connotations are as crucial as they are in advertising. Consider this sentence: "A new brand of journalism is being born, or spawned" (Dwight Macdonald writing in the *New York Review of Books*). The last word, by its associations with fish and crustaceans, suggests that this new journalism is scarcely the product of human beings.

Here is a famous poem rich in connotations.

William Blake (1757–1827)

London   1794

I wander through each chartered street,
Near where the chartered Thames does flow,
And mark in every face I meet
Marks of weakness, marks of woe.

In every cry of every man,   5
In every infant's cry of fear,
In every voice, in every ban,
The mind-forged manacles I hear.

How the chimney-sweeper's cry
Every black'ning church appalls   10
And the hapless soldier's sigh
Runs in blood down palace walls.

But most through midnight streets I hear
How the youthful harlot's curse
Blasts the new-born infant's tear   15
And blights with plagues the marriage hearse.

Here are only a few of the possible meanings of four of Blake's words:

- **chartered** (lines 1, 2)

  Denotations: Established by a charter (a written grant or a certificate of incorporation); leased or hired.

Connotations: Defined, limited, restricted, channeled, mapped, bound by law; bought and sold (like a slave or an inanimate object); Magna Carta; charters given to crown colonies by the King.

Other words in the poem with similar connotations: Ban, which can denote (1) a legal prohibition; (2) a churchman's curse or malediction; (3) in medieval times, an order summoning a king's vassals to fight for him. *Manacles,* or shackles, restrain movement. *Chimney-sweeper, soldier,* and *harlot* are all hirelings.

Interpretation of the lines: The street has had mapped out for it the direction in which it must go; the Thames has had laid down to it the course it must follow. Street and river are channeled, imprisoned, enslaved (like every inhabitant of London).

- *black'ning* (line 10)

Denotation: Becoming black.

Connotations: The darkening of something once light, the defilement of something once clean, the deepening of guilt, the gathering of darkness at the approach of night.

Other words in the poem with similar connotations: Objects becoming marked or smudged (*marks of weakness, marks of woe* in the faces of passersby; bloodied walls of a palace; marriage blighted with plagues); the word *appalls* (denoting not only "to overcome with horror" but "to make pale" and also "to cast a pall or shroud over"); *midnight streets.*

Interpretation of the line: Literally, every London church grows black from soot and hires a chimney-sweeper (a small boy) to help clean it. But Blake suggests too that by profiting from the suffering of the child laborer, the church is soiling its original purity.

- *Blasts, blights* (lines 15, 16)

Denotations: Both *blast* and *blight* mean "to cause to wither" or "to ruin and destroy." Both are terms from horticulture. Frost *blasts* a bud and kills it; disease *blights* a growing plant.

Connotations: Sickness and death; gardens shriveled and dying; gusts of wind and the ravages of insects; things blown to pieces or rotted and warped.

Other words in the poem with similar connotations: Faces marked with weakness and woe; the child becomes a chimney-sweep; the soldier killed by war; blackening church and bloodied palace; young girl turned harlot; wedding carriage transformed into a hearse.

Interpretation of the lines: Literally, the harlot spreads the plague of syphilis, which, carried into marriage, can cause a baby to be born blind. In a larger and more meaningful sense, Blake sees the prostitution of even one young girl corrupting the entire institution of matrimony and endangering every child.

Some of these connotations are more to the point than others; the reader of a poem nearly always has the problem of distinguishing relevant associations from irrelevant ones. We need to read a poem in its entirety and, when a word leaves us in doubt, look for other things in the poem to corroborate or refute what we think it means. Relatively simple and direct in its statement, Blake's account of his stroll through the city at night becomes an indictment of a whole social and religious order. The indictment could hardly be this effective if it were "mathematically plain," its every word restricted to one denotation clearly spelled out.

Wallace Stevens (1879–1955)

Disillusionment of Ten O'Clock   1923

The houses are haunted
By white night-gowns.
None are green,
Or purple with green rings,
Or green with yellow rings,   5
Or yellow with blue rings.
None of them are strange,
With socks of lace
And beaded ceintures.
People are not going   10
To dream of baboons and periwinkles.
Only, here and there, an old sailor,
Drunk and asleep in his boots,
Catches tigers
In red weather.   15

Questions

1. What are "beaded ceintures"? What does the phrase suggest?
2. What contrast does Stevens draw between the people who live in these houses and the old sailor? What do the connotations of "white night-gowns" and "sailor" add to this contrast?
3. What is lacking in these people who wear white night-gowns? Why should the poet's view of them be a "disillusionment"?

Gwendolyn Brooks (1917–2000)

The Bean Eaters   1960

They eat beans mostly, this old yellow pair.
Dinner is a casual affair.
Plain chipware on a plain and creaking wood,
Tin flatware.

Two who are Mostly Good.   5
Two who have lived their day,
But keep on putting on their clothes
And putting things away.

And remembering . . .
Remembering, with twinklings and twinges,   10
As they lean over the beans in their rented back room that is full of
        beads and receipts and dolls and cloths, tobacco crumbs, vases and fringes.

Questions

1. What do we infer about this old couple and their lifestyle from the details in lines 1–4 about their diet, dishes, dinner table, and cutlery?
2. How would you describe the tone of the second stanza? What attitude toward the couple does it seem to take?
3. In that long last line, what is suggested by the things they have saved and stored?

E. E. Cummings (1894–1962)

next to of course god america i

1926

"next to of course god america i
love you land of the pilgrims' and so forth oh
say can you see by the dawn's early my
country 'tis of centuries come and go
and are no more what of it we should worry   5
in every language even deafanddumb
thy sons acclaim your glorious name by gorry
by jingo by gee by gosh by gum
why talk of beauty what could be more beaut-
iful than these heroic happy dead   10
who rushed like lions to the roaring slaughter
they did not stop to think they died instead
then shall the voice of liberty be mute?"

He spoke. And drank rapidly a glass of water

Questions

1. How many allusions in this poem can you identify? What do all the sources of those allusions have in common?
2. Look up the origin of "jingo" (line 8). Is it used here as more than just a mindless exclamation?
3. Beyond what is actually said, what do the rhetoric of the first thirteen lines and the description in the last one suggest about the author's intentions in this poem?

Robert Frost (1874–1963)

Fire and Ice

1923

Some say the world will end in fire,
Some say in ice.
From what I've tasted of desire
I hold with those who favor fire.
But if it had to perish twice,   5
I think I know enough of hate
To say that for destruction ice
Is also great
And would suffice.

Questions

1. To whom does Frost refer in line 1? In line 2?
2. What connotations of "fire" and "ice" contribute to the richness of Frost's comparison?

Diane Thiel (b. 1967)

The Minefield

2000

He was running with his friend from town to town.
They were somewhere between Prague and Dresden.
He was fourteen. His friend was faster

and knew a shortcut through the fields they could take.
He said there was lettuce growing in one of them,   5
and they hadn't eaten all day. His friend ran a few lengths ahead,
like a wild rabbit across the grass,
turned his head, looked back once,
and his body was scattered across the field.

My father told us this, one night,   10
and then continued eating dinner.

He brought them with him—the minefields.
He carried them underneath his good intentions.
He gave them to us—in the volume of his anger,
in the bruises we covered up with sleeves.   15
In the way he threw anything against the wall—
a radio, that wasn't even ours,
a melon, once, opened like a head.
In the way we still expect, years later and continents away,
that anything might explode at any time,   20
and we would have to run on alone
with a vision like that
only seconds behind.

Questions

1. In the opening lines of the poem, a seemingly small decision—to take a shortcut and find something to eat—leads to a horrifying result. What does this suggest about the poem's larger view of what life is like?
2. The speaker tells the story of the minefield before letting us know that the other boy was her father. What is the effect of this narrative strategy?
3. How does the image of the melon reinforce the poem's intentions?

H.D. [*Hilda Doolittle*] (1886–1961)

Storm   1916

You crash over the trees,
you crack the live branch—
the branch is white,
the green crushed,
each leaf is rent like split wood.   5

You burden the trees
with black drops,
you swirl and crash—
you have broken off a weighted leaf
in the wind,   10
it is hurled out,
whirls up and sinks,
a green stone.

Questions

1. What effect is achieved by the speaker addressing the storm directly?
2. It could be maintained that the poem communicates principally through its verbs. After listing all the verbs, discuss whether you agree with this claim.
3. The poet addresses the storm as "you." What does this word choice imply?
4. The poem literally describes a violent storm. Does it suggest anything else to you?

Alfred, Lord Tennyson (1809–1892)

Tears, Idle Tears 1847

Tears, idle tears, I know not what they mean,
Tears from the depth of some divine despair
Rise in the heart, and gather to the eyes,
In looking on the happy Autumn-fields,
And thinking of the days that are no more. 5

Fresh as the first beam glittering on a sail,
That brings our friends up from the underworld,
Sad as the last which reddens over one
That sinks with all we love below the verge;
So sad, so fresh, the days that are no more. 10

Ah, sad and strange as in dark summer dawns
The earliest pipe of half-awakened birds
To dying ears, when unto dying eyes
The casement slowly grows a glimmering square;
So sad, so strange, the days that are no more. 15

Dear as remembered kisses after death,
And sweet as those by hopeless fancy feigned
On lips that are for others; deep as love,
Deep as first love, and wild with all regret;
O Death in Life, the days that are no more. 20

Richard Wilbur (b. 1921)

Love Calls Us to the Things of This World 1956

The eyes open to a cry of pulleys,
And spirited from sleep, the astounded soul
Hangs for a moment bodiless and simple
As false dawn.
         Outside the open window
The morning air is all awash with angels. 5

Some are in bed-sheets, some are in blouses,
Some are in smocks: but truly there they are.
Now they are rising together in calm swells
Of halcyon feeling, filling whatever they wear
With the deep joy of their impersonal breathing; 10

Now they are flying in place, conveying
The terrible speed of their omnipresence, moving
And staying like white water; and now of a sudden
They swoon down into so rapt a quiet
That nobody seems to be there.
                              The soul shrinks   15

From all that it is about to remember,
From the punctual rape of every blessèd day,
And cries,
          "Oh, let there be nothing on earth but laundry,
Nothing but rosy hands in the rising steam
And clear dances done in the sight of heaven."   20

Yet, as the sun acknowledges
With a warm look the world's hunks and colors,
The soul descends once more in bitter love
To accept the waking body, saying now
In a changed voice as the man yawns and rises,   25

"Bring them down from their ruddy gallows;
Let there be clean linen for the backs of thieves;
Let lovers go fresh and sweet to be undone,
And the heaviest nuns walk in a pure floating
Of dark habits,
                keeping their difficult balance."   30

LOVE CALLS US TO THE THINGS OF THIS WORLD. Wilbur once said that his title was taken from St. Augustine, but in a later interview he admitted that neither he nor any critic has ever been able to locate the quotation. Whatever its source, however, the title establishes the poem's central idea that love allows us to return from the divine world of the spirit to the imperfect world of our everyday lives. Wilbur's own comments on the poem appear after the questions that follow here.

Questions

1. What are the "angels" in line 5? Why does this metaphor seem appropriate to the situation?
2. What is "the punctual rape of every blessèd day?" Who is being raped? Who or what commits the rape? Why would Wilbur choose this particular word with all its violent associations?
3. Whom or what does the soul love in line 23, and why is that love bitter?
4. Is it merely obesity that make the nuns' balance "difficult" in the two final lines of the poem? What other "balance" does Wilbur's poem suggest?
5. The soul has two speeches in the poem. How do they differ in tone and imagery?
6. The spiritual world is traditionally considered invisible. What concrete images does Wilbur use to express its special character?

WRITING *effectively*

Richard Wilbur on Writing

Concerning "Love Calls Us to the Things of This World"

1966

Richard Wilbur

If I understand this poem rightly, it has a free and organic rhythm: that is to say, its movement arises naturally from the emotion, and from the things and actions described. At the same time, the lines are metrical and disposed in stanzas. The subject matter is both exalted and vulgar. There is, I should think, sufficient description to satisfy an Imagist, but there is also a certain amount of statement; my hope is that the statement seems to grow inevitably out of the situation described. The language of the poem is at one moment elevated and at the next colloquial or slangy: for example, the imposing word "omnipresence" occurs not far from the undignified word "hunks." A critic would find in this poem certain patterns of sound, but those patterns of sound do not constitute an abstract music; they are meant, at any rate, to be inseparable from what is being said, a subordinate aspect of the poem's meaning.

The title of the poem is a quotation from St. Augustine: "Love Calls Us to the Things of This World." You must imagine the poem as occurring at perhaps seven-thirty in the morning; the scene is a bedroom high up in a city apartment building; outside the bedroom window, the first laundry of the day is being yanked across the sky, and one has been awakened by the squeaking pulleys of the laundry-line.

From "On My Own Work"

THINKING ABOUT DENOTATION AND CONNOTATION

People often convey their feelings indirectly, through body language, facial expression, tone of voice, and other ways. Similarly, the imagery, tone, and diction of a poem can suggest a message so clearly that it doesn't need to be stated outright.

- **Pay careful attention to what a poem suggests.** Jot down a few key observations both about what the poem says directly and what you might want to know but aren't told. What important details are you left to infer for yourself?
- **Establish what the poem actually says.** When journalists write a news story, they usually try to cover the "five W's" in the opening paragraph—who,

what, when, where, and why. These questions are worthwhile ones to ask about a poem:

Who? Who is the speaker or central figure of the poem? (In William Blake's "London," for instance, the speaker is also the protagonist who witnesses the hellish horror of the city.) If the poem seems to be addressed not simply to the reader but to a more specific listener, identify that listener as well.

What? What objects or events are being seen or presented? Does the poem ever suddenly change its subject? (In Wallace Stevens's "Disillusionment of Ten O'Clock," for example, there are essentially two scenes—one dull and proper, the other wild and disreputable. What does that obvious shift suggest about Stevens's meaning?)

When? When does the poem take place? If a poet explicitly states a time of day or a season of the year, it is likely that the when of the poem is important. (The fact that Stevens's poem takes place at 10 P.M. and not 2 A.M. tells us a great deal about the people it describes.)

Where? Where is the poem set? Sometimes the setting suggests something important, or plays a part in setting a mood.

Why? If the poem describes some dramatic action but does not provide an overt reason for the occurrence, perhaps the reader is meant to draw his or her own conclusions on the subject. (Tennyson's "Tears, Idle Tears" becomes more evocative by not being explicit about why the speaker weeps.)

■ **Remember, it is almost as important to know what a poem does not tell us as what it does.**

CHECKLIST: Writing About What a Poem Says and Suggests

- ☐ Who speaks the words of the poem? Is it a voice close to the poet's own? A fictional character? A real person?
- ☐ Who is the poem's central figure?
- ☐ To whom—if anyone—is the poem addressed?
- ☐ What objects or events are depicted?
- ☐ When does the poem take place? Is that timing significant in any way?
- ☐ Where does the action of the poem take place?
- ☐ Why does the action of the poem take place? Is there some significant motivation?
- ☐ Does the poem leave any of the above information out? If so, what does that lack of information reveal about the poem's intentions?

WRITING ASSIGNMENT ON DENOTATION AND CONNOTATION

Search a poem of your own choosing for the answers to the "five W's"—*Who? What? When? Where? Why?* Indicate, with details, which of the questions are explicitly answered by the poem and which are left unaddressed.

MORE TOPICS FOR WRITING

1. Look closely at the central image of Richard Wilbur's "Love Calls Us to the Things of This World." Why does such an ordinary sight cause such intense feelings in the poem's speaker? Give evidence from the poem to back up your theory.

2. To which of the "five W's" does Robert Frost's brief poem "Fire and Ice" provide answers? In a brief essay, suggest why so many of the questions remain unanswered.

3. What do the various images in Tennyson's "Tears, Idle Tears" suggest about the speaker's reasons for weeping? Address each image, and explain what the images add up to.

4. Locate all the adjectives in Gwendolyn Brooks's "The Bean Eaters," and write one or two sentences on what each of these words contributes to the poem's thematic intent.

5. Paraphrase the literal content of H.D.'s "Storm," then analyze how her word choice suggests additional meanings.

6. Browse through a newspaper or magazine for an advertisement that tries to surround a product with an aura. A new car, for instance, might be described in terms of some powerful jungle cat ("purring power, ready to spring"). Clip or photocopy the ad and circle words in it that seem especially suggestive. Then, in an accompanying essay, unfold the suggestions in these words and try to explain the ad's appeal. What differences can you see between how poetry and advertising copy use connotative language?

▶ TERMS FOR *review*

Denotation ▶ The literal, dictionary meaning of a word.

Connotation ▶ An association or additional meaning that a word, image, or phrase may carry, apart from its literal denotation or dictionary definition. A word may pick up connotations from the uses to which it has been put in the past.

16 IMAGERY

*It is better to present one Image in a lifetime
than to produce voluminous works.*

—EZRA POUND

Ezra Pound (1885–1972)

In a Station of the Metro

1916

The apparition of these faces in the crowd;
Petals on a wet, black bough.

Pound said he wrote this poem to convey an experience: emerging one day from a train in the Paris subway (*Métro*), he beheld "suddenly a beautiful face, and then another and another." Originally he had described his impression in a poem thirty lines long. In this final version, each line contains an image, which, like a picture, may take the place of a thousand words.

Though the term **image** suggests a thing seen, when speaking of images in poetry, we generally mean *a word or sequence of words that refers to any sensory experience.* Often this experience is a sight (**visual imagery,** as in Pound's poem), but it may be a sound (**auditory imagery**) or a touch (**tactile imagery,** as a perception of roughness or smoothness). It may be an odor or a taste or perhaps a bodily sensation such as pain, the prickling of gooseflesh, the quenching of thirst, or—as in the following brief poem—the perception of something cold.

Taniguchi Buson (1716–1783)

The piercing chill I feel

(about 1760)

The piercing chill I feel:
   my dead wife's comb, in our bedroom,
    under my heel . . .

—*Translated by Harold G. Henderson*

As in this haiku (in Japanese, a poem of seventeen syllables) an image can convey a flash of understanding. Had he wished, the poet might have spoken of the dead woman, of the contrast between her death and his memory of her, of his feelings toward death in general. But such a discussion would be quite different from the poem he actually wrote. Striking his bare foot against the comb, now cold and motionless but associated with the living wife (perhaps worn in her hair), the widower feels a shock as if he had touched the woman's corpse. A literal, physical sense of death is conveyed; the abstraction "death" is understood through the senses. To render the abstract in concrete terms is what poets often try to do; in this attempt, an image can be valuable.

IMAGERY

An image may occur in a single word, a phrase, a sentence, or, as in this case, an entire short poem. To speak of the **imagery** of a poem—all its images taken together— is often more useful than to speak of separate images. To divide Buson's haiku into five images—*chill, wife, comb, bedroom, heel*—is possible, for any noun that refers to a visible object or a sensation is an image, but this is to draw distinctions that in themselves mean little and to disassemble a single experience.

Does an image cause a reader to experience a sense impression? Not quite. Reading the word *petals*, no one literally sees petals; but the occasion is given for imagining them. The image asks to be seen with the mind's eye. And although "In a Station of the Metro" records what Ezra Pound saw, it is of course not necessary for a poet actually to have lived through a sensory experience in order to write of it. Keats may never have seen a newly discovered planet through a telescope, despite the image in his sonnet "On first looking into Chapman's Homer."

It is tempting to think of imagery as mere decoration, particularly when we read Keats, who fills his poems with an abundance of sights, sounds, odors, and tastes. But a successful image is not just a dab of paint or a flashy bauble. When Keats opens "The Eve of St. Agnes" with what have been called the coldest lines in literature, he evokes by a series of images a setting and a mood:

> St. Agnes' eve—Ah, bitter chill it was!
> The owl, for all his feathers, was a-cold;
> The hare limped trembling through the frozen grass,
> And silent was the flock in woolly fold:
> Numb were the Beadsman's fingers, while he told
> His rosary, and while his frosted breath,
> Like pious incense from a censer old,
> Seemed taking flight for heaven, without a death . . .

Indeed, some literary critics look for much of the meaning of a poem in its imagery, wherein they expect to see the mind of the poet more truly revealed than in whatever the poet explicitly claims to believe. Though Shakespeare's Theseus (in *A Midsummer Night's Dream*) accuses poets of being concerned with "airy nothings," poets are usually very much concerned with what is in front of them. This concern is of use to us. Involved in our personal hopes and apprehensions, anticipating the future so hard that much of the time we see the present through a film of thought across our eyes, perhaps we need a poet occasionally to remind us that even the coffee we absentmindedly sip comes in (as Yeats put it) a "heavy spillable cup."

T. S. Eliot (1888–1965)

The winter evening settles down   1917

The winter evening settles down
With smell of steaks in passageways.
Six o'clock.
The burnt-out ends of smoky days.
And now a gusty shower wraps   5
The grimy scraps
Of withered leaves about your feet
And newspapers from vacant lots;
The showers beat
On broken blinds and chimney-pots,   10
And at the corner of the street
A lonely cab-horse steams and stamps.

And then the lighting of the lamps.

Questions

1. What mood is evoked by the images in Eliot's poem?
2. What kind of city neighborhood has the poet chosen to describe? How can you tell?

Theodore Roethke (1908–1963)

Root Cellar   1948

Nothing would sleep in that cellar, dank as a ditch,
Bulbs broke out of boxes hunting for chinks in the dark,
Shoots dangled and drooped,
Lolling obscenely from mildewed crates,
Hung down long yellow evil necks, like tropical snakes.   5
And what a congress of stinks!—
Roots ripe as old bait,
Pulpy stems, rank, silo-rich,
Leaf-mold, manure, lime, piled against slippery planks.
Nothing would give up life: 10
Even the dirt kept breathing a small breath.

Questions

1. As a boy growing up in Saginaw, Michigan, Theodore Roethke spent much of his time in a large commercial greenhouse run by his family. What details in his poem show more than a passing acquaintance with growing things?
2. What varieties of image does "Root Cellar" contain? Point out examples.
3. What do you understand to be Roethke's attitude toward the root cellar? Does he view it as a disgusting chamber of horrors? Pay special attention to the last two lines.

Elizabeth Bishop (1911–1979)

The Fish   1946

I caught a tremendous fish
and held him beside the boat
half out of water, with my hook
fast in a corner of his mouth.
He didn't fight.   5
He hadn't fought at all.
He hung a grunting weight,
battered and venerable
and homely. Here and there
his brown skin hung in strips   10
like ancient wallpaper,
and its pattern of darker brown
was like wallpaper:
shapes like full-blown roses
stained and lost through age.   15
He was speckled with barnacles,
fine rosettes of lime,
and infested
with tiny white sea-lice,
and underneath two or three   20
rags of green weed hung down.
While his gills were breathing in
the terrible oxygen
—the frightening gills,
fresh and crisp with blood,   25
that can cut so badly—
I thought of the coarse white flesh
packed in like feathers,
the big bones and the little bones,
the dramatic reds and blacks   30
of his shiny entrails,
and the pink swim-bladder
like a big peony.
I looked into his eyes
which were far larger than mine   35
but shallower, and yellowed,
the irises backed and packed
with tarnished tinfoil
seen through the lenses
of old scratched isinglass.   40
They shifted a little, but not
to return my stare.
—It was more like the tipping
of an object toward the light.
I admired his sullen face,   45

the mechanism of his jaw,
and then I saw
that from his lower lip
—if you could call it a lip—
grim, wet, and weaponlike,
hung five old pieces of fish-line,
or four and a wire leader
with the swivel still attached,
with all their five big hooks
grown firmly in his mouth.
A green line, frayed at the end
where he broke it, two heavier lines,
and a fine black thread
still crimped from the strain and snap
when it broke and he got away.
Like medals with their ribbons
frayed and wavering,
a five-haired beard of wisdom
trailing from his aching jaw.
I stared and stared
and victory filled up
the little rented boat,
from the pool of bilge
where oil had spread a rainbow
around the rusted engine
to the bailer rusted orange,
the sun-cracked thwarts,
the oarlocks on their strings,
the gunnels—until everything
was rainbow, rainbow, rainbow!
And I let the fish go.

Questions

1. How many abstract words does this poem contain? What proportion of the poem is imagery?
2. What is the speaker's attitude toward the fish? Comment in particular on lines 61–64.
3. What attitude do the images of the rainbow of oil (line 69), the orange bailer (bailing bucket, line 71), the "sun-cracked thwarts" (line 72) convey? Does the poet expect us to feel mournful because the boat is in such sorry condition?
4. What is meant by "rainbow, rainbow, rainbow"?
5. How do these images prepare us for the conclusion? Why does the speaker let the fish go?

Emily Dickinson (1830–1886)

A Route of Evanescence

A Route of Evanescence
With a revolving Wheel –
A Resonance of Emerald –
A Rush of Cochineal° –   *red dye*
And every Blossom on the Bush   5
Adjusts its tumbled Head –
The mail from Tunis, probably,
An easy Morning's Ride –

A ROUTE OF EVANESCENCE. Dickinson titled this poem "A Humming-bird" in an 1880 letter to a friend.
1 *Evanescence:* ornithologist's term for the luminous sheen of certain birds' feathers. 7 *Tunis:* capital city of
Tunisia, North Africa.

Questions
What is the subject of this poem? How can you tell?

Jean Toomer (1894–1967)

Reapers

1923

Black reapers with the sound of steel on stones
Are sharpening scythes. I see them place the hones
In their hip-pockets as a thing that's done,
And start their silent swinging, one by one.
Black horses drive a mower through the weeds,   5
And there, a field rat, startled, squealing bleeds,
His belly close to ground. I see the blade,
Blood-stained, continue cutting weeds and shade.

Questions
1. Imagine the scene Toomer describes. What details most vividly strike the mind's eye?
2. What kind of image is "silent swinging"?
3. Read the poem aloud. Notice especially the effect of the words "sound of steel on stones"
   and "field rat, startled, squealing bleeds." What interesting sounds are present in the very
   words that contain these images?
4. What feelings do you get from this poem as a whole? Besides appealing to our auditory
   and visual imagination, what do the images contribute?

Gerard Manley Hopkins (1844–1889)

Pied Beauty

(1877)

Glory be to God for dappled things—
    For skies of couple-color as a brinded° cow;   *streaked*
      For rose-moles all in stipple upon trout that swim;
Fresh-firecoal chestnut-falls; finches' wings;
    Landscape plotted and pieced—fold, fallow, and plow;   5
      And áll trádes, their gear and tackle and trim.°   *equipment*

All things counter, original, spare, strange;
   Whatever is fickle, freckled (who knows how?)
     With swift, slow; sweet, sour; adazzle, dim;
He fathers-forth whose beauty is past change: 10
       Praise him.

Questions

1. What does the word "pied" mean? (Hint: what does a Pied Piper look like?)
2. According to Hopkins, what do "skies," "cow," "trout," "ripe chestnuts," "finches' wings," and "landscapes" all have in common? What landscapes can the poet have in mind? (Have you ever seen any "dappled" landscape while looking down from an airplane, or from a mountain or high hill?)
3. What do you make of line 6: what can carpenters' saws and ditch-diggers' spades possibly have in common with the dappled things in lines 2–4?
4. Does Hopkins refer only to visual contrasts? What other kinds of variation interest him?
5. Try to state in your own words the theme of this poem. How essential to our understanding of this theme are Hopkins's images?

ABOUT HAIKU

Arakida Moritake   (1473–1549)

The falling flower

The falling flower
I saw drift back to the branch
Was a butterfly.

         —*Translated by Babette Deutsch*

Haiku means "beginning-verse" in Japanese—perhaps because the form may have originated in a game. Players, given a haiku, were supposed to extend its three lines into a longer poem. Haiku (the word can also be plural) consist mainly of imagery, but as we saw in Buson's lines about the cold comb, their imagery is not always only pictorial; it can involve any of the five senses. Haiku are so short that they depend on imagery to trigger associations and responses in the reader. A haiku in Japanese is rimeless; its seventeen syllables are traditionally arranged in three lines, usually following a pattern of five, seven, and five syllables. English haiku frequently ignore such a pattern, being rimed or unrimed as the poet prefers. What English haiku do try to preserve is the powerful way Japanese haiku capture the intensity of a particular moment, usually by linking two concrete images. There is little room for abstract thoughts or general observations. The following attempt, though containing seventeen syllables, is far from haiku in spirit:

Now that our love is gone
I feel within my soul
a nagging distress.

Unlike the author of those lines, haiku poets look out upon a literal world, seldom looking inward to *discuss* their feelings. Japanese haiku tend to be seasonal in subject, but because they are so highly compressed, they usually just *imply* a season: a blossom indicates spring; a crow on a branch, autumn; snow, winter. Not just pretty little sketches of nature (as some Westerners think), haiku assume a view of the universe in which observer and nature are not separated.

Haiku emerged in sixteenth-century Japan and soon developed into a deeply esteemed form. Even today, Japanese soldiers, stockbrokers, scientists, schoolchildren, and the emperor himself still find occasion to pen haiku. Soon after the form first captured the attention of Western poets at the end of the nineteenth century, it became immensely influential for modern poets such as Ezra Pound, William Carlos Williams, and H.D., as a model for the kind of verse they wanted to write—concise, direct, and imagistic.

The Japanese consider the poems of the "Three Masters"—Basho, Buson, and Issa—to be the pinnacle of the classical haiku. Each poet had his own personality: Basho, the ascetic seeker of Zen enlightenment; Buson, the worldly artist; Issa, the sensitive master of wit and pathos. Here are free translations of poems from each of the "Three Masters."

Matsuo Basho (1644–1694)

Heat-lightning streak

Heat-lightning streak—
through darkness pierces
the heron's shriek.

—*Translated by X. J. Kennedy*

In the old stone pool

In the old stone pool
a frogjump:
splishhhhh.

—*Translated by X. J. Kennedy*

Taniguchi Buson (1716–1783)

On the one-ton temple bell

On the one-ton temple bell
a moonmoth, folded into sleep,
sits still.

—*Translated by X. J. Kennedy*

Moonrise on mudflats

Moonrise on mudflats,
the line of water and sky
blurred by a bullfrog

—*Translated by Michael Stillman*

Kobayashi Issa (1763–1827)

only one guy

only one guy and
only one fly trying to
make the guest room do.

—*Translated by Cid Corman*

Cricket

Cricket, be
careful! I'm rolling
over!

—*Translated by Robert Bly*

HAIKU FROM JAPANESE INTERNMENT CAMPS

Japanese immigrants brought the tradition of haiku-writing to the United States, often forming local clubs to pursue their shared literary interests. During World War II, when Japanese Americans were unjustly considered "enemy aliens" and confined to federal internment camps, these poets continued to write in their bleak new surroundings. Today these haiku provide a vivid picture of the deprivations suffered by the poets, their families, and their fellow internees.

Suiko Matsushita

Rain shower from mountain

Rain shower from mountain
quietly soaking
bared wire fence

—*Translated by Violet Kazue de Cristoforo*

Cosmos in bloom

Cosmos in bloom
As if no war
were taking place

—*Translated by Violet Kazue de Cristoforo*

Hakuro Wada

Even the croaking of frogs

Even the croaking of frogs
comes from outside the barbed wire fence
this is our life

—*Translated by Violet Kazue de Cristoforo*

Neiji Ozawa

The war—this year

The war—this year
New Year midnight bell
ringing in the desert

—*Translated by Violet Kazue de Cristoforo*

CONTEMPORARY HAIKU

If you care to try your hand at haiku-writing, here are a few suggestions: make every word matter. Include few adjectives, shun needless conjunctions. Set your poem in the present. ("Haiku," said Basho, "is simply what is happening in this place at this moment.") Like many writers of haiku, you may wish to confine your poem to what can be seen, heard, smelled, tasted, or touched. Mere sensory reports, however, will be meaningless unless they make the reader feel something.

Here are four more recent haiku written in English. (Don't expect them all to observe a strict arrangement of seventeen syllables, however.) Haiku, in any language, is an art of few words, many suggestions. A haiku starts us thinking and telling.

Etheridge Knight (1931–1991)

Making jazz swing in

Making jazz swing in
Seventeen syllables AIN'T
No square poet's job.

Gary Snyder (b. 1930)

After weeks of watching the roof leak

After weeks of watching the roof leak
    I fixed it tonight
by moving a single board

Adelle Foley (b. 1940)

Learning to Shave
(Father Teaching Son)

    A nick on the jaw
The razor's edge of manhood
    Along the bloodline.

Garry Gay (b. 1951)

Hole in the ozone

Hole in the ozone
My bald spot . . .
sunburned

FOR REVIEW AND FURTHER STUDY

John Keats (1795–1821)

Bright star, would I were steadfast as thou art (1819)

Bright star, would I were steadfast as thou art—
    Not in lone splendor hung aloft the night,
And watching, with eternal lids apart,
    Like Nature's patient, sleepless Eremite,°   *hermit*
The moving waters at their priestlike task   5
    Of pure ablution round earth's human shores,
Or gazing on the new soft-fallen mask
    Of snow upon the mountains and the moors—
No—yet still steadfast, still unchangeable,
    Pillowed upon my fair love's ripening breast,   10
To feel for ever its soft swell and fall,
    Awake for ever in a sweet unrest,
Still, still to hear her tender-taken breath,
And so live ever—or else swoon to death.

Questions

1. Stars are conventional symbols for love and a loved one. (Love, Shakespeare tells us in a sonnet, "is the star to every wandering bark.") In this sonnet, why is it not possible for the star to have this meaning? How does Keats use it?
2. What seems concrete and particular in the speaker's observations?
3. Suppose Keats had said "slow and easy" instead of "tender-taken" in line 13. What would have been lost?

Experiment: Writing with Images

Taking the following poems as examples from which to start rather than as models to be slavishly copied, try to compose a brief poem that consists largely of imagery.

Walt Whitman (1819–1892)

The Runner 1867

On a flat road runs the well-train'd runner,
He is lean and sinewy with muscular legs,
He is thinly clothed, he leans forward as he runs,
With lightly closed fists and arms partially rais'd.

H.D. [*Hilda Doolittle*] (1886–1961)

Oread   1915

Whirl up, sea—
whirl your pointed pines,
splash your great pines
on our rocks,
hurl your green over us,   5
cover us with your pools of fir.

William Carlos Williams (1883–1963)

El Hombre   1917

It's a strange courage
You give me ancient star:

Shine alone in the sunrise
Toward which you lend no part!

Robert Bly (b. 1926)

Driving to Town Late to Mail a Letter   1962

It is a cold and snowy night. The main street is deserted.
The only things moving are swirls of snow.
As I lift the mailbox door, I feel its cold iron.
There is a privacy I love in this snowy night.
Driving around, I will waste more time.   5

Stevie Smith (1902–1971)

Not Waving but Drowning   1957

Nobody heard him, the dead man,
But still he lay moaning:
I was much further out than you thought
And not waving but drowning.

Poor chap, he always loved larking   5
And now he's dead
It must have been too cold for him his heart gave way,
They said.

Oh, no no no, it was too cold always
(Still the dead one lay moaning)   10
I was much too far out all my life
And not waving but drowning.

■ WRITING *effectively*

Ezra Pound on Writing

The Image   1913

An "Image" is that which presents an intellectual and emotional complex in an instant of
time. I use the term "complex" rather in the
technical sense employed by the newer psychologists, such as Hart, though we might not agree
absolutely in our application.

Ezra Pound

It is the presentation of such a "complex"
instantaneously which gives that sense of sudden
liberation; that sense of freedom from time limits
and space limits; that sense of sudden growth,
which we experience in the presence of the
greatest works of art.

It is better to present one Image in a lifetime than to produce voluminous works.

All this, however, some may consider open to debate. The immediate necessity
is to tabulate A LIST OF DON'TS for those beginning to write verses. I can not put all of
them into Mosaic negative.

• • •

Use no superfluous word, no adjective which does not reveal something.

Don't use such an expression as "dim lands *of peace*." It dulls the image. It mixes
an abstraction with the concrete. It comes from the writer's not realizing that the
natural object is always the *adequate* symbol.

Go in fear of abstractions. Do not retell in mediocre verse what has already been
done in good prose. Don't think any intelligent person is going to be deceived when
you try to shirk all the difficulties of the unspeakably difficult art of good prose by
chopping your composition into line lengths.

From "A Few Don'ts"

THINKING ABOUT IMAGERY

Images are powerful things—thus the old saw, "A picture is worth a thousand words."
A poem, however, must build its pictures from words. By taking note of its imagery,
and watching how the nature of those images evolves from start to finish, you can go
a long way toward a better understanding of the poem. The following steps can help:

- ■ **Make a short list of the poem's key images.** Be sure to write them down in
  the order they appear, because the sequence can be as important as the images
  themselves.
- ■ **Take the poem's title into account.** A title often points the way to important insights.

- ▪ **Remember: not all images are visual.** Images can draw on any or all of the five senses.
- ▪ **Jot down key adjectives or other qualifying words.**
- ▪ **Go back through your list and take notes about what moods or attitudes are suggested by each image.** What do you notice about the movement from the first image to the last?

Example: **Robert Bly's "Driving to Town Late to Mail a Letter"**

Let's try this method on a short poem. An initial list of images in Bly's "Driving to Town Late to Mail a Letter" (page 570) might look like this:

> cold and snowy night
> deserted main street
> mailbox door-cold iron
> snowy night (speaker loves its privacy)
> speaker drives around (to waste time)

Bly's title also contains several crucial images. Let's add them to the top of the list:

> driving (to town)
> late night
> a letter (to be mailed)

Looking over our list, we see how the images provide an outline of the poem's story. We also see how Bly begins the poem without providing an initial sense of how his speaker feels about the situation. Is driving to town late on a snowy evening a positive, negative, or neutral experience? By noting where (in line 4) the speaker reveals a subjective response to an image ("There is a privacy I love in this snowy night"), we may also begin to grasp the poem's overall emotional structure. We might also note on our list how the poem begins and ends with the same image (driving), but uses it for different effects. At the beginning, the speaker is driving for the practical purpose of mailing a letter but at the end purely for pleasure.

Simply by noting the images from start to finish, we have already worked out a rough essay outline—all on a single sheet of paper or a few inches of computer screen.

CHECKLIST: Writing About Imagery

- ☐ List a poem's key images, in the order in which they appear.
- ☐ What does the poem's title suggest?
- ☐ Remember, images can draw on all five senses—not just the visual.
- ☐ List key adjectives or other qualifying words.
- ☐ What emotions or attitudes are suggested by each image?
- ☐ Does the mood of the imagery change from start to finish?
- ☐ What is suggested by the movement from one image to the next? Remember that the order or sequence of images is almost as important as the images themselves.

WRITING ASSIGNMENT ON IMAGERY

Examining any poem in this chapter, demonstrate how its imagery helps communicate its general theme. Be specific in noting how each key image contributes to the poem's total effect. Feel free to consult criticism on the poem but make sure to credit any observation you borrow exactly from a critical source. Here is an essay written in response to this assignment by Becki Woods, a student of Mark Bernier's at Blinn College in Brenham, Texas.

SAMPLE STUDENT PAPER

Woods 1

Becki Woods

Professor Bernier

English 220

23 February 2012

Faded Beauty: Bishop's Use of Imagery in "The Fish"

Upon first reading, Elizabeth Bishop's "The Fish" appears to be a simple fishing tale. A close investigation of the imagery in Bishop's highly detailed description, however, reveals a different sort of poem. The real theme of Bishop's poem is a compassion and respect for the fish's lifelong struggle to survive. By carefully and effectively describing the captured fish, his reaction to being caught, and the symbols of his past struggles to stay alive, Bishop creates, through her images of beauty, victory, and survival, something more than a simple tale.

The first four lines of the poem are quite ordinary and factual:

> I caught a tremendous fish
> and held him beside the boat
> half out of water, with my hook
> fast in a corner of his mouth. (1–4)

Except for *tremendous*, Bishop's persona uses no exaggerations—unlike most fishing stories—to set up the situation of catching the fish. The detailed description begins as the speaker recounts the event further, noticing something signally important about the captive fish: "He didn't fight" (5). At this point the poem begins to seem unusual: most fish stories are about how ferociously the prey resists being captured. The speaker also notes that the "battered and venerable / and homely" fish offered no resistance to being caught (8–9). The image of the submissive attitude of the fish is essential to the theme of the poem. It is his "utter passivity [that] makes [the persona's] detailed scrutiny possible" (McNally 192).

First sentence gives name of author and work

Thesis sentence

Topic sentence

Quotation from secondary source

Topic sentence

Essay moves systematically through poem, from start to finish

Once the image of the passive fish has been established, the speaker begins an examination of the fish itself, noting that "Here and there / his brown skin hung in strips / like ancient wallpaper" (9–11). By comparing the fish's skin to wallpaper, the persona creates, as Sybil Estess argues, "implicit suggestions of both artistry and decay" (713). Images of peeling wallpaper are instantly brought to mind. The comparison of the fish's skin and wallpaper, though "helpful in conveying an accurate notion of the fish's color to anyone with memories of Victorian parlors and their yellowed wallpaper . . . is," according to Nancy McNally, "even more useful in evoking the associations of deterioration which usually surround such memories" (192). The fish's faded beauty has been hinted at in the comparison, thereby setting up the detailed imagery that soon follows:

> He was speckled with barnacles,
> fine rosettes of lime,
> and infested
> with tiny white sea-lice,
> and underneath two or three
> rags of green weed hung down. (16–21)

Textual evidence, mix of long and short quotations

The persona sees the fish as he is; the infestations and faults are not left out of the description. Yet, at the same time, the fisher "express[es] what [he/she] has sensed of the character of the fish" (Estess 714).

Bishop's persona notices "shapes like full-blown roses / stained and lost through age" on the fish's skin (14–15). The persona's perception of the fish's beauty is revealed along with a recognition of its faded beauty, which is best shown in the description of the fish's being speckled with barnacles and spotted with lime. However, the fisher observes these spots and sees them as rosettes—as objects of beauty, not just ugly brown spots. These images contribute to the persona's recognition of beauty's having become faded beauty.

Transitional phrase begins topic sentence

Textual evidence, mix of long and short quotations

(The poem next turns) to a description of the fish's gills. The imagery in "While his gills were breathing in / the terrible oxygen" (22-23) leads "to the very structure of the creature" that is now dying (Hopkins 201). The descriptions of the fish's interior beauty—"the coarse white flesh / packed in like feathers," the colors "of his shiny entrails," and his "pink swim-bladder / like a big peony"—are reminders of the life that seems about to end (27–28, 31–33).

Woods 3

The composite image of the fish's essential beauty—his being alive—is
developed further in the description of the five fish hooks that the captive,
living fish carries in his lip:

> grim, wet, and weaponlike,
>
> hung five old pieces of fish-line,
>
> . . . .
>
> with all their five big hooks
>
> grown firmly in his mouth. (50–51, 54–55)

Topic sentence

As if fascinated by them, the persona, observing how the lines must have
been broken during struggles to escape, sees the hooks as "medals with their
ribbons / frayed and wavering, / a five-haired beard of wisdom / trailing from
his aching jaw" (61–64), and the fisher becomes enthralled by re-created images
of the fish's fighting desperately for his life on at least five separate occasions—
and winning. Crale Hopkins suggests that "[i]n its capability not only for mere
existence, but for action, escaping from previous anglers, the fish shares the
speaker's humanity" (202), thus revealing the fisher's deepening understanding
of how he or she must now act. The persona has "all along," notes Estess,
"describe[d] the fish not just with great detail but with an imaginative empathy
for the aquatic creature. In her more-than-objective description, [the fisher]
relates what [he/she] has seen to be both the pride and poverty of the fish"
(715). It is at this point that the narrator of this fishing tale has a moment of
clarity. Realizing the fish's history and the glory the fish has achieved in
escaping previous hookings, the speaker sees everything become "rainbow,
rainbow, rainbow!" (75)—and then unexpectedly lets the fish go.

*Quotations from
secondary sources*

Bishop's "The Fish" begins by describing an event that might easily be a
conventional story's climax: "I caught a tremendous fish" (1). The poem,
however, develops into a highly detailed account of a fisher noticing both the
age and the faded beauty of the captive and his present beauty and past glory as
well. The fishing tale is not simply a recounting of a capture; it is a gradually
unfolding epiphany in which the speaker sees the fish in an entirely new light.
The intensity of this encounter between an apparently experienced fisher in a
rented boat and a battle-hardened fish is delivered through the poet's skillful use
of imagery. It is through the description of the capture of an aged fish that
Bishop offers her audience her theme of compassion derived from a respect for
the struggle for survival.

Conclusion

*Restatement of
thesis, in light of
all that comes
before it.*

Woods 4

Works Cited

Bishop, Elizabeth. "The Fish." *Literature: An Introduction to Fiction, Poetry, Drama, and Writing.* Ed. X. J. Kennedy and Dana Gioia. 7th Compact ed. New York: Pearson, 2013. 563–64. Print.

Estess, Sybil P. "Elizabeth Bishop: The Delicate Art of Map Making." *Southern Review* 13 (1977): 713–17. Print.

Hopkins, Crale D. "Inspiration as Theme: Art and Nature in the Poetry of Elizabeth Bishop." *Arizona Quarterly* 32 (1976): 200–202. Print.

McNally, Nancy L. "Elizabeth Bishop: The Discipline of Description." *Twentieth-Century Literature* 11 (1966): 192–94. Print.

MORE TOPICS FOR WRITING

1. Apply the steps listed in "Checklist: Writing About Imagery" to one of the poems in this chapter. Stevie Smith's "Not Waving but Drowning," John Keats's "Bright star, would I were steadfast as thou art," and Jean Toomer's "Reapers" would each make a good subject. Make a brief list of images, and jot down notes on what the images suggest. Now write a two-page description of this process—what it revealed about the poem itself, and about reading poetry in general.

2. Choose a small, easily overlooked object in your home that has special significance to you. Write a paragraph-long, excruciatingly detailed description of the item, putting at least four senses into play. Without making any direct statements about the item's importance to you, try to let the imagery convey the mood you associate with it. Bring your paragraph to class, exchange it with a partner, and see if he or she can identify the mood you were trying to convey.

3. Reread the section on haiku in this chapter. Write three or four haiku of your own and a brief prose account of your experience in writing them. Did anything about the process surprise you?

▶ TERMS FOR *review*

Image ▶ A word or series of words that refers to any sensory experience (usually sight, although also sound, smell, touch, or taste). An image is a direct or literal recreation of physical experience and adds immediacy to literary language.

Imagery ▶ The collective set of images in a poem or other literary work.

Haiku ▶ A Japanese verse form that has three unrhymed lines of five, seven, and five syllables. Traditional haiku is often serious and spiritual in tone, relying mostly on imagery, and usually set (often by implication instead of direct statement) in one of the four seasons. Modern haiku in English often ignore strict syllable count and may have a more playful, worldly tone.

17 FIGURES OF SPEECH

> *All slang is metaphor,*
> *and all metaphor is poetry.*
>
> —G. K. CHESTERTON

WHY SPEAK FIGURATIVELY?

"I will speak daggers to her, but use none," says Hamlet, preparing to confront his mother. His statement makes sense only because we realize that *daggers* is to be taken two ways: literally (denoting sharp, pointed weapons) and nonliterally (referring to something that can be used *like* weapons—namely, words). Reading poetry, we often meet comparisons between two things whose similarity we have never noticed before. When Marianne Moore observes that a fir tree has "an emerald turkey-foot at the top," the result is a pleasure that poetry richly affords: the sudden recognition of likenesses.

A treetop like a turkey-foot, words like daggers—such comparisons are called **figures of speech.** In its broadest definition, a figure of speech may be said to occur whenever a speaker or writer, for the sake of freshness or emphasis, departs from the usual denotations of words. Certainly, when Hamlet says he will speak daggers, no one expects him to release pointed weapons from his lips, for *daggers* is not to be read solely for its denotation. Its connotations—sharp, stabbing, piercing, wounding—also come to mind, and we see ways in which words and daggers work alike. (Words too can hurt: by striking through pretenses, possibly, or by wounding their hearer's self-esteem.) In the statement "A razor is sharper than an ax," there is no departure from the usual denotations of *razor* and *ax*, and no figure of speech results. Both objects are of the same class; the comparison is not offensive to logic. But in King Lear's "How sharper than a serpent's tooth it is / To have a thankless child," the objects—snake's tooth (fang) and ungrateful offspring—are so unlike that no reasonable comparison may be made between them. To find similarity, we attend to the connotations of *serpent's tooth*—biting, piercing, venom, pain—rather than to its denotations. If we are aware of the connotations of *red rose* (beauty, softness, freshness, and so forth), then the line "My love is like a red, red rose" need not call to mind a woman with a scarlet face and a thorny neck.

Figures of speech are not devices to state what is demonstrably untrue. Indeed they often state truths that more literal language cannot communicate; they call attention to such truths; they lend them emphasis.

Alfred, Lord Tennyson (1809–1892)

The Eagle   1851

He clasps the crag with crooked hands;
Close to the sun in lonely lands,
Ringed with the azure world, he stands.

The wrinkled sea beneath him crawls;
He watches from his mountain walls,   5
And like a thunderbolt he falls.

   This brief poem is rich in figurative language. In the first line, the phrase *crooked hands* may surprise us. An eagle does not have hands, we might protest; but the objection would be a quibble, for evidently Tennyson is indicating exactly how an eagle clasps a crag, in the way that human fingers clasp a thing. By implication, too, the eagle is a person. *Close to the sun,* if taken literally, is an absurd exaggeration, the sun being a mean distance of 93,000,000 miles from the earth. For the eagle to be closer to it by the altitude of a mountain is an approach so small as to be insignificant. But figuratively, Tennyson conveys that the eagle stands above the clouds, perhaps silhouetted against the sun, and for the moment belongs to the heavens rather than to the land and sea. The word *ringed* makes a circle of the whole world's horizons and suggests that we see the world from the eagle's height; the *wrinkled sea* becomes an aged, sluggish animal; *mountain walls,* possibly literal, also suggests a fort or castle; and finally the eagle itself is likened to a thunderbolt in speed and in power, perhaps also in that its beak is—like our abstract conception of a lightning bolt—pointed. How much of the poem can be taken literally? Only *he clasps the crag, he stands, he watches, he falls.* The rest is made of figures of speech. The result is that, reading Tennyson's poem, we gain a bird's-eye view of sun, sea, and land—and even of bird. Like imagery, figurative language refers us to the physical world.

William Shakespeare (1564–1616)

Shall I compare thee to a summer's day? (Sonnet 18)   1609

Shall I compare thee to a summer's day?
Thou art more lovely and more temperate.
Rough winds do shake the darling buds of May,
And summer's lease hath all too short a date.
Sometime too hot the eye of heaven shines,   5
And often is his gold complexion dimmed;
And every fair° from fair sometimes declines,   *fair one*
By chance, or nature's changing course, untrimmed:
But thy eternal summer shall not fade,
Nor lose possession of that fair thou ow'st,°   *ownest, have*   10
Nor shall death brag thou wand'rest in his shade,
When in eternal lines to time thou grow'st.
   So long as men can breathe or eyes can see,
   So long lives this, and this gives life to thee.

Howard Moss (1922–1987)

Shall I Compare Thee to a Summer's Day? 1976

Who says you're like one of the dog days?
You're nicer. And better.
Even in May, the weather can be gray,
And a summer sub-let doesn't last forever.
Sometimes the sun's too hot; 5
Sometimes it is not.
Who can stay young forever?
People break their necks or just drop dead!
But you? Never!
If there's just one condensed reader left 10
Who can figure out the abridged alphabet,
    After you're dead and gone,
    In this poem you'll live on!

SHALL I COMPARE THEE TO A SUMMER'S DAY? (Moss). 1 *Dog days:* the hottest days of summer. The ancient
Romans believed that the Dog-star, Sirius, added heat to summer months.

Questions

1. In Howard Moss's streamlined version of Shakespeare, from a series called "Modified Sonnets (Dedicated to adapters, abridgers, digesters, and condensers everywhere)," to what extent does the poet use figurative language? In Shakespeare's original sonnet, how high a proportion of Shakespeare's language is figurative?

2. Compare some of Moss's lines to the corresponding lines in Shakespeare's sonnet. Why is "Even in May, the weather can be gray" less interesting than the original? In the lines on the sun (5–6 in both versions), what has Moss's modification deliberately left out? Why is Shakespeare's seeing death as a braggart memorable? Why aren't you greatly impressed by Moss's last two lines?

3. Can you explain Shakespeare's play on the word "untrimmed" (line 8)? Evidently the word can mean "divested of trimmings," but what other suggestions do you find in it?

4. How would you answer someone who argued, "Maybe Moss's language isn't as good as Shakespeare's, but the meaning is still there. What's wrong with putting Shakespeare into up-to-date words that can be understood by everybody?"

METAPHOR AND SIMILE

Life, like a dome of many-colored glass,
Stains the white radiance of Eternity.

The first of these lines (from Shelley's "Adonais") is a **simile:** a comparison of two things, indicated by some connective, usually *like, as, than,* or a verb such as *resembles.* A simile expresses a similarity. Still, for a simile to exist, the things compared have to be dissimilar in kind. It is no simile to say "Your fingers are like mine"; it is a literal observation. But to say "Your fingers are like sausages" is to use a simile. Omit the connective—say "Your fingers are sausages"—and the result is a **metaphor,** a statement that one thing *is* something else, which, in a literal sense, it is not. In the second of Shelley's lines, it is *assumed* that Eternity is light or radiance, and we have an

implied metaphor, one that uses neither a connective nor the verb *to be.* Here are examples:

Oh, my love is like a red, red rose.	*Simile*
Oh, my love resembles a red, red rose.	*Simile*
Oh, my love is redder than a rose.	*Simile*
Oh, my love is a red, red rose.	*Metaphor*
Oh, my love has red petals and sharp thorns.	*Implied metaphor*
Oh, I placed my love into a long-stem vase and I bandaged my bleeding thumb.	*Implied metaphor*

Often you can tell a metaphor from a simile by much more than just the presence or absence of a connective. In general, a simile refers to only one characteristic that two things have in common, while a metaphor is not plainly limited in the number of resemblances it may indicate. To use the simile "He eats like a pig" is to compare man and animal in one respect: eating habits. But to say "He's a pig" is to use a metaphor that might involve comparisons of appearance and morality as well.

For scientists as well as poets, the making of metaphors is customary. In 1933 George Lemaitre, the Belgian priest and physicist credited with the big bang theory of the origin of the universe, conceived of a primal atom that existed before anything else, which expanded and produced everything. And so, he remarked, making a wonderful metaphor, the evolution of the cosmos as it is today "can be compared to a display of fireworks that has just ended." As astrophysicist and novelist Alan Lightman has noted, we can't help envisioning scientific discoveries in terms of things we know from daily life—spinning balls, waves in water, pendulums, weights on springs. "We have no other choice," Lightman reasons. "We cannot avoid forming mental pictures when we try to grasp the meaning of our equations, and how can we picture what we have not seen?"[1] In science as well as in poetry, it would seem, metaphors are necessary instruments of understanding.

Mixed Metaphors

In everyday speech, simile and metaphor occur frequently. We use metaphors ("She's a doll") and similes ("The tickets are selling like hotcakes") without being fully conscious of them. If, however, we are aware that words possess literal meanings as well as figurative ones, we do not write *died in the wool* for *dyed in the wool* or *tow the line* for *toe the line,* nor do we use **mixed metaphors** as did the writer who advised, "Water the spark of knowledge and it will bear fruit," or the speaker who urged, "To get ahead, keep your nose to the grindstone, your shoulder to the wheel, your ear to the ground, and your eye on the ball." Perhaps the unintended humor of these statements comes from our seeing that the writer, busy stringing together stale metaphors, was not aware that they had any physical reference.

Poetry and Metaphor

A poem may make a series of comparisons or the whole poem may be one extended comparison:

[1]"Physicists' Use of Metaphor," *The American Scholar* (Winter 1989): 99.

Emily Dickinson   (1830–1886)

My Life had stood – a Loaded Gun   (about 1863)

My Life had stood – a Loaded Gun –
In Corners – till a Day
The Owner passed – identified –
And carried Me away –

And now We roam in Sovereign Woods –   5
And now We hunt the Doe –
And every time I speak for Him –
The Mountains straight reply –

And do I smile, such cordial light
Upon the Valley glow –   10
It is as a Vesuvian face
Had let its pleasure through –

And when at Night – Our good Day done –
I guard My Master's Head –
'Tis better than the Eider-Duck's   15
Deep Pillow – to have shared –

To foe of His – I'm deadly foe –
None stir the second time –
On whom I lay a Yellow Eye –
Or an emphatic Thumb –   20

Though I than He – may longer live
He longer must – than I –
For I have but the power to kill,
Without – the power to die –

How much life metaphors bring to poetry may be seen by comparing two poems
by Tennyson and Blake.

Alfred, Lord Tennyson   (1809–1892)

Flower in the Crannied Wall   1869

Flower in the crannied wall,
I pluck you out of the crannies,
I hold you here, root and all, in my hand,
Little flower—but *if* I could understand
What you are, root and all, and all in all,   5
I should know what God and man is.

How many metaphors does this poem contain? None. Compare it with a briefer
poem on a similar theme: the quatrain that begins Blake's "Auguries of Innocence."

(We follow here the opinion of W. B. Yeats, who, in editing Blake's poems, thought the lines ought to be printed separately.)

William Blake (1757–1827)

To see a world in a grain of sand   (about 1803)

To see a world in a grain of sand
And a heaven in a wild flower,
Hold infinity in the palm of your hand
And eternity in an hour.

Set beside Blake's poem, Tennyson's—short though it is—seems lengthy. What contributes to the richness of "To see a world in a grain of sand" is Blake's use of a metaphor in every line. And every metaphor is loaded with suggestion. Our world does indeed resemble a grain of sand: in being round, in being stony, in being one of a myriad (the suggestions go on and on). Like Blake's grain of sand, a metaphor holds much, within a small circumference.

Sylvia Plath (1932–1963)

Metaphors   1960

I'm a riddle in nine syllables,
An elephant, a ponderous house,
A melon strolling on two tendrils.
O red fruit, ivory, fine timbers!
This loaf's big with its yeasty rising.   5
Money's new-minted in this fat purse.
I'm a means, a stage, a cow in calf.
I've eaten a bag of green apples,
Boarded the train there's no getting off.

Questions

1. To what central fact do all the metaphors in this poem refer?
2. In the first line, what has the speaker in common with a riddle? Why does she say she has *nine* syllables?

N. Scott Momaday (b. 1934)

Simile   1974

What did we say to each other
that now we are as the deer
who walk in single file
with heads high
with ears forward   5
with eyes watchful
with hooves always placed on firm ground
in whose limbs there is latent flight

Questions

1. Momaday never tells us what was said. Does this omission keep us from understanding the comparison?
2. The comparison is extended with each detail adding some new twist. Explain the implications of the last line.

Experiment: Likening

Write a poem that follows the method of N. Scott Momaday's "Simile," consisting of one long comparison between two objects. Possible subjects might include talking to a loved one long-distance; what you feel like going to a weekend job; being on a diet; not being noticed by someone you love; winning a lottery.

Jill Alexander Essbaum (b. 1971)

The Heart   2007

Four simple chambers.
A thousand complicated doors.

One of them is yours.

Questions

1. Which line contains a figure of speech?
2. Is that figure a metaphor or a simile? Explain.

Craig Raine (b. 1944)

A Martian Sends a Postcard Home   1979

Caxtons are mechanical birds with many wings
and some are treasured for their markings—

they cause the eyes to melt
or the body to shriek without pain.

I have never seen one fly, but   5
sometimes they perch on the hand.

Mist is when the sky is tired of flight
and rests its soft machine on ground:

then the world is dim and bookish
like engravings under tissue paper.   10

Rain is when the earth is television.
It has the property of making colors darker.

Model T is a room with the lock inside—
a key is turned to free the world

for movement, so quick there is a film   15
to watch for anything missed.

But time is tied to the wrist
or kept in a box, ticking with impatience.

In homes, a haunted apparatus sleeps,
that snores when you pick it up.   20

If the ghost cries, they carry it
to their lips and soothe it to sleep

with sounds. And yet, they wake it up
deliberately, by tickling with a finger.

Only the young are allowed to suffer   25
openly. Adults go to a punishment room

with water but nothing to eat.
They lock the door and suffer the noises

alone. No one is exempt
and everyone's pain has a different smell.   30

At night, when all the colors die,
they hide in pairs

and read about themselves—
in color, with their eyelids shut.

A MARTIAN SENDS A POSTCARD HOME. The title of this poem literally describes its contents. A Martian briefly describes everyday objects and activities on earth, but the visitor sees them all from an alien perspective. The Martian/author lacks a complete vocabulary and sometimes describes general categories of things with a proper noun (as in Model T in line 13). 1 *Caxtons:* Books, since William Caxton (c. 1422–1491) was the first person to print books in England.

Question

Can you recognize *everything* the Martian describes and translate it back into Earth-based English?

Exercise: What Is Similar?

Each of these quotations contains a simile or a metaphor. In each of these figures of speech, what two things is the poet comparing? Try to state exactly what you understand the two things to have in common: the most striking similarity or similarities that the poet sees.

1.   All the world's a stage,
   And all the men and women merely players:
   They have their exits and their entrances,
   And one man in his time plays many parts,
   His acts being seven ages.
        —William Shakespeare, *As You Like It*

2.   When the hounds of spring are on winter's traces . . .
        —Algernon Charles Swinburne, "Atalanta in Calydon"

3.   "Hope" is the thing with feathers –
   That perches in the soul –
   And sings the tune without the words –
   And never stops – at all –
        —Emily Dickinson, an untitled poem

4. Why should I let the toad *work*
      Squat on my life?
   Can't I use my wit as a pitchfork
   And drive the brute off?
   　　—Philip Larkin, "Toads"

5. I wear my patience like a light-green dress
   and wear it thin.
   　　—Emily Grosholz, "Remembering the Ardèche"

OTHER FIGURES OF SPEECH

When Shakespeare asks, in a sonnet,

> O! how shall summer's honey breath hold out
> Against the wrackful siege of batt'ring days,

it might seem at first that he mixes metaphors. How can a *breath* confront the batter-ing ram of an invading army? But it is summer's breath and, by giving it to summer, Shakespeare makes the season a man or woman. It is as if the fragrance of summer were the breath within a person's body, and winter were the onslaught of old age.

Personification

Such is Shakespeare's instance of **personification:** a figure of speech in which a thing, an animal, or an abstract term (*truth, nature*) is made human. A personification ex-tends throughout this short poem.

James Stephens (1882–1950)

The Wind   1915

The wind stood up, and gave a shout;
He whistled on his fingers, and

Kicked the withered leaves about,
And thumped the branches with his hand,

And said he'd kill, and kill, and kill;   5
And so he will! And so he will!

The wind is a wild man, and evidently it is not just any autumn breeze but a hurricane or at least a stiff gale. In poems that do not work as well as this one, personification may be employed mechanically. Hollow-eyed personifications walk the works of lesser English poets of the eighteenth century: Coleridge has quoted the beginning of one such neoclassical ode, "Inoculation! heavenly Maid, descend!" It is hard for the con-temporary reader to be excited by William Collins's "The Passions, An Ode for Music" (1747), which personifies, stanza by stanza, Fear, Anger, Despair, Hope, Revenge, Pity, Jealousy, Love, Hate, Melancholy, and Cheerfulness, and has them listen to Music, until even "Brown Exercise rejoiced to hear, / And Sport leapt up, and seized his beechen spear." Still, in "Two Sonnets on Fame" John Keats makes an abstraction come alive in seeing Fame as "a wayward girl."

Apostrophe

Hand in hand with personification often goes **apostrophe:** a way of addressing someone or something invisible or not ordinarily spoken to. In an apostrophe, a poet (in these examples Wordsworth) may address an inanimate object ("Spade! with which Wilkinson hath tilled his lands"), some dead or absent person ("Milton! thou shouldst be living at this hour"), an abstract thing ("Return, Delights!"), or a spirit ("Thou Soul that art the eternity of thought"). More often than not, the poet uses apostrophe to announce a lofty and serious tone. An "O" may even be put in front of it ("O moon!") since, according to W. D. Snodgrass, every poet has a right to do so at least once in a lifetime. But apostrophe doesn't have to be highfalutin. It is a means of giving life to the inanimate. It is a way of giving body to the intangible, a way of speaking to it person to person, as in the words of a moving American spiritual: "Death, ain't you got no shame?"

Robinson Jeffers   (1887–1962)

Hands   1929

Inside a cave in a narrow canyon near Tassajara
The vault of rock is painted with hands,
A multitude of hands in the twilight, a cloud of men's palms,
    no more,
No other picture. There's no one to say
Whether the brown shy quiet people who are dead intended   5
Religion or magic, or made their tracings
In the idleness of art; but over the division of years these
    careful
Signs-manual are now like a sealed message
Saying: "Look: we also were human; we had hands, not paws.
    All hail
You people with the cleverer hands, our supplanters   10
In the beautiful country; enjoy her a season, her beauty, and
    come down
And be supplanted; for you also are human."

Question

Identify examples of personification and apostrophe in "Hands."

Overstatement and Understatement

Most of us, from time to time, emphasize a point with a statement containing exaggeration: "Faster than greased lightning," "I've told him a thousand times." We speak, then, not literal truth but use a figure of speech called **overstatement** (or **hyperbole**). Poets too, being fond of emphasis, often exaggerate for effect. Instances are Marvell's profession of a love that should grow "Vaster than empires, and more slow" and John Burgon's description of Petra: "A rose-red city, half as old as Time." Overstatement can be used also for humorous purposes, as in a fat woman's boast (from a blues song): "Every time I shake, some skinny gal loses her home."[2] The opposite is

[2]Quoted by Amiri Baraka [LeRoi Jones] in *Blues People* (New York: Morrow, 1963).

understatement, implying more than is said. Mark Twain in *Life on the Mississippi* recalls how, as an apprentice steamboat-pilot asleep when supposed to be on watch, he was roused by the pilot and sent clambering to the pilot house: "Mr. Bixby was close behind, commenting." Another example is Robert Frost's line "One could do worse than be a swinger of birches"—the conclusion of a poem that has suggested that to swing on a birch tree is one of the most deeply satisfying activities in the world.

Metonymy and Synecdoche

In **metonymy,** the name of a thing is substituted for that of another closely associated with it. For instance, we say "The White House decided," and mean that the president did. When John Dyer writes in "Grongar Hill,"

> A little rule, a little sway,
> A sun beam in a winter's day,
> Is all the proud and mighty have
> Between the cradle and the grave,

we recognize that *cradle* and *grave* signify birth and death. A kind of metonymy, **synecdoche** is the use of a part of a thing to stand for the whole of it or vice versa. We say "She lent a hand," and mean that she lent her entire presence. Similarly, Milton in "Lycidas" refers to greedy clergymen as "blind mouths."

Paradox

Paradox occurs in a statement that at first strikes us as self-contradictory but that on reflection makes some sense. "The peasant," said G. K. Chesterton, "lives in a larger world than the globe-trotter." Here, two different meanings of *larger* are contrasted: "greater in spiritual values" versus "greater in miles." Some paradoxical statements, however, are much more than plays on words. In a moving sonnet, the blind John Milton tells how one night he dreamed he could see his dead wife. The poem ends in a paradox:

> But oh, as to embrace me she inclined,
> I waked, she fled, and day brought back my night.

Pun

Asked to tell the difference between men and women, Samuel Johnson replied, "I can't conceive, madam, can you?" The great dictionary-maker was using a figure of speech known to classical rhetoricians as *paronomasia*, better known to us as a **pun** or play on words. How does a pun operate? It reminds us of another word (or other words) of similar or identical sound but of very different denotation. Although puns at their worst can be mere piddling quibbles, at best they can sharply point to surprising but genuine resemblances. The name of a dentist's country estate, Tooth Acres, is accurate: aching teeth paid for the property. In his novel *Moby-Dick,* Herman Melville takes up questions about whales that had puzzled scientists: for instance, are the whale's spoutings water or gaseous vapor? And when Melville speaks pointedly of the great whale "sprinkling and mistifying the gardens of the deep," we catch his pun, and conclude that the creature both mistifies and mystifies at once.

In poetry, a pun may be facetious, as in Thomas Hood's ballad of "Faithless Nelly Gray":

> Ben Battle was a soldier bold,
>   And used to war's alarms;

> But a cannon-ball took off his legs,
>   So he laid down his arms!

Or it may be serious, as in these lines on war by E. E. Cummings:

> the bigness of cannon
> is skillful,

(*is skillful* becoming *is kill-ful* when read aloud), or perhaps, as in Shakespeare's song in *Cymbeline*, "Fear no more the heat o' th' sun," both facetious and serious at once:

> Golden lads and girls all must,
> As chimney-sweepers, come to dust.

Poets often make puns on images, thereby combining the sensory force of imagery with the verbal pleasure of wordplay. Find and explain the punning image in these two poems.

Margaret Atwood (b. 1939)

You fit into me   1971

you fit into me
like a hook into an eye

a fish hook
an open eye

To sum up: even though figures of speech are not to be taken *only* literally, they refer us to a tangible world. By *personifying* an eagle, Tennyson reminds us that the bird and humankind have certain characteristics in common. Through *metonymy*, a poet can focus our attention on a particular detail in a larger object; through *hyperbole* and *understatement*, make us see the physical actuality in back of words. *Pun* and *paradox* cause us to realize this actuality, too, and probably surprise us enjoyably at the same time. Through *apostrophe*, the poet animates the inanimate and asks it to listen—speaks directly to an immediate god or to the revivified dead. Put to such uses, figures of speech have power. They are more than just ways of playing with words.

Dana Gioia (b. 1950)

Money   1991

> *Money is a kind of poetry.*
>   *—Wallace Stevens*

Money, the long green,
cash, stash, rhino, jack
or just plain dough.

Chock it up, fork it over,
shell it out. Watch it   5
burn holes through pockets.

To be made of it! To have it
to burn! Greenbacks, double eagles,
megabucks and Ginnie Maes.

It greases the palm, feathers a nest,   10
holds heads above water,
makes both ends meet.

Money breeds money.
Gathering interest, compounding daily.
Always in circulation.   15

Money. You don't know where it's been,
but you put it where your mouth is.
And it talks.

Question

What figures of speech can you identify in this poem?

Carl Sandburg (1878–1967)

Fog   1916

The fog comes
on little cat feet.

It sits looking
over harbor and city
on silent haunches   5
and then moves on.

Questions

1. What figure of speech does this poem use?
2. Which specific feline qualities does the speaker impute to the fog?

FOR REVIEW AND FURTHER STUDY

Robert Frost (1874–1963)

The Silken Tent   1942

She is as in a field a silken tent
At midday when a sunny summer breeze
Has dried the dew and all its ropes relent,
So that in guys° it gently sways at ease,   *attachments that steady it*
And its supporting central cedar pole,   5
That is its pinnacle to heavenward
And signifies the sureness of the soul,
Seems to owe naught to any single cord,
But strictly held by none, is loosely bound
By countless silken ties of love and thought   10

To everything on earth the compass round,
And only by one's going slightly taut
In the capriciousness of summer air
Is of the slightest bondage made aware.

Questions

1. Is Frost's comparison of a woman and tent a simile or a metaphor?
2. What are the ropes or cords?
3. Does the poet convey any sense of this woman's character? What sort of person do you believe her to be?
4. Paraphrase the poem, trying to state its implied meaning. (To be refreshed about paraphrase, turn back to page 488.) Be sure to include the implications of the last three lines.

Jane Kenyon (1947–1995)

The Suitor   1978

We lie back to back. Curtains
lift and fall,
like the chest of someone sleeping.
Wind moves the leaves of the box elder;
they show their light undersides,   5
turning all at once
like a school of fish.
Suddenly I understand that I am happy.
For months this feeling
has been coming closer, stopping   10
for short visits, like a timid suitor.

Question

In each simile you find in "The Suitor," exactly what is the similarity?

Exercise: Figures of Speech

Identify the central figure of speech in the following short poems.

Robert Frost (1874–1963)

The Secret Sits   1942

We dance round in a ring and suppose,
But the Secret sits in the middle and knows.

A. R. Ammons (1926–2001)

Coward   1975

Bravery runs in my family.

Kay Ryan (b. 1945)

Turtle   1994

Who would be a turtle who could help it?
A barely mobile hard roll, a four-oared helmet,
she can ill afford the chances she must take
in rowing toward the grasses that she eats.
Her track is graceless, like dragging   5
a packing-case places, and almost any slope
defeats her modest hopes. Even being practical,
she's often stuck up to the axle on her way
to something edible. With everything optimal,
she skirts the ditch which would convert   10
her shell into a serving dish. She lives
below luck-level, never imagining some lottery
will change her load of pottery to wings.
Her only levity is patience,
the sport of truly chastened things.   15

Exercise: **Comparing Roses**

Here are two celebrated poems, both of which present roses as a symbol of love. What is similar
in the meaning each poet attaches to roses and what is different?

Emily Brontë (1818–1848)

Love and Friendship   (1839)

Love is like the wild rose-briar;
Friendship like the holly-tree—
The holly is dark when the rose-briar blooms
But which will bloom most constantly?

The wild rose-briar is sweet in spring,   5
Its summer blossoms scent the air;
Yet wait till winter comes again
And who will call the wild-briar fair?

Then scorn the silly rose-wreath now
And deck thee with the holly's sheen,   10
That when December blights thy brow
He still may leave thy garland green.

Robert Burns (1759–1796)

Oh, my love is like a red, red rose   (about 1788)

Oh, my love is like a red, red rose
    That's newly sprung in June;
My love is like the melody
    That's sweetly played in tune.

So fair art thou, my bonny lass,
   So deep in love am I;
And I will love thee still, my dear,
   Till a' the seas gang° dry.

Till a' the seas gang dry, my dear,
   And the rocks melt wi' the sun;
And I will love thee still, my dear,
   While the sands o' life shall run.

And fare thee weel, my only love!
   And fare thee weel awhile!
And I will come again, my love
   Though it were ten thousand mile.

■ WRITING *effectively*

Robert Frost on Writing

The Importance of Poetic Metaphor   1930

I do not think anybody ever knows the discreet use of metaphors, his own and other people's, the discreet handling of metaphor, unless he has been properly educated in poetry.

Poetry begins in trivial metaphors, pretty metaphors, "grace" metaphors, and goes on to the profoundest thinking that we have. Poetry provides the one permissible way of saying one thing and meaning another. People say, "Why don't you say what you mean?" We never do that, do we, being all of us too much poets. We like to talk in parables and in hints and in indirections—whether from diffidence or some other instinct.

Robert Frost

I have wanted in late years to go further and further in making metaphor the whole of thinking. I find someone now and then to agree with me that all thinking, except mathematical thinking, is metaphorical, or all thinking except scientific thinking. The mathematical might be difficult for me to bring in, but the scientific is easy enough.

• • •

What I am pointing out is that unless you are at home in the metaphor, unless you have had your proper poetical education in the metaphor, you are not safe anywhere. Because you are not at ease with figurative values: you don't know the metaphor in its strength and its weakness. You don't know how far you may expect to ride it and when it may break down with you. You are not safe in science; you are not safe in history.

From "Education by Poetry"

THINKING ABOUT METAPHORS

Metaphors are more than mere decoration. Sometimes, for example, they help us envision an unfamiliar thing more clearly by comparing it with another, more familiar item. A metaphor can reveal interesting aspects of both items. Usually we can see the main point of a good metaphor immediately, but in interpreting a poem, the practical issue sometimes arises of how far to extend a comparison.

- **To write effectively about a metaphorical poem, start by considering the general scope of its key metaphor.** In what ways, for instance, does the beloved resemble a rose in Robert Burns's "Oh, my love is like a red, red rose"?
- **Before you begin to write, clarify which aspects of the comparison are true and which are false.** The beloved in Burns's poem is probably beautiful, but might not have thorns, and she probably doesn't stand around in the dirt.
- **Make a list of metaphors and key images in the poem.** Then draw lines to connect the ones that seem to be related.
- **Notice whether there are obvious connections among all the metaphors or similes in a poem.** Perhaps all of them are threatening, or inviting, or nocturnal, or exaggerated. Such similarities, if they occur, will almost certainly be significant.

CHECKLIST: Writing About Metaphors

☐ Underline a poem's key comparisons. Look for both similes and metaphors.
☐ How are the two things being compared alike?
☐ In what ways are the two things unlike each other?
☐ Do the metaphors or similes in the poem have anything in common?
☐ If so, what does that commonality suggest?

WRITING ASSIGNMENT ON FIGURES OF SPEECH

In a brief essay of approximately 500 words, analyze the figures of speech to be found in any poem in this chapter. To what effect does the poem employ metaphors, similes, hyperbole, overstatement, paradox, or any other figure of speech?

MORE TOPICS FOR WRITING

1. Examine the extended implied metaphor that constitutes John Donne's "The Flea" (page 836). Paraphrase the poem's argument. In your opinion, does the use of metaphor strengthen the speaker's case?
2. Whip up some similes of your own. Choose someone likely to be unfamiliar to your classmates—your brother or your best friend from home, for example. Write a paragraph in which you use multiple metaphors and similes to communicate a sense of what that person looks, sounds, and acts like. Come up with at least one figure of speech in each sentence.
3. Write a paragraph on any topic, tossing in as many hyperbolic statements as possible. Then write another version, changing all your exaggeration to understatement. In one last paragraph, sum up what this experience taught you about figurative language.

4. Rewrite a short poem rich in figurative language: Sylvia Plath's "Metaphors," for example, or Robert Burns's "Oh, my love is like a red, red rose." Taking for your model Howard Moss's deliberately bepiddling version of "Shall I compare thee to a summer's day?," use language as flat and unsuggestive as possible. Eliminate every figure of speech. (Just ignore any rime or rhythm in the original.) Then, in a paragraph, indicate lines in your revised version that seem glaringly worsened. In conclusion, sum up what your barbaric rewrite tells you about the nature of poetry.

▶ TERMS FOR *review*

Simile and Metaphor

Simile ▶ A comparison of two things, indicated by some connective, usually *like, as,* or *than,* or a verb such as *resembles.* A simile usually compares two things that initially seem unlike but are shown to have a significant resemblance. "Cool as a cucumber" and "My love is like a red, red rose" are examples of similes.

Metaphor ▶ A statement that one thing *is* something else, which, in a literal sense, it is not. A metaphor creates a close association between the two entities and underscores some important similarity between them. An example of metaphor is "Richard is a pig."

Implied metaphor ▶ A metaphor that uses neither connectives nor the verb *to be.* If we say "John crowed over his victory," we imply metaphorically that John is a rooster but do not say so specifically.

Mixed metaphor ▶ The (usually unintentional) combining of two or more incompatible metaphors, resulting in ridiculousness or nonsense. For example, "Mary was such a tower of strength that she breezed her way through all the work" ("towers" do not "breeze").

Other Figures of Speech

Personification ▶ The endowing of a thing, an animal, or an abstract term with human characteristics. Personification dramatizes the nonhuman world in tangibly human terms.

Apostrophe ▶ A direct address to someone or something. In an apostrophe, a speaker may address an inanimate object, a dead or absent person, an abstract thing, or a spirit.

Overstatement ▶ Also called **hyperbole.** Exaggeration used to emphasize a point.

Understatement ▶ An ironic figure of speech that deliberately describes something in a way that is less than the case.

Metonymy ▶ Figure of speech in which the name of a thing is substituted for that of another closely associated with it. For instance, we might say "The White House decided" when we mean that the president did.

Synecdoche ▶ The use of a significant part of a thing to stand for the whole of it, or vice versa. Saying *wheels* for *car* is an example of synecdoche.

Paradox ▶ A statement that at first strikes one as self-contradictory, but that on reflection reveals some deeper sense. Paradox is often achieved by a play on words.

18 SONG

> *A bird doesn't sing because it has an answer,*
> *it sings because it has a song.*
>
> —MAYA ANGELOU

SINGING AND SAYING

Most poems are more memorable than most ordinary speech, and when music is combined with poetry, the result can be more memorable still. The differences between speech, poetry, and song may appear if we consider, first of all, this fragment of an imaginary conversation between two lovers:

> Let's not drink; let's just sit here and look at each other. Or put a kiss
>   inside my goblet and I won't want anything to drink.

Forgettable language, we might think; but let's try to make it a little more interesting:

> Drink to me only with your eyes, and I'll pledge my love to you with
>   my eyes;
> Or leave a kiss within the goblet, that's all I'll want to drink.

The passage is closer to poetry, but still has a distance to go. At least we now have a figure of speech—the metaphor that love is wine, implied in the statement that one lover may salute another by lifting an eye as well as by lifting a goblet. But the sound of the words is not yet especially interesting. Here is another try, by Ben Jonson:

> Drink to me only with thine eyes,
>   And I will pledge with mine;
> Or leave a kiss but in the cup,
>   And I'll not look for wine.

In these opening lines from Jonson's poem "To Celia," the improvement is noticeable. These lines are poetry; their language has become special. For one thing, the lines rime (with an additional rime sound on *thine*). There is interest, too, in the proximity of the words *kiss* and *cup*: the repetition (or alliteration) of the *k* sound. The rhythm of the lines has become regular; generally every other word (or syllable) is stressed:

DRINK to me ON-ly WITH thine EYES,
   And I will PLEDGE with MINE;
Or LEAVE a KISS but IN the CUP,
   And I'LL not LOOK for WINE.

All these devices of sound and rhythm, together with metaphor, produce a pleasing effect—more pleasing than the effect of "Let's not drink; let's look at each other." But the words became more pleasing still when later set to music:

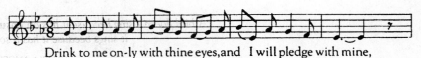

In this memorable form, the poem is still alive today.

Ben Jonson (1573?–1637)

To Celia   1616

Drink to me only with thine eyes,
   And I will pledge with mine;
Or leave a kiss but in the cup,
   And I'll not look for wine.
The thirst that from the soul doth rise   5
   Doth ask a drink divine;
But might I of Jove's nectar sup,
   I would not change for thine.

I sent thee late a rosy wreath,
   Not so much honoring thee   10
As giving it a hope that there
   It could not withered be.
But thou thereon didst only breathe,
   And sent'st it back to me;
Since when it grows, and smells, I swear,   15
   Not of itself but thee.

A compliment to a lady has rarely been put in language more graceful, more wealthy with interesting sounds. Other figures of speech besides metaphor make them unforgettable: for example, the hyperbolic tributes to the power of the lady's sweet breath, which can start picked roses growing again, and her kisses, which even surpass the nectar of the gods.

Stanza

"To Celia" falls into stanzas—as many poems that resemble songs also do. A **stanza** (Italian for "stopping-place" or "room") is a group of lines whose pattern is repeated throughout the poem. Most songs have more than one stanza. When printed, the stanzas of songs and poems usually are set off from one another by space. When sung, stanzas of songs are indicated by a pause or by the introduction of a refrain, or chorus (a line or lines repeated). The word **verse,** which strictly refers to one line of a poem, is sometimes loosely used to mean a whole stanza: "All join in and sing the second verse!" In speaking of a stanza, whether sung or read, it is customary to indicate by a convenient algebra its **rime scheme,** the order in which rimed words recur. For instance, the rime scheme of this stanza by Herrick is *a b a b;* the first and third lines rime and so do the second and fourth:

> For shame or pity now incline
>   To play a loving part,
> Either to send me kindly thine
>   Or give me back my heart.

Refrain

Refrains are words, phrases, or lines repeated at intervals in a song or songlike poem. A refrain usually follows immediately after a stanza, and when it does, it is sometimes called **terminal refrain.** Sometimes we also hear an **internal refrain:** one that appears within a stanza, generally in a position that stays fixed throughout a poem. James Weldon Johnson uses a blues-based stanza with both an internal refrain and a terminal refrain in "Sence You Went Away":

James Weldon Johnson (1871–1938)

Sence You Went Away

1917

Seems lak to me de stars don't shine so bright,
Seems lak to me de sun done loss his light,
Seems lak to me der's nothin' goin' right,
  Sence you went away.

Seems lak to me de sky ain't half so blue,
Seems lak to me dat ev'ything wants you,   5
Seems lak to me I don't know what to do,
  Sence you went away.

Seems lak to me dat ev'ything is wrong,
Seems lak to me de day's jes twice as long,
Seems lak to me de bird's forgot his song,   10
  Sence you went away.

Seems lak to me I jes can't he'p but sigh,
Seems lak to me ma th'oat keeps gittin' dry,
Seems lak to me a tear stays in ma eye,   15
  Sence you went away.

We usually meet poems as words on a page, but songs we generally first encounter as sounds in the air. Consequently, songs tend to be written in language simple enough to be understood on first hearing. But some contemporary songwriters have created songs that require listeners to pay close and repeated attention to their words. Beginning in the 1960s with performers such as Bob Dylan, Leonard Cohen, Joni Mitchell, and Frank Zappa, some pop songwriters crafted deliberately challenging songs. More recently, Sting, Aimee Mann, Beck, and Suzanne Vega have written complex lyrics, often full of strange, dreamlike imagery. To unravel them, a listener may have to play the recording many times, with the treble turned up all the way. Anyone who feels that literary criticism is solely an academic enterprise should listen to high school and college students discuss the lyrics of their favorite songs.

Madrigals

Many familiar poems began life as songs, but today, their tunes forgotten, they survive only in poetry anthologies. Shakespeare studded his plays with songs, and many of his contemporaries wrote verses to fit existing tunes. Some poets were themselves musicians (such as Thomas Campion), and composed both words and music. In Shakespeare's day, **madrigals,** short secular songs for three or more voices arranged in counterpoint, enjoyed great popularity. A madrigal is usually short, often just one stanza, and rarely exceeds twelve or thirteen lines. Elizabethans loved to sing, and a person was considered a dolt if he or she could not join in a three-part song. Here is an extended madrigal from one of Shakespeare's romances—sung as a funeral dirge by two characters in *Cymbeline*.

William Shakespeare (1564–1616)

Fear no more the heat o' the sun   1611

Fear no more the heat o' the sun,
 Nor the furious winter's rages;
Thou thy worldly task hast done,
 Home art gone, and ta'en thy wages.
Golden lads and girls all must,   5
As chimney sweepers, come to dust.

Fear no more the frown o' the great;
 Thou art past the tyrant's stroke.
Care no more to clothe and eat;
 To thee the reed is as the oak.   10
The scepter, learning, physic, must
All follow this, and come to dust.

Fear no more the lightning flash,
 Nor th' all-dreaded thunderstone.
Fear not slander, censure rash;   15
 Thou hast finished joy and moan.
All lovers young, all lovers must
Consign to thee, and come to dust.

FEAR NO MORE THE HEAT O' THE SUN. Song from *Cymbeline* (Act 4, Scene 2); notes by David Bevington. 10 *reed, oak:* contrasting symbols of a fragility that survives by being flexible and a mightiness often overthrown. 11 *Physic:* medical learning. 14 *thunderstone:* The supposed solid body accompanying a stroke of lightning. 18 *Consign:* share a similar fate with, submit to the same terms with.

Some poets who were not composers printed their work in madrigal books for others to set to music. In the seventeenth century, however, poetry and song seem to have fallen away from each other. By the end of the century, much new poetry, other than songs for plays, was written to be printed and to be silently read. Poets who wrote popular songs—such as Thomas D'Urfey, compiler of the collection *Pills to Purge Melancholy*—were considered somewhat disreputable. With the notable exceptions of John Gay, who took existing popular tunes for *The Beggar's Opera*, and Robert Burns, who rewrote folk songs or made completely new words for them, few important English poets since Campion have been first-rate songwriters.

Occasionally, a poet has learned a thing or two from music. "But for the opera I could never have written *Leaves of Grass*," said Walt Whitman, who loved the Italian art form for its expansiveness. Samuel Coleridge, Thomas Hardy, and W. H. Auden learned from folk ballads. Langston Hughes and Gwendolyn Brooks borrowed from blues, jazz, and boogie-woogie. T. S. Eliot patterned his thematically repetitive *Four Quartets* after the structure of a quartet in classical music. "Poetry," said Ezra Pound, "begins to atrophy when it gets too far from music." Still, even in the twentieth century, the poet was more often a corrector of printer's proofs than a tunesmith or performer.

From Troubadours to Rock Stars

Some people think that to write poems and to travel about singing them, as many rock singer-composers now do, is a return to the venerable tradition of the **troubadours,** minstrels of the late Middle Ages. But there are differences. No doubt the troubadours had to please their patrons, but for better or worse their songs were not affected by a producer's video promotion budget or by the technical resources of a sound studio. Bob Dylan has denied that he is a poet, and Paul Simon once told an interviewer, "If you want poetry read Wallace Stevens." Nevertheless, many rock lyrics have the verbal intensity of poetry. No rock lyric, however, can be judged independent of its musical accompaniment. Songwriters rarely create their lyrics to be read on the page. A song joins words and music; a great song joins them inseparably.

Although the words of a great song do not necessarily stand on their own without their music, they are not invalidated as lyrics. If the words seem rich and interesting in themselves, our enjoyment is only increased. Like most poems and songs of the past, most current songs may end up in the trash can of time. And yet, certain memorable rimed and rhythmic lines may live on, especially if they are expressed in stirring music and have been given wide exposure.

Exercise: Comparing Poem and Song

Compare the following poem by Edwin Arlington Robinson and a popular song lyric based on it. Notice what Paul Simon had to do to Robinson's original poem in order to make it into a song, and how Simon altered Robinson's conception.

Edwin Arlington Robinson (1869–1935)

Richard Cory   1897

Whenever Richard Cory went down town,
We people on the pavement looked at him:
He was a gentleman from sole to crown,
Clean favored, and imperially slim.

And he was always quietly arrayed,   5
And he was always human when he talked;
But still he fluttered pulses when he said,
"Good-morning," and he glittered when he walked.

And he was rich—yes, richer than a king—
And admirably schooled in every grace: 10
In fine,° we thought that he was everything   *in short*
To make us wish that we were in his place.

So on we worked, and waited for the light,
And went without the meat, and cursed the bread;
And Richard Cory, one calm summer night,   15
Went home and put a bullet through his head.

Paul Simon (b. 1941)

Richard Cory   1966

> *With Apologies to E. A. Robinson*

They say that Richard Cory owns
One half of this whole town,
With political connections
To spread his wealth around.
Born into Society,   5
A banker's only child,
He had everything a man could want:
Power, grace and style.

Refrain:

But I, I work in his factory
And I curse the life I'm livin'   10
And I curse my poverty
And I wish that I could be
Oh I wish that I could be
Oh I wish that I could be
Richard Cory.   15

The papers print his picture
Almost everywhere he goes:
Richard Cory at the opera,
Richard Cory at a show
And the rumor of his parties   20
And the orgies on his yacht—
Oh he surely must be happy
With everything he's got.   *(Refrain.)*

He freely gave to charity,
He had the common touch,   25

And they were grateful for his patronage
And they thanked him very much,
So my mind was filled with wonder
When the evening headlines read:
"Richard Cory went home last night   30
And put a bullet through his head."   *(Refrain.)*

RICHARD CORY by Paul Simon. If possible, listen to the ballad sung by Simon and Garfunkel on *Sounds of Silence* (Sony, 2001), © 1966 by Paul Simon. Used by permission.

BALLADS

Any narrative song, like Paul Simon's "Richard Cory," may be called a **ballad.** In English, some of the most famous ballads are **folk ballads,** loosely defined as anonymous story-songs transmitted orally before they were ever written down. Sir Walter Scott, a pioneer collector of Scottish folk ballads, drew the ire of an old woman whose songs he had transcribed: "They were made for singing and no' for reading, but ye ha'e broken the charm now and they'll never be sung mair." The old singer had a point. Print freezes songs and tends to hold them fast to a single version. If Scott and others had not written them down, however, many would have been lost.

Anonymous (traditional Scottish ballad)

Bonny Barbara Allan

It was in and about the Martinmas time,
   When the green leaves were afalling,
That Sir John Graeme, in the West Country,
   Fell in love with Barbara Allan.

He sent his men down through the town,   5
   To the place where she was dwelling;
"O haste and come to my master dear,
   Gin° ye be Barbara Allan."   *if*

O hooly,° hooly rose she up,   *slowly*
   To the place where he was lying,
And when she drew the curtain by: 10
   "Young man, I think you're dying."

"O it's I'm sick, and very, very sick,
   And 'tis a' for Barbara Allan."—
"O the better for me ye's never be,   15
   Tho your heart's blood were aspilling.

"O dinna ye mind,° young man," said she,   *don't you remember*
   "When ye was in the tavern adrinking,
That ye made the health° gae round and round,   *toasts*
   And slighted Barbara Allan?"   20

He turned his face unto the wall,
   And death was with him dealing:
"Adieu, adieu, my dear friends all,
   And be kind to Barbara Allan."

And slowly, slowly raise she up,   25
   And slowly, slowly left him,
And sighing said she could not stay,
   Since death of life had reft him.

She had not gane a mile but twa,
   When she heard the dead-bell ringing,   30
And every jow° that the dead-bell geid,   *stroke*
   It cried, "Woe to Barbara Allan!"

"O mother, mother, make my bed!
   O make it saft and narrow!
Since my love died for me today,   35
   I'll die for him tomorrow."

BONNY BARBARA ALLAN. 1 *Martinmas:* Saint Martin's Day, November 11.

Questions

1. In any line does the Scottish dialect cause difficulty? If so, try reading the line aloud.
2. Without ever coming out and explicitly calling Barbara hard-hearted, this ballad reveals that she is. In which stanza and by what means is her cruelty demonstrated?
3. At what point does Barbara evidently have a change of heart? Again, how does the poem dramatize this change without explicitly talking about it?
4. In many American versions of this ballad, noble knight John Graeme becomes an ordinary citizen. The gist of the story is the same, but at the end are these additional stanzas, incorporated from a different ballad:

   They buried Willie in the old churchyard
      And Barbara in the choir;
   And out of his grave grew a red, red rose,
      And out of hers a briar.

   They grew and grew to the steeple top
      Till they could grow no higher;
   And there they locked in a true love's knot,
      The red rose round the briar.

   Do you think this appendage heightens or weakens the final impact of the story? Can the American ending be defended as an integral part of a new song? Explain.

5. Paraphrase lines 9, 15–16, 22, 25–28. By putting these lines into prose, what has been lost?

As you can see from "Bonny Barbara Allan," in a traditional English or Scottish folk ballad the storyteller speaks of the lives and feelings of others. Even if the pronoun "I" occurs, it rarely has much personality. Characters often exchange dialogue, but no one character speaks all the way through. Events move rapidly, perhaps because some of the dull transitional stanzas have been forgotten. The events themselves, as ballad scholar Albert B. Friedman has said, are frequently "the stuff of tabloid journalism—sensational tales of lust, revenge and domestic crime. Unwed mothers slay their newborn babes; lovers unwilling to marry their pregnant mistresses brutally murder the poor women, for which, without fail, they are justly punished."[1] There are also many ballads of the supernatural and of gallant knights ("Sir Patrick Spence"), and there are a few humorous ballads, usually about unhappy marriages.

Ballad Stanza

A favorite pattern of ballad-makers is the so-called **ballad stanza,** four lines rimed *a b c b*, tending to fall into 8, 6, 8, and 6 syllables:

> Clerk Saunders and Maid Margaret
>   Walked owre yon garden green,
> And deep and heavy was the love   *between those two*
>   That fell thir twa between.°

Though not the only possible stanza for a ballad, this easily singable quatrain has continued to attract poets since the Middle Ages. Close kin to the ballad stanza is **common meter,** a stanza found in hymns such as "Amazing Grace," by the eighteenth-century English hymnist John Newton:

> Amazing grace! how sweet the sound
>   That saved a wretch like me!
> I once was lost, but now am found,
>   Was blind, but now I see.

Notice that its pattern is that of the ballad stanza except for its *two* pairs of rimes. That all its lines rime is probably a sign of more literate artistry than we usually hear in folk ballads. Another sign of schoolteachers' influence is that Newton's rimes are exact. (Rimes in folk ballads are often rough-and-ready, as if made by ear, rather than polished and exact, as if the riming words had been matched for their similar spellings. In "Barbara Allan," for instance, the hard-hearted lover's name rimes with *afalling, dwelling, aspilling, dealing,* and even with *ringing* and *adrinking.*) That so many hymns were written in common meter may have been due to convenience. If a congregation didn't know the tune to a hymn in common meter, they readily could sing its words to the tune of another such hymn they knew. Besides hymnists, many poets have favored common meter, among them A. E. Housman and Emily Dickinson.

Literary Ballads

Literary ballads, not meant for singing, are written by sophisticated poets for book-educated readers who enjoy being reminded of folk ballads. Literary ballads imitate certain features of folk ballads: they may tell of dramatic conflicts or of mortals who encounter the supernatural; they may use conventional figures of speech or ballad stanzas. Well-known poems of this kind include Keats's "La Belle Dame sans Merci" (see page 702), Coleridge's "Rime of the Ancient Mariner," and (more recently) Dudley Randall's "Ballad of Birmingham."

---

[1]Introduction to *The Viking Book of Folk Ballads of the English-Speaking World,* ed. Albert B. Friedman (New York: Viking, 1956).

Dudley Randall (1914–2000)

Ballad of Birmingham

1966

(On the Bombing of a Church in
Birmingham, Alabama, 1963)

"Mother dear, may I go downtown
Instead of out to play,
And march the streets of Birmingham
In a Freedom March today?"

"No, baby, no, you may not go,   5
For the dogs are fierce and wild,
And clubs and hoses, guns and jails
Aren't good for a little child."

"But, mother, I won't be alone.
Other children will go with me,   10
And march the streets of Birmingham
To make our country free."

"No, baby, no, you may not go,
For I fear those guns will fire.
But you may go to church instead   15
And sing in the children's choir."

She has combed and brushed her night-dark hair,
And bathed rose petal sweet,
And drawn white gloves on her small brown hands,
And white shoes on her feet.   20

The mother smiled to know her child
Was in the sacred place,
But that smile was the last smile
To come upon her face.

For when she heard the explosion,   25
Her eyes grew wet and wild.
She raced through the streets of Birmingham
Calling for her child.

She clawed through bits of glass and brick,
Then lifted out a shoe.   30
"O here's the shoe my baby wore,
But, baby, where are you?"

Questions

1. This poem, about a dynamite blast set off in an African American church by a racial terrorist (later convicted), delivers a message without preaching. How would you sum up this message, its implied theme?
2. What is ironic in the mother's denying her child permission to take part in a protest march?
3. How does this modern poem resemble a traditional ballad?

Exercise: **Seeing the Traits of Ballads**

Read the ballad "Sir Patrick Spence" (page 493). With this in mind, consider these modern poems:

> W. H. Auden, "As I Walked Out One Evening" (page 821)
> William Butler Yeats, "Crazy Jane Talks with the Bishop" (page 887)

What characteristics of folk ballads do you find in them? In what ways do these modern poets depart from the traditions of folk ballads of the Middle Ages?

BLUES

Among the many song forms to have shaped the way poetry is written in English, no recent form has been more influential than the **blues.** Originally a type of folk music developed by black slaves in the South, blues songs have both a distinctive form and tone. They traditionally consist of three-line stanzas in which the first two identical lines are followed by a concluding riming third line:

> To dream of muddy water—trouble is knocking at your door.
> To dream of muddy water—trouble is knocking at your door.
> Your man is sure to leave you and never return no more.

Early blues lyrics almost always spoke of some sadness, pain, or deprivation— often the loss of a loved one. The melancholy tone of the lyrics, however, is not only world-weary but also world-wise. The blues expound the hard-won wisdom of bitter life experience. They frequently create their special mood through down-to-earth, even gritty, imagery drawn from everyday life. Although blues reach back into the nineteenth century, they were not widely known outside African American communities before 1920, when the first commercial recordings appeared. Their influence on both music and song from that time on was rapid and extensive. By 1930 James Weldon Johnson could declare, "It is from the blues that all that may be called American music derives its most distinctive characteristic." Blues have not only become an enduring category of popular music, they have also helped shape virtually all the major styles of contemporary pop—jazz, rap, rock, gospel, country, and, of course, rhythm-and-blues.

The style and structure of blues have also influenced modern poets. Not only have African American writers such as Langston Hughes, Sterling A. Brown, Etheridge Knight, and Sonia Sanchez written blues poems, but white poets as dissimilar as W. H. Auden, Elizabeth Bishop, Donald Justice, and Sandra McPherson have employed the form. The classic touchstones of the blues, however, remain the early singers such as Robert Johnson, Ma Rainey, Blind Lemon Jefferson, Charley Patton, and—perhaps preeminently—Bessie Smith, "the Empress of the Blues." Any form that has fascinated Bishop and Auden as well as B. B. King, Mick Jagger, Tracy Chapman, and Eric Clapton surely deserves special notice.

The blues remind us of how closely related song and poetry will always be. Here are the lyrics of one of Bessie Smith's earliest songs, based on traditional folk blues, followed by a blues-influenced cabaret song written by W. H. Auden (with the composer Benjamin Britten) for a night-club singer.

Bessie Smith (1898?–1937)
with Clarence Williams (1898–1965)

Jailhouse Blues

1923

Thirty days in jail with my back turned to the wall.
Thirty days in jail with my back turned to the wall.
Look here, Mister Jailkeeper, put another gal in my stall.

I don't mind bein' in jail but I got to stay there so long.
I don't mind bein' in jail but I got to stay there so long.   5
Well, ev'ry friend I had has done shook hands and gone.

You better stop your man from ticklin' me under my chin.
You better stop your man from ticklin' me under my chin.
'Cause if he keep on ticklin' I'm sure gonna take him in.

Good mornin' blues, blues how do you do?   10
Good mornin' blues, blues how do you do?
Well, I just come here to have a few words with you.

W. H. Auden (1907–1973)

Funeral Blues

1940

Stop all the clocks, cut off the telephone,
Prevent the dog from barking with a juicy bone,
Silence the pianos and with muffled drum
bring out the coffin, let the mourners come.

Let aeroplanes circle moaning overhead   5
Scribbling on the sky the message He Is Dead,
Put crêpe bows round the white necks of the public doves,
let the traffic policemen wear black cotton gloves.

He was my North, my South, my East and West,
My working week and my Sunday rest,   10
My noon, my midnight, my talk, my song;
I thought that love would last for ever: I was wrong.

The stars are not wanted now: put out every one,
Pack up the moon and dismantle the sun,
Pour away the ocean and sweep up the woods;   15
For nothing now can ever come to any good.

Questions

What features of the traditional blues does Auden keep in his song? What does he discard?

RAP

One of the most interesting musical and literary developments of the 1980s was the emergence of **rap,** a form of popular music in which words are recited to a driving rhythmic beat. It differs from mainstream popular music in several ways, but, most interesting in literary terms, rap lyrics are *spoken* rather than sung. In that sense, rap is a form of popular poetry as well as popular music. In most rap songs, the lead performer or "M.C." talks or recites, usually at top speed, long, rhythmic, four-stress lines that end in rimes. Although today most rap singers and groups use electronic or sampled backgrounds, rap began on city streets in the game of "signifying," in which two poets aim rimed insults at each other, sometimes accompanying their tirades with a beat made by clapping or finger-snapping. This game also includes boasts made by the players on both sides about their own abilities.

Rap developed so rapidly that it now uses a variety of metrical forms, but it is interesting to look more closely at some of the early work that established the genre. Most rap still follows the initial formula of rimed couplets that casually mix full rime with assonance. Here are a few lines from one of the first popular raps:

I said, "By the way, baby, what's your name?"

She said, "I go by the name Lois Lane.

And you can be my boyfriend, you surely can,

Just let me quit my boyfriend, he's called Superman."

— "Rapper's Delight," Sugarhill Gang, 1979

Rap is not written in the standard meters of English literary verse, but its basic measure does come out of the English tradition. Rap's characteristic four-stress, accentual line has been the most common meter for spoken popular poetry in English from Anglo-Saxon verse and the folk ballads to the work of Robert W. Service and Rudyard Kipling.

What is a woman that you forsake her,

And the hearth-fire and the home-acre,

To go with the old grey Widow-maker?

— "Harp Song of the Dane Women," Rudyard Kipling, 1906

Rap deliberately makes use of stress-meter's ability to stretch and contract in syllable count. In fact, playing the syllable count against the beat is the basic metrical technique of rap. Like jazz, rap plays a flexible rhythm off against a fixed metrical beat, turning a traditional English folk meter into something distinctively African American. By hitting the beat hard while exploiting other elements of word music, rappers play interesting and elaborate games with the total rhythm of their lines.

FOR REVIEW AND FURTHER STUDY

Bob Dylan (b. 1941)

The Times They Are a-Changin'   1963

Come gather 'round people
Wherever you roam
And admit that the waters
Around you have grown
And accept it that soon   5
You'll be drenched to the bone.
If your time to you
Is worth savin'
Then you better start swimmin'
Or you'll sink like a stone   10
For the times they are a-changin'.

Come writers and critics
Who prophesize with your pen
And keep your eyes wide
The chance won't come again   15
And don't speak too soon
For the wheel's still in spin
And there's no tellin' who
That it's namin'.
For the loser now   20
Will be later to win
For the times they are a-changin'.

Come senators, congressmen
Please heed the call
Don't stand in the doorway   25
Don't block up the hall
For he that gets hurt
Will be he who has stalled
There's a battle outside
And it is ragin'.   30
It'll soon shake your windows
And rattle your walls
For the times they are a-changin'.

Come mothers and fathers
Throughout the land   35
And don't criticize
What you can't understand
Your sons and your daughters
Are beyond your command
Your old road is   40
Rapidly agin'.

Please get out of the new one
If you can't lend your hand
For the times they are a-changin'.

The line it is drawn   45
The curse it is cast
The slow one now
Will later be fast
As the present now
Will later be past   50
The order is
Rapidly fadin'.
And the first one now
Will later be last
For the times they are a-changin'.   55

Questions

1. What features does Dylan keep constant from stanza to stanza? What changes?
2. Who is addressed at the start of each stanza? How do those people affect what is said later in the same stanza?
3. Could the stanzas be sung in a different order without greatly changing the impact of the song? Or would any change undercut the structure of the song?
4. Do the words of this song work well on the page? Or is something essential lost when the music is taken away? Choose and defend one point of view.

Aimee Mann (b. 1960)

Deathly   1999

Now that I've met you
Would you object to
Never seeing each other again
Cause I can't afford to
Climb aboard you   5
No one's got that much ego to spend

So don't work your stuff
Because I've got troubles enough
No, don't pick on me
When one act of kindness could be   10
Deathly
Deathly
Definitely

Cause I'm just a problem
For you to solve and   15
Watch dissolve in the heat of your charm
But what will you do when

You run it through and
You can't get me back on the farm

So don't work your stuff   20
Because I've got troubles enough
No, don't pick on me
When one act of kindness could be
Deathly
Deathly
Definitely   25

You're on your honor
Cause I'm a goner
And you haven't even begun
So do me a favor
If I should waver   30
Be my savior
And get out the gun

Just don't work your stuff
Because I've got troubles enough   35
No, don't pick on me
When one act of kindness could be
Deathly
Deathly
Definitely   40

Questions

1. The first three lines of this lyric are quite arresting (so much so that they inspired Paul Thomas Anderson's ambitious 1999 film *Magnolia*). How well does the rest of the lyric sustain and develop this opening?

2. After reading "Deathly," listen to Aimee Mann's recording of the song. Are the melody, arrangement, and singing style what you would have expected from a reading of the words? Explain.

■ WRITING *effectively*

Bob Dylan on Writing

The Term "Protest Singer" Didn't Exist   2004

Greenwich Village was full of folk clubs, bars and coffee-houses, and those of us who played them all played the old-timey folk songs, rural blues and dance tunes. There were a few who wrote their own songs, like Tom Paxton and Len Chandler and because they used old melodies with new words they were pretty much accepted.

Both Len and Tom wrote topical songs—songs where you'd pick articles out of newspapers, fractured, demented stuff—some nun getting married, a high school teacher taking a flying leap off the Brooklyn Bridge, tourists who robbed a gas station, Broadway beauty being beaten and left in the snow, things like that. Len could usually fashion some song out of all that, found some kind of angle. Tom's songs were topical, too, even though his most famous song, "Last Thing on My Mind," was a yearning romantic ballad. I wrote a couple and slipped them into my repertoire but really didn't think they were here nor there.

Bob Dylan

• • •

Topical songs weren't protest songs. The term "protest singer" didn't exist any more than the term "singer-songwriter." You were a performer or you weren't, that was about it—a folksinger or not one. "Songs of dissent" was a term people used but even that was rare. I tried to explain later that I didn't think I was a protest singer, that there'd been a screw-up. I didn't think I was protesting anything any more than I thought that Woody Guthrie songs were protesting anything. I didn't think of Woody as a protest singer. If he is one, then so is Sleepy John Estes and Jelly Roll Morton. What I was hearing pretty regularly, though, were rebellion songs and those really moved me.

• • •

The rebellion songs were a really serious thing. The language was flashy and provocative—a lot of action in the words, all sung with great gusto. The singer always had a merry light in his eye, had to have it. I loved these songs and could still hear them in my head long after and into the next day. They weren't protest songs, though, they were rebel ballads—even in a simple, melodic wooing ballad there'd be rebellion waiting around the corner. You couldn't escape it. There were songs like that in my repertoire, too, where something lovely was suddenly upturned, but instead of rebellion showing up it would be death itself, the Grim Reaper. Rebellion spoke to me louder. The rebel was alive and well, romantic and honorable.

From Chronicles: Volume I

THINKING ABOUT POETRY AND SONG

Poetry and song were originally one art, and even today the two forms remain closely related. We celebrate the sounds of a poem by praising its "music" just as we compliment a great song lyric by calling it "poetic." And yet a very simple distinction separates the two arts: in a song the lyrics combine with music to create a collaborative work, whereas in a poem the author must create all the effects by words alone.

■ **To analyze song lyrics as poetry, you will need to separate the words temporarily from their music.**

▪ **Write out the lyrics and read them without the music playing in the background.** This can help you see how the words hold up on the page. While some lyrics stand well on their own, you may find that the song's power resides mostly in its music, or in the combination of words and music.

Remember, if you find yourself disappointed by the lyrics separated from their music, that song is no less powerful as a song just because the words don't stand on their own as poetry. A song, after all, *is* meant to be sung.

CHECKLIST: Writing About Song Lyrics

☐ Listen to the song and jot down the three or four moments that affect you most powerfully.

☐ Transcribe all of the lyrics onto the page. (Or find the lyrics on the Internet and print them out.)

☐ Compare the moments you remembered with the transcribed lyrics.

☐ Are the lyrics as moving without the music?

☐ Notice the form. Are there stanzas? A refrain? A rime scheme?

☐ What accounts for the song's power? Its music alone? Its lyrics? Its blend of words and music?

WRITING ASSIGNMENT ON SONG LYRICS

Write a short paper (750–1000 words) in which you analyze the lyrics of a favorite song. Discuss what the words alone provide and what they lack in re-creating the total power of the original song. The purpose of the paper is not to justify the song you have chosen as great poetry (though it may perhaps qualify); rather, it is to examine which parts of the song's power come solely from the words and which come from the music or performance. (Don't forget to provide your instructor with an accurate transcription of the song lyrics.)

MORE TOPICS FOR WRITING

1. Compare and contrast Edward Arlington Robinson's "Richard Cory" with Paul Simon's song of the same name. What changes did Simon make to the original? Why do you suppose he chose to make them? How did he alter Robinson's story and its characters?

2. Think of several recent popular songs. Can you think of any that qualify as ballads? Type out the lyrics of a narrative song you know well, and write a brief analysis of what those lyrics have in common with "Ballad of Birmingham" or "Bonny Barbara Allan."

3. What gives you the blues? Choose one of the blues songs in this chapter as a model, and write your own lyrics about a sad subject of your choice.

▶ TERMS FOR *review*

Components of Songs and Formal Poems

Stanza ▶ From the Italian, meaning "stopping-place" or "room." A recurring pattern of two or more lines of verse, poetry's equivalent to the paragraph in prose. The stanza is the basic organizational principle of most formal poetry.

Rime scheme ▶ Any recurrent pattern of rime within an individual poem. A rime scheme is usually described by using lowercase letters to represent each end rime—*a* for the first rime, *b* for the second, and so on—in the order in which the rimed words occur. The rime scheme of a stanza of common meter, for example, would be notated *a b a b*.

Refrain ▶ A word, phrase, line, or stanza repeated at intervals in a song or poem. The repeated chorus of a song is a refrain.

Ballads

Ballad ▶ Traditionally, a song that tells a story. Ballads are characteristically compressed, dramatic, and objective in their narrative style.

Folk ballads ▶ Anonymous narrative songs, usually in ballad meter. They were originally created for oral performance, often resulting in many versions of a single ballad.

Ballad stanza ▶ The most common pattern for a ballad, consisting of four lines rimed *a b c b*, in which the first and third lines have four metrical feet (usually eight syllables) and the second and fourth lines have three feet (usually six syllables). **Common meter,** often used in hymns, is a variation rimed *a b a b*.

Literary ballad ▶ A ballad not meant for singing, written by a sophisticated poet for educated readers, rather than arising from the anonymous oral tradition.

Other Kinds of Songs

Blues ▶ A type of folk music originally developed by African Americans in the South, often about some pain or loss. Blues lyrics traditionally consist of three-line stanzas in which two identical lines are followed by a third, riming line. The influence of the blues is fundamental in virtually all styles of contemporary pop—jazz, rap, rock, gospel, country, and rhythm and blues.

Rap ▶ A popular style of music that emerged in the 1980s in which lyrics are spoken or chanted over a steady beat, usually sampled or prerecorded. Rap lyrics are almost always rimed and very rhythmic—syncopating a heavy metrical beat in a manner similar to jazz.

19

SOUND

SOUND AS MEANING

Isak Dinesen, in a memoir of her life on a plantation in East Africa, tells how some Kikuyu tribesmen reacted to their first hearing of rimed verse:

> The Natives, who have a strong sense of rhythm, know nothing of verse, or at least did not know anything before the times of the schools, where they were taught hymns. One evening out in the maize-field, where we had been harvesting maize, breaking off the cobs and throwing them on to the ox-carts, to amuse myself, I spoke to the field laborers, who were mostly quite young, in Swahili verse. There was no sense in the verses, they were made for the sake of rime—"Ngumbe na-penda chumbe, Malaya mbaya. Wakamba na-kula mamba." The oxen like salt—whores are bad—The Wakamba eat snakes. It caught the interest of the boys, they formed a ring round me. They were quick to understand that meaning in poetry is of no consequence, and they did not question the thesis of the verse, but waited eagerly for the rime, and laughed at it when it came. I tried to make them themselves find the rime and finish the poem when I had begun it, but they could not, or would not, do that, and turned away their heads. As they had become used to the idea of poetry, they begged: "Speak again. Speak like rain." Why they should feel verse to be like rain I do not know. It must have been, however, an expression of applause, since in Africa rain is always longed for and welcomed.[1]

What the tribesmen had discovered is that poetry, like music, appeals to the ear. However limited it may be in comparison with the sound of an orchestra—or a tribal drummer—the sound of words in itself gives pleasure. However, we might doubt Isak Dinesen's assumption that "meaning in poetry is of no consequence." "Hey nonny-nonny" and such nonsense has a place in song lyrics and other poems, and we might take pleasure in hearing rimes in Swahili; but most good poetry has meaningful sound

---

[1] Isak Dinesen, *Out of Africa* (New York: Random, 1972).

614

as well as musical sound. Certainly the words of a song have an effect different from that of wordless music: they go along with their music and, by making statements, add more meaning. The French poet Isidore Isou, founder of a literary movement called *lettrisme*, maintained that poems can be written not only in words but also in letters (sample lines: *xyl, xyl, / prprali dryl / znglo trpylo pwi*). But the sound of letters alone, without denotation and connotation, has not been enough to make Letterist poems memorable. In the response of the Kikuyu tribesmen, there may have been not only the pleasure of hearing sounds but also the agreeable surprise of finding that things not usually associated had been brought together.

Euphony and Cacophony

More powerful when in the company of meaning, not apart from it, the sounds of consonants and vowels can contribute greatly to a poem's effect. The sound of *s*, which can suggest the swishing of water, has rarely been used more accurately than in Surrey's line "Calm is the sea, the waves work less and less." When, in a poem, the sound of words working together with meaning pleases mind and ear, the effect is **euphony,** as in the following lines from Tennyson's "Come down, O maid":

> Myriads of rivulets hurrying through the lawn,
> The moan of doves in immemorial elms,
> And murmuring of innumerable bees.

Its opposite is **cacophony:** a harsh, discordant effect. It too is chosen for the sake of meaning. We hear it in Milton's scornful reference in "Lycidas" to corrupt clergymen whose songs "Grate on their scrannel pipes of wretched straw." (Read that line and one of Tennyson's aloud and see which requires lips, teeth, and tongue to do more work.) But note that although Milton's line is harsh in sound, the line (when we meet it in his poem) is pleasing because it is artful.

Is sound identical with meaning in lines such as these? Not quite. In the passage from Tennyson, for instance, the cooing of doves is not *exactly* a moan. As John Crowe Ransom pointed out, the sound would be almost the same but the meaning entirely different in "The murdering of innumerable beeves." While it is true that the consonant sound *sl-* will often begin a word that conveys ideas of wetness and smoothness—*slick, slimy, slippery, slush*—we are so used to hearing it in words that convey nothing of the kind—*slave, slow, sledgehammer*—that it is doubtful whether, all by itself, the sound communicates anything definite. The most beautiful phrase in the English language, according to Dorothy Parker, is *cellar door*. Another wit once nominated, as our most euphonious word, not *sunrise* or *silvery* but *syphilis*.

Onomatopoeia

Relating sound more closely to meaning, the device called **onomatopoeia** is an attempt to represent a thing or action by a word that imitates the sound associated with it: *zoom, whiz, crash, bang, ding-dong, pitter-patter, yakety-yak*. Onomatopoeia is often effective in poetry, as in Emily Dickinson's line about the fly with its "uncertain stumbling Buzz," in which the nasal sounds *n, m, ng* and the sibilants *c, s* help make a droning buzz.

Like the Kikuyu tribesmen, others who care for poetry have discovered in the sound of words something of the refreshment of cool rain. Dylan Thomas, telling how he began to write poetry, said that from early childhood words were to him "as the notes of bells, the sounds of musical instruments, the noises of wind, sea, and rain, the rattle of milk carts, the clopping of hooves on cobbles, the fingering of branches on the window pane, might be to someone, deaf from birth, who has miraculously found his hearing."[2] For readers, too, the sound of words can have a magical spell, most powerful when it points to meaning.

William Butler Yeats (1865–1939)

Who Goes with Fergus? 1892

Who will go drive with Fergus now,
And pierce the deep wood's woven shade,
And dance upon the level shore?
Young man, lift up your russet brow,
And lift your tender eyelids, maid, 5
And brood on hopes and fear no more.

And no more turn aside and brood
Upon love's bitter mystery;
For Fergus rules the brazen cars,° *chariots*
And rules the shadows of the wood, 10
And the white breast of the dim sea
And all dishevelled wandering stars.

WHO GOES WITH FERGUS? *Fergus:* Irish king who gave up his throne to be a wandering poet.

Questions

1. In what lines do you find euphony?
2. In what line do you find cacophony?
3. How do the sounds of these lines stress what is said in them?

Exercise: Listening to Meaning

Read aloud the following two poems. In the sounds of which particular words are meanings well captured? Do you find examples of onomatopoeia?

William Wordsworth (1770–1850)

A Slumber Did My Spirit Seal 1800

A slumber did my spirit seal;
    I had no human fears—
She seemed a thing that could not feel
    The touch of earthly years.

[2]"Notes on the Art of Poetry," *Modern Poetics*, ed. James Scully (New York: McGraw-Hill, 1965).

No motion has she now, no force;   5
   She neither hears nor sees;
Rolled round in earth's diurnal course,
   With rocks, and stones, and trees.

Aphra Behn (1640?–1689)

When maidens are young   1687

When maidens are young, and in their spring,
Of pleasure, of pleasure let 'em take their full swing,
   Full swing, full swing,
And love, and dance, and play, and sing,
For Silvia, believe it, when youth is done,   5
There's nought but hum-drum, hum-drum, hum-drum,
There's nought but hum-drum, hum-drum, hum-drum.

ALLITERATION AND ASSONANCE

Listening to a symphony in which themes are repeated throughout each movement, we enjoy both their recurrence and their variation. We take similar pleasure in the repetition of a phrase or a single chord. Something like this pleasure is afforded us frequently in poetry.

Analogies between poetry and wordless music, it is true, tend to break down when carried far, since poetry—to mention a single difference—has denotation. But like musical compositions, poems have patterns of sounds. Among such patterns long popular in English poetry is **alliteration,** which has been defined as a succession of similar sounds. Alliteration occurs in the repetition of the same consonant sound at the beginning of successive words—"round and round the rugged rocks the ragged rascal ran," or in this delightful stanza by Witter Bynner, written nearly a century ago as part of an elaborate literary hoax:

> If I were only dafter
>   I might be making hymns
> To the liquor of your laughter
>   And the lacquer of your limbs.

Or it may occur inside the words, as in Milton's description of the gates of Hell:

> On a sudden open fly
> With impetuous recoil and jarring sound
> The infernal doors, and on their hinges grate
> Harsh thunder, that the lowest bottom shook
> Of Erebus.

The former kind is called **initial alliteration,** the latter **internal alliteration** or **hidden alliteration.** We recognize alliteration by sound, not by spelling: *know* and *nail* alliterate, *know* and *key* do not. In a line by E. E. Cummings, "colossal hoax of clocks and calendars," the sound of *x* within *hoax* alliterates with the *cks* in *clocks*. Incidentally, the letter *r* does not *always* lend itself to cacophony: elsewhere in *Paradise Lost* Milton says that

>   Heaven opened wide
> Her ever-during gates, harmonious sound
> On golden hinges moving . . .

By itself, a letter-sound has no particular meaning. This is a truth forgotten by people who would attribute the effectiveness of Milton's lines on the Heavenly Gates to, say, "the mellow o's and liquid *l* of *harmonious* and *golden*." Mellow o's and liquid *l*'s occur also in the phrase *moldy cold oatmeal*, which may have a quite different effect. Meaning depends on larger units of language than letters of the alphabet.

As we have seen, to repeat the sound of a consonant is to produce alliteration, but to repeat the sound of a *vowel* is to produce **assonance.** Like alliteration, assonance may occur either initially—"all the *awful auguries*"—or internally—Edmund Spenser's "Her goodly *eyes* like sapphires shining bright, / Her forehead *ivory* white . . ." and it can help make common phrases unforgettable: "eager beaver," "holy smoke." Like alliteration, it slows the reader down and focuses attention.

A. E. Housman (1859–1936)

Eight O'Clock   1922

He stood, and heard the steeple
  Sprinkle the quarters on the morning town.
One, two, three, four, to market-place and people
  It tossed them down.

Strapped, noosed, nighing his hour,   5
  He stood and counted them and cursed his luck;
And then the clock collected in the tower
  Its strength, and struck.

Questions

1. Why does the protagonist in this brief drama curse his luck? What is his situation?
2. For so short a poem, "Eight O'Clock" carries a great weight of alliteration. What patterns of initial alliteration do you find? What patterns of internal alliteration? What effect is created by all this heavy emphasis?

James Joyce (1882–1941)

All day I hear   1907

All day I hear the noise of waters
  Making moan,
Sad as the sea-bird is, when going
  Forth alone,
He hears the winds cry to the waters'   5
  Monotone.

The grey winds, the cold winds are blowing
  Where I go.

I hear the noise of many waters
    Far below.   10
All day, all night, I hear them flowing
    To and fro.

Questions

1. Find three instances of alliteration in the first stanza. Do any of them serve to reinforce meaning?
2. There is a great deal of assonance throughout the poem on a single vowel sound. What sound is it, and what effect is achieved by its repetition?

Experiment: Reading for Assonance

Try reading aloud as rapidly as possible the following poem by Tennyson. From the difficulties you encounter, you may be able to sense the slowing effect of assonance. Then read the poem aloud a second time, with consideration.

Alfred, Lord Tennyson (1809–1892)

The splendor falls on castle walls   1850

The splendor falls on castle walls
    And snowy summits old in story:
The long light shakes across the lakes,
    And the wild cataract leaps in glory.
Blow, bugle, blow, set the wild echoes flying,   5
Blow, bugle; answer, echoes, dying, dying, dying.

    O hark, O hear! how thin and clear,
        And thinner, clearer, farther going!
    O sweet and far from cliff and scar°   *jutting rock*
        The horns of Elfland faintly blowing!   10
Blow, let us hear the purple glens replying:
Blow, bugle; answer, echoes, dying, dying, dying.

    O love, they die in yon rich sky,
        They faint on hill or field or river:
    Our echoes roll from soul to soul,   15
        And grow for ever and for ever.
Blow, bugle, blow, set the wild echoes flying,
And answer, echoes, answer, dying, dying, dying.

RIME

Isak Dinesen's tribesmen, to whom rime was a new phenomenon, recognized at once that rimed language is special language. So do we, for, although much English poetry is unrimed, rime is one means to set poetry apart from ordinary conversation and bring it closer to music. A **rime** (or rhyme), defined most narrowly, occurs when two or more words or phrases contain an identical or similar vowel-sound, usually accented, and the consonant-sounds (if any) that follow the vowel-sound are identical: *hay* and *sleigh*, *prairie schooner* and *piano tuner*. From these examples it will be seen that rime depends not on spelling but on sound.

Excellent rimes surprise. It is all very well that a reader may anticipate which vowel-sound is coming next, for patterns of rime give pleasure by satisfying expectations; but riming becomes dull clunking if, at the end of each line, the reader can predict the word that will end the next. Hearing many a jukebox song for the first time, a listener can do so: *charms* lead to *arms*, *skies above* to *love*. As Alexander Pope observes of the habits of dull rimesters,

> Where'er you find "the cooling western breeze,"
> In the next line it "whispers through the trees";
> If crystal streams "with pleasing murmurs creep,"
> The reader's threatened (not in vain) with "sleep" . . .

But who—given the opening line of this comic poem—could predict the lines that follow?

William Cole (1919–2000)

On my boat on Lake Cayuga   1985

On my boat on Lake Cayuga
I have a horn that goes "Ay-oogah!"
I'm not the modern kind of creep
Who has a horn that goes "beep beep."

Robert Herrick, in a more subtle poem, made good use of rime to indicate a startling contrast:

> Then while time serves, and we are but decaying,
> Come, my Corinna, come, let's go a-Maying.

Though good rimes seem fresh, not all will startle, and probably few will call to mind things so unlike as *May* and *decay*, *Cayuga* and *Ay-oogah*. Some masters of rime often link words that, taken out of context, might seem common and unevocative. Here are the opening lines of Rachel Hadas's poem, "Three Silences," which describe an infant feeding at a mother's breast:

> Of all the times when not to speak is best,
> mother's and infant's is the easiest,
> the milky mouth still warm against her breast.

Hadas's rime words are not especially memorable in themselves, and yet these lines are—at least in part because they rime so well. The quiet echo of sound at the end of each line reinforces the intimate tone of the mother's moment with her child. Poetic invention may be driven home without rime, but it is rime sometimes that rings the doorbell. Admittedly, some rimes wear thin from too much use. More difficult to use freshly than before the establishment of Tin Pan Alley, rimes such as *moon*, *June*, *croon* seem leaden and would need an extremely powerful context to ring true. *Death* and *breath* are a rime that poets have used with wearisome frequency; another is *birth*, *earth*, *mirth*. And yet we cannot exclude these from the diction of poetry, for they might be the very words a poet would need in order to say something new and original.

Types of Rime

To have an **exact rime,** sounds following the vowel sound have to be the same: *red* and *bread, wealthily* and *stealthily, walk to her* and *talk to her.* If final consonant sounds are the same but the vowel sounds are different, the result is **slant rime,** also called **near rime, off rime,** or **imperfect rime:** *sun* riming with *bone, moon, rain, green, gone, thin.* By not satisfying the reader's expectation of an exact chime, but instead giving a clunk, a slant rime can help a poet say some things in a particular way. It works especially well for disappointed letdowns, negations, and denials, as in Blake's couplet:

> He who the ox to wrath has moved
> Shall never be by woman loved.

Consonance, a kind of slant rime, occurs when the rimed words or phrases have the same beginning and ending consonant sounds but a different vowel, as in *chitter* and *chatter.* Owen rimes *spoiled* and *spilled* in this way. Consonance is used in a traditional nonsense poem, "The Cutty Wren": "'O where are you going?' says *Milder* to *Malder.*" (W. H. Auden wrote a variation on it that begins, "'O where are you going?' said *reader* to *rider,*" thus keeping the consonance.)

End rime, as its name indicates, comes at the ends of lines, **internal rime** within them. Most rime tends to be end rime. Few recent poets have used internal rime so heavily as Wallace Stevens in the beginning of "Bantams in Pine-Woods": "Chieftain Iffucan of Azcan in caftan / Of tan with henna hackles, halt!" (lines also heavy on alliteration). A poet may employ both end rime and internal rime in the same poem, as in Robert Burns's satiric ballad "The Kirk's Alarm":

> Orthodox, Orthodox, wha believe in John Knox,
>   Let me sound an alarm to your conscience:
> There's a heretic blast has been blawn i' the wast,°   *west*
>   "That what is not sense must be nonsense."

Masculine rime is a rime of one-syllable words (*jail, bail*) or (in words of more than one syllable) stressed final syllables: *di-VORCE, re-MORSE,* or *horse, re-MORSE.*

Feminine rime is a rime of two or more syllables, with stress on a syllable other than the last: *TUR-tle, FER-tile,* or (to take an example from Byron) *in-tel-LECT-u-al, hen-PECKED you all.* Often it lends itself to comic verse, but can occasionally be valuable to serious poems, as in Wordsworth's "Resolution and Independence":

> We poets in our youth begin in gladness,
> But thereof come in the end despondency and madness.

Artfully used, feminine rime can give a poem a heightened musical effect for the simple reason that it offers the listener twice as many riming syllables in each line. In the wrong hands, however, that sonic abundance has the unfortunate ability of making a bad poem twice as painful to endure. Serious poems containing feminine rimes of three syllables have been attempted, notably by Thomas Hood in "The Bridge of Sighs":

> Take her up tenderly,
> Lift her with care;
> Fashioned so slenderly,
> Young, and so fair!

But the pattern is hard to sustain without lapsing into unintended comedy, as in the same poem:

> Still, for all slips of hers,
> One of Eve's family—
> Wipe those poor lips of hers,
> Oozing so clammily.

It works better when comedy is wanted.

Hilaire Belloc (1870–1953)

The Hippopotamus   1896

I shoot the Hippopotamus
   with bullets made of platinum,
Because if I use leaden ones
   his hide is sure to flatten 'em.

Bob Kaufman (1925–1986)

No More Jazz at Alcatraz   (1967)

No More Jazz
at Alcatraz
No more piano
for Lucky Luciano
No more trombone   5
for Al Capone
No More Jazz
at Alcatraz
No more cello
for Frank Costello   10
No more screeching of the
Seagulls
As they line up for
Chow
No More Jazz   15
at Alcatraz

NO MORE JAZZ AT ALCATRAZ. *Alcatraz:* maximum security federal prison on an island in the San Francisco Bay, closed down in 1963; now a popular tourist attraction. The prison once had an all-inmate jazz band. 4, 6, 10 *Lucky Luciano, Al Capone, Frank Costello:* famous Mafia gangsters.

Questions

1. What is unusual about Kaufman's rimes?
2. The poem describes one of the harshest prisons in American history. What is surprising about the poem's mood? How does the poet achieve that effect?

In **eye rime,** spellings look alike but pronunciations differ—*rough* and *dough*, *idea* and *flea*, *Venus* and *menus*. Strictly speaking, eye rime is not rime at all.

Rime in American poetry suffered a significant fall from favor in the early 1960s. A new generation of poets took for models the open forms of Whitman, Pound, and William Carlos Williams. In the last few decades, however, some poets have been skillfully using rime again in their work. Often called the **New Formalists,** these poets include Julia Alvarez, R. S. Gwynn, Mark Jarman, Paul Lake, Charles Martin, Marilyn Nelson, A. E. Stallings, and Timothy Steele. Their poems often use rime and meter to present unusual contemporary subjects, but they also sometimes write poems that recollect, converse with, and argue with the poetry of the past.

Still, most American poets don't write in rime; some even consider its possibilities exhausted. Such a view may be a reaction against the wearing thin of rimes by overuse or the mechanical and meaningless application of a rime scheme. Yet anyone who listens to children skipping rope in the street, making up rimes to delight themselves as they go along, may doubt that the pleasures of rime are ended; and certainly the practice of Yeats and Emily Dickinson, to name only two, suggests that the possibilities of slant rime may be nearly infinite. If successfully employed, as it has been at times by a majority of English-speaking poets whose work we care to save, rime runs through its poem like a spine: the creature moves by means of it.

William Butler Yeats (1865–1939)

Leda and the Swan
1928

A sudden blow: the great wings beating still
Above the staggering girl, her thighs caressed
By the dark webs, her nape caught in his bill,
He holds her helpless breast upon his breast.

How can those terrified vague fingers push   5
The feathered glory from her loosening thighs?
And how can body, laid in that white rush,
But feel the strange heart beating where it lies?

A shudder in the loins engenders there
The broken wall, the burning roof and tower   10
And Agamemnon dead.
                Being so caught up,
So mastered by the brute blood of the air,
Did she put on his knowledge with his power
Before the indifferent beak could let her drop?

Questions

1. According to Greek mythology, the god Zeus in the form of a swan descended on Leda, a Spartan queen. Among Leda's children were Clytemnestra, Agamemnon's unfaithful wife, who conspired in his murder, and Helen, on whose account the Trojan War was fought. What does a knowledge of these allusions contribute to our understanding of the poem's last two lines?
2. The slant rime *up* / *drop* (lines 11, 14) may seem accidental or inept. Is it? Would this poem have ended nearly so well if Yeats had made an exact rime like *up* / *cup* or *stop* / *drop*?

Gerard Manley Hopkins (1844–1889)

God's Grandeur (1877)

The world is charged with the grandeur of God.
　It will flame out, like shining from shook foil;
　It gathers to a greatness, like the ooze of oil
Crushed. Why do men then now not reck his rod?
Generations have trod, have trod, have trod; 5
　And all is seared with trade; bleared, smeared with toil;
　And wears man's smudge and shares man's smell: the soil
Is bare now, nor can foot feel, being shod.

And for all this, nature is never spent;
　There lives the dearest freshness deep down things; 10
And though the last lights off the black West went
　Oh, morning, at the brown brink eastward, springs—
Because the Holy Ghost over the bent
　World broods with warm breast and with ah! bright wings.

GOD'S GRANDEUR. 1 *charged*: as though with electricity. 3–4 *It gathers . . . Crushed*: The grandeur of God
will rise and be manifest, as oil rises and collects from crushed olives or grain. 4 *reck his rod*: heed His law.
10 *deep down things*: Tightly packing the poem, Hopkins omits the preposition *in* or *within* before *things*.
11 *last lights . . . went*: When in 1534 Henry VIII broke ties with the Roman Catholic Church and created
the Church of England.

Questions

1. In a letter Hopkins explained "shook foil" (line 2): "I mean foil in its sense of leaf or tinsel. . . .
Shaken goldfoil gives off broad glares like sheet lightning and also, and this is true of
nothing else, owing to its zigzag dints and creasings and network of small many cornered
facets, a sort of fork lightning too." What do you think he meant by the phrase "ooze of oil"
(line 3)? Would you call this phrase an example of alliteration?

2. What instances of internal rime does the poem contain? How would you describe their
effects?

3. Point out some of the poet's uses of alliteration and assonance. Do you believe that Hopkins
perhaps goes too far in his heavy use of devices of sound, or would you defend his practice?

4. Why do you suppose Hopkins, in the last two lines, says "over the bent / World" instead
of (as we might expect) *bent over the world*? How can the world be bent? Can you make
any sense out of this wording, or is Hopkins just trying to get his rime scheme to work out?

Robert Frost (1874–1963)

Desert Places 1936

Snow falling and night falling fast, oh, fast
In a field I looked into going past,
And the ground almost covered smooth in snow,
But a few weeds and stubble showing last.

The woods around it have it—it is theirs. 5
All animals are smothered in their lairs.
I am too absent-spirited to count;
The loneliness includes me unawares.

And lonely as it is that loneliness
Will be more lonely ere it will be less—— 10
A blanker whiteness of benighted snow
With no expression, nothing to express.

They cannot scare me with their empty spaces
Between stars—on stars where no human race is.
I have it in me so much nearer home 15
To scare myself with my own desert places.

Questions

1. What are these desert places that the speaker finds in himself? (More than one theory is possible. What is yours?)
2. Notice how many times, within the short space of lines 8–10, Frost says "lonely" (or "loneliness"). What other words in the poem contain similar sounds that reinforce these words?
3. In the closing stanza, the feminine rimes "spaces," "race is," and "places" might well occur in light or comic verse. Does "Desert Places" leave you laughing? If not, what does it make you feel?

READING AND HEARING POEMS ALOUD

Thomas Moore's "The light that lies in women's eyes"—a line rich in internal rime, alliteration, and assonance—is harder to forget than "The light burning in the gaze of a woman." Effective on the page, Moore's line becomes even more striking when heard aloud. There is no better way to understand a poem than to effectively read it aloud. Developing skill at reading poems aloud will not only deepen your understanding of literature, it will also improve your ability to speak in public.

Before trying to read a poem aloud to other people, understand its meaning as thoroughly as possible. If you know what the poet is saying and the poet's attitude toward it, you will be able to find an appropriate tone of voice and to give each part of the poem a proper emphasis.

Read more slowly than you would read aloud from a newspaper. Keep in mind that you are saying something to somebody. Don't race through the poem as if you are eager to get it over with.

Don't lapse into singsong. A poem may have a definite swing, but swing should never be exaggerated at the cost of sense. If you understand what the poem is saying and utter the poem as if you do, the temptation to fall into such a mechanical intonation should not occur. Observe the punctuation, making slight pauses for commas, longer pauses for full stops (periods, question marks, exclamation points).

If the poem is rimed, don't raise your voice and make the rimes stand out unnaturally. They should receive no more volume than other words in the poem, though a faint pause at the end of each line will call the listener's attention to them.

Listening to a poem, especially if it is unfamiliar, calls for concentration. Merciful people seldom read poetry uninterruptedly to anyone for more than a few minutes at a time. Robert Frost, always kind to his audiences, used to intersperse poems with many silences and seemingly casual remarks—shrewdly giving his hearers a chance to rest from their labors and giving his poems a chance to settle in.

If, in first listening to a poem, you don't take in all its meaning, don't be discouraged. With more practice in listening, your attention span and your ability to understand poems read aloud will increase. Incidentally, following the text of poems in a book while hearing them read aloud may increase your comprehension, but it may not necessarily help you to *listen*. At least some of the time, close your book and let your ears make the poems welcome. That way, their sounds may better work for you.

Exercise: Reading for Sound and Meaning

Read these brief poems aloud. What devices of sound do you find in each of them? Try to explain what sound contributes to the total effect of the poem and how it reinforces what the poet is saying.

Michael Stillman   (b. 1940)

In Memoriam John Coltrane   1972

   Listen to the coal
rolling, rolling through the cold
     steady rain, wheel on

   wheel, listen to the
turning of the wheels this night   5
     black as coal dust, steel

   on steel, listen to
these cars carry coal, listen
     to the coal train roll.

IN MEMORIAM JOHN COLTRANE. John Coltrane (1926–1967) was a saxophonist whose originality, passion, and technical wizardry have had a deep influence on the history of modern jazz.

Kevin Young   (b. 1970)

Doo Wop   2003

Honey baby
Lady lovely

Milk shake your
money maker

Shoo wah   5
Shoo wah

Countryfied
Sudden fried

Alabama
mamma jamma   10

Low bass
Fast pace

Past face
Femme postale

Penned pal   15
My gal

Corner song
Done wronged

Questions

1. What is the tone of this poem—comic? serious? both at once?
2. How many instances of plays on words, and playing with the sounds of words, can you find in the poem?
3. Beyond the author's exuberant delight in language, what do you think "Doo Wop" is about?

T. S. Eliot (1888–1965)

Virginia   1934

Red river, red river,
Slow flow heat is silence
No will is still as a river
Still. Will heat move
Only through the mocking-bird   5
Heard once? Still hills
Wait. Gates wait. Purple trees,
White trees, wait, wait,
Delay, decay. Living, living,
Never moving. Ever moving   10
Iron thoughts came with me
And go with me:
Red river, river, river.

VIRGINIA. This poem is one of a series entitled "Landscapes."

■ WRITING *effectively*

T. S. Eliot on Writing

The Music of Poetry   1942

I would remind you, first, that the music of poetry is not something which exists apart from the meaning. Otherwise, we could have poetry of great musical beauty which made no sense, and I have never come across such poetry. The apparent exceptions only show a difference of degree: there are poems in which we are moved by the music and take the sense for granted, just as there are poems in which we attend to the sense and are moved by the music without noticing it. Take an apparently extreme example—the non-sense verse of Edward Lear. His non-sense is not vacuity of sense: it is a parody of sense, and that is the sense of it.

• • •

So, while poetry attempts to convey something beyond what can be conveyed in prose rhythms, it remains, all the same, one person talking to another; and this is just as true if you sing it, for singing is another way of talking. The immediacy of poetry to conversation is not a matter on which we can lay down exact laws. Every revolution in poetry is apt to be, and sometimes to announce itself to be, a return to common speech. . . .

It would be a mistake, however, to assume that all poetry ought to be melodious, or that melody is more than one of the components of the music of words. Some poetry is meant to be sung; most poetry, in modern times, is meant to be spoken—and there are many other things to be spoken of besides the murmur of innumerable bees or the moan of doves in immemorial elms. Dissonance, even cacophony, has its place: just as, in a poem of any length, there must be transitions between passages of greater and less intensity, to give a rhythm of fluctuating emotion essential to the musical structure of the whole; and the passages of less intensity will be, in relation to the level on which the total poem operates, prosaic—so that, in the sense implied by that context, it may be said that no poet can write a poem of amplitude unless he is a master of the prosaic.

T. S. Eliot

From "The Music of Poetry"

THINKING ABOUT A POEM'S SOUND

A poem's music—the distinct way it sounds—is an important element of its effect and a large part of what separates it from prose. Describing a poem's sound can be tricky, though. Critics often disagree about the sonic effects of particular poems. Cataloguing every auditory element of a poem would be a huge, unwieldy job. The easiest way to write about sound is to focus your discussion. Concentrate on a single, clearly defined sonic element that strikes you as especially noteworthy. Simply try to understand how that element helps communicate the poem's main theme.

- **You might examine, for example, how certain features (such as rime, rhythm, meter, or alliteration) add force to the literal meaning of each line.** Or, for an ironic poem, you might look at how those same elements undercut and change the surface meaning of the poem.
- **Keep in mind that for a detailed analysis of this sort, it often helps to choose a short poem.** If you want to write about a longer poem, focus on a short passage that strikes you as especially rich in sonic effects.
- **Let your data build up before you force any conclusions about the poem's auditory effects.** As your list grows, a pattern should emerge, and ideas will probably occur to you that were not apparent earlier.

CHECKLIST: Writing About a Poem's Sound

☐ List the main auditory elements you find in the poem.

☐ Look for rime, meter, alliteration, assonance, euphony, cacophony, repetition, onomatopoeia.

☐ Is there a pattern in your list? Is the poem particularly heavy in alliteration or repetition, for example?

☐ Limit your discussion to one or two clearly defined sonic effects.

☐ How do your chosen effects help communicate the poem's main theme?

☐ How does the sound of the words add to the poem's mood?

WRITING ASSIGNMENT ON SOUND

Choose a brief poem from this chapter or the chapter "Poems for Further Reading" and examine how one or two elements of sound work throughout the poem to strengthen its meaning. Before you write, review the elements of sound described in this chapter. Back up your argument with specific quotations from the poem.

MORE TOPICS FOR WRITING

1. In a brief (500-word) essay, explore how wordplay contributes to the mood and meaning of T. S. Eliot's "Virginia."
2. Silently read Sylvia Plath's "Daddy" (in the chapter "Poems for Further Reading"). Now read the poem aloud, to yourself or to a friend. Now write briefly. What did you perceive about the poem from reading it aloud that you hadn't noticed before?
3. Consider the verbal music of Michael Stillman's "In Memoriam John Coltrane" (or a selection from the chapter "Poems for Further Reading"). Read the poem both silently and aloud, listening for sonic effects. Describe how the poem's sound underscores its meaning.

▶ TERMS FOR *review*

Sound Effects

Alliteration ▶ The repetition of a consonant sound in a line of verse or prose. Alliteration can be used at the beginning of words (**initial alliteration** as in "cool cats") or internally on stressed syllables (**internal alliteration** as in "I met a traveler from an antique land.").

Assonance ▶ The repetition of two or more vowel sounds in successive words, which creates a kind of rime. Like alliteration, the assonance may occur initially ("*all* the *awful* *auguries*") or internally ("white lilacs").

Cacophony ▶ A harsh, discordant sound often mirroring the meaning of the context in which it is used. The opposite of cacophony is **euphony.**

Euphony ▶ The harmonious effect when the sounds of the words connect with the meaning in a way pleasing to the ear and mind. The opposite of euphony is **cacophony.**

Onomatopoeia ▶ An attempt to represent a thing or action by a word that imitates the sound associated with it.

Rime

Rime ▶ Two or more words that contain an identical or similar vowel sound, usually accented, with following consonant sounds (if any) identical as well (*woo* and *stew*). An **exact rime** is a full rime in which the sounds following the initial letters of the words are identical in sound (*follow* and *hollow*).

Consonance ▶ Also called **Slant rime.** A kind of rime in which the linked words share similar consonant sounds but have different vowel sounds, as in *reason* and *raisin*, *mink* and *monk*. Sometimes only the final consonant sound is identical, as in *fame* and *room*.

End rime ▶ Rime that occurs at the ends of lines, rather than within them. End rime is the most common kind of rime in English-language poetry.

Internal rime ▶ Rime that occurs within a line of poetry, as opposed to **end rime.**

Masculine rime ▶ Either a rime of one-syllable words (*fox* and *socks*) or—in polysyllabic words—a rime on the stressed final syllables (con-*trive* and sur-*vive*).

Feminine rime ▶ A rime of two or more syllables with stress on a syllable other than the last (*tur*-tle and *fer*-tile).

Eye rime ▶ A "false" rime in which the spelling of the words is alike, but the pronunciations differ (*daughter* and *laughter*).

20

RHYTHM

*I would define, in brief, the Poetry of words as
the Rhythmical Creation of Beauty.*

—EDGAR ALLAN POE

STRESSES AND PAUSES

Rhythms affect us powerfully. We are lulled by a hammock's sway, awakened by an alarm clock's repeated yammer. Long after we come home from a beach, the rising and falling of waves and tides continue in memory. How powerfully the rhythms of poetry also move us may be felt in folk songs of railroad workers and chain gangs whose words were chanted in time to the lifting and dropping of a sledgehammer, and in verse that marching soldiers shout, putting a stress on every word that coincides with a footfall:

> Your LEFT! TWO! THREE! FOUR!
> Your LEFT! TWO! THREE! FOUR!
> You LEFT your WIFE and TWEN-ty-one KIDS
> And you LEFT! TWO! THREE! FOUR!
> You'll NEV-er get HOME to-NIGHT!

A rhythm is produced by a series of recurrences: the returns and departures of the seasons, the repetitions of an engine's stroke, the beats of the heart. A rhythm may be produced by the recurrence of a sound (the throb of a drum, a telephone's busy signal), but rhythm and sound are not identical. A totally deaf person at a parade can sense rhythm from the motions of the marchers' arms and feet, from the shaking of the pavement as they tramp. Rhythms inhere in the motions of the moon and stars, even though when they move, we hear no sound.

In poetry, several kinds of recurrent *sound* are possible, including (as we saw in the last chapter) rime, alliteration, and assonance. But most often when we speak of the **rhythm** of a poem, we mean the recurrence of stresses and pauses in it. When we hear a poem read aloud, stresses and pauses are, of course, part of its sound. It is possible to be aware of rhythms in poems read silently, too.

Stresses

A **stress** (or **accent**) is a greater amount of force given to one syllable in speaking than is given to another. We favor a stressed syllable with a little more breath and emphasis, with the result that it comes out slightly louder, higher in pitch, or longer in duration than other syllables. In this manner we place a stress on the first syllable of words such as *eagle, impact, open,* and *statue,* and on the second syllable in *cigar, mystique, precise,* and *until.* Each word in English carries at least one stress, except (usually) for the articles *a, an,* and *the,* the conjunction *and,* and one-syllable prepositions: *at, by, for, from, of, to, with.* Even these, however, take a stress once in a while: "Get WITH it!" "You're not THE Dolly Parton?" One word by itself is seldom long enough for us to notice a rhythm in it. Usually a sequence of at least a few words is needed for stresses to establish their pattern: a line, a passage, a whole poem. Strong rhythms may be seen in most Mother Goose rimes, to which children have been responding for hundreds of years. This rime is for an adult to chant while jogging a child up and down on a knee:

> Here goes my lord
> A trot, a trot, a trot, a trot!
> Here goes my lady
> A canter, a canter, a canter, a canter!
> Here goes my young master
> Jockey-hitch, jockey-hitch, jockey-hitch, jockey-hitch!
> Here goes my young miss
> An amble, an amble, an amble, an amble!
> The footman lags behind to tipple ale and wine
> And goes gallop, a gallop, a gallop, to make up his time.

More than one rhythm occurs in these lines, as the make-believe horse changes pace. How do these rhythms differ? From one line to the next, the interval between stresses lengthens or grows shorter. In "a TROT a TROT a TROT a TROT," the stress falls on every other syllable. But in the middle of the line "A CAN-ter a CAN-ter a CAN-ter a CAN-ter," the stress falls on every third syllable. When stresses recur at fixed intervals as in these lines, the result is called a **meter.**

Stresses embody meanings. Whenever two or more fall side by side, words gain in emphasis. Consider these hard-hitting lines from John Donne, in which accent marks have been placed, dictionary-fashion, to indicate the stressed syllables:

> Bat·ter my heart, three·per·soned God, for You
> As yet but knock, breathe, shine, and seek to mend.
> That I may rise and stand, o'er·throw me, and bend
> Your force to break, blow, burn, and make me new.

Unstressed (or **slack**) **syllables** also can direct our attention to what the poet means. In a line containing few stresses and a great many unstressed syllables, there can be an effect not of power and force but of hesitation and uncertainty. Yeats asks in "Among School Children" what young mother, if she could see her baby grown to be an old man, would think him:

> A com·pen·sa·tion for the pang of his birth,
> Or the un·cer·tain·ty of his set·ting forth?

When unstressed syllables recur in pairs, the result is a rhythm that trips and bounces, as in Robert Service's rollicking line:

A bunch of the boys were whoop·ing it up in the Ma·la·mute sa·loon . . .

or in Edgar Allan Poe's lines—also light but meant to be serious:

For the moon nev·er beams, with·out bring·ing me dreams

Of the beau·ti·ful An·na·bel Lee.

Apart from the words that convey it, the rhythm of a poem has no meaning. There are no essentially sad rhythms, nor any essentially happy ones. But some rhythms enforce certain meanings better than others do. The bouncing rhythm of Service's line seems fitting for an account of a merry night in a Klondike saloon; but it may be distracting when encountered in Poe's wistful elegy.

The special power of poetry comes from allowing us to hear simultaneously every level of meaning in language—denotation and connotation, image and idea, abstract content and physical sound. Since sound stress is one of the ways that the English language most clearly communicates meaning, any regular rhythmic pattern will affect the poem's effect. Poets learn to use rhythms that reinforce the meaning and the tone of a poem. As film directors know, any movie scene's effect can change dramatically if different background music accompanies the images. Master of the suspense film Alfred Hitchcock, for instance, could fill an ordinary scene with tension or terror just by playing nervous, grating music underneath it.

Exercise: Get with the Beat

In each of the following passages the author has established a strong rhythm. Describe how the rhythm helps establish the tone and meaning of the poem. How does each poem's beat seem appropriate to the tone and subject?

1. I sprang to the stirrup, and Joris and he;
    I galloped, Dirck galloped, we galloped all three;
    "Good speed!" cried the watch as the gate-bolts undrew;
    "Speed!" echoed the wall to us galloping through;
    Behind shut the postern, the lights sank to rest,
    And into the midnight we galloped abreast.
    —Robert Browning, from "How They Brought the Good News
    from Ghent to Aix"

2. I couldn't be cooler, I come from Missoula,
    And I rope and I chew and I ride.
    But I'm a heroin dealer, and I drive a four-wheeler
    With stereo speakers inside.
    My ol' lady Phoebe's out rippin' off C.B.'s
    From the rigs at the Wagon Wheel Bar,
    Near a Montana truck stop and a shit-outta-luck stop
    For a trucker who's driven too far.
    —Greg Keeler, from "There Ain't No Such Thing as a Montana
    Cowboy" (a song lyric)

3. Oh newsprint moonprint Marilyn!
    Rub ink from a finger
    to make your beauty mark.
    —Rachel Eisler, from "Marilyn's Nocturne" (a poem about a
    newspaper photograph of Marilyn Monroe)

Pauses

Rhythms in poetry are due not only to stresses but also to pauses. "Every nice ear," observed Alexander Pope (*nice* meaning "finely tuned"), "must, I believe, have observed that in any smooth English verse of ten syllables, there is naturally a pause either at the fourth, fifth, or sixth syllable." Such a light but definite pause within a line is called a **cesura** (or **caesura**), "a cutting." More liberally than Pope, we apply the name to any pause in a line of any length, after any word in the line. In studying a poem, we often indicate a cesura by double vertical lines (||). Usually, a cesura will occur at a mark of punctuation, but there can be a cesura even if no punctuation is present. Sometimes you will find it at the end of a phrase or clause or, as in these lines by William Blake, after an internal rime:

> And priests in black gowns || were walking their rounds
> And binding with briars || my joys and desires.

Lines of ten or twelve syllables (as Pope knew) tend to have just one cesura, though sometimes there are more as in John Webster's line from *The Duchess of Malfi*:

> Cover her face: || mine eyes dazzle: || she died young.

Pauses also tend to recur at more prominent places—namely, after each line. At the end of a verse (from *versus*, "a turning"), the reader's eye, before turning to go on to the next line, makes a pause, however brief. If a line ends in a full pause—usually indicated by some mark of punctuation—we call it **end-stopped.** All the lines in this passage from Christopher Marlowe's *Doctor Faustus* (in which Faustus addresses the apparition of Helen of Troy) are end-stopped:

> Was this the face that launch'd a thousand ships,
> And burnt the topless towers of Ilium?
> Sweet Helen, make me immortal with a kiss.
> Her lips suck forth my soul: see, where it flies!
> Come, Helen, come, give me my soul again.
> Here will I dwell, for heaven is in these lips,
> And all is dross that is not Helena.

A line that does not end in punctuation and that therefore is read with only a slight pause after it is called a **run-on line.** Because a run-on line gives us only part of a phrase, clause, or sentence, we have to read on to the line or lines following, in order to complete a thought. All these lines from Robert Browning's "My Last Duchess" are run-on lines:

> Sir, 'twas not
> Her husband's presence only, called that spot
> Of joy into the Duchess' cheek: perhaps
> Frà Pandolf chanced to say "Her mantle laps
> Over my lady's wrist too much," or "Paint
> Must never hope to reproduce the faint
> Half-flush that dies along her throat": such stuff
> Was courtesy, she thought . . .

A passage in run-on lines has a rhythm different from that of a passage like Marlowe's in end-stopped lines. When emphatic pauses occur in the quotation from Browning, they fall within a line rather than at the end of one. The passage by Marlowe and that by Browning are in lines of the same meter (iambic) and the same length (ten syllables). What makes the big difference in their rhythms is the running on, or lack of it.

To sum up: rhythm is recurrence. In poems, it is made of stresses and pauses. The poet can produce it by doing any of several things: making the intervals between stresses fixed or varied, long or short; indicating pauses (cesuras) within lines; end-stopping lines or running them over; writing in short or long lines. Rhythm in itself cannot convey meaning. And yet if a poet's words have meaning, their rhythm must be one with it.

Gwendolyn Brooks (1917–2000)

We Real Cool

1960

> *The Pool Players.*
> *Seven at the Golden Shovel.*

We real cool. We
Left school. We

Lurk late. We
Strike straight. We

Sing sin. We   5
Thin gin. We

Jazz June. We
Die soon.

Question

Describe the rhythms of this poem. By what techniques are they produced?

Alfred, Lord Tennyson (1809–1892)

Break, Break, Break

(1834)

Break, break, break,
  On thy cold gray stones, O Sea!
And I would that my tongue could utter
  The thoughts that arise in me.

O well for the fisherman's boy,   5
  That he shouts with his sister at play!
O well for the sailor lad,
  That he sings in his boat on the bay!

And the stately ships go on
  To their haven under the hill;   10
But O for the touch of a vanish'd hand,
  And the sound of a voice that is still!

Break, break, break,
At the foot of thy crags, O Sea!
But the tender grace of a day that is dead   15
Will never come back to me.

Questions

1. Read the first line aloud. What effect does it create at the beginning of the poem?
2. Is there a regular rhythmic pattern in this poem? If so, how would you describe it?
3. The speaker claims that his or her thoughts are impossible to utter. Using evidence from the poem, can you describe the speaker's thoughts and feelings?

Dorothy Parker (1893–1967)

Résumé   1926

Razors pain you;
Rivers are damp;
Acids stain you;
And drugs cause cramp.
Guns aren't lawful;   5
Nooses give;
Gas smells awful;
You might as well live.

Questions

1. Which of the following words might be used to describe the rhythm of this poem, and which might not—*flowing, jaunty, mournful, tender, abrupt*?
2. Is this light verse or a serious poem? Can it be both?

METER

Meter is the rhythmic pattern of stresses in verse. To enjoy the rhythms of a poem, no special knowledge of meter is necessary. All you need do is pay attention to stresses and where they fall, and you will perceive the basic pattern, if there is any. There is nothing occult about the study of meter. Most people find they can master its essentials in no more time than it takes to learn a complicated game such as chess. If you take the time, you will then have the pleasure of knowing what is happening in the rhythms of many a fine poem, and pleasurable knowledge may even deepen your insight into poetry. The following discussion, then, will be of interest only to those who care to go deeper into **prosody,** the study of metrical structures in poetry.

To make ourselves aware of a meter, we need only listen to a poem, or sound its words to ourselves. If we care to work out exactly what a poet is doing, we *scan* a line or a poem by indicating the stresses in it. **Scansion,** the art of so doing, is not just a matter of pointing to syllables; it is also a matter of listening to a poem and making sense of it. To scan a poem is one way to indicate how to read it aloud; in order to see where stresses fall, you have to see the places where the poet wishes to put emphasis. That is why, when scanning a poem, you may find yourself suddenly understanding it.

An objection might be raised against scanning: isn't it too simple to pretend that all language (and poetry) can be divided neatly into stressed syllables and unstressed syllables? Indeed it is. Language isn't binary; there are many levels of stress from a scream to a whisper. However, the idea in scanning a poem is not to reproduce the sound of a human voice. For that we would do better to buy a tape recorder. To scan a poem, rather, is to make a diagram of the stresses (and absences of stress) we find in it. Various marks are used in scansion; in this book we use *ˊ* for a stressed syllable and ⏑ for an unstressed syllable.

Types of Meter

There are four common accentual-syllabic meters in English—iambic, anapestic, trochaic, and dactylic. Each is named for its basic **foot** (usually a unit of two or three syllables that contains one strong stress) or building block. Here are some examples of each meter.

1. **Iambic**—a line made up primarily of **iambs,** an unstressed syllable followed by a stressed syllable, ⏑ˊ. The iambic measure is the most common meter in English poetry. Many writers, such as Robert Frost, feel iambs most easily capture the natural rhythms of our speech.

   But soft, | what light | through yon | der win | dow breaks?
   —*William Shakespeare*

   When I | have fears | that I | may cease | to be
   —*John Keats*

2. **Anapestic**—a line made up primarily of **anapests,** two unstressed syllables followed by a stressed syllable, ⏑⏑ˊ. Anapestic meter resembles iambic but contains an extra unstressed syllable. Totally anapestic lines often start to gallop, so poets sometimes slow them down by substituting an iambic foot (as Poe does in "Annabel Lee").

   Now this | is the Law | of the Jun | gle—as old | and as true | as the sky;

   And the Wolf | that shall keep | it may pros | per, | but the Wolf | that shall break | it must die.
   —*Rudyard Kipling*

   It was ma | ny and ma | ny a year | a go,
   In a king | dom by | the sea,
   That a maid | en there lived | whom you | may know
   By the name | of An | na·bel Lee.
   —*Edgar Allan Poe*

3. **Trochaic**—a line made up primarily of **trochees,** a stressed syllable followed by an unstressed syllable, ′◡. The trochaic meter is often associated with songs, chants, and magic spells in English. Trochees make a strong, emphatic meter that is often very mnemonic—that is, "helping, or meant to help, the memory." Shakespeare and Blake used trochaic meter to exploit its magical associations. Notice how Blake drops the unstressed syllable at the end of his lines from "The Tyger." (The location of a missing syllable in a metrical foot is usually marked with a caret sign, ∨.)

> ′ ◡ ′ ◡ ′ ◡ ′ ◡
> Dou·ble, | dou·ble, | toil and | trou·ble,
> ′ ◡ ′ ◡ ′ ◡ ′ ◡
> Fi·re | burn and | caul·dron | bub·ble.
> —*Shakespeare*

> ′ ◡ ′ ◡ ′ ◡ ′ ∨
> Ty·ger! | Ty·ger! | burn·ing | bright
> ′ ◡ ′ ◡ ′ ◡ ′ ∨
> In the | for·ests | of the | night
> —*William Blake*

4. **Dactylic**—a line made up primarily of **dactyls,** one stressed syllable followed by two unstressed syllables, ′◡◡. The dactylic meter is less common in English than in classical languages such as Greek or Latin. Used carefully, dactylic meter can sound stately, as in Longfellow's *Evangeline*.

> ′ ◡ ◡ ′ ◡ ◡ ′ ◡ ◡ ′ ◡ ◡ ′ ◡ ◡
> This is the | for·est pri | me·val. The | mur·mur·ing | pines and the
> ′ ◡
> | hem·lock
> —*Henry Wadsworth Longfellow*

But it also easily becomes a prancing, propulsive measure and is often used in comic verse.

> ′ ◡ ◡ ′ ◡ ◡ ′ ◡ ◡ ′ ∨
> Puss·y·cat, | puss·y·cat, | where have you | been?
> —*Mother Goose*

Iambic and anapestic meters are called **rising meters** because their movement rises from an unstressed syllable (or syllables) to stress; trochaic and dactylic meters are called **falling.** In the twentieth century, the bouncing meters—anapestic and dactylic—were used more often for comic verse than for serious poetry. Called feet, though they contain no unaccented syllables, are the **monosyllabic foot** (′) and the **spondee** (′′). Meters are not ordinarily made up of them; if one were, it would be like the steady impact of nails being hammered into a board—no pleasure to hear or to dance to. But inserted now and then, they can lend emphasis and variety to a meter, as Yeats well knew when he broke up the predominantly iambic rhythm of "Who Goes with Fergus?" (page 616) with the line in which two spondees occur:

> ◡ ◡ ′ ′ ◡ ◡ ′ ′
> And the white breast of the dim sea.

Line Lengths

Meters are classified also by line lengths: *trochaic monometer,* for instance, is a line one trochee long, as in this anonymous brief comment on microbes:

Adam
Had 'em.

A frequently heard metrical description is **iambic pentameter:** a line of five iambs, a meter especially familiar because it occurs in all blank verse (such as Shakespeare's plays and Milton's *Paradise Lost*), heroic couplets, and sonnets. The commonly used names for line lengths follow:

monometer	one foot
dimeter	two feet
trimeter	three feet
tetrameter	four feet
pentameter	five feet
hexameter	six feet
heptameter	seven feet
octameter	eight feet

Lines of more than eight feet are possible but are rare. They tend to break up into shorter lengths in the listening ear.

Like a basic dance step, a meter is not to be slavishly adhered to. The fun in reading a metrical poem often comes from watching the poet continually departing from perfect regularity, giving a few heel-kicks to display a bit of joy or ingenuity, then easing back into the basic step again. Because meter is orderly and the rhythms of living speech are unruly, poets can play one against the other, in a sort of counterpoint. Robert Frost, a master at pitting a line of iambs against a very natural-sounding and irregular sentence, declared, "I am never more pleased than when I can get these into strained relation. I like to drag and break the intonation across the meter as waves first comb and then break stumbling on the shingle."[1]

Evidently Frost's skilled effects would be lost to a reader who, scanning a Frost poem or reading it aloud, distorted its rhythms to fit the words exactly to the meter. With rare exceptions, a good poem can be read and scanned the way we would speak its sentences if they were ours. This, for example, is an unreal scansion:

That's my last Duch·ess paint·ed on the wall.

—because no speaker of English would say that sentence in that way. We are likely to stress *That's* and *last.*

Although in good poetry we seldom meet a very long passage of absolute metrical regularity, we sometimes find (in a line or so) a monotonous rhythm that is effective. Words fall meaningfully in Macbeth's famous statement of world-weariness: "Tomorrow and tomorrow and tomorrow . . ." and in the opening lines of Thomas Gray's "Elegy Written in a Country Churchyard":

The cur·few tolls the knell of part·ing day,
The low·ing herd wind slow·ly o'er the lea,

[1]Letter to John Cournos in 1914, in *Selected Letters of Robert Frost,* ed. Lawrance Thompson (New York: Holt, 1964) 128.

˘ ´ ˘ ´ ˘ ˘ ´ ˘ ´ ˘ ´
The plow·man home·ward plods his wear·y way,
˘ ´ ˘ ´ ˘ ˘ ´ ˘ ´ ˘ ´
And leaves the world to dark·ness and to me.

Although certain unstressed syllables in these lines seem to call for more emphasis than others—you might, for instance, care to throw a little more weight on the second syllable of *curfew* in the opening line—we can still say that the lines are notably iambic. Their almost unvarying rhythm seems just right to convey the tolling of a bell and the weary setting down of one foot after the other.

Accentual Meter

Besides the two rising meters (iambic, anapestic) and the two falling meters (trochaic, dactylic), English poets have another valuable meter. It is **accentual meter,** in which the poet does not write in feet (as in the other meters) but instead counts accents (stresses). The idea is to have the same number of stresses in every line. The poet may place them anywhere in the line and may include practically any number of unstressed syllables, which do not count. In "Christabel," for instance, Coleridge keeps four stresses to a line, though the first line has only eight syllables and the last line has eleven:

´ ´ ´ ´
There is not wind e·nough to twirl
´ ´ ´ ´
The one red leaf, the last of its clan,
´ ´ ´ ´
That dan·ces as of·ten as dance it can,
´ ´ ´ ´
Hang·ing so light, and hang·ing so high,
´ ´ ´ ´
On the top-most twig that looks up at the sky.

The history of accentual meter is long and honorable. Old English poetry was written in a kind of accentual meter, but its line was more rule-bound than Coleridge's: four stresses arranged two on either side of a cesura, plus alliteration of three of the stressed syllables. In "Junk," Richard Wilbur revives the pattern:

´ ´ ´ ´ ´
An axe an·gles ‖ from my neigh·bor's ash·can . . .

Many poets, from the authors of Mother Goose rimes to Gerard Manley Hopkins, have sometimes found accentual meters congenial. Recently, accentual meter has enjoyed huge popularity through rap poetry, which usually employs a four-stress line (see page 607 for further discussion of rap).

Although less popular among poets today than formerly, meter endures. Major poets from Shakespeare through Yeats have fashioned their work by it, and if we are to read their poems with full enjoyment, we need to be aware of it. To enjoy metrical poetry—even to write it—you do not have to slice lines into feet; you do need to recognize when a meter is present in a line, and when the line departs from it. An argument in favor of meter is that it reminds us of body rhythms such as breathing, walking, the beating of the heart. In an effective metrical poem, these rhythms cannot be separated from what the poet is saying—or, in the words of an old jazz song of Duke Ellington's, "It don't mean a thing if it ain't got that swing." As critic Paul Fussell has put it: "No element of a poem is more basic—and I mean physical—in its effect upon the reader than the metrical element, and perhaps no technical triumphs reveal more readily than the metrical the poet's sympathy with that universal human nature . . . which exists outside his own."[2]

Exercise: Recognizing Rhythms

Which of the following poems contain predominant meters? Which poems are not wholly metrical, but are metrical in certain lines? Point out any such lines. What reasons do you see, in such places, for the poet's seeking a metrical effect?

Edna St. Vincent Millay (1892–1950)

Counting-out Rhyme   1928

Silver bark of beech, and sallow
Bark of yellow birch and yellow
   Twig of willow.

Stripe of green in moosewood maple,
Color seen in leaf of apple,   5
   Bark of popple.

Wood of popple pale as moonbeam,
Wood of oak for yoke and barn-beam,
   Wood of hornbeam.

Silver bark of beech, and hollow   10
Stem of elder, tall and yellow
   Twig of willow.

A. E. Housman (1859–1936)

When I was one-and-twenty   1896

When I was one-and-twenty
   I heard a wise man say,
"Give crowns and pounds and guineas
   But not your heart away;
Give pearls away and rubies   5
   But keep your fancy free."
But I was one-and-twenty,
   No use to talk to me.

When I was one-and-twenty
   I heard him say again,   10
"The heart out of the bosom
   Was never given in vain;
'Tis paid with sighs a plenty
   And sold for endless rue."
And I am two-and-twenty,   15
   And oh, 'tis true, 'tis true.

[2]*Poetic Meter and Poetic Form* (New York: Random, 1965) 110.

William Carlos Williams (1883–1963)

Smell!   1917

Oh strong-ridged and deeply hollowed
nose of mine! what will you not be smelling?
What tactless asses we are, you and I, boney nose,
always indiscriminate, always unashamed,
and now it is the souring flowers of the bedraggled   5
poplars: a festering pulp on the wet earth
beneath them. With what deep thirst
we quicken our desires
to that rank odor of a passing springtime!
Can you not be decent? Can you not reserve your ardors   10
for something less unlovely? What girl will care
for us, do you think, if we continue in these ways?
Must you taste everything? Must you know everything?
Must you have a part in everything?

Walt Whitman (1819–1892)

Beat! Beat! Drums!   (1861)

Beat! beat! drums!—blow! bugles! blow!
Through the windows—through doors—burst like a ruthless force,
Into the solemn church, and scatter the congregation,
Into the school where the scholar is studying;
Leave not the bridegroom quiet—no happiness must he have now with   5
    his bride,
Nor the peaceful farmer any peace, ploughing his field or gathering his
    grain,
So fierce you whirr and pound you drums—so shrill you bugles blow.

Beat! beat! drums!—blow! bugles! blow!
Over the traffic of cities—over the rumble of wheels in the streets;
Are beds prepared for sleepers at night in the houses? no sleepers must   10
    sleep in those beds,
No bargainer's bargains by day—no brokers or speculators—would they
    continue?
Would the talkers be talking? would the singer attempt to sing?
Would the lawyer rise in the court to state his case before the judge?
Then rattle quicker, heavier drums—you bugles wilder blow.

Beat! beat! drums!—blow! bugles! blow!   15
Make no parley—stop for no expostulation,
Mind not the timid—mind not the weeper or prayer,
Mind not the old man beseeching the young man,
Let not the child's voice be heard, nor the mother's entreaties,
Make even the trestles to shake the dead where they lie awaiting the   20
    hearses.
So strong you thump O terrible drums—so loud you bugles blow.

David Mason (b. 1954)

Song of the Powers

1996

Mine, said the stone,
mine is the hour.
I crush the scissors,
such is my power.
Stronger than wishes,   5
my power, alone.

Mine, said the paper,
mine are the words
that smother the stone
with imagined birds,   10
reams of them, flown
from the mind of the shaper.

Mine, said the scissors,
mine all the knives
gashing through paper's   15
ethereal lives;
nothing's so proper
as tattering wishes.

As stone crushes scissors,
as paper snuffs stone   20
and scissors cut paper,
all end alone.
So heap up your paper
and scissor your wishes
and uproot the stone   25
from the top of the hill.
They all end alone
as you will, you will.

SONG OF THE POWERS. The three key images of this poem are drawn from the children's game of Scissors, Paper, Stone. In this game each object has a specific power: Scissors cuts paper, paper covers stone, and stone crushes scissors.

Langston Hughes (1902–1967)

Dream Boogie

1951

Good morning, daddy!
Ain't you heard
The boogie-woogie rumble
Of a dream deferred?

Listen closely: 5
You'll hear their feet
Beating out and beating out a—

> *You think*
> *It's a happy beat?*
>
> Listen to it closely: 10
> Ain't you heard
> something underneath
> like a—
> *What did I say?*
>
> Sure,   15
> I'm happy!
> Take it away!
>
> > *Hey, pop!*
> > *Re-bop!*
> > *Mop!*   20
> >
> > *Y-e-a-h!*

■ WRITING *effectively*

Gwendolyn Brooks on Writing

Hearing "We Real Cool"   1969

Interviewer: How about the seven pool players in the poem "We Real Cool"?

Brooks: They have no pretensions to any glamor. They are supposedly dropouts, or at least they're in the poolroom when they should be possibly in school, since they're probably young enough or at least those I saw were when I looked in a poolroom, and they. . . . First of all, let me tell you how that's supposed to be said, because there's a reason why I set it out as I did. These are people who are essentially saying, "Kilroy is here. We *are*." But they're a little uncertain of the strength of their identity. The "We"—you're supposed to stop after the "We" and think about *validity*; of course, there's no way for you to tell whether it

Gwendolyn Brooks

should be said softly or not, I suppose, but I say it rather softly because I want to represent their basic uncertainty, which they don't bother to question every day, of course.

Interviewer: Are you saying that the form of this poem, then, was determined by the colloquial rhythm you were trying to catch?

Brooks: No, determined by my feelings about these boys, these young men.

From "An Interview with Gwendolyn Brooks" by George Stavros

THINKING ABOUT RHYTHM

When we read casually, we don't need to think very hard about a poem's rhythm. We *feel* it as we read, even if we aren't consciously paying attention to matters such as iambs or anapests. When analyzing a poem, though, it helps to have a clear sense of how the rhythm works, and the best way to reach that understanding is through scansion. A scansion gives us a picture of the poem's most important sound patterns. Scanning a poem can seem a bit intimidating at first, but it really isn't all that difficult.

- **Read the poem aloud, marking the stressed syllables as you go.**
- **If you're having a hard time hearing the stresses, read the line a few different ways.** Try to detect which way seems most like natural speech.

Example: **Tennyson's "Break, Break, Break"**

A simple scansion of the opening of Tennyson's poem "Break, Break, Break" (on page 635) might look like this in your notes:

Break, break, break	(3 syllables)
On thy cold gray stones, O Sea!	(7 syllables)/rime
And I would that my tongue could utter	(9 syllables)
The thoughts that arise in me.	(7 syllables)/rime

By now some basic organizing principles of the poem have become clear. The lines are rimed *abcb*, but they contain an irregular number of syllables. The number of strong stresses, however, seems to be constant, at least in the opening stanza.

Now that you have a visual diagram of the poem's sound, the rhythm will be much easier to write about. This diagram will also lead you to a richer understanding of how the poet's artistry reinforces the poem's meaning. The three sharp syllables of the first line give the reader an immediate sense of the depth and intensity of the speaker's feelings. The sudden burst of syllables in the third line underscores the rush of passion that wells up in his breast and outstrips his ability to give voice to it. And the rhythm of the last two lines—the rising intensity of the third line followed by the ebb of the fourth—subtly suggests the effect of the surging and receding of the waves.

CHECKLIST: Scanning a Poem

☐ Read the poem aloud.

☐ Mark the syllables on which the main speech stresses fall. When in doubt, read the line aloud several different ways. Which way seems most natural?

☐ Are there rimes? Indicate where they occur.

☐ How many syllables are there in each line?

☐ Do any other recurring sound patterns strike you?

☐ Does the poem set up a reliable pattern and then diverge from it anywhere? If so, how does that irregularity underscore the line's meaning?

WRITING ASSIGNMENT ON RHYTHM

Scan the rhythm of a passage from any poem in this chapter, following the guidelines listed above. Discuss how the poem uses rhythm to create certain key effects. Be sure that your scansion shows all the elements you've chosen to discuss.

MORE TOPICS FOR WRITING

1. Pair up with a friend or classmate and take turns reading Langston Hughes's "Dream Boogie" out loud to each other. Now write briefly on what you learned about this poem's rhythm by speaking and hearing it.

2. How do rhythm and other kinds of sonic effects (alliteration and consonance, for example) combine to make meaning in Edna St. Vincent Millay's "Counting-out Rhyme"?

3. Scan a stanza of Walt Whitman's "Beat! Beat! Drums!" What do you notice about the poem's rhythms? How do the rhythms underscore the poem's meaning?

4. Scan two poems, one in free verse, and the other in regular meter. For a free verse poem you might pick William Carlos Williams's "Smell!" (page 642) or Hart Crane's "My Grandmother's Love Letters" (page 833); for a poem in regular meter you could go with one of the poems in this chapter, e.g., A. E. Housman's "When I was one-and-twenty" or David Mason's "Song of the Powers." Now write about the experience. Do you detect any particular strengths offered by regular meter? How about by free verse?

5. Robert Frost once claimed he tried to make poetry out of the "sound of sense." Writing to a friend, Frost discussed his notion that "the simple declarative sentence" in English often contained an abstract sound that helped communicate its meaning. "The best place to get the abstract sound of sense," wrote Frost, "is from voices behind a door that cuts off the words." Ask yourself how these sentences of dialogue would sound without the words in which they are embodied:

> You mean to tell me you can't read?
> I said no such thing.
> Well, read then.
> You're not my teacher.

Frost went on to say that "The reader must be at no loss to give his voice the posture proper to the sentence." Thinking about Frost's theory, can you see how it throws any light on one of his poems? In two or three paragraphs, discuss how Frost uses the "simple declarative sentence" as a distinctive rhythmic feature in his poetry.

▶ TERMS FOR *review*

Pattern and Structure

Stress ▶ An emphasis, or **accent,** placed on a syllable in speech. The unstressed syllable in a line of verse is called the **slack syllable.**

Rhythm ▶ The recurring pattern of stresses and pauses in a poem. A fixed rhythm in a poem is called **meter.**

Prosody ▶ The study of metrical structures in poetry.

Scansion ▶ A practice used to describe rhythmic patterns in a poem by separating the metrical feet, counting the syllables, marking the accents, and indicating the cesuras.

Cesura or caesura ▶ A light but definite pause within a line of verse. Cesuras often appear near the middle of a line, but their placement may be varied for rhythmic effect.

Run-on line ▶ A line of verse that does not end in punctuation, but carries on grammatically to the next line. The use of run-on lines is called *enjambment*.

End-stopped line ▶ A line of verse that ends in a full pause, often indicated by a mark of punctuation.

Meter

Foot ▶ The basic unit of measurement in metrical poetry. Each separate meter is identified by the pattern and order of stressed and unstressed syllables in its foot.

Iamb ▶ A metrical foot in verse in which an unaccented syllable is followed by an accented one (˘ ′). The iambic measure is the most common meter used in English poetry.

Iambic pentameter ▶ The most common meter in English verse, five iambic feet per line. Many fixed forms, such as the sonnet and heroic couplets, employ iambic pentameter.

Anapest ▶ A metrical foot in verse in which two unstressed syllables are followed by a stressed syllable (˘ ˘ ′).

Trochee ▶ A metrical foot in which a stressed syllable is followed by an unstressed one (′ ˘).

Dactyl ▶ A metrical foot in which one stressed syllable is followed by two unstressed ones (′ ˘ ˘). Dactylic meter is less common in English than in classical Greek and Latin.

Spondee ▶ A metrical foot of verse consisting of two stressed syllables (′ ′).

Accentual meter ▶ Verse meter based on the number of stresses per line, not the number of syllables.

21

CLOSED FORM

Anybody can write the first line of a poem,
but it is a very difficult task to make
the second line rhyme with the first.

—MARK TWAIN

Form, as a general idea, is the design of a thing as a whole, the configuration of all its parts. No poem can escape having some kind of form, whether its lines are as various in length as a tree's branches or all in hexameter. To put this point in another way: if you were to listen to a poem read aloud in a language unknown to you, or if you saw the poem printed in that foreign language, whatever in the poem you could see or hear would be the form of it.[1]

Writing in **closed form,** a poet follows (or finds) some sort of pattern, such as that of a sonnet with its rime scheme and its fourteen lines of iambic pentameter. On a page, poems in closed form tend to look regular and symmetrical, often falling into stanzas that indicate groups of rimes. Along with William Butler Yeats, who held that a successful poem will "come shut with a click, like a closing box," the poet who writes in closed form apparently strives for a kind of perfection—seeking, perhaps, to lodge words so securely in place that no word can be budged without a worsening. For the sake of meaning, though, a competent poet often will depart from a symmetrical pattern. As Robert Frost observed, there is satisfaction to be found in things not mechanically regular: "We enjoy the straight crookedness of a good walking stick."

The poet who writes in **open form** usually seeks no final click. Often, such a poet views the writing of a poem as a process, rather than a quest for an absolute. Free to use white space for emphasis, able to shorten or lengthen lines as the sense seems to require, the poet lets the poem discover its shape as it goes along, moving as water flows downhill, adjusting to its terrain, engulfing obstacles. (Open form will provide the focus of the next chapter.)

Most poetry of the past is in closed form, exhibiting at least a pattern of rime or meter, but since the early 1960s the majority of American poets have preferred forms that stay open. Lately, the situation has been changing yet again, with closed form

---

[1]For a good summary of the uses of the term *form* in criticism of poetry, see the article "Form" by G. N. G. Orsini in *Princeton Encyclopedia of Poetry and Poetics,* 2nd ed., ed. Alex Preminger, Frank Warnke, and O. B. Hardison (Princeton: Princeton UP, 1975).

reappearing in much recent poetry. Whatever the fashion of the moment, the reader who seeks a wide understanding of poetry of both the present and the past will need to know both the closed and open varieties.

Closed form gives some poems a valuable advantage: it makes them more easily memorable. The **epic** poems of nations—long narratives tracing the adventures of popular heroes: the Greek *Iliad* and *Odyssey,* the French *Song of Roland,* the Spanish *Cid*—tend to occur in patterns of fairly consistent line length or number of stresses because these works were sometimes transmitted orally. Sung to the music of a lyre or chanted to a drumbeat, they may have been easier to memorize because of their patterns. If a singer forgot something, the song would have a noticeable hole in it, so rime or fixed meter probably helped prevent an epic from deteriorating when passed along from one singer to another. It is no coincidence that so many English playwrights of Shakespeare's day favored iambic pentameter. Companies of actors, often called on to perform a different play each day, could count on a fixed line length to aid their burdened memories.

Some poets complain that closed form is a straitjacket, a limit to free expression. Other poets, however, feel that, like fires held fast in a narrow space, thoughts stated in a tightly binding form may take on a heightened intensity. "Limitation makes for power," according to one contemporary practitioner of closed form, Richard Wilbur; "the strength of the genie comes of his being confined in a bottle." Compelled by some strict pattern to arrange and rearrange words, delete, and exchange them, poets must focus on them the keenest attention. Often they stand a chance of discovering words more meaningful than the ones they started out with. And at times, in obedience to a rime scheme, the poet may be surprised by saying something quite unexpected.

FORMAL PATTERNS

The best-known one-line pattern for a poem in English is **blank verse:** unrimed iambic pentameter. (This pattern is not a stanza: stanzas have more than one line.) Most portions of Shakespeare's plays are in blank verse, and so are Milton's *Paradise Lost,* Tennyson's "Ulysses," certain dramatic monologues of Browning and Frost, and thousands of other poems. Here is a poem in blank verse that startles us by dropping out of its pattern in the final line. Keats appears to have written it late in his life to his fiancée, Fanny Brawne.

John Keats (1795–1821)

This living hand, now warm   (1819?)
and capable

This living hand, now warm and capable
Of earnest grasping, would, if it were cold
And in the icy silence of the tomb,
So haunt thy days and chill thy dreaming nights
That thou wouldst wish thine own heart dry of blood   5
So in my veins red life might stream again,
And thou be conscience-calmed—see here it is—
I hold it towards you.

The Couplet

The **couplet** is a two-line stanza, usually rimed. Its lines often tend to be equal in length, whether short or long. Here are two examples:

> Blow,
> Snow!

> As I in hoary winter's night stood shivering in the snow,
> Surprised I was with sudden heat which made my heart to glow.

Actually, any pair of rimed lines that contains a complete thought is called a couplet, even if it is not a stanza, such as the couplet that ends a sonnet by Shakespeare. Unlike other stanzas, couplets are often printed solid, one couplet not separated from the next by white space. This practice is usual in printing the **heroic couplet**—or **closed couplet**—two rimed lines of iambic pentameter, the first ending in a light pause, the second more heavily end-stopped. George Crabbe, in *The Parish Register*, described a shotgun wedding:

> Next at our altar stood a luckless pair,
> Brought by strong passions and a warrant there:
> By long rent cloak, hung loosely, strove the bride,
> From every eye, what all perceived, to hide;
> While the boy bridegroom, shuffling in his pace,
> Now hid awhile and then exposed his face.
> As shame alternately with anger strove
> The brain confused with muddy ale to move,
> In haste and stammering he performed his part,
> And looked the rage that rankled in his heart.

Though employed by Chaucer, the heroic couplet was named from its later use by Dryden and others in poems, translations of classical epics, and verse plays of epic heroes. It continued in favor through most of the eighteenth century. Much of our pleasure in reading good heroic couplets comes from the seemingly easy precision with which a skilled poet unites statements and strict pattern. In doing so, the poet may place a pair of words, phrases, clauses, or sentences side by side in agreement or similarity, forming a **parallel,** or in contrast and opposition, forming an **antithesis.** The effect is neat. For such skill in manipulating parallels and antitheses, John Denham's lines on the river Thames were much admired:

> O could I flow like thee, and make thy stream
> My great example, as it is my theme!
> Though deep, yet clear; though gentle, yet not dull;
> Strong without rage, without o'erflowing full.

These lines were echoed by Pope, ridiculing a poetaster, in two heroic couplets in *The Dunciad*:

> Flow, Welsted, flow! like thine inspirer, Beer:
> Though stale, not ripe; though thin, yet never clear;
> So sweetly mawkish, and so smoothly dull;
> Heady, not strong; o'erflowing, though not full.

Reading long poems in so exact a form, one may feel like a spectator at a Ping-Pong match, unless the poet skillfully keeps varying rhythms. One way of escaping such metronome-like monotony is to keep the cesura (see page 634) shifting about from place to place—now happening early in a line, now happening late—and at times unexpectedly to hurl in a second or third cesura.

The Tercet

A **tercet** is a group of three lines. If rimed, they usually keep to one rime sound, as in this anonymous English children's jingle:

> Julius Caesar,
> The Roman geezer,
> Squashed his wife with a lemon-squeezer.

(That, by the way, is a great demonstration of surprising and unpredictable rimes.) *Terza rima,* the form Dante employs in *The Divine Comedy,* is made of tercets linked together by the rime scheme *a b a, b c b, c d c, d e d, e f e,* and so on. Harder to do in English than in Italian—with its greater resources of riming words—the form nevertheless has been managed by Shelley in "Ode to the West Wind" (with the aid of some slant rimes):

> Make me thy lyre, even as the forest is:
> What if my leaves are falling like its own!
> The tumult of thy mighty harmonies
>
> Will take from both a deep, autumnal tone,
> Sweet though in sadness. Be thou, spirit fierce,
> My spirit! Be thou me, impetuous one!

The Quatrain

The workhorse of English poetry is the **quatrain,** a stanza consisting of four lines. Quatrains are used in rimed poems more often than any other form.

Robert Graves (1895–1985)

Counting the Beats   1959

You, love, and I,
(He whispers) you and I,
And if no more than only you and I
What care you or I?

Counting the beats,
Counting the slow heart beats,   5
The bleeding to death of time in slow heart beats,
Wakeful they lie.

Cloudless day,
Night, and a cloudless day,
Yet the huge storm will burst upon their heads one day   10
From a bitter sky.

Where shall we be,
(She whispers) where shall we be,
When death strikes home, O where then shall we be   15
Who were you and I?

Not there but here,
(He whispers) only here,
As we are, here, together, now and here,
Always you and I.   20

Counting the beats,
Counting the slow heart beats,
The bleeding to death of time in slow heart beats,
Wakeful they lie.

Questions

What elements of sound and rhythm are consistent from stanza to stanza? Do any features
change unpredictably from stanza to stanza?

Quatrains come in many line lengths, and sometimes contain lines of varying length, as
in the ballad stanza (see page 603). Most often, poets rime the second and fourth lines of
quatrains, as in the ballad, but the rimes can occur in any combination the poet chooses.

Longer and more complicated stanzas are, of course, possible, but couplet, tercet,
and quatrain have been called the building blocks of our poetry because most longer
stanzas are made up of them. What short stanzas does John Donne mortar together to
make the longer stanza of his "Song"?

John Donne (1572–1631)

Song   1633

Go and catch a falling star,
    Get with child a mandrake root,
Tell me where all past years are,
    Or who cleft the Devil's foot,
Teach me to hear mermaids singing,   5
    Or to keep off envy's stinging,
            And find
            What wind
Serves to advance an honest mind.

If thou be'st borne to strange sights,   10
    Things invisible to see,
Ride ten thousand days and nights,
    Till age snow white hairs on thee,
Thou, when thou return'st, wilt tell me
    All strange wonders that befell thee,   15
            And swear
            Nowhere
Lives a woman true, and fair.

If thou findst one, let me know,
   Such a pilgrimage were sweet—   20
Yet do not, I would not go,
   Though at next door we might meet;
Though she were true, when you met her,
   And last, till you write your letter,
      Yet she   25
      Will be
False, ere I come, to two, or three.

Syllabic Verse

Recently in vogue is a form known as **syllabic verse,** in which the poet establishes a pattern of a certain number of syllables to a line. Either rimed or rimeless but usually stanzaic, syllabic verse has been hailed as a way for poets to escape "the tyranny of the iamb" and discover less conventional rhythms, since, if they take as their line length an *odd* number of syllables, then iambs, being feet of *two* syllables, cannot fit perfectly into it. A well-known syllabic poem is Dylan Thomas's "Fern Hill" (page 878). Notice its shape on the page, count the syllables in its lines, and you'll perceive its perfect symmetry.

THE SONNET

When we speak of "traditional verse forms," we usually mean **fixed forms.** If written in a fixed form, a poem inherits from other poems certain familiar elements of structure: an unvarying number of lines, say, or a stanza pattern. In addition, it may display certain **conventions:** expected features such as themes, subjects, attitudes, or figures of speech. In medieval folk ballads a "milk-white steed" is a conventional figure of speech; and if its rider be a cruel and beautiful witch who kidnaps mortals, she is a conventional character.

    In the poetry of western Europe and America, the **sonnet** is the fixed form that has attracted for the longest time the largest number of noteworthy practitioners. Originally an Italian form (*sonetto:* "little song"), the sonnet owes much of its prestige to Petrarch (1304–1374), who wrote in it of his love for the unattainable Laura. So great was the vogue for sonnets in England at the end of the sixteenth century that a gentleman might have been thought a boor if he couldn't turn out a decent one. Not content to adopt merely the sonnet's fourteen-line pattern, English poets also tried on its conventional mask of the tormented lover. They borrowed some of Petrarch's similes (a lover's heart, for instance, is like a storm-tossed boat) and invented others.

    Soon after English poets imported the sonnet in the sixteenth century, they worked out their own rime scheme—one easier for them to follow than Petrarch's, which calls for a greater number of riming words than English can readily provide. (In Italian, according to an exaggerated report, practically everything rimes.) In the following **English sonnet,** sometimes called a **Shakespearean sonnet,** the rimes cohere in four clusters: *a b a b, c d c d, e f e f, g g.* Because a rime scheme tends to shape the poet's statements to it, the English sonnet has three places where the procession of thought is likely to turn in another direction. Within its form, a poet may pursue one idea throughout the three quatrains and then in the couplet end with a surprise.

William Shakespeare   (1564–1616)

Let me not to the marriage of true minds (Sonnet 116)   1609

Let me not to the marriage of true minds
Admit impediments; love is not love
Which alters when it alteration finds,
Or bends with the remover to remove.
O, no, it is an ever-fixèd mark   5
That looks on tempests and is never shaken;
It is the star to every wand'ring bark,
Whose worth's unknown, although his height be taken.
Love's not Time's fool, though rosy lips and cheeks
Within his bending sickle's compass° come;   *range*   10
Love alters not with his° brief hours and weeks,   *Time's*
But bears° it out even to the edge of doom.   *endures*
        If this be error and upon me proved,
        I never writ, nor no man ever loved.

LET ME NOT TO THE MARRIAGE OF TRUE MINDS. 5 *ever-fixèd mark:* a sea-mark like a beacon or a lighthouse
that provides mariners with safe bearings. 7 *the star:* presumably the North Star, which gave sailors the
most dependable bearing at sea. 12 *edge of doom:* either the brink of death or—taken more generally—
Judgment Day.

Less frequently met in English poetry, the **Italian sonnet,** or **Petrarchan sonnet,**
follows the rime scheme *a b b a, a b b a* in its first eight lines, the **octave,** and then
adds new rime sounds in the last six lines, the **sestet.** The sestet may rime *c d c d c d,
c d e c d e, c d c c d c,* or in almost any other variation that doesn't end in a couplet.
This organization into two parts sometimes helps arrange the poet's thoughts. In the
octave, the poet may state a problem, and then, in the sestet, may offer a resolution.
A lover, for example, may lament all octave long that a loved one is neglectful, then
in line 9 begin to foresee some outcome: the speaker will die, or accept unhappiness,
or trust that the beloved will have a change of heart.

Edna St. Vincent Millay   (1892–1950)

What lips my lips have kissed,   1923
and where, and why

What lips my lips have kissed, and where, and why,
I have forgotten, and what arms have lain
Under my head till morning; but the rain
Is full of ghosts tonight, that tap and sigh
Upon the glass and listen for reply,   5
And in my heart there stirs a quiet pain
For unremembered lads that not again
Will turn to me at midnight with a cry.
Thus in the winter stands the lonely tree,
Nor knows what birds have vanished one by one,   10

Yet knows its boughs more silent than before:
I cannot say what loves have come and gone,
I only know that summer sang in me
A little while, that in me sings no more.

In this Italian sonnet, the turn of thought comes at the traditional point—the beginning of the ninth line. Many English-speaking poets, however, feel free to vary its placement. In John Milton's commanding sonnet on his blindness ("When I consider how my light is spent" on page 863), the turn comes midway through line 8, and no one has ever thought the worse of it for bending the rules.

When we hear the terms *closed form* or *fixed form*, we imagine traditional poetic forms as a series of immutable rules. But, in the hands of the best poets, metrical forms are fluid concepts that change to suit the occasion. Here, for example, is a haunting poem by Robert Frost that simultaneously fulfills the rules of two traditional forms. Is it an innovative sonnet or a poem in *terza rima*? (See page 651 for a discussion of *terza rima*.) Frost combined the features of both forms to create a compressed and powerfully lyric poem.

Robert Frost (1874–1963)

Acquainted with the Night

1928

I have been one acquainted with the night.
I have walked out in rain—and back in rain.
I have outwalked the furthest city light.

I have looked down the saddest city lane.
I have passed by the watchman on his beat   5
And dropped my eyes, unwilling to explain.

I have stood still and stopped the sound of feet
When far away an interrupted cry
Came over houses from another street,

But not to call me back or say good-by;   10
And further still at an unearthly height,
One luminary clock against the sky

Proclaimed the time was neither wrong nor right.
I have been one acquainted with the night.

"The sonnet," quipped Robert Bly, a contemporary poet-critic, "is where old professors go to die." And certainly in the hands of an unskilled practitioner, the form can seem moribund. Considering the impressive number of powerful sonnets by modern poets such as Yeats, Frost, Auden, Millay, Cummings, Kees, and Heaney, however, the form hardly appears to be exhausted. Like the hero of the popular Irish ballad "Finnegan's Wake," literary forms (though not professors) declared dead have a startling habit of springing up again. No law compels sonnets to adopt an exalted tone, or confines them to an Elizabethan vocabulary. To see some of the surprising shapes contemporary sonnets take, read these three recent examples.

A. E. Stallings (b. 1968)

Sine Qua Non   2002

Your absence, father, is nothing. It is naught—
The factor by which nothing will multiply,
The gap of a dropped stitch, the needle's eye
Weeping its black thread. It is the spot
Blindly spreading behind the looking glass.   5
It is the startled silences that come
When the refrigerator stops its hum,
And crickets pause to let the winter pass.

Your absence, father, is nothing—for it is
Omega's long last O, memory's elision,   10
The fraction of impossible division,
The element I move through, emptiness,
The void stars hang in, the interstice of lace,
The zero that still holds the sum in place.

SINE QUA NON. *Sine qua non* is from Latin, meaning literally, "without which not." Used to describe something that is indispensable, an essential part, a prerequisite.

Questions

1. "Nothing" is a key concept in this poem. As used here, does it have its customary connotations of meaninglessness and unimportance? Explain.

2. In "Writing Effectively" at the end of this chapter, A. E. Stallings says that when she was young, she felt "that formal verse could not be contemporary, lacked spontaneity, had no room for the intimate." Discuss whether "Sine Qua Non" demonstrates the shortsightedness of that view.

Amit Majmudar (b. 1953)

Rites to Allay the Dead   2009

It is never enough to close their door.
You have to calm the ripples where they last slept.
The sandals that remember where they stepped
Out of the world must be picked up off the floor,
Their pictures not just folded to face the wood   5
But slid from the frames and snipped like credit cards.
Open the windows to air out the dark.
Closed blinds attract them, stopped clocks, cooling food.

They'll lick the doorstep like the cat come round,
Remembering you when they remember hunger.   10
They'll try to billow through their onetime sleeves
And point to your heart as in a lost and found.
The dead will know it, if you love much longer,
And whistle you near through the shuddering leaves.

Questions

1. To whom does the "they" in this poem refer?
2. Is there a change in this sonnet from the octave to the sestet?
3. What do the dead seem to want from the living?

R. S. Gwynn (b. 1948)

Shakespearean Sonnet   2002

With a first line taken from the TV listings

A man is haunted by his father's ghost.
Boy meets girl while feuding families fight.
A Scottish king is murdered by his host.
Two couples get lost on a summer night.
A hunchback slaughters all who block his way.   5
A ruler's rivals plot against his life.
A fat man and a prince make rebels pay.
A noble Moor has doubts about his wife.
An English king decides to conquer France.
A duke finds out his best friend is a she.   10
A forest sets the scene for this romance.
An old man and his daughters disagree.
A Roman leader makes a big mistake.
A sexy queen is bitten by a snake.

Questions

1. Explain the play on words in the title.
2. How many of the texts described in this sonnet can you identify?
3. Does this poem intend merely to amuse, or does it have a larger point?

THE EPIGRAM

Oscar Wilde said that a cynic is "a man who knows the price of everything and the value of nothing." Such a terse, pointed statement is called an epigram. In poetry, however, an **epigram** is a form: "A short poem ending in a witty or ingenious turn of thought, to which the rest of the composition is intended to lead up" (according to the *Oxford English Dictionary*). Often it is a malicious gibe with an unexpected stinger in the final line—perhaps in the very last word.

Sir John Harrington (1561?–1612)

Of Treason   1618

Treason doth never prosper; what's the reason?
For if it prosper, none dare call it treason.

Langston Hughes (1902–1967)

Two Somewhat Different Epigrams   1957

I

Oh, God of dust and rainbows, help us see
That without dust the rainbow would not be.

II

I look with awe upon the human race
And God, who sometimes spits right in its face.

Dorothy Parker (1893–1967)

The Actress   1931

Her name, cut clear upon this marble cross,
    Shines, as it shone when she was still on earth;
While tenderly the mild, agreeable moss
    Obscures the figures of her date of birth.

Limerick

In English the only other fixed form to rival the sonnet and the epigram in favor is the **limerick:** five anapestic lines usually riming *a a b b a*. The limerick was made popular by Edward Lear (1812–1888), English painter and author of such nonsense poems as "The Owl and the Pussycat." Here is a sample, attributed to President Woodrow Wilson (1856–1924):

    I sat next to the Duchess at tea;
    It was just as I feared it would be:
        Her rumblings abdominal
        Were truly phenomenal
    And everyone thought it was me!

POETWEETS

New technology creates new opportunities for poetic expression. The invention of writing and the phonetic alphabet, for example, allowed poets to create lyrics more complex and elaborate than the oral tradition, based on memory and improvisation, would allow. The poet literally became a *writer* for the first time in history—subtly changing the art in numerous ways. Likewise the invention of the shift-key typewriter, the first widely available keyboard, allowed poets to see how their work would look on the printed page. Not surprisingly, the first generation of poets who grew up using typewriters—authors such as William Carlos Williams and E. E. Cummings—created modernist free verse.

Today's digital communication technology offers new opportunities for literary experimentation. Recently poets have begun sending **poetweets**—poems in the form of Twitter messages. One of the first authors to pioneer this form was filmmaker/poet Lawrence Bridges who has defined the form as a short poem, sent on Twitter, of *exactly* 140 characters using standard English punctuation, without a title and "no line breaks other than the formatting imposed by a computer browser or mobile device." But other poets have printed their poetweets with conventional titles and the looser requirement of being no longer than 140 characters. Here are two of Bridges's poetweets in their original format, followed by a poetweet by Robert Pinsky in a more conventional literary format.

Lawrence Bridges (b. 1948)

Two Poetweets
2011

LawrenceBridges Snow on every field. I wonder at hands. Afternoon is night. We go into town, a clan. Ghosts of future ghosts play little league at the park.

LawrenceBridges All the friends who call you "best friend" are coming over thinking you live here. You live in a shadow house up the street, but don't tell.

Robert Pinsky (b. 1940)

Low Pay Piecework
2011

The fifth-grade teacher and her followers—
Five classes, twenty-eight in each, all hers:
One hundred-and-forty *different* characters.

Exercise: **Poetweets**
Write a poetweet using *exactly* 140 characters. Feel free to give it a title or leave it untitled.

OTHER FORMS

There are many other verse forms used in English. Some forms, like the villanelle and sestina, come from other European literatures. But English has borrowed fixed forms from an astonishing variety of sources. The rubaiyat stanza, for instance, comes from Persian poetry; the haiku (see page 566) and tanka originated in Japan. Other borrowed forms include the ghazal (Arabic), pantoum (Malay), and sapphics (Greek). Even blank verse (see page 649), which seems as English as the royal family, began as an attempt by Elizabethan poets to copy an Italian eleven-syllable line. To conclude this chapter, here are poems in three widely used closed forms— the villanelle, triolet, and sestina. Their patterns, which are sometimes called "French forms," have been particularly fascinating to English-language poets because they do not merely require the repetition of rime sounds; instead, they demand more elaborate echoing, involving the repetition of either full words or whole lines of verse. Sometimes difficult to master, these forms can create a powerful musical effect unlike ordinary riming.

Dylan Thomas (1914–1953)

Do not go gentle into that good night
1952

Do not go gentle into that good night,
Old age should burn and rave at close of day;
Rage, rage against the dying of the light.

Though wise men at their end know dark is right,
Because their words had forked no lightning they 5
Do not go gentle into that good night.

Good men, the last wave by, crying how bright
Their frail deeds might have danced in a green bay,
Rage, rage against the dying of the light.

Wild men who caught and sang the sun in flight, 10
And learn, too late, they grieved it on its way,
Do not go gentle into that good night.

Grave men, near death, who see with blinding sight
Blind eyes could blaze like meteors and be gay,
Rage, rage against the dying of the light. 15

And you, my father, there on the sad height,
Curse, bless, me now with your fierce tears, I pray,
Do not go gentle into that good night.
Rage, rage against the dying of the light.

Questions

1. "Do not go gentle into that good night" is a **villanelle:** a fixed form originated by French courtly poets of the Middle Ages. What are its rules?
2. Whom does the poem address? What is the speaker saying?
3. Villanelles are sometimes criticized as elaborate exercises in trivial wordplay. How would you defend Thomas's poem against this charge?

Robert Bridges (1844–1930)

Triolet   1890

When first we met we did not guess
That Love would prove so hard a master;
Of more than common friendliness
When first we met we did not guess.
Who could foretell this sore distress, 5
This irretrievable disaster
When first we met?—We did not guess
That Love would prove so hard a master.

TRIOLET. The **triolet** is a short lyric form borrowed from the French; its two opening lines are repeated according to a set pattern, as Bridges's poem illustrates. The triolet is often used for light verse, but Bridges's poem demonstrates how it can carry heavier emotional loads, if used with sufficient skill.

Question

How do the first two lines of "Triolet" change in meaning when they reappear at the end of the poem?

Elizabeth Bishop (1911–1979)

Sestina   1965

September rain falls on the house.
In the failing light, the old grandmother
sits in the kitchen with the child
beside the Little Marvel Stove,
reading the jokes from the almanac,   5
laughing and talking to hide her tears.

She thinks that her equinoctial tears
and the rain that beats on the roof of the house
were both foretold by the almanac,
but only known to a grandmother.   10
The iron kettle sings on the stove.
She cuts some bread and says to the child,

It's time for tea now; but the child
is watching the teakettle's small hard tears
dance like mad on the hot black stove,   15
the way the rain must dance on the house.
Tidying up, the old grandmother
hangs up the clever almanac

on its string. Birdlike, the almanac
hovers half open above the child,   20
hovers above the old grandmother
and her teacup full of dark brown tears.
She shivers and says she thinks the house
feels chilly, and puts more wood in the stove.

It was to be, says the Marvel Stove.   25
I know what I know, says the almanac.
With crayons the child draws a rigid house
and a winding pathway. Then the child
puts in a man with buttons like tears
and shows it proudly to the grandmother.   30

But secretly, while the grandmother
busies herself about the stove,
the little moons fall down like tears
from between the pages of the almanac
into the flower bed the child   35
has carefully placed in the front of the house.

Time to plant tears, says the almanac.
The grandmother sings to the marvellous stove
and the child draws another inscrutable house.

SESTINA. As its title indicates, this poem is written in the trickiest of medieval fixed forms, that of the **sestina** (or "song of sixes"), said to have been invented in Provence in the thirteenth century by the troubadour poet Arnaut Daniel. In six six-line stanzas, the poet repeats six end-words (in a prescribed order), then reintroduces the six repeated words (in any order) in a closing **envoy** of three lines. Elizabeth Bishop strictly follows the troubadour rules for the order in which the end-words recur. (If you care, you can figure out the formula: in the first stanza, the six words are arranged A B C D E F; in the second, F A E B D C; and so on.)

Questions

1. A perceptive comment from a student: "Something seems to be going on here that the child doesn't understand. Maybe some terrible loss has happened." Test this guess by reading the poem closely.

2. In the "little moons" that fall from the almanac (line 33), does the poem introduce dream or fantasy, or do you take these to be small round pieces of paper?

3. What is the tone of this poem—the speaker's apparent attitude toward the scene described?

4. In an essay, "The Sestina," in *A Local Habitation* (U of Michigan P, 1985), John Frederick Nims defends the form against an obvious complaint against it:

> A shallow view of the sestina might suggest that the poet writes a stanza, and then is stuck with six words which he has to juggle into the required positions through five more stanzas and an envoy—to the great detriment of what passion and sincerity would have him say. But in a good sestina the poet has six words, six images, six ideas so urgently in his mind that he cannot get away from them; he wants to test them in all possible combinations and come to a conclusion about their relationship.

How well does this description of a good sestina fit "Sestina"?

Experiment: Urgent Repetition

Write a sestina and see what you find out by doing so. (Even if you fail in the attempt, you just might learn something interesting.) To start, pick six words you think are worth repeating six times. This elaborate pattern gives you much help: as John Ashbery has pointed out, writing a sestina is "like riding downhill on a bicycle and having the pedals push your feet." Here is some encouragement from a poet and critic, John Heath-Stubbs: "I have never read a sestina that seemed to me a total failure."

■ WRITING *effectively*

A. E. Stallings on Writing

On Form and Artifice 2000

Is form artificial? Of course it is. I am all for the artificial. I am reminded of an anecdote. A lovely girl, with natural blonde hair, but of a rather dark, rather dingy shade, complains to a friend. She has wanted for a long time to get it highlighted, which she thinks will brighten her appearance, but with the qualms and vanity of a natural blonde, scruples about the artificiality of having her hair colored. At which point her friend laughs and declares, "Honey, the point is to *look* natural. Not to *be* natural."

It seems an obvious point for art. Art is effective and direct because of its use of artifice, not simply because the artist has something sincere or important to communicate. Anyone who has written a letter of condolence should be able to sympathize. When a close friend has lost a loved one, what can one say? "I cannot imagine your loss" "words cannot begin to" "our thoughts and prayers are with you" etc. That these phrases are threadbare does not make them less sincere. Phrases become threadbare *because* they are sincere.

A. E. Stallings

I had several revelations about the nature of poetry in a college Latin class on Catullus. I was shocked by how *modern*, how *contemporary* the poems seemed. And it was a revelation to see how a poet could at one and the same time be a supreme formal architect of verse, and write poems that seemed utterly spontaneous, candid, and confessional, with room for the sublime, the learned, the colloquial, and the frankly obscene.

I suppose at some point I had somehow imbibed the opposite notion, a notion still held by many, that formal verse could not be contemporary, lacked spontaneity, had no room for the intimate. At that time I did not see much formal work getting published: I wanted to publish, and therefore struggled in free verse. I did not have much luck. Eventually I gave up, wrote what I really wanted to write, which rhymed and scanned, and, oddly, *then* I had some success in publishing. Which leads to yet another little adage of mine, which is, don't write what you *know* (I think this is better fitted for prose writers), write what you *like*, the sort of stuff you actually enjoy reading, fashionable or not.

From "Crooked Roads Without Improvement:
Some Thoughts on Formal Verse"

THINKING ABOUT A SONNET

A poem's form is closely tied to its meaning. This is especially true of the sonnet, a form whose rules dictate not only the sound of a poem but also, to a certain extent, its sense. A sonnet traditionally looks at a single theme, but reverses its stance on the subject somewhere along the way. One possible definition of the sonnet might be a fourteen-line poem divided into two unequal parts. Traditionally, Italian sonnets divide their parts into an octave (the first eight lines) and a sestet (the last six), while English sonnets are more lopsided, with a final couplet balanced against three preceding quatrains. The moment when a sonnet changes its direction is commonly called "the turn."

- **Identifying the moment when the poem "turns" helps in understanding both its theme and its structure.** In a Shakespearean sonnet, the turn usually—but not always—comes in the final couplet. In modern sonnets, the turn is often less overt.

■ **To find that moment, study the poem's opening.** Latch on to the mood and manner of the opening lines. Is the feeling joyful or sad, loving or angry?

■ **Read the poem from this opening perspective until you feel it tug strongly in another direction.** Sometimes the second part of a sonnet will directly contradict the opening. More often it explains, augments, or qualifies the opening.

CHECKLIST: Writing About a Sonnet

☐ Read the poem carefully.

☐ What is the mood of its opening lines?

☐ Keep reading until you feel the mood shift. Where does that shift take place?

☐ What is the tone after the sonnet's turn away from its opening direction?

☐ What do the two alternative points of view add up to?

☐ How does the poem reconcile its contrasting sections?

WRITING ASSIGNMENT ON A SONNET

Examine a sonnet from anywhere in this book. Explain how its two parts combine to create a total effect neither part could achieve alone. Be sure to identify the turning point. Paraphrase what each of the poem's two sections says and describe how the poem as a whole reconciles the two contrasting parts.

(In addition to the sonnets in this chapter, you might consider any of the following from the chapter "Poems for Further Reading": Elizabeth Barrett Browning's "How Do I Love Thee?"; Gerard Manley Hopkins's "The Windhover"; John Keats's "When I have fears that I may cease to be"; John Milton's "When I consider how my light is spent"; Wilfred Owen's "Anthem for Doomed Youth"; or William Wordsworth's "Composed upon Westminster Bridge.")

MORE TOPICS FOR WRITING

1. Select a poem that incorporates rime from the chapter "Poems for Further Reading." Write a paragraph describing how the poem's rime scheme helps to advance its meaning.

2. Write ten lines of blank verse on a topic of your own choice. Then write about the experience. What aspects of writing in regular meter did you find most challenging? What did you learn about reading blank verse from trying your hand at writing it?

3. Discuss the use of form in Robert Bridges's "Triolet." What is the effect of so many repeated lines in so brief a poem?

4. Compare Dylan Thomas's "Do not go gentle into that good night" with Wendy Cope's "Lonely Hearts" (page 539). How can the same form be used to create such different kinds of poems?

▶ TERMS FOR *review*

Form

Form ▶ In a general sense, form is the means by which a literary work expresses its content. In poetry, form is usually used to describe the design of a poem.

Fixed form ▶ A traditional verse form requiring certain predetermined elements of structure—for example, a stanza pattern, set meter, or predetermined line length.

Closed form ▶ A generic term that describes poetry written in a pattern of meter, rime, lines, or stanzas. A closed form adheres to a set structure.

Open form ▶ Verse that has no set scheme—no regular meter, rime, or stanzaic pattern. Open form has also been called **free verse.**

Blank verse ▶ Blank verse contains five iambic feet per line (iambic pentameter) and is not rimed. ("Blank" means unrimed.)

Couplet ▶ A two-line stanza in poetry, usually rimed and with lines of equal length.

Closed couplet ▶ Two rimed lines of iambic pentameter that usually contain an independent and complete thought or statement. Also called **heroic couplet.**

Quatrain ▶ A stanza consisting of four lines, it is the most common stanza form used in English-language poetry.

Epic ▶ A long narrative poem tracing the adventures of a popular hero. Epic poems are usually written in a consistent form and meter throughout.

Epigram ▶ A very short, comic poem, often turning at the end with some sharp wit or unexpected stinger.

The Sonnet

Sonnet ▶ A fixed form of fourteen lines, traditionally written in iambic pentameter and rimed throughout.

Italian sonnet ▶ Also called **Petrarchan sonnet,** it rimes the **octave** (the first eight lines) *a b b a a b b a*; the **sestet** (the last six lines) may follow any rime pattern, as long as it does not end in a couplet. The poem traditionally turns, or shifts in mood or tone, after the octave.

English sonnet ▶ Also called **Shakespearean sonnet,** it has the following rime scheme organized into three quatrains and a concluding couplet: *a b a b c d c d e f e f g g.* The poem may turn—that is, shift in mood or tone—between any of the rime clusters.

22

OPEN FORM

All poetry is experimental poetry.

—WALLACE STEVENS

Writing in **open form,** a poet seeks to discover a fresh and individual arrangement for words in every poem. Such a poem, generally speaking, has neither a rime scheme nor a basic meter informing the whole of it. Doing without those powerful (some would say hypnotic) elements, the poet who writes in open form relies on other means to engage and to sustain the reader's attention. Novice poets often think that open form looks easy, not nearly so hard as riming everything; but in truth, formally open poems are easy to write only if written carelessly. To compose lines with keen awareness of open form's demands, and of its infinite possibilities, calls for skill: at least as much as that needed to write in meter and rime, if not more. Should the poet succeed, then the discovered arrangement will seem exactly right for what the poem is saying.

Denise Levertov (1923–1997)

Ancient Stairway

1999

Footsteps like water hollow
the broad curves of stone
ascending, descending
century by century.
Who can say if the last   5
to climb these stairs
will be journeying
downward or upward?

Open form, in this brief poem, affords Denise Levertov certain advantages. Able to break off a line at whatever point she likes (a privilege not available to the poet writing, say, a conventional sonnet, who has to break off each line after its tenth syllable), she selects her pauses artfully. Line breaks lend emphasis: a word or phrase at the end of a line takes a little more stress (and receives a little more attention), because the ending of the line compels the reader to make a slight pause, if only for the brief moment it takes to sling back one's eyes and fix them on the line following. Slight pauses, then, follow the words and phrases *hollow / stone / descending / century / last / stairs / journeying / upward*—all these being elements that apparently the poet wishes to call our attention to. (The pause after a line break also casts a little more weight on the *first* word or phrase of each succeeding line.) Levertov makes the most of white space—another means of calling attention to things, as any good picture-framer knows. She has greater control over the shape of the poem, its look on the page, than would be allowed by the demands of meter; she uses that control to stack on top of one another lines that appear much like the steps of a staircase. The opening line with its quick stresses might suggest to us the many feet passing over the steps. From there, Levertov slows the rhythm to the heavy beats of lines 3–4, which could communicate a sense of repeated trudging up and down the stairs (in a particularly effective touch, all four of the stressed syllables in these two lines make the same sound), a sense that is reinforced by the poem's last line, which echoes the rhythm of line 3. Note too how, without being restricted by the need of a rime, she can order the terms in that last line according to her intended thematic emphasis. In all likelihood, we perceive these effects instinctively, not consciously (which may also be the way the author created them), but no matter how we apprehend them, they serve to deepen our understanding of and pleasure in the text.

FREE VERSE

Poetry in open form used to be called **free verse** (from the French **vers libre**), suggesting a kind of verse liberated from the shackles of rime and meter. "Writing free verse," said Robert Frost, who wasn't interested in it, "is like playing tennis with the net down." And yet, as Denise Levertov and many other poets demonstrate, high scores can be made in such an unconventional game, provided it doesn't straggle all over the court. For a successful poem in open form, the term *free verse* seems inaccurate. "Being an art form," said William Carlos Williams, "verse cannot be 'free' in the sense of having *no* limitations or guiding principles."[1] Various substitute names have been suggested: organic poetry, composition by field, raw (as against cooked) poetry, open form poetry. "But what does it matter what you call it?" remark the editors of a 1969 anthology called *Naked Poetry*. "The best poems of the last thirty years don't rhyme (usually) and don't move on feet of more or less equal duration (usually). That nondescription moves toward the only technical principle they all have in common."[2]

Projective Verse

Yet many poems in open form have much more in common than absences and lacks. One positive principle has been Ezra Pound's famous suggestion that poets "compose in the sequence of the musical phrase, not in the sequence of the metronome"—good advice, perhaps, even for poets who write inside fixed forms. In Charles Olson's influential theory of **projective verse,** poets compose by listening to their own breathing. On paper, they indicate the rhythms of a poem by using a little white space or a lot, a slight indentation or a deep one, depending on whether a short pause or a long one is

---

[1]"Free Verse," *Princeton Encyclopedia of Poetry and Poetics*, 2nd ed., 1975.
[2]Stephen Berg and Robert Mezey, eds., foreword, *Naked Poetry: Recent American Poetry in Open Forms* (Indianapolis: Bobbs, 1969).

intended. Words can be grouped in clusters on the page (usually no more words than a lungful of air can accommodate). Heavy cesuras are sometimes shown by breaking a line in two and lowering the second part of it.[3]

Free Verse Lines

To the poet working in open form, no less than to the poet writing a sonnet, line length can be valuable. Walt Whitman, who loved to expand vast sentences for line after line, knew well that an impressive rhythm can accumulate if the poet will keep long lines approximately the same length, causing a pause to recur at about the same interval after every line. Sometimes, too, Whitman repeats the same words at each line's opening. An instance is the masterly sixth section of "When Lilacs Last in the Dooryard Bloom'd," an elegy for Abraham Lincoln:

> Coffin that passes through lanes and streets,
> Through day and night with the great cloud darkening the land,
> With the pomp of the inloop'd flags with the cities draped in black,
> With the show of the States themselves as of crape-veil'd women
>   standing,
> With processions long and winding and the flambeaus of the night,
> With the countless torches lit, with the silent sea of faces and the
>   unbared heads,
> With the waiting depot, the arriving coffin, and the somber faces,
> With dirges through the night, with the thousand voices rising
>   strong and solemn,
> With all the mournful voices of the dirges pour'd around the coffin,
> The dim-lit churches and the shuddering organs—where amid
>   these you journey,
> With the tolling tolling bells' perpetual clang,
> Here, coffin that slowly passes,
> I give you my sprig of lilac.

There is music in such solemn, operatic arias. Whitman's lines echo another model: the Hebrew **psalms,** or sacred songs, as translated in the King James Version of the Bible. In Psalm 150, repetition also occurs inside of lines:

> Praise ye the Lord. Praise God in his sanctuary: praise him in the
>   firmament of his power.
> Praise him for his mighty acts: praise him according to his excellent
>   greatness.
> Praise him with the sound of the trumpet: praise him with the
>   psaltery and harp.
> Praise him with the timbrel and dance: praise him with stringed
>   instruments and organs.
> Praise him upon the loud cymbals: praise him upon the high
>   sounding cymbals.
> Let every thing that hath breath praise the Lord. Praise ye the Lord.

[3]See Olson's essays "Projective Verse" and "Letter to Elaine Feinstein" in *Selected Writings*, edited by Robert Creeley (New York: New Directions, 1966). Olson's letters to Cid Corman are fascinating: *Letters for Origin, 1950–1955*, edited by Albert Glover (New York: Grossman, 1970).

Whitman was a more deliberate craftsman than he let his readers think, and to anyone interested in writing in open form, his work will repay close study. He knew that repetitions of any kind often make memorable rhythms, as in this passage from "Song of Myself," with every line ending on an *-ing* word (a stressed syllable followed by an unstressed syllable):

> Here and there with dimes on the eyes walking,
> To feed the greed of the belly the brains liberally spooning,
> Tickets buying, taking, selling, but in to the feast never once going,
> Many sweating, ploughing, thrashing, and then the chaff for
>   payment receiving,
> A few idly owning, and they the wheat continually claiming.

Much more than simply repetition, of course, went into the music of those lines—the internal rime *feed, greed*, the use of assonance, the trochees that begin the third and fourth lines, whether or not they were calculated.

Sound and Rhythm in Free Verse

In many classics of open form poetry, sound and rhythm are positive forces. When speaking a poem in open form, you often may find that it makes a difference for the better if you pause at the end of each line. Try pausing there, however briefly; but don't allow your voice to drop. Read just as you would normally read a sentence in prose (except for the pauses, of course). Why do the pauses matter? Open form poetry usually has no meter to lend it rhythm. *Some* lines in an open form poem, as we have seen in Whitman's "dimes on the eyes" passage, do fall into metrical feet; sometimes the whole poem does. Usually lacking meter's aid, however, open form, in order to have more and more noticeable rhythms, has need of all the recurring pauses it can get. As we can hear in recordings of them reading their work aloud, open form poets such as Robert Creeley and Allen Ginsberg would often pause very definitely at each line break—and so, for that matter, did Ezra Pound.

Some poems, to be sure, seem more widely open in form than others. A poet may wish to avoid the rigidity and predictability of fixed line lengths and stanzaic forms but still wish to hold a poem together through a strong rhythmic impulse and even a discernible metrical emphasis. A poet may employ rime, but have the rimes recur at various intervals, or perhaps rime lines of varying lengths. In a 1917 essay called "Reflections on *Vers Libre*" (French for "free verse"), T. S. Eliot famously observed, "No *vers* is *libre* for the man who wants to do a good job." In that same year, Eliot published his first collection of poems, whose title piece was the classic "The Love Song of J. Alfred Prufrock." Is "Prufrock" a closed poem left ajar or an open poem trying to slam itself?

W. S. Merwin (b. 1927)

For the Anniversary of My Death   1967

Every year without knowing it I have passed the day
When the last fires will wave to me
And the silence will set out
Tireless traveler
Like the beam of a lightless star   5

Then I will no longer
Find myself in life as in a strange garment
Surprised at the earth
And the love of one woman
And the shamelessness of men   10
As today writing after three days of rain
Hearing the wren sing and the falling cease
And bowing not knowing to what

Questions

1. Read the poem aloud. Try pausing for a fraction of a second at the end of every line. Is there a justification for each line break?

2. The poem is divided into two asymmetrical sections (a new stanza begins at line 6). Does this formal division reflect some change or difference of meaning between the two sections?

E. E. Cummings (1894–1962)

Buffalo Bill's   1923

Buffalo Bill's
defunct
            who used to
            ride a watersmooth-silver
                                            stallion   5
and break onetwothreefourfive pigeonsjustlikethat
                                                        Jesus
he was a handsome man
                        and what i want to know is
how do you like your blueeyed boy   10
Mister Death

Question

Cummings's poem would look like this if given conventional punctuation and set in a solid block like prose:

> Buffalo Bill's defunct, who used to ride a water-smooth silver stallion and break one, two, three, four, five pigeons just like that. Jesus, he was a handsome man. And what I want to know is: "How do you like your blue-eyed boy, Mister Death?"

If this were done, by what characteristics would it still be recognizable as poetry? But what would be lost?

William Carlos Williams (1883–1963)

The Dance   1944

In Brueghel's great picture, The Kermess,
the dancers go round, they go round and
around, the squeal and the blare and the
tweedle of bagpipes, a bugle and fiddles

tipping their bellies (round as the thick-
sided glasses whose wash they impound)
their hips and their bellies off balance
to turn them. Kicking and rolling about
the Fair Grounds, swinging their butts, those
shanks must be sound to bear up under such
rollicking measures, prance as they dance
in Brueghel's great picture, The Kermess.

THE DANCE. 1 *Brueghel:* Flemish painter known for his scenes of peasant activities. *The Kermess:* painting of a celebration on the feast day of a local patron saint.

Questions

1. Scan this poem and try to describe the effect of its rhythms.
2. Williams, widely admired for his free verse, insisted for many years that what he sought was a form not in the least bit free. What effect does he achieve by ending lines on such weak words as the articles "and" and "the"? By splitting "thick- / sided"? By splitting a prepositional phrase with the break at the end of line 8? By using line breaks to split "those" and "such" from what they modify? What do you think he is trying to convey?
3. Is there any point in his making line 12 a repetition of the opening line?
4. Look at the reproduction of Brueghel's painting *The Kermess* (also called *Peasant Dance*). Aware that the rhythms of dancers, the rhythms of a painting, and the rhythms of a poem are not all the same, can you put in your own words what Brueghel's dancing figures have in common with Williams's descriptions of them?
5. Compare "The Dance" with another poem that refers to a Brueghel painting: W. H. Auden's "Musée des Beaux Arts" on page 823. What seems to be each poet's main concern: to convey in words a sense of the painting, or to visualize the painting in order to state some theme?

The Kermess or Peasant Dance by Pieter Brueghel the Elder (1520?–1569).

Stephen Crane (1871–1900)

The Wayfarer
1899

The wayfarer,
Perceiving the pathway to truth,
Was struck with astonishment.
It was thickly grown with weeds.
"Ha," he said,   5
"I see that none has passed here
In a long time."
Later he saw that each weed
Was a singular knife.
"Well," he mumbled at last,   10
"Doubtless there are other roads."

Walt Whitman (1819–1892)

Cavalry Crossing a Ford
1865

A line in long array where they wind betwixt green islands,
They take a serpentine course, their arms flash in the sun—hark to the
    musical clank,
Behold the silvery river, in it the splashing horses loitering stop to drink,
Behold the brown-faced men, each group, each person a picture, the
    negligent rest on the saddles,
Some emerge on the opposite bank, others are just entering the   5
    ford—while,
Scarlet and blue and snowy white,
The guidon flags flutter gayly in the wind.

Questions: Crane Versus Whitman

The following nit-picking questions are intended to help you see exactly what makes these two open form poems by Crane and Whitman so different in their music.

1. What devices of sound occur in Whitman's phrase "silvery river" (line 3)? Where else in his poem do you find these devices?
2. Does Crane use any such devices?
3. In number of syllables, Whitman's poem is almost twice as long as Crane's. Which poem has more pauses in it? (Count pauses at the ends of lines, at marks of punctuation.)
4. Read the two poems aloud. In general, how would you describe the effect of their sounds and rhythms? Is Crane's poem necessarily an inferior poem for having less music?

Analyzing Line Breaks

Wallace Stevens's lineation in "Thirteen Ways of Looking at a Blackbird" allows us not only to see but also to savor the connections between the poem's ideas and images. Consider section II of the poem:

I was of three minds,
Like a tree
In which there are three blackbirds.

On a purely semantic level, these lines may mean the same as the prose statement, "I was of three minds like a tree in which there are three blackbirds," but Stevens's choice of line breaks adds special emphasis at several points. Each of these three lines isolates and presents a separate image (the speaker, the tree, and the blackbirds). The placement of *three* at the same position in the opening and closing lines helps us feel the similar nature of the two statements. The short middle line allows us to see the image of the tree before we fully understand why it is parallel to the divided mind—thus adding a touch of suspense that the prose version of this statement just can't supply. Ending each line with a key noun and image also gives the poem a concrete feel not altogether evident in the prose.

Wallace Stevens (1879–1955)

Thirteen Ways of Looking at a Blackbird   1923

I

Among twenty snowy mountains,
The only moving thing
Was the eye of the blackbird.

II

I was of three minds,
Like a tree   5
In which there are three blackbirds.

III

The blackbird whirled in the autumn winds.
It was a small part of the pantomime.

IV

A man and a woman
Are one.   10
A man and a woman and a blackbird
Are one.

V

I do not know which to prefer,
The beauty of inflections
Or the beauty of innuendoes,   15
The blackbird whistling
Or just after.

VI

Icicles filled the long window
With barbaric glass.

The shadow of the blackbird   20
Crossed it, to and fro.
The mood
Traced in the shadow
An indecipherable cause.

VII

O thin men of Haddam,   25
Why do you imagine golden birds?
Do you not see how the blackbird
Walks around the feet
Of the women about you?

VIII

I know noble accents   30
And lucid, inescapable rhythms;
But I know, too,
That the blackbird is involved
In what I know.

IX

When the blackbird flew out of sight,   35
It marked the edge
Of one of many circles.

X

At the sight of blackbirds
Flying in a green light,
Even the bawds of euphony   40
Would cry out sharply.

XI

He rode over Connecticut
In a glass coach.
Once, a fear pierced him,
In that he mistook   45
The shadow of his equipage
For blackbirds.

XII

The river is moving.
The blackbird must be flying.

XIII

It was evening all afternoon.
It was snowing
And it was going to snow.
The blackbird sat
In the cedar-limbs.

50

THIRTEEN WAYS OF LOOKING AT A BLACKBIRD. 25 *Haddam:* This biblical-sounding name is that of a town in Connecticut.

Questions

1. What is the speaker's attitude toward the men of Haddam? What attitude toward this world does he suggest they lack? What is implied by calling them "thin" (line 25)?

2. What do the landscapes of winter contribute to the poem's effectiveness? If Stevens had chosen images of summer lawns, what would have been lost?

3. In which sections of the poem does Stevens suggest that a unity exists between human being and blackbird, between blackbird and the entire natural world? Can we say that Stevens "philosophizes"? What role does imagery play in Stevens's statement of his ideas?

4. What sense can you make of Part X? Make an enlightened guess.

5. Consider any one of the thirteen parts. What patterns of sound and rhythm do you find in it? What kind of structure does it have?

6. If the thirteen parts were arranged in some different order, would the poem be just as good? Or can we find a justification for its beginning with Part I and ending with Part XIII?

7. Does the poem seem an arbitrary combination of thirteen separate poems? Or is there any reason to call it a whole?

PROSE POETRY

No law requires a poet to split thoughts into verse lines at all. Charles Baudelaire, Rainer Maria Rilke, Jorge Luis Borges, Alexander Solzhenitsyn, T. S. Eliot, and many others have written **prose poems,** in which, without caring that eye appeal and some of the rhythm of a line structure may be lost, the poet prints words in a block like a prose paragraph. To some, the term "prose poetry" is as oxymoronic as "jumbo shrimp" or "plastic glasses," if not a flat-out contradiction in terms. On the other hand, we might recall Samuel Johnson's response when told that Bishop Berkeley's theory that the material world is an illusion, while obviously false, could not be refuted; Johnson kicked a large stone, saying "I refute him *thus.*" Like stones, prose poems exist. To prove it, here is one by a contemporary American poet. As you read it, ask yourself: Is it a prose poem, or a very short piece of prose? If it is poetry, what features distinguish it from prose? If it should be considered prose, what essential features of poetry does it lack?

Charles Simic (b. 1939)

The Magic Study of Happiness

1992

In the smallest theater in the world the bread crumbs speak. It's a mystery play on the subject of a lost paradise. Once there was a kitchen with a table on which a few crumbs were left. Through the window you could see your young mother by the fence talking to a neighbor. She was cold and kept hugging her thin dress tighter and tighter. The clouds in the sky sailed on as she threw her head back to laugh.   5

Where the words can't go any further—there's the hard table. The crumbs are watching you as you in turn watch them. The unknown in you and the unknown in them attract each other. The two unknowns are like illicit lovers when they're exceedingly and unaccountably happy.

Questions

1. What is the effect of the phrases "the smallest theater in the world" and "mystery play"?
2. How do you interpret "Where the words can't go any further—there's the hard table"?
3. What is the significance of the simile in the last sentence?

VISUAL POETRY

Let's look at a famous poem with a distinctive visible shape. In the seventeenth century, ingenious poets trimmed their lines into the silhouettes of altars and crosses, pillars and pyramids. Here is one. Is it anything more than a demonstration of ingenuity?

George Herbert (1593–1633)

Easter Wings   1633

> Lord, who createdst man in wealth and store,
>   Though foolishly he lost the same,
>   Decaying more and more,
>   Till he became
>   Most poor;
>   With thee
>   Oh, let me rise
>   As larks, harmoniously,
>   And sing this day thy victories;
> Then shall the fall further the flight in me.

> My tender age in sorrow did begin;
>   And still with sicknesses and shame
>   Thou didst so punish sin,
>   That I became
>   Most thin.
>   With thee
>   Let me combine,
>   And feel this day thy victory;
>   For if I imp my wing on thine,
> Affliction shall advance the flight in me.

In the next-to-last line, *imp* is a term from falconry meaning to repair the wing of an injured bird by grafting feathers onto it.

If we see the poem merely as a picture, we will have to admit that Herbert's word design does not go far. It renders with difficulty shapes that a sketcher's pencil could set down in a flash, in more detail, more accurately. Was Herbert's effort wasted? It might have been, were there not more to his poem than meets the eye. The mind, too, is engaged by the visual pattern, by the realization that the words *most thin* are given emphasis by their narrow form. Here, visual pattern points out meaning. Heard aloud, too, "Easter Wings" gives further pleasure. Its rimes, its rhythm are perceptible.

Ever since George Herbert's day, poets have continued to experiment with the looks of printed poetry. Notable efforts to entertain the eye are Lewis Carroll's rimed mouse's tail in *Alice in Wonderland* and the *Calligrammes* of Guillaume Apollinaire, who arranged words in the shapes of a necktie, of the Eiffel Tower, of spears of falling rain. Here is a bird-shaped poem of more recent inspiration than Herbert's. What does its visual form have to do with what the poet is saying?

John Hollander (b. 1929)

Swan and Shadow   1969

```
                        Dusk
                      Above the
                  water hang the
                          loud
                          flies
                        Here
                          O so
                        gray
                        then
            What                         A pale signal will appear
            When                    Soon before its shadow fades
            Where                   Here in this pool of opened eye
           In us          No Upon us As at the very edges
              of where we take shape in the dark air
                this object bares its image awakening
                  ripples of recognition that will
                    brush darkness up into light
  even after this bird this hour both drift by atop the perfect sad instant now
                    already passing out of sight
                toward yet-untroubled reflection
              this image bears its object darkening
             into memorial shades Scattered bits of
            light        No of water Or something across
            water            Breaking up No Being regathered
            soon               Yet by then a swan will have
              gone                Yet out of mind into what
                        vast
                        pale
                        hush
                          of a
                        place
                          past
              sudden dark as
                if a swan
                    sang
```

At least some of our pleasure in silently reading a poem derives from the way it looks upon its page. A poem in an open form can engage the eye with snowfields of white space and thickets of close-set words. A poem in stanzas can please us by its visual symmetry. And, far from being merely decorative, the visual devices of a poem can be meaningful, too. White space—as poets who work in open forms demonstrate— can indicate pauses. If white space entirely surrounds a word or phrase or line, then that portion of the poem obviously takes special emphasis. Typographical devices such as capital letters and italics also can lay stress upon words. In most traditional poems, a capital letter at the beginning of each new line helps indicate the importance the poet places on line divisions, whose regular intervals make a rhythm out of pauses. And the poet may be trying to show us that certain lines rime by indenting them.

FOR REVIEW AND FURTHER STUDY

Exercise: Seeing the Logic of Open Form Verse

Read the following poems in open form silently to yourself, noticing what each poet does with white space, repetitions, line breaks, and indentations. Then read the poems aloud, trying to indicate by slight pauses where lines end and also pausing slightly at any space inside a line. Can you see any reasons for the poet's placing his or her words in this arrangement rather than in a prose paragraph? Do any of these poets seem to care also about visual effect? (As with other kinds of poetry, there may not be any obvious logical reason for everything that happens in these poems.)

E. E. Cummings (1894–1962)

in Just-   1923

in Just-
spring   when the world is mud-
luscious the little
lame balloonman

whistles   far   and wee   5

and eddieandbill come
running from marbles and
piracies and it's
spring

when the world is puddle-wonderful   10

the queer
old balloonman whistles
far   and   wee
and bettyandisbel come dancing

from hop-scotch and jump-rope and   15

it's
spring
and
   the

      goat-footed

balloonMan   whistles
far
and
wee

20

Francisco X. Alarcón (b. 1954)

Frontera	**Border**	2003
ninguna	no	
frontera	border	
podrá	can ever	
separanos	separate us	

Question

How would the meaning of this short poem change if you dropped one of the languages?

Carole Satyamurti (b. 1939)

I Shall Paint My Nails Red   1990

Because a bit of color is a public service.

Because I am proud of my hands.

Because it will remind me I'm a woman.

Because I will look like a survivor.

Because I can admire them in traffic jams.   5

Because my daughter will say ugh.

Because my lover will be surprised.

Because it is quicker than dyeing my hair.

Because it is a ten-minute moratorium.

Because it is reversible.   10

Question

"I Shall Paint My Nails Red" is written in free verse, but the poem has several organizing principles. How many can you discover?

Alice Fulton (b. 1952)

What I Like   1983

Friend—the face I wallow toward
through a scrimmage of shut faces.
Arms like towropes to haul me home, aide-
memoire, my lost childhood docks, a bottled ark
in harbor. *Friend*—I can't forget   5
how even the word contains an *end*.
We circle each other in a scared bolero,
imagining stratagems: postures and impostors.
Cold convictions keep us solo. I ahem
and hedge my affections. Who'll blow the first kiss,   10
land it like the lifeforces we feel
tickling at each wrist? It should be easy
easy to take your hand, whisper down this distance
labeled hers or his: what I like about you is

Questions

Does this poem have an ending? Does it need to have an ending to be a successful poem?

▪ WRITING *effectively*

Walt Whitman on Writing

The Poetry of the Future   1876

The poetry of the future, (a phrase open to
sharp criticism, and not satisfactory to me,
but significant, and I will use it)—the poetry
of the future aims at the free expression of
emotion, (which means far, far more than
appears at first,) and to arouse and initiate,
more than to define or finish. Like all modern tendencies, it has direct or indirect reference continually to the reader, to you or me,
to the central identity of everything, the
mighty Ego. (Byron's was a vehement dash,
with plenty of impatient democracy, but
lurid and introverted amid all its magnetism;
not at all the fitting, lasting song of a grand,
secure, free, sunny race.) It is more akin,
likewise, to outside life and landscape, (returning mainly to the antique feeling,) real

Walt Whitman

sun and gale, and woods and shores—to the elements themselves—not sitting at ease
in parlor or library listening to a good tale of them, told in good rhyme. Character, a

feature far above style or polish—a feature not absent at any time, but now first brought to the fore—gives predominant stamp to advancing poetry. . . .

Is there not even now, indeed, an evolution, a departure from the masters? Venerable and unsurpassable after their kind as are the old works, and always unspeakably precious as studies, (for Americans more than any other people,) is it too much to say that by the shifted combinations of the modern mind the whole underlying theory of first-class verse has changed?

From "Poetry To-day in America—Shakspere—The Future"

THINKING ABOUT FREE VERSE

"That's not poetry! It's just chopped-up prose." So runs one old-fashioned complaint about free verse. Such criticism may be true of inept poems, but in the best free verse the line endings transform language in ways beyond the possibilities of prose. A line break implies a slight pause so that the last word of each line receives special emphasis. The last word in a line is meant to linger, however briefly, in the listener's ear. With practice and attention, you can easily develop a better sense of how a poem's line breaks operate.

- **Note whether the breaks tend to come at the end of sentences or phrases, or in the middle of an idea.** An abundance of breaks in mid-thought can create a tumbling, headlong effect, forcing your eye to speed down the page. Conversely, lines that tend to break at the end of a full idea can give a more stately rhythm to a poem.
- **Determine whether the lines tend to be all brief, all long, or a mix.** A very short line forces us to pay special attention to its every word, no matter how small.
- **Ask yourself how the poet's choices about line breaks help to reinforce the poem's meaning.** Can you identify any example of a line break affecting the meaning of a phrase or sentence?

CHECKLIST: Writing About Line Breaks

- ☐ Reread a poem, paying attention to where its lines end.
- ☐ Do the breaks tend to come at the end of the sentences or phrases?
- ☐ Do they tend to come in the middle of an idea?
- ☐ Do the lines tend to be long? Short? A mix of both?
- ☐ Is the poem broken into stanzas? Are they long? Short? A mix of both?
- ☐ What mood is created by the breaks?
- ☐ How do line breaks and stanza breaks reinforce the poem's meaning as a whole?

WRITING ASSIGNMENT ON OPEN FORM

Retype a free verse poem as prose, adding conventional punctuation and capitalization if necessary. Then compare and contrast the prose version with the poem itself. How do the two texts differ in tone, rhythm, emphasis, and effect? How do they remain similar? Use any poem from this chapter or any of the following from the chapter "Poems for Further Reading": W. H. Auden's "Musée des Beaux Arts"; Robert Lowell's "Skunk Hour"; Ezra Pound's "The River Merchant's Wife: A Letter"; or William Carlos Williams's "Queen-Anne's-Lace."

MORE TOPICS FOR WRITING

1. Write a brief essay (approximately 500 words) on how the line breaks and white space (or lack thereof) in E. E. Cummings's "Buffalo Bill 's" contribute to the poem's effect.

2. Read aloud William Carlos Williams's "The Dance." Examine how the poem's line breaks and sonic effects underscore the poem's meaning.

3. Imagine Charles Simic's "The Magic Study of Happiness" broken into free-verse lines. What are the benefits of the prose-poem form to this particular text?

4. Compare any poem in this chapter with a poem in rime and meter. Discuss several key features that they have in common despite their apparent differences in style. Features it might be useful to compare include imagery, tone, figures of speech, and word choice.

5. Write an imitation of Wallace Stevens's "Thirteen Ways of Looking at a Blackbird." Come up with thirteen ways of looking at your car, a can opener, a housecat—or any object that intrigues you. Choose your line breaks carefully, to recreate some of the mood of the original. You might also have a look at Aaron Abeyta's parody "Thirteen Ways of Looking at a Tortilla" on page 816.

▶ TERMS FOR *review*

Open form ▶ Poems that have neither a rime scheme nor a basic meter are in open form. Open form has also been called free verse.

Free verse ▶ From the French *vers libre.* Free verse is poetry whose lines follow no consistent meter. It may be rimed, but usually is not. In the last hundred years, free verse has become a common practice.

Prose poetry ▶ Poetic language printed in prose paragraphs, but displaying the careful attention to sound, imagery, and figurative language characteristic of poetry.

23

SYMBOL

A symbol is like a rock dropped into a pool:
it sends out ripples in all directions,
and the ripples are in motion.

—JOHN CIARDI

The national flag is supposed to stir our patriotic feelings. When a black cat crosses his path, a superstitious man shivers, foreseeing bad luck. To each of these, by custom, our society expects a standard response. A flag, a black cat crossing one's path—each is a **symbol:** a visible object or action that suggests some further meaning in addition to itself. In literature, a symbol might be the word *flag* or the words *a black cat crossed his path* or every description of flag or cat in an entire novel, story, play, or poem.

A flag and the crossing of a black cat may be called **conventional symbols,** since they can have a conventional or customary effect on us. Conventional symbols are also part of the language of poetry, as we know when we meet the red rose, emblem of love, in a lyric, or the Christian cross in the devotional poems of George Herbert. More often, however, symbols in literature have no conventional, long-established meaning, but particular meanings of their own. In Melville's novel *Moby-Dick,* to take a rich example, whatever we associate with the great white whale is *not* attached unmistakably to white whales by custom. Though Melville tells us that men have long regarded whales with awe and relates Moby Dick to the celebrated fish that swallowed Jonah, the reader's response is to one particular whale, the creature of Herman Melville. Only the experience of reading the novel in its entirety can give Moby Dick his particular meaning.

THE MEANINGS OF A SYMBOL

As Eudora Welty has observed, it is a good thing Melville made Moby Dick a whale, a creature large enough to contain all that critics have found in him. A symbol in literature, if not conventional, has more than just one meaning. In "The Raven," by Edgar Allan Poe, the appearance of a strange black bird in the narrator's study is sinister; and indeed, if we take the poem seriously, we may even respond with a sympathetic shiver of dread. Does the bird mean death, fate, melancholy, the loss of a loved one, knowledge in the service of evil? All of these, perhaps. Like any well-chosen symbol, Poe's raven sets off within the reader an unending train of feelings and associations.

We miss the value of a symbol, however, if we think it can mean absolutely anything we wish. If a poet has any control over our reactions, the poem will guide our responses in a certain direction.

T. S. Eliot (1888–1965)

The *Boston Evening Transcript* 1917

The readers of the *Boston Evening Transcript*
Sway in the wind like a field of ripe corn.

When evening quickens faintly in the street,
Wakening the appetites of life in some
And to others bringing the *Boston Evening Transcript*, 5
I mount the steps and ring the bell, turning
Wearily, as one would turn to nod good-bye to La Rochefoucauld,
If the street were time and he at the end of the street,
And I say, "Cousin Harriet, here is the *Boston Evening Transcript*."

The newspaper, whose name Eliot purposely repeats so monotonously, indicates what this poem is about. Now defunct, the *Transcript* covered in detail the slightest activity of Boston's leading families and was noted for the great length of its obituaries. Eliot, then, uses the newspaper as a symbol for an existence of boredom, fatigue (*Wearily*), petty and unvarying routine (since an evening newspaper, like night, arrives on schedule). The *Transcript* evokes a way of life without zest or passion, for, opposed to people who read it, Eliot sets people who do not: those whose desires revive, not expire, when the working day is through. Suggestions abound in the ironic comparison of the *Transcript*'s readers to a cornfield late in summer. To mention only a few: the readers sway because they are sleepy; they vegetate; they are drying up; each makes a rattling sound when turning a page. It is not necessary that we know the remote and similarly disillusioned friend to whom the speaker might nod: La Rochefoucauld, whose cynical *Maxims* entertained Parisian society under Louis XIV (sample: "All of us have enough strength to endure the misfortunes of others"). We understand that the nod is symbolic of an immense weariness of spirit. We know nothing about Cousin Harriet, whom the speaker addresses, but imagine from the greeting she inspires that she is probably a bore.

If Eliot wishes to say that certain Bostonians lead lives of sterile boredom, why does he couch his meaning in symbols? Why doesn't he tell us directly what he means? These questions imply two assumptions not necessarily true: first, that Eliot has a message to impart; second, that he is concealing it. We have reason to think that Eliot did not usually have a message in mind when beginning a poem, for as he once told a critic: "The conscious problems with which one is concerned in the actual writing are more those of a quasi-musical nature . . . than of a conscious exposition of ideas." Poets sometimes discover what they have to say while in the act of saying it. And it may be that in his *Transcript* poem, Eliot is saying exactly what he means. By communicating his meaning through symbols instead of statements, he may be choosing the only kind of language appropriate to an idea of great subtlety and complexity. (The paraphrase "Certain Bostonians are bored" hardly begins to describe the poem in all its possible meanings.) And by his use of symbolism, Eliot affords us the pleasure of finding our own entrances to his poem.

This power of suggestion that a symbol contains is, perhaps, its greatest advantage. Sometimes, as in the following poem by Emily Dickinson, a symbol will lead us from a visible object to something too vast to be perceived.

Emily Dickinson (1830–1886)

The Lightning is a yellow Fork (about 1870)

The Lightning is a yellow Fork
From Tables in the sky
By inadvertent fingers dropt
The awful Cutlery

Of mansions never quite disclosed 5
And never quite concealed
The Apparatus of the Dark
To ignorance revealed.

If the lightning is a fork, then whose are the fingers that drop it, the table from
which it slips, the household to which it belongs? The poem implies this question
without giving an answer. An obvious answer is "God," but can we be sure? We
wonder, too, about these partially lighted mansions: if our vision were clearer, what
would we behold?

IDENTIFYING SYMBOLS

"But how am I supposed to know a symbol when I see one?" The best approach is to
read poems closely, taking comfort in the likelihood that it is better not to notice
symbols at all than to find significance in every literal stone and huge meanings in
every thing. In looking for the symbols in a poem, pick out all the references to concrete objects—newspapers, black cats, twisted pins. Consider these with special care.
Notice any that the poet emphasizes by detailed description, by repetition, or by
placing it at the very beginning or end of the poem. Ask: What is the poem about,
what does it add up to? If, when the poem is paraphrased, the paraphrase depends primarily on the meaning of certain concrete objects, these richly suggestive objects
may be the symbols.

There are some things a literary symbol usually is *not*. A symbol is not an abstraction. Such terms as *truth, death, love,* and *justice* cannot work as symbols (unless
personified, as in the traditional figure of Justice holding a scale). Most often, a symbol
is something we can see in the mind's eye: a newspaper, a lightning bolt, a gesture of
nodding good-bye.

In narratives, a well-developed character who speaks much dialogue and is not
the least bit mysterious is usually not a symbol. But watch out for an executioner in
a black hood; a character, named for a biblical prophet, who does little but utter a
prophecy; a trio of old women who resemble the Three Fates. (It has been argued,
with good reason, that Milton's fully rounded character of Satan in *Paradise Lost* is
a symbol embodying evil and human pride, but a narrower definition of symbol is
more frequently useful.) A symbol *may* be a part of a person's body (the baleful eye
of the murder victim in Poe's story "The Tell-Tale Heart") or a look, a voice, or a
mannerism.

A symbol usually is not the second term of a metaphor. In the line "The Lightning is a yellow Fork," the symbol is the lightning, not the fork.

Sometimes a symbol addresses a sense other than sight: the sound of a mysterious
snapping string at the end of Chekhov's play *The Cherry Orchard*; or, in William

Faulkner's tale "A Rose for Emily," the odor of decay that surrounds the house of the last survivor of a town's leading family—suggesting not only physical dissolution but also the decay of a social order. A symbol is a special kind of image, for it exceeds the usual image in the richness of its connotations. The dead wife's cold comb in the haiku of Buson (discussed on page 560) works symbolically, suggesting among other things the chill of the grave, the contrast between the living and the dead.

To sum up: a symbol radiates hints or casts long shadows (to use Henry James's metaphor). We are unable to say it "stands for" or "represents" a meaning. It evokes, it suggests, it manifests. It demands no single necessary interpretation, such as the interpretation a driver gives to a red traffic light. Rather, like Emily Dickinson's lightning bolt, it points toward an indefinite meaning, which may lie in part beyond the reach of words. In a symbol, as Thomas Carlyle said in *Sartor Resartus*, "the Infinite is made to blend with the Finite, to stand visible, and as it were, attainable there."

Thomas Hardy (1840–1928)

Neutral Tones

1898

We stood by a pond that winter day,
And the sun was white, as though chidden of° God,　　　　　°*rebuked by*
And a few leaves lay on the starving sod;
　　—They had fallen from an ash, and were gray.

Your eyes on me were as eyes that rove　　　　　　　　　　　　　　5
Over tedious riddles of years ago;
And some words played between us to and fro
　　On which lost the more by our love.

The smile on your mouth was the deadest thing
Alive enough to have strength to die;　　　　　　　　　　　　　　10
And a grin of bitterness swept thereby
　　Like an ominous bird a-wing. . . .

Since then, keen lessons that love deceives,
And wrings with wrong, have shaped to me
Your face, and the God-curst sun, and a tree,　　　　　　　　　　15
　　And a pond edged with grayish leaves.

Questions

1. Sum up the story told in this poem. In lines 1–12, what is the dramatic situation? What has happened in the interval between the experience related in these lines and the reflection in the last stanza?

2. What meanings do you find in the title?

3. Explain in your own words the metaphor in line 2.

4. What connotations appropriate to this poem does the "ash" (line 4) have that *oak* or *maple* would lack?

5. What visible objects in the poem function symbolically? What actions or gestures?

ALLEGORY

If we read of a ship, its captain, its sailors, and the rough seas, and we realize we are reading about a commonwealth and how its rulers and workers keep it going even in difficult times, then we are reading an **allegory.** Closely akin to symbolism, allegory is a description—usually narrative—in which persons, places, and things are employed in a continuous and consistent system of equivalents. In an allegory an object has a single additional significance, one largely determined by convention. When an allegory appears in a work, it usually has a one-to-one relationship to an abstract entity, recognizable to readers and audiences familiar with the cultural context of the work.

Although more strictly limited in its suggestions than symbolism, allegory need not be thought inferior. Few poems continue to interest readers more than Dante's allegorical *Divine Comedy.* Sublime evidence of the appeal of allegory may be found in Christ's use of the **parable:** a brief narrative—usually allegorical but sometimes not—that teaches a moral.

Matthew 13:24–30 (King James Version, 1611)

The Parable of the Good Seed

The kingdom of heaven is likened unto a man which sowed good seed in
   his field:
But while men slept, his enemy came and sowed tares among the wheat,
   and went his way.
But when the blade was sprung up, and brought forth fruit, then appeared
   the tares also.
So the servants of the householder came and said unto him, Sir, didst not
   thou sow good seed in thy field? From whence then hath it tares?
He said unto them, An enemy hath done this. The servants said unto him,   5
   Wilt thou then that we go and gather them up?
But he said, Nay; lest while ye gather up the tares, ye root up also the wheat
   with them.
Let both grow together until the harvest: and in the time of harvest I will
   say to the reapers, Gather ye together first the tares, and bind them in
   bundles to burn them: but gather the wheat into my barn.

The sower is the Son of man, the field is the world, the good seed are the children of the Kingdom, the tares are the children of the wicked one, the enemy is the devil, the harvest is the end of the world, the reapers are angels. "As therefore the tares are gathered and burned in the fire; so shall it be in the end of this world" (Matthew 13:36–42).

Usually, as in this parable, the meanings of an allegory are plainly labeled or thinly disguised. In John Bunyan's allegorical narrative *The Pilgrim's Progress*, it is clear that the hero Christian, on his journey through places with such pointed names as Vanity Fair, the Valley of the Shadow of Death, and Doubting Castle, is the soul, traveling the road of life on the way toward Heaven. An allegory, when carefully built, is systematic. It makes one principal comparison, the working out of whose details may lead to further comparisons, then still further comparisons: Christian, thrown by Giant Despair into the dungeon of Doubting Castle, escapes by means of a key called Promise. Such a complicated design may take great length to unfold, as in Spenser's *Faerie Queene*; but the method may be seen in a short poem.

George Herbert (1593–1633)

Redemption
1633

Having been tenant long to a rich Lord,
   Not thriving, I resolved to be bold,
   And make a suit unto him, to afford
A new small-rented lease, and cancel th' old.

In Heaven at his manor I him sought: 5
   They told me there, that he was lately gone
   About some land, which he had dearly bought
Long since on earth, to take possession.

I straight returned, and knowing his great birth,
   Sought him accordingly in great resorts;
   In cities, theaters, gardens, parks, and courts: 10
At length I heard a ragged noise and mirth

     Of thieves and murderers: there I him espied,
     Who straight, *Your suit is granted*, said, and died.

Questions

1. In this allegory, what equivalents does Herbert give each of these terms: "tenant," "Lord," "not thriving," "suit," "new lease," "old lease," "manor," "land," "dearly bought," "take possession," "his great birth"?
2. What scene is depicted in the last three lines?

An object in an allegory is like a bird whose cage is clearly lettered with its identity—"RAVEN, *Corvus corax*; habitat of specimen, Maine." A symbol, by contrast, is a bird with piercing eyes that mysteriously appears one evening in your library. It is there; you can touch it. But what does it mean? You look at it. It continues to look at you.

Whether an object in literature is a symbol, part of an allegory, or no such thing at all, it has at least one sure meaning. Moby Dick is first a whale, and the *Boston Evening Transcript* is a newspaper. Besides deriving a multitude of intangible suggestions from the title symbol in Eliot's long poem *The Waste Land*, its readers cannot fail to carry away a sense of the land's physical appearance: a river choked with sandwich papers and cigarette ends, London Bridge "under the brown fog of a winter dawn." A virtue of *The Pilgrim's Progress* is that its walking abstractions are no mere abstractions but are also human: Giant Despair is a henpecked husband. The most vital element of a literary work may pass us by, unless, before seeking further depths in a thing, we look to the thing itself.

Robert Frost (1874–1963)

The Road Not Taken   1916

Two roads diverged in a yellow wood,
And sorry I could not travel both
And be one traveler, long I stood
And looked down one as far as I could
To where it bent in the undergrowth;   5

Then took the other, as just as fair,
And having perhaps the better claim,
Because it was grassy and wanted wear;
Though as for that the passing there
Had worn them really about the same,   10

And both that morning equally lay
In leaves no step had trodden black.
Oh, I kept the first for another day!
Yet knowing how way leads on to way,
I doubted if I should ever come back.   15

I shall be telling this with a sigh
Somewhere ages and ages hence:
Two roads diverged in a wood, and I—
I took the one less traveled by,
And that has made all the difference.   20

Question

What symbolism do you find in this poem, if any? Back up your claim with evidence.

Antonio Machado (1875–1939)

Proverbios y Cantares (XXIX) 1912

Caminante, son tus huellas
el camino, y nada más;
caminante, no hay camino,
se hace camino al andar.
Al andar se hace camino,
y al volver la vista atrás
se ve la senda que nunca
se ha de volver a pisar.
Caminante, no hay camino,
sino estelas en la mar.

Traveler   2011

Traveler, your footsteps are
the road, there's nothing more;
traveler, there is no road,
the road is made by walking.
Walking makes the road,   5
and if you turn around,
you only see the path
you cannot walk again.
Traveler, there is no road,
only a track of foam upon the sea.   10

— *Translated by Michael Ortiz*

Questions

Compare Machado's poem with Robert Frost's "The Road Not Taken." In what ways does Machado's use of the road as a symbol resemble Frost's use? In what ways does it differ?

Christina Rossetti (1830–1894)

Uphill   1862

Does the road wind uphill all the way?
　　Yes, to the very end.
Will the day's journey take the whole long day?
　　From morn to night, my friend.

But is there for the night a resting-place?   5
　　A roof for when the slow dark hours begin.
May not the darkness hide it from my face?
　　You cannot miss that inn.

Shall I meet other wayfarers at night?
　　Those who have gone before.   10
Then must I knock, or call when just in sight?
　　They will not keep you standing at that door.

Shall I find comfort, travel-sore and weak?
　　Of labor you shall find the sum.
Will there be beds for me and all who seek?   15
　　Yea, beds for all who come.

Questions

1. In reading this poem, at what line did you realize that the poet is building an allegory?
2. For what does each thing stand?
3. What does the title of the poem suggest to you?
4. Recast the meaning of line 14, a knotty line, in your own words.
5. Discuss the possible identities of the two speakers—the apprehensive traveler and the character with all the answers. Are they specific individuals? Allegorical figures?
6. Compare "Uphill" with Robert Creeley's "Oh No" (page 514). What striking similarities do you find in these two dissimilar poems?

FOR REVIEW AND FURTHER STUDY

Exercise: Symbol Hunting

After you have read each of the following poems, decide which description best suits each one:

1. The poem has a central symbol.
2. The poem contains no symbolism, but it should be taken literally.

William Carlos Williams   (1883–1963)

The Young Housewife   1916

At ten A.M. the young housewife
moves about in negligee behind
the wooden walls of her husband's house.
I pass solitary in my car.

Then again she comes to the curb   5
to call the ice-man, fish-man, and stands
shy, uncorseted, tucking in
stray ends of hair, and I compare her
to a fallen leaf.

The noiseless wheels of my car   10
rush with a crackling sound over
dried leaves as I bow and pass smiling.

Ted Kooser   (b. 1939)

Carrie   1979

"There's never an end to dust
and dusting," my aunt would say
as her rag, like a thunderhead,
scudded across the yellow oak
of her little house. There she lived   5
seventy years with a ball
of compulsion closed in her fist,
and an elbow that creaked and popped
like a branch in a storm. Now dust
is her hands and dust her heart.   10
There is never an end to it.

Mary Oliver   (b. 1935)

Wild Geese   1986

You do not have to be good.
You do not have to walk on your knees
for a hundred miles through the desert, repenting.
You only have to let the soft animal of your body
    love what it loves.
Tell me about despair, yours, and I will tell you mine.   5
Meanwhile the world goes on.

Meanwhile the sun and the clear pebbles of the rain
are moving across the landscapes,
over the prairies and the deep trees,
the mountains and the rivers.
Meanwhile the wild geese, high in the clean blue air,   10
are heading home again.
Whoever you are, no matter how lonely,
the world offers itself to your imagination,
calls to you like the wild geese, harsh and exciting—   15
over and over announcing your place
in the family of things.

Questions

1. Is this poem addressed to a specific person?
2. What is meant by "good" in the first line?
3. What do the wild geese symbolize? What is the significance of the use of the term "wild"?
4. What other adjectives are used to describe the phenomena of nature? What thematic purpose is served by this characterization of the natural world?

Tami Haaland (b. 1960)

Lipstick   2001

I wonder how they do it, those women
who can slip lipstick over lips without
looking, after they've finished a meal
or when they ride in cars. Satin Claret
or Plum or Twig or Pecan. I can't stay   5
inside the lines, late comer to lipstick
that I am, and sometimes get messy
even in front of a mirror. But these
women know where lips end and plain
skin begins, probably know how to put   10
their hair in a knot with a single pin.

Questions

1. How does the speaker use lipstick differently from the way "those women" do?
2. Why do the other women know how to apply lipstick more accurately? What does this knowledge suggest about the difference between them and the speaker?
3. What does lipstick seem to suggest in the poem? Support your ideas with specific examples from the poem.

Lorine Niedecker (1903–1970)

Popcorn-can cover   (about 1959)

Popcorn-can cover
screwed to the wall
over a hole
      so the cold   5
can't mouse in

Wallace Stevens (1879–1955)

The Snow Man   1923

One must have a mind of winter
To regard the frost and the boughs
Of the pine-trees crusted with snow;

And have been cold a long time
To behold the junipers shagged with ice,   5
The spruces rough in the distant glitter

Of the January sun; and not to think
Of any misery in the sound of the wind,
In the sound of a few leaves,

Which is the sound of the land   10
Full of the same wind
That is blowing in the same bare place

For the listener, who listens in the snow,
And, nothing himself, beholds
Nothing that is not there and the nothing that is.   15

Wallace Stevens (1879–1955)

Anecdote of the Jar   1923

I placed a jar in Tennessee,
And round it was, upon a hill.
It made the slovenly wilderness
Surround that hill.

The wilderness rose up to it,   5
And sprawled around, no longer wild.
The jar was round upon the ground
And tall and of a port in air.

It took dominion everywhere.
The jar was gray and bare.   10
It did not give of bird or bush,
Like nothing else in Tennessee.

■ WRITING *effectively*

William Butler Yeats on Writing

Poetic Symbols   1901

Any one who has any experience of any
mystical state of the soul knows how there
float up in the mind profound symbols, whose
meaning, if indeed they do not delude one into
the dream that they are meaningless, one does
not perhaps understand for years. Nor I think
has any one, who has known that experience
with any constancy, failed to find some day, in
some old book or on some old monument, a
strange or intricate image that had floated up
before him, and to grow perhaps dizzy with the
sudden conviction that our little memories are
but a part of some great Memory that renews
the world and men's thoughts age after age,
and that our thoughts are not, as we suppose,
the deep, but a little foam upon the deep.

William Butler Yeats

• • •

    It is only by ancient symbols, by symbols that have numberless meanings besides
the one or two the writer lays an emphasis upon, or the half-score he knows of, that
any highly subjective art can escape from the barrenness and shallowness of a too
conscious arrangement, into the abundance and depth of Nature. The poet of
essences and pure ideas must seek in the half-lights that glimmer from symbol to symbol as if to the ends of the earth, all that the epic and dramatic poet finds of mystery
and shadow in the accidental circumstances of life.

From "The Philosophy of Shelley's Poetry"

THINKING ABOUT SYMBOLS

A symbol, to use poet John Drury's concise definition, is "an image that radiates
meanings." While images in a poem can and should be read as what they literally are,
images often do double duty, suggesting deeper meanings. Exactly what those meanings are, however, often differs from poem to poem.

    Some symbols have been used so often and effectively over time that a traditional
reading of them has developed. At times a poet clearly adopts an image's traditional
symbolic meaning. Some poems, however, deliberately play against a symbol's
conventional associations.

- **To determine the meaning (or meanings) of a symbol, start by asking if it
  has traditional associations.** If so, consider whether the symbol is being
  used in the expected way or if the poet is playing with those associations.

- **Consider the symbol's relationship to the rest of the poem.** Let context be your guide. The image might have a unique meaning to the poem's speaker.
- **Consider the emotions that the image evokes.** If the image recurs in the poem, pay attention to how it changes from one appearance to the next.
- **Keep in mind that not everything is a symbol.** If an image doesn't appear to radiate meanings above and beyond its literal sense, don't feel you have failed as a critic. As Sigmund Freud once said about symbol-hunting, "Sometimes a cigar is just a cigar."

CHECKLIST: Writing About Symbols

- ☐ Is the symbol a traditional one?
- ☐ If so, is it being used in the expected way? Or is the poet playing with its associations?
- ☐ What does the image seem to mean to the poem's speaker?
- ☐ What emotions are evoked by the image?
- ☐ If an image recurs in a poem, how does it change from one appearance to the next?
- ☐ Does the image radiate meaning beyond its literal sense? If not, it might not be intended as a symbol.

WRITING ASSIGNMENT ON SYMBOLISM

Do an in-depth analysis of the symbolism in a poem of your choice from the chapter "Poems for Further Reading." Some likely choices would be W. H. Auden's "As I Walked Out One Evening," Robert Lowell's "Skunk Hour," Sylvia Plath's "Daddy," and Adrienne Rich's "Living in Sin."

MORE TOPICS FOR WRITING

1. Compare and contrast the use of roads as symbols in Christina Rossetti's "Uphill" and Robert Frost's "The Road Not Taken." What does the use of this image suggest in each poem?
2. Discuss "The Snow Man" and "Anecdote of the Jar" in terms of Wallace Stevens's use of symbolism to portray the relationship between humanity and nature.
3. Write an explication of any poem from this chapter, paying careful attention to its symbols. Some good choices are Robert Frost's "The Road Not Taken," Tami Haaland's "Lipstick," Thomas Hardy's "Neutral Tones," and Christina Rossetti's "Uphill." For a further description of poetic explication, see the chapter "Writing About a Poem."
4. Take a relatively simple, straightforward poem, such as William Carlos Williams's "This Is Just to Say" (page 528), and write a burlesque critical interpretation of it. Claim to discover symbols that the poem doesn't contain. While running wild with your "reading into" the poem, don't invent anything that you can't somehow support from the text of the poem itself. At the end of your burlesque, sum up in a paragraph what this exercise taught you about how to read poems, or how not to.
5. Compare the symbols of the road in Robert Frost's "The Road Not Taken" with Antonio Machado's "Traveler." In what ways do the poets use the symbol similarly? In what ways does the symbol suggest different meanings?

▶ TERMS FOR *review*

Symbol ▶ A person, place, or thing in a narrative that suggests meanings beyond its literal sense. Symbol is related to *allegory*, but it works more complexly. A symbol bears multiple suggestions and associations. It is unique to the work, not common to a culture.

Allegory ▶ A description—often a narrative—in which the literal events (persons, places, and things) consistently point to a parallel sequence of ideas, values, or other recognizable abstractions. An allegory has two levels of meaning: a literal level that tells a surface story and a symbolic level in which the abstractions unfold.

Symbolic act ▶ An action whose significance goes well beyond its literal meaning. In literature, symbolic acts often involve a primal or unconscious ritual element such as rebirth, purification, forgiveness, vengeance, or initiation.

Conventional symbols ▶ Symbols that, because of their frequent use, have acquired a standard significance. They may range from complex metaphysical images such as those of Christian saints in Gothic art to social customs such as a young bride in a white dress. They are conventional symbols because they carry recognizable meanings and suggestions.

24 MYTH AND NARRATIVE

> *Myth does not mean something untrue,*
> *but a concentration of truth.*
>
> —DORIS LESSING

Poets have long been fond of retelling **myths,** narrowly defined as traditional stories about the exploits of immortal beings. Such stories taken collectively may also be called myth or **mythology.** In one of the most celebrated collections of myth ever assembled, the *Metamorphoses,* the Roman poet Ovid told—to take one example from many—how Phaeton, child of the sun god, rashly tried to drive his father's fiery chariot on its daily round, lost control of the horses, and caused disaster both to himself and to the world.

Our use of the term *myth* in discussing poetry, then, differs from its use in expressions such as "the myth of communism" and "the myth of democracy." In these examples, myth is used broadly to represent any idea people believe in, whether true or false. Nor do we mean—to take another familiar use of the word—a cock-and-bull story: "Judge Rapp doesn't roast speeders alive; that's just a *myth.*" In the following discussion, **myth** will mean a kind of story—either from ancient or modern sources—whose actions implicitly symbolize some profound truth about human or natural existence.

Traditional myths tell us stories of gods or heroes—their battles, their lives, their loves, and often their suffering—all on a scale of magnificence larger than our life. These exciting stories usually reveal part of a culture's worldview. Myths often try to explain universal natural phenomena, like the phases of the moon or the turning of the seasons. But some myths tell the stories of purely local phenomena; one Greek legend, for example, recounts how grief-stricken King Aegeus threw himself into the sea when he mistakenly believed his son, Theseus, had been killed; consequently, the body of water between Greece and Turkey was called the Aegean Sea.

Modern psychologists, such as Sigmund Freud and Carl Jung, have been fascinated by myth and legend, since they believe these stories symbolically enact deep truths about human nature. Our myths, psychologists believe, express our wishes, dreams, and nightmares. Whether or not we believe myths, we recognize their psychological power. Even in the first century B.C., Ovid did not believe in the literal truth of the legends he so suavely retold; he confessed, "I prate of ancient poets' monstrous lies."

And yet it is characteristic of a myth that it *can* be believed. Throughout history, myths have accompanied religious doctrines and rituals. They have helped sanction or recall the reasons for religious observances. A sublime instance is the New Testament account of the Last Supper. Because of its record of the words of Jesus, "Do this in remembrance of Me," Christians have continued to re-enact the offering and partaking of the body and blood of their Lord, under the appearances of bread and wine. It is essential to recall that, just because a myth narrates the acts of a god, we do not necessarily mean by the term a false or fictitious narrative. When we speak of "the myth of Islam" or "the Christian myth," we do so without implying either belief or disbelief.

Myths can also help sanction customs and institutions other than religious ones. At the same time that the baking of bread was introduced to ancient Greece—one theory goes—the myth of Demeter, goddess of grain, appeared. Demeter was a kindly deity who sent her emissary to teach humankind the valuable art of baking, thus helping to persuade the distrustful that bread was a good thing. Some myths seem designed to divert and regale, not to sanction anything. Such may be the story of the sculptor Pygmalion, who fell in love with the statue he had carved of a beautiful woman; so exquisite was his work, so deep was his feeling, that Aphrodite, the goddess of Love, brought the statue to life. And yet perhaps the story goes deeper than mere diversion: perhaps it is a way of saying that works of art achieve a reality of their own, that love can transform or animate its object.

ORIGINS OF MYTH

How does a myth begin? Several theories have been proposed, none universally accepted. One is that a myth is a way to explain some natural phenomenon. Winter comes and the vegetation perishes because Persephone, child of Demeter, must return to the underworld for several months every year. Many anthropologists emphasize the practical function of myth; in his influential work of comparative mythology, *The Golden Bough*, Sir James Frazer argued that most myths were originally expressions of human hope that nature would be fertile. Still another theory maintains that many myths began as real events; mythic heroes were real human beings whose deeds have been changed and exaggerated by posterity. Most present-day myth historians would say that different myths probably have different origins.

Poets have many coherent mythologies on which to draw; perhaps those most frequently consulted by British and American poets are the classical, the Christian, the Norse, the Native American, and the folktales of the American frontier (embodying the deeds of superhuman characters such as Paul Bunyan). Some poets have taken inspiration from other myths as well: T. S. Eliot's *The Waste Land*, for example, is enriched by allusions to Buddhism and to pagan vegetation cults. Robert Bly borrowed the terrifying Death Goddess of Aztec, Hindu, and Balinese mythology to make her the climactic figure of his long poem "The Teeth Mother Naked at Last."

A tour through any good art museum will demonstrate how thoroughly myth pervades the painting and sculpture of nearly every civilization. In literature, one evidence of its continuing value to recent poets and storytellers is how frequently ancient myths are retold. Even in modern society, writers often turn to myth when they try to tell stories of deep significance. Mythic structures still touch a powerful and primal part of the human imagination. William Faulkner's story "The Bear" recalls tales of Indian totem animals; John Updike's novel *The Centaur* presents the horse-man Chiron as a modern high-school teacher; James Joyce's *Ulysses* transposes the *Odyssey* to modern Dublin (and the Coen brothers' film *O Brother, Where Art Thou?* reimagines Homer's epic in Depression-era Mississippi); Rita Dove's play *The Darker Face of the Earth* recasts the story of Oedipus in the slave-era South; Bernard Shaw retells the story of Pygmalion in his popular Edwardian social comedy *Pygmalion*, later the basis of the hit musical *My Fair Lady*; Jean Cocteau's film *Orphée* shows us Eurydice riding to the underworld with an escort of motorcycles. Popular interest in such works may testify to the profound appeal myths continue to hold for us. Like other varieties of poetry, myth is a kind of knowledge, not at odds with scientific knowledge but existing in addition to it.

Robert Frost (1874–1963)

Nothing Gold Can Stay   1923

Nature's first green is gold,
Her hardest hue to hold.
Her early leaf's a flower;
But only so an hour.
Then leaf subsides to leaf.   5
So Eden sank to grief,
So dawn goes down to day.
Nothing gold can stay.

Questions

1. To what myth does this poem allude? Does Frost sound as though he believes in the myth or as though he rejects it?
2. When Frost says, "Nature's first green is gold," he is describing how many leaves first appear as tiny yellow buds and blossoms. But what else does this line imply?
3. What would happen to the poem's meaning if line 6 were omitted?

William Wordsworth (1770–1850)

The world is too much with us   1807

The world is too much with us; late and soon,
Getting and spending, we lay waste our powers:
Little we see in Nature that is ours;
We have given our hearts away, a sordid boon!
This Sea that bares her bosom to the moon;   5
The winds that will be howling at all hours,
And are up-gathered now like sleeping flowers;
For this, for everything, we are out of tune;
It moves us not.—Great God! I'd rather be
A Pagan suckled in a creed outworn;   10
So might I, standing on this pleasant lea,
Have glimpses that would make me less forlorn;
Have sight of Proteus rising from the sea;
Or hear old Triton blow his wreathèd horn.

Questions

1. What condition does the speaker complain of in this sonnet? To what does he attribute this condition?
2. How does this situation affect him personally?

H.D. [Hilda Doolittle] (1886–1961)

Helen   1924

All Greece hates
the still eyes in the white face,
the lustre as of olives
where she stands,
and the white hands.   5

All Greece reviles
the wan face when she smiles,
hating it deeper still
when it grows wan and white,
remembering past enchantments   10
and past ills.

Greece sees, unmoved,
God's daughter, born of love,
the beauty of cool feet
and slenderest knees,   15
could love indeed the maid,
only if she were laid,
white ash amid funereal cypresses.

HELEN. In Greek mythology, Helen, most beautiful of all women, was the daughter of a mortal, Leda, by the god Zeus. Her abduction set off the long and devastating Trojan War. While married to Menelaus, king of the Greek city-state of Sparta, Helen was carried off by Paris, prince of Troy. Menelaus and his brother, Agamemnon, raised an army, besieged Troy for ten years, and eventually recaptured her. One episode of the Trojan War is related in the *Iliad*, Homer's epic poem, composed before 700 B.C.

Questions

1. At what point in the Troy narrative does this poem appear to be set?
2. What connotations does the color white usually possess? Does it have those same associations here?
3. Reread Yeats's "Leda and the Swan" (page 623). Does his retelling of that myth add an ironic dimension to line 13 of "Helen"?

Edgar Allan Poe (1809–1849)

To Helen   1831

Helen, thy beauty is to me
   Like those Nicean barks of yore,
That gently, o'er a perfumed sea,
   The weary, way-worn wanderer bore
      To his own native shore.   5

On desperate seas long wont to roam,
    Thy hyacinth hair, thy classic face,
Thy Naiad airs have brought me home
    To the glory that was Greece
And the grandeur that was Rome.   10

Lo! in yon brilliant window-niche
    How statue-like I see thee stand!
    The agate lamp within thy hand,
Ah! Psyche, from the regions which
    Are Holy Land!   15

TO HELEN. 1 *Helen*: Helen of Troy, in legend the most beautiful woman in the world. 2 *Nicean barks*: boats from Nicea, an ancient trading city in Asia Minor. 7 *Naiad*: in classical mythology, a nymph of a lake or river. 14 *Psyche*: the beautiful mortal woman who was Cupid's lover.

Questions

1. Why does Poe invoke the name of Helen to address his beloved?
2. Compare Poe's Helen with H.D.'s in her poem "Helen." How do the two versions of the mythic woman differ?

ARCHETYPE

An important concept in understanding myth is the **archetype,** a basic image, character, situation, or symbol that appears so often in literature and legend that it evokes a deep universal response. (The Greek root of *archetype* means "original pattern.") The term was borrowed by literary critics from the writings of the Swiss psychologist Carl Jung, a serious scholar of myth and religion, who formulated a theory of the "collective unconscious," a set of primal memories common to the entire human race. Archetypal patterns emerged, he speculated, in prerational thought and often reflect key primordial experiences such as birth, growth, sexual awakening, family, generational struggle, and death, as well as primal elements such as fire, sun, moon, blood, and water. Jung also believed that these situations, images, and figures had actually been genetically coded into the human brain and are passed down to successive generations, but no one has ever been able to prove a biological base for the undeniable phenomenon of similar characters, stories, and symbols appearing across widely separated and diverse cultures.

Whatever their origin, archetypal images do seem verbally coded in most myths, legends, and traditional tales. One sees enough recurring patterns and figures from Greek myth to *Star Wars*, from Hindu epic to Marvel superhero comics, to strongly suggest that there is some common psychic force at work. Typical archetypal figures include the trickster, the cruel stepmother, the rebellious young man, the beautiful but destructive woman, and the stupid youngest son who succeeds through simple goodness. Any one of these figures can be traced from culture to culture. The trickster, for instance, appears in American Indian coyote tales, Norse myths about the fire god Loki, Marx Brothers films, and *Batman* comic books and movies featuring the Joker.

Archetypal myths are the basic conventions of human storytelling, which we learn without necessarily being aware of the process. The patterns we absorb in our first nursery rhymes and fairy tales, as mythological critic Northrop Frye has demonstrated, underlie—though often very subtly—the most sophisticated poems and novels. One powerful archetype seen across many cultures is the demon-goddess who immobilizes men by locking them into a deathly trance or—in the most primitive forms of the myth—turning them to stone. Here are modern versions of this ancient myth in the following two poems.

Louise Bogan (1897–1970)

Medusa 1923

I had come to the house, in a cave of trees,
Facing a sheer sky.
Everything moved,—a bell hung ready to strike,
Sun and reflection wheeled by.

When the bare eyes were before me   5
And the hissing hair,
Held up at a window, seen through a door.
The stiff bald eyes, the serpents on the forehead
Formed in the air.

This is a dead scene forever now.   10
Nothing will ever stir.
The end will never brighten it more than this,
Nor the rain blur.

The water will always fall, and will not fall,
And the tipped bell make no sound.   15
The grass will always be growing for hay
Deep on the ground.

And I shall stand here like a shadow
Under the great balanced day,
My eyes on the yellow dust, that was lifting in the wind,   20
And does not drift away.

MEDUSA. Medusa was one of the Gorgons of Greek mythology. Hideously ugly with snakes for hair, Medusa turned those who looked upon her face into stone.

Questions

1. Who is the speaker of the poem?
2. Why are the first two stanzas spoken in the past tense while the final three are mainly in the future tense?
3. What is the speaker's attitude toward Medusa? Is there anything surprising about his or her reaction to being transformed into stone?
4. Does Bogan merely dramatize an incident from classical mythology, or does the poem suggest other interpretations as well?

John Keats (1795–1821)

La Belle Dame sans Merci 1819

I

O what can ail thee, knight at arms,
    Alone and palely loitering?
The sedge has wither'd from the lake,
    And no birds sing.

II

O what can ail thee, knight at arms,
 So haggard and so woe-begone?
The squirrel's granary is full,
 And the harvest's done.   5

III

I see a lily on thy brow
 With anguish moist and fever dew,
And on thy cheeks a fading rose   10
 Fast withereth too.

IV

I met a lady in the meads,
 Full beautiful, a fairy's child;
Her hair was long, her foot was light,   15
 And her eyes were wild.

V

I made a garland for her head,
 And bracelets too, and fragrant zone;
She look'd at me as she did love,
 And made sweet moan.   20

VI

I set her on my pacing steed,
 And nothing else saw all day long,
For sidelong would she bend, and sing
 A fairy's song.

VII

She found me roots of relish sweet,   25
 And honey wild, and manna dew,
And sure in language strange she said—
 I love thee true.

VIII

She took me to her elfin grot,
 And there she wept, and sigh'd full sore,   30
And there I shut her wild wild eyes
 With kisses four.

IX

And there she lulled me asleep,
 And there I dream'd—Ah! woe betide!
The latest dream I ever dream'd   35
 On the cold hill's side.

X

I saw pale kings, and princes too,
  Pale warriors, death pale were they all;
They cried—"La belle dame sans merci
Hath thee in thrall!"   40

XI

I saw their starv'd lips in the gloam
  With horrid warning gaped wide,
And I awoke and found me here
  On the cold hill's side.

XII

And this is why I sojourn here,   45
  Alone and palely loitering,
Though the sedge is wither'd from the lake,
  And no birds sing.

LA BELLE DAME SANS MERCI. The title is French for "the beautiful woman without mercy." Keats borrowed the title from a fifteenth-century French poem.

Questions

1. What time of year is suggested by the details of the first two stanzas? What is the significance of the season in the larger context of the poem?
2. How many speakers are there? Where does the change of speaker occur?
3. What details throughout the text tell us that *la belle dame* is no ordinary woman?
4. Why do you think the poet chose to imitate the form of the folk ballad in this poem?

PERSONAL MYTH

Sometimes poets have been inspired to make up myths of their own, to embody their own visions of life. "I must create a system or be enslaved by another man's," said William Blake, who in his "prophetic books" peopled the cosmos with supernatural beings having names such as Los, Urizen, and Vala (side by side with recognizable figures from the Old and New Testaments). This kind of system-making probably has advantages and drawbacks. T. S. Eliot, in his essay on Blake, wishes that the author of *The Four Zoas* had accepted traditional myths, and he compares Blake's thinking to a piece of homemade furniture whose construction diverted valuable energy from the writing of poems. Others have found Blake's untraditional cosmos an achievement—notably William Butler Yeats, himself the author of an elaborate personal mythology. Although we need not know all of Yeats's mythology to enjoy his poems, to know of its existence can make a few great poems deeper for us and less difficult.

William Butler Yeats (1865–1939)

The Second Coming

1921

Turning and turning in the widening gyre°   *spiral*
The falcon cannot hear the falconer;
Things fall apart; the center cannot hold;
Mere anarchy is loosed upon the world,
The blood-dimmed tide is loosed, and everywhere   5
The ceremony of innocence is drowned;
The best lack all conviction, while the worst
Are full of passionate intensity.

Surely some revelation is at hand;
Surely the Second Coming is at hand.   10
The Second Coming! Hardly are those words out
When a vast image out of *Spiritus Mundi*
Troubles my sight: somewhere in sands of the desert
A shape with lion body and the head of a man,
A gaze blank and pitiless as the sun,   15
Is moving its slow thighs, while all about it
Reel shadows of the indignant desert birds.
The darkness drops again; but now I know
That twenty centuries of stony sleep
Were vexed to nightmare by a rocking cradle,   20
And what rough beast, its hour come round at last,
Slouches towards Bethlehem to be born?

What kind of Second Coming does Yeats expect? Evidently it is not to be a
Christian one. Yeats saw human history as governed by the turning of a Great
Wheel, whose phases influence events and determine human personalities—rather
like the signs of the Zodiac in astrology. Every two thousand years comes a horren-
dous moment: the Wheel completes a turn; one civilization ends and another begins.
Strangely, a new age is always announced by birds and by acts of violence. Thus the
Greek-Roman world arrives with the descent of Zeus in swan's form and the burning
of Troy, the Christian era with the descent of the Holy Spirit—traditionally depicted
as a dove—and the Crucifixion. In 1919 when Yeats wrote "The Second Coming,"
his Ireland was in the midst of turmoil and bloodshed; the Western Hemisphere had
been severely shaken by World War I and the Russian Revolution. A new millen-
nium seemed imminent. What sphinxlike, savage deity would next appear on earth,
with birds proclaiming it angrily? Yeats imagines it emerging from *Spiritus Mundi*,
Soul of the World, a collective unconscious from which a human being (since the
individual soul touches it) receives dreams, nightmares, and racial memories.

It is hard to say whether a poet who discovers a personal myth does so to have
something to live by or to have something to write about. Robert Graves, who professed his belief in a White Goddess ("Mother of All Living, the ancient power of
love and terror"), declared that he wrote his poetry in a trance, inspired by his Goddess-
Muse. Luckily, we do not have to know a poet's religious affiliation before we can
read his or her poems. Perhaps most personal myths that enter poems are not acts of
faith but works of art: stories that resemble traditional mythology.

MYTH AND POPULAR CULTURE

If one can find myths in an art museum, one can also find them abundantly in popular culture. Movies and comic books, for example, are full of myths in modern guise. What is Superman, if not a mythic hero who has adapted himself to modern urban life? Marvel Comics even made the Norse thunder god, Thor, into a superhero, although they initially obliged him, like Clark Kent, to get a job. We also see myths retold on the technicolor screen. Sometimes Hollywood presents the traditional story directly, as in Walt Disney's *Cinderella*; more often the ancient tales acquire contemporary settings, as in another celluloid Cinderella story, *Pretty Woman*. (See how Anne Sexton has retold the Cinderella story from a feminist perspective, later in this chapter, or find a recording of Dana Dane's Brooklyn housing-project version of the fairy tale done from a masculine perspective in his underground rap hit "Cinderfella.") George Lucas's *Star Wars* series borrowed the structure of medieval quest legends. In quest stories, young knights pursued their destiny, often by seeking the Holy Grail, the cup Christ used at the Last Supper; in *Star Wars*, Luke Skywalker searched for his own parentage and identity, but his interstellar quest brought him to a surprisingly similar cast of knights, monsters, princesses, and wizards. Medieval Grail romances, which influenced Eliot's *The Waste Land* and J. R. R. Tolkien's *The Lord of the Rings* trilogy, also shaped films such as *The Fisher King* and *The Matrix*. Science fiction also commonly uses myth to novel effect. Extraterrestrial visitors usually appear as either munificent mythic gods or nightmarish demons. Steven Spielberg's *E.T.*, for example, revealed a gentle, Christ-like alien recognized by innocent children, but persecuted by adults. E.T. even healed the sick, fell into a deathlike coma, and was resurrected.

Why do poets retell myths? Why don't they just make up their own stories? First, using myth allows poets to be concise. By alluding to stories that their audiences know, they can draw on powerful associations with just a few words. If someone describes an acquaintance, "He thinks he's James Bond," that one allusion speaks volumes. Likewise, when Robert Frost inserts the single line "So Eden sank to grief" in "Nothing Gold Can Stay," those five words summon up a wealth of associations. They tie the perishable quality of spring's beauty to the equally transient nature of human youth. They also suggest that everything in the human world is subject to time's ravages, that perfection is impossible for us to maintain, just as it was for Adam and Eve.

Second, poets know that many stories fall into familiar mythic patterns, and that the most powerful stories of human existence tend to be the same, generation after generation. Sometimes using an old story allows a writer to describe a new situation in a fresh and surprising way. Novels often try to capture the exact texture of a social situation; they need to present the everyday details to evoke the world in which their characters live. Myths tend to tell their stories more quickly and in more general terms. They give just the essential actions and leave out everything else. Narrative poems also work best when they focus on just the essential elements. Here are two modern narrative poems that retell traditional myths to make modern interpretations.

A. E. Stallings (b. 1968)

First Love: A Quiz   2006

He came up to me:

    a. in his souped-up Camaro

    b. to talk to my skinny best friend

    c. and bumped my glass of wine so I wore the ferrous stain on my sleeve

d. from the ground, in a lead chariot drawn by a team of stallions black as   5
crude oil and breathing sulfur; at his heart, he sported a tiny golden arrow

He offered me:
  a. a ride
  b. dinner and a movie, with a wink at the cliché
  c. an excuse not to go back alone to the apartment with its sink of dirty knives
  d. a narcissus with a hundred dazzling petals that breathed a sweetness   10
  as cloying as decay

I went with him because:
  a. even his friends told me to beware
  b. I had nothing to lose except my virginity
  c. he placed his hand in the small of my back and I felt the tread of honeybees
  d. he was my uncle, the one who lived in the half-finished basement, and   15
  he took me by the hair

The place he took me to:
  a. was dark as my shut eyes
  b. and where I ate bitter seed and became ripe
  c. and from which my mother would never take me wholly back, though she
  wept and walked the earth and made the bearded ears of barley wither on
  their stalks and the blasted flowers drop from their sepals
  d. is called by some men hell and others love   20
  e. all of the above

FIRST LOVE: A QUIZ. Stallings's poem alludes to the classical myth of Persephone. A beautiful young goddess, the daughter of Zeus and Demeter, she was abducted by Hades, the ruler of the Underworld (and the brother of Zeus). Her mother Demeter, the goddess of agriculture, became so grief-stricken that plants stopped growing. Eventually, Persephone was permitted to spend six months on the earth each year, which allows spring and summer to return, before descending again into Hades, which brings back winter.

Questions

1. How does Stallings adapt a classical myth of abduction and rape into a contemporary story? Give specific examples.
2. In each option, does the speaker see the man as dangerous? If so, why does she go with him?
3. What is your interpretation of the last line?

Anne Sexton (1928–1974)

Cinderella   1971

You always read about it:
the plumber with twelve children
who wins the Irish Sweepstakes.
From toilets to riches.
That story.

Or the nursemaid,
some luscious sweet from Denmark
who captures the oldest son's heart.
From diapers to Dior.
That story.   10

Or a milkman who serves the wealthy,
eggs, cream, butter, yogurt, milk,
the white truck like an ambulance
who goes into real estate
and makes a pile.   15
From homogenized to martinis at lunch.

Or the charwoman
who is on the bus when it cracks up
and collects enough from the insurance.
From mops to Bonwit Teller.   20
That story.

Once
the wife of a rich man was on her deathbed
and she said to her daughter Cinderella:
Be devout. Be good. Then I will smile   25
down from heaven in the seam of a cloud.
The man took another wife who had
two daughters, pretty enough
but with hearts like blackjacks.
Cinderella was their maid.   30
She slept on the sooty hearth each night
and walked around looking like Al Jolson.
Her father brought presents home from town,
jewels and gowns for the other women
but the twig of a tree for Cinderella.   35
She planted that twig on her mother's grave
and it grew to a tree where a white dove sat.
Whenever she wished for anything the dove
would drop it like an egg upon the ground.
The bird is important, my dears, so heed him.   40

Next came the ball, as you all know.
It was a marriage market.
The prince was looking for a wife.
All but Cinderella were preparing
and gussying up for the big event.   45
Cinderella begged to go too.
Her stepmother threw a dish of lentils
into the cinders and said: Pick them
up in an hour and you shall go.
The white dove brought all his friends;   50
all the warm wings of the fatherland came,
and picked up the lentils in a jiffy.
No, Cinderella, said the stepmother,
you have no clothes and cannot dance.
That's the way with stepmothers.   55

Cinderella went to the tree at the grave
and cried forth like a gospel singer:

Mama! Mama! My turtledove,
send me to the prince's ball!
The bird dropped down a golden dress   60
and delicate little gold slippers.
Rather a large package for a simple bird.
So she went. Which is no surprise.
Her stepmother and sisters didn't
recognize her without her cinder face   65
and the prince took her hand on the spot
and danced with no other the whole day.

As nightfall came she thought she'd better
get home. The prince walked her home
and she disappeared into the pigeon house   70
and although the prince took an axe and broke
it open she was gone. Back to her cinders.
These events repeated themselves for three days.
However on the third day the prince
covered the palace steps with cobbler's wax   75
and Cinderella's gold shoe stuck upon it.
Now he would find whom the shoe fit
and find his strange dancing girl for keeps.
He went to their house and the two sisters
were delighted because they had lovely feet.   80
The eldest went into a room to try the slipper on
but her big toe got in the way so she simply
sliced it off and put on the slipper.
The prince rode away with her until the white dove
told him to look at the blood pouring forth.   85
That is the way with amputations.
They don't just heal up like a wish.
The other sister cut off her heel
but the blood told as blood will.
The prince was getting tired.   90
He began to feel like a shoe salesman.
But he gave it one last try.
This time Cinderella fit into the shoe
like a love letter into its envelope.

At the wedding ceremony   95
the two sisters came to curry favor
and the white dove pecked their eyes out.
Two hollow spots were left
like soup spoons.

Cinderella and the prince   100
lived, they say, happily ever after,
like two dolls in a museum case
never bothered by diapers or dust,
never arguing over the timing of an egg,
never telling the same story twice,   105

never getting a middle-aged spread,
their darling smiles pasted on for eternity.
Regular Bobbsey Twins.
That story.

CINDERELLA. *32 Al Jolson:* Extremely popular American entertainer (1886–1950) who frequently performed in blackface.

Questions

1. Most of Sexton's "Cinderella" straightforwardly retells a version of the famous fairy tale. But in the beginning and ending of the poem, how does Sexton change the story?
2. How does Sexton's refrain of "That story" alter the meaning of the episodes it describes? What is the tone of this poem (the poet's attitude toward her material)?
3. What does Sexton's final stanza suggest about the way fairy tales usually end?

■ WRITING *effectively*

Anne Sexton on Writing

Transforming Fairy Tales   1970

October 14, 1970

Dear Paul [Brooks°],

. . . I realize that the "Transformations"° are a departure from my usual style. I would say that they lack the intensity and perhaps some of the confessional force of my previous work. I wrote them because I had to . . . because I wanted to . . . because it made me happy. I would want to publish them for the same reason. I would like my readers to see this side of me, and it is not in every case the lighter side. Some of the poems are grim. In fact I don't know how to typify them except to agree that I have made them very contemporary. It would further be a lie to say that they weren't about me, because they are just as much about me as my other poetry.

Anne Sexton

I look at my work in stages, and each new book is a kind of growth and reaching outward and as always backward. Perhaps the critics will be unhappy with this book and some of my readers maybe will not like it either. I feel I will gain new readers and critics who have always disliked my work (and too true, the critics are not always

Paul Brooks: Sexton's editor at Houghton Mifflin. He initially had reservations about Sexton's fairy tale poems.   *"Transformations"*: title of Sexton's 1971 volume of poems that contained "Cinderella."

kind to me) may come around. I have found the people I've shown them to apathetic in some cases and wildly excited in others. It often depends on their own feelings about Grimms' fairy tales.

November 17, 1970

Dear Kurt [Vonnegut Jr.°],

I meant to write you a postcard before your dentist appointment, but I was away at the time I should have sent it. Sorry. Your graph for "Cinderella" is right over my desk.

The enclosed manuscript is of my new book of poems. I've taken Grimms' Fairy Tales and "Transformed" them into something all of my own. The better books of fairy tales have introductions telling the value of these old fables. I feel my *Transformations* needs an introduction telling of the value of my (one could say) rape of them. Maybe that's an incorrect phrase. I do something very modern to them (have you ever tried to describe your own work? I find I am tongue-tied). They are small, funny and horrifying. Without quite meaning to I have joined the black humorists. I don't know if you know my other work, but humor was never a very prominent feature . . . terror, deformity, madness and torture were my bag. But this little universe of Grimm is not that far away. I think they end up being as wholly personal as my most intimate poems, in a different language, a different rhythm, but coming strangely, for all their story sound, from as deep a place.

From *Anne Sexton: A Self-Portrait in Letters*

THINKING ABOUT MYTH

Of the many myths conjured by the poets in these pages, you may know some by heart, some only vaguely, and others not at all. When reading a poem inspired by myth, there's no way around it: your understanding will be more precise if you know the mythic story the poem refers to. With the vast resources available on the Web, it's never hard to find a description of a myth, whether traditional or contemporary. While different versions of most myths exist, what usually remains fixed is the tale's basic pattern. A familiarity with that narrative is a key to the meaning—both intellectual and emotional—of any poem that makes reference to mythology.

- **Start with the underlying pattern of the narrative in question.** Does the basic shape of the poem's story seem familiar? Does it have some recognizable source in myth or legend? Even if the poem has no obvious narrative line, does it call to mind other stories?
- **Notice what new details the poem has added, and what it inevitably leaves out.** The difference between the poem and the source material will reveal something about the author's attitude toward the original, and may give you a sense of his or her intentions in reworking the original myth.
- **Read the section "Mythological Criticism" in the chapter "Critical Approaches to Literature."** A quick sense of how critics analyze myth in literature will help you approach a poem with mythological allusions.

Kurt Vonnegut Jr.: popular author of *Cat's Cradle* (1963) and other novels.

CHECKLIST: Writing About Myth

- ☐ Does the poem have a recognizable source in myth or legend?
- ☐ What new details has the poet added to the original myth?
- ☐ What do these details reveal about the poet's attitude toward the source material?
- ☐ Have important elements of the original been discarded? What does their absence suggest about the author's primary focus?
- ☐ Does the poem rely heavily on its mythic imagery? Or is myth tangential to the poem's theme?
- ☐ How do mythic echoes underscore the poem's meaning?

WRITING ASSIGNMENT ON MYTH

Provide a close reading of any poem from this book that uses a traditional myth or legend. In the course of your analysis, demonstrate how the author borrows or changes certain details of the myth to emphasize his or her meaning. In addition to the poems in this chapter, some selections to consider include: T. S. Eliot's "Journey of the Magi," Alfred, Lord Tennyson's "Ulysses," and William Butler Yeats's "The Magi" or "Leda and the Swan."

Here is an example of an essay on this assignment written by Heather Burke when she was a sophomore at Wesleyan University in Middletown, Connecticut.

SAMPLE STUDENT PAPER

Burke 1

Heather Burke
Professor Greene
English 150
18 January 2012

Title sets tone and draws reader in

Thesis sentence

Necessary background

The Bonds Between Love and Hatred in H.D.'s "Helen"

In her poem "Helen," H.D. examines the close connection between the emotions of love and hatred as embodied in the figure of Helen of Troy. Helen was the cause of the long and bloody Trojan War, and her homecoming is tainted by the memory of the suffering this war caused. As in many Imagist poems, the title is essential to the poem's meaning; it gives the reader both a specific mythic context and a particular subject. Without the title, it would be virtually impossible to understand the poem fully since Helen's name appears nowhere else in the text. The reader familiar with Greek myth knows that Helen, who was the wife of Menelaus, ran away with Paris. Their adultery

Burke 2

provoked the Trojan War, which lasted for ten years and resulted in the destruction of Troy.

What is unusual about the poem is H.D.'s perspective on Helen of Troy. The poem refuses to romanticize Helen's story, but its stark new version is easy for a reader to accept. After suffering so much for the sake of one adulterous woman, how could the Greeks not resent her? Rather than idealizing the situation, H.D. describes the enmity which defiles Helen's homecoming and explores the irony of the hatred which "All Greece" feels for her.

Topic sentence on poem's focus

The opening line of the poem sets its tone and introduces its central theme—hatred. Helen's beauty required thousands of men to face death in battle, but it cannot assuage the emotional aftermath of the war. Even though Helen is described as "God's daughter, born of love" (13), all she inspires now is resentment, and the poem explores the ways in which these two emotions are closely related.

Topic sentence on tone and theme

In the first stanza, the poet uses the color white, as well as the radiance or luster connected with it, in her description of Helen, and this color will be associated with her throughout the poem:

Topic sentence on specific image

> the still eyes in the white face,
>
> the lustre as of olives
>
> where she stands,
>
> and the white hands. (2–5)

As one of the foundations of agriculture and civilization, the olive was a crucial symbol in Greek culture. Helen's beauty is compared to the "lustre" of this olive. This word presumably refers to the radiance or light which the whiteness of her face reflects, but Helen's identification with this fruit also has an ironic connotation. The olive branch is a traditional symbol of peace, but the woman it is compared to was the cause of a bitter war.

Exploration of specific image

The majority of the imagery in the poem is connected with the color white. H.D. uses white to describe Helen's skin; white would have been seen as the appropriate color for a rich and beautiful woman's skin in pre-twentieth century poetry. This color also has several connotations, all of which operate simultaneously in the poem. The color white has a connection to Helen's paternity; her immortal father Zeus took the form of a white swan when he made love to her mortal mother Leda. At the same time, whiteness suggests a certain chilliness, as with snow or frost. In the third stanza, H.D.

Topic sentence (further analysis of imagery)

makes this suggestion explicit with her use of the phrase "the beauty of cool feet" (14). This image also suggests the barrenness connected with such frigidity. In this sense, it is a very accurate representation of Helen, because in *The Odyssey* Homer tells us that ". . . the gods had never after granted Helen / a child to bring into the sunlit world / after the first, rose-lipped Hermione" (4.13–15). Helen is returned to her rightful husband, but after her adulterous actions, she is unable to bear him any more children. She is a woman who is renowned for exciting passion in legions of men, but that passion is now sterile.

Another traditional connotation of the color white is purity, but this comparison only accentuates Helen's sexual transgressions; she is hardly pure. H.D. emphasizes her lasciviousness through the use of irony. In the third stanza, she refers to Helen as a "maid." A maid is a virgin, but Helen is most definitely not virginal in any sense. In the following line, the poet rhymes "maid" with the word "laid," which refers to the placement of Helen's body on the funeral pyre. This particular word, however, deliberately emphasized by the rhyme, also carries slangy associations with the act of sexual intercourse. This connotation presents another ironic contrast with the word "maid."

The first line of the second stanza is almost identical to that of the first, and again we are reminded of the intense animosity that Helen's presence inspires. This hatred is now made more explicit. The word *revile* is defined by the *American Heritage College Dictionary* as "to denounce with abusive language" ("Revile"). Helen is a queen, but she is subjected to the insults of her subjects as well as the rest of Greece.

Helen's homecoming is not joyous, but a time of exile and penance. The war is over, but no one, especially Helen, can forget the past. Her memories seem to cause her wanness, which the dictionary defines as "indicating weariness, illness, or unhappiness" ("Wan"). Her face now ". . . grows wan and white, / remembering past enchantments / and past ills" (9–11). The enchantment she remembers is that of Aphrodite, the goddess who lured her from her home and husband to Paris's bed. The "ills" which Helen remembers can be seen as both her sexual offenses and the human losses sustained in the Trojan War. The use of the word *ills* works in conjunction with the word *wan* to demonstrate Helen's spiritual sickness; she is plagued by regret.

Topic sentence (further analysis of specific image)

Topic sentence on effect of poem's form

Key word defined

Topic sentence/ textual analysis

Burke 4

As the opening of the third stanza shows, the woman who was famous for her beauty and perfection now leaves Greece "unmoved." This opening may not echo the sharpness of those of the first two stanzas, but it picks up on the theme of Helen as a devalued prize. In the eyes of the Greeks, she is not the beauty who called two armies to battle but merely an unfaithful wife for whom many died needlessly.

Topic sentence/ textual analysis

The final lines of the poem reveal the one condition which could turn the people's hatred into love again. They "could love indeed the maid, / only if she were laid, / white ash amid funereal cypresses" (16–18). The Greeks can only forgive Helen once her body has been burned on the funeral pyre. These disturbing lines illustrate the destructive power of hatred; it can only be conquered by death. These lines also reveal the final significance of the color white. It suggests Helen's death. As Helen's face is pale and white in life, so her ashes will be in death. The flames of the funeral pyre are the only way to purify the flesh that was tainted by the figurative flames of passion. Death is the only way to restore Helen's beauty and make it immortal. While she is alive, her beauty is only a reminder of lost fathers, sons, and brothers. The people of Greece can only despise her while she is living, but they can love and revere the memory of her beauty once she is dead.

Conclusion

More complex and specific restatement of thesis

Burke 5

Works Cited

H.D. "Helen." *Literature: An Introduction to Fiction, Poetry, Drama, and Writing.* Ed. X. J. Kennedy and Dana Gioia. 7th Compact ed. New York: Pearson, 2013. 700. Print.

Homer. *The Odyssey.* Trans. Robert Fitzgerald. New York: Noonday P, 1998. Print.

"Revile." *American Heritage College Dictionary.* 4th ed. 2002. Print.

"Wan." *American Heritage College Dictionary.* 4th ed. 2002. Print.

MORE TOPICS FOR WRITING

1. Anne Sexton's "Cinderella" freely mixes period detail and slang from twentieth-century American life with elements from the original fairy tale. (You can read the original in Charles Perrault's *Mother Goose Tales*.) Write an analysis of the effect of all this anachronistic mixing and matching. Be sure to look up any period details you don't recognize.

2. Provide an explication of Louise Bogan's "Medusa." For tips on poetic explication, refer to the chapter "Writing About a Poem."

3. Write an essay of approximately 750 words discussing A. E. Stallings's "First Love: A Quiz." How does the poet combine modern circumstances and mythological allusions to suggest personal meaning for the reader?

4. You're probably familiar with an urban legend or two—near-fantastical stories passed on from one person to another, with the suggestion that they really happened to a friend of a friend of the person who told you the tale. Retell an urban myth in free-verse form. If you don't know any urban myths, an Internet search engine can lead you to scores of them.

5. Compare and contrast H.D.'s portrait of Helen of Troy in "Helen" with Edgar Allan Poe's version in "To Helen." In what ways are the treatments similar? In what significant ways do they differ?

6. Retell a famous myth or fairy tale to reflect your personal worldview.

▶ TERMS FOR *review*

Myth ▶ A traditional narrative of anonymous authorship that arises out of a culture's oral tradition. The characters in traditional myths are often gods or heroic figures engaged in significant actions and decisions. Myth is usually differentiated from *legend*, which has a specific historical base.

Archetype ▶ A recurring symbol, character, landscape, or event found in myth and literature across different cultures and eras, one that appears so often that it evokes a universal response.

25 POETRY AND PERSONAL IDENTITY

All literature is, finally, autobiographical.

—JORGE LUIS BORGES

Only a naive reader assumes that all poems directly reflect the personal experience of their authors. That would be like believing that a TV sitcom actually describes the real family life of its cast. As you will recall if you read "The Person in the Poem" (page 507), poets often speak in voices other than their own. These voices may be borrowed or imaginary. Stevie Smith appropriates the voice of a dead swimmer in her poem "Not Waving but Drowning" (page 570), and Ted Hughes imagines a nonhuman voice in "Hawk Roosting" (page 510). Some poets also try to give their personal poems a universal feeling. Edna St. Vincent Millay's emotion-charged sonnet "Well, I Have Lost You; and I Lost You Fairly" describes the end of a difficult love affair with a younger man, but she dramatizes the situation in such a way that it seems deliberately independent of any particular time and place. Even her lover remains shadowy and nameless. No one has ever been able to identify the characters in Shakespeare's sonnets as actual people, but that fact does not diminish our pleasure in them as poems.

And yet there are times when poets try to speak openly in their own voices. What could be a more natural subject for a poet than examining his or her own life? The autobiographical elements in a poem may be indirect, as in Wilfred Owen's "Anthem for Doomed Youth" (page 865), which is clearly drawn from its author's battle experience in World War I, although it never refers to his own participation, or they may form the central subject, as in Sylvia Plath's "Lady Lazarus," which discusses her suicide attempts. In either case, the poem's autobiographical stance affects a reader's response.

Although we respond to a poem's formal elements, we also cannot help reacting to what we know about its human origins. Reading Plath's chilling exploration of her death wish while knowing that within a few months the poet would kill herself, we receive an extra jolt of emotion. In a good autobiographical poem, that shock of veracity adds to the poem's power. In an unsuccessful poem, the autobiographical facts become a substitute for emotions not credibly conveyed by the words themselves.

CONFESSIONAL POETRY

One literary movement, **Confessional poetry,** has made frank self-definition its main purpose. As the name implies, Confessional poetry renders personal experience as candidly as possible, even sharing confidences that may violate social conventions or propriety. Confessional poets sometimes shock their readers with admissions of experiences so intimate and painful—adultery, family violence, suicide attempts—that most people would try to suppress them, or at least not proclaim them to the world.

Some confessional poets, such as Anne Sexton, W. D. Snodgrass, and Robert Lowell, underwent psychoanalysis, and at times their poems sound like patients telling their analysts every detail of their personal lives. For this reason, confessional poems run the danger of being more interesting to their authors than to their readers. But when a poet successfully frames his or her personal experience so that the reader can feel an extreme emotion from the inside, the result can be powerful. Here is a chilling poem that takes us within the troubled psyche of a poet who contemplates suicide.

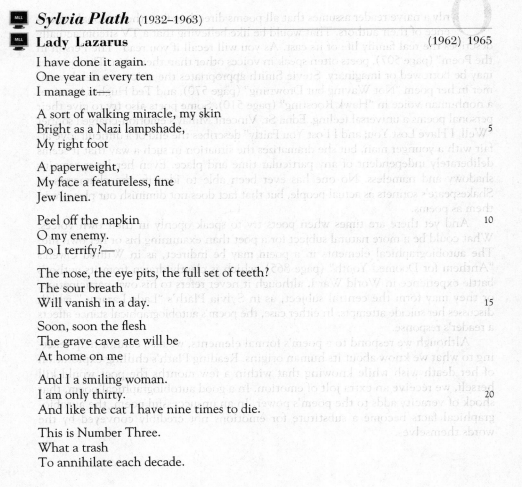

Sylvia Plath (1932–1963)

Lady Lazarus   (1962) 1965

I have done it again.
One year in every ten
I manage it——

A sort of walking miracle, my skin
Bright as a Nazi lampshade,   5
My right foot

A paperweight,
My face a featureless, fine
Jew linen.

Peel off the napkin   10
O my enemy.
Do I terrify?——

The nose, the eye pits, the full set of teeth?
The sour breath
Will vanish in a day.   15

Soon, soon the flesh
The grave cave ate will be
At home on me

And I am a smiling woman.
I am only thirty.   20
And like the cat I have nine times to die.

This is Number Three.
What a trash
To annihilate each decade.

What a million filaments.   25
The peanut-crunching crowd
Shoves in to see

Them unwrap me hand and foot—
The big strip tease.
Gentleman, ladies   30

These are my hands
My knees.
I may be skin and bone,

Nevertheless, I am the same, identical woman.
The first time it happened I was ten.   35
It was an accident.

The second time I meant
To last it out and not come back at all.
I rocked shut

As a seashell.   40
They had to call and call
And pick the worms off me like sticky pearls.

Dying
Is an art, like everything else.
I do it exceptionally well.   45

I do it so it feels like hell.
I do it so it feels real.
I guess you could say I've a call.

It's easy enough to do it in a cell.
It's easy enough to do it and stay put.   50
It's the theatrical

Comeback in broad day
To the same place, the same face, the same brute
Amused shout:

"A miracle!"   55
That knocks me out.
There is a charge

For the eyeing of my scars, there is a charge
For the hearing of my heart—
It really goes.   60

And there is a charge, a very large charge,
For the word or a touch
Or a bit of blood

Or a piece of my hair or my clothes.
So, so, Herr Doktor.   65
So, Herr Enemy.

I am your opus,°
I am your valuable,
The pure gold baby

That melts to a shriek.
I turn and burn.
Do not think I underestimate your great concern.

Ash, ash—
You poke and stir.
Flesh, bone, there is nothing there—

A cake of soap,
A wedding ring,
A gold filling,

Herr God, Herr Lucifer
Beware
Beware.

Out of the ash
I rise with my red hair
And I eat men like air.

Questions

1. Although the poem is openly autobiographical, Plath uses certain symbols to represent herself (Lady Lazarus, a Jew murdered in a concentration camp, a cat with nine lives, and so on). What do these symbols tell us about Plath's attitude toward herself and the world around her?

2. In her biography of Plath, *Bitter Fame*, the poet Anne Stevenson says that this poem penetrates "the furthest reaches of disdain and rage . . . bereft of all 'normal' human feelings." What do you think Stevenson means? Does anything in the poem strike you as particularly chilling?

3. The speaker in "Lady Lazarus" says, "Dying / Is an art, like everything else" (lines 43–44). What sense do you make of this metaphor?

4. Does the ending of "Lady Lazarus" imply that the speaker assumes that she will outlive her suicide attempts? Set forth your final understanding of the poem.

Not all autobiographical poetry needs to shock the reader, as Plath overtly does in "Lady Lazarus." Poets can also try to share the special moments that illuminate their day-to-day lives, as Elizabeth Bishop does in "Filling Station," when she describes a roadside gas station whose shabby bric-a-brac she sees as symbols of love. But when poets attempt to place their own lives under scrutiny, they face certain difficulties. Honest, thorough self-examination isn't as easy as it might seem. It is one thing to examine oneself in the mirror; it is quite another to sketch accurately what one sees there. Even if we have the skill to describe ourselves in words (or in paint) so that a stranger would recognize the self-portrait, there is the challenge of honesty. Drawing or writing our own self-portrait, most of us yield, often unconsciously, to the temptation of making ourselves a little nobler or better-looking than we really are. The best self-portraits, like Rembrandt's unflattering self-examinations, are usually critical. No one enjoys watching someone else preen in front of a dressing mirror, unless the intention is satiric.

IDENTITY POETICS

Autobiographical poetry requires a hunger for honest self-examination. Many poets find that, in order to understand themselves and who they are, they must scrutinize more than the self in isolation. Other forces may shape their identities: ethnic background, family, race, gender, sexual orientation, religion, economic status, and age. Aware of these elements, many recent poets have written memorable personal poems. Dominican-born Rhina Espaillat addresses these concerns in the following poem, which also examines the American experience from the viewpoint of individuals half inside and half outside mainstream society, a division intensified in this instance, as her title makes clear, by issues of language. Espaillat's poem also adds a new human dimension, the generation gap—familiar to anyone raised in an immigrant home—between those raised in "the old country" and those growing up (and feeling at home) in America.

Rhina Espaillat (b. 1932)

Bilingual/*Bilingüe*   1998

My father liked them separate, one there,
one here (*allá y aquí*), as if aware

that words might cut in two his daughter's heart
(*el corazón*) and lock the alien part

to what he was—his memory, his name   5
(*su nombre*)—with a key he could not claim.

"English outside this door, Spanish inside,"
he said, "*y basta*." But who can divide

the world, the word (*mundo y palabra*) from
any child? I knew how to be dumb   10

and stubborn (*testaruda*); late, in bed,
I hoarded secret syllables I read

until my tongue (*mi lengua*) learned to run
where his stumbled. And still the heart was one.

I like to think he knew that, even when,   15
proud (*orgulloso*) of his daughter's pen,

he stood outside *mis versos*, half in fear
of words he loved but wanted not to hear.

Questions

1. Espaillat's poem is full of Spanish words and phrases. (Even the title is given in both languages.) What does the Spanish add to the poem? Could we remove the phrases without changing the poem?
2. How does the father want to divide his daughter's world, at least in terms of language? Does his request suggest any other divisions he hopes to enforce in her life?
3. How does the daughter respond to her father's request to leave English outside their home?
4. "And still the heart was one," states the speaker of the poem. Should we take her statement at face value or do we sense a cost to her bilingual existence? Agree or disagree with the daughter's statement, but state the reasons for your opinion.

CULTURE, RACE, AND ETHNICITY

One of the personal issues Rhina Espaillat faces in "Bilingual/*Bilingüe*" is her dual identity as Dominican and American. The daughter of immigrants, she was born in the Dominican Republic but came to America at the age of seven and grew up in New York. Consequently, self-definition for her has meant resolving the claims of two potentially contradictory cultures, as well as dealing, on a more immediate level, with the conflicting demands of family love and loyalty, on the one hand, and personal growth and fulfillment, on the other. As much as she loves her father and wishes to honor him, she cannot be held back from what she is and what she needs to become, and "I hoarded secret syllables I read // until my tongue (*mi lengua*) learned to run / where his stumbled." Here Espaillat touches on the central issue facing the autobiographical poet—using *words* to embody experience. The tongue must "learn to run," even if where it runs, for an immigrant poet, is away from the language of one's parents.

American poetry is rich in immigrant cultures, as shown in the work of both first-generation writers such as Francisco X. Alarcón and John Ciardi and foreign-born authors such as Joseph Brodsky (Russia), Nina Cassian (Romania), Claude McKay (Jamaica), Eamon Grennan (Ireland), Thom Gunn (England), Shirley Geok-lin Lim (Malaysia), Emanuel di Pasquale (Italy), José Emilio Pacheco (Mexico), Herberto Padilla (Cuba), and Derek Walcott (St. Lucia). Some literary immigrants, such as the late Russian novelist and poet Vladimir Nabokov, make the difficult transition to writing in English. Others, such as Cassian and Pacheco, continue to write in their native languages. A few, such as Brodsky, write bilingually. Such texts often remind us of the multicultural nature of American poetry. Here is a poem by one literary immigrant that raises some important issues of personal identity.

Claude McKay (1890–1948)

America   1922

Although she feeds me bread of bitterness,
And sinks into my throat her tiger's tooth,
Stealing my breath of life, I will confess
I love this cultured hell that tests my youth!
Her vigor flows like tides into my blood,   5
Giving me strength erect against her hate.
Her bigness sweeps my being like a flood.
Yet, as a rebel fronts a king in state,
I stand within her walls with not a shred
Of terror, malice, not a word of jeer.   10
Darkly I gaze into the days ahead,
And see her might and granite wonders there,
Beneath the touch of Time's unerring hand,
Like priceless treasures sinking in the sand.

Questions

1. Is "America" written in a personal or public voice? What specific elements seem personal? What elements seem public?

2. McKay was a black immigrant from Jamaica, but he does not mention either his race or national origin in the poem. Is his personal background important to understanding "America"?

3. "America" is written in a traditional form. How does the poem's form contribute to its impact?

Claude McKay's "America" raises the question of how an author's race and ethnic identity influence the poetry he or she writes. In the 1920s, for instance, there was an ongoing discussion among black poets as to whether their poetry should deal specifically with the African American experience. Did black poetry exist apart from the rest of American poetry or was it, as Robert Hayden would later suggest, "shaped over some three centuries by social, moral, and literary forces essentially American"? Should black authors primarily address a black audience or should they try to engage a broader literary public? Should black poetry focus on specifically black subjects, forms, and idioms or should it rely mainly on the traditions of English literature? Black poets are divided into two camps. Claude McKay and Countee Cullen were among the writers who favored universal themes. (Cullen, for example, insisted he be called a "poet," not a "Negro poet.") Langston Hughes and Jean Toomer were among the "new" poets who felt that black poetry must reflect racial themes. They believed, as James Weldon Johnson had once said, that race was "perforce the thing that the American Negro Poet knows best." Writers on both sides of the debate produced excellent poems, but their work has a very different character.

The debate between ethnicity and universality has echoed among American writers of every racial and religious minority. Today, we find the same issues being discussed by Arab, Asian, Hispanic, Italian, Jewish, and Native American authors. There is no one correct answer to the questions of identity, for individual artists need the freedom to pursue their own imaginative vision. But considering the issues of race and ethnicity does help a poet think through the artist's sometimes conflicting responsibilities between group and personal identity. Even in poets who have pursued their individual vision, we often see how unmistakably they write from their racial, social, and cultural background. Sometimes a poet's ethnic background becomes part of his or her private mythology. In "Riding into California," Shirley Geok-lin Lim describes the dizzy mixture of alienation and acceptance an Asian immigrant might experience arriving in Southern California.

Shirley Geok-lin Lim (b. 1944)

Riding into California   1998

If you come to a land with no ancestors
to bless you, you have to be your own
ancestor. The veterans in the mobile home
park don't want to be there. It isn't easy.
Oil rigs litter the land like giant frozen birds.   5
Ghosts welcome us to a new life, and
an immigrant without home ghosts
cannot believe the land is real. So you're

grateful for familiarity, and Bruce Lee
becomes your hero. Coming into Fullerton,   10
everyone waiting at the station is white.
The good thing about being Chinese on Amtrak
is no one sits next to you. The bad thing is
you sit alone all the way to Irvine.

RIDING INTO CALIFORNIA. 9 *Bruce Lee:* Bruce Lee (1940–1973) was a martial arts and film star from Hong Kong.

Questions

1. What does the speaker find familiar in California?
2. Why does the speaker long for ancestors and ghosts in California? What does this wish
   tell us about the speaker's identity?

Sometimes a single word announces a new sort of voice, as in Judith Ortiz
Cofer's "Quinceañera." The title is a Spanish noun for which there is no one-word
English equivalent. That one word signals that we will be hearing a new voice.

Judith Ortiz Cofer (b. 1952)

Quinceañera   1987

My dolls have been put away like dead
children in a chest I will carry
with me when I marry.
I reach under my skirt to feel
a satin slip bought for this day. It is soft   5
as the inside of my thighs. My hair
has been nailed back with my mother's
black hairpins to my skull. Her hands
stretched my eyes open as she twisted
braids into a tight circle at the nape   10
of my neck. I am to wash my own clothes
and sheets from this day on, as if
the fluids of my body were poison, as if
the little trickle of blood I believe
travels from my heart to the world were   15
shameful. Is not the blood of saints and
men in battle beautiful? Do Christ's hands
not bleed into your eyes from His cross?
At night I hear myself growing and wake
to find my hands drifting of their own will   20
to soothe skin stretched tight
over my bones.
I am wound like the guts of a clock,
waiting for each hour to release me.

QUINCEAÑERA. The title refers to a fifteen-year-old girl's coming-out party in Latin cultures.

Questions

1. What items and actions are associated with the speaker's new life? What items are put away?
2. What is the speaker waiting to release in the final two lines?
3. If the poem's title were changed to "Fifteen-Year-Old Girl," what would the poem lose in meaning?

Yusef Komunyakaa (b. 1947)

Facing It   1988

My black face fades,
hiding inside the black granite.
I said I wouldn't,
dammit: No tears.
I'm stone. I'm flesh.   5
My clouded reflection eyes me
like a bird of prey, the profile of night
slanted against morning. I turn
this way—the stone lets me go.
I turn that way—I'm inside   10
the Vietnam Veterans Memorial
again, depending on the light
to make a difference.
I go down the 58,022 names,
half-expecting to find   15
my own in letters like smoke.
I touch the name Andrew Johnson;
I see the booby trap's white flash.
Names shimmer on a woman's blouse
but when she walks away   20
the names stay on the wall.
Brushstrokes flash, a red bird's
wings cutting across my stare.
The sky. A plane in the sky.
A white vet's image floats   25
closer to me, then his pale eyes
look through mine. I'm a window.
He's lost his right arm
inside the stone. In the black mirror
a woman's trying to erase names: 30
No, she's brushing a boy's hair.

Questions

1. How does the title of "Facing It" relate to the poem? Does it have more than one meaning?
2. The narrator describes the people around him by their reflections on the polished granite rather than by looking at them directly. What does this indirect way of scrutinizing contribute to the poem?
3. This poem comes out of the life experience of a black Vietnam veteran. Is Komunyakaa's writing closer to McKay's "universal" method or to Toomer's "ethnic" style?

GENDER

In her celebrated study *You Just Don't Understand: Women and Men in Conversation* (1990), Georgetown University linguist Deborah Tannen explored how men and women use language differently. Tannen compared many everyday conversations between husbands and wives to "cross-cultural communications," as if people from separate worlds lived under the same roof. While analyzing the divergent ways in which women and men converse, Tannen carefully emphasizes that neither linguistic style is superior, only that they are different.

While it would be simplistic to assume that all poems reveal the sex of their authors, many poems do become both richer and clearer when we examine their gender assumptions. Theodore Roethke's "My Papa's Waltz" (page 501) is hardly a macho poem, but it does reflect the complicated mix of love, authority, and violent horse-play that exists in many father-son relationships. By contrast, Sylvia Plath's "Metaphors" (page 582), which describes her own pregnancy through a series of images, deals with an experience that, by biological definition, only a woman can know first-hand. Feminist criticism has shown us how gender influences literary texts in subtler ways. (See the chapter "Critical Approaches to Literature" for a discussion of gender theory.) The central insight of feminist criticism seems inarguable—our gender does often influence how we speak, write, and interpret language. But that insight need not be intimidating. It can also invite us to bring our whole life experience, as women or men, to reading a poem. It reminds us that poetry, the act of using language with the greatest clarity and specificity, is a means to see the world through the eyes of the opposite sex. Or, it can demonstrate how deeply sexual orientation affects an individual's worldview. Sometimes the messages we get from this exchange are unsettling, but at least they may move us into better understanding the diversity of human behavior.

Carolyn Kizer (b. 1925)

Bitch   1984

Now, when he and I meet, after all these years,
I say to the bitch inside me, don't start growling.
He isn't a trespasser anymore,
Just an old acquaintance tipping his hat.
My voice says, "Nice to see you,"   5
As the bitch starts to bark hysterically.
He isn't an enemy now,
Where are your manners, I say, as I say,
"How are the children? They must be growing up."
At a kind word from him, a look like the old days,   10
The bitch changes her tone: she begins to whimper.
She wants to snuggle up to him, to cringe.
Down, girl! Keep your distance
Or I'll give you a taste of the choke-chain.
"Fine, I'm just fine," I tell him.   15
She slobbers and grovels.

After all, I am her mistress. She is basically loyal.
It's just that she remembers how she came running
Each evening, when she heard his step;
How she lay at his feet and looked up adoringly   20
Though he was absorbed in his paper;
Or, bored with her devotion, ordered her to the kitchen
Until he was ready to play.
But the small careless kindnesses
When he'd had a good day, or a couple of drinks,   25
Come back to her now, seem more important
Than the casual cruelties, the ultimate dismissal.
"It's nice to know you are doing so well," I say.
He couldn't have taken you with him;
You were too demonstrative, too clumsy,   30
Not like the well-groomed pets of his new friends.
"Give my regards to your wife," I say. You gag
As I drag you off by the scruff,
Saying, "Goodbye! Goodbye! Nice to have seen you again."

Questions

1. What is the pun in the title? What does the title tell us about the poem to follow?
2. What is the "bitch's" first reaction to the appearance of the speaker's old lover?
3. How does the speaker outwardly deal with her old lover? How does the reader know she feels differently inside?
4. How does the metaphor of a bitch-hound enhance the emotional meaning of the poem? Would the meaning of the poem be drastically different if it were titled "Dog" instead?

Rafael Campo (b. 1964)

For J.W.   1994

I know exactly what I want to say,
Except we're men. Except it's poetry,
And poetry is too precise. You know
That when we met on Robert's porch, I knew.
My paper plate seemed suddenly too small;   5

I stepped on a potato chip. I watched
The ordinary spectacle of birds
Become magnificent until the sky,
Which was an ordinary sky, was blue
And comforting across my face. At least   10

I thought I knew. I thought I'd seen your face
In poetry, in shapeless clouds, in ice—
Like staring deeply into frozen lakes.
I thought I'd heard your voice inside my chest,
And it was comforting, magnificent,   15

Like poetry but more precise. I knew,
Or thought I knew, exactly how I felt.
About the insects fizzing in the lawn.
About the stupid, ordinary birds,
About the poetry of Robert Frost,   20

Fragility and paper plates. I look at you.
Because we're men, and frozen hard as ice—
So hard from muscles spreading out our chests—
I want to comfort you, and say it all.
Except my poetry is imprecise.   25

Questions

1. One rhetorical strategy employed by Campo is the repetition of certain key terms in different contexts. Discuss the poem's use of the words "knew," "magnificent," and "ordinary."
2. What does Campo tell us about his sexual identity in line 2?
3. At the beginning, middle, and end of the poem, there are statements involving poetry and precision. How do the changes that occur in these statements help to communicate the poem's thematic intentions?
4. What point is the speaker making in lines 22-23?
5. If Campo had addressed "For J.W." to a woman, would he need to have changed anything in the poem?

Exercise: "Men at Forty"; "Women"

Rewrite either of the following poems from the perspective of the opposite sex. Then evaluate in what ways the new poem has changed the original's meaning and in what ways the original poem comes through more or less unaltered.

Donald Justice (1925–2004)

Men at Forty   1967

Men at forty
Learn to close softly
The doors to rooms they will not be
Coming back to.

At rest on a stair landing,   5
They feel it moving
Beneath them now like the deck of a ship,
Though the swell is gentle.

And deep in mirrors
They rediscover   10
The face of the boy as he practices tying
His father's tie there in secret,

And the face of that father,
Still warm with the mystery of lather.
They are more fathers than sons themselves now.   15
Something is filling them, something

That is like the twilight sound
Of the crickets, immense,
Filling the woods at the foot of the slope
Behind their mortgaged houses.   20

Adrienne Rich (1929-2012)

Women   1968

My three sisters are sitting
on rocks of black obsidian.
For the first time, in this light, I can see who they are.

My first sister is sewing her costume for the procession.
She is going as the Transparent Lady   5
and all her nerves will be visible.

My second sister is also sewing,
at the seam over her heart which has never healed entirely.
At last, she hopes, this tightness in her chest will ease.

My third sister is gazing   10
at a dark-red crust spreading westward far out on the sea.
Her stockings are torn but she is beautiful.

FOR REVIEW AND FURTHER STUDY

Brian Turner (b. 1967)

The Hurt Locker   2005

Nothing but the hurt left here.
Nothing but bullets and pain
and the bled-out slumping
and all the *fucks* and *goddamns*
and *Jesus Christs* of the wounded.   5
Nothing left here but the hurt.

Believe it when you see it.
Believe it when a twelve-year-old
rolls a grenade into the room.
Or when a sniper punches a hole   10
deep into someone's skull.
Believe it when four men
step from a taxicab in Mosul
to shower the street in brass
and fire. Open the hurt locker   15
and see what there is of knives
and teeth. Open the hurt locker and learn
how rough men come hunting for souls.

THE HURT LOCKER. Turner's title, based on military slang he learned in Iraq, is said to have inspired the title of the 2009 Academy Award-winning film *The Hurt Locker*. 13 *Mosul:* city in northern Iraq.

Questions

1. Who seems to be the speaker of the poem? What clues does the speaker give about his or her background?
2. Where do the memories surfacing in the poem take place?
3. How would you explain the title metaphor? What is a "hurt locker"?
4. Based on this poem, how would you say the experience of combat seems to affect personal identity?

Andrew Hudgins (b. 1951)

Elegy for My Father, Who Is Not Dead   1991

One day I'll lift the telephone
and be told my father's dead. He's ready.
In the sureness of his faith, he talks
about the world beyond this world
as though his reservations have   5
been made. I think he wants to go,
a little bit—a new desire
to travel building up, an itch
to see fresh worlds. Or older ones.
He thinks that when I follow him   10
he'll wrap me in his arms and laugh,
the way he did when I arrived
on earth. I do not think he's right.
He's ready. I am not. I can't
just say good-bye as cheerfully   15
as if he were embarking on a trip
to make my later trip go well.
I see myself on deck, convinced
his ship's gone down, while he's convinced
I'll see him standing on the dock   20
and waving, shouting, *Welcome back.*

Questions

1. The speaker describes his father's view of the afterlife in this poem. What image does he use to describe his father's vision of life after death?
2. What metaphor does the poet use to describe his own religious uncertainty?
3. How would the poem differ if the speaker shared his father's religious faith?

Philip Larkin (1922–1985)

Aubade   1977

I work all day, and get half-drunk at night.
Waking at four to soundless dark, I stare.
In time the curtain-edges will grow light.
Till then I see what's really always there:
Unresting death, a whole day nearer now,   5
Making all thought impossible but how
And where and when I shall myself die.
Arid interrogation: yet the dread
Of dying, and being dead,
Flashes afresh to hold and horrify.   10

The mind blanks at the glare. Not in remorse
—The good not done, the love not given, time
Torn off unused—nor wretchedly because
An only life can take so long to climb
Clear of its wrong beginnings, and may never;   15
But at the total emptiness for ever,
The sure extinction that we travel to
And shall be lost in always. Not to be here,
Not to be anywhere,
And soon; nothing more terrible, nothing more true.   20

This is a special way of being afraid
No trick dispels. Religion used to try,
That vast moth-eaten musical brocade
Created to pretend we never die,
And specious stuff that says *No rational being*   25
Can fear a thing it will not feel, not seeing
That this is what we fear—no sight, no sound,
No touch or taste or smell, nothing to think with,
Nothing to love or link with,
The anaesthetic from which none come round.   30

And so it stays just on the edge of vision,
A small unfocused blur, a standing chill
That slows each impulse down to indecision.
Most things may never happen: this one will,
And realisation of it rages out   35
In furnace-fear when we are caught without
People or drink. Courage is no good:
It means not scaring others. Being brave
Lets no one off the grave.
Death is no different whined at than withstood.   40

Slowly light strengthens, and the room takes shape.
It stands plain as a wardrobe, what we know,

Have always known, know that we can't escape,
Yet can't accept. One side will have to go.
Meanwhile telephones crouch, getting ready to ring   45
In locked-up offices, and all the uncaring
Intricate rented world begins to rouse.
The sky is white as clay, with no sun.
Work has to be done.
Postmen like doctors go from house to house.   50

Questions

1. Is "Aubade" a confessional poem? If so, what social taboo does it violate?
2. What embarrassing facts about the narrator does the poem reveal? Do these confessions lead us to trust or distrust him?
3. The narrator says that "Courage is no good" (line 37). How might he defend this statement?
4. Would a twenty-year-old reader respond differently to this poem than a seventy-year-old one? Would a devout Christian respond differently to the poem than an atheist?

▪ WRITING *effectively*

Rhina Espaillat on Writing

Being a Bilingual Writer   1998

Recent interest in the phenomenon known as "Spanglish" has led me to reexamine my own experience as a writer who works chiefly in her second language, and especially to recall my father's inflexible rule against the mixing of languages. In fact, no English was allowed in that midtown Manhattan apartment that became home after my arrival in New York in 1939. My father read the daily paper in English, taught himself to follow disturbing events in Europe through the medium of English-language radio, and even taught me to read the daily comic strips, in an effort to speed my learning of the language he knew I would need. But that necessary

Rhina Espaillat

language was banished from family conversation: it was the medium of the outer world, beyond the door; inside, among ourselves, only Spanish was permitted, and it had to be pure, grammatical, unadulterated Spanish.

At the age of seven, however, nothing seems more important than communicating with classmates and neighborhood children. For my mother, too, the new language was a way out of isolation, a means to deal with the larger world and with those American women for whom she sewed. But my father, a political exile waiting for changes in our native country, had different priorities: he lived in the hope of return, and believed that the new home, the new speech, were temporary. His theory was simple: if it could be said at all, it could be said best in the language of those authors whose words were the core of his education. But his insistence on pure Spanish made it difficult, sometimes impossible, to bring home and share the jokes of friends, puns, pop lyrics, and other staples of seven-year-old conversation. Table talk sometimes ended with tears or sullen silence.

And yet, despite the friction it caused from time to time, my native language was also a source of comfort—the reading that I loved, intimacy within the family, and a peculiar auditory delight best described as echoes in the mind. I learned early to relish words as counters in a game that could turn suddenly serious without losing the quality of play, and to value their sound as a meaning behind their meaning.

Nostalgia, a confusion of identity, the fear that if the native language is lost the self will somehow be altered forever: all are part of the subtle flavor of immigrant life, as well as the awareness that one owes gratitude to strangers for acts of communication that used to be simple and once imposed no such debt.

Memory, folklore, and food all become part of the receding landscape that language sets out to preserve. Guilt, too, adds to the mix, the suspicion that to love the second language too much is to betray those ancestors who spoke the first and could not communicate with us in the vocabulary of our education, our new thoughts. And finally, a sense of grievance and loss may spur hostility toward the new language and those who speak it, as if the common speech of the perceived majority could weld together a disparate population into a huge, monolithic, and threatening Other. That Other is then assigned traits and habits that preclude sympathy and mold "Us" into a unity whose cohesiveness gives comfort.

Luckily, there is another side to bilingualism: curiosity about the Other may be as natural and pervasive as group loyalty. If it weren't, travel, foreign residence, and intermarriage would be less common than they are. For some bilingual writers, the Other—and the language he speaks—are appealing. Some acknowledge and celebrate the tendency of languages to borrow from each other and produce something different in the process.

From Afterword to *Where Horizons Go*

THINKING ABOUT POETIC VOICE AND IDENTITY

Every writer strives to find his or her own voice, that distinct mix of subject matter and style that can make an author's work as instantly recognizable as a friend's voice on the phone. Poetic voice reflects matters of style—characteristic tone, word choice, figures of speech, and rhythms—as well as characteristic themes and subjects. Finding an authentic voice has long been a central issue among minority and female poets. In exploring their subjects, which often lie outside the existing poetic traditions, these writers sometimes need to find innovative forms of expression.

- **You will often find it illuminating to consider the author's personal identity when writing about voice in poetry.** Does the poem present any personal details of the author's life or background?
- **Consider whether the poem's subject matter is directly or indirectly shaped by race, gender, age, ethnicity, social class, sexual orientation, or religious beliefs.** If so, how is the viewpoint reflected in the poem's formal aspects (images, tone, metaphors, and so on)?
- **Read the section "Gender Criticism" in the chapter "Critical Approaches to Literature."** Although that section discusses only one aspect of identity, the general principles it explores relate to the broader question of how an author's life experience may influence the kinds of poetry he or she creates.

CHECKLIST: Writing About Voice and Personal Identity

☐ Is the poem's subject matter shaped by an aspect of the poet's identity?

☐ Does the poem address issues related to race, gender, social class, ethnicity, sexual orientation, age, or religious beliefs?

☐ Does personal identity reveal itself directly or indirectly in the poem's voice or content?

☐ If so, *how* does the voice reflect identity? Does it appear in the poem's diction, imagery, tone, metaphors, or sound?

WRITING ASSIGNMENT ON PERSONAL IDENTITY

Analyze any poem from this chapter from the perspective of its author's race, gender, ethnicity, age, or religious beliefs. Take into account the poem's style—its approach to tone, word choice, figures of speech, and rhythm—as well as its content. You may find it helpful to look at some biographical information on the poem's author, but focus your comments on the information provided by the poem itself.

MORE TOPICS FOR WRITING

1. Find another poem in the chapter "Poems for Further Reading" in which the poet, like Rhina Espaillat, considers his or her own family. In a paragraph or two, describe what the poem reveals about the author.
2. Write an explication of Adrienne Rich's "Women." What argument does the poem seem to be making?
3. Write a brief analysis (750 to 1,000 words) on how color imagery contributes to meaning in Yusef Komunyakaa's "Facing It."
4. Write a brief analysis (750 words) of the central metaphor in Carolyn Kizer's "Bitch." How does it help express the contradictory emotions of the poem?

5. Write an imitation of Shirley Geok-lin Lim's "Riding into California," about coming to terms with a place—a state, city, or neighborhood—in which you have lived and felt like an outsider.
6. Write about the personal identity of men and boys as explored in Donald Justice's "Men at Forty."
7. Compare Philip Larkin's "Aubade" with another poem about old age and death, such as William Butler Yeats's "Sailing to Byzantium" (page 754), or Dylan Thomas's "Do not go gentle into that good night" (page 659).

26

POETRY IN SPANISH: LITERATURE OF LATIN AMERICA

Poetry belongs to all epochs:
it is man's natural form of expression.

—OCTAVIO PAZ

Most Americans experience poetry in only one language—English. Because English is a world language, with its native speakers spread across every continent, it is easy for us to underestimate the significance of poetry written in other tongues. Why is it important to experience poetry in a different language or in translation? It matters because such poetry represents and illuminates a different cultural experience. Exposure to different cultures enriches our perspectives and challenges assumptions; it also helps us to understand our own culture better.

Latin American poetry is particularly relevant to the English speaker in the United States or Canada because of the long interconnected history of the Americas. Spanish is also an important world language, spoken by almost 400 million people and the primary language in over twenty countries. The vast spread of Spanish has created an enormous and prominent body of literature, an international tradition in which Latin America has gradually replaced Spain as the center. Poetry occupies a very significant place in Latin American culture—a more public place than in the United States. Poetry even forms an important part of the popular culture in Latin America, where the average person is able to name his or her favorite poets and can often recite some of their works from memory.

The tradition of Latin American poetry is long and rich. Many poets and scholars consider Sor Juana, a Catholic nun who lived in Mexico during the seventeenth century, to be the mother of Latin American poetry. Mexico's Nobel Laureate poet, Octavio Paz, acknowledges this lineage in his critical work on Sor Juana, *Traps of Faith* (1988), a quintessential book about her life and work. Sor Juana's writing was groundbreaking, not just in the context of Latin American poetry, but truly in the context of world literature, as she was the first writer in Latin America (and one of very few in her era) to address the rights of women to study and write. Her poems are also harbingers of important tendencies in Latin American poetry because of their heightened lyricism.

This lyrical quality finds new form and vitality in the works of the most widely known poets of Latin America—including César Vallejo, Pablo Neruda, Jorge Luis Borges, and Octavio Paz. Each of these poets addresses questions of cultural and personal identity in his work. Events of the twentieth century had great impact on both the subject matter and style of Latin American poets. The Spanish Civil War (1936–1939) sent many poets who had been living in Europe back to the Americas, conscious of the political and social values being tried and tested in Europe at the time.

Latin American poetry, particularly in the twentieth century, has been marked by a recognition of the region as a unique blending of different cultures, European and indigenous, among others. It has also been marked by a variety of artistic and political movements, of which surrealism is perhaps the most influential. The works of artists such as Mexican painter Frida Kahlo coincided with a body of new writing that emphasized a blurring of fantasy and reality. Some writers, such as Vallejo, became best known for their surrealist writing, while other poets, such as Neruda and Paz, incorporated some of the elements of the movement into their styles.

Three Latin American poets were awarded the Nobel Prize in Literature in the twentieth century: Paz, Neruda, and Gabriela Mistral. (Borges, to the astonishment of many critics, never won the award, though he captured nearly every other major international literary honor.) The importance of Spanish as a global language and in literature is reflected in the recognition of the stature of Latin American writers in the world. Even when decidedly political, Latin American poetry is known for its focus on the personal experience. One does not love one's country as a symbol, José Emilio Pacheco claims; rather, one loves its people, its mountains, and three or four of its rivers.

Sor Juana

Sor Juana Inés de la Cruz is said to have been born in Nepantla, Mexico, somewhere between 1648 and 1651. In 1667, she entered the convent of the "barefoot Carmelites," so named because of the austere way of life they adopted, either going barefoot or wearing rope sandals. In 1691 she wrote her famous Reply, *the first document in the Americas to argue for a woman's right to study and to write. She stated that she chose the convent life because it offered her more possibilities for engaging in intellectual pursuits than marriage at that time would allow. The Church responded by demanding she give up writing, and she renewed her vows to the Church, signing documents in her own blood. Sor Juana died during a devastating plague in 1695, after having given aid to a great number of the ill.*

Portrait of Sister Juana Inés de la Cruz
(by unknown Mexican artist, eighteenth century)

Presente en que el Cariño Hace Regalo la Llaneza 1689	A Simple Gift Made Rich by Affection 2004
Lysi: a tus manos divinas	Lysi, I give to your divine hand
doy castañas espinosas,	these chestnuts in their thorny guise
porque donde sobran rosas	because where velvet roses rise,
no pueden faltar espinas.	thorns also grow unchecked, unplanned.
Si a su aspereza te inclinas	If you're inclined toward their barbed brand 5
y con eso el gusto engañas,	and with this choice, betray your taste,
perdona las malas mañas	forgive the ill-bred lack of taste
de quien tal regalo te hizo;	of one who sends you such a missive—
perdona, pues que un erizo	Forgive me, only this husk can give
sólo puede dar castañas.	the chestnut, in its thorns embraced. 10

—Translated by Diane Thiel

Questions

1. How would you relate the title to the content of the poem?
2. Why does the speaker reject a gift of roses? Why does she fear that her gift may be rejected by its recipient?
3. How does the chestnut function as a metaphor? What does the thorny husk seem to represent? What does the chestnut represent?

Pablo Neruda

Pablo Neruda was born Neftali Ricardo Reyes Basoalto in 1904 in Parral, southern Chile. His mother died a month later, a fact which is said to have affected Neruda's choice of imagery throughout his life's work. He began writing poems as a child despite his family's disapproval, which led him to adopt the "working class" pen name Pablo Neruda. His early book Twenty Love Poems and a Song of Despair (1923) received vast attention, and Neruda decided to devote himself to writing poetry.

Pablo Neruda

Neruda served in a long line of diplomatic positions. He lived several years in Spain and chronicled the Spanish Civil War. He journeyed home to Chile in 1938, then served as consul to Mexico, and returned again to Chile in 1943. When the Chilean government moved to the right, Neruda, who was a communist, went into hiding.

In 1952, when the Chilean government ceased its persecution of leftist writers, Neruda returned to his native land, and in 1970 was a candidate for the presidency of Chile. He was awarded the Nobel Prize in Literature in 1971. Neruda died of cancer in Santiago in 1973.

Pablo Neruda

## Muchos Somos 1958	## We Are Many 1967

De tantos hombres que soy,
   que somos,
no puedo encontrar a ninguno:
se me pierden bajo la ropa,
se fueron a otra ciudad.
Cuando todo está preparado
para mostrarme inteligente
el tonto que llevo escondido
se toma la palabra en mi boca.

Otras veces me duermo en medio
de la sociedad distinguida
y cuando busco en mí al valiente,
un cobarde que no conozco
corre a tomar con mi esqueleto
mil deliciosas precauciones.

Cuando arde una casa estimada
en vez del bombero que llamo
se precipita el incendiario
y ése soy yo. No tengo arreglo.
Qué debo hacer para escogerme?
Cómo puedo rehabilitarme?

Todos los libros que leo
celebran héroes refulgentes
siempre seguros de sí mismos:
me muero de envidia por ellos,
y en los filmes de vientos y balas
me quedo envidiando al jinete,
me quedo admirando al caballo.

Pero cuando pido al intrépido
me sale el viejo perezoso,
y así yo no sé quién soy,
no sé cuántos soy o seremos.
Me gustaría tocar un timbre
y sacar el mí verdadero
porque si yo me necesito
no debo desaparecerme.

Of the many men who I am, who
   we are,
I can't find a single one;
they disappear among my clothes,
they've left for another city.
When everything seems to be set   5
to show me off as intelligent,
the fool I always keep hidden
takes over all that I say.

At other times, I'm asleep
among distinguished people,   10
and when I look for my brave self,
a coward unknown to me
rushes to cover my skeleton
with a thousand fine excuses.

When a decent house catches fire,   15
instead of the fireman I summon,
an arsonist bursts on the scene,
and that's me. What can I do?
What can I do to distinguish myself?
How can I pull myself together?   20

All the books I read
are full of dazzling heroes,
always sure of themselves.
I die with envy of them;
and in films full of wind and bullets,   25
I goggle at the cowboys,
I even admire the horses.

But when I call for a hero,
out comes my lazy old self;
so I never know who I am,   30
nor how many I am or will be.
I'd love to be able to touch a bell
and summon the real me,
because if I really need myself,
I mustn't disappear.   35

Mientras escribo estoy ausente	While I am writing, I'm far away;
y cuando vuelvo ya he partido:	and when I come back, I've gone.
voy a ver si a las otras gentes	I would like to know if others
les pasa lo que a mí me pasa,	go through the same things that I do,
si son tantos como soy yo,	have as many selves as I have, 40
si se parecen a sí mismos	and see themselves similarly;
y cuando lo haya averiguado	and when I've exhausted this problem,
voy a aprender tan bien las cosas	I'm going to study so hard
que para explicar mis problemas	that when I explain myself,
les hablaré de geografía.	I'll be talking geography. 45

—*Translated by Alastair Reid*

Questions

1. In line 26, Reid translates Neruda's phrase "me quedo envidiando al jinete" as "I goggle at the cowboys." What does Reid gain or lose with that version? (In Spanish, *jinete* means *horseman* or *rider* but not specifically *cowboy*, which is *vaquero* or even—thanks to Hollywood— *cowboy*.) Neruda once told Reid, "Alastair, don't just translate my poems. I want you to improve them." Is this line an improvement?

2. How many men are in the speaker of the poem? What seems to be their relationship to one another?

Jorge Luis Borges

Jorge Luis Borges (1899–1986), a blind librarian who became one of the most important writers ever to emerge from Latin America, was born in Buenos Aires. Borges's Protestant father and Catholic mother reflected Argentina's diverse background; their ancestry included Spanish, English, Italian, Portuguese, and Indian blood. In his youth, Borges lived in Switzerland and later Spain. On returning to Argentina in 1921, he edited a poetry magazine printed in the form of a poster and affixed to city walls. In 1937, to help support his mother and dying father, the thirty-seven-year-old Borges (who still lived at home) got his first job as an assistant librarian.

Jorge Luis Borges

During this decisive period, Borges encountered political trouble. For his opposition to the regime of Colonel Juan Perón, Borges was forced in 1946 to resign his post as a librarian and was mockingly offered a job as a chicken inspector. In 1955, after Perón was deposed, Borges became director of the National Library and a professor of English literature at the University of Buenos Aires. Suffering from poor eyesight since childhood, Borges eventually went blind. Probably the most influential short story writer of the last half-century, Borges considered himself first and foremost a poet.

Jorge Luis Borges

On his blindness 1985	On His Blindness 1994

Al cabo de los años me rodea
una terca neblina luminosa
que reduce las cosas a una cosa
sin forma ni color. Casi a una idea.
La vasta noche elemental y el día
lleno de gente son esa neblina
de luz dudosa y fiel que no declina
y que acecha en el alba. Yo querría
ver una cara alguna vez. Ignoro
la inexplorada enciclopedia, el goce
de libros que mi mano reconoce,
las altas aves y las lunas de oro.
A los otros les queda el universo;
a mi penumbra, el hábito del verso.

In the fullness of the years, like it or not,
a luminous mist surrounds me, unvarying,
that breaks things down into a single thing,
colorless, formless, Almost into a thought.
The elemental, vast night and the day   5
teeming with people have become that fog
of constant, tentative light that does not flag,
and lies in wait at dawn. I longed to see
just once a human face. Unknown to me
the closed encyclopedia, the sweet play   10
in volumes I can do no more than hold,
the tiny soaring birds, the moons of gold.
Others have the world, for better or worse;
I have this half-dark, and the toil of verse.

—Translated by Robert Mezey

Questions

1. Borges's Spanish original has an English title. Why would he use English? (Hint: Look at John Milton's poem on page 863.)
2. What is the form of the poem?
3. What images and metaphors does Borges use to describe his blindness?

Octavio Paz

Octavio Paz, the only Mexican author to win the Nobel Prize in Literature, was born in Mexico City in 1914. Paz once commented that he came from "a typical Mexican family" because it combined European and Indian ancestors. "Impoverished by the revolution and civil war," his family lived in his grandfather's huge, crumbling house in Mixoac, a suburb of Mexico City, where they abandoned rooms one by one as the roof collapsed. His grandfather had a library containing over six thousand books where the young author immersed himself. Joining his father in exile, the young Paz lived for two years in Los Angeles, and later went to Spain to fight in the Spanish Civil War. In the highly political world of Latin American letters, Paz refused to adopt the political opinions of the two

Octavio Paz

extremes—military dictatorship or Marxist revolution—but worked toward democracy, "the mystery of freedom," as he called it in an early poem.

In 1945 Paz became a diplomat, spending years in San Francisco, New York, Geneva, and Delhi. In 1968 he resigned his post as ambassador to India in protest of the Mexican government's massacre of student demonstrators shortly before the Mexico City Olympic games. Paz then taught abroad at several universities, but he always returned to Mexico City, where he died in 1998.

Con los ojos cerrados 1968	**With eyes closed** 1986
Con los ojos cerrados	With eyes closed
Te iluminas por dentro	you light up within
Ertes la piedra ciega	you are blind stone
Noche a noche te labro	Night after night I carve you
Con los ojos cerrados	with eyes closed 5
Eres la piedra franca	you are frank stone
Nos volvemos inmensos	We have become enormous
Sólo por conocernos	just knowing each other
Con los ojos cerrados	with eyes closed
	—*Translated by Eliot Weinberger*

Question

How does the refrain contribute to the musical quality of "With eyes closed"?

SURREALISM IN LATIN AMERICAN POETRY

Surrealism was one of the great artistic revolutions of the twentieth century. It first arose in the mockingly named "Dada" movement during World War I. (*Dada* is the French children's word for "rocking horse.") Dadaism announced itself as the radical rejection of the insanity perpetrated by the self-proclaimed "rational" world of the turbulent modern era. The approach was an attempt to shock the world out of its terrible self-destructive traditions. "The only way for Dada to continue," proclaimed poet André Breton, "is for it to cease to exist." Sure enough, the movement soon fell apart through its own excesses of energy, irreverence, and absurdism.

In 1922 **Surrealism** emerged as the successor to Dada, first as a literary movement, soon to spread to the visual arts. Surrealism also sought to free art from the bounds of rationality, promoting the creation of fantastic, dreamlike works that reflected the unconscious mind.

Surrealism emphasized spontaneity rather than craft as the essential element in literary creation. Not all Surrealist art, however, was spontaneous. Breton, for instance, spent six months on a poem of thirty words, in order to achieve what looked like spontaneity. And many Surrealist visual artists would do several versions of the same "automatic drawing" in pursuit of the effect of immediacy. Breton's famous "Manifesto of Surrealism" (1924) launched a movement that continues to influence a great number of writers and artists around the world.

The early Surrealists showed as much genius for absurd humor as for art, and their works often tried to shock and amuse. Marcel Duchamp once exhibited a huge printed reproduction of the *Mona Lisa* on which he had painted a large mustache. Louis Aragon's poem "Suicide" consisted only of the letters of the alphabet, and

Breton once published a poem made up of names and numbers copied from the telephone directory. Is it any wonder that the Surrealist motto was "The approval of the public must be shunned at all cost"?

Surrealism's greatest international literary influence was on Latin American poetry. In the early twentieth century, Latin America was much influenced by French culture, and literary innovations in Paris were quickly imported to Mexico City, Buenos Aires, and other New World capitals. In Latin America, however, Surrealism lost much of the playfulness it exhibited in Europe, and the movement often took on a darker and more explicitly political quality. According to Octavio Paz, many poets, such as himself, César Vallejo, and Pablo Neruda, adopted Surrealist processes, and their creative developments often coincided with the movement, although their work is not usually considered "Surrealist."

Surrealism also had a powerful effect on Latin American art. A tradition of Surrealist painting emerged parallel to the movement in literature. One of the best known Surrealist painters is the Mexican artist Frida Kahlo, whose work often created dreamlike visions of the human body, especially her own. In *The Two Fridas*, for example, she presents a frightening image of the body's interior exposed and mirrored. Kahlo's paintings are simultaneously personal and political—surrealistically portraying her own trauma as well as the schism in her native country.

The Two Fridas **by Frida Kahlo (1907–1954), c. 1939.**

César Vallejo (1892?–1938)

La cólera que quiebra al hombre en niños (1937) 1939

La cólera que quiebra al hombre en niños,
que quiebra al niño, en pájaros iguales,
y al pájaro, después, en huevecillos;
la cólera del pobre
tiene un aceite contra dos vinagres. 5

La cólera que el árbol quiebra en hojas,
a la hoja en botones desiguales
y al botón, en ranuras telescópicas;
la cólera del pobre
tiene dos ríos contra muchos mares. 10

La cólera que quiebra al bien en dudas,
a la duda, en tres arcos semejantes
y al arco, luego, en tumbas imprevistas;
la cólera del pobre
tiene un acero contra dos puñales. 15

La cólera que quiebra el alma en cuerpos,
al cuerpo en órganos desemejantes
y al órgano, en octavos pensamientos;
la cólera del pobre
tiene un fuego central contra dos cráteres. 20

Anger 1977

Anger which breaks a man into children,
Which breaks the child into two equal birds,
And after that the bird into a pair of little eggs:
The poor man's anger
Has one oil against two vinegars. 5

Anger which breaks a tree into leaves
And the leaf into unequal buds
And the bud into telescopic grooves;
The poor man's anger
Has two rivers against many seas. 10

Anger which breaks good into doubts
And doubt into three similar arcs
And then the arc into unexpected tombs;
The poor man's anger
Has one steel against two daggers. 15

Anger which breaks the soul into bodies
And the body into dissimilar organs
And the organ into octave thoughts;
The poor man's anger
Has one central fire against two craters. 20

—*Translated by Thomas Merton*

CONTEMPORARY MEXICAN POETRY

José Emilio Pacheco (b. 1939)

Alta Traición

1969

No amo mi Patria. Su fulgor abstracto
es inasible.
Pero (aunque suene mal) daría la vida
por diez lugares suyos, cierta gente.
Puertos, bosques de piños, fortalezas,   5
una ciudad deshecha, gris, monstruosa,
varias figuras de su historia,
montañas
(y tres o cuatro ríos)

High Treason

1978

I do not love my country. Its abstract lustre
is beyond my grasp.
But (although it sounds bad) I would give my life
for ten places in it, for certain people,
seaports, pinewoods, fortresses,   5
a run-down city, gray, grotesque,
various figures from its history,
mountains
(and three or four rivers).

—*Translated by Alastair Reid*

Pedro Serrano (b. 1957)

Golondrinas

2006

Enganchadas al cable como pinzas de ropa,
gaviotas de madera diminutas,
ágiles y minúsculas contra la brutalidad del azul,
fijas al mediodía cayendo una tras otra,
moviendo ropas, brazos, sonrisas,   5
el pecho blanco, la capucha negra,
las alas afiladas y en lista, mínima agitación.
Hasta que vuelan todas excepto una,
que se plantó un momento y arañó el regreso,
como una ligerísima despedida,   10
axila de golpe la mañana.
Quedan los cables, el cielo en abandono intenso,
una boda de domingo de pueblo,
después nada.

Swallows

2010

Pinned to the wire like clothes-pegs,
diminutive seagulls made of wood,
lithe and tiny in the brutal force of the blue,
motionless at noon, dropping one after another,
setting in motion clothes, arms, smiles,   5
with white breasts and black caps, streamlined
wings and in single file, with minimal fuss.
Until all have flown but one,
that perched for a moment and clung to its return,
as though to sketch the lightest of goodbyes,   10
with morning suddenly an armpit.
The wires remain, the sky never so empty,
like a village wedding on a Sunday,
then nothing.

—Translated by Anna Crowe

Questions

What is the simile Serrano uses initially to describe the swallows? What is his simile for their final absence?

Tedi López Mills (b. 1959)

Convalecencia   2000

Moscas de todas las horas.
—Antonio Machado

el rasguño de esta fiebre
y la mosca del aire
son como un ruido primario
en el espectro de sonidos
un estruendo rojo y sin matiz
el primer fierro en la oreja
el primer filo de la sierra
el primer chillido del garabato en la letra
la primera gota del agua
en un círculo vacío
el primer golpe del martillo
contra un muro y la piedra
el primer grito insumiso junto a la reja
el primer clavo en la luz del mediodía
el cristal predilecto del ojo
donde la mosca y yo
en la celda del cráneo
nos oímos

Convalescence   2000

Houseflies of all day long.
—Antonio Machado

this feverish scratch
and the fly in flight
are like primal noises
in the spectrum of sounds
a traceless red din   5
the first iron in the ear
the first cutting of the saw
the first screeching scribble of letters
the first drop of water
in an empty circle   10
the first blow of the hammer
against a wall and the stone
the first unruly scream beside the gate
the first nail in midday light
the favored windowpane of the eye   15
where the fly and I
inside the jail cell of the skull
hear each other

—Translated by Cheryl Clark

■ WRITING *effectively*

Alastair Reid on Writing (b. 1926)

Translating Neruda   1996

Translating someone's work, poetry in particular, has something about it akin to being possessed, haunted. Translating a poem means not only reading it deeply and deciphering it, but clambering about backstage among the props and the scaffolding. I found I could no longer read a poem of Neruda's simply as words on a page without hearing behind them that languid, caressing voice. Most important to me in translating these two writers [Neruda and Borges] was the sound of their voices in my memory, for it very much helped in finding the English appropriate to those voices. I found that if I learned poems of Neruda's by heart I could replay them at odd moments, on buses, at wakeful times in the night, until, at a certain point, the translation would somehow set. The voice was the clue: I felt that all Neruda's poems were fundamentally vocative—spoken poems, poems of direct address—and that Neruda's voice was in a sense the instrument for which he wrote. He once made a tape for me, reading pieces of different poems, in different tones and rhythms. I played it over so many times that I can hear it in my head at will. Two lines of his I used to repeat like a Zen koan, for they seemed to apply particularly to translating:

in this net it's not just the strings that count
but also the air that escapes through the meshes.

He often wrote of himself as having many selves, just as he had left behind him several very different poetic manners and voices.

From "Neruda and Borges"

WRITING ASSIGNMENT ON SPANISH POETRY

Compare the two love poems in this chapter—Sor Juana's "A Simple Gift Made Rich by Affection" and Octavio Paz's "With eyes closed." Analyze each poem's presentation of the beloved and contrast it to the presentations in the other poem.

MORE TOPICS FOR WRITING

1. Consider the surreal effects in César Vallejo's "Anger" as well as in Frida Kahlo's painting *The Two Fridas*.

2. Consider the way personal and political themes merge in José Emilio Pacheco's "High Treason" or César Vallejo's "Anger."

3. Compare Jorge Luis Borges's sonnet "On his blindness" with John Milton's sonnet "When I consider how my light is spent" on page 863 (from which Borges drew his title). How do their reactions to their disability differ? Are they similar in any significant ways?

27

Poetry is life distilled.

—GWENDOLYN BROOKS

Why do we call some poems "bad"? We are not talking about their moral implications. Rather, we mean that, for one or more of many possible reasons, the poem has failed to move us or to engage our sympathies. Instead, it has made us doubt that the poet is in control of language and vision; perhaps it has aroused our antipathies or unwittingly appealed to our sense of the comic, though the poet is serious. Some poems can be said to succeed despite burdensome faults. But in general such faults are symptoms of a deeper malady: some weakness in a poem's basic conception or in the poet's competence.

Nearly always, a bad poem reveals only a dim and distorted awareness of its probable effect on its audience. Perhaps the sound of words may clash with what a poem is saying, as in the jarring last word of this opening line of a tender lyric (author unknown, quoted by Richard Wilbur): "Come into the tent, my love, and close the flap." A bad poem usually overshoots or falls short of its mark by the poet's thinking too little or too much.

In a poem that has a rime scheme or a set line length, when all is well, pattern and structure move inseparably with the rest of the poem, the way a tiger's skin and bones move with the tiger. But sometimes, in a poem that fails, the poet evidently has had difficulty in fitting the statements into a formal pattern. English poets have long felt free to invert word order for a special effect (Milton: "ye myrtles brown"). This change of normal word order, usually done for purposes of meter or rime, is called **poetic inversion.** The poet having trouble keeping to a rime scheme may invert words for no apparent reason but convenience. Needing a rime for *barge* may lead to ending a line with *a police dog large* instead of *a large police dog*. Another sign of trouble is a profusion of adjectives. If a line of iambic pentameter reads "Her lovely skin, like dear sweet white old silk," we suspect the poet of stuffing the line to make it long enough.

Even great poets write awful poems, and after their deaths, their worst efforts are collected with their masterpieces with no consumer warning labels to inform the reader. Some lines in the canon of celebrated bards make us wonder, "How could they have written this?" Wordsworth, Shelley, Whitman, and Browning are among the great whose failures can be painful, and sometimes an excellent poem will have a bad spot in it. To be unwilling to read them, though, would be as ill advised as to refuse to see Venice just because the Grand Canal is said to contain impurities. The seasoned reader of poetry thinks no less of Tennyson for having written "Form, Form, Riflemen Form! . . . // Look to your butts, and take good aims!" The collected works of a duller poet may contain no such lines of unconscious double meaning, but neither do they contain any poem as good as "Ulysses." If the duller poet never had a spectacular failure, it may be because of a failure to take risks. "In poetry," said Ronsard, "the greatest vice is mediocrity."

Often, inept poems fall into familiar categories. At one extreme is the poem written entirely in conventional diction, dimly echoing Shakespeare, Wordsworth, and the Bible, but garbling them. Couched in a rhythm that ticks along like a metronome, this kind of poem shows no sign that its author has ever taken a hard look at anything that can be tasted, handled, or felt. It employs loosely and thoughtlessly the most abstract of words: *love, beauty, life, death, time, eternity*. Littered with old-fashioned contractions (*'tis, o'er, where'er*), it may end in a simple preachment or platitude. George Orwell's complaint against much contemporary writing (not only poetry) is applicable: "As soon as certain topics are raised"—and one thinks of such standard topics for poetry as spring, a first kiss, and stars—"the concrete melts into the abstract and no one seems able to think of turns of speech that are not hackneyed."

At the opposite extreme is the poem that displays no acquaintance with poetry of the past but manages, instead, to fabricate its own clichés. Slightly paraphrased, a manuscript once submitted to the *Paris Review* began:

Vile
    rottenflush
        o   —screaming—
        f CORPSEBLOOD!!   ooze
STRANGLE my
        eyes...
                    HELL's
          O, ghastly   stench**!!!

At most, such a work has only a private value. The writer has vented personal frustrations upon words, instead of kicking stray dogs. In its way, "Vile Rottenflush" is as self-indulgent as the oldfangled "first kiss in spring" kind of poem. "I dislike," said John Livingston Lowes, "poems that black your eyes, or put up their mouths to be kissed."

As jewelers tell which of two diamonds is fine by seeing which scratches the other, two poems may be tested by comparing them. This method works only on poems similar in length and kind: an epigram cannot be held up to test an epic. Most poems we meet are neither sheer trash nor obvious masterpieces. Because good diamonds to be proven need softer ones to scratch, in this chapter you will find a few clear-cut gems and a few clinkers.

Anonymous (English)

O Moon, when I gaze on thy beautiful face   (about 1900)

O Moon, when I gaze on thy beautiful face,
Careering along through the boundaries of space,
The thought has often come into my mind
If I ever shall see thy glorious behind.

O MOON. Sir Edmund Gosse, the English critic (1849–1928), offered this quatrain as the work of his servant, but there is reason to suspect him of having written it.

Questions

1. To what fact of astronomy does the last line refer?
2. Which words seem chosen with too little awareness of their denotations and connotations?
3. Even if you did not know that these lines probably were deliberately bad, how would you argue with someone who maintained that the opening "O" in the poem was admirable as a bit of concrete poetry?

Emily Dickinson (1830–1886)

A Dying Tiger – moaned for Drink   (about 1862)

A Dying Tiger – moaned for Drink –
I hunted all the Sand –
I caught the Dripping of a Rock
And bore it in my Hand –

His Mighty Balls – in death were thick –   5
But searching – I could see
A Vision on the Retina
Of Water – and of me –

'Twas not my blame – who sped too slow –
'Twas not his blame – who died   10
While I was reaching him –
But 'twas – the fact that He was dead –

Questions

How does this poem compare in success with other poems of Emily Dickinson that you know? Justify your opinion by pointing to some of this poem's particulars.

Exercise: Five Terrible Moments in Poetry

Here is a small anthology of bad moments in poetry.
For what reasons does each selection fail?
In which passages do you attribute the failure
    to inappropriate sound or diction?
    to awkward word order?
    to inaccurate metaphor?
    to excessive overstatement?
    to forced rime?
    to monotonous rhythm?
    to redundancy?
    to simple-mindedness or excessive ingenuity?

1. Last lines of *Enoch Arden* by Alfred, Lord Tennyson:

    So past the strong heroic soul away.
    And when they buried him, the little port
    Had seldom seen a costlier funeral.

2. From *Purely Original Verse* (1891) by J. Gordon Coogler (1865–1901), of Columbia, South Carolina:

    Alas for the South, her books have grown fewer –
    She never was much given to literature.

3. From "Lines Written to a Friend on the Death of His Brother, Caused by a Railway Train Running Over Him Whilst He Was in a State of Inebriation" by James Henry Powell:

> Thy mangled corpse upon the rails in frightful shape was found.
> The ponderous train had killed thee as its heavy wheels went round,
> And thus in dreadful form thou met'st a drunkard's awful death
> And I, thy brother, mourn thy fate, and breathe a purer breath.

4. From *Dolce Far Niente* by the American poet Francis Saltus Saltus, who flourished in the 1890s:

> Her laugh is like sunshine, full of glee,
> And her sweet breath smells like fresh-made tea.

5. From "Song to the Suliotes" by George Gordon, Lord Byron:

> Up to battle! Sons of Suli
>> Up, and do your duty duly!
> There the wall—and there the moat is:
>> Bouwah! Bouwah! Suliotes,
> There is booty—there is beauty!
>> Up my boys and do your duty!

SENTIMENTALITY

Sentimentality is a failure of writers who seem to feel a great emotion but who fail to give us sufficient grounds for sharing it. The emotion may be an anger greater than its object seems to call for, as in these lines by Ali Hilmi to a girl who caused scandal (the exact nature of her act never being specified): "The gossip in each hall / Will curse your name . . . / Go! better cast yourself right down the falls!" Or it may be an enthusiasm quite unwarranted by its subject: in *The Fleece* John Dyer temptingly describes the pleasures of life in a workhouse for the poor. The sentimental poet is especially prone to tenderness. Great tears fill his eyes at a glimpse of an aged grandmother sitting by a hearth. For all the poet knows, she may be the manager of a casino in Las Vegas who would be startled to find herself an object of pity, but the sentimentalist doesn't care to know about the woman herself. She is a general excuse for feeling maudlin. Any other conventional object will serve as well: a faded valentine, the strains of an old song, a baby's cast-off pacifier. An instance of such emotional self-indulgence is "The Old Oaken Bucket," by Samuel Woodworth, a stanza of which goes:

> How sweet from the green, mossy brim to receive it,
>> As, poised on the curb, it inclined to my lips!
> Not a full-flushing goblet could tempt me to leave it,
>> Tho' filled with the nectar that Jupiter sips.
> And now, far removed from the loved habitation,
>> The tear of regret will intrusively swell,
> As fancy reverts to my father's plantation,
>> And sighs for the bucket that hung in the well.

The staleness of the phrasing and imagery (Jove's nectar, *tear of regret*) suggests that the speaker is not even seeing the actual physical bucket, and the tripping meter of the lines is inappropriate to an expression of tearful regret. Perhaps the poet's nostalgia is genuine. Indeed, as Keith Waldrop has put it, "a bad poem is always sincere."

Bathos

However sincere in their feelings, sentimental poets fail as artists because they cannot separate their own emotional responses from those of the disinterested reader. Wet-eyed and sighing for a bucket, Woodworth achieves not pathos but **bathos:** a description that can move us to laughter instead of tears. Tears, of course, can be shed for good reason. A piece of sentimentality is not to be confused with a well-wrought poem whose tone is tenderness. Bathos in poetry can also mean an abrupt fall from the sublime to the trivial or incongruous. A sample, from Nicholas Rowe's play *The Fair Penitent:* "Is it the voice of thunder, or my father?" Another, from John Close, a minor Victorian: "Around their heads a dazzling halo shone, / No need of mortal robes, or any hat."

Rod McKuen (b. 1933)

Thoughts on Capital Punishment   1954

There ought to be capital punishment for cars
that run over rabbits and drive into dogs
and commit the unspeakable, unpardonable crime
of killing a kitty cat still in his prime.

Purgatory, at the very least   5
              should await the driver
   driving over a beast.

Those hurrying headlights coming out of the dark
that scatter the scampering squirrels in the park
should await the best jury that one might compose   10
of fatherless chipmunks and husbandless does.

And then found guilty, after too fair a trial
should be caged in a cage with a hyena's smile
or maybe an elephant with an elephant gun
should shoot out his eyes when the verdict is done.   15

There ought to be something, something that's fair
to avenge Mrs. Badger as she waits in her lair
for her husband who lies with his guts spilling out
cause he didn't know what automobiles are about.

Hell on the highway, at the very least   20
              should await the driver
   driving over a beast.

Who kills a man kills a bit of himself
But a cat too is an extension of God.

William Stafford (1914–1993)

Traveling Through the Dark   1962

Traveling through the dark I found a deer
dead on the edge of the Wilson River road.
It is usually best to roll them into the canyon:
that road is narrow; to swerve might make more dead.

By glow of the tail-light I stumbled back of the car   5
and stood by the heap, a doe, a recent killing;
she had stiffened already, almost cold.
I dragged her off; she was large in the belly.

My fingers touching her side brought me the reason—
her side was warm; her fawn lay there waiting,   10
alive, still, never to be born.
Beside that mountain road I hesitated.

The car aimed ahead its lowered parking lights;
under the hood purred the steady engine.
I stood in the glare of the warm exhaust turning red;   15
around our group I could hear the wilderness listen.

I thought hard for us all—my only swerving—
then pushed her over the edge into the river.

Questions

1. Compare these poems by Rod McKuen and William Stafford. How are they similar?
2. Explain Stafford's title. Who are all those traveling through the dark?
3. Comment on McKuen's use of language. Consider especially: *unspeakable, unpardonable crime* (line 3), *kitty cat* (4), *scatter the scampering squirrels* (9), and *cause he didn't know* (19).
4. Compare the meaning of Stafford's last two lines and McKuen's last two. Does either poem have a moral? Can either poem be said to moralize?
5. Which poem might be open to the charge of sentimentality? Why?

RECOGNIZING EXCELLENCE

How can we tell an excellent poem from any other? With poetry, explaining excellence is harder than explaining failure (so often due to familiar kinds of imprecision and sentimentality). A bad poem tends to be stereotyped, an excellent poem unique. In judging either, we can have no absolute specifications. A poem is not like an electric toaster that an inspector can test using a check-off list. It has to be judged on the basis of what it is trying to be and how well it succeeds in the effort.

To judge a poem, we first have to understand it. At least, we need to understand it *almost* all the way; to be sure, there are poems such as Hopkins's "The Windhover" (page 848), which most readers probably would call excellent even though its meaning is still being debated. Although it is a good idea to give a poem at least a couple of considerate readings before judging it, sometimes our first encounter starts turning into an act of evaluation. Moving along into the poem, becoming more deeply involved in it, we may begin forming an opinion. In general, the more a poem contains for us to understand, the more rewarding we are likely to find it. Of course, an obscure and highly demanding poem is not always to be preferred to a relatively simple one. Difficult poems can be pretentious and incoherent; still, there is something to be said for the poem complicated enough to leave us something to discover on our fifteenth reading (unlike most limericks, which yield their all at a look). Here is such a poem, one not readily fathomed and exhausted.

William Butler Yeats (1865–1939)

Sailing to Byzantium   1927

That is no country for old men. The young
In one another's arms, birds in the trees
—Those dying generations—at their song,
The salmon-falls, the mackerel-crowded seas,
Fish, flesh, or fowl, commend all summer long   5
Whatever is begotten, born, and dies.
Caught in that sensual music all neglect
Monuments of unaging intellect.

An aged man is but a paltry thing,
A tattered coat upon a stick, unless   10
Soul clap its hands and sing, and louder sing
For every tatter in its mortal dress,
Nor is there singing school but studying
Monuments of its own magnificence;
And therefore I have sailed the seas and come   15
To the holy city of Byzantium.

O sages standing in God's holy fire
As in the gold mosaic of a wall,
Come from the holy fire, perne in a gyre,°   *spin down a spiral*
And be the singing-masters of my soul.   20
Consume my heart away; sick with desire
And fastened to a dying animal
It knows not what it is; and gather me
Into the artifice of eternity.

Once out of nature I shall never take   25
My bodily form from any natural thing,
But such a form as Grecian goldsmiths make
Of hammered gold and gold enameling
To keep a drowsy Emperor awake;
Or set upon a golden bough to sing   30
To lords and ladies of Byzantium
Of what is past, or passing, or to come.

SAILING TO BYZANTIUM. Byzantium was the capital of the Byzantine Empire, the city now called Istanbul. Yeats means, though, not merely the physical city. Byzantium is also a name for his conception of paradise.

Though *salmon-falls* (line 4) suggests Yeats's native Ireland, the poem, as we find out in line 25, is about escaping from the entire natural world. If the poet desires this escape, then probably the *country* mentioned in the opening line is no political nation but the cycle of birth and death in which human beings are trapped; and, indeed, the poet says his heart is "fastened to a dying animal." Imaginary landscapes, it would seem, are merging with the historical Byzantium. Lines 17–18 refer to mosaic images, adornments of the Byzantine cathedral of St. Sophia, in which the figures of saints are inlaid against backgrounds of gold. The clockwork bird of the last stanza is also a reference to something actual. Yeats noted: "I have read somewhere that in the Emperor's palace at Byzantium was a tree made of gold and silver, and artificial birds that sang." This description of the role the poet would seek—that of a changeless, immortal singer—directs us back to the earlier references to music and singing. Taken all together, they point toward the central metaphor of the poem: the craft of poetry can be a kind of singing. One kind of everlasting monument is a great poem. To study masterpieces of poetry is the only "singing school"—the only way to learn to write a poem.

We have no more than skimmed through a few of this poem's suggestions, enough to show that, out of allusion and imagery, Yeats has woven at least one elaborate metaphor. Surely one thing the poem achieves is that, far from merely puzzling us, it makes us aware of relationships between what a person can imagine and the physical world. There is the statement that a human heart is bound to the body that perishes, and yet it is possible to see consciousness for a moment independent of flesh, to sing with joy at the very fact that the body is crumbling away. Much of the power of Yeats's poem comes from the physical terms with which he states the ancient quarrel between body and spirit, body being a "tattered coat upon a stick." There is all the difference in the world between the work of the poet like Yeats whose eye is on the living thing and whose mind is awake and passionate, and that of the slovenly poet whose dull eye and sleepy mind focus on nothing more than some book read hastily long ago. The former writes a poem out of compelling need, the latter as if it seems a nice idea to write something.

Yeats's poem has the three qualities essential to beauty, according to the definition of Thomas Aquinas: wholeness, harmony, and radiance. The poem is all one; its parts move in peace with one another; it shines with emotional intensity. There is an orderly progression going on in it: from the speaker's statement of his discontent with the world of "sensual music" to his statement that he is quitting this world, to his prayer that the sages will take him in, and his vision of future immortality. And the images of the poem relate to one another—*dying generations* (line 3), *dying animal* (line 22), and the undying golden bird (lines 27–32)—to mention just one series of related things. "Sailing to Byzantium" is not the kind of poem that has, in Pope's words, "One simile, that solitary shines / In the dry desert of a thousand lines." Rich in figurative language, Yeats's whole poem develops a metaphor, with further metaphors as its tributaries.

"Sailing to Byzantium" has a theme that matters to us. What human being does not long, at times, to shed timid, imperfect flesh, to live in a state of absolute joy, unperishing? Being human, perhaps we too are stirred by Yeats's prayer: "Consume my heart away; sick with desire / And fastened to a dying animal. . . ." If it is true that in poetry, as Ezra Pound declared, "only emotion endures," then Yeats's poem ought to endure. (If you happen not to feel moved by this poem, try another—but come back to "Sailing to Byzantium" after a while.)

Most excellent poems, it might be argued, contain significant themes, as does "Sailing to Byzantium." But the presence of such a theme is not enough to render a poem excellent. No theme alone makes an excellent poem, but rather how well the theme is stated.

Yeats's poem, some would say, is a match for any lyric in our language. Some might call it inferior to an epic (to Milton's *Paradise Lost*, say, or to the *Iliad*), but to make this claim is to lead us into a different argument: whether certain genres are innately better than others. Such an argument usually leads to a dead end. Evidently, *Paradise Lost* has greater range, variety, matter, length, and ambitiousness. But any poem—whether an epic or an epigram—may be judged by how well it fulfills the design it undertakes. God, who created both fleas and whales, pronounced all good. Fleas, like epigrams, have no reason to feel inferior.

Exercise: Two Poems to Compare

Here are two poems with a similar theme. Which contains more qualities of excellent poetry? Decide whether the other is bad or whether it may be praised for achieving something different.

Arthur Guiterman (1871–1943)

On the Vanity of Earthly Greatness   1936

The tusks that clashed in mighty brawls
Of mastodons, are billiard balls.

The sword of Charlemagne the Just
Is ferric oxide, known as rust.

The grizzly bear whose potent hug   5
Was feared by all, is now a rug.

Great Caesar's bust is on the shelf,
And I don't feel so well myself.

Percy Bysshe Shelley (1792–1822)

Ozymandias   1818

I met a traveler from an antique land
Who said: Two vast and trunkless legs of stone
Stand in the desert. . . . Near them, on the sand,
Half sunk, a shattered visage lies, whose frown,
And wrinkled lip, and sneer of cold command,   5
Tell that its sculptor well those passions read
Which yet survive, stamped on these lifeless things,
The hand that mocked° them, and the heart that fed: *imitated*
And on the pedestal these words appear:
"My name is Ozymandias, king of kings: 10
Look on my works, ye Mighty, and despair!"
Nothing beside remains. Round the decay
Of that colossal wreck, boundless and bare
The lone and level sands stretch far away.

Conventions and Conceits

Some excellent poems of the past will remain sealed to us unless we are willing to sympathize with their conventions. A **convention** is any established feature or technique that is commonly understood by both authors and readers. Pastoral poetry, for instance—Marlowe's "Passionate Shepherd" and Milton's "Lycidas"—asks us to accept certain conventions and situations that may seem old-fashioned: idle swains, oaten flutes. We are under no grim duty, of course, to admire poems whose conventions do not appeal to us. But there is no point in blaming a poet for playing a particular game or for observing its rules.

Bad poems, of course, can be woven together out of conventions, like patchwork quilts made of old unwanted words. In Shakespeare's England, poets were busily imitating the sonnets of Petrarch, the Italian poet whose praise of his beloved Laura had become well known. The result of their industry was a surplus of Petrarchan **conceits,** or elaborate comparisons (from the Italian *concetto*: concept, bright idea). In a famous sonnet ("My mistress' eyes are nothing like the sun," page 874), Shakespeare, who at times helped himself generously from the Petrarchan stockpile, pokes fun at poets who thoughtlessly use such handed-down figures of speech.

There is no predictable pattern for poetic excellence. A reader needs to remain open to surprise and innovation. Remember, too, that a superb poem is not necessarily an uplifting one—full of noble sentiments and inspiring ideas. Some powerful poems deal with difficult and even unpleasant subjects. What matters is the compelling quality of the presentation, the evocative power of the language, and the depth of feeling and perception achieved by the total work. William Trevor once defined the short story as "an explosion of truth"; the same notion applies to poetry, with a special reminder that not all truths are either pleasant or simple. Robert Hayden's powerful "Frederick Douglass," an unrimed sonnet, explores the slow and painful realization of the great abolitionist's dreams for African Americans. Masterfully, Hayden has created a poem with such sinuously complex syntax and rich verbal music that the lines cannot be read too quickly, allowing the broad vision of the poem to emerge.

Robert Hayden (1913–1980)

Frederick Douglass 1947

When it is finally ours, this freedom, this liberty, this beautiful
and terrible thing, needful to man as air,
usable as earth; when it belongs at last to all,
when it is truly instinct, brain matter, diastole, systole,
reflex action; when it is finally won; when it is more   5
than the gaudy mumbo jumbo of politicians:
this man, this Douglass, this former slave, this Negro
beaten to his knees, exiled, visioning a world
where none is lonely, none hunted, alien,
this man, superb in love and logic, this man   10
shall be remembered. Oh, not with statues' rhetoric,
not with legends and poems and wreaths of bronze alone,
but with the lives grown out of his life, the lives
fleshing his dream of the beautiful, needful thing.

FREDERICK DOUGLASS. Frederick Douglass (1818–1895), a freed slave, became the most influential African American abolitionist in America and later an eloquent advocate for civil rights for emancipated slaves.

Questions

1. What is unusual about the sentence structure of this poem?
2. What is the "it" repeatedly invoked in the poem?
3. When will this "it" be realized?

Sometimes poets use conventions in an innovative way, stretching the rules for new expressive ends. Here Elizabeth Bishop takes the form of the villanelle and bends the rules to give her poem a heartbreaking effect.

Elizabeth Bishop (1911–1979)

One Art   1976

The art of losing isn't hard to master;
so many things seem filled with the intent
to be lost that their loss is no disaster.

Lose something every day. Accept the fluster
of lost door keys, the hour badly spent.   5
The art of losing isn't hard to master.

Then practice losing farther, losing faster:
places, and names, and where it was you meant
to travel. None of these will bring disaster.

I lost my mother's watch. And look! my last, or   10
next-to-last, of three loved houses went.
The art of losing isn't hard to master.

I lost two cities, lovely ones. And, vaster,
some realms I owned, two rivers, a continent.
I miss them, but it wasn't a disaster.   15

—Even losing you (the joking voice, a gesture
I love) I shan't have lied. It's evident
the art of losing's not too hard to master
though it may look like (*Write* it!) like disaster.

Questions

1. What things has the speaker lost? Put together a complete list in the order she reveals them. What does the list suggest about her experience with loss?
2. Bishop varies the repeated lines that end with the word *disaster*. Look only at those lines: what do they suggest about the story being unfolded in the poem?
3. What effect does the parenthetical comment in the poem's last line create? Would the poem be different if it were omitted?

4. Compare this poem to other villanelles in this book, such as Dylan Thomas's "Do not go gentle into that good night" (page 659) and Wendy Cope's "Lonely Hearts" (page 539). In what ways does Bishop bend the rules of the form?

The best lyric poetry has the strange ability to seem both intensely personal and almost universal in its significance. In "Ode to a Nightingale" the English Romantic John Keats gave sublime expression to the complex and contradictory impulses of human desire and imagination. Vacillating between joy and melancholy, hope and despair, Keats recognized how such warring emotions lie at the heart of human experience. Originating in classical Greek and Latin literature, the **ode** is a special, exalted type of lyric poem, usually addressing a single subject in a stately and formal style. Odes have no set form; each one establishes its own stanza structure, sometimes very complex. The object is to create powerfully rhapsodic music. Keats's perpetually astonishing "Ode to a Nightingale," written one year before the poet's untimely death at twenty-five, is imbued with a sense of human suffering and mortality amid the enduring beauty of nature and art.

John Keats (1795–1821)

Ode to a Nightingale

1820

I

My heart aches, and a drowsy numbness pains
  My sense, as though of hemlock I had drunk,
Or emptied some dull opiate to the drains
  One minute past, and Lethe-wards had sunk:
'Tis not through envy of thy happy lot,   5
  But being too happy in thine happiness,—
    That thou, light-winged Dryad of the trees
      In some melodious plot
  Of beechen green, and shadows numberless,
    Singest of summer in full-throated ease.   10

II

O, for a draught of vintage! that hath been
  Cool'd a long age in the deep-delved earth,
Tasting of Flora and the country green,
  Dance, and Provençal song, and sunburnt mirth!
O for a beaker full of the warm South,   15
  Full of the true, the blushful Hippocrene,
    With beaded bubbles winking at the brim,
      And purple-stained mouth;
That I might drink, and leave the world unseen,
    And with thee fade away into the forest dim: 20

III

Fade far away, dissolve, and quite forget
  What thou among the leaves hast never known,
The weariness, the fever, and the fret
  Here, where men sit and hear each other groan;
Where palsy shakes a few, sad, last gray hairs,   25
  Where youth grows pale, and specter-thin, and dies;
    Where but to think is to be full of sorrow
      And leaden-eyed despairs,
  Where Beauty cannot keep her lustrous eyes,
    Or new Love pine at them beyond to-morrow.   30

IV

Away! away! for I will fly to thee,
  Not charioted by Bacchus and his pards,
But on the viewless wings of Poesy,
  Though the dull brain perplexes and retards:
Already with thee! tender is the night,   35
  And haply the Queen-Moon is on her throne,
    Cluster'd around by all her starry Fays;
      But here there is no light,
  Save what from heaven is with the breezes blown
    Through verdurous glooms and winding mossy ways.   40

V

I cannot see what flowers are at my feet,
  Nor what soft incense hangs upon the boughs,
But, in embalmed darkness, guess each sweet
  Wherewith the seasonable month endows
The grass, the thicket, and the fruit-tree wild;   45
  White hawthorn, and the pastoral eglantine;
    Fast fading violets cover'd up in leaves;
      And mid-May's eldest child,
  The coming musk-rose, full of dewy wine,
    The murmurous haunt of flies on summer eves.   50

VI

Darkling I listen; and, for many a time
  I have been half in love with easeful Death,
Call'd him soft names in many a mused rhyme,
  To take into the air my quiet breath;
Now more than ever seems it rich to die,   55
  To cease upon the midnight with no pain,
    While thou art pouring forth thy soul abroad
      In such an ecstasy!
  Still wouldst thou sing, and I have ears in vain—
    To thy high requiem become a sod.   60

VII

Thou wast not born for death, immortal Bird!
   No hungry generations tread thee down;
The voice I hear this passing night was heard
   In ancient days by emperor and clown:
Perhaps the self-same song that found a path   65
     Through the sad heart of Ruth, when, sick for home,
        She stood in tears amid the alien corn;
          The same that oft-times hath
   Charm'd magic casements, opening on the foam
     Of perilous seas, in faery lands forlorn.   70

VIII

Forlorn! the very word is like a bell
   To toll me back from thee to my sole self!
Adieu! the fancy cannot cheat so well
   As she is fam'd to do, deceiving elf.
Adieu! adieu! thy plaintive anthem fades   75
     Past the near meadows, over the still stream,
        Up the hill-side; and now 'tis buried deep
          In the next valley-glades:
   Was it a vision, or a waking dream?
     Fled is that music:—Do I wake or sleep?   80

ODE TO A NIGHTINGALE. 4 *Lethe-wards*: towards Lethe, the river of oblivion in Hades, the classical Underworld; dead souls drank the waters of Lethe to forget their past lives. 7 *Dryad*: wood nymph. 13 *Flora*: the classical goddess of flowers and spring. 16 *Hippocrene*: the sacred fountain of the Muses, whose waters have the power to inspire poetry. 32 *pards*: leopards, the animals who pull the chariot of Bacchus, the god of wine. 66-67 *Ruth...alien corn*: In the Old Testament, Ruth is a Moabite widow who gleans grain from the Israelite Boaz's field.

Questions

1. In the opening stanza to what things does the speaker compare the effect of the nightingale's song?
2. Why does the speaker desire wine in stanza two?
3. What are the worldly troubles and sorrows the speaker wishes to escape? (Cite specific lines.)
4. Why can't the speaker (in stanza V) see the flowers at his feet or in the branches above him?
5. What specifically is the attraction the speaker feels for death? (Cite specific lines.)
6. How could the nightingale singing in the poem be the same voice heard in the ancient world? What point is Keats making about the permanence of nature?
7. By the time Keats wrote this poem, he knew he would die young from tuberculosis. Do you see any evidence of this knowledge in the text of the poem?
8. What is your favorite line or lines from the ode? The choice is, of course, personal, but give your reasons, if possible, for your choice.

Excellent poetry might be easier to recognize if each poet had a fixed position on the slopes of Mount Parnassus, but, from one century to the next, the reputations of some poets have taken humiliating slides, or made impressive clambers. We decide for ourselves which poems to call excellent, but readers of the future may reverse our opinions. Most of us no longer would share this popular view of Walt Whitman held by one of his contemporaries:

> Walt Whitman (1819–1892), by some regarded as a great poet; by others, as no poet at all. Most of his so-called poems are mere catalogues of things, without meter or rime, but in a few more regular poems and in lines here and there he is grandly poetical, as in "O Captain! My Captain!"[1]

Walt Whitman (1819–1892)

O Captain! My Captain!   1865

O Captain! my Captain! our fearful trip is done,
The ship has weather'd every rack, the prize we sought is won,
The port is near, the bells I hear, the people all exulting,
While follow eyes the steady keel, the vessel grim and daring;
   But O heart! heart! heart!   5
     O the bleeding drops of red,
       Where on the deck my Captain lies,
        Fallen cold and dead.

O Captain! my Captain! rise up and hear the bells;
Rise up—for you the flag is flung—for you the bugle trills,   10
For you bouquets and ribbon'd wreaths—for you the shores a-crowding,
For you they call, the swaying mass, their eager faces turning;
   Here Captain! dear father!
     This arm beneath your head!
       It is some dream that on the deck,   15
        You've fallen cold and dead.

My Captain does not answer, his lips are pale and still,
My father does not feel my arm, he has no pulse nor will,
The ship is anchor'd safe and sound, its voyage closed and done,
From fearful trip the victor ship comes in with object won;   20
   Exult O shores, and ring O bells!
     But I with mournful tread,
       Walk the deck my Captain lies,
        Fallen cold and dead.

O CAPTAIN! MY CAPTAIN! Written soon after the death of Abraham Lincoln, this was, in Whitman's life-time, by far the most popular of his poems.

Questions

1. Compare this with other Whitman poems. In what ways is "O Captain! My Captain!" uncharacteristic of his works? Do you agree with J. Willis Westlake that this is one of the few occasions on which Whitman is "grandly poetical"?

2. Comment on the appropriateness of the poem's rhythms to its subject.

3. Do you find any evidence in this poem that an excellent poet wrote it?

[1]J. Willis Westlake, A. M., *Common-school Literature, English and American, with Several Hundred Extracts to be Memorized* (Philadelphia, 1898).

In a sense, all readers of poetry are constantly reexamining the judgments of the past by choosing those poems they care to go on reading. In the end, we have to admit that the critical principles set forth in this chapter are all very well for admiring excellent poetry we already know, but they cannot be carried like a yardstick in the hand, to go out looking for it. As Ezra Pound said in his *ABC of Reading*, "A classic is classic not because it conforms to certain structural rules, or fits certain definitions (of which its author had quite probably never heard). It is classic because of a certain eternal and irrepressible freshness."

The best poems, like "Sailing to Byzantium," may offer a kind of religious experience. At the beginning of the twenty-first century, some of us rarely set foot outside an artificial environment. Whizzing down four-lane superhighways, we observe lakes and trees in the distance. In a way our cities are to us as anthills are to ants: no less than anthills, they are "natural" structures. But the "unnatural" world of school or business is, as Wordsworth says, too much with us. Locked in the shells of our ambitions, our self-esteem, we forget our kinship to earth and sea. We fabricate self-justifications. Sometimes it takes a poet to remind us why—and for whom—poems are written.

Dylan Thomas (1914–1953)

In My Craft or Sullen Art   1946

In my craft or sullen art
Exercised in the still night
When only the moon rages
And the lovers lie abed
With all their griefs in their arms,   5
I labor by singing light
Not for ambition or bread
Or the strut and trade of charms
On the ivory stages
But for the common wages   10
Of their most secret heart.

Not for the proud man apart
From the raging moon I write
On these spindrift pages
Nor for the towering dead   15
With their nightingales and psalms
But for the lovers, their arms
Round the griefs of the ages,
Who pay no praise or wages
Nor heed my craft or art.   20

IN MY CRAFT OR SULLEN ART. 14 *spindrift*: spray blown from a rough sea or surf.

Questions

1. What plays on words do you find in *craft* (line 1), *trade* (line 8), and *charms* (line 8)?
2. Why does the speaker describe his art as *sullen*?
3. How would you interpret lines 15–16?
4. In light of the assumption made in the last two lines, why do you think the speaker goes on writing?

A great poem shocks us into another order of perception. It points beyond language to something still more essential. It ushers us into an experience so moving and true that we feel (to quote King Lear) "cut to the brain." In bad or indifferent poetry, words are all there is.

Exercise: Reevaluating Popular Classics

In this exercise you will read two of the most popular American poems of the nineteenth century: Emma Lazarus's "The New Colossus" and Edgar Allan Poe's "Annabel Lee." In their time, not only were these poems considered classics by serious critics, but thousands of ordinary readers knew them by heart. Recently, however, they have fallen out of critical favor. You will also read Paul Laurence Dunbar's "We Wear the Mask," which, while never as wildly popular as the others, enjoyed, along with its author, a higher esteem a century ago than it does today.

Your assignment is to read these poems carefully and make your own personal, tentative evaluation of each poem's merit. Here are some questions you might ask yourself as you consider them.

- Do these poems engage your sympathies? Do they stir you and touch your feelings?
- What, if anything, might make them memorable? Do they have any vivid images? Any metaphors, understatement, overstatement, or other figures of speech? Do these poems appeal to the ear?
- Do the poems exhibit any wild incompetence? Do you find any forced rimes, inappropriate words, or other unintentionally comic features? Can the poems be accused of bathos or sentimentality, or do you trust the poet to report honest feelings?
- How well does the poet seem in control of language? Does the poet's language reflect in any detail the physical world we know?
- Do these poems seem entirely drawn from other poetry of the past, or do you have a sense that the poet is thinking and feeling on her (or his) own? Does the poet show any evidence of having read other poets' poetry?
- What is the poet trying to do in each poem? How successful, in your opinion, is the attempt?

Try setting these poems next to similar poems you know and admire. (You might try comparing Emma Lazarus's "The New Colossus" to Percy Bysshe Shelley's "Ozymandias," found in this chapter; both are sonnets, and their subjects have interesting similarities and contrasts. Or read Paul Laurence Dunbar's "We Wear the Mask" in connection with Claude McKay's "America" (page 722). Or compare Edgar Allan Poe's "Annabel Lee" with A. E. Housman's "To an Athlete Dying Young" (page 849).

Are these poems sufficiently rich and interesting to repay more than one reading? Do you think that these poems still deserve to be considered classics? Or do they no longer speak powerfully to a contemporary audience?

Paul Laurence Dunbar (1872–1906)

We Wear the Mask   1895

We wear the mask that grins and lies,
It hides our cheeks and shades our eyes—
This debt we pay to human guile;
With torn and bleeding hearts we smile
And mouth with myriad subtleties,   5

Why should the world be over-wise,
In counting all our tears and sighs?

Nay, let them only see us, while
   We wear the mask.

We smile, but, oh great Christ, our cries   10
To Thee from tortured souls arise.
We sing, but oh the clay is vile
Beneath our feet, and long the mile,
But let the world dream otherwise,
   We wear the mask!   15

Emma Lazarus (1849–1887)

The New Colossus   1883

Not like the brazen giant of Greek fame,
With conquering limbs astride from land to land;
Here at our sea-washed, sunset gates shall stand
A mighty woman with a torch, whose flame
Is the imprisoned lightning, and her name   5
Mother of Exiles. From her beacon-hand
Glows world-wide welcome; her mild eyes command
The air-bridged harbor that twin cities frame.
"Keep, ancient lands, your storied pomp!" cries she
With silent lips. "Give me your tired, your poor,   10
Your huddled masses yearning to breathe free,
The wretched refuse of your teeming shore.
Send these, the homeless, tempest-tost to me,
I lift my lamp beside the golden door!"

THE NEW COLOSSUS. In 1883, a committee was formed to raise funds to build a pedestal for what would be the largest statue in the world, "Liberty Enlightening the World" by Fréderic-Auguste Bartholdi, which was a gift from the French people to celebrate America's centennial. American authors were asked to donate manuscripts for a fund-raising auction. The young poet Emma Lazarus sent in this sonnet composed for the occasion. When President Grover Cleveland unveiled the Statue of Liberty in October 1886, Lazarus's sonnet was read at the ceremony. In 1903, the poem was carved on the statue's pedestal. The reference in the opening line to "the brazen giant of Greek fame" is to the famous Colossus of Rhodes, a huge bronze statue that once stood in the harbor on the Aegean island of Rhodes. Built to commemorate a military victory, it was one of the so-called Seven Wonders of the World.

Edgar Allan Poe (1809–1849)

Annabel Lee   1849

It was many and many a year ago,
   In a kingdom by the sea,
That a maiden there lived whom you may know
   By the name of Annabel Lee;
And this maiden she lived with no other thought   5
   Than to love and be loved by me.

I was a child and *she* was a child,
   In this kingdom by the sea,
But we loved with a love that was more than love—
   I and my Annabel Lee—
With a love that the wingéd seraphs of Heaven
   Coveted her and me.   10

And this was the reason that, long ago,
   In this kingdom by the sea,
A wind blew out of a cloud, chilling
   My beautiful Annabel Lee;   15
So that her highborn kinsmen came
   And bore her away from me,
To shut her up in a sepulchre
   In this kingdom by the sea.   20

The angels, not half so happy in Heaven,
   Went envying her and me:—
Yes!—that was the reason (as all men know,
   In this kingdom by the sea)
That the wind came out of the cloud by night,   25
   Chilling and killing my Annabel Lee.

But our love it was stronger by far than the love
   Of those who were older than we—
   Of many far wiser than we—
And neither the angels in Heaven above,   30
   Nor the demons down under the sea,
Can ever dissever my soul from the soul
   Of the beautiful Annabel Lee:—

For the moon never beams, without bringing me dreams
   Of the beautiful Annabel Lee;   35
And the stars never rise, but I feel the bright eyes
   Of the beautiful Annabel Lee:
And so, all the night-tide, I lie down by the side
Of my darling—my darling—my life and my bride,
   In the sepulchre there by the sea—   40
   In her tomb by the sounding sea.

■ WRITING *effectively*

Edgar Allan Poe on Writing

A Long Poem Does Not Exist
1848

I hold that a long poem does not exist. I maintain that the phrase, "a long poem," is simply a flat contradiction in terms.

I need scarcely observe that a poem deserves its title only inasmuch as it excites, by elevating the soul. The value of the poem is in the ratio of this elevating excitement. But all excitements are, through a psychal necessity, transient. That degree of excitement which would entitle a poem to be so called at all, cannot be sustained throughout a composition of any great length. After the lapse of half an hour, at the very utmost, it flags—fails—a revulsion ensues—and then the poem is, in effect, and in fact, no longer such.

Edgar Allan Poe

From "The Poetic Principle"

THINKING ABOUT EVALUATING A POEM

Evaluating a poem begins with personal taste. Though your first impressions may become part of your ultimate judgment, they should usually end up being no more than a departure point. The question isn't merely whether a work pleases or moves you, but how well it manages the literary tasks it sets out to perform. A good critic is willing both to admire a strong poem that he or she doesn't like and to admit that a personal favorite might not really stand up to close scrutiny. Whatever your final opinion, the goal is to nourish your personal response with careful critical examination so that your evaluation will grow into an informed judgment.

- **In evaluating a poem, first try to understand your own subjective response.** Admit to yourself whether the poem delights, moves, bores, or annoys you.
- **Try to determine what the poem seems designed to make you think and feel.** If a poem is written within a genre, then you need to weigh the work against the generic expectations it sets up.
- **Consider how well it fulfills these expectations.** An epigram usually seeks to be witty and concise. If it proves tiresome and verbose, it can be fairly said to fail.
- **Focus on specific elements in the poem.** How well do its language, imagery, symbols, and figures of speech communicate its meanings? Are the metaphors or similes effective? Is the imagery fresh and precise? Is the language vague or verbose? Does the poem ever fall into clichés or platitudes?

CHECKLIST: Writing an Evaluation

☐ What is your subjective response to the poem?

☐ Highlight or underline moments that call up a strong reaction. Why do you think those passages elicit such a response?

☐ What task does the poem set for itself?

☐ Does it belong to some identifiable form or genre?

☐ If so, what are the expectations for that genre? How well does the poem fulfill the expectations it creates?

☐ How do its specific elements work to communicate meaning (e.g., language, imagery, symbols, figures of speech, rhythm, sound, rime)?

☐ Reread the poem. Does it seem better or worse than it did initially?

WRITING ASSIGNMENT ON EVALUATING A POEM

Look at a short poem to which you have a strong initial response—either positive or negative. Write an essay in which you begin by stating your response, then work through the steps outlined above. Does the poem succeed in fulfilling the task it sets for itself? Back up your opinion with specifics. Finally, state whether the process has changed your impression of the poem. Why or why not?

MORE TOPICS FOR WRITING

1. Choose a short poem that you admire from anywhere in this book. Write a brief essay defending the poem's excellence. Be specific in describing its particular strengths.

2. Write a brief evaluation of "The New Colossus" by Emma Lazarus, "We Wear the Mask" by Paul Laurence Dunbar, or "Annabel Lee" by Edgar Allan Poe. In what ways is the poem successful? In what ways is it unsuccessful?

3. Find a poem you admire in this book and wreck it. First, type the poem as is into a computer. Then go through it, substituting clichés and overly vague language for moments that are vivid and precise. Replace understatement with overstatement, restraint with sentimentality. Keep making changes until you've turned a perfectly good poem into a train wreck. Now write a brief explanation of your choices.

▶ TERMS FOR *review*

Bathos ▶ An unintentional lapse from the sublime to the ridiculous or trivial. An attempt to capture the grand and profound that comes off as inflated and fatuous.

Convention ▶ Any established feature or technique in literature that is commonly understood by both authors and readers. A convention is something generally agreed on to be appropriate for customary uses, such as the sonnet form for a love poem or the opening "Once upon a time" for a fairy tale.

Conceit ▶ A far-flung and often extended metaphor comparing dissimilar things. John Donne, for example, casts his doctors as cosmographers and his body as their map.

Poetic inversion ▶ The inversion of normal word order, usually done for purposes of meter and/or rime.

Sentimentality ▶ A term negatively applied to a literary work that tries to convey great feeling but fails to give the reader sufficient grounds for sharing it. Sentimentality involves an emotion that is excessive in relation to its cause, as opposed to *sentiment*, which connotes one proper to its cause.

28 WHAT IS POETRY?

> Poetry is a way of taking life by the throat.
>
> —ROBERT FROST

Archibald MacLeish (1892–1982)

Ars Poetica   1926

A poem should be palpable and mute
As a globed fruit,

Dumb
As old medallions to the thumb,

Silent as the sleeve-worn stone   5
Of casement ledges where the moss has grown—

A poem should be wordless
As the flight of birds.

         *   *

A poem should be motionless in time
As the moon climbs,   10

Leaving, as the moon releases
Twig by twig the night-entangled trees,

Leaving, as the moon behind the winter leaves,
Memory by memory the mind—

A poem should be motionless in time   15
As the moon climbs.

         *   *

A poem should be equal to:
Not true.

For all the history of grief
An empty doorway and a maple leaf.   20

For love
The leaning grasses and two lights above the sea—

A poem should not mean
But be.

The title of Archibald MacLeish's provocative poem is Latin for "the poetic art" or "the art of poetry," and it is not unusual for poets to speculate in verse about their art. MacLeish, in fact, borrowed his title from the Roman poet Horace, who wrote a brilliant verse epistle on the subject during the reign of Caesar Augustus. In the two thousand years since then, there has been no shortage of opinions from fellow poets. There is something alluring and mysterious about poetry, even to its practitioners.

SOME DEFINITIONS OF POETRY

What, then, is poetry? By now, perhaps, you have formed your own idea, whether or not you can define it. Robert Frost made a try at a definition: "A poem is an idea caught in the act of dawning." Just in case further efforts at definition may be useful, here are a few memorable ones (including, for a second look, some given earlier):

things that are true expressed in words that are beautiful.
> —*Dante*

the art of uniting pleasure with truth by calling imagination to the
help of reason.
> —*Samuel Johnson*

the best words in the best order.
> —*Samuel Taylor Coleridge*

the spontaneous overflow of powerful feelings.
> —*William Wordsworth*

emotion put into measure.
> —*Thomas Hardy*

If I feel physically as if the top of my head were taken off, I know *that* is
poetry.
> —*Emily Dickinson*

speech framed . . . to be heard for its own sake and interest even over
and above its interest of meaning.
> —*Gerard Manley Hopkins*

a way of remembering what it would impoverish us to forget.
> —*Robert Frost*

a revelation in words by means of the words.
> —*Wallace Stevens*

Poetry is prose bewitched.
> —*Mina Loy*

not the assertion that something is true, but the making of that truth
more fully real to us.
> —*T. S. Eliot*

the clear expression of mixed feelings.
> —*W. H. Auden*

an angel with a gun in its hand . . .
—*José García Villa*

the language in which man explores his own amazement.
—*Christopher Fry*

hundreds of things coming together at the right moment.
—*Elizabeth Bishop*

Poetry is a sound art.
—*Joy Harjo*

Poems come out of wonder, not out of knowing.
—*Lucille Clifton*

Poetry is always the cat concert under the window of the room in
which the official version of reality is being written.
—*Charles Simic*

A poem differs from most prose in several ways. For one, both writer and reader tend to regard it differently. The poet's attitude is something like this: I offer this piece of writing to be read not as prose but as a poem—that is, more perceptively, thoughtfully, and creatively, with more attention to sounds and connotations. This is a great deal to expect, but in return, the reader, too, has a right to certain expectations.

Approaching the poem in the anticipation of out-of-the-ordinary knowledge and pleasure, the reader assumes that the poem may use certain enjoyable devices not available to prose: rime, alliteration, meter, and rhythms—definite, various, or emphatic. (The poet may not *always* decide to use these things.) The reader expects the poet to make greater use, perhaps, of resources of meaning such as figurative language, allusion, symbol, and imagery. As readers of prose, we might seek no more than meaning: no more than what could be paraphrased without serious loss. Meeting any figurative language or graceful turns of word order, we think them pleasant extras. But in poetry all these "extras" matter as much as the paraphrasable content, if not more. For, when we finish reading a good poem, we cannot explain precisely to ourselves what we have experienced—without repeating, word for word, the language of the poem itself. Archibald MacLeish makes this point memorably in "Ars Poetica":

A poem should not mean
But be.

"Poetry is to prose as dancing is to walking," remarked Paul Valéry. It is doubtful, however, that anyone can draw an immovable boundary between poetry and prose. Throughout this book, we have been working on the assumption that the patient and conscious explication of poems will sharpen unconscious perceptions. We can only hope that it will; the final test lies in whether you care to go on by yourself, reading other poems, finding in them pleasure and enlightenment. Pedagogy must have a stop; so too must the viewing of poems as if their elements fell into chapters. For the total experience of reading a poem surpasses the mind's categories. The wind in the grass, says a proverb, cannot be taken into the house.

29 TWO CRITICAL CASEBOOKS
Emily Dickinson and Langston Hughes

Emily Dickinson
(Amherst College Archives and
Special Collections)

Langston Hughes

EMILY DICKINSON

Emily Dickinson (1830–1886) spent virtually all her life in her family home in Amherst, Massachusetts. Her father, Edward Dickinson, was a prominent lawyer who ranked as Amherst's leading citizen. (He even served a term in the U.S. Congress.) Dickinson attended one year of college at Mount Holyoke Female Seminary in South Hadley. She proved to be a good student, but, suffering from homesickness and poor health, she did not return for the second year. This brief period of study and a few trips to Boston, Philadelphia, and Washington, D.C., were the only occasions she left home in her fifty-five-year life. As the years passed, Dickinson became more reclusive. She stopped attending church (and refused to endorse the orthodox Congregationalist creed). She also spent increasing time alone in her room—often writing poems. Dickinson never married, but she had a significant romantic relationship with at least one unidentified man. Although scholars have suggested several likely candidates, the historical object of Dickinson's affections will likely never be known. What survives unmistakably, however, is the intensely passionate poetry written out of these private circumstances. By the end of her life, Dickinson had become a locally famous recluse; she rarely left home. She would greet visitors from her own upstairs room, clearly heard but never seen. In 1886 she was buried, according to her own instructions, within sight of the family home. Although Dickinson composed 1,789 known poems, only a handful were published in her lifetime. She often, however, sent copies of poems to friends in letters, but only after her death would the full extent of her writings become known when a cache of manuscripts was discovered in a trunk in the homestead attic—handwritten little booklets of poems sewn together by the poet with needle and thread. From 1890 until the mid-twentieth century, nine posthumous collections of her poems were published by friends and relatives, some of whom rewrote her work and changed her idiosyncratic punctuation to make it more conventional. Thomas H. Johnson's three-volume edition of the Poems *(1955) established a more accurate text. In relatively few and simple forms clearly indebted to the hymns she heard in church, Dickinson succeeded in being a true visionary and a poet of colossal originality.*

POEMS

Success is counted sweetest

(1859) Published 1878

Success is counted sweetest
By those who ne'er succeed.
To comprehend a nectar
Requires sorest need.

Not one of all the purple Host°   *an army*   5
Who took the Flag today
Can tell the definition
So clear of Victory

As he defeated – dying –
On whose forbidden ear   10
The distant strains of triumph
Burst agonized and clear!

I taste a liquor never brewed

Published 1861

I taste a liquor never brewed –
From Tankards scooped in Pearl –
Not all the Vats upon the Rhine
Yield such an Alcohol!

Inebriate of Air – am I –   5
And Debauchee of Dew –
Reeling – thro endless summer days –
From inns of Molten Blue –

When "Landlords" turn the drunken Bee
Out of the Foxglove's door –   10
When Butterflies – renounce their "drams" –
I shall but drink the more!

Till Seraphs swing their snowy Hats –
And Saints – to windows run –
To see the little Tippler   15
Leaning against the – Sun –

Wild Nights – Wild Nights!

(about 1861)

Wild Nights – Wild Nights!
Were I with thee
Wild Nights should be
Our luxury!

Futile – the Winds –   5
To a Heart in port –
Done with the Compass –
Done with the Chart!

Rowing in Eden –
Ah, the Sea!
Might I but moor – Tonight –   10
In Thee!

I felt a Funeral, in my Brain

(about 1861)

I felt a Funeral, in my Brain,
And Mourners to and fro
Kept treading – treading – till it seemed
That Sense was breaking through –

And when they all were seated,   5
A Service, like a Drum –
Kept beating – beating – till I thought
My Mind was going numb –

And then I heard them lift a Box
And creak across my Soul   10

With those same Boots of Lead, again,
Then Space – began to toll,

As all the Heavens were a Bell,
And Being, but an Ear,
And I, and Silence, some strange Race   15
Wrecked, solitary, here –

And Then a Plank in Reason, broke,
And I dropped down, and down –
And hit a World, at every plunge,
And Finished knowing – then –   20

I'm Nobody! Who are you?   (about 1861)

I'm Nobody! Who are you?
Are you – Nobody – Too?
Then there's a pair of us!
Don't tell! they'd advertise – you know!

How dreary – to be – Somebody!   5
How public – like a Frog –
To tell one's name – the livelong June –
To an admiring Bog!

The Soul selects her own Society   (about 1862)

The Soul selects her own Society –
Then – shuts the Door –
To her divine Majority –
Present no more –

Unmoved – she notes the Chariots – pausing –   5
At her low Gate –
Unmoved – an Emperor be kneeling
Upon her Mat –

I've known her – from an ample nation –
Choose One –   10
Then – close the Valves of her attention –
Like Stone –

After great pain, a formal feeling comes   (about 1862)

After great pain, a formal feeling comes –
The Nerves sit ceremonious, like Tombs –
The stiff Heart questions was it He, that bore,
And Yesterday, or Centuries before?

The Feet, mechanical, go round –   5
Of Ground, or Air, or Ought –
A Wooden way

Regardless grown,
A Quartz contentment, like a stone –

This is the Hour of Lead –   10
Remembered, if outlived,
As Freezing persons, recollect the Snow –
First – Chill – then Stupor – then the letting go –

Much Madness is divinest Sense   (about 1862)

Much Madness is divinest Sense –
To a discerning Eye –
Much Sense – the starkest Madness –
'Tis the Majority
In this, as All, prevail –   5
Assent – and you are sane –
Demur – you're straightway dangerous –
And handled with a Chain –

This is my letter to the World   (about 1862)

This is my letter to the World
That never wrote to Me –
The simple News that Nature told –
With tender Majesty

Her Message is committed   5
To Hands I cannot see –
For love of Her – Sweet – countrymen –
Judge tenderly – of Me

I heard a Fly buzz – when I died   (about 1862)

I heard a Fly buzz – when I died –
The Stillness in the Room
Was like the Stillness in the Air –
Between the Heaves of Storm –

The Eyes around – had wrung them dry –   5
And Breaths were gathering firm
For that last Onset – when the King
Be witnessed – in the Room –

I willed my Keepsakes – Signed away
What portion of me be   10
Assignable – and then it was
There interposed a Fly –

With Blue – uncertain stumbling Buzz –
Between the light – and me –
And then the Windows failed – and then   15
I could not see to see –

Because I could not stop for Death

Because I could not stop for Death –
He kindly stopped for me –
The Carriage held but just Ourselves –
And Immortality.

We slowly drove – He knew no haste   5
And I had put away
My labor and my leisure too,
For His Civility –

We passed the School, where Children strove
At Recess – in the Ring –   10
We passed the Fields of Gazing Grain –
We passed the Setting Sun –

Or rather – He passed Us –
The Dews drew quivering and chill –
For only Gossamer, my Gown –   15
My Tippet° – only Tulle –   *cape*

We paused before a House that seemed
A Swelling of the Ground –
The Roof was scarcely visible –
The Cornice – in the Ground –   20

Since then – 'tis Centuries – and yet
Feels shorter than the Day
I first surmised the Horses' Heads
Were toward Eternity –

Tell all the Truth but tell it slant

Tell all the Truth but tell it slant –
Success in Circuit lies
Too bright for our infirm Delight
The Truth's superb surprise
As Lightning to the Children eased   5
With explanation kind
The Truth must dazzle gradually
Or every man be blind –

Compare

Other poems by Emily Dickinson that are found in this book:

A Dying Tiger – moaned for Drink (page 750)
I like to see it lap the Miles (page 504)
The Lightning is a yellow Fork (page 685)
My Life had stood – a Loaded Gun (page 581)
A Route of Evanescence (page 565)

Emily Dickinson's room in Amherst, Massachusetts.

EMILY DICKINSON ON EMILY DICKINSON

Recognizing Poetry   (1870)

If I read a book [and] it makes my whole body so cold no fire ever can warm me I know *that* is poetry. If I feel physically as if the top of my head were taken off, I know *that* is poetry. These are the only ways I know it. Is there any other way.

How do most people live without any thoughts. There are many people in the world (you must have noticed them in the street). How do they live. How do they get strength to put on their clothes in the morning.

When I lost the use of my Eyes it was a comfort to think there were so few real *books* that I could easily find some one to read me all of them.

Truth is such a *rare* thing it is delightful to tell it.

I find ecstasy in living – the mere sense of living is joy enough.

From a conversation with Thomas Wentworth Higginson

Self-Description   (25 April 1862)

Mr. Higginson,

Your kindness claimed earlier gratitude – but I was ill – and write today, from my pillow.

Thank you for the surgery – it was not so painful as I supposed. I bring you others – as you ask – though they might not differ –

While my thought is undressed – I can make the distinction, but when I put them in the Gown – they look alike, and numb.

You asked how old I was? I made no verse – but one or two – until this winter – Sir –

I had a terror – since September – I could tell to none – and so I sing, as the Boy does by the Burying Ground – because I am afraid – You inquire my Books – For Poets – I have Keats – and Mr and Mrs Browning. For Prose – Mr Ruskin – Sir Thomas Browne – and the Revelations.° I went to school – but in your manner of the phrase – had no education. When a little Girl, I had a friend, who taught me Immortality – but venturing too near, himself – he never returned – Soon after, my Tutor, died – and for several years, my Lexicon – was my only companion – Then I found one more – but he was not contented I be his scholar – so he left the Land.

You ask of my Companions[.] Hills – Sir – and the Sundown – and a Dog – large as myself, that my Father bought me – They are better than Beings – because they know – but do not tell – and the noise in the Pool, at Noon – excels my Piano. I have a Brother and Sister – My Mother does not care for thought – and Father, too busy with his Briefs° – to notice what we do – He buys me many Books – but begs me not to read them – because he fears they joggle the Mind. They are religious – except me – and address an Eclipse, every morning – whom they call their "Father." But I fear my story fatigues you – I would like to learn – Could you tell me how to grow – or is it unconveyed – like Melody – or Witchcraft?

You speak of Mr Whitman – I never read his Book° – but was told that he was disgraceful –

I read Miss Prescott's "Circumstance,"° but it followed me, in the Dark – so I avoided her –

Two Editors of Journals came to my Father's House, this winter – and asked me for my Mind – and when I asked them "Why," they said I was penurious – and they, would use it for the World –

I could not weigh myself – Myself –

My size felt small – to me – I read your Chapters in the Atlantic – and experienced honor for you – I was sure you would not reject a confiding question –

Is this – Sir – what you asked me to tell you?

Your friend,

E – Dickinson

From *The Letters of Emily Dickinson*

SELF-DESCRIPTION. Emily Dickinson's letter was written to Thomas Wentworth Higginson, a noted writer. Dickinson had read his article of advice to young writers in the *Atlantic Monthly*. She sent him four poems and a letter asking if her verse was "alive." When he responded with comments and suggestions (the "surgery" Dickinson mentions in the second paragraph), she wrote him this letter about herself.

Mr Ruskin . . . Revelations: in listing her favorite prose authors Dickinson chose John Ruskin (1819–1900), an English art critic and essayist; Sir Thomas Browne (1605–1682), a doctor and philosopher with a magnificent prose style; and the final book of the New Testament. *Briefs*: legal papers (her father was a lawyer). *Whitman . . . book*: *Leaves of Grass* (1855) by Walt Whitman was considered an improper book for women at this time because of the volume's sexual candor. *Miss Prescott's "Circumstance"*: a story, also published in the *Atlantic Monthly*, that was full of violence.

CRITICS ON EMILY DICKINSON

Thomas H. Johnson (1902–1985)

The Discovery of Emily Dickinson's Manuscripts 1955

Shortly after Emily Dickinson's death on May fifteenth, 1886, her sister Lavinia discovered a locked box in which Emily had placed her poems. Lavinia's amazement seems to have been genuine. Though the sisters had lived intimately together under the same roof all their lives, and though Lavinia had always been aware that her sister wrote poems, she had not the faintest concept of the great number of them. The story of Lavinia's willingness to spare them because she found no instructions specifying that they be destroyed, and her search for an editor and a publisher to give them to the world has already been told in some detail.

Lavinia first consulted the two people most interested in Emily's poetry, her sister-in-law Susan Dickinson, and Mrs. Todd. David Peck Todd, a graduate of Amherst College in 1875, returned to Amherst with his young bride in 1881 as director of the college observatory and soon became professor of Astronomy and Navigation. These were the months shortly before Mrs. Edward Dickinson's death, when neighbors were especially thoughtful. Mrs. Todd endeared herself to Emily and Lavinia by small but understanding attentions, in return for which Emily sent Mrs. Todd copies of her poems. At first approach neither Susan Dickinson nor Mrs. Todd felt qualified for the editorial task which they both were hesitant to undertake. Mrs. Todd says of Lavinia's discovery: "She showed me the manuscripts and there were over sixty little 'volumes,' each composed of four or five sheets of note paper tied together with twine. In this box she discovered eight or nine hundred poems tied up in this way."

• • •

As the story can be reconstructed, at some time during the year 1858 Emily Dickinson began assembling her poems into packets. Always in ink, they are gatherings of four, five, or six sheets of letter paper usually folded once but sometimes single. They are loosely held together by thread looped through them at the spine at two points equidistant from the top and bottom. When opened up they may be read like a small book, a fact that explains why Emily's sister Lavinia, when she discovered them after Emily's death, referred to them as "volumes." All of the packet poems are either fair copies or semifinal drafts, and they constitute two-thirds of the entire body of her poetry.

For the most part the poems in a given packet seem to have been written and assembled as a unit. Since rough drafts of packet poems are almost totally lacking, one concludes that they were systematically discarded. If the poems were in fact composed at the time the copies were made, as the evidence now seems to point, one concludes that nearly two-thirds of her poems were created in the brief span of eight years, centering on her early thirties. Her interest in the packet method of assembling the verses thus coincides with the years of fullest productivity. In 1858 she gathered some fifty poems into packets. There are nearly one hundred so transcribed in 1859, some sixty-five in 1860, and in 1861 more than eighty. By 1862 the creative drive must have been almost frightening; during that year she transcribed into packets no fewer than three hundred and sixty-six poems, the greater part of them complete and final texts.

Whether this incredible number was in fact composed in that year or represents a transcription of earlier worksheet drafts can never be established by direct evidence. But the pattern established during the preceding four years reveals a gathering momentum, and the quality of tenseness and prosodic skill uniformly present in the poems of 1861–1862 bears scant likeness to the conventionality of theme and treatment in the poems of 1858–1859. Excepting a half dozen occasional verses written in the early fifties, there is not a single scrap of poetry that can be dated earlier than 1858.

From The Poems of Emily Dickinson

Richard Wilbur (b. 1921)

The Three Privations of Emily Dickinson   1959

Emily Dickinson never lets us forget for very long that in some respects life gave her short measure; and indeed it is possible to see the greater part of her poetry as an effort to cope with her sense of privation. I think that for her there were three major privations: she was deprived of an orthodox and steady religious faith; she was deprived of love; she was deprived of literary recognition.

At the age of seventeen, after a series of revival meetings at Mount Holyoke Seminary, Emily Dickinson found that she must refuse to become a professing Christian. To some modern minds this may seem to have been a sensible and necessary step; and surely it was a step toward becoming such a poet as she became. But for her, no pleasure in her own integrity could then eradicate the feeling that she had betrayed a deficiency, a want of grace. In her letters to Abiah Root she tells of the enhancing effect of conversion on her fellow-students, and says of herself in a famous passage:

> I am one of the lingering bad ones, and so do I slink away, and pause and ponder, and ponder and pause, and do work without knowing why, not surely for this brief world, and more sure it is not for heaven, and I ask what this message *means* that they ask for so very eagerly: *you* know of this depth and fulness, will you try to tell me about it?

There is humor in that, and stubbornness, and a bit of characteristic lurking pride: but there is also an anguished sense of having separated herself, through some dry incapacity, from spiritual community, from purpose, and from magnitude of life. As a child of evangelical Amherst, she inevitably thought of purposive, heroic life as requiring a vigorous faith. Out of such a thought she later wrote:

> The abdication of Belief
> Makes the Behavior small –
> Better an ignis fatuus
> Than no illume at all –

That hers *was* a species of religious personality goes without saying; but by her refusal of such ideas as original sin, redemption, hell, and election, she made it impossible for herself—as Whicher observed—"to share the religious life of her generation." She became an unsteady congregation of one.

Her second privation, the privation of love, is one with which her poems and her biographies have made us exceedingly familiar, though some biographical facts remain conjectural. She had the good fortune, at least once, to bestow her heart on another; but she seems to have found her life, in great part, a history of loneliness, separation, and bereavement.

As for literary fame, some will deny that Emily Dickinson ever greatly desired it, and certainly there is evidence, mostly from her latter years, to support such a view. She *did* write that "Publication is the auction / Of the mind of man." And she *did* say to Helen Hunt Jackson, "How can you print a piece of your soul?" But earlier, in 1861, she had frankly expressed to Sue Dickinson the hope that "sometime" she might make her kinfolk proud of her. The truth is, I think, that Emily Dickinson knew she was good, and began her career with a normal appetite for recognition. I think that she later came, with some reason, to despair of being understood or properly valued, and so directed against her hopes of fame what was by then a well-developed disposition to renounce. That she wrote a good number of poems about fame supports my view: the subjects to which a poet returns are those which vex him.

What did Emily Dickinson do, as a poet, with her sense of privation? One thing she quite often did was to pose as the laureate and attorney of the empty-handed, and question God about the economy of His creation. Why, she asked, is a fatherly God so sparing of His presence? Why is there never a sign that prayers are heard? Why does Nature tell us no comforting news of its Maker? Why do some receive a whole loaf, while others must starve on a crumb? Where is the benevolence in shipwreck and earthquake? By asking such questions as these, she turned complaint into critique, and used her own sufferings as experiential evidence about the nature of the deity. The God who emerges from these poems is a God who does not answer, an unrevealed God whom one cannot confidently approach through Nature or through doctrine.

From "Sumptuous Destitution"

Cynthia Griffin Wolff (b. 1935)

Dickinson and Death   1993

(A Reading of "Because I could not stop for Death": page 777)

Modern readers are apt to comment upon the frequency with which Dickinson returns to this subject of death—"How morbid," people say. Perhaps. But if Dickinson was morbid, so was everyone else in her culture. Poe's aestheticizing of death (along with the proliferation of Gothic fiction and poetry) reflects a pervasive real-world concern: in mid-nineteenth-century America death rates were high. It was a truism that men had three wives (two of them having predeceased the spouse); infant mortality was so common that parents often gave several of their children the same name so that at least one "John" or "Lavinia" might survive to adulthood; rapid urbanization had intensified the threat of certain diseases—cholera, typhoid, and tuberculosis.

Poe and the Gothic tradition were one response to society's anxiety about death. Another came from the pulpit: mid-nineteenth-century sermons took death as their almost constant subject. Somewhat later in the century, preachers would embrace a doctrine of consolation: God would be figured as a loving parent—almost motherly—who had prepared a home in heaven for us all, and ministers would tell the members of their congregation that they need not be apprehensive. However, stern traces of Puritanism still tinctured the religious discourse of Dickinson's young womanhood, and members of the Amherst congregation were regularly exhorted with blood-stirring urgency to reflect upon the imminence of their own demise. Repeatedly, then, in attempting to comprehend Dickinson's work, a reader must return to the fundamental tenets of Protestant Christianity, for her poetry echoes the Bible more often than any other single work or author.

In part this preoccupation with the doctrines of her day reflected a more general concern with the essential questions of human existence they addressed. In a letter to Higginson she once said, "To live is so startling, it leaves but little room for other occupations." And to her friend Mrs. Holland she wrote, "All this and more, though *is* there more? More than Love and Death? Then tell me its name." The religious thought and language of the culture was important to her poetry because it comprised the semiotic system that her society employed to discuss the mysteries of life and death. If she wished to contemplate these, what other language was there to employ?

In part, however, conventional Christianity—especially the latter-day Puritanism of Dickinson's New England—represented for Dickinson an ultimate expression of patriarchal power. Rebelling against its rule, upbraiding a "Father" in Heaven who required absolute "faith" from his followers, but gave no discernible response, became a way of attacking the very essence of unjust authority, especially male authority.

• • •

It is true that the stern doctrines of New England Protestantism offered hope for a life after death; yet in Dickinson's estimation, the trope that was used for this "salvation" revealed some of the most repellent features of God's power, for the invitation to accept "faith" had been issued in the context of a courtship with a macabre, sexual component. It was promised that those who had faith would be carried to Heaven by the "Bridegroom" Christ. "Blessed are they which are called unto the marriage supper of the Lamb" (Revelation 19:9). Nor did it escape Dickinson's notice that the perverse prurience of Poe's notions were essentially similar to this Christian idea of Christ's "love" for a "bride" which promised a reunion that must be "consummated" through death. Thus the poem that is, perhaps, the apotheosis of that distinctive Dickinson voice, "the speaking dead," offers an astonishing combination: this conventional promise of Christianity suffused with the tonalities of the Gothic tradition.

[*Griffin quotes the entire text of "Because I could not stop for Death."*]

The speaker is a beautiful woman (already dead!), and like some spectral Cinderella, she is dressed to go to a ball: "For only Gossamer, my Gown – / My Tippet – only Tulle –." Her escort recalls both the lover of Poe's configuration and the "Bridegroom" that had been promised in the Bible: "We slowly drove – He knew no haste / And I had put away / My labor and my leisure too, / For His Civility –". Their "Carriage" hovers in some surrealistic state that is exterior to both time and place: they are no longer earth-bound, not quite dead (or at least still possessed of consciousness), but they have not yet achieved the celebration that awaits them, the "marriage supper of the Lamb."

Yet the ultimate implication of this work turns precisely upon the *poet's* capacity to explode the finite temporal boundaries that generally define our existence, for there is a third member of the party—also exterior to time and location—and that is "Immortality." *True* immortality, the verse suggests, comes neither from the confabulations of a male lover nor from God's intangible Heaven. Irrefutable "Immortality" resides in the work of art itself, the creation of an empowered woman poet that continues to captivate readers more than one hundred years after her death. And this much-read, often-cited poem stands as patent proof upon the page of its own argument!

From "Emily Dickinson"

Judith Farr (b. 1937)

A Reading of "My Life had stood – a Loaded Gun"[1] 1992

One of the notable qualities of this poem is its formidable directness of statement. Both the substance and the shape of the rhetoric seem straightforward. The ideas of guns and killing are not, superficially, invested by the speaker with negative properties. Far from it. The speaker recounts life with her master in tones of heady confidence and pleasure. If we did not know that this poem had been written by a woman—perhaps especially by "Miss Emily"—some of its presumed complexity and ominousness would be reduced. Let us say that Emily "when a Boy" is speaking; then it may be easier to credit the open delight of the speaker. Liberated from corners in the poem, he/she is freed into a grown-up gunman's life of authority and power, and she likes the idea exceedingly. All the piled-up, dynamic "And"s tell us so.

Or, if we cast her as a woman, she is what has been called "a man's woman"; everything he likes, *she* likes. She likes hunting, and her instincts are not pacifist or nurturing—no ducks and does for her. She smiles at her work of killing; Nature smiles with her (the firing of the gun makes a glow like Vesuvius); and at night she can pronounce the day good. (Hunting is, after all, not always a selfish sport; often it is a protective measure. "Sovereign Woods," of course, suggests a royal preserve, an unfair advantage for the hunter.) Because of her identification with the man, she is nearly human, but with a "Yellow Eye"—the color of explosion in an oval gunbarrel—and "emphatic Thumb." The American hunting pictures of Dickinson's day, like the landscapes of Bowles's favorite painter, Sanford Gifford, present hunting scenes like Dickinson's. Her buoyancy of tone accords with them, depicting easy days roaming in the open air, taking from an apparently complaisant nature all that the Master wants. If we imagine the speaker as a boy with his designated sponsor or master, then she is—up to the last quatrain—learning how to be a man in the rustic world dreamed up by Fenimore Cooper.

"Owner," however, suggests sexual love, and to anyone versed in the language of Emily Dickinson, it inflects one of her central themes:

> 'Twas my one glory –
> Let it be
> Remembered
> I was owned of thee –

For that reason, and because there is such heroic intimacy between the gun and Master, one can see this as a poem of sexual love that emphasizes comradery, robust equality. It may be considered part of the Master cycle and related to "He touched me," where the speaker begins to "live" when Master touches her or carries her away. Although she is a woman, because the two are one in love she imagines herself like him; like him, empowered. . . . Here the speaker appropriates Master's masculinity; she is a loaded gun. Together they become one person, one royal We in a happy life of power. The speaker has always wanted to exercise her stored-up bullets or faculties; now she can. In a letter to her cousin Louise Norcross in 1880, Dickinson used these same images: "what is each instant but a gun, harmless because 'unloaded,' but that

---

[1]The full text of Dickinson's "My Life had stood – a Loaded Gun" appears on page 581.

touched 'goes off'?" Although she omits one step, loading the gun, she is describing in her letter what she may be describing in her poem: love, "touching," as a means of being empowered.

There remains the final quatrain. It reads as a tightly wrought riddle, inviting explication. In one way, the stanza points up the incontrovertible difference between the mechanical gun and the human owner. He is the complete being, having both the power to die and the power to kill (even without her help). For all her fusion with him in their acts of love and death, she must still depend on him; she must be "carried." Thus this poem is often read—and read brilliantly—as a revelation of the limitations experienced by women under patriarchy, or even of the dependency of the female artist who needs male masters like Higginson to help her exercise her powers.

In reading this poem, however, I think that emphasis should always be placed on the pleasure the speaker experiences. The Master may be carrying her, but she is also speaking for him. He cannot do without her. That the gun's firing is compared to the pleasure of "a Vesuvian face" accents destruction, certainly; and it is hard to exempt this use of Vesuvius from all the others, always destructive, in the Dickinson canon. But the speaker seems to welcome her own destructiveness. She has been waiting a long time in many "corners" until the right lover lets her speak. For Dickinson, love is always the muse. Her variant for "the *power* to kill" in the penultimate line is *art*— which could make others die, from love or from aesthetic rapture. She herself—the gun, the artist—can never "die" like a real woman, however. She is but the arresting voice that speaks to and for the Master.

From *The Passion of Emily Dickinson*

Sandra M. Gilbert (b. 1936)
and Susan Gubar (b. 1944)

The Freedom of Emily Dickinson   1985

[Emily Dickinson] defined herself as a *woman* writer, reading the works of female precursors with special care, attending to the implications of novels like Charlotte Brontë's *Jane Eyre,* Emily Brontë's *Wuthering Heights,* and George Eliot's *Middlemarch* with the same absorbed delight that characterized her devotion to Elizabeth Barrett Browning's *Aurora Leigh.* Finally, then, the key to her enigmatic identity as a "supposed person" who was called the "Myth of Amherst" may rest, not in investigations of her questionable romance, but in studies of her unquestionably serious reading as well as in analyses of her disquietingly powerful writing. Elliptically phrased, intensely compressed, her poems are more linguistically innovative than any other nineteenth-century verses, with the possible exception of some works by Walt Whitman and Gerard Manley Hopkins, her two most radical male contemporaries. Throughout her largely secret but always brilliant career, moreover, she confronted precisely the questions about the individual and society, time and death, flesh and spirit, that major precursors from Milton to Keats had faced. Dreaming of "Amplitude and Awe," she recorded sometimes vengeful, sometimes mystical visions of social and personal transformation in poems as inventively phrased and imaginatively constructed as any in the English language.

Clearly such accomplishments required not only extraordinary talent but also some measure of freedom. Yet because she was the unmarried daughter of conservative New Englanders, Dickinson was obliged to take on many household tasks; as a nineteenth-century New England wife, she would have had the same number of obligations, if not more. Some of these she performed with pleasure; in 1856, for instance, she was judge of a bread-baking contest, and in 1857 she won a prize in that contest. But as Higginson's "scholar," as a voracious reader and an ambitious writer, Dickinson had to win herself time for "Amplitude and Awe," and it is increasingly clear that she did so through a strategic withdrawal from her ordinary world. A story related by her niece Martha Dickinson Bianchi reveals that the poet herself knew from the first what both the price and the prize might be: on one occasion, said Mrs. Bianchi, Dickinson took her up to the room in which she regularly sequestered herself, and, mimicking locking herself in, "thumb and forefinger closed on an imaginary key," said "with a quick turn of her wrist, 'It's just a turn—and freedom, Matty!'"

In the freedom of her solitary, but not lonely, room, Dickinson may have become what her Amherst neighbors saw as a bewildering "myth." Yet there, too, she created myths of her own. Reading the Brontës and Barrett Browning, studying Transcendentalism and the Bible, she contrived a theology which is powerfully expressed in many of her poems. That it was at its most hopeful a female-centered theology is revealed in verses like those she wrote about the women artists she admired, as well as in more general works like her gravely pantheistic address to the "Sweet Mountains" who "tell me no lie," with its definition of the hills around Amherst as "strong Madonnas" and its description of the writer herself as "The Wayward Nun – beneath the Hill – / Whose service is to You – ." As Dickinson's admirer and descendant Adrienne Rich has accurately observed, this passionate poet consistently chose to confront her society—to "have it out"—"on her own premises."

From introduction to Emily Dickinson,
The Norton Anthology of Literature by Women

LANGSTON HUGHES

Langston Hughes

Langston Hughes was born in Joplin, Missouri, in 1902. After his parents separated during his early years, he and his mother often lived a life of itinerant poverty, mostly in Kansas. Hughes attended high school in Cleveland, where as a senior he wrote "The Negro Speaks of Rivers." Reluctantly supported by his father, he attended Columbia University for a year before withdrawing. After a series of menial jobs, Hughes became a merchant seaman in 1923 and visited the ports of West Africa. For a time he lived in Paris, Genoa, and Rome, before returning to the United States. The publication of The Weary Blues *(1926) earned him immediate fame, which he solidified a few months later with his pioneering essay "The Negro Artist and the Racial Mountain." In 1926 he also entered Lincoln University in Pennsylvania, from which he graduated in 1929. By then Hughes was already one of the central figures of the Harlem Renaissance, the flowering of African American arts and literature in the Harlem neighborhood of upper Manhattan in New York City during the 1920s. A strikingly versatile author, Hughes worked in fiction, drama, translation, criticism, opera libretti, memoir, cinema, and songwriting, as well as poetry. He also became a tireless promoter of African American culture, crisscrossing the United States on speaking tours as well as compiling twenty-eight anthologies of African American folklore and poetry. His newspaper columns, which often reported conversations with an imaginary Harlem friend named Jesse B. Semple, nicknamed "Simple," attracted an especially large following. During the 1930s Hughes became involved in radical politics and traveled to the Soviet Union, but after World War II he gradually shifted to mainstream progressive politics. In his last years he became a spokesman for the moderate wing of the civil rights movement. He died in Harlem in 1967.*

POEMS

The Negro Speaks of Rivers   (1921) 1926

I've known rivers:
I've known rivers ancient as the world and older than the flow of human
    blood in human veins.

My soul has grown deep like the rivers.

I bathed in the Euphrates when dawns were young.
I built my hut near the Congo and it lulled me to sleep.   5
I looked upon the Nile and raised the pyramids above it.
I heard the singing of the Mississippi when Abe Lincoln went down to New
    Orleans, and I've seen its muddy bosom turn all golden in the sunset.

I've known rivers:
Ancient, dusky rivers.

My soul has grown deep like the rivers.   10

My People

1922

Dream-singers,
Story-tellers,
Dancers,
Loud laughers in the hands of Fate—
    My People.   5
Dish-washers,
Elevator-boys,
Ladies' maids,
Crap-shooters,
Cooks,   10
Waiters,
Jazzers,
Nurses of babies,
Loaders of ships,
Porters,   15
Hairdressers,
Comedians in vaudeville
And band-men in circuses—
Dream-singers all,
Story-tellers all.   20
    Dancers—
God! What dancers!
Singers—
God! What singers!
Singers and dancers   25
Dancers and laughers.
Laughers?
Yes, laughers . . . laughers . . . laughers—
Loud-mouthed laughers in the hands
    Of Fate.   30

Mother to Son

(1922) 1932

Well, son, I'll tell you:
Life for me ain't been no crystal stair.
It's had tacks in it,
And splinters,
And boards torn up,   5
And places with no carpet on the floor—
Bare.
But all the time
I'se been a-climbin' on,
And reachin' landin's,   10
And turnin' corners,
And sometimes goin' in the dark
Where there ain't been no light.
So boy, don't you turn back.

Don't you set down on the steps   15
'Cause you finds it's kinder hard.
Don't you fall now—
For I'se still goin', honey,
I'se still climbin',
And life for me ain't been no crystal stair.   20

Dream Variations   (1924) 1926

To fling my arms wide
In some place of the sun,
To whirl and to dance
Till the white day is done.
Then rest at cool evening   5
Beneath a tall tree
While night comes on gently,
    Dark like me—
That is my dream!

To fling my arms wide   10
In the face of the sun,
Dance! Whirl! Whirl!
Till the quick day is done.
Rest at pale evening . . .
A tall, slim tree . . .   15
Night coming tenderly
    Black like me.

I, Too   1926

I, too, sing America.

I am the darker brother.
They send me to eat in the kitchen
When company comes,
But I laugh,   5
And eat well,
And grow strong.

Tomorrow,
I'll be at the table
When company comes.   10
Nobody'll dare
Say to me,
"Eat in the kitchen,"
Then.

Besides,   15
They'll see how beautiful I am
And be ashamed—

I, too, am America.

The Weary Blues

1926

Droning a drowsy syncopated tune,
Rocking back and forth to a mellow croon,
    I heard a Negro play.
Down on Lenox Avenue the other night
By the pale dull pallor of an old gas light   5
    He did a lazy sway. . . .
    He did a lazy sway. . . .
To the tune o' those Weary Blues.
With his ebony hands on each ivory key
He made that poor piano moan with melody.   10
    O Blues!
Swaying to and fro on his rickety stool
He played that sad raggy tune like a musical fool.
    Sweet Blues!
Coming from a black man's soul.   15
    O Blues!
In a deep song voice with a melancholy tone
I heard that Negro sing, that old piano moan—
    "Ain't got nobody in all this world,
    Ain't got nobody but ma self.   20
    I's gwine to quit ma frownin'
    And put ma troubles on the shelf."

Thump, thump, thump, went his foot on the floor.
He played a few chords then he sang some more—
    "I got the Weary Blues   25
    And I can't be satisfied.
    Got the Weary Blues
    And can't be satisfied—
    I ain't happy no mo'
    And I wish that I had died."   30
And far into the night he crooned that tune.
The stars went out and so did the moon.
The singer stopped playing and went to bed
While the Weary Blues echoed through his head.
He slept like a rock or a man that's dead.   35

THE WEARY BLUES. This poem quotes the first blues song Hughes had ever heard, "The Weary Blues,"
which begins, "I got the weary blues / And I can't be satisfied / . . . I ain't happy no mo' / And I wish that I
had died."

Song for a Dark Girl   1927

Way Down South in Dixie
  (Break the heart of me)
They hung my black young lover
  To a cross roads tree.

Way Down South in Dixie
  (Bruised body high in air)   5
I asked the white Lord Jesus
  What was the use of prayer.

Way Down South in Dixie
  (Break the heart of me)
Love is a naked shadow   10
  On a gnarled and naked tree.

Ballad of the Landlord   (1940) 1943

Landlord, landlord,
My roof has sprung a leak.
Don't you 'member I told you about it
Way last week?

Landlord, landlord,   5
These steps is broken down.
When you come up yourself
It's a wonder you don't fall down.

Ten Bucks you say I owe you?
Ten Bucks you say is due?   10
Well, that's Ten Bucks more'n I'll pay you
Till you fix this house up new.

What? You gonna get eviction orders?
You gonna cut off my heat?
You gonna take my furniture and   15
Throw it in the street?

Um-huh! You talking high and mighty.
Talk on—till you get through.
You ain't gonna be able to say a word
If I land my fist on you.   20

Police! Police!
Come and get this man!
He's trying to ruin the government
And overturn the land!

Copper's Whistle!   25
Patrol bell!
Arrest.

Precinct Station.
Iron cell.
Headlines in press: 30

MAN THREATENS LANDLORD

TENANT HELD NO BAIL

JUDGE GIVES NEGRO 90 DAYS IN COUNTY JAIL

 Theme for English B   1951

The instructor said,

    Go home and write
    a page tonight.
    And let that page come out of you—
    Then, it will be true.   5

I wonder if it's that simple?
I am twenty-two, colored, born in Winston-Salem.
I went to school there, then Durham, then here
to this college on the hill above Harlem.
I am the only colored student in my class.   10
The steps from the hill lead down into Harlem,
through a park, then I cross St. Nicholas,
Eighth Avenue, Seventh, and I come to the Y,
the Harlem Branch Y, where I take the elevator
up to my room, sit down, and write this page: 15

It's not easy to know what is true for you or me
at twenty-two, my age. But I guess I'm what
I feel and see and hear, Harlem, I hear you:
hear you, hear me—we two—you, me, talk on this page.
(I hear New York, too.) Me—who?   20
Well, I like to eat, sleep, drink, and be in love.
I like to work, read, learn, and understand life.
I like a pipe for a Christmas present,
or records—Bessie, bop, or Bach.
I guess being colored doesn't make me *not* like   25
the same things other folks like who are other races.
So will my page be colored that I write?
Being me, it will not be white.
But it will be
a part of you, instructor.   30
You are white—
yet a part of me, as I am a part of you.

That's American.
Sometimes perhaps you don't want to be a part of me.
Nor do I often want to be a part of you.   35
But we are, that's true!
As I learn from you,
I guess you learn from me—
although you're older—and white—
and somewhat more free.   40

This is my page for English B.

THEME FOR ENGLISH B. 9 *college on the hill above Harlem:* Columbia University, where Hughes was briefly a student. (Note, however, that this poem is not autobiographical. The young speaker is a character invented by the middle-aged author.) 24 *Bessie:* Bessie Smith (1898?–1937) was a popular blues singer often called the "Empress of the Blues."

Nightmare Boogie   1951

I had a dream
and I could see
a million faces
black as me!
A nightmare dream: 5
Quicker than light
All them faces
Turned dead white!
Boogie-woogie,
Rolling bass,   10
Whirling treble
Of cat-gut lace.

Harlem [Dream Deferred]   1951

What happens to a dream deferred?

    Does it dry up
    like a raisin in the sun?
    Or fester like a sore—
    And then run?   5
    Does it stink like rotten meat?
    Or crust and sugar over—
    like a syrupy sweet?

    Maybe it just sags
    like a heavy load.   10

    Or does it explode?

HARLEM. This famous poem appeared under two titles in the author's lifetime. Both titles appear above.

Homecoming

1959

I went back in the alley
And I opened up my door.
All her clothes was gone:
She wasn't home no more.

I pulled back the covers,   5
I made down the bed.
A *whole* lot of room
Was the only thing I had.

Compare

Other poems by Langston Hughes that are found in this book:

> Dream Boogie (page 643)
> Two Somewhat Different Epigrams (page 658)

LANGSTON HUGHES ON WRITING

Langston Hughes, c. 1945.

The Negro Artist and the Racial Mountain   1926

Most of my own poems are racial in theme and treatment, derived from the life I know. In many of them I try to grasp and hold some of the meanings and rhythms of jazz. I am as sincere as I know how to be in these poems and yet after every reading I answer questions like these from my own people: Do you think Negroes should always write about Negroes? I wish you wouldn't read some of your poems to white folks. How do you find anything interesting in a place like a cabaret? Why do you write about black people? You aren't black. What makes you do so many jazz poems?

But jazz to me is one of the inherent expressions of Negro life in America; the eternal tom-tom beating in the Negro soul—the tom-tom of revolt against weariness in a white world, a world of subway trains, and work, work, work; the tom-tom of joy and laughter, and pain swallowed in a smile. Yet the Philadelphia club-woman is ashamed to say that her race created it and she does not like me to write about it. The old subconscious "white is best" runs through her mind. Years of study under white teachers, a lifetime of white books, pictures, and papers, and white manners, morals, and Puritan standards made her dislike the spirituals. And now she turns up her nose at jazz and all its manifestations—likewise almost everything else distinctly racial. She doesn't care for the Winold Reiss portraits of Negroes because they are "too Negro." She does not want a true picture of herself from anybody. She wants the artist to flatter her, to make the white world believe that all Negroes are as smug and as near white in soul as she wants to be. But, to my mind, it is the duty of the younger Negro artist, if he accepts any duties at all from outsiders, to change through the force of his art that old whispering "I want to be white," hidden in the aspirations of his people, to "Why should I want to be white? I am a Negro—and beautiful."

So I am ashamed for the black poet who says, "I want to be a poet, not a Negro poet," as though his own racial world were not as interesting as any other world. I am ashamed, too, for the colored artist who runs from the painting of Negro faces to the painting of sunsets after the manner of the academicians because he fears the strange un-whiteness of his own features. An artist must be free to choose what he does, certainly, but he must also never be afraid to do what he might choose.

From "The Negro Artist and the Racial Mountain"

Compare

Hughes's comments on the African American artist with Darryl Pinckney's critical observations on Langston Hughes's public identity as a black poet (page 801).

The Harlem Renaissance   1940

White people began to come to Harlem in droves. For several years they packed the expensive Cotton Club on Lenox Avenue. But I was never there, because the Cotton Club was a Jim Crow club for gangsters and monied whites. They were not cordial to Negro patronage, unless you were a celebrity like Bojangles.° So Harlem Negroes did not like the Cotton Club and never appreciated its Jim Crow policy in the very heart of their dark community. Nor did ordinary Negroes like the growing influx of whites toward Harlem after sundown, flooding the little cabarets and bars where formerly only colored people laughed and sang, and where now the strangers were given the best ringside tables to sit and stare at the Negro customers—like amusing animals in a zoo.

The Negroes said: "We can't go downtown and sit and stare at you in your clubs. You won't even let us in your clubs." But they didn't say it out loud—for Negroes are practically never rude to white people. So thousands of whites came to Harlem night after night, thinking the Negroes loved to have them there, and firmly believing that all Harlemites left their houses at sundown to sing and dance in cabarets, because most of the whites saw nothing but the cabarets, not the houses.

Some of the owners of Harlem clubs, delighted at the flood of white patronage, made the grievous error of barring their own race, after the manner of the famous Cotton Club. But most of these quickly lost business and folded up, because they failed to realize that a large part of the Harlem attraction for downtown New Yorkers lay in simply watching the colored customers amuse themselves. And the smaller clubs, of course, had no big floor shows or a name band like the Cotton Club, where Duke Ellington usually held forth, so, without black patronage, they were not amusing at all.

Some of the small clubs, however, had people like Gladys Bentley, who was something worth discovering in those days, before she got famous, acquired an accompanist, specially written material, and conscious vulgarity. But for two or three amazing years, Miss Bentley sat, and played a big piano all night long, literally all night, without stopping—singing songs like "The St. James Infirmary," from ten in the evening until dawn, with scarcely a break between the notes, sliding from one song to another, with a powerful and continuous underbeat of jungle rhythm. Miss Bentley was an amazing exhibition of musical energy—a large, dark, masculine lady,

Bojangles: Bill "Bojangles" Robinson (1876–1949), dancer.

whose feet pounded the floor while her fingers pounded the keyboard—a perfect piece of African sculpture, animated by her own rhythm.

But when the place where she played became too well known, she began to sing with an accompanist, became a star, moved to a larger place, then downtown, and is now in Hollywood. The old magic of the woman and the piano and the night and the rhythm being one is gone. But everything goes, one way or another. The '20s are gone and lots of fine things in Harlem night life have disappeared like snow in the sun—since it became utterly commercial, planned for the downtown tourist trade, and therefore dull.

The lindy-hoppers at the Savoy even began to practice acrobatic routines, and to do absurd things for the entertainment of the whites, that probably never would have entered their heads to attempt merely for their own effortless amusement. Some of the lindy-hoppers had cards printed with their names on them and became dance professors teaching the tourists. Then Harlem nights became show nights for the Nordics.

Some critics say that that is what happened to certain Negro writers, too—that they ceased to write to amuse themselves and began to write to amuse and entertain white people, and in so doing distorted and overcolored their material, and left out a great many things they thought would offend their American brothers of a lighter complexion. Maybe—since Negroes have writer-racketeers, as has any other race. But I have known almost all of them, and most of the good ones have tried to be honest, write honestly, and express their world as they saw it.

From *The Big Sea*

Lenox Avenue, Harlem, in 1925.

CRITICS ON LANGSTON HUGHES

Arnold Rampersad (b. 1941)

Hughes as an Experimentalist   1991

From his first publication of verse in the *Crisis*, Hughes had reflected his admiration for Sandburg and Whitman by experimenting with free verse as opposed to committing himself conservatively to rhyme. Even when he employed rhyme in his verse, as he often did, Hughes composed with relative casualness—unlike other major black poets of the day, such as Countee Cullen and Claude McKay, with their highly wrought stanzas. He seemed to prefer, as Whitman and Sandburg had preferred, to write lines that captured the cadences of common American speech, with his ear always especially attuned to the variety of black American language. This last aspect was only a token of his emotional and aesthetic involvement in black American culture, which he increasingly saw as his prime source of inspiration, even as he regarded black Americans ("Loud laughers in the hands of Fate— / My People") as his only indispensable audience.

Early poems captured some of the sights and sounds of ecstatic black church worship ("Glory! Hallelujah!"), but Hughes's greatest technical accomplishment as a poet was in his fusing of the rhythms of blues and jazz with traditional poetry. This technique, which he employed his entire life, surfaced in his art around 1923 with the landmark poem "The Weary Blues," in which the persona recalls hearing a blues singer and piano player ("Sweet Blues! / Coming from a black man's soul") performing in what most likely is a speakeasy in Harlem. The persona recalls the plaintive verse intoned by the singer ("Ain't got nobody in all this world, / Ain't got nobody but ma self.") but finally surrenders to the mystery and magic of the blues singer's art. In the process, Hughes had taken an indigenous African American art form, perhaps the most vivid and commanding of all, and preserved its authenticity even as he formally enshrined it in the midst of a poem in traditional European form.

"The Weary Blues," a work virtually unprecedented in American poetry in its blending of black and white rhythms and forms, won Hughes the first prize for poetry in May 1925 in the epochal literary contest sponsored by *Opportunity* magazine, which marked the first high point of the Harlem Renaissance. The work also confirmed his leadership, along with Countee Cullen, of all the younger poets of the burgeoning movement. For Hughes, it was only the first step in his poetical tribute to blues and jazz. By the time of his second volume of verse, *Fine Clothes to the Jew* (1927), he was writing blues poems without either apology or framing devices taken from the traditional world of poetry. He was also delving into the basic subject matters of the blues—love and raw sexuality, deep sorrow and sudden violence, poverty and heartbreak. These subjects, treated with sympathy for the poor and dispossessed, and without false piety, made him easily the most controversial black poet of his time.

From "Langston Hughes"

Rita Dove (b. 1952)
and Marilyn Nelson (b. 1946)

The Voices in Langston Hughes   1998

Affectionately known for most of his life as "The Poet Laureate of Harlem," Langston Hughes was born in Missouri and raised in the Midwest, moving to Harlem only as a young man. There he discovered his spiritual home, in Harlem's heart of Blackness finding both his vocation—"to explain and illuminate the Negro condition in America"—and the proletarian voice of most of his best work. If Johnson was the Renaissance man of the Harlem Renaissance, Hughes was its greatest man of letters; he saw through publication more than a dozen collections of poems, ten plays, two novels, several collections of short fiction, one historical study, two autobiographical works, several anthologies, and many books for children. His essay, "The Negro Artist and the Racial Mountain," provided a personal credo and statement of direction for the poets of his generation, who, he says, "intend to express our individual dark-skinned selves without fear or shame . . . We know we are beautiful. And ugly too." His forthright commitment to the Negro people led him to explore with great authenticity the frustrated dreams of the Black masses and to experiment with diction, rhythm, and musical forms.

Hughes was ever quick to confess the influences of Whitman and Sandburg on his work, and his best poetry also reflects the influence of Sherwood Anderson's *Winesburg, Ohio*. Like these poets, Hughes collected individual voices; his work is a notebook of life-studies. In his best poems Hughes the man remains masked; his voices are the voices of the Negro race as a whole, or of individual Negro speakers. "The Negro Speaks of Rivers," a widely anthologized poem from his first book, *The Weary Blues* (1926), is a case in point. Here Hughes is visible only as spokesman for the race as he proclaims "I bathed in the Euphrates when dawns were young. / I built my hut near the Congo and it lulled me to sleep." Poems frequently present anonymous Black personae, each of whom shares a painful heritage and an ironic pride. As one humorous character announces:

> I do cooking,
> Day's work, too!
> Alberta K. Johnson—
> *Madam* to you.

Hughes took poetry out of what Cullen called "the dark tower"—which was, and even during the Harlem Renaissance, ivy-covered and distant and took it directly to the people. His blues and jazz experiments described and addressed an audience for which music was a central experience; he became a spokesman for their troubles, as in "Po' Boy Blues":

> When I was home de
> Sunshine seemed like gold.
> When I was home de
> Sunshine seemed like gold.
> Since I come up North de
> Whole damn world's turned cold.

American democracy appears frequently in Hughes's work as the unfulfilled but potentially realizable dream of the Negro, who says in "Let America Be America Again":

> O, yes,
> I say it plain,
> America never was America to me
> And yet I swear this oath—
> America will be!

There are many fine poems in the Hughes canon, but the strongest single work is *Montage of a Dream Deferred* (1951), a collection of sketches, captured voices, and individual lives unified by the jazzlike improvisations on the central theme of "a dream deferred." Like many of his individual poems, this work is intended for performance: think of it as a Harlem *Under Milk Wood*. Hughes moves rapidly from one voice or scene to the next; from the person in "Blues in Dawn" who says "I don't dare start thinking in the morning," to, in "Dime," a snatch of conversation: "Chile, these steps is hard to climb. / Grandma, lend me a dime."

The moods of the poems are as varied as their voices, for Hughes includes the daylight hours as well as the night. There are the bitter jump-rope rhymes of disillusioned children, the naive exclamations of young lovers, the gossip of friends. A college freshman writes in his "Theme for English B": "I guess being colored doesn't make me *not* like / the same things other folks like who are other races." A jaded woman offers in "Advice" the observation that "birthing is hard / and dying is mean," and advises youth to "get yourself / a little loving / in between." "Hope" is a miniature vignette in which a dying man asks for fish, and "His wife looked it up in her dream book / and played it." The changing voices, moods, and rhythms of this collection are, as Hughes wrote in a preface, "Like be-bop . . . marked by conflicting change, sudden nuances. . . ." We are reminded throughout that we should be hearing the poem as music; as boogie-woogie, as blues, as bass, as saxophone. Against the eighty-odd dreams collected here, the refrain insists that these frustrated dreams are potentially dangerous:

> What happens to a dream deferred?

> Does it dry up
> like a raisin in the sun?
> Or fester like a sore—
> And then run?
> Does it stink like rotten meat?
> Or crust and sugar over—
> like a syrupy sweet?

> Maybe it just sags
> like a heavy load.

> *Or does it explode?*

More than any other Black poet, Langston Hughes spoke for the Negro people. Most of those after him have emulated his ascent of the Racial Mountain, his painfully joyous declaration of pride and commonality. His work offers white readers a glimpse into the social and the personal lives of Black America; Black readers recognize a proud affirmation of self.

From "A Black Rainbow: Modern Afro-American Poetry"

Darryl Pinckney (b. 1953)

Black Identity in Langston Hughes 1989

Fierce identification with the sorrows and pleasures of the poor black—"I myself belong to that class"—propelled Hughes toward the voice of the black Everyman. He made a distinction between his lyric and his social poetry, the private and the public. In the best of his social poetry he turned himself into a transmitter of messages and made the "I" a collective "I":

> I've known rivers:
> I've known rivers ancient as the world and older than the flow of
>   human blood in human veins.
>
> My soul has grown deep like the rivers.
>
> I bathed in the Euphrates when dawns were young.
> I built my hut near the Congo and it lulled me to sleep.
> I looked upon the Nile and raised the pyramids above it.
> I heard the singing of the Mississippi when Abe Lincoln went down to
>   New Orleans, and I've seen its muddy bosom turn all golden in the
>   sunset.

> ("The Negro Speaks of Rivers")

The medium conveys a singleness of intention: to make the black known. The straightforward, declarative style doesn't call attention to itself. Nothing distracts from forceful statement, as if the shadowy characters Sandburg wrote about in, say, "When Mammy Hums" had at last their chance to come forward and testify. Poems like "Aunt Sue's Stories" reflect the folk ideal of black women as repositories of racial lore. The story told in dramatic monologues like "The Negro Mother" or "Mother to Son" is one of survival—life "ain't been no crystal stair." The emphasis is on the capacity of black people to endure, which is why Hughes's social poetry, though not strictly protest writing, indicts white America, even taunts it with the steady belief that blacks will overcome simply by "keeping on":

> I, too, sing America.
>
> I am the darker brother.
> They send me to eat in the kitchen
> When company comes,
> But I laugh,
> And eat well,
> And grow strong.

> ("I, Too")

Whites were not the only ones who could be made uneasy by Hughes's attempts to boldly connect past and future. The use of "black" and the invocation of Africa were defiant gestures back in the days when many blacks described themselves as brown. When Hughes answered Sandburg's "Nigger" ("I am the nigger, / Singer of Songs . . . ") with "I am a Negro, / Black as the night is black, / Black like the depths of my Africa" ("Negro") he challenged the black middle class with his absorption in slave heritage.

From "Suitcase in Harlem"

Onwuchekwa Jemie (b. 1940)

A Reading of "Dream Deferred"   1976

The deferred dream is examined through a variety of human agencies, of interlocking and recurring voices and motifs fragmented and scattered throughout the six sections of the poem. Much as in bebop, the pattern is one of constant reversals and contrasts. Frequently the poems are placed in thematic clusters, with poems within the cluster arranged in contrasting pairs. *Montage [of a Dream Deferred]* does not move in a straight line; its component poems move off in invisible directions, reappear and touch, creating a complex tapestry or mosaic.

The dream theme itself is carried in the musical motifs. It is especially characterized by the rumble ("The boogie-woogie rumble / Of a dream deferred")—that rapid thumping and tumbling of notes which so powerfully drives to the bottom of the emotions, stirring feelings too deep to be touched by the normal successions of notes and common rhythms. The rumble is an atomic explosion of musical energy, an articulate confusion, a moment of epiphany, a flash of blinding light in which all things are suddenly made clear. The theme is sounded at strategic times, culminating in the final section. . . .

The poet has taken us on a guided tour of microcosmic Harlem, day and night, past and present. And as a new day dawns and the poem moves into a summing up in the final section, he again poses the question and examines the possibilities:

What happens to a dream deferred?

  Does it dry up
  like a raisin in the sun?
  Or fester like a sore—
  And then run?
  Does it stink like rotten meat?
  Or crust and sugar over—
  like a syrupy sweet?

  Maybe it just sags
  like a heavy load.

  Or does it explode?

The images are sensory, domestic, earthy, like blues images. The stress is on deterioration—drying, rotting, festering, souring—on loss of essential natural quality. The raisin has fallen from a fresh, juicy grape to a dehydrated but still edible raisin to a sun-baked and inedible dead bone of itself. The Afro-American is not unlike the raisin, for he is in a sense a dessicated trunk of his original African self, used and abandoned in the American wilderness with the stipulation that he rot and disappear. Like the raisin lying neglected in the scorching sun, the black man is treated as a thing of no consequence. But the raisin refuses the fate assigned to it, metamorphoses instead into a malignant living sore that will not heal or disappear. Like the raisin, a sore is but a little thing, inconsequential on the surface but in fact symptomatic of a serious disorder. Its stink is like the stink of the rotten meat sold to black folks in so many ghetto groceries; meat no longer suitable for human use, deathly. And while a syrupy sweet is not central to the diet as meat might be, still it is a rounding-off final pleasure (dessert) at the end of a meal, or a delicious surprise that a child looks forward to at

Halloween or Christmas. But that final pleasure turns out to be a pain. Aged, spoiled candy leaves a sickly taste in the mouth; sweetness gone bad turns a treat into a trick.

The elements of the deferred dream are, like the raisin, sore, meat, and candy, little things of no great consequence in themselves. But their unrelieved accretion packs together considerable pressure. Their combined weight becomes too great to carry about indefinitely: not only does the weight increase from continued accumulation, but the longer it is carried the heavier it feels. The load sags from its own weight, and the carrier sags with it; and if he should drop it, it just might explode from all its strange, tortured, and compressed energies.

In short, a dream deferred can be a terrifying thing. Its greatest threat is its unpredictability, and for this reason the question format is especially fitting. Questions demand the reader's participation, corner and sweep him headlong to the final, inescapable conclusion.

From *Langston Hughes: An Introduction to the Poetry*

■ WRITING *effectively*

TOPICS FOR WRITING ABOUT EMILY DICKINSON

1. Focusing on one or two poems, demonstrate how Dickinson's idiosyncratic capitalization and punctuation add special impact to her work.

2. How do the poems by Dickinson in this chapter and elsewhere in the book illustrate her statement (in "Recognizing Poetry" on page 778) that "I find ecstasy in living—the mere sense of living is joy enough"?

3. In her work, Dickinson frequently adopts the stance of an outsider or nonconformist. Discuss this point through detailed discussion of at least two of her poems. What does she seem to find uncongenial about going along with the crowd?

4. Emily Dickinson is perhaps as famous for her reclusiveness as she is for her poetry. Discuss this element of her personality as it is reflected in at least three of the poems in this section. Do the poems suggest any reason—or reasons—for this tendency?

TOPICS FOR WRITING ABOUT LANGSTON HUGHES

1. Compare and contrast the use of first-person voices in two poems by Langston Hughes (such as "I, Too" and "Theme for English B" or "Mother to Son" and "The Negro Speaks of Rivers"). In what ways does the speaker's "I" differ in each poem and in what ways is it similar?

2. Discussing a single poem by Hughes, examine how musical forms (such as jazz, blues, or popular song) help shape the effect of the work.

3. Analyzing "Theme for English B" and "I, Too" as well as the excerpts from his essays in this casebook, discuss Hughes's vision of racial identity and integration in American society. What specific obstacles and opportunities does Hughes envision? What stereotypes and prejudices need to be overcome? (Cite from the text to find Hughes's opinion rather than expounding your own views.)

4. Write your own "Theme for English B," using autobiographical details and personal tastes to express both your sense of yourself and your relationship to your community.

30

CRITICAL CASEBOOK
T. S. Eliot's "The Love Song of J. Alfred Prufrock"

Eliot around 1910.

Yeats and Pound achieved modernity;
Eliot was modern from the start.

—LOUISE BOGAN

T. S. ELIOT

Thomas Stearns Eliot was born on September 26, 1888, in St. Louis, Missouri. Both his father, a brick manufacturer, and mother were descended from families that had emigrated from England to Massachusetts in the seventeenth century. Entering Harvard on his eighteenth birthday, he earned a B.A. in 1909 and an M.A. in English literature in 1910. After a year in Paris, he returned to Harvard, where he undertook graduate studies in philosophy and also served as a teaching assistant. Awarded a traveling fellowship, he intended to study in Germany, but the outbreak of World War I in August 1914 forced him to leave the country after only several weeks. He then went to London, England, which would be his home for the remaining fifty years of his life.

T. S. Eliot in his early twenties

In September 1914, Eliot met fellow poet Ezra Pound, who would be a great influence on his work and his literary career. In June 1915, Eliot married Vivienne Haigh-Wood after an acquaintance of two months. (The marriage was troubled from the start. He would separate from Vivienne in 1933; she was subsequently institutionalized and died in a nursing home in 1947.) The year 1915 also saw Eliot's first major publication, when "The Love Song of J. Alfred Prufrock" appeared in the June issue of Poetry. It became the central piece of his first collection, Prufrock and Other Observations (1917). During this period, he taught school briefly and worked in Lloyds Bank for several years. He secured permanent employment when he joined the publishing firm of Faber and Gwyer (later Faber and Faber) in 1925.

Eliot became one of the best-known and most controversial poets of his time with the publication of The Waste Land (1922). Conservative critics denounced it as impenetrable and incoherent; readers of more advanced tastes responded at once to the poem's depiction of a sordid society, empty of spiritual values, in the wake of World War I. Through the Criterion, a journal that he founded in 1922, and through his essays and volumes of literary and social criticism, Eliot came to exert immense influence as a molder of opinion.

Religious themes became increasingly important to his poetry, from "Journey of the Magi" (1927), through Ash-Wednesday (1930), to Murder in the Cathedral (1935), which dealt with the death of St. Thomas à Becket, and was the first of his several full-length verse dramas. Others included The Family Reunion (1939) and The Cocktail Party (1949), which became a remarkable popular success, estimated to have been seen by more than a million and a half people in Eliot's lifetime. Another of his works reached many more millions, at least indirectly: the light-verse pieces of Old Possum's Book of Practical Cats (1939) later became the basis of the record-breaking Broadway musical Cats (1982). Eliot's last major work of nondramatic poetry was Four Quartets (1943). In 1948, he was awarded the Nobel Prize in Literature.

In January 1957, Eliot married Valerie Fletcher, his secretary at Faber and Faber. After several years of declining health, he died of emphysema at his home in London on January 4, 1965.

The Love Song of J. Alfred Prufrock   1917

S'io credessi che mia risposta fosse
a persona che mai tornasse al mondo,
questa fiamma staria senza più scosse.
Ma per ciò che giammai di questo fondo
non tornò vivo alcun, s'i'odo il vero,
senza tema d'infamia ti rispondo.

Let us go then, you and I,
When the evening is spread out against the sky
Like a patient etherized upon a table;
Let us go, through certain half-deserted streets,
The muttering retreats   5
Of restless nights in one-night cheap hotels
And sawdust restaurants with oyster-shells:
Streets that follow like a tedious argument
Of insidious intent
To lead you to an overwhelming question . . .   10
Oh, do not ask, "What is it?"
Let us go and make our visit.

In the room the women come and go
Talking of Michelangelo.

The yellow fog that rubs its back upon the window-panes,   15
The yellow smoke that rubs its muzzle on the window-panes,
Licked its tongue into the corners of the evening,
Lingered upon the pools that stand in drains,
Let fall upon its back the soot that falls from chimneys,
Slipped by the terrace, made a sudden leap,   20
And seeing that it was a soft October night,
Curled once about the house, and fell asleep.

And indeed there will be time
For the yellow smoke that slides along the street
Rubbing its back upon the window-panes;   25
There will be time, there will be time
To prepare a face to meet the faces that you meet;
There will be time to murder and create,
And time for all the works and days of hands
That lift and drop a question on your plate;   30
Time for you and time for me,
And time yet for a hundred indecisions,
And for a hundred visions and revisions,
Before the taking of a toast and tea.

In the room the women come and go   35
Talking of Michelangelo.

And indeed there will be time
To wonder, "Do I dare?" and, "Do I dare?"
Time to turn back and descend the stair,
With a bald spot in the middle of my hair—   40
(They will say: "How his hair is growing thin!")
My morning coat, my collar mounting firmly to the chin,
My necktie rich and modest, but asserted by a simple pin—
(They will say: "But how his arms and legs are thin!")
Do I dare   45
Disturb the universe?
In a minute there is time
For decisions and revisions which a minute will reverse.

For I have known them all already, known them all—
Have known the evenings, mornings, afternoons,   50
I have measured out my life with coffee spoons;
I know the voices dying with a dying fall
Beneath the music from a farther room.
    So how should I presume?

And I have known the eyes already, known them all—   55
The eyes that fix you in a formulated phrase,
And when I am formulated, sprawling on a pin,
When I am pinned and wriggling on the wall,
Then how should I begin
To spit out all the butt-ends of my days and ways?   60
    And how should I presume?

And I have known the arms already, known them all—
Arms that are braceleted and white and bare
(But in the lamplight, downed with light brown hair!)
Is it perfume from a dress   65
That makes me so digress?
Arms that lie along a table, or wrap about a shawl.
    And should I then presume?
    And how should I begin?

                              • • •

Shall I say, I have gone at dusk through narrow streets   70
And watched the smoke that rises from the pipes
Of lonely men in shirt-sleeves, leaning out of windows? . . .

I should have been a pair of ragged claws
Scuttling across the floors of silent seas.

                              • • •

And the afternoon, the evening, sleeps so peacefully!   75
Smoothed by long fingers,
Asleep . . . tired . . . or it malingers,
Stretched on the floor, here beside you and me.
Should I, after tea and cakes and ices,
Have the strength to force the moment to its crisis?   80
But though I have wept and fasted, wept and prayed,
Though I have seen my head (grown slightly bald) brought in upon a platter,
I am no prophet—and here's no great matter;
I have seen the moment of my greatness flicker,
And I have seen the eternal Footman hold my coat, and snicker,   85
And in short, I was afraid.

And would it have been worth it, after all,
After the cups, the marmalade, the tea,
Among the porcelain, among some talk of you and me,
Would it have been worth while,   90
To have bitten off the matter with a smile,
To have squeezed the universe into a ball
To roll it toward some overwhelming question,
To say: "I am Lazarus, come from the dead,
Come back to tell you all, I shall tell you all"—   95
If one, settling a pillow by her head,
   Should say: "That is not what I meant at all.
   That is not it, at all."

And would it have been worth it, after all,
Would it have been worth while,   100
After the sunsets and the dooryards and the sprinkled streets,
After the novels, after the teacups, after the skirts that trail along the floor—
And this, and so much more?—
It is impossible to say just what I mean!
But as if a magic lantern threw the nerves in patterns on a screen: 105
Would it have been worth while
If one, settling a pillow or throwing off a shawl,
And turning toward the window, should say:
   "That is not it at all,
   That is not what I meant, at all."   110

     • • •

No! I am not Prince Hamlet, nor was meant to be;
Am an attendant lord, one that will do
To swell a progress, start a scene or two,
Advise the prince; no doubt, an easy tool,
Deferential, glad to be of use,   115
Politic, cautious, and meticulous;
Full of high sentence, but a bit obtuse;
At times, indeed, almost ridiculous—
Almost, at times, the Fool.

I grow old . . . I grow old . . .   120
I shall wear the bottoms of my trousers rolled.

Shall I part my hair behind? Do I dare to eat a peach?
I shall wear white flannel trousers, and walk upon the beach.
I have heard the mermaids singing, each to each.

I do not think that they will sing to me.   125

I have seen them riding seaward on the waves
Combing the white hair of the waves blown back
When the wind blows the water white and black.

We have lingered in the chambers of the sea
By sea-girls wreathed with seaweed red and brown   130
Till human voices wake us, and we drown.

THE LOVE SONG OF J. ALFRED PRUFROCK. The epigraph, from Dante's *Inferno*, is the speech of one dead and damned, who thinks that his hearer also is going to remain in Hell. Count Guido da Montefeltro, whose sin has been to give false counsel after a corrupt prelate had offered him prior absolution and whose punishment is to be wrapped in a constantly burning flame, offers to tell Dante his story:

> If I thought my answer were to someone who
>   might see the world again, then there would be
>   no more stirrings of this flame. Since it is true
> that no one leaves these depths of misery
>   alive, from all that I have heard reported,
>   I answer you without fear of infamy.

(Translation by Michael Palma from: Dante Alighieri, *Inferno: A New Verse Translation* [New York: Norton, 2002].) 29 *works and days*: title of a poem by Hesiod (eighth century B.C.), depicting his life as a hard-working Greek farmer and exhorting his brother to be like him. 82 *head . . . platter*: like that of John the Baptist, prophet and praiser of chastity, whom King Herod beheaded at the demand of Herodias, his unlawfully wedded wife (see Mark 6:17–28). 92–93 *squeezed . . . To roll it*: an echo from Marvell's "To His Coy Mistress," lines 41–42. 94 *Lazarus*: probably the Lazarus whom Jesus called forth from the tomb (John 11:1–44), but possibly the beggar seen in Heaven by the rich man in Hell (Luke 16:19–25). 105 *magic lantern*: an early type of projector used to display still pictures from transparent slides.

Questions

1. What expectations are created by the title of the poem? Are those expectations fulfilled by the text?

2. John Berryman wrote of line 3, "With this line, modern poetry begins." What do you think he meant?

3. It has been said that Prufrock suffers from a "morbid self-consciousness." How many references can you find in the poem to back up that statement?

4. In the total context of the poem, is the sense of lines 47–48 reassuring or disturbing? Explain your choice.

5. How do lines 70–72 relate to the questions that Prufrock raises in the three preceding stanzas (lines 49–69)?

6. What is the effect of riming "ices" and "crisis"? Can you find similar instances elsewhere in the poem?

7. Is the situation in the poem presented statically, or is there discernible development as the poem proceeds? Defend your answer with references to the text.

8. What, finally, is your attitude toward Prufrock—identification, sympathy, contempt, or something more complicated?

T. S. ELIOT ON WRITING

Poet T. S. Eliot teaching a class.

Poetry and Emotion   1919

It is not in his personal emotions, the emotions provoked by particular events in his life, that the poet is in any way remarkable or interesting. His particular emotions may be simple, or crude, or flat. The emotion in his poetry will be a very complex thing, but not with the complexity of the emotions of people who have very complex or unusual emotions in life. One error, in fact, of eccentricity in poetry is to seek for new human emotions to express; and in this search for novelty in the wrong place it discovers the perverse. The business of the poet is not to find new emotions, but to use the ordinary ones and, in working them up into poetry, to express feelings which are not in actual emotions at all. And emotions which he has never experienced will serve his turn as well as those familiar to him. Consequently, we must believe that "emotion recollected in tranquility"° is an inexact formula. For it is neither emotion, nor recollection, nor, without distortion of meaning, tranquility. It is a concentration, and a new thing resulting from the concentration, of a very great number of experiences which to the practical and active person would not seem to be experiences at all; it is a concentration which does not happen consciously or of deliberation. These experiences are not "recollected," and they finally unite in an atmosphere which is "tranquil" only in that it is a passive attending upon the event. Of course this is not quite the whole story. There is a great deal, in the writing of poetry, which must be conscious and deliberate. In fact, the bad poet is usually unconscious where he ought to be conscious, and conscious where he ought to be unconscious. Both errors tend to make him "personal." Poetry is not a turning loose of emotion, but an escape from emotion; it is not the expression of personality, but an escape from personality. But, of course, only those who have personality and emotions know what it means to want to escape from these things.

From "Tradition and the Individual Talent"

The Objective Correlative   1919

The only way of expressing emotion in the form of art is by finding an "objective correlative"; in other words, a set of objects, a situation, a chain of events which shall be the formula of that *particular* emotion; such that when the external facts, which must terminate in sensory experience, are given, the emotion is immediately evoked. If you examine any of Shakespeare's more successful tragedies, you will find this exact equivalence; you will find that the state of mind of Lady Macbeth walking in her sleep has been communicated to you by a skillful accumulation of imagined sensory impressions; the words of Macbeth on hearing of his wife's death strike us as if, given the sequence of events, these words were automatically released by the last event in the series. The artistic "inevitability" lies in this complete adequacy of the external to the emotion . . .

From "Hamlet and His Problems"

"*emotion recollected in tranquility*": Eliot is alluding to William Wordsworth's famous statement in his 1800 Preface to *Lyrical Ballads*: "I have said that Poetry is the spontaneous overflow of powerful feelings: it takes its origin from emotion recollected in tranquility."

CRITICS ON "PRUFROCK"

Denis Donoghue (b. 1928)

One of the Irrefutable Poets   2000

[Eliot] didn't come into my life till I went to university in Dublin. It is my impression that I first read "The Love Song of J. Alfred Prufrock" in the National Library, Kildare Street, my home-away-from-home. I knew that it was a different kind of poetry from Yeats's or Byron's and that I would never forget it. My criterion for poetry at that time was simple: a poem should be memorable. . . . "Prufrock" was one of those. At first reading, it took up residence in my mind. From that day to this I've never wavered from my conviction that it is a fully achieved poem or doubted that Eliot is one of the irrefutable poets. . . .

"Prufrock" seemed to me a poem about a man's dread of being no good. Later readings have made me think that it is about spiritual panic, the mind whirling in a void, or the penury of one's being in the world. No one instructed me to think of the poem in relation to Allen Tate's assertion that "in Mr. Eliot, puritan obligation withdraws into private conscience." Now that "Prufrock" seems to be the only poem of Eliot's that young people in America read, I find that my students at New York University take it as an uncanny description of themselves, their distress, their fear of having already failed. Prufrock is brooding on his insufficiency in mock-epic terms, but the terms don't remove his conviction of being inadequate. Growing up in Ireland, where there were no choices and one was lucky to get a job of any kind, I was likely to internalize the theme and to find Prufrock already defeated.

Knowing no Italian, I could make nothing of the epigraph to *Prufrock and Other Observations* or the further one to "Prufrock." The poem began for me with "Let us go then, you and I . . ." I'm still puzzled by the epigraph to the poem, but for different reasons. In *Inferno* xxvii Dante meets Guido da Montefeltro, confined in a single flame of punishment for having given false counsel to Pope Boniface. Guido answers Dante: "If I believed that my reply would be to someone who would return to earth, this flame would remain without further movement; but since no one has ever returned alive from this abyss, if what I hear is true, I answer you without fear of infamy." It's not clear what bearing this has on "Prufrock." In the "No! I am not Prince Hamlet" passage, Prufrock speaks of himself as if he were Polonius, but he doesn't confess to having given the king fraudulent advice. Perhaps the epigraph has him saying: I'll tell the truth about my life, however humiliating it turns out to be. Or it may be Eliot's device to clear a space for himself, ridding the reader's mind of extraneous matter, all the more effectively because the epigraph is in a foreign language. Or his way of insisting that what follows is a made poem, not what it might seem, a transcript of someone's confession. Eliot tended to choose an epigraph related to the poem it preceded by congruity or contradiction: either way, he enjoyed the latitude of keeping readers on their toes. I note, incidentally, that in his recording of the poem, he hasn't included the epigraph; he goes straight into "Let us go then . . ."

From *Words Alone: The Poet T. S. Eliot*

Philip R. Headings (1922–1982)

The Pronouns in the Poem: "One," "You," and "I"   1982

"One"

The "one"° of the poem presents no great problems. She seems to be a feminine counterpart of either "you" or "I," frequenting the same Boston teas, expressing on occasion dissatisfactions with the unfulfilling, conventionalized life of that whole milieu. Her
awarenesses may parallel theirs, though "I" is not sure. He probably does not even have a
particular lady in mind; if he had, he would likely have used "she" instead of "one." This
is not to deny the sexual component in his Love Song; it is rather to say that he is open
to various possibilities in that regard—to whatever lady demonstrates the qualities requi-
site to become his Lady, his Beatrice.°

"You" and "I"

The "you" and "I" of the first line present greater difficulties. Critics have commonly
interpreted them as referring to two parts of Prufrock, carrying on a conversation
with himself. This interpretation now seems to me both too clever and much simpler
than the actual situation in the poem. . . .
Sometime before 1949 Eliot wrote to Kristian Smidt:

> As for THE LOVE SONG OF J. ALFRED PRUFROCK anything I say now must be
> somewhat conjectural, as it was written so long ago that my memory may
> deceive me; but I am prepared to assert that the "you" in THE LOVE SONG is
> merely some friend or companion, *presumably of the male sex*, whom *the
> speaker* is at that moment addressing . . . [italics mine].

Having finally carefully compared "Prufrock" to Dante's *Inferno* and read dozens of
critiques of the poem, I now see no reason to dissent from Eliot's straightforward
statement. In fact, I see no other way of interpreting the poem that will fit all its
complexities. Old Possum's° delightful sense of humor is apparent in that phrase
"presumably of the male sex" and in "the speaker"; he knew very well that he himself,
allegorically projected to the age of thirty-five, or a persona very like that projection,
was the "friend or companion," the Dante-figure of the poem. The "I" who addresses
him is an unidentified friend.
  "You" and "I" are probably close friends and confidants who have attended such
teas together, though perhaps they have only discussed them.
  Though the presence of "you" is crucial to Eliot's Dantean intent, "Prufrock" is
a dramatic monologue, not a dialogue. It parallels monologues of Shakespeare's
Polonius, Dante's Pilgrim, Guido, and Ulysses. The only functions of the "you" are
to elicit confidences, set the Dantean tone, indicate Prufrock's equivalence with
Guido in the poem's epigraph, listen to the "I," and write the poem—bring back
the story.

From "Dantean Observations," *T. S. Eliot*

"one": The "one" of lines 96–98, "If one, settling a pillow by her head / Should say: 'That is not what I
meant at all. / That is not it, at all.'" *Beatrice*: Beatrice Portinari (1266–1290), Dante's inspiration in *The
New Life* and *The Divine Comedy*. *Old Possum*: Eliot's playful nickname for himself, used in the title *Old
Possum's Book of Practical Cats* (1939).

Maud Ellmann (b. 1954)

Will There Be Time?   1987

. . . Prufrock is etherized by *time*. This is the time that separates desire from fulfillment, motive from execution, thought from speech: in Eliot's words, "the awful separation between potential passion and any actualization possible in life." Time defers.

The way that time defers is through revision. Time itself becomes the object of revision, for the whole poem agonizes over writing time. The incessant repetition of "There will be time" is itself a way of losing time, as Nancy K. Gish[1] suggests; but also a way of gaining it, to prolong the re-editions of desire. "Stretched . . . beside you and me," time deflects Prufrock's ardor from his lover. But in this process time itself becomes the object of desire, in the form of the voluptuary sweetness of the evening. Indeed, Prufrock addresses time so constantly, in every tone of envy, rage, pain, impatience, longing, humor, flattery, seduction, that he can only really be in love with time.

Revisionary time: because revision has no present tense, and neither does "The Love Song." Instead, the poem hesitates between anticipation and regret for missed appointments with the self, the other or the muse. It begins in the future tense ("there will be time . . . " [23ff]); shifts into the perfect ("For I have known . . ." [49ff]); and finally subsides into the past conditional, the tense of wishful thinking: "I should have been . . . " (73). Because presence would mean speech, apocalypse, Prufrock only pauses in the present tense to say what he is not—"No! I am not Prince Hamlet" (a disavowal that conjures up the effigy that it denies, since Hamlet is the very spirit of theatricality). The poem concludes dreaming the future, faithful if only to its hopeless passion for postponement: "Till human voices wake us, and we drown." Prufrock feels the need to speak as a proof of his identity and as a rock to give him anchorage: yet speech would also mean his end, for voices are waters in which Prufrocks drown.

Through time, all Prufrock's aims have turned awry. His passion and his speech have lost themselves in detours, never to achieve satiety. Love becomes desire—tormenting, inexhaustible—while speech and revelation have surrendered to writing and revision, to the digressions which prolong his dalliance with time. Time is the greatest fetish of them all, the mother of all fetishes, since it is through time that all aims turn aside to revel in rehearsals, detours, transferences. What Prufrock longs for is a talking cure because, like Freud, he thinks that speech alone can transform repetition into memory. What talking remedies is *writing*: for his illness lies in his obsessive re-editions of the text of love. But Prufrock's very histrionics show he is condemned to reenactment, to forget what he repeats in a script that restlessly obliterates its history. It is by remembering the past that the subject can establish his identity, but only by forgetting it can he accede to his desire. Refusing to declare his love, or pop the overwhelming question, Prufrock renounces the position of the speaking subject, but he instigates the drama of revision in its stead. And it is by refusing sexual relation that he conjures up the theatre of desire. The love song Prufrock could not *sing* has been *writing* itself all the time, and the love that could not speak its name has been roving

---

[1]Nancy K. Gish, *Time in the Poetry of T. S. Eliot* (London: Macmillan, 1981) 15–16.

among all the fetishes his rhetoric has liberated to desire. We had the love song, even if we missed the meaning.

From *The Poetics of Impersonality: T. S. Eliot and Ezra Pound*

■ WRITING *effectively*

TOPICS FOR WRITING

1. "The Love Song of J. Alfred Prufrock" is very firmly grounded in upper-class society in the early twentieth century. Is the poem of purely historical value, opening a window on a society and a set of values that no longer exist, or are the attitudes and concerns that it expresses still relevant today?

2. In the excerpt entitled "Poetry and Emotion," Eliot says: "There is a great deal, in the writing of poetry, which must be conscious and deliberate. . . . Poetry is not a turning loose of emotion, but an escape from emotion; it is not the expression of personality, but an escape from personality." Discuss this statement, in terms of both its own meaning and its application to "The Love Song of J. Alfred Prufrock."

3. "The Love Song of J. Alfred Prufrock" features a speaker who expresses fear or ambivalence about love. What are the speaker's fears? Are there any sound reasons for his romantic uncertainty?

4. Eliot's poem mentions several famous cultural names—Michelangelo, John the Baptist, Lazarus, and Hamlet (as well as his epigraph from Dante's *Inferno*). What do these allusions tell the reader about Prufrock and his social environment? Would Eliot's poem be more accessible without them or would it be less effective?

5. Write your own version of the poem by substituting for Michelangelo, morning coats, coffee spoons, and other specific references in the text. The idea is not to parody Eliot or spoof the poem, but instead to do something more challenging—to come up with "objective correlatives" appropriate to contemporary society and culture, just as Eliot found them for his time and place.

31

POEMS FOR FURTHER READING

Aaron Abeyta (b. 1971)

thirteen ways of looking at a tortilla   2001

i.

among twenty different tortillas
the only thing moving
was the mouth of the niño

ii.

i was of three cultures
like a tortilla
for which there are three bolios   5

iii.

the tortilla grew on the wooden table
it was a small part of the earth

iv.

a house and a tortilla
are one
a man a woman and a tortilla   10
are one

v.

i do not know which to prefer
the beauty of the red wall
or the beauty of the green wall   15
the tortilla fresh
or just after

vi.

tortillas filled the small kitchen
with ancient shadows
the shadow of Maclovia   20
cooking long ago
the tortilla
rolled from the shadow
the innate roundness

vii.

o thin viejos of chimayo   25
why do you imagine biscuits
do you not see how the tortilla
lives with the hands
of the women about you

viii.

i know soft corn
and beautiful inescapable sopapillas
but i know too
that the tortilla
has taught me what I know

ix.

when the tortilla is gone
it marks the end
of one of many tortillas

x.

at the sight of tortillas
browning on a black comal°   *flat griddle pan*
even the pachucos of española
would cry out sharply

xi.

he rode over new mexico
in a pearl low rider
once he got a flat
in that he mistook
the shadow of his spare
for a tortilla

xii.

the abuelitas are moving
the tortilla must be baking

xiii.

it was cinco de mayo all year
it was warm
and it was going to get warmer
the tortilla sat
on the frijolito plate

Compare

"thirteen ways of looking at a tortilla" with "Thirteen Ways of Looking at a Blackbird" by
Wallace Stevens (page 673).

Anonymous (traditional Scottish ballad)

Lord Randall

"O where ha you been, Lord Randal, my son?
And where ha you been, my handsome young man?"
"I ha been at the greenwood; mother, mak my bed soon,
For I'm wearied wi hunting, and fain wad lie down."

"An wha° met ye there, Lord Randal, my son?   *who*   5
An wha met you there, my handsome young man?"

"O I met wi my true-love; mother, mak my bed soon,
For I'm wearied wi hunting, and fain wad lie down."

"And what did she give you, Lord Randal, my son?
And what did she give you, my handsome young man?"   10
"Eels fried in a pan; mother, mak my bed soon,
For I'm wearied wi hunting, and fain wad lie down."

"And wha gat° your leavins,° Lord Randal, my son?   *got; leftovers*
And wha gat your leavins, my handsome young man?"
"My hawks and my hounds; mother, mak my bed soon,   15
For I'm wearied wi hunting, and fain wad lie down."

"And what becam of them, Lord Randal, my son?
And what becam of them, my handsome young man?"
"They stretched their legs out an died; mother, mak my bed soon,
For I'm wearied wi hunting, and fain wad lie down."   20

"O I fear you are poisoned, Lord Randal, my son!
I fear you are poisoned, my handsome young man!"
"O yes, I am poisoned; mother, mak my bed soon,
For I'm sick at the heart, and I fain wad lie down."

"What d' ye leave to your mother, Lord Randal, my son?   25
What d' ye leave to your mother, my handsome young man?"
"Four and twenty milk kye;° mother, mak my bed soon,   *cows*
For I'm sick at the heart, and I fain wad lie down."

"What d' ye leave to your sister, Lord Randal, my son?
What d' ye leave to your sister, my handsome young man?"   30
"My gold and my silver; mother, mak my bed soon,
For I'm sick at the heart, and I fain wad lie down."

"What d' ye leave to your brother, Lord Randal, my son?
What d' ye leave to your brother, my handsome young man?"
"My house and my lands; mother, mak my bed soon,   35
For I'm sick at the heart, and I fain wad lie down."

"What d' ye leave to your true-love, Lord Randal, my son?
What d' ye leave to your true-love, my handsome young man?"
"I leave her hell and fire; mother, mak my bed soon,
For I'm sick at the heart, and I fain wad lie down."   40

Compare

"Lord Randall" with a modern ballad such as "Ballad of Birmingham" by Dudley Randall (page 604).

Matthew Arnold (1822–1888)

Dover Beach   1867

The sea is calm to-night.
The tide is full, the moon lies fair
Upon the straits; on the French coast the light

Gleams and is gone; the cliffs of England stand,
Glimmering and vast, out in the tranquil bay.   5
Come to the window, sweet is the night-air!
Only, from the long line of spray
Where the sea meets the moon-blanched land,
Listen! you hear the grating roar
Of pebbles which the waves draw back, and fling,   10
At their return, up the high strand,
Begin, and cease, and then again begin,
With tremulous cadence slow, and bring
The eternal note of sadness in.

Sophocles long ago   15
Heard it on the Aegean, and it brought
Into his mind the turbid ebb and flow
Of human misery; we
Find also in the sound a thought,
Hearing it by this distant northern sea.   20

The Sea of Faith
Was once, too, at the full, and round earth's shore
Lay like the folds of a bright girdle furled.
But now I only hear
Its melancholy, long, withdrawing roar,   25
Retreating, to the breath
Of the night-wind, down the vast edges drear
And naked shingles° of the world.   *gravel beaches*

Ah, love, let us be true
To one another! for the world, which seems   30
To lie before us like a land of dreams,
So various, so beautiful, so new,
Hath really neither joy, nor love, nor light,
Nor certitude, nor peace, nor help for pain;
And we are here as on a darkling° plain   *darkened or darkening* 35
Swept with confused alarms of struggle and flight,
Where ignorant armies clash by night.

Compare

"Dover Beach" with "Sea Grapes" by Derek Walcott (page 880).

John Ashbery (b. 1927)

At North Farm   1984

Somewhere someone is traveling furiously toward you,
At incredible speed, traveling day and night,
Through blizzards and desert heat, across torrents, through narrow passes.
But will he know where to find you,
Recognize you when he sees you,   5
Give you the thing he has for you?

Hardly anything grows here,
Yet the granaries are bursting with meal,
The sacks of meal piled to the rafters.
The streams run with sweetness, fattening fish;   10
Birds darken the sky. Is it enough
That the dish of milk is set out at night,
That we think of him sometimes,
Sometimes and always, with mixed feelings?

Compare

"At North Farm" with "Uphill" by Christina Rossetti (page 690).

Margaret Atwood (b. 1939)

Siren Song   1974

This is the one song everyone
would like to learn: the song
that is irresistible:

the song that forces men
to leap overboard in squadrons   5
even though they see the beached skulls

the song nobody knows
because anyone who has heard it
is dead, and the others can't remember.

Shall I tell you the secret   10
and if I do, will you get me
out of this bird suit?

Margaret Atwood

I don't enjoy it here
squatting on this island
looking picturesque and mythical

with these two feathery maniacs,
I don't enjoy singing
this trio, fatal and valuable.

I will tell the secret to you,
to you, only to you.   20
Come closer. This song

is a cry for help: Help me!
Only you, only you can,
you are unique

at last. Alas   25
it is a boring song
but it works every time.

SIREN SONG. In Greek mythology, sirens were half-woman, half-bird nymphs who lured sailors to their deaths by singing hypnotically beautiful songs.

Compare
"Siren Song" with "Her Kind" by Anne Sexton (page 513).

W. H. Auden (1907–1973)

As I Walked Out One Evening   1940

As I walked out one evening,
  Walking down Bristol Street,
The crowds upon the pavement
  Were fields of harvest wheat.

And down by the brimming river   5
  I heard a lover sing
Under an arch of the railway:
  "Love has no ending.

"I'll love you, dear, I'll love you
  Till China and Africa meet,   10
And the river jumps over the mountain
  And the salmon sing in the street,

"I'll love you till the ocean
  Is folded and hung up to dry
And the seven stars go squawking   15
  Like geese about the sky.

"The years shall run like rabbits,
  For in my arms I hold
The Flower of the Ages,
  And the first love of the world."   20

But all the clocks in the city
  Began to whirr and chime:
"O let not Time deceive you,
  You cannot conquer Time.

"In the burrows of the Nightmare   25
  Where Justice naked is,
Time watches from the shadow
  And coughs when you would kiss.

"In headaches and in worry
  Vaguely life leaks away,   30
And Time will have his fancy
  To-morrow or to-day.

"Into many a green valley
  Drifts the appalling snow;
Time breaks the threaded dances   35
  And the diver's brilliant bow.

"O plunge your hands in water,
  Plunge them in up to the wrist;

W. H. Auden

Stare, stare in the basin
    And wonder what you've missed.   40

"The glacier knocks in the cupboard,
    The desert sighs in the bed,
And the crack in the tea-cup opens
    A lane to the land of the dead.

"Where the beggars raffle the banknotes   45
    And the Giant is enchanting to Jack,
And the Lily-white Boy is a Roarer,
    And Jill goes down on her back.

"O look, look in the mirror,
    O look in your distress;   50
Life remains a blessing
    Although you cannot bless.

"O stand, stand at the window
    As the tears scald and start;
You shall love your crooked neighbor   55
    With your crooked heart."

It was late, late in the evening,
    The lovers they were gone;
The clocks had ceased their chiming,
    And the deep river ran on.   60

Compare

"As I Walked Out One Evening" with "Dover Beach" by Matthew Arnold (page 818) and
"anyone lived in a pretty how town" by E. E. Cummings (page 540).

The Fall of Icarus by Pieter Brueghel the Elder (1520?–1569).

W. H. Auden (1907–1973)

Musée des Beaux Arts   1940

About suffering they were never wrong,
The Old Masters: how well they understood
Its human position; how it takes place
While someone else is eating or opening a window or just walking
    dully along;
How, when the aged are reverently, passionately waiting   5
For the miraculous birth, there always must be
Children who did not specially want it to happen, skating
On a pond at the edge of the wood:
They never forgot
That even the dreadful martyrdom must run its course   10
Anyhow in a corner, some untidy spot
Where the dogs go on with their doggy life and the torturer's horse
Scratches its innocent behind on a tree.

In Brueghel's *Icarus*, for instance: how everything turns away
Quite leisurely from the disaster; the ploughman may   15
Have heard the splash, the forsaken cry,
But for him it was not an important failure; the sun shone
As it had to on the white legs disappearing into the green
Water; and the expensive delicate ship that must have seen
Something amazing, a boy falling out of the sky,   20
Had somewhere to get to and sailed calmly on.

Compare

"Musée des Beaux Arts" with "The Dance" by William Carlos Williams (page 670) and the
painting by Pieter Brueghel to which each poem refers.

Elizabeth Bishop (1911–1979)

Filling Station   1965

Oh, but it is dirty!
—this little filling station,
oil-soaked, oil-permeated
to a disturbing, over-all
black translucency.   5
Be careful with that match!

Father wears a dirty,
oil-soaked monkey suit
that cuts him under the arms,
and several quick and saucy   10
and greasy sons assist him

Elizabeth Bishop

(it's a family filling station),
all quite thoroughly dirty.

Do they live in the station?
It has a cement porch   15
behind the pumps, and on it
a set of crushed and grease-
impregnated wickerwork;
on the wicker sofa
a dirty dog, quite comfy.   20

Some comic books provide
the only note of color—
of certain color. They lie
upon a big dim doily
draping a taboret°   stool   25
(part of the set), beside
a big hirsute begonia.

Why the extraneous plant?
Why the taboret?
Why, oh why, the doily?   30
(Embroidered in daisy stitch
with marguerites, I think,
and heavy with gray crochet.)

Somebody embroidered the doily.
Somebody waters the plant,   35
or oils it, maybe. Somebody
arranges the rows of cans
so that they softly say:
ESSO—SO—SO—SO
to high-strung automobiles.   40
Somebody loves us all.

Compare

"Filling Station" with "The splendor falls on castle walls" by Alfred, Lord Tennyson (page 619).

William Blake (1757–1827)

The Tyger   1794

Tyger! Tyger! burning bright
In the forests of the night,
What immortal hand or eye
Could frame thy fearful symmetry?

In what distant deeps or skies   5
Burnt the fire of thine eyes?
On what wings dare he aspire?
What the hand dare seize the fire?

William Blake

And what shoulder, and what art,
Could twist the sinews of thy heart?
And when thy heart began to beat,
What dread hand? and what dread feet?

What the hammer? what the chain?
In what furnace was thy brain?
What the anvil? what dread grasp
Dare its deadly terrors clasp?

When the stars threw down their spears,
And watered heaven with their tears,
Did he smile his work to see?
Did he who made the Lamb make thee?

Tyger! Tyger! burning bright
In the forests of the night,
What immortal hand or eye
Dare frame thy fearful symmetry?

Detail of William Blake's *The Tyger.*

Compare
"The Tyger" with "The Windhover" by Gerard Manley Hopkins (page 848).

William Blake (1757–1827)

The Sick Rose   1794

O Rose, thou art sick!
The invisible worm
That flies in the night,
In the howling storm,

Has found out thy bed   5
Of crimson joy,
And his dark secret love
Does thy life destroy.

Compare

"The Sick Rose" with "Go, Lovely Rose" by Edmund Waller (page 881).

Gwendolyn Brooks (1917–2000)

the mother   1945

Abortions will not let you forget.
You remember the children you got that you did not
      get,
The damp small pulps with a little or with no hair,
The singers and workers that never handled the air.
You will never neglect or beat   5
Them, or silence or buy with a sweet.
You will never wind up the sucking-thumb
Or scuttle off ghosts that come.
You will never leave them, controlling your luscious sigh,
Return for a snack of them, with gobbling mother-eye.   10

Gwendolyn Brooks

I have heard in the voices of the wind the voices of my dim killed children.
I have contracted. I have eased
My dim dears at the breasts they could never suck.
I have said, Sweets, if I sinned, if I seized
Your luck   15
And your lives from your unfinished reach,
If I stole your births and your names,
Your straight baby tears and your games,
Your stilted or lovely loves, your tumults, your marriages, aches, and your deaths,
If I poisoned the beginnings of your breaths,   20
Believe that even in my deliberateness I was not deliberate.
Though why should I whine,
Whine that the crime was other than mine?—
Since anyhow you are dead.
Or rather, or instead,   25
You were never made.
But that too, I am afraid,

Is faulty: oh, what shall I say, how is the truth to be said?
You were born, you had body, you died.
It is just that you never giggled or planned or cried.   30

Believe me, I loved you all.
Believe me, I knew you, though faintly, and I loved, I loved you
All.

Compare

"the mother" with "Metaphors" by Sylvia Plath (page 582).

Gwendolyn Brooks   (1917–2000)

the rites for Cousin Vit

1949

Carried her unprotesting out the door.
Kicked back the casket-stand. But it can't hold her,
That stuff and satin aiming to enfold her,
The lid's contrition nor the bolts before.
Oh oh. Too much. Too much. Even now, surmise,   5
She rises in the sunshine. There she goes,
Back to the bars she knew and the repose
In love-rooms and the things in people's eyes.
Too vital and too squeaking. Must emerge.
Even now she does the snake-hips with a hiss,   10
Slops the bad wine across her shantung, talks
Of pregnancy, guitars and bridgework, walks
In parks or alleys, comes haply on the verge
Of happiness, haply hysterics. Is.

Compare

"the rites for Cousin Vit" with "Do not go gentle into that good night" by Dylan Thomas
(page 659).

Elizabeth Barrett Browning   (1806–1861)

How Do I Love Thee? Let Me Count the Ways

1850

How do I love thee? Let me count the ways.
I love thee to the depth and breadth and height
My soul can reach, when feeling out of sight
For the ends of Being and ideal Grace.
I love thee to the level of every day's   5
Most quiet need, by sun and candle-light.
I love thee freely, as men strive for Right.
I love thee purely, as they turn from Praise.
I love thee with the passion put to use

In my old griefs, and with my childhood's faith. 10
I love thee with a love I seemed to lose
With my lost saints,— I love thee with the breath,
Smiles, tears, of all my life!—and, if God choose,
I shall but love thee better after death.

Compare

"How Do I Love Thee?" with "What lips my lips have kissed" by Edna St. Vincent Millay
(page 654).

Robert Browning (1812–1889)

Soliloquy of the Spanish Cloister   1842

Gr-r-r—there go, my heart's abhorrence!
   Water your damned flower-pots, do!
If hate killed men, Brother Lawrence,
   God's blood, would not mine kill you!
What? your myrtle-bush wants trimming?   5
   Oh, that rose has prior claims—
Needs its leaden vase filled brimming?
   Hell dry you up with its flames!

At the meal we sit together;
   Salve tibi!° I must hear   *Hail to thee!*   10
Wise talk of the kind of weather,
   Sort of season, time of year:
Not a plenteous cork-crop: scarcely
   Dare we hope oak-galls, I doubt:
What's the Latin name for "parsley"?   15
   What's the Greek name for Swine's Snout?

Whew! We'll have our platter burnished,
   Laid with care on our own shelf!
With a fire-new spoon we're furnished,
   And a goblet for ourself,   20
Rinsed like something sacrificial
   Ere 'tis fit to touch our chaps—
Marked with L. for our initial!
   (He-he! There his lily snaps!)

Saint, forsooth! While brown Dolores   25
   Squats outside the Convent bank
With Sanchicha, telling stories,
   Steeping tresses in the tank,
Blue-black, lustrous, thick like horsehairs,
   —Can't I see his dead eye glow,   30
Bright as 'twere a Barbary corsair's?
   (That is, if he'd let it show!)

When he finishes refection,
    Knife and fork he never lays
Cross-wise, to my recollection,
    As I do, in Jesu's praise.
I the Trinity illustrate,   35
    Drinking watered orange-pulp—
In three sips the Arian frustrate;
    While he drains his at one gulp!

Oh, those melons! if he's able   40
    We're to have a feast; so nice!
One goes to the Abbot's table
    All of us get each a slice.
How go on your flowers? None double?
    Not one fruit-sort can you spy?   45
Strange!—And I, too, at such trouble,
    Keep them close-nipped on the sly!

There's a great text in Galatians,
    Once you trip on it, entails
Twenty-nine distinct damnations,   50
    One sure, if another fails:
If I trip him just a-dying,
    Sure of heaven as sure can be,
Spin him round and send him flying   55
    Off to hell, a Manichee?

Or, my scrofulous French novel
    On grey paper with blunt type!
Simply glance at it, you grovel
    Hand and foot in Belial's gripe: 60
If I double down its pages
    At the woeful sixteenth print,
When he gathers his greengages,
    Ope a sieve and slip it in't?

Or, there's Satan!—one might venture   65
    Pledge one's soul to him, yet leave
Such a flaw in the indenture
    As he'd miss till, past retrieve,
Blasted lay that rose-acacia
    We're so proud of! Hy, Zy, Hine. . . .   70
'St, there's Vespers! *Plena gratia*
    Ave, Virgo!° Gr-r-r—you swine!

    Hail, Virgin, full of grace!

SOLILOQUY OF THE SPANISH CLOISTER. 3 *Brother Lawrence:* one of the speaker's fellow monks. 31 *Barbary corsair:* a pirate operating off the Barbary Coast of Africa. 39 *Arian:* a follower of Arius, a heretic who denied the doctrine of the Trinity. 49 *a Great text in Galatians:* a difficult verse in this book of the Bible. Brother Lawrence will be damned as a heretic if he wrongly interprets it. 56 *Manichee:* another kind of heretic, one who (after the Persian philosopher Mani) sees in the world a constant struggle between good and evil, neither able to win. 60 *Belial:* here, not specifically Satan but (as used in the

Old Testament) a name for wickedness. 70 *Hy, Zy, Hine:* possibly the sound of a bell to announce evening devotions.

Compare

"Soliloquy of the Spanish Cloister" with "Down, Wanton, Down!" by Robert Graves (page 530).

Charles Bukowski (1920–1994)

Dostoevsky   1997

against the wall, the firing squad ready.
then he got a reprieve.
suppose they had shot Dostoevsky?
before he wrote all that?
I suppose it wouldn't have   5
mattered
not directly.
there are billions of people who have
never read him and never
will.   10
but as a young man I know that he   **Charles Bukowski**
got me through the factories,
past the whores,
lifted me high through the night
and put me down   15
in a better
place.
even while in the bar
drinking with the other
derelicts,   20
I was glad they gave Dostoevsky a
reprieve,
it gave me one,
allowed me to look directly at those
rancid faces   25
in my world,
death pointing its finger,
I held fast,
an immaculate drunk
sharing the stinking dark with   30
my
brothers.

DOSTOEVSKY. The Russian novelist Fyodor Dostoevsky (1821–1880), author of *Crime and Punishment* and *The Brothers Karamazov*, was arrested in 1849 in a czarist crackdown on liberal organizations and sentenced to death. It was not until the members of the firing squad had aimed their rifles and were awaiting the order to fire that he was informed that his sentence had been commuted to four years of hard labor in Siberia.

Compare

"Dostoevsky" with "When to the sessions of sweet silent thought" by William Shakespeare (page 873).

Lorna Dee Cervantes (b. 1954)

Cannery Town in August

1981

All night it humps the air.
Speechless, the steam rises
from the cannery columns. I hear
the night bird rave about work
or lunch, or sing the swing shift   5
home. I listen, while bodyless
uniforms and spinach specked shoes
drift in monochrome down the dark
moon-possessed streets. Women
who smell of whiskey and tomatoes,   10
peach fuzz reddening their lips and eyes—
I imagine them not speaking, dumbed
by the can's clamor and drop
to the trucks that wait, grunting
in their headlights below.   15
They spotlight those who walk
like a dream, with no one
waiting in the shadows
to palm them back to living.

Compare

"Cannery Town in August" with "London" by William Blake (page 550).

Samuel Taylor Coleridge (1772–1834)

Kubla Khan

(1797–1798)

Or, a Vision in a Dream. A Fragment.

In Xanadu did Kubla Khan
A stately pleasure-dome decree:
Where Alph, the sacred river, ran
Through caverns measureless to man
   Down to a sunless sea.   5
So twice five miles of fertile ground
With walls and towers were girdled round;
And here were gardens bright with sinuous rills,
Where blossomed many an incense-bearing tree;
And here were forests ancient as the hills,   10
Enfolding sunny spots of greenery.

But oh! that deep romantic chasm which slanted
Down the green hill athwart a cedarn cover!
A savage place! as holy and enchanted
As e'er beneath a waning moon was haunted   15
By woman wailing for her demon-lover!

And from this chasm, with ceaseless turmoil seething,
As if this earth in fast thick pants were breathing,
A mighty fountain momently was forced:
Amid whose swift half-intermitted burst 20
Huge fragments vaulted like rebounding hail,
Or chaffy grain beneath the thresher's flail:
And 'mid these dancing rocks at once and ever
It flung up momently the sacred river.
Five miles meandering with a mazy motion 25
Through wood and dale the sacred river ran,
Then reached the caverns measureless to man,
And sank in tumult to a lifeless ocean:
And 'mid this tumult Kubla heard from far
Ancestral voices prophesying war! 30

   The shadow of the dome of pleasure
   Floated midway on the waves;
   Where was heard the mingled measure
   From the fountain and the caves.
It was a miracle of rare device, 35
A sunny pleasure-dome with caves of ice!

   A damsel with a dulcimer
   In a vision once I saw:
   It was an Abyssinian maid,
   And on her dulcimer she played, 40
   Singing of Mount Abora.
   Could I revive within me
   Her symphony and song,
   To such a deep delight 'twould win me,
That with music loud and long, 45
I would build that dome in air,
That sunny dome! those caves of ice!
And all who heard should see them there,
And all should cry, Beware! Beware!
His flashing eyes, his floating hair! 50
Weave a circle round him thrice,
And close your eyes with holy dread,
For he on honey-dew hath fed,
And drunk the milk of Paradise.

KUBLA KHAN. There was an actual Kublai Khan, a thirteenth-century Mongol emperor, and a Chinese city of Xanadu; but Coleridge's dream vision also borrows from travelers' descriptions of such other exotic places as Abyssinia and America. 51 *circle:* a magic circle drawn to keep away evil spirits.

Compare

"Kubla Khan" with "The Second Coming" by William Butler Yeats (page 705).

Billy Collins (b. 1941)

Care and Feeding

2003

Billy Collins

Because I will turn 420 tomorrow
in dog years
I will take myself for a long walk
along the green shore of the lake,

and when I walk in the door,   5
I will jump up on my chest
and lick my nose and ears and eyelids
while I tell myself again and again to get down.

I will fill my metal bowl at the sink
with cold fresh water,   10
and lift a biscuit from the jar
and hold it gingerly with my teeth.

Then I will make three circles
and lie down at my feet on the wood floor
and close my eyes   15
while I type all morning and into the afternoon,

checking every once in a while
to make sure I am still there,
reaching down
to stroke my furry, venerable head.   20

Compare

"Care and Feeding" with "For the Anniversary of My Death" by W. S. Merwin (page 669).

Hart Crane (1899–1932)

My Grandmother's Love Letters

1926

There are no stars tonight
But those of memory.
Yet how much room for memory there is
In the loose girdle of soft rain.

There is even room enough   5
For the letters of my mother's mother,
Elizabeth,
That have been pressed so long
Into a corner of the roof
That they are brown and soft,   10
And liable to melt as snow.

Over the greatness of such space
Steps must be gentle.
It is all hung by an invisible white hair.
It trembles as birch limbs webbing the air.   15

And I ask myself:

"Are your fingers long enough to play
Old keys that are but echoes:
Is the silence strong enough
To carry back the music to its source   20
And back to you again
As though to her?"

Yet I would lead my grandmother by the hand
Through much of what she would not understand;
And so I stumble. And the rain continues on the roof   25
With such a sound of gently pitying laughter.

Compare

"My Grandmother's Love Letters" with "When You Are Old" by William Butler Yeats
(page 888).

E. E. Cummings (1894–1962)

somewhere i have never   1931
travelled,gladly beyond

somewhere i have never travelled,gladly beyond
any experience,your eyes have their silence:
in your most frail gesture are things which enclose me,
or which i cannot touch because they are too near

your slightest look easily will unclose me   5
though i have closed myself as fingers,
you open always petal by petal myself as Spring opens
(touching skilfully,mysteriously)her first rose

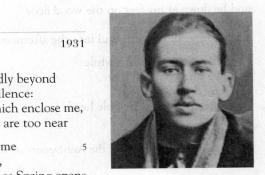

E. E. Cummings

or if your wish be to close me,i and
my life will shut very beautifully,suddenly,   10
as when the heart of this flower imagines
the snow carefully everywhere descending;

nothing which we are to perceive in this world equals
the power of your intense fragility:whose texture
compels me with the colour of its countries,   15
rendering death and forever with each breathing

(i do not know what it is about you that closes
and opens;only something in me understands
the voice of your eyes is deeper than all roses)
nobody,not even the rain,has such small hands   20

Compare

"somewhere i have never travelled,gladly beyond" with "Elegy for Jane" by Theodore Roethke
(page 872).

Marisa de los Santos

Marisa de los Santos (b. 1966)

Perfect Dress   2000

It's here in a student's journal, a blue confession
in smudged, erasable ink: "I can't stop hoping
I'll wake up, suddenly beautiful," and isn't it strange
how we want it, despite all we know? To be at last

the girl in the photograph, cobalt-eyed, hair puddling   5
like cognac, or the one stretched at the ocean's edge,
curved and light-drenched, more like a beach than
the beach. I confess I have longed to stalk runways,

leggy, otherworldly as a mantis, to balance a head
like a Fabergé egg on the longest, most elegant neck.   10
Today in the checkout line, I saw a magazine
claiming to know "How to Find the Perfect Dress

for that Perfect Evening," and I felt the old pull, flare
of the pilgrim's twin flames, desire and faith. At fifteen,
I spent weeks at the search. Going from store to store,   15
hands thirsty for shine, I reached for polyester satin,

machine-made lace, petunia- and Easter egg-colored,
brilliant and flammable. Nothing *haute* about this
couture but my hopes for it, as I tugged it on
and waited for my one, true body to emerge.   20

(Picture the angel inside uncut marble, articulation
of wings and robes poised in expectation of release.)
What I wanted was ordinary miracle, the falling away
of everything wrong. Silly maybe or maybe

I was right, that there's no limit to the ways eternity   25
suggests itself, that one day I'll slip into it, say
floor-length plum charmeuse. Someone will murmur,
"She is sublime," will be precisely right, and I will step,

with incandescent shoulders, into my perfect evening.

PERFECT DRESS. 10 *Fabergé*: Peter Carl Fabergé (1846–1920) was a Russian jeweler renowned for his elaborately decorated, golden, jeweled eggs.

Compare

"Perfect Dress" with "Cinderella" by Anne Sexton (page 707).

John Donne (1572–1631)

Death be not proud

(about 1610)

Death be not proud, though some have callèd thee
Mighty and dreadful, for thou art not so;
For those whom thou think'st thou dost overthrow
Die not, poor death, nor yet canst thou kill me.
From rest and sleep, which but thy pictures be,   5
Much pleasure, then from thee much more must flow,
And soonest our best men with thee do go,
Rest of their bones, and soul's delivery.
Thou art slave to fate, chance, kings, and desperate men,
And dost with poison, war, and sickness dwell,   10
And poppy, or charms can make us sleep as well,
And better than thy stroke; why swell'st thou then?
One short sleep past, we wake eternally,
And death shall be no more; death, thou shalt die.

John Donne

Compare

Compare Donne's personification of Death in "Death be not proud" with Emily Dickinson's in "Because I could not stop for Death" (page 777).

John Donne (1572–1631)

The Flea

1633

Mark but this flea, and mark in this
How little that which thou deny'st me is;
It sucked me first, and now sucks thee,
And in this flea our two bloods mingled be;
Thou know'st that this cannot be said   5
A sin, nor shame, nor loss of maidenhead,
    Yet this enjoys before it woo,
    And pampered swells with one blood made of two,
    And this, alas, is more than we would do.

Oh stay, three lives in one flea spare,   10
Where we almost, yea more than married are.
This flea is you and I, and this
Our marriage bed, and marriage temple is;
Though parents grudge, and you, we're met
And cloistered in these living walls of jet.   15
    Though use° make you apt to kill me,   *custom*
    Let not to that, self-murder added be,
    And sacrilege, three sins in killing three.

Cruel and sudden, hast thou since
Purpled thy nail in blood of innocence?
Wherein could this flea guilty be,
Except in that drop which it sucked from thee?
Yet thou triumph'st, and say'st that thou
Find'st not thyself, nor me, the weaker now;
    'Tis true; then learn how false, fears be;
    Just so much honor, when thou yield'st to me,
    Will waste, as this flea's death took life from thee.

                 20

                 25

Compare

"The Flea" with "To His Coy Mistress" by Andrew Marvell (page 861).

John Donne (1572–1631)

A Valediction: Forbidding Mourning   (1611)

As virtuous men pass mildly away,
 And whisper to their souls to go,
Whilst some of their sad friends do say
 The breath goes now, and some say no:

So let us melt, and make no noise,
 No tear-floods, nor sigh-tempests move;
'Twere profanation of our joys
 To tell the laity° our love.   *common people*

Moving of th' earth° brings harms and fears;   *earthquake*
 Men reckon what it did and meant;
But trepidation of the spheres,
 Though greater far, is innocent.°   *harmless*

Dull sublunary lovers' love
 (Whose soul is sense) cannot admit
Absence, because it doth remove
 Those things which elemented° it.   *constituted*

But we, by a love so much refined
 That ourselves know not what it is,
Inter-assurèd of the mind,
 Care less, eyes, lips, and hands to miss.

Our two souls, therefore, which are one,
 Though I must go, endure not yet
A breach, but an expansión,
 Like gold to airy thinness beat.

If they be two, they are two so
 As stiff twin compasses are two:
Thy soul, the fixed foot, makes no show
 To move, but doth, if th' other do.

                 5

                 10

                 15

                 20

                 25

And though it in the center sit,
   Yet when the other far doth roam,
It leans and harkens after it,
   And grows erect as that comes home.

Such wilt thou be to me, who must,   30
   Like th' other foot, obliquely run;
Thy firmness makes my circle just,°   *perfect*   35
   And makes me end where I begun.

A VALEDICTION: FORBIDDING MOURNING. According to Donne's biographer Izaak Walton, Donne's wife received this poem as a gift before the poet departed on a journey to France. 11 *spheres*: in Ptolemaic astronomy, the concentric spheres surrounding the earth. The trepidation or motion of the ninth sphere was thought to change the date of the equinox. 19 *Inter-assurèd of the mind*: each sure in mind that the other is faithful. 24 *gold to airy thinness*: gold is so malleable that, if beaten to the thickness of gold leaf (1/250,000 of one inch), one ounce of gold would cover 250 square feet.

Compare

"A Valediction: Forbidding Mourning" with "To Lucasta" by Richard Lovelace (page 521).

Rita Dove (b. 1952)

Daystar   1986

Rita Dove

She wanted a little room for thinking:
but she saw diapers steaming on the line,
a doll slumped behind the door.

So she lugged a chair behind the garage
to sit out the children's naps.   5

Sometimes there were things to watch—
the pinched armor of a vanished cricket,
a floating maple leaf. Other days
she stared until she was assured
when she closed her eyes   10
she'd see only her own vivid blood.

She had an hour, at best, before Liza appeared
pouting from the top of the stairs.
And just *what* was mother doing
out back with the field mice? Why,   15
building a palace. Later
that night when Thomas rolled over and
lurched into her, she would open her eyes
and think of the place that was hers
for an hour—where   20
she was nothing,
pure nothing, in the middle of the day.

Compare

"Daystar" with "The Lake Isle of Innisfree" by William Butler Yeats (page 489) or "Driving to Town Late to Mail a Letter" by Robert Bly (page 570).

T. S. Eliot (1888–1965)

Journey of the Magi

1927

"A cold coming we had of it,
Just the worst time of the year
For a journey, and such a long journey:
The ways deep and the weather sharp,
The very dead of winter."   5
And the camels galled, sore-footed, refractory,
Lying down in the melting snow.
There were times we regretted
The summer palaces on slopes, the terraces,
And the silken girls bringing sherbet.   10
Then the camel men cursing and grumbling
And running away, and wanting their liquor and women,
And the night-fires going out, and the lack of shelters,
And the cities hostile and the towns unfriendly
And the villages dirty and charging high prices: 15
A hard time we had of it.
At the end we preferred to travel all night,
Sleeping in snatches,
With the voices singing in our ears, saying
That this was all folly.   20

Then at dawn we came down to a temperate valley,
Wet, below the snow line, smelling of vegetation;
With a running stream and a water-mill beating the darkness,
And three trees on the low sky,
And an old white horse galloped away in the meadow.   25
Then we came to a tavern with vine-leaves over the lintel,
Six hands at an open door dicing for pieces of silver,
And feet kicking the empty wine-skins.
But there was no information, and so we continued
And arrived at evening, not a moment too soon   30
Finding the place; it was (you may say) satisfactory.

All this was a long time ago, I remember,
And I would do it again, but set down
This set down
This: were we led all that way for   35
Birth or Death? There was a Birth, certainly,
We had evidence and no doubt. I had seen birth and death,
But had thought they were different; this Birth was
Hard and bitter agony for us, like Death, our death.
We returned to our places, these Kingdoms,   40
But no longer at ease here, in the old dispensation,
With an alien people clutching their gods.
I should be glad of another death.

JOURNEY OF THE MAGI. The story of the Magi, the three wise men who traveled to Bethlehem to behold the baby Jesus, is told in Matthew 2:1–12. That the three were kings is a later tradition. 1–5 *A cold coming . . . winter:* Eliot quotes with slight changes from a sermon preached on Christmas Day, 1622, by Bishop Lancelot Andrewes. 24 *three trees:* foreshadowing the three crosses on Calvary (see Luke 23:32–33). 25 *white horse:* perhaps the steed that carried the conquering Christ in the vision of St. John the Divine (Revelation 19:11–16). 41 *old dispensation:* older, pagan religion about to be displaced by Christianity.

Compare

"Journey of the Magi" with "The Magi" by William Butler Yeats (page 887).

Robert Frost (1874–1963)

Birches   1916

When I see birches bend to left and right
Across the lines of straighter darker trees,
I like to think some boy's been swinging them.
But swinging doesn't bend them down to stay
As ice-storms do. Often you must have seen them   5
Loaded with ice a sunny winter morning
After a rain. They click upon themselves
As the breeze rises, and turn many-colored
As the stir cracks and crazes their enamel.
Soon the sun's warmth makes them shed crystal shells   10
Shattering and avalanching on the snow-crust—
Such heaps of broken glass to sweep away
You'd think the inner dome of heaven had fallen.
They are dragged to the withered bracken by the load,
And they seem not to break; though once they are bowed   15
So low for long, they never right themselves:
You may see their trunks arching in the woods
Years afterwards, trailing their leaves on the ground
Like girls on hands and knees that throw their hair
Before them over their heads to dry in the sun.   20
But I was going to say when Truth broke in
With all her matter-of-fact about the ice-storm
I should prefer to have some boy bend them
As he went out and in to fetch the cows—
Some boy too far from town to learn baseball,   25
Whose only play was what he found himself,
Summer or winter, and could play alone.
One by one he subdued his father's trees
By riding them down over and over again
Until he took the stiffness out of them,   30
And not one but hung limp, not one was left
For him to conquer. He learned all there was
To learn about not launching out too soon
And so not carrying the tree away
Clear to the ground. He always kept his poise   35

To the top branches, climbing carefully
With the same pains you use to fill a cup
Up to the brim, and even above the brim.
Then he flung outward, feet first, with a swish,
Kicking his way down through the air to the ground.   40
So was I once myself a swinger of birches.
And so I dream of going back to be.
It's when I'm weary of considerations,
And life is too much like a pathless wood
Where your face burns and tickles with the cobwebs   45
Broken across it, and one eye is weeping
From a twig's having lashed across it open.
I'd like to get away from earth awhile
And then come back to it and begin over.
May no fate willfully misunderstand me   50
And half grant what I wish and snatch me away
Not to return. Earth's the right place for love:
I don't know where it's likely to go better.
I'd like to go by climbing a birch tree,
And climb black branches up a snow-white trunk   55
Toward heaven, till the tree could bear no more,
But dipped its top and set me down again.
That would be good both going and coming back.
One could do worse than be a swinger of birches.

Compare

"Birches" with "Sailing to Byzantium" by William Butler Yeats (page 754).

Robert Frost (1874–1963)

Mending Wall   1914

Something there is that doesn't love a wall,
That sends the frozen-ground-swell under it,
And spills the upper boulders in the sun;
And makes gaps even two can pass abreast.
The work of hunters is another thing: 5
I have come after them and made repair
Where they have left not one stone on a stone,
But they would have the rabbit out of hiding,
To please the yelping dogs. The gaps I mean,
No one has seen them made or heard them made,   10
But at spring mending-time we find them there.
I let my neighbor know beyond the hill;
And on a day we meet to walk the line
And set the wall between us once again.
We keep the wall between us as we go.   15
To each the boulders that have fallen to each.

Robert Frost

And some are loaves and some so nearly balls
We have to use a spell to make them balance:
"Stay where you are until our backs are turned!"
We wear our fingers rough with handling them.   20
Oh, just another kind of outdoor game,
One on a side. It comes to little more:
There where it is we do not need the wall:
He is all pine and I am apple orchard.
My apple trees will never get across   25
And eat the cones under his pines, I tell him.
He only says, "Good fences make good neighbors."
Spring is the mischief in me, and I wonder
If I could put a notion in his head:
"Why do they make good neighbors? Isn't it   30
Where there are cows? But here there are no cows.
Before I built a wall I'd ask to know
What I was walling in or walling out,
And to whom I was like to give offence.
Something there is that doesn't love a wall,   35
That wants it down." I could say "Elves" to him,
But it's not elves exactly, and I'd rather
He said it for himself. I see him there
Bringing a stone grasped firmly by the top
In each hand, like an old-stone savage armed.   40
He moves in darkness as it seems to me,
Not of woods only and the shade of trees.
He will not go behind his father's saying,
And he likes having thought of it so well
He says again, "Good fences make good neighbors."   45

Compare

"Mending Wall" with "Digging" by Seamus Heaney (page 846).

Robert Frost (1874–1963)

Stopping by Woods on a Snowy Evening   1923

Whose woods these are I think I know.
His house is in the village though;
He will not see me stopping here
To watch his woods fill up with snow.

My little horse must think it queer   5
To stop without a farmhouse near
Between the woods and frozen lake
The darkest evening of the year.

He gives his harness bells a shake
To ask if there is some mistake.   10

The only other sound's the sweep
Of easy wind and downy flake.

The woods are lovely, dark and deep,
But I have promises to keep,
And miles to go before I sleep,   15
And miles to go before I sleep.

Compare

"Stopping by Woods on a Snowy Evening" with "Desert Places" by Robert Frost (page 624).

Allen Ginsberg (1926–1997)

A Supermarket in California   1956

What thoughts I have of you tonight, Walt Whitman, for I walked down the sidestreets under the trees with a headache self-conscious looking at the full moon.

In my hungry fatigue, and shopping for images, I went into the neon fruit supermarket, dreaming of your enumerations!

What peaches and what penumbras! Whole families shopping at night! Aisles full of husbands! Wives in the avocados, babies in the tomatoes!—and you, García Lorca, what were you doing down by the watermelons?

I saw you, Walt Whitman, childless, lonely old grubber, poking among the meats in the refrigerator and eyeing the grocery boys.

I heard you asking questions of each: Who killed the pork chops? What   5
price bananas? Are you my Angel?

I wandered in and out of the brilliant stacks of cans following you, and followed in my imagination by the store detective.

We strode down the open corridors together in our solitary fancy tasting artichokes, possessing every frozen delicacy, and never passing the cashier.

Where are we going, Walt Whitman? The doors close in an hour. Which way does your beard point tonight?

(I touch your book and dream of our odyssey in the supermarket and feel absurd.)

Will we walk all night through solitary streets? The trees add shade to   10
shade, lights out in the houses, we'll both be lonely.

Will we stroll dreaming of the lost America of love past blue automobiles in driveways, home to our silent cottage?

Ah, dear father, graybeard, lonely old courage-teacher, what America did you have when Charon quit poling his ferry and you got out on a smoking bank and stood watching the boat disappear on the black waters of Lethe?

A SUPERMARKET IN CALIFORNIA. 2 *enumerations:* many of Whitman's poems contain lists of observed details. 3 *García Lorca:* modern Spanish poet who wrote an "Ode to Walt Whitman" in his book-length sequence *Poet in New York.* 12 *Charon . . . Lethe:* Is the poet confusing two underworld rivers? Charon, in Greek and Roman mythology, is the boatman who ferries the souls of the dead across the river Styx. The river Lethe also flows through Hades, and a drink of its waters makes the dead lose their painful memories of loved ones they have left behind.

Compare

"A Supermarket in California" with Walt Whitman's "To a Locomotive in Winter" (page 504).

Thomas Hardy (1840–1928)

The Convergence of the Twain   1912

Lines on the Loss of the "Titanic"

I

In a solitude of the sea
Deep from human vanity,
And the Pride of Life that planned her, stilly couches she.

II

Steel chambers, late the pyres
Of her salamandrine fires,   5
Cold currents thrid,° and turn to rhythmic tidal lyres.   *thread*

III

Over the mirrors meant
To glass the opulent
The sea-worm crawls—grotesque, slimed, dumb, indifferent.

IV

Jewels in joy designed   10
To ravish the sensuous mind
Lie lightless, all their sparkles bleared and black and blind.

V

Dim moon-eyed fishes near
Gaze at the gilded gear
And query: "What does this vaingloriousness down here?" ...   15

VI

Well: while was fashioning
This creature of cleaving wing,
The Immanent Will that stirs and urges everything

VII

Prepared a sinister mate
For her—so gaily great—   20
A Shape of Ice, for the time far and dissociate.

VIII

And as the smart ship grew
In stature, grace, and hue,
In shadowy silent distance grew the Iceberg too.

IX

Alien they seemed to be: 25
No mortal eye could see
The intimate welding of their later history,

X

Or sign that they were bent
  By paths coincident
On being anon twin halves of one august event,   30

XI

Till the Spinner of the Years
  Said "Now!" And each one hears,
And consummation comes, and jars two hemispheres.

THE CONVERGENCE OF THE TWAIN. The luxury liner *Titanic*, supposedly unsinkable, went down
in 1912 after striking an iceberg on its first Atlantic voyage. 5 *salamandrine:* like the salamander, a
lizard that supposedly thrives in fires, or like a spirit of the same name that inhabits fire (according
to alchemists).

Compare

"The Convergence of the Twain" with "Song of the Powers" by David Mason (page 643).

Thomas Hardy (1840–1928)

The Darkling Thrush   1900

I leant upon a coppice gate
  When Frost was spectre-gray,
And Winter's dregs made desolate
  The weakening eye of day.
The tangled bine-stems scored the sky   5
  Like strings of broken lyres,
And all mankind that haunted nigh
  Had sought their household fires.

The land's sharp features seemed to be
  The Century's corpse outleant,   10
His crypt the cloudy canopy,
  The wind his death-lament.
The ancient pulse of germ and birth
  Was shrunken hard and dry,
And every spirit upon earth   15
  Seemed fervorless as I.

At once a voice arose among
  The bleak twigs overhead
In a full-hearted evensong
  Of joy illimited;   20
An aged thrush, frail, gaunt, and small,
  In blast-beruffled plume,

Thomas Hardy

Had chosen thus to fling his soul
   Upon the growing gloom.

So little cause for carolings   25
   Of such ecstatic sound
Was written on terrestrial things
   Afar or nigh around,
That I could think there trembled through
   His happy good-night air   30
Some blessed Hope, whereof he knew
   And I was unaware.

THE DARKLING THRUSH. Hardy set this poem on December 31, 1900, the last day of the nineteenth century.

Compare

"The Darkling Thrush" with "I Wandered Lonely as a Cloud" by William Wordsworth
(page 511).

Seamus Heaney (b. 1939)

Digging   1966

Between my finger and my thumb
The squat pen rests; snug as a gun.

Under my window, a clean rasping sound
When the spade sinks into gravelly ground:
My father, digging. I look down   5

Till his straining rump among the flowerbeds
Bends low, comes up twenty years away
Stooping in rhythm through potato drills
Where he was digging.

The coarse boot nestled on the lug, the shaft   10
Against the inside knee was levered firmly.
He rooted out tall tops, buried the bright edge deep
To scatter new potatoes that we picked
Loving their cool hardness in our hands.

By God, the old man could handle a spade.   15
Just like his old man.

My grandfather cut more turf in a day
Than any other man on Toner's bog.
Once I carried him milk in a bottle
Corked sloppily with paper. He straightened up   20

To drink it, then fell to right away
Nicking and slicing neatly, heaving sods
Over his shoulder, going down and down
For the good turf. Digging.

The cold smell of potato mould, the squelch and slap 25
Of soggy peat, the curt cuts of an edge
Through living roots awaken in my head.
But I've no spade to follow men like them.

Between my finger and my thumb
The squat pen rests. 30
I'll dig with it.

Compare

"Digging" with "The Writer" by Richard Wilbur (page 883).

George Herbert (1593–1633)

Love 1633

Love bade me welcome; yet my soul drew back,
    Guilty of dust and sin.
But quick-eyed Love, observing me grow slack
    From my first entrance in,
Drew nearer to me, sweetly questioning 5
    If I lacked anything.

"A guest," I answered, "worthy to be here";
    Love said, "You shall be he."
"I, the unkind, ungrateful? Ah, my dear,
    I cannot look on Thee." 10
Love took my hand, and smiling did reply,
    "Who made the eyes but I?"

"Truth, Lord, but I have marred them; let my shame
    Go where it doth deserve."
"And know you not," says Love, "who bore the blame?" 15
    "My dear, then I will serve."
"You must sit down," says Love, "and taste My meat."
    So I did sit and eat.

Compare

"Love" with "Batter my heart, three-personed God" by John Donne (page 531).

Robert Herrick (1591–1674)

To the Virgins, to Make Much of Time 1648

Gather ye rose-buds while ye may,
    Old Time is still a-flying;
And this same flower that smiles today,
    Tomorrow will be dying.

The glorious lamp of heaven, the sun, 5
    The higher he's a-getting,
The sooner will his race be run,
    And nearer he's to setting.

That age is best which is the first,
    When youth and blood are warmer;   10
But being spent, the worse, and worst
    Times still succeed the former.

Then be not coy, but use your time,
    And while ye may, go marry;
For having lost but once your prime,   15
    You may for ever tarry.

Compare

"To the Virgins, to Make Much of Time" with "To His Coy Mistress" by Andrew Marvell (page 861) and "Go, Lovely Rose" by Edmund Waller (page 881).

Gerard Manley Hopkins (1844–1889)

Spring and Fall   (1880)

    To a young child

Márgarét, áre you gríeving
Over Goldengrove unleaving°?   *shedding its leaves*
Leáves, líke the things of man, you
With your fresh thoughts care for, can you?
Áh! ás the heart grows older   5
It will come to such sights colder
By and by, nor spare a sigh
Though worlds of wanwood leafmeal lie;
And yet you wíll weep and know why.
Now no matter, child, the name: 10
Sórrow's spríngs áre the same.
Nor mouth had, no nor mind, expressed
What heart heard of, ghost° guessed: *spirit*
It ís the blight man was born for,
It is Margaret you mourn for.   15

Compare

"Spring and Fall" with "Aftermath" by Henry Wadsworth Longfellow (page 533).

Gerard Manley Hopkins (1844–1889)

The Windhover   (1877)

    To Christ Our Lord

I caught this morning morning's minion, king-
    dom of daylight's dauphin, dapple-dawn-drawn Falcon, in his riding
    Of the rolling level underneath him steady air, and striding
High there, how he rung upon the rein of a wimpling wing
In his ecstasy! then off, off forth on swing,   5
    As a skate's heel sweeps smooth on a bow-bend: the hurl and gliding
    Rebuffed the big wind. My heart in hiding
Stirred for a bird, —the achieve of, the mastery of the thing!

Brute beauty and valor and act, oh, air, pride, plume, here
    Buckle! AND the fire that breaks from thee then, a billion   10
Times told lovelier, more dangerous, O my chevalier!

    No wonder of it: shéer plód makes plough down sillion°   *furrow*
Shine, and blue-bleak embers, ah my dear,
    Fall, gall themselves, and gash gold-vermilion.

THE WINDHOVER. A windhover is a kestrel, or small falcon, so called because it can hover upon the wind.
4 *rung . . . wing:* A horse is "rung upon the rein" when its trainer holds the end of a long rein and has the
horse circle him. The possible meanings of *wimpling* include: (1) curving; (2) pleated, arranged in many
little folds one on top of another; (3) rippling or undulating like the surface of a flowing stream.

Compare
"The Windhover" with "Batter my heart, three-personed God" by John Donne (page 531).

A. E. Housman (1859–1936)

Loveliest of trees, the cherry now   1896

Loveliest of trees, the cherry now
Is hung with bloom along the bough,
And stands about the woodland ride°   *path*
Wearing white for Eastertide.

Now, of my threescore years and ten,   5
Twenty will not come again,
And take from seventy springs a score,
It only leaves me fifty more.

And since to look at things in bloom
Fifty springs are little room,   10
About the woodlands I will go
To see the cherry hung with snow.

Compare
"Loveliest of trees, the cherry now" with "To the Virgins, to Make Much of Time" by Robert
Herrick (page 847) and "Spring and Fall" by Gerard Manley Hopkins (page 848).

A. E. Housman (1859–1936)

To an Athlete Dying Young   1896

The time you won your town the race
We chaired you through the market-place;
Man and boy stood cheering by,
And home we brought you shoulder-high.

To-day, the road all runners come,   5
Shoulder-high we bring you home,
And set you at your threshold down,
Townsman of a stiller town.

Smart lad, to slip betimes away
From fields where glory does not stay   10
And early though the laurel grows
It withers quicker than the rose.

Eyes the shady night has shut
Cannot see the record cut,
And silence sounds no worse than cheers   15
After earth has stopped the ears:

Now you will not swell the rout
Of lads that wore their honors out,
Runners whom renown outran
And the name died before the man.   20

So set, before its echoes fade,
The fleet foot on the sill of shade,
And hold to the low lintel up
The still-defended challenge-cup.

And round that early-laureled head   25
Will flock to gaze the strengthless dead,
And find unwithered on its curls
The garland briefer than a girl's.

Compare

"To an Athlete Dying Young" with "Ex-Basketball Player" by John Updike (page 879).

Randall Jarrell (1914–1965)

The Death of the Ball Turret Gunner   1945

From my mother's sleep I fell into the State,
And I hunched in its belly till my wet fur froze.
Six miles from earth, loosed from its dream of life,
I woke to black flak and the nightmare fighters.
When I died they washed me out of the turret with a hose.   5

THE DEATH OF THE BALL TURRET GUNNER. Jarrell has written: "A ball turret was a plexiglass sphere set into the belly of a B-17 or B-24 and inhabited by two .50 caliber machine-guns and one man, a short small man. When this gunner tracked with his machine-guns a fighter attacking his bomber from below, he re-volved with the turret; hunched in his little sphere, he looked like the fetus in the womb. The fighters which attacked him were armed with cannon firing explosive shells. The hose was a steam hose."

Compare

"The Death of the Ball Turret Gunner" with "Dulce et Decorum Est" by Wilfred Owen (page 521).

Robinson Jeffers   (1887–1962)

Rock and Hawk   1935

Here is a symbol in which
Many high tragic thoughts
Watch their own eyes.

This gray rock, standing tall
On the headland, where the sea-wind   5
Lets no tree grow,

Earthquake-proved, and signatured
By ages of storms: on its peak
A falcon has perched.

Robinson Jeffers

I think, here is your emblem
To hang in the future sky;   10
Not the cross, not the hive,

But this; bright power, dark peace;
Fierce consciousness joined with final
Disinterestedness;   15

Life with calm death; the falcon's
Realist eyes and act
Married to the massive

Mysticism of stone,
Which failure cannot cast down   20
Nor success make proud.

Compare
"Rock and Hawk" with "The Windhover" by Gerard Manley Hopkins (page 848).

Ha Jin   (b. 1956)

Missed Time   2000

My notebook has remained blank for months
thanks to the light you shower
around me. I have no use
for my pen, which lies
languorously without grief.   5

Nothing is better than to live
a storyless life that needs
no writing for meaning—
when I am gone, let others say
they lost a happy man,   10
though no one can tell how happy I was.

Ha Jin

Compare
"Missed Time" with "somewhere i have never travelled,gladly beyond" by E. E. Cummings
(page 834).

Ben Jonson (1573?–1637)

On My First Son   (1603)

Farewell, thou child of my right hand, and joy.
My sin was too much hope of thee, loved boy;
Seven years thou wert lent to me, and I thee pay,
Exacted by thy fate, on the just day.
Oh, could I lose all father° now. For why   *fatherhood*   5
Will man lament the state he should envỳ—
To have so soon 'scaped world's and flesh's rage,
And, if no other misery, yet age?
Rest in soft peace, and asked, say, "Here doth lie
Ben Jonson his best piece of poetry,"   10
For whose sake henceforth all his vows be such
As what he loves may never like° too much.   *thrive*

ON MY FIRST SON. 1 *child of my right hand*: Jonson's son was named Benjamin; this phrase translates the
Hebrew name. 4 *the just day*: the very day. The boy had died on his seventh birthday. 10 *poetry*: Jonson
uses the word *poetry* here reflecting its Greek root *poiesis*, which means *creation*.

Compare

"On My First Son" with "'Out, Out—'" by Robert Frost (page 494).

Donald Justice (1925–2004)

On the Death of Friends in Childhood   1960

We shall not ever meet them bearded in heaven,
Nor sunning themselves among the bald of hell;
If anywhere, in the deserted schoolyard at twilight,
Forming a ring, perhaps, or joining hands
In games whose very names we have forgotten.   5
Come, memory, let us seek them there in the shadows.

Compare

"On the Death of Friends in Childhood" with "To an Athlete Dying Young" by A. E. Housman
(page 849).

John Keats (1795–1821)

Ode on a Grecian Urn   1820

I

Thou still unravished bride of quietness,
    Thou foster-child of silence and slow time,

Sylvan historian, who canst thus express
   A flowery tale more sweetly than our rhyme:
What leaf-fringed legend haunts about thy shape   5
   Of deities or mortals, or of both,
      In Tempe or the dales of Arcady?
   What men or gods are these? What maidens loth?
What mad pursuit? What struggle to escape?
      What pipes and timbrels? What wild ecstasy?   10

II

Heard melodies are sweet, but those unheard
   Are sweeter; therefore, ye soft pipes, play on;
Not to the sensual° ear, but, more endeared,   *physical*
   Pipe to the spirit ditties of no tone:
Fair youth, beneath the trees, thou canst not leave   15
   Thy song, nor ever can those trees be bare;
      Bold Lover, never, never canst thou kiss,
Though winning near the goal—yet, do not grieve;
      She cannot fade, though thou hast not thy bliss,
      For ever wilt thou love, and she be fair!   20

III

Ah, happy, happy boughs! that cannot shed
   Your leaves, nor ever bid the Spring adieu;
And, happy melodist, unwearièd,
   For ever piping songs for ever new;
More happy love! more happy, happy love!   25
   For ever warm and still to be enjoyed,
      For ever panting, and for ever young;
All breathing human passion far above,
   That leaves a heart high-sorrowful and cloyed,
      A burning forehead, and a parching tongue.   30

IV

Who are these coming to the sacrifice?
   To what green altar, O mysterious priest,
Lead'st thou that heifer lowing at the skies,
   And all her silken flanks with garlands drest?
What little town by river or sea shore,   35
   Or mountain-built with peaceful citadel,
      Is emptied of this folk, this pious morn?
And, little town, thy streets for evermore
   Will silent be; and not a soul to tell
      Why thou art desolate, can e'er return.   40

V

O Attic shape! Fair attitude! with brede°   *design*
    Of marble men and maidens overwrought,
With forest branches and the trodden weed;
    Thou, silent form, dost tease us out of thought
As doth eternity: Cold Pastoral!   45
    When old age shall this generation waste,
        Thou shalt remain, in midst of other woe
    Than ours, a friend to man, to whom thou say'st,
Beauty is truth, truth beauty,—that is all
    Ye know on earth, and all ye need to know.   50

ODE ON A GRECIAN URN. 7 *Tempe, dales of Arcady:* valleys in Greece. 41 *Attic:* Athenian, possessing a
classical simplicity and grace. 49–50: if Keats had put the urn's words in quotation marks, critics might
have been spared much ink. Does the urn say just "beauty is truth, truth beauty," or does its statement take
in the whole of the last two lines?

Compare

"Ode on a Grecian Urn" with "Musée des Beaux Arts" by W. H. Auden (page 823).

John Keats

John Keats (1795–1821)

When I have fears that   (1818)
I may cease to be

When I have fears that I may cease to be
    Before my pen has gleaned my teeming brain,
Before high-pilèd books, in charact'ry,°   *written language*
    Hold like rich garners° the full-ripened grain;   *storehouses*
When I behold, upon the night's starred face,   5
    Huge cloudy symbols of a high romance,
And think that I may never live to trace
    Their shadows with the magic hand of chance;
And when I feel, fair creature of an hour,
    That I shall never look upon thee more,   10
Never have relish in the fairy° power   *supernatural*
    Of unreflecting love;—then on the shore
Of the wide world I stand alone, and think
Till love and fame to nothingness do sink.

WHEN I HAVE FEARS THAT I MAY CEASE TO BE. 12 *unreflecting:* thoughtless and spontaneous, rather than
deliberate.

Compare

"When I have fears that I may cease to be" with Philip Larkin's "Aubade" (page 731).

John Keats (1795–1821)

To Autumn   1820

I

Season of mists and mellow fruitfulness,
　Close bosom-friend of the maturing sun;
Conspiring with him how to load and bless
　With fruit the vines that round the thatch-eaves run;
To bend with apples the mossed cottage-trees,   5
　And fill all fruit with ripeness to the core;
　　To swell the gourd, and plump the hazel shells
With a sweet kernel; to set budding more,
And still more, later flowers for the bees,
Until they think warm days will never cease,   10
　For Summer has o'er-brimmed their clammy cells.

II

Who hath not seen thee oft amid thy store?
　Sometimes whoever seeks abroad may find
Thee sitting careless on a granary floor,
　Thy hair soft-lifted by the winnowing wind;   15
Or on a half-reaped furrow sound asleep,
　Drowsed with the fume of poppies, while thy hook°   *sickle*
　　Spares the next swath and all its twinèd flowers:
And sometimes like a gleaner thou dost keep
　Steady thy laden head across a brook;   20
Or by a cider-press, with patient look,
　Thou watchest the last oozings hours by hours.

III

Where are the songs of Spring? Ay, where are they?
　Think not of them, thou hast thy music too,—
While barrèd clouds bloom the soft-dying day,   25
　And touch the stubble-plains with rosy hue;
Then in a wailful choir the small gnats mourn
　Among the river sallows,° borne aloft   *willows*
　　Or sinking as the light wind lives or dies;
And full-grown lambs loud bleat from hilly bourn;   30
　Hedge-crickets sing; and now with treble soft
　The red-breast whistles from a garden-croft;°   *garden plot*
　　And gathering swallows twitter in the skies.

To Autumn. 12 *thee:* Autumn personified. 15 *Thy hair . . . winnowing wind:* Autumn's hair is a billowing cloud of straw. In winnowing, whole blades of grain were laid on a granary floor and beaten with wooden flails, then the beaten mass was tossed in a blanket until the yellow straw (or *chaff*) drifted away on the air, leaving kernels of grain. 30 *bourn:* perhaps meaning a brook.

Compare

"To Autumn" with "Spring and Fall" by Gerard Manley Hopkins (page 848).

Ted Kooser (b. 1939)

Abandoned Farmhouse

1969/1974

He was a big man, says the size of his shoes
on a pile of broken dishes by the house;
a tall man too, says the length of the bed
in an upstairs room; and a good, God-fearing man,
says the Bible with a broken back   5
on the floor below the window, dusty with sun;
but not a man for farming, say the fields
cluttered with boulders and the leaky barn.

A woman lived with him, says the bedroom wall
papered with lilacs and the kitchen shelves   10
covered with oilcloth, and they had a child,
says the sandbox made from a tractor tire.
Money was scarce, say the jars of plum preserves
and canned tomatoes sealed in the cellar hole.
And the winters cold, say the rags in the window frames. 15
It was lonely here, says the narrow country road.

Something went wrong, says the empty house
in the weed-choked yard. Stones in the fields
say he was not a farmer; the still-sealed jars
in the cellar say she left in a nervous haste.   20
And the child? Its toys are strewn in the yard
like branches after a storm—a rubber cow,
a rusty tractor with a broken plow,
a doll in overalls. Something went wrong, they say.

Compare

"Abandoned Farmhouse" with "The Farm on the Great Plains" by William Stafford (page 875).

Philip Larkin (1922–1985)

Home is so Sad

1964

Home is so sad. It stays as it was left,
Shaped to the comfort of the last to go
As if to win them back. Instead, bereft
Of anyone to please, it withers so,
Having no heart to put aside the theft   5

And turn again to what it started as,
A joyous shot at how things ought to be,
Long fallen wide. You can see how it was:
Look at the pictures and the cutlery.
The music in the piano stool. That vase.   10

Compare

"Home is so Sad" with "Piano" by D. H. Lawrence (page 857).

Philip Larkin (1922–1985)

Philip Larkin

Poetry of Departures   1955

Sometimes you hear, fifth-hand,
As epitaph:
He chucked up everything
And just cleared off,
And always the voice will sound   5
Certain you approve
This audacious, purifying,
Elemental move.

And they are right, I think.
We all hate home   10
And having to be there:
I detest my room,
Its specially-chosen junk,
The good books, the good bed,
And my life, in perfect order: 15
So to hear it said

He walked out on the whole crowd
Leaves me flushed and stirred,
Like *Then she undid her dress*
Or *Take that you bastard;*   20
Surely I can, if he did?
And that helps me stay
Sober and industrious.
But I'd go today,

Yes, swagger the nut-strewn roads,   25
Crouch in the fo'c'sle
Stubbly with goodness, if
It weren't so artificial,
Such a deliberate step backwards
To create an object: 30
Books; china; a life
Reprehensibly perfect.

POETRY OF DEPARTURES. 26 *fo'c'sle*: nautical term, short for *forecastle*, the front upper deck of a sailing ship.

Compare

"Poetry of Departures" with "Miniver Cheevy" by Edwin Arlington Robinson (page 871).

D. H. Lawrence (1885–1930)

Piano   1918

Softly, in the dusk, a woman is singing to me;
Taking me back down the vista of years, till I see

A child sitting under the piano, in the boom of the tingling strings
And pressing the small, poised feet of a mother who smiles as she sings.

In spite of myself, the insidious mastery of song   5
Betrays me back, till the heart of me weeps to belong
To the old Sunday evenings at home, with winter outside
And hymns in the cozy parlor, the tinkling piano our guide.

So now it is vain for the singer to burst into clamor
With the great black piano appassionato. The glamour   10
Of childish days is upon me, my manhood is cast
Down in the flood of remembrance, I weep like a child for the past.

Compare

"Piano" with "Fern Hill" by Dylan Thomas (page 878).

Denise Levertov (1923–1997)

O Taste and See   1964

The world is
not with us enough.
O taste and see

the subway Bible poster said,
meaning **The Lord**, meaning   5
if anything all that lives
to the imagination's tongue,

grief, mercy, language,
tangerine, weather, to
breathe them, bite,   10
savor, chew, swallow, transform

into our flesh our
deaths, crossing the street, plum, quince,
living in the orchard and being

hungry, and plucking   15
the fruit.

Denise Levertov

Compare

"O Taste and See" with "Bread" by Samuel Menashe (page 535).

Li Po (701–762)

Drinking Alone by Moonlight   (about 750)   1919

A cup of wine, under the flowering trees;
I drink alone, for no friend is near.
Raising my cup I beckon the bright moon,

For he, with my shadow, will make three men.
The moon, alas, is no drinker of wine;   5
Listless, my shadow creeps about at my side.
Yet with the moon as friend and the shadow as slave
I must make merry before the Spring is spent.
To the songs I sing the moon flickers her beams;
In the dance I weave my shadow tangles and breaks.   10
While we were sober, three shared the fun;
Now we are drunk, each goes his way.
May we long share our odd, inanimate feast,
And meet at last on the Cloudy River of the sky.

—*Translated by Arthur Waley*

DRINKING ALONE BY MOONLIGHT. 14 *the Cloudy River of the sky:* the Milky Way.

Compare

"Drinking Alone by Moonlight" with "I taste a liquor never brewed" by Emily Dickinson (page 774).

Shirley Geok-lin Lim (b. 1944)

Learning to love America   1998

Shirley Geok-lin Lim

because it has no pure products

because the Pacific Ocean sweeps along the coastline
because the water of the ocean is cold
and because land is better than ocean

because I say we rather than they   5

because I live in California
I have eaten fresh artichokes
and jacarandas bloom in April and May

because my senses have caught up with my body
my breath with the air it swallows   10
my hunger with my mouth

because I walk barefoot in my house

because I have nursed my son at my breast
because he is a strong American boy
because I have seen his eyes redden when he is asked who he is   15
because he answers I don't know

because to have a son is to have a country
because my son will bury me here
because countries are in our blood and we bleed them

because it is late and too late to change my mind   20
because it is time.

LEARNING TO LOVE AMERICA. 1 *pure products:* an allusion to poem XVIII of *Spring and All* (1923) by
William Carlos Williams, which begins: "The pure products of America / go crazy—."

Compare

"Learning to love America" with "I Hear America Singing" by Walt Whitman (page 882).

Robert Lowell (1917–1977)

Skunk Hour

1959

For Elizabeth Bishop

Nautilus Island's hermit
heiress still lives through winter in her Spartan cottage;
her sheep still graze above the sea.
Her son's a bishop. Her farmer
is first selectman in our village;   5
she's in her dotage.

Thirsting for
the hierarchic privacy
of Queen Victoria's century,
she buys up all   10
the eyesores facing her shore,
and lets them fall.

The season's ill—
we've lost our summer millionaire,
who seemed to leap from an L. L. Bean   15
catalogue. His nine-knot yawl
was auctioned off to lobstermen.
A red fox stain covers Blue Hill.

And now our fairy
decorator brightens his shop for fall;   20
his fishnet's filled with orange cork,
orange, his cobbler's bench and awl;
there is no money in his work,
he'd rather marry.

One dark night,   25
my Tudor Ford climbed the hill's skull;
I watched for love-cars. Lights turned down,
they lay together, hull to hull,
where the graveyard shelves on the town. . . .
My mind's not right.   30

A car radio bleats,
"Love, O careless Love. . . ." I hear
my ill-spirit sob in each blood cell,
as if my hand were at its throat. . . .
I myself am hell;   35
nobody's here—

only skunks, that search
in the moonlight for a bite to eat.
They march on their soles up Main Street:
white stripes, moonstruck eyes' red fire   40
under the chalk-dry and spar spire
of the Trinitarian Church.

I stand on top
of our back steps and breathe the rich air—
a mother skunk with her column of kittens swills the garbage pail.   45
She jabs her wedge-head in a cup
of sour cream, drops her ostrich tail,
and will not scare.

Compare

"Skunk Hour" with "Desert Places" by Robert Frost (page 624).

Andrew Marvell (1621–1678)

To His Coy Mistress   1681

Had we but world enough, and time,
This coyness,° Lady, were no crime.   *modesty, reluctance*
We would sit down, and think which way
To walk, and pass our long love's day.
Thou by the Indian Ganges' side   5
Should'st rubies find; I by the tide
Of Humber would complain.° I would   *sing sad songs*
Love you ten years before the Flood,
And you should, if you please, refuse
Till the Conversion of the Jews.   10
My vegetable° love should grow   *vegetative, flourishing*
Vaster than empires, and more slow.
An hundred years should go to praise
Thine eyes, and on thy forehead gaze,
Two hundred to adore each breast,   15
But thirty thousand to the rest.
An age at least to every part,
And the last age should show your heart.
For, Lady, you deserve this state,°   *pomp, ceremony*
Nor would I love at lower rate.   20
    But at my back I always hear
Time's wingèd chariot hurrying near,
And yonder all before us lie
Deserts of vast eternity.
Thy beauty shall no more be found,   25
Nor, in thy marble vault, shall sound
My echoing song; then worms shall try
That long preserved virginity,

And your quaint honor turn to dust,
And into ashes all my lust.
The grave's a fine and private place,
But none, I think, do there embrace.   30
   Now therefore, while the youthful hue
Sits on thy skin like morning glew°   *glow*
And while thy willing soul transpires   35
At every pore with instant° fires,   *eager*
Now let us sport us while we may;
And now, like amorous birds of prey,
Rather at once our time devour,
Than languish in his slow-chapped° power.   *slow-jawed*   40
Let us roll all our strength, and all
Our sweetness, up into one ball
And tear our pleasures with rough strife,
Thorough° the iron gates of life.   *through*
Thus, though we cannot make our sun   45
Stand still, yet we will make him run.

TO HIS COY MISTRESS. 7 *Humber:* a river that flows by Marvell's town of Hull (on the side of the world opposite from the Ganges). 10 *conversion of the Jews:* an event that, according to St. John the Divine, is to take
place just before the end of the world. 35 *transpires:* exudes, as a membrane lets fluid or vapor pass through it.

Compare

"To His Coy Mistress" with "To the Virgins, to Make Much of Time" by Robert Herrick (page 847).

Edna St. Vincent Millay (1892–1950)

Recuerdo   1920

We were very tired, we were very merry—
We had gone back and forth all night on the ferry.
It was bare and bright, and smelled like a stable—
But we looked into a fire, we leaned across a table,
We lay on a hill-top underneath the moon;   5
And the whistles kept blowing, and the dawn came
    soon.

Edna St. Vincent Millay

We were very tired, we were very merry—
We had gone back and forth all night on the ferry;
And you ate an apple, and I ate a pear,
From a dozen of each we had bought somewhere;   10
And the sky went wan, and the wind came cold,
And the sun rose dripping, a bucketful of gold.

We were very tired, we were very merry,
We had gone back and forth all night on the ferry.
We hailed, "Good morrow, mother!" to a shawl-covered head,   15
And bought a morning paper, which neither of us read;

And she wept, "God bless you!" for the apples and pears,
And we gave her all our money but our subway fares.

RECUERDO. *The Spanish title means "a recollection" or "a memory."*

Compare

"Recuerdo" with "To the Virgins, to Make Much of Time" by Robert Herrick (page 847).

John Milton (1608–1674)

When I consider how my light is spent (1655?)

When I consider how my light is spent,
  Ere half my days in this dark world and wide,
  And that one talent which is death to hide
Lodged with me useless, though my soul more bent
To serve therewith my Maker, and present   5
  My true account, lest He returning chide;
  "Doth God exact day-labor, light denied?"
I fondly° ask. But Patience, to prevent   *foolishly*
That murmur, soon replies, "God doth not need
  Either man's work or his own gifts. Who best   10
  Bear his mild yoke, they serve him best. His state
Is kingly: thousands at his bidding speed,
  And post o'er land and ocean without rest;
  They also serve who only stand and wait."

WHEN I CONSIDER HOW MY LIGHT IS SPENT. *1 my light is spent:* Milton had become blind. *3 that one talent:* For Jesus' parable of the talents (measures of money), see Matthew 25:14–30.

Compare

"When I consider how my light is spent" with "On his blindness" by Jorge Luis Borges (page 741).

Marianne Moore (1887–1972)

Poetry 1921

I too, dislike it: there are things that are important beyond all this fiddle.
  Reading it, however, with a perfect contempt for it, one discovers
          that there is in
it after all, a place for the genuine.
      Hands that can grasp, eyes
         that can dilate, hair that can rise   5
            if it must, these things are important not because a

high sounding interpretation can be put upon them but because they are
  useful; when they become so derivative as to become
              unintelligible, the
same thing may be said for all of us—that we
      do not admire what   10

> we cannot understand. The bat,
>   holding on upside down or in quest of something to
>
> eat, elephants pushing, a wild horse taking a roll, a tireless wolf under
>   a tree, the immovable critic twinkling his skin like a horse that
>   feels a flea, the base-
>   ball fan, the statistician—case after case   15
>   could be cited did
>   one wish it; nor is it valid
>   to discriminate against "business documents and
>
> school-books"; all these phenomena are important. One must make a
>   distinction
>   however: when dragged into prominence by half poets, the result
>   is not poetry,   20
>   nor till the autocrats among us can be
>   "literalists of
>   the imagination"—above
>   insolence and triviality and can present
>
> for inspection, imaginary gardens with real toads in them, shall we have   25
>   it. In the meantime, if you demand on one hand, in defiance of
>   their opinion—
>   the raw material of poetry in
>   all its rawness and
>   that which is, on the other hand,
>   genuine then you are interested in poetry.   30

Compare

"Poetry" with "Ars Poetica" by Archibald MacLeish (page 769).

Marilyn Nelson

Marilyn Nelson (b. 1946)

A Strange Beautiful Woman   1985

A strange beautiful woman
met me in the mirror
the other night.
Hey,
I said,   5
What you doing here?
She asked me
the same thing.

Compare

"A Strange Beautiful Woman" with "Learning to Shave" by Adelle Foley (page 568).

Sharon Olds (b. 1942)

The One Girl at the Boys' Party

1983

Sharon Olds

When I take my girl to the swimming party
I set her down among the boys. They tower and
bristle, she stands there smooth and sleek,
her math scores unfolding in the air around her.
They will strip to their suits, her body hard and   5
indivisible as a prime number,
they'll plunge in the deep end, she'll subtract
her height from ten feet, divide it into
hundreds of gallons of water, the numbers
bouncing in her mind like molecules of chlorine   10
in the bright blue pool. When they climb out,
her ponytail will hang its pencil lead
down her back, her narrow silk suit
with hamburgers and french fries printed on it
will glisten in the brilliant air, and they will   15
see her sweet face, solemn and
sealed, a factor of one, and she will
see their eyes, two each,
their legs, two each, and the curves of their sexes,
one each, and in her head she'll be doing her   20
wild multiplying, as the drops
sparkle and fall to the power of a thousand from her body.

Compare

"The One Girl at the Boys' Party" with "My Papa's Waltz" by Theodore Roethke (page 501).

Wilfred Owen (1893–1918)

Anthem for Doomed Youth

(1917)

What passing-bells for these who die as cattle?
    Only the monstrous anger of the guns.
Only the stuttering rifles' rapid rattle
    Can patter out their hasty orisons.
No mockeries now for them; no prayers nor bells,   5
    Nor any voice of mourning save the choirs,—
The shrill, demented choirs of wailing shells;
    And bugles calling for them from sad shires.°   *counties*

What candles may be held to speed them all?
    Not in the hands of boys, but in their eyes   10
    Shall shine the holy glimmers of good-byes.
The pallor of girls' brows shall be their pall;

Their flowers the tenderness of patient minds,
And each slow dusk a drawing-down of blinds.

Compare

"Anthem for Doomed Youth" with "Facing It" by Yusef Komunyakaa (page 725).

Sylvia Plath (1932–1963)

Daddy   (1962) 1965

Sylvia Plath

You do not do, you do not do
Any more, black shoe
In which I have lived like a foot
For thirty years, poor and white,
Barely daring to breathe or Achoo.   5

Daddy, I have had to kill you.
You died before I had time—
Marble-heavy, a bag full of God,
Ghastly statue with one grey toe
Big as a Frisco seal   10

And a head in the freakish Atlantic
Where it pours bean green over blue
In the waters off beautiful Nauset.
I used to pray to recover you.
Ach, du.   15

In the German tongue, in the Polish town
Scraped flat by the roller
Of wars, wars, wars.
But the name of the town is common.
My Polack friend   20

Says there are a dozen or two.
So I never could tell where you
Put your foot, your root,
I never could talk to you.
The tongue stuck in my jaw.   25

It stuck in a barb wire snare.
Ich, ich, ich, ich,
I could hardly speak.
I thought every German was you.
And the language obscene   30

An engine, an engine
Chuffing me off like a Jew.
A Jew to Dachau, Auschwitz, Belsen.
I began to talk like a Jew.
I think I may well be a Jew.   35

The snows of the Tyrol, the clear beer of Vienna
Are not very pure or true.
With my gypsy ancestress and my weird luck
And my Taroc pack and my Taroc pack
I may be a bit of a Jew.   40

I have always been scared of *you*,
With your Luftwaffe, your gobbledygoo.
And your neat moustache
And your Aryan eye, bright blue.
Panzer-man, panzer-man, O You—   45

Not God but a swastika
So black no sky could squeak through.
Every woman adores a Fascist,
The boot in the face, the brute
Brute heart of a brute like you.   50

You stand at the blackboard, daddy,
In the picture I have of you,
A cleft in your chin instead of your foot
But no less a devil for that, no not
Any less the black man who   55

Bit my pretty red heart in two.
I was ten when they buried you.
At twenty I tried to die
And get back, back, back to you.
I thought even the bones would do.   60

But they pulled me out of the sack,
And they stuck me together with glue.
And then I knew what to do.
I made a model of you,
A man in black with a Meinkampf look   65

And a love of the rack and the screw.
And I said I do, I do.
So daddy, I'm finally through.
The black telephone's off at the root,
The voices just can't worm through.   70

If I've killed one man, I've killed two—
The vampire who said he was you
And drank my blood for a year,
Seven years, if you want to know.
Daddy, you can lie back now.   75

There's a stake in your fat black heart
And the villagers never liked you.
They are dancing and stamping on you.
They always *knew* it was you.
Daddy, daddy, you bastard, I'm through.   80

DADDY. 15 *Ach, du:* Oh, you. 27 *Ich, ich, ich, ich:* I, I, I, I. 51 *blackboard:* Otto Plath had been a professor of biology at Boston University. 65 *Meinkampf:* Adolf Hitler titled his autobiography *Mein Kampf* ("My Struggle").

Introducing this poem in a reading, Sylvia Plath remarked:

> The poem is spoken by a girl with an Electra complex. Her father died while she thought he was God. Her case is complicated by the fact that her father was also a Nazi and her mother very possibly part Jewish. In the daughter the two strains marry and paralyze each other—she has to act out the awful little allegory before she is free of it. (Quoted by A. Alvarez, *Beyond All This Fiddle* [New York: Random, 1968].)

In some details "Daddy" is autobiography: the poet's father, Otto Plath, a German, had come to the United States from Grabow, Poland. He died following the amputation of a gangrened foot and leg when Sylvia was eight years old. Politically, Otto Plath was a Republican, not a Nazi, but was apparently a somewhat domineering head of the household. (See the recollections of the poet's mother, Aurelia Schober Plath, in her edition of *Letters Home* by Sylvia Plath [New York: Harper, 1975].)

Compare

"Daddy" with "My Papa's Waltz" by Theodore Roethke (page 501).

Alexander Pope (1688–1744)

A little Learning is a dang'rous Thing (from *An Essay on Criticism*)

1711

A *little Learning* is a dang'rous Thing;
Drink deep, or taste not the *Pierian* Spring:
There *shallow Draughts* intoxicate the Brain,
And drinking *largely* sobers us again.
Fir'd at first Sight with what the *Muse* imparts,   5
In *fearless Youth* we tempt the Heights of Arts,
While from the bounded *Level* of our Mind,
Short Views we take, nor see the *Lengths behind,*
But *more advanc'd*, behold with strange Surprize
New, distant Scenes of *endless* Science rise!   10
So pleas'd at first, the towring *Alps* we try,
Mount o'er the Vales, and seem to tread the Sky;
Th' Eternal Snows appear already past,
And the first *Clouds* and *Mountains* seem the last:
But *those attain'd*, we tremble to survey   15
The growing Labours of the lengthen'd Way,
Th' *increasing* Prospect *tires* our wandring Eyes,
Hills peep o'er Hills, and *Alps* on *Alps* arise!

A LITTLE LEARNING IS A DANG'ROUS THING. 2 *Pierian Spring:* the spring of the Muses.

Compare

"A little Learning is a dang'rous Thing" with "The Writer" by Richard Wilbur (page 883).

Ezra Pound (1885–1972)

The River-Merchant's Wife: A Letter   1915

While my hair was still cut straight across my forehead
I played about the front gate, pulling flowers.
You came by on bamboo stilts, playing horse,
You walked about my seat, playing with blue plums.
And we went on living in the village of Chokan: 5
Two small people, without dislike or suspicion.

At fourteen I married My Lord you.
I never laughed, being bashful.
Lowering my head, I looked at the wall.
Called to, a thousand times, I never looked back.   10

At fifteen I stopped scowling,
I desired my dust to be mingled with yours
Forever and forever and forever.
Why should I climb the look out?

At sixteen you departed,   15
You went into far Ku-to-yen, by the river of swirling eddies,
And you have been gone five months.
The monkeys make sorrowful noise overhead.

You dragged your feet when you went out.
By the gate now, the moss is grown, the different mosses,   20
Too deep to clear them away!
The leaves fall early this autumn, in wind.
The paired butterflies are already yellow with August
Over the grass in the West garden;
They hurt me. I grow older.   25
If you are coming down through the narrows of the river Kiang,
Please let me know beforehand,
And I will come out to meet you
                    As far as Cho-fu-sa.

THE RIVER-MERCHANT'S WIFE: A LETTER. A free translation from the Chinese poet Li Po (eighth century).

Compare

"The River-Merchant's Wife: A Letter" with "A Valediction: Forbidding Mourning" by John
Donne (page 837).

Henry Reed (1914–1986)

Naming of Parts   1946

Today we have naming of parts. Yesterday,
We had daily cleaning. And tomorrow morning,
We shall have what to do after firing. But today,

Today we have naming of parts. Japonica
Glistens like coral in all of the neighboring gardens,   5
            And today we have naming of parts.

This is the lower sling swivel. And this
Is the upper sling swivel, whose use you will see,
When you are given your slings. And this is the piling swivel,
Which in your case you have not got. The branches   10
Hold in the gardens their silent, eloquent gestures,
            Which in our case we have not got.

This is the safety-catch, which is always released
With an easy flick of the thumb. And please do not let me
See anyone using his finger. You can do it quite easy   15
If you have any strength in your thumb. The blossoms
Are fragile and motionless, never letting anyone see
            Any of them using their finger.

And this you can see is the bolt. The purpose of this
Is to open the breech, as you see. We can slide it   20
Rapidly backwards and forwards: we call this
Easing the spring. And rapidly backwards and forwards
The early bees are assaulting and fumbling the flowers:
            They call it easing the Spring.

They call it easing the Spring: it is perfectly easy   25
If you have any strength in your thumb: like the bolt,
And the breech, and the cocking-piece, and the point of balance,
Which in our case we have not got; and the almond-blossom
Silent in all of the gardens and the bees going backwards and forwards,
            For today we have naming of parts.   30

Compare

"Naming of Parts" with "Musée des Beaux Arts" by W. H. Auden (page 823).

Adrienne Rich (1929-2012)

Living in Sin   1955

She had thought the studio would keep itself;
no dust upon the furniture of love.
Half heresy, to wish the taps less vocal,
the panes relieved of grime. A plate of pears,
a piano with a Persian shawl, a cat   5
stalking the picturesque amusing mouse
had risen at his urging.
Not that at five each separate stair would writhe
under the milkman's tramp; that morning light
so coldly would delineate the scraps   10
of last night's cheese and three sepulchral bottles;

that on the kitchen shelf among the saucers
a pair of beetle-eyes would fix her own—
envoy from some village in the moldings . . .
Meanwhile, he, with a yawn,   15
sounded a dozen notes upon the keyboard,
declared it out of tune, shrugged at the mirror,
rubbed at his beard, went out for cigarettes;
while she, jeered by the minor demons,
pulled back the sheets and made the bed and found   20
a towel to dust the table-top,
and let the coffee-pot boil over on the stove.
By evening she was back in love again,
though not so wholly but throughout the night
she woke sometimes to feel the daylight coming   25
like a relentless milkman up the stairs.

Compare

"Living in Sin" with "Let me not to the marriage of true minds" by William Shakespeare (page 654).

Edwin Arlington Robinson   (1869–1935)

Miniver Cheevy   1910

Miniver Cheevy, child of scorn,
    Grew lean while he assailed the seasons;
He wept that he was ever born,
    And he had reasons.

Miniver loved the days of old   5
    When swords were bright and steeds were prancing;
The vision of a warrior bold
    Would set him dancing.

Miniver sighed for what was not,
    And dreamed, and rested from his labors;   10
He dreamed of Thebes and Camelot,
    And Priam's neighbors.

Miniver mourned the ripe renown
    That made so many a name so fragrant;
He mourned Romance, now on the town,   15
    And Art, a vagrant.

Miniver loved the Medici,
    Albeit he had never seen one;
He would have sinned incessantly
    Could he have been one.   20

Miniver cursed the commonplace
    And eyed a khaki suit with loathing;
He missed the medieval grace
    Of iron clothing.

Miniver scorned the gold he sought,   25
  But sore annoyed was he without it;
Miniver thought, and thought, and thought,
  And thought about it.

Miniver Cheevy, born too late,
  Scratched his head and kept on thinking;   30
Miniver coughed, and called it fate,
  And kept on drinking.

MINIVER CHEEVY. 11 *Thebes:* a city in ancient Greece and the setting of many famous Greek myths; *Camelot:* the legendary site of King Arthur's Court. 12 *Priam:* the last king of Troy; his "neighbors" would have included Helen of Troy, Aeneas, and other famous figures. 17 *the Medici:* the ruling family of Florence during the high Renaissance, the Medici were renowned patrons of the arts.

Compare

"Miniver Cheevy" with "Ulysses" by Alfred, Lord Tennyson (page 876).

Theodore Roethke (1908–1963)

Elegy for Jane   1953

> My *Student, Thrown by a Horse*

I remember the neckcurls, limp and damp as tendrils;
And her quick look, a sidelong pickerel smile;
And how, once startled into talk, the light syllables leaped for her,
And she balanced in the delight of her thought,
A wren, happy, tail into the wind,   5
Her song trembling the twigs and small branches.
The shade sang with her;
The leaves, their whispers turned to kissing;
And the mold sang in the bleached valleys under the rose.

Oh, when she was sad, she cast herself down into such a pure depth,   10
Even a father could not find her:
Scraping her cheek against straw;
Stirring the clearest water.

My sparrow, you are not here,
Waiting like a fern, making a spiny shadow.   15
The sides of wet stones cannot console me,
Nor the moss, wound with the last light.

If only I could nudge you from this sleep,
My maimed darling, my skittery pigeon.
Over this damp grave I speak the words of my love: 20
I, with no rights in this matter,
Neither father nor lover.

Compare

"Elegy for Jane" with "Annabel Lee" by Edgar Allan Poe (page 765).

William Shakespeare (1564–1616)

When to the sessions of sweet silent thought (Sonnet 30) 1609

When to the sessions of sweet silent thought
I summon up remembrance of things past,
I sigh the lack of many a thing I sought,
And with old woes new wail my dear time's waste:
Then can I drown an eye, unused to flow,   5
For precious friends hid in death's dateless night,
And weep afresh love's long since cancelled woe,
And moan the expense of many a vanished sight;
Then can I grieve at grievances foregone,
And heavily from woe to woe tell o'er   10
The sad account of fore-bemoaned moan,
Which I new pay as if not paid before.
   But if the while I think on thee, dear friend,
   All losses are restored, and sorrows end.

William Shakespeare

Compare

"When to the sessions of sweet silent thought" with "Dostoevsky" by Charles Bukowski (page 830).

William Shakespeare (1564–1616)

That time of year thou mayst in me behold (Sonnet 73) 1609

That time of year thou mayst in me behold
When yellow leaves, or none, or few, do hang
Upon those boughs which shake against the cold,
Bare ruined choirs where late the sweet birds sang.
In me thou see'st the twilight of such day   5
As after sunset fadeth in the west,
Which by and by black night doth take away,
Death's second self that seals up all in rest.
In me thou see'st the glowing of such fire
That on the ashes of his youth doth lie,   10
As the deathbed whereon it must expire,
Consumed with that which it was nourished by.
   This thou perceiv'st, which makes thy love more strong,
   To love that well which thou must leave ere long.

Compare

"That time of year thou mayst in me behold" with "anyone lived in a pretty how town" by
E. E. Cummings (page 540).

William Shakespeare   (1564–1616)

My mistress' eyes are nothing like the sun (Sonnet 130)   1609

My mistress' eyes are nothing like the sun;
Coral is far more red than her lips' red;
If snow be white, why then her breasts are dun;
If hairs be wires, black wires grow on her head.
I have seen roses damasked, red and white,   5
But no such roses see I in her cheeks;
And in some perfumes is there more delight
Than in the breath that from my mistress reeks.
I love to hear her speak, yet well I know
That music hath a far more pleasing sound;   10
I grant I never saw a goddess go:
My mistress, when she walks, treads on the ground.
    And yet, by heaven, I think my love as rare
    As any she° belied with false compare.   *woman*

Compare

"My mistress' eyes are nothing like the sun" with "Crazy Jane Talks with the Bishop" by
William Butler Yeats (page 887).

Charles Simic   (b. 1938)

Butcher Shop   1971

Sometimes walking late at night
I stop before a closed butcher shop.
There is a single light in the store
Like the light in which the convict digs his tunnel.

An apron hangs on the hook: 5
The blood on it smeared into a map
Of the great continents of blood,
The great rivers and oceans of blood.

There are knives that glitter like altars
In a dark church   10
Where they bring the cripple and the imbecile
To be healed.

There's a wooden block where bones are broken,
Scraped clean—a river dried to its bed
Where I am fed,   15
Where deep in the night I hear a voice.

Compare

"Butcher Shop" with "Hawk Roosting" by Ted Hughes (page 510).

William Stafford (1914–1993)

The Farm on the Great Plains 1960

A telephone line goes cold;
birds tread it wherever it goes.
A farm back of a great plain
tugs an end of the line.

I call that farm every year, 5
ringing it, listening, still;
no one is home at the farm,
the line gives only a hum.

Some year I will ring the line
on a night at last the right one, 10
and with an eye tapered for braille
from the phone on the wall

I will see the tenant who waits—
the last one left at the place;
through the dark my braille eye 15
will lovingly touch his face.

"Hello, is Mother at home?"
No one is home today.
"But Father—he should be there."
No one—no one is here. 20

"But you—are you the one . . . ?"
Then the line will be gone
because both ends will be home:
no space, no birds, no farm.

My self will be the plain, 25
wise as winter is gray,
pure as cold posts go
pacing toward what I know.

Compare

"The Farm on the Great Plains" with "Piano" by D. H. Lawrence (page 857).

Wallace Stevens (1879–1955)

Wallace Stevens

The Emperor of Ice-Cream   1923

Call the roller of big cigars,
The muscular one, and bid him whip
In kitchen cups concupiscent curds.
Let the wenches dawdle in such dress
As they are used to wear, and let the boys   5
Bring flowers in last month's newspapers.
Let be be finale of seem.
The only emperor is the emperor of ice-cream.

Take from the dresser of deal,
Lacking the three glass knobs, that sheet   10
On which she embroidered fantails once
And spread it so as to cover her face.
If her horny feet protrude, they come
To show how cold she is, and dumb.
Let the lamp affix its beam.   15
The only emperor is the emperor of ice-cream.

THE EMPEROR OF ICE-CREAM. 9 *deal:* fir or pine wood used to make cheap furniture.

Compare

"The Emperor of Ice-Cream" with "This living hand, now warm and capable" by John Keats (page 649) and "A Slumber Did My Spirit Seal" by William Wordsworth (page 616).

Alfred, Lord Tennyson (1809–1892)

Ulysses   (1833)

It little profits that an idle king,
By this still hearth, among these barren crags,
Matched with an agèd wife, I mete and dole
Unequal laws unto a savage race
That hoard, and sleep, and feed, and know not me.   5
I cannot rest from travel; I will drink
Life to the lees. All times I have enjoyed
Greatly, have suffered greatly, both with those
That loved me, and alone; on shore, and when
Through scudding drifts the rainy Hyades   10
Vexed the dim sea. I am become a name;
For always roaming with a hungry heart
Much have I seen and known—cities of men
And manners, climates, councils, governments,
Myself not least, but honored of them all—   15
And drunk delight of battle with my peers,
Far on the ringing plains of windy Troy.
I am a part of all that I have met;

Yet all experience is an arch wherethrough
Gleams that untraveled world whose margin fades   20
Forever and forever when I move.
How dull it is to pause, to make an end,
To rust unburnished, not to shine in use!
As though to breathe were life! Life piled on life
Were all too little, and of one to me   25
Little remains; but every hour is saved
From that eternal silence, something more,
A bringer of new things; and vile it were
For some three suns to store and hoard myself,
And this grey spirit yearning in desire   30
To follow knowledge like a sinking star,
Beyond the utmost bound of human thought.
  This is my son, mine own Telemachus,
To whom I leave the scepter and the isle—
Well-loved of me, discerning to fulfill   35
This labor, by slow prudence to make mild
A rugged people, and through soft degrees
Subdue them to the useful and the good.
Most blameless is he, centered in the sphere
Of common duties, decent not to fail   40
In offices of tenderness, and pay
Meet adoration to my household gods,
When I am gone. He works his work, I mine.
  There lies the port; the vessel puffs her sail;
There gloom the dark, broad seas. My mariners,   45
Souls that have toiled, and wrought, and thought with me—
That ever with a frolic welcome took
The thunder and the sunshine, and opposed
Free hearts, free foreheads—you and I are old;
Old age hath yet his honor and his toil.   50
Death closes all; but something ere the end,
Some work of noble note, may yet be done,
Not unbecoming men that strove with Gods.
The lights begin to twinkle from the rocks;
The long day wanes; the slow moon climbs; the deep   55
Moans round with many voices. Come, my friends,
'Tis not too late to seek a newer world.
Push off, and sitting well in order smite
The sounding furrows; for my purpose holds
To sail beyond the sunset, and the baths   60
Of all the western stars, until I die.
It may be that the gulfs will wash us down;
It may be we shall touch the Happy Isles,
And see the great Achilles, whom we knew.
Though much is taken, much abides; and though   65
We are not now that strength which in old days

Moved earth and heaven, that which we are, we are—
One equal temper of heroic hearts,
Made weak by time and fate, but strong in will
To strive, to seek, to find, and not to yield.   70

ULYSSES. 10 *Hyades:* daughters of Atlas, who were transformed into a group of stars. Their rising with the sun was thought to be a sign of rain. 63 *Happy Isles:* Elysium, a paradise believed to be attainable by sailing west.

Compare

"Ulysses" with "Sir Patrick Spence" (page 493).

Dylan Thomas

Dylan Thomas   (1914–1953)

Fern Hill   1946

Now as I was young and easy under the apple boughs
About the lilting house and happy as the grass was
        green,
            The night above the dingle° starry,   *wooded valley*
                Time let me hail and climb
                Golden in the heydays of his eyes,   5
And honored among wagons I was prince of the apple towns
And once below a time I lordly had the trees and leaves
                Trail with daisies and barley
                Down the rivers of the windfall light.

And as I was green and carefree, famous among the barns   10
About the happy yard and singing as the farm was home,
            In the sun that is young once only,
                Time let me play and be
                Golden in the mercy of his means,
And green and golden I was huntsman and herdsman, the calves   15
Sang to my horn, the foxes on the hills barked clear and cold,
                And the sabbath rang slowly
                In the pebbles of the holy streams.

All the sun long it was running, it was lovely, the hay
Fields high as the house, the tunes from the chimneys, it was air   20
                And playing, lovely and watery
                And fire green as grass.
                And nightly under the simple stars
As I rode to sleep the owls were bearing the farm away,
All the moon long I heard, blessed among stables, the nightjars   25
                Flying with the ricks, and the horses
                Flashing into the dark.

And then to awake, and the farm, like a wanderer white
With the dew, come back, the cock on his shoulder: it was all
        Shining, it was Adam and maiden,   30
           The sky gathered again
        And the sun grew round that very day.
So it must have been after the birth of the simple light
In the first, spinning place, the spellbound horses walking warm
        Out of the whinnying green stable   35
           On to the fields of praise.

And honored among foxes and pheasants by the gay house
Under the new made clouds and happy as the heart was long,
        In the sun born over and over,
           I ran my heedless ways,   40
        My wishes raced through the house high hay
And nothing I cared, at my sky blue trades, that time allows
In all his tuneful turning so few and such morning songs
        Before the children green and golden
           Follow him out of grace,   45

Nothing I cared, in the lamb white days, that time would take me
Up to the swallow thronged loft by the shadow of my hand,
        In the moon that is always rising,
           Nor that riding to sleep
        I should hear him fly with the high fields   50
And wake to the farm forever fled from the childless land.
Oh as I was young and easy in the mercy of his means,
        Time held me green and dying
        Though I sang in my chains like the sea.

Compare

"Fern Hill" with "in Just-" by E. E. Cummings (page 678) and "The World Is Too Much with Us" by William Wordsworth (page 699).

John Updike (1932–2009)

Ex-Basketball Player   1958

Pearl Avenue runs past the high-school lot,
Bends with the trolley tracks, and stops, cut off
Before it has a chance to go two blocks,
At Colonel McComsky Plaza. Berth's Garage
Is on the corner facing west, and there,   5
Most days, you'll find Flick Webb, who helps Berth out.

Flick stands tall among the idiot pumps—
Five on a side, the old bubble-head style,
Their rubber elbows hanging loose and low.
One's nostrils are two S's, and his eyes   10
An E and O. And one is squat, without
A head at all—more of a football type.

Once Flick played for the high-school team, the Wizards.
He was good: in fact, the best. In '46
He bucketed three hundred ninety points,   15
A county record still. The ball loved Flick.
I saw him rack up thirty-eight or forty
In one home game. His hands were like wild birds.

He never learned a trade, he just sells gas,
Checks oil, and changes flats. Once in a while,   20
As a gag, he dribbles an inner tube,
But most of us remember anyway.
His hands are fine and nervous on the lug wrench.
It makes no difference to the lug wrench, though.

Off work, he hangs around Mae's luncheonette.   25
Grease-gray and kind of coiled, he plays pinball,
Smokes those thin cigars, nurses lemon phosphates.
Flick seldom says a word to Mae, just nods
Beyond her face toward bright applauding tiers
Of Necco Wafers, Nibs, and Juju Beads.   30

Compare

"Ex-Basketball Player" with "To an Athlete Dying Young" by A. E. Housman (page 849).

Derek Walcott (b. 1930)

Sea Grapes   1976

That sail which leans on light,
tired of islands,
a schooner beating up the Caribbean

Derek Walcott

for home, could be Odysseus,
home-bound on the Aegean;   5
that father and husband's

longing, under gnarled sour grapes, is
like the adulterer hearing Nausicaa's name
in every gull's outcry.

This brings nobody peace. The ancient war   10
between obsession and responsibility
will never finish and has been the same

for the sea-wanderer or the one on shore
now wriggling on his sandals to walk home,
since Troy sighed its last flame,   15

and the blind giant's boulder heaved the trough
from whose groundswell the great hexameters come
to the conclusions of exhausted surf.

The classics can console. But not enough.

SEA GRAPES. 4 *Odysseus*: Legendary king of Ithaca, the hero of Homer's *Odyssey*. 5 *Aegean*: Odysseus sailed over the Aegean Sea to return home after the Trojan war. 8 *Nausicaa*: beautiful young daughter of King Alcinous of Phaeacia, with whom Odysseus took refuge during his voyage home. 16 *blind giant*: allusion to the one-eyed cyclops whom Odysseus outwitted and blinded in order to avoid being eaten. 17 *hexameters*: dactylic hexameter is the meter in which Homer's *Odyssey* (as well as most classical epics) is written.

Compare

"Sea Grapes" with "Ulysses" by Alfred, Lord Tennyson (page 876).

Edmund Waller (1606–1687)

Go, Lovely Rose

1645

   Go, lovely rose,
Tell her that wastes her time and me
   That now she knows,
When I resemble° her to thee,   *compare*
How sweet and fair she seems to be.   5

   Tell her that's young
And shuns to have her graces spied,
   That hadst thou sprung
In deserts where no men abide,
Thou must have uncommended died.   10

   Small is the worth
Of beauty from the light retired:
   Bid her come forth,
Suffer herself to be desired,
And not blush so to be admired.   15

   Then die, that she
The common fate of all things rare
   May read in thee:
How small a part of time they share
That are so wondrous sweet and fair.   20

Compare

"Go, Lovely Rose" with "To the Virgins, to Make Much of Time" by Robert Herrick (page 847) and "To His Coy Mistress" by Andrew Marvell (page 861).

Walt Whitman (1819–1892)

from Song of the Open Road

1856, 1881

Allons! the road is before us!
It is safe—I have tried it—my own feet have tried it
    well—be not detain'd!

Let the paper remain on the desk unwritten, and the
    book on the shelf unopen'd!
Let the tools remain in the workshop! let the money remain unearn'd!
Let the school stand! mind not the cry of the teacher!   5
Let the preacher preach in his pulpit! let the lawyer plead in the court,
    and the judge expound the law.

Camerado, I give you my hand!
I give you my love more precious than money,
I give you myself before preaching or law;
Will you give me yourself? will you come travel with me?   10
Shall we stick by each other as long as we live?

SONG OF THE OPEN ROAD. This is part 15 of Whitman's long poem. 1 *Allons!*: French for "Come on!" or
"Let's go!"

Compare

"Song of the Open Road" with "Luke Havergal" by Edwin Arlington Robinson (page 509).

Walt Whitman (1819–1892)

I Hear America Singing   1860

I hear America singing, the varied carols I hear,
Those of mechanics, each one singing his as it should
    be blithe and strong,
The carpenter singing his as he measures his plank or
    beam,
The mason singing his as he makes ready for work, or
    leaves off work,

Walt Whitman

The boatman singing what belongs to him in his   5
    boat, the deckhand singing on the steamboat deck,
The shoemaker singing as he sits on his bench, the hatter singing as he stands,
The wood-cutter's song, the ploughboy's on his way in the morning, or at
    noon intermission or at sundown,
The delicious singing of the mother, or of the young wife at work, or of the
    girl sewing or washing,
Each singing what belongs to him or her and to none else,
The day what belongs to the day—at night the party of young fellows,   10
    robust, friendly,
Singing with open mouths their strong melodious songs.

Compare

"I Hear America Singing" with "I, Too" by Langston Hughes (page 789).

Richard Wilbur (b. 1921)

The Writer   1976

In her room at the prow of the house
Where light breaks, and the windows are tossed with linden,
My daughter is writing a story.

I pause in the stairwell, hearing
From her shut door a commotion of typewriter-keys   5
Like a chain hauled over a gunwale.

Young as she is, the stuff
Of her life is a great cargo, and some of it heavy:
I wish her a lucky passage.

But now it is she who pauses,   10
As if to reject my thought and its easy figure.
A stillness greatens, in which

The whole house seems to be thinking,
And then she is at it again with a bunched clamor
Of strokes, and again is silent.   15

I remember the dazed starling
Which was trapped in that very room, two years ago;
How we stole in, lifted a sash

And retreated, not to affright it;
And how for a helpless hour, through the crack of the door,   20
We watched the sleek, wild, dark

And iridescent creature
Batter against the brilliance, drop like a glove
To the hard floor, or the desk-top,

And wait then, humped and bloody,   25
For the wits to try it again; and how our spirits
Rose when, suddenly sure,

It lifted off from a chair-back,
Beating a smooth course for the right window
And clearing the sill of the world.   30

It is always a matter, my darling,
Of life or death, as I had forgotten. I wish
What I wished you before, but harder.

Compare

"The Writer" with "Digging" by Seamus Heaney (page 846).

William Carlos Williams (1883–1963)

William Carlos Williams

Spring and All   1923

By the road to the contagious hospital
under the surge of the blue
mottled clouds driven from the
northeast—a cold wind. Beyond, the
waste of broad, muddy fields   5
brown with dried weeds, standing and fallen

patches of standing water
the scattering of tall trees

All along the road the reddish
purplish, forked, upstanding, twiggy   10
stuff of bushes and small trees
with dead, brown leaves under them
leafless vines—

Lifeless in appearance, sluggish
dazed spring approaches—   15

They enter the new world naked,
cold, uncertain of all
save that they enter. All about them
the cold, familiar wind—

Now the grass, tomorrow   20
the stiff curl of wildcarrot leaf

One by one objects are defined—
It quickens: clarity, outline of leaf

But now the stark dignity of
entrance—Still, the profound change   25
has come upon them: rooted, they
grip down and begin to awaken

Compare

"Spring and All" with "in Just-" by E. E. Cummings (page 678) and "Root Cellar" by Theodore
Roethke (page 562).

William Carlos Williams (1883–1963)

Queen-Anne's-Lace   1921

Her body is not so white as
anemone petals nor so smooth—nor
so remote a thing. It is a field
of the wild carrot taking
the field by force; the grass   5
does not raise above it.

Here is no question of whiteness,
white as can be, with a purple mole
at the center of each flower.
Each flower is a hand's span
of her whiteness. Wherever
his hand has lain there is
a tiny purple blemish. Each part
is a blossom under his touch
to which the fibers of her being
stem one by one, each to its end,
until the whole field is a
white desire, empty, a single stem,
a cluster, flower by flower,
a pious wish to whiteness gone over—
or nothing.

Compare

"Queen-Anne's-Lace" with "Go, Lovely Rose" by Edmund Waller (page 881).

William Wordsworth (1770–1850)

Composed upon Westminster Bridge 1807

Earth has not anything to show more fair:
Dull would he be of soul who could pass by
A sight so touching in its majesty:
This City now doth, like a garment, wear
The beauty of the morning; silent, bare,   5
Ships, towers, domes, theatres, and temples lie
Open unto the fields, and to the sky;
All bright and glittering in the smokeless air.
Never did sun more beautifully steep
In his first splendor, valley, rock, or hill;   10
Ne'er saw I, never felt, a calm so deep!
The river glideth at his own sweet will:
Dear God! the very houses seem asleep;
And all that mighty heart is lying still!

William Wordsworth

Compare

"Composed upon Westminster Bridge" with "London" by William Blake (page 550).

James Wright (1927–1980)

Autumn Begins in Martins Ferry, Ohio   1963

In the Shreve High football stadium,
I think of Polacks nursing long beers in Tiltonsville,
And gray faces of Negroes in the blast furnace at Benwood,
And the ruptured night watchman of Wheeling Steel,
Dreaming of heroes.   5

All the proud fathers are ashamed to go home.
Their women cluck like starved pullets,
Dying for love.

Therefore,
Their sons grow suicidally beautiful   10
At the beginning of October,
And gallop terribly against each other's bodies.

Compare

"Autumn Begins in Martins Ferry, Ohio" with "Ex-Basketball Player" by John Updike (page 879).

Mary Sidney Wroth (1587?–1623?)

In this strange labyrinth   1621

In this strange labyrinth how shall I turn?
Ways are on all sides while the way I miss:
If to the right hand, there in love I burn;
Let me go forward, therein danger is;
If to the left, suspicion hinders bliss,   5
Let me turn back, shame cries I ought return
Nor faint though crosses with my fortunes kiss.
Stand still is harder, although sure to mourn;
Thus let me take the right, or left hand way;
Go forward, or stand still, or back retire;   10
I must these doubts endure without allay
Or help, but travail find for my best hire;
Yet that which most my troubled sense doth move
Is to leave all, and take the thread of love.

IN THIS STRANGE LABYRINTH. This sonnet comes from Wroth's *Urania* (1621), the first significant sonnet sequence by a woman. Wroth was the niece of Sir Philip Sidney and of the Countess of Pembroke as well as a distant relation of Sir Walter Raleigh. The *Labyrinth* of the title was the maze built by Minos to trap the young men and women sacrificed to the Minotaur. King Minos's daughter Ariadne saved her beloved Theseus by giving him a skein of thread to guide his way through the Labyrinth. (See the final line of the sonnet.)

Compare

"In this strange labyrinth" with Shakespeare's "Let me not to the marriage of true minds" (page 654).

William Butler Yeats (1865–1939)

Crazy Jane Talks with the Bishop   1933

I met the Bishop on the road
And much said he and I.
"Those breasts are flat and fallen now,
Those veins must soon be dry;
Live in a heavenly mansion,   5
Not in some foul sty."

"Fair and foul are near of kin,
And fair needs foul," I cried.
"My friends are gone, but that's a truth
Nor° grave nor bed denied,   *neither*   10
Learned in bodily lowliness
And in the heart's pride.

"A woman can be proud and stiff
When on love intent;
But Love has pitched his mansion in   15
The place of excrement;
For nothing can be sole or whole
That has not been rent."

William Butler Yeats

Compare

"Crazy Jane Talks with the Bishop" with "The Flea" by John Donne (page 836) or "Down, Wanton, Down!" by Robert Graves (page 530).

William Butler Yeats (1865–1939)

The Magi   1914

Now as at all times I can see in the mind's eye,
In their stiff, painted clothes, the pale unsatisfied ones
Appear and disappear in the blue depth of the sky
With all their ancient faces like rain-beaten stones,
And all their helms of silver hovering side by side,   5
And all their eyes still fixed, hoping to find once more,
Being by Calvary's turbulence unsatisfied,
The uncontrollable mystery on the bestial floor.

Compare

"The Magi" with "Journey of the Magi" by T. S. Eliot (page 839).

William Butler Yeats (1865–1939)

When You Are Old
1893

When you are old and grey and full of sleep,
And nodding by the fire, take down this book,
And slowly read, and dream of the soft look
Your eyes had once, and of their shadows deep;

How many loved your moments of glad grace, 5
And loved your beauty with love false or true,
But one man loved the pilgrim soul in you,
And loved the sorrows of your changing face;

And bending down beside the glowing bars,
Murmur, a little sadly, how Love fled 10
And paced upon the mountains overhead
And hid his face amid a crowd of stars.

Compare

"When You Are Old" with "Shall I compare thee to a summer's day?" by William Shakespeare (page 578).

Playwright David Ives.

DRAMA

TALKING WITH *David Ives*

"Comedy is just tragedy without the sentimentality."
Dana Gioia Interviews David Ives

Q: When did you first become interested in theater?

DAVID IVES: I played The Wolf opposite drop-dead-sexy Amy Skeehan in our third-grade production of "Little Red Riding Hood" at St. Mary Magdalene School in South Chicago. Basically it was all over after that. The show was so successful Amy and I took it on tour to the fourth and fifth grades. By then I had learned the Great Lesson of Theater, which is: *theater is a great way to hang out with girls.* It may be why Shakespeare became both an actor and a playwright: *more girls.*

Q: When did you discover that you could make people laugh?

DAVID IVES: There's some debate about this. An aunt of mine, a few years ago, said to me, "You're just like you were as a boy. Such a happy, funny child." I reported this to my mother, who said without a pause: "I wouldn't say that." She didn't seem to want to explain. One of my old high-school classmates recently mentioned that I was funny in high school. I only remember reading Russian novels about suicide in high school. Maybe I was funny between novels, but they were pretty thick.

Q: Tell us about your first play.

DAVID IVES: I wrote my first play when I was nine. It was about gangsters and had lots of gunfire and a girl I based on Amy Skeehan. I wrote my second play in high school. It was about Russian-like people talking about suicide a lot. My third play was at college and was The Worst Play Ever Written. From there, I had nowhere to go but up. My next play got produced, and suddenly I was a real live playwright. I've been faking it ever since.

Q: When you see one of your plays onstage, how different is it from what you imagined while writing it?

DAVID IVES: It's always better than I imagined it, unless it's worse.

Q: You are the master of the short comic play. What drew you to this unconventional form?

DAVID IVES: Probably a shorter and shorter attention span, like everybody else. Also, my wife Martha is on the short side and I am very drawn to her, so it is only a short (so to speak) way to short plays. I'm fond in general of the concise, the compact, the jeweled, the specific, and perfect as opposed to the verbose, the bloated, the baggy, and general. A good rock-and-roll song can be three or four minutes long and when it's over, if it's been made right and played right, you feel like you've gotten into a barfight, had a love affair, and ridden a convertible down Pacific Coast One on the most beautiful day of the year, all in three minutes. Imagine what you can do with a ten- or fifteen-minute play. You can make an audience feel like they've done all those things, plus they've gotten married, had kids, died, and went to heaven.

There they are, breathless just inside the pearly gates with their heads still spinning, and only ten minutes have passed. As far as I'm concerned, all plays, short or long, should aspire to the conditions of rock-and-roll, whose purpose is to make us aware of our mortality and the fact that we had better get with it before the song ends. Not a bad rule of thumb for art as a whole.

Q: Who are your favorite comic writers and comedians?

DAVID IVES: Nothing depresses me like comedians. Maybe it's because people who try to make me laugh instantly put me in a really bad mood. I once shot a man in Tucson and spent 38 years in the penitentiary because he tried to tell me a joke that started "A priest, a minister, and a rabbi walk into a bar. . . ." As for funny playwrights, Joe Orton and Noel Coward and Chris Durang do it for me because they're not just trying to be funny. They have a vision of life that happens to be comic. They've also got *style*, which is the outward and visible sign of having a vision of life.

Q: Why do people need comedy?

DAVID IVES: Comedy is important for three reasons. First, it's funny. Second, it makes us laugh. Third, it's easier to get a girl to go see a comedy than, let's say, *Hamlet*. Fourth, it shows us what frigging idiots we can be under the right circumstances. As Wendell Berry once said, "It is not from ourselves that we will learn to be better." Watching idiots cavort around onstage is one possible way to do that. First, of course, you have to be interested in being better.

Q: Comedy seems to get less critical respect than tragedy. Does that seem fair to you?

DAVID IVES: Nothing seems fair to me. That's why I write comedy. If you've ever met a critic you'll understand why they give more respect to sadder plays: because critics are the saddest dogs you'll ever meet. The fact is, comedy is much harder to do—to write, to act—than drama, the same way it's harder to look at life and say, *Okay*, than it is to mope around thinking about Russian roulette all the time. But let's get one thing clear: Comedy is not jokes. It certainly isn't sitcoms, which to me are about as funny as a sack of dead kittens. I'm talking about real comedy—human comedy, which is to say comedy that thinks and feels. I'm talking about *Twelfth Night*, or *The Marriage of Bette and Boo*, or *The Importance of Being Earnest*, where there's truth and sadness mixed in with the joy, just as there is in life. Theater *is* life, and fails when it settles for merely being funny, the same way life is not enough when it settles for just being funny. In the end, comedy is just tragedy without the sentimentality. Dostoyevsky, anyone?

Drama is life with the dull bits left out.

—ALFRED HITCHCOCK

Unlike a short story or a novel, a **play** is a work of storytelling in which actors represent the characters. A play also differs from a work of fiction in another essential way: it is addressed not to readers but to spectators.

To be part of an audience in a theater is an experience far different from reading a story in solitude. As the house lights dim and the curtain rises, we become members of a community. The responses of people around us affect our own responses. We, too, contribute to the community's response whenever we laugh, sigh, applaud, murmur in surprise, or catch our breath in excitement. In contrast, when we watch a movie by ourselves in our living room—say, a slapstick comedy—we probably laugh less often than if we were watching the same film in a theater, surrounded by a roaring crowd. On the other hand, no one is spilling popcorn down the backs of our necks. Each kind of theatrical experience, to be sure, has its advantages.

A theater of live actors has another advantage: a sensitive give-and-take between actors and audience. (Such rapport, of course, depends on the skill of the actors and the perceptiveness of the audience.) Although professional actors may try to give a first-rate performance on all occasions, it is natural for them to feel more keenly inspired by a lively, appreciative audience than by a lethargic one. As veteran playgoers well know, something unique and wonderful can happen when good actors and a good audience respond to each other.

In another sense, a play is more than actors and audience. Like a short story or a poem, a play is a work of art made of words. Watching a play, of course, we don't notice the playwright standing between us and the characters. If the play is absorbing, it flows before our eyes. In a silent reading, the usual play consists mainly of **dialogue**, exchanges of speech, punctuated by stage directions. In performance, though, stage directions vanish. And although the thoughtful efforts of perhaps a hundred people—actors, director, producer, stage designer, costumer, makeup artist, technicians—may have gone into a production, a successful play makes us forget its artifice. We may even forget that the play is literature, for its gestures, facial expressions, bodily stances, lighting, and special effects are as much a part of it as the playwright's written words. Even though words are not all there is to a living play, they are its bones. And the whole play, the finished production, is the total of whatever takes place on stage.

There is an aspect of theater related to both religious ritual and civic festival—a mixture of church service and rock concert. These are occasions when people gather for the special communal experiences of being reawakened emotionally and spiritually and celebrating their complex identities. Twice in the history of Europe, drama has sprung forth as a part of worship. In ancient Greece, plays were performed on feast days of Dionysus; and in the Christian Middle Ages, a play was introduced as an adjunct to the Easter mass with the enactment of the meeting between the three Marys and the angel at Jesus's empty tomb. Evidently, something in drama remains constant over the years—something as old, perhaps, as the deepest desires and highest aspirations of humanity.

32

READING A PLAY

*I regard the theatre as the greatest of all art forms,
the most immediate way in which a human being can share
with another the sense of what it is to be a human being.*

—OSCAR WILDE

Most plays are written not to be read in books but to be performed. Finding plays in a literature anthology, the student may well ask: Isn't there something wrong with the idea of reading plays on the printed page? Isn't that a perversion of their nature?

True, plays are meant to be seen on stage, but equally true, reading a play may afford advantages. One is that it is better to know some masterpieces by reading them than never to know them at all. Even if you live in a large city with many theaters, even if you attend a college with many theatrical productions, to succeed in your lifetime in witnessing, say, all the plays of Shakespeare might well be impossible. In print, they are as near to hand as a book on a shelf, ready to be enacted (if you like) on the stage of the mind.

After all, a play is literature before it comes alive in a theater, and it might be argued that when we read an unfamiliar play, we meet it in the same form in which it first appears to its actors and its director. If a play is rich and complex or if it dates from the remote past and contains difficulties of language and allusion, to read it on the page enables us to study it at our leisure and return to the parts that demand greater scrutiny.

But even if a play may be seen in a theater, sometimes to read it in print may be our way of knowing it as the author wrote it in its entirety. Far from regarding Shakespeare's words as holy writ, producers of *Hamlet*, *King Lear*, *Othello*, and other masterpieces often shorten or even leave out whole speeches and scenes. Besides, the nature of the play, as far as you can tell from a stage production, may depend on decisions of the director. In one production *Othello* may dress as a Renaissance Moor, in another as a modern general. Every actor who plays Iago in *Othello* makes his own interpretation of this knotty character. Some see Iago as a figure of pure evil; others, as a madman; still others, as a suffering human being consumed by hatred, jealousy, and pride. What do you think Shakespeare meant? You can always read the play and decide for yourself. If every stage production of a play is a fresh interpretation, so, too, is every reader's reading of it. Some readers, when silently reading a play to themselves, try to visualize a stage, imagining the characters in costume and under lights. If such a reader is an actor or a director and is reading the play with an eye toward staging it, then he or she may try to imagine every detail of a possible production, even shades of makeup and the loudness of sound effects. But the nonprofessional reader, who regards the play as literature, need not attempt such exhaustive imagining. Although some readers find it enjoyable to imagine the play taking place on a stage, others prefer to imagine the people and events that the play brings vividly to mind. Sympathetically following the tangled life of Nora in *A Doll's House* by Henrik Ibsen, we forget that we are reading printed stage directions and instead feel ourselves in the presence of human conflict. Thus regarded, a play becomes a form of storytelling, and the playwright's instructions to the actors and the director become a conventional mode of narrative that we accept much as we accept the methods of a novel or short story.

THEATRICAL CONVENTIONS

Most plays, whether seen in a theater or in print, employ some **conventions:** customary methods of presenting an action, usual and recognizable devices that an audience is willing to accept. In reading a great play from the past, such as *Oedipus the King* or *Othello*, it will help if we know some of the conventions of the classical Greek theater or the Elizabethan theater. When in *Oedipus the King* we encounter a character called the Chorus, it may be useful to be aware that this is a group of citizens who stand to one side of the action, conversing with the principal character and commenting. In *Othello*, when the sinister Iago, left on stage alone, begins to speak (at the end of Act I, Scene iii), we recognize the conventional device of a **soliloquy,** a monologue in which we seem to overhear the character's inmost thoughts uttered aloud. Another such device is the **aside,** in which a character addresses the audience directly, unheard by the other characters on stage, as when the villain in a melodrama chortles, "Heh! Heh! Now she's in my power!" Like conventions in poetry, such familiar methods of staging a narrative afford us a happy shock of recognition. Often, as in these examples, they are ways of making clear to us exactly what the playwright would have us know.

ELEMENTS OF A PLAY

When we read a play on the printed page and find ourselves swept forward by the motion of its story, we need not wonder how—and from what ingredients—the playwright put it together. Still, to analyze the structure of a play is one way to understand and appreciate a playwright's art. Analysis is complicated, however, because in an excellent play the elements (including plot, theme, and characters) do not stand in isolation. Often, deeds clearly follow from the kinds of people the characters are, and from those deeds it is left to the reader to infer the **theme** of the play—the general point or truth about human beings that may be drawn from it. Perhaps the most meaningful way to study the elements of a play (and certainly the most enjoyable) is to consider a play in its entirety.

Here is a short, famous one-act play worth reading for the boldness of its elements—and for its own sake. *Trifles* tells the story of a murder. As you will discover, the "trifles" mentioned in its title are not of trifling stature. In reading the play, you will probably find yourself imagining what you might see on stage if you were in a theater. You may also want to imagine what took place in the lives of the characters before the curtain rose. All this imagining may sound like a tall order, but don't worry. Just read the play for enjoyment the first time through, and then we will consider what makes it effective.

Susan Glaspell

Trifles

Susan Glaspell (1876–1948) grew up in her native Davenport, Iowa, daughter of a grain dealer. After four years at Drake University and a job as a reporter in Des Moines, she settled in New York's Greenwich Village. In 1915, with her husband, George Cram Cook, a theatrical director, she founded the Provincetown Players, the first influential noncommercial theater troupe in America. During the summers of 1915 and 1916, in a makeshift playhouse on a Cape Cod pier, the Players staged the earliest plays of Eugene O'Neill and works by John Reed, Edna St. Vincent Millay, and Glaspell herself. Transplanting the company to New York in the fall of 1916, Glaspell and Cook renamed it the Playwrights' Theater. Glaspell wrote several still-remembered plays, among them a pioneering work of feminist drama, The Verge *(1921), and the Pulitzer Prize-winning* Alison's House *(1930), about the family of a reclusive poet like Emily Dickinson who, after her death, squabble over the right to publish her poems. First widely known for her fiction with an Iowa background, Glaspell wrote ten novels, including* Fidelity *(1915) and* The Morning Is Near Us *(1939). Shortly after writing the play* Trifles, *she rewrote it as a short story, "A Jury of Her Peers."*

CHARACTERS

George Henderson, county attorney
Henry Peters, sheriff
Lewis Hale, a neighboring farmer
Mrs. Peters
Mrs. Hale

SCENE. *The kitchen in the now abandoned farmhouse of John Wright, a gloomy kitchen, and left without having been put in order—unwashed pans under the sink, a loaf of bread outside the breadbox, a dish towel on the table—other signs of incompleted work. At the rear the outer door opens and the Sheriff comes in followed by the County Attorney and Hale. The Sheriff and Hale are men in middle life, the County Attorney is a young man; all are much bundled up and go at once to the stove. They are followed by two women—the Sheriff's wife first; she is a slight wiry woman, a thin nervous face. Mrs. Hale is larger and would ordinarily be called more comfortable looking, but she is disturbed now and looks fearfully about as she enters. The women have come in slowly, and stand close together near the door.*

County Attorney (*rubbing his hands*): This feels good. Come up to the fire, ladies.

Mrs. Peters (*after taking a step forward*): I'm not—cold.

Sheriff (*unbuttoning his overcoat and stepping away from the stove as if to mark the beginning of official business*): Now, Mr. Hale, before we move things about, you explain to Mr. Henderson just what you saw when you came here yesterday morning.

County Attorney: By the way, has anything been moved? Are things just as you left them yesterday?

Sheriff (*looking about*): It's just the same. When it dropped below zero last night I thought I'd better send Frank out this morning to make a fire for us—no use getting pneumonia with a big case on, but I told him not to touch anything except the stove—and you know Frank.

County Attorney: Somebody should have been left here yesterday.

Sheriff: Oh—yesterday. When I had to send Frank to Morris Center for that man who went crazy—I want you to know I had my hands full yesterday, I knew you could get back from Omaha by today and as long as I went over everything here myself—

County Attorney: Well, Mr. Hale, tell just what happened when you came here yesterday morning.

Hale: Harry and I had started to town with a load of potatoes. We came along the road from my place and as I got here I said, "I'm going to see if I can't get John Wright to go in with me on a party telephone." I spoke to Wright about it once before and he put me off, saying folks talked too much anyway, and all he asked was peace and quiet—I guess you know about how much he talked himself; but I thought maybe if I went to the house and talked about it before his wife, though I said to Harry that I didn't know as what his wife wanted made much difference to John—

County Attorney: Let's talk about that later, Mr. Hale. I do want to talk about that, but tell now just what happened when you got to the house.

Hale: I didn't hear or see anything; I knocked at the door, and still it was all quiet in-side. I knew they must be up, it was past eight o'clock. So I knocked again, and I thought I heard somebody say, "Come in." I wasn't sure, I'm not sure yet, but I opened the door—this door (*indicating the door by which the two women are still standing*) and there in that rocker—(*pointing to it*) sat Mrs. Wright.

(*They all look at the rocker.*)

County Attorney: What—was she doing?

Hale: She was rockin' back and forth. She had her apron in her hand and was kind of—pleating it.

County Attorney: And how did she—look?

Hale: Well, she looked queer.

County Attorney: How do you mean—queer?

Hale: Well, as if she didn't know what she was going to do next. And kind of done up.

County Attorney: How did she seem to feel about your coming?

Hale: Why, I don't think she minded—one way or other. She didn't pay much at-tention. I said, "How do, Mrs. Wright, it's cold, ain't it?" And she said, "Is it?"—and went on kind of pleating at her apron. Well, I was surprised; she didn't ask me to come up to the stove, or to set down, but just sat there, not even looking at me, so I said, "I want to see John." And then she—laughed. I guess you would call it a laugh. I thought of Harry and the team outside, so I said a little sharp: "Can't I see John?" "No," she says, kind o' dull like. "Ain't he home?" says I. "Yes," says she, "he's home." "Then why can't I see him?" I asked her, out of pa-tience. "'Cause he's dead," says she. "*Dead?*" says I. She just nodded her head, not getting a bit excited, but rockin' back and forth. "Why—where is he?" says I, not knowing what to say. She just pointed upstairs—like that. (*Himself pointing to the room above.*) I got up, with the idea of going up there. I walked from there to here—then I says, "Why, what did he die of?" "He died of a rope round his neck," says she, and just went on pleatin' at her apron. Well, I went out and called Harry. I thought I might—need help. We went upstairs and there he was lyin'—

County Attorney: I think I'd rather have you go into that upstairs, where you can point it all out. Just go on now with the rest of the story.

Hale: Well, my first thought was to get that rope off. It looked . . . (*stops, his face twitches*) . . . but Harry, he went up to him, and he said, "No, he's dead all right, and we'd better not touch anything." So we went back down stairs. She was still sitting that same way. "Has anybody been notified?" I asked. "No," says she, unconcerned. "Who did this, Mrs. Wright?" said Harry. He said it businesslike—and she stopped pleatin' of her apron. "I don't know," she says. "You don't *know?*" says Harry. "No," says she. "Weren't you sleepin' in the bed with him?" says Harry. "Yes," says she, "but I was on the inside." "Somebody slipped a rope round his neck and strangled him and you didn't wake up?" says Harry. "I didn't wake up," she said after him. We must 'a looked as if we didn't see how that could be, for after a minute she said, "I sleep sound." Harry was going to ask her more questions but I said maybe we ought to let her tell her story first to the coroner, or the sheriff, so Harry went fast as he could to Rivers' place, where there's a telephone.

County Attorney: And what did Mrs. Wright do when she knew that you had gone for the coroner?

Hale: She moved from that chair to this one over here (*pointing to a small chair in the corner*) and just sat there with her hands held together and looking down. I got a feeling that I ought to make some conversation, so I said I had come in to see if John wanted to put in a telephone, and at that she started to laugh, and then she stopped and looked at me—scared. (*The County Attorney, who has had his notebook out, makes a note.*) I dunno, maybe it wasn't scared. I wouldn't like to say it was. Soon Harry got back, and then Dr. Lloyd came, and you, Mr. Peters, and so I guess that's all I know that you don't.

County Attorney (*looking around*): I guess we'll go upstairs first—and then out to the barn and around there. (*To the Sheriff*) You're convinced that there was nothing important here—nothing that would point to any motive.

Sheriff: Nothing here but kitchen things.

(*The County Attorney, after again looking around the kitchen, opens the door of a cupboard closet. He gets up on a chair and looks on a shelf. Pulls his hand away, sticky.*)

County Attorney: Here's a nice mess.

(*The women draw nearer.*)

Mrs. Peters (*to the other woman*): Oh, her fruit; it did freeze. (*To the County Attorney*) She worried about that when it turned so cold. She said the fire'd go out and her jars would break.

Sheriff: Well, can you beat the women! Held for murder and worryin' about her preserves.

County Attorney: I guess before we're through she may have something more serious than preserves to worry about.

Hale: Well, women are used to worrying over trifles.

(*The two women move a little closer together.*)

County Attorney (*with the gallantry of a young politician*): And yet, for all their worries, what would we do without the ladies? (*The women do not unbend. He goes to the sink, takes a dipperful of water from the pail and pouring it into a basin, washes his hands. Starts to wipe them on the roller towel, turns it for a cleaner place.*) Dirty towels! (*Kicks his foot against the pans under the sink.*) Not much of a housekeeper, would you say, ladies?

Mrs. Hale (*stiffly*): There's a great deal of work to be done on a farm.

County Attorney: To be sure. And yet (*with a little bow to her*) I know there are some Dickson County farmhouses which do not have such roller towels.

(*He gives it a pull to expose its full length again.*)

Mrs. Hale: Those towels get dirty awful quick. Men's hands aren't always as clean as they might be.

County Attorney: Ah, loyal to your sex, I see. But you and Mrs. Wright were neighbors. I suppose you were friends, too.

Mrs. Hale (*shaking her head*): I've not seen much of her of late years. I've not been in this house—it's more than a year.

County Attorney: And why was that? You didn't like her?

Mrs. Hale: I liked her all well enough. Farmers' wives have their hands full, Mr. Henderson. And then—

County Attorney: Yes—?

Mrs. Hale (*looking about*): It never seemed a very cheerful place.

County Attorney: No—it's not cheerful. I shouldn't say she had the home-making instinct.

Mrs. Hale: Well, I don't know as Wright had, either.

County Attorney: You mean that they didn't get on very well?

Mrs. Hale: No, I don't mean anything. But I don't think a place'd be any cheerfuller for John Wright's being in it.

County Attorney: I'd like to talk more of that a little later. I want to get the lay of things upstairs now.

(*He goes to the left, where three steps lead to a stair door.*)

Sheriff: I suppose anything Mrs. Peters does'll be all right. She was to take in some clothes for her, you know, and a few little things. We left in such a hurry yesterday.

County Attorney: Yes, but I would like to see what you take, Mrs. Peters, and keep an eye out for anything that might be of use to us.

Mrs. Peters: Yes, Mr. Henderson.

(*The women listen to the men's steps on the stairs, then look about the kitchen.*)

Mrs. Hale: I'd hate to have men coming into my kitchen, snooping around and criticizing.

(*She arranges the pans under sink which the County Attorney had shoved out of place.*)

Mrs. Peters: Of course it's no more than their duty.

Mrs. Hale: Duty's all right, but I guess that deputy sheriff that came out to make the fire might have got a little of this on. (*Gives the roller towel a pull.*) Wish I'd thought of that sooner. Seems mean to talk about her for not having things slicked up when she had to come away in such a hurry.

Mrs. Peters (*who has gone to a small table in the left rear corner of the room, and lifted one end of a towel that covers a pan*): She had bread set.

(*Stands still.*)

Mrs. Hale (*eyes fixed on a loaf of bread beside the breadbox, which is on a low shelf at the other side of the room; moves slowly toward it*): She was going to put this in there. (*Picks up loaf, then abruptly drops it. In a manner of returning to familiar things.*) It's a shame about her fruit. I wonder if it's all gone. (*Gets up on the chair and looks.*) I think there's some here that's all right, Mrs. Peters. Yes—here; (*holding it toward the window*) this is cherries, too. (*Looking again.*) I declare I believe that's the only one. (*Gets down, bottle in her hand. Goes to the sink and wipes it off on the outside.*) She'll feel awful bad after all her hard work in the hot weather. I remember the afternoon I put up my cherries last summer.

(*She puts the bottle on the big kitchen table, center of the room. With a sigh, is about to sit down in the rocking-chair. Before she is seated realizes what chair it is; with a slow look at it, steps back. The chair which she has touched rocks back and forth.*)

Mrs. Peters: Well, I must get those things from the front room closet. (*She goes to the door at the right, but after looking into the other room, steps back.*) You coming with me, Mrs. Hale? You could help me carry them.

(*They go in the other room; reappear, Mrs. Peters carrying a dress and skirt, Mrs. Hale following with a pair of shoes.*)

Mrs. Peters: My, it's cold in there.

(*She puts the clothes on the big table, and hurries to the stove.*)

Mrs. Hale (*examining her skirt*): Wright was close. I think maybe that's why she kept so much to herself. She didn't even belong to the Ladies Aid. I suppose she felt she couldn't do her part, and then you don't enjoy things when you feel shabby. She used to wear pretty clothes and be lively, when she was Minnie Foster, one of the town girls singing in the choir. But that—oh, that was thirty years ago. This all you was to take in?

Mrs. Peters: She said she wanted an apron. Funny thing to want, for there isn't much to get you dirty in jail, goodness knows. But I suppose just to make her feel more natural. She said they was in the top drawer in this cupboard. Yes, here. And then her little shawl that always hung behind the door. (*Opens stair door and looks.*) Yes, here it is.

(*Quickly shuts door leading upstairs.*)

Mrs. Hale (*abruptly moving toward her*): Mrs. Peters?

Mrs. Peters: Yes, Mrs. Hale?

Mrs. Hale: Do you think she did it?

Mrs. Peters (*in a frightened voice*): Oh, I don't know.

Mrs. Hale: Well, I don't think she did. Asking for an apron and her little shawl. Worrying about her fruit.

Mrs. Peters (starts to speak, glances up, where footsteps are heard in the room above; in a low voice): Mr. Peters says it looks bad for her. Mr. Henderson is awful sarcastic in a speech and he'll make fun of her sayin' she didn't wake up.

Mrs. Hale: Well, I guess John Wright didn't wake when they was slipping that rope under his neck.

Mrs. Peters: No, it's strange. It must have been done awful crafty and still. They say it was such a—funny way to kill a man, rigging it all up like that.

Mrs. Hale: That's just what Mr. Hale said. There was a gun in the house. He says that's what he can't understand.

Mrs. Peters: Mr. Henderson said coming out that what was needed for the case was a motive; something to show anger, or—sudden feeling.

Mrs. Hale (who is standing by the table): Well, I don't see any signs of anger around here. *(She puts her hand on the dish towel which lies on the table, stands looking down at table, one half of which is clean, the other half messy.)* It's wiped to here. *(Makes a move as if to finish work, then turns and looks at loaf of bread outside the breadbox. Drops towel. In that voice of coming back to familiar things.)* Wonder how they are finding things upstairs. I hope she had it a little more red-up° there. You know, it seems kind of sneaking. Locking her up in town and then coming out here and trying to get her own house to turn against her!

Mrs. Peters: But Mrs. Hale, the law is the law.

Mrs. Hale: I s'pose 'tis. *(Unbuttoning her coat.)* Better loosen up your things, Mrs. Peters. You won't feel them when you go out.

(Mrs. Peters takes off her fur tippet, goes to hang it on hook at back of room, stands looking at the under part of the small corner table.)

Mrs. Peters: She was piecing a quilt.

(She brings the large sewing basket and they look at the bright pieces.)

Mrs. Hale: It's a log cabin pattern. Pretty, isn't it? I wonder if she was goin' to quilt it or just knot it?

(Footsteps have been heard coming down the stairs. The Sheriff enters followed by Hale and the County Attorney.)

Sheriff: They wonder if she was going to quilt it or just knot it!

(The men laugh; the women look abashed.)

County Attorney (rubbing his hands over the stove): Frank's fire didn't do much up there, did it? Well, let's go out to the barn and get that cleared up.

(The men go outside.)

Mrs. Hale (resentfully): I don't know as there's anything so strange, our takin' up our time with little things while we're waiting for them to get the evidence. *(She sits*

---

red-up: (slang) readied up, ready to be seen.

down at the big table smoothing out a block with decision.) I don't see as it's anything to laugh about.

Mrs. Peters (*apologetically*): Of course they've got awful important things on their minds.

(*Pulls up a chair and joins Mrs. Hale at the table.*)

Mrs. Hale (*examining another block*): Mrs. Peters, look at this one. Here, this is the one she was working on, and look at the sewing! All the rest of it has been so nice and even. And look at this! It's all over the place! Why, it looks as if she didn't know what she was about!

(*After she has said this they look at each, then start to glance back at the door. After an instant Mrs. Hale has pulled at a knot and ripped the sewing.*)

Mrs. Peters: Oh, what are you doing, Mrs. Hale?

Mrs. Hale (*mildly*): Just pulling out a stitch or two that's not sewed very good. (*Threading a needle.*) Bad sewing always made me fidgety.

Mrs. Peters (*nervously*): I don't think we ought to touch things.

Mrs. Hale: I'll just finish up this end. (*Suddenly stopping and leaning forward.*) Mrs. Peters?

Mrs. Peters: Yes, Mrs. Hale?

Mrs. Hale: What do you suppose she was so nervous about?

Mrs. Peters: Oh—I don't know. I don't know as she was nervous. I sometimes sew awful queer when I'm just tired. (*Mrs. Hale starts to say something, looks at Mrs. Peters, then goes on sewing.*) Well, I must get these things wrapped up. They may be through sooner than we think. (*Putting apron and other things together.*) I wonder where I can find a piece of paper, and string.

Mrs. Hale: In that cupboard, maybe.

Mrs. Peters (*looking in cupboard*): Why, here's a birdcage. (*Holds it up.*) Did she have a bird, Mrs. Hale?

Mrs. Hale: Why, I don't know whether she did or not—I've not been here for so long. There was a man around last year selling canaries cheap, but I don't know as she took one; maybe she did. She used to sing real pretty herself.

Mrs. Peters (*glancing around*): Seems funny to think of a bird here. But she must have had one, or why would she have a cage? I wonder what happened to it.

Mrs. Hale: I s'pose maybe the cat got it.

Mrs. Peters: No, she didn't have a cat. She's got that feeling some people have about cats—being afraid of them. My cat got in her room and she was real upset and asked me to take it out.

Mrs. Hale: My sister Bessie was like that. Queer, ain't it?

Mrs. Peters (*examining the cage*): Why, look at this door. It's broke. One hinge is pulled apart.

Mrs. Hale (*looking too*): Looks as if someone must have been rough with it.

Mrs. Peters: Why, yes.

(*She brings the cage forward and puts it on the table.*)

Mrs. Hale: I wish if they're going to find any evidence they'd be about it. I don't like this place.

Mrs. Peters: But I'm awful glad you came with me, Mrs. Hale. It would be lonesome for me sitting here alone.

Mrs. Hale: It would, wouldn't it? (*Dropping her sewing.*) But I tell you what I do wish, Mrs. Peters. I wish I had come over sometimes when *she* was here. I—(*looking around the room*)—wish I had.

Mrs. Peters: But of course you were awful busy, Mrs. Hale—your house and your children.

Mrs. Hale: I could've come. I stayed away because it weren't cheerful—and that's why I ought to have come. I—I've never liked this place. Maybe because it's down in a hollow and you don't see the road. I dunno what it is but it's a lonesome place and always was. I wish I had come over to see Minnie Foster sometimes. I can see now—

(*Shakes her head.*)

Mrs. Peters: Well, you mustn't reproach yourself, Mrs. Hale. Somehow we just don't see how it is with other folks until—something comes up.

Mrs. Hale: Not having children makes less work—but it makes a quiet house, and Wright out to work all day, and no company when he did come in. Did you know John Wright, Mrs. Peters?

Mrs. Peters: Not to know him; I've seen him in town. They say he was a good man.

Mrs. Hale: Yes—good; he didn't drink, and kept his word as well as most, I guess, and paid his debts. But he was a hard man, Mrs. Peters. Just to pass the time of day with him—(*shivers*). Like a raw wind that gets to the bone. (*Pauses, her eye falling on the cage.*) I should think she would'a wanted a bird. But what do you suppose went with it?

Mrs. Peters: I don't know, unless it got sick and died.

(*She reaches over and swings the broken door, swings it again. Both women watch it.*)

Mrs. Hale: You weren't raised round here, were you? (*Mrs. Peters shakes her head.*) You didn't know—her?

Mrs. Peters: Not till they brought her yesterday.

Mrs. Hale: She—come to think of it, she was kind of like a bird herself—real sweet and pretty, but kind of timid and—fluttery. How—she—did—change. (*Silence; then as if struck by a happy thought and relieved to get back to everyday things.*) Tell you what, Mrs. Peters, why don't you take the quilt in with you? It might take up her mind.

Mrs. Peters: Why, I think that's a real nice idea, Mrs. Hale. There couldn't possibly be any objection to it, could there? Now, just what would I take? I wonder if her patches are in here—and her things.

(*They look in the sewing basket.*)

Mrs. Hale: Here's some red. I expect this has got sewing things in it. (*Brings out a fancy box.*) What a pretty box. Looks like something somebody would give you. Maybe her scissors are in here. (*Opens box. Suddenly puts her hand to her nose.*) Why—(*Mrs. Peters bends nearer, then turns her face away.*) There's something wrapped up in this piece of silk.

Mrs. Peters: Why, this isn't her scissors.

Mrs. Hale (*lifting the silk*): Oh, Mrs. Peters—it's—

(*Mrs. Peters bends closer.*)

Mrs. Peters: It's the bird.

2000 production of *Trifles*, by Echo Theatre of Dallas.

Mrs. Hale (*jumping up*): But, Mrs. Peters—look at it! Its neck! Look at its neck! It's all—other side *to*.

Mrs. Peters: Somebody—wrung—its—neck.

(*Their eyes meet. A look of growing comprehension, of horror. Steps are heard outside. Mrs. Hale slips box under quilt pieces, and sinks into her chair. Enter Sheriff and County Attorney. Mrs. Peters rises.*)

County Attorney (*as one turning from serious things to little pleasantries*): Well, ladies, have you decided whether she was going to quilt it or knot it?

Mrs. Peters: We think she was going to—knot it.

County Attorney: Well, that's interesting, I'm sure. (*Seeing the birdcage.*) Has the bird flown?

Mrs. Hale (*putting more quilt pieces over the box*): We think the—cat got it.

County Attorney (*preoccupied*): Is there a cat?

(*Mrs. Hale glances in a quick covert way at Mrs. Peters.*)

Mrs. Peters: Well, not *now*. They're superstitious, you know. They leave.

County Attorney (*to Sheriff Peters, continuing an interrupted conversation*): No sign at all of anyone having come from the outside. Their own rope. Now let's go up again and go over it piece by piece. (*They start upstairs.*) It would have to have been someone who knew just the—

(*Mrs. Peters sits down. The two women sit there not looking at one another, but as if peering into something and at the same time holding back. When they talk now it is in the manner of feeling their way over strange ground, as if afraid of what they are saying, but as if they cannot help saying it.*)

Mrs. Hale: She liked the bird. She was going to bury it in that pretty box.

Mrs. Peters (*in a whisper*): When I was a girl—my kitten—there was a boy took a hatchet, and before my eyes—and before I could get there—(*covers her face an instant*). If they hadn't held me back I would have—(*catches herself, looks upstairs where steps are heard, falters weakly*)—hurt him.

Mrs. Hale (*with a slow look around her*): I wonder how it would seem never to have had any children around. (*Pause.*) No, Wright wouldn't like the bird—a thing that sang. She used to sing. He killed that, too.

Mrs. Peters (*moving uneasily*): We don't know who killed the bird.

Mrs. Hale: I knew John Wright.

Mrs. Peters: It was an awful thing was done in this house that night, Mrs. Hale. Killing a man while he slept, slipping a rope around his neck that choked the life out of him.

Mrs. Hale: His neck. Choked the life out of him.

(*Her hand goes out and rests on the birdcage.*)

Mrs. Peters (*with rising voice*): We don't know who killed him. We don't *know*.

Mrs. Hale (*her own feeling not interrupted*): If there'd been years and years of nothing, then a bird to sing to you, it would be awful—still, after the bird was still.

Mrs. Peters (*something within her speaking*): I know what stillness is. When we homesteaded in Dakota, and my first baby died—after he was two years old, and me with no other then—

Mrs. Hale (*moving*): How soon do you suppose they'll be through looking for the evidence?

Mrs. Peters: I know what stillness is. (*Pulling herself back.*) The law has got to punish crime, Mrs. Hale.

Mrs. Hale (*not as if answering that*): I wish you'd seen Minnie Foster when she wore a white dress with blue ribbons and stood up there in the choir and sang. (*A look around the room.*) Oh, I wish I'd come over here once in a while! That was a crime! That was a crime! Who's going to punish that?

Mrs. Peters (*looking upstairs*): We mustn't—take on.

Mrs. Hale: I might have known she needed help! I know how things can be—for women. I tell you, it's queer, Mrs. Peters. We live close together and we live far apart. We all go through the same things—it's all just a different kind of the same thing. (*Brushes her eyes; noticing the bottle of fruit, reaches out for it.*) If I was you I wouldn't tell her her fruit was gone. Tell her it ain't. Tell her it's all right. Take this in to prove it to her. She—she may never know whether it was broke or not.

Mrs. Peters (*takes the bottle, looks about for something to wrap it in; takes petticoat from the clothes brought from the other room, very nervously begins winding this around the bottle; in a false voice*): My, it's a good thing the men couldn't hear us. Wouldn't they just laugh! Getting all stirred up over a little thing like a—dead canary. As if that could have anything to do with—with—wouldn't they *laugh!*

(*The men are heard coming down stairs.*)

Mrs. Hale (*under her breath*): Maybe they would—maybe they wouldn't.

County Attorney: No, Peters, it's all perfectly clear except a reason for doing it. But you know juries when it comes to women. If there was some definite thing. Something to show—something to make a story about—a thing that would connect up with this strange way of doing it—

(*The women's eyes meet for an instant. Enter Hale from outer door.*)

Hale: Well, I've got the team around. Pretty cold out there.

County Attorney: I'm going to stay here a while by myself. (*To the Sheriff*) You can send Frank out for me, can't you? I want to go over everything. I'm not satisfied that we can't do better.

Sheriff: Do you want to see what Mrs. Peters is going to take in?

(*The County Attorney goes to the table, picks up the apron, laughs.*)

County Attorney: Oh, I guess they're not very dangerous things the ladies have picked out. (*Moves a few things about, disturbing the quilt pieces which cover the box. Steps back.*) No, Mrs. Peters doesn't need supervising. For that matter, a sheriff's wife is married to the law. Ever think of it that way, Mrs. Peters?

Mrs. Peters: Not—just that way.

Sheriff (*chuckling*): Married to the law. (*Moves toward the other room.*) I just want you to come in here a minute, George. We ought to take a look at these windows.

County Attorney (*scoffingly*): Oh, windows!

Sheriff: We'll be right out, Mr. Hale.

(*Hale goes outside. The Sheriff follows the County Attorney into the other room. Then Mrs. Hale rises, hands tight together, looking intensely at Mrs. Peters, whose eyes make a slow turn, finally meeting Mrs. Hale's. A moment Mrs. Hale holds her, then her own eyes point the way to where the box is concealed. Suddenly Mrs. Peters throws back quilt pieces and tries to put the box in the bag she is wearing. It is too big. She opens box, starts to take bird out, cannot touch it, goes to pieces, stands there helpless. Sound of a knob turning in the other room. Mrs. Hale snatches the box and puts it in the pocket of her big coat. Enter County Attorney and Sheriff.*)

County Attorney (*facetiously*): Well, Henry, at least we found out that she was not going to quilt it. She was going to—what is it you call it, ladies?

Mrs. Hale (*her hand against her pocket*): We call it—knot it, Mr. Henderson.

CURTAIN

Questions

1. What attitudes toward women do the Sheriff and the County Attorney express? How do Mrs. Hale and Mrs. Peters react to these sentiments?
2. Why does the County Attorney care so much about discovering a motive for the killing?
3. What does Glaspell show us about the position of women in this early twentieth-century community?

4. What do we learn about the married life of the Wrights? By what means is this knowledge revealed to us?

5. What is the setting of this play, and how does it help us to understand Mrs. Wright's deed?

6. What do you infer from the wildly stitched block in Minnie's quilt? Why does Mrs. Hale rip out the crazy stitches?

7. What is so suggestive in the ruined birdcage and the dead canary wrapped in silk? What do these objects have to do with Minnie Foster Wright? What similarity do you notice between the way the canary died and John Wright's own death?

8. What thoughts and memories confirm Mrs. Peters and Mrs. Hale in their decision to help Minnie beat the murder rap?

9. In what places does Mrs. Peters show that she is trying to be a loyal, law-abiding sheriff's wife? How do she and Mrs. Hale differ in background and temperament?

10. What ironies does the play contain? Comment on Mrs. Hale's closing speech: "We call it—knot it, Mr. Henderson." Why is that little hesitation before "knot it" such a meaningful pause?

11. Point out some moments in the play when the playwright conveys much to the audience without needing dialogue.

12. How would you sum up the play's major theme?

13. How does this play, first produced in 1916, show its age? In what ways does it seem still remarkably new?

14. "*Trifles* is a lousy mystery. All the action took place before the curtain went up. Almost in the beginning, on the third page, we find out 'who done it.' So there isn't really much reason for us to sit through the rest of the play." Discuss this view.

ANALYZING *TRIFLES*

Some plays endure, perhaps because (among other reasons) actors take pleasure in performing them. *Trifles* is such a play, a showcase for the skills of its two principals. While the men importantly bumble about, trying to discover a motive, Mrs. Peters and Mrs. Hale solve the case right under their dull noses. The two players in these leading roles face a challenging task: to show both characters growing onstage before us. Discovering a secret that binds them, the two women must realize painful truths in their own lives, become aware of all they have in common with Minnie Wright, and gradually resolve to side with the accused against the men. That *Trifles* has enjoyed a revival of attention may reflect its evident feminist views, its convincing portrait of two women forced reluctantly to arrive at a moral judgment and to make a defiant move.

Conflict

Some critics say that the essence of drama is **conflict,** the central struggle between two or more forces in a play. Evidently, Glaspell's play is rich in this essential, even though its most violent conflict—the war between John and Minnie Wright—takes place before the play begins. Right away, when the menfolk barge through the door into the warm room, letting the women trail in after them; right away, when the sheriff makes fun of Minnie for worrying about "trifles" and the county attorney (that slick politician) starts crudely trying to flatter the "ladies," we sense a conflict between officious, self-important men and the women they expect to wait on them. What is the play's *theme*? Surely the title points to it: women, who men say worry over trifles, can find large meanings in those little things.

Plot

Like a carefully constructed traditional short story, *Trifles* has a **plot,** a term sometimes taken to mean whatever happens in a story, but more exactly referring to the unique arrangement of events that the author has made. (For more about plot in a story, see Chapter 1.) If Glaspell had elected to tell the story of John and Minnie Wright in chronological order, the sequence in which events took place in time, she might have written a much longer play, opening perhaps with a scene of Minnie's buying her canary and John's cold complaint, "That damned bird keeps twittering all day long!" She might have included scenes showing John strangling the canary and swearing when it beaks him; the Wrights in their loveless bed while Minnie knots her noose; and farmer Hale's entrance after the murder, with Minnie rocking. Only at the end would she have shown us what happened after the crime. That arrangement of events would have made for a quite different play than the short, tight one Glaspell wrote. By telling of events in retrospect, by having the women detectives piece together what happened, Glaspell leads us to focus not only on the murder but, more importantly, on the developing bond between the two women and their growing compassion for the accused.

Subplot

Tightly packed, the one-act *Trifles* contains but one plot: the story of how two women discover evidence that might hang another woman and then hide it. Some plays, usually longer ones, may be more complicated. They may contain a **double plot** (or **subplot**), a secondary arrangement of incidents, involving not the protagonist but someone less important. In Henrik Ibsen's *A Doll's House*, the main plot involves a woman and her husband; they are joined by a second couple, whose fortunes we also follow with interest and whose futures pose different questions.

Protagonist

If *Trifles* may be said to have a **protagonist,** a leading character—a word we usually save for the primary figure of a larger and more eventful play such as *Othello* or *Death of a Salesman*—then you would call the two women dual protagonists. They act in unison to make the plot unfold. Or you could argue that Mrs. Hale—because she destroys the wild stitching in the quilt, because she finds the dead canary, because she invents a cat to catch the bird (thus deceiving the county attorney), and because in the end when Mrs. Peters helplessly "goes to pieces" it is she who takes the initiative and seizes the evidence—deserves to be called the protagonist. More than anyone else in the play, you could claim, the more decisive Mrs. Hale makes things happen.

Exposition

A vital part of most plays is an **exposition,** the part in which we first meet the characters, learn what happened before the curtain rose, and find out what is happening now. For a one-act play, *Trifles* has a fairly long exposition, extending from the opening of the kitchen door through the end of farmer Hale's story. Clearly, this substantial exposition is necessary to set the situation and to fill in the facts of the crime. By comparison, Shakespeare's far longer *Tragedy of Richard III* begins almost abruptly, with its protagonist, a duke who yearns to be king, summing up history in an opening speech and revealing his evil character: "And therefore, since I cannot prove a lover . . . I am determinèd to prove a villain." But Glaspell, too, knows her craft. In the exposition, we are given a **foreshadowing** (or hint of what is to come) in Hale's dry remark, "I didn't know as what his wife wanted made much difference to John." The remark announces the play's theme that men often ignore women's feelings, and it hints at Minnie Wright's motive, later to be revealed. The county attorney, failing to pick up a valuable clue, tables the discussion. (Still another foreshadowing occurs in Mrs. Hale's ripping out the wild, panicky stitches in Minnie's quilt. In the end, Mrs. Hale will make a similar final move to conceal the evidence.)

Dramatic Question

With the county attorney's speech to the sheriff, "You're convinced that there was nothing important here—nothing that would point to any motive," we begin to understand what he seeks. As he will make even clearer later, the attorney needs a motive in order to convict the accused wife of murder in the first degree. Will Minnie's motive in killing her husband be discovered? Through the first two-thirds of *Trifles*, this is the play's **dramatic question.** Whether or not we state such a question in our minds (and it is doubtful that we do), our interest quickens as we sense that here is a problem to be solved, an uncertainty to be cleared up. When Mrs. Hale and Mrs. Peters find the dead canary with the twisted neck, the question is answered. We know that Minnie killed John to repay him for his act of gross cruelty. The playwright, however, now raises a *new* dramatic question. Having discovered Minnie's motive, will the women reveal it to the lawmen? Alternatively (if you care to phrase the new question differently), what will they do with the incriminating evidence? We keep reading, or stay clamped to our theater seats, because we want that question answered. We share the women's secret now, and we want to see what they will do with it.

Climax

Step by step, *Trifles* builds to a **climax:** a moment, usually coming late in a play, when tension reaches its greatest height. At such a moment, we sense that the play's dramatic question (or its final dramatic question, if the writer has posed more than one) is about to be answered. In *Trifles* this climax occurs when Mrs. Peters finds herself torn between her desire to save Minnie and her duty to the law. "It was an awful thing was done in this house that night," she reminds herself in one speech, suggesting that Minnie deserves to be punished; then in the next speech she insists, "We don't know who killed him. We don't *know*." Shortly after that, in one speech she voices two warring attitudes. Remembering the loss of her first child, she sympathizes with Minnie: "I know what stillness is." But in her next breath she recalls once more her duty to be a loyal sheriff's wife: "The law has got to punish crime, Mrs. Hale." For a moment, she is placed in conflict with Mrs. Hale, who knew Minnie personally. The two now stand on the edge of a fateful brink. Which way will they decide?

You will sometimes hear *climax* used in a different sense to mean any **crisis**— that is, a moment of tension when one or another outcome is possible. What *crisis* means will be easy to remember if you think of a crisis in medicine: the turning point in an illness when it becomes clear that a patient will either die or recover. In talking about plays, you will probably find both *crisis* and *climax* useful. You can say that a play has more than one crisis, perhaps several. In such a play, the last and most decisive crisis is the climax. A play has only one climax.

Resolution and Dénouement

From this moment of climax, the play, like its protagonist (or if you like, protagonists), will make a final move. Mrs. Peters takes her stand. Mrs. Hale, too, decides.

She owes Minnie something to make up for her own "crime"—her failure to visit the desperate woman. The plot now charges ahead to its outcome or **resolution,** also called the **conclusion** or **dénouement** (French for "untying of a knot"). The two women act: they scoop up the damaging evidence. Seconds before the very end, Glaspell heightens the **suspense,** our enjoyable anxiety, by making Mrs. Peters fumble with the incriminating box as the sheriff and the county attorney draw near. Mrs. Hale's swift grab for the evidence saves the day and presumably saves Minnie's life. The sound of the doorknob turning in the next room, as the lawmen return, is a small but effective bit of **stage business**—any nonverbal action that engages the attention of an audience. Earlier, when Mrs. Hale almost sits down in Minnie's place, the empty chair that ominously starts rocking is another brilliant piece of stage business. Not only does it give us something interesting to watch, but it also gives us something to think about.

Rising and Falling Action

The German critic Gustav Freytag maintained that events in a plot can be arranged in the outline of a pyramid. In his influential view, a play begins with a **rising action,** that part of the narrative (including the exposition) in which events start moving toward a climax. After the climax, the story tapers off in a **falling action**—that is, the subsequent events, including a resolution. In a tragedy, this falling action usually is recognizable: the protagonist's fortunes proceed downhill to an inevitable end.

Some plays indeed have demonstrable pyramids. In *Trifles*, we might claim that in the first two-thirds of the play a rising action builds in intensity. It proceeds through each main incident: the finding of the crazily stitched quilt, Mrs. Hale's ripping out the evidence, the discovery of the birdcage, then of the bird itself, and Mrs. Hale's concealing it. At the climax, the peak of the pyramid, the two women seem about to clash as Mrs. Peters wavers uncertainly. The action then falls to a swift resolution. If you outlined that pyramid on paper, however, it would look lopsided—a long rise and a short, steep fall. The pyramid metaphor seems more meaningfully to fit longer plays, among them some classic tragedies, such as *Oedipus the King*. Nevertheless, in most other plays, it is hard to find a symmetrical pyramid. (For a demonstration of another, quite different way to outline *Trifles*, see "Writing a Card Report" on page 1407.)

Unity of Time, Place, and Action

Because its action occurs all at one time and in one place, *Trifles* happens to observe the **unities,** certain principles of good drama laid down by Italian literary critics in the sixteenth century. Interpreting the theories of Aristotle as binding laws, these critics set down three basic principles: a good play, they maintained, should display unity of *action*, unity of *time*, and unity of *place*. In practical terms, this theory maintained that a play must represent a single series of interrelated actions that take place within twenty-four hours in a single location. Furthermore, they insisted, to have true unity of action, a play had to be entirely serious or entirely funny. Mixing tragic and comic elements was not allowed. That Glaspell consciously strove to obey those critics is doubtful, and certainly many great plays, such as Shakespeare's *Othello*, defy such arbitrary rules. Still, it is at least arguable that some of the power of *Trifles* (or Sophocles's *Oedipus the King*) comes from the intensity of the playwright's concentration on what happens in one place, in one short expanse of time.

Symbols in Drama

Brief though it is, *Trifles* has main elements you will find in much longer, more compli-cated plays. It even has **symbols,** things that hint at large meanings—for example, the broken birdcage and the dead canary, both suggesting the music and the joy that John Wright stifled in Minnie and the terrible stillness that followed his killing the one thing she loved. Perhaps the lone remaining jar of cherries, too, radiates suggestions: it is the one bright, cheerful thing poor Minnie has to show for a whole summer of toil. Plays can also contain symbolic characters (generally flat ones such as a prophet who croaks, "Be-ware the ides of March"), symbolic settings, and symbolic gestures. Symbols in drama may be as big as a house—the home in Ibsen's *A Doll's House,* for instance—or they may appear to be trifles. In Glaspell's rich art, such trifles aren't trifling at all.

WRITING *effectively*

Susan Glaspell on Writing

Creating *Trifles* 1927

We went to the theater, and for the most part we came away wishing we had gone somewhere else. Those were the days when Broadway flourished almost unchallenged. Plays, like magazine stories, were patterned. They might be pretty good within themselves, seldom did they open out to— where it surprised or thrilled your spirit to follow. They didn't ask much of *you,* those plays. Having paid for your seat, the thing was all done for you, and your mind came out where it went in, only tireder. An audience, Jig° said, had imagination. What was this "Broadway," which could make a thing as interesting as life into a thing as dull as a Broadway play?

Susan Glaspell

There was a meeting at the Liberal Club—Eddie Goodman, Phil Moeller, Ida Rauh, the Boni brothers, exciting talk about starting a theater.

• • •

He [Jig] wrote a letter to the people who had seen the plays, asking if they cared to become associate members of the Provincetown Players. The purpose was to give American playwrights of sincere purpose a chance to work out their ideas in freedom, to give all who worked with the plays their opportunity as artists. Were they inter-ested in this? One dollar for the three remaining bills.

Jig: the nickname of George Cram Cook (1873–1924), Glaspell's husband, who was the central founder and director of the Provincetown Players, perhaps the most influential theater company in the history of American drama.

The response paid for seats and stage, and for sets. A production need not cost a lot of money, Jig would say. The most expensive set at the Wharf Theater° cost thirteen dollars. There were sets at the Provincetown Playhouse which cost little more. . . .

"Now, Susan," he [Jig] said to me, briskly, "I have announced a play of yours for the next bill."

"But I have no play!"

"Then you will have to sit down to-morrow and begin one."

I protested. I did not know how to write a play. I had never "studied it."

"Nonsense," said Jig. "You've got a stage, haven't you?"

So I went out on the wharf, sat alone on one of our wooden benches without a back, and looked a long time at that bare little stage. After a time the stage became a kitchen—a kitchen there all by itself. I saw just where the stove was, the table, and the steps going upstairs. Then the door at the back opened, and people all bundled up came in—two or three men, I wasn't sure which, but sure enough about the two women, who hung back, reluctant to enter that kitchen. When I was a newspaper reporter out in Iowa, I was sent down-state to do a murder trial, and I never forgot going into the kitchen of a woman locked up in town. I had meant to do it as a short story, but the stage took it for its own, so I hurried in from the wharf to write down what I had seen. Whenever I got stuck, I would run across the street to the old wharf, sit in that leaning little theater under which the sea sounded, until the play was ready to continue. Sometimes things written in my room would not form on the stage, and I must go home and cross them out. "What playwrights need is a stage," said Jig, "their own stage."

Ten days after the director said he had announced my play, there was a reading at Mary Heaton Vorse's. I was late to the meeting, home revising the play. But when I got there the crowd liked "Trifles," and voted to put it in rehearsal next day.

From The Road to the Temple

THINKING ABOUT A PLAY

A good play almost always presents a conflict. Conflict creates suspense and keeps an audience from meandering out to the lobby water fountain. Without it, a play would be static and, most likely, dull. When a character intensely desires something but some obstacle—perhaps another character—stands in the way, the result is dramatic tension. To understand a play, it is essential to understand the basic conflicts motivating the plot.

- **Identify the play's protagonist.** Who is the central character of the play? What motivates this character? What does this character want most to achieve or avoid? Is this goal reasonable or does it reflect some delusion on the part of the protagonist?
- **Identify the antagonist.** Who prevents the main character from achieving his or her goal? Is the opposition conscious or accidental? What motivates this character to oppose the protagonist?
- **Identify the central dramatic conflict.** What does the struggle between the protagonist and antagonist focus on? Is it another person, a possession, an action, some sort of recognition, or honor?

Wharf Theater: the makeshift theater that Cook created from an old fish-house at the end of a Provincetown wharf.

▪ **How does the conflict influence the action of the play?** The central conflict usually fuels the plot, causing characters to do and say all sorts of things they might not otherwise undertake. What series of later events does the central conflict set in motion?

CHECKLIST: Writing About a Play

☐ List the play's three or four main characters. Jot down what each character wants most at the play's beginning.

☐ Which of these characters is the protagonist?

☐ What stands in the way of the protagonist achieving his or her goal?

☐ How do the other characters' motivations fit into the central conflict? Identify any double plots or subplots.

☐ What are the play's main events? How does each relate to the protagonist's struggle?

☐ Where do you find the play's climax?

☐ How is the conflict resolved? What qualities in the protagonist's character bring about the play's outcome?

☐ Does the protagonist achieve his or her goal? How does success or failure affect the protagonist?

WRITING ASSIGNMENT ON CONFLICT

Select any short play, and write a brief essay identifying the protagonist, central conflict, and dramatic question.

Here is a paper by Tara Mazzucca, a student of Beverly Schneller at Millersville University, that examines and compares the protagonists and dramatic questions of two short plays by Susan Glaspell.

SAMPLE STUDENT PAPER

Mazzucca 1

Tara Mazzucca

Professor Schneller

English 102

29 January 2012

Outside *Trifles*

Susan Glaspell was one of America's first feminist playwrights. A founder of the non-commercial Provincetown Players, she used this experimental company to present plays that realistically explored the lives of women. I would like to

Useful background

examine and compare two of Glaspell's early one-act plays, *Trifles* (1916) and *The Outside* (1917). I will discuss how they present women who are forced to survive in a world where men make most of the rules.

Both plays focus on female protagonists, and both realistically present the emotional hardships these women endure in their daily lives. Both plays have contemporary settings; they take place in the early twentieth century. Both plays present women who are isolated from society—Mrs. Wright in *Trifles* and the two protagonists of *The Outside*. And in both plays a pair of female characters work together to solve the central dramatic question.

In *Trifles* Glaspell ironically places two wives, one married to a farmer and the other to the sheriff, at the scene of a mysterious murder case. The play takes place entirely in familiar territory for women in the early 1900s—a kitchen. The kitchen becomes a symbol for the game of hot and cold that the characters unwittingly play. In the kitchen where it is hot, the women find all the clues necessary to solve the case. Meanwhile the men search the rest of the cold house and find nothing to suggest a motive for the crime.

The two wives soon recognize the story behind the murder by observing small details in the house. They see clues in what the men pass over as mere trifles. When the women mention the ruined fruit preserves in the kitchen, Mr. Hale dismisses the potential importance of housekeeping details and comments, "Well, women are used to worrying over trifles" (898). The two women, however, understand that small things can affect a person deeply.

The two women also recognize the importance of singing in Mrs. Wright's life. Singing was something she was known for when she was younger, only to have it taken away from her when she married John Wright. Doing housework alone all day in silence, Mrs. Wright became a different person. The stress of loneliness and depression finally got to Mrs. Wright. She bought a canary for company and enjoyment. She loved the singing bird, but her husband killed it. In desperation the woman decided to live without her husband.

Mrs. Hale and Mrs. Peters instinctively understand Mrs. Wright's worries. Their perspective gives them an advantage over their male counterparts. The women must work together, because if they did not, each would break under the pressure of the cold treatment they receive from their husbands—break like the glass jars of canned fruit Mrs. Wright stores away in her cabinet.

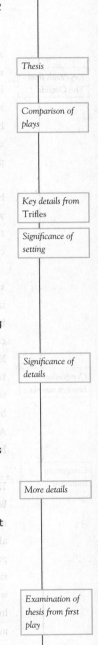

Thesis

Comparison of plays

Key details from Trifles

Significance of setting

Significance of details

More details

Examination of thesis from first play

Mazzucca 3

The plot of *The Outside* is relatively simple. The widowed Mrs. Patrick lives in a remote building that was once a life-saving station. Mrs. Patrick employs another widow, Allie Mayo, to help her with housekeeping. They lead lives of almost total isolation. One day three life-savers bring in the body of a drowned sailor and attempt unsuccessfully to revive him. Mrs. Patrick is furious that they have used her house as a rescue station and demands that they leave. Her behavior so upsets the usually silent Allie that the servant confronts Mrs. Patrick with a passionate speech about the futility of renouncing life.

Key details from The Outside

Allie also keeps to herself from grief. As a girl, she was talkative, but after her young husband vanished at sea, she resolved never to say an unnecessary word. Now twenty years later, she is notorious for her silence. The two women share a common grief of having lost the husbands they loved. Losing a husband changed each woman. Allie chose silence. Mrs. Patrick left society.

When the men bring the drowned young man into the former life-saving station, the incident upsets Mrs. Patrick, and she explodes with anger. This incident disturbs Allie in a different way. She realizes how isolated they have become. She knows that if they do not change, they will die without anyone caring. Deeply disturbed, Allie breaks her silence and argues with her employer. Mrs. Patrick initially resists Allie's remarks because she still has not come to terms with life without her husband. Allie resembles Mrs. Wright in *Trifles*. Both women keep quiet for years and do what they're told, until they reach a breaking point. A critical event forces each of them to take dramatic action. Allie violently argues with her employer; Mrs. Wright decides to murder her husband.

Comparison between two plays

Mrs. Hale and Mrs. Peters resemble Mrs. Patrick from *The Outside*. Throughout the play Mrs. Hale and Mrs. Peters try to understand why Mrs. Wright killed her husband. In the end, they recognize that their lives have much in common with that of the murderer. Their actions show their confusion about their own values. They do things that hinder the sheriff's investigation to protect an oppressed woman. First, Mrs. Hale rips out Mrs. Wright's erratic stitching so the men will not notice her nervous condition. Second, Mrs. Peters, who is—ironically—the sheriff's wife, hides the strangled bird from her husband and the other man. The women see a new side of Mrs. Wright's marriage and sympathize with her pathetic situation. By the end of *The Outside* Mrs. Patrick also sees a new side of Allie. Allie's outburst forces Mrs. Patrick to consider changing her life and reconsider her ideas.

Comparison continued

Mazzucca 4

Mrs. Patrick of *The Outside* and Mrs. Wright of *Trifles* are also alike because they are now isolated from the world they used to enjoy. One stopped living because of a harsh husband, the other because of a dead husband. Mrs. Hale and Allie also resemble one another because they both waited too late to understand the depression of their neighbor or living companion. In *Trifles*, Mrs. Hale decides to help her neighbor even though it means protecting a criminal. Allie speaks truthfully even though it might jeopardize her job. In the end, the actions Allie and Mrs. Hale take are helpful. The men never find a motive for the murder. Mrs. Patrick finally considers changing her way of life in *The Outside*. In the end each woman has found something new inside of her.

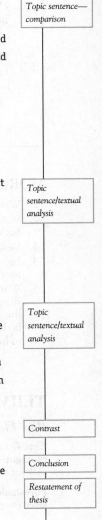

Topic sentence— comparison

Mrs. Hale and Mrs. Peters both realize the secret they must keep to protect Mrs. Wright. They also realize the injustices women go through to be accepted in society. Mrs. Hale says:

Topic sentence/textual analysis

> I might have known she needed help! I know how things can be—
> for women. I tell you, it's queer, Mrs. Peters. We live close
> together and we live far apart. We all go through the same
> things—it's all just a different kind of the same thing. (904)

In *The Outside*, the women don't feel socially oppressed by men, but they cannot define their lives except in relation to their husbands. When they become widows, they lose their reason to live. Allie realizes that their grief has gone too far. She finds her voice to say that life must be lived. Mrs. Patrick listens enough to feel uncertainty about her life of loneliness and isolation. Each play deals with death and its effects on the survivors.

Topic sentence/textual analysis

A major difference between the two plays is found in the way the central female characters treat one another. In *Trifles* the women work together to solve the mystery, but in *The Outside* the women clash and refuse to help one another. Glaspell did not have only one idealized image of female behavior. She realized that different women behave differently. Each play presents different ways women in the early twentieth century used to survive in a man's world. Trapped in the trifles of everyday life, many women felt as if they were living on the outside of the world.

Contrast

Conclusion

Restatement of thesis

Mazzucca 5

Works Cited

Glaspell, Susan. *The Outside. A Century of Plays by American Women*. Ed. Rachel
France. New York: Rosen, 1979. 48–54. Print.

Glaspell, Susan. *Trifles. Literature: An Introduction to Fiction, Poetry, Drama, and
Writing*. Ed. X. J. Kennedy and Dana Gioia. 7th Compact ed. New York:
Pearson, 2013. 895–905. Print.

MORE TOPICS FOR WRITING

1. Write a brief essay on the role gender differences play in Susan Glaspell's *Trifles*.
2. Write an analysis of the exposition—how the scene is set, characters introduced, and background information communicated—in *Trifles*.
3. Describe the significance of setting in *Trifles*.
4. Imagine you are a lawyer hired to defend Minnie Wright. Present your closing argument to the jury.
5. Watch any hour-long television drama. Write about the main conflict that drives the story. What motivates the protagonist? What stands in his or her way? How do each of the drama's main events relate to the protagonist's struggle? How is the conflict resolved? Is the show's outcome connected to the protagonist's character, or do events just happen to him or her? Do you believe the script is well written? Why or why not?

TERMS FOR *review*

Plot Elements

Exposition ► The opening portion of a narrative or drama in which the scene is set, the protagonist is introduced, and the author discloses any other background information necessary for the audience to understand the events that are to follow.

Foreshadowing ► The technique of arranging events and information in such a way that later events are prepared for beforehand, whether through specific words, images, or actions.

Double plot ► Also called **subplot**. A second story or plotline that is complete and interesting in its own right, often doubling or inverting the main plot.

Conflict ► The central struggle between two or more forces. Conflict generally occurs when some person or thing prevents the protagonist from achieving his or her goal.

Crisis ► A point when a crucial action, decision, or realization must be made, often marking a turning point or reversal of the protagonist's fortunes.

Climax ► The moment of greatest intensity, which almost inevitably occurs toward the end of the work. The climax often takes the form of a decisive confrontation between the protagonist and antagonist.

Resolution ▶ The final part of a narrative, the concluding action or actions that follow the climax.

Theatrical Conventions

Unities ▶ Unity of time, place, and action, the three formal qualities recommended by Renaissance critics to give a theatrical plot cohesion and integrity. According to this theory, a play should depict the causes and effects of a single action unfolding in one day in one place.

Soliloquy ▶ In drama, a speech by a character alone onstage in which he or she utters his or her thoughts aloud.

Aside ▶ A speech that a character addresses directly to the audience, unheard by the other characters on stage, as when the villain in a melodrama chortles: "Heh! Heh! Now she's in my power!"

Stage business ▶ Nonverbal action that engages the attention of an audience.

33 MODES OF DRAMA
Tragedy and Comedy

In 1770, Horace Walpole wrote, "the world is a comedy to those that think, a tragedy to those that feel." All of us, of course, both think and feel, and all of us have moments when we stand back and laugh, whether ruefully or with glee, at life's absurdities, just as we all have times when our hearts are broken by its pains and losses. Thus, the modes of tragedy and comedy, diametrically opposed to one another though they are, do not demand that we choose between them: both of them speak to something deep and real within us, and each of them has its own truth to tell about the infinitely complex experience of living in this world.

TRAGEDY

By **tragedy** we mean a play that portrays a serious conflict between human beings and some superior, overwhelming force. It ends sorrowfully and disastrously, and this outcome seems inevitable. Few spectators of *Oedipus the King* wonder how the play will turn out or wish for a happy ending. "In a tragedy," French playwright Jean Anouilh has remarked, "nothing is in doubt and everyone's destiny is known. . . . Tragedy is restful, and the reason is that hope, that foul, deceitful thing, has no part in it. There isn't any hope. You're trapped. The whole sky has fallen on you, and all you can do about it is shout."[1]

Many of our ideas of tragedy (from the Greek *tragoidia*, "goat song," referring to the goatskin dress of the performers), go back to ancient Athens; the plays of the Greek dramatists Sophocles, Aeschylus, and Euripides exemplify the art of tragedy. In the fourth century B.C., the philosopher Aristotle described Sophocles's *Oedipus the King* and other tragedies he had seen, analyzing their elements and trying to account for their power over our emotions. Aristotle's observations will make more sense after you read *Oedipus the King*, so we will save our principal discussion of them for the next chapter. But for now, to understand something of the nature of tragedy, let us take a brief overview of the subject.

---

[1]*Preface to Antigonê*, translated by Louis Galantière (New York: Random, 1946).

918

One of the oldest and most durable of literary genres, tragedy is also one of the simplest—the protagonist undergoes a reversal of fortune, from good to bad, ending in catastrophe. However simple, though, tragedy can be one of the most complex genres to explain satisfactorily, with almost every principal point of its definition open to differing and often hotly debated interpretations. It is a fluid and adaptive genre, and for every one of its defining points, we can cite a tragic masterpiece that fails to observe that particular convention. Its fluidity and adaptability can also be shown by the way in which the classical tragic pattern is played out in pure form in such unlikely places as Orson Welles's film *Citizen Kane* (1941) and Chinua Achebe's great novel *Things Fall Apart* (1958): in each of these works, a man of high position and character—one a multimillionaire newspaper publisher, the other a late nineteenth-century African warrior—moves inexorably to destruction, impelled by his rigidity and self-righteousness. Even a movie such as *King Kong*—despite its oversized and hirsute protagonist—exemplifies some of the principles of tragedy.

To gain a clearer understanding of what tragedy is, let us first take a moment to talk about what it is not. Consider the kinds of events that customarily bring the term "tragedy" to mind: the death of a child, a fire that destroys a family's home and possessions, the killing of a bystander caught in the crossfire of a shootout between criminals, and so on. What all of these unfortunate instances have in common, obviously, is that they involve the infliction of great and irreversible suffering. But what they also share is the sense that the sufferers are innocent, that they have done nothing to cause or to deserve their fate. This is what we usually describe as a tragedy in real life, but tragedy in a literary or dramatic context has a different meaning: most theorists take their lead from Aristotle (see the next chapter for a fuller discussion of several of the points raised here) in maintaining that the protagonist's reversal of fortune is brought about through some error or weakness on his part, generally referred to as his **tragic flaw.**

Despite this weakness, the hero is traditionally a person of nobility, of both social rank and personality. Just as the suffering of totally innocent people stirs us to sympathetic sorrow rather than a tragic response, so too the destruction of a purely evil figure, a tyrant or a murderer with no redeeming qualities, would inspire only feelings of relief and satisfaction—hardly the emotions that tragedy seeks to stimulate. In most tragedies, the catastrophe entails not only the loss of outward fortune—things such as reputation, power, and life itself, which even the basest villain may possess and then be deprived of—but also the erosion of the protagonist's moral character and greatness of spirit.

Tragic Style

In keeping with this emphasis on nobility of spirit, tragedies are customarily written in an elevated style, one characterized by dignity and seriousness. In the Middle Ages, just as *tragedy* meant a work written in a high style in which the central character went from good fortune to bad, *comedy* indicated just the opposite, a work written in a low or common style, in which the protagonist moved from adverse circumstances to happy ones—hence Dante's great triptych of hell, purgatory, and heaven, written in everyday Italian rather than scholarly Latin, is known as *The Divine Comedy*, despite the relative absence of humor, let alone hilarity, in its pages. The tragic view of life, clearly, presupposes that in the end we will prove unequal to the challenges we must face, while the comic outlook asserts a view of human possibility in which our common sense and resilience—or pure dumb luck—will enable us to win out.

Tragedy's complexity can be seen also in the response that, according to Aristotle, it seeks to arouse in the viewer: pity and fear. By its very nature, pity distances the one who pities from the object of that pity, since we can feel sorry only for those whom we perceive to be worse off than ourselves. When we watch or read a tragedy, moved as we may be, we observe the downfall of the protagonist with a certain detachment; "better him than me" may be a rather crude way of putting it, but perhaps not an entirely incorrect one. Fear, on the other hand, usually involves an immediate anxiety about our own well-being. Even as we regard the hero's destruction from the safety of a better place, we are made to feel our own vulnerability in the face of life's dangers and instability, because we see that neither position nor virtue can protect even the great from ruin.

The following is a scene from Christopher Marlowe's classic Elizabethan tragedy *Doctor Faustus*. Based on an anonymous pamphlet published in Germany in 1587 and translated into English shortly thereafter, this celebrated play tells the story of an elderly professor who feels that he has wasted his life in fruitless inquiry. Chafing at the limits of human understanding, he makes a pact with the devil to gain forbidden knowledge and power. The scene presented here is the decisive turning point of the play, in which Faustus seals the satanic bargain that will damn him. Stimulated by his thirst for knowledge and experience, spurred on by his pride to assume that the divinely ordained limits of human experience no longer apply to him, he rushes to embrace his own undoing. Marlowe dramatizes Faustus's situation by bringing a good angel and a fallen angel (i.e., a demon) to whisper conflicting advice in this pivotal scene. (This good angel versus bad angel device has proved popular for centuries. We still see it today in everything from TV commercials to cartoons such as *The Simpsons*.) Notice the dignified and often gorgeous language Marlowe employs to create the serious mood necessary for tragedy.

Christopher Marlowe

Scene from Doctor Faustus[2]
(about 1588)

Edited by Sylvan Barnet

Christopher Marlowe was born in Canterbury, England, in February 1564, about ten weeks before William Shakespeare. Marlowe, the son of a prosperous shoemaker, received a B.A. from Cambridge University in 1584 and an M.A. in 1587, after which he settled in London. The rest of his short life was marked by rumor, secrecy, and violence, including suspicions that he was a secret agent for Queen Elizabeth's government and allegations against him of blasphemy and atheism—no small matter in light of the political instability and religious controversies of the times. Peripherally implicated in several violent deaths, he met his own end in May 1593 when he was stabbed above the right eye during a tavern brawl, under circumstances that have never been fully explained. Brief and crowded as his life was, he wrote a number of intense, powerful, and highly influential tragedies— Tamburlaine the Great, Parts 1 and 2 (1587), Doctor Faustus (1588), The Jew of Malta (1589), Edward the Second (c. 1592), The Massacre at Paris (1593), and Dido, Queen of Carthage (c. 1593, with Thomas Nashe). He is also the author of the lyric poem "The Passionate Shepherd to His Love," with its universally known first line: "Come live with me and be my love."

[2]This scene is from the 1616 text, or "B-Text," published as *The Tragicall History of the Life and Death of Doctor Faustus*. Modernizations have been made in spelling and punctuation.

Doctor Faustus with the Bad Angel and the Good Angel, from the Utah Shakespearean Festival's 2005 production.

DRAMATIS PERSONAE

Doctor Faustus
Good Angel
Bad Angel
Mephistophilis, a devil

ACT II

SCENE I

(*Enter Faustus in his study.*)

Faustus: Now, Faustus, must thou needs be damned;
Canst thou not be saved!
What boots° it then to think on God or heaven?
Away with such vain fancies, and despair—
Despair in God and trust in Belzebub!   5
Now go not backward Faustus; be resolute!
Why waver'st thou? O something soundeth in mine ear,
"Abjure this magic, turn to God again."
Ay, and Faustus will turn to God again.
To God? He loves thee not.   10

3 *boots*: avails

The god thou serv'st is thine own appetite
Wherein is fixed the love of Belzebub!
To him I'll build an altar and a church,
And offer lukewarm blood of newborn babes!

(*Enter the two Angels.*)

Bad Angel: Go forward, Faustus, in that famous art.   15
Good Angel: Sweet Faustus, leave that execrable art.
Faustus: Contrition, prayer, repentance? What of these?
Good Angel: O, they are means to bring thee unto heaven.
Bad Angel: Rather illusions, fruits of lunacy,
    That make men foolish that do use them most.   20
Good Angel: Sweet Faustus, think of heaven and heavenly things.
Bad Angel: No, Faustus, think of honor and of wealth.

                                             (*Exeunt Angels.*)

Faustus: Wealth!
    Why, the signory of Emden° shall be mine!
    When Mephistophilis shall stand by me   25
    What power can hurt me? Faustus, thou art safe.
    Cast no more doubts! Mephistophilis, come,
    And bring glad tidings from great Lucifer.
    Is't not midnight? Come Mephistophilis,
    Veni, veni, Mephostophile!°   30

(*Enter Mephistophilis.*)

    Now tell me, what saith Lucifer thy lord?
Mephistophilis: That I shall wait on Faustus whilst he lives,
    So he will buy my service with his soul.
Faustus: Already Faustus hath hazarded that for thee.
Mephistophilis: But now thou must bequeath it solemnly   35
    And write a deed of gift with thine own blood,
    For that security craves Lucifer.
    If thou deny it I must back to hell.
Faustus: Stay Mephistophilis and tell me,
    What good will my soul do thy lord?   40
Mephistophilis: Enlarge his kingdom.
Faustus: Is that the reason why he tempts us thus?
Mephistophilis: *Solamen miseris socios habuisse doloris.*°
Faustus: Why, have you any pain that torture other?°
Mephistophilis: As great as have the human souls of men.   45
    But tell me, Faustus, shall I have thy soul—
    And I will be thy slave and wait on thee
    And give thee more than thou hast wit to ask?
Faustus: Ay Mephistophilis, I'll give it him.°

---

24 *signory of Emden:* lordship of the rich German port at the mouth of the Ems   30 *Veni, veni, Mephostophile!:* Come, come, Mephistophilis (Latin)   43 *Solamen . . . doloris:* Misery loves company (Latin)   44 *other:* others   49 *him:* i.e., to Lucifer

Mephistophilis: Then, Faustus, stab thy arm courageously, 50
　　And bind thy soul, that at some certain day
　　Great Lucifer may claim it as his own.
　　And then be thou as great as Lucifer!
Faustus: Lo, Mephistophilis: for love of thee
　　Faustus hath cut his arm, and with his proper° blood 55
　　Assures° his soul to be great Lucifer's,
　　Chief Lord and Regent of perpetual night.
　　View here this blood that trickles from mine arm,
　　And let it be propitious for my wish.
Mephistophilis: But, Faustus, 60
　　Write it in manner of a deed of gift.
Faustus: Ay, so I do—But Mephistophilis,
　　My blood congeals and I can write no more.
Mephistophilis: I'll fetch thee fire to dissolve it straight.

　　　　　　　　　　　　　　　　　　　　(*Exit.*)

Faustus: What might the staying of my blood portend? 65
　　Is it unwilling I should write this bill?°
　　Why streams it not that I may write afresh:
　　"Faustus gives to thee his soul"? O there it stayed.
　　Why should'st thou not? Is not thy soul thine own?
　　Then write again: "Faustus gives to thee his soul." 70

　　(*Enter Mephistophilis, with the chafer° of fire.*)

Mephistophilis: See, Faustus, here is fire. Set it° on.
Faustus: So, now the blood begins to clear again.
　　Now will I make an end immediately.
Mephistophilis (aside): What will not I do to obtain his soul!
Faustus: Consummatum est!° This bill is ended: 75
　　And Faustus hath bequeathed his soul to Lucifer.
　　—But what is this inscription on mine arm?
　　Homo fuge!° Whither should I fly?
　　If unto God, He'll throw me down to hell.
　　My senses are deceived; here's nothing writ. 80
　　O yes, I see it plain! Even here is writ
　　Homo fuge! Yet shall not Faustus fly!
Mephistophilis (aside): I'll fetch him somewhat° to delight his mind.

　　　　　　　　　　　　　　　　　(*Exit Mephistophilis.*)

　　(*Enter Devils, giving crowns and rich apparel to Faustus. They dance and then depart.*)

　　(*Enter Mephistophilis.*)

Faustus: What means this show? Speak, Mephistophilis.
Mephistophilis: Nothing, Faustus, but to delight thy mind, 85
　　And let thee see what magic can perform.
Faustus: But may I raise such spirits when I please?

55 *proper:* own   56 *Assures:* conveys by contract   66 *bill:* contract   70 *s.d. chafer:* portable grate
71 *it:* i.e., the receptacle containing the congealed blood   75 *Consummatum est:* It is finished. (Latin: a
blasphemous repetition of Christ's words on the Cross; see John 19:30.)   78 *Homo fuge:* fly, man
(Latin)   83 *somewhat:* something

Mephistophilis: Ay, Faustus, and do greater things than these.
Faustus: Then, Mephistophilis, receive this scroll,
    A deed of gift of body and of soul: 90
    But yet conditionally that thou perform
    All covenants and articles between us both.
Mephistophilis: Faustus, I swear by hell and Lucifer
    To effect all promises between us both.
Faustus: Then hear me read it, Mephistophilis: 95

"On these conditions following:

First, that Faustus may be a spirit° in form and substance.

Secondly, that Mephistophilis shall be his servant, and be by him commanded.

Thirdly, that Mephistophilis shall do for him and bring him whatsoever.   100

Fourthly, that he shall be in his chamber or house invisible.

Lastly, that he shall appear to the said John Faustus, at all times, in what shape and form soever he please.

I, John Faustus of Wittenberg, Doctor, by these presents, do give both body and soul to Lucifer, Prince of the East, and his minister Mephistophilis, and further-   105
more grant unto them that, four and twenty years being expired, and these articles written being inviolate,° full power to fetch or carry the said John Faustus, body and soul, flesh, blood, into their habitation wheresoever.

                                     By me John Faustus."

Mephistophilis: Speak, Faustus, do you deliver this as your deed?   110
Faustus: Ay, take it, and the devil give thee good of it!
Mephistophilis: So, now Faustus, ask me what thou wilt.
Faustus: First, I will question with thee about hell.
    Tell me, where is the place that men call hell?
Mephistophilis: Under the heavens.   115
Faustus: Ay, so are all things else, but whereabouts?
Mephistophilis: Within the bowels of these elements,
    Where we are tortured, and remain forever.
    Hell hath no limits, nor is circumscribed,
    In one self place, but where we are is hell,   120
    And where hell is there must we ever be.
    And to be short, when all the world dissolves,
    And every creature shall be purified,
    All places shall be hell that is not heaven!
Faustus: I think hell's a fable.   125
Mephistophilis: Ay, think so still—till experience change thy mind.
Faustus: Why, dost thou think that Faustus shall be damned?
Mephistophilis: Ay, of necessity, for here's the scroll
    In which thou hast given thy soul to Lucifer.

---

97 *spirit:* evil spirit, devil. (But to see Faustus as transformed now into a devil deprived of freedom to repent is to deprive the remainder of the play of much of its meaning.)   107 *inviolate:* unviolated

Faustus: Ay, and body too; but what of that?　　　　　　　　　　130
　　Think'st thou that Faustus is so fond° to imagine,
　　That after this life there is any pain?
　　No, these are trifles, and mere old wives' tales.
Mephistophilis: But I am an instance to prove the contrary,
　　For I tell thee I am damned, and now in hell!　　　　　　135
Faustus: Nay, and this be hell, I'll willingly be damned—
　　What, sleeping, eating, walking, and disputing?
　　But leaving this, let me have a wife,
　　The fairest maid in Germany,
　　For I am wanton and lascivious,　　　　　　　　　　　　140
　　And cannot live without a wife.
Mephistophilis: Well, Faustus, thou shalt have a wife.

　　(He fetches in a woman devil.)

Faustus: What sight is this?
Mephistophilis: Now, Faustus, wilt thou have a wife?
Faustus: Here's a hot whore indeed! No, I'll no wife.　　　　145
Mephistophilis: Marriage is but a ceremonial toy,°

　　　　　　　　　　　　　　　　　　　　(Exit she-devil.)

　　And if thou lov'st me, think no more of it.
　　I'll cull thee out° the fairest courtesans
　　And bring them every morning to thy bed.
　　She whom thine eye shall like, thy heart shall have,　　150
　　Were she as chaste as was Penelope,°
　　As wise as Saba,° or as beautiful
　　As was bright Lucifer before his fall.
　　Here, take this book and peruse it well.
　　The iterating° of these lines brings gold;　　　　　　　155
　　The framing° of this circle on the ground
　　Brings thunder, whirlwinds, storm, and lightning;
　　Pronounce this thrice devoutly to thyself,
　　And men in harness° shall appear to thee,
　　Ready to execute what thou command'st.　　　　　　　160
Faustus: Thanks, Mephistophilis, for this sweet book.
　　This will I keep as chary as my life.

　　　　　　　　　　　　　　　　　　　　　　　(Exeunt.)

Questions

1. What specifically motivates Faustus to make his satanic compact? Cite the text to back up your response.
2. How does his behavior constitute a compromise of his nobility?
3. "Is not thy soul thine own?" Faustus asks rhetorically (line 69). Discuss the implications of this statement in terms of the larger thematic concerns of the work.
4. Does Faustus inspire your pity and fear in this scene? Why or why not?

131 *fond:* foolish　146 *toy:* trifle　148 *cull thee out:* select for you　151 *Penelope:* wife of Ulysses, famed for her fidelity　152 *Saba:* the Queen of Sheba　155 *iterating:* repetition　156 *framing:* drawing　159 *harness:* armor

Traditional masks of Comedy and Tragedy.

COMEDY

The best-known traditional emblem of drama—a pair of masks, one sorrowful (representing tragedy) and one smiling (representing comedy)—suggests that tragedy and comedy, although opposites, are close relatives. Often, comedy shows people getting into trouble through error or weakness; in this respect it is akin to tragedy. An important difference between comedy and tragedy lies in the attitude toward human failing that is expected of us. When a main character in a comedy suffers from overweening pride, as does Oedipus, or if he fails to recognize that his bride-to-be is actually his mother, we laugh—something we would never do in watching a competent performance of *Oedipus the King*.

Comedy, from the Greek *komos,* "a revel," is thought to have originated in festivities to celebrate spring, ritual performances in praise of Dionysus, god of fertility and wine. In drama, comedy may be broadly defined as whatever makes us laugh. A comedy may be a name for one entire play, or we may say that there is comedy in only part of a play—as in a comic character or a comic situation.

Theories of Comedy

Many theories have been propounded to explain why we laugh; most of these notions fall into a few familiar types. One school, exemplified by French philosopher Henri Bergson, sees laughter as a form of ridicule, implying a feeling of disinterested superiority; all jokes are *on* somebody. Bergson suggests that laughter springs from situations in which we sense a conflict between some mechanical or rigid pattern of behavior and our sense of a more natural or "organic" kind of behavior that is possible. An example occurs in Buster Keaton's comic film *The Boat*. Having launched a little boat that springs a leak, Keaton rigidly goes down with it, with frozen face. (The more natural and organic thing to do would be to swim for shore.)

Other thinkers view laughter as our response to expectations fulfilled or to expectations set up but then suddenly frustrated. Some hold it to be the expression of our delight in seeing our suppressed urges acted out (as when a comedian hurls an egg at a pompous stuffed shirt); some, to be our defensive reaction to a painful and disturbing truth.

Satiric Comedy

Derisive humor is basic to **satiric comedy,** in which human weakness or folly is ridiculed from a vantage point of supposedly enlightened superiority. Satiric comedy may be coolly malicious and gently biting, but it tends to be critical of people, their manners, and their morals. It is at least as old as the comedies of Aristophanes, who thrived in the fifth century B.C. In *Lysistrata*, the satirist shows how the women of two warring cities speedily halt a war by agreeing to deny themselves to their husbands. (The satirist's target is men so proud that they go to war rather than make the slightest concession.)

High Comedy

Comedy is often divided into two varieties—"high" and "low." **High comedy** relies more on wit and wordplay than on physical action for its humor. It tries to address the audience's intelligence by pointing out the pretension and hypocrisy of human behavior. High comedy also generally avoids derisive humor. Jokes about physical appearance would, for example, be avoided. One technique it employs to appeal to a sophisticated, verbal audience is use of the **epigram,** a brief and witty statement that memorably expresses some truth, large or small. Oscar Wilde's plays such as *The Importance of Being Earnest* (1895) and *Lady Windermere's Fan* (1892) sparkle with such brilliant epigrams as: "I can resist everything except temptation"; "Experience is simply the name we give our mistakes"; "There is only one thing in the world worse than being talked about, and that is not being talked about."

A type of high comedy is the **comedy of manners,** a witty satire set in elite or fashionable society. Popular since the seventeenth-century Restoration period, splendid comedies of manners continue to be written to this day. Bernard Shaw's *Pygmalion* (1913), which eventually became the musical *My Fair Lady*, contrasts life in the streets of London with that in aristocratic drawing rooms. Contemporary playwrights such as Tom Stoppard, Michael Frayn, Tina Howe, and John Guare have all created memorable comedies of manners.

Low Comedy

Low comedy explores the opposite extreme of humor. It places greater emphasis on physical action and visual gags, and its verbal jokes do not require much intellect to appreciate (as in Groucho Marx's pithy put-down to his brother Chico, "You have the brain of a five-year-old, and I bet he was glad to get rid of it!"). Low comedy does not avoid derisive humor; rather, it revels in making fun of whatever will get a good laugh. Drunkenness, stupidity, lust, senility, trickery, insult, and clumsiness are inexhaustible staples of this style of comedy. Although it is all too easy for critics to dismiss low comedy, like high comedy it serves a valuable purpose in satirizing human failings. Shakespeare indulged in coarse humor in some of his noblest plays. Low comedy is usually the preferred style of popular culture, and it has inspired many incisive satires on modern life—from the classic films of W. C. Fields and the Marx Brothers to the weekly TV antics of Matt Groening's *The Simpsons* or Tina Fey's *30 Rock*.

Low comedy includes several distinct types. One is the **burlesque,** a broadly humorous parody or travesty of another play or kind of play. (In the United States, *burlesque* is something else: a once-popular form of show business featuring stripteases interspersed with bits of ribald low comedy.) Another valuable type of low comedy is the **farce,** a broadly humorous play whose action is usually fast-moving and improbable. The farce is a descendant of the Italian *commedia dell'arte* ("artistic comedy") of the late Renaissance, a kind of theater developed by comedians who traveled from town to town, regaling crowds at country fairs and in marketplaces. This popular art featured familiar stock characters in masks or whiteface: Harlequin, a clown; Columbine, his peppery sweetheart; and Pantaloon, a doddering duffer. Lately making a comeback, the more modern farces of French playwright Georges Feydeau (1862–1921) are practically all plot, with only the flattest of characters, mindless ninnies who play frantic games of hide-and-seek in order to deceive their spouses. **Slapstick comedy** (such as that of the Three Stooges) is a kind of farce. Featuring pratfalls, pie-throwing, fisticuffs, and other violent action, it takes its name from a circus clown's prop—a bat with two boards that loudly clap together when one clown swats another.

Romantic Comedy

Romantic comedy, another traditional sort of comedy, is subtler. Its main characters are generally lovers, and its plot unfolds their ultimately successful strivings to be united. Unlike satiric comedy, romantic comedy portrays its characters not with withering contempt but with kindly indulgence. It may take place in the everyday world, or perhaps in some never-never land, such as the forest of Arden in Shakespeare's *As You Like It*. Romantic comedy is also a popular staple of Hollywood, which depicts two people undergoing humorous mishaps on their way to falling in love. The characters often suffer humiliation and discomfort along the way, but these moments are funny rather than sad, and the characters are rewarded in the end by true love.

Here is a short contemporary comedy by one of America's most ingenious playwrights.

David Ives

Sure Thing   1988

David Ives (b. 1950) grew up on the South Side of Chicago. He attended Catholic schools before entering Northwestern University. Later Ives studied at the Yale Drama School—"a blissful time for me," he recalls, "in spite of the fact that there is slush on the ground in New Haven 238 days a year." Ives received his first professional production in Los Angeles at the age of twenty-one "at America's smallest, and possibly worst theater, in a storefront that had a pillar dead center in the middle of the stage." He continued writing for the theater while working as an editor at Foreign Affairs, and gradually achieved a reputation in theatrical circles for his wildly original and brilliantly written short comic plays. His public breakthrough came in 1993 with the New York staging of All in the Timing, which presented six short comedies, including Sure Thing. This production earned ecstatic reviews and a busy box office, and in the 1995–1996 season, All in the Timing was the most widely performed play in America (except for the works of Shakespeare). His second group of one-act comedies, Mere Mortals (1997), was produced with great success in New York City, followed by Lives of the Saints, a third group of one-act plays. Ives's full-length plays Don Juan in Chicago (1995), Ancient History (1996), The Red Address (1997), and Polish Joke (2000) are collected in the volume Polish Joke and Other Plays (2004). A talented adapter, Ives was chosen to rework a newly discovered play by Mark Twain, Is He Dead?, which had a successful run on Broadway in 2007. His most recent plays are Venus in Fur (2010) and a number of translations and adaptations of French theater, including Pierre Corneille's comedy The Liar (2010) and Molière's The Misanthrope which Ives titled The School For Lies (2011). He also writes short stories and screenplays for both motion pictures and television. Ives lives in New York City.

Original 1993 Off-Broadway production of *Sure Thing* by Primary Stages.

CHARACTERS

Betty
Bill

SCENE. *A café. Betty, a woman in her late twenties, is reading at a café table. An empty chair is opposite her. Bill, same age, enters.*

Bill: Excuse me. Is this chair taken?
Betty: Excuse me?
Bill: Is this taken?
Betty: Yes it is.
Bill: Oh. Sorry.
Betty: Sure thing.

  (*A bell rings softly.*)

Bill: Excuse me. Is this chair taken?
Betty: Excuse me?
Bill: Is this taken?
Betty: No, but I'm expecting somebody in a minute.
Bill: Oh. Thanks anyway.
Betty: Sure thing.

  (*A bell rings softly.*)

Bill: Excuse me. Is this chair taken?
Betty: No, but I'm expecting somebody very shortly.
Bill: Would you mind if I sit here till he or she or it comes?
Betty (glances at her watch): They do seem to be pretty late. . . .
Bill: You never know who you might be turning down.

Betty: Sorry. Nice try, though.
Bill: Sure thing.

(*Bell.*)

Is this seat taken?
Betty: No it's not.
Bill: Would you mind if I sit here?
Betty: Yes I would.
Bill: Oh.

(*Bell.*)

Is this chair taken?
Betty: No it's not.
Bill: Would you mind if I sit here?
Betty: No. Go ahead.
Bill: Thanks. (*He sits. She continues reading.*) Everyplace else seems to be taken.
Betty: Mm-hm.
Bill: Great place.
Betty: Mm-hm.
Bill: What's the book?
Betty: I just wanted to read in quiet, if you don't mind.
Bill: No. Sure thing.

(*Bell.*)

Everyplace else seems to be taken.
Betty: Mm-hm.
Bill: Great place for reading.
Betty: Yes, I like it.
Bill: What's the book?
Betty: *The Sound and the Fury.*
Bill: Oh. Hemingway.

(*Bell.*)

What's the book?
Betty: *The Sound and the Fury.*
Bill: Oh. Faulkner.
Betty: Have you read it?
Bill: Not . . . actually. I've sure read *about* it, though. It's supposed to be great.
Betty: It is great.
Bill: I hear it's great. (*Small pause.*) Waiter?

(*Bell.*)

What's the book?
Betty: *The Sound and the Fury.*
Bill: Oh. Faulkner.
Betty: Have you read it?
Bill: I'm a Mets fan, myself.

(*Bell.*)

Betty: Have you read it?
Bill: Yeah, I read it in college.
Betty: Where was college?
Bill: I went to Oral Roberts University.

(*Bell.*)

Betty: Where was college?
Bill: I was lying. I never really went to college. I just like to party.

(*Bell.*)

Betty: Where was college?
Bill: Harvard.
Betty: Do you like Faulkner?
Bill: I love Faulkner. I spent a whole winter reading him once.
Betty: I've just started.
Bill: I was so excited after ten pages that I went out and bought everything else he wrote. One of the greatest reading experiences of my life. I mean, all that incredible psychological understanding. Page after page of gorgeous prose. His profound grasp of the mystery of time and human existence. The smells of the earth . . . What do you think?
Betty: I think it's pretty boring.

(*Bell.*)

Bill: What's the book?
Betty: *The Sound and the Fury.*
Bill: Oh! Faulkner!
Betty: Do you like Faulkner?
Bill: I love Faulkner.
Betty: He's incredible.
Bill: I spent a whole winter reading him once.
Betty: I was so excited after ten pages that I went out and bought everything else he wrote.
Bill: All that incredible psychological understanding.
Betty: And the prose is so gorgeous.
Bill: And the way he's grasped the mystery of time—
Betty: —and human existence. I can't believe I've waited this long to read him.
Bill: You never know. You might not have liked him before.
Betty: That's true.
Bill: You might not have been ready for him. You have to hit these things at the right moment or it's no good.
Betty: That's happened to me.
Bill: It's all in the timing. (*Small pause.*) My name's Bill, by the way.
Betty: I'm Betty.
Bill: Hi.
Betty: Hi. (*Small pause.*)
Bill: Yes I thought reading Faulkner was . . . a great experience.
Betty: Yes. (*Small pause.*)
Bill: *The Sound and the Fury.* . . . (*Another small pause.*)

Betty: Well. Onwards and upwards. (*She goes back to her book.*)
Bill: Waiter—?

(*Bell.*)

You have to hit these things at the right moment or it's no good.
Betty: That's happened to me.
Bill: It's all in the timing. My name's Bill, by the way.
Betty: I'm Betty.
Bill: Hi.
Betty: Hi.
Bill: Do you come in here a lot?
Betty: Actually I'm just in town for two days from Pakistan.
Bill: Oh. Pakistan.

(*Bell.*)

My name's Bill, by the way.
Betty: I'm Betty.
Bill: Hi.
Betty: Hi.
Bill: Do you come in here a lot?
Betty: Every once in a while. Do you?
Bill: Not so much anymore. Not as much as I used to. Before my nervous breakdown.

(*Bell.*)

Do you come in here a lot?
Betty: Why are you asking?
Bill: Just interested.
Betty: Are you really interested, or do you just want to pick me up?
Bill: No, I'm really interested.
Betty: Why would you be interested in whether I come in here a lot?
Bill: I'm just . . . getting acquainted.
Betty: Maybe you're only interested for the sake of making small talk long enough
to ask me back to your place to listen to some music, or because you've just
rented this great tape for your VCR, or because you've got some terrific
unknown Django Reinhardt record, only all you really want to do is fuck—
which you won't do very well—after which you'll go into the bathroom and
pee very loudly, then pad into the kitchen and get yourself a beer from the
refrigerator without asking me whether I'd like anything, and then you'll proceed to lie back down beside me and confess that you've got a girlfriend named
Stephanie who's away at medical school in Belgium for a year, and that you've
been involved with her—*off and on*—in what you'll call a very "intricate" relationship, for the past *seven YEARS*. None of which *interests* me, mister!
Bill: Okay.

(*Bell.*)

Do you come in here a lot?
Betty: Every other day, I think.

Bill: I come in here quite a lot and I don't remember seeing you.

Betty: I guess we must be on different schedules.

Bill: Missed connections.

Betty: Yes. Different time zones.

Bill: Amazing how you can live right next door to somebody in this town and never even know it.

Betty: I know.

Bill: City life.

Betty: It's crazy.

Bill: We probably pass each other in the street every day. Right in front of this place, probably.

Betty: Yep.

Bill (looks around): Well the waiters here sure seem to be in some different time zone. I can't seem to locate one anywhere. . . . Waiter! *(He looks back.)* So what do you—*(He sees that she's gone back to her book.)*

Betty: I beg pardon?

Bill: Nothing. Sorry.

    (Bell.)

Betty: I guess we must be on different schedules.

Bill: Missed connections.

Betty: Yes. Different time zones.

Bill: Amazing how you can live right next door to somebody in this town and never even know it.

Betty: I know.

Bill: City life.

Betty: It's crazy.

Bill: You weren't waiting for somebody when I came in, were you?

Betty: Actually I was.

Bill: Oh. Boyfriend?

Betty: Sort of.

Bill: What's a sort-of boyfriend?

Betty: My husband.

Bill: Ah-ha.

    (Bell.)

    You weren't waiting for somebody when I came in, were you?

Betty: Actually I was.

Bill: Oh. Boyfriend?

Betty: Sort of.

Bill: What's a sort-of boyfriend?

Betty: We were meeting here to break up.

Bill: Mm-hm . . .

    (Bell.)

    What's a sort-of boyfriend?

Betty: My lover. Here she comes right now!

(*Bell.*)

Bill: You weren't waiting for somebody when I came in, were you?
Betty: No, just reading.
Bill: Sort of a sad occupation for a Friday night, isn't it? Reading here, all by yourself?
Betty: Do you think so?
Bill: Well sure. I mean, what's a good-looking woman like you doing out alone on a Friday night?
Betty: Trying to keep away from lines like that.
Bill: No, listen—

(*Bell.*)

You weren't waiting for somebody when I came in, were you?
Betty: No, just reading.
Bill: Sort of a sad occupation for a Friday night, isn't it? Reading here all by yourself?
Betty: I guess it is, in a way.
Bill: What's a good-looking woman like you doing out alone on a Friday night anyway? No offense, but . . .
Betty: I'm out alone on a Friday night for the first time in a very long time.
Bill: Oh.
Betty: You see, I just recently ended a relationship.
Bill: Oh.
Betty: Of rather long standing.
Bill: I'm sorry. (*Small pause.*) Well listen, since reading by yourself *is* such a sad occupation for a Friday night, would you like to go elsewhere?
Betty: No . . .
Bill: Do something else?
Betty: No thanks.
Bill: I was headed out to the movies in a while anyway.
Betty: I don't think so.
Bill: Big chance to let Faulkner catch his breath. All those long sentences get him pretty tired.
Betty: Thanks anyway.
Bill: Okay.
Betty: I appreciate the invitation.
Bill: Sure thing.

(*Bell.*)

You weren't waiting for somebody when I came in, were you?
Betty: No, just reading.
Bill: Sort of a sad occupation for a Friday night, isn't it? Reading here all by yourself?
Betty: I guess I was trying to think of it as existentially romantic. You know— cappuccino, great literature, rainy night . . .
Bill: That only works in Paris. We *could* hop the late plane to Paris. Get on a Concorde. Find a café . . .
Betty: I'm a little short on plane fare tonight.

Bill: Darn it, so am I.

Betty: To tell you the truth, I was headed to the movies after I finished this section. Would you like to come along? Since you can't locate a waiter?

Bill: That's a very nice offer, but . . .

Betty: Uh-huh. Girlfriend?

Bill: Two, actually. One of them's pregnant, and Stephanie—

(*Bell.*)

Betty: Girlfriend?

Bill: No, I don't have a girlfriend. Not if you mean the castrating bitch I dumped last night.

(*Bell.*)

Betty: Girlfriend?

Bill: Sort of. Sort of.

Betty: What's a sort-of girlfriend?

Bill: My mother.

(*Bell.*)

I just ended a relationship, actually.

Betty: Oh.

Bill: Of rather long standing.

Betty: I'm sorry to hear it.

Bill: This is my first night out alone in a long time. I feel a little bit at sea, to tell you the truth.

Betty: So you didn't stop to talk because you're a Moonie, or you have some weird political affiliation—?

Bill: Nope. Straight-down-the-ticket Republican.

(*Bell.*)

Straight-down-the-ticket Democrat.

(*Bell.*)

Can I tell you something about politics?

(*Bell.*)

I like to think of myself as a citizen of the universe.

(*Bell.*)

I'm unaffiliated.

Betty: That's a relief. So am I.

Bill: I vote my beliefs.

Betty: Labels are not important.

Bill: Labels are not important, exactly. Take me, for example. I mean, what does it matter if I had a two-point at—

(*Bell.*)

three-point at—

(*Bell.*)

four-point at college? Or if I did come from Pittsburgh—

(*Bell.*)

Cleveland—

(*Bell.*)

Westchester County?

Betty: Sure.
Bill: I believe that a man is what he is.

(*Bell.*)

A person is what he is.

(*Bell.*)

A person is . . . what they are.

Betty: I think so too.
Bill: So what if I admire Trotsky?

(*Bell.*)

So what if I once had a total-body liposuction?

(*Bell.*)

So what if I don't have a penis?

(*Bell.*)

So what if I spent a year in the Peace Corps? I was acting on my convictions.

Betty: Sure.
Bill: You just can't hang a sign on a person.
Betty: Absolutely. I'll bet you're a Scorpio.

(*Many bells ring.*)

Listen, I was headed to the movies after I finished this section. Would you like to come along?

Bill: That sounds like fun. What's playing?
Betty: A couple of the really early Woody Allen movies.
Bill: Oh.
Betty: You don't like Woody Allen?
Bill: Sure. I like Woody Allen.
Betty: But you're not crazy about Woody Allen.
Bill: Those early ones kind of get on my nerves.
Betty: Uh-huh.

(*Bell.*)

Bill: Y'know I was headed to the—
Betty (*simultaneously*): I was thinking about—
Bill: I'm sorry.

Betty: No, go ahead.

Bill: I was going to say that I was headed to the movies in a little while, and . . .

Betty: So was I.

Bill: The Woody Allen festival?

Betty: Just up the street.

Bill: Do you like the early ones?

Betty: I think anybody who doesn't ought to be run off the planet.

Bill: How many times have you seen *Bananas?*

Betty: Eight times.

Bill: Twelve. So are you still interested? (*Long pause.*)

Betty: Do you like Entenmann's crumb cake . . . ?

Bill: Last night I went out at two in the morning to get one. Did you have an Etch-a-Sketch as a child?

Betty: Yes! And do you like Brussels sprouts? (*Pause.*)

Bill: No, I think they're disgusting.

Betty: They *are* disgusting!

Bill: Do you still believe in marriage in spite of current sentiments against it?

Betty: Yes.

Bill: And children?

Betty: Three of them.

Bill: Two girls and a boy.

Betty: Harvard, Vassar, and Brown.

Bill: And will you love me?

Betty: Yes.

Bill: And cherish me forever?

Betty: Yes.

Bill: Do you still want to go to the movies?

Betty: Sure thing.

Bill and Betty (*together*): Waiter!

BLACKOUT

Questions

1. Ives originally planned to set *Sure Thing* at a bus stop. What does its current setting in a café suggest about the characters?
2. What happens on stage when the bell rings?
3. Who is the protagonist? What does the protagonist want?
4. Does the play have a dramatic question?
5. When does the climax of the play occur?
6. Is *Sure Thing* a romantic comedy or a farce? (See pages 927–28 for a discussion of these types of comedy.)
7. "*Sure Thing* was not a funny play because it isn't realistic. Conversations just don't happen this way." Discuss that opinion. Do you agree or disagree?

WRITING *effectively*

David Ives on Writing

On the One-Act Play
2006

Moss Hart said that you never really learn how to write a play, you only learn how to write *this* play. That is as true of one-acts as of two-, three-, four- or five-acts. To my mind the challenge of the one-act may be even greater than the challenge of larger and necessarily messier plays, in the same way that the sonnet with only fourteen lines remains the ever-attempted Everest of poetry. For what the one-act demands is a kind of concentrated perfection. "A play," said Lorca, "is a poem standing up," and I can't think of a better description of a one-act.

David Ives

The long play, like the symphony, luxuriates in development and recapitulation. The one-act has no time for them. Develop the story and you start to look overly melodramatic, forcing too much event into too little time. Develop the characters and you look like you're not doing them justice. (In fact you start to look like you want to write a larger play.) Develop your theme and you start to sound like one of those guys at a party trying to explain all of particle theory between two grabs at the canapés. Recapitulate and you're dead.

A one-act masterpiece like Pinter's *The Dumb Waiter* would be tedious and attenuated if stretched over two hours. It says all it needs to say—and that's volumes—in a quarter of that, then stops. *Death of a Salesman* as a one-act would look either like a character study or a short story transcribed for the stage. A full-length is a four-ton, cast-steel, Richard Serra ellipse that you can walk around in; a one-act, a piece of string draped by Richard Tuttle on a gallery wall. Not a ride on the *Titanic*, but a single suitcase left floating in the middle of a theatrical sea.

So what does a one-act like, if not development and recapitulation?

Compression, obviously. Think of a one-act and chances are good you're thinking of something short and sharp, a punch in the nose, the rug pulled out from under you, over before you know it—as if an actor had turned a camera on the audience and flashed a picture. A good one-act should leave you blinking. Think of a one-act and chances are also good you're picturing something like a small, bare, black-box stage with just a park bench, or a table and chair, or a bus-stop sign. One or two people. Minimal props. There is something necessarily stripped-down about the mere staging of one-acts, and this goes to the heart of the nature of one-acts themselves. They are *elemental*.

From *The Dramatist*

THINKING ABOUT COMEDY

If you have ever tried to explain a punch line to an uncomprehending friend, you know how hard it can be to convey the essence of humor. Too much explanation makes any joke fizzle out fast. We don't often stop to analyze why a joke strikes us as funny. It simply makes us laugh. For this reason, writing about comedy can be challenging.

- **What makes the play amusing?** Is there a central gag or situation (such as mistaken identity) that creates comic potential in every scene? Note that the central gag is often visual (such as a disguise), something that the audience constantly sees but is not equally apparent in the written text.

- **What is the flavor of the humor?** Is the comedy high or low? Is it verbal or visual, or both? Is there mostly slapstick action or clever wordplay? Is it a romantic comedy in which love plays a central role? A play often mixes types of comedy, but usually one style predominates. A farce may have a few moments of intellectual wit, but it will mostly keep silly jokes and pratfalls coming fast and furiously.

- **How do the personalities of the main characters intensify the humor?** Even when comedy arises out of a situation, character is likely to play an important role. In *A Midsummer Night's Dream*, for example, the fairy queen Titania is bewitched into falling in love with the weaver Bottom, whose head has been transformed into that of an ass. The situation is funny in its own right, but the humor is intensified by the personalities involved, the proud fairy queen pursuing the lowly and foolish tradesman. Humor often may be found in the unexpected, a twist on the normal and the logical.

CHECKLIST: Writing About Comedy

☐ What kind of comedy is the play? Romantic? Slapstick? Satire? How can you tell?

☐ Which style of comedy prevails? Is there more emphasis on high comedy or low? More emphasis on verbal humor or physical comedy?

☐ Focus on a key comic moment. Does the comedy grow out of situation? Character? A mix of both?

☐ How does the play end? In a wedding or romance? A reconciliation? Mutual understanding?

WRITING ASSIGNMENT ON COMEDY

Read *Sure Thing* and write a brief analysis of what makes the play amusing or humorous. Provide details to back up your argument. See pages 926–28 for more information on specific types of humor.

TOPICS FOR WRITING ABOUT TRAGEDY

1. According to Oscar Wilde, "In this world there are only two tragedies: one is not getting what one wants, and the other is getting it." Write an essay in which you discuss this statement in its application to the scene from *Doctor Faustus*.

2. Imagine that Faustus, after his death, has sought forgiveness and salvation with the claim, "The Devil tricked me. I didn't know what I was doing." Write a "judicial opinion" setting forth the grounds for the denial of his plea.

TOPICS FOR WRITING ABOUT COMEDY

1. What or who is being satirized in *Sure Thing*? How true or incisive do you find this satire? Why?

2. "*Sure Thing* isn't good drama because it doesn't have a plot or conflict." Write a two-page response to that complaint.

3. Write about a recent romantic comedy film. How does its plot fulfill the notion of comedy?

4. Write about a movie you've seen lately that was meant to be funny but fell short. What was lacking?

▶ TERMS FOR *review*

Dramatic Genres

Tragedy ▶ A play that portrays a serious conflict between human beings and some superior, overwhelming force. It ends sorrowfully and disastrously, an outcome that seems inevitable.

Comedy ▶ A literary work aimed at amusing an audience. In traditional comedy, the protagonist often faces obstacles and complications that threaten disaster but are overturned at the last moment to produce a happy ending.

Kinds of Comedy

High comedy ▶ A comic genre evoking thoughtful laughter from an audience in response to the play's depiction of the folly, pretense, and hypocrisy of human behavior.

Satiric comedy ▶ A genre using derisive humor to ridicule human weakness and folly or attack political injustices and incompetence. Satiric comedy often focuses on ridiculing overly serious characters who resist the festive mood of comedy.

Comedy of manners ▶ A realistic form of high comic drama. It deals with the social relations and romantic intrigues of sophisticated upper-class men and women, whose verbal fencing and witty repartee produce the principal comic effects.

Romantic comedy ▶ A form of comic drama in which the plot focuses on one or more pairs of young lovers who overcome difficulties to achieve a happy ending (usually marriage).

Low comedy ▶ A comic style arousing laughter through jokes, slapstick antics, sight gags, boisterous clowning, and vulgar humor.

Burlesque ▶ A broadly humorous parody or travesty of another play or kind of play.

Farce ▶ A broadly humorous play whose action is usually fast-moving and improbable.

Slapstick comedy ▶ A kind of farce. Featuring pratfalls, pie-throwing, fisticuffs, and other violent action, it takes its name from a circus clown's prop—a bat with two boards that loudly clap together when one clown swats another.

34

CRITICAL CASEBOOK
Sophocles

Oedipus with chorus in Tyrone Guthrie's 1957 film
Oedipus Rex.

None but a poet can write a tragedy.

—EDITH HAMILTON

THE THEATER OF SOPHOCLES

For the citizens of Athens in the fifth century B.C., theater was both a religious and a civic occasion. Plays were presented only twice a year at religious festivals, both associated with Dionysus, the god of wine and crops. In January there was the Lenaea, the festival of the winepress, when plays, especially comedies, were performed. But the major theatrical event of the year came in March at the Great Dionysia, a citywide celebration that included sacrifices, prize ceremonies, and spectacular processions as well as three days of drama.

Each day at dawn a different author presented a trilogy of tragic plays—three interrelated dramas that portrayed an important mythic or legendary event. Each intense tragic trilogy was followed by a **satyr play,** an obscene parody of a mythic story, performed with the chorus dressed as satyrs, unruly mythic attendants of Dionysus who were half goat or horse and half human.

The Greeks loved competition and believed it fostered excellence. Even theater was a competitive event—not unlike the Olympic games. A panel of five judges voted each year at the Great Dionysia for the best dramatic presentation, and a substantial cash prize was given to the winning poet-playwright (all plays were written in verse). Any aspiring writer who has ever lost a literary contest may be comforted to learn that Sophocles, who triumphed in the competition twenty-four times, seems not to have won the annual prize for *Oedipus the King*. Although this play ultimately proved to be the most celebrated Greek tragedy ever written, it lost the award to a revival of a popular trilogy by Aeschylus, who had recently died.

Staging

Seated in the open air in a hillside amphitheater, as many as 17,000 spectators could watch a performance that must have somewhat resembled an opera or musical. The audience was arranged in rows, with the Athenian governing council and young military cadets seated in the middle sections. Priests, priestesses, and foreign dignitaries were given special places of honor in the front rows. The performance space they watched was divided into two parts—the **orchestra,** a level circular "dancing space" (at the base of the amphitheater), and a slightly raised stage built in front of the *skene* or stage house, originally a canvas or wooden hut for costume changes.

The actors spoke and performed primarily on the stage, and the chorus sang and danced in the orchestra. The *skene* served as a general set or backdrop—the exterior of a palace, a temple, a cave, or a military tent, depending on the action of the play. The *skene* had a large door at its center that served as the major entrance for principal characters. When opened wide, the door could be used to frame a striking tableau, as when the body of Eurydicê is displayed at the end of Sophocles's play *Antigonê*. The *skene* supported a hook and pulley by which actors who played gods could be lowered or lifted—hence the Latin phrase *deus ex machina* ("god out of the machine") for any means of bringing a play quickly to a resolution.

What did the actors look like? They wore **masks** (*personae,* the source of our word *person,* "a thing through which sound comes"): some of these masks had exaggerated mouthpieces, possibly designed to project speech across the open air. Certainly, the masks, each of which covered an actor's entire head, helped spectators far away recognize the chief characters. The masks often represented certain

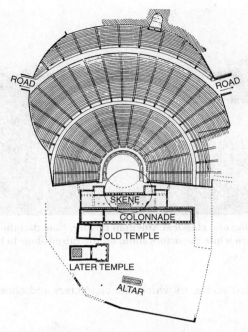

**The Theater of Dionysus in Athens during the time of Sophocles;
a modern drawing based on scholarly guesswork.
From R. C. Flickinger, *The Greek Theater and Its Drama* (1918).**

conventional types of characters: the old king, the young soldier, the shepherd, the beautiful girl (women's parts were played by male actors). Perhaps in order to gain in both increased dignity and visibility, actors in the Greek theater eventually came to wear **cothurni,** high, thick-soled elevator shoes that made them appear taller than ordinary men. All this equipment must have given the actors a slightly inhuman yet very imposing appearance, but we may infer that the spectators accepted such conventions as easily as opera lovers accept an opera's special artifice or today's football fans hardly notice the elaborate helmets, shoulderpads, kneepads, and garishly colored uniforms worn by their favorite teams.

Dramatic Structure

By Sophocles's time, the tragedy had a conventional structure understood by most of the citizens sitting in the audience. No more than three actors were allowed on stage at any one time, along with a chorus of fifteen (the number was fixed by Sophocles himself). The actors' spoken monologue and dialogue alternated with the chorus's singing and dancing. Each tragedy began with a **prologue,** a preparatory scene. In *Oedipus the King,* for example, the play begins with Oedipus asking the suppliants why they have come and the priest telling him about the plague ravaging Thebes. Next came the *párodos,* the song for the entrance of the chorus. Then the action was enacted in **episodes,** like the acts or scenes in modern plays; the episodes were separated by danced choral songs or **odes.** Finally, there was a

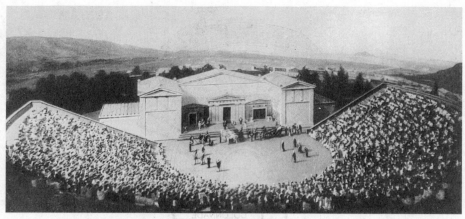

A modern reconstruction of a classical Athenian theater. Note that the chorus performs in the circular orchestra while the actors stand on the raised stage behind.

closing *éxodos,* the last scene, in which the characters and chorus concluded the action and departed.

THE CIVIC ROLE OF GREEK DRAMA

Athenian drama was supported and financed by the state. Administration of the Great Dionysia fell to the head civil magistrate. He annually appointed three wealthy citizens to serve as *choregoi,* or producers, for the competing plays. Each producer had to equip the chorus and rent the rehearsal space in which the poet-playwright would prepare the new work for the festival. The state covered the expenses of the theater, actors, and prizes (which went to author, actors, and *choregos* alike). Theater tickets were distributed free to citizens, which meant that every registered Athenian, even the poorest, could participate. The playwrights therefore addressed themselves to every element of the Athenian democracy. Only the size of the amphitheater limited the attendance. Holding between 14,000 and 17,000 spectators, it could accommodate slightly less than half of Athens's 40,000 citizens.

Greek theater was directed at the moral and political education of the community. The poet's role was the improvement of the *polis* or city-state (made up of a town and its surrounding countryside). Greek city-states traditionally sponsored public contests between *rhapsodes* (professional poetry performers) reciting stories from Homer's epics, the *Iliad* and *Odyssey.* As Greek society developed and urbanized, however, the competitive and individualized heroism of the Homeric epics had to be tempered with the values of cooperation and compromise necessary to a democracy. Civic theater provided the ideal medium to address these cultural needs.

Tragedy and Empathy

As a public art form, tragedy was not simply a stage for political propaganda to promote the status quo. Nor was it exclusively a celebration of idealized heroes nobly enduring the blows of harsh circumstance and misfortune. Tragedy often enabled its audience to reflect on personal values that might be in conflict with civic ideals, on the claims of minorities that it neglected or excluded from public life, on its own irrational prejudices toward the foreign or the unknown. Frequently a play challenged its audience to feel sympathy for a vanquished enemy (as in Euripides's *Trojan Women*, the greatest antiwar play of the period, which dramatizes the horrible fate of captured women). Some plays explored the problems facing members of the politically powerless groups that made up nearly three-fourths of the Athenian population—women, children, resident aliens, and slaves. A largely male audience also frequently watched male performers enact stories of the power and anger of women, such as Euripides's *Medea*, which made their tragic violence understandable (if not entirely pardonable) to an audience not particularly disposed to treat them sympathetically. Other plays such as Sophocles's *Oedipus the King* or Euripides's *Herakles* depicted powerful men undone by misfortune, their own bad judgment, or hubris, and thrown into defeat and exile.

Such tragic stories required performers and audience to put themselves in the places of persons quite unlike themselves, in situations that might engulf any unlucky citizen—war, political upheaval, betrayal, domestic crisis. The release of the powerful emotions of pity and fear through a carefully crafted plot in the orderly context of highly conventionalized performance accounts for the paradox of tragic drama—how a viewer takes aesthetic pleasure in witnessing the sufferings of others.

ARISTOTLE'S CONCEPT OF TRAGEDY

> *Tragedy is an imitation of an action of high importance, complete and of some amplitude; in language enhanced by distinct and varying beauties; acted not narrated; by means of pity and fear effecting its purgation of these emotions.*
>
> —ARISTOTLE, *POETICS*, CHAPTER VI

Aristotle's famous definition of tragedy, constructed in the fourth century B.C., is the testimony of one who probably saw many classical tragedies performed. In making his observations, Aristotle does not seem to be laying down laws for what a tragedy ought to be. More likely, he is drawing—from tragedies he has seen or read—a general description of them.

Tragic Hero

Aristotle observes that the protagonist, the hero or chief character of a tragedy, is a person of "high estate," apparently a king or queen or other member of a royal family. In thus being as keenly interested as are contemporary dramatists in the private lives of the powerful, Greek dramatists need not be accused of snobbery. It is the nature of tragedy that the protagonist must fall from power and from happiness; his high estate gives him a place of dignity to fall from and perhaps makes his fall seem all the more a calamity in that it involves an entire nation or people. Nor is the protagonist extraordinary merely by his position in society. Oedipus is not only a king but also a noble soul who suffers profoundly and who employs splendid eloquence to express his suffering.

The tragic hero, however, is not a superman; he is fallible. The hero's downfall is the result, as Aristotle said, of his **hamartia:** his error or transgression or (as some translators would have it) his flaw or weakness of character. The notion that a tragic hero has such a **tragic flaw** has often been attributed to Aristotle, but it is by no means clear that Aristotle meant just that. According to this interpretation, every tragic hero has some fatal weakness, some moral Achilles's heel, that brings him to a bad end. In some classical tragedies, his transgression is a weakness the Greeks called **hubris**—extreme pride, leading to overconfidence.

Whatever Aristotle had in mind, however, many later critics find value in the idea of the tragic flaw. In this view, the downfall of a hero follows from his very nature. Whatever view we take—whether we find the hero's sufferings due to a flaw of character or to an error of judgment—we will probably find that his downfall results from acts for which he himself is responsible. In a Greek tragedy, the hero is a character amply capable of making choices—capable, too, of accepting the consequences.

Katharsis

It may be useful to take another look at Aristotle's definition of *tragedy*, with which we began. By **purgation** (or *katharsis*), did the ancient theorist mean that after witnessing a tragedy we feel relief, having released our pent-up emotions? Or did he mean that our feelings are purified, refined into something more ennobling? Scholars continue to argue. Whatever his exact meaning, clearly Aristotle implies that after witnessing a tragedy we feel better, not worse—not depressed, but somehow elated. We take a kind of pleasure in the spectacle of a noble man being brought down, but surely this pleasure is a legitimate one. Part of that catharsis may also be based in our feeling of the "rightness" or accuracy of what we have just witnessed. The terrible but undeniable truth of the tragic vision of life is that blind overreaching and the destruction of hopes and dreams are very much a part of what really happens in the world.

Recognition and Reversal

Aristotle, in describing the workings of this inexorable force in *Oedipus the King*, uses terms that later critics have found valuable. One is **recognition,** or discovery (*anagnorisis*): the revelation of some fact not known before or some person's true identity. Oedipus makes such a discovery: he recognizes that he himself was the child whom his mother had given over to be destroyed. Such a recognition also occurs in Shakespeare's *Macbeth* when Macduff reveals himself to have been "from his mother's womb / Untimely ripped," thus disclosing a double meaning in the witches' prophecy that Macbeth could be harmed by "none of woman born," and sweeping aside Macbeth's last shred of belief that he is infallible. Modern critics have taken the term to mean also the terrible enlightenment that accompanies such a recognition with the protagonist's consequent awareness of his role in his own undoing. "To see things plain—that is *anagnorisis*," Clifford Leech observes, "It is what tragedy ultimately is about: the realization of the unthinkable."

Having made his discovery, Oedipus suffers a reversal in his fortunes; he goes off into exile, blinded and dethroned. Such a fall from happiness seems intrinsic to tragedy, but we should know that Aristotle has a more particular meaning for his term **reversal** (*peripeteia*, anglicized as **peripety**). He means an action that turns out to have the opposite effect from the one its doer had intended. One of his illustrations of such an ironic reversal is from *Oedipus the King*. The first messenger intends to cheer Oedipus with the partially good news that, contrary to the prophecy that Oedipus would kill his father, his father has died of old age. The reversal is in the fact that, when the messenger further reveals that old Polybus was Oedipus's father only by adoption, the king, instead of having his fears allayed, is stirred to new dread.

We are not altogether sorry, perhaps, to see an arrogant man such as Oedipus humbled, and yet it is difficult not to feel that the punishment of Oedipus is greater than he deserves. Possibly this feeling is what Aristotle meant in his observation that a tragedy arouses our pity and our fear—our compassion for Oedipus and our terror as we sense the remorselessness of a universe in which a man is doomed. Notice, however, that at the end of the play Oedipus does not curse God and die. Although such a complex play is open to many interpretations, it is probably safe to say that the play is not a bitter complaint against the universe. At last, Oedipus accepts the divine will, prays for blessings upon his children, and prepares to endure his exile—fallen from high estate but uplifted, through his newfound humility and piety, in moral dignity.

SOPHOCLES

Sophocles

Sophocles (496?–406 B.C.) tragic dramatist, priest, for a time one of ten Athenian generals, was one of the three great ancient Greek writers of tragedy whose work has survived. (The other two were his contemporaries: Aeschylus, his senior, and Euripides, his junior.) Sophocles won his first victory in the Athenian spring drama competition in 468 B.C., when a tragedy he had written defeated one by Aeschylus. He went on to win many prizes, writing more than 120 plays, of which only seven have survived in their entirety—Ajax, Antigonê, Oedipus the King, Electra, Philoctetes, The Trachinian Women, and Oedipus at Colonus. (Of the lost plays, about a thousand fragments remain.) In his long life, Sophocles saw Greece rise to supremacy over the Persian Empire. He enjoyed the favor of the statesman Pericles, who, making peace with enemy Sparta, ruled Athens during a Golden Age (461–429 B.C.), during which the Parthenon was built and music, art, drama, and philosophy flourished. The playwright lived on to see his native city-state in decline, its strength drained by the disastrous Peloponnesian War. His last play, Oedipus at Colonus, *set twenty years after the events of* Oedipus the King, *shows the former king in old age, ragged and blind, cast into exile by his sons, but still accompanied by his faithful daughter Antigonê. It was written when Sophocles was nearly ninety.* Oedipus the King *is believed to have been first produced in 425 B.C., five years after the plague had broken out in Athens.*

THE ORIGINS OF *OEDIPUS THE KING*

On a Great Dionysia feast day several years after Athens had survived a devastating plague, the audience turned out to watch a tragedy by Sophocles, set in the city of Thebes at the moment of another terrible plague. This timely play was *Oedipus*, later given the name (in Greek) *Oedipus Tyrannos* to distinguish it from Sophocles's last Oedipus play, *Oedipus at Colonus*, written many years later when the author was nearly ninety.

A folktale figure, Oedipus gets his name through a complex pun. *Oida* means "to know" (from the root *vid-*, "see"), pointing to the tale's contrasting themes of sight and blindness, wisdom and ignorance. *Oedipus* also means "swollen foot" or "club-foot," pointing to the injury sustained in the title character's infancy, when his

ankles were pinioned together like a goat's. Oedipus is the man who comes to knowledge of his true parentage through the evidence of his feet and his old injury. The term
tyrannos, in the context of the play, simply means a man who comes to rule through
his own intelligence and merit, though not related to the ruling family. The traditional Greek title might be translated, therefore, as *Clubfoot the Ruler.* (*Oedipus Rex,*
which means "Oedipus the King," is the conventional Latin title for the play.)

Presumably the audience already knew the story portrayed in the play. They
would have known that because a prophecy had foretold that Oedipus would grow up
to slay his father, he had been taken out as a newborn to perish in the wilderness of
Mount Cithaeron outside Thebes. (Exposure was the common fate of unwanted children in ancient Greece, though only in the most extraordinary circumstances would a
royal heir be exposed.) The audience would also have known that before he was left to
die, the baby's feet had been pinned together. And they would have known that later,
adopted by King Polybus and Queen Merope of Corinth and grown to maturity, Oedipus won both the throne and the recently widowed queen of Thebes as a reward for
ridding the city of the Sphinx, a winged, woman-headed lion. All who approached
the Sphinx were asked a riddle, and failure to solve it meant death. Her lethal riddle
was: "What goes on four legs in the morning, two at noon, and three at evening?"
Oedipus correctly answered, "Man." (As a baby he crawls on all fours, as a man he
walks erect, then as an old man he uses a cane.) Chagrined and outwitted, the Sphinx
leaped from her rocky perch and dashed herself to death. Familiarity with all these
events is necessary to understand *Oedipus the King,* which begins years later, after the
title character has long been established as ruler of Thebes.

Laurence Olivier in *Oedipus Rex.*

Oedipus the King   425 B.C.?

Translated by Dudley Fitts and Robert Fitzgerald

CHARACTERS°

Oedipus	*Messenger*
A Priest	*Shepherd of Laïos*
Creon	*Second Messenger*
Teiresias	*Chorus of Theban Elders*
Iocastê	

SCENE. *Before the palace of Oedipus, King of Thebes. A central door and two lateral doors open onto a platform which runs the length of the façade. On the platform, right and left, are altars; and three steps lead down into the "orchestra," or chorus-ground. At the beginning of the action these steps are crowded by suppliants° who have brought branches and chaplets of olive leaves and who lie in various attitudes of despair. Oedipus enters.*

PROLOGUE°

Oedipus: My children, generations of the living
In the line of Kadmos,° nursed at his ancient hearth:
Why have you strewn yourself before these altars
In supplication, with your boughs and garlands?
The breath of incense rises from the city   5
With a sound of prayer and lamentation.
                                                  Children,
I would not have you speak through messengers,
And therefore I have come myself to hear you—
I, Oedipus, who bear the famous name.
(*To a Priest.*) You, there, since you are eldest in the company,   10
Speak for them all, tell me what preys upon you,
Whether you come in dread, or crave some blessing:
Tell me, and never doubt that I will help you
In every way I can; I should be heartless
Were I not moved to find you suppliant here.   15
Priest: Great Oedipus, O powerful King of Thebes!
You see how all the ages of our people
Cling to your altar steps: here are boys
Who can barely stand alone, and here are priests
By weight of age, as I am a priest of God,   20
And young men chosen from those yet unmarried;
As for the others, all that multitude,
They wait with olive chaplets in the squares,

Characters: Some of these names are usually anglicized: Jocasta, Laius. In this version, the translators prefer spelling names more like the Greek originals.   *suppliants:* persons who come to ask some favor of the king.   *Prologue:* portion of the play containing the exposition.   *2 line of Kadmos:* according to legend the city of Thebes, where the play takes place, had been founded by the hero Cadmus.

At the two shrines of Pallas,° and where Apollo°
Speaks in the glowing embers.
Your own eyes   25
Must tell you: Thebes is tossed on a murdering sea
And can not lift her head from the death surge.
A rust consumes the buds and fruits of the earth;
The herds are sick; children die unborn,
And labor is vain. The god of plague and pyre   30
Raids like detestable lightning through the city,
And all the house of Kadmos is laid waste,
All emptied, and all darkened: Death alone
Battens upon the misery of Thebes.

You are not one of the immortal gods, we know;   35
Yet we have come to you to make our prayer
As to the man surest in mortal ways
And wisest in the ways of God. You saved us
From the Sphinx, that flinty singer, and the tribute
We paid to her so long; yet you were never   40
Better informed than we, nor could we teach you:
It was some god breathed in you to set us free.

Therefore, O mighty King, we turn to you:
Find us our safety, find us a remedy,
Whether by counsel of the gods or men.   45
A king of wisdom tested in the past
Can act in a time of troubles, and act well.
Noblest of men, restore
Life to your city! Think how all men call you
Liberator for your triumph long ago;   50
Ah, when your years of kingship are remembered,
Let them not say *We rose, but later fell*—
Keep the State from going down in the storm!
Once, years ago, with happy augury,
You brought us fortune; be the same again!   55
No man questions your power to rule the land:
But rule over men, not over a dead city!
Ships are only hulls, citadels are nothing,
When no life moves in the empty passageways.

Oedipus: Poor children! You may be sure I know   60
All that you longed for in your coming here.
I know that you are deathly sick; and yet,
Sick as you are, not one is as sick as I.
Each of you suffers in himself alone
His anguish, not another's; but my spirit   65
Groans for the city, for myself, for you.

---

24 *Pallas:* title for Athena, goddess of wisdom. *Apollo:* god of music, poetry, and prophecy. At his shrine near Thebes, the ashes of fires were used to divine the future.

I was not sleeping, you are not waking me.
No, I have been in tears for a long while
And in my restless thought walked many ways.
In all my search, I found one helpful course,   70
And that I have taken: I have sent Creon,
Son of Menoikeus, brother of the Queen,
To Delphi, Apollo's place of revelation,°
To learn there, if he can,
What act or pledge of mine may save the city.   75
I have counted the days, and now, this very day,
I am troubled, for he has overstayed his time.
What is he doing? He has been gone too long.
Yet whenever he comes back, I should do ill
To scant whatever duty God reveals.   80

Priest: It is a timely promise. At this instant
   They tell me Creon is here.

Oedipus: O Lord Apollo!
   May his news be fair as his face is radiant!

Priest: It could not be otherwise: he is crowned with bay,
   The chaplet is thick with berries.

Oedipus: We shall soon know;   85
   He is near enough to hear us now.

      Enter Creon.

                        O Prince:
   Brother: son of Menoikeus:
   What answer do you bring us from the god?

Creon: A strong one. I can tell you, great afflictions
   Will turn out well, if they are taken well.   90

Oedipus: What was the oracle? These vague words
   Leave me still hanging between hope and fear.

Creon: Is it your pleasure to hear me with all these
   Gathered around us? I am prepared to speak,
   But should we not go in?

Oedipus: Let them all hear it   95
   It is for them I suffer, more than for myself.

Creon: Then I will tell you what I heard at Delphi.

   In plain words
   The god commands us to expel from the land of Thebes
   An old defilement we are sheltering.   100
   It is a deathly thing, beyond cure.
   We must not let it feed upon us longer.

Oedipus: What defilement? How shall we rid ourselves of it?

---

73 *Delphi . . . revelation:* In the temple of Delphi at the foot of Mount Parnassus, a priestess of Dionysos, while in an ecstatic trance, would speak the wine god's words. Such a priestess was called an *oracle;* the word can also mean "a message from the god."

Creon: By exile or death, blood for blood. It was
   Murder that brought the plague-wind on the city.   105
Oedipus: Murder of whom? Surely the god has named him?
Creon: My lord: long ago Laïos was our king,
   Before you came to govern us.
Oedipus: I know;
   I learned of him from others; I never saw him.
Creon: He was murdered; and Apollo commands us now   110
   To take revenge upon whoever killed him.
Oedipus: Upon whom? Where are they? Where shall we find a clue
   To solve that crime, after so many years?
Creon: Here in this land, he said.
                                    If we make enquiry,
   We may touch things that otherwise escape us.   115
Oedipus: Tell me: Was Laïos murdered in his house,
   Or in the fields, or in some foreign country?
Creon: He said he planned to make a pilgrimage.
   He did not come home again.
Oedipus: And was there no one,
   No witness, no companion, to tell what happened?   120
Creon: They were all killed but one, and he got away
   So frightened that he could remember one thing only.
Oedipus: What was that one thing? One may be the key
   To everything, if we resolve to use it.
Creon: He said that a band of highwaymen attacked them,   125
   Outnumbered them, and overwhelmed the King.
Oedipus: Strange, that a highwayman should be so daring—
   Unless some faction here bribed him to do it.
Creon: We thought of that. But after Laïos' death
   New troubles arose and we had no avenger.   130
Oedipus: What troubles could prevent your hunting down the killers?
Creon: The riddling Sphinx's song
   Made us deaf to all mysteries but her own.
Oedipus: Then once more I must bring what is dark to light.
   It is most fitting that Apollo shows,   135
   As you do, this compunction for the dead.
   You shall see how I stand by you, as I should,
   To avenge the city and the city's god,
   And not as though it were for some distant friend,
   But for my own sake, to be rid of evil.   140
   Whoever killed King Laïos might—who knows?—
   Decide at any moment to kill me as well.
   By avenging the murdered king I protect myself.

   Come, then, my children: leave the altar steps,
   Lift up your olive boughs!
                                    One of you go   145
   And summon the people of Kadmos to gather here.
   I will do all that I can; you may tell them that.

Exit a Page.

So, with the help of God,
We shall be saved—or else indeed we are lost.

Priest: Let us rise, children. It was for this we came,   150
And now the King has promised it himself.
Phoibos° has sent us an oracle; may he descend
Himself to save us and drive out the plague.

Exeunt Oedipus and Creon into the palace by the central door. The Priest and the Suppliants disperse right and left. After a short pause the Chorus enters the orchestra.

PÁRODOS°

Strophe° 1

Chorus: What is God singing in his profound
Delphi of gold and shadow?
What oracle for Thebes, the sunwhipped city?

Fear unjoints me, the roots of my heart tremble.

Now I remember, O Healer, your power, and wonder: 5
Will you send doom like a sudden cloud, or weave it
Like nightfall of the past?

Speak, speak to us, issue of holy sound:
Dearest to our expectancy: be tender!

Antistrophe° 1

Let me pray to Athenê, the immortal daughter of Zeus,   10
And to Artemis her sister
Who keeps her famous throne in the market ring,
And to Apollo, bowman at the far butts of heaven—

O gods, descend! Like three streams leap against
The fires of our grief, the fires of darkness;   15
Be swift to bring us rest!

As in the old time from the brilliant house
Of air you stepped to save us, come again!

Strophe 2

Now our afflictions have no end,
Now all our stricken host lies down   20
And no man fights off death with his mind;

The noble plowland bears no grain,
And groaning mothers can not bear—

---

152 *Phoibos:* the sun god Phoebus Apollo.   *Párodos:* part to be sung by the chorus on first entering. *Strophe:* a strophe (according to theory) was sung while the chorus danced from stage right to stage left.   *Antistrophe:* part sung while the chorus danced back again across the stage, from left to right.

See, how our lives like birds take wing,
Like sparks that fly when a fire soars,   25
To the shore of the god of evening.

Antistrophe 2

The plague burns on, it is pitiless,
Though pallid children laden with death
Lie unwept in the stony ways,

And old gray women by every path   30
Flock to the strand about the altars

There to strike their breasts and cry
Worship of Phoibos in wailing prayers:
Be kind, God's golden child!

Strophe 3

There are no swords in this attack by fire,   35
No shields, but we are ringed with cries.

Send the besieger plunging from our homes
Into the vast sea-room of the Atlantic
Or into the waves that foam eastward of Thrace—

For the day ravages what the night spares—   40

Destroy our enemy, lord of the thunder!
Let him be riven by lightning from heaven!

Antistrophe 3

Phoibos Apollo, stretch the sun's bowstring,
That golden cord, until it sing for us,
Flashing arrows in heaven!
                              Artemis, Huntress,   45
Race with flaring lights upon our mountains!

O scarlet god, O golden-banded brow,
O Theban Bacchos in a storm of Maenads,°

Enter Oedipus, center.

Whirl upon Death, that all the Undying hate!
Come with blinding torches, come in joy!   50

SCENE I

Oedipus: Is this your prayer? It may be answered. Come,
        Listen to me, act as the crisis demands,
        And you shall have relief from all these evils.

        Until now I was a stranger to this tale,
        As I had been a stranger to the crime.   5
        Could I track down the murderer without a clue?
        But now, friends,

48 *Bacchos . . . Maenads:* god of wine with his attendant girl revelers.

As one who became a citizen after the murder,
I make this proclamation to all Thebans:

If any man knows by whose hand Laïos, son of Labdakos,   10
Met his death, I direct that man to tell me everything,
No matter what he fears for having so long withheld it.
Let it stand as promised that no further trouble
Will come to him, but he may leave the land in safety.

Moreover: If anyone knows the murderer to be foreign,   15
Let him not keep silent: he shall have his reward from me.
However, if he does conceal it; if any man
Fearing for his friend or for himself disobeys this edict,
Hear what I propose to do:

I solemnly forbid the people of this country,   20
Where power and throne are mine, ever to receive that man
Or speak to him, no matter who he is, or let him
Join in sacrifice, lustration,° or in prayer.
I decree that he be driven from every house,
Being, as he is, corruption itself to us: the Delphic   25
Voice of Zeus has pronounced this revelation.
Thus I associate myself with the oracle
And take the side of the murdered king.

As for the criminal, I pray to God—
Whether it be a lurking thief, or one of a number—   30
I pray that that man's life be consumed in evil and wretchedness.
And as for me, this curse applies no less
If it should turn out that the culprit is my guest here,
Sharing my hearth.
                    You have heard the penalty.
I lay it on you now to attend to this   35
For my sake, for Apollo's, for the sick
Sterile city that heaven has abandoned.
Suppose the oracle had given you no command:
Should this defilement go uncleansed for ever?
You should have found the murderer: your king,   40
A noble king, had been destroyed!
                    Now I,
Having the power that he held before me,
Having his bed, begetting children there
Upon his wife, as he would have, had he lived—
Their son would have been my children's brother,   45
If Laïos had had luck in fatherhood!
(But surely ill luck rushed upon his reign)—
I say I take the son's part, just as though
I were his son, to press the fight for him

---

23 *lustration:* propitiatory sacrifice.

And see it won! I'll find the hand that brought   50
Death to Labdakos' and Polydoros' child,
Heir of Kadmos' and Agenor's line.
And as for those who fail me,
May the gods deny them the fruit of the earth,
Fruit of the womb, and may they rot utterly!   55
Let them be wretched as we are wretched, and worse!

For you, for loyal Thebans, and for all
Who find my actions right, I pray the favor
Of justice, and of all the immortal gods.
Choragos:° Since I am under oath, my lord, I swear   60
I did not do the murder, I can not name
The murderer. Might not the oracle
That has ordained the search tell where to find him?
Oedipus: An honest question. But no man in the world
Can make the gods do more than the gods will.   65
Choragos: There is one last expedient—
Oedipus: Tell me what it is.
Though it seem slight, you must not hold it back.
Choragos: A lord clairvoyant to the lord Apollo,
As we all know, is the skilled Teiresias.
One might learn much about this from him, Oedipus.   70
Oedipus: I am not wasting time:
Creon spoke of this, and I have sent for him—
Twice, in fact; it is strange that he is not here.
Choragos: The other matter—that old report—seems useless.
Oedipus: Tell me. I am interested in all reports.   75
Choragos: The King was said to have been killed by highwaymen.
Oedipus: I know. But we have no witnesses to that.
Choragos: If the killer can feel a particle of dread,
Your curse will bring him out of hiding!
Oedipus: No.
The man who dared that act will fear no curse.   80

Enter the blind seer Teiresias, led by a Page.

Choragos: But there is one man who may detect the criminal.
This is Teiresias, this is the holy prophet
In whom, alone of all men, truth was born.
Oedipus: Teiresias: seer: student of mysteries,
Of all that's taught and all that no man tells,   85
Secrets of Heaven and secrets of the earth:
Blind though you are, you know the city lies
Sick with plague; and from this plague, my lord,
We find that you alone can guard or save us.

Possibly you did not hear the messengers?   90
Apollo, when we sent to him,

60 *Choragos:* spokesperson for the chorus.

Sent us back word that this great pestilence
Would lift, but only if we established clearly
The identity of those who murdered Laïos.
They must be killed or exiled.
                             Can you use   95
Birdflight or any art of divination
To purify yourself, and Thebes, and me
From this contagion? We are in your hands.
There is no fairer duty
Than that of helping others in distress.   100
Teiresias: How dreadful knowledge of the truth can be
    When there's no help in truth! I knew this well,
    But made myself forget. I should not have come.
Oedipus: What is troubling you? Why are your eyes so cold?
Teiresias: Let me go home. Bear your own fate, and I'll   105
    Bear mine. It is better so: trust what I say.
Oedipus: What you say is ungracious and unhelpful
    To your native country. Do not refuse to speak.
Teiresias: When it comes to speech, your own is neither temperate
    Nor opportune. I wish to be more prudent.   110
Oedipus: In God's name, we all beg you—
Teiresias: You are all ignorant.
    No; I will never tell you what I know.
    Now it is my misery; then, it would be yours.
Oedipus: What! You do know something, and will not tell us?
    You would betray us all and wreck the State?   115
Teiresias: I do not intend to torture myself, or you.
    Why persist in asking? You will not persuade me.
Oedipus: What a wicked old man you are! You'd try a stone's
    Patience! Out with it! Have you no feeling at all?
Teiresias: You call me unfeeling. If you could only see   120
    The nature of your own feelings . . . .
Oedipus: Why,
    Who would not feel as I do? Who could endure
    Your arrogance toward the city?
Teiresias: What does it matter!
    Whether I speak or not; it is bound to come.
Oedipus: Then, if "it" is bound to come, you are bound to tell me.   125
Teiresias: No, I will not go on. Rage as you please.
Oedipus: Rage? Why not!
               And I'll tell you what I think:
    You planned it, you had it done, you all but
    Killed him with your own hands: if you had eyes,
    I'd say the crime was yours, and yours alone.   130
Teiresias: So? I charge you, then,
    Abide by the proclamation you have made:
    From this day forth
    Never speak again to these men or to me;
    You yourself are the pollution of this country.   135

Oedipus: You dare say that! Can you possibly think you have
    Some way of going free, after such insolence?
Teiresias: I have gone free. It is the truth sustains me.
Oedipus: Who taught you shamelessness? It was not your craft.
Teiresias: You did. You made me speak. I did not want to.   140
Oedipus: Speak what? Let me hear it again more clearly.
Teiresias: Was it not clear before? Are you tempting me?
Oedipus: I did not understand it. Say it again.
Teiresias: I say that you are the murderer whom you seek.
Oedipus: Now twice you have spat out infamy. You'll pay for it!   145
Teiresias: Would you care for more? Do you wish to be really angry?
Oedipus: Say what you will. Whatever you say is worthless.
Teiresias: I say you live in hideous shame with those
    Most dear to you. You can not see the evil.
Oedipus: It seems you can go on mouthing like this for ever.   150
Teiresias: I can, if there is power in truth.
Oedipus: There is:
    But not for you, not for you,
    You sightless, witless, senseless, mad old man!
Teiresias: You are the madman. There is no one here
    Who will not curse you soon, as you curse me.   155
Oedipus: You child of endless night! You can not hurt me
    Or any other man who sees the sun.
Teiresias: True: it is not from me your fate will come.
    That lies within Apollo's competence,
    As it is his concern.
Oedipus: Tell me: 160
    Are you speaking for Creon, or for yourself?
Teiresias: Creon is no threat. You weave your own doom.
Oedipus: Wealth, power, craft of statesmanship!
    Kingly position, everywhere admired!
    What savage envy is stored up against these,   165
    If Creon, whom I trusted, Creon my friend,
    For this great office which the city once
    Put in my hands unsought—if for this power
    Creon desires in secret to destroy me!

    He has brought this decrepit fortune-teller, this   170
    Collector of dirty pennies, this prophet fraud—
    Why, he is no more clairvoyant than I am!
                                  Tell us:
    Has your mystic mummery ever approached the truth?
    When that hellcat the Sphinx was performing here,
    What help were you to these people?   175
    Her magic was not for the first man who came along:
    It demanded a real exorcist. Your birds—
    What good were they? or the gods, for the matter of that?
    But I came by,
    Oedipus, the simple man, who knows nothing—   180

I thought it out for myself, no birds helped me!
And this is the man you think you can destroy,
That you may be close to Creon when he's king!
Well, you and your friend Creon, it seems to me,
Will suffer most. If you were not an old man,   185
You would have paid already for your plot.
Choragos: We can not see that his words or yours
    Have been spoken except in anger, Oedipus,
    And of anger we have no need. How can God's will
    Be accomplished best? That is what most concerns us.   190
Teiresias: You are a king. But where argument's concerned
    I am your man, as much a king as you.
    I am not your servant, but Apollo's.
    I have no need of Creon to speak for me.

    Listen to me. You mock my blindness, do you?   195
    But I say that you, with both your eyes, are blind:
    You can not see the wretchedness of your life,
    Nor in whose house you live, no, nor with whom.
    Who are your father and mother? Can you tell me?
    You do not even know the blind wrongs   200
    That you have done them, on earth and in the world below.
    But the double lash of your parents' curse will whip you
    Out of this land some day, with only night
    Upon your precious eyes.
    Your cries then—where will they not be heard?   205
    What fastness of Kithairon will not echo them?
    And that bridal-descant of yours—you'll know it then,
    The song they sang when you came here to Thebes
    And found your misguided berthing.
    All this, and more, that you can not guess at now,   210
    Will bring you to yourself among your children.

    Be angry, then. Curse Creon. Curse my words.
    I tell you, no man that walks upon the earth
    Shall be rooted out more horribly than you.
Oedipus: Am I to bear this from him?—Damnation   215
    Take you! Out of this place! Out of my sight!
Teiresias: I would not have come at all if you had not asked me.
Oedipus: Could I have told that you'd talk nonsense, that
    You'd come here to make a fool of yourself, and of me?
Teiresias: A fool? Your parents thought me sane enough.   220
Oedipus: My parents again!—Wait: who were my parents?
Teiresias: This day will give you a father, and break your heart.
Oedipus: Your infantile riddles! Your damned abracadabra!
Teiresias: You were a great man once at solving riddles.
Oedipus: Mock me with that if you like; you will find it true.   225
Teiresias: It was true enough. It brought about your ruin.
Oedipus: But if it saved this town?
Teiresias (*to the Page*):   Boy, give me your hand.

Oedipus: Yes, boy; lead him away.
                                                    —While you are here
        We can do nothing. Go; leave us in peace.
Teiresias: I will go when I have said what I have to say.   230
        How can you hurt me? And I tell you again:
        The man you have been looking for all this time,
        The damned man, the murderer of Laïos,
        That man is in Thebes. To your mind he is foreign-born,
        But it will soon be shown that he is a Theban,   235
        A revelation that will fail to please.
                                        A blind man,
        Who has his eyes now; a penniless man, who is rich now;
        And he will go tapping the strange earth with his staff;
        To the children with whom he lives now he will be
        Brother and father—the very same; to her   240
        Who bore him, son and husband—the very same
        Who came to his father's bed, wet with his father's blood.

        Enough. Go think that over.
        If later you find error in what I have said,
        You may say that I have no skill in prophecy.   245

        Exit Teiresias, led by his Page. Oedipus goes into the palace.

ODE°I

                                                                    Strophe 1

Chorus: The Delphic stone of prophecies
        Remembers ancient regicide
        And a still bloody hand.
        That killer's hour of flight has come.
        He must be stronger than riderless   5
        Coursers of untiring wind,
        For the son of Zeus° armed with his father's thunder
        Leaps in lightning after him;
        And the Furies° follow him, the sad Furies.

                                                                Antistrophe 1

        Holy Parnassos' peak of snow   10
        Flashes and blinds that secret man,
        That all shall hunt him down:
        Though he may roam the forest shade
        Like a bull gone wild from pasture
        To rage through glooms of stone.   15
        Doom comes down on him; flight will not avail him;

Ode: a choral song. Here again (as in the *párodos*), *strophe* and *antistrophe* probably indicate the movements of a dance.   7 *son of Zeus:* Apollo.   9 *Furies:* three horrific female spirits whose task was to seek out and punish evildoers.

For the world's heart calls him desolate,
And the immortal Furies follow, for ever follow.

Strophe 2

But now a wilder thing is heard
From the old man skilled at hearing Fate in the wingbeat of a bird.   20
Bewildered as a blown bird, my soul hovers and can not find
Foothold in this debate, or any reason or rest of mind.
But no man ever brought—none can bring
Proof of strife between Thebes' royal house,
Labdakos' line,° and the son of Polybos;°   25
And never until now has any man brought word
Of Laïos' dark death staining Oedipus the King.

Antistrophe 2

Divine Zeus and Apollo hold
Perfect intelligence alone of all tales ever told;
And well though this diviner works, he works in his own night;   30
No man can judge that rough unknown or trust in second sight,
For wisdom changes hands among the wise.
Shall I believe my great lord criminal
At a raging word that a blind old man let fall?
I saw him, when the carrion woman faced him of old,   35
Prove his heroic mind! These evil words are lies.

SCENE II

Creon: Men of Thebes:
  I am told that heavy accusations
  Have been brought against me by King Oedipus.

  I am not the kind of man to bear this tamely.

  If in these present difficulties   5
  He holds me accountable for any harm to him
  Through anything I have said or done—why, then,
  I do not value life in this dishonor.

  It is not as though this rumor touched upon
  Some private indiscretion. The matter is grave.   10
  The fact is that I am being called disloyal
  To the State, to my fellow citizens, to my friends.
Choragos: He may have spoken in anger, not from his mind.
Creon: But did you not hear him say I was the one
  Who seduced the old prophet into lying?   15
Choragos: The thing was said; I do not know how seriously.
Creon: But you were watching him! Were his eyes steady?
  Did he look like a man in his right mind?

---

25 *Labdakos' line:* descendants of Laïos (true father of Oedipus, although the chorus does not know it).
Polybos: king who adopted the child Oedipus.

Choragos: I do not know.
    I can not judge the behavior of great men.
    But here is the King himself.

    Enter Oedipus.

Oedipus: So you dared come back.   20
    Why? How brazen of you to come to my house,
    You murderer!
                    Do you think I do not know
    That you plotted to kill me, plotted to steal my throne?
    Tell me, in God's name: am I coward, a fool,
    That you should dream you could accomplish this?   25
    A fool who could not see your slippery game?
    A coward, not to fight back when I saw it?
    You are the fool, Creon, are you not? hoping
    Without support or friends to get a throne?
    Thrones may be won or bought: you could do neither.   30
Creon: Now listen to me. You have talked; let me talk, too.
    You can not judge unless you know the facts.
Oedipus: You speak well: there is one fact; but I find it hard
    To learn from the deadliest enemy I have.
Creon: That above all I must dispute with you.   35
Oedipus: That above all I will not hear you deny.
Creon: If you think there is anything good in being stubborn
    Against all reason, then I say you are wrong.
Oedipus: If you think a man can sin against his own kind
    And not be punished for it, I say you are mad.   40
Creon: I agree. But tell me: what have I done to you?
Oedipus: You advised me to send for that wizard, did you not?
Creon: I did. I should do it again.
Oedipus: Very well. Now tell me:
    How long has it been since Laïos—
Creon: What of Laïos?
Oedipus: Since he vanished in that onset by the road?   45
Creon: It was long ago, a long time.
Oedipus: And this prophet,
    Was he practicing here then?
Creon: He was; and with honor, as now.
Oedipus: Did he speak of me at that time?
Creon: He never did;
    At least, not when I was present.
Oedipus: But . . . the enquiry?
    I suppose you held one?
Creon: We did, but we learned nothing.   50
Oedipus: Why did the prophet not speak against me then?
Creon: I do not know; and I am the kind of man
    Who holds his tongue when he has no facts to go on.
Oedipus: There's one fact that you know, and you could tell it.
Creon: What fact is that? If I know it, you shall have it.   55

Oedipus: If he were not involved with you, he could not say
    That it was I who murdered Laïos.
Creon: If he says that, you are the one that knows it!—
    But now it is my turn to question you.
Oedipus: Put your questions. I am no murderer.   60
Creon: First then: You married my sister?
Oedipus: I married your sister.
Creon: And you rule the kingdom equally with her?
Oedipus: Everything that she wants she has from me.
Creon: And I am the third, equal to both of you?
Oedipus: That is why I call you a bad friend.   65
Creon: No. Reason it out, as I have done.
    Think of this first: Would any sane man prefer
    Power, with all a king's anxieties,
    To that same power and the grace of sleep?
    Certainly not I.   70
    I have never longed for the king's power—only his rights.
    Would any wise man differ from me in this?
    As matters stand, I have my way in everything
    With your consent, and no responsibilities.
    If I were king, I should be a slave to policy.   75

    How could I desire a scepter more
    Than what is now mine—untroubled influence?
    No, I have not gone mad; I need no honors,
    Except those with the perquisites I have now.
    I am welcome everywhere; every man salutes me,   80
    And those who want your favor seek my ear,
    Since I know how to manage what they ask.
    Should I exchange this ease for that anxiety?
    Besides, no sober mind is treasonable.
    I hate anarchy   85
    And never would deal with any man who likes it.

    Test what I have said. Go to the priestess
    At Delphi, ask if I quoted her correctly.
    And as for this other thing: if I am found
    Guilty of treason with Teiresias,   90
    Then sentence me to death! You have my word
    It is a sentence I should cast my vote for—
    But not without evidence!
                  You do wrong
    When you take good men for bad, bad men for good.
    A true friend thrown aside—why, life itself   95
    Is not more precious!
                 In time you will know this well:
    For time, and time alone, will show the just man,
    Though scoundrels are discovered in a day.
Choragos: This is well said, and a prudent man would ponder it.
    Judgments too quickly formed are dangerous.   100

Oedipus: But is he not quick in his duplicity?
    And shall I not be quick to parry him?
    Would you have me stand still, hold my peace, and let
    This man win everything, through my inaction?
Creon: And you want—what is it, then? To banish me?   105
Oedipus: No, not exile. It is your death I want,
    So that all the world may see what treason means.
Creon: You will persist, then? You will not believe me?
Oedipus: How can I believe you?
Creon: Then you are a fool.
Oedipus: To save myself?
Creon: In justice, think of me.   110
Oedipus: You are evil incarnate.
Creon: But suppose that you are wrong?
Oedipus: Still I must rule.
Creon: But not if you rule badly.
Oedipus: O city, city!
Creon: It is my city, too!
Choragos: Now, my lords, be still. I see the Queen,
    Iocastê, coming from her palace chambers;   115
    And it is time she came, for the sake of you both.
    This dreadful quarrel can be resolved through her.

    Enter Iocastê.

Iocastê: Poor foolish men, what wicked din is this?
    With Thebes sick to death, is it not shameful
    That you should rake some private quarrel up?   120
    (*To Oedipus.*) Come into the house.
                   —And you, Creon, go now:
    Let us have no more of this tumult over nothing.
Creon: Nothing? No, sister: what your husband plans for me
    Is one of two great evils: exile or death.
Oedipus: He is right.
            Why, woman, I have caught him squarely   125
    Plotting against my life.
Creon: No! Let me die
    Accurst if ever I have wished you harm!
Iocastê: Ah, believe it, Oedipus!
    In the name of the gods, respect this oath of his
    For my sake, for the sake of these people here!   130

                              Strophe 1

Choragos: Open your mind to her, my lord. Be ruled by her, I beg you!
Oedipus: What would you have me do?
Choragos: Respect Creon's word. He has never spoken like a fool,
    And now he has sworn an oath.
Oedipus: You know what you ask?
Choragos: I do.
Oedipus: Speak on, then.

Choragos: A friend so sworn should not be baited so,   135
   In blind malice, and without final proof.
Oedipus: You are aware, I hope, that what you say
   Means death for me, or exile at the least.

                                                Strophe 2
Choragos: No, I swear by Helios, first in Heaven!
   May I die friendless and accurst,   140
   The worst of deaths, if ever I meant that!
      It is the withering fields
         That hurt my sick heart:
      Must we bear all these ills,
         And now your bad blood as well?   145
Oedipus: Then let him go. And let me die, if I must,
   Or be driven by him in shame from the land of Thebes.
   It is your unhappiness, and not his talk,
   That touches me.
             As for him—
   Wherever he goes, hatred will follow him.   150
Creon: Ugly in yielding, as you were ugly in rage!
   Natures like yours chiefly torment themselves.
Oedipus: Can you not go? Can you not leave me?
Creon: I can.
   You do not know me; but the city knows me,
   And in its eyes I am just, if not in yours.   155

   Exit Creon.

                                      Antistrophe 1
Choragos: Lady Iocastê, did you not ask the King to go to his chambers?
Iocastê: First tell me what has happened.
Choragos: There was suspicion without evidence; yet it rankled
   As even false charges will.
Iocastê: On both sides?
Choragos: On both.
Iocastê: But what was said?
Choragos: Oh let it rest, let it be done with!   160
   Have we not suffered enough?
Oedipus: You see to what your decency has brought you:
   You have made difficulties where my heart saw none.

                                      Antistrophe 2
Choragos: Oedipus, it is not once only I have told you—
   You must know I should count myself unwise   165
   To the point of madness, should I now forsake you—
      You, under whose hand,
         In the storm of another time,
      Our dear land sailed out free.
         But now stand fast at the helm!   170
Iocastê: In God's name, Oedipus, inform your wife as well:
   Why are you so set in this hard anger?

Oedipus: I will tell you, for none of these men deserves
    My confidence as you do. It is Creon's work,
    His treachery, his plotting against me.   175
Iocastê: Go on, if you can make this clear to me.
Oedipus: He charges me with the murder of Laïos.
Iocastê: Has he some knowledge? Or does he speak from hearsay?
Oedipus: He would not commit himself to such a charge,
    But he has brought in that damnable soothsayer   180
    To tell his story.
Iocastê: Set your mind at rest.
    If it is a question of soothsayers, I tell you
    That you will find no man whose craft gives knowledge
    Of the unknowable.

               Here is my proof:

    An oracle was reported to Laïos once   185
    (I will not say from Phoibos himself, but from
    His appointed ministers, at any rate)
    That his doom would be death at the hands of his own son—
    His son, born of his flesh and of mine!

    Now, you remember the story: Laïos was killed   190
    By marauding strangers where three highways meet;
    But his child had not been three days in this world
    Before the King had pierced the baby's ankles
    And left him to die on a lonely mountainside.

    Thus, Apollo never caused that child   195
    To kill his father, and it was not Laïos' fate
    To die at the hands of his son, as he had feared.
    This is what prophets and prophecies are worth!
    Have no dread of them.
               It is God himself
    Who can show us what he wills, in his own way.   200
Oedipus: How strange a shadowy memory crossed my mind,
    Just now while you were speaking; it chilled my heart.
Iocastê: What do you mean? What memory do you speak of?
Oedipus: If I understand you, Laïos was killed
    At a place where three roads meet.
Iocastê: So it was said;   205
    We have no later story.
Oedipus: Where did it happen?
Iocastê: Phokis, it is called: at a place where the Theban Way
    Divides into the roads toward Delphi and Daulia.
Oedipus: When?
Iocastê: We had the news not long before you came
    And proved the right to your succession here.   210
Oedipus: Ah, what net has God been weaving for me?
Iocastê: Oedipus! Why does this trouble you?

Oedipus: Do not ask me yet.
　　First, tell me how Laïos looked, and tell me
　　How old he was.
Iocastê: He was tall, his hair just touched
　　With white; his form was not unlike your own.   215
Oedipus: I think that I myself may be accurst
　　By my own ignorant edict.
Iocastê: You speak strangely.
　　It makes me tremble to look at you, my King.
Oedipus: I am not sure that the blind man can not see.
　　But I should know better if you were to tell me—   220
Iocastê: Anything—though I dread to hear you ask it.
Oedipus: Was the King lightly escorted, or did he ride
　　With a large company, as a ruler should?
Iocastê: There were five men with him in all: one was a herald,
　　And a single chariot, which he was driving.   225
Oedipus: Alas, that makes it plain enough!
　　　　　　　　　　　　　　　　But who—
　　Who told you how it happened?
Iocastê: A household servant,
　　The only one to escape.
Oedipus: And is he still
　　A servant of ours?
Iocastê: No; for when he came back at last
　　And found you enthroned in the place of the dead king,   230
　　He came to me, touched my hand with his, and begged
　　That I would send him away to the frontier district
　　Where only the shepherds go—
　　As far away from the city as I could send him.
　　I granted his prayer; for although the man was a slave,   235
　　He had earned more than this favor at my hands.
Oedipus: Can he be called back quickly?
Iocastê: Easily.
　　But why?
Oedipus: I have taken too much upon myself
　　Without enquiry; therefore I wish to consult him.
Iocastê: Then he shall come.
　　　　　　　　　　　But am I not one also   240
　　To whom you might confide these fears of yours?
Oedipus: That is your right; it will not be denied you,
　　Now least of all; for I have reached a pitch
　　Of wild foreboding. Is there anyone
　　To whom I should sooner speak?   245

　　Polybos of Corinth is my father.
　　My mother is a Dorian: Meropê.
　　I grew up chief among the men of Corinth
　　Until a strange thing happened—
　　Not worth my passion, it may be, but strange.   250

At a feast, a drunken man maundering in his cups
Cries out that I am not my father's son!

I contained myself that night, though I felt anger
And a sinking heart. The next day I visited
My father and mother, and questioned them. They stormed,   255
Calling it all the slanderous rant of a fool;
And this relieved me. Yet the suspicion
Remained always aching in my mind;
I knew there was talk; I could not rest;
And finally, saying nothing to my parents,   260
I went to the shrine at Delphi.
The god dismissed my question without reply;
He spoke of other things.
                         Some were clear,
Full of wretchedness, dreadful, unbearable:
As, that I should lie with my own mother, breed   265
Children from whom all men would turn their eyes;
And that I should be my father's murderer.

I heard all this, and fled. And from that day
Corinth to me was only in the stars
Descending in that quarter of the sky,   270
As I wandered farther and farther on my way
To a land where I should never see the evil
Sung by the oracle. And I came to this country
Where, so you say, King Laïos was killed.

I will tell you all that happened there, my lady.   275

There were three highways
Coming together at a place I passed;
And there a herald came towards me, and a chariot
Drawn by horses, with a man such as you describe
Seated in it. The groom leading the horses   280
Forced me off the road at his lord's command;
But as this charioteer lurched over towards me
I struck him in my rage. The old man saw me
And brought his double goad down upon my head
As I came abreast.
                    He was paid back, and more!   285
Swinging my club in this right hand I knocked him
Out of his car, and he rolled on the ground.
                                    I killed him.

I killed them all.
Now if that stranger and Laïos were—kin,
Where is a man more miserable than I?   290
More hated by the gods? Citizen and alien alike
Must never shelter me or speak to me—

I must be shunned by all.

          And I myself
Pronounced this malediction upon myself!

Think of it: I have touched you with these hands,   295
These hands that killed your husband. What defilement!

Am I all evil, then? It must be so,
Since I must flee from Thebes, yet never again
See my own countrymen, my own country,
For fear of joining my mother in marriage   300
And killing Polybos, my father.

               Ah,
If I was created so, born to this fate,
Who could deny the savagery of God?

O holy majesty of heavenly powers!
May I never see that day! Never!   305
Rather let me vanish from the race of men
Than know the abomination destined me!
Choragos: We too, my lord, have felt dismay at this.
    But there is hope: you have yet to hear the shepherd.
Oedipus: Indeed, I fear no other hope is left me.   310
Iocastê: What do you hope from him when he comes?
Oedipus: This much:
    If his account of the murder tallies with yours,
    Then I am cleared.
Iocastê: What was it that I said
    Of such importance?
Oedipus: Why, "marauders," you said,
    Killed the King, according to this man's story.   315
    If he maintains that still, if there were several,
    Clearly the guilt is not mine: I was alone.
    But if he says one man, singlehanded, did it,
    Then the evidence all points to me.
Iocastê: You may be sure that he said there were several;   320
    And can he call back that story now? He can not.
    The whole city heard it as plainly as I.
    But suppose he alters some detail of it:
    He can not ever show that Laïos' death
    Fulfilled the oracle: for Apollo said   325
    My child was doomed to kill him; and my child—
    Poor baby!—it was my child that died first.

    No. From now on, where oracles are concerned,
    I would not waste a second thought on any.
Oedipus: You may be right.
                   But come: let someone go   330
    For the shepherd at once. This matter must be settled.
Iocastê: I will send for him.

I would not wish to cross you in anything,
And surely not in this.—Let us go in.

Exeunt into the palace.

ODE II

Chorus: Let me be reverent in the ways of right,   *Strophe 1*
    Lowly the paths I journey on;
    Let all my words and actions keep
    The laws of the pure universe
    From highest Heaven handed down.   5
    For Heaven is their bright nurse,
    Those generations of the realms of light;
    Ah, never of mortal kind were they begot,
    Nor are they slaves of memory, lost in sleep:
    Their Father is greater than Time, and ages not.   10

    The tyrant is a child of Pride   *Antistrophe 1*
    Who drinks from his great sickening cup
    Recklessness and vanity,
    Until from his high crest headlong
    He plummets to the dust of hope.   15
    That strong man is not strong.
    But let no fair ambition be denied;
    May God protect the wrestler for the State
    In government, in comely policy,
    Who will fear God, and on His ordinance wait.   20

    Haughtiness and the high hand of disdain   *Strophe 2*
    Tempt and outrage God's holy law;
    And any mortal who dares hold
    No immortal Power in awe
    Will be caught up in a net of pain: 25
    The price for which his levity is sold.
    Let each man take due earnings, then,
    And keep his hands from holy things,
    And from blasphemy stand apart—
    Else the crackling blast of heaven   30
    Blows on his head, and on his desperate heart;
    Though fools will honor impious men,
    In their cities no tragic poet sings.

    Shall we lose faith in Delphi's obscurities,   *Antistrophe 2*
    We who have heard the world's core   35
    Discredited, and the sacred wood
    Of Zeus at Elis praised no more?
    The deeds and the strange prophecies
    Must make a pattern yet to be understood.
    Zeus, if indeed you are lord of all,   40

Throned in light over night and day,
Mirror this in your endless mind:
Our masters call the oracle
Words on the wind, and the Delphic vision blind!
Their hearts no longer know Apollo,   45
And reverence for the gods has died away.

SCENE III

Enter Iocastê.

Iocastê: Princes of Thebes, it has occurred to me
To visit the altars of the gods, bearing
These branches as a suppliant, and this incense.
Our King is not himself: his noble soul
Is overwrought with fantasies of dread,   5
Else he would consider
The new prophecies in the light of the old.
He will listen to any voice that speaks disaster,
And my advice goes for nothing.

She approaches the altar, right.

To you, then, Apollo,
Lycean lord, since you are nearest, I turn in prayer.   10
Receive these offerings, and grant us deliverance
From defilement. Our hearts are heavy with fear
When we see our leader distracted, as helpless sailors
Are terrified by the confusion of their helmsman.

Enter Messenger.

Messenger: Friends, no doubt you can direct me: 15
Where shall I find the house of Oedipus,
Or, better still, where is the King himself?
Choragos: It is this very place, stranger; he is inside.
This is his wife and mother of his children.
Messenger: I wish her happiness in a happy house,
Blest in all the fulfillment of her marriage.   20
Iocastê: I wish as much for you: your courtesy
Deserves a like good fortune. But now, tell me:
Why have you come? What have you to say to us?
Messenger: Good news, my lady, for your house and your husband.   25
Iocastê: What news? Who sent you here?
Messenger: I am from Corinth.
The news I bring ought to mean joy for you,
Though it may be you will find some grief in it.
Iocastê: What is it? How can it touch us in both ways?
Messenger: The word is that the people of the Isthmus   30
Intend to call Oedipus to be their king.
Iocastê: But old King Polybos—is he not reigning still?

Messenger: No. Death holds him in his sepulchre.

Iocastê: What are you saying? Polybos is dead?

Messenger: If I am not telling the truth, may I die myself.   35

Iocastê (to a Maidservant): Go in, go quickly; tell this to your master.

O riddlers of God's will, where are you now!
This was the man whom Oedipus, long ago,
Feared so, fled so, in dread of destroying him—
But it was another fate by which he died.   40

Enter Oedipus, center.

Oedipus: Dearest Iocastê, why have you sent for me?

Iocastê: Listen to what this man says, and then tell me
        What has become of the solemn prophecies.

Oedipus: Who is this man? What is his news for me?

Iocastê: He has come from Corinth to announce your father's death!   45

Oedipus: Is it true, stranger? Tell me in your own words.

Messenger: I can not say it more clearly: the King is dead.

Oedipus: Was it by treason? Or by an attack of illness?

Messenger: A little thing brings old men to their rest.

Oedipus: It was sickness, then?

Messenger: Yes, and his many years.   50

Oedipus: Ah!
        Why should a man respect the Pythian hearth,° or
        Give heed to the birds that jangle above his head?
        They prophesied that I should kill Polybos,
        Kill my own father; but he is dead and buried,   55
        And I am here—I never touched him, never,
        Unless he died of grief for my departure,
        And thus, in a sense, through me. No. Polybos
        Has packed the oracles off with him underground.
        They are empty words.

Iocastê: Had I not told you so?   60

Oedipus: You had; it was my faint heart that betrayed me.

Iocastê: From now on never think of those things again.

Oedipus: And yet—must I not fear my mother's bed?

Iocastê: Why should anyone in this world be afraid,
        Since Fate rules us and nothing can be foreseen?   65
        A man should live only for the present day.

        Have no more fear of sleeping with your mother:
        How many men, in dreams, have lain with their mothers!
        No reasonable man is troubled by such things.

Oedipus: That is true; only—   70
        If only my mother were not still alive!
        But she is alive. I can not help my dread.

Iocastê: Yet this news of your father's death is wonderful.

---

52 *Pythian hearth:* the shrine at Delphi, whose priestess was famous for her prophecies.

Oedipus: Wonderful. But I fear the living woman.
Messenger: Tell me, who is this woman that you fear?   75
Oedipus: It is Meropê, man; the wife of King Polybos.
Messenger: Meropê? Why should you be afraid of her?
Oedipus: An oracle of the gods, a dreadful saying.
Messenger: Can you tell me about it or are you sworn to silence?
Oedipus: I can tell you, and I will.   80
    Apollo said through his prophet that I was the man
    Who should marry his own mother, shed his father's blood
    With his own hands. And so, for all these years
    I have kept clear of Corinth, and no harm has come—
    Though it would have been sweet to see my parents again.   85
Messenger: And is this the fear that drove you out of Corinth?
Oedipus: Would you have me kill my father?
Messenger: As for that
    You must be reassured by the news I gave you.
Oedipus: If you could reassure me, I would reward you.
Messenger: I had that in mind, I will confess: I thought   90
    I could count on you when you returned to Corinth.
Oedipus: No: I will never go near my parents again.
Messenger: Ah, son, you still do not know what you are doing—
Oedipus: What do you mean? In the name of God tell me!
Messenger: —If these are your reasons for not going home.   95
Oedipus: I tell you, I fear the oracle may come true.
Messenger: And guilt may come upon you through your parents?
Oedipus: That is the dread that is always in my heart.
Messenger: Can you not see that all your fears are groundless?
Oedipus: How can you say that? They are my parents, surely?   100
Messenger: Polybos was not your father.
Oedipus: Not my father?
Messenger: No more your father than the man speaking to you.
Oedipus: But you are nothing to me!
Messenger: Neither was he.
Oedipus: Then why did he call me son?
Messenger: I will tell you:
    Long ago he had you from my hands, as a gift.   105
Oedipus: Then how could he love me so, if I was not his?
Messenger: He had no children, and his heart turned to you.
Oedipus: What of you? Did you buy me? Did you find me by chance?
Messenger: I came upon you in the crooked pass of Kithairon.
Oedipus: And what were you doing there?
Messenger: Tending my flocks.   110
Oedipus: A wandering shepherd?
Messenger: But your savior, son, that day.
Oedipus: From what did you save me?
Messenger: Your ankles should tell you that.
Oedipus: Ah, stranger, why do you speak of that childhood pain?
Messenger: I cut the bonds that tied your ankles together.
Oedipus: I have had the mark as long as I can remember.   115

Messenger: That was why you were given the name you bear.

Oedipus: God! Was it my father or my mother who did it?
    Tell me!

Messenger: I do not know. The man who gave you to me
    Can tell you better than I.

Oedipus: It was not you that found me, but another?   120

Messenger: It was another shepherd gave you to me.

Oedipus: Who was he? Can you tell me who he was?

Messenger: I think he was said to be one of Laïos' people.

Oedipus: You mean the Laïos who was king here years ago?

Messenger: Yes; King Laïos; and the man was one of his herdsmen.   125

Oedipus: Is he still alive? Can I see him?

Messenger: These men here
    Know best about such things.

Oedipus: Does anyone here
    Know this shepherd that he is talking about?
    Have you seen him in the fields, or in the town?
    If you have, tell me. It is time things were made plain.   130

Choragos: I think the man he means is that same shepherd
    You have already asked to see. Iocastê perhaps
    Could tell you something.

Oedipus: Do you know anything
    About him, Lady? Is he the man we have summoned?
    Is that the man this shepherd means?

Iocastê: Why think of him?   135
    Forget this herdsman. Forget it all.
    This talk is a waste of time.

Oedipus: How can you say that,
    When the clues to my true birth are in my hands?

Iocastê: For God's love, let us have no more questioning!
    Is your life nothing to you?   140
    My own is pain enough for me to bear.

Oedipus: You need not worry. Suppose my mother a slave,
    And born of slaves: no baseness can touch you.

Iocastê: Listen to me, I beg you: do not do this thing!

Oedipus: I will not listen; the truth must be made known.   145

Iocastê: Everything that I say is for your own good!

Oedipus: My own good
    Snaps my patience, then; I want none of it.

Iocastê: You are fatally wrong! May you never learn who you are!

Oedipus: Go, one of you, and bring the shepherd here.
    Let us leave this woman to brag of her royal name.   150

Iocastê: Ah, miserable!
    That is the only word I have for you now.
    That is the only word I can ever have.

    Exit into the palace.

Choragos: Why has she left us, Oedipus? Why has she gone
    In such a passion of sorrow? I fear this silence: 155
    Something dreadful may come of it.

Oedipus: Let it come!
   However base my birth, I must know about it.
   The Queen, like a woman, is perhaps ashamed
   To think of my low origin. But I
   Am a child of Luck; I can not be dishonored.   160
   Luck is my mother; the passing months, my brothers,
   Have seen me rich and poor.
                              If this is so,
   How could I wish that I were someone else?
   How could I not be glad to know my birth?

ODE III

Strophe

Chorus: If ever the coming time were known
   To my heart's pondering,
   Kithairon, now by Heaven I see the torches
   At the festival of the next full moon,
   And see the dance, and hear the choir sing   5
   A grace to your gentle shade:
   Mountain where Oedipus was found,
   O mountain guard of a noble race!
   May the god who heals us lend his aid,
   And let that glory come to pass   10
   For our king's cradling-ground.

Antistrophe

   Of the nymphs that flower beyond the years,
   Who bore you, royal child,
   To Pan of the hills or the timberline Apollo,
   Cold in delight where the upland clears,   15
   Or Hermês for whom Kyllenê's° heights are piled?
   Or flushed as evening cloud,
   Great Dionysos, roamer of mountains,
   He—was it he who found you there,
   And caught you up in his own proud   20
   Arms from the sweet god-ravisher
   Who laughed by the Muses' fountains?

SCENE IV

Oedipus: Sirs: though I do not know the man,
   I think I see him coming, this shepherd we want:
   He is old, like our friend here, and the men
   Bringing him seem to be servants of my house.
   But you can tell, if you have ever seen him.   5

   Enter Shepherd escorted by servants.

16 *Kyllenê:* a sacred mountain, birthplace of Hermês, the deities' messenger. The chorus assumes that the mountain was created in order to afford him birth.

Choragos: I know him, he was Laïos' man. You can trust him.
Oedipus: Tell me first, you from Corinth: is this the shepherd
    We were discussing?
Messenger: This is the very man.
Oedipus (to Shepherd): Come here. No, look at me. You must answer
    Everything I ask.—You belonged to Laïos?   10
Shepherd: Yes: born his slave, brought up in his house.
Oedipus: Tell me: what kind of work did you do for him?
Shepherd: I was a shepherd of his, most of my life.
Oedipus: Where mainly did you go for pasturage?
Shepherd: Sometimes Kithairon, sometimes the hills near-by.   15
Oedipus: Do you remember ever seeing this man out there?
Shepherd: What would he be doing there? This man?
Oedipus: This man standing here. Have you ever seen him before?
Shepherd: No. At least, not to my recollection.
Messenger: And that is not strange, my lord. But I'll refresh   20
    His memory: he must remember when we two
    Spent three whole seasons together, March to September,
    On Kithairon or thereabouts. He had two flocks;
    I had one. Each autumn I'd drive mine home
    And he would go back with his to Laïos' sheepfold.—   25
    Is this not true, just as I have described it?
Shepherd: True, yes; but it was all so long ago.
Messenger: Well, then: do you remember, back in those days
    That you gave me a baby boy to bring up as my own?
Shepherd: What if I did? What are you trying to say?   30
Messenger: King Oedipus was once that little child.
Shepherd: Damn you, hold your tongue!
Oedipus: No more of that!
    It is your tongue needs watching, not this man's.
Shepherd: My King, my Master, what is it I have done wrong?
Oedipus: You have not answered his question about the boy.   35
Shepherd: He does not know . . . He is only making trouble . . .
Oedipus: Come, speak plainly, or it will go hard with you.
Shepherd: In God's name, do not torture an old man!
Oedipus: Come here, one of you; bind his arms behind him.
Shepherd: Unhappy king! What more do you wish to learn?   40
Oedipus: Did you give this man the child he speaks of?
Shepherd: I did.
    And I would to God I had died that very day.
Oedipus: You will die now unless you speak the truth.
Shepherd: Yet if I speak the truth, I am worse than dead.
Oedipus: Very well; since you insist upon delaying—   45
Shepherd: No! I have told you already that I gave him the boy.
Oedipus: Where did you get him? From your house? From somewhere else?
Shepherd: Not from mine, no. A man gave him to me.
Oedipus: Is that man here? Do you know whose slave he was?
Shepherd: For God's love, my King, do not ask me any more!   50
Oedipus: You are a dead man if I have to ask you again.

Shepherd: Then . . . Then the child was from the palace of Laïos.
Oedipus: A slave child? or a child of his own line?
Shepherd: Ah, I am on the brink of dreadful speech!
Oedipus: And I of dreadful hearing. Yet I must hear.   55
Shepherd: If you must be told, then . . .
                              They said it was Laïos' child;
     But it is your wife who can tell you about that.
Oedipus: My wife!—Did she give it to you?
Shepherd: My lord, she did.
Oedipus: Do you know why?
Shepherd: I was told to get rid of it.
Oedipus: An unspeakable mother!
Shepherd: There had been prophecies . . .   60
Oedipus: Tell me.
Shepherd: It was said that the boy would kill his own father.
Oedipus: Then why did you give him over to this old man?
Shepherd: I pitied the baby, my King,
     And I thought that this man would take him far away   65
     To his own country.
                    He saved him—but for what a fate!
     For if you are what this man says you are,
     No man living is more wretched than Oedipus.
Oedipus: Ah God!
     It was true!
          All the prophecies!
                    —Now,   70
     O Light, may I look on you for the last time!
     I, Oedipus,
     Oedipus, damned in his birth, in his marriage damned,
     Damned in the blood he shed with his own hand!

     He rushes into the palace.

ODE IV

                                                        Strophe 1

Chorus: Alas for the seed of men.

     What measure shall I give these generations
     That breathe on the void and are void
     And exist and do not exist?

     Who bears more weight of joy   5
     Than mass of sunlight shifting in images,
     Or who shall make his thought stay on
     That down time drifts away?

     Your splendor is all fallen.

     O naked brow of wrath and tears,   10
     O change of Oedipus!

I who saw your days call no man blest—
Your great days like ghosts gone.

That mind was a strong bow.

Deep, how deep you drew it then, hard archer,   15
At a dim fearful range,
And brought dear glory down!

You overcame the stranger—
The virgin with her hooking lion claws—
And though death sang, stood like a tower   20
To make pale Thebes take heart.

Fortress against our sorrow!

True king, giver of laws,
Majestic Oedipus!
No prince in Thebes had ever such renown,   25
No prince won such grace of power.

And now of all men ever known
Most pitiful is this man's story:
His fortunes are most changed, his state
Fallen to a low slave's   30
Ground under bitter fate.

O Oedipus, most royal one!
The great door that expelled you to the light
Gave at night—ah, gave night to your glory:
As to the father, to the fathering son.   35

All understood too late.

How could that queen whom Laïos won,
The garden that he harrowed at his height,
Be silent when that act was done?

But all eyes fail before time's eye,   40
All actions come to justice there.
Though never willed, though far down the deep past,
Your bed, your dread sirings,
Are brought to book at last.

Child by Laïos doomed to die,   45
Then doomed to lose that fortunate little death,
Would God you never took breath in this air
That with my wailing lips I take to cry:

For I weep the world's outcast.

I was blind, and now I can tell why: 50
Asleep, for you had given ease of breath
To Thebes, while the false years went by.

ÉXODOS°

Enter, from the palace, Second Messenger.

Second Messenger: Elders of Thebes, most honored in this land,
　　What horrors are yours to see and hear, what weight
　　Of sorrow to be endured, if, true to your birth,
　　You venerate the line of Labdakos!
　　I think neither Istros nor Phasis, those great rivers, 5
　　Could purify this place of the corruption
　　It shelters now, or soon must bring to light—
　　Evil not done unconsciously, but willed.

　　The greatest griefs are those we cause ourselves.
Choragos: Surely, friend, we have grief enough already; 10
　　What new sorrow do you mean?
Second Messenger: 　　　　　　　　The Queen is dead.
Choragos: Iocastê? Dead? But at whose hand?
Second Messenger: 　　　　　　　　　　　Her own.
　　The full horror of what happened, you can not know,
　　For you did not see it; but I, who did, will tell you
　　As clearly as I can how she met her death. 15

　　When she had left us,
　　In passionate silence, passing through the court,
　　She ran to her apartment in the house,
　　Her hair clutched by the fingers of both hands.
　　She closed the doors behind her; then, by that bed 20
　　Where long ago the fatal son was conceived—
　　That son who should bring about his father's death—
　　We heard her call upon Laïos, dead so many years,
　　And heard her wail for the double fruit of her marriage,
　　A husband by her husband, children by her child. 25

　　Exactly how she died I do not know:
　　For Oedipus burst in moaning and would not let us
　　Keep vigil to the end: it was by him
　　As he stormed about the room that our eyes were caught.
　　From one to another of us he went, begging a sword, 30
　　Cursing the wife who was not his wife, the mother
　　Whose womb had carried his own children and himself.
　　I do not know: it was none of us aided him,
　　But surely one of the gods was in control!
　　For with a dreadful cry 35
　　He hurled his weight, as though wrenched out of himself,
　　At the twin doors: the bolts gave, and he rushed in.
　　And there we saw her hanging, her body swaying
　　From the cruel cord she had noosed about her neck.
　　A great sob broke from him, heartbreaking to hear, 40
　　As he loosed the rope and lowered her to the ground.

Éxodos: final scene, containing the resolution.

I would blot out from my mind what happened next!
For the King ripped from her gown the golden brooches
That were her ornament, and raised them, and plunged them down
Straight into his own eyeballs, crying, "No more,   45
No more shall you look on the misery about me,
The horrors of my own doing! Too long you have known
The faces of those whom I should never have seen,
Too long been blind to those for whom I was searching!
From this hour, go in darkness!" And as he spoke,   50
He struck at his eyes—not once, but many times;
And the blood spattered his beard,
Bursting from his ruined sockets like red hail.

So from the unhappiness of two this evil has sprung,
A curse on the man and woman alike. The old   55
Happiness of the house of Labdakos
Was happiness enough: where is it today?
It is all wailing and ruin, disgrace, death—all
The misery of mankind that has a name—
And it is wholly and for ever theirs.   60
Choragos: Is he in agony still? Is there no rest for him?
Second Messenger: He is calling for someone to lead him to the gates
So that all the children of Kadmos may look upon
His father's murderer, his mother's—no,
I can not say it!
                    And then he will leave Thebes,   65
Self-exiled, in order that the curse
Which he himself pronounced may depart from the house.
He is weak, and there is none to lead him,
So terrible is his suffering.
                        But you will see:
Look, the doors are opening; in a moment   70
You will see a thing that would crush a heart of stone.

The central door is opened; Oedipus, blinded, is led in.

Choragos: Dreadful indeed for men to see.
     Never have my own eyes
     Looked on a sight so full of fear.

Oedipus!   75
What madness came upon you, what daemon
Leaped on your life with heavier
Punishment than a mortal man can bear?
No: I can not even
Look at you, poor ruined one.
And I would speak, question, ponder,   80
If I were able. No.
     You make me shudder.
Oedipus: God. God.

Is there a sorrow greater?   85
Where shall I find harbor in this world?
My voice is hurled far on a dark wind.
What has God done to me?
Choragos: Too terrible to think of, or to see.

                                                                    Strophe 1

Oedipus: O cloud of night,   90
    Never to be turned away: night coming on,
    I can not tell how: night like a shroud!

My fair winds brought me here.
                                Oh God. Again
The pain of the spikes where I had sight,
The flooding pain   95
Of memory, never to be gouged out.
Choragos: This is not strange.
    You suffer it all twice over, remorse in pain,
    Pain in remorse.

                                                                  Antistrophe 1

Oedipus: Ah dear friend   100
    Are you faithful even yet, you alone?
    Are you still standing near me, will you stay here,
    Patient, to care for the blind?
                                The blind man!
    Yet even blind I know who it is attends me,
    By the voice's tone—   105
    Though my new darkness hide the comforter.
Choragos: Oh fearful act!
    What god was it drove you to rake black
    Night across your eyes?

                                                                    Strophe 2

Oedipus: Apollo. Apollo. Dear   110
    Children, the god was Apollo.
    He brought my sick, sick fate upon me.
    But the blinding hand was my own!
    How could I bear to see
    When all my sight was horror everywhere?   115
Choragos: Everywhere; that is true.
Oedipus: And now what is left?
    Images? Love? A greeting even,
    Sweet to the senses? Is there anything?
    Ah, no, friends: lead me away.   120
    Lead me away from Thebes.
                                Lead the great wreck
    And hell of Oedipus, whom the gods hate.
Choragos: Your fate is clear, you are not blind to that.
    Would God you had never found it out!

                                                                  Antistrophe 2

Oedipus: Death take the man who unbound   125
    My feet on that hillside
    And delivered me from death to life! What life?
    If only I had died,
    This weight of monstrous doom
    Could not have dragged me and my darlings down.   130
Choragos: I would have wished the same.
Oedipus: Oh never to have come here
    With my father's blood upon me! Never
    To have been the man they call his mother's husband!
    Oh accurst! Oh child of evil,   135
    To have entered that wretched bed—
                     the selfsame one!
    More primal than sin itself, this fell to me.
Choragos: I do not know how I can answer you.
    You were better dead than alive and blind.
Oedipus: Do not counsel me any more. This punishment   140
    That I have laid upon myself is just.
    If I had eyes,
    I do not know how I could bear the sight
    Of my father, when I came to the house of Death,
    Or my mother: for I have sinned against them both   145
    So vilely that I could not make my peace
    By strangling my own life.
                Or do you think my children,
    Born as they were born, would be sweet to my eyes?
    Ah never, never! Nor this town with its high walls,
    Nor the holy images of the gods.
                For I,   150
    Thrice miserable!—Oedipus, noblest of all the line
    Of Kadmos, have condemned myself to enjoy
    These things no more, by my own malediction
    Expelling that man whom the gods declared
    To be a defilement in the house of Laïos.   155
    After exposing the rankness of my own guilt,
    How could I look men frankly in the eyes?
    No, I swear it,
    If I could have stifled my hearing at its source,
    I would have done it and made all this body   160
    A tight cell of misery, blank to light and sound:
    So I should have been safe in a dark agony
    Beyond all recollection.
               Ah Kithairon!
    Why did you shelter me? When I was cast upon you,
    Why did I not die? Then I should never   165
    Have shown the world my execrable birth.

    Ah Polybos! Corinth, city that I believed
    The ancient seat of my ancestors: how fair
    I seemed, your child! And all the while this evil

Was cancerous within me!

                    For I am sick   170

In my daily life, sick in my origin.

O three roads, dark ravine, woodland and way
Where three roads met: you, drinking my father's blood,
My own blood, spilled by my own hand: can you remember
The unspeakable things I did there, and the things   175
I went on from there to do?

                        O marriage, marriage!
The act that engendered me, and again the act
Performed by the son in the same bed—

                          Ah, the net
Of incest, mingling fathers, brothers, sons,
With brides, wives, mothers: the last evil   180
That can be known by men: no tongue can say
How evil!

        No. For the love of God, conceal me
Somewhere far from Thebes; or kill me; or hurl me
Into the sea, away from men's eyes for ever.

Come, lead me. You need not fear to touch me.   185
Of all men, I alone can bear this guilt.

Enter Creon.

Choragos: We are not the ones to decide; but Creon here
    May fitly judge of what you ask. He only
    Is left to protect the city in your place.
Oedipus: Alas, how can I speak to him? What right have I   190
    To beg his courtesy whom I have deeply wronged?
Creon: I have not come to mock you, Oedipus,
    Or to reproach you, either.
    (*To Attendants.*)   —You, standing there:
    If you have lost all respect for man's dignity,
    At least respect the flame of Lord Helios: 195
    Do not allow this pollution to show itself
    Openly here, an affront to the earth
    And Heaven's rain and the light of day. No, take him
    Into the house as quickly as you can.
    For it is proper   200
    That only the close kindred see his grief.
Oedipus: I pray you in God's name, since your courtesy
    Ignores my dark expectation, visiting
    With mercy this man of all men most execrable:
    Give me what I ask—for your good, not for mine.   205
Creon: And what is it that you would have me do?
Oedipus: Drive me out of this country as quickly as may be
    To a place where no human voice can ever greet me.
Creon: I should have done that before now—only,
    God's will had not been wholly revealed to me.   210

Oedipus: But his command is plain: the parricide
    Must be destroyed. I am that evil man.
Creon: That is the sense of it, yes; but as things are,
    We had best discover clearly what is to be done.
Oedipus: You would learn more about a man like me?   215
Creon: You are ready now to listen to the god.
Oedipus: I will listen. But it is to you
    That I must turn for help. I beg you, hear me.

    The woman in there—
    Give her whatever funeral you think proper: 220
    She is your sister.
               —But let me go, Creon!
    Let me purge my father's Thebes of the pollution
    Of my living here, and go out to the wild hills,
    To Kithairon, that has won such fame with me,
    The tomb my mother and father appointed for me,   225
    And let me die there, as they willed I should.
    And yet I know
    Death will not ever come to me through sickness
    Or in any natural way: I have been preserved
    For some unthinkable fate. But let that be.   230

    As for my sons, you need not care for them.
    They are men, they will find some way to live.
    But my poor daughters, who have shared my table,
    Who never before have been parted from their father—
    Take care of them, Creon; do this for me.   235
    And will you let me touch them with my hands
    A last time, and let us weep together?
    Be kind, my lord,
    Great prince, be kind!
               Could I but touch them,
    They would be mine again, as when I had my eyes.   240

Enter Antigonê and Ismene, attended.

    Ah, God!
    Is it my dearest children I hear weeping?
    Has Creon pitied me and sent my daughters?
Creon: Yes, Oedipus: I knew that they were dear to you
    In the old days, and know you must love them still.   245
Oedipus: May God bless you for this—and be a friendlier
    Guardian to you than he has been to me!

    Children, where are you?
    Come quickly to my hands: they are your brother's—
    Hands that have brought your father's once clear eyes   250
    To this way of seeing—
               Ah dearest ones,
    I had neither sight nor knowledge then, your father

By the woman who was the source of his own life!
And I weep for you—having no strength to see you—,
I weep for you when I think of the bitterness
That men will visit upon you all your lives.
What homes, what festivals can you attend
Without being forced to depart again in tears?
And when you come to marriageable age,
Where is the man, my daughters, who would dare
Risk the bane that lies on all my children?
Is there any evil wanting? Your father killed
His father; sowed the womb of her who bore him;
Engendered you at the fount of his own existence!
That is what they will say of you.

                               Then, whom
Can you ever marry? There are no bridegrooms for you,
And your lives must wither away in sterile dreaming.

O Creon, son of Menoikeus!
You are the only father my daughters have,
Since we, their parents, are both of us gone for ever.
They are your own blood: you will not let them
Fall into beggary and loneliness;
You will keep them from the miseries that are mine!
Take pity on them; see, they are only children,
Friendless except for you. Promise me this,
Great Prince, and give me your hand in token of it.

Creon clasps his right hand.

Children:
I could say much, if you could understand me,
But as it is, I have only this prayer for you:
Live where you can, be as happy as you can—
Happier, please God, than God has made your father!

Creon: Enough. You have wept enough. Now go within.

Oedipus: I must; but it is hard.

Creon: Time eases all things.

Oedipus: But you must promise—

Creon: Say what you desire.

Oedipus: Send me from Thebes!

Creon: God grant that I may!

Oedipus: But since God hates me . . .

Creon: No, he will grant your wish.

Oedipus: You promise?

Creon: I can not speak beyond my knowledge.

Oedipus: Then lead me in.

Creon: Come now, and leave your children.

Oedipus: No! Do not take them from me!

Creon: Think no longer
That you are in command here, but rather think
How, when you were, you served your own destruction.

Exeunt into the house all but the Chorus; the Choragos chants directly to the audience.

Choragos: Men of Thebes: look upon Oedipus.

This is the king who solved the famous riddle
And towered up, most powerful of men.   295
No mortal eyes but looked on him with envy,
Yet in the end ruin swept over him.

Let every man in mankind's frailty
Consider his last day; and let none
Presume on his good fortune until he find   300
Life, at his death, a memory without pain.

Questions

1. How explicitly does the prophet Teiresias reveal the guilt of Oedipus? Does it seem to you stupidity on the part of Oedipus or a defect in Sophocles's play that the king takes so long to recognize his guilt and to admit to it?

2. How does Oedipus exhibit weakness of character? Point to lines that reveal him as imperfectly noble in his words, deeds, or treatment of others.

3. "Oedipus is punished not for any fault in himself, but for his ignorance. Not knowing his family history, unable to recognize his parents on sight, he is blameless; and in slaying his father and marrying his mother, he behaves as any sensible person might behave in the same circumstances." Do you agree with this interpretation?

4. Besides the predictions of Teiresias, what other foreshadowings of the shepherd's revelation does the play contain?

5. Consider the character of Iocastê. Is she a "flat" character—a generalized queen figure—or an individual with distinctive traits of personality? Point to speeches or details in the play to back up your opinion.

6. What is dramatic irony? Besides the example given on page 180, what other instances of dramatic irony do you find in *Oedipus the King*? What do they contribute to the effectiveness of the play?

7. In the drama of Sophocles, violence and bloodshed take place offstage; thus, the suicide of Iocastê is only reported to us. Nor do we witness Oedipus's removal of his eyes; this horror is only given in the report by the second messenger. Of what advantage or disadvantage to the play is this limitation?

8. For what reason does Oedipus blind himself? What meaning, if any, do you find in his choice of a surgical instrument?

9. What are your feelings toward him as the play ends?

10. Read the famous interpretation of this play offered by Sigmund Freud (page 988). How well does Freud explain why the play moves you?

11. With what attitude toward the gods does the play leave you? By inflicting a plague on Thebes, by causing barrenness, by cursing both the people and their king, do the gods seem cruel, unjust, or tyrannical? Does the play show any reverence toward them?

12. Does this play end in total gloom?

CRITICS ON SOPHOCLES

Aristotle (384–322 B.C.)

Defining Tragedy

330 B.C.?

Translated by L. J. Potts

Tragedy is an imitation of an action of high importance, complete and of some amplitude; in language enhanced by distinct and varying beauties; acted not narrated; by means of pity and fear effecting its purgation of these emotions. By the beauties enhancing the language I mean rhythm and melody; by "distinct and varying" I mean that some are produced by meter alone, and others at another time by melody.

• • •

What will produce the tragic effect? Since, then, tragedy, to be at its finest, requires a complex, not a simple, structure, and its structure should also imitate fearful and pitiful events (for that is the peculiarity of this sort of imitation), it is clear: first, that decent people must not be shown passing from good fortune to misfortune (for that is not fearful or pitiful but disgusting); again, vicious people must not be shown passing from misfortune to good fortune (for that is the most untragic situation possible—it has none of the requisites, it is neither humane, nor pitiful, nor fearful); nor again should an utterly evil man fall from good fortune into misfortune (for though a plot of that kind would be humane, it would not induce pity or fear—pity is induced by undeserved misfortune, and fear by the misfortunes of normal people, so that this situation will be neither pitiful nor fearful). So we are left with the man between these extremes: that is to say, the kind of man who neither is distinguished for excellence and virtue, nor comes to grief on account of baseness and vice, but on account of some error; a man of great reputation and prosperity, like Oedipus and Thyestes and conspicuous people of such families as theirs. So, to be well formed, a fable must be single rather than (as some say) double—there must be no change from misfortune to good fortune, but only the opposite, from good fortune to misfortune; the cause must not be vice, but a great error; and the man must be either of the type specified or better, rather than worse. This is borne out by the practice of poets; at first they picked a fable at random and made an inventory of its contents, but now the finest tragedies are plotted, and concern a few families—for example, the tragedies about Alcmeon, Oedipus, Orestes, Meleager, Thyestes, Telephus, and any others whose lives were attended by terrible experiences or doings.

This is the plot that will produce the technically finest tragedy. Those critics are therefore wrong who censure Euripides on this very ground—because he does this in his tragedies, and many of them end in misfortune; for it is, as I have said, the right thing to do. This is clearly demonstrated on the stage in the competitions, where such plays, if they succeed, are the most tragic, and Euripides, even if he is inefficient in every other respect, still shows himself the most tragic of our poets. The next best plot, which is said by some people to be the best, is the tragedy with a double plot, like the *Odyssey*, ending in one way for the better people and in the opposite way for the worse. But it is the weakness of theatrical performances that gives priority to this kind; when poets write what the audience would like to happen, they are in leading strings.° This is not the pleasure proper to tragedy, but rather to comedy, where the

---

in leading strings: each is led, by a string, wherever the audience wills.

greatest enemies in the fable, say Orestes and Aegisthus, make friends and go off at the end, and nobody is killed by anybody.

• • •

The pity and fear can be brought about by the *mise en scène;*° but they can also come from the mere plotting of the incidents, which is preferable, and better poetry. For, without seeing anything, the fable ought to have been so plotted that if one heard the bare facts, the chain of circumstances would make one shudder and pity. That would happen to any one who heard the fable of the *Oedipus.* To produce this effect by the *mise en scène* is less artistic and puts one at the mercy of the technician; and those who use it not to frighten but merely to startle have lost touch with tragedy altogether. We should not try to get all sorts of pleasure from tragedy, but the particular tragic pleasure. And clearly, since this pleasure coming from pity and fear has to be produced by imitation, it is by his handling of the incidents that the poet must create it.

From *Poetics, VI, XIII, XIV*

Sigmund Freud (1856–1939)

The Destiny of Oedipus   1900

Translated by James Strachey

If *Oedipus the King* moves a modern audience no less than it did the contemporary Greek one, the explanation can only be that its effect does not lie in the contrast between destiny and human will, but is to be looked for in the particular nature of the material on which that contrast is exemplified. There must be something which makes a voice within us ready to recognize the compelling force of destiny in the *Oedipus,* while we can dismiss as merely arbitrary such dispositions as are laid down in *Die Ahnfrau*° or other modern tragedies of destiny. And a factor of this kind is in fact involved in the story of King Oedipus. His destiny moves us only because it might have been ours—because the oracle laid the same curse upon us before our birth as upon him. It is the fate of all of us, perhaps, to direct our first sexual impulse towards our mother and our first hatred and our first murderous wish against our father. Our dreams convince us that that is so. King Oedipus, who slew his father Laius and married his mother Jocasta, merely shows us the fulfillment of our own childhood wishes. But, more fortunate than he, we have meanwhile succeeded, insofar as we have not become psychoneurotics, in detaching our sexual impulses from our mothers and in forgetting our jealousy of our fathers. Here is one in whom these primeval wishes of our childhood have been fulfilled, and we shrink back from him with the whole force of the repression by which those wishes have since that time been held down within us. While the poet, as he unravels the past, brings to light the guilt of Oedipus, he is at the same time compelling us to recognize our own inner minds, in which those same impulses, though suppressed, are still to be found. The contrast with which the closing Chorus leaves us confronted—

look upon Oedipus.

This is the king who solved the famous riddle
And towered up, most powerful of men.
No mortal eyes but looked on him with envy,
Yet in the end ruin swept over him.

mise en scène: arrangement of actors and scenery.   *Die Ahnfrau: The Foremother,* a play by Franz Grillparzer (1791–1872), Austrian dramatist and poet.

—strikes as a warning at ourselves and our pride, at us who since our childhood have grown so wise and so mighty in our own eyes. Like Oedipus, we live in ignorance of these wishes, repugnant to morality, which have been forced upon us by Nature, and after their revelation we may all of us well seek to close our eyes to the scenes of our childhood.

From *The Interpretation of Dreams*

E. R. Dodds (1893–1979)

On Misunderstanding Oedipus 1966

Some readers of the *Oedipus Rex* have told me that they find its atmosphere stifling and oppressive: they miss the tragic exaltation that one gets from the *Antigonê* or the *Prometheus Vinctus*. And I fear that what I have said here has done nothing to remove that feeling. Yet it is not a feeling which I share myself. Certainly the *Oedipus Rex* is a play about the blindness of man and the desperate insecurity of the human condition: in a sense every man must grope in the dark as Oedipus gropes, not knowing who he is or what he has to suffer; we all live in a world of appearance which hides from us who-knows-what dreadful reality. But surely the *Oedipus Rex* is also a play about human greatness. Oedipus is great, not in virtue of a great worldly position—for his worldly position is an illusion which will vanish like a dream—but in virtue of his inner strength: strength to pursue the truth at whatever personal cost, and strength to accept and endure it when found. "This horror is mine," he cries, "and none but I is *strong* enough to bear it." Oedipus is great because he accepts the responsibility for *all* his acts, including those which are objectively most horrible, though subjectively innocent.

To me personally Oedipus is a kind of symbol of the human intelligence which cannot rest until it has solved all the riddles—even the last riddle, to which the answer is that human happiness is built on an illusion. I do not know how far Sophocles intended that. But certainly in the last lines of the play (which I firmly believe to be genuine) he does generalize the case, does appear to suggest that in some sense Oedipus is every man and every man is potentially Oedipus. Freud felt this (he was not insensitive to poetry), but as we all know he understood it in a specific psychological sense. "Oedipus' fate," he says, "moves us only because it might have been our own, because the oracle laid upon us before birth is the very curse which rested upon him. It may be that we were all destined to direct our first sexual impulses towards our mothers, and our first impulses of hatred and violence towards our fathers; our dreams convince us that we were." Perhaps they do; but Freud did not ascribe his interpretation of the myth to Sophocles, and it is not the interpretation I have in mind. Is there not in the poet's view a much wider sense in which every man is Oedipus? If every man could tear away the last veils of illusion, if he could see human life as time and the gods see it, would he not see that against that tremendous background all the generations of men are as if they had not been, *isa kai to mēden zōsas*? That was how Odysseus saw it when he had conversed with Athena, the embodiment of divine wisdom. "In Ajax' condition," he says, "I recognize my own: I perceive that all men living are but appearance or un-substantial shadow."

From "On Misunderstanding the *Oedipus Rex*"

A. E. Haigh   (1855–1905)

The Irony of Sophocles   1896

The use of "tragic irony," as it has been called, is a favorite device in all dramatic literature. It is mostly employed when some catastrophe is about to happen, which is known and foreseen by the spectators, but concealed either from all, or from some, of the actors in the drama. In such cases the dialogue may be couched in terms which, though perfectly harmless upon the surface, carry an ominous significance to the initiated, and point suggestively to what is about to happen; and the contrast between the outer and the inner meaning of the language produces a deep effect upon the stage. Examples of this "irony" are to be found in most tragic writers, but especially in those of Greece, who use it with far greater frequency than the moderns; the reason being that, as the subjects of Greek tragedy were taken from the old legends with which everyone was familiar, it was far easier for the ancient dramatist to indulge in those ambiguous allusions which presuppose a certain knowledge on the part of the spectators. Sophocles, however, is distinguished even among the Greek poets for his predilection for this form of speech, and his "irony" has become proverbial. It figures so prominently in his dramas, and goes so far to determine their general tone, that a detailed consideration of the matter will not be out of place.

Tragic irony may be divided into two kinds, the conscious and the unconscious. Conscious irony occurs in those cases where the speaker is not himself the victim of any illusion, but foresees the calamity that is about to fall on others, and exults in the prospect. His language, though equivocal, is easily intelligible to the audience, and to those actors who are acquainted with the facts; and its dark humor adds to the horror of the situation. This kind of irony is the one more commonly met with in the modern drama.

• • •

The other kind of irony, the unconscious, is perhaps the more impressive of the two. Here the sufferer is himself the spokesman. Utterly blind as to the doom which overhangs him, he uses words which, to the mind of the audience, have an ominous suggestiveness, and without knowing it, probes his own wounds to the bottom. Such irony is not confined merely to the language, but runs through the whole situation; and the contrast between the cheerful heedlessness of the victim, and the dark shadows which surround him, produces an impression more terrible than that which any form of speech could convey. Scenes of this kind had a peculiar fascination for the ancients. The fear of a sudden reverse of fortune, and of some fatal Nemesis which waits upon pride and boastfulness, was of all ideas the one most deeply impressed upon the mind of antiquity. Hence the popularity upon the stage of those thrilling spectacles, in which confidence and presumption were seen advancing blindfold to destruction, and the bitterness of the doom was intensified by the unconscious utterances of the victim.

• • •

The greatest example of all is the *Oedipus Rex,* the masterpiece of Sophocles, and the most typical of all Greek tragedies. The irony of destiny is here exhibited with un-exampled force. In the opening scene Oedipus is depicted in the height of his prosper-ity, renowned and venerated, and surrounded by his suppliant countrymen; and the priest addresses him as the "wisest of men in dealing with life's chances and with the visitations of heaven." To the audience who know that within a few short hours the wrath of heaven will have crushed and shattered him, the pathetic meaning of these words is indescribable. From this first scene until the final catastrophe the speeches of Oedipus are all full of the same tragic allusiveness. He can scarcely open his lips with-out touching unconsciously on his own approaching fate. When he insists upon the fact that his search for the assassin is "not on behalf of strangers, but in his own cause," and when he cautiously warns Jocasta that, as his mother still lives, the guilt of incest is not yet an impossibility, every word that he utters has a concealed barb. Perhaps the most tragic passage of all is that in which, while cursing the murderer of Laius, he pro-nounces his own doom. "As for the man who did the deed of guilt, whether alone he lurks, or in league with others, I pray that he may waste his life away in suffering, per-ishing vilely for his vile actions. And if he should become a dweller in my house, I knowing it, may every curse I utter fall on my own head."

From *The Tragic Drama of the Greeks*

David Wiles

The Chorus as Democrat   2000

Oedipus becomes a political play when we focus on the interaction of actor and cho-rus, and see how the chorus forms a democratic mass jury. Each sequence of dialogue takes the form of a contest for the chorus' sympathy, with Oedipus sliding from the role of prosecutor to that of defendant, and each choral dance offers a provisional verdict. After Oedipus' set-to with Teiresias the soothsayer, the chorus decides to trust Oedipus on the basis of his past record; after his argument with his brother-in-law Creon, the chorus shows their distress and urges compromise. Once Oedipus has confessed to a killing and Iocastê has declared that oracles have no force, the chorus is forced to think about political tyranny, torn between respect for divine law and trust in their rulers. In the next dance they assume that the contradiction is resolved and Oedipus has turned out to be the son of a god. Finally a slave's evidence reveals that the man most honored by society is in fact the least to be envied. The political implications are clear: there is no space in democratic society for such as Oedipus. Athenians, like the chorus of the play, must reject the temptation to believe one man can calculate the future.

From *Greek Theatre Performance: An Introduction*

■ WRITING *effectively*

Robert Fitzgerald on Writing

Translating Sophocles into English   1941

The style of Sophocles was smooth. It has been likened by a modern critic to a molten flow of language, fitting and revealing every contour of the meaning, with no words wasted and no words poured on for effect. To approximate such purity I have sought a spare but felicitous manner of speech, not common and not "elevated" either, except by force of natural eloquence. The Greek writer did not disdain plainness when plainness was appropriate—appropriate, that is, both dramatically and within a context of verse very brilliant, mellifluous and powerful. As in every highly inflected language, the Greek order of words was controlled, by its masters, for special purposes of emphasis and even of meaning; and such of these as I have been acute enough to grasp I have tried to bring out by a comparable phrasing or rhythm in English. This I hold to be part of the business of "literal" rendering.

The difficulties involved in translating Greek dialogue are easily tripled when it comes to translating a chorus. Here the ellipses and compressions possible to the inflected idiom are particularly in evidence; and in the chorus, too, the poet concentrates his allusive power. For the modern reader, who has very little "literature" in the sense in which Samuel Johnson° used the term, two out of three allusions in the Greek odes will be meaningless. This is neither surprising nor deplorable. The Roman writer Ennius,° translating Euripides for a Latin audience two centuries after the Periclean period, found it advisable to omit many place names and to omit or explain many mythological references; and his public had greater reason to be familiar with such things than we have. My handling of this problem has been governed by the general wish to leave nothing in the English that would drive the literate reader to a library.

"Commentary" on Sophocles's The Oedipus Cycle

THINKING ABOUT GREEK TRAGEDY

Reading an ancient work of literature, such as Sophocles's *Oedipus the King* or *Antigonê*, you might have two contradictory reactions. On the one hand, you are likely to note how differently people thought, spoke, and conducted themselves in the ancient world from the way they do now. On the other hand, you might notice how many facets of human nature remain constant across the ages. Though Sophocles's characters are mythic, they also are recognizably human.

■ **Stay alert to both impulses.** Be open to the play's universal appeal, but never forget its foreignness. Take note of the basic beliefs and values that the characters hold that are different from your own. How do those elements influence their actions and motivations?

Samuel Johnson: Johnson (1709–1784) was the great eighteenth-century critic, lexicographer, poet, and conversationalist. His definition of *literature* would have referred mostly to the Greek and Latin classics. *Ennius:* Quintus Ennius (239–169 B.C.) was an early Latin epic poet and tragedian. He created Latin versions of the Greek tragic plays, especially those of Euripides.

- **Jot down something about each major character that seems odd or exotic to you.** Don't worry about being too basic; these notes are just a starting place. You might observe, for example, that Oedipus and Iocastê both believe in the power of prophecy. They also believe that Apollo and the other gods would punish the city with a plague because of an unsolved crime committed twenty years earlier. These are certainly not mainstream modern beliefs.
- **Focus on the differences themselves.** You do not need to understand the historical origins or cultural context of the differences you note. You can safely leave those things to scholars. But observing these differences—at least a few important ones—will keep you from making inappropriate modern assumptions about the characters, and keeping the differences in mind will give you greater insight into their behavior.

CHECKLIST: Writing About Greek Drama

- ☐ Identify the play's major characters.
- ☐ In what ways do they seem alien to you?
- ☐ What do you notice about a character's beliefs? About his or her values? How do these differ from your own?
- ☐ In what ways are the play's characters like the people you know?
- ☐ How do these qualities—both the alien and the familiar— influence the characters' motivations and actions?

WRITING ASSIGNMENT ON SOPHOCLES

Write a brief personality profile (two or three pages) of any major character in *Oedipus the King*. Describe the character's age, social position, family background, personality, and beliefs. What is his or her major motivation in the play? In what ways does the character resemble his or her modern equivalent? In what ways do they differ?

MORE TOPICS FOR WRITING

1. Suppose you were to direct and produce a new stage production of *Oedipus the King*. How would you go about it? Would you use masks? How would you render the chorus? Would you set the play in contemporary North America? Justify your decisions by referring to the play itself.

2. Write a brief comment on the play under the title "Does Sophocles's Oedipus Have an Oedipus Complex?" Consider Sigmund Freud's famous observations (quoted on page 988). Your comment can be either serious or light.

3. Write an essay explaining how Oedipus exemplifies or refutes Aristotle's definition of a tragic hero.

▶ TERMS FOR *review*

Stagecraft in Ancient Greece

Skene ▶ The canvas or wooden stage building in which actors changed masks and costumes when changing roles. Its façade, with double center doors and possibly two side doors, served as the setting for action taking place before a palace, temple, cave, or other interior space.

Orchestra ▶ "The place for dancing"; a circular, level performance space at the base of a horseshoe-shaped amphitheater, where twelve, then later (in Sophocles's plays) fifteen masked young male chorus members sang and danced the odes interspersed between dramatic episodes in a play. (Today the term *orchestra* refers to the ground-floor seats in a theater or concert hall.)

Deus ex machina ▶ (Latin for "god out of the machine.") Originally, the phrase referred to the Greek playwrights' frequent use of a god, mechanically lowered to the stage from the *skene* roof to resolve the human conflict. Today, *deus ex machina* refers to any forced or improbable device used to resolve a plot.

Masks ▶ (In Latin, *personae*.) Classical Greek theater masks covered an actor's entire head. Large, recognizable masks allowed far-away spectators to distinguish the conventional characters of tragedy and comedy.

Cothurni ▶ High, thick-soled elevator boots worn by tragic actors in late classical times to make them appear taller than ordinary men. (Earlier, in the fifth-century classical Athenian theater, actors wore soft shoes or boots or went barefoot.)

Elements of Classical Tragedy

Hamartia ▶ (Greek for "error.") An offense committed in ignorance of some material fact; a great mistake made as a result of an error by a morally good person.

Tragic flaw ▶ A fatal weakness or moral flaw in the protagonist that brings him or her to a bad end. Sometimes offered as an alternative understanding of *hamartia*, in contrast to the idea that the tragic hero's catastrophe is caused by an error in judgment.

Hubris ▶ Overweening pride, outrageous behavior, or the insolence that leads to ruin, the antithesis of moderation or rectitude.

Peripeteia ▶ (Anglicized as *peripety*; Greek for "sudden change.") A reversal of fortune, a sudden change of circumstance affecting the protagonist. According to Aristotle, the play's peripety occurs when a certain result is expected and instead its *opposite* effect is produced. In a tragedy, the reversal takes the protagonist from good fortune to catastrophe.

Recognition ▶ In tragic plotting, the moment of recognition occurs when ignorance gives way to knowledge, illusion to disillusion.

Katharsis, **catharsis** ▶ (Often translated from Greek as *purgation* or *purification*.) The feeling of emotional release or calm the spectator feels at the end of tragedy. The term is drawn from Aristotle's definition of tragedy, relating to the final cause or purpose of tragic art. Some feel that through *katharsis*, drama taught the audience compassion for the vulnerabilities of others and schooled it in justice and other civic virtues.

35

CRITICAL CASEBOOK
Shakespeare

"To be or not to be . . ." **Is it Shakespeare?** **In 2009 the Shakespeare Birthplace Trust unveiled this newly discovered portrait they believe is William Shakespeare. If authentic—and many scholars disagree—it is the only surviving portrait of the author painted during his lifetime.**

All the world's a stage

—WILLIAM SHAKESPEARE, *AS YOU LIKE IT* (II, vii, 139)

The reconstructed Globe Theatre in today's London—built in 1997 as an exact replica of the original.

THE THEATER OF SHAKESPEARE

Compared with the technical resources of a theater of today, those of a London public theater in the time of Queen Elizabeth I seem hopelessly limited. Plays had to be performed by daylight, and scenery had to be kept simple: a table, a chair, a throne, perhaps an artificial tree or two to suggest a forest. But these limitations were, in a sense, advantages. What the theater of today can spell out for us realistically, with massive scenery and electric lighting, Elizabethan playgoers had to imagine and the playwright had to make vivid for them by means of language. Not having a lighting technician to work a panel, Shakespeare had to indicate the dawn by having Horatio, in *Hamlet*, say in a speech rich in metaphor and descriptive detail:

> But look, the morn in russet mantle clad
> Walks o'er the dew of yon high eastward hill.

And yet the theater of Shakespeare was not bare, for the playwright did have *some* valuable technical resources. Costumes could be elaborate, and apparently some costumes conveyed recognized meanings: one theater manager's inventory included "a robe for to go invisible in." There could be musical accompaniment and sound effects such as gunpowder explosions and the beating of a pan to simulate thunder.

The stage itself was remarkably versatile. At its back were doors for exits and entrances and a curtained booth or alcove useful for hiding inside. Above the stage was a higher acting area—perhaps a porch or balcony—useful for a Juliet to stand upon and for a Romeo to raise his eyes to. In the stage floor was a trapdoor leading to a "hell" or cellar, especially useful for ghosts or devils who had to appear or disappear. The stage itself was a rectangular platform that projected into a yard enclosed by three-storied galleries.

The building was round or octagonal. In *Henry V*, Shakespeare calls it a "wooden O." The audience sat in these galleries or else stood in the yard in front of the stage and at its sides. A roof or awning protected the stage and the high-priced gallery seats, but in a sudden rain, the *groundlings*, who paid a penny to stand in the yard, must have been dampened.

Built by the theatrical company to which Shakespeare belonged, the Globe, most celebrated of Elizabethan theaters, was not in the city of London itself but on the south bank of the Thames River. This location had been chosen because earlier, in 1574, public plays had been banished from the city by an ordinance that blamed them for "corruptions of youth and other enormities" (such as providing opportunities for prostitutes and pickpockets).

A playwright had to please all members of the audience, not only the mannered and educated. This obligation may help to explain the wide range of subject matter and tone in an Elizabethan play: passages of subtle poetry, of deep philosophy, of coarse bawdry; scenes of sensational violence and of quiet psychological conflict (not that most members of the audience did not enjoy all these elements). Because he was an actor as well as a playwright, Shakespeare well knew what his company could do and what his audience wanted. In devising a play, he could write a part to take advantage of some actor's specific skills, or he could avoid straining the company's resources (some of his plays have few female parts, perhaps because of a shortage of competent boy actors). The company might offer as many as thirty plays in a season, customarily changing the program daily. The actors thus had to hold many parts in their heads, which may account for Elizabethan playwrights' fondness for blank verse. Lines of fixed length were easier for actors to commit to memory.

WILLIAM SHAKESPEARE

William Shakespeare (1564–1616), the supreme writer of English, was born, baptized, and buried in the market town of Stratford-on-Avon, eighty miles from London. Son of a glove maker and merchant who was high bailiff (or mayor) of the town, he probably attended grammar school and learned to read Latin authors in the original. At eighteen, he married Anne Hathaway, twenty-six, by whom he had three children, including twins. By 1592 he had become well known and envied as an actor and playwright in London. From 1594 until he retired, he belonged to the same theatrical company, the Lord Chamberlain's Men (later renamed the King's Men in honor of their patron, James I), for whom he wrote thirty-six plays—some of them, such as Hamlet *and*

William Shakespeare

King Lear, *profound reworkings of old plays. As an actor, Shakespeare is believed to have played supporting roles, such as the ghost of Hamlet's father. The company prospered, moved into the Globe in 1599, and in 1608 bought the fashionable Blackfriars as well; Shakespeare owned an interest in both theaters. When plagues shut down the theaters from 1592 to 1594, Shakespeare turned to story poems; his great Sonnets (published only in 1609) probably also date from the 1590s. Plays were regarded as entertainments of little literary merit, like comic books today, and Shakespeare did not bother to supervise their publication. After writing* The Tempest *(1611), the last play entirely from his hand, he retired to Stratford, where since 1597 he had owned the second-largest house in town. Most critics agree that when he wrote* Othello, *about 1604, Shakespeare was at the height of his powers.*

James Earl Jones as Othello.

A NOTE ON *OTHELLO*

Othello, the Moor of Venice, here offered for study, may be (if you are fortunate) new to you. It is seldom taught in high school, for it is ablaze with passion and violence. Even if you already know the play, we trust that you (like your instructor and your editors) still have much more to learn from it. Following his usual practice, Shakespeare based the play on a story he had appropriated—from a tale, "Of the Unfaithfulness of Husbands and Wives," by a sixteenth-century Italian writer, Giraldi Cinthio. As he could not help but do, Shakespeare freely transformed his source material. In the original tale, the heroine Disdemona (whose name Shakespeare so hugely improved) is beaten to death with a stocking full of sand—a shoddier death than the bard imagined for her.

Surely no character in literature can touch us more than Desdemona; no character can shock and disgust us more than Iago. Between these two extremes stands Othello, a black man of courage and dignity—and yet insecure, capable of being fooled, a pushover for bad advice. Besides breathing life into these characters and a host of others, Shakespeare—as brilliant a writer as any the world has known—enables them to speak poetry. Sometimes this poetry seems splendid and rich in imagery; at other times quiet and understated. Always, it seems to grow naturally from the nature of Shakespeare's characters and from their situations. *Othello, the Moor of Venice* has never ceased to grip readers and beholders alike. It is a safe bet that it will triumphantly live as long as fathers dislike whomever their daughters marry, as long as husbands suspect their wives of cheating, as long as blacks remember slavery, and as long as the ambitious court favor and the jealous practice deceit. The play may well make sense as long as public officials connive behind smiling faces, and it may even endure as long as the world makes room for the kind, the true, the beautiful—the blessed pure in heart.

PICTURING *Othello*

▲ Desdemona's father,
Brabantio, *page 1007*

▼ Othello and Desdemona,
page 1020

▲ Desdemona arrives in Cyprus,
page 1029

▲ Desdemona offers the
wrong handkerchief,
page 1061

▲ Iago's machinations, *page 1068*

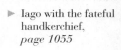

► Iago with the fateful
handkerchief,
page 1055

▶ Iago advises Cassio,
page 1040

▲ Drunken Cassio fights, *page 1036*

▲ Iago plants doubts about Desdemona,
page 1050

▼ Othello despairs, *page 1076*

▲ Othello
smothers
Desdemona,
page 1093

▶ Enter Othello, *page 1090*

Othello, the Moor of Venice

1604?

Edited by David Bevington

THE NAMES OF THE ACTORS

Othello, the Moor
Brabantio, [a senator,] father to Desdemona
Cassio, an honorable lieutenant [to Othello]
Iago, [Othello's ancient,] a villain
Roderigo, a gulled gentleman
Duke of Venice
Senators [of Venice]
Montano, governor of Cyprus
Gentlemen of Cyprus
Lodovico and Gratiano, [kinsmen to Brabantio,] two noble Venetians
Sailors
Clown
Desdemona, [daughter to Brabantio and] wife to Othello
Emilia, wife to Iago
Bianca, a courtesan [and mistress to Cassio]
[*A Messenger*
A Herald
A Musician
Servants, Attendants, Officers, Senators, Musicians, Gentlemen

SCENE. *Venice; a seaport in Cyprus*]

ACT I

SCENE I [VENICE. A STREET.]

Enter Roderigo and Iago.

Roderigo: Tush, never tell me!° I take it much unkindly
    That thou, Iago, who hast had my purse
    As if the strings were thine, shouldst know of this.°

NOTE ON THE TEXT: This text of *Othello* is based on that of the First Folio, or large collection, of Shakespeare's plays (1623). But there are many differences between the Folio text and that of the play's first printing in the Quarto, or small volume, of 1621 (eighteen or nineteen years after the play's first performance). Some readings from the Quarto are included. For the reader's convenience, some material has been added by the editor, David Bevington (some indications of scene, some stage directions). Such additions are enclosed in brackets. Mr. Bevington's text and notes were prepared for his book *The Complete Works of Shakespeare*, updated 4th ed. (New York: Longman, 1997).

PRODUCTION PHOTOS: The photos included are from the 2003 production of *Othello* by the Guthrie Theater of Minneapolis, with Lester Purry (Othello), Bill McCallum (Iago), Cheyenne Casebier (Desdemona), Robert O. Berdahl (Cassio), Virginia S. Burke (Emilia), Nathaniel Fuller (Brabantio), and Shawn Hamilton (Montano).

1 *never tell me* (An expression of incredulity, like "tell me another one.") 3 *this* i.e., Desdemona's elopement

Iago: 'Sblood,° but you'll not hear me.
>If ever I did dream of such a matter,   5
>Abhor me.
Roderigo: Thou toldst me thou didst hold him in thy hate.
Iago: Despise me
>If I do not. Three great ones of the city,
>In personal suit to make me his lieutenant,   10
>Off-capped to him;° and by the faith of man,
>I know my price, I am worth no worse a place.
>But he, as loving his own pride and purposes,
>Evades them with a bombast circumstance°
>Horribly stuffed with epithets of war,°   15
>And, in conclusion,
>Nonsuits° my mediators. For, "Certes,"° says he,
>"I have already chose my officer."
>And what was he?
>Forsooth, a great arithmetician,°   20
>One Michael Cassio, a Florentine,
>A fellow almost damned in a fair wife,°
>That never set a squadron in the field
>Nor the division of a battle° knows
>More than a spinster°—unless the bookish theoric,°   25
>Wherein the togaed° consuls° can propose°
>As masterly as he. Mere prattle without practice
>Is all his soldiership. But he, sir, had th' election;
>And I, of whom his° eyes had seen the proof
>At Rhodes, at Cyprus, and on other grounds   30
>Christened° and heathen, must be beleed and calmed°
>By debitor and creditor.° This countercaster,°
>He, in good time,° must his lieutenant be,
>And I—God bless the mark!°—his Moorship's ancient.°
Roderigo: By heaven, I rather would have been his hangman.°   35
Iago: Why, there's no remedy. 'Tis the curse of service;
>Preferment° goes by letter and affection,°

---

4 *'Sblood* by His (Christ's) blood   11 *him* i.e., Othello   14 *bombast circumstance* wordy evasion. (Bombast is cotton padding.)   15 *epithets of war* military expressions   17 *Nonsuits* rejects the petition of.   *Certes* certainly   20 *arithmetician* i.e., a man whose military knowledge is merely theoretical, based on books of tactics   22 *A . . . wife* (Cassio does not seem to be married, but his counterpart in Shakespeare's source does have a woman in his house. See also IV, i, 127.)   24 *division of a battle* disposition of a military unit   25 *a spinster* i.e., a housewife, one whose regular occupation is spinning.   *theoric* theory   26 *togaed* wearing the toga.   *consuls* counselors, senators.   *propose* discuss   29 *his* i.e., Othello's   31 *Christened* Christian.   *beleed and calmed* left to leeward without wind, becalmed. (A sailing metaphor.)   32 *debitor and creditor* (A name for a system of bookkeeping, here used as a contemptuous nickname for Cassio.)   *countercaster* i.e., bookkeeper, one who tallies with *counters*, or "metal disks." (Said contemptuously.)   33 *in good time* opportunely, i.e., forsooth   34 *God bless the mark* (Perhaps originally a formula to ward off evil; here an expression of impatience.)   *ancient* standard-bearer, ensign   35 *his hangman* his executioner   37 *Preferment* promotion.   *letter and affection* personal influence and favoritism

And not by old gradation,° where each second
Stood heir to th' first. Now, sir, be judge yourself
Whether I in any just term° am affined°   40
To love the Moor.
Roderigo: I would not follow him then.
Iago: O sir, content you.°
I follow him to serve my turn upon him.
We cannot all be masters, nor all masters   45
Cannot be truly° followed. You shall mark
Many a duteous and knee-crooking knave
That, doting on his own obsequious bondage,
Wears out his time, much like his master's ass,
For naught but provender, and when he's old, cashiered.°   50
Whip me° such honest knaves. Others there are
Who, trimmed in forms and visages of duty,°
Keep yet their hearts attending on themselves,
And, throwing but shows of service on their lords,
Do well thrive by them, and when they have lined their coats,°   55
Do themselves homage.° These fellows have some soul,
And such a one do I profess myself. For, sir,
It is as sure as you are Roderigo,
Were I the Moor I would not be Iago.°
In following him, I follow but myself—   60
Heaven is my judge, not I for love and duty,
But seeming so for my peculiar° end.
For when my outward action doth demonstrate
The native° act and figure° of my heart
In compliment extern,° 'tis not long after   65
But I will wear my heart upon my sleeve
For daws° to peck at. I am not what I am.°
Roderigo: What a full° fortune does the thick-lips° owe°
If he can carry 't thus!°
Iago: Call up her father.
Rouse him, make after him, poison his delight,   70
Proclaim him in the streets; incense her kinsmen,
And, though he in a fertile climate dwell,
Plague him with flies.° Though that his joy be joy,°

---

38 *old gradation* step-by-step seniority, the traditional way   40 *term* respect.   *affined* bound   43 *content you* don't you worry about that   46 *truly* faithfully   50 *cashiered* dismissed from service   51 *Whip me* whip, as far as I'm concerned   52 *trimmed . . . duty* dressed up in the mere form and show of dutifulness   55 *lined their coats* i.e., stuffed their purses   56 *Do themselves homage* i.e., attend to self-interest solely   59 *Were . . . Iago* i.e., if I were able to assume command, I certainly would not choose to remain a subordinate, or, I would keep a suspicious eye on a flattering subordinate   62 *peculiar* particular, personal   64 *native* innate.   *figure* shape, intent   65 *compliment extern* outward show. (Conforming in this case to the inner workings and intention of the heart.)   67 *daws* small crowlike birds, proverbially stupid and avaricious.   *I am not what I am* i.e., I am not one who wears his heart on his sleeve   68 *full* swelling.   *thick-lips* (Elizabethans often applied the term "Moor" to blacks.)   *owe* own   69 *carry 't thus* carry this off   72–73 *though . . . flies* though he seems prosperous and happy now, vex him with misery   73 *Though . . . be joy* although he seems fortunate and happy. (Repeats the idea of line 72.)

Yet throw such changes of vexation° on 't
As it may° lose some color.°   75
Roderigo: Here is her father's house. I'll call aloud.
Iago: Do, with like timorous° accent and dire yell
As when, by night and negligence,° the fire
Is spied in populous cities.
Roderigo: What ho, Brabantio! Signor Brabantio, ho!   80
Iago: Awake! What ho, Brabantio! Thieves, thieves, thieves!
Look to your house, your daughter, and your bags!
Thieves, thieves!

Brabantio [enters] above [at a window].°

Brabantio: What is the reason of this terrible summons?
What is the matter° there?   85
Roderigo: Signor, is all your family within?
Iago: Are your doors locked?
Brabantio: Why, wherefore ask you this?
Iago: Zounds,° sir, you're robbed. For shame, put on your gown!
Your heart is burst; you have lost half your soul.
Even now, now, very now, an old black ram   90
Is tupping° your white ewe. Arise, arise!
Awake the snorting° citizens with the bell,
Or else the devil° will make a grandsire of you.
Arise, I say!
Brabantio: What, have you lost your wits?
Roderigo: Most reverend signor, do you know my voice?   95
Brabantio: Not I. What are you?
Roderigo: My name is Roderigo.
Brabantio: The worser welcome.
I have charged thee not to haunt about my doors.
In honest plainness thou hast heard me say   100
My daughter is not for thee; and now, in madness,
Being full of supper and distempering° drafts,
Upon malicious bravery° dost thou come
To start° my quiet.
Roderigo: Sir, sir, sir—
Brabantio: But thou must needs be sure   105
My spirits and my place° have in° their power
To make this bitter to thee.
Roderigo: Patience, good sir.
Brabantio: What tell'st thou me of robbing? This is Venice;

---

74 *changes of vexation* vexing changes   75 *As it may* that may cause it to.   *some color* some of its fresh gloss
77 *timorous* frightening   78 *and negligence* i.e., by negligence   83 s.d. *at a window* (This stage direction,
from the Quarto, probably calls for an appearance on the gallery above and rearstage.)   85 *the matter* your
business   88 *Zounds* by His (Christ's) wounds   91 *tupping* covering, copulating with. (Said of sheep.)
92 *snorting* snoring   93 *the devil* (The devil was conventionally pictured as black.)   102 *distempering*
intoxicating   103 *Upon malicious bravery* with hostile intent to defy me   104 *start* startle, disrupt   106
My spirits and my place my temperament and my authority of office.   *have in* have it in

My house is not a grange.°

Roderigo: Most grave Brabantio,
In simple° and pure soul I come to you.   110

Iago: Zounds, sir, you are one of those that will not serve God if the devil bid you.
   Because we come to do you service and you think we are ruffians, you'll have your
   daughter covered with a Barbary° horse; you'll have your nephews° neigh to you;
   you'll have coursers° for cousins° and jennets° for germans.°

Brabantio: What profane wretch art thou?   115

Iago: I am one, sir, that comes to tell you your daughter and the Moor are now
   making the beast with two backs.

Brabantio: Thou art a villain.

Iago: You are—a senator.°

Brabantio: This thou shalt answer.° I know thee, Roderigo.

Roderigo: Sir, I will answer anything. But I beseech you,   120
   If't be your pleasure and most wise° consent—
   As partly I find it is—that your fair daughter,
   At this odd-even° and dull watch o' the night,
   Transported with° no worse nor better guard
   But with a knave° of common hire, a gondolier,   125
   To the gross clasps of a lascivious Moor—
   If this be known to you and your allowance°
   We then have done you bold and saucy° wrongs.
   But if you know not this, my manners tell me
   We have your wrong rebuke. Do not believe   130
   That, from° the sense of all civility,°
   I thus would play and trifle with your reverence.°
   Your daughter, if you have not given her leave,
   I say again, hath made a gross revolt,
   Tying her duty, beauty, wit,° and fortunes   135
   In an extravagant° and wheeling° stranger°
   Of here and everywhere. Straight° satisfy yourself.
   If she be in her chamber or your house,
   Let loose on me the justice of the state
   For thus deluding you.

Brabantio: Strike on the tinder,° ho!   140
   Give me a taper! Call up all my people!
   This accident° is not unlike my dream.
   Belief of it oppresses me already.
   Light, I say, light!   *Exit [above].*

---

109 *grange* isolated country house   110 *simple* sincere   113 *Barbary* from northern Africa (and hence
associated with Othello).   *nephews* i.e., grandsons   114 *coursers* powerful horses.   *cousins* kinsmen.
jennets small Spanish horses.   *germans* near relatives   118 *a senator* (Said with mock politeness, as though
the word itself were an insult.)   119 *answer* be held accountable for   121 *wise* well-informed   123 *odd-
even* between one day and the next, i.e., about midnight   124 *with* by   125 *But with a knave* than by a low
fellow, a servant   127 *allowance* permission   128 *saucy* insolent   131 *from* contrary to.   *civility* good
manners, decency   132 *your reverence* the respect due to you   135 *wit* intelligence   136 *extravagant*
expatriate, wandering far from home.   *wheeling* roving about, vagabond.   *stranger* foreigner   137 *Straight*
straightway   140 *tinder* charred linen ignited by a spark from flint and steel, used to light torches or *tapers*
(lines 141, 166)   142 *accident* occurrence, event

Roused from sleep, Desdemona's father, Brabantio, rushes to the street to search out his daughter (I, i, 160–180).

Iago:	Farewell, for I must leave you.
	It seems not meet° nor wholesome to my place° 145
	To be produced°—as, if I stay, I shall—
	Against the Moor. For I do know the state,
	However this may gall° him with some check,°
	Cannot with safety cast° him, for he's embarked°
	With such loud reason° to the Cyprus wars, 150
	Which even now stands in act,° that, for their souls,°
	Another of his fathom° they have none

---

145 *meet* fitting. *place* position (as ensign) 146 *produced* produced (as a witness) 148 *gall* rub; oppress. *check* rebuke 149 *cast* dismiss. *embarked* engaged 150 *loud reason* unanimous shout of confirmation (in the Senate) 151 *stands in act* are going on. *for their souls* to save themselves 152 *fathom* i.e., ability, depth of experience

To lead their business; in which regard,°
Though I do hate him as I do hell pains,
Yet for necessity of present life° 155
I must show out a flag and sign of love,
Which is indeed but sign. That you shall surely find him,
Lead to the Sagittary° the raisèd search,°
And there will I be with him. So farewell.

Exit.

Enter [below] Brabantio [in his nightgown°] with servants and torches.

Brabantio: It is too true an evil. Gone she is; 160
And what's to come of my despisèd time°
Is naught but bitterness. Now, Roderigo,
Where didst thou see her?—O unhappy girl!—
With the Moor, sayst thou?—Who would be a father!—
How didst thou know 'twas she?—O, she deceives me 165
Past thought!—What said she to you?—Get more tapers.
Raise all my kindred.—Are they married, think you?
Roderigo: Truly, I think they are.
Brabantio: O heaven! How got she out? O treason of the blood!
Fathers, from hence trust not your daughters' minds 170
By what you see them act. Is there not charms°
By which the property° of youth and maidhood
May be abused?° Have you not read, Roderigo,
Of some such thing?
Roderigo: Yes, sir, I have indeed.
Brabantio: Call up my brother.—O, would you had had her!— 175
Some one way, some another.—Do you know
Where we may apprehend her and the Moor?
Roderigo: I think I can discover° him, if you please
To get good guard and go along with me.
Brabantio: Pray you, lead on. At every house I'll call; 180
I may command° at most.—Get weapons, ho!
And raise some special officers of night.—
On, good Roderigo. I will deserve° your pains.

Exeunt.

SCENE II [VENICE. ANOTHER STREET, BEFORE OTHELLO'S LODGINGS.]

Enter Othello, Iago, attendants with torches.

Iago: Though in the trade of war I have slain men,
Yet do I hold it very stuff° o' the conscience

---

153 *in which regard* out of regard for which   155 *life* livelihood   158 *Sagittary* (An inn or house where Othello and Desdemona are staying, named for its sign of Sagittarius, or Centaur.)   *raisèd search* search party roused out of sleep   159 s.d. *nightgown* dressing gown. (This costuming is specified in the Quarto text.)   161 *time* i.e., remainder of life   171 *charms* spells   172 *property* special quality, nature   173 *abused* deceived   178 *discover* reveal, uncover   181 *command* demand assistance   183 *deserve* show gratitude for   2 *very stuff* essence, basic material (continuing the metaphor of *trade* from line 1)

To do no contrived° murder. I lack iniquity
    Sometimes to do me service. Nine or ten times
    I had thought t' have yerked° him° here under the ribs.   5
Othello: 'Tis better as it is.
Iago: Nay, but he prated,
    And spoke such scurvy and provoking terms
    Against your honor
    That, with the little godliness I have,
    I did full hard forbear him.° But, I pray you, sir,   10
    Are you fast married? Be assured of this,
    That the magnifico° is much beloved,
    And hath in his effect° a voice potential°
    As double as the Duke's. He will divorce you,
    Or put upon you what restraint or grievance   15
    The law, with all his might to enforce it on,
    Will give him cable.°
Othello: Let him do his spite.
    My services which I have done the seigniory°
    Shall out-tongue his complaints. 'Tis yet to know°—
    Which, when I know that boasting is an honor,   20
    I shall promulgate—I fetch my life and being
    From men of royal siege,° and my demerits°
    May speak unbonneted° to as proud a fortune
    As this that I have reached. For know, Iago,
    But that I love the gentle Desdemona,   25
    I would not my unhousèd° free condition
    Put into circumscription and confine°
    For the sea's worth.° But look, what lights come yond?

    Enter Cassio [and certain officers°] with torches.

Iago: Those are the raisèd father and his friends.
    You were best go in.
Othello: Not I. I must be found.   30
    My parts, my title, and my perfect soul°
    Shall manifest me rightly. Is it they?
Iago: By Janus,° I think no.
Othello: The servants of the Duke? And my lieutenant?
    The goodness of the night upon you, friends!   35
    What is the news?

---

3 *contrived* premeditated   5 *yerked* stabbed. *him* i.e., Roderigo   10 *I . . . him* I restrained myself with great difficulty from assaulting him   12 *magnifico* Venetian grandee, i.e., Brabantio   13 *in his effect* at his command. *potential* powerful   17 *cable* i.e., scope   18 *seigniory* Venetian government   19 *yet to know* not yet widely known   22 *siege* i.e., rank. (Literally, a seat used by a person of distinction.) *demerits* deserts   23 *unbonneted* without removing the hat, i.e., on equal terms (?) (Or "with hat off," "in all due modesty.")   26 *unhousèd* unconfined, undomesticated   27 *circumscription and confine* restriction and confinement   28 *the sea's worth* all the riches at the bottom of the sea. s.d. *officers* (The Quarto text calls for "Cassio with lights, officers with torches.")   31 *My . . . soul* my natural gifts, my position or reputation, and my unflawed conscience   33 *Janus* Roman two-faced god of beginnings

Cassio:	The Duke does greet you, General,

    And he requires your haste-post-haste appearance
    Even on the instant.

Othello:	What is the matter,° think you?

Cassio: Something from Cyprus, as I may divine.°
    It is a business of some heat.° The galleys   40
    Have sent a dozen sequent° messengers
    This very night at one another's heels,
    And many of the consuls,° raised and met,
    Are at the Duke's already. You have been hotly called for;
    When, being not at your lodging to be found,   45
    The Senate hath sent about° three several° quests
    To search you out.

Othello:	'Tis well I am found by you.

    I will but spend a word here in the house
    And go with you.   *[Exit.]*

Cassio:	Ancient, what makes° he here?

Iago: Faith, he tonight hath boarded° a land carrack.°   50
    If it prove lawful prize,° he's made forever.
Cassio: I do not understand.

Iago:	He's married.
Cassio:	To who?

    [Enter Othello.]

Iago: Marry,° to—Come, Captain, will you go?
Othello: Have with you.°
Cassio: Here comes another troop to seek for you.   55

    Enter Brabantio, Roderigo, with officers and torches.°

Iago: It is Brabantio. General, be advised.°
    He comes to bad intent.

Othello:	Holla! Stand there!

Roderigo: Signor, it is the Moor.

Brabantio:	Down with him, thief!

    [They draw on both sides.]

Iago: You, Roderigo! Come, sir, I am for you.
Othello: Keep up° your bright swords, for the dew will rust them.   60
    Good signor, you shall more command with years
    Than with your weapons.

---

38 *matter* business   39 *divine* guess   40 *heat* urgency   41 *sequent* successive   43 *consuls* senators
46 *about* all over the city.   *several* separate   49 *makes* does   50 *boarded* gone aboard and seized as an act
of piracy (with sexual suggestion).   *carrack* large merchant ship   51 *prize* booty   53 *Marry* (An oath,
originally "by the Virgin Mary"; here used with wordplay on *marry.*)   54 *Have with you* i.e., let's go
55 s.d. *officers and torches* (The Quarto text calls for "others with lights and weapons.")   56 *be advised* be
on your guard   60 *Keep up* keep in the sheath

Brabantio: O thou foul thief, where hast thou stowed my daughter?
　　　Damned as thou art, thou hast enchanted her!
　　　For I'll refer me° to all things of sense,°　　　　　　　　　65
　　　If she in chains of magic were not bound
　　　Whether a maid so tender, fair, and happy,
　　　So opposite to marriage that she shunned
　　　The wealthy curlèd darlings of our nation,
　　　Would ever have, t' incur a general mock,　　　　　　　　70
　　　Run from her guardage° to the sooty bosom
　　　Of such a thing as thou—to fear, not to delight.
　　　Judge me the world if 'tis not gross in sense°
　　　That thou hast practiced on her with foul charms,
　　　Abused her delicate youth with drugs or minerals°　　　　75
　　　That weaken motion.° I'll have 't disputed on;°
　　　'Tis probable and palpable to thinking.
　　　I therefore apprehend and do attach° thee
　　　For an abuser of the world, a practicer
　　　Of arts inhibited° and out of warrant.°—　　　　　　　　80
　　　Lay hold upon him! If he do resist,
　　　Subdue him at his peril.
Othello:　　　　　　　　Hold your hands,
　　　Both you of my inclining° and the rest.
　　　Were it my cue to fight, I should have known it
　　　Without a prompter.—Whither will you that I go　　　　85
　　　To answer this your charge?
Brabantio: To prison, till fit time
　　　Of law and course of direct session°
　　　Call thee to answer.
Othello:　　　　　　　What if I do obey?
　　　How may the Duke be therewith satisfied,　　　　　　　90
　　　Whose messengers are here about my side
　　　Upon some present business of the state
　　　To bring me to him?
Officer:　　　　　　　'Tis true, most worthy signor.
　　　The Duke's in council, and your noble self,
　　　I am sure, is sent for.
Brabantio:　　　　　　How? The Duke in council?　　　95
　　　In this time of the night? Bring him away.°
　　　Mine's not an idle° cause. The Duke himself,
　　　Or any of my brothers of the state,
　　　Cannot but feel this wrong as 'twere their own;

---

65 *refer me* submit my case.　*things of sense* commonsense understandings, or, creatures possessing common sense　71 *her guardage* my guardianship of her　73 *gross in sense* obvious　75 *minerals* i.e., poisons　76 *weaken motion* impair the vital faculties.　*disputed on* argued in court by professional counsel, debated by experts　78 *attach* arrest　80 *arts inhibited* prohibited arts, black magic.　*out of warrant* illegal　83 *inclining* following, party　88 *course of direct session* regular or specially convened legal proceedings　96 *away* right along　97 *idle* trifling

For if such actions may have passage free,°   100
Bondslaves and pagans shall our statesmen be.

Exeunt.

SCENE III [VENICE. A COUNCIL CHAMBER.]

*Enter Duke [and] Senators [and sit at a table, with lights], and Officers.° [The Duke
and Senators are reading dispatches.]*

Duke: There is no composition° in these news
    That gives them credit.
First Senator: Indeed, they are disproportioned.°
    My letters say a hundred and seven galleys.
Duke: And mine, a hundred forty.
Second Senator: And mine, two hundred.   5
    But though they jump° not on a just° account—
    As in these cases, where the aim° reports
    'Tis oft with difference—yet do they all confirm
    A Turkish fleet, and bearing up to Cyprus.
Duke: Nay, it is possible enough to judgment.   10
    I do not so secure me in the error
    But the main article I do approve°
    In fearful sense.
Sailor (within):   What ho, what ho, what ho!

    Enter Sailor.

Officer: A messenger from the galleys.
Duke: Now, what's the business?   15
Sailor: The Turkish preparation° makes for Rhodes.
    So was I bid report here to the state
    By Signor Angelo.
Duke: How say you by° this change?
First Senator: This cannot be
    By no assay° of reason. 'Tis a pageant°   20
    To keep us in false gaze.° When we consider
    Th' importancy of Cyprus to the Turk,
    And let ourselves again but understand
    That, as it more concerns the Turk than Rhodes,
    So may he with more facile question bear it,°   25
    For that° it stands not in such warlike brace,°
    But altogether lacks th' abilities°

---

100 *have passage free* are allowed to go unchecked   s.d. *Enter . . . Officers* (The Quarto text calls for the
Duke and senators to "sit at a table with lights and attendants.")   1 *composition* consistency   3 *disproportioned*
inconsistent   6 *jump* agree.   *just* exact   7 *the aim* conjecture   11–12 *I do not . . . approve* I do not take
such (false) comfort in the discrepancies that I fail to perceive the main point, i.e., that the Turkish fleet is
threatening   16 *preparation* fleet prepared for battle   19 *by* about   20 *assay* test.   *pageant* mere show
21 *in false gaze* looking the wrong way   25 *So may . . . it* so also he (the Turk) can more easily capture it
(Cyprus)   26 *For that* since.   *brace* state of defense   27 *abilities* means of self-defense

That Rhodes is dressed in°—if we make thought of this,
We must not think the Turk is so unskillful°
To leave that latest° which concerns him first,   30
Neglecting an attempt of ease and gain
To wake° and wage° a danger profitless.
Duke: Nay, in all confidence, he's not for Rhodes.
Officer: Here is more news.

    Enter a Messenger.

Messenger: The Ottomites, reverend and gracious,   35
    Steering with due course toward the isle of Rhodes,
    Have there injointed them° with an after° fleet.
First Senator: Ay, so I thought. How many, as you guess?
Messenger: Of thirty sail; and now they do restem
    Their backward course,° bearing with frank appearance°   40
    Their purposes toward Cyprus. Signor Montano,
    Your trusty and most valiant servitor,°
    With his free duty° recommends° you thus,
    And prays you to believe him.
Duke: 'Tis certain then for Cyprus.   45
    Marcus Luccicos, is not he in town?
First Senator: He's now in Florence.
Duke: Write from us to him, post-post-haste. Dispatch.
First Senator: Here comes Brabantio and the valiant Moor.

    Enter Brabantio, Othello, Cassio, Iago, Roderigo, and officers.

Duke: Valiant Othello, we must straight° employ you   50
    Against the general enemy° Ottoman.
    [*To Brabantio.*] I did not see you; welcome, gentle° signor.
    We lacked your counsel and your help tonight.
Brabantio: So did I yours. Good Your Grace, pardon me;
    Neither my place° nor aught I heard of business   55
    Hath raised me from my bed, nor doth the general care
    Take hold on me, for my particular° grief
    Is of so floodgate° and o'erbearing nature
    That it engluts° and swallows other sorrows
    And it is still itself.°
Duke: Why, what's the matter?   60
Brabantio: My daughter! O, my daughter!
Duke and Senators: Dead?
Brabantio: Ay, to me.
    She is abused,° stol'n from me, and corrupted

---

28 *dressed in* equipped with 29 *unskillful* deficient in judgment 30 *latest* last 32 *wake* stir up. *wage*
risk 37 *injointed them* joined themselves. *after* second, following 39–40 *restem . . . course* retrace their
original course 40 *frank appearance* undisguised intent 42 *servitor* officer under your command 43 *free
duty* freely given and loyal service. *recommends* commends himself and reports to 50 *straight* straightway 51 *general enemy* universal enemy to all Christendom 52 *gentle* noble 55 *place* official position
57 *particular* personal 58 *floodgate* i.e., overwhelming (as when floodgates are opened) 59 *engluts* engulfs
60 *is still itself* remains undiminished 62 *abused* deceived

Othello answers Brabantio's charges before the Duke (I, iii, 78–172).

By spells and medicines bought of mountebanks;
For nature so preposterously to err,
Being not deficient,° blind, or lame of sense,°   65
Sans° witchcraft could not.
Duke: Whoe'er he be that in this foul proceeding
Hath thus beguiled your daughter of herself,
And you of her, the bloody book of law
You shall yourself read in the bitter letter   70
After your own sense°—yea, though our proper° son
Stood in your action.°
Brabantio: Humbly I thank Your Grace.
Here is the man, this Moor, whom now it seems
Your special mandate for the state affairs
Hath hither brought.
All: We are very sorry for 't.   75
Duke [*to Othello*]: What, in your own part, can you say to this?
Brabantio: Nothing, but this is so.
Othello: Most potent, grave, and reverend signors,
My very noble and approved° good masters:
That I have ta'en away this old man's daughter,   80

65 *deficient* defective.   *lame of sense* deficient in sensory perception   66 *Sans* without   71 *After . . . sense*
according to your own interpretation.   *our proper* my own   72 *Stood . . . action* were under your accusation   79 *approved* proved, esteemed

It is most true; true, I have married her.
The very head and front° of my offending
Hath this extent, no more. Rude° am I in my speech,
And little blessed with the soft phrase of peace;
For since these arms of mine had seven years' pith,°   85
Till now some nine moons wasted,° they have used
Their dearest° action in the tented field;
And little of this great world can I speak
More than pertains to feats of broils and battle,
And therefore little shall I grace my cause   90
In speaking for myself. Yet, by your gracious patience,
I will a round° unvarnished tale deliver
Of my whole course of love—what drugs, what charms,
What conjuration, and what mighty magic,
For such proceeding I am charged withal,°   95
I won his daughter.

Brabantio: A maiden never bold;
Of spirit so still and quiet that her motion
Blushed at herself;° and she, in spite of nature,
Of years,° of country, credit,° everything,
To fall in love with what she feared to look on!   100
It is a judgment maimed and most imperfect
That will confess° perfection so could err
Against all rules of nature, and must be driven
To find out practices° of cunning hell
Why this should be. I therefore vouch° again   105
That with some mixtures powerful o'er the blood,°
Or with some dram conjured to this effect,°
He wrought upon her.

Duke: To vouch this is no proof,
Without more wider° and more overt test°
Than these thin habits° and poor likelihoods°   110
Of modern seeming° do prefer° against him.

First Senator: But Othello, speak.
Did you by indirect and forcèd courses°
Subdue and poison this young maid's affections?
Or came it by request and such fair question°   115
As soul to soul affordeth?

Othello: I do beseech you,
Send for the lady to the Sagittary

---

82 *head and front* height and breadth, entire extent   83 *Rude* unpolished   85 *since . . . pith* i.e., since I was seven. *pith* strength, vigor   86 *Till . . . wasted* until some nine months ago (since when Othello has evidently not been on active duty, but in Venice)   87 *dearest* most valuable   92 *round* plain   95 *withal* with 97–98 *her . . . herself* i.e., she blushed easily at herself. (*Motion* can suggest the impulse of the soul or of the emotions, or physical movement.)   99 *years* i.e., difference in age.   *credit* virtuous reputation   102 *confess* concede (that)   104 *practices* plots   105 *vouch* assert   106 *blood* passions   107 *dram . . . effect* dose made by magical spells to have this effect   109 *more wider* fuller.   *test* testimony   110 *habits* garments, i.e., appearances.   *poor likelihoods* weak inferences   111 *modern seeming* commonplace assumption.   *prefer* bring forth   113 *forcèd courses* means used against her will   115 *question* conversation

And let her speak of me before her father.
If you do find me foul in her report,
The trust, the office I do hold of you   120
Not only take away, but let your sentence
Even fall upon my life.
Duke: Fetch Desdemona hither.
Othello: Ancient, conduct them. You best know the place.

[*Exeunt Iago and attendants.*]

And, till she come, as truly as to heaven
I do confess the vices of my blood,°   125
So justly° to your grave ears I'll present
How I did thrive in this fair lady's love,
And she in mine.
Duke: Say it, Othello.
Othello: Her father loved me, oft invited me,   130
Still° questioned me the story of my life
From year to year—the battles, sieges, fortunes
That I have passed.
I ran it through, even from my boyish days
To th' very moment that he bade me tell it,   135
Wherein I spoke of most disastrous chances,
Of moving accidents° by flood and field,
Of hairbreadth scapes i' th' imminent deadly breach,°
Of being taken by the insolent foe
And sold to slavery, of my redemption thence,   140
And portance° in my travels' history,
Wherein of antres° vast and deserts idle,°
Rough quarries,° rocks, and hills whose heads touch heaven,
It was my hint° to speak—such was my process—
And of the Cannibals that each other eat,   145
The Anthropophagi,° and men whose heads
Do grow beneath their shoulders. These things to hear
Would Desdemona seriously incline;
But still the house affairs would draw her thence,
Which ever as she could with haste dispatch   150
She'd come again, and with a greedy ear
Devour up my discourse. Which I, observing,
Took once a pliant° hour, and found good means
To draw from her a prayer of earnest heart
That I would all my pilgrimage dilate,°   155
Whereof by parcels° she had something heard,

125 *blood* passions, human nature   126 *justly* truthfully, accurately   131 *Still* continually   137 *moving accident* stirring happenings   138 *imminent . . . breach* death-threatening gaps made in a fortification   141 *portance* conduct   142 *antres* caverns.   *idle* barren, desolate   143 *Rough quarries* rugged rock formations   144 *hint* occasion, opportunity   146 *Anthropophagi* man-eaters. (A term from Pliny's *Natural History.*)   153 *pliant* well-suiting   155 *dilate* relate in detail   156 *by parcels* piecemeal

But not intentively.° I did consent,
And often did beguile her of her tears,
When I did speak of some distressful stroke
That my youth suffered. My story being done,   160
She gave me for my pains a world of sighs.
She swore, in faith, 'twas strange, 'twas passing° strange,
'Twas pitiful, 'twas wondrous pitiful.
She wished she had not heard it, yet she wished
That heaven had made her° such a man. She thanked me,   165
And bade me, if I had a friend that loved her,
I should but teach him how to tell my story,
And that would woo her. Upon this hint° I spake.
She loved me for the dangers I had passed,
And I loved her that she did pity them.   170
This only is the witchcraft I have used.
Here comes the lady. Let her witness it.

Enter Desdemona, Iago, [and] attendants.

Duke: I think this tale would win my daughter too.
    Good Brabantio,
    Take up this mangled matter at the best.°   175
    Men do their broken weapons rather use
    Than their bare hands.
Brabantio: I pray you, hear her speak.
    If she confess that she was half the wooer,
    Destruction on my head if my bad blame
    Light on the man!—Come hither, gentle mistress.   180
    Do you perceive in all this noble company
    Where most you owe obedience?
Desdemona: My noble Father,
    I do perceive here a divided duty.
    To you I am bound for life and education;°
    My life and education both do learn° me   185
    How to respect you. You are the lord of duty;°
    I am hitherto your daughter. But here's my husband,
    And so much duty as my mother showed
    To you, preferring you before her father,
    So much I challenge° that I may profess   190
    Due to the Moor my lord.
Brabantio: God be with you! I have done.
    Please it Your Grace, on to the state affairs.
    I had rather to adopt a child than get° it.
    Come hither, Moor.   *[He joins the hands of Othello and Desdemona.]*   195

---

157 *intentively* with full attention, continuously   162 *passing* exceedingly   165 *made her* created her to be 168 *hint* opportunity. (Othello does not mean that she was dropping hints.)   175 *Take . . . best* make the best of a bad bargain   184 *education* upbringing   185 *learn* teach   186 *of duty* to whom duty is due   190 *challenge* claim   194 *get* beget

I here do give thee that with all my heart°
Which, but thou hast already, with all my heart°
I would keep from thee.—For your sake,° jewel,
I am glad at soul I have no other child,
For thy escape° would teach me tyranny,   200
To hang clogs° on them.—I have done, my lord.
Duke: Let me speak like yourself,° and lay a sentence°
   Which, as a grece° or step, may help these lovers
   Into your favor.
   When remedies° are past, the griefs are ended   205
   By seeing the worst, which late on hopes depended.°
   To mourn a mischief° that is past and gone
   Is the next° way to draw new mischief on.
   What° cannot be preserved when fortune takes,
   Patience her injury a mockery makes.°   210
   The robbed that smiles steals something from the thief;
   He robs himself that spends a bootless grief.°
Brabantio: So let the Turk of Cyprus us beguile,
   We lose it not, so long as we can smile.
   He bears the sentence well that nothing bears   215
   But the free comfort which from thence he hears,
   But he bears both the sentence and the sorrow
   That, to pay grief, must of poor patience borrow.°
   These sentences, to sugar or to gall,
   Being strong on both sides, are equivocal.°   220
   But words are words. I never yet did hear
   That the bruised heart was piercèd through the ear.°
   I humbly beseech you, proceed to th' affairs of state.
Duke: The Turk with a most mighty preparation makes for Cyprus. Othello, the
   fortitude° of the place is best known to you; and though we have there a   225
   substitute° of most allowed° sufficiency, yet opinion, a sovereign mistress
   of effects, throws a more safer voice on you.° You must therefore be content
   to slubber° the gloss of your new fortunes with this more stubborn° and boisterous expedition.
Othello: The tyrant custom, most grave senators,   230
   Hath made the flinty and steel couch of war

---

196 *with all my heart* wherein my whole affection has been engaged   197 *with all my heart* willingly, gladly
198 *For your sake* on your account   200 *escape* elopement   201 *clogs* (Literally, blocks of wood fastened to
the legs of criminals or convicts to inhibit escape.)   202 *like yourself* i.e., as you would, in your proper temper.
lay a sentence apply a maxim   203 *grece* step   205 *remedies* hopes of remedy   206 *which . . . depended*
which griefs were sustained until recently by hopeful anticipation   207 *mischief* misfortune, injury   208
next nearest   209 *What* whatever   210 *Patience . . . makes* patience laughs at the injury inflicted by fortune (and thus eases the pain)   212 *spends a bootless grief* indulges in unavailing grief   215–218 *He bears . . .
borrow* a person well bears out your maxim who can enjoy its platitudinous comfort, free of all genuine
sorrow, but anyone whose grief bankrupts his poor patience is left with your saying and his sorrow, too.
(*Bears the sentence* also plays on the meaning, "receives judicial sentence.")   219–220 *These . . . equivocal*
these fine maxims are equivocal, either sweet or bitter in their application   222 *piercèd . . . ear* i.e., surgi-
cally lanced and cured by mere words of advice   225 *fortitude* strength   226 *substitute* deputy.   *allowed*
acknowledged   226–227 *opinion . . . on you* general opinion, an important determiner of affairs, chooses
you as the best man   228 *slubber* soil, sully.   *stubborn* harsh, rough

My thrice-driven° bed of down. I do agnize°
A natural and prompt alacrity
I find in hardness,° and do undertake
These present wars against the Ottomites.   235
Most humbly therefore bending to your state,°
I crave fit disposition for my wife,
Due reference of place and exhibition,°
With such accommodation° and besort°
As levels° with her breeding.°   240
Duke: Why, at her father's.
Brabantio: I will not have it so.
Othello: Nor I.
Desdemona: Nor I. I would not there reside,
To put my father in impatient thoughts
By being in his eye. Most gracious Duke,
To my unfolding° lend your prosperous° ear,   245
And let me find a charter° in your voice,
T' assist my simpleness.
Duke: What would you, Desdemona?
Desdemona: That I did love the Moor to live with him,
My downright violence and storm of fortunes°   250
May trumpet to the world. My heart's subdued
Even to the very quality of my lord.°
I saw Othello's visage in his mind,
And to his honors and his valiant parts°
Did I my soul and fortunes consecrate.   255
So that, dear lords, if I be left behind
A moth° of peace, and he go to the war,
The rites° for why I love him are bereft me,
And I a heavy interim shall support
By his dear° absence. Let me go with him.   260
Othello: Let her have your voice.°
Vouch with me, heaven, I therefore beg it not
To please the palate of my appetite,
Nor to comply with heat°—the young affects°
In me defunct—and proper° satisfaction,   265
But to be free° and bounteous to her mind.
And heaven defend° your good souls that you think°

---

232 *thrice-driven* thrice sifted, winnowed. *agnize* know in myself, acknowledge 234 *hardness* hardship 236 *bending . . . state* bowing or kneeling to your authority 238 *reference . . . exhibition* provision of appropriate place to live and allowance of money 239 *accommodation* suitable provision. *besort* attendance 240 *levels* equals, suits. *breeding* social position, upbringing 245 *unfolding* explanation, proposal. *prosperous* propitious 246 *charter* privilege, authorization 250 *My . . . fortunes* my plain and total breach of social custom, taking my future by storm and disrupting my whole life 251–252 *My heart's . . . lord* my heart is brought wholly into accord with Othello's virtues; I love him for his virtues 254 *parts* qualities 257 *moth* i.e., one who consumes merely 258 *rites* rites of love (with a suggestion, too, of "rights," sharing) 260 *dear* (1) heartfelt (2) costly 261 *voice* consent 264 *heat* sexual passion. *young affects* passions of youth, desires 265 *proper* personal 266 *free* generous 267 *defend* forbid. *think* should think

Desdemona declares her loyalty to her husband Othello (I, iii, 182–301).

I will your serious and great business scant
When she is with me. No, when light-winged toys
Of feathered Cupid seel° with wanton dullness
My speculative and officed instruments,°   270
That° my disports° corrupt and taint° my business,
Let huswives make a skillet of my helm,
And all indign° and base adversities
Make head° against my estimation!°   275
Duke: Be it as you shall privately determine,
   Either for her stay or going. Th' affair cries haste,
   And speed must answer it.
A Senator: You must away tonight.
Desdemona: Tonight, my lord?
Duke: This night.
Othello: With all my heart.

270 *seel* i.e., make blind (as in falconry, by sewing up the eyes of the hawk during training) 271
speculative . . . instruments eyes and other faculties used in the performance of duty 272 *That* so that.
disports sexual pastimes. *taint* impair 274 *indign* unworthy, shameful 275 *Make head* raise an army.
estimation reputation

Duke: At nine i' the morning here we'll meet again.   280
    Othello, leave some officer behind,
    And he shall our commission bring to you,
    With such things else of quality and respect°
    As doth import° you.
Othello: So please Your Grace, my ancient;
    A man he is of honesty and trust.   285
    To his conveyance I assign my wife,
    With what else needful Your Good Grace shall think
    To be sent after me.
Duke: Let it be so.
    Good night to everyone. [*To Brabantio.*] And, noble signor,
    If virtue no delighted° beauty lack,   290
    Your son-in-law is far more fair than black.
First Senator: Adieu, brave Moor. Use Desdemona well.
Brabantio: Look to her, Moor, if thou hast eyes to see.
    She has deceived her father, and may thee.

                    Exeunt [Duke, Brabantio, Cassio, Senators, and officers].

Othello: My life upon her faith! Honest Iago,   295
    My Desdemona must I leave to thee.
    I prithee, let thy wife attend on her,
    And bring them after in the best advantage.°
    Come, Desdemona. I have but an hour
    Of love, of worldly matters and direction,°   300
    To spend with thee. We must obey the time.°

                                        Exit [with Desdemona].

Roderigo: Iago—
Iago: What sayst thou, noble heart?
Roderigo: What will I do, think'st thou?
Iago: Why, go to bed and sleep.   305
Roderigo: I will incontinently° drown myself.
Iago: If thou dost, I shall never love thee after. Why, thou silly gentleman?
Roderigo: It is silliness to live when to live is torment; and then have we a prescrip-
    tion° to die when death is our physician.
Iago: O villainous!° I have looked upon the world for four times seven years, and,   310
    since I could distinguish betwixt a benefit and an injury, I never found man that
    knew how to love himself. Ere I would say I would drown myself for the love of a
    guinea hen,° I would change my humanity with a baboon.
Roderigo: What should I do? I confess it is my shame to be so fond,° but it is not
    in my virtue° to amend it.   315

---

283 *of quality and respect* of importance and relevance 284 *import* concern 290 *delighted* capable of delighting 298 *in . . . advantage* at the most favorable opportunity 300 *direction* instructions 301 *the time*
the urgency of the present crisis 306 *incontinently* immediately, without self-restraint 308–309
prescription (1) right based on long-established custom (2) doctor's prescription 310 *villainous* i.e., what
perfect nonsense 313 *guinea hen* (A slang term for a prostitute.) 314 *fond* infatuated 315 *virtue*
strength, nature

Iago: Virtue? A fig!° 'Tis in ourselves that we are thus or thus. Our bodies are our gardens, to the which our wills are gardeners; so that if we will plant nettles or sow lettuce, set hyssop° and weed up thyme, supply it with one gender° of herbs or distract it with° many, either to have it sterile with idleness° or manured with industry—why, the power and corrigible authority° of this lies in our wills. If the 320 beam° of our lives had not one scale of reason to poise° another of sensuality, the blood° and baseness of our natures would conduct us to most preposterous conclusions. But we have reason to cool our raging motions,° our carnal stings, our unbitted° lusts, whereof I take this that you call love to be a sect or scion.°

Roderigo: It cannot be. 325

Iago: It is merely a lust of the blood and a permission of the will. Come, be a man. Drown thyself? Drown cats and blind puppies. I have professed me thy friend, and I confess me knit to thy deserving with cables of perdurable° toughness. I could never better stead° thee than now. Put money in thy purse. Follow thou the wars; defeat thy favor° with an usurped° beard. I say, put money in thy purse. 330 It cannot be long that Desdemona should continue her love to the Moor—put money in thy purse—nor he his to her. It was a violent commencement in her, and thou shalt see an answerable sequestration° —put but money in thy purse. These Moors are changeable in their wills°—fill thy purse with money. The food that to him now is as luscious as locusts° shall be to him shortly as bitter as 335 coloquintida.° She must change for youth; when she is sated with his body, she will find the error of her choice. She must have change, she must. Therefore put money in thy purse. If thou wilt needs damn thyself, do it a more delicate way than drowning. Make° all the money thou canst. If sanctimony° and a frail vow betwixt an erring° barbarian and a supersubtle Venetian be not too hard for my 340 wits and all the tribe of hell, thou shalt enjoy her. Therefore make money. A pox of drowning thyself! It is clean out of the way.° Seek thou rather to be hanged in compassing° thy joy than to be drowned and go without her.

Roderigo: Wilt thou be fast° to my hopes if I depend on the issue?°

Iago: Thou art sure of me. Go, make money. I have told thee often, and I retell thee 345 again and again, I hate the Moor. My cause is hearted;° thine hath no less reason. Let us be conjunctive° in our revenge against him. If thou canst cuckold him, thou dost thyself a pleasure, me a sport. There are many events in the womb of time which will be delivered. Traverse,° go, provide thy money. We will have more of this tomorrow. Adieu. 350

Roderigo: Where shall we meet i' the morning?

Iago: At my lodging.

---

316 *fig* (To give a fig is to thrust the thumb between the first and second fingers in a vulgar and insulting gesture.)   318 *hyssop* an herb of the mint family.   *gender* kind   319 *distract it with* divide it among.   *idleness* want of cultivation   320 *corrigible authority* power to correct   321 *beam* balance.   *poise* counterbalance   322 *blood* natural passions   323 *motions* appetites   324 *unbitted* unbridled, uncontrolled.   *sect or scion* cutting or offshoot   328 *perdurable* very durable   329 *stead* assist   330 *defeat thy favor* disguise your face.   *usurped* (The suggestion is that Roderigo is not man enough to have a beard of his own.)   333 *an answerable sequestration* a corresponding separation or estrangement   334 *wills* carnal appetites   335 *locusts* fruit of the carob tree (see Matthew 3:4), or perhaps honeysuckle.   336 *coloquintida* colocynth or bitter apple, a purgative   339 *Make* raise, collect.   *sanctimony* sacred ceremony   340 *erring* wandering, vagabond, unsteady   342 *clean . . . way* entirely unsuitable as a course of action   343 *compassing* encompassing, embracing   344 *fast* true.   *issue* (successful) outcome   346 *hearted* fixed in the heart, heartfelt   347 *conjunctive* united   349 *Traverse* (A military marching term.)

Roderigo: I'll be with thee betimes.°   [*He starts to leave.*]
Iago: Go to, farewell.—Do you hear, Roderigo?
Roderigo: What say you?   355
Iago: No more of drowning, do you hear?
Roderigo: I am changed.
Iago: Go to, farewell. Put money enough in your purse.
Roderigo: I'll sell all my land.   *Exit.*
Iago: Thus do I ever make my fool my purse;   360
    For I mine own gained knowledge should profane
    If I would time expend with such a snipe°
    But for my sport and profit. I hate the Moor;
    And it is thought abroad° that twixt my sheets
    He's done my office.° I know not if 't be true;   365
    But I, for mere suspicion in that kind,
    Will do as if for surety.° He holds me well;°
    The better shall my purpose work on him.
    Cassio's a proper° man. Let me see now:
    To get his place and to plume up° my will   370
    In double knavery—How, how?—Let's see:
    After some time, to abuse° Othello's ear
    That he° is too familiar with his wife.
    He hath a person and a smooth dispose°
    To be suspected, framed to make women false.   375
    The Moor is of a free° and open° nature,
    That thinks men honest that but seem to be so,
    And will as tenderly° be led by the nose
    As asses are.
    I have 't. It is engendered. Hell and night   380
    Must bring this monstrous birth to the world's light.

    [*Exit.*]

ACT II

SCENE I [A SEAPORT IN CYPRUS. AN OPEN PLACE NEAR THE QUAY.]

Enter Montano and two Gentlemen.

Montano: What from the cape can you discern at sea?
First Gentleman: Nothing at all. It is a high-wrought flood.°
    I cannot, twixt the heaven and the main,°
    Descry a sail.
Montano: Methinks the wind hath spoke aloud at land;   5
    A fuller blast ne'er shook our battlements.

---

353 *betimes* early   362 *snipe* woodcock, i.e., fool   364 *it is thought abroad* it is rumored   365 *my office* i.e., my sexual function as husband   367 *do . . . surety* act as if on certain knowledge. *holds me well* regards me favorably
369 *proper* handsome   370 *plume up* put a feather in the cap of, i.e., glorify, gratify   372 *abuse* deceive   373 *he* i.e., Cassio   374 *dispose* disposition   376 *free* frank, generous. *open* unsuspicious   378 *tenderly* readily 2 *high-wrought flood* very agitated sea   3 *main* ocean (also at line 41)

If it hath ruffianed° so upon the sea,
What ribs of oak, when mountains° melt on them,
Can hold the mortise?° What shall we hear of this?

Second Gentleman: A segregation° of the Turkish fleet.   10
For do but stand upon the foaming shore,
The chidden° billow seems to pelt the clouds;
The wind-shaked surge, with high and monstrous mane,°
Seems to cast water on the burning Bear°
And quench the guards of th' ever-fixèd pole.   15
I never did like molestation° view
On the enchafèd° flood.

Montano: If that° the Turkish fleet
Be not ensheltered and embayed,° they are drowned;
It is impossible to bear it out.°   20

Enter a [Third] Gentleman.

Third Gentleman: News, lads! Our wars are done.
The desperate tempest hath so banged the Turks
That their designment° halts.° A noble ship of Venice
Hath seen a grievous wreck° and sufferance°
On most part of their fleet.   25

Montano: How? Is this true?

Third Gentleman: The ship is here put in,
A Veronesa;° Michael Cassio,
Lieutenant to the warlike Moor Othello,
Is come on shore; the Moor himself at sea,   30
And is in full commission here for Cyprus.

Montano: I am glad on 't. 'Tis a worthy governor.

Third Gentleman: But this same Cassio, though he speak of comfort
Touching the Turkish loss, yet he looks sadly°
And prays the Moor be safe, for they were parted   35
With foul and violent tempest.

Montano: Pray heaven he be,
For I have served him, and the man commands
Like a full° soldier. Let's to the seaside, ho!
As well to see the vessel that's come in
As to throw out our eyes for brave Othello,   40
Even till we make the main and th' aerial blue°
An indistinct regard.°

---

7 *ruffianed* raged   8 *mountains* i.e., of water   9 *hold the mortise* hold their joints together. (A *mortise* is the socket hollowed out in fitting timbers.)   10 *segregation* dispersal   12 *chidden* i.e., rebuked, repelled (by the shore), and thus shot into the air   13 *monstrous mane* (The surf is like the mane of a wild beast.)   14 *the burning Bear* i.e., the constellation Ursa Minor or the Little Bear, which includes the polestar (and hence regarded as the *guards of th' ever-fixèd pole* in the next line; sometimes the term *guards* is applied to the two "pointers" of the Big Bear or Dipper, which may be intended here).   16 *like molestation* comparable disturbance   17 *enchafèd* angry   18 *If that* if   19 *embayed* sheltered by a bay   20 *bear it out* survive, weather the storm   23 *designment* design, enterprise. *halts* is lame   24 *wreck* shipwreck. *sufferance* damage, disaster   28 *Veronesa* i.e., fitted out in Verona for Venetian service, or possibly *Verennessa* (the Folio spelling), i.e., *verrinessa*, a cutter (from *verrinare*, "to cut through")   34 *sadly* gravely   38 *full* perfect   41 *the main . . . blue* the sea and the sky   42 *An indistinct regard* indistinguishable in our view

Third Gentleman:　　　　Come, let's do so,
　　For every minute is expectancy°
　　Of more arrivance.°

　Enter Cassio.

Cassio: Thanks, you the valiant of this warlike isle,　　　　45
　　That so approve° the Moor! O, let the heavens
　　Give him defense against the elements,
　　For I have lost him on a dangerous sea.
Montano: Is he well shipped?
Cassio: His bark is stoutly timbered, and his pilot　　　　50
　　Of very expert and approved allowance;°
　　Therefore my hopes, not surfeited to death,°
　　Stand in bold cure.°

　　[A cry] within:　　"A sail, a sail, a sail!"

Cassio: What noise?
A Gentleman: The town is empty. On the brow o' the sea°　　　55
　　Stand ranks of people, and they cry "A sail!"
Cassio: My hopes do shape him for° the governor.

　　[A shot within.]

Second Gentleman: They do discharge their shot of courtesy;°
　　Our friends at least.
Cassio:　　　　　　I pray you, sir, go forth,
　　And give us truth who 'tis that is arrived.　　　　60
Second Gentleman: I shall.　　　　　　　　　*Exit.*
Montano: But, good Lieutenant, is your general wived?
Cassio: Most fortunately. He hath achieved a maid
　　That paragons° description and wild fame,°
　　One that excels the quirks° of blazoning° pens,　　　　65
　　And in th' essential vesture of creation
　　Does tire the enginer.°

　Enter [Second] Gentleman.°

　　　　　　　　　How now? Who has put in?°
Second Gentleman: 'Tis one Iago, ancient to the General.
Cassio: He's had most favorable and happy speed.
　　Tempests themselves, high seas, and howling winds,　　　70
　　The guttered° rocks and congregated sands—

---

43 *is expectancy* gives expectation　44 *arrivance* arrival　46 *approve* admire, honor　51 *approved allowance* tested reputation　52 *surfeited to death* i.e., overextended, worn thin through repeated application or delayed fulfillment　53 *in bold cure* in strong hopes of fulfillment　55 *brow o' the sea* cliff-edge　57 *My . . . for* I hope it is　58 *discharge . . . courtesy* fire a salute in token of respect and courtesy　64 *paragons* surpasses. *wild fame* extravagant report　65 *quirks* witty conceits. *blazoning* setting forth as though in heraldic language　66–67 *in . . . enginer* in her real, God-given, beauty, (she) defeats any attempt to praise her. *enginer* engineer, i.e., poet, one who devises.　s.d. *[Second] Gentleman* (So identified in the Quarto text here and in lines 58, 61, 68, and 96; the Folio calls him a gentleman.)　67 *put in* i.e., to harbor　71 *guttered* jagged, trenched

Traitors ensteeped° to clog the guiltless keel—
As° having sense of beauty, do omit°
Their mortal° natures, letting go safely by
The divine Desdemona.
Montano: What is she?   75
Cassio: She that I spake of, our great captain's captain,
     Left in the conduct of the bold Iago,
     Whose footing° here anticipates our thoughts
     A sennight's° speed. Great Jove, Othello guard,
     And swell his sail with thine own powerful breath,   80
     That he may bless this bay with his tall° ship,
     Make love's quick pants in Desdemona's arms,
     Give renewed fire to our extincted spirits,
     And bring all Cyprus comfort!

     Enter Desdemona, Iago, Roderigo, and Emilia.

                              O, behold,
     The riches of the ship is come on shore!   85
     You men of Cyprus, let her have your knees.

     [The gentlemen make curtsy to Desdemona.]

     Hail to thee, lady! And the grace of heaven
     Before, behind thee, and on every hand
     Enwheel thee round!
Desdemona: I thank you, valiant Cassio.
     What tidings can you tell me of my lord?   90
Cassio: He is not yet arrived, nor know I aught
     But that he's well and will be shortly here.
Desdemona: O, but I fear—How lost you company?
Cassio: The great contention of the sea and skies
     Parted our fellowship.

     (*Within*)   "A sail, a sail!" [*A shot.*]

                              But hark. A sail!   95
Second Gentleman: They give their greeting to the citadel.
     This likewise is a friend.
Cassio: See for the news.

     [Exit Second Gentleman.]

     Good Ancient, you are welcome. [*Kissing Emilia.*] Welcome, mistress.
     Let it not gall your patience, good Iago,
     That I extend° my manners; 'tis my breeding°   100
     That gives me this bold show of courtesy.
Iago: Sir, would she give you so much of her lips
     As of her tongue she oft bestows on me,
     You would have enough.

72 *ensteeped* lying under water   73 *As* as if.   *omit* forbear to exercise   74 *mortal* deadly   78 *footing* landing
79 *sennight's* week's   81 *tall* splendid, gallant   100 *extend* give scope to.   *breeding* training in the
niceties of etiquette

Desdemona: Alas, she has no speech!° 105

Iago: In faith, too much.

I find it still,° when I have list° to sleep.

Marry, before your ladyship, I grant,

She puts her tongue a little in her heart

And chides with thinking.°

Emilia: You have little cause to say so. 110

Iago: Come on, come on. You are pictures out of doors,°

Bells° in your parlors, wildcats in your kitchens,°

Saints° in your injuries, devils being offended,

Players° in your huswifery,° and huswives° in your beds.

Desdemona: O, fie upon thee, slanderer! 115

Iago: Nay, it is true, or else I am a Turk.°

You rise to play, and go to bed to work.

Emilia: You shall not write my praise.

Iago: No, let me not.

Desdemona: What wouldst write of me, if thou shouldst praise me?

Iago: O gentle lady, do not put me to 't, 120

For I am nothing if not critical.°

Desdemona: Come on, essay.°—There's one gone to the harbor?

Iago: Ay, madam.

Desdemona: I am not merry, but I do beguile

The thing I am° by seeming otherwise. 125

Come, how wouldst thou praise me?

Iago: I am about it, but indeed my invention

Comes from my pate as birdlime° does from frieze°—

It plucks out brains and all. But my Muse labors,°

And thus she is delivered: 130

If she be fair and wise, fairness and wit,

The one's for use, the other useth it.°

Desdemona: Well praised! How if she be black° and witty?

Iago: If she be black, and thereto have a wit,

She'll find a white° that shall her blackness fit.° 135

Desdemona: Worse and worse.

Emilia: How if fair and foolish?

Iago: She never yet was foolish that was fair,

For even her folly° helped her to an heir.°

Desdemona: These are old fond° paradoxes to make fools laugh i' th' alehouse.

What miserable praise hast thou for her that's foul and foolish? 140

---

105 *she has no speech* i.e., she's not a chatterbox, as you allege   107 *still* always.   *list* desire   110 *with thinking* i.e., in her thoughts only   111 *pictures out of doors* i.e., silent and well-behaved in public   112 *Bells* i.e., jangling, noisy, and brazen.   *in your kitchens* i.e., in domestic affairs. (Ladies would not do the cooking.)   113 *Saints* martyrs   114 *Players* idlers, triflers, or deceivers.   *huswifery* housekeeping.   *huswives* hussies (i.e., women are "busy" in bed, or unduly thrifty in dispensing sexual favors)   116 *a Turk* an infidel, not to be believed   121 *critical* censorious   122 *essay* try   125 *The thing I am* i.e., my anxious self   128 *birdlime* sticky substance used to catch small birds.   *frieze* coarse woolen cloth   129 *labors* (1) exerts herself (2) prepares to deliver a child (with a following pun on *delivered* in line 130)   132 *The one's . . . it* i.e., her cleverness will make use of her beauty   133 *black* dark-complexioned, brunette   135 *a white* a fair person (with word-play on "wight," a person).   *fit* (with sexual suggestion of mating)   138 *folly* (with added meaning of "lechery, wantonness").   *to an heir* i.e., to bear a child   139 *fond* foolish

Iago: There's none so foul° and foolish thereunto,°
        But does foul° pranks which fair and wise ones do.
Desdemona: O heavy ignorance! Thou praisest the worst best. But what praise
        couldst thou bestow on a deserving woman indeed, one that, in the authority of
        her merit, did justly put on the vouch° of very malice itself?   145
Iago: She that was ever fair, and never proud,
        Had tongue at will, and yet was never loud,
        Never lacked gold and yet went never gay,°
        Fled from her wish, and yet said, "Now I may,"°
        She that being angered, her revenge being nigh,   150
        Bade her wrong stay° and her displeasure fly,
        She that in wisdom never was so frail
        To change the cod's head for the salmon's tail,°
        She that could think and ne'er disclose her mind,
        See suitors following and not look behind,   155
        She was a wight, if ever such wight were—
Desdemona: To do what?
Iago: To suckle fools° and chronicle small beer.°
Desdemona: O most lame and impotent conclusion! Do not learn of him, Emilia, though
        he be thy husband. How say you, Cassio? Is he not a most profane° and liberal°   160
        counselor?
Cassio: He speaks home,° madam. You may relish° him more in° the soldier than in
        the scholar.

        [Cassio and Desdemona stand together, conversing intimately.]

Iago [aside]:   He takes her by the palm. Ay, well said,° whisper. With as little a
        web as this will I ensnare as great a fly as Cassio. Ay, smile upon her, do; I will 165
        gyve° thee in thine own courtship.° You say true;° 'tis so, indeed. If such tricks as
        these strip you out of your lieutenantry, it had been better you had not kissed
        your three fingers so oft, which now again you are most apt to play the sir° in.
        Very good; well kissed! An excellent courtesy! 'Tis so, indeed. Yet again your
        fingers to your lips? Would they were clyster pipes° for your sake! [*Trumpet*   170
        within.] The Moor! I know his trumpet.
Cassio: 'Tis truly so.
Desdemona: Let's meet him and receive him.
Cassio: Lo, where he comes!

        Enter Othello and attendants.

Othello: O my fair warrior!
Desdemona: My dear Othello!   175

---

141 *foul* ugly.   *thereunto* in addition   142 *foul* sluttish   145 *put . . . vouch* compel the approval   148 *gay*
extravagantly clothed   149 *Fled . . . may* avoided temptation where the choice was hers   151 *Bade . . .
stay* i.e., resolved to put up with her injury patiently   153 *To . . . tail* i.e., to exchange a lackluster husband for a sexy lover (?) (*Cod's head* is slang for "penis," and *tail*, for "pudendum.")   158 *suckle fools*
breastfeed babies.   *chronicle small beer* i.e., keep petty household accounts, keep track of trivial matters
160 *profane* irreverent, ribald.   *liberal* licentious, free-spoken   162 *home* right to the target. (A term from
fencing.)   *relish* appreciate   *in* in the character of   164 *well said* well done   166 *gyve* fetter, shackle.
courtship courtesy, show of courtly manners.   *You say true* i.e., that's right, go ahead   168 *the sir* i.e., the
fine gentleman   170 *clyster pipes* tubes used for enemas and douches

Desdemona arrives in Cyprus and reunites with Othello as Cassio looks on (II, i, 175–208).

Othello: It gives me wonder great as my content
　　　To see you here before me. O my soul's joy,
　　　If after every tempest come such calms,
　　　May the winds blow till they have wakened death,
　　　And let the laboring bark climb hills of seas   180
　　　Olympus-high, and duck again as low
　　　As hell's from heaven! If it were now to die,
　　　'Twere now to be most happy, for I fear
　　　My soul hath her content so absolute
　　　That not another comfort like to this   185
　　　Succeeds in unknown fate.°
Desdemona:　　　　　　　　　　The heavens forbid
　　　But that our loves and comforts should increase
　　　Even as our days do grow!
Othello: Amen to that, sweet powers!
　　　I cannot speak enough of this content.   190
　　　It stops me here; it is too much of joy.
　　　And this, and this, the greatest discords be

　　　[*They kiss.*]°

　　　That e'er our hearts shall make!

186 *Succeeds . . . fate* i.e., can follow in the unknown future   192 s.d. *They kiss* (The direction is from the Quarto.)

Iago [aside]: O, you are well tuned now!
    But I'll set down° the pegs that make this music,   195
    As honest as I am.°
Othello: Come, let us to the castle.
    News, friends! Our wars are done, the Turks are drowned.
    How does my old acquaintance of this isle?—
    Honey, you shall be well desired° in Cyprus;   200
    I have found great love amongst them. O my sweet,
    I prattle out of fashion,° and I dote
    In mine own comforts.—I prithee, good Iago,
    Go to the bay and disembark my coffers.°
    Bring thou the master° to the citadel;   205
    He is a good one, and his worthiness
    Does challenge° much respect.—Come, Desdemona.—
    Once more, well met at Cyprus!

    Exeunt Othello and Desdemona [and all but Iago and Roderigo].

Iago [to an attendant]: Do thou meet me presently at the harbor. [*To Roderigo.*]
    Come hither. If thou be'st valiant—as, they say, base men° being in love have   210
    then a nobility in their natures more than is native to them—list° me. The Lieu-
    tenant tonight watches on the court of guard.° First, I must tell thee this: Desde-
    mona is directly in love with him.
Roderigo: With him? Why, 'tis not possible.
Iago: Lay thy finger thus,° and let thy soul be instructed. Mark me with what violence   215
    she first loved the Moor, but° for bragging and telling her fantastical lies. To love
    him still for prating? Let not thy discreet heart think it. Her eye must be fed; and
    what delight shall she have to look on the devil? When the blood is made dull
    with the act of sport,° there should be, again to inflame it and to give satiety
    a fresh appetite, loveliness in favor,° sympathy° in years, manners, and beauties—   220
    all which the Moor is defective in. Now, for want of these required conve-
    niences,° her delicate tenderness will find itself abused,° begin to heave the
    gorge,° disrelish and abhor the Moor. Very nature° will instruct her in it and com-
    pel her to some second choice. Now, sir, this granted—as it is a most pregnant° and
    unforced position—who stands so eminent in the degree of° this fortune as Cassio   225
    does? A knave very voluble,° no further conscionable° than in putting on the
    mere form of civil and humane° seeming for the better compassing of his salt°
    and most hidden loose affection.° Why, none, why, none. A slipper° and subtle
    knave, a finder out of occasions, that has an eye can stamp° and counterfeit

195 *set down* loosen (and hence untune the instrument)   196 *As . . . I am* for all my supposed honesty
200 *desired* welcomed   202 *out of fashion* irrelevantly, incoherently (?)   204 *coffers* chests, baggage   205
master ship's captain   207 *challenge* lay claim to, deserve   210 *base men* even lowly born men   211 *list* listen to   212 *court of guard* guardhouse. (Cassio is in charge of the watch.)   215 *thus* i.e., on your lips   216 *but*
only   219 *the act of sport* sex   220 *favor* appearance. *sympathy* correspondence, similarity
221–222 *required conveniences* things conducive to sexual compatibility   222 *abused* cheated, revolted
222–223 *heave the gorge* experience nausea   223 *Very nature* her very instincts   224 *pregnant* evident,
cogent   225 *in the degree of* as next in line for   226 *voluble* facile, glib.   *conscionable* conscientious,
conscience-bound   227 *humane* polite, courteous.   *salt* licentious   228 *affection* passion. *slipper* slippery
229 *an eye can stamp* an eye that can coin, create

advantages,° though true advantage never present itself; a devilish knave. Besides, 230
the knave is handsome, young, and hath all those requisites in him that folly°
and green° minds look after. A pestilent complete knave, and the woman hath
found him° already.

Roderigo: I cannot believe that in her. She's full of most blessed condition.°

Iago: Blessed fig's end!° The wine she drinks is made of grapes. If she had been 235
blessed, she would never have loved the Moor. Blessed pudding!° Didst thou not
see her paddle with the palm of his hand? Didst not mark that?

Roderigo: Yes, that I did; but that was but courtesy.

Iago: Lechery, by this hand. An index° and obscure° prologue to the history of lust
and foul thoughts. They met so near with their lips that their breaths embraced 240
together. Villainous thoughts, Roderigo! When these mutualities° so marshal
the way, hard at hand° comes the master and main exercise, th' incorporate°
conclusion. Pish! But, sir, be you ruled by me. I have brought you from Venice.
Watch you° tonight; for the command, I'll lay 't upon you.° Cassio knows you
not. I'll not be far from you. Do you find some occasion to anger Cassio, either by 245
speaking too loud, or tainting° his discipline, or from what other course you
please, which the time shall more favorably minister.°

Roderigo: Well.

Iago: Sir, he's rash and very sudden in choler,° and haply° may strike at you. Provoke
him that he may, for even out of that will I cause these of Cyprus to mutiny,° 250
whose qualification° shall come into no true taste° again but by the displanting
of Cassio. So shall you have a shorter journey to your desires by the means I shall
then have to prefer° them, and the impediment most profitably removed, without the which there were no expectation of our prosperity.

Roderigo: I will do this, if you can bring it to any opportunity. 255

Iago: I warrant° thee. Meet me by and by° at the citadel. I must fetch his necessaries
ashore. Farewell.

Roderigo: Adieu.   *Exit.*

Iago: That Cassio loves her, I do well believe 't;
That she loves him, 'tis apt° and of great credit.° 260
The Moor, howbeit that I endure him not,
Is of a constant, loving, noble nature,
And I dare think he'll prove to Desdemona
A most dear husband. Now, I do love her too,
Not out of absolute lust—though peradventure 265
I stand accountant° for as great a sin—
But partly led to diet° my revenge
For that I do suspect the lusty Moor
Hath leaped into my seat, the thought whereof

---

230 *advantages* favorable opportunities 231 *folly* wantonness 232 *green* immature 233 *found him* sized
him up, perceived his intent 234 *condition* disposition 235 *fig's end* (See Act I, Scene iii, line 316 for the
vulgar gesture of the fig.) 236 *pudding* sausage 239 *index* table of contents. *obscure* (i.e., the *lust and foul
thoughts* in lines 239–240 are secret, hidden from view) 241 *mutualities* exchanges, intimacies 242 *hard at
hand* closely following. *incorporate* carnal 244 *Watch you* stand watch. *for the command . . . you* I'll
arrange for you to be appointed, given orders 246 *tainting* disparaging 247 *minister* provide 249 *choler*
wrath. *haply* perhaps 250 *mutiny* riot 251 *qualification* appeasement. *true taste* i.e., acceptable state
253 *prefer* advance 256 *warrant* assure. *by and by* immediately 260 *apt* probable. *credit* credibility
266 *accountant* accountable 267 *diet* feed

Doth, like a poisonous mineral, gnaw my innards; 270
And nothing can or shall content my soul
Till I am evened with him, wife for wife,
Or failing so, yet that I put the Moor
At least into a jealousy so strong
That judgment cannot cure. Which thing to do, 275
If this poor trash of Venice, whom I trace°
For° his quick hunting, stand the putting on,°
I'll have our Michael Cassio on the hip,°
Abuse° him to the Moor in the rank garb°—
For I fear Cassio with my nightcap° too— 280
Make the Moor thank me, love me, and reward me
For making him egregiously an ass
And practicing upon° his peace and quiet
Even to madness. 'Tis here, but yet confused.
Knavery's plain face is never seen till used.   *Exit.* 285

SCENE II [CYPRUS. A STREET.]

Enter Othello's Herald with a proclamation.

Herald: It is Othello's pleasure, our noble and valiant general, that, upon certain tidings now arrived, importing the mere perdition° of the Turkish fleet, every man
put himself into triumph:° some to dance, some to make bonfires, each man to
what sport and revels his addiction° leads him. For, besides these beneficial
news, it is the celebration of his nuptial. So much was his pleasure should be pro- 5
claimed. All offices° are open, and there is full liberty of feasting from this present
hour of five till the bell have told eleven. Heaven bless the isle of Cyprus and our
noble general Othello!

Exit.

SCENE III [CYPRUS. THE CITADEL.]

Enter Othello, Desdemona, Cassio, and attendants.

Othello: Good Michael, look you to the guard tonight.
Let's teach ourselves that honorable stop°
Not to outsport° discretion.
Cassio: Iago hath direction what to do,
But notwithstanding, with my personal eye 5
Will I look to 't.

---

276 *trace* i.e., train, or follow (?), or perhaps *trash*, a hunting term, meaning to put weights on a hunting dog
in order to slow him down   277 *For* to make more eager.   *stand . . . on* respond properly when I incite him
to quarrel   278 *on the hip* at my mercy, where I can throw him. (A wrestling term.)   279 *Abuse* slander.
rank garb coarse manner, gross fashion   280 *with my nightcap* i.e., as a rival in my bed, as one who gives me
cuckold's horns   283 *practicing upon* plotting against   2 *mere perdition* complete destruction   3 *triumph* public celebration   4 *addiction* inclination   6 *offices* rooms where food and drink are kept   2 *stop* restraint   3
outsport celebrate beyond the bounds of

Othello: Iago is most honest.
 Michael, good night. Tomorrow with your earliest°
 Let me have speech with you. [*To Desdemona.*]
        Come, my dear love,
 The purchase made, the fruits are to ensue;
 That profit's yet to come 'tween me and you.°—   10
 Good night.

Exit [Othello, with Desdemona and attendants].

Enter Iago.

Cassio: Welcome, Iago. We must to the watch.
Iago: Not this hour,° Lieutenant; 'tis not yet ten o' the clock. Our general cast° us thus
 early for the love of his Desdemona; who° let us not therefore blame. He hath not
 yet made wanton the night with her, and she is sport for Jove.   15
Cassio: She's a most exquisite lady.
Iago: And, I'll warrant her, full of game.
Cassio: Indeed, she's a most fresh and delicate creature.
Iago: What an eye she has! Methinks it sounds a parley° to provocation.
Cassio: An inviting eye, and yet methinks right modest.   20
Iago: And when she speaks, is it not an alarum° to love?
Cassio: She is indeed perfection.
Iago: Well, happiness to their sheets! Come, Lieutenant, I have a stoup° of wine, and
 here without° are a brace° of Cyprus gallants that would fain have a measure° to
 the health of black Othello.   25
Cassio: Not tonight, good Iago. I have very poor and unhappy brains for drinking. I
 could well wish courtesy would invent some other custom of entertainment.
Iago: O, they are our friends. But one cup! I'll drink for you.°
Cassio: I have drunk but one cup tonight, and that was craftily qualified° too, and
 behold what innovation° it makes here.° I am unfortunate in the infirmity and 30
 dare not task my weakness with any more.
Iago: What, man? 'Tis a night of revels. The gallants desire it.
Cassio: Where are they?
Iago: Here at the door. I pray you, call them in.
Cassio: I'll do 't, but it dislikes me.°   *Exit.* 35
Iago: If I can fasten but one cup upon him,
 With that which he hath drunk tonight already,
 He'll be as full of quarrel and offense°
 As my young mistress' dog. Now, my sick fool Roderigo,
 Whom love hath turned almost the wrong side out,   40
 To Desdemona hath tonight caroused°

---

7 *with your earliest* at your earliest convenience 9–10 *The purchase . . . you* i.e., though married, we haven't yet consummated our love 13 *Not this hour* not for an hour yet. *cast* dismissed 14 *who* i.e., Othello 19 *sounds a parley* calls for a conference, issues an invitation 21 *alarum* signal calling men to arms (continuing the military metaphor of *parley,* line 19) 23 *stoup* measure of liquor, two quarts 24 *without* outside. *brace* pair. *fain have a measure* gladly drink a toast 28 *for you* in your place. (Iago will do the steady drinking to keep the gallants company while Cassio has only one cup.) 29 *qualified* diluted 30 *innovation* disturbance, insurrection. *here* i.e., in my head 35 *it dislikes me* i.e., I'm reluctant 38 *offense* readiness to take offense 41 *caroused* drunk off

Potations pottle-deep;° and he's to watch.°
Three lads of Cyprus—noble swelling° spirits,
That hold their honors in a wary distance,°
The very elements° of this warlike isle—   45
Have I tonight flustered with flowing cups,
And they watch° too. Now, 'mongst this flock of drunkards
Am I to put our Cassio in some action
That may offend the isle.—But here they come.

Enter Cassio, Montano, and gentlemen; [servants following with wine].

If consequence do but approve my dream,°   50
My boat sails freely both with wind and stream.°
Cassio: 'Fore God, they have given me a rouse° already.
Montano: Good faith, a little one; not past a pint, as I am a soldier.
Iago: Some wine, ho! [*He sings.*]
          "And let me the cannikin° clink, clink,   55
          And let me the cannikin clink.
          A soldier's a man,
          O, man's life's but a span;°
          Why, then, let a soldier drink."
      Some wine, boys!   60
Cassio: 'Fore God, an excellent song.
Iago: I learned it in England, where indeed they are most potent in potting.° Your
      Dane, your German, and your swag-bellied Hollander—drink, ho!—are nothing
      to your English.
Cassio: Is your Englishman so exquisite in his drinking?   65
Iago: Why, he drinks you,° with facility, your Dane° dead drunk; he sweats not° to
      overthrow your Almain;° he gives your Hollander a vomit ere the next pottle
      can be filled.
Cassio: To the health of our general!
Montano: I am for it, Lieutenant, and I'll do you justice.°   70
Iago: O sweet England! [*He sings.*]
          "King Stephen was and-a worthy peer,
          His breeches cost him but a crown;
          He held them sixpence all too dear,
          With that he called the tailor lown.°   75

          He was a wight of high renown,
          And thou art but of low degree.
          'Tis pride° that pulls the country down;
          Then take thy auld° cloak about thee."
      Some wine, ho!   80

42 *pottle-deep* to the bottom of the tankard.   *watch* stand watch   43 *swelling* proud   44 *hold . . . distance*
i.e., are extremely sensitive of their honor   45 *very elements* typical sort   47 *watch* are members of the
guard   50 *If . . . dream* if subsequent events will only substantiate my scheme   51 *stream* current
52 *rouse* full draft of liquor   55 *cannikin* small drinking vessel   58 *span* brief span of time. (Compare
Psalm 39:6 as rendered in the 1928 Book of Common Prayer: "Thou hast made my days as it were a span
long.")   62 *potting* drinking   66 *drinks you* drinks.   *your Dane* your typical Dane.   *sweats not* i.e., need
not exert himself   67 *Almain* German   70 *I'll . . . justice* i.e., I'll drink as much as you   75 *lown* lout, rascal
78 *pride* i.e., extravagance in dress   79 *auld* old

Cassio: 'Fore God, this is a more exquisite song than the other.

Iago: Will you hear 't again?

Cassio: No, for I hold him to be unworthy of his place that does those things. Well, God's above all; and there be souls must be saved, and there be souls must not be saved. 85

Iago: It's true, good Lieutenant.

Cassio: For mine own part—no offense to the General, nor any man of quality°—I hope to be saved.

Iago: And so do I too, Lieutenant.

Cassio: Ay, but, by your leave, not before me; the lieutenant is to be saved before the 90 ancient. Let's have no more of this; let's to our affairs.—God forgive us our sins!—Gentlemen, let's look to our business. Do not think, gentlemen, I am drunk. This is my ancient; this is my right hand, and this is my left. I am not drunk now. I can stand well enough, and speak well enough.

Gentlemen: Excellent well. 95

Cassio: Why, very well then; you must not think then that I am drunk. *Exit.*

Montano: To th' platform, masters. Come, let's set the watch.°

> [*Exeunt Gentlemen.*]

Iago: You see this fellow that is gone before.
    He's a soldier fit to stand by Caesar
    And give direction; and do but see his vice. 100
    'Tis to his virtue a just equinox,°
    The one as long as th' other. 'Tis pity of him.
    I fear the trust Othello puts him in,
    On some odd time of his infirmity,
    Will shake this island.

Montano: But is he often thus? 105

Iago: 'Tis evermore the prologue to his sleep.
    He'll watch the horologe a double set,°
    If drink rock not his cradle.

Montano: It were well
    The General were put in mind of it.
    Perhaps he sees it not, or his good nature 110
    Prizes the virtue that appears in Cassio
    And looks not on his evils. Is not this true?

> *Enter Roderigo.*

Iago [*aside to him*]: How now, Roderigo?
    I pray you, after the Lieutenant; go.   [*Exit Roderigo.*]

Montano: And 'tis great pity that the noble Moor 115
    Should hazard such a place as his own second
    With° one of an engraffed° infirmity.

---

87 *quality* rank   97 *set the watch* mount the guard   101 *just equinox* exact counterpart. (*Equinox* is an equal length of days and nights.)   107 *watch . . . set* stay awake twice around the clock or *horologe* 116–117 *hazard . . . With* risk giving such an important position as his second in command to   117 *engraffed* engrafted, inveterate

Cassio, encouraged to drink by Iago, starts a fight with Montano (II, iii, 130).

> It were an honest action to say so
> To the Moor.
> Iago: Not I, for this fair island.
> I do love Cassio well and would do much   120
> To cure him of this evil.   [*Cry within: "Help! Help!"*]
>   But, hark! What noise?
>
> *Enter Cassio, pursuing° Roderigo.*
>
> Cassio: Zounds, you rogue! You rascal!
> Montano: What's the matter, Lieutenant?
> Cassio: A knave teach me my duty?
>   I'll beat the knave into a twiggen° bottle.

121 s.d. *pursuing* (The Quarto text reads, "driving in.")   124 *twiggen* wicker-covered (Cassio vows to assail Roderigo until his skin resembles wickerwork or until he has driven Roderigo through the holes in a wickerwork.)

Roderigo: Beat me?   125
Cassio: Dost thou prate, rogue?   [*He strikes Roderigo.*]
Montano: Nay, good Lieutenant. [*Restraining him.*] I pray you, sir, hold your hand.
Cassio: Let me go, sir, or I'll knock you o'er the mazard.°
Montano: Come, come, you're drunk.
Cassio: Drunk?   [*They fight.*]   130
Iago [*aside to Roderigo*]: Away, I say. Go out and cry a mutiny.°

> [*Exit Roderigo.*]

> Nay, good Lieutenant—God's will, gentlemen—
> Help, ho!—Lieutenant—sir—Montano—sir—
> Help, masters!°—Here's a goodly watch indeed!

> [*A bell rings.*]°

> Who's that which rings the bell?—Diablo,° ho!   135
> The town will rise.° God's will, Lieutenant, hold!
> You'll be ashamed forever.

> *Enter Othello and attendants* [*with weapons*].

Othello: What is the matter here?
Montano: Zounds, I bleed still.
      I am hurt to th' death. He dies!   [*He thrusts at Cassio.*]
Othello: Hold, for your lives!
Iago: Hold, ho! Lieutenant—sir—Montano—gentlemen—   140
      Have you forgot all sense of place and duty?
      Hold! The General speaks to you. Hold, for shame!
Othello: Why, how now, ho! From whence ariseth this?
      Are we turned Turks, and to ourselves do that
      Which heaven hath forbid the Ottomites?°   145
      For Christian shame, put by this barbarous brawl!
      He that stirs next to carve for° his own rage
      Holds his soul light;° he dies upon his motion.°
      Silence that dreadful bell. It frights the isle
      From her propriety.° What is the matter, masters?   150
      Honest Iago, that looks dead with grieving,
      Speak. Who began this? On thy love, I charge thee.
Iago: I do not know. Friends all but now, even now,
      In quarter° and in terms° like bride and groom
      Devesting them° for bed; and then, but now—   155
      As if some planet had unwitted men—

---

128 *mazard* i.e., head. (Literally, a drinking vessel.)   131 *mutiny* riot   134 *masters* sirs.   s.d. *A bell rings* (This direction is from the Quarto, as are *Exit Roderigo* at line 114, *They fight* at line 130, and *with weapons* at line 137.)   135 *Diablo* the devil   136 *rise* grow riotous   144–145 *to ourselves . . . Ottomites* inflict on ourselves the harm that heaven has prevented the Turks from doing (by destroying their fleet)   147 *carve for* i.e., indulge, satisfy with his sword   148 *Holds . . . light* i.e., places little value on his life.   *upon his motion* if he moves   150 *propriety* proper state or condition   154 *In quarter* in friendly conduct, within bounds.   *in terms* on good terms   155 *Devesting them* undressing themselves

Swords out, and tilting one at others' breasts
In opposition bloody. I cannot speak°
Any beginning to this peevish odds;°
And would in action glorious I had lost
Those legs that brought me to a part of it!   160
Othello: How comes it, Michael, you are thus forgot?°
Cassio: I pray you, pardon me. I cannot speak.
Othello: Worthy Montano, you were wont be° civil;
The gravity and stillness° of your youth   165
The world hath noted, and your name is great
In mouths of wisest censure.° What's the matter
That you unlace° your reputation thus
And spend your rich opinion° for the name
Of a night-brawler? Give me answer to it.   170
Montano: Worthy Othello, I am hurt to danger.
Your officer, Iago, can inform you—
While I spare speech, which something° now offends° me—
Of all that I do know; nor know I aught
By me that's said or done amiss this night,   175
Unless self-charity be sometimes a vice,
And to defend ourselves it be a sin
When violence assails us.
Othello: Now, by heaven,
My blood° begins my safer guides° to rule,
And passion, having my best judgment collied,°   180
Essays° to lead the way. Zounds, if I stir,
Or do but lift this arm, the best of you
Shall sink in my rebuke. Give me to know
How this foul rout° began, who set it on;
And he that is approved in° this offense,   185
Though he had twinned with me, both at a birth,
Shall lose me. What? In a town of° war
Yet wild, the people's hearts brim full of fear,
To manage° private and domestic quarrel?
In night, and on the court and guard of safety?°   190
'Tis monstrous. Iago, who began 't?
Montano [*to Iago*]: If partially affined,° or leagued in office,°
Thou dost deliver more or less than truth,
Thou art no soldier.
Iago: Touch me not so near.
I had rather have this tongue cut from my mouth   195

---

158 *speak* explain   159 *peevish odds* childish quarrel   162 *are thus forgot* have forgotten yourself thus
164 *wont be* accustomed to be   165 *stillness* sobriety   167 *censure* judgment   168 *unlace* undo, lay open
(as one might loose the strings of a purse containing reputation)   169 *opinion* reputation   173 *something*
somewhat.   *offends* pains   179 *blood* passion (of anger).   *guides* i.e., reason   180 *collied* darkened   181
Essays undertakes   184 *rout* riot   185 *approved in* found guilty of   187 *town of* town garrisoned for
189 *manage* undertake   190 *on . . . safety* at the main guardhouse or headquarters and on watch   192
partially affined made partial by some personal relationship.   *leagued in office* in league as fellow officers

Than it should do offense to Michael Cassio;
Yet, I persuade myself, to speak the truth
Shall nothing wrong him. Thus it is, General.
Montano and myself being in speech,
There comes a fellow crying out for help,   200
And Cassio following him with determined sword
To execute° upon him. Sir, this gentleman

[*indicating Montano*]

Steps in to Cassio and entreats his pause.°
Myself the crying fellow did pursue,
Lest by his clamor—as it so fell out—   205
The town might fall in fright. He, swift of foot,
Outran my purpose, and I returned, the rather°
For that I heard the clink and fall of swords
And Cassio high in oath, which till tonight
I ne'er might say before. When I came back—   210
For this was brief—I found them close together
At blow and thrust, even as again they were
When you yourself did part them.
More of this matter cannot I report.
But men are men; the best sometimes forget.°   215
Though Cassio did some little wrong to him,
As men in rage strike those that wish them best,°
Yet surely Cassio, I believe, received
From him that fled some strange indignity,
Which patience could not pass.°
Othello: I know, Iago,   220
    Thy honesty and love doth mince this matter,
    Making it light to Cassio. Cassio, I love thee,
    But nevermore be officer of mine.

    Enter Desdemona, attended.

    Look if my gentle love be not raised up.
    I'll make thee an example.   225
Desdemona: What is the matter, dear?
Othello: All's well now, sweeting;
    Come away to bed. [*To Montano.*] Sir, for your hurts,
    Myself will be your surgeon.°—Lead him off.

    [*Montano is led off.*]

    Iago, look with care about the town
    And silence those whom this vile brawl distracted.   230

---

202 *execute* give effect to (his anger)   203 *his pause* him to stop   207 *rather* sooner   215 *forget* forget
themselves   217 *those . . . best* i.e., even those who are well disposed   220 *pass* pass over, overlook   228
be your surgeon i.e., make sure you receive medical attention

Iago advises Cassio to ask Desdemona to plead his cause with Othello (II, iii, 233–286).

Come, Desdemona. 'Tis the soldiers' life
To have their balmy slumbers waked with strife.

Exit [with all but Iago and Cassio].

Iago: What, are you hurt, Lieutenant?
Cassio: Ay, past all surgery.
Iago: Marry, God forbid!   235
Cassio: Reputation, reputation, reputation! O, I have lost my reputation! I have lost
the immortal part of myself, and what remains is bestial. My reputation, Iago, my
reputation!
Iago: As I am an honest man, I thought you had received some bodily wound; there
is more sense in that than in reputation. Reputation is an idle and most false   240
imposition,° oft got without merit and lost without deserving. You have lost no
reputation at all, unless you repute yourself such a loser. What, man, there are
more ways to recover° the General again. You are but now cast in his mood°—a
punishment more in policy° than in malice, even so as one would beat his
offenseless dog to affright an imperious lion.° Sue° to him again and he's yours.   245

240–241 *false imposition* thing artificially imposed and of no real value   243 *recover* regain favor with.
cast in his mood dismissed in a moment of anger   244 *in policy* done for expediency's sake and as a public
gesture   244–245 *would . . . lion* i.e., would make an example of a minor offender in order to deter more
important and dangerous offenders   245 *Sue* petition

Cassio: I will rather sue to be despised than to deceive so good a commander with so slight,° so drunken, and so indiscreet an officer. Drunk? And speak parrot?° And squabble? Swagger? Swear? And discourse fustian with one's own shadow? O thou invisible spirit of wine, if thou hast no name to be known by, let us call thee devil!   250

Iago: What was he that you followed with your sword? What had he done to you?

Cassio: I know not.

Iago: Is 't possible?

Cassio: I remember a mass of things, but nothing distinctly; a quarrel, but nothing wherefore.° O God, that men should put an enemy in their mouths to steal away   255 their brains! That we should, with joy, pleasance, revel, and applause° transform ourselves into beasts!

Iago: Why, but you are now well enough. How came you thus recovered?

Cassio: It hath pleased the devil drunkenness to give place to the devil wrath. One unperfectness shows me another, to make me frankly despise myself.   260

Iago: Come, you are too severe a moraler.° As the time, the place, and the condition of this country stands, I could heartily wish this had not befallen; but since it is as it is, mend it for your own good.

Cassio: I will ask him for my place again; he shall tell me I am a drunkard. Had I as many mouths as Hydra,° such an answer would stop them all. To be now a sensible   265 man, by and by a fool, and presently a beast! O, strange! Every inordinate cup is unblessed, and the ingredient is a devil.

Iago: Come, come, good wine is a good familiar creature, if it be well used. Exclaim no more against it. And, good Lieutenant, I think you think I love you.

Cassio: I have well approved° it, sir. I drunk!   270

Iago: You or any man living may be drunk at a time,° man. I'll tell you what you shall do. Our general's wife is now the general—I may say so in this respect, for that° he hath devoted and given up himself to the contemplation, mark, and denotement° of her parts° and graces. Confess yourself freely to her; importune her help to put you in your place again. She is of so free,° so kind, so apt, so blessed a dis-   275 position, she holds it a vice in her goodness not to do more than she is requested. This broken joint between you and her husband entreat her to splinter;° and, my fortunes against any lay° worth naming, this crack of your love shall grow stronger than it was before.

Cassio: You advise me well.   280

Iago: I protest,° in the sincerity of love and honest kindness.

Cassio: I think it freely;° and betimes in the morning I will beseech the virtuous Desdemona to undertake for me. I am desperate of my fortunes if they check° me here.

Iago: You are in the right. Good night, Lieutenant. I must to the watch.   285

---

247 *slight* worthless.   247–48 *speak parrot* talk nonsense, rant   255 *wherefore* why   256 *applause* desire for applause   261 *moraler* moralizer   265 *Hydra* the Lernaean Hydra, a monster with many heads and the ability to grow two heads when one was cut off, slain by Hercules as the second of his twelve labors   270 *approved* proved   271 *at a time* at one time or another   272 *in . . . . that* in view of this fact, that   273–274 *mark, and denotement* (Both words mean "observation.")   274 *parts* qualities   275 *free* generous   277 *splinter* bind with splints.   278 *lay* stake, wager   281 *protest* insist, declare   282 *freely* unreservedly   283 *check* repulse

Cassio: Good night, honest Iago.   *Exit Cassio.*

Iago: And what's he then that says I play the villain,
  When this advice is free° I give, and honest,
  Probal° to thinking, and indeed the course
  To win the Moor again? For 'tis most easy   290
  Th' inclining° Desdemona to subdue°
  In any honest suit; she's framed as fruitful°
  As the free elements.° And then for her
  To win the Moor—were 't to renounce his baptism,
  All seals and symbols of redeemèd sin—   295
  His soul is so enfettered to her love
  That she may make, unmake, do what she list,
  Even as her appetite° shall play the god
  With his weak function.° How am I then a villain,
  To counsel Cassio to this parallel° course   300
  Directly to his good? Divinity of hell!°
  When devils will the blackest sins put on,°
  They do suggest° at first with heavenly shows,
  As I do now. For whiles this honest fool
  Plies Desdemona to repair his fortune,   305
  And she for him pleads strongly to the Moor,
  I'll pour this pestilence into his ear,
  That she repeals him° for her body's lust;
  And by how much she strives to do him good,
  She shall undo her credit with the Moor.   310
  So will I turn her virtue into pitch,°
  And out of her own goodness make the net
  That shall enmesh them all.

  Enter Roderigo.

                                           How now, Roderigo?
Roderigo: I do follow here in the chase, not like a hound that hunts, but one that
  fills up the cry.° My money is almost spent; I have been tonight exceedingly 315
  well cudgeled; and I think the issue will be I shall have so much° experience
  for my pains, and so, with no money at all and a little more wit, return again
  to Venice.
Iago: How poor are they that have not patience!
  What wound did ever heal but by degrees?   320
  Thou know'st we work by wit, and not by witchcraft,
  And wit depends on dilatory time.

---

288 *free* (1) free from guile (2) freely given   289 *Probal* probable, reasonable   291 *inclining* favorably disposed.   *subdue* persuade   292 *framed as fruitful* created as generous   293 *free elements* i.e., earth, air, fire, and water, unrestrained and spontaneous   298 *her appetite* her desire, or, perhaps, his desire for her   299 *function* exercise of faculties (weakened by his fondness for her)   300 *parallel* corresponding to these facts and to his best interests   301 *Divinity of hell* inverted theology of hell (which seduces the soul to its damnation)   302 *put on* further, instigate   303 *suggest* tempt   308 *repeals him* attempts to get him restored   311 *pitch* i.e., (1) foul blackness (2) a snaring substance   315 *fills up the cry* merely takes part as one of the pack   316 *so much* just so much and no more

Does 't not go well? Cassio hath beaten thee,
And thou, by that small hurt, hast cashiered° Cassio.
Though other things grow fair against the sun,   325
Yet fruits that blossom first will first be ripe.°
Content thyself awhile. By the Mass, 'tis morning!
Pleasure and action make the hours seem short.
Retire thee; go where thou art billeted.
Away, I say! Thou shalt know more hereafter.   330
Nay, get thee gone.   *Exit Roderigo.*
     Two things are to be done.
My wife must move° for Cassio to her mistress;
I'll set her on;
Myself the while to draw the Moor apart
And bring him jump° when he may Cassio find   335
Soliciting his wife. Ay, that's the way.
Dull not device° by coldness° and delay.   *Exit.*

ACT III

SCENE I [BEFORE THE CHAMBER OF OTHELLO AND DESDEMONA.]

 Enter Cassio [and] Musicians.

Cassio: Masters, play here—I will content your pains°—
 Something that's brief, and bid "Good morrow, General." *[They play.]*

 [Enter] Clown.

Clown: Why, masters, have your instruments been in Naples, that they speak i' the
 nose° thus?
A Musician: How, sir, how?   5
Clown: Are these, I pray you, wind instruments?
A Musician: Ay, marry, are they, sir.
Clown: O, thereby hangs a tail.
A Musician: Whereby hangs a tale, sir?
Clown: Marry, sir, by many a wind instrument° that I know. But, masters, here's   10
 money for you. [*He gives money.*] And the General so likes your music that he
 desires you, for love's sake,° to make no more noise with it.
A Musician: Well, sir, we will not.
Clown: If you have any music that may not° be heard, to 't again; but, as they say, to
 hear music the General does not greatly care.   15

---

324 *cashiered* dismissed from service   325–326 *Though . . . ripe* i.e., plans that are well prepared and set
expeditiously in motion will soonest ripen into success   332 *move* plead   335 *jump* precisely   337 *device*
plot. *coldness* lack of zeal   1 *content your pains* reward your efforts   3–4 *speak i' the nose* (1) sound nasal
(2) sound like one whose nose has been attacked by syphilis. (Naples was popularly supposed to have a
high incidence of venereal disease.)   10 *wind instrument* (With a joke on flatulence. The *tail*, line 8, that
hangs nearby the *wind instrument* suggests the penis.)   12 *for love's sake* (1) out of friendship and affection
(2) for the sake of lovemaking in Othello's marriage   14 *may not* cannot

A Musician: We have none such, sir.

Clown: Then put up your pipes in your bag, for I'll away.° Go, vanish into air, away!

Exeunt Musicians.

Cassio: Dost thou hear, mine honest friend?

Clown: No, I hear not your honest friend; I hear you.   20

Cassio: Prithee, keep up° thy quillets.° There's a poor piece of gold for thee. [*He gives money.*] If the gentle-woman that attends the General's wife be stirring, tell her there's one Cassio entreats her a little favor of speech.° Wilt thou do this?

Clown: She is stirring, sir. If she will stir° hither, I shall seem° to notify unto her.

Cassio: Do, good my friend.   *Exit Clown.*

    Enter Iago.

In happy time,° Iago.   25

Iago: You have not been abed, then?

Cassio: Why, no. The day had broke
Before we parted. I have made bold, Iago,
To send in to your wife. My suit to her
Is that she will to virtuous Desdemona   30
Procure me some access.

Iago: I'll send her to you presently;
And I'll devise a means to draw the Moor
Out of the way, that your converse and business
May be more free.   35

Cassio: I humbly thank you for 't.   *Exit [Iago].*
I never knew
A Florentine° more kind and honest.

    Enter Emilia.

Emilia: Good morrow, good Lieutenant. I am sorry
For your displeasure;° but all will sure be well.
The General and his wife are talking of it,   40
And she speaks for you stoutly.° The Moor replies
That he you hurt is of great fame° in Cyprus
And great affinity,° and that in wholesome wisdom
He might not but refuse you; but he protests° he loves you
And needs no other suitor but his likings   45
To take the safest occasion by the front°
To bring you in again.

Cassio: Yet I beseech you,
If you think fit, or that it may be done,
Give me advantage of some brief discourse
With Desdemona alone.

---

17 *I'll away* (Possibly a misprint, or a snatch of song?)   21 *keep up* do not bring out, do not use.   *quillets* quibbles, puns   23 *a little . . . speech* the favor of a brief talk   24 *stir* bestir herself (with a play on *stirring,* "rousing herself from rest").   *seem* deem it good, think fit   25 *In happy time* i.e., well met   37 *Florentine* i.e., even a fellow Florentine. (Iago is a Venetian; Cassio is a Florentine.)   39 *displeasure* fall from favor   41 *stoutly* spiritedly   42 *fame* reputation, importance   43 *affinity* kindred, family connection   44 *protests* insists   46 *occasion . . . front* opportunity by the forelock

Emilia: Pray you, come in.   50
    I will bestow you where you shall have time
    To speak your bosom° freely.
Cassio: I am much bound to you.   [*Exeunt.*]

SCENE II [THE CITADEL.]

    Enter Othello, Iago, and Gentlemen.

Othello [*giving letters*]: These letters give, Iago, to the pilot,
    And by him do my duties° to the Senate.
    That done, I will be walking on the works;°
    Repair° there to me.
Iago: Well, my good lord, I'll do 't.
Othello: This fortification, gentlemen, shall we see 't?   5
Gentlemen: We'll wait upon° your lordship.   *Exeunt.*

SCENE III [THE GARDEN OF THE CITADEL.]

    Enter Desdemona, Cassio, and Emilia.

Desdemona: Be thou assured, good Cassio, I will do
    All my abilities in thy behalf.
Emilia: Good madam, do. I warrant it grieves my husband
    As if the cause were his.
Desdemona: O, that's an honest fellow. Do not doubt, Cassio,   5
    But I will have my lord and you again
    As friendly as you were.
Cassio: Bounteous madam,
    Whatever shall become of Michael Cassio,
    He's never anything but your true servant.
Desdemona: I know 't. I thank you. You do love my lord;   10
    You have known him long, and be you well assured
    He shall in strangeness° stand no farther off
    Than in a politic° distance.
Cassio: Ay, but, lady,
    That policy may either last so long,
    Or feed upon such nice and waterish diet,°   15
    Or breed itself so out of circumstance,°
    That, I being absent and my place supplied,°
    My general will forget my love and service.
Desdemona: Do not doubt° that. Before Emilia here
    I give thee warrant° of thy place. Assure thee,   20

---

52 *bosom* inmost thoughts   2 *do my duties* convey my respects   3 *works* breastworks, fortifications
4 *Repair* return, come   6 *wait upon* attend   12 *strangeness* aloofness   13 *politic* required by wise policy
15 *Or . . . diet* or sustain itself at length upon such trivial and meager technicalities   16 *breed . . . circum-*
stance continually renew itself so out of chance events, or yield so few chances for my being pardoned
17 *supplied* filled by another person   19 *doubt* fear   20 *warrant* guarantee

If I do vow a friendship I'll perform it
To the last article. My lord shall never rest.
I'll watch him tame° and talk him out of patience;°
His bed shall seem a school, his board° a shrift;°
I'll intermingle everything he does   25
With Cassio's suit. Therefore be merry, Cassio,
For thy solicitor° shall rather die
Than give thy cause away.°

    Enter Othello and Iago [at a distance].

Emilia: Madam, here comes my lord.
Cassio: Madam, I'll take my leave.   30
Desdemona: Why, stay, and hear me speak.
Cassio: Madam, not now. I am very ill at ease,
    Unfit for mine own purposes.
Desdemona: Well, do your discretion.°   *Exit Cassio.*
Iago: Ha? I like not that.   35
Othello: What dost thou say?
Iago: Nothing, my lord; or if—I know not what.
Othello: Was not that Cassio parted from my wife?
Iago: Cassio, my lord? No, sure, I cannot think it,
    That he would steal away so guiltylike,   40
    Seeing you coming.
Othello: I do believe 'twas he.
Desdemona: How now, my lord?
    I have been talking with a suitor here,
    A man that languishes in your displeasure.
Othello: Who is 't you mean?   45
Desdemona: Why, your lieutenant, Cassio. Good my lord,
    If I have any grace or power to move you,
    His present reconciliation take;°
    For if he be not one that truly loves you,
    That errs in ignorance and not in cunning,°   50
    I have no judgment in an honest face.
    I prithee, call him back.
Othello: Went he hence now?
Desdemona: Yes, faith, so humbled   55
    That he hath left part of his grief with me
    To suffer with him. Good love, call him back.
Othello: Not now, sweet Desdemon. Some other time.
Desdemona: But shall 't be shortly?
Othello: The sooner, sweet, for you.   60
Desdemona: Shall 't be tonight at supper?

---

23 *watch him tame* tame him by keeping him from sleeping. (A term from falconry.)   *out of patience* past
his endurance   24 *board* dining table.   *shrift* confessional   27 *solicitor* advocate   28 *away* up   34 *do
your discretion* act according to your own discretion   49 *His . . . take* let him be reconciled to you right
away   51 *in cunning* wittingly

Othello: No, not tonight.

Desdemona: Tomorrow dinner,° then?

Othello: I shall not dine at home.

    I meet the captains at the citadel.   65

Desdemona: Why, then, tomorrow night, or Tuesday morn,

    On Tuesday noon, or night, on Wednesday morn.

    I prithee, name the time, but let it not

    Exceed three days. In faith, he's penitent;

    And yet his trespass, in our common reason°—   70

    Save that, they say, the wars must make example

    Out of her best°—is not almost° a fault

    T' incur a private check.° When shall he come?

    Tell me, Othello. I wonder in my soul

    What you would ask me that I should deny,   75

    Or stand so mammering on.° What? Michael Cassio,

    That came a-wooing with you, and so many a time,

    When I have spoke of you dispraisingly,

    Hath ta'en your part—to have so much to do

    To bring him in!° By 'r Lady, I could do much—   80

Othello: Prithee, no more. Let him come when he will;

    I will deny thee nothing.

Desdemona: Why, this is not a boon.

    'Tis as I should entreat you wear your gloves,

    Or feed on nourishing dishes, or keep you warm,   85

    Or sue to you to do a peculiar° profit

    To your own person. Nay, when I have a suit

    Wherein I mean to touch° your love indeed,

    It shall be full of poise° and difficult weight,

    And fearful to be granted.   90

Othello: I will deny thee nothing.

    Whereon,° I do beseech thee, grant me this,

    To leave me but a little to myself.

Desdemona: Shall I deny you? No. Farewell, my lord.

Othello: Farewell, my Desdemona. I'll come to thee straight.°   95

Desdemona: Emilia, come.—Be as your fancies° teach you;

    Whate'er you be, I am obedient.   *Exit* [*with Emilia*]

Othello: Excellent wretch!° Perdition catch my soul

    But I do love thee! And when I love thee not,

    Chaos is come again.°   100

Iago: My noble lord—

---

63 *dinner* (The noontime meal.)   70 *common reason* everyday judgments   71–72 *Save . . . best* were it not that, as the saying goes, military discipline requires making an example of the very best men. (He refers to *wars* as a singular concept.)   72 *not almost* scarcely   73 *private check* even a private reprimand 76 *mammering on* wavering about   80 *bring him in* restore him to favor   86 *peculiar* particular, personal 88 *touch* test   89 *poise* weight, heaviness; or equipoise, delicate balance involving hard choice 92 *Whereon* in return for which   95 *straight* straightway   96 *fancies* inclinations   98 *wretch* (A term of affectionate endearment.)   99–100 *And . . . again* i.e., my love for you will last forever, until the end of time when chaos will return. (But with an unconscious, ironic suggestion that, if anything should induce Othello to cease loving Desdemona, the result would be chaos.)

Othello: What dost thou say, Iago?

Iago: Did Michael Cassio, when you wooed my lady,
Know of your love?

Othello: He did, from first to last. Why dost thou ask? 105

Iago: But for a satisfaction of my thought;
No further harm.

Othello: Why of thy thought, Iago?

Iago: I did not think he had been acquainted with her.

Othello: O, yes, and went between us very oft.

Iago: Indeed? 110

Othello: Indeed? Ay, indeed. Discern'st thou aught in that?
Is he not honest?

Iago: Honest, my lord?

Othello: Honest. Ay, honest.

Iago: My lord, for aught I know. 115

Othello: What dost thou think?

Iago: Think, my lord?

Othello: "Think, my lord?" By heaven, thou echo'st me,
As if there were some monster in thy thought
Too hideous to be shown. Thou dost mean something. 120
I heard thee say even now, thou lik'st not that,
When Cassio left my wife. What didst not like?
And when I told thee he was of my counsel°
In my whole course of wooing, thou criedst "Indeed?"
And didst contract and purse° thy brow together 125
As if thou then hadst shut up in thy brain
Some horrible conceit.° If thou dost love me,
Show me thy thought.

Iago: My lord, you know I love you.

Othello: I think thou dost; 130
And, for° I know thou'rt full of love and honesty,
And weigh'st thy words before thou giv'st them breath,
Therefore these stops° of thine fright me the more;
For such things in a false disloyal knave
Are tricks of custom,° but in a man that's just 135
They're close dilations,° working from the heart
That passion cannot rule.°

Iago: For° Michael Cassio,
I dare be sworn I think that he is honest.

Othello: I think so too.

Iago: Men should be what they seem;
Or those that be not, would they might seem none!° 140

Othello: Certain, men should be what they seem.

123 *of my counsel* in my confidence   125 *purse* knit   127 *conceit* fancy   131 *for* because   133 *stops* pauses
135 *of custom* customary   136 *close dilations* secret or involuntary expressions or delays   137 *That passion
cannot rule* i.e., that are too passionately strong to be restrained (referring to the workings), or that cannot
rule its own passions (referring to the heart).   *For* as for   140 *none* i.e., not to be men, or not seem to be
honest

Iago: Why, then, I think Cassio's an honest man.

Othello: Nay, yet there's more in this.
    I prithee, speak to me as to thy thinkings,
    As thou dost ruminate, and give thy worst of thoughts   145
    The worst of words.

Iago: Good my lord, pardon me.
    Though I am bound to every act of duty,
    I am not bound to that° all slaves are free to.°
    Utter my thoughts? Why, say they are vile and false,
    As where's the palace whereinto foul things   150
    Sometimes intrude not? Who has that breast so pure
    But some uncleanly apprehensions
    Keep leets and law days,° and in sessions sit
    With° meditations lawful?°

Othello: Thou dost conspire against thy friend,° Iago,   155
    If thou but think'st him wronged and mak'st his ear
    A stranger to thy thoughts.

Iago: I do beseech you,
    Though I perchance am vicious° in my guess—
    As I confess it is my nature's plague
    To spy into abuses, and oft my jealousy°   160
    Shapes faults that are not—that your wisdom then,°
    From one° that so imperfectly conceits,°
    Would take no notice, nor build yourself a trouble
    Out of his scattering° and unsure observance.
    It were not for your quiet nor your good,   165
    Nor for my manhood, honesty, and wisdom,
    To let you know my thoughts.

Othello: What dost thou mean?

Iago: Good name in man and woman, dear my lord,
    Is the immediate° jewel of their souls.
    Who steals my purse steals trash; 'tis something, nothing;   170
    'Twas mine, 'tis his, and has been slave to thousands;
    But he that filches from me my good name
    Robs me of that which not enriches him
    And makes me poor indeed.

Othello: By heaven, I'll know thy thoughts.   175

Iago: You cannot, if° my heart were in your hand,
    Nor shall not, whilst 'tis in my custody.

Othello: Ha?

Iago: O, beware, my lord, of jealousy.
    It is the green-eyed monster which doth mock
    The meat it feeds on.° That cuckold lives in bliss   180

---

148 *that* that which. *free to* free with respect to 153 *Keep leets and law days* i.e., hold court, set up their authority in one's heart. (*Leets* are a kind of manor court; *law days* are the days courts sit in session, or those sessions.) 154 *With* along with. *lawful* innocent 155 *thy friend* i.e., Othello 158 *vicious* wrong 160 *jealousy* suspicious nature 161 *then* on that account 162 *one* i.e., myself, Iago. *conceits* judges, conjectures 164 *scattering* random 169 *immediate* essential, most precious 176 *if* even if 179–180 *doth mock . . . on* mocks and torments the heart of its victim, the man who suffers jealousy

Iago plants doubts about Desdemona in Othello's mind (III, iii, 101–295).

> Who, certain of his fate, loves not his wronger;°
> But O, what damnèd minutes tells° he o'er
> Who dotes, yet doubts, suspects, yet fondly loves!
> *Othello:* O misery!
> *Iago:* Poor and content is rich, and rich enough,° 185
> But riches fineless° is as poor as winter
> To him that ever fears he shall be poor.
> Good God, the souls of all my tribe defend
> From jealousy!
> *Othello:* Why, why is this? 190
> Think'st thou I'd make a life of jealousy,
> To follow still the changes of the moon
> With fresh suspicions?° No! To be once in doubt
> Is once° to be resolved.° Exchange me for a goat

---

181 *his wronger* i.e., his faithless wife. (The unsuspecting cuckold is spared the misery of loving his wife only to discover she is cheating on him.)   182 *tells* counts   185 *Poor . . . enough* to be content with what little one has is the greatest wealth of all. (Proverbial.)   186 *fineless* boundless   192–193 *To follow . . . suspicions* to be constantly imagining new causes for suspicion, changing incessantly like the moon   194 *once* once and for all.   *resolved* free of doubt, having settled the matter

When I shall turn the business of my soul   195
To such exsufflicate and blown° surmises
Matching thy inference.° 'Tis not to make me jealous
To say my wife is fair, feeds well, loves company,
Is free of speech, sings, plays, and dances well;
Where virtue is, these are more virtuous.   200
Nor from mine own weak merits will I draw
The smallest fear or doubt of her revolt,°
For she had eyes, and chose me. No, Iago,
I'll see before I doubt; when I doubt, prove;
And on the proof, there is no more but this—   205
Away at once with love or jealousy.

Iago: I am glad of this, for now I shall have reason
To show the love and duty that I bear you
With franker spirit. Therefore, as I am bound,
Receive it from me. I speak not yet of proof.   210
Look to your wife; observe her well with Cassio.
Wear your eyes thus, not° jealous nor secure.°
I would not have your free and noble nature,
Out of self-bounty,° be abused.° Look to 't.
I know our country disposition well;   215
In Venice they do let God see the pranks
They dare not show their husbands; their best conscience
Is not to leave 't undone, but keep 't unknown.

Othello: Dost thou say so?

Iago: She did deceive her father, marrying you;   220
And when she seemed to shake and fear your looks,
She loved them most.

Othello: And so she did.

Iago: Why, go to,° then!
She that, so young, could give out such a seeming,°
To seel° her father's eyes up close as oak,°
He thought 'twas witchcraft! But I am much to blame.   225
I humbly do beseech you of your pardon
For too much loving you.

Othello: I am bound° to thee forever.

Iago: I see this hath a little dashed your spirits.

Othello: Not a jot, not a jot.

Iago: I' faith, I fear it has.   230
I hope you will consider what is spoke
Comes from my love. But I do see you're moved.
I am to pray you not to strain my speech

---

196 *exsufflicate and blown* inflated and blown up, rumored about, or, spat out and flyblown, hence, loathsome, disgusting   197 *inference* description or allegation   202 *doubt . . . revolt* fear of her unfaithfulness   212 *not* neither. *secure* free from uncertainty   214 *self-bounty* inherent or natural goodness and generosity. *abused* deceived   222 *go to* (An expression of impatience.)   223 *seeming* false appearance   224 *seel* blind. (A term from falconry.) *oak* (A close-grained wood.)   228 *bound* indebted (but perhaps with ironic sense of "tied")

      To grosser issues° nor to larger reach°

      Than to suspicion.   235

Othello: I will not.

Iago: Should you do so, my lord,

      My speech should fall into such vile success°

      Which my thoughts aimed not. Cassio's my worthy friend.

      My lord, I see you're moved.

Othello: No, not much moved.   240

      I do not think but Desdemona's honest.°

Iago: Long live she so! And long live you to think so!

Othello: And yet, how nature erring from itself—

Iago: Ay, there's the point! As—to be bold with you—

      Not to affect° many proposèd matches   245

      Of her own clime, complexion, and degree,°

      Whereto we see in all things nature tends—

      Foh! One may smell in such a will° most rank,

      Foul disproportion,° thoughts unnatural.

      But pardon me. I do not in position°   250

      Distinctly speak of her, though I may fear

      Her will, recoiling° to her better° judgment,

      May fall to match you with her country forms°

      And happily repent.°

Othello: Farewell, farewell!

      If more thou dost perceive, let me know more.   255

      Set on thy wife to observe. Leave me, Iago.

Iago [*going*]: My lord, I take my leave.

Othello: Why did I marry? This honest creature doubtless

      Sees and knows more, much more, than he unfolds.

Iago [*returning*]: My Lord, I would I might entreat your honor   260

      To scan° this thing no farther. Leave it to time.

      Although 'tis fit that Cassio have his place—

      For, sure, he fills it up with great ability—

      Yet, if you please to hold him off awhile,

      You shall by that perceive him and his means.°   265

      Note if your lady strain his entertainment°

      With any strong or vehement importunity;

      Much will be seen in that. In the meantime,

      Let me be thought too busy° in my fears—

      As worthy cause I have to fear I am—   270

      And hold her free,° I do beseech your honor.

Othello: Fear not my government.°

Iago: I once more take my leave.   *Exit.*

---

234 *issues* significances.   *reach* meaning, scope   238 *success* effect, result   241 *honest* chaste   245 *affect* prefer, desire   246 *clime . . . degree* country, color, and social position   248 *will* sensuality, appetite 249 *disproportion* abnormality   250 *position* argument, proposition   252 *recoiling* reverting. *better* i.e., more natural and reconsidered   253 *fall . . . forms* undertake to compare you with Venetian norms of handsomeness   254 *happily repent* happily repent her marriage   261 *scan* scrutinize   265 *his means* the method he uses (to regain his post)   266 *strain his entertainment* urge his reinstatement   269 *busy* interfering   271 *hold her free* regard her as innocent   272 *government* self-control, conduct

Othello: This fellow's of exceeding honesty,
    And knows all qualities,° with a learnèd spirit,   275
    Of human dealings. If I do prove her haggard,°
    Though that her jesses° were my dear heartstrings,
    I'd whistle her off and let her down the wind°
    To prey at fortune.° Haply, for° I am black
    And have not those soft parts of conversation°   280
    That chamberers° have, or for I am declined
    Into the vale of years—yet that's not much—
    She's gone. I am abused,° and my relief
    Must be to loathe her. O curse of marriage,
    That we can call these delicate creatures ours   285
    And not their appetites! I had rather be a toad
    And live upon the vapor of a dungeon
    Than keep a corner in the thing I love
    For others' uses. Yet, 'tis the plague of great ones;
    Prerogatived° are they less than the base.°   290
    'Tis destiny unshunnable, like death.
    Even then this forkèd° plague is fated to us
    When we do quicken.° Look where she comes.

Enter Desdemona and Emilia.

    If she be false, O, then heaven mocks itself!
    I'll not believe 't.
Desdemona: How now, my dear Othello?   295
    Your dinner, and the generous° islanders
    By you invited, do attend° your presence.
Othello: I am to blame.
Desdemona: Why do you speak so faintly?
    Are you not well?
Othello: I have a pain upon my forehead here.   300
Desdemona: Faith, that's with watching.° 'Twill away again.

    [*She offers her handkerchief.*]

    Let me but bind it hard, within this hour
    It will be well.
Othello: Your napkin° is too little.
    Let it alone.° Come, I'll go in with you.

    [*He puts the handkerchief from him, and it drops.*]

---

275 *qualities* natures, types   276 *haggard* wild (like a wild female hawk)   277 *jesses* straps fastened around the legs of a trained hawk   278 *I'd . . . wind* i.e., I'd let her go forever. (To release a hawk downwind was to invite it not to return.)   279 *prey at fortune* fend for herself in the wild. *Haply, for* perhaps because 280 *soft . . . conversation* pleasing graces of social behavior   281 *chamberers* gallants   283 *abused* deceived 290 *Prerogatived* privileged (to have honest wives). *the base* ordinary citizens. (Socially prominent men are especially prone to the unavoidable destiny of being cuckolded and to the public shame that goes with it.)   292 *forkèd* (An allusion to the horns of the cuckold.)   293 *quicken* receive life. (Quicken may also mean to swarm with maggots as the body festers, as in IV, ii, 69, in which case lines 292–293 suggest that *even then*, in death, we are cuckolded by *forkèd* worms.)   296 *generous* noble   297 *attend* await   301 *watching* too little sleep   303 *napkin* handkerchief   304 *Let it alone* i.e., never mind

Desdemona: I am very sorry that you are not well.   305

  Exit [with Othello].

Emilia [picking up the handkerchief]: I am glad I have found this napkin.
  This was her first remembrance from the Moor.
  My wayward° husband hath a hundred times
  Wooed me to steal it, but she so loves the token—
  For he conjured her she should ever keep it—   310
  That she reserves it evermore about her
  To kiss and talk to. I'll have the work ta'en out,°
  And give 't Iago. What he will do with it
  Heaven knows, not I;
  I nothing but to please his fantasy.°   315

  Enter Iago.

Iago: How now? What do you here alone?
Emilia: Do not you chide. I have a thing for you.
Iago: You have a thing for me? It is a common thing°—
Emilia: Ha?
Iago: To have a foolish wife.   320
Emilia: O, is that all? What will you give me now
  For that same handkerchief?
Iago: What handkerchief?
Emilia: What handkerchief?
  Why, that the Moor first gave to Desdemona;   325
  That which so often you did bid me steal.
Iago: Hast stolen it from her?
Emilia: No, faith. She let it drop by negligence,
  And to th' advantage° I, being here, took 't up.
  Look, here 'tis.
Iago: A good wench! Give it me.   330
Emilia: What will you do with 't, that you have been so earnest
  To have me filch it?
Iago [snatching it]:   Why, what is that to you?
Emilia: If it be not for some purpose of import,
  Give 't me again. Poor lady, she'll run mad
  When she shall lack° it.
Iago: Be not acknown on 't.°   335
  I have use for it. Go, leave me.   *Exit Emilia.*
  I will in Cassio's lodging lose° this napkin
  And let him find it. Trifles light as air
  Are to the jealous confirmations strong
  As proofs of Holy Writ. This may do something.   340

---

308 *wayward* capricious   312 *work ta'en out* design of the embroidery copied   315 *fantasy* whim
318 *common thing* (With bawdy suggestion; *common* suggests coarseness and availability to all comers, and
thing is a slang term for the pudendum.)   329 *to th' advantage* taking the opportunity   335 *lack* miss.   *Be
. . . on 't* do not confess knowledge of it   337 *lose* (The Folio spelling, *loose*, is a normal spelling for "lose,"
but it may also contain the idea of "let go," "release.")

Iago: "I have use for it. Go, leave me. / I will in Cassio's lodging
lose this napkin" (III, iii, 336–337).

The Moor already changes with my poison.
Dangerous conceits° are in their natures poisons,
Which at the first are scarce found to distaste,°
But with a little act° upon the blood
Burn like the mines of sulfur.

Enter Othello.

              I did say so.

Look where he comes! Not poppy nor mandragora°
Nor all the drowsy syrups of the world

345

---

342 *conceits* fancies, ideas   343 *distaste* be distasteful   344 *act* action, working   346 *mandragora* an
opiate made of the mandrake root

Shall ever medicine thee to that sweet sleep
Which thou owedst° yesterday.
Othello: Ha, ha, false to me?
Iago: Why, how now, General? No more of that.   350
Othello: Avaunt! Begone! Thou hast set me on the rack.
I swear 'tis better to be much abused
Than but to know 't a little.
Iago: How now, my lord?
Othello: What sense had I of her stolen hours of lust?
I saw 't not, thought it not, it harmed not me.   355
I slept the next night well, fed well, was free° and merry;
I found not Cassio's kisses on her lips.
He that is robbed, not wanting° what is stolen,
Let him not know 't and he's not robbed at all.
Iago: I am sorry to hear this.   360
Othello: I had been happy if the general camp,
Pioners° and all, had tasted her sweet body,
So° I had nothing known. O, now, forever
Farewell the tranquil mind! Farewell content!
Farewell the plumèd troops and the big° wars   365
That makes ambition virtue! O, farewell!
Farewell the neighing steed and the shrill trump,
The spirit-stirring drum, th' ear-piercing fife,
The royal banner, and all quality,°
Pride,° pomp, and circumstance° of glorious war!   370
And O, you mortal engines,° whose rude throats
Th' immortal Jove's dread clamors° counterfeit,
Farewell! Othello's occupation's gone.
Iago: Is 't possible, my lord?
Othello: Villain, be sure thou prove my love a whore!   375
Be sure of it. Give me the ocular proof,
Or, by the worth of mine eternal soul,
Thou hadst been better have been born a dog
Than answer my waked wrath!
Iago: Is 't come to this?
Othello: Make me to see 't, or at the least so prove it   380
That the probation° bear no hinge nor loop
To hang a doubt on, or woe upon thy life!
Iago: My noble lord—
Othello: If thou dost slander her and torture me,
Never pray more; abandon all remorse;°   385
On horror's head horrors accumulate;°
Do deeds to make heaven weep, all earth amazed;°

---

349 *thou owedst* you did own   356 *free* carefree   358 *wanting* missing   362 *Pioners* diggers of mines, the lowest grade of soldiers   363 *So* provided   365 *big* stately   369 *quality* character, essential nature 370 *Pride* rich display.   *circumstance* pageantry   371 *mortal engines* i.e., cannon. (*Mortal* means "deadly.") 372 *Jove's dread clamors* i.e., thunder   381 *probation* proof   385 *remorse* pity, penitent hope for salvation 386 *horrors accumulate* add still more horrors   387 *amazed* confounded with horror

For nothing canst thou to damnation add
Greater than that.
Iago: O grace! O heaven forgive me!
Are you a man? Have you a soul or sense?   390
God b' wi' you; take mine office. O wretched fool,°
That lov'st to make thine honesty a vice!°
O monstrous world! Take note, take note, O world,
To be direct and honest is not safe.
I thank you for this profit,° and from hence°   395
I'll love no friend, sith° love breeds such offense.°
Othello: Nay, stay. Thou shouldst be° honest.
Iago: I should be wise, for honesty's a fool
And loses that° it works for.
Othello: By the world,
I think my wife be honest and think she is not;   400
I think that thou art just and think thou art not.
I'll have some proof. My name, that was as fresh
As Dian's° visage, is now begrimed and black
As mine own face. If there be cords, or knives,
Poison, or fire, or suffocating streams,   405
I'll not endure it. Would I were satisfied!
Iago: I see, sir, you are eaten up with passion.
I do repent me that I put it to you.
You would be satisfied?
Othello: Would? Nay, and I will.
Iago: And may; but how? How satisfied, my lord?   410
Would you, the supervisor,° grossly gape on?
Behold her topped?
Othello: Death and damnation! O!
Iago: It were a tedious difficulty, I think,
To bring them to that prospect. Damn them then,°
If ever mortal eyes do see them bolster°   415
More° than their own.° What then? How then?
What shall I say? Where's satisfaction?
It is impossible you should see this,
Were they as prime° as goats, as hot as monkeys,
As salt° as wolves in pride,° and fools as gross   420
As ignorance made drunk. But yet I say,
If imputation and strong circumstances°
Which lead directly to the door of truth
Will give you satisfaction, you might have 't.

391 *O wretched fool* (Iago addresses himself as a fool for having carried honesty too far.) 392 *vice* failing, something overdone 395 *profit* profitable instruction. *hence* henceforth 396 *sith* since. *offense* i.e., harm to the one who offers help and friendship 397 *Thou shouldst be* it appears that you are. (But Iago replies in the sense of "ought to be.") 399 *that* what 403 *Dian* Diana, goddess of the moon and of chastity 411 *supervisor* onlooker 414 *Damn them then* i.e., they would have to be really incorrigible 415 *bolster* go to bed together, share a bolster 416 *More* other. *own* own eyes 419 *prime* lustful 420 *salt* wanton, sensual. *pride* heat 422 *imputation . . . circumstances* strong circumstantial evidence

Othello: Give me a living reason she's disloyal.   425
Iago: I do not like the office.
    But sith° I am entered in this cause so far,
    Pricked° to 't by foolish honesty and love,
    I will go on. I lay with Cassio lately,
    And being troubled with a raging tooth   430
    I could not sleep. There are a kind of men
    So loose of soul that in their sleeps will mutter
    Their affairs. One of this kind is Cassio.
    In sleep I heard him say, "Sweet Desdemona,
    Let us be wary, let us hide our loves!"   435
    And then, sir, would he grip and wring my hand,
    Cry "O sweet creature!" and then kiss me hard,
    As if he plucked up kisses by the roots
    That grew upon my lips; then laid his leg
    Over my thigh, and sighed, and kissed, and then   440
    Cried, "Cursèd fate that gave thee to the Moor!"
Othello: O monstrous! Monstrous!
Iago: Nay, this was but his dream.
Othello: But this denoted a foregone conclusion.°
    'Tis a shrewd doubt,° though it be but a dream.
Iago: And this may help to thicken other proofs   445
    That do demonstrate thinly.
Othello: I'll tear her all to pieces.
Iago: Nay, but be wise. Yet we see nothing done;
    She may be honest yet. Tell me but this:
    Have you not sometimes seen a handkerchief
    Spotted with strawberries° in your wife's hand?   450
Othello: I gave her such a one. 'Twas my first gift.
Iago: I know not that; but such a handkerchief—
    I am sure it was your wife's—did I today
    See Cassio wipe his beard with.
Othello: If it be that—
Iago: If it be that, or any that was hers,   455
    It speaks against her with the other proofs.
Othello: O, that the slave° had forty thousand lives!
    One is too poor, too weak for my revenge.
    Now do I see 'tis true. Look here, Iago,
    All my fond° love thus do I blow to heaven.   460
    'Tis gone.
    Arise, black vengeance, from the hollow hell!
    Yield up, O love, thy crown and hearted° throne
    To tyrannous hate! Swell, bosom, with thy freight,°
    For 'tis of aspics'° tongues!   465

---

427 *sith* since   428 *Pricked* spurred   443 *foregone conclusion* concluded experience or action   444 *shrewd doubt* suspicious circumstance   450 *Spotted with strawberries* embroidered with a strawberry pattern   457 *the slave* i.e., Cassio   460 *fond* foolish (but also suggesting "affectionate")   463 *hearted* fixed in the heart   464 *freight* burden   465 *aspics'* venomous serpents'

Iago: Yet be content.°
Othello: O, blood, blood, blood!
Iago: Patience, I say. Your mind perhaps may change.
Othello: Never, Iago. Like to the Pontic Sea,°
    Whose icy current and compulsive course   470
    Ne'er feels retiring ebb, but keeps due on
    To the Propontic° and the Hellespont,°
    Even so my bloody thoughts with violent pace
    Shall ne'er look back, ne'er ebb to humble love,
    Till that a capable° and wide revenge   475
    Swallow them up. Now, by yond marble° heaven,
    [*Kneeling*] In the due reverence of a sacred vow
    I here engage my words.
Iago: Do not rise yet.
    [*He kneels.*°] Witness, you ever-burning lights above,
    You elements that clip° us round about,   480
    Witness that here Iago doth give up
    The execution° of his wit,° hands, heart,
    To wronged Othello's service. Let him command,
    And to obey shall be in me remorse,°
    What bloody business ever.°   [*They rise.*]
Othello: I greet thy love,   485
    Not with vain thanks, but with acceptance bounteous,
    And will upon the instant put thee to 't.°
    Within these three days let me hear thee say
    That Cassio's not alive.
Iago: My friend is dead;
    'Tis done at your request. But let her live.   490
Othello: Damn her, lewd minx!° O, damn her, damn her!
    Come, go with me apart. I will withdraw
    To furnish me with some swift means of death
    For the fair devil. Now art thou my lieutenant.
Iago: I am your own forever.   *Exeunt.* 495

SCENE IV [BEFORE THE CITADEL.]

    Enter Desdemona, Emilia, and Clown.

Desdemona: Do you know, sirrah,° where Lieutenant Cassio lies?°
Clown: I dare not say he lies anywhere.
Desdemona: Why, man?
Clown: He's a soldier, and for me to say a soldier lies, 'tis stabbing.

---

466 *content* calm   469 *Pontic Sea* Black Sea   472 *Propontic* Sea of Marmara, between the Black Sea and
the Aegean. *Hellespont* Dardanelles, straits where the Sea of Marmara joins with the Aegean   475
capable ample, comprehensive   476 *marble* i.e., gleaming like marble and unrelenting   479 s.d. *He kneels*
(In the Quarto text, Iago kneels here after Othello has knelt at line 477.)   480 *clip* encompass   482
execution exercise, action. *wit* mind   484 *remorse* pity (for Othello's wrongs)   485 *ever* soever   487 *to 't*
to the proof   491 *minx* wanton   1 *sirrah* (A form of address to an inferior.) *lies* lodges. (But the Clown
makes the obvious pun.)

Desdemona: Go to. Where lodges he?   5

Clown: To tell you where he lodges is to tell you where I lie.

Desdemona: Can anything be made of this?

Clown: I know not where he lodges, and for me to devise a lodging and say he lies here, or he lies there, were to lie in mine own throat.°

Desdemona: Can you inquire him out, and be edified by report?   10

Clown: I will catechize the world for him; that is, make questions, and by them answer.

Desdemona: Seek him, bid him come hither. Tell him I have moved° my lord on his behalf and hope all will be well.

Clown: To do this is within the compass of man's wit, and therefore I will attempt   15
the doing it.   *Exit Clown.*

Desdemona: Where should I lose that handkerchief, Emilia?

Emilia: I know not, madam.

Desdemona: Believe me, I had rather have lost my purse
 Full of crusadoes;° and but my noble Moor   20
 Is true of mind and made of no such baseness
 As jealous creatures are, it were enough
 To put him to ill thinking.

Emilia: Is he not jealous?

Desdemona: Who, he? I think the sun where he was born
 Drew all such humors° from him.

Emilia: Look where he comes.   25

  Enter Othello.

Desdemona: I will not leave him now till Cassio
 Be called to him.—How is 't with you, my lord?

Othello: Well, my good lady. [*Aside.*] O, hardness to dissemble!—
 How do you, Desdemona?

Desdemona: Well, my good lord.

Othello: Give me your hand. [*She gives her hand.*] This hand is moist, my lady.   30

Desdemona: It yet hath felt no age nor known no sorrow.

Othello: This argues° fruitfulness° and liberal° heart.
 Hot, hot, and moist. This hand of yours requires
 A sequester° from liberty, fasting and prayer,
 Much castigation,° exercise devout;°   35
 For here's a young and sweating devil here
 That commonly rebels. 'Tis a good hand,
 A frank° one.

Desdemona: You may indeed say so,
 For 'twas that hand that gave away my heart.

Othello: A liberal hand. The hearts of old gave hands,°   40

---

9 *lie … throat* (1) lie egregiously and deliberately (2) use the windpipe to speak a lie   13 *moved* petitioned
20 *crusadoes* Portuguese gold coins   25 *humors* (Refers to the four bodily fluids thought to determine temperament.)   32 *argues* gives evidence of. *fruitfulness* generosity, amorousness, and fecundity. *liberal* generous and sexually free   34 *sequester* separation, sequestration   35 *castigation* corrective discipline. *exercise devout* i.e., prayer, religious meditation, etc.   38 *frank* generous, open (with sexual suggestion)   40 *The hearts . . . hands* i.e., in former times, people would give their hearts when they gave their hands to something

"She offers a handkerchief" (III, iv, 47 s.d.).

But our new heraldry is hands, not hearts.°
Desdemona: I cannot speak of this. Come now, your promise.
Othello: What promise, chuck?°
Desdemona: I have sent to bid Cassio come speak with you.
Othello: I have a salt and sorry rheum° offends me;   45
    Lend me thy handkerchief.
Desdemona: Here, my lord.   [*She offers a handkerchief.*]
Othello: That which I gave you.
Desdemona: I have it not about me.
Othello: Not?
Desdemona: No, faith, my lord.   50
Othello: That's a fault. That handkerchief
    Did an Egyptian to my mother give.
    She was a charmer,° and could almost read
    The thoughts of people. She told her, while she kept it
    'Twould make her amiable° and subdue my father   55
    Entirely to her love, but if she lost it
    Or made a gift of it, my father's eye
    Should hold her loathèd and his spirits should hunt

41 *But . . . hearts* i.e., in our decadent times, the joining of hands is no longer a badge to signify the giving of hearts   43 *chuck* (A term of endearment.)   45 *salt . . . rheum* distressful head cold or watering of the eyes   53 *charmer* sorceress   55 *amiable* desirable

After new fancies.° She, dying, gave it me,
And bid me, when my fate would have me wived,   60
To give it her.° I did so; and take heed on 't;
Make it a darling like your precious eye.
To lose 't or give 't away were such perdition°
As nothing else could match.
Desdemona: Is 't possible?
Othello: 'Tis true. There's magic in the web° of it.   65
A sibyl, that had numbered in the world
The sun to course two hundred compasses,°
In her prophetic fury° sewed the work;°
The worms were hallowed that did breed the silk,
And it was dyed in mummy° which the skillful   70
Conserved of° maidens' hearts.
Desdemona: I' faith! Is 't true?
Othello: Most veritable. Therefore look to 't well.
Desdemona: Then would to God that I had never seen 't!
Othello: Ha? Wherefore?
Desdemona: Why do you speak so startingly and rash?°   75
Othello: Is 't lost? Is 't gone? Speak, is 't out o' the way?°
Desdemona: Heaven bless us!
Othello: Say you?
Desdemona: It is not lost; but what an if° it were?
Othello: How?   80
Desdemona: I say it is not lost.
Othello: Fetch 't, let me see 't.
Desdemona: Why, so I can, sir, but I will not now.
This is a trick to put me from my suit.
Pray you, let Cassio be received again.
Othello: Fetch me the handkerchief! My mind misgives.   85
Desdemona: Come, come,
You'll never meet a more sufficient° man.
Othello: The handkerchief!
Desdemona: I pray, talk° me of Cassio.
Othello: The handkerchief!
Desdemona: A man that all his time°
Hath founded his good fortunes on your love,   90
Shared dangers with you—
Othello: The handkerchief!
Desdemona: I' faith, you are to blame.
Othello: Zounds!   *Exit Othello.*
Emilia: Is not this man jealous?   95

59 *fancies* loves   61 *her* i.e., to my wife   63 *perdition* loss   65 *web* fabric, weaving   67 *compasses* annual circlings. (The *sibyl*, or prophetess, was two hundred years old.)   68 *prophetic fury* frenzy of prophetic inspiration.   *work* embroidered pattern   70 *mummy* medicinal or magical preparation drained from mummified bodies   71 *Conserved of* prepared or preserved out of   75 *startingly and rash* disjointedly and impetuously, excitedly   76 *out o' the way* lost, misplaced   79 *an if* if   87 *sufficient* able, complete   88 *talk* talk to   89 *all his time* throughout his career

Desdemona: I ne'er saw this before.
  Sure, there's some wonder in this handkerchief.
  I am most unhappy in the loss of it.
Emilia: 'Tis not a year or two shows us a man.°
  They are all but stomachs, and we all but° food;   100
  They eat us hungerly,° and when they are full
  They belch us.

  Enter Iago and Cassio.

          Look you, Cassio and my husband.
Iago [*to Cassio*]: There is no other way; 'tis she must do 't.
  And, lo, the happiness!° Go and importune her.
Desdemona: How now, good Cassio? What's the news with you?   105
Cassio: Madam, my former suit. I do beseech you
  That by your virtuous° means I may again
  Exist and be a member of his love
  Whom I, with all the office° of my heart,
  Entirely honor. I would not be delayed.   110
  If my offense be of such mortal° kind
  That nor my service past, nor° present sorrows,
  Nor purposed merit in futurity
  Can ransom me into his love again,
  But to know so must be my benefit;°   115
  So shall I clothe me in a forced content,
  And shut myself up in° some other course,
  To fortune's alms.°
Desdemona: Alas, thrice-gentle Cassio,
  My advocation° is not now in tune.
  My lord is not my lord; nor should I know him,   120
  Were he in favor° as in humor° altered.
  So help me every spirit sanctified
  As I have spoken for you all my best
  And stood within the blank° of his displeasure
  For my free speech! You must awhile be patient.   125
  What I can do I will, and more I will
  Than for myself I dare. Let that suffice you.
Iago: Is my lord angry?
Emilia: He went hence but now,
  And certainly in strange unquietness.
Iago: Can he be angry? I have seen the cannon   130
  When it hath blown his ranks into the air,

---

99 *'Tis . . . man* i.e., you can't really know a man even in a year or two of experience (?), or, real men
come along seldom (?)   100 *but* nothing but   101 *hungerly* hungrily   104 *the happiness* in happy time,
fortunately met   107 *virtuous* efficacious   109 *office* loyal service   111 *mortal* fatal   112 *nor . . . nor*
neither . . . nor   115 *But . . . benefit* merely to know that my case is hopeless will have to content me
(and will be better than uncertainty)   117 *shut . . . in* confine myself to   118 *To fortune's alms* throwing
myself on the mercy of fortune   119 *advocation* advocacy   121 *favor* appearance.   *humor* mood   124
within the blank within point-blank range. (The *blank* is the center of the target.)

And like the devil from his very arm
Puffed his own brother—and is he angry?
Something of moment° then. I will go meet him.
There's matter in 't indeed, if he be angry.   135
Desdemona: I prithee, do so.   *Exit [Iago].*
      Something, sure, of state,°
Either from Venice, or some unhatched practice°
Made demonstrable here in Cyprus to him,
Hath puddled° his clear spirit; and in such cases
Men's natures wrangle with inferior things,   140
Though great ones are their object. 'Tis even so;
For let our finger ache, and it indues°
Our other, healthful members even to a sense
Of pain. Nay, we must think men are not gods,
Nor of them look for such observancy°   145
As fits the bridal.° Beshrew me° much, Emilia,
I was, unhandsome° warrior as I am,
Arraigning his unkindness with° my soul;
But now I find I had suborned the witness,°
And he's indicted falsely.
Emilia: Pray heaven it be   150
State matters, as you think, and no conception
Nor no jealous toy° concerning you.
Desdemona: Alas the day! I never gave him cause.
Emilia: But jealous souls will not be answered so;
They are not ever jealous for the cause,   155
But jealous for° they're jealous. It is a monster
Begot upon itself,° born on itself.
Desdemona: Heaven keep that monster from Othello's mind!
Emilia: Lady, amen.
Desdemona: I will go seek him. Cassio, walk hereabout.   160
If I do find him fit, I'll move your suit
And seek to effect it to my uttermost.
Cassio: I humbly thank your ladyship.

 Exit [Desdemona with Emilia].

 Enter Bianca.

Bianca: Save° you, friend Cassio!
Cassio: What make° you from home?
How is 't with you, my most fair Bianca?   165
I' faith, sweet love, I was coming to your house.

---

134 *of moment* of immediate importance, momentous   136 *of state* concerning state affairs   137 *unhatched practice* as yet unexecuted or undiscovered plot   139 *puddled* muddied   142 *indues* brings to the same condition   145 *observancy* attentiveness   146 *bridal* wedding (when a bridegroom is newly attentive to his bride).   *Beshrew me* (A mild oath.)   147 *unhandsome* insufficient, unskillful   148 *with* before the bar of   149 *suborned the witness* induced the witness to give false testimony   152 *toy* fancy   156 *for* because   157 *Begot upon itself* generated solely from itself   164 *Save* God save.   *make* do

Cassio explains to Bianca that he does not know how the handkerchief appeared in his room (III, iv, 175–186).

Bianca: And I was going to your lodging, Cassio.
　　　What, keep a week away? Seven days and nights?
　　　Eightscore-eight° hours? And lovers' absent hours
　　　More tedious than the dial° eightscore times?　　　　　　　170
　　　O weary reckoning!
Cassio: 　　　　　　　Pardon me, Bianca.
　　　I have this while with leaden thoughts been pressed;
　　　But I shall, in a more continuate° time,
　　　Strike off this score° of absence. Sweet Bianca,

169 *Eightscore-eight* one hundred sixty-eight, the number of hours in a week   170 *the dial* a complete revolution of the clock   173 *continuate* uninterrupted   174 *Strike . . . score* settle this account

[*giving her Desdemona's handkerchief*]

Take me this work out.°
Bianca: O Cassio, whence came this?   175
This is some token from a newer friend.°
To the felt absence now I feel a cause.
Is 't come to this? Well, well.
Cassio: Go to, woman!
Throw your vile guesses in the devil's teeth,
From whence you have them. You are jealous now   180
That this is from some mistress, some remembrance.
No, by my faith, Bianca.
Bianca: Why, whose is it?
Cassio: I know not, neither. I found it in my chamber.
I like the work well. Ere it be demanded°—
As like° enough it will—I would have it copied.   185
Take it and do 't, and leave me for this time.
Bianca: Leave you? Wherefore?
Cassio: I do attend here on the General,
And think it no addition,° nor my wish,
To have him see me womaned.   190
Bianca: Why, I pray you?
Cassio: Not that I love you not.
Bianca: But that you do not love me.
I pray you, bring° me on the way a little,
And say if I shall see you soon at night.   195
Cassio: 'Tis but a little way that I can bring you,
For I attend here; but I'll see you soon.
Bianca: 'Tis very good. I must be circumstanced.°

Exeunt omnes.

ACT IV

SCENE I [BEFORE THE CITADEL.]

Enter Othello and Iago.

Iago: Will you think so?
Othello: Think so, Iago?
Iago: What,
To kiss in private?
Othello: An unauthorized kiss!
Iago: Or to be naked with her friend in bed
An hour or more, not meaning any harm?
Othello: Naked in bed, Iago, and not mean harm?   5
It is hypocrisy against the devil.

175 *Take ... out* copy this embroidery for me   176 *friend* mistress   184 *demanded* inquired for   185 *like* likely   189 *addition* i.e., addition to my reputation   194 *bring* accompany   198 *be circumstanced* be governed by circumstance, yield to your conditions

They that mean virtuously and yet do so,
The devil their virtue tempts, and they tempt heaven.
Iago: If they do nothing, 'tis a venial° slip.
But if I give my wife a handkerchief—   10
Othello: What then?
Iago: Why then, 'tis hers, my lord, and being hers,
She may, I think, bestow 't on any man.
Othello: She is protectress of her honor too.
May she give that?   15
Iago: Her honor is an essence that's not seen;
They have it° very oft that have it not.
But, for the handkerchief—
Othello: By heaven, I would most gladly have forgot it.
Thou saidst—O, it comes o'er my memory   20
As doth the raven o'er the infectious house,°
Boding to all—he had my handkerchief.
Iago: Ay, what of that?
Othello: That's not so good now.
Iago: What
If I had said I had seen him do you wrong?
Or heard him say—as knaves be such abroad,°   25
Who having, by their own importunate suit,
Or voluntary dotage° of some mistress,
Convincèd or supplied° them, cannot choose
But they must blab—
Othello: Hath he said anything?
Iago: He hath, my lord; but, be you well assured,   30
No more than he'll unswear.
Othello: What hath he said?
Iago: Faith, that he did—I know not what he did.
Othello: What? What?
Iago: Lie—
Othello: With her?
Iago: With her, on her; what you will.
Othello: Lie with her? Lie on her? We say "lie on her" when they belie° her. Lie   35
with her? Zounds, that's fulsome.°—Handkerchief—confessions—handker-
chief!—To confess and be hanged for his labor—first to be hanged and then
to confess.°—I tremble at it. Nature would not invest herself in such shad-
owing passion without some instruction.° It is not words° that shakes me

---

9 *venial* pardonable   17 *They have it* i.e., they enjoy a reputation for it   21 *raven . . . house* (Allusion to the
belief that the raven hovered over a house of sickness or infection, such as one visited by the plague.)
25 *abroad* around about   27 *voluntary dotage* willing infatuation   28 *Convincèd or supplied* seduced or sexually
gratified   35 *belie* slander   36 *fulsome* foul   37–38 *first . . . to confess* (Othello reverses the proverbial
confess and *be hanged;* Cassio is to be given no time to confess before he dies.)   38–39 *Nature . . . instruction*
i.e., without some foundation in fact, nature would not have dressed herself in such an overwhelming passion that comes over me now and fills my mind with images, or in such a lifelike fantasy as Cassio had in his
dream of lying with Desdemona   39 *words* mere words

Iago lies to Cassio that Othello has "fall'n into an epilepsy" (IV, i, 48).

thus. Pish! Noses, ears, and lips.—Is 't possible?—Confess—handkerchief!—   40
O devil!

Falls in a trance.

Iago: Work on,
My medicine, work! Thus credulous fools are caught,
And many worthy and chaste dames even thus,
All guiltless, meet reproach.—What, ho! My lord!   45
My lord, I say! Othello!

Enter Cassio.

How now, Cassio?
Cassio: What's the matter?
Iago: My lord is fall'n into an epilepsy.
This is his second fit. He had one yesterday.

Cassio: Rub him about the temples.

Iago: No, forbear.   50

The lethargy° must have his° quiet course.
If not, he foams at mouth, and by and by
Breaks out to savage madness. Look, he stirs.
Do you withdraw yourself a little while.
He will recover straight. When he is gone,   55
I would on great occasion° speak with you.

[*Exit Cassio.*]

How is it, General? Have you not hurt your head?

Othello: Dost thou mock me?°

Iago: I mock you not, by heaven.

Would you would bear your fortune like a man!

Othello: A hornèd man's a monster and a beast.   60

Iago: There's many a beast then in a populous city,
And many a civil° monster.

Othello: Did he confess it?

Iago: Good sir, be a man.

Think every bearded fellow that's but yoked°   65
May draw with you.° There's millions now alive
That nightly lie in those unproper° beds
Which they dare swear peculiar.° Your case is better.°
O, 'tis the spite of hell, the fiend's arch-mock,
To lip° a wanton in a secure° couch   70
And to suppose her chaste! No, let me know,
And knowing what I am,° I know what she shall be.°

Othello: O, thou art wise. 'Tis certain.

Iago: Stand you awhile apart;

Confine yourself but in a patient list.°   75
Whilst you were here o'erwhelmèd with your grief—
A passion most unsuiting such a man—
Cassio came hither. I shifted him away,°
And laid good 'scuse upon your ecstasy,°
Bade him anon return and here speak with me,   80
The which he promised. Do but encave° yourself
And mark the fleers,° the gibes, and notable° scorns
That dwell in every region of his face;
For I will make him tell the tale anew,
Where, how, how oft, how long ago, and when   85
He hath and is again to cope° your wife.

---

51 *lethargy* coma. *his* its   56 *on great occasion* on a matter of great importance   58 *mock me* (Othello takes Iago's question about hurting his head to be a mocking reference to the cuckold's horns.)   62 *civil* i.e., dwelling in a city   65 *yoked* (1) married (2) put into the yoke of infamy and cuckoldry   66 *draw with you* pull as you do, like oxen who are yoked, i.e., share your fate as cuckold   67 *unproper* not exclusively their own   68 *peculiar* private, their own. *better* i.e., because you know the truth   70 *lip* kiss. *secure* free from suspicion   72 *what I am* i.e., a cuckold. *she shall be* will happen to her   75 *in . . . list* within the bounds of patience   78 *shifted him away* used a dodge to get rid of him   79 *ecstasy* trance   81 *encave* conceal   82 *fleers* sneers. *notable* obvious   86 *cope* encounter with, have sex with

I say, but mark his gesture. Marry, patience!
Or I shall say you're all-in-all in spleen,°
And nothing of a man.
Othello: Dost thou hear, Iago?
I will be found most cunning in my patience;   90
But—dost thou hear?—most bloody.
Iago: That's not amiss;
But yet keep time° in all. Will you withdraw?

[_Othello stands apart._]

Now will I question Cassio of Bianca,
A huswife° that by selling her desires
Buys herself bread and clothes. It is a creature   95
That dotes on Cassio—as 'tis the strumpet's plague
To beguile many and be beguiled by one.
He, when he hears of her, cannot restrain°
From the excess of laughter. Here he comes.

Enter Cassio.

As he shall smile, Othello shall go mad;   100
And his unbookish° jealousy must conster°
Poor Cassio's smiles, gestures, and light behaviors
Quite in the wrong.—How do you now, Lieutenant?
Cassio: The worser that you give me the addition°
Whose want° even kills me.   105
Iago: Ply Desdemona well and you are sure on 't.
[_Speaking lower._] Now, if this suit lay in Bianca's power,
How quickly should you speed!
Cassio [_laughing_]: Alas, poor caitiff!°
Othello [_aside_]: Look how he laughs already!   110
Iago: I never knew a woman love man so.
Cassio: Alas, poor rogue! I think, i' faith, she loves me.
Othello: Now he denies it faintly, and laughs it out.
Iago: Do you hear, Cassio?
Othello: Now he importunes him
To tell it o'er. Go to!° Well said,° well said.   115
Iago: She gives it out that you shall marry her.
Do you intend it?
Cassio: Ha, ha, ha!
Othello: Do you triumph, Roman?° Do you triumph?
Cassio: I marry her? What? A customer?° Prithee, bear some charity to my wit;°   120
do not think it so unwholesome. Ha, ha, ha!

---

88 _all-in-all in spleen_ utterly governed by passionate impulses   92 _keep time_ keep yourself steady (as in music)   94 _huswife_ hussy   98 _restrain_ refrain   101 _unbookish_ uninstructed.   _conster_ construe   104 _addition_ title   105 _Whose want_ the lack of which   109 _caitiff_ wretch   115 _Go to_ (An expression of remonstrance.)   _Well said_ well done   119 _Roman_ (The Romans were noted for their _triumphs_ or triumphal processions.)   120 _customer_ i.e., prostitute.   _bear . . . wit_ be more charitable to my judgment

Othello: So, so, so, so! They laugh that win.°
Iago: Faith, the cry° goes that you shall marry her.
Cassio: Prithee, say true.
Iago: I am a very villain else.°   125
Othello: Have you scored me?° Well.
Cassio: This is the monkey's own giving out. She is persuaded I will marry her out of
    her own love and flattery,° not out of my promise.
Othello: Iago beckons me.° Now he begins the story.
Cassio: She was here even now; she haunts me in every place. I was the other day 130
    talking on the seabank° with certain Venetians, and thither comes the bauble,°
    and, by this hand,° she falls me thus about my neck—

[*He embraces Iago.*]

Othello: Crying, "O dear Cassio!" as it were; his gesture imports it.
Cassio: So hangs and lolls and weeps upon me, so shakes and pulls me. Ha, ha, ha!
Othello: Now he tells how she plucked him to my chamber. O, I see that nose of 135
    yours, but not that dog I shall throw it to.°
Cassio: Well, I must leave her company.
Iago: Before me,° look where she comes.

Enter Bianca [*with Othello's handkerchief*].

Cassio: 'Tis such another fitchew!° Marry, a perfumed one.—What do you mean by
    this haunting of me?   140
Bianca: Let the devil and his dam° haunt you! What did you mean by that same
    handkerchief you gave me even now? I was a fine fool to take it. I must take out
    the work? A likely piece of work,° that you should find it in your chamber and
    know not who left it there! This is some minx's token, and I must take out the
    work? There; give it your hobbyhorse.° [*She gives him the handkerchief.*] Wheresoever 145
    you had it, I'll take out no work on 't.
Cassio: How now, my sweet Bianca? How now? How now?
Othello: By heaven, that should be° my handkerchief!
Bianca: If you'll come to supper tonight, you may; if you will not, come when you are
    next prepared for.°   *Exit.* 150
Iago: After her, after her.
Cassio: Faith, I must. She'll rail in the streets else.
Iago: Will you sup there?
Cassio: Faith, I intend so.
Iago: Well, I may chance to see you, for I would very fain speak with you.   155
Cassio: Prithee, come. Will you?
Iago: Go to.° Say no more.   [*Exit Cassio.*]

---

122 *They . . . win* i.e., they that laugh last laugh best   123 *cry* rumor   125 *I . . . else* call me a complete
rogue if I'm not telling the truth   126 *scored me* scored off me, beaten me, made up my reckoning, branded
me   128 *flattery* self-flattery, self-deception   129 *beckons* signals   131 *seabank* seashore. *bauble* play-
thing   132 *by this hand* I make my vow   136 *not . . . to* (Othello imagines himself cutting off Cassio's nose
and throwing it to a dog.)   138 *Before me* i.e., on my soul   139 *'Tis . . . fitchew* what a polecat she is! Just
like all the others. (Polecats were often compared with prostitutes because of their rank smell and presumed lechery.)   141 *dam* mother   143 *A likely . . . work* a fine story   145 *hobbyhorse* harlot   148 *should
be* must be   149–150 *when . . . for* when I'm ready for you (i.e., never)   157 *Go to* (An expression of
remonstrance.)

Othello [*advancing*]: How shall I murder him, Iago?

Iago: Did you perceive how he laughed at his vice?

Othello: O, Iago!   160

Iago: And did you see the handkerchief?

Othello: Was that mine?

Iago: Yours, by this hand. And to see how he prizes the foolish woman your wife!
She gave it him, and he hath given it his whore.

Othello: I would have him nine years a-killing. A fine woman! A fair woman! A   165
sweet woman!

Iago: Nay, you must forget that.

Othello: Ay, let her rot and perish, and be damned tonight, for she shall not live. No,
my heart is turned to stone; I strike it, and it hurts my hand. O, the world hath
not a sweeter creature! She might lie by an emperor's side and command him   170
tasks.

Iago: Nay, that's not your way.°

Othello: Hang her! I do but say what she is. So delicate with her needle! An admirable
musician! O, she will sing the savageness out of a bear. Of so high and plenteous
wit and invention!°   175

Iago: She's the worse for all this.

Othello: O, a thousand, a thousand times! And then, of so gentle a condition!°

Iago: Ay, too gentle.°

Othello: Nay, that's certain. But yet the pity of it, Iago! O, Iago, the pity of it, Iago!

Iago: If you are so fond° over her iniquity, give her patent° to offend, for if it touch   180
not you it comes near nobody.

Othello: I will chop her into messes.° Cuckold me?

Iago: O, 'tis foul in her.

Othello: With mine officer?

Iago: That's fouler.   185

Othello: Get me some poison, Iago, this night. I'll not expostulate with her, lest her
body and beauty unprovide° my mind again. This night, Iago.

Iago: Do it not with poison. Strangle her in her bed, even the bed she hath
contaminated.

Othello: Good, good! The justice of it pleases. Very good.   190

Iago: And for Cassio, let me be his undertaker.° You shall hear more by midnight.

Othello: Excellent good. [*A trumpet within.*] What trumpet is that same?

Iago: I warrant, something from Venice.

> *Enter Lodovico, Desdemona, and attendants.*

'Tis Lodovico. This comes from the Duke.
See, your wife's with him.

Lodovico: God save you, worthy General!

Othello: With all my heart,° sir.

Lodovico [*giving him a letter*]: The Duke and the senators of Venice greet you.

Othello: I kiss the instrument of their pleasures.

---

172 *your way* i.e., the way you should think of her   175 *invention* imagination   177 *gentle a condition* wellborn
and well-bred   178 *gentle* generous, yielding (to other men)   180 *fond* foolish.   *patent* license   182 *messes*
portions of meat, i.e., bits   187 *unprovide* weaken, render unfit   191 *be his undertaker* undertake to dispatch him
196 *With all my heart* i.e., I thank you most heartily

[*He opens the letter, and reads.*]

Desdemona: And what's the news, good cousin Lodovico?
Iago: I am very glad to see you, signor.   200
    Welcome to Cyprus.
Lodovico: I thank you. How does Lieutenant Cassio?
Iago: Lives, sir.
Desdemona: Cousin, there's fall'n between him and my lord
    An unkind° breach; but you shall make all well.   205
Othello: Are you sure of that?
Desdemona: My lord?
Othello [*reads*]: "This fail you not to do, as you will—"
Lodovico: He did not call; he's busy in the paper.
    Is there division twixt my lord and Cassio?   210
Desdemona: A most unhappy one. I would do much
    T' atone° them, for the love I bear to Cassio.
Othello: Fire and brimstone!
Desdemona: My lord?
Othello: Are you wise?   215
Desdemona: What, is he angry?
Lodovico: Maybe the letter moved him;
    For, as I think, they do command him home,
    Deputing Cassio in his government.°
Desdemona: By my troth, I am glad on 't.°
Othello: Indeed?   220
Desdemona: My lord?
Othello: I am glad to see you mad.°
Desdemona: Why, sweet Othello—
Othello [*striking her*]: Devil!
Desdemona: I have not deserved this.   225
Lodovico: My lord, this would not be believed in Venice,
    Though I should swear I saw 't. 'Tis very much.°
    Make her amends; she weeps.
Othello: O devil, devil!
    If that the earth could teem° with woman's tears,
    Each drop she falls would prove a crocodile.°   230
    Out of my sight!
Desdemona: I will not stay to offend you. [*Going.*]
Lodovico: Truly, an obedient lady.
    I do beseech your lordship, call her back.
Othello: Mistress!
Desdemona [*returning*]: My lord?   235
Othello: What would you with her, sir?°

---

205 *unkind* unnatural, contrary to their natures; hurtful 212 *atone* reconcile 218 *government* office
219 *on 't* of it 222 *I am . . . mad* i.e., I am glad to see that you are insane enough to rejoice in Cassio's
promotion (?) (Othello bitterly plays on Desdemona's *I am glad.*) 227 *very much* too much, outrageous
229 *teem* breed, be impregnated 230 *falls . . . crocodile* (Crocodiles were supposed to weep hypocritical
tears for their victims.) 236 *What . . . sir* (Othello implies that Desdemona is pliant and will do a *turn*,
lines 238–240, for any man.)

Lodovico: Who, I, my lord?
Othello: Ay, you did wish that I would make her turn.
　　Sir, she can turn, and turn, and yet go on
　　And turn again; and she can weep, sir, weep;　　　　　　　　240
　　And she's obedient,° as you say, obedient,
　　Very obedient.—Proceed you in your tears.—
　　Concerning this, sir—O well-painted passion!°—
　　I am commanded home.—Get you away;
　　I'll send for you anon.—Sir, I obey the mandate　　　　　245
　　And will return to Venice.—Hence, avaunt!

　　[*Exit Desdemona.*]

　　Cassio shall have my place. And, sir, tonight
　　I do entreat that we may sup together.
　　You are welcome, sir, to Cyprus.—Goats and monkeys!°　　　　*Exit.*
Lodovico: Is this the noble Moor whom our full Senate　　　　250
　　Call all in all sufficient? Is this the nature
　　Whom passion could not shake? Whose solid virtue
　　The shot of accident nor dart of chance
　　Could neither graze nor pierce?
Iago:　　　　　　　　　　　　　He is much changed.
Lodovico: Are his wits safe? Is he not light of brain?　　　　255
Iago: He's that he is. I may not breathe my censure
　　What he might be. If what he might he is not,
　　I would to heaven he were!°
Lodovico:　　　　　　　　　What, strike his wife?
Iago: Faith, that was not so well; yet would I knew
　　That stroke would prove the worst!
Lodovico:　　　　　　　　　　Is it his use?°　　　　260
　　Or did the letters work upon his blood°
　　And new-create his fault?
Iago:　　　　　　　　　　Alas, alas!
　　It is not honesty in me to speak
　　What I have seen and known. You shall observe him,
　　And his own courses will denote° him so　　　　　　　265
　　That I may save my speech. Do but go after,
　　And mark how he continues.
Lodovico: I am sorry that I am deceived in him.　　　　　*Exeunt.*

SCENE II [THE CITADEL.]

　　Enter Othello and Emilia.

Othello: You have seen nothing then?
Emilia: Nor ever heard, nor ever did suspect.

241 *obedient* (With much the same sexual connotation as *turn* in lines 238–240.)　243 *passion* i.e., grief
249 *Goats and monkeys* (See III, iii, 419.)　256–258 *I may . . . were* i.e., I dare not venture an opinion as
to whether he's of unsound mind, as you suggest, but, if he isn't, then it might be better to wish he were in
fact insane, since only that could excuse his wild behavior　260 *use* custom　261 *blood* passions　265
courses will denote actions will reveal

Othello: Yes, you have seen Cassio and she together.
Emilia: But then I saw no harm, and then I heard
    Each syllable that breath made up between them. 5
Othello: What, did they never whisper?
Emilia: Never, my lord.
Othello: Nor send you out o' the way?
Emilia: Never.
Othello: To fetch her fan, her gloves, her mask, nor nothing? 10
Emilia: Never, my lord.
Othello: That's strange.
Emilia: I durst, my lord, to wager she is honest,
    Lay down my soul at stake.° If you think other,
    Remove your thought; it doth abuse your bosom.° 15
    If any wretch have put this in your head,
    Let heaven requite it with the serpent's curse!°
    For if she be not honest, chaste, and true,
    There's no man happy; the purest of their wives
    Is foul as slander.
Othello: Bid her come hither. Go. 20

    Exit Emilia.

    She says enough; yet she's a simple bawd
    That cannot say as much.° This° is a subtle whore,
    A closet lock and key° of villainous secrets.
    And yet she'll kneel and pray; I have seen her do 't.

    Enter Desdemona and Emilia.

Desdemona: My lord, what is your will? 25
Othello: Pray you, chuck, come hither.
Desdemona: What is your pleasure?
Othello: Let me see your eyes.
    Look in my face.
Desdemona: What horrible fancy's this?
Othello [to Emilia]: Some of your function,° mistress.
    Leave procreants° alone and shut the door; 30
    Cough or cry "hem" if anybody come.
    Your mystery, your mystery!° Nay, dispatch.

    Exit Emilia.

Desdemona [kneeling]: Upon my knees, what doth your speech import?
    I understand a fury in your words,
    But not the words. 35
Othello: Why, what art thou?

14 *at stake* as the wager   15 *abuse your bosom* deceive you   17 *the serpent's curse* the curse pronounced by God on the serpent for deceiving Eve, just as some man has done to Othello and Desdemona. (See Genesis 3:14.)   21–22 *she's . . . much* i.e., any procuress or go-between who couldn't make up as plausible a story as Emilia's would have to be pretty stupid   22 *This* i.e., Desdemona   23 *closet lock and key* i.e., concealer   29 *Some . . . function* i.e., practice your chosen profession, that of bawd (by guarding the door) 30 *procreants* mating couples   32 *mystery* trade, occupation

"Ah, Desdemon! Away, away, away!" (IV, ii, 43).

Desdemona:	Your wife, my lord, your true
	And loyal wife.
Othello:	Come, swear it, damn thyself,

Lest, being like one of heaven,° the devils themselves
Should fear to seize thee. Therefore be double damned:
Swear thou art honest.

Desdemona: Heaven doth truly know it.   40
Othello: Heaven truly knows that thou art false as hell.
Desdemona: To whom, my lord? With whom? How am I false?
Othello [*weeping*]: Ah, Desdemon! Away, away, away!
Desdemona: Alas the heavy day! Why do you weep?
    Am I the motive° of these tears, my lord?   45

38 *being . . . heaven* looking like an angel   45 *motive* cause

If haply you my father do suspect
An instrument of this your calling back,
Lay not your blame on me. If you have lost him,
I have lost him too.
Othello: Had it pleased heaven
To try me with affliction, had they° rained   50
All kinds of sores and shames on my bare head,
Steeped me in poverty to the very lips,
Given to captivity me and my utmost hopes,
I should have found in some place of my soul
A drop of patience. But, alas, to make me   55
A fixèd figure for the time of scorn°
To point his° slow and moving finger° at!
Yet could I bear that too, well, very well.
But there where I have garnered° up my heart,
Where either I must live or bear no life,   60
The fountain° from the which my current runs
Or else dries up—to be discarded thence!
Or keep it as a cistern° for foul toads
To knot° and gender° in! Turn thy complexion there,°
Patience, thou young and rose-lipped cherubin—   65
Ay, there look grim as hell!°
Desdemona: I hope my noble lord esteems me honest.°
Othello: O, ay, as summer flies are in the shambles,°
That quicken° even with blowing.° O thou weed,
Who art so lovely fair and smell'st so sweet   70
That the sense aches at thee, would thou hadst ne'er been born!
Desdemona: Alas, what ignorant° sin have I committed?
Othello: Was this fair paper, this most goodly book,
Made to write "whore" upon? What committed?
Committed? O thou public commoner!°   75
I should make very forges of my cheeks,
That would to cinders burn up modesty,
Did I but speak thy deeds. What committed?
Heaven stops the nose at it and the moon winks;°
The bawdy° wind, that kisses all it meets,   80
Is hushed within the hollow mine° of earth
And will not hear 't. What committed?
Impudent strumpet!

---

50 *they* i.e., heavenly powers   56 *time of scorn* i.e., scornful world   57 *his* its *slow and moving finger* i.e., hour hand of the clock, moving so slowly it seems hardly to move at all. (Othello envisages himself as being eternally pointed at by the scornful world as the numbers on a clock are pointed at by the hour hand.)   59 *garnered* stored   61 *fountain* spring   63 *cistern* cesspool   64 *knot* couple. *gender* engender. *Turn . . . there* change your color, grow pale, at such a sight   65–66 *Patience . . . hell* (Even Patience, that rose-lipped cherub, will look grim and pale at this spectacle.)   67 *honest* chaste   68 *shambles* slaughterhouse   69 *quicken* come to life. *with blowing* i.e., with the puffing up of something rotten in which maggots are breeding   72 *ignorant sin* sin in ignorance   75 *commoner* prostitute   79 *winks* closes her eyes. (The moon symbolizes chastity.)   80 *bawdy* kissing one and all   81 *mine* cave (where the winds were thought to dwell)

Othello berates Desdemona as a "strumpet" and "cunning whore" (IV, ii, 73–98).

Desdemona: By heaven, you do me wrong.
Othello: Are not you a strumpet?
Desdemona: No, as I am a Christian.
   If to preserve this vessel° for my lord   85
   From any other foul unlawful touch
   Be not to be a strumpet, I am none.
Othello: What, not a whore?
Desdemona: No, as I shall be saved.
Othello: Is 't possible?   90
Desdemona: O, heaven forgive us!
Othello: I cry you mercy,° then.
   I took you for that cunning whore of Venice
   That married with Othello. [*Calling out.*] You, mistress,
   That have the office opposite to Saint Peter   95
   And keep the gate of hell!

   Enter Emilia.

              You, you, ay, you!
   We have done our course.° There's money for your pains.   [*He gives money.*]
   I pray you, turn the key and keep our counsel.

                                                              Exit.

86 *vessel* body   92 *cry you mercy* beg your pardon   97 *course* business (with an indecent suggestion of "trick," turn at sex)

Emilia: Alas, what does this gentleman conceive?°
How do you, madam? How do you, my good lady?   100
Desdemona: Faith, half asleep.°
Emilia: Good madam, what's the matter with my lord?
Desdemona: With who?
Emilia: Why, with my lord, madam.
Desdemona: Who is thy lord?
Emilia: He that is yours, sweet lady.   105
Desdemona: I have none. Do not talk to me, Emilia.
I cannot weep, nor answers have I none
But what should go by water.° Prithee, tonight
Lay on my bed my wedding sheets, remember;
And call thy husband hither.   110
Emilia: Here's a change indeed!   *Exit.*
Desdemona: 'Tis meet I should be used so, very meet.°
How have I been behaved, that he might stick°
The small'st opinion° on my least misuse?°

     Enter Iago.

Iago: What is your pleasure, madam? How is 't with you?   115
Desdemona: I cannot tell. Those that do teach young babes
Do it with gentle means and easy tasks.
He might have chid me so, for, in good faith,
I am a child to chiding.
Iago: What is the matter, lady?   120
Emilia: Alas, Iago, my lord hath so bewhored her,
Thrown such despite and heavy terms upon her,
That true hearts cannot bear it.
Desdemona: Am I that name, Iago?
Iago: What name, fair lady?   125
Desdemona: Such as she said my lord did say I was.
Emilia: He called her whore. A beggar in his drink
Could not have laid such terms upon his callet.°
Iago: Why did he so?
Desdemona [weeping]: I do not know. I am sure I am none such.   130
Iago: Do not weep, do not weep. Alas the day!
Emilia: Hath she forsook so many noble matches,
Her father and her country and her friends,
To be called whore? Would it not make one weep?
Desdemona: It is my wretched fortune.
Iago: Beshrew° him for 't!   135
How comes this trick° upon him?
Desdemona: Nay, heaven doth know.
Emilia: I will be hanged if some eternal° villain,

---

99 *conceive* suppose, think   101 *half asleep* i.e., dazed   108 *go by water* be expressed by tears   112 *meet*
fitting   113 *stick* attach   114 *opinion* censure. *least misuse* slightest misconduct   128 *callet* whore
135 *Beshrew* curse   136 *trick* strange behavior, delusion   137 *eternal* inveterate

Iago comforts Desdemona regarding Othello's accusations (IV, ii, 115–179).

    Some busy and insinuating° rogue,
    Some cogging,° cozening° slave, to get some office,
    Have not devised this slander. I will be hanged else.   140
Iago: Fie, there is no such man. It is impossible.
Desdemona: If any such there be, heaven pardon him!
Emilia: A halter° pardon him! And hell gnaw his bones!
    Why should he call her whore? Who keeps her company?
    What place? What time? What form?° What likelihood?   145
    The Moor's abused by some most villainous knave,
    Some base notorious knave, some scurvy fellow.
    O heaven, that° such companions° thou'dst unfold,°
    And put in every honest hand a whip
    To lash the rascals naked through the world   150
    Even from the east to th' west!
Iago: Speak within door.°
Emilia: O, fie upon them! Some such squire° he was
    That turned your wit the seamy side without°
    And made you to suspect me with the Moor.
Iago: You are a fool. Go to.°
Desdemona: Alas, Iago,   155
    What shall I do to win my lord again?

138 *insinuating* ingratiating, fawning, wheedling   139 *cogging* cheating.   *cozening* defrauding   143 *halter* hangman's noose   145 *form* appearance, circumstance   148 *that* would that.   *companions* fellows. *unfold* expose   151 *within door* i.e., not so loud   152 *squire* fellow   153 *seamy side without* wrong side out   155 *Go to* i.e., that's enough

Good friend, go to him; for, by this light of heaven,
I know not how I lost him. Here I kneel. [*She kneels.*]
If e'er my will did trespass 'gainst his love,
Either in discourse of thought° or actual deed,   160
Or that° mine eyes, mine ears, or any sense
Delighted them° in any other form;
Or that I do not yet,° and ever did,
And ever will—though he do shake me off
To beggarly divorcement—love him dearly,   165
Comfort forswear° me! Unkindness may do much,
And his unkindness may defeat° my life,
But never taint my love. I cannot say "whore."
It does abhor° me now I speak the word;
To do the act that might the addition° earn   170
Not the world's mass of vanity° could make me.

   [*She rises.*]

Iago: I pray you, be content. 'Tis but his humor.°
   The business of the state does him offense,
   And he does chide with you.
Desdemona: If 'twere no other—   175
Iago: It is but so, I warrant.   [*Trumpets within.*]
   Hark, how these instruments summon you to supper!
   The messengers of Venice stays the meat.°
   Go in, and weep not. All things shall be well.

   Exeunt Desdemona and Emilia.

   Enter Roderigo.

   How now, Roderigo?   180
Roderigo: I do not find that thou deal'st justly with me.
Iago: What in the contrary?
Roderigo: Every day thou daff'st me° with some device,° Iago, and rather, as it seems
   to me now, keep'st from me all conveniency° than suppliest me with the least
   advantage° of hope. I will indeed no longer endure it, nor am I yet persuaded to   185
   put up° in peace what already I have foolishly suffered.
Iago: Will you hear me, Roderigo?
Roderigo: Faith, I have heard too much, for your words and performances are no kin
   together.
Iago: You charge me most unjustly.   190
Roderigo: With naught but truth. I have wasted myself out of my means. The jewels
   you have had from me to deliver° Desdemona would half have corrupted a

---

160 *discourse of thought* process of thinking   161 *that* if. (Also in line 163.)   162 *Delighted them* took
delight   163 *yet still*   166 *Comfort forswear* may heavenly comfort forsake   167 *defeat* destroy   169
abhor (1) fill me with abhorrence (2) make me whorelike   170 *addition* title   171 *vanity* showy splendor
172 *humor* mood   178 *stays the meat* are waiting to dine   183 *thou daff'st me* you put me off.   *device*
excuse, trick   184 *conveniency* advantage, opportunity   185 *advantage* increase   186 *put up* submit to,
tolerate   192 *deliver* deliver to

votarist.° You have told me she hath received them and returned me expectations and comforts of sudden respect° and acquaintance, but I find none.

Iago: Well, go to, very well. 195

Roderigo: "Very well"! "Go to"! I cannot go to,° man, nor 'tis not very well. By this hand, I think it is scurvy, and begin to find myself fopped° in it.

Iago: Very well.

Roderigo: I tell you 'tis not very well.° I will make myself known to Desdemona. If she will return me my jewels, I will give over my suit and repent my unlawful 200 solicitation; if not, assure yourself I will seek satisfaction° of you.

Iago: You have said now?°

Roderigo: Ay, and said nothing but what I protest intendment° of doing.

Iago: Why, now I see there's mettle in thee, and even from this instant do build on thee a better opinion than ever before. Give me thy hand, Roderigo. Thou hast 205 taken against me a most just exception; but yet I protest I have dealt most directly in thy affair.

Roderigo: It hath not appeared.

Iago: I grant indeed it hath not appeared, and your suspicion is not without wit and judgment. But, Roderigo, if thou hast that in thee indeed which I have greater 210 reason to believe now than ever—I mean purpose, courage, and valor—this night show it. If thou the next night following enjoy not Desdemona, take me from this world with treachery and devise engines for° my life.

Roderigo: Well, what is it? Is it within reason and compass?

Iago: Sir, there is especial commission come from Venice to depute Cassio in Othello's 215 place.

Roderigo: Is that true? Why, then Othello and Desdemona return again to Venice.

Iago: O, no; he goes into Mauritania and takes away with him the fair Desdemona, unless his abode be lingered here by some accident; wherein none can be so determinate° as the removing of Cassio. 220

Roderigo: How do you mean, removing of him?

Iago: Why, by making him uncapable of Othello's place—knocking out his brains.

Roderigo: And that you would have me to do?

Iago: Ay, if you dare do yourself a profit and a right. He sups tonight with a harlotry,° and thither will I go to him. He knows not yet of his honorable fortune. If you 225 will watch his going thence, which I will fashion to fall out° between twelve and one, you may take him at your pleasure. I will be near to second your attempt, and he shall fall between us. Come, stand not amazed at it, but go along with me. I will show you such a necessity in his death that you shall think yourself bound to put it on him. It is now high° suppertime, and the night grows to waste.° 230 About it.

Roderigo: I will hear further reason for this.

Iago: And you shall be satisfied. *Exeunt.*

---

193 *votarist* nun   194 *sudden respect* immediate consideration   196 *I cannot go to* (Roderigo changes Iago's *go to,* an expression urging patience, to *I cannot go to,* "I have no opportunity for success in wooing.") 197 *fopped* fooled, duped   199 *not very well* (Roderigo changes Iago's *very well,* "all right, then," to *not very well,* "not at all good.")   201 *satisfaction* repayment. (The term normally means settling of accounts in a duel.)   202 *You . . . now* have you finished?   203 *intendment* intention   213 *engines for* plots against 220 *determinate* conclusive   224 *harlotry* slut   226 *fall out* occur   230 *high* fully.   *grows to waste* wastes away

SCENE III [THE CITADEL.]

Enter Othello, Lodovico, Desdemona, Emilia, and attendants.

Lodovico: I do beseech you, sir, trouble yourself no further.
Othello: O, pardon me; 'twill do me good to walk.
Lodovico: Madam, good night. I humbly thank your ladyship.
Desdemona: Your honor is most welcome.
Othello: Will you walk, sir?
    O, Desdemona!   5
Desdemona: My lord?
Othello: Get you to bed on th' instant. I will be returned
    forthwith. Dismiss your attendant there.
    Look 't be done.
Desdemona: I will, my lord.   10

    Exit [*Othello, with Lodovico and attendants*].

Emilia: How goes it now? He looks gentler than he did.
Desdemona: He says he will return incontinent,°
    And hath commanded me to go to bed,
    And bid me to dismiss you.
Emilia: Dismiss me?   15
Desdemona: It was his bidding. Therefore, good Emilia,
    Give me my nightly wearing, and adieu.
    We must not now displease him.
Emilia: I would you had never seen him!
Desdemona: So would not I. My love doth so approve him   20
    That even his stubbornness,° his checks,° his frowns—
    Prithee, unpin me—have grace and favor in them.

    [*Emilia prepares Desdemona for bed.*]

Emilia: I have laid those sheets you bade me on the bed.
Desdemona: All's one.° Good faith, how foolish are our minds!
    If I do die before thee, prithee shroud me   25
    In one of these same sheets.
Emilia: Come, come, you talk.°
Desdemona: My mother had a maid called Barbary.
    She was in love, and he she loved proved mad°
    And did forsake her. She had a song of "Willow."
    An old thing 'twas, but it expressed her fortune,   30
    And she died singing it. That song tonight
    Will not go from my mind; I have much to do
    But to go hang° my head all at one side
    And sing it like poor Barbary. Prithee, dispatch.
Emilia: Shall I go fetch your nightgown?°   35

---

12 *incontinent* immediately   21 *stubbornness* roughness.   *checks* rebukes   24 *All's one* all right. It doesn't
really matter   26 *talk* i.e., prattle   28 *mad* wild, i.e., faithless   32–33 *I . . . hang* I can scarcely keep myself from hanging   35 *nightgown* dressing gown

Desdemona: No, unpin me here.
　　This Lodovico is a proper° man.
Emilia: A very handsome man.
Desdemona: He speaks well.
Emilia: I know a lady in Venice would have walked barefoot to Palestine for a touch　　40
　　of his nether lip.
Desdemona [*singing*]:
　　　　"The poor soul sat sighing by a sycamore tree,
　　　　　Sing all a green willow;°
　　　　Her hand on her bosom, her head on her knee,
　　　　　Sing willow, willow, willow.　　45
　　　　The fresh streams ran by her and murmured her moans;
　　　　　Sing willow, willow, willow;
　　　　Her salt tears fell from her, and softened the stones—"
　　Lay by these.
　　　　[*Singing.*] "Sing willow, willow, willow—"　　50
　　Prithee, hie thee.° He'll come anon.°
　　　　[*Singing.*] "Sing all a green willow must be my garland.
　　　　Let nobody blame him; his scorn I approve—"
　　Nay, that's not next.—Hark! Who is 't that knocks?
Emilia: It's the wind.　　55
Desdemona [*singing*]:
　　　　"I called my love false love; but what said he then?
　　　　　Sing willow, willow, willow;
　　　　If I court more women, you'll couch with more men."

　　So, get thee gone. Good night. Mine eyes do itch;
　　Doth that bode weeping?
Emilia:　　　　　　　　　　'Tis neither here nor there.　　60
Desdemona: I have heard it said so. O, these men, these men!
　　Dost thou in conscience think—tell me, Emilia—
　　That there be women do abuse° their husbands
　　In such gross kind?
Emilia:　　　　　　　There be some such, no question.
Desdemona: Wouldst thou do such a deed for all the world?　　65
Emilia: Why, would not you?
Desdemona:　　　　　　　No, by this heavenly light!
Emilia: Nor I neither by this heavenly light;
　　I might do 't as well i' the dark.
Desdemona: Wouldst thou do such a deed for all the world?
Emilia: The world's a huge thing. It is a great price　　70
　　For a small vice.
Desdemona: Good troth, I think thou wouldst not.
Emilia: By my troth, I think I should, and undo 't when I had done. Marry, I would
　　not do such a thing for a joint ring,° nor for measures of lawn,° nor for gowns,
　　petticoats, nor caps, nor any petty exhibition.° But for all the whole world! Uds°　　75

---

37 *proper* handsome　43 *willow* (A conventional emblem of disappointed love.)　51 *hie thee* hurry.　*anon*
right away　63 *abuse* deceive　74 *joint ring* a ring made in separate halves.　*lawn* fine linen　75 *exhibition*
gift.　*Uds* God's

pity, who would not make her husband a cuckold to make him a monarch? I
should venture purgatory for 't.

Desdemona: Beshrew me if I would do such a wrong
For the whole world.

Emilia: Why, the wrong is but a wrong i' the world, and having the world for your   80
labor, 'tis a wrong in your own world, and you might quickly make it right.

Desdemona: I do not think there is any such woman.

Emilia: Yes, a dozen, and as many
To th' vantage° as would store° the world they played° for.
But I do think it is their husbands' faults   85
If wives do fall. Say that they slack their duties°
And pour our treasures into foreign laps,°
Or else break out in peevish jealousies,
Throwing restraint upon us?° Or say they strike us,
Or scant our former having in despite?°   90
Why, we have galls,° and though we have some grace,
Yet have we some revenge. Let husbands know
Their wives have sense° like them. They see, and smell,
And have their palates both for sweet and sour,
As husbands have. What is it that they do   95
When they change us for others? Is it sport?°
I think it is. And doth affection° breed it?
I think it doth. Is 't frailty that thus errs?
It is so, too. And have not we affections,
Desires for sport, and frailty, as men have?   100
Then let them use us well; else let them know,
The ills we do, their ills instruct us so.

Desdemona: Good night, good night. God me such uses° send
Not to pick bad from bad, but by bad mend!°

Exeunt.

ACT V

SCENE I [A STREET IN CYPRUS.]

Enter Iago and Roderigo.

Iago: Here stand behind this bulk.° Straight will he come.
Wear thy good rapier bare,° and put it home.
Quick, quick! Fear nothing. I'll be at thy elbow.
It makes us or it mars us. Think on that,
And fix most firm thy resolution.   5

Roderigo: Be near at hand. I may miscarry in 't.

84 *To th' vantage* in addition, to boot.   *store* populate.   *played* (1) gambled (2) sported sexually   86 *duties*
marital duties   87 *pour . . . laps* i.e., are unfaithful, give what is rightfully ours (semen) to other women
89 *Throwing . . . us* i.e., jealously restricting our freedom to see other men   90 *scant . . . despite* reduce
our allowance to spite us   91 *have galls* i.e., are capable of resenting injury and insult   93 *sense* physical
sense   96 *sport* sexual pastime   97 *affection* passion   103 *uses* habit, practice   104 *Not . . . mend* i.e.,
not to learn bad conduct from others' badness (as Emilia has suggested women learn from men), but to
mend my ways by perceiving what badness is, making spiritual benefit out of evil and adversity   1 *bulk*
framework projecting from the front of a shop   2 *bare* unsheathed

Iago: Here, at thy hand. Be bold, and take thy stand.

[*Iago stands aside. Roderigo conceals himself.*]

Roderigo: I have no great devotion to the deed;
    And yet he hath given me satisfying reasons.
    'Tis but a man gone. Forth, my sword! He dies.   10

[*He draws.*]

Iago: I have rubbed this young quat° almost to the sense,°
    And he grows angry. Now, whether he kill Cassio
    Or Cassio him, or each do kill the other,
    Every way makes my gain. Live Roderigo,°
    He calls me to a restitution large   15
    Of gold and jewels that I bobbed° from him
    As gifts to Desdemona.
    It must not be. If Cassio do remain,
    He hath a daily beauty in his life
    That makes me ugly; and besides, the Moor   20
    May unfold° me to him; there stand I in much peril.
    No, he must die. Be 't so. I hear him coming.

    Enter Cassio.

Roderigo [*coming forth*]: I know his gait, 'tis he.—Villain, thou diest!

[*He attacks Cassio.*]

Cassio: That thrust had been mine enemy indeed,
    But that my coat° is better than thou know'st.   25
    I will make proof° of thine.

[*He draws, and wounds Roderigo.*]

Roderigo: O, I am slain!   [*He falls.*]

[*Iago, from behind, wounds Cassio in the leg, and exits.*]

Cassio: I am maimed forever. Help, ho! Murder! Murder!

    Enter Othello.

Othello: The voice of Cassio! Iago keeps his word.
Roderigo: O, villain that I am!
Othello: It is even so.   30
Cassio: O, help, ho! Light! A surgeon!
Othello: 'Tis he. O brave Iago, honest and just,
    That hast such noble sense of thy friend's wrong!
    Thou teachest me. Minion,° your dear lies dead,

---

11 *quat* pimple, pustule.   *to the sense* to the quick   14 *Live Roderigo* if Roderigo lives   16 *bobbed* swindled
21 *unfold* expose   25 *coat* (Possibly a garment of mail under the outer clothing, or simply a tougher coat
than Roderigo expected.)   26 *proof* a test   34 *Minion* hussy (i.e., Desdemona)

And your unblest fate hies.° Strumpet, I come.   35
Forth of° my heart those charms, thine eyes, are blotted;
Thy bed, lust-stained, shall with lust's blood be spotted.   *Exit Othello.*

Enter Lodovico and Gratiano.

Cassio: What ho! No watch? No passage?° Murder! Murder!
Gratiano: 'Tis some mischance. The voice is very direful.
Cassio: O, help!   40
Lodovico: Hark!
Roderigo: O wretched villain!
Lodovico: Two or three groan. 'Tis heavy° night;
      These may be counterfeits. Let's think 't unsafe
      To come in to° the cry without more help.   45

[*They remain near the entrance.*]

Roderigo: Nobody come? Then shall I bleed to death.

Enter Iago [*in his shirtsleeves, with a light*].

Lodovico: Hark!
Gratiano: Here's one comes in his shirt, with light and weapons.
Iago: Who's there? Whose noise is this that cries on° murder?
Lodovico: We do not know.
Iago: Did not you hear a cry?   50
Cassio: Here, here! For heaven's sake, help me!
Iago: What's the matter?

[*He moves toward Cassio.*]

Gratiano [*to Lodovico*]: This is Othello's ancient, as I take it.
Lodovico [*to Gratiano*]: The same indeed, a very valiant fellow.
Iago [*to Cassio*]: What° are you here that cry so grievously?
Cassio: Iago? O, I am spoiled,° undone by villains!   55
      Give me some help.
Iago: O me, Lieutenant! What villains have done this?
Cassio: I think that one of them is hereabout,
      And cannot make° away.
Iago: O treacherous villains!

[*To Lodovico and Gratiano.*]

      What are you there? Come in, and give some help.   [*They advance.*] 60
Roderigo: O, help me there!
Cassio: That's one of them.
Iago: O murderous slave! O villain!

[*He stabs Roderigo.*]

---

35 *hies* hastens on   36 *Forth of* from out   38 *passage* people passing by   43 *heavy* thick, dark   45 *come in to* approach   49 *cries on* cries out   54 *What* who (also at lines 60 and 66)   55 *spoiled* ruined, done for   59 *make* get

Roderigo: O damned Iago! O inhuman dog!
Iago: Kill men i' the dark?—Where be these bloody thieves?—
    How silent is this town!—Ho! Murder, murder!—   65
    [*To Lodovico and Gratiano.*] What may you be? Are you of good or evil?
Lodovico: As you shall prove us, praise° us.
Iago: Signor Lodovico?
Lodovico: He, sir.
Iago: I cry you mercy.° Here's Cassio hurt by villains.   70
Gratiano: Cassio?
Iago: How is 't, brother?
Cassio: My leg is cut in two.
Iago: Marry, heaven forbid!
    Light, gentlemen! I'll bind it with my shirt.   75

    [*He hands them the light, and tends to Cassio's wound.*]

    Enter Bianca.

Bianca: What is the matter, ho? Who is 't that cried?
Iago: Who is 't that cried?
Bianca: O my dear Cassio!
    My sweet Cassio! O Cassio, Cassio, Cassio!
Iago: O notable strumpet! Cassio, may you suspect
    Who they should be that have thus mangled you?   80
Cassio: No.
Gratiano: I am sorry to find you thus. I have been to seek you.
Iago: Lend me a garter. [*He applies a tourniquet.*] So.—O, for a chair,°
    To bear him easily hence!
Bianca: Alas, he faints! O Cassio, Cassio, Cassio!   85
Iago: Gentlemen all, I do suspect this trash
    To be a party in this injury.—
    Patience awhile, good Cassio.—Come, come;
    Lend me a light.   [*He shines the light on Roderigo.*]
              Know we this face or no?
    Alas, my friend and my dear countryman
    Roderigo! No.—Yes, sure.—O heaven! Roderigo!   90
Gratiano: What, of Venice?
Iago: Even he, sir. Did you know him?
Gratiano: Know him? Ay.
Iago: Signor Gratiano? I cry your gentle° pardon.   95
    These bloody accidents° must excuse my manners
    That so neglected you.
Gratiano: I am glad to see you.
Iago: How do you, Cassio? O, a chair, a chair!
Gratiano: Roderigo!
Iago: He, he, 'tis he. [*A litter is brought in.*] O, that's well said;° the chair.   100
    Some good man bear him carefully from hence;

---

67 *praise* appraise   70 *I cry you mercy* I beg your pardon   83 *chair* litter   95 *gentle* noble   96 *accidents* sudden events   100 *well said* well done

I'll fetch the General's surgeon. [*To Bianca.*] For you, mistress,
Save you your labor.°—He that lies slain here, Cassio,
Was my dear friend. What malice° was between you?
Cassio: None in the world, nor do I know the man.   105
Iago [*to Bianca*]: What, look you pale?—O, bear him out o' th' air.°

    [*Cassio and Roderigo are borne off.*]

Stay you,° good gentlemen.—Look you pale, mistress?—
Do you perceive the gastness° of her eye?—
Nay, if you stare,° we shall hear more anon.—
Behold her well; I pray you, look upon her.   110
Do you see, gentlemen? Nay, guiltiness
Will speak, though tongues were out of use.

    [*Enter Emilia.*]

Emilia: 'Las, what's the matter? What's the matter, husband?
Iago: Cassio hath here been set on in the dark
By Roderigo and fellows that are scaped.   115
He's almost slain, and Roderigo dead.
Emilia: Alas, good gentleman! Alas, good Cassio!
Iago: This is the fruits of whoring. Prithee, Emilia,
Go know° of Cassio where he supped tonight.
[*To Bianca.*] What, do you shake at that?   120
Bianca: He supped at my house, but I therefore shake not.
Iago: O, did he so? I charge you go with me.
Emilia: O, fie upon thee, strumpet!
Bianca: I am no strumpet, but of life as honest°
As you that thus abuse me.   125
Emilia: As I? Faugh! Fie upon thee!
Iago: Kind gentlemen, let's go see poor Cassio dressed.°—
Come, mistress, you must tell's another tale.
Emilia, run you to the citadel
And tell my lord and lady what hath happed.—   130
Will you go on afore? [*Aside.*] This is the night
That either makes me or fordoes° me quite.   *Exeunt.*

SCENE II [A BEDCHAMBER IN THE CITADEL.]

    Enter Othello [*with a light*], *and Desdemona in her bed.*°

Othello: It is the cause,° it is the cause, my soul.
Let me not name it to you, you chaste stars!
It is the cause. Yet I'll not shed her blood,

---

103 *Save . . . labor* i.e., never you mind tending Cassio   104 *malice* enmity   106 *bear . . . air* (Fresh air was thought to be dangerous for a wound.)   107 *Stay you* (Lodovico and Gratiano are evidently about to leave.)   108 *gastness* terror   109 *stare* (Iago pretends to interpret Bianca's wild looks as an involuntary confession of guilt.)   119 *know* learn   124 *honest* chaste   127 *Cassio dressed* Cassio's wounds dressed   132 *fordoes* undoes, ruins   s.d. *in her bed* (Either the curtains are drawn back to reveal the bed in a recessed area backstage, or the bed is "thrust out" onstage as the scene begins.)   1 *cause* i.e., cause of justice, the offense itself, which Othello must correct as an agent of justice

"Enter Othello, and Desdemona in her bed" (V, ii, s.d.).

Nor scar that whiter skin of hers than snow,
And smooth as monumental° alabaster.   5
Yet she must die, else she'll betray more men.
Put out the light, and then put out the light.°
If I quench thee, thou flaming minister,°
I can again thy former light restore,
Should I repent me;° but once put out thy light,   10
Thou cunning'st pattern° of excelling nature,
I know not where is that Promethean heat°
That can thy light relume.° When I have plucked thy rose,
I cannot give it vital growth again;
It needs must wither. I'll smell thee on the tree.   15

[*He kisses her.*]

O balmy breath, that dost almost persuade
Justice to break her sword! One more, one more.
Be thus when thou art dead, and I will kill thee,
And love thee after. One more, and that's the last.

[*He kisses her.*]

5 *monumental* i.e., used in making tombs and funeral monuments;   7 *the light . . . light* the torch or lamp . . .
Desdemona's life   8 *flaming minister* torch or lamp that serves me   10 *repent me* change my mind   11 *Thou
. . . pattern* you skillfully wrought perfect example   12 *Promethean heat* divine fire. (Alluding to the theft of
fire from heaven by Prometheus.)   13 *relume* rekindle

So sweet was ne'er so fatal. I must weep,   20
But they are cruel° tears. This sorrow's heavenly;
It strikes where it doth love.° She wakes.
Desdemona: Who's there? Othello?
Othello: Ay, Desdemona.
Desdemona: Will you come to bed, my lord?   25
Othello: Have you prayed tonight, Desdemon?
Desdemona: Ay, my lord.
Othello: If you bethink yourself of any crime°
  Unreconciled as yet to heaven and grace,
  Solicit° for it straight.°   30
Desdemona: Alack, my lord, what may you mean by that?
Othello: Well, do it, and be brief. I will walk by.
  I would not kill thy unpreparèd spirit.
  No, heaven forfend!° I would not kill thy soul.
Desdemona: Talk you of killing?
Othello: Ay, I do.
Desdemona: Then heaven   35
  Have mercy on me!
Othello: Amen, with all my heart!
Desdemona: If you say so, I hope you will not kill me.
Othello: Humh!
Desdemona: And yet I fear you; for you're fatal then
  When your eyes roll so. Why I should fear I know not,   40
  Since guiltiness I know not; but yet I feel I fear.
Othello: Think on thy sins.
Desdemona: They are loves I bear to you.°
Othello: Ay, and for that thou diest.
Desdemona: That death's unnatural that kills for loving.
  Alas, why gnaw you so your nether lip?   45
  Some bloody passion shakes your very frame.
  These are portents; but yet I hope, I hope,
  They do not point on° me.
Othello: Peace, and be still!
Desdemona: I will so. What's the matter?   50
Othello: That handkerchief which I so loved and gave thee
  Thou gav'st to Cassio.
Desdemona: No, by my life and soul!
  Send for the man and ask him.
Othello: Sweet soul, take heed, take heed of perjury.
  Thou art on thy deathbed.   55
Desdemona: Ay, but not yet to die.
Othello: Yes, presently.°

---

21 *cruel* unrelenting   22 *It . . . love* (Compare Hebrews 12:6: "For whom the Lord loveth he chas-
teneth.")   28 *crime* sin   30 *Solicit* petition, pray.   *straight* immediately   34 *forfend* forbid   42 *They
are . . . you* i.e., if I sinned, it was in loving you more than my father or more than God   48 *point on* point
at, predict what is to happen to   56 *presently* immediately

Therefore confess thee freely of thy sin;
For to deny each article with oath
Cannot remove nor choke the strong conception°
That I do groan withal.° Thou art to die.   60
Desdemona: Then Lord have mercy on me!
Othello: I say, amen.
Desdemona: And have you mercy too! I never did
    Offend° you in my life; never loved Cassio
    But with such general warranty° of heaven
    As I might love. I never gave him token.   65
Othello: By heaven, I saw my handkerchief in 's hand.
    O perjured woman! Thou dost stone° my heart,
    And makes me call what I intend to do
    A murder, which I thought a sacrifice.
    I saw the handkerchief.
Desdemona: He found it, then.   70
    I never gave it him. Send for him hither;
    Let him confess a truth.
Othello: He hath confessed.
Desdemona: What, my lord?
Othello: That he hath used thee.
Desdemona: How? Unlawfully?
Othello: Ay.
Desdemona: He will not say so.
Othello: No, his mouth is stopped;   75
    Honest Iago hath ta'en order° for 't.
Desdemona: O, my fear interprets. What, is he dead?
Othello: Had all his hairs been lives, my great revenge
    Had stomach for them all.
Desdemona: Alas, he is betrayed and I undone!   [*She weeps.*]   80
Othello: Out, strumpet! Weep'st thou for him to my face?
Desdemona: O, banish me, my lord, but kill me not!
Othello: Down, strumpet!
Desdemona: Kill me tomorrow; let me live tonight!
Othello: Nay, if you strive—   85
Desdemona: But half an hour!
Othello: Being done,° there is no pause.
Desdemona: But while I say one prayer!
Othello: It is too late.

    Smothers her.

Emilia [*at the door*]: My lord, my lord! What, ho! My lord, my lord!
Othello: What noise is this? Not dead? Not yet quite dead?
    I that am cruel am yet merciful;   90
    I would not have thee linger in thy pain.

---

59 *conception* (1) belief in your guilt (2) plan in my mind   60 *groan withal* (1) groan at in sorrow (2) as in giving birth   63 *Offend* wrong   64 *warranty* sanction   67 *stone* turn to stone, harden   76 *ta'en order* taken measures   86 *Being done* i.e., since justice has begun its relentless course

Othello smothers Desdemona, (V, ii, 87–91).

[*He dispatches her*.]

                                                So, so.

Emilia [*within*]: What, ho! My lord, my lord!

Othello: Who's there?

Emilia [*within*]: O, good my lord, I would speak a word with you!

Othello: Yes, 'tis Emilia.—By and by.—She's dead.

    'Tis like° she comes to speak of Cassio's death.—   95

    The noise was here.° Ha! No more moving?

    Still as the grave. Shall she come in? Were 't good?—

    I think she stirs again. No. What's best to do?

    If she come in, she'll sure speak to my wife.

    My wife! My wife! What wife? I have no wife.   100

    O, insupportable! O heavy hour!

    Methinks it should be now a huge eclipse

    Of sun and moon, and that th' affrighted globe

    Should yawn° at alteration.°

Emilia [*within*]:   I do beseech you

    That I may speak with you, O, good my lord!   105

Othello: I had forgot thee. O, come in, Emilia.—

    Soft,° by and by. Let me the curtains draw.—

---

95 *like* likely that   96 *here* (The Folio's *high* is possible, suggesting that the commotion of the attack on Cassio was loud.)   104 *yawn* gape in amazement, i.e., move in an earthquake. (According to Pliny, earthquakes often happen during eclipses.)   *at alteration* at these cataclysmic events in nature, well suited to express the horror of Desdemona's death   107 *Soft* wait a minute

[*He closes the bed-curtains and opens the door.*]

Where art thou?

Enter Emilia.

What's the matter with thee now?
Emilia: O, my good lord, yonder's foul murders done!
Othello: What, now?   110
Emilia: But now, my lord.
Othello: It is the very error° of the moon;
    She comes more nearer earth than she was wont,
    And makes men mad.
Emilia: Cassio, my lord, hath killed a young Venetian   115
    Called Roderigo.
Othello: Roderigo killed?
    And Cassio killed?
Emilia: No, Cassio is not killed.
Othello: Not Cassio killed? Then murder's out of tune,
    And sweet revenge grows harsh.
Desdemona: O, falsely, falsely murdered!   120
Emilia: O Lord, what cry is that?
Othello: That? What?
Emilia: Out° and alas, that was my lady's voice.

[*She opens the bed-curtains.*]

Help, help, ho, help! O lady, speak again!
Sweet Desdemona! O sweet mistress, speak!   125
Desdemona: A guiltless death I die.
Emilia: O, who hath done this deed?
Desdemona: Nobody; I myself. Farewell.
    Commend me to my kind lord. O, farewell!   [*She dies.*]
Othello: Why, how should she be murdered?
Emilia: Alas, who knows?   130
Othello: You heard her say herself it was not I.
Emilia: She said so. I must needs report the truth.
Othello: She's like a liar gone to burning hell!
    'Twas I that killed her.
Emilia: O, the more angel she,
    And you the blacker devil!   135
Othello: She turned to folly,° and she was a whore.
Emilia: Thou dost belie° her, and thou art a devil.
Othello: She was false as water.
Emilia: Thou art rash as fire to say
    That she was false. O, she was heavenly true!   140
Othello: Cassio did top her. Ask thy husband else.°

---

112 *error* aberration, irregularity   123 *Out* (A cry of dismay, intensifying *alas*.)   136 *folly* i.e., wantonness, fleshly sin   137 *belie* slander   141 *else* i.e., if you don't believe me

Emilia declares Desdemona's innocence (V, ii, 134–164).

O, I were damned beneath all depth in hell
But that I did proceed upon just grounds
To this extremity. Thy husband knew it all.
Emilia: My husband?   145
Othello: Thy husband.
Emilia: That she was false to wedlock?
Othello: Ay, with Cassio. Nay, had she been true,
  If heaven would make me such another world
  Of one entire and perfect chrysolite,°   150
  I'd not have sold her for it.
Emilia: My husband?
Othello: Ay, 'twas he that told me on her first.
  An honest man he is, and hates the slime
  That sticks on filthy deeds.   155
Emilia: My husband?
Othello: What needs this iterance,° woman? I say thy husband.
Emilia: O mistress, villainy hath made mocks with° love!
  My husband say that she was false?
Othello: He, woman;

150 *chrysolite* precious topaz   157 *iterance* iteration, repetition   158 *made mocks with* derided, made sport of

I say thy husband. Dost understand the word?   160
My friend, thy husband, honest, honest Iago.
Emilia: If he say so, may his pernicious soul
   Rot half a grain a day! He lies to th' heart.
   She was too fond of her most filthy bargain.
Othello: Ha?   [*He draws.*]   165
Emilia: Do thy worst!
   This deed of thine is no more worthy heaven
   Than thou wast worthy her.
Othello: Peace, you were best.°
Emilia: Thou hast not half that power to do me harm
   As I have to be hurt.° O gull!° O dolt!   170
   As ignorant as dirt! Thou hast done a deed—
   I care not for thy sword; I'll make thee known,
   Though I lost twenty lives.—Help! Help, ho, help!
   The Moor hath killed my mistress! Murder, murder!

   Enter Montano, Gratiano, and Iago.

Montano: What is the matter? How now, General?   175
Emilia: O, are you come, Iago? You have done well,
   That men must lay their murders on your neck.
Gratiano: What is the matter?
Emilia [*to Iago*]: Disprove this villain, if thou be'st a man.
   He says thou toldst him that his wife was false.   180
   I know thou didst not; thou'rt not such a villain.
   Speak, for my heart is full.
Iago: I told him what I thought, and told no more
   Than what he found himself was apt° and true.
Emilia: But did you ever tell him she was false?   185
Iago: I did.
Emilia: You told a lie, an odious, damnèd lie!
   Upon my soul, a lie, a wicked lie.
   She false with Cassio? Did you say with Cassio?
Iago: With Cassio, mistress. Go to, charm° your tongue.   190
Emilia: I will not charm my tongue; I am bound to speak.
   My mistress here lies murdered in her bed—
All: O heavens forfend!
Emilia: And your reports have set the murder on.
Othello: Nay, stare not, masters. It is true indeed.   195
Gratiano: 'Tis a strange truth.
Montano: O monstrous act!
Emilia: Villainy, villainy, villainy!
   I think upon 't—I think I smell 't! O villainy!
   I thought so then°—I'll kill myself for grief—
   O villainy, villainy!   200

---

168 *you were best* it would be best for you   170 *to be hurt* i.e., to endure hurt.   *gull* dupe   184 *apt* plausible
190 *charm* keep silent (as though by a magic spell)   199 *then* (Perhaps at III, iii, 331–332 and IV, ii, 137–154.)

Iago: What, are you mad? I charge you, get you home.

Emilia: Good gentlemen, let me have leave to speak.
    'Tis proper I obey him, but not now.
    Perchance, Iago, I will ne'er go home.

Othello: O! O! O!   [*Othello falls on the bed.*°]

Emilia: Nay, lay thee down and roar,   205
    For thou hast killed the sweetest innocent
    That e'er did lift up eye.°

Othello [*rising*]:   O, she was foul!
    I scarce did know you, uncle. There lies your niece,
    Whose breath indeed these hands have newly stopped.
    I know this act shows° horrible and grim.   210

Gratiano: Poor Desdemon! I am glad thy father's dead.
    Thy match was mortal to him, and pure grief
    Shore his old thread° in twain. Did he live now,
    This sight would make him do a desperate turn,°
    Yea, curse his better angel from his side,   215
    And fall to reprobance.°

Othello: 'Tis pitiful. But yet Iago knows
    That she with Cassio hath the act of shame
    A thousand times committed. Cassio confessed it;
    And she did gratify° his amorous works   220
    With that recognizance° and pledge of love
    Which I first gave her. I saw it in his hand;
    It was a handkerchief, an antique token
    My father gave my mother.

Emilia: O God! O heavenly God!   225

Iago: Zounds, hold your peace.

Emilia: 'Twill out, 'twill out! I peace?
    No, I will speak as liberal as the north.°
    Let heaven and men and devils, let them all,
    All, all, cry shame against me, yet I'll speak.

Iago: Be wise, and get you home.

Emilia: I will not.

    [*Iago threatens Emilia.*]

Gratiano: Fie!   230
    Your sword upon a woman?

Emilia: O thou dull Moor! That handkerchief thou speak'st of
    I found by fortune and did give my husband;
    For often, with a solemn earnestness,
    More than indeed belonged° to such a trifle,   235
    He begged of me to steal 't.

---

205 s.d. *Othello . . . bed* (This direction is from the Quarto, as also *He kisses her* at line 19 and *She dies* at line 129.)   207 *lift up eye* i.e., lift her eyes to heaven   210 *shows* looks   213 *Shore . . . thread* sheared the thread of his old age (as Atropos, one of the three Fates, was thought to do)   214 *turn* deed   216 *reprobance* damnation, i.e., suicide   220 *gratify* reward   221 *recognizance* token   227 *liberal as the north* freely as the north wind (blows)   235 *belonged* was appropriate

Iago: Villainous whore!
Emilia: She give it Cassio? No, alas! I found it,
     And I did give 't my husband.
Iago: Filth, thou liest!
Emilia: By heaven, I do not, I do not, gentlemen.
     O murderous coxcomb!° What should such a fool   240
     Do with so good a wife?
Othello: Are there no stones° in heaven
     But what serves for the thunder?—Precious° villain!

     [*He runs at Iago; Montano disarms Othello. Iago, from behind, stabs Emilia.°*]

Gratiano: The woman falls! Sure he hath killed his wife.
Emilia: Ay, ay. O, lay me by my mistress' side.   245

     Exit [Iago.]

Gratiano: He's gone, but his wife's killed.
Montano: 'Tis a notorious villain. Take you this weapon,
     Which I have here recovered from the Moor.
     Come, guard the door without. Let him not pass,
     But kill him rather. I'll after that same villain,   250
     For 'tis a damnèd slave.

     Exit [with all but Othello and Emilia, who has been laid by Desdemona's side].

Othello: I am not valiant neither,
     But every puny whipster° gets my sword.
     But why should honor° outlive honesty?°
     Let it go all.
Emilia: What did thy song bode, lady?   255
     Hark, canst thou hear me? I will play the swan,
     And die in music. [*She sings.*] "Willow, willow, willow."
     Moor, she was chaste. She loved thee, cruel Moor.
     So come my soul to bliss as I speak true.
     So speaking as I think, alas, I die.   [*She dies.*]   260
Othello: I have another weapon in this chamber;
     It was a sword of Spain, the ice-brook's temper°—
     O, here it is. [*He finds a sword.*] Uncle, I must come forth.
Gratiano [*within*]: If thou attempt it, it will cost thee dear.
     Thou hast no weapon, and perforce must suffer.   265
Othello: Look in upon me then and speak with me,
     Or, naked° as I am, I will assault thee.

     [*Enter Gratiano.*]

---

240 *coxcomb* fool. (Addressed to Othello.)   242 *stones* bolts, such as those used for thunderbolts   243 *Precious* i.e., arrant, utter. s.d. *He . . . Emilia* (The Quarto text reads, "The Moor runs at Iago. Iago kills his wife." The Quarto also specifies the exit of Iago at line 245 and the death of Emilia at line 260.)   253 *whipster* contemptible fellow (one who is always ready to whip out his sword)   254 *honor* i.e., the bravery for which one enjoys a soldier's reputation.   *honesty* true integrity   262 *the ice-brook's temper* tempered in ice-cold water   267 *naked* unarmed

Gratiano: What is the matter?
Othello: Behold, I have a weapon;
   A better never did itself sustain
   Upon a soldier's thigh. I have seen the day   270
   That, with this little arm and this good sword,
   I have made my way through more impediments
   Than twenty times your stop.° But O, vain boast!
   Who can control his fate? 'Tis not so now.
   Be not afraid, though you do see me weaponed;   275
   Here is my journey's end, here is my butt°
   And very seamark° of my utmost sail.

   [*Gratiano steps back.*]

   Do you go back dismayed? 'Tis a lost° fear;
   Man but a rush° against Othello's breast
   And he retires. Where should Othello go?   280

   [*He turns to Desdemona.*]

   Now, how dost thou look now? O ill-starred wench!
   Pale as thy smock! When we shall meet at compt,°
   This look of thine will hurl my soul from heaven,
   And fiends will snatch at it. Cold, cold, my girl?
   Even like thy chastity. O cursèd, cursèd slave!°   285
   Whip me, ye devils,
   From the possession of this heavenly sight!
   Blow me about in winds! Roast me in sulfur!
   Wash me in steep-down gulfs of liquid fire!
   O Desdemon! Dead, Desdemon! Dead! O! O!   290

   *Enter Lodovico, Cassio [carried in a litter°], Montano, and Iago [prisoner], with
   officers.*

Lodovico: Where is this rash and most unfortunate man?
Othello: That's he that was Othello. Here I am.
Lodovico: Where is that viper? Bring the villain forth.

   [*Iago is led forward.*]

Othello: I look down towards his feet;° but that's a fable.
   If that thou be'st a devil, I cannot kill thee.   295

   [*He wounds Iago.*]

Lodovico: Wrench his sword from him.   [*Othello is disarmed.*]
Iago: I bleed, sir, but not killed.

---

273 *stop* power (to stop) 276 *butt* goal, limit. (An archery term.) 277 *seamark* beacon (marking his destination or limit) 278 *lost* wasted, unneeded 279 *Man . . . rush* wield no more than a reed 282 *compt* account,
judgment day 285 *slave* i.e., Othello himself 290 s.d. *in a litter* (The Quarto specifies that Cassio is "in a
chair.") 294 *towards his feet* i.e., to see if they are cloven, as the devil's are fabled to be

Lodovico confronts the prisoner Iago; Desdemona and Emilia lie dead in the background (V, ii, 296–314).

Othello: I am not sorry neither. I'd have thee live,
    For in my sense° 'tis happiness to die.
Lodovico: O thou Othello, that was once so good,
    Fall'n in the practice° of a cursèd slave,°   300
    What shall be said to thee?
Othello: Why, anything.
    An honorable murderer, if you will,
    For naught I did in hate, but all in honor.
Lodovico: This wretch hath part confessed his villainy.
    Did you and he consent° in Cassio's death?   305
Othello: Ay.
Cassio: Dear General, I never gave you cause.
Othello: I do believe it, and I ask your pardon.
    Will you, I pray, demand that demi-devil
    Why he hath thus ensnared my soul and body?   310
Iago: Demand me nothing. What you know, you know.
    From this time forth I never will speak word.
Lodovico: What, not to pray?
Gratiano: Torments° will ope your lips.
Othello: Well, thou dost best.   315
Lodovico: Sir, you shall understand what hath befall'n,

298 *in my sense* to one who feels as I do   300 *in the practice* through the plotting, into the snare.   *slave* villain   305 *consent* agree   314 *Torments* torture

Which, as I think, you know not. Here is a letter
Found in the pocket of the slain Roderigo;
And here another. [*He produces letters*.] The one of them imports
The death of Cassio, to be undertook   320
By Roderigo.
Othello: O villain!
Cassio: Most heathenish and most gross!°
Lodovico [*showing another paper*]: Now here's another discontented° paper
Found in his pocket too. And this, it seems,
Roderigo meant t' have sent this damnèd villain;   325
But that belike° Iago in the interim
Came in and satisfied him.°
Othello: O thou pernicious caitiff!—
How came you, Cassio, by that handkerchief
That was my wife's?
Cassio: I found it in my chamber;   330
And he himself confessed but even now
That there he dropped it for a special purpose
Which wrought to his desire.°
Othello: O fool, fool, fool!
Cassio: There is besides in Roderigo's letter
How he upbraids Iago, that he made him   335
Brave° me upon the watch, whereon it came°
That I was cast;° and even but now he spake,
After long seeming dead, Iago hurt him,
Iago set him on.
Lodovico [*to Othello*]: You must forsake this room and go with us.   340
Your power and your command is taken off,°
And Cassio rules in Cyprus. For this slave,
If there be any cunning cruelty
That can torment him much and hold him long,°
It shall be his. You shall close prisoner rest°   345
Till that the nature of your fault be known
To the Venetian state.—Come, bring away.
Othello: Soft you;° a word or two before you go.
I have done the state some service, and they know 't.
No more of that. I pray you, in your letters,   350
When you shall these unlucky° deeds relate,
Speak of me as I am; nothing extenuate,
Nor set down aught in malice. Then must you speak
Of one that loved not wisely but too well;
Of one not easily jealous but, being wrought,°   355

---

322 *gross* monstrous   323 *discontented* full of discontent   326 *belike* most likely   327 *Came . . . him* interposed and gave him satisfactory explanation   333 *wrought . . . desire* worked out as he wished, fitted in
with his plan   336 *Brave* defy.   *whereon it came* whereof it came about   337 *cast* dismissed   341 *taken off*
taken away   344 *hold him long* keep him alive a long time (during his torture)   345 *rest* remain   348 *Soft
you* one moment   351 *unlucky* unfortunate   355 *wrought* worked upon, worked into a frenzy

Perplexed° in the extreme; of one whose hand,
Like the base Indian,° threw a pearl away
Richer than all his tribe; of one whose subdued° eyes,
Albeit unusèd to the melting mood,
Drop tears as fast as the Arabian trees   360
Their medicinable gum.° Set you down this;
And say besides that in Aleppo once,
Where a malignant and a turbaned Turk
Beat a Venetian and traduced the state,
I took by th' throat the circumcisèd dog   365
And smote him, thus.   [*He stabs himself.*°]
Lodovico: O bloody period!°
Gratiano: All that is spoke is marred.
Othello: I kissed thee ere I killed thee. No way but this,
Killing myself, to die upon a kiss.   370

[*He kisses Desdemona and dies.*]

Cassio: This did I fear, but thought he had no weapon;
For he was great of heart.
Lodovico [*to Iago*]:   O Spartan dog,°
More fell° than anguish, hunger, or the sea!
Look on the tragic loading of this bed.
This is thy work. The object poisons sight;   375
Let it be hid.° Gratiano, keep° the house,

[*The bed curtains are drawn*]

And seize upon° the fortunes of the Moor,
For they succeed on° you. [*To Cassio.*] To you, Lord Governor,
Remains the censure° of this hellish villain,
The time, the place, the torture. O, enforce it!   380
Myself will straight aboard, and to the state
This heavy act with heavy heart relate.   *Exeunt.*

Questions

ACT I

1. What is Othello's position in society? How is he regarded by those who know him? By his own words, when we first meet him in Scene ii, what traits of character does he manifest?
2. How do you account for Brabantio's dismay on learning of his daughter's marriage, despite the fact that Desdemona has married a man so generally honored and admired?
3. What is Iago's view of human nature? In his fondness for likening men to animals (as in I, i, 49–50; I, i, 90–91; and I, iii, 378–379), what does he tell us about himself?
4. What reasons does Iago give for his hatred of Othello?

356 *Perplexed* distraught   357 *Indian* (This reading from the Quarto pictures an ignorant savage who cannot recognize the value of a precious jewel. The Folio reading, *Iudean* or *Judean*, i.e., infidel or disbeliever, may refer to Herod, who slew Miriamne in a fit of jealousy, or to Judas Iscariot, the betrayer of Christ.) 358 *subdued* i.e., overcome by grief   361 *gum* i.e., myrr   366 s.d. *He stabs himself* (This direction is in the Quarto text.)   367 *period* termination, conclusion   372 *Spartan dog* (Spartan dogs were noted for their savagery and silence.)   373 *fell* cruel   376 *Let it be hid* i.e., draw the bed curtains. (No stage direction specifies that the dead are to be carried offstage at the end of the play.)   *keep* remain in   377 *seize upon* take legal possession of   378 *succeed on* pass as though by inheritance to   379 *censure* sentencing

5. In Othello's defense before the senators (Scene iii), how does he explain Desdemona's gradual falling in love with him?
6. Is Brabantio's warning to Othello (I, iii, 293–294) an accurate or an inaccurate prophecy?
7. By what strategy does Iago enlist Roderigo in his plot against the Moor? In what lines do we learn Iago's true feelings toward Roderigo?

ACT II

1. What do the Cypriots think of Othello? Do their words (in Scene i) make him seem to us a lesser man or a larger one?
2. What cruelty does Iago display toward Emilia? How well founded is his distrust of his wife's fidelity?
3. In II, iii, 221, Othello speaks of Iago's "honesty and love." How do you account for Othello's being so totally deceived?
4. For what major events does the merrymaking (proclaimed in Scene ii) give opportunity?

ACT III

1. Trace the steps by which Iago rouses Othello to suspicion. Is there anything in Othello's character or circumstances that renders him particularly susceptible to Iago's wiles?
2. In III, iv, 49–98, Emilia knows of Desdemona's distress over the lost handkerchief. At this moment, how do you explain her failure to relieve Desdemona's mind? Is Emilia aware of her husband's villainy?

ACT IV

1. In this act, what circumstantial evidence is added to Othello's case against Desdemona?
2. How plausible do you find Bianca's flinging the handkerchief at Cassio just when Othello is looking on? How important is the handkerchief in this play? What does it represent? What suggestions or hints do you find in it?
3. What prevents Othello from being moved by Desdemona's appeal (IV, ii, 33–92)?
4. When Roderigo grows impatient with Iago (IV, ii, 181–201), how does Iago make use of his fellow plotter's discontent?
5. What does the conversation between Emilia and Desdemona (Scene iii) tell us about the nature of each?
6. In this act, what scenes (or speeches) contain memorable dramatic irony?

ACT V

1. Summarize the events that lead to Iago's unmasking.
2. How does Othello's mistaken belief that Cassio is slain (V, i, 27–34) affect the outcome of the play?
3. What is Iago's motive in stabbing Roderigo?
4. In your interpretation of the play, exactly what impels Othello to kill Desdemona? Jealousy? Desire for revenge? Excess idealism? A wish to be a public avenger who punishes, "else she'll betray more men"?
5. What do you understand by Othello's calling himself "one that loved not wisely but too well" (V, ii, 354)?
6. In your view, does Othello's long speech in V, ii, 348–366 succeed in restoring his original dignity and nobility? Do you agree with Cassio (V, ii, 372) that Othello was "great of heart"?

General Questions

1. What motivates Iago to carry out his schemes? Do you find him a devil incarnate, a madman, or a rational human being?

2. Whom besides Othello does Iago deceive? What is Desdemona's opinion of him? Emilia's? Cassio's (before Iago is found out)? To what do you attribute Iago's success as a deceiver?

3. How essential to the play is the fact that Othello is a black man, a Moor, and not a native of Venice?

4. In the introduction to his edition of the play in *The Complete Signet Classic Shakespeare*, Alvin Kernan remarks:

   > *Othello* is probably the most neatly, the most formally constructed of Shakespeare's plays. Every character is, for example, balanced by another similar or contrasting character. Desdemona is balanced by her opposite, Iago; love and concern for others at one end of the scale, hatred and concern for self at the other.

   Besides Desdemona and Iago, what other pairs of characters strike balances?

5. Consider any passage of the play in which there is a shift from verse to prose, or from prose to verse. What is the effect of this shift?

6. Indicate a passage that you consider memorable for its poetry. Does the passage seem introduced for its own sake? Does it in any way advance the action of the play, express theme, or demonstrate character?

7. Does the play contain any tragic *recognition*—as discussed on page 946 a moment of terrible enlightenment, a "realization of the unthinkable"?

8. Does the downfall of Othello proceed from any flaw in his nature, or is his downfall entirely the work of Iago?

CRITICS ON SHAKESPEARE

Oberon and Titania in the Ninagawa Company's 1996 production of *A Midsummer Night's Dream*.

Anthony Burgess (1917–1993)

An Asian Culture Looks at Shakespeare 1982

Is translation possible? I first found myself asking this question in the Far East, when I was given the task of translating T. S. Eliot's *The Waste Land* into Indonesian. The difficulties began with the first line: "April is the cruellest month . . . ." This I rendered as "*Bulan Abril ia-lah bulan yang dzalim sa-kali . . .*" I had to take *dzalim* from Arabic, since Indonesian did not, at that time, seem to possess a word for *cruel*. The term was accepted, but not the notion that a month, as opposed to a person or institution, could be cruel. Moreover, even if a month could be cruel, how—in the tropics where all the months are the same and the concepts of spring and winter do not exist— can one month be crueller than another? When I came to *forgetful snow*—rendered as *thalji berlupa*—I had to borrow a highly poetical word from the Persian, acceptable as a useful descriptive device for the brown skin of the beloved but not known in terms of a climatic reality. And, again, how could this inanimate substance possess the faculty of forgetting? I gave up the task as hopeless. Evidently the imagery of *The Waste Land* does not relate to a universal experience but applies only to the northern hemisphere, with its temperate climate and tradition of spring and fertility rituals.

As a teacher in Malaysia, I had to consider with a mixed group of Malay, Chinese, Indian, and Eurasian students, seasoned with the odd Buginese, Achinese, and Japanese, a piece of representative postwar British fiction. Although the setting of the book is West Africa, I felt that its story was of universal import. It was a novel by Graham Greene called *The Heart of the Matter*—a tragic story about a police officer named Scobie who is a Catholic convert. He is in love with his wife but falls in love with another woman, discovers that he cannot repent of this adultery, makes a sacrilegious communion so that his very Catholic wife will not suspect that a love affair is in progress, then commits suicide in despair, trusting that God will thrust him into the outer darkness and be no longer agonized by the exploits of sinning Scobie. To us this is a tragic situation. To my Muslim students it was extremely funny. One girl said: "Why cannot this Mr. Scobie become a Muslim? Then he can have four wives and there is no problem."

The only author who seemed to have the quality of universal appeal in Malaysia was William Shakespeare. Despite the problems of translating him, there is always an intelligible residue. I remember seeing in a Borneo kampong the film of *Richard III* made by Laurence Olivier, and the illiterate tribe which surrounded me was most appreciative. They knew nothing here of literary history and nothing of the great world outside this jungle clearing. They took this film about medieval conspiracy and tyranny to be a kind of newsreel representation of contemporary England. They approved the medieval costumes because they resembled their own ceremonial dress. This story of the assassination of innocents, including children, Machiavellian massacre, and the eventual defeat of a tyrant was typical of their own history, even their contemporary experience, and they accepted Shakespeare as a great poet. Eliot would not have registered with them at all. Translation is not a matter of words only; it is a matter of making intelligible a whole culture. Evidently the Elizabethan culture was still primitive enough to survive transportation over much time and space.

From spoken remarks on the "Importance of Translation"

W. H. Auden (1907–1973)

Iago as a Triumphant Villain   1962

Any consideration of the *Tragedy of Othello* must be primarily occupied, not with its official hero but with its villain. I cannot think of any other play in which only one character performs personal actions—all the *deeds* are Iago's—and all the others without exception only exhibit behavior. In marrying each other, Othello and Desdemona have performed a deed, but this took place before the play begins. Nor can I think of another play in which the villain is so completely triumphant: everything Iago sets out to do, he accomplishes—(among his goals, I include his self-destruction). Even Cassio, who survives, is maimed for life.

If *Othello* is a tragedy—and one certainly cannot call it a comedy—it is tragic in a peculiar way. In most tragedies the fall of the hero from glory to misery and death is the work, either of the gods, or of his own freely chosen acts, or, more commonly, a mixture of both. But the fall of Othello is the work of another human being; nothing he says or does originates with himself. In consequence we feel pity for him but no respect; our aesthetic respect is reserved for Iago.

Iago is a wicked man. The wicked man, the stage villain, as a subject of serious dramatic interest does not, so far as I know, appear in the drama of western Europe before the Elizabethans. In the mystery plays, the wicked characters, like Satan or Herod, are treated comically, but the theme of the triumphant villain cannot be treated comically because the suffering he inflicts is real.

From "The Joker in the Pack"

Maud Bodkin (1875–1967)

Lucifer in Shakespeare's Othello   1934

If we attempt to define the devil in psychological terms, regarding him as an archetype, a persistent or recurrent mode of apprehension, we may say that the devil is our tendency to represent in personal form the forces within and without us that threaten our supreme values. When Othello finds those values of confident love, of honor, and pride in soldiership, that made up his purposeful life, falling into ruin, his sense of the devil in all around him becomes acute. Desdemona has become "a fair devil"; he feels "a young and sweating devil" in her hand. The cry "O devil" breaks out among his incoherent words of raving. When Iago's falsehoods are disclosed, and Othello at last, too late, wrenches himself free from the spell of Iago's power over him, his sense of the devil incarnate in Iago's shape before him becomes overwhelming. If those who tell of the devil have failed to describe Iago, they have lied:

> I look down towards his feet; but that's a fable.
> If that thou be'st a devil, I cannot kill thee.

We also, watching or reading the play, experience the archetype. Intellectually aware, as we reflect, of natural forces, within a man himself as well as in society around, that betray or shatter his ideals, we yet feel these forces aptly symbolized for the imagination by such a figure as Iago—a being though personal yet hardly human, concentrated wholly on the hunting to destruction of its destined prey, the proud figure of the hero.

From Archetypal Patterns in Poetry

Virginia Mason Vaughan (b. 1947)

Black and White in Othello   1994

> If virtue no delighted beauty lack,
> Your son-in-law is far more fair than black.
> —Othello (1.3.290–291)

Black/white oppositions permeate Othello. Throughout the play, Shakespeare exploits a discourse of racial difference that by 1604 had become ingrained in the English psyche. From Iago's initial racial epithets at Brabantio's window ("old black ram," "barbary horse") to Emilia's cries of outrage in the final scene ("ignorant as dirt"), Shakespeare shows that the union of a white Venetian maiden and a black Moorish general is from at least one perspective emphatically unnatural. The union is of course a central fact of the play, and to some commentators, the spectacle of the pale-skinned woman caught in Othello's black arms has indeed seemed monstrous. Yet that spectacle is a major source of *Othello's* emotional power. From Shakespeare's day to the present, the sight has titillated and terrified predominantly white audiences.

The effect of *Othello* depends, in other words, on the essential fact of the hero's darkness, the visual signifier of his Otherness. To Shakespeare's original audience, this chromatic sign was probably dark black, although there were other signifiers as well. Roderigo describes the Moor as having "thick lips," a term many sixteenth-century explorers employed in their descriptions of Africans. But, as historian Winthrop Jordan notes, by the late sixteenth century, "Blackness became so generally associated with Africa that every African seemed a black man[,] . . . the terms *Moor* and *Negro* used almost interchangeably." "Moor" became, G. K. Hunter observes, "a word for 'people not like us,' so signaled by color." Richard Burbage's Othello was probably black. But in any production, whether he appears as a tawny Moor (as nineteenth-century actors preferred) or as a black man of African descent, Othello bears the visual signs of his Otherness, a difference that the play's language insists can never be eradicated.

From Othello: A Contextual History

Clare Asquith (b. 1951)

Shakespeare's Language as a Hidden Political Code   2005

Shakespeare was the one sixteenth-century writer who, it appears, never fell foul of the authorities. Yet in a strangely insistent passage, the editors of the First Folio of his work, published in 1623, urge us to look beneath the surface of the great universal plays to something hidden below. Though they are sure that his wit can "no more lie hid than it could be lost," they press us to "Read him therefore, and again, and again." We must seek help from his friends if we miss his "hidden wit," and we should act as guides to others if we find it. The insistence on readers acting as guides is striking and unusual.

● ● ●

Whatever its impact at the time, Shakespeare's cautious artistry was so great that his hidden language remained undetectable to succeeding generations that accepted the official version of England's Reformation. Yet the subterfuge was essential if he and his work were to survive. He was writing in a climate more dangerous and oppressive than anything experienced by his predecessors. By the 1580s, the censorship laws, regularly tightened under Elizabeth, were strictly enforced. Yet he could not remain silent. He was driven to write by a different fear, to which he returns throughout his work. This was the growing concern, shared by many contemporaries, that the true history of the age would never be told. . . . . Shakespeare not only needed to write; he needed to find a new method of writing, one capable of recording the whole unhappy story of the country's political and spiritual collapse against the background of a regime for whom the slightest topical reference was justification enough to imprison a playwright.

● ● ●

In these dramas, there would be no room for asides or explanations. Instead, Shakespeare worked out a set of simple markers, basic call-signs that would alert his audience to the entry point they needed to access the hidden story. Unlike Erasmus,

Sidney and Donne, who were poets and essayists, he was a seasoned actor addressing restless spectators, so he kept his signals simple and consistent. But he was also one of a brotherhood of dissident writers, and to them his pointers would have been as readily—even wittily—recognizable as they became baffling to later readers.

The master key to the hidden level is so simple that it is easy to miss. It takes the form of twin terms that identify the polar opposites in Elizabeth's England. They are not Shakespeare's only terms, and he uses them sparingly, but with pinpoint accuracy. They are the terms "high" and "fair," which always indicate Catholicism, and "low" and "dark," which always suggest Protestantism. Shakespeare's treatment of these words is sufficiently remarkable for critics to have wondered whether he was writing for a tall blond actor and a short dark one—but the theory is untenable. Shakespeare was not a dramatist who would have deliberately created casting problems, and the references span a ten-year period.

The opposition of high and low, representing the two opposing sides of the Reformation, was commonplace at the time. The modern Christian distinction between high and low church goes back to pre-Reformation days when High Mass, high day, and high altars involved full liturgical ceremony—Low Mass and low altars were for every day.

The opposition of dark and fair was equally recognizable. The glittering, skin-deep attractions of the scarlet woman were constantly under fire from Protestant plays, sermons, and literature: the sober reformers wore plain black, and the new Prayer Book was shorn of illuminated initials and, as far as possible, red print.

• • •

His markers are morally neutral. Fair, tall characters can be corrupt, while dark, low ones are often noble—the words merely identify the religious allegiance of one or two characters, providing a key compass-bearing from which alert readers and spectators can work out the rest of the shadowed plot. In the process an enjoyable trail of punning wordplay emerges, deepening and confirming the discovery.

From Shadowplay: The Hidden Beliefs and Coded Politics of William Shakespeare

■ WRITING *effectively*

Ben Jonson on Writing (1573?–1637)

On His Friend and Rival William Shakespeare   1640

Ben Jonson

I remember the players have often mentioned it as an honor to Shakespeare, that in his writing (whatsoever he penned) he never blotted out a line. My answer hath been, "Would he had blotted a thousand," which they thought a malevolent speech. I had not told posterity this but for their ignorance who chose that circumstance to commend their friend by wherein he most faulted; and to justify mine own candor, for I loved the man, and do honor his memory on this side idolatry as much as any. He was, indeed, honest, and of an open and free nature; had an excellent phantasy, brave notions, and gentle expressions, wherein he flowed with that facility that sometimes it was necessary he should be stopped. "*Sufflaminandus erat*,"° as Augustus° said of Haterius.° His wit was in his own power; would the rule of it had been so, too! Many times he fell into those things, could not escape laughter, as when he said in the person of Caesar,° one speaking to him, "Caesar, thou dost me wrong." He replied, "Caesar did never wrong but with just cause"; and such like, which were ridiculous. But he redeemed his vices with his virtues. There was ever more in him to be praised than to be pardoned.

From *Discoveries*

UNDERSTANDING SHAKESPEARE

The basic problem a modern reader faces with Shakespeare is language. Shakespeare's English is now four hundred years old, and it differs in innumerable small ways from contemporary American English. Although Shakespeare's idiom may at first seem daunting, it is easily mastered if you make the effort. To grow comfortable with his language, you must immerse yourself in it. Fortunately, doing so isn't all that hard; you might even find it pleasurable.

Sufflaminandus erat: Latin for "He ought to have been plugged up."   *Augustus:* the first emperor of Rome (63 B.C.–14 A.D.)   *Haterius:* a very verbose orator of the Augustan age.   *Caesar:* Shakespeare's tragedy *Julius Caesar*. Jonson misremembers the quotation, which (in the First Folio) actually reads "Know, Caesar doth not wrong, nor without cause will he be satisfied." (III, i, 47)

- **Let your ears do the work.** There is no substitute for hearing Shakespeare's words in performance. After all, the plays were written to be seen, not to be read silently on the page. After reading the play, listen to or watch a recording of it. It sometimes helps to read along as you listen or watch, hitting the pause button as needed. If you can attend a live performance of any Shakespearean play, do so.

- **But read the text first.** Watching a production is never a full substitute for reading an assigned play. Many productions abridge the play, leaving passages out. Even more important, directors and actors choose a particular interpretation of a play, and their choices might skew your understanding of events and motivation if you are unfamiliar with the original itself.

- **Before you write a paper, read the play again.** The first time through an Elizabethan-era text, you will almost certainly miss many things. As you grow more familiar with Shakespeare's language, you will be able to read it with greater comprehension. If you choose to write about a particular episode or character, carefully study the speeches and dialogue in question (and pay special attention to the footnotes) so that you understand each word.

- **Enjoy yourself.** From Beijing to Berlin, Buenos Aires to Oslo, Shakespeare is almost universally acknowledged as the world's greatest playwright, a master entertainer as well as a consummate artist.

CHECKLIST: Writing About Shakespeare

☐ Read closely. Work through passages with difficult language.

☐ Pay special attention to footnotes.

☐ Read the play more than once if necessary.

☐ Watch a DVD or listen to an audio recording after reading a play. Immerse yourself in Shakespeare's language until it becomes familiar.

☐ As you view or listen to a play, read along, or revisit the text afterward.

☐ Carefully study any speeches and dialogue you choose to write about.

☐ Be sure you understand each word of any passage you decide to discuss or quote.

WRITING ASSIGNMENT ON TRAGEDY

Select any tragedy found in the book and analyze it using Aristotle's definition of the form. Does the play measure up to Aristotle's requirements for a tragedy? In what ways does it meet the definition? In what ways does it depart from it? (Be sure to state clearly the Aristotelian rules by which drama is to be judged.)

Here is a paper written in response to this assignment by Janet Housden, a student of Melinda Barth at El Camino College.

Housden 1

Janet Housden

Professor Barth

English 201

3 January 2012

Othello: Tragedy or Soap Opera?

When we hear the word "tragedy," we usually think of either a terrible real-life disaster, or a dark and serious drama filled with pain, suffering, and loss that involves the downfall of a powerful person due to some character flaw or error in judgment. William Shakespeare's *Othello* is such a drama. Set in Venice and Cyprus during the Renaissance, the play tells the story of Othello, a Moorish general in the Venetian army, who has just married Desdemona, the daughter of a Venetian nobleman. Through the plotting of a jealous villain, Iago, Othello is deceived into believing that Desdemona has been unfaithful to him. He murders her in revenge, only to discover too late how he has been tricked. Overcome by shame and grief, Othello kills himself.

Dealing as it does with jealousy, murder, and suicide, the play is certainly dark, but is *Othello* a true tragedy? In the fourth century B.C., the Greek philosopher Aristotle proposed a formal definition of tragedy (Kennedy and Gioia 945–47), which only partially fits *Othello*.

The first characteristic of tragedy identified by Aristotle is that the protagonist is a person of outstanding quality and high social position. While Othello is not of royal birth as are many tragic heroes and heroines, he does occupy a sufficiently high position to satisfy this part of Aristotle's definition. Although Othello is a foreigner and a soldier by trade, he has risen to the rank of general and has married into a noble family, which is quite an accomplishment for an outsider. Furthermore, Othello is generally liked and respected by those around him. He is often described by others as being "noble," "brave," and "valiant." By virtue of his high rank and the respect he commands from others, Othello would appear to possess the high stature commonly given to the tragic hero in order to make his eventual fall seem all the more tragic.

While Othello displays the nobility and high status commonly associated with the tragic hero, he also possesses another, less admirable characteristic, the flaw or character defect shared by all heroes of classical tragedy. In Othello's case, it is a stunning gullibility, combined with a violent temper that once awakened overcomes all reason. These flaws permit Othello to be easily

---

Margin annotations:

First paragraph gives name of author and work

Key plot information avoids excessive retelling

Central question is raised

Thesis statement provides response

Topic sentence on Othello's social position

Essay systematically applies Aristotle's definition of tragedy to Othello

Topic sentence on Othello's tragic flaw

deceived and manipulated by the villainous Iago and make him easy prey for the "green-eyed monster" (3.3.179).

It is because of this tragic flaw, according to Aristotle, that the hero is at least partially to blame for his own downfall. While Othello's "free and open nature, / That thinks men honest that but seem to be so" (1.3.376–77) is not a fault in itself, it does allow Iago to convince the Moor of his wife's infidelity without one shred of concrete evidence. Furthermore, once Othello has been convinced of Desdemona's guilt, he makes up his mind to take vengeance, and says that his "bloody thoughts with violent pace / Shall ne'er look back, ne'er ebb to humble love" (3.3.473–74). He thereby renders himself deaf to the voice of reason, and ignoring Desdemona's protestations of innocence, brutally murders her, only to discover too late that he has made a terrible mistake. Although he is goaded into his crime by Iago, who is a master at manipulating people, it is Othello's own character flaws that lead to his horrible misjudgment.

Aristotle's definition also states that the hero's misfortune is not wholly deserved, that the punishment he receives exceeds his crime. Although it is hard to sympathize with a man as cruel as Othello is to the innocent Desdemona, Othello pays an extremely high price for his sin of gullibility. Othello loses everything—his wife, his position, even his life. Even though it's partially his fault, Othello is not entirely to blame, for without Iago's interference it's highly unlikely that things would turn out as they do. Though it seems incredibly stupid on Othello's part, that a man who has travelled the world and commanded armies should be so easily deceived, there is little evidence that Othello has had much experience with civilian society, and although he is "declined / Into the vale of years" (3.3.281–82) Othello has apparently never been married before. By his own admission, "little of this great world can I speak / More than pertains to feats of broils and battle" (1.3.88–89). Furthermore, Othello has no reason to suspect that "honest Iago" is anything but his loyal friend and supporter.

While it is understandable that Othello could be fooled into believing Desdemona unfaithful, the question remains whether his fate is deserved. In addition to his mistake of believing Iago's lies, Othello commits a more serious error: he lets himself be blinded by anger. Worse yet, in deciding to take vengeance, he also makes up his mind not be swayed from his course, even by his love for Desdemona. In fact, he refuses to listen to her at all, "lest her body and beauty unprovide my mind again" (4.1.186–87), therefore denying her the

Quotes from play as evidence to support point

Topic sentence elaborates on idea raised in previous paragraphs

Topic sentence on Othello's misfortune

Transitional words signal argument's direction

Topic sentence elaborates on Othello's misfortune

right to defend herself. Because of his rage and unfairness, perhaps Othello deserves his fate more than Aristotle's ideal tragic hero. Othello's punishment does exceed his crime, but just barely.

Topic sentence on whether Othello learns from his mistakes

According to Aristotle, the tragic hero's fall gives the protagonist deeper understanding and self-awareness. Othello departs from Aristotle's model in that Othello apparently learns nothing from his mistakes. He never realizes that he is partly at fault. He sees himself only as an innocent victim and blames his misfortune on fate rather than accepting responsibility for his actions. To be sure, he realizes he has been tricked and deeply regrets his mistake, but he seems to feel that he was justified under the circumstances, "For naught I did in hate, but all in honor" (5.2.303). Othello sees himself not as someone whose bad judgment and worse temper have resulted in the death of an innocent party, but as one who has "loved not wisely but too well" (5.2.354). This failure to grasp the true nature of his error indicates that Othello hasn't learned his lesson.

Topic sentence elaborating further on whether Othello learns from his errors

Neither accepting responsibility nor learning from his mistakes, Othello fails to fulfill yet another of Aristotle's requirements. Since the protagonist usually gains some understanding along with his defeat, classical tragedy conveys a sense of human greatness and of life's unrealized potentialities—a quality totally absent from *Othello*. Not only does Othello fail to learn from his mistakes, he never really realizes what those mistakes are, and it apparently never crosses his mind that things could have turned out any differently. "Who can control his fate?" Othello asks (5.2.274), and this defeatist attitude, combined with his failure to salvage any wisdom from his defeat, separates *Othello* from the tragedy as defined by Aristotle.

Topic sentence on catharsis

The last part of Aristotle's definition states that viewing the conclusion of a tragedy should result in catharsis for the audience, and that the audience should be left with a feeling of exaltation rather than depression. Unfortunately, the feeling we are left with after viewing *Othello* is neither catharsis nor exaltation but rather a feeling of horror, pity, and disgust at the senseless waste of human lives. The deaths of Desdemona and Othello, as well as those of Emilia and Roderigo, serve no purpose whatsoever. They die not in the service of a great cause but because of lies, treachery, jealousy, and spite. Their deaths don't even benefit Iago, who is directly or indirectly responsible for all of them. No lesson is learned, no epiphany is reached, and the audience, instead of experiencing catharsis, is left with its negative feeling unresolved.

Housden 4

Since *Othello* only partially fits Aristotle's definition of tragedy, it is
questionable whether or not it should be classified as one. Though it does
involve a great man undone by a defect in his own character, the hero gains
neither insight nor understanding from his defeat, and so there can be no
inspiration or catharsis for the audience, as there would be in a "true" tragedy.
Othello is tragic only in the everyday sense of the word, the way a plane crash
or fire is tragic. At least in terms of Aristotle's classic definition, *Othello*
ultimately comes across as more of a melodrama or soap opera than a tragedy.

Restatement of thesis

Conclusion

Housden 5

Works Cited

Kennedy, X. J., and Dana Gioia, eds. *Literature: An Introduction to Fiction,
    Poetry, Drama, and Writing.* 7th Compact ed. New York: Pearson, 2013.
    945–47. Print.

Shakespeare, William. *Othello, The Moor of Venice. Literature: An Introduction to
    Fiction, Poetry, Drama, and Writing.* Ed. X. J. Kennedy and Dana Gioia.
    7th Compact ed. New York: Pearson, 2013. 1290–1102. Print.

MORE TOPICS FOR WRITING

1. Write a defense of Iago.
2. "Never was any play fraught, like this of *Othello*, with improbabilities," wrote Thomas
   Rymer in a famous attack (*A Short View of Tragedy*, 1692). Consider Rymer's objection to
   the play, either answering it or finding evidence to back it up.
3. Suppose yourself a casting director assigned to a film version of *Othello*. What well-known
   actors would you cast in the principal roles? Write a report justifying your choices. Don't
   merely discuss the stars and their qualifications; discuss (with specific reference to the
   play) what Shakespeare appears to call for.
4. Emilia's long speech at the end of Act IV (iii, 83–102) has been called a Renaissance plea
   for women's rights. Do you agree? Write a brief, close analysis of this speech. How timely
   is it?
5. "The downfall of Oedipus is the work of the gods; the downfall of Othello is self-
   inflicted." Test this comment with reference to the two plays, and report your findings.

36

THE MODERN THEATER

*Speak of the moderns without contempt,
and of the ancients without idolatry.*

—LORD CHESTERFIELD

REALISM

The ancient art of the drama experienced a revival in the Renaissance and went through a number of changes over the next several centuries. The Elizabethan drama was marked by strong characterization, heightened and intense language, and crowded, sometimes sprawling plots. In the neoclassical period of the seventeenth and eighteenth centuries, greater emphasis was placed upon formality, decorum, and Aristotle's unities of time, place, and action. The early nineteenth century saw the rise of melodrama, with its florid dialogue, plots that relied heavily on often absurd coincidences, and crude stereotypes of good and evil characters. Through all these developments—from kings and generals to lords and ladies of high society to pure-hearted swashbucklers and craven villains—the one thing that seemed to remain constant was an absence of **realism**—the attempt to reproduce faithfully the surface appearance of life, especially that of ordinary people in everyday situations.

By the end of the nineteenth century, however, Realism had become the drama's dominant mode. The writer most responsible for that shift was the Norwegian playwright Henrik Ibsen. From *Pillars of Society* (1877) to *Hedda Gabler* (1890), he wrote a series of prose dramas in which realistically portrayed middle-class characters face conflicts in their lives and relationships. They are often called "problem plays" because of their engagement of social issues, such as women's place in society (*A Doll's House*) and inherited venereal disease (*Ghosts*). In actuality, the social problems in these plays serve as a context for Ibsen's real concern, an examination of the complexities of human personality and psychology, especially those aspects of our natures that are hidden or repressed because of society's expectations.

The attempt to use the theater to present the real lives of real people was taken even further by the Russian dramatist Anton Chekhov. In Chekhov's mature plays, the dialogue seems at times to meander and there appears to be little or no action. *The Cherry Orchard* (1904), his last and greatest play, presents a decayed aristocratic clan unable to deal with a threatened foreclosure on the family estate, despite advice from all quarters. The play has sparked debate for over a century: Is it a comedy or a tragedy? Are its characters foolish or sympathetic? Does it lament the passing of an old way of life or greet the dawn of a new age? The answer, of course, is *All of the above*—just like life itself.

Conventions of Realism

From Italian playhouses of the sixteenth century, the theater had inherited the **picture-frame stage:** a structure that holds the action within a **proscenium arch,** a gateway standing (as the word *proscenium* indicates) "in front of the scenery." This manner of constructing a playhouse in effect divided the actors from their audience; most commercial theaters even today are so constructed. But as the nineteenth century gave way to the twentieth, actors less often declaimed their passions in oratorical style in front of backdrops painted with waterfalls and volcanoes, while stationed exactly at the center of the stage as if to sing "duets meant to bring forth applause" (as Swedish playwright August Strindberg complained).

In the theater of Realism, a room was represented by a **box set**—three walls that joined in two corners and a ceiling that tilted as if seen in perspective—replacing drapery walls that had billowed and doors that had flapped, not slammed. Instead of posing at stage center and directly facing the audience to deliver key speeches, actors were instructed to speak from wherever the dramatic situation placed them, and now and then even to turn their backs upon the audience. They were to behave as if they were in a room with the fourth wall sliced away, unaware that they had an audience.

To encourage actors further to imitate reality, the influential director Constantin Stanislavsky of the Moscow Art Theater developed his famous system to help actors feel at home inside a playwright's characters. One of Stanislavsky's exercises was to have actors search their memories for personal experiences like those of the characters in the play; another was to have them act out things a character did *not* do in the play but might do in life. The system enabled Stanislavsky to bring authenticity to his productions of Chekhov's plays and of Maxim Gorky's *The Lower Depths* (1902), a play that showed the tenants of a sordid lodging house drinking themselves to death (and hanging themselves) in surroundings of realistic squalor. Stanislavsky's techniques are still used by stage and film actors today.

NATURALISM

Gorky's play is a masterpiece of **Naturalism,** a kind of realism in fiction and drama dealing with the more brutal or unpleasant aspects of reality. As codified by French novelist and playwright Émile Zola, who influenced Ibsen, Naturalism viewed a person as a creature whose acts are determined by heredity and environment; Zola urged writers to study their characters' behavior with the detachment of zoologists studying animals.

Another masterpiece of the naturalistic tradition is *The Hairy Ape* (1922) by the American playwright Eugene O'Neill. The title character is Yank, a brutish but good-natured engine-stoker on an ocean liner. After a rich young woman calls him a "filthy beast," he grows depressed and dislocated, trying and failing to find a comfortable place for himself in society. He ends up at the zoo, where he dies in a gorilla's embrace. (The play's enduring power was affirmed by a successful New York revival in 2006.) Universally regarded as the first true genius of the American theater, O'Neill greatly influenced several generations of American playwrights, including Arthur Miller. In many of his plays, Miller portrayed working-class characters whose lives are shaped and constrained by powerful social and cultural forces. Miller was also influenced by Ibsen, whose *Enemy of the People* he adapted for the Broadway stage in 1950.

SYMBOLISM AND EXPRESSIONISM

The ascendance of Realism had liberated drama from some outworn styles and opened rich new areas of artistic exploration, but when it became the dominant tradition, some writers began to feel confined by its themes and theatrical conventions, and new forms of drama emerged. One of these was the **Symbolist movement** in the French theater, most influentially expressed by Belgian playwright Maurice Maeterlinck, whose work conjures up a spirit world we cannot directly perceive, as in his play *The Intruder* (1890), when a blind man sees the approach of Death.

In Ireland, poet William Butler Yeats wrote (among other plays) "plays for dancers" to be performed in drawing rooms, often in friends' homes, with simple costumes and props, a few masked actors, and a very few musicians. In Sweden, August Strindberg, who earlier had won fame as a Naturalist, reversed direction and in *The Dream Play* (1902) and *The Ghost Sonata* (1907) introduced characters who change their identities and, ignoring space and time, move across dreamlike landscapes.

In these plays Strindberg anticipated the movement in German theater after World War I called **Expressionism.** Delighting in bizarre sets and exaggerated make-up and costuming, Expressionist playwrights and producers sought to reflect intense states of emotion and, sometimes, to depict the world through lunatic eyes. A classic film example is *The Cabinet of Dr. Caligari*, made in Berlin in 1919 and 1920, in which a hypnotist sends forth a subject to murder people. Garbed in jet black, the killer sleepwalks through a town of lopsided houses, twisted streets, and railings that tilt at gravity-defying angles. A restless experimenter throughout his career, Eugene O'Neill employed Expressionist techniques in his 1926 play *The Great God Brown*, in which characters speak through masks and wear one another's clothes (and identities).

AMERICAN MODERNISM

If modern American drama first came of age with Eugene O'Neill, it soon found powerful new voices. Thornton Wilder wrote experimental plays such as *Our Town* (1938) and *The Skin of Our Teeth* (1942) that were so carefully constructed, witty, and evocative that they achieved enormous popular and critical success. Wilder's plays, especially *Our Town*, have become so familiar to American audiences that we hardly realize how innovative his works were in their time.

It was not until the mid-1940s that two playwrights emerged who would rival O'Neill in the depth and artistry of their work—Arthur Miller and Tennessee Williams. Miller achieved his first major success with *All My Sons* (1947), in which an idealistic young man discovers that his father was guilty of supplying defective airplane parts to the government during World War II, resulting in the deaths of American servicemen. But it was his next play, *Death of a Salesman* (1949), that established Miller's work as a permanent part of America's literary heritage. In this emotionally devastating drama, Miller once again presents a tormented young man trying to come to terms with the deeply flawed father that he loves.

Tennessee Williams had made his mark a bit earlier, with *The Glass Menagerie*, produced in Chicago in December 1944 and on Broadway the following March. From there, Williams would go on to greater triumphs, especially in *A Streetcar Named Desire* (1947) and *Cat on a Hot Tin Roof* (1955). These two plays established the qualities most associated with Williams's name—strong but driven and sometimes brutal men who dominate their families; sensitive yet ambitious women; a kind of folk poetry grounded in vigorous speech rhythms (hinted at in the evocative titles of the plays); Southern settings in which contemporary decay embodies a nostalgia for a more refined past. But *The Glass Menagerie* is extraordinary for its tender lyricism and in the high quotient of human decency among its characters; partly for these reasons, it is still one of the most popular, if not *the* most popular, of Williams's works.

Below is one of the pioneering works of realism, Henrik Ibsen's *A Doll's House.* The play derives a good deal of its power from our ability to identify with its characters and the lives they live, an identification that Ibsen achieves in part by framing the action with the details of daily existence.

Henrik Ibsen

A Doll's House   1879

Translated by R. Farquharson Sharp
Revised by Viktoria Michelsen

Henrik Ibsen (1828–1906) was born in Skien, a seaport in Norway. When he was six, his father's business losses suddenly reduced his wealthy family to poverty. After a brief attempt to study medicine, young Ibsen worked as a stage manager in provincial Bergen; then, becoming known as a playwright, he moved to Oslo as artistic director of the National Theater—practical experiences that gained him firm grounding in his craft. Discouraged when his theater failed and the king turned down his plea for a grant to enable him to write, Ibsen left Norway and for twenty-seven years lived in Italy and Germany. There, in his middle years (1879–1891), he wrote most of his famed plays about small-town life, among them A Doll's House, Ghosts, An Enemy of the People, The Wild Duck, *and* Hedda Gabler. *Introducing social problems to the stage, these plays aroused storms of controversy. Although best known as a Realist, Ibsen early in his career wrote poetic dramas based on Norwegian history and folklore: the tragedy* Brand *(1866) and the powerful, wildly fantastic* Peer Gynt *(1867). He ended as a Symbolist in* John Gabriel Borkman *(1896) and* When We Dead Awaken *(1899), both encompassing huge mountains that heaven-assaulting heroes try to climb. Late in life Ibsen returned to Oslo, honored at last both at home and abroad.*

CHARACTERS

Torvald Helmer, a lawyer
Nora, his wife
Doctor Rank
Mrs. Kristine Linde
Nils Krogstad
The Helmers' three young children
Anne Marie, their nursemaid
Helene, the maid
A Porter

The action takes place in the Helmers' apartment.

ACT I

The scene is a room furnished comfortably and tastefully, but not extravagantly. At the back wall, a door to the right leads to the entrance hall. Another to the left leads to Helmer's study. Between the doors there is a piano. In the middle of the left-hand wall is a door, and

The 2009 adaptation of *A Doll's House* at the Donmar Warehouse in London, starring Gillian Anderson and Toby Stephens.

beyond it a window. Near the window are a round table, armchairs, and a small sofa. In the right-hand wall, at the farther end, is another door, and on the same side, nearer the footlights, a stove, two easy chairs and a rocking chair. Between the stove and the door there is a small table. There are engravings on the walls, a cabinet with china and other small objects, and a small bookcase with expensively bound books. The floors are carpeted, and a fire burns in the stove. It is winter.

A bell rings in the hall. A moment later, we hear the door being opened. Enter Nora, humming a tune and in high spirits. She is wearing a hat and coat and carries a number of packages, which she puts down on the table to the right. She leaves the outer door open behind her. Through the door we see a porter who is carrying a Christmas tree and a basket, which he gives to the maid, who has opened the door.

Nora: Hide the Christmas tree carefully, Helene. Make sure the children don't see it till it's decorated this evening. (*To the Porter, taking out her purse.*) How much?
Porter: Fifty ore.
Nora: Here's a krone. No, keep the change.

(*The Porter thanks her and goes out. Nora shuts the door. She is laughing to herself as she takes off her hat and coat. She takes a bag of macaroons from her pocket and eats one or two, then goes cautiously to the door of her husband's study and listens.*)

Yes, he's there. (*Still humming, she goes to the table on the right.*)

Helmer (*calls out from his study*): Is that my little lark twittering out there?
Nora (*busy opening some of the packages*): Yes, it is!
Helmer: Is it my little squirrel bustling around?

The 1896 production of *A Doll's House* at the Empire Theatre in New York.

Nora: Yes!

Helmer: When did my squirrel come home?

Nora: Just now. (*Puts the bag of macaroons into her pocket and wipes her mouth.*) Come in here, Torvald, and see what I bought.

Helmer: I'm very busy right now. (*A little later, he opens the door and looks into the room, pen in hand.*) Bought, did you say? All these things? Has my little spendthrift been wasting money again?

Nora: Yes, but, Torvald, this year we really can let ourselves go a little. This is the first Christmas that we don't have to watch every penny.

Helmer: Still, you know, we can't spend money recklessly.

Nora: Yes, Torvald, but we can be a little more reckless now, can't we? Just a tiny little bit! You're going to have a big salary and you'll be making lots and lots of money.

Helmer: Yes, after the New Year. But it'll still be a whole three months before the money starts coming in.

Nora: Pooh! We can borrow till then.

Helmer: Nora! (*Goes up to her and takes her playfully by the ear.*) The same little featherbrain! Just suppose that I borrowed a thousand kroner today, and you spent it all on Christmas, and then on New Year's Eve a roof tile fell on my head and killed me, and—

Nora (*putting her hand over his mouth*): Oh! Don't say such horrible things.

Helmer: Still, suppose that happened. What then?

Nora: If that happened, I don't suppose I'd care whether I owed anyone money or not.

Helmer: Yes, but what about the people who'd lent it to us?

Nora: Them? Who'd care about them? I wouldn't even know who they were.

Helmer: That's just like a woman! But seriously, Nora, you know how I feel about that. No debt, no borrowing. There can't be any freedom or beauty in a home life that depends on borrowing and debt. We two have managed to stay on the straight road so far, and we'll go on the same way for the short time that we still have to be careful.

Nora (moving towards the stove): As you wish, Torvald.

Helmer (following her): Now, now, my little skylark mustn't let her wings droop. What's the matter? Is my little squirrel sulking? (*Taking out his purse.*) Nora, what do you think I've got here?

Nora (turning round quickly): Money!

Helmer: There you are. (*Gives her some money.*) Do you think I don't know how much you need for the house at Christmastime?

Nora (counting): Ten, twenty, thirty, forty! Thank you, thank you, Torvald. That'll keep me going for a long time.

Helmer: It's going to have to.

Nora: Yes, yes, it will. But come here and let me show you what I bought. And all so cheap! Look, here's a new suit for Ivar, and a sword. And a horse and a trumpet for Bob. And a doll and doll's bed for Emmy. They're not the best, but she'll break them soon enough anyway. And here's dress material and handkerchiefs for the maids. Old Anne Marie really should have something nicer.

Helmer: And what's in this package?

Nora (crying out): No, no! You can't see that till this evening.

Helmer: If you say so. But now tell me, you extravagant little thing, what would you like for yourself?

Nora: For myself? Oh, I'm sure I don't want anything.

Helmer: But you must. Tell me something that you'd especially like to have—within reasonable limits.

Nora: No, I really can't think of anything. Unless, Torvald . . .

Helmer: Well?

Nora (playing with his coat buttons, and without raising her eyes to his): If you really want to give me something, you might . . . you might . . .

Helmer: Well, out with it!

Nora (speaking quickly): You might give me money, Torvald. Only just as much as you can afford. And then one of these days I'll buy something with it.

Helmer: But, Nora—

Nora: Oh, do! Dear Torvald, please, please do! Then I'll wrap it up in beautiful gold paper and hang it on the Christmas tree. Wouldn't that be fun?

Helmer: What do they call those little creatures that are always wasting money?

Nora: Spendthrifts. I know. Let's do as I suggest, Torvald, and then I'll have time to think about what I need most. That's a very sensible plan, isn't it?

Helmer (smiling): Yes, it is. That is, if you really did save some of the money I give you, and then really buy something for yourself. But if you spend it all on the housekeeping and all kinds of unnecessary things, then I just have to open my wallet all over again.

Nora: Oh, but, Torvald—

Helmer: You can't deny it, my dear little Nora. (*Puts his arm around her waist.*) She's a sweet little spendthrift, but she uses up a lot of money. One would hardly believe how expensive such little creatures are!

Nora: That's a terrible thing to say. I really do save all I can.

Helmer (laughing): That's true. All you can. But you can't save anything!

Nora (smiling quietly and happily): You have no idea how many bills skylarks and squirrels have, Torvald.

Helmer: You're an odd little soul. Just like your father. You always find some new way of wheedling money out of me, and, as soon as you've got it, it seems to melt in your hands. You never know where it's gone. Still, one has to take you as you are. It's in the blood. Because, you know, it's true that you can inherit these things, Nora.

Nora: Ah, I wish I'd inherited a lot of Papa's traits.

Helmer: And I wouldn't want you to be anything but just what you are, my sweet little skylark. But, you know, it seems to me that you look rather—how can I put it—rather uneasy today.

Nora: Do I?

Helmer: You do, really. Look straight at me.

Nora (looks at him): Well?

Helmer (wagging his finger at her): Has little Miss Sweet Tooth been breaking our rules in town today?

Nora: No, what makes you think that?

Helmer: Has she paid a visit to the bakery?

Nora: No, I assure you, Torvald—

Helmer: Not been nibbling pastries?

Nora: No, certainly not.

Helmer: Not even taken a bite of a macaroon or two?

Nora: No, Torvald, I assure you, really—

Helmer: Come on, you know I was only kidding.

Nora (going to the table on the right): I wouldn't dream of going against your wishes.

Helmer: No, I'm sure of that. Besides, you gave me your word. (*Going up to her.*) Keep your little Christmas secrets to yourself, my darling. They'll all be revealed tonight when the Christmas tree is lit, no doubt.

Nora: Did you remember to invite Doctor Rank?

Helmer: No. But there's no need. It goes without saying that he'll have dinner with us. All the same, I'll ask him when he comes over this morning. I've ordered some good wine. Nora, you have no idea how much I'm looking forward to this evening.

Nora: So am I! And how the children will enjoy themselves, Torvald!

Helmer: It's great to feel that you have a completely secure position and a big enough income. It's a delightful thought, isn't it?

Nora: It's wonderful!

Helmer: Do you remember last Christmas? For three whole weeks you hid yourself away every evening until long after midnight, making ornaments for the Christmas tree and all the other fine things that were going to be a surprise for us. It was the most boring three weeks I ever spent!

Nora: I wasn't bored.

Helmer (smiling): But there was precious little to show for it, Nora.

Nora: Oh, you're not going to tease me about that again. How could I help it that the cat went in and tore everything to pieces?

Helmer: Of course you couldn't, poor little girl. You had the best of intentions to make us all happy, and that's the main thing. But it's a good thing that our hard times are over.

Nora: Yes, it really is wonderful.

Helmer: This time I don't have to sit here and be bored all by myself, and you don't have to ruin your dear eyes and your pretty little hands—

Nora (clapping her hands): No, Torvald, I don't have to any more, do I! It's wonderfully lovely to hear you say so! (*Taking his arm.*) Now let me tell you how I've been thinking we should arrange things, Torvald. As soon as Christmas is over—(*A bell rings in the hall.*) There's the bell. (*She tidies the room a little.*) There's somebody at the door. What a nuisance!

Helmer: If someone's visiting, remember I'm not home.

Maid (in the doorway): A lady to see you, ma'am. A stranger.

Nora: Ask her to come in.

Maid (to Helmer): The doctor's here too, sir.

Helmer: Did he go straight into my study?

Maid: Yes, sir.

(*Helmer goes into his study. The maid ushers in Mrs. Linde, who is in traveling clothes, and shuts the door.*)

Mrs. Linde (in a dejected and timid voice): Hello, Nora.

Nora (doubtfully): Hello.

Mrs. Linde: You don't recognize me, I suppose.

Nora: No, I don't know . . . Yes, of course, I think so—(*Suddenly.*) Yes! Kristine! Is it really you?

Mrs. Linde: Yes, it is.

Nora: Kristine! Imagine my not recognizing you! And yet how could I—(*In a gentle voice.*) You've changed, Kristine!

Mrs. Linde: Yes, I certainly have. In nine, ten long years—

Nora: Is it that long since we've seen each other? I suppose it is. The last eight years have been a happy time for me, you know. And so now you've come to town, and you've taken this long trip in the winter. That was brave of you.

Mrs. Linde: I arrived by steamer this morning.

Nora: To have some fun at Christmastime, of course. How delightful! We'll have such fun together! But take off your things. You're not cold, I hope. (*Helps her.*) Now we'll sit down by the stove and be cozy. No, take this armchair. I'll sit here in the rocking chair. (*Takes her hands.*) Now you look like your old self again. It was only that first moment. You are a little paler, Kristine, and maybe a little thinner.

Mrs. Linde: And much, much older, Nora.

Nora: Maybe a little older. Very, very little. Surely not very much. (*Stops suddenly and speaks seriously.*) What a thoughtless thing I am, chattering away like this. My poor, dear Kristine, please forgive me.

Mrs. Linde: What do you mean, Nora?

Nora (gently): Poor Kristine, you're a widow.

Mrs. Linde: Yes. For three years now.

Nora: Yes, I knew. I saw it in the papers. I swear to you, Kristine, I kept meaning to write to you at the time, but I always put it off and something always came up.

Mrs. Linde: I understand completely, dear.

Nora: It was very bad of me, Kristine. Poor thing, how you must have suffered. And he left you nothing?

Mrs. Linde: No.

Nora: And no children?

Mrs. Linde: No.

Nora: Nothing at all, then?

Mrs. Linde: Not even any sorrow or grief to live on.

Nora (*looking at her in disbelief*): But, Kristine, is that possible?

Mrs. Linde (*smiles sadly and strokes Nora's hair*): It happens sometimes, Nora.

Nora: So you're completely alone. How terribly sad that must be. I have three beautiful children. You can't see them just now, because they're out with their nursemaid. But now you must tell me all about it.

Mrs. Linde: No, no, I want to hear about you.

Nora: No, you go first. I mustn't be selfish today. Today I should think only about you. But there is one thing I have to tell you. Do you know we've just had a fabulous piece of good luck?

Mrs. Linde: No, what is it?

Nora: Just imagine, my husband's been appointed manager of the bank!

Mrs. Linde: Your husband? That is good luck!

Nora: Yes, it's tremendous! A lawyer's life is so uncertain, especially if he won't take any cases that are the slightest bit shady, and of course Torvald has never been willing to do that, and I completely agree with him. You can imagine how delighted we are! He starts his job in the bank at New Year's, and then he'll have a big salary and lots of commissions. From now on we can live very differently. We can do just what we want. I feel so relieved and so happy, Kristine! It'll be wonderful to have heaps of money and not have to worry about anything, won't it?

Mrs. Linde: Yes. Anyway, I think it would be delightful to have what you need.

Nora: No, not only what you need, but heaps and heaps of money.

Mrs. Linde (*smiling*): Nora, Nora, haven't you learned any sense yet? Back in school you were a terrible spendthrift.

Nora (*laughing*): Yes, that's what Torvald says now. (*Wags her finger at her.*) But "Nora, Nora" isn't as silly as you think. We haven't been in a position for me to waste money. We've both had to work.

Mrs. Linde: You too?

Nora: Oh, yes, odds and ends, needlework, crocheting, embroidery, and that kind of thing. (*Dropping her voice.*) And other things too. You know Torvald left his government job when we got married? There was no chance of promotion, and he had to try to earn more money than he was making there. But in that first year he overworked himself terribly. You see, he had to make money any way he could, and he worked all hours, but he couldn't take it, and he got very sick, and the doctors said he had to go south, to a warmer climate.

Mrs. Linde: You spent a whole year in Italy, didn't you?

Nora: Yes. It wasn't easy to get away, I can tell you that. It was just after Ivar was born, but obviously we had to go. It was a wonderful, beautiful trip, and it saved Torvald's life. But it cost a tremendous amount of money, Kristine.

Mrs. Linde: I would imagine so.

Nora: It cost about four thousand, eight hundred kroner. That's a lot, isn't it?

Mrs. Linde: Yes, it is, and when you have an emergency like that it's lucky to have the money.

Nora: Well, the fact is, we got it from Papa.

Mrs. Linde: Oh, I see. It was just about that time that he died, wasn't it?

Nora: Yes, and, just think of it, I couldn't even go and take care of him. I was expecting little Ivar any day and I had my poor sick Torvald to look after. My dear, kind father. I never saw him again, Kristine. That was the worst experience I've gone through since we got married.

Mrs. Linde: I know how fond of him you were. And then you went off to Italy?

Nora: Yes. You see, we had money then, and the doctors insisted that we go, so we left a month later.

Mrs. Linde: And your husband came back completely recovered?

Nora: The picture of health!

Mrs. Linde: But . . . the doctor?

Nora: What doctor?

Mrs. Linde: Didn't your maid say that the gentleman who arrived here with me was the doctor?

Nora: Yes, that was Doctor Rank, but he doesn't come here professionally. He's our dearest friend, and he drops in at least once every day. No, Torvald hasn't been sick for an hour since then, and our children are strong and healthy, and so am I. (*Jumps up and claps her hands.*) Kristine! Kristine! It's good to be alive and happy! But how awful of me. I'm talking about nothing but myself. (*Sits on a nearby stool and rests her arms on her knees.*) Please don't be mad at me. Tell me, is it really true that you didn't love your husband? Why did you marry him?

Mrs. Linde: My mother was still alive then, and she was bedridden and helpless, and I had to provide for my two younger brothers, so I didn't think I had any right to turn him down.

Nora: No, maybe you did the right thing. So he was rich then?

Mrs. Linde: I believe he was quite well off. But his business wasn't very solid, and when he died, it all went to pieces and there was nothing left.

Nora: And then?

Mrs. Linde: Well, I had to turn my hand to anything I could find. First a small shop, then a small school, and so on. The last three years have seemed like one long workday, with no rest. Now it's over, Nora. My poor mother's gone and doesn't need me any more, and the boys don't need me, either. They've got jobs now and can manage for themselves.

Nora: What a relief it must be if—

Mrs. Linde: No, not at all. All I feel is an unbearable emptiness. No one to live for anymore. (*Gets up restlessly.*) That's why I couldn't stand it any longer in my little backwater. I hope it'll be easier to find something here that'll keep me busy and occupy my mind. If I could be lucky enough to find some regular work, office work of some kind—

Nora: But, Kristine, that's so awfully tiring, and you look tired out now. It'd be much better for you if you could get away to a resort.

Mrs. Linde (*walking to the window*): I don't have a father to give me money for a trip, Nora.

Nora (*rising*): Oh, don't be mad at me!

Mrs. Linde (*going up to her*): It's you who mustn't be mad at me, dear. The worst thing about a situation like mine is that it makes you so bitter. No one to work for, and yet you have to always be on the lookout for opportunities. You have to live, and so you grow selfish. When you told me about your good luck—you'll find this hard to believe—I was delighted less for you than for myself.

Nora: What do you mean? Oh, I understand. You mean that maybe Torvald could find you a job.

Mrs. Linde: Yes, that's what I was thinking.

Nora: He must, Kristine. Just leave it to me. I'll broach the subject very cleverly. I'll think of something that'll put him in a really good mood. It'll make me so happy to be of some use to you.

Mrs. Linde: How kind you are, Nora, to be so eager to help me! It's doubly kind of you, since you know so little of the burdens and troubles of life.

Nora: Me? I know so little of them?

Mrs. Linde (*smiling*): My dear! Small household cares and that sort of thing! You're a child, Nora.

Nora (*tosses her head and crosses the stage*): You shouldn't act so superior.

Mrs. Linde: No?

Nora: You're just like the others. They all think I'm incapable of anything really serious—

Mrs. Linde: Come on—

Nora: —that I haven't had to deal with any real problems in my life.

Mrs. Linde: But, my dear Nora, you've just told me all your troubles.

Nora: Pooh! That was nothing. (*Lowering her voice.*) I haven't told you the important thing.

Mrs. Linde: The important thing? What do you mean?

Nora: You really look down on me, Kristine, but you shouldn't. Aren't you proud of having worked so hard and so long for your mother?

Mrs. Linde: Believe me, I don't look down on anyone. But it's true, I'm proud and I'm glad that I had the privilege of making my mother's last days almost worry-free.

Nora: And you're proud of what you did for your brothers?

Mrs. Linde: I think I have the right to be.

Nora: I think so, too. But now, listen to this. I have something to be proud of and happy about too.

Mrs. Linde: I'm sure you do. But what do you mean?

Nora: Keep your voice down. If Torvald were to overhear! He can't find out, not under any circumstances. No one in the world must know, Kristine, except you.

Mrs. Linde: But what is it?

Nora: Come here. (*Pulls her down on the sofa beside her.*) Now I'll show you that I too have something to be proud and happy about. I'm the one who saved Torvald's life.

Mrs. Linde: Saved? How?

Nora: I told you about our trip to Italy. Torvald would never have recovered if he hadn't gone there—

Mrs. Linde: Yes, but your father gave you the money you needed.

Nora (*smiling*): Yes, that's what Torvald thinks, along with everybody else, but—

Mrs. Linde: But—

Nora: Papa didn't give us a penny. I was the one who raised the money.

Mrs. Linde: You? That huge amount?

Nora: That's right, four thousand, eight hundred kroner. What do you think of that?

Mrs. Linde: But, Nora, how could you possibly? Did you win the lottery?

Nora (*disdainfully*): The lottery? That wouldn't have been any accomplishment.

Mrs. Linde: But where did you get it from, then?

Nora (*humming and smiling with an air of mystery*): Hm, hm! Ha!

Mrs. Linde: Because you couldn't have borrowed it.

Nora: Couldn't I? Why not?

Mrs. Linde: No, a wife can't borrow money without her husband's consent.

Nora (*tossing her head*): Oh, if it's a wife with a head for business, a wife who has the brains to be a little clever—

Mrs. Linde: I don't understand this at all, Nora.

Nora: There's no reason why you should. I never said I'd borrowed the money. Maybe I got it some other way. (*Lies back on the sofa.*) Maybe I got it from an admirer. When a woman's as pretty as I am—

Mrs. Linde: You're crazy.

Nora: Now, you know you're dying of curiosity, Kristine.

Mrs. Linde: Listen to me, Nora dear. Have you done something rash?

Nora (*sits up straight*): Is it rash to save your husband's life?

Mrs. Linde: I think it's rash, without his knowledge, to—

Nora: But it was absolutely necessary that he not know! My goodness, can't you understand that? It was necessary he have no idea how sick he was. The doctors came to *me* and said his life was in danger and the only thing that could save him was to live in the south. Don't you think I tried first to get him to do it as if it was for me? I told him how much I would love to travel abroad like other young wives. I tried tears and pleading with him. I told him he should remember the condition I was in, and that he should be kind and indulgent to me. I even hinted that he might take out a loan. That almost made him mad, Kristine. He said I was thoughtless, and that it was his duty as my husband not to indulge me in my "whims and caprices," as I believe he called them. All right, I thought, you need to be saved. And that was how I came to think up a way out of the mess—

Mrs. Linde: And your husband never found out from your father that the money hadn't come from him?

Nora: No, never. Papa died just then. I'd meant to let him in on the secret and beg him never to reveal it. But he was so sick. Unfortunately, there never was any need to tell him.

Mrs. Linde: And since then you've never told your secret to your husband?

Nora: Good heavens, no! How could you think I would? A man with such strong opinions about these things! Besides, how painful and humiliating it would be for Torvald, with his masculine pride, to know that he owed me anything! It would completely upset the balance of our relationship. Our beautiful happy home would never be the same.

Mrs. Linde: Are you never going to tell him about it?

Nora (*meditatively, and with a half smile*): Yes, someday, maybe, in many years, when I'm not as pretty as I am now. Don't laugh at me! I mean, of course, when Torvald is no longer as devoted to me as he is now, when he's grown tired of my dancing and dressing up and reciting. Then it may be a good thing to have something in reserve—(*Breaking off.*) What nonsense! That time will never come. Now, what do you think of my great secret, Kristine? Do you still think I'm useless? And the fact is, this whole situation has caused me a lot of worry. It hasn't been easy for me to make my payments on time. I can tell you that there's something in business that's called quarterly interest, and something else called installment payments, and it's always so terribly difficult to keep up with them. I've had to save a little here and there, wherever I could, you understand. I haven't been able to put much aside from my housekeeping money, because Torvald has to live well. And I couldn't let my children be shabbily dressed. I feel I have to spend everything he gives me for them, the sweet little darlings!

Mrs. Linde: So it's all had to come out of your own allowance, poor Nora?

Nora: Of course. Besides, I was the one responsible for it. Whenever Torvald has given me money for new dresses and things like that, I've never spent more than half of it. I've always bought the simplest and cheapest things. Thank heaven, any clothes look good on me, and so Torvald's never noticed anything. But it was often very hard on me, Kristine, because it is delightful to be really well dressed, isn't it?

Mrs. Linde: I suppose so.

Nora: Well, then I've found other ways of earning money. Last winter I was lucky enough to get a lot of copying to do, so I locked myself up and sat writing every evening until late into the night. A lot of the time I was desperately tired, but all the same it was a tremendous pleasure to sit there working and earning money. It was like being a man.

Mrs. Linde: How much have you been able to pay off that way?

Nora: I can't tell you exactly. You see, it's very hard to keep a strict account of a business matter like that. I only know that I've paid out every penny I could scrape together. Many a time I was at my wits' end. (*Smiles.*) Then I used to sit here and imagine that a rich old gentleman had fallen in love with me—

Mrs. Linde: What! Who was it?

Nora: Oh, be quiet! That he had died, and that when his will was opened it said, in great big letters: "The lovely Mrs. Nora Helmer is to have everything I own paid over to her immediately in cash."

Mrs. Linde: But, my dear Nora, who could the man be?

Nora: Good gracious, can't you understand? There wasn't any old gentleman. It was only something that I used to sit here and imagine, when I couldn't think of any way of getting money. But it's all right now. The tiresome old gent can stay right where he is, as far as I'm concerned. I don't care about him or his will either, because now I'm worry-free. (*Jumps up.*) My goodness, it's delightful to think of, Kristine! Worry-free! To be able to have no worries, no worries at all! To be able to play and romp with the children! To be able to keep the house beautifully and have everything just the way Torvald likes it! And, just think of it, soon the spring will come and the big blue sky! Maybe we can take a little trip. Maybe I can see the sea again! Oh, it's a wonderful thing to be alive and happy.

(*A bell rings in the hall.*)

Mrs. Linde (*rising*): There's the bell. Perhaps I should be going.

Nora: No, don't go. No one will come in here. It's sure to be for Torvald.

Servant (*at the hall door*): Excuse me, ma'am. There's a gentleman to see the master, and as the doctor is still with him—

Nora: Who is it?

Krogstad (*at the door*): It's me, Mrs. Helmer.

(*Mrs. Linde starts, trembles, and turns toward the window.*)

Nora (*takes a step toward him, and speaks in a strained, low voice*): You? What is it? What do you want to see my husband for?

Krogstad: Bank business, in a way. I have a small position in the bank, and I hear your husband is going to be our boss now—

Nora: Then it's—

Krogstad: Nothing but dry business matters, Mrs. Helmer, that's all.

Nora: Then please go into the study.

(*She bows indifferently to him and shuts the door into the hall, then comes back and makes up the fire in the stove.*)

Mrs. Linde: Nora, who was that man?

Nora: A lawyer. His name is Krogstad.

Mrs. Linde: Then it really was him.

Nora: Do you know the man?

Mrs. Linde: I used to, many years ago. At one time he was a law clerk in our town.

Nora: That's right, he was.

Mrs. Linde: How much he's changed.

Nora: He had a very unhappy marriage.

Mrs. Linde: He's a widower now, isn't he?

Nora: With several children. There, now it's really caught. (*Shuts the door of the stove and moves the rocking chair aside.*)

Mrs. Linde: They say he's mixed up in a lot of questionable business.

Nora: Really? Maybe he is. I don't know anything about it. But let's not talk about business. It's so tiresome.

Doctor Rank (*comes out of Helmer's study. Before he shuts the door he calls to Helmer*): No, my dear fellow, I won't disturb you. I'd rather go in and talk to your wife for a little while.

(*Shuts the door and sees Mrs. Linde.*)

I beg your pardon. I'm afraid I'm in the way here too.

Nora: No, not at all. (*Introducing him:*) Doctor Rank, Mrs. Linde.

Rank: I've often heard that name in this house. I think I passed you on the stairs when I arrived, Mrs. Linde?

Mrs. Linde: Yes, I take stairs very slowly. I can't manage them very well.

Rank: Oh, some small internal problem?

Mrs. Linde: No, it's just that I've been overworking myself.

Rank: Is that all? Then I suppose you've come to town to get some rest by sampling our social life.

Mrs. Linde: I've come to look for work.

Rank: Is that a good cure for overwork?

Mrs. Linde: One has to live, Doctor Rank.

Rank: Yes, that seems to be the general opinion.

Nora: Now, now, Doctor Rank, you know you want to live.

Rank: Of course I do. However miserable I may feel, I want to prolong the agony for as long as possible. All my patients are the same way. And so are those who are morally sick. In fact, one of them, and a bad case too, is at this very moment inside with Helmer—

Mrs. Linde (sadly): Ah!

Nora: Who are you talking about?

Rank: A lawyer by the name of Krogstad, a fellow you don't know at all. He's a completely worthless creature, Mrs. Helmer. But even he started out by saying, as if it were a matter of the utmost importance, that he has to live.

Nora: Did he? What did he want to talk to Torvald about?

Rank: I have no idea. All I heard was that it was something about the bank.

Nora: I didn't know this—what's his name—Krogstad had anything to do with the bank.

Rank: Yes, he has some kind of a position there. (*To Mrs. Linde*) I don't know whether you find the same thing in your part of the world, that there are certain people who go around zealously looking to sniff out moral corruption, and, as soon as they find some, they put the person involved in some cushy job where they can keep an eye on him. Meanwhile, the morally healthy ones are left out in the cold.

Mrs. Linde: Still, I think it's the sick who are most in need of being taken care of.

Rank (shrugging his shoulders): Well, there you have it. That's the attitude that's turning society into a hospital.

(*Nora, who has been absorbed in her thoughts, breaks out into smothered laughter and claps her hands.*)

Rank: Why are you laughing at that? Do you have any idea what society really is?

Nora: What do I care about your boring society? I'm laughing at something else, something very funny. Tell me, Doctor Rank, are all the people who work in the bank dependent on Torvald now?

Rank: That's what's so funny?

Nora (smiling and humming): That's my business! (*Walking around the room.*) It's just wonderful to think that we have—that Torvald has—so much power over so many people. (*Takes the bag out of her pocket.*) Doctor Rank, what do you say to a macaroon?

Rank: Macaroons? I thought they were forbidden here.

Nora: Yes, but these are some Kristine gave me.

Mrs. Linde: What! Me?

Nora: Oh, well, don't be upset! How could you know that Torvald had forbidden them? I have to tell you, he's afraid they'll ruin my teeth. But so what? Once in a while, that's all right, isn't it, Doctor Rank? With your permission! (*Puts a macaroon into his mouth.*) You have to have one too, Kristine. And I'll have one, just a little one—or no more than two. (*Walking around.*) I am tremendously happy. There's just one thing in the world now that I would dearly love to do.

Rank: Well, what is it?

Nora: It's something I would dearly love to say, if Torvald could hear me.

Rank: Well, why can't you say it?

Nora: No, I don't dare. It's too shocking.

Mrs. Linde: Shocking?

Rank: Well then, I'd advise you not to say it. Still, in front of us you might risk it. What is it you'd so much like to say if Torvald could hear you?

Nora: I would just love to say—"Well, I'll be damned!"

Rank: Are you crazy?

Mrs. Linde: Nora, dear!

Rank: Here he is. Say it!

Nora (*hiding the bag*): Shh, shh, shh!

(*Helmer comes out of his room, with his coat over his arm and his hat in his hand.*)

Nora: Well, Torvald dear, did you get rid of him?

Helmer: Yes, he just left.

Nora: Let me introduce you. This is Kristine. She's just arrived in town.

Helmer: Kristine? I'm sorry, but I don't know any—

Nora: Mrs. Linde, dear, Kristine Linde.

Helmer: Oh, of course. A school friend of my wife's, I believe?

Mrs. Linde: Yes, we knew each other back then.

Nora: And just think, she's come all this way in order to see you.

Helmer: What do you mean?

Mrs. Linde: No, really, I—

Nora: Kristine is extremely good at bookkeeping, and she's very eager to work for some talented man, so she can perfect her skills—

Helmer: Very sensible, Mrs. Linde.

Nora: And when she heard that you'd been named manager of the bank—the news was sent by telegraph, you know—she traveled here as quickly as she could. Torvald, I'm sure you'll be able to do something for Kristine, for my sake, won't you?

Helmer: Well, it's not completely out of the question. I expect that you're a widow, Mrs. Linde?

Mrs. Linde: Yes.

Helmer: And you've had some bookkeeping experience?

Mrs. Linde: Yes, a fair amount.

Helmer: Ah! Well, there's a very good chance that I'll be able to find something for you—

Nora (*clapping her hands*): What did I tell you? What did I tell you?

Helmer: You've just come at a lucky moment, Mrs. Linde.

Mrs. Linde: How can I thank you?

Helmer: There's no need. (*Puts on his coat.*) But now you must excuse me—

Rank: Wait a minute. I'll come with you. (*Brings his fur coat from the hall and warms it at the fire.*)

Nora: Don't be long, Torvald dear.

Helmer: About an hour, that's all.

Nora: Are you leaving too, Kristine?

Mrs. Linde (putting on her cloak): Yes, I have to go and look for a place to stay.

Helmer: Oh, well then, we can walk down the street together.

Nora (helping her): It's too bad we're so short of space here. I'm afraid it's impossible for us—

Mrs. Linde: Please don't even think of it! Goodbye, Nora dear, and many thanks.

Nora: Goodbye for now. Of course you'll come back this evening. And you too, Dr. Rank. What do you say? If you're feeling up to it? Oh, you have to be! Wrap yourself up warmly.

(They go to the door all talking together. Children's voices are heard on the staircase.)

Nora: There they are! There they are!

(She runs to open the door. The nursemaid comes in with the children.)

Come in! Come in! *(Stoops and kisses them.)* Oh, you sweet blessings! Look at them, Kristine! Aren't they darlings?

Rank: Let's not stand here in the draft.

Helmer: Come along, Mrs. Linde. Only a mother will be able to stand it in here now!

(Rank, Helmer, and Mrs. Linde go downstairs. The Nursemaid comes forward with the children. Nora shuts the hall door.)

Nora: How fresh and healthy you look! Cheeks as red as apples and roses. *(The children all talk at once while she speaks to them.)* Did you have a lot of fun? That's wonderful! What, you pulled Emmy and Bob on the sled? Both at once? That was really something. You *are* a clever boy, Ivar. Let me take her for a little, Anne Marie. My sweet little baby doll! *(Takes the baby from the maid and dances her up and down.)* Yes, yes, mother will dance with Bob too. What! Have you been throwing snowballs? I wish I'd been there too! No, no, I'll take their things off, Anne Marie, please let me do it, it's such fun. Go inside now, you look half frozen. There's some hot coffee for you on the stove.

(The Nursemaid goes into the room on the left. Nora takes off the children's things and throws them around, while they all talk to her at once.)

Nora: Really! Did a big dog run after you? But it didn't bite you? No, dogs don't bite nice little dolly children. You mustn't look at the packages, Ivar. What are they? Oh, I'll bet you'd like to know. No, no, it's something boring! Come on, let's play a game! What should we play? Hide and seek? Yes, we'll play hide and seek. Bob will hide first. You want me to hide? All right, I'll hide first.

(She and the children laugh and shout, and romp in and out of the room. At last Nora hides under the table. The children rush in and out looking for her, but they don't see her. They hear her smothered laughter, run to the table, lift up the cloth and find her. Shouts of laughter. She crawls forward and pretends to scare them. More laughter. Meanwhile there has been a knock at the hall door, but none of them has noticed it. The door is opened halfway and Krogstad appears. He waits for a little while. The game goes on.)

Krogstad: Excuse me, Mrs. Helmer.

Nora (with a stifled cry, turns round and gets up onto her knees): Oh! What do you want?

Krogstad: Excuse me, the outside door was open. I suppose someone forgot to shut it.

Nora (rising): My husband is out, Mr. Krogstad.

Krogstad: I know that.

Nora: What do you want here, then?

Krogstad: A word with you.

Nora: With me? (*To the children, gently.*) Go inside to Anne Marie. What? No, the strange man won't hurt Mother. When he's gone we'll play another game. (*She takes the children into the room on the left, and shuts the door after them.*) You want to speak to me?

Krogstad: Yes, I do.

Nora: Today? It isn't the first of the month yet.

Krogstad: No, it's Christmas Eve, and it's up to you what kind of Christmas you're going to have.

Nora: What do you mean? Today it's absolutely impossible for me—

Krogstad: We won't talk about that until later on. This is something else. I presume you can spare me a moment?

Nora: Yes, yes, I can. Although . . .

Krogstad: Good. I was in Olsen's restaurant and I saw your husband going down the street—

Nora: Yes?

Krogstad: With a lady.

Nora: So?

Krogstad: May I be so bold as to ask if it was a Mrs. Linde?

Nora: It was.

Krogstad: Just arrived in town?

Nora: Yes, today.

Krogstad: She's a very good friend of yours, isn't she?

Nora: She is. But I don't see—

Krogstad: I knew her too, once upon a time.

Nora: I'm aware of that.

Krogstad: Are you? So you know all about it. I thought so. Then I can ask you, without beating around the bush. Is Mrs. Linde going to work in the bank?

Nora: What right do you have to question me, Mr. Krogstad? You're one of my husband's employees. But since you ask, I'll tell you. Yes, Mrs. Linde is going to work in the bank. And I'm the one who spoke up for her, Mr. Krogstad. So now you know.

Krogstad: So I was right, then.

Nora (walking up and down the stage): Sometimes one has a tiny little bit of influence, I should hope. Just because I'm a woman, it doesn't necessarily follow that—You know, when somebody's in a subordinate position, Mr. Krogstad, they should really be careful to avoid offending anyone who—who—

Krogstad: Who has influence?

Nora: Exactly.

Krogstad (changing his tone): Mrs. Helmer, may I ask you to use *your* influence on my behalf?

Nora: What? What do you mean?

Krogstad: Will you be kind enough to see to it that I'm allowed to keep my subordinate position in the bank?

Nora: What do you mean by that? Who's threatening to take your job away from you?

Krogstad: Oh, there's no need to keep up the pretence of ignorance. I can understand that your friend isn't very anxious to expose herself to the chance of rubbing shoulders with me. And now I realize exactly who I have to thank for pushing me out.

Nora: But I swear to you—

Krogstad: Yes, yes. But, to get right to the point, there's still time to prevent it, and I would advise you to use your influence to do so.

Nora: But, Mr. Krogstad, I have no influence.

Krogstad: Oh no? Didn't you yourself just say—

Nora: Well, obviously, I didn't mean for you to take it that way. Me? What would make you think I have that kind of influence with my husband?

Krogstad: Oh, I've known your husband since our school days. I don't suppose he's any more unpersuadable than other husbands.

Nora: If you're going to talk disrespectfully about my husband, I'll have to ask you to leave my house.

Krogstad: Bold talk, Mrs. Helmer.

Nora: I'm not afraid of you anymore. When the New Year comes, I'll soon be free of the whole thing.

Krogstad (*controlling himself*): Listen to me, Mrs. Helmer. If I have to, I'm ready to fight for my little job in the bank as if I were fighting for my life.

Nora: So it seems.

Krogstad: It's not just for the sake of the money. In fact, that matters the least to me. There's another reason. Well, I might as well tell you. Here's my situation. I suppose, like everybody else, you know that many years ago I did something pretty foolish.

Nora: I think I heard something about it.

Krogstad: It never got as far as the courtroom, but every door seemed closed to me after that. So I got involved in the business that you know about. I had to do something, and, honestly, I think there are many worse than me. But now I have to get myself free of all that. My sons are growing up. For their sake I have to try to win back as much respect as I can in this town. The job in the bank was like the first step up for me, and now your husband is going to kick me downstairs back into the mud.

Nora: But you have to believe me, Mr. Krogstad, it's not in my power to help you at all.

Krogstad: Then it's because you don't want to. But I have ways of making you.

Nora: You don't mean you'll tell my husband I owe you money?

Krogstad: Hm! And what if I did tell him?

Nora: That would be a terrible thing for you to do. (*Sobbing.*) To think he would learn my secret, which has been my pride and joy, in such an ugly, clumsy way— that he would learn it from you! And it would put me in a horribly uncomfortable position—

Krogstad: Just uncomfortable?

Nora (impetuously): Well, go ahead and do it, then! And it'll be so much the worse for you. My husband will see for himself how vile you are, and then you'll lose your job for sure.

Krogstad: I asked you if it's just an uncomfortable situation at home that you're afraid of.

Nora: If my husband does find out about it, of course he'll immediately pay you what I still owe, and then we'll be through with you once and for all.

Krogstad (coming a step closer): Listen to me, Mrs. Helmer. Either you have a very bad memory or you don't know much about business. I can see I'm going to have to remind you of a few details.

Nora: What do you mean?

Krogstad: When your husband was sick, you came to me to borrow four thousand, eight hundred kroner.

Nora: I didn't know anyone else to go to.

Krogstad: I promised to get you that amount—

Nora: Yes, and you did so.

Krogstad: I promised to get you that amount, on certain conditions. You were so preoccupied with your husband's illness, and you were so anxious to get the money for your trip, that you seem to have paid no attention to the conditions of our bargain. So it won't be out of place for me to remind you of them. Now, I promised to get the money on the security of a note which I drew up.

Nora: Yes, and which I signed.

Krogstad: Good. But underneath your signature there were a few lines naming your father as a co-signer who guaranteed the repayment of the loan. Your father was supposed to sign that part.

Nora: Supposed to? He did sign it.

Krogstad: I had left the date blank. That was because your father was supposed to fill in the date when he signed the paper. Do you remember that?

Nora: Yes, I think I remember. . . .

Krogstad: Then I gave you the note to mail to your father. Isn't that so?

Nora: Yes.

Krogstad: And obviously you mailed it right away, because five or six days later you brought me the note with your father's signature. And then I gave you the money.

Nora: Well, haven't I been paying it back regularly?

Krogstad: Fairly regularly, yes. But, to get back to the point, that must have been a very difficult time for you, Mrs. Helmer.

Nora: Yes, it was.

Krogstad: Your father was very sick, wasn't he?

Nora: He was very near the end.

Krogstad: And he died soon after?

Nora: Yes.

Krogstad: Tell me, Mrs. Helmer, can you by any chance remember what day your father died? On what day of the month, I mean.

Nora: Papa died on the 29th of September.

Krogstad: That's right. I looked it up myself. And, since that is the case, there's something extremely peculiar (*taking a piece of paper from his pocket*) that I can't account for.

Nora: Peculiar in what way? I don't know—

Krogstad: The peculiar thing, Mrs. Helmer, is the fact that your father signed this note three days after he died.

Nora: What do you mean? I don't understand—

Krogstad: Your father died on the 29th of September. But, look here. Your father dated his signature the 2nd of October. It is mighty peculiar, isn't it? (*Nora is silent.*) Can you explain it to me? (*Nora is still silent.*) And what's just as peculiar is that the words "October 2," as well as the year, are not in your father's handwriting, but in someone else's, which I think I recognize. Well, of course it can all be explained. Your father might have forgotten to date his signature, and someone else might have filled in the date before they knew that he had died. There's no harm in that. It all depends on the signature, and that's genuine, isn't it, Mrs. Helmer? It was your father himself who signed his name here?

Nora (after a short pause, lifts her head up and looks defiantly at him): No, it wasn't. I'm the one who wrote Papa's name.

Krogstad: Are you aware that you're making a very serious confession?

Nora: How so? You'll get your money soon.

Krogstad: Let me ask you something. Why didn't you send the paper to your father?

Nora: It was out of the question. Papa was too sick. If I had asked him to sign something, I'd have had to tell him what the money was for, and when he was so sick himself I couldn't tell him that my husband's life was in danger. It was out of the question.

Krogstad: It would have been better for you if you'd given up your trip abroad.

Nora: No, that was impossible. That trip was to save my husband's life. I couldn't give that up.

Krogstad: But didn't it ever occur to you that you were committing a fraud against me?

Nora: I couldn't take that into account. I didn't trouble myself about you at all. I couldn't stand you, because you put so many heartless difficulties in my way, even though you knew how seriously ill my husband was.

Krogstad: Mrs. Helmer, you evidently don't realize clearly what you're guilty of. But, believe me, my one mistake, which cost me my whole reputation, was nothing more and nothing worse than what you did.

Nora: You? You expect me to believe that you were brave enough to take a risk to save your wife's life?

Krogstad: The law doesn't care about motives.

Nora: Then the law must be very stupid.

Krogstad: Stupid or not, it's the law that's going to judge you, if I produce this paper in court.

Nora: I don't believe it. Isn't a daughter allowed to spare her dying father anxiety and concern? Isn't a wife allowed to save her husband's life? I don't know much about the law, but I'm sure there must be provisions for things like that. Don't you know anything about such provisions? You seem like a very poor excuse for a lawyer, Mr. Krogstad.

Krogstad: That's as may be. But business, the kind of business you and I have done together—do you think I don't know about that? Fine. Do what you want. But I can assure you of this. If I lose everything all over again, this time you're going down with me. (*He bows, and goes out through the hall.*)

Nora (*appears buried in thought for a short time, then tosses her head*): Nonsense! He's just trying to scare me! I'm not as naive as he thinks I am. (*Begins to busy herself putting the children's things in order.*) And yet . . . ? No, it's impossible! I did it for love.

Children (*in the doorway on the left*): Mother, the strange man is gone. He went out through the gate.

Nora: Yes, dears, I know. But don't tell anyone about the strange man. Do you hear me? Not even Papa.

Children: No, Mother. But will you come and play with us again?

Nora: No, no, not just now.

Children: But, Mother, you promised us.

Nora: Yes, but I can't right now. Go inside. I have too much to do. Go inside, my sweet little darlings.

(*She gets them into the room bit by bit and shuts the door on them. Then she sits down on the sofa, takes up a piece of needlework and sews a few stitches, but soon stops.*)

No! (*Throws down the work, gets up, goes to the hall door and calls out.*) Helene! Bring the tree in. (*Goes to the table on the left, opens a drawer, and stops again.*) No, no! It's completely impossible!

Maid (*coming in with the tree*): Where should I put it, ma'am?

Nora: Here, in the middle of the floor.

Maid: Do you need anything else?

Nora: No, thank you. I have everything I want.

(*Exit Maid.*)

Nora (*begins decorating the tree*): A candle here, and flowers here. That horrible man! It's all nonsense, there's nothing wrong. The tree is going to be magnificent! I'll do everything I can think of to make you happy, Torvald! I'll sing for you, dance for you—

(*Helmer comes in with some papers under his arm.*)

Oh! You're back already?

Helmer: Yes. Has anyone been here?

Nora: Here? No.

Helmer: That's strange. I saw Krogstad going out the gate.

Nora: You did? Oh yes, I forgot, Krogstad was here for a moment.

Helmer: Nora, I can tell from the way you're acting that he was here begging you to put in a good word for him.

Nora: Yes, he was.

Helmer: And you were supposed to pretend it was all your idea and not tell me that he'd been here to see you. Didn't he beg you to do that too?

Nora: Yes, Torvald, but—

Helmer: Nora, Nora, to think that you'd be a party to that sort of thing! To have any kind of conversation with a man like that, and promise him anything at all? And to lie to me in the bargain?

Nora: Lie?

Helmer: Didn't you tell me no one had been here? (*Shakes his finger at her.*) My little songbird must never do that again. A songbird must have a clean beak to chirp with. No false notes! (*Puts his arm round her waist.*) That's true, isn't it? Yes, I'm sure it is. (*Lets her go.*) We won't mention this again. (*Sits down by the stove.*) How warm and cozy it is here! (*Turns over his papers.*)

Nora (*after a short pause, during which she busies herself with the Christmas tree*): Torvald!

Helmer: Yes?

Nora: I'm really looking forward to the masquerade ball at the Stenborgs' the day after tomorrow.

Helmer: And I'm really curious to see what you're going to surprise me with.

Nora: Oh, it was very silly of me to want to do that.

Helmer: What do you mean?

Nora: I can't come up with anything good. Everything I think of seems so stupid and pointless.

Helmer: So my little Nora finally admits that?

Nora (*standing behind his chair with her arms on the back of it*): Are you very busy, Torvald?

Helmer: Well . . .

Nora: What are all those papers?

Helmer: Bank business.

Nora: Already?

Helmer: I've gotten the authority from the retiring manager to reorganize the work procedures and make the necessary personnel changes. I need to take care of it during Christmas week, so as to have everything in place for the new year.

Nora: Then that was why this poor Krogstad—

Helmer: Hm!

Nora (*leans against the back of his chair and strokes his hair*): If you weren't so busy, I would have asked you for a huge favor, Torvald.

Helmer: What favor? Tell me.

Nora: No one has such good taste as you. And I really want to look nice at the fancy-dress ball. Torvald, couldn't you take me in hand and decide what I should go as and what kind of costume I should wear?

Helmer: Aha! So my obstinate little woman has to get someone to come to her rescue?

Nora: Yes, Torvald, I can't get along at all without your help.

Helmer: All right, I'll think it over. I'm sure we'll come up with something.

Nora: That's so nice of you. (*Goes to the Christmas tree. A short pause.*) How pretty the red flowers look. But, tell me, was it really something very bad that this Krogstad was guilty of?

Helmer: He forged someone's name. Do you have any idea what that means?

Nora: Isn't it possible that he was forced to do it by necessity?

Helmer: Yes. Or, the way it is in so many cases, by foolishness. I'm not so heartless that I'd absolutely condemn a man because of one mistake like that.

Nora: No, you wouldn't, would you, Torvald?

Helmer: Many a man has been able to rehabilitate himself, if he's openly admitted his guilt and taken his punishment.

Nora: Punishment?

Helmer: But Krogstad didn't do that. He wriggled out of it with lies and trickery, and that's what completely undermined his moral character.

Nora: But do you think that that would—

Helmer: Just think how a guilty man like that has to lie and act like a hypocrite with everyone, how he has to wear a mask in front of the people closest to him, even with his own wife and children. And the children. That's the most terrible part of it all, Nora.

Nora: How so?

Helmer: Because an atmosphere of lies infects and poisons the whole life of a home. Every breath the children take in a house like that is full of the germs of moral corruption.

Nora (coming closer to him): Are you sure of that?

Helmer: My dear, I've seen it many times in my legal career. Almost everyone who's gone wrong at a young age had a dishonest mother.

Nora: Why only the mother?

Helmer: It usually seems to be the mother's influence, though naturally a bad father would have the same result. Every lawyer knows this. This Krogstad, now, has been systematically poisoning his own children with lies and deceit. That's why I say he's lost all moral character. (*Holds out his hands to her.*) And that's why my sweet little Nora must promise me not to plead his cause. Give me your hand on it. Come now, what's this? Give me your hand. There, that's settled. Believe me, it would be impossible for me to work with him. It literally makes me feel physically ill to be around people like that.

Nora (takes her hand out of his and goes to the opposite side of the Christmas tree): How hot it is in here! And I have so much to do.

Helmer (getting up and putting his papers in order): Yes, and I have to try to read through some of these before dinner. And I have to think about your costume, too. And it's just possible I'll have something wrapped in gold paper to hang up on the tree. (*Puts his hand on her head.*) My precious little songbird! (*He goes into his study and closes the door behind him.*)

Nora (after a pause, whispers): No, no, it's not true. It's impossible. It has to be impossible.

(*The nursemaid opens the door on the left.*)

Nursemaid: The little ones are begging so hard to be allowed to come in to see Mama.

Nora: No, no, no! Don't let them come in to me! You stay with them, Anne Marie.

Nursemaid: Very well, ma'am. (*Shuts the door.*)

Nora (pale with terror): Corrupt my little children? Poison my home? (*A short pause. Then she tosses her head.*) It's not true. It can't possibly be true.

ACT II

The same scene. The Christmas tree is in the corner by the piano, stripped of its ornaments and with burnt-down candle-ends on its disheveled branches. Nora's coat and hat are lying on the sofa. She is alone in the room, walking around uneasily. She stops by the sofa and picks up her coat.

Nora (*drops her coat*): Someone's coming! (*Goes to the door and listens.*) No, there's no one there. Of course, no one will come today. It's Christmas Day. And not tomorrow either. But maybe . . . (*opens the door and looks out*) No, nothing in the mailbox. It's empty. (*Comes forward.*) What nonsense! Of course he can't be serious about it. A thing like that couldn't happen. It's impossible. I have three little children.

(*Enter the nursemaid Anne Marie from the room on the left, carrying a big cardboard box.*)

Nursemaid: I finally found the box with the costume.

Nora: Thank you. Put it on the table.

Nursemaid (*doing so*): But it really needs to be mended.

Nora: I'd like to tear it into a hundred thousand pieces.

Nursemaid: What an idea! It can easily be fixed up. All you need is a little patience.

Nora: Yes, I'll go get Mrs. Linde to come and help me with it.

Nursemaid: What, going out again? In this horrible weather? You'll catch cold, Miss Nora, and make yourself sick.

Nora: Well, worse things than that might happen. How are the children?

Nursemaid: The poor little ones are playing with their Christmas presents, but—

Nora: Do they ask for me much?

Nursemaid: You see, they're so used to having their Mama with them.

Nora: Yes, but, Anne Marie, I won't be able to spend as much time with them now as I did before.

Nursemaid: Oh well, young children quickly get used to anything.

Nora: Do you think so? Do you think they'd forget their mother if she went away for good?

Nursemaid: Good heavens! Went away for good?

Nora: Anne Marie, I want you to tell me something I've often wondered about. How could you have the heart to let your own child be raised by strangers?

Nursemaid: I had to, if I wanted to be little Nora's nursemaid.

Nora: Yes, but how could you agree to it?

Nursemaid: What, when I was going to get such a good situation out of it? A poor girl who's gotten herself in trouble should be glad to. Besides, that worthless man didn't do a single thing for me.

Nora: But I suppose your daughter has completely forgotten you.

Nursemaid: No, she hasn't, not at all. She wrote to me when she was confirmed, and again when she got married.

Nora (*putting her arms round her neck*): Dear old Anne Marie, you were such a good mother to me when I was little.

Nursemaid: Poor little Nora, you had no other mother but me.

Nora: And if my little ones had no other mother, I'm sure that you would—What nonsense I'm talking! (*Opens the box.*) Go in and see to them. Now I have to . . . You'll see how lovely I'll look tomorrow.

Nursemaid: I'm sure there'll be no one at the ball as lovely as you, Miss Nora.

(*Goes into the room on the left.*)

Nora (*begins to unpack the box, but soon pushes it away from her*): If only I dared to go out. If only no one would come. If only I could be sure nothing would happen here in the meantime. What nonsense! No one's going to come. I just have to stop thinking about it. This muff needs to be brushed. What beautiful, beautiful gloves! Stop thinking about it, stop thinking about it! One, two, three, four, five, six—(*Screams.*) Aaah! Somebody *is* coming—(*Makes a movement towards the door, but stands in hesitation.*)

(*Enter Mrs. Linde from the hall, where she has taken off her coat and hat.*)

Nora: Oh, it's you, Kristine. There's no one else out in the hall, is there? How good of you to come!

Mrs. Linde: I heard you came by asking for me.

Nora: Yes, I was passing by. As a matter of fact, it's something you could help me with. Let's sit down here on the sofa. Listen, tomorrow evening there's going to be a fancy-dress ball at the Stenborgs'—they live upstairs from us—and Torvald wants me to go as a Neapolitan fisher-girl and dance the tarantella. I learned it when we were at Capri.

Mrs. Linde: I see. You're going to give them the whole show.

Nora: Yes, Torvald wants me to. Look, here's the dress. Torvald had it made for me there, but now it's all so torn, and I don't have any idea—

Mrs. Linde: We can easily fix that. Some of the trim has just come loose here and there. Do you have a needle and thread? That's all we need.

Nora: This is so nice of you.

Mrs. Linde (sewing): So you're going to be dressed up tomorrow, Nora. I'll tell you what. I'll stop by for a moment so I can see you in your finery. Oh, meanwhile I've completely forgotten to thank you for a delightful evening last night.

Nora (gets up, and crosses the stage): Well, I didn't think last night was as pleasant as usual. You should have come to town a little earlier, Kristine. Torvald really knows how to make a home pleasant and attractive.

Mrs. Linde: And so do you, if you ask me. You're not your father's daughter for nothing. But tell me, is Doctor Rank always as depressed as he was yesterday?

Nora: No, yesterday it was especially noticeable. But you have to understand that he has a very serious disease. He has tuberculosis of the spine, poor creature. His father was a horrible man who always had mistresses, and that's why his son has been sickly since childhood, if you know what I mean.

Mrs. Linde (dropping her sewing): But, my dear Nora, how do you know anything about such things?

Nora (walking around the room): Pooh! When you have three children, you get visits now and then from—from married women, who know something about medical matters, and they talk about one thing and another.

Mrs. Linde (goes on sewing. A short silence): Does Doctor Rank come here every day?

Nora: Every day, like clockwork. He's Torvald's best friend, and a great friend of mine too. He's just like one of the family.

Mrs. Linde: But tell me, is he really sincere? I mean, isn't he the kind of man who tends to play up to people?

Nora: No, not at all. What makes you think that?

Mrs. Linde: When you introduced him to me yesterday, he told me he'd often heard my name mentioned in this house, but later I could see that your husband didn't have the slightest idea who I was. So how could Doctor Rank—?

Nora: That's true, Kristine. Torvald is so ridiculously fond of me that he wants me completely to himself, as he says. At first he used to seem almost jealous if I even mentioned any of my friends back home, so naturally I stopped talking about them to him. But I often talk about things like that with Doctor Rank, because he likes hearing about them.

Mrs. Linde: Listen to me, Nora. You're still like a child in a lot of ways, and I'm older than you and more experienced. So pay attention. You'd better stop all this with Doctor Rank.

Nora: Stop all what?

Mrs. Linde: Two things, I think. Yesterday you talked some nonsense about a rich admirer who was going to leave you his money—

Nora: An admirer who doesn't exist, unfortunately! But so what?

Mrs. Linde: Is Doctor Rank a wealthy man?

Nora: Yes, he is.

Mrs. Linde: And he has no dependents?

Nora: No, no one. But—

Mrs. Linde: And he comes here every day?

Nora: Yes, I told you he does.

Mrs. Linde: But how can such a well-bred man be so tactless?

Nora: I don't understand what you mean.

Mrs. Linde: Don't try to play dumb, Nora. Do you think I didn't guess who lent you the four thousand, eight hundred kroner?

Nora: Are you out of your mind? How can you even think that? A friend of ours, who comes here every day! Don't you realize what an incredibly awkward position that would put me in?

Mrs. Linde: Then he's really not the one?

Nora: Absolutely not. It would never have come into my head for one second. Besides, he had nothing to lend back then. He inherited his money later on.

Mrs. Linde: Well, I think that was lucky for you, my dear Nora.

Nora: No, it would never have crossed my mind to ask Doctor Rank. Although I'm sure that if I had asked him—

Mrs. Linde: But of course you won't.

Nora: Of course not. I have no reason to think I could possibly need to. But I'm absolutely certain that if I told Doctor Rank—

Mrs. Linde: Behind your husband's back?

Nora: I have to finish up with the other one, and that'll be behind his back too. I've got to wash my hands of him.

Mrs. Linde: Yes, that's what I told you yesterday, but—

Nora (walking up and down): A man can take care of these things so much more easily than a woman.

Mrs. Linde: If he's your husband, yes.

Nora: Nonsense! (*Standing still.*) When you pay off a debt you get your note back, don't you?

Mrs. Linde: Yes, of course.

Nora: And you can tear it into a hundred thousand pieces and burn up the filthy, nasty piece of paper!

Mrs. Linde (*stares at her, puts down her sewing and gets up slowly*): Nora, you're hiding something from me.

Nora: You can tell by looking at me?

Mrs. Linde: Something's happened to you since yesterday morning. Nora, what is it?

Nora (*going nearer to her*): Kristine! (*Listens.*) Shh! I hear Torvald. He's come home. Would you mind going in to the children's room for a little while? Torvald can't stand to see all this sewing going on. You can get Anne Marie to help you.

Mrs. Linde (*gathering some of the things together*): All right, but I'm not leaving this house until we've talked this thing through.

(*She goes into the room on the left, as Helmer comes in from the hall.*)

Nora (*going up to Helmer*): I've missed you so much, Torvald dear.

Helmer: Was that the seamstress?

Nora: No, it was Kristine. She's helping me fix up my dress. You'll see how nice I'm going to look.

Helmer: Wasn't that a good idea of mine, now?

Nora: Wonderful! But don't you think it's nice of me, too, to do what you said?

Helmer: Nice, because you do what your husband tells you to? Go on, you silly little thing, I am sure you didn't mean it like that. But I'll stay out of your way. I imagine you'll be trying on your dress.

Nora: I suppose you're going to do some work.

Helmer: Yes. (*Shows her a stack of papers.*) Look at that. I've just been at the bank. (*Turns to go into his room.*)

Nora: Torvald.

Helmer: Yes?

Nora: If your little squirrel were to ask you for something in a very, very charming way—

Helmer: Well?

Nora: Would you do it?

Helmer: I'd have to know what it is, first.

Nora: Your squirrel would run around and do all her tricks if you would be really nice and do what she wants.

Helmer: Speak plainly.

Nora: Your skylark would chirp her beautiful song in every room—

Helmer: Well, my skylark does that anyhow.

Nora: I'd be a little elf and dance in the moonlight for you, Torvald.

Helmer: Nora, you can't be referring to what you talked about this morning.

Nora (*moving close to him*): Yes, Torvald, I'm really begging you—

Helmer: You really have the nerve to bring that up again?

Nora: Yes, dear, you have to do this for me. You have to let Krogstad keep his job in the bank.

Helmer: My dear Nora, his job is the one that I'm giving to Mrs. Linde.

Nora: Yes, you've been awfully sweet about that. But you could just as easily get rid of somebody else instead of Krogstad.

Helmer: This is just unbelievable stubbornness! Because you decided to foolishly promise that you'd speak up for him, you expect me to—

Nora: That's not the reason, Torvald. It's for your own sake. This man writes for the trashiest newspapers, you've told me so yourself. He can do you an incredible amount of harm. I'm scared to death of him—

Helmer: Oh, I see, it's bad memories that are making you afraid.

Nora: What do you mean?

Helmer: Obviously you're thinking about your father.

Nora: Yes. Yes, of course. You remember what those hateful creatures wrote in the papers about Papa, and how horribly they slandered him. I believe they'd have gotten him fired if the department hadn't sent you over to look into it, and if you hadn't been so kind and helpful to him.

Helmer: My little Nora, there's an important difference between your father and me. His reputation as a public official was not above suspicion. Mine is, and I hope it will continue to be for as long as I hold my office.

Nora: You never can tell what trouble these men might cause. We could be so well off, so snug and happy here in our peaceful home, without a care in the world, you and I and the children, Torvald! That's why I'm begging you to—

Helmer: And the more you plead for him, the more you make it impossible for me to keep him. They already know at the bank that I'm going to fire Krogstad. Do you think I'm going to let them all say that the new manager has changed his mind because his wife said to—

Nora: And what if they did?

Helmer: Right! What does it matter, as long as this stubborn little creature gets her own way! Do you think I'm going to make myself look ridiculous in front of my whole staff, and let people think that I can be pushed around by all sorts of outside influence? That would soon come back to haunt me, you can be sure! And besides, there's one thing that makes it totally impossible for me to have Krogstad working in the bank as long as I'm the manager.

Nora: What's that?

Helmer: I might have been able to overlook his moral failings, if need be—

Nora: Yes, you could do that, couldn't you?

Helmer: And I hear he's a good worker, too. But I knew him when we were boys. It was one of those rash friendships that so often turn out to be a millstone around the neck later on. I might as well tell you straight out, we were very close friends at one time. But he has no tact and no self-restraint, especially when other people are around. He thinks he has the right to still call me by my first name, and every minute it's Torvald this and Torvald that. I don't mind telling you, I find it extremely annoying. He would make my position at the bank intolerable.

Nora: Torvald, I can't believe you're serious.

Helmer: Oh no? Why not?

Nora: Because it's so petty.

Helmer: What do you mean, petty? You think I'm petty?

Nora: No, just the opposite, dear, and that's why I can't—

Helmer: It's the same thing. You say my attitude's petty, so I must be petty too! Petty! Fine! Well, I'll put a stop to this once and for all. (*Goes to the hall door and calls.*) Helene!

Nora: What are you going to do?

Helmer (*looking among his papers*): Settle it.

(*Enter Maid.*)

Here, take this letter downstairs right now. Find a messenger and tell him to deliver it, and to be quick about it. The address is on it, and here's the money.

Maid: Yes, sir. (*Exits with the letter.*)

Helmer (*putting his papers together*): There, Little Pigheaded Miss.

Nora (*breathlessly*): Torvald, what was that letter?

Helmer: Krogstad's notice.

Nora: Call her back, Torvald! There's still time. Oh, Torvald, call her back! Do it for my sake—for your own sake—for the children's sake! Do you hear me, Torvald? Call her back! You don't know what that letter can do to us.

Helmer: It's too late.

Nora: Yes, it's too late.

Helmer: My dear Nora, I can forgive this anxiety of yours, even though it's insulting to me. It really is. Don't you think it's insulting to suggest that I should be afraid of retaliation from a grubby pen-pusher? But I forgive you anyway, because it's such a beautiful demonstration of how much you love me. (*Takes her in his arms.*) And that is as it should be, my own darling Nora. Come what may, you can rest assured that I'll have both courage and strength if necessary. You'll see that I'm man enough to take everything on myself.

Nora (*in a horror-stricken voice*): What do you mean by that?

Helmer: Everything, I say.

Nora (*recovering herself*): You'll never have to do that.

Helmer: That's right, we'll take it on together, Nora, as man and wife. That's just how it should be. (*Caressing her.*) Are you satisfied now? There, there! Don't look at me that way, like a frightened dove! This whole thing is just your imagination running away with you. Now you should go and run through the tarantella and practice your tambourine. I'll go into my study and shut the door so I can't hear anything. You can make all the noise you want. (*Turns back at the door.*) And when Rank comes, tell him where I am.

(*Nods to her, takes his papers and goes into his room, and shuts the door behind him.*)

Nora (*bewildered with anxiety, stands as if rooted to the spot and whispers*): He's capable of doing it. He's going to do it. He'll do it in spite of everything. No, not that! Never, never! Anything but that! Oh, for somebody to help me find some way out of this! (*The doorbell rings.*) Doctor Rank! Anything but that—anything, whatever it is!

(*She puts her hands over her face, pulls herself together, goes to the door and opens it. Rank is standing in the hall, hanging up his coat. During the following dialogue it starts to grow dark.*)

Nora: Hello, Doctor Rank. I recognized your ring. But you'd better not go in and see Torvald just now. I think he's busy with something.

Rank: And you?

Nora (*brings him in and shuts the door behind him*): Oh, you know perfectly well I always have time for you.

Rank: Thank you. I'll make use of it for as long as I can.

Nora: What does that mean, for as long as you can?

Rank: Why, does that frighten you?

Nora: It was such a strange way of putting it. Is something going to happen?

Rank: Nothing but what I've been expecting for a long time. But I never thought it would happen so soon.

Nora (gripping him by the arm): What have you found out? Doctor Rank, you must tell me.

Rank (sitting down by the stove): I'm done for. And there's nothing I can do about it.

Nora (with a sigh of relief): Oh—you're talking about yourself?

Rank: Who else? And there's no use lying to myself. I'm the sickest patient I have, Mrs. Helmer. Lately I've been adding up my internal account. Bankrupt! In a month I'll probably be rotting in the ground.

Nora: What a horrible thing to say!

Rank: The thing itself is horrible, and the worst of it is all the horrible things I'll have to go through before it's over. I'm going to examine myself just once more. When that's done, I'll be pretty sure when I'm going to start breaking down. There's something I want to say to you. Helmer's sensitive nature makes him completely unable to deal with anything ugly. I don't want him in my sickroom.

Nora: Oh, but, Doctor Rank—

Rank: I won't have him there, period. I'll lock the door to keep him out. As soon as I'm quite sure that the worst has come, I'll send you my card with a black cross on it, and that way you'll know that the final stage of the horror has started.

Nora: You're being really absurd today. And I so much wanted you to be in a good mood.

Rank: With death stalking me? Having to pay this price for another man's sins? Where's the justice in that? In every single family, in one way or another, some such unavoidable retribution is being imposed.

Nora (putting her hands over her ears): Nonsense! Can't you talk about something cheerful?

Rank: Oh, this *is* something cheerful. In fact, it's hilarious. My poor innocent spine has to suffer for my father's youthful self-indulgence.

Nora (sitting at the table on the left): Yes, he did love asparagus and *pâté de foie gras*, didn't he?

Rank: Yes, and truffles.

Nora: Truffles, yes. And oysters too, I suppose?

Rank: Oysters, of course. That goes without saying.

Nora: And oceans of port and champagne. Isn't it sad that all those delightful things should take their revenge on our bones?

Rank: Especially that they should take their revenge on the unlucky bones of people who haven't even had the satisfaction of enjoying them.

Nora: Yes, that's the saddest part of all.

Rank (with a searching look at her): Hm!

Nora (after a short pause): Why did you smile?

Rank: No, it was you who laughed.

Nora: No, it was you who smiled, Doctor Rank!

Rank (rising): You're even more of a tease than I thought you were.

Nora: I am in a crazy mood today.

Rank: Apparently so.

Nora (*putting her hands on his shoulders*): Dear, dear Doctor Rank, we can't let death take you away from Torvald and me.

Rank: It's a loss that you'll easily recover from. Those who are gone are soon forgotten.

Nora (*looking at him anxiously*): Do you really believe that?

Rank: People make new friends, and then—

Nora: Who'll make new friends?

Rank: Both you and Helmer, when I'm gone. You yourself are already well on the way to it, I think. What was that Mrs. Linde doing here last night?

Nora: Oho! You're not telling me that you're jealous of poor Kristine, are you?

Rank: Yes, I am. She'll be my successor in this house. When I'm six feet under, this woman will—

Nora: Shh! Don't talk so loud. She's in that room.

Rank: Again today. There, you see.

Nora: She's just come to sew my dress for me. Goodness, how unreasonable you are! (*Sits down on the sofa.*) Be nice now, Doctor Rank, and tomorrow you'll see how beautifully I'll dance, and you can pretend that I'm doing it just for you—and for Torvald too, of course. (*Takes various things out of the box.*) Doctor Rank, come and sit down here, and I'll show you something.

Rank (*sitting down*): What is it?

Nora: Just look at these!

Rank: Silk stockings.

Nora: Flesh-colored. Aren't they lovely? It's so dark here now, but tomorrow—No, no, no! You're only supposed to look at the feet. Oh well, you have my permission to look at the legs too.

Rank: Hm!

Nora: Why do you look so critical? Don't you think they'll fit me?

Rank: I have no basis for forming an opinion on that subject.

Nora (*looks at him for a moment*): Shame on you! (*Hits him lightly on the ear with the stockings.*) That's your punishment. (*Folds them up again.*)

Rank: And what other pretty things do I have your permission to look at?

Nora: Not one single thing. That's what you get for being so naughty. (*She looks among the things, humming to herself.*)

Rank (*after a short silence*): When I'm sitting here, talking to you so intimately this way, I can't imagine for a moment what would have become of me if I'd never come into this house.

Nora (*smiling*): I believe you really do feel completely at home with us.

Rank (*in a lower voice, looking straight in front of him*): And to have to leave it all—

Nora: Nonsense, you're not going to leave it.

Rank (*as before*): And not to be able to leave behind the slightest token of my gratitude, hardly even a fleeting regret. Nothing but an empty place to be filled by the first person who comes along.

Nora: And if I were to ask you now for a—No, never mind!

Rank: For a what?

Nora: For a great proof of your friendship—

Rank: Yes, yes!

Nora: I mean a tremendously huge favor—

Rank: Would you really make me so happy, just this once?

Nora: But you don't know what it is yet.

Rank: No, but tell me.

Nora: I really can't, Doctor Rank. It's too much to ask. It involves advice, and help, and a favor—

Rank: So much the better. I can't imagine what you mean. Tell me what it is. You do trust me, don't you?

Nora: More than anyone. I know that you're my best and truest friend, so I'll tell you what it is. Well, Doctor Rank, it's something you have to help me prevent. You know how devoted Torvald is to me, how deeply he loves me. He wouldn't hesitate for a second to give his life for me.

Rank (leaning towards her): Nora, do you think that he's the only one—

Nora (with a slight start): The only one?

Rank: Who would gladly give his life for you.

Nora (sadly): Oh, is that it?

Rank: I'd made up my mind to tell you before I—I go away, and there'll never be a better opportunity than this. Now you know it, Nora. And now you know that you can trust me more than you can trust anyone else.

Nora (rises, deliberately and quietly): Let me by.

Rank (makes room for her to pass him, but sits still): Nora!

Nora (at the hall door): Helene, bring in the lamp. *(Goes over to the stove.)* Dear Doctor Rank, that was really horrible of you.

Rank: To love you just as much as somebody else does? Is that so horrible?

Nora: No, but to go and tell me like that. There was really no need—

Rank: What do you mean? Did you know—

(Maid enters with lamp, puts it down on the table, and goes out.)

Nora—Mrs. Helmer—tell me, did you have any idea I felt this way?

Nora: Oh, how do I know whether I did or I didn't? I really can't answer that. How could you be so clumsy, Doctor Rank? When we were getting along so nicely.

Rank: Well, at any rate, now you know that I'm yours to command, body and soul. So won't you tell me what it is?

Nora (looking at him): After what just happened?

Rank: I beg you to let me know what it is.

Nora: I can't tell you anything now.

Rank: Yes, yes. Please don't punish me that way. Give me permission to do anything for you that a man can do.

Nora: You can't do anything for me now. Besides, I really don't need any help at all. The whole thing is just my imagination. It really is. It has to be! *(Sits down in the rocking chair, and smiles at him.)* You're a nice man, Doctor Rank. Don't you feel ashamed of yourself, now that the lamp is lit?

Rank: Not a bit. But maybe it would be better if I left—and never came back?

Nora: No, no, you can't do that. You must keep coming here just as you always did. You know very well Torvald can't do without you.

Rank: But what about you?

Nora: Oh, I'm always extremely pleased to see you.

Rank: And that's just what gave me the wrong idea. You're a puzzle to me. I've often felt that you'd almost just as soon be in my company as in Helmer's.

Nora: Yes, you see, there are the people you love the most, and then there are the people whose company you enjoy the most.

Rank: Yes, there's something to that.

Nora: When I lived at home, of course I loved Papa best. But I always thought it was great fun to sneak down to the maids' room, because they never preached at me, and I loved listening to the way they talked to each other.

Rank: I see. So I'm their replacement.

Nora (jumping up and going to him): Oh, dear, sweet Doctor Rank, I didn't mean it that way. But surely you can understand that being with Torvald is a little like being with Papa—

(Enter Maid from the hall.)

Maid: Excuse me, ma'am. *(Whispers and hands her a card.)*

Nora (glancing at the card): Oh! *(Puts it in her pocket.)*

Rank: Is something wrong?

Nora: No, no, not at all. It's just—it's my new dress—

Rank: What? Your dress is lying right there.

Nora: Oh, yes, that one. But this is another one, one that I ordered. I don't want Torvald to find out about it—

Rank: Oh! So that was the big secret.

Nora: Yes, that's it. Why don't you just go inside and see him? He's in his study. Stay with him for as long as—

Rank: Put your mind at ease. I won't let him escape. *(Goes into Helmer's study.)*

Nora (to the maid): And he's waiting in the kitchen?

Maid: Yes, ma'am. He came up the back stairs.

Nora: Didn't you tell him no one was home?

Maid: Yes, but it didn't do any good.

Nora: He won't go away?

Maid: No, he says he won't leave until he sees you, ma'am.

Nora: Well, show him in, but quietly. Helene, I don't want you to say anything about this to anyone. It's a surprise for my husband.

Maid: Yes, ma'am. I understand. *(Exit.)*

Nora: This horrible thing is really going to happen! It's going to happen in spite of me! No, no, no, it can't happen! I can't let it happen!

(She bolts the door of Helmer's study. The maid opens the hall door for Krogstad and closes it behind him. He is wearing a fur coat, high boots, and a fur cap.)

Nora (advancing towards him): Speak quietly. My husband's home.

Krogstad: What do I care about that?

Nora: What do you want from me?

Krogstad: An explanation of something.

Nora: Be quick, then. What is it?

Krogstad: I suppose you're aware that I've been let go.

Nora: I couldn't prevent it, Mr. Krogstad. I fought for you as hard as I could, but it was no use.

Krogstad: Does your husband love you so little, then? He knows what I can expose you to, and he still goes ahead and—

Nora: How can you think that he knows any such thing?

Krogstad: I didn't think so for a moment. It wouldn't be at all like dear old Torvald Helmer to show that kind of courage——

Nora: Mr. Krogstad, a little respect for my husband, please.

Krogstad: Certainly—all the respect he deserves. But since you've kept everything so carefully to yourself, may I be bold enough to assume that you see a little more clearly than you did yesterday just what it is that you've done?

Nora: More than you could ever teach me.

Krogstad: Yes, such a poor excuse for a lawyer as I am.

Nora: What is it you want from me?

Krogstad: Only to see how you're doing, Mrs. Helmer. I've been thinking about you all day. A mere bill collector, a pen-pusher, a—well, a man like me—even he has a little of what people call feelings, you know.

Nora: Why don't you show some, then? Think about my little children.

Krogstad: Have you and your husband thought about mine? But never mind about that. I just wanted to tell you not to take this business too seriously. I won't make any accusations against you. Not for now, anyway.

Nora: No, of course not. I was sure you wouldn't.

Krogstad: The whole thing can be settled amicably. There's no need for anyone to know anything about it. It'll be our little secret, just the three of us.

Nora: My husband must never know anything about it.

Krogstad: How are you going to keep him from finding out? Are you telling me that you can pay off the whole balance?

Nora: No, not just yet.

Krogstad: Or that you have some other way of raising the money soon?

Nora: No way that I plan to make use of.

Krogstad: Well, in any case, it wouldn't be any use to you now even if you did. If you stood in front of me with a stack of bills in each hand, I still wouldn't give you back your note.

Nora: What are you planning to do with it?

Krogstad: I just want to hold onto it, just keep it in my possession. No one who isn't involved in the matter will ever know anything about it. So, if you've been thinking about doing something desperate—

Nora: I have.

Krogstad: If you've been thinking about running away—

Nora: I have.

Krogstad: Or doing something even worse—

Nora: How could you know that?

Krogstad: Stop thinking about it.

Nora: How did you know I'd thought of that?

Krogstad: Most of us think about that at first. I did, too. But I didn't have the courage.

Nora (faintly): Neither do I.

Krogstad (in a tone of relief): No, that's true, isn't it? You don't have the courage either?

Nora: No, I don't. I don't.

Krogstad: Besides, it would have been an incredibly stupid thing to do. Once the first storm at home blows over . . . I have a letter for your husband in my pocket.

Nora: Telling him everything?

Krogstad: As gently as possible.

Nora (quickly): He can't see that letter. Tear it up. I'll find some way of getting money.

Krogstad: Excuse me, Mrs. Helmer, but didn't I just tell you—

Nora: I'm not talking about what I owe you. Tell me how much you want from my husband, and I'll get the money.

Krogstad: I don't want any money from your husband.

Nora: Then what do you want?

Krogstad: I'll tell you what I want. I want a fresh start, Mrs. Helmer, and I want to move up in the world. And your husband's going to help me do it. I've steered clear of anything questionable for the last year and a half. In all that time I've been struggling along, pinching every penny. I was content to work my way up step by step. But now I've been fired, and it's not going to be enough just to get my job back, as if you people were doing me some huge favor. I want to move up, I tell you. I want to get back into the bank again, but with a promotion. Your husband's going to have to find me a position—

Nora: He'll never do it!

Krogstad: Oh yes, he will. I know him. He won't dare object. And as soon as I'm back there with him, then you'll see! Inside of a year I'll be the manager's right-hand man. It'll be Nils Krogstad, not Torvald Helmer, who's running the bank.

Nora: That's never going to happen!

Krogstad: Do you mean that you'll—

Nora: I have enough courage for it now.

Krogstad: Oh, you can't scare me. An elegant, spoiled lady like you—

Nora: You'll see, you'll see.

Krogstad: Under the ice, maybe? Down in the cold, coal-black water? And then floating up to the surface in the spring, all horrible and unrecognizable, with your hair fallen out—

Nora: You can't scare me.

Krogstad: And you can't scare me. People don't do that kind of thing, Mrs. Helmer. Besides, what good would it do? I'd still have him completely in my power.

Nora: Even then? When I'm no longer—

Krogstad: Have you forgotten that your reputation is completely in my hands? (*Nora stands speechless, looking at him.*) Well, now I've warned you. Don't do anything foolish. I'll be expecting an answer from Helmer after he reads my letter. And remember, it's your husband himself who's forced me to act this way again. I'll never forgive him for that. Goodbye, Mrs. Helmer. (*Exits through the hall.*)

Nora (goes to the hall door, opens it slightly and listens.): He's leaving. He isn't putting the letter in the box. Oh no, no! He couldn't! (*Opens the door little by little.*) What? He's standing out there. He's not going downstairs. He's hesitating? Is he?

(*A letter drops into the box. Then Krogstad's footsteps are heard, until they die away as he goes downstairs. Nora utters a stifled cry, and runs across the room to the table by the sofa. A short pause.*)

Nora: In the mailbox. (*Steals across to the hall door.*) It's there! Torvald, Torvald, there's no hope for us now!

(*Mrs. Linde comes in from the room on the left, carrying the dress.*)

Mrs. Linde: There, I can't find anything more to mend. Would you like to try it on?

Nora (*in a hoarse whisper*): Kristine, come here.

Mrs. Linde (*throwing the dress down on the sofa*): What's the matter with you? You look so agitated!

Nora: Come here. Do you see that letter? There, look. You can see it through the glass in the mailbox.

Mrs. Linde: Yes, I see it.

Nora: That letter is from Krogstad.

Mrs. Linde: Nora! It was Krogstad who lent you the money!

Nora: Yes, and now Torvald will know all about it.

Mrs. Linde: Believe me, Nora, that's the best thing for both of you.

Nora: You don't know the whole story. I forged a name.

Mrs. Linde: My God!

Nora: There's something I want to say to you, Kristine. I need you to be my witness.

Mrs. Linde: Your witness? What do you mean? What am I supposed to—

Nora: If I should go out of my mind—and it could easily happen—

Mrs. Linde: Nora!

Nora: Or if anything else should happen to me—anything, for instance, that might keep me from being here—

Mrs. Linde: Nora! Nora! What's the matter with you?

Nora: And if it turned out that somebody wanted to take all the responsibility, all the blame, you understand what I mean—

Mrs. Linde: Yes, yes, but how can you imagine—

Nora: Then you must be my witness that it's not true, Kristine. I'm not out of my mind at all. I'm perfectly rational right now, and I'm telling you that no one else ever knew anything about it. I did the whole thing all by myself. Remember that.

Mrs. Linde: I will. But I don't understand all this.

Nora: How could you understand it? Or the miracle that's going to happen!

Mrs. Linde: A miracle?

Nora: Yes, a miracle! But it's so terrible, Kristine. I can't let it happen, not for the whole world.

Mrs. Linde: I'll go and see Krogstad right this minute.

Nora: No, don't. He'll do something to hurt you too.

Mrs. Linde: There was a time when he would have gladly done anything for my sake.

Nora: What?

Mrs. Linde: Where does he live?

Nora: How should I know? Yes (*feeling in her pocket*), here's his card. But the letter, the letter—

Helmer (*calls from his room, knocking at the door*): Nora!

Nora (*cries out anxiously*): What is it? What do you want?

Helmer: Don't be so afraid. We're not coming in. You've locked the door. Are you trying on your dress?

Nora: Yes, that's it. Oh, it's going to look so nice, Torvald.

Mrs. Linde (who has read the card): Look, he lives right around the corner.

Nora: But it's no use. It's all over. The letter's lying right there in the box.

Mrs. Linde: And your husband has the key?

Nora: Yes, always.

Mrs. Linde: Krogstad can ask for his letter back unread. He'll have to make up some reason—

Nora: But now is just about the time that Torvald usually—

Mrs. Linde: You have to prevent him. Go in and talk to him. I'll be back as soon as I can.

(She hurries out through the hall door.)

Nora (goes to Helmer's door, opens it and peeps in): Torvald!

Helmer (from the inner room): Well? May I finally come back into my own room? Come along, Rank, now you'll see—(*Stopping in the doorway.*) But what's this?

Nora: What's what, dear?

Helmer: Rank led me to expect an amazing transformation.

Rank (in the doorway): So I understood, but apparently I was mistaken.

Nora: Yes, nobody gets to admire me in my dress until tomorrow.

Helmer: But, my dear Nora, you look exhausted. Have you been practicing too much?

Nora: No, I haven't been practicing at all.

Helmer: But you'll have to—

Nora: Yes, of course I will, Torvald. But I can't get anywhere without you helping me. I've completely forgotten the whole thing.

Helmer: Oh, we'll soon get you back up to form again.

Nora: Yes, help me, Torvald. Promise that you will! I'm so nervous about it—all those people. I need you to devote yourself completely to me this evening. Not even the tiniest little bit of business. You can't even pick up a pen. Do you promise, Torvald dear?

Helmer: I promise. This evening I will be wholly and absolutely at your service, you helpless little creature. But first I'm just going to—(*Goes towards the hall door.*)

Nora: Just going to what?

Helmer: To see if there's any mail.

Nora: No, no! Don't do that, Torvald!

Helmer: Why not?

Nora: Torvald, please don't. There's nothing there.

Helmer: Well, let me look. (*Turns to go to the mailbox. Nora, at the piano, plays the first bars of the tarantella. Helmer stops in the doorway.*) Aha!

Nora: I can't dance tomorrow if I don't practice with you.

Helmer (going up to her): Are you really so worried about it, dear?

Nora: Yes, terribly worried about it. Let me practice right now. We have time before dinner. Sit down and play for me, Torvald dear. Criticize me and correct me, the way you always do.

Helmer: With great pleasure, if you want me to. (*Sits down at the piano.*)

Nora (takes a tambourine and a long multicolored shawl out of the box. She hastily drapes the shawl around her. Then she bounds to the front of the stage and calls out): Now play for me! I'm going to dance!

(Helmer plays and Nora dances. Rank stands by the piano behind Helmer and watches.)

Helmer (as he plays): Slower, slower!

Nora: I can't do it any other way.

Helmer: Not so violently, Nora!

Nora: This is the way.

Helmer (stops playing): No, no, that's not right at all.

Nora (laughing and swinging the tambourine): Didn't I tell you so?

Rank: Let me play for her.

Helmer (getting up): Good idea. I can correct her better that way.

(*Rank sits down at the piano and plays. Nora dances more and more wildly. Helmer has taken up a position beside the stove, and as she dances, he gives her frequent instructions. She doesn't seem to hear him. Her hair comes undone and falls over her shoulders. She pays no attention to it, but goes on dancing. Enter Mrs. Linde.*)

Mrs. Linde (standing as if spellbound in the doorway): Oh!

Nora (as she dances): What fun, Kristine!

Helmer: My dear darling Nora, you're dancing as if your life depended on it.

Nora: It does.

Helmer: Stop, Rank. This is insane! I said stop!

(*Rank stops playing, and Nora suddenly stands still. Helmer goes up to her.*)

I never would have believed it. You've forgotten everything I taught you.

Nora (throwing the tambourine aside): There, you see.

Helmer: You're going to need a lot of coaching.

Nora: Yes, you see how much I need it. You have to coach me right up to the last minute. Promise me you will, Torvald!

Helmer: You can depend on me.

Nora: You can't think about anything but me, today or tomorrow. Don't open a single letter. Don't even open the mailbox—

Helmer: You're still afraid of that man—

Nora: Yes, yes, I am.

Helmer: Nora, I can tell from your face that there's a letter from him in the box.

Nora: I don't know. I think there is. But you can't read anything like that now. Nothing nasty must come between us until this is all over.

Rank (whispers to Helmer): Don't contradict her.

Helmer (taking her in his arms): The child shall have her way. But tomorrow night, after you've danced—

Nora: Then you'll be free.

(*The Maid appears in the doorway to the right.*)

Maid: Dinner is served, ma'am.

Nora: We'll have champagne, Helene.

Maid: Yes, ma'am. (*Exit.*)

Helmer: Oh, are we having a banquet?

Nora: Yes, a banquet. Champagne till dawn! (*Calls out.*) And a few macaroons, Helene. Lots of them, just this once!

Helmer: Come on, stop acting so wild and nervous. Be my own little skylark again.

Nora: Yes, dear, I will. But go inside now, and you too, Doctor Rank. Kristine, please help me do up my hair.

Rank (whispers to Helmer as they go out): There isn't anything—she's not expecting—?

Helmer: No, nothing like that. It's just this childish nervousness I was telling you about. (*They go into the right-hand room.*)

Nora: Well?

Mrs. Linde: Out of town.

Nora: I could tell from your face.

Mrs. Linde: He'll be back tomorrow evening. I wrote him a note.

Nora: You should have left it alone. Don't try to prevent anything. After all, it's exciting to be waiting for a miracle to happen.

Mrs. Linde: What is it that you're waiting for?

Nora: Oh, you wouldn't understand. Go inside with them, I'll be there in a moment.

(*Mrs. Linde goes into the dining room. Nora stands still for a little while, as if to compose herself. Then she looks at her watch.*)

Five o'clock. Seven hours till midnight, and another twenty-four hours till the next midnight. And then the tarantella will be over. Twenty-four plus seven? Thirty-one hours to live.

Helmer (from the doorway on the right): Where's my little skylark?

Nora (going to him with her arms outstretched): Here she is!

ACT III

The same scene. The table has been placed in the middle of the stage, with chairs around it. A lamp is burning on the table. The door into the hall stands open. Dance music is heard in the room above. Mrs. Linde is sitting at the table idly turning over the pages of a book. She tries to read, but she seems unable to concentrate. Every now and then she listens intently for a sound at the outer door.

Mrs. Linde (looking at her watch): Not yet—and the time's nearly up. If only he doesn't— (*Listens again.*) Ah, there he is. (*Goes into the hall and opens the outer door carefully. Light footsteps are heard on the stairs. She whispers.*) Come in. There's no one else here.

Krogstad (in the doorway): I found a note from you at home. What does this mean?

Mrs. Linde: It's absolutely necessary that I have a talk with you.

Krogstad: Really? And is it absolutely necessary that we have it here?

Mrs. Linde: It's impossible where I live. There's no private entrance to my apartment. Come in. We're all alone. The maid's asleep, and the Helmers are upstairs at a dance.

Krogstad (coming into the room): Are the Helmers really at a dance tonight?

Mrs. Linde: Yes. Why shouldn't they be?

Krogstad: Certainly—why not?

Mrs. Linde: Now, Nils, let's have a talk.

Krogstad: What can we two have to talk about?

Mrs. Linde: Quite a lot.

Krogstad: I wouldn't have thought so.

Mrs. Linde: Of course not. You've never really understood me.

Krogstad: What was there to understand, except what the whole world could see—a heartless woman drops a man when a better catch comes along?

Mrs. Linde: Do you think I'm really that heartless? And that I broke it off with you so lightly?

Krogstad: Didn't you?

Mrs. Linde: Nils, did you really think that?

Krogstad: If not, why did you write what you did to me?

Mrs. Linde: What else could I do? Since I had to break it off with you, I had an obligation to stamp out your feelings for me.

Krogstad (wringing his hands): So that was it. And all this just for the sake of money!

Mrs. Linde: Don't forget that I had an invalid mother and two little brothers. We couldn't wait for you, Nils. Success seemed a long way off for you back then.

Krogstad: That may be so, but you had no right to cast me aside for anyone else's sake.

Mrs. Linde: I don't know if I did or not. Many times I've asked myself if I had the right.

Krogstad (more gently): When I lost you, it was as if the earth crumbled under my feet. Look at me now—a shipwrecked man clinging to a bit of wreckage.

Mrs. Linde: But help may be on the way.

Krogstad: It *was* on the way, till you came along and blocked it.

Mrs. Linde: Without knowing it, Nils. It wasn't till today that I found out I'd be taking your job.

Krogstad: I believe you, if you say so. But now that you know it, are you going to step aside?

Mrs. Linde: No, because it wouldn't do you any good.

Krogstad: Good? *I* would quit whether it did any good or not.

Mrs. Linde: I've learned to be practical. Life and hard, bitter necessity have taught me that.

Krogstad: And life has taught me not to believe in fine speeches.

Mrs. Linde: Then life has taught you something very sensible. But surely you believe in actions?

Krogstad: What do you mean by that?

Mrs. Linde: You said you were like a shipwrecked man clinging to a piece of wreckage.

Krogstad: I had good reason to say so.

Mrs. Linde: Well, I'm like a shipwrecked woman clinging to a piece of wreckage, with no one to mourn for and no one to care for.

Krogstad: That was your own choice.

Mrs. Linde: I had no other choice—then.

Krogstad: Well, what about now?

Mrs. Linde: Nils, how would it be if we two shipwrecked people could reach out to each other?

Krogstad: What are you saying?

Mrs. Linde: Two people on the same piece of wreckage would stand a better chance than each one on their own.

Krogstad: Kristine, I . . .

Mrs. Linde: Why do you think I came to town?

Krogstad: You can't mean that you were thinking about me?

Mrs. Linde: Life is unendurable without work. I've worked all my life, for as long as I can remember, and it's been my greatest and my only pleasure. But now that I'm completely alone in the world, my life is so terribly empty and I feel so abandoned. There isn't the slightest pleasure in working only for yourself. Nils, give me someone and something to work for.

Krogstad: I don't trust this. It's just some romantic female impulse, a high-minded urge for self-sacrifice.

Mrs. Linde: Have you ever known me to be like that?

Krogstad: Could you really do it? Tell me, do you know all about my past?

Mrs. Linde: Yes.

Krogstad: And you know what they think of me around here?

Mrs. Linde: Didn't you imply that with me you might have been a very different person?

Krogstad: I'm sure I would have.

Mrs. Linde: Is it too late now?

Krogstad: Kristine, are you serious about all this? Yes, I'm sure you are. I can see it in your face. Do you really have the courage, then—

Mrs. Linde: I want to be a mother to someone, and your children need a mother. We two need each other. Nils, I have faith in your true nature. I can face anything together with you.

Krogstad (grasps her hands): Thank you, thank you, Kristine! Now I can find a way to clear myself in the eyes of the world. Ah, but I forgot—

Mrs. Linde (listening): Shh! The tarantella! You have to go!

Krogstad: Why? What's the matter?

Mrs. Linde: Do you hear them up there? They'll probably come home as soon as this dance is over.

Krogstad: Yes, yes, I'll go. But it won't make any difference. You don't know what I've done about my situation with the Helmers.

Mrs. Linde: Yes, I know all about that.

Krogstad: And in spite of that you still have the courage to—

Mrs. Linde: I understand completely what despair can drive a man like you to do.

Krogstad: If only I could undo it!

Mrs. Linde: You can't. Your letter's lying in the mailbox now.

Krogstad: Are you sure?

Mrs. Linde: Quite sure, but—

Krogstad (with a searching look at her): Is that what this is all about? That you want to save your friend, no matter what you have to do? Tell me the truth. Is that it?

Mrs. Linde: Nils, when a woman has sold herself for someone else's sake, she doesn't do it a second time.

Krogstad: I'll ask for my letter back.

Mrs. Linde: No, no.

Krogstad: Yes, of course I will. I'll wait here until Helmer comes home. I'll tell him he has to give me back my letter, that it's only about my being fired, that I don't want him to read it—

Mrs. Linde: No, Nils, don't ask for it back.

Krogstad: But wasn't that the reason why you asked me to meet you here?

Mrs. Linde: In my first moment of panic, it was. But twenty-four hours have gone by since then, and in the meantime I've seen some incredible things in this house. Helmer has to know all about it. This terrible secret has to come out. They have to have a complete understanding between them. It's time for all this lying and pretending to stop.

Krogstad: All right then, if you think it's worth the risk. But there's at least one thing I can do, and do right away—

Mrs. Linde (listening): You have to leave this instant! The dance is over. They could walk in here any minute.

Krogstad: I'll wait for you downstairs.

Mrs. Linde: Yes, please do. I want you to walk me home.

Krogstad: I've never been so happy in my entire life!

(*Goes out through the outer door. The door between the room and the hall remains open.*)

Mrs. Linde (straightening up the room and getting her hat and coat ready): How different things will be! Someone to work for and live for, a home to bring happiness into. I'm certainly going to try. I wish they'd hurry up and come home—(*Listens.*) Ah, here they are now. I'd better put on my things.

(*Picks up her hat and coat. Helmer's and Nora's voices are heard outside. A key is turned, and Helmer brings Nora into the hall almost by force. She is in an Italian peasant costume with a large black shawl wrapped around her. He is in formal wear and a black domino—a hooded cloak with an eye-mask—which is open.*)

Nora (hanging back in the doorway and struggling with him): No, no, no! Don't bring me inside. I want to go back upstairs. I don't want to leave so early.

Helmer: But, my dearest Nora—

Nora: Please, Torvald dear, please, please, only one more hour.

Helmer: Not one more minute, my sweet Nora. You know this is what we agreed on. Come inside. You'll catch cold standing out there.

(*He brings her gently into the room, in spite of her resistance.*)

Mrs. Linde: Good evening.

Nora: Kristine!

Helmer: What are you doing here so late, Mrs. Linde?

Mrs. Linde: You must excuse me. I was so anxious to see Nora in her dress.

Nora: Have you been sitting here waiting for me?

Mrs. Linde: Yes, unfortunately I came too late, you'd already gone upstairs. And I didn't want to go away again without seeing you.

Helmer (taking off Nora's shawl): Yes, take a good look at her. I think she's worth looking at. Isn't she charming, Mrs. Linde?

Mrs. Linde: Yes, indeed she is.

Helmer: Doesn't she look especially pretty? Everyone thought so at the dance. But this sweet little person is extremely stubborn. What are we going to do with her? Believe it or not, I almost had to drag her away by force.

Nora: Torvald, you'll be sorry you didn't let me stay, even if only for half an hour.

Helmer: Listen to her, Mrs. Linde! She danced her tarantella and it was a huge success, as it deserved to be, though maybe her performance was a tiny bit too realistic, a little more so than it might have been by strict artistic standards. But never mind about that! The main thing is, she was a success, a tremendous success. Do you think I was going to let her stay there after that, and spoil the effect? Not a chance! I took my charming little Capri girl—my capricious little Capri girl, I should say—I took her by the arm, one quick circle around the room, a curtsey to one and all, and, as they say in novels, the beautiful vision vanished. An exit should always make an effect, Mrs. Linde, but I can't make Nora understand that. Whew, this room is hot!

(*Throws his domino on a chair and opens the door to his study.*)

Why is it so dark in here? Oh, of course. Excuse me.

(*He goes in and lights some candles.*)

Nora (*in a hurried, breathless whisper*): Well?
Mrs. Linde (*in a low voice*): I talked to him.
Nora: And?
Mrs. Linde: Nora, you have to tell your husband the whole story.
Nora (*in an expressionless voice*): I knew it.
Mrs. Linde: You have nothing to fear from Krogstad, but you still have to tell him.
Nora: I'm not going to.
Mrs. Linde: Then the letter will.
Nora: Thank you, Kristine. Now I know what I have to do. Shh!
Helmer (*coming in again*): Well, Mrs. Linde, have you been admiring her?
Mrs. Linde: Yes, I have, and now I'll say goodnight.
Helmer: What, already? Is this your knitting?
Mrs. Linde (*taking it*): Yes, thank you, I'd almost forgotten it.
Helmer: So you knit?
Mrs. Linde: Yes, of course.
Helmer: You know, you ought to embroider.
Mrs. Linde: Really? Why?
Helmer: It's much more graceful-looking. Here, let me show you. You hold the embroidery this way in your left hand, and use the needle with your right, like this, with a long, easy sweep. Do you see?
Mrs. Linde: Yes, I suppose—
Helmer: But knitting, that can never be anything but awkward. Here, look. The arms close together, the knitting needles going up and down. It's sort of Chinese looking. That was really excellent champagne they gave us.
Mrs. Linde: Well, good night, Nora, and don't be stubborn anymore.
Helmer: That's right, Mrs. Linde.
Mrs. Linde: Good night, Mr. Helmer.
Helmer (*seeing her to the door*): Good night, good night. I hope you get home safely. I'd be very happy to—but you only have a short way to go. Good night, good night.

(*She goes out. He closes the door behind her, and comes in again.*)

Ah, rid of her at last! What a bore that woman is.
Nora: Aren't you tired, Torvald?
Helmer: No, not at all.
Nora: You're not sleepy?
Helmer: Not a bit. As a matter of fact, I feel very lively. And what about you? You really look tired *and* sleepy.
Nora: Yes, I am very tired. I want to go to sleep right away.

Helmer: So, you see how right I was not to let you stay there any longer.

Nora: You're always right, Torvald.

Helmer (*kissing her on the forehead*): Now my little skylark is talking sense. Did you notice what a good mood Rank was in this evening?

Nora: Really? Was he? I didn't talk to him at all.

Helmer: And I only talked to him for a little while, but it's a long time since I've seen him so cheerful. (*Looks at her for a while and then moves closer to her.*) It's delightful to be home again by ourselves, to be alone with you, you fascinating, charming little darling!

Nora: Don't look at me like that, Torvald.

Helmer: Why shouldn't I look at my dearest treasure? At all the beauty that is mine, all my very own?

Nora (*going to the other side of the table*): I wish you wouldn't talk that way to me tonight.

Helmer (*following her*): You've still got the tarantella in your blood, I see. And it makes you more captivating than ever. Listen, the guests are starting to leave now. (*In a lower voice.*) Nora, soon the whole house will be quiet.

Nora: Yes, I hope so.

Helmer: Yes, my own darling Nora. Do you know why, when we're out at a party like this, why I hardly talk to you, and keep away from you, and only steal a glance at you now and then? Do you know why I do that? It's because I'm pretending to myself that we're secretly in love, and we're secretly engaged, and no one suspects that there's anything between us.

Nora: Yes, yes, I know you're thinking about me every moment.

Helmer: And when we're leaving, and I'm putting the shawl over your beautiful young shoulders, on your lovely neck, then I imagine that you're my young bride and that we've just come from our wedding and I'm bringing you home for the first time, to be alone with you for the first time, all alone with my shy little darling! This whole night I've been longing for you alone. My blood was on fire watching you move when you danced the tarantella. I couldn't stand it any longer, and that's why I brought you home so early—

Nora: Stop it, Torvald! Let me go. I won't—

Helmer: What? You're not serious, Nora! You won't? You won't? I'm your husband—

(*There is a knock at the outer door.*)

Nora (*starting*): Did you hear—

Helmer (*going into the hall*): Who is it?

Rank (*outside*): It's me. May I come in for a moment?

Helmer (*in an irritated whisper*): What does he want now? (*Aloud.*) Wait a minute! (*Unlocks the door.*) Come in. It's good of you not to pass by our door without saying hello.

Rank: I thought I heard your voice, and I felt like dropping by. (*With a quick look around.*) Ah, yes, these dear familiar rooms. You two are very happy and cozy in here.

Helmer: You seemed to be making yourself pretty happy upstairs too.

Rank: Very much so. Why shouldn't I? Why shouldn't we enjoy everything in this world? At least as much as we can, for as long as we can. The wine was first-rate—

Helmer: Especially the champagne.

Rank: So you noticed that too? It's almost unbelievable how much of it I managed to put away!

Nora: Torvald drank a lot of champagne tonight too.

Rank: Did he?

Nora: Yes, and it always makes him so merry.

Rank: Well, why shouldn't a person have a merry evening after a well-spent day?

Helmer: Well-spent? I'm afraid I can't take credit for that.

Rank (clapping him on the back): But I can, you know!

Nora: Doctor Rank, you must have been busy with some scientific investigation today.

Rank: Exactly.

Helmer: Listen to this! Little Nora talking about scientific investigations!

Nora: And may I congratulate you on the result?

Rank: Indeed you may.

Nora: Was it favorable, then?

Rank: The best possible result, for both doctor and patient—certainty.

Nora (quickly and searchingly): Certainty?

Rank: Absolute certainty. So wasn't I entitled to make a merry evening of it after that?

Nora: Yes, you certainly were, Doctor Rank.

Helmer: I think so too, as long as you don't have to pay for it in the morning.

Rank: Oh well, you can't have anything in this life without paying for it.

Nora: Doctor Rank, are you fond of fancy-dress balls?

Rank: Yes, if there are a lot of pretty costumes.

Nora: Tell me, what should the two of us wear to the next one?

Helmer: Little featherbrain! You're thinking of the next one already?

Rank: The two of us? Yes, I can tell you. You'll go as a good-luck charm—

Helmer: Yes, but what would be the costume for that?

Rank: She just needs to dress the way she always does.

Helmer: That was very nicely put. But aren't you going to tell us what you'll be?

Rank: Yes, my dear friend, I've already made up my mind about that.

Helmer: Well?

Rank: At the next fancy-dress ball I'm going to be invisible.

Helmer: That's a good one!

Rank: There's a big black cap . . . Haven't you ever heard of the cap that makes you invisible? Once you put it on, no one can see you anymore.

Helmer (suppressing a smile): Yes, that's right.

Rank: But I'm clean forgetting what I came for. Helmer, give me a cigar. One of the dark Havanas.

Helmer: With the greatest pleasure. (*Offers him his case.*)

Rank (takes a cigar and cuts off the end): Thanks.

Nora (striking a match): Let me give you a light.

Rank: Thank you. (*She holds the match for him to light his cigar.*) And now goodbye!

Helmer: Goodbye, goodbye, my dear old friend.

Nora: Sleep well, Doctor Rank.

Rank: Thank you for that wish.

Nora: Wish me the same.

Rank: You? Well, if you want me to. Sleep well! And thanks for the light. (*He nods to them both and goes out.*)

Helmer (*in a subdued voice*): He's had too much to drink.

Nora (*absently*): Maybe.

(*Helmer takes a bunch of keys out of his pocket and goes into the hall.*)

Torvald! What are you going to do out there?

Helmer: Empty the mailbox. It's quite full. There won't be any room for the newspaper in the morning.

Nora: Are you going to work tonight?

Helmer: You know I'm not. What's this? Someone's been at the lock.

Nora: At the lock?

Helmer: Yes, it's been tampered with. What does this mean? I never would have thought the maid—Look, here's a broken hairpin. It's one of yours, Nora.

Nora (*quickly*): Then it must have been the children—

Helmer: Then you'd better break them of those habits. There, I've finally got it open.

(*Empties the mailbox and calls out to the kitchen.*)

Helene! Helene, put out the light over the front door.

(*Comes back into the room and shuts the door into the hall. He holds out his hand full of letters.*)

Look at that. Look what a pile of them there are. (*Turning them over.*) What's this?

Nora (*at the window*): The letter! No! Torvald, no!

Helmer: Two calling cards of Rank's.

Nora: Of Doctor Rank's?

Helmer (*looking at them*): Yes, Doctor Rank. They were on top. He must have put them in there when he left just now.

Nora: Is there anything written on them?

Helmer: There's a black cross over the name. Look. What a morbid thing to do! It looks as if he's announcing his own death.

Nora: That's exactly what he's doing.

Helmer: What? Do you know anything about it? Has he said anything to you?

Nora: Yes. He told me that when the cards came it would be his farewell to us. He means to close himself off and die.

Helmer: My poor old friend! Of course I knew we wouldn't have him for very long. But this soon! And he goes and hides himself away like a wounded animal.

Nora: If it has to happen, it's better that it be done without a word. Don't you think so, Torvald?

Helmer (*walking up and down*): He's become so much a part of our lives, I can't imagine him not being with us anymore. With his poor health and his loneliness, he was like a cloudy background to our sunlit happiness. Well, maybe it's all for the best. For him, anyway. (*Standing still.*) And maybe for us too, Nora. Now we have only each other to rely on. (*Puts his arms around her.*) My darling wife, I feel as though I can't possibly hold you tight enough. You know, Nora, I've often wished you were in some kind of serious danger, so that I could risk everything, even my own life, to save you.

Nora (*disengages herself from him, and says firmly and decidedly*): Now you must go and read your letters, Torvald.

Helmer: No, no, not tonight. I want to be with you, my darling wife.

Nora: With the thought of your friend's death—

Helmer: You're right, it has affected us both. Something ugly has come between us, the thought of the horrors of death. We have to try to put it out of our minds. Until we do, we'll each go to our own room.

Nora (*with her arms around his neck*): Good night, Torvald. Good night!

Helmer (*kissing her on the forehead*): Good night, my little songbird. Sleep well, Nora. Now I'll go read all my mail. (*He takes his letters and goes into his room, shutting the door behind him.*)

Nora (*gropes distractedly about, picks up Helmer's domino and wraps it around her, while she says in quick, hoarse, spasmodic whispers*): Never to see him again. Never! Never! (*Puts her shawl over her head.*) Never to see my children again either, never again. Never! Never! Oh, the icy, black water, the bottomless depths! If only it were over! He's got it now, now he's reading it. Goodbye, Torvald . . . children!

(*She is about to rush out through the hall when Helmer opens his door hurriedly and stands with an open letter in his hand.*)

Helmer: Nora!

Nora: Ah!

Helmer: What is this? Do you know what's in this letter?

Nora: Yes, I know. Let me go! Let me get out!

Helmer (*holding her back*): Where are you going?

Nora (*trying to get free*): You're not going to save me, Torvald!

Helmer (*reeling*): It's true? Is this true, what it says here? This is horrible! No, no, it can't possibly be true.

Nora: It is true. I've loved you more than anything else in the world.

Helmer: Don't start with your ridiculous excuses.

Nora (*taking a step towards him*): Torvald!

Helmer: You little fool, do you know what you've done?

Nora: Let me go. I won't let you suffer for my sake. You're not going to take it on yourself.

Helmer: Stop play-acting. (*Locks the hall door.*) You're going to stay right here and give me an explanation. Do you understand what you've done? Answer me! Do you understand what you've done?

Nora (*looks steadily at him and says with a growing look of coldness in her face*): Yes, I'm beginning to understand everything now.

Helmer (*walking around the room*): What a horrible awakening! The woman who was my pride and joy for eight years, a hypocrite, a liar, worse than that, much worse— a criminal! The unspeakable ugliness of it all! The shame of it! The shame!

(*Nora is silent and looks steadily at him. He stops in front of her.*)

I should have realized that something like this was bound to happen. I should have seen it coming. Your father's shifty nature—be quiet!—your father's shifty nature has come out in you. No religion, no morality, no sense of duty. This is my punishment for closing my eyes to what he did! I did it for your sake, and this is how you pay me back.

Nora: Yes, that's right.

Helmer: Now you've destroyed all my happiness. You've ruined my whole future. It's horrible to think about! I'm in the power of an unscrupulous man. He can do what he wants with me, ask me for anything he wants, give me any orders he wants, and I don't dare say no. And I have to sink to such miserable depths, all because of a feather-brained woman!

Nora: When I'm out of the way, you'll be free.

Helmer: Spare me the speeches. Your father had always plenty of those on hand, too. What good would it do me if you were out of the way, as you say? Not the slightest. He can tell everybody the whole story. And if he does, I could be wrongly suspected of having been in on it with you. People will probably think I was behind it all, that I put you up to it! And I have you to thank for all this, after I've cherished you the whole time we've been married. Do you understand what you've done to me?

Nora (coldly and quietly): Yes.

Helmer: It's so incredible that I can't take it all in. But we have to come to some understanding. Take off that shawl. Take it off, I said. I have to try to appease him some way or another. It has to be hushed up, no matter what it costs. And as for you and me, we have to make it look as if everything is just as it always was, but only for the sake of appearances, obviously. You'll stay here in my house, of course. But I won't let you bring up the children. I can't trust them to you. To think that I have to say these things to someone I've loved so dearly, and that I still—No, that's all over. From this moment on happiness is out of the question. All that matters now is to save the bits and pieces, to keep up the appearance—

(The front doorbell rings.)

Helmer (with a start): What's that? At this hour! Can the worst—Can he—Go and hide yourself, Nora. Say you don't feel well. *(Nora stands motionless. Helmer goes and unlocks the hall door.)*

Maid (half-dressed, comes to the door): A letter for Mrs. Helmer.

Helmer: Give it to me. *(Takes the letter, and shuts the door.)* Yes, it's from him. I'm not giving it to you. I'll read it myself.

Nora: Go ahead, read it.

Helmer (standing by the lamp): I barely have the courage to. It could mean ruin for both of us. No, I have to know. *(Tears open the letter, runs his eye over a few lines, looks at a piece of paper enclosed with it, and gives a shout of joy.)* Nora! *(She looks at him questioningly.)* Nora! No, I'd better read it again. Yes, it's true! I'm saved! Nora, I'm saved!

Nora: And what about me?

Helmer: You too, of course. We're both saved, you and I. Look, he's returned your note. He says he's sorry and he apologizes—that a happy change in his life—what difference does it make what he says! We're saved, Nora! Nobody can hurt you. Oh, Nora, Nora! No, first I have to destroy these horrible things. Let me see. . . . *(Glances at the note.)* No, no, I don't want to look at it. This whole business will be nothing but a bad dream to me.

(*Tears up the note and both letters, throws them all into the stove, and watches them burn.*)

There, now it doesn't exist anymore. He says that you've known since Christmas Eve. These must have been a horrible three days for you, Nora.

Nora: I fought a hard fight these three days.

Helmer: And suffered agonies, and saw no way out but—No, we won't dwell on any of those horrors. We'll just shout for joy and keep saying, "It's all over! It's all over!" Listen to me, Nora. You don't seem to realize that it's all over. What's this? Such a cold, hard face! My poor little Nora, I understand. You find it hard to believe that I've really forgiven you. But I swear that it's true, Nora. I forgive you for everything. I know that you did it all out of love for me.

Nora: That's true.

Helmer: You've loved me the way a wife ought to love her husband. You just didn't have the awareness to see what was wrong with the means you used. But do you think I love you any less because you don't understand how to deal with these things? No, of course not. I want you to lean on me. I'll advise you and guide you. I wouldn't be a man if this womanly helplessness didn't make you twice as attractive to me. Don't think anymore about the hard things I said when I was so upset at first, when I thought everything was going to crush me. I forgive you, Nora. I swear to you that I forgive you.

Nora: Thank you for your forgiveness. (*She goes out through the door to the right.*)

Helmer: No, don't go—(*Looks in.*) What are you doing in there?

Nora (from within): Taking off my costume.

Helmer (standing at the open door): Yes, do. Try to calm yourself, and ease your mind again, my frightened little songbird. I want you to rest and feel secure. I have wide wings for you to take shelter underneath. (*Walks up and down by the door.*) What a warm and cozy home we have, Nora: Here's a safe haven for you, and I'll protect you like a hunted dove that I've rescued from a hawk's claws. I'll calm your poor pounding heart. It will happen, little by little, Nora, believe me. In the morning you'll see it in a very different light. Soon everything will be exactly the way it was before. Before you know it, you won't need my reassurances that I've forgiven you. You'll know for certain that I have. You can't imagine that I'd ever consider rejecting you, or even blaming you? You have no idea what a man feels in his heart, Nora. A man finds it indescribably sweet and satisfying to know that he's forgiven his wife, freely and with all his heart. It's as if he's made her his own all over again. He's given her a new life, in a way, and she's become both wife and child to him. And from this moment on that's what you'll be to me, my little scared, helpless darling. Don't worry about anything, Nora. Just be honest and open with me, and I'll be your will and your conscience. What's this? You haven't gone to bed yet? Have you changed?

Nora (in everyday dress): Yes, Torvald, I've changed.

Helmer: But why—It's so late.

Nora: I'm not going to sleep tonight.

Helmer: But, my dear Nora—

Nora (looking at her watch): It's not that late. Sit down here, Torvald. You and I have a lot to talk about. (*She sits down at one side of the table.*)

Helmer: Nora, what is this? Why this cold, hard face?

Nora: Sit down. This is going to take a while. I have a lot to say to you.

Helmer (*sits down at the opposite side of the table*): You're making me nervous, Nora. And I don't understand you.

Nora: No, that's it exactly. You don't understand me, and I've never understood you either, until tonight. No, don't interrupt me. I want you to listen to what I have to say. Torvald, I'm settling accounts with you.

Helmer: What do you mean by that?

Nora (*after a short silence*): Doesn't anything strike you as odd about the way we're sitting here like this?

Helmer: No, what?

Nora: We've been married for eight years. Doesn't it occur to you that this is the first time the two of us, you and I, husband and wife, have had a serious conversation?

Helmer: What do you mean by serious?

Nora: In the whole eight years—longer than that, for the whole time we've known each other—we've never exchanged one word on any serious subject.

Helmer: Did you expect me to be constantly worrying you with problems that you weren't capable of helping me deal with?

Nora: I'm not talking about business. I mean we've never sat down together seriously to try to get to the bottom of anything.

Helmer: But, dearest Nora, what good would that have done you?

Nora: That's just it. You've never understood me. I've been treated badly, Torvald, first by Papa and then by you.

Helmer: What? The two people who've loved you more than anyone else?

Nora (*shaking her head*): You've never loved me. You just thought it was pleasant to be in love with me.

Helmer: Nora, what are you saying?

Nora: It's true, Torvald. When I lived at home with Papa, he gave me his opinion about everything, and so I had all the same opinions, and if I didn't, I kept my mouth shut, because he wouldn't have liked it. He used to call me his doll-child, and he played with me the way I played with my dolls. And when I came to live in your house—

Helmer: What kind of way is that to talk about our marriage?

Nora (*undisturbed*): I mean that I was just passed from Papa's hands to yours. You arranged everything according to your own taste, and so I had all the same tastes as you. Or else I pretended to, I'm not really sure which. Sometimes I think it's one way and sometimes the other. When I look back, it's as if I've been living here like a beggar, from hand to mouth. I've supported myself by performing tricks for you, Torvald. But that's the way you wanted it. You and Papa have committed a terrible sin against me. It's your fault that I've done nothing with my life.

Helmer: This is so unfair and ungrateful of you, Nora! Haven't you been happy here?

Nora: No, I've never really been happy. I thought I was, but it wasn't true.

Helmer: Not—not happy!

Nora: No, just cheerful. You've always been very kind to me. But our home's been nothing but a playroom. I've been your doll-wife, the same way that I was Papa's doll-child. And the children have been my dolls. I thought it was great fun when you played with me, the way they thought it was when I played with them. That's what our marriage has been, Torvald.

Helmer: There's some truth in what you're saying, even though your view of it is exaggerated and overwrought. But things will be different from now on. Playtime is over, and now it's lesson-time.

Nora: Whose lessons? Mine, or the children's?

Helmer: Both yours and the children's, my darling Nora.

Nora: I'm sorry, Torvald, but you're not the man to give me lessons on how to be a proper wife to you.

Helmer: How can you say that?

Nora: And as for me, who am I to be allowed to bring up the children?

Helmer: Nora!

Nora: Didn't you say so yourself a little while ago, that you don't dare trust them to me?

Helmer: That was in a moment of anger! Why can't you let it go?

Nora: Because you were absolutely right. I'm not fit for the job. There's another job I have to take on first. I have to try to educate myself. You're not the man to help me with that. I have to do that for myself. And that's why I'm going to leave you now.

Helmer (jumping up): What are you saying?

Nora: I have to stand completely on my own, if I'm going to understand myself and everything around me. That's why I can't stay here with you any longer.

Helmer: Nora, Nora!

Nora: I'm leaving right now. I'm sure Kristine will put me up for the night—

Helmer: You're out of your mind! I won't let you go! I forbid it!

Nora: It's no use forbidding me anything anymore. I'm taking only what belongs to me. I won't take anything from you, now or later.

Helmer: This is insanity!

Nora: Tomorrow I'm going home. Back to where I came from, I mean. It'll be easier for me to find something to do there.

Helmer: You're a blind, senseless woman!

Nora: Then I'd better try to get some sense, Torvald.

Helmer: But to desert your home, your husband, and your children! And aren't you concerned about what people will say?

Nora: I can't concern myself with that. I only know that this is what I have to do.

Helmer: This is outrageous! You're just going to walk away from your most sacred duties?

Nora: What do you consider to be my most sacred duties?

Helmer: Do you need me to tell you that? Aren't they your duties to your husband and your children?

Nora: I have other duties just as sacred.

Helmer: No, you do not. What could they be?

Nora: Duties to myself.

Helmer: First and foremost, you're a wife and a mother.

Nora: I don't believe that anymore. I believe that first and foremost I'm a human being, just as you are—or, at least, that I have to try to become one. I know very well, Torvald, that most people would agree with you, and that opinions like yours are in books, but I can't be satisfied anymore with what most people say, or with what's in books. I have to think things through for myself and come to understand them.

Helmer: Why can't you understand your place in your own home? Don't you have an infallible guide in matters like that? What about your religion?

Nora: Torvald, I'm afraid I'm not sure what religion is.

Helmer: What are you saying?

Nora: All I know is what Pastor Hansen said when I was confirmed. He told us that religion was this, that, and the other thing. When I'm away from all this and on my own, I'll look into that subject too. I'll see if what he said is true or not, or at least whether it's true for me.

Helmer: This is unheard of, coming from a young woman like you! But if religion doesn't guide you, let me appeal to your conscience. I assume you have some moral sense. Or do you have none? Answer me.

Nora: Torvald, that's not an easy question to answer. I really don't know. It's very confusing to me. I only know that you and I look at it in very different ways. I'm learning too that the law isn't at all what I thought it was, and I can't convince myself that the law is right. A woman has no right to spare her old dying father or to save her husband's life? I can't believe that.

Helmer: You talk like a child. You don't understand anything about the world you live in.

Nora: No, I don't. But I'm going to try. I'm going to see if I can figure out who's right, me or the world.

Helmer: You're sick, Nora. You're delirious. I'm half convinced that you're out of your mind.

Nora: I've never felt so clearheaded and sure of myself as I do tonight.

Helmer: Clearheaded and sure of yourself—and that's the spirit in which you forsake your husband and your children?

Nora: Yes, it is.

Helmer: Then there's only one possible explanation.

Nora: Which is?

Helmer: You don't love me anymore.

Nora: Exactly.

Helmer: Nora! How can you say that?

Nora: It's very painful for me to say it, Torvald, because you've always been so good to me, but I can't help it. I don't love you anymore.

Helmer (regaining his composure): Are you clearheaded and sure of yourself when you say that too?

Nora: Yes, totally clearheaded and sure of myself. That's why I can't stay here.

Helmer: Can you tell me what I did to make you stop loving me?

Nora: Yes, I can. It was tonight, when the miracle didn't happen. That's when I realized you're not the man I thought you were.

Helmer: Can you explain that more clearly? I don't understand you.

Nora: I've been waiting so patiently for the last eight years. Of course I knew that miracles don't happen every day. Then when I found myself in this horrible situation, I was sure that the miracle was about to happen at last. When Krogstad's letter was lying out there, never for a moment did I imagine that you would agree to his conditions. I was absolutely certain that you'd say to him: Go ahead, tell the whole world. And when he had—

Helmer: Yes, what then? After I'd exposed my wife to shame and disgrace?

Nora: When he had, I was absolutely certain you'd come forward and take the whole thing on yourself, and say: I'm the guilty one.

Helmer: Nora—!

Nora: You mean that I would never have let you make such a sacrifice for me? Of course I wouldn't. But who would have believed my word against yours? That was the miracle that I hoped for and dreaded. And it was to keep it from happening that made me want to kill myself.

Helmer: I'd gladly work night and day for you, Nora, and endure sorrow and poverty for your sake. But no man would sacrifice his honor for the one he loves.

Nora: Hundreds of thousands of women have done it.

Helmer: Oh, you think and talk like a thoughtless child.

Nora: Maybe so. But you don't think or talk like the man I want to be with for the rest of my life. As soon as your fear had passed—and it wasn't fear for what threatened me, but for what might happen to you—when the whole thing was past, as far as you were concerned it was just as if nothing at all had happened. I was still your little skylark, your doll, but now you'd handle me twice as gently and carefully as before, because I was so delicate and fragile. (*Getting up.*) Torvald, that's when it dawned on me that for eight years I'd been living here with a stranger and had borne him three children. Oh, I can't bear to think about it! I could tear myself into little pieces!

Helmer (*sadly*): I see, I see. An abyss has opened up between us. There's no denying it. But, Nora, can't we find some way to close it?

Nora: The way I am now, I'm no wife for you.

Helmer: I can find it in myself to become a different man.

Nora: Maybe so—if your doll is taken away from you.

Helmer: But to be apart!—to be apart from you! No, no, Nora, I can't conceive of it.

Nora (*going out to the right*): All the more reason why it has to be done.

(*She comes back with her coat and hat and a small suitcase which she puts on a chair by the table.*)

Helmer: Nora, Nora, not now! Wait till tomorrow.

Nora (*putting on her cloak*): I can't spend the night in a strange man's room.

Helmer: But couldn't we live here together like brother and sister?

Nora (*putting on her hat*): You know how long that would last. (*Puts the shawl around her.*) Goodbye, Torvald. I won't look in on the children. I know they're in better hands than mine. The way I am now, I'm no use to them.

Helmer: But someday, Nora, someday?

Nora: How can I tell? I have no idea what's going to become of me.

Helmer: But you're my wife, whatever becomes of you.

Nora: Listen, Torvald. I've heard that when a wife deserts her husband's house, the way I'm doing now, he's free of all legal obligations to her. In any event, I set you free from all your obligations. I don't want you to feel bound in the slightest, any more than I will. There has to be complete freedom on both sides. Look, here's your ring back. Give me mine.

Helmer: That too?

Nora: That too.

Helmer: Here it is.

Nora: Good. Now it's all over. I've left the keys here. The maids know all about how to run the house, much better than I do. Kristine will come by tomorrow after I leave her place and pack up my own things, the ones I brought with me from home. I'd like to have them sent to me.

Helmer: All over! All over! Nora, will you ever think about me again?

Nora: I know I'll often think about you, and the children, and this house.

Helmer: May I write to you, Nora?

Nora: No, never. You mustn't do that.

Helmer: But at least let me send you—

Nora: Nothing, nothing.

Helmer: Let me help you if you're in need.

Nora: No. I can't accept anything from a stranger.

Helmer: Nora . . . can't I ever be anything more than a stranger to you?

Nora (picking up her bag): Ah, Torvald, for that, the most wonderful miracle of all would have to happen.

Helmer: Tell me what that would be!

Nora: We'd both have to change so much that—Oh, Torvald, I've stopped believing in miracles.

Helmer: But I'll believe. Tell me! Change so much that . . . ?

Nora: That our life together would be a true marriage. Goodbye.

(*She goes out through the hall.*)

Helmer (sinks down into a chair at the door and buries his face in his hands): Nora! Nora! (*Looks around, and stands up.*) Empty. She's gone. (*A hope flashes across his mind.*) The most wonderful miracle of all . . . ?

(*The heavy sound of a closing door is heard from below.*)

Questions

ACT I

1. From the opening conversation between Helmer and Nora, what are your impressions of him? Of her? Of their marriage?
2. At what moment in the play do you understand why it is called *A Doll's House*?
3. In what ways does Mrs. Linde provide a contrast for Nora?
4. What in Krogstad's first appearance on stage, and in Dr. Rank's remarks about him, indicates that the bank clerk is a menace?
5. Of what illegal deed is Nora guilty? How does she justify it?
6. When the curtain falls on Act I, what problems now confront Nora?

ACT II

1. As Act II opens, what are your feelings on seeing the stripped, ragged Christmas tree? How is it suggestive?
2. What events that soon occur make Nora's situation even more difficult?
3. How does she try to save herself?
4. Why does Nora fling herself into the wild tarantella?

ACT III

1. For what possible reasons does Mrs. Linde pledge herself to Krogstad?
2. How does Dr. Rank's announcement of his impending death affect Nora and Helmer?

3. What is Helmer's reaction to learning the truth about Nora's misdeed? Why does he blame Nora's father? What is revealing (of Helmer's own character) in his remark, "From this moment on happiness is out of the question. All that matters now is to save the bits and pieces, to keep up the appearance—"?

4. When Helmer finds that Krogstad has sent back the note, what is his response? How do you feel toward him?

5. How does the character of Nora develop in this act?

6. How do you interpret her final slamming of the door?

General Questions

1. In what ways do you find Nora a victim? In what ways is she at fault?

2. Try to state the theme of the play. Does it involve women's rights? Self-fulfillment?

3. What dramatic question does the play embody? At what moment can this question first be stated?

4. What is the crisis? In what way is this moment or event a "turning point"? (In what new direction does the action turn?)

5. Eric Bentley, in an essay titled "Ibsen, Pro and Con" (*In Search of Theater* [New York: Knopf, 1953]), criticizes the character of Krogstad, calling him "a mere pawn of the plot." He then adds, "When convenient to Ibsen, he is a blackmailer. When inconvenient, he is converted." Do you agree or disagree?

6. Why is the play considered a work of realism? Is there anything in it that does not seem realistic?

7. In what respects does *A Doll's House* seem to apply to life today? Is it in any way dated? Could there be a Nora in North America today?

Henrik Ibsen on Writing

Correspondence on the Final Scene of *A Doll's House*   1880, 1891

Translated by John Nilsen Laurvik and Mary Morison

Munich, 17 February 1880

To the Editor of the *Nationaltidende*

Sir,
    In No. 1360 of your esteemed paper I have read a letter from Flensburg, in which it is stated that *A Doll's House* (in German *Nora*) has been acted there, and that the conclusion of the play has been changed—the alteration having been made, it is asserted, by my orders. This last statement is untrue. Immediately after the publication of *Nora*, I received from my translator, Mr. Wilhelm Lange of Berlin, the information that he had reason to fear that an "adaptation" of the play, giving it a different ending, was about to be published, and that this would probably be chosen in preference to the original by several of the North German theaters.

Henrik Ibsen

In order to prevent such a possibility, I sent to him, for use in case of absolute necessity, a draft of an altered last scene, according to which Nora does not leave the house, but is forcibly led by Helmer to the door of the children's bedroom; a short dialogue takes place, Nora sinks down at the door, and the curtain falls.

This change, I myself, in the letter to my translator, stigmatize as "barbaric violence" done to the play. Those who make use of the altered scene do so entirely against my wish. But I trust that it will not be used at very many German theaters. . . . When my works are threatened, I prefer, taught by experience, to commit the act of violence myself, instead of leaving them to be treated and "adapted" by less careful and less skilful hands.

Yours respectfully,

Henrik Ibsen

Dear Count Proznor,   1891

Mr. Luigi Capuana° has, I regret to see, given you a great deal of trouble by his proposal to alter the last scene of A Doll's House for performance in the Italian theaters. . . . [T]he fact is that I cannot possibly directly authorize any change whatever in the ending of the drama. I may almost say that it was for the sake of the last scene that the whole play was written.

And, besides, I believe that Mr. Capuana is mistaken in fearing that the Italian public would not be able to understand or approve of my work if it were put on the stage in its original form. The experiment, ought, at any rate, to be tried. If it turns out a failure, then let Mr. Capuana, on his own responsibility, employ your adaptation of the closing scene; for I cannot formally authorize, or approve of, such a proceeding.

I wrote to Mr. Capuana yesterday, briefly expressing my views on the subject; and I hope that he will disregard his misgivings until he has proved by experience that they are well founded.

At the time when A Doll's House was quite new, I was obliged to give my consent to an alteration of the last scene for Frau Hedwig Niemann-Raabe, who was to play the part of Nora in Berlin. At that time I had no choice. I was entirely unprotected by copyright law in Germany, and could, consequently prevent nothing. . . . With its altered ending it had only a short run. In its unchanged form it is still being played. . . .

Your sincere and obliged,

Henrik Ibsen

Luigi Capuana: Italian novelist and dramatic critic who translated A Doll's House into Italian. It was the famous actress Eleonora Duse who wished him to alter the last scene of the play, but she finally relented and acted it in the original form.

Tennessee Williams

The Glass Menagerie   1945

Tennessee Williams (1911–1983) was born Thomas Lanier Williams in Columbus, Mississippi, went to high school in St. Louis, and graduated from the University of Iowa. As an undergraduate, he saw a performance of Ibsen's Ghosts *and decided to become a playwright himself. His family bore a close resemblance to the Wingfields in* The Glass Menagerie: *his mother came from a line of Southern blue bloods (Tennessee pioneers); his sister Rose suffered from incapacitating shyness; and as a young man, Williams himself, like Tom, worked at a job he disliked (in a shoe factory where his father worked), wrote poetry, sought refuge in moviegoing, and finally left home to wander and hold odd jobs. He worked as a bellhop in a New Orleans hotel; a teletype operator in Jacksonville, Florida; an usher and a waiter in New York. In 1945* The Glass Menagerie *scored a success on Broadway, winning a Drama Critics Circle award. Two years later Williams received a Pulitzer Prize for* A Streetcar Named Desire, *a grim, powerful study of a woman's illusions and frustrations, set in New Orleans. In 1955 Williams was awarded another Pulitzer Prize for* Cat on a Hot Tin Roof. *Besides other plays, including* Summer and Smoke *(1948),* Sweet Bird of Youth *(1959),* The Night of the Iguana *(1961),* Small Craft Warnings *(1973),* Clothes for a Summer Hotel *(1980), and* A House Not Meant to Stand *(1981), Williams wrote two novels, poetry, essays, short stories, and* Memoirs *(1975).*

> Nobody, not even the rain, has such small hands.
>
> —E. E. CUMMINGS

CHARACTERS

Amanda Wingfield, the mother. A little woman of great but confused vitality clinging frantically to another time and place. Her characterization must be carefully created, not copied from type. She is not paranoiac, but her life is paranoia. There is much to admire in Amanda, and as much to love and pity as there is to laugh at. Certainly she has endurance and a kind of heroism, and though her foolishness makes her unwittingly cruel at times, there is tenderness in her slight person.

Laura Wingfield, her daughter. Amanda, having failed to establish contact with reality, continues to live vitally in her illusions, but Laura's situation is even graver. A childhood illness has left her crippled, one leg slightly shorter than the other, and held in a brace. This defect need not be more than suggested on the stage. Stemming from this, Laura's separation increases till she is like a piece of her own glass collection, too exquisitely fragile to move from the shelf.

Tom Wingfield, her son. And the narrator of the play. A poet with a job in a warehouse. His nature is not remorseless, but to escape from a trap he has to act without pity.

Jim O'Connor, the gentleman caller. A nice, ordinary, young man.

SCENE. *An alley in St. Louis.*
PART I. *Preparation for a Gentleman Caller.*
PART II. *The Gentleman Calls.*
TIME. *Now and the Past.*

SCENE I

The Wingfield apartment is in the rear of the building, one of those vast hive-like conglomerations of cellular living-units that flower as warty growths in overcrowded urban centers of lower middle-class population and are symptomatic of the impulse of this largest and fundamentally enslaved section of American society to avoid fluidity and differentiation and to exist and function as one interfused mass of automatism.

The apartment faces an alley and is entered by a fire-escape, a structure whose name is a touch of accidental poetic truth, for all of these huge buildings are always burning with the slow and implacable fires of human desperation. The fire-escape is included in the set—that is, the landing of it and steps descending from it.

The scene is memory and is therefore unrealistic. Memory takes a lot of poetic license. It omits some details; others are exaggerated, according to the emotional value of the articles it touches, for memory is seated predominantly in the heart. The interior is therefore rather dim and poetic.

At the rise of the curtain, the audience is faced with the dark, grim rear wall of the Wingfield tenement. This building, which runs parallel to the footlights, is flanked on both sides by dark, narrow alleys which run into murky canyons of tangled clotheslines, garbage cans, and the sinister latticework of neighboring fire-escapes. It is up and down these side alleys that exterior entrances and exits are made, during the play. At the end of Tom's opening commentary, the dark tenement wall slowly reveals (by means of a transparency) the interior of the ground floor Wingfield apartment.

Downstage is the living room, which also serves as a sleeping room for Laura, the sofa unfolding to make her bed. Upstage, center, and divided by a wide arch or second proscenium with transparent faded portieres (or second curtain), is the dining room. In an old-fashioned what-not in the living room are seen scores of transparent glass animals. A blown-up photograph of the father hangs on the wall of the living room, facing the audience, to the left of the archway. It is the face of a very handsome young man in a doughboy's First World War cap. He is gallantly smiling, ineluctably smiling, as if to say, "I will be smiling forever."

The audience hears and sees the opening scene in the dining room through both the transparent fourth wall of the building and the transparent gauze portieres of the dining room arch. It is during this revealing scene that the fourth wall slowly ascends, out of sight. This transparent exterior wall is not brought down again until the very end of the play, during Tom's final speech.

The narrator is an undisguised convention of the play. He takes whatever license with dramatic convention as is convenient to his purposes.

Tom enters dressed as a merchant sailor from the alley, stage left, and strolls across the front of the stage to the fire-escape. There he stops and lights a cigarette. He addresses the audience.

Tom: Yes, I have tricks in my pocket, I have things up my sleeve. But I am the opposite of a stage magician. He gives you illusion that has the appearance of truth. I give you truth in the pleasant disguise of illusion. To begin with, I turn back time. I reverse it to that quaint period, the thirties, when the huge middle class of America was matriculating in a school for the blind. Their eyes had failed them, or they had failed their eyes, and so they were having their fingers pressed forcibly down on the fiery Braille alphabet of a dissolving economy. In Spain there was revolution. Here there was only shouting and confusion. In Spain there was

Five years after *The Glass Menagerie's* Broadway debut, a movie version was filmed starring Kirk Douglas, Jane Wyman, Gertrude Lawrence, and Arthur Kennedy.

Guernica. Here there were disturbances of labor, sometimes pretty violent, in otherwise peaceful cities such as Chicago, Cleveland, St. Louis. . . . This is the social background of the play.

(Music.)

The play is memory. Being a memory play, it is dimly lighted, it is sentimental, it is not realistic. In memory everything seems to happen to music. That explains the fiddle in the wings. I am the narrator of the play, and also a character in it. The other characters are my mother, Amanda, my sister, Laura, and a gentleman caller who appears in the final scenes. He is the most realistic character in the play, being an emissary from a world of reality that we were somehow set apart from. But since I have a poet's weakness for symbols, I am using this character also as a symbol; he is the long delayed but always expected something that we live for. There is a fifth character in the play who doesn't appear except in this larger-than-life photograph over the mantel. This is our father who left us a long time ago. He was a telephone man who fell in love with long distances; he gave up his job with the telephone company and skipped the light fantastic out of town. . . . The last we heard of him was a picture post-card from Mazatlan, on the Pacific coast of Mexico, containing a message of two words—"Hello—Good-bye!" and an address. I think the rest of the play will explain itself. . . .

Amanda's voice becomes audible through the portieres.

Karen Allen and John Malkovich in a 1987 film of *The Glass Menagerie*, directed by Paul Newman.

(Screen Legend: "Où Sont Les Neiges.")°

He divides the portieres and enters the upstage area.

Amanda and Laura are seated at a drop-leaf table. Eating is indicated by gestures without food or utensils. Amanda faces the audience. Tom and Laura are seated in profile.

The interior has lit up softly and through the scrim we see Amanda and Laura seated at the table in the upstage area.

Amanda (calling): Tom?
Tom: Yes, Mother.
Amanda: We can't say grace until you come to the table!
Tom: Coming, Mother. (*He bows slightly and withdraws, reappearing a few moments later in his place at the table.*)
Amanda (to her son): Honey, don't *push* with your *fingers.* If you have to push with something, the thing to push with is a crust of bread. And chew—chew! Animals have sections in their stomachs which enable them to digest food without mastication, but human beings are supposed to chew their food before they swallow it

---

"*Où Sont Les Neiges*": A slide bearing this line is to be projected on a stage wall. The phrase is part of a famous line from French poet François Villon's *Ballad of the Dead Ladies.* The full line "*Où Sont Les Neiges D'antan?,*" meaning "But, where are the snows of yester-year?," is projected on the wall later in this scene.

down. Eat food leisurely, son, and really enjoy it. A well-cooked meal has lots of delicate flavors that have to be held in the mouth for appreciation. So chew your food and give your salivary glands a chance to function!

Tom deliberately lays his imaginary fork down and pushes his chair back from the table.

Tom: I haven't enjoyed one bite of this dinner because of your constant directions on how to eat it. It's you that makes me rush through meals with your hawk-like attention to every bite I take. Sickening—spoils my appetite—all this discussion of animals' secretion—salivary glands—mastication!
Amanda (*lightly*): Temperament like a Metropolitan star!

He rises and crosses downstage.

You're not excused from the table.

Tom: I am getting a cigarette.
Amanda: You smoke too much.

Laura rises.

Laura: I'll bring in the blanc mange.

He remains standing with his cigarette by the portieres during the following.

Amanda (*rising*): No, sister, no, sister—you be the lady this time and I'll be the darky.
Laura: I'm already up.
Amanda: Resume your seat, little sister—I want you to stay fresh and pretty—for gentlemen callers!
Laura (*sitting down*): I'm not expecting any gentlemen callers.
Amanda (*crossing out to kitchenette, airily*): Sometimes they come when they are least expected! Why, I remember one Sunday afternoon in Blue Mountain—(*Enters kitchenette.*)
Tom: I know what's coming!
Laura: Yes. But let her tell it.
Tom: Again?
Laura: She loves to tell it.

Amanda returns with bowl of dessert.

Amanda: One Sunday afternoon in Blue Mountain—your mother received— seventeen!—gentlemen callers! Why, sometimes there weren't chairs enough to accommodate them all. We had to send the nigger over to bring in folding chairs from the parish house.
Tom (*remaining at portieres*): How did you entertain those gentlemen callers?
Amanda: I understood the art of conversation!
Tom: I bet you could talk.
Amanda: Girls in those days *knew* how to talk, I can tell you.
Tom: Yes?

(Image: Amanda As A Girl On A Porch Greeting Callers.)

Amanda: They knew how to entertain their gentlemen callers. It wasn't enough for a girl to be possessed of a pretty face and a graceful figure—although I wasn't slighted in either respect. She also needed to have a nimble wit and a tongue to meet all occasions.

Tom: What did you talk about?

Amanda: Things of importance going on in the world! Never anything coarse or common or vulgar. (*She addresses Tom as though he were seated in the vacant chair at the table though he remains by portieres. He plays this scene as though reading from a script.*) My callers were gentlemen—all! Among my callers were some of the most prominent young planters of the Mississippi Delta—planters and sons of planters!

Tom motions for music and a spot of light on Amanda. Her eyes lift, her face glows, her voice becomes rich and elegiac.

(Screen Legend: "Où Sont Les Neiges D'antan?")

There was young Champ Laughlin who later became vice-president of the Delta Planters Bank. Hadley Stevenson who was drowned in Moon Lake and left his widow one hundred and fifty thousand in Government bonds. There were the Cutrere brothers, Wesley and Bates. Bates was one of my bright particular beaux! He got in a quarrel with that wild Wainright boy. They shot it out on the floor of Moon Lake Casino. Bates was shot through the stomach. Died in the ambulance on his way to Memphis. His widow was also well-provided for, came into eight or ten thousand acres, that's all. She married him on the rebound— never loved her—carried my picture on him the night he died! And there was that boy that every girl in the Delta had set her cap for! That beautiful, brilliant young Fitzhugh boy from Green County!

Tom: What did he leave his widow?

Amanda: He never married! Gracious, you talk as though all of my old admirers had turned up their toes to the daisies!

Tom: Isn't this the first you mentioned that still survives?

Amanda: That Fitzhugh boy went North and made a fortune—came to be known as the Wolf of Wall Street! He had the Midas touch, whatever he touched turned to gold! And I could have been Mrs. Duncan J. Fitzhugh, mind you! But—I picked your *father!*

Laura (rising): Mother, let me clear the table.

Amanda: No dear, you go in front and study your typewriter chart. Or practice your shorthand a little. Stay fresh and pretty!—It's almost time for our gentlemen callers to start arriving. (*She flounces girlishly toward the kitchenette.*) How many do you suppose we're going to entertain this afternoon?

Tom throws down the paper and jumps up with a groan.

Laura (alone in the dining room): I don't believe we're going to receive any, Mother.

Amanda (reappearing, airily): What? No one—not one? You must be joking! (*Laura nervously echoes her laugh. She slips in a fugitive manner through the half-open portieres and draws them gently behind her. A shaft of very clear light is thrown on her face against the jaded tapestry of the curtains.*) (**Music: "The Glass Menagerie"**

Under Faintly.) (*Lightly.*) Not one gentleman caller? It can't be true! There must be a flood, there must have been a tornado!

Laura: It isn't a flood, it's not a tornado, Mother. I'm just not popular like you were in Blue Mountain. . . . (*Tom utters another groan. Laura glances at him with a faint, apologetic smile. Her voice catching a little.*) Mother's afraid I'm going to be an old maid.

(The Scene Dims Out With "Glass Menagerie" Music.)

SCENE II

"Laura, Haven't You Ever Liked Some Boy?"

On the dark stage the screen is lighted with the image of blue roses.

Gradually Laura's figure becomes apparent and the screen goes out.

The music subsides.

Laura is seated in the delicate ivory chair at the small clawfoot table.

She wears a dress of soft violet material for a kimono—her hair tied back from her forehead with a ribbon.

She is washing and polishing her collection of glass.

Amanda appears on the fire-escape steps. At the sound of her ascent, Laura catches her breath, thrusts the bowl of ornaments away and seats herself stiffly before the diagram of the typewriter keyboard as though it held her spellbound. Something has happened to Amanda. It is written in her face as she climbs to the landing: a look that is grim and hopeless and a little absurd.

She has on one of those cheap or imitation velvety-looking cloth coats with imitation fur collar. Her hat is five or six years old, one of those dreadful cloche hats that were worn in the late twenties, and she is clasping an enormous black patent-leather pocketbook with nickel clasp and initials. This is her full-dress outfit, the one she usually wears to the D.A.R.

Before entering she looks through the door.

She purses her lips, opens her eyes wide, rolls them upward and shakes her head.

Then she slowly lets herself in the door. Seeing her mother's expression Laura touches her lips with a nervous gesture.

Laura: Hello, Mother, I was—(*She makes a nervous gesture toward the chart on the wall. Amanda leans against the shut door and stares at Laura with a martyred look.*)

Amanda: Deception? Deception? (*She slowly removes her hat and gloves, continuing the sweet suffering stare. She lets the hat and gloves fall on the floor—a bit of acting.*)

Laura (*shakily*): How was the D.A.R. meeting? (*Amanda slowly opens her purse and removes a dainty white handkerchief which she shakes out delicately and delicately touches to her lips and nostrils.*) Didn't you go to the D.A.R. meeting, Mother?

Amanda (*faintly, almost inaudibly*): —No.—No. (*Then more forcibly.*) I did not have the strength—to go to the D.A.R. In fact, I did not have the courage! I wanted to find a hole in the ground and hide myself in it forever! (*She crosses slowly to the wall and removes the diagram of the typewriter keyboard. She holds it in front of her for a second, staring at it sweetly and sorrowfully—then bites her lips and tears it in two pieces.*)

Laura (*faintly*): Why did you do that, Mother? (*Amanda repeats the same procedure with the chart of the Gregg Alphabet.*) Why are you—

Amanda: Why? Why? How old are you, Laura?

Laura: Mother, you know my age.

Amanda: I thought that you were an adult; it seems that I was mistaken. (*She crosses slowly to the sofa and sinks down and stares at Laura.*)

Laura: Please don't stare at me, Mother.

Amanda closes her eyes and lowers her head. Count ten.

Amanda: What are we going to do, what is going to become of us, what is the future?

   Count ten.

Laura: Has something happened, Mother? (*Amanda draws a long breath and takes out the handkerchief again. Dabbing process.*) Mother, has—something happened?

Amanda: I'll be all right in a minute. I'm just bewildered—(*count five*)—by life . . .

Laura: Mother, I wish that you would tell me what's happened.

Amanda: As you know, I was supposed to be inducted into my office at the D.A.R. this afternoon. (**Image: A Swarm of Typewriters.**) But I stopped off at Rubicam's Business College to speak to your teachers about your having a cold and ask them what progress they thought you were making down there.

Laura: Oh . . .

Amanda: I went to the typing instructor and introduced myself as your mother. She didn't know who you were. "Wingfield," she said, "We don't have any such student enrolled at the school!" I assured her she did, that you had been going to classes since early in January. "I wonder," she said, "if you could be talking about that terribly shy little girl who dropped out of school after only a few days' attendance?" "No," I said, "Laura, my daughter, has been going to school every day for the past six weeks!" "Excuse me," she said. She took the attendance book out and there was your name, unmistakably printed, and all the dates you were absent until they decided that you had dropped out of school. I still said, "No, there must have been some mistake! There must have been some mix-up in the records!" And she said, "No—I remember her perfectly now. Her hand shook so that she couldn't hit the right keys! The first time we gave a speed-test, she broke down completely—was sick at the stomach and almost had to be carried into the wash-room! After that morning she never showed up any more. We phoned the house but never got any answer"—While I was working at Famous-Barr, I suppose, demonstrating those—(*She indicates a brassiere with her hands.*) Oh! I felt so weak I could barely keep on my feet. I had to sit down while they got me a glass of water! Fifty dollars' tuition, all of our plans—my hopes and ambitions for you—just gone up the spout, just gone up the spout like that. (*Laura draws a long breath and gets awkwardly to her feet. She crosses to the victrola and winds it up.*) What are you doing?

Laura: Oh! (*She releases the handle and returns to her seat.*)

Amanda: Laura, where have you been going when you've gone out pretending that you were going to business college?

Laura: I've just been going out walking.

Amanda: That's not true.

Laura: It is. I just went walking.

Amanda: Walking? Walking? In winter? Deliberately courting pneumonia in that light coat? Where did you walk to, Laura?

Laura: All sorts of places—mostly in the park.

Amanda: Even after you'd started catching that cold?

Laura: It was the lesser of two evils, Mother. (**Image: Winter Scene In Park.**) I couldn't go back there. I—threw up—on the floor!

Amanda: From half past seven till after five every day you mean to tell me you walked around in the park, because you wanted to make me think that you were still going to Rubicam's Business College?

Laura: It wasn't as bad as it sounds. I went inside places to get warmed up.

Amanda: Inside where?

Laura: I went in the art museum and the bird-houses at the Zoo. I visited the penguins every day! Sometimes I did without lunch and went to the movies. Lately I've been spending most of my afternoons in the Jewel-box, that big glass house where they raise the tropical flowers.

Amanda: You did all this to deceive me, just for deception? (*Laura looks down.*) Why?

Laura: Mother, when you're disappointed, you get that awful suffering look on your face, like the picture of Jesus' mother in the museum!

Amanda: Hush!

Laura: I couldn't face it.

Pause. *A whisper of strings.*

(**Legend: "The Crust Of Humility."**)

Amanda (*hopelessly fingering the huge pocketbook*): So what are we going to do the rest of our lives? Stay home and watch the parades go by? Amuse ourselves with the glass menagerie, darling? Eternally play those worn-out phonograph records your father left as a painful reminder of him? We won't have a business career—we've given that up because it gave us nervous indigestion! (*Laughs wearily.*) What is there left but dependency all our lives? I know so well what becomes of unmarried women who aren't prepared to occupy a position. I've seen such pitiful cases in the South—barely tolerated spinsters living upon the grudging patronage of sister's husband or brother's wife!—stuck away in some little mouse-trap of a room—encouraged by one in-law to visit another—little birdlike women without any nest—eating the crust of humility all their life! Is that the future that we've mapped out for ourselves? I swear it's the only alternative I can think of! It isn't a very pleasant alternative, is it? Of course—some girls *do marry*. (*Laura twists her hands nervously.*) Haven't you ever liked some boy?

Laura: Yes. I liked one once. (*Rises.*) I came across his picture a while ago.

Amanda (*with some interest*): He gave you his picture?

Laura: No, it's in the year-book.

Amanda (disappointed): Oh—a high-school boy.

(Screen Image: Jim As A High-School Hero Bearing A Silver Cup.)

Laura: Yes. His name was Jim. (*Laura lifts the heavy annual from the clawfoot table.*) Here he is in *The Pirates of Penzance.*

Amanda (absently): The what?

Laura: The operetta the senior class put on. He had a wonderful voice and we sat across the aisle from each other Mondays, Wednesdays, and Fridays in the Aud. Here he is with the silver cup for debating! See his grin?

Amanda (absently): He must have had a jolly disposition.

Laura: He used to call me—Blue Roses.

(Image: Blue Roses.)

Amanda: Why did he call you such a name as that?

Laura: When I had that attack of pleurosis—he asked me what was the matter when I came back. I said pleurosis—he thought that I said Blue Roses! So that's what he always called me after that. Whenever he saw me, he'd holler, "Hello, Blue Roses!" I didn't care for the girl he went out with. Emily Meisenbach. Emily was the best-dressed girl at Soldan. She never struck me, though, as being sincere . . . It says in the Personal Section—they're engaged. That's—six years ago! They must be married by now.

Amanda: Girls that aren't cut out for business careers usually wind up married to some nice man. (*Gets up with a spark of revival.*) Sister, that's what you'll do!

Laura utters a startled, doubtful laugh. She reaches quickly for a piece of glass.

Laura: But, Mother—

Amanda: Yes? (*Crossing to photograph.*)

Laura (in a tone of frightened apology): I'm—crippled!

(Image: Screen.)

Amanda: Nonsense! Laura, I've told you never, never to use that word. Why, you're not crippled, you just have a little defect—hardly noticeable, even! When people have some slight disadvantage like that, they cultivate other things to make up for it—develop charm—and vivacity—and—*charm!* That's all you have to do! (*She turns again to the photograph.*) One thing your father had *plenty of*—was charm!

Tom motions to the fiddle in the wings.

(The Scene Fades Out With Music.)

SCENE III

(Legend On The Screen: "After The Fiasco—")

Tom speaks from the fire-escape landing.

Tom: After the fiasco at Rubicam's Business College, the idea of getting a gentleman caller for Laura began to play a more important part in Mother's calculations. It became an obsession. Like some archetype of the universal unconscious, the image of the gentleman caller haunted our small apartment. . . . (**Image: Young Man At Door With Flowers.**) An evening at home rarely passed without some allusion to this image, this specter, this hope. . . . Even when he wasn't mentioned, his presence hung in Mother's preoccupied look and in my sister's frightened, apologetic manner—hung like a sentence passed upon the Wingfields! Mother was a woman of action as well as words. She began to take logical steps in the planned direction. Late that winter and in the early spring—realizing that extra money would be needed to properly feather the nest and plume the bird— she conducted a vigorous campaign on the telephone, roping in subscribers to one of those magazines for matrons called *The Home-maker's Companion,* the type of journal that features the serialized sublimations of ladies of letters who think in terms of delicate cup-like breasts, slim, tapering waists, rich, creamy thighs, eyes like wood-smoke in autumn, fingers that soothe and caress like strains of music, bodies as powerful as Etruscan sculpture.

(Screen Image: Glamor Magazine Cover.)

Amanda enters with phone on long extension cord. She is spotted in the dim stage.

Amanda: Ida Scott? This is Amanda Wingfield! We *missed* you at the D.A.R. last Monday! I said to myself: She's probably suffering with that sinus condition! How is that sinus condition? Horrors! Heaven have mercy!—You're a Christian martyr, yes, that's what you are, a Christian martyr! Well, I just now happened to notice that your subscription to the *Companion's* about to expire! Yes, it expires with the next issue, honey!—just when that wonderful new serial by Bessie Mae Hopper is getting off to such an exciting start. Oh, honey, it's something that you can't miss! You remember how *Gone With the Wind* took everybody by storm? You simply couldn't go out if you hadn't read it. All everybody *talked* was Scarlett O'Hara. Well, this is a book that critics already compare to *Gone With the Wind.* It's the *Gone With the Wind* of the post-World War generation!— What?—Burning?—Oh, honey, don't let them burn, go take a look in the oven and I'll hold the wire! Heavens—I think she's hung up!

(Dim Out.)

(Legend On Screen: "You Think I'm In Love With Continental Shoemakers?")

Before the stage is lighted, the violent voices of Tom and Amanda are heard. They are quarreling behind the portieres. In front of them stands Laura with clenched hands and panicky expression.

A clear pool of light on her figure throughout this scene.

Tom: What in Christ's name am I—
Amanda (*shrilly*): Don't you use that—
Tom: —supposed to do!
Amanda: —expression! Not in my—
Tom: Ohhh!
Amanda: —presence! Have you gone out of your senses?
Tom: I have, that's true, *driven* out!
Amanda: What is the matter with you, you—big—big—IDIOT!

Tom: Look—I've got *no thing*, no single thing—

Amanda: Lower your voice!

Tom: —in my life here that I can call my OWN! Everything is—

Amanda: Stop that shouting!

Tom: Yesterday you confiscated my books! You had the nerve to—

Amanda: I took that horrible novel back to the library—yes! That hideous book by that insane Mr. Lawrence. (*Tom laughs wildly.*) I cannot control the output of diseased minds or people who cater to them—(*Tom laughs still more wildly.*) BUT I WON'T ALLOW SUCH FILTH BROUGHT INTO MY HOUSE! No, no, no, no, no!

Tom: House, house! Who pays rent on it, who makes a slave of himself to—

Amanda (*fairly screeching*): Don't you DARE to—

Tom: No, no, I mustn't say things! *I've* got to just—

Amanda: Let me tell you—

Tom: I don't want to hear any more! (*He tears the portieres open. The upstage area is lit with a turgid smoky red glow.*)

Amanda's hair is in metal curlers and she wears a very old bathrobe, much too large for her slight figure, a relic of the faithless Mr. Wingfield.

An upright typewriter and a wild disarray of manuscripts are on the drop-leaf table. The quarrel was probably precipitated by Amanda's interruption of his creative labor. A chair lying overthrown on the floor.

Their gesticulating shadows are cast on the ceiling by the fiery glow.

Amanda: You *will* hear more, you—

Tom: No, I won't hear more, I'm going out!

Amanda: You come right back in—

Tom: Out, out out! Because I'm—

Amanda: Come back here, Tom Wingfield! I'm not through talking to you!

Tom: Oh, go—

Laura (*desperately*): Tom!

Amanda: You're going to listen, and no more insolence from you! I'm at the end of my patience! (*He comes back toward her.*)

Tom: What do you think I'm at? Aren't I supposed to have any patience to reach the end of, Mother? I know, I know. It seems unimportant to you, what I'm *doing*—what I *want* to do—having a little *difference* between them! You don't think that—

Amanda: I think you've been doing things that you're ashamed of. That's why you act like this. I don't believe that you go every night to the movies. Nobody goes to the movies night after night. Nobody in their right minds goes to the movies as often as you pretend to. People don't go to the movies at nearly midnight, and movies don't let out at two A.M. Come in stumbling. Muttering to yourself like a maniac! You get three hours' sleep and then go to work. Oh, I can picture the way you're doing down there. Moping, doping, because you're in no condition.

Tom (*wildly*): No, I'm in no condition!

Amanda: What right have you got to jeopardize your job? Jeopardize the security of us all? How do you think we'd manage if you were—

Tom: Listen! You think I'm crazy about the *warehouse?* (*He bends fiercely toward her slight figure.*) You think I'm in love with the Continental Shoemakers? You think I want to spend fifty-five *years* down there in that—*celotex interior!* with—*fluorescent—tubes!* Look! I'd rather somebody picked up a crowbar and battered out my brains—than go back mornings! I *go!* Every time you come in yelling that God-damn *"Rise and Shine!" "Rise and Shine!"* I say to myself "How *lucky dead* people are!" But I get up. I *go!* For sixty-five dollars a month I give up all that I dream of doing and being *ever!* And you say self—*self's* all I ever think of. Why, listen, if self is what I thought of, Mother, I'd be where he is—GONE! (*Pointing to father's picture.*) As far as the system of transportation reaches! (*He starts past her. She grabs his arm.*) Don't grab at me, Mother!

Amanda: Where are you going?

Tom: I'm going to the *movies!*

Amanda: I don't believe that lie!

Tom (*crouching toward her, overtowering her tiny figure. She backs away, gasping*): I'm going to opium dens! Yes, opium dens, dens of vice and criminals' hangouts, Mother. I've joined the Hogan gang, I'm a hired assassin, I carry a tommy-gun in a violin case! I run a string of cat-houses in the Valley! They call me Killer, Killer Wingfield, I'm leading a double-life, a simple, honest warehouse worker by day, by night a dynamic *czar* of the *underworld,* Mother. I go to gambling casinos, I spin away fortunes on the roulette table! I wear a patch over one eye and a false mustache, sometimes I put on green whiskers. On those occasions they call me— *El Diablo!* Oh, I could tell you things to make you sleepless! My enemies plan to dynamite this place. They're going to blow us all sky-high some night! I'll be glad, very happy, and so will you! You'll go up, up on a broomstick, over Blue Mountain with seventeen gentlemen callers! You ugly—babbling old—*witch.* . . . (*He goes through a series of violent, clumsy movements, seizing his overcoat, lunging to the door, pulling it fiercely open. The women watch him, aghast. His arm catches in the sleeve of the coat as he struggles to pull it on. For a moment he is pinioned by the bulky garment. With an outraged groan he tears the coat off again, splitting the shoulders of it, and hurls it across the room. It strikes against the shelf of Laura's glass collection, there is a tinkle of shattering glass. Laura cries out as if wounded.*)

(Music Legend: "The Glass Menagerie.")

Laura (*shrilly*): My glass!—menagerie. . . . (*She covers her face and turns away.*)

But Amanda is still stunned and stupefied by the "ugly witch" so that she barely notices this occurrence. Now she recovers her speech.

Amanda (*in an awful voice*): I won't speak to you—until you apologize! (*She crosses through portieres and draws them together behind her. Tom is left with Laura. Laura clings weakly to the mantel with her face averted. Tom stares at her stupidly for a moment. Then he crosses to shelf. Drops awkwardly to his knees to collect the fallen glass, glancing at Laura as if he would speak but couldn't.*)

("The Glass Menagerie" Music Steals In As The Scene Dims Out.)

SCENE IV

The interior is dark. Faint in the alley.

A deep-voiced bell in a church is tolling the hour of five as the scene commences.

Tom appears at the top of the alley. After each solemn boom of the bell in the tower, he shakes a little noise-maker or rattle as if to express the tiny spasm of man in contrast to the sustained power and dignity of the Almighty. This and the unsteadiness of his advance make it evident that he has been drinking.

As he climbs the few steps to the fire-escape landing light steals up inside. Laura appears in night-dress, observing Tom's empty bed in the front room.

Tom fishes in his pockets for the door-key, removing a motley assortment of articles in the search, including a perfect shower of movie-ticket stubs and an empty bottle. At last he finds the key, but just as he is about to insert it, it slips from his fingers. He strikes a match and crouches below the door.

Tom (*bitterly*): One crack—and it falls through!

    Laura opens the door.

Laura: Tom! Tom, what are you doing?

Tom: Looking for a door-key.

Laura: Where have you been all this time?

Tom: I have been to the movies.

Laura: All this time at the movies?

Tom: There was a very long program. There was a Garbo picture and a Mickey Mouse and a travelogue and a newsreel and a preview of coming attractions. And there was an organ solo and a collection for the milk-fund—simultaneously—which ended up in a terrible fight between a fat lady and an usher!

Laura (*innocently*): Did you have to stay through everything?

Tom: Of course! And, oh, I forgot! There was a big stage show! The headliner on this stage show was Malvolio the Magician. He performed wonderful tricks, many of them, such as pouring water back and forth between pitchers. First it turned to wine and then it turned to beer and then it turned to whiskey. I know it was whiskey it finally turned into because he needed somebody to come up out of the audience to help him, and I came up—both shows! It was Kentucky Straight Bourbon. A very generous fellow, he gave souvenirs. (*He pulls from his back pocket a shimmering rainbow-colored scarf.*) He gave me this. This is his magic scarf. You can have it, Laura. You wave it over a canary cage and you get a bowl of gold-fish. You wave it over the gold-fish bowl and they fly away canaries. . . . But the wonderfullest trick of all was the coffin trick. We nailed him into a coffin and he got out of the coffin without removing one nail. (*He has come inside.*) There is a trick that would come in handy for me—get me out of this 2 by 4 situation! (*Flops onto bed and starts removing shoes.*)

Laura: Tom—shhh!

Tom: What're you shushing me for?

Laura: You'll wake up Mother.

Tom: Goody, goody! Pay 'er back for all those "Rise an' Shines." (*Lies down, groaning.*) You know it don't take much intelligence to get yourself into a nailed-up coffin, Laura. But who in hell ever got himself out of one without removing one nail?

As if in answer, the father's grinning photograph lights up.

(Scene Dims Out.)

Immediately following: The church bell is heard striking six. At the sixth stroke the alarm clock goes off in Amanda's room, and after a few moments we hear her calling: "Rise and Shine! Rise and Shine! Laura, go tell your brother to rise and shine!"

Tom (*sitting up slowly*): I'll rise—but I won't shine.

The light increases.

Amanda: Laura, tell your brother his coffee is ready.

Laura slips into front room.

Laura: Tom!—It's nearly seven. Don't make Mother nervous. (*He stares at her stupidly.*) (*Beseechingly*) Tom, speak to Mother this morning. Make up with her, apologize, speak to her!

Tom: She won't to me. It's her that started not speaking.

Laura: If you just say you're sorry she'll start speaking.

Tom: Her not speaking—is that such a tragedy?

Laura: Please—please!

Amanda (*calling from kitchenette*): Laura, are you going to do what I asked you to do, or do I have to get dressed and go out myself?

Laura: Going, going—soon as I get on my coat! (*She pulls on a shapeless felt hat with nervous, jerky movements, pleadingly glancing at Tom. Rushes awkwardly for coat. The coat is one of Amanda's inaccurately made-over, the sleeves too short for Laura.*) Butter and what else?

Amanda (*entering upstage*): Just butter. Tell them to charge it.

Laura: Mother, they make such faces when I do that.

Amanda: Sticks and stones may break my bones, but the expression on Mr. Garfinkel's face won't harm us! Tell your brother his coffee is getting cold.

Laura (*at door*): Do what I asked you, will you, will you, Tom?

He looks sullenly away.

Amanda: Laura, go now or just don't go at all!

Laura (*rushing out*): Going—going! (*A second later she cries out. Tom springs up and crosses to the door. Amanda rushes anxiously in. Tom opens the door.*)

Tom: Laura?

Laura: I'm all right. I slipped, but I'm all right.

Amanda (*peering anxiously after her*): If anyone breaks a leg on those fire-escape steps, the landlord ought to be sued for every cent he possesses! (*She shuts door. Remembers she isn't speaking and returns to other room.*)

As Tom enters listlessly for his coffee, she turns her back to him and stands rigidly facing the window on the gloomy gray vault of the areaway. Its light on her face with its aged but childish features is cruelly sharp, satirical as a Daumier print.

(Music Under: "Ave Maria.")

Tom glances sheepishly but sullenly at her averted figure and slumps at the table. The coffee is scalding hot; he sips it and gasps and spits it back in the cup. At his gasp, Amanda catches her breath and half turns. Then catches herself and turns back to window.

Tom blows on his coffee, glancing sidewise at his mother. She clears her throat. Tom clears his. He starts to rise. Sinks back down again, scratches his head, clears his throat again. Amanda coughs. Tom raises his cup in both hands to blow on it, his eyes staring over the rim of it at his mother for several moments. Then he slowly sets the cup down and awkwardly and hesitantly rises from the chair.

Tom (hoarsely): Mother. I—I apologize. Mother. (*Amanda draws a quick, shuddering breath. Her face works grotesquely. She breaks into childlike tears.*) I'm sorry for what I said, for everything that I said, I didn't mean it.

Amanda (sobbingly): My devotion has made me a witch and so I make myself hateful to my children!

Tom: No, you *don't.*

Amanda: I worry so much, don't sleep, it makes me nervous!

Tom (gently): I understand that.

Amanda: I've had to put up a solitary battle all these years. But you're my right-hand bower! Don't fall down, don't fail!

Tom (gently): I try, Mother.

Amanda (with great enthusiasm): Try and you will *succeed!* (*The notion makes her breathless.*) Why, you—you're just *full* of natural endowments! Both of my children—they're *unusual* children! Don't you think I know it? I'm so—*proud!* Happy and—feel I've—so much to be thankful for but—promise me one thing, son!

Tom: What, Mother?

Amanda: Promise, son you'll—never be a drunkard!

Tom (turns to her grinning): I will never be a drunkard, Mother.

Amanda: That's what frightened me so, that you'd be drinking! Eat a bowl of Purina!

Tom: Just coffee, Mother.

Amanda: Shredded wheat biscuit?

Tom: No. No, Mother, just coffee.

Amanda: You can't put in a day's work on an empty stomach. You've got ten minutes—don't gulp! Drinking too-hot liquids makes cancer of the stomach. . . . Put cream in.

Tom: No, thank you.

Amanda: To cool it.

Tom: No! No, thank you, I want it black.

Amanda: I know, but it's not good for you. We have to do all that we can to build ourselves up. In these trying times we live in, all that we have to cling to is— each other. . . . That's why it's so important to—Tom, I—I sent out your sister so I could discuss something with you. If you hadn't spoken I would have spoken to you. (*Sits down.*)

Tom (gently): What is it, Mother, that you want to discuss?

Amanda: Laura!

Tom puts his cup down slowly.

(Legend On Screen: "Laura.")

(Music: "The Glass Menagerie.")

Tom: —Oh.—Laura . . .

Amanda (touching his sleeve): You know how Laura is. So quiet but—still water runs deep! She notices things and I think she—broods about them. (*Tom looks up.*) A few days ago I came in and she was crying.

Tom: What about?

Amanda: You.

Tom: Me?

Amanda: She has an idea that you're not happy here.

Tom: What gave her that idea?

Amanda: What gives her any idea? However, you do act strangely. I—I'm not criticizing, understand *that!* I know your ambitions do not lie in the warehouse, that like everybody in the whole wide world—you've had to—make sacrifices, but— Tom—Tom—life's not easy, it calls for—Spartan endurance! There's so many things in my heart that I cannot describe to you! I've never told you but I—*loved* your father. . . .

Tom (gently): I know that, Mother.

Amanda: And you—when I see you taking after his ways! Staying out late—and— well, you *had* been drinking the night you were in that—terrifying condition! Laura says that you hate the apartment and that you go out nights to get away from it! Is that true, Tom?

Tom: No. You say there's so much in your heart that you can't describe to me. That's true of me, too. There's so much in my heart that I can't describe to *you!* So let's respect each other's—

Amanda: But, why—*why,* Tom—are you always so *restless?* Where do you go to, nights?

Tom: I—go to the movies.

Amanda: Why do you go to the movies so much, Tom?

Tom: I go to the movies because—I like adventure. Adventure is something I don't have much of at work, so I go to the movies.

Amanda: But, Tom, you go to the movies *entirely* too *much!*

Tom: I like a lot of adventure.

Amanda looks baffled, then hurt. As the familiar inquisition resumes he becomes hard and impatient again. Amanda slips back into her querulous attitude toward him.

(Image On Screen: Sailing Vessel With Jolly Roger.)

Amanda: Most young men find adventure in their careers.

Tom: Then most young men are not employed in a warehouse.

Amanda: The world is full of young men employed in warehouses and offices and factories.

Tom: Do all of them find adventure in their careers?

Amanda: They do or they do without it! Not everybody has a craze for adventure.

Tom: Man is by instinct a lover, a hunter, a fighter, and none of those instincts are given much play at the warehouse!

Amanda: Man is by instinct! Don't quote instinct to me! Instinct is something that people have got away from! It belongs to animals! Christian adults don't want it!

Tom: What do Christian adults want, then, Mother?

Amanda: Superior things! Things of the mind and the spirit! Only animals have to satisfy instincts! Surely your aims are somewhat higher than theirs! Than monkeys—pigs—

Tom: I reckon they're not.

Amanda: You're joking. However, that isn't what I wanted to discuss.

Tom (rising): I haven't much time.

Amanda (pushing his shoulder): Sit down.

Tom: You want me to punch in red at the warehouse, Mother?

Amanda: You have five minutes. I want to talk about Laura.

(Legend: "Plans And Provisions.")

Tom: All right! What about Laura?

Amanda: We have to be making some plans and provisions for her. She's older than you, two years, and nothing has happened. She just drifts along doing nothing. It frightens me terribly how she just drifts along.

Tom: I guess she's the type that people call home girls.

Amanda: There's no such type, and if there is, it's a pity! That is unless the home is hers, with a husband!

Tom: What?

Amanda: Oh, I can see the handwriting on the wall as plain as I see the nose in front of my face! It's terrifying! More and more you remind me of your father! He was out all hours without explanation—Then *left! Goodbye!* And me with the bag to hold. I saw that letter you got from the Merchant Marine. I know what you're dreaming of. I'm not standing here blindfolded. (*She pauses.*) Very well, then. Then *do* it! But not till there's somebody to take your place.

Tom: What do you mean?

Amanda: I mean that as soon as Laura has got somebody to take care of her, married, a home of her own, independent—why, then you'll be free to go wherever you please, on land, on sea, whichever way the wind blows! But until that time you've got to look out for your sister. I don't say me because I'm old and don't matter! I say for your sister because she's young and dependent. I put her in business college—a dismal failure! Frightened her so it made her sick to her stomach. I took her over to the Young People's League at the church. Another fiasco. She spoke to nobody, nobody spoke to her. Now all she does is fool with those pieces of glass and play those worn-out records. What kind of a life is that for a girl to lead!

Tom: What can I do about it?

Amanda: Overcome selfishness! Self, self, self is all that you ever think of! (*Tom springs up and crosses to get his coat. It is ugly and bulky. He pulls on a cap with earmuffs.*) Where is your muffler? Put your wool muffler on! (*He snatches it angrily from the closet and tosses it around his neck and pulls both ends tight.*) Tom! I haven't said what I had in mind to ask you.

Tom: I'm too late to—

Amanda (catching his arms—very importunately. Then shyly): Down at the warehouse, aren't there some—nice young men?

Tom: No!

Amanda: There *must be*—*some . . .*

Tom: Mother—

Gesture.

Amanda: Find one that's clean-living—doesn't drink—and ask him out for sister!

Tom: What?

Amanda: For *sister!* To *meet!* Get *acquainted!*

Tom (stamping to door): Oh, my go-osh!

Amanda: Will you? (*He opens door. Imploringly.*) Will you? (*He starts down.*) Will you? *Will* you, dear?

Tom (calling back): Yes!

Amanda closes the door hesitantly and with a troubled but faintly hopeful expression.

(Screen Image: Glamor Magazine Cover.)

Spot Amanda at phone.

Amanda: Ella Cartwright? This is Amanda Wingfield! How are you, honey? How is that kidney condition? (*Count five.*) Horrors! (*Count five.*) You're a Christian martyr, yes, honey, that's what you are, a Christian martyr! Well, I just happened to notice in my little red book that your subscription to the *Companion* has just run out! I knew that you wouldn't want to miss out on the wonderful serial starting in this new issue. It's by Bessie Mae Hopper, the first thing she's written since *Honeymoon for Three.* Wasn't that a strange and interesting story? Well, this one is even lovelier, I believe. It has a sophisticated society background. It's all about the horsey set on Long Island!

(Fade Out.)

SCENE V
(Legend On Screen: "Annunciation.") *Fade with music.*

It is early dusk of a spring evening. Supper has just been finished in the Wingfield apartment. Amanda and Laura in light colored dresses are removing dishes from the table, in the upstage area, which is shadowy, their movements formalized almost as a dance or ritual, their moving forms as pale and silent as moths.

Tom, in white shirt and trousers, rises from the table and crosses toward the fire-escape.

Amanda (as he passes her): Son, will you do me a favor?

Tom: What?

Amanda: Comb your hair! You look so pretty when your hair is combed! (*Tom slouches on sofa with evening paper. Enormous caption "Franco Triumphs."*) There is only one respect in which I would like you to emulate your father.

Tom: What respect is that?

Amanda: The care he always took of his appearance. He never allowed himself to look untidy. (*He throws down the paper and crosses to fire-escape.*) Where are you going?

Tom: I'm going out to smoke.

Amanda: You smoke too much. A pack a day at fifteen cents a pack. How much would that amount to in a month? Thirty times fifteen is how much, Tom? Figure it out and you will be astounded at what you could save. Enough to give you a night-school course in accounting at Washington U! Just think what a wonderful thing that would be for you, son!

Tom is unmoved by the thought.

Tom: I'd rather smoke. (*He steps out on landing, letting the screen door slam.*)

Amanda (*sharply*): I know! That's the tragedy of it. . . . (*Alone, she turns to look at her husband's picture.*)

(Dance Music: "All The World Is Waiting For The Sunrise.")

Tom (*to the audience*): Across the alley from us was the Paradise Dance Hall. On evenings in spring the windows and doors were open and the music came outdoors. Sometimes the lights were turned out except for a large glass sphere that hung from the ceiling. It would turn slowly about and filter the dusk with delicate rainbow colors. Then the orchestra played a waltz or a tango, something that had a slow and sensuous rhythm. Couples would come outside, to the relative privacy of the alley. You could see them kissing behind ash-pits and telephone poles. This was the compensation for lives that passed like mine, without any change or adventure. Adventure and change were imminent in this year. They were waiting around the corner for all these kids. Suspended in the mist over Berchtesgaden, caught in the folds of Chamberlain's umbrella. In Spain there was Guernica! But here there was only hot swing music and liquor, dance halls, bars, and movies, and sex that hung in the gloom like a chandelier and flooded the world with brief, deceptive rainbows. . . . All the world was waiting for bombardments!

Amanda turns from the picture and comes outside.

Amanda (*sighing*): A fire-escape landing's a poor excuse for a porch. (*She spreads a newspaper on a step and sits down, gracefully and demurely as if she were settling into a swing on a Mississippi veranda.*) What are you looking at?

Tom: The moon.

Amanda: Is there a moon this evening?

Tom: It's rising over Garfinkel's Delicatessen.

Amanda: So it is! A little silver slipper of a moon. Have you made a wish on it yet?

Tom: Um-hum.

Amanda: What did you wish for?

Tom: That's a secret.

Amanda: A secret, huh? Well, I won't tell mine either. I will be just as mysterious as you.

Tom: I bet I can guess what yours is.

Amanda: Is my head so transparent?

Tom: You're not a sphinx.

Amanda: No, I don't have secrets. I'll tell you what I wished for on the moon. Success and happiness for my precious children! I wish for that whenever there's a moon, and when there isn't a moon, I wish for it, too.

Tom: I thought perhaps you wished for a gentleman caller.

Amanda: Why do you say that?

Tom: Don't you remember asking me to fetch one?

Amanda: I remember suggesting that it would be nice for your sister if you brought home some nice young man from the warehouse. I think I've made that suggestion more than once.

Tom: Yes, you have made it repeatedly.

Amanda: Well?

Tom: We are going to have one.

Amanda: What?

Tom: A gentleman caller!

(The Annunciation Is Celebrated With Music.)

Amanda rises.

(Image On Screen: Caller With Bouquet.)

Amanda: You mean you have asked some nice young man to come over?

Tom: Yep. I've asked him to dinner.

Amanda: You really did?

Tom: I did!

Amanda: You did, and did he—*accept?*

Tom: He did!

Amanda: Well, well—well, well! That's—lovely!

Tom: I thought that you would be pleased.

Amanda: It's definite, then?

Tom: Very definite.

Amanda: Soon?

Tom: Very soon.

Amanda: For heaven's sake, stop putting on and tell me some things, will you?

Tom: What things do you want me to tell you?

Amanda: *Naturally* I would like to know when he's *coming!*

Tom: He's coming tomorrow.

Amanda: *Tomorrow?*

Tom: Yep. Tomorrow.

Amanda: But, Tom!

Tom: Yes, Mother?

Amanda: Tomorrow gives me no time!

Tom: Time for what?

Amanda: Preparations! Why didn't you phone me at once, as soon as you asked him, the minute that he accepted? Then, don't you see, I could have been getting ready!

Tom: You don't have to make any fuss.

Amanda: Oh, Tom, Tom, Tom, of course I have to make a fuss! I want things nice, not sloppy! Not thrown together. I'll certainly have to do some fast thinking, won't I?

Tom: I don't see why you have to think at all.

Amanda: You just don't know. We can't have a gentleman caller in a pig-sty! All my wedding silver has to be polished, the monogrammed table linen ought to be laundered! The windows have to be washed and fresh curtains put up. And how about clothes? We have to *wear* something, don't we?

Tom: Mother, this boy is no one to make a fuss over!

Amanda: Do you realize he's the first young man we've introduced to your sister? It's terrible, dreadful, disgraceful that poor little sister has never received a single gentleman caller! Tom, come inside! (*She opens the screen door.*)

Tom: What for?

Amanda: I want to ask you some things.

Tom: If you're going to make such a fuss, I'll call it off, I'll tell him not to come.

Amanda: You certainly won't do anything of the kind. Nothing offends people worse than broken engagements. It simply means I'll have to work like a Turk! We won't be brilliant, but we will pass inspection. Come on inside. (*Tom follows, groaning.*) Sit down.

Tom: Any particular place you would like me to sit?

Amanda: Thank heavens I've got that new sofa! I'm also making payments on a floor lamp I'll have sent out! And put the chintz covers on, they'll brighten things up! Of course I'd hoped to have these walls re-papered. . . . What is the young man's name?

Tom: His name is O'Connor.

Amanda: That, of course, means fish—tomorrow is Friday! I'll have that salmon loaf—with Durkee's dressing! What does he do? He works at the warehouse?

Tom: Of course! How else would I—

Amanda: Tom, he—doesn't drink?

Tom: Why do you ask me that?

Amanda: Your father *did*!

Tom: Don't get started on that!

Amanda: He *does* drink, then?

Tom: Not that I know of!

Amanda: Make sure, be certain! The last thing I want for my daughter's a boy who drinks!

Tom: Aren't you being a little premature? Mr. O'Connor has not yet appeared on the scene!

Amanda: But will tomorrow. To meet your sister, and what do I know about his character? Nothing! Old maids are better off than wives of drunkards!

Tom: Oh, my God!

Amanda: Be still!

Tom (*leaning forward to whisper*): Lots of fellows meet girls whom they don't marry!

Amanda: Oh, talk sensibly, Tom—and don't be sarcastic! (*She has gotten a hairbrush.*)

Tom: What are you doing?

Amanda: I'm brushing that cow-lick down! (*She attacks his hair with the brush.*) What is this young man's position at the warehouse?

Tom (*submitting grimly to the brush and the interrogation*): This young man's position is that of a shipping clerk, Mother.

Amanda: Sounds to me like a fairly responsible job, the sort of a job *you* would be in if you just had more *get-up*. What is his salary? Have you got any idea?

Tom: I would judge it to be approximately eighty-five dollars a month.

Amanda: Well—not princely, but—

Tom: Twenty more than I make.

Amanda: Yes, how well I know! But for a family man, eighty-five dollars a month is not much more than you can just get by on. . . .

Tom: Yes, but Mr. O'Connor is not a family man.

Amanda: He might be, mightn't he? Some time in the future?

Tom: I see. Plans and provisions.

Amanda: You are the only young man that I know of who ignores the fact that the future becomes the present, the present the past, and the past turns into everlasting regret if you don't plan for it!

Tom: I will think that over and see what I can make of it!

Amanda: Don't be supercilious with your mother! Tell me some more about this—what do you call him?

Tom: James D. O'Connor. The D. is for Delaney.

Amanda: Irish on *both* sides! *Gracious!* And doesn't drink?

Tom: Shall I call him up and ask him right this minute?

Amanda: The only way to find out about those things is to make discreet inquiries at the proper moment. When I was a girl in Blue Mountain and it was suspected that a young man drank, the girl whose attentions he had been receiving, if any girl *was*, would sometimes speak to the minister of his church, or rather her father would if her father was living, and sort of feel him out on the young man's character. That is the way such things are discreetly handled to keep a young woman from making a tragic mistake!

Tom: Then how did you happen to make a tragic mistake?

Amanda: That innocent look of your father's had everyone fooled! He *smiled*—the world was *enchanted!* No girl can do worse than put herself at the mercy of a handsome appearance! I hope that Mr. O'Connor is not too good-looking.

Tom: No, he's not too good-looking. He's covered with freckles and hasn't too much of a nose.

Amanda: He's not right-down homely, though?

Tom: Not right-down homely. Just medium homely, I'd say.

Amanda: Character's what to look for in a man.

Tom: That's what I've always said, Mother.

Amanda: You've never said anything of the kind and I suspect you would never give it a thought.

Tom: Don't be suspicious of me.

Amanda: At least I hope he's the type that's up and coming.

Tom: I think he really goes in for self-improvement.

Amanda: What reason have you to think so?

Tom: He goes to night school.

Amanda (beaming): Splendid! What does he do, I mean study?

Tom: Radio engineering and public speaking!

Amanda: Then he has visions of being advanced in the world! Any young man who studies public speaking is aiming to have an executive job some day! And radio engineering? A thing for the future! Both of these facts are very illuminating. Those are the sort of things that a mother should know concerning any young man who comes to call on her daughter. Seriously or—not.

Tom: One little warning. He doesn't know about Laura. I didn't let on that we had dark ulterior motives. I just said, why don't you come have dinner with us? He said okay and that was the whole conversation.

Amanda: I bet it was! You're eloquent as an oyster. However, he'll know about Laura when he gets here. When he sees how lovely and sweet and pretty she is, he'll thank his lucky stars he was asked to dinner.

Tom: Mother, you mustn't expect too much of Laura.

Amanda: What do you mean?

Tom: Laura seems all those things to you and me because she's ours and we love her. We don't even notice she's crippled any more.

Amanda: Don't say crippled! You know that I never allow that word to be used!

Tom: But face facts, Mother. She is and—that not's all—

Amanda: What do you mean "not all"?

Tom: Laura is very different from other girls.

Amanda: I think the difference is all to her advantage.

Tom: Not quite all—in the eyes of others—strangers—she's terribly shy and lives in a world of her own and those things make her seem a little peculiar to people outside the house.

Amanda: Don't say peculiar.

Tom: Face the facts. She is.

(The Dance-Hall Music Changes To A Tango That Has A Minor And Somewhat Ominous Tone.)

Amanda: In what way is she peculiar—may I ask?

Tom (gently): She lives in a world of her own—a world of—little glass ornaments, Mother. . . . (*Gets up. Amanda remains holding brush, looking at him, troubled.*) She plays old phonograph records and—that's about all—(*He glances at himself in the mirror and crosses to door.*)

Amanda (sharply): Where are you going?

Tom: I'm going to the movies. (*Out screen door.*)

Amanda: Not to the movies, every night to the movies! (*Follows quickly to screen door.*) I don't believe you always go to the movies! (*He is gone. Amanda looks worriedly after him for a moment. Then vitality and optimism return and she turns from the door. Crossing to portieres.*) Laura! Laura! (*Laura answers from kitchenette.*)

Laura: Yes, Mother.

Amanda: Let those dishes go and come in front! (*Laura appears with dish towel. Gaily.*) Laura, come here and make a wish on the moon!

Laura (entering): Moon—moon?

Amanda: A little silver slipper of a moon. Look over your left shoulder, Laura, and make a wish! (*Laura looks faintly puzzled as if called out of sleep. Amanda seizes her shoulders and turns her at an angle by the door.*) Now! Now, darling, wish!

Laura: What shall I wish for, Mother?

Amanda (her voice trembling and her eyes suddenly filling with tears): Happiness! Good fortune!

The violin rises and the stage dims out.

SCENE VI

(Image: High-School Hero.)

Tom: And so the following evening I brought him home to dinner. I had known Jim slightly in high school. In high school Jim was a hero. He had tremendous Irish good nature and vitality with the scrubbed and polished look of white chinaware. He seemed to move in a continual spotlight. He was a star in basketball, captain of the debating club, president of the senior class and the glee club and he sang the male lead in the annual light operas. He was always running or bounding, never just walking. He seemed always at the point of defeating the law of gravity. He was shooting with such velocity through his adolescence that you would logically expect him to arrive at nothing short of the White House by the time he was thirty. But Jim apparently ran into more interference after his graduation from Soldan. His speed had definitely slowed. Six years after he left high school he was holding a job that wasn't much better than mine.

(Image: Clerk.)

He was the only one at the warehouse with whom I was on friendly terms. I was valuable to him as someone who could remember his former glory, who had seen him win basketball games and the silver cup in debating. He knew of my secret practice of retiring to a cabinet of the washroom to work on my poems when business was slack in the warehouse. He called me Shakespeare. And while the other boys in the warehouse regarded me with suspicious hostility, Jim took a humorous attitude toward me. Gradually his attitude affected the others, their hostility wore off and they also began to smile at me as people smile at an oddly fashioned dog who trots across their path at some distance.

I knew that Jim and Laura had known each other at Soldan, and I had heard Laura speak admiringly of his voice. I didn't know if Jim remembered her or not. In high school Laura had been as unobtrusive as Jim had been astonishing. If he did remember Laura, it was not as my sister, for when I asked him to dinner, he grinned and said, "You know, Shakespeare, I never thought of you as having folks!"

He was about to discover that I did. . . .

(Light Up Stage.)

(Legend On Screen: "The Accent Of A Coming Foot.")

Friday evening. It is about five o'clock of a late spring evening which comes "scattering poems in the sky."

A delicate lemony light is in the Wingfield apartment.

Amanda has worked like a Turk in preparation for the gentleman caller. The results are astonishing. The new floor lamp with its rose-silk shade is in place, a colored paper lantern conceals the broken light fixture in the ceiling, new billowing white curtains are at the windows, chintz covers are on chairs and sofa, a pair of new sofa pillows make their initial appearance.

Open boxes and tissue paper are scattered on the floor.

Laura stands in the middle with lifted arms while Amanda crouches before her, adjusting the hem of the new dress, devout and ritualistic. The dress is colored and designed by memory. The arrangement of Laura's hair is changed; it is softer and more becoming. A fragile, unearthly prettiness has come out in Laura: she is like a piece of translucent glass touched by light, given a momentary radiance, not actual, not lasting.

Amanda (*impatiently*): Why are you trembling?

Laura: Mother, you've made me so nervous!

Amanda: How have I made you nervous?

Laura: By all this fuss! You make it seem so important!

Amanda: I don't understand you, Laura. You couldn't be satisfied with just sitting home, and yet whenever I try to arrange something for you, you seem to resist it. (*She gets up.*) Now take a look at yourself. No, wait! Wait just a moment—I have an idea!

Laura: What is it now?

Amanda produces two powder puffs which she wraps in handkerchiefs and stuffs in Laura's bosom.

Laura: Mother, what are you doing?

Amanda: They call them "Gay Deceivers"!

Laura: I won't wear them!

Amanda: You will!

Laura: Why should I?

Amanda: Because, to be painfully honest, your chest is flat.

Laura: You make it seem like we were setting a trap.

Amanda: All pretty girls are a trap, a pretty trap, and men expect them to be. (**Legend: "A Pretty Trap."**) Now look at yourself, young lady. This is the prettiest you will ever be! (*She stands back to admire Laura.*) I've got to fix myself now! You're going to be surprised by your mother's appearance! (*She crosses through the portieres, humming gaily.*)

Laura moves slowly to the long mirror and stares solemnly at herself.

A wind blows the white curtains inward in a slow, graceful motion and with a faint, sorrowful sighing.

Amanda (*offstage*): It isn't dark enough yet. (*She turns slowly before the mirror with a troubled look.*)

(**Legend On Screen: "This Is My Sister: Celebrate Her With Strings!" Music.**)

Amanda (*laughing, off*): I'm going to show you something. I'm going to make a spectacular appearance!

Laura: What is it, Mother?

Amanda: Possess your soul in patience—you will see! Something I've resurrected from that old trunk! Styles haven't changed so terribly much after all. . . . (*She parts the portieres.*) Now just look at your mother! (*She wears a girlish frock of yellowed voile with a blue silk sash. She carries a bunch of jonquils—the legend of her youth is nearly revived. Feverishly.*) This is the dress in which I led the cotillion. Won the cakewalk twice at Sunset Hill, wore one Spring to the Governor's Ball in Jackson! See how I sashayed around the ballroom, Laura? (*She raises her skirt and does a mincing step around the room.*) I wore it on Sundays for my gentlemen callers! I had it on the day I met your father . . . I had malaria fever all that Spring. The change of climate from East Tennessee to the Delta—weakened resistance—I had a little temperature all the time—not enough to be serious—just enough to make me restless and giddy! Invitations poured in—parties all over the Delta!—"Stay in bed," said Mother, "you have fever!"—but I just wouldn't. I took quinine but kept on going, going! Evenings, dances! Afternoons, long, long rides! Picnics—lovely!—So lovely, that country in May—all lacy with dogwood, literally flooded with jonquils! That was the spring I had the craze for jonquils. Jonquils became an absolute obsession. Mother said, "Honey, there's no more room for jonquils." And still I kept on bringing in more jonquils. Whenever, wherever I saw them, I'd say, "Stop! Stop! I see jonquils!" I made the young men help me gather the jonquils! It was a joke, Amanda and her jonquils! Finally there were no more vases to hold them, every available space was filled with jonquils. No vases to hold them? All right, I'll hold them myself! And then I—(*She stops in front of the picture.*) (**Music.**) met your father! Malaria fever and jonquils and then—this—boy. . . . (*She switches on the rose-colored lamp.*) I hope they get here before it starts to rain. (*She crosses upstage and places the jonquils in bowl on table.*) I gave your brother a little extra change so he and Mr. O'Connor could take the service car home.

Laura (*with altered look*): What did you say his name was?
Amanda: O'Connor.
Laura: What is his first name?
Amanda: I don't remember. Oh, yes, I do. It was—Jim!

Laura sways slightly and catches hold of a chair.

(**Legend On Screen. "Not Jim!"**)

Laura (*faintly*): Not—Jim!
Amanda: Yes, that was it, it was Jim! I've never known a Jim that wasn't nice!

(**Music: Ominous.**)

Laura: Are you sure his name is Jim O'Connor?
Amanda: Yes. Why?
Laura: Is he the one that Tom used to know in high school?
Amanda: He didn't say so. I think he just got to know him at the warehouse.
Laura: There was a Jim O'Connor we both knew in high school—(*Then, with effort.*) If that is the one that Tom is bringing to dinner—you'll have to excuse me, I won't come to the table.
Amanda: What sort of nonsense is this?
Laura: You asked me once if I'd ever liked a boy. Don't you remember I showed you this boy's picture?
Amanda: You mean the boy you showed me in the year-book?
Laura: Yes, that boy.
Amanda: Laura, Laura, were you in love with that boy?
Laura: I don't know, Mother. All I know is I couldn't sit at the table if it was him!

Amanda: It won't be him! It isn't the least bit likely. But whether it is or not, you will come to the table. You will not be excused.

Laura: I'll have to be, Mother.

Amanda: I don't intend to humor your silliness, Laura. I've had too much from you and your brother, both! So just sit down and compose yourself till they come. Tom has forgotten his key so you'll have to let them in, when they arrive.

Laura (*panicky*): Oh, Mother—*you* answer the door!

Amanda (*lightly*): I'll be in the kitchen—busy!

Laura: Oh, Mother, please answer the door, don't make me do it!

Amanda (*crossing into kitchenette*): I've got to fix the dressing for the salmon. Fuss, fuss—silliness!—over a gentleman caller!

Door swings shut. Laura is left alone.

(Legend: "Terror!")

She utters a low moan and turns off the lamp—sits stiffly on the edge of the sofa, knotting her fingers together.

(Legend On Screen: "The Opening Of A Door!")

Tom and Jim appear on the fire-escape steps and climb to landing. Hearing their approach, Laura rises with a panicky gesture. She retreats to the portieres.

The doorbell. Laura catches her breath and touches her throat. Low drums.

Amanda (*calling*): Laura, sweetheart! The door!

Laura stares at it without moving.

Jim: I think we just beat the rain.

Tom: Uh-huh. (*He rings again, nervously. Jim whistles and fishes for a cigarette.*)

Amanda (*very, very gaily*): Laura, that is your brother and Mr. O'Connor! Will you let them in, darling?

Laura crosses toward kitchenette door.

Laura (*breathlessly*): Mother—you go to the door!

Amanda steps out of kitchenette and stares furiously at Laura. She points imperiously at the door.

Laura: Please, please!

Amanda (*in a fierce whisper*): What is the matter with you, you silly thing?

Laura (*desperately*): Please, you answer it, *please!*

Amanda: I told you I wasn't going to humor you, Laura. Why have you chosen this moment to lose your mind?

Laura: Please, please, please, you go!

Amanda: You'll have to go to the door because I can't!

Laura (*despairingly*): I can't either!

Amanda: Why?

Laura: I'm *sick!*

Amanda: I'm sick, too—of your nonsense! Why can't you and your brother be normal people? Fantastic whims and behavior! (*Tom gives a long ring.*) Preposterous goings on! Can you give me one reason—(*Calls out lyrically.*) Coming! Just one second!—why should you be afraid to open a door? Now you answer it, Laura!

Laura: Oh, oh, oh . . . (*She returns through the portieres. Darts to the victrola and winds it frantically and turns it on.*)

Amanda: Laura Wingfield, you march right to that door!

Laura: Yes—yes, Mother!

A faraway, scratchy rendition of "Dardanella" softens the air and gives her strength to move through it. She slips to the door and draws it cautiously open. Tom enters with the caller, Jim O'Connor.

Tom: Laura, this is Jim. Jim, this is my sister, Laura.

Jim (stepping inside): I didn't know that Shakespeare had a sister!

Laura (retreating stiff and trembling from the door): How—how do you do?

Jim (heartily extending his hand): Okay!

Laura touches it hesitantly with hers.

Jim: Your hand's *cold*, Laura!

Laura: Yes, well—I've been playing the victrola. . . .

Jim: Must have been playing classical music on it! You ought to play a little hot swing music to warm you up!

Laura: Excuse me—I haven't finished playing the victrola. . . .

She turns awkwardly and hurries into the front room. She pauses a second by the victrola. Then catches her breath and darts through the portieres like a frightened deer.

Jim (grinning): What was the matter?

Tom: Oh—with Laura? Laura is—terribly shy.

Jim: Shy, huh? It's unusual to meet a shy girl nowadays. I don't believe you ever mentioned you had a sister.

Tom: Well, now you know. I have one. Here is the *Post Dispatch*. You want a piece of it?

Jim: Uh-huh.

Tom: What piece? The comics?

Jim: Sports! (*Glances at it.*) Ole Dizzy Dean is on his bad behavior.

Tom (disinterest): Yeah? (*Lights cigarette and crosses back to fire-escape door.*)

Jim: Where are you going?

Tom: I'm going out on the terrace.

Jim (goes after him): You know, Shakespeare—I'm going to sell you a bill of goods!

Tom: What goods?

Jim: A course I'm taking.

Tom: Huh?

Jim: In public speaking! You and me, we're not the warehouse type.

Tom: Thanks—that's good news. But what has public speaking got to do with it?

Jim: It fits you for—executive positions!

Tom: Awww.

Jim: I tell you it's done a helluva lot for me.

(Image: Executive At Desk.)

Tom: In what respect?

Jim: In every! Ask yourself what is the difference between you an' me and men in the office down front? Brains?—No!—Ability?—No! Then what? Just one little thing—

Tom: What is that one little thing?

Jim: Primarily it amounts to—social poise! Being able to square up to people and hold your own on any social level!

Amanda (offstage): Tom?

Tom: Yes, Mother?

Amanda: Is that you and Mr. O'Connor?

Tom: Yes, Mother.

Amanda: Well, you just make yourselves comfortable in there.

Tom: Yes, Mother.

Amanda: Ask Mr. O'Connor if he would like to wash his hands.

Jim: Aw—no—thank you—I took care of that at the warehouse. Tom—

Tom: Yes?

Jim: Mr. Mendoza was speaking to me about you.

Tom: Favorably?

Jim: What do you think?

Tom: Well—

Jim: You're going to be out of a job if you don't wake up.

Tom: I am waking up—

Jim: You show no signs.

Tom: The signs are interior.

(Image On Screen: The Sailing Vessel With Jolly Roger Again.)

Tom: I'm planning to change. (*He leans over the rail speaking with quiet exhilaration. The incandescent marquees and signs of the first-run movie houses light his face from across the alley. He looks like a voyager.*) I'm right at the point of committing myself to a future that doesn't include the warehouse and Mr. Mendoza or even a night-school course in public speaking.

Jim: What are you gassing about?

Tom: I'm tired of the movies.

Jim: Movies!

Tom: Yes, movies! Look at them—(*A wave toward the marvels of Grand Avenue.*) All of those glamorous people—having adventures—hogging it all, gobbling the whole thing up! You know what happens? People go to the *movies* instead of *moving!* Hollywood characters are supposed to have all the adventures for everybody in America, while everybody in America sits in a dark room and watches them have them! Yes, until there's a war. That's when adventure becomes available to the masses! *Everyone's* dish, not only Gable's! Then the people in the dark room come out of the dark room to have some adventures themselves—goody, goody! It's our turn now, to go to the South Sea Island—to make a safari—to be exotic, far-off—But I'm not patient. I don't want to wait till then. I'm tired of the *movies* and I am *about* to move!

Jim (*incredulously*): Move?

Tom: Yes!

Jim: When?

Tom: Soon!

Jim: Where? Where?

Theme three music seems to answer the question, while Tom thinks it over. He searches among his pockets.

Tom: I'm starting to boil inside. I know I seem dreamy, but inside—well, I'm boiling! Whenever I pick up a shoe, I shudder a little thinking how short life is and what I am doing!—Whatever that means. I know it doesn't mean shoes—except as something to wear on a traveler's feet! (*Finds paper.*) Look—

Jim: What?

Tom: I'm a member.

Jim (*reading*): The Union of Merchant Seamen.

Tom: I paid my dues this month, instead of the light bill.

Jim: You will regret it when they turn the lights off.

Tom: I won't be here.

Jim: How about your mother?

Tom: I'm like my father. The bastard son of a bastard! Did you notice how he is grinning in his picture in there? And he's been absent going on sixteen years!

Jim: You're just talking, you drip. How does your mother feel about it?

Tom: Shhh—Here comes Mother! Mother is not acquainted with my plans!

Amanda (*enters portieres*): Where are you all?

Tom: On the terrace, Mother.

They start inside. She advances to them. Tom is distinctly shocked at her appearance. Even Jim blinks a little. He is making his first contact with girlish Southern vivacity and in spite of the night-school course in public speaking is somewhat thrown off the beam by the unexpected outlay of social charm.

Certain responses are attempted by Jim but are swept aside by Amanda's gay laughter and chatter. Tom is embarrassed but after the first shock Jim reacts very warmly. He grins and chuckles, is altogether won over.

(Image: Amanda As A Girl.)

Amanda (*coyly smiling, shaking her girlish ringlets*): Well, well, well, so this is Mr. O'Connor. Introductions entirely unnecessary. I've heard so much about you from my boy. I finally said to him, Tom—good gracious!—why don't you bring this paragon to supper? I'd like to meet this nice young man at the warehouse!—Instead of just hearing him sing your praises so much! I don't know why my son is so stand-offish—that's not Southern behavior! Let's sit down and—I think we could stand a little more air in here! Tom, leave the door open. I felt a nice fresh breeze a moment ago. Where has it gone? Mmm, so warm already! And not quite summer, even. We're going to burn up when summer really gets started. However, we're having—we're having a very light supper. I think light things are better fo' this time of year. The same as light clothes are. Light clothes an' light food are what warm weather calls fo'. You know our blood gets so thick during th' winter—it takes a while fo' us to *adjust* ou'selves!—when the season changes . . . It's come so quick this year. I wasn't prepared. All of a sudden—heavens! Already summer!—I ran to the trunk an' pulled out this light dress—Terribly old! Historical almost! But feels so good—so good an' co-ol, y' know. . . .

Tom: Mother—

Amanda: Yes, honey?

Tom: How about—supper?

Amanda: Honey, you go ask Sister if supper is ready! You know that Sister is in full charge of supper! Tell her you hungry boys are waiting for it. (*To Jim*) Have you met Laura?

Jim: She—

Amanda: Let you in? Oh, good, you've met already! It's rare for a girl as sweet an' pretty as Laura to be domestic! But Laura is, thank heavens, not only pretty but also very domestic. I'm not at all. I never was a bit. I never could make a thing but angelfood cake. Well, in the South we had so many servants. Gone, gone, gone. All vestige of gracious living! Gone completely! I wasn't prepared for what the future brought me. All of my gentlemen callers were sons of planters and so of course I assumed that I would be married to one and raise my family on a large piece of land with plenty of servants. But man proposes—and woman accepts the proposal!—To vary that old, old saying a little bit—I married no planter! I married a man who worked for the telephone company! That gallantly smiling gentleman over there! (*Points to the picture.*) A telephone man who—fell in love with long-distance! Now he travels and I don't even know where!—But what am I going on for about my—tribulations? Tell me yours—I hope you don't have any! Tom?

Tom (*returning*): Yes, Mother?

Amanda: Is supper nearly ready?

Tom: It looks to me like supper is on the table.

Amanda: Let me look—(*She rises prettily and looks through portieres.*) Oh, lovely! But where is Sister?

Tom: Laura is not feeling well and she says that she thinks she'd better not come to the table.

Amanda: What? Nonsense! Laura? Oh, Laura!

Laura (*offstage, faintly*): Yes, Mother.

Amanda: You really must come to the table. We won't be seated until you come to the table! Come in, Mr. O'Connor. You sit over there and I'll . . . . Laura? Laura Wingfield! You're keeping us waiting, honey! We can't say grace until you come to the table!

The back door is pushed weakly open and Laura comes in. She is obviously quite faint, her lips trembling, her eyes wide and staring. She moves unsteadily toward the table.

(Legend: "Terror!")

Outside a summer storm is coming abruptly. The white curtains billow inward at the windows and there is a sorrowful murmur and deep blue dusk.

Laura suddenly stumbles—She catches at a chair with a faint moan.

Tom: Laura!

Amanda: Laura! (*There is a clap of thunder.*) (**Legend: "Ah!"**) (*Despairingly.*) Why, Laura, you *are* ill, darling! Tom, help your sister into the living room, dear! Sit in the living room, Laura—rest on the sofa. Well! (*To Jim as Tom helps his sister to the sofa in the living room*) Standing over the hot stove made her ill!—I told her that it was just too warm this evening, but—(*Tom comes back in. Laura is on the sofa.*) Is Laura all right now?

Tom: Yes.

Amanda: What *is* that? Rain? A nice cool rain has come up! (*She gives the gentleman caller a frightened look.*) I think we may—have grace—now . . . (*Tom looks at her stupidly.*) Tom, honey—you say grace!

Tom: Oh . . . "For these and all thy mercies—" (*They bow their heads, Amanda stealing a nervous glance at Jim. In the living room Laura, stretched on the sofa, clenches her hand to her lips, to hold back a shuddering sob.*) God's Holy Name be praised—

(The Scene Dims Out.)

SCENE VII

A Souvenir.

Half an hour later. Dinner is just being finished in the upstage area which is concealed by the drawn portieres.

As the curtain rises Laura is still huddled upon the sofa, her feet drawn under her, her head resting on a pale blue pillow, her eyes wide and mysteriously watchful. The new floor lamp with its shade of rose-colored silk gives a soft, becoming light to her face, bringing out the fragile, unearthly prettiness which usually escapes attention. There is a steady murmur of rain, but it is slackening and stops soon after the scene begins; the air outside becomes pale and luminous as the moon breaks out.

A moment after the curtain rises, the lights in both rooms flicker and go out.

Jim: Hey, there, Mr. Light Bulb!

Amanda laughs nervously.

(Legend: "Suspension Of A Public Service.")

Amanda: Where was Moses when the lights went out? Ha-ha. Do you know the answer to that one, Mr. O'Connor?

Jim: No, Ma'am, what's the answer?

Amanda: In the dark! (*Jim laughs appreciatively.*) Everybody sit still. I'll light the candles. Isn't it lucky we have them on the table? Where's a match? Which of you gentlemen can provide a match?

Jim: Here.

Amanda: Thank you, sir.

Jim: Not at all, Ma'am!

Amanda (*as she lights the candles*): I guess the fuse has burnt out. Mr. O'Connor, can you tell a burnt-out fuse? I know I can't and Tom is a total loss when it comes to mechanics. (**Sound: Getting Up: Voices Recede A Little To Kitchenette.**) Oh, be careful you don't bump into something. We don't want our gentleman caller to break his neck. Now wouldn't that be a fine howdy-do?

Jim: Ha-ha! Where is the fuse-box?

Amanda: Right here next to the stove. Can you see anything?

Jim: Just a minute.

Amanda: Isn't electricity a mysterious thing? Wasn't it Benjamin Franklin who tied a key to a kite? We live in such a mysterious universe, don't we? Some people say that science clears up all the mysteries for us. In my opinion it only creates more! Have you found it yet?

Jim: No, Ma'am. All these fuses look okay to me.

Amanda: Tom!

Tom: Yes, Mother?

Amanda: That light bill I gave you several days ago. The one I told you we got the notices about?

Tom: Oh—yeah.

(Legend: "Ha!")

Amanda: You didn't neglect to pay it by any chance?

Tom: Why, I—

Amanda: Didn't! I might have known it!

Jim: Shakespeare probably wrote a poem on that light bill, Mrs. Wingfield.

Amanda: I might have known better than to trust him with it! There's such a high price for negligence in this world!

Jim: Maybe the poem will win a ten-dollar prize.

Amanda: We'll just have to spend the remainder of the evening in the nineteenth century, before Mr. Edison made the Mazda lamp!

Jim: Candlelight is my favorite kind of light.

Amanda: That shows you're romantic! But that's no excuse for Tom. Well, we got through dinner. Very considerate of them to let us get through dinner before they plunged us into everlasting darkness, wasn't it, Mr. O'Connor?

Jim: Ha-ha!

Amanda: Tom, as a penalty for your carelessness you can help me with the dishes.

Jim: Let me give you a hand.

Amanda: Indeed you will not!

Jim: I ought to be good for something.

Amanda: Good for something? (*Her tone is rhapsodic.*) You? Why, Mr. O'Connor, nobody, *nobody's* given me this much entertainment in years—as you have!

Jim: Aw, now, Mrs. Wingfield!

Amanda: I'm not exaggerating, not one bit! But Sister is all by her lonesome. You go keep her company in the parlor! I'll give you this lovely old candelabrum that used to be on the altar at the church of the Heavenly Rest. It was melted a little out of shape when the church burnt down. Lightning struck it one spring. Gypsy Jones was holding a revival at the time and he intimated that the church was destroyed because the Episcopalians gave card parties.

Jim: Ha-ha.

Amanda: And how about coaxing Sister to drink a little wine? I think it would be good for her! Can you carry both at once?

Jim: Sure. I'm Superman!

Amanda: Now, Thomas, get into this apron!

Jim comes into the dining room, carrying the candelabrum, its candles lighted, in one hand and a glass of wine in the other. The door of kitchenette swings closed on Amanda's gay laughter; the flickering light approaches the portieres. Laura sits up nervously as he enters. Her speech at first is low and breathless from the almost intolerable strain of being alone with a stranger.

(The Legend: "I Don't Suppose You Remember Me At All!")

In her first speeches in this scene, before Jim's warmth overcomes her paralyzing shyness, Laura's voice is thin and breathless as though she has run up a steep flight of stairs. Jim's attitude is gently humorous. While the incident is apparently unimportant, it is to Laura the climax of her secret life.

Jim: Hello, there, Laura.

Laura (faintly): Hello. (*She clears her throat.*)

Jim: How are you feeling now? Better?

Laura: Yes. Yes, thank you.

Jim: This is for you. A little dandelion wine. (*He extends it toward her with extravagant gallantry.*)

Laura: Thank you.

Jim: Drink it—but don't get drunk! (*He laughs heartily. Laura takes the glass uncertainly; laughs shyly.*) Where shall I set the candles?

Laura: Oh—oh, anywhere . . .

Jim: How about here on the floor? Any objections?

Laura: No.

Jim: I'll spread a newspaper under to catch the drippings. I like to sit on the floor. Mind if I do?

Laura: Oh, no.

Jim: Give me a pillow?

Laura: What?

Jim: A pillow!

Laura: Oh . . . (*Hands him one quickly.*)

Jim: How about you? Don't you like to sit on the floor?

Laura: Oh—yes.

Jim: Why don't you, then?

Laura: I—will.

Jim: Take a pillow! (*Laura does. Sits on the other side of the candelabrum. Jim crosses his legs and smiles engagingly at her.*) I can't hardly see you sitting way over there.

Laura: I can—see you.

Jim: I know, but that's not fair, I'm in the limelight. (*Laura moves her pillow closer.*) Good! Now I can see you! Comfortable?

Laura: Yes.

Jim: So am I. Comfortable as a cow. Will you have some gum?

Laura: No, thank you.

Jim: I think that I will indulge, with your permission. (*Musingly unwraps it and holds it up.*) Think of the fortune made by the guy that invented the first piece of chewing gum. Amazing, huh? The Wrigley Building is one of the sights of Chicago—I saw it when I went up to the Century of Progress. Did you take in the Century of Progress?

Laura: No, I didn't.

Jim: Well, it was quite a wonderful exposition. What impressed me most was the Hall of Science. Gives you an idea of what the future will be in America, even more wonderful than the present time is! (*Pause. Smiling at her.*) Your brother tells me you're shy. Is that right, Laura?

Laura: I—don't know.

Jim: I judge you to be an old-fashioned type of girl. Well, I think that's a pretty good type to be. Hope you don't think I'm being too personal—do you?

Laura (*hastily, out of embarrassment*): I believe I *will* take a piece of gum, if you— don't mind. (*Clearing her throat.*) Mr. O'Connor, have you—kept up with your singing?

Jim: Singing? Me?

Laura: Yes. I remember what a beautiful voice you had.

Jim: When did you hear me sing?

(Voice Offstage In The Pause.)

Voice (*offstage*):

> O blow, ye winds, heigh-ho,
> A-roving I will go!
> I'm off to my love
> With a boxing glove—
> Ten thousand miles away!

Jim: You say you've heard me sing?

Laura: Oh, yes! Yes, very often . . . I—don't suppose you remember me—at all?

Jim (*smiling doubtfully*): You know I have an idea I've seen you before. I had that idea soon as you opened the door. It seemed almost like I was about to remember your name. But the name that I started to call you—wasn't a name! And so I stopped myself before I said it.

Laura: Wasn't it—Blue Roses?

Jim (*springs up, grinning*): Blue Roses! My gosh, yes—Blue Roses! That's what I had on my tongue when you opened the door! Isn't it funny what tricks your memory plays? I didn't connect you with the high school somehow or other. But that's where it was; it was high school. I didn't even know you were Shakespeare's sister! Gosh, I'm sorry.

Laura: I didn't expect you to. You—barely knew me!

Jim: But we did have a speaking acquaintance, huh?

Laura: Yes, we—spoke to each other.

Jim: When did you recognize me?

Laura: Oh, right away!

Jim: Soon as I came in the door?

Laura: When I heard your name I thought it was probably you. I knew that Tom used to know you a little in high school. So when you came in the door—well, then I was—sure.

Jim: Why didn't you *say* something, then?

Laura (*breathlessly*): I didn't know what to say, I was—too surprised!

Jim: For goodness sakes! You know, this sure is funny!

Laura: Yes! Yes, isn't it, though . . .

Jim: Didn't we have a class in something together?

Laura: Yes, we did.

Jim: What class was that?

Laura: It was—singing—chorus!

Jim: Aw!

Laura: I sat across the aisle from you in the Aud.

Jim: Aw.

Laura: Mondays, Wednesdays, and Fridays.

Jim: Now I remember—you always came in late.

Laura: Yes, it was so hard for me, getting upstairs. I had that brace on my leg—it clumped so loud!

Jim: I never heard any clumping.

Laura (*wincing at the recollection*): To me it sounded like—thunder!

Jim: Well, well, well. I never even noticed.

Laura: And everybody was seated before I came in. I had to walk in front of all those people. My seat was in the back row. I had to go clumping all the way up the aisle with everyone watching!

Jim: You shouldn't have been self-conscious.

Laura: I know, but I was. It was always such a relief when the singing started.

Jim: Aw, yes, I've placed you now! I used to call you Blue Roses. How was it that I got started calling you that?

Laura: I was out of school a little while with pleurosis. When I came back you asked me what was the matter. I said I had pleurosis—you thought I said *Blue Roses.* That's what you always called me after that!

Jim: I hope you didn't mind.

Laura: Oh, no—I liked it. You see, I wasn't acquainted with many—people. . . .

Jim: As I remember you sort of stuck by yourself.

Laura: I—I—never had much luck at—making friends.

Jim: I don't see why you wouldn't.

Laura: Well, I—started out badly.

Jim: You mean being—

Laura: Yes, it sort of—stood between me—

Jim: You shouldn't have let it!

Laura: I know, but it did, and—

Jim: You were shy with people!

Laura: I tried not to be but never could—

Jim: Overcome it?

Laura: No, I—I never could!

Jim: I guess being shy is something you have to work out of kind of gradually.

Laura (*sorrowfully*): Yes—I guess it—

Jim: Takes time!

Laura: Yes—

Jim: People are not so dreadful when you know them. That's what you have to re-member! And everybody has problems, not just you, but practically everybody has got some problems. You think of yourself as having the only problems, as being the only one who is disappointed. But just look around you and you will see lots of people as disappointed as you are. For instance, I hoped when I was going to high school that I would be further along at this time, six years later, than I am now—You remember that wonderful write-up I had in *The Torch?*

Laura: Yes! (*She rises and crosses to table.*)

Jim: It said I was bound to succeed in anything I went into! (*Laura returns with the annual.*) Holy Jeez! *The Torch!* (*He accepts it reverently. They smile across it with mutual wonder. Laura crouches beside him and they begin to turn through it. Laura's shyness is dissolving in his warmth.*)

Laura: Here you are in *Pirates of Penzance!*

Jim (*wistfully*): I sang the baritone lead in that operetta.

Laura (*rapidly*): So—*beautifully!*

Jim (*protesting*): Aw—

Laura: Yes, yes—beautifully—beautifully!

Jim: You heard me?

Laura: All three times!

Jim: No!

Laura: Yes!

Jim: All three performances?

Laura (*looking down*): Yes.

Jim: Why?

Laura: I—wanted to ask you to—autograph my program.

Jim: Why didn't you ask me to?

Laura: You were always surrounded by your own friends so much that I never had a chance to.

Jim: You should have just—

Laura: Well, I—thought you might think I was—

Jim: Thought I might think you was—what?

Laura: Oh—

Jim (*with reflective relish*): I was beleaguered by females in those days.

Laura: You were terribly popular!

Jim: Yeah—

Laura: You had such a—friendly way—

Jim: I was spoiled in high school.

Laura: Everybody—liked you!

Jim: Including you?

Laura: I—yes, I—did, too—(*She gently closes the book in her lap.*)

Jim: Well, well, well!—Give me that program, Laura. (*She hands it to him. He signs it with a flourish.*) There you are—better late than never!

Laura: Oh, I—what a—surprise!

Jim: My signature isn't worth very much right now. But some day—maybe—it will increase in value! Being disappointed is one thing and being discouraged is something else. I am disappointed but I'm not discouraged. I'm twenty-three years old. How old are you?

Laura: I'll be twenty-four in June.

Jim: That's not old age!

Laura: No, but—

Jim: You finished high school?

Laura (with difficulty): I didn't go back.

Jim: You mean you dropped out?

Laura: I made bad grades in my final examinations. (*She rises and replaces the book and the program. Her voice strained.*) How is—Emily Meisenbach getting along?

Jim: Oh, that kraut-head!

Laura: Why do you call her that?

Jim: That's what she was.

Laura: You're not still—going with her?

Jim: I never see her.

Laura: It said in the Personal Section that you were—engaged!

Jim: I know, but I wasn't impressed by that—propaganda!

Laura: It wasn't—the truth?

Jim: Only in Emily's optimistic opinion!

Laura: Oh—

(Legend: "What Have You Done Since High School?")

Jim lights a cigarette and leans indolently back on his elbows smiling at Laura with a warmth and charm which light her inwardly with altar candles. She remains by the table and turns in her hands a piece of glass to cover her tumult.

Jim (after several reflective puffs on a cigarette): What have you done since high school? (*She seems not to hear him.*) Huh? (*Laura looks up.*) I said what have you done since high school, Laura?

Laura: Nothing much.

Jim: You must have been doing something these six long years.

Laura: Yes.

Jim: Well, then, such as what?

Laura: I took a business course at business college—

Jim: How did that work out?

Laura: Well, not very—well—I had to drop out, it gave me—indigestion—

Jim laughs gently.

Jim: What are you doing now?

Laura: I don't do anything—much. Oh, please don't think I sit around doing nothing! My glass collection takes up a good deal of time. Glass is something you have to take good care of.

Jim: What did you say—about glass?

Laura: Collection I said—I have one—(*She clears her throat and turns away again, acutely shy.*)

Jim (abruptly): You know what I judge to be the trouble with you? Inferiority complex! Know what that is? That's what they call it when someone low-rates himself! I understand it because I had it, too. Although my case was not so aggravated as yours seems to be. I had it until I took up public speaking, developed my voice, and learned that I had an aptitude for science. Before that time I never thought of myself as being outstanding in any way whatsoever! Now I've never made a regular study of it, but I have a friend who says I can analyze people better than doctors that make a profession of it. I don't claim that to be necessarily true, but I can sure guess a person's psychology, Laura! (*Takes out his gum.*) Excuse me, Laura. I always take it out when the flavor is gone. I'll use this scrap of paper to wrap it in. I know how it is to get it stuck on a shoe. (*He wraps the gum in paper and puts it in his pocket.*) Yep—that's what I judge to be your principal trouble. A lack of confidence in yourself as a person. You don't have the proper amount of faith in yourself. I'm basing that fact on a number of your remarks and also on certain observations I've made. For instance that clumping you thought was so awful in high school. You say that you even dreaded to walk into class. You see what you did? You dropped out of school, you gave up an education because of a clump, which as far as I know was practically non-existent! A little physical defect is what you have. Hardly noticeable even! Magnified thousands of times by imagination! You know what my strong advice to you is? Think of yourself as *superior* in some way!

Laura: In what way would I think?

Jim: Why, man alive, Laura! Just look about you a little. What do you see? A world full of common people! All of 'em born and all of 'em going to die! Which of them has one-tenth of your good points! Or mine! Or anyone else's, as far as that goes—gosh! Everybody excels in some one thing. Some in many! (*Unconsciously glances at himself in the mirror.*) All you've got to do is discover in *what!* Take me, for instance. (*He adjusts his tie at the mirror.*) My interest happens to lie in electrodynamics. I'm taking a course in radio engineering at night school, Laura, on top of a fairly responsible job at the warehouse. I'm taking that course and studying public speaking.

Laura: Ohhhh.

Jim: Because I believe in the future of television! (*Turning back to her.*) I wish to be ready to go up right along with it. Therefore I'm planning to get in on the ground floor. In fact, I've already made the right connections and all that remains is for the industry itself to get under way! Full steam—(*His eyes are starry.*) Knowledge—Zzzzzp! Money—Zzzzzp!—Power! That's the cycle democracy is built on! (*His attitude is convincingly dynamic. Laura stares at him, even her shyness eclipsed in her absolute wonder. He suddenly grins.*) I guess you think I think a lot of myself!

Laura: No—o-o-o, I—

Jim: Now how about you? Isn't there something you take more interest in than anything else?

Laura: Well, I do—as I said—have my—glass collection—

A peal of girlish laughter from the kitchen.

Jim: I'm not right sure I know what you're talking about. What kind of glass is it?

Laura: Little articles of it, they're ornaments mostly! Most of them are little animals made out of glass, the tiniest little animals in the world. Mother calls them a glass menagerie! Here's an example of one, if you'd like to see it! This one is one of the oldest. It's nearly thirteen. (*He stretches out his hand.*) (**Music: "The Glass Menagerie."**) Oh, be careful—if you breathe, it breaks!

Jim: I'd better not take it. I'm pretty clumsy with things.

Laura: Go on, I trust you with him! (*Places it in his palm.*) There now—you're hold-ing him gently! Hold him over the light, he loves the light! You see how the light shines through him?

Jim: It sure does shine!

Laura: I shouldn't be partial, but he is my favorite one.

Jim: What kind of a thing is this one supposed to be?

Laura: Haven't you noticed the single horn on his forehead?

Jim: A unicorn, huh?

Laura: Mmm-hmmm!

Jim: Unicorns—aren't they extinct in the modern world?

Laura: I know!

Jim: Poor little fellow, he must feel sort of lonesome.

Laura (smiling): Well, if he does, he doesn't complain about it. He stays on a shelf with some horses that don't have horns and all of them seem to get along nicely together.

Jim: How do you know?

Laura (lightly): I haven't heard any arguments among them!

Jim (grinning): No arguments, huh? Well, that's a pretty good sign! Where shall I set him?

Laura: Put him on the table. They all like a change of scenery once in a while!

Jim: Well, well, well, well— (*He places the glass piece on the table, then raises his arms and stretches.*) Look how big my shadow is when I stretch!

Laura: Oh, oh, yes—it stretches across the ceiling!

Jim (crossing to door): I think it's stopped raining. (*Opens fire-escape door.*) Where does the music come from?

Laura: From the Paradise Dance Hall across the alley.

Jim: How about cutting the rug a little, Miss Wingfield?

Laura: Oh, I—

Jim: Or is your program filled up? Let me have a look at it. (*Grasps imaginary card.*) Why, every dance is taken! I'll just have to scratch some out. (**Waltz Music: "La Golondrina."**) Ahhh, a waltz! (*He executes some sweeping turns by himself, then holds his arms toward Laura.*)

Laura (breathlessly): I—can't dance!

Jim: There you go, that inferiority stuff!

Laura: I've never danced in my life!

Jim: Come on, try!

Laura: Oh, but I'd step on you!

Jim: I'm not made out of glass.

Laura: How—how—how do we start?

Jim: Just leave it to me. You hold your arms out a little.

Laura: Like this?

Jim (taking her in his arms): A little bit higher. Right. Now don't tighten up, that's the main thing about it—relax.

Laura (laughing breathlessly): It's hard not to.

Jim: Okay.

Laura: I'm afraid you can't budge me.

Jim: What do you bet I can't? (*He swings her into motion.*)

Laura: Goodness, yes, you can!

Jim: Let yourself go, now, Laura, just let yourself go.

Laura: I'm—

Jim: Come on!

Laura: —trying!

Jim: Not so stiff—easy does it!

Laura: I know but I'm—

Jim: Loosen th' backbone! There now, that's a lot better.

Laura: Am I?

Jim: Lots, lots better! (*He moves her about the room in a clumsy waltz.*)

Laura: Oh, my!

Jim: Ha-ha!

Laura: Oh, my goodness!

Jim: Ha-ha-ha! (*They suddenly bump into the table, and the glass piece on it falls to the floor. Jim stops.*) What did we hit on?

Laura: Table.

Jim: Did something fall off it? I think—

Laura: Yes. (*She stoops to pick it up.*)

Jim: I hope that it wasn't the little glass horse with the horn!

Laura: Yes. (*she stoops to pick it up.*)

Jim: Aw, aw, aw. Is it broken?

Laura: Now it is just like all the other horses.

Jim: It's lost its—

Laura: Horn! It doesn't matter. Maybe it's a blessing in disguise.

Jim: You'll never forgive me. I bet that that was your favorite piece of glass.

Laura: I don't have favorites much. It's no tragedy, Freckles. Glass breaks so easily. No matter how careful you are. The traffic jars the shelves and things fall off them.

Jim: Still I'm awfully sorry that I was the cause.

Laura (smiling): I'll just imagine he had an operation. The horn was removed to make him feel less—freakish! (*They both laugh.*) Now he will feel more at home with the other horses, the ones that don't have horns . . .

Jim: Ha-ha, that's very funny! (*Suddenly serious.*) I'm glad to see that you have a sense of humor. You know—you're—well—very different! Surprisingly different from anyone else I know! (*His voice becomes soft and hesitant with a genuine feeling.*) Do you mind me telling you that? (*Laura is abashed beyond speech.*) I mean it in a nice way. You make me feel sort of—I don't know how to put it! I'm usually pretty good at expressing things, but—this is something that I don't know how to say! (*Laura touches her throat and clears it—turns the broken unicorn in her hands.*) (*Even softer.*) Has anyone ever told you that you were pretty? (**Pause: Music.**) (*Laura looks up slowly, with wonder, and shakes her head.*) Well, you are! In a very different way from anyone else. And all the nicer because of the difference, too. (*His voice becomes low and husky. Laura turns away, nearly faint with the novelty of her emotions.*) I wish you were my sister. I'd teach you to have some confidence in yourself. The different people are not like other people, but being different is nothing to be ashamed of. Because other people are not such wonderful people. They're one hundred times one thousand. You're one times one!

They walk all over the earth. You just stay here. They're common as—weeds, but—you—well, you're—*Blue Roses!*

(Image On Screen: Blue Roses.)

(Music Changes.)

Laura: But blue is wrong for—roses . . .

Jim: It's right for you! You're—pretty!

Laura: In what respect am I pretty?

Jim: In all respects—believe me! Your eyes—your hair—are pretty! Your hands are pretty! (*He catches hold of her hand.*) You think I'm making this up because I'm invited to dinner and have to be nice. Oh, I could do that! I could put on an act for you, Laura, and say lots of things without being very sincere. But this time I am. I'm talking to you sincerely. I happened to notice you had this inferiority complex that keeps you from feeling comfortable with people. Somebody needs to build your confidence up and make you proud instead of shy and turning away and—blushing—Somebody ought to—ought to—*kiss you, Laura!* (*His hand slips slowly up her arm to her shoulder.*) (**Music Swells Tumultuously.**) (*He suddenly turns her about and kisses her on the lips. When he releases her Laura sinks on the sofa with a bright, dazed look. Jim backs away and fishes in his pocket for a cigarette.*) (**Legend On Screen: "Souvenir."**) Stumble-john! (*He lights the cigarette, avoiding her look. There is a peal of girlish laughter from Amanda in the kitchen. Laura slowly raises and opens her hand. It still contains the little broken glass animal. She looks at it with a tender, bewildered expression.*) Stumble-john! I shouldn't have done that—That was way off the beam. You don't smoke, do you? (*She looks up, smiling, not hearing the question. He sits beside her a little gingerly. She looks at him speechlessly—waiting. He coughs decorously and moves a little farther aside as he considers the situation and senses her feelings, dimly, with perturbation. Gently.*) Would you—care for a—mint? (*She doesn't seem to hear him but her look grows brighter even.*) Peppermint—Life Saver? My pocket's a regular drug store—wherever I go . . . (*He pops a mint in his mouth. Then gulps and decides to make a clean breast of it. He speaks slowly and gingerly.*) Laura, you know, if I had a sister like you, I'd do the same thing as Tom, I'd bring out fellows—and introduce her to them. The right type of boys—of a type to—appreciate her. Only—well—he made a mistake about me. Maybe I've got no call to be saying this. That may not have been the idea in having me over. But what if it was? There's nothing wrong about that. The only trouble is that in my case—I'm not in a situation to—do the right thing. I can't take down your number and say I'll phone. I can't call up next week and—ask for a date. I thought I had better explain the situation in case you—misunderstood it and—I hurt your feelings. . . . (*Pause. Slowly, very slowly, Laura's look changes, her eyes returning slowly from his to the ornament in her palm.*)

Amanda utters another gay laugh in the kitchen.

Laura (*faintly*): You—won't—call again?

Jim: No, Laura, I can't. (*He rises from the sofa.*) As I was just explaining, I've—got strings on me, Laura, I've—been going steady! I go out all the time with a girl named Betty. She's a home-girl like you, and Catholic, and Irish, and in a great many ways we—get along fine. I met her last summer on a moonlight boat trip up the river to Alton, on the *Majestic*. Well—right away from the start it was—love! **(Legend: Love!)** (*Laura sways slightly forward and grips the arm of the sofa. He fails to notice, now enrapt in his own comfortable being.*) Being in love has made a new man of me! (*Leaning stiffly forward, clutching the arm of the sofa, Laura struggles visibly with her storm. But Jim is oblivious, she is a long way off.*) The power of love is really pretty tremendous! Love is something that—changes the whole world, Laura! (*The storm abates a little and Laura leans back. He notices her again.*) It happened that Betty's aunt took sick, she got a wire and had to go to Centralia. So Tom—when he asked me to dinner—I naturally just accepted the invitation, not knowing that you—that he—that I—(*He stops awkwardly.*) Huh—I'm a stumble-john! (*He flops back on the sofa. The holy candles in the altar of Laura's face have been snuffed out! There is a look of almost infinite desolation. Jim glances at her uneasily.*) I wish that you would—say something. (*She bites her lip which was trembling and then bravely smiles. She opens her hand again on the broken glass ornament. Then she gently takes his hand and raises it level with her own. She carefully places the unicorn in the palm of his hand, then pushes his fingers closed upon it.*) What are you—doing that for? You want me to have him?—Laura? (*She nods.*) What for?

Laura: A—souvenir . . .

She rises unsteadily and crouches beside the victrola to wind it up.

(Legend On Screen: "Things Have A Way Of Turning Out So Badly.")

(Or Image: "Gentleman Caller Waving Good-bye! Gaily.")

At this moment Amanda rushes brightly back in the front room. She bears a pitcher of fruit punch in an old-fashioned cut-glass pitcher and a plate of macaroons. The plate has a gold border and poppies painted on it.

Amanda: Well, well, well! Isn't the air delightful after the shower? I've made you children a little liquid refreshment. (*Turns gaily to the gentleman caller.*) Jim, do you know that song about lemonade?
      "Lemonade, lemonade
      Made in the shade and stirred with a spade—
      Good enough for any old maid!"

Jim (uneasily): Ha-ha! No—I never heard it.
Amanda: Why, Laura! You look so serious!
Jim: We were having a serious conversation.
Amanda: Good! Now you're better acquainted!
Jim (uncertainly): Ha-ha! Yes.
Amanda: You modern young people are much more serious-minded than my generation. I was so gay as a girl!
Jim: You haven't changed, Mrs. Wingfield.
Amanda: Tonight I'm rejuvenated! The gaiety of the occasion, Mr. O'Connor! (*She tosses her head with a peal of laughter. Spills lemonade.*) Oooo! I'm baptizing myself!
Jim: Here—let me—
Amanda (setting the pitcher down): There now. I discovered we had some maraschino cherries. I dumped them in, juice and all!

Jim: You shouldn't have gone to that trouble, Mrs. Wingfield.

Amanda: Trouble, trouble? Why it was loads of fun! Didn't you hear me cutting up in the kitchen? I bet your ears were burning! I told Tom how outdone with him I was for keeping you to himself so long a time! He should have brought you over much, much sooner! Well, now that you've found your way, I want you to be a very frequent caller! Not just occasional but all the time. Oh, we're going to have a lot of gay times together! I see them coming! Mmm, just breathe that air! So fresh, and the moon's so pretty! I'll skip back out—I know where my place is when young folks are having a—serious conversation!

Jim: Oh, don't go out, Mrs. Wingfield. The fact of the matter is I've got to be going.

Amanda: Going, now? You're joking! Why, it's only the shank of the evening, Mr. O'Connor!

Jim: Well, you know how it is.

Amanda: You mean you're a young workingman and have to keep workingmen's hours. We'll let you off early tonight. But only on the condition that next time you stay later. What's the best night for you? Isn't Saturday night the best night for you workingmen?

Jim: I have a couple of time-clocks to punch, Mrs. Wingfield. One at morning, another one at night!

Amanda: My, but you *are* ambitious! You work at night, too?

Jim: No, Ma'am, not work but—Betty! (*He crosses deliberately to pick up his hat. The band at the Paradise Dance Hall goes into a tender waltz.*)

Amanda: Betty? Betty? Who's—Betty? (*There is an ominous cracking sound in the sky.*)

Jim: Oh, just a girl. The girl I go steady with! (*He smiles charmingly. The sky falls.*)

(Legend: "The Sky Falls.")

Amanda (*a long-drawn exhalation*): Ohhhh . . . Is it a serious romance, Mr. O'Connor?

Jim: We're going to be married the second Sunday in June.

Amanda: Ohhhh—how nice! Tom didn't mention that you were engaged to be married.

Jim: The cat's not out of the bag at the warehouse yet. You know how they are. They call you Romeo and stuff like that. (*He stops at the oval mirror to put on his hat. He carefully shapes the brim and the crown to give a discreetly dashing effect.*) It's been a wonderful evening, Mrs. Wingfield. I guess this is what they mean by Southern hospitality.

Amanda: It really wasn't anything at all.

Jim: I hope it don't seem like I'm rushing off. But I promised Betty I'd pick her up at the Wabash depot, an' by the time I get my jalopy down there her train'll be in. Some women are pretty upset if you keep 'em waiting.

Amanda: Yes, I know—The tyranny of women! (*Extends her hand.*) Goodbye, Mr. O'Connor. I wish you luck—and happiness—and success! All three of them, and so does Laura!—Don't you, Laura?

Laura: Yes!

Jim (*taking her hand*): Goodbye, Laura. I'm certainly going to treasure that souvenir. And don't you forget the good advice I gave you. (*Raises his voice to a cheery shout.*) So long, Shakespeare! Thanks again, ladies—Good night!

He grins and ducks jauntily out.

Still bravely grimacing, Amanda closes the door on the gentleman caller. Then she turns back to the room with a puzzled expression. She and Laura don't dare to face each other. Laura crouches beside the victrola to wind it.

Amanda (faintly): Things have a way of turning out so badly. I don't believe that I would play the victrola. Well, well—well—Our gentleman caller was engaged to be married! *(She raises her voice.)* Tom!

Tom (from back): Yes, Mother?

Amanda: Come in here a minute. I want to tell you something awfully funny.

Tom (enters with macaroon and a glass of the lemonade): Has the gentleman caller gotten away already?

Amanda: The gentleman caller has made an early departure. What a wonderful joke you played on us!

Tom: How do you mean?

Amanda: You didn't mention that he was engaged to be married.

Tom: Jim? Engaged?

Amanda: That's what he just informed us.

Tom: I'll be jiggered! I didn't know about that.

Amanda: That seems very peculiar.

Tom: What's peculiar about it?

Amanda: Didn't you call him your best friend down at the warehouse?

Tom: He is, but how did I know?

Amanda: It seems extremely peculiar that you wouldn't know your best friend was going to be married!

Tom: The warehouse is where I work, not where I know things about people!

Amanda: You don't know things anywhere! You live in a dream; you manufacture illusions! *(He crosses to door.)* Where are you going?

Tom: I'm going to the movies.

Amanda: That's right, now that you've had us make such fools of ourselves. The effort, the preparations, all the expense! The new floor lamp, the rug, the clothes for Laura! All for what? To entertain some other girl's fiancé! Go to the movies, go! Don't think about us, a mother deserted, an unmarried sister who's crippled and has no job! Don't let anything interfere with your selfish pleasure! Just go, go, go—to the movies!

Tom: All right, I will! The more you shout about my selfishness to me the quicker I'll go, and I won't go to the movies!

Amanda: Go, then! Then go to the moon—you selfish dreamer!

Tom smashes his glass on the floor. He plunges out on the fire-escape, slamming the door. Laura screams—cut by door.

Dance-hall music up. Tom goes to the rail and grips it desperately, lifting his face in the chill white moonlight penetrating the narrow abyss of the alley.

(Legend On Screen: "And So Good-bye . . .")

Tom's closing speech is timed with the interior pantomime. The interior scene is played as though viewed through sound-proof glass. Amanda appears to be making a comforting speech to Laura who is huddled upon the sofa. Now that we cannot hear the mother's speech, her silliness is gone and she has dignity and tragic beauty. Laura's dark hair hides her face until at the end of the speech she lifts it to smile at her mother. Amanda's gestures are slow and graceful, almost dancelike, as she comforts the daughter. At the end of her speech she glances a moment at the father's picture—then withdraws through the portieres. At close of Tom's speech, Laura blows out the candles, ending the play.

Tom: I didn't go to the moon, I went much further—for time is the longest distance between two places—Not long after that I was fired for writing a poem on the lid of a shoe-box. I left Saint Louis. I descended the steps of this fire-escape for a last time and followed, from then on, in my father's footsteps, attempting to find in motion what was lost in space. I traveled around a great deal. The cities swept about me like dead leaves, leaves that were brightly colored but torn away from the branches. I would have stopped, but I was pursued by something. It always came upon me unawares, taking me altogether by surprise. Perhaps it was a familiar bit of music. Perhaps it was only a piece of transparent glass. Perhaps I am walking along a street at night, in some strange city, before I have found companions. I pass the lighted window of a shop where perfume is sold. The window is filled with pieces of colored glass, tiny transparent bottles in delicate colors, like bits of a shattered rainbow. Then all at once my sister touches my shoulder. I turn around and look into her eyes. . . . Oh, Laura, Laura, I tried to leave you behind me, but I am more faithful than I intended to be! I reach for a cigarette, I cross the street, I run into the movies or a bar, I buy a drink, I speak to the nearest stranger—anything that can blow your candles out! *Laura bends over the candles.* For nowadays the world is lit by lightning! Blow out your candles, Laura— and so good-bye— .

She blows the candles out.

Questions

1. How do Amanda's dreams for her daughter contrast with the realities of the Wingfields' day-to-day existence?
2. What suggestions do you find in Laura's glass menagerie? In the glass unicorn?
3. In the cast of characters, Jim O'Connor is listed as "a nice, ordinary, young man." Why does his coming to dinner have such earthshaking implications for Amanda? For Laura?
4. Try to describe Jim's feelings toward Laura during their long conversation in Scene VII. After he kisses her, how do his feelings seem to change?
5. Near the end of the play, Amanda tells Tom, "You live in a dream; you manufacture illusions!" What is ironic about her speech? Is there any truth in it?
6. Who is the main character in *The Glass Menagerie*? Tom? Laura? Amanda? (It may be helpful to review the definition of a protagonist.)
7. Has Tom, at the conclusion of the play, successfully made his escape from home? Does he appear to have fulfilled his dream?
8. How effective is the device of accompanying the action by projecting slides on a screen, bearing titles and images? Do you think most producers of the play are wise to leave it out?

Tennessee Williams on Writing

How to Stage *The Glass Menagerie*   1945

Being a "memory play," *The Glass Menagerie* can be presented with unusual freedom of convention. Because of its considerably delicate or tenuous material, atmospheric touches and subtleties of direction play a particularly important part. Expressionism and all other unconventional techniques in drama have only one valid aim, and that is a closer approach to truth. When a play employs unconventional techniques, it is not, or certainly shouldn't be, trying to escape its responsibility of dealing with reality, or interpreting experience, but is actually or should be attempting to find a closer approach, a more penetrating and vivid expression of things as they are. The straight realistic play with its genuine Frigidaire and

Tennessee Williams

authentic ice-cubes, its characters that speak exactly as its audience speaks, corresponds to the academic landscape and has the same virtue of a photographic likeness. Everyone should know nowadays the unimportance of the photographic in art: that truth, life, or reality is an organic thing which the poetic imagination can represent or suggest, in essence, only through transformation, through changing into other forms than those which were merely present in appearance.

These remarks are not meant as a preface only to this particular play. They have to do with a conception of a new, plastic theater which must take the place of the exhausted theater of realistic conventions if the theater is to resume vitality as a part of our culture.

THE SCREEN DEVICE. There is *only one important difference between the original and acting version of the play* and that is the *omission* in the latter of the device which I tentatively included in my *original* script. This device was the use of a screen on which were projected magic-lantern slides bearing images or titles. I do not regret the omission of this device from the present Broadway production. The extraordinary power of Miss Taylor's performance° made it suitable to have the utmost simplicity in the physical production. But I think it may be interesting to some readers to see how this device was conceived. So I am putting it into the published manuscript. These images and legends, projected from behind, were cast on a section of wall between the front-room and dining-room areas, which should be indistinguishable from the rest when not in use.

The purpose of this will probably be apparent. It is to give accent to certain values in each case. Each scene contains a particular point (or several) which is structurally the most important. In an episodic play, such as this, the basic structure or narrative line may be obscured from the audience; the effect may seem fragmentary

Miss Taylor's performance: In the original Broadway production of the play in 1945 the role of Amanda Wingfield, the mother, was played by veteran actress Laurette Taylor.

rather than architectural. This may not be the fault of the play so much as a lack of attention in the audience. The legend or image upon the screen will strengthen the effect of what is merely allusion in the writing and allow the primary point to be made more simply and lightly than if the entire responsibility were on the spoken lines. Aside from this structural value, I think the screen will have a definite emotional appeal, less definable but just as important. An imaginative producer or director may invent many other uses for this device than those indicated in the present script. In fact the possibilities of the device seem much larger to me than the instance of this play can possibly utilize.

THE MUSIC. Another extra-literary accent in this play is provided by the use of music. A single recurring tune, "The Glass Menagerie," is used to give emotional emphasis to suitable passages. This tune is like circus music, not when you are on the grounds or in the immediate vicinity of the parade, but when you are at some distance and very likely thinking of something else. It seems under those circumstances to continue almost interminably and it weaves in and out of your preoccupied consciousness; then it is the lightest, most delicate music in the world and perhaps the saddest. It expresses the surface vivacity of life with the underlying strain of immutable and inexpressible sorrow. When you look at a piece of delicately spun glass you think of two things: how beautiful it is and how easily it can be broken. Both of those ideas should be woven into the recurring tune, which dips in and out of the play as if it were carried on a wind that changes. It serves as a thread of connection and allusion between the narrator with his separate point in time and space and the subject of his story. Between each episode it returns as reference to the emotion, nostalgia, which is the first condition of the play. It is primarily Laura's music and therefore comes out most clearly when the play focuses upon her and the lovely fragility of glass which is her image.

THE LIGHTING. The lighting in the play is not realistic. In keeping with the atmosphere of memory, the stage is dim. Shafts of light are focused on selected areas or actors, sometimes in contradistinction to what is the apparent center. For instance, in the quarrel scene between Tom and Amanda, in which Laura has no active part, the clearest pool of light is on her figure. This is also true of the supper scene, when her silent figure on the sofa should remain the visual center. The light upon Laura should be distinct from the others, having a peculiar pristine clarity such as light used in early religious portraits of female saints or madonnas. A certain correspondence to light in religious paintings, such as El Greco's, where the figures are radiant in atmosphere that is relatively dusky, could be effectively used throughout the play. (It will also permit a more effective use of the screen.) A free, imaginative use of light can be of enormous value in giving a mobile, plastic quality to plays of a more or less static nature.

From the author's production notes for *The Glass Menagerie*

TRAGICOMEDY AND THE ABSURD

One of the more prominent developments in mid-twentieth-century drama was the rise of **tragicomedies,** plays that stir us not only to pity and fear (echoing Aristotle's description of the effect of tragedy) but also to laughter. Although tragicomedy is a kind of drama we think distinctively modern, it is by no means new. The term was used (although jokingly) by the Roman writer of comedy Plautus in about 185 B.C.

Shakespeare's darker comedies such as *Measure for Measure* and *The Merchant of Venice* deal so forcefully with such stark themes as lust, greed, racism, revenge, and cruelty that they often seem like tragedies until their happy endings. In the tragedies of Shakespeare and others, passages of clownish humor are sometimes called **comic relief**, meaning that the section of comedy introduces a sharp contrast in mood. But such passages can do more than provide relief. In *Othello* (3.4.1–16) the clown's banter with Desdemona for a moment makes the surrounding tragedy seem, by comparison, more poignant and intense.

No one doubts that *Othello* is a tragedy, but some twentieth-century plays leave us both bemused and confused: should we laugh or cry? One of the most talked-about plays after World War II, Samuel Beckett's *Waiting for Godot* (1953) portrays two clownish tramps who mark time in a wasteland, wistfully looking for a savior who never arrives. Modern drama, by the way, has often featured such **antiheroes**: ordinary people, inglorious and inarticulate, who carry on not from bravery but from inertia. We cannot help laughing, in *Godot*, at the tramps' painful situation; but, turning the idea around, we also feel deeply moved by their ridiculous plight. Perhaps a modern tragicomedy like *Godot* does not show us great souls suffering greatly—as we observe in a classical tragedy—but Beckett's play nonetheless touches mysteriously on the universal sorrows of human existence.

Straddling the fence between tragedy and comedy, the plays of some modern playwrights portray people whose suffering seems ridiculous. These plays belong to the **theater of the absurd:** a general name for a type of play first staged in Paris in the 1950s. "For the modern critical spirit, nothing can be taken entirely seriously, nor entirely lightly," said Eugène Ionesco, one of the movement's leading playwrights. Behind the literary conventions of the theater of the absurd stands a philosophical fear that human existence has no meaning. Every person, such playwrights assume, is a helpless waif alone in a universe full of ridiculous obstacles. In Ionesco's *Rhinoceros* (1958), the human race starts turning into rhinos, except for one man, who remains human and isolated. A favorite theme in the theater of the absurd is that communication between people is impossible. Language is therefore futile. Ionesco's *The Bald Soprano* (1948) accordingly pokes fun at polite social conversation in a scene whose dialogue consists entirely of illogical strings of catchphrases.

RETURN TO REALISM

Trends in drama change along with playwrights' convictions, and during the 1970s and 1980s the theater of the absurd no longer seemed the dominant influence on new drama in America. Along with other protests of the 1960s, experimental theater seemed to have spent its force. During the later period most of the critically celebrated new plays were neither absurd nor experimental. David Mamet's *American Buffalo* (1975) realistically portrays three petty thieves in a junk shop as they plot to steal a coin collection. Albert Innaurato's *Gemini* (1977) takes a realistic (and comic) view of family life and sexual awakening in one of Philadelphia's Italian neighborhoods. Beth Henley's 1979 Pulitzer Prize–winning play *Crimes of the Heart* presents an eccentric but still believable group of sisters in a small Southern town. The dialogue in all three plays shows high fidelity to ordinary speech. Meanwhile, many of the most influential plays of **feminist theater,** which explores the lives, problems, and occasional triumphs of contemporary women, were also written in a realistic style. Notable success—with both critics and the ticket-buying public—greeted plays such as Marsha Norman's *'night, Mother* (1983), Tina Howe's *Painting Churches* (1983), and Wendy Wasserstein's *The Heidi Chronicles* (1988).

Some leading critics, among them Richard Gilman, believed that the American theater had entered an era of "new naturalism." Indeed many plays of this time subjected the lives of people, especially poor and unhappy people, to a realistic, searching light, showing the forces that shaped them. Sam Shepard in *Buried Child* (1978) explores violence and desperation in a family that dwells on the edge of poverty; while August Wilson in *Joe Turner's Come and Gone* (1988) convincingly portrays life in a Pittsburgh ghetto lodging house. But if these newly established playwrights sometimes showed life as frankly as did the earlier Naturalists, many also employed rich and suggestive symbolism.

EXPERIMENTAL DRAMA

In the latter part of the twentieth century, experimental drama, greatly influenced by the traditions of earlier Symbolist, Expressionist, and absurdist theater, continued to flourish. For example, David Hwang's work combines realistic elements with ritualistic and symbolic devices drawn from Asian theater (see his one-act play, *The Sound of a Voice*, in "Plays for Further Reading"). Caryl Churchill's *Top Girls* (1982) presents a dinner party in which a contemporary woman invites legendary women from history to a dinner party in a restaurant. Tony Kushner's *Angels in America* (1992) also mixes realism and fantasy to dramatize the plight of AIDS. Shel Silverstein, popular author of children's poetry, wrote a raucous one-man play, *The Devil and Billy Markham* (1991), entirely in rime, about a series of fantastic adventures in hell featuring a hard-drinking gambler and the Prince of Darkness. Silverstein's play is simultaneously experimental in form but traditional in content with its homage to American ballads and tall tales.

Experimental theater continues to exert a strong influence on contemporary drama. The following play, Milcha Sanchez-Scott's *The Cuban Swimmer*, deftly assimilates several dramatic styles—symbolism, new naturalism, ethnic drama, theater of the absurd—to create a brilliant original work. The play is simultaneously a family drama, a Latin comedy, a religious parable, and a critique of a media-obsessed American culture.

Milcha Sanchez-Scott

The Cuban Swimmer   1984

Milcha Sanchez-Scott was born in 1955 on the island of Bali. Her father was Colombian. Her mother was Chinese, Indonesian, and Dutch. Her father's work as an agronomist required constant travel, so when the young Sanchez-Scott reached school age, she was sent to a convent boarding school near London where she first learned English. Colombia, however, remained the family's one permanent home. Every Christmas and summer vacation was spent on a ranch in San Marta, Colombia, where four generations of family lived together. When she was fourteen, Sanchez-Scott's family moved to California. After attending the University of San Diego, where she majored in literature and philosophy, she worked at the San Diego Zoo and later at an employment agency in Los Angeles. Her first play, Latina, premiered in 1980 and won seven Drama-Logue awards. Dog Lady and The Cuban Swimmer followed in 1984. Sanchez-Scott then went to New York for a year to work with playwright Irene Fornes, in whose theater workshop she developed Roosters (1988). A feature-film version of Roosters, starring Edward James Olmos, was released in

1995. Her other plays include Evening Star (*1989*), El Dorado (*1990*), *and* The Old Matador (*1995*). *Sanchez-Scott lives in Los Angeles.*

CHARACTERS

Margarita Suárez, the swimmer
Eduardo Suárez, her father, the coach
Simón Suárez, her brother
Aída Suárez, her mother
Abuela, her grandmother
Voice of Mel Munson
Voice of Mary Beth White
Voice of Radio Operator

SETTING. *The Pacific Ocean between San Pedro and Catalina Island.*

TIME. *Summer.*

Live conga drums can be used to punctuate the action of the play.

SCENE I

Pacific Ocean. Midday. On the horizon, in perspective, a small boat enters upstage left, crosses to upstage right, and exits. Pause. Lower on the horizon, the same boat, in larger perspective, enters upstage right, crosses and exits upstage left. Blackout.

SCENE II

Pacific Ocean. Midday. The swimmer, Margarita Suárez, is swimming. On the boat following behind her are her father, Eduardo Suárez, holding a megaphone, and Simón, her brother, sitting on top of the cabin with his shirt off, punk sunglasses on, binoculars hanging on his chest.

Eduardo (leaning forward, shouting in time to Margarita's swimming): Uno, dos, uno, dos. Y uno, dos° . . . keep your shoulders parallel to the water.
Simón: I'm gonna take these glasses off and look straight into the sun.
Eduardo (through megaphone): Muy bien, muy bien° . . . but punch those arms in, baby.
Simón (looking directly at the sun through binoculars): Come on, come on, zap me. Show me something. (*He looks behind at the shoreline and ahead at the sea.*) Stop! Stop, *Papi!* Stop!

(*Aída Suárez and Abuela, the swimmer's mother and grandmother, enter running from the back of the boat.*)

Aída and Abuela: Qué? Qué es?°
Aída: Es un shark?°
Eduardo: Eh?
Abuela: Que es un shark dicen?°

(*Eduardo blows whistle. Margarita looks up at the boat.*)

Simón: No, *Papi,* no shark, no shark. We've reached the halfway mark.

Uno, dos, uno, dos. Y uno, dos: One, two, one, two. And one, two. *Muy bien, muy bien:* Very good, very good. *Qué? Qué es?:* What? What is it? *Es un shark?:* Is it a shark? *Que es un shark dicen?:* Did they say a shark?

2005 production of *The Cuban Swimmer* at the People's Light & Theatre, Malvern, Pennsylvania.

Abuela (looking into the water): A dónde está?°

Aída: It's not in the water.

Abuela: Oh, no? Oh, no?

Aída: No! A *poco* do you think they're gonna have signs in the water to say you are halfway to Santa Catalina? No. It's done very scientific. A *ver, hijo,*° explain it to your grandma.

Simón: Well, you see, Abuela—(*He points behind.*) There's San Pedro. (*He points ahead.*) And there's Santa Catalina. Looks halfway to me.

(*Abuela shakes her head and is looking back and forth, trying to make the decision, when suddenly the sound of a helicopter is heard.*)

Abuela (looking up): Virgencita de la Caridad del Cobre. Qué es eso?°

(*Sound of helicopter gets closer. Margarita looks up.*)

A dónde está?: Where is it?   A ver, hijo: Look here, son.   Virgencita de la Caridad del Cobre. Qué es eso?: Virgin of Charity! What is that?

Margarita: Papi, Papi!

(*A small commotion on the boat, with everybody pointing at the helicopter above. Shadows of the helicopter fall on the boat. Simón looks up at it through binoculars.*)

Papi—qué es? What is it?

Eduardo (*through megaphone*): Uh . . . uh . . . uh, *un momentico* . . . *mi hija.*° . . . Your papi's got everything under control, understand? Uh . . . you just keep stroking. And stay . . . uh . . . close to the boat.

Simón: Wow, *Papi!* We're on TV, man! Holy Christ, we're all over the fucking U.S.A.! It's Mel Munson and Mary Beth White!

Aída: Por Dios!° Simón, don't swear. And put on your shirt.

(*Aída fluffs her hair, puts on her sunglasses and waves to the helicopter. Simón leans over the side of the boat and yells to Margarita.*)

Simón: Yo, Margo! You're on TV, man.

Eduardo: Leave your sister alone. Turn on the radio.

Margarita: Papi! Qué está pasando?°

Abuela: Que es la televisión dicen? (*She shakes her head.*) Porque como yo no puedo ver nada sin mis espejuelos.°

(*Abuela rummages through the boat, looking for her glasses. Voices of Mel Munson and Mary Beth White are heard over the boat's radio.*)

Mel's Voice: As we take a closer look at the gallant crew of *La Havana* . . . and there . . . yes, there she is . . . the little Cuban swimmer from Long Beach, California, nineteen-year-old Margarita Suárez. The unknown swimmer is our Cinderella entry . . . a bundle of tenacity, battling her way through the choppy, murky waters of the cold Pacific to reach the Island of Romance . . . Santa Catalina . . . where should she be the first to arrive, two thousand dollars and a gold cup will be waiting for her.

Aída: Doesn't even cover our expenses.

Abuela: Qué dice?

Eduardo: Shhhh!

Mary Beth's Voice: This is really a family effort, Mel, and—

Mel's Voice: Indeed it is. Her trainer, her coach, her mentor, is her father, Eduardo Suárez. Not a swimmer himself, it says here, Mr. Suárez is head usher of the Holy Name Society and the owner-operator of Suárez Treasures of the Sea and Salvage Yard. I guess it's one of those places—

Mary Beth's Voice: If I might interject a fact here, Mel, assisting in this swim is Mrs. Suárez, who is a former Miss Cuba.

Mel's Voice: And a beautiful woman in her own right. Let's try and get a closer look.

(*Helicopter sound gets louder. Margarita, frightened, looks up again.*)

Margarita: Papi!

---

un momentico . . . mi hija: Just a second, my daughter.   *Por Dios!:* For God's Sake!   *Papi! Qué está pasando?:* Dad. What's happening?   *Que es la televisión dicen? Porque como yo no puedo ver nada sin mis espejuelos:* Did they say television? Because I can't see without my glasses.

Eduardo (*through megaphone*): *Mi hija,* don't get nervous . . . it's the press. I'm handling it.

Aída: I see how you're handling it.

Eduardo (*through megaphone*): Do you hear? Everything is under control. Get back into your rhythm. Keep your elbows high and kick and kick and kick and kick . . .

Abuela (*finds her glasses and puts them on*): *Ay sí, es la televisión* . . . (*She points to helicopter.*) *Qué lindo mira* . . . (*She fluffs her hair, gives a big wave.*) *Aló América! Viva mi Margarita, viva todo los Cubanos en los Estados Unidos!*°

Aída: *Ay por Dios,* Cecilia, the man didn't come all this way in his helicopter to look at you jumping up and down, making a fool of yourself.

Abuela: I don't care. I'm proud.

Aída: He can't understand you anyway.

Abuela: *Viva* . . . (*She stops.*) Simón, *cómo se dice viva?*°

Simón: Hurray.

Abuela: Hurray for *mi Margarita* y for all the Cubans living *en* the United States, *y un abrazo* . . . Simón, *abrazo* . . .

Simón: A big hug.

Abuela: *Sí,* a big hug to all my friends in Miami, Long Beach, Union City, except for my son Carlos, who lives in New York in sin! He lives . . . (*She crosses herself.*) in Brooklyn with a Puerto Rican woman in sin! *No decente* . . .

Simón: Decent.

Abuela: Carlos, *no decente.* This family, *decente.*

Aída: Cecilia, *por Dios.*

Mel's Voice: Look at that enthusiasm. The whole family has turned out to cheer little Margarita on to victory! I hope they won't be too disappointed.

Mary Beth's Voice: She seems to be making good time, Mel.

Mel's Voice: Yes, it takes all kinds to make a race. And it's a testimonial to the all-encompassing fairness . . . the greatness of this, the Wrigley Invitational Women's Swim to Catalina, where among all the professionals there is still room for the amateurs . . . like these, the simple people we see below us on the ragtag *La Havana,* taking their long-shot chance to victory. *Vaya con Dios!*°

(*Helicopter sound fading as family, including Margarita, watch silently. Static as Simón turns radio off. Eduardo walks to bow of boat, looks out on the horizon.*)

Eduardo (*to himself*): Amateurs.

Aída: Eduardo, that person insulted us. Did you hear, Eduardo? That he called us a simple people in a ragtag boat? Did you hear . . . ?

Abuela (*clenching her fist at departing helicopter*): *Mal-Rayo los parta!*°

Simón (*same gesture*): Asshole!

(*Aída follows Eduardo as he goes to side of boat and stares at Margarita.*)

Aída: This person comes in his helicopter to insult your wife, your family, your daughter . . .

Aló América! Viva mi Margarita, viva todo los Cubanos en los Estados Unidos!: Hello America! Hurray for my Margarita, hurray for all the Cubans in the United States! *cómo se dice viva?:* How do you say "viva" [in English]? *Vaya con Dios!:* Go with God. [God bless you.] *Mal-Rayo los parta!:* To hell with you!

Margarita (pops her head out of the water): Papi?

Aída: Do you hear me, Eduardo? I am not simple.

Abuela: Sí.

Aída: I am complicated.

Abuela: Sí, demasiada complicada.

Aída: Me and my family are not so simple.

Simón: Mom, the guy's an asshole.

Abuela (shaking her fist at helicopter): Asshole!

Aída: If my daughter was simple, she would not be in that water swimming.

Margarita: Simple? *Papi . . . ?*

Aída: Ahora, Eduardo, this is what I want you to do. When we get to Santa Catalina, I want you to call the TV station and demand an apology.

Eduardo: Cállete mujer! Aquí mando yo.° I will decide what is to be done.

Margarita: Papi, tell me what's going on.

Eduardo: Do you understand what I am saying to you, Aída?

Simón (leaning over side of boat, to Margarita): Yo Margo! You know that Mel Munson guy on TV? He called you a simple amateur and said you didn't have a chance.

Abuela (leaning directly behind Simón.): Mi hija, insultó a la familia. Desgraciado!

Aída (leaning in behind Abuela): He called us peasants! And your father is not doing anything about it. He just knows how to yell at me.

Eduardo (through megaphone): Shut up! All of you! Do you want to break her concentration? Is that what you are after? Eh?

(*Abuela, Aída and Simón shrink back. Eduardo paces before them.*)

Swimming is rhythm and concentration. You win a race *aquí.* (*Pointing to his head.*) Now . . . (*To Simón.*) you, take care of the boat, *Aída y Mama* . . . do something. Anything. Something practical.

(*Abuela and Aída get on knees and pray in Spanish.*)

Hija, give it everything, eh? . . . por la familia. Uno . . . dos. . . . You must win.

(*Simón goes into cabin. The prayers continue as lights change to indicate bright sunlight, later in the afternoon.*)

SCENE III

Tableau for a couple of beats. Eduardo on bow with timer in one hand as he counts strokes per minute. Simón is in the cabin steering, wearing his sunglasses, baseball cap on backward. Abuela and Aída are at the side of the boat, heads down, hands folded, still muttering prayers in Spanish.

Aída and Abuela (crossing themselves): En el nombre del Padre, del Hijo y del Espíritu Santo amén.°

Eduardo (through megaphone): You're stroking seventy-two!

Simón (singing): Mama's stroking, Mama's stroking seventy-two. . . .

Cállete mujer! Aquí mando yo: Quiet! I'm in charge here.   En el nombre del Padre, del Hijo y del Espíritu Santo amén: In the name of the Father, the Son, and the Holy Ghost, Amen.

Eduardo (through megaphone): You comfortable with it?

Simón (singing): Seventy-two, seventy-two, seventy-two for you.

Aída (looking at the heavens): Ay, Eduardo, *ven acá,°* we should be grateful that *Nuestro Señor°* gave us such a beautiful day.

Abuela (crosses herself): *Sí, gracias a Dios.°*

Eduardo: She's stroking seventy-two, with no problem *(He throws a kiss to the sky.)* It's a beautiful day to win.

Aída: *Qué hermoso!°* So clear and bright. Not a cloud in the sky. *Mira! Mira!°* Even rainbows on the water . . . a sign from God.

Simón (singing.): Rainbows on the water . . . you in my arms . . .

Abuela and Eduardo (looking the wrong way): *Dónde?*

Aída (pointing toward Margarita): There, dancing in front of Margarita, leading her on . . .

Eduardo: Rainbows on . . . Ay coño! It's an oil slick! You . . . you . . . *(To Simón.)* Stop the boat. *(Runs to bow, yelling.)* Margarita! Margarita!

(On the next stroke, Margarita comes up all covered in black oil.)

Margarita: Papi! Papi . . . !

(Everybody goes to the side and stares at Margarita, who stares back. Eduardo freezes.)

Aída: Apúrate, Eduardo, move . . . what's wrong with you . . . *no me oíste,°* get my daughter out of the water.

Eduardo (softly): We can't touch her. If we touch her, she's disqualified.

Aída: But I'm her mother.

Eduardo: Not even by her own mother. Especially by her own mother. . . . You always want the rules to be different for you, you always want to be the exception. *(To Simón.)* And you . . . you didn't see it, eh? You were playing again?

Simón: *Papi,* I was watching . . .

Aída (interrupting): *Pues,* do something Eduardo. You are the big coach, the monitor.

Simón: Mentor! Mentor!

Eduardo: How can a person think around you? *(He walks off to bow, puts head in hands.)*

Abuela (looking over side): Mira como todos los little birds are dead. *(She crosses herself)*

Aída: Their little wings are glued to their sides.

Simón: Christ, this is like the La Brea tar pits.

Aída: They can't move their little wings.

Abuela: *Esa niña tiene que moverse.°*

Simón: Yeah, Margo, you gotta move, man.

(Abuela and Simón gesture for Margarita to move. Aída gestures for her to swim.)

Abuela: Anda niña, muévete.°

---

ven acá: Look here.   *Nuestro Señor:* Our Father [God].   *Sí, gracias a Dios:* Yes, thanks be to God. *Qué hermoso!:* How beautiful!   *Mira!:* look.   *Apúrate . . . no me oíste:* Finish this! . . . didn't you hear me?   *Esa niña tiene que moverse:* That girl has to move.   *Anda niña, muévete:* Come on, girl, Move!

Aída: Swim, *hija*, swim or the *aceite*° will stick to your wings.
Margarita: Papi?
Abuela (taking megaphone): Your *papi* say "move it!"

   (*Margarita with difficulty starts moving.*)

Abuela, Aída and Simón (laboriously counting): Uno, dos . . . uno, dos . . . anda . . .
   uno, dos.
Eduardo (running to take megaphone from Abuela): Uno, dos . . .

   (*Simón races into cabin and starts the engine. Abuela, Aída and Eduardo count together.*)

Simón (looking ahead): Papi, it's over there!
Eduardo: Eh?
Simón (pointing ahead and to the right): It's getting clearer over there.
Eduardo (through megaphone): Now pay attention to me. Go to the right.

   (*Simón, Abuela, Aída and Eduardo all lean over side. They point ahead and to the right, except Abuela, who points to the left.*)

Family (shouting together): Para yá!° Para yá!

   (*Lights go down on boat. A special light on Margarita, swimming through the oil, and on Abuela, watching her.*)

Abuela: Sangre de mi sangre,° you will be another to save us. En Bolondron, where
   your great-grandmother Luz Suárez was born, they say one day it rained blood.
   All the people, they run into their houses. They cry, they pray, *pero* your great-
   grandmother Luz she had *cojones* like a man. She run outside. She look straight
   at the sky. She shake her fist. And she say to the evil one, "Mira . . . (*Beating her
   chest.*) coño, Diablo, aquí estoy si me quieres."° And she open her mouth, and she
   drunk the blood.

BLACKOUT

SCENE IV

*Lights up on boat. Aída and Eduardo are on deck watching Margarita swim. We hear the
gentle, rhythmic lap, lap, lap of the water, then the sound of inhaling and exhaling as Margarita's breathing becomes louder. Then Margarita's heartbeat is heard, with the lapping of
the water and the breathing under it. These sounds continue beneath the dialogue to the end
of the scene.*

Aída: Dios mío. Look how she moves through the water. . . .
Eduardo: You see, it's very simple. It is a matter of concentration.
Aída: The first time I put her in water she came to life, she grew before my eyes. She
   moved, she smiled, she loved it more than me. She didn't want my breast any
   longer. She wanted the water.

---

aceite: oil.   *Para yá:* over there.   *Sangre de mi sangre:* blood of my blood.   *Mira . . . coño, Diablo,
aquí estoy si me quieres:* Look . . . damn it Devil, here I am if you want me.

Eduardo: And of course, the rhythm. The rhythm takes away the pain and helps the concentration.

(*Pause. Aída and Eduardo watch Margarita.*)

Aída: Is that my child or a seal. . . .

Eduardo: Ah, a seal, the reason for that is that she's keeping her arms very close to her body. She cups her hands, and then she reaches and digs, reaches and digs.

Aída: To think that a daughter of mine. . . .

Eduardo: It's the training, the hours in the water. I used to tie weights around her little wrists and ankles.

Aída: A spirit, an ocean spirit, must have entered my body when I was carrying her.

Eduardo (to Margarita): Your stroke is slowing down.

(*Pause. We hear Margarita's heartbeat with the breathing under, faster now.*)

Aída: Eduardo, that night, the night on the boat . . .

Eduardo: Ah, the night on the boat again . . . the moon was . . .

Aída: The moon was full. We were coming to America. . . . *Qué romantico.*

(*Heartbeat and breathing continue.*)

Eduardo: We were cold, afraid, with no money, and on top of everything, you were hysterical, yelling at me, tearing at me with your nails. (*Opens his shirt, points to the base of his neck.*) Look, I still bear the scars . . . telling me that I didn't know what I was doing . . . saying that we were going to die. . . .

Aída: You took me, you stole me from my home . . . you didn't give me a chance to prepare. You just said we have to go now, now! Now, you said. You didn't let me take anything. I left everything behind. . . . I left everything behind.

Eduardo: Saying that I wasn't good enough, that your father didn't raise you so that I could drown you in the sea.

Aída: You didn't let me say even a good-bye. You took me, you stole me, you tore me from my home.

Eduardo: I took you so we could be married.

Aída: That was in Miami. But that night on the boat, Eduardo. . . . We were not married, that night on the boat.

Eduardo: *No pasó nada!°* Once and for all get it out of your head, it was cold, you hated me, and we were afraid. . . .

Aída: *Mentiroso!°*

Eduardo: A man can't do it when he is afraid.

Aída: Liar! You did it very well.

Eduardo: I did?

Aída: *Sí.* Gentle. You were so gentle and then strong . . . my passion for you so deep. Standing next to you . . . I would ache . . . looking at your hands I would forget to breathe, you were irresistible.

Eduardo: I was?

Aída: You took me into your arms, you touched my face with your fingertips . . . you kissed my eyes . . . *la esquina de la boca y* . . .

No pasó nada!: Nothing happened.   *Mentiroso!:* Liar!

Eduardo: Sí, Sí, and then . . .

Aída: I look at your face on top of mine, and I see the lights of Havana in your eyes. That's when you seduced me.

Eduardo: Shhh, they're gonna hear you.

(*Lights go down. Special on Aída.*)

Aída: That was the night. A woman doesn't forget those things . . . and later that night was the dream . . . the dream of a big country with fields of fertile land and big, giant things growing. And there by a green, slimy pond I found a giant pea pod and when I opened it, it was full of little, tiny baby frogs.

(*Aída crosses herself as she watches Margarita. We hear louder breathing and heartbeat.*)

Margarita: Santa Teresa. Little Flower of God, pray for me. San Martín de Porres, pray for me. Santa Rosa de Lima, *Virgencita de la Caridad del Cobre,* pray for me. . . . Mother pray for me.

SCENE V

Loud howling of wind is heard, as lights change to indicate unstable weather, fog and mist. Family on deck, braced and huddled against the wind. Simón is at the helm.

Aída: Ay Dios mío, qué viento.°

Eduardo (*through megaphone*): Don't drift out . . . that wind is pushing you out. (*To Simón.*) You! Slow down. Can't you see your sister is drifting out?

Simón: It's the wind, *Papi.*

Aída: Baby, don't go so far. . . .

Abuela (*to heaven*): Ay Gran Poder de Dios, quita este maldito viento.°

Simón: Margo! Margo! Stay close to the boat.

Eduardo: Dig in. Dig in hard. . . . Reach down from your guts and dig in.

Abuela (*to heaven*): Ay Virgen de la Caridad del Cobre, por lo más tú quieres a pararla.

Aída (*putting her hand out, reaching for Margarita*): Baby, don't go far.

(*Abuela crosses herself. Action freezes. Lights get dimmer, special on Margarita. She keeps swimming, stops, starts again, stops, then, finally exhausted, stops altogether. The boat stops moving.*)

Eduardo: What's going on here? Why are we stopping?

Simón: Papi, she's not moving! Yo Margo!

(*The family all run to the side.*)

Eduardo: Hija! . . . Hijita! You're tired, eh?

Aída: Por supuesto she's tired. I like to see you get in the water, waving your arms and legs from San Pedro to Santa Catalina. A person isn't a machine, a person has to rest.

Simón: Yo, Mama! Cool out, it ain't fucking brain surgery.

Ay Dios mío, qué viento: Oh my God, what wind!   Ay Gran Poder de Dios, quita este maldito viento: By the great power of God, keep the cursed winds away!

Eduardo (to Simón): Shut up, you. (*Louder to Margarita.*) I guess your mother's right for once, huh? . . . I guess you had to stop, eh? . . . Give your brother, the idiot . . . a chance to catch up with you.

Simón (clowning like Mortimer Snerd): Dum dee dum dee dum ooops, ah shucks . . .

Eduardo: I don't think he's Cuban.

Simón (like Ricky Ricardo): Oye, Lucy! I'm home! Ba ba lu!

Eduardo (joins in clowning, grabbing Simón in a headlock): What am I gonna do with this idiot, eh? I don't understand this idiot. He's not like us, Margarita. (*Laughing.*) You think if we put him into your bathing suit with a cap on his head . . . (*He laughs hysterically.*) You think anyone would know . . . huh? Do you think anyone would know? (*Laughs.*)

Simón (vamping): Ay, mi amor. Anybody looking for tits would know.

(*Eduardo slaps Simón across the face, knocking him down. Aída runs to Simón's aid. Abuela holds Eduardo back.*)

Margarita: Mía culpa!° Mía culpa!

Abuela: Qué dices hija?

Margarita: Papi, it's my fault, it's all my fault. . . . I'm so cold, I can't move. . . . I put my face in the water . . . and I hear them whispering . . . laughing at me. . . .

Aída: Who is laughing at you?

Margarita: The fish are all biting me . . . they hate me . . . they whisper about me. She can't swim, they say. She can't glide. She has no grace. . . . Yellowtails, bonita, tuna, man-o'-war, snub-nose sharks, *los baracudas* . . . they all hate me . . . only the dolphins care . . . and sometimes I hear the whales crying . . . she is lost, she is dead. I'm so numb, I can't feel. *Papi! Papi!* Am I dead?

Eduardo: Vamos, baby, punch those arms in. Come on . . . do you hear me?

Margarita: Papi . . . Papi . . . forgive me. . . .

(*All is silent on the boat. Eduardo drops his megaphone, his head bent down in dejection. Abuela, Aída, Simón, all leaning over the side of the boat. Simón slowly walks away.*)

Aída: Mi hija, qué tienes?

Simón: Oh, Christ, don't make her say it. Please don't make her say it.

Abuela: Say what? Qué cosa?

Simón: She wants to quit, can't you see she's had enough?

Abuela: Mira, para eso. Esta niña is turning blue.

Aída: Oyeme, mi hija. Do you want to come out of the water?

Margarita: Papi?

Simón (to Eduardo): She won't come out until *you* tell her.

Aída: Eduardo . . . answer your daughter.

Eduardo: Le dije to concentrate . . . concentrate on your rhythm. Then the rhythm would carry her . . . ay, it's a beautiful thing, Aída. It's like yoga, like meditation, the mind over matter . . . the mind controlling the body . . . that's how the great things in the world have been done. I wish you . . . I wish my wife could understand.

Margarita: Papi?

Simón (to Margarita): Forget him.

Mía culpa!: It's my fault.

Aída (imploring): Eduardo, *por favor.*

Eduardo (walking in circles): Why didn't you let her concentrate? Don't you understand, the concentration, the rhythm is everything. But no, you wouldn't listen. (*Screaming to the ocean.*) Goddamn Cubans, why, God, why do you make us go everywhere with our families? (*He goes to back of boat.*)

Aída (opening her arms): Mi hija, ven, come to Mami. (*Rocking.*) Your *mami* knows.

(*Abuela has taken the training bottle, puts it in a net. She and Simón lower it to Margarita.*)

Simón: Take this. Drink it. (*As Margarita drinks, Abuela crosses herself.*)

Abuela: Sangre de mi sangre.

(*Music comes up softly. Margarita drinks, gives the bottle back, stretches out her arms, as if on a cross. Floats on her back. She begins a graceful backstroke. Lights fade on boat as special lights come up on Margarita. She stops. Slowly turns over and starts to swim, gradually picking up speed. Suddenly as if in pain she stops, tries again, then stops in pain again. She becomes disoriented and falls to the bottom of the sea. Special on Margarita at the bottom of the sea.*)

Margarita: Ya no puedo . . . I can't. . . . A person isn't a machine . . . es mi culpa . . . Father forgive me . . . *Papi! Papi!* One, two. Uno, dos. (*Pause.*) Papi! A dónde estás? (*Pause.*) One, two, one, two. Papi! Ay, Papi! Where are you . . . ? Don't leave me. . . . Why don't you answer me? (*Pause. She starts to swim, slowly.*) Uno, dos, uno, dos. Dig in, dig in. (*Stops swimming.*) Por favor, Papi! (*Starts to swim again.*) One, two, one, two. Kick from your hip, kick from your hip. (*Stops swimming. Starts to cry.*) Oh God, please. . . . (*Pause.*) Hail Mary, full of grace . . . dig in, dig in . . . the Lord is with thee. . . . (*She swims to the rhythm of her Hail Mary.*) Hail Mary, full of grace . . . dig in, dig in . . . the Lord is with thee . . . dig in, dig in. . . . Blessed art thou among women. . . . Mami, it hurts. You let go of my hand. I'm lost. . . . And blessed is the fruit of thy womb, now and at the hour of our death. Amen. I don't want to die, I don't want to die.

(*Margarita is still swimming. Blackout. She is gone.*)

SCENE VI

Lights up on boat, we hear radio static. There is a heavy mist. On deck we see only black outline of Abuela with shawl over her head. We hear the voices of Eduardo, Aída, and Radio Operator.

Eduardo's Voice: La Havana! Coming from San Pedro. Over.

Radio Operator's Voice: Right, DT6-6, you say you've lost a swimmer.

Aída's Voice: Our child, our only daughter . . . listen to me. Her name is Margarita Inez Suárez, she is wearing a black one-piece bathing suit cut high in the legs with a white racing stripe down the sides, a white bathing cap with goggles and her whole body covered with a . . . with a . . .

Eduardo's Voice: With lanolin and paraffin.

Aída's Voice: Sí . . . con lanolin and paraffin.

(*More radio static. Special on Simón, on the edge of the boat.*)

Simón: Margo! Yo Margo! (*Pause.*) Man don't do this. (*Pause.*) Come on. . . . Come on. . . . (*Pause.*) God, why does everything have to be so hard? (*Pause.*) Stupid. You know you're not supposed to die for this. Stupid. It's his dream and he can't even swim. (*Pause.*) Punch those arms in. Come home. Come home. I'm your little brother. Don't forget what Mama said. You're not supposed to leave me behind. *Vamos,* Margarita, take your little brother, hold his hand tight when you cross the street. He's so little. (*Pause.*) Oh Christ, give us a sign. . . . I know! I know! Margo, I'll send you a message . . . like mental telepathy. I'll hold my breath, close my eyes, and I'll bring you home. (*He takes a deep breath; a few beats.*) This time I'll beep . . . I'll send out sonar signals like a dolphin. (*He imitates dolphin sounds.*)

(*The sound of real dolphins takes over from Simón, then fades into sound of Abuela saying the Hail Mary in Spanish, as full lights come up slowly.*)

SCENE VII

Eduardo coming out of cabin, sobbing, Aída holding him. Simón anxiously scanning the horizon. Abuela looking calmly ahead.

Eduardo: Es mi culpa, sí, es mi culpa.° (*He hits his chest.*)
Aída: Ya, ya viejo.° . . . it was my sin . . . I left my home.
Eduardo: Forgive me, forgive me. I've lost our daughter, our sister, our granddaughter, *mi carne, mi sangre, mis ilusiones.*° (*To heaven.*) *Dios mío,* take me . . . take me, I say . . . Goddammit, take me!
Simón: I'm going in.
Aída and Eduardo: No!
Eduardo (*grabbing and holding Simón, speaking to heaven*):   God, take me, not my children. They are my dreams, my illusions . . . and not this one, this one is my mystery . . . he has my secret dreams. In him are the parts of me I cannot see.

(*Eduardo embraces Simón. Radio static becomes louder.*)

Aída: I . . . I think I see her.
Simón: No, it's just a seal.
Abuela (*looking out with binoculars*):   Mi nietacita, dónde estás? (*She feels her heart.*) I don't feel the knife in my heart . . . my little fish is not lost.

(*Radio crackles with static. As lights dim on boat, Voices of Mel and Mary Beth are heard over the radio.*)

Mel's Voice: Tragedy has marred the face of the Wrigley Invitational Women's Race to Catalina. The Cuban swimmer, little Margarita Suárez, has reportedly been lost at sea. Coast Guard and divers are looking for her as we speak. Yet in spite of this tragedy the race must go on because . . .
Mary Beth's Voice (*interrupting loudly*):   Mel!
Mel's Voice (*startled*):   What!

Es mi culpa, sí, es mi culpa: It's my fault, yes, it's my fault.   *Ya, ya viejo:* Yes, yes, old man.   *mi carne, mi sangre, mis ilusiones:* My flesh, my blood, my dreams.

Mary Beth's Voice: Ah . . . excuse me, Mel . . . we have a winner. We've just received word from Catalina that one of the swimmers is just fifty yards from the breakers . . . it's, oh, it's . . . Margarita Suárez!

(*Special on family in cabin listening to radio.*)

Mel's Voice: What? I thought she died!

(*Special on Margarita, taking off bathing cap, trophy in hand, walking on the water.*)

Mary Beth's Voice: Ahh . . . unless . . . unless this is a tragic . . . No . . . there she is, Mel. Margarita Suárez! The only one in the race wearing a black bathing suit cut high in the legs with a racing stripe down the side.

(*Family cheering, embracing.*)

Simón (*screaming*): Way to go, Margo!

Mel's Voice: This is indeed a miracle! It's a resurrection! Margarita Suárez, with a flotilla of boats to meet her, is now walking on the waters, through the breakers . . . onto the beach, with crowds of people cheering her on. What a jubilation! This is a miracle!

(*Sound of crowds cheering. Lights and cheering sounds fade.*)

BLACKOUT

Milcha Sanchez-Scott on Writing

Writing *The Cuban Swimmer*   1989

From these women [recent immigrants Sanchez-Scott met at the employment agency where she worked] I got my material for Latina, my first play. I'd never tried to write. I was just collecting stories—for instance, a woman told me her child had died two years previously, and that at the mortuary she had lifted her child and put it across her face to give it a last goodbye. For two years, she said, the whole side of her face and her lips were cold. And being with my cousin again reminded me of the way we say things in Colombia: "Do you remember the summer when all the birds flew into the bedroom?" I was just writing things down.

About this time I was hired by Susan Loewenberg of L.A. Theatre Works to act in a project at the women's prison in Chino. I saw the way Doris Baizley, the writer, had put the women's stories together. When I offered Susan my notes, hoping she could make a piece out of them, she persuaded me to write it myself.

I'd found a channel to get all sorts of things flowing out. I liked controlling my own time, and *making* things—I've always admired architects. Acting seemed very airy to me because I could never take it home and show it to anybody. I had trouble being alone for long periods, but then I would go to the airport or someplace else busy to write. Doris and I used to do things like write under blankets by flashlight, which makes you feel like a little kid with a big secret.

L.A. Theatre Works got a grant and we toured *Latina* up and down the state with ten Latin actresses who were always feuding. We had one who was illegal, and wouldn't perform any place she thought Immigration might come, so I had to go on in her place. Then Susan commissioned me to write something else, which turned out to be *Dog Lady* and *Cuban Swimmer*. I saw the long-distance swimmer Diana Nyad on TV and I saw Salazar—the Cuban runner—and started thinking. I wanted to set a play in the water. So I put a family on a boat and a swimmer in the water and said, "Now, *what?*" I happened to be in a church and saw the most beautiful Stations of the Cross. It struck me as a good outline for anybody undertaking an endeavor—there's all this tripping and falling and rising. So that's what I used.

From *On New Ground*

DOCUMENTARY DRAMA

Some playwrights combine experimental and naturalistic elements, creating documentary works that dramatize actual events. British dramatist Michael Frayn presented the European physicists who did the work preceding the atom bomb in *Copenhagen* (1998) and explored the career of director Max Reinhardt in Nazi-era Austria in *Afterlife* (2008). Actress-playwright Anna Deavere Smith created an extremely innovative version of documentary drama in which she performed *all* of the roles herself in bravura one-woman shows. Using the actual words of real people, she constructed performance pieces to explore complex social events such as the race riots in Crown Heights, Brooklyn, in 1991 and in Los Angeles in 1992.

Anna Deavere Smith

Scenes from Twilight: Los Angeles, 1992   1994

Anna Deavere Smith was born in Baltimore, Maryland, in 1950, the daughter of a businessman and an elementary school principal. She graduated from Beaver College in 1971 and earned a Master of Fine Arts degree from the American Conservatory Theater in 1977. She taught drama at Stanford University from 1990 to 2000 and is presently a professor at both the Tisch School of the Arts at New York University and the NYU School of Law. Over many years Smith has conducted more than two thousand interviews; from them she has fashioned a number of works of "documentary theater," each of which is a stage presentation in which a single performer speaks a series of monologues using the actual words of her interview subjects. The best-known of these are Fires in the Mirror *(1993), drawn from the 1991 race riots in Crown Heights, Brooklyn,* Twilight: Los Angeles, 1992 *(1994), derived from the 1992 riot in that city, and* Let Me Down Easy *(2009), which examines health care issues. Smith has frequently performed these pieces herself, winning rave reviews both for the works and for her extraordinary ability to bring to life characters of both sexes and many ages and races. In its review of* Twilight: Los Angeles, 1992, *the New York Times said: "Anna Deavere Smith is the ultimate impressionist: she does people's souls." As an actress, she has also made many appearances on stage and in films, including* Philadelphia *and* The American President, *and has been seen on television in* The West Wing *and* Nurse Jackie. *Included here are three scenes from the over fifty monologues in* Twilight: Los Angeles, 1992.

CHARACTERS

Anonymous Young Man, former gang member
Mrs. Young-Soon Han, former liquor store owner, Korean American, 40s, heavy accent
Twilight Bey, gang truce organizer, African American, early 30s/late 20s, Crips gang.

GENERAL NOTE

This play is based on interviews conducted by Anna Deavere Smith soon after the race riots in Los Angeles of 1992. All words were spoken by real people and are verbatim from those interviews.

ANONYMOUS YOUNG MAN
Former Gang Member

Broad Daylight

(*Saturday, fall, sunny. He is wearing black pants and an oversized tee shirt. He is living with his mother after having recently gotten out of jail. His mother lives in a fancy apartment building, with pool, recreation room, etc. We are in one of the lounges. He has a goatee and wears his hair pulled back in a ponytail. He is black but looks Latino.*)

They kind of respected their elders,
as far as,
not robbing them,
but then a lot of . . .
as I got older I noticed,
like the younger ones,
the lot of the
respect,
it
just like
disappeared,
'cause I . . . when I was younger it was like
if the police had
me and a couple other guys in the middle of the street
on our knees,
the older people would
come out and question.
They like . . .
"Take 'em to jail,"
because of that loss of respect,
you know,
of the elders
by the younger ones,
losing the respect of the elders.
When I went to the Valley
I felt more respect,
because when
I was in the
Valley
I was right there with rivals.

It's like I could walk right over
and it was rivals
and the way I felt was like
strong,
'cause when I moved out there
I didn't bring
all my homeboys
with me
and it's like I used to tell them,
my rivals,
I used to tell 'em, "Man,
I'm a one-man army."
I would joke about it.
I say,
"I don't need my homeboys
and everything."
Me and my brother,
we used to call ourselves the Blues Brothers,
because it was two of us
and we
would go and we either have our blue rags hanging and go right up
there in their neighborhood where there are
Bloods
and go right up in the apartments
and there could be a crowd of 'em
and we would pass by—
"What's up, cuz?"—
and keep goin'
and every now and then
they might say
something
but the majority of 'em
knew that I keep a gun on me
and every now and then
there would be broad daylight like this.
Some of 'em
would try and test me and say,
"well, he ain't fixin' ta shoot me in this broad daylight,"
you know,
and then
when they do
then you know
I either end up chasin' 'em,
shootin' at 'em or shootin'
whatever.
'Cause they thought ain't nobody that stupid
to shoot people in broad daylight.
And I was the opposite.
My theory was when you shoot somebody in broad daylight

people gonna be mostly scared,
they not gonna just sit there and look at you,
you know, to identify you.
I figure there's gonna be like
"I gotta run"
and I figure they just gonna be too scared to see who you are to
identify you.
That's where the reputation
came,
'cause they didn't know when I was comin',
broad daylight
or at night.
My favorite song?
I like oldies.
My favorite song is by Atlantic Star.
It's called
"Am I Dreamin'?"

MRS. YOUNG-SOON HAN

Former Liquor Store Owner

Swallowing the Bitterness

(*A house on Sycamore Street in Los Angeles, just south of Beverly. A tree-lined street. A quiet street. It's in an area where many Hasidic Jews live as well as yuppie types. Mrs. Young-Soon Han's living room is impeccable. Dark pink-and-apricot rug and sofa and chairs. The sofa and chairs are made of a velour. On the back of the sofa and chairs is a Korean design. A kind of circle with lines in it, a geometric design. There is a glass coffee table in front of the sofa. There is nothing on the coffee table. There is a mantel with a bookcase, and a lot of books. The mantel has about thirty trophies. These are her nephew's. They may be for soccer. On the wall behind the sofa area, a series of citations and awards. These are her ex-husband's. They are civic awards. There are a couple of pictures of her husband shaking hands with official-looking people and accepting awards. In this area is also a large painting of Jesus Christ. There is another religious painting over the archway to the dining room. There are some objects hanging on the side of the archway. Long strips and oval shapes. It is very quiet. When we first came in, the television was on, but she turned it off.*

She is sitting on the floor and leaning on the coffee table. When she hits her hand on the table, it sounds very much like a drum. I am accompanied by two Korean-American graduate students from UCLA.)

Until last year
I believed America is the best.
I still believe it.
I don't deny that now.
because I'm a victim,
but
as
the year ends in '92
and we were still in turmoil

Anna Deavere Smith as Mrs. Young-Soon Han.

and having all the financial problems
and mental problems.
Then a couple months ago
I really realized that
Korean immigrants were left out
from this
society and we were nothing.
What is our right?
Is it because we are Korean?
Is it because we have no politicians?
Is it because we don't
speak good English?
Why?
Why do we have to be left out?

    (*She is hitting her hand on the coffee table*)

We are not qualified to have medical treatment.
We are not qualified to get, uh,
food stamp

    (*She hits the table once*),

not GR

    (*Hits the table once*),

no welfare

(*Hits the table once*).

Anything.
Many Afro-Americans

(*Two quick hits*)

who never worked

(*One hit*),

they get
at least minimum amount

(*One hit*)

of money

(*One hit*)

to survive

(*One hit*).

We don't get any!

(*Large hit with full hand spread*)

Because we have a car

(*One hit*)

and we have a house.

(*Pause six seconds*)

And we are high tax taxpayers.

(*One hit*)

(*Pause fourteen seconds*)

Where do I finda [*sic*] justice?
Okay, Black people
probably
believe they won
by the trial?
Even some complains only half right?
justice was there.
But I watched the television
that Sunday morning,
early morning as they started.
I started watch it all day.
They were having party and then they celebrated,
all of South Central,
all the churches.

They finally found that justice exists
in this society.
Then where is the victims' rights?
They got their rights.
By destroying innocent Korean merchants . . .
They have a lot of respect,
as I do,
for
Dr. Martin King?
He is the only model for Black community.
I don't care Jesse Jackson.
But
he was the model
of nonviolence.
Nonviolence?
They like to have hiseh [sic] spirits.
What about last year?
They destroyed innocent people.

 (Five-second pause)

And I wonder if that is really justice

 (And a very soft "uh" after "justice," like "justicah," but very quick)

to get their rights
in this way.

 (Thirteen-second pause)

I waseh swallowing the bitternesseh,
sitting here alone
and watching them.
They became all hilarious

 (Three-second pause)

and, uh,
in a way I was happy for them
and I felt glad for them.
At leasteh they got something back, you know.
Just let's forget Korean victims or other victims
who are destroyed by them.
They have fought
for their rights

 (One hit simultaneous with the word "rights")

over two centuries

 (One hit simultaneous with "centuries")

and I have a lot of sympathy and understanding for them.
Because of their effort and sacrificing,

other minorities, like Hispanic
or Asians,
maybe we have to suffer more
by mainstream.
You know,
that's why I understand,
and then
I like to be part of their
'joyment.
But . . .
That's why I had mixed feeling
as soon as I heard the verdict.
I wish I could
live together
with eh [*sic*] Blacks,
but after the riots
there were too much differences.
The fire is still there—
how do you call it?—
igni . . .
igniting fire.

> (*She says a Korean phrase phonetically: "Dashi yun gi ga nuh"*°)

It's still dere.
It canuh
burst out anytime.

TWILIGHT BEY
Organizer of Gang Truce

Limbo / Twilight #2

(*In a Denny's restaurant in a shopping center on a Saturday morning, February 1993. He is a gang member. He is short, graceful, very dark skinned. He is soft-spoken and even in his delivery. He is very confident.*)

Twilight Bey,
that's my name.
When I was
twelve and thirteen,
I stayed out until, they say,
until the sun come up.
Every night, you know,
and that was my thing.
I was a
watchdog.
You know, I stayed up in the neighborhood,
make sure we wasn't being rolled on and everything,
and when people

Dashi yun gi ga nuh: In a performance script, this stage direction reads, "She says a Korean word asking for translation. In Korean, she says 'igniting fire.'")

Anna Deavere Smith as Twilight Bey.

came into light
a what I knew,
a lot a people said,
"Well, Twilight, you know,
you a lot smarter and you have a lot more wisdom than those
twice your age."
And what I did, you know,
I was
at home writing one night
and I was writing my name
and I just looked at it and it came ta me:
"twi,"
abbreviation
of the word "twice."
You take a way the "ce."
You have the last word,
"light."
"Light" is a word that symbolizes knowledge, knowing,
wisdom,
within the Koran and the Holy Bible.
Twilight.
I have twice the knowledge of those my age,

twice the understanding of those my age.
So twilight
is
that time
between day and night.
Limbo,
I call it limbo.
So a lot of times when I've brought up ideas to my homeboys,
they say,
"Twilight,
that's before your time,
that's something you can't do now."
When I talked about the truce back in 1988,
that was something they considered before its time,
yet
in 1992
we made it
realistic.
So to me it's like I'm stuck in limbo,
like the sun is stuck between night and day
in the twilight hours.
You know,
I'm in an area not many people exist.
Nighttime to me
is like a lack of sun,
and I don't affiliate
darkness with anything negative.
I affiliate
darkness with what was first,
because it was first,
and then relative to my complexion.
I am a dark individual,
and with me stuck in limbo,
I see darkness as myself.
I see the light as knowledge and the wisdom of the world and
understanding others,
and in order for me to be a, to be a true human being,
I can't forever dwell in darkness,
I can't forever dwell in the idea,
of just identifying with people like me and understanding me and mine.
So I'm up twenty-four hours, it feels like,
and, you know,
what I see at nighttime
is,
like,
little kids
between the ages of
eight and eleven
out at three in the morning.

They beatin' up a old man on the bus stop,
a homeless old man.
You know,
I see these things.
I tell 'em, "Hey, man, what ya all doin'?
Whyn't ya go on home?
What ya doin' out this time of night?"
You know,
and then when I'm in my own neighborhood, I'm driving through and I
see the living dead, as we call them,
the base heads,
the people who are so addicted on crack,
if they need a hit they be up all night doin' whatever they have to do
to make the money to get the hit.
It's like gettin' a total dose
of what goes on in the daytime creates at night.

Questions

1. What does the speech by the Anonymous Young Man reveal about the escalation of street violence in Los Angeles?
2. Do you find Mrs. Young-Soon Han to be a sympathetic character? Why or why not?
3. Does the speech by Twilight Bey, which concludes the play, seem conciliatory or confrontational? Does it explain why the play is called *Twilight*?
4. Taking these monologues together, what do you see as the mood that emerges from the text—despair? hopefulness? resignation? Explain.

Anna Deavere Smith on Writing

A Call to the Community   1994

For over ten years now I have been creating performances based on actual events in a series I have titled *On the Road: A Search for American Character*. Each *On the Road* performance evolves from interviews I conduct with individuals directly or indirectly involved in the event I intend to explore. Basing my scripts entirely on this interview material, I perform the interviews onstage using their own words. *Twilight: Los Angeles, 1992* is the product of my search for the character of Los Angeles in the wake of the initial Rodney King verdict.

Anna Deavere Smith

• • •

The story of how Los Angeles came to experience what some call the worst riots in United States history is by now familiar. In the Spring of 1991, Rodney King, a black man, was severely beaten by four white Los Angeles police officers after a high-speed chase in which King was pursued for speeding. A nearby resident videotaped the beating from the balcony of his apartment. When the videotape was broadcast on national television, there was an immediate outcry from the community. The next year, the police officers who beat King were tried and found not guilty—and the city exploded. The verdict took the city by surprise, from public officials to average citizens. Even the defense lawyers, I was told, anticipated that there would be some convictions. Three days of burning, looting, and killing scarred Los Angeles and captured the attention of the world.

• • •

The video of the Rodney King beating, which seemed to "tell all," apparently did not tell enough, and the prosecution lost, as their lead attorney told me, "the slam-dunk case of the century." The city of Los Angeles lost much more. *Twilight* is an attempt to explore the shades of that loss. It is not really an attempt to find causes or to show where responsibility was lacking. That would be the task of a commission report. While I was in Los Angeles, and when I have returned since my initial performance of *Twilight* in the summer of 1993, I have been trying to look at the shifts in attitudes of citizens toward race relations. I have been particularly interested in the opportunity the events in Los Angeles give us to take stock of how the race canvas in America has *changed* since the Watts riots. Los Angeles shows us that the story of race in America is much larger and more complex than a story of black and white. There are new players in the race drama. Whereas Jewish merchants were hit during the Watts riots, Korean merchants were hit this time. Although the media tended to focus on blacks in South-Central, the Latino population was equally involved. We tend to think of race as us and them—us or them being black or white depending on one's own color. The relationships among peoples of color and *within* racial groups are getting more and more complicated.

• • •

When I did my research in Los Angeles, I was listening with an ear that was trained to hear stories for the specific purpose of repeating them with the elements of character intact. This becomes significant because sometimes there is the expectation that inasmuch as I am doing "social dramas," I am looking for *solutions* to social problems. In fact, though, I am looking at the *processes* of the problems. Acting is a constant process of becoming something. It is not a result, it is not an answer. It is not a solution. I am first looking for the humanness inside the problems, or the crises. The spoken word is evidence of the humanness. Perhaps the solutions come somewhere further down the road.

I see the work as a call. I played *Twilight* in Los Angeles as a call to the community. I performed it at a time when the community had not yet resolved the problems. I wanted to be a part of their examination of the problems. I believe that solutions to these problems will call for the participation of large and eclectic groups of people. I also believe that we are at a stage at which we must first break the silence about race and encourage many more people to participate in the dialogue.

One of the questions I was frequently asked when I was interviewed about *Twilight* was "Did you find any one voice that could speak for the entire city?" I think there is an expectation that in this diverse city, and in this diverse nation, a unifying voice would bring increased understanding and put us on the road to solutions. This expectation surprises me. There is little in culture or education that encourages the development of a unifying voice. In order to have real unity, all voices would have to first be heard or at least represented. Many of us who work in race relations do so from the point of view of our own ethnicity. This very fact inhibits our ability to hear more voices than those that are closest to us in proximity. Few people speak a language about race that is not their own. If more of us could actually speak from another point of view, like speaking another language, we could accelerate the flow of ideas.

Introduction to *Twilight: Los Angeles, 1992*

▪ WRITING *effectively*

THINKING ABOUT DRAMATIC REALISM

When critics use the word *realism* in relation to a play, are they claiming it is true to life? Not necessarily. Realism generally refers to certain dramatic conventions that emerged during the nineteenth century. A realistic play is not necessarily any truer to life than an experimental one, although the conventions of Realist drama have become so familiar to us that other kinds of drama—though no more artificial—can seem mannered and even bizarre to the casual viewer. Remember, though, that all drama—even the theater of Realism—is artifice.

- **Notice the conventions of Realist drama.** Compare, for example, a play by Henrik Ibsen with one by Sophocles. Ibsen's characters speak in prose, not verse. His settings are drawn from contemporary life, not a legendary past. His characters are ordinary middle-class citizens, not kings, queens, and aristocrats.
- **Be aware that the inner lives, memories, and motivations of the characters play a crucial role in the dramatic action.** Ibsen, like other Realist playwrights, seeks to portray the complexity of human psychology—especially motivation—in detailed, subtle ways. In contrast, Shakespeare appears less interested in the reason for Iago's villainy than its consequences. Did Iago have an unhappy childhood or a troubled adolescence? These questions do not greatly matter in Renaissance drama, but to Ibsen they become central. In *A Doll's House*, for example, we can infer that Nora's self-absorption and naiveté result from her father's overprotection.
- **Remember though, Realist drama does not necessarily come any closer than other dramatic styles to getting at the truths of human existence.** *A Doll's House*, for example, does not provide a more profound picture of psychological struggle than *Oedipus the King*. But Ibsen does offer a more detailed view of his protagonist's inner life and her daily routine.

CHECKLIST: Writing About a Realist Play

- ☐ List every detail the play gives about the protagonist's past. How does each detail affect the character's current behavior?
- ☐ What is the protagonist's primary motivation? What are the origins of that motivation?
- ☐ Do the other characters understand the protagonist's deeper motivations?
- ☐ How much of the plot arises from misunderstandings among characters?
- ☐ Do major plot events grow from characters' interactions? Or, do they occur at random?
- ☐ How does the protagonist's psychology determine his or her reactions to events?

WRITING ASSIGNMENT ON REALISM

Al Capovilla of Folsom Lake Center College has developed an ingenious assignment based on Ibsen's *A Doll's House* that asks you to combine the skills of a literary critic with those of a lawyer. Here is Professor Capovilla's assignment:

> You are the family lawyer for Torvald and Nora Helmer. The couple comes to you with a request. They want you to listen to an account of their domestic problems and recommend whether they should pursue a divorce or try to reconcile.
>
> You listen to both sides of the argument. (You also know everything that is said by every character.)
>
> Now, it is your task to write a short decision. In stating your opinion, provide a clear and organized explanation of your reasoning. Show both sides of the argument. You may employ as evidence anything said or done in the play.
>
> Conclude your paper with your recommendation. What do you advise under the circumstances—divorce or an attempt at reconciliation?

Following is a paper from Professor Capovilla's course written by Carlota Llarena, a student at Folsom Lake Center College.

Llarena 1

Carlota Llarena
Professor Capovilla
English 320
19 January 2012

Helmer vs. Helmer

In reaching a determination of whether Torvald and Nora Helmer should either get divorced or attempt reconciliation, I have carefully considered the events leading to the breakdown of their marriage in order to decide on an amicable solution to their present predicament. In my belief, marriage is a sacred institution—one that should not be taken lightly. Love and happiness in a marriage should be cultivated by the parties. Obstacles are often found throughout marriage, but in order to overcome those obstacles, a husband and wife should share responsibilities, discuss whatever problems arise, and jointly work on finding solutions to those problems. Based on this belief, I recommend that Torvald and Nora Helmer attempt a reconciliation of the marriage.

   In reviewing the testimony provided by both parties, I find it true that Torvald has treated Nora in such a manner as to make her feel she was considered a child rather than an equal partner. Torvald handled all their

Introduction establishes premise of essay

Thesis statement

Topic sentence weighing Torvald's faults

Llarena 2

Textual evidence

finances and solely resolved all their problems. Torvald never discussed any of their household problems with Nora or attempted to seek her advice. In that regard, I believe that Torvald treated Nora in that fashion because he felt Nora was incapable of handling these types of situations. Nora's every need had always been looked after by her father. She grew up with nannies, never had to take responsibility for herself, and never had to work to earn money as money was always given to her.

Topic sentence weighing Nora's flaws

I find it also true, however, that Nora has always acted like a child. She has the tendency to sulk if matters don't go her way, is happy when rewarded with gifts, hides treats (like macaroons) for herself when they are prohibited, and likes to play games. These characteristics are clearly evident in Nora. There are at least six examples of her child-like behaviors in the testimonies. First, Nora denied nibbling on a macaroon or two (1123) as a child would deny any wrongdoing. Second, Nora thought it would be "fun" to hang the money in pretty gold paper on the Christmas tree (1122) as a child would enjoy bright and colorful objects. Third, Nora considered it to be "a tremendous pleasure" to sit and work to earn money "like being a man" (1129) as a child would pretend and play-act adult roles. Fourth, Nora was excited when she received a gift of money from Torvald (1121) as a child would be excited when she receives a present. Fifth, Nora enjoyed dreaming of a rich old gentleman falling in love with her (1129) as a child would dream of getting married to a rich man who would take complete care of her. And, finally, Nora would "do everything I can think of . . . I'll sing for you, dance for you" (1138) as a child would always attempt to please her parents.

Textual evidence

More textual evidence

Topic sentence on how Torvald's character flaws encourage Nora's dependence

Unfortunately, Torvald reinforced Nora's child-like characteristics by calling her names such as "my little skylark" (1139), "my little squirrel" (1121), "little Miss Sweet Tooth" (1123), and "my little Nora" (1139). These nicknames seem more appropriate for a child than a grown woman. Torvald has also been very protective of Nora—just as a parent would be protective of a child. Torvald claimed that Nora had "precious eyes" and "fair little delicate hands" which indicates his belief that Nora was a fragile person, one who does not know how to take care of herself. Since Nora was treated in that same manner by her father, she has never experienced life in any other fashion other than that of a child.

As a further review of the testimony presented, I opine that Torvald is not solely to be blamed for the predicament at hand. Nora has allowed

Torvald to treat her in this manner during the eight years they were married. She never told Torvald that she wanted to be treated as an adult and as his equal or that she wanted to become more involved with family matters to help determine solutions to problems they may have. Nora was also guilty of not confiding in Torvald or discussing her problems with him. Did Nora discuss with Torvald the need for them to live in Italy for a year (1128)? Did she sit with her husband and discuss issues concerning money to make such a trip to Italy feasible and where the money actually came from (1128)? Did Nora ever tell Torvald the truth that she had borrowed the money from Krogstad, how she was repaying the loan and what she did to secure that loan (1128, 1135)? The answer to all these questions is no! Accordingly, it is quite clear that Nora and Torvald are both equally guilty of not discussing problems and issues with one another.

Topic sentence establishing mutual guilt

Conclusion

In summation, Nora and Torvald are equally at fault on the following issues. First, Torvald treated Nora as a child, and Nora allowed herself to be treated in that manner. Second, Torvald never confided in Nora regarding matters concerning the family or their finances. Nora, however, also did not confide in Torvald. Now that these issues and concerns are made known to the parties, the parties may work on resolving their differences, share the responsibility of handling both family and financial matters by discussing them with one another and finding amicable solutions, and cultivate the trust and judgment of one another. Accordingly, it is my ruling that Nora and Torvald attempt reconciling their marriage and forgo divorce as an immediate option. Only if the parties reach an impasse after an honest and sustained attempt at reconciliation would I suggest reconsidering the option of divorce.

Restatement of thesis

Work Cited

Ibsen, Henrik. *A Doll's House*. Trans. R. Farquharson Sharp. Rev. Viktoria Michelsen. *Literature: An Introduction to Fiction, Poetry, Drama, and Writing*. Ed. X. J. Kennedy and Dana Gioia. 7th Compact ed. New York: Pearson, 2013. 1119–71. Print.

MORE TOPICS FOR WRITING

1. How relevant is *A Doll's House* today? Do women like Nora still exist? How about men like Torvald? Build an argument, either that the concerns of *A Doll's House* are timeless and universal or that the issues addressed by the play are historical, not contemporary.

2. Placing yourself in the character of Ibsen's Torvald Helmer, write a defense of him and his attitudes as he himself might write it.

3. Who is the protagonist of *The Glass Menagerie*? Give the reasons for your choice. Is there an antagonist? If so, who is it, and why?

4. At the end of *The Glass Menagerie*, Amanda says to Tom, "You live in a dream; you manufacture illusions." Discuss the degree to which this is true of each of the characters in the play.

5. Choose a character from Milcha Sanchez-Scott's *The Cuban Swimmer* and examine his or her motivations. What makes your character act as he or she does? Present evidence from the play to back up your argument.

6. Describe some of the difficulties of staging *The Cuban Swimmer* as a play. What would be lost or gained by remaking it as a movie?

7. How effective is the technique of *Twilight: Los Angeles, 1992*? Does the lack of interplay between characters make it less dramatic, or is there sufficient drama in what the speakers say and the ways in which they present themselves?

8. Write a paper that compares and contrasts the different points of view of two characters in *Twilight: Los Angeles, 1992*.

9. Imagine you're a casting director. Choose a play from this chapter and cast it with well-known television and movie stars. Explain, in depth, what qualities in the characters you hope to emphasize by your casting choices.

▶ TERMS FOR *review*

Modern Theater Movements

Realism ▶ An attempt to reproduce faithfully on the stage the surface appearance of life, especially that of ordinary people in everyday situations. In a historical sense, Realism (usually capitalized) refers to a movement in nineteenth-century European theater. Realist drama customarily focused on the middle class (and occasionally the working class) rather than the aristocracy.

Naturalism ▶ A type of drama in which the characters are presented as products or victims of environment and heredity. Naturalism, considered an extreme form of Realism, customarily depicts the social, psychological, and economic milieu of the primary characters.

Symbolist drama ▶ A style of drama that avoids direct statement and exposition for powerful evocation and suggestion. In place of realistic stage settings and actions, Symbolist drama uses lighting, music, and dialogue to create a mystical atmosphere.

Expressionism ▶ A dramatic style developed between 1910 and 1924 in Germany in reaction against Realism's focus on surface details and external reality. Expressionist style used episodic plots, distorted lines, exaggerated shapes, abnormally intense coloring, mechanical physical movement, and telegraphic speech to create a dreamlike subjective realm.

Theater of the absurd ▶ Postwar European genre depicting the grotesquely comic plight of human beings thrown by accident into an irrational and meaningless world. The critic Martin Esslin coined the term to characterize plays by writers such as Samuel Beckett, Jean Genet, and Eugène Ionesco.

Aspects of Drama

Tragicomedy ▶ A type of drama that combines elements of both tragedy and comedy. Usually it creates potentially tragic situations that bring the protagonists to the brink of disaster but then ends happily.

Comic relief ▶ The appearance of a comic situation or character, or clownish humor in the midst of a serious action, introducing a sharp contrast in mood.

Antihero ▶ A protagonist who is lacking in one or more of the conventional qualities attributed to a hero. Instead of being dignified, brave, idealistic, or purposeful, for instance, the antihero may be buffoonish, cowardly, self-interested, or weak. The antihero is often considered an essentially modern form of characterization, a satiric or realistic commentary on traditional portrayals of idealized characters.

The Stage

Proscenium arch ▶ An architectural picture frame or gateway "standing in front of the scenery" (as the name *proscenium* indicates) that separates the auditorium from the raised stage and the world of the play.

Picture-frame stage ▶ A stage that holds the action within a proscenium arch, with painted scene panels (receding into the middle distance) designed to give the illusion of three-dimensional perspective. Picture-frame stages became the norm throughout Europe and England into the twentieth century.

Box set ▶ A stage set consisting of three walls joined in two corners and a ceiling that tilts, as if seen in perspective, to provide the illusion of scenic realism for interior rooms.

37

PLAYS FOR
FURTHER READING

A play isn't a text. It's an event.
—TOM STOPPARD

David Henry Hwang

The Sound of a Voice   1983

David Henry Hwang (b. 1957) grew up in San Gabriel, California, the son of first-generation Chinese immigrants. He was born into a family of musicians: his mother was a concert pianist, his sister plays cello in a string quartet, and he studied the violin. In 1979, as a senior at Stanford University, he directed his first play, F.O.B. (an acronym for "fresh off the boat"), in a dormitory lounge. F.O.B. was later staged at the New York Shakespeare Festival

American Repertory Theater's 2003 production of *The Sound of a Voice* in Cambridge, Massachusetts.

Public Theater and won a 1981 Obie Award. The Sound of a Voice was also produced at the Public Theater as part of a double bill with another one-act play by Hwang, The House of Sleeping Beauties. *Hwang enjoyed his greatest commercial and critical success with* M. Butterfly *(1988), which won the Tony Award for best play. His other plays include* Face Value *(1993),* Golden Child *(1997), and* Yellowface *(2007). While some of his plays are realistic in their approach, Hwang has always been fascinated by the possibilities of symbolic drama. In* The Sound of a Voice, *he creates a timeless, placeless scene in which two characters named Man and Woman act out a story reminiscent of a folk legend or a traditional Japanese Nō drama (a type of symbolic aristocratic drama developed in the fourteenth century in which a ghost recounts the struggles of his or her life for a traveler). Hwang's interest in nonrealistic and experimental drama has also led him to explore opera. He has collaborated with composer Philip Glass on three works:* 1000 Airplanes on the Roof *(1988), a science-fiction music drama;* The Voyage *(1992), an allegorical grand opera commissioned by New York's Metropolitan Opera for the 500th anniversary of Christopher Columbus's arrival in America; and* The Sound of a Voice *(2003), a combined staging of the following play with* The House of Sleeping Beauties. *He has also written the books for the shows* Aida *(2000), with music by Elton John and lyrics by Tim Rice, and* Tarzan *(2006), with music and lyrics by Phil Collins. Hwang lives in New York City.*

CHARACTERS

Man, fifties, Japanese
Woman, fifties, Japanese

SETTING. *Woman's house, in a remote corner of the forest.*

SCENE I

Woman pours tea for Man. Man rubs himself, trying to get warm.

Man: You're very kind to take me in.
Woman: This is a remote corner of the world. Guests are rare.
Man: The tea—you pour it well.
Woman: No.
Man: The sound it makes—in the cup—very soothing.
Woman: That is the tea's skill, not mine. (*She hands the cup to him.*) May I get you something else? Rice, perhaps?
Man: No.
Woman: And some vegetables?
Man: No, thank you.
Woman: Fish? (*Pause.*) It is at least two days' walk to the nearest village. I saw no horse. You must be very hungry. You would do a great honor to dine with me. Guests are rare.
Man: Thank you.
Woman (*Woman gets up, leaves. Man holds the cup in his hands, using it to warm himself. He gets up, walks around the room. It is sparsely furnished, drab, except for one shelf on which stands a vase of brightly colored flowers. The flowers stand out in sharp contrast to the starkness of the room. Slowly, he reaches out towards them. He touches them. Quickly, he takes one of the flowers from the vase, hides it in his clothes. He*

returns to where he had sat previously. He waits. Woman re-enters. She carries a tray with food.): Please. Eat. It will give me great pleasure.

Man: This—this is magnificent.

Woman: Eat.

Man: Thank you. (*He motions for Woman to join him.*)

Woman: No, thank you.

Man: This is wonderful. The best I've tasted.

Woman: You are reckless in your flattery. But anything you say, I will enjoy hearing. It's not even the words. It's the sound of a voice, the way it moves through the air.

Man: How long has it been since you last had a visitor? (*Pause.*)

Woman: I don't know.

Man: Oh?

Woman: I lose track. Perhaps five months ago, perhaps ten years, perhaps yesterday. I don't consider time when there is no voice in the air. It's pointless. Time begins with the entrance of a visitor, and ends with his exit.

Man: And in between? You don't keep track of the days? You can't help but notice—

Woman: Of course I notice.

Man: Oh.

Woman: I notice, but I don't keep track. (*Pause.*) May I bring out more?

Man: More? No. No. This was wonderful.

Woman: I have more.

Man: Really—the best I've had.

Woman: You must be tired. Did you sleep in the forest last night?

Man: Yes.

Woman: Or did you not sleep at all?

Man: I slept.

Woman: Where?

Man: By a waterfall. The sound of the water put me to sleep. It rumbled like the sounds of a city. You see, I can't sleep in too much silence. It scares me. It makes me feel that I have no control over what is about to happen.

Woman: I feel the same way.

Man: But you live here—alone?

Woman: Yes.

Man: It's so quiet here. How can you sleep?

Woman: Tonight, I'll sleep. I'll lie down in the next room, and hear your breathing through the wall, and fall asleep shamelessly. There will be no silence.

Man: You're very kind to let me stay here.

Woman: This is yours. (*She unrolls a mat; there is a beautiful design of a flower on the mat. The flower looks exactly like the flowers in the vase.*)

Man: Did you make it yourself?

Woman: Yes. There is a place to wash outside.

Man: Thank you.

Woman: Goodnight.

Man: Goodnight. (*Man starts to leave.*)

Woman: May I know your name?

Man: No. I mean, I would rather not say. If I gave you a name, it would only be made-up. Why should I deceive you? You are too kind for that.

Woman: Then what should I call you? Perhaps—"Man Who Fears Silence"?

Man: How about, "Man Who Fears Women"?

Woman: That name is much too common.

Man: And you?

Woman: Yokiko.

Man: That's your name?

Woman: It's what you may call me.

Man: Goodnight, Yokiko. You are very kind.

Woman: You are very smart. Goodnight.

(Man exits. Hanako° goes to the mat. She tidies it, brushes it off. She goes to the vase. She picks up the flowers, studies them. She carries them out of the room with her. Man re-enters. He takes off his outer clothing. He glimpses the spot where the vase used to sit. He reaches into his clothing, pulls out the stolen flower. He studies it. He puts it underneath his head as he lies down to sleep, like a pillow. He starts to fall asleep. Suddenly, a start. He picks up his head. He listens.)

SCENE II

Dawn. Man is getting dressed. Woman enters with food.

Woman: Good morning.

Man: Good morning, Yokiko.

Woman: You weren't planning to leave?

Man: I have quite a distance to travel today.

Woman: Please. (*She offers him food.*)

Man: Thank you.

Woman: May I ask where you're travelling to?

Man: It's far.

Woman: I know this region well.

Man: Oh? Do you leave the house often?

Woman: I used to. I used to travel a great deal. I know the region from those days.

Man: You probably wouldn't know the place I'm headed.

Woman: Why not?

Man: It's new. A new village. It didn't exist in "those days." (*Pause.*)

Woman: I thought you said you wouldn't deceive me.

Man: I didn't. You don't believe me, do you?

Woman: No.

Man: Then I didn't deceive you. I'm travelling. That much is true.

Woman: Are you in such a hurry?

Man: Travelling is a matter of timing. Catching the light. (*Woman exits; Man finishes eating, puts down his bowl. Woman re-enters with the vase of flowers.*) Where did you find those? They don't grow native around these parts, do they?

Hanako: The woman.

Woman: No; they've all been brought in. They were brought in by visitors. Such as yourself. They were left here. In my custody.

Man: But—they look so fresh, so alive.

Woman: I take care of them. They remind me of the people and places outside this house.

Man: May I touch them?

Woman: Certainly.

Man: These have just blossomed.

Woman: No; they were in bloom yesterday. If you'd noticed them before, you would know that.

Man: You must have received these very recently. I would guess—within five days.

Woman: I don't know. But I wouldn't trust your estimate. It's all in the amount of care you show to them. I create a world which is outside the realm of what you know.

Man: What do you do?

Woman: I can't explain. Words are too inefficient. It takes hundreds of words to describe a single act of caring. With hundreds of acts, words become irrelevant. (*Pause.*) But perhaps you can stay.

Man: How long?

Woman: As long as you'd like.

Man: Why?

Woman: To see how I care for them.

Man: I *am* tired.

Woman: Rest.

Man: The light?

Woman: It will return.

SCENE III

Man is carrying chopped wood. He is stripped to the waist. Woman enters.

Woman: You're very kind to do that for me.

Man: I enjoy it, you know. Chopping wood. It's clean. No questions. You take your axe, you stand up the log, you aim—pow!—you either hit it or you don't. Success or failure.

Woman: You seem to have been very successful today.

Man: Why shouldn't I be? It's a beautiful day. I can see to those hills. The trees are cool. The sun is gentle. Ideal. If a man can't be successful on a day like this, he might as well kick the dust up into his own face. (*Man notices Woman staring at him. Man pats his belly, looks at her.*) Protection from falls.

Woman: What? (*Man pinches his belly, showing some fat.*) Oh. Don't be silly. (*Man begins slapping the fat on his belly to a rhythm.*)

Man: Listen—I can make music—see?—that wasn't always possible. But now—that I've developed this—whenever I need entertainment.

Woman: You shouldn't make fun of your body.

Man: Why not? I saw you. You were staring.

Woman: I wasn't making fun. (*Man inflates his cheeks.*) I was just—stop that!

Man: Then why were you staring?

Woman: I was—

Man: Laughing?

Woman: No.

Man: Well?

Woman: I was—Your body. It's . . . strong. (*Pause.*)

Man: People say that. But they don't know. I've heard that age brings wisdom. That's a laugh. The years don't accumulate here. They accumulate here. (*Pause; he pinches his belly.*) But today is a day to be happy, right? The woods. The sun. Blue. It's a happy day. I'm going to chop wood.

Woman: There's nothing left to chop. Look.

Man: Oh. I guess . . . that's it.

Woman: Sit. Here.

Man: But—

Woman: There's nothing left. (*Man sits; Woman stares at his belly.*) Learn to love it.

Man: Don't be ridiculous.

Woman: Touch it.

Man: It's flabby.

Woman: It's strong.

Man: It's weak.

Woman: And smooth.

Man: Do you mind if I put on my shirt?

Woman: Of course not. Shall I get it for you?

Man: No. No. Just sit there. (*Man starts to put on his shirt. He pauses, studies his body.*) You think it's cute, huh?

Woman: I think you should learn to love it. (*Man pats his belly, talks to it.*)

Man (*to belly*): You're okay, sir. You hang onto my body like a great horseman.

Woman: Not like that.

Man (*ibid.*): You're also faithful. You'll never leave me for another man.

Woman: No.

Man: What do you want me to say? (*Woman walks over to Man. She touches his belly with her hand. They look at each other.*)

SCENE IV

Night. Man is alone. Flowers are gone from stand. Mat is unrolled. Man lies on it, sleeping. Suddenly, he starts. He lifts up his head. He listens. Silence. He goes back to sleep. Another start. He lifts up his head, strains to hear. Slowly, we begin to make out the strains of a single shakuhachi° playing a haunting line. It is very soft. He strains to hear it. The instrument slowly fades out. He waits for it to return, but it does not. He takes out the stolen flower. He stares into it.

SCENE V

Day. Woman is cleaning, while Man relaxes. She is on her hands and knees, scrubbing. She is dressed in a simple outfit, for working. Her hair is tied back. Man is sweating. He has not, however, removed his shirt.

shakuhachi: a Japanese bamboo flute.

Man: I heard your playing last night.

Woman: My playing?

Man: *Shakuhachi.*

Woman: Oh.

Man: You played very softly. I had to strain to hear it. Next time, don't be afraid. Play out. Fully. Clear. It must've been very beautiful, if only I could've heard it clearly. Why don't you play for me sometime?

Woman: I'm very shy about it.

Man: Why?

Woman: I play for my own satisfaction. That's all. It's something I developed on my own. I don't know if it's at all acceptable by outside standards.

Man: Play for me. I'll tell you.

Woman: No; I'm sure you're too knowledgeable in the arts.

Man: Who? Me?

Woman: You being from the city and all.

Man: I'm ignorant, believe me.

Woman: I'd play, and you'd probably bite your cheek.

Man: Ask me a question about music. Any question. I'll answer incorrectly. I guarantee it.

Woman: Look at this.

Man: What?

Woman: A stain.

Man: Where?

Woman: Here? See? I can't get it out.

Man: Oh. I hadn't noticed it before.

Woman: I notice it every time I clean.

Man: Here. Let me try.

Woman: Thank you.

Man: Ugh. It's tough.

Woman: I know.

Man: How did it get here?

Woman: It's been there as long as I've lived here.

Man: I hardly stand a chance. (*Pause.*) But I'll try. Uh—one—two—three—four! One—two—three—four! See, you set up . . . gotta set up . . . a rhythm—two—three—four. Like fighting! Like battle! One—two—three—four! Used to practice with a rhythm . . . beat . . . battle! Yes! (*The stain starts to fade away.*) Look—it's—yes!—whoo!—there it goes—got the sides—the edges—yes!—fading quick— fading away—ooo—here we come—towards the center—to the heart—two—three—four—slow—slow death—tough—dead! (*Man rolls over in triumphant laughter.*)

Woman: Dead.

Man: I got it! I got it! Whoo! A little rhythm! All it took! Four! Four!

Woman: Thank you.

Man: I didn't think I could do it—but there—it's gone—I did it!

Woman: Yes. You did.

Man: And you—you were great.

Woman: No—I was carried away.

Man: We were a team! You and me!

Woman: I only provided encouragement.

Man: You were great! You were! (*Man grabs Woman. Pause.*)

Woman: It's gone. Thank you. Would you like to hear me play *shakuhachi?*

Man: Yes I would.

Woman: I don't usually play for visitors. It's so . . . I'm not sure. I developed it—all by myself—in times when I was alone. I heard nothing—no human voice. So I learned to play *shakuhachi*. I tried to make these sounds resemble the human voice. The *shakuhachi* became my weapon. To ward off the air. It kept me from choking on many a silent evening.

Man: I'm here. You can hear my voice.

Woman: Speak again.

Man: I will.

SCENE VI

Night. Man is sleeping. Suddenly, a start. He lifts his head up. He listens. Silence. He strains to hear. The shakuhachi melody rises up once more. This time, however, it becomes louder and more clear than before. He gets up. He cannot tell from what direction the music is coming. He walks around the room, putting his ear to different places in the wall, but he cannot locate the sound. It seems to come from all directions at once, as omnipresent as the air. Slowly, he moves towards the wall with the sliding panel through which the Woman enters and exits. He puts his ear against it, thinking the music may be coming from there. Slowly, he slides the door open just a crack, ever so carefully. He peeks through the crack. As he peeks through, the Upstage wall of the set becomes transparent, and through the scrim, we are able to see what he sees. Woman is Upstage of the scrim. She is tending a room filled with potted and vased flowers of all variety. The lushness and beauty of the room Upstage of the scrim stands out in stark contrast to the barrenness of the main set. She is also transformed. She is a young woman. She is beautiful. She wears a brightly colored kimono. Man observes this scene for a long time. He then slides the door shut. The scrim returns to opaque. The music continues. He returns to his mat. He picks up the stolen flower. It is brown and wilted, dead. He looks at it. The music slowly fades out.

SCENE VII

Morning. Man is half-dressed. He is practicing sword maneuvers. He practices with the feel of a man whose spirit is willing, but the flesh is inept. He tries to execute deft movements, but is dissatisfied with his efforts. He curses himself, and returns to basic exercises. Suddenly, he feels something buzzing around his neck—a mosquito. He slaps his neck, but misses it. He sees it flying near him. He swipes at it with his sword. He keeps missing. Finally, he thinks he's hit it. He runs over, kneels down to recover the fallen insect. He picks up two halves of a mosquito on two different fingers. Woman enters the room. She looks as she normally does. She is carrying a vase of flowers, which she places on its shelf.

Man: Look.

Woman: I'm sorry?

Man: Look.

Woman: What? (*He brings over the two halves of mosquito to show her.*)

Man: See?

Woman: Oh.

Man: I hit it—chop!

Woman: These are new forms of target practice?

Man: Huh? Well—yes—in a way.

Woman: You seem to do well at it.

Man: Thank you. For last night. I heard your *shakuhachi*. It was very loud, strong—
good tone.

Woman: Did you enjoy it? I wanted you to enjoy it. If you wish, I'll play it for you
every night.

Man: Every night!

Woman: If you wish.

Man: No—I don't—I don't want you to treat me like a baby.

Woman: What? I'm not.

Man: Oh, yes. Like a baby. Who you must feed in the middle of the night or he cries.
Waaah! Waaah!

Woman: Stop that!

Man: You need your sleep.

Woman: I don't mind getting up for you. (*Pause.*) I would enjoy playing for you.
Every night. While you sleep. It will make me feel—like I'm shaping your
dreams. I go through long stretches when there is no one in my dreams. It's terrible. During those times, I avoid my bed as much as possible. I paint. I weave. I
play *shakuhachi*. I sit on mats and rub powder into my face. Anything to keep
from facing a bed with no dreams. It is like sleeping on ice.

Man: What do you dream of now?

Woman: Last night—I dreamt of you. I don't remember what happened. But you
were very funny. Not in a mocking way. I wasn't laughing at you. But you made
me laugh. And you were very warm. I remember that. (*Pause.*) What do you
remember about last night?

Man: Just your playing. That's all. I got up, listened to it, and went back to sleep.
(*Man gets up, resumes practicing with his sword.*)

Woman: Another mosquito bothering you?

Man: Just practicing. Ah! Weak! Too weak! I tell you, it wasn't always like this. I'm
telling you, there were days when I could chop the fruit from a tree without ever
taking my eyes off the ground. (*He continues practicing.*) You ever use one of
these?

Woman: I've had to pick one up, yes.

Man: Oh?

Woman: You forget—I live alone—out here—there is . . . not much to sustain me
but what I manage to learn myself. It wasn't really a matter of choice.

Man: I used to be very good, you know. Perhaps I can give you some pointers.

Woman: I'd really rather not.

Man: C'mon—a woman like you—you're absolutely right. You need to know how to
defend yourself.

Woman: As you wish.

Man: Do you have something to practice with?

Woman: Yes. Excuse me. (*She exits. He practices more. She re-enters with two wooden
sticks. He takes one of them.*) Will these do?

Man: Nice. Now, show me what you can do.

Woman: I'm sorry?

Man: Run up and hit me.

Woman: Please.

Man: Go on—I'll block it.

Woman: I feel so . . . undignified.

Man: Go on. (*She hits him playfully with stick.*) Not like that!

Woman: I'll try to be gentle.

Man: What?

Woman: I don't want to hurt you.

Man: You won't—Hit me! (*Woman charges at Man, quickly, deftly. She scores a hit.*) Oh!

Woman: Did I hurt you?

Man: No—you were—let's try that again. (*They square off again. Woman rushes forward. She appears to attempt a strike. He blocks that apparent strike, which turns out to be a feint. She scores.*) Huh?

Woman: Did I hurt you? I'm sorry.

Man: No.

Woman: I hurt you.

Man: No.

Woman: Do you wish to hit me?

Man: No.

Woman: Do you want me to try again?

Man: No.

Woman: Thank you.

Man: Just practice there—by yourself—let me see you run through some maneuvers.

Woman: Must I?

Man: Yes! Go! (*She goes to an open area.*) My greatest strength was always as a teacher. (*Woman executes a series of deft movements. Her whole manner is transformed. Man watches with increasing amazement. Her movements end. She regains her submissive manner.*)

Woman: I'm so embarrassed. My skills—they're so—inappropriate. I look like a man.

Man: Where did you learn that?

Woman: There is much time to practice here.

Man: But you—the techniques.

Woman: I don't know what's fashionable in the outside world. (*Pause.*) Are you unhappy?

Man: No.

Woman: Really?

Man: I'm just . . . . surprised.

Woman: You think it's unbecoming for a woman.

Man: No, no. Not at all.

Woman: You want to leave.

Man: No!

Woman: All visitors do. I know. I've met many. They say they'll stay. And they do. For a while. Until they see too much. Or they learn something new. There are boundaries outside of which visitors do not want to see me step. Only who knows what those boundaries are? Not I. They change with every visitor. You have to be careful not to cross them, but you never know where they are. And one day, inevitably, you step outside the lines. The visitor knows. You don't. You didn't know that you'd done anything different. You thought it was just another part of you. The visitor sneaks away. The next day, you learn that you had stepped outside his heart. I'm afraid you've seen too much.

Man: There are stories.

Woman: What?

Man: People talk.

Woman: Where? We're two days from the nearest village.

Man: Word travels.

Woman: What are you talking about?

Man: There are stories about you. I heard them. They say that your visitors never leave this house.

Woman: That's what you heard?

Man: They say you imprison them.

Woman: Then you were a fool to come here.

Man: Listen.

Woman: Me? Listen? You. Look! Where are these prisoners? Have you seen any?

Man: They told me you were very beautiful.

Woman: Then they are blind as well as ignorant.

Man: You are.

Woman: What?

Man: Beautiful.

Woman: Stop that! My skin feels like seaweed.

Man: I didn't realize it at first. I must confess—I didn't. But over these few days—your face has changed for me. The shape of it. The feel of it. The color. All changed. I look at you now, and I'm no longer sure you are the same woman who had poured tea for me just a week ago. And because of that I remembered—how little I know about a face that changes in the night. (*Pause.*) Have you heard those stories?

Woman: I don't listen to old wives' tales.

Man: But have you heard them?

Woman: Yes. I've heard them. From other visitors—young—hotblooded—or old—who came here because they were told great glory was to be had by killing the witch in the woods.

Man: I was told that no man could spend time in this house without falling in love.

Woman: Oh? So why did you come? Did you wager gold that you could come out untouched? The outside world is so flattering to me. And you—are you like the rest? Passion passing through your heart so powerfully that you can't hold onto it?

Man: No! I'm afraid!

Woman: Of what?

Man: Sometimes—when I look into the flowers, I think I hear a voice—from inside—a voice beneath the petals. A human voice.

Woman: What does it say? "Let me out"?

Man: No. Listen. It hums. It hums with the peacefulness of one who is completely imprisoned.

Woman: I understand that if you listen closely enough, you can hear the ocean.

Man: No. Wait. Look at it. See the layers? Each petal—hiding the next. Try and see where they end. You can't. Follow them down, further down, around—and as you come down—faster and faster—the breeze picks up. The breeze becomes a wail. And in that rush of air—in the silent midst of it—you can hear a voice.

Woman (grabs flower from Man): So, you believe I water and prune my lovers? How can you be so foolish? (*She snaps the flower in half, at the stem. She throws it to the ground.*) Do you come only to leave again? To take a chunk of my heart, then leave with your booty on your belt, like a prize? You say that I imprison hearts in these flowers? Well, bits of my heart are trapped with travellers across this land. I can't even keep track. So kill me. If you came here to destroy a witch, kill me now. I can't stand to have it happen again.

Man: I won't leave you.

Woman: I believe you. (*She looks at the flower that she has broken, bends to pick it up. He touches her. They embrace.*)

SCENE VIII

Day. Woman wears a simple undergarment, over which she is donning a brightly colored kimono, the same one we saw her wearing Upstage of the scrim. Man stands apart.

Woman: I can't cry. I don't have the capacity. Right from birth, I didn't cry. My mother and father were shocked. They thought they'd given birth to a ghost, a demon. Sometimes I've thought myself that. When great sadness has welled up inside me, I've prayed for a means to release the pain from my body. But my prayers went unanswered. The grief remained inside me. It would sit like water, still. (*Pause; she models her kimono.*) Do you like it?

Man: Yes, it's beautiful.

Woman: I wanted to wear something special today.

Man: It's beautiful. Excuse me. I must practice.

Woman: Shall I get you something?

Man: No.

Woman: Some tea, maybe?

Man: No. (*Man resumes swordplay.*)

Woman: Perhaps later today—perhaps we can go out—just around here. We can look for flowers.

Man: Alright.

Woman: We don't have to.

Man: No. Let's.

Woman: I just thought if—

Man: Fine. Where do you want to go?

Woman: There are very few recreational activities around here, I know.

Man: Alright. We'll go this afternoon. (*Pause.*)

Woman: Can I get you something?

Man (turning around): What?

Woman: You might be—

Man: I'm not hungry or thirsty or cold or hot.

Woman: Then what are you?

Man: Practicing. (*Man resumes practicing; Woman exits. As soon as she exits, he rests. He sits down. He examines his sword. He runs his finger along the edge of it. He takes the tip, runs it against the soft skin under his chin. He places the sword on the ground with the tip pointed directly upwards. He keeps it from falling by placing the tip under his chin. He experiments with different degrees of pressure. Woman re-enters. She sees him in this precarious position. She jerks his head upward; the sword falls.*)

Woman: Don't do that!

Man: What?

Woman: You can hurt yourself!

Man: I was practicing!

Woman: You were playing!

Man: I was practicing!

Woman: It's dangerous.

Man: What do you take me for—a child?

Woman: Sometimes wise men do childish things.

Man: I knew what I was doing!

Woman: It scares me.

Man: Don't be ridiculous. (*He reaches for the sword again.*)

Woman: Don't! Don't do that!

Man: Get back! (*He places the sword back in its previous position, suspended between the floor and his chin, upright.*)

Woman: But—

Man: Ssssh!

Woman: I wish—

Man: Listen to me! The slightest shock, you know—the slightest shock— surprise— it might make me jerk or—something—and then . . . so you must be perfectly still and quiet.

Woman: But I—

Man: Sssssh! (*Silence.*) I learned this exercise from a friend—I can't even remember his name—good swordsman—many years ago. He called it his meditation position. He said, like this, he could feel the line between this world and the others because he rested on it. If he saw something in another world that he liked better, all he would have to do is let his head drop, and he'd be there. Simple. No fuss. One day, they found him with the tip of his sword run clean out the back of his neck. He was smiling. I guess he saw something he liked. Or else he'd fallen asleep.

Woman: Stop that.

Man: Stop what?

Woman: Tormenting me.

Man: I'm not.

Woman: Take it away!

Man: You don't have to watch, you know.

Woman: Do you want to die that way—an accident?

Man: I was doing this before you came in.

Woman: If you do, all you need to do is tell me.

Man: What?

Woman: I can walk right over. Lean on the back of your head.

Man: Don't try to threaten—
Woman: Or jerk your sword up.
Man: Or scare me. You can't threaten—
Woman: I'm not. But if that's what you want.
Man: You can't threaten me. You wouldn't do it.
Woman: Oh?
Man: Then I'd be gone. You wouldn't let me leave that easily.
Woman: Yes, I would.
Man: You'd be alone.
Woman: No. I'd follow you. Forever. (*Pause.*) Now, let's stop this nonsense.
Man: No! I can do what I want! Don't come any closer!
Woman: Then release your sword.
Man: Come any closer and I'll drop my head.
Woman (*Woman slowly approaches Man. She grabs the hilt of the sword. She looks into his eyes. She pulls it out from under his chin.*): There will be no more of this. (*She exits with the sword. He starts to follow her, then stops. He touches under his chin. On his finger, he finds a drop of blood.*)

SCENE IX

Night. Man is leaving the house. He is just about out, when he hears a shakuhachi *playing. He looks around, trying to locate the sound. Woman appears in the doorway to the outside.* Shakuhachi *slowly fades out.*

Woman: It's time for you to go?
Man: Yes. I'm sorry.
Woman: You're just going to sneak out? A thief in the night? A frightened child?
Man: I care about you.
Woman: You express it strangely.
Man: I leave in shame because it is proper. (*Pause.*) I came seeking glory.
Woman: To kill me? You can say it. You'll be surprised at how little I blanch. As if you'd said, "I came for a bowl of rice," or "I came seeking love" or "I came to kill you."
Man: Weakness. All weakness. Too weak to kill you. Too weak to kill myself. Too weak to do anything but sneak away in shame. (*Woman brings out Man's sword.*)
Woman: Were you even planning to leave without this? (*He takes sword.*) Why not stay here?
Man: I can't live with someone who's defeated me.
Woman: I never thought of defeating you. I only wanted to take care of you. To make you happy. Because that made me happy and I was no longer alone.
Man: You defeated me.
Woman: Why do you think that way?
Man: I came here with a purpose. The world was clear. You changed the shape of your face, the shape of my heart—rearranged everything—created a world where I could do nothing.
Woman: I only tried to care for you.
Man: I guess that was all it took. (*Pause.*)

Woman: You still think I'm a witch. Just because old women gossip. You are so cruel. Once you arrived, there were only two possibilities: I would die or you would leave. (*Pause.*) If you believe I'm a witch, then kill me. Rid the province of one more evil.

Man: I can't—

Woman: Why not? If you believe that about me, then it's the right thing to do.

Man: You know I can't.

Woman: Then stay.

Man: Don't try and force me.

Woman: I won't force you to do anything. (*Pause.*) All I wanted was an escape—for both of us. The sound of a human voice—the simplest thing to find, and the hardest to hold onto. This house—my loneliness is etched into the walls. Kill me, but don't leave. Even in death, my spirit would rest here and be comforted by your presence.

Man: Force me to stay.

Woman: I won't. (*Man starts to leave.*) Beware.

Man: What?

Woman: The ground on which you walk is weak. It could give way at any moment. The crevice beneath is dark.

Man: Are you talking about death? I'm ready to die.

Woman: Fear for what is worse than death.

Man: What?

Woman: Falling. Falling through the darkness. Waiting to hit the ground. Picking up speed. Waiting for the ground. Falling faster. Falling alone. Waiting. Falling. Waiting. Falling.

(*Woman wails and runs out through the door to her room. Man stands, confused, not knowing what to do. He starts to follow her, then hesitates, and rushes out the door to the outside. Silence. Slowly, he re-enters from the outside. He looks for her in the main room. He goes slowly towards the panel to her room. He throws down his sword. He opens the panel. He goes inside. He comes out. He unrolls his mat. He sits on it, cross-legged. He looks out into space. He notices near him a shakuhachi. He picks it up. He begins to blow into it. He tries to make sounds. He continues trying through the end of the play. The Upstage scrim lights up. Upstage, we see the Woman. She is young. She is hanging from a rope suspended from the roof. She has hung herself. Around her are scores of vases with flowers in them whose blossoms have been blown off. Only the stems remain in the vases. Around her swirl the thousands of petals from the flowers. They fill the Upstage scrim area like a blizzard of color. Man continues to attempt to play. Lights fade to black.*)

David Henry Hwang on Writing

Multicultural Theater   1989

Interviewer: How did you begin . . . exploring your [Chinese American] heritage?

Hwang: A lot of that happened in college. I was in college in the mid-to-late 1970s, and whereas most people seem to associate collegiate life in the seventies with John

Travolta, there was at that time a third-world consciousness, a third-world power movement, in the universities, particularly among Hispanics and Asians. The blacks really started it in the late sixties and early seventies, and it took a while to trickle down into the other third-world communities. Asians probably picked it up last. . . . While I was never a very ardent Marxist, I studied the ideas and I was interested in the degree to which we all may have been affected by certain prejudices in the society without having realized it, and to what degree we had incorporated that into our persons by the time we'd reached our early twenties.

David Henry Hwang

The other thing that I think fascinated me about exploring my Chineseness at that time was consistent with my interest in play-writing. I had become very interested in Sam Shepard, particularly in the way in which Shepard likes to create a sort of American mythology. In his case it's the cowboy mythology, but nonetheless it's something that is larger than simply our present-day, fast-food existence. In my context, creating a mythology, creating a past for myself, involved going into Chinese history and Chinese American history. I think the combination of wanting to delve into those things for artistic reasons and being exposed to an active third-world-consciousness movement was what started to get me interested in my roots when I was in college.

Interviewer: I wonder if there will come a time when the expression "ethnic theater" won't have any meaning.

Hwang: I'm hopeful that there will be a time at some point, but I think it's going to be fifty years or so down the road. The whole idea of being ethnic only applies when it's clear what the dominant culture is. Once it becomes less clear and the culture is acknowledged to be more multicultural, then the idea of what's ethnic becomes irrelevant. I think even today we're starting to see that. The monoethnic theaters—that is, the Asian theaters, the black theaters, the Hispanic theaters— are really useful; they serve a purpose. But I think, if we do our jobs correctly, we will phase out our own need for existence, and the future of theaters will be in multicultural theaters, theaters that do a black play and a Jewish play and a classic and whatever . . .

There are so many people now who can't be labeled. I know a couple in which the man is Japanese and Jewish and the woman is Haitian and Filipino. They have a child, and sociologists have told them that a child of that stock probably hasn't existed before. When someone like that becomes a writer, what do we call him? Do we say he's an Asian writer, or what? As those distinctions become increasingly muddled, the whole notion of what is ethnic as opposed to what is mainstream is going to become more and more difficult to define.

From interview in *Contemporary Authors*

Edward Bok Lee

El Santo Americano   2001

Edward Bok Lee was born in Fargo, North Dakota, the son of Korean immigrants. He attended kindergarten in Seoul, South Korea, but grew up mostly in North Dakota and Minnesota. He received a B.A. in comparative literature from the University of Minnesota and an M.F.A. from Brown University. While enrolled in a graduate program in comparative literature at the University of California, Berkeley, he wrote his first full-length play, St. Petersburg: An Exodus *(2000). Lee writes plays, poetry, fiction, and memoir. A former bartender, custodian, journalist, and translator, Lee has performed his work in the United States, Europe, and Asia, as well as on public radio and on television, including MTV. His prose and poetry collection* Real Karaoke People *(2005) won the Asian American Literary Award and the PEN/Open Book Award. Lee currently teaches at Metropolitan State University.* El Santo Americano *(2001) was originally developed as part of a "ten-minute-play" project at the Guthrie Theater in Minneapolis. His other plays include* Athens County *(1997) and* History K *(2003). "Art can show you," Bok has observed, "the interior of another person's life and soul, if only just for a few minutes."*

CHARACTERS
Clay, *a man*
Evalana, *his wife*

TIME. *Present.*
PLACE. *The desert at night.*

Clay *(driving at night, 80 mph):* that's because in Mexico it's normal to wear a mask. almost everybody does. silk and satin and form-fitting lycra. it makes the whole body more aerodynamic. you ought see them flying around, doing triple flips in mid-air. they got these long flowing capes like colorful wings sprouting from their shoulders. they don't talk much, though. not the great ones. the silence is mysterious. it adds a kind of weight to them when they climb into the ring. get a guy with that much gold and glitter on him here and you know he'd have to talk shit. in Mexico they just wrestle. the masks come from thousands and thousands of years ago. fiestas. ancient rituals. slip one over your head and you could become a tiger or donkey, a bat or giant lizard. a corn spirit dancing under the clouds for rain. those were your gods if you lived back then. you'll like it there in Mexico. don't you think you'll like it there? Jesse?

(Evalana, brooding, eventually looks in the backseat then faces front again.)

Clay: he asleep back there?
    a growing boy needs his sleep.
        yes he does.
        you hungry?
Evalana: don't talk to me.
Clay: hard to fall asleep on an empty stomach.
Evalana: i can't sleep.

Clay: you ain't tried to.

> (*She checks her outburst, then looks in the backseat again, perhaps adjusting their son's blanket, then faces front. they drive on for a time.*)

Clay (looking in rearview mirror): hey there Jesse.
> you have a nice nap?
> we'll be there come morning, so you just sit back.
> how you like that comic book i got you?
> Jesse?
> what's the matter, boy? you not feeling well?
> Jesse?

Evalana: sometimes he sleeps with his eyes open.

Clay: like you.

Evalana: i do not sleep with my eyes open.

Clay: how do you know?

Evalana: i know.

Clay: how?

Evalana: 'cause someone would have said something. including you.

Clay: people do all kinds of things they're not aware of.
> my daddy used to wander through the house all night, buck naked,
> up and down the stairs. opening and closing windows.
> carrying only his briefcase chockfull of all the vending machine products he sold.
> combs. candy. chicken bouillon.
> my momma warned if we woke him up he'd have a heart attack.
> so we just let him sleepwalk.
> he didn't know.

Evalana: maybe somebody should have told him.

Clay: he didn't want to know.

> (*They drive on.*)

Evalana: you talk in your sleep.
> you snore.
> you drool.
> and you fart. all night.

> (*They drive on awhile.*)

Clay: i love you, Ev.

Evalana: jesus, Clay. listen to yourself.
> your whole life you been faking it.
> fake husband. fake father.
> fake man. that's what they ought to call you:
> Fake Man.

> (*Clay drives on for a little while longer through the night, then pulls the car to a stop on the side of the road and gets out. he walks a good ways away from the car, holding a flashlight in one hand and a gun in the other—not aimed at her, but clearly present, under the starlight. Evalana hesitates, then gets out, the flashlight's beam now on her.*)

Clay (*directs flashlight beam to a place in the brush*): there's a bush over there.

(*Evalana, hesitant at first, then grabs her purse and crosses past Clay.*)

Evalana (*off*): i won't run!
i promise!

(*Clay thinks, then lowers flashlight beam and switches it off. dim moonlight. sounds of desert at night.*)

Clay: you should have seen me last week, Ev!

Darton, he cut me a break! he didn't have to, but he did 'cause i been loyal to him all these years! you remember when we used to work at the turkey plant together! the smell on my hands when i'd come home and try to kiss you . . .

the match was against the eleventh-ranked contender! brand new guy, from Montreal! Kid Canuck they call him! long blonde hair, tan, all bulked up in white trunks with a red maple leaf you know where! some rich producer's nephew or something! he was scheduled to wrestle the Sheik in the opening match, but the old guy had a hernia while they was warming up, so Darton, he give me a break and put me on the bill against Kid Canuck at the last minute!

we didn't have time to choreograph much action! i think he was kind of nervous! two minutes in he starts grabbing my hair! hard! for real! trying to get the audience more into it! he wasn't telegraphing his head butts neither! soon enough my nose was a cherry caught under a dumptruck! the blood all over sure got the crowd into it boy! up till then they was pretty quiet, waiting for the main headliners to come out!

raking my eyes, slapping my face. i told him to ease up, it don't work like that here, but he wasn't listening. dancing around. cursing at me in French. winding his right arm up, then smacking me hard with the left until both my ears are firebells going off.

now i can take just about anything. you know me. i've been pile-drived, figure-foured, and suplexed into losses by the best of them. but on this particular night, something happened. and one pop i took in the mouth shot my adrenaline way up, my blood running all over hell now like carbolic acid, and him twisting my arm for real, not giving a flying fuck about my bad elbow, my bad back, or my five-year-old son, who don't even like to watch wrestling no more 'cause he's ashamed, 'cause his friends call his daddy a loser, and he don't know what to say or believe in, and the next thing i knew i had that pretty boy son of a bitch Kid Canuck down hard on the mat in a scorpion leg lock!!

they had to haul him off on a stretcher!

i was a little dazed yet, and the crowd, they didn't know what to think!

then the referee threw my arm up under the hot lights and before i knew it all the noise in the arena was more like cheering! it was a chemical thing! at first some people in the upper bleachers stood up! and then all of them did! everywhere! stomping, and starting to chant my name! and not 'cause they hated the other guy! they didn't! they was cheering 'cause i beat the guy fair and square! he gave up out of pain, right there in the middle of the ring! i had him wrenched in that scorpion leg lock a good two minutes screaming like a baby, like a cut pig, like a man in real pain! and they knew it!

you can't fake that! they'd seen so much phony bullshit through the years, and they could tell this match was different! and they appreciated that! they appreciated being shown the truth, just once in their sorry-ass lives!

Darton threw a wet towel at my face in the locker room.

i went out on a limb for you! he says. six months of planning and promotion! tens of thousands of dollars! t-shirts! coffee mugs! now who the hell's gonna believe Kid Canuck is a contender for the federation championship when he lost his debut match to you!!

i told him i was sorry, and after a while he put his hand on my shoulder. asked me what i'd been thinking there in the ring. tell me the truth, he says. so i can go home and feel at least a little bad about firing your dumb ass.

and i wanted to say that i did it for you.

for my wife, Evalana, who i never gave nothing to believe in.

and i did it for my boy, Jesse, who only ever got to see his daddy get beat time and again. i wanted to tell him i did it 'cause my wife and child was out there in the audience. not living in some other town. i wanted to say you was both out there watching over me. 'cause where else would you be?

Ev? Evalana!

(Clay switches on flashlight and directs its beam onto the "bush" in the desert. Evalana has run off. he directs the flashlight all around, searching in vain.)

shit.

(Clay turns off the flashlight and sits down on a stone. in the moonlight, he pulls out from his pocket a colorful Mexican wrestler's mask and slips it over his head. he sits there in the darkness alone for a moment. he then, as a little boy might, twirls the gun on his finger, and pretends what it'd be like to shoot himself in the head. he tries it from a couple different angles, in strange fun. eventually he places the gun in his mouth, holds it there for a second or two with his hand, then lets go. it remains stuck there in his mouth from here on out. eventually, out of the darkness of the desert, Evalana reappears.)

Evalana: once, when i was about Jesse's age, we took a trip to California. Disneyland. we drove all the way cross country in Daddy's Ford Falcon. Ma said it was the honeymoon she never got. a lot of the highway had just been tarred, and you could feel it. i thought we was gonna sail on forever into the future. it was somewhere in Arizona that Daddy woke us all up so we could see this great big dam at night. we stood there looking down at the bright lights and roaring darkness. Ma moved off to one side and stared down, a thousand feet.
i knew she wanted to jump.
then suddenly, she pointed at something. look, Ev, she said. a rainbow!

Shane and Darlene came running over, climbing up on the guard-rail but they couldn't see nothing. neither could Daddy.

a few hours later, somewhere outside of Flagstaff i told them i saw that rainbow too. it wasn't just Ma who saw it. i saw it too. Shane and Darlene were asleep now. Ma didn't say nothing. we drove on deeper into the night. then Daddy looked at me. i could see his eyes in the rear view mirror. hovering there in the blackness. "there's no such thing as a rainbow at night," he said. "not a real rainbow anyway."

the next day at dusk we camped on high ground. from where i stood looking down, you could see all the layers of sediment carved in the side of the mountains they cleared away for the highways a long time ago. red, black, brown, white, and sometimes almost blue, like a human vein in the side of a mountain, running parallel to the horizon. i stood there a long time, watching all the layers of earthen rainbows darkening all around me. then slowly, i noticed something. in the far distance, a cluster of fallen stars. only, it wasn't a cluster of stars, but a town. far off the highway, down there in the middle of nowhere. you wouldn't even notice it by day. but at night you could see something. twinkling. i imagined i'd been born in that town, and that that was where we was all heading back to. not Disneyland. but that town shining with tiny stars that weren't really stars, surrounded by rainbows that weren't really rainbows. but erosion. as far as the eye could see. for thousands and thousands of years. both real and imaginary. like that town down there in the valley at night. just barely shimmering. like . . . Eden.

(We hear the sound of their car start and drive off into the night. Clay in mask with gun still in mouth and Evalana slowly turn to watch the vehicle go, converging closer together as they walk and watch. "Jesse" has driven off into the night. once the sound of the car has faded into the distance, Clay in mask with gun in mouth and Evalana slowly turn to one another. after a moment, Evalana reaches up and removes the gun from Clay's mouth and slowly points it at him.

Fade to black.)

END OF PLAY

Edward Bok Lee on Writing

On Being a Korean American Writer 2006

Interviewer: Do you think of yourself as a Korean American writer?

Lee: What I'm doing, intentionally, is trying to participate in this thing we call Asian America, this Asian American culture, which is influenced by my parents and the way that they brought me up, their philosophies and their religious beliefs, their culture—everything from the food to the song to the art form.

I believe that a given culture has a given orientation of the soul. And you can hear it in a culture's music. It's live, it's right in front of you, it's all around you. I really believe that when I hear a culture—whether it's Irish or African or English or Hawaiian—when I hear the traditional songs

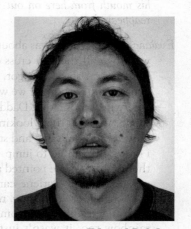

Edward Bok Lee

coming out of people, I definitely sense that there are differences of the soul. So in that way, I feel alive with some sort of Asian, and more Asian American sensibilities. I have no idea how to try and quantify those things, but I feel it.

It's sort of drenching the country when I go back to Korea—especially the countryside. It's tied to the land, it's tied to the history. It's a history, in Korea, of oppression, of colonization, and of survival. I feel, like it or not, that that ethos or whatever you want to call it, is infused in my work.

. . . I feel like a conduit between something going on in another realm. It might be something like the past, history, or something beyond memory. Voices. It's in the realm of intuition . . . and it's mysterious. And that's when I feel like I'm at my best in writing. Versus that I have things to say that I want to communicate. If that were the case, then I think I would do journalism, or write essays.

I think I'm in love with the unspeakable, the inarticulable. You're always coming up against this invisible wall, and putting a cup to it, trying to hear what's going on the other side. You're always trying to transcribe those things.

From "Thinking Souls: An Interview with Edward Bok Lee"
by Shannon Gibney

Jane Martin

Beauty   2001

The identity of Jane Martin is a closely guarded secret. No biographical details, public statements, or photographs of this Kentucky-based playwright have been published, nor has she given any interviews or made any public appearances. Often called "America's best known, unknown playwright," Martin first came to public notice in 1981 for Talking With, *a collection of monologues that received a number of productions worldwide and won a Best Foreign Play of the Year award in Germany. Of Martin's many plays, others include* What Mama Don't Know (1988), Cementville (1991), Keely and Du (*which was a finalist for the 1993 Pulitzer Prize*), Middle-Aged White Guys (1995), Jack and Jill (1996), Mr. Bundy (1998), Anton in Show Business (2000), Flaming Guns of the Purple Sage (2001), *and* Good Boys (2002). *Her most recent work is* Sez She (2005), *a monologue play for five actresses.*

CHARACTERS

Carla
Bethany

SCENE. *An apartment. Minimalist set. A young woman, Carla, on the phone.*

Carla: In love with me? You're in love with me? Could you describe yourself again? Uh-huh. Uh-huh. And you spoke to me? (*A knock at the door.*) Listen, I always hate to interrupt a marriage proposal, but . . . could you possibly hold that thought? (*Puts phone down and goes to door. Bethany, the same age as Carla and a friend, is there. She carries the sort of mid-eastern lamp we know of from Aladdin.*)
Bethany: Thank God you were home. I mean, you're not going to believe this!
Carla: Somebody on the phone. (*Goes back to it.*)
Bethany: I mean, I just had a beach urge, so I told them at work my uncle was dying . . .
Carla (*motions to Bethany for quiet*): And you were the one in the leather jacket with the tattoo? What was the tattoo? (*Carla again asks Bethany, who is gesturing wildly that she should hang up, to cool it.*) Look, a screaming eagle from shoulder to shoulder, maybe. There were a lot of people in the bar.

Bethany (*gesturing and mouthing*): I have to get back to work.

Carla (*on phone*): See, the thing is, I'm probably not going to marry someone I can't remember . . . particularly when I don't drink. Sorry. Sorry. Sorry. (*She hangs up.*) Madness.

Bethany: So I ran out to the beach . . .

Carla: This was some guy I never met who apparently offered me a beer . . .

Bethany: . . . low tide and this . . . (*The lamp*) . . . was just sitting there, lying there . . .

Carla: . . . and he tracks me down . . .

Bethany: . . . on the beach, and I lift this lid thing . . .

Carla: . . . and seriously proposes marriage.

Bethany: . . . and a genie comes out.

Carla: I mean, that's twice in a . . . what?

Bethany: A genie comes out of this thing.

Carla: A genie?

Bethany: I'm not kidding, the whole Disney kind of thing, swirling smoke, and then this twenty-foot-high, see-through guy in like an Arabian outfit.

Carla: Very funny.

Bethany: Yes, funny, but twenty feet high! I look up and down the beach, I'm alone. I don't have my pepper spray or my hand alarm. You know me, when I'm petrified I joke. I say his voice is too high for Robin Williams, and he says he's a castrati. Naturally. Who else would I meet?

Carla: What's a castrati?

Bethany: You know . . .

(*The appropriate gesture.*)

Carla: Bethany, dear one, I have three modeling calls. I am meeting Ralph Lauren!

Bethany: Okay, good. Ralph Lauren. Look, I am not kidding!

Carla: You're not kidding what?!

Bethany: There is a genie in this thingamajig.

Carla: Uh-huh. I'll be back around eight.

Bethany: And he offered me *wishes!*

Carla: Is this some elaborate practical joke because it's my birthday?

Bethany: No, happy birthday, but I'm like crazed because I'm on this deserted beach with a twenty-foot-high, see-through genie, so like sarcastically . . . you know how I need a new car . . . I said fine, gimme 25,000 dollars . . .

Carla: On the beach with the genie?

Bethany: Yeah, right, exactly, and it rains down out of the sky.

Carla: Oh sure.

Bethany (*pulling a wad out of her purse*): Count it, those are thousands. I lost one in the surf.

(*Carla sees the top bill. Looks at Bethany, who nods encouragement. Carla thumbs through them.*)

Carla: These look real.

Bethany: Yeah.

Carla: And they rained down out of the sky?

Bethany: Yeah.

Carla: You've been really strange lately, are you dealing?

Bethany: Dealing what, I've even given up chocolate.

Carla: Let me see the genie.

Bethany: Wait, wait.

Carla: Bethany, I don't have time to screw around. Let me see the genie or let me go on my appointments.

Bethany: Wait! So I pick up the money . . . see, there's sand on the money . . . and I'm like nuts so I say, you know, "Okay, look, ummm, big guy, my uncle is in the hospital" . . . because as you know when I said to the people at work my uncle was dying, I was on one level telling the truth although it had nothing to do with the beach, but he was in Intensive Care after the accident, and that's on my mind, so I say, okay, Genie, heal my uncle . . . which is like impossible given he was hit by two trucks, and the genie says, "Yes, Master" . . . like they're supposed to say, and he goes into this like kind of whirlwind, kicking up sand and stuff, and I'm like, "Oh my God!" and the air clears, and he bows, you know, and says, "It is done, Master," and I say, "Okay, whatever-you-are, I'm calling on my cell phone," and I get it out and I get this doctor who is like dumbstruck who says my uncle came to, walked out of Intensive Care and left the hospital! I'm not kidding, Carla.

Carla: On your mother's grave?

Bethany: On my mother's grave.

(They look at each other.)

Carla: Let me see the genie.

Bethany: No, no, look, that's the whole thing . . . I was just, like, reacting, you know, responding, and that's already two wishes . . . although I'm really pleased about my uncle, the $25,000 thing, I could have asked for $10 million, and there is only one wish left.

Carla: So ask for $10 million.

Bethany: I don't think so. I don't think so. I mean, I gotta focus in here. Do you have a sparkling water?

Carla: No. Bethany, I'm missing Ralph Lauren now. Very possibly my one chance to go from catalogue model to the very, very big time, so, if you are joking, stop joking.

Bethany: Not joking. See, see, the thing is, I know what I want. In my guts. Yes. Underneath my entire bitch of a life is this unspoken, ferocious, all-consuming urge . . .

Carla (trying to get her to move this along): Ferocious, all-consuming urge . . .

Bethany: I want to be like you.

Carla: Me?

Bethany: Yes.

Carla: Half the time you don't even like me.

Bethany: Jealous. The ogre of jealousy.

Carla: You're the one with the $40,000 job straight out of school. You're the one who has published short stories. I'm the one hanging on by her fingernails in modeling. The one who has creeps calling her on the phone. The one who had to have a nose job.

Bethany: I want to be beautiful.

Carla: You are beautiful.

Bethany: Carla, I'm not beautiful.

Carla: You have charm. You have personality. You know perfectly well you're pretty.

Bethany: "Pretty," see, that's it. Pretty is the minor leagues of beautiful. Pretty is what people discover about you after they know you. Beautiful is what knocks them out across the room. Pretty, you get called a couple of times a year; *beautiful* is 24 hours a day.

Carla: Yeah? So?

Bethany: So?! We're talking *beauty* here. Don't say "So?" Beauty is the real deal. You are the center of any moment of your life. People stare. Men flock. I've seen you get offered discounts on makeup for no reason. Parents treat beautiful children better. Studies show your income goes up. You can have sex anytime you want it. Men have to know me. That takes up to a year. I'm continually horny.

Carla: Bethany, I don't even like sex. I can't have a conversation without men coming on to me. I have no privacy. I get hassled on the street. They start pressuring me from the beginning. Half the time, it never occurs to them to start with a conversation. Smart guys like you. You've had three long-term relationships, and you're only twenty-three. I haven't had one. The good guys, the smart guys are scared to death of me. I'm surrounded by male bimbos who think a preposition is when you go to school away from home. I have no woman friends except you. I don't even want to talk about this!

Bethany: I knew you'd say something like this. See, you're "in the club" so you can say this. It's the way beauty functions as an elite. You're trying to keep it all for yourself.

Carla: I'm trying to tell you it's no picnic.

Bethany: But it's what everybody wants. It's the nasty secret at large in the world. It's the unspoken tidal desire in every room and on every street. It's the unspoken, the soundless whisper . . . millions upon millions of people longing hopelessly and forever to stop being whatever they are and be beautiful, but the difference between those ardent multitudes and me is that I have a goddamn genie and one more wish!

Carla: Well, it's not what I want. This is me, Carla. I have never read a whole book. Page 6, I can't remember page 4. The last thing I read was "The Complete Idiot's Guide to WordPerfect." I leave dinner parties right after the dessert because I'm out of conversation. You know the dumb blond joke about on the application where it says, "Sign here," she put Sagittarius? I've done that. Only beautiful guys approach me, and that's because they want to borrow my eye shadow. I barely exist outside a mirror! You don't want to *be me.*

Bethany: None of you tell the truth. That's why you have no friends. We can all see you're just trying to make us feel better because we aren't in your league. This only proves to me it should be my third wish. Money can only buy things. Beauty makes you the center of the universe.

(*Bethany picks up the lamp.*)

Carla: Don't do it. Bethany, don't wish it! I am telling you you'll regret it.

(*Bethany lifts the lid. There is a tremendous crash, and the lights go out. Then they flicker and come back up, revealing Bethany and Carla on the floor where they have been thrown by the explosion. We don't realize it at first, but they have exchanged places.*)

Carla/Bethany: Oh God.

Bethany/Carla: Oh God.

Carla/Bethany: Am I bleeding? Am I dying?

Bethany/Carla: I'm so dizzy. You're not bleeding.

Carla/Bethany: Neither are you.

Bethany/Carla: I feel so weird.

Carla/Bethany: Me too. I feel . . . (*Looking at her hands.*) Oh, my God, I'm wearing your jewelry. I'm wearing your nail polish.

Bethany/Carla: I know I'm over here, but I can see myself over there.

Carla/Bethany: I'm wearing your dress. I have your legs!!

Bethany/Carla: These aren't my shoes. I can't meet Ralph Lauren wearing these shoes!

Carla/Bethany: I wanted to be beautiful, but I didn't want to be you.

Bethany/Carla: Thanks a lot!!

Carla/Bethany: I've got to go. I want to pick someone out and get laid.

Bethany/Carla: You can't just walk out of here in my body!

Carla/Bethany: Wait a minute. Wait a minute. What's eleven eighteenths of 1,726?

Bethany/Carla: Why?

Carla/Bethany: I'm a public accountant. I want to know if you have my brain.

Bethany/Carla: One hundred thirty-two and a half.

Carla/Bethany: You have my brain.

Bethany/Carla: What shade of Rubenstein lipstick does Cindy Crawford wear with teal blue?

Carla/Bethany: Raging Storm.

Bethany/Carla: You have my brain. You poor bastard.

Carla/Bethany: I don't care. Don't you see?

Bethany/Carla: See what?

Carla/Bethany: We both have the one thing, the one and only thing everybody wants.

Bethany/Carla: What is that?

Carla/Bethany: It's better than beauty for me; it's better than brains for you.

Bethany/Carla: What? What?!

Carla/Bethany: Different problems.

BLACKOUT

August Wilson

Fences   1985

*August Wilson (1945–2005) was born in Pittsburgh, one of six children of a German Ameri-
can father and an African American mother. His parents separated early, and the young Wilson was raised on the Hill, a Pittsburgh ghetto neighborhood. Although he quit school in the
ninth grade when a teacher wrongly accused him of submitting a ghost-written paper, Wilson
continued his education in local libraries, supporting himself by working as a cook and stock
clerk. In 1968 he co-founded a community troupe, the Black Horizons Theater, staging plays
by LeRoi Jones and other militants; later he moved from Pittsburgh to Saint Paul, Minnesota,
where at last he saw a play of his own performed. Jitney, his first important work, won him entry to a 1982 playwrights' conference at the Eugene O'Neill Theater Center. There, Lloyd
Richards, dean of Yale University School of Drama, took an interest in Wilson's work and
offered to produce his plays at Yale. Ma Rainey's Black Bottom was the first to reach Broadway (in 1985), where it ran for ten months and received an award from the New York Drama
Critics Circle. In 1987 Fences, starring Mary Alice and James Earl Jones, won another Critics Circle Award, as well as a Tony Award and the Pulitzer Prize for best American play of its
year. It set a box office record for a Broadway nonmusical. Joe Turner's Come and Gone
(1988) also received high acclaim, and The Piano Lesson (1990) won Wilson a second
Pulitzer Prize. His subsequent plays were Two Trains Running (1992), Seven Guitars
(1995), King Hedley II (2000), Gem of the Ocean (2003), and Radio Golf (2005).*

*Wilson's ten plays, each one set in a different decade of the 1900s, constitute his "Cen-
tury Cycle" that traces the black experience in America throughout the twentieth century.
Seamlessly interweaving realistic and mythic approaches, filled with vivid characters, pun-
gent dialogue, and strong dramatic scenes, it is one of the most ambitious projects in the*

Viola Davis and Denzel Washington in 2010 Broadway production of *Fences*.

history of the American theater and an epic achievement in our literature. Wilson died of liver cancer in October 2005, a few months after completing the final play in his cycle. Two weeks after his death the Virginia Theater on Broadway was renamed the August Wilson Theater in his honor. A published poet as well as a dramatist, Wilson once told an interviewer, "After writing poetry for twenty-one years, I approach a play the same way. The mental process is poetic: you use metaphor and condense."

For Lloyd Richards, Who Adds to Whatever He Touches

When the sins of our fathers visit us
We do not have to play host.
We can banish them with forgiveness
As God, in His Largeness and Laws.

—AUGUST WILSON

LIST OF CHARACTERS

Troy Maxson
Jim Bono, Troy's friend
Rose, Troy's wife
Lyons, Troy's oldest son by previous marriage
Gabriel, Troy's brother
Cory, Troy and Rose's son
Raynell, Troy's daughter

Mary Alice, Ray Aranha, and James Earl Jones in Yale Repertory Theatre's 1985 world premiere of *Fences.*

SETTING. *The setting is the yard which fronts the only entrance to the Maxson household, an ancient two-story brick house set back off a small alley in a big-city neighborhood. The entrance to the house is gained by two or three steps leading to a wooden porch badly in need of paint.*

A relatively recent addition to the house and running its full width, the porch lacks congruence. It is a sturdy porch with a flat roof. One or two chairs of dubious value sit at one end where the kitchen window opens onto the porch. An old-fashioned icebox stands silent guard at the opposite end.

The yard is a small dirt yard, partially fenced, except for the last scene, with a wooden saw horse, a pile of lumber, and other fence-building equipment set off to the side. Opposite is a tree from which hangs a ball made of rags. A baseball bat leans against the tree. Two oil drums serve as garbage receptacles and sit near the house at right to complete the setting.

THE PLAY. *Near the turn of the century, the destitute of Europe sprang on the city with tenacious claws and an honest and solid dream. The city devoured them. They swelled its belly until it burst into a thousand furnaces and sewing machines, a thousand butcher shops and bakers' ovens, a thousand churches and hospitals and funeral parlors and money-lenders. The city grew. It nourished itself and offered each man a partnership limited only by his talent, his guile, and his willingness and capacity for hard work. For the immigrants of Europe, a dream dared and won true.*

The descendants of African slaves were offered no such welcome or participation. They came from places called the Carolinas and the Virginias, Georgia, Alabama, Mississippi, and Tennessee. They came strong, eager, searching. The city rejected them and they fled and settled along the riverbanks and under bridges in shallow, ramshackle houses made of sticks and tarpaper. They collected rags and wood. They sold the use of their muscles and their bodies. They cleaned houses and washed clothes, they shined shoes, and in quiet desperation and vengeful pride, they stole, and lived in pursuit of their own dream. That they could breathe free, finally, and stand to meet life with the force of dignity and whatever eloquence the heart could call upon.

By 1957, the hard-won victories of the European immigrants had solidified the industrial might of America. War had been confronted and won with new energies that used loyalty and patriotism as its fuel. Life was rich, full, and flourishing. The Milwaukee Braves won the World Series, and the hot winds of change that would make the sixties a turbulent, racing, dangerous, and provocative decade had not yet begun to blow full.

ACT I

SCENE I

It is 1957. Troy and Bono enter the yard, engaged in conversation. Troy is fifty-three years old, a large man with thick, heavy hands; it is this largeness that he strives to fill out and make an accommodation with. Together with his blackness, his largeness informs his sensibilities and the choices he has made in his life.

Of the two men, Bono is obviously the follower. His commitment to their friendship of thirty-odd years is rooted in his admiration of Troy's honesty, capacity for hard work, and his strength, which Bono seeks to emulate.

It is Friday night, payday, and the one night of the week the two men engage in a ritual of talk and drink. Troy is usually the most talkative and at times he can be crude and almost vulgar, though he is capable of rising to profound heights of expression. The men carry lunch buckets and wear or carry burlap aprons and are dressed in clothes suitable to their jobs as garbage collectors.

Bono: Troy, you ought to stop that lying!

Troy: I ain't lying! The nigger had a watermelon this big. (*He indicates with his hands.*) Talking about . . . "What watermelon, Mr. Rand?" I liked to fell out! "What watermelon, Mr. Rand?" . . . And it sitting there big as life.

Bono: What did Mr. Rand say?

Troy: Ain't said nothing. Figure if the nigger too dumb to know he carrying a watermelon, he wasn't gonna get much sense out of him. Trying to hide that great big old watermelon under his coat. Afraid to let the white man see him carry it home.

Bono: I'm like you . . . I ain't got no time for them kind of people.

Troy: Now what he look like getting mad cause he see the man from the union talking to Mr. Rand?

Bono: He come to me talking about . . . "Maxson gonna get us fired." I told him to get away from me with that. He walked away from me calling you a troublemaker. What Mr. Rand say?

Troy: Ain't said nothing. He told me to go down the Commissioner's office next Friday. They called me down there to see them.

Bono: Well, as long as you got your complaint filed, they can't fire you. That's what one of them white fellows tell me.

Troy: I ain't worried about them firing me. They gonna fire me cause I asked a question? That's all I did. I went to Mr. Rand and asked him, "Why? Why you got the white mens driving and the colored lifting?" Told him, "what's the matter, don't I count? You think only white fellows got sense enough to drive a truck. That ain't no paper job! Hell, anybody can drive a truck. How come you got all whites driving and the colored lifting?" He told me "take it to the union." Well, hell, that's what I done! Now they wanna come up with this pack of lies.

Bono: I told Brownie if the man come and ask him any questions . . . just tell the truth! It ain't nothing but something they done trumped up on you cause you filed a complaint on them.

Troy: Brownie don't understand nothing. All I want them to do is change the job description. Give everybody a chance to drive the truck. Brownie can't see that. He ain't got that much sense.

Bono: How you figure he be making out with that gal be up at Taylors' all the time . . . that Alberta gal?

Troy: Same as you and me. Getting just as much as we is. Which is to say nothing.

Bono: It is, huh? I figure you doing a little better than me . . . and I ain't saying what I'm doing.

Troy: Aw, nigger, look here . . . I know you. If you had got anywhere near that gal, twenty minutes later you be looking to tell somebody. And the first one you gonna tell . . . that you gonna want to brag to . . . is gonna be me.

Bono: I ain't saying that. I see where you be eyeing her.

Troy: I eye all the women. I don't miss nothing. Don't never let nobody tell you Troy Maxson don't eye the women.

Bono: You been doing more than eyeing her. You done bought her a drink or two.

Troy: Hell yeah, I bought her a drink! What that mean? I bought you one, too. What that mean cause I buy her a drink? I'm just being polite.

Bono: It's alright to buy her one drink. That's what you call being polite. But when you wanna be buying two or three . . . that's what you call eyeing her.

Troy: Look here, as long as you known me . . . you ever known me to chase after women?

Bono: Hell yeah! Long as I done known you. You forgetting I knew you when.

Troy: Naw, I'm talking about since I been married to Rose?

Bono: Oh, not since you been married to Rose. Now, that's the truth, there. I can say that.

Troy: Alright then! Case closed.

Bono: I see you be walking up around Alberta's house. You supposed to be at Taylors' and you be walking up around there.

Troy: What you watching where I'm walking for? I ain't watching after you.

Bono: I seen you walking around there more than once.

Troy: Hell, you liable to see me walking anywhere! That don't mean nothing cause you see me walking around there.

Bono: Where she come from anyway? She just kinda showed up one day.

Troy: Tallahassee. You can look at her and tell she one of them Florida gals. They got some big healthy women down there. Grow them right up out the ground. Got a little bit of Indian in her. Most of them niggers down in Florida got some Indian in them.

Bono: I don't know about that Indian part. But she damn sure big and healthy. Woman wear some big stockings. Got them great big old legs and hips as wide as the Mississippi River.

Troy: Legs don't mean nothing. You don't do nothing but push them out of the way. But them hips cushion the ride!

Bono: Troy, you ain't got no sense.

Troy: It's the truth! Like you riding on Goodyears!

(Rose enters from the house. She is ten years younger than Troy, her devotion to him stems from her recognition of the possibilities of her life without him: a succession of abusive men and their babies, a life of partying and running the streets, the Church, or aloneness with its attendant pain and frustration. She recognizes Troy's spirit as a fine and illuminating one and she either ignores or forgives his faults, only some of which she recognizes. Though she doesn't drink, her presence is an integral part of the Friday night rituals. She alternates between the porch and the kitchen, where supper preparations are under way.)

Rose: What you all out here getting into?

Troy: What you worried about what we getting into for? This is men talk, woman.

Rose: What I care what you all talking about? Bono, you gonna stay for supper?

Bono: No, I thank you, Rose. But Lucille say she cooking up a pot of pigfeet.

Troy: Pigfeet! Hell, I'm going home with you! Might even stay the night if you got some pigfeet. You got something in there to top them pigfeet, Rose?

Rose: I'm cooking up some chicken. I got some chicken and collard greens.

Troy: Well, go on back in the house and let me and Bono finish what we was talking about. This is men talk. I got some talk for you later. You know what kind of talk I mean. You go on and powder it up.

Rose: Troy Maxson, don't you start that now!

Troy (*puts his arm around her*): Aw, woman . . . come here. Look here, Bono . . . . when I met this woman . . . I got out that place, say, "Hitch up my pony, saddle up my mare . . . there's a woman out there for me somewhere. I looked here. Looked there. Saw Rose and latched on to her." I latched on to her and told her—I'm gonna tell you the truth—I told her, "Baby, I don't wanna marry, I just wanna be your man." Rose told me . . . tell him what you told me, Rose.

Rose: I told him if he wasn't the marrying kind, then move out the way so the marrying kind could find me.

Troy: That's what she told me. "Nigger, you in my way. You blocking the view! Move out the way so I can find me a husband." I thought it over two or three days. Come back—

Rose: Ain't no two or three days nothing. You was back the same night.

Troy: Come back, told her . . . "Okay, baby . . . but I'm gonna buy me a banty rooster and put him out there in the backyard . . . and when he see a stranger come, he'll flap his wings and crow . . ." Look here, Bono, I could watch the front door by myself . . . it was that back door I was worried about.

Rose: Troy, you ought not talk like that. Troy ain't doing nothing but telling a lie.

Troy: Only thing is . . . when we first got married . . . forget the rooster . . . we ain't had no yard!

Bono: I hear you tell it. Me and Lucille was staying down there on Logan Street. Had two rooms with the outhouse in the back. I ain't mind the outhouse none. But when that goddamn wind blow through there in the winter . . . that's what I'm talking about! To this day I wonder why in the hell I ever stayed down there for six long years. But see, I didn't know I could do no better. I thought only white folks had inside toilets and things.

Rose: There's a lot of people don't know they can do no better than they doing now. That's just something you got to learn. A lot of folks still shop at Bella's.

Troy: Ain't nothing wrong with shopping at Bella's. She got fresh food.

Rose: I ain't said nothing about if she got fresh food. I'm talking about what she charge. She charge ten cents more than the A&P.

Troy: The A&P ain't never done nothing for me. I spends my money where I'm treated right. I go down to Bella, say, "I need a loaf of bread, I'll pay you Friday." She give it to me. What sense that make when I got money to go and spend it somewhere else and ignore the person who done right by me? That ain't in the Bible.

Rose: We ain't talking about what's in the Bible. What sense it make to shop there when she overcharge?

Troy: You shop where you want to. I'll do my shopping where the people been good to me.

Rose: Well, I don't think it's right for her to overcharge. That's all I was saying.

Bono: Look here . . . I got to get on. Lucille going be raising all kind of hell.

Troy: Where you going, nigger? We ain't finished this pint. Come here, finish this pint.

Bono: Well, hell, I am . . . if you ever turn the bottle loose.

Troy (*hands him the bottle*): The only thing I say about the A&P is I'm glad Cory got that job down there. Help him take care of his school clothes and things. Gabe done moved out and things getting tight around here. He got that job . . . He can start to look out for himself.

Rose: Cory done went and got recruited by a college football team.

Troy: I told that boy about that football stuff. The white man ain't gonna let him get nowhere with that football. I told him when he first come to me with it. Now you come telling me he done went and got more tied up in it. He ought to go and get recruited in how to fix cars or something where he can make a living.

Rose: He ain't talking about making no living playing football. It's just something the boys in school do. They gonna send a recruiter by to talk to you. He'll tell you he ain't talking about making no living playing football. It's a honor to be recruited.

Troy: It ain't gonna get him nowhere. Bono'll tell you that.

Bono: If he be like you in the sports . . . he's gonna be alright. Ain't but two men ever played baseball as good as you. That's Babe Ruth and Josh Gibson.° Them's the only two men ever hit more home runs than you.

Troy: What it ever get me? Ain't got a pot to piss in or a window to throw it out of.

Rose: Times have changed since you was playing baseball, Troy. That was before the war. Times have changed a lot since then.

Troy: How in hell they done changed?

Rose: They got lots of colored boys playing ball now. Baseball and football.

Bono: You right about that, Rose. Times have changed, Troy. You just come along too early.

Troy: There ought not never have been no time called too early! Now you take that fellow . . . what's that fellow they had playing right field for the Yankees back then? You know who I'm talking about, Bono. Used to play right field for the Yankees.

Rose: Selkirk?°

Troy: Selkirk! That's it! Man batting .269, understand? .269. What kind of sense that make? I was hitting .432 with thirty-seven home runs! Man batting .269 and playing right field for the Yankees! I saw Josh Gibson's daughter yesterday. She walking around with raggedy shoes on her feet. Now I bet you Selkirk's daughter ain't walking around with raggedy shoes on her feet! I bet you that!

Rose: They got a lot of colored baseball players now. Jackie Robinson° was the first. Folks had to wait for Jackie Robinson.

Troy: I done seen a hundred niggers play baseball better than Jackie Robinson. Hell, I know some teams Jackie Robinson couldn't even make! What you talking about Jackie Robinson. Jackie Robinson wasn't nobody. I'm talking about if you could play ball then they ought to have let you play. Don't care what color you were. Come telling me I come along too early. If you could play . . . then they ought to have let you play.

(Troy takes a long drink from the bottle.)

Rose: You gonna drink yourself to death. You don't need to be drinking like that.

Josh Gibson: legendary catcher in the Negro Leagues whose batting average and home-run totals far outstripped Major League records; he died of a stroke at age 35 in January 1947, three months before Jackie Robinson's debut with the Brooklyn Dodgers. *Selkirk:* Andy Selkirk, Yankee outfielder who hit .269 in 118 games in 1940. *Jackie Robinson:* the first African American to play in major league baseball, joined the Brooklyn Dodgers in 1947.

Troy: Death ain't nothing. I done seen him. Done wrassled with him. You can't tell me nothing about death. Death ain't nothing but a fastball on the outside corner. And you know what I'll do to that! Lookee here, Bono . . . am I lying? You get one of them fastballs, about waist high, over the outside corner of the plate where you can get the meat of the bat on it . . . and good god! You can kiss it goodbye. Now, am I lying?

Bono: Naw, you telling the truth there. I seen you do it.

Troy: If I'm lying . . . that 450 feet worth of lying! (*Pause.*) That's all death is to me. A fastball on the outside corner.

Rose: I don't know why you want to get on talking about death.

Troy: Ain't nothing wrong with talking about death. That's part of life. Everybody gonna die. You gonna die, I'm gonna die. Bono's gonna die. Hell, we all gonna die.

Rose: But you ain't got to talk about it. I don't like to talk about it.

Troy: You the one brought it up. Me and Bono was talking about baseball . . . you tell me I'm gonna drink myself to death. Ain't that right, Bono? You know I don't drink this but one night out of the week. That's Friday night. I'm gonna drink just enough to where I can handle it. Then I cuts it loose. I leave it alone. So don't you worry about me drinking myself to death. 'Cause I ain't worried about Death. I done seen him. I done wrestled with him.

Look here, Bono . . . I looked up one day and Death was marching straight at me. Like Soldiers on Parade! The Army of Death was marching straight at me. The middle of July, 1941. It got real cold just like it be winter. It seem like Death himself reached out and touched me on the shoulder. He touch me just like I touch you. I got cold as ice and Death standing there grinning at me.

Rose: Troy, why don't you hush that talk.

Troy: I say . . . what you want, Mr. Death? You be wanting me? You done brought your army to be getting me? I looked him dead in the eye. I wasn't fearing nothing. I was ready to tangle. Just like I'm ready to tangle now. The Bible say be ever vigilant. That's why I don't get but so drunk. I got to keep watch.

Rose: Troy was right down there in Mercy Hospital. You remember he had pneumonia? Laying there with a fever talking plumb out of his head.

Troy: Death standing there staring at me . . . carrying that sickle in his hand. Finally he say, "You want bound over for another year?" See, just like that . . . "You want bound over for another year?" I told him, "Bound over hell! Let's settle this now!"

It seem like he kinda fell back when I said that, and all the cold went out of me. I reached down and grabbed that sickle and threw it just as far as I could throw it . . . and me and him commenced to wrestling.

We wrestled for three days and three nights. I can't say where I found the strength from. Everytime it seemed like he was gonna get the best of me, I'd reach way down deep inside myself and find the strength to do him one better.

Rose: Every time Troy tell that story he find different ways to tell it. Different things to make up about it.

Troy: I ain't making up nothing. I'm telling you the facts of what happened. I wrestled with Death for three days and three nights and I'm standing here to tell you about it. (*Pause.*) Alright. At the end of the third night we done weakened each other to where we can't hardly move. Death stood up, throwed on his robe

. . . had him a white robe with a hood on it. He throwed on that robe and went off to look for his sickle. Say, "I'll be back." Just like that. "I'll be back." I told him, say, "Yeah, but . . . you gonna have to find me!" I wasn't no fool. I wasn't going looking for him. Death ain't nothing to play with. And I know he's gonna get me. I know I got to join his army . . . his camp followers. But as long as I keep my strength and see him coming . . . as long as I keep up my vigilance . . . he's gonna have to fight to get me. I ain't going easy.

Bono: Well, look here, since you got to keep up your vigilance . . . let me have the bottle.

Troy: Aw hell, I shouldn't have told you that part. I should have left out that part.

Rose: Troy be talking that stuff and half the time don't even know what he be talking about.

Troy: Bono know me better than that.

Bono: That's right. I know you. I know you got some Uncle Remus in your blood. You got more stories than the devil got sinners.

Troy: Aw hell, I done seen him too! Done talked with the devil.

Rose: Troy, don't nobody wanna be hearing all that stuff.

(*Lyons enters the yard from the street. Thirty-four years old, Troy's son by a previous marriage, he sports a neatly trimmed goatee, sport coat, white shirt, tieless and buttoned at the collar. Though he fancies himself a musician, he is more caught up in the rituals and "idea" of being a musician than in the actual practice of the music. He has come to borrow money from Troy, and while he knows he will be successful, he is uncertain as to what extent his lifestyle will be held up to scrutiny and ridicule.*)

Lyons: Hey, Pop.

Troy: What you come "Hey, Popping" me for?

Lyons: How you doing, Rose? (*He kisses her.*) Mr. Bono. How you doing?

Bono: Hey, Lyons . . . how you been?

Troy: He must have been doing alright. I ain't seen him around here last week.

Rose: Troy, leave your boy alone. He come by to see you and you wanna start all that nonsense.

Troy: I ain't bothering Lyons. (*Offers him the bottle.*) Here . . . get you a drink. We got an understanding. I know why he come by to see me and he know I know.

Lyons: Come on, Pop . . . I just stopped by to say hi . . . see how you was doing.

Troy: You ain't stopped by yesterday.

Rose: You gonna stay for supper, Lyons? I got some chicken cooking in the oven.

Lyons: No, Rose . . . thanks. I was just in the neighborhood and thought I'd stop by for a minute.

Troy: You was in the neighborhood alright, nigger. You telling the truth there. You was in the neighborhood cause it's my payday.

Lyons: Well, hell, since you mentioned it . . . let me have ten dollars.

Troy: I'll be damned! I'll die and go to hell and play blackjack with the devil before I give you ten dollars.

Bono: That's what I wanna know about . . . that devil you done seen.

Lyons: What . . . Pop done seen the devil? You too much, Pops.

Troy: Yeah, I done seen him. Talked to him too!

Rose: You ain't seen no devil. I done told you that man ain't had nothing to do with the devil. Anything you can't understand, you want to call it the devil.

Troy: Look here, Bono . . . I went down to see Hertzberger about some furniture. Got three rooms for two-ninety-eight. That what it say on the radio. "Three rooms . . . two-ninety-eight." Even made up a little song about it. Go down there . . . man tell me I can't get no credit. I'm working every day and can't get no credit. What to do? I got an empty house with some raggedy furniture in it. Cory ain't got no bed. He's sleeping on a pile of rags on the floor. Working every day and can't get no credit. Come back here—Rose'll tell you—madder than hell. Sit down . . . try to figure what I'm gonna do. Come a knock on the door. Ain't been living here but three days. Who know I'm here? Open the door . . . devil standing there bigger than life. White fellow . . . got on good clothes and everything. Standing there with a clipboard in his hand. I ain't had to say nothing. First words come out of his mouth was . . . "I understand you need some furniture and can't get no credit." I liked to fell over. He say "I'll give you all the credit you want, but you got to pay the interest on it." I told him, "Give me three rooms worth and charge whatever you want." Next day a truck pulled up here and two men unloaded them three rooms. Man what drove the truck give me a book. Say send ten dollars, first of every month to the address in the book and every thing will be alright. Say if I miss a payment the devil was coming back and it'll be hell to pay. That was fifteen years ago. To this day . . . the first of the month I send my ten dollars, Rose'll tell you.

Rose: Troy lying.

Troy: I ain't never seen that man since. Now you tell me who else that could have been but the devil? I ain't sold my soul or nothing like that, you understand. Naw, I wouldn't have truck with the devil about nothing like that. I got my furniture and pays my ten dollars the first of the month just like clockwork.

Bono: How long you say you been paying this ten dollars a month?

Troy: Fifteen years!

Bono: Hell, ain't you finished paying for it yet? How much the man done charged you?

Troy: Aw hell, I done paid for it. I done paid for it ten times over! The fact is I'm scared to stop paying it.

Rose: Troy lying. We got that furniture from Mr. Glickman. He ain't paying no ten dollars a month to nobody.

Troy: Aw hell, woman. Bono know I ain't that big a fool.

Lyons: I was just getting ready to say . . . I know where there's a bridge for sale.

Troy: Look here, I'll tell you this . . . it don't matter to me if he was the devil. It don't matter if the devil give credit. Somebody has got to give it.

Rose: It ought to matter. You going around talking about having truck with the devil . . . God's the one you gonna have to answer to. He's the one gonna be at the Judgment.

Lyons: Yeah, well, look here, Pop . . . Let me have that ten dollars. I'll give it back to you. Bonnie got a job working at the hospital.

Troy: What I tell you, Bono? The only time I see this nigger is when he wants something. That's the only time I see him.

Lyons: Come on, Pop, Mr. Bono don't want to hear all that. Let me have the ten dollars. I told you Bonnie working.

Troy: What that mean to me? "Bonnie working." I don't care if she working. Go ask her for the ten dollars if she working. Talking about "Bonnie working." Why ain't you working?

Lyons: Aw, Pop, you know I can't find no decent job. Where am I gonna get a job at? You know I can't get no job.

Troy: I told you I know some people down there. I can get you on the rubbish if you want to work. I told you that the last time you came by here asking me for something.

Lyons: Naw, Pop . . . thanks. That ain't for me. I don't wanna be carrying nobody's rubbish. I don't wanna be punching nobody's time clock.

Troy: What's the matter, you too good to carry people's rubbish? Where you think that ten dollars you talking about come from? I'm just supposed to haul people's rubbish and give my money to you cause you too lazy to work. You too lazy to work and wanna know why you ain't got what I got.

Rose: What hospital Bonnie working at? Mercy?

Lyons: She's down at Passavant working in the laundry.

Troy: I ain't got nothing as it is. I give you that ten dollars and I got to eat beans the rest of the week. Naw . . . you ain't getting no ten dollars here.

Lyons: You ain't got to be eating no beans. I don't know why you wanna say that.

Troy: I ain't got no extra money. Gabe done moved over to Miss Pearl's paying her the rent and things done got tight around here. I can't afford to be giving you every payday.

Lyons: I ain't asked you to give me nothing. I asked you to loan me ten dollars. I know you got ten dollars.

Troy: Yeah, I got it. You know why I got it? Cause I don't throw my money away out there in the streets. You living the fast life . . . wanna be a musician . . . running around in them clubs and things . . . then, you learn to take care of yourself. You ain't gonna find me going and asking nobody for nothing. I done spent too many years without.

Lyons: You and me is two different people, Pop.

Troy: I done learned my mistake and learned to do what's right by it. You still trying to get something for nothing. Life don't owe you nothing. You owe it to yourself. Ask Bono. He'll tell you I'm right.

Lyons: You got your way of dealing with the world . . . I got mine. The only thing that matters to me is the music.

Troy: Yeah, I can see that! It don't matter how you gonna eat . . . where your next dollar is coming from. You telling the truth there.

Lyons: I know I got to eat. But I got to live too. I need something that gonna help me to get out of the bed in the morning. Make me feel like I belong in the world. I don't bother nobody. I just stay with my music cause that's the only way I can find to live in the world. Otherwise there ain't no telling what I might do. Now I don't come criticizing you and how you live. I just come by to ask you for ten dollars. I don't wanna hear all that about how I live.

Troy: Boy, your mama did a hell of a job raising you.

Lyons: You can't change me, Pop. I'm thirty-four years old. If you wanted to change me, you should have been there when I was growing up. I come by to see you . . . ask for ten dollars and you want to talk about how I was raised. You don't know nothing about how I was raised.

Rose: Let the boy have ten dollars, Troy.

Troy (to Lyons): What the hell you looking at me for? I ain't got no ten dollars. You know what I do with my money. (*To Rose.*) Give him ten dollars if you want him to have it.

Rose: I will. Just as soon as you turn it loose.

Troy (handing Rose the money): There it is. Seventy-six dollars and forty-two cents. You see this, Bono? Now, I ain't gonna get but six of that back.

Rose: You ought to stop telling that lie. Here, Lyons. (*She hands him the money.*)

Lyons: Thanks, Rose. Look . . . I got to run . . . I'll see you later.

Troy: Wait a minute. You gonna say, "thanks, Rose" and ain't gonna look to see where she got that ten dollars from? See how they do me, Bono?

Lyons: I know she got it from you, Pop. Thanks. I'll give it back to you.

Troy: There he go telling another lie. Time I see that ten dollars . . . he'll be owing me thirty more.

Lyons: See you, Mr. Bono.

Bono: Take care, Lyons!

Lyons: Thanks, Pop. I'll see you again.

(*Lyons exits the yard.*)

Troy: I don't know why he don't go and get him a decent job and take care of that woman he got.

Bono: He'll be alright, Troy. The boy is still young.

Troy: The *boy* is thirty-four years old.

Rose: Let's not get off into all that.

Bono: Look here . . . I got to be going. I got to be getting on. Lucille gonna be waiting.

Troy (puts his arm around Rose): See this woman, Bono? I love this woman. I love this woman so much it hurts. I love her so much . . . I done run out of ways of loving her. So I got to go back to basics. Don't you come by my house Monday morning talking about time to go to work . . . . 'cause I'm still gonna be stroking!

Rose: Troy! Stop it now!

Bono: I ain't paying him no mind, Rose. That ain't nothing but gin-talk. Go on, Troy. I'll see you Monday.

Troy: Don't you come by my house, nigger! I done told you what I'm gonna be doing.

(*The lights go down to black.*)

SCENE II

The lights come up on Rose hanging up clothes. She hums and sings softly to herself. It is the following morning.

Rose (sings):

>   Jesus, be a fence all around me every day
>   Jesus, I want you to protect me as I travel on my way.
>   Jesus, be a fence all around me every day.

(*Troy enters from the house.*)

>   Jesus, I want you to protect me
>   As I travel on my way.

(*To Troy.*) 'Morning. You ready for breakfast? I can fix it soon as I finish hanging up these clothes.

Troy: I got the coffee on. That'll be alright. I'll just drink some of that this morning.

Rose: That 651 hit yesterday. That's the second time this month. Miss Pearl hit for a dollar . . . seem like those that need the least always get lucky. Poor folks can't get nothing.

Troy: Them numbers don't know nobody. I don't know why you fool with them. You and Lyons both.

Rose: It's something to do.

Troy: You ain't doing nothing but throwing your money away.

Rose: Troy, you know I don't play foolishly. I just play a nickel here and a nickel there.

Troy: That's two nickels you done thrown away.

Rose: Now I hit sometimes . . . that makes up for it. It always comes in handy when I do hit. I don't hear you complaining then.

Troy: I ain't complaining now. I just say it's foolish. Trying to guess out of six hundred ways which way the number gonna come. If I had all the money niggers, these Negroes, throw away on numbers for one week—just one week—I'd be a rich man.

Rose: Well, you wishing and calling it foolish ain't gonna stop folks from playing numbers. That's one thing for sure. Besides . . . some good things come from playing numbers. Look where Pope done bought him that restaurant off of numbers.

Troy: I can't stand niggers like that. Man ain't had two dimes to rub together. He walking around with his shoes all run over bumming money for cigarettes. Alright. Got lucky there and hit the numbers . . .

Rose: Troy, I know all about it.

Troy: Had good sense, I'll say that for him. He ain't throwed his money away. I seen niggers hit the numbers and go through two thousand dollars in four days. Man bought him that restaurant down there . . . fixed it up real nice . . . . and then didn't want nobody to come in it! A Negro go in there and can't get no kind of service. I seen a white fellow come in there and order a bowl of stew. Pope picked all the meat out of the pot for him. Man ain't had nothing but a bowl of meat! Negro come behind him and ain't got nothing but the potatoes and carrots. Talking about what numbers do for people, you picked a wrong example. Ain't done nothing but make a worser fool out of him than he was before.

Rose: Troy, you ought to stop worrying about what happened at work yesterday.

Troy: I ain't worried. Just told me to be down there at the Commissioner's office on Friday. Everybody think they gonna fire me. I ain't worried about them firing me. You ain't got to worry about that. (*Pause.*) Where's Cory? Cory in the house? (*Calls.*) Cory?

Rose: He gone out.

Troy: Out, huh? He gone out 'cause he know I want him to help me with this fence. I know how he is. That boy scared of work.

(*Gabriel enters. He comes halfway down the alley and, hearing Troy's voice, stops.*)

Troy (continues): He ain't done a lick of work in his life.

Rose: He had to go to football practice. Coach wanted them to get in a little extra practice before the season start.

Troy: I got his practice . . . running out of here before he get his chores done.

Rose: Troy, what is wrong with you this morning? Don't nothing set right with you. Go on back in there and go to bed . . . get up on the other side.

Troy: Why something got to be wrong with me? I ain't said nothing wrong with me.

Rose: You got something to say about everything. First it's the numbers . . . then it's the way the man runs his restaurant . . . then you done got on Cory. What's it gonna be next? Take a look up there and see if the weather suits you . . . or is it gonna be how you gonna put up the fence with the clothes hanging in the yard?

Troy: You hit the nail on the head then.

Rose: I know you like I know the back of my hand. Go on in there and get you some coffee . . . see if that straighten you up. 'Cause you ain't right this morning.

(Troy starts into the house and sees Gabriel. Gabriel starts singing. Troy's brother, he is seven years younger than Troy. Injured in World War II, he has a metal plate in his head. He carries an old trumpet tied around his waist and believes with every fiber of his being that he is the Archangel Gabriel. He carries a chipped basket with an assortment of discarded fruits and vegetables he has picked up in the Strip District and which he attempts to sell.)

Gabriel (singing):

> Yes, ma'am, I got plums
> You ask me how I sell them
> Oh ten cents apiece
> Three for a quarter
> Come and buy now
> 'Cause I'm here today
> And tomorrow I'll be gone

(Gabriel enters.)

Hey, Rose!

Rose: How you doing, Gabe?

Gabriel: There's Troy . . . Hey, Troy!

Troy: Hey, Gabe.

(Exit into kitchen.)

Rose (to Gabriel): What you got there?

Gabriel: You know what I got, Rose. I got fruits and vegetables.

Rose (looking in basket): Where's all these plums you talking about?

Gabriel: I ain't got no plums today, Rose. I was just singing that. Have some tomorrow. Put me in a big order for plums. Have enough plums tomorrow for St. Peter and everybody.

(Troy reenters from kitchen, crosses to steps.)

(To Rose.) Troy's mad at me.

Troy: I ain't mad at you. What I got to be mad at you about? You ain't done nothing to me.

Gabriel: I just moved over to Miss Pearl's to keep out from in your way. I ain't mean no harm by it.

Troy: Who said anything about that? I ain't said anything about that.

Gabriel: You ain't mad at me, is you?

Troy: Naw . . . I ain't mad at you, Gabe. If I was mad at you I'd tell you about it.

Gabriel: Got me two rooms. In the basement. Got my own door too. Wanna see my key? (*He holds up a key.*) That's my own key! Ain't nobody else got a key like that. That's my key! My two rooms!

Troy: Well, that's good, Gabe. You got your own key . . . that's good.

Rose: You hungry, Gabe? I was just fixing to cook Troy his breakfast.

Gabriel: I'll take some biscuits. You got some biscuits? Did you know when I was in heaven . . . every morning me and St. Peter would sit down by the gate and eat some big fat biscuits? Oh, yeah! We had us a good time. We'd sit there and eat us them biscuits and then St. Peter would go off to sleep and tell me to wake him up when it's time to open the gates for the judgment.

Rose: Well, come on . . . I'll make up a batch of biscuits.

(*Rose exits into the house.*)

Gabriel: Troy . . . St. Peter got your name in the book. I seen it. It say . . . Troy Maxson. I say . . . I know him! He got the same name like what I got. That's my brother!

Troy: How many times you gonna tell me that, Gabe?

Gabriel: Ain't got my name in the book. Don't have to have my name. I done died and went to heaven. He got your name though. One morning St. Peter was looking at his book . . . marking it up for the judgment . . . and he let me see your name. Got it in there under M. Got Rose's name . . . I ain't seen it like I seen yours . . . but I know it's in there. He got a great big book. Got everybody's name what was ever been born. That's what he told me. But I seen your name. Seen it with my own eyes.

Troy: Go on in the house there. Rose going to fix you something to eat.

Gabriel: Oh, I ain't hungry. I done had breakfast with Aunt Jemimah. She come by and cooked me up a whole mess of flapjacks. Remember how we used to eat them flapjacks?

Troy: Go on in the house and get you something to eat now.

Gabriel: I got to sell my plums. I done sold some tomatoes. Got me two quarters. Wanna see? (*He shows Troy his quarters.*) I'm gonna save them and buy me a new horn so St. Peter can hear me when it's time to open the gates. (*Gabriel stops suddenly. Listens.*) Hear that? That's the hellhounds. I got to chase them out of here. Go on get out of here! Get out!

(*Gabriel exits singing.*)

> Better get ready for the judgment
> Better get ready for the judgment
> My Lord is coming down

(*Rose enters from the house.*)

Troy: He gone off somewhere.

Gabriel (*offstage*):

> Better get ready for the judgment
> Better get ready for the judgment morning
> Better get ready for the judgment
> My God is coming down

Rose: He ain't eating right. Miss Pearl say she can't get him to eat nothing.

Troy: What you want me to do about it, Rose? I done did everything I can for the man. I can't make him get well. Man got half his head blown away . . . what you expect?

Rose: Seem like something ought to be done to help him.

Troy: Man don't bother nobody. He just mixed up from that metal plate he got in his head. Ain't no sense for him to go back into the hospital.

Rose: Least he be eating right. They can help him take care of himself.

Troy: Don't nobody wanna be locked up, Rose. What you wanna lock him up for? Man go over there and fight the war . . . messin' around with them Japs, get half his head blown off . . . and they give him a lousy three thousand dollars. And I had to swoop down on that.

Rose: Is you fixing to go into that again?

Troy: That's the only way I got a roof over my head . . . cause of that metal plate.

Rose: Ain't no sense you blaming yourself for nothing. Gabe wasn't in no condition to manage that money. You done what was right by him. Can't nobody say you ain't done what was right by him. Look how long you took care of him . . . till he wanted to have his own place and moved over there with Miss Pearl.

Troy: That ain't what I'm saying, woman! I'm just stating the facts. If my brother didn't have that metal plate in his head . . . I wouldn't have a pot to piss in or a window to throw it out of. And I'm fifty-three years old. Now see if you can understand that!

(*Troy gets up from the porch and starts to exit the yard.*)

Rose: Where you going off to? You been running out of here every Saturday for weeks. I thought you was gonna work on this fence?

Troy: I'm gonna walk down to Taylors'. Listen to the ball game. I'll be back in a bit. I'll work on it when I get back.

(*He exits the yard. The lights go to black.*)

SCENE III

The lights come up on the yard. It is four hours later. Rose is taking down the clothes from the line. Cory enters carrying his football equipment.

Rose: Your daddy like to had a fit with you running out of here this morning without doing your chores.

Cory: I told you I had to go to practice.

Rose: He say you were supposed to help him with this fence.

Cory: He been saying that the last four or five Saturdays, and then he don't never do nothing, but go down to Taylors'. Did you tell him about the recruiter?

Rose: Yeah, I told him.

Cory: What he say?

Rose: He ain't said nothing too much. You get in there and get started on your chores before he gets back. Go on and scrub down them steps before he gets back here hollering and carrying on.

Cory: I'm hungry. What you got to eat, Mama?

Rose: Go on and get started on your chores. I got some meat loaf in there. Go on and make you a sandwich . . . and don't leave no mess in there.

(*Cory exits into the house. Rose continues to take down the clothes. Troy enters the yard and sneaks up and grabs her from behind.*)

Troy! Go on, now. You liked to scared me to death. What was the score of the game? Lucille had me on the phone and I couldn't keep up with it.

Troy: What I care about the game? Come here, woman. (*He tries to kiss her.*)

Rose: I thought you went down Taylors' to listen to the game. Go on, Troy! You supposed to be putting up this fence.

Troy (*attempting to kiss her again*): I'll put it up when I finish with what is at hand.

Rose: Go on, Troy. I ain't studying you.

Troy (*chasing after her*): I'm studying you . . . fixing to do my homework!

Rose: Troy, you better leave me alone.

Troy: Where's Cory? That boy brought his butt home yet?

Rose: He's in the house doing his chores.

Troy (*calling*): Cory! Get your butt out here, boy!

(*Rose exits into the house with the laundry. Troy goes over to the pile of wood, picks up a board, and starts sawing. Cory enters from the house.*)

Troy: You just now coming in here from leaving this morning?

Cory: Yeah, I had to go to football practice.

Troy: Yeah, what?

Cory: Yessir.

Troy: I ain't but two seconds off you noway. The garbage sitting in there overflowing . . . you ain't done none of your chores . . . and you come in here talking about "Yeah."

Cory: I was just getting ready to do my chores now, Pop . . .

Troy: Your first chore is to help me with this fence on Saturday. Everything else come after that. Now get that saw and cut them boards.

(*Cory takes the saw and begins cutting the boards. Troy continues working. There is a long pause.*)

Cory: Hey, Pop . . . why don't you buy a TV?

Troy: What I want with a TV? What I want one of them for?

Cory: Everybody got one. Earl, Ba Bra . . . Jesse!

Troy: I ain't asked you who had one. I say what I want with one?

Cory: So you can watch it. They got lots of things on TV. Baseball games and everything. We could watch the World Series.

Troy: Yeah . . . and how much this TV cost?

Cory: I don't know. They got them on sale for around two hundred dollars.

Troy: Two hundred dollars, huh?

Cory: That ain't that much, Pop.

Troy: Naw, it's just two hundred dollars. See that roof you got over your head at night? Let me tell you something about that roof. It's been over ten years since that roof was last tarred. See now . . . the snow come this winter and sit up there on that roof like it is . . . and it's gonna seep inside. It's just gonna be a little bit . . . ain't gonna hardly notice it. Then the next thing you know, it's gonna be leaking all over the house. Then the wood rot from all that water and you gonna need a whole new roof. Now, how much you think it cost to get that roof tarred?

Cory: I don't know.

Troy: Two hundred and sixty-four dollars . . . cash money. While you thinking about a TV, I got to be thinking about the roof . . . and whatever else go wrong here. Now if you had two hundred dollars, what would you do . . . fix the roof or buy a TV?

Cory: I'd buy a TV. Then when the roof started to leak . . . when it needed fixing . . . I'd fix it.

Troy: Where you gonna get the money from? You done spent it for a TV. You gonna sit up and watch the water run all over your brand new TV.

Cory: Aw, Pop. You got money. I know you do.

Troy: Where I got it at, huh?

Cory: You got it in the bank.

Troy: You wanna see my bankbook? You wanna see that seventy-three dollars and twenty-two cents I got sitting up in there?

Cory: You ain't got to pay for it all at one time. You can put a down payment on it and carry it on home with you.

Troy: Not me. I ain't gonna owe nobody nothing if I can help it. Miss a payment and they come and snatch it right out of your house. Then what you got? Now, soon as I get two hundred dollars clear, then I'll buy a TV. Right now, as soon as I get two hundred and sixty-four dollars, I'm gonna have this roof tarred.

Cory: Aw . . . Pop!

Troy: You go on and get you two hundred dollars and buy one if ya want it. I got better things to do with my money.

Cory: I can't get no two hundred dollars. I ain't never seen two hundred dollars.

Troy: I'll tell you what . . . you get you a hundred dollars and I'll put the other hundred with it.

Cory: Alright, I'm gonna show you.

Troy: You gonna show me how you can cut them boards right now.

(*Cory begins to cut the boards. There is a long pause.*)

Cory: The Pirates won today. That makes five in a row.

Troy: I ain't thinking about the Pirates. Got an all-white team. Got that boy . . . that Puerto Rican boy . . . Clemente.° Don't even half-play him. That boy could be something if they give him a chance. Play him one day and sit him on the bench the next.

Cory: He gets a lot of chances to play.

Clemente: Hall of Fame outfielder Roberto Clemente, a dark-skinned Puerto Rican, played 17 seasons with the Pittsburgh Pirates.

Troy: I'm talking about playing regular. Playing every day so you can get your timing. That's what I'm talking about.

Cory: They got some white guys on the team that don't play every day. You can't play everybody at the same time.

Troy: If they got a white fellow sitting on the bench . . . you can bet your last dollar he can't play! The colored guy got to be twice as good before he get on the team. That's why I don't want you to get all tied up in them sports. Man on the team and what it get him? They got colored on the team and don't use them. Same as not having them. All them teams the same.

Cory: The Braves got Hank Aaron and Wes Covington. Hank Aaron hit two home runs today. That makes forty-three.

Troy: Hank Aaron ain't nobody. That's what you supposed to do. That's how you supposed to play the game. Ain't nothing to it. It's just a matter of timing . . . getting the right follow-through. Hell, I can hit forty-three home runs right now!

Cory: Not off no major-league pitching, you couldn't.

Troy: We had better pitching in the Negro leagues. I hit seven home runs off of Satchel Paige.° You can't get no better than that!

Cory: Sandy Koufax.° He's leading the league in strikeouts.

Troy: I ain't thinking of no Sandy Koufax.

Cory: You got Warren Spahn° and Lew Burdette.° I bet you couldn't hit no home runs off of Warren Spahn.

Troy: I'm through with it now. You go on and cut them boards. (*Pause.*) Your mama tell me you done got recruited by a college football team? Is that right?

Cory: Yeah. Coach Zellman say the recruiter gonna be coming by to talk to you. Get you to sign the permission papers.

Troy: I thought you supposed to be working down there at the A&P. Ain't you suppose to be working down there after school?

Cory: Mr. Stawicki say he gonna hold my job for me until after the football season. Say starting next week I can work weekends.

Troy: I thought we had an understanding about this football stuff? You suppose to keep up with your chores and hold that job down at the A&P. Ain't been around here all day on a Saturday. Ain't none of your chores done . . . and now you telling me you done quit your job.

Cory: I'm going to be working weekends.

Troy: You damn right you are! And ain't no need for nobody coming around here to talk to me about signing nothing.

Cory: Hey, Pop . . . you can't do that. He's coming all the way from North Carolina.

Troy: I don't care where he coming from. The white man ain't gonna let you get nowhere with that football noway. You go on and get your book-learning so you can work yourself up in that A&P or learn how to fix cars or build houses or something, get you a trade. That way you have something can't nobody take

---

Satchel Paige . . . Sandy Koufax . . . Warren Spahn . . . Lew Burdette: The great Satchel Paige pitched many years in the Negro Leagues; beginning in 1948, when he was in his forties and long past his prime, he appeared in nearly 200 games in the American League. Star pitchers Sandy Koufax of the Dodgers and Warren Spahn and Lew Burdette of the Braves were all white.

away from you. You go on and learn how to put your hands to some good use. Besides hauling people's garbage.

Cory: I get good grades, Pop. That's why the recruiter wants to talk with you. You got to keep up your grades to get recruited. This way I'll be going to college. I'll get a chance . . .

Troy: First you gonna get your butt down there to the A&P and get your job back.

Cory: Mr. Stawicki done already hired somebody else 'cause I told him I was playing football.

Troy: You a bigger fool than I thought . . . . to let somebody take away your job so you can play some football. Where you gonna get your money to take out your girlfriend and whatnot? What kind of foolishness is that to let somebody take away your job?

Cory: I'm still gonna be working weekends.

Troy: Naw . . . naw. You getting your butt out of here and finding you another job.

Cory: Come on, Pop! I got to practice. I can't work after school and play football too. The team needs me. That's what Coach Zellman say . . .

Troy: I don't care what nobody else say. I'm the boss . . . you understand? I'm the boss around here. I do the only saying what counts.

Cory: Come on, Pop!

Troy: I asked you . . . did you understand?

Cory: Yeah . . .

Troy: What?!

Cory: Yessir.

Troy: You go on down there to that A&P and see if you can get your job back. If you can't do both . . . then you quit the football team. You've got to take the crookeds with the straights.

Cory: Yessir. (*Pause.*) Can I ask you a question?

Troy: What the hell you wanna ask me? Mr. Stawicki the one you got the questions for.

Cory: How come you ain't never liked me?

Troy: Liked you? Who the hell say I got to like you? What law is there say I got to like you? Wanna stand up in my face and ask a damn fool-ass question like that. Talking about liking somebody. Come here, boy, when I talk to you.

(*Cory comes over to where Troy is working. He stands slouched over and Troy shoves him on his shoulder.*)

Straighten up, goddammit! I asked you a question . . . . what law is there say I got to like you?

Cory: None.

Troy: Well, alright then! Don't you eat every day? (*Pause.*) Answer me when I talk to you! Don't you eat every day?

Cory: Yeah.

Troy: Nigger, as long as you in my house, you put that sir on the end of it when you talk to me.

Cory: Yes . . . sir.

Troy: You eat every day.

Cory: Yessir!

Troy: Got a roof over your head.

Cory: Yessir!

Troy: Got clothes on your back.

Cory: Yessir.

Troy: Why you think that is?

Cory: Cause of you.

Troy: Aw, hell I know it's cause of me . . . but why do you think that is?

Cory (hesitant): 'Cause you like me.

Troy: Like you? I go out of here every morning . . . bust my butt . . . putting up with them crackers every day . . . cause I like you? You about the biggest fool I ever saw. (*Pause.*) It's my job. It's my responsibility! You understand that? A man got to take care of his family. You live in my house . . . sleep you behind on my bed-clothes . . . fill you belly up with my food . . . cause you my son. You my flesh and blood. Not cause I like you! Cause it's my duty to take care of you. I owe a responsibility to you!

Let's get this straight right here . . . before it go along any further . . . I ain't got to like you. Mr. Rand don't give me my money come payday cause he likes me. He gives me cause he owe me. I done give you everything I had to give you. I gave you your life! Me and your mama worked that out between us. And liking your black ass wasn't part of the bargain. Don't you try and go through life worrying about if somebody like you or not. You best be making sure they doing right by you. You understand what I'm saying, boy?

Cory: Yessir.

Troy: Then get the hell out of my face, and get on down to that A&P.

(*Rose has been standing behind the screen door for much of the scene. She enters as Cory exits.*)

Rose: Why don't you let the boy go ahead and play football, Troy? Ain't no harm in that. He's just trying to be like you with the sports.

Troy: I don't want him to be like me! I want him to move as far away from my life as he can get. You the only decent thing that ever happened to me. I wish him that. But I don't wish him a thing else from my life. I decided seventeen years ago that boy wasn't getting involved in no sports. Not after what they did to me in the sports.

Rose: Troy, why don't you admit you was too old to play in the major leagues? For once . . . why don't you admit that?

Troy: What do you mean too old? Don't come telling me I was too old. I just wasn't the right color. Hell, I'm fifty-three years old and can do better than Selkirk's .269 right now!

Rose: How's was you gonna play ball when you were over forty? Sometimes I can't get no sense out of you.

Troy: I got good sense, woman. I got sense enough not to let my boy get hurt over playing no sports. You been mothering that boy too much. Worried about if people like him.

Rose: Everything that boy do . . . he do for you. He wants you to say "Good job, son." That's all.

Troy: Rose, I ain't got time for that. He's alive. He's healthy. He's got to make his own way. I made mine. Ain't nobody gonna hold his hand when he get out there in that world.

Rose: Times have changed from when you was young, Troy. People change. The world's changing around you and you can't even see it.

Troy (slow, methodical): Woman . . . I do the best I can do. I come in here every Friday. I carry a sack of potatoes and a bucket of lard. You all line up at the door with your hands out. I give you the lint from my pockets. I give you my sweat and my blood. I ain't got no tears. I done spent them. We go upstairs in that room at night . . . and I fall down on you and try to blast a hole into forever. I get up Monday morning . . . find my lunch on the table. I go out. Make my way. Find my strength to carry me through to the next Friday. (*Pause.*) That's all I got, Rose. That's all I got to give. I can't give nothing else.

(*Troy exits into the house. The lights go down to black.*)

SCENE IV

It is Friday. Two weeks later. Cory starts out of the house with his football equipment. The phone rings.

Cory (calling): I got it! (*He answers the phone and stands in the screen door talking.*) Hello? Hey, Jesse. Naw . . . I was just getting ready to leave now.

Rose (calling): Cory!

Cory: I told you, man, them spikes is all tore up. You can use them if you want, but they ain't no good. Earl got some spikes.

Rose (calling): Cory!

Cory (calling to Rose): Mam? I'm talking to Jesse. (*Into phone.*) When she say that? (*Pause.*) Aw, you lying, man. I'm gonna tell her you said that.

Rose (calling): Cory, don't you go nowhere!

Cory: I got to go to the game, Ma! (*Into the phone.*) Yeah, hey, look, I'll talk to you later. Yeah, I'll meet you over Earl's house. Later. Bye, Ma.

(*Cory exits the house and starts out the yard.*)

Rose: Cory, where you going off to? You got that stuff all pulled out and thrown all over your room.

Cory (in the yard): I was looking for my spikes. Jesse wanted to borrow my spikes.

Rose: Get up there and get that cleaned up before your daddy get back in here.

Cory: I got to go to the game! I'll clean it up when I get back.

(*Cory exits.*)

Rose: That's all he need to do is see that room all messed up.

(*Rose exits into the house. Troy and Bono enter the yard. Troy is dressed in clothes other than his work clothes.*)

Bono: He told him the same thing he told you. Take it to the union.

Troy: Brownie ain't got that much sense. Man wasn't thinking about nothing. He wait until I confront them on it . . . then he wanna come crying seniority. (*Calls.*) Hey, Rose!

Bono: I wish I could have seen Mr. Rand's face when he told you.

Troy: He couldn't get it out of his mouth! Liked to bit his tongue! When they called me down there to the Commissioner's office . . . he thought they was gonna fire me. Like everybody else.

Bono: I didn't think they was gonna fire you. I thought they was gonna put you on the warning paper.

Troy: Hey, Rose! (*To Bono.*) Yeah, Mr. Rand like to bit his tongue.

(*Troy breaks the seal on the bottle, takes a drink, and hands it to Bono.*)

Bono: I see you run right down to Taylors' and told that Alberta gal.

Troy (calling): Hey, Rose! (*To Bono.*) I told everybody. Hey, Rose! I went down there to cash my check.

Rose (entering from the house): Hush all that hollering, man! I know you out here. What they say down there at the Commissioner's office?

Troy: You supposed to come when I call you, woman. Bono'll tell you that. (*To Bono.*) Don't Lucille come when you call her?

Rose: Man, hush your mouth. I ain't no dog . . . talk about "come when you call me."

Troy (puts his arm around Rose): You hear this, Bono? I had me an old dog used to get uppity like that. You say, "C'mere, Blue!" . . . and he just lay there and look at you. End up getting a stick and chasing him away trying to make him come.

Rose: I ain't studying you and your dog. I remember you used to sing that old song.

Troy (he sings):
> Hear it ring! Hear it ring!
> I had a dog his name was Blue.

Rose: Don't nobody wanna hear you sing that old song.

Troy (sings):
> You know Blue was mighty true.

Rose: Used to have Cory running around here singing that song.

Bono: Hell, I remember that song myself.

Troy (sings):
> You know Blue was a good old dog.
> Blue treed a possum in a hollow log.

That was my daddy's song. My daddy made up that song.

Rose: I don't care who made it up. Don't nobody wanna hear you sing it.

Troy (makes a song like calling a dog): Come here, woman.

Rose: You come in here carrying on, I reckon they ain't fired you. What they say down there at the Commissioner's office?

Troy: Look here, Rose . . . Mr. Rand called me into his office today when I got back from talking to them people down there . . . it come from up top . . . he called me in and told me they was making me a driver.

Rose: Troy, you kidding!

Troy: No I ain't. Ask Bono.

Rose: Well, that's great, Troy. Now you don't have to hassle them people no more.

(*Lyons enters from the street.*)

Troy: Aw hell, I wasn't looking to see you today. I thought you was in jail. Got it all over the front page of the *Courier* about them raiding Sefus's place . . . where you be hanging out with all them thugs.

Lyons: Hey, Pop . . . that ain't got nothing to do with me. I don't go down there gambling. I go down there to sit in with the band. I ain't got nothing to do with the gambling part. They got some good music down there.

Troy: They got some rogues . . . is what they got.

Lyons: How you been, Mr. Bono? Hi, Rose.

Bono: I see where you playing down at the Crawford Grill tonight.

Rose: How come you ain't brought Bonnie like I told you? You should have brought Bonnie with you, she ain't been over in a month of Sundays.

Lyons: I was just in the neighborhood . . . thought I'd stop by.

Troy: Here he come . . .

Bono: Your daddy got a promotion on the rubbish. He's gonna be the first colored driver. Ain't got to do nothing but sit up there and read the paper like them white fellows.

Lyons: Hey, Pop . . . if you knew how to read you'd be alright.

Bono: Naw . . . naw . . . you mean if the nigger knew how to *drive* he'd be alright. Been fighting with them people about driving and ain't even got a license. Mr. Rand know you ain't got no driver's license?

Troy: Driving ain't nothing. All you do is point the truck where you want it to go. Driving ain't nothing.

Bono: Do Mr. Rand know you ain't got no driver's license? That's what I'm talking about. I ain't asked if driving was easy. I asked if Mr. Rand know you ain't got no driver's license.

Troy: He ain't got to know. The man ain't got to know my business. Time he find out, I have two or three driver's licenses.

Lyons (going into his pocket): Say, look here, Pop . . .

Troy: I knew it was coming. Didn't I tell you, Bono? I know what kind of "Look here, Pop" that was. The nigger fixing to ask me for some money. It's Friday night. It's my payday. All them rogues down there on the avenue . . . the ones that ain't in jail . . . and Lyons is hopping in his shoes to get down there with them.

Lyons: See, Pop . . . if you give somebody else a chance to talk sometime, you'd see that I was fixing to pay you back your ten dollars like I told you. Here . . . . I told you I'd pay you when Bonnie got paid.

Troy: Naw . . . you go ahead and keep that ten dollars. Put it in the bank. The next time you feel like you wanna come by here and ask me for something . . . you go on down there and get that.

Lyons: Here's your ten dollars, Pop. I told you I don't want you to give me nothing. I just wanted to borrow ten dollars.

Troy: Naw . . . you go on and keep that for the next time you want to ask me.

Lyons: Come on, Pop . . . here go your ten dollars.

Rose: Why don't you go on and let the boy pay you back, Troy?

Lyons: Here you go, Rose. If you don't take it I'm gonna have to hear about it for the next six months. (*He hands her the money.*)

Rose: You can hand yours over here too, Troy.

Troy: You see this, Bono. You see how they do me.

Bono: Yeah, Lucille do me the same way.

(Gabriel is heard singing offstage. He enters.)

Gabriel: Better get ready for the Judgment! Better get ready for . . . Hey! . . . Hey! . . . There's Troy's boy!

Lyons: How are you doing, Uncle Gabe?

Gabriel: Lyons . . . The King of the Jungle! Rose . . . hey, Rose. Got a flower for you. *(He takes a rose from his pocket.)* Picked it myself. That's the same rose like you is!

Rose: That's right nice of you, Gabe.

Lyons: What you been doing, Uncle Gabe?

Gabriel: Oh, I been chasing hellhounds and waiting on the time to tell St. Peter to open the gates.

Lyons: You been chasing hellhounds, huh? Well . . . you doing the right thing, Uncle Gabe. Somebody got to chase them.

Gabriel: Oh, yeah . . . I know it. The devil's strong. The devil ain't no pushover. Hellhounds snipping at everybody's heels. But I got my trumpet waiting on the judgment time.

Lyons: Waiting on the Battle of Armageddon, huh?

Gabriel: Ain't gonna be too much of a battle when God get to waving that Judgment sword. But the people's gonna have a hell of a time trying to get into heaven if them gates ain't open.

Lyons (putting his arm around Gabriel): You hear this, Pop. Uncle Gabe, you alright!

Gabriel (laughing with Lyons): Lyons! King of the Jungle.

Rose: You gonna stay for supper, Gabe? Want me to fix you a plate?

Gabriel: I'll take a sandwich, Rose. Don't want no plate. Just wanna eat with my hands. I'll take a sandwich.

Rose: How about you, Lyons? You staying? Got some short ribs cooking.

Lyons: Naw, I won't eat nothing till after we finished playing. *(Pause.)* You ought to come down and listen to me play, Pop.

Troy: I don't like that Chinese music. All that noise.

Rose: Go on in the house and wash up, Gabe . . . I'll fix you a sandwich.

Gabriel (to Lyons, as he exits): Troy's mad at me.

Lyons: What you mad at Uncle Gabe for, Pop?

Rose: He thinks Troy's mad at him cause he moved over to Miss Pearl's.

Troy: I ain't mad at the man. He can live where he want to live at.

Lyons: What he move over there for? Miss Pearl don't like nobody.

Rose: She don't mind him none. She treats him real nice. She just don't allow all that singing.

Troy: She don't mind that rent he be paying . . . that's what she don't mind.

Rose: Troy, I ain't going through that with you no more. He's over there cause he want to have his own place. He can come and go as he please.

Troy: Hell, he could come and go as he please here. I wasn't stopping him. I ain't put no rules on him.

Rose: It ain't the same thing, Troy. And you know it.

(Gabriel comes to the door.)

Now, that's the last I wanna hear about that. I don't wanna hear nothing else about Gabe and Miss Pearl. And next week . . .

Gabriel: I'm ready for my sandwich, Rose.

Rose: And next week . . . when that recruiter come from that school . . . I want you to sign that paper and go on and let Cory play football. Then that'll be the last I have to hear about that.

Troy (*to Rose as she exits into the house*): I ain't thinking about Cory nothing.

Lyons: What . . . Cory got recruited? What school he going to?

Troy: That boy walking around here smelling his piss . . . thinking he's grown. Thinking he's gonna do what he want, irrespective of what I say. Look here, Bono . . . I left the Commissioner's office and went down to the A&P . . . that boy ain't working down there. He lying to me. Telling me he got his job back . . . telling me he working weekends . . . telling me he working after school . . . Mr. Stawicki tell me he ain't working down there at all!

Lyons: Cory just growing up. He's just busting at the seams trying to fill out your shoes.

Troy: I don't care what he's doing. When he get to the point where he wanna disobey me . . . then it's time for him to move on. Bono'll tell you that. I bet he ain't never disobeyed his daddy without paying the consequences.

Bono: I ain't never had a chance. My daddy came on through . . . but I ain't never knew him to see him . . . or what he had on his mind or where he went. Just moving on through. Searching out the New Land. That's what the old folks used to call it. See a fellow moving around from place to place . . . woman to woman . . . called it searching out the New Land. I can't say if he ever found it. I come along, didn't want no kids. Didn't know if I was gonna be in one place long enough to fix on them right as their daddy. I figured I was going searching too. As it turned out I been hooked up with Lucille near about as long as your daddy been with Rose. Going on sixteen years.

Troy: Sometimes I wish I hadn't known my daddy. He ain't cared nothing about no kids. A kid to him wasn't nothing. All he wanted was for you to learn how to walk so he could start you to working. When it come time for eating . . . he ate first. If there was anything left over, that's what you got. Man would sit down and eat two chickens and give you the wing.

Lyons: You ought to stop that, Pop. Everybody feed their kids. No matter how hard times is . . . everybody care about their kids. Make sure they have something to eat.

Troy: The only thing my daddy cared about was getting them bales of cotton in to Mr. Lubin. That's the only thing that mattered to him. Sometimes I used to wonder why he was living. Wonder why the devil hadn't come and got him. "Get them bales of cotton in to Mr. Lubin" and find out he owe him money . . .

Lyons: He should have just went on and left when he saw he couldn't get nowhere. That's what I would have done.

Troy: How he gonna leave with eleven kids? And where he gonna go? He ain't knew how to do nothing but farm. No, he was trapped and I think he knew it. But I'll say this for him . . . he felt a responsibility toward us. Maybe he ain't treated us the way I felt he should have . . . but without that responsibility he could have walked off and left us . . . made his own way.

Bono: A lot of them did. Back in those days what you talking about . . . they walk out their front door and just take on down one road or another and keep on walking.

Lyons: There you go! That's what I'm talking about.

Bono: Just keep on walking till you come to something else. Ain't you never heard of nobody having the walking blues? Well, that's what you call it when you just take off like that.

Troy: My daddy ain't had them walking blues! What you talking about? He stayed right there with his family. But he was just as evil as he could be. My mama couldn't stand him. Couldn't stand that evilness. She run off when I was about eight. She sneaked off one night after he had gone to sleep. Told me she was coming back for me. I ain't never seen her no more. All his women run off and left him. He wasn't good for nobody.

When my turn come to head out, I was fourteen and got to sniffing around Joe Canewell's daughter. Had us an old mule we called Greyboy. My daddy sent me out to do some plowing and I tied up Greyboy and went to fooling around with Joe Canewell's daughter. We done found us a nice little spot, got real cozy with each other. She about thirteen and we done figured we was grown anyway . . . so we down there enjoying ourselves . . . ain't thinking about nothing. We didn't know Greyboy had got loose and wandered back to the house and my daddy was looking for me. We down there by the creek enjoying ourselves when my daddy come up on us. Surprised us. He had them leather straps off the mule and commenced to whupping me like there was no tomorrow. I jumped up, mad and embarrassed. I was scared of my daddy. When he commenced to whupping on me . . . quite naturally I run to get out of the way. (*Pause.*) Now I thought he was mad cause I ain't done my work. But I see where he was chasing me off so he could have the gal for himself. When I see what the matter of it was, I lost all fear of my daddy. Right there is where I become a man . . . at fourteen years of age. (*Pause.*) Now it was my turn to run him off. I picked up them same reins that he had used on me. I picked up them reins and commenced to whupping on him. The gal jumped up and run off . . . and when my daddy turned to face me, I could see why the devil had never come to get him . . . cause he was the devil himself. I don't know what happened. When I woke up, I was laying right there by the creek, and Blue . . . this old dog we had . . . was licking my face. I thought I was blind. I couldn't see nothing. Both my eyes were swollen shut. I layed there and cried. I didn't know what I was gonna do. The only thing I knew was the time had come for me to leave my daddy's house. And right there the world suddenly got big. And it was a long time before I could cut it down to where I could handle it.

Part of that cutting down was when I got to the place where I could feel him kicking in my blood and knew that the only thing that separated us was the matter of a few years.

(*Gabriel enters from the house with a sandwich.*)

Lyons: What you got there, Uncle Gabe?

Gabriel: Got me a ham sandwich. Rose gave me a ham sandwich.

Troy: I don't know what happened to him. I done lost touch with everybody except Gabriel. But I hope he's dead. I hope he found some peace.

Lyons: That's a heavy story, Pop. I didn't know you left home when you was fourteen.

Troy: And didn't know nothing. The only part of the world I knew was the forty-two acres of Mr. Lubin's land. That's all I knew about life.

Lyons: Fourteen's kinda young to be out on your own. (*Phone rings.*) I don't even think I was ready to be out on my own at fourteen. I don't know what I would have done.

Troy: I got up from the creek and walked on down to Mobile. I was through with farming. Figured I could do better in the city. So I walked the two hundred miles to Mobile.

Lyons: Wait a minute . . . you ain't walked no two hundred miles, Pop. Ain't nobody gonna walk no two hundred miles. You talking about some walking there.

Bono: That's the only way you got anywhere back in them days.

Lyons: Shhh. Damn if I wouldn't have hitched a ride with somebody!

Troy: Who you gonna hitch it with? They ain't had no cars and things like they got now. We talking about 1918.

Rose (entering): What you all out here getting into?

Troy (to Rose): I'm telling Lyons how good he got it. He don't know nothing about this I'm talking.

Rose: Lyons, that was Bonnie on the phone. She say you supposed to pick her up.

Lyons: Yeah, okay, Rose.

Troy: I walked on down to Mobile and hitched up with some of them fellows that was heading this way. Got up here and found out . . . not only couldn't you get a job . . . you couldn't find no place to live. I thought I was in freedom. Shhh. Colored folks living down there on the riverbanks in whatever kind of shelter they could find for themselves. Right down there under the Brady Street Bridge. Living in shacks made of sticks and tarpaper. Messed around there and went from bad to worse. Started stealing. First it was food. Then I figured, hell, if I steal money I can buy me some food. Buy me some shoes too! One thing led to another. Met your mama. I was young and anxious to be a man. Met your mama and had you. What I do that for? Now I got to worry about feeding you and her. Got to steal three times as much. Went out one day looking for somebody to rob . . . that's what I was, a robber. I'll tell you the truth. I'm ashamed of it today. But it's the truth. Went to rob this fellow . . . pulled out my knife . . . and he pulled out a gun. Shot me in the chest. It felt just like somebody had taken a hot branding iron and laid it on me. When he shot me I jumped at him with my knife. They told me I killed him and they put me in the penitentiary and locked me up for fifteen years. That's where I met Bono. That's where I learned how to play base-ball. Got out that place and your mama had taken you and went on to make life without me. Fifteen years was a long time for her to wait. But that fifteen years cured me of that robbing stuff. Rose'll tell you. She asked me when I met her if I had gotten all that foolishness out of my system. And I told her, "Baby, it's you and baseball all what count with me." You hear me, Bono? I meant it too. She say, "Which one comes first?" I told her, "Baby, ain't no doubt it's baseball . . . but you stick and get old with me and we'll both outlive this baseball." Am I right, Rose? And it's true.

Rose: Man, hush your mouth. You ain't said no such thing. Talking about, "Baby you know you'll always be number one with me." That's what you was talking.

Troy: You hear that, Bono. That's why I love her.

Bono: Rose'll keep you straight. You get off the track, she'll straighten you up.

Rose: Lyons, you better get on up and get Bonnie. She waiting on you.

Lyons (gets up to go): Hey, Pop, why don't you come on down to the Grill and hear me play?

Troy: I ain't going down there. I'm too old to be sitting around in them clubs.

Bono: You got to be good to play down at the Grill.

Lyons: Come on, Pop . . .

Troy: I got to get up in the morning.

Lyons: You ain't got to stay long.

Troy: Naw, I'm gonna get my supper and go on to bed.

Lyons: Well, I got to go. I'll see you again.

Troy: Don't you come around my house on my payday.

Rose: Pick up the phone and let somebody know you coming. And bring Bonnie with you. You know I'm always glad to see her.

Lyons: Yeah, I'll do that, Rose. You take care now. See you, Pop. See you, Mr. Bono. See you, Uncle Gabe.

Gabriel: Lyons! King of the Jungle!

(Lyons exits.)

Troy: Is supper ready, woman? Me and you got some business to take care of. I'm gonna tear it up too.

Rose: Troy, I done told you now!

Troy (puts his arm around Bono): Aw hell, woman . . . this is Bono. Bono like family. I done known this nigger since . . . how long I done know you?

Bono: It's been a long time.

Troy: I done know this nigger since Skippy was a pup. Me and him done been through some times.

Bono: You sure right about that.

Troy: Hell, I done know him longer than I known you. And we still standing shoulder to shoulder. Hey, look here, Bono . . . a man can't ask for no more than that. *(Drinks to him.)* I love you, nigger.

Bono: Hell, I love you too . . . but I got to get home see my woman. You got yours in hand. I got to go get mine.

(Bono starts to exit as Cory enters the yard, dressed in his football uniform. He gives Troy a hard, uncompromising look.)

Cory: What you do that for, Pop?

(He throws his helmet down in the direction of Troy.)

Rose: What's the matter? Cory . . . what's the matter?

Cory: Papa done went up to the school and told Coach Zellman I can't play football no more. Wouldn't even let me play the game. Told him to tell the recruiter not to come.

Rose: Troy . . .

Troy: What you Troying me for. Yeah, I did it. And the boy know why I did it.

Cory: Why you wanna do that to me? That was the one chance I had.

Rose: Ain't nothing wrong with Cory playing football, Troy.

Troy: The boy lied to me. I told the nigger if he wanna play football . . . to keep up his chores and hold down that job at the A&P. That was the conditions. Stopped down there to see Mr. Stawicki . . .

Cory: I can't work after school during the football season, Pop! I tried to tell you that Mr. Stawicki's holding my job for me. You don't never want to listen to nobody. And then you wanna go and do this to me!

Troy: I ain't done nothing to you. You done it to yourself.

Cory: Just cause you didn't have a chance! You just scared I'm gonna be better than you, that's all.

Troy: Come here.

Rose: Troy . . .

(*Cory reluctantly crosses over to Troy.*)

Troy: Alright! See. You done made a mistake.

Cory: I didn't even do nothing!

Troy: I'm gonna tell you what your mistake was. See . . . you swung at the ball and didn't hit it. That's strike one. See, you in the batter's box now. You swung and you missed. That's strike one. Don't you strike out!

(*Lights fade to black.*)

ACT II

SCENE I

The following morning. Cory is at the tree hitting the ball with the bat. He tries to mimic Troy, but his swing is awkward, less sure. Rose enters from the house.

Rose: Cory, I want you to help me with this cupboard.

Cory: I ain't quitting the team. I don't care what Poppa say.

Rose: I'll talk to him when he gets back. He had to go see about your Uncle Gabe. The police done arrested him. Say he was disturbing the peace. He'll be back directly. Come on in here and help me clean out the top of this cupboard.

(*Cory exits into the house. Rose sees Troy and Bono coming down the alley.*)

Troy . . . what they say down there?

Troy: Ain't said nothing. I give them fifty dollars and they let him go. I'll talk to you about it. Where's Cory?

Rose: He's in there helping me clean out these cupboards.

Troy: Tell him to get his butt out here.

(*Troy and Bono go over to the pile of wood. Bono picks up the saw and begins sawing.*)

Troy (to Bono): All they want is the money. That makes six or seven times I done went down there and got him. See me coming they stick out their *hands.*

Bono: Yeah. I know what you mean. That's all they care about . . . that money. They don't care about what's right. (*Pause.*) Nigger, why you got to go and get some hard wood? You ain't doing nothing but building a little old fence. Get you some soft pine wood. That's all you need.

Troy: I know what I'm doing. This is outside wood. You put pine wood inside the house. Pine wood is inside wood. This here is outside wood. Now you tell me where the fence is gonna be?

Bono: You don't need this wood. You can put it up with pine wood and it'll stand as long as you gonna be here looking at it.

Troy: How you know how long I'm gonna be here, nigger? Hell, I might just live forever. Live longer than old man Horsely.

Bono: That's what Magee used to say.

Troy: Magee's a damn fool. Now you tell me who you ever heard of gonna pull their own teeth with a pair of rusty pliers.

Bono: The old folks . . . my granddaddy used to pull his teeth with pliers. They ain't had no dentists for the colored folks back then.

Troy: Get clean pliers! You understand? Clean pliers! Sterilize them! Besides we ain't living back then. All Magee had to do was walk over to Doc Goldblum's.

Bono: I see where you and that Tallahassee gal . . . that Alberta . . . I see where you all done got tight.

Troy: What you mean "got tight"?

Bono: I see where you be laughing and joking with her all the time.

Troy: I laughs and jokes with all of them, Bono. You know me.

Bono: That ain't the kind of laughing and joking I'm talking about.

(*Cory enters from the house.*)

Cory: How you doing, Mr. Bono?

Troy: Cory? Get that saw from Bono and cut some wood. He talking about the wood's too hard to cut. Stand back there, Jim, and let that young boy show you how it's done.

Bono: He's sure welcome to it.

(*Cory takes the saw and begins to cut the wood.*)

Whew-e-e! Look at that. Big old strong boy. Look like Joe Louis. Hell, must be getting old the way I'm watching that boy whip through that wood.

Cory: I don't see why Mama want a fence around the yard noways.

Troy: Damn if I know either. What the hell she keeping out with it? She ain't got nothing nobody want.

Bono: Some people build fences to keep people out . . . and other people build fences to keep people in. Rose wants to hold on to you all. She loves you.

Troy: Hell, nigger, I don't need nobody to tell me my wife loves me. Cory . . . go on in the house and see if you can find that other saw.

Cory: Where's it at?

Troy: I said find it! Look for it till you find it!

(*Cory exits into the house.*)

What's that supposed to mean? Wanna keep us in?

Bono: Troy . . . I done known you seem like damn near my whole life. You and Rose both. I done know both of you all for a long time. I remember when you met Rose. When you was hitting them baseball out the park. A lot of them old gals was after you then. You had the pick of the litter. When you picked Rose, I was happy for you. That was the first time I knew you had any sense. I said . . . My man Troy knows what he's doing . . . I'm gonna follow this nigger . . . he might take me somewhere. I been following you too. I done learned a whole heap of things about life watching you. I done learned how to tell where the shit lies. How to tell it from the alfalfa. You done learned me a lot of things. You showed me how to not make the same mistakes . . . to take life as it comes along and keep putting one foot in front of the other. (*Pause.*) Rose a good woman, Troy.

Troy: Hell, nigger, I know she a good woman. I been married to her for eighteen years. What you got on your mind, Bono?

Bono: I just say she a good woman. Just like I say anything. I ain't got to have nothing on my mind.

Troy: You just gonna say she a good woman and leave it hanging out there like that? Why you telling me she a good woman?

Bono: She loves you, Troy. Rose loves you.

Troy: You saying I don't measure up. That's what you trying to say. I don't measure up cause I'm seeing this other gal. I know what you trying to say.

Bono: I know what Rose means to you, Troy. I'm just trying to say I don't want to see you mess up.

Troy: Yeah, I appreciate that, Bono. If you was messing around on Lucille I'd be telling you the same thing.

Bono: Well, that's all I got to say. I just say that because I love you both.

Troy: Hell, you know me . . . I wasn't out there looking for nothing. You can't find a better woman than Rose. I know that. But seems like this woman just stuck onto me where I can't shake her loose. I done wrestled with it, tried to throw her off me . . . but she just stuck on tighter. Now she's stuck on for good.

Bono: You's in control . . . that's what you tell me all the time. You responsible for what you do.

Troy: I ain't ducking the responsibility of it. As long as it sets right in my heart . . . then I'm okay. Cause that's all I listen to. It'll tell me right from wrong every time. And I ain't talking about doing Rose no bad turn. I love Rose. She done carried me a long ways and I love and respect her for that.

Bono: I know you do. That's why I don't want to see you hurt her. But what you gonna do when she find out? What you got then? If you try and juggle both of them . . . sooner or later you gonna drop one of them. That's common sense.

Troy: Yeah, I hear what you saying, Bono. I been trying to figure a way to work it out.

Bono: Work it out right, Troy. I don't want to be getting all up between you and Rose's business . . . but work it so it come out right.

Troy: Aw hell, I get all up between you and Lucille's business. When you gonna get that woman that refrigerator she been wanting? Don't tell me you ain't got no money now. I know who your banker is. Mellon° don't need that money bad as Lucille want that refrigerator. I'll tell you that.

Bono: Tell you what I'll do . . . when you finish building this fence for Rose . . . I'll buy Lucille that refrigerator.

Troy: You done stuck your foot in your mouth now!

(*Troy grabs up a board and begins to saw. Bono starts to walk out the yard.*)

Hey, nigger . . . where you going?

Mellon: banker and industrialist Andrew Mellon (1855–1937), U.S. Treasury Secretary 1921–32, was active in philanthropic enterprises, especially in his native Pittsburgh.

Bono: I'm going home. I know you don't expect me to help you now. I'm protecting my money. I wanna see you put that fence up by yourself. That's what I want to see. You'll be here another six months without me.

Troy: Nigger, you ain't right.

Bono: When it comes to my money . . . I'm right as fireworks on the Fourth of July.

Troy: Alright, we gonna see now. You better get out your bankbook.

(Bono exits, and Troy continues to work. Rose enters from the house.)

Rose: What they say down there? What's happening with Gabe?

Troy: I went down there and got him out. Cost me fifty dollars. Say he was disturbing the peace. Judge set up a hearing for him in three weeks. Say to show cause why he shouldn't be re-committed.

Rose: What was he doing that cause them to arrest him?

Troy: Some kids was teasing him and he run them off home. Say he was howling and carrying on. Some folks seen him and called the police. That's all it was.

Rose: Well, what's you say? What'd you tell the judge?

Troy: Told him I'd look after him. It didn't make no sense to recommit the man. He stuck out his big greasy palm and told me to give him fifty dollars and take him on home.

Rose: Where's he at now? Where'd he go off to?

Troy: He's gone on about his business. He don't need nobody to hold his hand.

Rose: Well, I don't know. Seem like that would be the best place for him if they did put him into the hospital. I know what you're gonna say. But that's what I think would be best.

Troy: The man done had his life ruined fighting for what? And they wanna take and lock him up. Let him be free. He don't bother nobody.

Rose: Well, everybody got their own way of looking at it I guess. Come on and get your lunch. I got a bowl of lima beans and some cornbread in the oven. Come on get something to eat. Ain't no sense you fretting over Gabe.

(Rose turns to go into the house.)

Troy: Rose . . . got something to tell you.

Rose: Well, come on . . . wait till I get this food on the table.

Troy: Rose!

(She stops and turns around.)

I don't know how to say this. *(Pause.)* I can't explain it none. It just sort of grows on you till it gets out of hand. It starts out like a little bush . . . and the next thing you know it's a whole forest.

Rose: Troy . . . what is you talking about?

Troy: I'm talking, woman, let me talk. I'm trying to find a way to tell you . . . I'm gonna be a daddy. I'm gonna be somebody's daddy.

Rose: Troy . . . you're not telling me this? You're gonna be . . . what?

Troy: Rose . . . now . . . see . . .

Rose: You telling me you gonna be somebody's daddy? You telling your *wife* this?

(Gabriel enters from the street. He carries a rose in his hand.)

Gabriel: Hey, Troy! Hey, Rose!

Rose: I have to wait eighteen years to hear something like this.

Gabriel: Hey, Rose . . . I got a flower for you. (*He hands it to her.*) That's a rose. Same rose like you is.

Rose: Thanks, Gabe.

Gabriel: Troy, you ain't mad at me is you? Them bad mens come and put me away. You ain't mad at me is you?

Troy: Naw, Gabe, I ain't mad at you.

Rose: Eighteen years and you wanna come with this.

Gabriel (*takes a quarter out of his pocket*)*:* See what I got? Got a brand new quarter.

Troy: Rose . . . it's just . . .

Rose: Ain't nothing you can say, Troy. Ain't no way of explaining that.

Gabriel: Fellow that give me this quarter had a whole mess of them. I'm gonna keep this quarter till it stop shining.

Rose: Gabe, go on in the house there. I got some watermelon in the Frigidaire. Go on and get you a piece.

Gabriel: Say, Rose . . . you know I was chasing hellhounds and them bad mens come and get me and take me away. Troy helped me. He come down there and told them they better let me go before he beat them up. Yeah, he did!

Rose: You go on and get you a piece of watermelon, Gabe. Them bad mens is gone now.

Gabriel: Okay, Rose . . . gonna get me some watermelon. The kind with the stripes on it.

(Gabriel exits into the house.)

Rose: Why, Troy? Why? After all these years to come dragging this in to me now. It don't make no sense at your age. I could have expected this ten or fifteen years ago, but not now.

Troy: Age ain't got nothing to do with it, Rose.

Rose: I done tried to be everything a wife should be. Everything a wife could be. Been married eighteen years and I got to live to see the day you tell me you been seeing another woman and done fathered a child by her. And you know I ain't never wanted no half nothing in my family. My whole family is half. Everybody got different fathers and mothers . . . my two sisters and my brother. Can't hardly tell who's who. Can't never sit down and talk about Papa and Mama. It's your papa and your mama and my papa and my mama . . .

Troy: Rose . . . stop it now.

Rose: I ain't never wanted that for none of my children. And now you wanna drag your behind in here and tell me something like this.

Troy: You ought to know. It's time for you to know.

Rose: Well, I don't want to know, goddamn it!

Troy: I can't just make it go away. It's done now. I can't wish the circumstance of the thing away.

Rose: And you don't want to either. Maybe you want to wish me and my boy away. Maybe that's what you want? Well, you can't wish us away. I've got eighteen years of my life invested in you. You ought to have stayed upstairs in my bed where you belong.

Troy: Rose . . . now listen to me . . . we can get a handle on this thing. We can talk this out . . . come to an understanding.

Rose: All of a sudden it's "we." Where was "we" at when you was down there rolling around with some godforsaken woman? "We" should have come to an understanding before you started making a damn fool of yourself. You're a day late and a dollar short when it comes to an understanding with me.

Troy: It's just . . . She gives me a different idea . . . a different understanding about myself. I can step out of this house and get away from the pressures and problems . . . be a different man. I ain't got to wonder how I'm gonna pay the bills or get the roof fixed. I can just be a part of myself that I ain't never been.

Rose: What I want to know . . . is do you plan to continue seeing her. That's all you can say to me.

Troy: I can sit up in her house and laugh. Do you understand what I'm saying. I can laugh out loud . . . and it feels good. It reaches all the way down to the bottom of my shoes. (*Pause.*) Rose, I can't give that up.

Rose: Maybe you ought to go on and stay down there with her . . . if she's a better woman than me.

Troy: It ain't about nobody being a better woman or nothing. Rose, you ain't the blame. A man couldn't ask for no woman to be a better wife than you've been. I'm responsible for it. I done locked myself into a pattern trying to take care of you all that I forgot about myself.

Rose: What the hell was I there for? That was my job, not somebody else's.

Troy: Rose, I done tried all my life to live decent . . . to live a clean . . . hard . . . useful life. I tried to be a good husband to you. In every way I knew how. Maybe I come into the world backwards, I don't know. But . . . you born with two strikes on you before you come to the plate. You got to guard it closely . . . always looking for the curve-ball on the inside corner. You can't afford to let none get past you. You can't afford a call strike. If you going down . . . you going down swinging. Everything lined up against you. What you gonna do. I fooled them, Rose. I bunted. When I found you and Cory and a halfway decent job . . . I was safe. Couldn't nothing touch me. I wasn't gonna strike out no more. I wasn't going back to the penitentiary. I wasn't gonna lay in the streets with a bottle of wine. I was safe. I had me a family. A job. I wasn't gonna get that last strike. I was on first looking for one of them boys to knock me in. To get me home.

Rose: You should have stayed in my bed, Troy.

Troy: Then when I saw that gal . . . she firmed up my backbone. And I got to thinking that if I tried . . . I just might be able to steal second. Do you understand after eighteen years I wanted to steal second.

Rose: You should have held me tight. You should have grabbed me and held on.

Troy: I stood on first base for eighteen years and I thought . . . well, goddamn it . . . go on for it!

Rose: We're not talking about baseball! We're talking about you going off to lay in bed with another woman . . . and then bring it home to me. That's what we're talking about. We ain't talking about no baseball.

Troy: Rose, you're not listening to me. I'm trying the best I can to explain it to you. It's not easy for me to admit that I been standing in the same place for eighteen years.

Rose: I been standing with you! I been right here with you, Troy. I got a life too. I gave eighteen years of my life to stand in the same spot with you. Don't you think I ever wanted other things? Don't you think I had dreams and hopes? What about my life? What about me. Don't you think it ever crossed my mind to want to know other men? That I wanted to lay up somewhere and forget about my responsibilities? That I wanted someone to make me laugh so I could feel good? You not the only one who's got wants and needs. But I held on to you, Troy. I took all my feelings, my wants and needs, my dreams . . . and I buried them inside you. I planted a seed and watched and prayed over it. I planted myself inside you and waited to bloom. And it didn't take me no eighteen years to find out the soil was hard and rocky and it wasn't never gonna bloom.

But I held on to you, Troy. I held you tighter. You was my husband. I owed you everything I had. Every part of me I could find to give you. And upstairs in that room . . . with the darkness falling in on me . . . I gave everything I had to try and erase the doubt that you wasn't the finest man in the world. And wherever you was going . . . I wanted to be there with you. Cause you was my husband. Cause that's the only way I was gonna survive as your wife. You always talking about what you give . . . and what you don't have to give. But you take too. You take . . . and don't even know nobody's giving!

(Rose turns to exit into the house; Troy grabs her arm.)

Troy: You say I take and don't give!

Rose: Troy! You're hurting me!

Troy: You say I take and don't give.

Rose: Troy . . . you're hurting my arm! Let go!

Troy: I done give you everything I got. Don't you tell that lie on me.

Rose: Troy!

Troy: Don't you tell that lie on me!

(Cory enters from the house.)

Cory: Mama!

Rose: Troy. You're hurting me.

Troy: Don't you tell me about no taking and giving.

(Cory comes up behind Troy and grabs him. Troy, surprised, is thrown off balance just as Cory throws a glancing blow that catches him on the chest and knocks him down. Troy is stunned, as is Cory.)

Rose: Troy. Troy. No!

(Troy gets to his feet and starts at Cory.)

Troy . . . no. Please! Troy!

(Rose pulls on Troy to hold him back. Troy stops himself.)

Troy (to Cory): Alright. That's strike two. You stay away from around me, boy. Don't you strike out. You living with a full count. Don't you strike out.

(Troy exits out the yard as the lights go down.)

SCENE II

It is six months later, early afternoon. Troy enters from the house and starts to exit the yard. Rose enters from the house.

Rose: Troy, I want to talk to you.

Troy: All of a sudden, after all this time, you want to talk to me, huh? You ain't wanted to talk to me for months. You ain't wanted to talk to me last night. You ain't wanted no part of me then. What you wanna talk to me about now?

Rose: Tomorrow's Friday.

Troy: I know what day tomorrow is. You think I don't know tomorrow's Friday? My whole life I ain't done nothing but look to see Friday coming and you got to tell me it's Friday.

Rose: I want to know if you're coming home.

Troy: I always come home, Rose. You know that. There ain't never been a night I ain't come home.

Rose: That ain't what I mean . . . . and you know it. I want to know if you're coming straight home after work.

Troy: I figure I'd cash my check . . . hang out at Taylors' with the boys . . . maybe play a game of checkers . . .

Rose: Troy, I can't live like this. I won't live like this. You livin' on borrowed time with me. It's been going on six months now you ain't been coming home.

Troy: I be here every night. Every night of the year. That's 365 days.

Rose: I want you to come home tomorrow after work.

Troy: Rose . . . I don't mess up my pay. You know that now. I take my pay and I give it to you. I don't have no money but what you give me back. I just want to have a little time to myself . . . a little time to enjoy life.

Rose: What about me? When's my time to enjoy life?

Troy: I don't know what to tell you, Rose. I'm doing the best I can.

Rose: You ain't been home from work but time enough to change your clothes and run out . . . and you wanna call that the best you can do?

Troy: I'm going over to the hospital to see Alberta. She went into the hospital this afternoon. Look like she might have the baby early. I won't be gone long.

Rose: Well, you ought to know. They went over to Miss Pearl's and got Gabe today. She said you told them to go ahead and lock him up.

Troy: I ain't said no such thing. Whoever told you that is telling a lie. Pearl ain't doing nothing but telling a big fat lie.

Rose: She ain't had to tell me. I read it on the papers.

Troy: I ain't told them nothing of the kind.

Rose: I saw it right there on the papers.

Troy: What it say, huh?

Rose: It said you told them to take him.

Troy: Then they screwed that up, just the way they screw up everything. I ain't worried about what they got on the paper.

Rose: Say the government send part of his check to the hospital and the other part to you.

Troy: I ain't got nothing to do with that if that's the way it works. I ain't made up the rules about how it work.

Rose: You did Gabe just like you did Cory. You wouldn't sign the paper for Cory . . . but you signed for Gabe. You signed that paper.

(The telephone is heard ringing inside the house.)

Troy: I told you I ain't signed nothing, woman! The only thing I signed was the re- lease form. Hell, I can't read, I don't know what they had on that paper! I ain't signed nothing about sending Gabe away.

Rose: I said send him to the hospital . . . you said let him be free . . . now you done went down there and signed him to the hospital for half his money. You went back on yourself, Troy. You gonna have to answer for that.

Troy: See now . . . you been over there talking to Miss Pearl. She done got mad cause she ain't getting Gabe's rent money. That's all it is. She's liable to say anything.

Rose: Troy, I seen where you signed the paper.

Troy: You ain't seen nothing I signed. What she doing got papers on my brother anyway? Miss Pearl telling a big fat lie. And I'm gonna tell her about it too! You ain't seen nothing I signed. Say . . . you ain't seen nothing I signed.

(Rose exits into the house to answer the telephone. Presently she returns.)

Rose: Troy . . . that was the hospital. Alberta had the baby.

Troy: What she have? What is it?

Rose: It's a girl.

Troy: I better get on down to the hospital to see her.

Rose: Troy . . .

Troy: Rose . . . I got to go see her now. That's only right . . . what's the matter . . . the baby's alright, ain't it?

Rose: Alberta died having the baby.

Troy: Died . . . you say she's dead? Alberta's dead?

Rose: They said they done all they could. They couldn't do nothing for her.

Troy: The baby? How's the baby?

Rose: They say it's healthy. I wonder who's gonna bury her.

Troy: She had family, Rose. She wasn't living in the world by herself.

Rose: I know she wasn't living in the world by herself.

Troy: Next thing you gonna want to know if she had any insurance.

Rose: Troy, you ain't got to talk like that.

Troy: That's the first thing that jumped out your mouth. "Who's gonna bury her?" Like I'm fixing to take on that task for myself.

Rose: I am your wife. Don't push me away.

Troy: I ain't pushing nobody away. Just give me some space. That's all. Just give me some room to breathe.

(Rose exits into the house. Troy walks about the yard.)

Troy (with a quiet rage that threatens to consume him): Alright . . . Mr. Death. See now . . . I'm gonna tell you what I'm gonna do. I'm gonna take and build me a fence around this yard. See? I'm gonna build me a fence around what belongs to me. And then I want you to stay on the other side. See? You stay over there until you're ready for me. Then you come on. Bring your army. Bring your sickle. Bring your wrestling clothes. I ain't gonna fall down on my vigilance this time.

You ain't gonna sneak up on me no more. When you ready for me . . . when the top of your list say Troy Maxson . . . that's when you come around here. You come up and knock on the front door. Ain't nobody else got nothing to do with this. This is between you and me. Man to man. You stay on the other side of that fence until you ready for me. Then you come up and knock on the front door. Anytime you want. I'll be ready for you.

(The lights go down to black.)

SCENE III

The lights come up on the porch. It is late evening three days later. Rose sits listening to the ball game waiting for Troy. The final out of the game is made and Rose switches off the radio. Troy enters the yard carrying an infant wrapped in blankets. He stands back from the house and calls.

Rose enters and stands on the porch. There is a long, awkward silence, the weight of which grows heavier with each passing second.

Troy: Rose . . . I'm standing here with my daughter in my arms. She ain't but a wee bittie little old thing. She don't know nothing about grownups' business. She innocent . . . and she ain't got no mama.
Rose: What you telling me for, Troy?

(She turns and exits into the house.)

Troy: Well . . . I guess we'll just sit out here on the porch.

(He sits down on the porch. There is an awkward indelicateness about the way he handles the baby. His largeness engulfs and seems to swallow it. He speaks loud enough for Rose to hear.)

A man's got to do what's right for him. I ain't sorry for nothing I done. It felt right in my heart. (*To the baby.*) What you smiling at? Your daddy's a big man. Got these great big old hands. But sometimes he's scared. And right now your daddy's scared cause we sitting out here and ain't got no home. Oh, I been homeless before. I ain't had no little baby with me. But I been homeless. You just be out on the road by your lonesome and you see one of them trains coming and you just kinda go like this . . .

(He sings as a lullaby.)

> Please, Mr. Engineer let a man ride the line
> Please, Mr. Engineer let a man ride the line
> I ain't got no ticket please let me ride the blinds

(Rose enters from the house. Troy, hearing her steps behind him, stands and faces her.)

She's my daughter, Rose. My own flesh and blood. I can't deny her no more than I can deny them boys. (*Pause.*) You and them boys is my family. You and them and this child is all I got in the world. So I guess what I'm saying is . . . I'd appreciate it if you'd help me take care of her.

Rose: Okay, Troy . . . you're right. I'll take care of your baby for you . . . cause . . . like you say . . . she's innocent . . . and you can't visit the sins of the father upon the child. A motherless child has got a hard time. (*She takes the baby from him.*) From right now . . . this child got a mother. But you a womanless man.

(*Rose turns and exits into the house with the baby. Lights go down to black.*)

SCENE IV

It is two months later. Lyons enters the street. He knocks on the door and calls.

Lyons: Hey, Rose! (*Pause.*) Rose!

Rose (from inside the house): Stop that yelling. You gonna wake up Raynell. I just got her to sleep.

Lyons: I just stopped by to pay Papa this twenty dollars I owe him. Where's Papa at?

Rose: He should be here in a minute. I'm getting ready to go down to the church. Sit down and wait on him.

Lyons: I got to go pick up Bonnie over her mother's house.

Rose: Well, sit it down there on the table. He'll get it.

Lyons (enters the house and sets the money on the table): Tell Papa I said thanks. I'll see you again.

Rose: Alright, Lyons. We'll see you.

(*Lyons starts to exit as Cory enters.*)

Cory: Hey, Lyons.

Lyons: What's happening, Cory? Say man, I'm sorry I missed your graduation. You know I had a gig and couldn't get away. Otherwise, I would have been there, man. So what you doing?

Cory: I'm trying to find a job.

Lyons: Yeah I know how that go, man. It's rough out here. Jobs are scarce.

Cory: Yeah, I know.

Lyons: Look here, I got to run. Talk to Papa . . . he know some people. He'll be able to help get you a job. Talk to him . . . see what he say.

Cory: Yeah . . . alright, Lyons.

Lyons: You take care. I'll talk to you soon. We'll find some time to talk.

(*Lyons exits the yard. Cory wanders over to the tree, picks up the bat, and assumes a batting stance. He studies an imaginary pitcher and swings. Dissatisfied with the result, he tries again. Troy enters. They eye each other for a beat. Cory puts the bat down and exits the yard. Troy starts into the house as Rose exits with Raynell. She is carrying a cake.*)

Troy: I'm coming in and everybody's going out.

Rose: I'm taking this cake down to the church for the bake sale. Lyons was by to see you. He stopped by to pay you your twenty dollars. It's laying in there on the table.

Troy (going into his pocket): Well . . . here go this money.

Rose: Put it in there on the table, Troy. I'll get it.

Troy: What time you coming back?

Rose: Ain't no use in you studying me. It don't matter what time I come back.

Troy: I just asked you a question, woman. What's the matter . . . can't I ask you a question?

Rose: Troy, I don't want to go into it. Your dinner's in there on the stove. All you
got to do is heat it up. And don't you be eating the rest of them cakes in there.
I'm coming back for them. We having a bake sale at the church tomorrow.

*(Rose exits the yard. Troy sits down on the steps, takes a pint bottle from his pocket,
opens it and drinks. He begins to sing.)*

Troy:

        Hear it ring! Hear it ring!
        Had an old dog his name was Blue
        You know Blue was mighty true
        You know Blue was a good old dog
        Blue trees a possum in a hollow log
        You know from that he was a good old dog

(Bono enters the yard.)

Bono: Hey, Troy.

Troy: Hey, what's happening, Bono?

Bono: I just thought I'd stop by to see you.

Troy: What you stop by and see me for? You ain't stopped by in a month of Sundays.
Hell, I must owe you money or something.

Bono: Since you got your promotion I can't keep up with you. Used to see you every
day. Now I don't even know what route you working.

Troy: They keep switching me around. Got me out in Greentree now . . . hauling
white folks' garbage.

Bono: Greentree, huh? You lucky, at least you ain't got to be lifting them barrels.
Damn if they ain't getting heavier. I'm gonna put in my two years and call it quits.

Troy: I'm thinking about retiring myself.

Bono: You got it easy. You can *drive* for another five years.

Troy: It ain't the same, Bono. It ain't like working the back of the truck. Ain't got
nobody to talk to . . . feel like you working by yourself. Naw, I'm thinking about
retiring. How's Lucille?

Bono: She alright. Her arthritis get to acting up on her sometime. Saw Rose on my
way in. She going down to the church, huh?

Troy: Yeah, she took up going down there. All them preachers looking for somebody
to fatten their pockets. *(Pause.)* Got some gin here.

Bono: Naw, thanks. I just stopped by to say hello.

Troy: Hell, nigger . . . you can take a drink. I ain't never known you to say no to a
drink. You ain't got to work tomorrow.

Bono: I just stopped by. I'm fixing to go over to Skinner's. We got us a domino game
going over his house every Friday.

Troy: Nigger, you can't play no dominoes. I used to whup you four games out of five.

Bono: Well, that learned me. I'm getting better.

Troy: Yeah? Well, that's alright.

Bono: Look here . . . I got to be getting on. Stop by sometime, huh?

Troy: Yeah, I'll do that, Bono. Lucille told Rose you bought her a new refrigerator.

Bono: Yeah, Rose told Lucille you had finally built your fence . . . so I figured we'd
call it even.

Troy: I knew you would.

Bono: Yeah . . . okay. I'll be talking to you.

Troy: Yeah, take care, Bono. Good to see you. I'm gonna stop over.

Bono: Yeah. Okay, Troy.

(*Bono exits. Troy drinks from the bottle.*)

Troy:

> Old Blue died and I dug his grave
> Let him down with a golden chain
> Every night when I hear old Blue bark
> I know Blue treed a possum in Noah's Ark.
> Hear it ring! Hear it ring!

(*Cory enters the yard. They eye each other for a beat. Troy is sitting in the middle of the steps. Cory walks over.*)

Cory: I got to get by.

Troy: Say what? What's you say?

Cory: You in my way. I got to get by.

Troy: You got to get by where? This is my house. Bought and paid for. In full. Took me fifteen years. And if you wanna go in my house and I'm sitting on the steps . . . you say excuse me. Like your mama taught you.

Cory: Come on, Pop . . . I got to get by.

(*Cory starts to maneuver his way past Troy. Troy grabs his leg and shoves him back.*)

Troy: You just gonna walk over top of me?

Cory: I live here too!

Troy (advancing toward him): You just gonna walk over top of me in my own house?

Cory: I ain't scared of you.

Troy: I ain't asked if you was scared of me. I asked you if you was fixing to walk over top of me in my own house? That's the question. You ain't gonna say excuse me? You just gonna walk over top of me?

Cory: If you wanna put it like that.

Troy: How else am I gonna put it?

Cory: I was walking by you to go into the house cause you sitting on the steps drunk, singing to yourself. You can put it like that.

Troy: Without saying excuse me???

(*Cory doesn't respond.*)

I asked you a question. Without saying excuse me???

Cory: I ain't got to say excuse me to you. You don't count around here no more.

Troy: Oh, I see . . . I don't count around here no more. You ain't got to say excuse me to your daddy. All of a sudden you done got so grown that your daddy don't count around here no more . . . Around here in his own house and yard that he done paid for with the sweat of his brow. You done got so grown to where you gonna take over. You gonna take over my house. Is that right? You gonna wear my pants. You gonna go in there and stretch out on my bed. You ain't got to say excuse me cause I don't count around here no more. Is that right?

Cory: That's right. You always talking this dumb stuff. Now, why don't you just get out my way?

Troy: I guess you got someplace to sleep and something to put in your belly. You got that, huh? You got that? That's what you need. You got that, huh?

Cory: You don't know what I got. You ain't got to worry about what I got.

Troy: You right! You one hundred percent right! I done spent the last seventeen years worrying about what you got. Now it's your turn, see? I'll tell you what to do. You grown . . . we done established that. You a man. Now, let's see you act like one. Turn your behind around and walk out this yard. And when you get out there in the alley . . . you can forget about this house. See? Cause this is my house. You go on and be a man and get your own house. You can forget about this. Cause this is mine. You go on and get yours cause I'm through with doing for you.

Cory: You talking about what you did for me . . . what'd you ever give me?

Troy: Them feet and bones! That pumping heart, nigger! I give you more than anybody else is ever gonna give you.

Cory: You ain't never gave me nothing! You ain't never done nothing but hold me back. Afraid I was gonna be better than you. All you ever did was try and make me scared of you. I used to tremble every time you called my name. Every time I heard your footsteps in the house. Wondering all the time . . . what's Papa gonna say if I do this? . . . What's he gonna say if I do that? . . . What's Papa gonna say if I turn on the radio? And Mama, too . . . she tries . . . but she's scared of you.

Troy: You leave your mama out of this. She ain't got nothing to do with this.

Cory: I don't know how she stand you . . . after what you did to her.

Troy: I told you to leave your mama out of this!

(*He advances toward Cory.*)

Cory: What you gonna do . . . give me a whupping? You can't whup me no more. You're too old. You just an old man.

Troy (*shoves him on his shoulder*): Nigger! That's what you are. You just another nigger on the street to me!

Cory: You crazy! You know that?

Troy: Go on now! You got the devil in you. Get on away from me!

Cory: You just a crazy old man . . . talking about I got the devil in me.

Troy: Yeah, I'm crazy! If you don't get on the other side of that yard . . . I'm gonna show you how crazy I am! Go on . . . get the hell out of my yard.

Cory: It ain't your yard. You took Uncle Gabe's money he got from the army to buy this house and then you put him out.

Troy (*advances on Cory*): Get your black ass out of my yard!

(*Troy's advance backs Cory up against the tree. Cory grabs up the bat.*)

Cory: I ain't going nowhere! Come on . . . put me out! I ain't scared of you.

Troy: That's my bat!

Cory: Come on!

Troy: Put my bat down!

Cory: Come on, put me out.

(*Cory swings at Troy, who backs across the yard.*)

What's the matter? You so bad . . . put me out!

(Troy advances toward Cory.)

Cory *(backing up):* Come on! Come on!

Troy: You're gonna have to use it! You wanna draw that bat back on me . . . you're gonna have to use it.

Cory: Come on! . . . Come on!

(Cory swings the bat at Troy a second time. He misses. Troy continues to advance toward him.)

Troy: You're gonna have to kill me! You wanna draw that bat back on me. You're gonna have to kill me.

(Cory, backed up against the tree, can go no farther. Troy taunts him. He sticks out his head and offers him a target.)

Come on! Come on!

(Cory is unable to swing the bat. Troy grabs it.)

Troy: Then I'll show you.

(Cory and Troy struggle over the bat. The struggle is fierce and fully engaged. Troy ultimately is the stronger, and takes the bat from Cory and stands over him ready to swing. He stops himself.)

Go on and get away from around my house.

(Cory, stung by his defeat, picks himself up, walks slowly out of the yard and up the alley.)

Cory: Tell Mama I'll be back for my things.
Troy: They'll be on the other side of that fence.

(Cory exits.)

Troy: I can't taste nothing. Helluljah! I can't taste nothing no more. *(Troy assumes a batting posture and begins to taunt Death, the fastball on the outside corner.)* Come on! It's between you and me now! Come on! Anytime you want! Come on! I be ready for you . . . but I ain't gonna be easy.

(The lights go down on the scene.)

SCENE V

The time is 1965. The lights come up in the yard. It is the morning of Troy's funeral. A funeral plaque with a light hangs beside the door. There is a small garden plot off to the side. There is noise and activity in the house as Rose, Lyons, and Bono have gathered. The door opens and Raynell, seven years old, enters dressed in a flannel nightgown. She crosses to the garden and pokes around with a stick. Rose calls from the house.

Rose: Raynell!
Raynell: Mam?
Rose: What you doing out there?
Raynell: Nothing.

(Rose comes to the door.)

Rose: Girl, get in here and get dressed. What you doing?
Raynell: Seeing if my garden growed.

Rose: I told you it ain't gonna grow overnight. You got to wait.

Raynell: It don't look like it never gonna grow. Dag!

Rose: I told you a watched pot never boils. Get in here and get dressed.

Raynell: This ain't even no pot, Mama.

Rose: You just have to give it a chance. It'll grow. Now you come on and do what I told you. We got to be getting ready. This ain't no morning to be playing around. You hear me?

Raynell: Yes, Mam.

> (*Rose exits into the house. Raynell continues to poke at her garden with a stick. Cory enters. He is dressed in a Marine corporal's uniform, and carries a duffelbag. His posture is that of a military man, and his speech has a clipped sternness.*)

Cory (to Raynell): Hi. (*Pause.*) I bet your name is Raynell.

Raynell: Uh huh.

Cory: Is your mama home?

> (*Raynell runs up on the porch and calls through the screen door.*)

Raynell: Mama . . . there's some man out here. Mama?

> (*Rose comes to the door.*)

Rose: Cory? Lord have mercy! Look here, you all!

> (*Rose and Cory embrace in a tearful reunion as Bono and Lyons enter from the house dressed in funeral clothes.*)

Bono: Aw, looka here . . .

Rose: Done got all grown up!

Cory: Don't cry, Mama. What you crying about?

Rose: I'm just so glad you made it.

Cory: Hey Lyons. How you doing, Mr. Bono.

> (*Lyons goes to embrace Cory.*)

Lyons: Look at you, man. Look at you. Don't he look good, Rose. Got them Corporal stripes.

Rose: What took you so long?

Cory: You know how the Marines are, Mama. They got to get all their paperwork straight before they let you do anything.

Rose: Well, I'm sure glad you made it. They let Lyons come. Your Uncle Gabe's still in the hospital. They don't know if they gonna let him out or not. I just talked to them a little while ago.

Lyons: A Corporal in the United States Marines.

Bono: Your daddy knew you had it in you. He used to tell me all the time.

Lyons: Don't he look good, Mr. Bono?

Bono: Yeah, he remind me of Troy when I first met him. (*Pause.*) Say, Rose, Lucille's down at the church with the choir. I'm gonna go down and get the pallbearers lined up. I'll be back to get you all.

Rose: Thanks, Jim.

Cory: See you, Mr. Bono.

Lyons (with his arm around Raynell): Cory . . . look at Raynell. Ain't she precious? She gonna break a whole lot of hearts.

Rose: Raynell, come and say hello to your brother. This is your brother, Cory. You remember Cory.

Raynell: No, Mam.

Cory: She don't remember me, Mama.

Rose: Well, we talk about you. She heard us talk about you. (*To Raynell.*) This is your brother, Cory. Come on and say hello.

Raynell: Hi.

Cory: Hi. So you're Raynell. Mama told me a lot about you.

Rose: You all come on into the house and let me fix you some breakfast. Keep up your strength.

Cory: I ain't hungry, Mama.

Lyons: You can fix me something, Rose. I'll be in there in a minute.

Rose: Cory, you sure you don't want nothing? I know they ain't feeding you right.

Cory: No, Mama . . . thanks. I don't feel like eating. I'll get something later.

Rose: Raynell . . . get on upstairs and get that dress on like I told you.

(*Rose and Raynell exit into the house.*)

Lyons: So . . . I hear you thinking about getting married.

Cory: Yeah, I done found the right one, Lyons. It's about time.

Lyons: Me and Bonnie been split up about four years now. About the time Papa re-tired. I guess she just got tired of all them changes I was putting her through. (*Pause.*) I always knew you was gonna make something out yourself. Your head was always in the right direction. So . . . you gonna stay in . . . make it a career . . . put in your twenty years?

Cory: I don't know. I got six already, I think that's enough.

Lyons: Stick with Uncle Sam and retire early. Ain't nothing out here. I guess Rose told you what happened with me. They got me down the workhouse. I thought I was being slick cashing other people's checks.

Cory: How much time you doing?

Lyons: They give me three years. I got that beat now. I ain't got but nine more months. It ain't so bad. You learn to deal with it like anything else. You got to take the crookeds with the straights. That's what Papa used to say. He used to say that when he struck out. I seen him strike out three times in a row . . . and the next time up he hit the ball over the grandstand. Right out there in Homestead Field. He wasn't satisfied hitting in the seats . . . he want to hit it over everything! After the game he had two hundred people standing around waiting to shake his hand. You got to take the crookeds with the straights. Yeah, Papa was something else.

Cory: You still playing?

Lyons: Cory . . . you know I'm gonna do that. There's some fellows down there we got us a band . . . we gonna try and stay together when we get out . . . but yeah, I'm still playing. It still helps me to get out of bed in the morning. As long as it do that I'm gonna be right there playing and trying to make some sense out of it.

Rose (calling): Lyons, I got these eggs in the pan.

Lyons: Let me go on and get these eggs, man. Get ready to go bury Papa. (*Pause.*) How you doing? You doing alright?

(Cory nods. Lyons touches him on the shoulder and they share a moment of silent grief. Lyons exits into the house. Cory wanders about the yard. Raynell enters.)

Raynell: Hi.

Cory: Hi.

Raynell: Did you used to sleep in my room?

Cory: Yeah . . . that used to be my room.

Raynell: That's what Papa call it. "Cory's room." It got your football in the closet.

(Rose comes to the door.)

Rose: Raynell, get in there and get them good shoes on.

Raynell: Mama, can't I wear these? Them other one hurt my feet.

Rose: Well, they just gonna have to hurt your feet for a while. You ain't said they hurt your feet when you went down to the store and got them.

Raynell: They didn't hurt then. My feet done got bigger.

Rose: Don't you give me no backtalk now. You get in there and get them shoes on.

(Raynell exits into the house.)

Ain't too much changed. He still got that piece of rag tied to that tree. He was out here swinging that bat. I was just ready to go back in the house. He swung that bat and then he just fell over. Seem like he swung it and stood there with this grin on his face . . . and then he just fell over. They carried him on down to the hospital, but I knew there wasn't no need . . . why don't you come on in the house?

Cory: Mama . . . I got something to tell you. I don't know how to tell you this . . . but I've got to tell you . . . I'm not going to Papa's funeral.

Rose: Boy, hush your mouth. That's your daddy you talking about. I don't want hear that kind of talk this morning. I done raised you to come to this? You standing there all healthy and grown talking about you ain't going to your daddy's funeral?

Cory: Mama . . . listen . . .

Rose: I don't want to hear it, Cory. You just get that thought out of your head.

Cory: I can't drag Papa with me everywhere I go. I've got to say no to him. One time in my life I've got to say no.

Rose: Don't nobody have to listen to nothing like that. I know you and your daddy ain't seen eye to eye, but I ain't got to listen to that kind of talk this morning. Whatever was between you and your daddy . . . the time has come to put it aside. Just take it and set it over there on the shelf and forget about it. Disrespecting your daddy ain't gonna make you a man, Cory. You got to find a way to come to that on your own. Not going to your daddy's funeral ain't gonna make you a man.

Cory: The whole time I was growing up . . . living in his house . . . Papa was like a shadow that followed you everywhere. It weighed on you and sunk into your flesh. It would wrap around you and lay there until you couldn't tell which one was you anymore. That shadow digging in your flesh. Trying to crawl in. Trying to live through you. Everywhere I looked, Troy Maxson was staring back at me . . . hiding under the bed . . . in the closet. I'm just saying I've got to find a way to get rid of that shadow, Mama.

Rose: You just like him. You got him in you good.

Cory: Don't tell me that, Mama.

Rose: You Troy Maxson all over again.

Cory: I don't want to be Troy Maxson. I want to be me.

Rose: You can't be nobody but who you are, Cory. That shadow wasn't nothing but you growing into yourself. You either got to grow into it or cut it down to fit you. But that's all you got to make life with. That's all you got to measure yourself against that world out there. Your daddy wanted you to be everything he wasn't . . . and at the same time he tried to make you into everything he was. I don't know if he was right or wrong . . . but I do know he meant to do more good than he meant to do harm. He wasn't always right. Sometimes when he touched he bruised. And sometimes when he took me in his arms he cut.

When I first met your daddy I thought . . . Here is a man I can lay down with and make a baby. That's the first thing I thought when I seen him. I was thirty years old and had done seen my share of men. But when he walked up to me and said, "I can dance a waltz that'll make you dizzy," I thought, Rose Lee, here is a man that you can open yourself up to and be filled to bursting. Here is a man that can fill all them empty spaces you been tipping around the edges of. One of them empty spaces was being somebody's mother.

I married your daddy and settled down to cooking his supper and keeping clean sheets on the bed. When your daddy walked through the house he was so big he filled it up. That was my first mistake. Not to make him leave some room for me. For my part in the matter. But at that time I wanted that. I wanted a house that I could sing in. And that's what your daddy gave me. I didn't know to keep up his strength I had to give up little pieces of mine. I did that. I took on his life as mine and mixed up the pieces so that you couldn't hardly tell which was which anymore. It was my choice. It was my life and I didn't have to live it like that. But that's what life offered me in the way of being a woman and I took it. I grabbed hold of it with both hands.

By the time Raynell came into the house, me and your daddy had done lost touch with one another. I didn't want to make my blessing off of nobody's misfortune . . . but I took on to Raynell like she was all them babies I had wanted and never had.

(The phone rings.)

Like I'd been blessed to relive a part of my life. And if the Lord see fit to keep up my strength . . . I'm gonna do her just like your daddy did you . . . I'm gonna give her the best of what's in me.

Raynell (entering, still with her old shoes): Mama . . . . Reverend Tolliver on the phone.

(Rose exits into the house.)

Raynell: Hi.
Cory: Hi.
Raynell: You in the Army or the Marines?
Cory: Marines.
Raynell: Papa said it was the Army. Did you know Blue?
Cory: Blue? Who's Blue?
Raynell: Papa's dog what he sing about all the time.
Cory (singing):
  Hear it ring! Hear it ring!
  I had a dog his name was Blue

You know Blue was mighty true
You know Blue was a good old dog
Blue treed a possum in a hollow log
You know from that he was a good old dog.
Hear it ring! Hear it ring!

(Raynell joins in singing.)

Cory and Raynell:

Blue treed a possum out on a limb
Blue looked at me and I looked at him
Grabbed that possum and put him in a sack
Blue stayed there till I came back
Old Blue's feets was big and round
Never allowed a possum to touch the ground.

Old Blue died and I dug his grave
I dug his grave with a silver spade
Let him down with a golden chain
And every night I call his name
Go on Blue, you good dog you
Go on Blue, you good dog you.

Raynell:

Blue laid down and died like a man
Blue laid down and died . . .

Both:

Blue laid down and died like a man
Now he's treeing possums in the Promised Land
I'm gonna tell you this to let you know
Blue's gone where the good dogs go
When I hear old Blue bark
When I hear old Blue bark
Blue treed a possum in Noah's Ark
Blue treed a possum in Noah's Ark.

(Rose comes to the screen door.)

Rose: Cory, we gonna be ready to go in a minute.

Cory *(to Raynell):* You go on in the house and change them shoes like Mama told you so we can go to Papa's funeral.

Raynell: Okay, I'll be back.

(Raynell exits into the house. Cory gets up and crosses over to the tree. Rose stands in the screen door watching him. Gabriel enters from the alley.)

Gabriel *(calling):* Hey, Rose!

Rose: Gabe?

Gabriel: I'm here, Rose. Hey, Rose, I'm here!

(Rose enters from the house.)

Rose: Lord . . . Look here, Lyons!

Lyons: See, I told you, Rose . . . I told you they'd let him come.

Cory: How you doing, Uncle Gabe?

Lyons: How you doing, Uncle Gabe?

Gabriel: Hey, Rose. It's time. It's time to tell St. Peter to open the gates. Troy, you ready? You ready, Troy. I'm gonna tell St. Peter to open the gates. You get ready now.

(Gabriel, with great fanfare, braces himself to blow. The trumpet is without a mouthpiece. He puts the end of it into his mouth and blows with great force, like a man who has been waiting some twenty-odd years for this single moment. No sound comes out of the trumpet. He braces himself and blows again with the same result. A third time he blows. There is a weight of impossible description that falls away and leaves him bare and exposed to a frightful realization. It is a trauma that a sane and normal mind would be unable to withstand. He begins to dance. A slow, strange dance, eerie and life-giving. A dance of atavistic signature and ritual. Lyons attempts to embrace him. Gabriel pushes Lyons away. He begins to howl in what is an attempt at song, or perhaps a song turning back into itself in an attempt at speech. He finishes his dance and the gates of heaven stand open as wide as God's closet.)

That's the way that go!

BLACKOUT

August Wilson on Writing

A Look into Black America

1999

Interviewer: Is it a concern to effect social change with your plays?

Wilson: I don't write primarily to effect social change. I believe writing can do that, but that's not why I write. I work as an artist. However, all art is political in the sense that it serves the politics of someone. Here in America whites have a particular view of blacks, and I think my plays offer them a different and new way to look at black Americans. For instance, in *Fences* they see a garbageman, a person they really don't look at, although they may see a garbageman every day. By looking at Troy's

August Wilson

life, white people find out that the content of this black garbageman's life is very similar to their own, that he is affected by the same things—love, honor, beauty, betrayal, duty. Recognizing that these things are as much a part of his life as of theirs can be revolutionary and can affect how they think about and deal with black people in their lives.

Interviewer: How would that same play, *Fences*, affect a black audience?

Wilson: Blacks see the content of their lives being elevated into art. They don't always know that it is possible, and it's important to know that.

From "Interview with August Wilson"
by Bonnie Lyons and George Plimpton

Susan Glaspell at work, around 1913.

WRITING

38 WRITING ABOUT LITERATURE

If one waits for the right time to come before writing,
the right time never comes.

——JAMES RUSSELL LOWELL

Assigned to write an essay on *Hamlet*, a student might well wonder, "What can I say that hasn't been said a thousand times before?" Often the most difficult aspect of writing about a story, poem, or play is the feeling that we have nothing of interest to contribute to the ongoing conversation about some celebrated literary work. There's always room, though, for a reader's fresh take on an old standby.

Remember that in the study of literature common sense is never out of place. For most of a class hour, a professor once rhapsodized about the arrangement of the contents of W. H. Auden's *Collected Poems*. Auden, he claimed, was a master of thematic continuity, who had brilliantly placed the poems in the order that they ingeniously complemented each other. Near the end of the hour, his theories were punctured—with a great inaudible pop—when a student, timidly raising a hand, pointed out that Auden had arranged the poems in the book not by theme but in alphabetical order according to the first word of each poem. The professor's jaw dropped: "Why didn't you say that sooner?" The student was apologetic: "I—I was afraid I'd sound too *ordinary*."

Don't be afraid to state a conviction, though it seems obvious. Does it matter that you may be repeating something that, once upon a time or even just the other day, has been said before? What matters more is that you are actively engaged in thinking about literature. There are excellent old ideas as well as new ones. You have something to say.

READ ACTIVELY

Most people read in a relaxed, almost passive way. They let the story or poem carry them along without asking too many questions. To write about literature well, however, you need to *read actively*, paying special attention to various aspects of the text. This special sort of attention will not only deepen your enjoyment of the story, poem, or play but will also help generate the information and ideas that will become your final paper. How do you become an active reader? Here are some steps to get you started:

▪ **Preview the text.** To get acquainted with a work of literature before you settle in for a closer reading, skim it for an overview of its content and organization. Take a quick look at all parts of the work. Even a book's cover, preface, introduction, footnotes, and biographical notes about the author can provide you with some context for reading the work itself.

▪ **Take notes. Annotate the text.** Read with a highlighter and pencil at hand, making appropriate annotations to the text. Later, you'll easily be able to review these highlights, and, when you write your paper, quickly refer to supporting evidence.

- Underline words, phrases, or sentences that seem interesting or important, or that raise questions.
- Jot down brief notes in the margin (*"key symbol—this foreshadows the ending,"* for example, or *"dramatic irony"*).
- Use lines or arrows to indicate passages that seem to speak to each other—for instance, all the places in which you find the same theme or related symbols.

Robert Frost

Nothing Gold Can Stay

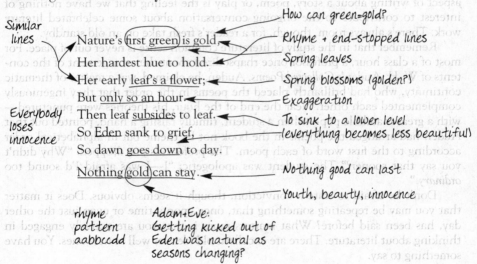

Similar lines

Nature's (first green) is gold,
Her hardest hue to hold.
Her early leaf's a flower;
But only so an hour.
Then leaf subsides to leaf.
So Eden sank to grief,
So dawn goes down to day.
Nothing (gold) can stay.

How can green=gold?
Rhyme + end-stopped lines
Spring leaves
Spring blossoms (golden?)
Exaggeration
To sink to a lower level (everything becomes less beautiful)
Nothing good can last
Youth, beauty, innocence

Everybody loses innocence

rhyme pattern aabbccdd

Adam+Eve:
Getting kicked out of Eden was natural as seasons changing?

▪ **Read closely.** Once you have begun reading in earnest, don't skim or skip over words you don't recognize; sometimes, looking up those very words will unlock a piece's meaning.

▪ **Reread as needed.** If a piece is short, read it several times. Often, knowing the ending of a poem or short story will allow you to extract new meaning from its beginning and middle. If the piece is longer, reread the passages you thought important enough to highlight.

PLAN YOUR ESSAY

If you have actively reread the work you plan to write about and have made notes or annotations, you are already well on your way to writing your paper. Your mind has already begun to work through some initial impressions and ideas. Now you need to arrange those early notions into an organized and logical essay. Here is some advice on how to manage the writing process:

- **Leave yourself time.** Good writing involves thought and revision. Anyone who has ever been a student knows what it's like to pull an all-nighter, churning out a term paper hours before it is due. Still, the best writing evolves over time. Your ideas need to marinate. Sometimes, you'll make false starts, and you'll need to salvage what you can and do the rest from scratch. For the sake of your writing—not to mention your health and sanity—it's far better to get the job started well before your deadline.

- **Choose a subject you care about.** If you have been given a choice of literary works to write about, always choose the play, story, or poem that evokes the strongest emotional response. Your writing will be liveliest if you feel engaged by your subject.

- **Know your purpose.** As you write, keep the assignment in mind. You may have been asked to write a response, in which you describe your reactions to a literary work. Perhaps your purpose is to interpret a work, analyzing how one or more of its elements contribute to its meaning. You may have been instructed to write an evaluation, in which you judge a work's merits. Whatever the assignment, how you approach your essay will depend in large part on your purpose.

- **Think about your audience.** When you write journal entries or rough drafts, you may be composing for your own eyes only. More often, though, you are likely to be writing for an audience, even if it is an audience of one: your professor. Whenever you write for others, you need to be conscious of your readers. Your task is to convince them that your take on a work of literature is a plausible one. To do so, you need to keep your audience's needs and expectations in mind.

- **Define your topic narrowly.** Worried about having enough to say, students sometimes frame their topic so broadly that they can't do justice to it in the allotted number of pages. Your paper will be stronger if you go more deeply into your subject than if you choose a gigantic subject and touch on most aspects of it only superficially. A thorough explication of a short story is hardly possible in a 250-word paper, but an explication of a paragraph or two could work in that space. A profound topic ("The Character of Hamlet") might overflow a book, but a more focused one ("Hamlet's View of Acting" or "Hamlet's Puns") could result in a manageable paper. A paper entitled "Female Characters in *Hamlet*" couldn't help being too general and vague, but one on "Ophelia's Relationship to Laertes" could make for a good marriage of length and subject.

PREWRITING: DISCOVER YOUR IDEAS

Topic in hand, you can begin to get your ideas on the page. To generate new ideas and clarify the thoughts you already have, try one or more of the following useful prewriting techniques:

- **Brainstorm.** Writing quickly, list everything that comes into your mind about your subject. Set a time limit—ten or fifteen minutes—and force yourself to keep adding items to the list, even when you think you have run out of things to say. Sometimes, if you press onward past the point where you feel you are finished, you will surprise yourself with new and fresh ideas.

> gold = early leaves/blossoms
> Or gold = something precious (both?)
> early leaf = flower (yellow blossoms)
> spring (lasts an hour)
> Leaves subside (sink to lower level)
> Eden = paradise = perfection = beauty
> Loss of innocence?
> What about original sin?
> Dawn becomes day (dawn is more precious?)
> Adam and Eve had to fall? Part of natural order.
> seasons/days/people's lives
> Title = last line: perfection can't last
> spring/summer/autumn
> dawn/day
> Innocence can't last

- **Cluster.** This prewriting technique works especially well for visual thinkers. In clustering, you build a diagram to help you explore the relationships among your ideas. To get started, write your subject at the center of a sheet of paper. Circle it. Then jot down ideas, linking each to the central circle with lines. As you write down each new idea, draw lines to link it to related old ideas. The result will look something like the following web.

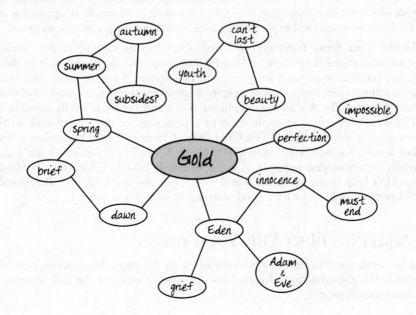

■ **List.** Look over the notes and annotations that you made in your active reading of the work. You have probably already underlined or noted more information than you can possibly use. One way to sort through your material to find the most useful information is to make a list of the important items. It helps to make several short lists under different headings. Here are some lists you might make after rereading Frost's "Nothing Gold Can Stay." Don't be afraid to add more comments or questions on the lists to help your thought process.

Images	Colors
leaf ("early leaf")	green
flower	gold ("hardest hue to hold")
dawn	
day	
Eden	
gold	

Key Actions
gold is hard to hold
early leaf lasts only an hour
leaf subsides to leaf (what does this mean???)
Eden sinks to grief (paradise is lost)
dawn goes down to day
gold can't stay (perfection is impossible?)

■ **Freewrite.** Most writers have snarky little voices in their heads, telling them that the words they're committing to paper aren't interesting or deep or elegant enough. To drown out those little voices, try freewriting. Give yourself a set amount of time (say, ten minutes) and write, nonstop, on your topic. Force your pen to keep moving or your fingers to keep typing, even if you have run out of things to say. If all you can think of to write is "I'm stuck" or "This is dumb," so be it. Keep writing and something else will most likely occur to you. Don't worry, yet, about grammar or spelling. When your time is up, read what you have written, highlighting the best ideas for later use.

How can green be gold? By nature's first green, I guess he means the first leaves in spring. Are those leaves gold? They're more delicate and yellow than summer leaves . . . so maybe in a sense they look gold. Or maybe he means spring blossoms. Sometimes they're yellow. Also the first line seems to connect with the third one, where he comes right out and says that flowers are like early leaves. Still, I think he also means that the first leaves are the most precious ones, like gold. I don't think the poem wants me to take all of these statements literally. Flowers on trees last more than an hour, but that really beautiful moment in spring when blossoms are everywhere always ends too quickly, so maybe that's what he means by "only so an hour." I had to look up "subsides." It means to sink to a lower level . . . as if the later leaves will be less perfect than the first ones. I don't know if I agree. Aren't fall leaves precious? Then he says, "So Eden sank to grief" which seems to be saying that Adam and Eve's fall would have happened no matter what they did, because everything that seems perfect falls apart . . . nothing gold can stay. Is he saying Adam and Eve didn't really have a choice? No matter what, everything gets older, less beautiful, less innocent . . . even people.

▪ **Journal.** Your instructor might ask you to keep a journal in which you jot down your ideas, feelings, and impressions before they are fully formulated. Sometimes a journal is meant for your eyes only; in other instances your instructor might read it. Either way, it is meant to be informal and immediate, and to provide raw material that you may later choose to refine into a formal essay. Here are some tips for keeping a useful journal:

- Get your ideas down as soon as they occur to you.
- Write quickly.
- Jot down your feelings about and first impressions of the story, poem, or play you are reading.
- Don't worry about grammar, spelling, or punctuation.
- Don't worry about sounding academic.
- Don't worry about whether your ideas are good or bad; sort that out later.
- Try out invention strategies such as freewriting, clustering, and outlining.
- Keep writing, even after you think you have run out of things to say. You might surprise yourself.
- Write about what interests you most.
- Write in your journal on a regular basis.

▪ **Outline.** Some topics by their very nature suggest obvious ways to organize a paper. "An Explication of a Sonnet by Wordsworth" might mean simply working through the poem line by line. If this isn't the case, some kind of outline will probably prove helpful. Your outline needn't be elaborate to be useful. While a long research paper on several literary works might call for a detailed outline, a 500-word analysis of a short story's figures of speech might call for just a simple list of points in the order that makes the most logical sense—not necessarily the order in which those thoughts first came to mind.

    1. Passage of time = fall from innocence
       blossoms
       gold
       dawn
       grief

    2. Innocence = perfection
       Adam and Eve
       loss of innocence = inevitable
       real original sin = passing of time
       paradise sinks to grief

    2. Grief = knowledge
       experience of sin & suffering
       unavoidable as grow older

DEVELOP A LITERARY ARGUMENT

Once you have finished a rough outline of your ideas, you need to refine it into a clear and logical shape. You need to state your thesis (or basic idea) clearly and then support it with logical and accurate evidence. Here is a practical approach to this crucial stage of the writing process:

- **Consider your purpose.** As you develop your argument, be sure to refer back to the specific assignment; let it guide you. Your instructor might request one of the following kinds of papers:
  - *Response*, in which you explore your reaction to a work of literature.
  - *Evaluation*, in which you assess the literary merits of a work.
  - *Interpretation*, in which you discuss a work's meaning. If your instructor has assigned an interpretation, he or she may have more specifically asked for an *analysis*, *explication*, or *comparison/contrast* essay, among other possibilities.

- **Remember your audience.** Practically speaking, your professor (and sometimes your classmates) will be your paper's primary audience. Some assignments may specify a particular audience beyond your professor and classmates. Keep your readers in mind. Be sure to adapt your writing to meet their needs and interests. If, for example, the audience has presumably already read a story under discussion, you won't need to relate the plot in its entirety. Instead, you will be free to bring up only those plot points that serve as evidence for your thesis.

- **Narrow your topic to fit the assignment.** Though you may be tempted to choose a broad topic so that you will have no shortage of things to say, remember that a good paper needs focus. Your choice should be narrow enough for you to do it justice in the space and time allotted.

- **Decide on a thesis.** Just as you need to know your destination before you set out on a trip, you need to decide what point you're traveling toward before you begin your first draft. Start by writing a provisional thesis sentence: a summing up of the main idea or argument your paper will explore. While your thesis doesn't need to be outrageous or deliberately provocative, it does need to take a stand. A clear, decisive statement gives you something to prove and lends vigor to your essay.

  ### WORKING THESIS

  The poem argues that like Adam and Eve we all lose our innocence and the passage of time is inevitable.

  This first stab at a thesis sentence gave its author a sense of purpose and direction that allowed him to finish his first draft. Later, as he revised his essay, he found he needed to refine his thesis to make more specific and focused assertions.

- **Build your argument.** Once you've formulated your thesis, your task will be clear: you need to convince your audience that your thesis is sound. To write persuasively, it helps to have an understanding of some key elements of argument:

- **Claims.** Anytime you make a statement you hope will be taken as true, you have made a claim. Some claims are unlikely to be contradicted ("the sky is blue" or "today is Tuesday"), but others are debatable ("every college sophomore dreams of running off to see the world"). Your essay's main claim—your thesis—should not be something entirely obvious. Having to support your point of view will cause you to clarify your ideas about a work of literature.

- **Persuasion.** If the word *argument* makes you think of raised voices and short tempers, it may help to think of your task as the gentler art of persuasion. To convince your audience of your thesis, you will need to present a cogent argument supported by evidence gathered from the text. If the assignment is a research paper, you will also need to cite what others have written on your topic.

- **Evidence.** When you write about a work of literature, the most convincing evidence will generally come from the text itself. Direct quotations from the poem, play, or story under discussion can provide particularly convincing support for your claims. Be sure to introduce any quotation by putting it in the context of the larger work. It is even more important to follow up each quotation with your own analysis of what it shows about the work.

- **Warrants.** Whenever you use a piece of evidence to support a claim, an underlying assumption connects one to the other. For instance, if you were to make the claim that today's weather is absolutely perfect and offer as your evidence the blue sky, your logic would include an unspoken warrant: sunny weather is perfect weather. Not everyone will agree with your warrant, though. Some folks (perhaps farmers) might prefer rain. In making any argument, including one about literature, you may find that you sometimes need to spell out your warrants to demonstrate that they are sound. This is especially true when the evidence you provide can lead to conclusions other than the one you are hoping to prove.

- **Credibility.** When weighing the merits of a claim, you will probably take into account the credibility of the person making the case. Often this happens almost automatically. You are more likely to listen to the opinion that you should take vitamins if it is expressed by your doctor than if it is put forth by a stranger you meet on the street. An expert on any given topic has a certain brand of authority not available to most of us. Fortunately, there are other ways to establish your own credibility:

  Keep your tone thoughtful. Your reader will develop a sense of who you are through your words. If you come across as belligerent or disrespectful to those inclined to disagree with your views, you may lose your reader's goodwill. Therefore, express your ideas calmly and thoughtfully. A level tone demonstrates that you are interested in thinking through an issue or idea, not in bullying your reader into submission.

  Take opposing arguments into account. To make an argument more convincing, demonstrate familiarity with other possible points of view.

Doing so indicates that you have taken other claims into account before arriving at your thesis; it reveals your fairness as well as your understanding of your subject matter. In laying out other points of view, though, be sure to represent them fairly but also to respectfully make clear why your thesis is the soundest claim; you don't want your reader to doubt where you stand.

Demonstrate your knowledge. To gain your reader's trust, it helps to demonstrate a solid understanding of your subject matter. Always check your facts; factual errors can call your knowledge into doubt. It also helps to have a command of the conventions of writing. Errors in punctuation and spelling can undermine a writer's credibility.

- **Organize your argument.** Unless you are writing an explication that works its way line by line through a work of literature, you will need to make crucial decisions about how to shape your essay. Its order should be driven by the logic of your argument, not by the structure of the story, play, or poem you're discussing. In other words, you need not work your way from start to finish through your source material, touching on each major point. Instead, choose only the points needed to prove your thesis, and present them in whatever order best makes your point. A rough outline can help you to determine that order.

- **Make sure your thesis is supported by the evidence.** If you find you can't support certain aspects of your thesis, then refine it so that you can. Remember: until you turn it in, your essay is a work in progress. Anything can and should be changed if it doesn't further the development of the paper's main idea.

CHECKLIST: DEVELOPING AN ARGUMENT

- ☐ What is your essay's purpose?
- ☐ Who is your audience?
- ☐ Is your topic narrow enough?
- ☐ Is your thesis interesting and thought-provoking?
- ☐ Does everything in your essay support your thesis?
- ☐ Have you considered and refuted alternative views?
- ☐ Is your tone thoughtful?
- ☐ Is your argument sensibly organized? Are similar ideas grouped together? Does one point lead logically to the next?

WRITE A ROUGH DRAFT

Seated at last, you prepare to write, only to find yourself besieged with petty distractions. All of a sudden you remember a friend you had promised to call, some double-A batteries you were supposed to pick up, a neglected Coke (in another room) growing warmer and flatter by the minute. If your paper is to be written, you have only one course of action: collar these thoughts and for the moment banish them. Here are a few tips for writing your rough draft:

- **Review your argument.** The shape of your argument, its support, and the evidence you have collected will form the basis of your rough draft.

- **Get your thoughts down.** The best way to draft a paper is to get your ideas down quickly. At this stage, don't fuss over details. The critical, analytical side of your mind can worry about spelling, grammar, and punctuation later. For now, let your creative mind take charge. This part of yourself has the good ideas, insight, and confidence. Forge ahead. Believe in yourself and in your ideas.

- **Write the part you feel most comfortable with first.** There's no need to start at the paper's beginning and work your way methodically through to the end. Instead, plunge right into the parts of the paper you feel most prepared to write. You can always go back later and fill in the blanks.

- **Leave yourself plenty of space.** As you compose, leave plenty of space between lines and set wide margins. When you print out your draft, you will easily be able to go back and squeeze other thoughts in.

- **Focus on the argument.** As you jot down your first draft, you might not want to look at the notes you have compiled. When you come to a place where a note will fit, just insert a reminder to yourself such as "See card 19" or "See Aristotle on comedy." Also, whenever you bring up a new point, it's good to tie it back to your thesis. If you can't find a way to connect a point to your thesis, it's probably better to leave it out of your paper and come up with a point that advances your central claim.

- **Does your thesis hold up?** If, as you write, you find that most of the evidence you uncover is not helping you prove your paper's thesis, it may be that the thesis needs honing. Adjust it as needed.

- **Be open to new ideas.** Writing rarely proceeds in a straight line. Even after you outline your paper and begin to write and revise, expect to discover new thoughts—perhaps the best thoughts of all. If you do, be sure to invite them in.

Here is a student's rough draft for an analytical essay on "Nothing Gold Can Stay."

On Robert Frost's "Nothing Gold Can Stay"

Most of the lines in the poem "Nothing Gold Can Stay" by Robert Frost focus on the changing of the seasons. The poem's first line says that the first leaves of spring are actually blossoms, and the actual leaves that follow are less precious. Those first blossoms only last a little while. The reader realizes that nature is a metaphor for a person's state of mind. People start off perfectly innocent, but as time passes, they can't help but lose that innocence. The poem argues that like Adam and Eve we all lose our innocence and the passage of time is inevitable.

The poem's first image is of the color found in nature. The early gold of spring blossoms is nature's "hardest hue to hold." The color gold is associated with the mineral gold, a precious commodity. There's a hint that early spring is nature in its perfect state, and perfection is impossible to hold on to. To the poem's speaker, the colors of early spring seem to last only an hour. If you blink, they are gone. Like early spring, innocence can't last.

The line "leaf subsides to leaf" brings us from early spring through summer and fall. The golden blossoms and delicate leaves of spring subside, or sink to a lower level, meaning they become less special and beautiful. There's nothing more special and beautiful than a baby, so people are the same way. In literature, summer often means the prime of your life, and autumn often means the declining years. These times are less beautiful ones. "So dawn goes down to day" is a similar kind of image. Dawns are unbelievably colorful and beautiful but they don't last very long. Day is nice, but not as special as dawn.

The most surprising line in the poem is the one that isn't about nature. Instead it's about human beings. Eden may have been a garden (a part of nature), but it also represents a state of mind. The traditional religious view is that Adam and Eve chose to disobey God and eat from the tree of knowledge. They could have stayed in paradise forever if they had followed God's orders. So it's surprising that Frost writes "So Eden sank to grief" in a poem that is all about how inevitable change is. It seems like he's saying that no matter what Adam and Eve had done, the Garden of Eden wouldn't stay the paradise it started out being. When Adam and Eve ate the apple, they lost their innocence. The apple is supposed to represent knowledge, so they became wiser but less perfect. But the poem implies that no matter what Adam and Eve had done, they would have grown sadder and wiser. That's true for all people. We can't stay young and innocent.

It's almost as if Frost is defying the Bible, suggesting that there is no such thing as sin. We can't help getting older and wiser. It's a natural process. Suffering happens not because we choose to do bad things but because passing time takes our innocence. The real original sin is that time has to pass and we all have to grow wiser and less innocent.

The poem "Nothing Gold Can Stay" makes the point that people can't stay innocent forever. Suffering is the inevitable result of the aging process. Like the first leaves of spring, we are at the best at the very beginning, and it's all downhill from there.

REVISE YOUR DRAFT

A writer rarely—if ever—achieves perfection on the first try. For most of us, good writing is largely a matter of revision. Once your first draft is done, you can—and should—turn on your analytical mind. Painstaking revision is more than just tidying up grammar and spelling. It might mean expanding your ideas or sharpening the focus by cutting out any unnecessary thoughts. To achieve effective writing, you must have the courage to be merciless. Tear your rough drafts apart and reassemble their pieces into a stronger order. As you revise, consider the following:

▪ **Be sure your thesis is clear, decisive, and thought-provoking.** The most basic ingredient in a good essay is a strong thesis—the sentence in which you summarize the claim you are making. Your thesis should say something more than just the obvious; it should be clear and decisive and make a point that requires evidence to persuade your reader to agree. A sharp, bold thesis lends energy to your argument. A revision of the working thesis used in the rough draft above provides a good example.

> **WORKING THESIS**
>
> The poem argues that like Adam and Eve we all lose our innocence and the passage of time is inevitable.

This thesis may not be bold or specific enough to make for an interesting argument. A careful reader would be hard pressed to disagree with the observation that Frost's poem depicts the passage of time or the loss of innocence. In a revision of his thesis, however, the essay's author pushes the claim further, going beyond the obvious to its implications.

> **REVISED THESIS**
>
> In "Nothing Gold Can Stay," Frost makes a bold claim: sin, suffering, and loss are inevitable because the passage of time causes everyone to fall from grace.

Instead of simply asserting that the poem looks with sorrow on the passage of time, the revised thesis raises the issue of why this is so. It makes a more thought-provoking claim about the poem. An arguable thesis can result in a more energetic, purposeful essay. A thesis that is obvious to everyone, on the other hand, leads to a static, dull paper.

▪ **Ascertain whether the evidence you provide supports your theory.** Does everything within your paper work to support its thesis sentence? While a solid paper might be written about the poetic form of "Nothing Gold Can Stay," the student paper above would not be well served by bringing the subject up unless the author could show how the poem's form contributes to its message that time causes everyone to lose his or her innocence. If you find yourself including information that doesn't serve your argument, consider going back into the poem, story, or play for more useful evidence. On the other hand, if you're beginning to have a sneaking feeling that your thesis itself is shaky, consider reworking *it* so that it more accurately reflects the evidence in the text.

▪ **Check whether your argument is logical.** Does one point lead naturally to the next? Reread the paper, looking for logical fallacies, moments in which the claims you make are not sufficiently supported by evidence, or the connection between one thought and the next seems less than rational. Classic logical fallacies include making hasty generalizations, confusing cause and effect, or using a non sequitur, a statement that doesn't follow from the statement that precedes it. An example of two seemingly unconnected thoughts may be found in the second paragraph of the draft above:

> To the poem's speaker, the colors of early spring seem to last only an hour.
> If you blink, they are gone. Like early spring, innocence can't last.

Though there may well be a logical connection between the first two sentences and the third one, the paper doesn't spell that connection out. Asked to clarify the warrant, or assumption, that makes possible the leap from the subject of spring to the subject of innocence, the author revised the passage this way:

> To the poem's speaker, the colors of early spring seem to last only an hour.
> When poets write of seasons, they often also are commenting on the life
> cycle. To make a statement that spring can't last more than an hour
> implies that a person's youth (often symbolically associated with spring) is
> all too short. Therefore, the poem implies that innocent youth, like spring,
> lasts for only the briefest time.

The revised version spells out the author's thought process, helping the reader to follow the argument.

■ **Supply transitional words and phrases.** To ensure that your reader's journey from one idea to the next is a smooth one, insert transitional words and phrases at the start of new paragraphs or sentences. Phrases such as "in contrast" and "however" signal a U-turn in logic, while those such as "in addition" and "similarly" alert the reader that you are continuing in the same direction you have been traveling. Seemingly inconsequential words and phrases such as "also" and "as well" or "as mentioned above" can smooth the reader's path from one thought to the next, as in the example below.

DRAFT

Though Frost is writing about nature, his real subject is humanity. In literature, spring often represents youth. Summer symbolizes young adulthood, autumn stands for middle age, and winter represents old age. The adult stages of life are, for Frost, less precious than childhood, which passes very quickly. The innocence of childhood is, like those spring leaves, precious as gold.

ADDING TRANSITIONAL WORDS AND PHRASES

Though Frost is writing about nature, his real subject is humanity. <u>As mentioned above,</u> in literature, spring often represents youth. <u>Similarly,</u> summer symbolizes young adulthood, autumn stands for middle age, and winter represents old age. The adult stages of life are, for Frost, less precious than childhood, which passes very quickly. <u>Also,</u> the innocence of childhood is, like those spring leaves, precious as gold.

■ **Make sure each paragraph contains a topic sentence.** Each paragraph in your essay should develop a single idea; this idea should be conveyed in a topic sentence. As astute readers often expect to get a sense of a paragraph's purpose from its first few sentences, a topic sentence is often well placed at or near a paragraph's start.

■ **Make a good first impression.** Your introductory paragraph may have seemed just fine as you began the writing process. Be sure to reconsider it in light of the entire paper. Does the introduction draw readers in and prepare them for what follows? If not, be sure to rework it, as the author of the rough draft above did. Look at his first paragraph again:

DRAFT OF OPENING PARAGRAPH

Most of the lines in the poem "Nothing Gold Can Stay" by Robert Frost focus on the changing of the seasons. The poem's first line says that the first leaves of spring are actually blossoms, and the actual leaves that follow are less precious. Those first blossoms only last a little while. The reader realizes that nature is a metaphor for a person's state of mind. People start off perfectly innocent, but as time passes, they can't help but lose that happy innocence. The poem argues that like Adam and Eve we all lose our innocence and the passage of time is inevitable.

While serviceable, this paragraph could be more compelling. Its author improved it by adding specifics to bring his ideas to more vivid life. For example, the rather pedestrian sentence "People start off perfectly innocent, but as time passes, they can't help but lose that innocence" became this livelier one: "As babies we are all perfectly innocent, but as time passes, we can't help but lose that innocence." By adding a specific image—the baby—the author gave the reader a visual picture to illustrate the abstract idea of innocence. He also sharpened his thesis sentence, making it less general and more thought-provoking. By varying the length of his sentences, he made the paragraph less monotonous.

REVISED OPENING PARAGRAPH

Most of the lines in Robert Frost's brief poem "Nothing Gold Can Stay" focus on nature: the changing of the seasons and the fading of dawn into day. The poem's opening line asserts that the first blossoms of spring are more precious than the leaves that follow. Likewise, dawn is more special than day. Though Frost's subject seems to be nature, the reader soon realizes that his real subject is human nature. As babies we are all perfectly innocent, but as time passes, we can't help but lose that happy innocence. In "Nothing Gold Can Stay," Frost makes a bold claim: sin, suffering, and loss are inevitable because the passage of time causes everyone to fall from grace.

■ **Remember that last impressions count too.** Your paper's conclusion should give the reader some closure, tying up the paper's loose ends without simply (and boringly) restating all that has come before. The author of the rough draft above initially ended his paper with a paragraph that repeated the paper's main ideas without pushing those ideas any further:

DRAFT OF CONCLUSION

The poem "Nothing Gold Can Stay" makes the point that people can't stay innocent forever. Grief is the inevitable result of the aging process. Like the first leaves of spring, we are at the best at the very beginning, and it's all downhill from there.

While revising his paper, the author realized that the ideas in his next-to-last paragraph would serve to sum up the paper. The new final paragraph doesn't simply restate the thesis; it pushes the idea further, in its last two sentences, by exploring the poem's implications.

REVISED CONCLUSION

Some people might view Frost's poem as sacrilegious because it seems to say that Adam and Eve had no choice; everything in life is doomed to fall. Growing less innocent and more knowing seems less a choice in Frost's view than a natural process like the changing of golden blossoms to green leaves. "Eden sank to grief" not because we choose to do evil things but because time takes away our innocence as we encounter the suffering and loss of human existence. Frost suggests that the real original sin is that time has to pass and we all must grow wiser and less innocent.

- **Give your paper a compelling title.** Like the introduction, a title should be inviting to readers, giving them a sense of what's coming. Avoid a nontitle such as "A Rose for Emily," which serves as a poor advertisement for your paper. Instead, provide enough specifics to pique your reader's interest. "On Robert Frost's 'Nothing Gold Can Stay'" is a duller, less informative title than "Lost Innocence in Robert Frost's 'Nothing Gold Can Stay,'" which may spark the reader's interest and prepare him or her for what is to come.

CHECKLIST: Revising Your Draft

- ☐ Is your thesis clear? Can it be sharpened?
- ☐ Does all your evidence serve to advance the argument put forth in your thesis?
- ☐ Is your argument logical?
- ☐ Do transitional words and phrases signal movement from one idea to the next?
- ☐ Does each paragraph contain a topic sentence?
- ☐ Does your introduction draw the reader in? Does it prepare the reader for what follows?
- ☐ Does your conclusion tie up the paper's loose ends? Does it avoid merely restating what has come before?
- ☐ Is your title compelling?

FINAL ADVICE ON REWRITING

- **Whenever possible, get feedback from a trusted reader.** In every project there comes a time when the writer has gotten so close to the work that he or she can't see it clearly. A talented roommate or a tutor in the campus writing center can tell you what isn't yet clear on the page, what questions still need answering, or what line of argument isn't yet as persuasive as it could be.

- **Be willing to refine your thesis.** Once you have fleshed out your whole paper, you may find that your original thesis is not borne out by the rest of your argument. If so, you will need to rewrite your thesis so that it more precisely fits the evidence at hand.

- **Be prepared to question your whole approach to a work of literature.** On occasion, you may even need to entertain the notion of throwing everything you have written into the wastebasket and starting over again. Occasionally having to start from scratch is the lot of any writer.

- **Rework troublesome passages.** Look for skimpy paragraphs of one or two sentences—evidence that your ideas might need more fleshing out. Can you supply more evidence, more explanation, more examples or illustrations?

- **Cut out any unnecessary information.** Everything in your paper should serve to further its thesis. Delete any sentences or paragraphs that detract from your focus.

- **Aim for intelligent clarity when you use literary terminology.** Critical terms can help sharpen your thoughts and make them easier to handle. Nothing is less sophisticated or more opaque, however, than too many technical terms thrown together for grandiose effect: "The mythic *symbolism* of this *archetype* is the *antithesis* of the *dramatic situation*." Choose plain words you're already at ease with. When you use specialized terms, do so to smooth the way for your reader— to make your meaning more precise. It is less cumbersome, for example, to refer to the *tone* of a story than to say, "the way the author makes you feel that she feels about what she is talking about."

- **Set your paper aside for a while.** Even an hour or two away from your essay can help you see it with fresh eyes. Remember that the literal meaning of "revision" is "seeing again."

- **Finally, carefully read your paper one last time to edit it.** Now it's time to sweat the small stuff. Check any uncertain spellings, scan for run-on sentences and fragments, pull out a weak word and send in a stronger one. Like soup stains on a job interviewee's tie, finicky errors distract from the overall impression and prejudice your reader against your essay.

Here is the revised version of the student paper we have been examining.

Gabriel 1

Noah Gabriel
Professor James
English 2171
6 January 2012

Lost Innocence in
Robert Frost's "Nothing Gold Can Stay"

Most of the lines in Robert Frost's brief poem "Nothing Gold Can Stay" focus on nature: the changing of the seasons and the fading of dawn into day. The poem's opening line asserts that the first blossoms of spring are more precious than the leaves that follow. Likewise, dawn is more special than day. Though Frost's subject seems to be nature, the reader soon realizes that his real subject is human nature. As babies we are all perfectly innocent, but as time passes, we can't help but lose that happy innocence. In "Nothing Gold Can Stay," Frost makes a bold claim: sin, suffering, and loss are inevitable because the passage of time causes everyone to fall from grace.

The poem begins with a deceptively simple sentence: "Nature's first green is gold." The subject seems to be the first, delicate leaves of spring which are less green and more golden than summer leaves. However, the poem goes on to say, "Her early leaf's a flower" (3), indicating that Frost is describing the first blossoms of spring. In fact, he's describing both the new leaves and blossoms. Both are as rare and precious as the mineral gold. They are precious because they don't last long; the early gold of spring blossoms is nature's "hardest hue to hold" (2). Early spring is an example of nature in its perfect state, and perfection is impossible to hold on to. To the poem's speaker, in fact, the colors of early spring seem to last only an hour. When poets write of seasons, they often also are commenting on the life cycle. To make a statement that spring can't last more than an hour implies that a person's youth (often symbolically associated with spring) is all too short. Therefore, the poem implies that innocent youth, like spring, lasts for only the briefest time.

While Frost takes four lines to describe the decline of the spring blossoms, he picks up the pace when he describes what happens next. The line "Then leaf subsides to leaf" (5) brings us from early spring through summer and fall, compressing three seasons into a single line. Just as time seems to pass slowly

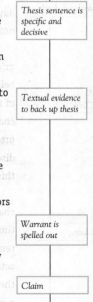

Thesis sentence is specific and decisive

Textual evidence to back up thesis

Warrant is spelled out

Claim

Gabriel 2

Significant word is looked at closely

when we are children, and then much more quickly when we grow up, the poem moves quickly once the first golden moment is past. The word "subsides" feels important. The golden blossoms and delicate leaves of spring subside, or sink to a lower level, meaning they become less special and beautiful.

Claim

Warrant spelled out

Though Frost is writing about nature, his real subject is humanity. As mentioned above, in literature, spring often represents youth. Similarly, summer symbolizes young adulthood, autumn stands for middle age, and winter represents old age. The adult stages of life are, for Frost, less precious than childhood, which passes very quickly, as we later realize. Also, the innocence of childhood is, like those spring leaves, precious as gold.

Frost shifts his view from the cycle of the seasons to the cycle of a single day to make a similar point. Just as spring turns to summer, "So dawn goes down to day" (7). Like spring, dawn is unbelievably colorful and beautiful but doesn't last very long. Like "subsides," the phrase "goes down" implies that full daylight is actually a falling off from dawn. As beautiful as daylight is, it's ordinary, while dawn is special because it is more fleeting.

Key phrase is analyzed closely

Among these natural images, one line stands out: "So Eden sank to grief" (6). This line is the only one in the poem that deals directly with human beings. Eden may have been a garden (a part of nature) but it represents a state of mind—perfect innocence. In the traditional religious view, Adam and Eve chose to disobey God by eating an apple from the tree of knowledge. They were presented with a choice: to be obedient and remain in paradise forever, or to disobey God's order. People often speak of that first choice as "original sin." In this religious view, "Eden sank to grief" because the first humans chose to sin.

Claim

Frost, however, takes a different view. He compares the Fall of Man to the changing of spring to summer, as though it was as inevitable as the passage of time. The poem implies that no matter what Adam and Eve did, they couldn't remain in paradise. Original sin in Frost's view seems less a voluntary moral action than a natural, if unhappy sort of maturation. The innocent perfection of the garden of Eden couldn't possibly last. The apple represents knowledge, so in a symbolic sense God wanted Adam and Eve to stay unknowing, or innocent. But the poem implies that it was inevitable that Adam and Eve would gain knowledge and lose their innocence, becoming wiser but less perfect. They lost Eden and encountered "grief," the knowledge of suffering and loss associated with the human condition. This is certainly true for the rest of us human beings. As much as we might like to, we can't stay young or innocent forever.

Claim

Gabriel 3

Some people might view Frost's poem as sacrilegious because it seems to say that Adam and Eve had no choice; everything in life is doomed to fall. Growing less innocent and more knowing seems less a choice in Frost's view than a natural process like the changing of golden blossoms to green leaves. "Eden sank to grief" not because we choose to do evil things but because time takes away our innocence as we encounter the suffering and loss of human existence. Frost suggests that the real original sin is that time has to pass and we all must grow wiser and less innocent.

Restatement of thesis

Gabriel 4

Work Cited

Frost, Robert. "Nothing Gold Can Stay." *Literature: An Introduction to Fiction, Poetry, Drama, and Writing.* Ed. X. J. Kennedy and Dana Gioia. 7th Compact ed. New York: Pearson, 2013. 699. Print.

DOCUMENT SOURCES TO AVOID PLAGIARISM

Certain literary works, because they offer intriguing difficulties, have attracted professional critics by the score. On library shelves, great phalanxes of critical books now stand at the side of James Joyce's *Ulysses* and T. S. Eliot's allusive poem *The Waste Land.* The student who undertakes to study such works seriously is well advised to profit from the critics' labors. Chances are, too, that even in discussing a relatively uncomplicated work, you will want to seek the aid of some critics.

If you do so, you may find yourself wanting to borrow quotations for your own papers. This is a fine thing to do—provided you give credit for those words to their rightful author. To do otherwise is plagiarism—a serious offense—and most English instructors are likely to recognize it when they see it. In any but the most superlative student paper, a brilliant (or even not so brilliant) phrase from a renowned critic is likely to stand out like a golf ball in a garter snake's midriff.

To avoid plagiarism, you must reproduce the text you are using with quotation marks around it, and give credit where it is due. Even if you summarize a critic's idea in your own words, rather than quoting his or her exact words, you have to give credit to your source. A later chapter, "Writing a Research Paper," will discuss the topic of properly citing your sources in greater depth. For now, students should simply remember that claiming another's work as one's own is the worst offense of the learning community. It negates the very purpose of education, which is to learn to think for oneself.

THE FORM OF YOUR FINISHED PAPER

If your instructor has not specified the form of your finished paper, follow the guidelines in the current edition of the *MLA Handbook for Writers of Research Papers*, which you will find more fully described in the chapter "Writing a Research Paper." In brief:

- Choose standard letter-size ($8\frac{1}{2} \times 11$) white paper.
- Use standard, easy-to-read type fonts, such as Times New Roman. Be sure the italic type style contrasts with the regular style.
- Give your name, your instructor's name, the course number, and the date at the top left-hand corner of your first page, starting one inch from the top.
- On all pages, give your last name and the page number in the upper right-hand corner, one-half inch from the top.
- Remember to give your paper a title that reflects your thesis.
- Leave one inch of margin on all four sides of each page and a few inches of space or an additional sheet of paper after your conclusion, so that your instructor can offer comments.
- If you include a works-cited section, begin it on a new page.
- Double-space all your text, including quotations, notes, and the works-cited page.
- Italicize the titles of longer works—books, plays, periodicals, and book-length poems such as *The Odyssey*. The titles of shorter works—poems, articles, or short stories—should appear in quotation marks.

SPELL-CHECK AND GRAMMAR-CHECK PROGRAMS

Most computer software includes a program to automatically check spelling. While such programs make proofreading easier, there are certain kinds of errors they won't catch. Words that are perfectly acceptable in other contexts but not the ones you intended ("is" where you meant "in," or "he" where you meant "the") will slip by undetected, making it clear to your instructor that your computer—and not you—did the proofreading. This is why it's still crucial that you proofread and correct your papers the old-fashioned way—read them yourself.

Another common problem is that the names of most authors, places, and special literary terms won't be in many standard spell-check memories. Unfamiliar words will be identified during the spell-check process, but you still must check all proper nouns carefully, so that Robert Forst, Gwendolyn Broks, or Emily Dickensen doesn't make an unauthorized appearance midway in your otherwise exemplary paper. As the well-known authors Dina Gioia, Dan Goia, Dana Glola, Dona Diora, and Dana Gioia advise, always check the spelling of all names.

As an example of the kinds of mistakes your spell-checker won't catch, here are some cautionary verses that have circulated on the Internet. (Based on a charming piece of light verse by Jerrold H. Zar, "Candidate for a Pullet Surprise," this version reflects additions and revisions by numerous anonymous Internet collaborators.)

A Little Poem Regarding Computer Spell-Checkers   2000?

Eye halve a spelling checker
    It came with my pea sea
It plainly marques four my revue
    Miss steaks eye kin knot sea.

Eye strike a key and type a word   5
    And weight four it two say
Weather eye am wrong oar write
    It shows me strait a weigh.

As soon as a mist ache is made
    It nose bee fore two long   10
And eye can put the error rite
    Its rare lea ever wrong.

Eye have run this poem threw it
    I am shore your pleased two no
Its letter perfect awl the weigh   15
    My checker tolled me sew.

Another mixed blessing is the grammar-check program that highlights sentences containing obvious grammatical mistakes. Unfortunately, if you don't know what is wrong with your sentence in the first place, the grammar program won't always tell you. You can try reworking the sentence until the highlighting disappears (indicating that it's now grammatically correct). Better still, you can take steps to ensure that you have a good grasp of grammar already. Most colleges offer brief refresher courses in grammar, and, of course, writers' handbooks with grammar rules are readily available. Still, the best way to improve your grammar, your spelling, and your general command of language is to read widely and well.

To that end, we urge you to read the works of literature collected in this book beyond those texts assigned to you by your teacher. A well-furnished mind is a great place to live, an address you'll want to have forever.

39 WRITING ABOUT A STORY

Don't write merely to be understood.
Write so that you cannot possibly be misunderstood.

—ROBERT LOUIS STEVENSON

Writing about fiction presents its own set of challenges and rewards. Because a well-wrought work of fiction can catch us up in the twists and turns of its plot, we may be tempted to read it in a trance, passively letting its plot wash over us, as we might watch an entertaining film. Or, because stories, even short ones, unfold over time, there is often so much to say about them that narrowing down and organizing your thoughts can seem daunting.

To write compellingly about fiction, you need to read actively, identify a meaningful topic, and focus on making a point about which you feel strongly. (For pointers on finding a topic, organizing, writing, and revising your paper, see the previous chapter, "Writing About Literature." Some methods especially useful for writing about stories are described in the present chapter.)

In this chapter much of the discussion and many of the examples refer to Edgar Allan Poe's short story "The Tell-Tale Heart" (page 52). If you haven't already read it, you can do so in only a few minutes, so that the rest of this chapter will make more sense to you.

READ ACTIVELY

Unlike a brief poem or a painting that you can take in with one long glance, a work of fiction—even a short story—may be too complicated to hold all at once in the mind's eye. Before you can write about it, you may need to give it two or more careful readings, and even then, as you begin to think further about it, you will probably have to thumb through it to reread passages. The first time through, it is best just to read attentively, open to whatever pleasure and wisdom the story may afford. The second time, you will find it useful to read with pencil in hand, either to mark your text or to take notes to jog your memory. To work out the design and meaning of a story need not be a boring chore, any more than it is to land a fighting fish and to study it with admiration.

- **Read the story at least twice.** The first time through, allow yourself just to enjoy the story—to experience surprise and emotion. Once you know how the tale ends, you'll find it easier to reread with some detachment, noticing details you may have glossed over the first time.

- **Annotate the text.** Reread the story, taking notes in the margins or highlighting key passages as you go. When you sit down to write, you probably will have to skim the story to refresh your memory, and those notes and highlighted passages should prove useful. Here is a sample of an annotated passage, from paragraph 3 of Edgar Allan Poe's "The Tell-Tale Heart."

who is his listener?

Now this is the point. You fancy me mad. Madmen know nothing. *Is this true?*

But you should have seen *me*. You should have seen how wisely I proceeded—with what caution—with what foresight—with what dissimulation I went to work! I was never kinder to the old man than during the *He's not so mad he doesn't know what he's doing* whole week before I killed him. And every night, about midnight, I turned the latch of his door and opened it—oh, so gently! And then, when I had made an opening sufficient for my head, I put in a dark lantern, all closed, closed, so that no light shone out, and then I thrust in my head. Oh, you would have laughed to see how cunningly I thrust it *He's strangely happy! excited* in! I moved it slowly—very, very slowly, so that I might not disturb the old man's sleep. It took me an hour to place my whole head within the opening so far that I could see him as he lay upon his bed. Ha!—would a *Careful planning* madman have been so wise as this? And then, when my head was well in the room, I undid the lantern cautiously—oh, so cautiously—cautiously (for the hinges creaked)—I undid it just so much that a single thin ray *Creepy image. Who is the vulture here?* fell upon the vulture eye. And this I did for seven long nights—every *What did he expect?!* night just at midnight—but I found the eye always closed; and so it was impossible to do the work; for it was not the old man who vexed me, but his Evil Eye. *Peculiar obsession*

THINK ABOUT THE STORY

Once you have reread the story, you can begin to process your ideas about it. To get started, try the following steps:

- **Identify the protagonist and the conflict.** Whose story is being told? What does that character desire more than anything else? What stands in the way of that character's achievement of his or her goal? The answers to these questions can give you a better handle on the story's plot.

- **Consider the story's point of view.** What does it contribute to the story? How might the tale change if told from another point of view?

- **Think about the setting.** Does it play a significant role in the plot? How does setting affect the story's tone?

- **Notice key symbols.** If any symbols catch your attention as you go, be sure to highlight each place in which they appear in the text. What do these symbols contribute to the story's meaning? (Remember, not every image is a symbol— only those important recurrent persons, places, or things that seem to suggest more than their literal meaning.)

- **Look for the theme.** Is the story's central meaning stated directly? If not, how does it reveal itself?

- **Think about tone and style.** How would you characterize the style in which the story is written? Consider elements such as diction, sentence structure, tone, and organization. How does the story's style contribute to its tone?

PREWRITING: DISCOVER YOUR IDEAS

Once you have given the story some preliminary thought, it is time to write as a means of discovering what it is you have to say. Brainstorming, clustering, listing, freewriting, keeping a journal, and outlining all can help you clarify your thoughts about the story and, in doing so, generate ideas for your paper. While you don't need to use *all* these techniques, try them to find the one or two that work best for you.

- **Brainstorm.** If you aren't sure what, exactly, to say about a story, try jotting down everything you can think of about it. Work quickly, without pausing to judge what you have written. Set yourself a time limit of ten or fifteen minutes and keep writing even if you think you have said it all. A list that results from brainstorming on "The Tell-Tale Heart" might look something like this:

> madness? seems crazy
> unreliable narrator
> Could story be a dream?
> Could heartbeat be supernatural?
> heartbeat = speaker's paranoia
> tone: dramatic, intense, quick mood changes
> glee/terror
> lots of exclamation points

telling his story to listener
old man = father? boss? friend?
old man's gold/treasures
old man's eye = motive
vulture eye = symbolic
Calls plotting murder "work"
careful/patient
Chops up body
perfect crime
Policemen don't hear heartbeat
Guilt makes him confess

- **Cluster.** Clustering involves generating ideas by diagramming the relationship among your many ideas. First, write your subject at the center of a sheet of paper and circle it. Then, jot down ideas as they occur to you, drawing lines to link each idea to related ones. Here is an example of how you might cluster your ideas about "The Tell-Tale Heart."

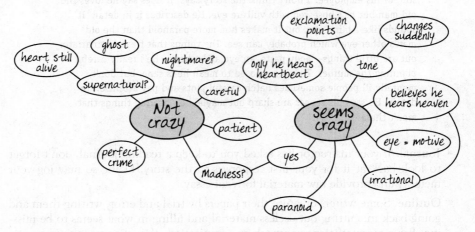

- **List.** Using your notes and annotations as a guide, list information that seems useful, adding any notes that help you to keep track of your thought process. Use different headings to organize related concepts. Your lists might look something like this:

Unreliable Narrator	Other Possibilities
mood swings	nightmare
insists too much on being sane	supernatural
confusion	heart still alive?
disease	ghost's heartbeat?
sharpened senses	
loved old man	
murder	
patience	
guilt	
hearing things	

▪ **Freewrite.** Before you try to write a coherent first draft of your essay, take time to write freely, exploring your ideas as they occur to you. Writing quickly, without thinking too hard about grammar or spelling, can call forth surprising new ideas that wouldn't arrive if you were composing in a more reflective, cautious manner. To freewrite, give yourself a set amount of time—fifteen or twenty minutes. Put your pen to paper (or your fingers to the keyboard) and write without pausing to think. Keep going even if you run out of things to say. A freewrite on "The Tell-Tale Heart" might look like this:

> The guy seems crazy. He keeps insisting he's sane, so maybe others have accused him of being insane. He's speaking to someone—a judge? a fellow inmate? The story feels spoken out loud, like a dramatic monologue. His mood changes really quickly. One minute he's gleeful, and then impatient, then terrified. The story is full of dashes and exclamation points. He says he can hear everything in heaven and earth and even some things in hell. That seems crazy. His disease has sharpened his senses. Is he the old man's son, or his employee? I don't think the story says. It does say he loves the old man but he's obsessed with vulture eye. He describes it in detail. It sounds like a blind eye, but it makes him more paranoid than the old man's other eye which probably can see. The things that freak the narrator out are little things—body parts, an eye and a heart. He's really careful in planning the murder. This is supposed to mean he is sane, but don't mentally ill people sometimes hatch careful plots and pay attention to detail? He says his senses are sharp but maybe he's hearing things that aren't there?

▪ **Journal.** If your instructor has asked you to keep a reading journal, don't forget to look back at it for your first responses to the story. Doing so may jog your memory and provide raw material for your essay.

▪ **Outline.** Some writers organize their papers by trial and error, writing them and going back in, cutting out useless material and filling in what seems to be missing. For a more efficient approach to organization, though, try making an outline—a simple list of points arranged in an order that makes logical sense. Such an outline might look like this:

1. Point of view is ironic (speaker is mad/unreliable)
   hears things in heaven/hell
   excited tone
   focus on strange detail
2. Can we trust story really happened?
   nightmare?
   more interesting if actual
3. Supernatural elements?
   ghost heartbeat?
   heart still alive?
4. More interesting/believable if speaker is mad

WRITE A ROUGH DRAFT

Once your prewriting exercises have sparked an idea or two, you will be ready to begin shaping your thoughts into a rough draft. Reread the section "Develop a Literary Argument" in the previous chapter for help getting started. You can still keep your approach loose and informal; don't worry yet about phrasing things perfectly or pinning down the ideal word. For now, your goal is to begin finding a shape for your argument.

- **Remember your purpose.** Before you begin work on your first draft, be sure to check the assignment you have been given. There is no sense in writing even the most elegant *analysis* (in which you focus on one particular element of a story) if you have been told to write an *explication* (a detailed, line-by-line interpretation of a passage).

- **Consider your audience.** Though your professor and classmates will likely be your paper's actual audience, the assignment might specify hypothetical readers. Whoever your audience may be, keep their needs in mind as you write.

- **Formulate your thesis.** Before you get going on your rough draft, you will need a thesis sentence summing up your paper's main idea. Begin with a provisional thesis to give your argument direction. As you write, be sure to keep your provisional thesis in mind; doing so will help you stay on track. Here is a working thesis for a paper on "The Tell-Tale Heart":

    WORKING THESIS

    The story contains many hints that the narrator of "The Tell-Tale Heart" is crazy.

    While this thesis gives its author something to work toward, it isn't yet as sharp as it could be. Most readers would agree that the story's narrator shows obvious signs of insanity. A more compelling thesis would go into the specifics of what, exactly, gives away the narrator's madness, or it might spell out the implications of this madness for the story. The following reworked version of this thesis sentence does both:

    REVISED THESIS

    The narrator's tenuous hold on reality and his wild shifts in mood indicate that he is insane and, therefore, that his point of view is untrustworthy.

    Like this statement, your thesis should be decisive and specific. As you write a rough draft, your task is to persuade readers of the wisdom of your thesis.

- **Back up your thesis with evidence.** The bulk of your essay should be spent providing evidence that proves your thesis. Because the most persuasive evidence tends to be that which comes from the story itself, be sure to quote as needed. As you flesh out your argument, check back frequently to make sure your thesis continues to hold up to the evidence. If you find that the facts of the story don't bear out your thesis, the problem may be with the evidence or with the thesis itself. Could your point be better proved by presenting different evidence? If so, exchange what you have for more convincing information. If not, go back in and refine your thesis sentence. Then make sure that the rest of the evidence bears out your new and improved thesis.

▪ **Organize your argument.** Choose the points you need to prove your thesis and present them, along with supporting evidence, in whatever order best makes your case. A rough outline is often a useful tool.

CHECKLIST: Writing a Rough Draft

☐ What is your essay's purpose?
☐ Who is your audience? What do they need to know?
☐ What is your thesis? Is it debatable?
☐ Does everything in your essay support your thesis?
☐ Is your argument sensibly organized?

REVISE YOUR DRAFT

Once your first draft has been committed to paper, you will need to begin revising—going back in and reworking it to make the argument as persuasive and the prose as seamless as can be. First, though, it is an excellent idea to get feedback on your draft from a trusted reader—a classmate, a roommate, a tutor in your school's writing center, or even your instructor—who can tell you which ideas are, and are not, coming across clearly, or where your argument is persuasive and where it could be more convincing. For writers at all levels of expertise, there simply is no substitute for constructive criticism from a thoughtful reader. If, however, you find readers are in short supply, put your rough draft away for at least an hour or two, and reread it with fresh eyes before you begin revising.

The following is an example of how one student used his instructor's comments to improve his paper's opening paragraph. (The final paper appears later in the chapter on page 1368.)

DRAFT OF OPENING PARAGRAPH

The narrator of Edgar Allan Poe's "The Tell-Tale Heart" is a very mysterious and murderous character. The reader doesn't know much about him, except for how he speaks and what he has to say for himself. There is one important fact revealed by evidence in the story. The story contains many hints that the narrator of "The Tell-Tale Heart" is crazy.

Provide specifics.

Tell me more!

Why is this important?

What are some of these?

REVISED OPENING PARAGRAPH

Although there are many things we do not know about the narrator of Edgar Allan Poe's story "The Tell-Tale Heart"—is he a son? a servant? a companion?—there is one thing we are sure of from the start. He is mad. In the opening paragraph, Poe makes the narrator's condition unmistakable, not only from his excited and worked-up speech (full of dashes and exclamation points), but also from his wild claims. He says it is merely some disease which has sharpened his senses that has made people call him crazy. Who but a madman, however, would say, "I heard all things in the heaven and in the earth," and brag how his ear is a kind of radio, listening in on hell? The narrator's tenuous hold on reality and his wild shifts in mood indicate that he is mad and, therefore, that his point of view is untrustworthy.

Remember that revision means more than just cleaning up typos and doing away with stray semicolons. Revision might mean fleshing out your ideas with new paragraphs, rearranging material, or paring away passages that detract from your focus. As you rewrite, make sure every paragraph has a topic sentence that announces its main idea. Feel free to link your ideas with transitional words and phrases such as "moreover," "in addition," or "in contrast" to help your reader understand how each new idea relates to the one that precedes it.

CHECKLIST: Revising Your Draft

- ☐ Is your thesis clear? Does it say something significant but not entirely obvious about the story?
- ☐ Does all your evidence serve to advance the argument put forth in your thesis?
- ☐ Is your argument clear and logical?
- ☐ Do transitional words and phrases help signal movement from one idea to the next?
- ☐ Does your introduction draw the reader in? Does it prepare the reader for what follows?
- ☐ Does your conclusion tie up the paper's loose ends? Does it avoid merely restating what has come before?
- ☐ Does each paragraph contain a topic sentence?
- ☐ Does the paper have an interesting and compelling title?

WHAT'S YOUR PURPOSE? COMMON APPROACHES TO WRITING ABOUT FICTION

It is crucial to keep your paper's purpose in mind. When you write an academic paper, you are likely to have been given a specific set of marching orders. Maybe you have been asked to write for a particular audience besides the obvious one (your professor, that is). Perhaps you have been asked to describe your personal reaction to a literary work. Maybe your purpose is to interpret a work, analyzing how one or more of its elements contribute to its meaning. You may have been instructed to write an evaluation in which you judge a work's merits. Let the assignment dictate your paper's tone and content. Below are several commonly used approaches to writing about fiction.

Explication

Explication is the patient unfolding of meanings in a work of literature. An explication proceeds carefully through a story, usually interpreting it line by line—perhaps even word by word—dwelling on details a casual reader might miss and illustrating how a story's smaller parts contribute to the whole. Alert and willing to take pains, the writer of such an essay notices anything meaningful that isn't obvious, whether it is a colossal theme suggested by a symbol or a little hint contained in a single word.

To write an honest explication of an entire story takes time and space, and it is a better assignment for a term paper, an honors thesis, or a dissertation than a short essay. A thorough explication of Nathaniel Hawthorne's "Young Goodman Brown," for example, would likely run much longer than the rich and intriguing short story itself. Ordinarily, explication is best suited to a short passage or section of a story: a key scene, a critical conversation, a statement of theme, or an opening or closing paragraph. In a long critical essay that doesn't adhere to one method all the way through, the method of explication may appear from time to time, as when the critic, in discussing a story, stops to unravel a particularly knotty passage. Here are tips for writing a successful explication of your own:

- **Focus on the details that strike you as most meaningful.** Do not try to cover everything.
- **Try working through the original passage sentence by sentence.** If you choose this method, be sure to vary your transitions from one point to the next, to avoid the danger of falling into a boring singsong: "In the first sentence I noticed . . . ," "In the next sentence . . . ," "Now in the third sentence . . . ," and "Finally, in the last sentence. . . ."
- **Consider working from a simple outline.** In writing the explication that follows of a passage from "The Tell-Tale Heart," the student began with a list of points she wanted to express:

  1. Speaker's extreme care and exactness—typical of some mental illnesses.
  2. Speaker doesn't act by usual logic but by a crazy logic.
  3. Dreamlike connection between latch and lantern and old man's eye.

Storytellers who are especially fond of language invite closer attention to their words than others might. Edgar Allan Poe, for one, was a poet sensitive to the rhythms of his sentences and a symbolist whose stories abound in potent suggestions. Here is a student's explication of a short but essential passage in "The Tell-Tale Heart." The passage occurs in the third paragraph of the story, and to help us follow the explication, the student quotes the passage in full at the paper's beginning.

Susan Kim
Professor A. M. Lundy
English 100
20 March 2012

By Lantern Light: An Explication
of a Passage in Poe's "The Tell-Tale Heart"

> And every night, about midnight, I turned the latch of his door and
> opened it—oh, so gently! And then, when I had made an opening
> sufficient for my head, I put in a dark lantern, all closed, closed, so
> that no light shone out, and then I thrust in my head. Oh, you would
> have laughed to see how cunningly I thrust it in! I moved it slowly—
> very, very slowly, so that I might not disturb the old man's sleep. It
> took me an hour to place my whole head within the opening so far
> that I could see him as he lay upon his bed. Ha!—would a madman
> have been so wise as this? And then, when my head was well in the
> room, I undid the lantern cautiously—oh, so cautiously—cautiously
> (for the hinges creaked)—I undid it just so much that a single thin
> ray fell upon the vulture eye. And this I did for seven long nights—
> every night just at midnight—but I found the eye always closed; and
> so it was impossible to do the work; for it was not the old man who
> vexed me, but his Evil Eye. (par. 3)

Quotes passage to be explicated

Although Edgar Allan Poe has suggested in the first lines of his story "The
Tell-Tale Heart" that the person who addresses us is insane, it is only when we
come to the speaker's account of his preparations for murdering the old man
that we find his madness fully revealed. Even more convincingly than his
earlier words (for we might possibly think that someone who claims to hear
things in heaven and hell is a religious mystic), these preparations reveal him
to be mad. What strikes us is that they are so elaborate and meticulous. A
significant detail is the exactness of his schedule for spying: "every night just
at midnight." The words with which he describes his motions also convey the
most extreme care (and I will indicate them by italics): "how wisely I
proceeded—with *what caution*," "I turned the latch of his door and opened
it—oh, so *gently*!" "how *cunningly* I thrust it [my head] in! I moved it
slowly—*very, very slowly*," "I undid the lantern *cautiously*—oh, *so cautiously—
cautiously*." Taking a whole hour to intrude his head into the room, he asks,
"Ha!—would a madman have been so wise as this?" But of course the word

Thesis sentence

Textual evidence supports thesis

Kim 2

wise is unconsciously ironic, for clearly it is not wisdom the speaker displays, but an absurd degree of care, an almost fiendish ingenuity. Such behavior, I understand, is typical of certain mental illnesses. All his careful preparations that he thinks prove him sane only convince us instead that he is mad.

Obviously his behavior is self-defeating. He wants to catch the "vulture eye" open, and yet he takes all these pains not to disturb the old man's sleep. If he behaved logically, he might go barging into the bedroom with his lantern ablaze, shouting at the top of his voice. And yet, if we can see things his way, there *is* a strange logic to his reasoning. He regards the eye as a creature in itself, quite apart from its possessor. "It was not," he says, "the old man who vexed me, but his Evil Eye." Apparently, to be inspired to do his deed, the madman needs to behold the eye—at least, this is my understanding of his remark, "I found the eye always closed; and so it was impossible to do the work." Poe's choice of the word *work*, by the way, is also revealing. Murder is made to seem a duty or a job; and anyone who so regards murder is either extremely cold-blooded, like a hired killer for a gangland assassination, or else deranged. Besides, the word suggests again the curious sense of detachment that the speaker feels toward the owner of the eye.

Topic sentence on narrator's mad logic

In still another of his assumptions, the speaker shows that he is madly logical, or operating on the logic of a dream. There seems a dreamlike relationship between his dark lantern "all closed, closed, so that no light shone out," and the sleeping victim. When the madman opens his lantern so that it emits a single ray, he is hoping that the eye in the old man's head will be open too, letting out its corresponding gleam. The latch that he turns so gently, too, seems like the eye, whose lid needs to be opened in order for the murderer to go ahead. It is as though the speaker is *trying* to get the eyelid to lift. By taking such great pains and by going through all this nightly ritual, he is practicing some kind of magic, whose rules are laid down not by our logic, but by the logic of dreams.

Conclusion pushes thesis further, making it more specific.

Kim 3

Work Cited

Poe, Edgar Allan. "The Tell-Tale Heart." *Literature: An Introduction to Fiction,*
Poetry, Drama, and Writing. Ed. X. J. Kennedy and Dana Gioia.
7th Compact ed. New York: Pearson, 2013. 52–55. Print.

An unusually well written essay, "By Lantern Light" cost its author two or three careful revisions. Rather than attempting to say something about *everything* in the passage from Poe, she selects only the details that strike her as most meaningful. In her very first sentence, she briefly shows us how the passage functions in the context of Poe's story: how it clinches our suspicions that the narrator is mad. Notice too that the student who wrote the essay doesn't inch through the passage sentence by sentence, but freely takes up its details in an order that seems appropriate to her argument.

Analysis

Examining a single component of a story can afford us a better understanding of the entire work. This is perhaps why in most literature classes students are asked to write at least one **analysis** (from the Greek: "breaking up"), an essay that breaks a story or novel into its elements and, usually, studies one part closely. One likely topic for an analysis might be "The Character of James Baldwin's Sonny," in which the writer would concentrate on showing us Sonny's highly individual features and traits of personality. Other topics for an analysis might be "Irony in Anne Tyler's 'Teenage Wasteland,'" or "Setting in Kate Chopin's 'The Storm,'" or "The Unidentified Narrator in 'A Rose for Emily.'"

To be sure, no element of a story dwells in isolation from the story's other elements. In "The Tell-Tale Heart," the madness of the leading character apparently makes it necessary to tell the story from a special point of view and probably helps determine the author's choice of theme, setting, symbolism, tone, style, and ironies. But it would be mind-boggling to try to study all those elements simultaneously. For this reason, when we write an analysis, we generally study just one element, though we may suggest—probably at the start of the essay—its relation to the whole story. Here are two points to keep in mind when writing an analysis:

- **Decide upon a thesis, and include only relevant insights.** As tempting as it might be to include your every idea, stick to those that will help to prove your point.
- **Support your contentions with specific references to the story you are analyzing.** Quotations can be particularly convincing.

The following paper is an example of a solid, brief analysis. Written by a student, it focuses on just one element of "The Tell-Tale Heart"—the story's point of view.

Frederick 1

Mike Frederick

Professor Stone

English 110

18 January 2012

The Hearer of the Tell-Tale Heart

> Although there are many things we do not know about the narrator of
Edgar Allan Poe's story "The Tell-Tale Heart"—is he a son? a servant? a
companion?—there is one thing we are sure of from the start. He is mad. In the
opening paragraph, Poe makes the narrator's condition unmistakable, not only
from his excited and worked-up speech (full of dashes and exclamation points),
but also from his wild claims. He says it is merely some disease which has
sharpened his senses that has made people call him crazy. Who but a madman,
however, would say, "I heard all things in the heaven and in the earth," and
brag how his ear is a kind of radio, listening in on hell? The narrator's tenuous
hold on reality and his wild shifts in mood indicate that he is insane and,
therefore, that his point of view is untrustworthy.

> Because the participant narrator is telling his story in the first person,
some details in the story stand out more than others. When the narrator goes
on to tell how he watches the old man sleeping, he rivets his attention on
the old man's "vulture eye." When a ray from his lantern finds the Evil Eye
open, he says, "I could see nothing else of the old man's face or person"
(par. 9). Actually, the reader can see almost nothing else about the old man
anywhere in the rest of the story. All we are told is that the old man treated
the younger man well, and we gather that the old man was rich, because his
house is full of treasures. We do not have a clear idea of what the old man
looks like, though, nor do we know how he talks, for we are not given any of
his words. Our knowledge of him is mainly confined to his eye and its effect
on the narrator. This confinement gives that symbolic eye a lot of importance
in the story. The narrator tells us all we know and directs our attention to
parts of it.

> This point of view raises an interesting question. Since we are dependent
on the narrator for all our information, how do we know the whole story isn't
just a nightmare in his demented mind? We have really no way to be sure it
isn't, as far as I can see. I assume, however, that there really is a dark shuttered
house and an old man and real policemen who start snooping around when

Marginal annotations:

States author and work

Thesis statement

Topic sentence—how point of view determines emphasis

Raises question, then explores answer

Frederick 2

screams are heard in the neighborhood because it is a more memorable story if it is a crazy man's view of reality than if it is all just a terrible dream. But we can't rely on the madman's interpretation of what happens. Poe keeps putting distances between what the narrator says and what we are apparently supposed to think. For instance: the narrator has boasted that he is calm and clear in the head, but as soon as he starts trying to explain why he killed the old man, we gather that he is confused, to say the least. "I think it was his eye!" the narrator exclaims, as if not quite sure (par. 2). As he goes on to explain how he conducted the murder, we realize that he is a man with a fixed idea working with a patience that is certainly mad, almost diabolical.

Some readers might wonder if "The Tell-Tale Heart" is a story of the supernatural. Is the heartbeat that the narrator hears a ghost come back to haunt him? Here, I think, the point of view is our best guide to what to believe. The simple explanation for the heartbeat is this: it is all in the madman's mind. Perhaps he feels such guilt that he starts hearing things. Another explanation is possible, one suggested by Daniel Hoffman, a critic who has discussed the story: the killer hears the sound of his *own* heart (227). Hoffman's explanation (which I don't like as well as mine) also is a natural one, and it fits the story as a whole. Back when the narrator first entered the old man's bedroom to kill him, the heartbeat sounded so loud to him that he was afraid the neighbors would hear it too. Evidently they didn't, and so Hoffman may be right in thinking that the sound was only that of his own heart pounding in his ears. Whichever explanation you take, it is a more down-to-earth and reasonable explanation than (as the narrator believes) that the heart is still alive, even though its owner has been cut to pieces. Then, too, the police keep chatting. If they heard the heartbeat, wouldn't they leap to their feet, draw their guns, and look all around the room? As the author keeps showing us in the rest of the story, the narrator's view of things is untrustworthy. You don't kill someone just because you dislike the look in his eye. You don't think that such a murder is funny. For all its Gothic atmosphere of the old dark house with a secret hidden inside, "The Tell-Tale Heart" is not a ghost story. We have only to see its point of view to know it is a study in abnormal psychology.

Topic sentence on how narrator's madness is revealed

Raises question, then explores answer

Secondary source paraphrase

Restatement of thesis

Frederick 3

Works Cited

Hoffman, Daniel. *Poe Poe Poe Poe Poe Poe Poe.* New York: Anchor, 1973. Print.

Poe, Edgar Allan. "The Tell-Tale Heart." *Literature: An Introduction to Fiction,*
    Poetry, Drama, and Writing. Ed. X. J. Kennedy and Dana Gioia.
    7th Compact ed. New York: Pearson, 2013. 52–55. Print.

The temptation in writing an analysis is to include all sorts of insights that the writer proudly wishes to display, even though they aren't related to the main idea. In the preceding essay, the student resists this temptation admirably. In fairly plump and ample paragraphs, he works out his ideas and supports his contentions with specific references to Poe's story. Although his paper is not brilliantly written and contains no insight so fresh as the suggestion (by the writer of the first paper) that the madman's lantern is like the old man's head, still, it is a good brief analysis. By sticking faithfully to his purpose and by confronting the problems he raises ("How do we know the whole story isn't just a nightmare?"), the writer persuades us that he understands not only the story's point of view but also the story in its entirety.

The Card Report

Another form of analysis, a **card report** breaks down a story into its various elements. Though card reports tend to include only as much information as can fit on both sides of a single 5- by 8-inch index card, they are at least as challenging to write as full-fledged essays. The author of a successful card report can dissect a story into its elements and describe them succinctly and accurately. A typical card report on "The Tell-Tale Heart" follows. In this assignment, the student was asked to include:

1. The story's title and the date of its original publication.
2. The author's name and dates of birth and death.
3. The name (if any) of the main character, along with a description of that character's dominant traits or features.
4. Similar information for other characters.
5. A short description of the setting.
6. The point of view from which the story is told.
7. A terse summary of the story's main events in chronological order.
8. A description of the general tone, or, in other words, the author's feelings toward the central character or the main event.
9. Some comments on the style in which the story is written. Brief illustrative quotations are helpful if space allows.
10. Whatever kinds of irony the story contains and what they contribute to the story.
11. The story's main theme, in a sentence.

12. Key symbols (if the story has any), with an educated guess at what each symbol suggests.
13. Finally, an evaluation of the story as a whole, concisely setting forth the student's opinion of it. (Some instructors consider this the most important part of the report, and most students find that, by the time they have so painstakingly separated the ingredients of the story, they have arrived at a definite opinion of its merits.)

Front of Card

Carly Grace   English 101

Story: "The Tell-Tale Heart," 1850

Author: Edgar Allan Poe (1809-1849)

Central character: An unnamed younger man whom people call mad, who claims that a nervous disease has greatly sharpened his sense perceptions. He is proud of his own cleverness.

Other characters: The old man, whose leading feature is one pale blue, filmed eye; said to be rich, kind, and lovable. Also three policemen, not individually described.

Setting: A shuttered house full of wind, mice, and treasures; pitch dark even in the afternoon.

Narrator: The madman himself.

Events in summary: (1) Dreading one vulture-like eye of the old man he shares a house with, a madman determines to kill its owner. (2) Each night he spies on the sleeping old man, but finding the eye shut, he stays his hand. (3) On the eighth night, finding the eye open, he suffocates its owner beneath the mattress and conceals the dismembered body under the floor of the bedchamber. (4) Entertaining some inquiring police officers in the very room where the body lies hidden, the killer again hears (or thinks he hears) the beat of the victim's heart. (5) Terrified, convinced that the police also hear the heartbeat growing louder, the killer confesses.

Tone: Horror at the events described, skepticism toward the narrator's claims to be sane, detachment from his gaiety and laughter.

Back of Card

> Style: Written as if told aloud by a deranged man eager to be believed, the story is punctuated by laughter, interjections ("Hearken!"), nervous halts, and fresh beginnings—indicated by dashes that grow more frequent as the story goes on and the narrator becomes more excited. Poe often relies on general adjectives ("mournful," "hideous," "hellish,") to convey atmosphere; also on exact details (the lantern that emits "a single dim ray, like the thread of a spider").
>
> Irony: The whole story is ironic in its point of view. Presumably the author is not mad, nor does he share the madman's self-admiration. Many of the narrator's statements therefore seem verbal ironies: his account of taking an hour to move his head through the bedroom door.
>
> Theme: Possibly "Murder will out," but I really don't find any theme either stated or clearly implied.
>
> Symbols: The vulture eye, called an Evil Eye (in superstition, one that can implant a curse), perhaps suggesting too the all-seeing eye of God the Father, from whom no guilt can be concealed. The ghostly heartbeat, sound of the victim's coming back to be avenged (or the God who cannot be slain?). Death watches: beetles said to be death omens, whose ticking sound foreshadows the sound of the tell-tale heart *"as a watch makes when enveloped in cotton."*
>
> Evaluation: Despite the overwrought style (to me slightly comic-bookish), a powerful story, admirable for its conclusion and for its memorable portrait of a deranged killer. Poe knows how it is to be mad.

As you might expect, fitting so much information on one card is like trying to engrave the Declaration of Independence on the head of a pin. The student who wrote this report had to spoil a few trial cards before she was able to complete the assignment. The card report is an extreme exercise in making every word count, a worthwhile discipline in almost any kind of writing. Some students enjoy the challenge, and most are surprised at how thoroughly they come to understand the story. A longer story, even a novel, may be analyzed in the same way, but insist on taking a second card if you are asked to analyze an especially hefty and complicated novel.

Comparison and Contrast

If you were to write on "The Humor of Alice Walker's 'Everyday Use' and John Updike's 'A & P,'" you would probably employ one or two methods. You might use **comparison,** placing the two stories side by side and pointing out their similarities, or **contrast,** pointing out their differences. Most of the time, in dealing with a pair of stories, you will find them similar in some ways and different in others, and you'll use both methods. Keep the following points in mind when writing a comparison-contrast paper:

- **Choose stories with something significant in common.** This will simplify your task and help ensure that your paper hangs together. Before you start writing, ask yourself if the two stories you've selected throw some light on each other. If the answer is no, rethink your story selection.

- **Choose a focus.** Simply ticking off every similarity and difference between two stories would make for a slack and rambling essay. More compelling writing would result from better-focused topics such as "The Experience of Coming of Age in James Joyce's 'Araby' and William Faulkner's 'Barn Burning'" or "Mother-Daughter Relationships in Alice Walker's 'Everyday Use' and Jamaica Kincaid's 'Girl.'"

- **Don't feel you need to spend equal amounts of time on comparing and contrasting.** If your chosen stories are more similar than different, you naturally will spend more space on comparison, and vice versa.

- **Don't devote the first half of your paper to one story and the second half to the other.** Such a paper wouldn't be a comparison or contrast so much as a pair of analyses yoked together. To reap the full benefits of the assignment, let the two stories mingle.

- **Before you start writing, draw up a brief list of points you would like to touch on.** Then address each point, first in one story and then in the other. A sample outline follows for a paper on William Faulkner's "A Rose for Emily" and Katherine Mansfield's "Miss Brill." The essay's topic is "Adapting to Change: The Characters of Emily Grierson and Miss Brill."

  1. Adapting to change (both women)
     Miss Brill more successful
  2. Portrait of women
     Miss Emily—unflattering
     Miss Brill—empathetic
  3. Imagery
     Miss Emily—morbid
     Miss Brill—cheerful
  4. Plot
     Miss Emily
     - loses sanity
     - refuses to adapt
     Miss Brill
     - finds place in society
     - adapts
  5. Summary: Miss Brill is more successful

- **Emphasize the points that interest you the most.** This strategy will help keep you from following your outline in a plodding fashion ("Well, now it's time to whip over to Miss Brill again . . .").

■ **If the assignment allows, consider applying comparison and contrast in an essay on a single story.** You might, for example, analyze the attitudes of the younger and older waiters in Hemingway's "A Clean, Well-Lighted Place." Or you might contrast Mrs. Turpin's smug view of herself with the young Mary Grace's merciless view of her in Flannery O'Connor's "Revelation."

The following student-written paper compares and contrasts the main characters in "A Rose for Emily" and "Miss Brill." Notice how the author focuses the discussion on a single aspect of each woman's personality—the ability to adapt to change and the passage of time. By looking through the lens of three different elements of the short story—diction, imagery, and plot—this clear and systematic essay convincingly argues its thesis.

Ortiz 1

Michelle Ortiz

Professor Gregg

English 200

25 February 2012

Successful Adaptation in

"A Rose for Emily" and "Miss Brill"

In William Faulkner's "A Rose for Emily" and Katherine Mansfield's "Miss Brill," the reader is given a glimpse into the lives of two old women living in different worlds but sharing many similar characteristics. Both Miss Emily and

> *Clear statement of thesis*

Miss Brill attempt to adapt to a changing environment as they grow older. Through the authors' use of language, imagery, and plot, it becomes clear to the reader that Miss Brill is more successful at adapting to the world around her and finding happiness.

> *Textual evidence on language supports thesis.*

In "A Rose for Emily," Faulkner's use of language paints an unflattering picture of Miss Emily. His tone evokes pity and disgust rather than sympathy. The reader identifies with the narrator of the story and shares the townspeople's opinion that Miss Emily is somehow "perverse" (par. 51). In "Miss Brill," however, the reader can identify with the title character and feel sympathy for her because of the lonely life she leads. Mansfield's attitude toward the young couple at the end makes the reader hate them for ruining the happiness that Miss Brill has found, however small it may be.

> *Imagery in Faulkner's story supports argument.*

The imagery in "A Rose for Emily" keeps the reader from further identifying with Miss Emily by creating several morbid images of her. For example, there are several images of decay throughout the story. The house she lived in is falling apart and described as "filled with dust and shadows" (par. 52), "an

Ortiz 2

eyesore among eyesores" (par. 2). Emily herself is described as looking "bloated, like a body long submerged in motionless water" (par. 6). Faulkner also uses words like "skeleton," "dank," "decay," and "cold" to reinforce these morbid, deathly images (par. 6, 5, 2, 8).

In "Miss Brill," however, Mansfield uses more cheerful imagery. The music and the lively action in the park make Miss Brill feel alive inside. She notices the other old people in the park are "still as statues," "odd," and "silent" (par. 5). She says they "looked as though they'd just come from dark little rooms or even—even cupboards!" (par. 5). In the final paragraph, her own room is described as "like a cupboard," but during the action of the story she does not include herself among those other old people. She still feels alive.

Contrasting imagery in Mansfield's story supports argument.

Through the plots of both stories the reader can also see that Miss Brill is more successful in adapting to her environment. Miss Emily loses her sanity and ends up committing a crime in order to control her environment. Throughout the story, she refuses to adapt to any of the changes going on in the town, such as the taxes or the mailboxes. Miss Brill is able to find her own special place in society where she can be happy and remain sane.

Characters contrasted with examples drawn from plots.

In "A Rose for Emily" and "Miss Brill" the authors' use of language and the plots of the stories illustrate that Miss Brill is more successful in her story. Instead of hiding herself away she emerges from the "cupboard" to participate in life. She adapts to the world that is changing as she grows older, without losing her sanity or committing crimes, as Miss Emily does. The language of "Miss Brill" allows the reader to sympathize with the main character. The imagery in the story is lighter and less morbid than in "A Rose for Emily." The resulting portrait is of an aging woman who has found creative ways to adjust to her lonely life.

The final conclusion is stated and the thesis is restated.

Ortiz 3

Works Cited

Faulkner, William. "A Rose for Emily." *Literature: An Introduction to Fiction, Poetry, Drama, and Writing.* Ed. X. J. Kennedy and Dana Gioia. 7th Compact ed. New York: Pearson, 2013. 31–37. Print.

Mansfield, Katherine. "Miss Brill." *Literature: An Introduction to Fiction, Poetry, Drama, and Writing.* Ed. X. J. Kennedy and Dana Gioia. 7th Compact ed. New York: Pearson, 2013. 100–103. Print.

Response Paper

One popular form of writing assignment is the **response paper,** a short essay that expresses your personal reaction to a work of literature. Both instructors and students often find the response paper an ideal introductory writing assignment. It provides you with an opportunity to craft a focused essay about a literary work, but it does not usually require any outside research. What it does require is careful reading, clear thinking, and honest writing.

The purpose of a response paper is to convey your thoughts and feelings about an aspect of a particular literary work. It isn't a book report (summarizing the work's content) or a book review (evaluating the quality of a work). A response paper expresses what you experienced in reading and thinking about the assigned text. Your reaction should reflect your background, values, and attitudes in response to the work, not what the instructor thinks about it. You might even consider your response paper a conversation with the work you have just read. What questions does it seem to ask you? What reactions does it elicit? You might also regard your paper as a personal message to your instructor telling him or her what you really think about one of the reading assignments.

Of course, you can't say everything you thought and felt about your reading in a short paper. Focus on an important aspect (such as a main character, setting, or theme) and discuss your reaction to it. Don't gush or meander. Personal writing doesn't mean disorganized writing. Identify your main ideas and present your point of view in a clear and organized way. Once you get started you might surprise yourself by discovering that it's fun to explore your own responses. Stranger things have happened.

Here are tips for writing a successful response paper of your own:

■ **Make quick notes as you read or reread the work.** Don't worry about writing anything organized at this point. Just write a word or two in the margin noting your reactions as you read (e.g., "very interesting" or "reminds me of my sister"). These little notes will jog your memory when you go back to write your paper.

■ **Consider which aspect of the work affected you the most.** That aspect will probably be a good starting point for your response.

■ **Be candid in your writing.** Remember that the literary work is only half of the subject matter of your paper. The other half is your reaction.

■ **Try to understand and explain why you have reacted the way you did.** It's not enough just to state your responses. You also want to justify or explain them.

■ **Refer to the text in your paper.** Demonstrate to the reader that your response is based on the text. Provide specific textual details and quotations wherever relevant.

The following paper is one student's response to Tim O'Brien's story "The Things They Carried" (page 462).

Ethan Martin

English 99

Professor Merrill

31 March 2012

"Perfect Balance and Perfect Posture":

Reflecting on "The Things They Carried"

Reading Tim O'Brien's short story "The Things They Carried" became a very personal experience. It reminded me of my father, who is a Vietnam veteran, and the stories he used to tell me. Growing up, I regularly asked my dad to share stories from his past, especially about his service in the United States Marine Corps. He would rarely talk about his tour during the Vietnam War for more than a few minutes, and what he shared was usually the same: the monsoon rain could chill to the bone, the mosquitoes would never stop biting, and the M-16 rifles often jammed in a moment of crisis. He dug a new foxhole where he slept every night, he traded the cigarettes from his C-rations for food, and—since he was the radio man of his platoon—the combination of his backpack and radio was very heavy during the long, daily walks through rice paddies and jungles. For these reasons, "The Things They Carried" powerfully affected me.

While reading the story, I felt as if I was "humping" (par. 4) through Vietnam with Lieutenant Jimmy Cross, Rat Kiley, Ted Lavender, and especially Mitchell Sanders—who carries the 26-pound radio and battery. Every day, we carry our backpacks to school. Inside are some objects that we need to use in class: books, paper, and pens. But most of us probably include "unnecessary" items that reveal something about who we are or what we value—photographs, perfume, or good-luck charms. O'Brien uses this device to tell his story. At times he lists the things that the soldiers literally carried, such as weapons, medicine, and flak jackets. These military items weigh between 30 and 70 pounds, depending on one's rank or function in the platoon. The narrator says, "They carried all they could bear, and then some, including a silent awe for the terrible power of the things they carried" (par. 12).

Some of this "terrible power" comes from the sentimental objects the men keep. Although these are relatively light, they weigh down the hearts of the soldiers. Lt. Jimmy Cross carries 10-ounce letters and a pebble from Martha, a girl in his hometown who doesn't love him back. Rat Kiley carries comic books, and Norman Bowker carries a diary. I now own the small, water-logged Bible that my father carried through his tour in Vietnam, which was a gift from his mother. When I open its pages, I can almost hear his voice praying to survive the war.

The price of such survival is costly. O'Brien's platoon carries ghosts, memories, and "the land itself" (par. 39). Their intangible burdens are heavier than what they carry in their backpacks. My father has always said that, while he was in Vietnam, an inexpressible feeling of death hung heavy in the air, which he could not escape. O'Brien notes that an emotional weight of fear and cowardice "could never be put down, it required perfect balance and perfect posture" (par. 77), and I wonder if this may be part of what my father meant.

Both Tim O'Brien and my father were wounded by shrapnel, and now they both carry a Purple Heart. They carry the weight of survival. They carry memories that I will never know. "The Things They Carried" is not a war story about glory and honor. It is a portrait of the psychological damage that war can bring. It is a story about storytelling and how hard it can be to find the truth. And it is a beautiful account of what the human heart can endure.

Work Cited

O'Brien, Tim. "The Things They Carried." *Literature: An Introduction to Fiction, Poetry, Drama, and Writing.* Ed. X. J. Kennedy and Dana Gioia. 7th Compact ed. New York: Pearson, 2013. 462–74. Print.

TOPICS FOR WRITING

What kinds of topics are likely to result in papers that will reveal something about works of fiction? Here is a list of typical topics, suitable for papers of various lengths, offered in the hope of stimulating your own ideas. For additional ideas, see "More Topics for Writing" at the end of most chapters in this book.

TOPICS FOR WRITING BRIEF PAPERS (250–500 WORDS)

1. Explicate the opening paragraph or first few lines of a story. Show how the opening prepares the reader for what will follow. In an essay of this length, you will need to limit your discussion to the most important elements of the passage you explicate; there won't be room to deal with everything. Or, as thoroughly as the word count allows, explicate the final paragraph of a story. What does the ending imply about the fates of the story's characters, and about the story's take on its central theme?

2. Select a story that features a first-person narrator. Write a concise yet thorough analysis of how that character's point of view colors the story.

3. Following the directions in this chapter, write a card report on any short story in this book.

4. Consider a short story in which the central character has to make a decision or must take some decisive step that will alter the rest of his or her life. Faulkner's "Barn Burning" is one such story; another is Updike's "A & P." As concisely and as thoroughly as you can, explain the nature of the character's decision, the reasons for it, and its probable consequences (as suggested by what the author tells us).

5. Choose two stories that might be interesting to compare and contrast. Write a brief defense of your choice. How might these two stories illuminate each other?

6. Choose a key passage from a story you admire. As closely as the word count allows, explicate that passage and explain why it strikes you as an important moment in the story. Concentrate on the aspects of the passage that seem most essential.

7. Write a new ending to a story of your choice. Try to imitate the author's writing style. Add a paragraph explaining how this exercise illuminates the author's choices in the original.

8. Drawing on your own experience, make the case that a character in any short story behaves (or doesn't behave) as people do in real life. Your audience for this assignment is your classmates; tailor your tone and argument accordingly.

TOPICS FOR WRITING MORE EXTENDED PAPERS (600–1,000 WORDS)

1. Write an analysis of a short story, focusing on a single element, such as point of view, theme, symbolism, character, or the author's voice (tone, style, irony). For a sample paper in response to this assignment, see "The Hearer of the Tell-Tale Heart" (page 1368).

2. Compare and contrast two stories with protagonists who share an important personality trait. Make character the focus of your essay.

3. Write a thorough explication of a short passage (preferably not more than four sentences) in a story you admire. Pick a crucial moment in the plot, or a passage

that reveals the story's theme. You might look to the paper "By Lantern Light" (page 1365) as a model.

4. Write an analysis of a story in which the protagonist experiences an epiphany or revelation of some sort. Describe the nature of this change of heart. How is the reader prepared for it? What are its repercussions in the character's life? Some possible story choices are Alice Walker's "Everyday Use," William Faulkner's "Barn Burning," Raymond Carver's "Cathedral," James Baldwin's "Sonny's Blues," and, not surprisingly, Flannery O'Connor's "Revelation."

5. Imagine you are given the task of teaching a story to your class. Write an explanation of how you would address this challenge.

6. Imagine a reluctant reader, one who would rather play video games than crack a book. Which story in this book would you recommend to him or her? Write an essay to that imagined reader, describing the story's merits.

TOPICS FOR WRITING LONG PAPERS (1,500 WORDS OR MORE)

1. Write an analysis of a longer work of fiction. Concentrate on a single element of the story, quoting as necessary to make your point.

2. Read three or four short stories by an author whose work you admire. Concentrating on a single element treated similarly in all of the stories, write an analysis of the author's work as exemplified by your chosen stories.

3. Adapt a short story in this book into a one-act play. This may prove harder than it sounds; be sure to choose a story in which most of the action takes place in the physical world and not in the protagonist's mind. Don't forget to include stage directions.

4. Describe the process of reading a story for the first time and gradually learning to understand and appreciate it. First, choose a story you haven't yet read. As you read it for the first time, take notes on aspects of the story you find difficult or puzzling. Read the story a second time. Now write about the experience. What uncertainties were resolved when you read the story the second time? What, if any, uncertainties remain? What has this experience taught you about reading fiction?

5. Choose two stories that treat a similar theme. Compare and contrast the stance each story takes toward that theme, marshalling quotations and specifics as necessary to back up your argument.

6. Browse through newspapers and magazines for a story with the elements of good fiction. Now rewrite the story *as* fiction. Then write a one-page accompanying essay explaining the challenges of the task. What did it teach you about the relative natures of journalism and fiction?

40

WRITING ABOUT A POEM

> *I love being a writer.*
> *What I can't stand is the paperwork.*
>
> —PETER DE VRIES

Many readers—even some enthusiastic ones—are wary of poems. "I don't know anything about poetry," some people say, if the subject arises. While poems aren't booby traps designed to trip up careless readers, it is true that poetry demands a special level of concentration. Poetry is language at its most intense and condensed, and in a good poem, every word counts. With practice, though, anyone can become a more confident reader—and critic—of poetry. Remember that the purpose of poetry isn't intimidation but wisdom and pleasure. Even writing a paper on poetry can occasion a certain enjoyment. Here are some tips.

- **Choose a poem that speaks to you.** Let pleasure be your guide in choosing the poem you write about. The act of writing is easier if your feelings are engaged. Write about something you dislike and don't understand, and your essay will be as dismal to read as it was for you to write. But write about something that interests you, and your essay will communicate that interest and enthusiasm.

- **Allow yourself time to get comfortable with your subject.** As most professors will tell you, when students try to fudge their way through a paper on a topic they don't fully understand, the lack of comfort shows, making for muddled, directionless prose. The more familiar you become with a poem, however, the easier and more pleasurable it will be to write about it. Expect to read the poem several times over before its meaning becomes clear. Better still, reread it over the course of several days.

READ ACTIVELY

A poem differs from most prose in that it should be read slowly, carefully, and attentively. Good poems yield more if read twice, and the best poems—after ten, twenty, or even thirty readings—keep on yielding. Here are some suggestions to enhance your reading of a poem you plan to write about.

■ **Read the poem aloud.** There is no better way to understand a poem than to effectively read it aloud. Read slowly, paying attention to punctuation cues. Listen for the auditory effects.

■ **Read closely and painstakingly, annotating as you go.** Keep your mind (and your pencil) sharp and ready. The subtleties of language are essential to a poem. Pay attention to the connotations or suggestions of words, and to the rhythm of phrases and lines. Underline words and images that jump out at you. Use arrows to link phrases that seem connected. Highlight key passages or take notes in the margins as ideas or questions occur to you.

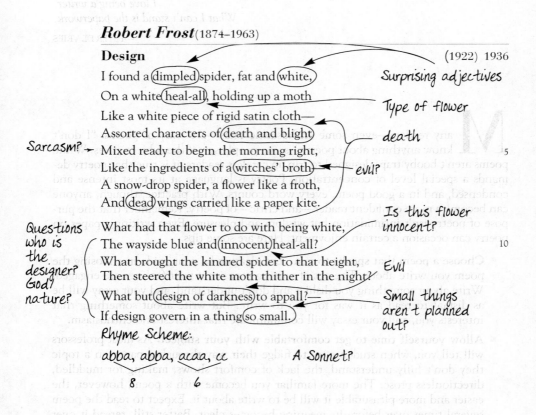

Robert Frost (1874–1963)

Design   (1922) 1936

I found a (dimpled) spider, fat and (white,)   *Surprising adjectives*
On a white (heal-all,) holding up a moth   *Type of flower*
Like a white piece of rigid satin cloth—
Assorted characters of (death and blight)   *death*
Sarcasm? → Mixed ready to begin the morning right,   5
Like the ingredients of a (witches' broth)   *evil?*
A snow-drop spider, a flower like a froth,
And (dead) wings carried like a paper kite.

Questions   What had that flower to do with being white,   *Is this flower innocent?*
who is   The wayside blue and (innocent) heal-all?   10
the   What brought the kindred spider to that height,
designer?   Then steered the white moth thither in the night?   *Evil*
God/
nature?   What but (design of darkness) to appall?—   *Small things aren't planned out?*
               If design govern in a thing (so small.)

Rhyme Scheme:
abba, abba, acaa, cc   *A Sonnet?*
        8   6

■ **Look up any unfamiliar words, allusions, or references.** Often the very words you may be tempted to skim over will provide the key to a poem's meaning. Thomas Hardy's "The Ruined Maid" will remain elusive to a reader unfamiliar with the archaic meaning of the word "ruin"—a woman's loss of virginity to a man other than her husband. Similarly, be sure to acquaint yourself with any references or allusions that appear in a poem. H.D.'s poem "Helen" will make sense only to readers who are familiar with the story of Helen of Troy.

THINK ABOUT THE POEM

Before you begin writing, take some time to collect your thoughts. The following steps can be useful in thinking about a poem.

- **Let your emotions guide you into the poem.** Do any images or phrases call up a strong emotional response? If so, try to puzzle out why those passages seem so emotionally loaded. In a word or two, describe the poem's tone.

- **Determine what's literally happening in the poem.** Separating literal language from figurative or symbolic language can be one of the trickiest—and most essential—tasks in poetic interpretation. Begin by working out the literal. Who is speaking the poem? To whom? Under what circumstances? What happens in the poem?

- **Ask what it all adds up to.** Once you've pinned down the literal action of the poem, it's time to take a leap into the figurative. What is the significance of the poem? Address symbolism, any figures of speech, and any language that means one thing literally but suggests something else. In "My Papa's Waltz," for example, Theodore Roethke tells a simple story of a father dancing his small son around a kitchen. The language of the poem suggests much more, however, implying that while the father is rough to the point of violence, the young boy hungers for his attention.

- **Consider the poem's shape on the page, and the way it sounds.** What patterns of sound do you notice? Are the lines long, short, or a mixture of both? How do these elements contribute to the poem's effect?

- **Pay attention to form.** If a poem makes use of rime or regular meter, ask yourself how those elements contribute to its meaning. If it is in a fixed form, such as a sonnet or villanelle, how do the demands of that form serve to set its tone? If the form calls for repetition—of sounds, words, or entire lines—how does that repetition underscore the poem's message? If, on the other hand, the poem is in free verse—without a consistent pattern of rime or regular meter—how does this choice affect the poem's feel?

- **Take note of line breaks.** If the poem is written in free verse, pay special attention to its line breaks. Poets break their lines with care, conscious that readers pause momentarily over the last word in any line, giving that word special emphasis. Notice whether the lines tend to be broken at the ends of whole phrases and sentences or in the middle of phrases. Then ask yourself what effect is created by the poet's choice of line breaks. How does that effect contribute to the poem's meaning?

PREWRITING: DISCOVER YOUR IDEAS

Now that you have thought the poem through, it's time to let your ideas crystallize on the page (or screen). Try one or more of the following prewriting techniques.

- **Brainstorm.** With the poem in front of you, jot down every single thing you can think of about it. Write quickly, without worrying about the value of your thoughts; you can sort that out later. Brainstorming works best if you set a time limit of ten or fifteen minutes and force yourself to keep working until the time is up. A list that results from brainstorming on "Design" might look something like this:

white spider	white = strangeness
heal-all/flower	heal-all usually blue
dead moth like a kite	flower doesn't heal all
white = innocence?	design = God or nature
death/blight	design of darkness = the devil?
begin the morning right=oddly cheerful	maybe no design (no God?)
irony	God doesn't govern small things
witches' broth/scary	

■ **Cluster.** If you are a visual thinker, you might find yourself drawn to clustering as a way to explore the relationships among your ideas. Begin by writing your subject at the center of a sheet of paper. Circle it. Then write ideas as they occur to you, drawing lines linking each new idea to ones that seem related. Here is an example of clustering on "Design."

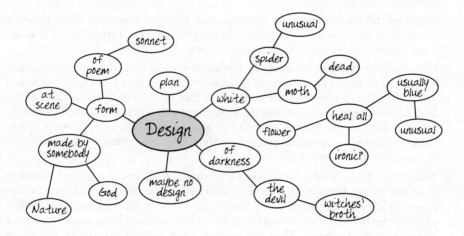

■ **List.** Make a list of information that seems useful. Feel free to add notes that will help you to remember what you meant by each item. Headings can help you to organize related concepts. A list might look like this:

Odd Coincidence	Questions
white spider	Accidental or by design?
white flower (not blue, innocent)	Whose design?
white moth (stiff, dead)	Nature or God?
characters of death/blight	Does God care?
morning (hopeful) = ironic	
witches' broth	Form of Poem
	sonnet (strict, orderly)
	form of universe =
	not so orderly?

■ **Freewrite.** Another approach to generating ideas is to let your thoughts pour out onto the page. To freewrite, give yourself a time limit: fifteen or twenty minutes will work well. Then write, without stopping to think, for that whole time. Keep writing. Don't worry about grammar or spelling or even logic; your task is to come up with fresh ideas that might evade you if you were writing more cautiously. Keep writing even (or especially) if you run out of ideas. New and surprising thoughts sometimes arrive when we least expect them. Here is a sample of freewriting on "Design."

> The scene seems strange. Spiders aren't usually white, and heal-alls are supposed to be blue. Moths are white, but this one is described as being like a rigid satin cloth or a paper kite. It's dead, which is why it is rigid, but the images seem to focus on its stiffness—its deadness—in a creepy way. The poet seems surprised at all this whiteness. Whiteness usually represents innocence, but here he says the flower would ordinarily be blue and innocent, so maybe it's not innocent now? I think he's saying this is a kind of deathly pageant; he calls the three things assorted characters though a flower can't be a character. The second part of the poem is all questions, no answers. What does he mean by "design of darkness"?
>
> Design seems to mean plan. It sounds like he's saying something sinister is going on. Like someone (God?) put the scene there for a purpose, maybe for him to notice. But then he seems to say no, God doesn't care about small things which maybe means he doesn't care about us either. I just noticed that this poem is (I think) a sonnet. It has rime and fourteen lines. It seems funny that a poem about there being no order to the universe is written in such a strict form.

■ **Journal.** A journal of your reactions to the works you read can be an excellent place to look for raw material for more formal writing. If your instructor has assigned such a journal, page through to remind yourself of your first reactions to a poem you plan to write about.

■ **Outline.** To think through your argument before you begin to flesh it out, make an outline (a list of points arranged in a logical order). Not all writers work from outlines, but some find them indispensable. Here is a sample outline.

1. Italian sonnet (define)
   two parts
   octave draws picture
   sestet asks questions
2. Rime
   "ite" sound stresses whiteness
3. Sonnet form = order
   poem's subject = order
   irony/no order in universe

4. Design of poem is unpredictable

     looks orderly but isn't

5. Design of universe is unpredictable

WRITE A ROUGH DRAFT

When your prewriting work has given you a sense of direction, you will be ready to begin forming your thoughts and writing a first draft of your essay. Reread the section "Develop a Literary Argument" in the chapter "Writing About Literature" for help getting started.

■ **Review your purpose and audience.** Begin by referring back to the exact assignment you have been given. No matter how crystal clear your prose or intriguing your ideas, an essay that fails to respond to the assignment is likely to fall flat. As you begin your first draft, consider how best to focus your essay to fulfill the instructor's requirements. Whatever the assignment, you need to keep your purpose in mind as you write. You also need to consider your audience's needs, whether that audience is your professor, your fellow students, or some hypothetical set of readers.

■ **Define your thesis.** To keep you focused on the task at hand, and to signal your intentions to your reader, you will need, first of all, to come up with a thesis. Like the rest of your first draft, that thesis sentence can be rough around the edges; you can refine it later in the process. For now, though, the thesis gives you something to work toward. You need to make a decisive statement that offers an insight that isn't entirely obvious about the work under discussion. In the final paper your task will be to convince readers that your thesis is sound. Here is a working thesis sentence for an analytical essay on Frost's poem "Design."

> **WORKING THESIS**
>
> The poem "Design" both is and isn't formal.

This rough thesis defines the essay's focus—the poem's form. But the statement is still very vague. A later, sharper version will clarify the idea and show what the author means by the claim that the poem both is and isn't formal. The revision also will push this idea further by connecting the poem's form to its meaning.

> **REVISED THESIS**
>
> Although Frost's sonnet "Design" is a well-designed formal poem, the conclusions it presents are not predictable but both surprising and disturbing.

In its revised form, this thesis makes a stronger and more specific claim. Because the revision says something specific about how the poem works, it is more compelling than the vaguer original.

■ **Supply evidence to prove your point.** Once you've settled on a working thesis, your next task is to decide what evidence will best prove your point. Be sure to quote from the poem to back up each point you make; there is no evidence more convincing than the words of the poem itself.

■ **Organize your argument.** You will need to make clear what each bit of evidence illustrates. Connect your argument back to the thesis as often as it takes to clarify your line of reasoning for the reader.

■ **Concentrate on getting your ideas onto the page.** Later you will go back and revise, making your prose clearer and more elegant. At that point, you can add information that seems to be missing and discard passages that seem beside the point. For now, though, the goal is to spell out your argument while it is clear in your mind.

CHECKLIST: Writing a Rough Draft

- ☐ What is your assignment? Does the essay fulfill it?
- ☐ Who is your audience?
- ☐ What is your thesis?
- ☐ Is your thesis thought-provoking rather than a statement of the obvious?
- ☐ Have you provided evidence to support your thesis?
- ☐ Does anything in your essay undercut your thesis?
- ☐ Have you quoted from the poem? Would more quotations strengthen your argument?
- ☐ Is your argument organized in a logical way?

REVISE YOUR DRAFT

■ **Have a reader review your paper.** Once you have completed your rough draft, consider enlisting the aid of a reader, professional (a writing center tutor) or otherwise (a trusted friend). The author of the paragraph below used her instructor's comments to improve her paper's introduction.

DRAFT OF OPENING PARAGRAPH

Robert Frost's poem "Design" is an Italian sonnet, a form that divides its argument into two parts, an octave and a sestet. The octave, or first part of the poem, concentrates on telling the reader about a peculiar scene the poet has noticed: a white spider holding a dead moth on a white flower. The sestet, or second part of the poem, asks what the scene means. It doesn't really provide any answers.

Good start. I'm glad you're thinking about the poem's form. How does the form suit the content?

Add a little more. Is the scene significant? How so?

Does it hint at answers? Be more specific.

REVISED OPENING PARAGRAPH

For Robert Frost's poem "Design," the sonnet form has at least two advantages. As in most Italian sonnets, the poem's argument falls into two parts. In the octave Frost's persona draws a still life of a spider, a flower, and a moth; then in the sestet he contemplates the meaning of his still life. The sestet focuses on a universal: the possible existence of a vindictive deity who causes the spider to catch the moth and, no doubt, also causes—when viewed anthropomorphically—other suffering.

To see this essay in its entirety, turn to page 1394. (It's worth noting that while the thesis sentence often appears in an essay's first paragraph, this paper takes a different tack. The first paragraph introduces the essay's focus—the benefits of the sonnet form for this particular poem—then builds carefully toward its thesis, which appears in the last paragraph.)

▪ **Make your argument more specific.** Use specifics instead of generalities in describing the poem. Writing imprecisely or vaguely, favoring the abstract over the concrete, is a common problem for student writers. When discussing ideas or principles, you can communicate more fully to your reader by supplying specific examples of those ideas or principles in action, as this student did when she reworked the ending of the paragraph above.

▪ **Make your language fresh and accurate.** It is easy to depend on habitual expressions and to overuse a few convenient words. Mechanical language may tempt you to think of the poem in mechanical terms. Here, for instance is a plodding discussion of Frost's "Design":

> DRAFT
>
> The symbols Frost uses in "Design" are very successful. Frost makes the
> spider <u>stand for</u> Nature. He <u>wants</u> us to see nature as blind and cruel. He
> also <u>employs</u> good sounds. He <u>uses</u> a lot of *i*'s because he is <u>trying</u> to make
> you think of falling rain.

What's wrong with this "analysis"? The underscored words are worth questioning here. While understandable, the words *employs* and *uses* seem to lead the writer to see Frost only as a conscious tool-manipulator. To be sure, Frost in a sense "uses" symbols, but did he grab hold of them and lay them into his poem? For all we know, perhaps the symbols arrived quite unbidden and used the poet. To write a good poem, Frost maintained, the poet himself has to be surprised. (How, by the way, can we hope to know what a poet wants to do? And there isn't much point in saying that the poet is *trying* to do something. He has already done it, if he has written a good poem.) At least it is likely that Frost didn't plan to fulfill a certain quota of *i*-sounds. Writing his poem, not by following a blueprint but probably by bringing it slowly to the surface of his mind, Frost no doubt had enough to do without trying to engineer the reactions of his possible audience. Like all true symbols, Frost's spider doesn't *stand for* anything. The writer would be closer to the truth in saying that the spider *suggests* or *reminds us* of nature or of certain forces in the natural world. (Symbols just hint; they don't indicate.)

After the student discussed the paper in a conference with her instructor, she rewrote her sentences:

> REVISION
>
> The symbols in Frost's "Design" are highly effective. The spider, for instance,
> suggests the blindness and cruelty of Nature. Frost's word-sounds, too, are
> part of the meaning of his poem, for the *i*'s remind the reader of falling rain.

Not every reader of "Design" will hear rain falling, but the student's revision probably comes closer to describing the experience of the poem most of us have.

▪ **Be clear and precise.** Another very real pitfall of writing literary criticism is the temptation to write in official-sounding Critic Speak. Writers who aren't quite sure about what to say may try to compensate for this uncertainty with un-necessarily ornate sentences that don't say much of anything. Other times, they will begin a sentence and find themselves completely entangled in its structure, unable to make a perfectly sound idea clear to the reader. Should you feel your-self being tugged out to sea by an undertow of fancy language, here is a trick for getting back ashore: speak your ideas aloud, in the simplest terms possible, to a friend, or a tape recorder, or your mirror. When you've formulated your idea sim-ply and clearly, write down your exact words. Most likely, your instructor will be grateful for the resulting clarity of expression.

CHECKLIST: Revising Your Draft

- ☐ Is your thesis clear and decisive?
- ☐ Does all your evidence advance your argument?
- ☐ Is information presented in the most logical order?
- ☐ Could your prose be clearer? More precise? More specific?
- ☐ Do transitional words and phrases signal movement from one idea to the next?
- ☐ Does your introduction draw the reader in? Does it prepare him or her for what follows?
- ☐ Does your conclusion tie up the essay's loose ends?
- ☐ Does each paragraph include a topic sentence?
- ☐ Does your title give a sense of the essay's subject?

COMMON APPROACHES TO WRITING ABOUT POETRY

Explication

In an **explication** (literally, "an unfolding"), a writer explains an entire poem in de-tail, unraveling its complexities. An explication, however, should not be confused with a paraphrase, which puts the poem's literal meaning into plain prose. While an explication might include some paraphrasing, it does more than simply restate. It ex-plains a poem, in great detail, showing how each part contributes to the whole. In writing an explication, keep the following tips in mind:

- **Start with the poem's first line, and keep working straight through to the end.** As needed, though, you can take up points out of order.
- **Read closely, addressing the poem's details.** You may choose to include allu-sions, the denotations or connotations of words, the possible meanings of symbols, the effects of certain sounds and rhythms and formal elements (rime schemes, for instance), the sense of any statements that contain irony, and other particulars.
- **Show how each part of the poem contributes to the meaning of the whole.** Your explication should go beyond dissecting the pieces of a poem; it should also bring them together in a way that casts light on the poem in its entirety.

Here is a successful student-authored explication of Frost's "Design." The assign-ment was to explain, in not more than 750 words, whatever in the poem seemed most essential.

Jasper 1

Ted Jasper

Professor Koss

English 130

21 November 2011

An Unfolding of Robert Frost's "Design"

"I always wanted to be very observing," Robert Frost once told an audience, after reading aloud his poem "Design." Then he added, "But I have always been afraid of my own observations" (qtd. in Cook 126–27). What could Frost have observed that could scare him? Let's examine the poem in question and see what we discover.

Starting with the title, "Design," any reader of this poem will find it full of meaning. As the *Merriam-Webster Dictionary* defines *design*, the word can denote among other things a plan, purpose, or intention ("Design"). Some arguments for the existence of God (I remember from Sunday School) are based on the "argument from design": that because the world shows a systematic order, there must be a Designer who made it. But the word design can also mean "a deliberate undercover project or scheme" such as we attribute to a "designing person" ("Design"). As we shall see, Frost's poem incorporates all of these meanings. His poem raises the old philosophic question of whether there is a Designer, an evil Designer, or no Designer at all.

Like many other sonnets, "Design" is divided into two parts. The first eight lines draw a picture centering on the spider, who at first seems almost jolly. It is *dimpled* and *fat* like a baby, or Santa Claus. The spider stands on a wildflower whose name, *heal-all*, seems ironic: a heal-all is supposed to cure any disease, but this flower has no power to restore life to the dead moth. (Later, in line ten, we learn that the heal-all used to be blue. Presumably, it has died and become bleached-looking.) In the second line we discover, too, that the spider has hold of another creature, a dead moth. We then see the moth described with an odd simile in line three: "Like a white piece of rigid satin cloth." Suddenly, the moth becomes not a creature but a piece of fabric—lifeless and dead—and yet *satin* has connotations of beauty. Satin is a luxurious material used in rich formal clothing, such as coronation gowns and brides' dresses. Additionally, there is great accuracy in the word: the smooth and slightly plush surface of satin is like the powder-smooth surface of moths' wings. But this "cloth," rigid and white, could be the lining to Dracula's coffin.

Jasper 2

In the fifth line an invisible hand enters. The characters are "mixed" like ingredients in an evil potion. Some force doing the mixing is behind the scene. The characters in themselves are innocent enough, but when brought together, their whiteness and look of *rigor mortis* are overwhelming. There is something diabolical in the spider's feast. The "morning right" echoes the word *rite*, a ritual—in this case apparently a Black Mass or a Witches' Sabbath. The simile in line seven ("a flower like a froth") is more ambiguous and harder to describe. Froth is white, foamy, and delicate—something found on a brook in the woods or on a beach after a wave recedes. However, in the natural world, froth also can be ugly: the foam on a polluted stream or a rabid dog's mouth. The dualism in nature—its beauty and its horror—is there in that one simile.

Refers to sound

(So far,) the poem has portrayed a small, frozen scene, with the dimpled killer holding its victim as innocently as a boy holds a kite. Already, Frost has hinted that Nature may be, as Radcliffe Squires suggests, "Nothing but an ash-white plain without love or faith or hope, where ignorant appetites cross by chance" (87). Now, in the last six lines of the sonnet, Frost comes out and directly states his theme. What else could bring these deathly pale, stiff things together "but design of darkness to appall"? The question is clearly rhetorical; we are meant to answer, "Yes, there does seem to be an evil design at work here!" I take the next-to-last line to mean, "What except a design so dark and sinister that we're appalled by it?" "Appall," by the way, is the second pun in the poem: it sounds like a pall or shroud. (The derivation of *appall*, according to *Merriam-Webster*, is ultimately from a Latin word meaning "to be pale"—an interesting word choice for a poem full of pale white images ["Appall"].) *Steered* carries the suggestion of a steering-wheel or rudder that some pilot had to control. Like the word *brought*, it implies that some invisible force charted the paths of spider, heal-all, and moth, so that they arrived together.

Transition words

Quotes secondary source

Discusses theme

Defines key word

Having suggested that the universe is in the hands of that sinister force (an indifferent God? Fate? the Devil?), Frost adds a note of doubt. The Bible tells us that "His eye is on the sparrow," but at the moment the poet doesn't seem sure. Maybe, he hints, when things in the universe drop below a certain size, they pass completely out of the Designer's notice. When creatures are this little, maybe God doesn't bother to govern them but just lets them run wild. And possibly the same mindless chance is all that governs human lives. And because this is even more senseless than having an angry God intent on punishing us, it is, Frost suggests, the worst suspicion of all.

Answers question raised in introduction

Conclusion

Jasper 3

Works Cited

"Appall." *Merriam-Webster Online Dictionary*. Merriam-Webster, 2011. Web.
13 November 2011.

Cook, Reginald. *Robert Frost: A Living Voice*. Amherst: U of Massachusetts P,
1974. Print.

"Design." *Merriam-Webster Online Dictionary*. Merriam-Webster, 2011. Web.
11 November 2011.

Frost, Robert. "Design." *Collected Poems, Prose and Plays*. New York: Library of
America, 1995. 275. Print.

Squires, Radcliffe. *The Major Themes of Robert Frost*. Ann Arbor: U of Michigan P,
1963. Print.

This excellent paper finds something worth unfolding in every line of Frost's poem, without seeming mechanical. Although the student proceeds sequentially through the poem from the title to the last line, he takes up some points out of order when it serves his purpose. In paragraph two, for example, he looks ahead to the poem's ending and briefly states its main theme in order to relate it to the poem's title. In the third paragraph, he explicates the poem's later image of the heal-all, relating it to the first image. He also comments on the poem's form ("Like many other sonnets"), on its similes and puns, and on its denotations and connotations.

This paper also demonstrates good use of manuscript form, following the *MLA Handbook*, 7th ed. Brief references (in parentheses) tell us where the writer found Frost's remarks and give the page number for his quotation from the book by Radcliffe Squires. At the end of the paper, a list of works cited uses abbreviations that the *MLA Handbook* recommends.

A Critic's Explication of Frost's "Design"

It might seem that to work through a poem line by line is a mechanical task, and yet there can be genuine excitement in doing so. Randall Jarrell once wrote an explication of "Design" in which he managed to convey just such excitement. See if you can sense Jarrell's joy in writing about the poem.

Frost's details are so diabolically good that it seems criminal to leave some unremarked; but notice how *dimpled, fat,* and *white* (all but one; all but one) come from our regular description of any baby; notice how the *heal-all,* because of its name, is the one flower in all the world picked to be the altar for this Devil's Mass; notice how *holding up* the moth brings something ritual and hieratic, a ghostly, ghastly formality, to this priest and its sacrificial victim; notice how terrible to the fingers, how full of the stilling rigor of death, that *white piece of rigid satin cloth* is. And *assorted characters of death and blight* is, like so many things in this poem, sharply ambiguous: *a mixed bunch of actors* or *diverse representative signs*. The tone of the phrase *assorted characters of death and blight* is beautifully developed in the ironic Breakfast-Club-calisthenics, Radio-Kitchen heartiness of *mixed ready to begin the morning right* (which assures us, so unreassuringly, that this isn't any sort of Strindberg *Spook Sonata,* but hard fact), and concludes in the *ingredients* of the witches' broth, giving the soup a sort of cuddly shimmer that the cauldron in *Macbeth* never had; the *broth,* even, is brought to life—we realize that witches' broth *is* broth, to be supped with a long spoon.[1]

Evidently, Jarrell's cultural interests are broad: ranging from August Strindberg's ground-breaking modern play down to *The Breakfast Club* (a once-popular radio program that cheerfully exhorted its listeners to march around their tables). And yet breadth of knowledge, however much it deepens and enriches Jarrell's writing, isn't all that he brings to the reading of poetry. For him an explication isn't a dull plod, but a voyage of discovery. His prose—full of figures of speech (*diabolically good, cuddly shimmer*)—conveys the apparent delight he takes in showing off his findings. Such a joy, of course, can't be acquired deliberately. But it can grow, the more you read and study poetry.

Analysis

Like a news commentator's analysis of a crisis in the Middle East or a chemist's analysis of an unknown fluid, an **analysis** separates a poem into elements as a means to understanding that subject. Usually, the writer of an analysis focuses on one particular element: "Imagery of Light and Darkness in Frost's 'Design'" or "The Character of Satan in Milton's *Paradise Lost.*" In this book, you probably already have encountered a few brief analyses: the discussion of connotations in William Blake's "London" (pages 550–51), for instance, or the examination of symbols in T. S. Eliot's "The Boston Evening Transcript" (page 684). In fact, most of the discussions in this book are analyses. To write an analysis, remember two key points:

- **Focus on a single, manageable element of a poem.** Some possible choices are tone, irony, literal meaning, imagery, figures of speech, sound, rhythm, theme, and symbolism.
- **Show how this element of the poem contributes to the meaning of the whole.** While no element of a poem exists apart from all the others, by taking a closer look at one particular aspect of the poem, you can see the whole more clearly.

The paper that follows analyzes a particularly tricky subject—the formal and technical elements of Frost's "Design." Long analyses of metrical feet, rime schemes, and indentations can make for ponderous reading, but this paper shows how formal analysis can be interesting and can cast light on a poem.

[1]*Poetry and the Age* (New York: Knopf, 1953), 42–43.

Guadalupe Lopez

Professor Faber

English 210

16 April 2012

The Design of Robert Frost's "Design"

Introduction gives overview of poem's form.

For Robert Frost's poem "Design," the sonnet form has at least two advantages. As in most Italian sonnets, the poem's argument falls into two parts. In the octave Frost's persona draws a still life of a spider, a flower, and a moth; then in the sestet he contemplates the meaning of his still life. Although

Thesis sentence

the poem is perfectly formal in its shape, the ideas it presents are not predictable, but are instead both surprising and disturbing. The sestet focuses on a universal: the possible existence of a vindictive deity who causes the spider to catch the moth and, no doubt, also causes—when viewed anthropomorphically—other suffering.

Topic sentence on how poem subtly makes its point

Frost's persona weaves his own little web. The unwary audience is led through the poem's argument from its opening "story" to a point at which something must be made of the story's symbolic significance. Even the rhyme scheme contributes to the poem's successful leading of the audience toward the sestet's theological questioning. The word *white* ends the first line of the sestet, and the same vowel sound is echoed in the lines that follow. All in all, half of the sonnet's lines end in the "ite" sound, as if to render significant the wh*ite*ness—the symbolic innocence—of nature's representation of a greater truth.

Topic sentence on how form relates to theme

A sonnet has a familiar design, and the poem's classical form points to the thematic concern that there seems to be an order to the universe that might be perceived by looking at even seemingly insignificant natural events. The sonnet must follow certain conventions, and nature, though not as readily apprehensible as a poetic form, is apparently governed by a set of laws. There is a ready-made irony in Frost's choosing such an order-driven form to meditate on whether or not there is any order in the universe. However, whether or not his questioning sestet is actually approaching an answer or, indeed, the answer, Frost has approached an order that seems to echo a larger order in his using the sonnet form. An approach through poetic form and substance is itself significant in Frost's own estimation, for he argues that what a poet achieves in writing poetry is "a momentary stay against confusion" (777).

Lopez 2

Although design clearly governs in this poem—in this "thing so small"—the design is not entirely predictable. The poem does start out in the form of an Italian sonnet, relying on only two rhyming sounds. However, unlike an Italian sonnet, one of the octave's rhyming sounds—the "ite"—continues into the sestet. And additionally, "Design" ends in a couplet, much in the manner of the Shakespearean sonnet, which frequently offers, in the final couplet, a summing up of the sonnet's argument. Perhaps not only nature's "story" of the spider, the flower, and the moth but also Frost's poem itself echoes the larger universe. It looks perfectly orderly until the details are given their due.

Conclusion

Lopez 3

Work Cited

Frost, Robert. "The Figure a Poem Makes." *Collected Poems, Prose and Plays*. New York: Library of America, 1995. 776–78. Print.

Comparison and Contrast

The process of **comparison and contrast** places two poems side by side and studies their differences and similarities in order to shed light on both works. Writing an effective comparison-contrast paper involves the following steps:

- **Pair two poems with much in common.** Comparing two poems with surface similarities—for example, Dorothy Parker's caustic "Résumé" and Ben Jonson's profoundly elegiac "On My First Son"—can be a futile endeavor. Though both poems are about death, the two seem hopelessly removed from each other in diction, tone, complexity, and scope. Instead, choose two poems with enough in common that their differences take on interesting weight.

- **Point to further, unsuspected resemblances.** Steer clear of the obvious ("'Design' and 'Wing-Spread' are both about bugs"). The interesting resemblances take some thought to discover.

- **Show noteworthy differences.** Avoid those your reader will see without any help.

- **Carefully consider your essay's organization.** While you may be tempted to discuss first one poem and then the other, this simple structure may weaken your essay if it leads you to keep the two poems in total isolation from each other. After all, the point is to see what can be learned by comparison. There is nothing wrong in discussing all of poem A first, then discussing poem B—if in discussing B you keep referring back to A. Another strategy is to do a point-by-point comparison of the two poems all the way through your paper, dealing first, perhaps, with their themes, then with their central metaphors, and finally with their respective merits.

A comparison-contrast essay is often a kind of analysis—a study of a theme common to two poems, perhaps, or of two poets' similar fondness for the myth of Eden. In some cases, though, a comparison can also involve evaluation—a judgment on the relative worth of two poems.

Here, for example, is a poem by Abbie Huston Evans, followed by a paper that considers the merits of that poem and Frost's "Design." Through comparison and contrast, this student makes a case for his view of which poet deserves the brighter laurels.

Abbie Huston Evans (1881–1983)

Wing-Spread	1938

The midge spins out to safety
Through the spider's rope;
But the moth, less lucky,
Has to grope.

Mired in glue-like cable   5
See him foundered swing
By the gap he opened
With his wing,

Dusty web enlacing
All that blue and beryl.   10
In a netted universe
Wing-spread is peril.

Munjee 1

Tom Munjee
Professor Mickey
English 110
21 February 2012
"Wing-Spread" Does a Dip
Abbie Huston Evans's "Wing-Spread" is an effective short poem, but it
lacks the complexity and depth of Robert Frost's "Design." These two poems
were published only two years apart, and both present a murderous spider and
an unlucky moth, but Frost's treatment differs from Evans's approach in at least

Thesis sentence

two important ways. First, Frost uses poetic language more evocatively than Evans. Second, "Design" digs more deeply into the situation to uncover a more memorable theme.

    If we compare the language of the two poems, we find "Design" is full of words and phrases rich with suggestions. The language of "Wing-Spread," by comparison, seems thinner. Frost's "dimpled spider, fat and white," for example, is certainly a more suggestive description. Actually, Evans does not describe her spider; she just says, "the spider's rope." (Evans does vividly show the spider and moth in action. In Frost's poem, they are already dead and petrified.) In "Design," the spider's dimples show that it is like a chubby little baby. This seems an odd way to look at a spider, but it is more original than Evans's conventional view (although I like her word *cable*, suggesting that the spider's web is a kind of high-tech food trap). Frost's word choice— his repetition of *white*—paints a more striking scene than Evans's slightly vague "All that blue and beryl." Except for her brief personification of the moth in the second stanza, Evans hardly uses any figures of speech, and even this one is not a clear personification—she simply gives the moth a sex by referring to it as "him." Frost's striking metaphors, similes, and even puns (*right*, *appall*) show him, as usual, to be a master of figures of speech. He calls the moth's wings "satin cloth" and "a paper kite"; Evans just refers in line 8 to a moth's wing. As far as the language of the two poems goes, we might as well compare a vase brimming with flowers and a single flower stuck in a vase. In fairness to Evans, I would say that her poem, while lacking complexity, still makes its point effectively. Her poem has powerful sounds: short lines with the riming words coming at us again and again.

    In theme, however, "Wing-Spread" seems much more narrow than "Design." The first time I read Evans's poem, all I felt was: Ho hum, the moth's wings were too wide and got stuck. The second time I read it, I realized that she was saying something with a universal application. This message comes out in line 11, in "a netted universe." That metaphorical phrase is the most interesting part of her poem. *Netted* makes me imagine the universe as being full of nets rigged by someone who is fishing for us. Maybe, like Frost, Evans sees an evil plan operating. She does not, though, investigate it. She says that the midge escapes because it is tiny. On the other hand, things with wide wing-spreads get stuck. Her theme as I read it is, "Be small and inconspicuous if you want to survive," or maybe, "Isn't it too bad that in this world the big beautiful types

Argument summary

Textual evidence— contrasts diction of two poems

Contrasts thematic approach

Munjee 3

crack up and die, while the little puny punks keep sailing?" Now, this is a valuable idea. I have often thought that very same thing myself. But Frost's closing note ("If design govern in a thing so small") is really devastating because it raises a huge uncertainty. "Wing-Spread" leaves us with not much besides a moth stuck in a web and a moral. In both language and theme, "Design" climbs to a higher altitude.

*Conclusion
restates thesis*

Munjee 4

Works Cited

Evans, Abbie Huston. "Wing-Spread." *Literature: An Introduction to Fiction,
   Poetry, Drama, and Writing.* Ed. X. J. Kennedy and Dana Gioia.
   7th Compact ed. New York: Pearson, 2013. 1396. Print.

Frost, Robert. "Design." *Collected Poems, Prose and Plays.* New York: Library of
   America, 1995. 275. Print.

HOW TO QUOTE A POEM

Quoted to illustrate some point, memorable lines can enliven your paper. Carefully chosen quotations can serve to back up your thesis, or to alert your readers to a phrase or passage they may have neglected. Quoting poetry accurately, however, raises certain difficulties you don't face in quoting prose. Poets choose their line breaks with deliberation, and part of a critic's job is to take those breaks into account. Here are guidelines for respecting a poet's line breaks and for making your essay more polished in the bargain.

▪ **Quoting a few lines.** If you are quoting fewer than four lines of poetry, transform the passage into prose form, separating each line by a space, diagonal (/), and another space. The diagonal (/) indicates where the poet's lines begin and end. Two diagonals (//) signal a new stanza. Do not change the poet's capitalization or punctuation. Be sure to identify the line numbers you are quoting, as follows:

   The color white preoccupies Frost. The spider is "fat and white, / On a

   white heal-all" (1–2), and even the victim moth is pale, too.

- **Quoting four or more lines.** If you are quoting four or more lines of verse, set them off from your text, and arrange them just as they occur on the page, white space and all. Be sure to identify the lines you are quoting. In general, follow these rules:

  - Indent the quotation one inch from the left-hand margin.
  - Double-space between the quoted lines.
  - Type the poem exactly as it appears in the original. You do not need to use quotation marks.
  - If you begin the quotation in the middle of a line of verse, position the starting word about where it occurs in the poem—not at the left-hand margin.
  - If a line you are quoting runs too long to fit on one line, indent the return one-quarter inch.
  - Cite the line numbers you are quoting in parentheses.

  > At the end of the poem, the poet asks what deity or fate cursed this
  > particular mutant flower
  >
  >   with being white,
  > The wayside blue and innocent heal-all?
  > What brought the kindred spider to that height,
  > Then steered the white moth thither in the
  >   night? (9–12)

- **Omitting words.** If you omit words from the lines you quote, indicate the omission with an ellipsis (. . .), as in the following example:

  > The color white preoccupies Frost in his description of the spider "fat and
  > white, / On a white heal-all . . . / Like a white piece of rigid satin cloth"
  > (1–3).

- **Quoting only a brief phrase.** There's no need for an ellipsis if it is obvious that only a phrase is being quoted.

  > The speaker says that he "found a dimpled spider," and he goes on to
  > portray it as a kite-flying boy.

- **Omitting full lines of verse.** If you leave out lines of verse, indicate the omission by spaced periods about the length of a line of the poem you are quoting.

  > Maybe, she hints, when things in the universe drop below a certain size,
  > they pass completely out of the Designer's notice:
  >
  >   The midge spins out to safety
  >   Through the spider's rope;
  >
  >   . . . .
  >
  >   In a netted universe
  >   Wing-spread is peril. (1–2, 11–12)

One last note: often a paper on a short poem will include the whole text of the poem at its beginning, with the lines numbered so that your reader can refer to it with ease. Ask your instructor whether he or she prefers the full text to be quoted this way.

TOPICS FOR WRITING BRIEF PAPERS (250–500 WORDS)

1. Write a concise *explication* of a short poem of your choice. Concentrate on those facets of the poem that you think most need explaining.
2. Write an *analysis* of a short poem, focusing on how a single key element shapes its meaning. Some possible topics are:

   - Tone in Edna St. Vincent Millay's "Recuerdo"
   - Imagery in Wallace Stevens's "The Emperor of Ice-Cream"
   - Kinds of irony in Thomas Hardy's "The Workbox"
   - Theme in W. H. Auden's "Musée des Beaux Arts"
   - Extended metaphor in Langston Hughes's "The Negro Speaks of Rivers" (Explain the one main comparison that the poem makes and show how the whole poem makes it. Other poems that would lend themselves to a paper on extended metaphor include: Emily Dickinson's "Because I could not stop for Death," Robert Frost's "The Silken Tent," Robert Lowell's "Skunk Hour," Adrienne Rich's "Aunt Jennifer's Tigers.")

   (To locate any of these poems, see the Index of Authors and Titles.)

3. Select a poem in which the main speaker is a character who for any reason interests you. You might consider, for instance, Robert Browning's "Soliloquy of the Spanish Cloister," T. S. Eliot's "The Love Song of J. Alfred Prufrock," or Rhina Espaillat's "Bilingual/*Bilingüe*." Then write a brief profile of this character, drawing only on what the poem tells you (or reveals). What is the character's age? Situation in life? Attitude toward self? Attitude toward others? General personality? Do you find this character admirable?
4. Choose a brief poem that you find difficult. Write an essay in which you begin by listing the points in the poem that strike you as most impenetrable. Next, reread the poem at least twice. In the essay's second half, describe how further readings changed your experience of the poem.
5. Although each of these poems tells a story, what happens in the poem isn't necessarily obvious: E. E. Cummings's "anyone lived in a pretty how town," T. S. Eliot's "The Love Song of J. Alfred Prufrock," Edwin Arlington Robinson's "Luke Havergal." Choose one of these poems, and in a paragraph sum up what you think happens in it. Then in a second paragraph, ask yourself: what, *besides* the element of story, did you consider in order to understand the poem?
6. Imagine a reader who categorically dislikes poetry. Choose a poem for that person to read, and, addressing your skeptical reader, explain the ways in which this particular poem rewards a careful reader.

TOPICS FOR WRITING MORE EXTENDED PAPERS (600–1,000 WORDS)

1. Perform a line-by-line explication of a brief poem of your choice. Imagine that your audience is unfamiliar with the poem and needs your assistance in interpreting it.
2. Explicate a passage from a longer poem. Choose a passage that is, in your opinion, central to the poem's meaning.
3. Compare and contrast any two poems that treat a similar theme. Let your comparison bring you to an evaluation of the poems. Which is the stronger, more satisfying one?
4. Write a comparison-contrast essay on any two or more poems by a single poet. Look for two poems that share a characteristic thematic concern. (This book contains multiple selections by Auden, Blake, Cummings, Dickinson, Donne, Eliot, Frost, Hardy, Hopkins, Hughes, Keats, Shakespeare, Stevens, Tennyson, Whitman, Williams, Wordsworth, Yeats, and many others.) Here are some possible topics:

   - Mortality in the work of John Keats
   - Nature in the poems of William Wordsworth
   - How Emily Dickinson's lyric poems resemble hymns
   - E. E. Cummings's approach to the free-verse line
   - Gerard Manley Hopkins's sonic effects

5. Evaluate by the method of comparison two versions of a poem, one an early draft and one a late draft, or perhaps two translations of the same poem from another language.
6. If the previous topic appeals to you, consider this. In 1912, ten years before he published "Design," Robert Frost sent a correspondent this early version:

In White

A dented spider like a snow drop white
On a white Heal-all, holding up a moth
Like a white piece of lifeless satin cloth—
Saw ever curious eye so strange a sight?
Portent in little, assorted death and blight
Like the ingredients of a witches' broth?
The beady spider, the flower like a froth,

And the moth carried like a paper kite.
What had that flower to do with being white,
The blue Brunella every child's delight.
What brought the kindred spider to that height?
(Make we no thesis of the miller's plight.)
What but design of darkness and of night?
Design, design! Do I use the word aright?

Compare "In White" with "Design." In what respects is the finished poem superior?

TOPICS FOR WRITING LONG PAPERS (1,500 WORDS OR MORE)

1. Review an entire poetry collection by a poet featured in this book. You will need to communicate to your reader a sense of the work's style and thematic preoccupations. Finally, make a value judgment about the work's quality.

2. Read five or six poems by a single author. Start with a poet featured in this book, and then find additional poems at the library or on the Internet. Write an analysis of a single element of that poet's work—for example, theme, imagery, diction, or form.

3. Write a line-by-line explication of a poem rich in matters to explain or of a longer poem that offers ample difficulty. While relatively short, John Donne's "A Valediction: Forbidding Mourning" and Gerard Manley Hopkins's "The Windhover" are poems that will take a good bit of time to explicate. Even a short, apparently simple poem such as Robert Frost's "Stopping by Woods on a Snowy Evening" can provide more than enough material to explicate thoughtfully in a longer paper.

4. Write an analysis of a certain theme (or other element) that you find in the work of two or more poets. It is probable that in your conclusion you will want to set the poets' works side by side, comparing or contrasting them, and perhaps making some evaluation. Here are some sample topics to consider:

   - Langston Hughes, Gwendolyn Brooks, and Dudley Randall as Prophets of Social Change
   - What It Is to Be a Woman: The Special Knowledge of Sylvia Plath, Anne Sexton, and Adrienne Rich
   - The Complex Relations Between Fathers and Children in the Poetry of Robert Hayden, Rhina Espaillat, Theodore Roethke, and A. E. Stallings
   - Making Up New Words for New Meanings: Neologisms in Lewis Carroll and Kay Ryan

5. Apply the ideas in one of the critical excerpts in the "Writing Effectively" section found at the end of each chapter to a poem by the same author. Formulate a thesis about whether or not the prose excerpt sheds any light on the poetry. How do T. S. Eliot's thoughts on the music of poetry, or William Butler Yeats's observations on poetic symbolism, help you to better understand their poems? Quote as needed to back up your argument.

41

WRITING
ABOUT A PLAY

> *The play was a great success,*
> *but the audience was a total failure.*
>
> —OSCAR WILDE

Writing about a play you've read is similar, in many ways, to writing about poetry or fiction. If your subject is a play you have actually seen performed, however, some differences will quickly become apparent. Although, like a story or a poem, a play in print is usually the work of a single author, a play on stage may be the joint effort of seventy or eighty people—actors, director, costumers, set designers, and technicians. Though a play on the page stays fixed and changeless, a play in performance changes in many details from season to season—and even from night to night.

Later in this chapter you will find advice on reviewing a performance of a play, as you might do for a class assignment or for publication in a campus newspaper. In a literature course, though, you will probably write about the plays you quietly read and behold only in the theater of your mind.

READ CRITICALLY

- **Read the whole play—not just the dialogue, but also everything in italics, including stage directions and descriptions of settings.** The meaning of a scene, or even of an entire play, may depend on the tone of voice in which an actor is supposed to deliver a significant line. At the end of *A Doll's House*, for example, we need to pay attention to *how* Helmer's last line is spoken—"*A hope flashes across his mind*"—if we are to understand that Nora ignores his last desperate hope for reconciliation when she closes the door. The meaning of a line may depend upon the actions described in the stage directions. If Nora did not leave the house or close the door, but hesitated at Helmer's last line, the meaning of the play would be slightly different.

- **Highlight key passages and take notes as you read.** Later you will want to quote or refer to important moments in the play, and marking those moments will simplify your job. Following is an example of a student's notes on a key scene in Susan Glaspell's *Trifles*.

Mrs. Peters (*to the other woman*): Oh, her fruit; it did freeze. (*To the County Attorney*) She worried about that when it turned so cold. She said the fire'd go out and her jars would break.

Sheriff: Well, can you beat the women! Held for murder and worryin' about her preserves.

> *Both men are insulting toward Mrs. Wright.*

County Attorney: I guess before we're through she may have something more serious than preserves to worry about.

> *He thinks he's being kind.*

Hale: Well, women are used to worrying over trifles.

> *Is housework really insignificant?*

(*The two women move a little closer together.*)

> *The women side with each other.*

County Attorney (with the gallantry of a young politician): And yet, for all their worries, what would we do without the ladies? (*The women do not unbend.* He goes to the sink, takes a dipperful of water from the pail and pouring it into a basin, washes his hands. Starts to wipe them on the roller towel, turns it for a cleaner place.) Dirty towels! (*Kicks his foot against the pans under the sink.*) Not much of a housekeeper, would you say, ladies?

> *Courtesy toward women, but condescending*
>
> *The two women aren't buying it.*

Mrs. Hale (stiffly): There's a great deal of work to be done on a farm.

> *She holds back, but she's mad.*

> *Small, insignificant things or not?*
>
> *Play's title. Significant word? The men miss the "clues"—too trifling.*

> *I don't like this guy!*

▪ **If your subject is a play in verse—such as those by Sophocles and Shakespeare—keep track of act, scene, and line numbers as you take notes.** This will help you to easily relocate any text you want to refer to or quote.

> Iago's hypocrisy is apparent in his speech defending his good name (3.3.168–74).

COMMON APPROACHES TO WRITING ABOUT DRAMA

The methods commonly used to write about fiction and poetry—for example, explication, analysis, or comparison and contrast—are all well suited to writing about drama. These methods are discussed in depth in earlier chapters. Here are a few suggestions for using these methods to write about plays in particular.

Explication

A whole play is too much to cover in an ordinary **explication,** a line-by-line unfolding of meaning in a literary work. In drama, explication is best suited to brief passages—a key soliloquy, for example, or a moment of dialogue that lays bare the play's theme. Closely examining a critical moment in a play can shed light on the play in its entirety. To be successful, an explication needs to concentrate on a passage probably not much more than 20 lines long.

Analysis

A separation of a literary work into elements, **analysis** is a very useful method for writing about drama. To write an analysis, choose a single element in a play—for example, animal imagery in some speeches from *Othello*, or the theme of fragility in *The Glass Menagerie*. Plays certainly offer many choices of elements for analysis: characters, themes, tone, irony, imagery, figures of speech, and symbols, for example. Keep in mind, though, that not all plays contain the same elements you would find in poetry or fiction. Few plays have a narrator, and in most cases the point of view is that of the audience, which perceives the events not through a narrator's eyes but through its own. And while we might analyze a short story's all-pervading style, a play might contain as many styles as there are speaking characters. (Noteworthy exceptions do exist, though: you might argue that in Susan Glaspell's *Trifles*, both main characters speak the same language.) As for traditional poetic devices such as metaphor and metrical pattern, they may be found in plays such as *Othello*, but not in most contemporary plays, in which the dialogue tends to sound like ordinary conversation.

Comparison and Contrast

The method of **comparison and contrast** involves setting two plays side by side and pointing out their similarities and differences. Because plays are complicated entities, you need to choose a narrow focus, or you will find yourself overwhelmed. A profound topic—"The Self-Deception of Othello and Oedipus"—might do for a three-hundred-page dissertation, but an essay of a mere thousand words could never do it justice. A large but finite topic—say, attitudes toward marriage in *A Doll's House* and *Trifles*—would best suit a long term paper. To apply this method to a shorter term paper, you might compare and contrast a certain aspect of personality in two characters within the same play—for example, Willy's and Biff's illusions in *Death of a Salesman*.

Card Report

In place of an essay, some instructors like to assign a **card report,** a succinct but thorough method of analyzing the components of a play. For more information on this kind of assignment, see "The Card Report" on page 1370. Keep in mind, though, that when dealing with a play, you will find some elements that differ from those in a short story. Specifying the work's narrator may not be relevant to a play, for example. Also, for a full-length play, you may need to write on both sides of two 5- × 8-inch index cards instead of on one card, as you might for a short story. Still, in order to write a good card report, you have to be both brief and specific. Before you start, sort out your impressions of the play and try to decide which characters, scenes, and lines of dialogue are the most memorable and important. Reducing your scattered impressions to essentials, you will have to reexamine what you have read. When you finish, you will know the play much more thoroughly.

Here is an example: a card report on Susan Glaspell's one-act play *Trifles*. By including only the elements that seemed most important, the writer managed to analyze the brief play on the front and back of one card. Still, he managed to work in a few pertinent quotations to give a sense of the play's remarkable language. Although the report does not say everything about Glaspell's little masterpiece, an adequate criticism of the play could hardly be much briefer. For this report, the writer was assigned to include the following:

1. The playwright's name, nationality, and dates.
2. The title of the play and the date of its first performance.
3. The central character or characters, with a brief description that includes leading traits.
4. Other characters, also described.
5. The scene or scenes and, if the play does not take place in the present, the time of its action.
6. The dramatic question. This question is whatever the play leads us to ask ourselves: some conflict whose outcome we wonder about, some uncertainty whose resolution we look forward to.
7. A brief summary of the play's principal events, in the order in which the playwright presents them. If you are reporting on a play longer than *Trifles*, you may find it simplest to sum up what happens in each act, perhaps in each scene.
8. The tone of the play, as best you can detect it. Try to describe the playwright's apparent feelings toward the characters or what happens to them.
9. The language spoken in the play. Try to describe it. Does any character speak with a choice of words or with figures of speech that strike you as unusual, distinctive, poetic—or maybe dull and drab? Does language indicate a character's background or place of birth? Brief quotations, in what space you have, will be valuable.
10. A one-sentence summary of the play's central theme. If you find none, say so. Plays often contain more than one theme. Which of them seems most clearly borne out by the main events?
11. Any symbols you notice and believe to be important. Try to state in a few words what each suggests.
12. A concise evaluation of the play. What did you think of it?

A card report on *Trifles* begins on the following page.

Front of Card

Ben Nelson   English 101

Susan Glaspell, American, 1876–1948   *Trifles*, 1916

Central characters: Mrs. Peters, the sheriff's nervous wife, dutiful but

independent, not "married to the law"—whose sorrows make her able to sympathize

with a woman accused of murder. Mrs. Hale, who knows the accused; more decisive.

Other characters: The County Attorney, self-important but short-sighted. The

Sheriff, a man of only middling intelligence, another sexist. Hale, a farmer, a cautious

man. Not seen on stage, two others are central: Minnie (Foster) Wright, the accused, a

music lover reduced to near despair by years of grim marriage and isolation; and

John Wright, the victim, known for his cruelty.

Scene: The kitchen of a gloomy farmhouse after the arrest of a wife on suspicion

of murder; little things left in disarray.

Major dramatic question: Why did Minnie Wright kill her husband? When this

question is answered, a new major dramatic question is raised: Will Mrs. Peters and

Mrs. Hale cover up incriminating evidence?

Events: In the exposition, Sheriff and C.A., investigating the death of Wright,

hear Hale tell how he found the body and a distracted Mrs. Wright. Then (1) C.A. starts

looking for a motive. (2) His jeering at Mrs. Wright (and all women) for their concern

with "trifles" causes Mrs. Peters and Mrs. Hale to rally to the woman's defense. (3) When

the two women find evidence that Mrs. Wright had panicked (a patch of wild sewing in

a quilt), Mrs. Hale destroys it. (4) Mrs. Peters finds more evidence: a wrecked birdcage.

[continued on back of card]

Back of Card

[<u>Events</u>, continued]

(5) The women find a canary with its neck wrung and realize that Minnie killed her husband in a similar way. (6) The women align themselves with Minnie when Mrs. Peters recalls her own sorrows, and Mrs. Hale decides her own failure to visit Minnie was "a crime." (7) The C.A. unwittingly provides Mrs. Peters with a means to smuggle out the canary. (8) The two women unite to seize the evidence.

<u>Tone</u>: Made clear in the women's dialogue: mingled horror and sadness at what has happened, compassion for a fellow woman, smoldering resentment toward men who crush women.

<u>Language</u>: The plain speech of farm people, with a dash of rural Midwestern slang (*red-up* for tidy; Hale's remark that the accused was "kind of done up"). Unschooled speech: Mrs. Hale says *ain't*—and yet her speech rises at moments to simple poetry: "She used to sing. He killed that too." Glaspell hints at the self-importance of the County Attorney by his heavy reliance on the first person.

<u>Central theme</u>: Women, in their supposed concern for trifles, see more deeply than men do.

<u>Symbols</u>: The broken birdcage and the dead canary, both suggesting the music and the joy that John Wright stifled in Minnie.

<u>Evaluation</u>: A powerful, successful, realistic play that conveys its theme with great economy—in its views, more than fifty years ahead of its time.

A Drama Review

Writing a **play review,** a brief critical account of an actual performance, involves going out on a limb and making an evaluation. It also can mean assessing various aspects of the production, including the acting, direction, sets, costumes, lighting, and possibly even the play itself. While reviews can be challenging to write, many students find them more stimulating—even more fun—than most writing assignments. There is no better way to understand—and appreciate—drama than by seeing live theater. Here are some tips for writing a review.

- **Clarify what you are evaluating.** Is it the play's script, or the performance? If the latter, are you concentrating on the performance in its entirety, or on certain elements, such as the acting or the direction? If the play is a classic one, the more urgent task for the reviewer will be not to evaluate the playwright's work but to comment on the success of the actors', director's, and production crew's particular interpretation of it. If the play is newer and less well established, you may profitably evaluate the script itself.

- **Don't simply sneer or gush; give reasons for your opinions.** Ground your praise or criticism of a production in specifics. Incidentally, harsh evaluations can tempt a reviewer to flashes of wit. One celebrated flash was writer Eugene Field's observation of an actor in a production of *King Lear*, that "he played the king as though he were in constant fear that someone else was about to play the ace." The comment isn't merely nasty; it implies that Field had closely watched the actor's performance and had discerned what was wrong with it.

- **Early in the review, provide the basic facts.** Give the play's title and author, the theatrical company producing it, and the theater in which it is performed.

- **Give the names of actors in lead roles, and evaluate their performances.** How well cast do the leads seem? If an actor stands out—for good or ill—in a supporting role, he or she may deserve a mention as well.

- **Provide a brief plot summary.** Your reader may be unacquainted with the play, and will certainly want a general sense of what it is about. Out of consideration to the reader, however, it is best not to reveal any plot surprises, unless the play is a classic one with an ending likely to be common knowledge.

- **If the play is unfamiliar, summarize its theme.** This exercise will not only help your reader understand your review but probably sharpen your analysis.

- **For a well-known play, evaluate the director's approach to familiar material.** Is the production exactly what you'd expect, or are there any fresh and apparently original innovations? If a production is unusual, does it achieve newness by violating the play? The director of one college production of *Othello* emphasized the play's being partly set in Venice by staging it in the campus swimming pool, with actors floating on barges and a homemade gondola—a fresh, but not entirely successful, innovation.

- **Comment on the director's work.** Can you discern the director's approach to the play? Do the actors hurry their lines or speak too slowly? Do they speak and gesture naturally, or in an awkward, stylized manner? Are these touches effective or distracting?

- **Pay attention to costumes, sets, and lighting.** Though such matters may seem small, they have an effect on the play's overall tone.

- **Finally, to prepare yourself, read a few professional play reviews.** Reviews appear regularly in magazines such as the *New Yorker*, *Time*, the *New Criterion*, and *American Theatre*, and also on the entertainment pages of most metropolitan newspapers. Newspaper reviews can often be accessed online; for example, *New York Times* reviews may be found at <http://theater.nytimes.com>.

Here is a good, concise review of an amateur production of *Trifles*, as it might be written for a college newspaper or as a course assignment.

Trifles Scores Mixed Success in Monday Players' Production

Opening paragraph gives information on play and production

Women have come a long way since 1916. At least, that impression was conveyed yesterday when the Monday Players presented Susan Glaspell's classic one-act play *Trifles* in Alpaugh Theater.

At first, in Glaspell's taut story of two subjugated farm women who figure out why a fellow farm woman strangled her husband, actors Lloyd Fox and Cal Federicci get to strut around. As a small-town sheriff and a county attorney, they lord it over the womenfolk, making sexist remarks about women in general. Fox and Federicci obviously enjoy themselves as the pompous types that Glaspell means them to be.

But of course it is the women with their keen eyes for small details who prove the superior detectives. In the demanding roles of the two Nebraska Miss Marples, Kathy Betts and Ruth Fine cope as best they can with what is asked of them. Fine is especially convincing. As Mrs. Hale, a

Evaluates performances

friend of the wife accused of the murder, she projects a growing sense of independence. Visibly smarting under the verbal lashes of the menfolk, she seems to straighten her spine inch by inch as the play goes on.

Unluckily for Betts, director Alvin Klein seems determined to view Mrs. Peters as a comedian. Though Glaspell's stage directions call the

Analyzes direction

woman "nervous," I doubt she is supposed to be quite so fidgety as Betts makes her. Betts vibrates like a tuning fork every time a new clue turns up, and when she is obliged to smell a dead canary bird (another clue), you would think she was whiffing a dead hippopotamus. Mrs. Peters, whose sad past includes a lost baby and a kitten some maniac chopped up with a hatchet, is no figure of fun to my mind. Played for laughs, her character fails to grow visibly on stage, as Fine makes Mrs. Hale grow.

Further elaborates on stage direction

Klein, be it said in his favor, makes the quiet action proceed at a brisk pace. Feminists in the audience must have been a little embarrassed, though, by his having Betts and Fine deliver every speech defending women in an extra-loud voice. After all, Glaspell makes her points clearly enough just by showing us what she shows. Not everything is overstated, however. As a farmer who found the murder victim, Ron Valdez acts his part with quiet authority.

Overall evaluation

Despite flaws in its direction, this powerful play still spellbinds an audience. Anna Winterbright's set, seen last week as a background for *Dracula* and just slightly touched up, provides appropriate gloom.

HOW TO QUOTE A PLAY

The guidelines for quoting prose or poetry generally apply to quoting from a play. Plays present certain challenges of their own, however. When you quote an extended section of a play or dialogue that involves more than one character, use the following MLA format to set the passage off from the body of your paper:

- Indent one inch.
- Type the character's name in all capitals, followed by a period.
- If a speech runs for more than a single line, indent any additional lines one-quarter inch.
- Provide a citation reference:

  If the play is written in prose, provide a page number.

  If the play is written in verse, provide the act, scene, and line numbers.

Here is an example of that format:

> The men never find a motive for the murder because, ironically, they
> consider all the real clues "trifles" that don't warrant their attention:
>
> > SHERIFF. Well, can you beat the women! Held for murder and
> > worryin' about her preserves.
> > COUNTY ATTORNEY. I guess before we're through she may have
> > something more serious than preserves to worry about.
> > HALE. Well, women are used to worrying over trifles. (897–98)

When you are quoting a verse play, be careful to respect the line breaks. For citation references, you should provide the act, scene, and line numbers, so that your reader will be able to find the quotation in any edition of the play. A quotation from a verse play should look like this:

> Even before her death, Othello will not confront Desdemona with his
> specific suspicions:
>
> > OTHELLO. Think on thy sins.
> > DESDEMONA.   They are loves I bear to you.
> > OTHELLO. Ay, and for that thou diest.
> > DESDEMONA. That death's unnatural that kills for loving.
> > Alas, why gnaw you so your nether lip?
> > Some bloody passion shakes your very frame.
> > These are portents; but yet I hope, I hope,
> > They do not point on me. (5.2.42–48)

TOPICS FOR WRITING BRIEF PAPERS (250–500 WORDS)

1. Analyze a key character from any play in this book. Some choices might be Tom Wingfield in *The Glass Menagerie*, Torvald Helmer in *A Doll's House*, or Mama in *Fences*. What motivates that character? Point to specific moments in the play to make your case.

2. When the curtain comes down on the conclusion of some plays, the audience is left to decide exactly what finally happened. In a short informal essay, state your interpretation of the conclusion of *El Santo Americano* or *The Glass Menagerie*. Don't just give a plot summary; tell what you think the conclusion means.

3. Sum up the main suggestions you find in one of these meaningful objects (or actions): the handkerchief in *Othello*; the Christmas tree in *A Doll's House* (or Nora's doing a wild tarantella); Laura's collection of figurines in *The Glass Menagerie*.

4. Here is an exercise in being terse. Write a card report on a short, one-scene play (other than *Trifles*), and confine your remarks to both sides of one 5- × 8-inch card. (For further instructions see page 1406.) Possible subjects include *The Sound of a Voice, Beauty, Sure Thing,* and *Andre's Mother*.

5. Attend a play and write a review. In an assignment this brief, you will need to concentrate your remarks on either the performance or the script itself. Be sure to back up your opinions with specific observations.

TOPICS FOR WRITING MORE EXTENDED PAPERS (600–1,000 WORDS)

1. From a play you have enjoyed, choose a passage that strikes you as difficult, worth reading closely. Try to pick a passage not longer than about 20 lines. Explicate it—give it a close, sentence-by-sentence reading—and explain how this small part of the play relates to the whole. For instance, any of the following passages might be considered memorable (and essential to their plays):

    • Othello's soliloquy beginning "It is the cause, it is the cause, my soul" (*Othello*, 5.2.1–22).
    • Oedipus to Teiresias, speech beginning "Wealth, power, craft of statemanship!" (*Oedipus the King*, 1.163–86).
    • Nora to Mrs. Linde, speech beginning "Yes, someday, maybe, in many years when I am not as pretty as I am now . . ." (*A Doll's House*, page 1129).

2. Analyze the complexities and contradictions to be found in a well-rounded character from a play of your choice. Some good subjects might be Othello, Nora Helmer (in *A Doll's House*), or Tom Wingfield (in *The Glass Menagerie*).

3. Take just a single line or sentence from a play, one that stands out for some reason as greatly important. Perhaps it states a theme, reveals a character, or serves as a crisis (or turning point). Write an essay demonstrating its importance—how it functions, why it is necessary. Two possible lines are:

    • Iago to Roderigo: "I am not what I am" (*Othello*, 1.1.67).
    • Amanda to Tom: "You live in a dream; you manufacture illusions!" (*The Glass Menagerie*, Scene vii).

4. Write an analysis essay in which you single out an element of a play for examination—character, plot, setting, theme, dramatic irony, tone, language, symbolism, conventions, or any other element. Try to relate this element to the play as a whole. Sample topics: "The Function of Teiresias in *Oedipus the King*," "Imagery of Poison in *Othello*," "Williams's Use of Magic-Lantern Slides in *The Glass Menagerie*," "The Theme of Success in *Fences*."

5. How would you stage an updated production of a play by Shakespeare, Sophocles, or Ibsen, transplanting it to our time? Choose a play, and describe the challenges and difficulties of this endeavor. How would you overcome them—or, if they cannot be overcome, why not?

6. Louis Phillips, of the School of Visual Arts in New York City, developed the following assignment. Read this statement from Woody Allen:

> Sports to me is like music. It's completely satisfying. There were times I would sit at a game with the old Knicks and think to myself in the fourth quarter, this is everything the theatre should be and isn't. There's an outcome that's unpredictable. The audience is not ahead of the dramatists. The drama is ahead of the audience.

What does Allen mean by the notion of the audience being ahead of (or behind) the dramatist? Apply that to a play you have read. If Woody Allen feels that sports are more satisfying than drama, why does he continue to make movies?

TOPICS FOR WRITING LONG PAPERS (1,500 WORDS OR MORE)

1. Choose a play you admire from this book, and read a second play by the same author. Compare and contrast the two plays with attention to a single element—a theme they have in common, or a particular kind of imagery, for example.

2. Read *Othello* and view a movie version of the play. You might choose Oliver Parker's 1995 take on the play with Laurence Fishburne and Kenneth Branagh, or even O (2001), an updated version that has a prep school as its setting and a basketball star as its protagonist. Review the movie. What does it manage to convey of the original? What gets lost in the translation?

3. Choosing any of the works in "Plays for Further Reading" or taking some other play your instructor suggests, report any difficulties you encountered in reading and responding to it. Explicate any troublesome passages for the benefit of other readers.

4. Attend a play and write an in-depth review, taking into account many elements of the drama: acting, direction, staging, costumes, lighting, and—if the work is relatively new and not a classic—the play itself.

5. Have you ever taken part in a dramatic production, either as an actor or a member of the crew? What did the experience teach you about the nature of drama and about what makes a play effective?

6. Write a one-act play of your own, featuring a minor character from one of the plays you have read for class. Think about what motivates that character, and let the play's central conflict grow from his or her preoccupations.

42

WRITING A RESEARCH PAPER

A writer is a person for whom writing is more difficult than it is for other people.

—THOMAS MANN

Oh no! You have been assigned a research paper, and every time you even think about starting it, your spirits sink and your blood pressure rises. You really liked the story by Ernest Hemingway, but when you entered his name in a search of the college library catalogue it listed 135 books about him. Time to switch authors, you decide. How about Emily Dickinson? She was fun to talk about in class, but when you Google her name, the computer states that there are over 8.4 million entries. What should you do? The paper is due in two weeks, not twenty years. Why would an otherwise very nice instructor put you through this mental trauma?

Why is it worthwhile to write a research paper? (Apart from the fact that you want a passing grade in the class, that is.) While you can learn much by exploring your own responses to a literary work, there is no substitute for entering into a conversation with others who have studied and thought about your topic. Literary criticism is that conversation. Your reading will expose you to the ideas of others who can shed light on a story, poem, or play. It will introduce you to the wide range of informed opinions that exist about literature, as about almost any subject. Sometimes, too, your research will uncover information about an author's life that leads you to new insights into a literary work. Undertaking a research paper gives you a chance to test your ideas against those of others, and in doing so to clarify your own opinions.

BROWSE THE RESEARCH

The most daunting aspect of the research paper may well be the mountains of information available on almost any literary subject. It can be hard to know where to begin. Sifting through books and articles is part of the research process. Unfortunately, the first material you uncover in the library or on the Internet is rarely the evidence you need to develop or support your thesis. Keep looking until you uncover helpful sources.

Another common pitfall in the process is the creeping feeling that your idea has already been examined a dozen times over. But take heart: like Odysseus, tie yourself to the mast so that when you hear the siren voices of published professors, you can listen without abandoning your own point of view. Your idea may have been treated, but not yet by you. Your particular take on a topic is bound to be different from someone else's. After all, thousands of books have been written on Shakespeare's plays, but people still find new things to say about them.

CHOOSE A TOPIC

- **Find a topic that interests you.** A crucial first step in writing a research paper is coming up with a topic that interests you. Start with a topic that bores you, and the process will be a chore and yield dull results. But if you come up with an intriguing research question, seeking the answer will be a more engaging process. The paper that results will inevitably be stronger and more interesting.

- **Find a way to get started.** Browsing through books of literary criticism in the library, or glancing at online journal articles, can help to spark an idea or two. Prewriting techniques such as brainstorming, freewriting, listing, and clustering can also help you to generate ideas on a specific work of literature. If you take notes and jot down ideas as they occur to you, when you start the formal writing process you will discover you have already begun.

- **Keep your purpose and audience in mind.** Refer often to the assignment, and approach your essay accordingly. Think of your audience as well. Is it your professor, your classmates, or some hypothetical reader? As you plan your essay, keep your audience's expectations and needs in mind.

- **Develop a general thesis that you hope to support with research, and look for material that will help you demonstrate its plausibility.** Remember: the ideal research paper is based on your own observations and interpretations of a literary text.

BEGIN YOUR RESEARCH

Print Resources

Writing a research paper on literature calls for two kinds of sources: primary sources, or the literary works that are your subject, and secondary sources, or the books, articles, and web resources that discuss your primary sources. When you are hunting down secondary sources, the best place to begin is your campus library. Plan to spend some time thumbing through scholarly books and journals, looking for passages that you find particularly interesting or that pertain to your topic. Begin your search with the online catalog to get a sense of where you might find the books and journals you need.

To choose from the many books available on your library's shelves and through interlibrary loan, you might turn to book reviews for a sense of which volumes would best suit your purpose. *Book Review Digest* contains the full texts of many book reviews and excerpts of others. The *Digest* may be found in printed form in the reference section of your campus library, which may also provide access to the online version. Whether you are using the online or print version, you will need the author's name, title, and date of first publication of any book for which you hope to find a review.

Scholarly journals are an excellent resource for articles on your topic. Indexes to magazines and journals may be found in your library's reference section. You may also find an index to print periodicals on your library's website.

Online Databases

Most college libraries subscribe to specialized online or CD-ROM database services covering all academic subjects—treasure troves of reliable sources. If you find yourself unsure how to use your library's database system, ask the reference librarian to help you get started. The following databases are particularly useful for literary research:

- The *MLA International Bibliography*, the Modern Language Association's database, is an excellent way to search for books and full-text articles on literary topics.

- *JSTOR*, a not-for-profit organization, indexes articles or abstracts from an archive of journals in over fifty disciplines.

- *Literature Resource Center* (Thomson Gale) provides biographies, bibliographies, and critical analyses of more than 120,000 authors and their work. This information is culled from journal articles and reference works.

- *Literature Online (LION)* provides a vast searchable database of critical articles and reference works as well as full texts of more than 300,000 works of prose, poetry, and drama.

- *Project Muse*, a collaboration between publishers and libraries, offers access to more than 400 journals in the humanities, arts, and social sciences.

- *EBSCO*, a multisubject resource, covers literature and the humanities, as well as the social sciences, medical sciences, linguistics, and other fields.

Your library may provide access to some or all of these databases, or it may offer other useful ones. Many college library home pages provide students with access to subscription databases, which means that if you really can't bear to leave your comfy desk at home, you can still pay a virtual visit.

Reliable Web Sources

While online databases are the most reliable source for high-quality information, you may find yourself looking to supplement journal articles with information and quotations from the Internet. If so, proceed with care. While the journal articles in online databases have been reviewed for quality by specialists and librarians, websites may be written and published by anybody for any purpose, with no oversight. Even the online reference site *Wikipedia*, for example, is an amalgamation of voluntary contributors, and is rife with small factual errors and contributor biases. Carefully analyze any material you gather online, or you may find yourself tangled in the spidery threads of a dubious website. To garner the best sources possible, take these steps:

- **Learn to use Internet search engines effectively.** If you enter general terms such as the author's name and story title into an Internet search engine, you may well find yourself bombarded with thousands of hits. For a more efficient approach to navigating the Internet, try using an "advanced" search option, entering keywords to get results that contain those words (LITERARY CRITICISM A DOLL'S HOUSE or SYMBOLISM THE LOTTERY).

- **Begin your search at a reliable website.** Helpful as an advanced search may be, it won't separate valuable sources from useless ones. To weed out sloppy and inaccurate sites, begin your search with one of the following excellent guides through cyberspace:

- *Library of Congress.* Fortunately, you don't have to trek to Washington to visit this venerable institution's annotated collection of websites in the Humanities and Social Sciences Division. For your purpose—writing a literary research paper—access the Subject Index <http://www.loc.gov/rr/main/alcove9>, click on "Literatures in English" and then on "Literary Criticism." This will take you to a list of metapages and websites with collections of reliable critical and biographical materials on authors and their works. (A metapage provides links to other websites.)
- *Internet Public Library.* Created and maintained by the University of Michigan School of Information and Library Studies, this site <http://www.ipl.org> lets you search for literary criticism by author, work, country of origin, or literary period.
- *Library Spot.* Visit <http://www.libraryspot.com> for a portal to over 5,000 libraries around the world, and to periodicals, online texts, reference works, and links to metapages and websites on any topic including literary criticism. This carefully maintained site is published by StartSpot Mediaworks, Inc., in the Northwestern University/Evanston Research Park in Evanston, Illinois.
- *Voice of the Shuttle.* Research links in over 25 categories in the humanities and social sciences, including online texts, libraries, academic websites, and metapages may be found at this site. Located at <http://vos.ucsb.edu> it was developed and is maintained by Dr. Alan Liu in the English Department of the University of California, Santa Barbara.

CHECKLIST: Finding Reliable Sources

☐ Begin at your campus library. Ask the reference librarian for advice.

☐ Check the library catalog for books and journals on your topic.

☐ Look into the online databases subscribed to by your library.

☐ Locate reputable websites by starting at a reputable website designed for that purpose.

Visual Images

The web is an excellent source of visual images. If a picture, chart, or graph will enhance your argument, you may find the perfect one via an image search on Google, PicSearch, or other search engines. The Library of Congress offers a wealth of images documenting American political, social, and cultural history—including portraits, letters, and original manuscripts—at <http://memory.loc.gov>. Remember, though, that not all images are available for use by the general public. Check for a copyright notice to see if its originator allows that image to be reproduced. If so, you may include the photograph, provided you credit your source as you would if you were quoting text.

One note on images: use them carefully. Choose visuals that provide supporting evidence for the point you are trying to make or that enhance your reader's understanding of the work. Label your images with captions. Your goal should be to make your argument more convincing. In the example below, a reproduction of Brueghel's painting helps to advance the author's argument and provide insight into Auden's poem.

Fig. 1. *Landscape with the Fall of Icarus* by Pieter Brueghel the Elder (c. 1558, Musées Royaux des Beaux-Arts de Belgique, Brussels)

W. H. Auden's poem "Musée des Beaux Arts" refers to a specific painting to prove its point that the most honest depictions of death take into account the way life simply goes on even after the most tragic of events. In line 14, Auden turns specifically to Pieter Brueghel the Elder's masterwork *The Fall of Icarus* (see Fig. 1), pointing to the painting's understated depiction of tragedy. In this painting, the death of Icarus does not take place on center stage. A plowman and his horse take up the painting's foreground, while the leg of Icarus falling into the sea takes up a tiny portion of the painting's lower-right corner. A viewer who fails to take the painting's title into account might not even notice Icarus at all.

CHECKLIST: Using Visual Images

- ☐ Use images as evidence to support your argument.
- ☐ Use images to enhance communication and understanding.
- ☐ Refer to the images in your text.
- ☐ Label image as "Fig. 1" and provide title or caption.
- ☐ Check copyrights.
- ☐ Include source in works-cited list.

EVALUATE YOUR SOURCES

Print Resources

It's an old saying, but a useful one: don't believe everything you read. The fact that a book or an article is printed and published doesn't necessarily mean it is accurate or unbiased. Be discriminating about printed resources.

Begin your search in a place that has taken some of the work out of quality control—your school library. Books and articles you find there are regarded by librarians as having some obvious merit. If your search takes you beyond the library, though, you will need to be discerning when choosing print resources. As you weigh the value of printed matter, take the following into account:

- **Look closely at information provided about the author.** Is he or she known for expertise in the field? What are the author's academic or association credentials? Is there any reason to believe that the author is biased in any way? For example, a biography of an author written by that author's son or daughter might not be as unbiased as one written by a scholar with no personal connections.

- **Determine the publisher's reliability.** Books or articles published by an advocacy group might be expected to take a particular—possibly biased—slant on an issue. Be aware also that some books are published by vanity presses, companies that are paid by an author to publish his or her books. As a result, vanity press-published books generally aren't subject to the same rigorous quality control as those put out by more reputable publishing houses.

- **Always check for a publication date.** If a document lists an edition number, check to see whether you are using the latest edition of the material.

- **For periodicals, decide whether a publication is an academic journal or a popular magazine.** What type of reputation does it have? Obviously, you do not want to use a magazine that periodically reports on Elvis sightings and alien births. And even articles on writers in magazines such as *Time* and *People* are likely to be too brief and superficial for purposes of serious research. Instead, choose scholarly journals designed to enhance the study of literature.

Web Resources

As handy and informative as the Internet is, it sometimes serves up some pretty iffy information. A website, after all, can be created by anyone with a computer and access to the Internet—no matter how poorly qualified that person might be. Be discerning when it comes to the Internet. Here are tips on choosing your sources wisely:

- **Check a site's author or sponsorship.** Is the site's creator or sponsor known to you or reputable by association? Look closely at information provided about the author. Is he or she known for expertise in the field? What are the author's academic or association credentials? Is the web entry unsigned and anonymous? If the website is sponsored by an organization, is it a reputable one? While government or university-sponsored sites may be considered reliable, think carefully about possible biases in sites sponsored by advocacy or special interest groups.

  A word of warning: individual student pages posted on university sites have not necessarily been reviewed by that university and are not reliable sources of information. Also, postings on the popular encyclopedia website *Wikipedia* are not subject to a scholarly review process and have been found to contain inaccuracies. It's safer to use a published encyclopedia.

■ **Look at the site's date of publication.** When was it last updated? In some cases you may want to base your essay on the most current information or theories, so you will want to steer toward the most recently published material.

■ **Is this an online version of a print publication?** If so, what type of reputation does it have?

■ **Make your own assessment of the site.** Does the content seem consistent with demonstrated scholarship? Does it appear balanced in its point of view?

■ **Consult experts.** Cornell University has two good documents with guidance for analyzing sources, posted at <http://www.olinuris.librarycornell.edu/content/ skill-guides>. The titles are "Critically Analyzing Information Sources" and "Distinguishing Scholarly from Non-Scholarly Periodicals." Your school's research librarian or library website may have similar resources.

CHECKLIST: Evaluating Your Sources

Print

☐ Who wrote it? What are the author's credentials?

☐ Is he or she an expert in the field?

☐ Does he or she appear to be unbiased toward the subject matter?

☐ Is the publisher reputable? Is it an advocacy group or a vanity press?

☐ When was it published? Do later editions exist? If so, would a later edition be more useful?

Web

☐ Who wrote it? What are the author's credentials?

☐ Is he or she an expert in the field?

☐ Who sponsors the website? Is the sponsor reputable?

☐ When was the website published? When was it last updated?

☐ Is the website an online journal or magazine? Is it scholarly or popular?

☐ Does content seem consistent with demonstrated scholarship?

☐ Can you detect obvious bias?

ORGANIZE YOUR RESEARCH

■ **Get your thoughts down on notecards or the equivalent on your laptop.** Once you have amassed your secondary sources, it will be time to begin reading in earnest. As you do so, be sure to take notes on any passage that pertains to your topic. A convenient way to organize your many thoughts is to write them down on index cards, which are easy to shuffle and rearrange. You'll need 3- × 5-inch cards for brief notes and titles and 5- × 8-inch cards for more in-depth notes. Confine your jottings to one side of the card; notes on the back can easily be overlooked. Write a single fact or opinion on each card. This will make it easier for you to shuffle the deck and re-envision the order in which you deliver information to your reader.

- **Keep careful track of the sources of quotations and paraphrases.** As you take notes, make it unmistakably clear which thoughts and phrases are yours and which derive from others. (Remember, *quotation* means using the exact words of your source and placing the entire passage in quotation marks and citing the author. *Paraphrase* means expressing the ideas of your source in your own words, again citing the author.) Bear in mind the cautionary tale of a well-known historian, Doris Kearns Goodwin. She was charged with plagiarizing sections of two of her famous books when her words were found to be jarringly similar to those published in other books. Because she had not clearly indicated on her notecards which ideas and passages were hers and which came from other sources, Goodwin was forced to admit to plagiarism. Her enormous reputation suffered from these charges, but you can learn from her mistakes and save your own reputation—and your grades.

- **Keep track of the sources of ideas and concepts.** When an idea is inspired by or directly taken from someone else's writing, be sure to jot down the source on that same card or in your computer file. Your deck of cards or computer list will function as a working bibliography, which later will help you put together a works-cited list. To save yourself work, keep a separate list of the sources you're using. Then, as you make the note, you need write only the material's author or title and page reference on the card in order to identify your source. It's also useful to classify the note in a way that will help you to organize your material, making it easy, for example, to separate cards that deal with a story's theme from cards that deal with point of view or symbolism.

- **Make notes of your own thoughts and reactions to your research.** When a critical article sparks your own original idea, be sure to capture that thought in your notes and mark it as your own. As you plan your paper, these notes may form the outline for your arguments.

Some useful note cards taken on a critical essay on page 1452 about Joyce Carol Oates's short story "Where Are You Going, Where Have You Been?" might look something like this:

Direct Quotation from Critic

THEME

Schulz and Rockwood, p. 1453

"There is a terrible irony here, for although the story is full of fairy tales, Connie, its protagonist, is not. Connie represents an entire generation of young people who have grown up—or tried to—without the help of those bedtime stories which not only entertain the child, but also enable him vicariously to experience and work through problems which he will encounter in adolescence."

Paraphrase of Critic

THEME

Schulz and Rockwood, p. 1453

Ironic that while story steeped in fairy tales, Connie is not. Connie stands for her whole generation that grew up without fairy tales.

Missed benefits of fairy tales for child: working through life's problems.

Critic's Idea

THEME

Schulz and Rockwood, p. 1453

Many fairy tales underlie "Where Are You Going ?" e.g.
Snow White
Cinderella
Sleeping Beauty
Little Red Riding Hood

Your Own Idea

THEME or CHARACTER?

My Idea

Is Arnold the big bad wolf?
Can I find clues in story?

▪ **Make photocopies or printouts to simplify the process and ensure accuracy.** Scholars once had to spend long hours copying out prose passages by hand. Luckily, for a small investment you can simply photocopy your sources to ensure accuracy in quoting and citing your sources. In fact, some instructors will require you to hand in photocopies of your original sources with the final paper, along with printouts of articles downloaded from an Internet database. Even if this is not the case, photocopying your sources and holding onto your printouts can help you to reproduce quotations accurately in your essay—and accuracy is crucial.

REFINE YOUR THESIS

As you read secondary sources and take notes, you should begin to refine your essay's thesis. This, in turn, will help you to winnow your stacks of source material down to the secondary sources that will best help you to make your point. Even your revised thesis doesn't have to be etched in stone. It should simply give you a sense of direction as you start to plan your essay.

- **Be willing to fine-tune your thesis or even rework it completely.** Your research may reveal that you have misinterpreted an idea, or that there is not much evidence to support your thesis. Of course, it is annoying to find that you may be wrong about something, but don't let these discoveries put you off. Use your research to refine your thoughts.

- **Let your initial idea be the jumping-off point to other, better ideas.** Say, for example, that you plan to write about the peculiar physical description of Arnold Friend in Joyce Carol Oates's story "Where Are You Going, Where Have You Been?" You may have noticed he has trouble standing in his shoes, and you want to explore that odd detail. If you research this character, you may find Arnold Friend likened to the devil (whose cloven hooves might give him similar problems with standard-issue cowboy boots), or to the wolf in "Little Red Riding Hood" (also a character who would have a hard time managing human clothes). Use your research to sharpen your focus. Can you think of other stories that deal with potentially supernatural, possibly even evil, characters? What about Nathaniel Hawthorne's "Young Goodman Brown"? Or Flannery O'Connor's "A Good Man Is Hard to Find"? How might you compare Arnold Friend with Hawthorne's devil or O'Connor's Misfit?

ORGANIZE YOUR PAPER

With your thesis in mind and your notes spread before you, draw up an outline—a rough map of how best to argue your thesis and present your material. Determine what main points you need to make, and look for quotations that support those points. Even if you generally prefer to navigate the paper-writing process without a map, you will find that an outline makes the research-paper writing process considerably smoother. When organizing information from many different sources, it pays to plan ahead.

WRITE AND REVISE

As with any other kind of essay, a research paper rarely, if ever, reaches its full potential in a single draft. Leave yourself time to rewrite. The knowledge that your first draft won't be your final one can free you up to take chances and to jot down your ideas as quickly as they occur to you. If your phrasing is less than elegant, it hardly matters in a first draft; the object is to work out your ideas on paper. Rough out the paper, working as quickly as you can. Later you can rearrange paragraphs and smooth out any rough patches.

Once you've got the first draft down, it's an excellent idea to run it by a friend, a writing center tutor, or even your instructor. A writer can't know how clear or persuasive his or her argument is without a trusted reader to give feedback.

When you do revise, be open to making both large and small changes. Sometimes revising means adding needed paragraphs, or even refining the thesis a bit further. Be willing to start from scratch if you need to, but even as you take the whole picture into account, remember that details are important too. Before you hand in that final draft, be sure to proofread for small errors that could detract from the finished product.

MAINTAIN ACADEMIC INTEGRITY

Papers for Sale Are Papers that "F"ail

Do not be seduced by the apparent ease of cheating by computer. Your Internet searches may turn up several sites that offer term papers to download (just as you can find pornography, political propaganda, and questionable get-rich-quick schemes!). Most of these sites charge money for what they offer, but a few do not, happy to strike a blow against the "oppressive" insistence of English teachers that students learn to think and write.

Plagiarized term papers are an old game: the fraternity file and the "research assistance" service have been around far longer than the computer. It may seem easy enough to download a paper, put your name at the head of it, and turn it in for an easy grade. As any writing instructor can tell you, though, such papers usually stick out like a sore thumb. The style will be wrong, the work will not be consistent with other work by the same student in any number of ways, and the teacher will sometimes even have seen the same phony paper before. The ease with which electronic texts are reproduced makes this last possibility increasingly likely.

The odds of being caught and facing the unpleasant consequences are reasonably high. It is far better to take the grade you have earned for your own effort, no matter how mediocre, than to try to pass off someone else's work as your own. Even if, somehow, your instructor does not recognize your submission as a plagiarized paper, you have diminished your character through dishonesty and lost an opportunity to learn something on your own.

A Warning Against Internet Plagiarism

Plagiarism detection services are a professor's newest ally in the battle against academic dishonesty. Questionable research papers can be sent to these services (such as Turnitin.com and EVE2), which perform complex searches of the Internet and of a growing database of purchased term papers. The research paper will be returned to the professor with plagiarized sections annotated and the sources documented. The end result will certainly be a failing grade on the essay, possibly a failing grade for the course, and, depending on the policies of your university, the very real possibility of expulsion.

ACKNOWLEDGE ALL SOURCES

The brand of straight-out dishonesty described above is one type of plagiarism. There is, however, another, subtler kind: when students incorporate somebody else's words *or* ideas into their papers without giving proper credit. To avoid this second—sometimes quite accidental—variety of plagiarism, familiarize yourself with the conventions for acknowledging sources. First and foremost, remember to give credit to any writer who supplies you with ideas, information, or specific words and phrases.

Using Quotations

■ **Acknowledge your source when you quote a writer's words or phrases.** When you use someone else's words or phrases, you should reproduce his or her exact words in quotation marks, and be sure to properly credit the source.

> Already, Frost has hinted that Nature may be, as Radcliffe Squires
> suggests, "Nothing but an ash-white plain without love or faith or hope,
> where ignorant appetites cross by chance" (87).

■ **If you quote more than four lines, set your quotation off from the body of the paper.** Start a new line; indent one inch and type the quotation, double-spaced. (You do not need to use quotation marks, as the format tells the reader the passage is a quotation.)

> Samuel Maio made an astute observation about the nature of Weldon Kees's
> distinctive tone:
>> Kees has therefore combined a personal subject matter with an
>> impersonal voice—that is, one that is consistent in its tone
>> evenly recording the speaker's thoughts without showing any
>> emotional intensity which might lie behind those thoughts. (136)

Citing Ideas

■ **Acknowledge your source when you mention a critic's ideas.** Even if you are not quoting exact words or phrases, be sure to acknowledge the source of any original ideas or concepts you have used.

> Another explanation is suggested by Daniel Hoffman, a critic who has
> discussed the story: the killer hears the sound of his *own* heart (227).

■ **Acknowledge your source when you paraphrase a writer's words.** To paraphrase a critic, you should do more than just rearrange his or her words: you should translate them into your own original sentences—again, always being sure to credit the original source. As an example, suppose you wish to refer to an insight of Randall Jarrell, who commented as follows on the images of spider, flower, and moth in Robert Frost's poem "Design":

RANDALL JARRELL'S ORIGINAL TEXT
Notice how the *heal-all*, because of its name, is the one flower in all the world picked to be the altar for this Devil's Mass; notice how *holding up* the moth brings something ritual and hieratic, a ghostly, ghastly formality, to this priest and its sacrificial victim.[1]

---

[1]*Poetry and the Age* (New York: Knopf, 1953) 42.

It would be too close to the original to write, without quotation marks, these sentences:

> **PLAGIARIZED REWORDING**
>
> Frost picks the *heal-all* as the one flower in all the world to be the altar for this Devil's Mass. There is a ghostly, ghastly formality to the spider *holding up* the moth, like a priest holding a sacrificial victim.

This rewording, although not exactly in Jarrell's language, manages to steal his memorable phrases without giving him credit. Nor is it sufficient just to include Jarrell's essay in the works-cited list at the end of your paper. If you do, you are still a crook; you merely point to the scene of the crime. Instead, think through Jarrell's words to the point he is making, so that it can be restated in your own original way. If you want to keep any of his striking phrases (and why not?), put them exactly as he wrote them in quotation marks:

> **APPROPRIATE PARAPHRASE, ACKNOWLEDGES SOURCE**
>
> As Randall Jarrell points out, Frost portrays the spider as a kind of priest in a Mass, or Black Mass, elevating the moth like an object for sacrifice, with "a ghostly, ghastly formality" (42).

Note also that this improved passage gives Jarrell the credit not just for his words but for his insight into the poem. Both the idea and the words in which it was originally expressed are the properties of their originator. Finally, notice the page reference that follows the quotation (this system of documenting your sources is detailed in the next section).

DOCUMENT SOURCES USING MLA STYLE

You must document everything you take from a source. When you quote from other writers, when you borrow their information, when you summarize or paraphrase their ideas, make sure you give them proper credit. Identify the writer by name and cite the book, magazine, newspaper, pamphlet, website, or other source you have used.

The conventions that govern the proper way to document sources are available in the *MLA Handbook for Writers of Research Papers*, 7th ed. (New York: MLA, 2009). The following brief list of pointers is not meant to take the place of the *MLA Handbook* itself, but give you a basic sense of the rules for documentation.

List of Sources

Keep a working list of your research sources—all the references from which you might quote, summarize, paraphrase, or take information. When your paper is in finished form, it will end with a neat copy of the works you actually used (once called a "Bibliography," now titled "Works Cited").

Parenthetical References

In the body of your paper, every time you refer to a source, you need to provide information to help a reader locate it in your works-cited list. You can usually give just the author's name and a page citation in parentheses. For example, if you are writing a paper on Weldon Kees's sonnet "For My Daughter" and want to include an observation you found on page 136 of Samuel Maio's book *Creating Another Self*, write:

> One critic has observed that the distinctive tone of "For My Daughter"
> depends on Kees's combination of "personal subject matter with an
> impersonal voice" (Maio 136).

If you mention the author's name in your sentence, you need give only the page number in your reference:

> As Samuel Maio has observed, Kees creates a distinctive tone in this sonnet
> by combining a "personal subject with an impersonal voice" (136).

If you have two books or magazine articles by Samuel Maio in your works-cited list, how will the reader tell them apart? In your text, refer to the title of each book or article by condensing it into a word or two. Condensed book titles are italicized, and condensed article titles are still placed within quotation marks.

> One critic has observed that the distinctive tone of "For My Daughter"
> depends on Kees's combination of "personal subject matter with an
> impersonal voice" (Maio, *Creating* 136).

Works-Cited List

Provide a full citation for each source on your works-cited page. At the end of your paper, in your list of works cited, your reader will find a full description of your source—for the above examples, a critical book:

> Maio, Samuel. *Creating Another Self: Voices in Modern American Personal*
> *Poetry*. 2nd ed. Kirksville: Thomas Jefferson UP, 2005. Print.

Put your works-cited list in proper form. The *MLA Handbook* provides detailed instructions for citing a myriad of different types of sources, from books to online databases. Here is a partial list of the *Handbook*'s recommendations for presenting your works-cited list.

1. Start a new page for the works-cited list, and continue the page numbering from the body of your paper.
2. Center the title, "Works Cited," one inch from the top of the page.
3. Double-space between all lines (including after title and between entries).
4. Type each entry beginning at the left-hand margin. If an entry runs longer than a single line, indent the following lines one-half inch from the left-hand margin.
5. Alphabetize each entry according to the author's last name.
6. Include three sections in each entry: author, title, publication or access information. (You will, however, give slightly different information for a book, journal article, online source, or other reference.)

Citing Print Sources in MLA Style

For a Book Citation

   a. **Author's full name** as it appears on the title page, last name first, followed by a period.

   b. **Book's full title** (and subtitle, if it has one, separated by a colon) followed by a period. Remember to italicize the title. Also provide edition and volume information, if applicable, followed by a period.

   c. **Publication information:** city of publication followed by a colon; name of publisher followed by a comma; year of publication followed by a period; and publication medium—*Print*—followed by a period.

   (1) **Make your citation of the city of publication brief, but clear.** If the title page lists more than one city, cite only the first. You need not provide the state, province, or country.

   (2) **Shorten the publisher's name.** Eliminate articles (*A, An, The*), business abbreviations (*Co., Corp., Inc., Ltd.*), and descriptive words (*Books, House, Press, Publishers*). The exception is a university press, for which you should use the letters *U* (for University) and *P* (for Press). Use only the first listed *surname* of the publisher.

Publisher's Name	Proper Citation
Harvard University Press	Harvard UP
University of Chicago Press	U of Chicago P
Farrar, Straus and Giroux, Inc.	Farrar
Alfred A. Knopf, Inc.	Knopf

   d. **Optional additional information:** Any additional information that may be helpful for your reader can be provided at the end of a citation. For example, if the book is part of an established series or part of a multivolume set, put the name of the series or the complete work here.

The citation for a book should read:

> Author's Last name, First name. *Book Title*. Ed. or vol. Publication city:
>
> Publisher, Year. Print.

For a Journal or Periodical Article Citation

   a. **Author's name,** last name first, followed by a period.

   b. **Title of article** followed by a period, all within quotation marks.

   c. **Journal publication information:** journal title (italicized); volume number followed by period, issue number; year of publication in parentheses followed by a colon; inclusive page numbers of the entire article followed by a period; and publication medium—*Print*—followed by a period.

or

   Periodical publication information: periodical title (italicized); day month year followed by a colon; page numbers of article (for continuous articles use inclusive pages, such as 31–33; for newspapers use starting page, such as C1+) followed by a period; and publication medium—*Print*—followed by a period.

The citation for a journal article should read:

Author's Last name, First name. "Article Title." *Journal* Volume.Issue
(Year): Pages. Print.

The citation for a periodical article should read:

Author's Last name, First name. "Article Title." *Periodical* Day Month Year:
Pages. Print.

Citing Web Sources in MLA Style

Like print sources, Internet sources should be documented with care. Before you begin your Internet search, be aware of the types of information you will want for your works-cited list. You can then record the information as you go. Keep track of the following information:

- Author's name
- Title of document
- Full information about publication in print form, when available
- Title of scholarly project, database, periodical, or professional or personal site
- Name of editor of project or database
- Date of electronic publication or last update
- Institution or organization sponsoring the website
- Date *you* accessed the source
- Website address or URL

Although many websites provide much of this information at the beginning or ending of an article or at the bottom of the home page, you will find that it is not always available. Also note that as web pages and even sites may sometimes disappear or change, you are well advised to print out important pages for future reference.

For a Web Resource Citation

a. **Author or editor's name,** last name first, followed by a period.
b. **Title of work,** within quotation marks or italicized as appropriate, followed by a period.
c. **Title of website,** in italics, followed by a period.
d. **Sponsor or publisher of website** followed by a comma. If not available, use *N.p.*
e. **Publication date** followed by a period. If data is not available, use *n.d.*
f. **Publication medium—*Web*—**followed by a period.
g. **Date *you* accessed information:** day month year that you viewed the document online.
h. **Optional URL:** if there is some reason your reader may not be able to access your web page with the information provided, you may include the full URL, enclosed in angle brackets< >.

The citation for a web source should read:

> Author's Last name, First name. "Document Title." *Website*. Website
> Sponsor, Publication date. Web. Access Day Month Year.

For a Print Journal Accessed on the Web
  a. **Provide information for standard print citation**
    (1) **Author's name,** last name first, followed by a period.
    (2) **Title of work,** within quotation marks or italicized as appropriate, followed by a period.
    (3) **Print publication information:** journal title in italics; volume and issue number; year; page references, as available. If no pages are available, use *n. pag.*
  b. **Provide web access information**
    (1) **Title of website or database,** italicized.
    (2) **Publication medium—*Web*—**followed by period.
    (3) **Date *you* accessed information:** day month year that you viewed document online.

The citation for a scholarly journal article obtained on the web should read:

> Author's Last name, First name. "Article Title." *Journal* Volume.Issue (Year):
> Pages. Website or Online Database. Web. Access Day Month Year.

Sample List of Works Cited

For a paper on Weldon Kees's "For My Daughter," a student's works-cited list might look as follows:

Works Cited

Grosholz, Emily. "The Poetry of Memory." *Weldon Kees: A Critical
  Introduction*. Ed. Jim Elledge. Metuchen: Scarecrow, 1985. 46–47.
  Print.

Kees, Weldon. *The Collected Poems of Weldon Kees*. Ed. Donald Justice.
  Lincoln: U of Nebraska P, 1975. Print.

Lane, Anthony. "The Disappearing Poet: What Ever Happened to Weldon
  Kees?" *New Yorker*. Condé Nast Digital, 4 July 2005. Web.
  22 Aug. 2011.

Maio, Samuel. *Creating Another Self: Voice in Modern American Personal
  Poetry*. 2nd ed. Kirksville: Thomas Jefferson UP, 2005. Print.

Nelson, Raymond. "The Fitful Life of Weldon Kees." *American Literary
  History* 1.3 (1989): 816–52. Print.

Reidel, James. *Vanished Act: The Life and Art of Weldon Kees*. Lincoln: U of
Nebraska P, 2003. Print.

---, ed. "Weldon Kees." *Nebraska Center for Writers*, Creighton University
n.d. Web. 26 Aug. 2011.

Ross, William T. *Weldon Kees*. Boston: Twayne, 1985. Print. Twayne's US
Authors Ser. 484.

"Weldon Kees." *Poetry Out Loud*. National Endowment for the Arts and the
Poetry Foundation, n.d. Web. 20 Sept. 2011.

See the Reference Guide for MLA Citations at the end of this chapter for additional examples of the types of citations that you are likely to need for your papers, or check the seventh edition of the *MLA Handbook*.

As you put together your works-cited list, keep in mind that the little things—page numbers, quotation marks—count. Documentation may seem tedious, but it has an important purpose: it's for the reader of your paper who wants to pursue a topic you have researched. Luckily, you don't have to know the rules by heart. You can refer as necessary to the *MLA Handbook* or to the examples in this book.

ENDNOTES AND FOOTNOTES

Citations and quotations in the text of your essay should be brief and snappy, lest they bog down your prose. You may, however, wish to provide your reader with passages of less important (yet possibly valuable) information, or make qualifying statements ("On the other hand, not every expert agrees. John Binks finds poets are often a little magazine's only cash customers, while Molly MacGuire maintains that . . ."). To insert such information without awkwardly interrupting your paper, put it into an **endnote** (placed at the end of a paper) or a **footnote** (placed at the bottom of the page). Footnotes and endnotes are now used mainly for such asides, but they are also a time-honored way to document sources.

Adding Footnotes

When an aside seems appropriate, insert a number in the text of your essay to send your reader to the corresponding note. Use the "Insert Footnote" option in your word processing program, or create a superscript number from the font menu. This will lift the number slightly above the level of your prose, so that it stands out.

> as many observers have claimed.[2]

Once you insert the number of your footnote into the text, your word processing program will cleverly take care of the formatting and placement of the footnote, automatically sending it to the bottom of the page.

> 2. On the other hand, not every expert agrees. John Binks, to name
> only one such observer, finds that poets are often a little magazine's only
> cash customers . . .

SAMPLE STUDENT RESEARCH PAPER—PAGE 300

Professor Michael Cass of Mercer University asked his class to select the fiction writer on their reading list whose work had seemed most impressive and write a research paper defending that author's claim to literary greatness. See page 300 to read the research essay Stephanie Crowe wrote to fulfill the assignment.

CONCLUDING THOUGHTS

A well-crafted research essay is a wondrous thing—as delightful, in its own way, as a well-crafted poem or short story or play. Good essays prompt thought and add to knowledge. Writing a research paper sharpens your own mind and exposes you to the honed insights of other thinkers. Think of anything you write as a piece that could be published for the benefit of other people interested in your topic. After all, such a goal is not as far-fetched as it seems: this textbook, for example, features a number of papers written by students. Why shouldn't yours number among them? Aim high.

REFERENCE GUIDE FOR MLA CITATIONS

Here are examples of the types of citations you are likely to need for most student papers. The formats follow current MLA style for works-cited lists.

PRINT PUBLICATIONS

Books

No Author Listed

The Chicago Manual of Style. 16th ed. Chicago: U of Chicago P, 2010. Print.

One Author

Middlebrook, Diane Wood. *Anne Sexton: A Biography.* Boston: Houghton, 1991. Print.

Two or Three Authors

Jarman, Mark, and Robert McDowell. *The Reaper: Essays.* Brownsville: Story Line, 1996. Print.

Four or More Authors

Phillips, Rodney, et al. *The Hand of the Poet.* New York: Rizzoli, 1997. Print.
or
Phillips, Rodney, Susan Benesch, Kenneth Benson, and Barbara Bergeron. *The Hand of the Poet.* New York: Rizzoli, 1997. Print.

Two Books by the Same Author

Bawer, Bruce. *The Aspect of Eternity.* St. Paul: Graywolf, 1993. Print.
---. *Diminishing Fictions: Essays on the Modern American Novel and Its Critics.* St. Paul: Graywolf, 1988. Print.

Corporate Author

Poets and Writers. *A Writer's Guide to Copyright.* New York: Poets and Writers, 1979. Print.

Author and Editor

Shakespeare, William. *The Sonnets.* Ed. G. Blakemore Evans. Cambridge: Cambridge UP, 1996. Print.

One Editor

Monteiro, George, ed. *Conversations with Elizabeth Bishop*. Jackson: UP of
    Mississippi, 1996. Print.

Two Editors

Craig, David, and Janet McCann, eds. *Odd Angles of Heaven: Contemporary Poetry by
    People of Faith*. Wheaton: Shaw, 1994. Print.

Translation

Dante Alighieri. *Inferno: A New Verse Translation*. Trans. Michael Palma. New York:
    Norton, 2002. Print.

Introduction, Preface, Foreword, or Afterword

Lapham, Lewis. Introduction. *Understanding Media: The Extensions of Man*. By
    Marshall McLuhan. Cambridge: MIT P, 1994. vi–x. Print.

Thwaite, Anthony. Preface. *Contemporary Poets*. Ed. Thomas Riggs. 6th ed. New
    York: St. James, 1996. vii–viii. Print.

Work in an Anthology

Rodriguez, Richard. "Aria: A Memoir of a Bilingual Childhood." *The Best American
    Essays of the Century*. Ed. Robert Atwan and Joyce Carol Oates. Boston:
    Houghton, 2001. 447–66. Print. Best American Ser.

Translation in an Anthology

Neruda, Pablo. "We Are Many." Trans. Alastair Reid. *Literature: An Introduction to
    Fiction, Poetry, Drama, and Writing*. Ed. X. J. Kennedy and Dana Gioia. 7th
    Compact ed. New York: Pearson, 2013. 739. Print.

Multivolume Work

Wellek, René. *A History of Modern Criticism, 1750–1950*. 8 vols. New Haven: Yale UP,
    1955–92. Print.

One Volume of a Multivolume Work

Wellek, René. *A History of Modern Criticism, 1750–1950*. Vol. 7. New Haven: Yale UP,
    1991. Print.

Book in a Series

Ross, William T. *Weldon Kees*. Boston: Twayne, 1985. Print. Twayne's US Authors
Ser. 484.

Republished Book

Ellison, Ralph. *Invisible Man*. 1952. New York: Vintage, 1995. Print.

Revised or Subsequent Edition

Janouch, Gustav. *Conversations with Kafka*. Trans. Goronwy Rees. Rev. ed. New
York: New Directions, 1971. Print.

Reference Books

Signed Article in a Reference Book

Cavoto, Janice E. "Harper Lee's *To Kill a Mockingbird*." *The Oxford Encyclopedia of
American Literature*. Ed. Jay Parini. Vol. 2. New York: Oxford UP, 2004.
418–21. Print.

Unsigned Encyclopedia Article—Standard Reference Book

"James Dickey." *The New Encyclopaedia Britannica: Micropaedia*. 15th ed. 1987.
Print.

Dictionary Entry

"Design." *Merriam-Webster's Collegiate Dictionary*. 11th ed. 2003. Print.

Periodicals

Journal

Salter, Mary Jo. "The Heart Is Slow to Learn." *New Criterion* 10.8 (1992): 23–29. Print.

Signed Magazine Article

Gioia, Dana. "Studying with Miss Bishop." *New Yorker* 5 Sept. 1986: 90–101. Print.

Unsigned Magazine Article

"The Real Test." *New Republic* 5 Feb. 2001: 7. Print.

Newspaper Article

Lyall, Sarah. "In Poetry, Ted Hughes Breaks His Silence on Sylvia Plath." *New York Times* 19 Jan. 1998, natl. ed.: A1+. Print.

Signed Book Review

Fugard, Lisa. "Divided We Love." Rev. of *Unaccustomed Earth*, by Jhumpa Lahiri. *Los Angeles Times* 30 Mar. 2008: R1. Print.

Unsigned, Untitled Book Review

Rev. of *Otherwise: New and Selected Poems*, by Jane Kenyon. *Virginia Quarterly Review* 72 (1996): 136. Print.

WEB PUBLICATIONS

Website

Liu, Alan, dir. Home Page. *Voice of the Shuttle*. Dept. of English, U of California, Santa Barbara, n.d. Web. 17 Oct. 2011.

Document on a Website

"A Hughes Timeline." *PBS Online*. Public Broadcasting Service, 2001. Web. 20 Sept. 2011.

"Wallace Stevens." *Poets.org*. Academy of American Poets, n.d. Web. 20 Sept. 2011.

Online Reference Database

"Brooks, Gwendolyn." *Encyclopaedia Britannica Online*. Encyclopaedia Britannica, 2011. Web. 15 Feb. 2011.

Entire Online Book, Previously Appeared in Print

Jewett, Sarah Orne. *The Country of the Pointed Firs*. 1896. *Project Gutenberg*, 8 July 2008. Web. 10 Oct. 2011.

Article in an Online Newspaper

Atwood, Margaret. "The Writer: A New Canadian Life-Form." *New York Times*. New York Times, 18 May 1997. Web. 20 Aug. 2008.

Article in an Online Magazine

Garner, Dwight. "Jamaica Kincaid: The *Salon* Interview." *Salon*. Salon Media Group,
13 Jan. 1996. Web. 15 Feb. 2011.

Article in an Online Scholarly Journal

Carter, Sarah. "From the Ridiculous to the Sublime: Ovidian and Neoplatonic
Registers in *A Midsummer Night's Dream*." *Early Modern Literary Studies* 12.1
(2006): 1–31. Web. 18 Jan. 2011.

Article from a Scholarly Journal, Part of an Archival Online Database

Finch, Annie. "My Father Dickinson: On Poetic Influence." *Emily Dickinson Journal*
17.2 (2008): 24–38. *Project Muse*. Web. 18 Jan. 2011.

Article Accessed via a Library Subscription Service

Seitler, Dana. "Unnatural Selection: Mothers, Eugenic Feminism, and Charlotte
Perkins Gilman's Regeneration Narratives." *American Quarterly* 55.1 (2003):
61–87. *ProQuest*. Web. 7 July 2011.

Online Blog

Gioia, Ted. "*The Road* by Cormac McCarthy." *The New Canon: The Best in Fiction
Since 1985*. N.p., n.d. Web. 11 May 2011.

Vellala, Rob. "Gilman: No Trouble to Anyone." *The American Literary Blog*. N.p.,
10 Sept. 2010. Web. 23 Feb. 2011.

Photograph or Painting Accessed Online

Alice Walker, Miami Book Fair International, 1989. *Wikimedia Commons*. Wikimedia
Foundation, 22 Jan. 2009. Web. 11 May 2011.

Brueghel, Pieter, *Landscape with the Fall of Icarus*. 1558. Musées Royaux des Beaux-
Arts de Belgique, Brussels. *ibiblio.org*. Center for the Public Domain and
UNC-CH. Web. 21 Nov. 2011.

Video Accessed Online

Ozymandias: Percy Bysshe Shelley. *YouTube*. E-Verse Radio, 13 Mar. 2007. Web.
21 January 2011. <http://www.youtube.com/watch?v=6xGa-fNSHaM>.

CD-ROM REFERENCE WORKS

CD-ROM Publication

"Appall." *The Oxford English Dictionary*. 2nd ed. Oxford: Oxford UP, 1992. CD-ROM.

Periodically Published Information, Collected on CD-ROM

Kakutani, Michiko. "Slogging Surreally in the Vietnamese Jungle." Rev. of *The Things They Carried*, by Tim O'Brien. *New York Times* 6 Mar. 1990: C6. CD-ROM. *New York Times Ondisc*. UMI-ProQuest. Oct. 1993.

MISCELLANEOUS SOURCES

Compact Disc (CD)

Shakespeare, William. *The Complete Arkangel Shakespeare: 38 Fully-Dramatized Plays*. Narr. Eileen Atkins and John Gielgud. Read by Imogen Stubbs, Joseph Fiennes, et al. Audio Partners, 2003. CD.

Audiocassette

Roethke, Theodore. *Theodore Roethke Reads His Poetry*. Caedmon, 1972. Audiocassette.

Videocassette

Henry V. By William Shakespeare. Dir. Laurence Olivier. Perf. Laurence Olivier. Two Cities Films. 1944. Paramount, 1988. Videocassette.

DVD

Hamlet. By William Shakespeare. Perf. Laurence Olivier, Eileen Herlie, and Basil Sydney. Two Cities Films. 1948. Criterion, 2000. DVD.

Film

Hamlet. By William Shakespeare. Dir. Franco Zeffirelli. Perf. Mel Gibson, Glenn Close, Helena Bonham Carter, Alan Bates, and Paul Scofield. Warner, 1991. Film.

Television or Radio Program

Moby Dick. By Herman Melville. Dir. Franc Roddam. Perf. Patrick Stewart and Gregory Peck. 2 episodes. USA Network. 16–17 Mar. 1998. Television.

43

WRITING AN ESSAY EXAM

The test of literature is, I suppose,
whether we ourselves live more intensely for the reading of it.

—ELIZABETH DREW

W hy might an instructor choose to give an essay examination? It may sometimes seem like sheer sadism, but there are good reasons for using essays to
test your knowledge of a subject. Longer, more involved answers can reveal not just
how well you have memorized course material but also how thoroughly you have
processed it. An essay exam allows you to demonstrate that you can think critically
about the literature you have read and the issues your reading has raised. It lets you
show how well you can marshal evidence to support your assertions. It also gives you
a chance to draw connections between the literary works you have read and the main
themes of the course.

Whether your exam is take-home or in-class, open-book or closed, the following
strategies will help you to show off what you know:

■ **Be prepared.** Before you take the exam, review the readings. If you have been
highlighting and annotating all semester, you will find yourself well rewarded for
that extra bit of effort. A glance at highlighted portions of text can help refresh
your memory about passages in a text that struck you as particularly important;
your marginalia can help you to recall why that was the case.

■ **Review your notes.** It is also a good idea to review any notes you have taken for
the course. If you kept a reading journal, go back and reread it. (You will be surprised how many specific memories rereading your journal will trigger.) Even if
you are permitted to use your books during the exam, reacquainting yourself with
the material beforehand can help you better recall what it is you are looking for
in those open books.

As you review, be sure to think about the big picture. How do the literary
works you have read relate to each other? If you have been reading theory and
criticism, how might it apply to the course's content? If you have been given historical background about the period in which a work was written, how does the
work embody its author's time? Sometimes it might help just to write down a few
of the central ideas the course has explored on a separate sheet of paper—to
summarize a few of the major insights the course has offered.

- **Think it through.** Once you have been given the exam, be sure to read it all the way through before you begin writing. Figure out how much time you can afford to spend per section. Pay attention to how many points each question is worth; you may well want to budget your time accordingly. Leave yourself time to proof-read your responses and add any missing information.

  When you are ready to start, you might find it helpful first to attack questions about which you feel more confident. Go ahead, but save enough time to tackle the tougher ones as well.

- **Read the questions carefully.** To ensure that you are answering the actual questions you have been asked, pay special attention to words in the directions that seem important. Verbs such as "analyze," "summarize," "explicate," "compare," "contrast," "evaluate," "interpret," and "explain" give clues to what your focus should be. Highlight or underline these action words so that you can more readily keep them in mind as you write. Understanding what you are being asked to do is crucial. Failing to follow directions might lose you precious points, no matter how brilliantly you write on your subject.

  Careful reading and highlighting can also help you remember to address all parts of any given question. Don't get so caught up in answering one part of a question that you neglect the other parts.

- **Understand your purpose.** Whenever you write, it pays to consider your audience and your purpose. Inevitably, the audience for an essay exam response will be your instructor. It's likely that he or she will be looking to see whether you have understood the material on which you are being tested. As you consider the questions you are about to answer, think back to concepts stressed by the instructor during in-class discussions. Try to touch on these concepts as you write, as long as you can do so without losing your focus. Also, since your instructor is familiar with the literary work under discussion, there's no need to relate the whole story in your exam response. Unless you are specifically asked to summarize, don't give any more plot details than are needed to accomplish the assigned task.

  For clues about what your purpose should be, pay attention to those action words you have highlighted in the directions. Here are some common ones:

Analyze	Consider how a single element of the text contributes to its full meaning or effect.
Compare	Explore how two or more things resemble each other.
Contrast	Explore how two or more things differ from each other.
Evaluate	Examine a work with the purpose of determining its quality or importance.
Explain	Clarify a concept.
Explicate	Explain a brief work or a passage from a longer work in detail to show how its parts contribute to the work as a whole.
Interpret	Express a literary work's meaning in your own words.
Paraphrase	Restate a passage in your own words.
Prove	Provide evidence of the truth of a claim, drawing on information from the literary work under study.
Relate	Show a connection between two or more items.
Summarize	Give a shortened version of a literary work, touching on key points.

- **Plan before you write. Start with a clear thesis that accurately addresses the exam question.** A critical step in writing a good essay exam is creating a thesis sentence that succinctly expresses your main point. Using the exam question to provide direction for your thesis, come up with a statement that is both decisive and specific.

  For example, if you have been asked to describe the grandmother's transformation in Flannery O'Connor's "A Good Man Is Hard to Find," your thesis should say something specific about *how* or *why* she gains insight in her last moments of life. The first thesis below does not address the assignment—it describes the grandmother, not the grandmother's transformation. It is accurate but incomplete since it does not lead anywhere useful.

  > IRRELEVANT THESIS
  > The grandmother in "A Good Man Is Hard to Find" is self-centered and silly.

  The rough thesis that follows sticks with the merely obvious.

  > ROUGH THESIS
  > The grandmother in "A Good Man Is Hard to Find" is a silly, self-centered woman who undergoes a transformation at the end of the story.

  The revised thesis makes a more decisive statement, providing specifics about what happens at the story's climax.

  > REVISED THESIS
  > In "A Good Man Is Hard to Find," the grandmother is transformed from a silly, self-centered woman into a wiser, more caring one.

  A final revision goes further, venturing to say not only what happens in the story but why it happens. It provides a good road map for writing an essay exam.

  > FINAL THESIS
  > In "A Good Man Is Hard to Find," the grandmother is transformed by her proximity to death from a silly, self-centered woman into a wiser, more caring one.

- **Create a rough outline.** Though an essay question might seem like an occasion for off-the-cuff writing, it's a good idea to sketch a rough outline before you plunge in. As you write, follow the outline point by point. An outline for an essay response based on the final thesis above might look something like this:

  1. Grandmother transformed by closeness to death
  2. Starts out silly
     Lives in the past
     Gets directions wrong
  3. Becomes wiser
     Sees her mistakes
     Sees her connection to the Misfit

4. Starts out self-centered
   Smuggles cat on trip
   Makes family drive out of way
5. Becomes caring
   Reaches out to Misfit
   Sees him as her own child
6. Nearness to death
   Hears her son get shot
   Misfit's quotation

▪ **Make it shapely.** Like a more formal piece of writing, your answer will need an introduction that establishes the point you will be making. It also should include a conclusion that summarizes your argument (preferably without too much bald-faced restatement) and reinforces your thesis. The paragraphs in between should be used to flesh out your argument.

▪ **Give evidence.** Back up your thesis, and any assertion you make along the way, with proof from the story, poem, or play you are discussing. Direct quotations generally make the most convincing evidence, but if you are working from memory, you can do the job with references to the text. To make your argument more convincing and establish how familiar you are with the material, be as specific as you can manage.

▪ **Keep your focus.** As you write, refer frequently to your outline. Be sure to keep your argument on track. Don't ramble or repeat yourself to fill up space; to do so will give the impression that you are uncertain about your response or the material.

▪ **Make smooth transitions.** Use transitional words and phrases to connect each new idea to the one that precedes it. These handy tools can signal your intentions. If your argument is changing directions, you might signal as much with words and phrases such as "in contrast," "on the other hand," "however," "yet," or "conversely." If you are continuing along the same track you've been traveling, try "in addition," "similarly," "furthermore," or "moreover." To indicate cause and effect, you might use "because," "therefore," "as a result," or "consequently." If you make it easy for your reader to follow your train of thought, the end result is likely to be a grateful reader.

▪ **Pay attention to detail.** Be sure to proofread your essay before handing it in. Nothing undermines a writer's authority faster than spelling mistakes and grammatical errors. Even illegible handwriting can try a reader's patience—never a good idea when a grade is involved.

CHECKLIST: Taking an Essay Exam

Exam Preparation

☐ Skim the literary works that will be on the exam.

☐ Reread all your notes and, if you have kept one, your reader's journal.

☐ Consider how the literary works on the exam relate to each other.

☐ Consider possible relationships between the literary works and any literary criticism, theory, or historical background you have been given in the course.

Taking the Exam

☐ When you are given the exam, quickly read it all the way through.

☐ Calculate how much time you can spend per question.

☐ Read each essay question carefully, underlining key words. Take note of multipart questions.

☐ Understand your purpose before you begin.

☐ Write a thesis sentence that accurately answers the exam question.

☐ Sketch an outline for the essay response.

☐ Include an introductory paragraph and a conclusion.

☐ Back up each point you make with evidence from the text.

☐ Don't give plot summaries unless asked to.

☐ Use transitional phrases to link paragraphs and ideas.

☐ Proofread your exam before handing it in.

44

CRITICAL APPROACHES TO LITERATURE

Literary criticism should arise out of a debt of love.

—GEORGE STEINER

Literary criticism is not an abstract, intellectual exercise; it is a natural human response to literature. If a friend informs you she is reading a book you have just finished, it would be odd indeed if you did not begin swapping opinions. Literary criticism is nothing more than discourse—spoken or written—about literature. A student who sits quietly in a morning English class, intimidated by the notion of literary criticism, will spend an hour that evening talking animatedly about the meaning of rock lyrics or comparing the relative merits of the *Star Wars* trilogies. It is inevitable that people will ponder, discuss, and analyze the works of art that interest them.

The informal criticism of friends talking about literature tends to be casual, unorganized, and subjective. Since Aristotle, however, philosophers, scholars, and writers have tried to create more precise and disciplined ways of discussing literature. Literary critics have borrowed concepts from other disciplines, such as philosophy, history, linguistics, psychology, and anthropology, to analyze imaginative literature more perceptively. Some critics have found it useful to work in the abstract area of **literary theory,** criticism that tries to formulate general principles rather than discuss specific texts. Mass media critics, such as newspaper reviewers, usually spend their time evaluating works—telling us which books are worth reading, which plays not to bother seeing. But most serious literary criticism is not primarily evaluative; it assumes we know that *Othello* or *The Metamorphosis* is worth reading. Instead, such criticism is analytic; it tries to help us better understand a literary work.

In the following pages you will find overviews of ten critical approaches to literature. While these ten methods do not exhaust the total possibilities of literary criticism, they represent the most widely used contemporary approaches. Although presented separately, the approaches are not necessarily mutually exclusive; many critics mix methods to suit their needs and interests. For example, a historical critic may use formalist techniques to analyze a poem; a biographical critic will frequently use psychological theories to analyze an author. The summaries try neither to provide a history of each approach nor to present the latest trends in each school. Their purpose is to give you a practical introduction to each critical method and then provide representative examples of it. If one of these critical methods interests you, why not try to write a class paper using the approach?

FORMALIST CRITICISM

Formalist criticism regards literature as a unique form of human knowledge that needs to be examined on its own terms. "The natural and sensible starting point for work in literary scholarship," René Wellek and Austin Warren wrote in their influential *Theory of Literature,* "is the interpretation and analysis of the works of literature themselves." To a formalist, a poem or story is not primarily a social, historical, or biographical document; it is a literary work that can be understood only by reference to its intrinsic literary features—that is, those elements found in the text itself. To analyze a poem or story, therefore, the formalist critic focuses on the words of the text rather than facts about the author's life or the historical milieu in which the text was written. The critic pays special attention to the formal features of the text—the style, structure, imagery, tone, and genre. These features, however, are usually not examined in isolation, because formalist critics believe that what gives a literary text its special status as art is how all its elements work together to create the reader's total experience. As Robert Penn Warren commented, "Poetry does not inhere in any particular element but depends upon the set of relationships, the structure, which we call the poem."

A key method that formalists use to explore the intense relationships within a poem is **close reading,** a careful step-by-step analysis and explication of a text. The purpose of close reading is to understand how various elements in a literary text work together to shape its effects on the reader. Since formalists believe that the various stylistic and thematic elements of a literary work influence each other, these critics insist that form and content cannot be meaningfully separated. The complete interdependence of form and content is what makes a text literary. When we extract a work's theme or paraphrase its meaning, we destroy the aesthetic experience of the work.

When Robert Langbaum examines Robert Browning's "My Last Duchess," he uses several techniques of formalist criticism. First, he places the poem in relation to its literary form, the dramatic monologue. Second, he discusses the dramatic structure of the poem—why the duke tells his story, whom he addresses, and the physical circumstances in which he speaks. Third, Langbaum analyzes how the duke tells his story—his tone, his manner, even the order in which he makes his disclosures. Langbaum neither introduces facts about Browning's life into his analysis, nor relates the poem to the historical period or social conditions that produced it. He focuses on the text itself to explain how it produces a complex effect on the reader.

Robert Langbaum (b. 1924)

On Robert Browning's "My Last Duchess" 1957

When we have said all the objective things about Browning's "My Last Duchess," we will not have arrived at the meaning until we point out what can only be substantiated by an appeal to effect—that moral judgment does not figure importantly in our response to the duke, that we even identify ourselves with him. But how is such an effect produced in a poem about a cruel Italian duke of the Renaissance who out of unreasonable jealousy has had his last duchess put to death, and is now about to contract a second marriage for the sake of dowry? Certainly, no summary or paraphrase would indicate that condemnation is not our principal response. The difference must be laid to form, to that extra quantity which makes the difference in artistic discourse between content and meaning.

The objective fact that the poem is made up entirely of the duke's utterance has of course much to do with the final meaning, and it is important to say that the poem is in form a monologue. But much more remains to be said about the way in which the content is laid out, before we can come near accounting for the whole meaning. It is important that the duke tells the story of his kind and generous last duchess to, of all people, the envoy from his prospective duchess. It is important that he tells his story while showing off to the envoy the artistic merits of a portrait of the last duchess. It is above all important that the duke carries off his outrageous indiscretion, proceeding triumphantly in the end downstairs to conclude arrangements for the dowry. All this is important not only as content but also as form, because it establishes a relation between the duke on the one hand, and the portrait and the envoy on the other, which determines the reader's relation to the duke and therefore to the poem—which determines, in other words, the poem's meaning.

The utter outrageousness of the duke's behavior makes condemnation the least interesting response, certainly not the response that can account for the poem's success. What interests us more than the duke's wickedness is his immense attractiveness. His conviction of matchless superiority, his intelligence and bland amorality, his poise, his taste for art, his manners—high-handed aristocratic manners that break the ordinary rules and assert the duke's superiority when he is being most solicitous of the envoy, waiving their difference of rank ("Nay, we'll go / Together down, sir"); these qualities overwhelm the envoy, causing him apparently to suspend judgment of the duke, for he raises no demur. The reader is no less overwhelmed. We suspend moral judgment because we prefer to participate in the duke's power and freedom, in his hard core of character fiercely loyal to itself. Moral judgment is in fact important as the thing to be suspended, as a measure of the price we pay for the privilege of appreciating to the full this extraordinary man.

It is because the duke determines the arrangement and relative subordination of the parts that the poem means what it does. The duchess's goodness shines through the duke's utterance; he makes no attempt to conceal it, so preoccupied is he with his own standard of judgment and so oblivious of the world's. Thus the duchess's case is subordinated to the duke's, the novelty and complexity of which engages our attention. We are busy trying to understand the man who can combine the connoisseur's pride in the lady's beauty with a pride that caused him to murder the lady rather than tell her in what way she displeased him, for in that

> would be some stooping; and I choose
Never to stoop.

> (lines 42–43)

The duke's paradoxical nature is fully revealed when, having boasted how at his command the duchess's life was extinguished, he turns back to the portrait to admire of all things its life-likeness:

> There she stands
As if alive.

> (lines 46–47)

This occurs ten lines from the end, and we might suppose we have by now taken the duke's measure. But the next ten lines produce a series of shocks that outstrip each time our understanding of the duke, and keep us panting after revelation with no opportunity to consolidate our impression of him for moral judgment. For it is at this point that we learn to whom he has been talking; and he goes on to talk about dowry, even allowing himself to murmur the hypocritical assurance that the new bride's self and not the dowry is of course his object. It seems to me that one side of the duke's nature is here stretched as far as it will go; the dazzling figure threatens to decline into paltriness admitting moral judgment, when Browning retrieves it with two brilliant strokes. First, there is the lordly waiving of rank's privilege as the duke and the envoy are about to proceed downstairs, and then there is the perfect all-revealing gesture of the last two and a half lines when the duke stops to show off yet another object in his collection:

> Notice Neptune, though,
> Taming a sea-horse, thought a rarity,
> Which Claus of Innsbruck cast in bronze for me!

(lines 54–56)

The lines bring all the parts of the poem into final combination, with just the relative values that constitute the poem's meaning. The nobleman does not hurry on his way to business, the connoisseur cannot resist showing off yet another precious object, the possessive egotist counts up his possessions even as he moves toward the acquirement of a new possession, a well-dowered bride; and most important, the last duchess is seen in final perspective. She takes her place as one of a line of objects in an art collection; her sad story becomes the *cicerone's* anecdote° lending piquancy to the portrait. The duke has taken from her what he wants, her beauty, and thrown the life away; and we watch with awe as he proceeds to take what he wants from the envoy and by implication from the new duchess. He carries all before him by sheer force of will so undeflected by ordinary compunctions as even, I think, to call into question—the question rushes into place behind the startling illumination of the last lines, and lingers as the poem's haunting afternote—the duke's sanity.

From The Poetry of Experience

BIOGRAPHICAL CRITICISM

Biographical criticism begins with the simple but central insight that literature is written by actual people and that understanding an author's life can help readers more thoroughly comprehend the work. Anyone who reads the biography of a writer quickly sees how much an author's experience shapes—both directly and indirectly—what he or she creates. Reading that biography will also change (and usually deepen) our response to the work. Sometimes even knowing a single important fact illuminates our reading of a poem or story. Learning, for example, that poet Josephine Miles was confined to a wheelchair or that Weldon Kees committed suicide at forty-one will certainly make us pay attention to certain aspects of their poems we might otherwise have missed or considered unimportant. A formalist critic might complain that we would also have noticed those things through careful textual analysis, but biographical information provides the practical assistance of underscoring subtle but important meanings in the poems. Though many literary theorists have assailed biographical criticism on philosophical grounds, the biographical approach to literature has never disappeared because of its obvious practical advantage in illuminating literary texts.

---

cicerone's anecdote: the Duke's tale. (In Italian, a *cicerone* is one who conducts guided tours for sightseers.)

It may be helpful here to make a distinction between biography and biographical criticism. **Biography** is, strictly speaking, a branch of history; it provides a written account of a person's life. To establish and interpret the facts of a poet's life, for instance, a biographer would use all the available information—not just personal documents such as letters and diaries but also the poems—for the possible light they might shed on the subject's life. A biographical *critic*, however, is not concerned with re-creating the record of an author's life. Biographical criticism focuses on explicating the literary work by using the insight provided by knowledge of the author's life. Quite often, biographical critics, such as Brett C. Millier in her discussion of Elizabeth Bishop's "One Art," will examine the drafts of a poem or story to see both how the work came into being and how it might have been changed from its autobiographical origins.

A reader, however, must use biographical interpretations cautiously. Writers are notorious for revising the facts of their own lives; they often delete embarrassments and invent accomplishments while changing the details of real episodes to improve their literary impact. John Cheever, for example, frequently told reporters about his sunny, privileged youth; after the author's death, his biographer Scott Donaldson discovered a childhood scarred by a distant mother; a failed, alcoholic father; and nagging economic uncertainty. Likewise, Cheever's outwardly successful adulthood was plagued by alcoholism, sexual promiscuity, and family tension. The unsettling facts of Cheever's life significantly changed the way critics read his stories. The danger in the case of a famous writer (Sylvia Plath and F. Scott Fitzgerald are two modern examples) is that the life story can overwhelm and eventually distort the work. A shrewd biographical critic always remembers to base an interpretation on what is in the text itself; biographical data should amplify the meaning of the text, not drown it out with irrelevant material.

Brett C. Millier (b. 1958)

On Elizabeth Bishop's "One Art"   1993

Elizabeth Bishop left seventeen drafts of the poem "One Art" among her papers. In the first draft, she lists all the things she's lost in her life—keys, pens, glasses, cities—and then she writes "One might think this would have prepared me / for losing one average-sized not exceptionally / beautiful or dazzlingly intelligent person . . . / But it doesn't seem to have at all. . . ." By the seventeenth draft, nearly every word has been transformed, but most importantly, Bishop discovered along the way that there might be a way to master this loss.

One way to read Bishop's modulation between the first and last drafts from "the loss of you is impossible to master" to something like "I am still the master of losing even though losing you looks like a disaster" is that in the writing of such a disciplined, demanding poem as this villanelle ("[*Write* it!]") lies the potential mastery of the loss. Working through each of her losses—from the bold, painful catalog of the first draft to the finely-honed and privately meaningful final version—is the way to overcome them or, if not to overcome them, then to see the way in which she might possibly master herself in the face of loss. It is all, perhaps "one art"—writing elegy, mastering loss, mastering grief, self-mastery. Bishop had a precocious familiarity with loss. Her father died before her first birthday, and four years later her mother disappeared into a sanitarium, never to be seen by her daughter again. The losses in the poem are real: time in the form of the "hour badly spent" and, more tellingly for the orphaned Bishop, "my mother's watch": the lost houses, in Key West, Petrópolis, and Ouro Prêto, Brazil. The city of Rio de Janeiro and the whole South American continent (where she had lived for nearly two decades) were lost to her with the suicide of her Brazilian companion. And currently, in the fall of 1975, she seemed to have lost her dearest friend and lover, who was trying to end their relationship. But each version of the poem distanced the pain a little more, depersonalized it, moved it away from the tawdry self-pity and "confession" that Bishop disliked in so many of her contemporaries.

Bishop's friends remained for a long time protective of her personal reputation, and unwilling to have her grouped among lesbian poets or even among the other great poets of her generation—Robert Lowell, John Berryman, Theodore Roethke—as they seemed to self-destruct before their readers' eyes. Bishop herself taught them this reticence by keeping her private life to herself, and by investing what "confession" there was in her poems deeply in objects and places, thus deflecting biographical inquiry. In the development of this poem, discretion is both a poetic method and a part of a process of self-understanding, the seeing of a pattern in her own life.

Adapted by the author from *Elizabeth Bishop: Life and the Memory of It*

HISTORICAL CRITICISM

Historical criticism seeks to understand a literary work by investigating the social, cultural, and intellectual context that produced it—a context that necessarily includes the artist's biography and milieu. Historical critics are less concerned with explaining a work's literary significance for today's readers than with helping us understand the work by recreating, as nearly as possible, the exact meaning and impact it had for its original audience. A historical reading of a literary work begins by exploring the possible ways in which the meaning of the text has changed over time. An analysis of William Blake's poem "London," for instance, carefully examines how certain words had different connotations for the poem's original readers than they do today. It also explores the probable associations an eighteenth-century English reader would have made with certain images and characters, like the poem's persona, the chimney sweep—a type of exploited child laborer who, fortunately, no longer exists in our society.

No one doubts the value of historical criticism in reading ancient literature. There have been so many social, cultural, and linguistic changes that some older texts are incomprehensible without scholarly assistance. But historical criticism can even help one better understand modern texts. To return to Weldon Kees's "For My Daughter," for example, one learns a great deal by considering two rudimentary historical facts—the year in which the poem was first published (1940) and the nationality of its author (American)—and then asking how this information has shaped the meaning of the poem. In 1940 war had already broken out in Europe, and most Americans realized that their country, still recovering from the Depression, would soon be drawn into it. For a young man like Kees, the future seemed bleak, uncertain, and personally dangerous. Even this simple historical analysis helps explain at least part of the bitter pessimism of Kees's poem, though a psychological critic would rightly insist that Kees's dark personality also played a crucial role. In writing a paper on a poem, story, or play, you might explore how the time and place of its creation affect its meaning as in this piece by Kathryn Lee Seidel on Zora Neale Hurston's story "Sweat."

Kathryn Lee Seidel

The Economics of Zora Neale Hurston's "Sweat"   1991

"Sweat" functions at one level as a documentary of the economic situation of Eatonville in the early decades of the twentieth century. Hurston uses a naturalistic narrator to comment on the roles of Delia and Sykes Jones as workers as well as marriage partners, but ultimately the story veers away from naturalistic fiction and becomes a modernist rumination on Delia as an artist figure. The story's coherence of theme and structure makes it one of Hurston's most powerful pieces of fiction.

Preserved not only as a place but as an idea of a place, Eatonville, Florida, retains the atmosphere of which Hurston wrote. As putatively the oldest town in the United States incorporated by blacks, Eatonville possesses understandable pride in its unique history. When Hurston writes of Eatonville in "How It Feels To Be Colored Me," she implies that her childhood place was idyllic because "it is exclusively a colored town," one in which the young Zora was happily unaware of the restrictions that race conferred elsewhere. However, this gloss of nostalgia can be read simultaneously with "Sweat," published only two years earlier . . . [where] Hurston reveals the somber and multifaced variations of life in Eatonville in the first part of this century.

Economically Eatonville in "Sweat" exists as a twin, a double with its neighbor, the town of Winter Park. Far from being identical, the twin towns are configured like Siamese twins, joined as they are by economic necessity. Winter Park is an all-white, wealthy town that caters to rich northerners from New England who journey south each fall to "winter" in Florida—"snowbirds," as the natives call them. Winter Park then as now boasts brick streets, huge oaks, landscaped lakes, and large, spacious houses. To clean these houses, tend these gardens, cook the meals, and watch the children of Winter Park, residents of Eatonville made a daily exodus across the railroad tracks on which Amtrak now runs to work as domestics. . . . What is unique about Eatonville and Winter Park is that they are not one town divided in two but two towns. Eatonville's self-governance, its pride in its historic traditions, and its social mores were thus able to develop far more autonomously than those in the many towns . . . where the black community had to struggle to develop a sense of independent identity.

In "Sweat" we see the results of this economic situation. On Saturdays the men of the town congregate on the porch of the general store chewing sugarcane and discussing the lamentable marriage of Delia and Sykes Jones. Although these men may be employed during the week, Sykes is not. Some working people mentioned besides Joe Clarke, the store owner, are the woman who runs a rooming house where Bertha, Sykes's mistress, stays, the minister of the church Delia attends, and the people who organize dances that Sykes frequents. Work as farm laborers on land owned by whites is probably available, but it pays very little and is seasonal. Jacqueline Jones points out that in 1900, not long before the time of the story, 50 to 70 percent of adult black women were employed full time as compared to only 20 percent of men.[1] A black man might be unemployed 50 percent of the time. One reason that unemployed men congregated at the local general store was not merely out of idleness, as whites alleged, nor out of a desire to create oral narratives, as we Hurston critics would like to imagine, but there they could be "visible to potential employers," as Jones asserts.

[1]Jacqueline Jones, *Labor of Love, Labor of Sorrow: Black Women, Work, and the Family from Slavery to the Present* (New York: Basic Books, 1985) 113.

There is not enough work for the men as it is, but the townspeople discuss Sykes's particular aversion to what work is available. Old man Anderson reports that Sykes was always "ovahbearin' . . . but since dat white 'oman from up north done teached 'im how to run a automobile, he done got too biggety to live—an' we oughter kill 'im." The identity of this woman and her exact role in Sykes's life is not referred to again, but if she was a Winter Park woman, then perhaps Sykes worked for a time as a driver for residents there. All the more ironic, then, his comment to Delia in which he berates her for doing white people's laundry: "ah done tole you time and again to keep them white folks' clothes outa this house." The comment suggests that Sykes does not work out of protest against the economic system of Eatonville in which blacks are dependent on whites for their livelihood. Has he chosen to be unemployed to resist the system? Within the story, this reading is fragile at best. The townspeople point out that Sykes has used and abused Delia; he has "squeezed" her dry, like a piece of sugarcane. They report that she was in her youth a pert, lively, and pretty girl, but that marriage to a man like Sykes has worn her out.

In fact, Delia's work is their only source of income. In the early days of their marriage Sykes was employed, but he "took his wages to Orlando," the large city about ten miles from Eatonville, where he spent every penny. At some point Sykes stopped working and began to rely entirely on Delia for income. As she says, "Mah tub of suds is filled yo' belly with vittles more times than yo' hands is filled it. Mah sweat is done paid for this house." Delia's sense of ownership is that of the traditional work ethic; if one works hard, one can buy a house and support a family. That Delia is the bread-winner, however, is a role reversal but not ostensibly a liberation; her sweat has brought her some meager material rewards but has enraged her husband.

Although she may at one time have considered stopping work so that Sykes might be impelled to "feel like man again" and become a worker once more, at the time of the story that possibility is long past. Sykes wants her to stop working so she can be dainty, not sweaty, fat, not thin. Moreover, he wants to oust her from the house so that he and his girlfriend can live there. . . . Sykes's brutality is a chosen compensation because he does not participate in the work of the community. He chooses instead to become the town's womanizer and bully who spends his earnings when he has them; he lives for the moment and for himself.

. . . With her house she possesses not only a piece of property, but she also gains the right to declare herself as a person, not a piece of property. Because Sykes has not shared in the labor that results in the purchase of this property, he remains in a dependent state. He is rebellious against Delia who he feels controls him by denying him the house he feels ought to be his; his only reason for this assertion is that he is a man and Delia is his wife.

Thus, the economics of slavery in "Sweat" becomes a meditation on marriage as an institution that perpetuates the possession of women for profit. Indeed, Sykes is the slaveholder here; he does not work, he is sustained by the harsh physical labor of a black woman, he relies on the work of another person to obtain his own pleasure (in this case buying presents for his mistress Bertha). He regards Delia's property and her body as his possessions to be disposed of as he pleases. Sykes's brutal beatings of Delia and his insulting remarks about her appearance are the tools with which he perpetuates her subordination to him for the sixteen years of their marriage.

From "The Artist in the Kitchen: The Economics of
Creativity in Hurston's 'Sweat'"

PSYCHOLOGICAL CRITICISM

Modern psychology has had an immense effect on both literature and literary criticism. The psychoanalytic theories of the Austrian neurologist Sigmund Freud changed our notions of human behavior by exploring new or controversial areas such as wish fulfillment, sexuality, the unconscious, and repression. Perhaps Freud's greatest contribution to literary study was his elaborate demonstration of how much human mental process was unconscious. He analyzed language, often in the form of jokes and conversational slips of the tongue (now often called "Freudian slips"), to show how it reflected the speaker's unconscious fears and desires. He also examined symbols, not only in art and literature but also in dreams, to study how the unconscious mind expressed itself in coded form to avoid the censorship of the conscious mind. His theory of human cognition asserted that much of what we apparently forget is actually stored deep in the unconscious mind, including painful traumatic memories from childhood that have been repressed.

Freud admitted that he himself had learned a great deal about psychology from studying literature. Sophocles, Shakespeare, Goethe, and Dostoyevsky were as important to the development of his ideas as were his clinical studies. Some of Freud's most influential writing was, in a broad sense, literary criticism, such as his psychoanalytic examination of Sophocles's Oedipus in *The Interpretation of Dreams* (1900). In analyzing Sophocles's tragedy *Oedipus the King,* Freud paid the classical Greek dramatist the considerable compliment that the playwright had such profound insight into human nature that his characters display the depth and complexity of real people. In focusing on literature, Freud and his disciples such as Carl Jung, Ernest Jones, Marie Bonaparte, and Bruno Bettelheim endorsed the belief that great literature truthfully reflects life.

Psychological criticism is a diverse category, but it often employs three approaches. First, it investigates the creative process of the arts: what is the nature of literary genius, and how does it relate to normal mental functions? Such analysis may also focus on literature's effects on the reader. How does a particular work register its impact on the reader's mental and sensory faculties? The second approach involves the psychological study of a particular artist. Most modern literary biographers employ psychology to understand their subject's motivations and behavior. One book, Diane Middlebrook's controversial *Anne Sexton: A Biography* (1991), actually used tapes of the poet's sessions with her psychiatrist as material for the study. The third common approach is the analysis of fictional characters. Freud's study of Oedipus is the prototype for this approach, which tries to bring modern insights about human behavior into the study of how fictional people act. While psychological criticism carefully examines the surface of the literary work, it customarily speculates on what lies underneath the text—the unspoken or perhaps even unspeakable memories, motives, and fears that covertly shape the work, especially in fictional characterizations.

Gretchen Schulz (b. 1943)
and R. J. R. Rockwood

Fairy Tale Motifs in "Where Are You Going, Where Have You Been?"   1980

In her fiction both short and long Miss Oates makes frequent use of fairy tale material. Again and again she presents characters and situations which parallel corresponding motifs from the world of folk fantasy. And never is this more true than in the present story ["Where Are You Going, Where Have You Been?"]—never in all the novels and collections of short stories which she has written at last count. Woven into the complex texture of "Where Are You Going, Where Have You Been?" are motifs from such tales as "The Spirit in the Bottle," "Snow White," "Cinderella," "Sleeping Beauty," "Rapunzel," "Little Red Riding Hood," and "The Three Little Pigs." *The Pied Piper of Hamelin,* which ends tragically and so according to [Bruno] Bettelheim does not qualify as a proper fairy tale, serves as the "frame device" that contains all the other tales.

There is a terrible irony here, for although the story is full of fairy tales, Connie, its protagonist, is not. Connie represents an entire generation of young people who have grown up—or tried to—without the help of those bedtime stories which not only entertain the child, but also enable him vicariously to experience and work through problems which he will encounter in adolescence. The only "stories" Connie knows are those of the sexually provocative but superficial lyrics of the popular songs she loves or of the equally insubstantial movies she attends. Such songs and movies provide either no models of behavior for her to imitate, or dangerously inappropriate ones. Connie has thus been led to believe that life and, in particular, love will be "sweet, gentle, the way it was in the movies and promised in songs." She has no idea that life actually can be just as grim as in folk fairy tales. The society that is depicted in "Where Are You Going, Where Have You Been?" has failed to make available to children like Connie maps of the unconscious such as fairy tales provide, because it has failed to recognize that in the unconscious past and future coalesce, and that, psychologically, where the child is going is where he has already been. Since Connie has been left—in the words of yet another of the popular songs—to "wander through that wonderland alone"—it is small wonder, considering her lack of spiritual preparation, that Connie's journey there soon becomes a terrifying schizophrenic separation from reality, with prognosis for recovery extremely poor.

• • •

Bettelheim points out that a fairy tale like "Spirit in the Bottle" deals with two problems that confront the child as he struggles to establish a sense of identity: parental belittlement, and integration of a divided personality. In Connie's case, her mother's belittling remarks that "Connie couldn't do a thing, her mind was all filled with trashy daydreams," certainly have contributed to Connie's two-sidedness, with her one personality "for home" and another for "anywhere that was not home," a division also apparent in the relationship between Connie and the "girl friend" who accompanies her to the bottle-shaped restaurant—the two are so poorly differentiated as to suggest a mere *doubling* of Connie, rather than two separate individuals. While such personality division may at first glance seem pathological, it is not, according to Bettelheim, necessarily abnormal, since the "manner in which the child can bring some order into his world view is by dividing everything into opposites," and that "in the late-oedipal and post-oedipal ages, this splitting extends to the child himself."

• • •

To be assured of safe passage through what Bettelheim terms "that thorniest of thickets, the oedipal period," a child like Connie would need to have absorbed the wisdom of the other fairy tales to which Miss Oates alludes, tales such as "Snow White," "Cinderella," "Rapunzel," and "Little Red Riding Hood." By their applicability to Connie's situation, these tales reveal that at its deepest level Connie's most compelling psychological problem is *unresolved oedipal conflict, aggravated by sibling rivalry.*

Suggestive of "Snow White" is Connie's "habit of craning her neck to glance into mirrors, or checking other people's faces to make sure her own was all right" (as though other people's faces were mirrors, too); and we are told also that her mother, "who noticed everything and knew everything"—as though with the wicked queen's magic power—"hadn't much reason any longer to look at her own face," and so was jealous of her daughter's beauty and "always after Connie." Arnold Friend's sunglasses also mirror everything, which means that, in this instance, he personifies the Magic Mirror and, of course, he finds Connie the fairest one of all. In his words, "Seen you that night and thought, that's the one, yes sir, I never needed to look anymore." Though he thus serves as Prince, there is a hint of the dwarf motif in Arnold's short stature and obvious phallicism; and most particularly is this true of his friend, Ellie Oscar, a case of arrested development, whose face is that of a "forty-year-old baby." Connie's "Someday My Prince Will Come" daydreams, plus the many references to how dazed and sleepy she always is, especially the day Arnold comes for her, when she "lay languidly about the airless little room" and "breathed in and breathed out with each gentle rise and fall of her chest"—these too, suggest "Snow White" and, for that matter, "Sleeping Beauty," whose heroine in the Brothers Grimm is, like Connie, fifteen.

The oedipal implications of "Snow White" are evident in the fact that, as Bettelheim points out, the queen's Magic Mirror speaks not with the mother's but the daughter's voice, revealing the jealous child's own sense of inferiority and frustration projected onto her mother. The father's romantic feelings for the daughter are never at issue in such a fairy tale and he is generally depicted as weak, ineffectual, and oblivious to the struggle that issues between mother and daughter—exactly as in Miss Oates's story.

From "In Fairyland Without a Map: Connie's Exploration Inward in Joyce Carol Oates's 'Where Are You Going, Where Have You Been?'"

MYTHOLOGICAL CRITICISM

Mythological critics look for the recurrent universal patterns underlying most literary works. **Mythological criticism** is an interdisciplinary approach that combines the insights of anthropology, psychology, history, and comparative religion. If psychological criticism examines the artist as an individual, mythological criticism explores the artist's common humanity by tracing how the individual imagination uses symbols and situations—consciously or unconsciously—in ways that transcend its own historical milieu and resemble the mythology of other cultures or epochs.

A central concept in mythological criticism is the **archetype,** a symbol, character, situation, or image that evokes a deep universal response. The idea of the archetype came into literary criticism from the Swiss psychologist Carl Jung, a lifetime student of myth and religion. Jung believed that all individuals share a "collective unconscious," a set of primal memories common to the human race, existing below each person's conscious mind. Archetypal images (which often relate to experiencing primordial phenomena like the sun, moon, fire, night, and blood), Jung believed, trigger the collective unconscious. We do not need to accept the literal truth of the collective unconscious, however, to endorse the archetype as a helpful critical concept.

Northrop Frye defined the archetype in considerably less occult terms as "a symbol, usually an image, which recurs often enough in literature to be recognizable as an element of one's literary experience as a whole."

Identifying archetypal symbols and situations in literary works, mythological critics almost inevitably link the individual text under discussion to a broader context of works that share an underlying pattern. In discussing Shakespeare's *Hamlet*, for instance, a mythological critic might relate Shakespeare's Danish prince to other mythic sons avenging the deaths of their fathers, like Orestes from Greek myth or Sigmund of Norse legend; or, in discussing *Othello*, relate the sinister figure of Iago to the devil in traditional Christian belief. Critic Joseph Campbell took such comparisons even further; his compendious study *The Hero with a Thousand Faces* demonstrates how similar mythic characters appear in virtually every culture on every continent.

Edmond Volpe (1922–2007)

Myth in Faulkner's "Barn Burning"   1964

"Barn Burning" however is not really concerned with class conflict. The story is centered upon Sarty's emotional dilemma. His conflict would not have been altered in any way if the person whose barn Ab burns had been a simple poor farmer, rather than an aristocratic plantation owner. The child's tension, in fact, begins to surface during the hearing in which a simple farmer accuses Ab of burning his barn. The moral antagonists mirrored in Sarty's conflict are not sharecropper and aristocrat. They are the father, Ab Snopes, versus the rest of mankind. Major De Spain is not developed as a character; his house is important to Sarty because it represents a totally new and totally different social and moral entity. Within the context of the society Faulkner is dealing with, the gap between the rich aristocrat and the poor sharecropper provides a viable metaphor for dramatizing the crisis Sarty is undergoing. Ab Snopes is by no means a social crusader. The De Spain manor is Sarty's first contact with a rich man's house, though he can recall, in the short span of his life, at least a dozen times the family had to move because Ab burned barns. Ab does not discriminate between rich and poor. For him there are only two categories: blood kin and "they," into which he lumps all the rest of mankind. Ab's division relates to Sarty's crisis and only by defining precisely the nature of the conflict the boy is undergoing can we determine the moral significance Faulkner sees in it. The clue to Sarty's conflict rests in its resolution.

• • •

The boy's anxiety is created by his awakening sense of his own individuality. Torn between strong emotional attachment to the parent and his growing need to assert his own identity, Sarty's crisis is psychological and his battle is being waged far below the level of his intellectual and moral awareness.

Faulkner makes this clear in the opening scene with imagery that might be described as synesthesia. The real smell of cheese is linked with the smell of the hermetic meat in the tin cans with the scarlet devils on the label that his "intestines believed he smelled coming in intermittent gusts momentary and brief between the other constant one, the smell and sense just a little of fear because mostly of despair and grief, the old fierce pull of blood." The smells below the level of the olfactory sense link the devil image and the blood image to identify the anxiety the father creates in the child's psyche. Tension is created by the blood demanding identification with his father against *"our enemy he thought in that despair; own! mine and hisn both! He's my father!"* Sarty's conflict is played out in terms of identification, not in moral terms. He does not think of his father as bad, his father's enemies as good.

Ab unjustly accuses Sarty of intending to betray him at the hearing, but he correctly recognizes that his son is moving out of childhood, developing a mind and will of his own and is no longer blindly loyal. In instructing the boy that everyone is the enemy and his loyalty belongs to his blood, Ab's phrasing is revealing: "'Don't you know all they wanted was a chance to get at me because they knew I had them beat?'" Ab does not use the plural "us." It is "I" and "they." Blood loyalty means total identification with Ab, and in the ensuing scenes, Snopes attempts to make his son an extension of himself by taking him to the De Spain house, having him rise up before dawn to be with Ab when he returns the rug, having him accompany Ab to the hearing against De Spain and finally making him an accomplice in the burning of De Spain's barn.

The moral import of Ab's insistence on blood loyalty is fully developed by the satanic imagery Faulkner introduces in the scene at the mansion. As they go up the drive, Sarty follows his father, seeing the stiff black form against the white plantation house. Traditionally the devil casts no shadow, and Ab's figure appears to the child as having "that impervious quality of something cut ruthlessly from tin, depthless, as though sidewise to the sun it would cast no shadow." The cloven hoof of the devil is suggested by Ab's limp upon which the boy's eyes are fixed as the foot unwaveringly comes down into the manure. Sarty's increasing tension resounds in the magnified echo of the limping foot on the porch boards, "a sound out of all proportion to the displacement of the body it bore, as though it had attained to a sort of vicious and ravening minimum not to be dwarfed by anything." At first Sarty thought the house was impervious to his father, but his burgeoning fear of the threat the father poses is reflected in his vision of Ab becoming magnified and monstrous as the black arm reaches up the white door and Sarty sees "the lifted hand like a curled claw."

The satanic images are projected out of the son's nightmarish vision of his father, but they are reinforced by the comments of the adult narrator. Sarty believes Snopes fought bravely in the Civil War, but Ab, we are told, wore no uniform, gave his fealty to no cause, admitted the authority of no man. He went to war for booty. Ab's ego is so great it creates a centripetal force into which everything must flow or be destroyed. The will-less, abject creature who is his wife symbolizes the power of his will. What Ab had done to his wife, he sets out to do to the emerging will of his son. Ab cannot tolerate any entity that challenges the dominance of his will. By allowing his hog to forage in the farmer's corn and by dirtying and ruining De Spain's rug, he deliberately creates a conflict that requires the assertion of primacy. Fire, the element of the devil, is the weapon for the preservation of his dominance. Ab's rage is not fired by social injustice. It is fired by a pride, like Lucifer's, so absolute it can accept no order beyond its own. In the satanic myth, Lucifer asserts his will against the divine order and is cast out of heaven. The angels who fall with Lucifer become extensions of his will. In the same way, Ab is an outcast and pariah among men. He accepts no order that is not of his blood.

From "'Barn Burning': A Definition of Evil"

SOCIOLOGICAL CRITICISM

Sociological criticism examines literature in the cultural, economic, and political context in which it is written or received. "Art is not created in a vacuum," critic Wilbur Scott observed, "it is the work not simply of a person, but of an author fixed in time and space, answering a community of which he is an important, because articulate part." Sociological criticism explores the relationships between the artist and society. Sometimes it looks at the sociological status of the author to evaluate how the profession of the writer in a particular milieu affected what was written. Sociological criticism also analyzes the social content of literary works—what cultural, economic, or political values a particular text implicitly or explicitly promotes. Finally, sociological criticism examines the role the audience has in shaping literature. A sociological view of Shakespeare, for example, might look at the economic position of Elizabethan playwrights and actors; it might also study the political ideas expressed in the plays or discuss how the nature of an Elizabethan theatrical audience (which was usually all male unless the play was produced at court) helped determine the subject, tone, and language of the plays.

An influential type of sociological criticism has been Marxist criticism, which focuses on the economic and political elements of art. Marxist criticism, as in the work of the Hungarian philosopher Georg Lukacs, often explores the ideological content of literature. Whereas a formalist critic would maintain that form and content are inextricably blended, Lukacs believed that content determines form and that, therefore, all art is political. Even if a work of art ignores political issues, it makes a political statement, Marxist critics believe, because it endorses the economic and political status quo. Consequently, Marxist criticism is frequently evaluative and judges some literary work better than others on an ideological basis; this tendency can lead to reductive judgment, as when Soviet critics rated Jack London a novelist superior to William Faulkner, Ernest Hemingway, Edith Wharton, and Henry James, because he illustrated the principles of class struggle more clearly. London was America's first major working-class writer. To examine the political ideas and observations found in his fiction can be illuminating, but to fault other authors for lacking his instincts and ideas is not necessarily helpful in understanding their particular qualities. There is always a danger in sociological criticism—Marxist or otherwise—of imposing the critic's personal politics on the work in question and then evaluating it according to how closely it endorses that ideology. As an analytical tool, however, Marxist criticism and sociological methods can illuminate political and economic dimensions of literature that other approaches overlook.

Alfred Kazin (1915–1998)

Walt Whitman and Abraham Lincoln   1984

In Lincoln's lifetime Whitman was the only major writer to describe him with love. Whitman identified Lincoln with himself in the worshipful fashion that became standard after Lincoln's death. That Lincoln was a class issue says a good deal about the prejudices of American society in the East. A leading New Yorker, George Templeton Strong, noted in his diary that while he never disavowed the "lank and hard featured man," Lincoln was "despised and rejected by a third of the community, and only tolerated by the other two-thirds." Whitman the professional man of the people had complicated reasons for loving Lincoln. The uneasiness about him among America's elite was based on the fear that this unknown, untried man, elected without administrative experience (and without a majority) might not be up to his "fearful task."

• • •

Whitman related himself to the popular passion released by war and gave himself to this passion as a political cause. He understood popular opinion in a way that Emerson, Thoreau, and Hawthorne did not attempt to understand it. Emerson said, like any conventional New England clergyman, that the war was holy. He could not speak for the masses who bore the brunt of the war. Whitman was able to get so much out of the war, to create a lasting image of it, because he knew what people were feeling. He was not above the battle like Thoreau and Hawthorne, not suspicious of the majority like his fellow New Yorker Herman Melville, who in "The House-top," the most personal poem in *Battle-Pieces*, denounced the "ship-rats" who had taken over the city in the anti-draft riots of 1863.

Despite Whitman's elusiveness—he made a career out of longings it would have ended that career to fulfill—he genuinely felt at home with soldiers and other "ordinary" people who were inarticulate by the standards of men "from the schools." He was always present, if far from available, presenting the picture of a nobly accessible and social creature. He certainly got on better with omnibus drivers, workingmen, and now "simple" soldiers (especially when they were wounded and open to his ministrations) than he did with "scribblers." By the time Whitman went down after Fredericksburg to look for brother George, the war was becoming a revolution of sorts and Whitman's old radical politics were becoming "the nation." This made him adore Lincoln as the symbol of the nation's unity. An essential quality of Whitman's Civil War "memoranda" is Whitman's libidinous urge to associate himself with the great, growing, ever more powerful federal cause. Whitman's characteristic lifelong urge to join, to combine, to see life as movement, unity, totality, became during the Civil War an actively loving association with the broad masses of the people and *their* war. In his cult of the Civil War, Whitman allies himself with a heroic and creative energy which sees itself spreading out from the people and their representative men, Lincoln and Whitman.

Hawthorne's and Thoreau's horror of America as the Big State did not reflect Whitman's image of the Union. His passion for the "cause" reflected his intense faith in democracy at a juncture when the United States at war represented the revolutionary principle to Marx, the young Ibsen, Mill, Browning, Tolstoy. Whitman's deepest feeling was that his own rise from the city streets, his future as a poet of democracy, was tied up with the Northern armies.

From *An American Procession*

GENDER CRITICISM

Gender criticism examines how sexual identity influences the creation and reception of literary works. Gender studies began with the feminist movement and was influenced by such works as Simone de Beauvoir's *The Second Sex* (1949) and Kate Millett's *Sexual Politics* (1970) as well as sociology, psychology, and anthropology. Feminist critics believe that culture has been so completely dominated by men that literature is full of unexamined "male-produced" assumptions. They see their criticism correcting this imbalance by analyzing and combating patriarchal attitudes. Feminist criticism has explored how an author's gender influences—consciously or unconsciously—his or her writing. While a formalist critic such as Allen Tate emphasized the universality of Emily Dickinson's poetry by demonstrating how powerfully the language, imagery, and mythmaking of her poems combine to affect a generalized reader, Sandra M. Gilbert, a leading feminist critic, has identified attitudes and assumptions in Dickinson's poetry that she believes are essentially female. Another important theme in feminist criticism is analyzing how sexual identity influences the reader of a text. If Tate's hypothetical reader was deliberately sexless, Gilbert's reader sees a text through the eyes of his or her sex. Finally, feminist critics carefully examine how the images of men and women in imaginative literature reflect or reject the social forces that have historically kept the sexes from achieving total equality.

Recently, gender criticism has expanded beyond its original feminist perspective. In the last twenty years or so, critics in the field of gay and lesbian studies—some of whom describe their discipline as "queer theory"—have explored the impact of different sexual orientations on literary creation and reception. Seeking to establish a canon of classic gay and lesbian authors, these critics argue that sexual orientation is so central a component of human personality (especially when it necessarily puts one at odds with established social and moral norms) that to ignore it in connection with such writers amounts to a fundamental misreading and misunderstanding of their work. A men's movement has also emerged in response to feminism, seeking not to reject feminism but to rediscover masculine identity in an authentic, contemporary way. Led by poet Robert Bly, the men's movement has paid special attention to interpreting poetry and fables as myths of psychic growth and sexual identity.

Nina Pelikan Straus

Transformations in *The Metamorphosis* 1989

Traditionally, critics of *Metamorphosis* have underplayed the fact that the story is about not only Gregor's but also his family's and, especially, Grete's metamorphosis. Yet it is mainly Grete, woman, daughter, sister, on whom the social and psychoanalytic resonances of the text depend. It is she who will ironically "blossom" as her brother deteriorates; it is she whose mirror reflects women's present situations as we attempt to critique patriarchal dominance in order to create new lives that avoid the replication of invalidation. . . .

If Grete is a symbol of anything, it is the irony of self-liberation in relation to the indeterminacy of gender roles. Grete's role as a woman unfolds as Gregor's life as a man collapses. It is no accident that this gender scrolling takes place in the literature of a writer who had curious experiences in his life with women—experiences of his own weakness and of women's strengths. Traditionally, the text has been read not as revealing brother-sister or gender-based relationships, however, but as revealing a father-son conflict or Oedipus complex.

• • •

The word "shame" is central to both Grete and Gregor's experiences. It is a shame that Gregor cannot get out of bed, that he cannot get up to go to work, that his voice fails him, that he cannot open the door of his room with his insect pincers, that he must be fed, that he stinks and must hide his body that is a shame to others. Shame comes from seeing oneself through another's eyes, from Gregor's seeing himself through Grete's eyes, and from the reader's seeing Grete through the narrator's eyes. The text graphically mirrors how we see each other in various shameful (and comic) conditions. Through Gregor's condition, ultimately shameful because he is reduced to the dependency of an ugly baby, Kafka imagines what it is like to be dependent on the care of women. And Kafka is impressed with women's efforts to keep their households and bodies clean and alive. This impression is enlarged with every detail that humiliates and weakens Gregor while simultaneously empowering Grete, who cares for Gregor, ironically, at his own—and perhaps at Kafka's—expense.

The change or metamorphosis is in this sense a literary experiment that plays with problems the story's title barely suggests. For Kafka there can be no change without an exchange, no flourishing of Grete without Gregor's withering; nor can the meaning of transformation entail a final closure that prevents further transformations. The metamorphosis occurs both in the first sentence of the text—"When Gregor Samsa awoke one morning from unsettling dreams, he found himself changed in his bed into a monstrous vermin"—and in the last paragraph of the story, which describes Grete's transformation into a woman "blossoming" and "stretching" toward the family's "new dreams" once Gregor has been transformed into garbage. Grete's final transformation, rendered in concrete bodily terms, is foreshadowed in Gregor's initial transformation from human into vermin. This deliberately reflective textual pattern implies that only when the distorting mirrors of the sexist fun house are dismantled can the sons of the patriarchs recognize themselves as dehumanized and dehumanizing. Only when Grete blooms into an eligible young woman, ripe for the job and marriage markets, can we recognize that her empowerment is also an ironic reification. She has been transformed at another's expense, and she will carry within her the marketplace value that has ultimately destroyed Gregor.

From "Transforming Franz Kafka's *Metamorphosis*"

READER-RESPONSE CRITICISM

Reader-response criticism attempts to describe what happens in the reader's mind while interpreting a text. If traditional criticism assumes that imaginative writing is a creative act, reader-response theory recognizes that reading is also a creative process. Reader-response critics believe that no text provides self-contained meaning; literary texts do not exist independently of readers' interpretations. A text, according to this critical school, is not finished until it is read and interpreted. As Oscar Wilde remarked in the preface to his novel *The Picture of Dorian Gray* (1891), "It is the spectator, and not life, that art really mirrors." The practical problem then arises, however, that no two individuals necessarily read a text in exactly the same way. Rather than declare one interpretation correct and the other mistaken, reader-response criticism recognizes the inevitable plurality of readings. Instead of trying to ignore or reconcile the contradictions inherent in this situation, it explores them.

The easiest way to explain reader-response criticism is to relate it to the common experience of rereading a favorite book after many years. Rereading a novel as an adult, for example, that "changed your life" as an adolescent, is often a shocking experience. The book may seem substantially different. The character you remembered liking most now seems less admirable, and another character you disliked now seems more sympathetic. Has the book changed? Very unlikely, but *you* certainly have in the intervening years. Reader-response criticism explores how different individuals (or classes of individuals) see the same text differently. It emphasizes how religious, cultural, and social values affect readings; it also overlaps with gender criticism in exploring how men and women read the same text with different assumptions.

While reader-response criticism rejects the notion that there can be a single correct reading for a literary text, it doesn't consider all readings permissible. Each text creates limits to its possible interpretations. As Stanley Fish admits in the following critical selection, we cannot arbitrarily place an Eskimo in William Faulkner's story "A Rose for Emily" (though Professor Fish does ingeniously imagine a hypothetical situation where this bizarre interpretation might actually be possible).

Stanley Fish (b. 1938)

An Eskimo "A Rose for Emily"   1980

The fact that it remains easy to think of a reading that most of us would dismiss out of hand does not mean that the text excludes it but that there is as yet no elaborated interpretive procedure for producing that text. . . . Norman Holland's analysis of Faulkner's "A Rose for Emily" is a case in point. Holland is arguing for a kind of psychoanalytic pluralism. The text, he declares, is "at most a matrix of psychological possibilities for its readers," but, he insists, "only some possibilities . . . truly fit the matrix": "One would not say, for example, that a reader of . . . 'A Rose for Emily' who thought the 'tableau' [of Emily and her father in the doorway] described an Eskimo was really responding to the story at all—only pursuing some mysterious inner exploration."

Holland is making two arguments: first, that anyone who proposes an Eskimo reading of "A Rose for Emily" will not find a hearing in the literary community. And that, I think, is right. ("We are right to rule out at least some readings.") His second argument is that the unacceptability of the Eskimo reading is a function of the text, of what he calls its "sharable promptuary," the public "store of structured language" that sets limits to the interpretations the words can accommodate. And that, I think, is wrong. The Eskimo reading is unacceptable because there is at present no interpretive strategy for producing it, no way of "looking" or reading (and remember, all acts of looking or reading are "ways") that would result in the emergence of obviously Eskimo meanings. This does not mean, however, that no such strategy could ever come into play, and it is not difficult to imagine the circumstances under which it would establish itself. One such circumstance would be the discovery of a letter in which Faulkner confides that he has always believed himself to be an Eskimo changeling. (The example is absurd only if one forgets Yeats's *Vision* or Blake's Swedenborgianism° or James Miller's recent elaboration of a homosexual reading of *The Waste Land*.) Immediately the workers in the Faulkner industry would begin to reinterpret the canon in the light of this newly revealed "belief" and the work of reinterpretation would involve the elaboration of a symbolic or allusive system (not unlike mythological or typological criticism) whose application would immediately transform the text into one informed everywhere by Eskimo meanings. It might seem that I am admitting that there is a text to be transformed, but the object of transformation would be the text (or texts) given by whatever interpretive strategies the Eskimo strategy was in

Yeats's Vision *or* Blake's Swedenborgianism: Irish poet William Butler Yeats and Swedish mystical writer Emanuel Swedenborg both claimed to have received revelations from the spirit world; some of Swedenborg's ideas are embodied in the long poems of William Blake.

the process of dislodging or expanding. The result would be that whereas we now have a Freudian "A Rose for Emily," a mythological "A Rose for Emily," a Christological "A Rose for Emily," a regional "A Rose for Emily," a sociological "A Rose for Emily," a linguistic "A Rose for Emily," we would in addition have an Eskimo "A Rose for Emily," existing in some relation of compatibility or incompatibility with the others.

Again the point is that while there are always mechanisms for ruling out readings, their source is not the text but the presently recognized interpretive strategies for producing the text. It follows, then, that no reading, however outlandish it might appear, is inherently an impossible one.

From *Is There a Text in This Class?*

DECONSTRUCTIONIST CRITICISM

Deconstructionist criticism rejects the traditional assumption that language can accurately represent reality. Language, according to deconstructionists, is a fundamentally unstable medium; consequently, literary texts, which are made up of words, have no fixed, single meaning. Deconstructionists insist, according to critic Paul de Man, on "the impossibility of making the actual expression coincide with what has to be expressed, of making the actual signs coincide with what is signified." Since they believe that literature cannot definitively express its subject matter, deconstructionists tend to shift their attention away from *what* is being said to *how* language is being used in a text.

Paradoxically, deconstructionist criticism often resembles formalist criticism; both methods usually involve close reading. But while a formalist usually tries to demonstrate how the diverse elements of a text cohere into meaning, the deconstructionist approach attempts to show how the text "deconstructs," that is, how it can be broken down—by a skeptical critic—into mutually irreconcilable positions. A biographical or historical critic might seek to establish the author's intention as a means to interpreting a literary work, but deconstructionists reject the notion that the critic should endorse the myth of authorial control over language. Deconstructionist critics like Roland Barthes and Michel Foucault have therefore called for "the death of the author," that is, the rejection of the assumption that the author, no matter how ingenious, can fully control the meaning of a text. They have also announced the death of literature as a special category of writing. In their view, poems and novels are merely words on a page that deserve no privileged status as art; all texts are created equal—equally untrustworthy, that is.

Deconstructionists focus on how language is used to achieve power. Since they believe, in the words of critic David Lehman, that "there are no truths, only rival interpretations," deconstructionists try to understand how some "interpretations" come to be regarded as truth. A major goal of deconstruction is to demonstrate how those supposed truths are at best provisional and at worst contradictory.

Deconstruction, as you may have inferred, calls for intellectual subtlety and skill. If you pursue your literary studies beyond the introductory stage, you will want to become more familiar with its assumptions. Deconstruction may strike you as a negative, even destructive, critical approach, and yet its best practitioners are adept at exposing the inadequacy of much conventional criticism. By patient analysis, they can sometimes open up the most familiar text and find unexpected significance.

Geoffrey Hartman (b. 1929)

On Wordsworth's "A Slumber Did My Spirit Seal" 1987

Take Wordsworth's well-known lyric of eight lines, one of the "Lucy" poems, which has been explicated so many times without its meaning being fully determined:

> A slumber did my spirit seal;
>   I had no human fears—
> She seemed a thing that could not feel
>   The touch of earthly years.
> No motion has she now, no force;
>   She neither hears nor sees;
> Rolled round in earth's diurnal course,
>   With rocks, and stones, and trees.

It does not matter whether you interpret the second stanza (especially its last line) as tending toward affirmation, or resignation, or a grief verging on bitterness. The tonal assignment of one rather than another possible meaning, to repeat Susanne Langer° on musical form, is curiously open or beside the point. Yet the lyric does not quite support Langer's general position, that "Articulation is its life, but not assertion," because the poem is composed of a series of short and definitive statements, very like assertions. You could still claim that the poem's life is not in the assertions but somewhere else: but where then? What would articulation mean in that case? Articulation is not anti-assertive here; indeed the sense of closure is so strong that it thematizes itself in the very first line.

Nevertheless, is not the harmony or aesthetic effect of the poem greater than this local conciseness; is not the sense of closure broader and deeper than our admiration for a perfect technical construct? The poem is surely something else than a fine box, a well-wrought coffin.

That it is a kind of epitaph is relevant, of course. We recognize, even if genre is not insisted on, that Wordsworth's style is laconic, even lapidary. There may be a mimetic or formal motive related to the ideal of epitaphic poetry. But the motive may also be, in a precise way, meta-epitaphic. The poem, first of all, marks the closure of a life that has never opened up: Lucy is likened in other poems to a hidden flower or the evening star. Setting overshadows rising, and her mode of existence is inherently inward, westering. I will suppose then, that Wordsworth was at some level giving expression to the traditional epitaphic wish: Let the earth rest lightly on the deceased. If so, his conversion of this epitaphic formula is so complete that to trace the process of conversion might seem gratuitous. The formula, a trite if deeply grounded figure of speech, has been catalyzed out of existence. Here it is formula itself, or better, the adjusted words of the mourner that lie lightly on the girl and everyone who is a mourner.

I come back, then, to the "aesthetic" sense of a burden lifted, rather than denied. A heavy element is made lighter. One may still feel that the term "elation" is inappropriate in this context; yet elation is, as a mood, the very subject of the first stanza. For the mood described is love or desire when it *eternizes* the loved person, when it makes her a star-like being that "could not feel / The touch of earthly years." This *naive* elation, this spontaneous movement of the spirit upward, is reversed in the

---

Susanne Langer: Langer (1895–1985) was an American philosopher who discussed the relationship between aesthetics and artistic form.

downturn or catastrophe of the second stanza. Yet this stanza does not close out the illusion; it preserves it within the elegiac form. The illusion is elated, in our use of the word: *aufgehoben*° seems the proper term. For the girl is still, and all the more, what she seemed to be: beyond touch, like a star, if the earth in its daily motion is a planetary and erring rather than a fixed star, and if all on this star of earth must partake of its sublunar, mortal, temporal nature.

• • •

To sum up: In Wordsworth's lyric the specific gravity of words is weighed in the balance of each stanza; and this balance is as much a judgment on speech in the context of our mortality as it is a meaningful response to the individual death. At the limit of the medium of words, and close to silence, what has been purged is not concreteness, or the empirical sphere of the emotions—shock, disillusion, trauma, recognition, grief, atonement—what has been purged is a series of flashy schematisms and false or partial mediations: artificial plot, inflated consolatory rhetoric, the coercive absolutes of logic or faith.

From "Elation in Hegel and Wordsworth"

CULTURAL STUDIES

Unlike the other critical approaches discussed in this chapter, cultural criticism (or **cultural studies**) does not offer a single way of analyzing literature. No central methodology is associated with cultural studies. Nor is cultural criticism solely, or even mainly, concerned with literary texts in the conventional sense. Instead, the term *cultural studies* refers to a relatively recent interdisciplinary field of academic inquiry. This field borrows methodologies from other approaches to analyze a wide range of cultural products and practices.

To understand cultural studies, it helps to know a bit about its origins. In the English-speaking world, the field was first defined at the Centre for Contemporary Cultural Studies of Birmingham University in Britain. Founded in 1964, this graduate program tried to expand the range of literary study beyond traditional approaches to canonic literature in order to explore a broader spectrum of historical, cultural, and political issues. The most influential teacher at the Birmingham Centre was Raymond Williams (1921–1983), a Welsh socialist with wide intellectual interests. Williams argued that scholars should not study culture as a canon of great works by individual artists but rather examine it as an evolutionary process that involves the entire society. "We cannot separate literature and art," Williams said, "from other kinds of social practice." The cultural critic, therefore, does not study fixed aesthetic objects so much as dynamic social processes. The critic's challenge is to identify and understand the complex forms and effects of the process of culture.

A Marxist intellectual, Williams called his approach cultural materialism (a reference to the Marxist doctrine of dialectical materialism), but later scholars soon discarded that name for two broader and more neutral terms, cultural criticism and cultural studies. From the start, this interdisciplinary field relied heavily on literary theory, especially Marxist and feminist criticism. It also employed the documentary techniques of historical criticism combined with political analysis focused on issues of social class, race, and gender. (This approach flourished in the United States,

---

aufgehoben: German for "taken up" or "lifted up," but this term can also mean "canceled" or "nullified." Hartman uses the term for its double meaning.

where it is called New Historicism.) Cultural studies is also deeply antiformalist, since the field concerns itself with investigating the complex relationships among history, politics, and literature. Cultural studies rejects the notion that literature exists in an aesthetic realm separate from ethical and political categories.

A chief goal of cultural studies is to understand the nature of social power as reflected in "texts." For example, if the object of analysis were a sonnet by Shakespeare, the cultural studies adherent might investigate the moral, psychological, and political assumptions reflected in the poem and then deconstruct them to see what individuals, social classes, or gender might benefit from having those assumptions perceived as true. The relevant mission of cultural studies is to identify both the overt and covert values reflected in a cultural practice. The cultural studies critic also tries to trace out and understand the structures of meaning that hold those assumptions in place and give them the appearance of objective representation. Any analytical technique that helps illuminate these issues is employed.

In theory, a cultural studies critic might employ any methodology. In practice, however, he or she will most often borrow concepts from deconstruction, Marxist analysis, gender criticism, race theory, and psychology. Each of these earlier methodologies provides particular analytical tools that cultural critics find useful. What cultural studies borrows from deconstructionism is its emphasis on uncovering conflict, dissent, and contradiction in the works under analysis. Whereas traditional critical approaches often sought to demonstrate the unity of a literary work, cultural studies often seeks to portray social, political, and psychological conflicts that the work masks. What cultural studies borrows from Marxist analysis is an attention to the ongoing struggle between social classes, each seeking economic (and therefore political) advantage. Cultural studies often asks questions about what social class created a work of art and what class (or classes) served as its audience. Among the many things that cultural studies borrowed from gender criticism and race theory is a concern with social inequality between the sexes and races. It seeks to investigate how these inequities have been reflected in the texts of a historical period or a society. Cultural studies is, above all, a political enterprise that views literary analysis as a means of furthering social justice.

Since cultural studies does not adhere to any single methodology (or even a consistent set of methodologies), it is impossible to characterize the field briefly, because there are exceptions to every generalization offered. What one sees most clearly are characteristic tendencies, especially the commitment to examining issues of class, race, and gender. There is also the insistence on expanding the focus of critical inquiry beyond traditional high literary culture. British cultural studies guru Anthony Easthope can, for example, analyze with equal aplomb Gerard Manley Hopkins's "The Windhover," Edgar Rice Burroughs's *Tarzan of the Apes*, a Benson and Hedges cigarette advertisement, and Sean Connery's eyebrows. Cultural studies is infamous—even among its practitioners—for its habitual use of literary jargon. It is also notorious for its complex intellectual analysis of mundane materials, such as Easthope's analysis of a cigarette ad, which may be interesting in its own right but remote from most readers' literary experience. Some scholars, such as Camille Paglia, however, use the principles of cultural studies to provide new social, political, and historical insights into canonic texts such as William Blake's "The Chimney Sweeper." Omnivorous, iconoclastic, and relentlessly analytic, cultural criticism has become a major presence in contemporary literary studies.

Camille Paglia (b. 1947)

A Reading of William Blake's "The Chimney Sweeper" 2005

Romantic writers glorified childhood as a state of innocence. Blake's "The Chimney Sweeper," written in the same year as the French Revolution, combines the Romantic cult of the child with the new radical politics, which can both be traced to social thinker Jean-Jacques Rousseau. It is the boy sweep, rather than Blake, who speaks: he acts as the poet's dramatic persona or mask. There is no anger in his tale. On the contrary, the sweep's gentle acceptance of his miserable life makes his exploitation seem all the more atrocious. Blake shifts responsibility for protest onto us.

The poem begins as autobiography, a favorite Romantic genre. Having lost his mother, his natural protector, the small child was "sold" into slavery by his father (1–2). That is, he was apprenticed to a chimney-sweeping firm whose young teams would probably have worked simply for food, lodging, and clothing—basics that the boy's widowed working-class father might well have been unable to provide for his family. Children, soberly garbed in practical black, were used for chimney sweeping because they could wriggle into narrow, cramped spaces. The health risks of this filthy job were many—deformation of a boy's growing skeleton as well as long-term toxic effects from coal dust, now known to be carcinogenic. Chronic throat and lung problems as well as skin irritation must have been common. (Among the specimens floating in formaldehyde at Philadelphia's Mütter Museum, a nineteenth-century medical collection, is a chimney sweep's foot deformed by a bulbous tumor on the instep.)

Blake's sweep was so young when indentured into service that, he admits, he still lisped (2–3). The hawking of products and services by itinerant street vendors was once a lively, raucous feature of urban life. "Sweep, sweep, sweep!" cried the wandering crews seeking a day's employment. But this tiny boy couldn't even form the word: "Weep weep weep weep!" is how it came out—inadvertently sending a damning message to the oblivious world. It's really the thundering indictment of Blake as poet-prophet: Weep, you callous society that enslaves and murders its young; weep for yourself and your defenseless victims.

"So your chimneys I sweep and in soot I sleep": this singsong, matter-of-fact line implicates the reader in the poem's crimes—a confrontational device ordinarily associated with ironically self-conscious writers like Baudelaire (4). The boy may be peacefully resigned to the horror of his everyday reality, but we, locked in our own routines and distanced by genteel book reading, are forced to face our collective indifference. The boy represents the invisible army of manual laborers, charwomen, and janitors who do our dirty work. Scrubbing the infernal warren of brick and stone tunnels, he absorbs soot (symbolizing social sin) into his own skin and clothes, while we stay neat and clean.

The anonymous sweep—made faceless by his role—chatters cheerfully away about his friend "little Tom Dacre," whom he has taken under his wing (5). In this moral vacuum, where parents and caretakers are absent or negligent, the children must nurture each other. When the newcomer's curly hair was shaved off (to keep it from catching fire from live coals), he cried at his disfigurement, experienced as loss of self. Head shaving is a familiar initiatory practice in military and religious settings to reduce individuality and enforce group norms. To soothe little Tom, the solicitous sweep resorts to consolation of pitiful illogic: "when your head's bare / You know that the soot cannot spoil your white hair" (7–8). That's like saying, "Good thing you lost your leg—now you'll never stub your toe!" Tom's white (that is, blond) "lamb's back" hair represents the innocence of the Christlike sacrificial lamb: children, according to Blake, have become scapegoats for society's amorality and greed (6). Their white hair seems unnatural, as if the boys have been vaulted forward to old age without enjoying the freedoms and satisfactions of virile adulthood. For modern readers, the bald children's caged sameness is disturbingly reminiscent of that of emaciated survivors of Nazi concentration camps, where liberation was met with blank stoicism.

Amazingly, the sweep's desperate reassurance works: Tom goes "quiet," and for the next three stanzas, the whole center of the text, we enter his dreams (9–20). The poem seems to crack open in an ecstatic allegory of rebirth: the children of industrial London escape by the "thousands" from a living death, the locked "coffins of black" that are their soot-stained bodies as well as the chimneys where they spend their days (11–12). Alas, Tom's vision of paradise is nothing more than a simple, playful childhood—the birthright that was robbed from them. The poem overflows with the boys' repressed energy and vitality, as "leaping, laughing, they run" across the "green plain" of nature, then plunge into the purifying "river." Bathed "white," they "shine" with their own inner light, bright as the "sun" (15–18).

But something goes terribly wrong. The "Angel" with the "bright key" who was their liberator inexplicably turns oppressor (13, 19). As the sweeps "rise upon clouds" toward heaven and "sport in the wind" like prankish cherubs casting off their burdens (the "bags" of brushes and collected soot), an officiously moralistic voice cuts into the dream and terminates it: "And the Angel told Tom, if he'd be a good boy, / He'd have God for his father, and never want joy" (17–20). That Tom wakes right up suggests that the voice actually belongs to the boss or overseer, briskly rousing his charges before dawn. The angel's homily, heavy with conventional piety, stops the children's fun and free motion dead: If you'll be good boys—that is, do what we say—you'll win God's approval and find your reward in heaven. (In British English, to "never want joy" means never to *lack* it.) But God is another false father in this poem.

The trusting, optimistic children grab their bags and brushes and get right to work in the "cold" and "dark" (21–23). They want to do right, and their spirit is unquenched. But they've been brainwashed into pliability by manipulative maxims such as the one recited by our first sweep in the ominous last line: "So if all do their duty they need not fear harm" (24). This bromide is an outrageous lie. If the children were to rebel, to run away to the green paradise lying just outside the city, they would be safe. Their naive goodwill leads straight to their ruin—a short, limited life of sickliness and toil. The final stanza's off rhymes ("dark"/"work," "warm"/"harm") subtly unbalance us and make us sense the fractures in the sweep's world. The poem shows him betrayed by an ascending row of duplicitous male authority figures—his father, the profiteering boss, the turncoat angel, and God himself, who tacitly endorses or tolerates an unjust social system. As Tom's dream suggests, the only deliverance for the sweep and his friends will be death.

From Break, Blow, Burn

► TERMS FOR *review*

Formalist criticism ► A school of criticism that focuses on the *form* of a literary work. A key method that formalists use is close reading, a step-by-step analysis of the elements in a text.

Biographical criticism ► The practice of analyzing a literary work by using knowledge of the author's life to gain insight. Although the work is understood as an independent creation, the *biography* of the author provides the practical assistance of underscoring subtle but important meanings.

Historical criticism ► The practice of analyzing a literary work by investigating the social, cultural, and intellectual context that produced it, including the author's biography and milieu.

Psychological criticism ► The application of the analytical tools of psychology and psychoanalysis to authors and/or fictional characters in order to understand the underlying motivations and meanings of a literary work.

Mythological criticism ► The practice of analyzing a literary work by looking for recurrent universal patterns. It explores the ways in which an individual imagination uses myths and symbols shared by different cultures and epochs.

Sociological criticism ► The practice of analyzing a literary work by examining the cultural, economic, and political context in which it was written or received. It primarily explores the relationship between the artist and society.

Gender criticism ► The examination of the ways in which sexual identity influences the creation, interpretation, and evaluation of literary works. Feminism, gay culture, and the men's movement all play key roles in gender criticism.

Reader-response criticism ► The practice of analyzing a literary work by describing what happens in the reader's mind while interpreting the text, on the assumption that no literary text exists independently of readers' interpretations and that there is no single fixed interpretation of any literary work.

Deconstructionist criticism ► A school of criticism that rejects the traditional assumption that language can accurately represent reality. Deconstructionists believe that literary texts can have no single meaning; therefore, they concentrate their attention on *how* language is being used in a text, rather than what is being said.

Cultural studies ► A contemporary interdisciplinary field of academic study that focuses on understanding the social power encoded in "texts"—which may include any analyzable phenomenon from a traditional poem to an advertising image or actor's face.

GLOSSARY
OF LITERARY TERMS

Abstract diction *See* **Diction.**

Accent An emphasis or stress placed on a syllable in speech. Clear pronunciation of polysyllabic words almost always depends on correct placement of their accents (e.g., *de-*sert and de-*sert* are two different words and parts of speech, depending on their accent). Accent or speech stress is the basis of most meters in English. (*See also* **Accentual meter, Meter.**)

Accentual meter A meter that uses a consistent number of strong speech stresses per line. The number of unstressed syllables may vary, as long as the accented syllables do not. Much popular poetry, such as rap and nursery rhymes, is written in accentual meter.

Acrostic A poem in which the initial letters of each line, when read downward, spell out a hidden word or words (often the name of a beloved person). Acrostics date back as far as the Hebrew Bible and classical Greek poetry.

Allegory A narrative in verse or prose in which the literal events (persons, places, and things) consistently point to a parallel sequence of symbolic ideas. This narrative strategy is often used to dramatize abstract ideas, historical events, religious systems, or political issues. An allegory has two levels of meaning: a literal level that tells a surface story and a symbolic level in which the abstract ideas unfold. The names of allegorical characters often hint at their symbolic roles. For example, in Nathaniel Hawthorne's "Young Goodman Brown," Faith is not only the name of the protagonist's wife but also a symbol of the protagonist's religious faith.

Alliteration The repetition of two or more consonant sounds in successive words in a line of verse or prose. Alliteration can be used at the beginning of words ("cool *cats*"—**initial alliteration**) or internally on stressed syllables ("In *kitchen cups* concupiscent curds"—which combines initial and **internal alliteration**). Alliteration was a central feature of Anglo-Saxon poetry and is still used by contemporary writers.

All-knowing narrator *See* **Omniscient narrator.**

Allusion A brief (and sometimes indirect) reference in a text to a person, place, or thing—fictitious or actual. An allusion may appear in a literary work as an initial quotation, a passing mention of a name, or as a phrase borrowed from another writer—often carrying the meanings and implications of the original. Allusions imply a common set of knowledge between reader and writer and operate as a literary shorthand to enrich the meaning of a text.

Analysis The examination of a piece of literature as a means of understanding its subject or structure. An effective analysis often clarifies a work by focusing on a single element such as tone, irony, symbolism, imagery, or rhythm in a way that enhances the reader's understanding of the whole. *Analysis* comes from the Greek word meaning to "undo," to "loosen."

Anapest A metrical foot in verse in which two unstressed syllables are followed by a stressed syllable, as in "on a *boat*" or "in a *slump*" (⌣ ⌣ ′). (*See also* **Meter.**)

Antagonist The most significant character or force that opposes the protagonist in a narrative or drama. The antagonist may be another character, society itself, a force of nature, or even—in modern literature—conflicting impulses within the protagonist.

Anticlimax An unsatisfying and trivial turn of events in a literary work that occurs in place of a genuine climax. An anticlimax often involves a surprising shift in tone from the lofty or serious into the petty or ridiculous. The term is often used negatively to denote a feeble moment in a plot in which an author fails to create an intended effect. Anticlimax, however, can also be a strong dramatic device when a writer uses it for humorous or ironic effect.

Antihero A protagonist who is lacking in one or more of the conventional qualities attributed to a hero. Instead of being dignified, brave, idealistic, or purposeful, for instance, the antihero may be buffoonish, cowardly, self-interested, or weak. The antihero is often considered an essentially modern form of characterization, a satiric or frankly realistic commentary on traditional portrayals of idealized heroes or heroines. Modern examples range from Kafka's many protagonists to Beckett's tramps in *Waiting for Godot*.

Antithesis Words, phrases, clauses, or sentences set in deliberate contrast to one another. Antithesis balances opposing ideas, tones, or structures, usually to heighten the effect of a statement.

Apostrophe A direct address to someone or something. In poetry an apostrophe often addresses something not ordinarily spoken to (e.g., "O mountain!"). In an apostrophe, a speaker may address an inanimate object, a dead or absent person, an abstract thing, or a spirit. Apostrophe is often used to provide a speaker with means to articulate thoughts aloud.

Apprenticeship novel *See **Bildungsroman.***

Archetype A recurring symbol, character, landscape, or event found in myth and literature across different cultures and eras. The idea of the archetype came into literary criticism from the Swiss psychologist Carl Jung, who believed that all individuals share a "collective unconscious," a set of primal memories common to the human race that exists in our subconscious. An example of an archetypal character is the devil who may appear in pure mythic form (as in John Milton's *Paradise Lost*) but occurs more often in a disguised form like Fagin in Charles Dickens's *Oliver Twist* or Abner Snopes in William Faulkner's "Barn Burning."

Aside In drama a few words or short passage spoken in an undertone or to the audience. By convention, other characters onstage are deaf to the aside.

Assonance The repetition of two or more vowel sounds in successive words, which creates a kind of rhyme. Like alliteration, the assonance may occur initially ("*all* the *awful auguries*") or internally ("white lilacs"). Assonance may be used to focus attention on key words or concepts. Assonance also helps make a phrase or line more memorable.

Atmosphere The dominant mood or feeling that pervades all or part of a literary work. Atmosphere is the total effect conveyed by the author's use of language, images, and physical setting. Atmosphere is often used to foreshadow the ultimate climax in a narrative.

Auditory imagery A word or sequence of words that refers to the sense of hearing. (*See also* **Imagery.**)

Ballad Traditionally, a song that tells a story. The ballad was originally an oral verse form—sung or recited and transmitted from performer to performer without being written down. Ballads are characteristically compressed, dramatic, and objective in their narrative style. There are many variations to the ballad form, most consisting of quatrains (made up of lines of three or four metrical feet) in a simple rhyme scheme. (*See also* **Ballad stanza.**)

Ballad stanza The most common pattern of ballad makers consists of four lines rhymed *abcb*, in which the first and third lines have four metrical feet and the second and fourth lines have three feet (4, 3, 4, 3).

Bathos In poetry, an unintentional lapse from the sublime to the ridiculous or trivial. Bathos differs from anticlimax, in that the latter is a deliberate effect, often for the purpose of humor or contrast, whereas bathos occurs through failure.

Bildungsroman German for "novel of growth and development." Sometimes called an **apprenticeship novel,** this genre depicts a youth who struggles toward maturity, forming a worldview or philosophy of life. Dickens's *David Copperfield* and Joyce's *Portrait of the Artist as a Young Man* are classic examples of the genre.

Biographical criticism The practice of analyzing a literary work by using knowledge of the author's life to gain insight.

Biography A factual account of a person's life, examining all available information or texts relevant to the subject.

Blank verse The most common and well-known meter of unrhymed poetry in English. Blank verse contains five iambic feet per line and is never rhymed. (*Blank* means "unrhymed.") Many literary works have been written in blank verse, including Tennyson's "Ulysses" and Frost's "Mending Wall." Shakespeare's plays are written primarily in blank verse. (*See also* **Iambic pentameter.**)

Blues A type of folk music originally developed by African Americans in the South, often about some pain or loss. Blues lyrics traditionally consist of three-line stanzas in which the first two identical lines are followed by a third concluding, rhyming line. The influence of the blues is fundamental in virtually all styles of contemporary pop—jazz, rap, rock, gospel, country, and rhythm and blues.

Box set The illusion of scenic realism for interior rooms was achieved in the early nineteenth century with the development of the box set, consisting of three walls that joined in two corners and a ceiling that tilted as if seen in perspective. The "fourth wall," invisible, ran parallel to the proscenium arch. By the middle of the nineteenth century, the addition of realistic props and furnishings made it possible for actors to behave onstage as if they inhabited private space, oblivious to the presence of an audience, even turning their backs to the audience if the dramatic situation required it.

Broadside ballads Poems printed on a single sheet of paper, often set to traditional tunes. Most broadside ballads, which originated in the late sixteenth century, were an early form of verse journalism, cheap to print, and widely circulated. Often they were humorous or pathetic accounts of sensational news events.

Burlesque Incongruous imitation of either the style or subject matter of a serious genre, humorous due to the disparity between the treatment and the subject. On the nineteenth-century English stage, the burlesque was a broad caricature, parody, travesty, or take-off of popular plays, opera, or current events. Gilbert and Sullivan's Victorian operettas, for example, burlesqued grand opera.

Cacophony A harsh, discordant sound often mirroring the meaning of the context in which it is used. For example, "Grate on the scrannel pipes of wretched straw" (Milton's "Lycidas"). The opposite of cacophony is **euphony.**

Caesura, cesura A pause within a line of verse. Traditionally, caesuras appear near the middle of a line, but their placement may be varied to create expressive rhythmic effects. A caesura will usually occur at a mark of punctuation, but there can be a caesura even if no punctuation is present.

Carpe diem Latin for "seize the day." Originally said in Horace's famous "Odes I (11)," this phrase has been applied to characterize much lyric poetry concerned with human mortality and the passing of time.

Central intelligence The character through whose sensibility and mind a story is told. Henry James developed this term to describe a narrator—not the author—whose perceptions shape the way a story is presented. (*See also* **Narrator.**)

Character An imagined figure inhabiting a narrative or drama. By convention, the reader or spectator endows the fictional character with moral, dispositional, and emotional qualities expressed in what the character says—the dialogue—and by what he or she does—the action. What a character says and does in any particular situation is motivated by his or her desires, temperament, and moral nature. (*See also* **Dynamic character** and **Flat character.**)

Character development The process in which a character is introduced, advanced, and possibly transformed in a story. This development can prove to be either static (the character's personality is unchanging throughout the narrative) or dynamic (the character's personality undergoes some meaningful change during the course of the narrative). (*See also* **Dynamic character.**)

Characterization The techniques a writer uses to create, reveal, or develop the characters in a narrative. (*See also* **Character.**)

Child ballads American scholar Francis J. Child compiled a collection of over three hundred authentic ballads in his book *The English and Scottish Popular Ballads* (1882–1898). He demonstrated that these ballads were the creations of oral folk culture. These works have come to be called Child ballads.

Clerihew A comic verse form named for its inventor, Edmund Clerihew Bentley. A clerihew begins with the name of a person and consists of two metrically awkward, rhymed couplets. Humorous and often insulting, clerihews serve as ridiculous biographies, usually of famous people.

Climax The moment of greatest intensity in a story, which almost inevitably occurs toward the end of the work. The climax often takes the form of a decisive confrontation between the protagonist and antagonist. In a conventional story, the climax is followed by the **resolution** or **dénouement** in which the effects and results of the climactic action are presented. (*See also* **Falling action, Rising action.**)

Closed couplet Two rhymed lines that contain an independent and complete thought or statement. The closed couplet usually pauses lightly at the end of the first line; the second is more heavily end-stopped, or "closed." When such couplets are written in rhymed iambic pentameter, they are called **heroic couplets.** (*See also* **Couplet.**)

Closed dénouement One of two types of conventional dénouement or resolution in a narrative. In closed dénouement, the author ties everything up at the end of the story so that little is left unresolved. (*See also* **Open dénouement.**)

Closed form A generic term that describes poetry written in some preexisting pattern of meter, rhyme, line, or stanza. A closed form produces a prescribed structure as in the triolet, with a set rhyme scheme and line length. Closed forms include the sonnet, sestina, villanelle, ballade, and rondeau.

Close reading A method of analysis involving careful step-by-step explication of a poem in order to understand how various elements work together. Close reading is a common practice of formalist critics in the study of a text.

Colloquial English The casual or informal but correct language of ordinary native speakers, which may include contractions, slang, and shifts in grammar, vocabulary, and diction. Wordsworth helped introduce colloquialism into English poetry, challenging the past constraints of highly formal language in verse and calling for the poet to become "a man speaking to men." Conversational in tone, *colloquial* is derived from the Latin *colloquium*, "speaking together." (*See also* **Diction, Levels of diction.**)

Comedy A literary work aimed at amusing an audience. Comedy is one of the basic modes of storytelling and can be adapted to most literary forms—from poetry to film. In traditional comic plotting, the action often involves the adventures of young lovers, who face obstacles and complications that threaten disaster but are overturned at the last moment to produce a happy ending. Comic situations or comic characters can provide humor in tragicomedy and even in tragedies (the gravediggers in *Hamlet*).

Comedy of manners A realistic form of comic drama that flourished with seventeenth-century playwrights such as Molière and English Restoration dramatists. It deals with the social relations and sexual intrigues of sophisticated, intelligent, upper-class men and women, whose verbal fencing and witty repartee produce the principal comic effects. Stereotyped characters from contemporary life, such as would-be wits, jealous husbands, conniving rivals, country bumpkins, and foppish dandies, reveal by their deviations from the norm the decorum and conventional behaviors expected in polite society. Modern examples include G. B. Shaw (*Arms and the Man*), Noel Coward (*Private Lives*), or Tom Stoppard (*Arcadia*).

Comic relief The appearance of a comic situation, character, or clownish humor in the midst of a serious action that introduces a sharp contrast in mood. The drunken porter in *Macbeth*, who imagines himself the doorkeeper of Hell, not only provides comic relief but intensifies the horror of Macbeth's murder of King Duncan.

Coming-of-age story *See* **Initiation story.**

Commedia dell'arte A form of comic drama developed by guilds of professional Italian actors in the mid-sixteenth century. Playing stock characters, masked *commedia* players improvised dialogue around a given scenario (a brief outline marking entrances of characters and the main course of action). In a typical play a pair of young lovers (played without masks), aided by a clever servant (Harlequin), outwit older masked characters.

Common meter A highly regular form of ballad meter with two sets of rhymes—*abab*. "Amazing Grace" and many other hymns are in common meter. (*See also* **Ballad stanza.**)

Comparison In the analysis or criticism of literature, one may place two works side-by-side to point out their similarities. The product of this, a comparison, may be more meaningful when paired with its counterpart, a **contrast.**

Complication The introduction of a significant development in the central conflict in a drama or narrative between characters (or between a character and his or her situation). Traditionally, a complication begins the rising action of a story's plot. Dramatic conflict (motivation versus obstacle) during the complication is the force that drives a literary work from action to action. Complications may be *external* or *internal* or a combination of the two. A fateful blow such as an illness or an accident that affects a character is a typical example of an *external* complication—a problem the characters cannot turn away from. An *internal* complication, in contrast, might not be immediately apparent, such as the result of some important aspect of a character's values or personality.

Conceit A poetic device using elaborate comparisons, such as equating a loved one with the graces and beauties of the world. Most notably used by the Italian poet Petrarch in praise of his beloved Laura, *conceit* comes from the Italian *concetto,* "concept" or "idea."

Conclusion In plotting, the logical end or outcome of a unified plot, shortly following the climax. Also called **resolution** or **dénouement** ("the untying of the knot"), as in resolving or untying the knots created by plot complications during the rising action. The action or intrigue ends in success or failure for the protagonist, the mystery is solved, or misunderstandings are dispelled. Sometimes a conclusion is ambiguous; at the climax of the story the characters are changed, but the conclusion suggests different possibilities for what that change is or means.

Concrete diction *See* **Diction.**

Concrete poetry A visual poetry composed exclusively for the page in which a picture or image is made of printed letters and words. Concrete poetry attempts to blur the line between language and visual art. Concrete poetry was especially popular as an experimental movement in the 1960s.

Confessional poetry A poetic genre emerging in the 1950s and 1960s primarily concerned with autobiography and the unexpurgated exposure of the poet's personal life. Notable practitioners included Robert Lowell, W. D. Snodgrass, and Anne Sexton.

Conflict In Greek, *agon,* or contest. The central struggle between two or more forces in a story. Conflict generally occurs when some person or thing prevents the protagonist from achieving his or her intended goal. Opposition can arise from another character, external events, preexisting situations, fate, or even some aspect of the main character's own personality. Conflict is the basic material out of which most plots are made. (*See also* **Antagonist, Character, Complication, Rising action.**)

Connotation An association or additional meaning that a word, image, or phrase may carry, apart from its literal denotation or dictionary definition. A word picks up connotations from all the uses to which it has been put in the past. For example, an owl in literature is not merely the literal bird. It also carries the many associations (connotations, that is) attached to it.

Consonance Also called **Slant rhyme.** A kind of rhyme in which the linked words share similar consonant sounds but different vowel sounds, as in *reason* and *raisin,* *mink* and *monk.* Sometimes only the final consonant sound is identical, as in *fame* and *room, crack* and *truck.* Used mostly by modern poets, consonance often registers more subtly than exact rhyme, lending itself to special poetic effects.

Contrast A contrast of two works of literature is developed by placing them side-by-side to point out their differences. This method of analysis works well with its opposite, a **comparison,** which focuses on likenesses.

Convention Any established feature or technique in literature that is commonly understood by both authors and readers. A convention is something generally agreed on to be appropriate for its customary uses, such as the sonnet form for a love poem or the opening "Once upon a time" for a fairy tale.

Conventional symbols Literary symbols that have a conventional or customary effect on most readers. We would respond similarly to a black cat crossing our path or a young bride in a white dress. These are conventional symbols because they carry recognizable connotations and suggestions.

Cosmic irony Also called **irony of fate,** it is the irony that exists between a character's aspiration and the treatment he or she receives at the hands of fate. Oedipus's ill-destined relationship with his parents is an example of cosmic irony.

Cothurni High thick-soled boots worn by Greek and Roman tragic actors in late classical times to make them appear taller than ordinary men. (Earlier, in the fifth-century classical Athenian theater, actors wore soft shoes or boots or went barefoot.)

Couplet A two-line stanza in poetry, usually rhymed, which tends to have lines of equal length. Shakespeare's sonnets were famous for ending with a summarizing, rhymed couplet: "Give my love fame faster than Time wastes life; / So thou prevent'st his scythe and crookèd knife." (*See also* **Closed couplet.**)

Cowboy poetry A contemporary genre of folk poetry written by people with firsthand experience in the life of horse, trail, and ranch. Plainspoken and often humorous, cowboy poetry is usually composed in rhymed ballad stanzas and meant to be recited aloud.

Crisis The point in a drama when the crucial action, decision, or realization must be made, marking the turning point or reversal of the protagonist's fortunes. From the Greek word *krisis*, meaning "decision." For example, Hamlet's decision to refrain from killing Claudius while the guilty king is praying is a crisis that leads directly to his accidental murder of Polonius, pointing forward to the catastrophe of Act V. Typically, the crisis inaugurates the falling action (after Hamlet's murder of Polonius, Claudius controls the events) until the catastrophe (or conclusion), which is decided by the death of the hero, King Claudius, Queen Gertrude, and Laertes. In *Oedipus*, the crisis occurs as the hero presses forward to the horrible truth, to realize he is an incestuous parricide and to take responsibility by blinding himself.

Cultural studies A contemporary interdisciplinary field of academic study that focuses on understanding the social power encoded in "texts." Cultural studies defines "texts" more broadly than literary works; they include any analyzable phenomenon from a traditional poem to an advertising image or an actor's face. Cultural studies has no central critical methodology but uses whatever intellectual tools are appropriate to the analysis at hand.

Dactyl A metrical foot of verse in which one stressed syllable is followed by two unstressed syllables (′ ⌣ ⌣, as in *bat*-ter-y or *par*-a-mour). The dactylic meter is less common to English than it was to classical Greek and Latin verse. Longfellow's *Evangeline* is the most famous English-language long dactylic poem.

Deconstructionist criticism A school of criticism that rejects the traditional assumption that language can accurately represent reality. Deconstructionists believe that literary texts can have no single meaning; therefore, they concentrate their attentions on *how* language is being used in a text, rather than on *what* is being said.

Decorum Propriety or appropriateness. In poetry, decorum usually refers to a level of diction that is proper to use in a certain occasion. Decorum can also apply to characters, setting, and the harmony that exists between the elements in a poem. For example, aged nuns speaking inner-city jive might violate decorum.

Denotation The literal, dictionary meaning of a word. (*See also* **Connotation.**)

Dénouement The resolution or conclusion of a literary work as plot complications are unraveled after the climax. In French, *dénouement* means "unknotting" or "untying." (*See also* **Closed dénouement, Conclusion, Open dénouement.**)

Deus ex machina Latin for "a god from a machine." The phrase refers to the Greek playwrights' frequent use of a god, mechanically lowered to the stage from the *skene* roof, to resolve human conflict with judgments and commands. Conventionally, the phrase now refers to any forced or improbable device in plot resolution.

Dialect A particular variety of language spoken by an identifiable regional group or social class of persons. Dialects are often used in literature in an attempt to present a character more realistically and to express significant differences in class or background.

Dialogue The direct representation of the conversation between two or more characters. (*See also* **Monologue.**)

Diction Word choice or vocabulary. Diction refers to the class of words that an author decides is appropriate to use in a particular work. Literary history is the story of diction being challenged, upheld, and reinvented. **Concrete diction** involves a highly specific word choice in the naming of something or someone. **Abstract diction** contains words that express more general ideas or concepts. More concrete diction would offer *boxer puppy* rather than *young canine*, *Lake Ontario* rather than *body of fresh water*. Concrete words refer to what we can immediately perceive with our senses. (*See also* **Levels of diction.**)

Didactic fiction A narrative that intends to teach a specific moral lesson or provide a model for proper behavior. This term is now often used pejoratively to describe a story in which the events seem manipulated in order to convey an uplifting idea, but much classic fiction has been written in the didactic mode—Aesop's *Fables*, John Bunyan's *The Pilgrim's Progress*, and Harriet Beecher Stowe's *Uncle Tom's Cabin*.

Didactic poetry A kind of poetry intended to teach the reader a moral lesson or impart a body of knowledge. Poetry that aims for education over art.

Dimeter A verse meter consisting of two metrical feet, or two primary stresses, per line.

Doggerel Verse full of irregularities often due to the poet's incompetence. Doggerel is crude verse that brims with cliché, obvious rhyme, and inept rhythm.

Double plot Also called **subplot.** Familiar in Elizabethan drama, a second story or plotline that is complete and interesting in its own right, often doubling or inverting the main plot. By analogy or counterpoint, a skillful subplot broadens perspective on the main plot to enhance rather than dilute its effect. In Shakespeare's *Othello*, for instance, Iago's duping of Rodrigo reflects the main plot of Iago's treachery to Othello.

Drama Derived from the Greek *dran*, "to do," *drama* means "action" or "deed." Drama is the form of literary composition designed for performance in the theater, in which actors take the roles of the characters, perform the indicated action, and speak the written dialogue. In the *Poetics*, Aristotle described tragedy or dramatic enactment as the most fully evolved form of the impulse to imitate or make works of art.

Dramatic irony A special kind of suspenseful expectation, when the audience or reader understands the implication and meaning of a situation onstage and foresees the oncoming disaster (in tragedy) or triumph (in comedy) but the character does not. The irony forms between the contrasting levels of knowledge of the character and the audience. Dramatic irony is pervasive throughout Sophocles's *Oedipus*, for example, because we know from the beginning what Oedipus does not. We watch with dread and fascination the spectacle of a morally good man, committed to the salvation of his city, unwittingly preparing undeserved suffering for himself.

Dramatic monologue A poem written as a speech made by a character at some decisive moment. The speaker is usually addressing a silent listener as in T. S. Eliot's "The Love Song of J. Alfred Prufrock" or Robert Browning's "My Last Duchess."

Dramatic poetry Any verse written for the stage, as in the plays of classical Greece, the Renaissance (Shakespeare), and neoclassical periods (Molière, Racine). Also a kind of poetry that presents the voice of an imaginary character (or characters) speaking directly, without any additional narration by the author. In poetry, the term usually refers to the dramatic monologue, a lyric poem written as a speech made by a character at some decisive moment, such as Lord, Alfred Tennyson's "Ulysses." (*See also* **Dramatic monologue.**)

Dramatic point of view A point of view in which the narrator merely reports dialogue and action with minimal interpretation or access to the characters' minds. The dramatic point of view, as the name implies, uses prose fiction to approximate the method of plays (where readers are provided only with set descriptions, stage directions, and dialogue, and thus must supply motivations based solely on this external evidence).

Dramatic question The primary unresolved issue in a drama as it unfolds. The dramatic question is the result of artful plotting, raising suspense and expectation in a play's action as it moves toward its outcome. Will the Prince in *Hamlet*, for example, achieve what he has been instructed to do and what he intends to do?

Dramatic situation The basic conflict that initiates a work or establishes a scene. It usually describes both a protagonist's motivation and the forces that oppose its realization. (*See also* **Antagonist, Character, Complication, Plot, Rising action.**)

Dumb show In Renaissance theater, a mimed dramatic performance whose purpose is to prepare the audience for the main action of the play to follow. Jacobean playwrights like John Webster used it to show violent events that occur some distance from the play's locale. The most famous Renaissance example is the dumb show preceding the presentation of "The Murder of Gonzago" in *Hamlet*.

Dynamic character A character who, during the course of the narrative, grows or changes in some significant way. (*See also* **Character development.**)

Echo verse A poetic form in which the final syllables of the lines are repeated back as a reply or commentary, often using puns. Echo verse dates back to late classical Greek poetry.

Editorial omniscience When an omniscient narrator goes beyond reporting the thoughts of his or her characters to make a critical judgment or commentary, making explicit the narrator's own thoughts or philosophies.

Editorial point of view The effect that occurs when a third-person narrator adds his or her own comments (which presumably represent the ideas and opinions of the author) into the narrative.

Elegy A lament or a sadly meditative poem, often written on the occasion of a death or other solemn theme. An elegy is usually a sustained poem in a formal style.

Endnote An additional piece of information that the author includes in a note at the end of a paper or chapter. Endnotes usually contain information that the author feels is important to convey but not appropriate to fit into the main body of text. (*See also* **Footnote.**)

End rhyme Rhyme that occurs at the ends of lines, rather than within them (as internal rhyme does). End rhyme is the most common kind of rhyme in English-language poetry.

End-stopped line A line of verse that ends in a full pause, usually indicated by a mark of punctuation.

English sonnet Also called **Shakespearean sonnet.** The English sonnet has a rhyme scheme organized into three quatrains with a final couplet: *abab cdcd efef gg.* The poem may turn, that is, shift in mood or tone, between any of the quatrains (although it usually occurs on the ninth line). (*See also* **Sonnet.**)

Envoy A short, often summarizing stanza that appears at the end of certain poetic forms (most notably the sestina, chant royal, and the French ballade). The envoy contains the poet's parting words. The word comes from the French *envoi*, meaning "sending forth."

Epic A long narrative poem usually composed in an elevated style tracing the adventures of a legendary or mythic hero. Epics are usually written in a consistent form and meter throughout. Famous epics include Homer's *Iliad* and *Odyssey*, Virgil's *Aeneid*, and Milton's *Paradise Lost*.

Epigram A very short poem, often comic, usually ending with some sharp turn of wit or meaning.

Epigraph A brief quotation preceding a story or other literary work. An epigraph usually suggests the subject, theme, or atmosphere the story will explore.

Epiphany A moment of insight, discovery, or revelation by which a character's life is greatly altered. An epiphany generally occurs near the end of a story. The term, which means "showing forth" in Greek, was first used in Christian theology to signify the manifestation of God's presence in the world. This theological idea was first borrowed by James Joyce to refer to a heightened moment of secular revelation.

Episode An incident in a large narrative that has unity in itself. An episode may bear close relation to the central narrative, but it can also be a digression.

Episodic plot, episodic structure A form of plotting where the individual scenes and events are presented chronologically without any profound sense of cause-and-effect relationship. In an episodic narrative the placement of many scenes could be changed without greatly altering the overall effect of the work.

Epistolary novel Novel in which the story is told by way of letters written by one or more of the characters. This form often lends an authenticity to the story, a sense that the author may have discovered these letters; but in fact they are a product of the author's invention.

Euphony The harmonious effect when the sounds of the words connect with the meaning in a way pleasing to the ear and mind. An example is found in Tennyson's lines, "The moan of doves in immemorial elms, / And murmuring of innumerable bees." The opposite of euphony is **cacophony.**

Exact rhyme A full rhyme in which the sounds following the initial letters of the words are identical in sound, as in *follow* and *hollow, go* and *slow, disband* and *this hand*.

Explication Literally, an "unfolding." In an explication an entire poem is explained in detail, addressing every element and unraveling any complexities as a means of analysis.

Exposition The opening portion of a narrative or drama. In the exposition, the scene is set, the protagonist is introduced, and the author discloses any other background information necessary to allow the reader to understand and relate to the events that are to follow.

Expressionism A dramatic style developed between 1910 and 1924 in Germany in reaction against realism's focus on surface details and external reality. To draw an audience into a dreamlike subjective realm, expressionistic artistic styles used episodic plots, distorted lines, exaggerated shapes, abnormally intense coloring, mechanical physical movement, and telegraphic speech (the broken syntax of a disordered psyche). Staging the contents of the unconscious, expressionist plays ranged from utopian visions of a fallen, materialistic world redeemed by the spirituality of "new men" to pessimistic nightmare visions of universal catastrophe.

Eye rhyme Rhyme in which the spelling of the words appears alike, but the pronunciations differ, as in *laughter* and *daughter, idea* and *flea*.

Fable A brief, often humorous narrative told to illustrate a moral. The characters in fables are traditionally animals whose personality traits symbolize human traits. Particular animals have conventionally come to represent specific human qualities or values. For example, the ant represents industry, the fox craftiness, and the lion nobility. A fable often concludes by summarizing its moral message in abstract terms. For example, Aesop's fable "The North Wind and the Sun" concludes with the moral "Persuasion is better than force." (*See also* **Allegory.**)

Fairy tale A traditional form of short narrative folklore, originally transmitted orally, that features supernatural characters such as witches, giants, fairies, or animals with human personality traits. Fairy tales often feature a hero or heroine who seems destined to achieve some desirable fate—such as marrying a prince or princess, becoming wealthy, or destroying an enemy.

Falling action The events in a narrative that follow the climax and bring the story to its conclusion, or dénouement.

Falling meter Trochaic and dactylic meters are called falling meters because their first syllable is accented, followed by one or more unaccented syllables. A foot of falling meter falls in its level of stress, as in the words *co*-medy or *aw*-ful.

Fantasy A narrative that depicts events, characters, or places that could not exist in the real world. Fantasy has limited interest in portraying experience realistically. Instead, it freely pursues the possibilities of the imagination. Fantasy usually includes elements of magic or the supernatural. Sometimes it is used to illustrate a moral message as in fables. Fantasy is a type of romance that emphasizes wish fulfillment (or nightmare fulfillment) instead of verisimilitude.

Farce A type of comedy featuring exaggerated character types in ludicrous and improbable situations, provoking belly laughs with sexual mix-ups, crude verbal jokes, pratfalls, and knockabout horseplay (like the comic violence of the Punch and Judy show).

Feminine rhyme A rhyme of two or more syllables with a stress on a syllable other than the last, as in *tur*-tle and *fer*-tile. (*See also* **Masculine rhyme, Rhyme.**)

Feminist criticism *See* **Gender criticism.**

Fiction From the Latin *ficio*, "act of fashioning, a shaping, a making." Fiction refers to any literary work that—although it might contain factual information—is not bound by factual accuracy, but creates a narrative shaped or made up by the author's imagination. Drama and poetry (especially narrative poetry) can be considered works of fiction, but the term now usually refers more specifically to prose stories and novels. Historical and other factual writing also requires shaping and making, but it is distinct from fiction because it is not free to invent people, places, and events; forays from documented fact must identify themselves as conjecture or hypothesis. Nonfiction, as the name suggests, is a category conventionally separate from fiction. Certainly an essay or work of literary journalism is "a made thing," and writers of nonfiction routinely employ the techniques used by fiction writers (moving forward and backward in time, reporting the inner thoughts of characters, etc.), but works of nonfiction must be not only true but factual. The truth of a work of fiction depends not on facts, but on how convincingly the writer creates the world of the story.

Figure of speech An expression or comparison that relies not on its literal meaning, but rather on its connotations and suggestions. For example, "He's dumber than dirt" is not literally true; it is a figure of speech. Major figures of speech include **metaphor, metonymy, simile,** and **synecdoche.**

First-person narrator A story in which the narrator is a participant in the action. Such a narrator refers to himself or herself as "I" and may be a major or minor character in the story. His or her attitude and understanding of characters and events shapes the reader's perception of the story being told.

Fixed form A traditional verse form requiring certain predetermined elements of structure, for example, a stanza pattern, set meter, or predetermined line length. A fixed form like the sonnet, for instance, must have no more nor less than fourteen lines, rhymed according to certain conventional patterns. (*See also* **Closed form.**)

Flashback A scene relived in a character's memory. Flashbacks can be related by the narrator in a summary or they can be experienced by the characters themselves. Flashbacks allow the author to include events that occurred before the opening of the story, which may show the reader something significant that happened in the character's past or give an indication of what kind of person the character used to be.

Flat character A term coined by English novelist E. M. Forster to describe a character with only one outstanding trait. Flat characters are rarely the central characters in a narrative and are often based on **stock characters.** Flat characters stay the same throughout a story. (*See also* **Dynamic character.**)

Folk ballads Anonymous narrative songs, usually in ballad meter, that were originally transmitted orally. Although most well-known ballads have been transcribed and published in order to protect them from being lost, they were originally created for oral performance, often resulting in many versions of a single ballad.

Folk epic Also called **Traditional epic.** A long narrative poem that traces the adventures of a tribe or nation's popular heroes. Some examples of epics are the *Iliad* and the *Odyssey* (Greek), *The Song of Roland* (French), and *The Cid* (Spanish). A folk epic originates in an oral tradition as opposed to a literary epic, which is written by an individual author consciously emulating earlier epic poetry.

Folklore The body of traditional wisdom and customs—including songs, stories, myths, and proverbs—of a people as collected and continued through oral tradition.

Folktale A short narrative drawn from folklore that has been passed down through an oral tradition. (*See also* **Fairy tale, Legend.**)

Foot The unit of measurement in metrical poetry. Different meters are identified by the pattern and order of stressed and unstressed syllables in their foot, usually containing two or three syllables, with one syllable accented.

Footnote An additional piece of information that the author includes at the bottom of a page, usually noted by a small reference number in the main text. A footnote might supply the reader with brief facts about a related historical figure or event, the definition of a foreign word or phrase, or any other relevant information that may help in understanding the text. (*See also* **Endnote.**)

Foreshadowing In plot construction, the technique of arranging events and information in such a way that later events are prepared for, or shadowed, beforehand. The author may introduce specific words, images, or actions in order to suggest significant later events. The effective use of foreshadowing by an author may prevent a story's outcome from seeming haphazard or contrived.

Form The means by which a literary work conveys its meaning. Traditionally, form refers to the way in which an artist expresses meaning rather than the content of that meaning, but it is now commonplace to note that form and content are inextricably related. Form, therefore, is more than the external framework of a literary work. It includes the totality of ways in which it unfolds and coheres as a structure of meaning and expression.

Formal English The heightened, impersonal language of educated persons, usually only written, although possibly spoken on dignified occasions. (*See also* **Levels of diction.**)

Formalist criticism A school of criticism which argues that literature may only be discussed on its own terms; that is, without outside influences or information. A key method that formalists use is close reading, a step-by-step analysis of the elements in a text.

Found poetry Poetry constructed by arranging bits of "found" prose. A found poem is a literary work made up of nonliterary language arranged for expressive effect.

Free verse From the French *vers libre.* Free verse describes poetry that organizes its lines without meter. It may be rhymed (as in some poems by H.D.), but it usually is not. There is no one means of organizing free verse, and different authors have used irreconcilable systems. What unites the two approaches is a freedom from metrical regularity. (*See also* **Open form.**)

Gender criticism Gender criticism examines how sexual identity influences the creation, interpretation, and evaluation of literary works. This critical approach began with feminist criticism in the 1960s and 1970s which stated that literary study had been so dominated by men that it contained many unexamined "male-produced" assumptions. Feminist criticism sought to address this imbalance in two ways: first in insisting that sexless interpretation was impossible, and second by articulating responses to the texts that were explicitly male or female. More recently, gender criticism has focused on gay and lesbian literary identity as interpretive strategies.

General English The ordinary speech of educated native speakers. Most literate speech and writing is general English. Its diction is more educated than **colloquial English,** yet not as elevated as **formal English.** (*See also* **Levels of diction.**)

Genre A conventional combination of literary form and subject matter, usually aimed at creating certain effects. A genre implies a preexisting understanding between the artist and the reader about the purpose and rules of the work. A horror story, for example, combines the form of the short story with certain conventional subjects, style, and theme with the expectation of frightening the reader. Major short story genres include science fiction, gothic, horror, and detective tales.

Gothic fiction A genre that creates terror and suspense, usually set in an isolated castle, mansion, or monastery populated by mysterious or threatening individuals. The Gothic form, invented by Horace Walpole in *The Castle of Otranto* (1764), has flourished in one form or another ever since. The term *Gothic* is also applied to medieval architecture, and Gothic fiction almost inevitably exploits claustrophobic interior architecture in its plotting—often featuring dungeons, crypts, torture chambers, locked rooms, and secret passageways. In the nineteenth century, writers such as Nathaniel Hawthorne, Edgar Allan Poe, and Charlotte Perkins Gilman brought the genre into the mainstream of American fiction.

Haiku A Japanese verse form that has three unrhymed lines of five, seven, and five syllables. Traditional haiku is often serious and spiritual in tone, relying mostly on imagery, and usually set in one of the four seasons.

Hamartia Greek for "error." An offense committed in ignorance of some material fact (without deliberate criminal intent) and therefore free of blameworthiness. A big mistake unintentionally made as a result of an intellectual error (not vice or criminal wickedness) by a morally good person, usually involving the identity of a blood relation. The *hamartia* of Oedipus, quite simply, is based on his ignorance of his true parentage; inadvertently and unwittingly, then, he commits the *hamartia* of patricide and incest. (*See also* **Recognition.**)

Heptameter A verse meter consisting of seven metrical feet, or seven primary stresses, per line.

Hero The central character in a narrative. The term is derived from the Greek epic tradition, in which *heroes* were the leading warriors among the princes. By extension, *hero* and *heroine* have come to mean the principal male and female figures in a narrative or dramatic literary work, although many today call protagonists of either sex *heroes*. When a critic terms the protagonist a *hero*, the choice of words often implies a positive moral assessment of the character. (*See also* **Antihero.**)

Heroic couplet *See* **Closed couplet.**

Hexameter A verse meter consisting of six metrical feet, or six primary stresses, per line.

High comedy A comic genre evoking so-called intellectual or thoughtful laughter from an audience that remains emotionally detached from the play's depiction of the folly, pretense, and incongruity of human behavior. The French playwright Molière and the English dramatists of the Restoration period developed a special form of high comedy in the **comedy of manners,** focused on the social relations and amorous intrigues of sophisticated upper-class men and women, conducted through witty repartee and verbal combat.

Historical criticism The practice of analyzing a literary work by investigating the social, cultural, and intellectual context that produced it—a context that necessarily includes the artist's biography and milieu. Historical critics strive to recreate the exact meaning and impact a work had on its original audience.

Historical fiction A type of fiction in which the narrative is set in another time or place. In historical fiction, the author usually attempts to recreate a faithful picture of daily life during the period. For example, Robert Graves's *I, Claudius* depicts the lives of the ancient Roman ruling class in the early Imperial age. Historical fiction sometimes introduces well-known figures from the past. More often it places imaginary characters in a carefully reconstructed version of a particular historical era.

Hubris Overweening pride, outrageous behavior, or the insolence that leads to ruin, hubris was in the Greek moral vocabulary the antithesis of moderation or rectitude. Creon, in Sophocles's *Antigonê,* is a good example of a character brought down by his hubris.

Hyperbole *See* **Overstatement.**

Iamb A metrical foot in verse in which an unaccented syllable is followed by an accented one, as in "ca-*ress*" or "a *cat*" (˘ ′). The iambic measure is the most common meter used in English poetry.

Iambic meter A verse meter consisting of a specific recurring number of iambic feet per line. (*See also* **Iamb, Iambic pentameter.**)

Iambic pentameter The most common meter in English verse—five iambic feet per line. Many fixed forms, such as the sonnet and heroic couplets, are written in iambic pentameter. Unrhymed iambic pentameter is called **blank verse.**

Image A word or series of words that refers to any sensory experience (usually sight, although also sound, smell, touch, or taste). An image is a direct or literal recreation of physical experience and adds immediacy to literary language.

Imagery The collective set of images in a poem or other literary work.

Impartial omniscience Refers to an omniscient narrator who, although he or she presents the thoughts and actions of the characters, does not judge them or comment on them. (Contrasts with **Editorial omniscience.**)

Implied metaphor A metaphor that uses neither connectives nor the verb *to be*. If we say, "John crowed over his victory," we imply metaphorically that John is a rooster but do not say so specifically. (*See also* **Metaphor.**)

In medias res A Latin phrase meaning "in the midst of things" that refers to a narrative device of beginning a story midway in the events it depicts (usually at an exciting or significant moment) before explaining the context or preceding actions. Epic poems such as Virgil's *Aeneid* or John Milton's *Paradise Lost* commonly begin *in medias res*, but the technique is also found in modern fiction.

Initial alliteration *See* **Alliteration.**

Initiation story Also called **Coming-of-age story.** A narrative in which the main character, usually a child or adolescent, undergoes an important experience or rite of passage—often a difficult or disillusioning one—that prepares him or her for adulthood. James Joyce's "Araby" is a classic example of an initiation story.

Innocent narrator Also called **naive narrator.** A character who fails to understand all the implications of the story he or she tells. Of course, virtually any narrator has some degree of innocence or naiveté, but the innocent narrator—often a child or childlike adult—is used by an author trying to generate irony, sympathy, or pity by creating a gap between what the narrator knows and what the reader knows. Mark Twain's Huckleberry Finn—despite his mischievous nature—is an example of an innocent narrator.

Interior monologue An extended presentation of a character's thoughts in a narrative. Usually written in the present tense and printed without quotation marks, an interior monologue reads as if the character were speaking aloud to himself or herself, for the reader to overhear. A famous example of interior monologue comes at the end of *Ulysses* when Joyce gives us the rambling memories and reflections of Molly Bloom.

Internal alliteration *See* **Alliteration.**

Internal refrain A refrain that appears within a stanza, generally in a position that stays fixed throughout a poem. (*See also* **Refrain.**)

Internal rhyme Rhyme that occurs within a line of poetry, as opposed to **end rhyme.** Read aloud, these Wallace Stevens lines are rich in internal rhyme: "Chieftain Iffucan of Azcan in caftan / Of tan with henna hackles, halt!" (from "Bantams in Pine-Woods").

Ironic point of view The perspective of a character or narrator whose voice or position is rich in ironic contradictions. (*See also* **Irony.**)

Irony A literary device in which a discrepancy of meaning is masked beneath the surface of the language. Irony is present when a writer says one thing but means something quite the opposite. There are many kinds of irony, but the two major varieties are **verbal irony** (in which the discrepancy is contained in words) and **situational irony** (in which the discrepancy exists when something is about to happen to a character or characters who expect the opposite outcome). (*See also* **Cosmic irony, Irony of fate, Sarcasm, Verbal irony.**)

Irony of fate A type of situational irony that can be used for either tragic or comic purposes. Irony of fate is the discrepancy between actions and their results, between what characters deserve and what they get, between appearance and reality. In Sophocles's tragedy, for instance, Oedipus unwittingly fulfills the prophecy even as he takes the actions a morally good man would take to avoid it. (*See also* **Cosmic irony.**)

Italian sonnet Also called **Petrarchan sonnet,** a sonnet with the following rhyme pattern for the first eight lines (the **octave**): *abba, abba*; the final six lines (the **sestet**) may follow any pattern of rhymes, as long as it does not end in a couplet. The poem traditionally turns, or shifts in mood or tone, after the octave. (*See also* **Sonnet.**)

Katharsis, **catharsis** Often translated as purgation or purification, the term is drawn from the last element of Aristotle's definition of tragedy, relating to the final cause or purpose of tragic art. Catharsis generally refers to the feeling of emotional release or calm the spectator feels at the end of tragedy. In Aristotle *katharsis* is the final effect of the playwright's skillful use of plotting, character, and poetry to elicit pity and fear from the audience. Through *katharsis,* drama taught the audience compassion for the vulnerabilities of others and schooled it in justice and other civic virtues.

Legend A traditional narrative handed down through popular oral tradition to illustrate and celebrate a remarkable character, an important event, or to explain the unexplainable. Legends, unlike other folktales, claim to be true and usually take place in real locations, often with genuine historical figures.

Levels of diction In English, there are conventionally four basic levels of formality in word choice, or four levels of diction. From the least formal to the most elevated they are **vulgate, colloquial English, general English,** and **formal English.** (*See also* **Diction.**)

Limerick A short and usually comic verse form of five anapestic lines usually rhyming *aabba*. The first, second, and fifth lines traditionally have three stressed syllables each; the third and fourth have two stresses each (3, 3, 2, 2, 3).

Limited omniscience Also called third-person limited point of view. A type of point of view in which the narrator sees into the minds of some but not all of the characters. Most typically, limited omniscience sees through the eyes of one major or minor character. In limited omniscience, the author can compromise between the immediacy of first-person narration and the mobility of third person.

Literary ballad Ballad not meant for singing, written for literate readers by sophisticated poets rather than arising from the anonymous oral tradition. (*See also* **Ballad.**)

Literary epic A crafted imitation of the oral folk epic written by an author living in a society where writing has been invented. Examples of the literary epic are *The Aeneid* by Virgil and *The Divine Comedy* by Dante Alighieri. (*See also* **Folk epic.**)

Literary genre *See* **Genre.**

Literary theory Literary criticism that tries to formulate general principles rather than discuss specific texts. Theory operates at a high level of abstraction and often focuses on understanding basic issues of language, communication, art, interpretation, culture, and ideological content.

Local color The use of specific regional material—unique customs, dress, habits, and speech patterns of ordinary people—to create atmosphere or realism in a literary work.

Locale The location where a story takes place.

Low comedy A comic style arousing laughter through jokes, slapstick humor, sight gags, and boisterous clowning. Unlike **high comedy,** it has little intellectual appeal. (*See also* **Comedy.**)

Lyric A short poem expressing the thoughts and feelings of a single speaker. Often written in the first person, lyric poetry traditionally has a songlike immediacy and emotional force.

Madrigal A short secular song for three or more voices arranged in counterpoint. The madrigal is often about love or pastoral themes. It originated in Italy in the fourteenth century and enjoyed great success during the Elizabethan Age.

Magic realism Also called **magical realism.** A type of contemporary narrative in which the magical and the mundane are mixed in an overall context of realistic storytelling. The term was coined by Cuban novelist Alejo Carpentier in 1949 to describe the matter-of-fact combination of the fantastic and everyday in Latin American fiction. Magic realism has become the standard name for an international trend in contemporary fiction such as Gabriel García Márquez's *One Hundred Years of Solitude*.

Masculine rhyme Either a rhyme of one syllable words (as in *fox* and *socks*) or—in polysyllabic words—a rhyme on the stressed final syllables: con-*trive* and sur-*vive*. (*See also* **Feminine rhyme.**)

Masks In Latin, *personae*. In classical Greek theater, full facial masks made of leather, linen, or light wood, with headdress, allowed male actors to embody the conventionalized characters (or *dramatis personae*) of the tragic and comic stage. Later, in the seventeenth and eighteenth centuries, stock characters of the ***commedia dell' arte*** wore characteristic half masks made of leather. (*See also* **Persona.**)

Melodrama Originally a stage play featuring background music and sometimes songs to underscore the emotional mood of each scene. Melodramas were notoriously weak in characterization and motivation but famously strong on action, suspense, and passion. Melodramatic characters were stereotyped villains, heroes, and young lovers. When the term *melodrama* is applied to fiction, it is almost inevitably a negative criticism implying that the author has sacrificed psychological depth and credibility for emotional excitement and adventurous plotting.

Metafiction Fiction that consciously explores its own nature as a literary creation. The Greek word *meta* means "upon"; metafiction consequently is a mode of narrative that does not try to create the illusion of verisimilitude but delights in its own fictional nature, often by speculating on the story it is telling. The term is usually associated with late-twentieth-century writers like John Barth, Italo Calvino, and Jorge Luis Borges.

Metaphor A statement that one thing *is* something else, which, in a literal sense, it is not. By asserting that a thing is something else, a metaphor creates a close association between the two entities and usually underscores some important similarity between them. An example of metaphor is "Richard is a pig."

Meter A recurrent, regular, rhythmic pattern in verse. When stresses recur at fixed intervals, the result is meter. Traditionally, meter has been the basic organizational device of world poetry. There are many existing meters, each identified by the different patterns of recurring sounds. In English most common meters involve the arrangement of stressed and unstressed syllables.

Metonymy Figure of speech in which the name of a thing is substituted for that of another closely associated with it. For instance, in saying "The White House decided," one could mean that the president decided.

Minimalist fiction Contemporary fiction written in a deliberately flat, unemotional tone and an appropriately unadorned style. Minimalist fiction often relies more on dramatic action, scene, and dialogue than complex narration or authorial summary. Examples of minimalist fiction can be found in the short stories of Raymond Carver and Bobbie Ann Mason.

Mixed metaphor A metaphor that trips over another metaphor—usually unconsciously—already in the statement. Mixed metaphors are the result of combining two or more incompatible metaphors resulting in ridiculousness or nonsense. For example, "Mary was such a tower of strength that she breezed her way through all the work" ("towers" do not "breeze").

Monologue An extended speech by a single character. The term originated in drama, where it describes a solo speech that has listeners (as opposed to a **soliloquy,** where the character speaks only to himself or herself). A short story or even a novel can be written in monologue form if it is an unbroken speech by one character to another silent character or characters.

Monometer A verse meter consisting of one metrical foot, or one primary stress, per line.

Monosyllabic foot A foot, or unit of meter, that contains only one syllable.

Moral A paraphrasable message or lesson implied or directly stated in a literary work. Commonly, a moral is stated at the end of a fable.

Motif An element that recurs significantly throughout a narrative. A motif can be an image, idea, theme, situation, or action (and was first commonly used as a musical term for a recurring melody or melodic fragment). A motif can also refer to an element that recurs across many literary works like a beautiful lady in medieval romances who turns out to be an evil fairy or three questions that are asked a protagonist to test his or her wisdom.

Motivation What a character in a story or drama wants. The reasons an author provides for a character's actions. Motivation can be either *explicit* (in which reasons are specifically stated in a story) or *implicit* (in which the reasons are only hinted at or partially revealed).

Myth A traditional narrative of anonymous authorship that arises out of a culture's oral tradition. The characters in traditional myths are usually gods or heroic figures. Myths characteristically explain the origins of things—gods, people, places, plants, animals, and natural events—usually from a cosmic view. A culture's values and belief systems are traditionally passed from generation to generation in myth. In literature, myth may also refer to boldly imagined narratives that embody primal truths about life. Myth is usually differentiated from legend, which has a specific historical base.

Mythological criticism The practice of analyzing a literary work by looking for recurrent universal patterns. Mythological criticism explores the artist's common humanity by tracing how the individual imagination uses myths and symbols that are shared by different cultures and epochs.

Naive narrator *See* **Innocent narrator.**

Narrative poem A poem that tells a story. Narrative is one of the four traditional modes of poetry, along with lyric, dramatic, and didactic. **Ballads** and **epics** are two common forms of narrative poetry.

Narrator A voice or character that provides the reader with information and insight about the characters and incidents in a narrative. A narrator's perspective and personality can greatly affect how a story is told. (*See also* **Omniscient narrator, Point of view.**)

Naturalism A type of fiction or drama in which the characters are presented as products or victims of environment and heredity. Naturalism, considered an extreme form of realism, customarily depicts the social, psychological, and economic milieu of the primary characters. Naturalism was first formally developed by French novelist Émile Zola in the 1870s. In promoting naturalism as a theory of animal behavior, Zola urged the modeling of naturalist literature and drama on the scientific case study. The writer, like the scientist, was to record objective reality with detachment;

events onstage should be reproduced with sufficient exactness to demonstrate the strict laws of material causality. Important American Naturalists include Jack London, Theodore Dreiser, and Stephen Crane. (*See also* **Realism.**)

New Formalism A term for a contemporary literary movement (begun around 1980) in which young poets began using rhyme, meter, and narrative again. New Formalists attempt to write poetry that appeals to an audience beyond academia. Timothy Steele, Vikram Seth, R. S. Gwynn, David Mason, A. E. Stallings, and Marilyn Nelson are poets commonly associated with the movement.

New naturalism A term describing some American plays of the 1970s and 1980s, frankly showing the internal and external forces that shape the lives of unhappy, alienated, dehumanized, and often impoverished characters. Examples include the plays of Sam Shepard, August Wilson, and David Mamet.

Nonfiction novel A genre in which actual events are presented as a novel-length story, using the techniques of fiction (flashback, interior monologues, etc.). Truman Capote's *In Cold Blood* (1966), which depicts a multiple murder and subsequent trial in Kansas, is a classic example of this modern genre.

Nonparticipant narrator A narrator who does not appear in the story as a character but is capable of revealing the thoughts and motives of one or more characters. A nonparticipant narrator is also capable of moving from place to place in order to describe action and report dialogue. (*See also* **Omniscient narrator.**)

Novel An extended work of fictional prose narrative. The term *novel* usually implies a book-length narrative (as compared to more compact forms of prose fiction such as the short story). Because of its extended length, a novel usually has more characters, more varied scenes, and a broader coverage of time than a short story.

Novella In modern terms, a prose narrative longer than a short story but shorter than a novel (approximately 30,000 to 50,000 words). Unlike a short story, a novella is long enough to be published independently as a brief book. Classic modern novellas include Franz Kafka's *The Metamorphosis*, Joseph Conrad's *Heart of Darkness*, and Thomas Mann's *Death in Venice*. During the Renaissance, however, the term *novella* originally referred to short prose narratives such as those found in Giovanni Boccaccio's *Decameron*.

Objective point of view *See* **Dramatic point of view.**

Observer A type of first-person narrator who is relatively detached from or plays only a minor role in the events described.

Octameter A verse meter consisting of eight metrical feet, or eight primary stresses, per line.

Octave A stanza of eight lines. *Octave* is a term usually used when speaking of sonnets to indicate the first eight-line section of the poem, as distinct from the *sestet* (the final six lines). Some poets also use octaves as separate stanzas as in W. B. Yeats's "Sailing to Byzantium," which employs the *ottava rima* ("eighth rhyme") stanza—*abababcc*.

Off rhyme *See* **Slant rhyme.**

Omniscient narrator Also called **all-knowing narrator.** A narrator who has the ability to move freely through the consciousness of any character. The omniscient narrator also has complete knowledge of all of the external events in a story. (*See also* **Nonparticipant narrator.**)

Onomatopoeia A literary device that attempts to represent a thing or action by the word that imitates the sound associated with it (e.g., *crash, bang, pitter-patter*).

Open dénouement One of the two conventional types of dénouement or resolution. In open dénouement, the author ends a narrative with a few loose ends, or unresolved matters, on which the reader is left to speculate. (*See also* **Closed dénouement.**)

Open form Verse that has no set formal scheme—no meter, rhyme, or even set stanzaic pattern. Open form is always in free verse. (*See also* **Free verse.**)

Oral tradition The tradition within a culture that transmits narratives by word of mouth from one generation to another. Fables, folktales, ballads, and songs are examples of some types of narratives found originally in an oral tradition.

Orchestra In classical Greek theater architecture, "the place for dancing," a circular, level performance space at the base of a horseshoe-shaped amphitheater, where twelve, then later (in Sophocles's plays) fifteen, young, masked, male chorus members sang and danced the odes interspersed between dramatic episodes making up the classical Greek play. Today the orchestra refers to the ground floor seats in a theater or concert hall.

Overstatement Also called **hyperbole.** Exaggeration used to emphasize a point.

Parable A brief, usually allegorical narrative that teaches a moral. The parables found in Christian literature, such as "The Parable of the Prodigal Son" (Luke 15:11–32), are classic examples of the form. In parables, unlike fables (where the moral is explicitly stated within the narrative), the moral themes are implicit and can often be interpreted in several ways. Modern parables can be found in the works of Franz Kafka and Jorge Luis Borges.

Paradox A statement that at first strikes one as self-contradictory, but that on reflection reveals some deeper sense. Paradox is often achieved by a play on words.

Parallelism An arrangement of words, phrases, clauses, or sentences side-by-side in a similar grammatical or structural way. Parallelism organizes ideas in a way that demonstrates their coordination to the reader.

Paraphrase The restatement in one's own words of what we understand a literary work to say. A paraphrase is similar to a summary, although not as brief or simple.

Parody A mocking imitation of a literary work or individual author's style, usually for comic effect. A parody typically exaggerates distinctive features of the original for humorous purposes.

Participant narrator A narrator that participates as a character within a story. (*See also* **First-person narrator.**)

Pentameter A verse meter consisting of five metrical feet, or five primary stresses, per line. In English, the most common form of pentameter is iambic.

Peripeteia Anglicized as *peripety*, Greek for "sudden change." Reversal of fortune. In a play's plotting, a sudden change of circumstance affecting the protagonist, often also including a reversal of intent on the protagonist's part. The play's peripety occurs usually when a certain result is expected and instead its opposite effect is produced. For example, at the beginning of *Oedipus*, the protagonist expects to discover the identity of the murderer of Laius. However, after the Corinthian messenger informs Oedipus that he was adopted, the hero's intent changes to encompass the search for his true parentage. A comedy's peripety restores a character to good fortune, when a moment in which the worst can happen is suddenly turned into happy circumstance.

Persona Latin for "mask." A fictitious character created by an author to be the speaker of a poem, story, or novel. A persona is always the narrator of the work and not merely a character in it.

Personification A figure of speech in which a thing, an animal, or an abstract term is endowed with human characteristics. Personification allows an author to dramatize the nonhuman world in tangibly human terms.

Petrarchan sonnet *See* **Italian sonnet.**

Picaresque A type of narrative, usually a novel, that presents the life of a likable scoundrel who is at odds with respectable society. The narrator of a picaresque was originally a *picaro* (Spanish for "rascal" or "rogue") who recounts his adventures tricking the rich and gullible. This type of narrative rarely has a tight plot, and the episodes or adventures follow in a loose chronological order.

Picture-frame stage Developed in sixteenth-century Italian playhouses, the picture-frame stage held the action within a proscenium arch, a gateway standing "in front of the scenery" (as the word *proscenium* indicates). The proscenium framed painted scene panels (receding into the middle distance) designed to give the illusion of three-dimensional perspective. Only one seat in the auditorium, reserved for the theater's royal patron or sponsor, enjoyed the complete perspectivist illusion. The raised and framed stage separated actors from the audience and the world of the play from the real world of the auditorium. Picture-frame stages became the norm throughout Europe and England up into the twentieth century.

Play review A critical account of a performance, providing the basic facts of the production, a brief plot summary, and an evaluation (with adequate rationale) of the chief elements of performance, including the acting, the direction, scene and light design, and the script, especially if the play is new or unfamiliar.

Plot The particular arrangement of actions, events, and situations that unfold in a narrative. A plot is not merely the general story of a narrative but the author's artistic pattern made from the parts of the narrative, including the exposition, complications, climax, and dénouement. How an author chooses to construct the plot determines the way the reader experiences the story. Manipulating a plot, therefore, can be the author's most important expressive device when writing a story. More than just a story made up of episodes or a bare synopsis of the temporal order of events, the plotting is the particular embodiment of an action that allows the audience to see the causal relationship between the parts of the action. (*See also* **Climax, Falling action, Rising action.**)

Poetic diction Strictly speaking, *poetic diction* means any language deemed suitable for verse, but the term generally refers to elevated language intended for poetry rather than common use. Poetic diction often refers to the ornate language used in literary periods such as the Augustan age, when authors employed a highly specialized vocabulary for their verse. (*See also* **Diction.**)

Point of view The perspective from which a story is told. There are many types of point of view, including first-person narrator (a story in which the narrator is a participant in the action) and third-person narrator (a type of narration in which the narrator is a nonparticipant).

Portmanteau word An artificial word that combines parts of other words to express some combination of their qualities. Sometimes portmanteau words prove so useful that they become part of the standard language. For example, *smog* from *smoke* and *fog;* or *brunch* from *breakfast* and *lunch.*

Print culture A culture that depends primarily on the printed word—in books, magazines, and newspapers—to distribute and preserve information. In recent decades the electronic media have taken over much of this role from print.

Projective verse Charles Olson's theory that poets compose by listening to their own breathing and using it as a rhythmic guide rather than poetic meter or form. (*See also* **Open form.**)

Proscenium arch Separating the auditorium from the raised stage and the world of the play, the architectural picture frame or gateway "standing in front of the scenery" (as the word *proscenium* indicates) in traditional European theaters from the sixteenth century on.

Prose poem Poetic language printed in prose paragraphs, but displaying the careful attention to sound, imagery, and figurative language characteristic of poetry.

Prosody The study of metrical structures in poetry. (*See also* **Scansion.**)

Protagonist The central character in a literary work. The protagonist usually initiates the main action of the story, often in conflict with the antagonist. (*See also* **Antagonist.**)

Psalms Sacred songs, usually referring to the 150 Hebrew poems collected in the Old Testament.

Psychological criticism The practice of analyzing a literary work through investigating three major areas: the nature of literary genius, the psychological study of a particular artist, and the analysis of fictional characters. This methodology uses the analytical tools of psychology and psychoanalysis to understand the underlying motivations and meanings of a literary work.

Pulp fiction A type of formulaic and quickly written fiction originally produced for cheap mass circulation magazines. The term *pulp* refers to the inexpensive wood-pulp paper developed in the mid-nineteenth century on which these magazines were printed. Most pulp fiction journals printed only melodramatic genre work—westerns, science fiction, romance, horror, adventure tales, or crime stories.

Pun A play on words in which one word is substituted for another similar or identical sound, but of very different meaning.

Purgation See **Katharsis.**

Quantitative meter A meter constructed on the principle of vowel length. Such quantities are difficult to hear in English, so this meter remains slightly foreign to our language. Classical Greek and Latin poetry were written in quantitative meters.

Quatrain A stanza consisting of four lines. Quatrains are the most common stanzas used in English-language poetry.

Rap A popular style of music that emerged in the 1980s in which lyrics are spoken or chanted over a steady beat, usually sampled or prerecorded. Rap lyrics are almost always rhymed and very rhythmic—syncopating a heavy metrical beat in a manner similar to jazz. Originally an African American form, rap is now international. In that way, rap can be seen as a form of popular poetry.

Reader-response criticism The practice of analyzing a literary work by describing what happens in the reader's mind while interpreting the text. Reader-response critics believe that no literary text exists independently of readers' interpretations and that there is no single fixed interpretation of any literary work.

Realism An attempt to reproduce faithfully the surface appearance of life, especially that of ordinary people in everyday situations. As a literary term, *realism* has two meanings—one general, the other historical. In a general sense, realism refers to the representation of characters, events, and settings in ways that the spectator will consider plausible, based on consistency and likeness to type. This sort of realism does not necessarily depend on elaborate factual description or documentation but more on the author's ability to draft plots and characters within a conventional framework of social, economic, and psychological reality. In a historical sense, Realism (usually capitalized) refers to a movement in nineteenth-century European literature and theater that rejected the idealism, elitism, and romanticism of earlier verse dramas and prose fiction in an attempt to represent life truthfully. Realist literature customarily focused on the middle class (and occasionally the working class) rather than the aristocracy, and it used social and economic detail to create an accurate account of human behavior. Realism began in France with Honoré de Balzac, Gustave Flaubert, and Guy de Maupassant and then moved internationally. Other major Realists include Leo Tolstoy, Henry James, Anton Chekhov, and Edith Wharton.

Recognition In tragic plotting, the moment of recognition occurs when ignorance gives way to knowledge, illusion to disillusion. In Aristotle's *Poetics*, this is usually a recognition of blood ties or kinship between the persons involved in grave actions involving suffering. According to Aristotle, the ideal moment of recognition coincides with *peripeteia* or reversal of fortune. The classic example occurs in *Oedipus* when Oedipus discovers that he had unwittingly killed his own father when defending himself at the crossroads and later married his own mother when assuming the Theban throne. (*See also* **Hamartia, Katharsis, Peripeteia.**)

Refrain A word, phrase, line, or stanza repeated at intervals in a song or poem. The repeated chorus of a song is a refrain.

Regionalism The literary representation of a specific locale that consciously uses the particulars of geography, custom, history, folklore, or speech. In regional narratives, the locale plays a crucial role in the presentation and progression of a story that could not be moved to another setting without artistic loss. Usually, regional narratives take place at some distance from the literary capital of a culture, often in small towns or rural areas. Examples of American regionalism can be found in the writing of Willa Cather, Kate Chopin, William Faulkner, and Eudora Welty.

Resolution The final part of a narrative, the concluding action or actions that follow the climax. (*See also* **Conclusion, Dénouement.**)

Retrospect *See* **Flashback.**

Reversal *See* **Peripeteia.**

Rhyme, Rime Two or more words that contain an identical or similar vowel sound, usually accented, with following consonant sounds (if any) identical as well: *queue* and *stew*, *prairie schooner* and *piano tuner*. (*See also* **Consonance, Exact rhyme.**)

Rhyme scheme, Rime scheme Any recurrent pattern of rhyme within an individual poem or fixed form. A rhyme scheme is usually described by using small letters to represent each end rhyme—*a* for the first rhyme, *b* for the second, and so on. The rhyme scheme of a stanza of **common meter** or hymn meter, for example, would be notated as *abab*.

Rhythm The pattern of stresses and pauses in a poem. A fixed and recurring rhythm in a poem is called **meter.**

Rising action That part of the play or narrative, including the exposition, in which events start moving toward a climax. In the rising action the protagonist usually faces the complications of the plot to reach his or her goal. In *Hamlet*, the rising action develops the conflict between Hamlet and Claudius, with Hamlet succeeding in controlling the course of events. Because the mainspring of the play's first half is the mystery of Claudius's guilt, the rising action reaches a climax when

Hamlet proves the king's guilt by the device of the play within a play (3.2—the "mousetrap" scene), when Hamlet as heroic avenger has positive proof of Claudius's guilt.

Rising meter A meter whose movement rises from an unstressed syllable (or syllables) to a stressed syllable (for-*get*, De-*troit*). Iambic and anapestic are examples of rising meter.

Romance In general terms, romance is a narrative mode that employs exotic adventure and idealized emotion rather than realistic depiction of character and action. In the romantic mode—out of which most popular genre fictions develop—people, actions, and events are depicted more as we wish them to be (heroes are very brave, villains are very bad) rather than the complex ways they usually are. Medieval romances (in both prose and verse) presented chivalric tales of kings, knights, and aristocratic ladies. Modern romances, emerging in the nineteenth century, were represented by adventure novels like Sir Walter Scott's *Ivanhoe* or Nathaniel Hawthorne's *The House of the Seven Gables*, which embodied the symbolic quests and idealized characters of earlier, chivalric tales in slightly more realistic terms, a tradition carried on in contemporary popular works like the *Star Wars* and James Bond films.

Romantic comedy A form of comic drama in which the plot focuses on one or more pairs of young lovers who overcome difficulties to achieve a happy ending (usually marriage). Shakespeare's *A Midsummer Night's Dream* is a classic example of the genre.

Rondel A thirteen-line English verse form consisting of three rhymed stanzas with a refrain.

Round character A term coined by English novelist E. M. Forster to describe a complex character who is presented in depth and detail in a narrative. Round characters are those who change significantly during the course of a narrative. Most often, round characters are the central characters in a narrative. (*See also* **Flat character.**)

Run-on line A line of verse that does not end in punctuation, but carries on grammatically to the next line. Such lines are read aloud with only a slight pause at the end. A run-on line is also called *enjambment*.

Sarcasm A conspicuously bitter form of irony in which the ironic statement is designed to hurt or mock its target. (*See also* **Irony.**)

Satiric comedy A genre using derisive humor to ridicule human weakness and folly or attack political injustices and incompetence. Satiric comedy often focuses on ridiculing characters or killjoys, who resist the festive mood of comedy. Such characters, called humors, are often characterized by one dominant personality trait or ruling obsession.

Satiric poetry Poetry that blends criticism with humor to convey a message. Satire characteristically uses irony to make its points. Usually, its tone is one of detached amusement, withering contempt, and implied superiority.

Satyr play A type of Greek comic play that was performed after the tragedies at the City Dionysia, the principal civic and religious festival of Athens. The playwrights winning the right to perform their works in the festival wrote three tragedies and one satyr play to form the traditional tetralogy, or group of four. The structure of a satyr play was similar to tragedy's. Its subject matter, treated in burlesque, was drawn from myth or the epic cycles. Its chorus was composed of satyrs (half human and half horse or goat) under the leadership of Silenus, the adoptive father of Dionysius. Rascals and revelers, satyrs represented wild versions of humanity, opposing the values of civilized men. Euripides's *Cyclops* is the only complete surviving example of the genre.

Scansion A practice used to describe rhythmic patterns in a poem by separating the metrical feet, counting the syllables, marking the accents, and indicating the pauses. Scansion can be very useful in analyzing the sound of a poem and how it should be read aloud.

Scene In drama, the scene is a division of the action in an act of the play. There is no universal convention as to what constitutes a scene, and the practice differs by playwright and period. Usually, a scene represents a single dramatic action that builds to a climax (often ending in the entrance or exit of a major character). In this last sense of a vivid and unified action, the term can be applied to fiction.

Selective omniscience The point of view that sees the events of a narrative through the eyes of a single character. The selectively omniscient narrator is usually a nonparticipant narrator.

Sentimentality A usually pejorative description of the quality of a literary work that tries to convey great emotion but fails to give the reader sufficient grounds for sharing it.

Sestet A poem or stanza of six lines. *Sestet* is a term usually used when speaking of sonnets, to indicate the final six-line section of the poem, as distinct from the octave (the first eight lines). (*See also* **Sonnet.**)

Sestina A complex verse form ("song of sixes") in which six end words are repeated in a prescribed order through six stanzas. A sestina ends with an **envoy** of three lines in which all six words appear—for a total of thirty-nine lines. Originally used by French and Italian poets, the sestina has become a popular modern form in English.

Setting The time and place of a literary work. The setting may also include the climate and even the social, psychological, or spiritual state of the participants.

Shakespearean sonnet *See* **English sonnet.**

Short Story A prose narrative too brief to be published in a separate volume—as novellas and novels frequently are. The short story is usually a focused narrative that presents one or two main characters involved in a single compelling action.

Simile A comparison of two things, indicated by some connective, usually *like*, *as*, *than*, or a verb such as *resembles*. A simile usually compares two things that initially seem unlike but are shown to have a significant resemblance. "Cool as a cucumber" and "My love is like a red, red rose" are examples of similes.

Situational Irony *See* **Irony.**

Skene In classical Greek staging of the fifth century B.C., the temporary wooden stage building in which actors changed masks and costumes when changing roles. Its facade, with double center doors and possibly two side doors, served as the setting for action taking place before a palace, temple, cave, or other interior space.

Slack syllable An unstressed syllable in a line of verse.

Slant rhyme A rhyme in which the final consonant sounds are the same but the vowel sounds are different, as in letter and litter, bone and bean. Slant rhyme may also be called *near rhyme*, *off rhyme*, or *imperfect rhyme*. (*See also* **Consonance.**)

Slapstick comedy A kind of farce, featuring pratfalls, pie throwing, fisticuffs, and other violent action. It takes its name originally from the slapstick carried by the *commedia dell'arte*'s main servant type, Harlequin.

Sociological criticism The practice of analyzing a literary work by examining the cultural, economic, and political context in which it was written or received. Sociological criticism primarily explores the relationship between the artist and society.

Soliloquy In drama, a speech by a character alone onstage in which he or she utters his or her thoughts aloud. The soliloquy is important in drama because it gives the audience insight into a character's inner life, private motivations, and uncertainties.

Sonnet From the Italian *sonnetto*: "little song." A traditional and widely used verse form, especially popular for love poetry. The sonnet is a fixed form of fourteen lines, traditionally written in iambic pentameter, usually made up of an **octave** (the first eight lines) and a concluding **sestet** (six lines). There are, however, several variations, most conspicuously the Shakespearean, or English sonnet, which consists of three quatrains and a concluding couplet. Most sonnets turn, or shift in tone or focus, after the first eight lines, although the placement may vary. (*See also* **English sonnet, Italian sonnet.**)

Spondee A metrical foot of verse containing two stressed syllables (′ ′) often substituted into a meter to create extra emphasis.

Stage business Nonverbal action that engages the attention of an audience. Expressing what cannot be said, stage business became a particularly important means of revealing the inner thoughts and feelings of a character in the development of Realism.

Stanza From the Italian, meaning "stopping-place" or "room." A recurring pattern of two or more lines of verse, poetry's equivalent to the paragraph in prose. The stanza is the basic organizational principle of most formal poetry.

Static character *See* **Flat character.**

Stock character A common or stereotypical character that occurs frequently in literature. Examples of stock characters are the mad scientist, the battle-scarred veteran, or the strong-but-silent cowboy. (*See also* **Archetype.**)

Stream of consciousness Not a specific technique, but a type of modern narration that uses various literary devices, especially interior monologue, in an attempt to duplicate the subjective and associative nature of human consciousness. Stream of consciousness often focuses on imagistic perception in order to capture the preverbal level of consciousness.

Stress An emphasis or accent placed on a syllable in speech. Clear pronunciation of polysyllabic words almost always depends on correct placement of their stress. (For instance, *de*-sert and de-*sert* are two different words and parts of speech, depending on their stress.) Stress is the basic principle of most English-language meter.

Style All the distinctive ways in which an author, genre, movement, or historical period uses language to create a literary work. An author's style depends on his or her characteristic use of diction, imagery, tone, syntax, and figurative language. Even sentence structure and punctuation can play a role in an author's style.

Subject The main topic of a poem, story, or play.

Subplot *See* **Double plot.**

Summary A brief condensation of the main idea or story of a literary work. A summary is similar to a paraphrase, but less detailed.

Surrealism A modernist movement in art and literature that tries to organize art according to the irrational dictates of the unconscious mind. Founded by the French poet André Breton, Surrealism sought to reach a higher plane of reality by abandoning logic for the seemingly absurd connections made in dreams and other unconscious mental activities.

Suspense Enjoyable anxiety created in the reader by the author's handling of plot. When the outcome of events is unclear, the author's suspension of resolution intensifies the reader's interest—particularly if the plot involves characters to whom the reader or audience is sympathetic. Suspense is also created when the fate of a character is clear to the audience, but not to the character. The suspense results from the audience's anticipation of how and when the character will meet his or her inevitable fate.

Syllabic verse A verse form in which the poet establishes a pattern of a certain number of syllables to a line. Syllabic verse is the most common meter in most Romance languages such as Italian, French, and Spanish; it is less common in English because it is difficult to hear syllable count. Syllabic verse was used by several Modernist poets, most conspicuously Marianne Moore.

Symbol A person, place, or thing in a narrative that suggests meanings beyond its literal sense. Symbol is related to allegory, but it works more complexly. In an allegory an object has a single additional significance. By contrast, a symbol usually contains multiple meanings and associations. In Herman Melville's *Moby-Dick*, for example, the great white whale does not have just a single significance but accrues powerful associations as the narrative progresses.

Symbolic act An action whose significance goes well beyond its literal meaning. In literature, symbolic acts usually involve some conscious or unconscious ritual element like rebirth, purification, forgiveness, vengeance, or initiation.

Symbolist movement An international literary movement that originated with nineteenth-century French poets such as Charles Baudelaire, Arthur Rimbaud, and Paul Verlaine. Symbolists aspired to make literature resemble music. They avoided direct statement and exposition for powerful evocation and suggestion. Symbolists also considered the poet as a seer who could look beyond the mundane aspects of the everyday world to capture visions of a higher reality.

Symbolists Members of the Symbolist movement.

Synecdoche The use of a significant part of a thing to stand for the whole of it or vice versa. To say *wheels* for *car* or *rhyme* for *poetry* are examples of synecdoche. (*See also* **Metonymy**.)

Synopsis A brief summary or outline of a story or dramatic work.

Tactile imagery A word or sequence of words that refers to the sense of touch. (*See also* **Imagery**.)

Tale A short narrative without a complex plot, the word originating from the Old English *talu*, or "speech." Tales are an ancient form of narrative found in folklore, and traditional tales often contain supernatural elements. A tale differs from a short story by its tendency toward less developed characters and linear plotting. British writer A. E. Coppard characterized the underlying difference by claiming that a story is something that is written and a tale is something that is told. The ambition of a tale is usually similar to that of a yarn: revelation of the marvelous rather than illumination of the everyday world.

Tall tale A humorous short narrative that provides a wildly exaggerated version of events. Originally an oral form, the tall tale assumes that its audience knows the narrator is distorting the events. The form is often associated with the American frontier.

Tercet A group of three lines of verse, usually all ending in the same rhyme. (*See also* **Terza rima**.)

Terminal refrain A refrain that appears at the end of each stanza in a song or poem. (*See also* **Refrain**.)

Terza rima A verse form made up of three-line stanzas that are connected by an overlapping rhyme scheme (*aba*, *bcb*, *cdc*, *ded*, etc.). Dante employs *terza rima* in *The Divine Comedy.*

Tetrameter A verse meter consisting of four metrical feet, or four primary stresses, per line.

Theater of the absurd Post–World War II European genre depicting the grotesquely comic plight of human beings thrown by accident into an irrational and meaningless world. The critic Martin Esslin coined the term to characterize plays by writers such as Samuel Beckett, Jean Genet, and Eugene Ionesco. Beckett's *Waiting for Godot* (1955), considered to be the greatest example of theater of the absurd, features in two nearly identical acts two tramps waiting almost without hope on a country road for an unidentified person, Godot. "Nothing happens, nobody comes, nobody goes, it's awful," one of them cries, perhaps echoing the unspoken thoughts of an audience confronted by a play that seemingly refuses to do anything.

Theme A generally recurring subject or idea conspicuously evident in a literary work. A short didactic work like a fable may have a single obvious theme, but longer works can contain multiple themes. Not all subjects in a work can be considered themes, only the central subject or subjects.

Thesis sentence A summing-up of the one main idea or argument that an essay or critical paper will embody.

Third-person narrator A type of narration in which the narrator is a nonparticipant. In a third-person narrative the characters are referred to as "he," "she," or "they." Third-person narrators are most commonly omniscient, but the level of their knowledge may vary from total omniscience (the narrator knows everything about the characters and their lives) to limited omniscience (the narrator is limited to the perceptions of a single character).

Tone The attitude toward a subject conveyed in a literary work. No single stylistic device creates tone; it is the net result of the various elements an author brings to creating the work's feeling and manner. Tone may be playful, sarcastic, ironic, sad, solemn, or any other possible attitude. A writer's tone plays an important role in establishing the reader's relationship to the characters or ideas presented in a literary work.

Total omniscience A type of point of view in which the narrator knows everything about all of the characters and events in a story. A narrator with total omniscience can also move freely from one character to another. Generally, a totally omniscient narrative is written in the third person.

Traditional epic *See* **Folk epic.**

Tragedy The representation of serious and important actions that lead to a disastrous end for the protagonist. The final purpose of tragedy in Aristotle's formulation is to evoke **katharsis** by means of events involving pity and fear. A unified tragic action, from beginning to end, brings a morally good but not perfect tragic hero from happiness to unhappiness because of a mistaken act, to which he or she is led by a **hamartia,** an error in judgment. Tragic heroes move us to pity because their misfortunes are greater than they deserve, because they are not evil, having committed the fateful deed or deeds unwittingly and involuntarily. They also move us to fear, because we recognize in ourselves similar possibilities of error. We share with the tragic hero a common world of mischance. (*See also* **Tragic flaw.**)

Tragic flaw A fatal weakness or moral flaw in the protagonist that brings him or her to a bad end, for example, Creon in *Antigonê* or Macbeth. Sometimes offered as an alternative translation of **hamartia,** in contrast to the idea that the tragic hero's catastrophe is caused by an error in judgment, the idea of a protagonist ruined by a tragic flaw makes more sense in relation to the Greek idea of *hubris,* commonly translated as "outrageous behavior," involving deliberate transgressions against moral or divine law.

Tragic irony A form of **dramatic irony** that ultimately arrives at some tragedy.

Tragicomedy A type of drama that combines elements of both tragedy and comedy. Usually, it creates potentially tragic situations that bring the protagonists to the brink of disaster but then ends happily. Tragicomedy can be traced as far back as the Renaissance (in plays likes Shakespeare's *Measure for Measure*), but it also refers to modern plays like Chekhov's *Cherry Orchard* and Beckett's *Waiting for Godot*.

Transferred epithet A figure of speech in which the poet attributes some characteristic of a thing to another thing closely associated with it. Transferred epithet is a kind of metonymy. It usually places an adjective next to a noun in which the connection is not strictly logical (Milton's phrase "blind mouths" or Hart Crane's "nimble blue plateaus") but has expressive power.

Trick ending A surprising climax that depends on a quick reversal of the situation from an unexpected source. The success of a trick ending is relative to the degree in which the reader is surprised but not left incredulous when it occurs. The American writer O. Henry popularized this type of ending.

Trimeter A verse meter consisting of three metrical feet, or three primary stresses, per line.

Triolet A short lyric form of eight rhymed lines borrowed from the French. The two opening lines are repeated according to a set pattern. Triolets are often playful, but dark lyric poems like Robert Bridge's "Triolet" demonstrate the form's flexibility.

Trochaic, trochee A metrical foot in which a stressed syllable is followed by an unstressed syllable (′ ⌣) as in the words *sum*-mer and *chor*-us. The trochaic meter is often associated with songs, chants, and magic spells in English.

Troubadours The minstrels of the late Middle Ages. Originally, troubadours were lyric poets living in southern France and northern Italy who sang to aristocratic audiences mostly of chivalry and love.

Understatement An ironic figure of speech that deliberately describes something in a way that is less than the true case.

Unities The three formal qualities recommended by Italian Renaissance literary critics to unify a plot in order to give it a cohesive and complete integrity. Traditionally, good plots honored the three unities—of action, time, and place. The action in neoclassical drama, therefore, was patterned by cause and effect to occur within a 24-hour period. The setting took place in one unchanging locale. In the *Poetics,* Aristotle urged only the requirement of unity of plot, with events patterned in a cause-and-effect relationship from beginning through middle to the end of the single action imitated.

Unreliable narrator A narrator who—intentionally or unintentionally—relates events in a subjective or distorted manner. The author usually provides some indication early on in such stories that the narrator is not to be completely trusted.

Verbal irony A statement in which the speaker or writer says the opposite of what is really meant. For example, a friend might comment, "How graceful you are!" after you trip clumsily on a stair.

Verisimilitude The quality in a literary work of appearing true to life. In fiction, verisimilitude is usually achieved by careful use of realistic detail in description, characterization, and dialogue. (*See also* **Realism.**)

Verse From the Latin *versum*, "to turn." Verse has two major meanings. First, it refers to any single line of poetry. Second, it refers to any composition in lines of more or less regular rhythm—in contrast to prose.

Vers libre *See* **Free verse.**

Villanelle A fixed form developed by French courtly poets of the Middle Ages in imitation of Italian folk song. A villanelle consists of six rhymed stanzas in which two lines are repeated in a prescribed pattern.

Visual imagery A word or sequence of words that refers to the sense of sight or presents something one may see.

Vulgate From the Latin word *vulgus*, "mob" or "common people." The lowest level of formality in language, vulgate is the diction of the common people with no pretensions at refinement or elevation. The vulgate is not necessarily vulgar in the sense of containing foul or inappropriate language; it refers simply to unschooled, everyday language.

LITERARY CREDITS

Fiction

Achebe, Chinua: "Dead Men's Path," copyright © 1972, 1973 by Chinua Achebe, from GIRLS AT WAR AND OTHER STORIES by Chinua Achebe. Used by permission of Doubleday, a division of Random House, Inc.

Alexie, Sherman: "This Is What It Means to Say Phoenix, Arizona" from THE LONE RANGER AND TONTO FISTFIGHT IN HEAVEN by Sherman Alexie. Copyright © 1993, 2005 by Sherman Alexie. Used by permission of Grove/Atlantic, Inc.

Allende, Isabel: "The Judge's Wife" reprinted with the permission of Scribner, an imprint of Simon & Schuster, Inc., from THE STORIES OF EVA LUNA by Isabel Allende, translated from the Spanish by Margaret Sayers Peden. Copyright © 1989 by Isabel Allende. English translation copyright © 1991 by Macmillan Publishing Company. All rights reserved.

Ammons, Elizabeth: "Biographical Echoes in 'The Yellow Wallpaper'" excerpted from CONFLICTING STORIES: AMERICAN WOMEN WRITERS AT THE TURN OF THE CENTURY, copyright © 1991. Reprinted by permission of Oxford University Press.

Atwood, Margaret: "Happy Endings" from GOOD BONES AND SIMPLE MURDERS by Margaret Atwood, copyright © 1983, 1992, 1994, by O. W. Toad Ltd. A Nan A. Talese Book. Used by permission of Doubleday, a division of Random House, Inc.

Baker, Houston A. and Charlotte Pierce-Baker: Excerpt from "Patches: Quilts and Community in Alice Walker's 'Everyday Use'" by Houston A. Baker and Charlotte Pierce-Baker from The Southern Review 21 (Summer 1985). Reprinted by permission of the authors.

Baldwin, James: "Sonny's Blues" © 1957 by James Baldwin was originally published in Partisan Review. Copyright renewed. Collected in GOING TO MEET THE MAN, published by Vintage Books. Reprinted by arrangement with the James Baldwin Estate.

Baldwin, James: From NOTES OF A NATIVE SON by James Baldwin. Copyright © 1955, renewed 1983, by James Baldwin. Reprinted by permission of Beacon Press, Boston.

Bidpai: "The Camel and His Friends" by Bidpai, retold in English by Arundhati Khanwalkar from The Panchatantra. (The Association of Grandparents of Indian Immigrants).

Borges, Jorge Luis: "The Gospel According to Mark" from COLLECTED FICTIONS by Jorge Luis Borges, translated by Andrew Hurley, copyright © 1998 by Maria Kodama; translation copyright © 1998 by Penguin Putnam Inc. Used by permission of Viking Penguin, a division of Penguin Group (USA) Inc.

Boyle, T. Coraghessan: "Greasy Lake," from GREASY LAKE AND OTHER STORIES by T. Coraghessan Boyle, © 1979, 1981, 1982, 1983, 1984, 1985 by T. Coraghessan Boyle. Used by permission of Viking Penguin, a division of Penguin Group (USA) Inc.

Bradbury, Ray: "A Sound of Thunder" by Ray Bradbury. Reprinted by permission of Don Congdon Associates, Inc. Copyright © 1952 by Crowell Collier Publishing Company, renewed 1980 by Ray Bradbury.

Carver, Raymond: "Cathedral," from CATHEDRAL by Raymond Carver, copyright © 1981, 1982, 1983 by Raymond Carver. Used by permission of Alfred A. Knopf, a division of Random House, Inc.

Carver, Raymond: Excerpt from "On Writing" from FIRES: Essays, Poems, Stories by Raymond Carver. Copyright © 1968, 1969, 1970, 1971, 1972, 1973, 1974, 1975, 1976, 1977, 1978, 1979, 1980, 1981, 1982, 1983 by Raymond Carver. Copyright © 1983, 1984 by the Estate of Raymond Carver. Used by permission of The Wylie Agency LLC.

Chopin, Kate: "The Storm," from THE COMPLETE WORKS OF KATE CHOPIN, edited by Per Seyersted (Louisiana State University Press, 1969). Reprinted by permission of the publisher.

Christian, Barbara: Excerpt from the Introduction to EVERYDAY USE by Alice Walker, edited by Barbara T. Christian, from THE WOMEN WRITERS: TEXT AND CONTEXT SERIES. Copyright © 1994 by Rutgers, the State University. Reprinted by permission of Rutgers University Press.

Cowan, Louise S.: From "Passing by the Dragon" by Louise S. Cowan in "Revelation" by Flannery O'Connor, The Trinity Forum Reading 40 (Summer 2005) (McLean, VA: The Trinity Forum, Inc., 2005). Used by permission.

Evans, Rob: Lyrics from "The Donut Song" by Rob Evans. Copyright © 1982 Integrity's Hosanna! Music (ASCAP) (adm. at EMICMG

Poetry

Majmudar, Amit: "Rites to Allay the Dead" from 0°, 0°: POEMS by Amit Majmudar. Copyright 2009 by Amit Majmudar. Published by Tri-Quarterly Books/Northwestern University Press. Reprinted by permission of the publisher.

Mann, Aimee: "Deathly" by Aimee Mann © 2000 Aimee Mann (ASCAP). Used by permission of Michael Hausman Artist Management. All Rights Reserved.

Mason, David: "Song of the Powers" from THE COUNTRY I REMEMBER by David Mason. Reprinted by permission of the author.

Matsushita, Suiko: "Rain shower from mountain" and "Cosmos in bloom," translated by Violet Kazue de Cristoforo, from MAY SKY: THERE IS ALWAYS TOMORROW. Reprinted by permission of Kimiko de Cristoforo.

McKuen, Rod: "Thoughts on Capital Punishment" from STANYAN STREET AND OTHER SORROWS by Rod McKuen, copyright 1954, 1960, 1961, 1962, 1963, 1964, 1965, 1966 by Rod McKuen. Used by permission of Random House, Inc.

Menashe, Samuel: "Bread" from COLLECTED POEMS by Samuel Menashe. Copyright © 1986 by Samuel Menashe. Reprinted by permission of the author.

Merwin, W.S.: "For the Anniversary of My Death" from MIGRATION by W.S. Merwin. Copyright © 1967, 2005 by W.S. Merwin, used by permission of The Wylie Agency LLC.

Mezey, Robert: "On his blindness" by Jorge Luis Borges, in LOS CONJURADOS (1985), English translation by Robert Mezey. Published in POETRY, 1994. Reprinted by permission of Robert Mezey.

Millay, Edna St. Vincent: "Counting-out Rhyme" from COLLECTED POEMS, HarperCollins. Copyright © 1928, 1955 by Edna St. Vincent Millay and Norma Millay Ellis. All rights reserved. Reprinted by permission of Elizabeth Barnett, literary executor.

Momaday, N. Scott: "Simile" from ANGLE OF GEESE AND OTHER POEMS by Scott Momaday. Copyright © 1972 by Scott Momaday. Reprinted by permission of the author.

Moore, Marianne: "Silence," reprinted with the permission of Scribner, a Division of Simon & Schuster Inc., from THE COLLECTED POEMS OF MARIANNE MOORE by Marianne Moore. Copyright © 1935 by Marianne Moore, renewed © 1963 by Marianne Moore & T. S. Eliot. All rights reserved.

Moss, Howard: "Shall I Compare Thee to a Summer's Day?" from A SWIM OFF THE ROCKS. Copyright © 1976 by Howard Moss. Reprinted by permission of Richard Evans.

Mullen, Harryette: "Dim Lady" from SLEEPING WITH THE DICTIONARY by Harryette Mullen. Copyright © 2002 The Regents of the University of California. Reprinted by permission.

Nelson, Marilyn: "A Strange Beautiful Woman" from THE FIELDS OF PRAISE by Marilyn Nelson. Copyright © 1997 by Marilyn Nelson. Reprinted by permission of Louisiana State University Press.

Neruda, Pablo: "Muchos Somos" from EXTRAVAGARIA by Pablo Neruda. Translated by Alastair Reid. Translation copyright © 1974 by Alastair Reid. Originally published as ESTRAVAGARIO, copyright © 1958 by Editorial Losada, S.A. Buenos Aires. Reprinted by permission of Farrar, Straus & Giroux, LLC.

Niedecker, Lorine: "Popcorn-can Cover" from FROM THIS CONDENSERY: THE COMPLETE WRITING OF LORINE NIEDECKER, edited by Robert J. Bertolf. Copyright © Cid Corman, Literary Executor of the Lorine Niedecker Estate. Reprinted by permission.

Nims, John Frederick: "Contemplation" reprinted by permission.

Olds, Sharon: "Rite of Passage" and "The One Girl at the Boys' Party" from THE DEAD AND THE LIVING by Sharon Olds, copyright © 1987 by Sharon Olds. Used by permission of Alfred A. Knopf, a division of Random House, Inc.

Oliver, Mary: "Wild Geese" from DREAM WORK by Mary Oliver. Copyright © 1986 by Mary Oliver. Used by permission of Grove/Atlantic, Inc.

Ozawa, Neiji: "The war—this year," translated by Violet Kazue de Cristoforo, from MAY SKY: THERE IS ALWAYS TOMORROW. Reprinted by permission of Kimiko de Cristoforo.

Pacheco, José Emilio: "Alta Traición" from DON'T ASK ME HOW THE TIME GOES BY: POEMS 1964–1968 by José Emilio Pacheco, translated by Alastair Reid. Copyright © 1978 Columbia University Press. Reprinted with permission of the publisher.

Parker, Dorothy: "Résumé," copyright 1926, 1928, renewed 1954, © 1956 by Dorothy Parker, "Tombstones in the Starlight," from THE PORTABLE DOROTHY PARKER by Dorothy Parker, edited by Marion Meade, copyright 1928, renewed © 1956 by Dorothy Parker; copyright © 1973, 2006 by The National Assoc. for the Advancement of Colored People. Used by permission of Viking Penguin, a division of Penguin Group (USA) Inc.

Paz, Octavio: "With Eyes Closed" by Octavio Paz, translated by Eliot Weinberger, from THE COLLECTED POEMS 1957–1987, copyright © 1986 by Octavio Paz and Eliot Weinberger. Reprinted by permission of New Directions Publishing Corp.

Pinckney, Darryl: Excerpted from "Suitcase in Harlem" by Darryl Pinckney, from THE NEW YORK REVIEW OF BOOKS, Vol. 36, Issue 2,

Williams, William Carlos: "Spring and All: Section I," "The Red Wheelbarrow," and "This Is Just to Say" by William Carlos Williams, from THE COLLECTED POEMS: VOLUME I, 1909–1939, copyright © 1938 by New Directions Publishing Corp. Reprinted by permission of New Directions Publishing Corp.

Williams, William Carlos: "The Dance (In Brueghel's)" by William Carlos Williams, from THE COLLECTED POEMS: VOLUME II, 1939–1962, copyright © 1944 by William Carlos Williams. Reprinted by permission of New Directions Publishing Corp.

Wolff, Cynthia Griffin: Excerpts from "Emily Dickinson" by Cynthia Griffin Wolff from THE COLUMBIA HISTORY OF AMERICAN POETRY edited by Jay Parini and Brett Millier. Copyright © 1993 Columbia University Press. Reprinted with permission of the publisher.

Wright, James: "Autumn Begins in Martins Ferry, Ohio" by James Wright from THE BRANCH WILL NOT BREAK (Wesleyan University Press, 1963). © 1963 by James Wright and reprinted by permission of Wesleyan University Press.

Yeats, W. B.: "Crazy Jane Talks with the Bishop" reprinted with the permission of Scribner, a Division of Simon & Schuster, Inc., from THE COLLECTED WORKS OF W. B. YEATS, VOLUME I: THE POEMS, REVISED edited by Richard J. Finneran. Copyright © 1933 by The Macmillan Company, renewed 1961 by Bertha Georgie Yeats. All rights reserved.

Yeats, W. B.: "Sailing to Byzantium" and "Leda and the Swan," reprinted with the permission of Scribner, a Division of Simon & Schuster, Inc., from THE COLLECTED WORKS OF W. B. YEATS, VOLUME I: THE POEMS, REVISED by W. B. Yeats, edited by Richard J. Finneran. Copyright © 1928 by The Macmillan Company, renewed 1956 by Georgie Yeats. All rights reserved.

Young, Kevin: "Doo Wop" from JELLY ROLL by Kevin Young, copyright © 2003 by Kevin Young. Used by permission of Alfred A. Knopf, a division of Random House, Inc.

Drama

Aristotle: Excerpts from "Poetics VI, XIII-XV" from ARISTOTLE ON THE ART OF FICTION, translated by L.J. Potts, Cambridge University Press, 1968. Reprinted with the permission of Cambridge University Press.

Asquith, Clare: Excerpt from SHADOWPLAY: THE HIDDEN BELIEFS AND CODED POLITICS OF WILLIAM SHAKESPEARE by Clare Asquith. Copyright © 2005 by Clare Asquith. Reprinted by permission of PublicAffairs, a member of the Perseus Books Group; permission conveyed through Copyright Clearance Center, Inc..

Auden, W.H.: "Iago as a Triumphant Villain" from "The Joker in the Pack," THE DYER'S HAND AND OTHER ESSAYS. London: Faber and Faber, 1975.

Bodkin, Maud: "Lucifer in Shakespeare's Othello" from ARCHETYPAL PATTERNS IN POETRY. London, Oxford University Press, 1934.

Burgess, Anthony: "An Asian Culture Looks at Shakespeare" excerpted from remarks on the "Importance of Translation" at a June 4, 1982 conference, as published in the Columbia University journal TRANSLATION. Copyright © 1982 by the Estate of Anthony Burgess. Reprinted by permission.

Dodds, E. R.: "On Misunderstanding Oedipus" from "On Misunderstanding the Oedipus Rex" by E. R. Dodds. Reprinted by permission.

Fitzgerald, Robert: Excerpt from "Commentary" in OEDIPUS AT COLONUS BY SOPHOCLES by Robert Fitzgerald. Harcourt, Inc., 1941.

Hwang, David Henry: "Multicultural Theater," excerpted from a June 28, 1989 interview with David Henry Hwang. From CONTEMPORARY AUTHORS, Vol. 132 & Index 0E. © 1991 Gale, a part of Cengage Learning, Inc. Reproduced by permission. www.cengage.com/ permissions

Hwang, David Henry: THE SOUND OF A VOICE copyright © 1990 by David Henry Hwang from FOB AND OTHER PLAYS by David Henry Hwang. Reprinted by permission of Writers and Artists Group International.

Ibsen, Henrik: A DOLL'S HOUSE, translated by R. Farquharson Sharp and Eleanor Marx-Aveling, revised 2008 by Viktoria Michelsen. Copyright © 2008 by Viktoria Michelsen. Reprinted by permission.

Ives, David: "Talking with David Ives." Copyright 2009 David Ives. Used by permission of the author.

Ives, David: SURE THING from ALL IN THE TIMING: FOURTEEN PLAYS by David Ives, copyright © 1989, 1990, 1992 by David Ives. Used by permission of Vintage Books, a division of Random House, Inc.

Ives, David: Excerpt from "The Exploding Rose" by David Ives is reprinted by permission of the author.

Lee, Edward Bok: EL SANTO AMERICANO, copyright © 2001 by Edward Bok Lee. Reprinted by permission of the author.

Lee, Edward Bok: "On Being a Korean American Writer" by Edward Bok Lee. Copyright © 2006 by Edward Bok Lee. Reprinted by permission of the author.

Martin, Jane: BEAUTY by Jane Martin, reprinted by permission of Jon Jory, Trustee, P.O. Box 66, Goshen, KY 40026.

Sanchez-Scott, Milcha: Introduction to "Roosters" by Milcha Sanchez-Scott from ON NEW GROUND. Copyright © 1989 by Milcha

Writing

PHOTO CREDITS

Fiction

1: Jim McHugh Photography; 2: Jim McHugh Photography; 3: Sara Krulwich/The New York Times/Redux; 8: Lebrecht Music and Arts Photo Library/Alamy; 9: Musée Condé, Chantilly, France/The Bridgeman Art Library; 12: Super-Stock; 22: Bettmann/Corbis; 31: Bettmann/Corbis; 38: Charles Hopkinson/Camera Press/Retna Ltd.; 52: Pearson; 77: Bettmann/Corbis; 83: Everett Collection; 90: Lebrecht Music and Arts Photo Library/Alamy; 100: Lebrecht Music and Arts Photo Library/Alamy; 114: Pearson; 121: Missouri Historical Society; 125: J.E. Purdy/Corbis; 135: Sophie Bassouls/Sygma/Corbis; 158: Nancy Crampton; 182: Bettmann/Corbis; 186: Time & Life Pictures/Getty Images; 193: Bettmann/Corbis; 199: b17/ZUMA Press/Newscom; 202: t14/ZUMA Press/Newscom; 215: World History Archive/Alamy; 221: Oliver Morris/Hulton Archive/Getty Images; 227: Pearson Scott Foresman; 235: Bettmann/Corbis; 245: Marion Wood Kolisch/Scripps Howard News Service/Newscom; 257: AP Photo; 268: Mary Evans Picture Library/Alamy; 307: Flannery O'Connor Collection, Georgia College & State University Library; 308: AP Photo; 333: Joe McTyre/The Atlanta Journal Constitution; 338: The Atlanta Journal Constitution; 344: The Granger Collection, NYC; 356: Charlotte Perkins Gilman: A Biography by Cynthia Davis. Copyright 2010 by the Board of Trustees of the Leland Stanford Jr. University. All rights reserved. Used with the permission of Stanford University Press, www.sup.org. 359: Library of Congress Prints and Photographs Division [LC-USZ62-60507]; 363: Bettmann/Corbis; 369: AP Photo/Noah Berger; 373: Courtesy of Suzanne England; 378: Christie's Images/Bridgeman Art Library; 380: Christopher Felver/Documentary/Corbis; 389: INTERFOTO/Alamy; 394: Sophie Bassouls/Sygma/Corbis; 397: The Granger Collection, NYC; 404: Bettmann/Corbis; 408: Nancy Crampton; 417: REUTERS/STR New; 422: Bettmann/Corbis; 430: Lebrecht Music and Arts Photo Library/Alamy; 435: Neal Boenzi/New York Times/Getty Images; 436: Aurora Photos/Alamy; 451: Everett Collection Inc/Alamy; 462: Peter Power/Toronto Star/ZUMA Press/Newscom; 474: AP Photo.

Poetry

481: Christopher Felver/Corbis; 482: AP Photo/Steve Yeater; 483: Courtesy of Tom Roster; 498: Everett Collection; 522: Fotosearch/Getty Images; 545: Library of Congress Prints and Photographs Division [LC-USZ62-70064]; 557: Bettmann/Corbis; 571: David Lees/Corbis; 592: Everett Collection; 611: Everett Collection; 628: AP Photo; 644: Bettmann/Corbis; 663: John Psarolpoulos; 671: Erich Lessing/Art Resource, NY; 680: Corbis; 694: Culver Pictures, Inc.; 710: Bettmann/Corbis; 732: Rhina P. Espaillat; 737: The Art Gallery Collection/Alamy; 738: RDA/Hulton Archive/Getty Images; 740: Charles H. Phillips/Time Life Pictures/Getty Images; 741: AP Photo/Mary Kent; 743: Schalkwijk/Art Resource, NY; 767: Pearson; 772: Amherst College Archives and Special Collections; 772: The Everett Collection; 778: Visions of America, LLC/Alamy; 787: MPI/Stringer/Archive Photos/Getty Images; 797: Underwood & Underwood/Corbis; 804: By permission of the Houghton Library, Harvard University; 805: Mary Evans Picture Library/Alamy; 810: Keystone Pictures USA/Alamy; 820: Sophie Bassouls/Sygma/Corbis; 821: Corbis; 823: Scala/Art Resource, NY; 823: Everett Collection; 824: Lebrecht Music and Arts Photo Library/Alamy; 825: The British Library/Heritage/The Image Works; 826: Bettmann/Corbis; 830: MAGNOLIA PICTURES/MONTFORT, MICHAEL/Album/Newscom; 833: Christopher Felver/Corbis; 834: Library of Congress Prints and Photographs Division [LC-USZ62-116342]; 835: Luigi Ciuffetelli; 836: Bettmann/Corbis; 838: Christopher Felver/Documentary/Corbis; 841: Eric Schaal/Time Life Pictures/Getty Images; 845: Archive Pics/Alamy; 851: Hulton Archive/Getty Images; 851: Reuters/Corbis; 854: GL Archive/Alamy; 857: Mirrorpix/Lebrecht Authors; 858: Christopher Felver/Corbis; 859: Shirley Geok-lin Lim; 862: Underwood & Underwood/Corbis; 864: Beowulf Sheehan/ZUMA Press/Corbis; 865: Thomas Victor/Harriet Spurlin; 866: Bettmann/Corbis; 873: Pictorial Press Ltd/Alamy; 876: Bettmann/Corbis; 878: Sueddeutsche Zeitung Photo/The Image Works; 880: Reuters/Corbis; 882: Library of Congress Prints and Photographs Division [LC-USZ62-82784]; 884: Hulton Archive/Getty Images; 885: Classic

Image/Alamy; 887: Lebrecht Music and Arts Photo Library/Alamy.

Drama

889: JM11 WENN Photos/Newscom; 890: AP Photo/Frank Franklin II; 891: Damon Winter /The New York Times/Redux Pictures; 903: Ellen Locy, Echo Theatre; 910: AP Photo; 921: Utah Shakespearean Festival; 926: The Granger Collection, NYC; 929: T. Charles Erickson Photography; 938: Janette Pellegrini/WireImage/Getty Images; 941: The Granger Collection, NYC; 944: Bettmann/Corbis; 947: Bettmann/Corbis; 948: Merlyn Severn/Stringer/Hulton Archive/Getty Images; 996: Oli Scarff/Getty Images; 997: Andrea Pistolesi/The Image Bank/Getty Images; 998: Georgios Kollidas/Alamy; 999: Martha Swope Studio; 1000–1001 (all): T. Charles Erickson Photography; 1007, 1014, 1020, 1029, 1036, 1040, 1050, 1055, 1061, 1065, 1068, 1076, 1078, 1080, 1090, 1093, 1095, 1100: T. Charles Erickson Pho-

tography; 1105: Utah Shakespearean Festival; 1110: Classic Image/Alamy; 1120: Geraint Lewis/Alamy; 1121: Harvard Theatre Collection; 1172: Hulton-Deutsch Collection/Corbis; 1176: The Everett Collection; 1177: Cineplex-Odeon Pictures/courtesy Everett Collection; 1221: Bettmann/Corbis; 1226: Mark Garvin; 1242, 1246: Jay Thompson/Center Theatre Group; 1248: Joe Kohen/WireImage/Getty Images; 1256: Richard Feldman/American Repertory Theater; 1271: Adam Rountree/Getty Images; 1276: Jeff Wheeler/ZUMA Press/Newscom; 1282: JM11 WENN Photos/Newscom; 1283: 1987 Ron Scherl/StageImage/The Image Works; 1331: RICH SUGG/KRT/Newscom; 1333: The New York Public Library Photographic Services/Art Resource, NY.

Writing

1418: Scala/Art Resource, NY.

INDEX OF MAJOR THEMES

If you prefer to study by theme or want to research possible subjects for an essay, here is a listing of stories, poems, and plays arranged into fifteen major themes.

Art, Language, and Imagination

Stories

BALDWIN, Sonny's Blues, 56
BORGES, The Gospel According to Mark, 404
BRADBURY, A Sound of Thunder, 135
CARVER, Cathedral, 103
GARCÍA MÁRQUEZ, A Very Old Man with Enormous Wings, 417
GILMAN, The Yellow Wallpaper, 345
LE GUIN, The Ones Who Walk Away from Omelas, 245
PORTER, The Jilting of Granny Weatherall, 83
WALKER, Everyday Use, 363

Poems

AUDEN, Musée des Beaux Arts, 823
BLAKE, The Tyger, 824
BRADSTREET, The Author to Her Book, 503
BUKOWSKI, Dostoevsky, 830
CARROLL, Jabberwocky, 544
DICKINSON, After great pain, a formal feeling comes, 775
DICKINSON, Tell all the Truth but tell it slant, 777
FULTON, What I Like, 680
HEANEY, Digging, 846
HUGHES, My People, 788
HUGHES, Theme for English B, 792
JEFFERS, Hands, 586
KAUFMAN, No More Jazz at Alcatraz, 622
KEATS, Ode on a Grecian Urn, 852
KEATS, Ode to a Nightingale, 759
MACLEISH, Ars Poetica, 769
MOORE, Poetry, 863
RAINE, A Martian Sends a Postcard Home, 583
SÁENZ, To the Desert, 505
SHAKESPEARE, My mistress' eyes, 874
SIMIC, The Butcher Shop, 874
STEVENS, Anecdote of the Jar, 693
STILLMAN, In Memoriam John Coltrane, 626
THOMAS, In My Craft or Sullen Art, 763
VALDÉS, English con Salsa, 543
WALCOTT, Sea Grapes, 880
WILBUR, The Writer, 883
WILLIAMS, The Dance, 670
YEATS, Sailing to Byzantium, 754
YOUNG, Doo Wop, 626

Play

WILLIAMS, The Glass Menagerie, 1174

Childhood and Adolescence

Stories

ALEXIE, This Is What It Means to Say Phoenix, Arizona, 380
JOYCE, Araby, 430
KINCAID, Girl, 435
LAWRENCE, The Rocking-Horse Winner, 234
MUNRO, How I Met My Husband, 202
OATES, Where Are You Going, Where Have You Been?, 451
PACKER, Brownies, 38

Poems

BISHOP, Sestina, 661
BLAKE, The Chimney Sweeper, 520
BROOKS, Speech to the Young. Speech to the Progress-Toward, 506
COFER, Quinceañera, 724
CUMMINGS, in Just-, 678
ESPAILLAT, Bilingual / Bilingüe, 721
FROST, Birches, 840
HAYDEN, Those Winter Sundays, 491
HOUSMAN, When I was one-and-twenty, 641
JUSTICE, On the Death of Friends in Childhood, 852
LAWRENCE, Piano, 857
OLDS, The One Girl at the Boys' Party, 865
OLDS, Rite of Passage, 516
ROETHKE, My Papa's Waltz, 501
SIMIC, The Magic Study of Happiness, 675
THIEL, The Minefield, 553
THOMAS, Fern Hill, 878
TRETHEWEY, White Lies, 507

Play

WILLIAMS, The Glass Menagerie, 1174

Comedy and Satire

Stories

ATWOOD, Happy Endings, 394
CHUANG TZU, Independence, 11
KINCAID, Girl, 435
MUNRO, How I Met My Husband, 202
PACKER, Brownies, 38

TYLER, Teenage Wasteland, 186
VONNEGUT, Harrison Bergeron, 216

Poems
ABEYTA, thirteen ways of looking at a tortilla, 816
AMMONS, Coward, 590
ANONYMOUS, Carnation Milk, 543
ANONYMOUS, Dog Haiku, 510
ATWOOD, Siren Song, 820
AUDEN, The Unknown Citizen, 515
R. BROWNING, Soliloquy of the Spanish Cloister, 828
COPE, Lonely Hearts, 539
CULLEN, For a Lady I Know, 502
DONNE, The Flea, 836
GRAVES, Down, Wanton, Down!, 530
HARDY, The Ruined Maid, 538
HOUSMAN, When I was one-and-twenty, 641
HUGHES, Dream Boogie, 643
MARVELL, To His Coy Mistress, 861
MOSS, Shall I Compare Thee to a Summer's Day?, 519
PARKER, The Actress, 658
PARKER, Résumé, 636
SHAKESPEARE, My mistress' eyes, 874
SHEEHAN, Hate Poem, 517
YEATS, Crazy Jane Talks with the Bishop, 887

Plays
IVES, Sure Thing, 928
MARTIN, Beauty, 1277

Death

Stories
ACHEBE, Dead Men's Path, 199
ALEXIE, This Is What It Means to Say Phoenix, Arizona, 380
BIERCE, An Occurrence at Owl Creek Bridge, 397
BORGES, The Gospel According to Mark, 404
FAULKNER, A Rose for Emily, 31
GARCÍA MÁRQUEZ, A Very Old Man with Enormous Wings, 417
GRIMM, Godfather Death, 12
HURSTON, Sweat, 421
LONDON, To Build a Fire, 125
MAUGHAM, The Appointment in Samarra, 6
O'CONNOR, A Good Man Is Hard to Find, 308
POE, The Tell-Tale Heart, 52
PORTER, The Jilting of Granny Weatherall, 83

Poems
ASHBERY, At North Farm, 819
AUDEN, Funeral Blues, 606
BROOKS, the mother, 826
BROOKS, the rites for Cousin Vit, 827
COLLINS, The Names, 541
DICKINSON, Because I could not stop for Death, 777
DICKINSON, I heard a Fly buzz – when I died, 776
DONNE, Death be not proud, 836
FROST, "Out, Out—," 494
FROST, Birches, 840
HOUSMAN, To an Athlete Dying Young, 849

JONSON, On My First Son, 852
JUSTICE, On the Death of Friends in Childhood, 852
KEATS, Ode to a Nightingale, 759
KEATS, This living hand, now warm and capable, 649
KEATS, When I have fears that I may cease to be, 854
LARKIN, Aubade, 731
MAJMUDAR, Rites to Allay the Dead, 656
MERWIN, For the Anniversary of my Death, 669
OWEN, Anthem for Doomed Youth, 865
PLATH, Lady Lazarus, 718
POE, Annabel Lee, 765
ROBINSON, Luke Havergal, 509
ROETHKE, Elegy for Jane, 872
ROSSETTI, Uphill, 690
SHAKESPEARE, Fear no more the heat o' the sun, 598
STEVENS, The Emperor of Ice-Cream, 876
STILLMAN, In Memoriam John Coltrane, 626
TENNYSON, Break, Break, Break, 635
TENNYSON, Tears, Idle Tears, 555
THOMAS, Do not go gentle into that good night, 659
WHITMAN, O Captain! My Captain!, 762
WORDSWORTH, A Slumber Did My Spirit Seal, 619

Plays
GLASPELL, Trifles, 895
HWANG, The Sound of a Voice, 1256
SHAKESPEARE, Othello, 1002

Faith, Doubt, and Religious Vision

Stories
ALEXIE, This Is What It Means to Say Phoenix, Arizona, 380
BORGES, The Gospel According to Mark, 404
GARCÍA MÁRQUEZ, A Very Old Man with Enormous Wings, 417
HAWTHORNE, Young Goodman Brown, 90
LUKE, The Parable of the Prodigal Son, 214
O'CONNOR, A Good Man Is Hard to Find, 308
O'CONNOR, Revelation, 319

Poems
ARNOLD, Dover Beach, 818
BORGES, On his blindness, 741
S. CRANE, The Wayfarer, 672
DICKINSON, Because I could not stop for Death, 777
DONNE, Batter my heart, three-personed God, 531
DONNE, Death be not proud, 836
ELIOT, Journey of the Magi, 839
FROST, Fire and Ice, 553
HERBERT, Easter Wings, 676
HERBERT, Love, 847
HERBERT, Redemption, 688
HOPKINS, God's Grandeur, 624

HOPKINS, Pied Beauty, 565
HOPKINS, The Windhover, 848
LARKIN, Aubade, 731
LEVERTOV, O Taste and See, 858
MATTHEW, The Parable of the Good Seed, 687
MENASHE, Bread, 535
MILTON, When I consider how my light is spent, 863
OLIVER, Wild Geese, 691
ROSSETTI, Uphill, 690
SÁENZ, To the Desert, 505
WILBUR, Love Calls Us to the Things of This World, 555
WORDSWORTH, The World Is Too Much with Us, 699
YEATS, The Magi, 887
YEATS, The Second Coming, 705

Plays
MARLOWE, Doctor Faustus, 920
SANCHEZ-SCOTT, The Cuban Swimmer, 1224

Families/Parents and Children

Stories
ALEXIE, This Is What It Means to Say Phoenix, Arizona, 380
CHOPIN, The Storm, 121
FAULKNER, Barn Burning, 168
KAFKA, The Metamorphosis, 268
KINCAID, Girl, 435
LAHIRI, Interpreter of Maladies, 436
LAWRENCE, The Rocking-Horse Winner, 234
LUKE, The Parable of the Prodigal Son, 214
O'CONNOR, A Good Man Is Hard to Find, 308
PORTER, The Jilting of Granny Weatherall, 83
TAN, A Pair of Tickets, 144
TYLER, Teenage Wasteland, 186
WALKER, Everyday Use, 363
WELTY, A Worn Path, 474

Poems
BROOKS, Speech to the Young. Speech to the Progress-Toward, 506
H. CRANE, My Grandmother's Love Letters, 833
DOVE, Daystar, 838
ESPAILLAT, Bilingual / *Bilingüe*, 721
HAYDEN, Those Winter Sundays, 491
HEANEY, Digging, 846
HUDGINS, Elegy for my Father, Who Is Not Dead, 730
KEES, For My Daughter, 506
LARKIN, Home is so Sad, 856
LAWRENCE, Piano, 857
OLDS, Rite of Passage, 516
PLATH, Daddy, 866
ROETHKE, My Papa's Waltz, 501
STALLINGS, Sine Qua Non, 656
THIEL, The Minefield, 553
WILBUR, The Writer, 883

Plays
SANCHEZ-SCOTT, The Cuban Swimmer, 1224
SOPHOCLES, Oedipus, 949

WILLIAMS, The Glass Menagerie, 1174
WILSON, Fences, 1282

Immigration and Assimilation

Stories
LAHIRI, Interpreter of Maladies, 436
TAN, A Pair of Tickets, 144

Poems
ABEYTA, thirteen ways of looking at a tortilla, 816
ALARCÓN, Frontera / Border, 679
COFER, Quinceañera, 724
ESPAILLAT, Bilingual / *Bilingüe*, 721
LAZARUS, The New Colossus, 765
LIM, Learning to love America, 859
LIM, Riding into California, 723
MATSUSHITA, Rain shower from mountain, 568
OZAWA, The war—this year, 568
RAINE, A Martian Sends a Postcard Home, 583
THIEL, The Minefield, 553
VALDÉS, English con Salsa, 543
WADA, Even the croaking of frogs, 568

Plays
SANCHEZ-SCOTT, The Cuban Swimmer, 1224
SMITH, Twilight: Los Angeles, 1992, 1238

Individual Versus Society

Stories
ACHEBE, Dead Men's Path, 199
ALEXIE, This Is What It Means to Say Phoenix, Arizona, 380
CHUANG TZU, Independence, 11
FAULKNER, Barn Burning, 168
FAULKNER, A Rose for Emily, 31
GARCÍA MÁRQUEZ, A Very Old Man with Enormous Wings, 417
HAWTHORNE, Young Goodman Brown, 90
JACKSON, The Lottery, 250
LE GUIN, The Ones Who Walk Away from Omelas, 245
UPDIKE, A & P, 17
VONNEGUT, Harrison Bergeron, 216

Poems
AUDEN, Musée des Beaux Arts, 823
AUDEN, The Unknown Citizen, 515
BLAKE, London, 550
BLAKE, The Sick Rose, 826
BROOKS, We Real Cool, 833
BUKOWSKI, Dostoevsky, 830
CUMMINGS, anyone lived in a pretty how town, 540
CUMMINGS, next to of course god america i, 553
DICKINSON, I'm Nobody! Who are you?, 775
DICKINSON, Much madness Is Divinest Sense, 776
DICKINSON, The Soul selects her own Society, 775
DYLAN, The Times They Are a-Changin', 608
ELIOT, The Love Song of J. Alfred Prufrock, 806
FROST, Acquainted with the Night, 655

FROST, Mending Wall, 841
FROST, Stopping by Woods on a Snowy Evening, 842
HAYDEN, Frederick Douglass, 757
HUGHES, I, Too, 789
HUGHES, Theme for English B, 792
MACHADO, The Traveler, 689
MCKAY, America, 722
MILTON, When I consider how my light is spent, 863
NERUDA, Muchos Somos / We Are Many, 739
STEVENS, Disillusionment of Ten O'Clock, 552

Plays
GLASPELL, Trifles, 895
IBSEN, A Doll's House, 1119
SANCHEZ-SCOTT, The Cuban Swimmer, 1224
SMITH, Twilight: Los Angeles, 1992, 1238
WILLIAMS, The Glass Menagerie, 1174
WILSON, Fences, 1282

Loneliness and Alienation

Stories
ALEXIE, This Is What It Means to Say Phoenix, Arizona, 380
GILMAN, The Yellow Wallpaper, 345
HEMINGWAY, A Clean, Well-Lighted Place, 165
JOYCE, Araby, 430
KAFKA, The Metamorphosis, 268
MANSFIELD, Miss Brill, 100
MUNRO, How I Met My Husband, 202
STEINBECK, The Chrysanthemums, 227

Poems
BOGAN, Medusa, 702
DICKINSON, After great pain, a formal feeling comes, 775
DICKINSON, I felt a Funeral, in my Brain, 774
DICKINSON, I'm Nobody! Who are you?, 775
DICKINSON, The Soul selects her own Society, 775
DICKINSON, Success is counted sweetest, 773
DOVE, Daystar, 838
ELIOT, The Love Song of J. Alfred Prufrock, 806
ELIOT, The winter evening settles down, 562
FROST, Acquainted with the Night, 655
FROST, Desert Places, 624
GINSBERG, A Supermarket in California, 843
HUGHES, Homecoming, 794
JOHNSON, Sence You Went Away, 597
KOOSER, Abandoned Farmhouse, 856
LARKIN, Home is so Sad, 856
LARKIN, Poetry of Departures, 857
LI PO, Drinking Alone by Moonlight, 858
LOWELL, Skunk Hour, 860
MANN, Deathly, 609
MILLAY, What lips my lips have kissed, 654
NELSON, A Strange Beautiful Woman, 864
OLIVER, Wild Geese, 691
ROBINSON, Luke Havergal, 509
SHAKESPEARE, When to the sessions of sweet silent thought, 873
STAFFORD, The Farm on the Great Plains, 875

STEVENS, The Snow Man, 693
WILLIAMS, El Hombre, 570
WILLIAMS, Smell!, 642

Plays
GLASPELL, Trifles, 895
IBSEN, A Doll's House, 1119
LEE, El Santo Americano, 1272
WILLIAMS, The Glass Menagerie, 1174

Love and Desire

Stories
ATWOOD, Happy Endings, 394
CHOPIN, The Storm, 121
CHOPIN, The Story of an Hour, 415
FAULKNER, A Rose for Emily, 31
JOYCE, Araby, 430
LAHIRI, Interpreter of Maladies, 436
MUNRO, How I Met My Husband, 202
PORTER, The Jilting of Granny Weatherall, 83
STEINBECK, The Chrysanthemums, 227
UPDIKE, A & P, 17

Poems
ANONYMOUS, Bonny Barbara Allen, 601
ARNOLD, Dover Beach, 818
AUDEN, As I Walked Out One Evening, 821
BRIDGES, Triolet, 660
BURNS, Oh, my love is like a red, red rose, 591
CAMPO, For J. W., 727
COPE, Lonely Hearts, 539
CUMMINGS, somewhere i have never travelled, gladly beyond, 834
DICKINSON, The Soul selects her own Society, 775
DICKINSON, Wild Nights – Wild Nights!, 774
DONNE, The Flea, 836
DONNE, A Valediction: Forbidding Mourning, 837
ESSBAUM, The Heart, 583
FROST, The Silken Tent, 589
FULTON, What I Like, 680
GRAVES, Counting the Beats, 651
GRAVES, Down, Wanton, Down!, 530
H.D., Oread, 570
HARDY, Neutral Tones, 686
HAYDEN, Those Winter Sundays, 491
HOUSMAN, When I was one-and-twenty, 641
JOHNSON, Sence You Went Away, 597
JONSON, To Celia, 596
KEATS, La Belle Dame sans Merci, 702
MARVELL, To His Coy Mistress, 861
MILLAY, What lips my lips have kissed, 654
POE, Annabel Lee, 765
POE, To Helen, 700
POUND, The River Merchant's Wife: A Letter, 869
SEXTON, Cinderella, 707
SHAKESPEARE, My mistress' eyes, 874
SHAKESPEARE, Shall I compare thee to a summer's day?, 578
SHEEHAN, Hate Poem, 517

STALLINGS, First Love: A Quiz, 706
THOMAS, In My Craft or Sullen Art, 763
WALLER, Go, Lovely Rose, 881
WILLIAMS, Queen-Anne's-Lace, 884
YEATS, Crazy Jane Talks with the Bishop, 887
YEATS, When You Are Old, 888

Plays
HWANG, The Sound of a Voice, 1256
IBSEN, A Doll's House, 1119
IVES, Sure Thing, 928
SHAKESPEARE, Othello, 1002

Men and Women/Marriage

Stories
ATWOOD, Happy Endings, 394
CARVER, Cathedral, 103
CHOPIN, The Storm, 121
GILMAN, The Yellow Wallpaper, 345
HENRY, The Gift of the Magi, 182
HURSTON, Sweat, 421
LAHIRI, Interpreter of Maladies, 436
STEINBECK, The Chrysanthemums, 227
UPDIKE, A & P, 17

Poems
E. BROWNING, How Do I Love Thee?, 827
R. BROWNING, My Last Duchess, 496
DONNE, A Valediction: Forbidding Mourning, 837
DOVE, Daystar, 838
ELIOT, The Love Song of J. Alfred Prufrock, 806
HARDY, The Workbox, 519
HERRICK, To the Virgins, to make much of time, 847
JUSTICE, Men at Forty, 728
LOVELACE, To Lucasta, 521
MARVELL, To His Coy Mistress, 861
POUND, The River-Merchant's Wife: a Letter, 869
RICH, Living in Sin, 870
SEXTON, Cinderella, 707
SHAKESPEARE, Let me not to the marriage of true minds, 654
WILLIAMS, The Young Housewife, 691

Plays
GLASPELL, Trifles, 895
HWANG, The Sound of a Voice, 1256
IBSEN, A Doll's House, 1119
IVES, Sure Thing, 928
LEE, El Santo Americano, 1272
SHAKESPEARE, Othello, 1002
WILLIAMS, The Glass Menagerie, 1174
WILSON, Fences, 1282

Nature

Stories
BRADBURY, A Sound of Thunder, 135
CHOPIN, The Storm, 121
LONDON, To Build a Fire, 125

Poems
BISHOP, The Fish, 563
BLAKE, The Tyger, 824
BLAKE, To see a world in a grain of sand, 582
BUSON, Moonrise on mudflats, 567
DICKINSON, The Lightning is a yellow Fork, 685
DICKINSON, A Route of Evanescence, 565
FROST, Desert Places, 624
H.D., Oread, 570
H.D., Storm, 554
HARDY, The Darkling Thrush, 845
HOLLANDER, Swan and Shadow, 677
HOPKINS, Pied Beauty, 565
HOPKINS, Spring and Fall, 848
HOPKINS, The Windhover, 848
HOUSMAN, Loveliest of trees, the cherry now, 849
T. HUGHES, Hawk Roosting, 510
JEFFERS, Rock and Hawk, 851
KEATS, Ode to a Nightingale, 759
KEATS, To Autumn, 855
MATSUSHITA, Cosmos in Bloom, 568
OLIVER, Wild Geese, 691
ROETHKE, Root Cellar, 562
RYAN, Mockingbird, 533
RYAN, Turtle, 591
SÁENZ, To the Desert, 505
SANDBURG, Fog, 589
STAFFORD, Traveling Through the Dark, 753
STEPHENS, The Wind, 585
STEVENS, Anecdote of the Jar, 693
STEVENS, The Snow Man, 693
STEVENS, Thirteen Ways of Looking at a Blackbird, 673
TENNYSON, The Eagle, 578
TENNYSON, Flower in the Crannied Wall, 581
WILLIAMS, Spring and All, 884
WORDSWORTH, I Wandered Lonely as a Cloud, 511
YEATS, Lake Isle of Innisfree, 489

Play
SANCHEZ-SCOTT, The Cuban Swimmer, 1224

Race, Class, and Culture

Stories
ACHEBE, Dead Men's Path, 199
ALEXIE, This Is What It Means to Say Phoenix, Arizona, 380
ALLENDE, The Judge's Wife, 388
BALDWIN, Sonny's Blues, 56
CHUANG TZU, Independence, 11
FAULKNER, Barn Burning, 168
HURSTON, Sweat, 421
O'CONNOR, Revelation, 319
PACKER, Brownies, 38
TAN, A Pair of Tickets, 144
WALKER, Everyday Use, 363
WELTY, A Worn Path, 474

Poems

BLAKE, The Chimney Sweeper, 520
BROOKS, The Bean Eaters, 552
BROOKS, the mother, 826
BROOKS, Speech to the Young. Speech to the Progress-Toward, 506
BROOKS, We Real Cool, 635
CERVANTES, Cannery Town in August, 831
COFER, Quinceañera, 724
CULLEN, For a Lady I Know, 502
DUNBAR, We Wear the Mask, 764
HAYDEN, Frederick Douglass, 757
HAYDEN, Those Winter Sundays, 491
HUGHES, Dream Boogie, 643
HUGHES, Harlem [Dream Deferred], 793
HUGHES, I, Too, 789
HUGHES, My People, 788
HUGHES, The Negro Speaks of Rivers, 787
HUGHES, Nightmare Boogie, 793
HUGHES, Song for a Dark Girl, 791
HUGHES, Theme for English B, 792
LIM, Learning to Love America, 859
McKAY, America, 722
RANDALL, Ballad of Birmingham, 604
SEXTON, Her Kind, 513
B. SMITH, Jailhouse Blues, 606
STILLMAN, In Memoriam John Coltrane, 626
TOOMER, Reapers, 565
TRETHEWEY, White Lies, 507
VALDÉS, English con Salsa, 543

Plays

HWANG, The Sound of a Voice, 1256
SANCHEZ-SCOTT, The Cuban Swimmer, 1224
SMITH, Twilight: Los Angeles, 1992, 1238
WILSON, Fences, 1282

War, Murder, and Violence

Stories

ALLENDE, The Judge's Wife, 388
BIERCE, An Occurrence at Owl Creek Bridge, 397
BORGES, The Gospel According to Mark, 404
BOYLE, Greasy Lake, 408
BRADBURY, A Sound of Thunder, 135
FAULKNER, A Rose for Emily, 31
HURSTON, Sweat, 421
OATES, Where Are You Going, Where Have You Been?, 451
O'BRIEN, The Things They Carried, 462
O'CONNOR, A Good Man Is Hard to Find, 308
POE, The Tell-Tale Heart, 52

Poems

ARNOLD, Dover Beach, 818
HUGHES, Song for a Dark Girl, 791
JARRELL, The Death of the Ball Turret Gunner, 850

KEES, For My Daughter, 506
KOMUNYAKAA, Facing It, 725
LOVELACE, To Lucasta, 521
OWEN, Anthem for Doomed Youth, 865
OWEN, Dulce et Decorum Est, 521
OZAWA, The war—this year, 568
RANDALL, Ballad of Birmingham, 604
REED, Naming of Parts, 869
SANDBURG, Grass, 535
STAFFORD, At the Un-National Monument Along the Canadian Border, 520
THIEL, The Minefield, 553
TURNER, The Hurt Locker, 725
WHITMAN, Beat! Beat! Drums!, 642
WHITMAN, Cavalry Crossing a Ford, 672
YEATS, Leda and the Swan, 623

Plays

GLASPELL, Trifles, 895
LEE, El Santo Americano, 1272
SHAKESPEARE, Othello, 1002
SMITH, Twilight: Los Angeles, 1992, 1238
SOPHOCLES, Oedipus, 949

Woman's Identity

Stories

GILMAN, The Yellow Wallpaper, 345
STEINBECK, The Chrysanthemums, 227

Poems

BROOKS, the mother, 826
BROOKS, the rites for Cousin Vit, 827
COFER, Quinceañera, 724
DE LOS SANTOS, Perfect Dress, 835
DICKINSON, My Life had stood – a Loaded Gun, 581
DOVE, Daystar, 838
HAALAND, Lipstick 692
KIZER, Bitch, 726
NELSON, A Strange Beautiful Woman, 864
OLDS, The One Girl at the Boys' Party, 865
PLATH, Daddy, 866
RICH, Aunt Jennifer's Tigers, 492
RICH, Women, 729
SATYAMURTI, I Shall Paint My Nails Red, 679
SEXTON, Cinderella, 707
SEXTON, Her Kind, 513
STALLINGS, First Love: A Quiz, 706
WILLIAMS, The Young Housewife, 691

Plays

GLASPELL, Trifles, 895
IBSEN, A Doll's House, 1119
IVES, Sure Thing, 928
MARTIN, Beauty, 1277

INDEX OF FIRST LINES OF POETRY

A cup of wine, under the flowering trees, 858
A cold coming we had of it, 839
A Dying Tiger – moaned for Drink –, 750
A line in long array where they wind betwixt green islands, 672
A *little Learning* is a dang'rous Thing, 868
A man is haunted by his father's ghost, 657
A nick on the jaw, 568
A poem should be palpable and mute, 769
A Route of Evanescence, 565
A slumber did my spirit seal, 616
A strange beautiful woman, 864
A sudden blow: the great wings beating still, 623
A telephone line goes cold, 875
Abortions will not let you forget, 826
About suffering they were never wrong, 823
After great pain, a formal feeling comes –, 775
After weeks of watching the roof leak, 568
against the wall, the firing squad ready, 830
Al cabo de los años me rodea, 741
All day I hear the noise of waters, 618
All Greece hates, 700
All night it humps the air, 831
All the friends, 659
Allons! the road is before us!, 881
Although she feeds me bread of bitterness, 722
among twenty different tortillas, 816
Among twenty snowy mountains, 673
Anger which breaks a man into children, 744
anyone lived in a pretty how town, 540
As I walked out one evening, 821
As the guests arrive at my son's party, 516
As virtuous men pass mildly away, 837
At ten A.M. the young housewife, 691
Aunt Jennifer's tigers prance across a screen, 492

Batter my heart, three-personed God, for You, 531
Beat! beat! drums!—blow! bugles! blow!, 642
Because a bit of color is a public service, 679
Because I could not stop for Death –, 777
Because I will turn 420 tomorrow, 833
because it has no pure products, 859
Bent double, like old beggars under sacks, 521
Between my finger and my thumb, 846
Black reapers with the sound of steel on stones, 565
Bravery runs in my family, 590
Break, break, break, 635
Bright star, would I were steadfast as thou art—, 569

Buffalo Bill 's, 669
By the road to the contagious hospital, 884

Call the roller of big cigars, 876
Caminante, son tus huellas, 689
Can someone make my simple wish come true?, 539
Carnation Milk is the best in the land, 543
Carried her unprotesting out the door, 827
Caxtons are mechanical birds with many wings, 583
Come gather 'round people, 608
Con los ojos cerrados, 742
Cosmos in bloom, 568
Cricket, be, 567

De tantos hombres que soy, 739
Death be not proud, though some have callèd thee, 836
Do not go gentle into that good night, 659
Does the road wind uphill all the way?, 690
Down, wanton, down! Have you no shame, 530
Dream-singers, 788
Drink to me only with thine eyes, 596
Droning a drowsy syncopated tune, 790
Dusk, 677

Earth has not anything to show more fair, 885
el rasguño de esta fiebre, 746
Enganchadas al cable como pinzas de ropa, 745
Even the croaking of frogs, 568
Every year without knowing it I have passed the day, 669

Farewell, thou child of my right hand, and joy, 852
Fear no more the heat o' the sun, 598
Flower in the crannied wall, 581
Footsteps like water hollow, 666
Four simple chambers, 583
Friend, on this scaffold Thomas More lies dead, 535
Friend—the face I wallow toward, 680
From my mother's sleep I fell into the State, 850

Gather ye rose-buds while ye may, 847
Glory be to God for dappled things—, 565
Go, lovely rose, 881
Go and catch a falling star, 652
Go to the western gate, Luke Havergal, 509

Good morning, daddy!, 643
Gr-r-r—there go, my heart's abhorrence!, 828

Had we but world enough, and time, 861
Having been tenant long to a rich Lord, 688
He came up to me, 706
He clasps the crag with crooked hands, 578
He stood, and heard the steeple, 618
He was a big man, says the size of his shoes, 856
He was found by the Bureau of Statistics to be, 515
He was running with his friend from town to
    town, 553
Heat-lightning streak—, 567
Helen, thy beauty is to me, 700
Her body is not so white as, 884
Her name, cut clear upon this marble cross, 658
Here is a symbol in which, 851
Hole in the ozone, 568
Home is so sad. It stays as it was left, 856
Honey baby, 626
How do I love thee? Let me count the ways, 827

I, too, sing America, 789
I came to you one rainless August night, 505
I caught a tremendous fish, 563
I caught this morning morning's minion, king-, 848
I do not love my country. Its abstract lustre, 745
I felt a Funeral, in my Brain, 774
I had a dream, 793
I had come to the house, in a cave of trees, 702
I hate you truly. Truly I do, 517
I have been one acquainted with the night, 655
I have done it again, 718
I have eaten, 528
I have gone out, a possessed witch, 513
I hear America singing, the varied carols I hear, 882
I heard a Fly buzz – when I died –, 776
I know exactly what I want to say, 727
I leant upon a coppice gate, 845
I like to see it lap the Miles –, 504
I met a traveler from an antique land, 756
I met the Bishop on the road, 887
I placed a jar in Tennessee, 693
I remember the neckcurls, limp and damp as
    tendrils, 872
I shoot the Hippopotamus, 622
I sit in the top of the wood, my eyes closed, 510
I taste a liquor never brewed –, 774
I too, dislike it: there are things that are important
    beyond all this fiddle, 863
I wander through each chartered street, 550
I wandered lonely as a cloud, 511
I went back in the alley, 794
I will arise and go now, and go to Innisfree, 489
I wonder how they do it, those women, 692
I work all day, and get half-drunk at night, 731
If you come to a land with no ancestors, 723
If you wander far enough, 514
I'm a riddle in nine syllables, 582
I'm Nobody! Who are you?, 775
In a solitude of the sea, 844
In Brueghel's great picture, The Kermess, 670

In her room at the prow of the house, 883
in Just-, 678
In my craft or sullen art, 763
In the fullness of the years, like it or not, 741
In the old stone pool, 567
In the Shreve High football stadium, 886
In the smallest theater in the world, 675
In this strange labyrinth how shall I turn?, 886
In Xanadu did Kubla Khan, 831
Inside a cave in a narrow canyon near Tassajara, 586
It is a cold and snowy night. The main street is
    deserted, 570
It is never enough to close their door, 656
It little profits that an idle king, 876
It was in and about the Martinmas time, 601
It was many and many a year ago, 765
It's a strange courage, 570
It's here in a student's journal, a blue confession,
    835
I've known rivers, 787

Julius Caesar, 651

La cólera que quiebra al hombre en niños, 744
Landlord, landlord, 791
Let me not to the marriage of true minds, 654
Let us go then, you and I, 806
Listen to the coal, 626
Looking into my daughter's eyes I read, 506
Lord, who createdst man in wealth and
    store, 676
Love bade me welcome; yet my soul drew back,
    847
Love is like the wild rose-briar, 591
Loveliest of trees, the cherry now, 849
Lysi, I give to your divine hand, 738
Lysi: a tus manos divinas, 738

Make me thy lyre, even as the forest is, 651
Making jazz swing in, 568
Márgarét, áre you grieving, 848
Mark but this flea, and mark in this, 836
Men at forty, 728
Mine, said the stone, 643
Miniver Cheevy, child of scorn, 871
Money, the long green, 588
Moonrise on mudflats, 567
Mother dear, may I go downtown, 604
Much Madness is divinest Sense –, 776
My black face fades, 725
My dolls have been put away like dead, 724
My father liked them separate, one there, 721
My father used to say, 530
My heart aches, and a drowsy numbness
    pains, 759
My Life had stood – a Loaded Gun –, 581
My mistress' eyes are nothing like the sun, 874
My notebook has remained blank for months, 851
My three sisters are sitting, 729

Nature's first green is gold, 699
Nautilus Island's hermit, 860

next to of course god america i, 553
ninguna, 679
no, 679
No amo mi Patria. Su fulgor abstracto, 745
No More Jazz, 622
Nobody heard him, the dead man, 570
Not like the brazen giant of Greek fame, 765
Nothing but the hurt left here, 729
Nothing whole, 533
Nothing would sleep in that cellar, dank as a
     ditch, 562
Now, when he and I meet, after all these years, 726
Now as at all times I can see in the mind's eye, 887
Now as I was young and easy under the apple
     boughs, 878
Now that I've met you, 609

O Captain! my Captain! our fearful trip is done,
     762
O 'Melia, my dear, this does everything crown!,
     538
O Moon, when I gaze on thy beautiful face, 749
O Rose, thou art sick!, 826
O what can ail thee, knight at arms, 702
O where ha you been, Lord Randal, my son?, 817
Of the many men who I am, who we are, 739
Oh, but it is dirty!, 823
Oh, God of dust and rainbows, help us see, 658
Oh, my love is like a red, red rose, 591
Oh strong-ridged and deeply hollowed, 642
On a flat road runs the well-train'd runner, 569
On my boat on Lake Cayuga, 620
On the one-ton temple bell, 567
One day I'll lift the telephone, 730
One must have a mind of winter, 693
only one guy and, 567

Pearl Avenue runs past the high-school lot, 879
Pile the bodies high at Austerlitz and Waterloo,
     535
Pinned to the wire like clothes-pegs, 746
Popcorn-can cover, 693
Praise ye the Lord, 668

Rain shower from mountain, 568
Razors pain you, 636
Red river, red river, 627

Safe upon the solid rock the ugly houses stand, 518
Say to them, 506
Season of mists and mellow fruitfulness, 855
See, here's the workbox, little wife, 519
Seems lak to me de stars don't shine so bright, 597
September rain falls on the house, 661
Shall I compare thee to a summer's day?, 578
She even thinks that up in heaven, 502
She had thought the studio would keep itself, 870
She is as in a field a silken tent, 589
She wanted a little room for thinking, 838
Silver bark of beech, and sallow, 641
Snow falling and night falling fast, oh, fast, 624
Snow on every field, 659

so much depends, 513
Softly, in the dusk, a woman is singing to me, 857
Some say the world will end in fire, 553
Some time when the river is ice ask me, 499
Something there is that doesn't love a wall, 841
Sometimes walking late at night, 874
Sometimes you hear, fifth-hand, 857
somewhere i have never travelled,gladly
     beyond, 834
Somewhere someone is traveling furiously toward
     you, 819
Stop all the clocks, cut off the telephone, 606
Success is counted sweetest, 773
Sundays too my father got up early, 491

Tears, idle tears, I know not what they mean, 555
Tell all the Truth but tell it slant –, 777
Tell me not, Sweet, I am unkind, 521
That is no country for old men. The young, 754
That sail which leans on light, 880
That time of year thou mayst in me behold, 873
That's my last Duchess painted on the wall, 496
The apparition of these faces in the crowd, 560
The art of losing isn't hard to master, 758
The buzz-saw snarled and rattled in the yard, 494
The eyes open to a cry of pulleys, 555
The falling flower, 566
The fifth-grade teacher and her followers—, 659
The fog comes, 589
The houses are haunted, 552
The instructor said, 792
The king sits in Dumferling toune, 493
The kingdom of heaven is likened unto a man
     which sowed good seed in his field, 687
The lies I could tell, 507
The Lightning is a yellow Fork, 685
The piercing chill I feel, 560
The readers of the *Boston Evening Transcript*, 684
The sea is calm to-night, 818
The Soul selects her own Society –, 775
The splendor falls on castle walls, 619
The time you won your town the race, 849
The tusks that clashed in mighty brawls, 756
The war—this year, 568
The wayfarer, 672
The whiskey on your breath, 501
The wind stood up, and gave a shout, 585
The winter evening settles down, 562
The world is, 858
The world is charged with the grandeur of God, 624
The world is too much with us; late and soon, 699
Thee for my recitative, 504
There are no stars tonight, 833
There ought to be capital punishment for cars, 752
There's never an end to dust, 691
They eat beans mostly, this old yellow pair, 552
They say that Richard Cory owns, 600
Thirty days hath September, 487
Thirty days in jail with my back turned to the
     wall, 606
this feverish scratch, 746
This is my letter to the World, 776

This is the field where the battle did not happen, 520
This is the one song everyone, 820
This living hand, now warm and capable, 649
Thou ill-formed offspring of my feeble brain, 503
Thou still unravished bride of quietness, 852
Thy will be done, 535
To fling my arms wide, 789
To see a world in a grain of sand, 582
Today I sniffed, 510
Today we have naming of parts. Yesterday, 869
Traveler, your footsteps are, 689
Traveling through the dark I found a deer, 753
Treason doth never prosper; what's the reason?, 657
Turning and turning in the widening gyre, 705
Twas brillig, and the slithy toves, 544
Two roads diverged in a yellow wood, 689
Tyger! Tyger! burning bright, 824

Way Down South in Dixie, 791
We dance round in a ring and suppose, 590
We lie back to back. Curtains, 590
We real cool. We, 635
We shall not ever meet them bearded in heaven, 852
We stood by a pond that winter day, 686
We wear the mask that grins and lies, 764
We were very tired, we were very merry—, 862
Welcome to ESL 100, English Surely Latinized, 543
Well, son, I'll tell you, 788
What did we say to each other, 582
What happens to a dream deferred?, 793
What lips my lips have kissed, and where, and why, 654
What passing-bells for these who die as cattle?, 865

What thoughts I have of you tonight, Walt Whitman, 843
When first we met we did not guess, 660
When I consider how my light is spent, 863
When I have fears that I may cease to be, 854
When I see birches bend to left and right, 840
When I take my girl to the swimming party, 865
When I was one-and-twenty, 641
When it is finally ours, this freedom, this liberty, this beautiful, 757
When maidens are young, and in their spring, 617
When my mother died I was very young, 520
When the summer fields are mown, 533
When to the sessions of sweet silent thought, 873
When you are old and grey and full of sleep, 888
Whenas in silks my Julia goes, 537
Whenever Richard Cory went down town, 599
While my hair was still cut straight across my forehead, 869
Whirl up, sea—, 570
Who says you're like one of the dog days?, 579
Who will go drive with Fergus now, 616
Who would be a turtle who could help it?, 591
Whose woods these are I think I know, 842
Wild Nights – Wild Nights!, 774
With eyes closed, 742

Yesterday, I lay awake in the palm of the night, 541
You, love, and I, 651
You always read about it, 707
You crash over the trees, 554
You do not do, you do not do, 866
You do not have to be good, 691
you fit into me, 588
Your absence, father, is nothing. It is naught—, 656

INDEX OF AUTHORS
AND TITLES

Every page number immediately following a writer's name indicates a quotation or reference to that writer. A number in **bold** refers you to the page on which you will find the writer's biography.

A & P, 17
Abandoned Farmhouse, 856
ABEYTA, AARON
   thirteen ways of looking at a tortilla, 816
ACHEBE, CHINUA, **199**, 222, 919
   Dead Men's Path, 199
Acquainted with the Night, 655
Actress, The, 658
ADAMS, RICHARD, 81
AESCHYLUS, 918, 942, 947
AESOP, **7**, 197
   Fox and the Grapes, The, 7
After great pain, a formal feeling comes, 775
Aftermath, 533
After weeks of watching the roof leak, 568
ALARCÓN, FRANCISCO X., 722
   Frontera / Border, 679
ALDRICH, THOMAS BAILEY, 4
ALEXIE, SHERMAN, **380**
   This Is What It Means to Say Phoenix,
     Arizona, 380
All day I hear, 618
ALLENDE, ISABEL, **388**
   Judge's Wife, The, 388
Alta Traición, 745
ALVAREZ, JULIA, 623
America, 722
AMMONS, A. R.
   Coward, 590
AMMONS, ELIZABETH
   Biographical Echoes in "The Yellow
     Wallpaper," 361
Ancient Stairway, 666
ANDERSEN, HANS CHRISTIAN, 12
Anecdote of the Jar, 693
ANGELOU, MAYA, 595
Anger, 744
Annabel Lee, 765
ANONYMOUS
   Bonny Barbara Allan, 601
   Carnation Milk, 543
   Dog Haiku, 510
   Little Poem Regarding Computer Spell-
     Checkers, A, 1355
   Lord Randall, 817
   O Moon, when I gaze on thy beautiful face, 749
   Sir Patrick Spence, 493
ANOUILH, JEAN, 918
Anthem for Doomed Youth, 865

anyone lived in a pretty how town, 540
Appointment in Samarra, The, 6
AQUINAS, THOMAS, 755
Araby, 430
ARAGON, LOUIS, 742
ARISTOPHANES, 927
ARISTOTLE, 909, 918, 920, 945–47, 1116, 1222
   Defining Tragedy, 987
ARMSTRONG, LOUIS, 484
ARNOLD, MATTHEW
   Dover Beach, 818
Ars Poetica, 769
ASHBERY, JOHN
   At North Farm, 819
Asian Culture Looks at Shakespeare, An, 1105
As I Walked Out One Evening, 821
Ask Me, 499
ASQUITH, CLARE
   Shakespeare's Language as a Hidden Political
     Code, 1108
At North Farm, 819
At the Un-National Monument Along the
   Canadian Border, 520
ATWOOD, MARGARET, 81, 194, **394**
   Happy Endings, 394
   Siren Song, 820
   You fit into me, 588
Aubade, 731
AUDEN, W. H., 301, 621, 770, 1335, 1345
   As I Walked Out One Evening, 821
   Funeral Blues, 606
   Iago as a Triumphant Villain, 1106
   Musée des Beaux Arts, 823
   Unknown Citizen, The, 515
AUGUSTINE, 557
Aunt Jennifer's Tigers, 492
AUSTEN, JANE, 268
Author to Her Book, The, 503
Autumn Begins in Martins Ferry, Ohio, 886

BAKER, HOUSTON A.
   Stylish vs. Sacred in "Everyday Use," 375
BALDWIN, JAMES, **56**
   Race and the African American Writer, 77
   Sonny's Blues, 56
Ballad of Birmingham, 604
Ballad of the Landlord, 791
BALZAC, HONORÉ DE, 16, 82, 118
Barn Burning, 168

BARTHES, ROLAND, 1462
BASHO, MATSUO, 567, 568
 Heat-lightning streak, 567
 In the old stone pool, 567
Batter my heart, three-personed God, for You, 531
Bean Eaters, The, 552
Beat! Beat! Drums!, 642
BEATTIE, ANN, 163
Beauty, 1277
BEAUVOIR, SIMONE DE, 1458
Because I could not stop for Death, 777
BECKETT, SAMUEL, 1223
BEHN, APHRA
 When maidens are young, 617
Being a Bilingual Writer, 732
BELLOC, HILAIRE
 Hippopotamus, The, 622
BERENDT, JOHN, 266
BERGSON, HENRI, 926
BETTELHEIM, BRUNO, 1452, 1453
BEVINGTON, DAVID, 1002
BIBLE, 10, 224, 668, 687, 698
 Parable of the Good Seed, The, 687
 Parable of the Prodigal Son, The, 214
BIDPAI, 8
 Camel and His Friends, The, 8
BIERCE, AMBROSE, 264, 397
 Occurrence at Owl Creek Bridge, An, 397
Bilingual/Bilingüe, 721
Biographical Echoes in "The Yellow Wallpaper," 361
Biography of a Story, 257
Birches, 840
BISHOP, ELIZABETH, 532, 573–76, 720, 771, 1448–49
 Filling Station, 823
 Fish, The, 563
 One Art, 758
 Sestina, 661
Bitch, 726
Black and White in Othello, 1107
Black Identity in Langston Hughes, 801
Black Woman Writer in America, The, 369
BLAKE, WILLIAM, 508, 550–51, 558, 621, 634, 638, 704, 1466–67
 Chimney Sweeper, The, 520
 London, 550
 Sick Rose, The, 826
 To see a world in a grain of sand, 582
 Tyger, The, 824
BLY, ROBERT, 572, 655, 698, 1459
 Cricket (translation), 567
 Driving to Town Late to Mail a Letter, 570
BODKIN, MAUD
 Lucifer in Shakespeare's Othello, 1107
BOGAN, LOUISE, 804
 Medusa, 702
Bonny Barbara Allan, 601
BORGES, JORGE LUIS, 17, 194, 404, 717, 737, 740
 Gospel According to Mark, The, 404
 On his blindness, 741
Boston Evening Transcript, The, 684

BOSWELL, JAMES, 536
BOTTOME, PHYLLIS, 115
BOWLES, PAUL, 29
BOYLE, T. CORAGHESSAN, 408
 Greasy Lake, 408
BRADBURY, RAY, 135
 Sound of Thunder, A, 135
BRADSTREET, ANNE, 503–4, 507
 Author to Her Book, The, 503
Bread, 535
Break, Break, Break, 635
BRETON, ANDRÉ, 742
BRIDGES, LAWRENCE, 658–59
 Two Poetweets, 659
BRIDGES, ROBERT
 Triolet, 660
Bright star, would I were steadfast as thou art, 569
BRONTË, EMILY
 Love and Friendship, 591
BROOKS, GWENDOLYN, 748
 Bean Eaters, The, 552
 Hearing "We Real Cool," 644
 mother, the, 826
 rites for Cousin Vit, the, 827
 Speech to the Young. Speech to the Progress-Toward, 506
 We Real Cool, 635
Brownies, 38
BROWNING, ELIZABETH BARRETT
 How Do I Love Thee? Let Me Count the Ways, 827
BROWNING, ROBERT, 490, 495, 514, 633, 634–35, 748, 1445–47
 My Last Duchess, 496
 Soliloquy of the Spanish Cloister, 828
BRUEGEL, PIETER, 671, 822, 1418
Buffalo Bill 's, 670
BUKOWSKI, CHARLES
 Dostoevsky, 830
BUNYAN, JOHN, 225, 687–88
BURGESS, ANTHONY
 Asian Culture Looks at Shakespeare, An, 1105
BURGON, JOHN, 586
BURNS, ROBERT, 593, 599, 621
 Oh, my love is like a red, red rose, 591
BURROUGHS, WILLIAM, 266
BUSON, TANIGUCHI, 560–61, 567, 686
 Moonrise on mudflats, 567
 On the one-ton temple bell, 567
 piercing chill I feel, The, 560
Butcher Shop, 874
BYNNER, WITTER, 617
BYRON, GEORGE GORDON, LORD, 621, 751

Call to the Community, A, 1248
Camel and His Friends, The, 8
CAMERON, JAMES, 119
CAMPBELL, JOSEPH, 1455
CAMPION, THOMAS, 598
CAMPO, RAFAEL
 For J. W., 727

CAMUS, ALBERT, 83
Cannery Town in August, 831
CAPOTE, TRUMAN, 266
Care and Feeding, 833
CARLYLE, THOMAS, 686
Carnation Milk, 543
Carrie, 691
CARROLL, LEWIS [CHARLES LUTWIDGE DODGSON]
  Humpty Dumpty Explicates "Jabberwocky," 545
  Jabberwocky, 544
CARVER, RAYMOND, **103**, 163
  Cathedral, 103
  Commonplace but Precise Language, 114
Cathedral, 103
CATHER, WILLA, 120
Cavalry Crossing a Ford, 672
CERVANTES, LORNA DEE
  Cannery Town in August, 831
Character of Mrs. Turpin in "Revelation," The,
  341
CHEEVER, JOHN, 1448
CHEKHOV, ANTON, 16, 161–62, 685, 1116
CHESTERFIELD, PHILIP STANHOPE, LORD, 1116
CHESTERTON, G. K., 577, 587
Chimney Sweeper, The, 520
CHOPIN, KATE, 120, **121**, 194
  Storm, The, 121
  Story of an Hour, The, 415
Chorus as Democrat, The, 991
CHRISTIAN, BARBARA T.
  "Everyday Use" and the Black Power
    Movement, 371
Chrysanthemums, The, 227
CHUANG TZU, **11**
  Independence, 11
CHURCHILL, CARYL, 1224
CIARDI, JOHN, 683, 722
Cinderella, 707
CINTHIO, GIRALDI, 999
CLARK, CHERYL
  Convalescence (translation), 746
Clean, Well-Lighted Place, A, 165
CLIFTON, LUCILLE, 771
CLOSE, JOHN, 752
COCTEAU, JEAN, 699
COFER, JUDITH ORTIZ
  Quinceañera, 724
COLE, WILLIAM
  On my boat on Lake Cayuga, 620
COLERIDGE, SAMUEL, 487, 490, 536, 538, 585,
  603, 640, 770
  Kubla Khan, 831
COLLINS, BILLY
  Care and Feeding, 833
  Names, The, 541
COLLINS, WILLIAM, 585
Commonplace but Precise Language, 114
Composed upon Westminster Bridge, 885
Concerning "Love Calls Us to the Things of This
  World," 557
Con los ojos cerrados, 742
CONNOLLY, CYRIL, 264

CONRAD, JOSEPH, 162, 225
Convalecencia, 746
Convalescence, 746
Convergence of the Twain, The, 844
COOGLER, J. GORDON, 750
COPE, WENDY
  Lonely Hearts, 539
CORMAN, CID
  only one guy (translation), 567
Correspondence on the Final Scene of A Doll's
  House, 1172
Cosmos in bloom, 568
Counting-out Rhyme, 641
Counting the Beats, 651
COWAN, LOUISE S.
  Character of Mrs. Turpin in "Revelation," The,
    341
Coward, 590
CRABBE, GEORGE, 650
CRANE, HART, 528
  My Grandmother's Love Letters, 833
CRANE, STEPHEN, 5, 120, 264–65, 266
  Wayfarer, The, 672
Crazy Jane Talks with the Bishop, 887
Creating Trifles, 910
CREELEY, ROBERT, 515, 669
  Oh No, 514
Cricket, 567
CROWE, ANNA
  Swallows (translation), 746
Cuban Swimmer, The, 1224
CULLEN, COUNTEE, 723
  For a Lady I Know, 502
CUMMINGS, E. E., 536, 588, 617, 1174
  anyone lived in a pretty how town, 540
  Buffalo Bill 's, 670
  in Just-, 678
  next to of course god america i, 553
  somewhere i have never travelled,gladly
    beyond, 834
CUNNINGHAM, J. V.
  Friend, on this scaffold Thomas More lies dead,
    535

Daddy, 866
Dance, The, 670
DANTE (DANTE ALIGHIERI), 225, 651, 687, 770,
  919
Darkling Thrush, The, 845
Daystar, 838
Dead Men's Path, 199
Death be not proud, 836
Deathly, 609
Death of the Ball Turret Gunner, The, 850
Deconstructing "A Good Man Is Hard to Find,"
  340
DE CRISTOFORO, VIOLET KAZUE
  Cosmos in bloom (translation), 568
  Even the croaking of frogs (translation), 568
  Rain shower from mountain (translation), 568
  War—this year (translation), The, 568
Defining Tragedy, 987

DEFOE, DANIEL, 5, 265
DEGAS, EDGAR, 528
DE LOS SANTOS, MARISA
   Perfect Dress, 835
DE MAN, PAUL, 1462
DENHAM, JOHN, 650
Desert Places, 624
Design, 1382
Destiny of Oedipus, The, 988
DEUTSCH, BABETTE
   falling flower (*translation*), The, 566
DE VRIES, PETER, 1381
DICK, PHILIP K., 268
DICKENS, CHARLES, 81, 82
DICKINSON, EMILY, 512, 584, 603, 615, 686, 770,
   772, **773**, 780–86, 1459
   After great pain, a formal feeling comes, 775
   Because I could not stop for Death, 777
   Dying Tiger – moaned for Drink, A, 750
   I felt a Funeral, in my Brain, 774
   I heard a Fly buzz – when I died, 776
   I like to see it lap the Miles, 504
   I'm Nobody! Who are you?, 775
   I taste a liquor never brewed, 774
   Lightning is a yellow Fork, The, 685
   Much Madness is divinest Sense, 776
   My Life had stood – a Loaded Gun, 581
   Recognizing Poetry, 778
   Route of Evanescence, A, 565
   Self-Description, 778
   Soul selects her own Society, The, 775
   Success is counted sweetest, 773
   Tell all the Truth but tell it slant, 777
   This is my letter to the World, 776
   Wild Nights – Wild Nights!, 774
Dickinson and Death, 782
Digging, 846
DINESEN, ISAK, 614–15
Direct Style, The, 193
DISCH, M. THOMAS, 268
Discovery of Emily Dickinson's Manuscripts, The,
   780
Discussing *The Metamorphosis*, 298
Disillusionment of Ten O'Clock, 552
Doctor Faustus, 920
DODDS, E. R.
   On Misunderstanding Oedipus, 989
Dog Haiku, 510
Doll's House, A, 1119
DONNE, JOHN, 632
   Batter my heart, three-personed God, for You,
   531
   Death be not proud, 836
   Flea,The, 836
   Song, 652
   Valediction: Forbidding Mourning, A, 837
DONOGHUE, DENIS
   One of the Irrefutable Poets, 812
Do not go gentle into that good night, 659
DOOLITTLE, HILDA. *See* H. D.
Doo Wop, 626
Dostoevsky, 830

DOVE, RITA, 699
   Daystar, 838
   Voices in Langston Hughes, The, 799
Dover Beach, 818
Down, Wanton, Down!, 530
Dream Boogie, 643
Dream Deferred. *See* Harlem
Dream Variations, 789
DREISER, THEODORE, 120, 266
DREW, ELIZABETH, 1439
Drinking Alone by Moonlight, 858
Driving to Town Late to Mail a Letter, 570
DRURY, JOHN, 694
Dulce et Decorum Est, 521
DUNBAR, PAUL LAURENCE, 491
   We Wear the Mask, 764
DYER, JOHN, 497, 587, 751
Dying Tiger – moaned for Drink, A, 750
DYLAN, BOB, 599
   Term "Protest Singer" Didn't Exist, The, 610
   Times They Are a-Changin', The, 608

Eagle, The, 578
Easter Wings, 676
EASTHOPE, ANTHONY, 1465
Economics of Zora Neale Hurston's "Sweat," The,
   1450
Eight O'Clock, 618
EISLER, RACHEL, 633
Elegy for Jane, 872
Elegy for My Father, Who Is Not Dead, 730
El Hombre, 570
ELIOT, GEORGE, 161, 264
ELIOT, T. S., 488, 495, 503, 530, 534, 538, 599,
   669, 684, 688, 698, 704, 706, 770, 804, **805,**
   812–15
   Boston Evening Transcript, The, 684
   Journey of the Magi, 839
   Love Song of J. Alfred Prufrock, The, 806
   Music of Poetry, The, 627
   Objective Correlative, The, 811
   Poetry and Emotion, 810
   Virginia, 627
   winter evening settles down, The, 562
ELLINGTON, DUKE, 640
ELLMANN, MAUD
   Will There Be Time?, 814
El Santo Americano, 1272
EMERSON, RALPH WALDO, 5, 532
Emperor of Ice-Cream, The, 876
English con Salsa, 543
Eskimo "A Rose for Emily," An, 1461
ESPAILLAT, RHINA, 721, 722
   Being a Bilingual Writer, 732
   Bilingual/*Bilingüe*, 721
ESSBAUM, JILL ALEXANDER
   Heart, The, 583
EURIPIDES, 918, 945, 947
EVANS, ABBIE HUSTON, 1396–98
   Wing-Spread, 1396
Even the croaking of frogs, 568
Everyday Use, 363

"Everyday Use" and the Black Power Movement, 371
"Everyday Use" as a Portrait of the Artist, 374
Ex-Basketball Player, 879
Excerpt from "On Her Own Work": Insights into "A Good Man Is Hard to Find, 333
Excerpt from "The Grotesque in Southern Fiction": The Serious Writer and the Tired Reader, 336

Facing It, 725
Fairy Tale Motifs in "Where Are You Going, Where Have You Been?", 1452
falling flower, The, 566
Farm on the Great Plains, The, 875
FARR, JUDITH
    Reading of "My Life had stood – a Loaded Gun," A, 784
FAULKNER, WILLIAM, 16, 29, 30, **31**, 82, 119, 120, 163, 164, 168, 194, 198, 225, 226, 685–86, 698, 1373–75, 1455–56, 1461–62
    Barn Burning, 168
    Rose for Emily, A, 31
Fear no more the heat o' the sun, 598
Fences, 1282
Fern Hill, 878
FERRIS, WILLIAM R., 371
FEYDEAU, GEORGES, 928
FIELDING, HENRY, 82, 267
FIELDS, W. C., 115
Filling Station, 823
Fire and Ice, 553
First Love: A Quiz, 706
FISH, STANLEY
    Eskimo "A Rose for Emily, An," 1461
Fish, The, 563
FITTS, DUDLEY
    Oedipus the King (translation), 949
FITZGERALD, F. SCOTT, 28, 224, 918
FITZGERALD, ROBERT
    Oedipus the King (translation), 949
    Translating Sophocles into English, 992
FLAUBERT, GUSTAVE, 27
Flea, The, 836
FLEENOR, JULIANN
    Gender and Pathology in "The Yellow Wallpaper," 358
FLOWER, DEAN
    Listening to Flannery O'Connor, 342
Flower in the Crannied Wall, 581
Fog, 589
FOLEY, ADELLE
    Learning to Shave, 568
For a Lady I Know, 502
For J. W., 727
For My Daughter, 506
FORSTER, E. M., 82, 267
For the Anniversary of My Death, 669
FOUCAULT, MICHEL, 1462
FOWLES, JOHN, 528
Fox and the Grapes, The, 7
FRAYN, MICHAEL, 927, 1238
FRAZER, SIR JAMES, 698

Frederick Douglass, 757
Freedom of Emily Dickinson, The, 785
FREUD, SIGMUND, 83, 695, 697, 1452
    Destiny of Oedipus, The, 988
FREYTAG, GUSTAV, 909
FRIEDMAN, ALBERT B., 602
Friend, on this scaffold Thomas More lies dead, 535
Frontera / Border, 679
FROST, ROBERT, 484, 587, 625, 637, 639, 646, 667, 706, 769, 770, 1338–41, 1344–49, 1351–53, 1382, 1384–86, 1390–92, 1394–95, 1396–98
    Acquainted with the Night, 655
    Birches, 840
    Desert Places, 624
    Design, 1382
    Fire and Ice, 553
    Importance of Poetic Metaphor, The, 592
    In White, 1401
    Mending Wall, 841
    Nothing Gold Can Stay, 699, 1336
    "Out, Out–," 494
    Road Not Taken, The, 689
    Secret Sits, The, 590
    Silken Tent, The, 589
    Stopping by Woods on a Snowy Evening, 842
FRY, CHRISTOPHER, 771
FRYE, NORTHROP, 701, 1455
FULTON, ALICE
    What I Like, 680
Funeral Blues, 606
FUSSELL, PAUL, 640

GARCÍA MÁRQUEZ, GABRIEL, 17, **417**
    Very Old Man with Enormous Wings, A, 417
GASCOIGNE, GEORGE, 532
GASS, WILLIAM, 82
GAY, GARRY
    Hole in the ozone, 568
GAY, JOHN, 599
Gender and Pathology in "The Yellow Wallpaper," 358
Gift of the Magi, The, 182
GILBERT, SANDRA M., 1459
    Freedom of Emily Dickinson, The, 785
    Imprisonment and Escape: The Psychology of Confinement, 360
GILES, HERBERT
    Independence (translation), 11
GILGAMESH, 492
GILMAN, CHARLOTTE PERKINS, **344**, 358–62
    Nervous Breakdown of Women, The, 357
    Whatever Is, 357
    Why I Wrote "The Yellow Wallpaper," 356
    Yellow Wallpaper, The, 345
GILMAN, RICHARD, 1224
GINSBERG, ALLEN, 669
    Supermarket in California, A, 843
GIOIA, DANA, 2, 482, 890
    Godfather Death (translation), 12
    Money, 588

Girl, 435

GLASPELL, SUSAN, **895,** 906–10, 912–16, 1333, 1404–5, 1407–8, 1410

Creating *Trifles*, 910

Trifles, 895

Glass Menagerie, The, 1174

Go, Lovely Rose, 881

Godfather Death, 12

God's Grandeur, 624

GOETHE, JOHANN WOLFGANG VON, 266, 501

Golondrinas, 745

Good Man Is Hard to Find, A, 308

Good Source Is Not So Hard to Find: The Real Life Misfit, A, 337

GORKY, MAXIM, 1117

Gospel According to Mark, The, 404

GOSSE, SIR EDMUND, 749

Grass, 535

GRAVES, ROBERT, 119, 266, 705

Counting the Beats, 651

Down, Wanton, Down!, 530

GRAY, THOMAS, 639

Greasy Lake, 408

GRIMM, JAKOB AND WILHELM, **12,** 14–16, 27, 29

Godfather Death, 12

GROSHOLZ, EMILY, 585

GUARE, JOHN, 927

GUBAR, SUSAN

Freedom of Emily Dickinson, The, 785

Imprisonment and Escape: The Psychology of Confinement, 360

GUITERMAN, ARTHUR

On the Vanity of Earthly Greatness, 756

GWYNN, R. S., 623

Shakespearean Sonnet, 657

HAALAND, TAMI

Lipstick, 692

HADAS, RACHEL, 620

HAIGH, A. E.

Irony of Sophocles, The, 990

HAMILTON, EDITH, 941

HAMMETT, DASHIELL, 29

Hands, 586

HANSEN, RON, 119

Happy Endings, 394

HARDY, THOMAS, 181, 495, 515, 770

Convergence of the Twain, The, 844

Darkling Thrush, The, 845

Neutral Tones, 686

Ruined Maid, The, 538

Workbox, The, 519

HARJO, JOY, 771

Harlem [Dream Deferred], 793

Harlem Renaissance, The, 796

HARRINGTON, SIR JOHN

Of Treason, 657

Harrison Bergeron, 216

HARTMAN, GEOFFREY

On Wordsworth's "A Slumber Did My Spirit Seal," 1463

Hate Poem, 517

Hawk Roosting, 510

HAWTHORNE, NATHANIEL, **90,** 118, 224, 264, 266

Young Goodman Brown, 90

HAYDEN, ROBERT, 723, 757

Frederick Douglass, 757

Those Winter Sundays, 491

H.D. [HILDA DOOLITTLE], 567, 712–15

Helen, 700

Oread, 570

Storm, 554

HEADINGS, PHILIP R.

Pronouns in the Poem: "One," "You," and "I," The, 813

HEANEY, SEAMUS

Digging, 846

Hearing "We Real Cool," 644

Heart, The, 583

Heat-lightning streak, 567

Helen, 700

HEMINGWAY, ERNEST, 164, **165,** 181, 194, 197–98, 225, 264

Clean, Well-Lighted Place, A, 165

Direct Style, The, 193

HENDERSON, HAROLD G.

piercing chill I feel (*translation*), The, 560

HENLEY, BETH, 1223

HENRY, O. [WILLIAM SYDNEY PORTER], **182**

Gift of the Magi, The, 182

HERBERT, GEORGE, 676–77, 683

Easter Wings, 676

Love, 847

Redemption, 688

Her Kind, 513

HERRICK, ROBERT, 537, 597, 620

To the Virgins, to Make Much of Time, 847

Upon Julia's Clothes, 537

HERSEY, JOHN, 266

High Treason, 745

HILMI, ALI, 751

Hippopotamus, The, 622

HITCHCOCK, ALFRED, 633, 892

Hole in the ozone, 568

HOLLANDER, JOHN

Swan and Shadow, 677

Homecoming, 794

Home is so Sad, 856

HOMER, 82–83, 263, 492

HOOD, THOMAS, 587, 621–22

HOPKINS, GERARD MANLEY, 487, 491, 536, 640, 753, 770

God's Grandeur, 624

Pied Beauty, 565

Spring and Fall, 848

Windhover, The, 848

HORACE, 770

HOUSMAN, A. E., 501, 603

Eight O'Clock, 618

Loveliest of trees, the cherry now, 849

To an Athlete Dying Young, 849

When I was one-and-twenty, 641

How Do I Love Thee? Let Me Count the Ways, 827

HOWE, TINA, 927, 1224
How I Met My Husband, 202
How to Stage *The Glass Menagerie*, 1221
HUDGINS, ANDREW
   Elegy for My Father, Who Is Not Dead, 730
HUGHES, LANGSTON, 723, 772, **787**, 798–803
   Ballad of the Landlord, 791
   Dream Boogie, 643
   Dream Deferred. *See* Harlem
   Dream Variations, 789
   Harlem [Dream Deferred], 793
   Harlem Renaissance, The, 796
   Homecoming, 794
   I, Too, 789
   Mother to Son, 788
   My People, 788
   Negro Artist and the Racial Mountain, The, 795
   Negro Speaks of Rivers, The, 787
   Nightmare Boogie, 793
   Song for a Dark Girl, 791
   Theme for English B, 792
   Two Somewhat Different Epigrams, 658
   Weary Blues, The, 790
HUGHES, TED, 717
   Hawk Roosting, 510
Hughes as an Experimentalist, 798
Humpty Dumpty Explicates "Jabberwocky," 545
HURLEY, ANDREW
   Gospel According to Mark (*translation*), The,
      404
HURSTON, ZORA NEALE, 198, 370–71, **421**,
   1450–51
   Sweat, 421
Hurt Locker, The, 729
HWANG, DAVID HENRY, 1224, **1256**
   Multicultural Theater, 1270
   Sound of a Voice, The, 1256

I, Too, 789
Iago as a Triumphant Villain, 1106
IBSEN, HENRIK, 894, 907, 1116, 1117, **1119**, 1250,
   1251–53
   Correspondence on the Final Scene of *A Doll's
      House*, 1172
   Doll's House, A, 1119
I felt a Funeral, in my Brain, 774
I Hear America Singing, 882
I heard a Fly buzz – when I died, 776
I like to see it lap the Miles, 504
Image, The, 571
I'm Nobody! Who are you?, 775
Importance of Poetic Metaphor, The, 592
Imprisonment and Escape: The Psychology of
   Confinement, 360
In a Station of the Metro, 560
Independence, 11
in Just-, 678
In Memoriam John Coltrane, 626
In My Craft or Sullen Art, 763
INNAURATO, ALBERT, 1223
Interpreter of Maladies, 436
In the old stone pool, 567

In this strange labyrinth, 886
In White, 1401
IONESCO, EUGÈNE, 1223
Irony of Sophocles, The, 990
I Shall Paint My Nails Red, 679
ISOU, ISIDORE, 615
ISSA, KOBAYASHI, 567
   Cricket, 567
   only one guy, 567
I taste a liquor never brewed, 774
IVES, DAVID, 889, **928**
   On the One-Act Play, 938
   Sure Thing, 928
   Talking With David Ives, 890
I Wandered Lonely as a Cloud, 511

Jabberwocky, 544
JACKSON, SHIRLEY, 198, **250**
   Biography of a Story, 257
   Lottery, The, 250
Jailhouse Blues, 606
JAMES, HENRY, 31, 224, 268, 686
JAMES, WILLIAM, 30
JARMAN, MARK, 623
JARRELL, RANDALL, 1392–93
   Death of the Ball Turret Gunner, The, 850
JEFFERS, ROBINSON
   Hands, 586
   Rock and Hawk, 851
JEMIE, ONWUCHEKWA
   Reading of "Dream Deferred," A, 802
Jilting of Granny Weatherall, The, 83
JIN, HA
   Missed Time, 851
JOHNSON, JAMES WELDON, 605, 723
   Sence You Went Away, 597
JOHNSON, SAMUEL, 497, 536, 587, 675, 770
JOHNSON, THOMAS H.
   Discovery of Emily Dickinson's Manuscripts,
      The, 780
JONES, V. S. VERNON
   Fox and the Grapes (*translation*), The, 7
JONSON, BEN, 595–96
   On His Friend and Rival William Shakespeare,
      1110
   On My First Son, 852
   To Celia, 596
Journal Entry, 512
Journey of the Magi, 839
JOYCE, JAMES, 16, 30, 82, 120, 198, 225, 266, **430**,
   698–99
   All day I hear, 618
   Araby, 430
Judge's Wife, The, 388
JUNG, CARL, 697, 701, 1452, 1454
JUSTICE, DONALD
   Men at Forty, 728
   On the Death of Friends in Childhood, 852

KAFKA, FRANZ, 83, 264, **268**, 300–05, 1459–60
   Discussing *The Metamorphosis*, 298
   Metamorphosis, The, 268

KAHLO, FRIDA, 737, 743
  Two Fridas, The, 743
KAUFMAN, BOB
  No More Jazz at Alcatraz, 622
KAZIN, ALFRED
  Walt Whitman and Abraham Lincoln, 1457
KEATS, JOHN, 561, 585, 603, 637
  Bright star, would I were steadfast as thou art, 569
  La Belle Dame sans Merci, 702
  Ode on a Grecian Urn, 852
  Ode to a Nightingale, 759
  This living hand, now warm and capable, 649
  To Autumn, 855
  When I have fears that I may cease to be, 854
KEELER, GREG, 633
KEES, WELDON, 1430–31, 1447, 1449
  For My Daughter, 506
KENNEDY, X. J.
  Heat-lightning streak (translation), 567
  In the old stone pool (translation), 567
  On the one-ton temple bell (translation), 567
  To the Muse, 486
KENYON, JANE
  Suitor, The, 590
KHANWALKAR, ARUNDHATI
  Camel and His Friends (translation), The, 8
KINCAID, JAMAICA, 435
  Girl, 435
KIPLING, RUDYARD, 607, 637
KIZER, CAROLYN
  Bitch, 726
KNIGHT, ETHERIDGE
  Making jazz swing in, 568
KOMUNYAKAA, YUSEF
  Facing It, 725
KOOSER, TED
  Abandoned Farmhouse, 856
  Carrie, 691
Kubla Khan, 831
KUSHNER, TONY, 1224

La Belle Dame sans Merci, 702
La cólera que quiebra al hombre en niños, 744
Lady Lazarus, 718
LAHIRI, JHUMPA, 225, 436
  Interpreter of Maladies, 436
LAKE, PAUL, 623
Lake Isle of Innisfree, The, 489
LANGBAUM, ROBERT
  On Robert Browning's "My Last Duchess," 1445
LARKIN, PHILIP, 585
  Aubade, 731
  Home is so Sad, 856
  Poetry of Departures, 857
LAWRENCE, D. H., 234, 263
  Piano, 857
  Rocking-Horse Winner, The, 234
LAZARUS, EMMA
  New Colossus, The, 765

LEAR, EDWARD, 658
Learning to love America, 859
Learning to Shave, 568
Leda and the Swan, 623
LEE, EDWARD BOK, 1272
  El Santo Americano, 1272
  On Being a Korean American Writer, 1276
LEECH, CLIFFORD, 946
LE GUIN, URSULA K., 245
  Ones Who Walk Away from Omelas, The, 245
LEHMAN, DAVID, 1462
LEMAITRE, GEORGE, 580
LESSING, DORIS, 697
Let me not to the marriage of true minds, 654
LEVERTOV, DENISE, 666–67
  Ancient Stairway, 666
  O Taste and See, 858
LIGHTMAN, ALAN, 580
Lightning is a yellow Fork, The, 685
LIM, SHIRLEY GEOK-LIN, 722
  Learning to love America, 859
  Riding Into California, 723
LINCOLN, ABRAHAM, 668, 1457–58
LI PO
  Drinking Alone by Moonlight, 858
Lipstick, 692
Listening to Flannery O'Connor, 342
little Learning is a dang'rous Thing, A, 868
Little Poem Regarding Computer Spell-Checkers, A, 1355
Living in Sin, 870
London, 550
LONDON, JACK, 120, 125, 181, 264, 1457
  To Build a Fire, 125
Lonely Hearts, 539
LONGFELLOW, HENRY WADSWORTH, 492, 638
  Aftermath, 533
Long Poem Does Not Exist, A, 767
Look Into Black America, A, 1331
Lord Randall, 817
Lottery, The, 250
Love, 847
Love and Friendship, 591
Love Calls Us to the Things of This World, 555
LOVELACE, RICHARD
  To Lucasta, 521
Loveliest of trees, the cherry now, 849
Love Song of J. Alfred Prufrock, The, 806
LOWELL, JAMES RUSSELL, 1335
LOWELL, ROBERT, 718
  Skunk Hour, 860
LOWES, JOHN LIVINGSTON, 749
Low Pay Piecework, 659
LOY, MINA, 770
LUCAS, GEORGE, 706
Lucifer in Shakespeare's Othello, 1107
LUCRETIUS, 497
LUKACS, GEORG, 1457
LUKE, 214
  Parable of the Prodigal Son, The, 214
Luke Havergal, 509

MACDONALD, DWIGHT, 550
MACHADO, ANTONIO
    Traveler, 689
MACLEISH, ARCHIBALD, 770, 771
    Ars Poetica, 769
MAETERLINCK, MAURICE, 1118
Magi, The, 887
Magic Study of Happiness, The, 675
MAILER, NORMAN, 266
MAJMUDAR, AMIT
    Rites to Allay the Dead, 656
Making jazz swing in, 568
MALLARMÉ, STÉPHANE, 528, 549
MAMET, DAVID, 1223
MANN, AIMEE
    Deathly, 609
MANN, THOMAS, 1414
MANSFIELD, KATHERINE, **100**, 1373–75
    Miss Brill, 100
MARLOWE, CHRISTOPHER, 634–35, 757, **920**
    Doctor Faustus, 920
MÁRQUEZ, GABRIEL GARCÍA. See GARCÍA
    MÁRQUEZ, GABRIEL
Martian Sends a Postcard Home, A, 583
MARTIN, CHARLES, 623
MARTIN, JANE, **1277**
    Beauty, 1277
MARVELL, ANDREW, 503, 532, 586
    To His Coy Mistress, 861
MARX, GROUCHO, 927
MASON, BOBBIE ANN, 163
MASON, DAVID
    Song of the Powers, 643
MATSUSHITA, SUIKO
    Cosmos in bloom, 568
    Rain shower from mountain, 568
MATTHEW
    Parable of the Good Seed, The, 687
MAUGHAM, W. SOMERSET, 7, 120, 181
    Appointment in Samarra, The, 6
MAUPASSANT, GUY DE, 16
MCEWAN, IAN, 119
MCINERNEY, JAY, 30
MCKAY, CLAUDE, 722, 723
    America, 722
MCKUEN, ROD
    Thoughts on Capital Punishment, 752
Medusa, 702
MELVILLE, HERMAN, 82, 197, 224, 226, 587,
    683
MENASHE, SAMUEL
    Bread, 535
Men at Forty, 728
Mending Wall, 841
MERTON, THOMAS
    Anger (*translation*), 744
MERWIN, W. S.
    For the Anniversary of My Death, 669
Metamorphosis, The, 268
Metaphors, 582
MEZEY, ROBERT
    On His Blindness (*translation*), 741

MICHENER, JAMES A., 265
MIDDLEBROOK, DIANA, 1452
MILES, JOSEPHINE, 1445
MILLAY, EDNA ST. VINCENT, 717
    Counting-out Rhyme, 641
    Recuerdo, 862
    Second Fig, 518
    What lips my lips have kissed, and where, and
      why, 654
MILLER, ARTHUR, 1117, 1118
MILLETT, KATE, 1458
MILLIER, BRETT C.
    On Elizabeth Bishop's "One Art," 1448
MILLS, TEDI LÓPEZ
    Convalecencia, 746
MILTON, JOHN, 498, 538, 587, 615, 617–18, 655,
    685, 748, 757
    When I consider how my light is spent, 863
Minefield, The, 553
Miniver Cheevy, 871
Miss Brill, 100
Missed Time, 851
MISTRAL, GABRIELA, 737
Mockingbird, 533
MOLIÈRE (JEAN-BAPTISTE POQUELIN), 495
MOMADAY, N. SCOTT
    Simile, 582
Money, 588
Moonrise on mudflats, 567
MOORE, MARIANNE, 577
    Poetry, 863
    Silence, 530
MOORE, THOMAS, 625
MORITAKE, ARAKIDA
    falling flower, The, 566
MOSS, HOWARD
    Shall I Compare Thee to a Summer's Day?,
      579
mother, the, 826
MOTHER GOOSE, 632, 638, 640
Mother to Son, 788
Much Madness is divinest Sense, 776
Muchos Somos, 739
Multicultural Theater, 1270
MUNRO, ALICE, **202**
    How I Met My Husband, 202
Musée des Beaux Arts, 823
Music of Poetry, The, 627
My Grandmother's Love Letters, 833
My Last Duchess, 496
My Life had stood – a Loaded Gun, 581
My mistress' eyes are nothing like the sun, 874
My Papa's Waltz, 501
My People, 788
Myth in Faulkner's "Barn Burning," 1455

NABOKOV, VLADIMIR, 722
Names, The, 541
Naming of Parts, 869
NASHE, THOMAS, 529
Negro Artist and the Racial Mountain, The, 795
Negro Speaks of Rivers, The, 787

NELSON, MARILYN, 623
    Strange Beautiful Woman, A, 864
    Voices in Langston Hughes, The, 799
NERUDA, PABLO, 737, **738**, 743, 747
    Muchos Somos, 739
Nervous Breakdown of Women, The, 357
Neutral Tones, 686
New Colossus, The, 765
NEWTON, JOHN, 603
next to of course god america i, 553
NIEDECKER, LORINE
    Popcorn-can cover, 693
Nightmare Boogie, 793
NIMS, JOHN FREDERICK, 662
No More Jazz at Alcatraz, 622
NORMAN, MARSHA, 1224
Nothing Gold Can Stay, 699, 1336
Not Waving but Drowning, 570

OATES, JOYCE CAROL, 16, **451**, 1421–22, 1423,
    1452–54
    Where Are You Going, Where Have You
      Been?, 451
Objective Correlative, The, 811
O'BRIEN, JOHN, 369
O'BRIEN, TIM, **462**, 1377–78
    Things They Carried, The, 462
O Captain! My Captain!, 762
Occurrence at Owl Creek Bridge, An, 397
O'CONNOR, FLANNERY, 307, **308**, 337–43,
    1441–42
    Excerpt from "On Her Own Work": Insights
      into "A Good Man Is Hard to Find," 333
    Excerpt from "The Grotesque in Southern
      Fiction": The Serious Writer and the Tired
      Reader, 336
    Good Man Is Hard to Find, A, 308
    On Her Catholic Faith, 335
    Revelation, 319
Ode on a Grecian Urn, 852
Ode to a Nightingale, 759
Oedipus the King, 949
O'FAOLAIN, SEAN, 82
Of Treason, 657
Oh, my love is like a red, red rose, 591
Oh No, 514
OLDS, SHARON
    One Girl at the Boys' Party, The, 865
    Rite of Passage, 516
OLIVER, MARY
    Wild Geese, 691
OLSON, CHARLES, 667
O Moon, when I gaze on thy beautiful face, 749
On Being a Korean American Writer, 1276
One Art, 758
One Girl at the Boys' Party, The, 865
O'NEILL, EUGENE, 1117, 1118
On Elizabeth Bishop's "One Art," 1448
One of the Irrefutable Poets, 812
Ones Who Walk Away from Omelas, The, 245
On Form and Artifice, 662
On Her Catholic Faith, 335

On his blindness (*Borges*), 741
On His Blindness (*Mezey*), 741
On His Friend and Rival William Shakespeare,
    1110
only one guy, 567
On Misunderstanding Oedipus, 989
On my boat on Lake Cayuga, 620
On My First Son, 852
On Robert Browning's "My Last Duchess,"
    1445
On the Death of Friends in Childhood, 852
On the One-Act Play, 938
On the one-ton temple bell, 567
On the Vanity of Earthly Greatness, 756
On Wordsworth's "A Slumber Did My Spirit
    Seal," 1463
Oread, 570
ORTIZ, MICHAEL
    Traveler (*translation*), 689
ORWELL, GEORGE, 225, 749
O Taste and See, 858
Othello, the Moor of Venice, 1002
"Out, Out—," 494
OVID, 497, 697
OWEN, WILFRED, **522**, 717
    Anthem for Doomed Youth, 865
    Dulce et Decorum Est, 521
    War Poetry, 523
OZAWA, NEIJI
    War—this year, The, 568
Ozymandias, 756

PACHECO, JOSÉ EMILIO, 722, 737
    Alta Traición, 745
PACKER, ZZ, **38**
    Brownies, 38
PAGLIA, CAMILLE
    Reading of William Blake's "The Chimney
      Sweeper," A, 1466
Pair of Tickets, A, 144
Parable of the Good Seed, The, 687
Parable of the Prodigal Son, The, 214
Paraphrase of "Ask Me," A, 499
PARKER, DOROTHY, 615
    Actress, The, 658
    Résumé, 636
PAZ, OCTAVIO, 736, **741**, 743
    Con los ojos cerrados, 742
PEDEN, MARGARET SAYERS
    Judge's Wife (*translation*), The, 388
Perfect Dress, 835
PETRARCH, 653, 757
Piano, 857
Pied Beauty, 565
PIERCE-BAKER, CHARLOTTE
    Stylish vs. Sacred in "Everyday Use," 375
piercing chill I feel, The, 560
PINCKNEY, DARRYL
    Black Identity in Langston Hughes, 801
PINSKY, ROBERT
    Low Pay Piecework, 659

PLATH, SYLVIA, 717, 726, 1448
  Daddy, 866
  Lady Lazarus, 718
  Metaphors, 582
PLAUTUS, 1222
PLIMPTON, GEORGE, 1331
POE, EDGAR ALLAN, **52**, 119, 226, 534, 631, 633,
  637, 683, 685, 1357–60, 1365–70, 1371–72
  Annabel Lee, 765
  Long Poem Does Not Exist, A, 767
  Tell-Tale Heart, The, 52
  To Helen, 700
Poetic Symbols, 694
Poetry, 863
Poetry and Emotion, 810
Poetry of Departures, 857
Poetry of the Future, The, 680
Popcorn-can cover, 693
POPE, ALEXANDER, 614, 620, 634, 650
  little Learning is a dang'rous Thing, A, 868
PORTER, KATHERINE ANNE, **83**
  Jilting of Granny Weatherall, The, 83
PORTER, WILLIAM. See HENRY, O.
POTTS, L. J.
  Defining Tragedy (translation), 987
POUND, EZRA, 530, 560, 561, 567, 599, 623, 667,
  669, 763
  Image, The, 571
  In a Station of the Metro, 560
  River-Merchant's Wife: A Letter, The, 869
POWELL, JAMES HENRY, 751
Presente en que el Cariño Hace Regalo la
  Llaneza, 738
PRITCHETT, V. S., 380
Pronouns in the Poem: "One," "You," and "I,"
  The, 813

Queen-Anne's-Lace, 884
Quilt as Metaphor in "Everyday Use," 377
Quinceañera, 724

RABASSA, GREGORY
  Very Old Man with Enormous Wings
  (translation), A, 417
Race and the African American Writer, 77
RAINE, CRAIG
  Martian Sends a Postcard Home, A, 583
Rain shower from mountain, 568
RAMPERSAD, ARNOLD
  Hughes as an Experimentalist, 798
RANDALL, DUDLEY
  Ballad of Birmingham, 604
RANSOM, JOHN CROWE, 615
RATUSHINSKAYA, IRINA, 484
Reading of "Dream Deferred, A," 802
Reading of "My Life had stood – a Loaded Gun,"
  A, 784
Reading of William Blake's "The Chimney
  Sweeper," A, 1466
Reapers, 565
Recalling "Aunt Jennifer's Tigers," 498
Recognizing Poetry, 778

Recuerdo, 862
Redemption, 688
Red Wheelbarrow, The, 513
REED, HENRY
  Naming of Parts, 869
REEVE, CLARA, 263
Reflections on Writing and Women's Lives, 371
REID, ALASTAIR
  High Treason, 745
  Translating Neruda, 747
  We Are Many (translation), 739
Résumé, 636
Revelation, 319
RICH, ADRIENNE
  Aunt Jennifer's Tigers, 492
  Living in Sin, 870
  Recalling "Aunt Jennifer's Tigers," 498
  Women, 729
Richard Cory (Robinson), 599
Richard Cory (Simon), 600
RICHARDSON, SAMUEL, 265
Riding Into California, 723
Rite of Passage, 516
rites for Cousin Vit, the, 827
Rites to Allay the Dead, 656
River-Merchant's Wife: A Letter, The, 869
Road Not Taken, The, 689
ROBBE-GRILLET, ALAIN, 83
ROBINSON, EDWIN ARLINGTON, 508, 515
  Luke Havergal, 509
  Miniver Cheevy, 871
  Richard Cory, 599
Rock and Hawk, 851
Rocking-Horse Winner, The, 234
ROCKWOOD, R. J. R.
  Fairy Tale Motifs in "Where Are You Going,
  Where Have You Been?", 1452
ROETHKE, THEODORE, 491, 502, 524–26, 726
  Elegy for Jane, 872
  My Papa's Waltz, 501
  Root Cellar, 562
ROOSEVELT, THEODORE, 508
Root Cellar, 562
Rose for Emily, A, 31
ROSSETTI, CHRISTINA
  Uphill, 690
Route of Evanescence, A, 565
ROWE, NICHOLAS, 752
Ruined Maid, The, 538
Runner, The, 569
RYAN, KAY, 481
  Mockingbird, 533
  Talking With Kay Ryan, 482
  Turtle, 591

SÁENZ, BENJAMIN ALIRE
  To the Desert, 505
Sailing to Byzantium, 754
SALTUS, FRANCIS SALTUS, 751
SANCHEZ-SCOTT, MILCHA, **1224**
  Cuban Swimmer, The, 1224
  Writing The Cuban Swimmer, 1237

SANDBURG, CARL
Fog, 589
Grass, 535
SATYAMURTI, CAROLE
I Shall Paint My Nails Red, 679
SCHENCK, MARY JANE
Deconstructing "A Good Man Is Hard to Find", 340
SCHULZ, GRETCHEN
Fairy Tale Motifs in "Where Are You Going, Where Have You Been?", 1452
SCOTT, RIDLEY, 119
SCOTT, SIR WALTER, 264, 601
SCOTT, WILBUR, 1457
Sea Grapes, 880
Second Coming, The, 705
Second Fig, 518
Secret Sits, The, 590
SEIDEL, KATHRYN LEE
Economics of Zora Neale Hurston's "Sweat," The, 1450
Self-Description, 778
Sence You Went Away, 597
SENECA, 161
SERRANO, PEDRO
Golondrinas, 745
SERVICE, ROBERT, 632–33
Sestina, 661
Setting the Voice, 158
SEXTON, ANNE, 718, 1452
Cinderella, 707
Her Kind, 513
Transforming Fairy Tales, 710
SHAKESPEARE, WILLIAM, 487, 495, 514, 561, 577, 584, 585, 588, 637, 638, 639, 649, 717, 893, 907, 927, 928, 939, 946, 996–99, **998**, 1105–15, 1223, 1455, 1457
Fear no more the heat o' the sun, 598
Let me not to the marriage of true minds, 654
My mistress' eyes are nothing like the sun, 874
Othello, the Moor of Venice, 1002
Shall I compare thee to a summer's day?, 578
That time of year thou mayst in me behold, 873
When to the sessions of sweet silent thought, 873
Shakespearean Sonnet, 657
Shakespeare's Language as a Hidden Political Code, 1108
Shall I Compare Thee to a Summer's Day? (Moss), 579
Shall I compare thee to a summer's day? (Shakespeare), 578
SHARP, R. FARQUHARSON
Doll's House (translation), A, 1119
SHAW, GEORGE BERNARD, 699, 927
SHEEHAN, JULIE
Hate Poem, 517
SHELLEY, PERCY BYSSHE, 579, 651, 748
Ozymandias, 756

SHEPARD, SAM, 1224
SHOWALTER, ELAINE
Quilt as Metaphor in "Everyday Use," 377
Sick Rose, The, 826
Silence, 530
Silken Tent, The, 589
SILVERSTEIN, SHEL, 1224
SIMIC, CHARLES, 771
Butcher Shop, 874
Magic Study of Happiness, The, 675
Simile, 582
SIMON, PAUL, 599
Richard Cory, 600
Simple Gift Made Rich by Affection, A, 738
Sine Qua Non, 656
SINGER, ISAAC BASHEVIS, 180
Siren Song, 820
Sir Patrick Spence, 493
SISCOE, JOHN
Metamorphosis (translation), The, 268
Skunk Hour, 860
Slumber Did My Spirit Seal, A, 616
Smell!, 642
SMITH, ANNA DEAVERE, **1238**
Call to the Community, A, 1248
Twilight: Los Angeles, 1992, 1238
SMITH, BESSIE
Jailhouse Blues, 606
SMITH, STEVIE, 717
Not Waving but Drowning, 570
SNODGRASS, W. D., 586, 718
Snow Man, The, 693
SNYDER, GARY
After weeks of watching the roof leak, 568
SOCRATES, 485
Soliloquy of the Spanish Cloister, 828
somewhere i have never travelled,gladly beyond, 834
Song, 652
Song for a Dark Girl, 791
Song of the Open Road, 881
Song of the Powers, 643
Sonny's Blues, 56
SOPHOCLES, 180–81, 515, 894, 909, 918, 926, 942–48, **947**, 987–91, 1250, 1452
Oedipus the King, 949
SOR JUANA, 736, **737**
Presente en que el Cariño Hace Regalo la Llaneza, 738
Soul selects her own Society, The, 775
Sound of a Voice, The, 1256
Sound of Thunder, A, 135
Speech to the Young. Speech to the Progress-Toward, 506
SPENSER, EDMUND, 618, 688
SPIELBERG, STEVEN, 706
splendor falls on castle walls, The, 619
Spring and All, 884
Spring and Fall, 848
SPRINGSTEEN, BRUCE, 408
STAFFORD, WILLIAM
Ask Me, 499

At the Un-National Monument Along the
Canadian Border, 520
Farm on the Great Plains, The, 875
Paraphrase of "Ask Me," A, 499
Traveling Through the Dark, 753
STALLINGS, A. E., 623
First Love: A Quiz, 706
On Form and Artifice, 662
Sine Qua Non, 656
STANISLAVSKY, CONSTANTIN, 1117
STAVROS, GEORGE, 644
STEELE, TIMOTHY, 623
STEINBECK, JOHN, 16, 120, **227**, 260–61
Chrysanthemums, The, 227
STEINER, GEORGE, 1444
STEPHENS, JAMES
Wind, The, 585
STEVENS, WALLACE, 558, 588, 621, 666, 672–73,
770
Anecdote of the Jar, 693
Disillusionment of Ten O'Clock, 552
Emperor of Ice-Cream, The, 876
Snow Man, The, 693
Thirteen Ways of Looking at a Blackbird, 673
STEVENSON, ROBERT LOUIS, 1356
STEWART, GEORGE, 81
STILLMAN, MICHAEL
In Memoriam John Coltrane, 626
Moonrise on mudflats (translation), 567
STOPPARD, TOM, 927, 1256
Stopping by Woods on a Snowy Evening, 842
Storm (Chopin), The, 123
Storm (H.D.), 554
Story of an Hour, The, 415
STRACHEY, JAMES
Destiny of Oedipus (translation), The, 988
Strange Beautiful Woman, A, 864
STRAUS, NINA PELIKAN
Transformations in The Metamorphosis, 1459
STRINDBERG, AUGUST, 1117, 1118
STUDENT PAPERS
Analysis of the Symbolism in Steinbeck's "The
Chrysanthemums," An, 260
Bonds Between Love and Hatred in H.D.'s
"Helen," The, 712
By Lantern Light: An Explication of a Passage
in Poe's "The Tell-Tale Heart," 1365
Card Report: "The Tell-Tale Heart," 1371
Card Report: Trifles, 1407
Design of Robert Frost's "Design," The, 1394
Faded Beauty: Bishop's Use of Imagery in "The
Fish," 573
Hearer of the Tell-Tale Heart, The, 1368
Helmer vs. Helmer, 1251
Kafka's Greatness, 300
Lost Innocence in Robert Frost's "Nothing
Gold Can Stay," 1351
Othello: Tragedy or Soap Opera?, 1112
Outside Trifles, 912
"Perfect Balance and Perfect Posture":
Reflecting on "The Things They Carried,"
1377

Successful Adaptation in "A Rose for Emily"
and "Miss Brill," 1374
Trifles Scores Mixed Success in Monday
Player's Production, 1410
Unfolding of Robert Frost's "Design," An, 1390
"Wing-Spread" Does a Dip, 1396
Word Choice, Tone, and Point of View in
Roethke's "My Papa's Waltz," 524
Stylish vs. Sacred in "Everyday Use," 375
Success is counted sweetest, 773
SUGARHILL GANG, 607
Suitor, The, 590
Supermarket in California, A, 843
Sure Thing, 928
Swallows, 746
Swan and Shadow, 677
Sweat, 421
SWIFT, JONATHAN, 263, 514
SWINBURNE, ALGERNON, 584

Talking With Amy Tan, 2
Talking With David Ives, 890
Talking With Kay Ryan, 482
TAN, AMY, 1, **144**, 194, 264
Pair of Tickets, A, 144
Setting the Voice, 158
Talking With Amy Tan, 2
TANNEN, DEBORAH, 726
TATE, J. O.
Good Source Is Not So Hard to Find: The Real
Life Misfit, A, 337
Tears, Idle Tears, 555
Teenage Wasteland, 186
Tell all the Truth but tell it slant, 777
Tell-Tale Heart, The, 52
TENNYSON, ALFRED, LORD, 492, 558, 578, 588,
615, 645, 649, 749, 750
Break, Break, Break, 635
Eagle, The, 578
Flower in the Crannied Wall, 581
splendor falls on castle walls, The, 619
Tears, Idle Tears, 555
Ulysses, 876
Term "Protest Singer" Didn't Exist, The, 610
That time of year thou mayst in me behold,
873
Theme for English B, 792
Themes of Science Fiction, The, 221
THIEL, DIANE
Minefield, The, 553
Simple Gift Made Rich by Affection
(translation), A, 738
Things They Carried, The, 462
Thirteen Ways of Looking at a Blackbird, 673
thirteen ways of looking at a tortilla, 816
This Is Just to Say, 528
This is my letter to the World, 776
This Is What It Means to Say Phoenix, Arizona,
380
This living hand, now warm and capable, 649
THOMAS, DYLAN, 616, 653
Do not go gentle into that good night, 659

THOMAS, DYLAN (*continued*)
Fern Hill, 878
In My Craft or Sullen Art, 763
Those Winter Sundays, 491
Thoughts on Capital Punishment, 752
Three Privations of Emily Dickinson, The, 781
Times They Are a-Changin', The, 608
To a Locomotive in Winter, 504
To an Athlete Dying Young, 849
To Autumn, 855
To Build a Fire, 125
To Celia, 596
To Helen, 700
To His Coy Mistress, 861
TOLKIEN, J. R. R., 264, 706
TOLSTOY, LEO, 28
To Lucasta, 521
TOOMER, JEAN, 723
Reapers, 565
To see a world in a grain of sand, 582
To the Desert, 505
To the Muse, 486
To the Virgins, to Make Much of Time, 847
Transformations in *The Metamorphosis*, 1459
Transforming Fairy Tales, 710
Translating Neruda, 747
Translating Sophocles into English, 992
Traveler, 689
Traveling Through the Dark, 753
TRETHEWEY, NATASHA, 508
White Lies, 507
TREVOR, WILLIAM, 757
Trifles, 895
Triolet, 660
TROLLOPE, ANTHONY, 161
TURNER, BRIAN
Hurt Locker, The, 729
Turtle, 591
TWAIN, MARK, 16, 27, 30, 267, 587, 648
Twilight: Los Angeles, 1992, 1238
Two Fridas, The, 743
Two Poetweets, 659
Two Somewhat Different Epigrams, 658
Tyger, The, 824
TYLER, ANNE, 181, **186**
Teenage Wasteland, 186

Ulysses, 876
Unknown Citizen, The, 515
UPDIKE, JOHN, **17**, 162, 181, 698
A & P, 17
Ex-Basketball Player, 879
Why Write?, 22
Uphill, 690
Upon Julia's Clothes, 537

VALDÉS, GINA
English con Salsa, 543
Valediction: Forbidding Mourning, A, 837
VALÉRY, PAUL, 771

VALLEJO, CÉSAR, 737, 743
La cólera que quiebra al hombre en niños, 744
VAUGHAN, VIRGINIA MASON
Black and White in *Othello*, 1107
Very Old Man with Enormous Wings, A, 417
VILLA, JOSÉ GARCIA, 771
Virginia, 627
Voices in Langston Hughes, The, 799
VOLPE, EDMOND
Myth in Faulkner's "Barn Burning," 1455
VONNEGUT, KURT JR., **216**
Harrison Bergeron, 216
Themes of Science Fiction, The, 221

WADA, HAKURO
Even the croaking of frogs, 568
WALCOTT, DEREK, 722
Sea Grapes, 880
WALDROP, KEITH, 751
WALEY, ARTHUR
Drinking Alone by Moonlight (*translation*), 858
WALKER, ALICE, 265, **363**, 371–79
Black Woman Writer in America, The, 369
Everyday Use, 363
Reflections on Writing and Women's Lives, 371
WALLER, EDMUND
Go, Lovely Rose, 881
WALPOLE, HORACE, 918
Walt Whitman and Abraham Lincoln, 1457
War Poetry, 523
WARREN, AUSTIN, 1444
WARREN, ROBERT PENN, 1445
War—this year, The, 568
WASHINGTON, MARY HELEN
"Everyday Use" as a Portrait of the Artist, 374
WASSERSTEIN, WENDY, 1224
Wayfarer, The, 672
We Are Many, 739
Weary Blues, The, 790
WEBSTER, JOHN, 634
WEINBERGER, ELIOT
With eyes closed (*translation*), 742
WELLEK, RENÉ, 1445
WELLES, ORSON, 919
WELTY, EUDORA, **474, 683**
Worn Path, A, 474
We Real Cool, 635
We Wear the Mask, 764
Whatever Is, 357
What I Like, 680
What lips my lips have kissed, and where, and why, 654
When I consider how my light is spent, 863
When I have fears that I may cease to be, 854
When I was one-and-twenty, 641
When maidens are young, 617
When to the sessions of sweet silent thought, 873
When You Are Old, 888

Where Are You Going, Where Have You Been?, 451

White Lies, 507

WHITMAN, WALT, 599, 623, 668, 669, 748, 762, 1457–58

Beat! Beat! Drums!, 642

Cavalry Crossing a Ford, 672

I Hear America Singing, 882

O Captain! My Captain!, 762

Poetry of the Future, The, 680

Runner, The, 569

Song of the Open Road, 881

To a Locomotive in Winter, 504

Who Goes with Fergus?, 616

Why I Wrote "The Yellow Wallpaper," 356

Why Write?, 22

WILBUR, RICHARD, 640, 649, 748

Concerning "Love Calls Us to the Things of This World, 557

Love Calls Us to the Things of This World, 555

Three Privations of Emily Dickinson, The, 781

Writer, The, 883

WILDE, OSCAR, 657, 893, 927, 1403, 1460

WILDER, THORNTON, 119, 1118

Wild Geese, 691

Wild Nights – Wild Nights!, 774

WILES, DAVID

Chorus as Democrat, The, 991

WILLIAMS, CLARENCE

Jailhouse Blues, 606

WILLIAMS, MILLER, 487

WILLIAMS, RAYMOND, 1464

WILLIAMS, TENNESSEE, 224, 1118–19, **1174**

Glass Menagerie, The, 1174

How to Stage The Glass Menagerie, 1221

WILLIAMS, WILLIAM CARLOS, 529, 567, 623, 667

Dance, The, 670

El Hombre, 570

Queen-Anne's-Lace, 884

Red Wheelbarrow, The, 513

Smell!, 642

Spring and All, 884

This Is Just to Say, 528

Young Housewife, The, 691

Will There Be Time?, 814

WILSON, AUGUST, 1224, **1282**

Fences, 1282

Look Into Black America, A, 1331

WILSON, WOODROW, 658

Wind, The, 585

Windhover, The, 848

Wing-Spread, 1396

winter evening settles down, The, 562

With eyes closed, 742

WOLFF, CYNTHIA GRIFFIN

Dickinson and Death, 782

WOLFF, TOBIAS, 266

Women, 729

WOODWORTH, SAMUEL, 751, 752

WOOLF, VIRGINIA, 29, 30

WORDSWORTH, DOROTHY

Journal Entry, 512

WORDSWORTH, WILLIAM, 511–12, 586, 576, 621, 748, 763, 770, 1463–64

Composed upon Westminster Bridge, 885

I Wandered Lonely as a Cloud, 511

Slumber Did My Spirit Seal, A, 616

world is too much with us, The, 699

Workbox, The, 519

world is too much with us, The, 699

Worn Path, A, 474

WRIGHT, JAMES

Autumn Begins in Martins Ferry, Ohio, 886

WRIGHT, RICHARD, 266

Writer, The, 883

Writing The Cuban Swimmer, 1237

WROTH, MARY SIDNEY

In this strange labyrinth, 886

YEATS, WILLIAM BUTLER, 489, 490, 491, 529, 561, 632, 638, 648, 704, 705, 754–56, 1118

Crazy Jane Talks with the Bishop, 887

Lake Isle of Innnisfree, The, 489

Leda and the Swan, 623

Magi, The, 887

Poetic Symbols, 694

Sailing to Byzantium, 754

Second Coming, The, 705

When You Are Old, 888

Who Goes with Fergus?, 616

Yellow Wallpaper, The, 345

You fit into me, 588

YOUNG, KEVIN

Doo Wop, 626

Young Goodman Brown, 90

Young Housewife, The, 691

ZAR, JERROLD H., 1355

ZOLA, ÉMILE, 1117

INDEX OF LITERARY TERMS

Page numbers indicate discussion of terms in anthology. A page number in **bold** indicates entry in the Glossary of Literary Terms. n following a page number indicates entry in a note.

abstract diction, 529, 548, **1469**
accent, 631, 647, **1469**
accentual meter, 640, 647, **1469**
acrostic, **1469**
allegory, 224, 262, 687, 696, **1469**
alliteration, 617, 629, **1469**
all-knowing narrator, 28, 29, 79, **1469**
allusion, 82, 534, 548, **1469**
analysis, 1367, 1393, 1405, **1469**
anapest, anapestic, 637, 647, **1469**
antagonist, 15, 25, **1470**
anticlimax, **1470**
antihero, 82, 1223, 1255, **1470**
antithesis, 650, **1470**
apostrophe, 586, 594, **1470**
apprenticeship novel, 266, 306, **1470**
archetype, 701, 716, 1454, **1470**
aside, 894, 917, **1470**
assonance, 618, 629, **1470**
atmosphere 119, 160, **1470**
auditory imagery, 560, **1470**

ballad, 500, 601, 613, **1470**
ballad stanza, 603, 613, **1471**
bathos, 752, 768, **1471**
Bildungsroman, 266, 306, **1471**
biographical criticism, 1447, 1468, **1471**
biography, 1448, **1471**
blank verse, 649, 665, **1471**
blues, 605, 613, **1471**
box set, 1117, 1255, **1471**
broadside ballad, **1471**
burlesque, 927, 940, **1471**

cacophony, 615, 629, **1471**
card report, 1370, 1405
carpe diem, **1472**
catharsis. *See katharsis*
central intelligence, **1472**
cesura, caesura, 634, 647, **1472**
character, 81, **1472**
character description, 117
character development, 117, **1472**
characterization, 117, **1472**
Child ballad, **1472**

clerihew, **1472**
climax, 15, 25, 908, 916, **1472**
closed couplet, 650, 665, **1472**
closed dénouement, **1472**
closed form, 648, 665, **1472**
close reading, 1445, **1472**
colloquial English, 536, 548, **1473**
comedy, 926, 940, **1473**
comedy of manners, 927, 940 **1473**
comic relief, 1223, 1255, **1473**
coming-of-age story, 25, **1473**
commedia dell'arte, 927, **1473**
common meter, 603, 613, **1473**
comparison, 1372, 1395, 1405, **1473**
complication, 15, 25, **1473**
conceit, 757, 768, **1474**
conclusion, 15, 26, 909, **1474**
concrete diction, 529, 548, **1474**
concrete poetry, **1474**
Confessional poetry, 718, **1474**
conflict, 15, 25, 906, 916, **1474**
connotation, 549, 559, **1474**
consonance, 621, 630, **1474**
contrast, 1373, 1395, 1405, **1474**
convention, 653, 757, 768, 894, **1474**
conventional symbol, 262, 683, 696, **1474**
cosmic irony, 181, 196, 515, **1474**
cothurni, 943, 994, **1475**
couplet, 650, 665, **1475**
cowboy poetry, **1475**
crisis, 15, 25, 908, 916, **1475**
cultural studies, 1464, 1468, **1475**

dactyl, dactylic, 638, 647, **1475**
deconstructionist criticism, 1462, 1468, **1475**
decorum, 536, **1475**
denotation, 549, 559, **1475**

dénouement, 15, 26, 909, **1475**
deus ex machina, 942, 994, **1475**
dialect, 537, 548, **1476**
dialogue, 892, **1476**
diction, 163, 196, 529, 548, **1476**
didactic fiction, didactic poetry, 497, 500, **1476**
dimeter, 639, **1476**
doggerel, **1476**
double plot, 907, 916, **1476**
drama, **1476**
dramatic irony, 180, 196, 515, 527, **1476**
dramatic monologue, 495, 500, **1476**
dramatic poetry, 495, **1476**
dramatic point of view, **1477**
dramatic question, 908, **1477**
dramatic situation, 15, **1477**
dumb show, **1477**
dynamic character, 82, **1477**

echo verse, **1477**
editorial omniscience, 29, 79, **1477**
editorial point of view, **1477**
elegy, **1477**
endnote, **1477**
end rime, 621, 630, **1477**
end-stopped line, 634, 647, **1477**
English sonnet, 653, 665, **1477**
envoy, 662n, **1477**
epic, 500, 649, 665, **1478**
epigram, 657, 665, 927, **1478**
epigraph, **1478**
epiphany, 16, 26, **1478**
episode, 943, **1478**
episodic plot, **1478**
epistolary novel, 265, 306, **1478**
euphony, 615, 629, **1478**
exact rime, 621, 630, **1478**
éxodos, 944
explication, 1364, 1389, 1405, **1478**
exposition, 15, 25, 907, 916, **1478**
Expressionism, 1118, 1254, **1478**
eye rime, 623, 630, **1478**

fable, 6, 25, **1479**
fairy tale, 12, 25, **1479**

falling action, 909, **1479**
falling meter, 638, **1479**
fantasy, **1479**
farce, 927, 940, **1479**
feminine rime, 621, 630, **1479**
feminist criticism, **1479**
feminist theater, 1223
fiction, 5, **1479**
figure of speech, 577, **1479**
first-person narrator, 79, **1479**
fixed form, 653, 665, **1480**
flashback, 16, 26, **1480**
flat character, 82, 117, **1480**
folk ballad, 601, 613, **1480**
folk epic, **1480**
folklore, **1480**
folktale, 25, **1480**
foot, 637, 647, **1480**
footnote, **1480**
foreshadowing, 16, 26, 907, 916, **1480**
form, 648, 665, **1480**
formal English, 537, 548, **1480**
formalist criticism, 1445, 1468, **1481**
found poetry, **1481**
free verse 665, 667, 682, **1481**

gender criticism, 1458, 1468, **1481**
general English, 536, 548, **1481**
genre, **1481**
Gothic fiction, **1481**

haiku, 566, 576, **1481**
hamartia, 945, 994, **1481**
heptameter, 639, **1482**
hero, 15, 82, **1482**
heroic couplet, 650, 665, **1482**
hexameter, 639, **1482**
hidden alliteration, 617
high comedy, 927, 940, **1482**
historical criticism, 1449, 1468, **1482**
historical fiction, historical novel, 119, 266, 306, **1482**
hubris, 946, 995, **1482**
hyperbole, 586, 594, **1482**

iamb, iambic, 637, 647, **1482**
iambic meter, **1482**
iambic pentameter, 639, 647, **1482**

image, 560, 576, **1482**
imagery, 561, 576, **1482**
impartial omniscience, 29, 79, **1482**
imperfect rime, 621
implied metaphor, 580, 594, **1483**
in medias res, 16, 26, **1483**
initial alliteration, 617, 629
initiation story, 16, 25, **1483**
innocent narrator, 30, 80, **1483**
interior monologue, 30, 80, **1483**
internal alliteration, 617, 629, **1483**
internal refrain, 597, **1483**
internal rime, 621, 630, **1483**
ironic point of view, 181, 514, **1483**
irony, 180, 196, 514, 527, **1483**
irony of fate, 181, 196, 515, 527, **1483**
Italian sonnet, 654, 665, **1484**

katharsis, 946, 995, **1484**

legend, **1484**
levels of diction, 536, **1484**
limerick, 658, **1484**
limited omniscience, 28, 29, 79, **1484**
literary ballad, 603, 613, **1484**
literary epic, **1484**
literary genre, **1484**
literary theory, 1444, **1484**
local color, **1484**
locale, 118, 160, **1484**
low comedy, 927, 940, **1484**
lyric poem, 491, 500, **1484**

madrigal, 598, **1485**
magic (or magical) realism, **1485**
masculine rime, 621, 630, **1485**
masks, 942, 994, **1485**
melodrama, **1485**
metafiction, **1485**
metaphor, 579, 594, **1485**
meter, 632, 636, **1485**
metonymy, 587, 594, **1485**
minimalist fiction, 163, **1485**
mixed metaphor, 580, 594, **1485**
monologue, **1486**
monometer, 639, **1486**
monosyllabic foot, 638, **1486**
moral, 7, **1486**
motif, **1486**
motivation, 81, 117, **1486**
myth, 697, 716, **1486**
mythological criticism, 1454, 1468, **1486**
mythology, 697

naive narrator, 30, 80, **1486**
narrative poem, 492, 500, **1486**
narrator, 27, **1486**

naturalism, 120, 160, 1117, 1254, **1486**
near rime, 621
New Formalism, 623, **1487**
new naturalism, **1487**
nonfiction novel, 266, 306, **1487**
nonparticipant narrator, 28, 80, **1487**
novel, 263, 306, **1487**
novelette, 266
novella, 266, 306, **1487**

objective point of view, 29, 79, **1487**
observer, 28, 79, **1487**
octameter, 639, **1487**
ode, 759, 943
octave, 654, 665, **1487**
off rime, 621, **1487**
omniscient narrator, 28, 29, 79, **1487**
onomatopoeia, 615, 629, **1487**
open dénouement, **1488**
open form, 648, 665, 666, 682, **1488**
oral tradition, **1488**
orchestra, 942, 994, **1488**
overstatement, 586, 594, **1488**

parable, 10, 25, **1488**
paradox, 587, 594, **1488**
parallel, parallelism, 650, **1488**
paraphrase, 488, 500, **1488**
párodos, 943
parody, **1488**
participant narrator, 28, 79, **1488**
pentameter, 639, **1488**
peripeteia, peripety, 946, 995, **1488**
persona, 508, 527, **1488**
personification, 585, 594, **1489**
Petrarchan sonnet, 654, 665, **1489**
picaresque, 266, 306, **1489**
picture-frame stage, 1117, 1255, **1489**
play, 892
play review, 1408, **1489**
plot, 15, 907, **1489**
poetic diction, 536, 548, **1489**
poetic inversion, 748, 768
poetweet, 658
point of view, 28, **1489**
portmanteau word, 546n, **1489**
print culture, **1489**
projective verse, 667, **1490**
prologue, 943
proscenium arch, 1117, 1255, **1490**
prose poem, 675, 682, **1490**
prosody, 636, 647, **1490**
protagonist, 15, 25, 907, **1490**
psalms, 668, **1490**

psychological criticism, 1452, 1468, **1490**
pulp fiction, **1490**
pun, 587, **1490**
purgation, 946, **1490**

quantitative meter, **1490**
quatrain, 651, 665, **1490**

rap, 607, 613, **1490**
reader-response criticism, 1460, 1468, **1490**
realism, 160, 1116, 1254, **1490**
recognition, 946, 995, **1491**
refrain, 597, 613, **1491**
regional writer, 120
regionalism, 160, **1491**
resolution, 15, 26, 909, 917, **1491**
response paper, 1376
retrospect, 16, **1491**
reversal, 946
rhyme, rime, 619, 630, **1491**
rhythm, 631, 647, **1491**
rime, rhyme, 619, 630, **1491**
rime scheme, 597, 613, **1491**
rising action, 909, **1491**
rising meter, 638, **1492**
romance, 264, 306, **1492**
romantic comedy, 928, 940, **1492**
rondel, roundel, **1492**
round character, 82, 117, **1492**
run-on line, 634, 647, **1492**

sarcasm, 180, 196, 514, 527, **1492**
satiric comedy, 926, 940, **1492**
satiric poetry, 502, 527, **1492**
satyr play, 942, **1492**
scansion, 636, 647, **1493**
scene, 16, **1493**
selective omniscience, 29, 79, **1493**
sentimentality, 751, 768, **1493**
sestet, 654, 665, **1493**
sestina, 662n, **1493**
setting, 118, 160, **1493**
Shakespearean sonnet, 653, 665, **1493**
short novel, 267
short story, 16, 25, **1493**
simile, 579, 594, **1493**
situational irony, **1493**
skene, 942, 994, **1493**
slack syllable, 632, 647, **1493**
slant rime, 621, 630, **1493**
slapstick comedy, 928, 940, **1493**
sociological criticism, 1457, 1468, **1493**
soliloquy, 894, 917, **1494**
sonnet, 653, 665, **1494**
spondee, 638, 647, **1494**
stage business, 909, 917, **1494**
stanza, 597, 613, **1494**

static character, 82, **1494**
stock character, 81, 117, **1494**
story of initiation, 16, 25
stream of consciousness, 30, 80, **1494**
stress, 631, 647, **1494**
style, 162, 196, **1494**
subject, 490, 500, **1494**
subplot, 907, 916
summary, 16, 197, 223, 488, 500, **1494**
Surrealism, 742, **1494**
suspense, 15, 909, **1494**
syllabic verse, 653, **1495**
symbol, 224, 262, 683, 696, 910, **1495**
symbolic act, 226, 262, 696, **1495**
symbolist drama, 1254
Symbolist movement, 1118, **1495**
synecdoche, 587, 594, **1495**
synopsis, **1495**

tactile imagery, 560, **1495**
tale, 11, 25, **1495**
tall tale, 12, 25, **1495**
tercet, 651, **1495**
terminal refrain, 597, **1495**
terza rima, 651, **1496**
tetrameter, 639, **1496**
theater of the absurd, 1223, 1254, **1496**
theme, 197, 223, 490, 500, 894, **1496**
thesis sentence, **1496**
third-person narrator, 80, **1496**
tone, 162, 196, 501, 527, **1496**
total omniscience, 31, 79, **1496**
traditional epic, **1496**
tragedy, 918, 940, **1496**
tragic flaw, 919, 945, 994, **1496**
tragic irony, **1497**
tragicomedy, 1222, 1255, **1497**
transferred epithet, **1497**
trick ending, **1497**
trimeter, 639, **1497**
triolet, 660n, **1497**
trochaic, trochee, 638, 647, **1497**
troubadour, 599, **1487**

understatement, 587, 594, **1497**
unities, 909, 917, **1497**
unreliable narrator, 30, 80, **1497**

verbal irony, 180, 196, 514, 527, **1497**
verisimilitude, **1498**
verse, 487, 500, 597, **1498**
vers libre, 667, 682, **1498**
villanelle, 539n, 660n, **1498**
visual imagery, 560, **1498**
vulgate, 536, 548, **1498**

WRITING RESOURCES IN *Literature*
COMPACT EDITION

Chapters 1 to 36
"WRITING EFFECTIVELY" FEATURE

Each major chapter in Fiction, Poetry, and Drama includes a **"Writing Effectively"** feature with material on writing specially focused on the chapter's topic.

Each chapter contains:
Writers on Writing ■ insights about writing from a famous author on an aspect of the chapter's topic
Writing Advice ■ focused, practical advice on writing
Writing Checklist ■ easy-to-use summaries of key points
Writing Assignment ■ paper topic related to the chapter theme or selections
More Topics for Writing ■ additional paper topics related to the chapter contents

Chapter 38
WRITING ABOUT LITERATURE

Read Actively
Plan Your Essay
Prewriting: Discover Your Ideas
Develop a Literary Argument:
■ Purpose   ■ Thesis
■ Audience   ■ Argument
■ Topic   ■ Organization

Write a Rough Draft
Revise Your Draft
Document Sources to Avoid Plagiarism
Format of Finished Paper

Chapter 39
WRITING ABOUT A STORY

Read Actively
Prewriting: Discover Your Ideas
Write a Rough Draft
Revise Your Draft

Common Approaches to Writing About Fiction:
■ Explication   ■ Comparison and Contrast
■ Analysis   ■ Response Paper
■ Card Report
Topics for Writing

Chapter 40
WRITING ABOUT A POEM

Read Actively
Prewriting: Discover Your Ideas
Write a Rough Draft
Revise Your Draft

Common Approaches to Writing About Poetry
How to Quote a Poem
Topics for Writing

Chapter 41
WRITING ABOUT A PLAY

Read Critically
Common Approaches to Writing About Drama

How to Quote a Play
Topics for Writing